£5

THIS BOOK BELONGS TO THE REFERENCE SECTION AND IS NOT TO BE REMOVED

EUROPEAN DICTIONARY

French – English – German
Spanish – Italian – Portuguese

Henri and Monique Goursau

Mosaik

We take pleasure in expressing our thanks to all those who have contributed to the production of this first European dictionary. In particular our thanks go to Mr. Jean Froidure, Miss Suzan Gilzmer, as well as Mr. Rainer Kubis from the Goethe Institute, Mrs. Monique Zoppi from L'ENSAE, Mrs. Lolin Fuertès and Mrs. Almut Plays.

Special edition 1992 published by Mosaik Books, a division of GeoCenter International UK Ltd.
Printing and binding: Mohndruck Graphische Betriebe GmbH, Gütersloh
Printed in Germany
ISBN 3-576-80000-X

INTRODUCTION

This dictionary is your ideal companion for travelling and studying.

For all travellers to England, France, Italy, Spain and Portugal, here is the dictionary you will need!

The dictionary also gives the user a selection of 8000 colloquial words.

The word at the beginning of each line corresponds to the words and paraphrases that follow in the other European languages.

An important part of the preparation of this dictionary was the development of a type of memory aid, so that the user would be immediately able to cope with the different cultures and traditions likely to be encountered when visiting the various European countries.

This dictionary contains both the spoken and written word of many specific areas such as business, technical, cultural, sport and tourism.

Due to lack of space we have had to omit grammatical and semantic references as well as parts of speech, gender and phonetic transcription. We apologise for any inconvenience this may cause.

Our objective has been to produce both a handy and practical dictionary. For this reason we have chosen the typography to suit this particular format, that still enables the users to read it both quickly and easily.

It was also our aim to produce an interesting book which will continue to develop and help strengthen the bridges between the different European languages. We would therefore be grateful if you would let us have your observations and comments, please send these to:

GeoCenter International UK Ltd.
The Viables Centre
Harrow Way
Basingstoke
Hampshire RG22 4BJ

We assure you that we will take these into consideration when preparing future editions.

PREFACE

A travel companion and a school companion.

This is the dictionary you need if you travel in France, Germany, and Spain, and sometimes in Italy or Portugal.

It contains a selection of 8,000 words taken from everyday conversation.

The entry in the first column is followed by its equivalent in each of the other European languages.

In compiling this dictionary our main aim was to produce a handbook which could come to the immediate aid of the user in countries with different languages and cultures.

We hope that you will forgive our lack of precision and the omission of grammatical and semantic information: the function and gender of words for example, the absence of context and of phonetic transcription for pronunciation.

This is a dictionary of everyday language and reflects the spoken and written word as used in many fields of activity such as economics, the technical sector, culture, sport, and tourism.

We wanted it to be easy to use and carry. We have, therefore, selected a practical format and lay-out that will enable you to consult it easily and quickly.

It is planned that the dictionary will evolve and include other European languages. We should be most grateful if you would send us any observations, comments and criticisms you may wish to make. We will take these into serious consideration when working on later editions.

Henri GOURSAU and Monique GOURSAU

A

French	English	German	Spanish	Italian	Portuguese
à	at; to; in	zu; nach; in; bei; von	en; a; de; por; con	a; in; da; con; di	em; a; para
abaisser	lower	nieder = lassen	bajar	abbassare	abaixar
abandonner	abandon, leave	preis = geben; auf = geben	abandonar	abbandonare	abandonar
abbaye	abbey	Abtei(f)	abadía	abbazia, badia	abadia
abcès	abscess(-es)	Geschwür(n)	absceso	ascesso	abcesso
abdiquer	abdicate	ab = danken	abdicar	abdicare	abdicar
abdomen	abdomen	Unterleib(m)	abdomen	addome	abdómen
abeille	bee	Biene(f)	abeja	ape	abelha
à bientôt	see you soon, bye	bis bald	hasta pronto	a presto	até breve; até já
abîmer	damage, spoil, ruin	beschädigen	estropear	sciupare, rovinare	estragar
abolir	abolish	ab = schaffen	abolir	abolire	abolir
abominable	awful	scheußlich	abominable	abominevole	abominável
abondance	abundance	Uberfluß(m)	abundancia	abbondanza	abundância
abondant, e	plentiful, abundant	reichlich	abundante	abbondante	abundante
abonné, e	subscriber	Abonnent(m)	suscriptor, a	abbonato, a	assinante
abonnement	subscription	Abonnement(n)	subscripción	abbonamento	assinatura
abord(d')	first(at)	zunächst	primero	anzitutto	primeiro
à bord	aboard	an Bord	a bordo	a bordo	a bordo
aboutir à	lead to	führen zu	conducir a	arrivare a	conduzir a
aboyer	bark	bellen	ladrar	abbaiare	ladrar
abréviation	abbreviation	Abkürzung(f)(Wort)	abreviatura	abbreviazione	abreviatura
abri, refuge	shelter	Obdach(n), Schutz(m)	abrigo, refugio	riparo, rifugio	abrigo, refúgio
abrupt, e	steep	steil	abrupto, a	ripido, a; scosceso, a	abrupto, a
abrutir	exhaust; stupefy	ab = stumpfen	embrutecer	abbrutire	embrutecer
absent, e	absent	abwesend	ausente	assente	ausente
absolu, e	absolute	unbedingt	absoluto, a	assoluto, a	absoluto, a
absolument	absolutely	unbedingt, absolut	absolutamente	assolutamente	absolutamente
absorber	absorb	verzehren	absorber	assorbire	absorver
abstrait, e	abstract	abstrakt	abstracto, a	astratto, a	abstracto, a
absurde	absurd	unsinnig	absurdo, a	assurdo, a	absurdo, a
abus	abuse, misuse	Mißbrauch(m)	abuso	abuso	abuso
abuser	take advantage of	mißbrauchen	abusar	abusare	abusar
académie	academy	Akademie(f)	academia	accademia	academia
accalmie	lull	Wetterberuhigung(f)	calma	schiarita, tregua	acalmia
accéder	accede to	gelangen zu/kommen an	acceder	assurgere	chegar
accéder à	reach	Zugang haben zu	llegar a	accedere a	chegar a
accélérer	accelerate	beschleunigen	acelerar	accelerare	acelerar
accent	accent	Akzent(m), Tonfall(m)	dejo	accento	sotaque
accent(')	accent	Akzent(m)	acento	accento	acento
accentuation	stress(ing)	Betonung(f)	acentuación	accentazione	acentuação
accepter	accept, agree	akzeptieren, an = nehmen	aceptar	accettare	aceitar
accès	access	Zugang(m)	acceso	accesso	acesso
accessible	accessible	zugänglich	accesible	accessibile	acessível
accessoire	accessory	Zubehör(n)	accesorio	accessorio	acessório
accident	accident	Unfall(m)	accidente	incidente	acidente
accidenté, e	injured person	Verunglückte(f, m)	accidentado, a	accidentato, a	acidentado, a
acclamer	cheer	zu = jubeln	aclamar	acclamare	aclamar
accompagner	accompany	begleiten	acompañar	accompagnare	acompanhar
accomplir	accomplish	vollführen	realizar, efectuar	compiere, effettuare	realizar
accomplir	perform, accomplish	aus = führen, vollenden	cumplir, realizar	compiere	realizar
accomplir	achieve	vollbringen	ejecutar, realizar	realizzare, compiere	realizar
accord	agreement	Einverständnis(n)	acuerdo	accordo	acordo
accord(d')	all right, O.K	einverstanden, okay	vale, de acuerdo	accordo(d')	acordo(de)
accord(être d')	agree	überein = stimmen	acuerdo(estar de)	accordo(essere d')	acordo(estar de)
accorder	grant	bewilligen	conceder	concedere, accordare	conceder
accoster	berth	an = legen	abordar	accostare, attraccare	acostar
accouchement	delivery; birth	Entbindung(f)	parto	parto	parto

9

French	English	German	Spanish	Italian	Portuguese
accoucher	birth(give)	entbinden	dar a luz	partorire	dar à luz
accoupler(s')	mate	paaren, sich	aparearse	accoppiarsi	acasalar-se
accoutumance	habituation	Gewöhnung(f)	hábito	abitudine	habituação
accoutumance	addiction	Abhängigkeit(f)	adicto, dependencia	assuefazione	dependência
accrocher	hang	auf = hängen	colgar	appendere	pendurar
accrocher	connect, link	an = hängen	enganchar	agganciare	engatar
accroissement	increase	Zuwachs(m)	crecimiento	crescita	crescimento
accroître	increase	zu = nehmen	incrementar	accrescere	aumentar
accueil	reception; welcome	Empfang(m), Aufnahme f	recepción	accoglienza	recepção
accueillant, e	hospitable	gastfreundlich	acogedor, a	accogliente	acolhedor, a
accueillir	welcome	empfangen, auf = nehmen	acoger, recibir	accogliere	acolher, receber
accumuler	accumulate	an = häufen	acumular	accumulare	acumular
accusation	accusation, charge	Anklage(f)	acusación	accusa	acusação
accusé, e	accused(the)	Angeklagte(f, m)	acusado, a; reo	accusato, a	acusado, a; réu(ré)
accuser	accuse	an = klagen	acusar	accusare	acusar
acharner(s')	persist	beharren	empeñarse	accanirsi	insistir
achat	purchase	Kauf(m)	compra	acquisto	compra
acheter	buy	kaufen	comprar	comprare	comprar
acheteur, se	buyer; shopper	Käufer(in f)m	comprador, a	acquirente	comprador, a
achever	complete, finish	beenden	acabar	terminare, finire	acabar
acide	acid	Säure(f)	ácido	acido	ácido
acier	steel	Stahl(m)	acero	acciaio	aço
à côté	next to, beside	neben, daneben	al lado	accanto; vicino, a	ao lado
acoustique	acoustics	Akustik(f)	acústica	acustica	acústica
acquérir	acquire	erwerben; erlangen	adquirir	acquistare	adquirir, obter
acquis, e	acquired	erworben	adquirido, a	acquisito, a	adquirido, a
acrobate	acrobat	Akrobat(in f)m	acróbata	acrobata	acrobata
acrobatie	acrobatics, stunts	Akrobatik(f)	acrobacia	acrobazia	acrobacia
acrylique	acrylic	Akryl(n)	acrílico	acrilico	acrílico
acte	action, act	Handlung(f)	acto	atto	acto, acção
acteur, actrice	actor, actress(-es)	Schauspieler(in f)m	actor, actriz	attore, attrice	actor, actriz
actif, ive	active	aktiv, tatkräftig	activo, a	attivo, a	activo, a
action	action	Vorgehen(n), Handlung	acción	azione	acção
action	share	Aktie(f)	acción	azione	acção
actionnaire	shareholder	Aktionär(m)	accionista	azionista	accionista
activer	activate	beschleunigen	activar	attivare	activar
activité	activity	Tätigkeit(f)	actividad	attività	actividade
actualiser	update	aktualisieren	actualizar	attualizzare	actualizar
actualités(T.V)	news	Nachrichten(pl.)	telediario	telegiornale	telejornal
actuel, le	present, current	aktuell, gegenwärtig	actual	attuale	actual
actuellement	now, at present	zur Zeit	actualmente	attualmente	actualmente
acuponcture	acupuncture	Akupunktur(f)	acupuntura	agopuntura	acupunctura
adaptation	adaptation	Anpassung(f)	adaptación	adattamento	adaptação
adapter	adapt, adjust	an = passen	adaptar	adattare	adaptar
adapter(s')	adapt(to)	an = passen, sich	adaptarse(a)	adattarsi(a)	adaptar-se(a)
addition, somme	addition, sum	Addition(f), Summe(f)	adición, suma	addizione, somma	adição, soma
additionnel, le	additional	hinzugefügt	adicional	addizionale	adicional
adepte	follower	Anhänger(in f)m	adepto, a; seguidor	seguace, adepto, a	adepto, a; seguidor, a
adéquat, e	appropriate	passend	adecuado, a	adeguato, a	adequado, a
adhérent, e	member	Mitglied(n)	adherente	aderente, socio	aderente
adhérer	join	Mitglied werden	adherir a	aderire a	aderir a
adhésif, ive	adhesive	klebrig, anhaftend	adhesivo, a	adesivo, a	adesivo, a
adhésion	membership	Beitritt(m)	adhesión	adesione	adesão
adieu!	good bye!	tschüß!, lebe wohl!	adiós(!)	addio!	adeus!
adjectif	adjective	Adjektiv(n)	adjetivo	aggettivo	adjectivo
adjoint, e	assistant	Gehilfe(m); Hilfs-	adjunto, a	aggiunto, a; vice	adjunto, a
adjoint, e	deputy	Stellvertreter(in f)m	substituto, a	assessore	adjunto, a
adjudication	auction	Versteigerung(f)	adjudicación	aggiudicazione	adjudicação
admettre	admit	zu = geben; zu = lassen	admitir	ammettere	admitir
administratif, ve	administrative	Verwaltungs-	administrativo, a	amministrativo, a	administrativo, a
administration	administration	Verwaltung(f)	administración	amministrazione	administração
administrer	manage, run	verwalten	administrar	amministrare	administrar
admirateur, trice	admirer, fan	Bewunderer(in f)m	admirador, a	ammiratore, trice	admirador, a
admiration	admiration	Bewunderung(f)	admiración	ammirazione	admiração
admissible	admissible	zulässig, annehmbar	admisible	ammissibile	admissível
admission	admission	Zulassung, Einweisung	admisión	ammissione	admissão
adolescent, e	teenager	Jugendliche(m, f)	adolescente	adolescente	adolescente
adopter	adopt	adoptieren	adoptar	adottare	adoptar

French	English	German	Spanish	Italian	Portuguese
adorable	adorable, lovely	reizend	adorable	adorabile	adorável
adorer	adore	an = beten	adorar	adorare	adorar
adresse	address(-es)	Anschrift(f), Adresse	dirección	indirizzo	endereço, morada
adroit, e	skilled	geschickt	diestro, a	abile	destro, a; hábil
adulte	adult	Erwachsene(f, m)	adulto, a	adulto, a	adulto, a
adultère	adultery	Ehebruch(m)	adulterio	adulterio	adultério
adverbe	adverb	Umstandswort, Adverb	adverbio	avverbio	advérbio
adversaire	opponent	Gegner(in f)m	adversario, a	avversario, a	adversário, a
adverse	adverse, opposing	feindlich, gegnerisch	adverso, a	avverso, a	adverso, a
aérer	air, ventilate	lüften	airear, ventilar	arieggiare	arejar, ventilar
aérien, ne	aerial, air	Luft-	aéreo, a	aereo, a	aéreo, a
aérogramme	aerogram	Funkspruch(m)	aerograma	aerogramma	aerograma
aéronautique	aeronautics	Luftfahrt(f)	aeronáutica	aeronautica	aeronáutica
aéroport	airport	Flughafen(m)	aeropuerto	aeroporto	aeroporto
affaiblir	weaken	schwächen	debilitar	indebolire	enfraquecer
affaire	affair, matter	Affäre(f), Sache(f)	asunto	faccenda, affare	assunto
affaires	business	Geschäfte(n, pl.)	negocios	affari	negócios
affaires	things	Sachen(pl)	cosas	roba, oggetti	coisas
affamé, e	starving, hungry	hungrig	hambriento, a	affamato, a	esfomeado, a
affection	affection, love	Zuneigung(f)	afecto; afección	affetto	afeição; afecto
affectueux, se	affectionate	liebevoll	afectuoso, a	affettuoso, a	afectuoso, a
affichage	putting up posters	Anschlag, Plakatierung	anuncios(fijación)	affissione	afixação
affiche	poster, placard	Plakat(n)	cartel	manifesto	cartaz
afficher	post up, put up	an = schlagen	anunciar	affiggere	afixar
afficher(s')	display	erscheinen	visualizar	apparire	mostrar, dar
affinité	affinity	Ähnlichkeit(f)	afinidad	affinità	afinidade
affirmer	assert, maintain	behaupten	afirmar	affermare	afirmar
affliger	distress, afflict	heim = suchen; betrüben	afligir	affliggere	afligir
affluence	rush	Andrang(m)	afluencia	affluenza	afluência
affluence	crowd	Gedränge(n)	afluencia	afflusso	afluência
affolement	panic	Panik(f)	pánico	panico	pânico
affoler(s')	panic	Panik geraten(in)	ponerse nervioso, a	disorientarsi	afligir-se
affranchir	stamp	frankieren, freimachen	franquear	affrancare	franquear
affreux, se	awful	schrecklich	horrendo, a	spaventoso, a	horrível
affrontement	confrontation	Konfrontation(f)	enfrentamiento	affrontamento	afrontamento
affronter	confront, face	entgegen = treten	afrontar	affrontare	afrontar
affût	wait for(in)	Versteck(n)	acecho(al)	agguato	espreita de(à)
afin de	in order to	um...zu	a fin de	per; allo scopo di	a fim de
afin que	so that	damit	a fin de que	affinché	a fim de que
agacement	irritation	Ärger(m)	fastidio	irritazione	irritação
âge	age	Alter(n)	edad	età	idade
âgé, e	old	alt	anciano, a	anziano, a	idoso, a
agence	agency	Agentur(f); Filiale(f)	agencia	agenzia	agência
agencement	layout	Anlage(f)	disposición	disposizione	disposição
agenda	diary	Taschenkalender(m)	agenda	agenda	agenda
agenouiller(s')	kneel	hin = knien, sich	arrodillarse	inginocchiare(-rsi)	ajoelhar-se
agent	agent	Agent(in f)m	agente	agente	agente
aggraver	worsen, aggravate	verschlimmern	empeorar	aggravare	agravar
agile	agile, nimble	flink	ágil	agile	ágil
agir	act	handeln	actuar	agire	agir
agitation	agitation; unrest	Aufregung(f); Unruhe f	agitación	agitazione	agitação
agiter	shake	schütteln	agitar	agitare	agitar
agiter	wave	schwenken	agitar	agitare	agitar
agneau	lamb	Lamm(n)	cordero	agnello	cordeiro
agonie	agony	Todeskampf(m), Agonie	agonía	agonia	agonia
agrandir	enlarge	vergrößern	ampliar	ingrandire	ampliar
agréable	pleasant, nice	angenehm	agradable	gradevole, piacevole	agradável
agréer	accept, approve	genehmigen, zu = lassen	aceptar	gradire, accettare	aceitar
agrément	approval, consent	Zustimmung(f)(verbal)	consentimiento	consenso	consentimento
agresser	attack, assault	an = greifen	agredir	aggredire	agredir
agresseur	attacker	Angreifer(in f)m	agresor, a	aggressore	agressor, a
agression	attack	Aggression(f), Angriff	agresión	aggressione	agressão
agricole	agricultural	landwirtschaftlich	agrícola	agricolo, a	agrícola
agriculteur	farmer	Landwirt(in f)m	agricultor, a	agricoltore	agricultor, a
agriculture	agriculture	Landwirtschaft(f)	agricultura	agricoltura	agricultura
ahuri, e	stupefied	verdutzt	espantado, a	attonito, a	pasmado, a
aide	help	Hilfe(f)	ayuda	aiuto	ajuda
aider	help, assist, aid	helfen	ayudar	aiutare	ajudar

French	English	German	Spanish	Italian	Portuguese
aïeux	ancestors	Ahnen(pl.)	antepasados	antenati	antepassados
aigle	eagle	Adler(m)	águila	aquila	águia
aigre	sour	sauer	agrio, a	aspro, a; agro, a	azedo, a
aigu, ë	sharp, shrill	hoch, schrill	agudo, a	acuto, a	agudo, a
aigue-marine	aquamarine	Aquamarin(m)	aguamarina	acquamarina	água marinha
aiguille	needle	Nadel(f)	aguja	ago	agulha
aiguisé, e	sharp	scharf	afilado, a	affilato, a	afiado, a
aiguiser	sharpen	schärfen	afilar	affilare	afiar
aile	wing	Flügel(m)	ala	ala	asa
ailleurs	somewhere else	woanders	otra parte(en)	altrove	noutro sítio
ailleurs(d')	moreover, besides	übrigens	por otra parte	del resto, d'altronde	aliás
aimable	nice	lieb, nett	amable	amabile	amável
aimant	magnet	Magnet(m)	imán	calamita	íman
aimer	love	lieben	amar, querer	amare, volere bene	amar, gostar de
aimer	like	gern haben	gustar(le)	piacere, amare	gostar(de)
aimer	enjoy	mögen; gern mögen	gustar	piacere	gostar
aîné, e	oldest, eldest	Ältere(f, m)	primogénito, a	primogenito, a	velho, a(o, a mais)
ainsi	so, thus	so	así	così	assim
air	air	Luft(f)	aire	aria	ar
air	tune	Melodie(f)	melodía	melodia	melodia
aire, zone	area	Bereich(m), Gebiet(n)	área, zona	area, zona	área, zona
aise(être à l')	ease(be at)	wohl fühlen, sich	gusto(estar a)	agio(essere a)	vontade(estar à)
ajourner	postpone, adjourn	vertagen	aplazar	rimandare, aggiornare	adiar
ajouter	add	hinzu = fügen	añadir	aggiungere	ajuntar, juntar
ajuster	adjust	ein = stellen	ajustar	aggiustare	ajustar
à la fois	both	beide, beides	ambos, ambas	entrambi	ambos, os dois
alarme	alarm	Alarm(m)	alarma	allarme	alarme
album	album	Album(n)	álbum	album	álbum
alcool	alcohol	Alkohol(m)	alcohol	alcol, alcool	álcool
alcool(s)	spirit(s)	Alkohol(m)	alcohol	alcolico	álcool
alcoolisme	alcoholism	Alkoholmißbrauch(m)	alcoholismo	alcolismo	alcoolismo
aléa	hazard	Zufall(m)	riesgo, azar	rischio	acaso
aléatoire	aleatory, uncertain	unsicher, ungewiß	aleatorio, a	aleatorio, a	aleatório, a; incerto
alentours	surroundings	Umgebung(f)	alrededores	dintorni	arredores
alerte	alert	Alarm(m)	alerta	allarme	alerta, alarme
algèbre	algebra	Algebra(f)	álgebra	algebra	álgebra
algue	seaweed, alga(ae)	Alge(f)	alga	alga	alga
alibi	alibi	Alibi(n)	coartada	alibi	alibi
alignement	alignment	Ausrichtung(f)	alineación	allineamento	alinhamento
aliment	food	Lebensmittel(n, pl)	alimento	alimento, cibo	alimento
alimentation	feeding; food	Ernährung(f)	alimentación	alimentazione	alimentação
alimentation	food shop	Lebensmittelladen(m)	alimentación	alimentari(negozio)	mercearia
alimentation	supplying	Versorgung(f)	abastecimiento	rifornimento	abastecimento
allaiter	feed	stillen	pecho(dar el)	allattare	aleitar
allée	path, lane	Allee(f)	paseo, calle	viale	alameda
alléger	lighten	erleichtern	aliviar	alleggerire	aliviar
allégresse	elation	Heiterkeit(f)	júbilo, alegría	esultanza	júbilo, alegria
aller	go	gehen, fahren nach	ir(a, por, hacia)	andare, recarsi	ir
aller chercher	go to fetch/get	ab = holen	ir a buscar	andare a prendere	ir buscar
allergie	allergy	Allergie(f)	alergia	allergia	alergia
alliage	alloy	Legierung(f)	aleación	lega	liga
alliance	alliance	Bündnis(n)	alianza	alleanza	aliança
allier	ally	verbünden	aliar, unir	alleare, unire	aliar, unir
allô!	hello!	Ja, bitte?	dígame(!)	pronto!	está lá?; estou?
allocation	allowance	Beihilfe(f), Zulage(f)	subsidio	assegnazione; assegno	subsídio, abono
allocution	speech(short)	Ansprache(kurze)(f)	alocución	allocuzione	alocução
allonger	lengthen	verlängern	alargar	allungare	alongar
allonger(s')	lie down	hin = legen, sich	acostarse	sdraiarsi	estender-se
allopathie	allopathy	Allopathie(f)	alopatía	allopatia	alopatia
allouer	allocate	zu = teilen, bewilligen	conceder	assegnare	conceder
allumage	ignition	Zündung(f)	encendido	accensione	ignição
allumer	switch on	an = machen	encender	accendere	acender
allumer	light	an = zünden	encender	accendere	acender
allumette	match(-es)	Streichholz(n)	cerilla	fiammifero	fósforo
alors	then	dann	entonces	allora	então
alourdir	make heavy	erschweren	pesado(hacer)	appesantire	pesado(tornar)
alphabet	alphabet	Alphabet(n)	alfabeto	alfabeto	alfabeto
alpiniste	mountaineer	Alpinist(m)	alpinista	alpinista	alpinista

French	English	German	Spanish	Italian	Portuguese
alternatif, ive	alternating(ive)	alternativ	alternativo, a	alternativo, a	alternativo, a
alterner	alternate	ab = wechseln	alternar	alternare	alternar
altitude	altitude, height	Höhe(f)	altitud, altura	altitudine	altitude
aluminium	aluminium	Aluminium(n)	aluminio	alluminio	alumínio
amande	almond	Mandel(f)	almendra	mandorla	amêndoa
amant, e	lover	Geliebte(f, m)	amante	amante	amante
amas	pile	Haufen(m)	montón	mucchio	amontoado
amateur	amateur	Amateur(in f)m	aficionado, a	dilettante	amador, a
amateur de	lover of	Liebhaber(in f)m	amante de	appassionato, a	apreciador, a
ambassade	embassy	Botschaft(f)	embajada	ambasciata	embaixada
ambassadeur	ambassador	Botschafter(in f)m	embajador	ambasciatore	embaixador
ambiance	atmosphere	Stimmung(f)	ambiente	atmosfera	ambiente
ambigu, ë	ambiguous	zweideutig, mehrdeutig	ambiguo, a	ambiguo, a	ambíguo, a
ambitieux, se	ambitious	ehrgeizig	ambicioso, a	ambizioso, a	ambicioso, a
ambition	ambition	Ehrgeiz(m)	ambición	ambizione	ambição
ambulance	ambulance	Krankenwagen(m)	ambulancia	ambulanza	ambulância
âme	soul	Seele(f)	alma	anima	alma
amélioration	improvement	Verbesserung(f)	mejora; mejoría	miglioramento	melhoramento
améliorer	improve	verbessern	mejorar	migliorare	melhorar
aménager	fit out; convert	ein = richten	acondicionar	sistemare	arranjar, dispor
amener	bring	mit = bringen	traer	portare	trazer
amende	fine	Geldstrafe(f)	multa	multa	multa
amender	amend	verbessern, ändern	enmendar	emendare	emendar
amer, ère	bitter	bitter; sauer	amargo, a	amaro, a	amargo, a
ameublement	furnishing	Einrichtung(f)	mobiliario	arredamento, mobilio	mobiliário
ami, e	friend	Freund(in f)m	amigo, a	amico, a	amigo, a
amical, e	friendly	freundschaftlich	amistoso, a	amichevole	amigável
amiral	admiral	Admiral(m)	almirante	ammiraglio	almirante
amitié	friendship	Freundschaft(f)	amistad	amicizia	amizade
amnésie	amnesia	Gedächtnisschwund(m)	amnesia	amnesia	amnésia
amnistie	amnesty	Amnestie(f)	amnistía	amnistia	amnistia
amortir	absorb, cushion	dämpfen	amortiguar	attutire	amortecer
amortisseur	shock absorber	Stoßdämpfer(m)	amortiguador	ammortizzatore	amortecedor
amour	love	Liebe(f)	amor	amore	amor
amoureux, se	love(in)	verliebt	enamorado, a	innamorato, a	apaixonado, a
amovible	removable	auswechselbar	amovible	amovibile	amovível
ample	ample; loose	weit	amplio, a	ampio, a	amplo, a
ampleur	scale, size	Weite(f), Größe(f)	amplitud	ampiezza	amplidão
amplitude	amplitude	Amplitude(f)	amplitud	ampiezza	amplitude
ampoule	bulb	Glühbirne(f)	bombilla	lampadina	lâmpada
ampoule	blister	Blase(f)	ampolla	bolla, vescica	empola
amputer	amputate	amputieren	amputar	amputare	amputar
amusant, e	funny, amusing	lustig, amüsant	divertido, a	buffo, a; divertente	divertido, a
amusant, e	amusing, funny	amüsant, drollig	divertido, a	divertente	engraçado, a
amusement	amusement, fun	Vergnügen(n)	diversión	divertimento	divertimento
amuser(s')	fun(have)	amüsieren, sich	divertir(se)	divertire(-rsi)	divertir-se
amygdale(s)	tonsils	Mandeln(f, pl)	amígdalas	tonsilla	amígdala
an	year	Jahr(n)	año	anno	ano
analogue	analogous, similar	analog	análogo, a	analogo, a	análogo, a
analyse	analysis(-ses)	Analyse(f)	análisis	analisi	análise
analyser	analyse	analysieren	analizar	analizzare	analisar
ananas	pineapple	Ananas(f)	piña	ananas	ananás
anarchie	anarchy	Anarchie(f)	anarquía	anarchia	anarquia
anatomie	anatomy	Anatomie(f)	anatomía	anatomia	anatomia
ancêtre	ancestor	Ahn(m)	antepasado, a	antenato, a	antepassado, a
ancien, ne	old	alt	antiguo, a	vecchio, a; antico, a	antigo, a
ancien, ne	ancient	alt	antiguo, a	antico, a	antigo, a
ancien, ne	former	ehemalig	ex, antiguo, a	ex	antigo, a
ancre	anchor	Anker(m)	ancla	àncora	âncora
anéantir	annihilate, destroy	vernichten	aniquilar	annientare	aniquilar
anecdote	anecdote	Anekdote(f)	anécdota	aneddoto	anedota
anémie	anaemia	Blutarmut(f)	anemia	anemia	anemia
anesthésie	anaesthetic	Narkose(f)	anestesia	anestesia	anestesia
ange	angel	Engel(m)	ángel	angelo	anjo
angine	sore throat	Angina(f)	angina	angina, tonsillite	angina
angle	angle	Winkel(m)	ángulo	angolo	ângulo
angoisse	anguish, distress	Angst(f)	angustia	angoscia	angústia
animal	animal	Tier(n)	animal	animale	animal

13

French	English	German	Spanish	Italian	Portuguese
animateur, trice	leader, organiser	Leiter/in, Unterhalter	animador, a	animatore, trice	animador, a
animé, e	lively	lebhaft	animado, a	animato, a	animado, a
animer	animate	beleben	animar	animare	animar
animer	liven up	Stimmung machen	animar	animare	animar
anneau	ring	Ring(m)	anilla, anillo	anello	anel
année	year	Jahr(n)	año	annata, anno	ano
annexe	annexe	Anhang(m), Anlage(f)	anexo; anejo	annesso	anexo
anniversaire	birthday	Geburtstag(m)	cumpleaños	compleanno	aniversário
anniversaire	anniversary	Jahrestag(m)	aniversario	anniversario	aniversário
annonce	notice	Anzeige(f)	anuncio	annuncio	anúncio
annoncer	announce	an = kündigen	anunciar	annunciare	anunciar
annuaire	directory	Adreßbuch; Telefonbuch	anuario, guía	elenco, annuario	anuário
annuel, le	yearly, annual	jährlich	anual	annuale	anual
annulaire	annular, ring-	ringförmig	anular	anulare	anelar
annuler	cancel	annullieren	cancelar, anular	annullare	anular
annuler	delete	streichen	borrar	annullare	suprimir
annuler	quash	auf = heben	anular	annullare	anular
annuler	annul	ungültig erklären	anular	annullare	anular
anomalie	anomaly	Anomalie(f)	anomalía	anomalia	anomalia
anonymat	anonymity	Anonymität(f)	anonimato	anonimato	anonimato
anonyme	anonymous	anonym, unbekannt	anónimo, a	anonimo, a	anónimo, a
anormal, e	not normal	anormal	anormal	anormale	anormal
anse	handle	Griff(m)	asa	ansa	asa
antécédent, e	previous	vorhergehend	antecedente	antecedente	antecedente
antenne	aerial, antenna(e)	Antenne(f)	antena	antenna	antena
antérieur, e	previous, former	vorhergehend	anterior	anteriore	anterior
antérieur, e	prior	früher	anterior	anteriore	anterior
antibiotique	antibiotic	Antibiotikum(n)	antibiótico	antibiotico	antibiótico
anticiper	anticipate	vor = greifen	anticipar	anticipare	antecipar
antique	antique, ancient	antik	antiguo, a	antico, a	antigo, a
antiquité	antiquity	Antiquität(f)	antigüedad	antichità	antiguidade
antiquités	antique shop	Antiquitäten	anticuario	antiquariato	antiguidades
antiseptique	antiseptic	antiseptisch	antiséptico, a	antisettico, a	antiséptico, a
antivol	anti-theft lock	Diebstahlsicherung(f)	antirrobo	antifurto	alarme
anxieux, se	anxious	ängstlich	ansioso, a	ansioso, a	ansioso, a
août	August	August(m)	agosto	agosto	Agosto
apaiser	calm, soothe	beruhigen	apaciguar	calmare	acalmar
apercevoir	perceive, notice	bemerken	avistar, divisar	scorgere	avistar
apéritif	aperitif, drink	Aperitif(m)	aperitivo	aperitivo	aperitivo
aphone	lose one's voice	stimmlos, heiser	afónico, a	áfono, a	áfono, a
aplanir	level	ebnen	aplanar	spianare	aplanar
aplatir	flatten	glätten, ab = flachen	allanar, aplastar	appiattire	achatar, alisar
apparaître	appear	erscheinen	aparecer	apparire	aparecer
appareil	appliance, device	Apparat(m)	aparato	apparecchio	aparelho
appareil photo	camera	Kamera(f)	cámara fotográfica	macchina fotografica	máquina fotográfica
apparence	appearance, look	Aussehen(n)	apariencia	apparenza	aparência
appartement	flat, apartment	Wohnung(f)	piso	appartamento	apartamento
appartenir(à)	belong to	gehören	pertenecer	appartenere	pertencer
appât	bait	Köder(m)	cebo	esca	engodo, isca
appel	call	Ruf(m)(Zu-, An-)	llamada	chiamata	chamada
appel	appeal	Berufung(f)	apelación	appello	apelação
appeler	call	rufen(an =), heißen	llamar	chiamare	chamar
appétit	appetite	Appetit(m)	apetito	appetito	apetite
applaudir	applaud, clap	klatschen	aplaudir	applaudire	aplaudir
appliquer	apply	an = wenden	aplicar	applicare	aplicar
apporter	bring	bringen	traer	apportare, portare	trazer
appréciation	appreciation	Beurteilung(f)	apreciación	giudizio	apreciação
apprécier	appreciate	schätzen	apreciar	apprezzare	apreciar
appréhension	apprehension	Furcht(f)	aprensión, recelo	apprensione	apreensão
apprendre	learn	lernen	aprender	imparare	aprender
apprendre	hear(of)	erfahren	enterarse	apprendere, sapere	saber
apprentissage	apprenticeship	Lehre(f), Lehrjahre(f)	aprendizaje	apprendistato	aprendizagem
apprentissage	learning	Lernen(n)	estudio	tirocinio	aprendizagem
apprivoiser	tame	zähmen	domesticar	addomesticare	domesticar
approcher(s')	approach	nähern, sich	acercar(se)	avvicinarsi	aproximar-se
approuver	approve	genehmigen	aprobar	approvare	aprovar
approvisionner	supply	versorgen	aprovisionar	rifornire	abastecer
approximatif, ive	approximate	ungefähr	aproximativo, a	approssimativo, a	aproximado, a

14

French	English	German	Spanish	Italian	Portuguese
appui	support	Stütze(f)	apoyo	appoggio	apoio
appuyer(s')	lean on(against)	stützen, sich	apoyar(se)	appoggiarsi	apoiar-se
après	after; afterwards	nach	después	dopo	depois
après-midi	afternoon	Nachmittag(m)	tarde	pomeriggio	tarde
apte	able, qualified	fähig; tauglich	apto, a	adatto, a	apto, a
aptitude	ability, aptitude	Fähigkeit(f)	aptitud(es)	attitudine	aptidão, talento
aquarium	aquarium	Aquarium(n)	acuario	acquario	aquário
aquatique	aquatic	Wasser-	acuático, a	acquatico, a	aquático, a
araignée	spider	Spinne(f)	araña	ragno	aranha
arbitraire	arbitrary	willkürlich	arbitrario, a	arbitrario, a	arbitrário, a
arbitre	referee	Schiedsrichter(in f)m	árbitro	arbitro	árbitro
arbre	tree	Baum(m)	árbol	albero	árvore
arc	bow	Bogen(m)	arco	arco	arco
arc	arc	Halbkreis(m)	arco	arco	arco
arc-en-ciel	rainbow	Regenbogen(m)	arco iris	arcobaleno	arco-íris
archaïque	archaic	archaisch	arcaico, a	arcaico, a	arcaico, a
arche	arch	Bogen(m), Gewölbe(n)	arca	arco, volta	arco
archéologie	archaeology	Archeologie(f)	arqueología	archeologia	arqueologia
archipel	archipelago	Inselgruppe(f)	archipiélago	arcipelago	arquipélago
architecte	architect	Architekt(in f)m	arquitecto, a	architetto	arquitecto, a
architecture	architecture	Architektur(f)	arquitectura	architettura	architectura
archives	archives	Archiv(n)	archivos	archivi	arquivo
ardoise	slate	Schiefer(m)	pizarra	ardesia	ardósia, lousa
arène	arena	Arena(f)	arena	arena	arena
arène(s)	bull ring, arena	Kampfbahn(f)	plaza de toros	arena	praça de touros
arête	fish-bone, bone	Gräte(f)	espina	lisca	espinha
argent	money	Geld(n)	dinero	denaro; soldi	dinheiro
argent	silver	Silber(n)	plata	argento	prata
argile	clay	Ton(m), Lehm(m)	arcilla	argilla	argila
argument	argument	Argument(n)	argumento	argomento	argumento
argumenter	argue	verhandeln	argüir, argumentar	argomentare	argumentar
aride	arid	dürr, trocken	árido, a	arido, a	árido, a
aristocrate	aristocrat	Adlige(f, m)	aristócrata	aristocratico, a	aristocrata
arithmétique	arithmetic	Arithmetik(f)	aritmética	aritmetica	aritmética
armateur	ship-owner	Reeder(m)	armador	armatore	armador
arme	weapon, arm	Waffe(f)	arma	arma	arma
arme	arm	Waffe(f)	arma	arma; armi	arma
armée	army	Armee(f)	ejército	esercito	exército
armement	armament, weapons	Bewaffnung(f)	armamento	armamento	armamento
armoire	wardrobe	Schrank(m)(Kleider-)	armario	armadio	armário
armoire	cupboard	Schrank(m)	armario	armadio	armário
arôme	aroma	Aroma(n)	aroma	aroma	aroma, cheiro
arracher	tear out; tear off	weg = reißen, aus = reißen	arrancar	strappare, togliere	arrancar
arrangement	arrangement	Anordnung(f)	arreglo	ordinamento	arranjo
arrangement	arrangement	Abmachung(f)	arreglo, acuerdo	accordo	compromisso
arranger	arrange	arrangieren	arreglar	sistemare	arranjar
arrestation	arrest	Verhaftung(f)	arresto	arresto	detenção
arrêt	stop	Pause(f), Stillstand	parada	fermata	paragem
arrêt, cessation	stop, cessation	Stillstand(m)	cese	cessazione, tregua	cessação
arrêter	stop	halten(an-, auf-)	parar	fermare	parar
arrêter(s')	stop	stehen = bleiben	pararse	fermarsi	parar
arrhes	deposit	Anzahlung(f)	señal(dejar)	caparra	sinal
arrière, derrière	behind, back	hinten, zurück	atrás	dietro, posteriore	atrás
arrière(en)	backward(s)	rückwärts	atrás(para)	indietro	trás(para)
arrivée	arrival	Ankunft(f)	llegada; meta	arrivo	chegada
arriver	arrive, come	an = kommen	llegar	arrivare	chegar
arriver	occur, happen	geschehen	ocurrir, suceder	succedere	acontecer
arriver(à)	attain	erlangen, erreichen	lograr, alcanzar	raggiungere	alcançar, atingir
arroser	water	gießen, begießen	regar	innaffiare	regar
arsenal	arsenal, armoury	Arsenal(n)	arsenal	arsenale	arsenal
art	art	Kunst(f)	arte	arte	arte
artère	artery	Ader(f); Arterie(f)	arteria	arteria	artéria
arthrose	arthritis	Arthrose(f)	artrosis	artrosi	artrose
article	article	Artikel(m)	artículo	articolo	artigo
article	article	Gesetzesartikel(m)	artículo	articolo	artigo
article	item	Artikel(m)	artículo	articolo	artigo
articulation	joint	Gelenk(n)	articulación	articolazione	articulação
artificiel, le	artificial	künstlich	artificial	artificiale	artificial

French	English	German	Spanish	Italian	Portuguese
artisan	craftsman(-men)	Handwerker(in f)m	artesano	artigiano	artesão
artiste	artist	Künstler(in f)m	artista	artista	artista
arts martiaux	martial arts	Kriegskunst(f)	artes marciales	arti marziali	artes marciais
ascenseur	lift, elevator	Aufzug(m)	ascensor	ascensore	elevador
asile	mental hospital	Irrenhaus(n)	manicomio	manicomio	manicômio
asile	asylum(political)	Asyl(n)	asilo	asilo	asilo
aspect	aspect	Aussehen(n)	aspecto	aspetto	aspecto
asphyxie	suffocation	Ersticken(n)	asfixia	asfissia	asfixia
aspirateur	vacuum-cleaner	Staubsauger(m)	aspirador	aspirapolvere	aspirador
aspirer	inhale, suck in(up)	ein = atmen, saugen	aspirar	aspirare	aspirar
aspirine	aspirin	Aspirin(n)	aspirina	aspirina	aspirina
assaisonnement	seasoning	Würze(f)	aliño	condimento	tempero
assassin	murderer	Mörder(in f)m	asesino, a	assassino, a	assassino, a
assassinat	murder	Mord(m)	asesinato	assassinio	assassínio
assaut	assault, attack	Angriff(m)	asalto	assalto	assalto
assemblage	assembly	Montage(f)	ensambladura	assemblaggio	montagem
assemblée	meeting, assembly	Versammlung(f)	asamblea	assemblea	assembleia
assembler	assemble	zusammen = setzen	ensamblar	assemblare	juntar
assembler	assemble	versammeln	reunir	radunare, riunire	reunir
asseoir(s')	sit(down)	setzen, sich	sentarse	sedersi	sentar-se
assez	enough; rather	genug	bastante(s)	abbastanza	bastante
assez!; suffit!	enough!(that's)	das langt, jetzt langt	basta(!)	basta così!	basta!, chega!
assiette	plate	Teller(m)	plato	piatto	prato
assis, e	seated	sitzen	sentado, a	seduto, a	sentado, a
assistance	assistance	Hilfe(f)	asistencia	assistenza	assistência
assistant, e	assistant	Assistent(in f)m	asistente, a	assistente	assistente
assister	attend	assistieren	asistir	assistere	assistir
assister	attend	bei = wohnen	concurrir a	presenziare	assistir a
association	association	Verband(m)	asociación	associazione	associação
associé, e	associate, partner	Teilhaber(in f)m	socio, a, asociado	socio, a	sócio, a
associer	combine, associate	verbinden	asociar	associarsi	associar
associer à(s')	join	an = schließen, sich	asociarse(a, con)	associarsi(a, con)	associar-se a
assommer	knock out	nieder = schlagen	dejar k.o.	stordire	espancar
assortiment	assortment, set	sortiment(n)	surtido	assortimento	sortimento
assujettir	subject(to)	unterwerfen	someter, sujetar	assoggettare	sujeitar
assumer	assume	übernehmen, nehmen	asumir	assumere	assumir
assurance	insurance	Versicherung(f)	seguro	assicurazione	seguro
assuré, e	insured	versichert	asegurado, a	assicurato, a	segurado, a
assuré, e	assured	sicher	seguro, a	sicuro, a; certo, a	certo, a
assurer(s')	make sure	überzeugen, sich	cerciorarse	accertarsi	verificar
assurer(s')	ensure; insure	versichern; zu = sichern	asegurarse	assicurarsi	assegurar-se
asthme	asthma	Asthma(n)	asma	asma	asma
astre	star	Stern(m), Gestirn(n)	astro	astro	astro
astrologie	astrology	Astrologie(f)	astrología	astrologia	astrologia
astronautique	astronautics	Weltraumfahrt(f)	astronaútica	astronautica	astronáutica
astronomie	astronomy	Astronomie(f)	astronomía	astronomia	astronomia
astuce	trick	List(f), Trick(m)	astucia	astuzia	astúcia
astucieux, se	astute, clever	verschmitzt, schlau	astuto, a	astuto, a	astucioso, a
atelier	workshop	Werkstatt(f)	taller	officina	oficina
athlète	athlete	Athlet(in f)m	atleta	atleta	atleta
athlétisme	athletics	Leichtathletik(f)	atletismo	atletismo	atletismo
Atlantique	Atlantic	Atlantik(m)	Atlántico	Atlantico	Atlântico
atmosphère	atmosphere	Atmosphäre(f)	atmósfera	atmosfera	atmosfera
atoll	atoll	Atoll(n)	atolón	atollo	atol
atome	atom	Atom(n)	átomo	atomo	átomo
atomique	atomic	atomar	atómico, a	atomico, a	atómico, a
atomiseur	spray, atomizer	Zerstäuber(m)	atomizador	nebulizzatore	pulverizador
atout, avantage	asset	Trumpf(m), Vorteil(m)	ventaja	vantaggio	vantagem
atroce	atrocious	grausam	atroz	atroce	atroz
attaché, e	attaché	Attaché(m)	agregado, a	addetto, a	adido, a
attaché-case	attaché-case	Aktenkoffer(m)	maletín	valigetta	maleta
attachement	attachment	Verbundenheit(f)	apego, cariño	attaccamento	apego
attacher	attach, tie, fasten	fest = binden, binden	atar	legare	atar
attacher	fasten	befestigen	atar, fijar	attaccare, legare	atar, amarrar
attaque	attack	Angriff(m)	ataque	attacco	ataque
attaquer	attack	an = greifen	atacar	attaccare	atacar
atteindre	reach	erreichen	alcanzar, lograr	raggiungere	atingir
attendant(en)	meanwhile	inzwischen	mientras	attesa(in)	entretanto

16

French	English	German	Spanish	Italian	Portuguese
attendez!	wait!	Moment bitte!	espere(!)	aspetti!	espere!
attendre	wait(for)	warten	esperar	aspettare	esperar
attendre	expect	erwarten	esperar	aspettare	esperar
attendre à(s')	expect	rechnen, mit etwas	esperar(se)	aspettarsi	esperar
attentat	attempt, attack	Attentat(n)	atentado	attentato	atentado
attente	wait(ing)	Warten(n)	espera	attesa	espera
attentif, ive	attentive, careful	aufmerksam	atento, a	attento, a	atento, a
attention	care, caution	Sorgfalt(f)	cuidado	accuratezza	atenção, cuidado
attention!	careful!(be)	Achtung!(f)	cuidado(!)	attenzione!, attento!	atenção!, cuidado!
attention(à l')	attention	Aufmerksamkeit(f)	atención a(en)	attenzione	cuidado(ao)
atténuer	attenuate	ab = schwächen; lindern	atenuar	attenuare	atenuar
atterrir	land	landen	aterrizar	atterrare	aterrar
attirant, e	attractive	anziehend	atrayente	attraente	atraente
attirer	attract	an = ziehen	atraer	attirare	atrair
attirer, séduire	entice	verführen	atraer, seducir	attirare, sedurre	atrair, seduzir
attitude	attitude	Haltung(f)	actitud	atteggiamento	atitude
attraction	attraction	Anziehung(f)	atracción	attrazione	atracção
attraper	catch	fangen	agarrar, coger	acchiappare	agarrar, apanhar
attribuer	attribute	bei = messen	atribuir	attribuire	atribuir
attribuer	assign	zu = teilen	asignar	assegnare	destinar
aube	dawn	Morgendämmerung(f)	alba	alba	amanhecer
auberge	inn	Gasthaus(n)	posada; albergue	locanda	estalagem
aucun, e	no, not any; no one	keiner, keine	ningún, o, a	nessuno, a	nenhum, a
audace	audacity	Kühnheit(f)	audacia	audacia	audácia
au-delà de	beyond	jenseits	más allá de	al di là	além de(para)
au-dessous	below, under(neath)	unter	debajo(de)	sotto(al di)	baixo(por); abaixo
au-dessus	above	über	encima(por, de)	sopra(al di)	cima(por); acima de
au-dessus	overhead	oben	arriba	sopra, in alto	cima(por, em)
audience	audience	Audienz(f)	audiencia	udienza	audiência
auditeur, trice	listener	Zuhörer(in f)m	auditor, a	uditore, uditrice	ouvinte
augmentation	increase, rise	Zunahme(f)	aumento	aumento	aumento
augmentation	increment	Zunahme(f)	incremento	incremento	incremento
augmenter	increase, raise	zu = nehmen	aumentar	aumentare	aumentar
aujourd'hui	today	heute	hoy	oggi	hoje
au lieu de	instead(of)	anstatt	en vez de/lugar de	invece di	em vez de/lugar de
auparavant	before	vorher, zuvor	antes	prima	dantes
auprès de	close to	bei	cerca de	vicino a	perto de
au revoir	good bye, bye-bye	auf Wiedersehen	hasta luego	arrivederci	até logo, adeus!
aurore	dawn	Morgenröte(f)	aurora	aurora	aurora
ausculter	examine	ab = horchen	auscultar	auscultare	auscultar
aussi	also, too; as	auch	también	anche, pure	também
aussitôt	straight away	sofort, sogleich	seguida(en)	subito, appena	imediatamente
austère	austere	streng, hart	austero, a	austero, a	austero, a
auteur	author	Autor(in f)m	autor, a	autore, autrice	autor, a
authentique	authentic, genuine	authentisch	auténtico, a	autentico, a	autêntico, a
authentique	genuine	echt	genuino, a	genuino, a	autêntico, a
autobus	bus	Bus(m)	autobús	autobus	autocarro
autocar	coach	Reisebus(m)	autocar	pullman	autocarro
autographe	autograph	Autogramm(n)	autógrafo	autografo	autógrafo
automate	automaton	Automat(m)	autómata	automa	autómato
automatique	automatic	automatisch	automático, a	automatico, a	automático, a
automne	autumn	Herbst(m)	otoño	autunno	outono
automobile	car	Auto(n)	automóvil	automobile	automóvel
autonome	autonomous	autonom; unabhängig	autónomo, a	autonomo, a	autónomo, a
autonomie	autonomy	Autonomie(f)	autonomía	autonomia	autonomia
autopsie	autopsy	Autopsie(f)	autopsia	autopsia	autópsia
autoriser	authorize	erlauben	autorizar	autorizzare	autorizar
autoritaire	authoritarian	autoritär	autoritario, a	autoritario, a	autoritário, a
autorité	authority	Autorität(f)	autoridad	autorità	autoridade
autoroute	motorway	Autobahn(f)	autopista	autostrada	auto-estrada
auto-stop	hitch-hiking	trampen	autostop, a dedo	autostop	boleia(pedir)
autour	around	um	alrededor	intorno, attorno	redor de(em)
autre	other	andere, sonstige	otro, a	altro, a	outro, a
autre(d')	else	ander; anders	otro, a	altro, a	outro, a
autre	further; other	weiter	otro, a	altro, a	mais
autrefois	past(in the)	früher	antaño	volta(una)	antigamente
autrement	otherwise	anders; sonst	otro modo(de)	altrimenti	outro modo(de)
auxiliaire	auxiliary	Hilfs-; Hilfe(f)	auxiliar	ausiliare	auxiliar

French	English	German	Spanish	Italian	Portuguese
avalanche	avalanche	Lawine(f)	avalancha	valanga	avalanche
avaler	swallow	schlucken	tragar	inghiottire, ingoiare	engolir
avance	advance	Vorsprung(m)	adelanto	anticipo	avanço
avance(être en)	early(to be)	zu früh (sein)	adelantado(estar)	anticipo(essere in)	adiantado(estar)
avancer	advance, move fwd	weiter = gehen	avanzar	procedere	avançar
avancer	advance	voran = gehen; vorrücken	adelantar	avanzare	adiantar
avant	before	vor, vorher	antes(de)	prima	antes(de)
avant	forward(s)	vorwärts	adelante(hacia)	davanti	frente(para a)
avant	front, fore	Vorderteil(n)	delantero, a	anteriore	dianteira
avant(en)	ahead	voran, voraus	adelante	avanti	adiante
avantage	advantage	Vorteil(m)	ventaja	vantaggio	vantagem
avant-bras	fore-arm	Unterarm(m)	antebrazo	avambraccio	antebraço
avare	miserly, mean	geizig	avaro, a	avaro, a	avarento, a
avec	with	mit	con	con	com
avenir	future	Zukunft(f)	porvenir, futuro	avvenire	futuro
aventure	adventure	Abenteuer(n)	aventura	avventura	aventura
avenue	avenue	Allee(f)	avenida	viale	avenida
avertir	warn	warnen	advertir	avvertire	avisar, prevenir
avertissement	warning	Warnung(f)	advertencia	ammonizione	aviso
aveu	confession	Geständnis(n)	confesión	confessione	confissão
aveugle	blind	blind	ciego, a	cieco, a	cego, a
aviateur, trice	aviator	Flieger(m), Pilot(m)	aviador, a	aviatore, trice	aviador, a
aviation	aviation	Luftfahrt(f)	aviación	aviazione	aviação
avide, impatient	eager	begierig	deseoso, a	desideroso, a	ávido, a; desejoso, a
avion	plane, aeroplane	Flugzeug(n)	avión	aereo	avião
aviron	rowing	Rudersport(m)	remo, piragua	canottaggio	remo
avis	opinion	Meinung(f)	opinión	avviso, parere	opinião, parecer
avis	notice	Mitteilung(f)	aviso	avviso	aviso, notícia
avocat, e	lawyer, barrister	Anwalt(m), Anwältin(f)	abogado, a	avvocato, tessa	advogado, a
avoir	have	haben	tener	avere	ter, possuir
avoir	have	haben	haber; tener	avere	haver; ter
avorter	abort	ab = treiben	abortar	abortire	abortar
avortement	abortion	Abtreibung(f)	aborto	aborto	aborto
avouer	confess, admit	gestehen	confesar	confessare	confessar
avril	April	April(m)	abril	aprile	Abril
axe	axis(axes)	Achse(f)	eje	asse	eixo

B

French	English	German	Spanish	Italian	Portuguese
bac	ferry	Fähre(f)	transbordador	traghetto, ferry	barco
baccalauréat	G.C.E. A.Level(s)	Abitur(n)	bachillerato	maturità	bacharelato
bâche	cover	Plane(f)	toldo, lona	telone	toldo
bactérie	bacterium(-eria)	Bakterie(f)	bacteria	batterio	bactéria
baffle	speaker	Lautsprecher(m)	altavoz	altoparlante	alto-falante
bafouiller	splutter, stammer	stammeln	balbucear	farfugliare	balbuciar
bagage(s)	luggage, baggage	Gepäck(n)	equipaje	bagaglio	bagagem
bagages à main	hand luggage	Handgepäck(n)	equipaje de mano	bagaglio a mano	bagagem de mão
bagarre	fight	Schlägerei(f)	riña	rissa, zuffa	briga
bague	ring	Ring(m)	anillo, sortija	anello	anel
baguette	stick	Stöckchen(n)	varilla	bacchetta	vara
bahut, coffre	chest	Truhe(f)	arca, cajón	cassone	baú, arca, armário
baie	bay	Bucht(f)	bahía	baia	baía
baignade	swimming, bathing	Baden(n)	baño	bagno	banho
baigner(se)	bathe; swim	baden; schwimmen	bañarse	bagno(fare il)	banho(tomar)
baignoire	bath	Badewanne(f)	bañera	vasca da bagno	banheira
bâiller	yawn	gähnen	bostezar	sbadigliare	bocejar
bain	bath	Bad(n)	baño	bagno	banho
baiser	kiss	Kuß(m)	beso(dar un)	bacio	beijo
baisse	fall, drop	Senkung(f)	baja	calo	baixa

French	English	German	Spanish	Italian	Portuguese
baisser	drop, lower; fall	senken	rebajar	abbassare, calare	baixar
baisser, abaisser	lower	herunter = lassen	bajar	calare, abbassare	baixar, abaixar
baisser(se)	bend down	bücken, sich	agacharse	abbassarsi	baixar-se
bal	dance, ball	Ball(m)	baile	ballo	baile
balafre	gash	Schmiß(m), Schnitt(m)	cuchillada	sfregio	corte, cutilada
balai	brush, broom	Besen(m)	escoba	scopa	vassoura
balance	scales	Waage(f)	balanza	bilancia	balança
balançoire	swing; see-saw	Schaukel(f)	columpio	altalena	baloiço
balayer	sweep	fegen	barrer	spazzare	varrer
balcon	balcony	Balkon(m)	balcón	balcone	varanda
baleine	whale	Wal(m)	ballena	balena	baleia
balle	ball	Ball(m)	pelota	palla	bola
balle	bullet	Kugel(f)	bala	pallottola	bala
ballet	ballet	Ballet(n)	ballet	balletto	ballet, bailado
ballon	ball	Ball(m)(Fußball m)	balón	pallone	bola
ballon	balloon	Heißluftballon(m)	globo	pallone	balão
banal, e	banal	banal	común	banale	banal
banane	banana	Banane(f)	plátano, banana	banana	banana
banc	bench	Bank(f)	banco	panca; panchina	banco
bancaire	bank, banking	Bank-	bancario, a	bancario, a	bancário, a
bandage	bandage	Bandage(f), Verband(m)	vendaje, venda	fasciatura	ligadura
bande	band, strip	Streifen(m)	faja, tira	striscia	tira
bande	tape	Band(n)	cinta	nastro	fita
bande	gang	Bande(f)	pandilla	banda	quadrilha
bande dessinée	cartoon(strip)	Comic Strip(m)	comics, tebeos	fumetto	banda desenhada
bandit	bandit	Bandit(m)	bandido	bandito	bandido
banlieue	suburbs	Vorort(m)	afueras	periferia	arredores
bannir	banish	verbannen	desterrar	bandire	desterrar
banque	bank	Bank(f)	banco, banca	banca	banco
banquet	banquet	Bankett(n)	banquete	banchetto	banquete
banquier	banker	Bankier(m)	banquero	banchiere	banqueiro
banquise	ice-floe	Packeis(n)	banco de hielo	banchisa	campo de gelo
baptême	baptism	Taufe(f)	bautizo	battesimo	baptismo
bar	bar, pub	Kneipe(f)	bar, café	bar	bar, café
barbare	barbaric	barbarisch	bárbaro, a	barbaro, a	bárbaro, a
barbe	beard	Bart(m)	barba	barba	barba
barème	scale	Liste(f)	baremo	tariffario	tabela
baromètre	barometer	Barometer(n)	barómetro	barometro	barómetro
baron, ne	baron, baroness	Baron(in, f)m	barón, baronesa	barone, baronessa	barão, baronesa
barque	boat(small)	Barke(f), Kahn(m)	barca	barca	barca
barrage	dam	Damm(m)	embalse, presa	diga	barragem
barrage	blockade	Sperre(f)	cordón(policía)	posto di blocco	barreira
barre	bar	Stange(f)	barra	sbarra	barra
barré, e	blocked	gesperrt	cortado, a	sbarrato, a	impedido, a
barricade	barricade	Barrikade(f)	barricada	barricata	barricada
barrière	barrier; gate	Schranke(f)	barrera	barriera	barreira
bas, basse	low	niedrig	bajo, a	basso, a	baixo, a
bas	down	hinunter	abajo	giù	baixo
bas(en)	downstairs	unten; hinunter	abajo	basso, giù	baixo(de)
bas	stocking	Strumpf(m)(Nylon-)	media	calza	meias
bascule	scales	Waage(f)	báscula	basculla, bilancia	báscula
base	base	Grundlage(f)	base	base	base
base(de)	basic	Grund-; Grundlage	básico	base	base(de)
base(militaire)	base	Stützpunkt(m)	base(militar)	base(militar)	base(militar)
basket-ball	basket-ball	Basketball(m)	baloncesto	pallacanestro	basquetebol
bassin	pond	Bassin(n), Teich(m)	estanque	bacino	lago
bassine	bowl	Wanne(f); Schüssel(f)	barreño	bacinella	bacia
bataille	battle	Gefecht(n)	batalla	battaglia	batalha
bateau	boat, ship	Schiff(n)	barco	imbarcazione, nave	barco
bâtiment	building	Gebäude(n)	edificio	edificio, palazzo	edifício
bâtir	build	bauen	edificar	costruire	construir
bâton	stick	Stock(m)	palo	bastone	pau, bastão
batterie	battery	Batterie(f)	batería	batteria	bateria
battre	beat; hit	schlagen	batir; golpear	battere; picchiare	bater; golpear
battre(se)	fight	kämpfen	pelearse	battersi, lottare	lutar
bavard, e	talkative	geschwätzig	parlanchín, a	chiacchierone, a	falador, a
bavarder	chat, talk	schwätzen, schwatzen	charlar	chiacchierare	falar, conversar
baver	dribble	sabbern	babear	sbavare	babar-se

French	English	German	Spanish	Italian	Portuguese
beau, belle	beautiful, fine	schön	hermoso, a; bello, a	bello, a	belo, a; bonito, a
beau, belle	handsome	ansehnlich, schön	bello, a	bello, a	bonito, a
beaucoup	much, many	viel(e)	mucho	molto	muito
beaucoup	lots of, a lot of	viel(e)	mucho, a	molto, a, i, e	muito, a
beaucoup	many	viele	muchos, as	molti	muitos, as
beau-frère	brother-in-law	Schwager(m)	cuñado	cognato	cunhado
beau-père	father-in-law	Schwiegervater(m)	suegro	suocero	sogro
beau temps	fine weather	schönes Wetter	buen tiempo	bel tempo	bom tempo
beauté	beauty	Schönheit(f)	belleza	bellezza	beleza
beaux-arts	fine arts	Kunst(f)	bellas artes	belle arti	belas-artes
beaux-parents	parents-in-law	Schwiegereltern(pl.)	suegros	suoceri	sogros
bébé	baby	Baby(n)	bebé	bebè, bambino, a	bebé
bec	beak	Schnabel(m)	pico	becco	bico
bégayer	stutter, stammer	stottern	tartamudear	balbettare	gaguejar
beige	beige	beige	crema, beis	beige	bege
beignets	fritters	Krapfen, Pfannkuchen	buñuelos	frittella	pastéis
belle	beautiful	schön	bella	bella	bela
belle	beautiful, fine	schön, e, er, es	hermosa	bella	bonita, bela
belle-fille	daughter-in-law	Schwiegertochter(f)	nuera	nuora	nora
belle-mère	mother-in-law	Schwiegermutter(f)	suegra	suocera	sogra
belle-soeur	sister-in-law	Schwägerin(f)	cuñada	cognata	cunhada
belliqueux, se	aggressive	kriegerisch	belicoso, a	bellicoso, a	belicoso, a
bénéfice	benefit; profit	Gewinn(m)	beneficio	beneficio; utile	lucro, proveito
bénéficier	profit, benefit	profitieren, gewinnen	beneficiar	beneficiare	beneficiar
bénévole	voluntary	unentgeltlich	benévolo, a	benevolo, a	benévolo, a
bénin, bénigne	benign	gutartig	benigno, a	benigno, a	benigno, a
bénir	bless	segnen	bendecir	benedire	benzer
béquille	crutch(-es)	Krücke(f)	muleta	stampella	muleta
berceau	cradle	Wiege(f)	cuna	culla	berço
bercer	rock	wiegen	mecer	cullare	embalar
berge	bank	Ufer(n)	ribera, orilla	sponda	margem
berger, ère	shepherd, -ess	Schäfer(in f)m	pastor, a	pastore, pastorella	pastor, a
besoin	need	Bedürfnis(n)	necesidad	bisogno	necessidade
besoin(avoir)	require, need	brauchen	necesitar	bisogno(avere)	necessidade(ter)
bétail, bestiaux	cattle	Vieh(n)	ganado	bestiame	gado
bête	animal, beast	Biest(n), Tier(n)	bestia	bestia	bicho, animal
bête; sot, te	silly, foolish	dumm	tonto, a	sciocco, a	tolo, a; burro, a
bêtise	stupid thing(do a)	Dummheit(f)	estupidez	sciocchezza	asneira
béton	concrete	Beton(m)	hormigón	calcestruzzo	betão
beurre	butter	Butter(f)	mantequilla	burro	manteiga
biberon	bottle(baby's -)	Fläschchen(n)	biberón	biberon	biberão
Bible	Bible	Bibel(f)	Biblia	Bibbia	Bíblia
bibliographie	bibliography	Bibliographie(f)	bibliografía	bibliografia	bibliografia
bibliothèque	library	Bibliothek(f)	biblioteca	biblioteca	biblioteca
bibliothèque	bookcase	Bücherschrank(m)	biblioteca	libreria	estante
biceps	biceps	Bizeps(m)	bíceps	bicipite	biceps
bicyclette	bicycle	Fahrrad(n)	bicicleta	bicicletta	bicicleta
bidon	can	Kanister(m)	bidón, lata	bidone	cantil
bidonville	shanty-town	Elendsviertel(n)	chabolas	bidonville	bairro de lata
bien	well	gut	bien	bene	bem
bien	well	wohl	bien	bene	bem
bien	good	Gut(n)	bien	bene	bem
bien-être	well-being	Wohlbefinden(n)	bienestar	benessere	bem-estar
bien que	though, although	obwohl, obgleich	aunque	benché	ainda que
bien sûr	of course	natürlich	claro	certamente	claro
biens	possessions, estate	Besitz(m), Güter(pl)	bienes	beni; averi	bens
bientôt	soon	bald	pronto	presto	logo, brevemente
bienveillant, e	benevolent	wohlwollend	benévolo, a	benevolo, a	benévolo, a
bienvenu, e	welcome(to be)	Willkommen(n)	bienvenido, a	benvenuto, a	bem-vindo, a
bière	beer	Bier(n)	cerveza	birra	cerveja
bifteck	steak	Beefsteak(n)	bistec	bistecca	bife
bijou(x)	jewel	Schmuck(m)(-stück n)	joya	gioiello	jóia
bijouterie	jeweller's	Schmuckgeschäft(n)	joyería	gioielleria	joalharia
bilan	balance-sheet	Bilanz(f)	balance	bilancio	balanço
bilingue	bilingual	zweisprachig	bilingüe	bilingue	bilingue
billard	billiards	Billard(n)	billar	biliardo	bilhar
bille	marble	Murmel(f)	bola	biglia	berlinde
bille	ball	Kugel(f)	bola	sfera	esfera

French	English	German	Spanish	Italian	Portuguese
billet(banque)	bank-note	Geldschein(m)	billete(de banco)	banconota	nota(de banco)
billet	ticket	Fahrkarte(f)	billete	biglietto	bilhete
billet	ticket	Los(n)	billete	biglietto	bilhete
billet Aller/R	return ticket	Rückfahrkarte(f)	billete ida/vuelta	andata e ritorno	bilhete ida/volta
billet simple	single ticket	einfache Fahrkarte(f)	billete de ida	andata	bilhete de ida
biographie	biography	Lebensbeschreibung(f)	biografía	biografia	biografia
biologie	biology	Biologie(f)	biología	biologia	biologia
biscuit	biscuit	Keks(m)	galleta	biscotto	biscoito
bise	kiss	Küßchen(n)	besito	bacio	beijinho
bistouri	scalpel, bistoury	Skalpell(n)	bisturí	bisturi	bisturi
bitume	asphalt, tarmac	Asphalt(m)	asfalto	bitume	asfalto
bivouac	bivouac	Biwak(m)	vivaque	bivacco	acampamento
bizarre	strange, odd	seltsam	raro, a	strano, a	estranho, a
blague	joke	Witz(m)	chiste	scherzo	anedota, chalaça
blâme	blame; reprimand	Rüge(f)	reprobación	biasimo	censura
blanc, blanche	white	weiß	blanco, a	bianco, a	branco, a
blanchisserie	laundry	Wäscherei(f)	lavandería	lavanderia	lavandaria
blasphème	blasphemy	Lästerung(f)(Gottes-)	blasfemia	bestemmia	blasfémia
blé	corn	Weizen(m)	trigo	grano	trigo
blesser	injure, wound	verletzen	herir	ferire	ferir
blesser, offenser	hurt, offend	kränken	lastimar, ofender	ferire, offendere	magoar, ofender
blesser(se)	injured(to be)	verletzen, sich	herir(se)	ferirsi	ferir-se
blessure	injury, wound	Verletzung(f)	herida	ferita	ferida
bleu, e	blue	blau	azul	blu	azul
blindé, e	armoured	gepanzert	blindado, a	blindato, a	blindado, a
bloc	block	Block(m)	bloque	blocco	bloco
bloc	pad	Block(m)	bloc	blocco	bloco
blocage	jamming	Blockierung(f), Sperre	bloqueo	bloccaggio	bloqueamento
blocage	freeze	Preisstopp(m)	congelación	blocco	congelamento
blocus	blockade	Blockade(f)	bloqueo	blocco	bloqueio
blond, e	fair, blond	blond	rubio(pelo)	biondo, a	louro, a
bloquer	block	blockieren	bloquear	bloccare	bloquear
blottir(se)	huddle	an = schmiegen, sich	acurrucar(se)	rannicchiarsi	aninhar-se
blouse	overall	Kittel(m)	bata, blusa	blusa, camice	bata
bobine	reel	Spule(f)	bobina, carrete	bobina	bobina
bocal	jar	Glasgefäß(n)	tarro, bocal	boccale, vaso	boião
boeuf	bullock; beef	Ochse(m); Rind(n)	buey; carne de vaca	bue; manzo	boi; carne de vaca
boire	drink	trinken	beber	bere	beber
bois	wood	Brennholz(n)	leña	legna	lenha
bois	wood	Wald(n)	bosque	bosco	bosque
bois	timber	Holz(n)	madera	legno	madeira
boisson	drink	Getränk(n)	bebida	bibita; bevanda	bebida
boîte	box(-es)	Schachtel(f)	caja	scatola	caixa
boîte	tin	Dose(f)	lata	latta, scatola	lata
boîte(lettres)	letter box	Briefkasten(m)	buzón	buca delle lettere	caixa do correio
boîte de nuit	night-club	Diskothek(f)	discoteca	discoteca, night	boîte
boiter	limp	hinken	cojear	zoppicare	coxear
bol	bowl	Trinkschale(f)	tazón	scodella	tigela; malga
bombe	bomb	Bombe(f)	bomba	bomba	bomba
bombé, e	convex	gewölbt	abombado, a	convesso, a	convexo, a
bon, ne	good	gut	bueno, a	buono, a	bom, boa
bon, aimable	kind, kindly	gütig, liebvoll	bueno, a	buono, a	bom, boa
bon	form, slip, voucher	Bestellschein(m)	orden, pedido	bolla, buono, bolletta	nota
bon appétit!	enjoy your meal!	Guten Appetit!	que aproveche(!)	buon appetito!	bom proveito!
bon marché	cheap	billig	barato, a	buon prezzo	barato, a
bon voyage	good trip(have a)	gute Reise	buen viaje	buon viaggio	boa viagem
bonbon	sweet	Bonbon(n, m)	caramelo; bombón	caramella	rebuçado
bondir	jump, leap	springen	saltar	saltare, balzare	saltar
bonheur	happiness	Glück(n).	felicidad	felicità	felicidade
bonjour	hello	guten Tag	buenos días	buongiorno	bom dia
bonjour!	good morning!/aft-	guten Morgen!/-Tag	hola(!)	buongiorno!	bom dia!
bonjour!	good afternoon!	guten Tag!	hola(!)	buona sera!	bom dia!
bonne	maid	Haushaltshilfe(f).	criada	domestica	criada
bonne chance	good luck	viel Glück	buena suerte	buona fortuna	boa sorte
bonne nuit	good night	gute Nacht	buenas noches	buona notte	boa noite
bonnet	cap, hat	Mütze(f).	gorro	berretto, cuffia	barrete
bonsoir	good evening	guten Abend	buenas tardes	buonasera	boa tarde
bonté	kindness	Güte(f)	bondad	bontà	bondade

French	English	German	Spanish	Italian	Portuguese
bord	side; edge	Rand(m)	borde	bordo, riva, orlo	borda
bord de mer	sea-side	Küste(f)	orilla del mar	riva	beira-mar
bordure	edge, border	Rand(m)	bordura; ribete	bordo, lungo	borda, orla
borgne	one-eyed	einäugig	tuerto, a	guercio, a	zarolho, a
bosse	lump, bump	Beule(f)	chichón	bernoccolo, gobba	bossa; alto
bosse	bump	Unebenheit(f); Buckel	bache	gobba, dosso, cunetta	bossa; alto
bossu, e	hunch-backed	buckelig	jorobado, a	gobbo, a	corcunda
botanique	botany	Botanik(f)	botánica	botanica	botânica
botte	boot	Stiefel(m)	bota	stivale	bota
bouche	mouth	Mund(m)	boca	bocca	boca
bouchée	mouthful	Bissen(m)	bocado	boccone	bocado
boucherie	butcher's(shop)	Metzgerei(f)	carnicería	macelleria	talho
bouchon	cork	Korken(m)	corcho	tappo, turacciolo	rolha
bouchon	cap, plug	Pfropfen(m), Stöpsel	tapón	tappo	rolha; tampa
boucle	buckle	Schnalle(f)	hebilla	fibbia	fivela; argola
boucle	loop	Schleife(f)	lazo	cappio; occhiello	laço
boucle	curl	Locke(f)	rizo	ricciolo	caracóis
boucle(s)	earring	Ohrring(m)	pendientes	orecchini	brincos, argolas
boue	mud	Schlamm(m)	barro	fango, melma	lama
bouée	lifebelt	Rettungsring(m)	salvavidas	salvagente	bóia
bouée	buoy	Boje(f)	boya	boa	bóia
bouffée	puff, breath	Hauch(m), Atemzug(m)	bocanada	ventata	baforada
bouger	move	bewegen	moverse	muovere	mexer-se
bougie	candle	Kerze(f)	vela	candela	vela
bougie	sparking plug	Zündkerze(f)	bujía	candela	vela
bouillant, e	boiling	kochend	hirviente	bollente	fervente
bouillir	boil	kochen	hervir	bollire	ferver
bouilloire	kettle	Wasserkessel(m)	hervidor	bollitore	chaleira
bouillon	stock, broth	Brühe(f)	caldo	brodo	caldo
boulangerie	baker's(shop)	Bäckerei(f)	panadería	panificio	padaria
boule	bowl	Kugel(f)	bola	boccia	bola
boule	ball	Ball(m)(Schneeball)	bola	palla	bola
boulevard	boulevard	Boulevard(m)	bulevar	viale	avenida
bouleversé, e	overwhelmed	erschüttert	conmocionado, a	sconvolto, a	perturbado, a
boulon	bolt	Bolzen(m)	perno, tornillo	bullone	parafuso; cavilha
bouquet	bunch; bouquet	Strauß(m)	ramo	mazzo	ramo
bouquet	bouquet	Blume(f), Bukett(n)	buqué, aroma, boca	bouquet, aroma	aroma
bourgeois, e	middle class	Bürger(in f)m	burgués, a	borghese	burguês, a
bourgeoisie	middle class	Bürgertum(n)	burguesía	borghesia	burguesia
bourgeon	bud	Knospe(f)	brote, botón	gemma	rebento, botão
bourrasque	squall	Windstoß(m)	borrasca	burrasca	borrasca
bourse	grant; scholarship	Stipendium(n)	beca	borsa di studio	bolsa
Bourse(la)	Stock Exchange	Börse(f)	Bolsa	Borsa	Bolsa
bousculer	push	drängeln	empujar	spingere, urtare	empurrar
boussole	compass	Kompaß(m)	brújula	bussola	bússola
bout	tip, end	Zipfel(m), Ende(n)	punta	punta, estremità	ponta
bout, extrémité	end, tip	Ende(n)	cabo	capo, estremità	cabo
bouteille	bottle	Flasche(f)	botella	bottiglia	garrafa
boutique	boutique, shop	Geschäft(n)	tienda	negozio, boutique	loja
bouton	spot, pimple	Pickel(m)	grano	brufolo, foruncolo	borbulha
bouton	button	Knopf(m)	botón	bottone	botão
bouton	button	Taste(f)	pulsador	pulsante, bottone	botão
bouton	knob	Knopf(m)	botón	manopola, pomello	botão
bouton	switch(-es)	Schalter(m)	interruptor, botón	bottone, pulsante	interruptor
boxe	boxing	Boxen(n)	boxeo	pugilato	boxe
boxeur	boxer	Boxer(m)	boxeador	pugile	pugilista
bracelet	bracelet	Armband(n)	pulsera	braccialetto	pulseira
bracelet	strap	Armband(n)	correa	cinturino	pulseira
braise	embers	Glut(f)	brasa	brace	brasa
branche	branch(-es)	Ast(m)	rama	ramo	ramo
brancher	plug in	ein = stecken	enchufar	innestare	ligar
brancher	connect	an = schließen	empalmar	allacciare	ligar
branle-bas	upheaval	Durcheinander(n)	zafarrancho	scompiglio	agitação
braquer	aim	richten auf	apuntar	puntare	apontar
bras	arm	Arm(m)	brazo	braccio	braço
brave	decent, nice	brav, nett, angenehm	bueno, a	bravo, a	amável
braver	defy	trotzen	desafiar	sfidare	defrontar
brèche	breach, gap	Spalt(m), Bresche(f)	brecha	breccia	brecha

French	English	German	Spanish	Italian	Portuguese
bref, brève	brief, short	kurz	breve	breve	breve
bretelle(s)	braces	Hosenträger(m)	tirantes	bretella	suspensórios
brevet	patent	Patent(n)	patente	brevetto	patente
bricolage	odd-jobs	Basteln(n)	bricolage, maña	bricolage	bricolage
brigade	brigade	Brigade(f)	brigada	brigata, squadra	brigada
brigand	bandit	Räuber(in f)m	maleante	brigante	bandido
brillant, e	bright, shining	glänzend	brillante	brillante	brilhante
brillant, e	brilliant	prächtig, brillant	brillante	brillante	brilhante
briller	shine	glänzen	brillar	brillare	brilhar
brique	brick	Ziegel(m)	ladrillo	mattone	tijolo
briquet	lighter	Feuerzeug(n)	mechero	accendino	isqueiro
briser	break	brechen, zerbrechen	romper	spezzare, rompere	quebrar
broche	brooch(-es)	Brosche(f)	broche	spilla	broche
broche	spit	Spieß(m)	asador	spiedo	espeto
broder	embroider	sticken	bordar	ricamare	bordar
bronche(s)	bronchial tubes	Bronchie(f)	bronquios	bronco(bronchi)	brônquios
bronchite	bronchitis	Bronchitis(f)	bronquitis	bronchite	bronquite
bronzage	sun-tan	Bräune(f)	bronceado	abbronzatura	bronzeamento
bronze	bronze	Bronze(f)	bronce	bronzo	bronze
bronzer	tan	bräunen	broncear	abbronzare	bronzear
brosse	brush(-es)	Bürste(f)	cepillo	spazzola	escova
brosse à dents	toothbrush(-es)	Zahnbürste(f)	cepillo de dientes	spazzolino	escova de dentes
brouette	wheelbarrow	Schubkarre(f)	carretilla	carriola	carro de mão
brouillard	fog	Nebel(m)	niebla	nebbia	nevoeiro
brouillon	rough paper	Schmierzettel(m)	borrador	brutta copia	rascunho
broussaille	undergrowth	Gestrüpp(n)	zarzal, maleza	macchia, cespugli	mato, brenha
brousse	bush(the)	Busch(m)	maleza	boscaglia	mato
broyer	crush, grind	mahlen	triturar	stritolare, macinare	triturar; moer
bruine	drizzle	Sprühregen(m)	llovizna	pioggerella	chuvisco
bruit	noise	Geräusch(m)	ruido	rumore	ruído, barulho
brûlant, e	boiling hot	brennend, kochend	ardiente	ardente, bollente	ardente
brûler	burn	verbrennen	quemar	bruciare	queimar, arder
brûlure	burn	Verbrennung(f)	quemadura	bruciatura	queimadura
brume	mist, haze	Nebel(m)	bruma	foschia	bruma
brun, ne	brown	braun	pardo, a	bruno, a	castanho, a
brusque	abrupt, sudden	brüsk	brusco, a	brusco, a	brusco, a
brut, e	raw; crude	roh	bruto, a	grezzo, a	bruto, a
brutal, e	brutal	brutal	brutal	brutale	brutal
brutalité	brutality	Brutalität, Roheit(f)	brutalidad	brutalità	brutalidade
bruyant, e	noisy; loud	laut	ruidoso, a	rumoroso, a	barulhento, a
bûche	log	Scheit(n)	leño	tronco, ceppo	acha
budget	budget	Budget(n)	presupuesto	bilancio	orçamento
buffet	dresser; sideboard	Büfett(n)	aparador	credenza, buffè	aparador
buisson	bush	Gebüsch(n)	matorral	cespuglio	moita
bulle	bubble	Blase(f)	burbuja	bolla	bolha
bulletin	bulletin, report	Bericht(m)	boletín	bollettino, bolletta	boletim
bureau	desk	Schreibtisch(m)	escritorio	scrivania	secretária
bureau	office	Büro(n)	despacho	ufficio	escritório
bureau de tabac	tobacconist's	Tabakladen(m)	estanco	tabaccheria	estanco, tabacaria
buste	bust	Oberkörper(m)	busto	busto	busto
but	aim, purpose	Ziel(n)	propósito	scopo	fim, intento
but	goal	Tor(n)	gol	goal, rete	golo
butin	spoils	Beute(f)	botín	bottino	despojo
buveur, se	drinker	Trinker(in f)m	bebedor, a	bevitore, trice	bebedor, a

C

French	English	German	Spanish	Italian	Portuguese
cabaret	cabaret; nightclub	Kabarett(n)	cabaret	cabaret	cabaret
cabine	cabin	Kabine(f)	cabina	cabina	cabine

French	English	German	Spanish	Italian	Portuguese
cabine(téléph.)	phone box	Telefonzelle(f)	cabina(telefónica)	cabina(telefonica)	cabine(telefónica)
cabinet(médecin)	surgery	Praxis(f)(Arztpraxis)	consulta(-torio)	studio(medico)	consultório
cabinet(avocat)	practice	Büro(n)(Anwaltsbüro)	despacho; bufete	studio(avvocato)	escritório
cabinet(pol.)	cabinet	Kabinett(n)	gabinete	gabinetto	gabinete
câble	cable	Kabel(n)	cable	cavo	cabo
cacahuète	peanut	Erdnuß(f)	cacahuete, maní	arachide	amendoim
cacao	cocoa, cacao	Kakao(m)	cacao	cacao	cacau
cache-nez	scarf	Schal(m)	bufanda	sciarpa	cachecol
cacher	hide	verstecken	esconder	nascondere	esconder
cacher	conceal	verbergen, verhehlen	esconder, ocultar	nascondere	ocultar
cachet	tablet	Tablette(f)	pastilla	pastiglia	comprimido
cachet	postmark; seal	Stempel(m), Siegel(n)	sello	sigillo, bollo	selo
cachet	fee	Honorar(n); Gage(f)	remuneración	cachet, compenso	remuneração
cadastre	land register	Grundbuch(n)	catastro	catasto	cadastro
cadavre	corpse	Leiche(f)	cadáver	cadavere	cadáver
cadeau	present, gift	Geschenk(n)	regalo	regalo	prenda, presente
cadenas	padlock	Vorhängeschloß(n)	candado	lucchetto, catenaccio	cadeado
cadence	rate, rhythm	Rhythmus(m)	cadencia	cadenza	cadência
cadet, te	younger; youngest	Jüngere(r)mf	menor	cadetto, a	novo, a(o, a mais)
cadran	dial	Zifferblatt(n)	esfera	quadrante	mostrador
cadre	frame	Rahmen(m)	marco	cornice, quadro	moldura
cadre	executive	leitende Angestellte	ejecutivo	dirigente	quadro
cafard	miserable(feel)	Trübsinn(m)	melancolía	malinconia	tristeza
café	coffee	Kaffee(m)	café	caffè	café
cafetière	coffee-pot	Kaffeemaschine(f)	cafetera	caffettiera	cafeteira
cage	cage	Käfig(m)	jaula	gabbia	gaiola, jaula
cahier	exercise book	Heft(n)	cuaderno	quaderno	caderno
caillot	clot	Blutgerinnsel(n)	coágulo	grumo	coágulo
caillou	stone, pebble	Stein(m)	piedra	sasso	calhau
caisse	chest, case	Kiste(f)	cajón, caja	cassa	caixa
caisse	cash-desk	Kasse(f)	caja	cassa	caixa
caissier, ière	cashier	Kassierer(in f)m	cajero, a	cassiere, a	caixa(o)
calcium	calcium	Kalzium(n)	calcio	calcio	cálcio
calcul	calculation	Berechnung(f)	cálculo	calcolo	cálculo
calculatrice	calculator	Rechenmaschine(f)	calculadora	calcolatrice	calculadora
calculer	calculate, reckon	rechnen, berechnen	calcular	calcolare	calcular
cale	wedge, chock	Keil(m)	cuña	zeppa	cunha
cale	hold	Laderaum(m)	bodega	stiva	porão
calendrier	calendar	Kalender(m)	calendario	calendario	calendário
calibre	bore, calibre	Kaliber(n)	calibre	calibro	calibre
calmant	sedative	Beruhigungsmittel(n)	calmante	calmante	calmante
calme	calm, quiet, still	ruhig, still	tranquilo, a	calmo, a	calmo, a
calme	calm, quiet, still	Ruhe(f), Stille(f)	calma, sosiego	calma, quiete	calma, sossego
calmer	calm	beruhigen	calmar	calmare	acalmar
calomnie	slander	Verleumdung(f)	calumnia	calunnia	calúnia
calorie	calorie	Kalorie(f)	caloría	caloria	caloria
camarade	friend	Kamerad(in f)m	compañero, a	compagno, a	camarada
cambré, e	arched	krumm, gebeugt	arqueado, a	inarcato, a; arcuato, a	arqueado, a
cambriolage	burglary	Einbruch(m)	robo, atraco	furto con scasso	roubo, assalto
caméra	cine-camera	Kamera(f)	cámara	cinepresa	câmara
camion	lorry	Lastwagen(m)	camión	camion	camião
campagne	country(side)	Land(n)	campo	campagna	campo
campagne	campaign	Wahlkampf(m)	campaña	campagna	campanha
camper	camp	zelten	acampar	campeggiare	acampar
camping(aire de)	camp(ing) site	Campingplatz(m)	camping	campeggio	campismo
canal	canal	Kanal(m)	canal	canale	canal
canapé	sofa	Sofa(n)	sofá, canapé	divano, canapè	canapé, sofá
canalisation	pipe	Leitung(f)(-snetz n)	canalización	canalizzazione	canalização
canard	duck	Ente(f)	pato	anatra	pato, a
cancer	cancer	Krebs(m)	cáncer	cancro	cancro
cancéreux, se	cancerous	krebsartig	canceroso, se	canceroso, a	canceroso, a
candidat, e	candidate	Kandidat(in f)m	candidato, a	candidato, a	candidato, a
candidature	application	Bewerbung(f)	candidatura	candidatura	candidatura
candide	ingenuous	naiv, aufrichtig	cándido, a	candido, a	cândido, a
caniveau	gutter	Rinnstein(m)	arroyo	canaletto di scolo	valeta
canne	stick	Stock(m)	bastón	bastone	bengala
canne à pêche	fishing rod	Angelrute(f)	caña de pescar	canna da pesca	cana de pesca
canoë	canoe	Kanu(n)	canoa	canoa	canoa

| --- | --- | --- | --- | --- | --- |
canon	cannon	Kanone(f)	cañón	cannone	canhão
canot	dinghy	Boot(n)	bote	canotto	canoa
canular	joke, hoax	Ulk(m), Witz(m)	broma	scherzo, burla	partida
caoutchouc	rubber	Gummi(m, n)	caucho	gomma	borracha
cap	head for	Kurs(m)	rumbo a	rotta	rumo
cap	cape	Kap(n)	cabo	capo	cabo
capable de	able to(be)	fähig	capaz de	capace di	capaz de
capitaine	captain	Hauptmann(m); Kapitän	capitán	capitano	capitão
capital	capital, assets	Kapital(n)	capital	capitale	capital(o)
capitale	capital	Hauptstadt(f)	capital	capitale	capital(a)
capitalisme	capitalism	Kapitalismus(m)	capitalismo	capitalismo	capitalismo
capituler	capitulate	kapitulieren	capitular	capitolare	capitular
caporal	corporal	Gefreiter(m); Korporal	cabo(mil.)	caporale	cabo
capot	bonnet, hood	Motorhaube(f)	capó	cofano	capota
caprice	caprice, whim	Laune(f)	capricho	capriccio	capricho, birra
capturer	capture	fangen	capturar	catturare	capturar
capuchon	cap	Kappe(f)	capuchón	cappuccio	capuz
car	because, for	weil, denn	porque, pues	perché	porque, pois
carabine	rifle	Gewehr(n), Karabiner m	carabina	carabina	espingarda
caractère	letter, character	Schrifttyp(m)	letra	carattere, lettera	carácter
caractère	character	Charakter(m)	carácter	carattere	carácter
caractéristique	characteristic	charakteristisch	característico, a	caratteristico, a	característico, a
caractéristique	feature	Merkmal(n)	característica	caratteristica	característica
carafe	jug, carafe	Karaffe(f)	jarra	caraffa	jarro, caneca
carat	carat	Karat(n)	quilate	carato	quilate
caravane	caravan	Wohnwagen(m)	caravana	roulotte	caravana
carbone	carbon	Kohlenstoff(m)	carbono	carbonio	carbono
carbonique	carbonic	Kohlensäure(f)	carbónico, a	carbonico, a	carbónico, a
carburant	fuel	Treibstoff(m)	carburante	carburante	carburante
carburateur	carburettor	Vergaser(m)	carburador	carburatore	carburador
cardiaque	heart-trouble...	herzkrank	cardíaco, a	cardiaco, a	cardíaco, a
cardinal	cardinal	Kardinal(m)	cardenal	cardinale	cardeal
cardiologie	cardiology	Kardiologie(f)	cardiología	cardiologia	cardiologia
carence	deficiency	Fehlen(n), Mangel(m)	carencia	carenza	carência
caresse	caress	Streicheln(n)	caricia	carezza	carícia
caresser	caress	liebkosen, streicheln	acariciar	accarezzare	acariciar
caresser	stroke	streicheln	acariciar	carezzare	afagar
cargaison	cargo, freight	Ladung(f)	cargamento	carico	carga
cargo	cargo(-boat)	Frachter(m)	carguero, buque	cargo, nave da carico	cargueiro
caricaturer	caricature	karikieren	caricaturar	caricaturare	caricaturar
carie	tooth decay	Karies(f)	caries	carie	cárie
carnaval	carnival	Karneval(m)	carnaval	carnevale	carnaval
carnet	note-book	Notizbuch(n)	libreta	taccuino	bloco, canhenho
carnivore	carnivorous	fleischfressend	carnívoro, a	carnivoro, a	carnívoro, a
carotte	carrot	Möhre(f)	zanahoria	carota	cenoura
carré	square	Viereck(n)	cuadrado	quadrato	quadrado
carreau	tile	Fliese(f), Kachel(f)	baldosa, azulejo	piastrella	ladrilho, azulejo
carrefour	cross-road(s)	Kreuzung(f)	encrucijada	incrocio	cruzamento
carrelage	tiling; tiles	Fliesen(n); Fliese(f)	embaldosado	pavimento	ladrilho
carrière	quarry	Steinbruch(m)	cantera	cava	pedreira
carrière	career	Karriere(f)	carrera	carriera	carreira
carrosserie	body(-work)	Karosserie(f)	carrocería	carrozzeria	carroçaria
cartable	briefcase; satchel	Ranzen(m)	cartera	cartella	pasta
carte à jouer	card	Spielkarte(f)	carta	carta da gioco	carta
carte(géo)	map	Landkarte(f)	mapa	mappa, carta	mapa
carte	card, ticket	Karte(f)	tarjeta	tessera	bilhete
carte de crédit	credit card	Kreditkarte(f)	carta de crédito	carta di credito	cartão de crédito
carte d'identité	identity card	Personalausweis(m)	carné de identidad	carta d'identità	bilhete(identidade)
carte de visite	visiting card	Visitenkarte(f)	tarjeta de visita	biglietto da visita	cartão de visita
carte postale	post-card	Postkarte(f)	tarjeta postal	cartolina	bilhete-postal
carte(resto)	menu	Karte(f)(Speisekarte)	menú	menù, carta	lista
carte de voeux	greeting(s) card	Glückwunschkarte(f)	postal, carta	biglietto di auguri	cartão(festas)
carte des vins	wine-list	Weinkarte(f)	carta de vinos	lista dei vini	lista dos vinhos
carte grise	log-book	KFZ-Schein(m)	cédula iden-fiscal	libretto di circola-	livrete(circulação)
cartilage	cartilage	Knorpel(m)	cartílago	cartilagine	cartilagem
carton	cardboard	Pappe(f)	cartón	cartone	cartão
cartouche	cartridge	Patrone(f)	cartucho	cartuccia	cartucho
cas	case	Fall(m)	caso	caso	caso

French	English	German	Spanish	Italian	Portuguese
cascade	waterfall	Wasserfall(m)	cascada	cascata	cascata
case	hut	Hütte(f)	cabaña	capanna	palhota
caserne	barracks	Kaserne(f)	cuartel	caserma	quartel
casino	casino	Kasino(n)	casino	casinò	casino
casque	helmet	Helm(m)	casco	casco, elmetto	capacete
casquette	cap	Mütze(f)	gorra	berretto	boné
cassant, e	brittle	brüchig, spröde	quebradizo, a	fragile	quebradiço, a
casser, briser	break	zerbrechen	romper	rompere	quebrar, partir
casserole	pan, saucepan	Topf(m)	cazo, cacerola	casseruola	tacho, caçarola
cassette	cassette	Kassette(f)	casete	cassetta	cassete
cassure, rupture	break	Bruch(m)	rotura	frattura, rottura	ruptura, quebra
caste	caste	Kaste(f)	casta	casta	casta
cataclysme	cataclysm	Katastrophe(f)	cataclismo	cataclisma	cataclismo
catalogue	catalogue	Katalog(m)	catálogo	catalogo	catálogo
catastrophe	catastrophe	Katastrophe(f)	catástrofe	catastrofe	catástrofe
catégorie	category	Kategorie(f)	categoría	categoria	categoria
cathédrale	cathedral	Kathedrale(f), Dom(m)	catedral	cattedrale, duomo	catedral
catholique	Catholic	katholisch	católico, a	cattolico, a	católico, a
cauchemar	nightmare	Alptraum(m)	pesadilla	incubo	pesadelo
cause	cause	Ursache(f), Grund(m)	causa	causa	causa
causer, provoquer	cause	verursachen	causar, provocar	causare, provocare	causar, provocar
cavalier, ière	rider	Reiter(in f)m	jinete, a	cavaliere, a	cavaleiro, a
cave	cellar	Keller(m)	bodega, sótano	cantina	adega
caverne	cave, cavern	Höhle(f)	caverna	caverna	caverna
caviar	caviar	Kaviar(m)	caviar	caviale	caviar
cavité	cavity	Hohlraum(m)	cavidad	cavità	cavidade
ce, cette	this, that	dieser, diese	este; esta; estos, as	questo, a; quello, a	este, a; esse, a
ce, cette, ces	that, those	dieser, diese, dieses	ese, esa, esos(as)	quello, a; questo, a	este, esta, estes
ceci	this	dies(es); das	esto	questo, ciò	isto
céder, renoncer	give up	auf = geben; nach = geben	ceder	cedere	ceder
ceinture	belt	Gürtel(m)	cinturón	cintura	cinto
cela, ça	that	das, jene(r, s)	eso, aquello, ello	ciò, questo, quello	isso, aquilo
célèbre	famous, well-known	berühmt	célebre, famoso, a	celebre; famoso, a	célebre
célébrer	celebrate	feiern	celebrar	celebrare	celebrar
céleste	heavenly	himmlisch	celeste	celeste	celeste
célibataire	bachelor; single -	Junggeselle m/-sellin	soltero, a	scapolo, nubile	solteiro, a
célibataire	single, unmarried	ledig	soltero, a	scapolo; nubile	solteiro, a
cellulite	fat, cellulitis	Zellulitis(f)	celulitis	cellulite	celulite
celui, celle	the one	derjenige, die-, das-	él, la	quello, a	o, a
celui-ci, celle-	this one	diese(r, s)(hier)	éste, ésta	questo, questa	este, esta
celui-là, celle-	that one	der(jenige); die( )	ése, ésa, éso(s)	quello, quella	esse(a); aquele(a)
cendre(s)	ash(es)	Asche(f)	ceniza(s)	cenere(-ri)	cinza
cendrier	ash-tray	Aschenbecher(m)	cenicero	portacenere	cinzeiro
censure	censorship	Zensur(f)	censura	censura	censura
cent	hundred(one)	hundert	cien, ciento	cento	cem, cento
centaine	hundred(about a)	Hundert(n)	centena	centinaio	centena
centimètre	centimetre	Zentimeter(n, m)	centímetro	centimetro	centímetro
central, e	central	zentral	central	centrale	central
centrale	power-station	Kraftwerk(n), Zentrale	central	centrale	central
centre	centre	Mitte(f)	centro	centro	centro
centre	centre	Zentrum(n)	centro	centro	centro
centre	hub	Mittelpunkt(m)	centro	centro	centro
centre ville	city/town centre	Stadtzentrum(n)	centro(ciudad)	centro della città	centro(cidade)
centrifuge	centrifugal	zentrifugal	centrífugo, a	centrifugo, a	centrífugo, a
cependant	however, but	jedoch	sin embargo	eppure, tuttavia	todavia, porém
cercle	circle	Kreis(m)	círculo	cerchio	círculo
cercueil	coffin	Sarg(m)	ataúd	bara	caixão
céréale	cereal	Getreide(n)	cereal	cereale	cereal
cérébral, e	cerebral	Gehirn-; zerebral	cerebral	cerebrale	cerebral
cérémonie	ceremony	Zeremonie(f)	ceremonia	cerimonia	cerimónia
cerise	cherry	Kirsche(f)	cereza	ciliegia	cereja
cerne	ring, circle	Augenringe(pl.)	ojeras	occhiaia	olheiras
certain, e	certain, sure	sicher	cierto, a	certo, a; sicuro, a	certo, a
certainement	certainly	sicherlich	ciertamente	certamente	certamente
certaines	certain; some	manche	algunos, as	certi, e; alcuni, e	certos, as
certificat	certificate	Bescheinigung(f)	certificado	certificato	certificado
certifier	certify	bescheinigen	certificar	certificare	certificar
certitude	certainty	Gewißheit(f)	certeza	certezza	certeza

| --- | --- | --- | --- | --- | --- |
cerveau	brain	Gehirn(n)	cerebro	cervello	cérebro
ces	these, those	diese(pl)	estos, as; esos, as	questi, e	estes, as; esses, as
césarienne	Caesarean	Kaiserschnitt(m)	cesárea	taglio cesareo	cesariana
cesser	stop, cease	auf = hören	cesar, parar	cessare, smettere	cessar, parar
c'est-à-dire	that is(to say)	das heißt	es decir	cioè	quer dizer
cet, cette	this, that	dieser, diese	éste; ésta; éstos	questo, a; quello, a	este; esta; estes, as
ceux, celles, ces	these, those	diese	esos, aquellos	questi, e	aqueles, aquelas
ceux-ci, celles-	these; those	diese; jene	éstos; ésos	questi; quelli	estes(as); esses(as)
chacun, e; chaque	each, every(one)	jeder, jede	cada uno(una)	ciascuno, a	cada um(uma)
chagrin	grief, sorrow	Kummer(m)	pena	dispiacere	desgosto, pena
chaîne	chain	Kette(f)	cadena	catena	cadeia, corrente
chaîne	channel	Programm, Fernseh-	cadena	canale	canal
chaîne(montagne)	range(mountain)	Bergkette(f)	sierra	catena(monti)	serra
chair	flesh	Fleisch(n)	carne	carne	carne
chaise	chair	Stuhl(m)	silla	sedia	cadeira
chaise longue	deck-chair	Liegestuhl(m)	hamaca	sdraio	preguiceira
châle	shawl	Schal(m)	chal	scialle	xale
chaleur	heat	Hitze(f)	calor	caldo; calore	calor
chaleureux, se	hearty, warm	herzlich	caluroso, a	caloroso, a	caloroso, a
challenge	challenge, contest	Wettkampf(m)	trofeo, challenge	gara, sfida	desafio, torneio
chambre	bedroom, room	Zimmer(n)(Schlaf-)	cuarto	camera, stanza	quarto
chambre d'hôtel	room, hotel room	Hotelzimmer(n)	habitación	camera	quarto
chambre à 1 lit	single room	Einzelzimmer(n)	habitación(1 cama)	camera singola	quarto individual
chambre	chamber	Kammer(f)	cámara	camera	câmara
Chambre(députés)	House, Chamber	Abgeordnetenhaus(n)	cámara(diputados)	camera	câmara
chameau	camel	Kamel(n)	camello	cammello	camelo
champ	field	Feld(n)	campo	campo	campo
champagne	champagne	Champagner(m)	champaña	champagne	champanhe
champignon	mushroom	Pilz(m)	champiñón, seta	fungo	cogumelo
champion, ne	champion	Meister(in f)m	campeón, a	campione, -essa	campeão, campeã
championnat	championship	Meisterschaft(f)	campeonato	campionato	campeonato
chance	luck; chance	Glück(n), Chance(f)	suerte, fortuna	fortuna	sorte
chance(avoir)	fortunate(be)	Glück haben	suerte(tener)	fortuna(avere)	sorte(ter)
chanceler	stagger	taumeln	tambalearse	barcollare	vacilar
chancelier	chancellor	Kanzler(in f)m	canciller	cancelliere	chanceler
chanceux, se	lucky	Glückspilz(m)	afortunado, a	fortunato, a	afortunado, a
chandail	jumper, sweater	Pullover(m)	jersey	maglione	camisola
change	exchange	Wechsel(m)(Geld-)	cambio	cambio	câmbio
changement	change	Veränderung(f)	cambio	cambiamento	mudança
changer	change	ändern	mudar	cambiare	mudar; trocar
changer	shift	wechseln	cambiar	cambiare	mudar; remover
chanson, chant	song	Lied(n)	canción; cante	canzone; canto	canção; canto
chanter	sing	singen	cantar	cantare	cantar
chanteur, se	singer	Sänger(in f)m	cantante	cantante	cantor, a
chantier	work-site	Baustelle(f)	obra	cantiere	obra
chapeau	hat	Hut(m)	sombrero	cappello	chapéu
chapelle	chapel	Kapelle(f)	capilla	cappella	capela
chapitre	chapter	Kapitel(n)	capítulo	capitolo	capítulo
chaque	every, each	jede(r, s)	cada	ogni	cada
charbon	coal	Kohle(f)	carbón	carbone	carvão
charcuterie	delicatessen shop	Metzgerei(f)	salchichería	salumeria	salsicharia
charge	load	Last(f)	carga, peso	carico	carga, peso
charge	contribution	Abgaben(pl.)	carga	onere	encargo
charge	charge	Anklage(f)(punkt m)	cargo	indizio	acusação
charger	load	laden	cargar	caricare	carregar
chargement	load, loading	Ladung(f)	cargamento	carico	carregamento
chariot	trolley	Karre(f)	carro	carrello	carroça, carro
charité	charity	Mildtätigkeit(f)	caridad	carità	caridade
charmant, e	charming, lovely	liebenswert	encantador, a	affascinante	encantador, a
charmant, e	delightful	entzückend, reizend	delicioso, a	delizioso, a	delicioso, a
charme	charm	Charme(m), Reiz(m)	encanto	fascino	encanto
charnière	hinge	Scharnier(n)	bisagra	cerniera	gonzo, dobradiça
charpente	framework	Holzgerüst(n)	armazón	ossatura, travatura	madeiramento
charpentier	carpenter	Zimmermann(m)	carpintero	carpentiere	carpinteiro
charrette	cart	Karren(m)	carreta, carro	carretta	carroça, carreta
chasse	hunting	Jagd(f)	caza	caccia	caça
chasser	hunt	jagen	cazar	cacciare	caçar
chasseur	hunter	Jäger(in f)m	cazador	cacciatore	caçador

French	English	German	Spanish	Italian	Portuguese
chasseur(hôtel)	page(boy), bellboy	Page(m), Hotelboy(m)	botones	fattorino	paquete
châssis	frame, chassis	Rahmen(m), Chassis(n)	chasis	telaio	chassis
chaste	pure	keusch	casto, a	casto, a	casto, a
chat, te	cat	Kater(m), Katze(f)	gato, a	gatto, a	gato, a
châtain	chestnut brown	kastanienbraun	castaño, a	castano, a	castanho, a
château	castle; mansion	Schloß(n)	castillo	castello	castelo
châtiment	punishment	Bestrafung(f)	castigo	castigo	castigo
chatouille(s)	tickle	Kitzeln(n)	cosquillas	solletico	cócegas
chaud, e	hot	heiß	caliente	caldo, a	quente
chaud, e	warm	warm	cálido, a	caldo, a	cálido, a
chauffage	heating	Heizung(f)	calefacción	riscaldamento	aquecimento
chauffer	heat	heizen	calentar	riscaldare	aquecer
chauffeur	driver; chauffeur	Fahrer m; Chauffeur m	chófer	autista	motorista
chauffeur(taxi)	taxi-driver	Taxifahrer(in f)m	taxista	tassista	motorista
chaussée	road	Fahrbahn(f)	calzada	carreggiata	calçada
chausser(se)	put on(shoes)	Schuhe anziehen, sich	calzarse	calzarsi	calçar-se
chaussette(s)	sock	Socke(f), Strumpf(m)	calcetín(es)	calza, e; calzini	peúga
chaussure	shoe	Schuh(m)	calzado	scarpa, e	sapato
chauve	bald	glatzköpfig	calvo, a	calvo, a	calvo, a; careca
chavirer	capsize	kentern, um = kippen	zozobrar	capovolgersi	soçobrar
chef	head; chief; leader	Chef(in f)m	jefe	capo	chefe
chef, dirigeant	leader	Leiter(m), Führer(m)	jefe	capo, dirigente	chefe, líder
chef(entreprise)	manager, head	Betriebsführer(m)	jefe de empresa	dirigente d'azienda	chefe de empresa
chef(orchestre)	conductor	Dirigent(in f)m	director(orquesta)	direttore(orchestra)	maestro(orquestra)
chef d'état	head of state	Staatsoberhaupt(n)	jefe de estado	capo di stato	chefe de estado
chef-d'oeuvre	masterpiece	Meisterwerk(n)	obra maestra	capolavoro	obra-prima
chemin	path; way	Weg(m)	camino	cammino	caminho
chemin, voie	way	Weg(m)	camino	cammino, strada	caminho
chemin de fer	railway	Eisenbahn(f)	ferrocarril	ferrovia	caminho de ferro
cheminée	chimney; fire-place	Kamin(m)	chimenea	camino	chaminé
chemise	shirt	Hemd(n)	camisa	camicia	camisa
chemise de nuit	nightdress(-es)	Nachthemd(n)	camisón	camicia da notte	camisa de noite
chenal	channel	Fahrwasser(n)	canal	canale	canal
chèque	cheque	Scheck(m)	cheque, talón	assegno	cheque
chéquier	cheque book	Scheckheft(n)	talonario(cheques)	libretto di assegni	livro de cheques
cher, ère	dear	liebe(r)	querido, a	caro, a	caro, a; querido, a
cher, ère	expensive, dear	teuer	caro, a	caro, a	caro, a
chercher	look for, search -	suchen	buscar	cercare	procurar; buscar
chercher	seek	holen, suchen	buscar, investigar	cercare	procurar, buscar
chercheur, euse	research worker	Forscher(in f)m	investigador, a	cercatore	investigador, a
chéri, e	dear, darling	Liebling(m)	querido, a	caro, a	querido, a
chétif, ive	puny, weak	schwächlich, kümmer-	endeble	gracile	débil
cheval	horse	Pferd(n)	caballo	cavallo	cavalo
cheveu(x)	hair	Haar(n)	pelo, cabello	capello	cabelo
cheville	ankle	Knöchel(m)	tobillo	caviglia	tornozelo
chèvre	goat	Ziege(f)	cabra	capra	cabra
chez	at, to	bei	en casa de	da	em casa de
chic	smart, chic	schick	elegante	elegante	elegante
chien, ne	dog, bitch(-es)	Hund(m)	perro, a	cane, cagna	cão, cadela
chiffon	rag	Lappen(m)	trapo	straccio	trapo
chiffre	figure, number	Zahl(f), Ziffer(f)	cifra, número	cifra, numero	número
chiffre(affaire)	turnover	Umsatz(m)	volumen(negocios)	fatturato	volume(negócios)
chignon	chignon, bun	Haarknoten(m)	moño	crocchia	carrapicho
chimie	chemistry	Chemie(f)	química	chimica	química
chimique	chemical	chemisch	químico, a	chimico, a	químico, a
chirurgie	surgery	Chirurgie(f)	cirugía	chirurgia	cirurgia
chirurgien	surgeon	Chirurg(in f)m	cirujano	chirurgo	cirurgião
choc	shock, impact	Stoß(m), Aufprall(m)	choque	urto, scontro	choque
choc	shock	Schock(m)	choque	choc, colpo	choque
chocolat	chocolate	Schokolade(f)	chocolate	cioccolato, a	chocolate
choeur	choir	Chor(m)	coro	coro	coro
choisir	choose, select	aus = wählen	escoger	scegliere	escolher
choix	choice	Wahl(f)	escogimiento	scelta	escolha
choléra	cholera	Cholera(f)	cólera	colera	cólera
chômage	unemployment	Arbeitslosigkeit(f)	paro, desempleo	disoccupazione	desemprego
chômeur, euse	unemployed person	Arbeitslose(f, m)	parado, a	disoccupato, a	desempregado, a
choquant, e	shocking	anstößig	chocante	urtante	chocante
chose	thing	Ding(n)	cosa	cosa	coisa

French	English	German	Spanish	Italian	Portuguese
chou	cabbage	Kohl(m)	col	cavolo	couve
chrétien, ne	Christian	Christ(in f)m	cristiano, a	cristiano, a	cristão, cristã
chromosome	chromosome	Chromosom(n)	cromosoma	cromosoma	cromossoma
chronique	chronic	chronisch	crónico, a	cronico, a	crónico, a
chronique	chronicle	Chronik(f)	crónica	cronaca	crónica
chronologie	chronology	Chronologie(f)	cronología	cronologia	cronologia
chronomètre	chronometer	Stoppuhr(f)	cronómetro	cronometro	cronómetro
chuchoter	whisper	flüstern	susurrar	bisbigliare	sussurrar
chut!	hush!, sh!	pst!	chitón(!)	sst!, zitto!	chut!
chute	fall	Fall(m)	caída	caduta	queda
cible	target	Zielscheibe(f)	blanco	bersaglio	alvo
cicatrice	scar	Narbe(f)	cicatriz	cicatrice	cicatriz
ci-dessous	below	unten(-stehend)	abajo(más)	sotto(qui)	abaixo
ci-dessus	above	oben(-stehend)	arriba(más)	sopra(qui)	acima
cidre	cider	Apfelwein(m)	sidra	sidro	sidra
ciel	sky	Himmel(m)	cielo	cielo	céu
ciel, paradis	heaven	Himmel(m)	cielo, paraíso	cielo, paradiso	céu, paraíso
cierge	candle	Kerze(f)	cirio	cero	círio
cigare	cigar	Zigarre(f)	cigarro, puro	sigaro	charuto
cigarette	cigarette	Zigarette(f)	cigarrillo	sigaretta	cigarro
ci-joint, e	enclosed	anbei	adjunto, a	allegato, a	anexo(em)
cil	eyelash(-es)	Wimper(f)	pestaña	ciglio(a)	pestana
cime	summit, peak, top	Gipfel(m)	cima	cima, vetta	cimo, cume
ciment	cement	Zement(m)	cemento	cemento	cimento
cimetière	cemetery	Friedhof(m)	cementerio	cimitero	cemitério
cinéaste	film-producer	Filmproduzent(in f)m	cineasta	cineasta	cineasta
cinéma	cinema	Kino(n)	cine	cinema	cinema
cinglé, e	mad, nuts, barmy	verrückt	chiflado, a	tocco, a; picchiato, a	doido, a; louco, a
cinq	five	fünf	cinco	cinque	cinco
cinquante	fifty	fünfzig	cincuenta	cinquanta	cinquenta
cintre	hanger, coat-hanger	Bügel(m)	percha	gruccia, attaccapanni	cabide
circonférence	circumference	Kreisumfang(m)	circunferencia	circonferenza	circunferência
circonstance	circumstance	Umstand(m)	circunstancia	circostanza	circunstância
circuit	circuit	Strecke(f)(Renn-)	circuito	circuito	circuito
circuit	circuit, system	Stromkreis(m)	circuito	circuito	circuito
circuit	tour	Rundfahrt(f)(-reise)	circuito	giro, circuito	circuito
circulaire	circular	rund	circular	circolare	circular
circulation	traffic	Verkehr(m)	tráfico	traffico	trânsito
circulation	circulation	Kreislauf(m)	circulación	circolazione	circulação
circuler	circulate	umher = gehen	circular	circolare	circular
circuler	circulate	zirkulieren	circular	circolare	circular
cire	wax, polish	Wachs(n)	cera	cera	cera
cirer	polish	polieren, wachsen	dar crema	lucidare	encerar
cirque	circus	Zirkus(m)	circo	circo	circo
cirrhose	cirrhosis	Zirrhose(f)	cirrosis	cirrosi	cirrose
ciseaux	scissors	Schere(f)	tijeras	forbici	tesoura
citadin, e	town/city dweller	Städter(in f)m	ciudadano, a	cittadino, a	citadino, a
cité	city	Stadt(f)	ciudad	città	cidade
citer	quote	zitieren	citar	citare	citar
citoyen, ne	citizen	Bürger(in f)m	ciudadano, a	cittadino, a	cidadão, cidadã
citron	lemon	Zitrone(f)	limón	limone	limão
civière	stretcher	Bahre(f)	camilla	barella	maca
civil, e	civil	zivil	civil	civile	civil
civilisation	civilization	Zivilisation(f)	civilización	civiltà	civilização
civiliser	civilize	zivilisieren	civilizar	civilizzare	civilizar
civique	civic	staatsbürgerlich	cívico, a	civico, a	cívico, a
clair, e	light	hell	claro, a	chiaro, a	claro, a
clair, e	clear	klar	claro, a	chiaro, a; limpido, a	claro, a
clan	clan	Sippe(f)	clan	clan	clã
clandestin, e	clandestine	heimlich	clandestino, a	clandestino, a	clandestino, a
clapet	valve	Klappenventil(n)	válvula	valvola	válvula
claque	slap	Ohrfeige(f)	bofetada	schiaffo	bofetada
clarifier	clarify	klären	clarificar	chiarificare	clarificar
clarinette	clarinet	Klarinette(f)	clarinete	clarinetto	clarinete
clarté	brightness	Helligkeit(f)	claridad	chiarezza	claridade
classe	class	Klasse(f)	clase	classe, ceto	classe
classe	class, form	Klassenstufe(f)	clase, curso	classe	classe
classe(salle)	classroom	Klassenzimmer(n)	aula	aula	aula(sala de)

French	English	German	Spanish	Italian	Portuguese
classement	filing	Einorden(n)	clasificación	classificazione	classificação
classer	classify, file	ordnen	clasificar	classificare	classificar
classeur	file	Ordner(m)	clasificador	schedario	classificador
classique	classical	klassisch	clásico, a	classico, a	clássico, a
clause	clause	Klausel(f)	cláusula	clausola	cláusula
clavicule	collar-bone	Schlüsselbein(n)	clavícula	clavicola	clavícula
clavier	keyboard	Tastatur(f)	teclado	tastiera	teclado
clef, clé	key	Schlüssel(m)	llave	chiave	chave
clé	spanner, wrench	Schraubenschlüssel(m)	llave	chiave	chave
clergé	clergy	Klerus(m)	clero	clero	clero
cliché, négatif	negative	Negativ(n)	cliché	negativo	cliché
client, e	customer	Kunde(m), Kundin(f)	cliente	cliente	cliente
client, e	client	Klient(in f)m	cliente	cliente	cliente
clignotant	indicator	Blinklicht(n)	intermitente	freccia	pisca
clignoter	flash	blinken	pestañear	lampeggiare	piscar
climat	climate	Klima(n)	clima	clima	clima
climatiseur	air conditioner	Klimaanlage(f)	climatizador	condizionatore	climatizador
clinique	nursing-home	Klinik(f)	clínica	clinica	clínica
clochard, e	tramp	Penner(m)	vagabundo, a	barbone, a; vagabondo	vagabundo, a
cloche	bell	Glocke(f)	campana	campana	sino
cloison	partition	Trennwand(f)	tabique	tramezzo	tabique
cloque	blister	Blase(f)(Brandblase)	ampolla	vescica	bolha
clôture	fence, railings	Zaun(m)	valla, cerca	recinzione, muro	cerca, vedação
clôture	closure, closing	Schluß(m)(Abschluß m)	clausura	chiusura	encerramento
clou	nail	Nagel(m)	clavo	chiodo	prego
clouer	nail	nageln	clavar	inchiodare	pregar, cravar
clown	clown	Clown(m)	payaso	pagliaccio, clown	palhaço
club	club	Klub(m)	club	club	clube
coaguler	coagulate, clot	gerinnen	coagular	coagulare	coagular
coalition	coalition	Koalition(f)	coalición	coalizione	coligação
cobaye	guinea-pig(be a)	Versuchskaninchen(n)	conejillo(Indias)	cavia	cobaia
cobra	cobra	Kobra(f)	cobra	cobra	cobra
cocaïne	cocaine	Kokain(n)	cocaína	cocaina	cocaína
cocher	tick	an = kreuzen	marcar	segnare	marcar
cocktail	cocktail	Cocktail(m)	cóctel	cocktail	coquetel
cocktail	party(cocktail -)	Party(f)	cóctel	party	recepção
cocotier	coconut palm(tree)	Kokuspalme(f)	cocotero	palma da cocco	coqueiro
code	code	Kod(m)	código	codice	código
coder	code, encode	verschlüsseln	codificar	cifrare	codificar
codifier	codify	kodifizieren	codificar	codificare	codificar
coefficient	coefficient	Koeffizient(m)	coeficiente	coefficiente	coeficiente
coeur	heart	Herz(n)	corazón	cuore	coração
coffre	boot	Kofferraum(m)	maletero	bagagliaio	mala
coffre-fort	safe	Safe(m)	caja fuerte	cassaforte	cofre-forte
coffret	box, case	Schmuckkasten(m)	estuche	portagioie	estojo
cogner(se)	knock	stoßen, sich	golpe(darse un)	sbattere	chocar com
cohérent, e	coherent	zusammenhängend	coherente	coerente	coerente
cohésion	cohesion	Zusammenhalt(m)	cohesión	coesione	coesão
cohue, foule	crush, crowd	Menge(f)	barullo, jaleo	ressa, affollamento	multidão, confusão
coiffer(se)	hair(do one's)	frisieren, sich	peinar(se)	pettinare(-rsi)	pentear-se
coiffeur, se	hairdresser	Friseur(m), Friseuse f	peluquero, a	parrucchiere, a	cabeleireiro, a
coiffure	hair-style	Frisur(f)	peinado	pettinatura	penteado
coin	corner	Ecke(f)	esquina, rincón	angolo	canto, esquina
coincer	jam	ein = klemmen	apretar, apiñar	schiacciare, stipare	apertar, comprimir
coincidence	coincidence	Zusammentreffen(n)	coincidencia	coincidenza	coincidência
col	collar	Kragen(m)	cuello	collo, colletto	colarinho; gola
col	pass	Paß(m)	puerto	colle, passo	desfiladeiro
colère	anger(be angry)	Wut(f)	cólera, ira	collera, ira	cólera, ira
colique	colic	Kolik(f)	cólico	colica	cólica
colis	parcel	Paket(n)	paquete	pacco, collo	pacote
collaborateur	assistant	Mitarbeiter(in f)m	colaborador, a	collaboratore, -trice	colaborador, a
collaboration	collaboration	Mitarbeit(f)	colaboración	collaborazione	colaboração
collants	tights(pair of)	Strumpfhose(f)	pantys	collant	meias
colle	glue	Klebstoff(m)	cola, pegamento	colla	cola
collectif, ive	collective	gemeinschaftlich	colectivo, a	collettivo, a	colectivo, a
collection	collection	Kollektion(f)	colección	collezione	colecção
collection	collection	Sammlung(f)	colección	collezione	colecção
collectionner	collect	sammeln	coleccionar	collezionare	coleccionar

30

French	English	German	Spanish	Italian	Portuguese
collège	comprehensive(Jnr)	Oberschule(f)	escuela(EGB)	scuola media	escola preparatória
collège	college	Kollegium(n)	colegio	collegio	colégio
collègue	colleague	Kollege(m), Kollegin f	colega	collega	colega
coller	stick, glue	kleben	pegar	incollare	colar, pegar
collier	necklace	Halskette(f); Kette(f)	collar	collana	colar
colline	hill	Hügel(m)	colina	collina	colina
collision	collision	Zusammenstoß(m)	colisión, choque	collisione	colisão, choque
colloque	symposium	Symposium(n)	coloquio	colloquio	colóquio
colonel	colonel	Oberst(m)	coronel	colonnello	coronel
colonie	colony	Kolonie(f)	colonia	colonia	colónia
colonisation	colonization	Kolonisierung(f)	colonización	colonizzazione	colonização
colonne	column	Säule(f)	columna	colonna	coluna
colonne(vertéb-)	spine	Wirbelsäule(f)	columna vertebral	colonna vertebrale	coluna vertebral
colorant	colouring	Farbstoff(m)	colorante	colorante	corante
colorer	colour	färben	colorear	colorare	colorir
colorier	colour(in)	an = malen	colorear	colorare	colorir
colossal, e	colossal	riesig	colosal	colossale	colossal
coma	coma	Koma(n)	coma	coma	coma
combat	combat, fight	Kampf(m)	combate	combattimento	combate
combattant, e	fighting-man	Kämpfer(m)	combatiente	combattente	combatente
combattre	fight	streiten, kämpfen	combatir	combattere	combater
combien	how much, how many	wieviel	cuánto; cuanto	quanto	quanto
combinaison	combination	Kombination(f)	combinación	combinazione	combinação
combinaison	suit(ski-)	Anzug(m)(Ski-)	traje	tuta, completo	fato
combinaison	suit(space-)	Anzug(Raum-)(m)	traje(espacial)	tuta(spaziale)	fato(espacial)
combinaison	slip	Unterrock(m)	combinación	sottoveste	combinação
combustible	combustible	verbrennbar	combustible	combustibile	combustível
comédie	comedy	Komödie(f)	comedia	commedia	comédia
comédien, ne	actor, actress(-es)	Schauspieler(in f)m	actor, actriz	attore, attrice	actor, actriz
comédien, ne	comedian	Komödiant(in f)m	comediante, a	commediante	comediante, a
comestible	edible	eßbar	comestible	commestibile	comestível
comète	comet	Komet(m)	cometa	cometa	cometa
comique	comic, funny	komisch	cómico, a	comico, a	cómico, a
comique	comedian, comic	Komiker(in f)m	cómico	comico	cómico
comité	committee	Komitee(n), Ausschuß m	comité	comitato	comissão
commandant	major	Kommandant(m), Major m	comandante	comandante	comandante
commande	order	Bestellung(f)	encargo, pedido	ordinazione	encomenda
commandement	command	Befehl(m)(-sgewalt f)	mando	comando	comando
commander	order	bestellen	pedir, encargar	ordinare	encomendar
commander	command	befehlen, befehligen	ordenar, mandar	comandare	comandar
commando	commando	Kommando(n)	comando	comando	comando
comme	as; like	wie	como	come	como
commémorer	commemorate	gedenken	conmemorar	commemorare	comemorar
commencement	beginning, start	Anfang(m)	comienzo, principio	principio, inizio	começo, princípio
commencer	begin, start	an = fangen	comenzar	cominciare	começar
commencer	start	an = fangen	principiar	cominciare, iniziare	principiar
comment	how	wie	cómo	come	como
comment?	pardon?	wie bitte?	cómo(?)	come?, come dice?	como disse?
commentaire	commentary	Kommentar(m)	comentario	commentario	comentário
commentaire	comment	Anmerkung(f)	comentario	commento	comentário
commenter	comment(on)	erläutern	comentar	commentare	comentar
commerçant, e	tradesman(-men)	Geschäftsmann m/-frau	comerciante	commerciante	comerciante
commerçant, e	shop-keeper	Kaufmann m, Kauffrau f	tendero, a	negoziante	comerciante
commerce	trade, commerce	Handel(m)	comercio	commercio	comércio
commerce	shop, business	Geschäft(n)	tienda, negocio	negozio	loja
commercial, e	commercial	geschäftlich	comercial	commerciale	comercial
commercialiser	market	vermarkten	comercializar	commercializzare	comercializar
commettre	commit	begehen, verüben	cometer	commettere	cometer
commissariat	police station	Kommissariat(n)	comisaría	commissariato	esquadra(polícia)
commission	commission	Kommission(f)	comisión	commissione	comissão
commission	committee	Ausschuß(m)	comisión	commissione	comissão
commode	convenient	praktisch	cómodo, a	comodo, a	cómodo, a
commun, e	common, usual	gewöhnlich	común	comune	comum
commun, e	common	Gemeinschafts-	común	comune	comum
communauté	community	Gemeinschaft(f)	comunidad	comunità	comunidade
communication	communication	Verständigung(f)	comunicación	comunicazione	comunicação
communiquer	communicate	mitteilen	comunicar	comunicare	comunicar
communisme	communism	Kommunismus(m)	comunismo	comunismo	comunismo

French	English	German	Spanish	Italian	Portuguese
commutateur	switch	Schalter(m)	conmutador	commutatore	comutador
compact, e	compact	kompakt	compacto, a	compatto, a	compacto, a
compagnie	company	Gesellschaft(f)	compañía	compagnia	companhia
compagnie(en)	company of(in the)	Gesellschaft(in)	compañía(en)	compagnia(in)	companhia(em)
compagnon, agne	companion	Begleiter(in f)m	compañero, a	compagno, a	companheiro, a
comparer	compare	vergleichen	comparar	paragonare	comparar
compartiment	compartment	Abteil(n)	compartimiento	compartimento	compartimento
compas	compass(es)	Kompaß(m)	compás	compasso	compasso
compatir	sympathize	mit = fühlen	compadecer	compatire	apiedar-se
compensation	compensation	Kompensation(f)	compensación	compenso	compensação
compétence	competence	Zuständigkeit(f)	competencia	competenza	competência
compétent, e	competent	kompetent	competente, capaz	competente	competente, capaz
compétition	competition	Wettbewerb(m)	competición	competizione, gara	competição
complément	complement	Ergänzung(f)	complemento	complemento	complemento
complet, ète	complete, full	vollständig, voll	completo, a	completo, a	completo, a
complètement	completely	völlig	completamente	completamente	completamente
complexe	complex	Komplex(m)	complejo	complesso	complexo
complice	accomplice	Komplize(m), Komplizin	cómplice	complice	cúmplice
compliment	compliment	Kompliment(n)	cumplido	complimento	cumprimento
compliqué, e	complicated	kompliziert	complicado, a	complicato, a	complicado, a
complot	conspiracy, plot	Verschwörung(f)	complot	complotto	conspiração
comportement	behaviour	Verhalten(n)	comportamiento	comportamento	comportamento
composant	component	Bestandteil(m)	componente	componente	componente
composer	compose	zusammen = stellen	componer	comporre	compor
composer(n°tél)	dial	Nummer(f)(wählen)	marcar un número	comporre(numero)	discar, marcar
compositeur	composer	Komponist(in f)m	compositor	compositore	compositor
composition	composition	Zusammensetzung(f)	composición	composizione	composição
compote	stewed fruit	Kompott(n)	compota	frutta cotta	compota
comprendre	understand	verstehen	comprender	capire	compreender
comprendre	understand	begreifen, verstehen	entender	comprendere	entender
comprendre	comprise	ein = begreifen	comprender	comprendere	compreender
compression	compression	Druck(m)	compresión	compressione	compressão
comprimé	tablet, pill	Tablette(f)	comprimido	compressa	comprimido
comprimer	compress	drücken	comprimir	comprimere	comprimir
compromettre	compromise	bloß = stellen(jdn.)	comprometer	compromettere	comprometer
compromis	compromise	Kompromiß(m)	compromiso	compromesso	compromisso
compromission	compromising	Kompromittierung(f)	compromiso	compromissione	comprometimento
comptabilité	accountancy	Buchhaltung(f)	contabilidad	contabilità	contabilidade
comptable	accountant	Buchhalter(in f)m	contable	ragioniere	contabilista
comptant	cash	Barzahlung(f)	contado(al)	contanti	pronto(a)
compte	account	Konto(n)	cuenta	conto	conta
compte	account	Rechnung(f)	cuenta	conto	conta
compter	count	zählen	contar	contare	contar
compter sur	rely on	zählen, auf jdn	contar con	contare su	contar com
compte rendu	report, minutes	Bericht(m)	informe, acta	resoconto	relatório, acta
compteur	meter	Zähler(m)	contador	contatore	contador
comptoir	counter	Ladentisch(m)	mostrador	banco	balcão
comptoir	counter, bar	Theke(f)	barra	banco	balcão
concentrer	concentrate	konzentrieren	concentrar	concentrare	concentrar
concentrer(se)	concentrate	konzentrieren, sich	concentrar(se)	concentrarsi	concentrar-se
concept	concept	Begriff(m)	concepto	concetto	conceito
conception	conception	Konzeption(f)	concepción	concezione	concepção
concerner	concern	betreffen	concernir	riguardare	dizer respeito a
concert	concert	Konzert(n)	concierto	concerto	concerto
concertation	cooperation	Zusammenarbeit(f)	concertación	concertazione	concertação
concevoir	conceive(of)	vor = stellen, sich	concebir	concepire	conceber
concevoir	design	entwerfen	concebir	ideare	conceber
concierge	porter, caretaker	Hausmeister(in f)m	conserje	portiere, a	porteiro, a
conclure	conclude	schließen, abschließen	concluir	concludere	concluir
conclusion	conclusion	Abschluß(m)	conclusión	conclusione	conclusão
concorder	tally, agree	überein = stimmen	concordar	concordare	concordar
concours	competition	Wettbewerb(m)	concurso	concorso	concurso
concours	contest	Wettbewerb(m)	concurso	gara	concurso
concours	competitive exam	Prüfung(f)	oposiciones	concorso	concurso
concours	cooperation, help	Mitwirkung(unter)	ayuda	concorso	colaboração
concret, ète	concrete	konkret	concreto, a	concreto, a	concreto, a
concubinage	co-habitation	wilde Ehe(f)	concubinato	concubinato	concubinato
concurrence	competition	Konkurrenz(f)	competencia	concorrenza	concorrência

32

concurrent, e	competitor	konkurrent(in f)m	competidor, a	concorrente	concorrente
condamnation	sentence	Verurteilung(f)	condenación	condanna	condenação
condamner	condemn	verurteilen	condenar	condannare	condenar
condamner	convict, sentence	verurteilen	condenar	condannare	condenar
condensation	condensation	Kondensierung(f)	condensación	condensazione	condensação
condition	condition	Bedingung(f)	condición	condizione	condição
conducteur, trice	driver	Fahrer(in f)m	conductor, a	conducente	condutor, a
conduire	drive	fahren	conducir	guidare	conduzir
conduit(e)	pipe	Röhre(f), Leitung(f)	caño, conducto	condotto(a)	cano, tubo
cône	cone	Kegel(m)	cono	cono	cone
confection	clothing industry	Anfertigung(f)	confección	confezione	confecção
conférence	conference; lecture	Konferenz(f)	conferencia	conferenza	conferência
conférence	lecture	Vorlesung(f), Vortrag	conferencia	conferenza	conferência
confiance	confidence, trust	Vertrauen(n)	confianza	fiducia	confiança
confiance(avoir)	trust	vertrauen(jdm.)	confianza(tener)	fiducia(aver)	confiar
confidence	confidence, secret	Vertrauen(im)	confidencia	confidenza	confidência
confidentiel, le	confidential	vertraulich	confidencial	confidenziale	confidencial
confier	entrust	an = vertrauen	confiar	affidare	confiar
confirmer	confirm	bestätigen	confirmar	confermare	confirmar, comprovar
confiserie	sweet shop	Süßwarenladen(m)	confitería	confetteria	confeitaria
confiture	jam	Marmelade(f)	mermelada	marmellata	doce, compota
conflit	conflict	Konflikt(m)	conflicto	conflitto	conflito
confondre	confuse, mistake	verwechseln	confundir	confondere	confundir
conforme à	in accordance with	entsprechend	conforme a/con	conforme a	conforme com
confort	comfort	Bequemlichkeit(f)	confort	comodità	conforto
confortable	comfortable	bequem	cómodo, a	confortevole	confortável
confronter	confront	konfrontieren	confrontar	confrontare	confrontar
confusion	confusion	Verwechslung(f)	confusión	confusione	confusão
congé	holiday, vacation	Urlaub(m)	vacaciones	ferie(le)	férias
congélateur	freezer	Kühltruhe(f)	congelador	congelatore	congelador
congestion	congestion	Blutandrang(m)	congestión	congestione	congestão
congratuler	congratulate	gratulieren	congratular	congratulare	congratular
congrès	congress	Kongress(m)	congreso	congresso	congresso
conifère	conifer	Nadelbaum(m)	conifera	conifera	conífera
conique	conical	kegelförmig	cónico, a	conico, a	cónico, a
conjoncture	conjuncture	Konjunktur(f)	coyuntura	congiuntura	conjuntura
conjugaison	conjugation	Konjugation(f)	conjugación	coniugazione	conjugação
conjugal, e	married, marriage-	ehelich	conyugal	coniugale	conjugal
connaissance	knowledge	Kenntnis(f)	conocimiento	conoscenza	conhecimento
connaître	know	kennen	conocer, saber	conoscere, sapere	conhecer, saber
connecter	connect	kuppeln, verbinden	conectar	connettere	ligar
connexion	connection	Verbindung; Anschluß	conexión	connessione	conexão
conquête	conquest	Eroberung(f)	conquista	conquista	conquista
consacrer	consecrate	weihen	consagrar	consacrare	consagrar
consacrer	devote	widmen	dedicar	dedicare	dedicar
conscience	conscience	Bewußtsein(n)	conciencia	coscienza	consciência
conscient, e	conscious	bewußt	consciente	cosciente, conscio, a	consciente
consécration	consecration	Weihe(f)	consagración	consacrazione	consagração
consécutif, ive	consecutive	folgend	consecutivo, a	consecutivo, a	consecutivo, a
conseil	advice	Rat(m)	consejo	consiglio	conselho
conseil	council	Rat(m)(Europrat m)	consejo	consiglio	conselho
conseil	council	Rat(m)(Stadtrat m)	concejo	giunta, consiglio	município
conseiller	advise	beraten	aconsejar	consigliare	aconselhar
conseiller, ère	adviser	Berater(in f)m	consejero, a	consigliere, a	conselheiro, a
conseiller, ère	councillor	Rat(m)(Staatsrat m)	concejal, a	consigliere, a	conselheiro, a
consentir	agree	ein = willigen	consentir	consentire	consentir
consentir	consent	zu = stimmen	consentir	consentire	consentir
conséquence	consequence	Konsequenz(f)	consecuencia	conseguenza	consequência
conséquent(par)	therefore	folglich; deshalb	consiguiente(por)	perciò	conseguinte(por)
conservation	conservation	Konservierung(f)	conservación	conservazione	conservação
conserve(s)	tinned food	Konserve(f)	conserva	conserva	conserva
conserver	preserve, keep	konservieren	conservar	conservare	conservar
considérable	considerable	erheblich	considerable	considerevole	considerável
considération	consideration	Betrachtung(f)	consideración	considerazione	consideração
considérer	consider	an = sehen(als)	considerar	considerare	considerar
considérer	regard	betrachten	considerar	considerare	considerar
consigne	orders, instruction	Anweisung(f)	consigna, orden	direttiva, ordine	ordem, instruções
consigne	luggage lockers	Schließfach(n)	consigna	cassetta, deposito	depósito

33

French	English	German	Spanish	Italian	Portuguese
consigne(bagage)	left luggage	Gepäckaufbewahrung(f)	consigna(equipaje)	deposito bagagli	depósito(bagagem)
consister à	consist(in, of)	bestehen aus	consistir en	consistere in	consistir em
consoler	console, comfort	trösten	consolar	consolare	consolar
consolider	strengthen	verstärken	consolidar	consolidare	consolidar
consommateur	consumer	Verbraucher(in f)m	consumidor, a	consumatore, trice	consumidor, a
consommation	consumption	Verbrauch(m)	consumo	consumo	consumo
consommer	consume	verbrauchen	consumir	consumare	consumir
consonne	consonant	Mitlaut(m)	consonante	consonante	consoante
conspiration	plot, conspiracy	Komplott(n)	conspiración	cospirazione	conspiração
constant, e	constant	beständig	constante	costante	constante
constater	state; note	fest = stellen	constatar	constatare	constatar
constellation	constellation	Konstellation(f)	constelación	costellazione	constelação
constipation	constipation	Verstopfung(f)	estreñimiento	stitichezza	prisão de ventre
constituer	constitute	bilden	constituir	costituire	constituir
constitution	constitution	Verfassung(f)	constitución	costituzione	constituição
construction	construction	Bau(m)	construcción	costruzione	construção
construire	construct, build	bauen	construir	costruire	construir
consul	consul	Konsul(m)	cónsul	console	cônsul
consulat	consulate	Konsulat(n)	consulado	consolato	consulado
consulter	consult	befragen	consultar	consultare	consultar
contact	contact	Kontakt(m)	contacto	contatto	contacto
contact(prendre)	contact	Kontakt(auf = nehmen)	contacto(entrar en)	contattare	contactar
contagieux, se	contagious	ansteckend	contagioso, a	contagioso, a	contagioso, a
contagion	contagion	Ansteckung(f)	contagio	contagio	contágio
contamination	contamination	Ansteckung(f)	contaminación	contaminazione	contaminação
conte	tale, story	Märchen(n)	cuento	racconto, fiaba	conto
contempler	contemplate	betrachten	contemplar	contemplare	contemplar
contemporain, e	contemporary	zeitgenössisch	contemporáneo, a	contemporaneo, a	contemporâneo, a
contenance	capacity, content	Fassungsvermögen(n)	capacidad	capacità	capacidade
contenir	contain	enthalten	contener	contenere	conter
content, e	pleased, glad	froh	contento, a	contento, a	contente
content, e	glad, happy, pleased	froh, erfreut	contento, a	contento, a	contente
contenu	content(s)	Inhalt(m)	contenido	contenuto	conteúdo
contester	contest	bestreiten	impugnar, objetar	contestare	contestar
continent	continent	Kontinent(m)	continente	continente	continente
continu, e	continuous	ununterbrochen	continuo, a	continuo, a	contínuo, a
continuel, le	continual	ständig	continuo, a	continuo, a	contínuo, a
continuer	continue, go on	fort = setzen	continuar	continuare	continuar
contour	outline, contour	Umriß(m)	contorno	contorno	contorno
contourner	bypass	umgehen	contornear	aggirare	contornar
contraceptif	contraceptive	Verhütungsmittel(n)	anticonceptivo	anticoncezionale	contraceptivo
contraction	contraction	Zusammenziehen(n)	contracción	contrazione	contracção
contradiction	contradiction	Widerspruch(m)	contradicción	contraddizione	contradição
contraindre	force, compel	zwingen	obligar a	costringere	obrigar
contrainte	restraint	Zwang(m)	obligación	costrizione	obrigação
contraire	contrary	entgegengesetzt	contrario, a	contrario, a	contrário, a
contraire	opposite, contrary	Gegenteil(n)	contrario	contrario	contrário
contrarié, e	upset	ärgerlich sein	contrariado, a	contrariato, a	contrariado, a
contrariété	annoyance	Verdruß(m)	molestia	seccatura	contrariedade
contraste	contrast	Gegensatz(m)	contraste	contrasto	contraste
contrat	contract	Vertrag(m), Kontrakt m	contrato	contratto	contrato
contre	against	gegen, an	contra	contro	encostado a
contre	against	wider, gegen	contra(en)	contro	contra
contre-attaque	counter-attack	Gegenangriff(m)	contraataque	contro-attacco	contra-ataque
contrebande	smuggling	Schmuggel(m)	contrabando	contrabbando	contrabando
contredire	contradict	widersprechen	contradecir	contraddire	contradizer
contrer	counter	Kontra geben	oponerse(a)	opporsi(a)	contrariar
contribuer	contribute	bei = tragen	contribuir	contribuire	contribuir
contrôle	control, check	Aufsicht(f), Prüfung f	control	controllo	controlo
contrôle	examination	Kontrolle(f)	control	controllo	controlo
contrôler	control, check	kontrollieren	controlar	controllare	controlar
contrôler	inspect	besichtigen	controlar, examinar	esaminare	examinar
contrôleur	inspector	Kontrolleur(m)	revisor	controllore	revisor; fiscal
contusion	bruise	Quetschung(f)	contusión	contusione	contusão
convaincre	convince	überzeugen	convencer	convincere	convencer
convalescence	convalescence	Genesung(f)	convalecencia	convalescenza	convalescência
convenable	suitable, fitting	angemessen	conveniente	conveniente	conveniente
convenir	suit, fit	passen	convenir	convenire	estar bem

French	English	German	Spanish	Italian	Portuguese
convenir	agree	überein = kommen	acordar	convenire	convir, combinar
convention	agreement	Übereinstimmung(f)	convención	convenzione	convenção
converger	converge	konvergieren	converger	convergere	convergir
conversation	conversation	Gespräch(n)	conversación	conversazione	conversação
convertir(se)	convert	konvertieren	convertirse	convertirsi	converter-se
conviction	conviction	Überzeugung(f)	convicción	convinzione	convicção
convive	guest	Gast(m)	convidado, a	commensale	conviva
convocation	notification	Einberufung(f); Ladung	convocatoria	convocazione	convocação
convoi	convoy	Konvoi(m)	convoy	convoglio	comboio
convoiter	covet	begehren	codiciar	ambire, desiderare	cobiçar
convoquer	summon; invite	vor = laden	convocar	convocare	convocar
convulsion	convulsion	Zuckung(f), Krampf(m)	convulsión	convulsione	convulsão
coordonner	coordinate	koordinieren	coordinar	coordinare	coordenar
coopération	cooperation	Mitarbeit(f)	cooperación	cooperazione	cooperação
coopérative	cooperative	Genossenschaft(f)	cooperativa	cooperativa	cooperativa
coopérer	cooperate	mit = arbeiten	cooperar	cooperare	cooperar
copie	copy	Kopie(f)	copia	copia	cópia
copier	copy	kopieren	copiar	copiare	copiar
copieux, se	copious	reichlich	copioso, a	abbondante	copioso, a
coq	cock	Hahn(m)	gallo	gallo	galo
coque	hull	Rumpf(m)	casco	scafo	casco
coquet, te	pretty; coquettish	kokett; eitel	presumido, a	civettuolo, a	vaidoso, a
coquillage	shell-fish; shell	Muschel(f)	marisco	conchiglia	concha
coquille, coque	shell	Schale(f)	cáscara	guscio	casca
coquille	shell	Schale(f), Muschel(f)	concha	conchiglia	concha
coquin, e	mischievous	schelmisch	travieso, a	birbante, birichino, a	travesso, a; maroto, a
corail	coral	Koralle(f)	coral	corallo	coral
Coran	Koran	Koran(der)	Corán	Corano	Alcorão
corbeau	crow	Rabe(m)	cuervo	corvo	corvo
corbeille	basket; bin	Korb(m)(Papierkorb m)	cesto(a); cestillo	cestino	cesto, a
corde	rope	Tau(n)	cuerda	corda	corda
cordial, e	cordial, hearty	herzlich, freundlich	cordial	cordiale	cordial
cordon	cord, string	Kordel(f)	cordón, cable	cordone	cordão
corne	horn	Horn(n)	cuerno	corno	corno; chifre
corporation	corporation	Körperschaft(f)	corporación	corporazione	corporação
corporel, le	bodily	körperlich	corporal	corporale	corporal
corps	body	Körper(m)	cuerpo	corpo	corpo
correct, e	correct; proper	richtig	correcto, a	corretto, a	correcto, a
correctement	properly	richtig	correctamente	correttamente	correctamente
correction	correction	Verbesserung(f)	corrección	correzione	correcção
correspondance	correspondence	Korrespondenz(f)	correspondencia	corrispondenza	correspondência
correspondance	connection	Verbindung, Anschluß	empalme	coincidenza	correspondência
correspondre	correspond, tally	entsprechen	corresponder	corrispondere	corresponder
corrida	bull-fight	Stierkampf(m)	corrida	corrida	toirada
corriger	correct, rectify	korrigieren	corregir	correggere	corrigir
corriger	rectify, correct	berichtigen	corregir	correggere	rectificar
corrompu, e	corrupt	verdorben, korrupt	corrompido, a	corrotto, a	corrupto, a
corrosion	corrosion	Korrosion(f)	corrosión	corrosione	corrosão
corruption	corruption	Korruption(f)	corrupción	corruzione	corrupção
cortège	procession	Umzug(m), Festzug(m)	cortejo	corteo	cortejo
cosmétique	cosmetic	Kosmetik(f)	cosmético	cosmetico	cosmético
cosmonaute	astronaut	Astronaut(m)	cosmonauta	cosmonauta	cosmonauta
cosmopolite	cosmopolitan	kosmopolitisch	cosmopolita	cosmopolita	cosmopolita
costume	suit	Anzug(m)	traje	abito, vestito	fato, traje
cotation	quotation	Kurswert(m)	cotización	quotazione	cotação
côte	coast	Küste(f)	costa	costa	costa
côte	rib	Rippe(f)	costilla	costola	costela
côte	hill, slope	Abhang(m), Steigung(f)	cuesta	salita, pendio	ladeira, encosta
côté	side	Seite(f)	lado	lato	lado
coteau	hill(side)	Anhöhe(f), Hang(m)	ladera	colle, collinetta	encosta; colina
côtier, ère	coastal	Küsten-	costero, a	costiero, a	costeiro, a
cotisation	contribution	Beitrag(m)	cotización	contributo	contribuição
cotisation	subscription, dues	Beitrag m(Mitglieds-)	cuota	quota	quota
coton	cotton	Baumwolle(f)	algodón	cotone	algodão
cou	neck	Hals(m), Nacken(m)	cuello	collo	pescoço
couche	layer	Schicht(f)	capa	strato	camada
couche	coat	Anstrich(m)	capa	strato	camada
coucher(se)	go to bed	schlafen gehen	ir a la cama	andare a letto	deitar-se

35

French	English	German	Spanish	Italian	Portuguese
coucher(soleil)	sunset	Sonnenuntergang(m)	puesta de sol	tramonto	pôr do sol
couchette	couchette	Liegeplatz(m)	litera	cuccetta	couchette
coude	elbow	Ellenbogen(m)	codo	gomito	cotovelo
coudre	sew	nähen	coser	cucire	coser
couler	flow, run	fließen	correr, fluir	scorrere	correr
couler, enfoncer	sink	sinken, versenken	hundir	affondare	afundar
couleur	colour	Farbe(f)	color	colore	côr
coulisses	wings	Kulisse(f)	bastidores	quinte(le)	bastidores
couloir	corridor	Flur(m)	pasillo	corridoio	corredor
coup	knock, blow	Schlag(m)	golpe	colpo	golpe
coup de poing	punch	Faustschlag(m)	puñetazo	pugno	soco; murro
coup de pied	kick	Fußtritt(m)	patada	calcio	pontapé
coup de soleil	sunburn	Sonnenbrand(m)	insolación	scottatura	insolação
coupable	guilty	schuldig	culpable	colpevole	culpado, a
coupe	glass(-es)	Kelch(m), Schale(f)	copa	calice	taça
coupe	cup	Pokal(m)	copa	coppa	taça
coupé, e	cut	geschnitten	cortado, a	tagliato, a	cortado, a
couper	cut	schneiden	cortar	tagliare	cortar
couple	couple	Paar(n)	pareja	coppia	casal
coupole	dome	Kuppel(f)	cúpula, bóveda	cupola	cúpula
coupure(peau)	cut	Schnitt(m)	corte, tajo	taglio	corte, golpe
cour	yard	Hof(m)	patio	cortile	pátio
cour	court	Hof(m)	corte	corte	corte
courage	courage	Mut(m)	valentía	coraggio	coragem
courageux, brave	brave	mutig	valiente, valeroso	coraggioso, a	corajoso, a
couramment	fluently	fließend	soltura(con)	correntemente	fluentemente
courant, e	common	geläufig	corriente	corrente, comune	corrente
courant, e	current	laufend, heutig	corriente	corrente	corrente, vulgar
courant	current	Strom(m)	corriente	corrente	corrente
courbe	curve	Kurve(f)	curva	curva	curva
courbure	bend, curve	Krümmung(f)	curvatura	curvatura	curvatura
coureur, se	runner	Läufer(in f)m	corredor, a	corridore	corredor, a
courir	run	laufen	correr	correre	correr
couronne	crown	Krone(f)	corona	corona	coroa
courrier	mail, post	Post(f)	correo	posta	correio
courroie	belt; strap	Riemen(m)	correa	cinghia	correia
cours	rate, quotation	Kurs(m)	cotización	corso	índice, tabela
cours	lesson	Unterricht(m)	curso, clase	corso, lezione	curso, aula
course	race	Rennen(n)	carrera	corsa	corrida
course	running	Wettrennen(n)	carrera	corsa	corrida
courses	races	Pferderennen(n)	carreras	corsa	corridas
courses	shopping	Einkäufe(pl)	compras	spesa	compras
court, e	short	kurz	corto, a	corto, a	curto, a
courtois, e	courteous	höflich	cortés	cortese	cortês
cousin, e	cousin	Cousin(m), Cousine(f)	primo, a	cugino, a	primo, a
coussin	cushion	Kissen(n)	cojín	cuscino	almofada
coût	cost	Kosten(pl)	costo, coste	costo	custo, preço
couteau	knife(-ives)	Messer(n)	cuchillo	coltello	faca
coûter	cost	kosten	costar	costare	custar
coûteux, se	costly, expensive	teuer	costoso, a	costoso, a	custoso, a
coutume	custom	Brauch(m)	costumbre	costume, usanza	costume
couture	sewing	Naht(f)	costura	cucito	costura
couture	seam	Saum(m)	costura	cucito	costura
couturier, ière	dressmaker, tailor	Schneider(in f)m	modista	sarto, a	costureiro, a
couvée	brood	Brut(f)	pollada	covata	ninhada
couvent	convent	Kloster(n)	convento	convento	convento
couvercle	lid, cover	Deckel(m)	tapa, tapadera	coperchio	tampa
couvert	table(lay the)	Gedeck(n)	cubierto	coperto	talher
couverture	blanket; cover	Decke(f)(Woll-, Bett-)	manta	coperta	manta, cobertor
couvrir	cover	zu = decken	cubrir	coprire	cobrir
crabe	crab	Krebs(m)	cangrejo	granchio	caranguejo
cracher	spit	spucken	escupir	sputare	cuspir
craindre	fear, be afraid of	befürchten, fürchten	temer, tener miedo	temere	temer
crainte	fear	Furcht(f)	temor, miedo	timore	temor, receio
crampe	cramp	Krampf(m)	calambre	crampo	cãibra
crampons	crampons, irons	Steigeisen(n)	crampones	rampone	grampo
crâne	skull	Schädel(m)	cráneo	cranio	crâneo
crapule	crook, villain	Lump(m)	granuja; pillo, a	canaglia	crápula

French	English	German	Spanish	Italian	Portuguese
craquelé, e	crackled, cracked	rissig	agrietado, a	screpolato, a	estalado, a
craquer	crack	krachen	crujir	scricchiolare	estalar
crasse	filth, dirt	Dreck(m)	roña, mugre	sporcizia	sujidade
cratère	crater	Krater(m)	cráter	cratere	cratera
cravate	tie	Kravatte(f)	corbata	cravatta	gravata
crayon	pencil	Bleistift(m)	lápiz	matita, lapis	lápis
crayon-feutre	felt-tip pen	Filzschreiber(m)	rotulador	pennarello	marcador
créateur, trice	creator(creative)	Schöpfer(in f)m	creador, a	creatore, trice	criador, a
création	creation	Erschaffung; Schöpfung	creación	creazione, creato	criação
crédit	credit	Kredit(m)	crédito	credito	crédito
créer	create	schöpfen	crear	creare	criar
crème	cream	Sahne(f)	crema	crema	creme
crème(peau)	cream	Creme(f)	crema	crema	creme
crépuscule	twilight, dusk	Abenddämmerung(f)	crepúsculo	crepuscolo	crepúsculo
crête	crest	Kamm(m)	cresta	cresta	crista, cimo
creuser	dig	graben	cavar	scavare	cavar
creux, se	hollow	hohl	hueco, a	vuoto, a; cavo, a	oco, a
crevaison	puncture	Reifenpanne(f)	pinchazo	foratura	furo
crevasse	crevice	Spalte(f)	grieta	crepa, crepaccio	fenda
crever	puncture, burst	platzen, bersten	reventar	bucare, scoppiare	rebentar; furar
crever, éclater	burst	bersten	estallar, reventar	scoppiare	furar, rebentar
crevette	prawn, shrimp	Krabbe(f)	gamba, camarón	gamberetto	camarão
cri	shout	Schrei(m)	grito	grido	grito
cric	jack	Wagenheber(m)	gato	cric, cricco	macaco
crier	shout, scream	schreien	gritar	gridare	gritar
crime	crime	Verbrechen(n)	crimen	crimine	crime
criminel, le	criminal	Verbrecher(in f)m	criminal	criminale	criminoso, a
crinière	mane	Mähne(f)	crines, melena	criniera	crina
crise	crisis(-ses)	Krise(f)	crisis	crisi	crise
crise cardiaque	heart attack	Herzattacke(f)	crisis cardíaca	infarto	ataque
cristal	crystal	Kristall(n)	cristal	cristallo	cristal
critère	criterion(-ia)	Kriterium(n)	criterio	criterio	critério
critique	criticism	Kritik(f)	crítica	critica	crítica
critiquer	criticize	kritisieren	criticar	criticare	criticar
crochet	hook	Haken(m)	gancho	gancio, uncino	gancho
crocodile	crocodile	Krokodil(n)	cocodrilo	coccodrillo	crocodilo
croire	believe	glauben	creer	credere	crer
croisement	crossing	Kreuzung(f)	cruce	incrocio	cruzamento
croiser(se)	cross, intersect	kreuzen, sich	cruzarse	incrociarsi	cruzar-se
croiser	interbreed, cross	kreuzen	cruzar	incrociare	cruzar
croisière	cruise	Kreuzfahrt(f)	crucero	crociera	cruzeiro
croissance	growth	Wachstum(n)	crecimiento	crescita	crescimento
croître	grow, increase	wachsen	crecer	crescere	crescer
croix	cross(-es)	Kreuz(n)	cruz	croce	cruz
croquer	crunch	knabbern	mascar	sgranocchiare	trincar
croquis	sketch(-es)	Skizze(f)	croquis	schizzo	esboço
crosse	butt; grip, handle	Gewehrkolben(m)	culata	calcio	coronha
crotte	dropping, dung	Häufchen(n), Kot(m)	caca	sterco	bosta
croupier, ière	croupier	Croupier(m)	crupier	croupier	croupier
croûte	crust	Kruste(f)	costra, corteza	crosta	crosta
croyance	belief	Glaube(m)	creencia	credenza	crença
croyant, e	believer	Gläubige(f, m)	creyente	credente	crente
cru, e	raw	roh	crudo, a	crudo, a	cru, a
crudité	salad, crudité	Rohkost(f)	ensalada	insalata mista	salada
cruel, le	cruel	grausam	cruel	crudele	cruel
crustacé	shell-fish	Schalentier(n)	crustáceo	crostaceo	crustáceo
cube	cube	Würfel(m)	cubo	cubo	cubo
cueillir	pick, gather	pflücken	coger; recoger	cogliere, raccogliere	colher
cuillère	spoon	Löffel(m)	cuchara	cucchiaio	colher
cuiller à café	teaspoon	Kaffeelöffel(m)	cucharilla	cucchiaino	colher de chá
cuir	leather	Leder(n)	cuero	cuoio, pelle	couro
cuirassé	warship	Kriegsschiff(n)	acorazado	corazzata	couraçado
cuire	cook	kochen	cocer	cuocere	cozer
cuisine	kitchen	Küche(f)	cocina	cucina	cozinha
cuisiner	cook	kochen	cocinar	cucinare	cozinhar
cuisinier, ière	cook; chef	Koch(m), Köchin(f)	cocinero, a	cuoco, a	cozinheiro, a
cuisinière	cooker, stove	Herd(m)	cocina	cucina	fogão
cuisse	thigh	Schenkel(m)	muslo	coscia	coxa

French	English	German	Spanish	Italian	Portuguese
cuisse	leg	Schenkel(m)	muslo; pierna	coscia	perna
cuisson	cooking	Kochen(n), Sieden(n)	cocción	cottura	cozedura, cocção
cuit, e	cooked	gar, gekocht	cocido, a	cotto, a	cozido, a
cuivre	copper	Kupfer(n)	cobre	rame	cobre
culbuter	somersault	überrennen	volcar	ribaltare	cambalhotas(dar)
culotte	briefs, knickers	Unterhose(f), Slip(m)	bragas	mutandine, slip	cuecas
culpabilité	guilt	Schuld(f)	culpabilidad	colpevolezza	culpabilidade
culte	worship	Kult(m)	culto	culto	culto
cultivateur	farmer	Landwirt(in f)m	cultivador, a	coltivatore, trice	lavrador, a
cultivé, e	cultured, learned	gebildet	culto, a	colto, a	culto, a
cultiver	cultivate	bebauen, züchten	cultivar	coltivare	cultivar
cultiver	cultivate, grow	an = bauen, an = pflanzen	cultivar	coltivare	cultivar
culture	cultivation	Anbau(m)	cultivo	coltura	cultura
culture	culture	Kultur(f)	cultura	cultura	cultura
culturel, le	cultural	kulturell	cultural	culturale	cultural
cumuler	accumulate	an = häufen	acaparar	cumulare	acumular
cure	treatment	Kur(f)	cura	cura	cura
cure-dents	tooth-pick	Zahnstocher(m)	palillo	stuzzicadenti	palito
curieux, se	curious	neugierig	curioso, a	curioso, a	curioso, a
cutané, e	cutaneous, skin	Haut-	cutáneo, a	cutaneo, a	cutâneo, a
cuve	tank; vat	Wanne(f), Faß(n)	cuba	tino	cuba
cuvette	basin, bowl	Schale(f)	palangana	catino	bacia
cycle	cycle	Zyklus(m)	ciclo	ciclo	ciclo
cyclisme	cycling	Radfahren(n)	ciclismo	ciclismo	ciclismo
cycliste	cyclist	Radfahrer(in f)m	ciclista	ciclista	ciclista
cyclone	cyclone	Wirbelwind(m)	ciclón	ciclone	ciclone
cygne	swan	Schwan(m)	cisne	cigno	cisne
cylindre	cylinder	Zylinder(m)	cilindro	cilindro	cilindro
cylindrique	cylindrical	zylindrisch	cilíndrico, a	cilindrico, a	cilíndrico, a
cynique	cynical	zynisch	cínico, a	cinico, a	cínico, a

D

French	English	German	Spanish	Italian	Portuguese
dame	lady	Dame(f)	señora	signora	senhora
damner	damn	verdammen	condenar	dannare	condenar
dancing	dance-hall	Tanzlokal(n)	sala de baile	sala da ballo	dancing
danger	danger	Gefahr(f)	peligro	pericolo	perigo
dangereux, se	dangerous	gefährlich	peligroso, a	pericoloso, a	perigoso, a
dans	in, into	in	dentro, en	in	dentro(de), em
danse	dance	Tanz(m)	danza, baile	ballo, danza	dança
danser	dance	tanzen	bailar	ballare	dançar, bailar
danseur, se	dancer	Tänzer(in f)m	bailarín, a	ballerino, a	bailarino, a
date	date	Datum(n)	fecha	data	data
datte	date	Dattel(f)	dátil	dattero	tâmara
dauphin	dolphin	Delphin(m)	delfín	delfino	golfinho
davantage, plus	more	mehr	más	più, di più	mais
de	from	aus; von	de, desde	da	de
de	of	von	de	di; del; dello, a	de
dé(jeux)	die(dice)	Würfel(m)	dado	dado	dado
débarquer	disembark, land	Land gehen(an)	desembarcar	sbarcare	desembarcar
débarquer	unload	aus = laden	descargar	sbarcare	descarregar
débarrasser	clear, rid	weg = räumen	quitar, tirar	sbarazzare	desembaraçar
débarrasser(se)	get rid of	beseitigen	quitarse	liberarsi	livrar-se
débat	debate	Debatte(f)	debate	dibattito	debate
débile	crazy, mad	verrückt; schwach	débil	scemo, a; minorato, a	parvo, a
débloquer	release	deblockieren, lösen	desbloquear	sbloccare	desbloquear

French	English	German	Spanish	Italian	Portuguese
déborder	overflow	über = laufen	desbordar	traboccare	transbordar
déborder	overflow	über die Ufer treten	salirse de madre	straripare	extravasar
débourser	spend	aus = geben	desembolsar	sborsare	desembolsar
debout	standing(up)	stehend, aufrecht	de pie, en pie	in piedi	de pé, em pé
débrancher	disconnect, unplug	aus = machen, abschalten	desenchufar	disinserire	desligar
débrancher	unplug	raus = ziehen	desenchufar	staccare	desligar
débris	remains, debris	Trümmer(m, pl)	resto, residuo	resti, cocci	resto, destroços
débrouiller	clear up	entwirren	desenredar	sbrogliare	desenredar
débrouiller(se)	manage	zu helfen wissen, sich	desenredarse	cavarsela	desenredar-se
début	beginning	Anfang(m)	comienzo	inizio	princípio
débutant, e	beginner	Anfänger(in f)m	principiante	principiante	principiante
débuter	begin, start	an = fangen	principiar	esordire	principiar
décadence	decadence, decline	Verfall(m), Untergang	decadencia	decadenza	decadência
décéder	die	versterben, sterben	fallecer	decedere	falecer
déceler	discover; reveal	auf = decken, entdecken	descubrir	svelare, scoprire	descobrir
décélérer	decelerate	ab = bremsen	reducir, aminorar	decelerare	desacelerar
décembre	December	Dezember(m)	diciembre	dicembre	Dezembro
décennie	decade	Jahrzehnt(n)	decenio, década	decennio	década
décent, e	decent	anständig	decente	decente	decente
déception	disappointment	Enttäuschung(f)	decepción	delusione	decepção
décerner	award	zu = erkennen, erteilen	otorgar	conferire	atribuir
décès	death	Tod(m)	fallecimiento	decesso	falecimento
décevoir	disappoint	enttäuschen	decepcionar	deludere	desapontar
déchargement	unloading	Ausladen(n)	descarga	scarico	descarga
décharger	unload	ab = laden, aus = laden	descargar	scaricare	descarregar
déchéance	downfall	Untergang(m), Verfall	decaimiento	decadenza	decadência
déchet	waste	Abfall(m)	residuo	scarto	resíduo
déchiqueter	tear to pieces	zerstückeln	despedazar	dilaniare	despedaçar
déchirer	tear	zerreißen	rasgar, romper	strappare	rasgar
déchu, e	fallen, deposed	abgesetzt, verfallen	decaído, a	destituito, a	decaído, a
décider	decide	entscheiden	decidir	decidere	decidir
décimal, e	decimal	dezimal	decimal	decimale	decimal
décision	decision	Entscheidung(f)	decisión	decisione	decisão
déclaration	declaration	Erklärung(f)	declaración	dichiarazione	declaração
déclarer	declare	bekannt = geben	declarar	dichiarare	declarar
déclencher	trigger off	aus = lösen	iniciar	scattare, attivare	desencadear
déclin	decline	Untergang(m)	decadencia, ocaso	declino	declínio
décoder	decode	dekodieren	descifrar	decifrare	decifrar
décoller	take off	ab = heben	despegar	decollare	descolar
décoller	unstick	ab = lösen	despegar	staccare, scollare	descolar
décoloniser	decolonize	entkolonisieren	descolonizar	decolonizzare	descolonizar
décoloration	discolouration	Entfärbung(f)	descoloramiento	decolorazione	descoloração
décombres	ruins	Trümmer(m, pl)	escombros	macerie, rovine	escombros
décomposer	decompose	zerlegen	descomponer	decomporre	decompor
déconcertant, e	disconcerting	verwirrend	desconcertante	sconcertante	desconcertante
décongeler	thaw	auf = tauen	descongelar	scongelare	descongelar
déconseiller	advise against	ab = raten	desaconsejar	sconsigliare	desaconselhar
décontaminer	decontaminate	entseuchen	descontaminar	decontaminare	descontaminar
décontracté, e	relaxed	lässig, entspannt	relajado, a	rilassato, a	descontraído, a
décoration	decoration	Dekoration(f)	decoración	decorazione	decoração
décorer	decorate	schmücken	decorar, adornar	ornare, adornare	ornar, adornar
décorer	decorate	aus = zeichnen	condecorar	decorare	condecorar
décors	set, scenery	Dekor(m), Bühnenbild n	decorado	scenografia	cenários
découper	cut up	zerschneiden	recortar	tagliare	recortar
découragé, e	discouraged	entmutigt	desanimado, a	scoraggiato, a	desalentado, a
découragé, e	disheartened	mutlos, verzagt	desalentado, a	scoraggiato, a	desalentado, a
décourageant, e	discouraging	entmutigend	desalentador, a	scoraggiante	desanimador, a
décourager	discourage	entmutigen	desalentar	scoraggiare	desalentar
décousu, e	unstitched	abgetrennt	descosido, a	scucito, a	descosido, a
découverte	discovery	Entdeckung(f)	descubrimiento	scoperta	descoberta
découvrir	discover	entdecken	descubrir	scoprire	descobrir
décret	decree	Erlaß(m), Verordnung f	decreto	decreto	decreto
décrire	describe	beschreiben	describir	descrivere	descrever
décroître	decrease	ab = nehmen	decrecer	decrescere	decrescer
déçu, e	disappointed	enttäuscht	decepcionado, a	deluso, a	desiludido, a
dédaigner	disdain	mißachten	desdeñar	disprezzare	desdenhar
dedans	inside	in, drinnen, innen	dentro, adentro	dentro	dentro
dédier	dedicate	widmen	dedicar	dedicare	dedicar

F

French	English	German	Spanish	Italian	Portuguese
dédommager	compensate	entschädigen	indemnizar	indennizzare	indemnizar
dédouaner	clear(customs)	verzollen	retirar aduana	sdoganare	desalfandegar
déduction	deduction	Abzug(m)	deducción	deduzione	dedução
déduction	deduction	Rückschluß(m)	deducción	deduzione	dedução
déduire	deduct	folgern, schließen aus	deducir	detrarre	deduzir
défaillance	weakness(-es)	Schwäche(f), Versagen	desfallecimiento	svenimento	desfalecimento
défaillance	failure, fault	Versagen(n)	fallo	difetto	falha
défaire	dismantle, undo	ab = bauen	deshacer	disfare	desfazer
défaite	defeat	Niederlage(f)	derrota	sconfitta	derrota
défaut	defect, fault	Fehler(m)	defecto	difetto	defeito
défavorisé, e	underprivileged	benachteiligt	desfavorecido, a	svantaggiato, a	desfavorecido, a
défectueux, se	defective, faulty	defekt	defectuoso, a	difettoso, a	defeituoso, a
défendre	defend	verteidigen	defender	difendere	defender
défendre	forbid	verbieten	prohibir	proibire	proibir
défense	defence	Verteidigung(f)	defensa	difesa	defesa
déferler	break	branden	romper	infrangersi	quebrar-se
défi	challenge	Herausforderung(f)	desafío	sfida	desafio
déficient, e	deficient	mangelhaft	deficiente	deficiente	deficiente
déficit	deficit	Verlust(m), Defizit(n)	déficit	deficit	défice
défier	challenge	heraus = fordern	desafiar	sfidare	desafiar
défilé	parade	Parade(f)	desfile	sfilata	desfile
définir	define	definieren	definir	definire	definir
définitif, ive	definitive, final	endgültig	definitivo, a	definitivo, a	definitivo, a
définition	definition	Definition(f)	definición	definizione	definição
déflagration	explosion	Knall(m), Explosion(f)	deflagración	deflagrazione	deflagração
déflation	deflation	Deflation(f)	deflación	deflazione	deflação
déformation	distortion	Mißbildung(f)	deformación	deformazione	deformação
déformer	distort, deform	verformen	deformar	deformare	deformar
défunt, e	deceased person	Verstorbene(f, m)	difunto, a	defunto, a	defunto, a
dégager	clear	frei = machen	despejar	sgomberare	desimpedir
dégât(s)	damage	Schaden(m)	daño(s), estrago(s)	danno	estrago
dégel	thaw	Auftauen(n)	deshielo	disgelo	degelo
dégénérer	degenerate	degenerieren	degenerar	degenerare	degenerar
dégivrer	de-ice; defrost	ab = tauen	descongelar	sbrinare	descongelar
dégonflé, e	deflated, flat	platt, ohne Luft	desinflado, a	sgonfio, a	vazio, a
dégonfler	deflate	Luft raus = lassen	desinflar	sgonfiare	desinchar
dégoûtant, e	disgusting	ekelhaft	asqueroso, a	disgustoso, a	nojento, a
dégoûter	disgust	an = widern	asco(dar)	disgustare	enojar
dégradation	degradation	Beschädigung(f)	degradación	degradazione	degradação
dégrader	degrade	degradieren	degradar	degradare	degradar
dégrafer	undo, unfasten	auf = machen	desabrochar	slacciare	desapertar
degré	degree	Grad(m)	grado	grado	grau
degré(alcool)	proof(per cent)	Prozent(n)	graduación	grado	grau
dégressif, ive	decreasing	abnehmend	decreciente	decrescente	decrescente
déguiser	disguise	verkleiden	disfrazar	mascherare	disfarçar
déguster	taste, sample	kosten	saborear, catar	gustare	provar
dehors	outside, outdoors	draußen	fuera, afuera	fuori	fora
déjà	already	schon	ya	giá	já
déjeuner	lunch, have lunch	Mittag essen(zu)	almorzar	pranzare	almoçar
déjeuner(petit)	breakfast	Frühstück(n)	desayuno	colazione(prima)	almoço(pequeno)
délai	delay	Frist(f)	plazo	termine	prazo
délégation	delegation	Delegation(f)	delegación	delegazione	delegação
délégué, e	delegate	Abgesandte(f, m)	delegado, a	delegato, a	delegado, a
déléguer	delegate	beauftragen	delegar	delegare	delegar
délibéré, e	deliberate	gewollt, absichtlich	deliberado, a	deliberato, a	deliberado, a
délibérer	deliberate	beraten	deliberar	deliberare	deliberar
délicat, e	delicate	schwierig	delicado, a	delicato, a	delicado, a
délicat, e	delicate	zart; fein	delicado, a	delicato, a	delicado, a
délicatesse	delicacy	Aufmerksamkeit(f)	delicadeza	delicatezza	delicadeza
délicieux, se	delicious	köstlich	delicioso, a	delizioso, a	delicioso, a
délimiter	delimit	ab = grenzen	delimitar	delimitare	delimitar
délinquance	delinquency	Kriminalität(f)	delincuencia	delinquenza	delinquência
délinquant, e	delinquent	Kriminelle(f, m)	delincuente	delinquente	delinquente
délire	delirium	Fieberwahn(m)	delirio	delirio	delírio
délit	offence	Vergehen(n), Delikt(n)	delito	delitto	delito
délivrer	free	befreien	libertar	rilasciare, liberare	libertar
déluge	flood; downpour	Überschwemmung(f)	diluvio	diluvio	dilúvio
démagogie	demagogy	Demagogie(f)	demagogia	demagogia	demagogia

French	English	German	Spanish	Italian	Portuguese
demain	tomorrow	morgen	mañana	domani	amanhã
demande	request	Anfrage(f)	pedido	richiesta	pedido
demande	request; demand	Bitte(f); Gesuch(n)	petición	richiesta	pedido
demande(emploi)	application	Bewerbung(f)	solicitud	domanda	pedido
demander	ask(for)	fragen	pedir	chiedere	pedir
demander	ask	fragen	preguntar	domandare	perguntar
demander	beg	bitten	pedir	domandare	pedir
demander(se)	wonder	fragen, sich	preguntarse	domandarsi	perguntar-se
démangeaison	itch, itching	Juckreiz(m)	picazón	prurito	comichão
démarrer	start	starten	arrancar	avviare, iniziare	arrancar
démarreur	starter	Starter(m)	arranque	motorino(avviamento)	motor de arranque
déménager	move	um = ziehen	mudar(se)	traslocare	mudar, mudar-se
démence	insanity, madness	Wahnsinn(m)	demencia	demenza, follia	demência
dément, e	insane, crazy, mad	verrückt	demente	demente	demente
démentir	refute, deny	dementieren, leugnen	desmentir	smentire	desmentir
demeure	residence, dwelling	Wohnung(f), Haus(n)	morada, casa	dimora	habitação, casa
demeurer	live, stay, remain	wohnen, bleiben	residir, vivir	dimorare, stare	habitar
demi, e	half	halb	medio, a	mezzo, a	meio, a
demi-heure	half an hour	halbe Stunde	media hora	mezz'ora	meia-hora
démission	resignation	Rücktritt(m)	dimisión	dimissione	demissão
démissionner	resign	zurück = treten	dimitir	dimettere(-rsi)	demitir-se
démobiliser	demobilize	demobilisieren	desmovilizar	smobilitare	desmobilizar
démocrate	democrat	Demokrat(in f)m	demócrata	democratico, a	democrata
démocratie	democracy	Demokratie(f)	democracia	democrazia	democracia
démodé, e	old-fashioned	altmodisch	pasado de moda	passato di moda	fora de moda
démodé, e; désuet	obsolete	veraltet	anticuado, a	antiquato, a	antiquado, a
démographie	demography	Demographie(f)	demografía	demografia	demografia
démolir	demolish	zerstören	demoler	demolire	demolir
démon	demon, devil	Teufel(m)	demonio	demonio	demónio
démonstration	demonstration	Vorführung(f)	demostración	dimostrazione	demonstração
démontage	dismantling	Zerlegung(f), Abbau(m)	desmontaje	smontaggio	desmontagem
démonter	remove, dismantle	ab = bauen	desmontar	smontare	desmontar
démontrer	demonstrate	beweisen	demostrar	dimostrare	demonstrar
démoraliser	demoralize	entmutigen	desmoralizar	demoralizzare	desmoralizar
dénigrer	denigrate	verleumden	denigrar	denigrare	denegrir
dénoncer	denounce	denunzieren	denunciar	denunziare	denunciar
denrée	foodstuff	Eßware(f)	comestibles	derrata	género; víveres
dense	dense	dicht	denso, a	denso, a	denso, a
densité	density	Dichte(f)	densidad	densità	densidade
dent	tooth(teeth)	Zahn(m)	diente	dente	dente
dentelle	lace	Spitze(f)	puntilla	merletto	renda
dentier	denture	Gebiß(n)	dentadura	dentiera	dentadura
dentifrice	tooth-paste	Zahnpasta(f)	dentífrico	dentifricio	dentífrico
dentiste	dentist	Zahnarzt(in f)m	dentista	dentista	dentista
dénuder	strip, bare	entblößen	desnudar	denudare	desnudar
déodorant	deodorant	Deo(n)	desodorante	deodorante	desodorisante
départ	departure, start	Abfahrt(f)	salida, partida	partenza	partida
départ	start	Anfang(m)	marcha, partida	inizio	princípio
département	department	Bezirk(m), Bereich(m)	departamento	dipartimento	departamento
dépasser	go beyond, exceed	überholen	sobresalir	oltrepassare	ultrapassar
dépasser	protrude	hervor = stehen	sobresalir	sporgere	sobressair
dépasser	exceed	überschreiten	adelantar	superare	ultrapassar
dépêcher(se)	hurry(up)	beeilen, sich	darse prisa	sbrigarsi	despachar-se
dépendant, e	dependent(on)	abhängig	dependiente	dipendente	dependente
dépendre(de)	depend(on)	ab = hängen	depender	dipendere	depender
dépense	expenditure	Ausgabe(f)	gasto	spesa	despesa, gasto
dépenser	spend	aus = geben	gastar	spendere	gastar
dépit	spite; vexation	Groll(m), Trotz(m)	despecho	dispetto	despeito
déplacement	transfer, moving	Umstellung(f)	desplazamiento	spostamento	deslocação
déplacer	shift, move	versetzen, -schieben	trasladar	spostare	deslocar
déplacer(se)	move, shift	bewegen, sich	desplazar(se)	spostare(-arsi)	deslocar-se
déplaisant, e	unpleasant	unangenehm	desagradable	sgradevole	desagradável
déplier	unfold	auf = falten	desdoblar	spiegare, aprire	desdobrar
déplorable	deplorable	beklagenswert	deplorable	deplorevole	deplorável
déplorer	deplore	beklagen	deplorar	deplorare	deplorar
déportation	deportation	Deportation(f)	deportación	deportazione	deportação
déposer	deposit	deponieren	depositar	depositare	depositar
déposer	put down, lay down	legen, stellen	depositar	depositare, porre	pousar

French	English	German	Spanish	Italian	Portuguese
déposition	statement	Aussage(f)	deposición	deposizione	deposição
dépôt	deposit	Satz(m)	depósito	deposito	depósito
dépression(atm.)	depression	Tief(n)	depresión	depressione	depressão
dépression	breakdown	Nervenzusammenbruch m	depresión	esaurimento(nerv.)	depressão
déprimé, e	depressed	deprimiert	deprimido, a	depresso, a	deprimido, a
depuis	since; for	seit	desde	da	desde
député	Member(Parliament)	Abgeordnete(f, m)	diputado	deputato	deputado
déranger	disturb, bother	stören	molestar	disturbare	incomodar
déraper	skid	schleudern	patinar	slittare	derrapar
dériver	drift	ab = treiben	derivar	derivare	derivar
dernier, ière	last	letzter, letzte	último, a	ultimo, a	último, a
dernier	last	Letzte(f, m)	último, a	ultimo, a	último, a
dérober	steal	entwenden	robar	derubare	roubar, furtar
dérouler	unroll	ab = rollen	desenrollar	svolgere, srotolare	desenrolar
derrière	behind	hinter	detrás, tras	dietro	atrás, detrás
derrière, arrière	rear	Rück-; Hinter-	trasero, a; de atrás	dietro, indietro	traseiro, a
derrière	back, rear	Hinter-, Rückseite(f)	trasero, a	retro	trazeiro
dès(que)	as soon as	sobald	desde	fin da	logo que
désaccord	disagreement	Uneinigkeit(f), Streit	discrepancia	disaccordo	desacordo
désagréable	unpleasant	unangenehm	desagradable	sgradevole	desagradável
désamorcer	defuse	entschärfen	desactivar	disinnescare	despoletar
désapprouver	disapprove	mißbilligen	desaprobar	disapprovare	desaprovar
désarmement	disarmament	Abrüstung(f)	desarme	disarmo	desarmamento
désarmer	disarm	ab = rüsten, entwaffnen	desarmar	disarmare	desarmar
désastre	disaster	Unheil(n)	desastre	disastro	desastre
désavantage	disadvantage	Nachteil(m)	desventaja	svantaggio	desvantagem
descendance	descendants	Nachkommenschaft(f)	descendencia	discendenza	descendência
descendre	go down, descend	herunter = gehen	descender, bajar	scendere	descer, baixar
descendre	fall, drop	fallen	bajar	abbassare	baixar
descendre	get out of; get off	aus = steigen	bajarse	scendere	descer
descente	descent	Abstieg(m)	descenso, bajada	discesa	descida
description	description	Beschreibung(f)	descripción	descrizione	descrição
désemparé, e	distraught	ratlos	desamparado, a	smarrito, a; sgomento	desamparado, a
désert	desert	Wüste(f)	desierto	deserto	deserto
désertique	desert, barren	öde; einsam	desértico, a	desertico, a	desértico, a
désespoir	despair	Verzweiflung(f)	desesperación	disperazione	desespero
déshabiller(se)	undress	aus = ziehen, sich	desnudar(se)	svestire(-irsi)	despir-se
déshériter	disinherit	enterben	desheredar	diseredare	deserdar
déshonneur	dishonour	Schande(f)	deshonor	disonore	desonra
déshydrater	dehydrate	aus = trocknen	deshidratar	disidratare	desidratar
désigner	indicate	bezeichnen	señalar, indicar	indicare	indicar
désigner	appoint	ernennen	designar	designare	designar
désinfecter	disinfect	desinfizieren	desinfectar	disinfettare	desinfectar
désintégrer	disintegrate	auf = lösen	desintegrar	disintegrare	desintegrar
désir	wish(-es)	Wunsch(m)	deseo	desiderio	desejo
désirer	desire, want	wünschen	desear	desiderare	desejar
désister(se)	withdraw, give up	zurück = treten	desistir	desistere, rinunziare	desistir
désobéir	disobey	ungehorsam sein	desobedecer	disobbedire	desobedecer
désodorisant	air-freshener	Deodorant(n)	desodorante	deodorante	desodorisante
désolé, e	sorry	betrübt	desolado, a	spiacente	desolado, a
désolé, e	regret(I)	bedauern	siento(lo)	rammaricato, a	lamento(eu)
désordre	disorder, mess	Unordnung(f)	desorden	disordine	desordem
désorganiser	disorganize	desorganisieren	desorganizar	disorganizzare	desorganizar
despote	despot	Despot(m)	déspota	despota	déspota
dessein	purpose, aim	Absicht(f)	propósito	proposito	propósito
desserré, e	slack	schlaff, lose	flojo, a	allentato, a	frouxo, a
desserrer	loosen	lockern	aflojar	allentare	desapertar
desserrer	loosen	lösen	aflojar	allentare	afrouxar
dessert	dessert	Nachtisch(m)	postre	dessert	sobremesa
dessin	drawing; design	Zeichnung(f)	dibujo; diseño	disegno	desenho
dessin, plan	design	Entwurf(m)	diseño	disegno	desenho
dessin animé	cartoon	Trickfilm(m)Zeichen-	dibujo animado	cartone animato	desenho animado
dessinateur	drawer; designer	Zeichner(in f)m	dibujante	disegnatore, trice	desenhador, a
dessiner	draw; design	zeichnen	dibujar; diseñar	disegnare	desenhar
dessous	under, beneath	unter	debajo, abajo	sotto	debaixo, sob
dessous	lower part	Unterteil(n)	inferior(parte)	sotto, disotto	baixo(parte de)
dessus(au-, par-)	above, on, over	über	arriba, encima	sopra	em cima, sobre
dessus	top	Oberteil(n)	superior(parte)	disopra	cima(parte de)

French	English	German	Spanish	Italian	Portuguese
destin	fate, destiny	Schicksal(n)	destino, sino	destino	destino
destinataire	addressee	Empfänger(in f)m	destinatario, a	destinatario, a	destinatário, a
destination	destination	Bestimmungsort(m)	destinación	destinazione	destino
destinée	destiny	Schicksal(n)	destino	destino	destino
destiner	intended to(be)	bestimmen für	destinar	destinare	destinar
destruction	destruction	Zerstörung(f)	destrucción	distruzione	destruição
désuet, ète	obsolete	altmodisch	desusado, a	antiquato, a; desueto	desusado, a
détacher	detach, unfasten	lösen, ab = trennen	desatar	staccare	desatar
détail	detail	Einzelheit(f)	detalle	particolare	pormenor
détaillé, e	detailed	einzelnen(im)	detallado, a	dettagliato, a	detalhado, a
détaxé, e	duty(tax)-free	steuerfrei	desgravado, a	sgravio fiscale	isento de taxa
détecteur	detector	Anzeiger(m)	detector	rivelatore	detector
détection	detection	Aufspüren(n)	detección	rivelazione	detecção
détective	detective	Detektiv(m)	detective	detective	detective
détendu, e	relaxed	entspannt	descansado, a	disteso, a; rilassato	descontraído, a
détendu, e	slack, loose	schlaff, lose	aflojado, a	allentato, a	frouxo, a; lasso, a
détention	detention	Haft(f)	detención	detenzione	detenção
détenu, e	prisoner	Häftling(m)	detenido, a; preso, a	detenuto, a	preso, a; detido, a
détérioration	deterioration	Verschlechterung(f)	deterioración	deteriorazione	deterioração
déterminer	determine	fest = legen	determinar	determinare	determinar
déterrer	dig up	aus = graben	desenterrar	dissotterrare	desenterrar
détester	detest, hate	hassen	detestar, odiar	detestare, odiare	detestar
détonation	detonation	Knall(m)	detonación	detonazione	detonação
détourner	hijack	entführen	secuestrar	dirottare	sequestrar
détresse	distress	Verzweiflung(f)	angustia	sconforto	aflição, angústia
détritus	rubbish, garbage	Unrat(m)	desperdicios	detrito	detrito, lixo
détroit	strait	Meerenge(f)	estrecho	stretto	estreito
détruire	destroy	zerstören	destruir	distruggere	destruir
dette	debt	Schuld(f)	deuda	debito	dívida
deuil	mourning(be in)	Trauer(f)	duelo; luto	lutto	luto
deux	two	zwei	dos	due	dois, duas
deuxième	second	zweite	segundo, a	secondo, a	segundo, a
dévaliser	rob, burgle	aus = rauben	desvalijar	svaligiare	roubar
dévaluation	devaluation	Abwertung(f)	devaluación	svalutazione	desvalorização
dévaluer	devalue	entwerten, ab = werten	devaluar	svalutare	desvalorizar
devant	in front(ahead)of	vor	delante, ante	davanti a	diante de
devant	front, fore	Front(f)	frente, delantera	davanti	frente(a)
dévaster	ravage, devastate	verwüsten, zerstören	devastar	devastare	devastar
développement	development	Entwicklung(f)	desarrollo	sviluppo	desenvolvimento
développer	develop	entwickeln	desarrollar	sviluppare	desenvolver
devenir	become	werden	volverse	diventare	tornar-se
devenir	become	werden	llegar a ser	diventare	vir a ser
devenir	become	werden	ponerse	diventare	pôr-se
déverser	pour out, tip	aus = gießen	verter	riversare, scaricare	despejar
déviation	diversion	Umleitung(f)	desviación	deviazione	desvio
dévier	divert	um = leiten	desviar	deviare	desviar
deviner	guess	raten	adivinar	indovinare	adivinhar
devis	estimate	Kostenvoranschlag(m)	presupuesto	preventivo	orçamento
devise	currency	Währung(f)	divisa	valuta	moeda, divisa
devoir	must, have to	müssen	deber	dovere	dever
devoir	duty	Pflicht(f)	deber	dovere	dever
devoir	homework; exercise	Aufgabe(f)	deber, tarea	compito	dever
dévorer	devour	verschlingen	devorar	divorare	devorar
dévotion	devotion	Frömmigkeit(f)	devoción	devozione	devoção
dévouement	devotion	Ergebenheit(f)	consagración a	dedizione	dedicação
dévoué, e	devoted	ergeben	servicial	devoto, a	dedicado, a
diabète	diabetes	Zuckerkrankheit(f)	diabetes	diabete	diabetes
diable	devil	Teufel(m)	diablo	diavolo	diabo
diagnostic	diagnosis(-oses)	Diagnose(f)	diagnóstico	diagnosi	diagnóstico
diagonal, e	diagonal	diagonal	diagonal	diagonale	diagonal
diagramme	diagram	Diagramm(n)	diagrama	diagramma	diagrama
dialecte	dialect	Dialekt(m)	dialecto	dialetto	dialecto
dialogue	dialogue	Dialog(m)	diálogo	dialogo	diálogo
diamant	diamond	Diamant(m)	diamante	diamante	diamante
diamètre	diameter	Durchmesser(m)	diámetro	diametro	diâmetro
diaphragme	diaphragm	Zwerchfell(n)	diafragma	diaframma	diafragma
diapo(sitives)	slide	Diapositiv(n), Dia(n)	diapositiva	diapositiva	diapositivos
diarrhée	diarrhoea	Durchfall(m)	diarrea	diarrea	diarreia

French	English	German	Spanish	Italian	Portuguese
dictateur	dictator	Diktator(m)	dictador	dittatore	ditador
dictature	dictatorship	Diktatur(f)	dictadura	dittatura	ditadura
dictionnaire	dictionary	Wörterbuch(n)	diccionario	dizionario	dicionário
diesel	diesel	Diesel(m)	diesel	diesel	diesel
diététique	dietetic	diätetisch	dietético, a	dietetico, a	dietético, a
dieu	God	Gott(m)	dios, Dios	dio, Dio (dio, dei)	Deus
Dieu(mon)	Goodness(my)	Gott!(Mein Gott!)	Dios(mío)	Dio(mio)	Deus(meu)
diffamation	slander	Verleumdung(f)	difamación	diffamazione	difamação
différence	difference	Unterschied(m)	diferencia	differenza	diferença
différent, e	different	verschieden	diferente	differente	diferente
différer	postpone	auf = schieben	diferir, demorar	differire, rimandare	diferir, adiar
difficile	difficult	schwer	difícil	difficile	difícil
difficulté	difficulty	Schwierigkeit(f)	dificultad	difficoltá	dificuldade
diffuser	diffuse	verbreiten	difundir	diffondere	difundir
diffuser	broadcast	senden	difundir	trasmettere	transmitir
diffusion	diffusion	Verbreitung; Sendung	difusión	diffusione	difusão
digestion	digestion	Verdauung(f)	digestión	digestione	digestão
digne	worthy; dignified	würdig	digno, a	degno, a	digno, a
dignité	dignity	Würde(f)	dignidad	dignità	dignidade
dilatation	expansion	Ausdehnung(f)	dilatación	dilatazione	dilatação
diluer	dilute	verdünnen	diluir	diluire	diluir
dimanche	Sunday	Sonntag(m)	domingo	domenica	domingo
dimension	dimension, size	Maß(f)	dimensión	dimensione	dimensão
diminuer	reduce, decrease	verringern	disminuir	diminuire	diminuir
diminution	reduction	Verminderung(f)	disminución	diminuzione	diminuição
dîner	dinner(have)	Abend essen(zu)	cenar	cenare	jantar
dîner	dinner	Abendessen(n)	cena	cena	jantar
diphtérie	diphtheria	Diphterie(f)	difteria	difterite	difteria
diplomate	diplomat	Diplomat(in f)m	diplomático	diplomatico	diplomata
diplomatie	diplomacy	Diplomatie(f)	diplomacia	diplomazia	diplomacia
diplomatique	diplomatic	diplomatisch	diplomático, a	diplomatico, a	diplomático, a
diplôme	diploma	Diplom(n)	diploma, título	diploma	diploma
diplômé, e	qualified	staatlich geprüft	graduado, a	diplomato, a	diplomado, a
diplômé, e	graduate	Diplom-	titulado, a	diplomato, a	diplomado, a
dire	say	sagen	decir	dire	dizer
dire	tell	sagen	decir	dire	contar
direct, e	direct	direkt	directo, a	diretto, a	directo, a
directement	directly	direkt	directamente	direttamente	directamente
directeur, trice	director, head	Direktor(in f)m	director, a	direttore, -trice	director, a
directeur(école)	headmaster	Schuldirektor(m)	director(escuela)	direttore(scuola)	director(escola)
direction	direction	Richtung(f)	dirección	direzione	direcção
direction	management	Direktion(f)	dirección	direzione	direcção
dirigeant, e	leader, manager	Leiter(m), Führer(m)	dirigente	dirigente	dirigente
diriger	manage, run	leiten, führen	dirigir	dirigere	dirigir
diriger	direct, guide, point	richten, steuern	dirigir, guiar	dirigere	dirigir
disciple	disciple	Jünger(m)	discípulo	discepolo	discípulo
discerner	discern	unterscheiden	discernir	discernere	discernir
discipline	discipline	Disziplin(f)	disciplina	disciplina	disciplina
discothèque	disco(theque)	Diskothek(f)	discoteca	discoteca	discoteca
discours	speech, talk	Rede(f)	discurso	discorso	discurso
discréditer	discredit	Verruf bringen(in)	desacreditar	discreditare	desacreditar
discret, ète	discreet	diskret	discreto, a	discreto, a	discreto, a
discussion	discussion, talk	Diskussion(f)	discusión	discussione	discussão
discuter	discuss	besprechen	discutir	discutere	discutir
disgrâce	disgrace	Ungnade(f)	desgracia	disgrazia	desvalimento
disparaître	disappear	verschwinden	desaparecer	sparire	desaparecer
disperser	disperse; scatter	zerstreuen	dispersar	disperdere	dispersar
disponible	available	verfügbar	disponible	disponibile	disponível
disposer	arrange	auf = stellen	disponer	disporre	dispor
disposition	arrangement	Anordnung(f)	disposición	disposizione	disposição
dispute	dispute, argument	Streit(m)	disputa	disputa, lite	disputa
disputer(se)	quarrel, argue	streiten, sich	reñir(con)	litigare	disputar-se
disque	record	Schallplatte(f)	disco	disco	disco
dissident, e	dissident	Dissident(m)	disidente	dissidente	dissidente
dissimuler	conceal	verbergen, verhehlen	disimular	dissimulare	dissimular
dissipé, e	unruly	unaufmerksam	indisciplinado, a	indisciplinato, a	indisciplinado, a
dissiper	dissipate, clear	verziehen, sich	disipar	dissipare	dissipar
dissocier	dissociate	trennen	disociar	dissociare	dissociar

French	English	German	Spanish	Italian	Portuguese
dissolvant	solvent, remover	Lösungsmittel(n)	disolvente	solvente	acetona
dissoudre	dissolve	auf = lösen	disolver	sciogliere	dissolver
dissuader	dissuade	ab = raten	disuadir	dissuadere	dissuadir
dissuasion	dissuasion	Abschreckung(f)	disuasión	dissuasione	dissuasão
distance	distance	Entfernung(f)	distancia	distanza	distância
distillation	distillation	Destillation(f)	destilación	distillazione	distilação
distinct, e	distinct	deutlich	distinto, a	distinto, a	distinto, a
distinguer	distinguish	unterscheiden	distinguir	distinguere	distinguir
distraction(s)	entertainment	Zeitvertreib(m)	distracción	svago, distrazione	distracção, -ões
distraire	distract, divert	ab = lenken	distraer	distrarre	distrair
distraire	entertain	unterhalten	entretener	distrarre	distrair
distrait, e	absent-minded	zerstreut	distraído, a	distratto, a	distraído, a
distribuer	distribute; deal	verteilen	distribuir	distribuire	distribuir
distribution	distribution	Verteilung(f)	distribución	distribuzione	distribuição
district, région	district	Bezirk(m)	distrito, área	distretto	distrito
divan	couch(-es)	Couch(f), Sofa(n)	diván	divano	divã
diverger	diverge	ab = weichen	divergir	divergere	divergir
divers, e	diverse, various	verschieden	diverso, a	diverso, a	diverso, a
divers, e	various, varied	mannigfach	vario, a	vario, a	variado, a
diversifier	diversify	variieren	diversificar	diversificare	diversificar
diversité	diversity	Verschiedenheit(f)	diversidad	diversità	diversidade
divin, e	divine	göttlich	divino, a	divino, a	divino, a
diviser	divide	teilen	dividir	dividere	dividir
division	division	Division(f)	división	divisione	divisão
division	partition	Trennung(f)	división	divisione	partilha
divorce	divorce	Scheidung(f)	divorcio	divorzio	divórcio
divorcer	divorce	scheiden lassen, sich	divorciar(se)	divorziare	divorciar-se
divulguer	divulge, reveal	aus = plaudern	divulgar	divulgare	divulgar
dix	ten	zehn	diez	dieci	dez
dix-sept	seventeen	siebzehn	diecisiete	diciassette	dezassete
dix-huit	eighteen	achtzehn	dieciocho	diciotto	dezoito
dix-neuf	nineteen	neunzehn	diecinueve	diciannove	dezanove
dixième	tenth	zehnte	décimo, a	decimo, a	décimo, a
docile	docile	gehorsam	dócil	docile	dócil, manso
docteur(toresse)	doctor	Arzt(m); Doktor(m)	doctor, a	dottore, -essa	doutor, a
docteur	doctor	Doktor(m)	doctor, a	dottore, -essa	doutor, a
doctrine	doctrine	Lehre(f)	doctrina	dottrina	doutrina
document	document	Dokument(n)	documento	documento	documento
documentation	documentation	Dokumentation(f)	documentación	documentazione	documentação
dogmatique	dogmatic	dogmatisch	dogmático, a	dogmatico, a	dogmático, a
doigt	finger	Finger(m)	dedo	dito	dedo
domaine	domain, estate	Gut(n), Besitzung(f)	dominio, terreno	tenuta, fondo	terreno
domaine	field, scope	Bereich(m)	campo, área	campo, settore	domínio
dôme	dome	Kuppel(f)	cúpula	duomo	cúpula
domestique	domestic, home	Haus-	doméstico, a	domestico, a	doméstico, a
domestique	servant	Hausangestellte(m, f)	criado, a	domestico, a	empregado, a
domicile	home	Wohnsitz(m), Wohnort m	domicilio	domicilio	domicílio
dominer	dominate, rule	beherrschen	dominar	dominare	dominar
dommage	damage	Schaden(m)	perjuicio, daño	danno	prejuízo, dano
dommage(c'est)	pity(it is a)	schade!	pena(es una)	peccato(è)	pena(e')
dommage(quel)	pity(what a)	schade !(wie ---)	lástima(qué)	peccato(che)	pena(que)
dompter	tame	zähmen	domar	domare	domar
don	gift, talent	Talent(n)	don, talento	dono	dom, talento
donc	therefore; so	also	por tanto, pues	dunque	portanto, pois
donnée(s)	data	Daten(pl)	datos	dati	dados
donner	give	geben	dar	dare	dar
dont	whose, of which	dessen; deren	cuyo, a; del cual	di cui	cujo, a; do qual
doper(se)	take stimulants	dopen, sich	doparse	drogarsi	drogar-se
dormir	sleep	schlafen	dormir	dormire	dormir
dos	back	Rücken(m)	espalda	schiena	costas
dosage	proportion	Dosierung(f)	dosificación	dosaggio, dose	dosagem
dose	dose	Dosis(f)	dosis	dose	dose
dossier	record, file	Akte(f)	expediente	dossier	processo
douane	customs	Zoll(m)	aduana	dogana	alfândega
douanier	customs officer	Zöllner(m)	aduanero	doganiere	guarda-fiscal
double	double	doppelt	doble	doppio, a	duplo, a
double	dual	doppelt	doble	doppio, a	duplo, a
doubler	overtake	überholen	adelantar	sorpassare	ultrapassar

45

French	English	German	Spanish	Italian	Portuguese
doucement	gently; slowly	langsam, sanft	despacio	piano, adagio	devagar
douche	shower	Dusche(f)	ducha	doccia	duche, chuveiro
doué, e	gifted, talented	begabt	dotado, a	dotato, a	dotado, a; capaz
douleur	pain, ache	Schmerz(m)	dolor	dolore	dor
douloureux, se	painful, aching	schmerzhaft	doloroso, a	doloroso, a	doloroso, a
doute	doubt	Zweifel(m)	duda	dubbio	dúvida
douter	doubt	zweifeln	dudar	dubitare	duvidar
douter(se)	suspect, mistrust	ahnen, vermuten	sospechar	sospettare	suspeitar
douteux, se	dubious; doubtful	zweifelhaft	dudoso, a	dubbio, a	duvidoso, a
doux, ce	soft	sanft	suave	morbido, a	macio, a
doux, ce	mild	mild	templado, a	mite	ameno, a
doux, ce	sweet	süß	dulce	dolce	doce
douzaine	dozen	Dutzend(n)	docena	dozzina	dúzia
douze	twelve	zwölf	doce	dodici	doze
doyen, ne	oldest person	Älteste(f, m)	decano, a	decano, a	decano, a
drainer	drain	entwässern	drenar	drenare	drenar
dramatique	dramatic	dramatisch	dramático, a	drammatico, a	dramático, a
drame	drama	Drama(n)	drama	dramma	drama
drap	sheet	Laken(n)	sábana	lenzuolo	lençol
drapeau	flag	Flagge(f)	bandera	bandiera	bandeira
drapeau	flag	Fahne(f)	bandera	bandiera	bandeira
dresser	erect, put up	auf = richten, errichten	erigir	drizzare	erigir, erguer
dresser	train	ab = richten, dressieren	amaestrar	addestrare	amestrar
drogue	drug	Droge(f)	droga	droga	droga
drogué, e	drug addict	Drogenabhängige(m, f)	drogado, a	drogato, a	drogado, a
droguerie	hardware shop	Kramwarenhandel(m)	droguería	mesticheria	drogaria
droit	law	Recht(n)	derecho	diritto	direito
droit	right	Recht(n)	derecho	diritto	direito
droit, e	right	rechte(r, s); rechts	derecho, a	destro, a	direito, a
droit, e	straight	gerade	recto, a	diritto, a	recto, a
droite	straight line	Gerade(f)	recta	retta	recta
drôle	funny	lustig	gracioso, a	buffo, a	divertido, a
duc, duchesse	duke, duchess	Herzog(m), Herzogin(f)	duque, duquesa	duca, duchessa	duque, duquesa
duel	duel	Duell(n)	duelo	duello	duelo
dune	dune	Düne(f)	duna	duna	duna
dur, e	hard	hart	duro, a	duro, a	duro, a
durant, pendant	during, for	während	durante	durante	durante
durée	duration, length	Dauer(f)	duración	durata	duração
durer	last	dauern	durar	durare	durar
dynamique	dynamic	dynamisch	dinámico, a	dinamico, a	dinâmico, a
dynamisme	dynamism	Tatkraft(f), Schwung m	dinamismo	dinamismo	dinamismo
dynamite	dynamite	Dynamit(n)	dinamita	dinamite	dinamite
dynastie	dynasty	Herrscherhaus(n)	dinastía	dinastia	dinastia

E

French	English	German	Spanish	Italian	Portuguese
eau	water	Wasser(n)	agua	acqua	água
eau bénite	holy water	Weihwasser(n)	agua bendita	acqua santa	água benta
eau de toilette	toilet water	Eau de Toilette(n)	colonia(agua de)	acqua di toeletta	água de colónia
eau-de-vie	spirits	Schnaps(m)	aguardiente	grappa, acquavite	aguardente
eau gazeuse	sparkling water	Sprudelwasser(n)	gaseosa	acqua gassata	água gaseificada
éblouir	dazzle, glare	blenden	deslumbrar	abbagliare	encandear
éboulement	landslide	Erdrutsch(m)	desprendimiento	frana, slavina	desmoronamento
éboulis	scree	Geröll(n)	escombros	detriti	escombros
ébullition	boiling	Kochen(n)	ebullición	ebollizione	fervura
écaille	scale	Schuppe(f)	escama	squama	escama
écart	gap, margin	Abstand(m)	diferencia, margen	margine, differenza	desvio, margem

French	English	German	Spanish	Italian	Portuguese
écarter	separate, part	entfernen	apartar	allontanare; scartare	afastar
échafaudage	scaffolding	Gerüst(n)	andamio	impalcatura	andaime
échange	exchange	Tausch(Aus-, Um-)(m)	cambio	scambio	troca; câmbio
échanger	exchange	tauschen	intercambiar	scambiare	trocar
échantillon	sample	Probe(f), Muster(n)	muestra	campione	amostra
échapper	drop	entgleiten	irse, escaparse	sfuggire, scappare	escapar
échapper(s')	escape	fliehen	escapar(se)	scappare	escapar-se
écharpe	scarf	Halstuch(n), Schal(m)	bufanda	sciarpa	cachecol, cachené
échauffement	heating	Aufwärmen(n)	calentamiento	riscaldamento	aquecimento
échéance	expiration	Fälligkeitstermin(m)	vencimiento	scadenza	vencimento
échec	failure	Mißerfolg(m)	fracaso, revés	smacco, sconfitta	fracasso
échecs	chess	Schachspiel(n)	ajedrez	scacchi	xadrês
échelle	ladder	Leiter(f)	escalera	scala	escada
échelle	scale	Tabelle(f), Skala(f)	escala	scala	escala
écho	echo(-es)	Echo(n)	eco	eco	eco
échouer	fail	scheitern	fracasar	fallire	falhar
échouer(examen)	fail	durch = fallen	suspender	bocciare	ficar mal(exame)
éclair	lightning; flash	Blitz(m)	relámpago	lampo	relâmpago
éclairage	lighting	Beleuchtung(f)	iluminación	illuminazione	iluminação
éclairer	light; illuminate	beleuchten	iluminar	illuminare	iluminar
éclater	burst	platzen	reventar	scoppiare	rebentar
éclipse	eclipse	Finsternis(f)	eclipse	eclisse	eclipse
éclore	hatch	aus = schlüpfen	abrirse	schiudere, uscire	abrir-se
écoeurer	disgust	an = ekeln, an = widern	asquear	nauseare	enjoar
école	school	Schule(f)	escuela	scuola	escola
écolier, ière	schoolboy/girl	Schüler(in f)m	colegial, a	scolaro, a	aluno, a
écologie	ecology	Naturschutz(m)	ecología	ecologia	ecologia
économie, épargne	saving	Ersparnis(f)	economía, ahorro	risparmio	economia
économie	economy	Wirtschaft(f)	economía	economia	economia
économique	economic(al)	wirtschaftlich	económico, a	economico, a	económico, a
économiser	save, economise	sparen	economizar	economizzare	economizar
économiste	economist	Volkswirt(in f)m	economista	economista	economista
écorce	bark	Rinde(f)	corteza	scorza, buccia	casca
écoulement	flow, outflow	Abfluß(m)	derrame, flujo	deflusso, scolo	escoamento
écouler(s')	run, flow	ab = fließen	correr, fluir	scorrere, defluire	escorrer
écouler(s')	elapse	vergehen, verfließen	transcurrir	trascorrere	decorrer
écouter	listen(to)	zu = hören, horchen	escuchar	ascoltare	escutar
écouteurs, casque	ear/headphones	Kopfhörer(m)	casco	cuffia	auscultadores
écran	screen	Bildschirm; Leinwand	pantalla	schermo	écran
écran	screen	Wandschirm(m)	pantalla	schermo	painel
écraser	crush, flatten	zerquetschen	aplastar	schiacciare	esmagar
écraser(s')	crash	ab = stürzen	estrellarse	schiantare	esmagar-se
écrevisse	crayfish	Flußkrebs(m)	cangrejo(de río)	gambero(di fiume)	caranguejo
écrire	write	schreiben	escribir	scrivere	escrever
écriture	writing	Schrift(f)	escritura	scrittura	escrita
écrivain	writer	Schriftsteller(in f)m	escritor, a	scrittore, -trice	escritor, a
écrou	nut	Mutter(f)(Schrauben-)	tuerca	dado	porca
écrouler(s')	collapse, crumble	zusammen = brechen	derrumbar(se)	crollare	desmoronar-se
écume	foam, froth	Schaum(m), Gischt(f)	espuma	schiuma	espuma
écureuil	squirrel	Eichhörnchen(n)	ardilla	scoiattolo	esquilo
écurie	stable	Pferdestall(m)	cuadra	scuderia	cavalariça
eczéma	eczema	Ekzem(n)	eczema	eczema	eczema
édifice	edifice, building	Gebäude(n)	edificio	edificio	edifício
éditeur, trice	publisher; editor	Herausgeber(in f)m	editor, a	editore, trice	editor, a
édition	publishing	Verlagswesen(n)	industria editor-	edizione	indústria livro
édition	edition	Auflage(f), Ausgabe(f)	edición	edizione	edição
éditorial	editorial	Leitartikel(m)	editorial	editoriale	editorial
éducateur, trice	instructor	Erzieher(in f)m	educador, a	educatore, trice	educador, a
éducation	education	Erziehung(f)	educación	educazione	educação
éduquer	educate	erziehen, bilden	educar	educare	educar
effacer	erase, rub out	radieren	borrar	cancellare	apagar
effarer, effrayer	terrify	erschrecken	espantar, asustar	sgomentare	apavorar
effectif, ive	effective	tatsächlich, wirklich	efectivo, a	effettivo, a	efectivo, a
effectif	number of people	Personalbestand(m)	efectivo	effettivo	efectivo
effectuer	carry out, perform	aus = führen	efectuar	effettuare	efectuar
effet	effect	Wirkung(f)	efecto	effetto	efeito
effet(en)	indeed	tatsächlich	efecto(en)	infatti	efeito(com)
efficace	efficient	tüchtig, fähig	eficiente	efficiente	eficiente

F

French	English	German	Spanish	Italian	Portuguese
efficace	effective	wirkungsvoll	eficaz	efficace	eficaz
effondrer(s')	collapse	zusammen = brechen	hundirse	crollare	desabar
effort	effort	Anstrengung(f)	esfuerzo	sforzo	esforço
effrayer	frighten	erschrecken	asustar	spaventare	assustar
égal, e	equal	gleich	igual	uguale	igual
également	too, also, as well	ebenfalls, auch	igualmente	ugualmente	igualmente
égalité	equality	Gleichheit(f)	igualdad	uguaglianza	igualdade
église	church(-es)	Kirche(f)	iglesia	chiesa	igreja
égoïste	selfish	egoïstisch	egoísta	egoista	egoísta
égout	sewer, drain	Gulli, Abwasserkanäle	cloaca	fogna	esgoto
égratigner	scratch	kratzen, schrammen	rasguñar	scalfire	arranhar
éjecter	eject	aus = stoßen	eyectar, expulsar	espellere	expelir
élaborer	elaborate	aus = arbeiten	elaborar	elaborare	elaborar
élan	spring, bound	Anlauf(m), Schwung(m)	impulso	slancio	impulso
élargir	widen, enlarge	verbreiten	ensanchar	allargare	alargar
élastique	rubber band	Gummiband(n)	goma elástica	elastico	elástico
élastique	elastic; flexible	elastisch	elástico, a	elastico, a	elástico, a
électeur, trice	voter	Wähler(in f)m	elector, a	elettore, -trice	eleitor, a
élection	election	Wahl(f)	elección	elezione	eleição
électricien	electrician	Elektriker(in f)m	electricista	elettricista	electricista
électricité	electricity	Elektrizität(f)	electricidad	elettricità	electricidade
électrique	electric(al)	elektrisch	eléctrico, a	elettrico, a	eléctrico, a
électronique	electronic	elektronisch	electrónico, a	elettronico, a	electrónico, a
électronique	electronics	Elektronik(f)	electrónica	elettronica	electrónica
élégance	elegance	Eleganz(f)	elegancia	eleganza	elegância
élégant, e	elegant, smart	elegant	elegante	elegante	elegante
élément	element	Element(n)	elemento	elemento	elemento
éléphant	elephant	Elefant(m)	elefante	elefante	elefante
élevage	breeding; rearing	Zucht(f); Aufzucht(f)	ganadería	allevamento	criação de gado
élève	pupil	Schüler(in f)m	alumno, a	alunno, a	aluno, a
élevé, e	high	hoch, erhöht	alto, a	elevato, a; alto, a	alto, a
élever	elevate	erhöhen	elevar, alzar	elevare	elevar
élever	bring up	erziehen, auf = ziehen	criar, educar	allevare, educare	criar, educar
élever	breed, rear	züchten	criar	allevare	criar
élever, hausser	raise	an = heben	elevar	elevare, alzare	elevar
élever(s')	rise	an = steigen	subir	elevarsi	subir
élimination	elimination	Beseitigung(f)	eliminación	eliminazione	eliminação
éliminer	eliminate	aus = scheiden	eliminar	eliminare	eliminar
élire	elect	wählen	elegir	eleggere	eleger
élite	élite	Elite(f)	élite	elite	elite
elle	she	sie	ella	essa; lei; ella	ela
elles	they	sie	ellas	esse, loro	elas
ellipse	ellipse	Ellipse(f)	elipse	ellisse	elipse
élocution	elocution	Sprechweise(f)	elocución	eloquio	elocução
éloge	praise	Lob(n)	elogio	elogio	elogio
éloignement	distance	Entfernung(f)	alejamiento	lontananza	afastamento
éloquence	eloquence	Redegewandtheit(f)	elocuencia	eloquenza	eloquência
élu, e	elected, chosen	gewählt	elegido, a	eletto, a	eleito, a
émail	enamel	Emaille(f), Glasur(f)	esmalte	smalto	esmalte
emballage	packing, wrapping	Verpackung(f)	embalaje, envase	imballaggio	embalagem
embargo	embargo(-es)	Embargo(n)	embargo	embargo	embargo
embarquer	board, embark	ein = steigen	embarcar	imbarcare	embarcar
embarquer	load	ein = laden	embarcar	imbarcare	carregar
embarras	embarrassment	Verlegenheit(f)	apuro	imbarazzo	embaraço
embaucher	employ, take on	ein = stellen	dar trabajo	assumere	empregar
embêter	bother, annoy	ärgern	fastidiar	infastidire	aborrecer
emblème	emblem	Emblem(n)	emblema	emblema	emblema
embout	tip, end	Endstück(n)	punta; remate	estremità; punta	ponta; remate
embrasser	kiss; embrace	küssen, umarmen	abrazar, besar	baciare	abraçar, beijar
embrayage	clutch	Kupplung(f)	embrague	frizione	embraiagem
embryon	embryo	Embryo(m)	embrión	embrione	embrião
embuscade	ambush	Hinterhalt(m)	emboscada	imboscata	emboscada
émeraude	emerald	Smaragd(m)	esmeralda	smeraldo	esmeralda
émerger	emerge	auf = tauchen	emerger	emergere	emergir
émerveiller	amaze	entzücken	maravillar	meravigliare	maravilhar
émetteur	transmitter	Sender(m)	emisor	emittente	emissor
émeute	riot	Aufruhr(m)	motín	sommossa	motim
émettre	emit	aus = strahlen	emitir	emettere	emitir

French	English	German	Spanish	Italian	Portuguese
émigration	emigration	Auswanderung(f)	emigración	emigrazione	emigração
émigré, e	emigrant	Emigrant(in f)m	emigrante	emigrato, a	emigrante
émigrer	emigrate	aus = wandern	emigrar	emigrare	emigrar
éminent, e	eminent	hervorragend	eminente	eminente	eminente
émissaire	emissary	Bote(m)	emisario	emissario	emissário
émission	sending	Sendung(f)	envío	emissione	envio
émission	programme	Sendung(f)	emisión	programma	emissão
emmêler(s')	tangle(up)	verwickeln, verwirren	enmarañar(se)	aggrovigliare(-rsi)	emaranhar-se
emmener	take	mit = nehmen	llevar	portare, condurre	levar
émotif, ive	emotional	empfindsam	emotivo, a	emotivo, a	emotivo, a
émotion	emotion	Rührung(f)	emoción	emozione	emoção
émouvant, e	moving	ergreifend	emocionante	commovente	comovente
émouvoir	move	rühren	conmover	commuovere	comover
empaqueter	pack, wrap	ein = packen, verpacken	empaquetar	impacchettare	empacotar
empêcher	prevent	verhindern	impedir	impedire	impedir
empereur	emperor	Kaiser(m)	emperador	imperatore	imperador
empiler	pile up, stack	stapeln	apilar, amontonar	accatastare	empilhar, amontoar
emplacement	location, site	Lage(f), Stelle(f)	sitio	posto, sito, luogo	lugar; sítio
empire	empire	Reich(n)	imperio	impero	império
emploi	employment	Stelle(f)	empleo	impiego	emprego
emploi	job, work	Beruf(m)	empleo	impiego	emprego
emploi	use	Gebrauch(m)	uso, empleo	uso	uso
employé, e	employee	Angestellte(f, m)	empleado, a	impiegato, a	empregado, a
employé, e	clerk	Angestellte(f, m)	oficinista	impiegato, a	empregado, a
employer	employ	an = stellen	emplear	impiegare	empregar
employer	use	benützen	usar, emplear	usare, adoperare	usar
employeur	employer	Arbeitgeber(in f)m	patrón	datore di lavoro	patrão
empoigner, saisir	grab, grasp	greifen	empuñar	agguantare	agarrar
empoisonnement	poisoning	Vergiftung(f)	envenenamiento	avvelenamento	envenenamento
emporter	take(away)	mit = nehmen	llevar	portar via	levar
empreinte	print	Abdruck(m)	huella	impronta	impressão; marca
emprisonnement	imprisonment	Haft(f), Verhaftung(f)	encarcelamiento	incarcerazione	prisão
emprunt	loan	Anleihe(f)	préstamo	prestito	empréstimo
emprunter	borrow	borgen	pedir prestado	prendere in prestito	pedir emprestado
ému, e	moved, affected	gerührt	emocionado, a	commosso, a	comovido, a
émulsion	emulsion	Emulsion(f)	emulsión	emulsione	emulsão
en	in	in	en	in	em
encaisser	cash	ein = kassieren	cobrar	incassare	receber
encastrer	set in	ein = setzen	empotrar	incastrare	embutir
enceinte	fence; enclosure	Einzäunung(f)	muralla	cinta, recinto	muralha, recinto
enceinte	pregnant	schwanger	encinta	incinta	grávida
enchère	bid, bidding	Auktion(f); Gebot(n)	subasta	asta	leilão
enclencher	engage	ein = legen, = schalten	engranar	ingranare, avviare	engrenar
encoche	notch	Kerbe(f), Einschnitt m	muesca	tacca, intacco	entalhe
encombrant, e	bulky, cumbersome	sperrig, lästig	voluminoso, a	imgombrante	volumoso, a
encombrement	congestion, jam	Gedränge(n)	estorbo	affollamento, ingorgo	engarrafamento
encore	still	noch, wieder	todavía, aún	ancora	ainda
encore	again	noch einmal	otra vez	ancora	mais(uma vez)
encore	more	noch	más	ancora	mais
encore	still; yet	noch, noch mehr	aún	ancora	ainda
encore(pas)	yet(not)	noch(nicht)	todavía no	ancora(non)	ainda não
encourager	encourage, urge	ermutigen	alentar, animar	incoraggiare	encorajar
encre	ink	Tinte(f)	tinta	inchiostro	tinta
encyclopédie	encyclopaedia	Enzyklopädie(f)	enciclopedia	enciclopedia	enciclopédia
endoctriner	indoctrinate	indoktrinieren	adoctrinar	addottrinare	doutrinar
endommager	damage	beschädigen	dañar	danneggiare	estragar
endormi, e	asleep	schlafend	dormido, a	addormentato, a	adormecido, a
endroit	place, spot	Stelle(f)	lugar, sitio	luogo, posto	lugar, sítio
endurance	endurance	Ausdauer(f)	resistencia	resistenza	resistência
endurer	endure, bear	aus = halten, ertragen	aguantar, pasar	patire, resistere	aguentar
énergie	energy	Energie(f)	energía	energia	energia
énervé, e	edgy, worked up	erregt, nervös	excitado, a	nervoso, a	enervado, a
énerver(s')	edgy, irritable(be)	auf = regen, sich	ponerse nervioso, a	innervosirsi	enervar-se
enfance	childhood	Kindheit(f)	infancia	infanzia	infância
enfant	child, children(pl)	Kind(n)	niño, a; chico, a	bambino, a	criança
enfer	hell	Hölle(f)	infierno	inferno	inferno
enfermer	shut in	ein = schließen	encerrar	rinchiudere	encerrar, fechar
enfler	swell	an = schwellen	hinchar	gonfiare	inchar

49

French	English	German	Spanish	Italian	Portuguese
enfoncer	drive in	ein = schlagen	clavar	piantare	cravar
enfuir(s')	run away	fliehen	huir	fuggire	fugir
engagement	commitment	Verpflichtung(f)	compromiso	impegno	compromisso
engager	engage	engagieren	empeñar	impegnare	empenhar
engager(s')	join, enter	bei = treten	ingresar, meterse	impegnarsi	aderir, ligar-se
engager(s')	commit oneself	engagieren, sich	comprometerse	impegnarsi a	comprometer-se
engelure	chilblain	Frostbeule(f)	sabañón	gelone	frieira
engendrer	generate	zeugen, erzeugen	engendrar	generare	engendrar
engrais	fertilizer, manure	Dünger(m)	abono	concime	adubo
énigme	enigma	Rätsel(n)	enigma	enigma	enigma
enjeu	stake	Einsatz(m)(Spiel-)	apuesta	posta	aposta
enlever	take away, remove	entfernen	sacar, quitar	togliere	retirar, tirar
enlever	take off	aus = ziehen	quitar	togliere	tirar
enlever, retirer	remove	ab = nehmen	quitar, retirar	rimuovere	remover, retirar
ennemi, e	enemy	Feind(in f)m	enemigo, a	nemico, a	inimigo, a
ennui	boredom	Langeweile(f)	aburrimiento	noia	aborrecimento
ennui, problème	trouble, problem	Ärger(m)	problema	guaio	aborrecimento
ennuyer(s')	bored(be)	langweilen, sich	aburrir(se)	annoiarsi	aborrecer-se
ennuyeux, se	boring; annoying	langweilig	aburrido, a	noioso, a	aborrecido, a
énorme	enormous, huge	riesig	enorme	enorme	enorme
enquête	inquiry, inquest	Untersuchung(f)	investigación	indagine, inchiesta	inquérito
enquête, étude	survey	Umfrage(f)	encuesta	inchiesta	inquérito
enquêter	investigate	untersuchen	investigar	investigare, indagare	investigar
enregistrement	registration	Registrierung(f)	registro	registrazione	registo
enregistrement	recording	Aufnahme(f)	grabación	registrazione	gravação
enregistrer	record	auf = nehmen	grabar	registrare	gravar
enregistrer	register, check in	auf = geben	registrar	registrare	registar
enrhumer(s')	catch a cold	erkälten, sich	constipar(se)	raffreddarsi	constipar-se
enrichir	enrich	bereichern	enriquecer	arricchire	enriquecer
enroué, e	hoarse	heiser	ronco, a	rauco, a	rouco, a
enrouler	roll up	auf = wickeln	enrollar	arrotolare	enrolar
enseignant, e	teacher	Lehrer(in f)m	profesor, a	insegnante	professor, a
enseigne	sign	Schild(m)(Reklame-)	letrero	insegna	letreiro
enseignement	teaching	Unterricht(m), Lehre f	enseñanza	insegnamento	ensino
enseigner	teach	lehren, unterrichten	enseñar	insegnare	ensinar
ensemble	together	zusammen	juntos	insieme	junto
ensemble	whole; all the	Ganze(n); Gesamtheit f	conjunto	insieme	conjunto
ensemble	set	Satz(m)	conjunto	insieme	conjunto
ensoleillé, e	sunny	sonnig	soleado, a	soleggiato, a	soalheiro, a
ensuite, puis	then, next	danach	después	poi, dopo	em seguida
entaille	cut, nick, notch	Kerbe(f)	cortadura	incisione	incisão, golpe
entasser	pile up	stapeln	amontonar	ammucchiare	amontoar
entendre	hear	hören	oír	sentire	ouvir
enterrement	burial, funeral	Beerdigung(f)	entierro	funerale	enterro
enthousiasme	enthusiasm	Begeisterung(f)	entusiasmo	entusiasmo	entusiasmo
entier, ière	whole, entire	ganz	entero, a	intero, a	inteiro, a
entièrement	entirely	ganz	completamente	interamente	inteiramente
entonnoir	funnel	Trichter(m)	embudo	imbuto	funil
entorse	sprain	Verrenkung(f)	esguince	storta	entorse
entourer	surround	um = geben	rodear	circondare	rodear, cercar
entracte	interval	Pause(f)	intermedio	intervallo	intervalo
entrain	liveliness	Schwung(m)	vivacidad	brio	entusiasmo
entraînement	training, practice	Training(n)	entrenamiento	allenamento	treino
entraîner(s')	train, practise	üben; trainieren	entrenarse	allenare(-rsi)	treinar-se
entraîner	entail	mit sich bringen	ocasionar	comportare	acarretar
entraîneur	trainer	Trainer(m)	entrenador	allenatore	treinador
entre	between	zwischen	entre	tra, fra	entre
entrée	entry, entrance	Eintritt(m), Eingang m	entrada	ingresso	entrada
entrée	admission	Eintrittskarte(f)	entrada	ingresso	entrada, bilhete
entrepôt	warehouse	Lager(n)	almacén	magazzino	armazém
entreprendre	undertake	unternehmen	emprender	intraprendere	empreender
entrepreneur	contractor	Unternehmer(in f)m	empresario	imprenditore	empresário
entreprise	company, firm	Unternehmen(n)	empresa	impresa, ditta	empresa
entrer	enter, come/go in	ein = treten	entrar	entrare	entrar
entre-temps	meanwhile, meantime	inzwischen	entretanto	intanto, frattanto	entretanto
entretien	upkeep	Instandhaltung(f)	cuidado	mantenimento	manutenção
entretien	maintenance	Wartung(f)	mantenimiento	manutenzione	manutenção
entretien	talk, conversation	Gespräch(n)	conversación	colloquio	entrevista

French	English	German	Spanish	Italian	Portuguese
entrevoir	glimpse	flüchtig sehen	entrever	intravedere	entrever
entrevue	interview	Treffen(n), Gespräch n	entrevista	intervista	entrevista
entrez!	come in!	herein!	pase(!), adelante!	avanti!, prego!	entre!
énumérer	enumerate	auf = zählen	enumerar	enumerare	enumerar
envahir	invade	ein = fallen	invadir	invadere	invadir
enveloppe	envelope	Umschlag(m)(Brief-)	sobre	busta	envelope
envelopper	wrap, envelop	ein = hüllen, ein = packen	envolver	avvolgere	envolver
envers	reverse, back	Rückseite(f)	revés	rovescio	avesso
envie	desire	Lust(f)	ganas	voglia	vontade
environ	about	ungefähr	aproximadamente	circa	cerca de
environnement	surroundings	Umgebung(f)	ambiente(medio)	ambiente	ambiente
envisager	envisage	beabsichtigen	enfocar	prevedere	encarar
envoi	sending	Sendung(f), Versand(m)	envío	invio	envio
envoyer	send	schicken, senden(ab =)	enviar	inviare	enviar
envoyer	send	senden	mandar, enviar	mandare, inviare	mandar, enviar
épais, se	thick	dick	espeso, a	spesso, a	espesso, a
épaisseur	thickness	Stärke(f), Dicke(f)	espesor	spessore	espessura
épargnant, e	saver, investor	Sparer(in f)m	ahorrador, a	risparmiatore, trice	aforrador, a
épargner	save	sparen	ahorrar	risparmiare	poupar
épatant, e	wonderful, super	großartig, fabelhaft	estupendo, a	straordinario, a	estupendo, a
épaule	shoulder	Schulter(f)	hombro	spalla	ombro
épave	wreck	Wrack(n)	ruina, restos	relitto	destroços
épée	sword	Schwert(n)	espada	spada	espada
épeler	spell	buchstabieren	deletrear	compitare, sillabare	soletrar
épervier	sparrow-hawk	Habicht(m)	gavilán	sparviere	gavião
éphémère	ephemeral	vergänglich	efímero, a	effimero, a	efémero, a
épice(s)	spice	Gewürz(n)	especia	spezie	especiaria
épicé, e	spicy	gewürzt, würzig	picante	piccante	picante
épicerie	grocer's(shop)	Lebensmittelladen(m)	ultramarinos	drogheria	mercearia
épicier, ière	grocer	Lebensmittelhändler m	tendero, a	droghiere, a	merceeiro, a
épidémie	epidemic	Seuche(f)	epidemia	epidemia	epidemia
épiderme	epidermis, skin	Oberhaut(f), Haut(f)	epidermis	epidermide	epiderme
épilepsie	epilepsy	Epilepsie(f)	epilepsia	epilessia	epilepsia
épiler	remove hair	enthaaren	depilar	depilare	depilar
épine	thorn	Dorn(m); Stachel(m)	espina	spina	espinho
épingle	pin	Stecknadel(f)	alfiler	spillo	alfinete
épisode	episode	Episode(f)	episodio	episodio	episódio
éplucher	peel	schälen	pelar	sbucciare	descascar
éponge	sponge	Schwamm(m)	esponja	spugna	esponja
épopée	epic	Epos(n)	epopeya	epopea	epopeia
époque	epoch, era, time	Epoche(f), Ära(f), Zeit	época	epoca	época
épouse	wife(wives)	Gattin, Frau, Ehefrau f	esposa	sposa, consorte	esposa
épouvantable	dreadful	entsetzlich	horroroso, a	spaventoso, a	horroroso, a
époux	husband	Gatte, Mann, Ehemann(m)	esposo	sposo, consorte	esposo
épreuve, essai	test	Test(m), Probe(f)	prueba	prova, test	prova
éprouver	feel	spüren, fühlen	sentir	provare	sentir
épuisé, e	exhausted	erschöpft	agotado, a	esausto, a	esgotado, a
épuisé, e	exhausted, run out	ausverkauft	agotado, a	esaurito, a	esgotado, a
épuisette	fishing net	Fangnetz(n)	manguilla	guadino, retino	rede
équateur	equator	Äquator(m)	ecuador	equatore	equador
équatorial, e	equatorial	äquatorial	ecuatorial	equatoriale	equatorial
équerre	square(set -)	Zeichendreieck(n)	escuadra	squadra	esquadro
équestre	equestrian	Reiter-	ecuestre	equestre	equestre
équilibre	balance	Gleichgewicht(n)	equilibrio	equilibrio	equilíbrio
équilibrer	balance	aus = gleichen	equilibrar	equilibrare	equilibrar
équipage	crew	Besatzung(f)	tripulación	equipaggio	equipagem
équipe	team	Mannschaft(f), Team(n)	equipo	squadra; équipe	equipa, grupo
équipement	equipment	Ausstattung(f)	equipo	equipaggiamento	equipamento
équiper	equip, fit out	aus = rüsten	equipar	equipaggiare	equipar
équitation	riding(horse -)	Reiten(n)	equitación	equitazione	equitação
équité	equity	Gerechtigkeit(f)	equidad	equità	equidade
équivalent, e	equivalent	gleichwertig	equivalente	equivalente	equivalente
équivoque	equivocal	zweideutig	equívoco, a	equivoco, a	equívoco, a
éraflure	scratch, graze	Kratzer(m), Schramme f	rasguño	scalfittura	arranhadura
ère	era	Ära(f)	era	era	era
ériger	erect	errichten	erigir, levantar	erigere	erigir
ermite	hermit	Einsiedler(in f)m	ermitaño	eremita	eremita
érosion	erosion	Abtragung(f)	erosión	erosione	erosão

érotique	erotic	erotisch	erótico, a	erotico, a	erótico, a
érotisme	eroticism	Erotik(f)	erotismo	erotismo	erotismo
erreur	error, mistake	Irrtum(m), Fehler(m)	error	errore	erro
erreur(faire)	mistake(make a)	Irrtum(m)(machen)	error(cometer un)	errore(fare un)	erro(dar um)
érudit, e	erudite, learned	gelehrt	erudito, a	erudito, a	erudito, a
érudit, e	scholar	Gelehrte(f, m)	erudito, a	dotto, a; erudito, a	erudito, a
éruption	eruption	Ausbruch(m)	erupción	eruzione	erupção
escabeau	stool	Schemel(m)	escabel, taburete	sgabello	escabelo, mocho
escadron	squadron	Schwadron; Eskadron(f)	escuadrón	squadrone; squadra	esquadrão
escale	stop(over)	Zwischenlandung(f)	escala	scalo	escala
escalier	staircase, stairs	Treppe(f)	escalera	scala	escada
escamotable	fold-away	zusammenklappbar	plegable	ribaltabile	escamoteável
escargot	snail	Schnecke(f)	caracol	lumaca, chiocciola	caracol
escarpé, e	steep	steil	escarpado, a	scosceso, a	escarpado, a
esclavage	slavery	Sklaverei(f)	esclavitud	schiavitú	escravatura
esclave	slave	Sklave(m), Sklavin(f)	esclavo, a	schiavo, a	escravo, a
escompte	discount	Skonto(m)	descuento	sconto	desconto
escorte	escort	Gefolge(n)	escolta	scorta	escolta
escrime	fencing	Fechten(n)	esgrima	scherma	esgrima
escroc	crook, swindler	Gauner(m)	estafador	imbroglione	gatuno, escroque
escroquerie	swindle	Schwindel(m), Gaunerei	estafa, timo	truffa, imbroglio	trapaça, burla
espace	space, gap	Zwischenraum(m)	espacio	spazio	espaço
espace	space	Raum(m)	espacio	spazio	espaço
espèce	kind, sort	Gattung(f), Art(f)	especie	specie	espécie
espèce	species	Art(f)	especie	specie	espécie
espérer	hope	hoffen	esperar, desear	sperare	esperar, desejar
espion, ne	spy	Spion(m), Spionin(f)	espía	spia	espião, espia
espionnage	spying, espionage	Spionage(f)	espionaje	spionaggio	espionagem
espoir	hope	Hoffnung(f)	esperanza	speranza	esperança
esprit	mind	Sinn(m)	espíritu	mente	espírito
esprit	spirit	Geist(m)	espíritus	spirito	espírito
esquimau	Eskimo	Eskimo(m)	esquimal	eschimese	esquimó
essai	trial, test	Versuch(m)	prueba	prova, collaudo	ensaio
essayer	try	versuchen	probar, intentar	provare	tentar; provar
essence	petrol	Benzin(n)	gasolina	benzina	gasolina
essence super	four-star petrol	Superbenzin(n)	supercarburante	benzina super	super
essentiel, le	essential	wesentlich	esencial	essenziale	essencial
essentiel	main thing(the)	Hauptsache(f)	esencial	essenziale	essencial
essor	expansion, boom	Aufschwung(m)	auge, desarrollo	sviluppo	progresso
essuyer	wipe, dry	ab = wischen, abtrocknen	limpiar, secar	asciugare	limpar, secar
Est	East	Osten(m)	Este	Est	Este, Leste
esthétique	aesthetic	ästhetisch	estético, a	estetico, a	estético, a
estimation	estimate	Schätzung(f)	estimación	stima, valutazione	estimativa
estime	esteem	Achtung(f)	estima	stima	estima
estimer	estimate, value	schätzen	valorar, estimar	stimare, valutare	estimar
estival, e	summer	sommerlich	estival	estivo, a	estival
estomac	stomach	Magen(m)	estómago	stomaco	estômago
estropié, e	crippled	verkrüppelt	lisiado, a	storpio, a	aleijado, a
et	and	und	y	e, ed	e
établir	establish	festsetzen, aufstellen	establecer	stabilire	estabelecer
établir(s')	settle; set up	an = siedeln, sich	establecerse	stabilirsi	estabelecer-se
établissement	establishment	Anstalt(f)	establecimiento	stabilimento	estabelecimento
étage	floor, storey	Etage(f)	piso, planta	piano	andar
étagère	shelf(-ves)	Regal(n)	estantería	scaffale	prateleira
étain	tin; pewter	Zinn(n)	estaño	stagno	estanho
étaler	spread(out)	aus = breiten	exponer	stendere, spalmare	expor
étanche	watertight(air-)	undurchlässig	estanco, a	stagno, a	estanque
étang	pond	Teich(m)	estanque	stagno	lago; tanque
étape	stage	Strecke(f)	etapa	tappa	etapa
état	condition	Zustand(m)	condición	condizione	estado
état	state	Staat(m)	estado	stato	estado
été	summer	Sommer(m)	verano	estate	verão
éteindre	turn/switch off	aus = schalten	apagar	spegnere	apagar
éteindre	extinguish	löschen	apagar	spegnere	apagar
étendre	extend, spread	aus = breiten	extender	stendere	estender
étendre, agrandir	expand	aus = dehnen	extender(se)	estendere	estender
étendre(s')	stretch	erstrecken, sich	extenderse	estendersi	estender-se
étendue	extent	Umfang(m)	extensión, amplitud	estensione, ampiezza	extensão

French	English	German	Spanish	Italian	Portuguese
éternel, le	eternal	ewig	eterno, a	eterno, a	eterno, a
éternité	eternity	Ewigkeit(f)	eternidad	eternità	eternidade
éternuer	sneeze	niesen	estornudar	starnutire	espirrar
éthique	ethical	ethisch	ético, a	etico, a	ético, a
ethnique	ethnic(al)	ethnisch	étnico, a	etnico, a	étnico, a
étincelle	spark	Funken(m)	chispa	scintilla	faísca
étiquette	label, tag	Schild(n)	etiqueta	etichetta	rótulo
étirer	stretch	aus = dehnen	estirar	stirare	esticar
étoffe	material	Stoff(m)	tejido, tela	stoffa	tecido, estofo
étoile	star	Stern(m)	estrella	stella	estrela
étonnant, e	surprising	erstaunlich	asombroso, a	sorprendente	espantoso, a
étonner	astonish, amaze	überraschen	sorprender	sorprendere	espantar
étonner(s')	astonished(be -)	wundern, sich	sorprenderse	meravigliarsi	espantar-se
étouffer	suffocate; choke	ersticken	sofocar, ahogar	soffocare	sufocar
étourdir	stun, daze	betäuben	aturdir; atontar	stordire	aturdir; atordoar
étourdissant, e	deafening	betäubend	aturdidor, a	sbalorditivo, a	atroador, a
étrange	strange, odd	seltsam	extraño, a; raro, a	strano, a	estranho, a
étranger, ère	foreigner	Ausländer(in f)m	extranjero, a	straniero, a	estrangeiro, a
étranger, ère	foreign	ausländisch	extranjero, a	estero, a	estrangeiro, a
étranger(l')	foreign country	Ausland(n)	extranjero	estero	estrangeiro
étranger(à l')	abroad	Ausland(im)	extranjero(en el)	estero(all')	estrangeiro(ao)
étranglement	strangling	Erwürgen(n)	estrangulación	strangolamento	estrangulamento
être	be	sein	ser, estar	essere	ser, estar
être	be	sein	estar	essere	estar
étroit, e	narrow	eng	estrecho, a	stretto, a	estreito, a
étude	study; survey	Studie(f)	estudio	studio	estudo
étudiant, e	student	Student(in f)m	estudiante	studente, -essa	estudante
étudier	study	studieren	estudiar	studiare	estudar
étudier, examiner	investigate	prüfen, erforschen	estudiar	studiare	estudar, examinar
étui	case	Etui(n)	estuche	astuccio	estojo
euphorique	euphoric	euphorisch	eufórico, a	euforico, a	eufórico, a
euthanasie	euthanasia	Euthanasie(f)	eutanasia	eutanasia	eutanásia
évacuer	evacuate	räumen, leeren	evacuar	evacuare	evacuar
évaluation	assessment	Schätzung(f)	evaluación	valutazione	avaliação
évaluation	assessment	Einschätzung(f)	valoración	valutazione	avaliação
évaluer, estimer	assess	ein = schätzen	tasar, valorar	valutare, stimare	avaliar, fixar
évanouir(s')	faint	ohnmächtig werden	desmayarse	svenire	desmaiar
évaporation	evaporation	Verdunstung(f)	evaporación	evaporazione	evaporação
évasion	escape	Flucht(f)	evasión	evasione	evasão
éveiller(s')	wake up	auf = wachen	despertar(se)	svegliarsi	despertar
événement	event	Ereignis(n)	acontecimiento	avvenimento	acontecimento
éventail	fan	Fächer(m)	abanico	ventaglio	leque
éventualité	contingency	Eventualität(f)	eventualidad	eventualità	eventualidade
éventuel, le	possible	möglich	eventual	eventuale	eventual
évêque	bishop	Bischof(m)	obispo	vescovo	bispo
évidemment	of course	natürlich	desde luego	evidentemente	evidentemente
évidence, preuve	evidence, proof	Beweis(m)	evidencia, prueba	evidenza, prova	evidência, prova
évident, e	obvious, evident	offensichtlich	evidente	evidente	evidente
évier	sink	Spülbecken(n)	fregadero	acquaio, lavandino	pia, banca
éviter	avoid	vermeiden	evitar	evitare	evitar
évoluer	evolve	entwickeln, sich	evolucionar	evolvere	evoluir
évolution	evolution	Entwicklung(f)	evolución	evoluzione	evolução
évoquer	evoke	wach = rufen, erinnern	evocar	evocare	evocar
exact, e	exact, right	genau, richtig	exacto, a	esatto, a	exacto, a
exact, e; précis, e	accurate	genau, richtig	exacto, a; preciso, a	accurato, a; preciso, a	exacto, a; preciso, a
exact(c'est)	right(that 's)	stimmt !	exacto(es)	esatto(è)	exacto(é)
exactement	exactly	genau, richtig; gerade	exactamente	esattamente	exactamente
exactitude	accuracy	Genauigkeit(f)	exactitud	esattezza	exactidão
exagérer	exaggerate	übertreiben	exagerar	esagerare	exagerar
examen	examination, exam	Prüfung(f)	examen	esame	exame
examen(médical)	examination	Untersuchung(f)	examen, chequeo	esame	exame
examiner	examine, inspect	untersuchen	examinar	esaminare	examinar
excédent	surplus, excess	Überschuß(m)	excedente	eccedente	excedente
Excellence, Votre	Excellency(Your)	Exzellenz(f)	Excelencia(Su)	Eccellenza(Sua)	Excelência(Vossa)
excellent, e	excellent	vorzüglich	excelente	eccellente	excelente
excepté	except	außer	excepto, salvo	tranne	excepto
exception	exception	Ausnahme(f)	excepción	eccezione	excepção
exceptionnel, le	exceptional	außergewöhnlich	excepcional	eccezionale	excepcional

French	English	German	Spanish	Italian	Portuguese
excès	excess	Übermaß(n)	exceso	eccesso	excesso
excessif, ive	excessive	übermäßig	excesivo, a	eccessivo, a	excessivo, a
excitant, e	exciting	aufregend	excitante	eccitante	excitante
excité, e	worked up	gereizt	excitado, a	eccitato, a	excitado, a
exciter	excite	auf = regen	excitar	eccitare	excitar
exclamer(s')	exclaim	aus = rufen	exclamar	esclamare	exclamar
exclure	exclude	aus = schließen	excluir	escludere	excluir
exclusif, ive	exclusive	ausschließlich	exclusivo, a	esclusivo, a	exclusivo, a
exclusivité	exclusive rights	Alleinvertrieb(m)	exclusiva(-ividad)	esclusività	exclusividade
excrément	excrement	Ausscheidung(f)	excremento	escremento	excremento
excursion	excursion	Ausflug(m)	excursión	gita, escursione	excursão
excuse	excuse; apology	Entschuldigung(f)	excusa, disculpa	scusa	desculpa
excuse(je m')	sorry(I am)	es tut mir leid	siento(lo)	scusi(mi)	desculpe!
excuser(s')	apologize	entschuldigen, sich	disculpar(se)	scusarsi	desculpar-se
excusez-moi!	excuse me!; sorry!	Entschuldigung!	perdone(!)	scusi!	desculpe!; perdão!
exécuter	perform, carry out	aus = führen	ejecutar	eseguire	executar
exécutif, ive	executive	ausübend, vollziehend	ejecutivo, a	esecutivo, a	executivo, a
exécution	execution	Hinrichtung(f)	ejecución	esecuzione	execução
exemple	example	Beispiel(n)	ejemplo	esempio	exemplo
exemple(par)	instance(for)	Beispiel(zum)	ejemplo(por)	esempio(per)	exemplo(por)
exercer	exercise, practise	aus = üben	ejercitar	esercitare	exercitar
exercice	exercise	Übung(f)	ejercicio	esercizio	exercício
exhibition	exhibition	Schau, Ausstellung(f)	exhibición	esibizione	exibição
exigence	demand, requirement	Forderung(f)	exigencia	esigenza	exigência
exiger	demand, require	fordern	exigir	esigere	exigir
exiger, demander	demand	verlangen, fordern	exigir, demandar	esigere, domandare	exigir, pedir
exil	exile	Verbannung(f)	exilio	esilio	exílio
exilé, e	exile	Verbannte(f, m)	exiliado, a	esiliato, a	exilado, a
existence	existence, life	Dasein(n)	existencia	esistenza	existência
exister	exist	existieren	existir	esistere	existir
exode	exodus	Massenauswanderung(f)	éxodo	esodo	êxodo
exotique	exotic	exotisch	exótico, a	esotico, a	exótico, a
expansion	expansion	Ausdehnung(f)	expansión	espansione	expansão
expatriation	expatriation	Vertreibung(f)	expatriación	espatrio	expatriação
expatrier(s')	expatriate	aus = wandern	expatriarse	espatriare	expatriar-se
expédier	dispatch, send	verschicken	expedir	spedire	expedir
expédier, livrer	consign	übersenden	enviar, expedir	inviare	enviar, expedir
expéditeur	sender	Absender(in f)m	remitente	mittente	expedidor
expédition	expedition	Expedition(f)	expedición	spedizione	expedição
expérience	experience	Erfahrung(f)	experiencia	esperienza	experiência
expérience	experiment	Versuch(m)	experimento	esperimento	experiência
expérimental, e	experimental	experimentell	experimental	sperimentale	experimental
expérimentation	experimentation	Experimentieren(n)	experimentación	sperimentazione	experimentação
expert, e	expert	Experte(m), Expertin f	experto, a; perito, a	esperto, a	perito, a
expirer	die	verscheiden	expirar	spirare	expirar
expirer	breathe out	aus = atmen	espirar	espirare	expirar
expirer	expire	ab = laufen	expirar; vencer	scadere	expirar
explication	explanation	Erklärung(f)	explicación	spiegazione	explicação
expliquer	explain	erklären	explicar	spiegare	explicar
exploit	exploit	Glanzleistung(f)	hazaña	impresa, prodezza	proeza, feito
exploiter	exploit	aus = nutzen	explotar	sfruttare	explorar
explorateur	explorer	Forscher(in f)m	explorador, a	esploratore, trice	explorador, a
exploration	exploration	Erforschung(f)	exploración	esplorazione	exploração
explorer	explore	erforschen	explorar	esplorare	explorar
exploser	explode, blow up	explodieren	estallar	esplodere	explodir
explosion	explosion	Explosion(f)	explosión	esplosione	explosão
exportation	export(ing)	Export(m), Ausfuhr(f)	exportación	esportazione	exportação
exporter	export	exportieren	exportar	esportare	exportar
exposant, e	exhibitor	Aussteller(in f)m	expositor, a	espositore, trice	expositor, a
exposé	talk, commentary	Referat(n)	exposición	relazione; esposto	exposição
exposition	exhibition, show	Ausstellung(f)	exposición	esposizione, mostra	exposição
exprès	purpose(on)	absichtlich	expresamente	apposta	propósito(de)
expression	expression	Ausdruck(m)	expresión	espressione	expressão
exprimer(s')	express oneself	aus = drücken, sich	expresar(se)	esprimersi	exprimir-se
expulser	expel, eject	aus = weisen	expulsar	espellere	expulsar
extase	ecstasy	Entzückung(f)	éxtasis	estasi	êxtase
extension	extension	Ausdehnung(f)	extensión	estensione	extensão
exténué, e	exhausted	erschöpft	extenuado, a	spossato, a	extenuado, a

French	English	German	Spanish	Italian	Portuguese
extérieur, e	outer, outside	äußere	externo, a	esterno, a	exterior; externo, a
extérieur, e	outside	äußer; Außen-	exterior	esteriore	exterior
extérieur, e	foreign	Außen-	exterior	estero, a	exterior
extérieur	outside; exterior	Außenseite(f)	exterior	esterno	exterior
externe	external	äußerlich	externo, a	esterno, a	externo, a
extincteur	extinguisher	Feuerlöscher(m)	extintor	estintore	extintor
extinction	extinction	Löschen(Aus-)(n)	extinción	estinzione	extinção
extraction	extraction	Kohlenförderung(f)	extracción	estrazione	extracção
extraction	extraction	Zahnziehen(n)	extracción	estrazione	extracção
extrait	extract	Auszug(m)	pasaje, trozo	brano, estratto	excerto, trecho
extraire	extract	heraus = ziehen, ziehen	extraer	estrarre	extrair
extraordinaire	extraordinary	außergewöhnlich	extraordinario, a	straordinario, a	extraordinário, a
extrême	extreme	extrem	extremo, a	estremo, a	extremo, a
extrémité	extremity, end	Extremität(f)	extremidad	estremità	extremidade

F

French	English	German	Spanish	Italian	Portuguese
fabricant, e	manufacturer	Hersteller(in f)m	fabricante	fabbricante	fabricante
fabrication	manufacture	Herstellung(f)	fabricación	fabbricazione	fabrico
fabriquer	manufacture, make	her = stellen	fabricar	fabbricare	fabricar
fabuleux, se	fabulous	phantastisch	fabuloso, a	favoloso, a	fabuloso, a
façade	front(age)	Fassade(f)	fachada	facciata	fachada
face	face	Gesicht(n)	cara	faccia	face; cara
face	side	Seite(f)	cara	faccia	face; lado
facile	easy	leicht	fácil	facile	fácil
facilement	easily	leicht	fácilmente	facilmente	fácilmente
façon, manière	way, manner, fashion	Weise(f), Art(f)	modo, manera	modo, maniera	modo, maneira
facteur, trice	postman/-woman	Briefträger(in f)m	cartero, a	postino, a	carteiro, a
facteur	factor	Faktor(m)	factor	fattore	factor
facture	invoice, bill	Rechnung(f)	factura	fattura	factura
facultatif, ive	optional	wahlfrei, beliebig	facultativo, a	facoltativo, a	facultativo, a
faculté	Faculty	Fakultät(f)	facultad	facoltà	faculdade
faculté	possibility	Fähigkeit(f)	facultad	facoltà	faculdade
faible	weak	schwach	débil	debole, fragile	fraco, a
faible	dim	matt	flojo, a	debole	fraco, a
faiblesse	weakness(-es)	Schwäche(f)	debilidad	debolezza	fraqueza
faille	break, fault	Spalte(f)	falla	faglia	falha
faillite	failure; bankruptcy	Konkurs(m)	quiebra, ruina	fallimento	falência
faillite(faire)	bankrupt(go)	bankrott sein	quiebra(hacer)	fallire	falir
faim(avoir)	hunger(hungry be)	Hunger(m)(haben)	hambre(tener)	fame(aver)	fome(ter)
fainéant, e	lazy	faul	holgazán, a	fannullone, a	preguiçoso, a
faire	do, make	tun, machen	hacer	fare	fazer
faire	make, do	machen, tun	hacer	fare	fazer
faisan	pheasant	Fasan(m)	faisán	fagiano	faisão
faisceau	beam	Strahl(m)(Licht)	haz	fascio	foco
fait	fact	Tatsache(f)	hecho	fatto	facto
falaise	cliff	Steilküste(f)	acantilado	scogliera	falésia
falloir	have to, must	müssen	necesario(ser)	bisognare	preciso(ser)
falsifier	falsify	fälschen	falsificar	falsificare	falsificar
fameux, se	excellent	großartig	famoso, a	ottimo, a	famoso, a
familial, e	family	Familien-	familiar	familiare	familiar
familier, ière	familiar	familiär	familiar	familiare	familiar
famille	family	Familie(f)	familia	famiglia	família
famine	famine	Hungersnot(f)	hambre	fame, carestia	fome
fanatique	fanatic(al)	fanatisch	fanático, a	fanatico, a	fanático, a
fanfare	brass band	Fanfare(f)	banda	banda	fanfarra, banda
fantaisie	fancy; fantasy	Spielerei(f)	fantasía	fantasia	fantasia

French	English	German	Spanish	Italian	Portuguese
fantasme	fantasy	Phantasievorstellung	fantasma	fantasia	fantasma
fantastique	fantastic	phantastisch	fantástico, a	fantastico, a	fantástico, a
fantôme	ghost	Gespenst(n)	fantasma	fantasma	fantasma
farce	joke; farce	Streich(m)	broma	scherzo	partida
fardeau	burden	Last(f)	carga	fardello	fardo
farine	flour	Mehl(n)	harina	farina	farinha
farouche	wild	wild	feroz	selvatico, a	arisco, a
fascinant, e	fascinating	faszinierend	fascinante	affascinante	fascinante
fasciné, e	fascinated	fasziniert	fascinado, a	affascinato, a	fascinado, a
fasciste	fascist	Faschist(in f)m	fascista	fascista	fascista
fastueux, se	sumptuous	prunkvoll	ostentoso, a	fastoso, a	faustoso, a
fatal, e	fatal	tödlich	fatal	fatale	fatal
fatalité	fatality, fate	Schicksal(n)	fatalidad	fatalità	fatalidade
fatigant, e	tiring	anstrengend	fatigante	faticoso, a	cansativo, a
fatigue	tiredness	Müdigkeit(f)	cansancio	stanchezza	fatiga, cansaço
fatigué, e	tired	müde, ermüdet	cansado, a	stanco, a	cansado, a
fatiguer	tire, make tired	ermüden	cansar, fatigar	stancare	cansar, fatigar
faubourg	suburb	Vorstadt(f)	suburbio	sobborgo	subúrbio
faune	fauna	Fauna(f), Tierwelt(f)	fauna	fauna	fauna
faute, erreur	mistake, error	Fehler(m), Irrtum(m)	falta, error	fallo, errore	falta, erro
faute	fault	Fehler(m)	culpa	colpa	culpa
fauteuil	arm-chair	Sessel(m)	sillón	poltrona	poltrona
fautif, ive	wrong(in the)	schuldig	culpable	colpevole	culpado, a
faux, fausse	wrong, false	falsch	falso, a	falso, a	falso, a
faveur	favour	Gunst(f)	favor	favore	favor
favorable	favourable	günstig	favorable	favorevole	favorável
favori, ite	favourite	Favorit(in f)m	favorito, a	favorito, a	favorito, a
favoriser	favour	begünstigen	favorecer	favorire	favorecer
fécondation	fertilization	Befruchtung(f)	fecundación	fecondazione	fecundação
fécondité	fertility	Fruchtbarkeit(f)	fecundidad	fecondità	fecundidade
fédération	federation	Verband(m)	federación	federazione	federação
fée	fairy	Fee(f)	hada	fata	fada
félicitations!	congratulations!	Glückwunsch!	enhorabuena(!)	congratulazioni!	parabéns!
féliciter	congratulate	gratulieren	felicitar	congratularsi	felicitar
félure	crack	Sprung(m), Riß(m)	raja, grieta	incrinatura	estaladela
femelle	female	Weibchen(n)	hembra	femmina	fêmea
féminin	feminine	weiblich	femenino	femminile	feminino
féminin, e	feminine	fraulich	femenino, a	femminile	feminino, a
femme	woman(women)	Frau(f)	mujer	donna	mulher
femme, épouse	wife(wives)	Ehefrau(f), Frau(f)	mujer	moglie	mulher
femme de chambre	chambermaid	Zimmermädchen(n)	camarera	cameriera	empregada
femme de ménage	domestic help	Putzfrau(f)	asistenta	donna di servizio	mulher a dias
fendre	split, slit	spalten	rajar, partir	spaccare	fender, rachar
fenêtre	window	Fenster(n)	ventana	finestra	janela
fendre	slit	auf = schlitzen	rajar, hender	fendere	rachar, fender
fente	split; slot; slit	Spalt(m)	grieta	fessura	fenda
fente	slit	Schlitz(m)	raja	fessura; spacco	fenda
fer	iron	Eisen(n)	hierro	ferro	ferro
fer à repasser	iron	Bügeleisen(n)	plancha	ferro da stiro	ferro de passar
férié(jour)	public holiday	Feiertag(m)	festivo(día)	festivo(giorno)	feriado(dia)
ferme	firm	fest	firme	fermo, a; solido, a	firme
ferme	farm	Bauernhof(m)	granja	fattoria	quinta
fermé, e	closed, shut	zu, geschlossen	cerrado, a	chiuso, a	fechado, a
fermenter	ferment	gären	fermentar	fermentare	fermentar
fermer	close, shut	schließen	cerrar	chiudere	fechar, cerrar
fermer	shut	zu = machen	cerrar	chiudere	fechar
fermer à clé	lock	ab = schließen	cerrar con llave	chiudere a chiave	fechar à chave
fermeté	firmness	Entschlossenheit(f)	firmeza	fermezza	firmeza
fermier, ière	farmer	Bauer(m), Bäuerin(f)	granjero, a	contadino, a	caseiro, a
féroce	ferocious, fierce	wild, furchtbar	feroz	feroce	feroz
ferraille	scrap iron	Alteisen(n)	chatarra	ferraglia, rottame	sucata
fertile	fertile	fruchtbar	fértil	fertile	fértil
fesse	bottom, buttock	Gesäß(n), Po(m)	nalga	natica	nádega
fessée	spanking	Hinternvoll(m)	azotaina, paliza	sculacciata	surra, açoite
festin	feast, banquet	Festmahl(n)	festín	festino	festim, banquete
festival	festival	Festspiel(n)	festival	festival	festival
fête	celebration	Feier(f)	fiesta	festa	festa
feu	fire	Feuer(n)	fuego	fuoco	fogo

French	English	German	Spanish	Italian	Portuguese
feuille	leaf(leaves)	Blatt(n)	hoja	foglia	folha
feuille	sheet	Blatt(n)	hoja	foglio	folha
février	February	Februar(m)	febrero	febbraio	Fevereiro
fiable	reliable	zuverlässig	fiable, seguro, a	sicuro, a; affidabile	seguro, a
fiancé, e	fiancé(e)	Verlobte(f, m)	novio, a	fidanzato, a	noivo, a
fiancer(se)	engaged(get)	verloben, sich	prometerse	fidanzarsi	ficar noivo, a
fibre	fibre	Faser(f)	fibra	fibra	fibra
ficelle	string, cord	Schnur(f)	cordel	spago	cordel, guita
fiche	card	Karteikarte(f)	ficha	scheda, cartella	ficha
fichier	card-index	Kartei(f)	fichero	schedario	ficheiro
fiction	fiction	Fiktion(f)	ficción	finzione	ficção
fidèle	faithful	treu	fiel	fedele	fiel
fier, fière	proud	stolz	altivo, a	fiero, a	altivo, a
fierté	pride	Stolz(m)	orgullo	fierezza	orgulho
fièvre	fever, temperature	Fieber(n)	fiebre	febbre	febre
figure	face	Gesicht(n)	rostro	faccia	rosto
figure	figure	Figur(f)	figura	figura	figura
fil	thread	Faden(m)	hilo	filo	fio
fil(de fer)	wire	Draht(m)	alambre	filo(di ferro)	arame
filament	filament	Faser(f), Faden(m)	filamento	filamento	filamento
file	queue, line	Schlange(f)	fila	fila, coda	fila, bicha
file	lane	Spur(f)	fila	fila, corsia	fila
filet	net	Netz(n)	red	rete	rede
filiale	subsidiary	Filiale(f)	filial, sucursal	filiale	filial, sucursal
fille	girl	Mädchen(n)	chica	ragazza	rapariga
fille	daughter	Tochter(f)	hija	figlia	filha
film	film, movie	Film(m)	película	film	filme
filmer	film	filmen	rodar, filmar	filmare	filmar
fils	son	Sohn(m)	hijo	figlio	filho
filtre	filter	Filter(m)	filtro	filtro	filtro
fin, e	fine, thin	fein, dünn	fino, a	fine, sottile	fino, a
fin	end	Ende(n)	fin	fine	fim
final, e	final	letzte, Schluß-	final	finale	final
finance	finance	Finanzwelt, Finanzen	finanza	finanza	finança
financement	financing	Finanzierung(f)	financiación	finanziamento	financiamento
financer	finance	finanzieren	financiar	finanziare	financiar
financier, ière	financial	finanziell	financiero, a	finanziario, a	financeiro, a
finir	finish, end	beenden	acabar, terminar	finire	acabar, terminar
firme	firm	Firma(f)	firma	firma, ditta, azienda	firma
fisc	Inland Revenue	Fiskus(m), Finanzamt	fisco	fisco	fisco
fiscal, e	fiscal, tax	fiskalisch, Steuer-	fiscal	fiscale	fiscal
fiscalité	tax system	Steuerwesen(n)	fiscalidad	fiscalità	fiscalidade
fission	fission	Spaltung(f)(Atom)	fisión	fissione	fissão
fissure, fente	crack, fissure	Riß(m), Spalte(f)	fisura, grieta	fessura, crepa	fissura; fenda
fixation	fixing, fixation	Befestigung(f)	fijación	fissazione	fixação
fixe	fixed	fest	fijo, a	fisso, a	fixo, a
fixer	fix, attach	befestigen	fijar	fissare	fixar
flacon	bottle(small)	Fläschchen(n)	frasco	boccetta	frasco
flairer	sniff; scent; sense	wittern, schnüffeln	olfatear, husmear	annusare	farejar, cheirar
flamme	flame	Flamme(f)	llama	fiamma	chama
flash	flash	Blitz(m)	flash	flash	flash
flatter	flatter	schmeicheln	halagar	adulare	lisonjear
flèche	arrow	Pfeil(m)	flecha	freccia	flecha, seta
flétrir	wilt, wither	verwelken	marchitar	appassire	murchar
fleur	flower	Blume(f)	flor	fiore	flor
fleuriste	florist	Blumenhändler(in f)m	florista	fioraio	florista
fleuve	river	Strom(m)	río	fiume	rio
flexible	flexible	flexibel	flexible	flessibile	flexível
flocon	flake	Flocke(f)	copo	fiocco	floco
flore	flora	Flora(f), Pflanzenwelt	flora	flora	flora
flot	wave; flood	Welle(f); Flut(f)	oleada	flutto	corrente
flotte	fleet	Flotte(f)	flota	flotta	frota
flotter	float	schwimmen, treiben	flotar	galleggiare	flutuar
flou, e	fuzzy, blurred	verschwommen	borroso, a	sfumato, a	vago, a
fluctuation	fluctuation	Schwanken(n)	fluctuación	fluttuazione	flutuação
fluide	fluid	Flüssigkeit(f)	fluido	fluido	fluido
flûte	flute	Flöte(f)	flauta	flauto	flauta
flux	flow	Fluß(m), Strömung(f)	flujo	flusso	fluxo

F

French	English	German	Spanish	Italian	Portuguese
foetus	foetus	Fötus(m)	feto	feto	feto
foi	faith	Glaube(m)	fe	fede	fé
foie	liver	Leber(f)	hígado	fegato	fígado
foire	fair	Messe(f)	feria	fiera	feira
fois	time	Mal(n)	vez	volta	vez
fois(une)	once	einmal	vez(una)	volta(una)	vez(uma)
folie	madness, folly	Wahnsinn(m), Wahn(m)	locura	follia, pazzia	loucura
folklore	folklore	Folklore(f)	folklore	folclore	folclore
fonction	function	Funktion(f)	función	funzione	função
fonction	function	Stellung(f), Amt(n)	función	funzione	função
fonctionnaire	state employee	Beamter(m), Beamtin(f)	funcionario, a	impiegato statale	funcionário, a
fonctionnaire	civil servant	Beamte(r)m, Beamtin(f)	funcionario, a	funzionario, a	funcionário, a
fonctionnement	functioning	Betrieb(m)	funcionamiento	funzionamento	funcionamento
fonctionner	function, work, run	funktionieren	funcionar	funzionare	funcionar
fond	bottom; back	Boden(m), Grund(m)	fondo	fondo	fundo
fondamental, e	fundamental	fundamental	fundamental	fondamentale	fundamental
fondateur, trice	founder	Gründer(in f)m	fundador, a	fondatore, trice	fundador, a
fonder	found	gründen	fundar	fondare	fundar
fondre	melt	schmelzen	fundir	fondere	fundir
fondre	melt	schmilzen	derretir	sciogliere(-rsi)	derreter
fonds	funds	Fonds(m), Kapital(n)	fondos	fondi	fundos, capital
fondu, e	melted	geschmolzen	derretido, a	sciolto, a	derretido, a
fontaine	fountain	Springbrunnen(m)	fuente	fontana	fonte
football	football, soccer	Fußball(m)	fútbol	calcio	futebol
forage	boring	Bohrung(f)	perforación	perforazione	perfuração
force	strength	Stärke(f), Kraft(f)	fuerza	forza	força
force	force	Gewalt(f); Kraft(f)	fuerza	forza	força
forcer	force	zwingen	forzar	forzare	forçar
forêt	forest	Wald(m)	bosque	foresta, bosco	floresta, bosque
forfaitaire	inclusive	pauschal	global; convenido, a	forfettario, a	preço fixo(a)
formalité	formality	Formalität(f)	formalidad	formalità	formalidade
format	format, size	Format(n)	formato, tamaño	formato	formato
formation	formation	Entstehung(f)	formación	formazione	formação
formation	training	Ausbildung(f)	formación	formazione	formação
forme	shape, form	Form(f), Aussehen(n)	forma	forma	forma
forme	design, style	Schnitt(m)	hechura	taglio, stile	corte, design
forme	form	Verfassung(f)	forma(en)	forma	forma
former	form	bilden, formen	formar	formare	formar
formidable	tremendous	großartig	formidable	formidabile	formidável
formulaire	form	Formular(n), Vordruck	formulario	modulo, formulario	formulário
formule	formula	Formel(f)	fórmula	formula	fórmula
fort, e	strong	stark	fuerte	forte	forte
fort, e	loud	laut	fuerte; alto, a	forte; alto, a	forte; alto, a
fortifiant	tonic	Stärkungsmittel(n)	fortificante	ricostituente	fortificante
fortune	fortune	Vermögen(n)	fortuna	fortuna	fortuna
fosse	pit	Grube(f)	fosa, hoyo	fossa; buca	fossa
fossé	ditch	Graben(m)	cuneta	fossato, fosso	fosso
fossile	fossil	Fossil(n)	fósil	fossile	fóssil
fou, folle	mad, foolish, crazy	verrückt	loco, a	matto, a; pazzo, a	louco, a; maluco, a
foudre	lightning	Blitz(m)	rayo	fulmine	raio
fouet	whip	Peitsche(f)	látigo	frusta	chicote
fougère	fern	Farn(-kraut n)m	helecho	felce	feto
fouiller	search	suchen, durchsuchen	registrar	frugare	rebuscar
fouiller	excavate	aus = graben	excavar	scavare	escavar
foulard	scarf	Seidentuch, Halstuch	fular, pañuelo	foulard	lenço, cachecol
foule	crowd	Menge(f)	muchedumbre	folla	multidão
foulure	sprain	Verstauchung(f)	esguince	slogatura	entorse
four	oven	Ofen(m)	horno	forno	forno
fourche	pitchfork, fork	Gabel(f)(Heu-; Mist-)	horca	forca	forcado
fourchette	fork	Gabel(f)	tenedor	forchetta	garfo
fourmi	ant	Ameise(f)	hormiga	formica	formiga
fournir	supply, provide	beliefern	proveer, dar	fornire	fornecer
fournir	provide	versorgen, liefern	proveer	fornire	fornecer
fournisseur, se	supplier	Lieferant(in f)m	abastecedor, a	fornitore, trice	fornecedor, a
fourniture	supply(ing)	Lieferung(f)	abastecimiento	fornitura	fornecimento
fourrage	fodder	Futter(n)	forraje	foraggio	forragem
fourrure	fur	Pelz(m)	piel	pelliccia	pele; peliça
foyer	home	Heim(n)	hogar	focolare	lar

French	English	German	Spanish	Italian	Portuguese
foyer, âtre	fire-place, hearth	Feuerstelle(f), Herd m	hogar, chimenea	focolare	lareira
fraction	fraction	Bruchteil(m)	fracción	frazione	fracção
fracture	fracture	Bruch(m)	fractura	frattura	fractura
fragile	fragile	zerbrechlich	frágil	fragile	frágil
fragment	fragment	Fragment(n)	fragmento	frammento	fragmento
frais, fraîche	fresh	frisch	fresco, a	fresco, a	fresco, a
frais	expenses	Kosten(pl.)	gastos	spese(le)	gastos, despesas
frais(scolarité)	fee	Kosten(pl.)	gastos(escolares)	spese	despesas
fraise	strawberry	Erdbeere(f)	fresa	fragola	morango
franc, che	frank	offen, ehrlich	franco, a	franco, a; sincero, a	franco, a
franchir	cross	überqueren	atravesar	varcare, passare	atravessar
franco de port	carriage-paid	portofrei	porte pago	porto franco	porte pago
frapper	hit, knock, strike	schlagen, prügeln	golpear	picchiare	bater
frapper	knock	an = klopfen	llamar	bussare	bater
fraternité	brotherhood	Brüderlichkeit(f)	fraternidad	fraternità	fraternidade
fraude	fraud	Betrug(m)	fraude	frode	fraude
fraude(fiscale)	tax evasion	Steuerhinterziehung f	fraude(fiscal)	frode(fiscale)	fraude(fiscal)
frayeur	fright	Schreck(m), Angst(f)	espanto	spavento	temor
frein	brake	Bremse(f)	freno	freno	travão
freiner	brake	bremsen	frenar	frenare	travar
fréquence	frequency	Frequenz(f)	frecuencia	frequenza	frequência
fréquent, e	frequent	häufig	frecuente	frequente	frequente
frère	brother	Bruder(m)	hermano	fratello	irmão
fret	freight	Fracht(f)	flete	nolo, carico	frete
friandise	delicacy	Nascherei(f)	golosina	dolciume	guloseima
frigo, frigidaire	fridge	Kühlschrank(m)	frigorífico	frigorifero	frigorífico
frigorifique	refrigerating	Kühl-; kalt, kühl	frigorífico, a	frigorifero, a	frigorífico, a
frire	fry	braten	freír	friggere	fritar
frisé, e	curly	lockig	rizado, a	ricciuto, a	ondulado, a
frisson	shiver	Schauer(m)	escalofrío	brivido	arrepio
frites	chips	Pommes Frites	patatas fritas	patatine fritte	batatas fritas
frivole	frivolous	frivol, leichtsinnig	frívolo, a	frivolo, a	frívolo, a
froid, e	cold	kalt	frío, a	freddo, a	frio, a
froid(avoir)	cold(to be)	frieren	frío(tener)	freddo(avere)	frio(ter)
fromage	cheese	Käse(m)	queso	formaggio	queijo
front	forehead	Stirn(f)	frente	fronte	testa
frontière	border, frontier	Grenze(f)	frontera	confine, frontiera	fronteira
frontière, limite	boundary	Grenze(f)	frontera, límite	frontiera, limite	fronteira, limite
frottement	friction, rubbing	Reibung(f)	frotamiento	strofinio	fricção
frotter	rub	reiben	frotar	strofinare, sfregare	esfregar
fruit(s)	fruit	Frucht(f)	fruta	frutto; frutta	fruta
fruits de mer	seafood	Meeresfrüchte(f, pl.)	marisco	frutti di mare	marisco
frustration	frustration	Enttäuschung(f)	frustración	frustrazione	frustração
fugitif, ive	fugitive	flüchtig	fugitivo, a	fuggitivo, a	fugitivo, a
fuir	run away, flee	fliehen	huir	fuggire	fugir
fuite	flight, escape	Flucht(f)	huída	fuga	fuga
fuite	leak	Leck(n)	escape	perdita	fuga
fumé, e	smoked	geräuchert	ahumado, a	affumicato, a	fumado, a
fumée	smoke	Rauch(m)	humo	fumo	fumo
fumée	smoke, fumes	Rauch(m)	humo	smog, fumo	fumo
fumer	smoke	rauchen	fumar	fumare	fumar
fumeurs	smokers	Raucher(m)	fumadores	fumatore, trice	fumadores
fumier	manure	Mist(m)	estiércol	letame	estrume
funérailles	funeral	Begräbnis(n)	funerales	funerale	funeral
fureur	fury	Wut(f)	furor	furore	furor
furieux, se	furious	wütend	furioso, a	furioso, a	furioso, a
furoncle	boil	Furunkel(m)	furúnculo	foruncolo	furúnculo
fusée	rocket	Rakete(f)	cohete	razzo	foguete
fusil	shot-gun, rifle	Gewehr(n)	fusil	fucile	espingarda
fusion	merger	Vereinigung(f), Fusion	fusión	fusione, alleanza	fusão
fusion	fusion, melting	Schmelzen(n)(Ver-)	fusión	fusione	fusão
fût	barrel	Faß(n)	barril	fusto, barile	barril
futur, e	future	zukünftig	futuro, a	futuro, a	futuro, a
futur	future	Zukunft(f)	futuro	futuro	futuro

G

French	English	German	Spanish	Italian	Portuguese
gâchette	trigger	Abzug(m)	gatillo	grilletto	gatilho
gadget	gadget	Spielerei(f)	chisme, mecanismo	gadget	aparelho
gage	pledge	Pfand(n)	prenda	pegno	penhor
gagner	win	gewinnen	ganar	vincere	ganhar
gagner	earn; win	verdienen	ganar	guadagnare	ganhar
gagner	save	sparen	ganar	guadagnare	ganhar
gai, e	happy, merry	froh	alegre	allegro, a	alegre
gain(s)	earnings	Gewinn(m)	ganancia(s)	lucro, profitto	lucro
gaine	sheath	Hülle(f)	funda, estuche	guaina, astuccio	invólucro
gaine	girdle	Korsett(n)	faja	guaina, corsetto	cinta elástica
galant, e	gallant	galant	galante	galante	galante
galaxie	galaxy	Galaxie(f)	galaxia	galassia	galáxia
gale	scabies	Krätze(f)	sarna	scabbia, rogna	sarna
galerie	arcade	Passage(f)	galería	galleria	galeria
galerie	gallery	Galerie, Ausstellung	galería	galleria	galeria
galet	pebble	Kieselstein(m)	canto rodado	ciottolo	seixo
galon	stripe	Galone(f)	galón	gallone, grado	galão
galop	gallop	Galopp(m)	galope	galoppo	galope
gamin, e	kid, child	Kind(n)	chiquillo, a	ragazzino, a	miúdo
ganglion	ganglion, gland	Ganglien(pl.)	ganglio	ganglio	gânglio
gangrène	gangrene	Brand(m), Wundbrand(m)	gangrena	cancrena	gangrena
gangster	gangster	Gangster(m)	gángster	gangster	gangster
gant	glove	Handschuh(m)	guante	guanto	luva
gant	flannel	Waschlappen(m)	manopla	guanto	luva
garage	garage	Garage(f)	garaje, garage	garage	garagem
garagiste	garage mechanic	Autoschlosser(m)	garajista	garagista	garagista
garantie	guarantee; warranty	Garantie(f)	garantía	garanzia	garantia
garantir	guarantee, warrant	gewährleisten	garantizar	garantire	garantir
garçon	boy	Junge(m)	muchacho, mozo	ragazzo	rapaz
garçon, enfant	boy	kleiner Junge(m)	chico	ragazzo, bambino	rapaz
garçon	waiter	Ober(m)	camarero	cameriere	criado
garde	guard	Wache(f)	guardia	guardia, custodia	guarda
garde	guard	Wächter(m), Hüter(m)	guarda	guardia	guarda
garde-à-vous!	attention!	Stillgestanden!	firmes(!)	attenti!	sentido!
garder	keep	behalten	guardar	tenere	guardar
garder	look after	hüten	vigilar, guardar	custodire	cuidar de, vigiar
garder	guard, watch over	hüten, bewachen	guardar	custodire, guardare	guardar, vigiar
gardien, ne	keeper, caretaker	Wärter(in f)m	guardián, ana	custode, guardia	guarda
gardien, ne; garde	guard; keeper	Wächter(in f)m	guardián, guarda	guardiano, a; custode	guarda
gare	station	Bahnhof(m)	estación	stazione	estação, gare
garer	park	parken	aparcar	posteggiare	estacionar
garnir	garnish	garnieren	guarnecer	guarnire	guarnecer
gas-oil	diesel oil	Diesel(n), Dieselöl(n)	gasoil	gasolio	gasóleo
gaspillage	waste	Verschwendung(f)	despilfarro	spreco	desperdício
gaspiller, perdre	waste	verschwenden	despilfarrar	sprecare	desperdiçar
gaspiller	waste	verschwenden	desperdiciar	sperperare	desperdiçar
gastrique	gastric	Magen-	gástrico, a	gastrico, a	gástrico, a
gastronomie	gastronomy	Gastronomie(f)	gastronomía	gastronomia	gastronomia
gâteau	cake; pastry	Kuchen(m)	pastel	dolce	bolo
gauche	left	links; linke(r, s)	izquierdo, a	sinistro, a	esquerdo, a
gaz	gas	Gas(n)	gas	gas	gás
gazeux, se	gaseous	gasförmig	gaseoso, a	gassoso, a	gasoso, a
gazeux, se	fizzy, sparkling	sprudeln; Sprudel-	gaseoso, a	gassato, a	gasoso, a
gazon	grass	Rasen(m)	césped	prato, erba	relva
géant, e	giant	riesig, gigantisch	gigante	gigante	gigante
gelée	jelly	Gelee(n)	jalea	gelatina	geleia
geler	freeze	frieren	helar	gelare	gelar
gélure	frostbite	Erfrierung(f)	heladura	congelamento	frieira
gémir	moan	stöhnen	gemir	gemere	gemer
gencive	gum	Zahnfleisch(n)	encía	gengiva	gengiva
gendarme	policeman(-men)	Polizist(m)	guardia civil	carabiniere	guarda-republicano

French	English	German	Spanish	Italian	Portuguese
gendre	son-in-law	Schwiegersohn(m)	yerno	genero	genro
gêne	embarrassment	Verlegenheit(f)	molestia	disagio, imbarazzo	embaraço
généalogie	genealogy	Genealogie(f)	genealogía	genealogia	genealogia
gêner	obstruct	stören	molestar	imbarazzare	incomodar
général, e	general	allgemein, generell	general	generale	geral
général(en)	usually, in general	allgemeinen(im)	general(en)	genere(in)	geral(em)
général	general	General(m)	general	generale	general
générateur	generator	Generator(m)	generador	generatore	gerador
génération	generation	Generation(f)	generación	generazione	geração
générer	generate	erzeugen	engendrar	generare	gerar
généreux, se	generous	freigebig	generoso, a	generoso, a	generoso, a
génétique	genetics	Genetik(f)	genética	genetica	genética
génial, e	brilliant	genial	genial	geniale	genial
génie	genius	Genie(n)	genio	genio	génio
génital, e	genital	Genital-	genital	genitale	genital
génocide	genocide	Völkermord(m)	genocidio	genocidio	genocídio
genou	knee	Knie(n)	rodilla	ginocchio	joelho
genre	kind, sort	Art(f), Sorte(f)	género	genere	género
gens	people	Leute(pl.)	gente	gente(la)	gente, pessoas
gentil, le	kind, nice	nett	gentil, amable	gentile	gentil, amável
géographie	geography	Erdkunde(f)	geografía	geografia	geografia
géologie	geology	Geologie(f)	geología	geologia	geologia
géométrie	geometry	Geometrie(f)	geometría	geometria	geometria
gérant, e	manager	Geschäftsführer(m)	gerente	gerente, gestore	gerente
gérant, e	manager	Verwalter(in f)m	gerente, director, a	gestore, gerente	gerente, director, a
gerçure	chap(ped)	Riß(m), Hautriß(m)	grieta	screpolatura	greta
gérer	manage	verwalten, führen	administrar	amministrare	gerir
germe	germ, seed	Keim(m)	germen	germe	germe
germe	seed	Keim(m)	germen, grano	germoglio	germe
geste	gesture	Geste(f)	gesto	gesto	gesto
gestion	management	Verwaltung(f)	gestión	gestione	gestão
gestionnaire	manager	Verwalter(in f)m	gestor, a	gestore	gestor, a
gibier	game	Wild(n)	caza	selvaggina	caça
gicler, jaillir	squirt, spurt	spritzen	salpicar	sprizzare, schizzare	salpicar
gifle	slap	Ohrfeige(f)	bofetada	schiaffo	bofetada
gigantesque	gigantic, huge	gigantisch, riesig	gigantesco, a	gigantesco, a	gigantesco, a
gilet	cardigan	Weste(f), Jacke(f)	chaleco	gilè; golf	casaco de malha
girafe	giraffe	Giraffe(f)	jirafa	giraffa	girafa
gisant, e	lying	liegend	yacente	giacente	jacente
givre	frost	Reif(m)	escarcha	brina	geada
glace	ice	Eis(n)	hielo	ghiaccio	gelo
glace; miroir	window; mirror	Scheibe(f); Spiegel(m)	luna; cristal	vetro; specchio	vidro; espelho
glace	ice cream	Eis(n)	helado	gelato	gelado
glacé, e; gelé, e	icy	eisig	helado, a	gelato, a; ghiacciato	gelado, a
glacier	glacier	Gletscher(m)	glaciar	ghiacciaio	glaciar
glande	gland	Drüse(f)	glándula	ghiandola	glândula
glisser	slip, slide	rutschen	resbalar	scivolare	escorregar
glissière	slide	Gleitschiene(f)	corredera, guía	guida, scivolo	corrediça
global, e	global, overall	Gesamt-; pauschal	global	globale	global
globe	globe	Globus(m)	globo	globo	globo
globule(sang)	corpuscle, globule	Blutkörperchen(n)	glóbulo	globulo	glóbulo
gloire	glory	Ruhm(m)	gloria	gloria	glória
glorieux, se	glorious	glorreich	glorioso, a	glorioso, a	glorioso, a
glossaire	glossary	Glossar(n)	glosario	glossario	glossário
gluant, e	sticky	klebrig	viscoso, a	viscido, a	viscoso, a
glucose	glucose	Traubenzucker(m)	glucosa	glucosio	glicose
goal	goalkeeper	Torwärter(m)	portero	portiere	guarda-redes
goéland	gull	Silbermöwe(f)	gaviota	gabbiano	gaivota
golf	golf	Golf(n)	golf	golf	golfe
golf(terrain)	golf course	Golfplatz(m)	golf	golf	campo de golfe
golfe	gulf	Golf(m)	golfo	golfo	golfo
gomme	rubber	Radiergummi(m)	goma	gomma	borracha
gondolé, e	warped, buckled	verbogen	combado, a	incurvato, a	empenado, a
gonfler	inflate, blow up	auf = blasen	inflar	gonfiare	inchar, encher
gorge	throat	Hals(m)	garganta	gola	garganta
gorille	gorilla	Gorilla(m)	gorila	gorilla	gorila
goudron	tar	Teer(m)	alquitrán	asfalto	alcatrão
gouffre	chasm, pit	Abgrund(m), Kluft(f)	abismo, sima	baratro	abismo

French	English	German	Spanish	Italian	Portuguese
goulot	neck(bottle)	Hals(m)(Flaschen)	gollete	collo	gargalo
gourmand, e	greedy	erpicht auf	goloso, a	goloso, a	guloso, a
goût	taste	Geschmack(m)	gusto	gusto, sapore	gosto
goûter	taste	kosten	probar	assaggiare	provar
goutte	drop	Tropfen(m)	gota	goccia	gota
gouttière	gutter	Dachrinne(f)	canalón	grondaia	goteira
gouvernail	rudder	Ruder(n), Steur(n)	timón	timone	leme
gouvernement	government	Regierung(f)	gobierno	governo	governo
gouverner	govern	regieren	gobernar	governare	governar
gouverneur	governor	Gouverneur(m)	gobernador	governatore	governador
grâce	grace	Gnade(f); Anmut(f)	gracia	grazia	graça
grâce à	thanks to	dank	gracias a	grazie a	graças a
gracieux, se	good natured	lieb	simpático, a	grazioso, a	gracioso, a
gracieux, se	graceful	graziös	gracioso, a	grazioso, a	gracioso, a
grade	rank	Rang(m)	grado	grado	grau
grain	grain	Korn(n)	grano	chicco, grano	grão
grain(café)	bean(coffee-)	Bohne(Kaffee-)(f)	grano	chicco	grão
graine	seed	Samenkorn(n)	semilla	seme	semente
graisse	fat	Fett(n)	gordo; grasa	grasso	gordura
graisse	grease	Schmiere(f)	grasa	grasso	massa
graisseux, se	fatty, greasy	schmierig, fettig	grasiento, a	unto, a	gorduroso, a
grammaire	grammar	Grammatik(f)	gramática	grammatica	gramática
grand, e	tall	groß	alto, a	alto, a	alto, a; grande
grand, e	large, big	weit	gran, grande	grande, ampio, a	grande
grand, e	big	groß	gran, grande	grande	grande
grand, e	great	groß	gran, grande	grand(e)	grande
grand, e	high	hoch	alto, a	forte; alto, a	alto, a
grand-mère	grandmother	Großmutter(f)	abuela	nonna	avó
grand-père	grandfather	Großvater(m)	abuelo	nonno	avô
grands-parents	grandparents	Großeltern(pl.)	abuelos	nonni	avós
grandir	grow	wachsen	crecer	crescere	crescer
grange	barn	Scheune(f)	granero	fienile	celeiro
granule	granule	Körnchen(n)	gránulo	granulo	grânulo
graphique	graph	Graphik(f)	gráfico, a	grafico	gráfico
graphologie	graphology	Graphologie(f)	grafología	grafologia	grafologia
grappe	bunch(-es)	Traube(f)	racimo	grappolo	cacho
gras, se	fat(ty), greasy	fett	graso, a	grasso, a	gordo, a
gratitude	gratitude	Dankbarkeit(f)	gratitud	gratitudine	gratidão
gratte-ciel	skyscraper	Wolkenkratzer(m)	rascacielos	grattacielo	arranha-céus
gratter	scrape, scratch	kratzen	raspar, rascar	grattare	raspar
gratter(se)	scratch oneself	kratzen, sich	rascarse	grattarsi	coçar-se
gratuit, e	free	kostenlos	gratis; gratuito, a	gratuito, a; gratis	grátis; gratuito, a
grave	grave, serious	schwer; ernst	grave	grave	grave
gravier	gravel	Kies(m)	grava	ghiaia	cascalho
gravité	gravity	Schwere(f)	gravedad	gravità	gravidade
gravure	engraving	Gravieren(n)	grabado	incisione	gravura
gravure	print	Gravur(f)	grabado	stampa	gravura
greffe	transplant, graft	Verpflanzung(f)	trasplante	trapianto	enxerto
greffe	graft	Veredelung; Pfropfen	injerto	innesto	enxerto
grêle	hail	Hagel(m)	granizo	grandine	granizo
grelotter	shiver	zittern	tiritar	tremare(di freddo)	tiritar
grenade	grenade	Handgranate(f)	granada	bomba a mano	granada
grenier	attic, loft	Speicher(m), Dachboden	desván	solaio; granaio	sótão
grenouille	frog	Frosch(m)	rana	rana	rã
grève	strike	Streik(m)	huelga	sciopero	greve
griffe	claw	Kralle(f), Klaue(f)	garra	artiglio	garra
griffer	scratch, claw	kratzen	arañar	graffiare	arranhar
grignoter	nibble	knabbern	mordisquear	sgranocchiare	petiscar
grillage	wire fencing	Gitter(n)	reja	reticolato	gradeamento
griller	grill	grillen	asar(parrilla)	arrostire	grelhar
griller	toast	toasten	tostar	abbrustolire	torrar
grimace	grimace	Grimasse(f)	mueca	smorfia	careta
grimper	climb	klettern	escalar, subir	arrampicarsi	trepar, escalar
grincer	grind, grate	knirschen	chirriar	stridere	ranger
grippe	flu, influenza	Grippe(f)	gripe	influenza	gripe
gris, e	grey	grau	gris	grigio, a	cinzento, a
grognon, ne	grumpy	quengelig	gruñon, a	brontolone	rabugento, a
gronder	scold, tell off	schimpfen	regañar	sgridare	ralhar

French	English	German	Spanish	Italian	Portuguese
gros, se	big	groß	grueso, a; grande	grosso, a; grande	grande
gros, se	fat	dick	grueso, a; gordo, a	grosso, a	gordo, a
gros, se	big	geräumig	grande	grosso, a	grande
gros mot	bad word	Schimpfwort(n)	palabrota	parolaccia	palavrão
grossesse	pregnancy	Schwangerschaft(f)	embarazo	gravidanza	gravidez
grossier, ière	rude; crude	grob	grosero, a	grossolano, a	grosseiro, a
grossir	put on weight	zu = nehmen	engordar	ingrassare	engordar
grossir	increase	vermehren	agrandar	ingrandire	aumentar
grotte	cave, grotto	Grotte(f)	cueva, gruta	grotta	gruta
grouiller	crawl with	wimmeln	hormiguear	brulicare	pulular
groupe	group	Gruppe(f)	grupo	gruppo	grupo
grue	crane	Kran(m)	grúa	gru	grua
guêpe	wasp	Wespe(f)	avispa	vespa	vespa
guérilla	guerilla	Guerilla(f)	guerrilla	guerriglia	guerrilha
guérir	cure, heal	heilen	curar	guarire	curar
guérison	cure, recovery	Heilung(f)	curación	guarigione	cura
guérisseur, se	healer	Heilpraktiker(in f)m	curandero, a	guaritore, -trice	curandeiro, a
guerre	war	Krieg(m)	guerra	guerra	guerra
gueule	mouth	Maul(n)	hocico	muso	goela, garganta
guichet	counter, position	Schalter(m)	ventanilla	sportello	guichê, postigo
guichet	booking office	Fahrkartenschalter(m)	taquilla	biglietteria	bilheteira
guide	guide	Führer(in f)m	guía	guida	guia
guide	guide-book	Führer(Reise-)(m)	guía	guida	guia
guider	guide	führen	guiar	guidare	guiar
guirlande	garland	Girlande(f)	guirnalda	ghirlanda	grinalda
guitare	guitar	Gitarre(f)	guitarra	chitarra	guitarra
gymnastique	gymnastics	Gymnastik(f)	gimnasia	ginnastica	ginástica
gynécologie	gynaecology	Gynäkologie(f)	ginecología	ginecologia	ginecologia

H

French	English	German	Spanish	Italian	Portuguese
habile; adroit, e	clever, skilful	geschickt	hábil; diestro, a	abile	hábil; destro, a
habileté	ability, skill	Geschicklichkeit(f)	habilidad	abilità	habilidade
habillé, e	dressed	angezogen	vestido, a	vestito, a	vestido, a
habillement	clothing	Bekleidung(f)	ropa	abbigliamento	vestuário
habiller(s')	dress	an = ziehen, sich	vestirse	vestirsi	vestir-se
habiller(s')	dress up	an = kleiden	vestirse, ataviar	vestire(-rsi)	vestir-se
habit(s)	clothes	Kleidung(f)	vestido, traje	vestito(i), abiti	fato, traje
habitant, e	inhabitant	Einwohner(in f)m	habitante	abitante	habitante
habitation	dwelling; living	Wohnung(f)	vivienda, morada	abitazione	habitação, morada
habiter	live(in), inhabit	bewohnen, wohnen	vivir, habitar	abitare	morar
habitude	habit	Gewohnheit(f)	costumbre	abitudine	hábito, costume
habituel, le	usual	gewöhnlich	habitual	abituale	habitual
habituellement	usually	üblich, gewönnlich	generalmente	abitualmente	habitualmente
habituer(s')	get used to	gewöhnen, sich	acostumbrarse	abituarsi	habituar-se
hache	axe	Axt(f)	hacha	ascia	machado
haie	hedge	Hecke(f)	seto, valla	siepe	sebe
haine	hate	Haß(m)	odio	odio	ódio
haïr	hate, detest	hassen	odiar	odiare	odiar
haleine	breath	Atem(m)	aliento	alito	hálito
haleter	pant, gasp	keuchen	jadear	ansimare	arquejar
hall	foyer, hall	Eingangshalle(f)	vestíbulo	hall, ingresso	vestíbulo
hallucination	hallucination	Sinnestäuschung(f)	alucinación	allucinazione	alucinação
halte, arrêt	halt, stop	Halt(m)	alto, parada	sosta, fermata	alto, paragem
hamac	hammock	Hängematte(f)	hamaca	amaca	rede
hameçon	hook	Angelhaken(m)	anzuelo	amo	anzol
hanche	hip	Hüfte(f)	cadera	anca	anca

French	English	German	Spanish	Italian	Portuguese
handicap	handicap	Handikap(n)	hándicap	handicap	handicap
handicapé, e	handicapped	behindert	minusválido, a	andicappato, a	deficiente
hangar	shed	Schuppen(m)	cobertizo	hangar, capannone	alpendre
hanté, e	haunted	verflucht	embrujado, a	spiritato, a	assombrado, a
hantise	obsessive fear	Zwangsvorstellung(f)	obsesión	ossessione	obsessão
harceler	harass	quälen	acosar	assillare	perseguir
harem	harem	Harem(m)	harén	harem	harém
hareng	herring	Hering(m)	arenque	aringa	arenque
haricot	bean	Bohne(f)	judía	fagiolo; fagiolino	feijão
harmonie	harmony	Harmonie(f)	armonía	armonia	harmonia
harmonieux, se	harmonious	harmonisch	armonioso, a	armonioso, a	harmonioso, a
harnais	harness	Geschirr(n)	arnés	finimenti	arnês
harpe	harp	Harfe(f)	arpa	arpa	harpa
harpon	harpoon	Harpune(f)	arpón	arpione	arpão
hasard	chance, luck	Zufall(m)	azar, casualidad	caso	acaso, azar
hasard(au)	random(at)	aufs Geratewohl	azar(al)	casaccio(a)	acaso(ao)
hâte	haste, hurry	Eile(f)	prisa	fretta	pressa
hausse	rise, increase	Steigerung(f)	subida	aumento	subida
haut, e	high, tall	hoch	alto, a	alto, a	alto, a
haut	up	Oben-; Hoch-; auf	arriba	alto, a	cima(em, para)
haut	top	Oberteil(n)	alto	alto	alto, cimo
haut(en)	upstairs	oben	arriba	alto(in)	cima(em)
hauteur	height	Höhe(f)	altura	altezza	altura
haut-parleur	loud-speaker	Lautsprecher(m)	altavoz	altoparlante	alto-falante
hebdomadaire	weekly	wöchentlich	semanal	settimanale	semanal
hébergement	accommodation	Unterbringung(f)	alojamiento	alloggio	alojamento
hectare	hectare	Hektar(m)	hectárea	ettaro	hectare
hélice	propeller	Propeller(m)	hélice	elica	hélice
hélicoptère	helicopter	Hubschrauber(m)	helicóptero	elicottero	helicóptero
hémisphère	hemisphere	Halbkreis(m)	hemisferio	emisfero	hémisfério
hémorragie	haemorrhage	Blutsturz(m)	hemorragia	emorragia	hemorragia
hémorroïde(s)	haemorrhoids	Hämorrhoiden(f, pl)	hemorroides	emorroide	hemorróidas
hépatite	hepatitis	Hepatitis, Gelbsucht f	hepatitis	epatite	hepatite
herbe	grass	Gras(n)	hierba, yerba	erba	erva
herbe(s)	herb(s)	Kraut(n), Kräuter(pl.)	hierbas	erbe(aromatiche)	erva
héréditaire	hereditary	erblich	hereditario, a	ereditario, a	hereditário, a
hérédité	heredity	Vererbung(f)	herencia	ereditarietà	hereditariedade
héritage	inheritance, legacy	Erbschaft(f), Erbe(n)	herencia	eredità	herança
héritier, ière	heir, heiress	Erbe(m), Erbin(f)	heredero, a	erede	herdeiro, a
hermétique	hermetic	hermetisch	hermético, a	ermetico, a	hermético, a
hernie	hernia	Bruch(m)	hernia	ernia	hérnia
héroïne	heroin	Heroin(n)	heroína	eroina	heroína
héroïque	heroic	heldenhaft	heroico, a	eroico, a	heróico, a
héros, héroïne	hero, heroine	Held(m), Heldin(f)	héroe, heroína	eroe, eroina	herói, heroína
hésitation	hesitation	Zögern(n)	vacilación	esitazione	hesitação
hésiter	hesitate	zögern	dudar	esitare	hesitar
hétérosexuel, le	heterosexual	heterosexuell	heterosexual	eterosessuale	heterossexual
heure	hour; time	Stunde(f); Zeit(f)	hora	ora	hora
heureux, se	happy, glad	glücklich	feliz	felice	feliz
heureusement	fortunately	glücklicherweise	afortunadamente	fortunatamente	felizmente
heurter	knock(against)	stoßen	tropezar con	urtare	chocar, bater
hier	yesterday	gestern	ayer	ieri	ontem
hiérarchie	hierarchy	Hierarchie(f)	jerarquía	gerarchia	hierarquia
hiérarchique	hierarchical	hierarchisch	jerárquico, a	gerarchico, a	hierárquico, a
hippie, y	hippy	Hippie(m)	hippy, jipi	capellone, hippy	hippie
hippopotame	hippopotamus	Nilpferd(n)	hipopótamo	ippopotamo	hipopótamo
hirondelle	swallow	Schwalbe(f)	golondrina	rondine	andorinha
histoire	story	Geschichte(f)	historia	storia	história
histoire	history	Geschichte(f)	historia	storia	História
historien	historian	Geschichtschreiber(m)	historiador	storico	historiador
historique	historic(al)	historisch	histórico, a	storico, a	histórico, a
hiver	winter	Winter(m)	invierno	inverno	inverno
hockey	hockey	Hockeyspiel(n)	hockey	hockey	hóquei
hold-up	hold-up	Raubüberfall(m)	atraco	rapina	assalto
homard	lobster	Hummer(m)	bogavante	gambero(di mare)	lavagante
homéopathie	homoeopathy	Homöopathie(f)	homeopatía	omeopatia	homeopatia
homicide	murder, homicide	Totschlag(m)	homicidio	omicidio	homicídio
hommage	homage, tribute	Huldigung(f); Ehrung f	homenaje	omaggio	homenagem

French	English	German	Spanish	Italian	Portuguese
homme	man(men)	Mann(m), Mensch(m)	hombre	uomo; uomini	homem
homme politique	politician	Politiker(in f)m	político	uomo politico	político
homogène	homogeneous	homogen	homogéneo, a	omogeneo, a	homogéneo, a
homologation	certification	Zulassung(f)	homologación	omologazione	homologação
homonyme	homonym	Homonym(n)	homónimo, a	omonimo, a	homónimo, a
homosexuel, le	homosexual	homosexuell	homosexual	omosessuale	homossexual
honnête	honest	ehrlich	honrado, a	onesto, a	honesto, a
honneur	honour	Ehre(f)	honor	onore	honra
honorable	honourable	ehrwürdig	honorable	onorabile	honroso, a
honoraires	fee	Honorar(n)	honorarios	onorario	honorários
honte	shame	Scham(f), Schande(f)	vergüenza	vergogna	vergonha
honte(avoir)	ashamed(be)	schämen, sich	vergüenza(tener)	vergognarsi	vergonha(ter)
honteux, se	shameful	beschämend	vergonzoso, a	vergognoso, a	vergonhoso, a
hôpital	hospital	Krankenhaus(n)	hospital	ospedale	hospital
horaire(s)	timetable	Fahrplan(m)	horario(s)	orario	horário
horizon	horizon, sky-line	Horizont(m)	horizonte	orizzonte	horizonte
horizontal, e	horizontal	waagerecht	horizontal	orizzontale	horizontal
horloge	clock	Uhr(f)	reloj	orologio	relógio
hormone	hormone	Hormon(n)	hormona	ormone	hormona
horoscope	horoscope	Horoskop(n)	horóscopo	oroscopo	horóscopo
horreur	horror	Grausen(n)	horror	orrore	horror
horrible	horrible	grausig	horrible	orribile, orrendo, a	horrível
hors-bord	speed-boat	Außenbordmotor(m)	fuera borda	fuoribordo	fora de borda
hors de	out of	außer(+dat)	fuera de	fuori, fuori di	fora de
hors-d'oeuvre	starter	Vorspeise(f)	entremeses	antipasto	acepipe, entrada
hors-taxe	duty-free	zollfrei	libre impuestos	duty-free	sem imposto
horticulture	horticulture	Gartenbau(m)	horticultura	orticultura	horticultura
hospice	hospice; home	Hospiz(n)	hospicio	ospizio	hospício, asilo
hospitalité	hospitality	Gastfreundlichkeit(f)	hospitalidad	ospitalità	hospitalidade
hostile	hostile	feindlich	hostil	ostile	hostil
hôte, tesse	host; guest	Gastgeber(m); Gast(m)	anfitrión; huésped	ospite	anfitrião; hóspede, a
hôte	guest	Gast(m)	huésped, a	ospite	hóspede, a
hôtel	hotel	Hotel(n)	hotel	albergo, hotel	hotel
hôtellerie	hotel trade	Hotelwesen(n)	hostelería	alberghiera(indust-)	hotelaria
hôtesse de l'air	hostess(air -)	Stewardess(f)	azafata	hostess	hospedeira
houle	swell, surge	Brandung(f)	marejada	ondosità	vaga
housse	cover	Bezug(m)	funda	fodera	cobertura
hublot	window	Bullauge(n), Luke(f)	ventanilla	oblò	vigia
huer	boo	aus=pfeifen	abuchear	fischiare, urlare	vaiar
huile	oil	Öl(n); Speiseöl(n)	aceite	olio	óleo; azeite
huile	oil	Öl(n); Motoröl(n)	aceite; óleo	olio	óleo
huit	eight	acht	ocho	otto	oito
huître	oyster	Auster(f)	ostra	ostrica	ostra
humain, e	human	menschlich	humano, a	umano, a	humano, a
humanité	humanity	Menschheit(f)	humanidad	umanità	humanidade
humeur	mood	Laune(f)	humor	umore	humor
humide	damp, humid, moist	feucht	húmedo, a	umido, a	húmido, a
humidité	humidity	Feuchtigkeit(f)	humedad	umidità	humidade
humilier	humiliate	erniedrigen	humillar	umiliare	humilhar
humoristique	humorous	humoristisch	humorístico, a	umoristico, a	humorístico, a
humour	humour	Humor(m)	humor	umorismo	humor
hurler	scream, yell	brüllen	chillar	urlare	gritar; berrar
hurler	howl	heulen	aullar	ululare, guaire	uivar; urrar
hybride	hybrid	zwitterhaft	híbrido, a	ibrido, a	híbrido, a
hydraulique	hydraulic	hydraulisch	hidráulico, a	idraulico, a	hidráulico, a
hydrogène	hydrogen	Wasserstoff(m)	hidrógeno	idrogeno	hidrogénio
hyène	hyena	Hyäne(f)	hiena	iena	hiena
hygiène	hygiene	Hygiene(f)	higiene	igiene	higiene
hygiénique	hygienic	hygienisch	higiénico, a	igienico, a	higiénico, a
hymne	hymn	Hymne(f)	himno	inno	hino
hypertension	blood pressure	Bluthochdruck(m)	hipertensión	ipertensione	hipertensão
hypnose	hypnosis	Hypnose(f)	hipnosis	ipnosi	hipnose
hypnotisme	hypnotism	Hypnotismus(m)	hipnotismo	ipnotismo	hipnotismo
hypocrisie	hypocrisy	Heuchelei(f)	hipocresía	ipocrisia	hipocrisia
hypocrite	hypocrite	Heuchler(in f)m	hipócrita	ipocrita	hipócrita
hypothèque	mortgage	Hypothek(f)	hipoteca	ipoteca	hipoteca
hypothèse	hypothesis(-es)	Hypothese(f)	hipótesis	ipotesi	hipótese
hystérique	hysteric(al)	hysterisch	histérico, a	isterico, a	histérico, a

F

I

French	English	German	Spanish	Italian	Portuguese
iceberg	iceberg	Eisberg(m)	iceberg	iceberg	iceberg
ici	here	hier	aquí	qui	aqui
idéal, e	ideal	ideal	ideal	ideale	ideal
idéal	ideal	Ideal(n)	ideal	ideale	ideal
idée	idea	Idee(f)	idea	idea	ideia
identifier	identify	identifizieren	identificar	identificare	identificar
identique	identical	identisch	idéntico, a	identico, a	idêntico, a
identité	identity	Identität(f)	identidad	identità	identidade
idéologie	ideology	Ideologie(f)	ideología	ideologia	ideologia
idiot, e	idiot, fool	Idiot(m), Dummkopf(m)	idiota	idiota; scemo, a	idiota
idiot, e	idiotic, stupid	idiotisch, dumm	idiota; tonto, a	idiota; stupido, a	idiota
idiotie	stupidity	Dummheit(f)	idiotez	idiozia	idiotice, asneira
idole	idol	Idol(n)	ídolo	idolo	ídolo
igloo	igloo	Iglu(n)	iglú	igloo	iglu
ignorance	ignorance	Unwissenheit(f)	ignorancia	ignoranza	ignorância
ignorer	ignorant of(be)	nicht wissen	ignorar	ignorare	ignorar
il	he; it	er; es	él	egli, lui, esso	ele
il y a	there is, there are	es gibt	hay	c'è; ci sono	há
il y a	ago	vor	hace	fa	há
île	island, isle	Insel(f)	isla	isola	ilha
illégal, e	illegal	illegal	ilegal	illegale	ilegal
illégitime	illegitimate	unehelich	ilegítimo, a	illegittimo, a	ilegítimo, a
illettré, e	illiterate	ungebildet	analfabeto, a	analfabeta	iletrado, a
illogique	illogical	unlogisch	ilógico, a	illogico, a	ilógico, a
illuminé, e	illuminated	erleuchtet	iluminado, a	illuminato, a	iluminado, a
illusion	illusion	Illusion(f)	ilusión	illusione	ilusão
illustration	illustration	Illustration(f)	ilustración	illustrazione	ilustração
illustre	illustrious	berühmt	ilustre	illustre	ilustre
illustré, e	illustrated	illustriert	ilustrado, a	illustrato, a	ilustrado, a
îlot	islet	Inselchen(n)	islote	isolotto	ilhéu, ilhota
ils	they	sie	ellos	essi; loro	eles
image	image, picture	Bild(n)	imagen	immagine	imagem
image	picture	Bild(n)	imagen	illustrazione	gravura
imaginaire	imaginary	eingebildet	imaginario, a	immaginario, a	imaginário, a
imagination	imagination	Einbildung(f)	imaginación	immaginazione	imaginação
imaginer	imagine	vor = stellen, sich	imaginar	immaginare	imaginar
imaginer(s')	imagine	ein = bilden, sich	imaginarse	immaginarsi	julgar
imbécile	fool, idiot	Idiot(in f)m	imbécil	imbecille	imbecil; parvo, a
imbiber	soak	durchtränken	empapar	imbevere	embeber
imitation	imitation	Nachahmung(f)	imitación	imitazione	imitação
imiter	imitate	nach = ahmen	imitar	imitare	imitar
immatriculation	registration	Eintragung(f)	matrícula	immatricolazione	matrícula
immédiat, e	immediate	unverzüglich	inmediato, a	immediato, a	imediato, a
immédiatement	immediately	sofort	inmediatamente	immediatamente	imediatamente
immense	immense, vast	unendlich groß	inmenso, a	immenso, a	imenso, a
immerger	immerse	versenken	sumergir	immergere	imergir
immersion	immersion	Versenkung(f)	inmersión	immersione	imersão
immeuble	block of flats	Gebäude(n)	inmueble	palazzo, edificio	edifício, imóvel
immigration	immigration	Einwanderung(f)	inmigración	immigrazione	imigração
immigré, e	immigrant	Einwanderer(in f)m	inmigrado, a	immigrato, a	imigrante
immobile	motionless	unbeweglich	inmóvil	immobile	imóvel
immobilier	property	Immobilien(f, pl)	inmobiliario	immobiliare	imobiliário
immortel, le	immortal	unsterblich	inmortal	immortale	imortal
immuniser	immunize	immunisieren	inmunizar	immunizzare	imunizar
immunité	immunity	Immunität(f)	inmunidad	immunità	imunidade
impact	impact	Stoß(m)	impacto	impatto	impacto
impact	impact	Einfluß(m)	impacto	impatto	impacto
impair	odd	ungerade	impar	dispari	ímpar
impartial, e	impartial	unparteiisch	imparcial	imparziale	imparcial
impatience	impatience	Ungeduld(f)	impaciencia	impazienza	impaciência
impatient, e	impatient	ungeduldig	impaciente	impaziente	impaciente

French	English	German	Spanish	Italian	Portuguese
impensable	unthinkable	undenkbar	increíble	impensabile	impensável
impératif, ive	imperative, urgent	bindend, zwingend	imperativo, a	imperativo, a	imperativo, a
impératrice	empress	Kaiserin(f)	emperatriz	imperatrice	imperatriz
imperfection	imperfection	Unvollkommenheit(f)	imperfección	imperfezione	imperfeição
impérialisme	imperialism	Imperialismus(m)	imperialismo	imperialismo	imperialismo
imperméable	rain-coat, mac	Regenmantel(m)	gabardina	impermeabile	gabardina
imperméable	water-proof	wasserdicht	impermeable	impermeabile	impermeável
impertinent, e	impertinent	unverschämt	impertinente	impertinente	impertinente
impétueux, se	impetuous	ungestüm, stürmisch	impetuoso, a	impetuoso, a	impetuoso, a
impitoyable	pitiless	unbarmherzig	despiadado, a	spietato, a	impiedoso, a
implantation	setting up(of)	Niederlassung	implantación	impianto	implantação
implanter	establish, set up	etablieren, gründen	implantar	impiantare	implantar
implication	implication	Verwicklung(f)	implicación	implicazione	implicação
impliquer	involve	verwickeln	implicar	implicare	implicar
impliquer	imply	bedeuten; an = deuten	implicar	implicare	implicar
implorer	implore, beg	an = flehen	implorar	implorare	implorar
impoli, e	impolite, rude	unhöflich	maleducado, a	maleducato, a	mal educado, a
impopulaire	unpopular	unbeliebt	impopular	impopolare	impopular
importance	importance	Bedeutung(f)	importancia	importanza	importância
important, e	important	wichtig	importante	importante	importante
importation	import; importing	Einfuhr(f)	importación	importazione	importação
importer	import	ein = führen	importar	importare	importar
imposer	impose	auf = zwingen	imponer	imporre	impor
imposer(s')	impose oneself on	auf = drängen, sich	imponerse	imporsi	impor-se
impossible	impossible	unmöglich	imposible	impossibile	impossível
impôt	tax(-es)	Steuer(f)	impuesto	tassa	imposto
imprégner	impregnate	imprägnieren	impregnar	impregnare	impregnar
imprésario	impresario	Manager(m)	empresario	impresario	empresário
impression	impression	Eindruck(m)	impresión	impressione	impressão
impression	printing	Druck(m)	impresión	stampa	impressão
impressionnant, e	impressive	beeindruckend	impresionante	impressionante	impressionante
impressionner	impress	beeindrucken	impresionar	impressionare	impressionar
imprévu, e	unexpected	unvorhergesehen	imprevisto, a	imprevisto, a	imprevisto, a
imprimé	printed form	Formular(n)	impreso	stampato	impresso
imprimer	print	drucken	imprimir	stampare	imprimir
imprimerie	printing works	Druckerei(f)	imprenta	tipografia	tipografia
improviser	improvise	improvisieren	improvisar	improvvisare	improvisar
imprudence	imprudence	Unvorsichtigkeit(f)	imprudencia	imprudenza	imprudência
imprudent, e	careless	unvorsichtig	imprudente	imprudente	imprudente
impuissant, e	powerless	machtlos	impotente	impotente	impotente
impulsion	impulse	Impuls(m)	impulso	impulso	impulso
impuni, e	unpunished	unbestraft	impune	impunito, a	impune
impureté	impurity	Unreinheit(f)	impureza	impurità	impureza
inaccessible	inaccessible	unerreichbar	inaccesible	inaccessibile	inacessível
inactif, ive	inactive	untätig, inaktiv	inactivo, a	inattivo, a	inactivo, a
inadapté, e	unsuitable	ungeeignet	inadaptado, a	inadatto, a	inadaptado, a
inadmissible	inadmissible	unzulässig	inadmisible	inammissibile	inadmissível
inanimé, e	lifeless	unbelebt, leblos	inanimado, a	inanimato, a	inanimado, a
inapte	unsuited, unfit	ungeeignet	inapto, a	inabile	inapto, a
inattention	carelessness	Unachtsamkeit(f)	descuido	disattenzione	distracção
inauguration	inauguration	Einweihung(f)	inauguración	inaugurazione	inauguração
inaugurer	inaugurate	ein = weihen	inaugurar	inaugurare	inaugurar
incandescent, e	incandescent	glühend	incandescente	incandescente	incandescente
incapable	incapable, unable	unfähig, untauglich	incapaz	incapace	incapaz
incarcérer	imprison	ein = sperren	encarcelar	incarcerare	encarcerar
incendie	fire	Brand(m)	incendio	incendio	incêndio
incertain, e	uncertain	unsicher	inseguro, a	incerto, a	incerto, a
inceste	incest	Inzucht(f)	incesto	incesto	incesto
inchangé, e	unchanged	unverändert	inalterado, a	immutato, a	inalterado, a
incident	incident	Zwischenfall(m)	incidente	incidente	incidente
incinérer	incinerate	ein = äschern	incinerar	incenerire	incinerar
inciter	incite	an = regen	incitar	incitare	incitar
inclinaison	slant, incline	Neigung(f), Gefälle(n)	inclinación	inclinazione	inclinação
incliner	incline, tilt	neigen	inclinar	inclinare	inclinar
inclure	include	ein = schließen	incluir	includere	incluir
inclus, e	included	inklusiv	incluido, a	incluso, a	incluso, a
incolore	colourless	farblos	incoloro, a	incolore	incolor
incommoder	bother	stören	incomodar	incomodare	incomodar

French	English	German	Spanish	Italian	Portuguese
incompatible	incompatible	unvereinbar	incompatible	incompatibile	incompatível
incompétence	incompetence	Inkompetenz(f)	incompetencia	incompetenza	incompetência
incomplet, ète	incomplete	unvollständig	incompleto, a	incompleto, a	incompleto, a
inconnu, e	unknown	unbekannt	desconocido, a	sconosciuto, a	desconhecido, a
inconscient, e	unconscious	unbewußt	inconsciente	incosciente	inconsciente
incontestable	incontestable	unbestreitbar	indiscutible	incontestabile	incontestável
inconvénient	disadvantage	Nachteil(m)	inconveniente	inconveniente	inconveniente
incorporation	incorporation	Eingliederung(f)	incorporación	incorporazione	incorporação
incorporer	incorporate	ein = verleiben	incorporar	incorporare	incorporar
incorrect, e	incorrect, wrong	unrichtig, falsch	incorrecto, a	scorretto, a	incorrecto, a
incriminer	incriminate	beschuldigen	incriminar	incriminare	incriminar
incroyable	unbelievable	unglaublich	increíble	incredibile	incrível
inculpé, e	accused(the)	Angeklagte(f, m)	inculpado, a	imputato, a	acusado, a
inculper	charge, accuse	beschuldigen	inculpar, acusar	incolpare, accusare	inculpar, acusar
incurable	incurable	unheilbar	incurable	incurabile	incurável
incursion	incursion	Überfall(m)	incursión	incursione	incursão
indécent, e	indecent	unanständig	indecente	indecente	indecente
indéfini, e	indefinite	unbestimmt	indefinido, a	indefinito, a	indefinido, a
indemniser	compensate	entschädigen	indemnizar	indennizzare	indemnizar
indemnité	compensation	Entschädigung(f)	indemnidad	risarcimento	indemnização
indemnité	allowance	Schadenersatz(m)	dietas	indennità	ajuda de custo
indépendance	independence	Unabhängigkeit(f)	independencia	indipendenza	independência
indépendant, e	independent	unabhängig	independiente	indipendente	independente
index	index	Index(m)	índice	indice	índice
indicateur	indicator	Anzeiger(m)	indicador	indicatore	indicador
indicatif(tél.)	dialling code	Vorwählnummer(f)	prefijo	prefisso	indicativo, prefixo
indication	indication	Angabe(f), Hinweis(m)	indicación	indicazione	indicação
indice	indication, sign	Anzeichen(n)	indicio	indizio	indício
indice	index	Index m(Preisindex m)	índice	indice	índice
indifférent, e	indifferent	gleichgültig	indiferente	indifferente	indiferente
indigène	native, indigenous	Eingeborene(f, m)	indígena	indigeno, a	indígena
indigeste	indigestible	unverdaulich	indigesto, a	indigesto, a	indigesto, a
indignation	indignation	Empörung(f)	indignación	indignazione	indignação
indigne	unworthy	unwürdig	indigno, a	indegno, a	indigno, a
indiquer	indicate, show	an = deuten, zeigen	indicar	indicare	indicar
indirect, e	indirect	indirekt	indirecto, a	indiretto, a	indirecto, a
indiscrétion	indiscretion	Indiskretion(f)	indiscreción	indiscrezione	indiscrição
indispensable	indispensable	unentbehrlich	indispensable	indispensabile	indispensável
individu	individual	Individuum(n)	individuo	individuo	indivíduo
individuel, le	individual	individuell	individual	individuale	individual
indolore	painless	schmerzlos	indoloro, a	indolore	indolor
induire	induce	veranlassen	inducir	indurre	induzir
indulgence	indulgence	Nachsicht(f)	indulgencia	indulgenza	indulgência
industrie	industry	Industrie(f)	industria	industria	indústria
industriel	industrialist	Industrielle(m)	industrial	industriale	industrial
industriel, le	industrial	industriell	industrial	industriale	industrial
inédit, e	unpublished	unveröffentlicht	inédito, a	inedito, a	inédito, a
inefficace	inefficient	unwirksam, unfähig	ineficaz	inefficace	ineficaz
inégal, e	unequal	ungleich	desigual	ineguale	desigual
inégal, e	uneven	uneben	desigual	disuguale	desigual
inégalité	inequality	Ungleichheit(f)	desigualdad	disuguaglianza	desigualdade
inerte	inert	regungslos	inerte	inerte	inerte
inertie	inertia	Trägheit(f)	inercia	inerzia	inércia
inespéré, e	unexpected	unerwartet, unverhofft	inesperado, a	insperato, a	inesperado, a
inexact, e	inexact, inaccurate	ungenau	inexacto, a	inesatto, a	inexacto, a
inexistant, e	non-existent	nicht existierend	inexistente	inesistente	inexistente
infaillible	infallible	unfehlbar	infalible	infallibile	infalível
infâme	vile, infamous	niederträchtig	infame	infame	infame
infantile	infantile, child	Kinder-, kindisch	infantil	infantile	infantil
infarctus	coronary	Infarkt(m)	infarto	infarto	enfarte
infatigable	tireless	unermüdlich	incansable	instancabile	infatigável
infect, e	foul, vile	ekelhaft, stinkig	asqueroso, a	fetido, a	asqueroso, a
infection	infection	Infektion(f)	infección	infezione	infecção
inférieur, e	inferior	minderwertig	inferior	inferiore	inferior
inférieur, e	lower	untere(r)	inferior	inferiore	inferior
infernal, e	infernal	Höllen-; höllisch	infernal	infernale	infernal
infidèle	unfaithful	untreu	infiel	infedele	infiel
infiltration	infiltration	Einsickern(n)	infiltración	infiltrazione	infiltração

68

French	English	German	Spanish	Italian	Portuguese
infini, e	infinite	unendlich	infinito, a	infinito, a	infinito, a
infinitif	infinitive	Infinitiv(m)	infinitivo	infinito	infinitivo
infirme	disabled	behindert	inválido, a	infermo, a	doente
infirmerie	infirmary	Krankenraum(m)	enfermería	infermeria	enfermaria
infirmier, ière	nurse	Krankenpfleger(in f)m	enfermero, a	infermiere, a	enfermeiro, a
inflammable	inflammable	brennbar	inflamable	infiammabile	inflamável
inflation	inflation	Inflation(f)	inflación	inflazione	inflação
inflexible	inflexible	starr	inflexible	inflessibile	inflexível
infliger	inflict	auf = erlegen	infligir	infliggere	infligir
influence	influence	Einfluß(m)	influencia	influenza	influência
influent, e	influential	einflußreich	influyente	influente	influente
information	information	Information(f)	información	informazione	informação
informatique	data processing	Informatik(f)	informática	informatica	informática
informer	inform	informieren	informar	imformare	informar
informer(s')	inquire	erkundigen, sich	informarse	informarsi	informar-se
infraction	offence, violation	Verstoß(m)	infracción	infrazione	infracção
ingénierie	engineering	Ingenieurkunst(f)	ingeniería	ingegneria	engenharia
ingénieur	engineer	Ingenieur(in f)m	ingeniero, a	ingegnere	engenheiro, a
ingénieux, se	ingenious	sinnreich	ingenioso, a	ingegnoso, a	engenhoso, a
ingérence	interference	Einmischung(f)	ingerencia	ingerenza	ingerência
ingrat, e	ungrateful	undankbar	ingrato, a	ingrato, a	ingrato, a
inhaler, respirer	inhale	ein = atmen	inhalar	inalare	inalar
inhumain, e	inhuman	unmenschlich	inhumano, a	inumano, a	desumano, a
inimaginable	inconceivable	undenkbar	inimaginable	inimmaginabile	inimaginável
ininflammable	fire-proof	unbrennbar	ininflamable	ininfiammabile	prova de fogo(à)
initial, e	initial	anfänglich; Anfangs-	inicial	iniziale	inicial
initiation	initiation	Einführung(f)	iniciación	iniziazione	iniciação
initiative	initiative	Initiative(f)	iniciativa	iniziativa	iniciativa
injecter	inject	spritzen, ein = spritzen	inyectar	iniettare	injectar
injure	insult	Beleidigung(f)	injuria	ingiuria	injúria
injustice	injustice	Ungerechtigkeit(f)	injusticia	ingiustizia	injustiça
inné, e	innate	angeboren	innato, a	innato, a	inato, a
innocent, e	innocent	unschuldig	inocente	innocente	inocente
innovation	innovation	Neuerung(f)(Er-)	innovación	innovazione	inovação
innover	innovate	innovieren, erneuern	innovar	innovare	inovar
inoccupé, e	unoccupied	untätig	desocupado, a	inoperoso, a	desocupado, a
inoffensif, ive	inoffensive	harmlos	inofensivo, a	inoffensivo, a	inofensivo, a
inondation	flooding, flood	Überschwemmung(f)	inundación	inondazione	inundação
inorganique	inorganic	anorganisch	inorgánico, a	inorganico, a	inorgânico, a
inquiet, ète	worried	besorgt	inquieto, a	inquieto, a	inquieto, a
inquiéter(s')	worry	beunruhigen, sich	preocuparse	preoccuparsi	preocupar-se
inquiétude	anxiety, worry	Sorge(f)	inquietud	inquietudine	inquietação
insatisfait, e	not satisfied	unzufrieden	insatisfecho, a	insoddisfatto, a	insatisfeito, a
inscription	inscription	Inschrift(f)	inscripción	iscrizione	inscrição
inscription	registration	Einschreibung(f)	matrícula	iscrizione	matrícula
inscrire, noter	note, write	ein = schreiben	inscribir	iscrivere	inscrever
inscrire(s')	join	bei = treten	inscribirse	iscriversi	inscrever-se
inscrire(s')	register	ein = schreiben, sich	matricularse	iscriversi	matricular-se
insecte	insect	Insekt(n)	insecto	insetto	insecto
insémination	insemination	Befruchtung(f)	inseminación	inseminazione	inseminação
insensible	insensitive	unempfindlich	insensible	insensibile	insensível
insérer	insert	ein = setzen, ein = fügen	insertar	inserire	inserir
insertion	insertion	Einfügung(f)	inserción	inserzione	inserção
insigne	badge	Zeichen(n), Abzeichen	insignia	distintivo	insígnia
insignifiant, e	insignificant	unbedeutend	insignificante	insignificante	insignificante
insister	insist	bestehen, beharren	insistir	insistere	insistir
insolation	sunstroke	Sonnenstich(m)	insolación	insolazione	insolação
insolence	insolence	Frechheit(f)	insolencia	insolenza	insolência
insolent, e	insolent	unverschämt, frech	insolente	insolente	insolente
insolite	unusual	seltsam, ungewohnt	insólito, a	insolito, a	insólito, a
insomnie	insomnia	Schlaflosigkeit(f)	insomnio	insonnia	insónia
insonore	sound-proof	schalldicht	insonoro, a	insonoro, a	insonoro, a
insouciant, e	carefree	unbekümmert	despreocupado, a	noncurante	descuidado, a
inspecteur, trice	inspector	Inspektor(in f)m	inspector, a	ispettore, trice	inspector, a
inspection	inspection	Überprüfung(f)	inspección	ispezione	inspecção
inspiration	inspiration	Anregung(f)	inspiración	ispirazione	inspiração
instable	unstable	unbeständig	inestable	instabile	instável
installation	installation	Einrichtung(f)	instalación	installazione	instalação

French	English	German	Spanish	Italian	Portuguese
installer	install	ein = richten	instalar	installare	instalar
installer(s')	settle	nieder = lassen, sich	instalarse	stabilirsi	instalar-se
instant	moment, instant	Moment(m)	instante	istante	instante
instinct	instinct	Instinkt(m)	instinto	istinto	instinto
instinctif, ive	instinctive	instinktiv	instintivo, a	istintivo, a	instintivo, a
institut	institute	Institut(n)	instituto	istituto	instituto
instituteur	teacher(primary)	Grundschullehrer/in	maestro, a	maestro, a	professor primário
institution	institution	Institution(f)	institución	istituzione	instituição
institutionnel	institutional	gesetzlich	institucional	istituzionale	institucional
instructeur	instructor	Ausbilder(m)	instructor	istruttore, trice	instrutor, a
instruction	instruction	Ausbildung(f)	instrucción	istruzione	instrução
instruire	teach	aus = bilden	instruir	istruire	instruir
instrument	instrument	Instrument(n)	instrumento	strumento	instrumento
insuffisant, e	insufficient	ungenügend	insuficiente	insufficiente	insuficiente
insuline	insulin	Insulin(n)	insulina	insulina	insulina
insulte	insult	Beleidigung(f)	insulto	insulto	insulto
insulter	insult	beleidigen	insultar	insultare	insultar
insurger(s')	rebel(against)	empören, sich	rebelarse	ribellarsi	insurgir-se
insurger(s')	rise up, revolt	auf = lehnen gegen, sich	sublevarse	insorgere	insurgir-se
intact, e	intact	intakt	intacto, a	intatto, a	intacto, a
intégral, e	integral	vollständig	íntegro, a	integrale	integral
intégrer	integrate	integrieren	integrar	integrare	integrar
intégrité	integrity	Integrität(f)	integridad	integrità	integridade
intellectuel, le	intellectual	intellektuell	intelectual	intellettuale	intelectual
intelligence	intelligence	Intelligenz(f)	inteligencia	intelligenza	inteligência
intelligent, e	intelligent	intelligent	inteligente	intelligente	inteligente
intelligent, e	clever	klug, gescheit	inteligente	intelligente	inteligente
intense	intense	heftig, stark	intenso, a	intenso, a	intenso, a
intensif, ive	intensive	intensiv	intensivo, a	intensivo, a	intensivo, a
intensité	intensity	Intensität(f)	intensidad	intensità	intensidade
intention	intention	Absicht(f)	intención	intenzione	intenção
intention, but	purpose, aim, goal	Absicht(f)	intención	intento, fine, scopo	intenção
intention(avoir)	intend	beabsichtigen	intención(tener)	intenzione(avere)	tencionar
intercepter	intercept	auf = fangen, ab = fangen	interceptar	intercettare	interceptar
interdiction	ban	Verbot(n)	prohibición	proibizione	proibição
interdire	forbid, ban	verbieten	prohibir	vietare, proibire	proibir
interdit, e	forbidden	verboten	prohibido, a	proibito, a	proibido, a
intéressant, e	interesting	interessant	interesante	interessante	interessante
intéresser(s')	interested in(be)	interessieren, sich	interesarse	interessarsi	interessar-se
intérêt	interest	Interesse(n)	interés	interesse	interesse
intérêt	interest	Zins(m)	interés	interesse	juro
interférence	interference	Einmischung; Störung	interferencia	interferenza	interferência
intérieur, e	inside, inner	innere(r, s); innen	interior	interno, a	interior
intérieur, e	inner, interior	inner	interior	interiore	interior
intérieur, e	domestic, home	Innen-	interior	interno, a	interno, a
intérieur	interior	Innere(n)	interior	interiore	interior
interlocuteur	interlocutor	Gesprächspartner/in	interlocutor, a	interlocutore, trice	interlocutor, a
intermédiaire	intermediate	Zwischen-, Mittel-	intermediario, a	intermediario, a	intermediário, a
intermittent, e	intermittent	aussetzend	intermitente	intermittente	intermitente
international, e	international	international	internacional	internazionale	internacional
interne	internal, inner	intern	interno, a	interno, a	interno, a
interprète	interpreter	Dolmetscher(in f)m	intérprete	interprete	intérprete
interpréter	interpret	deuten, aus = legen	interpretar	interpretare	interpretar
interroger	question, ask	fragen, befragen	interrogar	interrogare	interrogar
interrompre	interrupt	unterbrechen	interrumpir	interrompere	interromper
interrupteur	switch(-es)	Schalter(m)	interruptor	interruttore	interruptor
interruption	interruption	Unterbrechung(f)	interrupción	interruzione	interrupção
intersection	intersection	Kreuzung(f)	intersección	intersezione	intersecção
intervalle	interval	Abstand(m)	intervalo	intervallo	intervalo
intervalle	gap	Abstand(m)	intervalo	intervallo	intervalo
intervenir	intervene	dazwischen = treten	intervenir	intervenire	intervir
intervention	intervention	Eingriff(m)	intervención	intervento	intervenção
interview	interview	Interview(n)	interviú	intervista	entrevista
intestin	intestine	Darm(m)	intestino	intestino	intestino
intime	close, intimate	intim	íntimo, a	íntimo, a	íntimo, a
intime	intimate	vertraut, intim	íntimo, a	íntimo, a	íntimo, a
intimider	intimidate	ein = schüchtern	intimidar	intimidire	intimidar
intolérance	intolerance	Intoleranz(f)	intolerancia	intolleranza	intolerância

French	English	German	Spanish	Italian	Portuguese
intonation	intonation	Tonfall(m)	entonación	intonazione	entoação
intoxication	poisoning	Vergiftung(f)	intoxicación	intossicazione	intoxicação
intrépide	intrepid	kühn, mutig	intrépido, a	intrepido, a	intrépido, a
intrigue	intrigue	Intrige(f)	intriga	intrigo	intriga
intriguer	intrigue	intrigieren	intrigar	intrigare	intrigar
introduire	insert; introduce	ein = führen	introducir	introdurre	introduzir
introduire	introduce	vor = stellen	presentar	introdurre	apresentar
intrusion	intrusion	Eindringen(n)	intrusión	intrusione	intrusão
intuition	intuition	Intuition(f)	intuición	intuizione	intuição
inutile	useless	nutzlos	inútil	inutile	inútil
invalide	disabled	behindert	inválido, a	invalido, a	inválido, a
invariable	invariable	unveränderlich	invariable	invariabile	invariável
invasion	invasion	Invasion(f)	invasión	invasione	invasão
inventaire	inventory	Inventar(n)	inventario	inventario	inventário
inventaire	stock-list(taking)	Inventur(f)	inventario	inventario	inventário
inventer	invent	erfinden	inventar	inventare	inventar
inventeur	inventor	Erfinder(in f)m	inventor	inventore	inventor
invention	invention	Erfindung(f)	invención	invenzione	invenção
inverse	opposite	umgekehrt	inverso, a	inverso, a	inverso, a
inverser	reverse, invert	um = kehren	invertir	invertire	inverter
inversion	inversion	Umkehrung(f)	inversión	inversione	inversão
investir	invest	investieren	invertir	investire	investir
investissement	investment	Investition(f)	inversión	investimento	investimento
investiture	investiture	Investitur(f)	investidura	investitura	investidura
invincible	invincible	unbesiegbar	invencible	invincibile	invencível
invisible	invisible	unsichtbar	invisible	invisibile	invisível
invitation	invitation	Einladung(f)	invitación	invito	convite
invité, e	guest	Gast(m)	invitado, a	invitato, a	convidado, a
inviter	invite	ein = laden	invitar	invitare	convidar
invoquer	invoke	beziehen auf, sich	invocar	invocare	invocar
iris	iris	Iris(f)	iris	iride	íris
ironie	irony	Ironie(f)	ironía	ironia	ironia
irradiation	irradiation	Bestrahlung(f)	irradiación	irradiazione	irradiação
irrégulier, e	irregular	unregelmäßig	irregular	irregolare	irregular
irriguer	irrigate	bewässern	irrigar	irrigare	irrigar
irritant, e	irritating	ärgerlich; aufregend	irritante	irritante	irritante
irriter	irritate	reizen, irritieren	irritar	irritare	irritar
irruption	irruption	Eindringen(n)	irrupción	irruzione	irrupção
islamique	Islamic	islamisch	islámico, a	islamico, a	islâmico, a
isolation	insulation	Isolierung(f)	aislamiento	isolamento	isolação
isolé, e	isolated, lonely	allein, einsam	aislado, a	isolato, a	isolado, a; só, a
isoler	isolate	ab = sondern; isolieren	aislar	isolare	isolar
isoler	insulate; isolate	isolieren	aislar	isolare	isolar
issue(sortie)	way out, exit	Ausgang(m)	salida	uscita	saída
itinéraire	itinerary, route	Route(f), Strecke(f)	itinerario	itinerario	itinerário
itinéraire, route	route	Route(f), Weg(m)	ruta, itinerario	rotta, itinerario	caminho, rota
ivoire	ivory	Elfenbein(n)	marfil	avorio	marfim
ivresse	drunkenness	Trunkenheit(f)	ebriedad	ubriachezza	embriaguez
ivrogne	drunkard	Trunkenbold(m)	borracho, a	ubriaco, a	bêbedo, a; ébrio, a

J

French	English	German	Spanish	Italian	Portuguese
jaillir	spring	springen; sprudeln	brotar, surgir	schizzare	brotar
jalousie	jealousy	Eifersucht(f)	celos	gelosia	ciúme
jaloux, se	jealous	eifersüchtig	celoso, a	geloso, a	ciumento, a
jamais	never; ever	niemals, jemals	jamás, nunca	mai	nunca, jamais
jambe	leg	Bein(n)	pierna	gamba	perna

French	English	German	Spanish	Italian	Portuguese
jambon	ham	Schinken(m)	jamón	prosciutto	fiambre
jante	rim	Felge(f), Radkranz(m)	llanta	cerchione	jante, camba
janvier	January	Januar(m)	enero	gennaio	Janeiro
jardin	garden	Garten(m)	jardín	giardino	jardim
jardin	garden	Gemüsegarten(m)	huerto	orto	horta
jardinier, ière	gardener	Gärtner(in f)m	jardinero, a	giardiniere, a	jardineiro, a
jargon	jargon	Fachsprache(f)	jerga	gergo	calão, gíria
jaune	yellow	gelb	amarillo, a	giallo, a	amarelo, a
jaunisse	jaundice	Gelbsucht(f)	ictericia	itterizia	ictericia
jazz	jazz	Jazz(m)	jazz	jazz	jazz
je	I	ich	yo	io	eu
jet	spray, jet	Strahl(m)	surtidor, chorro	getto, zampillo	jacto, repuxo
jetée	jetty	Hafendamm(m)	escollera	molo, gettata	molhe
jeter	throw	werfen	arrojar, lanzar	gettare	atirar, lançar
jeter	throw away(out)	weg = werfen	echar, tirar	buttare	deitar fora
jeton	counter, token	Spielmarke(f)	ficha	gettone	ficha
jeu	game	Spiel(n)	juego	gioco	jogo
jeudi	Thursday	Donnerstag(m)	jueves	giovedì	quinta-feira
jeune	young	jung	joven	giovane	jovem
jeunes	young people	jungen Leute(pl)	jóvenes	giovani	jovens
jeunesse	youth	Jugend(f)	juventud	gioventù, giovinezza	juventude
jockey	jockey	Jockey(m)	jockey	jockey, fantino	jockey
joie	joy	Freude(f)	alegría	gioia	alegria
joindre à(se)	join	an = schließen, sich	juntarse con	unirsi, associarsi	juntar-se
joint, e	joined, linked	zusammengefügt	junto, a	giunto, a	junto, a
joint	joint, join, seal	Dichtung(f)	junta	giunto, guarnizione	junta, anilha
joli, e	pretty	hübsch	bonito, a	carino, a	bonito, a
joli, e	nice	nett	lindo, a	bello, a	bonito, a
joue	cheek	Wange(f)	mejilla	guancia	bochecha, face
jouer	play	spielen	jugar	giocare	jogar, brincar
jouer	play	spielen	tocar	suonare	tocar
jouer	gamble	spielen	jugar	giocare	jogar
jouer	act	spielen	desempeñar	recitare	representar
jouet	toy	Spielzeug(n)	juguete	giocattolo	brinquedo
joueur, se	player	Spieler(in f)m	jugador, a	giocatore, trice	jogador, a
jouir	enjoy	genießen	gozar	godere	gozar
jour, journée	day	Tag(m)	día; jornada	giorno; giornata	dia
jour de congé	day off	Urlaubstag(m)	día libre	giorno di vacanza	dia de folga
journal	newspaper, paper	Zeitung(f)	periódico, diario	giornale	jornal
journalier, ière	daily	täglich	diario, a	giornaliero, a	diário, a
journalisme	journalism	Journalismus(m)	periodismo	giornalismo	jornalismo
journaliste	journalist	Journalist(in f)m	periodista	giornalista	jornalista
joyau	jewel	Juwel(n), Schmuckstück	joya	gioiello	jóia
joyeux, se	merry, joyful	lustig, fröhlich	alegre	allegro, a; felice	alegre
judiciaire	judicial, legal	gerichtlich	judicial	giudiziario, a	judiciário, a
judiciaire, légal	legal	rechtmäßig	judicial	giudiziario, a	judicial
judicieux, se	judicious	scharfsinnig	juicioso, a	giudizioso, a	judicioso, a
judo	judo	Judo(n)	judo, yudo	judò	judo
juge	judge	Richter(in f)m	juez	giudice	juíz
jugement	judgement	Urteil(n)	juicio	giudizio	julgamento
jugement	sentence	Urteil(n)	sentencia	sentenza	sentença
juger	judge	beurteilen	juzgar	giudicare	julgar
juif, juive	Jew, Jewess(-es)	Jude(m), Jüdin(f)	judío, judía	ebreo, a	judeu, judia
juillet	July	Juli(m)	julio	luglio	Julho
juin	June	Juni(m)	junio	giugno	Junho
jumeau, jumelle	twin	Zwilling(m)	gemelo, a	gemello, a	gémeo, a
jumelles	binoculars	Fernglas(n)	gemelos	binocolo	binóculos
jungle	jungle	Dschungel(m)	selva, jungla	giungla	selva
junte	junta	Junta(f)	junta	giunta	junta
jupe	skirt	Rock(m)	falda	gonna	saia
jupon	petticoat, slip	Unterrock(m)	enagua	sottana	saiote
juré	juryman, juror	Geschworene(f, m)	jurado	giurato	jurado
jurer	swear	schwören	jurar	giurare	jurar
juridique	juridical, legal	juristisch	jurídico, a	giuridico, a	jurídico, a
jurisprudence	jurisprudence	Rechtsprechung(f)	jurisprudencia	giurisprudenza	jurisprudência
juriste	jurist; lawyer	Jurist(in f)m	jurista	giurista	jurista
juron	swear-word	Fluch(m)	juramento, taco	bestemmia	palavrão
jury	jury	Jury(f)	jurado; tribunal	giuria	júri

French	English	German	Spanish	Italian	Portuguese
jus	juice	Saft(m)	jugo	succo	sumo
jus de fruit	fruit-juice	Obstsaft(m)	zumo de fruta	succo di frutta	sumo de fruta
jusqu'à	until, till	bis	hasta	fino a, sino a	até
jusqu'à	as far as	bis	hasta	fino	até
juste	just	gerecht	justo, a	giusto, a	justo, a
juste; exact, e	right	richtig	exacto, a	giusto, a	certo, a
justement	exactly	genau	justamente	appunto	justamente
justice	justice	Gerechtigkeit(f)	justicia	giustizia	justiça
justification	justification	Rechtfertigung(f)	justificación	giustificazione	justificação
justifier	justify	begründen, belegen	justificar	giustificare	justificar

K

French	English	German	Spanish	Italian	Portuguese
kangourou	kangaroo	Känguruh(n)	canguro	canguro	cangurú
karaté	karate	Karate(n)	karate	karatè	karaté
kayac	kayak	Kajak(m)	kayac, piragua	kayak	kayac
kidnapper	kidnap	entführen	secuestrar	rapire	raptar
kilogramme	kilogram(me)	Kilo(gramm n)n	kilogramo	chilogrammo, chilo	quilograma, quilo
kilomètre	kilometre	Kilometer(m)	kilómetro	chilometro	quilómetro
kimono	kimono	Kimono(m)	quimono, kimono	chimono	quimono
kiosque	news-stand	Zeitungskiosk(m)	quiosco	edicola; chiosco	quiosque
klaxon	horn, hooter	Hupe(f)	claxon, bocina	clacson	buzina
klaxonner	hoot	hupen	pitar	suonare(clacson)	buzinar
kyste	cyst	Zyste(f)	quiste	ciste	quisto

L

French	English	German	Spanish	Italian	Portuguese
la, l', les	the	die	la, las	la; l'; le	a, as
là	there	da	ahí; allí	là	aí; ali; lá
là	there	da; dort	allí; allá	là; lì	aí; lá
là-bas	over there	da; dort	allá	là, laggiù	além, acolá
laboratoire	laboratory	Labor(n)	laboratorio	laboratorio	laboratório
labour	ploughing	Feldarbeit(f)	labranza	aratura	lavoura
labyrinthe	labyrinth, maze	Labyrinth(n)	laberinto	labirinto	labirinto
lac	lake	See(m)	lago	lago	lago
lacet	lace	Schnürsenkel(m)	cordón	laccio	cordão
lâche	cowardly	feig(e)	cobarde	vigliacco, a	cobarde
lâche, détendu, e	loose, slack	locker, lose	flojo, a	allentato, a	frouxo, a
lâcher	release	los = lassen	soltar	lasciare	soltar
lâcheté	cowardliness	Feigheit(f)	cobardía	vigliaccheria	cobardia
lacrymogène	tear-gas	Tränengas(n)	lacrimógeno	lacrimogeno	lacrimogéneo
lagune	lagoon	Binnensee(m)	laguna	laguna	laguna
là-haut	up there	da oben	arriba	in alto	lá em cima
laid, e; moche	ugly, hideous	häßlich, gräßlich	feo, a	brutto, a	feio, a
laine	wool	Wolle(f)	lana	lana	lã
laisser	leave	lassen(zurück = -, ver-)	dejar	lasciare	deixar

F

French	English	German	Spanish	Italian	Portuguese
laisser	let; leave	lassen	dejar	lasciare	deixar
laissez-passer	pass	Ausweis(m)	salvoconducto	lascia-passare	salvo-conduto
lait	milk	Milch(f)	leche	latte	leite
laitue, salade	lettuce	Kopfsalat(m)	lechuga	lattuga	alface
lama	llama	Lama(n)	llama	lama	lama
lame	blade	Schneide(f)	hoja	lama	lâmina
lame	wave	Welle(f)	ola	ondata	vaga
lamenter(se)	lament	jammern	lamentarse	lamentarsi	lamentar-se
lampadaire	street-lamp	Straßenlaterne(f)	lámpara de pie	lampione	candeeiro
lampe	lamp	Lampe(f)	lámpara	lampada	candeeiro
lampe de poche	torch(-es)	Taschenlampe(f)	linterna	lampadina tascabile	pilha
lance	spear, lance	Lanze(f)	lanza	lancia	lança
lancement	launch(ing)	Start(m)	lanzamiento	lancio	lançamento
lancer	throw	werfen	lanzar	lanciare	lançar; atirar
lancer	launch, start up	lancieren, starten	lanzar	lanciare	lançar
landau	pram	Kinderwagen(m)	cochecito	carrozzina	carrinho(bebé)
lande	moor, heath	Heide(f)	landa	landa	charneca
langage	language	Sprache(f)	lenguaje	linguaggio	linguagem
langouste	crayfish	Languste(f)	langosta	aragosta	lagosta
langoustine	Dublin Bay prawn	Langustine(f)	langostino	scampo	lagostim
langue	tongue	Zunge(f)	lengua	lingua	língua
langue	language	Sprache(f)	idioma, lengua	lingua	língua, idioma
lanterne	lantern	Laterne(f)	linterna	lanterna	lanterna
lapin, e	rabbit	Kaninchen(n)	conejo, a	coniglio, a	coelho, a
laque	lacquer	Lack(m)	laca	lacca	laca
laque	hair-spray	Haarspray(m, n)	laca	lacca	laca
laquelle	which; who; whom	welche	cual(la)	quale(la)	qual(a)
large	wide, broad	weit, breit	ancho, a	largo, a	largo, a
large	broad	breit, weit	ancho, a	largo, a; ampio, a	largo, a; amplo, a
largeur	width, breadth	Breite(f)	anchura	larghezza	largura
larguer	let go, release	weg = werfen, auf = geben	largar	lasciare, mollare	largar, deixar
larme	tear	Träne(f)	lágrima	lacrima	lágrima
larve	larva(-vae)	Larve(f)	larva	larva	larva
laryngite	laryngitis	Halsentzündung(f)	laringitis	laringite	laringite
larynx	larynx	Kehlkopf(m)	laringe	laringe	laringe
laser	laser	Laser(m)	láser	laser	laser
latéral, e	lateral	seitlich	lateral	laterale	lateral
latitude	latitude	Breitengrad(m)	latitud	latitudine	latitude
lauréat, e	prize-winner	Preisträger(in f)m	galardonado, a	premiato, a	galardoado, a
lavabo	wash-basin	Waschbecken(n)	lavabo	lavabo, lavandino	lavabo
lavage	washing	Waschen(n)	lavado	lavaggio	lavagem
laver	wash	waschen	lavar	lavare	lavar
laver(se)	wash	waschen, sich	lavarse	lavarsi	lavar-se
laxatif, ive	laxative	abführend	laxante	lassativo, a	laxante
le, l', les	the	der, die, das, die	el, lo, los	il, lo, l'; i, gli	o, os
le	the	das	lo	lo	o
leader, chef	leader	Führer(in f)m	jefe, guía	capo, guida	chefe
lécher	lick	lecken	lamer	leccare	lamber
leçon	lesson	Stunde(f); Lektion(f)	lección	lezione	lição
lecteur, trice	reader	Leser(in f)m	lector, a	lettore, trice	leitor, a
lecture	reading	Lesen(n)	lectura	lettura	leitura
légal, e	legal	gesetzlich	legal	legale	legal
légalité	legality	Rechtmäßigkeit(f)	legalidad	legalità	legalidade
légende	legend	Legende(f)	leyenda	leggenda	lenda
léger, ère	light	leicht	ligero, a	leggero, a	ligeiro, a; leve
légèrement	lightly, slightly	leicht	ligeramente	leggermente	ligeiramente
législatif, ive	legislative	gesetzgebend	legislativo, a	legislativo, a	legislativo, a
législation	legislation	Gesetzgebung(f)	legislación	legislazione	legislação
légitime	legitimate	legitim	legítimo, a	legittimo, a	legítimo, a
légitime, légal	rightful, lawful	rechtmäßig	legítimo, a	legittimo, a	legítimo, a
léguer	bequeath, leave	vermachen	legar	legare	legar
légume	vegetable	Gemüse(n)	legumbre, verdura	verdura; legume	legume
lendemain	next day	folgenden Tag(m)	día siguiente	indomani(l')	dia seguinte
lent, e	slow	langsam	lento, a	lento, a	lento, a
lentement	slowly	langsam	lentamente	lentamente	lentamente
lentille	lens(contact -)	Kontaktlinse(f)	lentilla	lente a contatto	lente
lentille	lentil	Linse(f)(Pflanze)	lenteja	lenticchia	lentilha
lequel	which; who; whom	welcher	cúal, cual	quale(il)	qual(o)

74

French	English	German	Spanish	Italian	Portuguese
les	the	die	los, las	i, gli; le	os, as
lesbienne	lesbian	lesbisch	lesbiana	lesbica	lésbica
lésion	lesion, injury	Verletzung(f)	lesión	lesione	lesão
lessive	washing powder	Waschpulver(n)	detergente	detersivo	detergente
lettre	letter	Buchstabe(m)	letra	lettera	letra
lettre	letter	Brief(m)	carta	lettera	carta
leucémie	leukaemia	Leukämie(f)	leucemia	leucemia	leucemia
leur	them(to -)	ihnen	les	loro; gli	lhes
leur(s)	their	ihr/ihre	su, sus, suyo	loro(il/la, i/le)	seu, sua, deles
leur(le, la)	theirs	ihrige(der, die, das)	suyo, a(el, la)	loro(il, la)	seu(o), a sua; dele, a
leurre, appât	lure, bait	Lockmittel(n)	señuelo	esca	isca, engodo
lever	lift(up), raise	heben	levantar	alzare	levantar
lever(se)	stand up, get up	auf = stehen	levantarse	alzarsi	levantar-se
lever(se)	get up	erheben, sich	levantar(se)	alzarsi	levantar-se
lever(se)	rise	auf = gehen	amanecer	sorgere	nascer
lever(se)	break, dawn	an = brechen	amanecer	sorgere	nascer
levier	lever	Hebel(m)	palanca	leva	alavanca
lèvre	lip	Lippe(f)	labio	labbro(a)	lábio
lézard	lizard	Eidechse(f)	lagarto	lucertola	lagarto
liaison	connection, link	Verbindung(f)	relación; enlace	collegamento	ligação, junção
liaison	link	Verbindung(f)	enlace	collegamento	conexão
libéral, e	liberal	liberal	liberal	liberale	liberal
libéralisme	liberalism	Liberalismus(m)	liberalismo	liberalismo	liberalismo
libérer	liberate, free	befreien	liberar	liberare	libertar
liberté	liberty, freedom	Freiheit(f)	libertad	libertà	liberdade
libido	libido	Libido(f)	líbido	libido	líbido
librairie	book-shop	Buchhandlung(f)	librería	libreria	livraria
libre	free	frei	libre	libero, a	livre
libre	clear	frei	libre	libero, a	livre
licence	licence	Lizenz(f)	licencia	licenza	licença
licence	degree	Lizenz(f)	licenciatura	laurea	licenciatura
licenciement	dismissal, lay-off	Entlassung(f)	despido	licenziamento	despedimento
licencier	lay off, dismiss	entlassen	despedir	licenziare	despedir
liège	cork	Kork(m)	corcho	sughero	cortiça
lier	tie, bind	binden, verbinden	ligar, amarrar	legare	ligar
lieu	place, spot	Ort(m)	lugar	luogo	lugar
lieutenant	lieutenant	Leutnant(m)	teniente	tenente	tenente
ligne	line	Linie(f)	línea	linea	linha
ligne	line	Angelschnur(f)	caña	lenza	linha
lime	file	Feile(f)	lima	lima	lima
limite	limit	Grenze(f)	límite	limite	limite
limiter	limit	begrenzen	limitar	limitare	limitar
limitrophe	border(ing)	angrenzend	limítrofe	limitrofo	limítrofe
limoger	dismiss	entlassen	destituir	silurare	destituir
linéaire	linear	linear	lineal	lineare	linear
linge	linen	Wäsche(f)	ropa	biancheria	roupa
lingot	ingot, bullion	Barren(m)	lingote	lingotto	lingote
lion, ne	lion, lioness	Löwe(m), Löwin(f)	león, leona	leone, leonessa	leão, leoa
liqueur	liqueur	Likör(m)	licor	liquore	licor
liquide	liquid	flüssig	líquido, a	liquido, a	líquido, a
liquide	liquid	Flüssigkeit(f)	líquido	liquido	líquido
liquider	liquidate	liquidieren	liquidar	liquidare	liquidar
lire	read	lesen	leer	leggere	ler
lisible	legible	leserlich	legible	leggibile	legível
lisse	smooth	glatt	liso, a	liscio, a	liso, a
liste	list	Liste(f)	lista	lista	lista
lit	bed	Bett(n)	cama	letto	cama
lit de camp	camp-bed	Feldbett(n)	cama de campaña	letto da campo	cama de campismo
lithographie	lithograph(y)	Steindruck(m)	litografía	litografia	litografia
litige	litigation	Streitfall(m)	litigio	litigio	litígio
litre	litre	Liter(m, n)	litro	litro	litro
littéraire	literary	literarisch	literario, a	letterario, a	literário, a
littérature	literature	Literatur(f)	literatura	letteratura	literatura
littoral	coast	Küstenstreifen(m)	litoral	litorale	litoral
livide	livid, pallid	blaß, fahl	lívido, a	livido, a	lívido, a
livraison	delivery	Lieferung(f)	entrega	consegna	entrega
livre	book	Buch(n)	libro	libro	livro
livrer	deliver	liefern	entregar	consegnare	entregar

French	English	German	Spanish	Italian	Portuguese
lobe	lobe	Ohrläppchen(n)	lóbulo	lobo	lóbulo
local	premises	Gebäude(n), Lokal(n)	local	locale	local
local, e	local	lokal	local	locale	local
localiser	localize; locate	lokalisieren	localizar	localizzare	localizar
localité	locality	Ortschaft(f)	localidad	località	localidade
locataire	tenant	Mieter(in f)m	inquilino, a	inquilino, a	inquilino, a
location	rental, hiring	Vermietung(f)	alquiler	noleggio, affitto	aluguer
locomotive	locomotive	Lokomotive(f)	locomotiva	locomotiva	locomotiva
locution	phrase, locution	Redensart(f)	locución	locuzione	locução
loge	box	Loge(f)	camerino	camerino	camarim
logement	accommodation	Wohnung(f)	alojamiento	alloggio	alojamento
loger	accommodate	unter = bringen	alojar	alloggiare	alojar, morar
logiciel	software	Software(f)	logicial	software	software
logique	logical	logisch	lógico, a	logico, a	lógico, a
loi	law	Gesetz(n)	ley	legge	lei
loin	far(away), distant	weit, fern	lejos	lontano, a	longe
loin(au)	away, far away	weg(fort); weit weg	lejos(a lo)	lontano	longe(ao)
loisir	leisure	Freizeit(f)	tiempo libre	tempo libero, hobby	tempo livre
long, longue	long	lang	largo, a	lungo, a	longo, a
long(le)	along	entlang	largo(a lo)	lungo	longo(ao)
longitude	longitude	Längengrad(m)	longitud	longitudine	longitude
longitudinal, e	longitudinal	Längs-	longitudinal	longitudinale	longitudinal
longtemps	long time(a)	lange	mucho tiempo	molto/molto tempo	muito tempo
longueur	length	Länge(f)	longitud	lunghezza	comprimento
lorsque	when; as	als; wenn	cuando	quando	quando
losange	diamond-shaped	Raute(f), Rhombus(m)	rombo	rombo	losango
lot	prize	Los(n)	premio	premio	prémio
lot	batch, assortment	Assortiment(n)	lote	assortimento	lote
loterie	lottery	Lotterie(f)	lotería	lotteria	lotaria
lotion	lotion	Gesichtswasser(n)	loción	lozione	loção
loucher	squint	schielen	bizquear	strabico, a(essere)	estrábico, a(ser)
louer	hire, rent	mieten; vermieten	alquilar	noleggiare	alugar
louer	rent	vermieten; mieten	alquilar	affittare	alugar
louer à bail	lease	mieten; pachten	arrendar	noleggiare	arrendar, alugar
loup	wolf(-lves)	Wolf(m)	lobo	lupo	lobo
loupe	magnifying-glass	Lupe(f)	lupa	lente(ingrandimento)	lupa
lourd, e	heavy	schwer	pesado, a	pesante	pesado, a
loyal, e	loyal	loyal, treu	leal	leale	leal
loyer	rent	Miete(f)	alquiler	affitto	aluguer
lucide	lucid	klar	lúcido, a	lucido, a	lúcido, a
lueur	gleam, glow	Schimmer(m)	resplandor	chiarore, luce	luz, clarão
lui	him, her, it	ihm, ihr, ihm	le, él; ella; se	lui; gli; le	ele(a); lhe
luisant, e	shining, bright	leuchtend	reluciente	brillante	brilhante
lumbago	lumbago	Hexenschuß(m)	lumbago	lombaggine	lumbago
lumière	light	Licht(n)	luz	luce	luz
lumineux, se	luminous	leuchtend, hell	luminoso, a	luminoso, a	luminoso, a
lundi	Monday	Montag(m)	lunes	lunedì	segunda-feira
lune	moon	Mond(m)	luna	luna	lua
lunettes	glasses	Brille(f)	gafas	occhiali	óculos
lutte	struggle, fight	Kampf(m)	lucha	lotta	luta
lutter	fight, struggle	kämpfen	luchar	lottare	lutar
lutteur, se	wrestler; fighter	Kämpfer(m); Ringer(m)	luchador, a	lottatore, trice	lutador, a
luxe	luxury	Luxus(m)	lujo	lusso	luxo
luxueux, se	luxurious	üppig	lujoso, a	lussuoso, a	luxuoso, a
luxuriant, e	luxuriant, lush	üppig	exuberante	lussureggiante	luxuriante
lycée	comprehensive sch.	Gymnasium(n)	instituto, liceo	liceo	liceu
lyncher	lynch	lynchen	linchar	linciare	linchar

M

French	English	German	Spanish	Italian	Portuguese
ma	my	meine	mi	mia(la)	minha
macabre	macabre	makaber	macabro, a	macabro, a	macabro, a

macchabée	corpse	Leiche(f)	cadáver	cadavere	cadáver
mâcher	chew	kauen	masticar	masticare	mastigar
machine	machine	Maschine(f)	máquina	macchina	máquina
mâchoire	jaw	Kiefer(m)	mandíbula	mascella	maxila
maçon	builder	Maurer(m)	albañil	muratore	pedreiro, trolha
madame	Mrs; Madam	Frau(f)	señora	signora	senhora
mademoiselle	Miss	Fräulein(n)	señorita	signorina	menina
mafia	Mafia	Mafia(f)	mafia	mafia	mafia
magasin	shop	Geschäft(n), Laden(m)	tienda	negozio; bottega	loja
magasin	store	Warenlager(n)	almacén	magazzino; negozio	armazém
magazine	magazine	Illustrierte(f)	revista	rivista	revista
magie	magic	Zauberei(f)	magia	magia	magia
magique	magic	magisch	mágico, a	magico, a	mágico, a
magistrat	magistrate	Magistrat(m)	magistrado	magistrato	magistrado
magnétique	magnetic	magnetisch	magnético, a	magnetico, a	magnético, a
magnétophone	tape recorder	Kassettenrecorder(m)	magnetófono	registratore	gravador
magnétoscope	video recorder	Videorecorder(m)	magnetoscopio	videoregistratore	gravador video
magnifique	magnificent	prächtig	magnífico, a	magnifico, a	magnífico, a
mai	May	Mai(m)	mayo	maggio	Maio
maigre	thin	mager	delgado, a	magro, a	magro, a
maigrir	lose weight	ab = nehmen	adelgazar	dimagrire	emagrecer
maillot de bain	swimsuit; trunks	Badeanzug(m)	traje de baño	costume da bagno	fato de banho
maillot de corps	vest	Trikot(n)	camiseta	maglia intima	camisola interior
main	hand	Hand(f)	mano	mano	mão
main-d'oeuvre	workforce, labour	Arbeitskraft(f)	mano de obra	manodopera	mão-de-obra
main-d'oeuvre	manpower, labour	Arbeitskräfte(pl.)	mano de obra	manodopera	mão-de-obra
maintenant	now	jetzt	ahora	ora, adesso	agora
maintenir	maintain	erhalten	mantener	mantenere	manter
maire	mayor	Bürgermeister(m)	alcalde	sindaco	President.da Câmara
mairie	town hall	Rathaus(n)	ayuntamiento	municipio, comune	câmara
mais	but	aber	pero; sino; mas	ma	mas
mais, cependant	but, yet, however	aber, jedoch	pero	però	porém
mais	maize, corn	Mais(m)	maíz	granturco, mais	milho
maison	house	Haus(n)	casa	casa	casa
maison(à la)	home(at)	Hause(zu)	casa(en)	casa(a)	casa(em)
maître, esse	master, mistress	Herr(in f)m	señor, señora	maestro, a; padrone, a	dono, a; senhor, a
maître d'hôtel	head-waiter	Oberkellner(m)	jefe de hotel	capocameriere	mordomo
maître-nageur	life-guard	Bademeister(in f)m	maestro(natación)	bagnino	nadador-salvador
maîtriser	control, master	beherrschen	dominar	dominare	dominar
majesté	majesty	Majestät(f)	majestad	maestà	majestade
majestueux, se	majestic	majestätisch	majestuoso, a	maestoso, a	majestoso, a
majorité	majority	Mehrheit(f)	mayoría	maggioranza	maioria
mal	evil	Böse(n)	mal	male	mal
mal	harm, hurt	Weh(n)	daño	male	mal
mal	ache, pain	Schmerz(m), Weh(n)	dolor	male	dor
mal	badly	schlecht	mal	male	mal
mal de tête	headache	Kopfschmerzen(m, pl)	dolor de cabeza	mal di testa	dor de cabeça
mal de gorge	sore throat	Halsschmerzen(m, pl)	dolor de garganta	mal di gola	dor de garganta
mal aux dents	toothache	Zahnschmerzen(m, pl)	dolor de dientes	mal di denti	dor de dentes
mal de mer	sea-sickness	Seekrankheit(f)	mareo	mal di mare	enjôo
mal(faire)	ache, hurt	weh tun, schmerzen	doler	male(fare)	doer
mal(avoir)	hurts(it)	Schmerzen haben	dolerle a uno	male(aver)	doer
malade	sick person	Kranke(f, m)	enfermo, a	malato, a	doente
malade	ill	krank	enfermo, a	malato, a	doente; enfermo, a
maladie	illness(-es)	Krankheit(f)	enfermedad	malattia	doença
maladroit, e	clumsy, awkward	ungeschickt	torpe	maldestro, a	desajeitado, a
malaise	faintness	Unwohlsein, Schwäche	malestar	malessere	indisposição
malchance	misfortune	Unglück(n)	mala suerte	sventura; sfortuna	desventura
malchance	ill luck, bad luck	Pech(n), Unglück(n)	mala suerte	sfortuna	má sorte
malchanceux, se	unlucky	unglücklich	desafortunado, a	sfortunato, a	azarento, a
mâle	male	Männchen(n)	macho	maschio	macho
malfaiteur	criminal	Missetäter(in f)m	malhechor	malvivente	malfeitor
malgré	despite	trotz	a pesar de	malgrado	apesar de
malheur	misfortune	Unglück(n)	desgracia	disgrazia	desgraça
malheureux, se	unhappy, miserable	unglücklich, betrübt	desgraciado, a	infelice	infeliz
malheureux, se	unhappy, sorrowful	betrübt, unglücklich	infeliz, triste	infelice, triste	infeliz, triste
malheureux, se	unfortunate	unglücklich	desgraciado, a	disgraziato, a	infeliz
malhonnête	dishonest	unehrlich	deshonesto, a	disonesto, a	desonesto, a

F

French	English	German	Spanish	Italian	Portuguese
malin, igne	smart, clever	gerissen, schlau	pillo, a; astuto, a	furbo, a	esperto, a; astuto, a
malle	trunk	Koffer(großer)(m)	baúl	baule	mala
malnutrition	malnutrition	Unterernährung(f)	desnutrición	malnutrizione	malnutrição
malsain, e	unhealthy	ungesund	malsano, a	malsano, a	doentio, a
malveillance	ill will	Böswilligkeit(f)	malevolencia	malanimo	malevolência
malveillant, e	malevolent	böswillig	malévolo, a	malevolo, a	malévolo, a
maman	Mummy, Mum	Mama(f)	mamá	mamma	mamã
mamelle	udder	Euter(n)	mama, teta	mammella	mama
mammifère	mammal	Säugetier(n)	mamífero	mammifero	mamífero
manche	sleeve	Ärmel(m)	manga(la)	manica	manga
manche	handle	Stiel(m)	mango(el)	manico	cabo
mandarine	tangerine	Mandarine(f)	mandarina	mandarino	tangerina
mandat-lettre	postal order	Postanweisung(f)	giro postal	vaglia(postale)	vale postal
manège	roundabout	Karussell(n)	tiovivo, noria	giostra	carrossel
manette	handle	Griff(m)	manecilla	leva	manípulo
manger	eat	essen	comer	mangiare	comer
maniable	handy, manageable	handlisch	manuable	maneggevole	manejável
maniaque	maniac	Verrückte(f, m)	maníaco, a	maniaco, a	maníaco, a
maniaque	fussy	übergenau sein	maniático, a	pignolo, a	meticuloso, a
manie	mania	Sucht(f)	manía	mania	mania
manière	manner, way	Art(f)	manera, modo	maniera, modo	maneira, modo
manifestant, e	demonstrator	Demonstrant(in f)m	manifestante	manifestante	manifestante
manifestation	demonstration	Demonstration(f)	manifestación	manifestazione	manifestação
manipuler	manipulate	manipulieren	manipular	manipolare	manipular
manivelle	crank	Handkurbel(f)	manivela	manovella	manivela
mannequin	model	Mannequin(n)	maniquí, modelo	indossatore, trice	modelo
mannequin	dummy; model	Schaufensterpuppe(f)	maniquí	manichino	manequim
manoeuvre	manoeuvre	Manöver(n)	maniobra	manovra	manobra
manoeuvre	labourer	Hilfsarbeiter(in f)m	peón, obrero	manovale	servente
manoir, château	mansion	Herrensitz(m), -haus n	mansión, morada	maniero, castello	mansão, palacete
manque	lack, shortage	Mangel(m)	falta, carencia	mancanza	falta, carência
manquer	lack, be short of	fehlen	faltar	mancare	falta(ter)
manquer	miss	verpassen	perder	perdere; mancare	perder
manteau	coat	Mantel(m)	abrigo	cappotto	casaco, manto
manucure	manicure	Maniküre(f)	manicura	manicure	manicura
manuel, elle	manual; hand-	manuell; Hand-	manual	manuale	manual
manuscrit, e	handwritten	handgeschrieben	manuscrito, a	manoscritto, a	manuscrito, a
maquereau	mackerel	Makrele(f)	caballa	sgombro	cavala
maquette	model	Modell(n)	maqueta	modello	maqueta
maquillage	make-up	Schminke(f)	maquillaje	trucco	maquilhagem
maquiller(se)	make-up(put on)	schminken, sich	maquillarse	truccarsi	maquilhar-se
marais	marsh	Sumpf(m)	pantano	palude	pântano
marathon	marathon	Marathonlauf(m)	maratón	maratona	maratona
marbre	marble	Marmor(m)	mármol	marmo	mármore
marchander	bargain, haggle	feilschen, handeln	regatear	contrattare	regatear
marchand, e	tradesman, dealer	Händler(in f)m	vendedor, a	mercante	negociante
marchand, e	shop-keeper	Kaufmann(m), Kauffrau	vendedor, a	negoziante	comerciante
marchandise	goods, merchandise	Ware(f)	mercancía	merce	mercadoria
marche	step	Stufe(f)	peldaño, escalón	scalino	degrau
marche	walk(ing)	Wanderung(f)	marcha	marcia	marcha
marché	market	Markt(m)	mercado	mercato	mercado
marcher	walk	gehen	andar	andare	andar
marcher, cheminer	walk	laufen, gehen	caminar	camminare	caminhar
marcher	work, run	in Betrieb sein	marchar	funzionare	funcionar
marcher(faire)	operate	bedienen	funcionar(hacer)	funzionare(fare)	funcionar(fazer)
mardi	Tuesday	Dienstag(m)	martes	martedì	terça-feira
mare	pond, pool	Tümpel(m)	charca	stagno	charco
marécageux, se	marshy, boggy	sumpfig	pantanoso, a	paludoso, a	pantanoso, a
marée	tide	Gezeiten(pl.)	marea	marea	maré
marge	margin	Rand(m)	margen	margine	margem
marginal, e	fringe(on the)	Außenseiter(in f)m	marginal	marginale	marginal
mari	husband	Ehemann(m)	marido	marito	marido
mariage	wedding; marriage	Hochzeit(f); Heirat(f)	matrimonio	matrimonio	casamento
marié, e	married	verheiratet	casado, a	sposato, a	casado, a
marié, mariée	bridegroom, bride	Bräutigam(m), Braut(f)	novio, novia	sposo, sposa	noivo, noiva
marier(se)	married(get)	heiraten	casarse	sposarsi	casar-se
marin	sailor	Seemann(m)	marino	marinaio	marinheiro
marine	navy	Marine(f)	marina	marina	marinha

French	English	German	Spanish	Italian	Portuguese
maritime	maritime, sea-	See-	marítimo, a	marittimo, a	marítimo, a
marmite	cooking-pot	Kochtopf(m)	marmita, olla	pentola, marmitta	marmita
marque, trace	mark	Spur(f)	señal, marca	segno, marca	marca, vestígio
marque	brand, make	Marke(f)	marca	marchio, marca	marca
marquer	mark	markieren	marcar	segnare, marcare	marcar
marquer	score	schießen(Tor-)	marcar	segnare	marcar
marraine	godmother	Patin(f)	madrina	madrina	madrinha
mars	March	März(m)	marzo	marzo	Março
marteau	hammer	Hammer(m)	martillo	martello	martelo
martyr, e	martyr	Märtyrer(in f)m	mártir	martire	mártir
marxisme	Marxism	Marxismus(m)	marxismo	marxismo	marxismo
masculin, e	masculine, male	männlich	masculino, a	maschile	masculino, a
masque	mask	Maske(f)	máscara	maschera	máscara
massacre	slaughter	Blutbad(n)	masacre	massacro	massacre
massage	massage	Massage(f)	masaje	massaggio	massagem
masse	mass	Masse(f)	masa	massa	massa
massif, ive	massive; solid	massiv	masivo, a	massiccio, a	maciço, a
mastic	putty	Kitt(m)	masilla	mastice	betume
mat, e	dull, matt	glanzlos, matt	mate	opaco, a	mate
mât	mast	Mast(m)	mástil	albero	mastro
matador	matador	Matador(m)	matador	matador	matador
match	match(-es), game	Spiel(n)	partido	partita	desafio, partida
matelas	mattress(-es)	Matraze(f)	colchón	materasso	colchão
matelot	sailor	Matrose(m)	marinero	marinaio	marinheiro
matériau	material	Material(n)	material	materiale	material
matériel	material	Material(n)	material	materiale	material
maternel, le	maternal, motherly	mütterlich	materno, a; maternal	materno, a	maternal
mathématique(s)	mathematics	Mathematik(f)	matemáticas	matematica	matemáticas
matière	matter, material	Stoff(m), Material(n)	materia	materia	matéria
matière	material	Material(n)	material; materia	materiale; materia	material; matéria
matière	subject	Fach(n)	asignatura	materia	matéria
matière	subject matter	Thema(n)	materia, tema	materia, tema	assunto
matin	morning	Morgen(m)	mañana	mattino	manhã
matinal, e	early	früh	matutino, a	mattutino, a	matinal
matraquer	beat up, club	prügeln	aporrear	manganellare	espancar
matricule	roll, register	Matrikel(f)	matrícula	matricola	matrícula
maturité	maturity	Reife(f)	madurez	maturità	maturidade
maudit, e	cursed, damned	verdammt	maldito, a	maledetto, a	maldito, a
mauvais, e	bad	schlecht	malo, a	cattivo, a	mau, má
mauvais, mal	evil, bad	übel	malo, a	cattivo, a; male	mau, má
maximum	maximum	Maximum(n)	máximo	massimo	máximo
mazout	fuel oil	Heizöl(n)	fuel-oil	nafta	fuel, óleo
me, m'; moi	me	mich; mir	me	mi, me	me
mécanicien, ne	mechanic	Mechaniker(in f)m	mecánico, a	meccanico, a	mecânico, a
mécanique	mechanical	mechanisch	mecánico, a	meccanico, a	mecânico, a
mécanique	mechanics	Mechanik(f)	mecánica	meccanica	mecânica
mécanisme	mechanism	Mechanismus(m)	mecanismo	meccanismo	mecanismo
mécène	patron	Mäzen(m), Sponsor(m)	mecenas	mecenate	mecenas
méchant, e	naughty	böse, boshaft	malo, a	cattivo, a	mau, má
mèche	lock(of hair)	Locke(f)	mechón	ciocca	madeixa
mécontent, e	displeased	unzufrieden	descontento, a	scontento, a	descontente
mécontentement	displeasure	Unzufriedenheit(f)	descontento	scontento	descontentamento
médaille	medal	Medaille(f)	medalla	medaglia	medalha
médecin	doctor	Arzt(m), Ärztin(f)	médico	medico	médico
médecine	medicine	Medizin(f)	medicina	medicina	medicina
médical, e	medical	medizinisch	médico, a	medico, a	médico, a
médicament	drug, medicine	Medikament(n)	medicina	medicina	medicamento
médiocre	mediocre	mittelmäßig, schlecht	mediocre	mediocre	medíocre
méditer	meditate	nach = denken, sinnen	meditar	meditare	meditar
méfiance	distrust, mistrust	Mißtrauen(n)	desconfianza	diffidenza	desconfiança
méfiant, e	suspicious	mißtrauisch	desconfiado, a	diffidente	desconfiado, a
méfier(se)	mistrust	mißtrauen	desconfiar	diffidare	desconfiar
meilleur, e	better	besser(sein)	mejor	migliore	melhor
meilleur, e	best	Beste(f, m)	mejor	migliore	melhor
mélancolie	melancholy	Wehmut(f)	melancolía	malinconia	melancolia
mélange	mixture; mixing	Mischung(f)	mezcla	miscuglio	mistura
mélange	blend, mixture	Mischung(f)	mezcla	mescolanza	mistura
mélanger	mix	mischen	mezclar	mescolare	misturar

French	English	German	Spanish	Italian	Portuguese
mêler de(se)	interfere	ein = mischen, sich	implicarse	immischiare(-rsi)	envolver-se
mélodie	melody, tune	Melodie(f)	melodía	melodia	melodia
melon	melon	Melone(f)	melón	melone	melão
membrane	membrane	Membran(f)	membrana	membrana	membrana
membre	limb	Glied(n)	miembro	membro, arto	membro
membre(de)	member(of)	Mitglied(n)	miembro, a; socio, a	membro, i	membro, a; sócio, a
même	same	selbe; gleich(der -)	mismo, a	stesso, a	mesmo, a
même	even	sogar; selbst	aun; incluso	anche; perfino	mesmo(que)
même(lui, elle)	self(him, her, it)	selbst(er, sie, es)	mismo, a(él, ella)	stesso, a(lui, lei)	próprio, a(ele, a)
même pas	even(not)	einmal(nicht)	siquiera(ni)	neanche	sequer(nem)
mémoire	memory	Gedächtnis(n)	memoria	memoria	memória
menace	threat	Drohung(f)	amenaza	minaccia	ameaça
menacer	threaten	bedrohen	amenazar	minacciare	ameaçar
ménage	housework	Haushalt(m)	limpieza	pulizie	limpeza
ménagère	housewife(-ives)	Hausfrau(f)	ama de casa	casalinga	dona de casa
mendiant, e	beggar	Bettler(in f)m	mendigo, a	mendicante	mendigo, a
mener, conduire	lead	führen	guiar, conducir	condurre	levar, conduzir
ménopause	menopause	Wechseljahre(n, pl)	menopausia	menopausa	menopausa
menottes	handcuffs	Handschellen(f, pl)	esposas	manette	algemas
mensonge	lie, fib	Lüge(f)	mentira	bugia	mentira
mensuel, le	monthly	monatlich	mensual	mensile	mensal
mental, e	mental	geistig	mental	mentale	mental
mentalité	mentality	Mentalität(f)	mentalidad	mentalità	mentalidade
menteur, se	liar	Lügner(in f)m	mentiroso, a	bugiardo, a	mentiroso, a
menthe	mint	Minze(f)	menta	menta	hortelã
mention	mention	Vermerk(m)	mención	menzione	menção
mentir	lie	lügen	mentir	mentire	mentir
menton	chin	Kinn(n)	barbilla	mento	queixo
menu	menu	Menü(n); Speisekarte f	menú	menù	ementa
menuisier	joiner, carpenter	Tischler(m)	carpintero	falegname	carpinteiro
mépris	contempt, scorn	Verachtung(f)	desprecio	disprezzo	desprezo
mer	sea	Meer(n)	mar	mare	mar
mer	sea	See(f)	mar	mare	mar
mercenaire	mercenary	Söldner(m)	mercenario	mercenario	mercenário
merci	thank you, thanks	danke	gracias	grazie	obrigado, a
mercredi	Wednesday	Mittwoch(m)	miércoles	mercoledì	quarta-feira
mercure	mercury	Quecksilber(n)	mercurio	mercurio	mercúrio
mère	mother	Mutter(f)	madre	madre	mãe
méridien	meridian	Meridian(m)	meridiano	meridiano	meridiano
mérite	merit, worth	Verdienst(n)	mérito	merito	mérito
mériter	deserve, merit	verdienen	merecer	meritare	merecer
merveilleux, se	marvellous	wunderbar	maravilloso, a	meraviglioso, a	maravilhoso, a
merveilleux, se	wonderful	wunderbar	maravilloso, a	meraviglioso, a	maravilhoso, a
mes	my	meine	mis	miei, mie(i, le)	meus
mésaventure	mishap	Mißgeschick(n)	contratiempo	disavventura	contratempo
mesdames	ladies	meine Damen	señoras	signore	senhoras
message	message	Nachricht(f)	mensaje	messaggio	mensagem, recado
messe	mass	Messe(f)	misa	messa	missa
messieurs	gentlemen	meine Herren	señores	signori	senhores
mesurer	measure	messen	medir	misurare	medir
métal	metal	Metal(n)	metal	metallo	metal
métallique	metallic	metallisch	metálico, a	metallico, a	metálico, a
métamorphose	metamorphosis(-es)	Verwandlung(f)	metamorfosis	metamorfosi	metamorfose
métastase	metastasis(-es)	Tochtergeschwulst(f)	metástasis	metastasi	metástase
météorologie	weather forecast	Wetterkunde(f)	meteorología	meteorologia	meteorologia
méthode	method	Methode(f)	método	metodo	método
méticuleux, se	meticulous	sorgfältig	meticuloso, a	meticoloso, a	meticuloso, a
métier	profession, job	Beruf(m)	oficio	mestiere	ofício
métis, se	half-caste	Mischling(m)	mestizo, a	meticcio, a	mestiço, a
mètre	metre	Meter(m, n)	metro	metro	metro
métrique	metric	metrisch	métrico, a	metrico, a	métrico, a
métro	underground, tube	U-Bahn(f)	metro	metropolitana	metropolitano
mettre	put	legen, stellen	poner	mettere	pôr
mettre, placer	lay	legen	poner, colocar	porre, mettere	pôr, colocar
mettre, placer	set	setzen, stellen	poner, colocar	porre, mettere	pôr, colocar
meuble	furniture	Möbelstück(n)	mueble	mobile	móvel
meurtre	murder	Mord(m)	asesinato	assassinio	homicídio, crime
meurtrier, ière	murderer	Mörder(in f)m	homicida	omicida	assassino, a

French	English	German	Spanish	Italian	Portuguese
mi-	half(-); mid-	halb-	medio, a	semi-; mezzo-	meio, a
miauler	mew	miauen	maullar	miagolare	miar
micro(phone)	microphone, mike	Mikrophon(n)	micrófono	microfono	microfone
microbe	germ, microbe	Mikrobe(f)	microbio	microbo	micróbio
microscope	microscope	Mikroskop(n)	microscopio	microscopio	microscópio
midi	midday, noon	Mittag(m)	mediodía	mezzogiorno	meio-dia
miel	honey	Honig(m)	miel	miele	mel
mien, ne	mine	meine, meiner	mío, mía	mio(il); mia(la)	meu, minha
mieux	better	besser	mejor	meglio	melhor
migraine	migraine, headache	Migräne(f)	jaqueca	emicrania	enxaqueca
migrateur, trice	migrant	wandernd; Wander-	migratorio, a	migratore, trice	migrador, a
migration	migration	Wanderung(f)	migración	migrazione	migração
milice	militia	Miliz(f)	milicia	milizia	milícia
milieu	middle	Mitte(f)	medio	mezzo	meio
milieu	milieu, background	Milieu(n)	ambiente, medio	ambiente	meio
militaire	military	militärisch	militar	militare	militar
militant, e	militant	Militant(m)	militante	militante	militante
militer	militate	kämpfen für	militar	militare	militar
mille	thousand	tausend	mil	mille; mila(pl.)	mil
millésime	vintage	Jahrgang(m)	cosecha(año)	annata	vintage
milliard	thousand million	Milliarde(f)	mil millones	miliardo	bilião
millième	thousandth	tausendste	milésimo, a	millesimo, a	milésimo, a
millier	thousand	Tausend(n)	millar	migliaio(a)	milhar
million	million	Million(f)	millón	milione	milhão
mince	slim; slender	schlank	delgado, a	snello, a	magro, a; delgado, a
mince	thin	dünn	delgado, a	sottile	fino, a
mine	mine	Bergwerk(n)	mina	miniera	mina
mine	look	Aussehen(n)	semblante, cara	cera, aspetto	aparência
minerai	ore	Erz(n)	mineral	minerale	minério
minéral, e	mineral	mineralisch	mineral	minerale	mineral
mineur, e	minor	unbedeutend	menor	minore	menor
mineur, e	minor	Minderjährige(f, m)	menor	minore, minorenne	menor
miniature	miniature	Miniatur(f)	miniatura	miniatura	miniatura
minimum	minimum	Minimum(n)	mínimo, a	minimo, a	mínimo, a
ministère	ministry	Ministerium(n)	ministerio	ministero	ministério
ministre	minister	Minister(in f)m	ministro	ministro	ministro
minorité	minority	Minderheit(f)	minoría	minoranza	minoria
minuit	midnight	Mitternacht(f)	medianoche	mezzanotte	meia-noite
minuscule	minute, tiny	winzig	minúsculo, a	minuscolo, a	minúsculo, a
minute	minute	Minute(f)	minuto	minuto	minuto
miracle	miracle	Wunder(n)	milagro	miracolo	milagre
mirage	mirage	Fata Morgana(f)	espejismo	miraggio	miragem
miroir	mirror	Spiegel(m)	espejo	specchio	espelho
misère	poverty	Elend(n)	miseria	miseria	miséria
missile	missile	Rakete(f)	misil	missile	míssil
mission	mission	Mission(f)	misión	missione	missão
mixte	mixed	gemischt	mixto, a	misto, a	misto, a
mobile	mobile, movable	beweglich, mobil	móvil, movible	mobile	móvel
mobilier	furniture	Möbel(pl)	mobiliario	mobilio	mobiliário
mobiliser	mobilize	mobilisieren	mobilizar	mobilitare	mobilizar
mobilité	mobility	Beweglichkeit(f)	mobilidad	mobilità	mobilidade
mobylette	moped	Mofa(n)	velomotor	motorino, scooter	motorizada
mode	fashion	Mode(f)	moda	moda	moda
mode, manière	mode, manner	Weise(f)	modo, manera	modo, maniera	modo, maneira
modèle	model, pattern	Modell(n)	modelo	modello	modelo
modèle	design	Muster(n), Modell(n)	modelo, patrón	modello	modelo
modèle	pattern	Muster(n)	modelo	modello	modelo
modérer	moderate	mäßigen	moderar	moderare	moderar
moderne	modern	modern	moderno, a	moderno, a	moderno, a
modeste	modest	bescheiden	modesto, a	modesto, a	modesto, a
modification	modification	Abänderung(f)	modificación	modifica	modificação
modifier	modify	verändern	modificar	modificare	modificar
moelle	marrow(-bone)	Mark(n)	médula, tuétano	midollo	medula, tutano
moeurs	morals	Sitten(f, pl)	costumbres	costumi	costumes
moi	me; I	mich; mir; ich	mí, me; yo	io; me	eu; me; mim
moi(à)	mine, to me	mir	mío, a(el, la)	mio, mia(è)	meu(é)
moine	monk	Mönch(m)	monje, fraile	monaco, frate	monge, frade
moineau	sparrow	Spatz(m)	gorrión	passero	pardal

moins	less	weniger	menos	meno	menos
moins(le)	least(the)	wenigsten(am)	menos(lo)	meno(il)	menos(o)
mois	month	Monat(m)	mes	mese	mês
moisir	mouldy(to go)	verschimmeln	enmohecer	ammuffire	bolor(criar)
moisson	harvest	Ernte(f)	cosecha	mietitura	ceifa, colheita
moitié	half(-lves)	Hälfte(f)	mitad	metà	metade
molaire	molar	Backenzahn(m)	molar	molare	molar
molécule	molecule	Molekül(n)	molécula	molecola	molécula
mollet	calf(-lves)	Wade(f)	pantorrilla	polpaccio	barriga(perna)
mollusque	mollusc	Weichtier(n)	molusco	mollusco	molusco
moment	moment	Augenblick(m)	momento	momento, attimo	momento
moment, instant	while, time	Moment(m)	rato	attimo, momento	momento, instante
mon	my	mein	mi	mio, mia(il, la)	meu, minha
monarchie	monarchy	Monarchie(f)	monarquía	monarchia	monarquia
monastère	monastery	Kloster(n)	monasterio	monastero	mosteiro
monde	world	Welt(f)	mundo	mondo	mundo
mondial, e	world-wide, world	weltlich	mundial	mondiale	mundial
monétaire	monetary	Währungs-, Geld-	monetario, a	monetario, a	monetário, a
moniteur, trice	instructor	Leiter/in; Lehrer/in	monitor, a	istruttore, trice	monitor, a
monnaie	money	Geld(n)	moneda, dinero	moneta	moeda
monnaie	change	Kleingeld(n); Klein-	cambio	resto	troco
monnaie	currency	Währung(f), Devisen pl	moneda	valuta; moneta	moeda
monogamie	monogamy	Monogamie(f)	monogamia	monogamia	monogamia
monopole	monopoly	Monopol(n)	monopolio	monopolio	monopólio
monotone	monotonous	monoton, eintönig	monótono, a	monotono, a	monótono, a
monsieur(Mr)	Mr	Herr(m)	señor	signor	senhor
monsieur(Mr)	Mr	Herr(m)	Don	Signor	Senhor
monsieur	Sir	Herr(m)	señor	signore	senhor
monsieur	man, gentleman(men)	Gentleman(m)	caballero	signore	cavalheiro
monstre	monster	Monster(n)	monstruo	mostro	monstro
mont, montagne	mount	Berg(m)	monte	monte	monte
montage	mounting, assembly	Montage(f)	montaje	montaggio	montagem
montagne	mountain	Gebirge(n), Berg(m)	montaña	montagna	montanha
montant	amount	Betrag(m)	importe	ammontare	montante
montée	rise	Steigung(f)	subida	salita	subida
monter	climb; rise; go up	steigen	subir	salire	subir
monter	get into, get on	ein = steigen	subir	salire	subir a, entrar
montre	watch	Uhr(f), Armbanduhr(f)	reloj	orologio	relógio
montrer	show	zeigen	enseñar, mostrar	mostrare	mostrar
monument	monument	Denkmal(n)	monumento	monumento	monumento
moquer(se)	make fun of, mock	verspotten	mofarse, burlarse	burlarsi	troçar
moquerie	mockery	Spott(m)	burla, mofa	canzonatura, beffa	zombaria, troça
moquette	carpet	Teppichboden(m)	moqueta	moquette	alcatifa
moral	morale	Stimmung(f), Moral(f)	moral, ánimo	morale	moral
moral, e	moral	moralisch	moral	morale	moral
morale	moral	Moral(f)	moral	morale	moral
morceau, bout	piece, bit	Stück(n)	pedazo, trozo	pezzo	pedaço
mordre	bite	beißen	morder	mordere	morder
morgue	mortuary	Leichenschauhaus(n)	depósito(cadáver.)	obitorio	morgue
morphine	morphine	Morphium(n)	morfina	morfina	morfina
morphologie	morphology	Morphologie(f)	morfología	morfologia	morfologia
mort	death	Tod(m)	muerte	morte	morte
mort, e	dead man/woman	Tote(f, m)	muerto, a	morto, a	morto, a
mort, e	dead	tot	muerto, a	morto, a	morto, a
mortalité	mortality	Sterblichkeit(f)	mortalidad	mortalità	mortalidade
mortel, le	mortal; deadly	tödlich	mortal	mortale	mortal
mortel, le	fatal	tödlich	mortal	mortale	mortal
mortier	mortar	Mörtel(m)	argamasa	malta, calcina	argamassa
morue	cod	Schellfisch(m)	bacalao	baccalà; merluzzo	bacalhau
mosaïque	mosaic	Mosaik(n)	mosaico	mosaico	mosaico
mosquée	mosque	Moschee(f)	mezquita	moschea	mesquita
mot	word	Wort(n)	palabra	parola	palavra
motard	motorcyclist	Motorradfahrer(in f)m	motorista	motociclista	motociclista
motel	motel	Motel(n)	motel	motel	motel
moteur	engine; motor	Motor(m)	motor	motore	motor
motif	motive	Motiv(n)	motivo	motivo	motivo
motiver	motivate	motivieren	motivar	motivare	motivar
moto	motor-bike	Motorrad(n)	moto	moto	mota

French	English	German	Spanish	Italian	Portuguese
mots croisés	crossword	Kreuzworträtsel(n)	crucigrama	cruciverba	palavras cruzadas
mou, molle	soft	weich	blando, a	molle; tenero, a	mole
mou, molle	lethargic	schlaff	fofo, a	molle; fiacco, a	mole; fraco, a
mouche	fly	Fliege(f)	mosca	mosca	mosca
moucher(se)	blow one's nose	Nase putzen	sonarse	soffiarsi il naso	assoar-se
mouchoir	handkerchief	Taschentuch(n)	pañuelo	fazzoletto	lenço
moudre	grind	mahlen	moler	macinare	moer
mouette	seagull	Möve(f)	gaviota	gabbiano	gaivota
mouillé, e	wet	naß	mojado, a	bagnato, a	molhado, a
mouiller	wet	an = feuchten	mojar	bagnare	molhar
moule	mould	Form(f)	molde	stampo, forma	molde; forma
moule	mussel	Muschel(f)	mejillón	cozza	mexilhão
moulin	mill	Mühle(f)	molino	mulino	moinho
mourir	die	sterben	morir	morire	morrer
mousse	moss	Moos(n)	musgo	muschio	musgo
mousse	froth, foam	Schaum(m)	espuma	schiuma	espuma
mousson	monsoon	Monsun(m)	monzón	monsone	monção
moustache	moustache	Schnurrbart(m)	bigote	baffo	bigode
moustique	mosquito(-es)	Mücke(f)	mosquito	zanzara	mosquito
moutarde	mustard	Senf(m)	mostaza	senape	mostarda
mouton	sheep; mutton	Schaf(n)	carnero; oveja	pecora; montone	carneiro; ovelha
mouvement	movement, motion	Bewegung(f)	movimiento	movimento	movimento
moyen, ne	middle	mittel	medio, a	medio, a	médio, a
moyen, ne	medium	mittlere(r, s)	medio, a	medio, a	médio, a
moyen	means	Mittel(n)	medio(s)	mezzo	meio
moyenne	average	Durchschnitt(m)	media	media	média
muet, te	dumb; silent	stumm	mudo, a	muto, a	mudo, a
multiple	multiple, numerous	viel-; vielfältig	múltiple	multiplo, a	múltiplo, a
multiplier	multiply	multiplizieren	multiplicar	moltiplicare	multiplicar
multitude	multitude	Menge(f)	multitud	moltitudine	multidão
municipal, e	municipal; town -	städtisch; Stadt-	municipal	municipale	municipal
munitions	ammunition	Munition(f)	municiones	munizioni	munições
mur	wall	Mauer(f)	muro, pared	muro	muro, parede
mûr, e	ripe	reif	maduro, a	maturo, a	maduro, a
mûr, e	mature	reif	maduro, a	maturo, a	maduro, a
murmurer	murmur, whisper	flüstern	murmurar	mormorare	murmurar
muscle	muscle	Muskel(m)	músculo	muscolo	músculo
musclé, e	muscular	muskulös	musculoso, a	muscoloso, a	musculado, a
musculaire	muscular	Muskel-	muscular	muscolare	muscular
museau	muzzle	Schnauze(f)	hocico	muso	focinho
musée	museum	Museum(n)	museo	museo	museu
musical, e	musical	musikalisch	musical	musicale	musical
musicien, ne	musician	Musiker(in f)m	músico, a	musicista	músico, a
musique	music	Musik(f)	música	musica	música
musulman, e	Moslem, Muslim	Mohammedaner(in f)m	musulmán, a	musulmano, a	muçulmano, a
mutation	transfer	Versetzung(f)	traslado	trasferimento	transferência
mutilé, e	disabled	verstümmelt	mutilado, a	mutilato, a	mutilado, a
mutuel, le	mutual	gegenseitig	mútuo, a	mutuo, a	mútuo, a
myope	short-sighted	kurzsichtig	miope	miope	míope
mystère	mystery	Geheimnis(n); Rätsel n	misterio	mistero	mistério
mystérieux, se	mysterious	mysteriös	misterioso, a	misterioso, a	misterioso, a
mystique	mystic(al)	mystisch	místico, a	mistico, a	místico, a
mythe	myth	Mythos(m); Sage(f)	mito	mito	mito

N

French	English	German	Spanish	Italian	Portuguese
nageoire	fin	Flosse(f)	aleta	pinna	barbatana
nager	swim	schwimmen	nadar	nuotare	nadar
nageur, se	swimmer	Schwimmer(in f)m	nadador, a	nuotatore, trice	nadador, a

French	English	German	Spanish	Italian	Portuguese
naïf, ïve	naïve	naïv	ingenuo, a	ingenuo, a	ingénuo, a
nain, e	dwarf	Zwerg(m)	enano, a	nano, a	anão, anã
naissance	birth	Geburt(f)	nacimiento	nascita	nascimento
naître	born(be)	geboren werden	nacer	nascere	nascer
nappe(eau)	sheet, expanse	Wasserfläche(f)	capa(de agua)	falda	lençol(de água)
nappe	table-cloth	Tischdecke(f)	mantel	tovaglia	toalha
narine	nostril	Nasenloch(n)	nariz	narice	narina
narcotique	narcotic	Betäubungsmittel(n)	narcótico	narcotico	narcótico
nasal, e	nasal	nasal	nasal	nasale	nasal
natal, e	native	Heimat-; Geburts-	natal	natale	natal
natalité	birth-rate	Geburtenrate(f)	natalidad	natalità	natalidade
natation, nage	swimming	Schwimmen(n)	natación	nuoto	natação
natif, ive	native	gebürtig	nativo, a	nativo, a	nativo, a
nation	nation	Nation(f)	nación	nazione	nação
national, e	national	national	nacional	nazionale	nacional
nationalisme	nationalism	Nationalismus(m)	nacionalismo	nazionalismo	nacionalismo
nationalité	nationality	Nationalität(f)	nacionalidad	nazionalità	nacionalidade
natte	plait	Zopf(m)	trenza	treccia	trança
naturalisé, e	naturalized	eingebürgert	nacionalizado, a	naturalizzato, a	naturalizado, a
nature	nature	Natur(f)	naturaleza	natura	natureza
naturel, le	natural	natürlich	natural	naturale	natural
naturiste	nudist	Nudist(in f)m	naturista	nudista	naturista
naufrage	wreck	Schiffbruch(m)	naufragio	naufragio	naufrágio
nausée	nausea, feel sick	Brechreiz(m)	náusea	nausea	naúsea
nautique	nautical, water-	nautisch, Wasser-	náutico, a	nautico, a	naútico, a
naval, e	naval	See-	naval	navale	naval
navigateur	navigator	Seefahrer(m)	navegante	navigatore	navegador
navigation	navigation	Seefahrt(f)	navegación	navigazione	navegação
navire	ship	Schiff(n)	navío	nave	navio
navré, e	sorry	leid tun	desconsolado, a	spiacente	desolado, a
né, e	born(be)	geboren	nacido, a	nato, a	nascido, a
nécessaire	necessary	nötig, notwendig	necesario, a	necessario, a	necessário, a
nécessité	necessity	Notwendigkeit(f)	necesidad	necessità	necessidade
négatif, ive	negative	negativ	negativo, a	negativo, a	negativo, a
négligence	negligence	Nachlässigkeit(f)	negligencia	negligenza	negligência
négligent, e	careless	nachlässig	descuidado, a	negligente	descuidado, a
négliger	neglect	vernachlässigen	descuidar	trascurare	descuidar
négociateur	negotiator	Unterhändler(in f)m	negociador, a	negoziatore, trice	negociador, a
négociation	negotiation	Verhandlung(f)	negociación	negoziato	negociação
négocier	negotiate	verhandeln	negociar	negoziare	negociar
négocier, traiter	deal	handeln	comerciar, tratar	negoziare, trattare	negociar, tratar
nègre, esse	negro(-ress), black	Neger(in f)m	negro, a	negro, a	negro, a
neige	snow	Schnee(m)	nieve	neve	neve
nerf	nerve	Nerv(m)	nervio	nervo	nervo
nerveux, se	nervous	nervös; Nerven-	nervioso, a	nervoso, a	nervoso, a
nerveux, se	nervy	nervös	nervioso, a	nervoso, a	nervoso, a
nettoyage	cleaning	Reinigung(f)	limpieza	pulizia	limpeza
nettoyer	clean	reinigen	limpiar	pulire	limpar
neuf	nine	neun	nueve	nove	nove
neuf, neuve	new	neu	nuevo, a	nuovo, a	novo, a
neurologie	neurology	Neurologie(f)	neurología	neurologia	neurologia
neutraliser	neutralize	neutralisieren	neutralizar	neutralizzare	neutralizar
neutre	neutral	neutral	neutro, a	neutro, a	neutro, a
neveu	nephew	Neffe(m)	sobrino	nipote(il)	sobrinho
névrose	neurosis(-ses)	Neurose(f)	neurosis	nevrosi	nevrose
nez	nose	Nase(f)	nariz	naso	nariz
ni	neither, nor	weder, noch	ni	né	nem
nickel	nickel	Nickel(n)	níquel	nichel	níquel
nicotine	nicotine	Nikotin(n)	nicotina	nicotina	nicotina
nid	nest	Nest(n)	nido	nido	ninho
nièce	niece	Nichte(f)	sobrina	nipote(la)	sobrinha
nier	deny	verneinen, leugnen	negar	negare	negar
niveau	level	Stand(m), Niveau(n)	nivel	livello	nível
niveau(de vie)	standard of living	Standard(m)	nivel(de vida)	tenore(di vita)	nível(de vida)
noble	noble	edel; nobel	noble	nobile	nobre
noble	nobleman/-woman	Edelmann m, Edelfrau f	noble	nobile	nobre
noce	wedding	Hochzeit(f)	boda	nozze	boda
nocif, ive	harmful	schädlich	nocivo, a	nocivo, a	nocivo, a

84

French	English	German	Spanish	Italian	Portuguese
nocturne	nocturnal, night-	nächtlich	nocturno, a	notturno, a	nocturno, a
Noël	Christmas	Weihnachten(n)	Navidad	Natale	Natal
noeud	knot	Knoten(m)	nudo	nodo	nó, laço
noeud papillon	bow tie	Fliege(f)	pajarita	papillon	laço
noir, e	black	schwarz	negro, a	nero, a	preto, a
noir, e	black(person)	Schwarze(f, m)	negro, a	negro, a	negro, a
noix	walnut	Walnuß(f)	nuez	noce	noz
noix de coco	coconut	Kokosnuß(f)	coco	noce di cocco	coco
nom	name	Name(m)	nombre	nome	nome
nom	surname	Familienname(m)	apellido	cognome	apelido
nom, substantif	noun	Hauptwort(n)	nombre	nome, sostantivo	substantivo
nomade	nomad	Nomade(m)	nómada	nomade	nómada
nombre	number	Anzahl(f), Zahl(f)	número	numero	número
nombreux, se	numerous, many	zahlreich	numeroso, a	numeroso, a	numeroso, a
nombril	navel	Nabel(m)	ombligo	ombelico	umbigo
nomination	nomination	Ernennung(f)	nombramiento	nomina	nomeação
nommer	name	nennen	llamar	chiamare	chamar
nommer	appoint	ernennen	nombrar	nominare	nomear
nommer(se)	called(be)	heißen	llamarse	chiamarsi	chamar-se
non	no	nein	no	no	não
non-fumeur	non-smoker	Nichtraucher(m)	no-fumadores	non-fumatore	não-fumador
non merci	no thank you	nein, danke	no, gracias	no, grazie	não, obrigado
Nord	North	Norden(m)	Norte	Nord	Norte
nordique	nordic; northern	nordisch; nördlich	nórdico, a	nordico, a	nórdico, a
normal, e	normal; usual	normal	normal	normale	normal
norme	norm, standard	Norm(f)	norma	norma	norma
nos	our	unser(e)	nuestros, nuestras	nostri, e(i, le)	nossos, nossas
nostalgie	homesickness	Heimweh(n)	nostalgia	nostalgia	nostalgia
notaire	solicitor, lawyer	Notar(m)	notario	notaio	notário
notamment	particular(in)	besonders, nämlich	particularmente	particolarmente	particularmente
note	note	Vermerk(m)	nota	appunto	nota
note	bill	Rechnung(f)	cuenta	conto	conta
note	note	Note(f)	nota	nota	nota
note	mark	Note(f)	nota	voto	nota
noter	note; notice	notieren; bemerken	anotar	notare	anotar, notar
notifier	notify	bekannt = geben	notificar	notificare	notificar
notion	notion	Kenntnis(f), Begriff m	noción	nozione	noção
notoriété	notoriety	Offenkundigkeit(f)	notoriedad	notorietà	notoriedade
notre	our	unser, unsere	nuestro, a	nostro, a(il, la)	nosso, a
nôtre(le, la)	ours	unsere(der, die, das)	nuestro, a(el, la)	nostro, a(il, la)	nosso, a(o, a)
nouilles	noodles	Nudeln(f, pl)	macarrones	tagliatelle, pasta	massa
nourrir	feed, nourish	ernähren	alimentar	nutrire	alimentar
nourriture	food	Nahrung(f)	alimento	cibo; nutrimento	alimentação
nous	we	wir	nosotros	noi	nós
nous	us	uns	nos	ci, ce	nos
nouveau, nouvelle	new	neu	nuevo, a	nuovo, a	novo, a
nouveau-né, e	new-born baby	Neugeborene(n)	recién nacido, a	neonato, a	recém-nascido, a
nouvelles	news	Nachrichten(f, pl)	noticias	notizie	notícias
nouveauté	novelty	Neuheit(f)	novedad	novità	novidade
novembre	November	November(m)	noviembre	novembre	Novembro
novice, débutant	novice	Neuling(m)	novicio, a; novato, a	novizio, a	principiante
noyau	stone	Kern(m)	hueso	nocciolo	caroço
noyau	nucleus(-ei)	Kern(m)	núcleo	nucleo	núcleo
noyer(se)	drown	ertrinken	ahogar(se)	annegare	afogar-se
nu, e	naked; bare	nackt	desnudo, a	nudo, a	nu, nua
nuage	cloud	Wolke(f)	nube	nuvola	nuvem
nuance, ton	shade, nuance	Farbenton(m)	matiz	sfumatura	matiz, tom
nucléaire	nuclear	Kern-, Atom-	nuclear	nucleare	nuclear
nuisible	harmful	schädlich	dañino, a	nocivo, a	nocivo, a
nuit	night	Nacht(f)	noche	notte	noite
nul, le	worthless; useless	wertlos	nulo, a	nullo, a	nulo, a
numérique	numerical	numerisch	numérico, a	numerico, a	numérico, a
numéro	number	Nummer(f)	número	numero	número
nuque	nape of the neck	Nacken(m)	nuca	nuca	nuca
numéro, tirage	issue	Auflage(f)	número, edición	numero, pubblicazione	número
nurse	nanny	Kindermädchen(n)	niñera	bambinaia	ama
nutritif, ive	nutritious	nahrhaft	nutritivo, a	nutritivo, a	nutritivo, a
nylon	nylon	Nylon(m)	nilón	nylon	nylon

F

O

French	English	German	Spanish	Italian	Portuguese
oasis	oasis(oases pl.)	Oase(f)	oasis	oasi	oásis
obéir	obey	gehorchen	obedecer	obbedire	obedecer
obèse	obese	füllig, fettleibig	obeso, a	obeso, a	obeso, a
objectif, ive	objective	objektiv, sachlich	objetivo, a	oggettivo, a	objectivo, a
objectif	objective	Objektiv(n), Ziel(n)	objetivo	obiettivo	objectivo
objectif	lens	Objektiv(n)	objetivo	obiettivo	objectiva
objection	objection, protest	Einwand(m)	objeción, reparo	obiezione	objecção
objet	object	Objekt(n), Ding(n)	objeto	oggetto	objecto
objet, thème	theme, subject	Thema(n), Objekt(n)	objeto, tema	oggetto, scopo	tema, assunto
objets de valeur	valuables	Wertsachen(f pl)	objetos de valor	oggetti di valore	objectos de valor
obligation	obligation	Verpflichtung(f)	obligación	obbligo	obrigação
obligatoire	compulsory	obligatorisch	obligatorio, a	obbligatorio, a	obrigatório, a
obligatoire	mandatory	obligatorisch	obligatorio, a	obbligatorio, a	obrigatório, a
obliger	oblige, force	zwingen	obligar	obbligare	obrigar
oblique	oblique, slanting	schräg, schief	oblicuo, a	obliquo, a	oblíquo, a
obscène	obscene	obszön	obsceno, a	osceno, a	obsceno, a
obscurité	darkness	Dunkelheit(f)	oscuridad	oscurità, buio	obscuridade
obsédé, e	maniac	Besessene(m, f)	obseso, a	maniaco, a	obcecado, a
obséder	obsess	verfolgen, quälen	obsesionar	ossessionare	obcecar
observateur	observer	Beobachter(in f)m	observador, a	osservatore, trice	observador, a
observer	observe	beobachten	observar	osservare	observar
obsession	obsession	fixe Idee(f)	obsesión	ossessione	obsessão
obstacle	obstacle	Hindernis(n)	obstáculo	ostacolo	obstáculo
obstruction	obstruction	Störung(f)	obstrucción	ostruzione	obstrucção
obtenir	obtain, get	erhalten	obtener	ottenere	obter
obtenir, recevoir	get, obtain	bekommen	obtener	ottenere	obter
obus	shell	Geschoß(n), Granate(f)	obús	proiettile	obus
occasion	opportunity	Gelegenheit(f)	oportunidad	occasione	oportunidade
occasion	second-hand, used	gebraucht	segunda mano	seconda mano	segunda mão(em)
occasionnel, le	occasional	gelegentlich	ocasional, a	occasionale	ocasional
occasionner	cause, bring about	verursachen	ocasionar, causar	causare	ocasionar, causar
occidental, e	Western	westlich	occidental	occidentale	ocidental
occupé, e	busy	beschäftigt	ocupado, a	impegnato, a	ocupado, a
occupé, e	engaged; taken	besetzt	ocupado, a	occupato, a	ocupado, a
occupé, e	occupied	besetzt	ocupado, a	occupato, a	ocupado, a
occuper	occupy, fill	ein = nehmen	ocupar	occupare	ocupar
occuper(s')	deal with	beschäftigen, sich	dedicarse a	occuparsi	tratar de
occuper(s')	look after	kümmern sich/um	ocuparse	occuparsi	tomar conta
occurence(en l')	case(in this)	vorliegenden Fall(im)	caso(en este)	nella circostanza	caso(neste)
océan	ocean	Ozean(m)	océano	oceano	oceano
océanique	oceanic	ozeanisch	oceánico, a	oceanico, a	oceânico, a
octobre	October	Oktober(m)	octubre	ottobre	Outubro
oculiste	oculist	Augenarzt m/-ärztin f	oculista	oculista	oftalmologista
odeur	odour, smell	Geruch(m)	olor	odore	cheiro, odor
odieux, se	odious, obnoxious	widerwärtig	odioso, a	odioso, a	odioso, a
odorat	smell(sense of)	Geruchssinn(m)	olfato	odorato	olfacto
oeil	eye	Auge(n)	ojo	occhio	olho
oesophage	oesophagus	Speiseröhre(f)	esófago	esofago	esófago
oeuf	egg	Ei(n)	huevo	uovo(a)	ovo
oeuvre, travail	work	Werk(n)	obra	opera	obra
offensive	offensive	Offensive(f)	ofensiva	offensiva	ofensiva
officiel, le	official	offiziell	oficial	ufficiale	oficial
officier	officer	Offizier(m)	oficial	ufficiale	oficial
officieux, se	unofficial	halbamtlich	oficioso, a	ufficioso, a	oficioso, a
offre	offer	Angebot(n)	oferta	offerta	oferta
offrir	give; offer	schenken, an = bieten	ofrecer	offrire, regalare	oferecer
oie	goose(geese pl.)	Gans(f)	oca	oca	ganso
oignon	onion	Zwiebel(f)	cebolla	cipolla	cebola
oiseau	bird	Vogel(m)	pájaro, ave	uccello	pássaro, ave
olive	olive	Olive(f)	aceituna, oliva	oliva	azeitona
olympique	Olympic	olympisch	olímpico, a	olimpico, a	olímpico, a

French	English	German	Spanish	Italian	Portuguese
ombre	shadow	Schatten(m)	sombra	ombra	sombra
ombrelle	sunshade, parasol	Sonnenschirm(m)	sombrilla	ombrello, parasole	sombrinha
omettre	omit	aus = lassen	omitir	omettere	omitir
oncle	uncle	Onkel(m)	tío	zio	tio
onctueux, se	unctuous	cremig, sahnig	untuoso, a	untuoso, a	untuoso, a
onde	wave	Welle(f)	onda	onda	onda
ongle	nail	Fingernagel(m)	uña	unghia	unha
onze	eleven	elf	once	undici	onze
opaque	opaque	undurchsichtig; trüb	opaco, a	opaco, a	opaco, a
opéra	opera	Oper(f)	ópera	opera	ópera
opération	operation	Operation(f)	operación	operazione	operação
opérer	operate	wirken	efectuar	operare	fazer
opérer	operate(on)	operieren	operar	operare	operar
opérette	operetta	Operette(f)	zarzuela, opereta	operetta	opereta
ophtalmologie	ophthalmology	Augenheilkunde(f)	oftalmología	oftalmologia	oftalmologia
opinion	opinion	Meinung(f)	opinión	opinione	opinião
opportun, e	opportune	günstig	oportuno, a	opportuno, a	oportuno, a
opposé, e	opposed to	entgegengesetzt	opuesto, a	opposto, a	contra(ser)
opposé, e	opposing	entgegengesetzt	opuesto, a	opposto, a	oposto, a
opposé, e	opposite	gegenüberliegend	opuesto, a	opposto, a	oposto, a
opposer(s')	oppose	widersetzen, sich	oponerse	opporsi	opor-se
opposition	opposition	Opposition(f)	oposición	opposizione	oposição
opprimé, e	oppressed	unterdrückt	oprimido, a	oppresso, a	oprimido, a
opticien, ne	optician	Optiker(in f)m	óptico, a	ottico, a	oculista
optimiste	optimistic	optimistisch	optimista	ottimista	optimista
option, choix	option	Wahl(f)	opción	opzione	opção
optique	optic(al)	optisch	óptico, a	ottico, a	óptico, a
or	gold	Gold(n)	oro	oro	ouro
orage	storm, thunderstorm	Gewitter(n)	tormenta	temporale	tempestade
oral, e	oral	mündlich	oral	orale	oral
orange	orange	Apfelsine(f)	naranja	arancia	laranja
orange	orange	orangefarben	anaranjado, a	arancione	cor-de-laranja
orateur, trice	speaker, orator	Redner(in f)m	orador, a; locutor, a	oratore, trice	orador, a
orbite	orbit	Umlaufbahn(f)	órbita	orbita	órbita
orchestre	orchestra; band	Orchester(n)	orquesta	orchestra	orquestra
orchidée	orchid	Orchidee(f)	orquídea	orchidea	orquídia
ordinaire	ordinary	gewöhnlich	ordinario, a	ordinario, a	ordinário, a
ordinateur	computer	Computer(m)	ordenador	computer	computador
ordonnance	prescription	Rezept(n)	receta	ricetta medica	receita
ordonner	order	befehlen, verordnen	ordenar	ordinare	ordenar
ordonner	command, order	befehlen, beherrschen	mandar, ordenar	comandare, ordinare	mandar, ordenar
ordre	order	Ordnung(f)	orden	ordine	ordem
ordre	order	Rangordnung(f)	orden	ordine	ordem
ordre	order	Befehl(m)	orden	ordine	ordem
ordure(s)	rubbish, garbage	Abfall(m)	basura	immondizia	lixo
oreille	ear	Ohr(n)	oreja	orecchio	orelha
oreiller	pillow	Kopfkissen(n)	almohada	guanciale	travesseiro
oreillons	mumps	Mumps(m)	paperas	orecchioni	trasorelho
organe	organ	Organ(n)	órgano	organo	órgão
organique	organic	organisch	orgánico, a	organico, a	orgânico, a
organisateur	organizer	Organisator(in f)m	organizador, a	organizzatore, trice	organizador, a
organisation	organization	Organisation(f)	organización	organizzazione	organização
organiser	organize	organisieren	organizar	organizzare	organizar
organisme	organism	Organismus(m)	organismo	organismo	organismo
orgasme	orgasm	Orgasmus(m)	orgasmo	orgasmo	orgasmo
orgie	orgy	Orgie(f)	orgía	orgia	orgia
orgue	organ	Orgel(f)	órgano	organo	órgão
orgueil	pride, arrogance	Stolz(m)	orgullo	orgoglio	orgulho
orgueilleux, se	proud, arrogant	stolz, arrogant	orgulloso, a	orgoglioso, a	orgulhoso, a
oriental, e	oriental	orientalisch	oriental	orientale	oriental
orientation	orientation	Orientierung(f)	orientación	orientamento	orientação
orienter	position	orientieren	orientar	orientare	orientar
orifice	orifice, aperture	Öffnung(f), Mündung(f)	orificio	orifizio	orifício
originaire	native(of)	gebürtig	oriundo, a	originario, a	oriundo, a
original, e	original	original	original	originale	original
original	original	Original(n)	original	originale	original
origine	origin	Ursprung(m)	origen	origine	origem
ornement	ornament	Verzierung; Schmuck	adorno	ornamento	ornamento

87

French	English	German	Spanish	Italian	Portuguese
orphelin, e	orphan	Waise(f, m)	huérfano, a	orfano, a	órfão, órfã
orteil	toe	Zehe(f)	dedo del pie	dito del piede	dedo do pé
orthodoxe	orthodox	orthodox	ortodoxo, a	ortodosso, a	ortodoxo, a
orthographe	spelling	Rechtschreibung(f)	ortografía	ortografia	ortografia
os	bone	Knochen(m)	hueso	osso	osso
osciller	oscillate	schwanken	oscilar	oscillare	oscilar
oser	dare	wagen	osar, atreverse	osare	ousar, atrever-se
ossature	structure	Struktur(f)	armazón	ossatura	ossatura
otage	hostage	Geisel(f)	rehén	ostaggio	refém
ôter, enlever	remove, take away	ab = nehmen	quitar	togliere	tirar
otite	ear-ache	Mittelohrentzündung f	otitis	otite	otite
ou	or	oder	o; u	o	ou
où	where	wo	donde, dónde	dove	onde
oublier	forget	vergessen	olvidar	dimenticare	esquecer
Ouest	West	Westen(m)	Oeste	Ovest	Oeste
oui	yes	ja	sí	sì	sim
ouïe	hearing, audition	Gehör(n)	oído	udito	ouvido
ouragan	hurricane	Orkan(m)	huracán	uragano	furacão
ours	bear	Bär(m)	oso	orso	urso
outil	tool	Werkzeug(n)	herramienta	attrezzo	ferramenta
outillage	tools, equipment	Werkzeug(n)	herramientas	attrezzatura	ferramentas
outre(en)	besides	außerdem; außer	además(de)	inoltre; per di più	além disso; além de
outre-mer	overseas	überseeisch	ultramar	oltremare	ultramar
ouvert, e	open	offen; geöffnet	abierto, a	aperto, a	aberto, a
ouverture	opening	Öffnungszeiten(f, pl)	apertura	apertura	abertura
ouvrage	work	Arbeit(f)	tarea, trabajo	opera, lavoro	obra, trabalho
ouvrage	work	Werk(n)	obra	lavoro	obra
ouvre-boîte(s)	tin/can opener	Büchsenöffner(m)	abrelatas	apriscatole	abre-latas
ouvrier, ière	worker, workman	Arbeiter(in f)m	obrero, a	operaio, a	operário, a
ouvrir	open	öffnen	abrir	aprire	abrir
ovaire	ovary	Eierstock(m)	ovario	ovaia	ovário
ovale	oval	oval	oval, ovalado, a	ovale	oval
ovin	ovine	Schaf-	ovino	ovino	ovino
ovule	ovule	Ei(zelle f)n	óvulo	ovulo	óvulo
oxydation	oxidization	Oxydierung(f)	oxidación	ossidazione	oxidação
oxygène	oxygen	Sauerstoff(m)	oxígeno	ossigeno	oxigénio
ozone	ozone	Ozon(n)	ozono	ozono	ozone

P

French	English	German	Spanish	Italian	Portuguese
pacifique	peaceful, pacific	friedlich	pacífico, a	pacifico, a	pacífico, a
Pacifique	Pacific Ocean	Pazifik(m)	Pacífico	Pacifico	Pacífico
pacte	pact	Pakt(m)	pacto	patto	pacto
pagaille	mess	Durcheinander(n)	follón, lío	caos, confusione	desordem
page	page	Seite(f)	página	pagina	página
paie(paye)	pay	Lohn(m)	paga	paga, stipendio	paga, ordenado
paiement	payment	Bezahlung(f)	pago, abono	pagamento	pagamento
paille	straw	Stroh(n)	paja	paglia	palha
paillette	glitter, spangle	Flitter(m)	lentejuela	lustrino	lentejoula
paillotte	hut(straw-hut)	Strohhütte(f)	choza	capanna	palhota
pain	bread	Brot(n)	pan	pane	pão
pain grillé	toast	Toast(m)	tostadas	pane tostato	pão torrado
pair	even	gerade	par	pari	par
paire	pair(of)	Paar(n)	par	paio	par
paisible	peaceful, quiet	friedlich, ruhig	apacible	pacifico a; placido, a	pacífico, a
paix	peace	Frieden(m)	paz	pace	paz
palais	palace	Palast(m)	palacio	palazzo	palácio

French	English	German	Spanish	Italian	Portuguese
pâle	pale	blaß	pálido, a	pallido, a	pálido, a
palmarès	list of winners	Preisträgerliste(f)	lista de premios	albo dei premiati	quadro de honra
palme	flipper	Flosse(f)	aleta	pinna	barbatanas
palmier	palm-tree	Palme(f)	palmera	palma	palmeira
palper, tâter	feel, finger	betasten	palpar	palpare	apalpar
palpitation	palpitation	Herzklopfen(n)	palpitación	palpitazione	palpitação
paludisme	malaria	Sumpffieber(n)	paludismo	malaria, paludismo	paludismo
pamplemousse	grapefruit	Pampelmuse(f)	pomelo	pompelmo	toranja
pancarte	sign, notice	Plakat(n), Schild(n)	pancarta	cartello	cartaz
panier	basket	Korb(m)	cesto	paniere, cesto	cesto
panique	panic	Panik(f)	pánico	panico	pânico
panne	breakdown	Panne(f)	avería	guasto, panna	avaria
panneau	panel	Brett(n)	tablero	cartello	painel
panneau	sign, notice	Schild(n)	señal, letrero	cartello	sinal
panse	belly, paunch	Bauch(m); Pansen(m)	panza	pancia	pança
pansement	plaster, bandage	Verband(m)	cura, vendaje	medicazione	penso, curativo
pantalon	trousers	Hose(f)	pantalón	pantalone	calças
panthère	panther	Panther(m)	pantera	pantera	pantera
pantin	puppet	Hampelmann(m)	títere	burattino	fantoche
pantoufle	slipper	Pantoffel(m)	zapatilla	pantofola	pantufa, chinelo
papa	Daddy, Dad	Papa	papá	papà, babbo	papá
Pape	Pope	Papst(m)	Papa	Papa	Papa
papeterie	stationer's	Schreibwarenladen(m)	papelería	cartoleria	papelaria
papier	paper	Papier(n)	papel	carta	papel
papiers(les)	papers	Papiere(pl); Ausweise	documentación	documenti	documentos
papier toilette	toilet paper	Toilettenpapier(n)	papel higiénico	carta igienica	papel higiénico
papillon	butterfly	Schmetterling(m)	mariposa	farfalla	borboleta
paquebot	liner	Passagierdampfer(m)	buque	transatlantico	paquete
Pâques	Easter	Ostern(n)	Pascua	Pasqua	Páscoa
paquet	packet; package	Paket(n)	paquete	pacco	pacote
par	by, through	durch	por	per, da	por
par	per	per	por	per	por
parachute	parachute	Fallschirm(m)	paracaídas	paracadute	pára-quedas
parade	parade	Parade(f)	parada, desfile	parata	parada
paradis	paradise	Paradies(n)	paraíso	paradiso	paraíso
paradoxe	paradox	Paradox(n)	paradoja	paradosso	paradoxo
paragraphe	paragraph	Absatz(m), Abschnitt m	párrafo	paragrafo	parágrafo
paraître	seem, appear, look	scheinen, erscheinen	parecer	parere, sembrare	parecer
parallèle	parallel	parallel	paralelo, a	parallelo, a	paralelo, a
paralysé, e	paralysed	gelähmt	paralítico, a	paralitico, a	paralítico, a
paralysie	paralysis	Lähmung(f)	parálisis	paralisi	paralisia
paranoïa	paranoia	Paranoia(f)	paranoia	paranoia	paranóia
parapluie	umbrella	Regenschirm(m)	paraguas	ombrello	chapéu de chuva
parasite	parasite	Parasit(m)	parásito	parassita	parasita
parasol	parasol, sunshade	Sonnenschirm(m)	parasol	ombrellone	guarda-sol
parc	park	Park(m)	parque	parco	parque
parcelle	plot	Parzelle(f)	parcela	parcella	parcela
parce que	because	weil, da	porque	perché	porque
parcours	journey; course	Strecke(f), Route(f)	recorrido	percorso	percurso
pardessus	overcoat	Mantel(m)	abrigo	soprabito	sobretudo
pardon	forgiveness	Vergebung(f)	perdón	scusa, perdono	perdão
pardon!	sorry!, excuse me!	Verzeihung!	perdón (!), disculpe	scusi!	perdão!, desculpe!
pardonner	forgive, pardon	verzeihen, vergeben	perdonar	perdonare	perdoar
pare-brise	windscreen	Windschutzscheibe(f)	parabrisas	parabrezza	pára-brisas
pareil, le	same, similar, like	gleich, wie	igual	uguale, pari	igual
parent, e	relative, relation	verwandt	pariente	parente	parente
parenté	relationship	Verwandtschaft(f)	parentesco	parentela	parentesco
parenthèse	bracket	Klammer(f)	paréntesis	parentesi	parêntesis
parents	parents	Eltern(pl)	padres	genitori	pais
paresseux, se	lazy	faul	perezoso, a	pigro, a	preguiçoso, a
parfait, e	perfect	einwandfrei	perfecto, a	perfetto, a	perfeito, a
parfois	sometimes	manchmal	a veces	talvolta	às vezes
parfum	perfume, scent	Parfüm(n)	perfume	profumo	perfume
parfumerie	perfume shop	Parfümerie(f)	perfumería	profumeria	perfumaria
pari	bet	Wette(f)	apuesta	scommessa	aposta
parking	car park	Parkplatz(m)	aparcamiento	parcheggio	p.estacionamento
parlement	parliament	Parlament(n)	parlamento	parlamento	parlamento
parler	speak, talk	sprechen, reden	hablar	parlare	falar

French	English	German	Spanish	Italian	Portuguese
parler à	talk to, speak to	reden(mit jdm)	hablar con	parlare a	falar com
parler(le)	speech	Sprechen(n); Sprache f	habla(el)	parlare(il)	fala(a)
parmi	among	unter	entre	fra, tra	entre
paroi, mur	wall	Wand(f)	pared	parete	parede
parole	word; speech	Wort(n)	palabra	parola	palavra
parrain	godfather	Pate(m)	padrino	padrino	padrinho
parrainer	sponsor	sponsorisieren	patrocinar	sponsorizzare	apadrinhar
part, partie	share; part	Anteil(m); Teil(m, n)	parte	parte	parte
partager	share, divide	teilen	repartir	dividere	repartir
partenaire	partner	Partner(in f)m	pareja	socio, a; partner	parceiro, a
parterre	flower-bed	Beet(n)	arriate	aiuola	canteiro
parti	party	Partei(f)	partido	partito	partido
participer à	participate in	beteiligen, sich	participar en	partecipare a	participar a
participer(à)	take part(in)	teil = nehmen	participar(en)	partecipare(a)	participar(em)
particule	particle	Teilchen(n)	partícula	particella	partícula
particulier, ière	particular	eigentümlich	particular	particolare	particular
particulier	individual	Privatmann(m)	particular	privato	particular
particulièrement	especially	besonders	especialmente	particolarmente	especialmente
partie, part	part	Teil(m n)	parte	pezzo, parte	parte
partie	game	Spiel(n)	partida	partita	jogada, jogo
partir	leave, go away	weg = gehen	salir, marcharse	partire	partir, abalar
partisan, e	partisan	Anhänger(in f)m	partidario, a	partigiano, a	partidário, a
partition	score(music)	Partitur(f)	partitura	spartito	partitura
partout	everywhere	überall	por todas partes	dappertutto	por toda a parte
parure	finery, jewellery	Schmuck(m)	adorno	parure	adorno
parvenir	reach, arrive at	erreichen	conseguir	giungere	chegar; conseguir
pas	step; pace	Schritt(m)	paso	passo	passo
pas	not	nicht	no	non	não, nem
passage	passage	Durchgang(m)	pasaje, paso	passaggio	passagem
passager, ère	passenger	Passagier(in f)m	pasajero, a	passeggero, a	passageiro, a
passé, e	past	vergangen	pasado, a	passato, a	passado, a
passé	past	Vergangenheit(f)	pasado	passato	passado
passeport	passport	Paß(m)	pasaporte	passaporto	passaporte
passer	pass, go(through)	fahren über	pasar	passare	passar(por; em)
passer	call, drop in	vorbei = kommen	pasar	passare	passar
passer	spend	verbringen	pasar	trascorrere	passar
passer(examen)	take(an exam)	ab = legen(Prüfung f)	pasar(un examen)	dare(un esame)	fazer(exame)
passe-temps	hobby, pastime	Hobby(n)	pasatiempo	passatempo	passatempo
passif, ive	passive	passiv	pasivo, a	passivo, a	passivo, a
passion	passion	Leidenschaft(f)	pasión	passione	paixão
passionnant, e	fascinating	spannend	apasionante	appassionante	apaixonante
passionné, e	interested(very)	leidenschaftlich	apasionado, a	appassionato, a	apaixonado, a
pasteur	vicar, minister	Pastor(in f)m	pastor	pastore	padre; pastor
pâte	paste	Paste(f); Masse(f)	masa, pasta	impasto, pasta	massa
pâte	pastry, dough	Teig(m)	masa	pasta	massa
pâté	paté	Pastete(f)	paté	patè	paté
paternel, le	paternal	väterlich	paterno, a	paterno, a	paterno, a
pâtes	pasta, noodles	Nudeln(f, pl)	pastas(aliment.)	pasta	massa
pâteux, se	pasty	pappig	pastoso, a	pastoso, a	pastoso, a
patience	patience	Geduld(f)	paciencia	pazienza	paciência
patient, e	patient	geduldig	paciente	paziente	paciente
patinage	skating	Eiskunstlauf(m)	patinaje	pattinaggio	patinagem
patiner	skate	Schlittschuh laufen	patinar	pattinare	patinar
patinoire	skating rink	Eisbahn(f)	pista de patinar	pista da pattinaggio	pista de patinagem
pâtisserie	cake shop	Konditorei(f)	pastelería	pasticceria	pastelaria
pâtisserie(s)	pastry, cake	Backwaren(f, pl)	pasteles	dolci	pastelaria
patriarche	patriarch	Patriarch(m)	patriarca	patriarca	patriarca
patrie	native land	Vaterland(n)	patria	patria	pátria
patrimoine	patrimony	Familiengut(n)	patrimonio	patrimonio	património
patron, ne	boss; employer	Chef(m), Arbeitgeber m	patrón, a; dueño, a	padrone, a	patrão, patroa
patron, dirigeant	manager, boss	Unternehmer(in f)m	director, jefe	manager, padrone	director, patrão
patrouille	patrol	Patrouille(f), Streife	patrulla	pattuglia	patrulha
patte	paw; leg; foot	Pfote(f); Bein(n)	pata	zampa	pata
paume	palm	Handfläche(f)	palma	palma	palma
paupière	eyelid	Lid(n)	párpado	palpebra	pálpebra
pause	pause, break	Pause(f)	pausa	pausa	pausa
pauvre	poor	arm	pobre	povero, a	pobre
pauvreté	poverty	Armut(f)	pobreza	povertà	pobreza

French	English	German	Spanish	Italian	Portuguese
pavé	paving-stone	Pflasterstein(m)	adoquín	selce, selciato	pedra de calçada
payement	payment	Zahlung(f)	abono, pago	pagamento	pagamento
payer	pay	bezahlen	pagar	pagare	pagar
pays	country	Land(n)	país	paese	país
paysage	landscape	Landschaft(f)	paisaje	paesaggio	paisagem
paysan, ne	farmer	Bauer(m), Bäuerin(f)	campesino, a	contadino, a	camponês, a
péage	toll	Autobahngebühr(f)	peaje	pedaggio	portagem
peau	skin	Haut(f)	piel	pelle	pele
pêche	peach(-es)	Pfirsich(m)	melocotón	pesca	pêssego
pêche	fishing, angling	Fischen n; Fischfang m	pesca	pesca	pesca
pêche	angling	Angeln(n)	pesca(con caña)	pesca(con lenza)	pesca(à linha)
péché	sin	Sünde(f)	pecado	peccato	pecado
pêcheur	fisherman(-men)	Fischer(m)	pescador	pescatore	pescador
pédale	pedal	Pedal(n)	pedal	pedale	pedal
pédant, e	pedantic	pedantisch	pedante	pedante	pedante; vaidoso, a
pédiatre	paediatrician	Kinderarzt(m)/-ärztin	pediatra	pediatra	pediatra
pédicure	chiropodist	Fußpfleger(in f)m	pedicuro, a	pedicure	pedicuro
pédigree	pedigree	Stammbaum(Tier-)(m)	pedigrí	pedigree	pedigree
pègre	underworld	Unterwelt(f)	hampa	teppa, malviventi	súcia, ladroagem
peigne	comb	Kamm(m)	peine	pettine	pente
peigner(se)	comb(one's hair)	kämmen	peinar(se)	pettinarsi	pentear-se
peignoir	dressing gown	Morgenmantel(m)	bata	accappatoio	roupão
peindre	paint	streichen	pintar	imbiancare	pintar
peindre	paint	malen	pintar	dipingere	pintar
peine	sorrow, grief	Schmerz(m), Kummer(m)	pena	pena; dolore	pena; tristeza
peine	trouble, effort	Anstrengung(f)	dificultad	fatica	esforço
peine	sentence	Bestrafung(f)	pena, castigo	punizione, castigo	pena
peintre	painter	Anstreicher; Maler(m)	pintor, a	pittore, trice	pintor, a
peinture	painting	Malerei(f)	pintura	pittura; dipinto	pintura
peinture	paint	Farbe(f)	pintura	vernice, pittura	tinta
pelage	coat, fur	Fell(n)	pelaje, pelo	pelo	pêlo
peler	peel	schälen	mondar	sbucciare	descascar
pèlerin	pilgrim	Pilger(in f)m	peregrino	pellegrino, a	peregrino
pèlerinage	pilgrimage	Wallfahrt(f)	peregrinación	pellegrinaggio	peregrinação
pelle	spade; shovel	Schaufel(f); Spaten(m)	pala	pala	pá
pellicule	dandruff	Schuppe(f)	caspa	forfora	caspa
pellicule	film	Film(m)	película	pellicola	película
pelouse	lawn	Rasenfläche(f)	césped	prato inglese	relvado
pénal, e	penal	strafrechtlich	penal	penale	penal
pénalité	penalty	Strafe(f), Strafpunkt	penalidad	penalità	penalidade
pencher	tilt, lean	neigen	inclinar	inclinare	inclinar
pencher(se)	bend, lean	bücken, sich	inclinarse	chinarsi	inclinar-se
pencher(se)	lean out	hinaus = lehnen	asomarse	sporgersi	debruçar-se
pendant	during; for	während	durante	durante	durante
pendant que	while	während	mientras	mentre; già che	enquanto
pendre	hang	hängen, auf = hängen	colgar	appendere	pendurar
pénétrer	enter, penetrate	ein = dringen	penetrar	penetrare	penetrar
pénible	hard, arduous	mühsam, schwierig	penoso, a; duro, a	penoso, a	penoso, a
pénicilline	penicillin	Penizillin(n)	penicilina	penicillina	penicilina
péninsule	peninsula	Halbinsel(f)	península	penisola	península
pensée	thought	Gedanke(m)	pensamiento	pensiero	pensamento
penser	think	denken	pensar	pensare	pensar
pension	guest-house	Gasthaus(n)	pensión	pensione	pensão
pension	pension; allowance	Pension(f)	pensión	pensione	pensão
pensionnaire	lodger	Untermieter(in f)m	huésped	ospite	hóspede
pensionnaire	resident	Pensionsgast(m)	pensionista	pensionante	hóspede
pensionnaire	boarder	Internatsschüler(m)	interno, a	collegiale	interno, a
pente	slope	Hang(m), Abhang(m)	declive	pendio, discesa	declive
pénurie	shortage	Mangel(m)	penuria, escasez	penuria	penúria
pépin	pip	Kern(m)	pepita	seme	caroço
perceptible	perceptible	wahrnehmbar	perceptible	percettibile	perceptível
percer	drill; pierce	bohren	perforar	bucare, forare	furar
percevoir	perceive	wahr = nehmen	percibir	percepire	perceber
perdre	lose	verlieren	perder	perdere	perder
perdu, e	lost	verloren	perdido, a	perso, a; smarrito, a	perdido, a
père	father	Vater(m)	padre	padre	pai
perfection	perfection	Vollkommenheit(f)	perfección	perfezione	perfeição
perfectionner	improve; perfect	vervollkommnen	perfeccionar	perfezionare	aperfeiçoar

French	English	German	Spanish	Italian	Portuguese
perfide	treacherous	heimtückisch	pérfido, a	perfido, a	pérfido, a
perforer	perforate	durchbohren	perforar	perforare	perfurar
performance	performance	Leistung(f)	proeza, hazaña	prestazione	desempenho
péril	peril, danger	Gefahr(f)	peligro, riesgo	pericolo	perigo
périmé, e	expired	verfallen	caducado, a	scaduto, a	caducado, a
périmètre	perimeter	Umfang(m)	perímetro	perimetro	perímetro
période	period	Periode(f)	período	periodo	período
périodique	periodic(al)	periodisch	periódico, a	periodico, a	periódico, a
périphérie	periphery	Umkreis(m), Umfang(m)	periferia	periferia	periferia
perle	pearl	Perle(f)	perla	perla	pérola
permanent, e	permanent	andauernd	permanente	permanente	permanente
permettre	allow, enable	erlauben	permitir	permettere	permitir
permettre(se)	afford	leisten, sich	permitirse	permettersi	permitir-se
permis	licence; permit	Schein(m), Genehmigung	permiso	permesso, licenza	licença
permis(auto)	driving licence	Führerschein(m)	permiso conducir	patente di guida	carta de condução
permission	permission	Erlaubnis(f)	permiso	permesso	permissão
perpendiculaire	perpendicular	senkrecht	perpendicular	perpendicolare	perpendicular
perpétuel, le	perpetual	fortdauernd	perpetuo, a	perpetuo, a	perpétuo, a
perroquet	parrot	Papagei(m)	loro	pappagallo	papagaio
perruque	wig	Perücke(f)	peluca	parrucca	peruca
persécuter	persecute	verfolgen	perseguir	perseguitare	perseguir
persévérance	perseverance	Ausdauer(f)	perseverancia	perseveranza	perseverança
persévérer	persevere	beharren, aus = halten	perseverar	perseverare	perseverar
persistance	persistence	Beharrlichkeit(f)	persistencia	persistenza	persistência
personnalité	personality	Persönlichkeit(f)	personalidad	personalità	personalidade
personne	person	Person(f)	persona	persona	pessoa
personne	nobody, no one	niemand	nadie	nessuno	ninguém
personnel, le	personal	persönlich	personal	personale	pessoal
personnel	staff, personnel	Personal(n)	personal, plantilla	personale	pessoal
perspective	perspective	Perspektive(f)	perspectiva	prospettiva	perspectiva
perspective	prospect	Aussicht(f)	perspectiva	prospettiva	perspectiva
persuader	persuade	überreden	persuadir	persuadere	persuadir
perte	loss, waste	Verlust(m)	pérdida	perdita	perda, prejuizo
perturber	disturb, perturb	stören	perturbar	perturbare	perturbar
pervers, e	perverse	pervers	perverso, a	perverso, a	perverso, a
peser	weigh	wiegen	pesar	pesare	pesar
pessimiste	pessimistic	pessimistisch	pesimista	pessimista	pessimista
pétale	petal	Blütenblatt(n)	pétalo	petalo	pétala
pétard	banger, cracker	Knallkörper(m)	petardo	petardo	bomba, foguete
petit, e	small, little	klein	pequeño, a	piccolo, a	pequeno, a
petit, e	little	klein	pequeño, a	piccolo, a	pequeno, a
petit-fils/fille	grandson-/daughter	Enkel(m), Enkelin(f)	nieto, a	nipote	neto, a
pétition	petition	Bittschrift(f), Gesuch	petición	petizione	petição
pétrir	knead	kneten	amasar	impastare	amassar
pétrole	oil	Erdöl(n)	petróleo	petrolio	petróleo
peu	some; a little	etwas; wenig	poco	poco, pó	pouco
peu	little, few	wenig(e)	poco, a	poco, a	pouco, a
peuple	people	Volk(n)	pueblo	popolo	povo
peuplé, e	populated	bevölkert	poblado, a	popolato, a	povoado, a
peur	fear	Angst(f)	miedo	paura	medo
peur(avoir)	afraid(to be)	Angst(haben)	miedo(tener)	paura(avere)	medo(ter)
peut-être	perhaps, maybe	vielleicht	quizá(s)	forse	talvez
phare	lighthouse	Leuchtturm(m)	faro	faro	farol
phare(s)	headlight	Scheinwerfer(m)	faro(s)	fanale, faro(-ri)	faróis
pharmacie	chemist's	Apotheke(f)	farmacia	farmacia	farmácia
pharmacien, ne	chemist, pharmacist	Apotheker(in f)m	farmacéutico, a	farmacista	farmacêutico, a
pharynx	pharynx	Rachen(m)	faringe	faringe	faringe
phase	phase, stage	Phase(f)	fase	fase	fase
phénomène	phenomenon(-mena)	Phänomen(n)	fenómeno	fenomeno	fenómeno
philosophie	philosophy	Philosophie(f)	filosofía	filosofia	filosofia
phonétique	phonetic	phonetisch	fonético, a	fonetico, a	fonético, a
phoque	seal	Seehund(m)	foca	foca	foca
photo	photo(graph)	Foto(n)	foto	foto, fotografia	fotografia
photographie	photography	Fotografie(f)	fotografía	fotografia	fotografia
photographier	take a photo	fotografieren	fotografiar	fotografare	fotografar
phrase	sentence	Satz(m)	frase	frase	frase
physicien, ne	physicist	Physiker(in f)m	físico, a	fisico, a	físico, a
physionomie	physiognomy	Gesichtsausdruck(m)	fisionomía	fisionomia	fisionomia

French	English	German	Spanish	Italian	Portuguese
physique	physical	physisch	físico, a	fisico, a	físico, a
physique	physics	Physik(f)	física	fisica	fisíca
physique	physique	Äußere(n), Aussehen(n)	físico	fisico	físico
pianiste	pianist	Pianist(in f)m	pianista	pianista	pianista
piano	piano	Klavier(n)	piano	pianoforte	piano
pic	peak	Gipfel(m)	pico	picco	pico
pièce	room	Raum(m)	cuarto	stanza	divisão
pièce	coin	Geldstück(n)	moneda	spiccioli, moneta	moeda
pièce	part, component	Teil(n)	pieza	pezzo	peça
pièce	play	Stück(n)	obra	commedia	peça
pied	foot(feet pl.)	Fuß(m)	pie	piede	pé
piège	trap, snare	Falle(f)	trampa	trappola	armadilha
pierre	stone	Stein(m)	piedra	pietra	pedra
piéton	pedestrian	Fußgänger(m)	peatón	pedone	peão
pieu, poteau	stake, post	Pfahl(m)	estaca	palo, piolo	estaca
pigeon	pigeon	Taube(f)	paloma	piccione	pombo, a
pile	battery	Batterie(f)	pila	pila	pilha
pile	pile	Stapel(m)	pila	pila	pilha, montão
pilier	pillar	Pfeiler(m)	pilar	pilastro	pilar
pillage	plunder, pillage	Plünderung(f)	saqueo	saccheggio	pilhagem
pilote	pilot	Pilot(m)	piloto	pilota	piloto
piloter	pilot; fly; drive	fliegen; lotsen; fahren	pilotar	pilotare	pilotar
pilule	pill	Pille(f)	píldora	pillola	pílula
pince	pincers, pliers	Zange(f)	pinza(s), tenazas	pinza	pinça, alicate
pinceau	brush	Pinsel(m)	pincel	pennello	pincel
pincer	pinch, nip	kneifen	pellizcar	pizzicare	beliscar
pinces	pliers, pincers	Zangen(pl)	alicates, tenazas	pinze	alicate; tenaz
pion(échecs)	pawn(chess)	Bauer(m)(Schach)	peón(ajedrez)	pedone(scacchi)	peão(xadrez)
pion(dames)	draught	Stein(m)(Spiel)	ficha(damas)	pedina(dama)	peça, tábula(dama)
pionnier	pioneer	Pionier, Bahnbrecher	pionero	pioniere	pioneiro
pipe	pipe	Pfeife(f)	pipa	pipa	cachimbo
piquant, e	spicy, hot	scharf	picante	piccante	picante
piquer	prick, sting	stechen	pinchar	pungere	picar
piquet	post, stake, peg	Pfahl(m)	estaca	picchetto	estaca
piqûre	sting, bite	Stich(m)	picadura	puntura	picada
piqûre	injection	Spritze(f)	inyección	iniezione	injecção
pirate	pirate	Pirat(in f)m	pirata	pirata	pirata
pire	worse	schlimmer	peor	peggio	pior
pirogue	pirogue	Piroge(f), Kanu(n)	piragua	piroga	piroga
piscine	swimming-pool	Schwimmbad(n)	piscina	piscina	piscina
piste	track	Spur(f)	pista	pista	pista
piste	slope	Piste(f)	pista	pista	pista
piste	runway	Bahn(Lande-, Start-)	pista	pista	pista
pistolet	gun, pistol	Pistole(f)	pistola	pistola	pistola
piston	piston	Kolben(m)	pistón	pistone	pistão
pitié	pity	Mitleid(n)	piedad	pietà	piedade
pittoresque	picturesque	malerisch	pintoresco, a	pittoresco, a	pitoresco, a
pivoter	revolve, pivot	schwenken	girar	girare, ruotare	girar; rodar
placard	cupboard	Wandschrank(m)	armario	armadio a muro	armário
place	place	Ort(m), Platz(m)	lugar	posto	lugar; sítio
place	square	Platz(m)	plaza	piazza	praça
place	room	Platz(m)	sitio, espacio	spazio	espaço
place	seat	Sitzplatz(m)	sitio, asiento	posto	lugar
placer	place, install	setzen, stellen	colocar	collocare, porre	colocar; pôr
placer	invest	an = legen	invertir	investire	pôr a render
plafond	ceiling	Decke(f)(Zimmer-)	techo	soffitto	tecto
plage	beach(-es)	Strand(m)	playa	spiaggia	praia
plaider	plead	plädieren	litigar	patrocinare	defender(causa)
plaie	wound; cut	Wunde(f)	llaga, herida	piaga	ferida
plaindre	pity	bedauern	compadecer	compatire	lastimar
plaindre(se)	complain	beklagen, sich	quejarse	lamentarsi	queixar-se
plaine	plain	Ebene(f)	llanura, llano	pianura	planície
plainte	complaint	Klage(f)	queja	lamento	queixume, queixa
plainte(porter)	complaint(lodge a)	an = zeigen	denunciar	querelare	queixa(apresentar)
plaire	please; like	gefallen(jdm)	gustar, agradar	piacere	agradar
plaisant, e	pleasant	gefällig	agradable	piacevole	agradável
plaisanter	joke	scherzen	bromear	scherzare	gracejar
plaisanterie	joke	Witz(m)	chiste, gracia	scherzo	brincadeira

French	English	German	Spanish	Italian	Portuguese
plaisir	pleasure	Vergnügen(n)	placer	piacere	prazer
plaisir(faire)	please	Freude machen	gusto(dar)	piacere(fare)	gosto(dar)
plan	plan; drawing	Plan(m)	plan; plano	piano; schema	plano; desenho
plan	map	Plan(m)(Stadtplan m)	plano	pianta; stradario	planta
plan, projet	scheme, plan	Plan(m)	plan, proyecto	schema, piano	plano, projecto
planche	board	Brett(n)	tabla	tavola, asse	tábua
planche à voile	windsurf(ing)	Windsurfen(n)	tabla a vela, surf	windsurf	wind-surf
plancher	floor	Fußboden(m)	suelo	pavimento	soalho, sobrado
planer	glide	schweben, gleiten	planear	planare	planar
planète	planet	Planet(m)	planeta	pianeta	planeta
planeur	glider	Segelflugzeug(n)	planeador	aliante	planador
plante	plant	Pflanze(f)	planta	pianta	planta
planter	plant	pflanzen	plantar	piantare	plantar
plaque	plate, plaque	Platte(f)	placa	lastra, piastra	placa
plastique	plastic	Plastik(n)	plástico	plastica	plástico
plastique	plastic	plastisch	plástico, a	plastico, a	plástico, a
plat, e	flat	platt	llano, a	piatto, a	plano, a
plat	dish, plate	Schüssel(f)	fuente, plato	vassoio, piatto	travessa
plateau	tray	Tablett(n), Platte(f)	bandeja	vassoio	tabuleiro
plateau	plateau	Hochebene(f)	meseta	altipiano	planalto
plate-forme	platform	Plattform(f)	plataforma	piattaforma	plataforma
plâtre	plaster	Gips(m)	yeso	gesso	gesso
plein, e	full	voll	lleno, a	pieno, a	cheio, a
pleurer	cry	weinen	llorar	piangere	chorar
pleuvoir	rain	regnen	llover	piovere	chover
pli	fold; pleat	Falte(f); Kniff(m)	pliegue	piega	prega
plier	fold	falten	doblar	piegare	dobrar
plier	bend	biegen	plegar, doblar	piegare	vergar
plomb	lead	Blei(n)	plomo	piombo	chumbo
plombier	plumber	Klempner(m)	fontanero	idraulico	canalizador
plongeon	dive	Kopfsprung(m)	zambullida	tuffo	mergulho
plonger	plunge, dive	tauchen	zambullirse	tuffarsi	mergulhar
pluie	rain	Regen(m)	lluvia	pioggia	chuva
plume	feather	Feder(f)	pluma	penna, piuma	pluma; pena
plupart(la)	most(of the)	meisten(die)	mayoría(la)	maggior parte(la)	maior parte(a)
pluriel	plural	Mehrzahl(f)	plural	plurale	plural
plus	more	mehr	más	più	mais
plus	plus	plus	más	più	mais
plus	plus	und, plus	más	più	mais
plus(de)	further, moreover	ferner, überdies	además	più(di, in)	além disso
plus(de)	moreover, further	überdies, ferner	más de	più(di, in)	além do mais
plus loin	further	weiter	más lejos	più in là	mais longe
plus tard	later	später	más tarde	più tardi	mais tarde
plusieurs	several	mehrere	varios, as	parecchi	vários, as
plutôt	rather	eher, lieber	más bien	piuttosto	antes; mais
pluvieux, se	rainy	regnerisch	lluvioso, a	piovoso, a	chuvoso, a
pneu	tyre	Reifen(m)	neumático	pneumatico, gomma	pneu
pneumonie	pneumonia	Lungenentzündung(f)	neumonía	polmonite	pneumonia
poche	pocket	Tasche(f)	bolsillo	tasca	bolso
podium	podium, stage	Podest(n)	podio	podio	estrado
poêle	frying pan	Pfanne(f)	sartén	padella	frigideira
poêle	stove	Ofen(m)	estufa	stufa	fogão
poème	poem	Gedicht(n)	poema	poema	poema
poésie	poetry	Poesie(f)	poesía	poesia	poesia
poids	weight	Gewicht(n)	peso	peso	peso
poignard	dagger	Dolch(m)	puñal	pugnale	punhal
poignée	handful	Handvoll(f)	puñado	manciata, pugno	punhado
poignée	handle	Griff(m)	manilla, mango	maniglia	fecho
poignée	handle	Griff(m)	asa, mango	manico	asa
poignet	wrist	Handgelenk(n)	muñeca	polso	punho
poil	hair	Haar(n)	pelo	pelo	pêlo
poilu, e	hairy	behaart	peludo, a	peloso, a	peludo, a
poing	fist	Faust(f)	puño	pugno	punho
point	point	Punkt(m)	punto	punto	ponto
point	dot	Punkt(m)	punto	punto	ponto
point	spot	Fleck(m); Ort; Stelle	lugar, punto	punto	ponto
point	stitch	Stich(m); Masche(f)	puntada	punto	ponto
point de vue	viewpoint	Aussichtspunkt(m)	punto de vista	punto di vista	ponto de vista

French	English	German	Spanish	Italian	Portuguese
pointe	point	Spitze(f)	punta	punta	ponta
pointu, e	pointed, sharp	spitz	puntiagudo, a	appuntito, a	pontiagudo, a
pointure	size	Größe(f)	número	numero	tamanho; número
poire	pear	Birne(f)	pera	pera	pêra
poison	poison	Gift(n)	veneno	veleno	veneno
poisson	fish	Fisch(m)	pescado	pesce	peixe
poissonnerie	fishmonger's	Fischgeschäft(n)	pescadería	pescheria	peixaria
poitrine	chest; breast	Brust(f)	pecho	petto	peito
poivre	pepper	Pfeffer(m)	pimienta	pepe	pimenta
polaire	polar	polar; Polar-	polar	polare	polar
pôle	pole	Pol(m)	polo	polo	polo
polémique	controversy	Polemik(f)	polémica	polemica	polémica
poli, e	polished	poliert	pulido, a	levigato, a	polido, a
poli, e	polite	höflich	educado, a; cortés	educato, a	educado, a
police	police	Polizei(f)	policía	polizia	polícia
policier	policeman(-men)	Polizist(in f)m	policía	poliziotto	polícia
poliomyélite	polio(myelitis)	Kinderlähmung(f)	poliomielitis	poliomelite	poliomielite
polir	polish	polieren	pulir	lucidare, levigare	polir
politesse	politeness	Höflichkeit(f)	cortesía	educazione	delicadeza
politicien, ne	politician	Politiker(in f)m	político, a	politico, a	político, a
politique	political	politisch	político, a	politico, a	político, a
politique	politics	Politik(f)	política	politica	política
politique	policy	Politik(f)	política	politica	política
polluer	pollute	verunreinigen	contaminar	inquinare	poluir
pollution	pollution	Verschmutzung(f)	contaminación	inquinamento	poluição
polygamie	polygamy	Polygamie(f)	poligamia	poligamia	poligamia
polype	polyp	Polyp(m)	pólipo	polipo	pólipo
polyvalent, e	polyvalent	vielseitig	polivalente	polivalente	polivalente
pommade	ointment, cream	Salbe(f)	pomada	pomata	pomada
pomme	apple	Apfel(m)	manzana	mela	maçã
pomme de terre	potato(-es)	Kartoffel(f)	patata	patata	batata
pompe	pump	Pumpe(f)	bomba	pompa	bomba
pompier(sapeur-)	fireman(-men)	Feuerwehrmann(m)	bombero	pompiere	bombeiro
ponction	puncture	Punktion(f)	punción	puntura, prelievo	punção
ponctuation	punctuation	Zeichensetzung(f)	puntuación	punteggiatura	pontuação
ponctuel, le	punctual	pünktlich	puntual	puntuale	pontual
pondre	lay	Eier legen	poner(huevos)	fare l'uovo	pôr(ovos)
pont	bridge	Brücke(f)	puente	ponte	ponte
pont	deck; bridge	Deck(n)	puente	ponte	convés
populaire	popular	populär	popular	popolare	popular
population	population	Bevölkerung(f)	población	popolazione	população
porc	pig; pork(meat)	Schwein(n)	cerdo	porco, maiale	porco
porcelaine	porcelain, china	Porzellan(n)	porcelana	porcellana	porcelana
porche	porch	Portal(n)	soportal, porche	atrio, portico	pórtico
pore	pore	Pore(f)	poro	poro	poro
poreux, se	porous	porös	poroso, a	poroso, a	poroso, a
pornographie	pornography	Pornographie(f)	pornografía	pornografia	pornografia
port	port, harbour	Hafen(m)	puerto	porto	porto
port	postage	Porto(-kosten)(n/pl)	porte	porto	porte
portail	gate	Tor(n)	portal	portone	portal
portatif, ive	portable	tragbar	portátil	portatile	portátil
porte	door	Tür(f)	puerta	porta	porta
porte	gate	Pforte(f)	puerta, entrada	porta, uscita	porta
porte-clefs	key-ring	Schlüsselring(m)	llavero	portachiavi	porta-chaves
porte-documents	document case	Aktenmappe(f)	portadocumentos	portadocumenti	carteira
portée	range, reach	Reichweite(f)	alcance	portata, gittata	alcance
portefeuille	wallet	Brieftasche(f)	cartera	portafoglio	carteira
portemanteau	hat stand	Kleiderständer(m)	colgador, percha	attaccapanni	cabide
porte-monnaie	purse	Geldbörse(f)	monedero	portamonete	porta-moedas
porter	carry	tragen	llevar	portare	levar
porter	wear	tragen	llevar	indossare, portare	usar; trazer
portier	porter	Portier(m)	portero	portiere	porteiro
portière	door(car)	Wagentür(f)	puerta	sportello	porta
portion	portion, piece	Stück(n), Portion(f)	porción	porzione	porção
portrait	portrait	Portrait(n)	retrato	ritratto	retrato
poser	put, lay(down)	legen	poner, colocar	posare, porre	pôr, colocar
poser, placer	place	stellen	poner, colocar	collocare	pôr, colocar
poser(photo)	pose	Modell stehen	posar	posare	posar

French	English	German	Spanish	Italian	Portuguese
poser(question)	ask	fragen	preguntar	porre(domanda)	perguntar
positif, ive	positive	positiv	positivo, a	positivo, a	positivo, a
position	position	Position(f)	posición	posizione	posição
posséder	own, possess	besitzen	poseer	possedere	possuír
possibilité	possibility	Möglichkeit(f)	posibilidad	possibilità	possibilidade
possible	possible	möglich	posible	possibile	possível
poste	post-office	Post(f)	correos	posta	correios
poste d'essence	petrol station	Tankstelle(f)	gasolinera	distributore(benzina)	bomba de gasolina
poste de police	police station	Polizeiwache(f)	cuartelillo	posto di guardia	esquadra
poste radio	radio set	Radio(n)	aparato de radio	radio	rádio
poster	post, mail	ein=werfen	echar al correo	impostare, imbucare	pôr no correio
poster	poster	Plakat(n)	cartel, póster	poster, manifesto	cartaz
postérieur, e	later	spätere(r, s)	posterior	posteriore	posterior
pot	pot	Topf(m)	maceta	vaso	vaso; pote
potable	drinking	trinkbar, genießbar	potable	potabile	potável
pot-de-vin	bribe	Schmiergelder(pl.)	soborno	bustarella	suborno
poteau	post, pole	Pfosten(m)	poste	palo	poste
potentiel, le	potential	potentiell	potencial	potenziale	potencial
poubelle	bin, dustbin	Abfalleimer(m)	cubo de basura	pattumiera	caixote do lixo
pouce	thumb	Daumen(m)	pulgar	pollice	polegar
poudre	powder	Puder(m); Pulver(n)	polvo	polvere	pó
poudre	powder	Pulver(n)(Schieß-)	pólvora	polvere	pólvora
poulain	foal	Fohlen(n)	potro	puledro	potro
poule	hen	Huhn(n)	gallina	gallina	galinha
poulet	chicken	Hähnchen, Hühnchen(n)	pollo	pollo	frango
poulie	pulley	Flaschenzug(m)	polea	puleggia	polia
pouls	pulse	Puls(m)	pulso	polso	pulso
poumon	lung	Lunge(f)	pulmón	polmone	pulmão
poupée	doll	Puppe(f)	muñeca	bambola	boneca
pour	for	für	para; por	per	para; por
pour	for	für	por	per	por
pourboire	tip	Trinkgeld(n)	propina	mancia	gorgeta
pour cent	per cent	Prozent(n)	por ciento	per cento	por cento
pourcentage	percentage	Prozentsatz(m)	porcentaje	percentuale	percentagem
pourparlers	talks	Verhandlungen(pl)	negociaciones	trattative	negociações
pourquoi	why	warum	por qué	perché	porquê
pourquoi(le--de)	reason(the--for)	Grund(m)(der--für)	porqué(el--de)	perché(il--di)	porquê(o--de)
pourri, e	rotten	verfault	podrido, a	marcio, a	podre
pourrir	rot	verfaulen	pudrir	marcire	apodrecer
poursuivre	pursue	verfolgen	perseguir	inseguire	perseguir
pourtant	yet, however	dennoch, doch	sin embargo	però, tuttavia	contudo, todavia
pourtour	periphery	Umkreis(m)	contorno	giro, circuito	perímetro
pourvu que	provided that	wenn nur, sofern, daß	ojalá	purché	oxalá
pousser	push	schieben, stoßen	empujar	spingere	empurrar
pousser, croître	grow	wachsen	crecer	crescere	crescer
poussette	push-chair	Sportwagen(m)	silla de bebé	passeggino	cadeira de bebé
poussière	dust	Staub(m)	polvo	polvere	poeira
poussin	chick	Küken(n)	pollito	pulcino	pinto
poutre	beam	Balken(m)	viga	trave	trave
pouvoir	power	Macht(f)	poder	potere	poder
pouvoir	can, able to(be)	können	poder	potere	poder
prairie	meadow	Wiese(f)	pradera	prateria	pradaria, prado
pratique	practical	praktisch	práctico, a	pratico, a	prático, a
pratiquer	practise	betreiben, üben	practicar	praticare	praticar
pré	meadow, field	Weide(f), Wiese(f)	prado	prato	prado
préalable	preliminary	vorhergehend	previo, a	preliminare	prévio, a
précaution	precaution	Vorsicht(f)	precaución	precauzione	precaução
précédent, e	previous	vorherig	precedente	precedente	precedente
prêcher	preach	predigen	predicar	predicare	pregar
précieux, se	precious	wertvoll, kostbar	precioso, a	prezioso, a	precioso, a
précipice	precipice	Abgrund(m)	precipicio	precipizio	precipício
précipitation	hurry, haste	Eile(f), Hast(f)	precipitación	precipitazione	precipitação
précipiter(se)	rush	stürzen, sich	precipitarse	precipitarsi	precipitar-se
précis, e	precise, accurate	genau	preciso, a	preciso, a	exacto, a
précisément	precisely	genau	precisamente	precisamente, appunto	precisamente
préciser	specify	genau fest=legen	precisar	precisare	precisar
précision	precision	Genauigkeit(f)	precisión	precisione	precisão
précision	clarification	Klarstellung(f)	aclaración	precisazione	explicação, precisão

French	English	German	Spanish	Italian	Portuguese
précoce	precocious	frühreif, frühzeitig	precoz	precoce	precoce
prédécesseur	predecessor	Vorgänger(in f)m	predecesor, a	predecessore	predecessor, a
prédire	predict	vorher = sagen	predecir	predire	predizer
prédominant, e	predominant	vorherrschend	predominante	predominante	predominante
préface	preface	Vorwort(n)	prefacio	prefazione	prefácio
préférence	preference	Vorliebe(f)	preferencia	preferenza	preferência
préféré, e	favourite	Lieblings-	preferido, a	preferito, a	preferido, a
préférer	prefer	bevorzugen	preferir	preferire	preferir
préfixe	prefix	Vorsilbe(f)	prefijo	prefisso	prefixo
préhistoire	prehistory	Vorgeschichte(f)	prehistoria	preistoria	pré-história
préjudice	wrong, harm	Schaden(m)	perjuicio	pregiudizio, danno	prejuízo
préjugé	prejudice	Vorurteil(n)	prejuicio	pregiudizio	preconceito
prélever	take from	entnehmen	sacar	prelevare	tirar
préliminaire	preliminary	einleitend	preliminar	preliminare	preliminar
prématuré, e	premature(baby)	Frühgeburt(f)	prematuro, a	prematuro, a	prematuro, a
prémédité, e	premeditated	vorsätzlich	premeditado, a	premeditato, a	premeditado, a
préméditer	premeditate	vor = setzen	premeditar	premeditare	premeditar
premier, ière	first	erste(r, s)	primero, a; primer	primo, a	primeiro, a
premier ministre	prime minister	Premierminister(m)	primer ministro	primo ministro	primeiro ministro
premier ministre	prime minister	Ministerpräsident(m)	primer ministro	primo ministro	primeiro ministro
prendre	take	nehmen	tomar, coger	prendere	tomar
prendre(leçon)	have(a lesson)	nehmen	recibir(clases)	prendere(lezione)	ter(lição)
prénom	first name	Vorname(m)	nombre	nome	nome próprio
préoccuper	worry, preoccupy	beunruhigen	preocupar	preoccupare	preocupar
préparation	preparation	Vorbereitung(f)	preparación	preparazione	preparação
préparer	prepare	vor = bereiten	preparar	preparare	preparar
préposition	preposition	Präposition(f)	preposición	preposizione	preposição
près, proche	near, close to	nah(e)	cerca	vicino, a	perto
presbyte	long-sighted	weitsichtig	présbita	presbite	présbita
prescrire	prescribe	vor = schreiben	prescribir	prescrivere	prescrever
présence	presence	Anwesenheit(f)	presencia	presenza	presença
présent, e	present	anwesend	presente	presente	presente
présent, e	present	gegenwärtig, aktuell	presente, actual	presente, attuale	presente, actual
présent	present	Gegenwart(f)	presente	presente	presente
présentation	presentation	Vorführung(f)	presentación	presentazione	apresentação
présenter	present	vor = zeigen, - = stellen	presentar	presentare	apresentar
présenter	introduce	vor = stellen	presentar	presentare	apresentar
préservatif	condom, sheath	Präservativ(n)	preservativo	preservativo	preservativo
présidence	presidency	Präsidium n, Vorsitz m	presidencia	presidenza	presidência
président, e	president	Präsident(in f)m	presidente	presidente, essa	presidente
président, e	chairman/-woman	Vorsitzende(m, f)	presidente	presidente, essa	presidente
presque	almost, nearly	fast	casi	quasi	quase
presse	press	Presse(f)	prensa	stampa	imprensa
presser	press, squeeze	drücken(zusammen-)	apretar	premere	prensar
pressé, e(être)	hurry(be in a)	eilig(es...haben)	prisa(tener)	fretta(avere)	pressa(ter)
pression	pressure	Druck(m)	presión	pressione	pressão
prestige	prestige	Ansehen(n)	prestigio	prestigio	prestigio
prestigieux, se	prestigious	wunderbar	prestigioso, a	prestigioso, a	prestigioso, a
présumer	presume	vermuten	presumir	presumere	presumir
prêt, e	ready	fertig	dispuesto, a	pronto, a	pronto, a
prêt	loan	Darlehen(n)	préstamo	prestito	empréstimo
prétentieux, se	pretentious	eingebildet	presuntuoso, a	pretenzioso, a	pretencioso, a
prêter	lend	leihen, verleihen	prestar	prestare	emprestar
prêtre	priest	Priester(m)	sacerdote, padre	prete	padre
preuve	proof, evidence	Beweis(m)	prueba	prova	prova
prévaloir	prevail	vor = herrschen	prevalecer	prevalere	prevalecer
prévenir	warn, inform	warnen	prevenir, avisar	prevenire	prevenir, avisar
prévision	forecast	Vorhersage(f)	previsión	previsione	previsão
prévoir	foresee; plan	vorher = sehen; planen	prever	prevedere	prever
prier	pray	beten	rezar	pregare	rezar, orar
prière	prayer	Gebet(n)	oración	preghiera	oração
primaire	primary	Primär-	primario, a	primario, a	primário, a
prime	bonus	Zulage(f)	prima	premio, sussidio	gratificação
primitif, ive	primitive	primitiv	primitivo, a	primitivo, a	primitivo, a
prince	prince	Prinz(m)	príncipe	principe	príncipe
princesse	princess(-es)	Prinzessin(f)	princesa	principessa	princesa
principal, e	principal, main	hauptsächlich	principal	principale	principal
principe	principle	Grundsatz(m)	principio	principio	princípio

French	English	German	Spanish	Italian	Portuguese
printemps	spring	Frühling(m)	primavera	primavera	primavera
prioritaire	priority(have)	vorrangig; Prioritäts-	prioritario, a	prioritario, a	prioritário, a
priorité	priority	Vorrang(m)	prioridad	precedenza; priorità	prioridade
prise	plug; socket	Steckdose(f)	enchufe	presa	tomada
prison	prison, jail	Gefängnis(n)	prisión, cárcel	prigione, carcere	prisão, cadeia
prisonnier, ière	prisoner	Gefangene(f, m)	prisionero, a	prigioniero, a	prisioneiro, a
privé, e	private	privat	privado, a	privato, a	privado, a
priver	deprive	berauben, entziehen	privar	privare	privar
privilège	privilege	Vorrecht(n)	privilegio	privilegio	privilégio
privilégié, e	privileged	bevorzugt	privilegiado, a	privilegiato, a	privilegiado, a
prix	price	Preis(m)	precio	prezzo	preço
prix	prize	Preis(m)	premio	premio	prémio
probable	probable, likely	wahrscheinlich	probable	probabile	provável
probablement	probably	wahrscheinlich	probablemente	probabilmente	provavelmente
problème	problem	Problem(n)	problema	problema	problema
procédé	process(-es)	Verfahren(n)	procedimiento	procedimento	procedimento
précéder	precede	voran = gehen, voraus = -	preceder	precedere	preceder
procédure	procedure	Verfahren(n)	procedimiento	procedimento	procedimento
procès	lawsuit, trial	Prozeß(m)	proceso, juicio	processo	processo
procès	lawsuit	Prozeß(m)	pleito	causa	pleito, processo
procession	procession	Prozession(f)	procesión	processione	procissão
procès-verbal	minutes, report	Protokoll(n)	acta	verbale	acta
procès-verbal	ticket, penalty	Strafmandat(n)	multa	contravvenzione	multa
prochain, e	next	nächste	próximo, a	prossimo, a	próximo, a
proche	near, close	nah(e)	cercano, a; próximo	prossimo, a	próximo, a; perto
proclamer	proclaim	bekannt = geben	proclamar	proclamare	proclamar
procréation	procreation	Zeugung(f)	procreación	procreazione	procriação
procréer	procreate	erzeugen	procrear	procreare	procriar
procurer(se)	obtain, get	besorgen, sich	procurarse	procurarsi	arranjar; obter
prodigieux, se	prodigious	wunderbar	prodigioso, a	prodigioso, a	prodigioso, a
producteur, trice	producer	Hersteller(in f)m	productor, a	produttore, trice	produtor, a
producteur, trice	producer	Produzent(in f)m	productor, a	produttore, trice	produtor, a
productif, ive	productive	leistungsfähig	productivo, a	produttivo, a	produtivo, a
production	production	Produktion(f)	producción	produzione	produção
produire	produce	produzieren	producir	produrre	produzir
produire	produce	her = stellen	producir	produrre	produzir
produire(se)	happen, occur	passieren	suceder, ocurrir	accadere	ocorrer
produit	product	Produkt(n)	producto	prodotto	produto
profaner	desecrate	entweihen	profanar	profanare	profanar
professeur	teacher	Lehrer(in f)m	profesor, a	professore, essa	professor, a
professeur	professor	Professor(in f)m	catedrático, a	professore, essa	professor, a
profession	profession	Beruf(m)	profesión	professione	profissão
professionnel, le	professional	professionell	profesional	professionale	profissional
professionnel	professional	Profi(m)	profesional	professionista	profissional
profil	profile	Profil(n)	perfil	profilo	perfil
profit	profit, benefit	Gewinn(m)	ganancia	profitto, guadagno	lucro
profit(au--de)	in aid of	zugunsten von	beneficio(en--de)	beneficio(al--di)	proveito(em--de)
profiter	take advantage of	profitieren	aprovechar	approffittare	aproveitar
profond, e	deep	tief	profundo, a	profondo, a	profundo, a
profondeur	depth	Tiefe(f)	profundidad	profondità	profundidade
progéniture	offspring	Nachkomme(m)	progenitura	progenitura	progenitura
programme	programme	Programm(n)	programa	programma	programa
programmeur, se	programmer	Programmierer(in f)m	programador, a	programmatore, trice	programador, a
progrès	progress	Fortschritt(m)	progreso	progresso	progresso
progressif, ive	progressive	fortschreitend	progresivo, a	progressivo, a	progressivo, a
progression	progression	Fortschreiten(n)	progresión	progressione	progressão
proie	prey	Beute(f)	presa	preda	presa
projecteur	projector	Scheinwerfer(m)	proyector	proiettore	projector
projectile	projectile	Geschoß(n)	proyectil	proiettile	projéctil
projet	project, plan	Vorhaben(n)	proyecto, plan	progetto	projecto
projet	plan	Plan(m)	plan, proyecto	progetto	projecto
projeter	plan	planen	proyectar, planear	progettare	projectar
prolongation	prolongation	Verlängerung(f)	prolongación	prolungazione	prolongamento
proliférer	proliferate	vermehren, sich	proliferar	prolificare	proliferar
prolongement	extension	Verlängerung(f)	prolongamiento	prolungamento	prolongamento
prolonger	extend	verlängern	prolongar	prolungare	prolongar
promenade	walk; drive; ride	Spaziergang(m)	paseo	passeggiata	passeio
promener	walk(go for a)	spazieren = gehen	pasear	passeggiare	passear

98

French	English	German	Spanish	Italian	Portuguese
promesse	promise	Versprechen(n)	promesa	promessa	promessa
promettre	promise	versprechen	prometer	promettere	prometer
promis, e	promised	versprochen	prometido, a	promesso, a	prometido, a
promotion	promotion	Beförderung(f)	promoción	promozione	promoção
promouvoir	promote	befördern	promover	promuovere	promover
prompt, e	quick, prompt	schnell, rasch	pronto, a	pronto, a	pronto, a
pronom	pronoun	Fürwort(n)	pronombre	pronome	pronome
prononcer	pronounce	aus = sprechen	pronunciar	pronunziare	pronunciar
pronostic	prognosis(-ses)	Prognose(f)	pronóstico	prognosi	prognóstico
pronostic	forecast	Vorhersage(f)	pronóstico	pronostico	prognóstico
propagande	propaganda	Propaganda(f)	propaganda	propaganda	propaganda
propager	spread	verbreiten	propagar	propagare	propagar
propice	favourable	günstig	propicio, a	propizio, a	propício, a
proportion	proportion, ratio	Verhältnis(n)	proporción	proporzione	proporção
propos	words, talk	Worte(pl.)	palabras	parole, discorsi	fala, conversa
propos, intention	intention, aim	Absicht(f)	propósito	proposito	propósito
proposer	propose; offer	vor = schlagen	proponer	proporre	propor
proposition	proposal	Vorschlag(m)	propuesta	proposta	proposta
propre	clean	sauber	limpio, a	pulito, a	limpo, a
propre	own	eigen	propio, a	proprio, a	próprio, a
propreté	clean(li)ness	Reinlichkeit(f)	limpieza	pulizia	limpeza
propriétaire	owner	Eigentümer(in f)m	propietario, a	proprietario, a	proprietário, a
propriétaire	landowner	Gutsherr(-sbesitzer)	propietario, a	proprietario, a	proprietário, a
propriétaire	landlord	Besitzer/in; (Haus-)	dueño, a	proprietario, a	senhorio, a; dono, a
propriété	property	Eigentum(n)	propiedad	proprietà	propriedade
propulsion	propulsion	Antrieb(m)	propulsión	propulsione	propulsão
prospectus	leaflet	Flugblatt(n)	folleto	prospetto	prospecto
prospère	flourishing	erfolgreich, blühend	próspero, a	prospero, a	próspero, a
prostate	prostate	Prostata(f)	próstata	prostata	próstata
prostituée	prostitute	Prostituierte(f)	prostituta	prostituta	prostituta
prostitution	prostitution	Prostitution(f)	prostitución	prostituzione	prostituição
protection	protection	Schutz(m)	protección	protezione	protecção
protéger	protect	beschützen	proteger	proteggere	proteger
protestant, e	Protestant	Protestant(in f)m	protestante	protestante	protestante
protester	protest, contest	protestieren	protestar	protestare	protestar
prothèse	artificial-, false-	Prothese(f)	prótesis	protesi	prótese
protocole	protocol	Protokoll(n)	protocolo	protocollo	protocolo
prototype	prototype	Prototyp(m)	prototipo	prototipo	protótipo
protubérance	protuberance	Beule(f), Buckel(m)	protuberancia	protuberanza	protuberância
prouver	prove	beweisen	probar	provare	provar
provenance	origin	Herkunft(f)	procedencia	provenienza	proveniência
proverbe	proverb	Sprichwort(n)	proverbio	proverbio	provérbio
province	province	Provinz(f)	provincia	provincia	província
provision	stock, supply	Vorrat(m)	provisión	provvista	provisão
provisoire	provisional	provisorisch	provisional	provvisorio, a	provisório, a
provocation	provocation	Herausforderung(f)	provocación	provocazione	provocação
provoquer	provoke	heraus = fordern, reizen	provocar	provocare	provocar
proxénète	pimp	Zuhälter(m)	proxeneta	ruffiano, prosseneta	proxeneta
proxénétisme	pimping	Kuppelei(f)	proxenetismo	prossenetismo	proxenetismo
proximité	proximity	Nähe(f)	proximidad	prossimità	proximidade
proximité(à)	close, near	nahe bei	cerca de	vicinanze(nelle)	próximo a
prudence	caution, prudence	Vorsicht(f)	prudencia	prudenza	prudência
prudent, e	careful, prudent	vorsichtig	prudente	prudente	prudente
prune	plum	Pflaume(f)	ciruela	prugna, susina	ameixa
pseudonyme	pseudonym	Pseudonym(n)	seudónimo	pseudonimo	pseudónimo
psychanalyste	psychoanalyst	Psychoanalytiker(m)	sicoanalista	psicanalista	psicanalista
psychiatre	psychiatrist	Psychiater(in f)m	siquiatra	psichiatra	psiquiatra
psychique	psychological	psychisch	síquico, a	psichico, a	psíquico, a
psychologie	psychology	Psychologie(f)	sicología	psicologia	psicologia
psychologue	psychologist	Psychologe(m)/-gin(f)	sicólogo, a	psicologo, a	psicólogo, a
psychose	psychosis(-ses)	Psychose(f)	sicosis	psichosi	psicose
puanteur	stench, stink	Gestank(m)	hedor, peste	puzza, fetore	fedor
puberté	puberty	Pubertät(f)	pubertad	pubertà	puberdade
public, ique	public	öffentlich	público, a	pubblico, a	público, a
public	public; audience	Publikum(n)	público	pubblico	público
publication	publication	Veröffentlichung(f)	publicación	pubblicazione	publicação
publicité	advertising	Werbung(f), Anzeige(f)	publicidad	pubblicità	publicidade
publier	publish, issue	veröffentlichen	publicar	pubblicare	publicar

99

French	English	German	Spanish	Italian	Portuguese
puce	flea	Floh(m)	pulga	pulce	pulga
pudique	modest	keusch	púdico, a	pudico, a	púdico, a
puer	stink	stinken	apestar	puzzare	cheirar mal
puis, ensuite	then	dann	después	poi	depois
puiser	draw(from)	schöpfen	sacar	attingere	tirar, extraír
puisque	since	da, weil	ya que; pues	poichè	já que
puissance, force	power, strength	Macht(f), Kraft(f)	potencia, fuerza	potenza, forza	potência, poder
puissant, e	powerful, strong	mächtig, kräftig	poderoso, a	poderoso, a; potente	poderoso, a
puissant, e	potent, powerful	kräftig, stark	potente	potente	potente
puits	well	Brunnen(m)	pozo	pozzo	poço
pull-over	pullover, sweater	Pullover(m)	jersey	maglione, pullover	pulover
pulsation	beating, pulsation	Pulsschlag(m)	pulsación	pulsazione	pulsação
pulvérisation	spraying	Zerstäubung(f)	pulverización	nebulizzazione	pulverização
punaise	drawing-pin	Heftzwecke(f)	chincheta	puntina(disegno)	percevejo
punir	punish	bestrafen	castigar	punire	castigar
punition	punishment	Strafe(f)	castigo	punizione	castigo
pupille	pupil	Pupille(f)	pupila	pupilla	pupila
pur, e	pure	rein	puro, a	puro, a	puro, a
purge	purge	Säuberungsaktion(f)	purga	purga	purga
purifier	purify	reinigen	purificar	purificare	purificar
pus	pus	Eiter(m)	pus	pus	pus
puzzle	jigsaw(puzzle)	Puzzle(n)	rompecabezas	puzzle	puzzle
pyjama	pyjamas	Schlafanzug(m)	pijama	pigiama	pijama
pyramide	pyramid	Pyramide(f)	pirámide	piramide	pirâmide
python	python	Python(m)	pitón	pitone	jibóia

Q

French	English	German	Spanish	Italian	Portuguese
quai	platform	Bahnsteig(m)	andén	binario, marciapiede	plataforma
quai	quay	Kai((m)	muelle	molo	cais
qualifié, e	qualified	qualifiziert	calificado, a	qualificato, a	qualificado, a
qualité	quality	Qualität(f)	calidad; cualidad	qualità	qualidade
qualité	quality	Eigenschaft(f)	cualidad	qualità	qualidade
quand	when	wann	cuándo, cuando	quando	quando
quantité	quantity, amount	Quantität(f)	cantidad	quantità	quantidade
quarante	forty	vierzig	cuarenta	quaranta	quarenta
quart	quarter	Viertel(n)	cuarto	quarto	quarto
quartier	district	Viertel(n)	barrio	quartiere	bairro
quatorze	fourteen	vierzehn	catorce	quattordici	catorze
quatre	four	vier	cuatro	quattro	quatro
quatre-vingts	eighty	achtzig	ochenta	ottanta	oitenta
quatre-vingt-dix	ninety	neunzig	noventa	novanta	noventa
quatuor	quartet	Quartett(n)	cuarteto	quartetto	quarteto
que	that; whom; which	was, das	que, qué	che	que
quel, le	what; which	welch(e, er, es)	cuál; que	quale; che	qual; que
quelconque	any, whatever	beliebig	cualquier(a)	qualunque	qualquer
quelque	some, any	einige	alguno, a	qualche	algum, a
quelques	few(a), some	einige	algunos, as	alcuni, e	alguns, algumas
quelque chose	something	etwas	algo	qualche cosa	qualquer coisa
quelquefois	sometimes	manchmal	a veces	qualche volta	às vezes
quelque part	somewhere	irgendwo	alguna parte(en)	qualche parte(da)	algures
quel que soit	whatever	was auch immer	cualquiera que sea	qualunque sia	seja qual for
quelqu'un, e	someone, somebody	jemand	alguien	qualcuno, a	alguém
question	question	Frage(f)	pregunta	domanda	pergunta
question	question	Frage(f)	cuestión	questione	questão
queue	tail	Schwanz(m)	rabo	coda	cauda
queue	queue	Schlange(f)	cola	coda, fila	bicha; fila

French	English	German	Spanish	Italian	Portuguese
qui	who(m); which; that	wer; wen	quién, que	chi, che	quem
quiconque	anyone(who)	jeder	quienquiera	chiunque	qualquer(um)
quille	skittle	Kegel(f)	bolos(juego)	birillo	paulitos
quincaillerie	ironmonger's	Eisenwarenhandlung(f)	ferretería	ferramenta	loja de ferragens
quinze	fifteen	fünfzehn	quince	quindici	quinze
quittance	receipt	Quittung(f)	recibo	ricevuta	recibo
quitter	leave	verlassen	dejar, abandonar	lasciare	deixar
quoi	what	was	que, qué	cosa, che cosa	quê
quoique	although, though	obgleich, obwohl	aunque	sebbene	embora
quota	quota	Quote(f)	cuota	quota	cota
quotidien, ne	daily	täglich	cotidiano, a	quotidiano, a	quotidiano, a
quotidien	daily	Tageszeitung(f)	diario	quotidiano	diário
quotient	quotient	Quotient(m), Bruch(m)	cociente	quoziente	quociente

R

French	English	German	Spanish	Italian	Portuguese
rabais, remise	discount	Rabatt(m)	rebaja, descuento	ribasso, sconto	desconto, saldo
rabbin	rabbi	Rabbiner(m)	rabino	rabbino	rabino
raccommodage	mending	Flicken(n)	remiendo	rammendo	remendo
raccourci	short cut	Abkürzung(f)	atajo	scorciatoia	atalho
race	race, breed	Rasse(f)	raza	razza	raça
race	breed	Rasse(f)	casta, raza	razza	casta, raça
rachitique	rickety	rachitisch	raquítico, a	rachitico, a	raquítico, a
racial, e	racial	rassisch	racial	raziale	racial
racine	root	Wurzel(f)	raíz	radice	raiz
racisme	racism	Rassismus(m)	racismo	razzismo	racismo
racket	racket(-eering)	Erpressung(f)	extorsión	racket	vigarice
raconter	relate, tell	erzählen	contar	raccontare	contar
radar	radar	Radar(m)	radar	radar	radar
radeau	raft	Floß(n)	balsa	zattera	jangada
radiateur	radiator, heater	Heizkörper(m)	radiador	termosifone	aquecedor
radiation	radiation	Bestrahlung(f)	radiación	radiazione	radiação
radio	radio	Radio(n)	radio	radio	rádio
radioactivité	radioactivity	Radioaktivität(f)	radiactividad	radioattività	radioactividade
radiodiffusion	broadcasting	Radioübertragung(f)	radiodifusión	radiodiffusione	radiodifusão
radiographie	X-ray; radiography	Röntgenbild(n)	radiografía	radiografia	radiografia
rafale	gust, gale	Windstoß(m)	ráfaga	raffica	rajada
rafale	burst, hail	Salve(f)	ráfaga	raffica	rajada
rafle	raid, round-up	Razzia(f)	redada	retata	rusga
rafraîchir	cool	ab = kühlen	refrescar	rinfrescare	refrescar
rage	rabies	Tollwut(f)	rabia	rabbia	raiva
rage, fureur	rage	Wut(f)	rabia, furia	rabbia	raiva, furor
raide	stiff	starr, steif	tieso, a; rígido, a	rigido, a	teso, a; hirto, a
raide; escarpé, e	steep	steil	empinado, a	ripido, a	empinado, a
raie	line	Strich(m)	raya	riga	linha; risca
rail	rail; track	Schiene(f)	carril	rotaia	carril
rainure	groove	Rille(f), Nute(f)	ranura	scanalatura	ranhura
raisin	grape	Traube(f)(Wein-)	uva(s)	uva	uva
raison	reason	Grund(m)	razón, causa	ragione	razão
raison(avoir)	right(to be)	Recht(n)(haben)	razón(tener)	ragione(avere)	razão(ter)
raisonnable	reasonable	vernünftig	razonable	ragionevole	razoável
raisonnement	reasoning	Überlegung(f)	razonamiento	ragionamento	raciocínio
ralentir	slow down	verlangsamen	aminorar	rallentare	abrandar
râler	moan, groan	nörgeln	refunfuñar	brontolare	resmungar
ramadan	Ramadan	Ramadan(m)	ramadán	ramadan	ramadão
ramasser	pick up	auf = heben	recoger	raccogliere	apanhar, recolher
rame	oar	Ruder(n)	remo	remo	remo

French	English	German	Spanish	Italian	Portuguese
ramener	bring back	wieder = bringen	devolver, traer	riportare	trazer
ramer	row	rudern	remar	remare	remar
rampe	banister, handrail	Geländer(n)	barandilla	rampa	corrimão
ramper	crawl	kriechen	arrastrarse	strisciare	rastejar
rançon	ransom	Lösegeld(n)	rescate	riscatto	resgate
rancune	grudge, spite	Rachsucht(f)	rencor	rancore	rancor
randonnée	ramble	Tour(f), Fußtour(f)	caminata, paseo	gita, escursione	caminhada
rang	rank	Rang(m)	puesto	rango	posição
rangée	row	Reihe(f)	hilera, fila	fila	fileira, renque
rangé, e	tidy	ordentlich	ordenado, a	ordinato, a	arrumado, a
ranger, ordonner	tidy, put in order	ein = räumen	ordenar, colocar	sistemare	arrumar
ranger	tidy up	auf = räumen	ordenar	ordinare	ordenar
rapace	bird of prey	Raubvogel(m)	rapaz	rapace	ave de rapina
rapatriement	repatriation	Repatriierung(f)	repatriación	rimpatrio	repatriação
rapide	rapid, fast, quick	schnell	rápido, a	rapido, a; veloce	rápido, a
rappel	reminder	Erinnerung(f); Mahnung	llamada	richiamo	aviso; lembrança
rappel	recall	Rückruf(m)	recuerdo	richiamo	lembrança
rappeler(se)	recall, remember	erinnern, sich	recordar, acordarse	ricordarsi	lembrar-se
rapport	ratio, proportion	Beziehung(f)	razón, relación	rapporto	razão
rapport	report	Bericht(m)	informe	rapporto, relazione	relatório
rapport	yield, return	Ertrag(m)	renta; ganancia	frutto, rendita	renda; ganho
rapporter	bring back	zurück = bringen	traer	riportare	trazer
rapporter	bring in, yield	ein = bringen	proporcionar	fruttare	render
rapprocher	bring nearer	heran = rücken	acercar	avvicinare	acercar
raquette	racket	Schläger(Tennis-)(m)	raqueta	racchetta	raqueta
raquette	bat	Schläger(m)	raqueta, pala	racchetta	raqueta
rare	rare	selten	raro, a	raro, a	raro, a
raser(se)	shave	rasieren, sich	afeitar(se)	radersi	barbear-se
rasoir	razor	Rasierapparat(m)	navaja de afeitar	rasoio	navalha, gilete
rassemblement	gathering	Versammlung(f)	concentración	raduno, adunanza	ajuntamento
rassembler	gather(together)	sammeln	juntar	radunare	juntar
rassurer	reassure	beruhigen	tranquilizar	rassicurare	tranquilizar
rat	rat	Ratte(f)	rata	topo, ratto	rato, a
rate	spleen	Milz(f)	bazo	milza	baço
râteau	rake	Rechen(m)	rastrillo	rastrello	ancinho
rater	fail	mißlingen	fallar	mancare	falhar
rater	miss	verpassen	perder	perdere; mancare	perder
ratifier	ratify	ratifizieren	ratificar	ratificare	ratificar
ration, portion	ration	Ration(f); Stück(n)	ración	razione	ração
rationnel, le	rational	rational	racional	razionale	racional
rationnement	rationing	Rationierung(f)	racionamiento	razionamento	racionamento
rature	deletion	Streichung(f)	tachadura	cancellatura	rasura
rauque	hoarse	rauh, heiser	ronco, a	rauco, a	rouco, a
ravage	devastation	Verwüstung(f)	destrozo	devastazione	estrago
ravager	devastate, ravage	verwüsten	asolar, devastar	devastare	assolar
ravi, e	delighted	hocherfreut	encantado, a	lietissimo, a	encantado, a
ravin	ravine	Schlucht(f); Graben(m)	barranco	burrone	barranco
ravissant, e	ravishing, lovely	entzückend	encantador, a	incantevole	encantador, a
ravitailler	supply	versorgen	abastecer	rifornire	abastecer
rayé, e	scratched	zerkratzt	rayado, a	rigato, a	riscado, a
rayer	cross out	durch = streichen	rayar	cancellare	riscar; cortar
rayon	radius(-ii)	Radius(m)	radio	raggio	raio
rayon	ray	Strahl(m)	rayo	raggio	raio
rayon	spoke	Speiche(f)	radio	raggio	raio
rayon	department	Abteilung(f)	sección	reparto	secção
rayonnement	radiance	Strahlung(f)	irradiación	irradiazione	irradiação
rayures(à)	striped	gestreift	rayas(a)	righe(a)	riscas(às)
réacteur	reactor; engine	Reaktor(m)	reactor	reattore	reactor
réaction	reaction	Reaktion(f)	reacción	reazione	reacção
réactionnaire	reactionary	reaktionär	reaccionario, a	reazionario, a	reaccionário, a
réadaptation	readjustment	Umstellung(f)	readaptación	riadattamento	readaptação
réagir	react	reagieren	reaccionar	reagire	reagir
réalisation	realization	Verwirklichung(f)	realización	realizzazione	realização
réaliser	realize	begreifen	darse cuenta	realizzare	aperceber-se
réaliser	carry out, perform	verwirklichen	realizar	realizzare	realizar, fazer
réalité	reality	Wirklichkeit(f)	realidad	realtà	realidade
réanimation	resuscitation	Wiederbelebung(f)	reanimación	rianimazione	reanimação
rebelle	rebel	Rebell(m)	rebelde	ribelle	rebelde

French	English	German	Spanish	Italian	Portuguese
rébellion	rebellion	Aufstand(m)	rebelión	ribellione	rebelião
rebondir	bounce, rebound	ab=prallen, aufprallen	rebotar	rimbalzare	ressaltar
récemment	recently	kürzlich	recientemente	recentemente	recentemente
recensement	census	Volkszählung(f)	censo	censimento	recenseamento
récent, e	recent	neu	reciente	recente	recente
réceptacle	receptacle	Sammelbecken(n)	receptáculo	ricettacolo	receptáculo
récepteur	receiver	Empfänger(m)	receptor	ricevitore	receptor
réception	reception	Empfang(m)	recepción	ricezione	recepção
réception	reception	Rezeption(f)	recepción	reception	recepção
réception	party, reception	Empfang(m)	recepción	ricevimento	recepção
réception	receipt	Empfang(m)	recibo	ricevuta	recepção
recette	recipe	Rezept(n)	receta	ricetta	receita
recette	receipts; takings	Einnahmen(f, pl)	ingresos	incasso	receita
recevoir	receive, get	empfangen	recibir	ricevere	receber
réchaud	stove	Kocher(m)	hornillo	fornello	fogão
réchauffer	warm, (re)heat	auf=wärmen	recalentar	riscaldare	aquecer
recherche	search	Suche(f)	busca	ricerca	busca
recherche	research	Forschung(f)	investigación	ricerca	investigação
rechercher	search/look for	suchen	buscar, indagar	ricercare	buscar, procurar
récif	reef	Riff(n)	arrecife	scoglio	recife
récipient	container	Behälter(m)	recipiente	recipiente	recipiente
récit	story	Bericht(m)	narración	racconto	narração
récital	recital	Konzert(n), Vortrag(m)	recital	recital	recital
récitation	recitation	Vortrag(m)	recitación	recita	recitação
réclamation	complaint, claim	Beschwerde(f)	reclamo, claim	reclamo	reclamação
réclame(s), pub	advertisement	Reklame(f)	publicidad	reclame	publicidade
réclame(en)	offer(on)	Sonderangebot(n)	reclamo(de)	offerta(in)	promoção(em)
réclamer à	ask(for)	bitten um	reclamar	reclamare	reclamar
récolte	crop; harvest	Ernte(f)	cosecha	raccolta	colheita
récolter	harvest, gather	ernten	cosechar, recoger	raccogliere	colher, apanhar
recommandation	recommendation	Empfehlung(f)	recomendación	raccomandazione	recomendação
récompense	reward; award	Belohnung(f)	recompensa	ricompensa	recompensa
réconciliation	reconciliation	Versöhnung(f)	reconciliación	riconciliazione	reconciliação
réconfortant, e	comforting	tröstlich	reconfortante	riconfortante	reconfortante
reconnaissant, e	grateful	dankbar	agradecido, a	grato, a	reconhecido, a
reconnaître	recognize	erkennen	reconocer	riconoscere	reconhecer
record	record	Rekord(m)	récord	record	recorde
recourir à	appeal to	Berufung(f)ein=legen	recurrir, apelar	ricorrere, appellarsi	recorrer, apelar
recours	recourse	Zuflucht(f), Berufung	recurso	ricorso	recurso
récréation	break	Pause(f)	recreo	ricreazione	recreio
recrutement	recruitment	Rekrutierung(f)	reclutamiento	reclutamento	recrutamento
recruter	recruit	an=werben	contratar, reclutar	assumere	recrutar
rectangle	rectangle	Rechteck(n)	rectángulo	rettangolo	rectângulo
rectifier	rectify	berichtigen	rectificar	rettificare	rectificar
reçu	receipt	Quittung(f)	recibo	ricevuta	recibo
recul	recoil	Rückstoß(m)	retroceso	rinculo	recuo
reculer	move back, reverse	zurück=gehen	retroceder	indietreggiare	recuar
récupérer	recover, get back	wieder=bekommen	recuperar	recuperare	recuperar
rédaction	editorial staff	Redaktion(f)	redacción	redazione	redacção
redevance	tax; royalty	Gebühr(f)	impuesto, tasa	cànone	taxa
redoutable	formidable	furchtbar	temible	temibile	temível
redresser	straighten out/up	gerade=biegen	enderezar	raddrizzare	endireitar
réduction	reduction	Verringerung(f)	reducción	riduzione	redução
réduction	reduction	Senkung(f)	rebaja	riduzione	desconto
réduire	reduce	reduzieren	reducir	ridurre	reduzir
rééducation	therapy	Heilgymnastik(f)	reeducación	rieducazione	reeducação
réel, le	real, actual	wirklich	real	reale; vero, a	real
réellement	truly	wirklich	realmente	realmente	realmente
référence	reference	Referenz(f)	referencia	riferimento	referência
référer(se)	refer to	beziehen, sich	referirse	riferirsi	referir-se
réfléchi, e	thoughtful	bedächtig	reflexivo, a	riflessivo, a	ponderado, a
réfléchir(à)	reflect, think	überlegen	reflexionar	riflettere	reflectir; pensar
réfléchir(se)	reflected(be)	reflektieren	reflejar	riflettere(-ersi)	reflectir
reflet	reflection	Widerschein(m), Reflex	reflejo	riflesso	reflexo
réflexe	reflex	Reflex(m)	reflejo	riflesso	reflexo
reflux	ebb	Ebbe(f)	reflujo	riflusso	refluxo
réforme	reform	Reform(f)	reforma	riforma	reforma
refrain	refrain, chorus	Refrain(m)	estribillo	ritornello	refrão

F

103

French	English	German	Spanish	Italian	Portuguese
réfrigérateur	refrigerator	Kühlschrank(m)	nevera	frigorifero	frigorífico
refroidir	cool(down)	ab = kühlen	enfriar	raffreddare	arrefecer
refuge, asile	refuge	Zufluchtsort(m)	refugio, asilo	rifugio, asilo	refúgio, asilo
réfugié, e	refugee	Flüchtling(m)	refugiado, a	rifugiato, a	refugiado, a
refus	refusal	Verweigerung(f)	rechazo	rifiuto	recusa
refuser	refuse	verweigern	rehusar	rifiutare	recusar
refuser, rejeter	reject	ab = lehnen, verwerfen	rechazar	rigettare	rejeitar
réfuter	refute	widerlegen	refutar	confutare	refutar
regard	look, expression	Blick(m)	mirada	sguardo	olhar
regard	glance	Blick(m)	ojeada	occhiata	olhada
regarder	look(at)	schauen, an = sehen	mirar	guardare	olhar
regarder	watch, look(at)	fern = sehen	mirar	guardare	ver
regardez!	look!	seht!, schauen Sie!	mire(!)	guardi!, guardate!	olhe!
régime	régime	Regime(n)	régimen	regime	regime
régime	speed	Drehzahl(f)	régimen	regime	velocidade
régime	diet(be on a)	Diät(f)	dieta	dieta	dieta
régiment	regiment	Regiment(n)	regimiento	reggimento	regimento
région	region, area	Gegend(f)	región	regione	região
registre	register	Register(m)	registro	registro	registo
réglage	adjustment	Einstellung(f)	reglaje, ajuste	regolazione	afinação
règle	ruler	Lineal(n)	regla	riga	régua
règle	rule	Regel(f)	regla, norma	regola, norma	regra, norma
règlement	regulation	Bestimmung(f)	reglamento	regolamento	regulamento
règlement	settlement	Begleichung(f)	liquidación	saldo	pagamento
réglementation	regulation(s)	Regelung(f)	reglamentación	regolamentazione	regulamentação
régler	settle	regeln; erledigen	resolver	risolvere	resolver
régler	settle	bezahlen	liquidar, pagar	regolare, saldare	pagar
régler	adjust, tune	ein = stellen	ajustar, arreglar	regolare	afinar, regular
règne	reign	Herrschaft(f)	reino	regno	reinado
régression	regression	Rückgang(m)	regresión	regresso	regressão
regret	regret	Bedauern(n)	lamento(lo)	rimpianto	pena; pesar
regretter	regret	nach = trauern(jdm/etw)	lamentar, añorar	rimpiangere	lamentar
regretter	sorry(be), regret	bedauern	sentir(lo)	dispiacere(-ersi)	sentir, lamentar
régularisation	regularization	Regulierung(f)	regularización	regolarizzazione	regularização
régulier, ière	regular	regelmäßig	regular	regolare	regular
rein	kidney	Niere(f)	riñón	rene	rim
reine	queen	Königin(f)	reina	regina	rainha
réintégrer	return	zurück = kehren	reintegrar	reintegrare	voltar
réintégrer	reinstate	wiederein = setzen	rehabilitar	reintegrare	reintegrar
rejoindre	rejoin, return to	an = schließen, sich	reunirse con	raggiungere	reunir-se
réjouir(se)	delighted(be)	erfreuen, sich	alegrarse	rallegrare(-arsi)	alegrar-se
réjouissance	rejoicing	Fröhlichkeit(f)	regocijo	gioia, giubilo	regozijo; alegria
relâcher	release	frei = lassen	soltar	rilasciare	libertar
relâcher	loosen	lockern	aflojar	allentare	largar; soltar
relater	relate, recount	erzählen	relatar	riferire	relatar
relatif, ive	relative	relativ	relativo, a	relativo, a	relativo, a
relation	relation(-ship)	Beziehung(f)	relación	relazione	relação
relaxation	relaxation	Entspannung(f)	relajamiento	rilassamento	relaxação
relevé	statement	Aufstellung(f)machen	extracto	estratto	levantamento
relevé(compte)	statement(bank)	Kontoauszug(m)	estado(cuentas)	estratto conto	extracto(conta)
relief	relief	Relief(n)	relieve	rilievo	relevo
relier	link, connect	verbinden	enlazar, unir	collegare	ligar
religieux, se	religious	religiös	religioso, a	religioso, a	religioso, a
religion	religion	Religion(f)	religión	religione	religião
reliure	binding(book-)	Einband(m)	encuadernación	rilegatura	encadernação
remarquable	remarkable	bemerkenswert	notable	notevole	notável
remarque	remark, comment	Bemerkung(f)	observación	osservazione	observação
remarquer	notice	bemerken	notar, señalar	notare, osservare	notar, reparar
remboursement	repayment	Rückzahlung(f)	reembolso	rimborso	reembolso
rembourser	pay back, reimburse	zurück = zahlen	reembolsar	rimborsare	reembolsar
remède	remedy	Heilmittel(n)	remedio	rimedio	remédio
remerciement	thanks	Dank(m)	agradecimiento	ringraziamento	agradecimento
remercier	thank	danken; bedanken, sich	agradecer	ringraziare	agradecer
remise, rabais	reduction	Nachlaß, Ermäßigung	descuento	rimessa, sconto	desconto
remontage	reassembly	Zusammensetzen(n)	volver a montar	rimontaggio	nova montagem
remonter	reassemble	wieder montieren	volver a montar	rimontare	tornar a montar
remords	remorse	Gewissensbiß(m)	remordimiento	rimorso	remorso
remorque	trailer	Anhänger(m)	remolque	rimorchio	reboque

French	English	German	Spanish	Italian	Portuguese
remorquer	tow	ab = schleppen	remolcar	rimorchiare	rebocar
remous	eddy, swirl	Wirbel(m)	remolino	mulinello, gorgo	redemoinho
remplaçant, e	substitute	Stellvertreter(in f)m	sustituto, a	sostituto, a	substituto, a
remplacer	replace	ersetzen	sustituir	sostituire	substituir
remplir	fill	füllen	llenar	riempire	encher
remporter, gagner	achieve	erringen	lograr, triunfar	raggiungere, ottenere	alcançar, obter
remuer	move	bewegen, sich	mover	muovere(-rsi)	mexer-se
remuer	stir	rühren	remover	mescolare	mexer
rémunération	remuneration	Entlohnung(f), Lohn(m)	remuneración	rimunerazione	remuneração
renard	fox(-es)	Fuchs(m)	zorro	volpe	raposa
rencontre	meeting	Begegnung(f)	encuentro	incontro	encontro
rencontrer	meet	treffen	encontrar	incontrare	encontrar
rendement	output, yield	Ertrag(m), Leistung(f)	rendimiento	rendimento	rendimento
rendement	yield	Ertrag(m)	rendimiento	rendimento	rendimento; produto
rendez-vous	appointment	Verabredung(f)	cita	appuntamento	encontro
rendre	give back	zurück = geben	devolver	rendere	devolver
renforcer	reinforce	verstärken	reforzar	rinforzare	reforçar
renfort	reinforcement	Verstärkung(f)	refuerzo	rinforzo	reforço
renier	disown; renounce	verleugnen, verneinen	renegar	rinnegare	renegar
renifler	sniff	schnüffeln	resoplar	tirar su col naso	fungar
renommée	fame	Ruhm(m)	fama	fama	fama
renoncer	give up	auf = geben	renunciar	rinunciare	desistir; renunciar
renouveler	renew	erneuern	renovar	rinnovare	renovar
renouvellement	renewal	Erneuerung(f)	renovación	rinnovo	renovação
rénovation	renovation	Renovation(f)	renovación	rinnovazione	restauração
renseignement	information	Auskunft(f)	información	informazione	informação
renseigner(se)	inquire	erkundigen, sich	informar(se)	informare(-arsi)	informar-se
rentabilité	profitability	Rentabilität(f)	rentabilidad	redditività	rentabilidade
rentable	profitable	einträglich	rentable	redditizio, a	rentável
rente	income, pension	Einkommen(n)	renta	rendita	renda
rentrer	go back, come back	zurück = kommen	regresar	tornare, rientrare	voltar
renverser	spill, knock over	verschütten	derramar, volcar	rovesciare	entornar
renverser	knock over/down	um = stoßen	derribar	travolgere	derrubar
renverser(se)	overturn	überschlagen, sich	volcarse	rovesciarsi	virar; cair
renvoyer	send back, return	zurück = schicken	devolver	rinviare	devolver
renvoyer	dismiss	entlassen	despedir	dimettere	despedir
répandre	spread; spill	verschütten	derramar	spargere	espalhar
réparation	repair	Reparation(f)	reparación	riparazione	reparação
réparer	repair, mend	reparieren	reparar	riparare	reparar
répartir	share out	auf = teilen	repartir	ripartire	repartir
répartition	distribution	Verteilung(f)	reparto	ripartizione	repartição
repas	meal	Mahlzeit(f)	comida	pasto	refeição
repassage	ironing	Bügeln(n)	planchado	stirare	passar a ferro
repère	mark, landmark	Markierung(f)	señal, indicio	contrassegno	sinal, marca
repérer	locate	lokalisieren	localizar	localizzare	localizar
répertoire	index; repertoire	Repertoire(n)	repertorio	repertorio	repertório
répéter	repeat	wieder = holen	repetir	ripetere	repetir
répit	respite	Atempause(f)	tregua, respiro	tregua, riposo	trégua, espera
répliquer	reply	erwidern, entgegnen	replicar	replicare	replicar
répondre	answer, reply	antworten	contestar	rispondere	responder
répondre	reply, answer	erwidern	responder	rispondere	responder
réponse	answer, reply	Antwort(f)	respuesta	risposta	resposta
reportage	report	Reportage(f)	reportaje	cronaca	reportagem
reporter	postpone	verschieben	postergar	rinviare	adiar
repos	rest	Ruhe(f)	descanso	riposo	descanço
reposer(se)	rest	aus = ruhen, sich	descansar	riposarsi	descançar
représaille(s)	reprisal	Vergeltung(f)	represalia	rappresaglia	represália
représentant, e	representative, rep	Vertreter(in f)m	representante	rappresentante	representante
représentation	representation	Darstellung(f)	representación	rappresentazione	representação
représentation	performance	Vorstellung(f)	representación	rappresentazione	representação
représenter	represent	dar = stellen	representar	rappresentare	representar
répression	repression	Unterdrückung(f)	represión	repressione	repressão
reprocher	reproach	vor = werfen	reprochar	rimproverare	censurar
reproduction	reproduction	Reproduktion(f)	reproducción	riproduzione	reprodução
reproduire	reproduce	reproduzieren	reproducir	riprodurre	reproduzir
reproduire(se)	breed(animals)	fort = pflanzen, sich	reproducir(se)	riprodurre(-rsi)	reproduzir-se
reptile	reptile	Reptil(n)	reptil	rettile	réptil
république	republic	Republik(f)	república	repubblica	república

French	English	German	Spanish	Italian	Portuguese
réputation	reputation	Ansehen(n), Ruf(m)	reputación, fama	reputazione, fama	reputação, fama
requête	request	Ersuchen(n), Gesuch(n)	demanda	richiesta	pedido
requin	shark	Hai(m)	tiburón	squalo	tubarão
réquisitoire	indictment	Anklagerede(f)	requisitoria	requisitoria	requisitório
rescapé, e	survivor	Überlebende(f, m)	superviviente	scampato, a	sobrevivente
réseau	network	Netz(n)	red	rete	rede
réservation	reservation	Reservierung(f)	reserva	prenotazione	reserva
réserve	reserve	Reserve(f)	reserva	riserva	reserva
réservé, e	reserved	reserviert	reservado, a	prenotato, a	reservado, a
réserver	reserve	reservieren	reservar	riservare	reservar
réserver	book, reserve	vor = bestellen	reservar	prenotare	reservar
réservoir	tank	Tank(m)	depósito	serbatoio	depósito
résidence	residence	Wohnsitz(m)	residencia	residenza	residência
résider	reside	wohnen	residir	risiedere	residir
résidu	residue	Rückstand(m)	residuo	residuo	resíduo
résigner(se)	resign oneself	entsagen, ergeben, sich	resignarse	rassegnarsi	resignar-se
résine	resin	Harz(m)	resina	resina	resina
résistance	resistance	Widerstand(m)	resistencia	resistenza	resistência
résistant, e	resistant	widerstandsfähig	resistente	resistente	resistente
résister	resist; withstand	widerstehen	resistir	resistere	resistir
résister à	withstand	widerstehen	resistir a	resistere a	resistir a
résonner	resound, sound	klingen	resonar	rimbombare	ressoar, ecoar
résoudre	solve, resolve	lösen	resolver	risolvere	resolver
respect	respect	Respekt(m)	respeto	rispetto	respeito
respectable	respectable	achtbar	respetable	rispettabile	respeitável
respecter	respect	respektieren	respetar	rispettare	respeitar
respectivement	respectively	beziehungsweise	respectivamente	rispettivamente	respectivamente
respiration	breathing	Atmung(f)	respiración	respirazione	respiração
respirer	breathe	atmen	respirar	respirare	respirar
responsabilité	responsibility	Verantwortung(f)	responsabilidad	responsabilità	responsabilidade
responsable	responsible	verantwortlich	responsable	responsabile	responsável
responsable	liable(to be)	haftbar	responsable	responsabile	responsável
responsable	person in charge	Verantwortliche(f, m)	encargado, a	responsabile	responsável
ressemblance	resemblance	Ähnlichkeit(f)	parecido	somiglianza	semelhança
ressembler(à)	look like	ähneln, aussehen wie	parecerse(a)	somigliare a	parecer-se
ressentir	feel	empfinden	sentir	sentire	sentir
resserrer	narrow	verengen	estrechar	ristringere	estreitar
ressort	spring	Feder(f)(Sprung-)	muelle	molla	mola
ressource(s)	resources	Mittel(n, pl)	recurso	risorsa	recurso
restaurant	restaurant	Restaurant(n)	restaurante	ristorante	restaurante
restaurer	restore	wiederher = stellen	restaurar	restaurare	restaurar
reste	rest, remainder	Rest(m)	resto	resto	resto
rester	left(be), remain	übrig = bleiben, bleiben	quedar	rimanere, avanzare	sobrar
rester	remain	bleiben	sobrar, quedar	restare, rimanere	sobejar, sobrar
rester	stay, remain	bleiben	quedarse	restare	ficar
restituer	return	zurück = erstatten	restituir	restituire	restituir
restreindre	restrict	beschränken	restringir	restringere	restringir
restriction	restriction	Einschränkung(f)	restricción	restrizione	restrição
résultat	result	Ergebnis(n)	resultado	risultato, esito	resultado
résulter, être	result, be	ergeben, sich	resultar	risultare	resultar
résumé	summary	Zusammenfassung(f)	resumen	riassunto	resumo
retard	delay; lateness	Verspätung(f)	atraso	ritardo	atraso
retard(être en)	late(to be)	zu spät kommen	retrasado, a(estar)	ritardo(essere in)	atrasado, a(estar)
retarder	delay	verzögern	retrasar, demorar	ritardare	atrasar, demorar
retenir	hold back; retain	zurück = halten	retener	trattenere	reter
rétine	retina	Netzhaut(f)	retina	retina	retina
retirer	withdraw	zurück = ziehen	retirar	ritirare	retirar
retirer, tirer	draw	ab = heben	cobrar	prelevare	tirar
retirer	draw out, withdraw	ab = heben	sacar	prelevare	levantar
retour	return	Rückkehr(f)	regreso, vuelta	ritorno	regresso, volta
retourner	return(to)	zurück = gehen	regresar	tornare	voltar(a)
retraite	retirement	Pensionierung(f)	jubilación	pensione	reforma
retraité, e(être)	retired(be)	pensioniert sein	jubilado, a(estar)	pensione(essere in)	reformado, a(estar)
retraité, e	retired person	Rentner(in f)m	retirado, a	pensionato, a	reformado, a
rétrécir	shrink	schrumpfen	encoger	restringere	encolher
rétrécir(se)	narrow	enger machen/werden	estrechar(se)	restringersi	estreitar-se
rétroviseur	rear-view mirror	Rückspiegel(m)	retrovisor	retrovisore	retrovisor
réunion	meeting; reunion	Treffen(n)	reunión	riunione	reunião

French	English	German	Spanish	Italian	Portuguese
réunir	gather(together)	sammeln	reunir	riunire	reunir
réunir(se)	meet	treffen, sich	reunirse	riunirsi	reunir-se
réussir	succeed	gelingen	lograr, conseguir	riuscire	conseguir
réussite	success(-es)	Erfolg(m)	éxito, logro	riuscita	êxito
rêve	dream	Traum(m)	sueño	sogno	sonho
réveil	alarm clock	Wecker(m)	despertador	sveglia	despertador
réveiller	wake(up)	wecken	despertar	svegliare	acordar
révéler	reveal	auf = decken	revelar	rivelare	revelar
revendication	claim, demand	Forderung(f)	reivindicación	rivendicazione	reivindicação
revendiquer	claim	beanspruchen	reivindicar	rivendicare	reivindicar
revenir	come back, return	zurück = kommen	volver	ritornare	voltar
revenu	income, revenue	Einkommen(n)	renta, ingresos	reddito	rendimento
rêver	dream	träumen	soñar	sognare	sonhar
révision	revision	Revision(f)	revisión	revisione	revisão
révision	service, overhaul	Überholung(f)	revisión	revisione	revisão
revoir	see again	wieder = sehen	volver a ver	rivedere	voltar a ver
révolte	revolt	Revolte(f)	revuelta	rivolta	revolta
révolution	revolution	Revolution(f)	revolución	rivoluzione	revolução
révolutionnaire	revolutionary	revolutionär	revolucionario, a	rivoluzionario, a	revolucionário, a
révolver	revolver, gun	Revolver(m)	revólver	revolver	revólver
révoquer	dismiss	ab = setzen, entlassen	revocar	revocare	demitir
revue, magazine	review, magazine	Zeitschrift, Revue(f)	revista	rivista, periodico	revista
rez-de-chaussée	ground floor	Erdgeschoß(n)	planta baja, bajo	piano terra	rés-do-chão
rhumatisme	rheumatism	Rheumatismus(m)	reumatismo	reumatismo	reumatismo
rhume	cold	Schnupfen(m)	resfriado	raffreddore	constipação
ricaner	snigger	grinsen, kichern	burlarse	sogghignare	troçar
riche	rich, wealthy	reich	rico, a	ricco, a	rico, a
richesse	wealth, richness	Reichtum(m)	riqueza	ricchezza	riqueza
ride	wrinkle	Falte(f)	arruga	ruga	ruga
rideau	curtain	Vorhang(m)	cortina	tenda, tapparella	cortina
ridicule	ridiculous	lächerlich	ridículo, a	ridicolo, a	ridículo, a
rien	nothing	nichts	nada	niente, nulla	nada
rigide	rigid, stiff	steif	rígido, a	rigido, a	rígido, a
rigoureux, se	rigorous	streng	riguroso, a	rigoroso, a	rigoroso, a
riposte	counter-attack	Gegenangriff(m)	réplica	risposta	réplica
rire	laugh	lachen	reir	ridere	rir
rire	laugh, laughter	Lachen(n)	risa	riso, ridere	riso
risque	risk	Risiko(n)	riesgo	rischio	risco
risquer	risk	riskieren	arriesgar	rischiare	arriscar
rite	rite; ritual	Brauch(m), Ritus(m)	rito	rito	rito
rivage	shore	Küstenstrich(m)	orilla	riva	beira-mar
rival, e	rival; competitor	Rivale(m), Rivalin(f)	rival	rivale	rival
rivalité	rivalry	Rivalität(f)	rivalidad	rivalità	rivalidade
rive	bank	Ufer(n)	orilla, margen	riva	margem
rivière	river	Fluß(m)	río, ribera	fiume	rio, ribeira
riz	rice	Reis(m)	arroz	riso	arroz
robe	dress	Kleid(n)	vestido	vestito	vestido
robe de chambre	dressing gown	Schlafrock(m)	bata	vestaglia	roupão
robe de soirée	evening dress	Abendkleid(n)	traje de noche	abito da sera	vestido de noite
robinet	tap; stop-cock	Wasserhahn(m), Hahn(m)	grifo	rubinetto	torneira
robinet	cock, tap	Hahn(m)(Wasser-; Gas-)	llave, grifo	rubinetto	torneira
robot	robot	Roboter(m)	robot	robot	robot
robuste	robust, sturdy	robust, stark	robusto, a	robusto, a	robusto, a
robuste, solide	sturdy	kräftig, fest	vigoroso, a; fuerte	robusto, a; forte	robusto, a; forte
roche, rocher	rock	Fels(m)	roca	roccia	rocha
rocher	rock	Felsen(m)	peñasco, roca	masso, roccia	rochedo, rocha
rodage	running in	Einfahren(n)	rodaje	rodaggio	rodagem
rôdeur, se	prowler	Herumstreicher(m)	vagabundo, a	vagabondo, a	vagabundo, a
roi	king	König(m)	rey	re	rei
rôle	role	Rolle(f)	papel	parte, ruolo	papel
rôle	role, part	Rolle(f)	cometido, función	ruolo, parte	função
roman	novel	Roman(m)	novela	romanzo	romance
roman policier	detective novel	Kriminalroman(m)	novela policíaca	giallo	romance policial
romancier, ière	novelist	Schriftsteller(in f)m	novelista	romanziere, a	romancista
romantique	romantic	romantisch	romántico, a	romantico, a	romântico, a
rompre	break	brechen(ab = -; zer-)	romper	rompere	romper
rond, e	round	rund	redondo, a	rotondo, a	redondo, a
rondelle	slice	Scheibe(f)	rodaja	fettina, fetta	rodela

French	English	German	Spanish	Italian	Portuguese
rondelle	washer	Scheibe(f)	arandela	rondella	anilha
rond-point	roundabout	Kreisverkehr(m)	glorieta	rotonda, rotatoria	rotunda
ronfler	snore	schnarchen	roncar	russare	ressonar, roncar
ronger	gnaw	zernagen	roer	rodere	roer
rose	pink	rosafarben	rosa	rosa	cor-de-rosa
rose	rose	Rose(f)	rosa	rosa	rosa
rosée	dew	Tau(m)	rocío	rugiada	orvalho
rotation	rotation	Drehung(f)	rotación	rotazione	rotação
roter	burp	auf = stoßen, rülpsen	eructar	ruttare	arrotar
rôti	roast; joint	Braten(m)	asado	arrosto	assado
rotule	knee-cap	Kniescheibe(f)	rótula	rotula	rótula
roue	wheel	Rad(n)	rueda	ruota	roda
rouge	red	rot	rojo, a	rosso, a	vermelho, a
rouge à lèvres	lipstick	Lippenstift(m)	barra de labios	rossetto	baton
rougeole	measles	Masern(pl.)	sarampión	morbillo	sarampo
rougir	blush, flush	erröten	sonrojarse	arrossire	corar
rouille	rust	Rost(m)	herrumbre	ruggine	ferrugem
rouleau	roll	Rolle(f), Walze(f)	rollo	rotolo; rullo	rolo
rouler	roll	rollen	rodar	rotolare	rolar
rouler	run, drive, go	fahren	correr, rodar	correre, andare	andar; rolar
rouspéter	grouse, moan	meckern, murren	refunfuñar	brontolare	rezingar
route	road	Straße(f)	carretera	strada	estrada
route nationale	main/trunk road	Landstraße(f)	carretera	strada statale	estrada
routine	routine	Routine(f)	rutina	routine, tran tran	rotina
roux, rousse	auburn; reddish	rothaarig	pelirrojo, a	rosso, a	ruivo, a
royal, e	royal	königlich	real	reale	real
royaume	kingdom	Königreich(n)	reino	reame	reino
royauté	royalty, monarchy	Königstum(n)	realeza	sovranità	realeza
ruban	ribbon; tape; band	Band(n)	cinta, banda	nastro	fita
rubéole	German measles	Röteln(pl)	rubéola	rosolia	rubéola
rubis	ruby	Rubin(m)	rubí	rubino	rubi
ruche	hive	Bienenstock(m)	colmena	alveare	colmeia
rue	street	Straße(f)	calle	via	rua
ruée	rush	Ansturm(m)	riada	ressa	corrida
ruelle	alley	Gäßchen(n), Gasse(f)	callejuela	viuzza, vicolo	viela
rugueux, se	rough, harsh	rauh	rugoso, a	rugoso, a	rugoso, a
ruine	ruin	Ruine(f)	ruina	rovina	ruína
ruine	ruin	Trümmer(m, pl)	ruina	rovina	ruína
ruiner	ruin	ruinieren	arruinar	rovinare	arruinar
ruisseau	stream, brook	Bach(m)	riachuelo, arroyo	ruscello	regato, ribeiro
rumeur	rumour	Gerücht(n)	rumor	voce, diceria	rumor
rupture	rupture	Bruch(m)	ruptura	rottura	ruptura
rural, e	rural	ländlich	rural	rurale	rural
ruse	trick, craftiness	List(f)	ardid; astucia	furbizia	astúcia
rusé, e	crafty, cunning	schlau, gerissen	astuto, a	astuto, a	astuto, a; fino, a
rustique	rustic	ländlich, einfach	rústico, a	rustico, a	rústico, a
rythme	rhythm	Takt(m), Rhythmus(m)	ritmo	ritmo	ritmo

S

French	English	German	Spanish	Italian	Portuguese
sa	her; his; its	sein, e; ihr, ihre	su	sua(la)	sua
sable	sand	Sand(m)	arena	sabbia	areia
sabot	hoof	Huf(m)	pezuña, casco	zoccolo	casco
sabotage	sabotage	Sabotage(f)	sabotaje	sabotaggio	sabotagem
saboter	sabotage	sabotieren	sabotear	sabotare	sabotar
sabre	sabre	Säbel(m)	sable	sciabola	sabre
sac	bag	Tasche(f)	bolsa, saco	borsa	saco

French	English	German	Spanish	Italian	Portuguese
sac	sack	Sack(m)	saco	sacco	saco
sac à dos	rucksack	Rucksack(m)	mochila	zaino	mochila
sac à main	handbag	Handtasche(f)	bolso	borsetta	carteira
sac de couchage	sleeping bag	Schlafsack(m)	saco de dormir	sacco a pelo	saco-cama
sac de voyage	travel-bag	Reisetasche(f)	bolso de viaje	borsa da viaggio	saco de viagem
saccager	ransack	verwüsten	saquear	saccheggiare	saquear
sachet	bag(small), sachet	Beutel(m), Tütchen(n)	bolsita	bustina	pacote; carteira
sacoche	bag	Tasche(f)(Umhänge-)	cartera	saccoccia, borsa	saco
sacré, e	holy; sacred	heilig	sagrado, a	sacro, a	sagrado, a
sacrifice	sacrifice	Opfer(n)	sacrificio	sacrificio	sacrifício
sacrifier	sacrifice	opfern	sacrificar	sacrificare	sacrificar
sacrilège	sacrilege	Entweihung(f)	sacrilegio	sacrilegio	sacrilégio
sadique	sadistic	sadistisch	sádico, a	sadico, a	sádico, a
sadique	sadist	Sadist(in f)m	sádico, a	sadico, a	sádico, a
sage	good	brav	bueno, a	buono, a; bravo, a	ajuizado, a
sage	sage, wise man	Weise(m)	sabio	saggio, a; savio, a	sábio
sage-femme	midwife(-ives)	Hebamme(f)	comadrona	levatrice	parteira
saignement	bleeding	Blutung(f)	desangramiento	emorragia	perda de sangue
saigner	bleed	bluten	sangrar	sanguinare	sangrar
sain, e	healthy	gesund	sano, a	sano, a	são, sã
saint, e	holy	heilig	santo, a; san	santo, a	santo, a
saint, e	saint	Heilige(m, f)	santo, a	santo, a	santo, a
saisir	seize	ergreifen	coger, agarrar	afferrare	agarrar
saison	season	Jahreszeit(f)	estación	stagione	estação
saisonnier, ière	seasonal	saisonbedingt	temporero, a	stagionale	sazonal
salade	salad; lettuce	Salat(m); Kopfsalat(m)	ensalada; lechuga	insalata	salada
salaire	salary, wage	Lohn(m), Gehalt(n)	salario	salario	salário
salarié, e	salaried employee	Arbeitnehmer(in f)m	asalariado, a	salariato, a	assalariado, a
sale	dirty	dreckig	sucio, a	sporco, a	sujo, a
salé, e	salty	salzig	salado, a	salato, a	salgado, a
saleté	dirt	Schmutz(m)	suciedad	sporcizia	sujidade, porcaria
salir	dirty	verschmutzen	ensuciar	sporcare	sujar
salive	saliva	Speichel(m)	saliva	saliva	saliva
salle	room	Saal(m), Raum(m)	sala	sala, stanza	sala
salle à manger	dining-room	Eßzimmer(n)	comedor	sala da pranzo	sala de jantar
salle d'attente	waiting-room	Wartezimmer(n)	sala de espera	sala d'attesa	sala de espera
salle de bains	bathroom	Badezimmer(n)	cuarto de baño	bagno	quarto de banho
salle de séjour	living-room	Wohnzimmer(n)	sala de estar	soggiorno	sala de estar
salon	lounge	Herrenzimmer(n)	sala	salotto	sala de estar
salon de thé	tea-room	Café(n), Konditorei(f)	salón de té	sala da tè	casa de chá
salon(coiffure)	salon	Friseurladen(m)	peluquería	parrucchiere, a(da)	salão
salon	show, exhibition	Messe(f)	salón	salone	salão
saluer	greet; say hello	begrüßen	saludar	salutare	saudar
salut!	hi!, hello!	Hallo!; tschüs!; tschüß	hola(!)	ciao!	olá!
samedi	Saturday	Samstag(m)	sábado	sabato	sábado
sanction	sanction	Strafe(f)	sanción	sanzione	sanção
sanctuaire	sanctuary	Heiligtum(n)	santuario	santuario	santuário
sandale	sandal	Sandale(f)	sandalia	sandalo	sandália
sandwich	sandwich(-es)	Butterbrot(n)	bocadillo	panino	sande, sanduíche
sang	blood	Blut(n)	sangre	sangue	sangue
sang-froid	cool, calm	Kaltblütigkeit(f)	sangre fría	sangue freddo	sangue-frio
sangle	strap	Riemen(m), Gurt(m)	cincha, correa	cinghia	correia
sanglot	sob	Schluchzer(m)	sollozo	singhiozzo	soluço
sanitaire	sanitary	Gesundheits-	sanitario, a	sanitario, a	sanitário, a
sans	without	ohne	sin	senza	sem
santé	health	Gesundheit(f)	salud	salute	saúde
saphir	sapphire	Saphir(m)	zafiro	zaffiro	safira
sapin	fir-tree	Tanne(f)	abeto	abete	abeto
sardine	sardine	Sardine(f)	sardina	sardina	sardinha
satellite	satellite	Satellit(m)	satélite	satellite	satélite
satin	satin	Satin(m)	raso, satén	raso	cetim
satisfaction	satisfaction	Zufriedenheit(f)	satisfacción	soddisfazione	satisfação
satisfait, e	satisfied	zufrieden	satisfecho, a	soddisfatto, a	satisfeito, a
saturation	saturation	Übersättigung(f)	saturación	saturazione	saturação
saturer	saturate	sättigen	saturar	saturare	saturar
sauce	sauce	Soße(f)	salsa	sugo; salsa	molho
saucisse	sausage	Wurst(f)	salchicha	salsiccia	salsicha
sauf	except	außer	excepto	salvo	salvo, excepto

French	English	German	Spanish	Italian	Portuguese
sauf, ve	safe	sicher	salvo, a	salvo, a	salvo, a
saumon	salmon	Lachs(m)	salmón	salmone	salmão
sauna	sauna	Sauna(f)	sauna	sauna	sauna
saut, bond	jump, leap, spring	Sprung(m)	salto, brinco	salto, balzo	salto, pulo
sauter	jump	springen	saltar	saltare	saltar, pular
sauvage	wild	wild	salvaje	selvaggio, a	selvagem
sauver	save	retten	salvar	salvare	salvar
sauvetage	rescue	Rettung(f)	salvamento	salvataggio	salvamento
sauvetage	salvage	Bergung(f)	salvamento	salvataggio	salvamento
sauveteur	rescuer	Retter(in f)m	socorrista	soccorritore	socorrista
savane	savannah	Savanne(f)	sabana	savana	savana
savant, e	learned person	Wissenschaftler(m)	sabio, a	studioso, a; dotto, a	sábio, a
savant	scientist	Gelehrte(f, m)	científico	scienziato	cientista
saveur	flavour	Geschmack(m)	sabor	sapore	sabor
savoir	know	wissen	saber	sapere	saber
savoir	knowledge	Wissen(n)	saber	sapere	sabedoria
savoir-faire	know-how	Geschick(n)	tacto, maña	savoir-faire	habilidade
savon	soap	Seife(f)	jabón	sapone	sabão
savourer	savour	kosten, genießen	saborear	assaporare	saborear
savoureux, se	tasty	schmackhaft	sabroso, a	saporito, a	saboroso, a
scandale	scandal	Skandal(m)	escándalo	scandalo	escândalo
scaphandre	diving-suit	Taucheranzug(m)	escafandra	scafandro	escafandro
sceau	seal	Siegel(n)	sello	sigillo	selo
scénario	script(film -)	Drehbuch(n)	guión	scenario	guião
scénariste	script-writer	Drehbuchautor(in f)m	guionista	scenarista	cenarista
scène	scene	Szene(f)	escena	scena	cena
scène	stage	Szene(f), Bühne(f)	escena	scena	cena
sceptique	sceptic(al)	skeptisch	escéptico, a	scettico, a	céptico, a
schéma	diagram	Schema(n)	esquema	schema	esquema
sciatique	sciatica	Ischias(m)	ciática	sciatica	ciática
scie	saw	Säge(f)	sierra	sega	serra
scier	saw	sägen	serrar, aserrar	segare	serrar
science	science	Wissenschaft(f)	ciencia	scienza	ciência
scientifique	scientific	wissenschaftlich	científico, a	scientifico, a	científico, a
scientifique	scientist	Wissenschaftler(m)	científico	scienziato	cientista
scintiller	sparkle	flimmern	centellear	scintillare	cintilar
sclérose	sclerosis(-ses)	Sklerose(f)	esclerósis	sclerosi	esclerose
scolarité	schooling	Schulzeit(f)	escolaridad	scolarità	escolaridade
scoliose	scoliosis	Skoliose(f)	escoliosis	scoliosi	escoliose
score	score	Punktzahl(f)	marca, tanteo	punteggio	resultado
scorpion	scorpion	Skorpion(m)	escorpión	scorpione	escorpião
scotch	sellotape	Tesafilm(m)	papel celo	scotch	fita adesiva
scrupule	scruple	Skrupel(m)	escrúpulo	scrupolo	escrúpulo
scruter	scan, scrutinize	erforschen	escudriñar	scrutare	perscrutar
scrutin, vote	poll; ballot	Wahl(f), Abstimmung(f)	escrutinio	scrutinio	escrutínio
sculpture	sculpture	Skulptur(f)	escultura	scultura	escultura
séance	session; meeting	Sitzung(f)	sesión	seduta	sessão
seau	bucket, pail	Eimer(m)	cubo	secchio	balde
sec, sèche	dry	trocken	seco, a	secco, a; asciutto, a	seco, a
sèche-cheveux	hair-dryer	Fön(m), Haartrockner m	secador	asciugacapelli	secador
sécher	dry	trocknen	secar	asciugare; seccare	secar
sécheresse	drought	Trockenheit(f)	sequía	siccità	seca
second, e	second	zweite	segundo, a	secondo, a	segundo, a
secondaire	secondary	nebensächlich	secundario, a	secondario, a	secundário, a
seconde	second	Sekunde(f)	segundo	secondo	segundo
secouer	shake	schütteln	sacudir	scuotere	sacudir
secourir	rescue	retten	socorrer	soccorrere	socorrer
secourir	help, assist, aid	helfen	socorrer	soccorrere	socorrer
secours	help, aid	Hilfe(f)	socorro	soccorso	socorro
secousse	jolt, jerk	Ruck(m), Stoß(m)	sacudida	scossa	abalo
secret	secret	Geheimnis(n)	secreto	segreto	segredo
secret, ète	secret	geheim	secreto, a	segreto, a	secreto, a
secrétaire	secretary	Sekretär(in f)m	secretario, a	segretario, a	secretário, a
sécrétion	secretion	Ausscheidung(f)	secreción	secrezione	secreção
secte	sect	Sekte(f)	secta	setta	seita
secteur	sector	Bereich(m)	sector	settore	sector
section	section	Schnitt(m)	sección	sezione	secção
sectionner	cut, divide	schneiden	seccionar	sezionare	seccionar

French	English	German	Spanish	Italian	Portuguese
sécurité	security; safety	Sicherheit(f)	seguridad	sicurezza	segurança
sédatif, ive	sedative	schmerzlindernd	sedativo, a	sedativo, a	sedativo, a
séduction	seduction	Verführung(f)	seducción	seduzione	sedução
séduire	charm; seduce	verführen, verleiten	seducir	sedurre	seduzir
séduisant, e	attractive	reizend, anziehend	atractivo, a	seducente	atraente
segment	segment	Abschnitt(m)	segmento	segmento	segmento
ségrégation	segregation	Trennung(f)	segregación	segregazione	segregação
seigle	rye	Roggen(m)	centeno	segale	centeio
Seigneur	Lord	Herr(m)	Señor	Signore	Senhor
sein(s)	breast	Busen(m)	seno, pecho	seno	seio
séisme	earthquake	Erdbeben(n)	seismo	sisma	sismo
séisme	earthquake	Erdbeben(n)	terremoto	terremoto	terremoto
seize	sixteen	sechzehn	dieciséis	sedici	dezasseis
séjour	stay	Aufenthalt(m)	estancia	soggiorno	estadia, estada
sel	salt	Salz(n)	sal	sale	sal
sélection	selection	Auslese(f); Auswahl(f)	selección	selezione	selecção
sélectionner	select	aus = lesen	seleccionar	selezionare	seleccionar
selle	saddle	Sattel(m)	silla	sella	sela
selle	saddle	Sattel(m)	sillín	sellino	selim
selon	according to	gemäß	según	secondo	segundo
semaine	week	Woche(f)	semana	settimana	semana
semblable	similar	ähnlich	semejante	simile, uguale	semelhante
sembler	seem	scheinen	parecer	sembrare	parecer
semelle	sole	Sohle(f)	suela	suola	sola
semence	seed	Samen(m)	simiente	seme, semente	semente
semer	sow	säen	sembrar	seminare	semear
semi	semi, half	halb	semi	semi	semi
sénat	senate	Senat(m), Bundesrat(m)	senado	senato	senado
sénateur	senator	Senator(m)	senador	senatore	senador
sens	direction, way	Richtung(f)	sentido	senso	sentido
sens	meaning, sense	Bedeutung(f)	sentido	senso	sentido
sens unique	one-way	Einbahnstraße(f)	dirección única	senso unico	sentido único
sensation	sensation; feeling	Empfindung(f)	sensación	sensazione	sensação
sensé, e	sensible	vernünftig	sensato, a	sensato, a	sensato, a
sensibiliser	sensitive(make sb)	sensibilisieren	sensibilizar	sensibilizzare	sensibilizar
sensibilité	sensitivity	Sensibilität(f)	sensibilidad	sensibilità	sensibilidade
sensible	sensitive	empfindlich	sensible	sensibile	sensível
sensualité	sensuality	Sinnlichkeit(f)	sensualidad	sensualità	sensualidade
sensuel, le	sensual	sinnlich	sensual	sensuale	sensual
sentier	footpath, path	Weg(m)	sendero, senda	sentiero	vereda, atalho
sentiment	feeling	Gefühl(n)	sentimiento	sentimento	sentimento
sentimental, e	sentimental	sentimental	sentimental	sentimentale	sentimental
sentinelle	sentry	Wache(f)	centinela	sentinela	sentinela
sentir	smell	riechen	oler	odorare, annusare	cheirar
sentir	feel	fühlen	sentir	sentire	sentir
séparation	separation	Trennung(f)	separación	separazione	separação
séparer	separate, part	trennen	separar	separare, dividere	separar
sept	seven	sieben	siete	sette	sete
septembre	September	September(m)	septiembre	settembre	Setembro
sépulture	burial(-place)	Grab(n)	sepultura	sepoltura	sepultura
séquence	sequence	Folge(f), Sequenz(f)	secuencia	sequenza	sequência
séquestrer	lock away	ein = sperren	secuestrar	sequestrare	sequestrar
serein, e	serene	heiter	sereno, a	sereno, a	sereno, a
sérénité	serenity	Heiterkeit(f)	serenidad	serenità	serenidade
sergent	sergeant	Unteroffizier(m)	sargento	sergente	sargento
série	series	Serie(f)	serie	serie	série
sérieux, se	serious	ernst, ernsthaft	serio, a	serio, a	sério, a
seringue	syringe	Spritze(f)	jeringa	siringa	seringa
serment	oath, pledge	Eid(m)	juramento	giuramento	juramento
serpent	snake	Schlange(f)	serpiente	serpente	serpente
serrer	grip, hold tight	greifen, packen	apretar	stringere	apertar
serrer, resserrer	tighten	an = ziehen	apretar	stringere	apertar
serrer la main	shake hands	Hand schütteln	estrechar la mano	stringere la mano	apertar a mão
serrure	lock	Schloß(Tür-)(n)	cerradura	serratura	fechadura
sérum	serum	Serum(n)	suero	siero	soro
serveur, se	waiter, waitress	Kellner(in f)m	camarero, a	cameriere, a	criado, a; moço
service	service	Dienstleistung(f)	servicio	servizio	serviço
service	service	Bedienung(f)	servicio	servizio	serviço

111

serviette	serviette, napkin	Serviette(f)	servilleta	tovagliolo	guardanapo
serviette	towel	Handtuch(n)	toalla	asciugamano	toalha
servir	serve	dienen, bedienen	servir	servire	servir
servir de(se)	use	benutzen	servirse	adoperare	servir-se
ses	his; her; its	seine; ihre	sus	suoi(i); sue(le)	seus, suas
session	session	Sitzung(f)	sesión	sessione	sessão
seul, e	alone	allein	solo, a	solo, a	só
seul, e	lonely	einsam	aislado, a; solo, a	isolato, a; solo, a	isolado, a
seul, e	only	einzig	solo, a	solo, a	só
seulement	only	nur	solamente, sólo	solo, soltanto	somente, só
sève	sap	Saft(m)	savia	linfa	seiva
sévère	severe, strict	streng	severo, a	severo, a	severo, a
sévices	cruelty	Mißhandlung(f)	malos tratos	sevizie	sevícias
sexe	sex	Geschlecht(n)	sexo	sesso	sexo
sexualité	sexuality	Sexualität(f)	sexualidad	sessualità	sexualidade
sexuel, le	sexual	geschlechtlich	sexual	sessuale	sexual
shampooing	shampoo	Shampoo(n)	champú	shampoo	champô
short	shorts	kurze Hose(f)	pantalón corto	shorts, calzoncini	calções; calção
si	if; whether	wenn; ob	si	se	se
si	so	so	tan	così	tão
siècle	century	Jahrhundert(n)	siglo	secolo	século
siège	seat	Sitz(m)	asiento	sedia	assento
siège	head office	Firmensitz(m)	sede	sede	sede
siège	siege	Belagerung(f)	sitio	assedio	cerco
sien, ne	his; hers; its	seine, ihre	suyo, suya	suo, sua(il, la)	seu, sua
sieste	nap, snooze	Mittagsschlaf(m)	siesta	siesta, riposino	sesta
siffler	whistle	pfeifen	silbar	fischiare	assobiar
sifflet	whistle	Pfeife(f)	pito	fischietto	apito
sigle	initials	Abkürzung(f)	sigla	sigla	sigla
signal	signal	Signal(n)	señal	segnale	sinal
signaler	point out	melden; an = zeigen	señalar	segnalare	assinalar
signalisation	sign	Beschilderung(f)	señalización	segnalazione	sinalização
signature	signature	Unterschrift(f)	firma	firma	assinatura
signe	sign	Zeichen(n)	signo	segno	sinal, signo
signer	sign	unterschreiben	firmar	firmare	assinar
significatif, ive	significant	bezeichnend	significativo, a	significativo, a	significativo, a
signification	meaning	Bedeutung(f)	significación	significato	significação
signifier	mean, signify	bedeuten	significar	significare	significar
silence	silence	Stille(f)	silencio	silenzio	silêncio
silencieux, se	silent, quiet	still, leise, ruhig	silencioso, se	silenzioso, a	silencioso, a
silhouette	outline	Silhouette(f)	silueta	sagoma; silhouette	silhueta
sillage	wake	Kielwasser(n)	estela	scia	esteira
sillon	furrow	Furche(f)	surco	solco	rego
s'il vous plaît!	please!	bitte!	por favor(!)	per favore!	se faz favor!
similaire	similar	ähnlich, gleichartig	similar	similare	similar
simple	simple	einfach	simple	semplice	simples
simplement	simply	einfach	simplemente	semplicemente	simplesmente
simplicité	simplicity	Einfachheit(f)	sencillez	semplicità	simplicidade
simplifier	simplify	vereinfachen	simplificar	semplificare	simplificar
simulation	simulation	Vortäuschung(f)	simulación	simulazione	simulação
simultané, e	simultaneous	gleichzeitig	simultáneo, a	simultaneo, a	simultâneo, a
sincère	sincere, candid	aufrichtig	sincero, a	sincero, a	sincero, a
singe	monkey	Affe(m)	mono	scimmia	macaco
singulier	singular	Einzahl(f)	singular	singolare	singular
sinistre	sinister	unheilvoll	siniestro, a	sinistro, a	sinistro, a
sinistré, e	victim(disaster -)	Geschädigte(r)m f	siniestrado, a	sinistrato, a	sinistrado, a
sinon	otherwise, or else	andernfalls, sonst	si no	se no; altrimenti	senão
sinueux, se	winding, sinuous	kurvenreich	sinuoso, a	sinuoso, a	sinuoso, a
sirène	siren	Sirene(f)	sirena	sirena	sirene
sirop	syrup, medicine	Sirup(m)	jarabe	sciroppo	xarope
sirop	cordial, squash	Saft(m), Sirup(m)	almíbar	sciroppo	xarope
sismique	seismic	seismisch	sísmico, a	sismico, a	sísmico, a
site	site	Ort(m), Lage(f)	paraje, vista	sito	sítio
situation	situation	Lage(f)	situación	situazione	situação
situation	location, position	Lage(f)	situación	situazione	situação
situation	position, job	Stellung, Position(f)	situación	situazione	situação
situé, e	located	gelegen	situado, a	situato, a	situado, a
situer	situate, locate	stellen, setzen	situar, localizar	situare, localizzare	situar, localizar

French	English	German	Spanish	Italian	Portuguese
six	six	sechs	seis	sei	seis
ski	ski	Ski(m)	esquí	sci	esqui
skier	ski	skifahren	esquiar	sciare	esquiar
ski nautique	water-skiing	Wasserski(m)	esquí acuático	sci nautico	esqui aquático
slip	briefs, pants	Unterhose(f)	calzoncillos	mutande, slip	cuecas
slow	smooch, slow dance	Blues(m), Slow(m)	lento	lento, slow	slow
smoking	dinner-jacket	Smoking(m)	esmoquin	smoking	smoking
snobisme	snobbery	Snobismus(m)	esnobismo	snobismo	snobismo
sociable	sociable	gesellig	sociable	socievole	sociável
social, e	social	sozial	social	sociale	social
socialisme	socialism	Sozialismus(m)	socialismo	socialismo	socialismo
société	society	Gesellschaft(f)	sociedad	società	sociedade
société	company, firm	Gesellschaft(f)	sociedad	società	sociedade
sociologie	sociology	Soziologie(f)	sociología	sociologia	sociologia
socle	base	Sockel(m)	zócalo	zoccolo	soco, pedestal
socquette	sock(ankle-)	Socke(f)	calcetín	calzino	meias
soeur	sister	Schwester(f)	hermana	sorella	irmã
soeur	nun, sister	Nonne(f), Schwester(f)	monja	suora	freira
soi(-même)	oneself	sich, selbst	sí(mismo)	se(stesso)	si(mesmo)
soie	silk	Seide(f)	seda	seta	seda
soif	thirst	Durst(m)	sed	sete	sede
soigner	nurse; tend; treat	pflegen	curar	curare	cuidar
soigneux, se	neat, tidy	sorgfältig	cuidadoso, a	accurato, a	cuidadoso, a
soin	care	Pflege(f)	cuidado	cura	cuidado
soins de beauté	beauty treatment	Schönheitspflege(f)	cosmética	cura	tratamento
soir	evening	Abend(m)	tarde, noche	sera	tarde, noite
soir(ce)	tonight	heute abend	noche(esta)	sera(questa)	noite(esta)
soixante	sixty	sechzig	sesenta	sessanta	sessenta
soixante-dix	seventy	siebzig	setenta	settanta	setenta
sol, terre	ground	Boden(m)	suelo	suolo	solo
solaire	solar	Sonnen-	solar	solare	solar
soldat	soldier	Soldat(m)	soldado	soldato	soldado
solder	sell off	aus = verkaufen	saldar	saldare, liquidare	saldar
soldes	sales	Ausverkauf(m)	saldos, rebajas	saldi	saldos
soleil	sun	Sonne(f)	sol	sole	sol
soleil(il fait)	sunny(it's)	Sonne scheint(die)	sol(hace)	sole(c'è il)	sol(está)
solennel, le	solemn	feierlich	solemne	solenne	solene
solfège	sol-fa, theory	Tonleiter(f)	solfeo	solfeggio	solfejo
solidarité	solidarity	Solidarität(f)	solidaridad	solidarietà	solidaridade
solide	solid, strong	solide, fest	sólido, a	solido, a	sólido, a
solitaire	solitary, lonely	einsam	solitario, a	solitario, a	solitário, a
solitude	loneliness	Einsamkeit(f)	soledad	solitudine	solidão
solliciter	appeal to, request	ersuchen	solicitar	sollecitare	solicitar
soluble	soluble	löslich	soluble	solubile	solúvel
solution	solution	Lösung(f)	solución	soluzione	solução
solutionner	solve	lösen	solucionar	risolvere	solucionar
sombre; obscur, e	dark	dunkel	oscuro, a	scuro, a	escuro, a; sombrio, a
somme	sum, amount	Summe(f)	suma; cantidad	somma	soma; quantia
sommeil	sleep	Schlaf(m)	sueño	sonno	sono
sommeiller	doze	schlummern	dormitar	sonnecchiare	dormitar
sommet	summit, top	Gipfel(m)	cumbre; cima	cima; vetta	cimo; cume
sommité	V.I.P.	Prominente(f, m)	eminencia	sommità	sumidade
somnambule	sleep-walker	Schlafwandler(in f)m	sonámbulo, a	sonnambulo, a	sonâmbulo, a
somnifère	sleeping tablet	Schlaftablette(f)	somnífero	sonnifero	soporífero
somnolence	drowsiness	Schläfrigkeit(f)	somnolencia	sonnolenza	sonolência
somptueux, se	sumptuous	prächtig	suntuoso, a	sontuoso, a	sumptuoso, a
son	his; her; its	sein, seine, ihr, ihre	su	suo(il)	seu
son	sound	Ton(m)	sonido	suono	som
sonate	sonata	Sonate(f)	sonata	sonata	sonata
sondage	poll(opinion)	Umfrage(f)	sondeo	sondaggio	sondagem
sonde	probe	Sonde(f)	sonda	sonda	sonda
sonner	ring	klingeln	sonar, tocar	suonare, sonare	soar, tocar
sonnerie	ring	Klingel(f)	campana, timbre	squillo, soneria	campainha, toque
sonnette	bell	Klingel(f)	timbre	campanello	campainha
sophistiqué, e	sophisticated	hochkompliziert	sofisticado, a	sofisticato, a	sofisticado, a
sorcellerie	witchcraft	Hexerei(f)	brujería	stregoneria	bruxaria
sorcier, ière	wizard; witch(-es)	Hexer(m); Hexe(f)	brujo, a	stregone, strega	bruxo, a
sordide	sordid	schäbig	sórdido, a	squallido, a	sórdido, a

sort	fate	Schicksal(n)	suerte, destino	sorte, destino	sorte, destino
sorte, espèce	sort, kind, type	Sorte(f), Art(f)	especie, género	specie, genere	espécie, género
sortie	exit, way out	Ausgang(m)	salida	uscita	saída
sortie(secours)	emergency exit	Notausgang(m)	salida(emergencia)	uscita(sicurezza)	saída de emergência
sortir	go out, come out	aus = gehen	salir	uscire	sair
sosie	double	Doppelgänger(in f)m	sosia	sosia	sósia
sottise	silliness	Dummheit(f)	tontería	sciocchezza	estupidez
souci	worry	Sorge(f)	preocupación	preoccupazione	preocupação
soucier(se)	worry	sorgen, sich; plagen, s.	preocuparse	preoccuparsi	preocupar-se
soucieux, se	worried	sorgenvoll	preocupado, a	preoccupato, a	preocupado, a
soucoupe	saucer	Untertasse(f)	platillo	piattino	pires
soudain	sudden(ly)	plötzlich	pronto(de)	ad un tratto	súbito(de)
soudure	welding	Schweißen(n)	soldadura	saldatura	soldadura
souffle	breath	Luft(f), Puste(f)	soplo, aliento	fiato, soffio	sopro, fôlego
souffler	blow	blasen	soplar	soffiare	soprar
souffler	blow	wehen	soplar	soffiare	soprar
souffrance	suffering	Leiden(n)	sufrimiento	sofferenza	sofrimento
souffrir	suffer	leiden	sufrir	soffrire	sofrer
souhaiter	wish, desire	wünschen	desear	augurare	desejar
soûl, e; saoul, e	drunk	betrunken	embriagado, a	ubriaco, a	bêbado, a; ébrio, a
soulagement	relief	Erleichterung(f)	alivio, desahogo	sollievo	alívio
soulager(se)	relieve	lindern	aliviar	sollevare, lenire	aliviar
soulager	relieve	erleichtern	aliviar	alleggerire	aliviar
soulever	lift, raise	an = heben, hoch = heben	levantar, elevar	sollevare	levantar, erguer
soulier	shoe	Schuh(m)	zapato	scarpa	sapato
souligner	underline	unterstreichen	subrayar	sottolineare	sublinhar
souligner	emphasize	betonen	recalcar, subrayar	accentuare	acentuar
soumettre	submit	unterwerfen	someter	sottomettere	submeter
soumission	submission	Unterwerfung(f)	sumisión	sottomissione	submissão
soupçon	suspicion	Argwohn(m), Verdacht m	sospecha	sospetto	suspeita
soupçonner	suspect	verdächtigen	sospechar	sospettare	suspeitar
soupe	soup	Suppe(f)	sopa	minestra	sopa
souper	supper(have)	Abend essen(zu)	cenar	cenare	cear
soupirer	sigh	seufzen	suspirar	sospirare	suspirar
souple	supple; flexible	biegsam	flexible	flessibile	maleável
souplesse	suppleness	Biegsamkeit(f)	flexibilidad	flessibilità	flexibilidade
source	spring	Quelle(f)	fuente	sorgente	fonte, nascente
source, origine	source	Ursprung(m)	fuente, origen	fonte, origine	fonte, origem
sourcil	eyebrow	Augenbraue(f)	ceja	sopracciglio(a)	sobrolho
sourd, e	deaf	taub	sordo, a	sordo, a	surdo, a
sourd-muet, te	deaf and dumb	taubstumm	sordomudo, a	sordomuto, a	surdo-mudo, a
souriant, e	cheerful	lächelnd	sonriente	sorridente	sorridente
sourire	smile	lächeln	sonreír	sorridere	sorrir
sourire	smile	Lächeln(n)	sonrisa	sorriso	sorriso
souris	mouse(mice pl.)	Maus(f)	ratón	topo	rato
sous	under	unter	debajo, bajo	sotto	debaixo, sob
sous, au-dessous	beneath	unter(halb); unten	bajo; debajo; abajo	sotto	baixo(de-; a-)
souscription	subscription	Subskription(f)	suscripción	sottoscrizione	subscrição
sous-marin	submarine	Unterseeboot(n)	submarino	sottomarino	submarino
sous-sol	subsoil	Unterboden(m)	subsuelo	sottosuolo	sub-solo
sous-sol	basement	Untergeschoß(n)	sótano	scantinato	cave
sous-titré, e	subtitled	Untertiteln(mit)	subtitulado, a	didascalie(con)	legendado, a
soustraction	subtraction	Subtraktion(f)	resta	sottrazione	subtração
soustraire	subtract	ab = ziehen	sustraer, restar	sottrarre	subtrair, deduzir
soutenir	support	unterstützen	sostener	sostenere	sustentar
souterrain, e	underground	unterirdisch	subterráneo, a	sotterraneo, a	subterrâneo, a
soutien, appui	support	Unterstützung(f)	sostén, apoyo	sostegno, appoggio	apoio, socorro
soutien-gorge	bra	Büstenhalter(m)	sostén	reggiseno	soutien
souvenir	memory	Erinnerung(f)	recuerdo	ricordo	recordação
souvenir	souvenir	Andenken(n)	recuerdo	ricordo, souvenir	recordação
souvenir(se)	remember, recall	erinnern, sich	acordarse	ricordarsi	recordar-se
souvent	often	oft	frecuentemente	spesso	frequentemente
souverain, e	sovereign, monarch	Herrscher(in f)m	soberano, a; monarca	sovrano, a; monarca	soberano, a; monarca
souveraineté	sovereignty	Souveränität(f)	soberanía	sovranità	soberania
spacieux, se	spacious	weiträumig	espacioso, a	spazioso, a	espaçoso, a
sparadrap	plaster	Pflaster(n)	esparadrapo	cerotto	esparadrapo
spasme	spasm	Krampf(m)	espasmo	spasma	espasmo
spatial, e	space	Raum-	espacial	spaziale	espacial

French	English	German	Spanish	Italian	Portuguese
spatule	spatula	Spachtel(f)	espátula	spatola	espátula
spécial, e	special	speziell, eigen	especial	speciale	especial
spécialiste	specialist	Spezialist(in f)m	especialista	specialista	especialista
spécialiste	expert, specialist	Fachmann(m)	especialista	specialista	especialista
spécialité	speciality	Spezialität(f)	especialidad	specialità	especialidade
spécimen	specimen	Muster(n); Exemplar(n)	espécimen	specimen	espécime
spécifier	specify, state	spezifieren	especificar	specificare	especificar
spécifique	specific	spezifisch	específico, a	specifico, a	específico, a
spectacle	show	Aufführung(f)	espectáculo	spettacolo	espectáculo
spectacles	entertainment	Unterhaltung(f)	espectáculos	spettacoli	espectáculos
spectateur, trice	spectator	Zuschauer(in f)m	espectador, a	spettatore, trice	espectador, a
spéculation	speculation	Spekulation(f)	especulación	speculazione	especulação
spéléologie	pot-holing	Höhlenforschung(f)	espeleología	speleologia	espeleologia
sperme	sperm	Sperma(n)	esperma	sperma	esperma
sphère	sphere	Sphäre(f)	esfera	sfera	esfera
spirale	spiral	Spirale(f)	espiral	spirale	espiral
spirituel, le	spiritual	geistreich	espiritual	spirituale	espiritual
splendide	splendid	glänzend	espléndido, a	splendido, a	esplêndido, a
spongieux, se	spongy	schwammig	esponjoso, a	spugnoso, a	esponjoso, a
sponsor	sponsor	Sponsor(m)	patrocinador	sponsor	patrocinador
spontané, e	spontaneous	spontan	espontáneo, a	spontaneo, a	espontâneo, a
sport	sport	Sport(m)	deporte	sport	desporto
sportif, ive	sportsman/-woman	Sportler(in f)m	deportista	sportivo, a	desportista
sportif, ive	sporty, athletic	sportlich; Sport-	deportivo, a	sportivo, a	desportivo, a
squelette	skeleton	Skelett(n)	esqueleto	scheletro	esqueleto
stabilité	stability	Stabilität(f)	estabilidad	stabilità	estabilidade
stade	stadium	Stadium(n)	estadio	stadio	estádio
stage	training period	Praktikum(n)	cursillo	tirocinio, stage	estágio
stagiaire	trainee	Praktikant(in f)m	cursillista	apprendista	estagiário
station	station	Station(f)	estación	stazione	estação
station	resort	Erholungsort(m)	estación	stazione	estação
station-service	service station	Tankstelle(f)	estación(servicio)	stazione di servizio	estação de serviço
stationnement	parking	Parken(n)	estacionamiento	sosta	estacionamento
stationner	park	parken	estacionarse	stazionare	estacionar
statique	static	statisch	estático, a	statico, a	estático, a
statistique(s)	statistics	Statistik(f)	estadística	statistica	estatística
statue	statue	Statue(f)	estatua	statua	estátua
statut	status; statute	Status(m); Statut(n)	estatuto	statuto	estatuto
steppe	steppe	Steppe(f)	estepa	steppa	estepe
stéréo	stereo	Stereo(f)	estéreo	stereo	estereofonia
stérile	sterile	steril	estéril	sterile	estéril
stérilet	coil	Spirale(f)	espiral	spirale	esterilete
stimuler	stimulate	reizen, an = regen	estimular	stimolare	estimular
stocker	stock, store	lagern	almacenar	immagazzinare	armazenar
store	blind	Vorhang m; Jalousie f	toldo; persiana	tapparella	estore
strapontin	folding seat	Klappstuhl(m)	traspuntín	strapuntino	banco dobrável
stratégie	strategy	Strategie(f)	estrategia	strategia	estratégia
strict, e	strict	streng	estricto, a	stretto, a	estrito, a
structure	structure	Struktur(f)	estructura	struttura	estrutura
studieux, se	studious	fleißig	estudioso, a	studioso, a	estudioso, a
studio	studio	Studio(n)	estudio	studio	estúdio
stupéfait, e	amazed	verblüfft	estupefacto, a	stupefatto, a	estupefacto, a
stupéfiant	narcotic	Betäubungsmittel(n)	narcótico	stupefacente	narcótico
stupeur	stupor	Erstaunen(n)	estupor	stupore	estupefacção
stupide	stupid, silly	dumm	estúpido, a	stupido, a	estúpido, a
style	style	Stil(m)	estilo	stile	estilo
stylo	pen, fountain-pen	Füller(m)	estilográfica	stilografica	caneta
stylo à bille	ball-point pen	Kugelschreiber(m)	bolígrafo	penna a sfera	esferográfica
subconscient	subconscious	Unterbewußtsein(n)	subconsciente	subcosciente	subconsciente
subir	undergo	ertragen	sufrir, padecer	subire	sofrer
sublime	sublime	erhaben	sublime	sublime	sublime
subordonné, e	subordinate	Untergebene(f m)	subordinado, a	subalterno, a	subordinado, a
subsister	subsist, remain	fort = bestehen	subsistir	sussistere	subsistir
substance	substance	Substanz(f)	sustancia	sostanza	substância
substance	matter, material	Materie(f)	materia	materia	matéria
substantif	substantive, noun	Hauptwort(n)	sustantivo	sostantivo	substantivo
substituer	substitute	vertauschen	sustituir	sostituire	substituir
subtil, e	subtle	scharfsinnig, listig	sutil	sottile	subtil

French	English	German	Spanish	Italian	Portuguese
subvention	grant, subsidy	Zuschuß(m)	subvención	sovvenzione	subvenção
subvention	subsidy	Subvention(f)	subvención	sussidio	subvenção
succéder	succeed	nach = folgen	suceder	succedere	suceder
succès	success(-es)	Erfolg(m)	éxito	successo	sucesso, êxito
successeur	successor	Nachfolger(in f)m	sucesor	successore	sucessor
successif, ive	successive	aufeinanderfolgend	sucesivo, a	successivo, a	sucessivo, a
succinct, e	succinct, brief	bündig	sucinto, a	succinto, a	sucinto, a
succomber	succumb	erliegen	sucumbir	soccombere	sucumbir
succursale	branch(-es)	Zweigstelle(f)	sucursal	succursale	sucursal
sucer	suck	lutschen	chupar	succhiare	chupar
sucette	lollipop	Lutscher(m)	pirulí	lecca lecca	chupa-chupa
sucette	dummy	Schnuller(m)	chupete	succhiotto	chupeta
sucre	sugar	Zucker(m)	azúcar	zucchero	açúcar
sucré, e	sweet	süß	azucarado, a	zuccherato, a	açucarado, a; doce
Sud	South	Süden(m)	Sur	Sud	Sul
suer	sweat	schwitzen	sudar	sudare	suar
sueur	sweat	Schweiß(m)	sudor	sudore	suor
suffisant, e	sufficient	genügend	suficiente	sufficiente	suficiente
suffrage	vote	Wahl(f)	sufragio	suffragio	sufrágio
suggérer	suggest	vor = schlagen	sugerir	suggerire	sugerir, propôr
suicide	suicide	Selbstmord(m)	suicidio	suicidio	suicídio
suicider(se)	commit suicide	um = bringen, sich	suicidarse	suicidarsi	suicidar-se
suite	continuation	Folge(f)	continuación	seguito	continuação
suite	suite	Suite(f)	suite	appartamento	suite
suite(à la)	following	hinter, nach	después de	seguito a(in)	seguir a(a)
suite(tout de)	once(at)	sogleich, sofort	seguida(en)	subito	imediatamente
suite à	further to	Anschluß an(im)	contestación(en)	seguito(facendo)	consequência(em)
suivant, e	following, next	nächste	siguiente	seguente	seguinte
suivre	follow	folgen	seguir	seguire	seguir
sujet	subject	Subjekt(n)	sujeto	soggetto	sujeito
sujet, thème	subject, theme	Thema(n)	tema	tema	assunto, tema
sultan	sultan	Sultan(m)	sultán	sultano	sultão
superbe	superb	großartig	soberbio, a	splendido, a	soberbo, a
superficie	area	Oberfläche(f)	superficie	superficie	superfície
supérieur, e	superior	höher, besser	superior, a	superiore	superior, a
supérieur, e	upper	obere(r, s); Ober-	superior, a	superiore	superior, a
supérieur	superior	Vorgesetzte(m, f)	superior	superiore	superior
supériorité	superiority	Überlegenheit(f)	superioridad	superiorità	superioridade
supermarché	supermarket	Supermarkt(m)	supermercado	supermercato	supermercado
superposer	superpose	aufeinander = legen	sobreponer	sovrapporre	sobrepor
supersonique	supersonic	Überschall-	supersónico, a	supersonico, a	supersónico, a
superstitieux, se	superstitious	abergläubisch	supersticioso, a	superstizioso, a	supersticioso, a
superviser	supervise	überprüfen	supervisar	soprintendere	supervisar
suppléant, e	substitute	Stellvertreter(in f)m	suplente	supplente	suplente
supplément	supplement	Ergänzung(f); Zulage f	suplemento	supplemento	suplemento
supplément(en)	extra-, additional-	Extra-; Neben-	más(de)	più(in)	mais(a)
supplémentaire	additional, extra	zusätzlich	suplementario, a	supplementare	suplementar
supplice	torture	Qual(f)	suplicio	supplizio	suplício
supplier	implore	an = flehen	suplicar	supplicare	suplicar
support	support	Stütze(f)	soporte	supporto	suporte
supporter	support	stützen, unterstützen	soportar	sopportare	suportar
supposer	suppose	an = nehmen	suponer	supporre	supor
suppositoire	suppository	Zäpfchen(n)	supositorio	supposta	supositório
supprimer	suppress	ab = schaffen	suprimir	sopprimere	suprimir
supprimer	delete	beseitigen	suprimir	sopprimere	suprimir
suprématie	supremacy	Obergewalt(f)	supremacía	supremazia	supremacia
suprême	supreme	oberst-, höchst-	supremo, a	supremo, a	supremo, a
sur	on	auf	en, encima, sobre	sopra, su	em cima de; sobre
sur	on, upon	über; auf	sobre	su, sopra	sobre
sûr, e; certain, e	sure, certain	sicher	seguro, a	sicuro, a	seguro, a
surdité	deafness	Taubheit(f)	sordera	sordità	surdez
surdose	overdose	Überdosis(f)	sobredosis	overdose	overdose
sûrement	surely, certainly	gewiß, sicherlich	ciertamente	sicuramente	certamente
sûreté	safety	Sicherheit(f)	seguridad	sicurezza	segurança
surface	surface	Oberfläche(f)	superficie	superficie	superfície
surgelés	frozen food	Tiefkühlkost(f)	congelados	surgelati	congelados
surmenage	overwork(ing)	Überarbeitung(f)	agotamiento	esaurimento	esgotamento
surmonter	overcome	überwinden	superar	superare	superar

French	English	German	Spanish	Italian	Portuguese
surnaturel, le	supernatural	überirdisch	sobrenatural	soprannaturale	sobrenatural
surnom	nickname	Spitzname(m)	apodo, mote	soprannome	alcunha, apelido
surpris, e	surprised	überrascht	sorprendido, a	sorpreso, a	surpreendido, a
surprise	surprise	Überraschung(f)	sorpresa	sorpresa	surpresa
surtout	above all	besonders	sobre todo	soprattutto	sobretudo
surveillance	watch; supervision	Überwachung(f)	vigilancia	sorveglianza	vigilância
surveillant, e	supervisor	Aufseher m, Supervisor	vigilante	sorvegliante	vigia
surveiller	watch; supervise	überwachen	vigilar	sorvegliare	vigiar
survivant, e	survivor	Überlebende(f, m)	superviviente	superstite	sobrevivente
survivre	survive	überleben	sobrevivir	sopravvivere	sobreviver
survol	flight over	Überfliegen(n)	sobrevuelo	sorvolo	sobrevôo
suspect, e	suspicious	verdächtig	sospechoso, a	sospetto, a	suspeito, a
suspendre	hang up	auf = hängen	colgar, suspender	appendere	pendurar
suspendre	suspend, defer	verschieben	suspender	sospendere	suspender
suspense	suspense	Spannung(f)	suspense	suspense	suspense
suspension	suspension	Federung(f)	suspensión	sospensione	suspensão
svelte	slim, slender	schlank	esbelto, a	slanciato, a; snello, a	esbelto, a
syllabe	syllable	Silbe(f)	sílaba	sillaba	sílaba
symbole	symbol	Symbol(n)	símbolo	simbolo	símbolo
symbolique	symbolic(al)	symbolisch	simbólico, a	simbolico, a	simbólico, a
symétrie	symmetry	Symetrie(f)	simetría	simmetria	simetria
sympathique	pleasant, nice	sympathisch	simpático, a	simpatico, a	simpático, a
symphonie	symphony	Symphonie(f)	sinfonía	sinfonia	sinfonia
symptôme	symptom	Symptom(n)	síntoma	sintomo	sintoma
synagogue	synagogue	Synagoge(f)	sinagoga	sinagoga	sinagoga
synchroniser	synchronize	synchronisieren	sincronizar	sincronizzare	sincronizar
syncope	black-out	Ohnmacht(f)	síncope	sincope	síncope
syndicalisme	trade unionism	Gewerkschaftswesen	sindicalismo	sindacalismo	sindicalismo
syndicat	trade union	Gewerkschaft(f)	sindicato	sindacato	sindicato
synonyme	synonym	Synonym(n)	sinónimo	sinonimo	sinónimo
syntaxe	syntax	Syntax(f), Satzlehre f	sintaxis	sintassi	sintaxe
synthèse	synthesis(-ses)	Synthese(f)	síntesis	sintesi	síntese
synthétique	synthetic	synthetisch	sintético, a	sintetico, a	sintético, a
syphilis	syphilis	Syphilis(f)	sífilis	sifilide	sífilis
systématique	systematic	systematisch	sistemático, a	sistematico, a	sistemático, a
système	system	System(n)	sistema	sistema	sistema

T

French	English	German	Spanish	Italian	Portuguese
ta	your	dein(e)	tu	tua(la)	tua, teu
tabac	tobacco	Tabak(m)	tabaco	tabacco	tabaco
table	table	Tisch(m)	mesa	tavolo; tavola	mesa
tableau	board, panel	Tafel(f)	tablero, tablón	pannello, quadro	painel, quadro
tableau	painting, picture	Gemälde(n)	cuadro	dipinto, quadro	quadro
tableau noir	blackboard	Tafel(f)	pizarra	lavagna	quadro
tablier	apron	Schürze(f)	delantal	grembiule	avental
tabouret	stool	Hocker(m)	taburete	sgabello	escabelo, banco
tache	stain	Fleck(m)	mancha	macchia	mancha, nódoa
tâche	task	Aufgabe(f)	tarea	compito	tarefa
tacher	stain, dirty	beflecken, beschmutzen	manchar	macchiare	manchar, sujar
tachycardie	tachycardia	Herzjagen(n)	taquicardia	tachicardia	taquicardia
tact	tact	Takt(m)	tacto	tatto	tacto
tactique	tactical	taktisch	táctico, a	tattico, a	táctico, a
tactique	tactic	Taktik(f)	táctica	tattica	táctica
taille	size	Größe(f)	tamaño	misura	tamanho
taille	size	Größe(f)	talla, número	taglia, misura	tamanho
taille	waist	Taille(f)	cintura, talle	vita	cinta

French	English	German	Spanish	Italian	Portuguese
taille, grandeur	height, size	Größe(f)	talla, estatura	statura	estatura
tailleur	tailor	Schneider(m)	sastre	sarto	alfaiate
tailleur	suit	Kostüm(n)	traje	tailleur	saia-casaco
taire(se)	silent(to be)	schweigen	callarse	tacere	calar-se
talent	talent	Talent(n)	talento	talento	talento
talon	heel	Ferse(f); Absatz(m)	talón	tallone	calcanhar
tamponner	stamp	stempeln	sellar	timbrare	carimbar
tamponner	bump, crash into	zusammen = stoßen	chocar con	tamponare	chocar, esbarrar
tandis que	while, whilst	während	mientras	mentre	enquanto
tangent, e	tangent	berührend	tangente	tangente	tangente
tanguer	pitch	schaukeln	cabecear	beccheggiare	balouçar-se
tant	so much, so many	so viel, e	tanto, tan	tanto	tanto
tante	aunt	Tante(f)	tía	zia	tia
tape, fessée	smack	Schlag(m)	cachete	schiaffo	palmada
tapis	mat, rug, carpet	Teppich(m)	alfombra, tapiz	tappeto	tapete, carpete
tapisserie	tapestry	Wandteppich; Gobelin m	tapiz; tapicería	arazzo; tappezzeria	tapeçaria
tapisserie	wallpaper	Tapete(f)	empapelado	carta da parati	papel de parede
taquiner	tease	necken	hacer rabiar	stuzzicare	arreliar
tard	late	spät	tarde	tardi	tarde
tarif	tariff, price	Tarif(m)	tarifa	tariffa	tarifa
tarif	fare	Tarif(m)	tarifa	tariffa	tarifa
tarte	tart	Torte(f)	tarta	torta, crostata	torta
tartine de pain	slice of bread	Brotscheibe(f)	rebanada de pan	fetta di pane	fatia de pão
tas	pile	Haufen(m)	montón	mucchio	montão, pilha
tasse	cup	Tasse(f)	taza	tazza	chávena
tâter	feel, touch	berühren	tantear	tastare	tatear, apalpar
tatouage	tattoo	Tätowierung(f)	tatuaje	tatuaggio	tatuagem
taudis	slum	Bruchbude(f)	tugurio	topaia	antro, tugúrio
taureau	bull	Stier(m)	toro	toro	touro; toiro
taux	rate	Rate(f)	tasa	tasso	taxa
taxe	tax; duty	Steuer(f)	tasa, impuesto	tassa, imposta	taxa, imposto
taxi	taxi, cab	Taxi(n)	taxi	taxi, tassi	táxi
taxi-/publiphone	public call-box	Telefonzelle(f)	teléfono público	telefono pubblico	telefone público
te, t'	you	dich; dir	te	ti, te	te
technicien, ne	technician	Techniker(in f)m	técnico, a	tecnico, a	técnico, a
technique	technical	technisch	técnico, a	tecnico, a	técnico, a
technocrate	technocrat	Technokrat(m)	tecnócrata	tecnocrate	tecnocrata
technologie	technology	Technologie(f)	tecnología	tecnologia	tecnologia
teindre, colorer	dye	färben	teñir	tingere	tingir
teint	complexion, colour	Teint(m)	tez, color	carnagione	tez
teinte	tint, colour	Färbung(f), Farbe(f)	tinte, color	tinta	tinta
tel, le	such a, such(pl.)	solche(r, s); so ein	tal	tale	tal
télécommande	remote control	Fernsteuerung(f)	telemando	telecomando	telecomando
télégramme	telegram, cable	Telegramm(n)	telegrama	telegramma	telegrama
télépathie	telepathy	Telepathie(f)	telepatía	telepatia	telepatia
téléphérique	cable-car	Seilbahn(f)	teleférico	teleferica	teleférico
téléphone	telephone, phone	Telefon(n)	teléfono	telefono	telefone
téléphoner	phone, ring, call	telefonieren	telefonear	telefonare	telefonar
télescope	telescope	Teleskop(n)	telescopio	telescopio	telescópio
téléspectateur	viewer	Fernsehzuschauer/in	telespectador, a	telespettatore, trice	telespectador, a
téléviser	televise	übertragen	televisar	teletrasmettere	televisionar
téléviseur	television set	Fernseher(m)	televisor	televisore	televisor
télévision	television	Fernsehen(n)	televisión	televisione	televisão; TV
télex	telex	Telex(n)	telex	telex	telex
tellement	so(-much, -many)	so(sehr), derartig	tanto, a; tan	talmente	tanto, a
téméraire	rash, reckless	waghalsig	temerario, a	temerario, a	temerário, a
témoignage	testimony, evidence	Zeugenaussage(f)	testimonio	testimonianza	testemunho
témoigner	testify	aus = sagen	testimoniar	testimoniare	testemunhar
témoigner	witness	zeugen, bezeugen	atestiguar	testificare	testemunhar
témoin	witness(-es)	Zeuge(m), Zeugin(f)	testigo	testimone	testemunha
tempe	temple	Schläfe(f)	sien	tempia	têmpora
tempérament	temperament	Temperament(n)	temperamento	temperamento	temperamento
température	temperature	Temperatur(f)	temperatura	temperatura	temperatura
tempéré, e	temperate	gemäßigt	templado, a	temperato, a	temperado, a
tempête	storm	Unwetter(n)	tempestad	tempesta	tempestade
temple	temple	Tempel(m)	templo	tempio	templo
temporaire	temporary	vorübergehend	temporario, a	temporaneo, a	temporário, a
temps	time	Zeit(f)	tiempo	tempo	tempo

French	English	German	Spanish	Italian	Portuguese
temps	weather	Wetter(n)	tiempo	tempo	tempo
ténacité	tenacity	Hartnäckigkeit(f)	tenacidad	tenacità; tenacia	tenacidade
tendance	tendency; trend	Tendenz(f), Neigung(f)	tendencia	tendenza	tendência
tendance	trend, tendency	Neigung(f)	inclinación	inclinazione	inclinação
tendre	soft; tender	weich	blando, a	morbido, a; tenero, a	tenro, a
tendre	tender	zärtlich	tierno, a	tenero, a	terno, a
tendre	tighten; stretch	spannen	tender	tendere	estender, esticar
tendresse	tenderness	Zärtlichkeit(f)	ternura	tenerezza	ternura
tendu, e	tight	gespannt	tenso, a	teso, a	esticado, a
ténèbres	darkness	Finsternis(f)	tinieblas	tenebre	trevas
tenir	hold	halten	tener	tenere	ter, segurar
tennis	tennis	Tennis(n)	tenis	tennis	ténis
tennis de table	table-tennis	Tischtennis(n)	ping-pong	ping pong	ténis de mesa
ténor	tenor	Tenor(m)	tenor	tenore	tenor
tension	tension	Spannung(f)	tensión	tensione	tensão
tentacule	tentacle	Fangarm(m)	tentáculo	tentacolo	tentáculo
tentation	temptation	Versuchung(f)	tentación	tentazione	tentação
tentative	attempt	Versuch(m)	tentativa	tentativo	tentativa
tente	tent	Zelt(n)	tienda	tenda	tenda
tenter	attempt, try	versuchen; wagen	intentar	tentare	tentar
terme	term	Ausdruck(m)	término	parola	termo
terme	end	Ende(n), Ziel(n)	término	termine	termo
terminal, e	terminal, final	letzte(r, s); End-	terminal	terminale	terminal
terminer	end, finish	beenden	terminar	terminare	terminar
terne	dull	matt	sin brillo, mate	spento, a; smorto, a	baço, a
terrain	ground	Gelände(n)	terreno	terreno	terreno
terrain(sport)	field; court	Sportplatz(m)	campo	terreno	campo
terre	soil	Erde(f)	tierra	terra	terra
terre	earth	Erde(f)	tierra	terra	Terra
terre	land	Land(n)	tierra	terra	terra
terrestre	terrestrial	irdisch	terrestre	terrestre	terrestre
terreur	terror	Schrecken(m)	terror	terrore	terror
terrible	terrible	schrecklich	terrible	terribile	terrível
territoire	territory	Gebiet(n), Land(n)	territorio	territorio	território
terroriser	terrorize	terrorisieren	aterrorizar	terrorizzare	aterrorizar
terrorisme	terrorism	Terrorismus(m)	terrorismo	terrorismo	terrorismo
terroriste	terrorist	Terrorist(in f)m	terrorista	terrorista	terrorista
tes	your	deine	tus	tuoi, tue(i, le)	teus, tuas
testament	will, testament	Testament(n)	testamento	testamento	testamento
tester	test	testen	ensayar, probar	testare	testar
testicule	testicle	Hoden(m)	testículo	testicolo	testículo
tétanie	tetany	Starrkrampf(m)	tetania	tetania	tetania
tétanos	tetanus	Tetanus(m)	tétanos	tetano	tétano
tête	head	Kopf(m)	cabeza	testa, capo	cabeça
téter	suck	saugen	mamar	poppare	mamar
têtu, e	stubborn	dickköpfig	tozudo, a	testardo, a	cabeçudo, a
texte	text	Text(m)	texto	testo	texto
textile	textile	Textil-; Web-	textil	tessile	têxtil
thé	tea	Tee(m)	té	tè	chá
théâtre	theatre	Theater(n)	teatro	teatro	teatro
théière	teapot	Teekanne(f)	tetera	teiera	bule
thème	theme	Thema(n)	tema	tema	tema
théologie	theology	Theologie(f)	teología	teologia	teologia
théorème	theorem	Lehrsatz(m)	teorema	teorema	teorema
théorie	theory	Theorie(f)	teoría	teoria	teoria
thermal, e	thermal	Thermal-	termal	termale	termal
théorique	theoretical	theoretisch	teórico, a	teorico, a	teórico, a
thérapie	therapy	Therapie(f)	terapia	terapia	terapia
thermique	thermic, thermal	thermisch	térmico, a	termico, a	térmico, a
thermomètre	thermometer	Thermometer(n)	termómetro	termometro	termómetro
thèse	thesis(theses)	These(f)	tesis	tesi	tese
thon	tuna(fish)	Thunfisch(m)	atún, bonito	tonno	atum
thorax	thorax	Brustkasten(m)	tórax	torace	tórax
thyroïde	thyroid(gland)	Schilddrüse(f)	tiroides	tiroide	tiróide
tibia	tibia	Schienbein(n)	tibia	tibia	tíbia
tic	twitch(ing)	Tick(m)	tic	tic	tique
ticket	ticket	Karte(f); Fahrkarte(f)	ticket, billete	biglietto	bilhete
tiède	lukewarm, tepid	lauwarm, lau	tibio, a	tiepido, a	tépido, a; morno, a

119

French	English	German	Spanish	Italian	Portuguese
tien, ne	yours	deine(r, s), deine	tuyo, a	tuo, a	teu, tua
tiers	third	Drittel(n)	tercio, a; tercero	terzo, a	terço, a; terceiro
tiers-monde	third world	dritte Welt(f)	tercer mundo	terzo mondo	terceiro mundo
tige	stem	Stiel(m)	tallo	stelo	caule
tige	rod	Stange(f)	tallo, vástago	asta, barra	haste
tigre	tiger	Tiger(m)	tigre	tigre	tigre
timbre(-poste)	stamp	Briefmarke(f)	sello	francobollo	selo
timide	shy, timid	schüchtern	tímido, a	timido, a	tímido, a
timidité	shyness, timidity	Schüchternheit(f)	timidez	timidezza	timidez
tintement	ringing, jingle	Klimpern, Klingeln(n)	tañido	tintinnio	tilintar
tir	shooting, firing	Schießen(n)	tiro	tiro	tiro
tire-bouchon	corkscrew	Korkenzieher(m)	sacacorchos	cavatappi	saca-rolhas
tirer	pull	ziehen	tirar	tirare	puxar
tirer	draw	ziehen	tirar	tirare	puxar
tirer	fire, shoot	feuern, schießen	tirar	sparare, tirare	disparar, atirar
tirer	shoot, fire	schießen, feuern	disparar	tirare, sparare	atirar, disparar
tiret	dash	Gedankenstrich(m)	raya, guión	trattino	travessão, hífen
tiroir	drawer	Schublade(f)	cajón	cassetto	gaveta
tisane	herb tea	Kräutertee(m)	tisana	tisana	tisana
tisser	weave	weben	tejer	tessere	tecer
tissu	material, fabric	Stoff(m)	tela	tessuto	tecido
titre	title	Titel(m)	título	titolo	título
tituber	stagger	wanken	titubear	barcollare	titubear
titulaire	holder	Inhaber(in f)m	titular	titolare	titular
titulaire	tenured	festangestellt	numerario	titolare	titular
toboggan	slide, chute	Rutschbahn(f)	tobogán	scivolo	escorrega
toi	you	du; dich	tú; te	tu; te	tu; ti
toi(à)	yours	dir	tuyo, a	tuo, a; tuoi, tue	teu, tua
toile	canvas, material	Tuch(n)	tela, lienzo	tela	tela
toile	canvas, painting	Gemälde(n)(Leinwand)	lienzo, cuadro	tela, dipinto	tela, quadro
toilettes(W.C)	toilet, lavatory	Toiletten(f pl)	servicios(W.C)	toilettes; W.C	lavabos; sanita
toit	roof	Dach(n)	tejado	tetto	telhado
tôle	sheet-metal	Blech(n)	chapa	lamiera	chapa
tolérance	tolerance	Toleranz(f)	tolerancia	tolleranza	tolerância
tolérer	tolerate	dulden, ertragen	tolerar	tollerare	tolerar
tomate	tomato(-es)	Tomate(f)	tomate	pomodoro	tomate
tombe	grave	Grab(n)	tumba	tomba	túmulo, sepultura
tombeau	tomb	Grabmal(n)	tumba	tomba	túmulo
tomber	fall	fallen	caer	cadere	cair
tomber(laisser)	drop	fallenlassen	caer(dejar)	cadere(lasciar)	cair(deixar)
ton	your	dein(e)	tu	tuo(il)	teu
ton, son, timbre	tone	Ton(m), Klang(m)	tono, sonido	tono	tom, som, timbre
tonalité	tonality, tone	Tonart(f), Klangfarbe	tonalidad	tonalità	tonalidade
tonne	ton	Tonne(f)	tonelada	tonnellata	tonelada
tonneau	barrel	Faß(n)	tonel; barril	botte, barile	tonel; barril
tonnerre	thunder	Donner(m)	trueno	tuono	trovão
topaze	topaz	Topas(m)	topacio	topazio	topázio
torche	torch(-es)	Fackel(f)	antorcha	torcia	tocha, archote
tordre	twist	verbiegen, verdrehen	torcer	torcere, piegare	torcer
toréador	bull-fighter	Stierkämpfer(m)	torero	torero	toureiro
tornade	tornado(-es)	Wirbelsturm(m)	tornado	tornado	tornado
torpeur	torpor	Erstarrungszustand(m)	torpor	torpore	torpor
torpille	torpedo(-es)	Torpedo(m)	torpedo	torpedine	torpedo
torrent	torrent	Wildbach(m)	torrente	torrente	torrente
torsion	twist(ing)	Drehung(f), Torsion(f)	torsión	torsione	torção
tort(avoir)	wrong(to be)	Unrecht(haben)	culpa(tener)	torto(aver)	razão(não ter)
tortue	tortoise; turtle	Schildkröte(f)	tortuga	tartaruga	tartaruga
torture	torture	Folter(f)	tortura	tortura	tortura
tôt	early	früh	temprano	presto	cedo
total, e	total	ganz; Gesamt-	total	totale	total
total, e	overall	Gesamt-	total	complessivo, a	total
total	total	Summe(f), Ganze(s)(n)	total	totale	total
touche	key	Taste(f)	tecla	tasto	tecla
toucher	touch	an = fassen, berühren	tocar	toccare	tocar
toucher	cash, earn, win	kassieren(ein =)	cobrar	incassare	receber
toucher, émouvoir	affect	rühren	afectar	commuovere	afectar
toujours	always	immer	siempre	sempre	sempre
toujours	still	immer noch	todavía	sempre	ainda

120

French	English	German	Spanish	Italian	Portuguese
toujours(pour)	forever	immer(für)	siempre(para, por)	sempre(per)	sempre(para)
tour	tower	Turm(m)	torre	torre	torre
tour	turn	Umdrehung(f)	vuelta	giro	volta, giro
tour	turn	Reihe(f)	turno	turno	vez
tourbillon	whirlwind, swirl	Wirbel(wind)(m)	torbellino	vortice	turbilhão
tourisme	tourism	Tourismus(m)	turismo	turismo	turismo
touriste	tourist	Tourist(m)	turista	turista	turista
tourmenté, e	tormented	beunruhigt	atormentado, a	tormentato, a	atormentado, a
tourmenter	torment	quälen	atormentar	tormentare	atormentar
tournage	shooting	Filmaufnahme(f)	rodaje	riprese	filmagem
tourne-disque	record-player	Plattenspieler(m)	tocadiscos	giradischi	gira-discos
tourner	turn	drehen	girar	girare	girar; rodar
tourner	turn	drehen	volver	girare	virar
tourner	turn	wenden	girar	svoltare, girare	virar
tourner(faire)	rotate, revolve	drehen	girar(hacer)	roteare	girar(fazer)
tournevis	screwdriver	Schraubenzieher(m)	destornillador	cacciavite	chave de parafusos
tournoi	tournament	Turnier(n)	torneo	torneo	torneio
tourte	pie	Pastete(f)	pastel, tortada	torta salata	empada
tousser	cough	husten	toser	tossire	tossir
tout, e	all(the)	alles	todo, a	tutto, a	todo, a
toute	whole(the)	ganz	toda	tutta	toda
tous	all(the)	alle	todos	tutti	todos
tout à fait	quite	ganz	totalmente	affatto	totalmente
toutefois	however	jedoch	sin embargo	tuttavia	todavia
toux	cough	Husten(m)	tos	tosse	tosse
toxicologie	toxicology	Toxikologie(f)	toxicología	tossicologia	toxicologia
toxicomane	drug addict	Rauschgiftsüchtige(r)	drogadicto, a	tossicomane	toxicómano, drogado
toxique	toxic	giftig	tóxico, a	tossico, a	tóxico, a
trace	trace, track	Spur(f)	huella, rastro	traccia	traço; vestígio
tracer	draw	entwerfen	trazar	tracciare	traçar
trachée-artère	trachea	Luftröhre(f)	traquearteria	trachea	traqueia
tract	handout, leaflet	Flugblatt(n)	octavilla	volantino	panfleto
tracter	tug, tow	ab = schleppen	tirar	trainare, tirare	puxar
tracteur	tractor	Traktor(m)	tractor	trattore	tractor
tradition	tradition	Tradition(f)	tradición	tradizione	tradição
traducteur, trice	translator	Übersetzer(in f)m	traductor, a	traduttore, trice	tradutor, a
traduction	translation	Übersetzung(f)	traducción	traduzione	tradução
trafic	traffic	Verkehr(m)	tráfico	traffico	tráfego, tráfico
trafiquant, e	trafficker; pedlar	Schwarzhändler(in f)m	traficante	trafficante	traficante
tragédie	tragedy	Tragödie(f)	tragedia	tragedia	tragédia
tragique	tragic	tragisch	trágico, a	tragico, a	trágico, a
trahir	betray	verraten	traicionar	tradire	trair
trahison	betrayal; treason	Verrat(m)	traición	tradimento	traição
train	train	Zug(m), Eisenbahn(f)	tren	treno	comboio
traîneau	sleigh, sledge	Schlitten(m)	trineo	slitta	trenó
traîner	drag, trail, haul	schleppen	arrastrar	trascinare	arrastar
trait	line	Strich(m)	raya	tratto, riga	traço, risco
trait(s)	feature	Zug(m)(Gesichts-)	rasgos	tratto, lineamento	feição
traité	treaty	Vertrag(m)	tratado	trattato	tratado
traitement	treatment	Behandlung(f)	tratamiento	trattamento	tratamento
traiter	treat; deal with	behandeln	tratar	trattare	tratar
traître, esse	traitor, -tress	Verräter(in f)m	traidor, a	traditore, trice	traidor, a
trajectoire	trajectory	Bahn(f), Kurs(m)	trayectoria	traiettoria	trajectória
trajet	journey, trip	Strecke(f)	trayecto	tragitto	trajecto
tramway	tram-car	Straßenbahn(f)	tranvía	tram	carro eléctrico
tranche	slice	Scheibe(f)	rebanada	fetta	fatia
tranchée	trench(-es)	Graben(m)	trinchera, zanja	trincea	trincheira
tranquille	quiet, still, calm	ruhig	tranquilo, a	tranquillo, a	tranquilo, a
tranquillisant	tranquillizer	Beruhigungsmittel(n)	tranquilizante	tranquillante	tranquilizante
transaction	transaction	Transaktion(f)	transacción	transazione	transacção
transférer	transfer	überführen	transferir	trasferire	transferir
transfert	transfer	Verlegung(f)	transferencia	trasferimento	transferência
transformation	transformation	Veränderung(f)	transformación	trasformazione	transformação
transformer	transform, change	verändern	transformar	trasformare	transformar
transfuge	defector	Überläufer(in f)m	transfuga	transfuga	trânsfuga
transfusion	transfusion	Transfusion(f)	transfusión	trasfusione	transfusão
transmettre	transmit	übertragen	transmitir	trasmettere	transmitir
transmission	transmission	Übertragung(f)	transmisión	trasmissione	transmissão

121

French	English	German	Spanish	Italian	Portuguese
transparent, e	transparent	durchsichtig	transparente	trasparente	transparente
transpercer	pierce	durchbohren	atravesar	trapassare	trespassar
transpiration	perspiration	Schweiß(m)	transpiración	traspirazione	transpiração
transpirer	perspire, sweat	schwitzen	transpirar	traspirare	transpirar
transport	transport	Transport(m)	transporte	trasporto	transporte
transporter	transport, carry	transportieren	transportar	trasportare	transportar
transversal, e	transversal	Quer-; schräg	transversal	trasversale	transversal
trapèze	trapezium; trapeze	Trapez(n)	trapecio	trapezio	trapézio
traumatisme	traumatism	Trauma(n)	traumatismo	trauma	traumatismo
travail	work	Arbeit(f)	trabajo	lavoro	trabalho
travail	labour	Arbeit(f)	trabajo	lavoro	trabalho
travailler	work	arbeiten	trabajar	lavorare	trabalhar
travailleur, se	worker	Arbeiter(in f)m	trabajador, a	lavoratore, trice	trabalhador, a
travers(à)	across; through	durch	través de(a)	attraverso	através de
travers(de)	askew	schief	través(de)	traverso(di)	través(de)
traverser	cross	überqueren	atravesar, cruzar	attraversare	atravessar
travesti	transvestite	Transvestit(m)	travesti	travestito	travesti
trébucher	stumble, trip	stolpern	tropezar	inciampare	tropeçar
treize	thirteen	dreizehn	trece	tredici	treze
trembler	tremble	zittern	temblar	tremare	tremer
tremper	soak	ein = weichen	mojar	inzuppare	molhar
tremper	dip	ein = tauchen	sumergir	intingere	mergulhar
trente	thirty	dreißig	treinta	trenta	trinta
très	very	sehr	muy	molto	muito
trésor	treasure	Schatz(m)	tesoro	tesoro	tesouro
trésorier, ière	treasurer	Schatzmeister(in f)m	tesorero, a	tesoriere, a	tesoureiro, a
tresse	plait, braid	Zopf(m)	trenza	treccia	trança
trêve	truce	Waffenstillstand(m)	tregua	tregua	trégua
triangle	triangle	Dreieck(n)	triángulo	triangolo	triângulo
tribu	tribe	Stamm(m)	tribu	tribù	tribo
tribunal	court, tribunal	Gericht(n)	tribunal	tribunale	tribunal
tricher	cheat	fuschen, mogeln	trampas(hacer)	barare	batota(fazer)
tricot	sweater, jumper	Trikot(m), Strickweste	prenda de punto	maglia	malha
tricoter	knit	stricken	hacer punto	lavorare a maglia	tricotar
trier	sort(out)	sortieren	escoger, separar	scegliere, smistare	escolher, triar
trimestre	term, quarter	Vierteljahr(n)	trimestre	trimestre	trimestre
trimestriel, le	quarterly	vierteljährlich	trimestral	trimestrale	trimestral
triomphe	triumph	Triumph(m)	triunfo	trionfo	triunfo
triste	sad, unhappy	traurig	triste	triste	triste
tristesse	sadness	Traurigkeit(f)	tristeza	tristezza	tristeza
trois	three	drei	tres	tre	três
troisième	third	dritte	tercero, a	terzo, a	terceiro, a
tromper	deceive, cheat	betrügen	engañar	ingannare	enganar
tromper(se)	mistaken(be)	täuschen, sich	equivocarse	sbagliarsi	enganar-se
trompette	trumpet	Trompete(f)	trompeta	trombetta	trombeta
tronc	trunk	Stamm(m)	tronco	tronco	tronco
trône	throne	Thron(m)	trono	trono	trono
trop	too(much, many)	zuviel	demasiado, a	troppo, a	demasiado, a
trophée	trophy	Trophäe(f)	trofeo	trofeo	troféu
tropical, e	tropical	tropisch	tropical	tropicale	tropical
trotter	trot	traben	trotar	trottare	trotar
trottoir	pavement	Bürgersteig(m)	acera	marciapiede	passeio
trou	hole	Loch(n)	agujero	buco(a), foro	buraco, furo
trou	pit, hole	Grube(f)	hoyo	buca	cova
trouble	troubled	verworren	confuso, a	confuso, a; torbido, a	confuso, a
trouble	cloudy; muddy	trüb	turbio, a	torbido, a	turvo, a
trouble	blurred	verwackelt	desenfocado, a	sfocato, a	tremido, a
troubler	disturb; trouble	stören	perturbar	turbare, disturbare	perturbar
troubles	troubles	Unruhen(f, pl)	disturbios	disordini	perturbação
troupe	troop	Truppe(f)	tropa	truppa	tropa
troupeau	flock	Herde(f)	rebaño	gregge	rebanho
troupeau	herd	Herde(f)	ganado	branco	manada
trousse	kit, case, bag	Etui(n), Tasche(f)	maletín, estuche	borsa, astuccio	estojo
trouver	find	finden	encontrar	trovare	achar, encontrar
truand, e	crook	Ganove(m), Gauner(m)	granuja, bandido	teppista	bandido
truite	trout	Forelle(f)	trucha	trota	truta
truquage	faking	Trickaufnahme(f)	falsificación	trucco	falsificação
tu	you	du	tú	tu	tu

French	English	German	Spanish	Italian	Portuguese
tube	tube	Tube(f)	tubo	tubo	tubo
tuberculose	tuberculosis, T.B.	Tuberkulose(f)	tuberculosis	tubercolosi	tuberculose
tué, e	killed	getötet	muerto, a	ucciso, a	morto, a
tuer	kill	töten	matar	uccidere	matar
tueur, se	killer	Mörder(in f)m	asesino, a	assassino, a	assassino, a
tuile	tile	Ziegel(m)	teja	tegola	telha
tulipe	tulip	Tulpe(f)	tulipán	tulipano	tulipa
tumeur	tumour	Tumor(m)	tumor	tumore	tumor
tumulte	tumult, uproar	Tumult(m)	tumulto	tumulto	tumulto
tunique	tunic	Tunika(f)	túnica	tunica	túnica
tunnel	tunnel	Tunnel(m)	túnel	tunnel	túnel
turbine	turbine	Turbine(f)	turbina	turbina	turbina
turbulence	turbulence	Turbulenz(f)	turbulencia	turbolenza	turbulência
tutelle	trusteeship	Treuhandschaft(f)	tutela	tutela	tutela
tuteur, tutrice	guardian	Vormund(m)	tutor, a	tutore, trice	tutor, a
tuyau(terie)	pipe	Röhre(f), Schlauch(m)	tubo, caño	tubo, tubazione	tubo, cano
tuyau	hose	Schlauch(m)	manguera	tubo	mangueira
tympan	eardrum	Trommelfell(n)	tímpano	timpano	tímpano
type	type	Typ(m)	tipo	tipo	tipo
typhoïde	typhoid	Typhus(m)	tifoidea	tifoide	tifóide
typhon	typhoon	Taifun(m)	tifón	tifone	tufão
typique	typical	typisch	típico, a	tipico, a	típico, a
tyran	tyrant	Tyrann(m)	tirano, a	tiranno, a	tirano, a

U

French	English	German	Spanish	Italian	Portuguese
ulcère	ulcer	Geschwür(n)	úlcera	ulcera	úlcera
ultérieur, e	later	später	ulterior	ulteriore	ulterior
ultime	ultimate, final	allerletzte(r, s)	último, a	ultimo, a	último, a
un	one	eins	un, uno	un, uno	um
un, e	a, an	ein, e	uno, una	uno, una	um, uma
un, e(à); unique	single	einzeln; einzig	solo, a; único, a	singolo, a	único, a
un(l')ou l'autre	either	eine(der) der andere	uno u otro, cada	uno(l') o l'altro	um ou outro, cada
unanime	unanimous	einstimmig	unánime	unanime	unânime
unifié, e	unified, united	vereinigt	unificado, a	unificato, a	unificado, a
uniforme	uniform	Uniform(f)	uniforme	uniforme; divisa	uniforme
uniforme	uniform	gleichförmig	uniforme	uniforme	uniforme
union	union	Bund(m), Vereinigung f	unión	unione	união
unique	unique; only	einzig, einzeln	único, a	unico, a	único, a
unique	unique, exceptional	einmalig	único, a	unico, a	único, a
uniquement	only	ausschließlich	únicamente	unicamente	somente
unir	unite	vereinen	unir	unire	unir, juntar
unitaire	unitary, per unit	unitarisch	unitario, a	unitario, a	unitário, a
unité	unity	Einigkeit(f)	unidad	unità	unidade
unité	unit	Einheit(f)	unidad	unità	unidade
univers	universe	Universum(n)	universo	universo	universo
universel, le	universal	universell	universal	universale	universal
universitaire	academic	Universität-	universitario, a	universitario, a	universitário, a
université	university	Universität(f)	universidad	università	universidade
uranium	uranium	Uran(n)	uranio	uranio	urânio
urbain, e	urban	städtisch, Stadt-	urbano, a	urbano, a	urbano, a
urbanisme	town-planning	Städtebau(m)	urbanismo	urbanistica	urbanismo
urée	urea	Harnstoff(m)	urea	urea	ureia
urgence	emergency, urgency	Notfall(m)	urgencia	urgenza	urgência
urgence	urgency	Dringlichkeit(f)	urgencia	urgenza	urgência
urgent, e	urgent	dringend	urgente	urgente	urgente
urine	urine	Urin(m)	orina	urina	urina

French	English	German	Spanish	Italian	Portuguese
usage	usage, use	Gebrauch(m)	uso, empleo	uso	uso
usager, ère	user	Benutzer(in f)m	usuario, a	utente	utente
usé, e	worn, worn out	verbraucht	usado, a	logoro, a	usado, a
usine	factory, plant	Fabrik(f)	fábrica	fabbrica	fábrica
usine	plant	Anlage(f)	fábrica	fabbrica	fábrica
ustensile	utensil	Gerät(n)	utensilios	utensile	utensílio
usuel, le	usual	gebräuchlich	usual	usuale	usual
usure	wear	Abnützung(f)	desgaste	usura; logorio	usura, desgaste
utérus	uterus, womb	Gebärmutter(f)	útero	utero	útero
utile	useful	nützlich	útil	utile	útil
utilisateur	user	Benutzer(in f)m	utilizador, a	utilizzatore, trice	utilizador, a
utilisation	utilization, use	Benutzung(f)	utilización	utilizzazione	utilização
utiliser	use	benutzen	utilizar	utilizzare	utilizar
utopique	Utopian	utopisch	utópico, a	utopico, a	utópico, a

V

French	English	German	Spanish	Italian	Portuguese
vacances	holidays	Ferien(pl.)	vacaciones	vacanze	férias
vacances	vacation	Ferien(pl.)	vacaciones	vacanze	férias
vacarme	uproar, din	Krach(m)	alboroto, jaleo	chiasso	barulho
vaccin	vaccine	Impfstoff(m)	vacuna	vaccino	vacina
vaccination	vaccination	Impfung(f)	vacunación	vaccinazione	vacinação
vache	cow	Kuh(f)	vaca	vacca, mucca	vaca
vaciller	sway, wobble	taumeln	vacilar	vacillare	vacilar
vaciller	flicker	flackern	oscilar, vacilar	vacillare	tremer
vagabond, e	vagabond; tramp	Landstreicher(in f)m	vagabundo, a	vagabondo, a	vagabundo, a
vagin	vagina	Scheide(f)(Anat.)	vagina	vagina	vagina
vague	wave	Welle(f)	ola	onda	onda, vaga
vaillant, e	brave	tapfer	valiente	valoroso, a	valente; bravo, a
vaincre	defeat	besiegen	vencer	vincere	vencer
vainqueur	winner; victor	Sieger(in f)m	vencedor, a	vincitore, trice	vencedor, a
vaisseau	vessel, ship	Schiff(n)	nave, navío	vascello, nave	navio
vaisseau	vessel(blood)	Gefäß(Blut-)(n)	vaso(sanguíneo)	vaso(sanguigno)	vaso(sanguíneo)
vaisselle	crockery, dishes	Geschirr(n)	vajilla	stoviglie, vasellame	loiça, louça
valable	valid, good	gültig; annehmbar	válido, a; valedero	valido, a	válido, a
valeur	value, worth	Wert(m)	valor	valore	valor
valeur, mérite	worth, merit	Wert(m)	valor, mérito	valore, merito	valor, mérito
validité	validity	Gültigkeit(f)	validez	validità	validade
valise	suitcase, case	Koffer(m)	maleta	valigia	mala
vallée	valley	Tal(n)	valle	valle	vale
valoir	worth(be)	wert sein	valer	valere	valer
valse	waltz	Walzer(m)	vals	valzer	valsa
vanille	vanilla	Vanille(f)	vainilla	vaniglia	baunilha
vanité	vanity	Eitelkeit(f)	vanidad	vanità	vaidade
vanne	gate; valve	Klappe(f)	compuerta	saracinesca	comporta
vanter(se)	boast	prahlen	jactarse	vantarsi	gabar-se
vapeur	steam	Dampf(m)	vapor	vapore	vapor
vapeur	vapour, fumes	Dunst(m)	vapor	vapore	vapor
vaporiser	spray	sprühen	vaporizar	vaporizzare	vaporizar
variable	variable	veränderlich	variable	variabile	variável
variation	variation	Abwandlung(f)	variación	variazione	variação
varicelle	chicken-pox	Windpocken(f, pl).	varicela	varicella	varicela
varié, e	varied, various	vielfältig	variado, a	vario, a	variado, a
variété	variety	Vielfalt(f)	variedad	varietà	variedade
variole	smallpox	Pocken(f, pl)	viruela	vaiolo	varíola
vasculaire	vascular	Gefäß-	vascular	vascolare	vascular
vase	vase	Vase(f)	jarrón	vaso	jarra

F

French	English	German	Spanish	Italian	Portuguese
vase	sludge, mud	Schlamm(m)	limo, fango	melma	lodo
vaseline	vaseline	Vaseline(f)	vaselina	vasellina	vaselina
vaste	vast	weit	vasto, a	vasto, a	vasto, a
vaut la peine	worthwhile	der Mühe wert	vale la pena	vale la pena	vale a pena
vautour	vulture	Geier(m)	buitre	avvoltoio	abutre
veau	calf(-lves); veal	Kalb(n)	becerro; ternera	vitello(a)	bezerro; vitelo
vedette	star	Star(m)	estrella; divo, a	vedette; divo, a	vedeta, estrela
végétal	vegetable, plant	Pflanze(f)	vegetal	vegetale	vegetal
végétation	vegetation	Pflanzenwuchs(m)	vegetación	vegetazione	vegetação
véhicule	vehicle	Fahrzeug(n)	vehículo	veicolo	veículo
veine	vein	Vene(f)	vena	vena	veia
vélo	bike	Fahrrad(n)	bici	bici, bicicletta	bicicleta
vélocité, vitesse	velocity	Schnelligkeit(f)	velocidad	velocità	velocidade
velours	velvet	Samt(m)	terciopelo	velluto	veludo
vendeur, se	sales assistant	Verkäufer(in f)m	vendedor, a	commesso, a	vendedor, a
vendeur, se	salesman(-men)	Verkäufer(in f)m	vendedor, a	venditore, trice	vendedor, a
vendre	sell	verkaufen	vender	vendere	vender
vendredi	Friday	Freitag(m)	viernes	venerdì	sexta-feira
vénéneux, se	poisonous	giftig	venenoso, a	velenoso, a	venenoso, a
vénérien, ne	venereal	Geschlechts-	venéreo, a	venereo, a	venéreo, a
venez!	come(on)!	kommen Sie!	venga(!)	venga!, venite!	venha!
venez ici!	come here!	kommen Sie her!	venga aquí(!).	venga qui!, venite!	venha cá!
vengeance	revenge	Rache(f)	venganza	vendetta	vingança
venger	avenge	rächen	vengar	vendicare	vingar
venin	venom, poison	Gift(n)	veneno	veleno	veneno
venir	come	kommen	venir	venire	vir
vent	wind	Wind(m)	viento	vento	vento
vente	sale	Verkauf(m)	venta	vendita	venda
ventilateur	fan, ventilator	Ventilator(m)	ventilador	ventilatore	ventilador
ventilation	ventilation	Belüftung(f)	ventilación	ventilazione	ventilação
ventouse	suction disc	Saugnapf(m)	ventosa	ventosa	ventosa
ventre	stomach, abdomen	Bauch(m)	barriga, vientre	pancia, ventre	barriga
ver	worm	Wurm(m)	gusano	verme	verme
verbe	verb	Verb(n)	verbo	verbo	verbo
verdict	verdict	Urteil(n)	veredicto	verdetto	veredicto
verdure	greenery	Grün(n)	verdor, verdura	verdura	verdura
vérification	verification	Überprüfung(f)	verificación	verifica	verificação
vérifier	check, verify	überprüfen	comprobar	verificare	verificar
vérin, cric	jack	Winde(f)	gato, cric	martinetto, binda	macaco
vérifier	verify	bestätigen, nachweisen	verificar	verificare	verificar
véritable	real, genuine	wahrhaftig	verdadero, a	vero, a	verdadeiro, a
vérité	truth	Wahrheit(f)	verdad	verità	verdade
vernis	varnish	Lack(m)	barniz	vernice	verniz
verre	glass(-es)	Glas(n)	vaso	bicchiere	copo
verre	glass	Glas(n)	vidrio	vetro	vidro
verrou	bolt, lock	Riegel(m), Schloß(n)	cerrojo	catenaccio	ferrolho
verrue	wart	Warze(f)	verruga	verruca, porro	verruga
vers	to, towards	nach, zu	hacia	verso	para
vers	towards, to	gegen, in Richtung	hacia	verso	direcção a(em)
vers	line	Vers(m)	verso	verso	verso
verser	pour	aus = gießen	verter	versare	verter
verser	pay(in)	ein = zahlen	ingresar	versare	pagar
vert, e	green	grün	verde	verde	verde
vertèbre	vertebra(-ae)	Wirbel(m)	vértebra	vertebra	vértebra
vertical, e	vertical	senkrecht	vertical	verticale	vertical
vertige	dizziness	Schwindel(m)	vértigo	vertigine	vertigem
vertu	virtue	Tugend(f)	virtud	virtù	virtude
vertueux, se	virtuous	tugendhaft	virtuoso, a	virtuoso, a	virtuoso, a
vésicule	gall-bladder	Blase(f)	vesícula	cistifellea	vesícula
vessie	bladder	Harnblase(f)	vejiga	vescica	bexiga
veste	jacket	Jacke(f)	chaqueta	giacca	jaqueta, casaco
vestiaire	cloak-room	Garderobe(f)	vestuario	vestiario	vestiário
vestibule	hall	Flur(m)	vestíbulo	ingresso, anticamera	vestíbulo; hall
vestige	remains	Überrest(m)	vestigio	vestigia	vestígio
vêtement	garment	Kleidungsstück(n)	traje, ropa	vestito	peça de roupa
vêtements	clothes	Kleidung(f)	ropa, prenda	vestiti	roupa(s)
vétérinaire	vet	Tierarzt(m)	veterinario	veterinario	veterinário
vêtir	clothe, dress	an = ziehen, an = kleiden	vestir	vestire	vestir

French	English	German	Spanish	Italian	Portuguese
veto	veto	Veto(n)	veto	veto	veto
veuf, veuve	widower, widow	Witwer(m), Witwe(f)	viudo, a	vedovo, a	viúvo, a
vexation	vexation	Ärger(m)	vejación	vessazione	vexame
vexer	offend, vex	beleidigen	ofender, picar	offendere	ofender
vexer(se)	get upset	beleidigt sein	ofenderse	offendersi	ofender-se
viande	meat	Fleisch(n)	carne	carne	carne
vibrer	vibrate	schwingen	vibrar	vibrare	vibrar
vice	vice	Laster(n)	vicio	vizio	vício
vice-président	vice-president	Vize-Präsident(m)	vicepresidente	vicepresidente	vice-presidente
vicieux, se	vicious	lasterhaft	vicioso, a	vizioso, a	vicioso, a
victime	victim	Opfer(n)	víctima	vittima	vítima
victoire	victory	Sieg(m)	victoria	vittoria	vitória
vide	empty	leer	vacío, a	vuoto, a	vazio, a
vide	vacuum; void	Vakuum(n), Leere(f)	vacío	vuoto	vazio, vácuo
vider	empty	leeren	vaciar	vuotare	esvaziar
vie	life(lives)	Leben(n)	vida	vita	vida
vieillard	old man(men)	Alte(m), alter Mann(m)	viejo, anciano	vecchio, anziano	velho, ancião
vierge	virgin	unberührt	virgen	vergine	virgem
vieux, vieille	old	alt	viejo, a	vecchio, a	velho, a
vif, vive	lively	lebendig	vivo, a	vivace; vivo, a	vivo, a
vif, vive	keen	scharf	agudo, a; vivo, a	vivo, a	vivo, a
vigilant, e	vigilant	wachsam	vigilante	vigilante	vigilante
vigueur	vigour	Kraft(f)	vigor	vigore	vigor
vigueur(en)	force(in), current	Kraft(in), geltend	vigente	vigore(in), vigente	vigente
vigoureux, se	vigorous, strong	rüstig, kräftig	vigoroso, a	vigoroso, a	vigoroso, a
village	village	Dorf(n)	aldea, pueblo	paese, villaggio	aldeia, povoado
ville	town	Stadt(f)	ciudad	città	cidade
vin	wine	Wein(m)	vino	vino	vinho
vinaigre	vinegar	Essig(m)	vinagre	aceto	vinagre
vingt	twenty	zwanzig	veinte	venti	vinte
vingt-et-un	twenty one	einundzwanzig	veintiún(o)	ventuno	vinte e um
viol	rape	Vergewaltigung(f)	violación	stupro	violação
violation	violation	Verstoß(m)	violación	violazione	violação
violence	violence	Gewalt(f)	violencia	violenza	violência
violent, e	violent	gewalttätig, gewaltsam	violento, a	violento, a	violento, a
violent, e	violent	heftig, stark	violento, a	violento, a	violento, a
violer	rape	vergewaltigen	violar	violentare	violentar
violer	violate	verraten	violar	violare	violar
violet, te	violet, purple	violett, lila	violeta	viola	roxo, a; violeta
violon	violin	Geige(f)	violín	violino	violino
violoncelle	cello	Cello(n)	violoncelo	violoncello	violoncelo
vipère	viper	Viper(f), Otter(f)	víbora	vipera	víbora
virage	bend, turn	Kurve(f)	curva	curva	curva
virginité	virginity	Jungfräulichkeit(f)	virginidad	verginità	virgindade
virgule	comma	Komma(n)	coma	virgola	vírgula
viril, e	virile, manly	männlich, mannhaft	viril	virile	viril
virilité	virility	Männlichkeit(f)	virilidad	virilità	virilidade
virtuose	virtuoso	Meister(m), Virtuose m	virtuoso, a	virtuoso, a	virtuoso, a
virus	virus	Virus(m)	virus	virus	vírus
vis	screw	Schraube(f)	tornillo	vite	parafuso
visa	visa	Visum(n)	visado	visto	visto
visage	face	Gesicht(n)	rostro, cara	viso	cara
viser	aim	zielen	apuntar	mirare	apontar
visibilité	visibility	Sicht(-weite)(f)	visibilidad	visibilità	visibilidade
visible	visible	sichtbar	visible	visibile	visível
visite	visit	Besuch(m)	visita	visita	visita
visiter	visit	besichtigen, reisen	visitar	visitare	visitar
visiter	visit	besuchen	visitar	andare a trovare	visitar
visiteur, se	visitor	Besucher(in f)m	visitante	visitatore, trice	visitante
vison	mink	Nerz(m)	visón	visone	marta
visqueux, se	viscous	zähflüssig	viscoso, a	vischioso, a	viscoso, a
visualiser	display	sichtbar machen	visualizar	visualizzare	visualizar
visuel, le	visual	visuell	visual	visivo, a; visuale	visual
vital, e	vital	wesentlich	vital	vitale	vital
vitalité	vitality	Lebenskraft(f)	vitalidad	vitalità	vitalidade
vitamine	vitamin	Vitamin(n)	vitamina	vitamina	vitamina
vite	quickly, fast	schnell, rasch	rápido, pronto	fretta(in), presto	rápido, a; depressa
vite	fast, quickly	rasch	pronto; rápido, a	presto	depressa; rápido, a

French	English	German	Spanish	Italian	Portuguese
vitesse	speed	Geschwindigkeit(f)	velocidad	velocità	velocidade
vitre	pane, window	Scheibe(f)(Fenster-)	cristal, vidrio	vetro	vidro
vitrine	shop-window	Schaufenster(n)	escaparate	vetrina	montra, vitrina
vivace	hardy	immergrün; ausdauernd	vivaz	vivace	vivaz
vivant, e	alive	lebendig	vivo, a	vivo, a; vivente	vivo, a
vive!	hurrah!; Long live!	Es lebe!; Lang lebe!	viva(!)	viva!, evviva!	viva!
vivre	live	leben	vivir	vivere	viver
vocabulaire	vocabulary	Vokabular(n)	vocabulario	vocabolario	vocabulário
vocal, e	vocal	Stimm-	vocal	vocale	vocal
vocation	vocation	Berufung(f)	vocación	vocazione	vocação
voeu	wish(-es)	Wunsch(m)	deseo	augurio	voto
voeu	vow	Gelübde(n)	voto	voto	promessa
voici	here is; here are	hier(ist/sind)	he aquí	ecco	aqui está
voie	way; track	Weg(m)	vía; camino	via; binario	via; caminho
voie	lane	Spur(f)(Straßen-)	vía	corsia	faixa(rua)
voile	sail	Segel(n)	vela	vela	vela
voile	sailing	Segeln(n)	vela	vela	vela
voile	veil	Schleier(m)	velo	velo	véu
voilier	yacht, sailing boat	Segelboot(n)	velero	veliero	veleiro
voir	see	sehen	ver	vedere	ver
voisin, e	neighbour	Nachbar(in f)m	vecino, a	vicino, a	vizinho, a
voisinage	neighbourhood	Nachbarschaft(f)	vecindario	vicinanza	vizinhança
voiture	car	Wagen(m)	coche	macchina, auto	carro
voiture(course)	racing car	Rennwagen(m)	coche de carreras	macchina da corsa	carro de corrida
voix	voice	Stimme(f)	voz	voce	voz
vol	flight	Flug(m)	vuelo	volo	voo
vol	theft, robbery	Diebstahl(m)	robo	furto	roubo
volaille	poultry	Geflügel(n)	aves de corral	pollame	aves de capoeira
volant	steering-wheel	Steuer(n)	volante	volante	volante
volcan	volcano(-es)	Vulkan(m)	volcán	vulcano	vulcão
voler	fly	fliegen	volar	volare	voar
voler, se	steal, rob	stehlen	robar	rubare	roubar
voleur, se	thief(-ves), robber	Dieb(in f)m	ladrón, a	ladro, a	ladrão, ladra
volontaire	voluntary	freiwillig	voluntario, a	volontario, a	voluntário, a
volontaire	volunteer	Freiwillige(f, m)	voluntario, a	volontario, a	voluntário, a
volonté	will, determination	Wille(m)	voluntad	volontà	vontade
volontiers	willingly	gern	buena gana(de)	volentieri	bom grado(de)
volume	volume	Volumen(n)	volumen	volume	volume
vomir	vomit	erbrechen, sich	vomitar	vomitare	vomitar
vorace	voracious	gefräßig, gierig	voraz	vorace	voraz
vos	your	eure, Ihre	vuestros, as	vostri, e	vossos, as
vote	vote	Wahl(f)	voto	voto	voto
voter	vote	wählen	votar	votare	votar
votre	your	Ihr(e); euer, eure	vuestro, a	vostro, a(il, la)	vosso, a
vôtre(le, la)	yours	eure(r, s); Ihre(r, s)	vuestro, a; suyo, a	vostro, a; suo, sua	vosso, a; seu, sua
voudrais(je)	would like(I)	möchte(ich)	quisiera(yo)	vorrei	gostava
vouloir	want	wollen	querer	volere	querer
vous	you	ihr; Sie	vosotros; ustedes	voi; lei	vós; você
vous	you	Sie	usted(es)	lei, loro(pl.)	você
vous; te	you	euch; Sie; Ihnen	os; les; le; te	vi; ve; ti; te	vos; vosco; lhe
voûte	vault, arch	Gewölbe(n)	bóveda	arco, volta	abóbada
voyage	trip; journey	Reise(f)	viaje	viaggio	viagem
voyager	travel	reisen	viajar	viaggiare	viajar
voyageur, se	traveller	Reisende(r)m f	viajero, a	viaggiatore, trice	viajante
voyelle	vowel	Vokal(m), Selbstlaut m	vocal	vocale	vogal
voyou	hooligan	Strolch(m)	canalla	mascalzone, a	patife
vrai, e	true	wahr	verdadero, a	vero, a	verdadeiro, a
vraiment	really	wirklich	verdaderamente	veramente	verdadeiramente
vraisemblable	likely, probable	wahrscheinlich	verosímil	verosimile	verosímil
vue	sight	Sehkraft(f)	vista	vista	vista
vue	view	Ausblick(m)	vista	veduta	vista
vulgaire	vulgar	vulgär	vulgar	volgare	vulgar
vulnérable	vulnerable	verwundbar	vulnerable	vulnerabile	vulnerável

F

W

French	English	German	Spanish	Italian	Portuguese
wagon	coach, carriage	Wagen(m)	vagón	vagone, carrozza	vagão
wagon	truck, wag(g)on	Waggon(m)(Güterwagen)	vagón	vagone	vagão
water-closet	toilets	Toilette(f)	water, retretes	WC; gabinetto	retrete, sanita
week-end	weekend	Wochenende(n)	fin de semana	fine settimana	fim de semana

Y

French	English	German	Spanish	Italian	Portuguese
yeux	eyes	Augen(n, pl)	ojos	occhi	olhos
yoga	yoga	Yoga(n), Joga(n)	yoga	yoga	yoga

Z

French	English	German	Spanish	Italian	Portuguese
zèbre	zebra	Zebra(n)	cebra	zebra	zebra
zéro	zero, nought	Null(f)	cero	zero	zero
zone	zone	Zone(f)	zona	zona	zona
zoo	zoo	Zoo(m)	zoológico	zoo	jardim zoológico
zoologique	zoological	zoologisch	zoológico, a	zoologico, a	zoológico, a

A

English	French	German	Spanish	Italian	Portuguese
a, an	un, e	ein, e	uno, una	uno, una	um, uma
abandon, leave	abandonner	preis = geben; auf = geben	abandonar	abbandonare	abandonar
abbey	abbaye	Abtei(f)	abadía	abbazia, badia	abadia
abbreviation	abréviation	Abkürzung(f)(Wort)	abreviatura	abbreviazione	abreviatura
abdicate	abdiquer	ab = danken	abdicar	abdicare	abdicar
abdomen	abdomen	Unterleib(m)	abdomen	addome	abdómen
ability, aptitude	aptitude	Fähigkeit(f)	aptitud(es)	attitudine	aptidão, talento
ability, skill	habileté	Geschicklichkeit(f)	habilidad	abilità	habilidade
able, qualified	apte, compétent	fähig; tauglich	apto, a	adatto, a	apto, a
able to(be)	capable de	fähig	capaz de	capace di	capaz de
aboard	à bord	an Bord	a bordo	a bordo	a bordo
abolish	abolir	ab = schaffen	abolir	abolire	abolir
abort	avorter	ab = treiben	abortar	abortire	abortar
abortion	avortement	Abtreibung(f)	aborto	aborto	aborto
about	environ	ungefähr	aproximadamente	circa	cerca de
above	au-dessus	über	encima(por, de)	sopra(al di)	cima(por); acima de
above	ci-dessus	oben(-stehend)	arriba(más)	sopra(qui)	acima
above, on, over	dessus(au-; par-)	über	arriba, encima	sopra	em cima, sobre
above all	surtout	besonders	sobre todo	soprattutto	sobretudo
abroad	étranger(à l')	Ausland(im)	extranjero(en el)	estero(all')	estrangeiro(ao)
abrupt, sudden	brusque	brüsk	brusco, a	brusco, a	brusco, a
abscess(-es)	abcès	Geschwür(n)	absceso	ascesso	abcesso
absent	absent, e	abwesend	ausente	assente	ausente
absent-minded	distrait, e	zerstreut	distraído, a	distratto, a	distraído, a
absolute	absolu, e	unbedingt	absoluto, a	assoluto, a	absoluto, a
absolutely	absolument	unbedingt, absolut	absolutamente	assolutamente	absolutamente
absorb	absorber	verzehren	absorber	assorbire	absorver
absorb, cushion	amortir	dämpfen	amortiguar	attutire	amortecer
abstract	abstrait, e	abstrakt	abstracto, a	astratto, a	abstracto, a
absurd	absurde	unsinnig	absurdo, a	assurdo, a	absurdo, a
abundance	abondance	Uberfluß(m)	abundancia	abbondanza	abundância
abuse, misuse	abus	Mißbrauch(m)	abuso	abuso	abuso
academic	universitaire	Universität-	universitario, a	universitario, a	universitário, a
academy	académie	Akademie(f)	academia	accademia	academia
accede to	accéder	gelangen zu/kommen an	acceder	assurgere	chegar
accelerate	accélérer	beschleunigen	acelerar	accelerare	acelerar
accent	accent	Akzent(m), Tonfall(m)	dejo	accento	sotaque
accent	accent(')	Akzent(m)	acento	accento	acento
accept, agree	accepter	akzeptieren, an = nehmen	aceptar	accettare	aceitar
accept, approve	agréer	genehmigen, zu = lassen	aceptar	gradire, accettare	aceitar
access	accès	Zugang(m)	acceso	accesso	acesso
accessible	accessible	zugänglich	accesible	accessibile	acessível
accessory	accessoire	Zubehör(n)	accesorio	accessorio	acessório
accident	accident	Unfall(m)	accidente	incidente	acidente
accommodate	loger	unter = bringen	alojar	alloggiare	alojar, morar
accommodation	logement	Wohnung(f)	alojamiento	alloggio	alojamento
accommodation	hébergement	Unterbringung(f)	alojamiento	alloggio	alojamento
accompany	accompagner	begleiten	acompañar	accompagnare	acompanhar
accomplice	complice	Komplize(m)	cómplice	complice	cúmplice
accomplish	accomplir	vollführen	realizar, efectuar	compiere, effettuare	realizar
according to	selon	gemäß	según	secondo	segundo
account	compte	Konto(n)	cuenta	conto	conta
account	compte	Rechnung(f)	cuenta	conto	conta
accountancy	comptabilité	Buchhaltung(f)	contabilidad	contabilità	contabilidade
accountant	comptable	Buchhalter(in f)m	contable	ragioniere	contabilista
accumulate	accumuler	an = häufen	acumular	accumulare	acumular
accumulate	cumuler	an = häufen	acaparar	cumulare	acumular

129

English	French	German	Spanish	Italian	Portuguese
accuracy	exactitude	Genauigkeit(f)	exactitud	esattezza	exactidão
accurate	exact, e; précis, e	genau; richtig	exacto, a; preciso, a	accurato, a; preciso, a	exacto, a; preciso, a
accusation, charge	accusation	Anklage(f)	acusación	accusa	acusação
accuse	accuser	an = klagen	acusar	accusare	acusar
accused(the)	accusé, e	Angeklagte(f, m)	acusado, a; reo	accusato, a	acusado, a; réu(ré)
accused(the)	inculpé, e	Angeklagte(f, m)	inculpado, a	imputato, a	acusado, a
ache, pain	mal	Schmerz(m), Weh(n)	dolor	male	dor
ache, hurt	mal(faire)	weh tun, schmerzen	doler	male(fare)	doer
achieve	accomplir	vollbringen	ejecutar, realizar	realizzare, compiere	realizar
achieve	remporter, gagner	erringen	lograr, triunfar	raggiungere, ottenere	alcançar, obter
acid	acide	Säure(f)	ácido	acido	ácido
acoustics	acoustique	Akustik(f)	acústica	acustica	acústica
acquire	acquérir	erwerben; erlangen	adquirir	acquistare	adquirir, obter
acquired	acquis, e	erworben	adquirido, a	acquisito, a	adquirido, a
acrobat	acrobate	Akrobat(in f)m	acróbata	acrobata	acrobata
acrobatics, stunts	acrobatie	Akrobatik(f)	acrobacia	acrobazia	acrobacia
across; through	travers(à)	durch	través de(a)	attraverso	através de
acrylic	acrylique	Akryl(n)	acrílico	acrilico	acrílico
act	agir	handeln	actuar	agire	agir
act	jouer	spielen	desempeñar	recitare	representar
action	action	Vorgehen(n), Handlung	acción	azione	acção
action, act	acte	Handlung(f)	acto	atto	acto, acção
activate	activer	beschleunigen	activar	attivare	activar
active	actif, ive	aktiv, tatkräftig	activo, a	attivo, a	activo, a
activity	activité	Tätigkeit(f)	actividad	attività	actividade
actor, actress(-es)	acteur, actrice	Schauspieler(in f)m	actor, actriz	attore, attrice	actor, actriz
actor, actress(-es)	comédien, ne	Schauspieler(in f)m	actor, actriz	attore, attrice	actor, actriz
acupuncture	acuponcture	Akupunktur(f)	acupuntura	agopuntura	acupunctura
adapt, adjust	adapter	an = passen	adaptar	adattare	adaptar
adapt(to)	adapter(s')	an = passen, sich	adaptarse(a)	adattarsi(a)	adaptar-se(a)
adaptation	adaptation	Anpassung(f)	adaptación	adattamento	adaptação
add	ajouter	hinzu = fügen	añadir	aggiungere	ajuntar, juntar
addiction	accoutumance	Abhängigkeit(f)	adicto, dependencia	assuefazione	dependência
addition, sum	addition, somme	Addition(f), Summe(f)	adición, suma	addizione, somma	adição, soma
additional	additionnel, le	hinzugefügt	adicional	addizionale	adicional
additional, extra	supplémentaire	zusätzlich	suplementario, a	supplementare	suplementar
address(-es)	adresse	Anschrift(f), Adresse	dirección	indirizzo	endereço, morada
addressee	destinataire	Empfänger(in f)m	destinatario, a	destinatario, a	destinatário, a
adhesive	adhésif, ive	klebrig, anhaftend	adhesivo, a	adesivo, a	adesivo, a
adjective	adjectif	Adjektiv(n)	adjetivo	aggettivo	adjectivo
adjust	ajuster	ein = stellen	ajustar	aggiustare, adattare	ajustar
adjust, tune	régler	ein = stellen	ajustar, arreglar	regolare	afinar, regular
adjustment	réglage	Einstellung(f)	reglaje, ajuste	regolazione	afinação
administration	administration	Verwaltung(f)	administración	amministrazione	administração
administrative	administratif, ve	Verwaltungs-	administrativo, a	amministrativo, a	administrativo, a
admiral	amiral	Admiral(m)	almirante	ammiraglio	almirante
admiration	admiration	Bewunderung(f)	admiración	ammirazione	admiração
admirer, fan	admirateur, trice	Bewunderer(in f)m	admirador, a	ammiratore, trice	admirador, a
admissible	admissible	zulässig, annehmbar	admisible	ammissibile	admissível
admission	admission	Zulassung, Einweisung	admisión	ammissione	admissão
admission	entrée	Eintrittskarte(f)	entrada	ingresso	entrada, bilhete
admit	admettre	zu = geben; zu = lassen	admitir	ammettere	admitir
adopt	adopter	adoptieren	adoptar	adottare	adoptar
adorable, lovely	adorable	reizend	adorable	adorabile	adorável
adore	adorer	an = beten	adorar	adorare	adorar
adult	adulte	Erwachsene(f, m)	adulto, a	adulto, a	adulto, a
adultery	adultère	Ehebruch(m)	adulterio	adulterio	adultério
advance	avance	Vorsprung(m)	adelanto	anticipo	avanço
advance, move fwd	avancer	weiter = gehen	avanzar	procedere	avançar
advance	avancer	voran = gehen; vorrücken	adelantar	avanzare	adiantar
advantage	avantage	Vorteil(m)	ventaja	vantaggio	vantagem
adventure	aventure	Abenteuer(n)	aventura	avventura	aventura
adverb	adverbe	Umstandswort, Adverb	adverbio	avverbio	advérbio
adverse, opposing	adverse	feindlich, gegnerisch	adverso, a	avverso, a	adverso, a
advertisement	réclame(s), pub	Reklame(f)	publicidad	reclame	publicidade
advertising	publicité	Werbung(f), Anzeige(f)	publicidad	pubblicità	publicidade
advice	conseil	Rat(m)	consejo	consiglio	conselho
advise	conseiller	beraten	aconsejar	consigliare	aconselhar

English	French	German	Spanish	Italian	Portuguese
advise against	déconseiller	ab = raten	desaconsejar	sconsigliare	desaconselhar
adviser	conseiller, ère	Berater(in f)m	consejero, a	consigliere, a	conselheiro, a
aerial, air	aérien, ne	Luft-	aéreo, a	aereo, a	aéreo, a
aerial, antenna(e)	antenne	Antenne(f)	antena	antenna	antena
aerogram	aérogramme	Funkspruch(m)	aerograma	aerogramma	aerograma
aeronautics	aéronautique	Luftfahrt(f)	aeronáutica	aeronautica	aeronáutica
aeroplane, plane	avion	Flugzeug(n)	avión	aereo, aeroplano	avião
aesthetic	esthétique	ästhetisch	estético, a	estetico, a	estético, a
affair, matter	affaire	Affäre(f), Sache(f)	asunto	faccenda, affare	assunto
affect	toucher, émouvoir	rühren	afectar	commuovere	afectar
affection, love	affection	Zuneigung(f)	afecto; afección	affetto	afeição; afecto
affectionate	affectueux, se	liebevoll	afectuoso, a	affettuoso, a	afectuoso, a
affinity	affinité	Ähnlichkeit(f)	afinidad	affinità	afinidade
afford	permettre(se)	leisten, sich	permitirse	permettersi	permitir-se
afraid(to be)	peur(avoir)	Angst(haben)	miedo(tener)	paura(avere)	medo(ter)
after; afterwards	après	nach	después	dopo	depois
afternoon	après-midi	Nachmittag(m)	tarde	pomeriggio	tarde
again	encore	noch einmal	otra vez	ancora	mais(uma vez)
against	contre	gegen, an	contra	contro	encostado a
against	contre	wider, gegen	contra(en)	contro	contra
age	âge	Alter(n)	edad	età	idade
agency	agence	Agentur(f); Filiale(f)	agencia	agenzia	agência
agent	agent	Agent(in f)m	agente	agente	agente
aggressive	belliqueux, se	kriegerisch	belicoso, a	bellicoso, a	belicoso, a
agile, nimble	agile	flink	ágil	agile	ágil
agitation; unrest	agitation	Aufregung(f); Unruhe f	agitación	agitazione	agitação
ago	il y a	vor	hace	fa	há
agony	agonie	Todeskampf(m), Agonie	agonía	agonia	agonia
agree	accord(être d')	überein = stimmen	acuerdo(estar de)	accordo(essere d')	acordo(estar de)
agree	convenir	überein = kommen	acordar	convenire	convir, combinar
agree	consentir	ein = willigen	consentir	consentire	consentir
agreement	accord	Einverständnis(n)	acuerdo	accordo	acordo
agreement	convention	Übereinstimmung(f)	convención	convenzione	convenção
agricultural	agricole	landwirtschaftlich	agrícola	agricolo, a	agrícola
agriculture	agriculture	Landwirtschaft(f)	agricultura	agricoltura	agricultura
ahead	avant(en)	voran, voraus	adelante	avanti	adiante
aim	viser	zielen	apuntar	mirare	apontar
aim	braquer	richten auf	apuntar	puntare	apontar
aim, purpose	but	Ziel(n)	propósito	scopo	fim, intento
air	air	Luft(f)	aire	aria	ar
air, ventilate	aérer	lüften	airear, ventilar	arieggiare	arejar, ventilar
air conditioner	climatiseur	Klimaanlage(f)	climatizador	condizionatore	climatizador
air-freshener	désodorisant	Deodorant(n)	desodorante	deodorante	desodorisante
airport	aéroport	Flughafen(m)	aeropuerto	aeroporto	aeroporto
alarm	alarme	Alarm(m)	alarma	allarme	alarme
alarm clock	réveil	Wecker(m)	despertador	sveglia	despertador
album	album	Album(n)	álbum	album	álbum
alcohol	alcool	Alkohol(m)	alcohol	alcol, alcool	álcool
alcoholism	alcoolisme	Alkoholmißbrauch(m)	alcoholismo	alcolismo	alcoolismo
aleatory, uncertain	aléatoire	unsicher, ungewiß	aleatorio, a	aleatorio, a	aleatório, a; incerto
alert	alerte	Alarm(m)	alerta	allarme	alerta, alarme
algebra	algèbre	Algebra(f)	álgebra	algebra	álgebra
alibi	alibi	Alibi(n)	coartada	alibi	alibi
alignment	alignement	Ausrichtung(f)	alineación	allineamento	alinhamento
alive	vivant, e	lebendig	vivo, a	vivo, a; vivente	vivo, a
all(the)	tout, e	alles	todo, a	tutto, a	todo, a
all(the)	tous	alle	todos	tutti	todos
allergy	allergie	Allergie(f)	alergia	allergia	alergia
alley	ruelle	Gäßchen(n), Gasse(f)	callejuela	viuzza, vicolo	viela
alliance	alliance	Bündnis(n)	alianza	alleanza	aliança
allocate	allouer	zu = teilen, bewilligen	conceder	assegnare	conceder
allopathy	allopathie	Allopathie(f)	alopatía	allopatia	alopatia
allow, enable	permettre	erlauben	permitir	permettere	permitir
allowance	allocation	Beihilfe(f), Zulage(f)	subsidio	assegnazione; assegno	subsídio, abono
allowance	indemnité	Schadenersatz(m)	dietas	indennità	ajuda de custo
alloy	alliage	Legierung(f)	aleación	lega	liga
all right, O.K	accord(d')	einverstanden, okay	vale, de acuerdo	accordo(d')	acordo(de)
ally	allier	verbünden	aliar, unir	alleare, unire	aliar, unir

131

English	French	German	Spanish	Italian	Portuguese
almond	amande	Mandel(f)	almendra	mandorla	amêndoa
almost, nearly	presque	fast	casi	quasi	quase
alone	seul, e	allein	solo, a	solo, a	só
along	long(le)	entlang	largo(a lo)	lungo	longo(ao)
alphabet	alphabet	Alphabet(n)	alfabeto	alfabeto	alfabeto
already	déjà	schon	ya	giá	já
also, too; as	aussi	auch	también	anche, pure	também
alternate	alterner	ab = wechseln	alternar	alternare	alternar
alternating(ive)	alternatif, ive	alternativ	alternativo, a	alternativo, a	alternativo, a
although, though	quoique	obgleich, obwohl	aunque	sebbene	embora
altitude, height	altitude	Höhe(f)	altitud, altura	altitudine	altitude
aluminium	aluminium	Aluminium(n)	aluminio	alluminio	alumínio
always	toujours	immer	siempre	sempre	sempre
amateur	amateur	Amateur(in f)m	aficionado, a	dilettante	amador, a
amaze	émerveiller	entzücken	maravillar	meravigliare	maravilhar
amazed	stupéfait, e	verblüfft	estupefacto, a	stupefatto, a	estupefacto, a
ambassador	ambassadeur	Botschafter(in f)m	embajador	ambasciatore	embaixador
ambiguous	ambigu, ë	zweideutig, mehrdeutig	ambiguo, a	ambiguo, a	ambíguo, a
ambition	ambition	Ehrgeiz(m)	ambición	ambizione	ambição
ambitious	ambitieux, se	ehrgeizig	ambicioso, a	ambizioso, a	ambicioso, a
ambulance	ambulance	Krankenwagen(m)	ambulancia	ambulanza	ambulância
ambush	embuscade	Hinterhalt(m)	emboscada	imboscata	emboscada
amend	amender	verbessern, ändern	enmendar	emendare	emendar
ammunition	munitions	Munition(f)	municiones	munizioni	munições
amnesia	amnésie	Gedächtnisschwund(m)	amnesia	amnesia	amnésia
amnesty	amnistie	Amnestie(f)	amnistía	amnistia	amnistia
among	parmi	unter	entre	fra, tra	entre
amount	montant	Betrag(m)	importe	ammontare	montante
ample; loose	ample	weit	amplio, a	ampio, a	amplo, a
amplitude	amplitude	Amplitude(f)	amplitud	ampiezza	amplitude
amputate	amputer	amputieren	amputar	amputare	amputar
amusement, fun	amusement	Vergnügen(n)	diversión	divertimento	divertimento
amusing, funny	amusant, e	amüsant, drollig	divertido, a	divertente	engraçado, a
anaemia	anémie	Blutarmut(f)	anemia	anemia	anemia
anaesthetic	anesthésie	Narkose(f)	anestesia	anestesia	anestesia
analogous, similar	analogue	analog	análogo, a	analogo, a	análogo, a
analyse	analyser	analysieren	analizar	analizzare	analisar
analysis(-ses)	analyse	Analyse(f)	análisis	analisi	análise
anarchy	anarchie	Anarchie(f)	anarquía	anarchia	anarquia
anatomy	anatomie	Anatomie(f)	anatomía	anatomia	anatomia
ancestor	ancêtre	Ahn(m)	antepasado, a	antenato, a	antepassado, a
ancestors	aïeux	Ahnen(pl.)	antepasados	antenati	antepassados
anchor	ancre	Anker(m)	ancla	àncora	âncora
ancient	ancien, ne	alt	antiguo, a	antico, a	antigo, a
and	et	und	y	e, ed	e
anecdote	anecdote	Anekdote(f)	anécdota	aneddoto	anedota
angel	ange	Engel(m)	ángel	angelo	anjo
anger(be angry)	colère	Wut(f)	cólera, ira	collera, ira	cólera, ira
angle	angle	Winkel(m)	ángulo	angolo	ângulo
angling	pêche	Angeln(n)	pesca(con caña)	pesca(con lenza)	pesca(à linha)
anguish, distress	angoisse	Angst(f)	angustia	angoscia	angústia
animal	animal	Tier(n)	animal	animale	animal
animal, beast	bête	Biest(n), Tier(n)	bestia	bestia	bicho, animal
animate	animer	beleben	animar	animare	animar
ankle	cheville	Knöchel(m)	tobillo	caviglia	tornozelo
annexe	annexe	Anhang(m), Anlage(f)	anexo; anejo	annesso	anexo
annihilate, destroy	anéantir	vernichten	aniquilar	annientare	aniquilar
anniversary	anniversaire	Jahrestag(m)	aniversario	anniversario	aniversário
announce	annoncer	an = kündigen	anunciar	annunciare	anunciar
annoyance	contrariété	Verdruß(m)	molestia	seccatura	contrariedade
annul	annuler	ungültig erklären	anular	annullare	anular
annular, ring-	annulaire	ringförmig	anular	anulare	anelar
anomaly	anomalie	Anomalie(f)	anomalía	anomalia	anomalia
anonymity	anonymat	Anonymität(f)	anonimato	anonimato	anonimato
anonymous	anonyme	anonym, unbekannt	anónimo, a	anonimo, a	anónimo, a
answer, reply	réponse	Antwort(f)	respuesta	risposta	resposta
answer, reply	répondre	antworten	contestar	rispondere	responder
ant	fourmi	Ameise(f)	hormiga	formica	formiga

English	French	German	Spanish	Italian	Portuguese
antibiotic	antibiotique	Antibiotikum(n)	antibiótico	antibiotico	antibiótico
anticipate	anticiper	vor = greifen	anticipar	anticipare	antecipar
antique, ancient	antique	antik	antiguo, a	antico, a	antigo, a
antique shop	antiquités	Antiquitäten	anticuario	antiquariato	antiguidades
antiquity	antiquité	Antiquität(f)	antigüedad	antichità	antiguidade
antiseptic	antiseptique	antiseptisch	antiséptico, a	antisettico, a	antiséptico, a
anti-theft lock	antivol	Diebstahlsicherung(f)	antirrobo	antifurto	alarme
anxiety, worry	inquiétude	Sorge(f)	inquietud	inquietudine	inquietação
anxious	anxieux, se	ängstlich	ansioso, a	ansioso, a	ansioso, a
any, whatever	quelconque	beliebig	cualquier(a)	qualunque	qualquer
anyone(who)	quiconque	jeder	quienquiera	chiunque	qualquer(um)
aperitif, drink	apéritif	Apéritif(m)	aperitivo	aperitivo	aperitivo
aperture	orifice	Öffnung(f)	abertura, orificio	apertura, orifizio	abertura, orifício
apologize	excuser(s')	entschuldigen, sich	disculpar(se)	scusarsi	desculpar-se
appeal	appel	Berufung(f)	apelación	appello	apelação
appeal to	recourir à	Berufung(f)ein = legen	recurrir, apelar	ricorrere, appellarsi	recorrer, apelar
appeal to, request	solliciter	ersuchen	solicitar	sollecitare	solicitar
appear	apparaître	erscheinen	aparecer	apparire	aparecer
appearance, look	apparence	Aussehen(n)	apariencia	apparenza	aparência
appetite	appétit	Appetit(m)	apetito	appetito	apetite
applaud, clap	applaudir	klatschen	aplaudir	applaudire	aplaudir
apple	pomme	Apfel(m)	manzana	mela	maçã
appliance, device	appareil	Apparat(m)	aparato	apparecchio	aparelho
application	demande(emploi)	Bewerbung(f)	solicitud	domanda	pedido
application	candidature	Bewerbung(f)	candidatura	candidatura	candidatura
apply	appliquer	an = wenden	aplicar	applicare	aplicar
appoint	nommer	ernennen	nombrar	nominare	nomear
appoint	désigner	ernennen	designar	designare	designar
appointment	rendez-vous	Verabredung(f)	cita	appuntamento	encontro
appreciate	apprécier	schätzen	apreciar	apprezzare	apreciar
appreciation	appréciation	Beurteilung(f)	apreciación	giudizio	apreciação
apprehension	appréhension	Furcht(f)	aprensión, recelo	apprensione	apreensão
apprenticeship	apprentissage	Lehre(f), Lehrjahre(f)	aprendizaje	apprendistato	aprendizagem
approach	approcher(s')	nähern, sich	acercar(se)	avvicinarsi	aproximar-se
appropriate	adéquat, e	passend	adecuado, a	adeguato, a	adequado, a
approval, consent	agrément	Zustimmung(f)(verbal)	consentimiento	consenso	consentimento
approve	approuver	genehmigen	aprobar	approvare	aprovar
approximate	approximatif, ive	ungefähr	aproximativo, a	approssimativo, a	aproximado, a
April	Avril	April(m)	Abril	Aprile	Abril
apron	tablier	Schürze(f)	delantal	grembiule	avental
aquamarine	aigue-marine	Aquamarin(m)	aguamarina	acquamarina	água marinha
aquarium	aquarium	Aquarium(n)	acuario	acquario	aquário
aquatic	aquatique	Wasser-	acuático, a	acquatico, a	aquático, a
arbitrary	arbitraire	willkürlich	arbitrario, a	arbitrario, a	arbitrário, a
arc	arc	Halbkreis(m)	arco	arco	arco
arcade	galerie	Passage(f)	galería	galleria	galeria
arch	arche	Bogen(m), Gewölbe(n)	arca	arco, volta	arco
archaeology	archéologie	Archeologie(f)	arqueología	archeologia	arqueologia
archaic	archaïque	archaisch	arcaico, a	arcaico, a	arcaico, a
arched	cambré, e	krumm, gebeugt	arqueado, a	inarcato, a; arcuato, a	arqueado, a
archipelago	archipel	Inselgruppe(f)	archipiélago	arcipelago	arquipélago
architect	architecte	Architekt(in f)m	arquitecto, a	architetto, a	arquitecto, a
architecture	architecture	Architektur(f)	arquitectura	architettura	arquitectura
archives	archives	Archiv(n)	archivos	archivi	arquivo
area	aire, zone, région	Bereich(m), Gebiet(n)	área, zona	area, zona	área, zona
area	superficie	Oberfläche(f)	superficie	superficie	superfície
arena	arène	Arena(f)	arena	arena	arena
argue	argumenter	verhandeln	argüir, argumentar	argomentare	argumentar
argue	disputer	disputieren	disputar; discutir	disputare; discutere	disputar; discutir
argument	argument	Argument(n)	argumento	argomento	argumento
arid	aride	dürr, trocken	árido, a	arido, a	árido, a
aristocrat	aristocrate	Adlige(f, m)	aristócrata	aristocratico, a	aristocrata
arithmetic	arithmétique	Arithmetik(f)	aritmética	aritmetica	aritmética
arm	bras	Arm(m)	brazo	braccio	braço
arm	arme	Waffe(f)	arma	arma; armi	arma
arm-chair	fauteuil	Sessel(m)	sillón	poltrona	poltrona
armament, weapons	armement	Bewaffnung(f)	armamento	armamento	armamento
armoured	blindé, e	gepanzert	blindado, a	blindato, a	blindado, a

E

133

English	French	German	Spanish	Italian	Portuguese
army	armée	Armee(f)	ejército	esercito	exército
aroma	arôme	Aroma(n)	aroma	aroma	aroma, cheiro
around	autour	um	alrededor	intorno, attorno	redor de(em)
arrange	arranger	arrangieren	arreglar	sistemare	arranjar
arrange	disposer	auf = stellen	disponer	disporre	dispor
arrangement	arrangement	Anordnung(f)	arreglo	ordinamento	arranjo
arrangement	disposition	Anordnung(f)	disposición	disposizione	disposição
arrangement	arrangement	Abmachung(f)	arreglo, acuerdo	accordo	compromisso
arrest	arrestation	Verhaftung(f)	arresto	arresto	detenção
arrival	arrivée	Ankunft(f)	llegada; meta	arrivo	chegada
arrive, come	arriver	an = kommen	llegar	arrivare	chegar
arrow	flèche	Pfeil(m)	flecha	freccia	flecha, seta
arsenal, armoury	arsenal	Arsenal(n)	arsenal	arsenale	arsenal
art	art	Kunst(f)	arte	arte	arte
artery	artère	Ader(f); Arterie(f)	arteria	arteria	artéria
arthritis	arthrose	Arthrose(f)	artrosis	artrosi	artrose
article	article	Artikel(m)	artículo	articolo	artigo
article	article	Gesetzesartikel(m)	artículo	articolo	artigo
artificial	artificiel, le	künstlich	artificial	artificiale	artificial
artificial-, false-	prothèse	Prothese(f)	prótesis	protesi	prótese
artist	artiste	Künstler(in f)m	artista	artista	artista
as; like	comme	wie	como	come	como
as far as	jusqu'à	bis	hasta	fino	até
as soon as	dès(que)	sobald	desde	fin da	logo que
ash(es)	cendre(s)	Asche(f)	ceniza(s)	cenere(-ri)	cinza
ashamed(be)	honte(avoir)	schämen, sich	vergüenza(tener)	vergognarsi	vergonha(ter)
ash-tray	cendrier	Aschenbecher(m)	cenicero	portacenere	cinzeiro
ask	poser(question)	fragen	preguntar	porre(domanda)	perguntar
ask	demander	fragen	preguntar	domandare	perguntar
ask(for)	demander	fragen	pedir	chiedere	pedir
ask(for)	réclamer à	bitten um	reclamar	reclamare	reclamar
askew	travers(de)	schief	través(de)	traverso(di)	través(de)
asleep	endormi, e	schlafend	dormido, a	addormentato, a	adormecido, a
aspect	aspect	Aussehen(n)	aspecto	aspetto	aspecto
asphalt, tarmac	bitume	Asphalt(m)	asfalto	bitume	asfalto
aspirin	aspirine	Aspirin(m)	aspirina	aspirina	aspirina
assault, attack	assaut	Angriff(m)	asalto	assalto	assalto
assemble	assembler	zusammen = setzen	ensamblar	assemblare	juntar
assemble	assembler	versammeln	reunir	radunare, riunire	reunir
assembly	assemblage	Montage(f)	ensambladura	assemblaggio	montagem
assert, maintain	affirmer	behaupten	afirmar	affermare	afirmar
assess	évaluer, estimer	ein = schätzen	tasar, valorar	valutare, stimare	avaliar, fixar
assessment	évaluation	Schätzung(f)	evaluación	valutazione	avaliação
assessment	évaluation	Einschätzung(f)	valoración	valutazione	avaliação
asset	atout, avantage	Trumpf(m), Vorteil(m)	ventaja	vantaggio	vantagem
assign	attribuer	zu = teilen	asignar	assegnare	destinar
assist	aider, assister	helfen	ayudar, asistir	assistere, aiutare	auxiliar, ajudar
assistance	assistance	Hilfe(f)	asistencia	assistenza	assistência
assistant	assistant, e	Assistent(in f)m	asistente, a	assistente	assistente
assistant	adjoint, e	Gehilfe(m); Hilfs-	adjunto, a	aggiunto, a; vice	adjunto, a
assistant	collaborateur	Mitarbeiter(in f)m	colaborador, a	collaboratore, -trice	colaborador, a
associate, partner	associé, e	Teilhaber(in f)m	socio, a, asociado	socio, a	sócio, a
association	association	Verband(m)	asociación	associazione	associação
assortment, set	assortiment	Sortiment(n)	surtido	assortimento	sortimento
assume	assumer	übernehmen, nehmen	asumir	assumere	assumir
assured	assuré, e	sicher	seguro, a	sicuro, a; certo, a	certo, a
asthma	asthme	Asthma(n)	asma	asma	asma
astonish, amaze	étonner	überraschen	sorprender	sorprendere	espantar
astonished(be -)	étonner(s')	wundern, sich	sorprenderse	meravigliarsi	espantar-se
astrology	astrologie	Astrologie(f)	astrología	astrologia	astrologia
astronaut	cosmonaute	Astronaut(m)	cosmonauta	cosmonauta	cosmonauta
astronautics	astronautique	Weltraumfahrt(f)	astronaútica	astronautica	astronáutica
astronomy	astronomie	Astronomie(f)	astronomía	astronomia	astronomia
astute, clever	astucieux, se	verschmitzt, schlau	astuto, a	astuto, a	astucioso, a
asylum(political)	asile	Asyl(n)	asilo	asilo	asilo
at	à; au; de; par; sur	an; zu; bei; in	a; en; de; con; sobre	a; in; da	a; em
at, to	chez	bei	en casa de	da	em casa de
athlete	athlète	Athlet(in f)m	atleta	atleta	atleta

English	French	German	Spanish	Italian	Portuguese
athletics	athlétisme	Leichtathletik(f)	atletismo	atletismo	atletismo
Atlantic	Atlantique	Atlantik(m)	Atlántico	Atlantico	Atlântico
atmosphere	atmosphère	Atmosphäre(f)	atmósfera	atmosfera	atmosfera
atmosphere	ambiance	Stimmung(f)	ambiente	atmosfera	ambiente
atoll	atoll	Atoll(n)	atolón	atollo	atol
atom	atome	Atom(n)	átomo	atomo	átomo
atomic	atomique	atomar	atómico, a	atomico, a	atómico, a
atrocious	atroce	grausam	atroz	atroce	atroz
attach, tie, fasten	attacher	fest = binden, binden	atar	legare	atar
attaché	attaché, e	Attaché(m)	agregado, a	addetto, a	adido, a
attaché-case	attaché-case	Aktenkoffer(m)	maletín	valigetta	maleta
attachment	attachement	Verbundenheit(f)	apego, cariño	attaccamento	apego
attack	attaquer	an = greifen	atacar	attaccare	atacar
attack, assault	agresser	an = greifen	agredir	aggredire	agredir
attack	attaque	Angriff(m)	ataque	attacco	ataque
attack	agression	Aggression(f), Angriff	agresión	aggressione	agressão
attacker	agresseur	Angreifer(in f)m	agresor, a	aggressore	agressor, a
attain	arriver(à)	erlangen, erreichen	lograr, alcanzar	raggiungere	alcançar, atingir
attempt	tentative	Versuch(m)	tentativa	tentativo	tentativa
attempt, attack	attentat	Attentat(n)	atentado	attentato	atentado
attempt, try	tenter	versuchen; wagen	intentar	tentare	tentar
attend	assister	assistieren	asistir	assistere	assistir
attend	assister	bei = wohnen	concurrir a	presenziare	assistir a
attention	attention(à l')	Aufmerksamkeit(f)	atención a(en)	attenzione	cuidado(ao)
attention!	garde-à-vous!	Stillgestanden!	firmes(!)	attenti!	sentido!
attentive, careful	attentif, ive	aufmerksam	atento, a	attento, a	atento, a
attenuate	atténuer	ab = schwächen; lindern	atenuar	attenuare	atenuar
attic, loft	grenier	Speicher(m), Dachboden	desván	solaio; granaio	sótão
attitude	attitude	Haltung(f)	actitud	atteggiamento	atitude
attract	attirer	an = ziehen	atraer	attirare	atrair
attraction	attraction	Anziehung(f)	atracción	attrazione	atracção
attractive	attirant, e	anziehend	atrayente	attraente	atraente
attractive	séduisant, e	reizend, anziehend	atractivo, a	seducente	atraente
attribute	attribuer	bei = messen	atribuir	attribuire	atribuir
auburn; reddish	roux, rousse	rothaarig	pelirrojo, a	rosso, a	ruivo, a
auction	adjudication	Versteigerung(f)	adjudicación	aggiudicazione	adjudicação
audacity	audace	Kühnheit(f)	audacia	audacia	audácia
audience	audience, public	Audienz(f)	audiencia	udienza	audiência
August	Août	August(m)	Agosto	Agosto	Agosto
aunt	tante	Tante(f)	tía	zia	tia
austere	austère	streng, hart	austero, a	austero, a	austero, a
authentic, genuine	authentique	authentisch	auténtico, a	autentico, a	autêntico, a
author	auteur	Autor(in f)m	autor, a	autore, autrice	autor, a
authoritarian	autoritaire	autoritär	autoritario, a	autoritario, a	autoritário, a
authority	autorité	Autorität(f)	autoridad	autorità	autoridade
authorize	autoriser	erlauben	autorizar	autorizzare	autorizar
autograph	autographe	Autogramm(n)	autógrafo	autografo	autógrafo
automatic	automatique	automatisch	automático, a	automatico, a	automático, a
automaton	automate	Automat(m)	autómata	automa	autómato
autonomous	autonome	autonom; unabhängig	autónomo, a	autonomo, a	autónomo, a
autonomy	autonomie	Autonomie(f)	autonomía	autonomia	autonomia
autopsy	autopsie	Autopsie(f)	autopsia	autopsia	autópsia
autumn	automne	Herbst(m)	otoño	autunno	outono
auxiliary	auxiliaire	Hilfs-; Hilfe(f)	auxiliar	ausiliare	auxiliar
available	disponible	verfügbar	disponible	disponibile	disponível
avalanche	avalanche	Lawine(f)	avalancha	valanga	avalanche
avenge	venger	rächen	vengar	vendicare	vingar
avenue	avenue	Allee(f)	avenida	viale	avenida
average	moyenne	Durchschnitt(m)	media	media	média
aviation	aviation	Luftfahrt(f)	aviación	aviazione	aviação
aviator	aviateur, trice	Flieger(m), Pilot(m)	aviador, a	aviatore, trice	aviador, a
avoid	éviter	vermeiden	evitar	evitare	evitar
award	décerner	zu = erkennen, erteilen	otorgar	conferire	atribuir
away, far away	loin(au)	weg(fort); weit weg	lejos(a lo)	lontano	longe(ao)
awful	affreux, se	schrecklich	horrendo, a	spaventoso, a	horrível
awful	abominable	scheußlich	abominable	abominevole	abominável
axe	hache	Axt(f)	hacha	ascia	machado
axis(axes)	axe	Achse(f)	eje	asse	eixo

135

B

English	French	German	Spanish	Italian	Portuguese
baby	bébé	Baby(n)	bebé	bebè, bambino, a	bebé
bachelor; single -	célibataire	Junggeselle m/-sellin	soltero, a	scapolo, nubile	solteiro, a
back	dos	Rücken(m)	espalda	schiena	costas
back, rear	derrière, arrière	Hinter-, Rückseite(f)	trasero, a	retro	trazeiro
backward(s)	arrière(en)	rückwärts	atrás(para)	indietro	trás(para)
bacterium(-eria)	bactérie	Bakterie(f)	bacteria	batterio	bactéria
bad	mauvais, e	schlecht	malo, a	cattivo, a	mau, má
badge	insigne	Zeichen(n), Abzeichen	insignia	distintivo	insígnia
badly	mal	schlecht	mal	male	mal
bad word	gros mot	Schimpfwort(n)	palabrota	parolaccia	palavrão
bag	sac	Tasche(f)	bolsa, saco	borsa	saco
bag	sacoche	Tasche(f)(Umhänge-)	cartera	saccoccia, borsa	saco
bag(small), sachet	sachet	Beutel(m), Tütchen(n)	bolsita	bustina	pacote; carteira
bait	appât	Köder(m)	cebo	esca	engodo, isca
baker's(shop)	boulangerie	Bäckerei(f)	panadería	panificio	padaria
balance	équilibre	Gleichgewicht(n)	equilibrio	equilibrio	equilíbrio
balance	équilibrer	aus = gleichen	equilibrar	equilibrare	equilibrar
balance-sheet	bilan	Bilanz(f)	balance	bilancio	balanço
balcony	balcon	Balkon(m)	balcón	balcone	varanda
bald	chauve	glatzköpfig	calvo, a	calvo, a	calvo, a; careca
ball	balle	Ball(m)	pelota	palla	bola
ball	ballon	Ball(m)(Fußball m)	balón	pallone	bola
ball	boule	Ball(m)(Schneeball)	bola	palla	bola
ball	bille	Kugel(f)	bola	sfera	esfera
ballet	ballet	Ballet(n)	ballet	balletto	ballet, bailado
balloon	ballon	Heißluftballon(m)	globo	pallone	balão
ball-point pen	stylo à bille	Kugelschreiber(m)	bolígrafo	penna a sfera	esferográfica
ban	interdiction	Verbot(n)	prohibición	proibizione	proibição
banal	banal, e	banal	común	banale	banal
banana	banane	Banane(f)	plátano, banana	banana	banana
band, strip	bande	Streifen(m)	faja, tira	striscia	tira
bandage	bandage	Bandage(f), Verband(m)	vendaje, venda	fasciatura	ligadura
bandit	bandit	Bandit(m)	bandido	bandito	bandido
bandit	brigand	Räuber(in f)m	maleante	brigante	bandido
banger, cracker	pétard	Knallkörper(m)	petardo	petardo	bomba, foguete
banish	bannir	verbannen	desterrar	bandire	desterrar
banister, handrail	rampe	Geländer(n)	barandilla	rampa	corrimão
bank	banque	Bank(f)	banco, banca	banca	banco
bank, banking	bancaire	Bank-	bancario, a	bancario, a	bancário, a
bank	berge	Ufer(n)	ribera, orilla	sponda	margem
bank	rive	Ufer(n)	orilla, margen	riva	margem
banker	banquier	Bankier(m)	banquero	banchiere	banqueiro
bank-note	billet de banque	Geldschein(m)	billete(de banco)	banconota	nota(de banco)
bankrupt(go)	faillite(faire)	bankrott sein	quiebra(hacer)	fallire	falir
banquet	banquet	Bankett(n)	banquete	banchetto	banquete
baptism	baptême	Taufe(f)	bautizo	battesimo	baptismo
bar	barre	Stange(f)	barra	sbarra	barra
bar, pub	bar	Kneipe(f)	bar, café	bar	bar, café
barbaric	barbare	barbarisch	bárbaro, a	barbaro, a	bárbaro, a
bargain, haggle	marchander	feilschen, handeln	regatear	contrattare	regatear
bark	écorce	Rinde(f)	corteza	scorza, buccia	casca
bark	aboyer	bellen	ladrar	abbaiare	ladrar
barn	grange	Scheune(f)	granero	fienile	celeiro
barometer	baromètre	Barometer(n)	barómetro	barometro	barómetro
baron, baroness	baron, ne	Baron(in, f)m	barón, baronesa	barone, baronessa	barão, baronesa
barracks	caserne	Kaserne(f)	cuartel	caserma	quartel
barrel	fût	Faß(n)	barril	fusto, barile	barril
barrel	tonneau	Faß(n)	tonel; barril	botte, barile	tonel; barril
barricade	barricade	Barrikade(f)	barricada	barricata	barricada
barrier; gate	barrière	Schranke(f)	barrera	barriera	barreira
base	base	Grundlage(f)	base	base	base

English	French	German	Spanish	Italian	Portuguese
base	socle	Sockel(m)	zócalo	zoccolo	soco, pedestal
base	base(militaire)	Stützpunkt(m)	base(militar)	base(militare)	base(militar)
basement	sous-sol	Untergeschoß(n)	sótano	scantinato	cave
basic	base(de)	Grund-; Grundlage	básico	base	base(de)
basin, bowl	cuvette	Schale(f)	palangana	catino	bacia
basket	panier	Korb(m)	cesto	paniere, cesto	cesto
basket; bin	corbeille	Korb(m)(Papierkorb m)	cesto(a); cestillo	cestino	cesto, a
basket-ball	basket-ball	Basketball(m)	baloncesto	pallacanestro	basquetebol
bat	raquette	Schläger(m)	raqueta, pala	racchetta	raqueta
batch, assortment	lot	Assortiment(n)	lote	assortimento	lote
bath	bain	Bad(n)	baño	bagno	banho
bath	baignoire	Badewanne(f)	bañera	vasca da bagno	banheira
bathe, swim	baigner(se)	baden; schwimmen	bañarse	bagno(fare il)	banho(tomar)
bathroom	salle de bains	Badezimmer(n)	cuarto de baño	bagno	quarto de banho
battery	batterie	Batterie(f)	batería	batteria	bateria
battery	pile	Batterie(f)	pila	pila	pilha
battle	bataille	Gefecht(n)	batalla	battaglia	batalha
bay	baie	Bucht(f)	bahía	baia	baía
be	être	sein	ser, estar	essere	ser, estar
be	être	sein	estar	essere	estar
beach(-es)	plage	Strand(m)	playa	spiaggia	praia
beak	bec	Schnabel(m)	pico	becco	bico
beam	poutre	Balken(m)	viga	trave	trave
beam	faisceau, rayon	Strahl(m)(Licht)	haz	fascio	foco
bean	haricot	Bohne(f)	judía	fagiolo; fagiolino	feijão
bean(coffee-)	grain(café)	Bohne(Kaffee-)(f)	grano	chicco	grão
bear	ours	Bär(m)	oso	orso	urso
beard	barbe	Bart(m)	barba	barba	barba
beat	battre	schlagen	batir, golpear	battere; picchiare	bater, golpear
beat up, club	matraquer	prügeln	aporrear	manganellare	espancar
beating, pulsation	pulsation	Pulsschlag(m)	pulsación	pulsazione	pulsação
beautiful, fine	beau, belle	schön	hermoso, a; bello, a	bello, a	belo, a; bonito, a
beautiful, fine	belle	schön, e, er, es	hermosa	bella	bonita, bela
beautiful	belle	schön	bella	bella	bela
beauty	beauté	Schönheit(f)	belleza	bellezza	beleza
beauty treatment	soins de beauté	Schönheitspflege(f)	cosmética	cura	tratamento
because	parce que	weil, da	porque	perché	porque
because, for	car	weil, denn	porque, pues	perché	porque, pois
become	devenir	werden	volverse	diventare	tornar-se
become	devenir	werden	llegar a ser	diventare	vir a ser
become	devenir	werden	ponerse	diventare	pôr-se
bed	lit	Bett(n)	cama	letto	cama
bedroom, room	chambre	Zimmer(n)(Schlaf-)	cuarto	camera, stanza	quarto
bee	abeille	Biene(f)	abeja	ape	abelha
beer	bière	Bier(n)	cerveza	birra	cerveja
before	avant	vor, vorher	antes(de)	prima	antes(de)
before	auparavant	vorher, zuvor	antes	prima	dantes
beg	demander; mendierbitten; betteln	pedir; mendigar	domandare; mendicare	pedir; mendigar
beggar	mendiant, e	Bettler(in f)m	mendigo, a	mendicante	mendigo, a
begin, start	commencer	an = fangen	comenzar	cominciare	começar
begin, start	débuter	an = fangen	principiar	esordire	principiar
beginner	débutant, e	Anfänger(in f)m	principiante	principiante	principiante
beginning	début	Anfang(m)	comienzo	inizio	princípio
beginning, start	commencement	Anfang(m)	comienzo, principio	principio, inizio	começo, princípio
behaviour	comportement	Verhalten(n)	comportamiento	comportamento	comportamento
behind	derrière	hinter	detrás, tras	dietro	atrás, detrás
behind, back	arrière, derrière	hinten, zurück	atrás	dietro, posteriore	atrás
beige	beige	beige	crema, beis	beige	bege
belief	croyance	Glaube(m)	creencia	credenza	crença
believe	croire	glauben	creer	credere	crer
believer	croyant, e	Gläubige(f, m)	creyente	credente	crente
bell	cloche	Glocke(f)	campana	campana	sino
bell	sonnette	Klingel(f)	timbre	campanello	campainha
belly, paunch	panse	Bauch(m); Pansen(m)	panza	pancia	pança
belong to	appartenir(à)	gehören	pertenecer	appartenere	pertencer
below, under(neath)	au-dessous(de)	unter	debajo(de)	sotto(al di)	baixo(por); abaixo
below	ci-dessous	unten(-stehend)	abajo(más)	sotto(qui)	abaixo
belt	ceinture	Gürtel(m)	cinturón	cintura	cinto

English	French	German	Spanish	Italian	Portuguese
belt; strap	courroie	Riemen(m)	correa	cinghia	correia
bench	banc	Bank(f)	banco	panca; panchina	banco
bend	plier, courber	biegen	plegar, doblar	piegare	vergar
bend, lean	pencher(se)	bücken, sich	inclinarse	chinarsi	inclinar-se
bend down	baisser(se)	bücken, sich	agacharse	abbassarsi	baixar-se
bend, curve	courbure	Krümmung(f)	curvatura	curvatura	curvatura
bend, turn	virage	Kurve(f)	curva	curva	curva
beneath	sous, au-dessous	unter(halb); unten	bajo; debajo; abajo	sotto	baixo; baixo(de-; a-)
benefit; profit	bénéfice	Gewinn(m)	beneficio	beneficio; utile	lucro, proveito
benevolent	bienveillant, e	wohlwollend	benévolo, a	benevolo, a	benévolo, a
benign	bénin, bénigne	gutartig	benigno, a	benigno, a	benigno, a
bequeath, leave	léguer	vermachen	legar	legare	legar
berth	accoster	an = legen	abordar	accostare, attraccare	acostar
beside	à côté de	neben	al lado de, cerca	accanto a	ao lado de, junto de
besides	de plus, en outre	außerdem; außer	además(de)	inoltre; per di più	além disso; além de
best	meilleur, e	Beste(f, m)	mejor	migliore	melhor
bet	pari	Wette(f)	apuesta	scommessa	aposta
betray	trahir	verraten	traicionar	tradire	trair
betrayal; treason	trahison	Verrat(m)	traición	tradimento	traição
better	meilleur, e	besser(sein)	mejor	migliore	melhor
better	mieux	besser	mejor	meglio	melhor
between	entre	zwischen	entre	tra, fra	entre
beyond	au-delà de	jenseits	más allá de	al di là	além de(para)
Bible	Bible	Bibel(f)	Biblia	Bibbia	Bíblia
bibliography	bibliographie	Bibliographie(f)	bibliografía	bibliografia	bibliografia
biceps	biceps	Bizeps(m)	bíceps	bicipite	biceps
bicycle	bicyclette	Fahrrad(n)	bicicleta	bicicletta	bicicleta
bid, bidding	enchère	Auktion(f); Gebot(n)	subasta	asta	leilão
big	grand, e	groß	gran, grande	grande	grande
big	gros, se	groß	grueso, a; grande	grosso, a; grande	grande
big	gros, se	geräumig	grande	grosso, a	grande
bike	vélo	Fahrrad(n)	bici	bici, bicicletta	bicicleta
bilingual	bilingue	zweisprachig	bilingüe	bilingue	bilingue
bill	note	Rechnung(f)	cuenta	conto	conta
billiards	billard	Billard(n)	billar	biliardo	bilhar
bin, dustbin	poubelle	Abfalleimer(m)	cubo de basura	pattumiera	caixote do lixo
binding(book-)	reliure	Einband(m)	encuadernación	rilegatura	encadernação
binoculars	jumelles	Fernglas(n)	gemelos	binocolo	binóculos
biography	biographie	Lebensbeschreibung(f)	biografía	biografia	biografia
biology	biologie	Biologie(f)	biología	biologia	biologia
bird	oiseau	Vogel(m)	pájaro, ave	uccello	pássaro, ave
bird of prey	rapace	Raubvogel(m)	rapaz	rapace	ave de rapina
birth	naissance	Geburt(f)	nacimiento	nascita	nascimento
birth(give)	accoucher	entbinden	dar a luz	partorire	dar à luz
birthday	anniversaire	Geburtstag(m)	cumpleaños	compleanno	aniversário
birth-rate	natalité	Geburtenrate(f)	natalidad	natalità	natalidade
biscuit	biscuit	Keks(m)	galleta	biscotto	biscoito
bishop	évêque	Bischof(m)	obispo	vescovo	bispo
bite	mordre	beißen	morder	mordere	morder
bitter	amer, ère	bitter; sauer	amargo, a	amaro, a	amargo, a
bivouac	bivouac	Biwak(m)	vivaque	bivacco	acampamento
black	noir, e	schwarz	negro, a	nero, a	preto, a
black(person)	noir, e	Schwarze(f, m)	negro, a	negro, a	negro, a
blackboard	tableau noir	Tafel(f)	pizarra	lavagna	quadro
black-out	syncope	Ohnmacht(f)	síncope	sincope	síncope
bladder	vessie	Harnblase(f)	vejiga	vescica	bexiga
blade	lame	Schneide(f)	hoja	lama	lâmina
blame; reprimand	blâme	Rüge(f)	reprobación	biasimo	censura
blanket; cover	couverture	Decke(f)(Woll-, Bett-)	manta	coperta	manta, cobertor
blasphemy	blasphème	Lästerung(f)(Gottes-)	blasfemia	bestemmia	blasfémia
bleed	saigner	bluten	sangrar	sanguinare	sangrar
bleeding	saignement	Blutung(f)	desangramiento	emorragia	perda de sangue
blend, mixture	mélange	Mischung(f)	mezcla	mescolanza	mistura
bless	bénir	segnen	bendecir	benedire	benzer
blind	aveugle	blind	ciego, a	cieco, a	cego, a
blind	store	Vorhang m; Jalousie f	toldo; persiana	tapparella	estore
blister	ampoule	Blase(f)	ampolla	bolla, vescica	empola
blister	cloque	Blase(f)(Brandblase)	ampolla	vescica	bolha

| --- | --- | --- | --- | --- | --- |
block	bloquer	blockieren	bloquear	bloccare	bloquear
block	bloc	Block(m)	bloque	blocco	bloco
block of flats	immeuble	Gebäude(n)	inmueble	palazzo, edificio	edifício, imóvel
blockade	blocus	Blockade(f)	bloqueo	blocco	bloqueio
blockade	barrage	Sperre(f)	cordón(policía)	posto di blocco	barreira
blocked	barré, e	gesperrt	cortado, a	sbarrato, a	impedido, a
blood	sang	Blut(n)	sangre	sangue	sangue
blood pressure	hypertension	Bluthochdruck(m)	hipertensión	ipertensione	hipertensão
blow	souffler	blasen	soplar	soffiare	soprar
blow	souffler	wehen	soplar	soffiare	soprar
blow one's nose	moucher(se)	Nase putzen	sonarse	soffiarsi il naso	assoar-se
blow up	exploser, sauter	sprengen, explodieren	estallar	scoppiare	explodir
blue	bleu, e	blau	azul	blu	azul
blurred	trouble	verwackelt	desenfocado, a	sfocato, a	tremido, a
blush, flush	rougir	erröten	sonrojarse	arrossire	corar
board	planche	Brett(n)	tabla	tavola, asse	tábua
board, panel	tableau	Tafel(f)	tablero, tablón	pannello, quadro	painel, quadro
board, embark	embarquer	ein = steigen	embarcar	imbarcare	embarcar
boarder	pensionnaire	Internatsschüler(m)	interno, a	collegiale	interno, a
boast	vanter(se)	prahlen	jactarse	vantarsi	gabar-se
boat, ship	bateau	Schiff(n)	barco	imbarcazione, nave	barco
boat(small)	barque	Barke(f), Kahn(m)	barca	barca	barca
bodily	corporel, le	körperlich	corporal	corporale	corporal
body	corps	Körper(m)	cuerpo	corpo	corpo
body(-work)	carrosserie	Karosserie(f)	carrocería	carrozzeria	carroçaria
boil	bouillir	kochen	hervir	bollire	ferver
boil	furoncle	Furunkel(m)	furúnculo	foruncolo	furúnculo
boiling	ébullition	Kochen(n)	ebullición	ebollizione	fervura
boiling	bouillant, e	kochend	hirviente	bollente	fervente
boiling hot	brûlant, e	brennend, kochend	ardiente	ardente, bollente	ardente
bolt	boulon	Bolzen(m)	perno, tornillo	bullone	parafuso; cavilha
bolt, lock	verrou	Riegel(m), Schloß(n)	cerrojo	catenaccio	ferrolho
bomb	bombe	Bombe(f)	bomba	bomba	bomba
bone	os	Knochen(m)	hueso	osso	osso
bonnet, hood	capot	Motorhaube(f)	capó	cofano	capota
bonus	prime	Zulage(f)	prima	premio, sussidio	gratificação
boo	huer	aus = pfeifen	abuchear	fischiare, urlare	vaiar
book	livre	Buch(n)	libro	libro	livro
bookcase	bibliothèque	Bücherschrank(m)	biblioteca	libreria	estante
book-shop	librairie	Buchhandlung(f)	librería	libreria	livraria
book, reserve	réserver	vor = bestellen	reservar	prenotare	reservar
booking office	guichet	Fahrkartenschalter(m)	taquilla	biglietteria	bilheteira
boot	botte	Stiefel(m)	bota	stivale	bota
boot	coffre	Kofferraum(m)	maletero	bagagliaio	mala
border, frontier	frontière	Grenze(f)	frontera	confine, frontiera	fronteira
border(ing)	limitrophe	angrenzend	limítrofe	limitrofo	limítrofe
bore, calibre	calibre	Kaliber(n)	calibre	calibro	calibre
bored(be)	ennuyer(s')	langweilen, sich	aburrir(se)	annoiarsi	aborrecer-se
boredom	ennui	Langeweile(f)	aburrimiento	noia	aborrecimento
boring; annoying	ennuyeux, se	langweilig	aburrido, a	noioso, a	aborrecido, a
boring	forage	Bohrung(f)	perforación	perforazione	perfuração
born(be)	naître	geboren werden	nacer	nascere	nascer
born(be)	né, e	geboren	nacido, a	nato, a	nascido, a
borrow	emprunter	borgen	pedir prestado	prendere in prestito	pedir emprestado
boss; employer	patron, ne	Chef(m), Arbeitgeber m	patrón, a; dueño, a	padrone, a	patrão, patroa
botany	botanique	Botanik(f)	botánica	botanica	botânica
both	à la fois	beide, beides	ambos, ambas	entrambi	ambos, os dois
bother, annoy	embêter	ärgern	fastidiar	infastidire	aborrecer
bother	déranger, ennuyer	plagen; bemühen	fastidiar, molestar	infastidire, seccare	preocupar, molestar
bother	incommoder	stören	incomodar, molestar	incomodare, molestare	incomodar, molestar
bottle	bouteille	Flasche(f)	botella	bottiglia	garrafa
bottle(small)	flacon	Fläschchen(n)	frasco	boccetta	frasco
bottle(baby's -)	biberon	Fläschchen(n)	biberón	biberon	biberão
bottom; back	fond	Boden(m), Grund(m)	fondo	fondo	fundo
bottom, buttock	fesse	Gesäß(n), Po(m)	nalga	natica	nádega
boulevard	boulevard	Boulevard(m)	bulevar	viale	avenida
bounce, rebound	rebondir	ab = prallen, aufprallen	rebotar	rimbalzare	ressaltar
boundary	frontière, limite	Grenze(f)	frontera, límite	frontiera, limite	fronteira, limite

English	French	German	Spanish	Italian	Portuguese
bouquet	bouquet	Blume(f), Bukett(n)	buqué, aroma, boca	bouquet, aroma	aroma
boutique, shop	boutique	Geschäft(n)	tienda	negozio, boutique	loja
bow	arc	Bogen(m)	arco	arco	arco
bow tie	noeud papillon	Fliege(f)	pajarita	papillon	laço
bowl	bol	Trinkschale(f)	tazón	scodella	tigela; malga
bowl	bassine	Wanne(f); Schüssel(f)	barreño	bacinella	bacia
bowl	boule	Kugel(f)	bola	boccia	bola
box(-es)	boîte	Schachtel(f)	caja	scatola	caixa
box, case	coffret	Schmuckkasten(m)	estuche	portagioie	estojo
box	loge	Loge(f)	camerino	camerino	camarim
boxer	boxeur	Boxer(m)	boxeador	pugile	pugilista
boxing	boxe	Boxen(n)	boxeo	pugilato	boxe
boy	garçon	Junge(m)	muchacho, mozo	ragazzo	rapaz
boy	garçon, enfant	kleiner Junge(m)	chico	ragazzo, bambino	rapaz
bra	soutien-gorge	Büstenhalter(m)	sostén	reggiseno	soutien
bracelet	bracelet	Armband(n)	pulsera	braccialetto	pulseira
braces	bretelle(s)	Hosenträger(m)	tirantes	bretella	suspensórios
bracket	parenthèse	Klammer(f)	paréntesis	parentesi	parêntesis
brain	cerveau	Gehirn(n)	cerebro	cervello	cérebro
brake	frein	Bremse(f)	freno	freno	travão
brake	freiner	bremsen	frenar	frenare	travar
branch(-es)	branche	Ast(m)	rama	ramo	ramo
branch(-es)	succursale	Zweigstelle(f)	sucursal	succursale	sucursal
brand, make	marque	Marke(f)	marca	marchio, marca	marca
brass band	fanfare	Fanfare(f)	banda	banda	fanfarra, banda
brave	courageux, brave	mutig	valiente, valeroso	coraggioso, a	corajoso, a
brave	vaillant, e	tapfer	valiente	valoroso, a	valente; bravo, a
breach, gap	brèche	Spalt(m), Bresche(f)	brecha	breccia	brecha
bread	pain	Brot(n)	pan	pane	pão
break	casser, briser	zerbrechen	romper	rompere	quebrar, partir
break	briser	brechen, zerbrechen	romper	spezzare, rompere	quebrar
break	rompre	brechen(ab = -; zer-)	romper	rompere	romper
break	déferler	branden	romper	infrangersi	quebrar-se
break, dawn	lever(se)	an = brechen	amanecer	sorgere	nascer
break	cassure, rupture	Bruch(m)	rotura	frattura, rottura	ruptura, quebra
break, fault	faille	Spalte(f)	falla	faglia	falha
break	récréation	Pause(f)	recreo	ricreazione	recreio
breakdown	panne	Panne(f)	avería	guasto, panna	avaria
breakdown	dépression	Nervenzusammenbruch m	depresión	esaurimento(nerv.)	depressão
breakfast	déjeuner(petit)	Frühstück(n)	desayuno	colazione(prima)	almoço(pequeno)
breast	sein(s)	Busen(m)	seno, pecho	seno	seio
breath	haleine	Atem(m)	aliento	alitó	hálito
breath	souffle	Luft(f), Puste(f)	soplo, aliento	fiato, soffio	sopro, fôlego
breathe	respirer	atmen	respirar	respirare	respirar
breathe out	expirer	aus = atmen	espirar	espirare	expirar
breathing	respiration	Atmung(f)	respiración	respirazione	respiração
breed	race	Rasse(f)	casta, raza	razza	casta, raça
breed, rear	élever	züchten	criar	allevare	criar
breed(animals)	reproduire(se)	fort = pflanzen, sich	reproducir(se)	riprodurre(-rsi)	reproduzir-se
breeding; rearing	élevage	Zucht(f); Aufzucht(f)	ganadería	allevamento	criação de gado
bribe	pot-de-vin	Schmiergelder(pl.)	soborno	bustarella	suborno
brick	brique	Ziegel(m)	ladrillo	mattone	tijolo
bridegroom, bride	marié, mariée	Bräutigam(m), Braut(f)	novio, novia	sposo, sposa	noivo, noiva
bridge	pont	Brücke(f)	puente	ponte	ponte
brief, short	bref, brève	kurz	breve	breve	breve
briefcase; satchel	cartable	Ranzen(m)	cartera	cartella	pasta
briefs, knickers	culotte	Unterhose(f), Slip(m)	bragas	mutandine, slip	cuecas
briefs, pants	slip	Unterhose(f)	calzoncillos	mutande, slip	cuecas
brigade	brigade	Brigade(f)	brigada	brigata, squadra	brigada
bright, shining	brillant, e	glänzend	brillante	brillante	brilhante
brightness	clarté	Helligkeit(f)	claridad	chiarezza	claridade
brilliant	brillant, e	prächtig, brillant	brillante	brillante	brilhante
brilliant	génial, e	genial	genial	geniale	genial
bring	apporter	bringen	traer	apportare, portare	trazer
bring	amener	mit = bringen	traer	portare	trazer
bring back	rapporter	zurück = bringen	traer	riportare	trazer
bring back	ramener	wieder = bringen	devolver, traer	riportare	trazer
bring in, yield	rapporter	ein = bringen	proporcionar	fruttare	render

English	French	German	Spanish	Italian	Portuguese
bring nearer	rapprocher	heran = rücken	acercar	avvicinare	acercar
bring up	élever	erziehen, auf = ziehen	criar, educar	allevare, educare	criar, educar
brittle	cassant, e	brüchig, spröde	quebradizo, a	fragile	quebradiço, a
broad	large	breit, weit	ancho, a	largo, a; ampio, a	largo, a; amplo, a
broadcast	diffuser	senden	difundir	trasmettere	transmitir
broadcasting	radiodiffusion	Radioübertragung(f)	radiodifusión	radiodiffusione	radiodifusão
bronchial tubes	bronche(s)	Bronchie(f)	bronquios	bronco(bronchi)	brônquios
bronchitis	bronchite	Bronchitis(f)	bronquitis	bronchite	bronquite
bronze	bronze	Bronze(f)	bronce	bronzo	bronze
brooch(-es)	broche	Brosche(f)	broche	spilla	broche
brood	couvée	Brut(f)	pollada	covata	ninhada
brother	frère	Bruder(m)	hermano	fratello	irmão
brotherhood	fraternité	Brüderlichkeit(f)	fraternidad	fraternità	fraternidade
brother-in-law	beau-frère	Schwager(m)	cuñado	cognato	cunhado
brown	brun, ne	braun	pardo, a	bruno, a	castanho, a
bruise	contusion, bleu	Quetschung(f)	contusión	contusione	contusão
brush(-es)	brosse	Bürste(f)	cepillo	spazzola	escova
brush, broom	balai	Besen(m)	escoba	scopa	vassoura
brush	pinceau	Pinsel(m)	pincel	pennello	pincel
brutal	brutal, e	brutal	brutal	brutale	brutal
brutality	brutalité	Brutalität, Roheit(f)	brutalidad	brutalità	brutalidade
bubble	bulle	Blase(f)	burbuja	bolla	bolha
bucket, pail	seau	Eimer(m)	cubo	secchio	balde
buckle	boucle	Schnalle(f)	hebilla	fibbia	fivela; argola
bud	bourgeon	Knospe(f)	brote, botón	gemma	rebento, botão
budget	budget	Budget(n)	presupuesto	bilancio	orçamento
build	bâtir	bauen	edificar	costruire	construir
builder	maçon	Maurer(m)	albañil	muratore	pedreiro, trolha
building	bâtiment	Gebäude(n)	edificio	edificio, palazzo	edifício
bulb	ampoule	Glühbirne(f)	bombilla	lampadina	lâmpada
bulky, cumbersome	encombrant, e	sperrig, lästig	voluminoso, a	imgombrante	volumoso, a
bull	taureau	Stier(m)	toro	toro	touro; toiro
bullet	balle	Kugel(f)	bala	pallottola	bala
bulletin, report	bulletin	Bericht(m)	boletín	bollettino, bolletta	boletim
bull-fight	corrida	Stierkampf(m)	corrida	corrida	toirada
bull-fighter	toréador	Stierkämpfer(m)	torero	torero	toureiro
bullock; beef	boeuf	Ochse(m); Rind(n)	buey; carne de vaca	bue; manzo	boi; carne de vaca
bull ring, arena	arène(s)	Kampfbahn(f)	plaza de toros	arena	praça de touros
bump	bosse	Unebenheit(f); Buckel	bache	gobba, dosso, cunetta	bossa; alto
bump, crash into	tamponner	zusammen = stoßen	chocar con	tamponare	chocar, esbarrar
bunch; bouquet	bouquet	Strauß(m)	ramo	mazzo	ramo
bunch(-es)	grappe	Traube(n)	racimo	grappolo	cacho
buoy	bouée	Boje(f)	boya	boa	bóia
burden	fardeau	Last(f)	carga	fardello	fardo
burglary	cambriolage	Einbruch(m)	robo, atraco	furto con scasso	roubo, assalto
burial, funeral	enterrement	Beerdigung(f)	entierro	funerale	enterro
burial(-place)	sépulture	Grab(n)	sepultura	sepoltura	sepultura
burn	brûler	verbrennen	quemar	bruciare	queimar, arder
burn	brûlure	Verbrennung(f)	quemadura	bruciatura	queimadura
burp	roter	auf = stoßen, rülpsen	eructar	ruttare	arrotar
burst	crever, éclater	bersten	estallar, reventar	scoppiare	furar, rebentar
burst	éclater	platzen	reventar	scoppiare	rebentar
burst, hail	rafale	Salve(f)	ráfaga	raffica	rajada
bus	autobus	Bus(m)	autobús	autobus	autocarro
bush	buisson	Gebüsch(n)	matorral	cespuglio	moita
bush(the)	brousse	Busch(m)	maleza	boscaglia	mato
business	affaires	Geschäfte(n, pl.)	negocios	affari	negócios
bust	buste	Oberkörper(m)	busto	busto	busto
busy	occupé, e	beschäftigt	ocupado, a	impegnato, a	ocupado, a
but	mais	aber	pero; sino; mas	ma	mas
but, yet, however	mais, cependant	aber, jedoch	pero	però	porém
butcher's(shop)	boucherie	Metzgerei(f)	carnicería	macelleria	talho
butt; grip, handle	crosse	Gewehrkolben(m)	culata	calcio	coronha
butter	beurre	Butter(f)	mantequilla	burro	manteiga
butterfly	papillon	Schmetterling(m)	mariposa	farfalla	borboleta
button	bouton	Knopf(m)	botón	bottone	botão
button	bouton	Taste(f)	pulsador	pulsante, bottone	botão
buy	acheter	kaufen	comprar	comprare	comprar

E

141

English	French	German	Spanish	Italian	Portuguese
buyer; shopper	acheteur, se	Käufer(in f)m	comprador, a	acquirente	comprador, a
by, through	par	durch	por	per, da	por
bypass	contourner	umgehen	contornear	aggirare	contornar

C

English	French	German	Spanish	Italian	Portuguese
cabaret; nightclub	cabaret	Kabarett(n)	cabaret	cabaret	cabaret
cabbage	chou	Kohl(m)	col	cavolo	couve
cabin	cabine	Kabine(f)	cabina	cabina	cabine
cabinet	cabinet(pol.)	Kabinett(n)	gabinete	gabinetto	gabinete
cable	câble	Kabel(n)	cable	cavo	cabo
cable-car	téléphérique	Seilbahn(f)	teleférico	teleferica	teleférico
Caesarean	césarienne	Kaiserschnitt(m)	cesárea	taglio cesareo	cesariana
cage	cage	Käfig(m)	jaula	gabbia	gaiola, jaula
cake; pastry	gâteau	Kuchen(m)	pastel	dolce	bolo
cake shop	pâtisserie	Konditorei(f)	pastelería	pasticceria	pastelaria
calcium	calcium	Kalzium(n)	calcio	calcio	cálcio
calculate, reckon	calculer	rechnen, berechnen	calcular	calcolare	calcular
calculation	calcul	Berechnung(f)	cálculo	calcolo	cálculo
calculator	calculatrice	Rechenmaschine(f)	calculadora	calcolatrice	calculadora
calendar	calendrier	Kalender(m)	calendario	calendario	calendário
calf(-lves)	mollet	Wade(f)	pantorrilla	polpaccio	barriga(perna)
calf(-lves); veal	veau	Kalb(n)	becerro; ternera	vitello(a)	bezerro; vitelo
call	appel	Ruf(m)(Zu-, An-)	llamada	chiamata	chamada
call	appeler	rufen(an =), heißen	llamar	chiamare	chamar
call, drop in	passer	vorbei = kommen	pasar	passare	passar
called(be)	nommer(se)	heißen	llamarse	chiamarsi	chamar-se
calm, quiet, still	calme	Ruhe(f), Stille(f)	calma, sosiego	calma, quiete	calma, sossego
calm, quiet, still	calme	ruhig, still	tranquilo, a	calmo, a	calmo, a
calm	calmer	beruhigen	calmar	calmare	acalmar
calm, soothe	apaiser	beruhigen	apaciguar	calmare	acalmar
calorie	calorie	Kalorie(f)	caloría	caloria	caloria
camel	chameau	Kamel(n)	camello	cammello	camelo
camera	appareil photo	Kamera(f)	cámara fotográfica	macchina fotografica	máquina fotográfica
camp(ing) site	camping(aire de)	Campingplatz(m)	camping	campeggio	campismo
camp	camper	zelten	acampar	campeggiare	acampar
campaign	campagne	Wahlkampf(m)	campaña	campagna	campanha
camp-bed	lit de camp	Feldbett(n)	cama de campaña	letto da campo	cama de campismo
can, able to(be)	pouvoir	können	poder	potere	poder
can	bidon	Kanister(m)	bidón, lata	bidone	cantil
canal	canal	Kanal(m)	canal	canale	canal
cancel	annuler	annullieren	cancelar, anular	annullare	anular
cancer	cancer	Krebs(m)	cáncer	cancro	cancro
cancerous	cancéreux, se	krebsartig	canceroso, a	canceroso, a	canceroso, a
candidate	candidat, e	Kandidat(in f)m	candidato, a	candidato, a	candidato, a
candle	bougie	Kerze(f)	vela	candela	vela
candle	cierge	Kerze(f)	cirio	cero	círio
cannon	canon	Kanone(f)	cañón	cannone	canhão
canoe	canoë	Kanu(n)	canoa	canoa	canoa
canvas, material	toile	Tuch(n)	tela, lienzo	tela	tela
canvas, painting	toile	Gemälde(n)(Leinwand)	lienzo, cuadro	tela, dipinto	tela, quadro
cap	casquette	Mütze(f)	gorra	berretto	boné
cap, hat	bonnet	Mütze(f)	gorro	berretto, cuffia	barrete
cap	capuchon, capsule	Kappe(f)	capuchón	cappuccio	capuz
cap, plug	bouchon	Pfropfen(m), Stöpsel	tapón	tappo	rolha; tampa
capacity, content	contenance	Fassungsvermögen(n)	capacidad	capacità	capacidade
cape	cap	Kap(n)	cabo	capo	cabo

English	French	German	Spanish	Italian	Portuguese
capital	capitale	Hauptstadt(f)	capital	capitale	capital(a)
capital, assets	capital	Kapital(n)	capital	capitale	capital(o)
capitalism	capitalisme	Kapitalismus(m)	capitalismo	capitalismo	capitalismo
capitulate	capituler	kapitulieren	capitular	capitolare	capitular
caprice, whim	caprice	Laune(f)	capricho	capriccio	capricho, birra
capsize	chavirer	kentern, um = kippen	zozobrar	capovolgersi	soçobrar
captain	capitaine	Hauptmann(m); Kapitän	capitán	capitano	capitão
capture	capturer	fangen	capturar	catturare	capturar
car	voiture	Wagen(m)	coche	macchina, auto	carro
car	automobile	Auto(n)	automóvil	automobile	automóvel
car park	parking	Parkplatz(m)	aparcamiento	parcheggio	p.estacionamento
carat	carat	Karat(n)	quilate	carato	quilate
caravan	caravane	Wohnwagen(m)	caravana	roulotte	caravana
carbon	carbone	Kohlenstoff(m)	carbono	carbonio	carbono
carbonic	carbonique	Kohlensäure(f)	carbónico, a	carbonico, a	carbónico, a
carburettor	carburateur	Vergaser(m)	carburador	carburatore	carburador
card	carte à jouer	Spielkarte(f)	carta	carta da gioco	carta
card	fiche	Karteikarte(f)	ficha	scheda, cartella	ficha
card, ticket	carte	Karte(f)	tarjeta	tessera	bilhete
cardboard	carton	Pappe(f)	cartón	cartone	cartão
cardigan	gilet	Weste(f), Jacke(f)	chaleco	gilè; golf	casaco de malha
cardinal	cardinal	Kardinal(m)	cardenal	cardinale	cardeal
card-index	fichier	Kartei(f)	fichero	schedario	ficheiro
cardiology	cardiologie	Kardiologie(f)	cardiología	cardiologia	cardiologia
care	soin	Pflege(f)	cuidado	cura	cuidado
care, caution	attention	Sorgfalt(f)	cuidado	accuratezza	atenção, cuidado
career	carrière	Karriere(f)	carrera	carriera	carreira
carefree	insouciant, e	unbekümmert	despreocupado, a	noncurante	descuidado, a
careful; tidy	soigneux, se	sorgfältig	cuidadoso, a	accurato, a	cuidadoso, a
careful, prudent	prudent, e	vorsichtig	prudente	prudente	prudente
careful!(be)	attention!	Achtung!(f)	cuidado(!)	attenzione!, attento!	atenção!, cuidado!
careless	négligent, e	nachlässig	descuidado, a	negligente	descuidado, a
careless	imprudent, e	unvorsichtig	imprudente	imprudente	imprudente
carelessness	inattention	Unachtsamkeit(f)	descuido	disattenzione	distracção
caress	caresse	Streicheln(n)	caricia	carezza	carícia
caress	caresser	liebkosen, streicheln	acariciar	accarezzare	acariciar
cargo, freight	cargaison	Ladung(f)	cargamento	carico	carga
cargo(-boat)	cargo	Frachter(m)	carguero, buque	cargo, nave da carico	cargueiro
caricature	caricaturer	karikieren	caricaturar	caricaturare	caricaturar
carnival	carnaval	Karneval(m)	carnaval	carnevale	carnaval
carnivorous	carnivore	fleischfressend	carnívoro, a	carnivoro, a	carnívoro, a
carpenter	charpentier	Zimmermann(m)	carpintero	carpentiere	carpinteiro
carpet	moquette, tapis	Teppichboden(m)	moqueta	moquette	alcatifa
carpet	tapis	alfombra	Teppich(m)	tappeto	tapete
carriage-paid	franco de port	portofrei	porte pago	porto franco	porte pago
carrot	carotte	Möhre(f)	zanahoria	carota	cenoura
carry	porter	tragen	llevar	portare	levar
carry out, perform	effectuer	aus = führen	efectuar	effettuare	efectuar
carry out, perform	réaliser	verwirklichen	realizar	realizzare	realizar, fazer
cart	charrette	Karren(m)	carreta, carro	carretta	carroça, carreta
cartilage	cartilage	Knorpel(m)	cartílago	cartilagine	cartilagem
cartoon	dessin animé	Trickfilm(m)Zeichen-	dibujo animado	cartone animato	desenho animado
cartoon(strip)	bande dessinée	Comic Strip(m)	comics, teveos	fumetto	banda desenhada
cartridge	cartouche	Patrone(f)	cartucho	cartuccia	cartucho
case	cas	Fall(m)	caso	caso	caso
case	caisse, boîte	Kiste(f), Etui(n)	caja, estuche	cassa, cassetta	caixa, estojo
case(in this)	occurence(en l')	vorliegenden Fall(im)	caso(en este)	nella circostanza	caso(neste)
cash	comptant	Barzahlung(f)	contado(al)	contanti	pronto(a)
cash	encaisser	ein = kassieren	cobrar	incassare	receber
cash; earn; win	toucher	kassieren(ein =)	cobrar	incassare	receber
cash-desk	caisse	Kasse(f)	caja	cassa	caixa
cashier	caissier, ière	Kassierer(in f)m	cajero, a	cassiere, a	caixa(o)
casino	casino	Kasino(n)	casino	casinò	casino
cassette	cassette	Kassette(f)	casete	cassetta	cassete
caste	caste	Kaste(f)	casta	casta	casta
castle; mansion	château	Schloß(n)	castillo	castello	castelo
cat	chat, te	Kater(m), Katze(f)	gato, a	gatto, a	gato, a
cataclysm	cataclysme	Katastrophe(f)	cataclismo	cataclisma	cataclismo

E

143

English	French	German	Spanish	Italian	Portuguese
catalogue	catalogue	Katalog(m)	catálogo	catalogo	catálogo
catastrophe	catastrophe	Katastrophe(f)	catástrofe	catastrofe	catástrofe
catch	attraper	fangen	agarrar, coger	acchiappare	agarrar, apanhar
catch a cold	enrhumer(s')	erkälten, sich	constipar(se)	raffreddarsi	constipar-se
category	catégorie	Kategorie(f)	categoría	categoria	categoria
cathedral	cathédrale	Kathedrale(f), Dom(m)	catedral	cattedrale, duomo	catedral
Catholic	catholique	katholisch	católico, a	cattolico, a	católico, a
cattle	bétail, bestiaux	Vieh(n)	ganado	bestiame	gado
cause	cause	Ursache(f), Grund(m)	causa	causa	causa
cause	causer, provoquer	verursachen	causar, provocar	causare, provocare	causar, provocar
cause, bring about	occasionner	verursachen	ocasionar, causar	causare	ocasionar, causar
caution	prudence	Vorsicht(f)	prudencia	prudenza	prudência
cave, cavern	caverne	Höhle(f)	caverna	caverna	caverna
cave, grotto	grotte	Grotte(f)	cueva, gruta	grotta	gruta
caviar	caviar	Kaviar(m)	caviar	caviale	caviar
cavity	cavité	Hohlraum(m)	cavidad	cavità	cavidade
ceiling	plafond	Decke(f)(Zimmer-)	techo	soffitto	tecto
celebrate	célébrer	feiern	celebrar	celebrare	celebrar
celebration	fête	Feier(f)	fiesta	festa	festa
cellar	cave	Keller(m)	bodega, sótano	cantina	adega
cello	violoncelle	Cello(n)	violoncelo	violoncello	violoncelo
cement	ciment	Zement(m)	cemento	cemento	cimento
cemetery	cimetière	Friedhof(m)	cementerio	cimitero	cemitério
censorship	censure	Zensur(f)	censura	censura	censura
census	recensement	Volkszählung(f)	censo	censimento	recenseamento
centimetre	centimètre	Zentimeter(n, m)	centímetro	centimetro	centímetro
central	central, e	zentral	central	centrale	central
centre	centre	Mitte(f)	centro	centro	centro
centre	centre	Zentrum(n)	centro	centro	centro
centrifugal	centrifuge	zentrifugal	centrífugo, a	centrifugo, a	centrífugo, a
century	siècle	Jahrhundert(n)	siglo	secolo	século
cereal	céréale	Getreide(n)	cereal	cereale	cereal
cerebral	cérébral, e	Gehirn-; zerebral	cerebral	cerebrale	cerebral
ceremony	cérémonie	Zeremonie(f)	ceremonia	cerimonia	cerimónia
certain, sure	certain, e	sicher	cierto, a	certo, a; sicuro, a	certo, a
certain; some	certaines	manche	algunos, as	certi, e; alcuni, e	certos, as
certainly	certainement	sicherlich	ciertamente	certamente	certamente
certainty	certitude	Gewißheit(f)	certeza	certezza	certeza
certificate	certificat	Bescheinigung(f)	certificado	certificato	certificado
certification	homologation	Zulassung(f)	homologación	omologazione	homologação
certify	certifier	bescheinigen	certificar	certificare	certificar
chain	chaîne	Kette(f)	cadena	catena	cadeia, corrente
chair	chaise	Stuhl(m)	silla	sedia	cadeira
chairman/-woman	président, e	Vorsitzende(m, f)	presidente	presidente, essa	presidente
challenge, contest	challenge	Wettkampf(m)	trofeo, challenge	gara, sfida	desafio, torneio
challenge	défi	Herausforderung(f)	desafío	sfida	desafio
challenge	défier	heraus = fordern	desafiar	sfidare	desafiar
chamber	chambre	Kammer(f)	cámara	camera	câmara
chambermaid	femme de chambre	Zimmermädchen(n)	camarera	cameriera	empregada
champagne	champagne	Champagner(m)	champaña	champagne	champanhe
champion	champion, ne	Meister(in f)m	campeón, a	campione, -essa	campeão, campeã
championship	championnat	Meisterschaft(f)	campeonato	campionato	campeonato
chance, luck	hasard	Zufall(m)	azar, casualidad	caso	acaso, azar
chancellor	chancelier	Kanzler(in f)m	canciller	cancelliere	chanceler
change	changer	ändern	mudar	cambiare	mudar; trocar
change	changement	Veränderung(f)	cambio	cambiamento	mudança
change	monnaie	Kleingeld(n); Klein-	cambio	resto	troco
channel	chaîne	Programm, Fernseh-	cadena	canale	canal
channel	chenal	Fahrwasser(n)	canal	canale	canal
chap(ped)	gerçure	Riß(m), Hautriß(m)	grieta	screpolatura	greta
chapel	chapelle	Kapelle(f)	capilla	cappella	capela
chapter	chapitre	Kapitel(n)	capítulo	capitolo	capítulo
character	caractère	Charakter(m)	carácter	carattere	carácter
characteristic	caractéristique	charakteristisch	característico, a	caratteristico, a	característico, a
charge	charge	Anklage(f)(punkt m)	cargo	indizio	acusação
charge, accuse	inculper	beschuldigen	inculpar, acusar	incolpare, accusare	inculpar, acusar
charity	charité	Mildtätigkeit(f)	caridad	carità	caridade
charm	charme	Charme(m), Reiz(m)	encanto	fascino	encanto

English	French	German	Spanish	Italian	Portuguese
charm; seduce	séduire	verführen, verleiten	seducir	sedurre	seduzir
charming, lovely	charmant, e	liebenswert	encantador, a	affascinante	encantador, a
chasm, pit	gouffre	Abgrund(m), Kluft(f)	abismo, sima	baratro	abismo
chat, talk	bavarder	schwätzen, schwatzen	charlar	chiacchierare	falar, conversar
cheap	bon marché	billig	barato, a	buon prezzo	barato, a
cheat	tricher	fuschen, mogeln	trampas(hacer)	barare	batota(fazer)
check, verify	vérifier	überprüfen	comprobar	verificare	verificar
check in	enregistrer	auf = geben	facturar	spedire appresso	entregar
cheek	joue	Wange(f)	mejilla	guancia	bochecha, face
cheer	acclamer	zu = jubeln	aclamar	acclamare	aclamar
cheerful	souriant, e	lächelnd	sonriente	sorridente	sorridente
cheese	fromage	Käse(m)	queso	formaggio	queijo
chemical	chimique	chemisch	químico, a	chimico, a	químico, a
chemist, pharmacist	pharmacien, ne	Apotheker(in f)m	farmacéutico, a	farmacista	farmacêutico, a
chemist's	pharmacie	Apotheke(f)	farmacia	farmacia	farmácia
chemistry	chimie	Chemie(f)	química	chimica	química
cheque	chèque	Scheck(m)	cheque, talón	assegno	cheque
cheque book	chéquier	Scheckheft(n)	talonario(cheques)	libretto di assegni	livro de cheques
cherry	cerise	Kirsche(f)	cereza	ciliegia	cereja
chess	échecs	Schachspiel(n)	ajedrez	scacchi	xadrês
chest; breast	poitrine	Brust(f)	pecho	petto	peito
chest	bahut, coffre	Truhe(f)	arca, cajón	cassone	baú, arca, armário
chest, case	caisse	Kiste(f)	cajón, caja	cassa	caixa
chestnut brown	châtain	kastanienbraun	castaño, a	castano, a	castanho, a
chew	mâcher	kauen	masticar	masticare	mastigar
chick	poussin	Küken(n)	pollito	pulcino	pinto
chicken	poulet	Hähnchen, Hühnchen(n)	pollo	pollo	frango
chicken-pox	varicelle	Windpocken(f, pl)	varicela	varicella	varicela
chignon, bun	chignon	Haarknoten(m)	moño	crocchia	carrapicho
chilblain	engelure	Frostbeule(f)	sabañón	gelone	frieira
child, children(pl)	enfant	Kind(n)	niño, a; chico, a	bambino, a	criança
childhood	enfance	Kindheit(f)	infancia	infanzia	infância
chimney; fire-place	cheminée	Kamin(m)	chimenea	camino	chaminé
chin	menton	Kinn(n)	barbilla	mento	queixo
chips	frites	Pommes Frites	patatas fritas	patatine fritte	batatas fritas
chiropodist	pédicure	Fußpfleger(in f)m	pedicuro, a	pedicure	pedicuro
chocolate	chocolat	Schokolade(f)	chocolate	cioccolato, a	chocolate
choice	choix	Wahl(f)	escogimiento	scelta	escolha
choir	choeur	Chor(m)	coro	coro	coro
cholera	choléra	Cholera(f)	cólera	colera	cólera
choose, select	choisir	aus = wählen	escoger	scegliere	escolher
Christian	chrétien, ne	Christ(in f)m	cristiano, a	cristiano, a	cristão, cristã
Christmas	Noël	Weihnachten(n)	Navidad	Natale	Natal
chromosome	chromosome	Chromosom(n)	cromosoma	cromosoma	cromossoma
chronic	chronique	chronisch	crónico, a	cronico, a	crónico, a
chronicle	chronique	Chronik(f)	crónica	cronaca	crónica
chronology	chronologie	Chronologie(f)	cronología	cronologia	cronologia
chronometer	chronomètre	Stoppuhr(f)	cronómetro	cronometro	cronómetro
church(-es)	église	Kirche(f)	iglesia	chiesa	igreja
cider	cidre	Apfelwein(m)	sidra	sidro	sidra
cigar	cigare	Zigarre(f)	cigarro, puro	sigaro	charuto
cigarette	cigarette	Zigarette(f)	cigarrillo	sigaretta	cigarro
cine-camera	caméra	Kamera(f)	cámara	cinepresa	câmara
cinema	cinéma	Kino(n)	cine	cinema	cinema
circle	cercle	Kreis(m)	círculo	cerchio	círculo
circuit	circuit	Strecke(f)(Renn-)	circuito	circuito	circuito
circuit, system	circuit	Stromkreis(m)	circuito	circuito	circuito
circular	circulaire	rund	circular	circolare	circular
circulate	circuler	umher = gehen	circular	circolare	circular
circulate	circuler	zirkulieren	circular	circolare	circular
circulation	circulation	Kreislauf(m)	circulación	circolazione	circulação
circumference	circonférence	Kreisumfang(m)	circunferencia	circonferenza	circunferência
circumstance	circonstance	Umstand(m)	circunstancia	circostanza	circunstância
circus	cirque	Zirkus(m)	circo	circo	circo
cirrhosis	cirrhose	Zirrhose(f)	cirrosis	cirrosi	cirrose
citizen	citoyen, ne	Bürger(in f)m	ciudadano, a	cittadino, a	cidadão, cidadã
city	cité	Stadt(f)	ciudad	città	cidade
city/town centre	centre ville	Stadtzentrum(n)	centro(ciudad)	centro della città	centro(cidade)

E

English	French	German	Spanish	Italian	Portuguese
civic	civique	staatsbürgerlich	cívico, a	civico, a	cívico, a
civil	civil, e	zivil	civil	civile	civil
civil servant	fonctionnaire	Beamte(r)m, Beamtin(f)	funcionario, a	funzionario, a	funcionário, a
civilization	civilisation	Zivilisation(f)	civilización	civiltà	civilização
civilize	civiliser	zivilisieren	civilizar	civilizzare	civilizar
claim	revendiquer	beanspruchen	reivindicar	rivendicare	reivindicar
claim, demand	revendication	Forderung(f)	reivindicación	rivendicazione	reivindicação
clan	clan	Sippe(f)	clan	clan	clã
clandestine	clandestin, e	heimlich	clandestino, a	clandestino, a	clandestino, a
clarification	précision	Klarstellung(f)	aclaración	precisazione	explicação, precisão
clarify	clarifier	klären	clarificar	chiarificare	clarificar
clarinet	clarinette	Klarinette(f)	clarinete	clarinetto	clarinete
class	classe	Klasse(f)	clase	classe, ceto	classe
class, form	classe	Klassenstufe(f)	clase, curso	classe	classe
classical	classique	klassisch	clásico, a	classico, a	clássico, a
classify, file	classer	ordnen	clasificar	classificare	classificar
classroom	classe(salle)	Klassenzimmer(n)	aula	aula	aula(sala de)
clause	clause	Klausel(f)	cláusula	clausola	cláusula
claw	griffe	Kralle(f), Klaue(f)	garra	artiglio	garra
clay	argile	Ton(m), Lehm(m)	arcilla	argilla	argila
clean	propre	sauber	limpio, a	pulito, a	limpo, a
clean	nettoyer	reinigen	limpiar	pulire	limpar
cleaning	nettoyage	Reinigung(f)	limpieza	pulizia	limpeza
clean(li)ness	propreté	Reinlichkeit(f)	limpieza	pulizia	limpeza
clear	clair, e	klar	claro, a	chiaro, a; limpido, a	claro, a
clear	libre; dégagé, e	frei	libre	libero, a	livre
clear	dégager	frei = machen	despejar	sgomberare	desimpedir
clear, rid	débarrasser	weg = räumen	quitar, tirar	sbarazzare	desembaraçar
clear(customs)	dédouaner	verzollen	retirar aduana	sdoganare	desalfandegar
clear up	débrouiller	entwirren	desenredar	sbrogliare	desenredar
clergy	clergé	Klerus(m)	clero	clero	clero
clerk	employé, e	Angestellte(f, m)	oficinista	impiegato, a	empregado, a
clever	intelligent, e	klug, gescheit	inteligente	intelligente	inteligente
clever, skilful	habile; adroit, e	geschickt	hábil; diestro, a	abile	hábil; destro, a
client	client, e	Klient(in f)m	cliente	cliente	cliente
cliff	falaise	Steilküste(f)	acantilado	scogliera	falésia
climate	climat	Klima(n)	clima	clima	clima
climb	grimper	klettern	escalar, subir	arrampicarsi	trepar, escalar
climb; rise; go up	monter	steigen	subir	salire	subir
cloak-room	vestiaire	Garderobe(f)	vestuario	vestiario	vestiário
clock	horloge	Uhr(f)	reloj	orologio	relógio
close, shut	fermer	schließen	cerrar	chiudere	fechar, cerrar
closed, shut	fermé, e	zu, geschlossen	cerrado, a	chiuso, a	fechado, a
close, near	près, proche	nahe; bei	cerca; próximo	vicino; prossimo	perto; próximo
close, near	proximité(à)	nahe bei	cerca de	vicinanze(nelle)	próximo a
close to	auprès de	bei	cerca de	vicino a	perto de
close, intimate	intime	intim	íntimo, a	intimo, a	íntimo, a
closure, closing	clôture	Schluß(m)(Abschluß m)	clausura	chiusura	encerramento
clot	caillot	Blutgerinnsel(n)	coágulo	grumo	coágulo
clothe, dress	vêtir, habiller	an = ziehen, an = kleiden	vestir	vestire	vestir
clothes	vêtements	Kleidung(f)	ropa, prenda	vestiti	roupa(s)
clothes	habit(s)	Kleidung(f)	vestido, traje	vestito(i), abiti	fato, traje
clothing	habillement	Bekleidung(f)	ropa	abbigliamento	vestuário
clothing industry	confection	Anfertigung(f)	confección	confezione	confecção
cloud	nuage	Wolke(f)	nube	nuvola	nuvem
cloudy; muddy	trouble	trüb	turbio, a	torbido, a	turvo, a
clown	clown	Clown(m)	payaso	pagliaccio, clown	palhaço
club	club	Klub(m)	club	club	clube
clumsy, awkward	maladroit, e	ungeschickt	torpe	maldestro, a	desajeitado, a
clutch	embrayage	Kupplung(f)	embrague	frizione	embraiagem
coach	autocar	Reisebus(m)	autocar	pullman	autocarro
coach, carriage	wagon	Wagen(m)	vagón	vagone, carrozza	vagão
coagulate, clot	coaguler	gerinnen	coagular	coagulare	coagular
coal	charbon	Kohle(f)	carbón	carbone	carvão
coalition	coalition	Koalition(f)	coalición	coalizione	coligação
coast	côte	Küste(f)	costa	costa	costa
coast	littoral	Küstenstreifen(m)	litoral	litorale	litoral
coastal	côtier, ère	Küsten-	costero, a	costiero, a	costeiro, a

| --- | --- | --- | --- | --- | --- |
coat	manteau	Mantel(m)	abrigo	cappotto	casaco, manto
coat, fur	pelage	Fell(n)	pelaje, pelo	pelo	pêlo
coat	couche	Anstrich(m)	capa	strato	camada
cobra	cobra	Kobra(f)	cobra	cobra	cobra
cocaine	cocaïne	Kokain(n)	cocaína	cocaina	cocaína
cock	coq	Hahn(m)	gallo	gallo	galo
cock, tap	robinet	Hahn(m)(Wasser-; Gas-)	llave, grifo	rubinetto	torneira
cocktail	cocktail	Cocktail(m)	cóctel	cocktail	coquetel
cocoa, cacao	cacao	Kakao(m)	cacao	cacao	cacau
coconut	noix de coco	Kokosnuß(f)	coco	noce di cocco	coco
coconut palm(tree)	cocotier	Kokuspalme(f)	cocotero	palma da cocco	coqueiro
cod	morue	Schellfisch(m)	bacalao	baccalà; merluzzo	bacalhau
code	code	Kod(m)	código	codice	código
code, encode	coder	verschlüsseln	codificar	cifrare	codificar
codify	codifier	kodifizieren	codificar	codificare	codificar
coefficient	coefficient	Koeffizient(m)	coeficiente	coefficiente	coeficiente
coffee	café	Kaffee(m)	café	caffè	café
coffee-pot	cafetière	Kaffeemaschine(f)	cafetera	caffettiera	cafeteira
coffin	cercueil	Sarg(m)	ataúd	bara	caixão
co-habitation	concubinage	wilde Ehe(f)	concubinato	concubinato	concubinato
coherent	cohérent, e	zusammenhängend	coherente	coerente	coerente
cohesion	cohésion	Zusammenhalt(m)	cohesión	coesione	coesão
coil	stérilet	Spirale(f)	espiral	spirale	esterilete
coin	pièce	Geldstück(n)	moneda	spiccioli, moneta	moeda
coincidence	coincidence	Zusammentreffen(n)	coincidencia	coincidenza	coincidência
cold	froid, e	kalt	frío, a	freddo, a	frio, a
cold	rhume	Schnupfen(m)	resfriado	raffreddore	constipação
cold(to be)	froid(avoir)	frieren	frío(tener)	freddo(avere)	frio(ter)
colic	colique	Kolik(f)	cólico	colica	cólica
collaboration	collaboration	Mitarbeit(f)	colaboración	collaborazione	colaboração
collapse	effondrer(s')	zusammen = brechen	hundirse	crollare	desabar
collapse, crumble	écrouler(s')	zusammen = brechen	derrumbar(se)	crollare	desmoronar-se
collar	col	Kragen(m)	cuello	collo, colletto	colarinho; gola
collar-bone	clavicule	Schlüsselbein(n)	clavícula	clavicola	clavícula
colleague	collègue	Kollege(m), Kollegin f	colega	collega	colega
collect	collectionner	sammeln	coleccionar	collezionare	coleccionar
collection	collection	Kollektion(f)	colección	collezione	colecção
collection	collection	Sammlung(f)	colección	collezione	colecção
collective	collectif, ive	gemeinschaftlich	colectivo, a	collettivo, a	colectivo, a
college	collège	Kollegium(n)	colegio	collegio	colégio
collision	collision	Zusammenstoß(m)	colisión, choque	collisione	colisão, choque
colonel	colonel	Oberst(m)	coronel	colonnello	coronel
colonization	colonisation	Kolonisierung(f)	colonización	colonizzazione	colonização
colony	colonie	Kolonie(f)	colonia	colonia	colónia
colossal	colossal, e	riesig	colosal	colossale	colossal
colour	couleur	Farbe(f)	color	colore	côr
colour(in)	colorier	an = malen	colorear	colorare	colorir
colouring	colorant	Farbstoff(m)	colorante	colorante	corante
colourless	incolore	farblos	incoloro, a	incolore	incolor
column	colonne	Säule(f)	columna	colonna	coluna
coma	coma	Koma(n)	coma	coma	coma
comb	peigne	Kamm(m)	peine	pettine	pente
comb(one's hair)	peigner(se)	kämmen	peinar(se)	pettinarsi	pentear-se
combat, fight	combat	Kampf(m)	combate	combattimento	combate
combination	combinaison	Kombination(f)	combinación	combinazione	combinação
combine, associate	associer	verbinden	asociar	associare	associar
combustible	combustible	verbrennbar	combustible	combustibile	combustível
come	venir	kommen	venir	venire	vir
come(on)!	venez!	kommen Sie!	venga(!)	venga!, venite!	venha!
come back, return	revenir	zurück = kommen	volver	ritornare	voltar
come here!	venez ici!	kommen Sie her!	venga aquí(!)	venga qui!, venite!	venha cá!
come in!	entrez!	herein!	pase(!), adelante!	avanti!, prego!	entre!
comedian, comic	comique	Komiker(in f)m	cómico	comico	cómico
comedian	comédien, ne	Komödiant(in f)m	comediante, a	commediante	comediante, a
comedy	comédie	Komödie(f)	comedia	commedia	comédia
comet	comète	Komet(m)	cometa	cometa	cometa
comfort	confort	Bequemlichkeit(f)	confort	comodità	conforto
comfortable	confortable	bequem	cómodo, a	confortevole	confortável

English	French	German	Spanish	Italian	Portuguese
comforting	réconfortant, e	tröstlich	reconfortante	riconfortante	reconfortante
comic, funny	comique	komisch	cómico, a	comico, a	cómico, a
comma	virgule	Komma(n)	coma	virgola	vírgula
command	commandement	Befehl(m)(-sgewalt f)	mando	comando	comando
command	commander	befehlen, befehligen	ordenar, mandar	comandare	comandar
command, order	ordonner	befehlen, beherrschen	mandar, ordenar	comandare, ordinare	mandar, ordenar
commando	commando	Kommando(n)	comando	commando	comando
commemorate	commémorer	gedenken	conmemorar	commemorare	comemorar
comment	commentaire	Anmerkung(f)	comentario	commento	comentário
comment(on)	commenter	erläutern	comentar	commentare	comentar
commentary	commentaire	Kommentar(m)	comentario	commentario	comentário
commercial	commercial, e	geschäftlich	comercial	commerciale	comercial
commission	commission	Kommission(f)	comisión	commissione	comissão
commit	commettre	begehen, verüben	cometer	commettere	cometer
commitment	engagement	Verpflichtung(f)	compromiso	impegno	compromisso
commit oneself	engager(s')	engagieren, sich	comprometerse	impegnarsi a	comprometer-se
commit suicide	suicider(se)	um = bringen, sich	suicidarse	suicidarsi	suicidar-se
committee	comité	Komitee(n), Ausschuß m	comité	comitato	comissão
committee	commission	Ausschuß(m)	comisión	commissione	comissão
common, usual	commun, e	gewöhnlich	común	comune	comum
common	commun, e	Gemeinschafts-	común	comune	comum
common	courant, e	geläufig	corriente	corrente, comune	corrente
communicate	communiquer	mitteilen	comunicar	comunicare	comunicar
communication	communication	Verständigung(f)	comunicación	comunicazione	comunicação
communism	communisme	Kommunismus(m)	comunismo	comunismo	comunismo
community	communauté	Gemeinschaft(f)	comunidad	comunità	comunidade
compact	compact, e	kompakt	compacto, a	compatto, a	compacto, a
companion	compagnon, agne	Begleiter(in f)m	compañero, a	compagno, a	companheiro, a
company	compagnie	Gesellschaft(f)	compañía	compagnia	companhia
company of(in the)	compagnie(en)	Gesellschaft(in)	compañía(en)	compagnia(in)	companhia(em)
company, firm	entreprise	Unternehmen(n)	empresa	impresa, ditta	empresa
company, firm	société	Gesellschaft(f)	sociedad	società	sociedade
compare	comparer	vergleichen	comparar	paragonare	comparar
compartment	compartiment	Abteil(n)	compartimiento	compartimento	compartimento
compass	boussole	Kompaß(m)	brújula	bussola	bússola
compass(es)	compas	Kompaß(m)	compás	compasso	compasso
compensate	indemniser	entschädigen	indemnizar	indennizzare	indemnizar
compensate	dédommager	entschädigen	indemnizar	indennizzare	indemnizar
compensation	compensation	Kompensation(f)	compensación	compenso	compensação
compensation	indemnité	Entschädigung(f)	indemnidad	risarcimento	indemnização
competence	compétence	Zuständigkeit(f)	competencia	competenza	competência
competent	compétent, e	kompetent	competente, capaz	competente	competente, capaz
competition	compétition	Wettbewerb(m)	competición	competizione, gara	competição
competition	concours	Wettbewerb(m)	concurso	concorso	concurso
competition	concurrence	Konkurrenz(f)	competencia	concorrenza	concorrência
competitive exam	concours	Prüfung(f)	oposiciones	concorso	concurso
competitor	concurrent, e	konkurrent(in f)m	competidor, a	concorrente	concorrente
complain	plaindre(se)	beklagen, sich	quejarse	lamentarsi	queixar-se
complaint	plainte	Klage(f)	queja	lamento	queixume, queixa
complaint, claim	réclamation	Beschwerde(f)	reclamación	reclamo	reclamação
complaint(lodge a)	plainte(porter)	an = zeigen	denunciar	querelare	queixa(apresentar)
complement	complément	Ergänzung(f)	complemento	complemento	complemento
complete, full	complet, ète	vollständig, voll	completo, a	completo, a	completo, a
complete, finish	achever	beenden	acabar	terminare, finire	acabar
completely	complètement	völlig	completamente	completamente	completamente
complex	complexe	Komplex(m)	complejo	complesso	complexo
complexion, colour	teint	Teint(m)	tez, color	carnagione	tez
complicated	compliqué, e	kompliziert	complicado, a	complicato, a	complicado, a
compliment	compliment	Kompliment(n)	cumplido	complimento	cumprimento
component	composant	Bestandteil(m)	componente	componente	componente
compose	composer	zusammen = stellen	componer	comporre	compor
composer	compositeur	Komponist(in f)m	compositor	compositore	compositor
composition	composition	Zusammensetzung(f)	composición	composizione	composição
comprehensive(Jnr)	collège	Oberschule(f)	escuela(EGB)	scuola media	escola preparatória
comprehensive sch.	lycée	Gymnasium(n)	instituto, liceo	liceo	liceu
compress	comprimer	drücken	comprimir	comprimere	comprimir
compression	compression	Druck(m)	compresión	compressione	compressão
comprise	comprendre	ein = begreifen	comprender	comprendere	compreender

English	French	German	Spanish	Italian	Portuguese
compromise	compromis	Kompromiß(m)	compromiso	compromesso	compromisso
compromise	compromettre	bloß = stellen(jdn.)	comprometer	compromettere	comprometer
compromising	compromission	Kompromittierung(f)	compromiso	compromissione	comprometimento
compulsory	obligatoire	obligatorisch	obligatorio, a	obbligatorio, a	obrigatório, a
computer	ordinateur	Computer(m)	ordenador	computer	computador
conceal	cacher	verbergen, verhehlen	esconder, ocultar	nascondere	ocultar
conceal	dissimuler	verbergen, verhehlen	disimular	dissimulare	dissimular
conceive(of)	concevoir	vor = stellen, sich	concebir	concepire	conceber
concentrate	concentrer(se)	konzentrieren, sich	concentrar(se)	concentrarsi	concentrar-se
concentrate	concentrer	konzentrieren	concentrar	concentrare	concentrar
concept	concept	Begriff(m)	concepto	concetto	conceito
conception	conception	Konzeption(f)	concepción	concezione	concepção
concern	concerner	betreffen	concernir	riguardare	dizer respeito a
concert	concert	Konzert(n)	concierto	concerto	concerto
conclude	conclure	schließen, abschließen	concluir	concludere	concluir
conclusion	conclusion	Abschluß(m)	conclusión	conclusione	conclusão
concrete	béton	Beton(m)	hormigón	calcestruzzo	betão
concrete	concret, ète	konkret	concreto, a	concreto, a	concreto, a
condemn	condamner	verurteilen	condenar	condannare	condenar
condensation	condensation	Kondensierung(f)	condensación	condensazione	condensação
condition	condition	Bedingung(f)	condición	condizione	condição
condition	état	Zustand(m)	condición	condizione	estado
condom, sheath	préservatif	Präservativ(n)	preservativo	preservativo	preservativo
conductor	chef(orchestre)	Dirigent(in f)m	director(orquesta)	direttore(orchestra)	maestro(orquestra)
cone	cône	Kegel(m)	cono	cono	cone
conference; lecture	conférence	Konferenz(f)	conferencia	conferenza	conferência
confess, admit	avouer	gestehen	confesar	confessare	confessar
confession	aveu	Geständnis(n)	confesión	confessione	confissão
confidence, trust	confiance	Vertrauen(n)	confianza	fiducia	confiança
confidence, secret	confidence	Vertrauen(im)	confidencia	confidenza	confidência
confidential	confidentiel, le	vertraulich	confidencial	confidenziale	confidencial
confirm	confirmer	bestätigen	confirmar	confermare	confirmar
conflict	conflit	Konflikt(m)	conflicto	conflitto	conflito
confront	confronter	konfrontieren	confrontar	confrontare	confrontar
confront, face	affronter	entgegen = treten	afrontar	affrontare	afrontar
confrontation	affrontement	Konfrontation(f)	enfrentamiento	affrontamento	afrontamento
confuse, mistake	confondre	verwechseln	confundir	confondere	confundir
confusion	confusion	Verwechslung(f)	confusión	confusione	confusão
congestion	congestion	Blutandrang(m)	congestión	congestione	congestão
congestion, jam	encombrement	Gedränge(n)	estorbo	affollamento, ingorgo	engarrafamento
congratulate	congratuler	gratulieren	congratular	congratulare	congratular
congratulate	féliciter	gratulieren	felicitar	congratularsi	felicitar
congratulations!	félicitations!	Glückwunsch!	enhorabuena(!)	congratulazioni!	parabéns!
congress	congrès	Kongress(m)	congreso	congresso	congresso
conical	conique	kegelförmig	cónico, a	conico, a	cónico, a
conifer	conifère	Nadelbaum(m)	conífera	conifera	conífera
conjugation	conjugaison	Konjugation(f)	conjugación	coniugazione	conjugação
conjuncture	conjoncture	Konjunktur(f)	coyuntura	congiuntura	conjuntura
connect	connecter	kuppeln, verbinden	conectar	connettere	ligar
connect	brancher	an = schließen	empalmar	allacciare	ligar
connect, link	accrocher	an = hängen	enganchar	agganciare	engatar
connection	connexion	Verbindung; Anschluß	conexión	connessione	conexão
connection	correspondance	Verbindung, Anschluß	empalme	coincidenza	correspondência
connection, link	liaison	Verbindung(f)	relación; enlace	collegamento	ligação, junção
conquest	conquête	Eroberung(f)	conquista	conquista	conquista
conscience	conscience	Bewußtsein(n)	conciencia	coscienza	consciência
conscious	conscient, e	bewußt	consciente	cosciente, conscio, a	consciente
consecrate	consacrer	weihen	consagrar	consacrare	consagrar
consecration	consécration	Weihe(f)	consagración	consacrazione	consagração
consecutive	consécutif, ive	folgend	consecutivo, a	consecutivo, a	consecutivo, a
consent	consentir	zu = stimmen	consentir	consentire	consentir
consequence	conséquence	Konsequenz(f)	consecuencia	conseguenza	consequência
conservation	conservation	Konservierung(f)	conservación	conservazione	conservação
consider	considérer	an = sehen(als)	considerar	considerare	considerar
considerable	considérable	erheblich	considerable	considerevole	considerável
consideration	considération	Betrachtung(f)	consideración	considerazione	consideração
consign	expédier, livrer	übersenden	enviar, expedir	inviare	enviar, expedir
consist(in, of)	consister à	bestehen aus	consistir en	consistere in	consistir em

E

English	French	German	Spanish	Italian	Portuguese
console, comfort	consoler	trösten	consolar	consolare	consolar
consonant	consonne	Mitlaut(m)	consonante	consonante	consoante
conspiracy, plot	complot	Verschwörung(f)	complot	complotto	conspiração
constant	constant, e	beständig	constante	costante	constante
constellation	constellation	Konstellation(f)	constelación	costellazione	constelação
constipation	constipation	Verstopfung(f)	estreñimiento	stitichezza	prisão de ventre
constitute	constituer	bilden	constituir	costituire	constituir
constitution	constitution	Verfassung(f)	constitución	costituzione	constituição
construct, build	construire	bauen	construir	costruire	construir
construction	construction	Bau(m)	construcción	costruzione	construção
consul	consul	Konsul(m)	cónsul	console	cônsul
consulate	consulat	Konsulat(n)	consulado	consolato	consulado
consult	consulter	befragen	consultar	consultare	consultar
consume	consommer	verbrauchen	consumir	consumare	consumir
consumer	consommateur	Verbraucher(in f)m	consumidor, a	consumatore, trice	consumidor, a
consumption	consommation	Verbrauch(m)	consumo	consumo	consumo
contact	contact	Kontakt(m)	contacto	contatto	contacto
contact	contact(prendre)	Kontakt(auf = nehmen)	contacto(entrar en)	contattare	contactar
contagion	contagion	Ansteckung(f)	contagio	contagio	contágio
contagious	contagieux, se	ansteckend	contagioso, a	contagioso, a	contagioso, a
contain	contenir	enthalten	contener	contenere	conter
container	récipient	Behälter(m)	recipiente	recipiente	recipiente
contamination	contamination	Ansteckung(f)	contaminación	contaminazione	contaminação
contemplate	contempler	betrachten	contemplar	contemplare	contemplar
contemporary	contemporain, e	zeitgenössisch	contemporáneo, a	contemporaneo, a	contemporâneo, a
contempt, scorn	mépris	Verachtung(f)	desprecio	disprezzo	desprezo
content(s)	contenu	Inhalt(m)	contenido	contenuto	conteúdo
contest	concours	Wettbewerb(m)	concurso	gara	concurso
contest	contester	bestreiten	impugnar, objetar	contestare	contestar
continent	continent	Kontinent(m)	continente	continente	continente
contingency	éventualité	Eventualität(f)	eventualidad	eventualità	eventualidade
continual	continuel, le	ständig	continuo, a	continuo, a	contínuo, a
continuation	suite	Folge(f)	continuación	seguito	continuação
continue, go on	continuer	fort = setzen	continuar	continuare	continuar
continuous	continu, e	ununterbrochen	continuo, a	continuo, a	contínuo, a
contraceptive	contraceptif	Verhütungsmittel(n)	anticonceptivo	anticoncezionale	contraceptivo
contract	contrat	Vertrag(m), Kontrakt m	contrato	contratto	contrato
contraction	contraction	Zusammenziehen(n)	contracción	contrazione	contracção
contractor	entrepreneur	Unternehmer(in f)m	empresario	imprenditore	empresário
contradict	contredire	widersprechen	contradecir	contraddire	contradizer
contradiction	contradiction	Widerspruch(m)	contradicción	contraddizione	contradição
contrary	contraire	entgegengesetzt	contrario, a	contrario, a	contrário, a
contrast	contraste	Gegensatz(m)	contraste	contrasto	contraste
contribute	contribuer	bei = tragen	contribuir	contribuire	contribuir
contribution	charge	Abgaben(pl.)	carga	onere	encargo
contribution	cotisation	Beitrag(m)	cotización	contributo	contribuição
control, check	contrôle	Aufsicht(f), Prüfung f	control	controllo	controlo
control, check	contrôler	kontrollieren	controlar	controllare	controlar
control, master	maîtriser	beherrschen	dominar	dominare	dominar
controversy	polémique	Polemik(f)	polémica	polemica	polémica
convalescence	convalescence	Genesung(f)	convalecencia	convalescenza	convalescência
convenient	commode	praktisch	cómodo, a	comodo, a	cómodo, a
convent	couvent	Kloster(n)	convento	convento	convento
converge	converger	konvergieren	converger	convergere	convergir
conversation	conversation	Gespräch(n)	conversación	conversazione	conversação
convert	convertir(se)	konvertieren	convertirse	convertirsi	converter-se
convex	bombé, e	gewölbt	abombado, a	convesso, a	convexo, a
convict, sentence	condamner	verurteilen	condenar	condannare	condenar
conviction	conviction	Überzeugung(f)	convicción	convinzione	convicção
convince	convaincre	überzeugen	convencer	convincere	convencer
convoy	convoi	Konvoi(m)	convoy	convoglio	comboio
convulsion	convulsion	Zuckung(f), Krampf(m)	convulsión	convulsione	convulsão
cook	cuire	kochen	cocer	cuocere	cozer
cook	cuisiner	kochen	cocinar	cucinare	cozinhar
cook; chef	cuisinier, ière	Koch(m), Köchin(f)	cocinero, a	cuoco, a	cozinheiro, a
cooked	cuit, e	gar, gekocht	cocido, a	cotto, a	cozido, a
cooker, stove	cuisinière	Herd(m)	cocina	cucina	fogão
cooking	cuisson	Kochen(n), Sieden(n)	cocción	cottura	cozedura, cocção

English	French	German	Spanish	Italian	Portuguese
cooking-pot	marmite	Kochtopf(m)	marmita, olla	pentola, marmitta	marmita
cool	rafraîchir	ab = kühlen	refrescar	rinfrescare	refrescar
cool(down)	refroidir	ab = kühlen	enfriar	raffreddare	arrefecer
cool, calm	sang-froid	Kaltblütigkeit(f)	sangre fría	sangue freddo	sangue-frio
cooperate	coopérer	mit = arbeiten	cooperar	cooperare	cooperar
cooperation	coopération	Mitarbeit(f)	cooperación	cooperazione	cooperação
cooperation, help	concours	Mitwirkung(unter)	ayuda	concorso	colaboração
cooperation	concertation	Zusammenarbeit(f)	concertación	concertazione	concertação
cooperative	coopérative	Genossenschaft(f)	cooperativa	cooperativa	cooperativa
coordinate	coordonner	koordinieren	coordinar	coordinare	coordenar
copious	copieux, se	reichlich	copioso, a	abbondante	copioso, a
copper	cuivre	Kupfer(n)	cobre	rame	cobre
copy	copie	Kopie(f)	copia	copia	cópia
copy	copier	kopieren	copiar	copiare	copiar
coral	corail	Koralle(f)	coral	corallo	coral
cord, string	cordon	Kordel(f)	cordón, cable	cordone	cordão
cordial, hearty	cordial, e	herzlich, freundlich	cordial	cordiale	cordial
cordial, squash	sirop	Saft(m), Sirup(m)	almíbar	sciroppo	xarope
cork	liège	Kork(m)	corcho	sughero	cortiça
cork	bouchon	Korken(m)	corcho	tappo, turacciolo	rolha
corkscrew	tire-bouchon	Korkenzieher(m)	sacacorchos	cavatappi	saca-rolhas
corn	blé	Weizen(m)	trigo	grano	trigo
corner	coin	Ecke(f)	esquina, rincón	angolo	canto, esquina
coronary	infarctus	Infarkt(m)	infarto	infarto	enfarte
corporal	caporal	Gefreiter(m); Korporal	cabo(mil.)	caporale	cabo
corporation	corporation	Körperschaft(f)	corporación	corporazione	corporação
corpse	cadavre	Leiche(f)	cadáver	cadavere	cadáver
corpse	macchabée	Leiche(f)	cadáver	cadavere	cadáver
corpuscle, globule	globule(sang)	Blutkörperchen(n)	glóbulo	globulo	glóbulo
correct; proper	correct, e	richtig	correcto, a	corretto, a	correcto, a
correct, rectify	corriger	korrigieren	corregir	correggere	corrigir
correction	correction	Verbesserung(f)	corrección	correzione	correcção
correspond, tally	correspondre	entsprechen	corresponder	corrispondere	corresponder
correspondence	correspondance	Korrespondenz(f)	correspondencia	corrispondenza	correspondência
corridor	couloir	Flur(m)	pasillo	corridoio	corredor
corrosion	corrosion	Korrosion(f)	corrosión	corrosione	corrosão
corrupt	corrompu, e	verdorben, korrupt	corrompido, a	corrotto, a	corrupto, a
corruption	corruption	Korruption(f)	corrupción	corruzione	corrupção
cosmetic	cosmétique	Kosmetik(f)	cosmético	cosmetico	cosmético
cosmopolitan	cosmopolite	kosmopolitisch	cosmopolita	cosmopolita	cosmopolita
cost	coût	Kosten(pl)	costo, coste	costo	custo, preço
cost	coûter	kosten	costar	costare	custar
costly, expensive	coûteux, se	teuer	costoso, a	costoso, a	custoso, a
cotton	coton	Baumwolle(f)	algodón	cotone	algodão
couch(-es)	divan	Couch(f), Sofa(n)	diván	divano	divã
couchette	couchette	Liegeplatz(m)	litera	cuccetta	couchette
cough	toux	Husten(m)	tos	tosse	tosse
cough	tousser	husten	toser	tossire	tossir
council	conseil	Rat(m)(Europrat m)	consejo	consiglio	conselho
council	conseil	Rat(m)(Stadtrat m)	concejo	giunta, consiglio	município
councillor	conseiller, ère	Rat(m)(Staatsrat m)	concejal, a	consigliere, a	conselheiro, a
count	compter	zählen	contar	contare	contar
counter	comptoir	Ladentisch(m)	mostrador	banco	balcão
counter, bar	comptoir	Theke(f)	barra	banco	balcão
counter, position	guichet	Schalter(m)	ventanilla	sportello	guichê, postigo
counter, token	jeton	Spielmarke(f)	ficha	gettone	ficha
counter	contrer	Kontra geben	oponerse(a)	opporsi(a)	contrariar
counter-attack	contre-attaque	Gegenangriff(m)	contraataque	contro-attacco	contra-ataque
counter-attack	riposte	Gegenangriff(m)	réplica	risposta	réplica
country	pays	Land(n)	país	paese	país
country(side)	campagne	Land(n)	campo	campagna	campo
couple	couple	Paar(n)	pareja	coppia	casal
courage	courage	Mut(m)	valentía	coraggio	coragem
court, tribunal	tribunal	Gericht(n)	tribunal	tribunale	tribunal
court	cour	Hof(m)	corte	corte	corte
courteous	courtois, e	höflich	cortés	cortese	cortês
cousin	cousin, e	Cousin(m), Cousine(f)	primo, a	cugino, a	primo, a
cover	couvrir	zu = decken	cubrir	coprire	cobrir

cover	bâche	Plane(f)	toldo, lona	telone	toldo
cover	housse	Bezug(m)	funda	fodera	cobertura
covet	convoiter	begehren	codiciar	ambire, desiderare	cobiçar
cow	vache	Kuh(f)	vaca	vacca, mucca	vaca
cowardliness	lâcheté	Feigheit(f)	cobardía	vigliaccheria	cobardia
cowardly	lâche	feig(e)	cobarde	vigliacco, a	cobarde
crab	crabe	Krebs(m)	cangrejo	granchio	caranguejo
crack, fissure	fissure, fente	Riß(m), Spalte(f)	fisura, grieta	fessura, crepa	fissura; fenda
crack	félure	Sprung(m), Riß(m)	raja, grieta	incrinatura	estaladela
crack	craquer	krachen	crujir	scricchiolare	estalar
crackled, cracked	craquelé, e	rissig	agrietado, a	screpolato, a	estalado, a
cradle	berceau	Wiege(f)	cuna	culla	berço
craftsman(-men)	artisan	Handwerker(in f)m	artesano	artigiano	artesão
crafty, cunning	rusé, e	schlau, gerissen	astuto, a	astuto, a	astuto, a; fino, a
cramp	crampe	Krampf(m)	calambre	crampo	càibra
crampons, irons	crampons	Steigeisen(n)	crampones	rampone	grampo
crane	grue	Kran(m)	grúa	gru	grua
crank	manivelle	Handkurbel(f)	manivela	manovella	manivela
crash	écraser(s')	ab=stürzen	estrellarse	schiantare	esmagar-se
crater	cratère	Krater(m)	cráter	cratere	cratera
crawl	ramper	kriechen	arrastrarse	strisciare	rastejar
crawl with	grouiller	wimmeln	hormiguear	brulicare	pulular
crayfish	langouste	Languste(f)	langosta	aragosta	lagosta
crayfish	écrevisse	Flußkrebs(m)	cangrejo(de río)	gambero(di fiume)	caranguejo
crazy, mad	débile	verrückt; schwach	débil	scemo, a; minorato, a	parvo, a
cream	crème	Sahne(f)	crema	crema	creme
cream	crème(peau)	Creme(f)	crema	crema	creme
create	créer	schöpfen	crear	creare	criar
creation	création	Erschaffung; Schöpfung	creación	creazione, creato	criação
creator(creative)	créateur, trice	Schöpfer(in f)m	creador, a	creatore, trice	criador, a
credit	crédit	Kredit(m)	crédito	credito	crédito
credit card	carte de crédit	Kreditkarte(f)	carta de crédito	carta di credito	cartão de crédito
crest	crête	Kamm(m)	cresta	cresta	crista, cimo
crevice	crevasse	Spalte(f)	grieta	crepa, crepaccio	fenda
crew	équipage	Besatzung(f)	tripulación	equipaggio	equipagem
crime	crime	Verbrechen(n)	crimen	crimine	crime
criminal	criminel, le	Verbrecher(in f)m	criminal	criminale	criminoso, a
criminal	malfaiteur	Missetäter(in f)m	malhechor	malvivente	malfeitor
crippled	estropié, e	verkrüppelt	lisiado, a	storpio, a	aleijado, a
crisis(-ses)	crise	Krise(f)	crisis	crisi	crise
criterion(-ia)	critère	Kriterium(n)	criterio	criterio	critério
criticism	critique	Kritik(f)	crítica	critica	crítica
criticize	critiquer	kritisieren	criticar	criticare	criticar
crockery, dishes	vaisselle	Geschirr(n)	vajilla	stoviglie, vasellame	loiça, louça
crocodile	crocodile	Krokodil(n)	cocodrilo	coccodrillo	crocodilo
crook, swindler	escroc	Gauner(m)	estafador	imbroglione	gatuno, escroque
crook	truand, e	Ganove(m), Gauner(m)	granuja, bandido	teppista	bandido
crook, villain	crapule	Lump(m)	granuja; pillo, a	canaglia	crápula
crop; harvest	récolte	Ernte(f)	cosecha	raccolta	colheita
cross(-es)	croix	Kreuz(n)	cruz	croce	cruz
cross, intersect	croiser(se)	kreuzen, sich	cruzarse	incrociarsi	cruzar-se
cross	traverser	überqueren	atravesar, cruzar	attraversare	atravessar
cross	franchir	überqueren	atravesar	varcare, passare	atravessar
crossing	croisement	Kreuzung(f)	cruce	incrocio	cruzamento
cross out	rayer	durch=streichen	rayar	cancellare	riscar; cortar
cross-road(s)	carrefour	Kreuzung(f)	encrucijada	incrocio	cruzamento
crossword	mots croisés	Kreuzworträtsel(n)	crucigrama	cruciverba	palavras cruzadas
croupier	croupier, ière	Croupier(m)	crupier	croupier	croupier
crow	corbeau	Rabe(m)	cuervo	corvo	corvo
crowd	foule	Menge(f)	muchedumbre	folla	multidão
crowd	affluence	Gedränge(n)	afluencia	afflusso	afluência
crown	couronne	Krone(f)	corona	corona	coroa
cruel	cruel, le	grausam	cruel	crudele	cruel
cruelty	sévices	Mißhandlung(f)	malos tratos	sevizie	sevícias
cruise	croisière	Kreuzfahrt(f)	crucero	crociera	cruzeiro
crunch	croquer	knabbern	mascar	sgranocchiare	trincar
crush, crowd	cohue, foule	Menge(f)	barullo, jaleo	ressa, affollamento	multidão, confusão
crush, grind	broyer	mahlen	triturar	stritolare, macinare	triturar; moer

English	French	German	Spanish	Italian	Portuguese
crush, flatten	écraser	zerquetschen	aplastar	schiacciare	esmagar
crust	croûte	Kruste(f)	costra, corteza	crosta	crosta
crutch(-es)	béquille	Krücke(f)	muleta	stampella	muleta
cry	pleurer	weinen	llorar	piangere	chorar
crystal	cristal	Kristall(n)	cristal	cristallo	cristal
cube	cube	Würfel(m)	cubo	cubo	cubo
cultivate	cultiver	bebauen, züchten	cultivar	coltivare	cultivar
cultivate, grow	cultiver	an = bauen, an = pflanzen	cultivar	coltivare	cultivar
cultivation	culture	Anbau(m)	cultivo	coltura	cultura
cultural	culturel, le	kulturell	cultural	culturale	cultural
culture	culture	Kultur(f)	cultura	cultura	cultura
cultured, learned	cultivé, e	gebildet	culto, a	colto, a	culto, a
cup	tasse	Tasse(f)	taza	tazza	chávena
cup	coupe	Pokal(m)	copa	coppa	taça
cupboard	armoire	Schrank(m)	armario	armadio	armário
cupboard	placard	Wandschrank(m)	armario	armadio a muro	armário
cure, heal	guérir	heilen	curar	guarire	curar
cure, recovery	guérison	Heilung(f)	curación	guarigione	cura
curious	curieux, se	neugierig	curioso, a	curioso, a	curioso, a
curl	boucle	Locke(f)	rizo	ricciolo	caracóis
curly	frisé, e	lockig	rizado, a	ricciuto, a	ondulado, a
currency	monnaie	Währung(f), Devisen pl	moneda	valuta; moneta	moeda
currency	devise	Währung(f)	divisa	valuta	moeda, divisa
current	courant	Strom(m)	corriente	corrente	corrente
current	courant, e	laufend, heutig	corriente	corrente	corrente, vulgar
cursed, damned	maudit, e	verdammt	maldito, a	maledetto, a	maldito, a
curtain	rideau	Vorhang(m)	cortina	tenda, tapparella	cortina
curve	courbe	Kurve(f)	curva	curva	curva
cushion	coussin	Kissen(n)	cojín	cuscino	almofada
custom	coutume	Brauch(m)	costumbre	costume, usanza	costume
customer	client, e	Kunde(m), Kundin(f)	cliente	cliente	cliente
customs	douane	Zoll(m)	aduana	dogana	alfândega
customs officer	douanier	Zöllner(m)	aduanero	doganiere	guarda-fiscal
cut	couper	schneiden	cortar	tagliare	cortar
cut up	découper	zerschneiden	recortar	tagliare	recortar
cut, divide	sectionner	schneiden	seccionar	sezionare	seccionar
cut	coupé, e	geschnitten	cortado, a	tagliato, a	cortado, a
cut	coupure(peau)	Schnitt(m)	corte, tajo	taglio	corte, golpe
cut, nick, notch	entaille	Kerbe(f)	cortadura	incisione	incisão, golpe
cutaneous, skin	cutané, e	Haut-	cutáneo, a	cutaneo, a	cutâneo, a
cycle	cycle	Zyklus(m)	ciclo	ciclo	ciclo
cycling	cyclisme	Radfahren(n)	ciclismo	ciclismo	ciclismo
cyclist	cycliste	Radfahrer(in f)m	ciclista	ciclista	ciclista
cyclone	cyclone	Wirbelwind(m)	ciclón	ciclone	ciclone
cylinder	cylindre	Zylinder(m)	cilindro	cilindro	cilindro
cylindrical	cylindrique	zylindrisch	cilíndrico, a	cilindrico, a	cilíndrico, a
cynical	cynique	zynisch	cínico, a	cinico, a	cínico, a
cyst	kyste	Zyste(f)	quiste	ciste	quisto

D

English	French	German	Spanish	Italian	Portuguese
Daddy, Dad	papa	Papa	papá	papà, babbo	papá
dagger	poignard	Dolch(m)	puñal	pugnale	punhal
daily	journalier, ière	täglich	diario, a	giornaliero, a	diário, a
daily	quotidien, ne	täglich	cotidiano, a	quotidiano, a	quotidiano, a
daily	quotidien	Tageszeitung(f)	diario	quotidiano	diário
dam	barrage	Damm(m)	embalse, presa	diga	barragem

English	French	German	Spanish	Italian	Portuguese
damage	dégât(s)	Schaden(m)	daño(s), estrago(s)	danno	estrago
damage	dommage	Schaden(m)	perjuicio, daño	danno	prejuízo, dano
damage	endommager	beschädigen	dañar	danneggiare	estragar
damage, spoil, ruin	abîmer	beschädigen	estropear	sciupare, rovinare	estragar
damn	damner	verdammen	condenar	dannare	condenar
damp, humid, moist	humide	feucht	húmedo, a	umido, a	húmido, a
dance	danse	Tanz(m)	danza, baile	ballo, danza	dança
dance, ball	bal	Ball(m)	baile	ballo	baile
dance	danser	tanzen	bailar	ballare	dançar, bailar
dance-hall	dancing	Tanzlokal(n)	sala de baile	sala da ballo	dancing
dancer	danseur, se	Tänzer(in f)m	bailarín, a	ballerino, a	bailarino, a
dandruff	pellicule	Schuppe(f)	caspa	forfora	caspa
danger	danger	Gefahr(f)	peligro	pericolo	perigo
dangerous	dangereux, se	gefährlich	peligroso, a	pericoloso, a	perigoso, a
dare	oser	wagen	osar, atreverse	osare	ousar, atrever-se
dark	sombre; obscur, e	dunkel	oscuro, a	scuro, a	escuro, a; sombrio, a
darkness	obscurité	Dunkelheit(f)	oscuridad	oscurità, buio	obscuridade
darkness	ténèbres	Finsternis(f)	tinieblas	tenebre	trevas
dash	tiret	Gedankenstrich(m)	raya, guión	trattino	travessão, hífen
data	donnée(s)	Daten(pl)	datos	dati	dados
data processing	informatique	Informatik(f)	informática	informatica	informática
date	date	Datum(n)	fecha	data	data
date	datte	Dattel(f)	dátil	dattero	tâmara
daughter	fille	Tochter(f)	hija	figlia	filha
daughter-in-law	belle-fille	Schwiegertochter(f)	nuera	nuora	nora
dawn	aube	Morgendämmerung(f)	alba	alba	amanhecer
dawn	aurore	Morgenröte(f)	aurora	aurora	aurora
day	jour, journée	Tag(m)	día; jornada	giorno; giornata	dia
day off	jour de congé	Urlaubstag(m)	día libre	giorno di vacanza	dia de folga
dazzle, glare	éblouir	blenden	deslumbrar	abbagliare	encandear
dead	mort, e	tot	muerto, a	morto, a	morto, a
dead man/woman	mort, e	Tote(f, m)	muerto, a	morto, a	morto, a
deaf	sourd, e	taub	sordo, a	sordo, a	surdo, a
deaf and dumb	sourd-muet, te	taubstumm	sordomudo, a	sordomuto, a	surdo-mudo, a
deafening	étourdissant, e	betäubend	aturdidor, a	sbalorditivo, a	atroador, a
deafness	surdité	Taubheit(f)	sordera	sordità	surdez
deal	distribuer	geben	distribuir, dar	distribuire	dar
deal	négocier, traiter	handeln	comerciar, tratar	negoziare, trattare	negociar, tratar
deal with	occuper(s')	beschäftigen, sich	dedicarse a	occuparsi	tratar de
dear	cher, ère	liebe(r)	querido, a	caro, a	caro, a; querido, a
dear, darling	chéri, e	Liebling(m)	querido, a	caro, a	querido, a
death	mort	Tod(m)	muerte	morte	morte
death	décès	Tod(m)	fallecimiento	decesso	falecimento
debate	débat	Debatte(f)	debate	dibattito	debate
debt	dette	Schuld(f)	deuda	debito	dívida
decade	décennie	Jahrzehnt(n)	decenio, década	decennio	década
decadence, decline	décadence	Verfall(m), Untergang	decadencia	decadenza	decadência
deceased person	défunt, e	Verstorbene(f, m)	difunto, a	defunto, a	defunto, a
deceive, cheat	tromper	betrügen	engañar	ingannare	enganar
decelerate	décélérer	ab = bremsen	reducir, aminorar	decelerare	desacelerar
December	Décembre	Dezember(m)	Diciembre	Dicembre	Dezembro
decent	décent, e	anständig	decente	decente	decente
decent, nice	brave	brav, nett, angenehm	bueno, a	bravo, a	amável
decide	décider	entscheiden	decidir	decidere	decidir
decimal	décimal, e	dezimal	decimal	decimale	decimal
decision	décision	Entscheidung(f)	decisión	decisione	decisão
deck; bridge	pont	Deck(n)	puente	ponte	convés
deck-chair	chaise longue	Liegestuhl(m)	hamaca	sdraio	preguiceira
declaration	déclaration	Erklärung(f)	declaración	dichiarazione	declaração
declare	déclarer	bekannt = geben	declarar	dichiarare	declarar
decline	déclin	Untergang(m)	decadencia, ocaso	declino	declínio
decode	décoder	dekodieren	descifrar	decifrare	decifrar
decolonize	décoloniser	entkolonisieren	descolonizar	decolonizzare	descolonizar
decompose	décomposer	zerlegen	descomponer	decomporre	decompor
decontaminate	décontaminer	entseuchen	descontaminar	decontaminare	descontaminar
decorate	décorer	schmücken	decorar, adornar	ornare, adornare	ornar, adornar
decorate	décorer	aus = zeichnen	condecorar	decorare	condecorar
decoration	décoration	Dekoration(f)	decoración	decorazione	decoração

English	French	German	Spanish	Italian	Portuguese
decrease	décroître	ab = nehmen	decrecer	decrescere	decrescer
decreasing	dégressif, ive	abnehmend	decreciente	decrescente	decrescente
decree	décret	Erlaß(m), Verordnung f	decreto	decreto	decreto
dedicate	dédier	widmen	dedicar	dedicare	dedicar
deduct	déduire	folgern, schließen aus	deducir	detrarre	deduzir
deduction	déduction	Abzug(m)	deducción	deduzione	dedução
deduction	déduction	Rückschluß(m)	deducción	deduzione	dedução
deep	profond, e	tief	profundo, a	profondo, a	profundo, a
defeat	défaite	Niederlage(f)	derrota	sconfitta	derrota
defeat	vaincre	besiegen	vencer	vincere	vencer
defect, fault	défaut	Fehler(m)	defecto	difetto	defeito
defective, faulty	défectueux, se	defekt	defectuoso, a	difettoso, a	defeituoso, a
defector	transfuge	Überläufer(in f)m	transfuga	transfuga	trânsfuga
defence	défense	Verteidigung(f)	defensa	difesa	defesa
defend	défendre	verteidigen	defender	difendere	defender
deficiency	carence	Fehlen(n), Mangel(m)	carencia	carenza	carência
deficient	déficient, e	mangelhaft	deficiente	deficiente	deficiente
deficit	déficit	Verlust(m), Defizit(n)	déficit	deficit	défice
define	définir	definieren	definir	definire	definir
definition	définition	Definition(f)	definición	definizione	definição
definitive, final	définitif, ive	endgültig	definitivo, a	definitivo, a	definitivo, a
deflate	dégonfler	Luft raus = lassen	desinflar	sgonfiare	desinchar
deflated, flat	dégonflé, e	platt, ohne Luft	desinflado, a	sgonfio, a	vazio, a
deflation	déflation	Deflation(f)	deflación	deflazione	deflação
defuse	désamorcer	entschärfen	desactivar	disinnescare	despoletar
defy	braver	trotzen	desafiar	sfidare	defrontar
degenerate	dégénérer	degenerieren	degenerar	degenerare	degenerar
degradation	dégradation	Beschädigung(f)	degradación	degradazione	degradação
degrade	dégrader	degradieren	degradar	degradare	degradar
degree	degré	Grad(m)	grado	grado	grau
degree	licence	Lizenz(f)	licenciatura	laurea	licenciatura
dehydrate	déshydrater	aus = trocknen	deshidratar	disidratare	desidratar
de-ice; defrost	dégivrer	ab = tauen	descongelar	sbrinare	descongelar
delay	délai	Frist(f)	plazo	termine	prazo
delay; lateness	retard	Verspätung(f)	atraso	ritardo	atraso
delay	retarder	verzögern	retrasar, demorar	ritardare	atrasar, demorar
delegate	délégué, e	Abgesandte(f, m)	delegado, a	delegato, a	delegado, a
delegate	déléguer	beauftragen	delegar	delegare	delegar
delegation	délégation	Delegation(f)	delegación	delegazione	delegação
delete	annuler	streichen	borrar	annullare	suprimir
delete	supprimer	beseitigen	suprimir	sopprimere	suprimir
deletion	rature	Streichung(f)	tachadura	cancellatura	rasura
deliberate	délibérer	beraten	deliberar	deliberare	deliberar
deliberate	délibéré, e	gewollt, absichtlich	deliberado, a	deliberato, a	deliberado, a
delicacy	délicatesse	Aufmerksamkeit(f)	delicadeza	delicatezza	delicadeza
delicacy	friandise	Nascherei(f)	golosina	dolciume	guloseima
delicate	délicat, e	schwierig	delicado, a	delicato, a	delicado, a
delicate	délicat, e	zart; fein	delicado, a	delicato, a	delicado, a
delicatessen shop	charcuterie	Metzgerei(f)	salchichería	salumeria	salsicharia
delicious	délicieux, se	köstlich	delicioso, a	delizioso, a	delicioso, a
delighted	ravi, e	hocherfreut	encantado, a	lietissimo, a	encantado, a
delighted(be)	réjouir(se)	erfreuen, sich	alegrarse	rallegrare(-arsi)	alegrar-se
delightful	charmant, e	entzückend, reizend	delicioso, a	delizioso, a	delicioso, a
delimit	délimiter	ab = grenzen	delimitar	delimitare	delimitar
delinquency	délinquance	Kriminalität(f)	delincuencia	delinquenza	delinquência
delinquent	délinquant, e	Kriminelle(f, m)	delincuente	delinquente	delinquente
delirium	délire	Fieberwahn(m)	delirio	delirio	delirio
deliver	livrer, délivrer	liefern	entregar	consegnare	entregar
delivery	livraison	Lieferung(f)	entrega	consegna	entrega
delivery; birth	accouchement	Entbindung(f)	parto	parto	parto
demagogy	démagogie	Demagogie(f)	demagogia	demagogia	demagogia
demand, requirement	exigence	Forderung(f)	exigencia	esigenza	exigência
demand	exiger, demander	verlangen, fordern	exigir, demandar	esigere, domandare	exigir, pedir
demand, require	exiger, réclamer	fordern	exigir	esigere	exigir
demobilize	démobiliser	demobilisieren	desmovilizar	smobilitare	desmobilizar
democracy	démocratie	Demokratie(f)	democracia	democrazia	democracia
democrat	démocrate	Demokrat(in f)m	demócrata	democratico, a	democrata
demography	démographie	Demographie(f)	demografía	demografia	demografia

English	French	German	Spanish	Italian	Portuguese
demolish	démolir	zerstören	demoler	demolire	demolir
demon, devil	démon	Teufel(m)	demonio	demonio	demónio
demonstrate	démontrer	beweisen	demostrar	dimostrare	demonstrar
demonstration	démonstration	Vorführung(f)	demostración	dimostrazione	demonstração
demonstration	manifestation	Demonstration(f)	manifestación	manifestazione	manifestação
demonstrator	manifestant, e	Demonstrant(in f)m	manifestante	manifestante	manifestante
demoralize	démoraliser	entmutigen	desmoralizar	demoralizzare	desmoralizar
denigrate	dénigrer	verleumden	denigrar	denigrare	denegrir
denounce	dénoncer	denunzieren	denunciar	denunziare	denunciar
dense	dense	dicht	denso, a	denso, a	denso, a
density	densité	Dichte(f)	densidad	densità	densidade
dentist	dentiste	Zahnarzt(in f)m	dentista	dentista	dentista
denture	dentier	Gebiß(n)	dentadura	dentiera	dentadura
deny	nier	verneinen, leugnen	negar	negare	negar
deodorant	déodorant	Deo(n)	desodorante	deodorante	desodorisante
department	département	Bezirk(m), Bereich(m)	departamento	dipartimento	departamento
department	rayon	Abteilung(f)	sección	reparto	secção
departure, start	départ	Abfahrt(f)	salida, partida	partenza	partida
depend(on)	dépendre(de)	ab = hängen	depender	dipendere	depender
dependent(on)	dépendant, e	abhängig	dependiente	dipendente	dependente
deplorable	déplorable	beklagenswert	deplorable	deplorevole	deplorável
deplore	déplorer	beklagen	deplorar	deplorare	deplorar
deportation	déportation	Deportation(f)	deportación	deportazione	deportação
deposit	dépôt	Satz(m)	depósito	deposito	depósito
deposit	arrhes	Anzahlung(f)	señal(dejar)	caparra	sinal
deposit	déposer	deponieren	depositar	depositare	depositar
depressed	déprimé, e	deprimiert	deprimido, a	depresso, a	deprimido, a
depression	dépression(atm.)	Tief(n)	depresión	depressione	depressão
deprive	priver	berauben, entziehen	privar	privare	privar
depth	profondeur	Tiefe(f)	profundidad	profondità	profundidade
deputy	adjoint, e	Stellvertreter(in f)m	substituto, a	assessore	adjunto, a
descendants	descendance	Nachkommenschaft(f)	descendencia	discendenza	descendência
descent	descente	Abstieg(m)	descenso, bajada	discesa	descida
describe	décrire	beschreiben	describir	descrivere	descrever
description	description	Beschreibung(f)	descripción	descrizione	descrição
desecrate	profaner	entweihen	profanar	profanare	profanar
desert	désert	Wüste(f)	desierto	deserto	deserto
desert, barren	désertique	öde; einsam	desértico, a	desertico, a	desértico, a
deserve, merit	mériter	verdienen	merecer	meritare	merecer
design	dessin, plan	Entwurf(m)	diseño	disegno	desenho
design, style	forme	Schnitt(m)	hechura	taglio, stile	corte, design
design	modèle	Muster(n), Modell(n)	modelo, patrón	modello	modelo
design	concevoir	entwerfen	concebir	ideare	conceber
desire, want	désirer	wünschen	desear	desiderare	desejar
desire	envie	Lust(f)	ganas	voglia	vontade
desk	bureau	Schreibtisch(m)	escritorio	scrivania	secretária
despair	désespoir	Verzweiflung(f)	desesperación	disperazione	desespero
despite	malgré	trotz	a pesar de	malgrado	apesar de
despot	despote	Despot(m)	déspota	despota	déspota
dessert	dessert	Nachtisch(m)	postre	dessert	sobremesa
destination	destination	Bestimmungsort(m)	destinación	destinazione	destino
destiny	destinée	Schicksal(n)	destino	destino	destino
destroy	détruire	zerstören	destruir	distruggere	destruir
destruction	destruction	Zerstörung(f)	destrucción	distruzione	destruição
detach, unfasten	détacher	lösen, ab = trennen	desatar	staccare	desatar
detail	détail	Einzelheit(f)	detalle	particolare	pormenor
detailed	détaillé, e	einzelnen(im)	detallado, a	dettagliato, a	detalhado, a
detection	détection	Aufspüren(n)	detección	rivelazione	detecção
detective	détective	Detektiv(m)	detective	detective	detective
detective novel	roman policier	Kriminalroman(m)	novela policíaca	giallo	romance policial
detector	détecteur	Anzeiger(m)	detector	rivelatore	detector
detention	détention	Haft(f)	detención	detenzione	detenção
deterioration	détérioration	Verschlechterung(f)	deterioración	deteriorazione	deterioração
determine	déterminer	fest = legen	determinar	determinare	determinar
detest, hate	détester	hassen	detestar, odiar	detestare, odiare	detestar
detonation	détonation	Knall(m)	detonación	detonazione	detonação
devaluation	dévaluation	Abwertung(f)	devaluación	svalutazione	desvalorização
devalue	dévaluer	entwerten, ab = werten	devaluar	svalutare	desvalorizar

156

English	French	German	Spanish	Italian	Portuguese
devastate, ravage	ravager	verwüsten	asolar, devastar	devastare	assolar
devastation	ravage	Verwüstung(f)	destrozo	devastazione	estrago
develop	développer	entwickeln	desarrollar	sviluppare	desenvolver
development	développement	Entwicklung(f)	desarrollo	sviluppo	desenvolvimento
devil	diable	Teufel(m)	diablo	diavolo	diabo
devote	consacrer	widmen	dedicar	dedicare	dedicar
devoted	dévoué, e	ergeben	servicial	devoto, a	dedicado, a
devotion	dévouement	Ergebenheit(f)	consagración a	dedizione	dedicação
devotion	dévotion	Frömmigkeit(f)	devoción	devozione	devoção
devour	dévorer	verschlingen	devorar	divorare	devorar
dew	rosée	Tau(m)	rocío	rugiada	orvalho
diabetes	diabète	Zuckerkrankheit(f)	diabetes	diabete	diabetes
diagnosis(-oses)	diagnostic	Diagnose(f)	diagnóstico	diagnosi	diagnóstico
diagonal	diagonal, e	diagonal	diagonal	diagonale	diagonal
diagram	diagramme	Diagramm(n)	diagrama	diagramma	diagrama
diagram	schéma	Schema(n)	esquema	schema	esquema
dial	cadran	Zifferblatt(n)	esfera	quadrante	mostrador
dial	composer(n°tél)	Nummer(f)(wählen)	marcar un número	comporre(numero)	discar, marcar
dialling code	indicatif(tél.)	Vorwählnummer(f)	prefijo	prefisso	indicativo, prefixo
dialect	dialecte	Dialekt(m)	dialecto	dialetto	dialecto
dialogue	dialogue	Dialog(m)	diálogo	dialogo	diálogo
diameter	diamètre	Durchmesser(m)	diámetro	diametro	diâmetro
diamond	diamant	Diamant(m)	diamante	diamante	diamante
diamond-shaped	losange	Raute(f), Rhombus(m)	rombo	rombo	losango
diaphragm	diaphragme	Zwerchfell(n)	diafragma	diaframma	diafragma
diarrhoea	diarrhée	Durchfall(m)	diarrea	diarrea	diarreia
diary	agenda	Taschenkalender(m)	agenda	agenda	agenda
dictator	dictateur	Diktator(m)	dictador	dittatore	ditador
dictatorship	dictature	Diktatur(f)	dictadura	dittatura	ditadura
dictionary	dictionnaire	Wörterbuch(n)	diccionario	dizionario	dicionário
die	mourir	sterben	morir	morire	morrer
die	décéder	versterben, sterben	fallecer	decedere	falecer
die	expirer	verscheiden	expirar	spirare	expirar
die(dice)	dé(jeux)	Würfel(m)	dado	dado	dado
diesel oil	diesel	Diesel(m)	diesel	diesel	diesel
diesel oil	gas-oil	Diesel(n), Dieselöl(n)	gasoil	gasolio	gasóleo
diet(be on a)	régime	Diät(f)	dieta	dieta	dieta
dietetic	diététique	diätetisch	dietético, a	dietetico, a	dietético, a
difference	différence	Unterschied(m)	diferencia	differenza	diferença
different	différent, e	verschieden	diferente	differente	diferente
difficult	difficile	schwer	difícil	difficile	difícil
difficulty	difficulté	Schwierigkeit(f)	dificultad	difficoltà	dificuldade
diffuse	diffuser	verbreiten	difundir	diffondere	difundir
diffusion	diffusion	Verbreitung; Sendung	difusión	diffusione	difusão
dig	creuser	graben	cavar	scavare	cavar
dig up	déterrer	aus = graben	desenterrar	dissotterrare	desenterrar
digestion	digestion	Verdauung(f)	digestión	digestione	digestão
digit	chiffre	Ziffer(f), Zahl(f)	cifra	cifra	cifra
dignity	dignité	Würde(f)	dignidad	dignità	dignidade
dilute	diluer	verdünnen	diluir	diluire	diluir
dim	faible	matt	flojo, a	debole	fraco, a
dimension, size	dimension	Maß(n)	dimensión	dimensione	dimensão
dinghy	canot	Boot(n)	bote	canotto	canoa
dining-room	salle à manger	Eßzimmer(n)	comedor	sala da pranzo	sala de jantar
dinner	dîner	Abendessen(n)	cena	cena	jantar
dinner(have)	dîner	Abend essen(zu)	cenar	cenare	jantar
dinner-jacket	smoking	Smoking(m)	esmoquin	smoking	smoking
dip	tremper, plonger	ein = tauchen	sumergir	intingere	mergulhar
diphtheria	diphtérie	Diphterie(f)	difteria	difterite	difteria
diploma	diplôme	Diplom(n)	diploma, título	diploma	diploma
diplomacy	diplomatie	Diplomatie(f)	diplomacia	diplomazia	diplomacia
diplomat	diplomate	Diplomat(in f)m	diplomático	diplomatico	diplomata
diplomatic	diplomatique	diplomatisch	diplomático, a	diplomatico, a	diplomático, a
direct	direct, e	direkt	directo, a	diretto, a	directo, a
direct, guide, point	diriger	richten, steuern	dirigir, guiar	dirigere	dirigir
direction	direction	Richtung(f)	dirección	direzione	direcção
direction, way	sens	Richtung(f)	sentido	senso	sentido
directly	directement	direkt	directamente	direttamente	directamente

director, head . . . . directeur, trice . . . . Direktor(in f)m . . . . director, a . . . . direttore, -trice . . . . director, a
directory . . . . annuaire . . . . Adreßbuch; Telefonbuch . . . anuario, guía . . . . elenco, annuario . . . . . . anuário
dirt . . . . saleté . . . . Schmutz(m) . . . . suciedad . . . . sporcizia . . . . sujidade, porcaria
dirty . . . . sale . . . . dreckig . . . . sucio, a . . . . sporco, a . . . . sujo, a
dirty . . . . salir . . . . verschmutzen . . . . ensuciar . . . . sporcare . . . . sujar
disabled . . . . infirme . . . . behindert . . . . inválido, a . . . . infermo, a . . . . doente
disabled . . . . invalide . . . . behindert . . . . inválido, a . . . . invalido, a . . . . inválido, a
disabled . . . . mutilé, e . . . . verstümmelt . . . . mutilado, a . . . . mutilato, a . . . . mutilado, a
disadvantage . . . . désavantage . . . . . . Nachteil(m) . . . . desventaja . . . . svantaggio . . . . desvantagem
disadvantage . . . . inconvénient . . . . . . Nachteil(m) . . . . inconveniente . . . . inconveniente . . . . inconveniente
disagreement . . . . désaccord . . . . Uneinigkeit(f), Streit . . . . discrepancia . . . . disaccordo . . . . desacordo
disappear . . . . disparaître . . . . verschwinden . . . . desaparecer . . . . sparire . . . . desaparecer
disappoint . . . . décevoir . . . . enttäuschen . . . . decepcionar . . . . deludere . . . . desapontar
disappointed . . . . déçu, e . . . . enttäuscht . . . . decepcionado, a . . . . . deluso, a . . . . desiludido, a
disappointment . . . . . . déception . . . . Enttäuschung(f) . . . . decepción . . . . delusione . . . . decepção
disapprove . . . . désapprouver . . . . . . mißbilligen . . . . desaprobar . . . . disapprovare . . . . desaprovar
disarm . . . . désarmer . . . . ab = rüsten, entwaffnen . . . . desarmar . . . . disarmare . . . . desarmar
disarmament . . . . désarmement . . . . . . Abrüstung(f) . . . . desarme . . . . disarmo . . . . desarmamento
disaster . . . . désastre . . . . Unheil(n) . . . . desastre . . . . disastro . . . . desastre
discern . . . . discerner . . . . unterscheiden . . . . discernir . . . . discernere . . . . discernir
disciple . . . . disciple . . . . Jünger(m) . . . . discípulo . . . . discepolo . . . . discípulo
discipline . . . . discipline . . . . Disziplin(f) . . . . disciplina . . . . disciplina . . . . disciplina
disco(theque) . . . . discothèque . . . . Diskothek(f) . . . . discoteca . . . . discoteca . . . . discoteca
discolouration . . . . décoloration . . . . Entfärbung(f) . . . . descoloramiento . . . . . decolorazione . . . . descoloração
disconcerting . . . . déconcertant, e . . . . verwirrend . . . . desconcertante . . . . . . sconcertante . . . . desconcertante
disconnect, unplug . . . débrancher . . . . aus = machen, abschalten . . . desenchufar . . . . disinserire . . . . desligar
discount . . . . escompte . . . . Skonto(m) . . . . descuento . . . . sconto . . . . desconto
discount . . . . rabais, remise . . . . . Rabatt(m) . . . . rebaja, descuento . . . . ribasso, sconto . . . . desconto, saldo
discourage . . . . décourager . . . . entmutigen . . . . desalentar . . . . scoraggiare . . . . desalentar
discouraged . . . . découragé, e . . . . . . entmutigt . . . . desanimado, a . . . . scoraggiato, a . . . . desalentado, a
discouraging . . . . décourageant, e . . . . entmutigend . . . . desalentador, a . . . . . . scoraggiante . . . . desanimador, a
discover . . . . découvrir . . . . entdecken . . . . descubrir . . . . scoprire . . . . descobrir
discover; reveal . . . . . . déceler . . . . auf = decken, entdecken . . . . descubrir . . . . svelare, scoprire . . . . . . descobrir
discovery . . . . découverte . . . . Entdeckung(f) . . . . descubrimiento . . . . . . scoperta . . . . descoberta
discredit . . . . discréditer . . . . Verruf bringen(in) . . . . desacreditar . . . . discreditare . . . . desacreditar
discreet . . . . discret, ète . . . . diskret . . . . discreto . . . . discreto, a . . . . discreto, a
discuss . . . . discuter . . . . besprechen . . . . discutir . . . . discutere . . . . discutir
discussion, talk . . . . . . discussion . . . . Diskussion(f) . . . . discusión . . . . discussione . . . . discussão
disdain . . . . dédaigner . . . . mißachten . . . . desdeñar . . . . disprezzare . . . . desdenhar
disembark, land . . . . . . débarquer . . . . Land gehen(an) . . . . desembarcar . . . . sbarcare . . . . desembarcar
disgrace . . . . disgrâce . . . . Ungnade(f) . . . . desgracia . . . . disgrazia . . . . desvalimento
disguise . . . . déguiser . . . . verkleiden . . . . disfrazar . . . . mascherare . . . . disfarçar
disgust . . . . dégoûter . . . . an = widern . . . . asco(dar) . . . . disgustare . . . . enojar
disgust . . . . écoeurer . . . . an = ekeln, an = widern . . . . asquear . . . . nauseare . . . . enjoar
disgusting . . . . dégoûtant, e . . . . . . ekelhaft . . . . asqueroso, a . . . . disgustoso, a . . . . nojento, a
dish, plate . . . . plat . . . . Schüssel(f) . . . . fuente, plato . . . . vassoio, piatto . . . . travessa
disheartened . . . . découragé, e . . . . . . mutlos, verzagt . . . . desalentado, a . . . . scoraggiato, a . . . . desalentado, a
dishonest . . . . malhonnête . . . . unehrlich . . . . deshonesto, a . . . . disonesto, a . . . . desonesto, a
dishonour . . . . déshonneur . . . . Schande(f) . . . . deshonor . . . . disonore . . . . desonra
disinfect . . . . désinfecter . . . . desinfizieren . . . . desinfectar . . . . disinfettare . . . . desinfectar
disinherit . . . . déshériter . . . . enterben . . . . desheredar . . . . diseredare . . . . deserdar
disintegrate . . . . désintégrer . . . . auf = lösen . . . . desintegrar . . . . disintegrare . . . . desintegrar
dismantle, undo . . . . . . défaire, démonter . . . ab = bauen . . . . deshacer . . . . disfare . . . . desfazer
dismantling . . . . démontage . . . . Zerlegung(f), Abbau(m) . . . . desmontaje . . . . smontaggio . . . . desmontagem
dismiss . . . . limoger . . . . entlassen . . . . destituir . . . . silurare . . . . destituir
dismiss . . . . révoquer . . . . ab = setzen, entlassen . . . . . . revocar . . . . revocare . . . . demitir
dismiss . . . . renvoyer . . . . entlassen . . . . despedir . . . . dimettere . . . . despedir
dismissal, lay-off . . . . . licenciement . . . . . . Entlassung(f) . . . . despido . . . . licenziamento . . . . despedimento
disobey . . . . désobéir . . . . ungehorsam sein . . . . desobedecer . . . . disobbedire . . . . desobedecer
disorder, mess . . . . désordre . . . . Unordnung(f) . . . . desorden . . . . disordine . . . . desordem
disorganize . . . . désorganiser . . . . . . desorganisieren . . . . desorganizar . . . . disorganizzare . . . . desorganizar
disown; renounce . . . . . renier . . . . verleugnen, verneinen . . . . . renegar . . . . rinnegare . . . . renegar
dispatch, send . . . . expédier . . . . verschicken . . . . expedir . . . . spedire . . . . expedir
disperse; scatter . . . . . . disperser . . . . zerstreuen . . . . dispersar . . . . disperdere . . . . dispersar
display . . . . visualiser . . . . sichtbar machen . . . . visualizar . . . . visualizzare . . . . visualizar
display . . . . afficher(s') . . . . erscheinen . . . . visualizar . . . . apparire . . . . mostrar, dar
displeased . . . . mécontent, e . . . . . . unzufrieden . . . . descontento, a . . . . scontento, a . . . . descontente
displeasure . . . . mécontentement . . . . Unzufriedenheit(f) . . . . descontento . . . . scontento . . . . descontentamento

English	French	German	Spanish	Italian	Portuguese
dispute, argument	dispute	Streit(m)	disputa	disputa, lite	disputa
dissident	dissident, e	Dissident(m)	disidente	dissidente	dissidente
dissipate, clear	dissiper	verziehen, sich	disipar	dissipare	dissipar
dissociate	dissocier	trennen	disociar	dissociare	dissociar
dissolve	dissoudre	auf = lösen	disolver	sciogliere	dissolver
dissuade	dissuader	ab = raten	disuadir	dissuadere	dissuadir
dissuasion	dissuasion	Abschreckung(f)	disuasión	dissuasione	dissuasão
distance	distance	Entfernung(f)	distancia	distanza	distância
distance	éloignement	Entfernung(f)	alejamiento	lontananza	afastamento
distillation	distillation	Destillation(f)	destilación	distillazione	distilação
distinct	distinct, e	deutlich	distinto, a	distinto, a	distinto, a
distinguish	distinguer	unterscheiden	distinguir	distinguere	distinguir
distort, deform	déformer	verformen	deformar	deformare	deformar
distortion	déformation	Mißbildung(f)	deformación	deformazione	deformação
distract, divert	distraire	ab = lenken	distraer	distrarre	distrair
distraught	désemparé, e	ratlos	desamparado, a	smarrito, a; sgomento	desamparado, a
distress	détresse	Verzweiflung(f)	angustia	sconforto	aflição, angústia
distress, afflict	affliger	heim = suchen; betrüben	afligir	affliggere	afligir
distribute; deal	distribuer	verteilen	distribuir	distribuire	distribuir
distribution	distribution	Verteilung(f)	distribución	distribuzione	distribuição
distribution	répartition	Verteilung(f)	reparto	ripartizione	repartição
district	quartier	Viertel(n)	barrio	quartiere	bairro
district	district, région	Bezirk(m)	distrito, área	distretto	distrito
distrust, mistrust	méfiance	Mißtrauen(n)	desconfianza	diffidenza	desconfiança
disturb; trouble	troubler	stören	perturbar	turbare, disturbare	perturbar
disturb, bother	déranger	stören	molestar	disturbare	incomodar
disturb, perturb	perturber	stören	perturbar	perturbare	perturbar
ditch	fossé	Graben(m)	cuneta	fossato, fosso	fosso
dive	plongeon	Kopfsprung(m)	zambullida	tuffo	mergulho
diverge	diverger	ab = weichen	divergir	divergere	divergir
diverse, various	divers, e	verschieden	diverso, a	diverso, a	diverso, a
diversify	diversifier	variieren	diversificar	diversificare	diversificar
diversion	déviation	Umleitung(f)	desviación	deviazione	desvio
diversity	diversité	Verschiedenheit(f)	diversidad	diversità	diversidade
divert	dévier	um = leiten	desviar	deviare	desviar
divide	diviser	teilen	dividir	dividere	dividir
divine	divin, e	göttlich	divino, a	divino, a	divino, a
diving-suit	scaphandre	Taucheranzug(m)	escafandra	scafandro	escafandro
division	division	Division(f)	división	divisione	divisão
divorce	divorce	Scheidung(f)	divorcio	divorzio	divórcio
divorce	divorcer	scheiden lassen, sich	divorciar(se)	divorziare	divorciar-se
divulge, reveal	divulguer	aus = plaudern	divulgar	divulgare	divulgar
dizziness	vertige	Schwindel(m)	vértigo	vertigine	vertigem
do, make	faire	tun, machen	hacer	fare	fazer
docile	docile	gehorsam	dócil	docile	dócil, manso
doctor	médecin	Arzt(m), Ärztin(f)	médico	medico	médico
doctor	docteur(toresse)	Arzt(m); Doktor(m)	doctor, a	dottore, -essa	doutor, a
doctor	docteur	Doktor(m)	doctor, a	dottore, -essa	doutor, a
doctrine	doctrine	Lehre(f)	doctrina	dottrina	doutrina
document	document	Dokument(n)	documento	documento	documento
document case	porte-documents	Aktenmappe(f)	portadocumentos	portadocumenti	carteira
documentation	documentation	Dokumentation(f)	documentación	documentazione	documentação
dog, bitch(-es)	chien, ne	Hund(m)	perro, a	cane, cagna	cão, cadela
dogmatic	dogmatique	dogmatisch	dogmático, a	dogmatica, a	dogmático, a
doll	poupée	Puppe(f)	muñeca	bambola	boneca
dolphin	dauphin	Delphin(m)	delfín	delfino	golfinho
domain, estate	domaine	Gut(n), Besitzung(f)	dominio, terreno	tenuta, fondo	terreno
dome	dôme	Kuppel(f)	cúpula	duomo	cúpula
dome	coupole	Kuppel(f)	cúpula, bóveda	cupola	cúpula
domestic, home	domestique	Haus-	doméstico, a	domestico, a	doméstico, a
domestic, home	intérieur, e	Innen-	interior	interno, a	interno, a
domestic help	femme de ménage	Putzfrau(f)	asistenta	donna di servizio	mulher a dias
dominate, rule	dominer	beherrschen	dominar	dominare	dominar
door	porte	Tür(f)	puerta	porta	porta
door(car)	portière	Wagentür(f)	puerta	sportello	porta
dose	dose	Dosis(f)	dosis	dose	dose
dot	point	Punkt(m)	punto	punto	ponto
double	double	doppelt	doble	doppio, a	duplo, a

English	French	German	Spanish	Italian	Portuguese
double	sosie	Doppelgänger(in f)m	sosia	sosia	sósia
doubt	doute	Zweifel(m)	duda	dubbio	dúvida
doubt	douter	zweifeln	dudar	dubitare	duvidar
down	bas	hinunter	abajo	giù	baixo
downfall	déchéance	Untergang(m), Verfall	decaimiento	decadenza	decadência
downstairs	bas(en)	unten; hinunter	abajo	basso, giù	baixo(de)
doze	sommeiller	schlummern	dormitar	sonnecchiare	dormitar
dozen	douzaine	Dutzend(n)	docena	dozzina	dúzia
drag, trail, haul	traîner	schleppen	arrastrar	trascinare	arrastar
drain	drainer	entwässern	drenar	drenare	drenar
drama	drame	Drama(n)	drama	dramma	drama
dramatic	dramatique	dramatisch	dramático, a	drammatico, a	dramático, a
draught	pion(dames)	Stein(m)(Spiel)	ficha(damas)	pedina(dama)	peça, tábula(dama)
draw; design	dessiner	zeichnen	dibujar; diseñar	disegnare	desenhar
draw	tracer	entwerfen	trazar	tracciare	traçar
draw	tirer	ziehen	tirar	tirare	puxar
draw(from)	puiser, tirer	schöpfen	sacar	attingere	tirar, extraír
draw out, withdraw	retirer	ab = heben	sacar	prelevare	levantar
drawer	tiroir	Schublade(f)	cajón	cassetto	gaveta
drawer; designer	dessinateur	Zeichner(in f)m	dibujante	disegnatore, trice	desenhador, a
drawing; design	dessin	Zeichnung(f)	dibujo; diseño	disegno	desenho
drawing-pin	punaise	Heftzwecke(f)	chincheta	puntina(disegno)	percevejo
dreadful	épouvantable	entsetzlich	horroroso, a	spaventoso, a	horroroso, a
dream	rêve	Traum(m)	sueño	sogno	sonho
dream	rêver	träumen	soñar	sognare	sonhar
dress	robe	Kleid(n)	vestido	vestito	vestido
dress	habiller(s')	an = ziehen, sich	vestirse	vestirsi	vestir-se
dress up	habiller(s')	an = kleiden	vestirse, ataviar	vestire(-rsi)	vestir-se
dressed	habillé, e	angezogen	vestido, a	vestito, a	vestido, a
dresser; sideboard	buffet	Büfett(n)	aparador	credenza, buffè	aparador
dressing gown	robe de chambre	Schlafrock(m)	bata	vestaglia	roupão
dressing gown	peignoir	Morgenmantel(m)	bata	accappatoio	roupão
dressmaker, tailor	couturier, ière	Schneider(in f)m	modista	sarto, a	costureiro, a
dribble	baver	sabbern	babear	sbavare	babar-se
drift	dériver	ab = treiben	derivar	derivare	derivar
drill; pierce	percer	bohren	perforar	bucare, forare	furar
drink	boisson	Getränk(n)	bebida	bibita; bevanda	bebida
drink	boire	trinken	beber	bere	beber
drinker	buveur, se	Trinker(in f)m	bebedor, a	bevitore, trice	bebedor, a
drinking	potable	trinkbar, genießbar	potable	potabile	potável
drive	conduire	fahren	conducir	guidare	conduzir
drive in	enfoncer	ein = schlagen	clavar	piantare	cravar
driver	conducteur, trice	Fahrer(in f)m	conductor, a	conducente	condutor, a
driver; chauffeur	chauffeur	Fahrer m; Chauffeur m	chófer	autista	motorista
driving licence	permis(auto)	Führerschein(m)	permiso conducir	patente di guida	carta de condução
drizzle	bruine	Sprühregen(m)	llovizna	pioggerella	chuvisco
drop	goutte	Tropfen(m)	gota	goccia	gota
drop, fall	baisse, chute	Sinken(n), Fallen(n)	baja, caída	abbassamento	baixa, queda
drop	tomber(laisser)	fallenlassen	caer(dejar)	cadere(lasciar)	cair(deixar)
drop	échapper	entgleiten	irse, escaparse	sfuggire, scappare	escapar
drop, lower; fall	baisser	senken	rebajar	abbassare, calare	baixar
dropping, dung	crotte	Häufchen(n), Kot(m)	caca	sterco	bosta
drought	sécheresse	Trockenheit(f)	sequía	siccità	seca
drown	noyer(se)	ertrinken	ahogar(se)	annegare	afogar-se
drowsiness	somnolence	Schläfrigkeit(f)	somnolencia	sonnolenza	sonolência
drug, medicine	médicament	Medikament(n)	medicina	medicina	medicamento
drug	drogue	Droge(f)	droga	droga	droga
drug addict	drogué, e	Drogenabhängige(m, f)	drogado, a	drogato, a	drogado, a
drug addict	toxicomane	Rauschgiftsüchtige(r)	drogadicto, a	tossicomane	toxicómano, drogado
drunk	soûl, e; ivre	betrunken	embriagado, a	ubriaco, a	bêbado, a; ébrio, a
drunkard	ivrogne	Trunkenbold(m)	borracho, a	ubriaco, a	bêbedo, a; ébrio, a
drunkenness	ivresse	Trunkenheit(f)	ebriedad	ubriachezza	embriaguez
dry	sec, sèche	trocken	seco, a	secco, a; asciutto, a	seco, a
dry	sécher	trocknen	secar	asciugare; seccare	secar
dual	double	doppelt	doble	doppio, a	duplo, a
dubious; doubtful	douteux, se	zweifelhaft	dudoso, a	dubbio, a	duvidoso, a
Dublin Bay prawn	langoustine	Langustine(f)	langostino	scampo	lagostim
duck	canard	Ente(f)	pato	anatra	pato, a

English	French	German	Spanish	Italian	Portuguese
duel	duel	Duell(n)	duelo	duello	duelo
duke, duchess	duc, duchesse	Herzog(m), Herzogin(f)	duque, duquesa	duca, duchessa	duque, duquesa
dull	terne	matt	sin brillo, mate	spento, a; smorto, a	baço, a
dull, matt	mat, e	glanzlos, matt	mate	opaco, a	mate
dumb; silent	muet, te	stumm	mudo, a	muto, a	mudo, a
dummy; model	mannequin	Schaufensterpuppe(f)	maniquí	manichino	manequim
dummy	sucette	Schnuller(m)	chupete	succhiotto	chupeta
dune	dune	Düne(f)	duna	duna	duna
duration, length	durée	Dauer(f)	duración	durata	duração
during; for	pendant, durant	während	durante	durante	durante
dust	poussière	Staub(m)	polvo	polvere	poeira
duty	devoir	Pflicht(f)	deber	dovere	dever
duty(tax)-free	détaxé, e	steuerfrei	desgravado, a	sgravio fiscale	isento de taxa
duty-free	hors-taxe	zollfrei	libre impuestos	duty-free	sem imposto
dwarf	nain, e	Zwerg(m)	enano, a	nano, a	anão, anã
dwelling; living	habitation	Wohnung(f)	vivienda, morada	abitazione	habitação, morada
dye	teindre, colorer	färben	teñir	tingere	tingir
dynamic	dynamique	dynamisch	dinámico, a	dinamico, a	dinâmico, a
dynamism	dynamisme	Tatkraft(f), Schwung m	dinamismo	dinamismo	dinamismo
dynamite	dynamite	Dynamit(n)	dinamita	dinamite	dinamite
dynasty	dynastie	Herrscherhaus(n)	dinastía	dinastia	dinastia

E

English	French	German	Spanish	Italian	Portuguese
each, every(one)	chacun, e; chaque	jeder, jede	cada uno(una)	ciascuno, a	cada um(uma)
eager	avide, impatient	begierig	deseoso, a	desideroso, a	ávido, a; desejoso, a
eagle	aigle	Adler(m)	águila	aquila	águia
ear	oreille	Ohr(n)	oreja	orecchio	orelha
ear-ache	otite	Mittelohrentzündung f	otitis	otite	otite
eardrum	tympan	Trommelfell(n)	tímpano	timpano	tímpano
ear/headphones	écouteurs, casque	Kopfhörer(m)	casco	cuffia	auscultadores
early	matinal, e	früh	matutino, a	mattutino, a	matinal
early	tôt	früh	temprano	presto	cedo
early(to be)	avance(être en)	zu früh (sein)	adelantado(estar)	anticipo(essere in)	adiantado(estar)
earn; win	gagner	verdienen	ganar	guadagnare	ganhar
earnings	gain(s)	Gewinn(m)	ganancia(s)	lucro, profitto	lucro
earring	boucle(s)	Ohrring(m)	pendientes	orecchini	brincos, argolas
earth	terre	Erde(f)	tierra	terra	Terra
earthquake	séisme	Erdbeben(n)	seismo	sisma	sismo
earthquake	séisme	Erdbeben(n)	terremoto	terremoto	terremoto
ease(be at)	aise(être à l')	wohl fühlen, sich	gusto(estar a)	agio(essere a)	vontade(estar à)
easily	facilement	leicht	fácilmente	facilmente	fácilmente
East	Est	Osten(m)	Este	Est	Este, Leste
Easter	Pâques	Ostern(n)	Pascua	Pasqua	Páscoa
easy	facile	leicht	fácil	facile	fácil
eat	manger	essen	comer	mangiare	comer
ebb	reflux	Ebbe(f)	reflujo	riflusso	refluxo
echo(-es)	écho	Echo(n)	eco	eco	eco
eclipse	éclipse	Finsternis(f)	eclipse	eclisse	eclipse
ecology	écologie	Naturschutz(m)	ecología	ecologia	ecologia
economic(al)	économique	wirtschaftlich	económico, a	economico, a	económico, a
economist	économiste	Volkswirt(in f)m	economista	economista	economista
economy	économie	Wirtschaft(f)	economía	economia	economia
ecstasy	extase	Entzückung(f)	éxtasis	estasi	êxtase
eczema	eczéma	Ekzem(n)	eczema	eczema	eczema
eddy, swirl	remous	Wirbel(m)	remolino	mulinello, vortice	redemoinho
edge, border	bord, bordure	Rand(m)	bordura; ribete	bordo, lungo	borda, orla

English	French	German	Spanish	Italian	Portuguese
edgy, worked up	énervé, e	erregt, nervös	excitado, a	nervoso, a	enervado, a
edgy, irritable(be)	énerver(s')	auf = regen, sich	ponerse nervioso, a	innervosirsi	enervar-se
edible	comestible	eßbar	comestible	commestibile	comestível
edifice, building	édifice	Gebäude(n)	edificio	edificio	edifício
edition	édition	Auflage(f), Ausgabe(f)	edición	edizione	edição
editorial	éditorial	Leitartikel(m)	editorial	editoriale	editorial
editorial staff	rédaction	Redaktion(f)	redacción	redazione	redacção
educate	éduquer	erziehen, bilden	educar	educare	educar
education	éducation	Erziehung(f)	educación	educazione	educação
effect	effet	Wirkung(f)	efecto	effetto	efeito
effective	effectif, ive	tatsächlich, wirklich	efectivo, a	effettivo, a	efectivo, a
effective	efficace	wirkungsvoll	eficaz	efficace	eficaz
efficient	efficace	tüchtig, fähig	eficiente, a	efficiente	eficiente
effort	effort	Anstrengung(f)	esfuerzo	sforzo	esforço
egg	oeuf	Ei(n)	huevo	uovo(a)	ovo
eight	huit	acht	ocho	otto	oito
eighteen	dix-huit	achtzehn	dieciocho	diciotto	dezoito
eighty	quatre-vingts	achtzig	ochenta	ottanta	oitenta
either	un(l')ou l'autre	eine(der) der andere	uno u otro, cada	uno(l') o l'altro	um ou outro, cada
eject	éjecter	aus = stoßen	eyectar, expulsar	espellere	expelir
elaborate	élaborer	aus = arbeiten	elaborar	elaborare	elaborar
elapse	écouler(s')	vergehen, verfließen	transcurrir	trascorrere	decorrer
elastic; flexible	élastique	elastisch	elástico, a	elastico, a	elástico, a
elation	allégresse	Heiterkeit(f)	júbilo, alegría	esultanza	júbilo, alegria
elbow	coude	Ellenbogen(m)	codo	gomito	cotovelo
elect	élire	wählen	elegir	eleggere	eleger
elected, chosen	élu, e	gewählt	elegido, a	eletto, a	eleito, a
election	élection	Wahl(f)	elección	elezione	eleição
electric(al)	électrique	elektrisch	eléctrico, a	elettrico, a	eléctrico, a
electrician	électricien	Elektriker(in f)m	electricista	elettricista	electricista
electricity	électricité	Elektrizität(f)	electricidad	elettricità	electricidade
electronic	électronique	elektronisch	electrónico, a	elettronico, a	electrónico, a
electronics	électronique	Elektronik(f)	electrónica	elettronica	electrónica
elegance	élégance	Eleganz(f)	elegancia	eleganza	elegância
elegant, smart	élégant, e	elegant	elegante	elegante	elegante
element	élément	Element(n)	elemento	elemento	elemento
elephant	éléphant	Elefant(m)	elefante	elefante	elefante
elevate	élever	erhöhen	elevar, alzar	elevare	elevar
eleven	onze	elf	once	undici	onze
eliminate	éliminer	aus = scheiden	eliminar	eliminare	eliminar
elimination	élimination	Beseitigung(f)	eliminación	eliminazione	eliminação
élite	élite	Elite(f)	élite	elite	elite
ellipse	ellipse	Ellipse(f)	elipse	ellisse	elipse
elocution	élocution	Sprechweise(f)	elocución	eloquio	elocução
eloquence	éloquence	Redegewandtheit(f)	elocuencia	eloquenza	eloquência
else	autre(d')	ander; anders	otro, a	altro, a	outro, a
embargo(-es)	embargo	Embargo(n)	embargo	embargo	embargo
embarrassment	embarras	Verlegenheit(f)	apuro	imbarazzo	embaraço
embarrassment	gêne	Verlegenheit(f)	molestia	disagio, imbarazzo	embaraço
embassy	ambassade	Botschaft(f)	embajada	ambasciata	embaixada
embers	braise	Glut(f)	brasa	brace	brasa
emblem	emblème	Emblem(n)	emblema	emblema	emblema
embroider	broder	sticken	bordar	ricamare	bordar
embryo	embryon	Embryo(m)	embrión	embrione	embrião
emerald	émeraude	Smaragd(m)	esmeralda	smeraldo	esmeralda
emerge	émerger	auf = tauchen	emerger	emergere	emergir
emergency, urgency	urgence	Notfall(m)	urgencia	urgenza	urgência
emergency exit	sortie(secours)	Notausgang(m)	salida(emergencia)	uscita(sicurezza)	saída de emergência
emigrant	émigré, e	Emigrant(in f)m	emigrante	emigrato, a	emigrante
emigrate	émigrer	aus = wandern	emigrar	emigrare	emigrar
emigration	émigration	Auswanderung(f)	emigración	emigrazione	emigração
eminent	éminent, e	hervorragend	eminente	eminente	eminente
emissary	émissaire	Bote(m)	emisario	emissario	emissário
emit	émettre	aus = strahlen	emitir	emettere	emitir
emotion	émotion	Rührung(f)	emoción	emozione	emoção
emotional	émotif, ive	empfindsam	emotivo, a	emotivo, a	emotivo, a
emperor	empereur	Kaiser(m)	emperador	imperatore	imperador
emphasize	souligner	betonen	recalcar, subrayar	accentuare	acentuar

English	French	German	Spanish	Italian	Portuguese
empire	empire	Reich(n)	imperio	impero	império
employ	employer	an = stellen	emplear	impiegare	empregar
employ, take on	embaucher	ein = stellen	dar trabajo	assumere	empregar
employee	employé, e	Angestellte(f, m)	empleado, a	impiegato, a	empregado, a
employer	employeur	Arbeitgeber(in f)m	patrón	datore di lavoro	patrão
employment	emploi	Stelle(f)	empleo	impiego	emprego
empress	impératrice	Kaiserin(f)	emperatriz	imperatrice	imperatriz
empty	vide	leer	vacío, a	vuoto, a	vazio, a
empty	vider	leeren	vaciar	vuotare	esvaziar
emulsion	émulsion	Emulsion(f)	emulsión	emulsione	emulsão
enamel	émail	Emaille(f), Glasur(f)	esmalte	smalto	esmalte
enclosed	ci-joint, e	anbei	adjunto, a	allegato, a	anexo(em)
encourage, urge	encourager	ermutigen	alentar, animar	incoraggiare	encorajar
encyclopaedia	encyclopédie	Enzyklopädie(f)	enciclopedia	enciclopedia	enciclopédia
end	fin	Ende(n)	fin	fine	fim
end, tip	bout, extrémité	Ende(n)	cabo	capo, estremità	cabo
end	terme	Ende(n), Ziel(n)	término	termine	termo
end, finish	terminer, finir	beenden	terminar	terminare	terminar
endurance	endurance	Ausdauer(f)	resistencia	resistenza	resistência
endure, bear	endurer	aus = halten, ertragen	aguantar, pasar	patire, resistere	aguentar
enemy	ennemi, e	Feind(in f)m	enemigo, a	nemico, a	inimigo, a
energy	énergie	Energie(f)	energía	energia	energia
engage	engager	engagieren	empeñar	impegnare	empenhar
engage	enclencher	ein = legen, = schalten	engranar	ingranare, avviare	engrenar
engaged(get)	fiancer(se)	verloben, sich	prometerse	fidanzarsi	ficar noivo, a
engaged; taken	occupé, e	besetzt	ocupado, a	occupato, a	ocupado, a
engine; motor	moteur; réacteur	Motor(m)	motor	motore	motor
engineer	ingénieur	Ingenieur(in f)m	ingeniero, a	ingegnere	engenheiro, a
engineering	ingénierie	Ingenieurkunst(f)	ingeniería	ingegneria	engenharia
engraving	gravure	Gravieren(n)	grabado	incisione	gravura
enigma	énigme	Rätsel(n)	enigma	enigma	enigma
enjoy	aimer	mögen; gern mögen	gustar	piacere	gostar
enjoy	jouir	genießen	gozar	godere	gozar
enjoy your meal!	bon appétit!	Guten Appetit!	que aproveche(!)	buon appetito!	bom proveito!
enlarge	agrandir	vergrößern	ampliar	ingrandire	ampliar
enormous, huge	énorme	riesig	enorme	enorme	enorme
enough; rather	assez	genug	bastante(s)	abbastanza	bastante
enough!(that's)	assez!; suffit!	das langt, jetzt langt	basta(!)	basta così!	basta!, chega!
enrich	enrichir	bereichern	enriquecer	arricchire	enriquecer
ensure; insure	assurer(s')	versichern; zu = sichern	asegurarse	assicurarsi	assegurar-se
entail	entraîner	mit sich bringen	ocasionar	comportare	acarretar
enter, come/go in	entrer	ein = treten	entrar	entrare	entrar
enter, penetrate	pénétrer	ein = dringen	penetrar	penetrare	penetrar
entertain	distraire	unterhalten	entretener	distrarre	distrair
entertainment	distraction(s)	Zeitvertreib(m)	distracción	svago, distrazione	distracção, -ões
entertainment	spectacles	Unterhaltung(f)	espectáculos	spettacoli	espectáculos
enthusiasm	enthousiasme	Begeisterung(f)	entusiasmo	entusiasmo	entusiasmo
entice	attirer, séduire	verführen	atraer, seducir	attirare, sedurre	atrair, seduzir
entirely	entièrement	ganz	completamente	interamente	inteiramente
entrust	confier	an = vertrauen	confiar	affidare	confiar
entry, entrance	entrée	Eintritt(m), Eingang m	entrada	ingresso	entrada
enumerate	énumérer	auf = zählen	enumerar	enumerare	enumerar
envelope	enveloppe	Umschlag(m)(Brief-)	sobre	busta	envelope
envisage	envisager	beabsichtigen	enfocar	prevedere	encarar
ephemeral	éphémère	vergänglich	efímero, a	effimero, a	efémero, a
epic	épopée	Epos(n)	epopeya	epopea	epopeia
epidemic	épidémie	Seuche(f)	epidemia	epidemia	epidemia
epidermis, skin	épiderme	Oberhaut(f), Haut(f)	epidermis	epidermide	epiderme
epilepsy	épilepsie	Epilepsie(f)	epilepsia	epilessia	epilepsia
episode	épisode	Episode(f)	episodio	episodio	episódio
epoch, era, time	époque	Epoche(f), Ära(f), Zeit	época	epoca	época
equal	égal, e	gleich	igual	uguale	igual
equality	égalité	Gleichheit(f)	igualdad	uguaglianza	igualdade
equator	équateur	Äquator(m)	ecuador	equatore	equador
equatorial	équatorial, e	äquatorial	ecuatorial	equatoriale	equatorial
equestrian	équestre	Reiter-	ecuestre	equestre	equestre
equip, fit out	équiper	aus = rüsten	equipar	equipaggiare	equipar
equipment	équipement	Ausstattung(f)	equipo	equipaggiamento	equipamento

E

English	French	German	Spanish	Italian	Portuguese
equity	équité	Gerechtigkeit(f)	equidad	equità	equidade
equivalent	équivalent, e	gleichwertig	equivalente	equivalente	equivalente
equivocal	équivoque	zweideutig	equívoco, a	equivoco, a	equívoco, a
era	ère	Ära(f)	era	era	era
erase, rub out	effacer	radieren	borrar	cancellare	apagar
erect	ériger	errichten	erigir, levantar	erigere	erigir
erect, put up	dresser	auf = richten, errichten	erigir	drizzare	erigir, erguer
erosion	érosion	Abtragung(f)	erosión	erosione	erosão
erotic	érotique	erotisch	erótico, a	erotico, a	erótico, a
eroticism	érotisme	Erotik(f)	erotismo	erotismo	erotismo
error, mistake	erreur	Irrtum(m), Fehler(m)	error	errore	erro
erudite, learned	érudit, e	gelehrt	erudito, a	erudito, a	erudito, a
eruption	éruption	Ausbruch(m)	erupción	eruzione	erupção
escape	évasion	Flucht(f)	evasión	evasione	evasão
escape	échapper(s')	fliehen	escapar(se)	scappare	escapar-se
escort	escorte	Gefolge(n)	escolta	scorta	escolta
Eskimo	esquimau	Eskimo(m)	esquimal	eschimese	esquimó
especially	particulièrement	besonders	especialmente	particolarmente	especialmente
essential	essentiel, le	wesentlich	esencial	essenziale	essencial
establish	établir	festsetzen, aufstellen	establecer	stabilire	estabelecer
establish, set up	implanter	etablieren, gründen	implantar	impiantare	implantar
establishment	établissement	Anstalt(f)	establecimiento	stabilimento	estabelecimento
esteem	estime	Achtung(f)	estima	stima	estima
estimate	estimation	Schätzung(f)	estimación	stima, valutazione	estimativa
estimate	devis	Kostenvoranschlag(m)	presupuesto	preventivo	orçamento
estimate, value	estimer	schätzen	valorar, estimar	stimare, valutare	estimar
eternal	éternel, le	ewig	eterno, a	eterno, a	eterno, a
eternity	éternité	Ewigkeit(f)	eternidad	eternità	eternidade
ethical	éthique	ethisch	ético, a	etico, a	ético, a
ethnic(al)	ethnique	ethnisch	étnico, a	etnico, a	étnico, a
euphoric	euphorique	euphorisch	eufórico, a	euforico, a	eufórico, a
euthanasia	euthanasie	Euthanasie(f)	eutanasia	eutanasia	eutanásia
evacuate	évacuer	räumen, leeren	evacuar	evacuare	evacuar
evaporation	évaporation	Verdunstung(f)	evaporación	evaporazione	evaporação
even	même	sogar; selbst	aun; incluso	anche; perfino	mesmo(que)
even(not)	même pas	einmal(nicht)	siquiera(ni)	neanche	sequer(nem)
even	pair	gerade	par	pari	par
evening	soir	Abend(m)	tarde, noche	sera	tarde, noite
evening dress	robe de soirée	Abendkleid(n)	traje de noche	abito da sera	vestido de noite
event	événement	Ereignis(n)	acontecimiento	avvenimento	acontecimento
every, each	chaque	jede(r, s)	cada	ogni	cada
everywhere	partout	überall	por todas partes	dappertutto	por toda a parte
evidence, proof	preuve	Beweis(m)	evidencia, prueba	testimonianza, prova	evidência, prova
evident	évident, e	offenbar	evidente	evidente	evidente
evil	mal	Böse(n)	mal	male	mal
evil, bad	mauvais, mal	übel	malo, a	cattivo, a; male	mau, má
evoke	évoquer	wach = rufen, erinnern	evocar	evocare	evocar
evolution	évolution	Entwicklung(f)	evolución	evoluzione	evolução
evolve	évoluer	entwickeln, sich	evolucionar	evolvere	evoluir
exact, right	exact, e	genau, richtig	exacto, a	esatto, a	exacto, a
exactly	exactement	genau, richtig; gerade	exactamente	esattamente	exactamente
exactly	justement	genau	justamente	appunto	justamente
exaggerate	exagérer	übertreiben	exagerar	esagerare	exagerar
examination, exam	examen	Prüfung(f)	examen	esame	exame
examination	examen(médical)	Untersuchung(f)	examen, chequeo	esame	exame
examination	contrôle	Kontrolle(f)	control	controllo	controlo
examine, inspect	examiner	untersuchen	examinar	esaminare	examinar
examine	ausculter	ab = horchen	auscultar	auscultare	auscultar
example	exemple	Beispiel(n)	ejemplo	esempio	exemplo
excavate	fouiller	aus = graben	excavar	scavare	escavar
exceed	dépasser	überschreiten	adelantar	superare	ultrapassar
Excellency(Your)	Excellence, Votre	Exzellenz(f)	Excelencia(Su)	Eccellenza(Sua)	Excelência(Vossa)
excellent	excellent, e	vorzüglich	excelente	eccellente	excelente
excellent	fameux, se	großartig	famoso, a	ottimo, a	famoso, a
except	sauf	außer	excepto	salvo	salvo, excepto
except	excepté	außer	excepto, salvo	tranne	excepto
exception	exception	Ausnahme(f)	excepción	eccezione	excepção
exceptional	exceptionnel, le	außergewöhnlich	excepcional	eccezionale	excepcional

| --- | --- | --- | --- | --- | --- |
excess	excès	Übermaß(n)	exceso	eccesso	excesso
excessive	excessif, ive	übermäßig	excesivo, a	eccessivo, a	excessivo, a
exchange	échange	Tausch(Aus-, Um-)(m)	cambio	scambio	troca; câmbio
exchange	change	Wechsel(m)(Geld-)	cambio	cambio	câmbio
exchange	échanger	tauschen	intercambiar	scambiare	trocar
excite	exciter	auf = regen	excitar	eccitare	excitar
exciting	excitant, e	aufregend	excitante	eccitante	excitante
exclaim	exclamer(s')	aus = rufen	exclamar	esclamare	exclamar
exclude	exclure	aus = schließen	excluir	escludere	excluir
exclusive	exclusif, ive	ausschließlich	exclusivo, a	esclusivo, a	exclusivo, a
exclusive rights	exclusivité	Alleinvertrieb(m)	exclusiva(-ividad)	esclusività	exclusividade
excrement	excrément	Ausscheidung(f)	excremento	escremento	excremento
exculpate	disculper	entschuldigen, sich	disculpar	discolpare	desculpar
excursion	excursion	Ausflug(m)	excursión	gita, escursione	excursão
excuse; apology	excuse	Entschuldigung(f)	excusa, disculpa	scusa	desculpa
excuse me!; sorry!	excusez-moi!	Entschuldigung!	perdone(!)	scusi!	desculpe!; perdão!
execution	exécution	Hinrichtung(f)	ejecución	esecuzione	execução
executive	cadre	leitende Angestellte	ejecutivo	dirigente	quadro
executive	exécutif, ive	ausübend, vollziehend	ejecutivo, a	esecutivo, a	executivo, a
exercise	exercice	Übung(f)	ejercicio	esercizio	exercício
exercise, practise	exercer	aus = üben	ejercitar	esercitare	exercitar
exercise book	cahier	Heft(n)	cuaderno	quaderno	caderno
exhaust; stupefy	abrutir	ab = stumpfen	embrutecer	abbrutire	embrutecer
exhausted	épuisé, e	erschöpft	agotado, a	esausto, a	esgotado, a
exhausted	exténué, e	erschöpft	extenuado, a	spossato, a	extenuado, a
exhausted, run out	épuisé, e	ausverkauft	agotado, a	esaurito, a	esgotado, a
exhibition	exhibition	Schau, Ausstellung(f)	exhibición	esibizione	exibição
exhibition, show	exposition	Ausstellung(f)	exposición	esposizione, mostra	exposição
exhibitor	exposant, e	Aussteller(in f)m	expositor, a	espositore, trice	expositor, a
exile	exil	Verbannung(f)	exilio	esilio	exílio
exile	exilé, e	Verbannte(f, m)	exiliado, a	esiliato, a	exilado, a
exist	exister	existieren	existir	esistere	existir
existence, life	existence	Dasein(n)	existencia	esistenza	existência
exit, way out	sortie	Ausgang(m)	salida	uscita	saída
exodus	exode	Massenauswanderung(f)	éxodo	esodo	êxodo
exotic	exotique	exotisch	exótico, a	esotico, a	exótico, a
expand	étendre, agrandir	aus = dehnen	extender(se)	estendere	estender
expansion	expansion	Ausdehnung(f)	expansión	espansione	expansão
expansion, boom	essor	Aufschwung(m)	auge, desarrollo	sviluppo	progresso
expansion	dilatation	Ausdehnung(f)	dilatación	dilatazione	dilatação
expatriate	expatrier(s')	aus = wandern	expatriarse	espatriare	expatriar-se
expatriation	expatriation	Vertreibung(f)	expatriación	espatrio	expatriação
expect	attendre à(s')	rechnen, mit etwas	esperar(se)	aspettarsi	esperar
expect	attendre	erwarten	esperar	aspettare	esperar
expedition	expédition	Expedition(f)	expedición	spedizione	expedição
expel, eject	expulser	aus = weisen	expulsar	espellere	expulsar
expenditure	dépense	Ausgabe(f)	gasto	spesa	despesa, gasto
expenses	frais	Kosten(pl.)	gastos	spese(le)	gastos, despesas
expensive, dear	cher, ère	teuer	caro, a	caro, a	caro, a
experience	expérience	Erfahrung(f)	experiencia	esperienza	experiência
experiment	expérience	Versuch(m)	experimento	esperimento	experiência
experimental	expérimental, e	experimentell	experimental	sperimentale	experimental
experimentation	expérimentation	Experimentieren(n)	experimentación	sperimentazione	experimentação
expert	expert, e	Experte(m), Expertin f	experto, a; perito, a	esperto, a	perito, a
expert, specialist	spécialiste	Fachmann(m)	especialista	specialista	especialista
expiration	échéance	Fälligkeitstermin(m)	vencimiento	scadenza	vencimento
expire	expirer	ab = laufen	expirar; vencer	scadere	expirar
expired	périmé, e	verfallen	caducado, a	scaduto, a	caducado, a
explain	expliquer	erklären	explicar	spiegare	explicar
explanation	explication	Erklärung(f)	explicación	spiegazione	explicação
explode, blow up	exploser	explodieren	estallar	esplodere	explodir
exploit	exploit	Glanzleistung(f)	hazaña	impresa, prodezza	proeza, feito
exploit	exploiter	aus = nutzen	explotar	sfruttare	explorar
exploration	exploration	Erforschung(f)	exploración	esplorazione	exploração
explore	explorer	erforschen	explorar	esplorare	explorar
explorer	explorateur	Forscher(in f)m	explorador, a	esploratore, trice	explorador, a
explosion	explosion	Explosion(f)	explosión	esplosione	explosão
explosion	déflagration	Knall(m), Explosion(f)	deflagración	deflagrazione	deflagração

E

English	French	German	Spanish	Italian	Portuguese
export	exporter	exportieren	exportar	esportare	exportar
export(ing)	exportation	Export(m), Ausfuhr(f)	exportación	esportazione	exportação
expression	expression	Ausdruck(m)	expresión	espressione	expressão
express oneself	exprimer(s')	aus = drücken, sich	expresar(se)	esprimersi	exprimir-se
extend	prolonger	verlängern	prolongar	prolungare	prolongar
extend, spread	étendre	aus = breiten	extender	stendere	estender
extension	extension	Ausdehnung(f)	extensión	estensione	extensão
extension	prolongement	Verlängerung(f)	prolongamiento	prolungamento	prolongamento
extent	étendue	Umfang(m)	extensión, amplitud	estensione, ampiezza	extensão
external	externe	äußerlich	externo, a	esterno, a	externo, a
extinction	extinction	Löschen(Aus-)(n)	extinción	estinzione	extinção
extinguish	éteindre	löschen	apagar	spegnere	apagar
extinguisher	extincteur	Feuerlöscher(m)	extintor	estintore	extintor
extra-, additional-	supplément(en)	Extra-; Neben-	más(de)	più(in)	mais(a)
extract	extraire	heraus = ziehen, ziehen	extraer	estrarre	extrair
extract	extrait	Auszug(m)	pasaje, trozo	brano, estratto	excerto, trecho
extraction	extraction	Kohlenförderung(f)	extracción	estrazione	extracção
extraction	extraction	Zahnziehen(n)	extracción	estrazione	extracção
extraordinary	extraordinaire	außergewöhnlich	extraordinario, a	straordinario, a	extraordinário, a
extreme	extrême	extrem	extremo, a	estremo, a	extremo, a
extremity, end	extrémité	Extremität(f)	extremidad	estremità	extremidade
eye	oeil	Auge(n)	ojo	occhio	olho
eyebrow	sourcil	Augenbraue(f)	ceja	sopracciglio(a)	sobrolho
eyelash	cil	Wimper(f)	pestaña	ciglio(a)	pestana
eyelid	paupière	Lid(n)	párpado	palpebra	pálpebra
eyes	yeux	Augen(n, pl)	ojos	occhi	olhos

F

English	French	German	Spanish	Italian	Portuguese
fabulous	fabuleux, se	phantastisch	fabuloso, a	favoloso, a	fabuloso, a
face	face	Gesicht(n)	cara	faccia	face; cara
face	figure	Gesicht(n)	rostro	faccia	rosto
face	visage	Gesicht(n)	rostro, cara	viso	cara
fact	fait	Tatsache(f)	hecho	fatto	facto
factor	facteur	Faktor(m)	factor	fattore	factor
factory, plant	usine	Fabrik(f)	fábrica	fabbrica	fábrica
Faculty	faculté	Fakultät(f)	facultad	facoltà	faculdade
fail	échouer	scheitern	fracasar	fallire	falhar
fail	rater	mißlingen	fallar	mancare	falhar
fail	échouer(examen)	durch = fallen	suspender	bocciare	ficar mal(exame)
failure	échec	Mißerfolg(m)	fracaso, revés	smacco, sconfitta	fracasso
failure, fault	défaillance	Versagen(n)	fallo	difetto	falha
failure; bankruptcy	faillite	Konkurs(m)	quiebra, ruina	fallimento	falência
faint	évanouir(s')	ohnmächtig werden	desmayarse	svenire	desmaiar
faintness	malaise	Unwohlsein, Schwäche	malestar	malessere	indisposição
fair, blond	blond, e	blond	rubio(pelo)	biondo, a	louro, a
fair	foire	Messe(f)	feria	fiera	feira
fairy	fée	Fee(f)	hada	fata	fada
faith	foi	Glaube(m)	fe	fede	fé
faithful	fidèle	treu	fiel	fedele	fiel
faking	truquage	Trickaufnahme(f)	falsificación	trucco	falsificação
fall	chute	Fall(m)	caída	caduta	queda
fall, drop	baisse	Senkung(f)	baja	calo	baixa
fall	tomber	fallen	caer	cadere	cair
fall, drop	descendre	fallen	bajar	abbassare	baixar
fallen, deposed	déchu, e	abgesetzt, verfallen	decaído, a	destituito, a	decaído, a
falsify	falsifier	fälschen	falsificar	falsificare	falsificar

English	French	German	Spanish	Italian	Portuguese
fame	renommée	Ruhm(m)	fama	fama	fama
familiar	familier, ière	familiär	familiar	familiare	familiar
family	famille	Familie(f)	familia	famiglia	família
family	familial, e	Familien-	familiar	familiare	familiar
famine	famine	Hungersnot(f)	hambre	fame, carestia	fome
famous, well-known	célèbre	berühmt	célebre, famoso, a	celebre; famoso, a	célebre
fan	éventail	Fächer(m)	abanico	ventaglio	leque
fan, ventilator	ventilateur	Ventilator(m)	ventilador	ventilatore	ventilador
fanatic(al)	fanatique	fanatisch	fanático, a	fanatico, a	fanático, a
fancy; fantasy	fantaisie	Spielerei(f)	fantasía	fantasia	fantasia
fantastic	fantastique	phantastisch	fantástico, a	fantastico, a	fantástico, a
fantasy	fantasme	Phantasievorstellung	fantasma	fantasia	fantasma
far(away), distant	loin	weit, fern	lejos	lontano, a	longe
fare	tarif	Tarif(m)	tarifa	tariffa	tarifa
farm	ferme	Bauernhof(m)	granja	fattoria	quinta
farmer	fermier, ière	Bauer(m), Bäuerin(f)	granjero, a	contadino, a	caseiro, a
farmer	cultivateur	Landwirt(in f)m	cultivador, a	coltivatore, trice	lavrador, a
farmer	agriculteur	Landwirt(in f)m	agricultor, a	agricoltore	agricultor, a
farmer	paysan, ne	Bauer(m), Bäuerin(f)	campesino, a	contadino, a	camponês, a
fascinated	fasciné, e	fasziniert	fascinado, a	affascinato, a	fascinado, a
fascinating	fascinant, e	faszinierend	fascinante	affascinante	fascinante
fascinating	passionnant, e	spannend	apasionante	appassionante	apaixonante
fascist	fasciste	Faschist(in f)m	fascista	fascista	fascista
fashion	mode	Mode(f)	moda	moda	moda
fast, quickly	vite	rasch	pronto; rápido, a	presto	depressa; rápido, a
fasten	attacher	befestigen	atar, fijar	attaccare, legare	atar, amarrar
fat	gros, se	dick	grueso, a; gordo, a	grosso, a	gordo, a
fat(ty), greasy	gras, se	fett	graso, a	grasso, a	gordo, a
fat	graisse	Fett(n)	gordo; grasa	grasso	gordura
fat, cellulitis	cellulite	Zellulitis(f)	celulitis	cellulite	celulite
fatal	fatal, e	tödlich	fatal	fatale	fatal
fatal	mortel, le	tödlich	mortal	mortale	mortal
fatality, fate	fatalité	Schicksal(n)	fatalidad	fatalità	fatalidade
fate, destiny	destin	Schicksal(n)	destino, sino	destino	destino
fate	sort	Schicksal(n)	suerte, destino	sorte, destino	sorte, destino
father	père	Vater(m)	padre	padre	pai
father-in-law	beau-père	Schwiegervater(m)	suegro	suocero	sogro
fatty, greasy	graisseux, se	schmierig, fettig	grasiento, a	unto, a	gorduroso, a
fault	faute	Fehler(m)	culpa	colpa	culpa
fauna	faune	Fauna(f), Tierwelt(f)	fauna	fauna	fauna
favour	faveur	Gunst(f)	favor	favore	favor
favour	favoriser	begünstigen	favorecer	favorire	favorecer
favourable	favorable	günstig	favorable	favorevole	favorável
favourable	propice	günstig	propicio, a	propizio, a	propício, a
favourite	favori, ite	Favorit(in f)m	favorito, a	favorito, a	favorito, a
favourite	préféré, e	Lieblings-	preferido, a	preferito, a	preferido, a
fear	crainte	Furcht(f)	temor, miedo	timore	temor, receio
fear	peur	Angst(f)	miedo	paura	medo
fear, be afraid of	craindre	befürchten, fürchten	temer, tener miedo	temere	temer
feast, banquet	festin	Festmahl(n)	festín	festino	festim, banquete
feather	plume	Feder(f)	pluma	penna, piuma	pluma; pena
feature	caractéristique	Merkmal(n)	característica	caratteristica	característica
feature	trait(s)	Zug(m)(Gesichts-)	rasgos	tratto, lineamento	feição
February	Février	Februar(m)	Febrero	Febbraio	Fevereiro
federation	fédération	Verband(m)	federación	federazione	federação
fee	honoraires	Honorar(n)	honorarios	onorario	honorários
fee	cachet	Honorar(n); Gage(f)	remuneración	cachet, compenso	remuneração
fee	frais(scolarité)	Kosten(pl.)	gastos(escolares)	spese	despesas
feed, nourish	nourrir	ernähren	alimentar	nutrire	alimentar
feed	allaiter	stillen	pecho(dar el)	allattare	aleitar
feeding; food	alimentation	Ernährung(f)	alimentación	alimentazione	alimentação
feel, touch	tâter	berühren	tantear	tastare	tatear, apalpar
feel, finger	palper, tâter	betasten	palpar	palpare	apalpar
feel	sentir	fühlen	sentir	sentire	sentir
feel	ressentir	empfinden	sentir	sentire	sentir
feel	éprouver	spüren, fühlen	sentir	provare	sentir
feeling	sentiment	Gefühl(n)	sentimiento	sentimento	sentimento
felt-tip pen	crayon-feutre	Filzschreiber(m)	rotulador	pennarello	marcador

E

English	French	German	Spanish	Italian	Portuguese
female	femelle	Weibchen(n)	hembra	femmina	fêmea
feminine	féminin, e	fraulich	femenino, a	femminile	feminino, a
feminine	féminin	weiblich	femenino	femminile	feminino
fence, railings	clôture	Zaun(m)	valla, cerca	recinzione, muro	cerca, vedação
fence; enclosure	enceinte	Einzäunung(f)	muralla	cinta, recinto	muralha, recinto
fence	barrière	Zaun(m); Schranke(f)	barrera, valla	barriera	barreira
fencing	escrime	Fechten(n)	esgrima	scherma	esgrima
ferment	fermenter	gären	fermentar	fermentare	fermentar
fern	fougère	Farn(-kraut n)m	helecho	felce	feto
ferocious, fierce	féroce	wild, furchtbar	feroz	feroce	feroz
ferry	bac	Fähre(f)	transbordador	traghetto, ferry	barco
fertile	fertile	fruchtbar	fértil	fertile	fértil
fertility	fécondité	Fruchtbarkeit(f)	fecundidad	fecondità	fecundidade
fertilization	fécondation	Befruchtung(f)	fecundación	fecondazione	fecundação
fertilizer, manure	engrais	Dünger(m)	abono	concime	adubo
festival	festival	Festspiel(n)	festival	festival	festival
fever, temperature	fièvre	Fieber(n)	fiebre	febbre	febre
few(a), some	quelques	einige	algunos, as	alcuni, e	alguns, algumas
fiancé(e)	fiancé, e	Verlobte(f, m)	novio, a	fidanzato, a	noivo, a
fibre	fibre	Faser(f)	fibra	fibra	fibra
fiction	fiction	Fiktion(f)	ficción	finzione	ficção
field	champ	Feld(n)	campo	campo	campo
field, scope	domaine	Bereich(m)	campo, área	campo, settore	domínio
field; court	terrain(sport)	Sportplatz(m)	campo	terreno	campo
fifteen	quinze	fünfzehn	quince	quindici	quinze
fifty	cinquante	fünfzig	cincuenta	cinquanta	cinquenta
fight	bagarre	Schlägerei(f)	riña	rissa, zuffa	briga
fight	battre(se)	kämpfen	pelearse	battersi, lottare	lutar
fight	combattre	streiten, kämpfen	combatir	combattere	combater
fight, struggle	lutter	kämpfen	luchar	lottare	lutar
fighting-man	combattant, e	Kämpfer(m)	combatiente	combattente	combatente
figure	figure	Figur(f)	figura	figura	figura
figure, number	chiffre	Zahl(f), Ziffer(f)	cifra, número	cifra, numero	número
filament	filament	Faser(f), Faden(m)	filamento	filamento	filamento
file	lime	Feile(f)	lima	lima	lima
file	classeur	Ordner(m)	clasificador	schedario	classificador
filing	classement	Einorden(n)	clasificación	classificazione	classificação
fill	remplir	füllen	llenar	riempire	encher
film, movie	film	Film(m)	película	film	filme
film	pellicule	Film(m)	película	pellicola	película
film	filmer	filmen	rodar, filmar	filmare	filmar
film-producer	cinéaste	Filmproduzent(in f)m	cineasta	cineasta	cineasta
filter	filtre	Filter(m)	filtro	filtro	filtro
filth, dirt	crasse	Dreck(m)	roña, mugre	sporcizia	sujidade
fin	nageoire	Flosse(f)	aleta	pinna	barbatana
final	final, e	letzte, Schluß-	final	finale	final
finance	finance	Finanzwelt, Finanzen	finanza	finanza	finança
finance	financer	finanzieren	financiar	finanziare	financiar
financial	financier, ière	finanziell	financiero, a	finanziario, a	financeiro, a
financing	financement	Finanzierung(f)	financiación	finanziamento	financiamento
find	trouver	finden	encontrar	trovare	achar, encontrar
fine, thin	fin, e	fein, dünn	fino, a	fine, sottile	fino, a
fine	amende	Geldstrafe(f)	multa	multa	multa
fine arts	beaux-arts	Kunst(f)	bellas artes	belle arti	belas-artes
fine weather	beau temps	schönes Wetter	buen tiempo	bel tempo	bom tempo
finery, jewellery	parure	Schmuck(m)	adorno	parure	adorno
finger	doigt	Finger(m)	dedo	dito	dedo
finish, end	finir, terminer	beenden	acabar, terminar	finire	acabar, terminar
fire	feu	Feuer(n)	fuego	fuoco	fogo
fire	incendie	Brand(m)	incendio	incendio	incêndio
fire, shoot	tirer	feuern, schießen	tirar	sparare, tirare	disparar, atirar
fireman(-men)	pompier(sapeur-)	Feuerwehrmann(m)	bombero	pompiere	bombeiro
fire-place, hearth	foyer, âtre	Feuerstelle(f), Herd m	hogar, chimenea	focolare	lareira
fire-proof	ininflammable	unbrennbar	ininflamable	ininfiammabile	prova de fogo(à)
firm	firme	Firma(f)	firma	firma, ditta, azienda	firma
firm	ferme	fest	firme	fermo, a; solido, a	firme
firmness	fermeté	Entschlossenheit(f)	firmeza	fermezza	firmeza
first	premier, ière	erste(r, s)	primero, a; primer	primo, a	primeiro, a

English	French	German	Spanish	Italian	Portuguese
first(at)	abord(d')	zunächst	primero	anzitutto	primeiro
first name	prénom	Vorname(m)	nombre	nome	nome próprio
fir-tree	sapin	Tanne(f)	abeto	abete	abeto
fiscal, tax	fiscal, e	fiskalisch, Steuer-	fiscal	fiscale	fiscal
fish	poisson	Fisch(m)	pescado	pesce	peixe
fish-bone, bone	arête	Gräte(f)	espina	lisca	espinha
fisherman(-men)	pêcheur	Fischer(m)	pescador	pescatore	pescador
fishing, angling	pêche	Fischen n; Fischfang m	pesca	pesca	pesca
fishing net	épuisette	Fangnetz(n)	manguilla	guadino, retino	rede
fishing rod	canne à pêche	Angelrute(f)	caña de pescar	canna da pesca	cana de pesca
fishmonger's	poissonnerie	Fischgeschäft(n)	pescadería	pescheria	peixaria
fission	fission	Spaltung(f)(Atom)	fisión	fissione	fissão
fist	poing	Faust(f)	puño	pugno	punho
fit	aller bien	passen	convenir, sentar	andar bene	ficar bem
fit	ajuster, monter	montieren	ajustar, adaptar	adattarsi	ajustar, adaptar
fit out; convert	aménager	ein = richten	acondicionar	sistemare	arranjar, dispor
five	cinq	fünf	cinco	cinque	cinco
fix, attach	fixer	befestigen	fijar	fissare	fixar
fixed	fixe	fest	fijo, a	fisso, a	fixo, a
fixing, fixation	fixation	Befestigung(f)	fijación	fissazione	fixação
fizzy, sparkling	gazeux, se	sprudelnd; Sprudel-	gaseoso, a	gassato, a	gasoso, a
flag	drapeau	Fahne(f)	bandera	bandiera	bandeira
flag	drapeau	Flagge(f)	bandera	bandiera	bandeira
flake	flocon	Flocke(f)	copo	fiocco	floco
flame	flamme	Flamme(f)	llama	fiamma	chama
flannel	gant	Waschlappen(m)	manopla	guanto	luva
flash	flash, éclair	Blitz(m)	flash	flash	flash
flash	clignoter	blinken	pestañear	lampeggiare	piscar
flat	plat, e	platt	llano, a	piatto, a	plano, a
flat, apartment	appartement	Wohnung(f)	piso	appartamento	apartamento
flatten	aplatir	glätten, ab = flachen	allanar, aplastar	appiattire	achatar, alisar
flatter	flatter	schmeicheln	halagar	adulare	lisonjear
flavour	saveur	Geschmack(m)	sabor	sapore	sabor
flea	puce	Floh(m)	pulga	pulce	pulga
fleet	flotte	Flotte(f)	flota	flotta	frota
flesh	chair	Fleisch(n)	carne	carne	carne
flexible	flexible	flexibel	flexible	flessibile	flexível
flicker	vaciller	flackern	oscilar, vacilar	vacillare	tremer
flight, escape	fuite	Flucht(f)	huída	fuga	fuga
flight	vol	Flug(m)	vuelo	volo	voo
flight over	survol	Überfliegen(n)	sobrevuelo	sorvolo	sobrevôo
flipper	palme	Flosse(f)	aleta	pinna	barbatanas
float	flotter	schwimmen, treiben	flotar	galleggiare	flutuar
flock	troupeau	Herde(f)	rebaño	gregge	rebanho
flood; downpour	déluge	Überschwemmung(f)	diluvio	diluvio	dilúvio
flooding, flood	inondation	Überschwemmung(f)	inundación	inondazione	inundação
floor	plancher, sol	Fußboden(m)	suelo	pavimento	soalho, sobrado
floor, storey	étage	Etage(f)	piso, planta	piano	andar
flora	flore	Flora(f), Pflanzenwelt	flora	flora	flora
florist	fleuriste	Blumenhändler(in f)m	florista	fioraio	florista
flour	farine	Mehl(n)	harina	farina	farinha
flourishing	prospère	erfolgreich, blühend	próspero, a	prospero, a	próspero, a
flow	flux	Fluß(m), Strömung(f)	flujo	flusso	fluxo
flow, outflow	écoulement	Abfluß(m)	derrame, flujo	deflusso, scolo	escoamento
flow, run	couler	fließen	correr, fluir	scorrere	correr
flower	fleur	Blume(f)	flor	fiore	flor
flower-bed	parterre	Beet(n)	arriate	aiuola	canteiro
flu, influenza	grippe	Grippe(f)	gripe	influenza	gripe
fluctuation	fluctuation	Schwanken(n)	fluctuación	fluttuazione	flutuação
fluently	couramment	fließend	soltura(con)	correntemente	fluentemente
fluid	fluide	Flüssigkeit(f)	fluido	fluido	fluido
flute	flûte	Flöte(f)	flauta	flauto	flauta
fly	mouche	Fliege(f)	mosca	mosca	mosca
fly	voler	fliegen	volar	volare	voar
foal	poulain	Fohlen(n)	potro	puledro	potro
foam, froth	écume	Schaum(m), Gischt(f)	espuma	schiuma	espuma
fodder	fourrage	Futter(n)	forraje	foraggio	forragem
foetus	foetus	Fötus(m)	feto	feto	feto

E

English	French	German	Spanish	Italian	Portuguese
fog	brouillard	Nebel(m)	niebla	nebbia	nevoeiro
fold	plier	falten	doblar	piegare	dobrar
fold; pleat	pli	Falte(f); Kniff(m)	pliegue	piega	prega
fold-away	escamotable	zusammenklappbar	plegable	ribaltabile	escamoteável
folding seat	strapontin	Klappstuhl(m)	traspuntín	strapuntino	banco dobrável
folklore	folklore	Folklore(f)	folklore	folclore	folclore
follow	suivre	folgen	seguir	seguire	seguir
follower	adepte	Anhänger(in f)m	adepto, a; seguidor	seguace, adepto, a	adepto, a; seguidor, a
following, next	suivant, e	nächste	siguiente	seguente	seguinte
following	suite(à la)	hinter, nach	después de	seguito a(in)	seguir a(a)
food	nourriture	Nahrung(f)	alimento	cibo; nutrimento	alimentação
food	aliment	Lebensmittel(n, pl)	alimento	alimento, cibo	alimento
food shop	alimentation	Lebensmittelladen(m)	alimentación	alimentari(negozio)	mercearia
foodstuff	denrée	Eßware(f)	comestibles	derrata	género; víveres
fool, idiot	imbécile	Idiot(in f)m	imbécil	imbecille	imbecil; parvo, a
foot(feet pl.)	pied	Fuß(m)	pie	piede	pé
football, soccer	football	Fußball(m)	fútbol	calcio	futebol
footpath, path	sentier	Weg(m)	sendero, senda	sentiero	vereda, atalho
for	pour	für	para; por	per	para; por
for	pour	für	por	per	por
for; during	pendant	während	durante	durante	durante
forbid	défendre	verbieten	prohibir	proibire	proibir
forbid, ban	interdire	verbieten	prohibir	vietare, proibire	proibir
forbidden	interdit, e	verboten	prohibido, a	proibito, a	proibido, a
force	force	Gewalt(f); Kraft(f)	fuerza	forza	força
force	forcer	zwingen	forzar	forzare	forçar
force, compel	contraindre	zwingen	obligar a	costringere	obrigar
force(in), current	vigueur(en)	Kraft(in), geltend	vigente	vigore(in), vigente	vigente
fore-arm	avant-bras	Unterarm(m)	antebrazo	avambraccio	antebraço
forecast	prévision	Vorhersage(f)	previsión	previsione	previsão
forecast	pronostic	Vorhersage(f)	pronóstico	pronostico	prognóstico
forehead	front	Stirn(f)	frente	fronte	testa
foreign	étranger, ère	ausländisch	extranjero, a	estero, a	estrangeiro, a
foreign	extérieur, e	Außen-	exterior	estero, a	exterior
foreign country	étranger(l')	Ausland(n)	extranjero	estero	estrangeiro
foreigner	étranger, ère	Ausländer(in f)m	extranjero, a	straniero, a	estrangeiro, a
foresee; plan	prévoir	vorher = sehen; planen	prever	prevedere	prever
forest	forêt	Wald(m)	bosque	foresta, bosco	floresta, bosque
forever	toujours(pour)	immer(für)	siempre(para, por)	sempre(per)	sempre(para)
forget	oublier	vergessen	olvidar	dimenticare	esquecer
forgive, pardon	pardonner	verzeihen, vergeben	perdonar	perdonare	perdoar
forgiveness	pardon	Vergebung(f)	perdón	scusa, perdono	perdão
fork	fourchette	Gabel(f)	tenedor	forchetta	garfo
form	forme	Verfassung(f)	forma(en)	forma	forma
form	formulaire	Formular(n), Vordruck	formulario	modulo, formulario	formulário
form, slip, voucher	bon	Bestellschein(m)	orden, pedido	bolla, buono, bolletta	nota
form	former	bilden, formen	formar	formare	formar
formality	formalité	Formalität(f)	formalidad	formalità	formalidade
format, size	format	Format(n)	formato, tamaño	formato	formato
formation	formation	Entstehung(f)	formación	formazione	formação
former	ancien, ne	ehemalig	ex, antiguo, a	ex	antigo, a
formidable	redoutable	furchbar	temible	temibile	temível
formula	formule	Formel(f)	fórmula	formula	fórmula
fortunate(be)	chance(avoir)	Glück haben	suerte(tener)	fortuna(avere)	sorte(ter)
fortunately	heureusement	glücklicherweise	afortunadamente	fortunatamente	felizmente
fortune	fortune	Vermögen(n)	fortuna	fortuna	fortuna
forty	quarante	vierzig	cuarenta	quaranta	quarenta
forward(s)	avant	vorwärts	adelante(hacia)	davanti	frente(para a)
fossil	fossile	Fossil(n)	fósil	fossile	fóssil
foul, vile	infect, e	ekelhaft, stinkig	asqueroso, a	fetido, a	asqueroso, a
found	fonder	gründen	fundar	fondare	fundar
founder	fondateur, trice	Gründer(in f)m	fundador, a	fondatore, trice	fundador, a
fountain	fontaine	Springbrunnen(m)	fuente	fontana	fonte
four	quatre	vier	cuatro	quattro	quatro
four-star petrol	essence super	Superbenzin(n)	supercarburante	benzina super	super
fourteen	quatorze	vierzehn	catorce	quattordici	catorze
fox(-es)	renard	Fuchs(m)	zorro	volpe	raposa
foyer, hall	hall	Eingangshalle(f)	vestíbulo	hall, ingresso	vestíbulo

English	French	German	Spanish	Italian	Portuguese
fraction	fraction	Bruchteil(m)	fracción	frazione	fracção
fracture	fracture	Bruch(m)	fractura	frattura	fractura
fragile	fragile	zerbrechlich	frágil	fragile	frágil
fragment	fragment	Fragment(n)	fragmento	frammento	fragmento
frame	cadre	Rahmen(m)	marco	cornice, quadro	moldura
frame, chassis	châssis	Rahmen(m), Chassis(n)	chasis	telaio	chassis
framework	charpente	Holzgerüst(n)	armazón	ossatura, travatura	madeiramento
frank	franc, che	offen, ehrlich	franco, a	franco, a; sincero, a	franco, a
fraud	fraude	Betrug(m)	fraude	frode	fraude
free	libre	frei	libre	libero, a	livre
free	gratuit, e	kostenlos	gratis; gratuito, a	gratuito, a; gratis	grátis; gratuito, a
free	délivrer	befreien	libertar	rilasciare, liberare	libertar
freeze	blocage	Preisstopp(m)	congelación	blocco	congelamento
freeze	geler	frieren	helar	gelare	gelar
freezer	congélateur	Kühltruhe(f)	congelador	congelatore	congelador
freight	fret	Fracht(f)	flete	nolo, carico	frete
frequency	fréquence	Frequenz(f)	frecuencia	frequenza	frequência
frequent	fréquent, e	häufig	frecuente	frequente	frequente
fresh	frais, fraîche	frisch	fresco, a	fresco, a	fresco, a
friction, rubbing	frottement	Reibung(f)	frotamiento	strofinio	fricção
Friday	Vendredi	Freitag(m)	Viernes	Venerdì	Sexta-feira
fridge	frigo, frigidaire	Kühlschrank(m)	frigorífico	frigorifero	frigorífico
friend	ami, e	Freund(in f)m	amigo, a	amico, a	amigo, a
friend	camarade	Kamerad(in f)m	compañero, a	compagno, a	camarada
friendly	amical, e	freundschaftlich	amistoso, a	amichevole	amigável
friendship	amitié	Freundschaft(f)	amistad	amicizia	amizade
fright	frayeur	Schreck(m), Angst(f)	espanto	spavento	temor
frighten	effrayer	erschrecken	asustar	spaventare	assustar
fringe(on the)	marginal, e	Außenseiter(in f)m	marginal	marginale	marginal
fritters	beignets	Krapfen, Pfannkuchen	buñuelos	frittella	pastéis
frivolous	frivole	frivol, leichtsinnig	frívolo, a	frivolo, a	frívolo, a
frog	grenouille	Frosch(m)	rana	rana	rã
from	de	aus; von	de, desde	da	de
front, fore	devant	Front(f)	frente, delantera	davanti	frente(a)
front, fore	avant	Vorderteil(n)	delantero, a	anteriore	dianteira
front(age)	façade	Fassade(f)	fachada	facciata	fachada
frost	givre	Reif(m)	escarcha	brina	geada
frostbite	gélure	Erfrierung(f)	heladura	congelamento	frieira
froth, foam	mousse	Schaum(m)	espuma	schiuma	espuma
frozen food	surgelés	Tiefkühlkost(f)	congelados	surgelati	congelados
fruit	fruit(s)	Frucht(f)	fruta	frutto; frutta	fruta
fruit-juice	jus de fruit	Obstsaft(m)	zumo de fruta	succo di frutta	sumo de fruta
frustration	frustration	Enttäuschung(f)	frustración	frustrazione	frustração
fry	frire	braten	freír	friggere	fritar
frying pan	poêle	Pfanne(f)	sartén	padella	frigideira
fuel	carburant	Treibstoff(m)	carburante	carburante	carburante
fuel oil	mazout	Heizöl(n)	fuel-oil	nafta	fuel, óleo
fugitive	fugitif, ive	flüchtig	fugitivo, a	fuggitivo, a	fugitivo, a
full	plein, e; complet	voll	lleno, a	pieno, a	cheio, a
fun(have)	amuser(s')	amüsieren, sich	divertir(se)	divertire(-rsi)	divertir-se
function	fonction	Funktion(f)	función	funzione	função
function	fonction	Stellung(f), Amt(n)	función	funzione	função
function, work, run	fonctionner	funktionieren	funcionar	funzionare	funcionar
functioning	fonctionnement	Betrieb(m)	funcionamiento	funzionamento	funcionamento
fundamental	fondamental, e	fundamental	fundamental	fondamentale	fundamental
funds	fonds	Fonds(m), Kapital(n)	fondos	fondi	fundos, capital
funeral	funérailles	Begräbnis(n)	funerales	funerale	funeral
funnel	entonnoir	Trichter(m)	embudo	imbuto	funil
funny, amusing	amusant, e	lustig, amüsant	divertido, a	buffo, a; divertente	divertido, a
funny	drôle	lustig	gracioso, a	buffo, a	divertido, a
fur	fourrure	Pelz(m)	piel	pelliccia	pele; peliça
furious	furieux, se	wütend	furioso, a	furioso, a	furioso, a
furnishing	ameublement	Einrichtung(f)	mobiliario	arredamento, mobilio	mobiliário
furniture	mobilier	Möbel(pl)	mobiliario	mobilio	mobiliário
furniture	meuble	Möbelstück(n)	mueble	mobile	móvel
furrow	sillon	Furche(f)	surco	solco	rego
further; other	autre	weiter	otro, a	altro, a	mais
further, moreover	plus(de)	ferner, überdies	además	più(di, in)	além disso

E

English	French	German	Spanish	Italian	Portuguese
further	plus loin	weiter	más lejos	più in là	mais longe
further to	suite à	Anschluß an(im)	contestación(en)	seguito(facendo)	consequência(em)
fury	fureur	Wut(f)	furor	furore	furor
fusion, melting	fusion	Schmelzen(n)(Ver-)	fusión	fusione	fusão
fussy	maniaque	übergenau sein	maniático, a	pignolo, a	meticuloso, a
future	futur, e	zukünftig	futuro, a	futuro, a	futuro, a
future	avenir	Zukunft(f)	porvenir, futuro	avvenire	futuro
future	futur	Zukunft(f)	futuro	futuro	futuro
fuzzy, blurred	flou, e	verschwommen	borroso, a	sfumato, a	vago, a

G

English	French	German	Spanish	Italian	Portuguese
gadget	gadget	Spielerei(f)	chisme, mecanismo	gadget	aparelho
galaxy	galaxie	Galaxie(f)	galaxia	galassia	galáxia
gallant	galant, e	galant	galante	galante	galante
gall-bladder	vésicule	Blase(f)	vesícula	cistifellea	vesícula
gallery	galerie	Galerie, Ausstellung	galería	galleria	galeria
gallop	galop	Galopp(m)	galope	galoppo	galope
gamble	jouer	spielen	jugar	giocare	jogar
game	jeu	Spiel(n)	juego	gioco	jogo
game	partie	Spiel(n)	partida	partita	jogada, jogo
game	gibier	Wild(n)	caza	selvaggina	caça
gang	bande	Bande(f)	pandilla	banda	quadrilha
ganglion, gland	ganglion	Ganglien(pl.)	ganglio	ganglio	gânglio
gangrene	gangrène	Brand(m), Wundbrand(m)	gangrena	cancrena	gangrena
gangster	gangster	Gangster(m)	gángster	gangster	gangster
gap, margin	écart	Abstand(m)	diferencia, margen	margine, differenza	desvio, margem
gap	intervalle	Abstand(m)	intervalo	intervallo	intervalo
garage	garage	Garage(f)	garaje, garage	garage	garagem
garage mechanic	garagiste	Autoschlosser(m)	garajista	garagista	garagista
garden	jardin	Garten(m)	jardín	giardino	jardim
garden	jardin	Gemüsegarten(m)	huerto	orto	horta
gardener	jardinier, ière	Gärtner(in f)m	jardinero, a	giardiniere, a	jardineiro, a
garland	guirlande	Girlande(f)	guirnalda	ghirlanda	grinalda
garment	vêtement	Kleidungsstück(n)	traje, ropa	vestito	peça de roupa
garnish	garnir	garnieren	guarnecer	guarnire	guarnecer
gas	gaz	Gas(n)	gas	gas	gás
gaseous	gazeux, se	gasförmig	gaseoso, a	gassoso, a	gasoso, a
gash	balafre	Schmiß(m), Schnitt(m)	cuchillada	sfregio	corte, cutilada
gastric	gastrique	Magen-	gástrico, a	gastrico, a	gástrico, a
gastronomy	gastronomie	Gastronomie(f)	gastronomía	gastronomia	gastronomia
gate	portail	Tor(n)	portal	portone	portal
gate	porte	Pforte(f)	puerta, entrada	porta, uscita	porta
gate; valve	vanne	Klappe(f)	compuerta	saracinesca	comporta
gather(together)	rassembler	sammeln	juntar	radunare	juntar
gather(together)	réunir	sammeln	reunir	riunire	reunir
gathering	rassemblement	Versammlung(f)	concentración	raduno, adunanza	ajuntamento
G.C.E. A.Level(s)	baccalauréat	Abitur(n)	bachillerato	maturità	bacharelato
genealogy	généalogie	Genealogie(f)	genealogía	genealogia	genealogia
general	général, e	allgemein, generell	general	generale	geral
general	général	General(m)	general	generale	general
generate	engendrer	zeugen, erzeugen	engendrar	generare	engendrar
generate	générer	erzeugen	engendrar	generare	gerar
generation	génération	Generation(f)	generación	generazione	geração
generator	générateur	Generator(m)	generador	generatore	gerador
generous	généreux, se	freigebig	generoso, a	generoso, a	generoso, a
genetics	génétique	Genetik(f)	genética	genetica	genética

English	French	German	Spanish	Italian	Portuguese
genital	génital, e	Genital-	genital	genitale	genital
genius	génie	Genie(n)	genio	genio	génio
genocide	génocide	Völkermord(m)	genocidio	genocidio	genocídio
gentlemen	messieurs	meine Herren	señores	signori	senhores
gently; slowly	doucement	langsam, sanft	despacio	piano, adagio	devagar
genuine	authentique	echt	genuino, a	genuino, a	autêntico, a
geography	géographie	Erdkunde(f)	geografía	geografia	geografia
geology	géologie	Geologie(f)	geología	geologia	geologia
geometry	géométrie	Geometrie(f)	geometría	geometria	geometria
germ, microbe	microbe	Mikrobe(f)	microbio	microbo	micróbio
germ, seed	germe	Keim(m)	germen	germe	germe
German measles	rubéole	Röteln(pl)	rubéola	rosolia	rubéola
gesture	geste	Geste(f)	gesto	gesto	gesto
get, obtain	obtenir, recevoir	bekommen	obtener	ottenere	obter
get into; get on	monter	ein = steigen	subir	salire	subir a, entrar
get out of; get off	descendre	aus = steigen	bajarse	scendere	descer
get rid of	débarrasser(se)	beseitigen	quitarse	liberarsi	livrar-se
get up	lever(se)	erheben, sich	levantar(se)	alzarsi	levantar-se
get upset	vexer(se)	beleidigt sein	ofenderse	offendersi	ofender-se
get used to	habituer(s')	gewöhnen, sich	acostumbrarse	abituarsi	habituar-se
ghost	fantôme	Gespenst(n)	fantasma	fantasma	fantasma
giant	géant, e	riesig, gigantisch	gigante	gigante	gigante
gift, talent	don	Talent(n)	don, talento	dono	dom, talento
gifted, talented	doué, e	begabt	dotado, a	dotato, a	dotado, a; capaz
gigantic, huge	gigantesque	gigantisch, riesig	gigantesco, a	gigantesco, a	gigantesco, a
giraffe	girafe	Giraffe(f)	jirafa	giraffa	girafa
girdle	gaine	Korsett(n)	faja	guaina, corsetto	cinta elástica
girl	fille	Mädchen(n)	chica	ragazza	rapariga
give	donner	geben	dar	dare	dar
give; offer	offrir	schenken, an = bieten	ofrecer	offrire, regalare	oferecer
give back	rendre	zurück = geben	devolver	rendere	devolver
give up	renoncer	auf = geben	renunciar	rinunciare	desistir; renunciar
give up	céder, renoncer	auf = geben; nach = geben	ceder	cedere	ceder
glacier	glacier	Gletscher(m)	glaciar	ghiacciaio	glaciar
glad, happy, pleased	content, e	froh, erfreut	contento, a	contento, a	contente
glance	regard	Blick(m)	ojeada	occhiata	olhada
gland	glande	Drüse(f)	glándula	ghiandola	glândula
glass	verre	Glas(n)	vidrio	vetro	vidro
glass(-es)	verre	Glas(n)	vaso	bicchiere	copo
glass(-es)	coupe	Kelch(m), Schale(f)	copa	calice	taça
glasses	lunettes	Brille(f)	gafas	occhiali	óculos
gleam, glow	lueur	Schimmer(m)	resplandor	chiarore, luce	luz, clarão
glide	planer	schweben, gleiten	planear	planare	planar
glider	planeur	Segelflugzeug(n)	planeador	aliante	planador
glimpse	entrevoir	flüchtig sehen	entrever	intravedere	entrever
glitter, spangle	paillette	Flitter(m)	lentejuela	lustrino	lentejoula
global, overall	global, e	Gesamt-; pauschal	global	globale	global
globe	globe	Globus(m)	globo	globo	globo
glorious	glorieux, se	glorreich	glorioso, a	glorioso, a	glorioso, a
glory	gloire	Ruhm(m)	gloria	gloria	glória
glossary	glossaire	Glossar(n)	glosario	glossario	glossário
glove	gant	Handschuh(m)	guante	guanto	luva
glucose	glucose	Traubenzucker(m)	glucosa	glucosio	glicose
glue	colle	Klebstoff(m)	cola, pegamento	colla	cola
gnaw	ronger	zernagen	roer	rodere	roer
go	aller	gehen, fahren nach	ir(a, por, hacia)	andare, recarsi	ir
go back, come back	rentrer	zurück = kommen	regresar	tornare, rientrare	voltar
go beyond, exceed	dépasser	überholen	sobresalir	oltrepassare	ultrapassar
go down, descend	descendre	herunter = gehen	descender, bajar	scendere	descer, baixar
go out, come out	sortir	aus = gehen	salir	uscire	sair
go to bed	coucher(se)	schlafen gehen	ir a la cama	andare a letto	deitar-se
go to fetch/get	aller chercher	ab = holen	ir a buscar	andare a prendere	ir buscar
goal	but	Tor(n)	gol	goal, rete	golo
goalkeeper	goal	Torwärter(m)	portero	portiere	guarda-redes
goat	chèvre	Ziege(f)	cabra	capra	cabra
God	dieu	Gott(m)	dios, Dios	dio, Dio (dio, dei)	Deus
godfather	parrain	Pate(m)	padrino	padrino	padrinho
godmother	marraine	Patin(f)	madrina	madrina	madrinha

English	French	German	Spanish	Italian	Portuguese
gold	or	Gold(n)	oro	oro	ouro
golf	golf	Golf(n)	golf	golf	golfe
golf course	golf(terrain)	Golfplatz(m)	golf	golf	campo de golfe
good	bon, ne	gut	bueno, a	buono, a	bom, boa
good	sage	brav	bueno, a	buono, a; bravo, a	ajuizado, a
good	bien	Gut(n)	bien	bene	bem
good afternoon!	bonjour!	guten Tag!	hola(!)	buona sera!	bom dia!
good bye!	adieu!	tschüß!, lebe wohl!	adiós(!)	addio!	adeus!
good bye, bye-bye	au revoir	auf Wiedersehen	hasta luego	arrivederci	até logo, adeus!
good evening	bonsoir	guten Abend	buenas tardes	buonasera	boa tarde
good luck	bonne chance	viel Glück	buena suerte	buona fortuna	boa sorte
good morning!/aft-	bonjour!	guten Morgen!/-Tag	hola(!)	buongiorno!	bom dia!
good natured	gracieux, se	lieb	simpático, a	grazioso, a	gracioso, a
Goodness(my)	Dieu(mon)	Gott!(Mein Gott!)	Dios(mío)	Dio(mio)	Deus(meu)
good night	bonne nuit	gute Nacht	buenas noches	buona notte	boa noite
good trip(have a)	bon voyage	gute Reise	buen viaje	buon viaggio	boa viagem
goods, merchandise	marchandise	Ware(f)	mercancía	merce	mercadoria
goose(geese pl.)	oie	Gans(f)	oca	oca	ganso
gorilla	gorille	Gorilla(m)	gorila	gorilla	gorila
govern	gouverner	regieren	gobernar	governare	governar
government	gouvernement	Regierung(f)	gobierno	governo	governo
governor	gouverneur	Gouverneur(m)	gobernador	governatore	governador
grab, grasp	empoigner, saisir	greifen	empuñar	agguantare	agarrar
grace	grâce	Gnade(f); Anmut(f)	gracia	grazia	graça
graceful	gracieux, se	graziös	gracioso, a	grazioso, a	gracioso, a
graduate	diplômé, e	Diplom-	titulado, a	diplomato, a	diplomado, a
graft	greffe	Veredelung; Pfropfen	injerto	innesto	enxerto
grain	grain	Korn(n)	grano	chicco, grano	grão
grammar	grammaire	Grammatik(f)	gramática	grammatica	gramática
grandfather	grand-père	Großvater(m)	abuelo	nonno	avô
grandmother	grand-mère	Großmutter(f)	abuela	nonna	avó
grandparents	grands-parents	Großeltern(pl.)	abuelos	nonni	avós
grandson/-daughter	petit-fils/fille	Enkel(m), Enkelin(f)	nieto, a	nipote	neto, a
grant	accorder	bewilligen	conceder	concedere, accordare	conceder
grant; scholarship	bourse	Stipendium(n)	beca	borsa di studio	bolsa
grant, subsidy	subvention	Zuschuß(m)	subvención	sovvenzione	subvenção
granule	granule	Körnchen(n)	gránulo	granulo	grânulo
grape	raisin	Traube(f)(Wein-)	uva(s)	uva	uva
grapefruit	pamplemousse	Pampelmuse(f)	pomelo	pompelmo	toranja
graph	graphique	Graphik(f)	gráfico, a	grafico	gráfico
graphology	graphologie	Graphologie(f)	grafología	grafologia	grafologia
grass	herbe	Gras(n)	hierba, yerba	erba	erva
grass	gazon	Rasen(m)	césped	prato, erba	relva
grateful	reconnaissant, e	dankbar	agradecido, a	grato, a	reconhecido, a
gratitude	gratitude	Dankbarkeit(f)	gratitud	gratitudine	gratidão
grave	tombe	Grab(n)	tumba	tomba	túmulo, sepultura
grave, serious	grave	schwer; ernst	grave	grave	grave
gravel	gravier	Kies(m)	grava	ghiaia	cascalho
gravity	gravité	Schwere(f)	gravedad	gravità	gravidade
grease	graisse	Schmiere(f)	grasa	grasso	massa
great	grand, e	groß	gran, grande	grand(e)	grande
greedy	gourmand, e	erpicht auf	goloso, a	goloso, a	guloso, a
green	vert, e	grün	verde	verde	verde
greenery	verdure	Grün(n)	verdor, verdura	verdura	verdura
greet; say hello	saluer	begrüßen	saludar	salutare	saudar
greeting(s) card	carte de voeux	Glückwunschkarte(f)	postal, carta	biglietto di auguri	cartão(festas)
grenade	grenade	Handgranate(f)	granada	bomba a mano	granada
grey	gris, e	grau	gris	grigio, a	cinzento, a
grief, sorrow	chagrin	Kummer(m)	pena	dispiacere	desgosto, pena
grill	griller	grillen	asar(parrilla)	arrostire	grelhar
grimace	grimace	Grimasse(f)	mueca	smorfia	careta
grind	moudre, écraser	mahlen	moler	macinare	moer
grind, grate	grincer	knirschen	chirriar	stridere	ranger
grip	saisir, empoigner	greifen, packen	agarrar, empuñar	afferrare	agarrar, empunhar
grip, hold tight	serrer	greifen, packen	apretar	stringere	apertar
grocer	épicier, ière	Lebensmittelhändler m	tendero, a	droghiere, a	merceeiro, a
grocer's(shop)	épicerie	Lebensmittelladen(m)	ultramarinos	drogheria	mercearia
groove	rainure	Rille(f), Nute(f)	ranura	scanalatura	ranhura

English	French	German	Spanish	Italian	Portuguese
ground	sol, terre	Boden(m)	suelo	suolo	solo
ground	terrain	Gelände(n)	terreno	terreno	terreno
ground floor	rez-de-chaussée	Erdgeschoß(n)	planta baja, bajo	piano terra	rés-do-chão
group	groupe	Gruppe(f)	grupo	gruppo	grupo
grouse, moan	rouspéter	meckern, murren	refunfuñar	brontolare	rezingar
grow, increase	croître	wachsen	crecer	crescere	crescer
grow	pousser, croître	wachsen	crecer	crescere	crescer
grow	grandir	wachsen	crecer	crescere	crescer
growth	croissance	Wachstum(n)	crecimiento	crescita	crescimento
grudge, spite	rancune	Rachsucht(f)	rencor	rancore	rancor
grumpy	grognon, ne	quengelig	gruñon, a	brontolone	rabugento, a
guarantee	garantie	Garantie(f)	garantía	garanzia	garantia
guarantee, warrant	garantir	gewährleisten	garantizar	garantire	garantir
guard	garde	Wache(f)	guardia	guardia, custodia	guarda
guard	garde	Wächter(m), Hüter(m)	guarda	guardia	guarda
guard, watch over	garder	hüten, bewachen	guardar	custodire, guardare	guardar, vigiar
guard; keeper	gardien, ne; garde	Wächter(in f)m	guardián, guarda	guardiano, a; custode	guarda
guardian	tuteur, tutrice	Vormund(m)	tutor, a	tutore, trice	tutor, a
guerilla	guérilla	Guerilla(f)	guerrilla	guerriglia	guerrilha
guess	deviner	raten	adivinar	indovinare	adivinhar
guest	invité, e	Gast(m)	invitado, a	invitato, a	convidado, a
guest	convive	Gast(m)	convidado, a	commensale	conviva
guest	hôte	Gast(m)	huésped, a	ospite	hóspede, a
guest-house	pension	Gasthaus(n)	pensión	pensione	pensão
guide	guide	Führer(in f)m	guía	guida	guia
guide	guider	führen	guiar	guidare	guiar
guide-book	guide	Führer(Reise-)(m)	guía	guida	guia
guilt	culpabilité	Schuld(f)	culpabilidad	colpevolezza	culpabilidade
guilty	coupable	schuldig	culpable	colpevole	culpado, a
guinea-pig(be a)	cobaye	Versuchskaninchen(n)	conejillo(Indias)	cavia	cobaia
guitar	guitare	Gitarre(f)	guitarra	chitarra	guitarra
gulf	golfe	Golf(m)	golfo	golfo	golfo
gull	goéland	Silbermöwe(f)	gaviota	gabbiano	gaivota
gum	gencive	Zahnfleisch(n)	encía	gengiva	gengiva
gun, pistol	pistolet	Pistole(f)	pistola	pistola	pistola
gust, gale	rafale	Windstoß(m)	ráfaga	raffica	rajada
gutter	gouttière	Dachrinne(f)	canalón	grondaia	goteira
gutter	caniveau	Rinnstein(m)	arroyo	canaletto di scolo	valeta
gymnastics	gymnastique	Gymnastik(f)	gimnasia	ginnastica	ginástica
gynaecology	gynécologie	Gynäkologie(f)	ginecología	ginecologia	ginecologia

H

English	French	German	Spanish	Italian	Portuguese
habit	habitude	Gewohnheit(f)	costumbre	abitudine	hábito, costume
habituation	accoutumance	Gewöhnung(f)	hábito	abitudine	habituação
haemorrhage	hémorragie	Blutsturz(m)	hemorragia	emorragia	hemorragia
haemorrhoids	hémorroïde(s)	Hämorrhoiden(f, pl)	hemorroides	emorroide	hemorróidas
hail	grêle	Hagel(m)	granizo	grandine	granizo
hair	cheveu(x)	Haar(n)	pelo, cabello	capello	cabelo
hair	poil	Haar(n)	pelo	pelo	pêlo
hair(do one's)	coiffer(se)	frisieren, sich	peinar(se)	pettinare(-rsi)	pentear-se
hairdresser	coiffeur, se	Friseur(m), Friseuse f	peluquero, a	parrucchiere, a	cabeleireiro, a
hair-dryer	sèche-cheveux	Fön(m), Haartrockner m	secador	asciugacapelli	secador
hair-spray	laque	Haarspray(m, n)	laca	lacca	laca
hair-style	coiffure	Frisur(f)	peinado	pettinatura	penteado
hairy	poilu, e	behaart	peludo, a	peloso, a	peludo, a
half(-lves)	moitié	Hälfte(f)	mitad	metà	metade

English	French	German	Spanish	Italian	Portuguese
half	demi, e	halb	medio, a	mezzo, a	meio, a
half(-); mid-	mi-	halb-	medio, a	semi-; mezzo-	meio, a
half an hour	demi-heure	halbe Stunde	media hora	mezz'ora	meia-hora
half-caste	métis, se	Mischling(m)	mestizo, a	meticcio, a	mestiço, a
hall	vestibule	Flur(m)	vestíbulo	ingresso, anticamera	vestíbulo; hall
hallucination	hallucination	Sinnestäuschung(f)	alucinación	allucinazione	alucinação
halt, stop	halte, arrêt	Halt(m)	alto, parada	sosta, fermata	alto, paragem
ham	jambon	Schinken(m)	jamón	prosciutto	fiambre
hammer	marteau	Hammer(m)	martillo	martello	martelo
hammock	hamac	Hängematte(f)	hamaca	amaca	rede
hand	main	Hand(f)	mano	mano	mão
hand luggage	bagages à main	Handgepäck(n)	equipaje de mano	bagaglio a mano	bagagem de mão
handbag	sac à main	Handtasche(f)	bolso	borsetta	carteira
handcuffs	menottes	Handschellen(f, pl)	esposas	manette	algemas
handful	poignée	Handvoll(f)	puñado	manciata, pugno	punhado
handicap	handicap	Handikap(n)	hándicap	handicap	handicap
handicapped	handicapé, e	behindert	minusválido, a	andicappato, a	deficiente
handkerchief	mouchoir	Taschentuch(n)	pañuelo	fazzoletto	lenço
handle	poignée	Griff(m)	manilla, mango	maniglia	fecho
handle	poignée	Griff(m)	asa, mango	manico	asa
handle	manette	Griff(m)	manecilla	leva	manípulo
handle	manche	Stiel(m)	mango(el)	manico	cabo
handle	anse	Griff(m)	asa	ansa	asa
handout, leaflet	tract	Flugblatt(n)	octavilla	volantino	panfleto
handsome	beau, belle	ansehnlich, schön	bello, a	bello, a	bonito, a
handwritten	manuscrit, e	handgeschrieben	manuscrito, a	manoscritto, a	manuscrito, a
handy, manageable	maniable	handlich	manuable	maneggevole	manejável
hang	accrocher	auf = hängen	colgar	appendere	pendurar
hang	pendre	hängen, auf = hängen	colgar	appendere	pendurar
hang up	suspendre	auf = hängen	colgar, suspender	appendere	pendurar
hanger, coat-hanger	cintre	Bügel(m)	percha	gruccia, attaccapanni	cabide
happen, occur	produire(se)	passieren	suceder, ocurrir	accadere	ocorrer
happiness	bonheur	Glück(n)	felicidad	felicità	felicidade
happy, glad	heureux, se	glücklich	feliz	felice	feliz
happy, merry	gai, e	froh	alegre	allegro, a	alegre
harass	harceler	quälen	acosar	assillare	perseguir
hard	dur, e	hart	duro, a	duro, a	duro, a
hard, arduous	pénible	mühsam, schwierig	penoso, a; duro, a	penoso, a	penoso, a
hardware shop	droguerie	Kramwarenhandel(m)	droguería	mesticheria	drogaria
hardy	vivace	immergrün; ausdauernd	vivaz	vivace	vivaz
harem	harem	Harem(m)	harén	harem	harém
harm, hurt	mal	Weh(n)	daño	male	mal
harmful	nuisible	schädlich	dañino, a	nocivo, a	nocivo, a
harmful	nocif, ive	schädlich	nocivo, a	nocivo, a	nocivo, a
harmonious	harmonieux, se	harmonisch	armonioso, a	armonioso, a	harmonioso, a
harmony	harmonie	Harmonie(f)	armonía	armonia	harmonia
harness	harnais	Geschirr(n)	arnés	finimenti	arnês
harp	harpe	Harfe(f)	arpa	arpa	harpa
harpoon	harpon	Harpune(f)	arpón	arpione	arpão
harvest	moisson	Ernte(f)	cosecha	mietitura	ceifa, colheita
harvest, gather	récolter	ernten	cosechar, recoger	raccogliere	colher, apanhar
haste, hurry	hâte	Eile(f)	prisa	fretta	pressa
hat	chapeau	Hut(m)	sombrero	cappello	chapéu
hat stand	portemanteau	Kleiderständer(m)	colgador, percha	attaccapanni	cabide
hatch	éclore	aus = schlüpfen	abrirse	schiudere, uscire	abrir-se
hate, detest	haïr, détester	hassen	odiar	odiare	odiar
hate	haine	Haß(m)	odio	odio	ódio
haunted	hanté, e	verflucht	embrujado, a	spiritato, a	assombrado, a
have	avoir	haben	tener	avere	ter, possuir
have	avoir	haben	haber; tener	avere	haver; ter
have(a lesson)	prendre(leçon)	nehmen	recibir(clases)	prendere(lezione)	ter(lição)
have to, must	falloir	müssen	necesario(ser)	bisognare	preciso(ser)
hazard	aléa, hasard	Zufall(m)	riesgo, azar	rischio	acaso
he; it	il	er; es	él	egli, lui, esso	ele
head	tête	Kopf(m)	cabeza	testa, capo	cabeça
head for	cap	Kurs(m)	rumbo a	rotta	rumo
head; chief; leader	chef	Chef(in f)m)	jefe	capo	chefe
head of state	chef d'état	Staatsoberhaupt(n)	jefe de estado	capo di stato	chefe de estado

English	French	German	Spanish	Italian	Portuguese
head office	siège	Firmensitz(m)	sede	sede	sede
headache	mal de tête	Kopfschmerzen(m, pl)	dolor de cabeza	mal di testa	dor de cabeça
headlight	phare(s)	Scheinwerfer(m)	faro(s)	fanale, faro(-ri)	faróis
headmaster	directeur(école)	Schuldirektor(m)	director(escuela)	direttore(scuola)	director(escola)
head-waiter	maître d'hôtel	Oberkellner(m)	jefe de hotel	capocameriere	mordomo
healer	guérisseur, se	Heilpraktiker(in f)m	curandero, a	guaritore, -trice	curandeiro, a
health	santé	Gesundheit(f)	salud	salute	saúde
healthy	sain, e	gesund	sano, a	sano, a	são, sã
hear	entendre	hören	oír	sentire	ouvir
hear(of)	apprendre	erfahren	enterarse	apprendere, sapere	saber
hearing, audition	ouïe	Gehör(n)	oído	udito	ouvido
heart	coeur	Herz(n)	corazón	cuore	coração
heart attack	crise cardiaque	Herzattacke(f)	crisis cardíaca	infarto	ataque
heart-trouble...	cardiaque	herzkrank	cardíaco, a	cardiaco, a	cardíaco, a
hearty, warm	chaleureux, se	herzlich	caluroso, a	caloroso, a	caloroso, a
heat	chaleur	Hitze(f)	calor	caldo; calore	calor
heat	chauffer	heizen	calentar	riscaldare	aquecer
heating	chauffage	Heizung(f)	calefacción	riscaldamento	aquecimento
heating	échauffement	Aufwärmen(n)	calentamiento	riscaldamento	aquecimento
heaven	ciel, paradis	Himmel(m)	cielo, paraíso	cielo, paradiso	céu, paraíso
heavenly	céleste	himmlisch	celeste	celeste	celeste
heavy	lourd, e	schwer	pesado, a	pesante	pesado, a
hectare	hectare	Hektar(m)	hectárea	ettaro	hectare
hedge	haie	Hecke(f)	seto, valla	siepe	sebe
heel	talon	Ferse(f); Absatz(m)	talón	tallone	calcanhar
height	hauteur	Höhe(f)	altura	altezza	altura
height, size	taille, grandeur	Größe(f)	talla, estatura	statura	estatura
heir, heiress	héritier, ière	Erbe(m), Erbin(f)	heredero, a	erede	herdeiro, a
helicopter	hélicoptère	Hubschrauber(m)	helicóptero	elicottero	helicóptero
hell	enfer	Hölle(f)	infierno	inferno	inferno
hello	bonjour	guten Tag	buenos días	buongiorno	bom dia
hello!	allô!	Ja, bitte?	dígame(!)	pronto!	está lá?; estou?
helmet	casque	Helm(m)	casco	casco, elmetto	capacete
help	aide	Hilfe(f)	ayuda	aiuto	ajuda
help, aid	secours	Hilfe(f)	socorro	soccorso	socorro
help, assist, aid	aider	helfen	ayudar	aiutare	ajudar
help, assist, aid	secourir	helfen	socorrer	soccorrere	socorrer
hemisphere	hémisphère	Halbkreis(m)	hemisferio	emisfero	hémisfério
hen	poule	Huhn(n)	gallina	gallina	galinha
hepatitis	hépatite	Hepatitis, Gelbsucht f	hepatitis	epatite	hepatite
her; his; its	sa	sein, e; ihr, ihre	su	sua(la)	sua
herb(s)	herbe(s)	Kraut(n), Kräuter(pl.)	hierbas	erbe(aromatiche)	erva
herb tea	tisane	Kräutertee(m)	tisana	tisana	tisana
herd	troupeau	Herde(f)	ganado	branco	manada
here	ici	hier	aquí	qui	aqui
here is; here are	voici	hier(ist/sind)	he aquí	ecco	aqui está
hereditary	héréditaire	erblich	hereditario, a	ereditario, a	hereditário, a
heredity	hérédité	Vererbung(f)	herencia	ereditarietà	hereditariedade
heritage; legacy	héritage	Erbe(n), Erbschaft(f)	herencia	eredità	herança
hermetic	hermétique	hermetisch	hermético, a	ermetico, a	hermético, a
hermit	ermite	Einsiedler(in f)m	ermitaño	eremita	eremita
hernia	hernie	Bruch(m)	hernia	ernia	hérnia
hero, heroine	héros, héroïne	Held(m), Heldin(f)	héroe, heroína	eroe, eroina	herói, heroína
heroic	héroïque	heldenhaft	heroico, a	eroico, a	heróico, a
heroin	héroïne	Heroin(n)	heroína	eroina	heroína
herring	hareng	Hering(m)	arenque	aringa	arenque
hesitate	hésiter	zögern	dudar	esitare	hesitar
hesitation	hésitation	Zögern(n)	vacilación	esitazione	hesitação
heterosexual	hétérosexuel, le	heterosexuell	heterosexual	eterosessuale	heterossexual
hi!, hello!	salut!	Hallo!; tschüs!; tschüß	hola(!)	ciao!	olá!
hide	cacher	verstecken	esconder	nascondere	esconder
hierarchical	hiérarchique	hierarchisch	jerárquico, a	gerarchico, a	hierárquico, a
hierarchy	hiérarchie	Hierarchie(f)	jerarquía	gerarchia	hierarquia
high, tall	haut, e	hoch	alto, a	alto, a	alto, a
high	grand, e	hoch	alto, a	forte; alto, a	alto, a
high	élevé, e	hoch, erhöht	alto, a	elevato, a; alto, a	alto, a
hijack	détourner	entführen	secuestrar	dirottare	sequestrar
hill	colline	Hügel(m)	colina	collina	colina

English	French	German	Spanish	Italian	Portuguese
hill(side)	coteau	Anhöhe(f), Hang(m)	ladera	colle, collinetta	encosta; colina
hill, slope	côte	Abhang(m), Steigung(f)	cuesta	salita, pendio	ladeira, encosta
him, her, it	lui	ihm, ihr, ihm	le, él; ella; se	lui; gli; le	ele(a); lhe
hinge	charnière	Scharnier(n)	bisagra	cerniera	gonzo, dobradiça
hip	hanche	Hüfte(f)	cadera	anca	anca
hippopotamus	hippopotame	Nilpferd(n)	hipopótamo	ippopotamo	hipopótamo
hippy	hippie, y	Hippie(m)	hippy, jipi	capellone, hippy	hippie
hire, rent	louer	mieten; vermieten	alquilar	noleggiare	alugar
his; her; its	son	sein, seine, ihr, ihre	su	suo(il)	seu
his; her; its	ses	seine; ihre	sus	suoi(i); sue(le)	seus, suas
his; hers; its	sien, ne	seine, ihre	suyo, suya	suo, sua(il, la)	seu, sua
historian	historien	Geschichtschreiber(m)	historiador	storico	historiador
historic(al)	historique	historisch	histórico, a	storico, a	histórico, a
history	histoire	Geschichte(f)	historia	storia	História
hit, knock, strike	frapper	schlagen, prügeln	golpear	picchiare	bater
hitch-hiking	auto-stop	trampen	autostop, a dedo	autostop	boleia(pedir)
hive	ruche	Bienenstock(m)	colmena	alveare	colmeia
hoarse	enroué, e	heiser	ronco, a	rauco, a	rouco, a
hoarse	rauque	rauh, heiser	ronco, a	rauco, a	rouco, a
hobby, pastime	passe-temps	Hobby(n)	pasatiempo	passatempo	passatempo
hockey	hockey	Hockeyspiel(n)	hockey	hockey	hóquei
hold	cale	Laderaum(m)	bodega	stiva	porão
hold	tenir	halten	tener	tenere	ter, segurar
hold back; retain	retenir	zurück = halten	retener	trattenere	reter
holder	titulaire	Inhaber(in f)m	titular	titolare	titular
hold-up	hold-up	Raubüberfall(m)	atraco	rapina	assalto
hole	trou	Loch(n)	agujero	buco(a), foro	buraco, furo
holiday, vacation	congé	Urlaub(m)	vacaciones	ferie(le)	férias
holidays	vacances	Ferien(pl.)	vacaciones	vacanze	férias
hollow	creux, se	hohl	hueco, a; cavo, a	vuoto, a; cavo, a	oco, a
holy	saint, e	heilig	santo, a; san	santo, a	santo, a
holy; sacred	sacré, e	heilig	sagrado, a	sacro, a	sagrado, a
holy water	eau bénite	Weihwasser(n)	agua bendita	acqua santa	água benta
homage, tribute	hommage	Huldigung(f); Ehrung f	homenaje	omaggio	homenagem
home	foyer, maison	Heim(n)	hogar	focolare	lar
home	domicile	Wohnsitz(m), Wohnort m	domicilio	domicilio	domicílio
home(at)	maison(à la)	Hause(zu)	casa(en)	casa(a)	casa(em)
homesickness	nostalgie	Heimweh(n)	nostalgia	nostalgia	nostalgia
homework; exercise	devoir	Aufgabe(f)	deber, tarea	compito	dever
homoeopathy	homéopathie	Homöopathie(f)	homeopatía	omeopatia	homeopatia
homogeneous	homogène	homogen	homogéneo, a	omogeneo, a	homogéneo, a
homonym	homonyme	Homonym(n)	homónimo, a	omonimo, a	homónimo, a
homosexual	homosexuel, le	homosexuell	homosexual	omosessuale	homossexual
honest	honnête	ehrlich	honrado, a	onesto, a	honesto, a
honey	miel	Honig(m)	miel	miele	mel
honour	honneur	Ehre(f)	honor	onore	honra
honourable	honorable	ehrwürdig	honorable	onorabile	honroso, a
hoof	sabot	Huf(m)	pezuña, casco	zoccolo	casco
hook	crochet	Haken(m)	gancho	gancio, uncino	gancho
hook	hameçon	Angelhaken(m)	anzuelo	amo	anzol
hooligan	voyou	Strolch(m)	canalla	mascalzone, a	patife
hoot	klaxonner	hupen	pitar	suonare(clacson)	buzinar
hope	espérer	hoffen	esperar, desear	sperare	esperar, desejar
hope	espoir	Hoffnung(f)	esperanza	speranza	esperança
horizon, sky-line	horizon	Horizont(m)	horizonte	orizzonte	horizonte
horizontal	horizontal, e	waagerecht	horizontal	orizzontale	horizontal
hormone	hormone	Hormon(n)	hormona	ormone	hormona
horn	corne	Horn(n)	cuerno	corno	corno; chifre
horn, hooter	klaxon	Hupe(f)	claxon, bocina	clacson	buzina
horoscope	horoscope	Horoskop(n)	horóscopo	oroscopo	horóscopo
horrible	horrible	grausig	horrible	orribile, orrendo, a	horrível
horror	horreur	Grausen(n)	horror	orrore	horror
horse	cheval	Pferd(n)	caballo	cavallo	cavalo
horticulture	horticulture	Gartenbau(m)	horticultura	orticultura	horticultura
hose	tuyau	Schlauch(m)	manguera	tubo	mangueira
hospice; home	hospice	Hospiz(n)	hospicio	ospizio	hospício, asilo
hospitable	accueillant, e	gastfreundlich	acogedor, a	accogliente	acolhedor, a
hospital	hôpital	Krankenhaus(n)	hospital	ospedale	hospital

178

English	French	German	Spanish	Italian	Portuguese
hospitality	hospitalité	Gastfreundlichkeit(f)	hospitalidad	ospitalità	hospitalidade
host; guest	hôte, tesse	Gastgeber(m); Gast(m)	anfitrión; huésped	ospite	anfitrião; hóspede, a
hostage	otage	Geisel(f)	rehén	ostaggio	refém
hostess(air -)	hôtesse	Stewardess(f)	azafata	hostess	hospedeira
hostile	hostile	feindlich	hostil	ostile	hostil
hot	chaud, e	heiß	caliente	caldo, a	quente
hotel	hôtel	Hotel(n)	hotel	albergo, hotel	hotel
hotel trade	hôtellerie	Hotelwesen(n)	hostelería	alberghiera(indust-)	hotelaria
hour; time	heure	Stunde(f); Zeit(f)	hora	ora	hora
house	maison	Haus(n)	casa	casa	casa
House, Chamber	Chambre(députés)	Abgeordnetenhaus(n)	cámara(diputados)	camera	câmara
housewife(-ives)	ménagère	Hausfrau(f)	ama de casa	casalinga	dona de casa
housework	ménage	Haushalt(m)	limpieza	pulizie	limpeza
how	comment	wie	cómo	come	como
how much, how many	combien	wieviel	cuánto; cuanto	quanto	quanto
however, but	cependant	jedoch	sin embargo	eppure, tuttavia	todavia, porém
however	toutefois	jedoch	sin embargo	tuttavia	todavia
howl	hurler	heulen	aullar	ululare, guaire	uivar; urrar
hub	centre	Mittelpunkt(m)	centro	centro	centro
huddle	blottir(se)	an = schmiegen, sich	acurrucar(se)	rannicchiarsi	aninhar-se
hull	coque	Rumpf(m)	casco	scafo	casco
human	humain, e	menschlich	humano, a	umano, a	humano, a
humanity	humanité	Menschheit(f)	humanidad	umanità	humanidade
humidity	humidité	Feuchtigkeit(f)	humedad	umidità	humidade
humiliate	humilier	erniedrigen	humillar	umiliare	humilhar
humorous	humoristique	humoristisch	humorístico, a	umoristico, a	humorístico, a
humour	humour	Humor(m)	humor	umorismo	humor
hunch-backed	bossu, e	buckelig	jorobado, a	gobbo, a	corcunda
hundred(one)	cent	hundert	cien, ciento	cento	cem, cento
hundred(about a)	centaine	Hundert(n)	centena	centinaio	centena
hunger(hungry be)	faim(avoir)	Hunger(m)(haben)	hambre(tener)	fame(aver)	fome(ter)
hunt	chasser	jagen	cazar	cacciare	caçar
hunter	chasseur	Jäger(in f)m	cazador	cacciatore	caçador
hunting	chasse	Jagd(f)	caza	caccia	caça
hurrah!; Long live!	vive!	Es lebe!; Lang lebe!	viva(!)	viva!, evviva!	viva!
hurricane	ouragan	Orkan(m)	huracán	uragano	furacão
hurry, haste	précipitation	Eile(f), Hast(f)	precipitación	precipitazione	precipitação
hurry(up)	dépêcher(se)	beeilen, sich	darse prisa	sbrigarsi	despachar-se
hurry(be in a)	pressé, e(être)	eilig(es...haben)	prisa(tener)	fretta(avere)	pressa(ter)
hurt, offend	blesser, offenser	kränken	lastimar, ofender	ferire, offendere	magoar, ofender
hurts(it)	mal(avoir)	Schmerzen haben	dolerle a uno	male(aver)	doer
husband	mari	Ehemann(m)	marido	marito	marido
husband	époux	Gatte, Mann, Ehemann m	esposo	sposo, consorte	esposo
hush!, sh!	chut!	pst!	chitón(!)	sst!, zitto!	chut!
hut	case, hutte	Hütte(f)	cabaña	capanna	palhota
hut(straw-hut)	paillotte	Strohhütte(f)	choza	capanna	palhota
hybrid	hybride	zwitterhaft	híbrido, a	ibrido, a	híbrido, a
hydraulic	hydraulique	hydraulisch	hidráulico, a	idraulico, a	hidráulico, a
hydrogen	hydrogène	Wasserstoff(m)	hidrógeno	idrogeno	hidrogénio
hyena	hyène	Hyäne(f)	hiena	iena	hiena
hygiene	hygiène	Hygiene(f)	higiene	igiene	higiene
hygienic	hygiénique	hygienisch	higiénico, a	igienico, a	higiénico, a
hymn	hymne	Hymne(f)	himno	inno	hino
hypnosis	hypnose	Hypnose(f)	hipnosis	ipnosi	hipnose
hypnotism	hypnotisme	Hypnotismus(m)	hipnotismo	ipnotismo	hipnotismo
hypocrisy	hypocrisie	Heuchelei(f)	hipocresía	ipocrisia	hipocrisia
hypocrite	hypocrite	Heuchler(in f)m	hipócrita	ipocrita	hipócrita
hypothesis(-es)	hypothèse	Hypothese(f)	hipótesis	ipotesi	hipótese
hysteric(al)	hystérique	hysterisch	histérico, a	isterico, a	histérico, a

E

I

English	French	German	Spanish	Italian	Portuguese
I	je	ich	yo	io	eu
ice	glace	Eis(n)	hielo	ghiaccio	gelo
iceberg	iceberg	Eisberg(m)	iceberg	iceberg	iceberg
ice cream	glace	Eis(n)	helado	gelato	gelado
ice-floe	banquise	Packeis(n)	banco de hielo	banchisa	campo de gelo
icy	glacé, e; gelé, e	eisig	helado, a	gelato, a; ghiacciato	gelado, a
idea	idée	Idee(f)	idea	idea	ideia
ideal	idéal, e	ideal	ideal	ideale	ideal
ideal	idéal	Ideal(n)	ideal	ideale	ideal
identical	identique	identisch	idéntico, a	identico, a	idêntico, a
identify	identifier	identifizieren	identificar	identificare	identificar
identity	identité	Identität(f)	identidad	identità	identidade
identity card	carte d'identité	Personalausweis(m)	carné de identidad	carta d'identità	bilhete(identidade)
ideology	idéologie	Ideologie(f)	ideología	ideologia	ideologia
idiot, fool	idiot, e	Idiot(m), Dummkopf(m)	idiota	idiota; scemo, a	idiota
idiotic, stupid	idiot, e	idiotisch, dumm	idiota; tonto, a	idiota; stupido, a	idiota
idol	idole	Idol(n)	ídolo	idolo	ídolo
if; whether	si	wenn; ob	si	se	se
igloo	igloo	Iglu(n)	iglú	igloo	iglu
ignition	allumage	Zündung(f)	encendido	accensione	ignição
ignorance	ignorance	Unwissenheit(f)	ignorancia	ignoranza	ignorância
ignorant of(be)	ignorer	nicht wissen	ignorar	ignorare	ignorar
ill	malade	krank	enfermo, a	malato, a	doente; enfermo, a
ill will	malveillance	Böswilligkeit(f)	malevolencia	malanimo	malevolência
illegal	illégal, e	illegal	ilegal	illegale	ilegal
illegitimate	illégitime	unehelich	ilegítimo, a	illegittimo, a	ilegítimo, a
illiterate	illettré, e	ungebildet	analfabeto, a	analfabeta	iletrado, a
ill luck, bad luck	malchance	Pech(n), Unglück(n)	mala suerte	sfortuna	má sorte
illness(-es)	maladie	Krankheit(f)	enfermedad	malattia	doença
illogical	illogique	unlogisch	ilógico, a	illogico, a	ilógico, a
illuminated	illuminé, e	erleuchtet	iluminado, a	illuminato, a	iluminado, a
illusion	illusion	Illusion(f)	ilusión	illusione	ilusão
illustrated	illustré, e	illustriert	ilustrado, a	illustrato, a	ilustrado, a
illustration	illustration	Illustration(f)	ilustración	illustrazione	ilustração
illustrious	illustre	berühmt	ilustre	illustre	ilustre
image, picture	image	Bild(n)	imagen	immagine	imagem
imaginary	imaginaire	eingebildet	imaginario, a	immaginario, a	imaginário, a
imagination	imagination	Einbildung(f)	imaginación	immaginazione	imaginação
imagine	imaginer	vor = stellen, sich	imaginar	immaginare	imaginar
imagine	imaginer(s')	ein = bilden, sich	imaginarse	immaginarsi	julgar
imitate	imiter	nach = ahmen	imitar	imitare	imitar
imitation	imitation	Nachahmung(f)	imitación	imitazione	imitação
immediate	immédiat, e	unverzüglich	inmediato, a	immediato, a	imediato, a
immediately	immédiatement	sofort	inmediatamente	immediatamente	imediatamente
immense, vast	immense	unendlich groß	inmenso, a	immenso, a	imenso, a
immerse	immerger	versenken	sumergir	immergere	imergir
immersion	immersion	Versenkung(f)	inmersión	immersione	imersão
immigrant	immigré, e	Einwanderer(in f)m	inmigrado, a	immigrato, a	imigrante
immigration	immigration	Einwanderung(f)	inmigración	immigrazione	imigração
immortal	immortel, le	unsterblich	inmortal	immortale	imortal
immunity	immunité	Immunität(f)	inmunidad	immunità	imunidade
immunize	immuniser	immunisieren	inmunizar	immunizzare	imunizar
impact	impact	Stoß(m)	impacto	impatto	impacto
impact	impact	Einfluß(m)	impacto	impatto	impacto
impartial	impartial, e	unparteiisch	imparcial	imparziale	imparcial
impatience	impatience	Ungeduld(f)	impaciencia	impazienza	impaciência
impatient	impatient, e	ungeduldig	impaciente	impaziente	impaciente
imperative, urgent	impératif, ive	bindend, zwingend	imperativo, a	imperativo, a	imperativo, a
imperfection	imperfection	Unvollkommenheit(f)	imperfección	imperfezione	imperfeição
imperialism	impérialisme	Imperialismus(m)	imperialismo	imperialismo	imperialismo
impertinent	impertinent, e	unverschämt	impertinente	impertinente	impertinente

English	French	German	Spanish	Italian	Portuguese
impetuous	impétueux, se	ungestüm, stürmisch	impetuoso, a	impetuoso, a	impetuoso, a
implication	implication	Verwicklung(f)	implicación	implicazione	implicação
implore, beg	implorer	an = flehen	implorar	implorare	implorar
implore	supplier	an = flehen	suplicar	supplicare	suplicar
imply	impliquer	bedeuten; an = deuten	implicar	implicare	implicar
impolite, rude	impoli, e	unhöflich	maleducado, a	maleducato, a	mal educado, a
import; importing	importation	Einfuhr(f)	importación	importazione	importação
import	importer	ein = führen	importar	importare	importar
importance	importance	Bedeutung(f)	importancia	importanza	importância
important	important, e	wichtig	importante	importante	importante
impose	imposer	auf = zwingen	imponer	imporre	impor
impose oneself on	imposer(s')	auf = drängen, sich	imponerse	imporsi	impor-se
impossible	impossible	unmöglich	imposible	impossibile	impossível
impregnate	imprégner	imprägnieren	impregnar	impregnare	impregnar
impresario	imprésario	Manager(m)	empresario	impresario	empresário
impress	impressionner	beeindrucken	impresionar	impressionare	impressionar
impression	impression	Eindruck(m)	impresión	impressione	impressão
impressive	impressionnant, e	beeindruckend	impresionante	impressionante	impressionante
imprison	incarcérer	ein = sperren	encarcelar	incarcerare	encarcerar
imprisonment	emprisonnement	Haft(f), Verhaftung(f)	encarcelamiento	incarcerazione	prisão
improve	améliorer	verbessern	mejorar	migliorare	melhorar
improve; perfect	perfectionner	vervollkommnen	perfeccionar	perfezionare	aperfeiçoar
improvement	amélioration	Verbesserung(f)	mejora; mejoría	miglioramento	melhoramento
improvise	improviser	improvisieren	improvisar	improvvisare	improvisar
imprudence	imprudence	Unvorsichtigkeit(f)	imprudencia	imprudenza	imprudência
impulse	impulsion	Impuls(m)	impulso	impulso	impulso
impurity	impureté	Unreinheit(f)	impureza	impurità	impureza
in, into	dans	in	dentro, en	in	dentro(de), em
in	en	in	en	in	em
in	à	in	en	a	em
in accordance with	conforme à	entsprechend	conforme a/con	conforme a	conforme com
in aid of	profit(au--de)	zugunsten von	beneficio(en--de)	beneficio(al--di)	proveito(em--de)
in front(ahead)of	devant	vor	delante, ante	davanti a	diante de
in order to	afin de	um...zu	a fin de	per; allo scopo di	a fim de
inaccessible	inaccessible	unerreichbar	inaccesible	inaccessibile	inacessível
inactive	inactif, ive	untätig, inaktiv	inactivo, a	inattivo, a	inactivo, a
inadmissible	inadmissible	unzulässig	inadmisible	inammissibile	inadmissível
inaugurate	inaugurer	ein = weihen	inaugurar	inaugurare	inaugurar
inauguration	inauguration	Einweihung(f)	inauguración	inaugurazione	inauguração
incandescent	incandescent, e	glühend	incandescente	incandescente	incandescente
incapable, unable	incapable	unfähig, untauglich	incapaz	incapace	incapaz
incest	inceste	Inzucht(f)	incesto	incesto	incesto
incident	incident	Zwischenfall(m)	incidente	incidente	incidente
incinerate	incinérer	ein = äschern	incinerar	incenerire	incinerar
incite	inciter	an = regen	incitar	incitare	incitar
incline, tilt	incliner	neigen	inclinar	inclinare	inclinar
include	inclure	ein = schließen	incluir	includere	incluir
included	inclus, e	inklusiv	incluido, a	incluso, a	incluso, a
inclusive	forfaitaire	pauschal	global; convenido, a	forfettario, a	preço fixo(a)
income, revenue	revenu	Einkommen(n)	renta, ingresos	reddito	rendimento
income, pension	rente	Einkommen(n)	renta	rendita	renda
incompatible	incompatible	unvereinbar	incompatible	incompatibile	incompatível
incompetence	incompétence	Inkompetenz(f)	incompetencia	incompetenza	incompetência
incomplete	incomplet, ète	unvollständig	incompleto, a	incompleto, a	incompleto, a
inconceivable	inimaginable	undenkbar	inimaginable	inimmaginabile	inimaginável
incontestable	incontestable	unbestreitbar	indiscutible	incontestabile	incontestável
incorporate	incorporer	ein = verleiben	incorporar	incorporare	incorporar
incorporation	incorporation	Eingliederung(f)	incorporación	incorporazione	incorporação
incorrect, wrong	incorrect, e	unrichtig, falsch	incorrecto, a	scorretto, a	incorrecto, a
increase, rise	augmentation	Zunahme(f)	aumento	aumento	aumento
increase	accroissement	Zuwachs(m)	crecimiento	crescita	crescimento
increase, raise	augmenter	zu = nehmen	aumentar	aumentare	aumentar
increase	accroître	zu = nehmen	incrementar	accrescere	aumentar
increase	grossir	vermehren	agrandar	ingrandire	aumentar
increment	augmentation	Zunahme(f)	incremento	incremento	incremento
incriminate	incriminer	beschuldigen	incriminar	incriminare	incriminar
incurable	incurable	unheilbar	incurable	incurabile	incurável
incursion	incursion	Überfall(m)	incursión	incursione	incursão

181

English	French	German	Spanish	Italian	Portuguese
indecent	indécent, e	unanständig	indecente	indecente	indecente
indeed	effet(en)	tatsächlich	efecto(en)	infatti	efeito(com)
indefinite	indéfini, e	unbestimmt	indefinido, a	indefinito, a	indefinido, a
independence	indépendance	Unabhängigkeit(f)	independencia	indipendenza	independência
independent	indépendant, e	unabhängig	independiente	indipendente	independente
index	index	Index(m)	índice	indice	índice
index	indice	Index m(Preisindex m)	índice	indice	índice
index; repertoire	répertoire	Repertoire(n)	repertorio	repertorio	repertório
indicate, show	indiquer	an = deuten, zeigen	indicar	indicare	indicar
indicate	désigner	bezeichnen	señalar, indicar	indicare	indicar
indication	indication	Angabe(f), Hinweis(m)	indicación	indicazione	indicação
indication, sign	indice	Anzeichen(n)	indicio	indizio	indício
indicator	indicateur	Anzeiger(m)	indicador	indicatore	indicador
indicator	clignotant	Blinklicht(n)	intermitente	freccia	pisca
indictment	réquisitoire	Anklagerede(f)	requisitoria	requisitoria	requisitório
indifferent	indifférent, e	gleichgültig	indiferente	indifferente	indiferente
indigestible	indigeste	unverdaulich	indigesto, a	indigesto, a	indigesto, a
indignation	indignation	Empörung(f)	indignación	indignazione	indignação
indirect	indirect, e	indirekt	indirecto, a	indiretto, a	indirecto, a
indiscretion	indiscrétion	Indiskretion(f)	indiscreción	indiscrezione	indiscrição
indispensable	indispensable	unentbehrlich	indispensable	indispensabile	indispensável
individual	individuel, le	individuell	individual	individuale	individual
individual	individu	Individuum(n)	individuo	individuo	indivíduo
individual	particulier	Privatmann(m)	particular	privato	particular
indoctrinate	endoctriner	indoktrinieren	adoctrinar	addottrinare	doutrinar
induce	induire	veranlassen	inducir	indurre	induzir
indulgence	indulgence	Nachsicht(f)	indulgencia	indulgenza	indulgência
industrial	industriel, le	industriell	industrial	industriale	industrial
industrialist	industriel	Industrielle(m)	industrial	industriale	industrial
industry	industrie	Industrie(f)	industria	industria	indústria
inefficient	inefficace	unwirksam, unfähig	ineficaz	inefficace	ineficaz
inequality	inégalité	Ungleichheit(f)	desigualdad	disuguaglianza	desigualdade
inert	inerte	regungslos	inerte	inerte	inerte
inertia	inertie	Trägheit(f)	inercia	inerzia	inércia
inexact, inaccurate	inexact, e	ungenau	inexacto, a	inesatto, a	inexacto, a
infallible	infaillible	unfehlbar	infalible	infallibile	infalível
infantile, child	infantile	Kinder-, kindisch	infantil	infantile	infantil
infection	infection	Infektion(f)	infección	infezione	infecção
inferior	inférieur, e	minderwertig	inferior	inferiore	inferior
infernal	infernal, e	Höllen-; höllisch	infernal	infernale	infernal
infiltration	infiltration	Einsickern(n)	infiltración	infiltrazione	infiltração
infinite	infini, e	unendlich	infinito, a	infinito, a	infinito, a
infinitive	infinitif	Infinitiv(m)	infinitivo	infinito	infinitivo
infirmary	infirmerie	Krankenraum(m)	enfermería	infermeria	enfermaria
inflammable	inflammable	brennbar	inflamable	infiammabile	inflamável
inflate, blow up	gonfler	auf = blasen	inflar	gonfiare	inchar, encher
inflation	inflation	Inflation(f)	inflación	inflazione	inflação
inflexible	inflexible	starr	inflexible	inflessibile	inflexível
inflict	infliger	auf = erlegen	infligir	infliggere	infligir
influence	influence	Einfluß(m)	influencia	influenza	influência
influential	influent, e	einflußreich	influyente	influente	influente
inform	informer	informieren	informar	imformare	informar
information	information	Information(f)	información	informazione	informação
information	renseignement	Auskunft(f)	información	informazione	informação
ingenious	ingénieux, se	sinnreich	ingenioso, a	ingegnoso, a	engenhoso, a
ingenuous	candide	naiv, aufrichtig	cándido, a	candido, a	cândido, a
ingot, bullion	lingot	Barren(m)	lingote	lingotto	lingote
inhabitant	habitant, e	Einwohner(in f)m	habitante	abitante	habitante
inhale	inhaler, respirer	ein = atmen	inhalar	inalare	inalar
inhale, suck in(up)	aspirer	ein = atmen, saugen	aspirar	aspirare	aspirar
inheritance, legacy	héritage	Erbschaft(f)	herencia	eredità	herança
inhuman	inhumain, e	unmenschlich	inhumano, a	inumano, a	desumano, a
initial	initial, e	anfänglich; Anfangs-	inicial	iniziale	inicial
initials	sigle	Abkürzung(f)	sigla	sigla	sigla
initiation	initiation	Einführung(f)	iniciación	iniziazione	iniciação
initiative	initiative	Initiative(f)	iniciativa	iniziativa	iniciativa
inject	injecter	spritzen, ein = spritzen	inyectar	iniettare	injectar
injection	piqûre	Spritze(f)	inyección	iniezione	injecção

English	French	German	Spanish	Italian	Portuguese
injure, wound	blesser	verletzen	herir	ferire	ferir
injured(to be)	blesser(se)	verletzen, sich	herir(se)	ferirsi	ferir-se
injured person	accidenté, e	Verunglückte(f, m)	accidentado, a	accidentato, a	acidentado, a
injury, wound	blessure	Verletzung(f)	herida	ferita	ferida
injustice	injustice	Ungerechtigkeit(f)	injusticia	ingiustizia	injustiça
ink	encre	Tinte(f)	tinta	inchiostro	tinta
Inland Revenue	fisc	Fiskus(m), Finanzamt	fisco	fisco	fisco
inn	auberge	Gasthaus(n)	posada; albergue	locanda	estalagem
innate	inné, e	angeboren	innato, a	innato, a	inato, a
inner, interior	intérieur, e	inner	interior	interiore	interior
innocent	innocent, e	unschuldig	inocente	innocente	inocente
innovate	innover	innovieren, erneuern	innovar	innovare	inovar
innovation	innovation	Neuerung(f)(Er-)	innovación	innovazione	inovação
inoffensive	inoffensif, ive	harmlos	inofensivo, a	inoffensivo, a	inofensivo, a
inorganic	inorganique	anorganisch	inorgánico, a	inorganico, a	inorgânico, a
inquire	informer(s')	erkundigen, sich	informarse	informarsi	informar-se
inquire	renseigner(se)	erkundigen, sich	informar(se)	informare(-arsi)	informar-se
inquiry, inquest	enquête	Untersuchung(f)	investigación	indagine, inchiesta	inquérito
insane, crazy, mad	dément, e	verrückt	demente	demente	demente
insanity, madness	démence	Wahnsinn(m)	demencia	demenza, follia	demência
inscription	inscription	Inschrift(f)	inscripción	iscrizione	inscrição
insect	insecte	Insekt(n)	insecto	insetto	insecto
insemination	insémination	Befruchtung(f)	inseminación	inseminazione	inseminação
insensitive	insensible	unempfindlich	insensible	insensibile	insensível
insert	insérer	ein = setzen, ein = fügen	insertar	inserire	inserir
insert; introduce	introduire	ein = führen	introducir	introdurre	introduzir
insertion	insertion	Einfügung(f)	inserción	inserzione	inserção
inside	dedans	in, drinnen, innen	dentro, adentro	dentro	dentro
inside, inner	intérieur, e	innere(r, s); innen	interior	interno, a	interior
insignificant	insignifiant, e	unbedeutend	insignificante	insignificante	insignificante
insist	insister	bestehen, beharren	insistir	insistere	insistir
insolence	insolence	Frechheit(f)	insolencia	insolenza	insolência
insolent	insolent, e	unverschämt, frech	insolente	insolente	insolente
insomnia	insomnie	Schlaflosigkeit(f)	insomnio	insonnia	insónia
inspect	contrôler	besichtigen	controlar, examinar	esaminare	examinar
inspection	inspection	Überprüfung(f)	inspección	ispezione	inspecção
inspector	inspecteur, trice	Inspektor(in f)m	inspector, a	ispettore, trice	inspector, a
inspector	contrôleur	Kontrolleur(m)	revisor	controllore	revisor; fiscal
inspiration	inspiration	Anregung(f)	inspiración	ispirazione	inspiração
install	installer	ein = richten	instalar	installare	instalar
installation	installation	Einrichtung(f)	instalación	installazione	instalação
instance(for)	exemple(par)	Beispiel(zum)	ejemplo(por)	esempio(per)	exemplo(por)
instead(of)	au lieu de	anstatt	en vez de/lugar de	invece di	em vez de/lugar de
instinct	instinct	Instinkt(m)	instinto	istinto	instinto
instinctive	instinctif, ive	instinktiv	instintivo, a	istintivo, a	instintivo, a
institute	institut	Institut(n)	instituto	istituto	instituto
institution	institution	Institution(f)	institución	istituzione	instituição
institutional	institutionnel	gesetzlich	institucional	istituzionale	institucional
instruction	instruction	Ausbildung(f)	instrucción	istruzione	instrução
instructor	instructeur	Ausbilder(m)	instructor	istruttore, trice	instrutor, a
instructor	moniteur, trice	Leiter/in; Lehrer/in	monitor, a	istruttore, trice	monitor, a
instructor	éducateur, trice	Erzieher(in f)m	educador, a	educatore, trice	educador, a
instrument	instrument	Instrument(n)	instrumento	strumento	instrumento
insufficient	insuffisant, e	ungenügend	insuficiente	insufficiente	insuficiente
insulate; isolate	isoler	isolieren	aislar	isolare	isolar
insulation	isolation	Isolierung(f)	aislamiento	isolamento	isolação
insulin	insuline	Insulin(n)	insulina	insulina	insulina
insult	insulte	Beleidigung(f)	insulto	insulto	insulto
insult	injure	Beleidigung(f)	injuria	ingiuria	injúria
insult	insulter	beleidigen	insultar	insultare	insultar
insurance	assurance	Versicherung(f)	seguro	assicurazione	seguro
insured	assuré, e	versichert	asegurado, a	assicurato, a	segurado, a
intact	intact, e	intakt	intacto, a	intatto, a	intacto, a
integral	intégral, e	vollständig	íntegro, a	integrale	integral
integrate	intégrer	integrieren	integrar	integrare	integrar
integrity	intégrité	Integrität(f)	integridad	integrità	integridade
intellectual	intellectuel, le	intellektuell	intelectual	intellettuale	intelectual
intelligence	intelligence	Intelligenz(f)	inteligencia	intelligenza	inteligência

English	French	German	Spanish	Italian	Portuguese
intelligent	intelligent, e	intelligent	inteligente	intelligente	inteligente
intend	intention(avoir)	beabsichtigen	intención(tener)	intenzione(avere)	tencionar
intended to(be)	destiner	bestimmen für	destinar	destinare	destinar
intense	intense	heftig, stark	intenso, a	intenso, a	intenso, a
intensity	intensité	Intensität(f)	intensidad	intensità	intensidade
intensive	intensif, ive	intensiv	intensivo, a	intensivo, a	intensivo, a
intention	intention	Absicht(f)	intención	intenzione	intenção
intention, aim	propos, intention	Absicht(f)	propósito	proposito	propósito
interbreed, cross	croiser	kreuzen	cruzar	incrociare	cruzar
intercept	intercepter	auf = fangen, ab = fangen	interceptar	intercettare	interceptar
interest	intérêt	Interesse(n)	interés	interesse	interesse
interest	intérêt	Zins(m)	interés	interesse	juro
interested in(be)	intéresser(s')	interessieren, sich	interesarse	interessarsi	interessar-se
interested(very)	passionné, e	leidenschaftlich	apasionado, a	appassionato, a	apaixonado, a
interesting	intéressant, e	interessant	interesante	interessante	interessante
interfere	mêler de(se)	ein = mischen, sich	implicarse	immischiare(-rsi)	envolver-se
interference	interférence	Einmischung; Störung	interferencia	interferenza	interferência
interference	ingérence	Einmischung(f)	ingerencia	ingerenza	ingerência
interior	intérieur	Innere(n)	interior	interiore	interior
interlocutor	interlocuteur	Gesprächspartner/in	interlocutor, a	interlocutore, trice	interlocutor, a
intermediate	intermédiaire	Zwischen-, Mittel-	intermediario, a	intermediario, a	intermediário, a
intermittent	intermittent, e	aussetzend	intermitente	intermittente	intermitente
internal, inner	interne	intern	interno, a	interno, a	interno, a
international	international, e	international	internacional	internazionale	internacional
interpret	interpréter	deuten, aus = legen	interpretar	interpretare	interpretar
interpreter	interprète	Dolmetscher(in f)m	intérprete	interprete	intérprete
interrupt	interrompre	unterbrechen	interrumpir	interrompere	interromper
interruption	interruption	Unterbrechung(f)	interrupción	interruzione	interrupção
intersection	intersection	Kreuzung(f)	intersección	intersezione	intersecção
interval	intervalle	Abstand(m)	intervalo	intervallo	intervalo
interval	entracte	Pause(f)	intermedio	intervallo	intervalo
intervene	intervenir	dazwischen = treten	intervenir	intervenire	intervir
intervention	intervention	Eingriff(m)	intervención	intervento	intervenção
interview	interview	Interview(n)	interviú	intervista	entrevista
interview	entrevue	Treffen(n), Gespräch n	entrevista	intervista	entrevista
intestine	intestin	Darm(m)	intestino	intestino	intestino
intimate	intime	vertraut, intim	íntimo, a	íntimo, a	íntimo, a
intimidate	intimider	ein = schüchtern	intimidar	intimidire	intimidar
intolerance	intolérance	Intoleranz(f)	intolerancia	intolleranza	intolerância
intonation	intonation	Tonfall(m)	entonación	intonazione	entoação
intrepid	intrépide	kühn, mutig	intrépido, a	intrepido, a	intrépido, a
intrigue	intrigue	Intrige(f)	intriga	intrigo	intriga
intrigue	intriguer	intrigieren	intrigar	intrigare	intrigar
introduce	introduire	vor = stellen	presentar	introdurre	apresentar
introduce	présenter	vor = stellen	presentar	presentare	apresentar
intrusion	intrusion	Eindringen(n)	intrusión	intrusione	intrusão
intuition	intuition	Intuition(f)	intuición	intuizione	intuição
invade	envahir	ein = fallen	invadir	invadere	invadir
invariable	invariable	unveränderlich	invariable	invariabile	invariável
invasion	invasion	Invasion(f)	invasión	invasione	invasão
invent	inventer	erfinden	inventar	inventare	inventar
invention	invention	Erfindung(f)	invención	invenzione	invenção
inventor	inventeur	Erfinder(in f)m	inventor	inventore	inventor
inventory	inventaire	Inventar(n)	inventario	inventario	inventário
inversion	inversion	Umkehrung(f)	inversión	inversione	inversão
invest	investir	investieren	invertir	investire	investir
invest	placer	an = legen	invertir	investire	pôr a render
investigate	enquêter	untersuchen	investigar	investigare, indagare	investigar
investigate	étudier, examiner	prüfen, erforschen	estudiar	studiare	estudar, examinar
investiture	investiture	Investitur(f)	investidura	investitura	investidura
investment	investissement	Investition(f)	inversión	investimento	investimento
invincible	invincible	unbesiegbar	invencible	invincibile	invencível
invisible	invisible	unsichtbar	invisible	invisibile	invisível
invitation	invitation	Einladung(f)	invitación	invito	convite
invite	inviter	ein = laden	invitar	invitare	convidar
invoice, bill	facture	Rechnung(f)	factura	fattura	factura
invoke	invoquer	beziehen auf, sich	invocar	invocare	invocar
involve	impliquer	verwickeln	implicar	implicare	implicar

English	French	German	Spanish	Italian	Portuguese
iris	iris	Iris(f)	iris	iride	íris
iron	fer	Eisen(n)	hierro	ferro	ferro
iron	fer à repasser	Bügeleisen(n)	plancha	ferro da stiro	ferro de passar
ironing	repassage	Bügeln(n)	planchado	stirare	passar a ferro
ironmonger's	quincaillerie	Eisenwarenhandlung(f)	ferretería	ferramenta	loja de ferragens
irony	ironie	Ironie(f)	ironía	ironia	ironia
irradiation	irradiation	Bestrahlung(f)	irradiación	irradiazione	irradiação
irregular	irrégulier, e	unregelmäßig	irregular	irregolare	irregular
irrigate	irriguer	bewässern	irrigar	irrigare	irrigar
irritate	irriter	reizen, irritieren	irritar	irritare	irritar
irritating	irritant, e	ärgerlich; aufregend	irritante	irritante	irritante
irritation	agacement	Ärger(m)	fastidio	irritazione	irritação
irruption	irruption	Eindringen(n)	irrupción	irruzione	irrupção
Islamic	islamique	islamisch	islámico, a	islamico, a	islâmico, a
island, isle	île	Insel(f)	isla	isola	ilha
islet	îlot	Inselchen(n)	islote	isolotto	ilhéu, ilhota
isolate	isoler	ab = sondern; isolieren	aislar	isolare	isolar
isolated, lonely	isolé, e	allein, einsam	aislado, a	isolato, a	isolado, a; só, a
issue	numéro, tirage	Auflage(f)	número, edición	numero, pubblicazione	número
itch, itching	démangeaison	Juckreiz(m)	picazón	prurito	comichão
item	article	Artikel(m)	artículo	articolo	artigo
itinerary, route	itinéraire	Route(f), Strecke(f)	itinerario	itinerario	itinerário
ivory	ivoire	Elfenbein(n)	marfil	avorio	marfim

J

English	French	German	Spanish	Italian	Portuguese
jack	cric	Wagenheber(m)	gato	cric, cricco	macaco
jack	vérin, cric	Winde(f)	gato, cric	martinetto, binda	macaco
jacket	veste	Jacke(f)	chaqueta	giacca	jaqueta, casaco
jam	confiture	Marmelade(f)	mermelada	marmellata	doce, compota
jam	coincer	ein = klemmen	apretar, apiñar	schiacciare, bloccare	apertar, comprimir
jamming	blocage	Blockierung(f), Sperre	bloqueo	bloccaggio	bloqueamento
January	Janvier	Januar(m)	Enero	Gennaio	Janeiro
jar	bocal	Glasgefäß(n)	tarro, bocal	boccale, vaso	boião
jargon	jargon	Fachsprache(f)	jerga	gergo	calão, gíria
jaundice	jaunisse	Gelbsucht(f)	ictericia	itterizia	icterícia
jaw	mâchoire	Kiefer(m)	mandíbula	mascella	maxila
jazz	jazz	Jazz(m)	jazz	jazz	jazz
jealous	jaloux, se	eifersüchtig	celoso, a	geloso, a	ciumento, a
jealousy	jalousie	Eifersucht(f)	celos	gelosia	ciúme
jelly	gelée	Gelee(n)	jalea	gelatina	geleia
jetty	jetée	Hafendamm(m), Mole(f)	escollera	molo, gettata	molhe
Jew, Jewess(-es)	juif, juive	Jude(m), Jüdin(f)	judío, judía	ebreo, a	judeu, judia
jewel	bijou(x)	Schmuck(m)(-stück n)	joya	gioiello	jóia
jewel	joyau	Juwel(n), Schmuckstück	joya	gioiello	jóia
jeweller's	bijouterie	Schmuckgeschäft(n)	joyería	gioielleria	joalharia
jigsaw(puzzle)	puzzle	Puzzle(n)	rompecabezas	puzzle	puzzle
job, work	emploi	Beruf(m)	empleo	impiego	emprego
jockey	jockey	Jockey(m)	jockey	jockey, fantino	jockey
join	inscrire(s')	bei = treten	inscribirse	iscriversi	inscrever-se
join	joindre à(se)	an = schließen, sich	juntarse con	unirsi, associarsi	juntar-se
join	adhérer	Mitglied werden	adherir a	aderire a	aderir a
join	associer à(s')	an = schließen, sich	asociarse(a, con)	associarsi(a, con)	associar-se a
join, enter	engager(s')	bei = treten	ingresar, meterse	impegnarsi	aderir, ligar-se
joined, linked	joint, e	zusammengefügt	junto, a	giunto, a	junto, a
joiner, carpenter	menuisier	Tischler(m)	carpintero	falegname	carpinteiro
joint, join, seal	joint	Dichtung(f)	junta	giunto, guarnizione	junta, anilha

English	French	German	Spanish	Italian	Portuguese
joint	articulation	Gelenk(n)	articulación	articolazione	articulação
joke	plaisanterie	Witz(m)	chiste, gracia	scherzo	brincadeira
joke; farce	farce	Streich(m)	broma	scherzo	partida
joke	blague	Witz(m)	chiste	scherzo	anedota, chalaça
joke, hoax	canular	Ulk(m), Witz(m)	broma	scherzo, burla	partida
joke	plaisanter	scherzen	bromear	scherzare	gracejar
jolt, jerk	secousse	Ruck(m), Stoß(m)	sacudida	scossa	abalo
journalism	journalisme	Journalismus(m)	periodismo	giornalismo	jornalismo
journalist	journaliste	Journalist(in f)m	periodista	giornalista	jornalista
journey, trip	trajet, voyage	Strecke(f)	trayecto	tragitto	trajecto
journey; course	parcours	Strecke(f), Route(f)	recorrido	percorso	percurso
joy	joie	Freude(f)	alegría	gioia	alegria
judge	juge	Richter(in f)m	juez	giudice	juíz
judge	juger	beurteilen	juzgar	giudicare	julgar
judgement	jugement	Urteil(n)	juicio	giudizio	julgamento
judicial, legal	judiciaire	gerichtlich	judicial	giudiziario, a	judiciário, a
judicious	judicieux, se	scharfsinnig	juicioso, a	giudizioso, a	judicioso, a
judo	judo	Judo(n)	judo, yudo	judò	judo
jug, carafe	carafe	Karaffe(f)	jarra	caraffa	jarro, caneca
juice	jus	Saft(m)	jugo	succo	sumo
July	Juillet	Juli(m)	Julio	Luglio	Julho
jump	sauter	springen	saltar	saltare	saltar, pular
jump, leap	bondir	springen	saltar	saltare, balzare	saltar
jump	saut	Sprung(m)	salto	salto	salto
jumper, sweater	chandail	Pullover(m)	jersey	maglione	camisola
June	Juin	Juni(m)	Junio	Giugno	Junho
jungle	jungle	Dschungel(m)	selva, jungla	giungla	selva
junta	junte	Junta(f)	junta	giunta	junta
juridical, legal	juridique	juristisch	jurídico, a	giuridico, a	jurídico, a
jurisprudence	jurisprudence	Rechtsprechung(f)	jurisprudencia	giurisprudenza	jurisprudência
jurist; lawyer	juriste	Jurist(in f)m	jurista	giurista	jurista
jury	jury	Jury(f)	jurado; tribunal	giuria	júri
juryman, juror	juré	Geschworene(f, m)	jurado	giurato	jurado
just	juste	gerecht	justo, a	giusto, a	justo, a
justice	justice	Gerechtigkeit(f)	justicia	giustizia	justiça
justification	justification	Rechtfertigung(f)	justificación	giustificazione	justificação
justify	justifier	begründen, belegen	justificar	giustificare	justificar

K

English	French	German	Spanish	Italian	Portuguese
kangaroo	kangourou	Känguruh(n)	canguro	canguro	cangurú
karate	karaté	Karate(n)	karate	karatè	karaté
kayak	kayac	Kajak(m)	kayac, piragua	kayak	kayac
keen	vif, vive	scharf	agudo, a; vivo, a	vivo, a	vivo, a
keep	garder	behalten	guardar	tenere	guardar
keeper, caretaker	gardien, ne	Wärter(in f)m	guardián, ana	custode, guardia	guarda
kettle	bouilloire	Wasserkessel(m)	hervidor	bollitore	chaleira
key	clef, clé	Schlüssel(m)	llave	chiave	chave
key	touche	Taste(f)	tecla	tasto	tecla
keyboard	clavier	Tastatur(f)	teclado	tastiera	teclado
key-ring	porte-clefs	Schlüsselring(m)	llavero	portachiavi	porta-chaves
kick	coup de pied	Fußtritt(m)	patada	calcio	pontapé
kid, child	gamin, e	Kind(n)	chiquillo, a	ragazzino, a	miúdo
kidnap	kidnapper	entführen	secuestrar	rapire	raptar
kidney	rein	Niere(f)	riñón	rene	rim
kill	tuer	töten	matar	uccidere	matar
killed	tué, e	getötet	muerto, a	ucciso, a	morto, a

English	French	German	Spanish	Italian	Portuguese
killer	tueur, se	Mörder(in f)m	asesino, a	assassino, a	assassino, a
kilogram(me)	kilogramme	Kilo(gramm n)n	kilogramo	chilogrammo, chilo	quilograma, quilo
kilometre	kilomètre	Kilometer(m)	kilómetro	chilometro	quilómetro
kimono	kimono	Kimono(m)	quimono, kimono	chimono	quimono
kind, kindly	bon, aimable	gütig, liebvoll	bueno, a	buono, a	bom, boa
kind, nice	gentil, le	nett	gentil, amable	gentile	gentil, amável
kind, sort	espèce	Gattung(f), Art(f)	especie	specie	espécie
kind, sort	genre	Art(f), Sorte(f)	género	genere	género
kindness	bonté	Güte(f)	bondad	bontà	bondade
king	roi	König(m)	rey	re	rei
kingdom	royaume	Königreich(n)	reino	reame	reino
kiss	bise	Küßchen(n)	besito	bacio	beijinho
kiss	baiser	Kuß(m)	beso(dar un)	bacio	beijo
kiss; embrace	embrasser	küssen, umarmen	abrazar, besar	baciare	abraçar, beijar
kit, case, bag	trousse	Etui(n), Tasche(f)	maletín, estuche	borsa, astuccio	estojo
kitchen	cuisine	Küche(f)	cocina	cucina	cozinha
knead	pétrir	kneten	amasar	impastare	amassar
knee	genou	Knie(n)	rodilla	ginocchio	joelho
knee-cap	rotule	Kniescheibe(f)	rótula	rotula	rótula
kneel	agenouiller(s')	hin = knien, sich	arrodillarse	inginocchiare(-rsi)	ajoelhar-se
knife(-ives)	couteau	Messer(n)	cuchillo	coltello	faca
knit	tricoter	stricken	hacer punto	lavorare a maglia	tricotar
knob	bouton	Knopf(m)	botón	manopola, pomello	botão
knock, blow	coup	Schlag(m)	golpe	colpo	golpe
knock	frapper, heurter	an = klopfen	llamar	bussare	bater
knock(against)	heurter	stoßen	tropezar con	urtare	chocar, bater
knock	cogner(se)	stoßen, sich	golpe(darse un)	sbattere	chocar com
knock out	assommer	nieder = schlagen	dejar k.o.	stordire	espancar
knock over/down	renverser	um = stoßen	derribar	travolgere	derrubar
knot	noeud	Knoten(m)	nudo	nodo	nó, laço
know	savoir	wissen	saber	sapere	saber
know	connaître	kennen	conocer, saber	conoscere, sapere	conhecer, saber
know-how	savoir-faire	Geschick(n)	tacto, maña	savoir-faire	habilidade
knowledge	savoir	Wissen(n)	saber	sapere	sabedoria
knowledge	connaissance	Kenntnis(f)	conocimiento	conoscenza	conhecimento
Koran	Coran	Koran(der)	Corán	Corano	Alcorão

L

English	French	German	Spanish	Italian	Portuguese
label, tag	étiquette	Schild(n)	etiqueta	etichetta	rótulo
laboratory	laboratoire	Labor(n)	laboratorio	laboratorio	laboratório
labour	travail	Arbeit(f)	trabajo	lavoro	trabalho
labourer	manoeuvre	Hilfsarbeiter(in f)m	peón, obrero	manovale	servente
labyrinth, maze	labyrinthe	Labyrinth(n)	laberinto	labirinto	labirinto
lace	dentelle	Spitze(f)	puntilla	merletto	renda
lace	lacet	Schnürsenkel(m)	cordón	laccio	cordão
lack, shortage	manque	Mangel(m)	falta, carencia	mancanza	falta, carência
lack, be short of	manquer	fehlen	faltar	mancare	falta(ter)
lacquer	laque	Lack(m)	laca	lacca	laca
ladder	échelle	Leiter(f)	escalera	scala	escada
ladies	mesdames	meine Damen	señoras	signore	senhoras
lady	dame	Dame(f)	señora	signora	senhora
lagoon	lagune	Binnensee(m)	laguna	laguna	laguna
lake	lac	See(m)	lago	lago	lago
lamb	agneau	Lamm(n)	cordero	agnello	cordeiro
lament	lamenter(se)	jammern	lamentarse	lamentarsi	lamentar-se
lamp	lampe	Lampe(f)	lámpara	lampada	candeeiro

English	French	German	Spanish	Italian	Portuguese
land	terre	Land(n)	tierra	terra	terra
land	atterrir	landen	aterrizar	atterrare	aterrar
landowner	propriétaire	Gutsherr(-sbesitzer)	propietario, a	proprietario, a	proprietário, a
landlord	propriétaire	Besitzer/in; (Haus-)	dueño, a	proprietario, a	senhorio, a; dono, a
land register	cadastre	Grundbuch(n)	catastro	catasto	cadastro
landscape	paysage	Landschaft(f)	paisaje	paesaggio	paisagem
landslide	éboulement	Erdrutsch(m)	desprendimiento	frana, slavina	desmoronamento
lane	voie	Spur(f)(Straßen-)	vía	corsia	faixa(rua)
lane	file	Spur(f)	fila	fila, corsia	fila
language	langage	Sprache(f)	lenguaje	linguaggio	linguagem
language	langue	Sprache(f)	idioma, lengua	lingua	língua, idioma
lantern	lanterne	Laterne(f)	linterna	lanterna	lanterna
large, big	grand, e	weit	gran, grande	grande, ampio, a	grande
larva(-vae)	larve	Larve(f)	larva	larva	larva
laryngitis	laryngite	Halsentzündung(f)	laringitis	laringite	laringite
larynx	larynx	Kehlkopf(m)	laringe	laringe	laringe
laser	laser	Laser(m)	láser	laser	laser
last	dernier, ière	letzter, letzte	último, a	ultimo, a	último, a
last	dernier	Letzte(f, m)	último, a	ultimo, a	último, a
last	durer	dauern	durar	durare	durar
late	tard	spät	tarde	tardi	tarde
late(to be)	retard(être en)	zu spät kommen	retrasado, a(estar)	ritardo(essere in)	atrasado, a(estar)
later	plus tard	später	más tarde	più tardi	mais tarde
later	ultérieur, e	später	ulterior	ulteriore	ulterior
later	postérieur, e	spätere(r, s)	posterior	posteriore	posterior
lateral	latéral, e	seitlich	lateral	laterale	lateral
latitude	latitude	Breitengrad(m)	latitud	latitudine	latitude
laugh	rire	lachen	reir	ridere	rir
laugh, laughter	rire	Lachen(n)	risa	riso, ridere	riso
launch, start up	lancer	lancieren, starten	lanzar	lanciare	lançar
launch(ing)	lancement	Start(m)	lanzamiento	lancio	lançamento
laundry	blanchisserie	Wäscherei(f)	lavandería	lavanderia	lavandaria
law	loi	Gesetz(n)	ley	legge	lei
law	droit	Recht(n)	derecho	diritto	direito
lawn	pelouse	Rasenfläche(f)	césped	prato inglese	relvado
lawsuit, trial	procès	Prozeß(m)	proceso, juicio	processo	processo
lawsuit	procès	Prozeß(m)	pleito	causa	pleito, processo
lawyer, barrister	avocat, e	Anwalt(m), Anwältin(f)	abogado, a	avvocato, tessa	advogado, a
laxative	laxatif, ive	abführend	laxante	lassativo, a	laxante
lay	mettre, placer	legen	poner, colocar	porre, mettere	pôr, colocar
lay	pondre	Eier legen	poner(huevos)	fare l'uovo	pôr(ovos)
lay off, dismiss	licencier	entlassen	despedir	licenziare	despedir
layer	couche	Schicht(f)	capa	strato	camada
layout	agencement	Anlage(f)	disposición	disposizione	disposição
lazy	paresseux, se	faul	perezoso, a	pigro, a	preguiçoso, a
lazy	fainéant, e	faul	holgazán, a	fannullone, a	preguiçoso, a
lead	plomb	Blei(n)	plomo	piombo	chumbo
lead	mener, conduire	führen	guiar, conducir	condurre	levar, conduzir
lead to	aboutir à	führen zu	conducir a	arrivare a	conduzir a
leader	chef, dirigeant	Leiter(m), Führer(m)	jefe	capo, dirigente	chefe, líder
leader, manager	dirigeant, leader	Leiter(m), Führer(m)	dirigente	dirigente	dirigente
leader, organiser	animateur, trice	Leiter/in, Unterhalter	animador, a	animatore, trice	animador, a
leaf(leaves)	feuille	Blatt(n)	hoja	foglia	folha
leaflet	prospectus	Flugblatt(n)	folleto	prospetto	prospecto
leak	fuite	Leck(n)	escape	perdita	fuga
lean on(against)	appuyer(s')	stützen, sich	apoyar(se)	appoggiarsi	apoiar-se
lean out	pencher(se)	hinaus = lehnen	asomarse	sporgersi	debruçar-se
learn	apprendre	lernen	aprender	imparare	aprender
learned person	savant, e	Wissenschaftler(m)	sabio, a	studioso, a; dotto, a	sábio, a
learning	apprentissage	Lernen(n)	estudio	tirocinio	aprendizagem
lease	louer à bail	mieten; pachten	arrendar	noleggiare	arrendar, alugar
least((the)	moins(le)	wenigsten(am)	menos(lo)	meno(il)	menos(o)
leather	cuir	Leder(n)	cuero	cuoio, pelle	couro
leave	laisser	lassen(zurück = -, ver-)	dejar	lasciare	deixar
leave	quitter	verlassen	dejar, abandonar	lasciare	deixar
leave, go away	partir	weg = gehen	salir, marcharse	partire	partir, abalar
lecture	conférence	Vorlesung(f), Vortrag	conferencia	conferenza	conferência
left	gauche	links; linke(r, s)	izquierdo, a	sinistro, a	esquerdo, a

English	French	German	Spanish	Italian	Portuguese
left(be), remain	rester	übrig = bleiben, bleiben	quedar	rimanere, avanzare	sobrar
left luggage	consigne(bagage)	Gepäckaufbewahrung(f)	consigna(equipaje)	deposito bagagli	depósito(bagagem)
leg	jambe	Bein(n)	pierna	gamba	perna
leg	cuisse	Schenkel(m)	muslo; pierna	coscia	perna
legal	légal, e	gesetzlich	legal	legale	legal
legal	judiciaire, légal	rechtmäßig	judicial	giudiziario, a	judicial
legality	légalité	Rechtmäßigkeit(f)	legalidad	legalità	legalidade
legend	légende	Legende(f)	leyenda	leggenda	lenda
legible	lisible	leserlich	legible	leggibile	legível
legislation	législation	Gesetzgebung(f)	legislación	legislazione	legislação
legislative	législatif, ive	gesetzgebend	legislativo, a	legislativo, a	legislativo, a
legitimate	légitime	legitim	legítimo, a	legittimo, a	legítimo, a
leisure	loisir	Freizeit(f)	tiempo libre	tempo libero, hobby	tempo livre
lemon	citron	Zitrone(f)	limón	limone	limão
lend	prêter	leihen, verleihen	prestar	prestare	emprestar
length	longueur	Länge(f)	longitud	lunghezza	comprimento
lengthen	allonger	verlängern	alargar	allungare	alongar
lens	objectif	Objektiv(n)	objetivo	obiettivo	objectiva
lens(contact -)	lentille	Kontaktlinse(f)	lentilla	lente a contatto	lente
lentil	lentille	Linse(f)(Pflanze)	lenteja	lenticchia	lentilha
lesbian	lesbienne	lesbisch	lesbiana	lesbica	lésbica
lesion, injury	lésion	Verletzung(f)	lesión	lesione	lesão
less	moins	weniger	menos	meno	menos
lesson	leçon	Stunde(f); Lektion(f)	lección	lezione	lição
lesson	cours	Unterricht(m)	curso, clase	corso, lezione	curso, aula
let; leave	laisser	lassen	dejar	lasciare	deixar
let go, release	larguer	weg = werfen, auf = geben	largar	lasciare, mollare	largar, deixar
lethargic	mou, molle	schlaff	fofo, a	molle; fiacco, a	mole; fraco, a
letter	lettre	Buchstabe(m)	letra	lettera	letra
letter	lettre	Brief(m)	carta	lettera	carta
letter, character	caractère	Schrifttyp(m)	letra	carattere, lettera	carácter
letter box	boîte(lettres)	Briefkasten(m)	buzón	buca delle lettere	caixa do correio
lettuce	laitue, salade	Kopfsalat(m)	lechuga	lattuga	alface
leukaemia	leucémie	Leukämie(f)	leucemia	leucemia	leucemia
level	niveau	Stand(m), Niveau(n)	nivel	livello	nível
level	aplanir	ebnen	aplanar	spianare	aplanar
lever	levier	Hebel(m)	palanca	leva	alavanca
liable(to be)	responsable	haftbar	responsable	responsabile	responsável
liar	menteur, se	Lügner(in f)m	mentiroso, a	bugiardo, a	mentiroso, a
liberal	libéral, e	liberal	liberal	liberale	liberal
liberalism	libéralisme	Liberalismus(m)	liberalismo	liberalismo	liberalismo
liberate, free	libérer	befreien	liberar	liberare	libertar
liberty, freedom	liberté	Freiheit(f)	libertad	libertà	liberdade
libido	libido	Libido(f)	líbido	libido	líbido
library	bibliothèque	Bibliothek(f)	biblioteca	biblioteca	biblioteca
licence	licence	Lizenz(f)	licencia	licenza	licença
licence; permit	permis	Schein(m), Genehmigung	permiso	permesso, licenza	licença
lick	lécher	lecken	lamer	leccare	lamber
lid, cover	couvercle	Deckel(m)	tapa, tapadera	coperchio	tampa
lie, fib	mensonge	Lüge(f)	mentira	bugia	mentira
lie	mentir	lügen	mentir	mentire	mentir
lie down	allonger(s')	hin = legen, sich	acostarse	sdraiarsi	estender-se
lieutenant	lieutenant	Leutnant(m)	teniente	tenente	tenente
life(lives)	vie	Leben(n)	vida	vita	vida
lifebelt	bouée	Rettungsring(m)	salvavidas	salvagente	bóia
life-guard	maître-nageur	Bademeister(in f)m	maestro(natación)	bagnino	nadador-salvador
lifeless	inanimé, e	unbelebt, leblos	inanimado, a	inanimato, a	inanimado, a
lift, elevator	ascenseur	Aufzug(m)	ascensor	ascensore	elevador
lift(up), raise	lever	heben	levantar	alzare	levantar
lift, raise	soulever	an = heben, hoch = heben	levantar, elevar	sollevare	levantar, erguer
light	lumière	Licht(n)	luz	luce	luz
light	feu	Licht(n)	luz(luces)	luce; faro	luz; farol
light	allumer	an = zünden	encender	accendere	acender
light; illuminate	éclairer	beleuchten	iluminar	illuminare	iluminar
light	clair, e	hell	claro, a	chiaro, a	claro, a
light	léger, ère	leicht	ligero, a	leggero, a	ligeiro, a; leve
lighten	alléger	erleichtern	aliviar	alleggerire	aliviar
lighter	briquet	Feuerzeug(n)	mechero	accendino	isqueiro

English	French	German	Spanish	Italian	Portuguese
lighthouse	phare	Leuchtturm(m)	faro	faro	farol
lighting	éclairage	Beleuchtung(f)	iluminación	illuminazione	iluminação
lightly, slightly	légèrement	leicht	ligeramente	leggermente	ligeiramente
lightning; flash	éclair	Blitz(m)	relámpago	lampo	relâmpago
lightning	foudre	Blitz(m)	rayo	fulmine	raio
like	aimer	gern haben	gustar(le)	piacere, amare	gostar(de)
likely, probable	vraisemblable	wahrscheinlich	verosímil	verosimile	verosímil
limb	membre	Glied(n)	miembro	membro, arto	membro
limit	limite	Grenze(f)	límite	limite	limite
limit	limiter	begrenzen	limitar	limitare	limitar
limp	boiter	hinken	cojear	zoppicare	coxear
line	ligne	Linie(f)	línea	linea	linha
line	trait	Strich(m)	raya	tratto, riga	traço, risco
line	raie	Strich(m)	raya	riga	linha; risca
line	ligne	Angelschnur(f)	caña	lenza	linha
line	vers	Vers(m)	verso	verso	verso
linear	linéaire	linear	lineal	lineare	linear
linen	linge	Wäsche(f)	ropa	biancheria	roupa
liner	paquebot	Passagierdampfer(m)	buque	transatlantico	paquete
link	liaison	Verbindung(f)	enlace	collegamento	conexão
link, connect	relier	verbinden	enlazar, unir	collegare	ligar
lion, lioness	lion, ne	Löwe(m), Löwin(f)	león, leona	leone, leonessa	leão, leoa
lip	lèvre	Lippe(f)	labio	labbro(a)	lábio
lipstick	rouge à lèvres	Lippenstift(m)	barra de labios	rossetto	baton
liqueur	liqueur	Likör(m)	licor	liquore	licor
liquid	liquide	flüssig	líquido, a	liquido, a	líquido, a
liquid	liquide	Flüssigkeit(f)	líquido	liquido	líquido
liquidate	liquider	liquidieren	liquidar	liquidare	liquidar
list	liste	Liste(f)	lista	lista	lista
list of winners	palmarès	Preisträgerliste(f)	lista de premios	albo dei premiati	quadro de honra
listen(to)	écouter	zu = hören, horchen	escuchar	ascoltare	escutar
listener	auditeur, trice	Zuhörer(in f)m	auditor, a	uditore, uditrice	ouvinte
literary	littéraire	literarisch	literario, a	letterario, a	literário, a
literature	littérature	Literatur(f)	literatura	letteratura	literatura
lithograph(y)	lithographie	Steindruck(m)	litografía	litografia	litografia
litigation	litige	Streitfall(m)	litigio	litigio	litígio
litre	litre	Liter(m, n)	litro	litro	litro
little	petit, e	klein	pequeño, a	piccolo, a	pequeno, a
little, few	peu	wenig(e)	poco, a	poco, a	pouco, a
live	vivre	leben	vivir	vivere	viver
live(in), inhabit	habiter	bewohnen, wohnen	vivir, habitar	abitare	morar
live, stay, remain	demeurer	wohnen, bleiben	residir, vivir	dimorare, stare	habitar
liveliness	entrain	Schwung(m)	vivacidad	brio	entusiasmo
lively	vif, vive	lebendig	vivo, a	vivace; vivo, a	vivo, a
lively	animé, e	lebhaft	animado, a	animato, a	animado, a
liven up	animer	Stimmung machen	animar	animare	animar
liver	foie	Leber(f)	hígado	fegato	fígado
livid, pallid	livide	blaß, fahl	lívido, a	livido, a	lívido, a
living-room	salle de séjour	Wohnzimmer(n)	sala de estar	soggiorno	sala de estar
lizard	lézard	Eidechse(f)	lagarto	lucertola	lagarto
llama	lama	Lama(n)	llama	lama	lama
load	charger	laden	cargar	caricare	carregar
load	charge	Last(f)	carga, peso	carico	carga, peso
load, loading	chargement	Ladung(f)	cargamento	carico	carregamento
load	embarquer	ein = laden	embarcar	imbarcare	carregar
loan	prêt	Darlehen(n)	préstamo	prestito	empréstimo
loan	emprunt	Anleihe(f)	préstamo	prestito	empréstimo
lobe	lobe	Ohrläppchen(n)	lóbulo	lobo	lóbulo
lobster	homard	Hummer(m)	bogavante	gambero(di mare)	lavagante
local	local, e	lokal	local	locale	local
locality	localité	Ortschaft(f)	localidad	località	localidade
localize; locate	localiser	lokalisieren	localizar	localizzare	localizar
locate	repérer	lokalisieren	localizar	localizzare	localizar
located	situé, e	gelegen	situado, a	situato, a	situado, a
location, site	emplacement	Lage(f), Stelle(f)	sitio	posto, sito, luogo	lugar; sítio
location, position	situation	Lage(f)	situación	situazione	situação
lock	serrure	Schloß(Tür-)(n)	cerradura	serratura	fechadura
lock	fermer à clé	ab = schließen	cerrar con llave	chiudere a chiave	fechar à chave

lock(of hair)	mèche	Locke(f)	mechón	ciocca	madeixa
lock away	séquestrer	ein = sperren	secuestrar	sequestrare	sequestrar
locomotive	locomotive	Lokomotive(f)	locomotiva	locomotiva	locomotiva
lodger	pensionnaire	Untermieter(in f)m	huésped	ospite	hóspede
log	bûche	Scheit(n)	leño	tronco, ceppo	acha
log-book	carte grise	KFZ-Schein(m)	cédula iden-fiscal	libretto di circola-	livrete(circulação)
logical	logique	logisch	lógico, a	logico, a	lógico, a
lollipop	sucette	Lutscher(m)	pirulí	lecca lecca	chupa-chupa
loneliness	solitude	Einsamkeit(f)	soledad	solitudine	solidão
lonely	seul, e	einsam	aislado, a; solo, a	isolato, a; solo, a	isolado, a
long	long, longue	lang	largo, a	lungo, a	longo, a
longitude	longitude	Längengrad(m)	longitud	longitudine	longitude
longitudinal	longitudinal, e	Längs-	longitudinal	longitudinale	longitudinal
long-sighted	presbyte	weitsichtig	présbita	presbite	présbita
long time(a)	longtemps	lange	mucho tiempo	molto/molto tempo	muito tempo
look(at)	regarder	schauen, an = sehen	mirar	guardare	olhar
look, expression	regard	Blick(m)	mirada	sguardo	olhar
look	mine	Aussehen(n)	semblante, cara	cera, aspetto	aparência
look!	regardez!	seht !, schauen Sie!	mire(!)	guardi !, guardate!	olhe!
look after	occuper(s')	kümmern sich/um	ocuparse	occuparsi	tomar conta
look after	garder	hüten	vigilar, guardar	custodire	cuidar de, vigiar
look for, search -	chercher	suchen	buscar	cercare	procurar; buscar
look like	ressembler(à)	ähneln, aussehen wie	parecerse(a)	somigliare a	parecer-se
loop	boucle	Schleife(f)	lazo	cappio; occhiello	laço
loose, slack	lâche, détendu, e	locker, lose	flojo, a	allentato, a	frouxo, a
loosen	desserrer	lockern	aflojar	allentare	desapertar
loosen	desserrer	lösen	aflojar	allentare	afrouxar
loosen	relâcher	lockern	aflojar	allentare	largar; soltar
Lord	Seigneur	Herr(m)	Señor	Signore	Senhor
lorry	camion	Lastwagen(m)	camión	camion	camião
lose	perdre	verlieren	perder	perdere	perder
lose one's voice	aphone	stimmlos, heiser	afónico, a	afono, a	áfono, a
lose weight	maigrir	ab = nehmen	adelgazar	dimagrire	emagrecer
loss, waste	perte	Verlust(m)	pérdida	perdita	perda, prejuizo
lost	perdu, e	verloren	perdido, a	perso, a; smarrito, a	perdido, a
lotion	lotion	Gesichtswasser(n)	loción	lozione	loção
lots of, a lot of	beaucoup de	viel(e)	mucho, a	molto, a, i, e	muito, a
lottery	loterie	Lotterie(f)	lotería	lotteria	lotaria
loud	fort, e	laut	fuerte; alto, a	forte; alto, a	forte; alto, a
loud	bruyant, e	laut	ruidoso, a	rumoroso, a	ruidoso, a
loud-speaker	haut-parleur	Lautsprecher(m)	altavoz	altoparlante	alto-falante
lounge	salon	Herrenzimmer(n)	sala	salotto	sala de estar
love	aimer	lieben	amar, querer	amare, volere bene	amar, gostar de
love	amour	Liebe(f)	amor	amore	amor
love(in)	amoureux, se	verliebt	enamorado, a	innamorato, a	apaixonado, a
lover	amant, e	Geliebte(f, m)	amante	amante	amante
lover of	amateur de	Liebhaber(in f)m	amante de	appassionato, a	apreciador, a
low	bas, basse	niedrig	bajo, a	basso, a	baixo, a
lower	inférieur, e	untere(r)	inferior	inferiore	inferior
lower	baisser, abaisser	herunter = lassen	bajar	calare, abbassare	baixar, abaixar
lower	abaisser	nieder = lassen	bajar	abbassare	abaixar
lower part	dessous	Unterteil(n)	inferior(parte)	sotto, disotto	baixo(parte de)
loyal	loyal, e	loyal, treu	leal	leale	leal
lucid	lucide	klar	lúcido, a	lucido, a	lúcido, a
luck; chance	chance	Glück(n), Chance(f)	suerte, fortuna	fortuna	sorte
lucky	chanceux, se	Glückspilz(m)	afortunado, a	fortunato, a	afortunado, a
luggage, baggage	bagage(s)	Gepäck(n)	equipaje	bagaglio	bagagem
luggage lockers	consigne	Schließfach(n)	consigna	cassetta, deposito	depósito
lukewarm, tepid	tiède	lauwarm, lau	tibio, a	tiepido, a	tépido, a; morno, a
lull	accalmie	Wetterberuhigung(f)	calma	schiarita, tregua	acalmia
lumbago	lumbago	Hexenschuß(m)	lumbago	lombaggine	lumbago
luminous	lumineux, se	leuchtend, hell	luminoso, a	luminoso, a	luminoso, a
lump, bump	bosse	Beule(f)	chichón	bernoccolo, gobba	bossa; alto
lunch, have lunch	déjeuner	Mittag essen(zu)	almorzar	pranzare	almoçar
lung	poumon	Lunge(f)	pulmón	polmone	pulmão
lure, bait	leurre, appât	Lockmittel(n)	señuelo	esca	isca, engodo
luxuriant, lush	luxuriant, e	üppig	exuberante	lussureggiante	luxuriante
luxurious	luxueux, se	üppig	lujoso, a	lussuoso, a	luxuoso, a

E

English	French	German	Spanish	Italian	Portuguese
luxury	luxe	Luxus(m)	lujo	lusso	luxo
lying	gisant, e	liegend	yacente	giacente	jacente
lynch	lyncher	lynchen	linchar	linciare	linchar

M

English	French	German	Spanish	Italian	Portuguese
macabre	macabre	makaber	macabro, a	macabro, a	macabro, a
machine	machine	Maschine(f)	máquina	macchina	máquina
mackerel	maquereau	Makrele(f)	caballa	sgombro	cavala
mad, foolish, crazy	fou, folle	verrückt	loco, a	matto, a; pazzo, a	louco, a; maluco, a
mad, nuts, barmy	cinglé, e	verrückt	chiflado, a	tocco, a; picchiato, a	doido, a; louco, a
madness, folly	folie	Wahnsinn(m), Wahn(m)	locura	follia, pazzia	loucura
Mafia	mafia	Mafia(f)	mafia	mafia	mafia
magazine	magazine	Illustrierte(f)	revista	rivista	revista
magic	magique	magisch	mágico, a	magico, a	mágico, a
magic	magie	Zauberei(f)	magia	magia	magia
magistrate	magistrat	Magistrat(m)	magistrado	magistrato	magistrado
magnet	aimant	Magnet(m)	imán	calamita	íman
magnetic	magnétique	magnetisch	magnético, a	magnetico, a	magnético, a
magnificent	magnifique	prächtig	magnífico, a	magnifico, a	magnífico, a
magnifying-glass	loupe	Lupe(f)	lupa	lente(ingrandimento)	lupa
maid	bonne	Haushaltshilfe(f)	criada	domestica	criada
mail, post	courrier	Post(f)	correo	posta	correio
maintain	maintenir	erhalten	mantener	mantenere	manter
maintenance	entretien	Wartung(f)	mantenimiento	manutenzione	manutenção
main	principal	hauptsächlich	principal	principale	principal
main thing(the)	essentiel	Hauptsache(f)	esencial	essenziale	essencial
main/trunk road	route nationale	Landstraße(f)	carretera	strada statale	estrada
maize, corn	maïs	Mais(m)	maíz	granturco, mais	milho
majestic	majestueux, se	majestätisch	majestuoso, a	maestoso, a	majestoso, a
majesty	majesté	Majestät(f)	majestad	maestà	majestade
major	commandant	Kommandant(m), Major m	comandante	comandante	comandante
majority	majorité	Mehrheit(f)	mayoría	maggioranza	maioria
make, do	faire	machen, tun	hacer	fare	fazer
make fun of, mock	moquer(se)	verspotten	mofarse, burlarse	burlarsi	troçar
make heavy	alourdir	erschweren	pesado(hacer)	appesantire	pesado(tornar)
make sure	assurer(s')	überzeugen, sich	cerciorarse	accertarsi	verificar
make-up	maquillage	Schminke(f)	maquillaje	trucco	maquilhagem
make-up(put on)	maquiller(se)	schminken, sich	maquillarse	truccarsi	maquilhar-se
malaria	paludisme	Sumpffieber(n)	paludismo	malaria, paludismo	paludismo
male	mâle	Männchen(n)	macho	maschio	macho
malevolent	malveillant, e	böswillig	malévolo, a	malevolo, a	malévolo, a
malnutrition	malnutrition	Unterernährung(f)	desnutrición	malnutrizione	malnutrição
mammal	mammifère	Säugetier(n)	mamífero	mammifero	mamífero
man(men)	homme	Mann(m), Mensch(m)	hombre	uomo; uomini	homem
man, gentleman(men)	monsieur	Gentleman(m)	caballero	signore	cavalheiro
manage	débrouiller(se)	zu helfen wissen, sich	desenredarse	cavarsela	desenredar-se
manage	gérer	verwalten, führen	administrar	amministrare	gerir
manage, run	diriger	leiten, führen	dirigir	dirigere	dirigir
manage, run	administrer	verwalten	administrar	amministrare	administrar
management	direction	Direktion(f)	dirección	direzione	direcção
management	gestion	Verwaltung(f)	gestión	gestione	gestão
manager, head	chef(entreprise)	Betriebsführer(m)	jefe de empresa	dirigente d'azienda	chefe de empresa
manager, boss	patron, dirigeant	Unternehmer(in f)m	director, jefe	manager, padrone	director, patrão
manager	gestionnaire	Verwalter(in f)m	gestor, a	gestore	gestor, a
manager	gérant, e	Geschäftsführer(m)	gerente	gerente, gestore	gerente
manager	gérant, e	Verwalter(in f)m	gerente, director, a	gestore, gerente	gerente, director, a

English	French	German	Spanish	Italian	Portuguese
mandatory	obligatoire	obligatorisch	obligatorio, a	obbligatorio, a	obrigatório, a
mane	crinière	Mähne(f)	crines, melena	criniera	crina
mania	manie	Sucht(f)	manía	mania	mania
maniac	maniaque	Verrückte(f, m)	maníaco, a	maniaco, a	maníaco, a
maniac	obsédé, e	Besessene(f, m)	obseso, a	maniaco, a	obcecado, a
manicure	manucure	Maniküre(f)	manicura	manicure	manicura
manipulate	manipuler	manipulieren	manipular	manipolare	manipular
manner, way	manière	Art(f)	manera, modo	maniera, modo	maneira, modo
manoeuvre	manoeuvre	Manöver(n)	maniobra	manovra	manobra
manpower, labour	main-d'oeuvre	Arbeitskräfte(pl.)	mano de obra	manodopera	mão-de-obra
mansion	manoir, château	Herrensitz(m), -haus n	mansión, morada	maniero, castello	mansão, palacete
manual; hand-	manuel, elle	manuell; Hand-	manual	manuale	manual
manufacture, make	fabriquer	her = stellen	fabricar	fabbricare	fabricar
manufacture	fabrication	Herstellung(f)	fabricación	fabbricazione	fabrico
manufacturer	fabricant, e	Hersteller(in f)m	fabricante	fabbricante	fabricante
manure	fumier	Mist(m)	estiércol	letame	estrume
many	beaucoup	viele	muchos, as	molti	muitos, as
map	carte(géo)	Landkarte(f)	mapa	mappa, carta	mapa
map	plan	Plan(m)(Stadtplan m)	plano	pianta; stradario	planta
marathon	marathon	Marathonlauf(m)	maratón	maratona	maratona
marble	marbre	Marmor(m)	mármol	marmo	mármore
marble	bille	Murmel(f)	bola	biglia	berlinde
March	Mars	März(m)	Marzo	Marzo	Março
margin	marge	Rand(m)	margen	margine	margem
maritime, sea-	maritime	See-	marítimo, a	marittimo, a	marítimo, a
mark	marque, trace	Spur(f)	señal, marca	segno, marca	marca, vestígio
mark, landmark	repère	Markierung(f)	señal, indicio	contrassegno	sinal, marca
mark	note	Note(f)	nota	voto	nota
mark	marquer	markieren	marcar	segnare, marcare	marcar
market	marché	Markt(m)	mercado	mercato	mercado
market	commercialiser	vermarkten	comercializar	commercializzare	comercializar
married	marié, e	verheiratet	casado, a	sposato, a	casado, a
married(get)	marier(se)	heiraten	casarse	sposarsi	casar-se
married, marriage-	conjugal, e	ehelich	conyugal	coniugale	conjugal
marrow(-bone)	moelle	Mark(n)	médula, tuétano	midollo	medula, tutano
marsh	marais	Sumpf(m)	pantano	palude	pântano
marshy, boggy	marécageux, se	sumpfig	pantanoso, a	paludoso, a	pantanoso, a
martial arts	arts martiaux	Kriegskunst(f)	artes marciales	arti marziali	artes marciais
martyr	martyr, e	Märtyrer(in f)m	mártir	martire	mártir
marvellous	merveilleux, se	wunderbar	maravilloso, a	meraviglioso, a	maravilhoso, a
Marxism	marxisme	Marxismus(m)	marxismo	marxismo	marxismo
masculine, male	masculin, e	männlich	masculino, a	maschile	masculino, a
mask	masque	Maske(f)	máscara	maschera	máscara
mass	masse	Masse(f)	masa	massa	massa
mass	messe	Messe(f)	misa	messa	missa
massage	massage	Massage(f)	masaje	massaggio	massagem
massive; solid	massif, ive	massiv	masivo, a	massiccio, a	maciço, a
mast	mât	Mast(m)	mástil	albero	mastro
master, mistress	maître, esse	Herr(in f)m	señor, señora	maestro, a; padrone, a	dono, a; senhor, a
masterpiece	chef-d'oeuvre	Meisterwerk(n)	obra maestra	capolavoro	obra-prima
mat, rug, carpet	tapis	Teppich(m)	alfombra, tapiz	tappeto	tapete, carpete
matador	matador	Matador(m)	matador	matador	matador
match(-es)	allumette	Streichholz(n)	cerilla	fiammifero	fósforo
match(-es), game	match, partie	Spiel(n)	partido	partita	desafio, partida
mate	accoupler(s')	paaren, sich	aparearse	accoppiarsi	acasalar-se
material	matière	Material(n)	material; materia	materiale; materia	material; matéria
material	matériau	Material(n)	material	materiale	material
material	matériel	Material(n)	material	materiale	material
material	étoffe	Stoff(m)	tejido, tela	stoffa	tecido, estofo
material, fabric	tissu	Stoff(m)	tela	tessuto	tecido
maternal, motherly	maternel, le	mütterlich	materno, a; maternal	materno, a	maternal
mathematics	mathématique(s)	Mathematik(f)	matemáticas	matematica	matemáticas
matter, material	matière	Stoff(m), Material(n)	materia	materia	matéria
matter, material	substance	Materie(f)	materia	materia	matéria
mattress(-es)	matelas	Matraze(f)	colchón	materasso	colchão
mature	mûr, e	reif	maduro, a	maturo, a	maduro, a
maturity	maturité	Reife(f)	madurez	maturità	maturidade
maximum	maximum	Maximum(n)	máximo	massimo	máximo

English	French	German	Spanish	Italian	Portuguese
May	Mai	Mai(m)	Mayo	Maggio	Maio
maybe	peut-être	möglicherweise	acaso, tal vez	forse, può darsi(che)	talvez
mayor	maire	Bürgermeister(m)	alcalde	sindaco	President.da Câmara
me	me, m'; moi	mich; mir	me	mi, me	me
me; I	moi	mich; mir; ich	mí, me; yo	io; me	eu; me; mim
meadow, field	pré	Weide(f), Wiese(f)	prado	prato	prado
meadow	prairie	Wiese(f)	pradera	prateria	pradaria, prado
meal	repas	Mahlzeit(f)	comida	pasto	refeição
mean, signify	signifier	bedeuten	significar	significare	significar
meaning	signification	Bedeutung(f)	significación	significato	significação
meaning, sense	sens	Bedeutung(f)	sentido	senso	sentido
means	moyen	Mittel(n)	medio(s)	mezzo	meio
meanwhile	attendant(en)	inzwischen	mientras	attesa(in)	entretanto
meanwhile, meantime	entre-temps	inzwischen	entretanto	intanto, frattanto	entretanto
measles	rougeole	Masern(pl.)	sarampión	morbillo	sarampo
measure	mesurer	messen	medir	misurare	medir
meat	viande	Fleisch(n)	carne	carne	carne
mechanic	mécanicien, ne	Mechaniker(in f)m	mecánico, a	meccanico, a	mecânico, a
mechanical	mécanique	mechanisch	mecánico, a	meccanico, a	mecânico, a
mechanics	mécanique	Mechanik(f)	mecánica	meccanica	mecânica
mechanism	mécanisme	Mechanismus(m)	mecanismo	meccanismo	mecanismo
medal	médaille	Medaille(f)	medalla	medaglia	medalha
medical	médical, e	medizinisch	médico, a	medico, a	médico, a
medicine	médecine	Medizin(f)	medicina	medicina	medicina
medicine, drug	médicament	Medikament(n)	medicamento	medicina	medicamento
mediocre	médiocre	mittelmäßig, schlecht	mediocre	mediocre	medíocre
meditate	méditer	nach = denken, sinnen	meditar	meditare	meditar
medium	moyen, ne	mittlere(r, s)	medio, a	medio, a	médio, a
meet	rencontrer	treffen	encontrar	incontrare	encontrar
meet	réunir(se)	treffen, sich	reunirse	riunirsi	reunir-se
meeting	rencontre	Begegnung(f)	encuentro	incontro	encontro
meeting; reunion	réunion	Treffen(n)	reunión	riunione	reunião
meeting, assembly	assemblée	Versammlung(f)	asamblea	assemblea	assembleia
melancholy	mélancolie	Wehmut(f)	melancolía	malinconia	melancolia
melody, tune	mélodie	Melodie(f)	melodía	melodia	melodia
melon	melon	Melone(f)	melón	melone	melão
melt	fondre	schmelzen	fundir	fondere	fundir
melt	fondre	schmilzen	derretir	sciogliere(-rsi)	derreter
melted	fondu, e	geschmolzen	derretido, a	sciolto, a	derretido, a
member	adhérent, e	Mitglied(n)	adherente	aderente, socio	aderente
member(of)	membre(de)	Mitglied(n)	miembro, a; socio, a	membro, i	membro, a; sócio, a
Member(Parliament)	député	Abgeordnete(f, m)	diputado	deputato	deputado
membership	adhésion	Beitritt(m)	adhesión	adesione	adesão
membrane	membrane	Membran(f)	membrana	membrana	membrana
memory	mémoire	Gedächtnis(n)	memoria	memoria	memória
memory	souvenir	Erinnerung(f)	recuerdo	ricordo	recordação
mending	raccommodage	Flicken(n)	remiendo	rammendo	remendo
menopause	ménopause	Wechseljahre(n, pl)	menopausia	menopausa	menopausa
mental	mental, e	geistig	mental	mentale	mental
mental hospital	asile	Irrenhaus(n)	manicomio	manicomio	manicômio
mentality	mentalité	Mentalität(f)	mentalidad	mentalità	mentalidade
mention	mention	Vermerk(m)	mención	menzione	menção
menu	menu	Menü(n), Speisekarte f	menú	menù	ementa
menu	carte(resto)	Karte(f)(Speisekarte)	menú	menù, carta	lista
mercenary	mercenaire	Söldner(m)	mercenario	mercenario	mercenário
mercury	mercure	Quecksilber(n)	mercurio	mercurio	mercúrio
merger	fusion	Vereinigung(f), Fusion	fusión	fusione, alleanza	fusão
meridian	méridien	Meridian(m)	meridiano	meridiano	meridiano
merit, worth	mérite	Verdienst(n)	mérito	merito	mérito
merry, joyful	joyeux, se	lustig, fröhlich	alegre	allegro, a; felice	alegre
mess	pagaille	Durcheinander(n)	follón, lío	caos, confusione	desordem
message	message	Nachricht(f)	mensaje	messaggio	mensagem, recado
metal	métal	Metal(n)	metal	metallo	metal
metallic	métallique	metallisch	metálico, a	metallico, a	metálico, a
metamorphosis(-es)	métamorphose	Verwandlung(f)	metamorfosis	metamorfosi	metamorfose
metastasis(-es)	métastase	Tochtergeschwulst(f)	metástasis	metastasi	metástase
meter	compteur	Zähler(m)	contador	contatore	contador
method	méthode	Methode(f)	método	metodo	método

English	French	German	Spanish	Italian	Portuguese
meticulous	méticuleux, se	sorgfältig	meticuloso, a	meticoloso, a	meticuloso, a
metre	mètre	Meter(m, n)	metro	metro	metro
metric	métrique	metrisch	métrico, a	metrico, a	métrico, a
mew	miauler	miauen	maullar	miagolare	miar
microphone, mike	micro(phone)	Mikrophon(n)	micrófono	microfono	microfone
microscope	microscope	Mikroskop(n)	microscopio	microscopio	microscópio
midday, noon	midi	Mittag(m)	mediodía	mezzogiorno	meio-dia
middle	milieu	Mitte(f)	medio	mezzo	meio
middle	moyen, ne	mittel	medio, a	medio, a	médio, a
middle class	bourgeoisie	Bürgertum(n)	burguesía	borghesia	burguesia
middle class	bourgeois, e	Bürger(in f)m	burgués, a	borghese	burguês, a
midnight	minuit	Mitternacht(f)	medianoche	mezzanotte	meia-noite
midwife(-ives)	sage-femme	Hebamme(f)	comadrona	levatrice	parteira
migraine, headache	migraine	Migräne(f)	jaqueca	emicrania	enxaqueca
migrant	migrateur, trice	wandernd; Wander-	migratorio, a	migratore, trice	migrador, a
migration	migration	Wanderung(f)	migración	migrazione	migração
mild	doux, ce	mild	templado, a	mite	ameno, a
milieu, background	milieu	Milieu(n)	ambiente, medio	ambiente	meio
militant	militant, e	Militant(m)	militante	militante	militante
military	militaire	militärisch	militar	militare	militar
militate	militer	kämpfen für	militar	militare	militar
militia	milice	Miliz(f)	milicia	milizia	milícia
milk	lait	Milch(f)	leche	latte	leite
mill	moulin	Mühle(f)	molino	mulino	moinho
million	million	Million(f)	millón	milione	milhão
mind	esprit	Sinn(m)	espíritu	mente	espírito
mine	mine	Bergwerk(n)	mina	miniera	mina
mine	mien, ne	meine, meiner	mío, mía	mio(il); mia(la)	meu, minha
mine, to me	moi(à)	mir	mío, a(el, la)	mio, mia(è)	meu(é)
mineral	minéral, e	mineralisch	mineral	minerale	mineral
miniature	miniature	Miniatur(f)	miniatura	miniatura	miniatura
minimum	minimum	Minimum(n)	mínimo, a	minimo, a	mínimo, a
minister	ministre	Minister(in f)m	ministro	ministro	ministro
ministry	ministère	Ministerium(n)	ministerio	ministero	ministério
mink	vison	Nerz(m)	visón	visone	marta
minor	mineur, e	unbedeutend	menor	minore	menor
minor	mineur, e	Minderjährige(f, m)	menor	minore, minorenne	menor
minority	minorité	Minderheit(f)	minoría	minoranza	minoria
mint	menthe	Minze(f)	menta	menta	hortelã
minute	minute	Minute(f)	minuto	minuto	minuto
minute, tiny	minuscule	winzig	minúsculo, a	minuscolo, a	minúsculo, a
minutes, report	procès-verbal	Protokoll(n)	acta	verbale	acta
miracle	miracle	Wunder(n)	milagro	miracolo	milagre
mirage	mirage	Fata Morgana(f)	espejismo	miraggio	miragem
mirror	miroir, glace	Spiegel(m)	espejo	specchio	espelho
mischievous	coquin, e	schelmisch	travieso, a	birbante, birichino, a	travesso, a; maroto, a
miserable(feel)	cafard	Trübsinn(m)	melancolía	malinconia	tristeza
miserly, mean	avare	geizig	avaro, a	avaro, a	avarento, a
misfortune	malchance	Unglück(n)	mala suerte	sventura, sfortuna	desventura
misfortune	malheur	Unglück(n)	desgracia	disgrazia	desgraça
mishap	mésaventure	Mißgeschick(n)	contratiempo	disavventura	contratempo
Miss	mademoiselle	Fräulein(n)	señorita	signorina	menina
miss	manquer	verpassen	perder	perdere; mancare	perder
miss	rater	verpassen	perder	perdere; mancare	perder
missile	missile	Rakete(f)	misil	missile	míssil
mission	mission	Mission(f)	misión	missione	missão
mist, haze	brume	Nebel(m)	bruma	foschia	bruma
mistake, error	faute, erreur	Fehler(m), Irrtum(m)	falta, error	fallo, errore	falta, erro
mistake(make a)	erreur(faire)	Irrtum(m)(machen)	error(cometer un)	errore(fare un)	erro(dar um)
mistaken(be)	tromper(se)	täuschen, sich	equivocarse	sbagliarsi	enganar-se
mistrust	méfier(se)	mißtrauen	desconfiar	diffidare	desconfiar
misuse	abus	Mißbrauch(m)	abuso	abuso	abuso
mix	mélanger	mischen	mezclar	mescolare	misturar
mixed	mixte	gemischt	mixto, a	misto, a	misto, a
mixture; mixing	mélange	Mischung(f)	mezcla	miscuglio	mistura
moan	gémir	stöhnen	gemir	gemere	gemer
moan, groan	râler	nörgeln	refunfuñar	brontolare	resmungar
mobile, movable	mobile	beweglich, mobil	móvil, movible	mobile	móvel

English	French	German	Spanish	Italian	Portuguese
mobility	mobilité	Beweglichkeit(f)	mobilidad	mobilità	mobilidade
mobilize	mobiliser	mobilisieren	mobilizar	mobilitare	mobilizar
mockery	moquerie	Spott(m)	burla, mofa	canzonatura, beffa	zombaria, troça
mode, manner	mode, manière	Weise(f)	modo, manera	modo, maniera	modo, maneira
model, pattern	modèle	Modell(n)	modelo	modello	modelo
model	maquette	Modell(n)	maqueta	modello	maqueta
model	mannequin	Mannequin(n)	maniquí, modelo	indossatore, trice	modelo
moderate	modérer	mäßigen	moderar	moderare	moderar
modern	moderne	modern	moderno, a	moderno, a	moderno, a
modest	modeste	bescheiden	modesto, a	modesto, a	modesto, a
modest	pudique	keusch	púdico, a	pudico, a	púdico, a
modification	modification	Abänderung(f)	modificación	modifica	modificação
modify	modifier	verändern	modificar	modificare	modificar
molar	molaire	Backenzahn(m)	molar	molare	molar
molecule	molécule	Molekül(n)	molécula	molecola	molécula
mollusc	mollusque	Weichtier(n)	molusco	mollusco	molusco
moment	moment	Augenblick(m)	momento	momento, attimo	momento
moment, instant	instant	Moment(m)	instante	istante	instante
monarchy	monarchie	Monarchie(f)	monarquía	monarchia	monarquia
monastery	monastère	Kloster(n)	monasterio	monastero	mosteiro
Monday	Lundi	Montag(m)	Lunes	Lunedì	Segunda-feira
monetary	monétaire	Währungs-, Geld-	monetario, a	monetario, a	monetário, a
money	argent	Geld(n)	dinero	denaro; soldi	dinheiro
money	monnaie	Geld(n)	moneda, dinero	moneta	moeda
monk	moine	Mönch(m)	monje, fraile	monaco, frate	monge, frade
monkey	singe	Affe(m)	mono	scimmia	macaco
monogamy	monogamie	Monogamie(f)	monogamia	monogamia	monogamia
monopoly	monopole	Monopol(n)	monopolio	monopolio	monopólio
monotonous	monotone	monoton, eintönig	monótono, a	monotono, a	monótono, a
monsoon	mousson	Monsun(m)	monzón	monsone	monção
monster	monstre	Monster(n)	monstruo	mostro	monstro
month	mois	Monat(m)	mes	mese	mês
monthly	mensuel, le	monatlich	mensual	mensile	mensal
monument	monument	Denkmal(n)	monumento	monumento	monumento
mood	humeur	Laune(f)	humor	umore	humor
moon	lune	Mond(m)	luna	luna	lua
moor, heath	lande	Heide(f)	landa	landa	charneca
moped	mobylette	Mofa(n)	velomotor	motorino, scooter	motorizada
moral	moral, e	moralisch	moral	morale	moral
moral	morale	Moral(f)	moral	morale	moral
morale	moral	Stimmung(f), Moral(f)	moral, ánimo	morale	moral
morals	moeurs	Sitten(f, pl)	costumbres	costumi	costumes
more	plus	mehr	más	più	mais
more	davantage, plus	mehr	más	più, di più	mais
more	encore	noch	más	ancora	mais
moreover, further	plus(de)	überdies, ferner	más de	più(di, in)	além do mais
moreover, besides	ailleurs(d')	übrigens	por otra parte	del resto, d'altronde	aliás
morning	matin	Morgen(m)	mañana	mattino	manhã
morphine	morphine	Morphium(n)	morfina	morfina	morfina
morphology	morphologie	Morphologie(f)	morfología	morfologia	morfologia
mortal; deadly	mortel, le	tödlich	mortal	mortale	mortal
mortality	mortalité	Sterblichkeit(f)	mortalidad	mortalità	mortalidade
mortar	mortier	Mörtel(m)	argamasa	malta, calcina	argamassa
mortgage	hypothèque	Hypothek(f)	hipoteca	ipoteca	hipoteca
mortgage	emprunt-logement	Darlehen(n)	préstamo	prestito, credito	empréstimo
mortuary	morgue	Leichenschauhaus(n)	depósito(cadáver.)	obitorio	morgue
mosaic	mosaïque	Mosaik(n)	mosaico	mosaico	mosaico
Moslem, Muslim	musulman, e	Mohammedaner(in f)m	musulmán, a	musulmano, a	muçulmano, a
mosque	mosquée	Moschee(f)	mezquita	moschea	mesquita
mosquito(-es)	moustique	Mücke(f)	mosquito	zanzara	mosquito
moss	mousse	Moos(n)	musgo	muschio	musgo
most(of the)	plupart(la)	meisten(die)	mayoría(la)	maggior parte(la)	maior parte(a)
motel	motel	Motel(n)	motel	motel	motel
mother	mère	Mutter(f)	madre	madre	mãe
mother-in-law	belle-mère	Schwiegermutter(f)	suegra	suocera	sogra
motion	mouvement	Bewegung(f); Gang(m)	movimiento	moto, movimento	movimento
motionless	immobile	unbeweglich	inmóvil	immobile	imóvel
motivate	motiver	motivieren	motivar	motivare	motivar

English	French	German	Spanish	Italian	Portuguese
motive	motif	Motiv(n)	motivo	motivo	motivo
motor-bike	moto	Motorrad(n)	moto	moto	mota
motorcyclist	motard	Motorradfahrer(in f)m	motorista	motociclista	motociclista
motorway	autoroute	Autobahn(f)	autopista	autostrada	auto-estrada
mould	moule	Form(f)	molde	stampo, forma	molde; forma
mouldy(to go)	moisir	verschimmeln	enmohecer	ammuffire	bolor(criar)
mount	mont, montagne	Berg(m)	monte	monte	monte
mountain	montagne	Gebirge(n), Berg(m)	montaña	montagna	montanha
mountaineer	alpiniste	Alpinist(m)	alpinista	alpinista	alpinista
mounting, assembly	montage	Montage(f)	montaje	montaggio	montagem
mourning(be in)	deuil	Trauer(f)	duelo; luto	lutto	luto
mouse(mice pl.)	souris	Maus(f)	ratón	topo	rato
moustache	moustache	Schnurrbart(m)	bigote	baffo	bigode
mouth	bouche	Mund(m)	boca	bocca	boca
mouth	gueule	Maul(n)	hocico	muso	goela, garganta
mouthful	bouchée	Bissen(m)	bocado	boccone	bocado
move	bouger	bewegen	moverse	muovere	mexer-se
move, shift	déplacer(se)	bewegen, sich	desplazar(se)	spostare(-arsi)	deslocar-se
move	remuer	bewegen, sich	mover	muovere(-rsi)	mexer-se
move	déménager	um = ziehen	mudar(se)	traslocare	mudar, mudar-se
move	émouvoir	rühren	conmover	commuovere	comover
move back, reverse	reculer	zurück = gehen	retroceder	indietreggiare	recuar
moved, affected	ému, e	gerührt	emocionado, a	commosso, a	comovido, a
movement, motion	mouvement	Bewegung(f)	movimiento	movimento	movimento
moving	émouvant, e	ergreifend	emocionante	commovente	comovente
Mr	monsieur(Mr)	Herr(m)	señor	signor	senhor
Mr	monsieur(Mr)	Herr(m)	Don	Signor	Senhor
Mrs; Madam	madame	Frau(f)	señora	signora	senhora
much, many	beaucoup	viel(e)	mucho	molto	muito
mud	boue	Schlamm(m)	barro	fango, melma	lama
multiple, numerous	multiple	viel-; vielfältig	múltiple	multiplo, a	múltiplo, a
multiply	multiplier	multiplizieren	multiplicar	moltiplicare	multiplicar
multitude	multitude	Menge(f)	multitud	moltitudine	multidão
Mummy, Mum	maman	Mama(f)	mamá	mamma	mamã
mumps	oreillons	Mumps(m)	paperas	orecchioni	trasorelho
municipal; town -	municipal, e	städtisch; Stadt-	municipal	municipale	municipal
murder	meurtre	Mord(m)	asesinato	assassinio	homicídio, crime
murder	assassinat	Mord(m)	asesinato	assassinio	assassínio
murder, homicide	homicide	Totschlag(m)	homicidio	omicidio	homicídio
murderer	assassin	Mörder(in f)m	asesino, a	assassino, a	assassino, a
murderer	meurtrier, ière	Mörder(in f)m	homicida	omicida	assassino, a
murmur, whisper	murmurer	flüstern	murmurar	mormorare	murmurar
muscle	muscle	Muskel(m)	músculo	muscolo	músculo
muscular	musculaire	Muskel-	muscular	muscolare	muscular
muscular	musclé, e	muskulös	musculoso, a	muscoloso, a	musculado, a
museum	musée	Museum(n)	museo	museo	museu
mushroom	champignon	Pilz(m)	champiñón, seta	fungo	cogumelo
music	musique	Musik(f)	música	musica	música
musical	musical, e	musikalisch	musical	musicale	musical
musician	musicien, ne	Musiker(in f)m	músico, a	musicista	músico, a
mussel	moule	Muschel(f)	mejillón	cozza	mexilhão
must, have to	devoir	müssen	deber	dovere	dever
mustard	moutarde	Senf(m)	mostaza	senape	mostarda
mutual	mutuel, le	gegenseitig	mútuo, a	mutuo, a	mútuo, a
muzzle	museau	Schnauze(f)	hocico	muso	focinho
my	ma	meine	mi	mia(la)	minha
my	mon	mein	mi	mio, mia(il, la)	meu, minha
my	mes	meine	mis	miei, mie(i, le)	meus
mysterious	mystérieux, se	mysteriös	misterioso, a	misterioso, a	misterioso, a
mystery	mystère	Geheimnis(n); Rätsel n	misterio	mistero	mistério
mystic(al)	mystique	mystisch	místico, a	mistico, a	místico, a
myth	mythe	Mythos(m); Sage(f)	mito	mito	mito

E

N

English	French	German	Spanish	Italian	Portuguese
nail	ongle	Fingernagel(m)	uña	unghia	unha
nail	clou	Nagel(m)	clavo	chiodo	prego
nail	clouer	nageln	clavar	inchiodare	pregar, cravar
naïve	naïf, ive	naiv	ingenuo, a	ingenuo, a	ingénuo, a
naked; bare	nu, e	nackt	desnudo, a	nudo, a	nu, nua
name	nom	Name(m)	nombre	nome	nome
name	nommer	nennen	llamar	chiamare	chamar
nanny	nurse	Kindermädchen(n)	niñera	bambinaia	ama
nap, snooze	sieste	Mittagsschlaf(m)	siesta	siesta, riposino	sesta
nape of the neck	nuque	Nacken(m)	nuca	nuca	nuca
narcotic	narcotique	Betäubungsmittel(n)	narcótico	narcotico	narcótico
narcotic	stupéfiant	Betäubungsmittel(n)	narcótico	stupefacente	narcótico
narrow	étroit, e	eng	estrecho, a	stretto, a	estreito, a
narrow	rétrécir(se)	enger machen/werden	estrechar(se)	restringersi	estreitar-se
narrow	resserrer	verengen	estrechar	ristringere	estreitar
nasal	nasal, e	nasal	nasal	nasale	nasal
nation	nation	Nation(f)	nación	nazione	nação
national	national, e	national	nacional	nazionale	nacional
nationalism	nationalisme	Nationalismus(m)	nacionalismo	nazionalismo	nacionalismo
nationality	nationalité	Nationalität(f)	nacionalidad	nazionalità	nacionalidade
native	natif, ive	gebürtig	nativo, a	nativo, a	nativo, a
native	natal, e	Heimat-; Geburts-	natal	natale	natal
native(of)	originaire	gebürtig	oriundo, a	originario, a	oriundo, a
native, indigenous	indigène	Eingeborene(f, m)	indígena	indigeno, a	indígena
native land	patrie	Vaterland(n)	patria	patria	pátria
natural	naturel, le	natürlich	natural	naturale	natural
naturalized	naturalisé, e	eingebürgert	nacionalizado, a	naturalizzato, a	naturalizado, a
nature	nature	Natur(f)	naturaleza	natura	natureza
naughty	méchant, e	böse, boshaft	malo, a	cattivo, a	mau, má
nausea, feel sick	nausée	Brechreiz(m)	náusea	nausea	naúsea
nautical, water-	nautique	nautisch, Wasser-	náutico, a	nautico, a	naútico, a
naval	naval, e	See-	naval	navale	naval
navel	nombril	Nabel(m)	ombligo	ombelico	umbigo
navigation	navigation	Seefahrt(f)	navegación	navigazione	navegação
navigator	navigateur	Seefahrer(m)	navegante	navigatore	navegador
navy	marine	Marine(f)	marina	marina	marinha
near, close to	près, proche	nah(e)	cerca	vicino, a	perto
near, close	proche	nah(e)	cercano, a; próximo	prossimo, a	próximo, a; perto
near(to)	auprès de	bei	cerca(de)	vicino(a)	perto(de)
neat, tidy	soigneux, se	sorgfältig	cuidadoso, a	accurato, a	cuidadoso, a
necessary	nécessaire	nötig, notwendig	necesario, a	necessario, a	necessário, a
necessity	nécessité	Notwendigkeit(f)	necesidad	necessità	necessidade
neck	cou	Hals(m), Nacken(m)	cuello	collo	pescoço
neck(bottle)	goulot	Hals(m)(Flaschen)	gollete	collo	gargalo
necklace	collier	Halskette(f); Kette(f)	collar	collana	colar
need	besoin	Bedürfnis(n)	necesidad	bisogno	necessidade
need	besoin(avoir)	brauchen	necesitar	occorrere	necessitar
needle	aiguille	Nadel(f)	aguja	ago	agulha
negative	négatif, ive	negativ	negativo, a	negativo, a	negativo, a
negative	cliché, négatif	Negativ(n)	cliché	negativo	cliché
neglect	négliger	vernachlässigen	descuidar	trascurare	descuidar
negligence	négligence	Nachlässigkeit(f)	negligencia	negligenza	negligência
negotiate	négocier	verhandeln	negociar	negoziare	negociar
negotiation	négociation	Verhandlung(f)	negociación	negoziazione	negociação
negotiator	négociateur	Unterhändler(in f)m	negociador, a	negoziatore, trice	negociador, a
negro(-ress), black	nègre, esse	Neger(in f)m	negro, a	negro, a	negro, a
neighbour	voisin, e	Nachbar(in f)m	vecino, a	vicino, a	vizinho, a
neighbourhood	voisinage	Nachbarschaft(f)	vecindario	vicinanza	vizinhança
neither, nor	ni	weder, noch	ni	né	nem
nephew	neveu	Neffe(m)	sobrino	nipote	sobrinho
nerve	nerf	Nerv(m)	nervio	nervo	nervo

English	French	German	Spanish	Italian	Portuguese
nervous	nerveux, se	nervös; Nerven-	nervioso, a	nervoso, a	nervoso, a
nervy	nerveux, se	nervös	nervioso, a	nervoso, a	nervoso, a
nest	nid	Nest(n)	nido	nido	ninho
net	filet	Netz(n)	red	rete	rede
network	réseau	Netz(n)	red	rete	rede
neurology	neurologie	Neurologie(f)	neurología	neurologia	neurologia
neurosis(-ses)	névrose	Neurose(f)	neurosis	nevrosi	nevrose
neutral	neutre	neutral	neutro, a	neutro, a	neutro, a
neutralize	neutraliser	neutralisieren	neutralizar	neutralizzare	neutralizar
never; ever	jamais	niemals, jemals	jamás, nunca	mai	nunca, jamais
new	nouveau, nouvelle	neu	nuevo, a	nuovo, a	novo, a
new	neuf, neuve	neu	nuevo, a	nuovo, a	novo, a
new-born baby	nouveau-né, e	Neugeborene(n)	recién nacido, a	neonato, a	recém-nascido, a
news	nouvelles	Nachrichten(f, pl)	noticias	notizie	notícias
news	actualités(T.V)	Nachrichten(pl.)	telediario	telegiornale	telejornal
newspaper, paper	journal	Zeitung(f)	periódico, diario	giornale	jornal
news-stand	kiosque	Zeitungskiosk(m)	quiosco	edicola; chiosco	quiosque
next	prochain, e	nächste	próximo, a	prossimo, a	próximo, a
next day	lendemain	folgenden Tag(m)	día siguiente	indomani(l')	dia seguinte
next to, beside	à côté	neben, daneben	al lado	accanto; vicino, a	ao lado
nibble	grignoter	knabbern	mordisquear	sgranocchiare	petiscar
nice	aimable, gentil	lieb, nett	amable	amabile	amável
nice	joli, e	nett	lindo, a	bello, a	bonito, a
nickel	nickel	Nickel(n)	níquel	nichel	níquel
nickname	surnom	Spitzname(m)	apodo, mote	soprannome	alcunha, apelido
nicotine	nicotine	Nikotin(n)	nicotina	nicotina	nicotina
niece	nièce	Nichte(f)	sobrina	nipote	sobrinha
night	nuit	Nacht(f)	noche	notte	noite
night-club	boîte de nuit	Diskothek(f)	discoteca	discoteca, night	boîte
nightdress(-es)	chemise de nuit	Nachthemd(n)	camisón	camicia da notte	camisa de noite
nightmare	cauchemar	Alptraum(m)	pesadilla	incubo	pesadelo
nine	neuf	neun	nueve	nove	nove
nineteen	dix-neuf	neunzehn	diecinueve	diciannove	dezanove
ninety	quatre-vingt-dix	neunzig	noventa	novanta	noventa
no	non	nein	no	no	não
no, not any; no one	aucun, e	keiner, keine	ningún, o, a	nessuno, a	nenhum, a
no thank you	non merci	nein, danke	no, gracias	no, grazie	não, obrigado
noble	noble	edel; nobel	noble	nobile	nobre
nobleman/-woman	noble	Edelmann m, Edelfrau f	noble	nobile	nobre
nobody, no one	personne	niemand	nadie	nessuno	ninguém
nocturnal, night-	nocturne	nächtlich	nocturno, a	notturno, a	nocturno, a
noise	bruit	Geräusch(n)	ruido	rumore	ruído, barulho
noisy; loud	bruyant, e	laut	ruidoso, a	rumoroso, a	barulhento, a
nomad	nomade	Nomade(m)	nómada	nomade	nómada
nomination	nomination	Ernennung(f)	nombramiento	nomina	nomeação
non-existent	inexistant, e	nicht existierend	inexistente	inesistente	inexistente
non-smoker	non-fumeur	Nichtraucher(m)	no-fumadores	non-fumatore	não-fumador
noodles	nouilles	Nudeln(f, pl)	macarrones	tagliatelle, pasta	massa
nordic; northern	nordique	nordisch; nördlich	nórdico, a	nordico, a	nórdico, a
norm, standard	norme	Norm(f)	norma	norma	norma
normal; usual	normal, e	normal	normal	normale	normal
North	Nord	Norden(m)	Norte	Nord	Norte
nose	nez	Nase(f)	nariz	naso	nariz
nostril	narine	Nasenloch(n)	nariz	narice	narina
not	pas	nicht	no	non	não, nem
not normal	anormal, e	anormal	anormal	anormale	anormal
not satisfied	insatisfait, e	unzufrieden	insatisfecho, a	insoddisfatto, a	insatisfeito, a
notch	encoche	Kerbe(f), Einschnitt m	muesca	tacca, intacco	entalhe
note	note	Vermerk(m)	nota	appunto	nota
note	note	Note(f)	nota	nota	nota
note; notice	noter	notieren; bemerken	anotar	notare	anotar, notar
note, write	inscrire, noter	ein = schreiben	inscribir	iscrivere	inscrever
note-book	carnet	Notizbuch(n)	libreta	taccuino	bloco, canhenho
nothing	rien	nichts	nada	niente, nulla	nada
notice	avis	Mitteilung(f)	aviso	avviso	aviso, notícia
notice	annonce	Anzeige(f)	anuncio	annuncio	anúncio
notice	remarquer	bemerken	notar, señalar	notare, osservare	notar, reparar
notification	convocation	Einberufung(f); Ladung	convocatoria	convocazione	convocação

English	French	German	Spanish	Italian	Portuguese
notify	notifier	bekannt = geben	notificar	notificare	notificar
notion	notion	Kenntnis(f), Begriff m	noción	nozione	noção
notoriety	notoriété	Offenkundigkeit(f)	notoriedad	notorietà	notoriedade
noun	nom, substantif	Hauptwort(n)	nombre	nome, sostantivo	substantivo
novel	roman	Roman(m)	novela	romanzo	romance
novelist	romancier, ière	Schriftsteller(in f)m	novelista	romanziere, a	romancista
novelty	nouveauté	Neuheit(f)	novedad	novità	novidade
November	Novembre	November(m)	Noviembre	Novembre	Novembro
novice	novice, débutant	Neuling(m)	novicio, a; novato, a	novizio, a	principiante
now	maintenant	jetzt	ahora	ora, adesso	agora
now, at present	actuellement	zur Zeit	actualmente	attualmente	actualmente
nuclear	nucléaire	Kern-, Atom-	nuclear	nucleare	nuclear
nucleus(-ei)	noyau	Kern(m)	núcleo	nucleo	núcleo
nudist	naturiste	Nudist(in f)m	naturista	nudista	naturista
number	nombre, chiffre	Anzahl(f), Zahl(f)	número	numero	número
number	numéro	Nummer(f)	número	numero	número
number of people	effectif	Personalbestand(m)	efectivo	effettivo	efectivo
numerical	numérique	numerisch	numérico, a	numerico, a	numérico, a
numerous, many	nombreux, se	zahlreich	numeroso, a	numeroso, a	numeroso, a
nun, sister	soeur	Nonne(f), Schwester(f)	monja	suora	freira
nurse	infirmier, ière	Krankenpfleger(in f)m	enfermero, a	infirmiere, a	enfermeiro, a
nurse; tend; treat	soigner	pflegen	curar	curare	cuidar
nursing-home	clinique	Klinik(f)	clínica	clinica	clínica
nut	écrou	Mutter(f)(Schrauben-)	tuerca	dado	porca
nutritious	nutritif, ive	nahrhaft	nutritivo, a	nutritivo, a	nutritivo, a
nylon	nylon	Nylon(m)	nilón	nylon	nylon

O

English	French	German	Spanish	Italian	Portuguese
oar	rame	Ruder(n)	remo	remo	remo
oasis(oases pl.)	oasis	Oase(f)	oasis	oasi	oásis
oath, pledge	serment	Eid(m)	juramento	giuramento	juramento
obese	obèse	füllig, fettleibig	obeso, a	obeso, a	obeso, a
obey	obéir	gehorchen	obedecer	obbedire	obedecer
object	objet	Objekt(n), Ding(n)	objeto	oggetto	objecto
objection, protest	objection	Einwand(m)	objeción, reparo	obiezione	objecção
objective	objectif, ive	objektiv, sachlich	objetivo, a	oggettivo, a	objectivo, a
objective	objectif	Objektiv(n), Ziel(n)	objetivo	obiettivo	objectivo
obligation	obligation	Verpflichtung(f)	obligación	obbligo	obrigação
oblige, force	obliger	zwingen	obligar	obbligare	obrigar
oblique, slanting	oblique	schräg, schief	oblicuo, a	obliquo, a	oblíquo, a
obscene	obscène	obszön	obsceno, a	osceno, a	obsceno, a
observe	observer	beobachten	observar	osservare	observar
observer	observateur	Beobachter(in f)m	observador, a	osservatore, trice	observador, a
obsess	obséder	verfolgen, quälen	obsesionar	ossessionare	obcecar
obsession	obsession	fixe Idee(f)	obsesión	ossessione	obsessão
obsessive fear	hantise	Zwangsvorstellung(f)	obsesión	ossessione	obsessão
obsolete	démodé, e; désuet	veraltet	anticuado, a	antiquato, a	antiquado, a
obsolete	désuet, ète	altmodisch	desusado, a	antiquato, a; desueto	desusado, a
obstacle	obstacle	Hindernis(n)	obstáculo	ostacolo	obstáculo
obstruct	gêner	stören	molestar	imbarazzare	incomodar
obstruction	obstruction	Störung(f)	obstrucción	ostruzione	obstrucção
obtain, get	obtenir	erhalten	obtener	ottenere	obter
obtain, get	procurer(se)	besorgen, sich	procurarse	procurarsi	arranjar; obter
obvious, evident	évident, e	offensichtlich	evidente	evidente	evidente
occasional	occasionnel, le	gelegentlich	ocasional	occasionale	ocasional
occupied	occupé, e	besetzt	ocupado, a	occupato, a	ocupado, a

English	French	German	Spanish	Italian	Portuguese
occupy, fill	occuper	ein = nehmen	ocupar	occupare	ocupar
occur, happen	arriver	geschehen	ocurrir, suceder	succedere	acontecer
ocean	océan	Ozean(m)	océano	oceano	oceano
oceanic	océanique	ozeanisch	oceánico, a	oceanico, a	oceânico, a
October	Octobre	Oktober(m)	Octubre	Ottobre	Outubro
oculist	oculiste	Augenarzt m/-ärztin f	oculista	oculista	oftalmologista
odd	impair	ungerade	impar	dispari	ímpar
odd-jobs	bricolage	Basteln(n)	bricolage, maña	bricolage	bricolage
odious, obnoxious	odieux, se	widerwärtig	odioso, a	odioso, a	odioso, a
odour, smell	odeur	Geruch(m)	olor	odore	cheiro, odor
oesophagus	oesophage	Speiseröhre(f)	esófago	esofago	esófago
of	de	von	de; en; con; por	di; del; dello, della	de
of course	bien sûr	natürlich	claro	certamente	claro
of course	évidemment	natürlich	desde luego	evidentemente	evidentemente
offence	délit	Vergehen(n), Delikt(n)	delito	delitto	delito
offence, violation	infraction	Verstoß(m)	infracción	infrazione	infracção
offend, vex	vexer	beleidigen	ofender, picar	offendere	ofender
offensive	offensive	Offensive(f)	ofensiva	offensiva	ofensiva
offer	offre	Angebot(n)	oferta	offerta	oferta
offer	offrir, proposer	an = bieten	ofrecer, obsequiar	offrire	oferecer, ofertar
offer(on)	réclame(en)	Sonderangebot(n)	reclamo(de)	offerta(in)	promoção(em)
office	bureau	Büro(n)	despacho	ufficio	escritório
officer	officier	Offizier(m)	oficial	ufficiale	oficial
official	officiel, le	offiziell	oficial	ufficiale	oficial
offspring	progéniture	Nachkomme(m)	progenitura	progenitura	progenitura
often	souvent	oft	frecuentemente	spesso	frequentemente
oil	huile	Öl(n); Speiseöl(n)	aceite	olio	óleo; azeite
oil	huile	Öl(n); Motoröl(n)	aceite; óleo	olio	óleo
oil	pétrole	Erdöl(n)	petróleo	petrolio	petróleo
ointment, cream	pommade	Salbe(f)	pomada	pomata	pomada
old	vieux, vieille	alt	viejo, a	vecchio, a	velho, a
old	âgé, e	alt	anciano	anziano, a	idoso, a
old	ancien, ne	alt	antiguo, a	vecchio, a; antico, a	antigo, a
oldest, eldest	aîné, e	Ältere(f, m)	primogénito, a	primogenito, a	velho, a(o, a mais)
oldest person	doyen, ne	Älteste(f, m)	decano, a	decano, a	decano, a
old-fashioned	démodé, e	altmodisch	pasado de moda	passato di moda	fora de moda
old man(men)	vieillard	Alte(m), alter Mann(m)	viejo, anciano	vecchio, anziano	velho, ancião
olive	olive	Olive(f)	aceituna, oliva	oliva	azeitona
Olympic	olympique	olympisch	olímpico, a	olimpico, a	olímpico, a
omit	omettre	aus = lassen	omitir	omettere	omitir
on	sur	auf	en, encima, sobre	sopra, su	em cima de; sobre
on, upon	sur	über; auf	sobre	sopra, su	sobre
once	fois(une)	einmal	vez(una)	volta(una)	vez(uma)
once(at)	suite(tout de)	sogleich, sofort	seguida(en)	subito	imediatamente
one	un	eins	un, uno	un, uno	um
one-eyed	borgne	einäugig	tuerto, a	guercio, a	zarolho, a
oneself	soi(-même)	sich, selbst	sí(mismo)	se(stesso)	si(mesmo)
one-way	sens unique	Einbahnstraße(f)	dirección única	senso unico	sentido único
onion	oignon	Zwiebel(f)	cebolla	cipolla	cebola
only	seul, e	einzig	solo, a	solo, a	só
only	seulement	nur	solamente, sólo	solo, soltanto	somente, só
only	uniquement	ausschließlich	únicamente	unicamente	somente
opaque	opaque	undurchsichtig; trüb	opaco, a	opaco, a	opaco, a
open	ouvert, e	offen; geöffnet	abierto, a	aperto, a	aberto, a
open	ouvrir	öffnen	abrir	aprire	abrir
opening	ouverture	Öffnungszeiten(f, pl)	apertura	apertura	abertura
opera	opéra	Oper(f)	ópera	opera	ópera
operate	marcher(faire)	bedienen	funcionar(hacer)	funzionare(fare)	funcionar(fazer)
operate	opérer	wirken	efectuar	operare	fazer
operate(on)	opérer	operieren	operar	operare	operar
operation	opération	Operation(f)	operación	operazione	operação
operetta	opérette	Operette(f)	zarzuela, opereta	operetta	opereta
ophthalmology	ophtalmologie	Augenheilkunde(f)	oftalmología	oftalmologia	oftalmologia
opinion	opinion	Meinung(f)	opinión	opinione	opinião
opinion	avis	Meinung(f)	opinión	avviso, parere	opinião, parecer
opponent	adversaire	Gegner(in f)m	adversario, a	avversario, a	adversário, a
opportune	opportun, e	günstig	oportuno, a	opportuno, a	oportuno, a
opportunity	occasion	Gelegenheit(f)	oportunidad	occasione	oportunidade

English	French	German	Spanish	Italian	Portuguese
oppose	opposer(s')	widersetzen, sich	oponerse	opporsi	opor-se
opposed to	opposé, e	entgegengesetzt	opuesto, a	opposto, a	contra(ser)
opposing	opposé, e	entgegengesetzt	opuesto, a	opposto, a	oposto, a
opposite	opposé, e	gegenüberliegend	opuesto, a	opposto, a	oposto, a
opposite, contrary	contraire	Gegenteil(n)	contrario	contrario	contrário
opposite	inverse	umgekehrt	inverso, a	inverso, a	inverso, a
opposition	opposition	Opposition(f)	oposición	opposizione	oposição
oppressed	opprimé, e	unterdrückt	oprimido, a	oppresso, a	oprimido, a
optic(al)	optique	optisch	óptico, a	ottico, a	óptico, a
optician	opticien, ne	Optiker(in f)m	óptico, a	ottico	oculista
optimistic	optimiste	optimistisch	optimista	ottimista	optimista
option	option, choix	Wahl(f)	opción	opzione	opção
optional	facultatif, ive	wahlfrei, beliebig	facultativo, a	facoltativo, a	facultativo, a
or	ou	oder	o; u	o	ou
oral	oral, e	mündlich	oral	orale	oral
orange	orange	Apfelsine(f)	naranja	arancia	laranja
orange	orange	orangefarben	anaranjado, a	arancione	cor-de-laranja
orbit	orbite	Umlaufbahn(f)	órbita	orbita	órbita
orchestra; band	orchestre	Orchester(n)	orquesta	orchestra	orquestra
orchid	orchidée	Orchidee(f)	orquídea	orchidea	orquídia
order	ordre	Ordnung(f)	orden	ordine	ordem
order	ordre	Rangordnung(f)	orden	ordine	ordem
order	ordre	Befehl(m)	orden	ordine	ordem
order	commande	Bestellung(f)	encargo, pedido	ordinazione	encomenda
order	ordonner	befehlen, verordnen	ordenar	ordinare	ordenar
order	commander	bestellen	pedir, encargar	ordinare	encomendar
orders, instruction	consigne(s)	Anweisung(f)	consigna, orden	direttiva, ordine	ordem, instruções
ordinary	ordinaire	gewöhnlich	ordinario, a	ordinario, a	ordinário, a
ore	minerai	Erz(n)	mineral	minerale	minério
organ	orgue	Orgel(f)	órgano	organo	órgão
organ	organe	Organ(n)	órgano	organo	órgão
organic	organique	organisch	orgánico, a	organico, a	orgánico, a
organism	organisme	Organismus(m)	organismo	organismo	organismo
organization	organisation	Organisation(f)	organización	organizzazione	organização
organize	organiser	organisieren	organizar	organizzare	organizar
organizer	organisateur	Organisator(in f)m	organizador, a	organizzatore, trice	organizador, a
orgasm	orgasme	Orgasmus(m)	orgasmo	orgasmo	orgasmo
orgy	orgie	Orgie(f)	orgía	orgia	orgia
oriental	oriental, e	orientalisch	oriental	orientale	oriental
orientation	orientation	Orientierung(f)	orientación	orientamento	orientação
orifice, aperture	orifice	Öffnung(f), Mündung(f)	orificio	orifizio	orifício
origin	origine	Ursprung(m)	origen	origine	origem
origin	provenance	Herkunft(f)	procedencia	provenienza	proveniência
original	original, e	original	original	originale	original
original	original	Original(n)	original	originale	original
ornament	ornement	Verzierung; Schmuck	adorno	ornamento	ornamento
orphan	orphelin, e	Waise(f, m)	huérfano, a	orfano, a	órfão, órfã
orthodox	orthodoxe	orthodox	ortodoxo, a	ortodosso, a	ortodoxo, a
oscillate	osciller	schwanken	oscilar	oscillare	oscilar
other	autre	andere, sonstige	otro, a	altro, a	outro, a
otherwise	autrement	anders; sonst	otro modo(de)	altrimenti	outro modo(de)
otherwise, or else	sinon	andernfalls, sonst	si no	se no; altrimenti	senão
our	notre	unser, unsere	nuestro, a	nostro, a(il, la)	nosso, a
our	nos	unser(e)	nuestros, nuestras	nostri, e(i, le)	nossos, nossas
ours	nôtre(le, la)	unsere(der, die, das)	nuestro, a(el, la)	nostro, a(il, la)	nosso, a(o, a)
out of	hors de	außer(+ dat)	fuera de	fuori, fuori di	fora de
outdoors	dehors	(dr)außen; hinaus	fuera(de casa)	all'aperto	fora
outer, outside	extérieur, e	äußere	externo, a	esterno, a	exterior; externo, a
outline, contour	contour	Umriß(m)	contorno	contorno	contorno
outline	silhouette	Silhouette(f)	silueta	sagoma; silhouette	silhueta
output, yield	rendement	Ertrag(m), Leistung(f)	rendimiento	rendimento	rendimento
outside; exterior	extérieur	Außenseite(f)	exterior	esterno	exterior
outside, outdoors	dehors	draußen	fuera, afuera	fuori	fora
outside	extérieur, e	äußer; Außen-	exterior	esteriore	exterior
oval	ovale	oval	oval, ovalado, a	ovale	oval
ovary	ovaire	Eierstock(m)	ovario	ovaia	ovário
oven	four	Ofen(m)	horno	forno	forno
over	dessus(par-)	über	sobre, por encima	al di sopra; al di là	sobre, por cima

English	French	German	Spanish	Italian	Portuguese
over there	là-bas	da; dort	allá	là, laggiù	além, acolá
overall	total, e	Gesamt-	total	complessivo, a	total
overall	blouse	Kittel(m)	bata, blusa	blusa, camice	bata
overcoat	pardessus	Mantel(m)	abrigo	soprabito	sobretudo
overcome	surmonter	überwinden	superar	superare	superar
overdose	surdose	Überdosis(f)	sobredosis	overdose	overdose
overflow	déborder	über = laufen	desbordar	traboccare	transbordar
overflow	déborder	über die Ufer treten	salirse de madre	straripare	extravasar
overhead	au-dessus	oben	arriba	sopra, in alto	cima(por, em)
overseas	outre-mer	überseeisch	ultramar	oltremare	ultramar
overtake	doubler	überholen	adelantar	sorpassare	ultrapassar
overturn	renverser(se)	überschlagen, sich	volcarse	rovesciarsi	virar; cair
overwhelmed	bouleversé, e	erschüttert	conmocionado, a	sconvolto, a	perturbado, a
overwork(ing)	surmenage	Überarbeitung(f)	agotamiento	esaurimento	esgotamento
ovine	ovin	Schaf-	ovino	ovino	ovino
ovule	ovule	Ei(zelle f)n	óvulo	ovulo	óvulo
own, possess	posséder	besitzen	poseer	possedere	possuír
own	propre	eigen	propio, a	proprio, a	próprio, a
owner	propriétaire	Eigentümer(in f)m	propietarío, a	proprietario, a	proprietárío, a
oxidization	oxydation	Oxydierung(f)	oxidación	ossidazione	oxidação
oxygen	oxygène	Sauerstoff(m)	oxígeno	ossigeno	oxigénio
oyster	huître	Auster(f)	ostra	ostrica	ostra
ozone	ozone	Ozon(n)	ozono	ozono	ozone

P

English	French	German	Spanish	Italian	Portuguese
pace	pas, allure	Schritt(m)	paso	passo, andatura	passo
Pacific Ocean	Pacifique	Pazifik(m)	Pacífico	Pacifico	Pacífico
pack, wrap	empaqueter	ein = packen, verpacken	empaquetar	impacchettare	empacotar
packet; package	paquet	Paket(n)	paquete	pacco	pacote
packing, wrapping	emballage	Verpackung(f)	embalaje, envase	imballaggio	embalagem
pact	pacte	Pakt(m)	pacto	patto	pacto
pad	bloc	Block(m)	bloc	blocco	bloco
padlock	cadenas	Vorhängeschloß(n)	candado	lucchetto, catenaccio	cadeado
paediatrician	pédiatre	Kinderarzt(m)/-ärztin	pediatra	pediatra	pediatra
page	page	Seite(f)	página	pagina	página
page(boy), bellboy	chasseur(hôtel)	Page(m), Hotelboy(m)	botones	fattorino	paquete
pain, ache	douleur	Schmerz(m)	dolor	dolore	dor
painful, aching	douloureux, se	schmerzhaft	doloroso, a	doloroso, a	doloroso, a
painless	indolore	schmerzlos	indoloro, a	indolore	indolor
paint	peinture	Farbe(f)	pintar	vernice, pittura	tinta
paint	peindre	streichen	pintar	imbiancare	pintar
paint	peindre	malen	pintar	dipingere	pintar
painter	peintre	Anstreicher; Maler(m)	pintor, a	pittore, trice	pintor, a
painting	peinture	Malerei(f)	pintura	pittura; dipinto	pintura
painting, picture	tableau	Gemälde(n)	cuadro	dipinto, quadro	quadro
pair(of)	paire	Paar(n)	par	paio	par
palace	palais	Palast(m)	palacio	palazzo	palácio
pale	pâle	blaß	pálido, a	pallido, a	pálido, a
palm	paume	Handfläche(f)	palma	palma	palma
palm-tree	palmier	Palme(f)	palmera	palma	palmeira
palpitation	palpitation	Herzklopfen(n)	palpitación	palpitazione	palpitação
pan, saucepan	casserole	Topf(m)	cazo, cacerola	casseruola	tacho, caçarola
pane, window	vitre	Scheibe(f)(Fenster-)	cristal, vidrio	vetro	vidro
panel	panneau	Brett(n)	tablero	cartello	painel
panic	panique	Panik(f)	pánico	panico	pânico
panic	affolement	Panik(f)	pánico	panico	pânico

English	French	German	Spanish	Italian	Portuguese
panic	affoler(s')	Panik geraten(in)	ponerse nervioso, a	disorientarsi	afligir-se
pant, gasp	haleter	keuchen	jadear	ansimare	arquejar
panther	panthère	Panther(m)	pantera	pantera	pantera
paper	papier	Papier(n)	papel	carta	papel
papers	papiers(les)	Papiere(pl); Ausweise	documentación	documenti	documentos
parachute	parachute	Fallschirm(m)	paracaídas	paracadute	pára-quedas
parade	défilé	Parade(f)	desfile	sfilata	desfile
parade	parade	Parade(f)	parada, desfile	parata	parada
paradise	paradis	Paradies(n)	paraíso	paradiso	paraíso
paradox	paradoxe	Paradox(n)	paradoja	paradosso	paradoxo
paragraph	paragraphe	Absatz(m), Abschnitt m	párrafo	paragrafo	parágrafo
parallel	parallèle	parallel	paralelo, a	parallelo, a	paralelo, a
paralysed	paralysé, e	gelähmt	paralítico, a	paralitico, a	paralítico, a
paralysis	paralysie	Lähmung(f)	parálisis	paralisi	paralisia
paranoia	paranoïa	Paranoia(f)	paranoia	paranoia	paranóia
parasite	parasite	Parasit(m)	parásito	parassita	parasita
parasol, sunshade	parasol	Sonnenschirm(m)	parasol	ombrellone	guarda-sol
parcel	colis	Paket(n)	paquete	pacco, collo	pacote
pardon?	comment?	wie bitte?	cómo(?)	come?, come dice?	como disse?
parents	parents	Eltern(pl)	padres	genitori	pais
parents-in-law	beaux-parents	Schwiegereltern(pl.)	suegros	suoceri	sogros
park	parc, jardin	Park(m)	parque	parco	parque
park	garer	parken	aparcar	posteggiare	estacionar
park	stationner	parken	estacionarse	stazionare	estacionar
parking	stationnement	Parken(n)	estacionamiento	sosta	estacionamento
parliament	parlement	Parlament(n)	parlamento	parlamento	parlamento
parrot	perroquet	Papagei(m)	loro	pappagallo	papagaio
part	partie, part	Teil(m n)	parte	pezzo, parte	parte
part, component	pièce	Teil(n)	pieza	pezzo	peça
participate in	participer à	beteiligen, sich	participar en	partecipare a	participar em
particle	particule	Teilchen(n)	partícula	particella	partícula
particular	particulier, ière	eigentümlich	particular	particolare	particular
particular(in)	notamment	besonders, nämlich	particularmente	particolarmente	particularmente
partisan	partisan, e	Anhänger(in f)m	partidario, a	partigiano, a	partidário, a
partition	division	Trennung(f)	división	divisione	partilha
partition	cloison	Trennwand(f)	tabique	tramezzo	tabique
partner	partenaire	Partner(in f)m	pareja	socio, a; partner	parceiro, a
party	parti	Partei(f)	partido	partito	partido
party, reception	réception	Empfang(m)	recepción	ricevimento	recepção
party(cocktail -)	cocktail	Party(f)	cóctel	party	recepção
pass, go(through)	passer	fahren über	pasar	passare	passar(por; em)
pass	laissez-passer	Ausweis(m)	salvoconducto	lascia-passare	salvo-conduto
pass	col	Paß(m)	puerto	colle, passo	desfiladeiro
passage	passage	Durchgang(m)	pasaje, paso	passaggio	passagem
passenger	passager, ère	Passagier(in f)m	pasajero, a	passeggero, a	passageiro, a
passion	passion	Leidenschaft(f)	pasión	passione	paixão
passive	passif, ive	passiv	pasivo, a	passivo, a	passivo, a
passport	passeport	Paß(m)	pasaporte	passaporto	passaporte
past	passé	Vergangenheit(f)	pasado	passato	passado
past	passé, e	vergangen	pasado, a	passato, a	passado, a
past(in the)	autrefois	früher	antaño	volta(una)	antigamente
pasta, noodles	pâtes	Nudeln(f, pl)	pastas(aliment.)	pasta	massa
paste	pâte	Paste(f); Masse(f)	masa, pasta	impasto, pasta	massa
pastry; dough	pâte	Teig(m)	masa	pasta	massa
pastry, cake	pâtisserie(s)	Backwaren(f, pl)	pasteles	dolci	pastelaria
pasty	pâteux, se	pappig	pastoso, a	pastoso, a	pastoso, a
paté	pâté	Pastete(f)	paté	patè	paté
patent	brevet	Patent(n)	patente	brevetto	patente
paternal	paternel, le	väterlich	paterno, a	paterno, a	paterno, a
path; way	chemin	Weg(m)	camino	cammino	caminho
path, lane	allée	Allee(f)	paseo, calle	viale	alameda
patience	patience	Geduld(f)	paciencia	pazienza	paciência
patient	patient, e	geduldig	paciente	paziente	paciente
patriarch	patriarche	Patriarch(m)	patriarca	patriarca	patriarca
patrimony	patrimoine	Familiengut(n)	patrimonio	patrimonio	património
patrol	patrouille	Patrouille(f), Streife	patrulla	pattuglia	patrulha
patron	mécène	Mäzen(m), Sponsor(m)	mecenas	mecenate	mecenas
pattern	modèle	Muster(n)	modelo	modello	modelo

English	French	German	Spanish	Italian	Portuguese
pause, break	pause	Pause(f)	pausa	pausa	pausa
pavement	trottoir	Bürgersteig(m)	acera	marciapiede	passeio
paving-stone	pavé	Pflasterstein(m)	adoquín	selce, selciato	pedra de calçada
paw; leg; foot	patte	Pfote(f); Bein(n)	pata	zampa	pata
pawn(chess)	pion(échecs)	Bauer(m)(Schach)	peón(ajedrez)	pedone(scacchi)	peão(xadrez)
pay	paie(paye)	Lohn(m)	paga	paga, stipendio	paga, ordenado
pay	payer	bezahlen	pagar	pagare	pagar
pay(in)	verser	ein = zahlen	ingresar	versare	pagar
pay back, reimburse	rembourser	zurück = zahlen	reembolsar	rimborsare	reembolsar
payment	paiement	Bezahlung(f)	pago, abono	pagamento	pagamento
payment	payement	Zahlung(f)	abono, pago	pagamento	pagamento
peace	paix	Frieden(m)	paz	pace	paz
peaceful, pacific	pacifique	friedlich	pacífico, a	pacifico, a	pacífico, a
peaceful, quiet	paisible	friedlich, ruhig	apacible	pacifico, a; placido, a	pacífico, a
peach(-es)	pêche	Pfirsich(m)	melocotón	pesca	pêssego
peak	pic	Gipfel(m)	pico	picco	pico
peanut	cacahuète	Erdnuß(f)	cacahuete, maní	arachide	amendoim
pear	poire	Birne(f)	pera	pera	pêra
pearl	perle	Perle(f)	perla	perla	pérola
pebble	galet	Kieselstein(m)	canto rodado	ciottolo	seixo
pedal	pédale	Pedal(n)	pedal	pedale	pedal
pedantic	pédant, e	pedantisch	pedante	pedante	pedante; vaidoso, a
pedestrian	piéton	Fußgänger(m)	peatón	pedone	peão
pedigree	pédigree	Stammbaum(Tier-)(m)	pedigrí	pedigree	pedigree
peel	peler	schälen	mondar	sbucciare	descascar
peel	éplucher	schälen	pelar	sbucciare	descascar
pen, fountain-pen	stylo	Füller(m)	estilográfica	stilografica	caneta
penal	pénal, e	strafrechtlich	penal	penale	penal
penalty	pénalité	Strafe(f), Strafpunkt	penalidad	penalità	penalidade
pencil	crayon	Bleistift(m)	lápiz	matita, lapis	lápis
penicillin	pénicilline	Penizillin(n)	penicilina	penicillina	penicilina
peninsula	péninsule	Halbinsel(f)	península	penisola	península
pension; allowance	pension	Pension(f)	pensión	pensione	pensão
people	gens	Leute(pl.)	gente	gente(la)	gente, pessoas
people	peuple	Volk(n)	pueblo	popolo	povo
pepper	poivre	Pfeffer(m)	pimienta	pepe	pimenta
per	par	per	por	per	por
perceive	percevoir	wahr = nehmen	percibir	percepire	perceber
perceive, notice	apercevoir	bemerken	avistar, divisar	scorgere	avistar
per cent	pour cent	Prozent(n)	por ciento	per cento	por cento
percentage	pourcentage	Prozentsatz(m)	porcentaje	percentuale	percentagem
perceptible	perceptible	wahrnehmbar	perceptible	percettibile	perceptível
perfect	parfait, e	einwandfrei	perfecto, a	perfetto, a	perfeito, a
perfection	perfection	Vollkommenheit(f)	perfección	perfezione	perfeição
perforate	perforer	durchbohren	perforar	perforare	perfurar
perform, accomplish	accomplir	aus = führen, vollenden	cumplir, realizar	compiere	realizar
perform, carry out	exécuter	aus = führen	ejecutar	eseguire	executar
performance	performance	Leistung(f)	proeza, hazaña	prestazione	desempenho
performance	représentation	Vorstellung(f)	representación	rappresentazione	representação
perfume, scent	parfum	Parfüm(n)	perfume	profumo	perfume
perfume shop	parfumerie	Parfümerie(f)	perfumería	profumeria	perfumaria
perhaps, maybe	peut-être	vielleicht	quizá(s)	forse	talvez
peril, danger	péril	Gefahr(f)	peligro, riesgo	pericolo	perigo
perimeter	périmètre	Umfang(m)	perímetro	perimetro	perímetro
period	période	Periode(f)	período	periodo	período
periodic(al)	périodique	periodisch	periódico, a	periodico, a	periódico, a
periphery	périphérie	Umkreis(m), Umfang(m)	periferia	periferia	periferia
periphery	pourtour	Umkreis(m)	contorno	giro, circuito	perímetro
permanent	permanent, e	andauernd	permanente	permanente	permanente
permission	permission	Erlaubnis(f)	permiso	permesso	permissão
perpendicular	perpendiculaire	senkrecht	perpendicular	perpendicolare	perpendicular
perpetual	perpétuel, le	fortdauernd	perpetuo, a	perpetuo, a	perpétuo, a
persecute	persécuter	verfolgen	perseguir	perseguitare	perseguir
perseverance	persévérance	Ausdauer(f)	perseverancia	perseveranza	perseverança
persevere	persévérer	beharren, aus = halten	perseverar	perseverare	perseverar
persist	acharner(s')	beharren	empeñarse	accanirsi	insistir
persistence	persistance	Beharrlichkeit(f)	persistencia	persistenza	persistência
person	personne	Person(f)	persona	persona	pessoa

English	French	German	Spanish	Italian	Portuguese
person in charge	responsable	Verantwortliche(f, m)	encargado, a	responsabile	responsável
personal	personnel, le	persönlich	personal	personale	pessoal
personality	personnalité	Persönlichkeit(f)	personalidad	personalità	personalidade
personnel	personnel	Personal(n)	personal	personale	pessoal
perspective	perspective	Perspektive(f)	perspectiva	prospettiva	perspectiva
perspiration	transpiration	Schweiß(m)	transpiración	traspirazione	transpiração
perspire, sweat	transpirer	schwitzen	transpirar	traspirare, sudare	transpirar
persuade	persuader	überreden	persuadir	persuadere	persuadir
perverse	pervers, e	pervers	perverso, a	perverso, a	perverso, a
pessimistic	pessimiste	pessimistisch	pesimista	pessimista	pessimista
petal	pétale	Blütenblatt(n)	pétalo	petalo	pétala
petition	pétition	Bittschrift(f), Gesuch	petición	petizione	petição
petrol	essence	Benzin(n)	gasolina	benzina	gasolina
petrol station	poste d'essence	Tankstelle(f)	gasolinera	distributore(benzina)	bomba de gasolina
petticoat, slip	jupon	Unterrock(m)	enagua	sottana	saiote
pharynx	pharynx	Rachen(m)	faringe	faringe	faringe
phase, stage	phase	Phase(f)	fase	fase	fase
pheasant	faisan	Fasan(m)	faisán	fagiano	faisão
phenomenon(-mena)	phénomène	Phänomen(n)	fenómeno	fenomeno	fenómeno
philosophy	philosophie	Philosophie(f)	filosofía	filosofia	filosofia
phone, ring, call	téléphoner	telefonieren	telefonear	telefonare	telefonar
phone box	cabine(téléph.)	Telefonzelle(f)	cabina(telefónica)	cabina(telefonica)	cabine(telefónica)
phonetic	phonétique	phonetisch	fonético, a	fonetico, a	fonético, a
photo(graph)	photo	Foto(n)	foto	foto, fotografia	fotografia
photography	photographie	Fotografie(f)	fotografía	fotografia	fotografia
phrase, locution	locution	Redensart(f)	locución	locuzione	locução
physical	physique	physisch	físico, a	fisico, a	físico, a
physicist	physicien, ne	Physiker(in f)m	físico, a	fisico, a	físico, a
physics	physique	Physik(f)	física	fisica	física
physiognomy	physionomie	Gesichtsausdruck(m)	fisionomía	fisionomia	fisionomia
physique	physique	Äußere(n), Aussehen(n)	físico	fisico	físico
pianist	pianiste	Pianist(in f)m	pianista	pianista	pianista
piano	piano	Klavier(n)	piano	pianoforte	piano
pick, gather	cueillir	pflücken	coger, recoger	cogliere, raccogliere	colher
pick up	ramasser	auf = heben	recoger	raccogliere	apanhar, recolher
picture	image	Bild(n)	imagen	illustrazione	gravura
picturesque	pittoresque	malerisch	pintoresco, a	pittoresco, a	pitoresco, a
pie	tourte	Pastete(f)	pastel, tortada	torta salata	empada
piece, bit	morceau, bout	Stück(n)	pedazo, trozo	pezzo	pedaço
pierce	transpercer	durchbohren	atravesar	trapassare	trespassar
pig; pork(meat)	porc	Schwein(n)	cerdo	porco, maiale	porco
pigeon	pigeon	Taube(f)	paloma	piccione	pombo, a
pile	pile	Stapel(m)	pila	pila	pilha, montão
pile	tas	Haufen(m)	montón	mucchio	montão, pilha
pile	amas	Haufen(m)	montón	mucchio	amontoado
pile up, stack	empiler	stapeln	apilar, amontonar	accatastare	empilhar, amontoar
pile up	entasser	stapeln	amontonar	ammucchiare	amontoar
pilgrim	pèlerin	Pilger(in f)m	peregrino	pellegrino, a	peregrino
pilgrimage	pèlerinage	Wallfahrt(f)	peregrinación	pellegrinaggio	peregrinação
pill	pilule	Pille(f)	píldora	pillola	pílula
pillar	pilier	Pfeiler(m)	pilar	pilastro	pilar
pillow	oreiller	Kopfkissen(n)	almohada	guanciale	travesseiro
pilot	pilote	Pilot(m)	piloto	pilota	piloto
pilot; fly; drive	piloter	fliegen; lotsen; fahren	pilotar	pilotare	pilotar
pimp	proxénète	Zuhälter(m)	proxeneta	ruffiano, prosseneta	proxeneta
pimping	proxénétisme	Kuppelei(f)	proxenetismo	prossenetismo	proxenetismo
pimple	bouton	Pickel(m)	grano, espinilla	brufolo, foruncolo	borbulha
pin	épingle	Stecknadel(f)	alfiler	spillo	alfinete
pincers, pliers	pince	Zange(f)	pinza(s), tenazas	pinza	pinça, alicate
pinch, nip	pincer	kneifen	pellizcar	pizzicare	beliscar
pineapple	ananas	Ananas(f)	piña	ananas	ananás
pink	rose	rosafarben	rosa	rosa	cor-de-rosa
pioneer	pionnier	Pionier, Bahnbrecher	pionero	pioniere	pioneiro
pip	pépin	Kern(m)	pepita	seme	caroço
pipe	tuyau(terie)	Röhre(f), Schlauch(m)	tubo, caño	tubo, tubazione	tubo, cano
pipe	conduit(e)	Röhre(f), Leitung(f)	caño, conducto	condotto(a)	cano, tubo
pipe	canalisation	Leitung(f)(-snetz n)	canalización	canalizzazione	canalização
pipe	pipe	Pfeife(f)	pipa	pipa	cachimbo

English	French	German	Spanish	Italian	Portuguese
pirate	pirate	Pirat(in f)m	pirata	pirata	pirata
pirogue	pirogue	Piroge(f), Kanu(n)	piragua	piroga	piroga
piston	piston	Kolben(m)	pistón	pistone	pistão
pit	fosse	Grube(f)	fosa, hoyo	fossa; buca	fossa
pit, hole	trou	Grube(f)	hoyo	buca	cova
pitch	tanguer	schaukeln	cabecear	beccheggiare	balouçar-se
pitchfork, fork	fourche	Gabel(f)(Heu-; Mist-)	horca	forca	forcado
pitiless	impitoyable	unbarmherzig	despiadado, a	spietato, a	impiedoso, a
pity	pitié	Mitleid(n)	piedad	pietà	piedade
pity	plaindre	bedauern	compadecer	compatire	lastimar
pity(what a)	dommage(quel)	schade!(wie ---)	lástima(qué)	peccato(che)	pena(que)
pity(it is a)	dommage(c'est)	schade!	pena(es una)	peccato(è)	pena(e')
place, spot	endroit	Stelle(f)	lugar, sitio	luogo, posto	lugar, sítio
place, spot	lieu	Ort(m)	lugar	luogo	lugar
place	place	Ort(m), Platz(m)	lugar	posto	lugar; sítio
place, install	placer	setzen, stellen	colocar	collocare, porre	colocar; pôr
place	poser, placer	stellen	poner, colocar	collocare	pôr, colocar
plain	plaine	Ebene(f)	llanura, llano	pianura	planície
plait	natte	Zopf(m)	trenza	treccia	trança
plait, braid	tresse	Zopf(m)	trenza	treccia	trança
plan; drawing	plan	Plan(m)	plan; plano	piano; schema	plano; desenho
plan	projet	Plan(m)	plan, proyecto	progetto	projecto
plan	projeter	planen	proyectar, planear	progettare	projectar
plane, aeroplane	avion	Flugzeug(n)	avión	aereo	avião
planet	planète	Planet(m)	planeta	pianeta	planeta
plant	plante	Pflanze(f)	planta	pianta	planta
plant	usine	Anlage(f)	fábrica	fabbrica	fábrica
plant	planter	pflanzen	plantar	piantare	plantar
plaster	plâtre	Gips(m)	yeso	gesso	gesso
plaster, bandage	pansement	Verband(m)	cura, vendaje	medicazione	penso, curativo
plaster	sparadrap	Pflaster(n)	esparadrapo	cerotto	esparadrapo
plastic	plastique	plastisch	plástico, a	plastico, a	plástico, a
plastic	plastique	Plastik(n)	plástico	plastica	plástico
plate	assiette	Teller(m)	plato	piatto	prato
plate, plaque	plaque	Platte(f)	placa	lastra, piastra	placa
plateau	plateau	Hochebene(f)	meseta	altipiano	planalto
platform	quai	Bahnsteig(m)	andén	binario, marciapiede	plataforma
platform	plate-forme	Plattform(f)	plataforma	piattaforma	plataforma
play	jouer	spielen	jugar	giocare	jogar, brincar
play	jouer	spielen	tocar	suonare	tocar
play	pièce	Stück(n)	obra	commedia	peça
player	joueur, se	Spieler(in f)m	jugador, a	giocatore, trice	jogador, a
plead	plaider	plädieren	litigar	patrocinare	defender(causa)
pleasant	plaisant, e	gefällig	agradable	piacevole	agradável
pleasant, nice	agréable	angenehm	agradable	gradevole, piacevole	agradável
pleasant, nice	sympathique	sympathisch	simpático, a	simpatico, a	simpático, a
please; like	plaire	gefallen(jdm)	gustar, agradar	piacere	agradar
please	plaisir(faire)	Freude machen	gusto(dar)	piacere(fare)	gosto(dar)
please!	s'il vous plaît!	bitte!	por favor(!)	per favore!	se faz favor!
pleased, glad	content, e	froh	contento, a	contento, a	contente
pleasure	plaisir	Vergnügen(n)	placer	piacere	prazer
pledge	gage	Pfand(n).	prenda	pegno	penhor
plentiful, abundant	abondant, e	reichlich	abundante	abbondante	abundante
pliers, pincers	pinces	Zangen(pl)	alicates, tenazas	pinze	alicate; tenaz
plot, conspiracy	conspiration	Komplott(n)	conspiración	cospirazione	conspiração
plot	parcelle	Parzelle(f)	parcela	parcella	parcela
ploughing	labour	Feldarbeit(f)	labranza	aratura	lavoura
plug; socket	prise	Steckdose(f)	enchufe	presa	tomada
plug in	brancher	ein = stecken	enchufar	innestare	ligar
plum	prune	Pflaume(f)	ciruela	prugna, susina	ameixa
plumber	plombier	Klempner(m)	fontanero	idraulico	canalizador
plunder, pillage	pillage	Plünderung(f)	saqueo	saccheggio	pilhagem
plunge, dive	plonger	tauchen	zambullirse	tuffarsi	mergulhar
plural	pluriel	Mehrzahl(f)	plural	plurale	plural
plus	plus	und, plus	más	più	mais
plus	plus	plus	más	più	mais
pneumonia	pneumonie	Lungenentzündung(f)	neumonía	polmonite	pneumonia
pocket	poche	Tasche(f)	bolsillo	tasca	bolso

E

English	French	German	Spanish	Italian	Portuguese
podium, stage	podium	Podest(n)	podio	podio	estrado
poem	poème	Gedicht(n)	poema	poema	poema
poetry	poésie	Poesie(f)	poesía	poesia	poesia
point	point	Punkt(m)	punto	punto	ponto
point	pointe	Spitze(f)	punta	punta	ponta
pointed, sharp	pointu, e	spitz	puntiagudo, a	appuntito, a	pontiagudo, a
point out	signaler	melden; an = zeigen	señalar	segnalare	assinalar
poison	poison	Gift(n)	veneno	veleno	veneno
poisoning	empoisonnement	Vergiftung(f)	envenenamiento	avvelenamento	envenenamento
poisoning	intoxication	Vergiftung(f)	intoxicación	intossicazione	intoxicação
poisonous	vénéneux, se	giftig	venenoso, a	velenoso, a	venenoso, a
polar	polaire	polar; Polar-	polar	polare	polar
pole	pôle	Pol(m)	polo	polo	polo
police	police	Polizei(f)	policía	polizia	polícia
policeman(-men)	policier	Polizist(in f)m	policía	poliziotto	polícia
policeman(-men)	gendarme	Polizist(in f)m	guardia civil	carabiniere	guarda-republicano
police station	commissariat	Kommissariat(n)	comisaría	commissariato	esquadra(polícia)
police station	poste de police	Polizeiwache(f)	cuartelillo	posto di guardia	esquadra
policy	politique	Politik(f)	política	politica	política
polio(myelitis)	poliomyélite	Kinderlähmung(f)	poliomielitis	poliomelite	poliomielite
polish	polir	polieren	pulir	lucidare, levigare	polir
polish	cirer	polieren, wachsen	dar crema	lucidare	encerar
polished	poli, e	poliert	pulido, a	levigato, a	polido, a
polite	poli, e	höflich	educado, a; cortés	educato, a	educado, a
politeness	politesse	Höflichkeit(f)	cortesía	educazione	delicadeza
political	politique	politisch	político, a	politico, a	político, a
politician	homme politique	Politiker(in f)m	político	uomo politico	político
politician	politicien, ne	Politiker(in f)m	político, a	politico, a	político, a
politics	politique	Politik(f)	política	politica	política
poll; ballot	scrutin, vote	Wahl(f), Abstimmung(f)	escrutinio	scrutinio	escrutínio
poll(opinion)	sondage	Umfrage(f)	sondeo	sondaggio	sondagem
pollute	polluer	verunreinigen	contaminar	inquinare	poluir
pollution	pollution	Verschmutzung(f)	contaminación	inquinamento	poluição
polygamy	polygamie	Polygamie(f)	poligamia	poligamia	poligamia
polyp	polype	Polyp(m)	pólipo	polipo	pólipo
polyvalent	polyvalent, e	vielseitig	polivalente	polivalente	polivalente
pond	bassin	Bassin(n), Teich(m)	estanque	bacino	lago
pond	étang	Teich(m)	estanque	stagno	lago; tanque
pond, pool	mare	Tümpel(m)	charca	stagno	charco
poor	pauvre	arm	pobre	povero, a	pobre
Pope	Pape	Papst(m)	Papa	Papa	Papa
popular	populaire	populär	popular	popolare	popular
populated	peuplé, e	bevölkert	poblado, a	popolato, a	povoado, a
population	population	Bevölkerung(f)	población	popolazione	população
porcelain, china	porcelaine	Porzellan(n)	porcelana	porcellana	porcelana
porch	porche	Portal(n)	soportal, porche	atrio, portico	pórtico
pore	pore	Pore(f)	poro	poro	poro
pornography	pornographie	Pornographie(f)	pornografía	pornografia	pornografia
porous	poreux, se	porös	poroso, a	poroso, a	poroso, a
port, harbour	port	Hafen(m)	puerto	porto	porto
portable	portatif, ive	tragbar	portátil	portatile	portátil
porter	portier	Portier(m)	portero	portiere	porteiro
porter, caretaker	concierge	Hausmeister(in f)m	conserje	portiere, a	porteiro, a
portion, piece	portion	Stück(n), Portion(f)	porción	porzione	porção
portrait	portrait	Portrait(n)	retrato	ritratto	retrato
pose	poser(photo)	Modell stehen	posar	posare	posar
position	position	Position(f)	posición	posizione	posição
position, job	situation	Stellung, Position(f)	situación	situazione	situação
position	orienter	orientieren	orientar	orientare	orientar
positive	positif, ive	positiv	positivo, a	positivo, a	positivo, a
possessions, estate	biens	Besitz(m), Güter(pl)	bienes	beni; averi	bens
possibility	possibilité	Möglichkeit(f)	posibilidad	possibilità	possibilidade
possibility	faculté	Fähigkeit(f)	facultad	facoltà	faculdade
possible	possible	möglich	posible	possibile	possível
possible	éventuel, le	möglich	eventual	eventuale	eventual
post, pole	poteau	Pfosten(m)	poste	palo	poste
post, stake, peg	piquet	Pfahl(m)	estaca	picchetto	estaca
post, mail	poster	ein = werfen	echar al correo	impostare, imbucare	pôr no correio

English	French	German	Spanish	Italian	Portuguese
post-card	carte postale	Postkarte(f)	tarjeta postal	cartolina	bilhete-postal
postage	port	Porto(-kosten)(n/pl)	porte	porto	porte
postal order	mandat-lettre	Postanweisung(f)	giro postal	vaglia(postale)	vale postal
post up, put up	afficher	an = schlagen	anunciar	affiggere	afixar
poster	poster	Plakat(n)	cartel, póster	poster, manifesto	cartaz
poster, placard	affiche	Plakat(n)	cartel	manifesto	cartaz
postman/-woman	facteur, trice	Briefträger(in f)m	cartero, a	postino, a	carteiro, a
postmark; seal	cachet	Stempel(m), Siegel(n)	sello	sigillo, bollo	selo
post-office	poste	Post(f)	correos	posta	correios
postpone, adjourn	ajourner	vertagen	aplazar	rimandare, aggiornare	adiar
postpone	différer	auf = schieben	diferir, demorar	differire, rimandare	diferir, adiar
postpone	reporter	verschieben	postergar	rinviare	adiar
pot	pot	Topf(m)	maceta	vaso	vaso; pote
potato(-es)	pomme de terre	Kartoffel(f)	patata	patata	batata
potent, powerful	puissant, e	kräftig, stark	potente	potente	potente
potential	potentiel, le	potentiell	potencial	potenziale	potencial
pot-holing	spéléologie	Höhlenforschung(f)	espeleología	speleologia	espeleologia
poultry	volaille	Geflügel(n)	aves de corral	pollame	aves de capoeira
pour	verser	aus = gießen	verter	versare	verter
pour out, tip	déverser	aus = gießen	verter	riversare, scaricare	despejar
poverty	pauvreté	Armut(f)	pobreza	povertà	pobreza
poverty	misère	Elend(n)	miseria	miseria	miséria
powder	poudre	Puder(m); Pulver(n)	polvo	polvere	pó
powder	poudre	Pulver(n)(Schieß-)	pólvora	polvere	pólvora
power	pouvoir	Macht(f)	poder	potere	poder
power, strength	puissance, force	Macht(f), Kraft(f)	potencia, fuerza	potenza, forza	potência, poder
powerful, strong	puissant, e	mächtig, kräftig	poderoso, a	poderoso, a; potente	poderoso, a
powerless	impuissant, e	machtlos	impotente	impotente	impotente
power-station	centrale	Kraftwerk(n), Zentrale	central	centrale	central
practical	pratique	praktisch	práctico, a	pratico, a	prático, a
practice	cabinet(avocat)	Büro(n)(Anwaltsbüro)	despacho; bufete	studio(avvocato)	escritório
practise	pratiquer	betreiben, üben	practicar	praticare	praticar
praise	éloge	Lob(n)	elogio	elogio	elogio
pram	landau	Kinderwagen(m)	cochecito	carrozzina	carrinho(bebé)
prawn, shrimp	crevette	Krabbe(f)	gamba, camarón	gamberetto	camarão
pray	prier	beten	rezar	pregare	rezar, orar
prayer	prière	Gebet(n)	oración	preghiera	oração
preach	prêcher	predigen	predicar	predicare	pregar
precaution	précaution	Vorsicht(f)	precaución	precauzione	precaução
precede	précéder	voran = gehen, voraus = -	preceder	precedere	preceder
precious	précieux, se	wertvoll, kostbar	precioso, a	prezioso, a	precioso, a
precipice	précipice	Abgrund(m)	precipicio	precipizio	precipício
precise, accurate	précis, e	genau	preciso, a	preciso, a	exacto, a
precisely	précisément	genau	precisamente	precisamente, appunto	precisamente
precision	précision	Genauigkeit(f)	precisión	precisione	precisão
precocious	précoce	frühreif, frühzeitig	precoz	precoce	precoce
predecessor	prédécesseur	Vorgänger(in f)m	predecesor, a	predecessore	predecessor, a
predict	prédire	vorher = sagen	predecir	predire	predizer
predominant	prédominant, e	vorherrschend	predominante	predominante	predominante
preface	préface	Vorwort(n)	prefacio	prefazione	prefácio
prefer	préférer	bevorzugen	preferir	preferire	preferir
preference	préférence	Vorliebe(f)	preferencia	preferenza	preferência
prefix	préfixe	Vorsilbe(f)	prefijo	prefisso	prefixo
pregnancy	grossesse	Schwangerschaft(f)	embarazo	gravidanza	gravidez
pregnant	enceinte	schwanger	encinta	incinta	grávida
prehistory	préhistoire	Vorgeschichte(f)	prehistoria	preistoria	pré-história
prejudice	préjugé	Vorurteil(n)	prejuicio	pregiudizio, danno	preconceito
preliminary	préliminaire	einleitend	preliminar	preliminare	preliminar
preliminary	préalable	vorhergehend	previo, a	preliminare	prévio, a
premature(baby)	prématuré, e	Frühgeburt(f)	prematuro, a	prematuro, a	prematuro, a
premeditate	préméditer	vor = setzen	premeditar	premeditare	premeditar
premeditated	prémédité, e	vorsätzlich	premeditado, a	premeditato, a	premeditado, a
premises	local	Gebäude(n), Lokal(n)	local	locale	local
preparation	préparation	Vorbereitung(f)	preparación	preparazione	preparação
prepare	préparer	vor = bereiten	preparar	preparare	preparar
preposition	préposition	Präposition(f)	preposición	preposizione	preposição
prescribe	prescrire	vor = schreiben	prescribir	prescrivere	prescrever
prescription	ordonnance	Rezept(n)	receta	ricetta medica	receita

English	French	German	Spanish	Italian	Portuguese
presence	présence	Anwesenheit(f)	presencia	presenza	presença
present	présent, e	anwesend	presente	presente	presente
present	présent, e	gegenwärtig, aktuell	presente, actual	presente, attuale	presente, actual
present, current	actuel, le	aktuell, gegenwärtig	actual	attuale	actual
present	présent	Gegenwart(f)	presente	presente	presente
present, gift	cadeau	Geschenk(n)	regalo	regalo	prenda, presente
present	présenter	vor = zeigen, - = stellen	presentar	presentare	apresentar
presentation	présentation	Vorführung(f)	presentación	presentazione	apresentação
preserve, keep	conserver	konservieren	conservar	conservare	conservar
presidency	présidence	Präsidium n, Vorsitz m	presidencia	presidenza	presidência
president	président, e	Präsident(in f)m	presidente	presidente, essa	presidente
press	presse	Presse(f)	prensa	stampa	imprensa
press, squeeze	presser	drücken(zusammen-)	apretar	premere	prensar
pressure	pression	Druck(m)	presión	pressione	pressão
prestige	prestige	Ansehen(n)	prestigio	prestigio	prestigio
prestigious	prestigieux, se	wunderbar	prestigioso, a	prestigioso, a	prestigioso, a
presume	présumer	vermuten	presumir	presumere	presumir
pretentious	prétentieux, se	eingebildet	presuntuoso, a	pretenzioso, a	pretencioso, a
pretty	joli, e	hübsch	bonito, a	carino, a	bonito, a
pretty; coquettish	coquet, te	kokett; eitel	presumido, a	civettuolo, a	vaidoso, a
prevail	prévaloir	vor = herrschen	prevalecer	prevalere	prevalecer
prevent	empêcher	verhindern	impedir	impedire	impedir
previous	précédent, e	vorherig	precedente	precedente	precedente
previous, former	antérieur, e	vorhergehend	anterior	anteriore	anterior
previous	antécédent, e	vorhergehend	antecedente	antecedente	antecedente
prey	proie	Beute(f)	presa	preda	presa
price	prix	Preis(m)	precio	prezzo	preço
prick, sting	piquer	stechen	pinchar	pungere	picar
pride, arrogance	orgueil	Stolz(m)	orgullo	orgoglio	orgulho
pride	fierté	Stolz(m)	orgullo	fierezza	orgulho
priest	prêtre	Priester(m)	sacerdote, padre	prete	padre
primary	primaire	Primär-	primario, a	primario, a	primário, a
prime minister	premier ministre	Premierminister(m)	primer ministro	primo ministro	primeiro ministro
prime minister	premier ministre	Ministerpräsident(m)	primer ministro	primo ministro	primeiro ministro
primitive	primitif, ive	primitiv	primitivo, a	primitivo, a	primitivo, a
prince	prince	Prinz(m)	príncipe	principe	príncipe
princess(-es)	princesse	Prinzessin(f)	princesa	principessa	princesa
principal, main	principal, e	hauptsächlich	principal	principale	principal
principle	principe	Grundsatz(m)	principio	principio	princípio
print	empreinte	Abdruck(m)	huella	impronta	impressão; marca
print	gravure	Gravur(f)	grabado	stampa	gravura
print	imprimer	drucken	imprimir	stampare	imprimir
printed form	imprimé	Formular(n)	impreso	stampato	impresso
printing	impression	Druck(m)	impresión	stampa	impressão
printing works	imprimerie	Druckerei(f)	imprenta	tipografia	tipografia
prior	antérieur, e	früher	anterior	anteriore	anterior
priority	priorité	Vorrang(m)	prioridad	precedenza; priorità	prioridade
priority(have)	prioritaire	vorrangig; Prioritäts-	prioritario, a	prioritario, a	prioritário, a
prison, jail	prison	Gefängnis(n)	prisión, cárcel	prigione, carcere	prisão, cadeia
prisoner	prisonnier, ière	Gefangene(f, m)	prisionero, a	prigioniero, a	prisioneiro, a
prisoner	détenu, e	Häftling(m)	detenido, a; preso, a	detenuto, a	preso, a; detido, a
private	privé, e	privat	privado, a	privato, a	privado, a
privilege	privilège	Vorrecht(n)	privilegio	privilegio	privilégio
privileged	privilégié, e	bevorzugt	privilegiado, a	privilegiato, a	privilegiado, a
prize	prix	Preis(m)	premio	premio	prémio
prize	lot	Los(n)	premio	premio	prémio
prize-winner	lauréat, e	Preisträger(in f)m	galardonado, a	galardoado, a	galardoado, a
probable, likely	probable	wahrscheinlich	probable	probabile	provável
probably	probablement	wahrscheinlich	probablemente	probabilmente	provavelmente
probe	sonde	Sonde(f)	sonda	sonda	sonda
problem	problème	Problem(m)	problema	problema	problema
procedure	procédure	Verfahren(n)	procedimiento	procedimento	procedimento
process(-es)	procédé	Verfahren(n)	procedimiento	procedimento	procedimento
procession	cortège	Umzug(m), Festzug(m)	cortejo	corteo	cortejo
procession	procession	Prozession(f)	procesión	processione	procissão
proclaim	proclamer	bekannt = geben	proclamar	proclamare	proclamar
procreate	procréer	erzeugen	procrear	procreare	procriar
procreation	procréation	Zeugung(f)	procreación	procreazione	procriação

English	French	German	Spanish	Italian	Portuguese
prodigious	prodigieux, se	wunderbar	prodigioso, a	prodigioso, a	prodigioso, a
produce	produire	her = stellen	producir	produrre	produzir
produce	produire	produzieren	producir	produrre	produzir
producer	producteur, trice	Produzent(in f)m	productor, a	produttore, trice	produtor, a
producer	producteur, trice	Hersteller(in f)m	productor, a	produttore, trice	produtor, a
product	produit	Produkt(n)	producto	prodotto	produto
production	production	Produktion(f)	producción	produzione	produção
productive	productif, ive	leistungsfähig	productivo, a	produttivo, a	produtivo, a
profession	profession	Beruf(m)	profesión	professione	profissão
profession, job	métier	Beruf(m)	oficio	mestiere	ofício
professional	professionnel, le	professionell	profesional	professionale	profissional
professional	professionnel	Profi(m)	profesional	professionista	profissional
professor	professeur	Professor(in f)m	catedrático, a	professore, essa	professor, a
profile	profil	Profil(n)	perfil	profilo	perfil
profit, benefit	profit	Gewinn(m)	ganancia	profitto, guadagno	lucro
profit, benefit	bénéficier	profitieren, gewinnen	beneficiar	beneficiare	beneficiar
profitability	rentabilité	Rentabilität(f)	rentabilidad	redditività	rentabilidade
profitable	rentable	einträglich	rentable	redditizio, a	rentável
prognosis(-ses)	pronostic	Prognose(f)	pronóstico	prognosi	prognóstico
programme	programme	Programm(n)	programa	programma	programa
programme	émission	Sendung(f)	emisión	programma	emissão
programmer	programmeur, se	Programmierer(in f)m	programador, a	programmatore, trice	programador, a
progress	progrès	Fortschritt(m)	progreso	progresso	progresso
progression	progression	Fortschreiten(n)	progresión	progressione	progressão
progressive	progressif, ive	fortschreitend	progresivo, a	progressivo, a	progressivo, a
project, plan	projet	Vorhaben(n)	proyecto, plan	progetto	projecto
projectile	projectile	Geschoß(n)	proyectil	proiettile	projéctil
projector	projecteur	Scheinwerfer(m)	proyector	proiettore	projector
proliferate	proliférer	vermehren, sich	proliferar	prolificare	proliferar
prolongation	prolongation	Verlängerung(f)	prolongación	prolungazione	prolongamento
promise	promesse	Versprechen(n)	promesa	promessa	promessa
promise	promettre	versprechen	prometer	promettere	prometer
promised	promis, e	versprochen	prometido, a	promesso, a	prometido, a
promote	promouvoir	befördern	promover	promuovere	promover
promotion	promotion	Beförderung(f)	promoción	promozione	promoção
pronoun	pronom	Fürwort(n)	pronombre	pronome	pronome
pronounce	prononcer	aus = sprechen	pronunciar	pronunziare	pronunciar
proof, evidence	preuve	Beweis(m)	prueba	prova	prova
proof(per cent)	degré(alcool)	Prozent(n)	graduación	grado	grau
propaganda	propagande	Propaganda(f)	propaganda	propaganda	propaganda
propeller	hélice	Propeller(m)	hélice	elica	hélice
properly	correctement	richtig	correctamente	correttamente	correctamente
property	propriété	Eigentum(n)	propiedad	proprietà	propriedade
property	immobilier	Immobilien(f, pl)	inmobiliario	immobiliare	imobiliário
proportion, ratio	proportion	Verhältnis(n)	proporción	proporzione	proporção
proportion	dosage	Dosierung(f)	dosificación	dosaggio, dose	dosagem
proposal	proposition	Vorschlag(m)	propuesta	proposta	proposta
propose; offer	proposer	vor = schlagen	proponer	proporre	propor
propulsion	propulsion	Antrieb(m)	propulsión	propulsione	propulsão
prospect	perspective	Aussicht(f)	perspectiva	prospettiva	perspectiva
prostate	prostate	Prostata(f)	próstata	prostata	próstata
prostitute	prostituée	Prostituierte(f)	prostituta	prostituta	prostituta
prostitution	prostitution	Prostitution(f)	prostitución	prostituzione	prostituição
protect	protéger	beschützen	proteger	proteggere	proteger
protection	protection	Schutz(m)	protección	protezione	protecção
protest, contest	protester	protestieren	protestar	protestare	protestar
Protestant	protestant, e	Protestant(in f)m	protestante	protestante	protestante
protocol	protocole	Protokoll(n)	protocolo	protocollo	protocolo
prototype	prototype	Prototyp(m)	prototipo	prototipo	protótipo
protrude	dépasser	hervor = stehen	sobresalir	sporgere	sobressair
protuberance	protubérance	Beule(f), Buckel(m)	protuberancia	protuberanza	protuberância
proud	fier, fière	stolz	altivo, a	fiero, a	altivo, a
proud, arrogant	orgueilleux, se	stolz, arrogant	orgulloso, a	orgoglioso, a	orgulhoso, a
prove	prouver	beweisen	probar	provare	provar
proverb	proverbe	Sprichwort(n)	proverbio	proverbio	provérbio
provide	fournir	versorgen, liefern	proveer	fornire	fornecer
provided that	pourvu que	wenn nur, sofern, daß	ojalá	purché	oxalá
province	province	Provinz(f)	provincia	provincia	província

English	French	German	Spanish	Italian	Portuguese
provisional	provisoire	provisorisch	provisional	provvisorio, a	provisório, a
provocation	provocation	Herausforderung(f)	provocación	provocazione	provocação
provoke	provoquer	heraus = fordern, reizen	provocar	provocare	provocar
prowler	rôdeur, se	Herumstreicher(m)	vagabundo, a	vagabundo, a	vagabundo, a
proximity	proximité	Nähe(f)	proximidad	prossimità	proximidade
prudence	prudence	Vorsicht(f)	prudencia	prudenza	prudência
pseudonym	pseudonyme	Pseudonym(n)	seudónimo	pseudonimo	pseudônimo
psychiatrist	psychiatre	Psychiater(in f)m	siquiatra	psichiatra	psiquiatra
psychoanalyst	psychanalyste	Psychoanalytiker(m)	sicoanalista	psicanalista	psicanalista
psychological	psychique	psychisch	síquico, a	psichico, a	psíquico, a
psychologist	psychologue	Psychologe(m)/-gin(f)	sicólogo, a	psicologo, a	psicólogo, a
psychology	psychologie	Psychologie(f)	sicología	psicologia	psicologia
psychosis(-ses)	psychose	Psychose(f)	sicosis	psichosi	psicose
puberty	puberté	Pubertät(f)	pubertad	pubertà	puberdade
public	public, ique	öffentlich	público, a	pubblico, a	público, a
public; audience	public	Publikum(n)	público	pubblico	público
publication	publication	Veröffentlichung(f)	publicación	pubblicazione	publicação
public call-box	taxi-/publiphone	Telefonzelle(f)	teléfono público	telefono pubblico	telefone público
public holiday	férié(jour)	Feiertag(m)	festivo(día)	festivo(giorno)	feriado(dia)
publish, issue	publier	veröffentlichen	publicar	pubblicare	publicar
publisher; editor	éditeur, trice	Herausgeber(in f)m	editor, a	editore, trice	editor, a
publishing	édition	Verlagswesen(n)	industria editor-	edizione	indústria livro
puff, breath	bouffée	Hauch(m), Atemzug(m)	bocanada	ventata	baforada
pull	tirer	ziehen	tirar	tirare	puxar
pulley	poulie	Flaschenzug(m)	polea	puleggia	polia
pullover, sweater	pull-over	Pullover(m)	jersey	maglione, pullover	pulover
pulse	pouls	Puls(m)	pulso	polso	pulso
pump	pompe	Pumpe(f)	bomba	pompa	bomba
punch	coup de poing	Faustschlag(m)	puñetazo	pugno	soco; murro
punctual	ponctuel, le	pünktlich	puntual	puntuale	pontual
punctuation	ponctuation	Zeichensetzung(f)	puntuación	punteggiatura	pontuação
puncture, burst	crever	platzen, bersten	reventar	bucare, scoppiare	rebentar; furar
puncture	crevaison	Reifenpanne(f)	pinchazo	foratura	furo
puncture	ponction	Punktion(f)	punción	puntura, prelievo	punção
punish	punir	bestrafen	castigar	punire	castigar
punishment	punition	Strafe(f)	castigo	punizione	castigo
punishment	châtiment	Bestrafung(f)	castigo	castigo	castigo
puny, weak	chétif, ive	schwächlich, kümmer-	endeble	gracile	débil
pupil	élève	Schüler(in f)m	alumno, a	alunno, a	aluno, a
pupil	pupille	Pupille(f)	pupila	pupilla	pupila
puppet	pantin	Hampelmann(m)	títere	burattino	fantoche
purchase	achat	Kauf(m)	compra	acquisto	compra
pure	pur, e	rein	puro, a	puro, a	puro, a
pure	chaste	keusch	casto, a	casto, a	casto, a
purge	purge	Säuberungsaktion(f)	purga	purga	purga
purify	purifier	reinigen	purificar	purificare	purificar
purpose, aim, goal	intention, but	Absicht(f)	intención	intento, fine, scopo	intenção
purpose, aim	dessein	Absicht(f)	propósito	proposito	propósito
purpose(on)	exprès	absichtlich	expresamente	apposta	propósito(de)
purse	porte-monnaie	Geldbörse(f)	monedero	portamonete	porta-moedas
pursue	poursuivre	verfolgen	perseguir	inseguire	perseguir
pus	pus	Eiter(m)	pus	pus	pus
push	pousser	schieben, stoßen	empujar	spingere	empurrar
push	bousculer	drängeln	empujar	spingere, urtare	empurrar
push-chair	poussette	Sportwagen(m)	silla de bebé	passeggino	cadeira de bebé
put	mettre	legen, stellen	poner	mettere	pôr
put, lay(down)	poser	legen	poner, colocar	posare, porre	pôr, colocar
put down, lay down	déposer	legen, stellen	depositar	depositare, porre	pousar
put in order, tidy	ranger	auf = räumen	ordenar	ordinare	ordenar
put on(shoes)	chausser(se)	Schuhe anziehen, sich	calzarse	calzarsi	calçar-se
put on weight	grossir	zu = nehmen	engordar	ingrassare	engordar
putting up posters	affichage	Anschlag, Plakatierung	anuncios(fijación)	affissione	afixação
putty	mastic	Kitt(m)	masilla	mastice	betume
pyjamas	pyjama	Schlafanzug(m)	pijama	pigiama	pijama
pyramid	pyramide	Pyramide(f)	pirámide	piramide	pirâmide
python	python	Python(m)	pitón	pitone	jibóia

Q

English	French	German	Spanish	Italian	Portuguese
qualified	qualifié, e	qualifiziert	calificado, a	qualificato, a	qualificado, a
qualified	diplômé, e	staatlich geprüft	graduado, a	diplomato, a	diplomado, a
quality	qualité	Qualität(f)	calidad; cualidad	qualità	qualidade
quality	qualité	Eigenschaft(f)	cualidad	qualità	qualidade
quantity, amount	quantité	Quantität(f)	cantidad	quantità	quantidade
quarrel, argue	disputer(se)	streiten, sich	reñir(con)	litigare	disputar-se
quarry	carrière	Steinbruch(m)	cantera	cava	pedreira
quarter	quart	Viertel(n)	cuarto	quarto	quarto
quarterly	trimestriel, le	vierteljährlich	trimestral	trimestrale	trimestral
quartet	quatuor	Quartett(n)	cuarteto	quartetto	quarteto
quash	annuler	auf = heben	anular	annullare	anular
quay	quai	Kai((m)	muelle	molo	cais
queen	reine	Königin(f)	reina	regina	rainha
question	question	Frage(f)	pregunta	domanda	pergunta
question	question	Frage(f)	cuestión	questione	questão
question, ask	interroger	fragen, befragen	interrogar	interrogare	interrogar
queue	queue	Schlange(f)	cola	coda, fila	bicha; fila
queue, line	file	Schlange(f)	fila	fila, coda	fila, bicha
quick, prompt	prompt, e; rapide	schnell, rasch	pronto, a	pronto, a	pronto, a
quickly, fast	vite	schnell, rasch	rápido, pronto	fretta(in), presto	rápido, a; depressa
quiet, still, calm	tranquille	ruhig	tranquilo, a	tranquillo, a	tranquilo, a
quite	tout à fait	ganz	totalmente	affatto	totalmente
quota	quota	Quote(f)	cuota	quota	cota
quotation	cotation	Kurswert(m)	cotización	quotazione	cotação
quote	citer	zitieren	citar	citare	citar
quotient	quotient	Quotient(m), Bruch(m)	cociente	quoziente	quociente

R

English	French	German	Spanish	Italian	Portuguese
rabbi	rabbin	Rabbiner(m)	rabino	rabbino	rabino
rabbit	lapin, e	Kaninchen(n)	conejo, a	coniglio, a	coelho, a
rabies	rage	Tollwut(f)	rabia	rabbia	raiva
race, breed	race	Rasse(f)	raza	razza	raça
race	course	Rennen(n)	carrera	corsa	corrida
races	courses	Pferderennen(n)	carreras	corsa	corridas
racial	racial, e	rassisch	racial	raziale	racial
racing car	voiture(course)	Rennwagen(m)	coche de carreras	macchina da corsa	carro de corrida
racism	racisme	Rassismus(m)	racismo	razzismo	racismo
racket	raquette	Schläger(Tennis-)(m)	raqueta	racchetta	raqueta
racket(-eering)	racket	Erpressung(f)	extorsión	racket	vigarice
radar	radar	Radar(m)	radar	radar	radar
radiance	rayonnement	Strahlung(f)	irradiación	irradiazione	irradiação
radiation	radiation	Bestrahlung(f)	radiación	radiazione	radiação
radiator, heater	radiateur	Heizkörper(m)	radiador	termosifone	aquecedor
radio	radio	Radio(n)	radio	radio	rádio
radioactivity	radioactivité	Radioaktivität(f)	radiactividad	radioattività	radioactividade
radio set	poste radio	Radio(n)	aparato de radio	radio	rádio
radius(-ii)	rayon	Radius(m)	radio	raggio	raio
raft	radeau	Floß(n)	balsa	zattera	jangada
rag	chiffon	Lappen(m)	trapo	straccio	trapo

English	French	German	Spanish	Italian	Portuguese
rage	rage, fureur	Wut(f)	rabia, furia	rabbia	raiva, furor
raid, round-up	rafle	Razzia(f)	redada	retata	rusga
rail; track	rail	Schiene(f)	carril	rotaia	carril
railway	chemin de fer	Eisenbahn(f)	ferrocarril	ferrovia	caminho de ferro
rain	pluie	Regen(m)	lluvia	pioggia	chuva
rain	pleuvoir	regnen	llover	piovere	chover
rainbow	arc-en-ciel	Regenbogen(m)	arco iris	arcobaleno	arco-íris
rain-coat, mac	imperméable	Regenmantel(m)	gabardina	impermeabile	gabardina
rainy	pluvieux, se	regnerisch	lluvioso, a	piovoso, a	chuvoso, a
raise	élever, hausser	an = heben	elevar	elevare, alzare	elevar
rake	râteau	Rechen(m)	rastrillo	rastrello	ancinho
Ramadan	ramadan	Ramadan(m)	ramadán	ramadan	ramadão
ramble	randonnée	Tour(f), Fußtour(f)	caminata, paseo	gita, escursione	caminhada
random(at)	hasard(au)	aufs Geratewohl	azar(al)	casaccio(a)	acaso(ao)
range, reach	portée	Reichweite(f)	alcance	portata, gittata	alcance
range(mountain)	chaîne(montagne)	Bergkette(f)	sierra	catena(monti)	serra
rank	rang	Rang(m)	puesto	rango	posição
rank	grade	Rang(m)	grado	grado	grau
ransack	saccager	verwüsten	saquear	saccheggiare	saquear
ransom	rançon	Lösegeld(n)	rescate	riscatto	resgate
rape	viol	Vergewaltigung(f)	violación	stupro	violação
rape	violer	vergewaltigen	violar	violentare	violentar
rapid, fast, quick	rapide	schnell	rápido, a	rapido, a; veloce	rápido, a
rare	rare	selten	raro, a	raro, a	raro, a
rash, reckless	téméraire	waghalsig	temerario, a	temerario, a	temerário, a
rat	rat	Ratte(f)	rata	topo, ratto	rato, a
rate	taux	Rate(f)	tasa	tasso	taxa
rate, quotation	cours	Kurs(m)	cotización	corso	índice, tabela
rate, rhythm	cadence	Rhythmus(m)	cadencia	cadenza	cadência
rather	plutôt	eher, lieber	más bien	piuttosto	antes; mais
ratify	ratifier	ratifizieren	ratificar	ratificare	ratificar
ratio, proportion	rapport	Beziehung(f)	razón, relación	rapporto	razão
ration	ration, portion	Ration(f); Stück(n)	ración	razione	ração
rational	rationnel, le	rational	racional	razionale	racional
rationing	rationnement	Rationierung(f)	racionamiento	razionamento	racionamento
ravage, devastate	dévaster	verwüsten, zerstören	devastar	devastare	devastar
ravine	ravin	Schlucht(f); Graben(m)	barranco	burrone	barranco
ravishing, lovely	ravissant, e	entzückend	encantador, a	incantevole	encantador, a
raw	cru, e	roh	crudo, a	crudo, a	cru, a
raw; crude	brut, e	roh	bruto, a	grezzo, a	bruto, a
ray	rayon	Strahl(m)	rayo	raggio	raio
razor	rasoir	Rasierapparat(m)	navaja de afeitar	rasoio	navalha, gilete
reach	accéder à	Zugang haben zu	llegar a	accedere a	chegar a
reach	atteindre	erreichen	alcanzar, lograr	raggiungere	atingir
reach, arrive at	parvenir	erreichen	conseguir	giungere	chegar; conseguir
react	réagir	reagieren	reaccionar	reagire	reagir
reaction	réaction	Reaktion(f)	reacción	reazione	reacção
reactionary	réactionnaire	reaktionär	reaccionario, a	reazionario, a	reaccionário, a
reactor; engine	réacteur	Reaktor(m)	reactor	reattore	reactor
read	lire	lesen	leer	leggere	ler
reader	lecteur, trice	Leser(in f)m	lector, a	lettore, trice	leitor, a
reading	lecture	Lesen(n)	lectura	lettura	leitura
readjustment	réadaptation	Umstellung(f)	readaptación	riadattamento	readaptação
ready	prêt, e	fertig	dispuesto, a	pronto, a	pronto, a
real, actual	réel, le	wirklich	real	reale; vero, a	real
real, genuine	véritable	wahrhaftig	verdadero, a	vero, a	verdadeiro, a
reality	réalité	Wirklichkeit(f)	realidad	realtà	realidade
realization	réalisation	Verwirklichung(f)	realización	realizzazione	realização
realize	réaliser	begreifen	darse cuenta	realizzare	aperceber-se
really	vraiment	wirklich	verdaderamente	veramente	verdadeiramente
rear	derrière, arrière	Rück-; Hinter-	trasero, a; de atrás	dietro, indietro	traseiro, a
rear-view mirror	rétroviseur	Rückspiegel(m)	retrovisor	retrovisore	retrovisor
reason	raison	Grund(m)	razón, causa	ragione	razão
reason(the--for)	pourquoi(le--de)	Grund(m)(der--für)	porqué(el--de)	perché(il--di)	porquê(o--de)
reasonable	raisonnable	vernünftig	razonable	ragionevole	razoável
reasoning	raisonnement	Überlegung(f)	razonamiento	ragionamento	raciocínio
reassemble	remonter	wieder montieren	volver a montar	rimontare	tornar a montar
reassembly	remontage	Zusammensetzen(n)	volver a montar	rimontaggio	nova montagem

English	French	German	Spanish	Italian	Portuguese
reassure	rassurer	beruhigen	tranquilizar	rassicurare	tranquilizar
rebel	rebelle	Rebell(m)	rebelde	ribelle	rebelde
rebel(against)	insurger(s')	empören, sich	rebelarse	ribellarsi	insurgir-se
rebellion	rébellion	Aufstand(m)	rebelión	ribellione	rebelião
recall	rappel	Rückruf(m)	recuerdo	richiamo	lembrança
recall, remember	rappeler(se)	erinnern, sich	recordar, acordarse	ricordarsi	lembrar-se
receipt	réception	Empfang(m)	recibo	ricevuta	recepção
receipt	reçu	Quittung(f)	recibo	ricevuta	recibo
receipt	quittance	Quittung(f)	recibo	ricevuta	recibo
receipts; takings	recette	Einnahmen(f, pl)	ingresos	incasso	receita
receive, get	recevoir	empfangen	recibir	ricevere	receber
receiver	récepteur	Empfänger(m)	receptor	ricevitore	receptor
recent	récent, e	neu	reciente	recente	recente
recently	récemment	kürzlich	recientemente	recentemente	recentemente
receptacle	réceptacle	Sammelbecken(n)	receptáculo	ricettacolo	receptáculo
reception; welcome	accueil	Empfang(m), Aufnahme f	recepción	accoglienza	recepção
reception	réception	Empfang(m)	recepción	ricezione	recepção
reception	réception	Rezeption(f)	recepción	reception	recepção
recipe	recette	Rezept(n)	receta	ricetta	receita
recital	récital	Konzert(n), Vortrag(m)	recital	recital	recital
recitation	récitation	Vortrag(m)	recitación	recita	recitação
recognize	reconnaître	erkennen	reconocer	riconoscere	reconhecer
recoil	recul	Rückstoß(m)	retroceso	rinculo	recuo
recommendation	recommandation	Empfehlung(f)	recomendación	raccomandazione	recomendação
reconciliation	réconciliation	Versöhnung(f)	reconciliación	riconciliazione	reconciliação
record, file	dossier	Akte(f)	expediente	dossier	processo
record	rapport	Protokoll(n)	acta, protocolo	atto, protocollo	acta
record	disque	Schallplatte(f)	disco	disco	disco
record	record	Rekord(m)	récord	record	recorde
record	enregistrer	auf = nehmen	grabar	registrare	gravar
recording	enregistrement	Aufnahme(f)	grabación	registrazione	gravação
record-player	tourne-disque	Plattenspieler(m)	tocadiscos	giradischi	gira-discos
recourse	recours	Zuflucht(f), Berufung	recurso	ricorso	recurso
recover, get back	récupérer	wieder = bekommen	recuperar	recuperare	recuperar
recruit	recruter	an = werben	contratar, reclutar	assumere	recrutar
recruitment	recrutement	Rekrutierung(f)	reclutamiento	reclutamento	recrutamento
rectangle	rectangle	Rechteck(n)	rectángulo	rettangolo	rectângulo
rectify	rectifier	berichtigen	rectificar	rettificare	rectificar
rectify, correct	corriger	berichtigen	corregir	correggere	rectificar
red	rouge	rot	rojo, a	rosso, a	vermelho, a
reduce	réduire	reduzieren	reducir	ridurre	reduzir
reduce, decrease	diminuer	verringern	disminuir	diminuire	diminuir
reduction	réduction	Verringerung(f)	reducción	riduzione	redução
reduction	diminution	Verminderung(f)	disminución	diminuzione	diminuição
reduction	réduction	Senkung(f)	rebaja	riduzione	desconto
reduction	remise, rabais	Nachlaß, Ermäßigung	descuento	rimessa, sconto	desconto
reef	récif	Riff(n)	arrecife	scoglio	recife
reel	bobine	Spule(f)	bobina, carrete	bobina	bobina
refer to	référer(se)	beziehen, sich	referirse	riferirsi	referir-se
referee	arbitre	Schiedsrichter(in f)m	árbitro	arbitro	árbitro
reference	référence	Referenz(f)	referencia	riferimento	referência
reflect, think	réfléchir(à)	überlegen	reflexionar	riflettere	reflectir; pensar
reflected(be)	réfléchir(se)	reflektieren	reflejar	riflettere(-ersi)	reflectir
reflection	reflet	Widerschein(m), Reflex	reflejo	riflesso	reflexo
reflex	réflexe	Reflex(m)	reflejo	riflesso	reflexo
reform	réforme	Reform(f)	reforma	riforma	reforma
refrain, chorus	refrain	Refrain(m)	estribillo	ritornello	refrão
refrigerating	frigorifique	Kühl-; kalt, kühl	frigorífico, a	frigorifero, a	frigorífico, a
refrigerator	réfrigérateur	Kühlschrank(m)	nevera	frigorifero	frigorífico
refuge	refuge, asile	Zufluchtsort(m)	refugio, asilo	rifugio, asilo	refúgio, asilo
refugee	réfugié, e	Flüchtling(m)	refugiado, a	rifugiato, a	refugiado, a
refusal	refus	Verweigerung(f)	rechazo	rifiuto	recusa
refuse	refuser	verweigern	rehusar	rifiutare	recusar
refute	réfuter	widerlegen	refutar	confutare	refutar
refute, deny	démentir	dementieren, leugnen	desmentir	smentire	desmentir
regard	considérer	betrachten	considerar	considerare	considerar
régime	régime	Regime(n)	régimen	regime	regime
regiment	régiment	Regiment(n)	regimiento	reggimento	regimento

region	région	Gegend(f)	región	regione	região
register	registre	Register(n)	registro	registro	registo
register, check in	enregistrer	auf = geben	registrar	registrare	registar
register	inscrire(s')	ein = schreiben, sich	matricularse	iscriversi	matricular-se
registration	enregistrement	Registrierung(f)	registro	registrazione	registo
registration	inscription	Einschreibung(f)	matrícula	iscrizione	matrícula
registration	immatriculation	Eintragung(f)	matrícula	immatricolazione	matrícula
regression	régression	Rückgang(m)	regresión	regresso	regressão
regret	regret	Bedauern(n)	lamento(lo)	rimpianto	pena; pesar
regret	regretter	nach = trauern(jdm/etw)	lamentar, añorar	rimpiangere	lamentar
regret(I)	désolé, e	bedauern	siento(lo)	rammaricato, a	lamento(eu)
regular	régulier, ière	regelmäßig	regular	regolare	regular
regularization	régularisation	Regulierung(f)	regularización	regolarizzazione	regularização
regulation	règlement	Bestimmung(f)	reglamento	regolamento	regulamento
regulation(s)	réglementation	Regelung(f)	reglamentación	regolamentazione	regulamentação
reign	règne	Herrschaft(f)	reino	regno	reinado
reinforce	renforcer	verstärken	reforzar	rinforzare	reforçar
reinforcement	renfort	Verstärkung(f)	refuerzo	rinforzo	reforço
reinstate	réintégrer	wiederein = setzen	rehabilitar	reintegrare	reintegrar
reject	refuser, rejeter	ab = lehnen, verwerfen	rechazar	rigettare	rejeitar
rejoicing	réjouissance	Fröhlichkeit(f)	regocijo	gioia, giubilo	regozijo; alegria
rejoin, return to	rejoindre	an = schließen, sich	reunirse con	raggiungere	reunir-se
relate, tell	raconter	erzählen	contar	raccontare	contar
relate, recount	relater	erzählen	relatar	riferire	relatar
relation(-ship)	relation	Beziehung(f)	relación	relazione	relação
relationship	parenté	Verwandtschaft(f)	parentesco	parentela	parentesco
relative	relatif, ive	relativ	relativo, a	relativo, a	relativo, a
relative, relation	parent, e	verwandt	pariente	parente	parente
relaxation	relaxation	Entspannung(f)	relajamiento	rilassamento	relaxação
relaxed	détendu, e	entspannt	descansado, a	disteso, a; rilassato	descontraído, a
relaxed	décontracté, e	lässig, entspannt	relajado, a	rilassato, a	descontraído, a
release	débloquer	deblockieren, lösen	desbloquear	sbloccare	desbloquear
release	lâcher	los = lassen	soltar	lasciare	soltar
release	relâcher	frei = lassen	soltar	rilasciare	libertar
reliable	fiable	zuverlässig	fiable, seguro, a	sicuro, a; affidabile	seguro, a
relief	soulagement	Erleichterung(f)	alivio, desahogo	sollievo	alívio
relief	relief	Relief(n)	relieve	rilievo	relevo
relieve	soulager	lindern	aliviar	sollevare, lenire	aliviar
relieve	soulager	erleichtern	aliviar	alleggerire	aliviar
religion	religion	Religion(f)	religión	religione	religião
religious	religieux, se	religiös	religioso, a	religioso, a	religioso, a
rely on	compter sur	zählen, auf jdn	contar con	contare su	contar com
remain	rester	bleiben	sobrar, quedar	restare, rimanere	sobejar, sobrar
remains, debris	débris, restes	Trümmer(m, pl)	resto, residuo	resti, cocci	resto, destroços
remains	vestige	Überrest(m)	vestigio	vestigia	vestígio
remark, comment	remarque	Bemerkung(f)	observación	osservazione	observação
remarkable	remarquable	bemerkenswert	notable	notevole	notável
remedy	remède	Heilmittel(n)	remedio	rimedio	remédio
remember, recall	souvenir(se)	erinnern, sich	acordarse	ricordarsi	recordar-se
reminder	rappel	Erinnerung(f); Mahnung	llamada	richiamo	aviso; lembrança
remorse	remords	Gewissensbiß(m)	remordimiento	rimorso	remorso
remote control	télécommande	Fernsteuerung(f)	telemando	telecomando	telecomando
removable	amovible	auswechselbar	amovible	amovibile	amovível
remove	enlever, retirer	ab = nehmen	quitar, retirar	rimuovere	remover, retirar
remove, take away	ôter, enlever	ab = nehmen	quitar	togliere	tirar
remove, dismantle	démonter	ab = bauen	desmontar	smontare	desmontar
remove hair	épiler	enthaaren	depilar	depilare	depilar
remuneration	rémunération	Entlohnung(f), Lohn(m)	remuneración	rimunerazione	remuneração
renew	renouveler	erneuern	renovar	rinnovare	renovar
renewal	renouvellement	Erneuerung(f)	renovación	rinnovo	renovação
renovation	rénovation	Renovation(f)	renovación	rinnovazione	restauração
rent	louer	vermieten; mieten	alquilar	affittare	alugar
rent	loyer	Miete(f)	alquiler	affitto	aluguer
rental, hiring	location	Vermietung(f)	alquiler	noleggio, affitto	aluguer
repair	réparation	Reparation(f)	reparación	riparazione	reparação
repair, mend	réparer	reparieren	reparar	riparare	reparar
repatriation	rapatriement	Repatriierung(f)	repatriación	rimpatrio	repatriação
repayment	remboursement	Rückzahlung(f)	reembolso	rimborso	reembolso

repeat	répéter	wieder = holen	repetir	ripetere	repetir
replace	remplacer	ersetzen	sustituir	sostituire	substituir
reply, answer	répondre	erwidern	responder	rispondere	responder
reply	répliquer	erwidern, entgegnen	replicar	replicare	replicar
report	rapport	Bericht(m)	informe	rapporto, relazione	relatório
report, minutes	compte rendu	Bericht(m)	informe, acta	resoconto	relatório, acta
report	reportage	Reportage(f)	reportaje	cronaca	reportagem
represent	représenter	dar = stellen	representar	rappresentare	representar
representation	représentation	Darstellung(f)	representación	rappresentazione	representação
representative, rep	représentant, e	Vertreter(in f)m	representante	rappresentante	representante
repression	répression	Unterdrückung(f)	represión	repressione	repressão
reprisal	représaille(s)	Vergeltung(f)	represalia	rappresaglia	represália
reproach	reprocher	vor = werfen	reprochar	rimproverare	censurar
reproduce	reproduire	reproduzieren	reproducir	riprodurre	reproduzir
reproduction	reproduction	Reproduktion(f)	reproducción	riproduzione	reprodução
reptile	reptile	Reptil(n)	reptil	rettile	réptil
republic	république	Republik(f)	república	repubblica	república
reputation	réputation	Ansehen(n), Ruf(m)	reputación, fama	reputazione, fama	reputação, fama
request	demande	Anfrage(f)	pedido	richiesta	pedido
request; demand	demande	Bitte(f); Gesuch(n)	petición	richiesta	pedido
request	requête	Ersuchen(n), Gesuch(n)	demanda	richiesta	pedido
require, need	besoin(avoir)	brauchen	necesitar	bisogno(avere)	necessidade(ter)
rescue	sauvetage	Rettung(f)	salvamento	salvataggio	salvamento
rescue	secourir	retten	socorrer	soccorrere	socorrer
rescuer	sauveteur	Retter(in f)m	socorrista	soccorritore	socorrista
research	recherche	Forschung(f)	investigación	ricerca	investigação
research worker	chercheur, euse	Forscher(in f)m	investigador, a	cercatore	investigador, a
resemblance	ressemblance	Ähnlichkeit(f)	parecido	somiglianza	semelhança
reservation	réservation	Reservierung(f)	reserva	prenotazione	reserva
reserve	réserve	Reserve(f)	reserva	riserva	reserva
reserve	réserver	reservieren	reservar	riservare	reservar
reserved	réservé, e	reserviert	reservado, a	prenotato, a	reservado, a
reside	résider	wohnen	residir	risiedere	residir
residence	résidence	Wohnsitz(m)	residencia	residenza	residência
residence, dwelling	demeure	Wohnung(f), Haus(n)	morada, casa	dimora	habitação, casa
resident	pensionnaire	Pensionsgast(m)	pensionista	pensionante	hóspede
residue	résidu	Rückstand(m)	residuo	residuo	resíduo
resign	démissionner	zurück = treten	dimitir	dimettere(-rsi)	demitir-se
resign oneself	résigner(se)	entsagen, ergeben, sich	resignarse	rassegnarsi	resignar-se
resignation	démission	Rücktritt(m)	dimisión	dimissione	demissão
resin	résine	Harz(m)	resina	resina	resina
resist; withstand	résister	widerstehen	resistir	resistere	resistir
resistance	résistance	Widerstand(m)	resistencia	resistenza	resistência
resistant	résistant, e	widerstandsfähig	resistente	resistente	resistente
resort	station	Erholungsort(m)	estación	stazione	estação
resound, sound	résonner	klingen	resonar	rimbombare	ressoar, ecoar
resources	ressource(s)	Mittel(n, pl)	recurso	risorsa	recurso
respect	respect	Respekt(m)	respeto	rispetto	respeito
respect	respecter	respektieren	respetar	rispettare	respeitar
respectable	respectable	achtbar	respetable	rispettabile	respeitável
respectively	respectivement	beziehungsweise	respectivamente	rispettivamente	respectivamente
respite	répit	Atempause(f)	tregua, respiro	tregua, riposo	trégua, espera
responsibility	responsabilité	Verantwortung(f)	responsabilidad	responsabilità	responsabilidade
responsible	responsable	verantwortlich	responsable	responsabile	responsável
rest	reposer(se)	aus = ruhen, sich	descansar	riposarsi	descançar
rest	repos	Ruhe(f)	descanso	riposo	descanço
rest, remainder	reste	Rest(m)	resto	resto	resto
restaurant	restaurant	Restaurant(n)	restaurante	ristorante	restaurante
restore	restaurer	wiederher = stellen	restaurar	restaurare	restaurar
restraint	contrainte	Zwang(m)	obligación	costrizione	obrigação
restrict	restreindre	beschränken	restringir	restringere	restringir
restriction	restriction	Einschränkung(f)	restricción	restrizione	restrição
result	résultat	Ergebnis(n)	resultado	risultato, esito	resultado
result, be	résulter, être	ergeben, sich	resultar	risultare	resultar
resuscitation	réanimation	Wiederbelebung(f)	reanimación	rianimazione	reanimação
retina	rétine	Netzhaut(f)	retina	retina	retina
retired(be)	retraité, e(être)	pensioniert sein	jubilado, a(estar)	pensione(essere in)	reformado, a(estar)
retired person	retraité, e	Rentner(in f)m	retirado, a	pensionato, a	reformado, a

English	French	German	Spanish	Italian	Portuguese
retirement	retraite	Pensionierung(f)	jubilación	pensione	reforma
return	retour	Rückkehr(f)	regreso, vuelta	ritorno	regresso, volta
return(to)	retourner	zurück = gehen	regresar	tornare	voltar(a)
return	réintégrer	zurück = kehren	reintegrar	reintegrare	voltar
return	restituer	zurück = erstatten	restituir	restituire	restituir
return ticket	billet Aller/R	Rückfahrkarte(f)	billete ida/vuelta	andata e ritorno	bilhete ida/volta
reveal	révéler	auf = decken	revelar	rivelare	revelar
revenge	vengeance	Rache(f)	venganza	vendetta	vingança
reverse, back	envers	Rückseite(f)	revés	rovescio	avesso
reverse, invert	inverser	um = kehren	invertir	invertire	inverter
review, magazine	revue, magazine	Zeitschrift, Revue(f)	revista	rivista, periodico	revista
revision	révision	Revision(f)	revisión	revisione	revisão
revolt	révolte	Revolte(f)	revuelta	rivolta	revolta
revolution	révolution	Revolution(f)	revolución	rivoluzione	revolução
revolutionary	révolutionnaire	revolutionär	revolucionario, a	rivoluzionario, a	revolucionário, a
revolve, pivot	pivoter	schwenken	girar	girare, ruotare	girar; rodar
revolver, gun	révolver	Revolver(m)	revólver	revolver	revólver
reward; award	récompense	Belohnung(f)	recompensa	ricompensa	recompensa
rheumatism	rhumatisme	Rheumatismus(m)	reumatismo	reumatismo	reumatismo
rhythm	rythme	Takt(m), Rhythmus(m)	ritmo	ritmo	ritmo
rib	côte	Rippe(f)	costilla	costola	costela
ribbon; tape; band	ruban	Band(n)	cinta, banda	nastro	fita
rice	riz	Reis(m)	arroz	riso	arroz
rich, wealthy	riche	reich	rico, a	ricco, a	rico, a
rickety	rachitique	rachitisch	raquítico, a	rachitico, a	raquítico, a
rider	cavalier, ière	Reiter(in f)m	jinete, a	cavaliere, a	cavaleiro, a
ridiculous	ridicule	lächerlich	ridículo, a	ridicolo, a	ridículo, a
riding(horse -)	équitation	Reiten(n)	equitación	equitazione	equitação
rifle	carabine	Gewehr(n), Karabiner m	carabina	carabina	espingarda
right	juste; exact, e	richtig	exacto, a	giusto, a	certo, a
right	droit, e	rechte(r, s); rechts	derecho, a	destro, a	direito, a
right	droit	Recht(n)	derecho	diritto	direito
right(that 's)	exact(c'est)	stimmt!	exacto(es)	esatto(è)	exacto(é)
right(to be)	raison(avoir)	Recht(n)(haben)	razón(tener)	ragione(avere)	razão(ter)
rightful, lawful	légitime, légal	rechtmäßig	legítimo, a	legittimo, a	legítimo, a
rigid, stiff	rigide	steif	rígido, a	rigido, a	rígido, a
rigorous	rigoureux, se	streng	riguroso, a	rigoroso, a	rigoroso, a
rim	jante	Felge(f), Radkranz(m)	llanta	cerchione	jante, camba
ring	anneau	Ring(m)	anilla, anillo	anello	anel
ring	bague	Ring(m)	anillo, sortija	anello	anel
ring, circle	cerne	Augenringe(pl.)	ojeras	occhiaia	olheiras
ring	sonnerie	Klingel(f)	campana, timbre	squillo, soneria	campainha, toque
ring	sonner, retentir	klingeln	sonar, tocar	suonare, sonare	soar, tocar
ringing, jingle	tintement	Klimpern, Klingeln(n)	tañido	tintinnio	tilintar
riot	émeute	Aufruhr(m)	motín	sommossa	motim
ripe	mûr, e	reif	maduro, a	maturo, a	maduro, a
rise	montée	Steigung(f)	subida	salita	subida
rise, increase	hausse	Steigerung(f)	subida	aumento	subida
rise	augmentation	Zulage(f)	aumento, subida	aumento, crescita	aumento, subida
rise	élever(s')	an = steigen	subir	elevarsi	subir
rise	lever(se)	auf = gehen	amanecer	sorgere	nascer
rise up, revolt	insurger(s')	auf = lehnen gegen, sich	sublevarse	insorgere	insurgir-se
risk	risque	Risiko(n)	riesgo	rischio	risco
risk	risquer	riskieren	arriesgar	rischiare	arriscar
rite; ritual	rite	Brauch(m), Ritus(m)	rito	rito	rito
rival; competitor	rival, e	Rivale(m), Rivalin(f)	rival	rivale	rival
rivalry	rivalité	Rivalität(f)	rivalidad	rivalità	rivalidade
river	rivière	Fluß(m)	río, ribera	fiume	rio, ribeira
river	fleuve	Strom(m)	río	fiume	rio
road	route	Straße(f)	carretera	strada	estrada
road	chaussée	Fahrbahn(f)	calzada	carreggiata	calçada
roast; joint	rôti	Braten(m)	asado	arrosto	assado
rob, burgle	dévaliser, voler	aus = rauben	desvalijar	svaligiare	roubar
robot	robot	Roboter(m)	robot	robot	robot
robust, sturdy	robuste	robust, stark	robusto, a	robusto, a	robusto, a
rock	roche, rocher	Fels(m)	roca	roccia	rocha
rock	rocher	Felsen(m)	peñasco, roca	masso, roccia	rochedo, rocha
rock	bercer	wiegen	mecer	cullare	embalar

English	French	German	Spanish	Italian	Portuguese
rocket	fusée	Rakete(f)	cohete	razzo	foguete
rod	tige	Stange(f)	tallo, vástago	asta, barra	haste
role, part	rôle	Rolle(f)	cometido, función	ruolo, parte	função
role	rôle	Rolle(f)	papel	parte, ruolo	papel
roll	rouleau	Rolle(f), Walze(f)	rollo	rotolo; rullo	rolo
roll, register	matricule	Matrikel(f)	matrícula	matricola	matrícula
roll	rouler	rollen	rodar	rotolare	rolar
roll up	enrouler	auf = wickeln	enrollar	arrotolare	enrolar
romantic	romantique	romantisch	romántico, a	romantico, a	romântico, a
roof	toit	Dach(n)	tejado	tetto	telhado
room	pièce	Raum(m)	cuarto	stanza	divisão
room	salle	Saal(m), Raum(m)	sala	sala, stanza	sala
room	place	Platz(m)	sitio, espacio	spazio	espaço
room, hotel room	chambre d'hôtel	Hotelzimmer(n)	habitación	camera	quarto
root	racine	Wurzel(f)	raíz	radice	raiz
rope	corde	Tau(n)	cuerda	corda	corda
rose	rose	Rose(f)	rosa	rosa	rosa
rot	pourrir	verfaulen	pudrir	marcire	apodrecer
rotate, revolve	tourner(faire)	drehen	girar(hacer)	roteare	girar(fazer)
rotation	rotation	Drehung(f)	rotación	rotazione	rotação
rotten	pourri, e	verfault	podrido, a	marcio, a	podre
rough, harsh	rugueux, se	rauh	rugoso, a	rugoso, a	rugoso, a
rough paper	brouillon	Schmierzettel(m)	borrador	brutta copia	rascunho
round	rond, e	rund	redondo, a	rotondo, a	redondo, a
roundabout	rond-point	Kreisverkehr(m)	glorieta	rotonda, rotatoria	rotunda
roundabout	manège	Karussell(n)	tiovivo, noria	giostra	carrossel
route	itinéraire, route	Route(f), Weg(m)	ruta, itinerario	rotta, itinerario	caminho, rota
routine	routine	Routine(f)	rutina	routine, tran tran	rotina
row	rangée	Reihe(f)	hilera, fila	fila	fileira, renque
row	ramer	rudern	remar	remare	remar
rowing	aviron	Rudersport(m)	remo; piragua	canottaggio	remo
royal	royal, e	königlich	real	reale	real
royalty, monarchy	royauté	Königstum(n)	realeza	sovranità	realeza
rub	frotter	reiben	frotar	strofinare, sfregare	esfregar
rubber	caoutchouc	Gummi(m, n)	caucho	gomma	borracha
rubber	gomme	Radiergummi(m)	goma	gomma	borracha
rubber band	élastique	Gummiband(n)	goma elástica	elastico	elástico
rubbish, garbage	ordure(s)	Abfall(m)	basura	immondizia	lixo
rubbish, garbage	détritus	Unrat(m)	desperdicios	detrito	detrito, lixo
ruby	rubis	Rubin(m)	rubí	rubino	rubi
rucksack	sac à dos	Rucksack(m)	mochila	zaino	mochila
rudder	gouvernail	Ruder(n), Steur(n)	timón	timone	leme
rude; crude	grossier, ière	grob	grosero, a	grossolano, a	grosseiro, a
ruin	ruiner	ruinieren	arruinar	rovinare	arruinar
ruin	ruine	Ruine(f)	ruina	rovina	ruína
ruin	ruine	Trümmer(m, pl)	ruina	rovina	ruína
ruins	décombres	Trümmer(m, pl)	escombros	macerie, rovine	escombros
rule	règle	Regel(f)	regla, norma	regola, norma	regra, norma
ruler	règle	Lineal(m)	regla	riga	régua
rumour	rumeur	Gerücht(n)	rumor	voce, diceria	rumor
run	courir	laufen	correr	correre	correr
run away, flee	fuir	fliehen	huir	fuggire	fugir
run away	enfuir(s')	fliehen	huir	fuggire	fugir
run, drive, go	rouler	fahren	correr, rodar	correre, andare	andar; rolar
run, flow	écouler(s')	ab = fließen	correr, fluir	scorrere, defluire	escorrer
runner	coureur, se	Läufer(in f)m	corredor, a	corridore	corredor, a
running	course	Wettrennen(n)	carrera	corsa	corrida
running in	rodage	Einfahren(n)	rodaje	rodaggio	rodagem
runway	piste	Bahn(Lande-, Start-)	pista	pista	pista
rupture	rupture	Bruch(m)	ruptura	rottura	ruptura
rural	rural, e	ländlich	rural	rurale	rural
rush	ruée	Ansturm(m)	riada	ressa	corrida
rush	affluence	Andrang(m)	afluencia	affluenza	afluência
rush	précipiter(se)	stürzen, sich	precipitarse	precipitarsi	precipitar-se
rust	rouille	Rost(m)	herrumbre	ruggine	ferrugem
rustic	rustique	ländlich, einfach	rústico, a	rustico, a	rústico, a
rye	seigle	Roggen(m)	centeno	segale	centeio

S

English	French	German	Spanish	Italian	Portuguese
sabotage	sabotage	Sabotage(f)	sabotaje	sabotaggio	sabotagem
sabotage	saboter	sabotieren	sabotear	sabotare	sabotar
sabre	sabre	Säbel(m)	sable	sciabola	sabre
sack	sac	Sack(m)	saco	sacco	saco
sacrifice	sacrifice	Opfer(n)	sacrificio	sacrificio	sacrifício
sacrifice	sacrifier	opfern	sacrificar	sacrificare	sacrificar
sacrilege	sacrilège	Entweihung(f)	sacrilegio	sacrilegio	sacrilégio
sad, unhappy	triste	traurig	triste	triste	triste
saddle	selle	Sattel(m)	silla	sella	sela
saddle	selle	Sattel(m)	sillín	sellino	selim
sadist	sadique	Sadist(in f)m	sádico, a	sadico, a	sádico, a
sadistic	sadique	sadistisch	sádico, a	sadico, a	sádico, a
sadness	tristesse	Traurigkeit(f)	tristeza	tristezza	tristeza
safe	sauf, ve	sicher	salvo, a	salvo, a	salvo, a
safe	coffre-fort	Safe(m)	caja fuerte	cassaforte	cofre-forte
safety	sûreté; sécurité	Sicherheit(f)	seguridad	sicurezza	segurança
sage, wise man	sage	Weise(m)	sabio	saggio, a; savio, a	sábio
sail	voile	Segel(n)	vela	vela	vela
sailing	voile	Segeln(n)	vela	vela	vela
sailor	marin	Seemann(m)	marino	marinaio	marinheiro
sailor	matelot	Matrose(m)	marinero	marinaio	marinheiro
saint	saint, e	Heilige(m, f)	santo, a	santo, a	santo, a
salad; lettuce	salade	Salat(m); Kopfsalat(m)	ensalada; lechuga	insalata	salada
salad, crudité	crudité	Rohkost(f)	ensalada	insalata mista	salada
salaried employee	salarié, e	Arbeitnehmer(in f)m	asalariado, a	salariato, a	assalariado, a
salary, wage	salaire	Lohn(m), Gehalt(n)	salario	salario	salário
sale	vente	Verkauf(m)	venta	vendita	venda
sales	soldes	Ausverkauf(m)	saldos, rebajas	saldi	saldos
sales assistant	vendeur, se	Verkäufer(in f)m	vendedor, a	commesso, se	vendedor, a
salesman(-men)	vendeur, se	Verkäufer(in f)m	vendedor, a	venditore, trice	vendedor, a
saliva	salive	Speichel(m)	saliva	saliva	saliva
salmon	saumon	Lachs(m)	salmón	salmone	salmão
salon	salon(coiffure)	Friseurladen(m)	peluquería	parrucchiere, a(da)	salão
salt	sel	Salz(n)	sal	sale	sal
salty	salé, e	salzig	salado, a	salato, a	salgado, a
salvage	sauvetage	Bergung(f)	salvamento	salvataggio	salvamento
same	même	selbe; gleich(der -)	mismo, a	stesso, a	mesmo, a
same, similar, like	pareil, le	gleich, wie	igual	uguale, pari	igual
sample	échantillon	Probe(f), Muster(n)	muestra	campione	amostra
sanction	sanction	Strafe(f)	sanción	sanzione	sanção
sanctuary	sanctuaire	Heiligtum(n)	santuario	santuario	santuário
sand	sable	Sand(m)	arena	sabbia	areia
sandal	sandale	Sandale(f)	sandalia	sandalo	sandália
sandwich(-es)	sandwich	Butterbrot(n)	bocadillo	panino	sande, sanduiche
sanitary	sanitaire	Gesundheits-	sanitario, a	sanitario, a	sanitário, a
sap	sève	Saft(m)	savia	linfa	seiva
sapphire	saphir	Saphir(m)	zafiro	zaffiro	safira
sardine	sardine	Sardine(f)	sardina	sardina	sardinha
satellite	satellite	Satellit(m)	satélite	satellite	satélite
satin	satin	Satin(m)	raso, satén	raso	cetim
satisfaction	satisfaction	Zufriedenheit(f)	satisfacción	soddisfazione	satisfação
satisfied	satisfait, e	zufrieden	satisfecho, a	soddisfatto, a	satisfeito, a
saturate	saturer	sättigen	saturar	saturare	saturar
saturation	saturation	Übersättigung(f)	saturación	saturazione	saturação
Saturday	Samedi	Samstag(m)	Sábado	Sabato	Sábado
sauce	sauce	Soße(f)	salsa	sugo; salsa	molho
saucer	soucoupe	Untertasse(f)	platillo	piattino	pires
sauna	sauna	Sauna(f)	sauna	sauna	sauna
sausage	saucisse	Wurst(f)	salchicha	salsiccia	salsicha
savannah	savane	Savanne(f)	sabana	savana	savana
save	sauver	retten	salvar	salvare	salvar

English	French	German	Spanish	Italian	Portuguese
save, economise	économiser	sparen	economizar	economizzare	economizar
save	épargner	sparen	ahorrar	risparmiare	poupar
save	gagner	sparen	ganar	guadagnare	ganhar
saver, investor	épargnant, e	Sparer(in f)m	ahorrador, a	risparmiatore, trice	aforrador, a
saving	économie, épargne	Ersparnis(f)	economía, ahorro	risparmio	economia
savour	savourer	kosten, genießen	saborear	assaporare	saborear
saw	scie	Säge(f)	sierra	sega	serra
saw	scier	sägen	serrar, aserrar	segare	serrar
say	dire	sagen	decir	dire	dizer
scabies	gale	Krätze(f)	sarna	scabbia, rogna	sarna
scaffolding	échafaudage	Gerüst(n)	andamio	impalcatura	andaime
scale, size	ampleur	Weite(f), Größe(f)	amplitud	ampiezza	amplidão
scale	échelle	Tabelle(f), Skala(f)	escala	scala	escala
scale	barème	Liste(f)	baremo	tariffario	tabela
scale	écaille	Schuppe(f)	escama	squama	escama
scales	balance	Waage(f)	balanza	bilancia	balança
scales	bascule	Waage(f)	báscula	basculla, bilancia	báscula
scalpel, bistoury	bistouri	Skalpell(n)	bisturí	bisturi	bisturi
scan, scrutinize	scruter	erforschen	escudriñar	scrutare	perscrutar
scandal	scandale	Skandal(m)	escándalo	scandalo	escândalo
scar	cicatrice	Narbe(f)	cicatriz	cicatrice	cicatriz
scarf	écharpe	Halstuch(n), Schal(m)	bufanda	sciarpa	cachecol, cachené
scarf	cache-nez	Schal(m)	bufanda	sciarpa	cachecol
scarf	foulard	Seidentuch, Halstuch	fular, pañuelo	foulard	lenço, cachecol
scene	scène	Szene(f)	escena	scena	cena
sceptic(al)	sceptique	skeptisch	escéptico, a	scettico, a	céptico, a
scheme, plan	plan, projet	Plan(m)	plan, proyecto	schema, piano	plano, projecto
scholar	érudit, e	Gelehrte(f, m)	erudito, a	dotto, a; erudito, a	erudito, a
school	école	Schule(f)	escuela	scuola	escola
schoolboy/girl	écolier, ière	Schüler(in f)m	colegial, a	scolaro, a	aluno, a
schooling	scolarité	Schulzeit(f)	escolaridad	scolarità	escolaridade
sciatica	sciatique	Ischias(m)	ciática	sciatica	ciática
science	science	Wissenschaft(f)	ciencia	scienza	ciência
scientific	scientifique	wissenschaftlich	científico, a	scientifico, a	científico, a
scientist	scientifique	Wissenschaftler(m)	científico	scienziato	cientista
scientist	savant	Gelehrte(f, m)	científico	scienziato	cientista
scissors	ciseaux	Schere(f)	tijeras	forbici	tesoura
sclerosis(-ses)	sclérose	Sklerose(f)	esclerósis	sclerosi	esclerose
scold, tell off	gronder	schimpfen	regañar	sgridare	ralhar
scoliosis	scoliose	Skoliose(f)	escoliosis	scoliosi	escoliose
score	score	Punktzahl(f)	marca, tanteo	punteggio	resultado
score	marquer	schießen(Tor-)	marcar	segnare	marcar
score(music)	partition	Partitur(f)	partitura	spartito	partitura
scorpion	scorpion	Skorpion(m)	escorpión	scorpione	escorpião
scrap iron	ferraille	Alteisen(n)	chatarra	ferraglia, rottame	sucata
scrape, scratch	gratter	kratzen	raspar, rascar	grattare	raspar
scratch, graze	éraflure	Kratzer(m), Schramme f	rasguño	scalfittura	arranhadura
scratch	égratigner	kratzen, schrammen	rasguñar	scalfire	arranhar
scratch, claw	griffer	kratzen	arañar	graffiare	arranhar
scratch oneself	gratter(se)	kratzen, sich	rascarse	grattarsi	coçar-se
scratched	rayé, e	zerkratzt	rayado, a	rigato, a	riscado, a
scream, yell	hurler	brüllen	chillar	urlare	gritar; berrar
scree	éboulis	Geröll(n)	escombros	detriti	escombros
screen	écran	Bildschirm; Leinwand	pantalla	schermo	écran
screen	écran	Wandschirm(m)	pantalla	schermo	painel
screw	vis	Schraube(f)	tornillo	vite	parafuso
screwdriver	tournevis	Schraubenzieher(m)	destornillador	cacciavite	chave de parafusos
script(film -)	scénario	Drehbuch(n)	guión	scenario	guião
script-writer	scénariste	Drehbuchautor(in f)m	guionista	scenarista	cenarista
scruple	scrupule	Skrupel(m)	escrúpulo	scrupolo	escrúpulo
sculpture	sculpture	Skulptur(f)	escultura	scultura	escultura
sea	mer	Meer(n)	mar	mare	mar
sea	mer	See(f)	mar	mare	mar
sea-sickness	mal de mer	Seekrankheit(f)	mareo	mal di mare	enjôo
sea-side	bord de mer	Küste(f)	orilla del mar	riva	beira-mar
seafood	fruits de mer	Meeresfrüchte(f, pl.)	marisco	frutti di mare	marisco
seagull	mouette	Möve(f)	gaviota	gabbiano	gaivota
seal	phoque	Seehund(m)	foca	foca	foca

English	French	German	Spanish	Italian	Portuguese
seal	sceau	Siegel(n)	sello	sigillo	selo
seam	couture	Saum(m)	costura	cucito	costura
search	recherche	Suche(f)	busca	ricerca	busca
search/look for	rechercher	suchen	buscar, indagar	ricercare	buscar, procurar
search	fouiller	suchen, durchsuchen	registrar	frugare	rebuscar
season	saison	Jahreszeit(f)	estación	stagione	estação
seasonal	saisonnier, ière	saisonbedingt	temporero, a	stagionale	sazonal
seasoning	assaisonnement	Würze(f)	aliño	condimento	tempero
seat	siège	Sitz(m)	asiento	sedia	assento
seat	place	Sitzplatz(m)	sitio, asiento	posto	lugar
seated	assis, e	sitzen	sentado, a	seduto, a	sentado, a
seaweed, alga(ae)	algue	Alge(f)	alga	alga	alga
second	second, e	zweite	segundo, a	secondo, a	segundo, a
second	deuxième	zweite	segundo, a	secondo, a	segundo, a
second	seconde	Sekunde(f)	segundo	secondo	segundo
secondary	secondaire	nebensächlich	secundario, a	secondario, a	secundário, a
second-hand, used	occasion	gebraucht	segunda mano	seconda mano	segunda mão(em)
secret	secret	Geheimnis(n)	secreto	segreto	segredo
secret	secret, ète	geheim	secreto, a	segreto, a	secreto, a
secretary	secrétaire	Sekretär(in f)m	secretario, a	segretario, a	secretário, a
secretion	sécrétion	Ausscheidung(f)	secreción	secrezione	secreção
sect	secte	Sekte(f)	secta	setta	seita
section	section	Schnitt(m)	sección	sezione	secção
sector	secteur	Bereich(m)	sector	settore	sector
security; safety	sécurité	Sicherheit(f)	seguridad	sicurezza	segurança
sedative	sédatif, ive	schmerzlindernd	sedativo, a	sedativo, a	sedativo, a
sedative	calmant	Beruhigungsmittel(n)	calmante	calmante	calmante
seduction	séduction	Verführung(f)	seducción	seduzione	sedução
see	voir	sehen	ver	vedere	ver
see again	revoir	wieder = sehen	volver a ver	rivedere	voltar a ver
see you soon, bye	à bientôt	bis bald	hasta pronto	a presto	até breve; até já
seed	germe	Keim(m)	germen, grano	germoglio	germe
seed	graine	Samenkorn(n)	semilla	seme	semente
seed	semence	Samen(m)	simiente	seme, semente	semente
seek	chercher	holen, suchen	buscar, investigar	cercare	procurar, buscar
seem	sembler	scheinen	parecer	sembrare	parecer
seem, appear, look	paraître	scheinen, erscheinen	parecer	parere, sembrare	parecer
segment	segment	Abschnitt(m)	segmento	segmento	segmento
segregation	ségrégation	Trennung(f)	segregación	segregazione	segregação
seismic	sismique	seismisch	sísmico, a	sismico, a	sísmico, a
seize	saisir	ergreifen	coger, agarrar	afferrare	agarrar
select	sélectionner	aus = lesen	seleccionar	selezionare	seleccionar
selection	sélection	Auslese(f); Auswahl(f)	selección	selezione	selecção
self(him, her, it)	même(lui, elle)	selbst(er, sie, es)	mismo, a(él, ella)	stesso, a(lui, lei)	próprio, a(ele, a)
selfish	égoïste	egoistisch	egoísta	egoista	egoísta
sell	vendre	verkaufen	vender	vendere	vender
sell off	solder	aus = verkaufen	saldar	saldare, liquidare	saldar
sellotape	scotch	Tesafilm(m)	papel celo	scotch	fita adesiva
semi, half	semi	halb	semi	semi	semi
senate	sénat	Senat(m), Bundesrat(m)	senado	senato	senado
senator	sénateur	Senator(m)	senador	senatore	senador
send	envoyer	senden	mandar, enviar	mandare, inviare	mandar, enviar
send	envoyer	schicken, senden(ab =)	enviar	inviare	enviar
send back, return	renvoyer	zurück = schicken	devolver	rinviare	devolver
sender	expéditeur	Absender(in f)m	remitente	mittente	expedidor
sending	envoi	Sendung(f), Versand(m)	envío	invio	envio
sending	émission	Sendung(f)	envio	emissione	envio
sensation; feeling	sensation	Empfindung(f)	sensación	sensazione	sensação
sensible	sensé, e	vernünftig	sensato, a	sensato, a	sensato, a
sensitive	sensible	empfindlich	sensible	sensibile	sensível
sensitive(make sb)	sensibiliser	sensibilisierend	sensibilizar	sensibilizzare	sensibilizar
sensitivity	sensibilité	Sensibilität(f)	sensibilidad	sensibilità	sensibilidade
sensual	sensuel, le	sinnlich	sensual	sensuale	sensual
sensuality	sensualité	Sinnlichkeit(f)	sensualidad	sensualità	sensualidade
sentence	phrase	Satz(m)	frase	frase	frase
sentence	condamnation	Verurteilung(f)	condenación	condanna	condenação
sentence	peine	Bestrafung(f)	pena, castigo	punizione, castigo	pena
sentence	jugement	Urteil(n)	sentencia	sentenza	sentença

English	French	German	Spanish	Italian	Portuguese
sentimental	sentimental, e	sentimental	sentimental	sentimentale	sentimental
sentry	sentinelle	Wache(f)	centinela	sentinella	sentinela
separate, part	séparer	trennen	separar	separare, dividere	separar
separate, part	écarter	entfernen	apartar	allontanare; scartare	afastar
separation	séparation	Trennung(f)	separación	separazione	separação
September	Septembre	September(m)	Septiembre	Settembre	Setembro
sequence	séquence	Folge(f), Sequenz(f)	secuencia	sequenza	sequência
serene	serein, e	heiter	sereno, a	sereno, a	sereno, a
serenity	sérénité	Heiterkeit(f)	serenidad	serenità	serenidade
sergeant	sergent	Unteroffizier(m)	sargento	sergente	sargento
series	série	Serie(f)	serie	serie	série
serious	sérieux, se	ernst, ernsthaft	serio, a	serio, a	sério, a
serum	sérum	Serum(n)	suero	siero	soro
servant	domestique	Hausangestellte(m, f)	criado, a	domestico, a	empregado, a
serve	servir	dienen, bedienen	servir	servire	servir
service	service	Dienstleistung(f)	servicio	servizio	serviço
service	service	Bedienung(f)	servicio	servizio	serviço
service, overhaul	révision	Überholung(f)	revisión	revisione	revisão
service station	station-service	Tankstelle(f)	estación(servicio)	stazione di servizio	estação de serviço
serviette, napkin	serviette	Serviette(f)	servilleta	tovagliolo	guardanapo
session	session	Sitzung(f)	sesión	sessione	sessão
session; meeting	séance	Sitzung(f)	sesión	seduta	sessão
set	ensemble	Satz(m)	conjunto	insieme	conjunto
set, scenery	décors	Dekor(m), Bühnenbild n	decorado	scenografia	cenários
set	mettre, placer	setzen, stellen	poner, colocar	porre, mettere	pôr, colocar
set in	encastrer	ein = setzen	empotrar	incastrare	embutir
setting up(of)	implantation	Niederlassung	implantación	impianto	implantação
settle	régler	regeln; erledigen	resolver	risolvere	resolver
settle	régler	bezahlen	liquidar, pagar	regolare, saldare	pagar
settle	installer(s')	nieder = lassen, sich	instalarse	stabilirsi	instalar-se
settle; set up	établir(s')	an = siedeln, sich	establecerse	stabilirsi	estabelecer-se
settlement	règlement	Begleichung(f)	liquidación	saldo	pagamento
seven	sept	sieben	siete	sette	sete
seventeen	dix-sept	siebzehn	diecisiete	diciassette	dezassete
seventy	soixante-dix	siebzig	setenta	settanta	setenta
several	plusieurs	mehrere	varios, as	parecchi	vários, as
severe, strict	sévère	streng	severo, a	severo, a	severo, a
sew	coudre	nähen	coser	cucire	coser
sewer, drain	égout	Gulli, Abwasserkanäle	cloaca	fogna	esgoto
sewing	couture	Naht(f)	costura	cucito	costura
sex	sexe	Geschlecht(n)	sexo	sesso	sexo
sexual	sexuel, le	geschlechtlich	sexual	sessuale	sexual
sexuality	sexualité	Sexualität(f)	sexualidad	sessualità	sexualidade
shade, nuance	nuance, ton	Farbenton(m)	matiz	sfumatura	matiz, tom
shadow	ombre	Schatten(m)	sombra	ombra	sombra
shake	agiter	schütteln	agitar	agitare	agitar
shake	secouer	schütteln	sacudir	scuotere	sacudir
shake hands	serrer la main	Hand schütteln	estrechar la mano	stringere la mano	apertar a mão
shame	honte	Scham(f), Schande(f)	vergüenza	vergogna	vergonha
shameful	honteux, se	beschämend	vergonzoso, a	vergognoso, a	vergonhoso, a
shampoo	shampooing	Shampoo(n)	champú	shampoo	champô
shanty-town	bidonville	Elendsviertel(n)	chabolas	bidonville	bairro de lata
shape, form	forme	Form(f), Aussehen(n)	forma	forma	forma
share; part	part, partie	Anteil(m); Teil(m, n)	parte	parte	parte
share	action	Aktie(f)	acción	azione	acção
share, divide	partager	teilen	repartir	dividere	repartir
shareholder	actionnaire	Aktionär(m)	accionista	azionista	accionista
share out	répartir	auf = teilen	repartir	ripartire	repartir
shark	requin	Hai(m)	tiburón	squalo	tubarão
sharp	aiguisé, e	scharf	afilado, a	affilato, a	afiado, a
sharp, shrill	aigu, ë	hoch, schrill	agudo, a	acuto, a	agudo, a
sharpen	aiguiser	schärfen	afilar	affilare	afiar
shave	raser(se)	rasieren, sich	afeitar(se)	radersi	barbear-se
shawl	châle	Schal(m)	chal	scialle	xale
she	elle	sie	ella	essa; lei; ella	ela
sheath	gaine	Hülle(f)	funda, estuche	guaina, astuccio	invólucro
shed	hangar	Schuppen(m)	cobertizo	hangar, capannone	alpendre
sheep; mutton	mouton	Schaf(n)	carnero; oveja	pecora; montone	carneiro; ovelha

E

English	French	German	Spanish	Italian	Portuguese
sheet	drap	Laken(n)	sábana	lenzuolo	lençol
sheet	feuille	Blatt(n)	hoja	foglio	folha
sheet, expanse	nappe(eau)	Wasserfläche(f)	capa(de agua)	falda	lençol(de água)
sheet-metal	tôle	Blech(n)	chapa	lamiera	chapa
shelf(-ves)	étagère, rayon	Regal(n)	estantería	scaffale	prateleira
shell	coquille	Schale(f), Muschel(f)	concha	conchiglia	concha
shell	coquille, coque	Schale(f)	cáscara	guscio	casca
shell	obus	Geschoß(n), Granate(f)	obús	proiettile	obus
shell-fish; shell	coquillage	Muschel(f)	marisco	conchiglia	concha
shell-fish	crustacé	Schalentier(n)	crustáceo	crostaceo	crustáceo
shelter	abri, refuge	Obdach(n), Schutz(m)	abrigo, refugio	riparo, rifugio	abrigo, refúgio
shepherd, -ess	berger, ère	Schäfer(in f)m	pastor, a	pastore, pastorella	pastor, a
shift, move	déplacer	versetzen, -schieben	trasladar	spostare	deslocar
shift	changer	wechseln	cambiar	cambiare	mudar; remover
shine	briller	glänzen	brillar	brillare	brilhar
shining, bright	luisant, e	leuchtend	reluciente	brillante	brilhante
ship	navire	Schiff(n)	navío	nave	navio
ship-owner	armateur	Reeder(m)	armador	armatore	armador
shirt	chemise	Hemd(n)	camisa	camicia	camisa
shiver	frisson	Schauer(m)	escalofrío	brivido	arrepio
shiver	grelotter	zittern	tiritar	tremare(di freddo)	tiritar
shock	choc	Schock(m)	choque	choc, colpo	choque
shock, impact	choc	Stoß(m), Aufprall(m)	choque	urto, scontro	choque
shock absorber	amortisseur	Stoßdämpfer(m)	amortiguador	ammortizzatore	amortecedor
shocking	choquant, e	anstößig	chocante	urtante	chocante
shoe	chaussure	Schuh(m)	calzado	scarpa, e	sapato
shoe	soulier	Schuh(m)	zapato	scarpa	sapato
shoot, fire	tirer	schießen, feuern	disparar	tirare, sparare	atirar, disparar
shooting, firing	tir	Schießen(n)	tiro	tiro	tiro
shooting	tournage	Filmaufnahme(f)	rodaje	riprese	filmagem
shop	magasin	Geschäft(n), Laden(m)	tienda	negozio; bottega	loja
shop, business	commerce	Geschäft(n)	tienda, negocio	negozio	loja
shop-keeper	commerçant, e	Kaufmann m, Kauffrau f	tendero, a	negoziante	comerciante
shop-keeper	marchand, e	Kaufmann m, Kauffrau f	vendedor, a	negoziante	comerciante
shopping	courses	Einkäufe(pl)	compras	spesa	compras
shop-window	vitrine	Schaufenster(n)	escaparate	vetrina	montra, vitrina
shore	rivage	Küstenstrich(m)	orilla	riva	beira-mar
short	court, e	kurz	corto, a	corto, a	curto, a
short cut	raccourci	Abkürzung(f)	atajo	scorciatoia	atalho
shortage	pénurie	Mangel(m)	penuria, escasez	penuria	penúria
shorts	short	kurze Hose(f)	pantalón corto	shorts, calzoncini	calções; calção
short-sighted	myope	kurzsichtig	miope	miope	míope
shot-gun, rifle	fusil	Gewehr(n)	fusil	fucile	espingarda
shoulder	épaule	Schulter(f)	hombro	spalla	ombro
shout	cri	Schrei(m)	grito	grido	grito
shout, scream	crier	schreien	gritar	gridare	gritar
show	montrer	zeigen	enseñar, mostrar	mostrare	mostrar
show	spectacle	Aufführung(f)	espectáculo	spettacolo	espectáculo
show, exhibition	salon	Messe(f)	salón	salone	salão
shower	douche	Dusche(f)	ducha	doccia	duche, chuveiro
shrimp, prawn	crevette	Garnele(f)	gamba, camarón	gamberetto(di mare)	camarão
shrink	rétrécir	schrumpfen	encoger	restringere	encolher
shut	fermer	zu = machen	cerrar	chiudere	fechar
shut in	enfermer	ein = schließen	encerrar	rinchiudere	encerrar, fechar
shy, timid	timide	schüchtern	tímido, a	timido, a	tímido, a
shyness, timidity	timidité	Schüchternheit(f)	timidez	timidezza	timidez
sick person	malade	Kranke(f, m)	enfermo, a	malato, a	doente
side	côté	Seite(f)	lado	lato	lado
side	face	Seite(f)	cara	faccia	face; lado
side; edge	bord	Rand(m)	borde	bordo, riva, orlo	borda
siege	siège	Belagerung(f)	sitio	assedio	cerco
sigh	soupirer	seufzen	suspirar	sospirare	suspirar
sight	vue	Sehkraft(f)	vista	vista	vista
sign	enseigne	Schild(n)(Reklame-)	letrero	insegna	letreiro
sign	signe	Zeichen(n)	signo	segno	sinal, signo
sign	signalisation	Beschilderung(f)	señalización	segnalazione	sinalização
sign, notice	panneau	Schild(n)	señal, letrero	cartello	sinal
sign, notice	pancarte	Plakat(n), Schild(n)	pancarta	cartello	cartaz

English	French	German	Spanish	Italian	Portuguese
sign	signer	unterschreiben	firmar	firmare	assinar
signal	signal	Signal(n)	señal	segnale	sinal
signature	signature	Unterschrift(f)	firma	firma	assinatura
significant	significatif, ive	bezeichnend	significativo, a	significativo, a	significativo, a
silence	silence	Stille(f)	silencio	silenzio	silêncio
silent, quiet	silencieux, se	still, leise, ruhig	silencioso, a	silenzioso, a	silencioso, a
silent(to be)	taire(se)	schweigen	callarse	tacere	calar-se
silk	soie	Seide(f)	seda	seta	seda
silliness	sottise	Dummheit(f)	tontería	sciocchezza	estupidez
silly, foolish	bête; sot, te	dumm	tonto, a	sciocco, a	tolo, a; burro, a
silver	argent	Silber(n)	plata	argento	prata
similar	semblable	ähnlich	semejante	simile, uguale	semelhante
similar	similaire	ähnlich, gleichartig	similar	similare	similar
simple	simple	einfach	simple	semplice	simples
simplicity	simplicité	Einfachheit(f)	sencillez	semplicità	simplicidade
simplify	simplifier	vereinfachen	simplificar	semplificare	simplificar
simply	simplement	einfach	simplemente	semplicemente	simplesmente
simulation	simulation	Vortäuschung(f)	simulación	simulazione	simulação
simultaneous	simultané, e	gleichzeitig	simultáneo, a	simultaneo, a	simultâneo, a
sin	péché	Sünde(f)	pecado	peccato	pecado
since; for	depuis	seit	desde	da	desde
since	puisque	da, weil	ya que; pues	poichè	já que
sincere, candid	sincère	aufrichtig	sincero, a	sincero, a	sincero, a
sing	chanter	singen	cantar	cantare	cantar
singer	chanteur, se	Sänger(in f)m	cantante	cantante	cantor, a
single, unmarried	célibataire	ledig	soltero, a	scapolo; nubile	solteiro, a
single	un, e(à); unique	einzeln; einzig	solo, a; único, a	singolo, a	único, a
single room	chambre à 1 lit	Einzelzimmer(n)	habitación(1 cama)	camera singola	quarto individual
single ticket	billet simple	einfache Fahrkarte(f)	billete de ida	andata	bilhete de ida
singular	singulier	Einzahl(f)	singular	singolare	singular
sinister	sinistre	unheilvoll	siniestro, a	sinistro, a	sinistro, a
sink	évier	Spülbecken(n)	fregadero	acquaio, lavandino	pia, banca
sink	couler, enfoncer	sinken, versenken	hundir	affondare	afundar
Sir	monsieur	Herr(m)	señor	signore	senhor
siren	sirène	Sirene(f)	sirena	sirena	sirene
sister	soeur	Schwester(f)	hermana	sorella	irmã
sister-in-law	belle-soeur	Schwägerin(f)	cuñada	cognata	cunhada
sit(down)	asseoir(s')	setzen, sich	sentarse	sedersi	sentar-se
site	site	Ort(m), Lage(f)	paraje, vista	sito	sítio
situate, locate	situer	stellen, setzen	situar, localizar	situare, localizzare	situar, localizar
situation	situation	Lage(f)	situación	situazione	situação
six	six	sechs	seis	sei	seis
sixteen	seize	sechzehn	dieciséis	sedici	dezasseis
sixty	soixante	sechzig	sesenta	sessanta	sessenta
size	taille	Größe(f)	tamaño	misura	tamanho
size	taille	Größe(f)	talla, número	taglia, misura	tamanho
size	pointure	Größe(f)	número	numero	tamanho; número
skate	patiner	Schlittschuh laufen	patinar	pattinare	patinar
skating	patinage	Eiskunstlauf(m)	patinaje	pattinaggio	patinagem
skating rink	patinoire	Eisbahn(f)	pista de patinar	pista da pattinaggio	pista de patinagem
skeleton	squelette	Skelett(n)	esqueleto	scheletro	esqueleto
sketch(-es)	croquis	Skizze(f)	croquis	schizzo	esboço
ski	ski	Ski(m)	esquí	sci	esqui
ski	skier	skifahren	esquiar	sciare	esquiar
skid	déraper	schleudern	patinar	slittare	derrapar
skilled, skilful	adroit, e	geschickt	diestro, a	abile	destro, a; hábil
skin	peau	Haut(f)	piel	pelle	pele
skirt	jupe	Rock(m)	falda	gonna	saia
skittle	quille	Kegel(f)	bolos(juego)	birillo	paulitos
skull	crâne	Schädel(m)	cráneo	cranio	crâneo
sky	ciel	Himmel(m)	cielo	cielo	céu
skyscraper	gratte-ciel	Wolkenkratzer(m)	rascacielos	grattacielo	arranha-céus
slack	desserré, e	schlaff, lose	flojo, a	allentato, a	frouxo, a
slack, loose	détendu, e	schlaff, lose	aflojado, a	allentato, a	frouxo, a; lasso, a
slander	calomnie	Verleumdung(f)	calumnia	calunnia	calúnia
slander	diffamation	Verleumdung(f)	difamación	diffamazione	difamação
slant, incline	inclinaison	Neigung(f), Gefälle(n)	inclinación	inclinazione	inclinação
slap	claque	Ohrfeige(f)	bofetada	schiaffo	bofetada

E

225

English	French	German	Spanish	Italian	Portuguese
slap	gifle	Ohrfeige(f)	bofetada	schiaffo	bofetada
slate	ardoise	Schiefer(m)	pizarra	ardesia	ardósia, lousa
slaughter	massacre	Blutbad(n)	masacre	massacro	massacre
slave	esclave	Sklave(m), Sklavin(f)	esclavo, a	schiavo, a	escravo, a
slavery	esclavage	Sklaverei(f)	esclavitud	schiavitú	escravatura
sleep	sommeil	Schlaf(m)	sueño	sonno	sono
sleep	dormir	schlafen	dormir	dormire	dormir
sleeping bag	sac de couchage	Schlafsack(m)	saco de dormir	sacco a pelo	saco-cama
sleeping tablet	somnifère	Schlaftablette(f)	somnífero	sonnifero	soporífero
sleep-walker	somnambule	Schlafwandler(in f)m	sonámbulo, a	sonnambulo, a	sonâmbulo, a
sleeve	manche	Ärmel(m)	manga(la)	manica	manga
sleigh, sledge	traîneau	Schlitten(m)	trineo	slitta	trenó
slender	svelte, mince	schlank	esbelto, a; delgado	snello, a; sottile	esbelto, a; delgado
slice	tranche	Scheibe(f)	rebanada	fetta	fatia
slice	rondelle	Scheibe(f)	rodaja	fettina, fetta	rodela
slice of bread	tartine de pain	Brotscheibe(f)	rebanada de pan	fetta di pane	fatia de pão
slide	glissière	Gleitschiene(f)	corredera, guía	guida, scivolo	corrediça
slide, chute	toboggan	Rutschbahn(f)	tobogán	scivolo	escorrega
slide	diapo(sitives)	Diapositiv(n), Dia(n)	diapositiva	diapositiva	diapositivos
slim; slender	mince	schlank	delgado, a	snello, a	magro, a; delgado, a
slim; slender	svelte	schlank	esbelto, a	slanciato, a; snello, a	esbelto, a
slip	combinaison	Unterrock(m)	combinación	sottoveste	combinação
slip, slide	glisser	rutschen	resbalar	scivolare	escorregar
slipper	pantoufle	Pantoffel(m)	zapatilla	pantofola	pantufa, chinelo
slit	fente	Schlitz(m)	raja	fessura; spacco	fenda
slit	fendre	auf = schlitzen	rajar, hender	fendere	rachar, fender
slope	pente, côte	Hang(m), Abhang(m)	declive	pendio, discesa	declive
slope	piste	Piste(f)	pista	pista	pista
slow	lent, e	langsam	lento, a	lento, a	lento, a
slow down	ralentir	verlangsamen	aminorar	rallentare	abrandar
slowly	lentement	langsam	lentamente	lentamente	lentamente
sludge, mud	vase	Schlamm(m)	limo, fango	melma	lodo
slum	taudis	Bruchbude(f)	tugurio	topaia	antro, tugúrio
smack	tape, fessée	Schlag(m)	cachete	schiaffo	palmada
small, little	petit, e	klein	pequeño, a	piccolo, a	pequeno, a
smallpox	variole	Pocken(f, pl)	viruela	vaiolo	varíola
smart, chic	chic, élégant, e	schick	elegante	elegante	elegante
smart, clever	malin, igne	gerissen, schlau	pillo, a; astuto, a	furbo, a	esperto, a; astuto, a
smell(sense of)	odorat	Geruchssinn(m)	olfato	odorato	olfacto
smell	sentir	riechen	oler	odorare, annusare	cheirar
smile	sourire	lächeln	sonreír	sorridere	sorrir
smile	sourire	Lächeln(n)	sonrisa	sorriso	sorriso
smoke	fumée	Rauch(m)	humo	fumo	fumo
smoke, fumes	fumée	Rauch(m)	humo	smog, fumo	fumo
smoke	fumer	rauchen	fumar	fumare	fumar
smoked	fumé, e	geräuchert	ahumado, a	affumicato, a	fumado, a
smokers	fumeurs	Raucher(m)	fumadores	fumatore, trice	fumadores
smooch, slow dance	slow	Blues(m), Slow(m)	lento	lento, slow	slow
smooth	lisse	glatt	liso, a	liscio, a	liso, a
smuggling	contrebande	Schmuggel(m)	contrabando	contrabbando	contrabando
snail	escargot	Schnecke(f)	caracol	lumaca, chiocciola	caracol
snake	serpent	Schlange(f)	serpiente	serpente	serpente
sneeze	éternuer	niesen	estornudar	starnutire	espirrar
sniff	renifler	schnüffeln	resoplar	tirar su col naso	fungar
sniff; scent; sense	flairer	wittern, schnüffeln	olfatear, husmear	annusare	farejar, cheirar
snigger	ricaner	grinsen, kichern	burlarse	sogghignare	troçar
snobbery	snobisme	Snobismus(m)	esnobismo	snobismo	snobismo
snore	ronfler	schnarchen	roncar	russare	ressonar, roncar
snow	neige	Schnee(m)	nieve	neve	neve
so(-much, -many)	si, tellement	so(sehr), derartig	tanto, a; tan	talmente	tanto, a
so much, so many	tant	so viel, e	tanto, tan	tanto	tanto
so	si	so	tan	così	tão
so, thus	ainsi	so	así	così	assim
so that	afin que	damit	a fin de que	affinché	a fim de que
soak	tremper	ein = weichen	mojar	inzuppare	molhar
soak	imbiber	durchtränken	empapar	imbevere	embeber
soap	savon	Seife(f)	jabón	sapone	sabão
sob	sanglot	Schluchzer(m)	sollozo	singhiozzo	soluço

English	French	German	Spanish	Italian	Portuguese
sociable	sociable	gesellig	sociable	socievole	sociável
social	social, e	sozial	social	sociale	social
socialism	socialisme	Sozialismus(m)	socialismo	socialismo	socialismo
society	société	Gesellschaft(f)	sociedad	società	sociedade
sociology	sociologie	Soziologie(f)	sociología	sociologia	sociologia
sock	chaussette(s)	Socke(f), Strumpf(m)	calcetín(es)	calza, e; calzini	peúga
sock(ankle-)	socquette	Socke(f)	calcetín	calzino	meias
sofa	canapé	Sofa(n)	sofá, canapé	divano, canapè	canapé, sofá
soft	doux, ce	sanft	suave	morbido, a	macio, a
soft	mou, molle	weich	blando, a	molle; tenero, a	mole
soft; tender	tendre	weich	blando, a	morbido, a; tenero, a	tenro, a
software	logiciel	Software(f)	logicial	software	software
soil	terre	Erde(f)	tierra	terra	terra
solar	solaire	Sonnen-	solar	solare	solar
soldier	soldat	Soldat(m)	soldado	soldato	soldado
sole	semelle	Sohle(f)	suela	suola	sola
solemn	solennel, le	feierlich	solemne	solenne	solene
sol-fa, theory	solfège	Tonleiter(f)	solfeo	solfeggio	solfejo
solicitor, lawyer	notaire	Notar(m)	notario	notaio	notário
solid, strong	solide	solide, fest	sólido, a	solido, a	sólido, a
solidarity	solidarité	Solidarität(f)	solidaridad	solidarietà	solidaridade
solitary, lonely	solitaire	einsam	solitario, a	solitario, a	solitário, a
soluble	soluble	löslich	soluble	solubile	solúvel
solution	solution	Lösung(f)	solución	soluzione	solução
solve	solutionner	lösen	solucionar	risolvere	solucionar
solve, resolve	résoudre	lösen	resolver	risolvere	resolver
solvent, remover	dissolvant	Lösungsmittel(n)	disolvente	solvente	acetona
some; a little	peu	etwas; wenig	poco	poco, pó	pouco
some, any	quelque	einige	alguno, a	qualche	algum, a
someone, somebody	quelqu'un, e	jemand	alguien	qualcuno, a	alguém
somersault	culbuter	überrennen	volcar	ribaltare	cambalhotas(dar)
something	quelque chose	etwas	algo	qualche cosa	qualquer coisa
sometimes	quelquefois	manchmal	a veces	qualche volta	às vezes
sometimes	parfois	manchmal	a veces	talvolta	às vezes
somewhere	quelque part	irgendwo	alguna parte(en)	qualche parte(da)	algures
somewhere else	ailleurs	woanders	otra parte(en)	altrove	noutro sítio
son	fils	Sohn(m)	hijo	figlio	filho
son-in-law	gendre	Schwiegersohn(m)	yerno	genero	genro
sonata	sonate	Sonate(f)	sonata	sonata	sonata
song	chanson, chant	Lied(n)	canción; cante	canzone; canto	canção; canto
soon	bientôt	bald	pronto	presto	logo, brevemente
sophisticated	sophistiqué, e	hochkompliziert	sofisticado, a	sofisticato, a	sofisticado, a
sordid	sordide	schäbig	sórdido, a	squallido, a	sórdido, a
sore throat	mal de gorge	Halsschmerzen(m, pl)	dolor de garganta	mal di gola	dor de garganta
sore throat	angine	Angina(f)	angina	angina, tonsillite	angina
sorrow, grief	peine	Schmerz(m), Kummer(m)	pena	pena; dolore	pena; tristeza
sorry	désolé, e	betrübt	desolado, a	spiacente	desolado, a
sorry	navré, e	leid tun	desconsolado, a	spiacente	desolado, a
sorry(I am)	excuse(je m')	es tut mir leid	siento(lo)	scusi(mi)	desculpe!
sorry!, excuse me!	pardon!	Verzeihung!	perdón(!), disculpe	scusi!	perdão!, desculpe!
sorry(be), regret	regretter	bedauern	sentir(lo)	dispiacere(-ersi)	sentir, lamentar
sort, kind, type	sorte, espèce	Sorte(f), Art(f)	especie, género	specie, genere	espécie, género
sort(out)	trier	sortieren	escoger, separar	scegliere, smistare	escolher, triar
soul	âme	Seele(f)	alma	anima	alma
sound	son	Ton(m)	sonido	suono	som
sound-proof	insonore	schalldicht	insonoro, a	insonoro, a	insonoro, a
soup	soupe	Suppe(f)	sopa	minestra	sopa
sour	aigre	sauer	agrio, a	aspro, a; agro, a	azedo, a
source	source, origine	Ursprung(m)	fuente, origen	fonte, origine	fonte, origem
South	Sud	Süden(m)	Sur	Sud	Sul
souvenir	souvenir	Andenken(n)	recuerdo	ricordo, souvenir	recordação
sovereign, monarch	souverain, e	Herrscher(in f)m)	soberano, a; monarca	sovrano, a; monarca	soberano, a; monarca
sovereignty	souveraineté	Souveränität(f)	soberanía	sovranità	soberania
sow	semer	säen	sembrar	seminare	semear
space	espace	Raum(m)	espacio	spazio	espaço
space, gap	espace	Zwischenraum(m)	espacio	spazio	espaço
space	spatial, e	Raum-	espacial	spaziale	espacial
spacious	spacieux, se	weiträumig	espacioso, a	spazioso, a	espaçoso, a

English	French	German	Spanish	Italian	Portuguese
spade; shovel	pelle	Schaufel(f); Spaten(m)	pala	pala	pá
spanking	fessée	Hinternvoll(m)	azotaina, paliza	sculacciata	surra, açoite
spanner, wrench	clé	Schraubenschlüssel(m)	llave	chiave	chave
spark	étincelle	Funken(m)	chispa	scintilla	faísca
sparking plug	bougie	Zündkerze(f)	bujía	candela	vela
sparkle	scintiller	flimmern	centellear	scintillare	cintilar
sparkling water	eau gazeuse	Sprudelwasser(n)	gaseosa	acqua gassata	água gaseificada
sparrow	moineau	Spatz(m)	gorrión	passero	pardal
sparrow-hawk	épervier	Habicht(m)	gavilán	sparviere	gavião
spasm	spasme	Krampf(m)	espasmo	spasma	espasmo
spatula	spatule	Spachtel(f)	espátula	spatola	espátula
speak, talk	parler	sprechen, reden	hablar	parlare	falar
speaker	baffle	Lautsprecher(m)	altavoz	altoparlante	alto-falante
speaker, orator	orateur, trice	Redner(in f)m	orador, a; locutor, a	oratore, trice	orador, a
spear, lance	lance	Lanze(f)	lanza	lancia	lança
special	spécial, e	speziell, eigen	especial	speciale	especial
specialist	spécialiste	Spezialist(in f)m	especialista	specialista	especialista
speciality	spécialité	Spezialität(f)	especialidad	specialità	especialidade
species	espèce	Art(f)	especie	specie	espécie
specific	spécifique	spezifisch	específico, a	specifico, a	específico, a
specify, state	spécifier	spezifieren	especificar	specificare	especificar
specify	préciser	genau fest = legen	precisar	precisare	precisar
specimen	spécimen	Muster(n); Exemplar(n)	espécimen	specimen	espécime
spectator	spectateur, trice	Zuschauer(in f)m	espectador, a	spettatore, trice	espectador, a
speculation	spéculation	Spekulation(f)	especulación	speculazione	especulação
speech, talk	discours	Rede(f)	discurso	discorso	discurso
speech(short)	allocution	Ansprache(kurze)(f)	alocución	allocuzione	alocução
speech	parler(le)	Sprechen(n); Sprache f	habla(el)	parlare(il)	fala(a)
speed	vitesse	Geschwindigkeit(f)	velocidad	velocità	velocidade
speed	régime	Drehzahl(f)	régimen	regime	velocidade
speed-boat	hors-bord	Außenbordmotor(m)	fuera borda	fuoribordo	fora de borda
spell	épeler	buchstabieren	deletrear	compitare, sillabare	soletrar
spelling	orthographe	Rechtschreibung(f)	ortografía	ortografia	ortografia
spend	dépenser	aus = geben	gastar	spendere	gastar
spend	débourser	aus = geben	desembolsar	sborsare	desembolsar
spend	passer	verbringen	pasar	trascorrere	passar
sperm	sperme	Sperma(n)	esperma	sperma	esperma
sphere	sphère	Sphäre(f)	esfera	sfera	esfera
spice	épice(s)	Gewürz(n)	especia	spezie	especiaria
spicy	épicé, e	gewürzt, würzig	picante	piccante	picante
spicy, hot	piquant, e	scharf	picante	piccante	picante
spider	araignée	Spinne(f)	araña	ragno	aranha
spill, knock over	renverser	verschütten	derramar, volcar	rovesciare	entornar
spine	colonne(vertéb-)	Wirbelsäule(f)	columna vertebral	colonna vertebrale	coluna vertebral
spiral	spirale	Spirale(f)	espiral	spirale	espiral
spirit	esprit	Geist(m)	espíritus	spirito	espírito
spirit(s)	alcool(s)	Alkohol(m)	alcohol	alcolico	álcool
spirits	eau-de-vie	Schnaps(m)	aguardiente	grappa, acquavite	aguardente
spiritual	spirituel, le	geistreich	espiritual	spirituale	espiritual
spit	broche	Spieß(m)	asador	spiedo	espeto
spit	cracher	spucken	escupir	sputare	cuspir
spite; vexation	dépit	Groll(m), Trotz(m)	despecho	dispetto	despeito
spleen	rate	Milz(f)	bazo	milza	baço
splendid	splendide	glänzend	espléndido, a	splendido, a	esplêndido, a
split; slot; slit	fente	Spalt(m)	grieta	fessura	fenda
split, slit	fendre	spalten	rajar, partir	spaccare	fender, rachar
splutter, stammer	bafouiller	stammeln	balbucear	farfugliare	balbuciar
spoils	butin	Beute(f)	botín	bottino	despojo
spoke	rayon	Speiche(f)	radio	raggio	raio
sponge	éponge	Schwamm(m)	esponja	spugna	esponja
spongy	spongieux, se	schwammig	esponjoso, a	spugnoso, a	esponjoso, a
sponsor	sponsor	Sponsor(m)	patrocinador	sponsor	patrocinador
sponsor	parrainer	sponsorisieren	patrocinar	sponsorizzare	apadrinhar
spontaneous	spontané, e	spontan	espontáneo, a	spontaneo, a	espontâneo, a
spoon	cuillère	Löffel(m)	cuchara	cucchiaio	colher
sport	sport	Sport(m)	deporte	sport	desporto
sportsman/-woman	sportif, ive	Sportler(in f)m	deportista	sportivo, a	desportista
sporty, athletic	sportif, ive	sportlich; Sport-	deportivo, a	sportivo, a	desportivo, a

English	French	German	Spanish	Italian	Portuguese
spot, pimple	bouton	Pickel(m)	grano	brufolo, foruncolo	borbulha
spot	point	Fleck(m); Ort; Stelle	lugar, punto	punto	ponto
sprain	entorse	Verrenkung(f)	esguince	storta	entorse
sprain	foulure	Verstauchung(f)	esguince	slogatura	entorse
spray, jet	jet	Strahl(m)	surtidor, chorro	getto, zampillo	jacto, repuxo
spray, atomizer	atomiseur	Zerstäuber(m)	atomizador	nebulizzatore	pulverizador
spray	vaporiser	sprühen	vaporizar	vaporizzare	vaporizar
spraying	pulvérisation	Zerstäubung(f)	pulverización	nebulizzazione	pulverização
spread	propager	verbreiten	propagar	propagare	propagar
spread; spill	répandre	verschütten	derramar	spargere	espalhar
spread(out)	étaler	aus = breiten	exponer	stendere, spalmare	expor
spring, leap	bond, saut	Sprung(m)	salto, brinco	salto, balzo	salto, pulo
spring	ressort	Feder(f)(Sprung-)	muelle	molla	mola
spring	printemps	Frühling(m)	primavera	primavera	primavera
spring	source	Quelle(f)	fuente	sorgente	fonte, nascente
spring, bound	élan	Anlauf(m), Schwung(m)	impulso	slancio	impulso
spring	jaillir, surgir	springen; sprudeln	brotar, surgir	schizzare	brotar
spy	espion, ne	Spion(m), Spionin(f)	espía	spia	espião, espia
spying, espionage	espionnage	Spionage(f)	espionaje	spionaggio	espionagem
squadron	escadron	Schwadron; Eskadron(f)	escuadrón	squadrone; squadra	esquadrão
squall	bourrasque	Windstoß(m)	borrasca	burrasca	borrasca
square	carré	Viereck(n)	cuadrado	quadrato	quadrado
square	place	Platz(m)	plaza	piazza	praça
square(set -)	équerre	Zeichendreieck(n)	escuadra	squadra	esquadro
squint	loucher	schielen	bizquear	strabico(essere)	estrábico(ser)
squirrel	écureuil	Eichhörnchen(n)	ardilla	scoiattolo	esquilo
squirt, spurt	gicler, jaillir	spritzen	salpicar	sprizzare, schizzare	salpicar
stability	stabilité	Stabilität(f)	estabilidad	stabilità	estabilidade
stable	écurie	Pferdestall(m)	cuadra	scuderia	cavalariça
stack	pile	Stapel(m), Stoß(m)	pila	mucchio	pilha, montão
stadium	stade	Stadium(n)	estadio	stadio	estádio
staff, personnel	personnel	Personal(n)	personal	personale	pessoal
staff	personnel	Personal(n)	plantilla, personal	personale	pessoal
stage	scène	Szene(f), Bühne(f)	escena	scena	cena
stage	étape	Strecke(f)	etapa	tappa	etapa
stagger	chanceler	taumeln	tambalearse	barcollare	vacilar
stagger	tituber	wanken	titubear	barcollare	titubear
stain	tache	Fleck(m)	mancha	macchia	mancha, nódoa
stain, dirty	tacher	beflecken, beschmutzen	manchar	macchiare	manchar, sujar
staircase, stairs	escalier	Treppe(f)	escalera	scala	escada
stake, post	pieu, poteau	Pfahl(m)	estaca	palo, piolo	estaca
stake	enjeu	Einsatz(m)(Spiel-)	apuesta	posta	aposta
stamp	timbre(-poste)	Briefmarke(f)	sello	francobollo	selo
stamp	tamponner	stempeln	sellar	timbrare	carimbar
stamp	affranchir	frankieren, freimachen	franquear	affrancare	franquear
stand up, get up	lever(se)	auf = stehen	levantarse	alzarsi	levantar-se
standard of living	niveau(de vie)	Standard(m)	nivel(de vida)	tenore(di vita)	nível(de vida)
standing(up)	debout	stehend, aufrecht	de pie, en pie	in piedi	de pé, em pé
star	étoile	Stern(m)	estrella	stella	estrela
star	astre	Stern(m), Gestirn(n)	astro	astro	astro
star	vedette	Star(m)	estrella; divo, a	vedette; divo, a	vedeta, estrela
start	commencer	an = fangen	principiar	cominciare	principiar, começar
start	démarrer	starten	arrancar	avviare, iniziare	arrancar
start; departure	départ	Anfang(m); Abfahrt(f)	marcha; partida	inizio; partenza	princípio; partida
starter	démarreur	Starter(m)	arranque	motorino(avviamento)	motor de arranque
starter	hors-d'oeuvre	Vorspeise(f)	entremeses	antipasto	acepipe, entrada
starving, hungry	affamé, e	hungrig	hambriento, a	affamato, a	esfomeado, a
state	état	Staat(m)	estado	stato	estado
state; note	constater	fest = stellen	constatar	constatare	constatar
state employee	fonctionnaire	Beamter(m), Beamtin(f)	funcionario, a	impiegato statale	funcionário, a
statement	déclaration	Erklärung(f)	declaración	dichiarazione	declaração
statement	déposition	Aussage(f)	deposición	deposizione	deposição
statement	relevé	Aufstellung(f)machen	extracto	estratto	levantamento
statement(bank)	relevé(compte)	Kontoauszug(m)	estado(cuentas)	estratto conto	extracto(conta)
static	statique	statisch	estático, a	statico, a	estático, a
station	station	Station(f)	estación	stazione	estação
station	gare	Bahnhof(m)	estación	stazione	estação, gare
stationer's	papeterie	Schreibwarenladen(m)	papelería	cartoleria	papelaria

English	French	German	Spanish	Italian	Portuguese
statistics	statistique(s)	Statistik(f)	estadística	statistica	estatística
statue	statue	Statue(f)	estatua	statua	estátua
status; statute	statut	Status(m); Statut(n)	estatuto	statuto	estatuto
stay	séjour	Aufenthalt(m)	estancia	soggiorno	estadia, estada
stay, remain	rester	bleiben	quedarse	restare	ficar
steak	bifteck	Beefsteak(n)	bistec	bistecca	bife
steal, rob	voler	stehlen	robar	rubare	roubar
steal	dérober	entwenden	robar	derubare	roubar, furtar
steam	vapeur	Dampf(m)	vapor	vapore	vapor
steel	acier	Stahl(m)	acero	acciaio	aço
steep	abrupt, e	steil	abrupto, a	ripido, a; scosceso, a	abrupto, a
steep	escarpé, e	steil	escarpado, a	scosceso, a	escarpado, a
steep	raide; escarpé, e	steil	empinado, a	ripido, a	empinado, a
steering-wheel	volant	Steuer(n)	volante	volante	volante
stem	tige	Stiel(m)	tallo	stelo	caule
stench, stink	puanteur	Gestank(m)	hedor, peste	puzza, fetore	fedor
step	pas	Schritt(m)	paso	passo	passo
step	marche	Stufe(f)	peldaño, escalón	scalino	degrau
steppe	steppe	Steppe(f)	estepa	steppa	estepe
stereo	stéréo	Stereo(f)	estéreo	stereo	estereofonia
sterile	stérile	steril	estéril	sterile	estéril
stewed fruit	compote	Kompott(n)	compota	frutta cotta	compota
stick	bâton	Stock(m)	palo	bastone	pau, bastão
stick	canne	Stock(m)	bastón	bastone	bengala
stick	baguette	Stöckchen(n)	varilla	bacchetta	vara
stick, glue	coller	kleben	pegar	incollare	colar, pegar
sticky	gluant, e	klebrig	viscoso, a	viscido, a	viscoso, a
stiff	raide	starr, steif	tieso, a; rígido, a	rigido, a	teso, a; hirto, a
still	encore	noch, wieder	todavía, aún	ancora	ainda
still; yet	encore	noch, noch mehr	aún	ancora	ainda
still	toujours	immer noch	todavía	sempre	ainda
still	calme, tranquille	still	quieto, a; tranquilo	calmo, a	quieto, a
stimulate	stimuler	reizen, an = regen	estimular	stimolare	estimular
sting, bite	piqûre	Stich(m)	picadura	puntura	picada
stink	puer	stinken	apestar	puzzare	cheirar mal
stir	remuer	rühren	remover	mescolare	mexer
stitch	point	Stich(m); Masche(f)	puntada	punto	ponto
stock, broth	bouillon	Brühe(f)	caldo	brodo	caldo
stock, supply	provision	Vorrat(m)	provisión	provvista	provisão
stock, store	stocker	lagern	almacenar	immagazzinare	armazenar
stock-list(taking)	inventaire	Inventur(f)	inventario	inventario	inventário
Stock Exchange	Bourse(la)	Börse(f)	Bolsa	Borsa	Bolsa
stocking	bas	Strumpf(m)(Nylon-)	media	calza	meias
stomach	estomac	Magen(m)	estómago	stomaco	estômago
stomach, abdomen	ventre	Bauch(m)	barriga, vientre	pancia, ventre	barriga
stone	pierre	Stein(m)	piedra	pietra	pedra
stone, pebble	caillou	Stein(m)	piedra	sasso	calhau
stone	noyau	Kern(m)	hueso	nocciolo	caroço
stool	tabouret	Hocker(m)	taburete	sgabello	escabelo, banco
stop	arrêt	Pause(f), Stillstand	parada	fermata	paragem
stop, cessation	arrêt, cessation	Stillstand(m)	cese	cessazione, tregua	cessação
stop	arrêter	halten(an-, auf-)	parar	fermare	parar
stop	arrêter(s')	stehen = bleiben	pararse	fermarsi	parar
stop, cease	cesser	auf = hören	cesar, parar	cessare, smettere	cessar, parar
stop(over)	escale	Zwischenlandung(f)	escala	scalo	escala
store	magasin	Warenlager(n)	almacén	magazzino; negozio	armazém
storm, thunderstorm	orage	Gewitter(n)	tormenta	temporale	tempestade
storm	tempête	Unwetter(n)	tempestad	tempesta	tempestade
story	histoire	Geschichte(f)	historia	storia	história
story	récit	Bericht(m)	narración	racconto	narração
stove	réchaud	Kocher(m)	hornillo	fornello	fogão
stove	poêle, cuisinière	Ofen(m)	estufa	stufa	fogão
straight	droit, e	gerade	recto, a	diritto, a	recto, a
straight away	aussitôt	sofort, sogleich	seguida(en)	subito, appena	imediatamente
straight line	droite	Gerade(f)	recta	retta	recta
straighten out/up	redresser	gerade = biegen	enderezar	raddrizzare	endireitar
strait	détroit	Meerenge(f)	estrecho	stretto	estreito
strange, odd	étrange	seltsam	extraño, a; raro, a	strano, a	estranho, a

230

English	French	German	Spanish	Italian	Portuguese
strange, odd	bizarre	seltsam	raro, a	strano, a	estranho, a
strangling	étranglement	Erwürgen(n)	estrangulación	strangolamento	estrangulamento
strap	sangle	Riemen(m), Gurt(m)	cincha, correa	cinghia	correia
strap	bracelet	Armband(n)	correa	cinturino	pulseira
strategy	stratégie	Strategie(f)	estrategia	strategia	estratégia
straw	paille	Stroh(n)	paja	paglia	palha
strawberry	fraise	Erdbeere(f)	fresa	fragola	morango
stream, brook	ruisseau	Bach(m)	riachuelo, arroyo	ruscello	regato, ribeiro
street	rue	Straße(f)	calle	via	rua
street-lamp	lampadaire	Straßenlaterne(f)	lámpara de pie	lampione	candeeiro
strength	force	Stärke(f), Kraft(f)	fuerza	forza	força
strengthen	consolider	verstärken	consolidar	consolidare	consolidar
stress(ing)	accentuation	Betonung(f)	acentuación	accentazione	acentuação
stretch	étirer	aus = dehnen	estirar	stirare	esticar
stretch	étendre(s')	erstrecken, sich	extenderse	estendersi	estender-se
stretcher	civière	Bahre(f)	camilla	barella	maca
strict	strict, e	streng	estricto, a	stretto, a	estrito, a
strike	grève	Streik(m)	huelga	sciopero	greve
string, cord	ficelle	Schnur(f)	cordel	spago	cordel, guita
strip, bare	dénuder	entblößen	desnudar	denudare	desnudar
stripe	galon	Galone(f)	galón	gallone, grado	galão
striped	rayures(à)	gestreift	rayas(a)	righe(a)	riscas(às)
stroke	caresser	streicheln	acariciar	carezzare	afagar
strong	fort, e	stark	fuerte	forte	forte
structure	structure	Struktur(f)	estructura	struttura	estrutura
structure	ossature	Struktur(f)	armazón	ossatura	ossatura
struggle, fight	lutte	Kampf(m)	lucha	lotta	luta
stubborn	têtu, e	dickköpfig	tozudo, a	testardo, a	cabeçudo, a
student	étudiant, e	Student(in f)m	estudiante	studente, -essa	estudante
studio	studio	Studio(n)	estudio	studio	estúdio
studious	studieux, se	fleißig	estudioso, a	studioso, a	estudioso, a
study; survey	étude	Studie(f)	estudio	studio	estudo
study	étudier	studieren	estudiar	studiare	estudar
stumble, trip	trébucher	stolpern	tropezar	inciampare	tropeçar
stun, daze	étourdir	betäuben	aturdir; atontar	stordire	aturdir; atordoar
stupefied	ahuri, e	verdutzt	espantado, a	attonito, a	pasmado, a
stupid, silly	stupide	dumm	estúpido, a	stupido, a	estúpido, a
stupid thing(do a)	bêtise	Dummheit(f)	estupidez	sciocchezza	asneira
stupidity	idiotie	Dummheit(f)	idiotez	idiozia	idiotice, asneira
stupor	stupeur	Erstaunen(n)	estupor	stupore	estupefacção
sturdy	robuste, solide	kräftig, fest	vigoroso, a; fuerte	robusto, a; forte	robusto, a; forte
stutter, stammer	bégayer	stottern	tartamudear	balbettare	gaguejar
style	style	Stil(m)	estilo	stile	estilo
subconscious	subconscient	Unterbewußtsein(n)	subconsciente	subcosciente	subconsciente
subject	sujet	Subjekt(n)	sujeto	soggetto	sujeito
subject, theme	sujet, thème	Thema(n)	tema	tema	assunto, tema
subject	matière	Fach(n)	asignatura	materia	matéria
subject matter	matière	Thema(n)	materia, tema	materia, tema	assunto
subject(to)	assujettir	unterwerfen	someter, sujetar	assoggettare	sujeitar
sublime	sublime	erhaben	sublime	sublime	sublime
submarine	sous-marin	Unterseeboot(n)	submarino	sottomarino	submarino
submission	soumission	Unterwerfung(f)	sumisión	sottomissione	submissão
submit	soumettre	unterwerfen	someter	sottomettere	submeter
subordinate	subordonné, e	Untergebene(f m)	subordinado, a	subalterno, a	subordinado, a
subscriber	abonné, e	Abonnent(m)	suscriptor, a	abbonato, a	assinante
subscription	souscription	Subskription(f)	suscripción	sottoscrizione	subscrição
subscription	abonnement	Abonnement(n)	subscripción	abbonamento	assinatura
subscription, dues	cotisation	Beitrag m(Mitglieds-)	cuota	quota	quota
subsidiary	filiale	Filiale(f)	filial, sucursal	filiale	filial, sucursal
subsidy	subvention	Subvention(f)	subvención	sussidio	subvenção
subsist, remain	subsister	fort = bestehen	subsistir	sussistere	subsistir
subsoil	sous-sol	Unterboden(m)	subsuelo	sottosuolo	sub-solo
substance	substance	Substanz(f)	sustancia	sostanza	substância
substantive, noun	substantif	Hauptwort(n)	sustantivo	sostantivo	substantivo
substitute	suppléant, e	Stellvertreter(in f)m	suplente, a	supplente	suplente
substitute	remplacant, e	Stellvertreter(in f)m	sustituto, a	sostituto, a	substituto, a
substitute	substituer	vertauschen	sustituir	sostituire	substituir
subtitled	sous-titré, e	Untertiteln(mit)	subtitulado, a	didascalie(con)	legendado, a

E

English	French	German	Spanish	Italian	Portuguese
subtle	subtil, e	scharfsinnig, listig	sutil	sottile	subtil
subtract	soustraire	ab = ziehen	sustraer, restar	sottrarre	subtrair, deduzir
subtraction	soustraction	Subtraktion(f)	resta	sottrazione	subtração
suburb	faubourg	Vorstadt(f)	suburbio	sobborgo	subúrbio
suburbs	banlieue	Vorort(m)	afueras	periferia	arredores
succeed	réussir	gelingen	lograr, conseguir	riuscire	conseguir
succeed	succéder	nach = folgen	suceder	succedere	suceder
success(-es)	succès	Erfolg(m)	éxito	successo	sucesso, êxito
success(-es)	réussite	Erfolg(m)	éxito, logro	riuscita	êxito
successive	successif, ive	aufeinanderfolgend	sucesivo, a	successivo, a	sucessivo, a
successor	successeur	Nachfolger(in f)m	sucesor	successore	sucessor
succinct, brief	succinct, e	bündig	sucinto, a	succinto, a	sucinto, a
succumb	succomber	erliegen	sucumbir	soccombere	sucumbir
such a, such(pl.)	tel, le	solche(r, s); so ein	tal	tale	tal
suck	sucer	lutschen	chupar	succhiare	chupar
suck	téter	saugen	mamar	poppare	mamar
suction disc	ventouse	Saugnapf(m)	ventosa	ventosa	ventosa
sudden(ly)	soudain	plötzlich	pronto(de)	ad un tratto	súbito(de)
suffer	souffrir	leiden	sufrir	soffrire	sofrer
suffering	souffrance	Leiden(n)	sufrimiento	sofferenza	sofrimento
sufficient	suffisant, e	genügend	suficiente	sufficiente	suficiente
suffocate; choke	étouffer	ersticken	sofocar, ahogar	soffocare	sufocar
suffocation	asphyxie	Ersticken(n)	asfixia	asfissia	asfixia
sugar	sucre	Zucker(m)	azúcar	zucchero	açúcar
suggest	suggérer	vor = schlagen	sugerir	suggerire	sugerir, propôr
suicide	suicide	Selbstmord(m)	suicidio	suicidio	suicídio
suit	costume	Anzug(m)	traje	abito, vestito	fato, traje
suit	tailleur	Kostüm(n)	traje	tailleur	saia-casaco
suit(ski-)	combinaison	Anzug(m)(Ski-)	traje	tuta, completo	fato
suit(space-)	combinaison	Anzug(Raum-)(m)	traje(espacial)	tuta(spaziale)	fato(espacial)
suit, fit	convenir	passen	convenir	convenire	estar bem
suitable, fitting	convenable	angemessen	conveniente	conveniente	conveniente
suitcase, case	valise	Koffer(m)	maleta	valigia	mala
suite	suite	Suite(f)	suite	appartamento	suite
sultan	sultan	Sultan(m)	sultán	sultano	sultão
sum, amount	somme	Summe(f)	suma; cantidad	somma	soma; quantia
summary	résumé	Zusammenfassung(f)	resumen	riassunto	resumo
summer	été	Sommer(m)	verano	estate	verão
summer	estival, e	sommerlich	estival	estivo, a	estival
summit, top	sommet	Gipfel(m)	cumbre; cima	cima; vetta	cimo; cume
summit, peak, top	cime	Gipfel(m)	cima	cima, vetta	cimo, cume
summon; invite	convoquer	vor = laden	convocar	convocare	convocar
sumptuous	somptueux, se	prächtig	suntuoso, a	sontuoso, a	sumptuoso, a
sumptuous	fastueux, se	prunkvoll	ostentoso, a	fastoso, a	faustoso, a
sun	soleil	Sonne(f)	sol	sole	sol
sunburn	coup de soleil	Sonnenbrand(m)	insolación	scottatura	insolação
Sunday	Dimanche	Sonntag(m)	Domingo	Domenica	Domingo
sunny	ensoleillé, e	sonnig	soleado, a	soleggiato, a	soalheiro, a
sunny(it's)	soleil(il fait)	Sonne scheint(die)	sol(hace)	sole(c'è il)	sol(está)
sunset	coucher(soleil)	Sonnenuntergang(m)	puesta de sol	tramonto	pôr do sol
sunshade, parasol	ombrelle	Sonnenschirm(m)	sombrilla	ombrello, parasole	sombrinha
sunstroke	insolation	Sonnenstich(m)	insolación	insolazione	insolação
sun-tan	bronzage	Bräune(f)	bronceado	abbronzatura	bronzeamento
superb	superbe	großartig	soberbio, a	splendido, a	soberbo, a
superior	supérieur, e	höher, besser	superior, a	superiore	superior, a
superior	supérieur	Vorgesetzte(f, m)	superior	superiore	superior
superiority	supériorité	Überlegenheit(f)	superioridad	superiorità	superioridade
supermarket	supermarché	Supermarkt(m)	supermercado	supermercato	supermercado
supernatural	surnaturel, le	überirdisch	sobrenatural	soprannaturale	sobrenatural
superpose	superposer	aufeinander = legen	sobreponer	sovrapporre	sobrepor
supersonic	supersonique	Überschall-	supersónico, a	supersonico, a	supersónico, a
superstitious	superstitieux, se	abergläubisch	supersticioso, a	superstizioso, a	supersticioso, a
supervise	superviser	überprüfen	supervisar	soprintendere	supervisar
supervisor	surveillant, e	Aufseher m, Supervisor	vigilante	sorvegliante	vigia
supper(have)	souper	Abend essen(zu)	cenar	cenare	cear
supple; flexible	souple	biegsam	flexible	flessibile	maleável
supplement	supplément	Ergänzung(f); Zulage f	suplemento	supplemento	suplemento
suppleness	souplesse	Biegsamkeit(f)	flexibilidad	flessibilità	flexibilidade

English	French	German	Spanish	Italian	Portuguese
supplier	fournisseur, se	Lieferant(in f)m	abastecedor, a	fornitore, trice	fornecedor, a
supply, provide	fournir	beliefern	proveer, dar	fornire	fornecer
supply	approvisionner	versorgen	aprovisionar	rifornire	abastecer
supply	ravitailler	versorgen	abastecer	rifornire	abastecer
supply(ing)	fourniture	Lieferung(f)	abastecimiento	fornitura	fornecimento
supplying	alimentation	Versorgung(f)	abastecimiento	rifornimento	abastecimento
support	soutien, appui	Unterstützung(f)	sostén, apoyo	sostegno, appoggio	apoio, socorro
support	appui	Stütze(f)	apoyo	appoggio	apoio
support	support	Stütze(f)	soporte	supporto	suporte
support	soutenir	unterstützen	sostener	sostenere	sustentar
support	supporter	stützen, unterstützen	soportar	sopportare	suportar
suppose	supposer	an = nehmen	suponer	supporre	supor
suppository	suppositoire	Zäpfchen(n)	supositorio	supposta	supositório
suppress	supprimer	ab = schaffen	suprimir	sopprimere	suprimir
supremacy	suprématie	Obergewalt(f)	supremacía	supremazia	supremacia
supreme	suprême	oberst-, höchst-	supremo, a	supremo, a	supremo, a
sure, certain	sûr, e; certain, e	sicher	seguro, a	sicuro, a	seguro, a
surely, certainly	sûrement	gewiß, sicherlich	ciertamente	sicuramente	certamente
surface	surface	Oberfläche(f)	superficie	superficie	superfície
surgeon	chirurgien	Chirurg(in f)m	cirujano	chirurgo	cirurgião
surgery	chirurgie	Chirurgie(f)	cirugía	chirurgia	cirurgia
surgery	cabinet(médecin)	Praxis(f)(Arztpraxis)	consulta(-torio)	studio(medico)	consultório
surname	nom	Familienname(m)	apellido	cognome	apelido
surplus, excess	excédent	Überschuß(m)	excedente	eccedente	excedente
surprise	surprise	Überraschung(f)	sorpresa	sorpresa	surpresa
surprised	surpris, e	überrascht	sorprendido, a	sorpreso, a	surpreendido, a
surprising	étonnant, e	erstaunlich	asombroso, a	sorprendente	espantoso, a
surround	entourer	um = geben	rodear	circondare	rodear, cercar
surroundings	alentours	Umgebung(f)	alrededores	dintorni	arredores
surroundings	environnement	Umgebung(f)	ambiente(medio)	ambiente	ambiente
survey	enquête, étude	Umfrage(f)	encuesta	inchiesta	inquérito
survive	survivre	überleben	sobrevivir	sopravvivere	sobreviver
survivor	survivant, e	Überlebende(r)mf	superviviente	superstite	sobrevivente
survivor	rescapé, e	Überlebende(r)mf	superviviente	scampato, a	sobrevivente
suspect	soupçonner	verdächtigen	sospechar	sospettare	suspeitar
suspect, mistrust	douter(se)	ahnen, vermuten	sospechar	sospettare	suspeitar
suspend, defer	suspendre	verschieben	suspender	sospendere	suspender
suspense	suspense	Spannung(f)	suspense	suspense	suspense
suspension	suspension	Federung(f)	suspensión	sospensione	suspensão
suspicion	soupçon; méfiance	Argwohn(m), Verdacht m	sospecha	sospetto	suspeita
suspicious	méfiant, e	mißtrauisch	desconfiado, a	diffidente	desconfiado, a
suspicious	suspect, e	verdächtig	sospechoso, a	sospetto, a	suspeito, a
swallow	hirondelle	Schwalbe(f)	golondrina	rondine	andorinha
swallow	avaler	schlucken	tragar	inghiottire, ingoiare	engolir
swan	cygne	Schwan(m)	cisne	cigno	cisne
sway, wobble	vaciller	taumeln	vacilar	vacillare	vacilar
swear	jurer	schwören	jurar	giurare	jurar
swear-word	juron	Fluch(m)	juramento, taco	bestemmia	palavrão
sweat	sueur	Schweiß(m)	sudor	sudore	suor
sweat	suer	schwitzen	sudar	sudare	suar
sweater, jumper	tricot	Trikot(m), Strickweste	prenda de punto	maglia	malha
sweep	balayer	fegen	barrer	spazzare	varrer
sweet	bonbon	Bonbon(n, m)	caramelo; bombón	caramella	rebuçado
sweet	doux, ce	süß	dulce	dolce	doce
sweet	sucré, e	süß	azucarado, a	zuccherato, a	açucarado, a; doce
sweet shop	confiserie	Süßwarenladen(m)	confitería	confetteria	confeitaria
swell, surge	houle	Brandung(f)	marejada	ondosità	vaga
swell	enfler	an = schwellen	hinchar	gonfiare	inchar
swim	nager	schwimmen	nadar	nuotare	nadar
swimmer	nageur, se	Schwimmer(in f)m	nadador, a	nuotatore, trice	nadador, a
swimming	natation, nage	Schwimmen(n)	natación	nuoto	natação
swimming, bathing	baignade	Baden(n)	baño	bagno	banho
swimming-pool	piscine	Schwimmbad(n)	piscina	piscina	piscina
swimsuit; trunks	maillot de bain	Badeanzug(m)	traje de baño	costume da bagno	fato de banho
swindle	escroquerie	Schwindel(m), Gaunerei	estafa	truffa, imbroglio	trapaça, burla
swing; see-saw	balançoire	Schaukel(f)	columpio	altalena	baloiço
switch(-es)	bouton	Schalter(m)	interruptor, botón	bottone, pulsante	interruptor
switch(-es)	interrupteur	Schalter(m)	interruptor	interruttore	interruptor

233

English	French	German	Spanish	Italian	Portuguese
switch on	allumer	an = machen	encender	accendere	acender
sword	épée	Schwert(n)	espada	spada	espada
syllable	syllabe	Silbe(f)	sílaba	sillaba	sílaba
symbol	symbole	Symbol(n)	símbolo	simbolo	símbolo
symbolic(al)	symbolique	symbolisch	simbólico, a	simbolico, a	simbólico, a
symmetry	symétrie	Symetrie(f)	simetría	simmetria	simetria
sympathize	compatir	mit = fühlen	compadecer	compatire	apiedar-se
symphony	symphonie	Symphonie(f)	sinfonía	sinfonia	sinfonia
symposium	colloque	Symposium(n)	coloquio	colloquio	colóquio
symptom	symptôme	Symptom(n)	síntoma	sintomo	sintoma
synagogue	synagogue	Synagoge(f)	sinagoga	sinagoga	sinagoga
synchronize	synchroniser	synchronisieren	sincronizar	sincronizzare	sincronizar
synonym	synonyme	Synonym(n)	sinónimo	sinonimo	sinónimo
syntax	syntaxe	Syntax(f), Satzlehre f	sintaxis	sintassi	sintaxe
synthesis(-ses)	synthèse	Synthese(f)	síntesis	sintesi	síntese
synthetic	synthétique	synthetisch	sintético, a	sintetico, a	sintético, a
syphilis	syphilis	Syphilis(f)	sífilis	sifilide	sífilis
syringe	seringue	Spritze(f)	jeringa	siringa	seringa
syrup, medicine	sirop	Sirup(m)	jarabe	sciroppo	xarope
system	système	System(n)	sistema	sistema	sistema
systematic	systématique	systematisch	sistemático, a	sistematico, a	sistemático, a

T

English	French	German	Spanish	Italian	Portuguese
table	table	Tisch(m)	mesa	tavolo; tavola	mesa
table(lay the)	couvert	Gedeck(n)	cubierto	coperto	talher
table-cloth	nappe	Tischdecke(f)	mantel	tovaglia	toalha
table-tennis	tennis de table	Tischtennis(n)	ping-pong	ping pong	ténis de mesa
tablet	cachet	Tablette(f)	pastilla	pastiglia	comprimido
tablet, pill	comprimé	Tablette(f)	comprimido	compressa	comprimido
tachycardia	tachycardie	Herzjagen(n)	taquicardia	tachicardia	taquicardia
tact	tact	Takt(m)	tacto	tatto	tacto
tactic	tactique	Taktik(f)	táctica	tattica	táctica
tactical	tactique	taktisch	táctico, a	tattico, a	táctico, a
tail	queue	Schwanz(m)	rabo	coda	cauda
tailor	tailleur	Schneider(m)	sastre	sarto	alfaiate
take	prendre	nehmen	tomar, coger	prendere	tomar
take	emmener	mit = nehmen	llevar	portare, condurre	levar
take(away)	emporter	mit = nehmen	llevar	portar via	levar
take away, remove	enlever	entfernen	sacar, quitar	togliere	retirar, tirar
take from	prélever	entnehmen	sacar	prelevare	tirar
take off	enlever	aus = ziehen	quitar	togliere	tirar
take off	décoller	ab = heben	despegar	decollare	descolar
take(an exam)	passer(examen)	ab = legen(Prüfung f)	pasar(un examen)	dare(un esame)	fazer(exame)
take advantage of	abuser	mißbrauchen	abusar	abusare	abusar
take advantage of	profiter	profitieren	aprovechar	approfittare	aproveitar
take a photo	photographier	fotografieren	fotografiar	fotografare	fotografar
take part(in)	participer(à)	teil = nehmen	participar(en)	partecipare(a)	participar(em)
take stimulants	doper(se)	dopen, sich	doparse	drogarsi	drogar-se
tale, story	conte	Märchen(n)	cuento	racconto, fiaba	conto
talent	talent	Talent(n)	talento	talento	talento
talk, conversation	entretien	Gespräch(n)	conversación	colloquio	entrevista
talk, commentary	exposé	Referat(n)	exposición	relazione; esposto	exposição
talk to, speak to	parler à	reden(mit jdm)	hablar con	parlare a	falar com
talkative	bavard, e	geschwätzig	parlanchín, a	chiacchierone, a	falador, a
talks	pourparlers	Verhandlungen(pl)	negociaciones	trattative	negociações
tall	grand, e	groß	alto, a	alto, a	alto, a; grande

English	French	German	Spanish	Italian	Portuguese
tally, agree	concorder	überein = stimmen	concordar	concordare	concordar
tame	apprivoiser	zähmen	domesticar	addomesticare	domesticar
tame	dompter	zähmen	domar	domare	domar
tan	bronzer	bräunen	broncear	abbronzare	bronzear
tangent	tangent, e	berührend	tangente	tangente	tangente
tangerine	mandarine	Mandarine(f)	mandarina	mandarino	tangerina
tangle(up)	emmêler(s')	verwickeln, verwirren	enmarañar(se)	aggrovigliare(-rsi)	emaranhar-se
tank	réservoir	Tank(m)	depósito	serbatoio	depósito
tank; vat	cuve	Wanne(f), Faß(n)	cuba	tino	cuba
tap; stop-cock	robinet	Wasserhahn(m), Hahn(m)	grifo	rubinetto	torneira
tape	bande	Band(n)	cinta	nastro	fita
tape recorder	magnétophone	Kassettenrecorder(m)	magnetófono	registratore	gravador
tapestry	tapisserie	Wandteppich; Gobelin m	tapiz; tapicería	arazzo; tappezzeria	tapeçaria
tar	goudron	Teer(m)	alquitrán	asfalto	alcatrão
target	cible	Zielscheibe(f)	blanco	bersaglio	alvo
tariff, price	tarif	Tarif(m)	tarifa	tariffa	tarifa
tart	tarte	Torte(f)	tarta	torta, crostata	torta
task	tâche	Aufgabe(f)	tarea	compito	tarefa
taste	goût	Geschmack(m)	gusto	gusto, sapore	gosto
taste	goûter	kosten	probar	assaggiare	provar
taste, sample	déguster	kosten	saborear, catar	gustare	provar
tasty	savoureux, se	schmackhaft	sabroso, a	saporito, a	saboroso, a
tattoo	tatouage	Tätowierung(f)	tatuaje	tatuaggio	tatuagem
tax(-es); duty	taxe	Steuer(f)	tasa, impuesto	tassa, imposta	taxa, imposto
tax(-es)	impôt	Steuer(f)	impuesto	tassa	imposto
tax(-es); royalty	redevance	Gebühr(f)	impuesto, tasa	cànone	taxa
tax evasion	fraude(fiscale)	Steuerhinterziehung f	fraude(fiscal)	frode(fiscale)	fraude(fiscal)
tax system	fiscalité	Steuerwesen(n)	fiscalidad	fiscalità	fiscalidade
taxi, cab	taxi	Taxi(n)	taxi	taxi, tassì	táxi
taxi-driver	chauffeur(taxi)	Taxifahrer(in f)m	taxista	tassista	motorista
tea	thé	Tee(m)	té	tè	chá
tea-room	salon de thé	Café(n), Konditorei(f)	salón de té	sala da tè	casa de chá
teach	enseigner	lehren, unterrichten	enseñar	insegnare	ensinar
teach	instruire	aus = bilden	instruir	istruire	instruir
teacher	enseignant, e	Lehrer(in f)m	profesor, a	insegnante	professor, a
teacher	professeur	Lehrer(in f)m	profesor, a	professore, essa	professor, a
teacher(primary)	instituteur	Grundschullehrer/in	maestro, a	maestro, a	professor primário
teaching	enseignement	Unterricht(m), Lehre f	enseñanza	insegnamento	ensino
team	équipe	Mannschaft(f), Team(n)	equipo	squadra; équipe	equipa, grupo
teapot	théière	Teekanne(f)	tetera	teiera	bule
tear	larme	Träne(f)	lágrima	lacrima	lágrima
tear-gas	lacrymogène	Tränengas(n)	lacrimógeno	lacrimogeno	lacrimogéneo
tear	déchirer	zerreißen	rasgar, romper	strappare	rasgar
tear out; tear off	arracher	weg = reißen, aus = reißen	arrancar	strappare, togliere	arrancar
tear to pieces	déchiqueter	zerstückeln	despedazar	dilaniare	despedaçar
tease	taquiner	necken	hacer rabiar	stuzzicare	arreliar
teaspoon	cuiller à café	Kaffeelöffel(m)	cucharilla	cucchiaino	colher de chá
technical	technique	technisch	técnico, a	tecnico, a	técnico, a
technician	technicien, ne	Techniker(in f)m	técnico, a	tecnico, a	técnico, a
technocrat	technocrate	Technokrat(m)	tecnócrata	tecnocrate	tecnocrata
technology	technologie	Technologie(f)	tecnología	tecnologia	tecnologia
teenager	adolescent, e	Jugendliche(m, f)	adolescente	adolescente	adolescente
telegram, cable	télégramme	Telegramm(n)	telegrama	telegramma	telegrama
telepathy	télépathie	Telepathie(f)	telepatía	telepatia	telepatia
telephone, phone	téléphone	Telefon(n)	teléfono	telefono	telefone
telescope	télescope	Teleskop(n)	telescopio	telescopio	telescópio
televise	téléviser	übertragen	televisar	teletrasmettere	televisionar
television	télévision	Fernsehen(n)	televisión	televisione	televisão; TV
television set	téléviseur	Fernseher(m)	televisor	televisore	televisor
telex	télex	Telex(n)	telex	telex	telex
tell	dire	sagen	decir	dire	contar
temperament	tempérament	Temperament(n)	temperamento	temperamento	temperamento
temperate	tempéré, e	gemäßigt	templado, a	temperato, a	temperado, a
temperature	température	Temperatur(f)	temperatura	temperatura	temperatura
temple	temple	Tempel(m)	templo	tempio	templo
temple	tempe	Schläfe(f)	sien	tempia	têmpora
temporary	temporaire	vorübergehend	temporario, a	temporaneo, a	temporário, a
temptation	tentation	Versuchung(f)	tentación	tentazione	tentação

E

235

English	French	German	Spanish	Italian	Portuguese
ten	dix	zehn	diez	dieci	dez
tenacity	ténacité	Hartnäckigkeit(f)	tenacidad	tenacità; tenacia	tenacidade
tenant	locataire	Mieter(in f)m	inquilino, a	inquilino, a	inquilino, a
tendency; trend	tendance	Tendenz(f), Neigung(f)	tendencia	tendenza	tendência
tender	tendre	zärtlich	tierno, a	tenero, a	terno, a
tenderness	tendresse	Zärtlichkeit(f)	ternura	tenerezza	ternura
tennis	tennis	Tennis(n)	tenis	tennis	ténis
tenor	ténor	Tenor(m)	tenor	tenore	tenor
tension	tension	Spannung(f)	tensión	tensione	tensão
tent	tente	Zelt(n)	tienda	tenda	tenda
tentacle	tentacule	Fangarm(m)	tentáculo	tentacolo	tentáculo
tenth	dixième	zehnte	décimo, a	decimo, a	décimo, a
tenured	titulaire	festangestellt	numerario	titolare	titular
term	terme	Ausdruck(m)	término	parola	termo
term; quarter	trimestre	Vierteljahr(n)	trimestre	trimestre	trimestre
terminal, final	terminal, e	letzte(r, s); End-	terminal	terminale	terminal
terrestrial	terrestre	irdisch	terrestre	terrestre	terrestre
terrible	terrible	schrecklich	terrible	terribile	terrível
terrify	effarer, effrayer	erschrecken	espantar, asustar	sgomentare	apavorar
territory	territoire	Gebiet(n), Land(n)	territorio	territorio	território
terror	terreur	Schrecken(m)	terror	terrore	terror
terrorism	terrorisme	Terrorismus(m)	terrorismo	terrorismo	terrorismo
terrorist	terroriste	Terrorist(in f)m	terrorista	terrorista	terrorista
terrorize	terroriser	terrorisieren	aterrorizar	terrorizzare	aterrorizar
test	épreuve, essai	Test(m), Probe(f)	prueba	prova, test	prova
test	tester	testen	ensayar, probar	testare	testar
testicle	testicule	Hoden(m)	testículo	testicolo	testículo
testify	témoigner	aus = sagen	testimoniar	testimoniare	testemunhar
testimony, evidence	témoignage	Zeugenaussage(f)	testimonio	testimonianza	testemunho
tetanus	tétanos	Tetanus(m)	tétanos	tetano	tétano
tetany	tétanie	Starrkrampf(m)	tetania	tetania	tetania
text	texte	Text(m)	texto	testo	texto
textile	textile	Textil-; Web-	textil	tessile	textil
thank	remercier	danken; bedanken, sich	agradecer	ringraziare	agradecer
thank you, thanks	merci	danke	gracias	grazie	obrigado, a
thanks	remerciement	Dank(m)	agradecimiento	ringraziamento	agradecimento
thanks to	grâce à	dank	gracias a	grazie a	graças a
that, those	ce, cette, ces	dieser, diese, dieses	ese, esa, esos(as)	quello, a; questo, a	este, esta, estes
that	cela, ça	das, jene(r, s)	eso, aquello, ello	ciò, questo, quello	isso, aquilo
that; whom; which	que	was, das	que, qué	che	que
that is(to say)	c'est-à-dire	das heißt	es decir	cioè	quer dizer
that one	celui-là, celle-	der(jenige); die( )	ése, ésa, éso(s)	quello, quella	esse(a); aquele(a)
thaw	dégel	Auftauen(n)	deshielo	disgelo	degelo
thaw	décongeler	auf = tauen	descongelar	scongelare	descongelar
the	le, l', les	der, die, das, die	el, lo, los	il, lo, l'; i, gli	o, os
the	la, l', les	die	la, las	la; l'; le	a, as
the	le	das	lo	lo	o
the	les	die	los, las	i, gli; le	os, as
the one	celui, celle	derjenige, die-, das-	él, la	quello, a	o, a
theatre	théâtre	Theater(n)	teatro	teatro	teatro
theft, robbery	vol	Diebstahl(m)	robo	furto	roubo
their	leur(s)	ihr/ihre	su, sus, suyo	loro(il/la, i/le)	seu, sua, deles
theirs	leur(le, la)	ihrige(der, die, das)	suyo, a(el, la)	loro(il, la)	seu(o) a sua; dele, a
them	leur	ihnen	les	loro; gli	lhes
theme	thème	Thema(n)	tema	tema	tema
theme, subject	objet, thème	Thema(n), Objekt(n)	objeto, tema	oggetto, scopo	tema, assunto
then	alors	dann	entonces	allora	então
then, next	ensuite, puis	danach	después	poi, dopo	em seguida
then	puis, ensuite	dann	después	poi	depois
theology	théologie	Theologie(f)	teología	teologia	teologia
theorem	théorème	Lehrsatz(m)	teorema	teorema	teorema
theoretical	théorique	theoretisch	teórico, a	teorico, a	teórico, a
theory	théorie	Theorie(f)	teoría	teoria	teoria
therapy	thérapie	Therapie(f)	terapia	terapia	terapia
therapy	rééducation	Heilgymnastik(f)	reeducación	rieducazione	reeducação
there	là	da	ahí; allí	là	aí; ali; lá
there	là	da; dort	allí; allá	là; lì	aí; lá
there is, there are	il y a	es gibt	hay	c'è; ci sono	há

236

therefore; so	donc	also	por tanto, pues	dunque	portanto, pois
therefore	conséquent(par)	folglich; deshalb	consiguiente(por)	perciò	conseguinte(por)
thermal	thermal, e	Thermal-	termal	termale	termal
thermic, thermal	thermique	thermisch	térmico, a	termico, a	térmico, a
thermometer	thermomètre	Thermometer(n)	termómetro	termometro	termómetro
these, those	ces	diese(pl)	estos, as; esos, as	questi, e	estes, as; esses, as
these, those	ceux, celles, ces	diese	esos, aquellos	questi, e	aqueles, aquelas
these, those	ceux-ci, celles-	diese, jene	éstos, ésos	questi, quelli	estes(as), esses(as)
thesis(theses)	thèse	These(f)	tesis	tesi	tese
they	ils	sie	ellos	essi; loro	eles
they	elles	sie	ellas	esse, loro	elas
thick	épais, se	dick	espeso, a	spesso, a	espesso, a
thickness	épaisseur	Stärke(f), Dicke(f)	espesor	spessore	espessura
thief(-ves), robber	voleur, se	Dieb(in f)m	ladrón, a	ladro, a	ladrão, ladra
thigh	cuisse	Schenkel(m)	muslo	coscia	coxa
thin	mince	dünn	delgado, a	sottile	fino, a
thin	maigre	mager	delgado, a	magro, a	magro, a
thing	chose	Ding(n)	cosa	cosa	coisa
things	affaires	Sachen(pl)	cosas	roba, oggetti	coisas
think	penser	denken	pensar	pensare	pensar
third	troisième	dritte	tercero, a	terzo, a	terceiro, a
third	tiers	Drittel(n)	tercio, a; tercero	terzo, a	terço, a; terceiro
third world	tiers-monde	dritte Welt(f)	tercer mundo	terzo mondo	terceiro mundo
thirst	soif	Durst(m)	sed	sete	sede
thirteen	treize	dreizehn	trece	tredici	treze
thirty	trente	dreißig	treinta	trenta	trinta
this, that	ce, cette	dieser, diese	este; estos, as	questo, a; quello, a	este, a; esse, a
this, that	cet, cette	dieser, diese	éste; ésta; éstos	questo, a; quello, a	este; esta; estes, as
this	ceci	dies(es); das	esto	questo, ciò	isto
this one	celui-ci, celle-	diese(r, s)(hier)	éste, ésta	questo, questa	este, esta
thorax	thorax	Brustkasten(m)	tórax	torace	tórax
thorn	épine	Dorn(m); Stachel(m)	espina	spina	espinho
though, although	bien que	obwohl, obgleich	aunque	benché	ainda que
thought	pensée	Gedanke(m)	pensamiento	pensiero	pensamento
thoughtful	réfléchi, e	bedächtig	reflexivo, a	riflessivo, a	ponderado, a
thousand	mille	tausend	mil	mille; mila(pl.)	mil
thousand	millier	Tausend(n)	millar	migliaio(a)	milhar
thousand million	milliard	Milliarde(f)	mil millones	miliardo	bilião
thousandth	millième	tausendste	milésimo, a	millesimo, a	milésimo, a
thread	fil	Faden(m)	hilo	filo	fio
threat	menace	Drohung(f)	amenaza	minaccia	ameaça
threaten	menacer	bedrohen	amenazar	minacciare	ameaçar
three	trois	drei	tres	tre	três
throat	gorge	Hals(m)	garganta	gola	garganta
throne	trône	Thron(m)	trono	trono	trono
throw	lancer	werfen	lanzar	lanciare	lançar; atirar
throw	jeter	werfen	arrojar, lanzar	gettare	atirar, lançar
throw away(out)	jeter	weg = werfen	echar, tirar	buttare	deitar fora
thumb	pouce	Daumen(m)	pulgar	pollice	polegar
thunder	tonnerre	Donner(m)	trueno	tuono	trovão
Thursday	Jeudi	Donnerstag(m)	Jueves	Giovedì	Quinta-feira
thyroid(gland)	thyroïde	Schilddrüse(f)	tiroides	tiroide	tiróide
tibia	tibia	Schienbein(n)	tibia	tibia	tíbia
tick	cocher	an = kreuzen	marcar	segnare	marcar
ticket	ticket	Karte(f); Fahrkarte(f)	ticket, billete	biglietto	bilhete
ticket	billet	Fahrkarte(f)	billete	biglietto	bilhete
ticket	billet	Los(n)	billete	biglietto	bilhete
ticket, penalty	procès-verbal	Strafmandat(n)	multa	contravvenzione	multa
tickle	chatouille(s)	Kitzeln(n)	cosquillas	solletico	cócegas
tide	marée	Gezeiten(pl.)	marea	marea	maré
tidy	rangé, e	ordentlich	ordenado, a	ordinato, a	arrumado, a
tidy, put in order	ranger, ordonner	ein = räumen	ordenar, colocar	sistemare	arrumar
tie	cravate	Krawatte(f)	corbata	cravatta	gravata
tie, bind	lier	binden, verbinden	ligar, amarrar	legare	ligar
tiger	tigre	Tiger(m)	tigre	tigre	tigre
tight	tendu, e	gespannt	tenso, a	teso, a	esticado, a
tighten; stretch	tendre	spannen	tender	tendere	estender, esticar
tighten	serrer, resserrer	an = ziehen	apretar	stringere	apertar

English	French	German	Spanish	Italian	Portuguese
tights(pair of)	collants	Strumpfhose(f)	pantys	collant	meias
tile	tuile	Ziegel(m)	teja	tegola	telha
tile	carreau	Fliese(f), Kachel(f)	baldosa, azulejo	piastrella	ladrilho, azulejo
tiling; tiles	carrelage	Fliesen(n); Fliese(f)	embaldosado	pavimento	ladrilho
tilt, lean	pencher, incliner	neigen	inclinar	inclinare	inclinar
timber	bois	Holz(n)	madera	legno	madeira
time	temps; heure	Zeit(f); Uhr(f)	tiempo; hora	tempo; ora	tempo; hora
time	fois	Mal(n)	vez	volta	vez
timetable	horaire(s)	Fahrplan(m)	horario(s)	orario	horário
tin; pewter	étain	Zinn(n)	estaño	stagno	estanho
tin	boîte	Dose(f)	lata	latta, scatola	lata
tin/can opener	ouvre-boîte(s)	Büchsenöffner(m)	abrelatas	apriscatole	abre-latas
tinned food	conserve(s)	Konserve(f)	conserva	conserva	conserva
tint, colour	teinte	Färbung(f), Farbe(f)	tinte, color	tinta	tinta
tip, end	bout	Zipfel(m), Ende(n)	punta	punta, estremità	ponta
tip, end	embout	Endstück(n)	punta; remate	estremità; punta	ponta; remate
tip	pourboire	Trinkgeld(n)	propina	mancia	gorgeta
tire, make tired	fatiguer	ermüden	cansar, fatigar	stancare	cansar, fatigar
tired	fatigué, e	müde, ermüdet	cansado, a	stanco, a	cansado, a
tiredness	fatigue	Müdigkeit(f)	cansancio	stanchezza	fatiga, cansaço
tireless	infatigable	unermüdlich	incansable	instancabile	infatigável
tiring	fatigant, e	anstrengend	fatigante	faticoso, a	cansativo, a
title	titre	Titel(m)	título	titolo	título
to	à	nach	a; en	a	a; para
to, towards	vers	nach, zu	hacia	verso	para
toast	griller	toasten	tostar	abbrustolire	torrar
toast	pain grillé	Toast(m)	tostadas	pane tostato	pão torrado
tobacco	tabac	Tabak(m)	tabaco	tabacco	tabaco
tobacconist's	bureau de tabac	Tabakladen(m)	estanco	tabaccheria	estanco, tabacaria
today	aujourd'hui	heute	hoy	oggi	hoje
toe	orteil	Zehe(f)	dedo del pie	dito del piede	dedo do pé
together	ensemble	zusammen	juntos	insieme	junto
toilet, lavatory	toilettes(W.C)	Toiletten(f pl)	servicios(W.C)	toilettes; W.C	lavabos; sanita
toilet paper	papier toilette	Toilettenpapier(n)	papel higiénico	carta igienica	papel higiénico
toilet water	eau de toilette	Eau de Toilette(n)	colonia(agua de)	acqua di toeletta	água de colónia
toilets	water-closet	Toilette(f)	water, retretes	WC; gabinetto	retrete, sanita
tolerance	tolérance	Toleranz(f)	tolerancia	tolleranza	tolerância
tolerate	tolérer	dulden, ertragen	tolerar	tollerare	tolerar
toll	péage	Autobahngebühr(f)	peaje	pedaggio	portagem
tomato(-es)	tomate	Tomate(f)	tomate	pomodoro	tomate
tomb	tombeau	Grabmal(n)	tumba	tomba	túmulo
tomorrow	demain	morgen	mañana	domani	amanhã
ton	tonne	Tonne(f)	tonelada	tonnellata	tonelada
tonality, tone	tonalité	Tonart(f), Klangfarbe	tonalidad	tonalità	tonalidade
tone	ton, son, timbre	Ton(m), Klang(m)	tono, sonido	tono	tom, som, timbre
tongue	langue	Zunge(f)	lengua	lingua	língua
tonic	fortifiant	Stärkungsmittel(n)	fortificante	ricostituente	fortificante
tonight	soir(ce)	heute abend	noche(esta)	sera(questa)	noite(esta)
tonsils	amygdale(s)	Mandeln(f, pl)	amígdalas	tonsilla	amígdala
too(much, many)	trop	zuviel	demasiado, a	troppo, a	demasiado, a
too, also, as well	également, aussi	ebenfalls, auch	igualmente	ugualmente	igualmente
tool	outil	Werkzeug(n)	herramienta	attrezzo	ferramenta
tools, equipment	outillage	Werkzeug(n)	herramientas	attrezzatura	ferramentas
tooth(teeth)	dent	Zahn(n)	diente	dente	dente
toothache	mal aux dents	Zahnschmerzen(m, pl)	dolor de dientes	mal di denti	dor de dentes
toothbrush(-es)	brosse à dents	Zahnbürste(f)	cepillo de dientes	spazzolino	escova de dentes
tooth decay	carie	Karies(f)	caries	carie	cárie
tooth-paste	dentifrice	Zahnpasta(f)	dentífrico	dentifricio	dentífrico
tooth-pick	cure-dents	Zahnstocher(m)	palillo	stuzzicadenti	palito
top	haut	Oberteil(n)	alto	alto	alto, cimo
top	dessus	Oberteil(n)	superior(parte)	disopra	cima(parte de)
topaz	topaze	Topas(m)	topacio	topazio	topázio
torch(-es)	torche	Fackel(f)	antorcha	torcia	tocha, archote
torch(-es)	lampe de poche	Taschenlampe(f)	linterna	lampadina tascabile	pilha
torment	tourmenter	quälen	atormentar	tormentare	atormentar
tormented	tourmenté, e	beunruhigt	atormentado, a	tormentato, a	atormentado, a
tornado(-es)	tornade	Wirbelsturm(m)	tornado	tornado	tornado
torpedo(-es)	torpille	Torpedo(m)	torpedo	torpedine	torpedo

English	French	German	Spanish	Italian	Portuguese
torpor	torpeur	Erstarrungszustand(m)	torpor	torpore	torpor
torrent	torrent	Wildbach(m)	torrente	torrente	torrente
tortoise; turtle	tortue	Schildkröte(f)	tortuga	tartaruga	tartaruga
torture	torture	Folter(f)	tortura	tortura	tortura
torture	supplice	Qual(f)	suplicio	supplizio	suplício
total	total, e	ganz; Gesamt-	total	totale	total
total	total	Summe(f), Ganze(s)(n)	total	totale	total
touch	toucher	an = fassen, berühren	tocar	toccare	tocar
tour	circuit	Rundfahrt(f)(-reise)	circuito	giro, circuito	circuito
tourism	tourisme	Tourismus(m)	turismo	turismo	turismo
tourist	touriste	Tourist(m)	turista	turista	turista
tournament	tournoi	Turnier(m)	torneo	torneo	torneio
tow	remorquer	ab = schleppen	remolcar	rimorchiare	rebocar
towards, to	vers	gegen, in Richtung	hacia	verso	direcção a(em)
towel	serviette	Handtuch(n)	toalla	asciugamano	toalha
tower	tour	Turm(m)	torre	torre	torre
town	ville	Stadt(f)	ciudad	città	cidade
town hall	mairie	Rathaus(n)	ayuntamiento	municipio, comune	câmara
town-planning	urbanisme	Städtebau(m)	urbanismo	urbanistica	urbanismo
town/city dweller	citadin, e	Städter(in f)m	ciudadano, a	cittadino, a	citadino, a
toxic	toxique	giftig	tóxico, a	tossico, a	tóxico, a
toxicology	toxicologie	Toxikologie(f)	toxicología	tossicologia	toxicologia
toy	jouet	Spielzeug(n)	juguete	giocattolo	brinquedo
trace, track	trace	Spur(f)	huella, rastro	traccia	traço; vestígio
trachea	trachée-artère	Luftröhre(f)	traquearteria	trachea	traqueia
track	piste	Spur(f)	pista	pista	pista
tractor	tracteur	Traktor(m)	tractor	trattore	tractor
trade, commerce	commerce	Handel(m)	comercio	commercio	comércio
tradesman(-men)	commerçant, e	Geschäftsmann(m)	comerciante	commerciante	comerciante
tradesman, dealer	marchand, e	Händler(in f)m	vendedor, a	mercante	negociante
trade union	syndicat	Gewerkschaft(f)	sindicato	sindacato	sindicato
trade unionism	syndicalisme	Gewerkschaftswesen	sindicalismo	sindacalismo	sindicalismo
tradition	tradition	Tradition(f)	tradición	tradizione	tradição
traffic	circulation	Verkehr(m)	tráfico	traffico	trânsito
traffic	trafic	Verkehr(m)	tráfico	traffico	tráfego, tráfico
traffic	trafic	Schleichhandel(m)	tráfico	traffico	tráfico
trafficker; pedlar	trafiquant, e	Schwarzhändler(in f)m	traficante	trafficante	traficante
tragedy	tragédie	Tragödie(f)	tragedia	tragedia	tragédia
tragic	tragique	tragisch	trágico, a	tragico, a	trágico, a
trailer	remorque	Anhänger(m)	remolque	rimorchio	reboque
train	train	Zug(m), Eisenbahn(f)	tren	treno	comboio
train, practise	entraîner(s')	üben; trainieren	entrenarse	allenare(-rsi)	treinar-se
train	dresser	ab = richten, dressieren	amaestrar	addestrare	amestrar
trainee	stagiaire	Praktikant(in f)m	cursillista	apprendista	estagiário
trainer	entraîneur	Trainer(m)	entrenador	allenatore	treinador
training	formation	Ausbildung(f)	formación	formazione	formação
training, practice	entraînement	Training(n)	entrenamiento	allenamento	treino
training period	stage	Praktikum(n)	cursillo	tirocinio, stage	estágio
traitor, -tress	traître, esse	Verräter(in f)m	traidor, a	traditore, trice	traidor, a
trajectory	trajectoire	Bahn(f), Kurs(m)	trayectoria	traiettoria	trajectória
tram-car	tramway	Straßenbahn(f)	tranvía	tram	carro eléctrico
tramp	clochard, e	Penner(m)	vagabundo, a	barbone, a; vagabundo	vagabundo, a
tranquillizer	tranquillisant	Beruhigungsmittel(n)	tranquilizante	tranquillante	tranquilizante
transaction	transaction	Transaktion(f)	transacción	transazione	transacção
transfer, moving	déplacement	Umstellung(f)	desplazamiento	spostamento	deslocação
transfer	transfert	Verlegung(f)	transferencia	trasferimento	transferência
transfer	mutation	Versetzung(f)	traslado	trasferimento	transferência
transfer	transférer	überführen	transferir	trasferire	transferir
transform, change	transformer	verändern	transformar	trasformare	transformar
transformation	transformation	Veränderung(f)	transformación	trasformazione	transformação
transfusion	transfusion	Transfusion(f)	transfusión	trasfusione	transfusão
translation	traduction	Übersetzung(f)	traducción	traduzione	tradução
translator	traducteur, trice	Übersetzer(in f)m	traductor, a	traduttore, trice	tradutor, a
transmission	transmission	Übertragung(f)	transmisión	trasmissione	transmissão
transmit	transmettre	übertragen	transmitir	trasmettere	transmitir
transmitter	émetteur	Sender(m)	emisor	emittente	emissor
transparent	transparent, e	durchsichtig	transparente	trasparente	transparente
transplant, graft	greffe	Verpflanzung(f)	trasplante	trapianto	enxerto

E

English	French	German	Spanish	Italian	Portuguese
transport	transport	Transport(m)	transporte	trasporto	transporte
transport, carry	transporter	transportieren	transportar	trasportare	transportar
transversal	transversal, e	Quer-; schräg	transversal	trasversale	transversal
transvestite	travesti	Transvestit(m)	travesti	travestito	travesti
trap, snare	piège	Falle(f)	trampa	trappola	armadilha
trapezium; trapeze	trapèze	Trapez(n)	trapecio	trapezio	trapézio
traumatism	traumatisme	Trauma(n)	traumatismo	trauma	traumatismo
travel	voyager	reisen	viajar	viaggiare	viajar
travel-bag	sac de voyage	Reisetasche(f)	bolso de viaje	borsa da viaggio	saco de viagem
traveller	voyageur, se	Reisende(r)m f	viajero, a	viaggiatore, trice	viajante
tray	plateau	Tablett(n), Platte(f)	bandeja	vassoio	tabuleiro
treacherous	perfide	heimtückisch	pérfido, a	perfido, a	pérfido, a
treasure	trésor	Schatz(m)	tesoro	tesoro	tesouro
treasurer	trésorier, ière	Schatzmeister(in f)m	tesorero, a	tesoriere, a	tesoureiro, a
treat; deal with	traiter	behandeln	tratar	trattare	tratar
treat	soigner	behandeln	tratar, curar	curare	tratar, cuidar
treatment	traitement	Behandlung(f)	tratamiento	trattamento	tratamento
treatment	cure	Kur(f)	cura	cura	cura
treaty	traité	Vertrag(m)	tratado	trattato	tratado
tree	arbre	Baum(m)	árbol	albero	árvore
tremble	trembler	zittern	temblar	tremare	tremer
tremendous	formidable	großartig	formidable	formidabile	formidável
trench(-es)	tranchée	Graben(m)	trinchera, zanja	trincea	trincheira
trend, tendency	tendance	Neigung(f)	inclinación	inclinazione	inclinação
trial, test	essai	Versuch(m)	prueba	prova, collaudo	ensaio
triangle	triangle	Dreieck(n)	triángulo	triangolo	triângulo
tribe	tribu	Stamm(m)	tribu	tribù	tribo
trick, craftiness	ruse	List(f)	ardid; astucia	furbizia	astúcia
trick	astuce	List(f), Trick(m)	astucia	astuzia	astúcia
trigger	gâchette	Abzug(m)	gatillo	grilletto	gatilho
trigger off	déclencher	aus = lösen	iniciar	scattare, attivare	desencadear
trip; journey	voyage	Reise(f)	viaje	viaggio	viagem
triumph	triomphe	Triumph(m)	triunfo	trionfo	triunfo
trolley	chariot	Karre(f)	carro	carrello	carroça, carro
troop	troupe	Truppe(f)	tropa	truppa	tropa
trophy	trophée	Trophäe(f)	trofeo	trofeo	troféu
tropical	tropical, e	tropisch	tropical	tropicale	tropical
trot	trotter	traben	trotar	trottare	trotar
trouble, problem	ennui, problème	Ärger(m)	problema	guaio	aborrecimento
trouble, effort	peine	Anstrengung(f)	dificultad	fatica	esforço
troubled	trouble	verworren	confuso, a	confuso, a; torbido, a	confuso, a
troubles	troubles	Unruhen(f, pl)	disturbios	disordini	perturbação
trousers	pantalon	Hose(f)	pantalón	pantalone	calças
trout	truite	Forelle(f)	trucha	trota	truta
truce	trêve	Waffenstillstand(m)	tregua	tregua	trégua
truck, wag(g)on	wagon	Waggon(m)(Güterwagen)	vagón	vagone	vagão
true	vrai, e	wahr	verdadero, a	vero, a	verdadeiro, a
truly	réellement	wirklich	realmente	realmente	realmente
trumpet	trompette	Trompete(f)	trompeta	trombetta	trombeta
trunk	tronc	Stamm(m)	tronco	tronco	tronco
trunk	malle	Koffer(großer)(m)	baúl	baule	mala
trust	confiance(avoir)	vertrauen(jdm.)	confianza(tener)	fiducia(aver)	confiar
trusteeship	tutelle	Treuhandschaft(f)	tutela	tutela	tutela
truth	vérité	Wahrheit(f)	verdad	verità	verdade
try	essayer	versuchen	probar, intentar	provare	tentar; provar
tube	tube	Tube(f)	tubo	tubo	tubo
tuberculosis, T.B.	tuberculose	Tuberkulose(f)	tuberculosis	tubercolosi	tuberculose
Tuesday	Mardi	Dienstag(m)	Martes	Martedì	Terça-feira
tug, tow	tracter	ab = schleppen	tirar	trainare, tirare	puxar
tulip	tulipe	Tulpe(f)	tulipán	tulipano	tulipa
tumour	tumeur	Tumor(m)	tumor	tumore	tumor
tumult, uproar	tumulte	Tumult(m)	tumulto	tumulto	tumulto
tuna(fish)	thon	Thunfisch(m)	atún, bonito	tonno	atum
tune	air	Melodie(f)	melodía	melodia	melodia
tunic	tunique	Tunika(f)	túnica	tunica	túnica
tunnel	tunnel	Tunnel(m)	túnel	tunnel	túnel
turbine	turbine	Turbine(f)	turbina	turbina	turbina
turbulence	turbulence	Turbulenz(f)	turbulencia	turbolenza	turbulência

English	French	German	Spanish	Italian	Portuguese
turn	tour	Umdrehung(f)	vuelta	giro	volta, giro
turn	tour	Reihe(f)	turno	turno	vez
turn	tourner	drehen	girar	girare	girar; rodar
turn	tourner	drehen	volver	girare	virar
turn	tourner	wenden	girar	svoltare, girare	virar
turn/switch off	éteindre	aus = schalten	apagar	spegnere	apagar
turnover	chiffre(affaire)	Umsatz(m)	volumen(negocios)	fatturato	volume(negócios)
twelve	douze	zwölf	doce	dodici	doze
twenty	vingt	zwanzig	veinte	venti	vinte
twenty one	vingt-et-un	einundzwanzig	veintiún(o)	ventuno	vinte e um
twilight, dusk	crépuscule	Abenddämmerung(f)	crepúsculo	crepuscolo	crepúsculo
twin	jumeau, jumelle	Zwilling(m)	gemelo, a	gemello, a	gémeo, a
twist(ing)	torsion, tour	Drehung(f), Torsion(f)	torsión	torsione	torção
twist	tordre	verbiegen, verdrehen	torcer	torcere, piegare	torcer
twitch(ing)	tic	Tick(m)	tic	tic	tique
two	deux	zwei	dos	due	dois, duas
type	type	Typ(m)	tipo	tipo	tipo
typhoid	typhoïde	Typhus(m)	tifoidea	tifoide	tifóide
typhoon	typhon	Taifun(m)	tifón	tifone	tufão
typical	typique	typisch	típico, a	tipico, a	típico, a
tyrant	tyran	Tyrann(m)	tirano, a	tiranno, a	tirano, a
tyre	pneu	Reifen(m)	neumático	pneumatico, gomma	pneu

U

English	French	German	Spanish	Italian	Portuguese
udder	mamelle	Euter(n)	mama, teta	mammella	mama
ugly, hideous	laid, e; moche	häßlich, gräßlich	feo, a	brutto, a	feio, a
ulcer	ulcère	Geschwür(n)	úlcera	ulcera	úlcera
ultimate, final	ultime	allerletzte(r, s)	último, a	ultimo, a	último, a
umbrella	parapluie	Regenschirm(m)	paraguas	ombrello	chapéu de chuva
unanimous	unanime	einstimmig	unánime	unanime	unânime
unbelievable	incroyable	unglaublich	increíble	incredibile	incrível
uncertain	incertain, e	unsicher	inseguro, a	incerto, a	incerto, a
unchanged	inchangé, e	unverändert	inalterado, a	immutato, a	inalterado, a
uncle	oncle	Onkel(m)	tío	zio	tio
unconscious	inconscient, e	unbewußt	inconsciente	incosciente	inconsciente
unctuous	onctueux, se	cremig, sahnig	untuoso, a	untuoso, a	untuoso, a
under	sous	unter	debajo, bajo	sotto	debaixo, sob
under, beneath	dessous	unter	debajo, abajo	sotto	debaixo, sob
undergo	subir	ertragen	sufrir, padecer	subire	sofrer
underground	souterrain, e	unterirdisch	subterráneo, a	sotterraneo, a	subterrâneo, a
underground, tube	métro	U-Bahn(f)	metro	metropolitana	metropolitano
undergrowth	broussaille	Gestrüpp(n)	zarzal, maleza	macchia, cespugli	mato, brenha
underline	souligner	unterstreichen	subrayar	sottolineare	sublinhar
underprivileged	défavorisé, e	benachteiligt	desfavorecido, a	svantaggiato, a	desfavorecido, a
understand	comprendre	verstehen	comprender	capire	compreender
understand	comprendre	begreifen, verstehen	entender	comprendere	entender
undertake	entreprendre	unternehmen	emprender	intraprendere	empreender
underworld	pègre	Unterwelt(f)	hampa	teppa, malviventi	súcia, ladroagem
undo, unfasten	dégrafer	auf = machen	desabrochar	slacciare	desapertar
undress	déshabiller(se)	aus = ziehen, sich	desnudar(se)	svestire(-irsi)	despir-se
unemployed person	chômeur, euse	Arbeitslose(f, m)	parado, a	disoccupato, a	desempregado, a
unemployment	chômage	Arbeitslosigkeit(f)	paro, desempleo	disoccupazione	desemprego
unequal	inégal, e	ungleich	desigual	ineguale	desigual
uneven	inégal, e	uneben	desigual	disuguale	desigual
unexpected	imprévu, e	unvorhergesehen	imprevisto, a	imprevisto, a	imprevisto, a
unexpected	inespéré, e	unerwartet, unverhofft	inesperado, a	insperato, a	inesperado, a

English	French	German	Spanish	Italian	Portuguese
unfaithful	infidèle	untreu	infiel	infedele	infiel
unfold	déplier	auf = falten	desdoblar	spiegare, aprire	desdobrar
unfortunate	malheureux, se	unglücklich	desgraciado, a	disgraziato, a	infeliz
ungrateful	ingrat, e	undankbar	ingrato, a	ingrato, a	ingrato, a
unhappy, miserable	malheureux, se	unglücklich, betrübt	desgraciado, a	infelice	infeliz
unhappy, sorrowful	malheureux, se	betrübt, unglücklich	infeliz, triste	infelice, triste	infeliz, triste
unhealthy	malsain, e	ungesund	malsano, a	malsano, a	doentio, a
unified, united	unifié, e	vereinigt	unificado, a	unificato, a	unificado, a
uniform	uniforme	gleichförmig	uniforme	uniforme	uniforme
uniform	uniforme	Uniform(f)	uniforme	uniforme; divisa	uniforme
union	union	Bund(m), Vereinigung f	unión	unione	união
unique; only	unique	einzig, einzeln	único, a	unico, a	único, a
unique, exceptional	unique	einmalig	único, a	unico, a	único, a
unit	unité	Einheit(f)	unidad	unità	unidade
unitary, per unit	unitaire	unitarisch	unitario, a	unitario, a	unitário, a
unite	unir	vereinen	unir	unire	unir, juntar
unity	unité	Einigkeit(f)	unidad	unità	unidade
universal	universel, le	universell	universal	universale	universal
universe	univers	Universum(n)	universo	universo	universo
university	université	Universität(f)	universidad	università	universidade
unknown	inconnu, e	unbekannt	desconocido, a	sconosciuto, a	desconhecido, a
unload	décharger	ab = laden, aus = laden	descargar	scaricare	descarregar
unload	débarquer	aus = laden	descargar	sbarcare	descarregar
unloading	déchargement	Ausladen(n)	descarga	scarico	descarga
unlucky	malchanceux, se	unglücklich	desafortunado, a	sfortunato, a	azarento, a
unoccupied	inoccupé, e	untätig	desocupado, a	inoperoso, a	desocupado, a
unofficial	officieux, se	halbamtlich	oficioso, a	ufficioso, a	oficioso, a
unpleasant	déplaisant, e	unangenehm	desagradable	sgradevole	desagradável
unpleasant	désagréable	unangenehm	desagradable	sgradevole	desagradável
unplug	débrancher	raus = ziehen	desenchufar	staccare	desligar
unpopular	impopulaire	unbeliebt	impopular	impopolare	impopular
unpublished	inédit, e	unveröffentlicht	inédito, a	inedito, a	inédito, a
unpunished	impuni, e	unbestraft	impune	impunito, a	impune
unroll	dérouler	ab = rollen	desenrollar	svolgere, srotolare	desenrolar
unruly	dissipé, e	unaufmerksam	indisciplinado, a	indisciplinato, a	indisciplinado, a
unstable	instable	unbeständig	inestable	instabile	instável
unstick	décoller	ab = lösen	despegar	staccare, scollare	descolar
unstitched	décousu, e	abgetrennt	descosido, a	scucito, a	descosido, a
unsuitable	inadapté, e	ungeeignet	inadaptado, a	inadatto, a	inadaptado, a
unsuited, unfit	inapte	ungeeignet	inapto, a	inabile	inapto, a
unthinkable	impensable	undenkbar	increíble	impensabile	impensável
until, till	jusqu'à	bis	hasta	fino a, sino a	até
unusual	insolite	seltsam, ungewohnt	insólito, a	insolito, a	insólito, a
unworthy	indigne	unwürdig	indigno, a	indegno, a	indigno, a
up	haut	Oben-; Hoch-; auf	arriba	alto, a	cima(em, para)
update	actualiser	aktualisieren	actualizar	attualizzare	actualizar
upheaval	branle-bas	Durcheinander(n)	zafarrancho	scompiglio	agitação
upkeep	entretien	Instandhaltung(f)	cuidado	mantenimento	manutenção
upper	supérieur, e	obere(r, s); Ober-	superior, a	superiore	superior, a
uproar, din	vacarme	Krach(m)	alboroto, jaleo	chiasso	barulho
upset	contrarié, e	ärgerlich sein	contrariado, a	contrariato, a	contrariado, a
upstairs	haut(en)	oben	arriba	alto(in)	cima(em)
up there	là-haut	da oben	arriba	in alto	lá em cima
uranium	uranium	Uran(n)	uranio	uranio	urânio
urban	urbain, e	städtisch, Stadt-	urbano, a	urbano, a	urbano, a
urea	urée	Harnstoff(m)	urea	urea	ureia
urgency	urgence	Dringlichkeit(f)	urgencia	urgenza	urgência
urgent	urgent, e	dringend	urgente	urgente	urgente
urine	urine	Urin(m)	orina	urina	urina
us	nous	uns	nos	ci, ce	nos
usage, use	usage	Gebrauch(m)	uso, empleo	uso	uso
use	emploi	Gebrauch(m)	uso, empleo	uso	uso
use	servir de(se)	benutzen	servirse	adoperare	servir-se
use	utiliser	benutzen	utilizar	utilizzare	utilizar
use	employer	benützen	usar, emplear	usare, adoperare	usar
useful	utile	nützlich	útil	utile	útil
useless	inutile	nutzlos	inútil	inutile	inútil
user	usager, ère	Benutzer(in f)m	usuario, a	utente	utente

English	French	German	Spanish	Italian	Portuguese
user	utilisateur	Benutzer(in f)m	utilizador, a	utilizzatore, trice	utilizador, a
usual	habituel, le	gewöhnlich	habitual	abituale	habitual
usual	usuel, le	gebräuchlich	usual	usuale	usual
usually	habituellement	üblich, gewöhnlich	generalmente	abitualmente	habitualmente
usually, in general	général(en)	allgemeinen(im)	general(en)	genere(in)	geral(em)
utensil	ustensile	Gerät(n)	utensilios	utensile	utensílio
uterus, womb	utérus	Gebärmutter(f)	útero	utero	útero
utilization, use	utilisation	Benutzung(f)	utilización	utilizzazione	utilização
Utopian	utopique	utopisch	utópico, a	utopico, a	utópico, a

V

English	French	German	Spanish	Italian	Portuguese
vacation	vacances	Ferien(pl.)	vacaciones	vacanze	férias
vaccination	vaccination	Impfung(f)	vacunación	vaccinazione	vacinação
vaccine	vaccin	Impfstoff(m)	vacuna	vaccino	vacina
vacuum; void	vide	Vakuum(n), Leere(f)	vacío	vuoto	vazio, vácuo
vacuum-cleaner	aspirateur	Staubsauger(m)	aspirador	aspirapolvere	aspirador
vagabond; tramp	vagabond, e	Landstreicher(in f)m	vagabundo, a	vagabondo, a	vagabundo, a
vagina	vagin	Scheide(f)(Anat.)	vagina	vagina	vagina
valid, good	valable	gültig; annehmbar	válido, a; valedero	valido, a	válido, a
validity	validité	Gültigkeit(f)	validez	validità	validade
valley	vallée	Tal(n)	valle	valle	vale
valuables	objets de valeur	Wertsachen(f pl)	objetos de valor	oggetti di valore	objectos de valor
value, worth	valeur	Wert(m)	valor	valore	valor
valve	clapet	Klappenventil(n)	válvula	valvola	válvula
vanilla	vanille	Vanille(f)	vainilla	vaniglia	baunilha
vanity	vanité	Eitelkeit(f)	vanidad	vanità	vaidade
vapour, fumes	vapeur	Dunst(m)	vapor	vapore	vapor
variable	variable	veränderlich	variable	variabile	variável
variation	variation	Abwandlung(f)	variación	variazione	variação
varied, various	varié, e	vielfältig	variado, a	vario, a	variado, a
variety	variété	Vielfalt(f)	variedad	varietà	variedade
various, varied	divers, e	mannigfach	vario, a	vario, a	variado, a
varnish	vernis	Lack(m)	barniz	vernice	verniz
vascular	vasculaire	Gefäß-	vascular	vascolare	vascular
vase	vase	Vase(f)	jarrón	vaso	jarra
vaseline	vaseline	Vaseline(f)	vaselina	vasellina	vaselina
vast	vaste	weit	vasto, a	vasto, a	vasto, a
vault, arch	voûte	Gewölbe(n)	bóveda	arco, volta	abóbada
vegetable	légume	Gemüse(n)	legumbre, verdura	verdura; legume	legume
vegetable, plant	végétal	Pflanze(f)	vegetal	vegetale	vegetal
vegetation	végétation	Pflanzenwuchs(m)	vegetación	vegetazione	vegetação
vehicle	véhicule	Fahrzeug(n)	vehículo	veicolo	veículo
veil	voile	Schleier(m)	velo	velo	véu
vein	veine	Vene(f)	vena	vena	veia
velocity	vélocité, vitesse	Schnelligkeit(f)	velocidad	velocità	velocidade
velvet	velours	Samt(m)	terciopelo	velluto	veludo
venereal	vénérien, ne	Geschlechts-	venéreo, a	venereo, a	venéreo, a
venom, poison	venin	Gift(n)	veneno	veleno	veneno
ventilation	ventilation	Belüftung(f)	ventilación	ventilazione	ventilação
verb	verbe	Verb(n)	verbo	verbo	verbo
verdict	verdict	Urteil(n)	veredicto	verdetto	veredicto
verification	vérification	Überprüfung(f)	verificación	verifica	verificação
verify	vérifier	bestätigen, nachweisen	verificar	verificare	verificar
vertebra(-ae)	vertèbre	Wirbel(m)	vértebra	vertebra	vértebra
vertical	vertical, e	senkrecht	vertical	verticale	vertical
very	très	sehr	muy	molto	muito

English	French	German	Spanish	Italian	Portuguese
vessel(blood)	vaisseau	Gefäß(Blut-)(n)	vaso(sanguíneo)	vaso(sanguigno)	vaso(sanguíneo)
vessel, ship	vaisseau	Schiff(n)	nave, navío	vascello, nave	navio
vest	maillot de corps	Trikot(n)	camiseta	maglia intima	camisola interior
vet	vétérinaire	Tierarzt(m)	veterinario	veterinario	veterinário
veto	veto	Veto(n)	veto	veto	veto
vexation	vexation	Ärger(m)	vejación	vessazione	vexame
vibrate	vibrer	schwingen	vibrar	vibrare	vibrar
vicar, minister	pasteur	Pastor(in f)m	pastor	pastore	padre; pastor
vice	vice	Laster(n)	vicio	vizio	vício
vice-president	vice-président	Vize-Präsident(m)	vicepresidente	vicepresidente	vice-presidente
vicious	vicieux, se	lasterhaft	vicioso, a	vizioso, a	vicioso, a
victim	victime	Opfer(n)	víctima	vittima	vítima
victim(disaster -)	sinistré, e	Geschädigte(r)m f	siniestrado, a	sinistrato, a	sinistrado, a
victory	victoire	Sieg(m)	victoria	vittoria	vitória
video recorder	magnétoscope	Videorecorder(m)	magnetoscopio	videoregistratore	gravador video
view	vue	Ausblick(m)	vista	veduta	vista
viewer	téléspectateur	Fernsehzuschauer/in	telespectador, a	telespettatore, trice	telespectador, a
viewpoint	point de vue	Aussichtspunkt(m)	punto de vista	punto di vista	ponto de vista
vigilant	vigilant, e	wachsam	vigilante	vigilante	vigilante
vigorous, strong	vigoureux, se	rüstig, kräftig	vigoroso, a	vigoroso, a	vigoroso, a
vigour	vigueur	Kraft(f)	vigor	vigore	vigor
vile, infamous	infâme	niederträchtig	infame	infame	infame
village	village	Dorf(n)	aldea, pueblo	paese, villaggio	aldeia, povoado
vinegar	vinaigre	Essig(m)	vinagre	aceto	vinagre
vintage	millésime	Jahrgang(m)	cosecha(año)	annata	vintage
violate	violer	verraten	violar	violare	violar
violation	violation	Verstoß(m)	violación	violazione	violação
violence	violence	Gewalt(f)	violencia	violenza	violência
violent	violent, e	gewalttätig, gewaltsam	violento, a	violento, a	violento, a
violent	violent, e	heftig, stark	violento, a	violento, a	violento, a
violet, purple	violet, te	violett, lila	violeta	viola	roxo, a; violeta
violin	violon	Geige(f)	violín	violino	violino
V.I.P	sommité	Prominente(f, m)	eminencia	sommità	sumidade
viper	vipère	Viper(f), Otter(f)	víbora	vipera	víbora
virgin	vierge	unberührt	virgen	vergine	virgem
virginity	virginité	Jungfräulichkeit(f)	virginidad	verginità	virgindade
virile, manly	viril, e	männlich, mannhaft	viril	virile	viril
virility	virilité	Männlichkeit(f)	virilidad	virilità	virilidade
virtue	vertu	Tugend(f)	virtud	virtù	virtude
virtuoso	virtuose	Meister(m), Virtuose m	virtuoso, a	virtuoso, a	virtuoso, a
virtuous	vertueux, se	tugendhaft	virtuoso, a	virtuoso, a	virtuoso, a
virus	virus	Virus(m)	virus	virus	virus
visa	visa	Visum(n)	visado	visto	visto
viscous	visqueux, se	zähflüssig	viscoso, a	vischioso, a	viscoso, a
visibility	visibilité	Sicht(-weite)(f)	visibilidad	visibilità	visibilidade
visible	visible	sichtbar	visible	visibile	visível
visit	visite	Besuch(m)	visita	visita	visita
visit	visiter	besichtigen, reisen	visitar	visitare	visitar
visit	visiter	besuchen	visitar	andare a trovare	visitar
visiting card	carte de visite	Visitenkarte(f)	tarjeta de visita	biglietto da visita	cartão de visita
visitor	visiteur, se	Besucher(in f)m	visitante	visitatore, trice	visitante
visual	visuel, le	visuell	visual	visivo, a; visuale	visual
vital	vital, e	wesentlich	vital	vitale	vital
vitality	vitalité	Lebenskraft(f)	vitalidad	vitalità	vitalidade
vitamin	vitamine	Vitamin(n)	vitamina	vitamina	vitamina
vocabulary	vocabulaire	Vokabular(n)	vocabulario	vocabolario	vocabulário
vocal	vocal, e	Stimm-	vocal	vocale	vocal
vocation	vocation	Berufung(f)	vocación	vocazione	vocação
voice	voix	Stimme(f)	voz	voce	voz
volcano(-es)	volcan	Vulkan(m)	volcán	vulcano	vulcão
volume	volume	Volumen(n)	volumen	volume	volume
voluntary	volontaire	freiwillig	voluntario, a	volontario, a	voluntário, a
voluntary	bénévole	unentgeltlich	benévolo, a	benevolo, a	benévolo, a
volunteer	volontaire	Freiwillige(f, m)	voluntario, a	volontario, a	voluntário, a
vomit	vomir	erbrechen, sich	vomitar	vomitare	vomitar
voracious	vorace	gefräßig, gierig	voraz	vorace	voraz
vote	vote	Wahl(f)	voto	voto	voto
vote	suffrage	Wahl(f)	sufragio	suffragio	sufrágio

English	French	German	Spanish	Italian	Portuguese
vote	voter	wählen	votar	votare	votar
voter	électeur, trice	Wähler(in f)m	elector, a	elettore, -trice	eleitor, a
vow	voeu	Gelübde(n)	voto	voto	promessa
vowel	voyelle	Vokal(m), Selbstlaut m	vocal	vocale	vogal
vulgar	vulgaire	vulgär	vulgar	volgare	vulgar
vulnerable	vulnérable	verwundbar	vulnerable	vulnerabile	vulnerável
vulture	vautour	Geier(m)	buitre	avvoltoio	abutre

W

English	French	German	Spanish	Italian	Portuguese
wag(g)on	wagon	Wagen(m)(Güter-)	vagón	vagone, carro	vagão, carruagem
wage(s)	salaire, paye	Lohn(m)	salario, sueldo	salario, paga	salário, paga
waist	taille	Taille(f)	cintura, talle	vita	cinta
wait(ing)	attente	Warten(n)	espera	attesa	espera
wait(for)	attendre	warten	esperar	aspettare	esperar
wait!	attendez!	Moment bitte!	espere(!)	aspetti!	espere!
wait for(in)	affût	Versteck(n)	acecho(al)	agguato	espreita de(à)
waiter	garçon	Ober(m)	camarero	cameriere	criado
waiter, waitress	serveur, se	Kellner(in f)m	camarero, a	cameriere, a	criado, a; moço
waiting-room	salle d'attente	Wartezimmer(n)	sala de espera	sala d'attesa	sala de espera
wake(up)	réveiller	wecken	despertar	svegliare	acordar
wake up	éveiller(s')	auf = wachen	despertar(se)	svegliarsi	despertar
wake	sillage	Kielwasser(n)	estela	scia	esteira
walk	marcher	gehen	andar	andare	andar
walk	marcher, cheminer	laufen, gehen	caminar	camminare	caminhar
walk(go for a)	promener	spazieren = gehen	pasear	passeggiare	passear
walk; drive; ride	promenade	Spaziergang(m)	paseo	passeggiata	passeio
walk(ing)	marche	Wanderung(f)	marcha	marcia	marcha
wall	mur	Mauer(f)	muro, pared	muro	muro, parede
wall	paroi	Wand(f)	pared	parete	parede
wallet	portefeuille	Brieftasche(f)	cartera	portafoglio	carteira
wallpaper	tapisserie	Tapete(f)	empapelado	carta da parati	papel de parede
walnut	noix	Walnuß(f)	nuez	noce	noz
waltz	valse	Walzer(m)	vals	valzer	valsa
want	vouloir	wollen	querer	volere	querer
war	guerre	Krieg(m)	guerra	guerra	guerra
wardrobe	armoire	Schrank(m)(Kleider-)	armario	armadio	armário
warehouse	entrepôt	Lager(n)	almacén	magazzino	armazém
warm	chaud, e	warm	cálido, a	caldo, a	cálido, a
warm, (re)heat	réchauffer	auf = wärmen	recalentar	riscaldare	aquecer
warn	avertir	warnen	advertir	avvertire	avisar, prevenir
warn, inform	prévenir	warnen	prevenir, avisar	prevenire	prevenir, avisar
warning	avertissement	Warnung(f)	advertencia	ammonizione	aviso
warped, buckled	gondolé, e	verbogen	combado, a	incurvato, a	empenado, a
warrant(y)	garantie	Garantie(f)	garantía	garanzia	garantia
warship	cuirassé	Kriegsschiff(n)	acorazado	corazzata	couraçado
wart	verrue	Warze(f)	verruga	verruca, porro	verruga
wash	laver	waschen	lavar	lavare	lavar
wash	laver(se)	waschen, sich	lavarse	lavarsi	lavar-se
wash-basin	lavabo	Waschbecken(n)	lavabo	lavabo, lavandino	lavabo
washer	rondelle	Scheibe(f)	arandela	rondella	anilha
washing	lavage	Waschen(n)	lavado	lavaggio	lavagem
washing powder	lessive	Waschpulver(n)	detergente	detersivo	detergente
wasp	guêpe	Wespe(f)	avispa	vespa	vespa
waste	gaspillage	Verschwendung(f)	despilfarro	spreco	desperdício
waste	déchet	Abfall(m)	residuo	scarto	resíduo
waste	gaspiller, perdre	verschwenden	despilfarrar	sprecare	desperdiçar

245

English	French	German	Spanish	Italian	Portuguese
waste	gaspiller	verschwenden	desperdiciar	sperperare	desperdiçar
watch	montre	Uhr(f), Armbanduhr(f)	reloj	orologio	relógio
watch, look(at)	regarder	fern = sehen	mirar	guardare	ver
watch; supervise	surveiller	überwachen	vigilar	sorvegliare	vigiar
watch; supervision	surveillance	Überwachung(f)	vigilancia	sorveglianza	vigilância
water	eau	Wasser(n)	agua	acqua	água
water	arroser	gießen, begießen	regar	innaffiare	regar
waterfall	cascade	Wasserfall(m)	cascada	cascata	cascata
water-proof	imperméable	wasserdicht	impermeable	impermeabile	impermeável
water-skiing	ski nautique	Wasserski(m)	esquí acuático	sci nautico	esqui aquático
watertight(air-)	étanche	undurchlässig	estanco, a	stagno, a	estanque
wave	vague	Welle(f)	ola	onda	onda, vaga
wave	onde	Welle(f)	onda	onda	onda
wave	lame	Welle(f)	ola	ondata	vaga
wave; flood	flot	Welle(f); Flut(f)	oleada	flutto	corrente
wave	agiter	schwenken	agitar	agitare	agitar
wax, polish	cire	Wachs(n)	cera	cera	cera
way	chemin, voie	Weg(m)	camino	cammino, strada	caminho
way; track	voie	Weg(m)	vía; camino	via; binario	via; caminho
way, manner, fashion	façon, manière	Weise(f), Art(f)	modo, manera	modo, maniera	modo, maneira
way out, exit	issue(sortie)	Ausgang(m)	salida	uscita	saída
we	nous	wir	nosotros	noi	nós
weak	faible	schwach	débil	debole, fragile	fraco, a
weaken	affaiblir	schwächen	debilitar	indebolire	enfraquecer
weakness(-es)	défaillance	Schwäche(f), Versagen	desfallecimiento	svenimento	desfalecimento
weakness(-es)	faiblesse	Schwäche(f)	debilidad	debolezza	fraqueza
wealth, richness	richesse	Reichtum(m)	riqueza	ricchezza	riqueza
weapon, arm	arme	Waffe(f)	arma	arma	arma
wear	usure	Abnützung(f)	desgaste	usura; logorio	usura, desgaste
wear	porter	tragen	llevar	indossare, portare	usar; trazer
weather	temps	Wetter(n)	tiempo	tempo	tempo
weather forecast	météorologie	Wetterkunde(f)	meteorología	meteorologia	meteorologia
weave	tisser	weben	tejer	tessere	tecer
wedding; marriage	mariage	Hochzeit(f); Heirat(f)	matrimonio	matrimonio	casamento
wedding	noce	Hochzeit(f)	boda	nozze	boda
wedge, chock	cale	Keil(m)	cuña	zeppa	cunha
Wednesday	Mercredi	Mittwoch(m)	Miércoles	Mercoledì	Quarta-feira
week	semaine	Woche(f)	semana	settimana	semana
weekend	week-end	Wochenende(n)	fin de semana	fine settimana	fim de semana
weekly	hebdomadaire	wöchentlich	semanal	settimanale	semanal
weigh	peser	wiegen	pesar	pesare	pesar
weight	poids	Gewicht(n)	peso	peso	peso
welcome	accueillir	empfangen, auf = nehmen	acoger, recibir	accogliere	acolher, receber
welcome(to be)	bienvenu, e	Willkommen(n)	bienvenido, a	benvenuto, a	bem-vindo, a
welding	soudure	Schweißen(n)	soldadura	saldatura	soldadura
well	bien	wohl	bien	bene	bem
well	bien	gut	bien	bene	bem
well	puits	Brunnen(m)	pozo	pozzo	poço
well-being	bien-être	Wohlbefinden(n)	bienestar	benessere	bem-estar
West	Ouest	Westen(m)	Oeste	Ovest	Oeste
Western	occidental, e	westlich	occidental	occidentale	ocidental
wet	mouillé, e; humide naß	mojado, a; húmedo, a	bagnato, a; umido, a	molhado, a; húmido, a
wet	mouiller	an = feuchten	mojar	bagnare	molhar
whale	baleine	Wal(m)	ballena	balena	baleia
what	quoi	was	que, qué	cosa, che cosa	quê
what; which	quel, le	welch(e, er, es)	cuál; que	quale; che	qual; que
whatever	quel que soit	was auch immer	cualquiera que sea	qualunque sia	seja qual for
wheel	roue	Rad(n)	rueda	ruota	roda
wheelbarrow	brouette	Schubkarre(f)	carretilla	carriola	carro de mão
when	quand	wann	cuándo, cuando	quando	quando
when; as	lorsque	als; wenn	cuando	quando	quando
where	où	wo	donde, dónde	dove	onde
whether	si	ob	si	se	se
which; who; whom	lequel	welcher	cúal, cual	quale(il)	qual(o)
which; who; whom	laquelle	welche	cual(la)	quale(la)	qual(a)
while, time	moment, instant	Moment(m)	rato	attimo, momento	momento, instante
while	pendant que	während	mientras	mentre; già che	enquanto
while, whilst	tandis que	während	mientras	mentre	enquanto

English	French	German	Spanish	Italian	Portuguese
whip	fouet	Peitsche(f)	látigo	frusta	chicote
whirlwind, swirl	tourbillon	Wirbel(wind)(m)	torbellino	vortice	turbilhão
whisper	chuchoter	flüstern	susurrar	bisbigliare	sussurrar
whistle	sifflet	Pfeife(f)	pito	fischietto	apito
whistle	siffler	pfeifen	silbar	fischiare	assobiar
white	blanc, blanche	weiß	blanco, a	bianco, a	branco, a
who(m); which; that	qui	wer; wen	quién, que	chi, che	quem
whole, entire	entier, ière	ganz	entero, a	intero, a	inteiro, a
whole; all the	ensemble	Ganze(n); Gesamtheit f	conjunto	insieme	conjunto
whole(the)	toute	ganz	toda	tutta	toda
whose, of which	dont	dessen; deren	cuyo, a; del cual	di cui	cujo, a; do qual
why	pourquoi	warum	por qué	perché	porquê
wide, broad	large	weit, breit	ancho, a	largo, a	largo, a
widen, enlarge	élargir	verbreiten	ensanchar	allargare	alargar
widower, widow	veuf, veuve	Witwer(m), Witwe(f)	viudo, a	vedovo, a	viúvo, a
width, breadth	largeur	Breite(f)	anchura	larghezza	largura
wife(wives)	épouse	Gattin, Frau, Ehefrau f	esposa	sposa, consorte	esposa
wife(wives)	femme, épouse	Ehefrau(f), Frau(f)	mujer	moglie	mulher
wig	perruque	Perücke(f)	peluca	parrucca	peruca
wild	sauvage	wild	salvaje	selvaggio, a	selvagem
wild	farouche	wild	feroz	selvatico, a	arisco, a
will, determination	volonté	Wille(m)	voluntad	volontà	vontade
will, testament	testament	Testament(n)	testamento	testamento	testamento
willingly	volontiers	gern	buena gana(de)	volentieri	bom grado(de)
wilt, wither	flétrir	verwelken	marchitar	appassire	murchar
win	gagner	gewinnen	ganar	vincere	ganhar
wind	vent	Wind(m)	viento	vento	vento
winding, sinuous	sinueux, se	kurvenreich	sinuoso, a	sinuoso, a	sinuoso, a
window	fenêtre	Fenster(n)	ventana	finestra	janela
window	hublot	Bullauge(n), Luke(f)	ventanilla	oblò	vigia
window; mirror	glace; miroir	Scheibe(f); Spiegel(m)	cristal; luna	vetro; specchio	vidro; espelho
windscreen	pare-brise	Windschutzscheibe(f)	parabrisas	parabrezza	pára-brisas
windsurf(ing)	planche à voile	Windsurfen(n)	tabla a vela, surf	windsurf	wind-surf
wine	vin	Wein(m)	vino	vino	vinho
wine-list	carte des vins	Weinkarte(f)	carta de vinos	lista dei vini	lista dos vinhos
wing	aile	Flügel(m)	ala	ala	asa
wings	coulisses	Kulisse(f)	bastidores	quinte(le)	bastidores
winner; victor	vainqueur	Sieger(in f)m	vencedor, a	vincitore, trice	vencedor, a
winter	hiver	Winter(m)	invierno	inverno	inverno
wipe, dry	essuyer	ab = wischen, abtrocknen	limpiar, secar	asciugare	limpar, secar
wire	fil(de fer)	Draht(m)	alambre	filo(di ferro)	arame
wire fencing	grillage	Gitter(n)	reja	reticolato	gradeamento
wish(-es)	désir	Wunsch(m)	deseo	desiderio	desejo
wish(-es)	voeu	Wunsch(m)	deseo	augurio	voto
wish, desire	souhaiter	wünschen	desear	augurare	desejar
witchcraft	sorcellerie	Hexerei(f)	brujería	stregoneria	bruxaria
with	avec	mit	con	con	com
withdraw	retirer	zurück = ziehen	retirar	ritirare	retirar
withdraw, give up	désister(se)	zurück = treten	desistir	desistere, rinunziare	desistir
without	sans	ohne	sin	senza	sem
withstand	résister à	widerstehen	resistir a	resistere a	resistir a
witness(-es)	témoin	Zeuge(m), Zeugin(f)	testigo	testimone	testemunha
witness	témoigner	zeugen, bezeugen	atestiguar	testificare	testemunhar
wizard; witch(-es)	sorcier, ière	Hexer(m); Hexe(f)	brujo, a	stregone, strega	bruxo, a
wolf(-lves)	loup	Wolf(m)	lobo	lupo	lobo
woman(women)	femme	Frau(f)	mujer	donna	mulher
wonder	demander(se)	fragen, sich	preguntarse	domandarsi	perguntar-se
wonderful	merveilleux, se	wunderbar	maravilloso, a	meraviglioso, a	maravilhoso, a
wonderful, super	épatant, e	großartig, fabelhaft	estupendo, a	straordinario, a	estupendo, a
wood	bois	Brennholz(n)	leña	legna	lenha
wood	bois	Wald(m)	bosque	bosco	bosque
wool	laine	Wolle(f)	lana	lana	lã
word	mot	Wort(n)	palabra	parola	palavra
word; speech	parole	Wort(n)	palabra	parola	palavra
words, talk	propos	Worte(pl.)	palabras	parole, discorsi	fala, conversa
work	travail	Arbeit(f)	trabajo	lavoro	trabalho
work	ouvrage	Arbeit(f)	tarea, trabajo	opera, lavoro	obra, trabalho
work	ouvrage	Werk(n)	obra	lavoro	obra

E

English	French	German	Spanish	Italian	Portuguese
work	oeuvre	Werk(n)	obra	opera	obra
work	travailler	arbeiten	trabajar	lavorare	trabalhar
work, run	marcher	in Betrieb sein	marchar	funzionare	funcionar
worked up	excité, e	gereizt	excitado, a	eccitato, a	excitado, a
worker	travailleur, se	Arbeiter(in f)m	trabajador, a	lavoratore, trice	trabalhador, a
worker, workman	ouvrier, ière	Arbeiter(in f)m	obrero, a	operaio, a	operário, a
workforce, labour	main-d'oeuvre	Arbeitskraft(f)	mano de obra	manodopera	mão-de-obra
workshop	atelier	Werkstatt(f)	taller	officina	oficina
work-site	chantier	Baustelle(f)	obra	cantiere	obra
world	monde	Welt(f)	mundo	mondo	mundo
world-wide, world	mondial, e	weltlich	mundial	mondiale	mundial
worm	ver	Wurm(m)	gusano	verme	verme
worn, worn out	usé, e	verbraucht	usado, a	logoro, a	usado, a
worried	inquiet, ète	besorgt	inquieto, a	inquieto, a	inquieto, a
worried	soucieux, se	sorgenvoll	preocupado, a	preoccupato, a	preocupado, a
worry	souci	Sorge(f)	preocupación	preoccupazione	preocupação
worry	inquiéter(s')	beunruhigen, sich	preocuparse	preoccuparsi	preocupar-se
worry	soucier(se)	sorgen, sich; plagen, s.	preocuparse	preoccuparsi	preocupar-se
worry, preoccupy	préoccuper	beunruhigen	preocupar	preoccupare	preocupar
worse	pire	schlimmer	peor	peggio	pior
worsen, aggravate	aggraver	verschlimmern	empeorar	aggravare	agravar
worship	culte	Kult(m)	culto	culto	culto
worth, merit	valeur, mérite	Wert(m)	valor, mérito	valore, merito	valor, mérito
worth(be)	valoir	wert sein	valer	valere	valer
worthless; useless	nul, le	wertlos	nulo, a	nullo, a	nulo, a
worthwhile	vaut la peine	der Mühe wert	vale la pena	vale la pena	vale a pena
worthy; dignified	digne	würdig	digno, a	degno, a	digno, a
would like(I)	voudrais(je)	möchte(ich)	quisiera(yo)	vorrei	gostava
wound; cut	plaie	Wunde(f)	llaga, herida	piaga	ferida
wrap, envelop	envelopper	ein = hüllen, ein = packen	envolver	avvolgere	envolver
wreck	naufrage	Schiffbruch(m)	naufragio	naufragio	naufrágio
wreck	épave	Wrack(n)	ruina, restos	relitto	destroços
wrestler; fighter	lutteur, se	Kämpfer(m); Ringer(m)	luchador, a	lottatore, trice	lutador, a
wrinkle	ride	Falte(f)	arruga	ruga	ruga
wrist	poignet	Handgelenk(n)	muñeca	polso	punho
write	écrire	schreiben	escribir	scrivere	escrever
writer	écrivain	Schriftsteller(in f)m	escritor, a	scrittore, -trice	escritor, a
writing	écriture	Schrift(f)	escritura	scrittura	escrita
wrong, false	faux, fausse	falsch	falso, a	falso, a	falso, a
wrong(in the)	fautif, ive	schuldig	culpable	colpevole	culpado, a
wrong(to be)	tort(avoir)	Unrecht(haben)	culpa(tener)	torto(aver)	razão(não ter)
wrong, harm	préjudice	Schaden(m)	perjuicio	pregiudizio	prejuízo

X

English	French	German	Spanish	Italian	Portuguese
X-ray; radiography	radiographie	Röntgenbild(n)	radiografía	radiografia	radiografia

Y

English	French	German	Spanish	Italian	Portuguese
yacht, sailing boat	voilier	Segelboot(n)	velero	veliero	veleiro
yard	cour	Hof(m)	patio	cortile	pátio
yawn	baîller	gähnen	bostezar	sbadigliare	bocejar
year	an	Jahr(n)	año	anno	ano
year	année	Jahr(n)	año	annata, anno	ano
yearly, annual	annuel, le	jährlich	anual	annuale	anual
yellow	jaune	gelb	amarillo, a	giallo, a	amarelo, a
yes	oui	ja	sí	sì	sim
yesterday	hier	gestern	ayer	ieri	ontem
yet, however	pourtant	dennoch, doch	sin embargo	però, tuttavia	contudo, todavia
yet(not)	encore(pas)	noch(nicht)	todavía no	ancora(non)	ainda não
yield	rendement	Ertrag(m)	rendimiento	rendimento	rendimento; produto
yield, return	rapport	Ertrag(m)	renta; ganancia	frutto, rendita	renda; ganho
yoga	yoga	Yoga(n), Joga(n)	yoga	yoga	yoga
you	tu	du	tú	tu	tu
you	vous	ihr; Sie	vosotros; ustedes	voi; lei	vós; você
you	vous	Sie	usted(es)	lei, loro(pl.)	você
you	vous; te	euch; Sie; Ihnen	os; les; le; te	vi; ve; le; ti; te	vos; vosco; lhe
you	te, t'	dich; dir	te	ti, te	te
you	toi	du; dich	tú; te	tu; te	tu; ti
young	jeune	jung	joven	giovane	jovem
younger; youngest	cadet, te	Jüngere(m, f)	menor	cadetto, a	novo, a(o, a mais)
young people	jeunes	jungen Leute(pl)	jóvenes	giovani	jovens
your	ton	dein(e)	tu	tuo(il)	teu
your	ta	dein(e)	tu	tua(la)	tua, teu
your	tes	deine	tus	tuoi, tue(i, le)	teus, tuas
your	votre	Ihr(e); euer, eure	vuestro, a	vostro, a(il, la)	vosso, a
your	vos	eure, Ihre	vuestros, as	vostri, e	vossos, as
yours	vôtre(le, la)	eure(r, s); Ihre(r, s)	vuestro, a; suyo, a	vostro, a; suo, sua	vosso, a; seu, sua
yours	tien, ne; vôtre(s)	deine(r, s), deine	tuyo, a	tuo, a	teu, tua
yours	toi(à); vous(à)	dir	tuyo, a	tuo, a; tuoi, tue	teu, tua
youth	jeunesse	Jugend(f)	juventud	gioventù, giovinezza	juventude

Z

English	French	German	Spanish	Italian	Portuguese
zebra	zèbre	Zebra(n)	cebra	zebra	zebra
zero, nought	zéro	Null(f)	cero	zero	zero
zone	zone	Zone(f)	zona	zona	zona
zoo	zoo	Zoo(m)	zoológico	zoo	jardim zoológico
zoological	zoologique	zoologisch	zoológico, a	zoologico, a	zoológico, a

E

Notes

Notes

Notes

Notes

Notes

Notes

Notes

A

German	French	English	Spanish	Italian	Portuguese
Abänderung(f)	modification	modification	modificación	modifica	modificação
Abbau(m)	démontage	dismantling	desmontaje	smontaggio	desmontagem
ab = bauen	défaire	dismantle, undo	deshacer	disfare	desfazer
ab = bauen	démonter	remove, dismantle	desmontar	smontare	desmontar
ab = bremsen	décélérer	decelerate	reducir, aminorar	decelerare	desacelerar
ab = danken	abdiquer	abdicate	abdicar	abdicare	abdicar
Abdruck(m)	empreinte	print	huella	impronta	impressão; marca
Abend(m)	soir	evening	tarde, noche	sera	tarde, noite
Abenddämmerung(f)	crépuscule	twilight, dusk	crepúsculo	crepuscolo	crepúsculo
Abend essen(zu)	dîner	dinner(have)	cenar	cenare	jantar
Abend essen(zu)	souper	supper(have)	cenar	cenare	cear
Abendessen(n)	dîner	dinner	cena	cena	jantar
Abendkleid(n)	robe de soirée	evening dress	traje de noche	abito da sera	vestido de noite
Abenteuer(n)	aventure	adventure	aventura	avventura	aventura
aber	mais	but	pero; sino; mas	ma	mas
abergläubisch	superstitieux, se	superstitious	supersticioso, a	superstizioso, a	supersticioso, a
Abfahrt(f)	départ	departure, start	salida, partida	partenza	partida
Abfall(m)	déchet	waste	residuo	scarto	resíduo
Abfall(m)	ordure(s)	rubbish, garbage	basura	immondizia	lixo
Abfalleimer(m)	poubelle	bin, dustbin	cubo de basura	pattumiera	caixote do lixo
ab = fließen	écouler(s')	run, flow	correr, fluir	scorrere, defluire	escorrer
Abfluß(m)	écoulement	flow, outflow	derrame, flujo	deflusso, scolo	escoamento
abführend	laxatif, ive	laxative	laxante	lassativo, a	laxante
Abgaben(pl.)	charge	contribution	carga	onere	encargo
Abgeordnete(r)mf	député	Member(Parliament)	diputado	deputato	deputado
Abgeordnetenhaus(n)	Chambre(députés)	House, Chamber	cámara(diputados)	camera	câmara
Abgesandte(r)mf	délégué, e	delegate	delegado, a	delegato, a	delegado, a
abgesetzt, verfallen	déchu, e	fallen, deposed	decaído, a	destituito, a	decaído, a
abgetrennt	décousu, e	unstitched	descosido, a	scucito, a	descosido, a
ab = grenzen	délimiter	delimit	delimitar	delimitare	delimitar
Abgrund(m), Kluft(f)	gouffre	chasm, pit	abismo, sima	baratro	abismo
Abgrund(m)	précipice	precipice	precipicio	precipizio	precipício
Abhang(m), Steigung(f)	côte	hill, slope	cuesta	salita, pendio	ladeira, encosta
ab = hängen	dépendre(de)	depend(on)	depender	dipendere	depender
abhängig	dépendant, e	dependent(on)	dependiente	dipendente	dependente
Abhängigkeit(f)	accoutumance	addiction	adicto, dependencia	assuefazione	dependência
ab = heben	retirer	draw out, withdraw	sacar	prelevare	levantar
ab = heben	décoller	take off	despegar	decollare	descolar
ab = holen	aller chercher	go to fetch/get	ir a buscar	andare a prendere	ir buscar
ab = horchen	ausculter	examine	auscultar	auscultare	auscultar
Abitur(n)	baccalauréat	G.C.E. A.Level(s)	bachillerato	maturità	bacharelato
ab = kühlen	rafraîchir	cool	refrescar	rinfrescare	refrescar
ab = kühlen	refroidir	cool(down)	enfriar	raffreddare	arrefecer
Abkürzung(f)(Wort)	abréviation	abbreviation	abreviatura	abbreviazione	abreviatura
Abkürzung(f)	sigle	initials	sigla	sigla	sigla
Abkürzung(f)	raccourci	short cut	atajo	scorciatoia	atalho
ab = laden, aus = laden	décharger	unload	descargar	scaricare	descarregar
ab = laufen	expirer	expire	expirar; vencer	scadere	expirar
ab = legen(Prüfung f)	passer(examen)	take(an exam)	pasar(un examen)	dare(un esame)	fazer(exame)
ab = lehnen, verwerfen	refuser, rejeter	reject	rechazar	rigettare	rejeitar
ab = lenken	distraire	distract, divert	distraer	distrarre	distrair
ab = lösen	décoller	unstick	despegar	staccare, scollare	descolar
Abmachung(f)	arrangement	arrangement	arreglo, acuerdo	accordo	compromisso
ab = nehmen	ôter, enlever	remove, take away	quitar	togliere	tirar
ab = nehmen	enlever, retirer	remove	quitar, retirar	rimuovere	remover, retirar
ab = nehmen	décroître	decrease	decrecer	decrescere	decrescer
ab = nehmen	maigrir	lose weight	adelgazar	dimagrire	emagrecer

German	French	English	Spanish	Italian	Portuguese
abnehmend	dégressif, ive	decreasing	decreciente	decrescente	decrescente
Abnützung(f)	usure	wear	desgaste	usura; logorio	usura, desgaste
Abonnement(n)	abonnement	subscription	subscripción	abbonamento	assinatura
Abonnent(m)	abonné, e	subscriber	suscriptor, a	abbonato, a	assinante
ab = prallen, aufprallen	rebondir	bounce, rebound	rebotar	rimbalzare	ressaltar
ab = raten	déconseiller	advise against	desaconsejar	sconsigliare	desaconselhar
ab = raten	dissuader	dissuade	disuadir	dissuadere	dissuadir
ab = richten, dressieren	dresser	train	amaestrar	addestrare	amestrar
ab = rollen	dérouler	unroll	desenrollar	svolgere, srotolare	desenrolar
ab = rüsten, entwaffnen	désarmer	disarm	desarmar	disarmare	desarmar
Abrüstung(f)	désarmement	disarmament	desarme	disarmo	desarmamento
Absatz(m), Abschnitt m	paragraphe	paragraph	párrafo	paragrafo	parágrafo
ab = schaffen	supprimer	suppress	suprimir	sopprimere	suprimir
ab = schaffen	abolir	abolish	abolir	abolire	abolir
ab = schleppen	remorquer	tow	remolcar	rimorchiare	rebocar
ab = schleppen	tracter	tug, tow	tirar	trainare, tirare	puxar
ab = schließen	fermer à clé	lock	cerrar con llave	chiudere a chiave	fechar à chave
Abschluß(m)	conclusion	conclusion	conclusión	conclusione	conclusão
Abschnitt(m)	segment	segment	segmento	segmento	segmento
Abschreckung(f)	dissuasion	dissuasion	disuasión	dissuasione	dissuasão
ab = schwächen; lindern	atténuer	attenuate	atenuar	attenuare	atenuar
Absender(in f)m	expéditeur	sender	remitente	mittente	expedidor
ab = setzen, entlassen	révoquer	dismiss	revocar	revocare	demitir
Absicht(f)	intention	intention	intención	intenzione	intenção
Absicht(f)	intention, but	purpose, aim, goal	intención	intento, fine, scopo	intenção
Absicht(f)	propos, intention	intention, aim	propósito	proposito	propósito
Absicht(f)	dessein	purpose, aim	propósito	proposito	propósito
absichtlich	exprès	purpose(on)	expresamente	apposta	propósito(de)
ab = sondern; isolieren	isoler	isolate	aislar	isolare	isolar
Abstand(m)	écart	gap, margin	diferencia, margen	margine, differenza	desvio, margem
Abstand(m)	intervalle	gap	intervalo	intervallo	intervalo
Abstand(m)	intervalle	interval	intervalo	intervallo	intervalo
Abstieg(m)	descente	descent	descenso, bajada	discesa	descida
abstrakt	abstrait, e	abstract	abstracto, a	astratto, a	abstracto, a
ab = stumpfen	abrutir	exhaust; stupefy	embrutecer	abbrutire	embrutecer
ab = stürzen	écraser(s')	crash	estrellarse	schiantare	esmagar-se
ab = tauen	dégivrer	de-ice; defrost	descongelar	sbrinare	descongelar
Abtei(f)	abbaye	abbey	abadía	abbazia, badia	abadia
Abteil(n)	compartiment	compartment	compartimiento	compartimento	compartimento
Abteilung(f)	rayon	department	sección	reparto	secção
Abtragung(f)	érosion	erosion	erosión	erosione	erosão
ab = treiben	dériver	drift	derivar	derivare	derivar
ab = treiben	avorter	abort	abortar	abortire	abortar
Abtreibung(f)	avortement	abortion	aborto	aborto	aborto
Abwandlung(f)	variation	variation	variación	variazione	variação
ab = wechseln	alterner	alternate	alternar	alternare	alternar
ab = weichen	diverger	diverge	divergir	divergere	divergir
Abwertung(f)	dévaluation	devaluation	devaluación	svalutazione	desvalorização
abwesend	absent, e	absent	ausente	assente	ausente
ab = wischen, abtrocknen	essuyer	wipe, dry	limpiar, secar	asciugare	limpar, secar
ab = ziehen	soustraire	subtract	sustraer, restar	sottrarre	subtrair, deduzir
Abzug(m)	déduction	deduction	deducción	deduzione	dedução
Abzug(m)	gâchette	trigger	gatillo	grilletto	gatilho
Achse(f)	axe	axis	eje	asse	eixo
acht	huit	eight	ocho	otto	oito
achtbar	respectable	respectable	respetable	rispettabile	respeitável
Achtung!(f)	attention!	careful!(be)	cuidado(!)	attenzione!, attento!	atenção!, cuidado!
Achtung(f)	estime	esteem	estima	stima	estima
achtzehn	dix-huit	eighteen	dieciocho	diciotto	dezoito
achtzig	quatre-vingts	eighty	ochenta	ottanta	oitenta
Addition(f), Summe(f)	addition, somme	addition, sum	adición, suma	addizione, somma	adição, soma
Ader(f); Arterie(f)	artère	artery	arteria	arteria	artéria
Adjektiv(n)	adjectif	adjective	adjetivo	aggettivo	adjectivo
Adler(m)	aigle	eagle	águila	aquila	águia
Adlige(f, m)	aristocrate	aristocrat	aristócrata	aristocratico, a	aristocrata
Admiral(m)	amiral	admiral	almirante	ammiraglio	almirante
adoptieren	adopter	adopt	adoptar	adottare	adoptar
Adreßbuch; Telefonbuch	annuaire	directory	anuario, guía	elenco, annuario	anuário

German	French	English	Spanish	Italian	Portuguese
Affäre(f), Sache(f)	affaire	affair, matter	asunto	faccenda, affare	assunto
Affe(m)	singe	monkey	mono	scimmia	macaco
Agent(in f)m	agent	agent	agente	agente	agente
Agentur(f); Filiale(f)	agence	agency	agencia	agenzia	agência
Aggression(f), Angriff	agression	attack	agresión	aggressione	agressão
Ahn(m)	ancêtre	ancestor	antepasado, a	antenato, a	antepassado, a
ähneln, aussehen wie	ressembler(à)	look like	parecerse(a)	somigliare a	parecer-se
ahnen, vermuten	douter(se)	suspect, mistrust	sospechar	sospettare	suspeitar
Ahnen(pl.)	aïeux	ancestors	antepasados	antenati	antepassados
ähnlich	semblable	similar	semejante	simile, uguale	semelhante
ähnlich, gleichartig	similaire	similar	similar	similare	similar
Ähnlichkeit(f)	ressemblance	resemblance	parecido	somiglianza	semelhança
Ähnlichkeit(f)	affinité	affinity	afinidad	affinità	afinidade
Akademie(f)	académie	academy	academia	accademia	academia
Akrobat(in f)m	acrobate	acrobat	acróbata	acrobata	acrobata
Akrobatik(f)	acrobatie	acrobatics, stunts	acrobacia	acrobazia	acrobacia
Akryl(n)	acrylique	acrylic	acrílico	acrilico	acrílico
Akte(f)	dossier	record, file	expediente	dossier	processo
Aktenkoffer(m)	attaché-case	attaché-case	maletín	valigetta	maleta
Aktenmappe(f)	porte-documents	document case	portadocumentos	portadocumenti	carteira
Aktie(f)	action	share	acción	azione	acção
Aktionär(m)	actionnaire	shareholder	accionista	azionista	accionista
aktiv, tatkräftig	actif, ive	active	activo, a	attivo, a	activo, a
aktualisieren	actualiser	update	actualizar	attualizzare	actualizar
aktuell, gegenwärtig	actuel, le	present, current	actual	attuale	actual
Akupunktur(f)	acuponcture	acupuncture	acupuntura	agopuntura	acupunctura
Akustik(f)	acoustique	acoustics	acústica	acustica	acústica
Akzent(m), Tonfall(m)	accent	accent	dejo	accento	sotaque
Akzent(m)	accent(')	accent	acento	accento	acento
akzeptieren, an = nehmen	accepter	accept, agree	aceptar	accettare	aceitar
Alarm(m)	alarme	alarm	alarma	allarme	alarme
Alarm(m)	alerte	alert	alerta	allarme	alerta, alarme
Album(n)	album	album	álbum	álbum	álbum
Alge(f)	algue	seaweed, alga(ae)	alga	alga	alga
Algebra(f)	algèbre	algebra	álgebra	algebra	álgebra
Alibi(n)	alibi	alibi	coartada	alibi	alibi
Alkohol(m)	alcool	alcohol	alcohol	alcol, alcool	álcool
Alkohol(m)	alcool(s)	spirit(s)	alcohol	alcolico	álcool
Alkoholmißbrauch(m)	alcoolisme	alcoholism	alcoholismo	alcolismo	alcoolismo
alle	tous	all(the)	todos	tutti	todos
Allee(f)	allée	path, lane	paseo, calle	viale	alameda
Allee(f)	avenue	avenue	avenida	viale	avenida
allein	seul, e	alone	solo, a	solo, a	só
allein, einsam	isolé, e	isolated, lonely	aislado, a	isolato, a	isolado, a; só, a
Alleinvertrieb(m)	exclusivité	exclusive rights	exclusiva(-ividad)	esclusività	exclusividade
Allergie(f)	allergie	allergy	alergia	allergia	alergia
allerletzte(r, s)	ultime	ultimate, final	último, a	ultimo, a	último, a
alles	tout, e	all(the)	todo, a	tutto, a	todo, a
allgemein, generell	général, e	general	general	generale	geral
allgemeinen(im)	général(en)	usually, in general	general(en)	genere(in)	geral(em)
Allopathie(f)	allopathie	allopathy	alopatía	allopatia	alopatia
Alphabet(n)	alphabet	alphabet	alfabeto	alfabeto	alfabeto
Alpinist(m)	alpiniste	mountaineer	alpinista	alpinista	alpinista
Alptraum(m)	cauchemar	nightmare	pesadilla	incubo	pesadelo
als; wenn	lorsque	when; as	cuando	quando	quando
also	donc	therefore; so	por tanto, pues	dunque	portanto, pois
alt	vieux, vieille	old	viejo, a	vecchio, a	velho, a
alt	âgé, e	old	anciano, a	anziano, a	idoso, a
alt	ancien, ne	old	antiguo, a	vecchio, a; antico, a	antigo, a
alt	ancien	ancient	antiguo, a	antico, a	antigo, a
Alte(m), alter Mann(m)	vieillard	old man(men)	viejo, anciano	vecchio, anziano	velho, ancião
Alteisen(n)	ferraille	scrap iron	chatarra	ferraglia, rottame	sucata
Alter(n)	âge	age	edad	età	idade
Ältere(f, m)	aîné, e	oldest, eldest	primogénito, a	primogenito, a	velho, a(o, a mais)
alternativ	alternatif, ive	alternating(ive)	alternativo, a	alternativo, a	alternativo, a
Älteste(f, m)	doyen, ne	oldest person	decano, a	decano, a	decano, a
altmodisch	démodé, e	old-fashioned	pasado de moda	passato di moda	fora de moda
altmodisch	désuet, ète	obsolete	desusado, a	antiquato, a; desueto	desusado, a

259

Aluminium(n)	aluminium	aluminium	aluminio	alluminio	alumínio
Amateur(in f)m	amateur	amateur	aficionado, a	dilettante	amador, a
Ameise(f)	fourmi	ant	hormiga	formica	formiga
Amnestie(f)	amnistie	amnesty	amnistía	amnistia	amnistia
Amplitude(f)	amplitude	amplitude	amplitud	ampiezza	amplitude
amputieren	amputer	amputate	amputar	amputare	amputar
amüsant, drollig	amusant, e	amusing, funny	divertido, a	divertente	engraçado, a
amüsieren, sich	amuser(s')	fun(have)	divertir(se)	divertire(-rsi)	divertir-se
an	à; sur; près de	at; on; near; by	a; sobre; cerca de	a; su; vicino a	a; sobre; perto de
analog	analogue	analogous, similar	análogo, a	analogo, a	análogo, a
Analyse(f)	analyse	analysis(-ses)	análisis	analisi	análise
analysieren	analyser	analyse	analizar	analizzare	analisar
Ananas(f)	ananas	pineapple	piña	ananas	ananás
Anarchie(f)	anarchie	anarchy	anarquía	anarchia	anarquia
Anatomie(f)	anatomie	anatomy	anatomía	anatomia	anatomia
Anbau(m)	culture	cultivation	cultivo	coltura	cultura
an = bauen, an = pflanzen	cultiver	cultivate, grow	cultivar	coltivare	cultivar
anbei	ci-joint, e	enclosed	adjunto, a	allegato, a	anexo(em)
an = bieten	offrir, proposer	offer	ofrecer, obsequiar	offrire	oferecer, ofertar
an = beten	adorer	adore	adorar	adorare	adorar
an Bord	à bord	aboard	a bordo	a bordo	a bordo
an = brechen	lever(se)	break, dawn	amanecer	sorgere	nascer
andauernd	permanent, e	permanent	permanente	permanente	permanente
Andenken(n)	souvenir	souvenir	recuerdo	ricordo, souvenir	recordação
andere, sonstige	autre	other	otro, a	altro, a	outro, a
ander; anders	autre(d')	else	otro, a	altro, a	outro, a
ändern	changer	change	mudar	cambiare	mudar; trocar
andernfalls, sonst	sinon	otherwise, or else	si no	se no; altrimenti	senão
anders; sonst	autrement	otherwise	otro modo(de)	altrimenti	outro modo(de)
an = deuten, zeigen	indiquer	indicate, show	indicar	indicare	indicar
Andrang(m)	affluence	rush	afluencia	affluenza	afluência
Anekdote(f)	anecdote	anecdote	anécdota	aneddoto	anedota
an = ekeln, an = widern	écoeurer	disgust	asquear	nauseare	enjoar
Anfang(m)	commencement	beginning, start	comienzo, principio	principio, inizio	começo, princípio
Anfang(m)	début	beginning	comienzo	inizio	princípio
Anfang(m)	départ	start	partida; marcha	inizio	princípio
an = fangen	commencer	begin, start	comenzar	cominciare	começar
an = fangen	débuter	begin, start	principiar	esordire	principiar
Anfänger(in f)m	débutant, e	beginner	principiante	principiante	principiante
anfänglich; Anfangs-	initial, e	initial	inicial	iniziale	inicial
an = fassen, berühren	toucher	touch	tocar	toccare	tocar
Anfertigung(f)	confection	clothing industry	confección	confezione	confecção
an = feuchten	mouiller	wet	mojar	bagnare	molhar
an = flehen	supplier	implore	suplicar	supplicare	suplicar
an = flehen	implorer	implore, beg	implorar	implorare	implorar
Anfrage(f)	demande	request	pedido	richiesta	pedido
Angabe(f), Hinweis(m)	indication	indication	indicación	indicazione	indicação
angeboren	inné, e	innate	innato, a	innato, a	inato, a
Angebot(n)	offre	offer	oferta	offerta	oferta
Angeklagte(r)mf	accusé, e	accused(the)	acusado, a; reo	accusato, a	acusado, a; réu(ré)
Angeklagte(r)mf	inculpé, e	accused(the)	inculpado, a	imputato, a	acusado, a
Angelhaken(m)	hameçon	hook	anzuelo	amo	anzol
Angeln(n)	pêche	angling	pesca(con caña)	pesca(con lenza)	pesca(à linha)
Angelrute(f)	canne à pêche	fishing rod	caña de pescar	canna da pesca	cana de pesca
Angelschnur(f)	ligne	line	caña	lenza	linha
angemessen	convenable	suitable, fitting	conveniente	conveniente	conveniente
angenehm	agréable	pleasant, nice	agradable	gradevole, piacevole	agradável
Angestellte(r)mf	employé, e	employee	empleado, a	impiegato, a	empregado, a
Angestellte(r)mf	employé, e	clerk	oficinista	impiegato, a	empregado, a
angezogen	habillé, e	dressed	vestido, a	vestito, a	vestido, a
Angina(f)	angine	sore throat	angina	angina, tonsillite	angina
an = greifen	attaquer	attack	atacar	attaccare	atacar
an = greifen	agresser	attack, assault	agredir	aggredire	agredir
Angreifer(in f)m	agresseur	attacker	agresor, a	aggressore	agressor, a
angrenzend	limitrophe	border(ing)	limítrofe	limitrofo	limítrofe
Angriff(m)	attaque	attack	ataque	attacco	ataque
Angriff(m)	assaut	assault, attack	asalto	assalto	assalto
Angst(f)	peur	fear	miedo	paura	medo

German	French	English	Spanish	Italian	Portuguese
Angst(f)	angoisse	anguish, distress	angustia	angoscia	angústia
Angst(haben)	peur(avoir)	afraid(to be)	miedo(tener)	paura(avere)	medo(ter)
ängstlich	anxieux, se	anxious	ansioso, a	ansioso, a	ansioso, a
Anhang(m), Anlage(f)	annexe	annexe	anexo; anejo	annesso	anexo
an = hängen	accrocher	connect, link	enganchar	agganciare	engatar
Anhänger(in f)m	partisan, e	partisan	partidario, a	partigiano, a	partidário, a
Anhänger(in f)m	adepte	follower	adepto, a; seguidor	seguace, adepto, a	adepto, a; seguidor, a
Anhänger(m)	remorque	trailer	remolque	rimorchio	reboque
an = häufen	accumuler	accumulate	acumular	accumulare	acumular
an = häufen	cumuler	accumulate	acaparar	cumulare	acumular
an = heben	élever, hausser	raise	elevar	elevare, alzare	elevar
an = heben, hoch = heben	soulever	lift, raise	levantar, elevar	sollevare	levantar, erguer
Anhöhe(f), Hang(m)	coteau	hill(side)	ladera	colle, collinetta	encosta; colina
Anker(m)	ancre	anchor	ancla	àncora	âncora
Anklage(f)	accusation	accusation, charge	acusación	accusa	acusação
Anklage(f)(punkt m)	charge	charge	cargo	indizio	acusação
an = klagen	accuser	accuse	acusar	accusare	acusar
Anklagerede(f)	réquisitoire	indictment	requisitoria	requisitoria	requisitório
an = kleiden	habiller(s')	dress up	vestirse, ataviar	vestire(-rsi)	vestir-se
an = klopfen	frapper	knock	llamar	bussare	bater
an = kommen	arriver	arrive, come	llegar	arrivare	chegar
an = kreuzen	cocher	tick	marcar	segnare	marcar
an = kündigen	annoncer	announce	anunciar	annunciare	anunciar
Ankunft(f)	arrivée	arrival	llegada; meta	arrivo	chegada
Anlage(f)	agencement	layout	disposición	disposizione	disposição
Anlage(f)	usine	plant	fábrica	fabbrica	fábrica
Anlauf(m), Schwung(m)	élan	spring, bound	impulso	slancio	impulso
an = legen	placer	invest	invertir	investire	pôr a render
an = legen	accoster	berth	abordar	accostare, attraccare	acostar
Anleihe(f)	emprunt	loan	préstamo	prestito	empréstimo
an = machen	allumer	switch on	encender	accendere	acender
an = malen	colorier	colour(in)	colorear	colorare	colorir
Anmerkung(f)	commentaire	comment	comentario	commento	comentário
an = nehmen	supposer	suppose	suponer	supporre	supor
annullieren	annuler	cancel	cancelar, anular	annullare	anular
Anomalie(f)	anomalie	anomaly	anomalía	anomalia	anomalia
anonym, unbekannt	anonyme	anonymous	anónimo, a	anonimo, a	anónimo, a
Anonymität(f)	anonymat	anonymity	anonimato	anonimato	anonimato
Anordnung(f)	disposition	arrangement	disposición	disposizione	disposição
Anordnung(f)	arrangement	arrangement	arreglo	ordinamento	arranjo
anorganisch	inorganique	inorganic	inorgánico, a	inorganico, a	inorgânico, a
anormal	anormal, e	not normal	anormal	anormale	anormal
an = passen	adapter	adapt, adjust	adaptar	adattare	adaptar
an = passen, sich	adapter(s')	adapt(to)	adaptarse(a)	adattarsi(a)	adaptar-se(a)
Anpassung(f)	adaptation	adaptation	adaptación	adattamento	adaptação
an = regen	inciter	incite	incitar	incitare	incitar
Anregung(f)	inspiration	inspiration	inspiración	ispirazione	inspiração
Anschlag, Plakatierung	affichage	putting up posters	anuncios(fijación)	affissione	afixação
an = schlagen	afficher	post up, put up	anunciar	affiggere	afixar
an = schließen	brancher	connect	empalmar	allacciare	ligar
an = schließen, sich	joindre à(se)	join	juntarse con	unirsi, associarsi	juntar-se
an = schließen, sich	rejoindre	rejoin, return to	reunirse con	raggiungere	reunir-se
an = schließen, sich	associer à(s')	join	asociarse(a, con)	associarsi(a, con)	associar-se a
Anschluß an(im)	suite à	further to	contestación(en)	seguito(facendo)	consequência(em)
an = schmiegen, sich	blottir(se)	huddle	acurrucar(se)	rannicchiarsi	aninhar-se
Anschrift(f), Adresse	adresse	address	dirección	indirizzo	endereço, morada
an = schwellen	enfler	swell	hinchar	gonfiare	inchar
an = sehen(als)	considérer	consider	considerar	considerare	considerar
Ansehen(n)	prestige	prestige	prestigio	prestigio	prestígio
Ansehen(n), Ruf(m)	réputation	reputation	reputación, fama	reputazione, fama	reputação, fama
ansehnlich, schön	beau, belle	handsome	bello, a	bello, a	bonito, a
an = siedeln, sich	établir(s')	settle; set up	establecerse	stabilirsi	estabelecer-se
Ansprache(kurze)(f)	allocution	speech(short)	alocución	allocuzione	alocução
Anstalt(f)	établissement	establishment	establecimiento	stabilimento	estabelecimento
anständig	décent, e	decent	decente	decente	decente
anstatt	au lieu de	instead(of)	en vez de/lugar de	invece di	em vez de/lugar de
ansteckend	contagieux, se	contagious	contagioso, a	contagioso, a	contagioso, a
Ansteckung(f)	contagion	contagion	contagio	contagio	contágio

G

German	French	English	Spanish	Italian	Portuguese
Ansteckung(f)	contamination	contamination	contaminación	contaminazione	contaminação
an = steigen	élever(s')	rise	subir	elevarsi	subir
an = stellen	employer	employ	emplear	impiegare	empregar
anstößig	choquant, e	shocking	chocante	urtante	chocante
Anstreicher; Maler(m)	peintre	painter	pintor, a	pittore, trice	pintor, a
anstrengend	fatigant, e	tiring	fatigante	faticoso, a	cansativo, a
Anstrengung(f)	effort	effort	esfuerzo	sforzo	esforço
Anstrengung(f)	peine	trouble, effort	dificultad	fatica	esforço
Anstrich(m)	couche	coat	capa	strato	camada
Ansturm(m)	ruée	rush	riada	ressa	corrida
Anteil(m); Teil(m, n)	part, partie	share; part	parte	parte	parte
Antenne(f)	antenne	aerial, antenna(e)	antena	antenna	antena
Antibiotikum(n)	antibiotique	antibiotic	antibiótico	antibiotico	antibiótico
antik	antique	antique, ancient	antiguo, a	antico, a	antigo, a
Antiquität(f)	antiquité	antiquity	antigüedad	antichità	antiguidade
Antiquitäten	antiquités	antique shop	anticuario	antiquariato	antiguidades
antiseptisch	antiseptique	antiseptic	antiséptico, a	antisettico, a	antiséptico, a
Antrieb(m)	propulsion	propulsion	propulsión	propulsione	propulsão
Antwort(f)	réponse	answer, reply	respuesta	risposta	resposta
antworten	répondre	answer, reply	contestar	rispondere	responder
an = vertrauen	confier	entrust	confiar	affidare	confiar
Anwalt(m), Anwältin(f)	avocat, e	lawyer, barrister	abogado, a	avvocato, tessa	advogado, a
Anweisung(f)	consigne	orders, instruction	consigna, orden	direttiva, ordine	ordem, instruções
an = wenden	appliquer	apply	aplicar	applicare	aplicar
an = werben	recruter	recruit	contratar, reclutar	assumere	recrutar
anwesend	présent, e	present	presente	presente	presente
Anwesenheit(f)	présence	presence	presencia	presenza	presença
an = widern	dégoûter	disgust	asco(dar)	disgustare	enojar
Anzahl(f), Zahl(f)	nombre	number	número	numero	número
Anzahlung(f)	arrhes	deposit	señal(dejar)	caparra	sinal
Anzeichen(n)	indice	indication, sign	indicio	indizio	indício
Anzeige(f)	annonce	notice	anuncio	annuncio	anúncio
an = zeigen	plainte(porter)	complaint(lodge a)	denunciar	querelare	queixa(apresentar)
Anzeiger(m)	indicateur	indicator	indicador	indicatore	indicador
Anzeiger(m)	détecteur	detector	detector	rivelatore	detector
an = ziehen	attirer	attract	atraer	attirare	atrair
an = ziehen	serrer, resserrer	tighten	apretar	stringere	apertar
an = ziehen, sich	habiller(s')	dress	vestirse	vestirsi	vestir-se
an = ziehen, an = kleiden	vêtir, habiller	clothe, dress	vestir	vestire	vestir
anziehend	attirant, e	attractive	atrayente	attraente	atraente
Anziehung(f)	attraction	attraction	atracción	attrazione	atracção
Anzug(m)	costume	suit	traje	abito, vestito	fato, traje
Anzug(m)(Ski-)	combinaison	suit(ski-)	traje	tuta, completo	fato
Anzug(Raum-)(m)	combinaison	suit(space-)	traje(espacial)	tuta(spaziale)	fato(espacial)
an = zünden	allumer	light	encender	accendere	acender
Apéritif(m)	apéritif	aperitif, drink	aperitivo	aperitivo	aperitivo
Apfel(m)	pomme	apple	manzana	mela	maçã
Apfelsine(f)	orange	orange	naranja	arancia	laranja
Apfelwein(m)	cidre	cider	sidra	sidro	sidra
Apotheke(f)	pharmacie	chemist's	farmacia	farmacia	farmácia
Apotheker(in f)m	pharmacien, ne	chemist, pharmacist	farmacéutico, a	farmacista	farmacêutico, a
Apparat(m)	appareil	appliance, device	aparato	apparecchio	aparelho
Appetit(m)	appétit	appetite	apetito	appetito	apetite
April(m)	avril	April	abril	aprile	Abril
Aquamarin(m)	aigue-marine	aquamarine	aguamarina	acquamarina	água marinha
Aquarium(n)	aquarium	aquarium	acuario	acquario	aquário
Äquator(m)	équateur	equator	ecuador	equatore	equador
äquatorial	équatorial, e	equatorial	ecuatorial	equatoriale	equatorial
Ära(f)	ère	era	era	era	era
Arbeit(f)	travail	work	trabajo	lavoro	trabalho
Arbeit(f)	travail	labour	trabajo	lavoro	trabalho
Arbeit(f)	ouvrage	work	tarea, trabajo	opera, lavoro	obra, trabalho
arbeiten	travailler	work	trabajar	lavorare	trabalhar
Arbeiter(in f)m	travailleur, se	worker	trabajador, a	lavoratore, trice	trabalhador, a
Arbeiter(in f)m	ouvrier, ière	worker, workman	obrero, a	operaio, a	operário, a
Arbeitgeber(in f)m	employeur	employer	patrón	datore di lavoro	patrão
Arbeitnehmer(in f)m	salarié, e	salaried employee	asalariado, a	salariato, a	assalariado, a
Arbeitskraft(f)	main-d'oeuvre	workforce, labour	mano de obra	manodopera	mão-de-obra

German	French	English	Spanish	Italian	Portuguese
Arbeitskräfte(pl.)	main-d'oeuvre	manpower, labour	mano de obra	manodopera	mão-de-obra
Arbeitslose(r)mf	chômeur, euse	unemployed person	parado, a	disoccupato, a	desempregado, a
Arbeitslosigkeit(f)	chômage	unemployment	paro, desempleo	disoccupazione	desemprego
archaisch	archaïque	archaic	arcaico, a	arcaico, a	arcaico, a
Archeologie(f)	archéologie	archaeology	arqueología	archeologia	arqueologia
Architekt(in f)m	architecte	architect	arquitecto, a	architetto	arquitecto, a
Architektur(f)	architecture	architecture	arquitectura	architettura	arquitectura
Archiv(n)	archives	archives	archivos	archivi	arquivo
Arena(f)	arène	arena	arena	arena	arena
Ärger(m)	agacement	irritation	fastidio	irritazione	irritação
Ärger(m)	ennui, problème	trouble, problem	problema	guaio	aborrecimento
Ärger(m)	vexation	vexation	vejación	vessazione	vexame
ärgerlich; aufregend	irritant, e	irritating	irritante	irritante	irritante
ärgerlich sein	contrarié, e	upset	contrariado, a	contrariato, a	contrariado, a
ärgern	embêter	bother, annoy	fastidiar	infastidire	aborrecer
Argument(n)	argument	argument	argumento	argomento	argumento
Argwohn(m), Verdacht m	soupçon; méfiance	suspicion	sospecha	sospetto	suspeita
Arithmetik(f)	arithmétique	arithmetic	aritmética	aritmetica	aritmética
arm	pauvre	poor	pobre	povero, a	pobre
Arm(m)	bras	arm	brazo	braccio	braço
Armband(n)	bracelet	strap	correa	cinturino	pulseira
Armband(n)	bracelet	bracelet	pulsera	braccialetto	pulseira
Armee(f)	armée	army	ejército	esercito	exército
Ärmel(m)	manche	sleeve	manga(la)	manica	manga
Armut(f)	pauvreté	poverty	pobreza	povertà	pobreza
Aroma(n)	arôme	aroma	aroma	aroma	aroma, cheiro
arrangieren	arranger	arrange	arreglar	sistemare	arranjar
Arsenal(n)	arsenal	arsenal, armoury	arsenal	arsenale	arsenal
Art(f)	manière	manner, way	manera, modo	maniera, modo	maneira, modo
Art(f)	espèce	species	especie	specie	espécie
Art(f), Sorte(f)	genre	kind, sort	género	genere	género
Arthrose(f)	arthrose	arthritis	artrosis	artrosi	artrose
Artikel(m)	article	article	artículo	articolo	artigo
Artikel(m)	article	item	artículo	articolo	artigo
Arzt(m), Ärztin(f)	médecin, docteur	doctor	médico	medico	médico
Arzt(m); Doktor(m)	docteur(toresse)	doctor	doctor, a	dottore, -essa	doutor, a
Asche(f)	cendre(s)	ash(es)	ceniza(s)	cenere(-ri)	cinza
Aschenbecher(m)	cendrier	ash-tray	cenicero	portacenere	cinzeiro
Asphalt(m)	bitume	asphalt, tarmac	asfalto	bitume	asfalto
Aspirin(n)	aspirine	aspirin	aspirina	aspirina	aspirina
Assistent(in f)m	assistant, e	assistant	asistente, a	assistente	assistente
assistieren	assister	attend	asistir	assistere	assistir
Assortiment(n)	lot	batch, assortment	lote	assortimento	lote
Ast(m)	branche	branch	rama	ramo	ramo
ästhetisch	esthétique	aesthetic	estético, a	estetico, a	estético, a
Asthma(n)	asthme	asthma	asma	asma	asma
Astrologie(f)	astrologie	astrology	astrología	astrologia	astrologia
Astronaut(m)	cosmonaute	astronaut	cosmonauta	cosmonauta	cosmonauta
Astronomie(f)	astronomie	astronomy	astronomía	astronomia	astronomia
Asyl(n)	asile	asylum(political)	asilo	asilo	asilo
Atem(m)	haleine	breath	aliento	alito	hálito
Atempause(f)	répit	respite	tregua, respiro	tregua, riposo	trégua, espera
Athlet(in f)m	athlète	athlete	atleta	atleta	atleta
Atlantik(m)	Atlantique	Atlantic	Atlántico	Atlantico	Atlântico
atmen	respirer	breathe	respirar	respirare	respirar
Atmosphäre(f)	atmosphère	atmosphere	atmósfera	atmosfera	atmosfera
Atmung(f)	respiration	breathing	respiración	respirazione	respiração
Atoll(n)	atoll	atoll	atolón	atollo	atol
Atom(n)	atome	atom	átomo	atomo	átomo
atomar	atomique	atomic	atómico, a	atomico, a	atómico, a
Attaché(m)	attaché, e	attaché	agregado, a	addetto	adido, a
Attentat(n)	attentat	attempt, attack	atentado	attentato	atentado
auch	aussi	also, too; as	también	anche, pure	também
Audienz(f)	audience	audience	audiencia	udienza	audiência
auf	sur	on	en, encima, sobre	sopra, su	em cima de; sobre
auf = blasen	gonfler	inflate, blow up	inflar	gonfiare	inchar, encher
auf = decken, entdecken	déceler	discover; reveal	descubrir	svelare, scoprire	descobrir
auf = decken	révéler	reveal	revelar	rivelare	revelar

German	French	English	Spanish	Italian	Portuguese
auf = drängen, sich	imposer(s')	impose oneself on	imponerse	imporsi	impor-se
aufeinanderfolgend	successif, ive	successive	sucesivo, a	successivo, a	sucessivo, a
aufeinander = legen	superposer	superpose	sobreponer	sovrapporre	sobrepor
Aufenthalt(m)	séjour	stay	estancia	soggiorno	estadia, estada
auf = erlegen	infliger	inflict	infligir	infliggere	infligir
auf = falten	déplier	unfold	desdoblar	spiegare, aprire	desdobrar
auf = fangen, ab = fangen	intercepter	intercept	interceptar	intercettare	interceptar
Aufführung(f)	spectacle	show	espectáculo	spettacolo	espectáculo
Aufgabe(f)	devoir	homework; exercise	deber, tarea	compito	dever
Aufgabe(f)	tâche	task	tarea	compito	tarefa
auf = geben	enregistrer	register, check in	registrar	registrare	registar
auf = geben	renoncer	give up	renunciar	rinunciare	desistir; renunciar
auf = geben; nach = geben	céder, renoncer	give up	ceder	cedere	ceder
auf = gehen	lever(se)	rise	amanecer	sorgere	nascer
auf = hängen	suspendre	hang up	colgar, suspender	appendere	pendurar
auf = hängen	accrocher	hang	colgar	appendere	pendurar
auf = heben	ramasser	pick up	recoger	raccogliere	apanhar, recolher
auf = heben	annuler	quash	anular	annullare	anular
auf = hören	cesser	stop, cease	cesar, parar	cessare, smettere	cessar, parar
Auflage(f), Ausgabe(f)	édition	edition	edición	edizione	edição
Auflage(f)	numéro, tirage	issue	número, edición	numero, pubblicazione	número
auf = lehnen gegen, sich	insurger(s')	rise up, revolt	sublevarse	insorgere	insurgir-se
auf = lösen	dissoudre	dissolve	disolver	sciogliere	dissolver
auf = lösen	désintégrer	disintegrate	desintegrar	disintegrare	desintegrar
auf = machen	dégrafer	undo, unfasten	desabrochar	slacciare	desapertar
aufmerksam	attentif, ive	attentive, careful	atento, a	attento, a	atento, a
Aufmerksamkeit(f)	attention(à l')	attention	atención a(en)	attenzione	cuidado(ao)
Aufmerksamkeit(f)	délicatesse	delicacy	delicadeza	delicatezza	delicadeza
Aufnahme(f)	enregistrement	recording	grabación	registrazione	gravação
auf = nehmen	enregistrer	record	grabar	registrare	gravar
auf = räumen	ranger	tidy up	ordenar	ordinare	ordenar
auf = regen	exciter	excite	excitar	eccitare	excitar
auf = regen, sich	énerver(s')	edgy, irritable(be)	ponerse nervioso, a	innervosirsi	enervar-se
aufregend	excitant, e	exciting	excitante	eccitante	excitante
Aufregung(f); Unruhe f	agitation	agitation; unrest	agitación	agitazione	agitação
auf = richten, errichten	dresser	erect, put up	erigir	drizzare	erigir, erguer
aufrichtig	sincère	sincere, candid	sincero, a	sincero, a	sincero, a
Aufruhr(m)	émeute	riot	motín	sommossa	motim
auf = schieben	différer	postpone	diferir, demorar	differire, rimandare	diferir, adiar
auf = schlitzen	fendre	slit	rajar, hender	fendere	rachar, fender
Aufschwung(m)	essor	expansion, boom	auge, desarrollo	sviluppo	progresso
Aufseher m, Supervisor	surveillant, e	supervisor	vigilante	sorvegliante	vigia
aufs Geratewohl	hasard(au)	random(at)	azar(al)	casaccio(a)	acaso(ao)
Aufsicht(f), Prüfung f	contrôle	control, check	control	controllo	controlo
Aufspüren(n)	détection	detection	detección	rivelazione	detecção
Aufstand(m)	rébellion	rebellion	rebelión	ribellione	rebelião
auf = stehen	lever(se)	stand up, get up	levantarse	alzarsi	levantar-se
auf = stellen	disposer	arrange	disponer	disporre	dispor
Aufstellung(f)machen	relevé	statement	extracto	estratto	levantamento
auf = stoßen, rülpsen	roter	burp	eructar	ruttare	arrotar
auf = tauchen	émerger	emerge	emerger	emergere	emergir
Auftauen(n)	dégel	thaw	deshielo	disgelo	degelo
auf = tauen	décongeler	thaw	descongelar	scongelare	descongelar
auf = teilen	répartir	share out	repartir	ripartire	repartir
auf = wachen	éveiller(s')	wake up	despertar(se)	svegliarsi	despertar
Aufwärmen(n)	échauffement	heating	calentamiento	riscaldamento	aquecimento
auf = wärmen	réchauffer	warm, (re)heat	recalentar	riscaldare	aquecer
auf = wickeln	enrouler	roll up	enrollar	arrotolare	enrolar
auf Wiedersehen	au revoir	good bye, bye-bye	hasta luego	arrivederci	até logo, adeus!
auf = zählen	énumérer	enumerate	enumerar	enumerare	enumerar
Aufzug(m)	ascenseur	lift, elevator	ascensor	ascensore	elevador
auf = zwingen	imposer	impose	imponer	imporre	impor
Auge(n)	oeil	eye	ojo	occhio	olho
Augen(n, pl)	yeux	eyes	ojos	occhi	olhos
Augenarzt(m)(-ärztin)	oculiste	oculist	oculista	oculista	oftalmologista
Augenblick(m)	moment	moment	momento	momento, attimo	momento
Augenbraue(f)	sourcil	eyebrow	ceja	sopracciglio(a)	sobrolho
Augenheilkunde(f)	ophtalmologie	ophthalmology	oftalmología	oftalmologia	oftalmologia

German	French	English	Spanish	Italian	Portuguese
Augenringe(pl)	cerne	ring, circle	ojeras	occhiaia	olheiras
August(m)	août	August	agosto	agosto	Agosto
Auktion(f); Gebot(n)	enchère	bid, bidding	subasta	asta	leilão
aus; von	de	from	de, desde	da	de
aus = arbeiten	élaborer	elaborate	elaborar	elaborare	elaborar
aus = atmen	expirer	breathe out	espirar	espirare	expirar
aus = bilden	instruire	teach	instruir	istruire	instruir
Ausbilder(m)	instructeur	instructor	instructor	istruttore, trice	instructor, a
Ausbildung(f)	formation	training	formación	formazione	formação
Ausbildung(f)	instruction	instruction	instrucción	istruzione	instrução
Ausblick(m)	vue	view	vista	veduta	vista
aus = breiten	étendre	extend, spread	extender	stendere	estender
aus = breiten	étaler	spread(out)	exponer	stendere, spalmare	expor
Ausbruch(m)	éruption	eruption	erupción	eruzione	erupção
Ausdauer(f)	endurance	endurance	resistencia	resistenza	resistência
Ausdauer(f)	persévérance	perseverance	perseverancia	perseveranza	perseverança
aus = dehnen	étendre, agrandir	expand	extender(se)	estendere	estender
aus = dehnen	étirer	stretch	estirar	stirare	esticar
Ausdehnung(f)	extension	extension	extensión	estensione	extensão
Ausdehnung(f)	expansion	expansion	expansión	espansione	expansão
Ausdehnung(f)	dilatation	expansion	dilatación	dilatazione	dilatação
Ausdruck(m)	expression	expression	expresión	espressione	expressão
Ausdruck(m)	terme	term	término	parola	termo
aus = drücken, sich	exprimer(s')	express oneself	expresar(se)	esprimersi	exprimir-se
Ausflug(m)	excursion	excursion	excursión	gita, escursione	excursão
aus = führen	effectuer	carry out, perform	efectuar	effettuare	efectuar
aus = führen	exécuter	perform, carry out	ejecutar	eseguire	executar
aus = führen, vollenden	accomplir	perform, accomplish	cumplir, realizar	compiere	realizar
Ausgabe(f)	dépense	expenditure	gasto	spesa	despesa, gasto
Ausgang(m)	sortie	exit, way out	salida	uscita	saída
Ausgang(m)	issue(sortie)	way out, exit	salida	uscita	saída
aus = geben	dépenser	spend	gastar	spendere	gastar
aus = geben	débourser	spend	desembolsar	sborsare	desembolsar
aus = gehen	sortir	go out, come out	salir	uscire	sair
aus = gießen	verser	pour	verter	versare	verter
aus = gießen	déverser	pour out, tip	verter	riversare, scaricare	despejar
aus = gleichen	équilibrer	balance	equilibrar	equilibrare	equilibrar
aus = graben	déterrer	dig up	desenterrar	dissotterrare	desenterrar
aus = graben	fouiller	excavate	excavar	scavare	escavar
aus = halten, ertragen	endurer	endure, bear	aguantar, pasar	patire, resistere	aguentar
Auskunft(f)	renseignement	information	información	informazione	informação
aus = laden	débarquer	unload	descargar	sbarcare	descarregar
Ausladen(n)	déchargement	unloading	descarga	scarico	descarga
Ausland(n)	étranger(l')	foreign country	extranjero	estero	estrangeiro
Ausland(im)	étranger(à l')	abroad	extranjero(en el)	estero(all')	estrangeiro(ao)
Ausländer(in f)m	étranger, ère	foreigner	extranjero, a	straniero, a	estrangeiro, a
ausländisch	étranger, ère	foreign	extranjero, a	estero, a	estrangeiro, a
aus = lassen	omettre	omit	omitir	omettere	omitir
Auslese(f); Auswahl(f)	sélection	selection	selección	selezione	selecção
aus = lesen	sélectionner	select	seleccionar	selezionare	seleccionar
aus = lösen	déclencher	trigger off	iniciar	scattare, attivare	desencadear
aus = machen, abschalten	débrancher	disconnect, unplug	desenchufar	disinserire	desligar
Ausnahme(f)	exception	exception	excepción	eccezione	excepção
aus = nutzen	exploiter	exploit	explotar	sfruttare	explorar
aus = pfeifen	huer	boo	abuchear	fischiare, urlare	vaiar
aus = plaudern	divulguer	divulge, reveal	divulgar	divulgare	divulgar
aus = rauben	dévaliser	rob, burgle	desvalijar	svaligiare	roubar
Ausrichtung(f)	alignement	alignment	alineación	allineamento	alinhamento
aus = rufen	exclamer(s')	exclaim	exclamar	esclamare	exclamar
aus = ruhen, sich	reposer(se)	rest	descansar	riposarsi	descançar
aus = rüsten	équiper	equip, fit out	equipar	equipaggiare	equipar
Aussage(f)	déposition	statement	deposición	deposizione	deposição
aus = sagen	témoigner	testify	testimoniar	testimoniare	testemunhar
aus = schalten	éteindre	turn/switch off	apagar	spegnere	apagar
aus = scheiden	éliminer	eliminate	eliminar	eliminare	eliminar
Ausscheidung(f)	sécrétion	secretion	secreción	secrezione	secreção
Ausscheidung(f)	excrément	excrement	excremento	escremento	excremento
aus = schließen	exclure	exclude	excluir	escludere	excluir

German	French	English	Spanish	Italian	Portuguese
ausschließlich	uniquement	only	únicamente	unicamente	somente
ausschließlich	exclusif, ive	exclusive	exclusivo, a	esclusivo, a	exclusivo, a
aus = schlüpfen	éclore	hatch	abrirse	schiudere, uscire	abrir-se
Ausschuß(m)	commission	committee	comisión	commissione	comissão
Aussehen(n)	apparence	appearance, look	apariencia	apparenza	aparência
Aussehen(n)	aspect	aspect	aspecto	aspetto	aspecto
Aussehen(n)	mine	look	semblante, cara	cera, aspetto	aparência
Außen-	extérieur, e	foreign	exterior	estero, a	exterior
Außenbordmotor(m)	hors-bord	speed-boat	fuera borda	fuoribordo	fora de borda
Außenseite(f)	extérieur	outside; exterior	exterior	esterno	exterior
Außenseiter(in f)m	marginal, e	fringe(on the)	marginal	marginale	marginal
außer	excepté	except	excepto, salvo	tranne	excepto
außer	sauf	except	excepto	salvo	salvo, excepto
außer(+dat)	hors de	out of	fuera de	fuori, fuori di	fora de
äußer; Außen-	extérieur, e	outside	exterior	esteriore	exterior
außerdem; außer	de plus, en outre	besides	además(de)	inoltre; per di più	além disso; além de
äußere	extérieur, e	outer, outside	externo, a	esterno, a	exterior; externo, a
Äußere(n), Aussehen(n)	physique	physique	físico	fisico	físico
außergewöhnlich	exceptionnel, le	exceptional	excepcional	eccezionale	excepcional
außergewöhnlich	extraordinaire	extraordinary	extraordinario, a	straordinario, a	extraordinário, a
äußerlich	externe	external	externo, a	esterno, a	externo, a
aussetzend	intermittent, e	intermittent	intermitente	intermittente	intermitente
Aussicht(f)	perspective	prospect	perspectiva	prospettiva	perspectiva
Aussichtspunkt(m)	point de vue	viewpoint	punto de vista	punto di vista	ponto de vista
aus = sprechen	prononcer	pronounce	pronunciar	pronunziare	pronunciar
Ausstattung(f)	équipement	equipment	equipo	equipaggiamento	equipamento
aus = steigen	descendre	get out of, get off	bajarse	scendere	descer
Aussteller(in f)m	exposant, e	exhibitor	expositor, a	espositore, trice	expositor, a
Ausstellung(f)	exposition	exhibition, show	exposición	esposizione, mostra	exposição
aus = stoßen	éjecter	eject	eyectar, expulsar	espellere	expelir
aus = strahlen	émettre	emit	emitir	emettere	emitir
Auster(f)	huître	oyster	ostra	ostrica	ostra
aus = trocknen	déshydrater	dehydrate	deshidratar	disidratare	desidratar
aus = üben	exercer	exercise, practise	ejercitar	esercitare	exercitar
ausübend, vollziehend	exécutif, ive	executive	ejecutivo, a	esecutivo, a	executivo, a
Ausverkauf(m)	soldes	sales	saldos, rebajas	saldi	saldos
aus = verkaufen	solder	sell off	saldar	saldare, liquidare	saldar
ausverkauft	épuisé, e	exhausted, run out	agotado, a	esaurito, a	esgotado, a
aus = wählen	choisir	choose, select	escoger	scegliere	escolher
aus = wandern	émigrer	emigrate	emigrar	emigrare	emigrar
aus = wandern	expatrier(s')	expatriate	expatriarse	espatriare	expatriar-se
Auswanderung(f)	émigration	emigration	emigración	emigrazione	emigração
auswechselbar	amovible	removable	amovible	amovibile	amovível
Ausweis(m)	laissez-passer	pass	salvoconducto	lascia-passare	salvo-conduto
aus = weisen	expulser	expel, eject	expulsar	espellere	expulsar
aus = zeichnen	décorer	decorate	condecorar	decorare	condecorar
aus = ziehen	enlever	take off	quitar	togliere	tirar
aus = ziehen, sich	déshabiller(se)	undress	desnudar(se)	svestire(-irsi)	despir-se
Auszug(m)	extrait	extract	pasaje, trozo	brano, estratto	excerto, trecho
authentisch	authentique	authentic, genuine	auténtico, a	autentico, a	autêntico, a
Auto(n)	automobile	car	automóvil	automobile	automóvel
Autobahn(f)	autoroute	motorway	autopista	autostrada	auto-estrada
Autobahngebühr(f)	péage	toll	peaje	pedaggio	portagem
Autogramm(n)	autographe	autograph	autógrafo	autografo	autógrafo
Automat(m)	automate	automaton	autómata	automa	autómato
automatisch	automatique	automatic	automático, a	automatico, a	automático, a
autonom; unabhängig	autonome	autonomous	autónomo, a	autonomo, a	autónomo, a
Autonomie(f)	autonomie	autonomy	autonomía	autonomia	autonomia
Autopsie(f)	autopsie	autopsy	autopsia	autopsia	autópsia
Autor(in f)m	auteur	author	autor, a	autore, autrice	autor, a
autoritär	autoritaire	authoritarian	autoritario, a	autoritario, a	autoritário, a
Autorität(f)	autorité	authority	autoridad	autorità	autoridade
Autoschlosser(m)	garagiste	garage mechanic	garajista	garagista	garagista
Axt(f)	hache	axe	hacha	ascia	machado

B

German	French	English	Spanish	Italian	Portuguese
Baby(n)	bébé	baby	bebé	bebè, bambino, a	bebé
Bach(m)	ruisseau	stream, brook	riachuelo, arroyo	ruscello	regato, ribeiro
Backenzahn(m)	molaire	molar	molar	molare	molar
Bäckerei(f)	boulangerie	baker's(shop)	panadería	panificio	padaria
Backwaren(f, pl)	pâtisserie(s)	pastry, cake	pasteles	dolci	pastelaria
Bad(n)	bain	bath	baño	bagno	banho
Badeanzug(m)	maillot de bain	swimsuit; trunks	traje de baño	costume da bagno	fato de banho
Bademeister(in f)m	maître-nageur	life-guard	maestro(natación)	bagnino	nadador-salvador
Baden(n)	baignade	swimming, bathing	baño	bagno	banho
baden; schwimmen	baigner(se)	bathe; swim	bañarse	bagno(fare il)	banho(tomar)
Badewanne(f)	baignoire	bath	bañera	vasca da bagno	banheira
Badezimmer(n)	salle de bains	bathroom	cuarto de baño	bagno	quarto de banho
Bahn(Lande-, Start-)	piste	runway	pista	pista	pista
Bahn(f), Kurs(m)	trajectoire	trajectory	trayectoria	traiettoria	trajectória
Bahnhof(m)	gare	station	estación	stazione	estação, gare
Bahnsteig(m)	quai	platform	andén	binario, marciapiede	plataforma
Bahre(f)	civière	stretcher	camilla	barella	maca
Bakterie(f)	bactérie	bacterium(-eria)	bacteria	batterio	bactéria
bald	bientôt	soon	pronto	presto	logo, brevemente
Balken(m)	poutre	beam	viga	trave	trave
Balkon(m)	balcon	balcony	balcón	balcone	varanda
Ball(m)	balle	ball	pelota	palla	bola
Ball(m)(Fußball m)	ballon	ball	balón	pallone	bola
Ball(m)(Schneeball)	boule	ball	bola	palla	bola
Ball(m)	bal	dance, ball	baile	ballo	baile
Ballett(n)	ballet	ballet	ballet	balletto	ballet, bailado
banal	banal, e	banal	común	banale	banal
Banane(f)	banane	banana	plátano, banana	banana	banana
Band(n)	ruban	ribbon; tape; band	cinta, banda	nastro	fita
Band(n)	bande	tape	cinta	nastro	fita
Bandage(f), Verband(m)	bandage	bandage	vendaje, venda	fasciatura	ligadura
Bande(f)	bande	gang	pandilla	banda	quadrilha
Bandit(m)	bandit	bandit	bandido	bandito	bandido
Bank(f)	banc	bench	banco	panca; panchina	banco
Bank(f)	banque	bank	banco, banca	banca	banco
Bank-	bancaire	bank, banking	bancario, a	bancario, a	bancário, a
Bankett(n)	banquet	banquet	banquete	banchetto	banquete
Bankier(m)	banquier	banker	banquero	banchiere	banqueiro
bankrott sein	faillite(faire)	bankrupt(go)	quiebra(hacer)	fallire	falir
Bär(m)	ours	bear	oso	orso	urso
barbarisch	barbare	barbaric	bárbaro, a	barbaro, a	bárbaro, a
Barke(f), Kahn(m)	barque	boat(small)	barca	barca	barca
Barometer(n)	baromètre	barometer	barómetro	barometro	barómetro
Baron(in, f)m	baron, ne	baron, baroness	barón, baronesa	barone, baronessa	barão, baronesa
Barren(m)	lingot	ingot, bullion	lingote	lingotto	lingote
Barrikade(f)	barricade	barricade	barricada	barricata	barricada
Bart(m)	barbe	beard	barba	barba	barba
Barzahlung(f)	comptant	cash	contado(al)	contanti	pronto(a)
Basketball(m)	basket-ball	basket-ball	baloncesto	pallacanestro	basquetebol
Bassin(n), Teich(m)	bassin	pond	estanque	bacino	lago
Basteln(n)	bricolage	odd-jobs	bricolaje, maña	bricolage	bricolage
Batterie(f)	batterie	battery	batería	batteria	bateria
Batterie(f)	pile	battery	pila	pila	pilha
Bau(m)	construction	construction	construcción	costruzione	construção
Bauch(m)	ventre	stomach, abdomen	barriga, vientre	pancia, ventre	barriga
Bauch(m); Pansen(m)	panse	belly, paunch	panza	pancia	pança
bauen	bâtir	build	edificar	costruire	construir
bauen	construire	construct, build	construir	costruire	construir
Bauer(m), Bäuerin(f)	paysan, ne	farmer	campesino, a	contadino, a	camponês, a
Bauer(m), Bäuerin(f)	fermier, ière	farmer	granjero, a	contadino, a	caseiro, a
Bauer(m)(Schach)	pion(échecs)	pawn(chess)	peón(ajedrez)	pedone(scacchi)	peão(xadrez)

G

267

German	French	English	Spanish	Italian	Portuguese
Bauernhof(m)	ferme	farm	granja	fattoria	quinta
Baum(m)	arbre	tree	árbol	albero	árvore
Baumwolle(f)	coton	cotton	algodón	cotone	algodão
Baustelle(f)	chantier	work-site	obra	cantiere	obra
beabsichtigen	envisager	envisage	enfocar	prevedere	encarar
beabsichtigen	intention(avoir)	intend	intención(tener)	intenzione(avere)	tencionar
Beamter(m), Beamtin(f)	fonctionnaire	state employee	funcionario, a	impiegato statale	funcionário, a
Beamte(r)m, Beamtin(f)	fonctionnaire	civil servant	funcionario, a	funzionario, a	funcionário, a
beanspruchen	revendiquer	claim	reivindicar	rivendicare	reivindicar
beauftragen	déléguer	delegate	delegar	delegare	delegar
bebauen, züchten	cultiver	cultivate	cultivar	coltivare	cultivar
bedächtig	réfléchi, e	thoughtful	reflexivo, a	riflessivo, a	ponderado, a
bedauern	regretter	sorry(be), regret	sentir(lo)	dispiacere(-ersi)	sentir, lamentar
bedauern	plaindre	pity	compadecer	compatire	lastimar
bedauern	désolé, e	regret(I)	siento(lo)	rammaricato, a	lamento(eu)
Bedauern(n)	regret	regret	lamento(lo)	rimpianto	pena; pesar
bedeuten	signifier	mean, signify	significar	significare	significar
bedeuten; an = deuten	impliquer	imply	implicar	implicare	implicar
Bedeutung(f)	signification	meaning	significación	significato	significação
Bedeutung(f)	sens	meaning, sense	sentido	senso	sentido
Bedeutung(f)	importance	importance	importancia	importanza	importância
bedienen	marcher(faire)	operate	funcionar(hacer)	funzionare(fare)	funcionar(fazer)
Bedienung(f)	service	service	servicio	servizio	serviço
Bedingung(f)	condition	condition	condición	condizione	condição
bedrohen	menacer	threaten	amenazar	minacciare	ameaçar
Bedürfnis(n)	besoin	need	necesidad	bisogno	necessidade
Beefsteak(n)	bifteck	steak	bistec	bistecca	bife
beeilen, sich	dépêcher(se)	hurry(up)	darse prisa	sbrigarsi	despachar-se
beeindrucken	impressionner	impress	impresionar	impressionare	impressionar
beeindruckend	impressionnant, e	impressive	impresionante	impressionante	impressionante
beenden	terminer	end, finish	terminar	terminare	terminar
beenden	finir	finish, end	acabar, terminar	finire	acabar, terminar
beenden	achever	complete, finish	acabar	terminare, finire	acabar
Beerdigung(f)	enterrement	burial, funeral	entierro	funerale	enterro
Beet(n)	parterre	flower-bed	arriate	aiuola	canteiro
Befehl(m)	ordre	order	orden	ordine	ordem
Befehl(m)(-sgewalt f)	commandement	command	mando	comando	comando
befehlen, verordnen	ordonner	order	ordenar	ordinare	ordenar
befehlen, befehligen	commander	command	ordenar, mandar	comandare	comandar
befehlen, beherrschen	ordonner	command, order	mandar, ordenar	comandare, ordinare	mandar, ordenar
befestigen	fixer	fix, attach	fijar	fissare	fixar
befestigen	attacher	fasten	atar, fijar	attaccare, legare	atar, amarrar
Befestigung(f)	fixation	fixing, fixation	fijación	fissazione	fixação
beflecken, beschmutzen	tacher	stain, dirty	manchar	macchiare	manchar, sujar
befördern	promouvoir	promote	promover	promuovere	promover
Beförderung(f)	promotion	promotion	promoción	promozione	promoção
befragen	consulter	consult	consultar	consultare	consultar
befreien	libérer	liberate, free	liberar	liberare	libertar
befreien	délivrer	free	libertar	rilasciare, liberare	libertar
Befruchtung(f)	fécondation	fertilization	fecundación	fecondazione	fecundação
Befruchtung(f)	insémination	insemination	inseminación	inseminazione	inseminação
befürchten, fürchten	craindre	fear, be afraid of	temer, tener miedo	temere	temer
begabt	doué, e	gifted, talented	dotado, a	dotato, a	dotado, a; capaz
Begegnung(f)	rencontre	meeting	encuentro	incontro	encontro
begehen, verüben	commettre	commit	cometer	commettere	cometer
begehren	convoiter	covet	codiciar	ambire, desiderare	cobiçar
Begeisterung(f)	enthousiasme	enthusiasm	entusiasmo	entusiasmo	entusiasmo
begierig	avide, impatient	eager	deseoso, a	desideroso, a	ávido, a; desejoso, a
Begleichung(f)	règlement	settlement	liquidación	saldo	pagamento
begleiten	accompagner	accompany	acompañar	accompagnare	acompanhar
Begleiter(in f)m	compagnon, agne	companion	compañero, a	compagno, a	companheiro, a
Begräbnis(n)	funérailles	funeral	funerales	funerale	funeral
begreifen, verstehen	comprendre	understand	entender	comprendere	entender
begreifen	réaliser	realize	darse cuenta	realizzare	aperceber-se
begrenzen	limiter	limit	limitar	limitare	limitar
Begriff(m)	concept	concept	concepto	concetto	conceito
begründen, belegen	justifier	justify	justificar	giustificare	justificar
begrüßen	saluer	greet; say hello	saludar	salutare	saudar

German	French	English	Spanish	Italian	Portuguese
begünstigen	favoriser	favour	favorecer	favorire	favorecer
behaart	poilu, e	hairy	peludo, a	peloso, a	peludo, a
behalten	garder	keep	guardar	tenere	guardar
Behälter(m)	récipient	container	recipiente	recipiente	recipiente
behandeln	traiter	treat; deal with	tratar	trattare	tratar
behandeln	soigner	treat	tratar, curar	curare	tratar, cuidar
Behandlung(f)	traitement	treatment	tratamiento	trattamento	tratamento
beharren, aus = halten	persévérer	persevere	perseverar	perseverare	perseverar
beharren	acharner(s')	persist	empeñarse	accanirsi	insistir
Beharrlichkeit(f)	persistance	persistence	persistencia	persistenza	persistência
behaupten	affirmer	assert, maintain	afirmar	affermare	afirmar
beherrschen	dominer	dominate, rule	dominar	dominare	dominar
beherrschen	maîtriser	control, master	dominar	dominare	dominar
behindert	handicapé, e	handicapped	minusválido, a	andicappato, a	deficiente
behindert	infirme	disabled	inválido, a	infermo, a	doente
behindert	invalide	disabled	inválido, a	invalido, a	inválido, a
bei	auprès de	close to	cerca de	vicino a	perto de
bei	chez	at, to	en casa de	da	em casa de
beide, beides	à la fois	both	ambos, ambas	entrambi	ambos, os dois
beige	beige	beige	crema, beis	beige	bege
Beihilfe(f), Zulage(f)	allocation	allowance	subsidio	assegnazione; assegno	subsídio, abono
bei = messen	attribuer	attribute	atribuir	attribuire	atribuir
Bein(n)	jambe	leg	pierna	gamba	perna
Beispiel(n)	exemple	example	ejemplo	esempio	exemplo
Beispiel(zum)	exemple(par)	instance(for)	ejemplo(por)	esempio(per)	exemplo(por)
beißen	mordre	bite	morder	mordere	morder
Beitrag(m)	cotisation	contribution	cotización	contributo	contribuição
Beitrag m(Mitglieds-)	cotisation	subscription, dues	cuota	quota	quota
bei = tragen	contribuer	contribute	contribuir	contribuire	contribuir
bei = treten	inscrire(s')	join	inscribirse	iscriversi	inscrever-se
bei = treten	engager(s')	join, enter	ingresar, meterse	impegnarsi	aderir, ligar-se
Beitritt(m)	adhésion	membership	adhésion	adesione	adesão
bei = wohnen	assister	attend	concurrir a	presenziare	assistir a
bekannt = geben	déclarer	declare	declarar	dichiarare	declarar
bekannt = geben	notifier	notify	notificar	notificare	notificar
bekannt = geben	proclamer	proclaim	proclamar	proclamare	proclamar
beklagen	déplorer	deplore	deplorar	deplorare	deplorar
beklagen, sich	plaindre(se)	complain	quejarse	lamentarsi	queixar-se
beklagenswert	déplorable	deplorable	deplorable	deplorevole	deplorável
Bekleidung(f)	habillement	clothing	ropa	abbigliamento	vestuário
bekommen	obtenir, recevoir	get, obtain	obtener	ottenere	obter
Belagerung(f)	siège	siege	sitio	assedio	cerco
beleben	animer	animate	animar	animare	animar
beleidigen	vexer	offend, vex	ofender, picar	offendere	ofender
beleidigen	insulter	insult	insultar	insultare	insultar
beleidigt sein	vexer(se)	get upset	ofenderse	offendersi	ofender-se
Beleidigung(f)	insulte	insult	insulto	insulto	insulto
Beleidigung(f)	injure	insult	injuria	ingiuria	injúria
beleuchten	éclairer	light; illuminate	iluminar	illuminare	iluminar
Beleuchtung(f)	éclairage	lighting	iluminación	illuminazione	iluminação
beliebig	quelconque	any, whatever	cualquier(a)	qualunque	qualquer
beliefern	fournir	supply, provide	proveer, dar	fornire	fornecer
bellen	aboyer	bark	ladrar	abbaiare	ladrar
Belohnung(f)	récompense	reward; award	recompensa	ricompensa	recompensa
Belüftung(f)	ventilation	ventilation	ventilación	ventilazione	ventilação
bemerken	apercevoir	perceive, notice	avistar, divisar	scorgere	avistar
bemerken	remarquer	notice	notar, señalar	notare, osservare	notar, reparar
bemerkenswert	remarquable	remarkable	notable	notevole	notável
Bemerkung(f)	remarque	remark, comment	observación	osservazione	observação
benachteiligt	défavorisé, e	underprivileged	desfavorecido, a	svantaggiato, a	desfavorecido, a
benutzen	utiliser	use	utilizar	utilizzare	utilizar
benützen	employer	use	usar, emplear	usare, adoperare	usar
benutzen	servir de(se)	use	servirse	adoperare	servir-se
Benutzer(in f)m	usager, ère	user	usuario, a	utente	utente
Benutzer(in f)m	utilisateur	user	utilizador, a	utilizzatore, trice	utilizador, a
Benutzung(f)	utilisation	utilization, use	utilización	utilizzazione	utilização
Benzin(n)	essence	petrol	gasolina	benzina	gasolina
beobachten	observer	observe	observar	osservare	observar

G

269

German	French	English	Spanish	Italian	Portuguese
Beobachter(in f)m	observateur	observer	observador, a	osservatore, trice	observador, a
bequem	confortable	comfortable	cómodo, a	confortevole	confortável
Bequemlichkeit(f)	confort	comfort	confort	comodità	conforto
beraten	conseiller	advise	aconsejar	consigliare	aconselhar
beraten	délibérer	deliberate	deliberar	deliberare	deliberar
Berater(in f)m	conseiller, ère	adviser	consejero, a	consigliere, a	conselheiro, a
berauben, entziehen	priver	deprive	privar	privare	privar
Berechnung(f)	calcul	calculation	cálculo	calcolo	cálculo
Bereich(m), Gebiet(n)	aire, zone	area	área, zona	area, zona	área, zona
Bereich(m)	domaine	field, scope	campo, área	campo, settore	domínio
Bereich(m)	secteur	sector	sector	settore	sector
bereichern	enrichir	enrich	enriquecer	arricchire	enriquecer
Berg(m)	mont, montagne	mount	monte	monte	monte
Bergkette(f)	chaîne(montagne)	range(mountain)	sierra	catena(monti)	serra
Bergung(f)	sauvetage	salvage	salvamento	salvataggio	salvamento
Bergwerk(n)	mine	mine	mina	miniera	mina
Bericht(m)	rapport	report	informe	rapporto, relazione	relatório
Bericht(m)	compte rendu	report, minutes	informe, acta	resoconto	relatório, acta
Bericht(m)	récit	story	narración	racconto	narração
Bericht(m)	bulletin	bulletin, report	boletín	bollettino, bolletta	boletim
berichtigen	corriger	rectify, correct	corregir	correggere	rectificar
berichtigen	rectifier	rectify	rectificar	rettificare	rectificar
bersten	crever, éclater	burst	estallar, reventar	scoppiare	furar, rebentar
Beruf(m)	profession	profession	profesión	professione	profissão
Beruf(m)	métier	profession, job	oficio	mestiere	ofício
Beruf(m)	emploi	job, work	empleo	impiego	emprego
Berufung(f)	appel	appeal	apelación	appello	apelação
Berufung(f)	vocation	vocation	vocación	vocazione	vocação
Berufung(f)ein = legen	recourir à	appeal to	recurrir, apelar	ricorrere, appellarsi	recorrer, apelar
beruhigen	calmer	calm	calmar	calmare	acalmar
beruhigen	apaiser	calm, soothe	apaciguar	calmare	acalmar
beruhigen	rassurer	reassure	tranquilizar	rassicurare	tranquilizar
Beruhigungsmittel(n)	calmant	sedative	calmante	calmante	calmante
Beruhigungsmittel(n)	tranquillisant	tranquillizer	tranquilizante	tranquillante	tranquilizante
berühmt	célèbre	famous, well-known	célèbre, famoso, a	celebre; famoso, a	célebre
berühmt	illustre	illustrious	ilustre	illustre	ilustre
berühren	tâter	feel, touch	tantear	tastare	tatear, apalpar
berührend	tangent, e	tangent	tangente	tangente	tangente
Besatzung(f)	équipage	crew	tripulación	equipaggio	equipagem
beschädigen	abîmer	damage, spoil, ruin	estropear	sciupare, rovinare	estragar
beschädigen	endommager	damage	dañar	danneggiare	estragar
Beschädigung(f)	dégradation	degradation	degradación	degradazione	degradação
beschäftigen, sich	occuper(s')	deal with	dedicarse a	occuparsi	tratar de
beschäftigt	occupé, e	busy	ocupado, a	impegnato, a	ocupado, a
beschämend	honteux, se	shameful	vergonzoso, a	vergognoso, a	vergonhoso, a
bescheiden	modeste	modest	modesto, a	modesto, a	modesto, a
bescheinigen	certifier	certify	certificar	certificare	certificar
Bescheinigung(f)	certificat	certificate	certificado	certificato	certificado
Beschilderung(f)	signalisation	sign	señalización	segnalazione	sinalização
beschleunigen	accélérer	accelerate	acelerar	accelerare	acelerar
beschleunigen	activer	activate	activar	attivare	activar
beschränken	restreindre	restrict	restringir	restringere	restringir
beschreiben	décrire	describe	describir	descrivere	descrever
Beschreibung(f)	description	description	descripción	descrizione	descrição
beschuldigen	inculper	charge, accuse	inculpar, acusar	incolpare, accusare	inculpar, acusar
beschuldigen	incriminer	incriminate	incriminar	incriminare	incriminar
beschützen	protéger	protect	proteger	proteggere	proteger
Beschwerde(f)	réclamation	complaint, claim	reclamación	reclamo	reclamação
beseitigen	supprimer	delete	suprimir	sopprimere	suprimir
beseitigen	débarrasser(se)	get rid of	quitarse	liberarsi	livrar-se
Beseitigung(f)	élimination	elimination	eliminación	eliminazione	eliminação
Besen(m)	balai	brush, broom	escoba	scopa	vassoura
Besessene(r)mf	obsédé, e	maniac	obseso, a	maniaco, a	obcecado, a
besetzt	occupé, e	occupied	ocupado, a	occupato, a	ocupado, a
besetzt	occupé, e	engaged; taken	ocupado, a	occupato, a	ocupado, a
besichtigen, reisen	visiter	visit	visitar	visitare	visitar
besichtigen	contrôler	inspect	controlar, examinar	esaminare	examinar
besiegen	vaincre	defeat	vencer	vincere	vencer

270

German	French	English	Spanish	Italian	Portuguese
Besitz(m), Güter(pl)	biens	possessions, estate	bienes	beni; averi	bens
besitzen	posséder	own, possess	poseer	possedere	possuír
Besitzer/in; (Haus-)	propriétaire	landlord	dueño, a	proprietario, a	senhorio, a; dono, a
besonders	surtout	above all	sobre todo	soprattutto	sobretudo
besonders	particulièrement	especially	especialmente	particolarmente	especialmente
besonders, nämlich	notamment	particular(in)	particularmente	particolarmente	particularmente
besorgen, sich	procurer(se)	obtain, get	procurarse	procurarsi	arranjar; obter
besorgt	inquiet, ète	worried	inquieto, a	inquieto, a	inquieto, a
besprechen	discuter	discuss	discutir	discutere	discutir
besser(sein)	meilleur, e	better	mejor	migliore	melhor
besser	mieux	better	mejor	meglio	melhor
beständig	constant, e	constant	constante	costante	constante
Bestandteil(m)	composant	component	componente	componente	componente
bestätigen	confirmer	confirm	confirmar	confermare	confirmar
Beste(f, m)	meilleur, e	best	mejor	migliore	melhor
bestehen, beharren	insister	insist	insistir	insistere	insistir
bestehen aus	consister à	consist(in, of)	consisir en	consistere in	consistir em
bestellen	commander	order	pedir, encargar	ordinare	encomendar
Bestellschein(m)	bon	form, slip, voucher	orden, pedido	bolla, buono, bolletta	nota
Bestellung(f)	commande	order	encargo, pedido	ordinazione	encomenda
bestimmen für	destiner	intended to(be)	destinar	destinare	destinar
Bestimmung(f)	règlement	regulation	reglamento	regolamento	regulamento
Bestimmungsort(m)	destination	destination	destinación	destinazione	destino
bestrafen	punir	punish	castigar	punire	castigar
Bestrafung(f)	châtiment	punishment	castigo	castigo	castigo
Bestrafung(f)	peine	sentence	pena, castigo	punizione, castigo	pena
Bestrahlung(f)	irradiation	irradiation	irradiación	irradiazione	irradiação
Bestrahlung(f)	radiation	radiation	radiación	radiazione	radiação
bestreiten	contester	contest	impugnar, objetar	contestare	contestar
Besuch(m)	visite	visit	visita	visita	visita
besuchen	visiter	visit	visitar	andare a trovare	visitar
Besucher(in f)m	visiteur, se	visitor	visitante	visitatore, trice	visitante
betasten	palper, tâter	feel, finger	palpar	palpare	apalpar
betäuben	étourdir	stun, daze	aturdir; atontar	stordire	aturdir; atordoar
betäubend	étourdissant, e	deafening	aturdidor, a	sbalorditivo, a	atroador, a
Betäubungsmittel(n)	narcotique	narcotic	narcótico	narcotico	narcótico
Betäubungsmittel(n)	stupéfiant	narcotic	narcótico	stupefacente	narcótico
beteiligen, sich	participer à	participate in	participar en	partecipare a	participar em
beten	prier	pray	rezar	pregare	rezar, orar
Beton(m)	béton	concrete	hormigón	calcestruzzo	betão
betonen	souligner	emphasize	recalcar, subrayar	accentuare	acentuar
Betonung(f)	accentuation	stress(ing)	acentuación	accentazione	acentuação
betrachten	contempler	contemplate	contemplar	contemplare	contemplar
betrachten	considérer	regard	considerar	considerare	considerar
Betrachtung(f)	considération	consideration	consideración	considerazione	consideração
Betrag(m)	montant	amount	importe	ammontare	montante
betreffen	concerner	concern	concernir	riguardare	dizer respeito a
betreiben, üben	pratiquer	practise	practicar	praticare	praticar
Betrieb(m)	fonctionnement	functioning	funcionamiento	funzionamento	funcionamento
Betriebsführer(m)	chef(entreprise)	manager, head	jefe de empresa	dirigente d'azienda	chefe de empresa
betrübt	désolé, e	sorry	desolado, a	spiacente	desolado, a
betrübt, unglücklich	malheureux, se	unhappy, sorrowful	infeliz, triste	infelice, triste	infeliz, triste
Betrug(m)	fraude	fraud	fraude	frode	fraude
betrügen	tromper	deceive, cheat	enga ñ ar	ingannare	enganar
betrunken	soûl, e; saoul, e	drunk	embriagado, a	ubriaco, a	bêbado, a; ébrio, a
Bett(n)	lit	bed	cama	letto	cama
Bettler(in f)m	mendiant, e	beggar	mendigo, a	mendicante	mendigo, a
Beule(f)	bosse	lump, bump	chichón	bernoccolo, gobba	bossa; alto
Beule(f), Buckel(m)	protubérance	protuberance	protuberancia	protuberanza	protuberância
beunruhigen	préoccuper	worry, preoccupy	preocupar	preoccupare	preocupar
beunruhigen, sich	inquiéter(s')	worry	preocuparse	preoccuparsi	preocupar-se
beunruhigt	tourmenté, e	tormented	atormentado, a	tormentato, a	atormentado, a
beurteilen	juger	judge	juzgar	giudicare	julgar
Beurteilung(f)	appréciation	appreciation	apreciación	giudizio	apreciação
Beute(f)	butin	spoils	botín	bottino	despojo
Beute(f)	proie	prey	presa	preda	presa
Beutel(m), Tütchen(n)	sachet	bag(small), sachet	bolsita	bustina	pacote; carteira
bevölkert	peuplé, e	populated	poblado, a	popolato, a	povoado, a

G

German	French	English	Spanish	Italian	Portuguese
Bevölkerung(f)	population	population	población	popolazione	população
bevorzugen	préférer	prefer	preferir	preferire	preferir
bevorzugt	privilégié, e	privileged	privilegiado, a	privilegiato, a	privilegiado, a
Bewaffnung(f)	armement	armament, weapons	armamento	armamento	armamento
bewässern	irriguer	irrigate	irrigar	irrigare	irrigar
bewegen	bouger	move	moverse	muovere	mexer-se
bewegen, sich	remuer	move	mover	muovere(-rsi)	mexer-se
bewegen, sich	déplacer(se)	move, shift	desplazar(se)	spostare(-arsi)	deslocar-se
beweglich, mobil	mobile	mobile, movable	móvil, movible	mobile	móvel
Beweglichkeit(f)	mobilité	mobility	mobilidad	mobilità	mobilidade
Bewegung(f)	mouvement	movement, motion	movimiento	movimento	movimento
Beweis(m)	preuve	proof, evidence	prueba	prova	prova
Beweis(m)	évidence, preuve	evidence, proof	evidencia, prueba	evidenza, prova	evidência, prova
beweisen	prouver	prove	probar	provare	provar
beweisen	démontrer	demonstrate	demostrar	dimostrare	demonstrar
Bewerbung(f)	candidature	application	candidatura	candidatura	candidatura
Bewerbung(f)	demande(emploi)	application	solicitud	domanda	pedido
bewilligen	accorder	grant	conceder	concedere, accordare	conceder
bewohnen, wohnen	habiter	live(in), inhabit	vivir, habitar	abitare	morar
Bewunderer(in f)m	admirateur, trice	admirer, fan	admirador, a	ammiratore, trice	admirador, a
Bewunderung(f)	admiration	admiration	admiración	ammirazione	admiração
bewußt	conscient, e	conscious	consciente	cosciente, conscio, a	consciente
Bewußtsein(n)	conscience	conscience	conciencia	coscienza	consciência
bezahlen	payer	pay	pagar	pagare	pagar
bezahlen	régler	settle	liquidar, pagar	regolare, saldare	pagar
Bezahlung(f)	paiement	payment	pago, abono	pagamento	pagamento
bezeichnen	désigner	indicate	señalar, indicar	indicare	indicar
bezeichnend	significatif, ive	significant	significativo, a	significativo, a	significativo, a
beziehen, sich	référer(se)	refer to	referirse	riferirsi	referir-se
beziehen auf, sich	invoquer	invoke	invocar	invocare	invocar
Beziehung(f)	relation	relation(-ship)	relación	relazione	relação
Beziehung(f)	rapport	ratio, proportion	razón, relación	rapporto	razão
beziehungsweise	respectivement	respectively	respectivamente	rispettivamente	respectivamente
Bezirk(m)	district, région	district	distrito, área	distretto	distrito
Bezirk(m), Bereich(m)	département	department	departamento	dipartimento	departamento
Bezug(m)	housse	cover	funda	fodera	cobertura
Bibel(f)	Bible	Bible	Biblia	Bibbia	Bíblia
Bibliographie(f)	bibliographie	bibliography	bibliografía	bibliografia	bibliografia
Bibliothek(f)	bibliothèque	library	biblioteca	biblioteca	biblioteca
biegen	plier, courber	bend	plegar, doblar	piegare	vergar
biegsam	souple	supple; flexible	flexible	flessibile	maleável
Biegsamkeit(f)	souplesse	suppleness	flexibilidad	flessibilità	flexibilidade
Biene(f)	abeille	bee	abeja	ape	abelha
Bienenstock(m)	ruche	hive	colmena	alveare	colmeia
Bier(n)	bière	beer	cerveza	birra	cerveja
Biest(n), Tier(n)	bête	animal, beast	bestia	bestia	bicho, animal
Bilanz(f)	bilan	balance-sheet	balance	bilancio	balanço
Bild(n)	image	picture	imagen	illustrazione	gravura
Bild(n)	image	image, picture	imagen	immagine	imagem
bilden, formen	former	form	formar	formare	formar
bilden	constituer	constitute	constituir	costituire	constituir
Bildschirm; Leinwand	écran	screen	pantalla	schermo	écran
Billard(n)	billard	billiards	billar	biliardo	bilhar
billig	bon marché	cheap	barato, a	buon prezzo	barato, a
binden, verbinden	lier	tie, bind	ligar, amarrar	legare	ligar
bindend, zwingend	impératif, ive	imperative, urgent	imperativo, a	imperativo, a	imperativo, a
Binnensee(m)	lagune	lagoon	laguna	laguna	laguna
Biologie(f)	biologie	biology	biología	biologia	biologia
Birne(f)	poire	pear	pera	pera	pêra
bis	jusqu'à	until, till	hasta	fino a, sino a	até
bis	jusqu'à	as far as	hasta	fino	até
bis bald	à bientôt	see you soon, bye	hasta pronto	a presto	até breve; até já
Bischof(m)	évêque	bishop	obispo	vescovo	bispo
Bissen(m)	bouchée	mouthful	bocado	boccone	bocado
Bitte(f); Gesuch(n)	demande	request; demand	petición	richiesta	pedido
bitte!	s'il vous plaît!	please!	por favor(!)	per favore!	se faz favor!
bitten	demander	beg	pedir	domandare	pedir
bitten um	réclamer à	ask(for)	reclamar	reclamare	reclamar

German	French	English	Spanish	Italian	Portuguese
bitter; sauer	amer, ère	bitter	amargo, a	amaro, a	amargo, a
Bittschrift(f), Gesuch	pétition	petition	petición	petizione	petição
Biwak(m)	bivouac	bivouac	vivaque	bivacco	acampamento
Bizeps(m)	biceps	biceps	bíceps	bicipite	biceps
Blase(f)	bulle	bubble	burbuja	bolla	bolha
Blase(f)	ampoule	blister	ampolla	bolla, vescica	empola
Blase(f)(Brandblase)	cloque	blister	ampolla	vescica	bolha
Blase(f)	vésicule	gall-bladder	vesícula	cistifellea	vesícula
blasen	souffler	blow	soplar	soffiare	soprar
blaß	pâle	pale	pálido, a	pallido, a	pálido, a
blaß, fahl	livide	livid, pallid	lívido, a	livido, a	lívido, a
Blatt(n)	feuille	sheet	hoja	foglio	folha
Blatt(n)	feuille	leaf(leaves)	hoja	foglia	folha
blau	bleu, e	blue	azul	blu	azul
Blech(n)	tôle	sheet-metal	chapa	lamiera	chapa
Blei(n)	plomb	lead	plomo	piombo	chumbo
bleiben	rester	stay, remain	quedarse	restare	ficar
bleiben	rester	remain	sobrar, quedar	restare, rimanere	sobejar, sobrar
Bleistift(m)	crayon	pencil	lápiz	matita, lapis	lápis
blenden	éblouir	dazzle, glare	deslumbrar	abbagliare	encandear
Blick(m)	regard	look, expression	mirada	sguardo	olhar
Blick(m)	regard	glance	ojeada	occhiata	olhada
blind	aveugle	blind	ciego, a	cieco, a	cego, a
blinken	clignoter	flash	pestañear	lampeggiare	piscar
Blinklicht(n)	clignotant	indicator	intermitente	freccia	pisca
Blitz(m)	éclair	lightning; flash	relámpago	lampo	relâmpago
Blitz(m)	foudre	lightning	rayo	fulmine	raio
Blitz(m)	flash	flash	flash	flash	flash
Block(m)	bloc	block	bloque	blocco	bloco
Block(m)	bloc	pad	bloc	blocco	bloco
Blockade(f)	blocus	blockade	bloqueo	blocco	bloqueio
blockieren	bloquer	block	bloquear	bloccare	bloquear
Blockierung(f), Sperre	blocage	jamming	bloqueo	bloccaggio	bloqueamento
blond	blond, e	fair, blond	rubio(pelo)	biondo, a	louro, a
bloß – stellen(jdn.)	compromettre	compromise	comprometer	compromettere	comprometer
Blues(m), Slow(m)	slow	smooch, slow dance	lento	lento, slow	slow
Blume(f)	fleur	flower	flor	fiore	flor
Blume(f), Bukett(n)	bouquet	bouquet	buqué, aroma, boca	bouquet, aroma	aroma
Blumenhändler(in f)m	fleuriste	florist	florista	fioraio	florista
Blut(n)	sang	blood	sangre	sangue	sangue
Blutandrang(m)	congestion	congestion	congestión	congestione	congestão
Blutarmut(f)	anémie	anaemia	anemia	anemia	anemia
Blutbad(n)	massacre	slaughter	masacre	massacro	massacre
bluten	saigner	bleed	sangrar	sanguinare	sangrar
Blütenblatt(n)	pétale	petal	pétalo	petalo	pétala
Blutgerinnsel(n)	caillot	clot	coágulo	grumo	coágulo
Bluthochdruck(m)	hypertension	blood pressure	hipertensión	ipertensione	hipertensão
Blutkörperchen(n)	globule(sang)	corpuscle, globule	glóbulo	globulo	glóbulo
Blutsturz(m)	hémorragie	haemorrhage	hemorragia	emorragia	hemorragia
Blutung(f)	saignement	bleeding	desangramiento	emorragia	perda de sangue
Boden(m)	sol, terre	ground	suelo	suolo	solo
Boden(m), Grund(m)	fond	bottom; back	fondo	fondo	fundo
Bogen(m)	arc	bow	arco	arco	arco
Bogen(m), Gewölbe(n)	arche	arch	arca	arco, volta	arco
Bohne(f)	haricot	bean	judía	fagiolo; fagiolino	feijão
Bohne(Kaffee-)(f)	grain(café)	bean(coffee-)	grano	chicco	grão
bohren	percer	drill; pierce	perforar	bucare, forare	furar
Bohrung(f)	forage	boring	perforación	perforazione	perfuração
Boje(f)	bouée	buoy	boya	boa	bóia
Bolzen(m)	boulon	bolt	perno, tornillo	bullone	parafuso; cavilha
Bombe(f)	bombe	bomb	bomba	bomba	bomba
Bonbon(n, m)	bonbon	sweet	caramelo; bombón	caramella	rebuçado
Boot(n)	canot	dinghy	bote	canotto	canoa
borgen	emprunter	borrow	pedir prestado	prendere in prestito	pedir emprestado
Börse(f)	Bourse(la)	Stock Exchange	Bolsa	Borsa	Bolsa
Böse(n)	mal	evil	mal	male	mal
böse, boshaft	méchant, e	naughty	malo, a	cattivo, a	mau, má
böswillig	malveillant, e	malevolent	malévolo, a	malevolo, a	malévolo, a

273

German	French	English	Spanish	Italian	Portuguese
Böswilligkeit(f)	malveillance	ill will	malevolencia	malanimo	malevolência
Botanik(f)	botanique	botany	botánica	botanica	botânica
Bote(m)	émissaire	emissary	emisario	emissario	emissário
Botschaft(f)	ambassade	embassy	embajada	ambasciata	embaixada
Botschafter(in f)m	ambassadeur	ambassador	embajador	ambasciatore	embaixador
Boulevard(m)	boulevard	boulevard	bulevar	viale	avenida
Boxen(n)	boxe	boxing	boxeo	pugilato	boxe
Boxer(m)	boxeur	boxer	boxeador	pugile	pugilista
Brand(m)	incendie, feu	fire	incendio	incendio	incêndio
Brand(m), Wundbrand(m)	gangrène	gangrene	gangrena	cancrena	gangrena
branden	déferler	break	romper	infrangersi	quebrar-se
Brandung(f)	houle	swell, surge	marejada	ondosità	vaga
braten	frire	fry	freír	friggere	fritar
Braten(m)	rôti	roast; joint	asado	arrosto	assado
Brauch(m)	coutume	custom	costumbre	costume, usanza	costume
Brauch(m), Ritus(m)	rite	rite; ritual	rito	rito	rito
brauchen	besoin(avoir)	require, need	necesitar	bisogno(avere)	necessidade(ter)
braun	brun, ne	brown	pardo, a	bruno, a	castanho, a
Bräune(f)	bronzage	sun-tan	bronceado	abbronzatura	bronzeamento
bräunen	bronzer	tan	broncear	abbronzare	bronzear
Bräutigam(m), Braut(f)	marié, mariée	bridegroom, bride	novio, novia	sposo, sposa	noivo, noiva
brav, nett, angenehm	brave	decent, nice	bueno, a	bravo, a	amável
brav	sage	good	bueno, a	buono, a; bravo, a	ajuizado, a
brechen, zerbrechen	briser	break	romper	spezzare, rompere	quebrar
brechen(ab = -; zer-)	rompre	break	romper	rompere	romper
Brechreiz(m)	nausée	nausea, feel sick	náusea	nausea	náusea
breit, weit	large	broad	ancho, a	largo, a; ampio, a	largo, a; amplo, a
Breite(f)	largeur	width, breadth	anchura	larghezza	largura
Breitengrad(m)	latitude	latitude	latitud	latitudine	latitude
Bremse(f)	frein	brake	freno	freno	travão
bremsen	freiner	brake	frenar	frenare	travar
brennbar	inflammable	inflammable	inflamable	infiammabile	inflamável
brennend, kochend	brûlant, e	boiling hot	ardiente	ardente, bollente	ardente
Brennholz(n)	bois	wood	leña	legna	lenha
Brett(n)	planche	board	tabla	tavola, asse	tábua
Brett(n)	panneau	panel	tablero	cartello	painel
Brief(m)	lettre	letter	carta	lettera	carta
Briefkasten(m)	boîte(lettres)	letter box	buzón	buca delle lettere	caixa do correio
Briefmarke(f)	timbre(-poste)	stamp	sello	francobollo	selo
Brieftasche(f)	portefeuille	wallet	cartera	portafoglio	carteira
Briefträger(in f)m	facteur, trice	postman/-woman	cartero, a	postino, a	carteiro, a
Brigade(f)	brigade	brigade	brigada	brigata, squadra	brigada
Brille(f)	lunettes	glasses	gafas	occhiali	óculos
bringen	apporter	bring	traer	apportare, portare	trazer
Bronchie(f)	bronche(s)	bronchial tubes	bronquios	bronco(bronchi)	brônquios
Bronchitis(f)	bronchite	bronchitis	bronquitis	bronchite	bronquite
Bronze(f)	bronze	bronze	bronce	bronzo	bronze
Brosche(f)	broche	brooch	broche	spilla	broche
Brot(n)	pain	bread	pan	pane	pão
Brotscheibe(f)	tartine de pain	slice of bread	rebanada de pan	fetta di pane	fatia de pão
Bruch(m)	cassure, rupture	break	rotura	frattura, rottura	ruptura, quebra
Bruch(m)	rupture	rupture	ruptura	rottura	ruptura
Bruch(m)	fracture	fracture	fractura	frattura	fractura
Bruch(m)	hernie	hernia	hernia	ernia	hérnia
Bruchbude(f)	taudis	slum	tugurio	topaia	antro, tugúrio
brüchig, spröde	cassant, e	brittle	quebradizo, a	fragile	quebradiço, a
Bruchteil(m)	fraction	fraction	fracción	frazione	fracção
Brücke(f)	pont	bridge	puente	ponte	ponte
Bruder(m)	frère	brother	hermano	fratello	irmão
Brüderlichkeit(f)	fraternité	brotherhood	fraternidad	fraternità	fraternidade
Brühe(f)	bouillon	stock, broth	caldo	brodo	caldo
brüllen	hurler	scream, yell	chillar	urlare	gritar; berrar
Brunnen(m)	puits	well	pozo	pozzo	poço
brüsk	brusque	abrupt, sudden	brusco, a	brusco, a	brusco, a
Brust(f)	poitrine	chest; breast	pecho	petto	peito
Brustkasten(m)	thorax	thorax	tórax	torace	tórax
Brut(f)	couvée	brood	pollada	covata	ninhada
brutal	brutal, e	brutal	brutal	brutale	brutal

German	French	English	Spanish	Italian	Portuguese
Brutalität, Roheit(f)	brutalité	brutality	brutalidad	brutalità	brutalidade
Buch(n)	livre	book	libro	libro	livro
Bücherschrank(m)	bibliothèque	bookcase	biblioteca	libreria	estante
Buchhalter(in f)m	comptable	accountant	contable	ragioniere	contabilista
Buchhaltung(f)	comptabilité	accountancy	contabilidad	contabilità	contabilidade
Buchhandlung(f)	librairie	book-shop	librería	libreria	livraria
Büchsenöffner(m)	ouvre-boîte(s)	tin/can opener	abrelatas	apriscatole	abre-latas
Buchstabe(m)	lettre	letter	letra	lettera	letra
buchstabieren	épeler	spell	deletrear	compitare, sillabare	soletrar
Bucht(f)	baie	bay	bahía	baia	baía
buckelig	bossu, e	hunch-backed	jorobado, a	gobbo, a	corcunda
bücken, sich	baisser(se)	bend down	agacharse	abbassarsi	baixar-se
bücken, sich	pencher(se)	bend, lean	inclinarse	chinarsi	inclinar-se
Budget(n)	budget	budget	presupuesto	bilancio	orçamento
Büfett(n)	buffet	dresser; sideboard	aparador	credenza, buffè	aparador
Bügel(m)	cintre	hanger, coat-hanger	percha	gruccia, attaccapanni	cabide
Bügeleisen(n)	fer à repasser	iron	plancha	ferro da stiro	ferro de passar
Bügeln(n)	repassage	ironing	planchado	stirare	passar a ferro
Bullauge(n), Luke(f)	hublot	window	ventanilla	oblò	vigia
Bund(m), Vereinigung f	union	union	unión	unione	união
bündig	succinct, e	succinct, brief	sucinto, a	succinto, a	sucinto, a
Bündnis(n)	alliance	alliance	alianza	alleanza	aliança
Bürger(in f)m	bourgeois, e	middle class	burgués	borghese	burguês, a
Bürger(in f)m	citoyen, ne	citizen	ciudadano, a	cittadino, a	cidadão, cidadã
Bürgermeister(m)	maire	mayor	alcalde	sindaco	President.da Câmara
Bürgersteig(m)	trottoir	pavement	acera	marciapiede	passeio
Bürgertum(n)	bourgeoisie	middle class	burguesía	borghesia	burguesia
Büro(n)	bureau	office	despacho	ufficio	escritório
Büro(n)(Anwaltsbüro)	cabinet(avocat)	practice	despacho; bufete	studio(avvocato)	escritório
Bürste(f)	brosse	brush	cepillo	spazzola	escova
Bus(m)	autobus	bus	autobús	autobus	autocarro
Busch(m)	brousse	bush(the)	maleza	boscaglia	mato
Busen(m)	sein(s)	breast	seno, pecho	seno	seio
Büstenhalter(m)	soutien-gorge	bra	sostén	reggiseno	soutien
Butter(f)	beurre	butter	mantequilla	burro	manteiga
Butterbrot(n)	sandwich	sandwich(-es)	bocadillo	panino	sande, sanduiche

C

German	French	English	Spanish	Italian	Portuguese
Café(n), Konditorei(f)	salon de thé	tea-room	salón de té	sala da tè	casa de chá
Campingplatz(m)	camping(aire de)	camp(ing) site	camping	campeggio	campismo
Cello(n)	violoncelle	cello	violoncelo	violoncello	violoncelo
Champagner(m)	champagne	champagne	champaña	champagne	champanhe
Charakter(m)	caractère	character	carácter	carattere	carácter
charakteristisch	caractéristique	characteristic	característico, a	caratteristico, a	característico, a
Charme(m), Reiz(m)	charme	charm	encanto	fascino	encanto
Chef(in f)m	chef	head; chief; leader	jefe	capo	chefe
Chef(m), Arbeitgeber m	patron, ne	boss; employer	patrón, a; dueño, a	padrone, a	patrão, patroa
Chemie(f)	chimie	chemistry	química	chimica	química
chemisch	chimique	chemical	químico, a	chimico, a	químico, a
Chirurg(in f)m	chirurgien	surgeon	cirujano	chirurgo	cirurgião
Chirurgie(f)	chirurgie	surgery	cirugía	chirurgia	cirurgia
Cholera(f)	choléra	cholera	cólera	colera	cólera
Chor(m)	choeur	choir	coro	coro	coro
Christ(in f)m	chrétien, ne	Christian	cristiano, a	cristiano, a	cristão, cristã
Chromosom(n)	chromosome	chromosome	cromosoma	cromosoma	cromossoma
Chronik(f)	chronique	chronicle	crónica	cronaca	crónica

German	French	English	Spanish	Italian	Portuguese
chronisch	chronique	chronic	crónico, a	cronico, a	crónico, a
Chronologie(f)	chronologie	chronology	cronología	cronologia	cronologia
Clown(m)	clown	clown	payaso	pagliaccio, clown	palhaço
Cocktail(m)	cocktail	cocktail	cóctel	cocktail	coquetel
Comic Strip(m)	bande dessinée	cartoon(strip)	comics, tebeos	fumetto	banda desenhada
Computer(m)	ordinateur	computer	ordenador	computer	computador
Couch(f), Sofa(n)	divan	couch(-es)	diván	divano	divã
Cousin(m), Cousine(f)	cousin, e	cousin	primo, a	cugino, a	primo, a
Creme(f)	crème(peau)	cream	crema	crema	creme
cremig, sahnig	onctueux, se	unctuous	untuoso, a	untuoso, a	untuoso, a
Croupier(m)	croupier, ière	croupier	crupier	croupier	croupier

D

German	French	English	Spanish	Italian	Portuguese
da	là	there	ahí; allí	là	aí; ali; lá
da oben	là-haut	up there	arriba	in alto	lá em cima
da; dort	là	there	allí; allá	là; lì	aí; lá
da; dort	là-bas	over there	allá	là, laggiù	além, acolá
da, weil	puisque	since	ya que; pues	poichè	já que
Dach(n)	toit	roof	tejado	tetto	telhado
Dachrinne(f)	gouttière	gutter	canalón	grondaia	goteira
Dame(f)	dame	lady	señora	signora	senhora
damit	afin que	so that	a fin de que	affinché	a fim de que
Damm(m)	barrage	dam	embalse, presa	diga	barragem
Dampf(m)	vapeur	steam	vapor	vapore	vapor
dämpfen	amortir	absorb, cushion	amortiguar	attutire	amortecer
danach	ensuite, puis	then, next	después	poi, dopo	em seguida
dank	grâce à	thanks to	gracias a	grazie a	graças a
Dank(m)	remerciement	thanks	agradecimiento	ringraziamento	agradecimento
dankbar	reconnaissant, e	grateful	agradecido, a	grato, a	reconhecido, a
Dankbarkeit(f)	gratitude	gratitude	gratitud	gratitudine	gratidão
danke	merci	thank you, thanks	gracias	grazie	obrigado, a
danken; bedanken, sich	remercier	thank	agradecer	ringraziare	agradecer
dann	alors	then	entonces	allora	então
dann	puis, ensuite	then	después	poi	depois
Darlehen(n)	prêt	loan	préstamo	prestito	empréstimo
Darm(m)	intestin	intestine	intestino	intestino	intestino
dar = stellen	représenter	represent	representar	rappresentare	representar
Darstellung(f)	représentation	representation	representación	rappresentazione	representação
das	le	the	lo	lo	o
das, jene(r, s)	cela, ça	that	eso, aquello, ello	ciò, questo, quello	isso, aquilo
das heißt	c'est-à-dire	that is(to say)	es decir	cioè	quer dizer
das langt, jetzt langt	assez!; suffit!	enough!(that's)	basta(!)	basta così!	basta!, chega!
Dasein(n)	existence	existence, life	existencia	esistenza	existência
Daten(pl)	donnée(s)	data	datos	dati	dados
Dattel(f)	datte	date	dátil	dattero	tâmara
Datum(n)	date	date	fecha	data	data
Dauer(f)	durée	duration, length	duración	durata	duração
dauern	durer	last	durar	durare	durar
Daumen(m)	pouce	thumb	pulgar	pollice	polegar
dazwischen = treten	intervenir	intervene	intervenir	intervenire	intervir
Debatte(f)	débat	debate	debate	dibattito	debate
deblockieren, lösen	débloquer	release	desbloquear	sbloccare	desbloquear
Deck(n)	pont	deck; bridge	puente	ponte	convés
Decke(f)(Woll-, Bett-)	couverture	blanket; cover	manta	coperta	manta, cobertor
Decke(f)(Zimmer-)	plafond	ceiling	techo	soffitto	tecto
Deckel(m)	couvercle	lid, cover	tapa, tapadera	coperchio	tampa

German	French	English	Spanish	Italian	Portuguese
defekt	défectueux, se	defective, faulty	defectuoso, a	difettoso, a	defeituoso, a
definieren	définir	define	definir	definire	definir
Definition(f)	définition	definition	definición	definizione	definição
Deflation(f)	déflation	deflation	deflación	deflazione	deflação
degenerieren	dégénérer	degenerate	degenerar	degenerare	degenerar
degradieren	dégrader	degrade	degradar	degradare	degradar
dein(e)	ton	your	tu	tuo(il)	teu
dein(e)	ta	your	tu	tua(la)	tua, teu
deine	tes	your	tus	tuoi, tue(i, le)	teus, tuas
deine(r, s), deine	tien, ne; vôtre	yours	tuyo, a	tuo, a	teu, tua
dekodieren	décoder	decode	descifrar	decifrare	decifrar
Dekor(m), Bühnenbild n	décors	set, scenery	decorado	scenografia	cenários
Dekoration(f)	décoration	decoration	decoración	decorazione	decoração
Delegation(f)	délégation	delegation	delegación	delegazione	delegação
Delphin(m)	dauphin	dolphin	delfín	delfino	golfinho
Demagogie(f)	démagogie	demagogy	demagogia	demagogia	demagogia
dementieren, leugnen	démentir	refute, deny	desmentir	smentire	desmentir
demobilisieren	démobiliser	demobilize	desmovilizar	smobilitare	desmobilizar
Demographie(f)	démographie	demography	demografía	demografia	demografia
Demokrat(in f)m	démocrate	democrat	demócrata	democratico, a	democrata
Demokratie(f)	démocratie	democracy	democracia	democracia	democracia
Demonstrant(in f)m	manifestant, e	demonstrator	manifestante	manifestante	manifestante
Demonstration(f)	manifestation	demonstration	manifestación	manifestazione	manifestação
denken	penser	think	pensar	pensare	pensar
Denkmal(n)	monument	monument	monumento	monumento	monumento
dennoch, doch	pourtant	yet, however	sin embargo	però, tuttavia	contudo, todavia
denunzieren	dénoncer	denounce	denunciar	denunziare	denunciar
Deo(n)	déodorant	deodorant	desodorante	deodorante	desodorisante
Deodorant(n)	désodorisant	air-freshener	desodorante	deodorante	desodorisante
deponieren	déposer	deposit	depositar	depositare	depositar
Deportation(f)	déportation	deportation	deportación	deportazione	deportação
deprimiert	déprimé, e	depressed	deprimido, a	depresso, a	deprimido, a
der, die, das, die	le, l', les	the	el, lo, los	il, lo, l'; i, gli	o, os
derjenige, die-, das-	celui, celle	the one	él, la	quello, a	o, a
der(jenige); die( )	celui-là, celle-	that one	ése, ésa, éso(s)	quello, quella	esse(a); aquele(a)
der Mühe wert	vaut la peine	worthwhile	vale la pena	vale la pena	vale a pena
desinfizieren	désinfecter	disinfect	desinfectar	disinfettare	desinfectar
desorganisieren	désorganiser	disorganize	desorganizar	disorganizzare	desorganizar
Despot(m)	despote	despot	déspota	despota	déspota
dessen; deren	dont	whose, of which	cuyo, a; del cual	di cui	cujo, a; do qual
Destillation(f)	distillation	distillation	destilación	distillazione	distilação
Detektiv(m)	détective	detective	detective	detective	detective
deuten, aus = legen	interpréter	interpret	interpretar	interpretare	interpretar
deutlich	distinct, e	distinct	distinto, a	distinto, a	distinto, a
Dezember(m)	décembre	December	diciembre	dicembre	Dezembro
dezimal	décimal, e	decimal	decimal	decimale	decimal
Diagnose(f)	diagnostic	diagnosis(-oses)	diagnóstico	diagnosi	diagnóstico
diagonal	diagonal, e	diagonal	diagonal	diagonale	diagonal
Diagramm(n)	diagramme	diagram	diagrama	diagramma	diagrama
Dialekt(m)	dialecte	dialect	dialecto	dialetto	dialecto
Dialog(m)	dialogue	dialogue	diálogo	dialogo	diálogo
Diamant(m)	diamant	diamond	diamante	diamante	diamante
Diapositiv(n), Dia(n)	diapo(sitives)	slide	diapositiva	diapositiva	diapositivos
Diät(f)	régime	diet(be on a)	dieta	dieta	dieta
diätetisch	diététique	dietetic	dietético, a	dietetico, a	dietético, a
dich; dir	te, t'	you	te	ti, te	te
dicht	dense	dense	denso, a	denso, a	denso, a
Dichte(f)	densité	density	densidad	densità	densidade
Dichtung(f)	joint	joint, join, seal	junta	giunto, guarnizione	junta, anilha
dick	épais, se	thick	espeso, a	spesso, a	espesso, a
dick	gros, se	fat	grueso, a; gordo, a	grosso, a	gordo, a
dickköpfig	têtu, e	stubborn	tozudo, a	testardo, a	cabeçudo, a
die	la, l', les	the	la, las	la, l', le	a, as
die	les	the	los, las	i, gli; le	os, as
Dieb(in f)m	voleur, se	thief(-ves), robber	ladrón, a	ladro, a	ladrão, ladra
Diebstahl(m)	vol	theft, robbery	robo	furto	roubo
Diebstahlsicherung(f)	antivol	anti-theft lock	antirrobo	antifurto	alarme
dienen, bedienen	servir	serve	servir	servire	servir

German	French	English	Spanish	Italian	Portuguese
Dienstag(m)	mardi	Tuesday	martes	martedì	terça-feira
Dienstleistung(f)	service	service	servicio	servizio	serviço
dies(es); das	ceci	this	esto	questo, ciò	isto
diese(pl)	ces	these, those	estos, as; esos, as	questi, e	estes, as; esses, as
diese	ceux, celles, ces	these, those	esos, aquellos	questi, e	aqueles, aquelas
diese(r, s)(hier)	celui-ci, celle-	this one	éste, ésta	questo, questa	este, esta
diese; jene	ceux-ci, celles-	these; those	éstos; ésos	questi; quelli	estes(as); esses(as)
Diesel(m)	diesel	diesel	diesel	diesel	diesel
Diesel(n), Dieselöl(n)	gas-oil	diesel oil	gasoil	gasolio	gasóleo
dieser, diese	ce, cette	this, that	este; esta; estos, as	questo, a; quello, a	este, a; esse, a
dieser, diese	cet, cette	this, that	éste; ésta; éstos	questo, a; quello, a	este; esta; estes, as
dieser, diese, dieses	ce, cette, ces	that, those	ese, esa, esos(as)	quello, a; questo, a	este, esta, estes
Diktator(m)	dictateur	dictator	dictador	dittatore	ditador
Diktatur(f)	dictature	dictatorship	dictadura	dittatura	ditadura
Ding(n)	chose	thing	cosa	cosa	coisa
Diphterie(f)	diphtérie	diphtheria	difteria	difterite	difteria
Diplom(n)	diplôme	diploma	diploma, título	diploma	diploma
Diplomat(in f)m	diplomate	diplomat	diplomático	diplomatico	diplomata
Diplomatie(f)	diplomatie	diplomacy	diplomacia	diplomazia	diplomacia
diplomatisch	diplomatique	diplomatic	diplomático, a	diplomatico, a	diplomático, a
Diplom-	diplômé, e	graduate	titulado, a	diplomato, a	diplomado, a
dir	toi(à), vous(à)	yours	tuyo, a	tuo, a; tuoi, tue	teu, tua
direkt	direct	direct	directo, a	diretto, a	directo, a
direkt	directement	directly	directamente	direttamente	directamente
Direktion(f)	direction	management	dirección	direzione	direcção
Direktor(in f)m	directeur, trice	director, head	director, a	direttore, -trice	director, a
Dirigent(in f)m	chef(orchestre)	conductor	director(orquesta)	direttore(orchestra)	maestro(orquestra)
Diskothek(f)	discothèque	disco(theque)	discoteca	discoteca	discoteca
Diskothek(f)	boîte de nuit	night-club	discoteca	discoteca, night	boîte
diskret	discret, ète	discreet	discreto, a	discreto, a	discreto, a
Diskussion(f)	discussion	discussion, talk	discusión	discussione	discussão
Dissident(m)	dissident, e	dissident	disidente	dissidente	dissidente
Disziplin(f)	discipline	discipline	disciplina	disciplina	disciplina
Division(f)	division	division	división	divisione	divisão
dogmatisch	dogmatique	dogmatic	dogmático, a	dogmatico, a	dogmático, a
Doktor(m)	docteur	doctor	doctor, a	dottore, -essa	doutor, a
Dokument(n)	document	document	documento	documento	documento
Dokumentation(f)	documentation	documentation	documentación	documentazione	documentação
Dolch(m)	poignard	dagger	puñal	pugnale	punhal
Dolmetscher(in f)m	interprète	interpreter	intérprete	interprete	intérprete
Donner(m)	tonnerre	thunder	trueno	tuono	trovão
Donnerstag(m)	jeudi	Thursday	jueves	giovedì	quinta-feira
dopen, sich	doper(se)	take stimulants	doparse	drogarsi	drogar-se
Doppelgänger(in f)m	sosie	double	sosia	sosia	sósia
doppelt	double	double	doble	doppio, a	duplo, a
doppelt	double	dual	doble	doppio, a	duplo, a
Dorf(n)	village	village	aldea, pueblo	paese, villaggio	aldeia, povoado
Dorn(m); Stachel(m)	épine	thorn	espina	spina	espinho
Dose(f)	boîte	tin	lata	latta, scatola	lata
Dosierung(f)	dosage	proportion	dosificación	dosaggio, dose	dosagem
Dosis(f)	dose	dose	dosis	dose	dose
Draht(m)	fil(de fer)	wire	alambre	filo(di ferro)	arame
Drama(n)	drame	drama	drama	dramma	drama
dramatisch	dramatique	dramatic	dramático, a	drammatico, a	dramático, a
drängeln	bousculer	push	empujar	spingere, urtare	empurrar
draußen	dehors	outside, outdoors	fuera, afuera	fuori	fora
Dreck(m)	crasse	filth, dirt	roña, mugre	sporcizia	sujidade
dreckig	sale	dirty	sucio, a	sporco, a	sujo, a
Drehbuch(n)	scénario	script(film -)	guión	scenario	guião
Drehbuchautor(in f)m	scénariste	script-writer	guionista	scenarista	cenarista
drehen	tourner	turn	volver	girare	virar
drehen	tourner	turn	girar	girare	girar; rodar
drehen	tourner(faire)	rotate, revolve	girar(hacer)	roteare	girar(fazer)
Drehung(f)	rotation	rotation	rotación	rotazione	rotação
Drehung(f), Torsion(f)	torsion	twist(ing)	torsión	torsione	torção
Drehzahl(f)	régime	speed	régimen	regime	velocidade
drei	trois	three	tres	tre	três
Dreieck(n)	triangle	triangle	triángulo	triangolo	triângulo

278

German	French	English	Spanish	Italian	Portuguese
dreißig	trente	thirty	treinta	trenta	trinta
dreizehn	treize	thirteen	trece	tredici	treze
dringend	urgent, e	urgent	urgente	urgente	urgente
drinnen, innen, in	dedans	inside	dentro, adentro	dentro	dentro
Dringlichkeit(f)	urgence	urgency	urgencia	urgenza	urgência
dritte	troisième	third	tercero, a	terzo, a	terceiro, a
Drittel(n)	tiers	third	tercio, a; tercero	terzo, a	terço, a; terceiro
dritte Welt(f)	tiers-monde	third world	tercer mundo	terzo mondo	terceiro mundo
Droge(f)	drogue	drug	droga	droga	droga
Drogenabhängige(r)mf	drogué, e	drug addict	drogado, a	drogato, a	drogado, a
Drohung(f)	menace	threat	amenaza	minaccia	ameaça
Druck(m)	pression	pressure	presión	pressione	pressão
Druck(m)	compression	compression	compresión	compressione	compressão
Druck(m)	impression	printing	impresión	stampa	impressão
drucken	imprimer	print	imprimir	stampare	imprimir
drücken(zusammen-)	presser	press, squeeze	apretar	premere	prensar
drücken	comprimer	compress	comprimir	comprimere	comprimir
Druckerei(f)	imprimerie	printing works	imprenta	tipografia	tipografia
Drüse(f)	glande	gland	glándula	ghiandola	glândula
Dschungel(m)	jungle	jungle	selva, jungla	giungla	selva
du	tu	you	tú	tu	tu
du; dich	toi	you	tú; te	tu; te	tu; ti
Duell(n)	duel	duel	duelo	duello	duelo
dulden, ertragen	tolérer	tolerate	tolerar	tollerare	tolerar
dumm	stupide	stupid, silly	estúpido, a	stupido, a	estúpido, a
dumm	bête; sot, te	silly, foolish	tonto, a	sciocco, a	tolo, a; burro, a
Dummheit(f)	sottise	silliness	tontería	sciocchezza	estupidez
Dummheit(f)	bêtise	stupid thing(do a)	estupidez	sciocchezza	asneira
Dummheit(f)	idiotie	stupidity	idiotez	idiozia	idiotice, asneira
Düne(f)	dune	dune	duna	duna	duna
Dünger(m)	engrais	fertilizer, manure	abono	concime	adubo
dunkel	sombre; obscur, e	dark	oscuro, a	scuro, a	escuro, a; sombrio, a
Dunkelheit(f)	obscurité	darkness	oscuridad	oscurità, buio	obscuridade
dünn	mince	thin	delgado, a	sottile	fino, a
Dunst(m)	vapeur	vapour, fumes	vapor	vapore	vapor
durch	par	by, through	por	per, da	por
durch	travers(à)	across; through	través de(a)	attraverso	através de
durchbohren	perforer	perforate	perforar	perforare	perfurar
durchbohren	transpercer	pierce	atravesar	trapassare	trespassar
Durcheinander(n)	branle-bas	upheaval	zafarrancho	scompiglio	agitação
Durcheinander(n)	pagaille	mess	follón, lío	caos, confusione	desordem
Durchfall(m)	diarrhée	diarrhoea	diarrea	diarrea	diarreia
durch = fallen	échouer(examen)	fail	suspender	bocciare	ficar mal(exame)
Durchgang(m)	passage	passage	pasaje, paso	passaggio	passagem
Durchmesser(m)	diamètre	diameter	diámetro	diametro	diâmetro
Durchschnitt(m)	moyenne	average	media	media	média
durchsichtig	transparent, e	transparent	transparente	trasparente	transparente
durch = streichen	rayer	cross out	rayar	cancellare	riscar; cortar
durchtränken	imbiber	soak	empapar	imbevere	embeber
dürr, trocken	aride	arid	árido, a	arido, a	árido, a
Durst(m)	soif	thirst	sed	sete	sede
Dusche(f)	douche	shower	ducha	doccia	duche, chuveiro
Dutzend(n)	douzaine	dozen	docena	dozzina	dúzia
dynamisch	dynamique	dynamic	dinámico, a	dinamico, a	dinâmico, a
Dynamit(n)	dynamite	dynamite	dinamita	dinamite	dinamite

G

E

German	French	English	Spanish	Italian	Portuguese
Eau de Toilette(n)	eau de toilette	toilet water	colonia(agua de)	acqua di toeletta	água de colónia
Ebbe(f)	reflux	ebb	reflujo	riflusso	refluxo
Ebene(f)	plaine	plain	llanura, llano	pianura	planície
ebenfalls, auch	également, aussi	too, also, as well	igualmente	ugualmente	igualmente
ebnen	aplanir	level	aplanar	spianare	aplanar
Echo(n)	écho	echo(-es)	eco	eco	eco
echt	authentique	genuine	genuino, a	genuino, a	autêntico, a
Ecke(f)	coin	corner	esquina, rincón	angolo	canto, esquina
edel; nobel	noble	noble	noble	nobile	nobre
Edelmann m, Edelfrau f	noble	nobleman/-woman	noble	nobile	nobre
egoistisch	égoïste	selfish	egoísta	egoista	egoísta
Ehebruch(m)	adultère	adultery	adulterio	adulterio	adultério
Ehefrau(f), Frau(f)	femme, épouse	wife(wives)	mujer	moglie	mulher
ehelich	conjugal, e	married, marriage-	conyugal	coniugale	conjugal
ehemalig	ancien, ne	former	ex, antiguo, a	ex	antigo, a
Ehemann(m)	mari	husband	marido	marito	marido
eher, lieber	plutôt	rather	más bien	piuttosto	antes; mais
Ehre(f)	honneur	honour	honor	onore	honra
Ehrgeiz(m)	ambition	ambition	ambición	ambizione	ambição
ehrgeizig	ambitieux, se	ambitious	ambicioso, a	ambizioso, a	ambicioso, a
ehrlich	honnête	honest	honrado, a	onesto, a	honesto, a
ehrwürdig	honorable	honourable	honorable	onorabile	honroso, a
Ei(n)	oeuf	egg	huevo	uovo(a)	ovo
Ei(zelle f)n	ovule	ovule	óvulo	ovulo	óvulo
Eichhörnchen(n)	écureuil	squirrel	ardilla	scoiattolo	esquilo
Eid(m)	serment	oath, pledge	juramento	giuramento	juramento
Eidechse(f)	lézard	lizard	lagarto	lucertola	lagarto
Eier legen	pondre	lay	poner(huevos)	fare l'uovo	pôr(ovos)
Eierstock(m)	ovaire	ovary	ovario	ovaia	ovário
Eifersucht(f)	jalousie	jealousy	celos	gelosia	ciúme
eifersüchtig	jaloux, se	jealous	celoso, a	geloso, a	ciumento, a
eigen	propre	own	propio, a	proprio, a	próprio, a
Eigenschaft(f)	qualité	quality	cualidad	qualità	qualidade
Eigentum(n)	propriété	property	propiedad	proprietà	propriedade
Eigentümer(in f)m	propriétaire	owner	propietario, a	proprietario, a	proprietário, a
eigentümlich	particulier, ière	particular	particular	particolare	particular
Eile(f)	hâte	haste, hurry	prisa	fretta	pressa
Eile(f), Hast(f)	précipitation	hurry, haste	precipitación	precipitazione	precipitação
eilig(es...haben)	pressé, e(être)	hurry(be in a)	prisa(tener)	fretta(avere)	pressa(ter)
Eimer(m)	seau	bucket, pail	cubo	secchio	balde
ein, e	un, e	a, an	uno, una	uno, una	um, uma
eine(der) der andere	un(l')ou l'autre	either	uno u otro, cada	uno(l') o l'altro	um ou outro, cada
ein = äschern	incinérer	incinerate	incinerar	incenerire	incinerar
ein = atmen, saugen	aspirer	inhale, suck in(up)	aspirar	aspirare	aspirar
ein = atmen	inhaler, respirer	inhale	inhalar	inalare	inalar
einäugig	borgne	one-eyed	tuerto, a	guercio, a	zarolho, a
Einbahnstraße(f)	sens unique	one-way	dirección única	senso unico	sentido único
Einband(m)	reliure	binding(book-)	encuadernación	rilegatura	encadernação
ein = begreifen	comprendre	comprise	comprender	comprendere	compreender
Einberufung(f); Ladung	convocation	notification	convocatoria	convocazione	convocação
ein = bilden, sich	imaginer(s')	imagine	imaginarse	immaginarsi	julgar
Einbildung(f)	imagination	imagination	imaginación	immaginazione	imaginação
ein = bringen	rapporter	bring in, yield	proporcionar	fruttare	render
Einbruch(m)	cambriolage	burglary	robo, atraco	furto con scasso	roubo, assalto
Eindringen(n)	irruption	irruption	irrupción	irruzione	irrupção
Eindringen(n)	intrusion	intrusion	intrusión	intrusione	intrusão
ein = dringen	pénétrer	enter, penetrate	penetrar	penetrare	penetrar
Eindruck(m)	impression	impression	impresión	impressione	impressão
einfach	simple	simple	simple	semplice	simples
einfach	simplement	simply	simplemente	semplicemente	simplesmente
einfache Fahrkarte(f)	billet simple	single ticket	billete de ida	andata	bilhete de ida

German	French	English	Spanish	Italian	Portuguese
Einfachheit(f)	simplicité	simplicity	sencillez	semplicità	simplicidade
Einfahren(n)	rodage	running in	rodaje	rodaggio	rodagem
ein = fallen	envahir	invade	invadir	invadere	invadir
Einfluß(m)	influence	influence	influencia	influenza	influência
Einfluß(m)	impact	impact	impacto	impatto	impacto
einflußreich	influent, e	influential	influyente	influente	influente
Einfügung(f)	insertion	insertion	inserción	inserzione	inserção
Einfuhr(f)	importation	import; importing	importación	importazione	importação
ein = führen	introduire	insert; introduce	introducir	introdurre	introduzir
ein = führen	importer	import	importar	importare	importar
Einführung(f)	initiation	initiation	iniciación	iniziazione	iniciação
Eingangshalle(f)	hall	foyer, hall	vestíbulo	hall, ingresso	vestíbulo
eingebildet	imaginaire	imaginary	imaginario, a	immaginario, a	imaginário, a
eingebildet	prétentieux, se	pretentious	presuntuoso, a	pretenzioso, a	pretencioso, a
Eingeborene(r)mf	indigène	native, indigenous	indígena	indigeno, a	indígena
eingebürgert	naturalisé, e	naturalized	nacionalizado, a	naturalizzato, a	naturalizado, a
Eingliederung(f)	incorporation	incorporation	incorporación	incorporazione	incorporação
Eingriff(m)	intervention	intervention	intervención	intervento	intervenção
Einheit(f)	unité	unit	unidad	unità	unidade
ein = hüllen, ein = packen	envelopper	wrap, envelop	envolver	avvolgere	envolver
einige	quelque	some, any	alguno, a	qualche	algum, a
einige	quelques	few(a), some	algunos, as	alcuni, e	alguns, algumas
Einigkeit(f)	unité	unity	unidad	unità	unidade
ein = kassieren	encaisser	cash	cobrar	incassare	receber
Einkäufe(pl)	courses	shopping	compras	spesa	compras
ein = klemmen	coincer	jam	apretar, apiñar	schiacciare, stipare	apertar
Einkommen(n)	revenu	income, revenue	renta, ingresos	reddito	rendimento
Einkommen(n)	rente	income, pension	renta	rendita	renda
ein = laden	embarquer	load	embarcar	imbarcare	carregar
ein = laden	inviter	invite	invitar	invitare	convidar
Einladung(f)	invitation	invitation	invitación	invito	convite
ein = legen, = schalten	enclencher	engage	engranar	ingranare, avviare	engrenar
einleitend	préliminaire	preliminary	preliminar	preliminare	preliminar
einmal	fois(une)	once	vez(una)	volta(una)	vez(uma)
einmal(nicht)	même pas	even(not)	siquiera(ni)	neanche	sequer(nem)
einmalig	unique	unique, exceptional	único, a	unico, a	único, a
ein = mischen, sich	mêler de(se)	interfere	implicarse	immischiare(-rsi)	envolver-se
Einmischung(f)	ingérence	interference	ingerencia	ingerenza	ingerência
Einmischung; Störung	interférence	interference	interferencia	interferenza	interferência
Einnahmen(f, pl)	recette	receipts; takings	ingresos	incasso	receita
ein = nehmen	occuper	occupy, fill	ocupar	occupare	ocupar
Einorden(n)	classement	filing	clasificación	classificazione	classificação
ein = packen, verpacken	empaqueter	pack, wrap	empaquetar	impacchettare	empacotar
ein = räumen	ranger, ordonner	tidy, put in order	ordenar, colocar	sistemare	arrumar
ein = richten	aménager	fit out; convert	acondicionar	sistemare	arranjar, dispor
ein = richten	installer	install	instalar	installare	instalar
Einrichtung(f)	ameublement	furnishing	mobiliario	arredamento, mobilio	mobiliário
Einrichtung(f)	installation	installation	instalación	installazione	instalação
eins	un	one	un, uno	un, uno	um
einsam	seul, e	lonely	aislado, a; solo, a	isolato, a; solo, a	isolado, a
einsam	solitaire	solitary, lonely	solitario, a	solitario, a	solitário, a
Einsamkeit(f)	solitude	loneliness	soledad	solitudine	solidão
Einsatz(m)(Spiel-)	enjeu	stake	apuesta	posta	aposta
ein = schätzen	évaluer, estimer	assess	tasar, valorar	valutare, stimare	avaliar, fixar
Einschätzung(f)	évaluation	assessment	valoración	valutazione	avaliação
ein = schlagen	enfoncer	drive in	clavar	piantare	cravar
ein = schließen	enfermer	shut in	encerrar	rinchiudere	encerrar, fechar
ein = schließen	inclure	include	incluir	includere	incluir
Einschränkung(f)	restriction	restriction	restricción	restrizione	restrição
ein = schreiben	inscrire, noter	note, write	inscribir	iscrivere	inscrever
ein = schreiben, sich	inscrire(s')	register	matricularse	iscriversi	matricular-se
Einschreibung(f)	inscription	registration	matrícula	iscrizione	matrícula
ein = schüchtern	intimider	intimidate	intimidar	intimidire	intimidar
ein = setzen	encastrer	set in	empotrar	incastrare	embutir
ein = setzen, ein = fügen	insérer	insert	insertar	inserire	inserir
Einsickern(n)	infiltration	infiltration	infiltración	infiltrazione	infiltração
Einsiedler(in f)m	ermite	hermit	ermitaño	eremita	eremita
ein = sperren	incarcérer	imprison	encarcelar	incarcerare	encarcerar

G

ein = sperren	séquestrer	lock away	secuestrar	sequestrare	sequestrar
ein = stecken	brancher	plug in	enchufar	innestare	ligar
ein = steigen	embarquer	board, embark	embarcar	imbarcare	embarcar
ein = steigen	monter	get into, get on	subir	salire	subir a, entrar
ein = stellen	embaucher	employ, take on	dar trabajo	assumere	empregar
ein = stellen	régler	adjust, tune	ajustar, arreglar	regolare	afinar, regular
ein = stellen	ajuster	adjust	ajustar	aggiustare, adattare	ajustar
Einstellung(f)	réglage	adjustment	reglaje, ajuste	regolazione	afinação
einstimmig	unanime	unanimous	unánime	unanime	unânime
ein = tauchen	tremper, plonger	dip	sumergir	intingere	mergulhar
einträglich	rentable	profitable	rentable	redditizio, a	rentável
Eintragung(f)	immatriculation	registration	matrícula	immatricolazione	matrícula
ein = treten	entrer	enter, come/go in	entrar	entrare	entrar
Eintritt(m), Eingang m	entrée	entry, entrance	entrada	ingresso	entrada
Eintrittskarte(f)	entrée	admission	entrada	ingresso	entrada, bilhete
einundzwanzig	vingt-et-un	twenty one	veintiún(o)	ventuno	vinte e um
ein = verleiben	incorporer	incorporate	incorporar	incorporare	incorporar
einverstanden, okay	accord(d')	all right, O.K	vale, de acuerdo	accordo(d')	acordo(de)
Einverständnis(n)	accord	agreement	acuerdo	accordo	acordo
Einwand(m)	objection	objection, protest	objeción, reparo	obiezione	objecção
Einwanderer(in f)m	immigré, e	immigrant	inmigrado, a	immigrato, a	imigrante
Einwanderung(f)	immigration	immigration	inmigración	immigrazione	imigração
einwandfrei	parfait, e	perfect	perfecto, a	perfetto, a	perfeito, a
ein = weichen	tremper	soak	mojar	inzuppare	molhar
ein = weihen	inaugurer	inaugurate	inaugurar	inaugurare	inaugurar
Einweihung(f)	inauguration	inauguration	inauguración	inaugurazione	inauguração
ein = werfen	poster	post, mail	echar al correo	impostare, imbucare	pôr no correio
ein = willigen	consentir	agree	consentir	consentire	consentir
Einwohner(in f)m	habitant, e	inhabitant	habitante	abitante	habitante
Einzahl(f)	singulier	singular	singular	singolare	singular
ein = zahlen	verser	pay(in)	ingresar	versare	pagar
Einzäunung(f)	enceinte	fence; enclosure	muralla	cinta, recinto	muralha, recinto
Einzelheit(f)	détail	detail	detalle	particolare	pormenor
einzeln; einzig	un, e(à); unique	single	solo, a; único, a	singolo, a	único, a
einzelnen(im)	détaillé, e	detailed	detallado, a	dettagliato, a	detalhado, a
Einzelzimmer(n)	chambre à 1 lit	single room	habitación(l cama)	camera singola	quarto individual
einzig	seul, e	only	solo, a	solo, a	só
einzig, einzeln	unique	unique; only	único, a	unico, a	único, a
Eis(n)	glace	ice	hielo	ghiaccio	gelo
Eis(n)	glace	ice cream	helado	gelato	gelado
Eisbahn(f)	patinoire	skating rink	pista de patinar	pista da pattinaggio	pista de patinagem
Eisberg(m)	iceberg	iceberg	iceberg	iceberg	iceberg
Eisen(n)	fer	iron	hierro	ferro	ferro
Eisenbahn(f)	chemin de fer	railway	ferrocarril	ferrovia	caminho de ferro
Eisenwarenhandlung(f)	quincaillerie	ironmonger's	ferretería	ferramenta	loja de ferragens
eisig	glacé, e; gelé, e	icy	helado, a	gelato, a; ghiacciato	gelado, a
Eiskunstlauf(m)	patinage	skating	patinaje	pattinaggio	patinagem
Eitelkeit(f)	vanité	vanity	vanidad	vanità	vaidade
Eiter(m)	pus	pus	pus	pus	pus
ekelhaft	dégoûtant, e	disgusting	asqueroso, a	disgustoso, a	nojento, a
ekelhaft, stinkig	infect, e	foul, vile	asqueroso, a	fetido, a	asqueroso, a
Ekzem(n)	eczéma	eczema	eczema	eczema	eczema
elastisch	élastique	elastic; flexible	elástico, a	elastico, a	elástico, a
Elefant(m)	éléphant	elephant	elefante	elefante	elefante
elegant	élégant, e	elegant, smart	elegante	elegante	elegante
Eleganz(f)	élégance	elegance	elegancia	eleganza	elegância
Elektriker(in f)m	électricien	electrician	electricista	elettricista	electricista
elektrisch	électrique	electric(al)	eléctrico, a	elettrico, a	eléctrico, a
Elektrizität(f)	électricité	electricity	electricidad	elettricità	electricidade
Elektronik(f)	électronique	electronics	electrónica	elettronica	electrónica
elektronisch	électronique	electronic	electrónico, a	elettronico, a	electrónico, a
Element(n)	élément	element	elemento	elemento	elemento
Elend(n)	misère	poverty	miseria	miseria	miséria
Elendsviertel(n)	bidonville	shanty-town	chabolas	bidonville	bairro de lata
elf	onze	eleven	once	undici	onze
Elfenbein(n)	ivoire	ivory	marfil	avorio	marfim
Elite(f)	élite	élite	élite	elite	elite
Ellenbogen(m)	coude	elbow	codo	gomito	cotovelo

German	French	English	Spanish	Italian	Portuguese
Ellipse(f)	ellipse	ellipse	elipse	ellisse	elipse
Eltern(pl.)	parents	parents	padres	genitori	pais
Emaille(f), Glasur(f)	émail	enamel	esmalte	smalto	esmalte
Embargo(n)	embargo	embargo	embargo	embargo	embargo
Emblem(n)	emblème	emblem	emblema	emblema	emblema
Embryo(m)	embryon	embryo	embrión	embrione	embrião
Emigrant(in f)m	émigré, e	emigrant	emigrante	emigrato, a	emigrante
Empfang(m), Aufnahme f	accueil	reception; welcome	recepción	accoglienza	recepção
Empfang(m)	réception	reception	recepción	ricezione	recepção
Empfang(m)	réception	party, reception	recepción	ricevimento	recepção
Empfang(m)	réception	receipt	recibo	ricevuta	recepção
empfangen, auf = nehmen	accueillir	welcome	acoger, recibir	accogliere	acolher, receber
empfangen	recevoir	receive, get	recibir	ricevere	receber
Empfänger(in f)m	destinataire	addressee	destinatario, a	destinatario, a	destinatário, a
Empfänger(m)	récepteur	receiver	receptor	ricevitore	receptor
Empfehlung(f)	recommandation	recommendation	recomendación	raccomandazione	recomendação
empfinden	ressentir	feel	sentir	sentire	sentir
empfindlich	sensible	sensitive	sensible	sensibile	sensível
empfindsam	émotif, ive	emotional	emotivo, a	emotivo, a	emotivo, a
Empfindung(f)	sensation	sensation; feeling	sensación	sensazione	sensação
empören, sich	insurger(s')	rebel(against)	rebelarse	ribellarsi	insurgir-se
Empörung(f)	indignation	indignation	indignación	indignazione	indignação
Emulsion(f)	émulsion	emulsion	emulsión	emulsione	emulsão
Ende(n)	fin	end	fin	fine	fim
Ende(n), Ziel(n)	terme	end	término	termine	termo
Ende(n)	bout, extrémité	end, tip	cabo	capo, estremità	cabo
endgültig	définitif, ive	definitive, final	definitivo, a	definitivo, a	definitivo, a
Endstück(n)	embout	tip, end	punta; remate	estremità; punta	ponta; remate
Energie(f)	énergie	energy	energía	energia	energia
eng	étroit, e	narrow	estrecho, a	stretto, a	estreito, a
engagieren	engager	engage	empeñar	impegnare	empenhar
engagieren, sich	engager(s')	commit oneself	comprometerse	impegnarsi a	comprometer-se
Engel(m)	ange	angel	ángel	angelo	anjo
enger machen/werden	rétrécir(se)	narrow	estrechar(se)	restringersi	estreitar-se
Enkel(m), Enkelin(f)	petit-fils/fille	grandson/-daughter	nieto, a	nipote	neto, a
entbinden	accoucher	birth(give)	dar a luz	partorire	dar à luz
Entbindung(f)	accouchement	delivery; birth	parto	parto	parto
entblößen	dénuder	strip, bare	desnudar	denudare	desnudar
entdecken	découvrir	discover	descubrir	scoprire	descobrir
Entdeckung(f)	découverte	discovery	descubrimiento	scoperta	descoberta
Ente(f)	canard	duck	pato	anatra	pato, a
enterben	déshériter	disinherit	desheredar	diseredare	deserdar
Entfärbung(f)	décoloration	discolouration	descoloramiento	decolorazione	descoloração
entfernen	écarter	separate, part	apartar	allontanare; scartare	afastar
entfernen	enlever	take away, remove	sacar, quitar	togliere	retirar, tirar
Entfernung(f)	éloignement	distance	alejamiento	lontananza	afastamento
Entfernung(f)	distance	distance	distancia	distanza	distância
entführen	kidnapper	kidnap	secuestrar	rapire	raptar
entführen	détourner	hijack	secuestrar	dirottare	sequestrar
entgegengesetzt	contraire	contrary	contrario, a	contrario, a	contrário, a
entgegengesetzt	opposé, e	opposing	opuesto, a	opposto, a	oposto, a
entgegengesetzt	opposé, e	opposed to	opuesto, a	opposto, a	contra(ser)
entgegen = treten	affronter	confront, face	afrontar	affrontare	afrontar
entgleiten	échapper	drop	irse, escaparse	sfuggire, scappare	escapar
enthaaren	épiler	remove hair	depilar	depilare	depilar
enthalten	contenir	contain	contener	contenere	conter
entkolonisieren	décoloniser	decolonize	descolonizar	decolonizzare	descolonizar
entlang	long(le)	along	largo(a lo)	lungo	longo(ao)
entlassen	licencier	lay off, dismiss	despedir	licenziare	despedir
entlassen	limoger	dismiss	destituir	silurare	destituir
entlassen	renvoyer	dismiss	despedir	dimettere	despedir
Entlassung(f)	licenciement	dismissal, lay-off	despido	licenziamento	despedimento
Entlohnung(f), Lohn(m)	rémunération	remuneration	remuneración	rimunerazione	remuneração
entmutigen	décourager	discourage	desalentar	scoraggiare	desalentar
entmutigen	démoraliser	demoralize	desmoralizar	demoralizzare	desmoralizar
entmutigend	décourageant, e	discouraging	desalentador, a	scoraggiante	desanimador, a
entmutigt	découragé, e	discouraged	desanimado, a	scoraggiato, a	desalentado, a
entnehmen	prélever	take from	sacar	prelevare	tirar

G

283

German	French	English	Spanish	Italian	Portuguese
entsagen, ergeben, sich	résigner(se)	resign oneself	resignarse	rassegnarsi	resignar-se
entschädigen	dédommager	compensate	indemnizar	indennizzare	indemnizar
entschädigen	indemniser	compensate	indemnizar	indennizzare	indemnizar
Entschädigung(f)	indemnité	compensation	indemnidad	risarcimento	indemnização
entschärfen	désamorcer	defuse	desactivar	disinnescare	despoletar
entscheiden	décider	decide	decidir	decidere	decidir
Entscheidung(f)	décision	decision	decisión	decisione	decisão
Entschlossenheit(f)	fermeté	firmness	firmeza	fermezza	firmeza
entschuldigen, sich	excuser(s')	apologize	disculpar(se)	scusarsi	desculpar-se
Entschuldigung(f)	excuse	excuse; apology	excusa, disculpa	scusa	desculpa
Entschuldigung!	excusez-moi!	excuse me!; sorry!	perdone(!)	scusi!	desculpe!; perdão!
entsetzlich	épouvantable	dreadful	horroroso, a	spaventoso, a	horroroso, a
entseuchen	décontaminer	decontaminate	descontaminar	decontaminare	descontaminar
entspannt	détendu, e	relaxed	descansado, a	disteso, a; rilassato	descontraído, a
Entspannung(f)	relaxation	relaxation	relajamiento	rilassamento	relaxação
entsprechen	correspondre	correspond, tally	corresponder	corrispondere	corresponder
entsprechend	conforme à	in accordance with	conforme a/con	conforme a	conforme com
Entstehung(f)	formation	formation	formación	formazione	formação
enttäuschen	décevoir	disappoint	decepcionar	deludere	desapontar
enttäuscht	déçu, e	disappointed	decepcionado, a	deluso, a	desiludido, a
Enttäuschung(f)	déception	disappointment	decepción	delusione	decepção
Enttäuschung(f)	frustration	frustration	frustración	frustrazione	frustração
entwässern	drainer	drain	drenar	drenare	drenar
entweihen	profaner	desecrate	profanar	profanare	profanar
Entweihung(f)	sacrilège	sacrilege	sacrilegio	sacrilegio	sacrilégio
entwenden	dérober	steal	robar	derubare	roubar, furtar
entwerfen	tracer	draw	trazar	tracciare	traçar
entwerfen	concevoir	design	concebir	ideare	conceber
entwerten, ab = werten	dévaluer	devalue	devaluar	svalutare	desvalorizar
entwickeln	développer	develop	desarrollar	sviluppare	desenvolver
entwickeln, sich	évoluer	evolve	evolucionar	evolvere	evoluir
Entwicklung(f)	développement	development	desarrollo	sviluppo	desenvolvimento
Entwicklung(f)	évolution	evolution	evolución	evoluzione	evolução
entwirren	débrouiller	clear up	desenredar	sbrogliare	desenredar
Entwurf(m)	dessin, plan	design	diseño	disegno	desenho
entzücken	émerveiller	amaze	maravillar	meravigliare	maravilhar
entzückend	ravissant, e	ravishing, lovely	encantador, a	incantevole	encantador, a
entzückend, reizend	charmant, e	delightful	delicioso, a	delizioso, a	delicioso, a
Entzückung(f)	extase	ecstasy	éxtasis	estasi	êxtase
Enzyklopädie(f)	encyclopédie	encyclopaedia	enciclopedia	enciclopedia	enciclopédia
Epilepsie(f)	épilepsie	epilepsy	epilepsia	epilessia	epilepsia
Episode(f)	épisode	episode	episodio	episodio	episódio
Epoche(f), Ära(f), Zeit	époque	epoch, era, time	época	epoca	época
Epos(n)	épopée	epic	epopeya	epopea	epopeia
er; es	il	he; it	él	egli, lui, esso	ele
Erbe(m), Erbin(f)	héritier, ière	heir, heiress	heredero, a	erede	herdeiro, a
erblich	héréditaire	hereditary	hereditario, a	ereditario, a	hereditário, a
erbrechen, sich	vomir	vomit	vomitar	vomitare	vomitar
Erbschaft(f)	héritage	inheritance, legacy	herencia	eredità	herança
Erdbeben(n)	séisme	earthquake	terremoto	terremoto	terremoto
Erdbeben(n)	séisme	earthquake	seismo	sisma	sismo
Erdbeere(f)	fraise	strawberry	fresa	fragola	morango
Erde(f)	terre	earth	tierra	terra	Terra
Erde(f)	terre	soil	tierra	terra	terra
Erdgeschoß(n)	rez-de-chaussée	ground floor	planta baja, bajo	piano terra	rés-do-chão
Erdkunde(f)	géographie	geography	geografía	geografia	geografia
Erdnuß(f)	cacahuète	peanut	cacahuete, maní	arachide	amendoim
Erdöl(n)	pétrole	oil	petróleo	petrolio	petróleo
Erdrutsch(m)	éboulement	landslide	desprendimiento	frana, slavina	desmoronamento
Ereignis(n)	événement	event	acontecimiento	avvenimento	acontecimento
erfahren	apprendre	hear(of)	enterarse	apprendere, sapere	saber
Erfahrung(f)	expérience	experience	experiencia	esperienza	experiência
erfinden	inventer	invent	inventar	inventare	inventar
Erfinder(in f)m	inventeur	inventor	inventor	inventore	inventor
Erfindung(f)	invention	invention	invención	invenzione	invenção
Erfolg(m)	succès	success(-es)	éxito	successo	sucesso, êxito
Erfolg(m)	réussite	success(-es)	éxito, logro	riuscita	êxito
erfolgreich, blühend	prospère	flourishing	próspero, a	prospero, a	próspero, a

284

German	French	English	Spanish	Italian	Portuguese
erforschen	explorer	explore	explorar	esplorare	explorar
erforschen	scruter	scan, scrutinize	escudriñar	scrutare	perscrutar
Erforschung(f)	exploration	exploration	exploración	esplorazione	exploração
erfreuen, sich	réjouir(se)	delighted(be)	alegrarse	rallegrare(-arsi)	alegrar-se
Erfrierung(f)	gélure	frostbite	heladura	congelamento	frieira
Ergänzung(f)	complément	complement	complemento	complemento	complemento
Ergänzung(f); Zulage f	supplément	supplement	suplemento	supplemento	suplemento
ergeben, sich	résulter, être	result, be	resultar	risultare	resultar
ergeben	dévoué, e	devoted	servicial	devoto, a	dedicado, a
Ergebenheit(f)	dévouement	devotion	consagración a	dedizione	dedicação
Ergebnis(n)	résultat	result	resultado	risultato, esito	resultado
ergreifen	saisir	seize	coger, agarrar	afferrare	agarrar
ergreifend	émouvant, e	moving	emocionante	commovente	comovente
erhaben	sublime	sublime	sublime	sublime	sublime
erhalten	obtenir	obtain, get	obtener	ottenere	obter
erhalten	maintenir	maintain	mantener	mantenere	manter
erheben, sich	lever(se)	get up	levantar(se)	alzarsi	levantar-se
erheblich	considérable	considerable	considerable	considerevole	considerável
erhöhen	élever	elevate	elevar, alzar	elevare	elevar
Erholungsort(m)	station	resort	estación	stazione	estação
erinnern, sich	rappeler(se)	recall, remember	recordar, acordarse	ricordarsi	lembrar-se
erinnern, sich	souvenir(se)	remember, recall	acordarse	ricordarsi	recordar-se
Erinnerung(f)	souvenir	memory	recuerdo	ricordo	recordação
Erinnerung(f); Mahnung	rappel	reminder	llamada	richiamo	aviso; lembrança
erkälten, sich	enrhumer(s')	catch a cold	constipar(se)	raffreddarsi	constipar-se
erkennen	reconnaître	recognize	reconocer	riconoscere	reconhecer
erklären	expliquer	explain	explicar	spiegare	explicar
Erklärung(f)	explication	explanation	explicación	spiegazione	explicação
Erklärung(f)	déclaration	declaration	declaración	dichiarazione	declaração
erkundigen, sich	informer(s')	inquire	informarse	informarsi	informar-se
erkundigen, sich	renseigner(se)	inquire	informar(se)	informare(-arsi)	informar-se
erlangen, erreichen	arriver(à)	attain	lograr, alcanzar	raggiungere	alcançar, atingir
Erlaß(m), Verordnung f	décret	decree	decreto	decreto	decreto
erlauben	permettre	allow, enable	permitir	permettere	permitir
erlauben	autoriser	authorize	autorizar	autorizzare	autorizar
Erlaubnis(f)	permission	permission	permiso	permesso	permissão
erläutern	commenter	comment(on)	comentar	commentare	comentar
erleichtern	alléger	lighten	aliviar	alleggerire	aliviar
erleichtern	soulager	relieve	aliviar	alleggerire	aliviar
Erleichterung(f)	soulagement	relief	alivio, desahogo	sollievo	alívio
erleuchtet	illuminé, e	illuminated	iluminado, a	illuminato, a	iluminado, a
erliegen	succomber	succumb	sucumbir	soccombere	sucumbir
ermüden	fatiguer	tire, make tired	cansar, fatigar	stancare	cansar, fatigar
ermutigen	encourager	encourage, urge	alentar, animar	incoraggiare	encorajar
ernähren	nourrir	feed, nourish	alimentar	nutrire	alimentar
Ernährung(f)	alimentation	feeding; food	alimentación	alimentazione	alimentação
ernennen	nommer	appoint	nombrar	nominare	nomear
ernennen	désigner	appoint	designar	designare	designar
Ernennung(f)	nomination	nomination	nombramiento	nomina	nomeação
erneuern	renouveler	renew	renovar	rinnovare	renovar
Erneuerung(f)	renouvellement	renewal	renovación	rinnovo	renovação
erniedrigen	humilier	humiliate	humillar	umiliare	humilhar
ernst, ernsthaft	sérieux, se	serious	serio, a	serio, a	sério, a
Ernte(f)	récolte	crop; harvest	cosecha	raccolta	colheita
Ernte(f)	moisson	harvest	cosecha	mietitura	ceifa, colheita
ernten	récolter	harvest, gather	cosechar, recoger	raccogliere	colher, apanhar
Eroberung(f)	conquête	conquest	conquista	conquista	conquista
Erotik(f)	érotisme	eroticism	erotismo	erotismo	erotismo
erotisch	érotique	erotic	erótico, a	erotico, a	erótico, a
erpicht auf	gourmand, e	greedy	goloso, a	goloso, a	guloso, a
Erpressung(f)	racket	racket(-eering)	extorsión	racket	vigarice
erregt, nervös	énervé, e	edgy, worked up	excitado, a	nervoso, a	enervado, a
erreichen	atteindre	reach	alcanzar, lograr	raggiungere	atingir
erreichen	parvenir	reach, arrive at	conseguir	giungere	chegar; conseguir
errichten	ériger	erect	erigir, levantar	erigere	erigir
erringen	remporter, gagner	achieve	lograr, triunfar	raggiungere, ottenere	alcançar, obter
erröten	rougir	blush, flush	sonrojarse	arrossire	corar
Erschaffung; Schöpfung	création	creation	creación	creazione, creato	criação

German	French	English	Spanish	Italian	Portuguese
erscheinen	apparaître	appear	aparecer	apparire	aparecer
erscheinen	afficher(s')	display	visualizar	apparire	mostrar, dar
erschöpft	épuisé, e	exhausted	agotado, a	esausto, a	esgotado, a
erschöpft	exténué, e	exhausted	extenuado, a	spossato, a	extenuado, a
erschrecken	effrayer	frighten	asustar	spaventare	assustar
erschrecken	effarer, effrayer	terrify	espantar, asustar	sgomentare	apavorar
erschüttert	bouleversé, e	overwhelmed	conmocionado, a	sconvolto, a	perturbado, a
erschweren	alourdir	make heavy	pesado(hacer)	appesantire	pesado(tornar)
ersetzen	remplacer	replace	sustituir	sostituire	substituir
Ersparnis(f)	économie, épargne	saving	economía, ahorro	risparmio	economia
Erstarrungszustand(m)	torpeur	torpor	torpor	torpore	torpor
Erstaunen(n)	stupeur	stupor	estupor	stupore	estupefacção
erstaunlich	étonnant, e	surprising	asombroso, a	sorprendente	espantoso, a
erste(r, s)	premier, ière	first	primero, a; primer	primo, a	primeiro, a
Ersticken(n)	asphyxie	suffocation	asfixia	asfissia	asfixia
ersticken	étouffer	suffocate; choke	sofocar, ahogar	soffocare	sufocar
erstrecken, sich	étendre(s')	stretch	extenderse	estendersi	estender-se
Ersuchen(n), Gesuch(n)	requête	request	demanda	richiesta	pedido
ersuchen	solliciter	appeal to, request	solicitar	sollecitare	solicitar
Ertrag(m)	rapport	yield, return	renta; ganancia	frutto, rendita	renda; ganho
Ertrag(m), Leistung(f)	rendement	output, yield	rendimiento	rendimento	rendimento
Ertrag(m)	rendement	yield	rendimiento	rendimento	rendimento; produto
ertragen	subir	undergo	sufrir, padecer	subire	sofrer
ertrinken	noyer(se)	drown	ahogar(se)	annegare	afogar-se
Erwachsene(f, m)	adulte	adult	adulto, a	adulto, a	adulto, a
erwarten	attendre	expect	esperar	aspettare	esperar
erwerben; erlangen	acquérir	acquire	adquirir	acquistare	adquirir, obter
erwidern	répondre	reply, answer	responder	rispondere	responder
erwidern, entgegnen	répliquer	reply	replicar	replicare	replicar
erworben	acquis, e	acquired	adquirido, a	acquisito, a	adquirido, a
Erwürgen(n)	étranglement	strangling	estrangulación	strangolamento	estrangulamento
Erz(n)	minerai	ore	mineral	minerale	minério
erzählen	raconter	relate, tell	contar	raccontare	contar
erzählen	relater	relate, recount	relatar	riferire	relatar
erzeugen	procréer	procreate	procrear	procreare	procriar
erzeugen	générer	generate	engendrar	generare	gerar
erziehen, auf = ziehen	élever	bring up	criar, educar	allevare, educare	criar, educar
erziehen, bilden	éduquer	educate	educar	educare	educar
Erzieher(in f)m	éducateur, trice	instructor	educador, a	educatore, trice	educador, a
Erziehung(f)	éducation	education	educación	educazione	educação
es gibt	il y a	there is, there are	hay	c'è; ci sono	há
Es lebe!; Lang lebe!	vive!	hurrah!; Long live!	viva(!)	viva!, evviva!	viva!
es tut mir leid	excuse(je m')	sorry(I am)	siento(lo)	scusi(mi)	desculpe!
Eskimo(m)	esquimau	Eskimo	esquimal	eschimese	esquimó
eßbar	comestible	edible	comestible	commestibile	comestível
essen	manger	eat	comer	mangiare	comer
Essig(m)	vinaigre	vinegar	vinagre	aceto	vinagre
Eßware(f)	denrée	foodstuff	comestibles	derrata	género; víveres
Eßzimmer(n)	salle à manger	dining-room	comedor	sala da pranzo	sala de jantar
etablieren, gründen	implanter	establish, set up	implantar	impiantare	implantar
Etage(f)	étage	floor, storey	piso, planta	piano	andar
ethisch	éthique	ethical	ético, a	etico, a	ético, a
ethnisch	ethnique	ethnic(al)	étnico, a	etnico, a	étnico, a
Etui(n)	étui	case	estuche	astuccio	estojo
Etui(n), Tasche(f)	trousse	kit, case, bag	maletín, estuche	borsa, astuccio	estojo
etwas	quelque chose	something	algo	qualche cosa	qualquer coisa
etwas; wenig	peu	some; a little	poco	poco, pó	pouco
euch; Sie; Ihnen	vous; te	you	os; les; le; te	vi; ve; le; ti; te	vos; vosco; lhe
euphorisch	euphorique	euphoric	eufórico, a	euforico, a	eufórico, a
eure, Ihre	vos	your	vuestros, as	vostri, e	vossos, as
eure(r, s); Ihre(r, s)	vôtre(le, la)	yours	vuestro, a; suyo, a	vostro, a; suo, sua	vosso, a; seu, sua
Euter(n)	mamelle	udder	mama, teta	mammella	mama
Euthanasie(f)	euthanasie	euthanasia	eutanasia	eutanasia	eutanásia
Eventualität(f)	éventualité	contingency	eventualidad	eventualità	eventualidade
ewig	éternel, le	eternal	eterno, a	eterno, a	eterno, a
Ewigkeit(f)	éternité	eternity	eternidad	eternità	eternidade
existieren	exister	exist	existir	esistere	existir
exotisch	exotique	exotic	exótico, a	esotico, a	exótico, a

German	French	English	Spanish	Italian	Portuguese
Expedition(f)	expédition	expedition	expedición	spedizione	expedição
experimentell	expérimental, e	experimental	experimental	sperimentale	experimental
Experimentieren(n)	expérimentation	experimentation	experimentación	sperimentazione	experimentação
Experte(m), Expertin f	expert, e	expert	experto, a; perito, a	esperto, a	perito, a
explodieren	exploser	explode, blow up	estallar	esplodere	explodir
Explosion(f)	explosion	explosion	explosión	esplosione	explosão
Export(m), Ausfuhr(f)	exportation	export(ing)	exportación	esportazione	exportação
exportieren	exporter	export	exportar	esportare	exportar
Extra-; Neben-	supplément(en)	extra-, additional-	más(de)	più(in)	mais(a)
extrem	extrême	extreme	extremo, a	estremo, a	extremo, a
Extremität(f)	extrémité	extremity, end	extremidad	estremità	extremidade
Exzellenz(f)	Excellence, Votre	Excellency(Your)	Excelencia(Su)	Eccellenza(Sua)	Excelência(Vossa)

F

German	French	English	Spanish	Italian	Portuguese
Fabrik(f)	usine	factory, plant	fábrica	fabbrica	fábrica
Fach(n)	matière	subject	asignatura	materia	matéria
Fächer(m)	éventail	fan	abanico	ventaglio	leque
Fachmann(m)	spécialiste	expert, specialist	especialista	specialista	especialista
Fachsprache(f)	jargon	jargon	jerga	gergo	calão, gíria
Fackel(f)	torche	torch	antorcha	torcia	tocha, archote
Faden(m)	fil	thread	hilo	filo	fio
fähig	capable de	able to(be)	capaz de	capace di	capaz de
fähig; tauglich	apte, compétent	able, qualified	apto, a	adatto, a	apto, a
Fähigkeit(f)	aptitude	ability, aptitude	aptitud(es)	attitudine	aptidão, talento
Fähigkeit(f)	faculté	possibility	facultad	facoltà	faculdade
Fahne(f)	drapeau	flag	bandera	bandiera	bandeira
Fahrbahn(f)	chaussée	road	calzada	carreggiata	calçada
Fähre(f)	bac	ferry	transbordador	traghetto, ferry	barco
fahren	rouler	run, drive, go	correr, rodar	correre, andare	andar; rolar
fahren	conduire	drive	conducir	guidare	conduzir
fahren über	passer	pass, go(through)	pasar	passare	passar(por; em)
Fahrer(in f)m	conducteur, trice	driver	conductor, a	conducente	condutor, a
Fahrer m; Chauffeur m	chauffeur	driver; chauffeur	chófer	autista	motorista
Fahrkarte(f)	billet	ticket	billete	biglietto	bilhete
Fahrkartenschalter(m)	guichet	booking office	taquilla	biglietteria	bilheteira
Fahrplan(m)	horaire(s)	timetable	horario(s)	orario	horário
Fahrrad(n)	bicyclette	bicycle	bicicleta	bicicletta	bicicleta
Fahrrad(n)	vélo	bike	bici	bici, bicicletta	bicicleta
Fahrwasser(n)	chenal	channel	canal	canale	canal
Fahrzeug(n)	véhicule	vehicle	vehículo	veicolo	veículo
Faktor(m)	facteur	factor	factor	fattore	factor
Fakultät(f)	faculté	Faculty	facultad	facoltà	faculdade
Fall(m)	chute	fall	caída	caduta	queda
Fall(m)	cas	case	caso	caso	caso
Falle(f)	piège	trap, snare	trampa	trappola	armadilha
fallen	tomber	fall	caer	cadere	cair
fallen	descendre	fall, drop	bajar	abbassare	baixar
fallenlassen	tomber(laisser)	drop	caer(dejar)	cadere(lasciar)	cair(deixar)
Fälligkeitstermin(m)	échéance	expiration	vencimiento	scadenza	vencimento
Fallschirm(m)	parachute	parachute	paracaídas	paracadute	pára-quedas
falsch	faux, fausse	wrong, false	falso, a	falso, a	falso, a
fälschen	falsifier	falsify	falsificar	falsificare	falsificar
Falte(f); Kniff(m)	pli	fold; pleat	pliegue	piega	prega
Falte(f)	ride	wrinkle	arruga	ruga	ruga
falten	plier	fold	doblar	piegare	dobrar
familiär	familier, ière	familiar	familiar	familiare	familiar

G

German	French	English	Spanish	Italian	Portuguese
Familie(f)	famille	family	familia	famiglia	família
Familiengut(n)	patrimoine	patrimony	patrimonio	patrimonio	patrimónío
Familienname(m)	nom	surname	apellido	cognome	apelido
Familien-	familial, e	family	familiar	familiare	familiar
fanatisch	fanatique	fanatic(al)	fanático, a	fanatico, a	fanático, a
Fanfare(f)	fanfare	brass band	banda	banda	fanfarra, banda
Fangarm(m)	tentacule	tentacle	tentáculo	tentacolo	tentáculo
fangen	attraper	catch	agarrar, coger	acchiappare	agarrar, apanhar
fangen	capturer	capture	capturar	catturare	capturar
Fangnetz(n)	épuisette	fishing net	manguilla	guadino, retino	rede
Farbe(f)	couleur	colour	color	colore	côr
Farbe(f)	peinture	paint	pintura	vernice, pittura	tinta
färben	colorer	colour	colorear	colorare	colorir
färben	teindre, colorer	dye	teñir	tingere	tingir
Farbenton(m)	nuance, ton	shade, nuance	matiz	sfumatura	matiz, tom
farblos	incolore	colourless	incoloro, a	incolore	incolor
Farbstoff(m)	colorant	colouring	colorante	colorante	corante
Färbung(f), Farbe(f)	teinte	tint, colour	tinte, color	tinta	tinta
Farn(-kraut n)m	fougère	fern	helecho	felce	feto
Fasan(m)	faisan	pheasant	faisán	fagiano	faisão
Faschist(in f)m	fasciste	fascist	fascista	fascista	fascista
Faser(f)	fibre	fibre	fibra	fibra	fibra
Faser(f), Faden(m)	filament	filament	filamento	filamento	filamento
Faß(n)	tonneau	barrel	tonel; barril	botte, barile	tonel; barril
Faß(n)	fût	barrel	barril	fusto, barile	barril
Fassade(f)	façade	front(age)	fachada	facciata	fachada
Fassungsvermögen(n)	contenance	capacity, content	capacidad	capacità	capacidade
fast	presque	almost, nearly	casi	quasi	quase
faszinierend	fascinant, e	fascinating	fascinante	affascinante	fascinante
fasziniert	fasciné, e	fascinated	fascinado, a	affascinato, a	fascinado, a
Fata Morgana(f)	mirage	mirage	espejismo	miraggio	miragem
faul	paresseux, se	lazy	perezoso, a	pigro, a	preguiçoso, a
faul	fainéant, e	lazy	holgazán, a	fannullone, a	preguiçoso, a
Fauna(f), Tierwelt(f)	faune	fauna	fauna	fauna	fauna
Faust(f)	poing	fist	puño	pugno	punho
Faustschlag(m)	coup de poing	punch	puñetazo	pugno	soco; murro
Favorit(in f)m	favori, ite	favourite	favorito, a	favorito, a	favorito, a
Februar(m)	février	February	febrero	febbraio	Fevereiro
Fechten(n)	escrime	fencing	esgrima	scherma	esgrima
Feder(f)	plume	feather	pluma	penna, piuma	pluma; pena
Feder(f)(Sprung-)	ressort	spring	muelle	molla	mola
Federung(f)	suspension	suspension	suspensión	sospensione	suspensão
Fee(f)	fée	fairy	hada	fata	fada
fegen	balayer	sweep	barrer	spazzare	varrer
Fehlen(n), Mangel(m)	carence	deficiency	carencia	carenza	carência
fehlen	manquer	lack, be short of	faltar	mancare	falta(ter)
Fehler(m)	défaut	defect, fault	defecto	difetto	defeito
Fehler(m)	faute, erreur	fault	culpa	colpa	culpa
Fehler(m), Irrtum(m)	faute	mistake, error	falta, error	fallo, errore	falta, erro
Feier(f)	fête	celebration	fiesta	festa	festa
feierlich	solennel, le	solemn	solemne	solenne	solene
feiern	célébrer	celebrate	celebrar	celebrare	celebrar
Feiertag(m)	férié(jour)	public holiday	festivo(día)	festivo(giorno)	feriado(dia)
feig(e)	lâche	cowardly	cobarde	vigliacco, a	cobarde
Feigheit(f)	lâcheté	cowardliness	cobardía	vigliaccheria	cobardia
Feile(f)	lime	file	lima	lima	lima
feilschen, handeln	marchander	bargain, haggle	regatear	contrattare	regatear
fein, dünn	fin, e	fine, thin	fino, a	fine, sottile	fino, a
Feind(in f)m	ennemi, e	enemy	enemigo, a	nemico, a	inimigo, a
feindlich	hostile	hostile	hostil	ostile	hostil
feindlich, gegnerisch	adverse	adverse, opposing	adverso, a	avverso, a	adverso, a
Feld(n)	champ	field	campo	campo	campo
Feldarbeit(f)	labour	ploughing	labranza	aratura	lavoura
Feldbett(n)	lit de camp	camp-bed	cama de campaña	letto da campo	cama de campismo
Felge(f), Radkranz(m)	jante	rim	llanta	cerchione	jante, camba
Fell(n)	pelage	coat, fur	pelaje, pelo	pelo	pêlo
Fels(m)	roche, rocher	rock	roca	roccia	rocha
Felsen(m)	rocher	rock	peñasco, roca	masso, roccia	rochedo, rocha

German	French	English	Spanish	Italian	Portuguese
Fenster(n)	fenêtre	window	ventana	finestra	janela
Ferien(pl.)	vacances	holidays	vacaciones	vacanze	férias
Ferien(pl.)	vacances	vacation	vacaciones	vacanze	férias
ferner, überdies	plus(de)	further, moreover	además	più(di, in)	além disso
Fernglas(n)	jumelles	binoculars	gemelos	binocolo	binóculos
fern = sehen	regarder	watch, look(at)	mirar	guardare	ver
Fernsehen(n)	télévision	television	televisión	televisione	televisão; TV
Fernseher(m)	téléviseur	television set	televisor	televisore	televisor
Fernsehzuschauer/in	télespectateur	viewer	telespectador, a	telespettatore, trice	telespectador, a
Fernsteuerung(f)	télécommande	remote control	telemando	telecomando	telecomando
Ferse(f); Absatz(m)	talon	heel	talón	tallone	calcanhar
fertig	prêt, e	ready	dispuesto, a	pronto, a	pronto, a
fest	ferme	firm	firme	fermo, a; solido, a	firme
fest	fixe	fixed	fijo, a	fisso, a	fixo, a
festangestellt	titulaire	tenured	numerario	titolare	titular
fest = binden, binden	attacher	attach, tie, fasten	atar	legare	atar
fest = legen	déterminer	determine	determinar	determinare	determinar
Festmahl(n)	festin	feast, banquet	festín	festino	festim, banquete
festsetzen, aufstellen	établir	establish	establecer	stabilire	estabelecer
Festspiel(n)	festival	festival	festival	festival	festival
fest = stellen	constater	state; note	constatar	constatare	constatar
Fett(n)	graisse	fat	gordo; grasa	grasso	gordura
fett	gras, se	fat(ty), greasy	graso, a	grasso, a	gordo, a
feucht	humide	damp, humid, moist	húmedo, a	umido, a	húmido, a
Feuchtigkeit(f)	humidité	humidity	humedad	umidità	humidade
Feuer(n)	feu	fire	fuego	fuoco	fogo
Feuerlöscher(m)	extincteur	extinguisher	extintor	estintore	extintor
feuern, schießen	tirer	fire, shoot	tirar	sparare, tirare	disparar, atirar
Feuerstelle(f), Herd m	foyer, âtre	fire-place, hearth	hogar, chimenea	focolare	lareira
Feuerwehrmann(m)	pompier(sapeur-)	fireman(-men)	bombero	pompiere	bombeiro
Feuerzeug(n)	briquet	lighter	mechero	accendino	isqueiro
Fieber(n)	fièvre	fever, temperature	fiebre	febbre	febre
Fieberwahn(m)	délire	delirium	delirio	delirio	delirio
Figur(f)	figure	figure	figura	figura	figura
Fiktion(f)	fiction	fiction	ficción	finzione	ficção
Filiale(f)	filiale	subsidiary	filial, sucursal	filiale	filial, sucursal
Film(m)	film	film, movie	película	film	filme
Film(m)	pellicule	film	película	pellicola	película
Filmaufnahme(f)	tournage	shooting	rodaje	riprese	filmagem
filmen	filmer	film	rodar, filmar	filmare	filmar
Filmproduzent(in f)m	cinéaste	film-producer	cineasta	cineasta	cineasta
Filter(m)	filtre	filter	filtro	filtro	filtro
Filzschreiber(m)	crayon-feutre	felt-tip pen	rotulador	pennarello	marcador
finanziell	financier, ière	financial	financiero, a	finanziario, a	financeiro, a
finanzieren	financer	finance	financiar	finanziare	financiar
Finanzierung(f)	financement	financing	financiación	finanziamento	financiamento
Finanzwelt, Finanzen	finance	finance	finanza	finanza	finança
finden	trouver	find	encontrar	trovare	achar, encontrar
Finger(m)	doigt	finger	dedo	dito	dedo
Fingernagel(m)	ongle	nail	uña	unghia	unha
Finsternis(f)	ténèbres	darkness	tinieblas	tenebre	trevas
Finsternis(f)	éclipse	eclipse	eclipse	eclisse	eclipse
Firma(f)	firme	firm	firma	firma, ditta, azienda	firma
Firmensitz(m)	siège	head office	sede	sede	sede
Fisch(m)	poisson	fish	pescado	pesce	peixe
Fischen n; Fischfang m	pêche	fishing, angling	pesca	pesca	pesca
Fischer(m)	pêcheur	fisherman(-men)	pescador	pescatore	pescador
Fischgeschäft(n)	poissonnerie	fishmonger's	pescadería	pescheria	peixaria
fiskalisch, Steuer-	fiscal, e	fiscal, tax	fiscal	fiscale	fiscal
Fiskus(m), Finanzamt	fisc	Inland Revenue	fisco	fisco	fisco
fixe Idee(f)	obsession	obsession	obsesión	ossessione	obsessão
flackern	vaciller	flicker	oscilar, vacilar	vacillare	tremer
Flagge(f)	drapeau	flag	bandera	bandiera	bandeira
Flamme(f)	flamme	flame	llama	fiamma	chama
Fläschchen(n)	flacon	bottle(small)	frasco	boccetta	frasco
Fläschchen(n)	biberon	bottle(baby's -)	biberón	biberon	biberão
Flasche(f)	bouteille	bottle	botella	bottiglia	garrafa
Flaschenzug(m)	poulie	pulley	polea	puleggia	polia

G

289

Fleck(m)	tache	stain	mancha	macchia	mancha, nódoa
Fleck(m); Ort; Stelle	point	spot	lugar, punto	punto	ponto
Fleisch(n)	chair	flesh	carne	carne	carne
Fleisch(n)	viande	meat	carne	carne	carne
fleischfressend	carnivore	carnivorous	carnívoro, a	carnivoro, a	carnívoro, a
fleißig	studieux, se	studious	estudioso, a	studioso, a	estudioso, a
flexibel	flexible	flexible	flexible	flessibile	flexível
Flicken(n)	raccommodage	mending	remiendo	rammendo	remendo
Fliege(f)	mouche	fly	mosca	mosca	mosca
Fliege(f)	noeud papillon	bow tie	pajarita	papillon	laço
fliegen	voler	fly	volar	volare	voar
fliegen; lotsen; fahren	piloter	pilot; fly; drive	pilotar	pilotare	pilotar
Flieger(m), Pilot(m)	aviateur, trice	aviator	aviador, a	aviatore, trice	aviador, a
fliehen	fuir	run away, flee	huir	fuggire	fugir
fliehen	enfuir(s')	run away	huir	fuggire	fugir
fliehen	échapper(s')	escape	escapar(se)	scappare	escapar-se
Fliese(f), Kachel(f)	carreau	tile	baldosa, azulejo	piastrella	ladrilho, azulejo
Fliesen(n); Fliese(f)	carrelage	tiling; tiles	embaldosado	pavimento	ladrilho
fließen	couler	flow, run	correr, fluir	scorrere	correr
fließend	couramment	fluently	soltura(con)	correntemente	fluentemente
flimmern	scintiller	sparkle	centellear	scintillare	cintilar
flink	agile	agile, nimble	ágil	agile	ágil
Flitter(m)	paillette	glitter, spangle	lentejuela	lustrino	lentejoula
Flocke(f)	flocon	flake	copo	fiocco	floco
Floh(m)	puce	flea	pulga	pulce	pulga
Flora(f), Pflanzenwelt	flore	flora	flora	flora	flora
Floß(n)	radeau	raft	balsa	zattera	jangada
Flosse(f)	nageoire	fin	aleta	pinna	barbatana
Flosse(f)	palme	flipper	aleta	pinna	barbatanas
Flöte(f)	flûte	flute	flauta	flauto	flauta
Flotte(f)	flotte	fleet	flota	flotta	frota
Fluch(m)	juron	swear-word	juramento, taco	bestemmia	palavrão
Flucht(f)	évasion	escape	evasión	evasione	evasão
Flucht(f)	fuite	flight, escape	huída	fuga	fuga
flüchtig	fugitif, ive	fugitive	fugitivo, a	fuggitivo, a	fugitivo, a
flüchtig sehen	entrevoir	glimpse	entrever	intravedere	entrever
Flüchtling(m)	réfugié, e	refugee	refugiado, a	rifugiato, a	refugiado, a
Flug(m)	vol	flight	vuelo	volo	voo
Flugblatt(n)	prospectus	leaflet	folleto	prospetto	prospecto
Flugblatt(n)	tract	handout, leaflet	octavilla	volantino	panfleto
Flügel(m)	aile	wing	ala	ala	asa
Flughafen(m)	aéroport	airport	aeropuerto	aeroporto	aeroporto
Flugzeug(n)	avion	plane, aeroplane	avión	aereo	avião
Flur(m)	couloir	corridor	pasillo	corridoio	corredor
Flur(m)	vestibule	hall	vestíbulo	ingresso, anticamera	vestíbulo; hall
Fluß(m)	rivière	river	río, ribera	fiume	rio, ribeira
Fluß(m), Strömung(f)	flux	flow	flujo	flusso	fluxo
flüssig	liquide	liquid	líquido, a	liquido, a	líquido, a
Flußkrebs(m)	écrevisse	crayfish	cangrejo(de río)	gambero(di fiume)	caranguejo
Flüssigkeit(f)	liquide	liquid	líquido	liquido	líquido
Flüssigkeit(f)	fluide	fluid	fluido	fluido	fluido
flüstern	chuchoter	whisper	susurrar	bisbigliare	sussurrar
flüstern	murmurer	murmur, whisper	murmurar	mormorare	murmurar
Fohlen(n)	poulain	foal	potro	puledro	potro
Folge(f)	suite	continuation	continuación	seguito	continuação
Folge(f), Sequenz(f)	séquence	sequence	secuencia	sequenza	sequência
folgen	suivre	follow	seguir	seguire	seguir
folgend	consécutif, ive	consecutive	consecutivo, a	consecutivo, a	consecutivo, a
folgenden Tag(m)	lendemain	next day	día siguiente	indomani(l')	dia seguinte
folgern, schließen aus	déduire	deduct	deducir	detrarre	deduzir
folglich; deshalb	conséquent(par)	therefore	consiguiente(por)	perciò	conseguinte(por)
Folklore(f)	folklore	folklore	folklore	folclore	folclore
Folter(f)	torture	torture	tortura	tortura	tortura
Fön(m), Haartrockner m	sèche-cheveux	hair-dryer	secador	asciugacapelli	secador
Fonds(m), Kapital(n)	fonds	funds	fondos	fondi	fundos, capital
fordern	exiger, réclamer	demand, require	exigir	esigere	exigir
Forderung(f)	exigence	demand, requirement	exigencia	esigenza	exigência
Forderung(f)	revendication	claim, demand	reivindicación	rivendicazione	reivindicação

German	French	English	Spanish	Italian	Portuguese
Forelle(f)	truite	trout	trucha	trota	truta
Form(f), Aussehen(n)	forme	shape, form	forma	forma	forma
Form(f)	moule	mould	molde	stampo, forma	molde; forma
Formalität(f)	formalité	formality	formalidad	formalità	formalidade
Format(n)	format	format, size	formato, tamaño	formato	formato
Formel(f)	formule	formula	fórmula	formula	fórmula
Formular(n), Vordruck	formulaire	form	formulario	modulo, formulario	formulário
Formular(n)	imprimé	printed form	impreso	stampato	impresso
Forscher(in f)m	chercheur, euse	research worker	investigador, a	cercatore	investigador, a
Forscher(in f)m	explorateur	explorer	explorador, a	esploratore, trice	explorador, a
Forschung(f)	recherche	research	investigación	ricerca	investigação
fort = bestehen	subsister	subsist, remain	subsistir	sussistere	subsistir
fortdauernd	perpétuel, le	perpetual	perpetuo, a	perpetuo, a	perpétuo, a
fort = pflanzen, sich	reproduire(se)	breed(animals)	reproducir(se)	riprodurre(-rsi)	reproduzir-se
Fortschreiten(n)	progression	progression	progresión	progressione	progressão
fortschreitend	progressif, ive	progressive	progresivo, a	progressivo, a	progressivo, a
Fortschritt(m)	progrès	progress	progreso	progresso	progresso
fort = setzen	continuer	continue, go on	continuar	continuare	continuar
Fossil(n)	fossile	fossil	fósil	fossile	fóssil
Foto(n)	photo	photo(graph)	foto	foto, fotografia	fotografia
Fotografie(f)	photographie	photography	fotografía	fotografia	fotografia
fotografieren	photographier	take a photo	fotografiar	fotografare	fotografar
Fötus(m)	foetus	foetus	feto	feto	feto
Fracht(f)	fret	freight	flete	nolo, carico	frete
Frachter(m)	cargo	cargo(-boat)	carguero, buque	cargo, nave da carico	cargueiro
Frage(f)	question	question	pregunta	domanda	pergunta
Frage(f)	question	question	cuestión	questione	questão
fragen	demander	ask(for)	pedir	chiedere	pedir
fragen	demander	ask	preguntar	domandare	perguntar
fragen, sich	demander(se)	wonder	preguntarse	domandarsi	perguntar-se
fragen, befragen	interroger	question, ask	interrogar	interrogare	interrogar
fragen	poser(question)	ask	preguntar	porre(domanda)	perguntar
Fragment(n)	fragment	fragment	fragmento	frammento	fragmento
frankieren, freimachen	affranchir	stamp	franquear	affrancare	franquear
Frau(f)	femme	woman(women)	mujer	donna	mulher
Frau(f)	madame	Mrs; Madam	señora	signora	senhora
Fräulein(n)	mademoiselle	Miss	señorita	signorina	menina
fraulich	féminin, e	feminine	femenino, a	femminile	feminino, a
Frechheit(f)	insolence	insolence	insolencia	insolenza	insolência
frei	libre	free	libre	libero, a	livre
frei	libre; dégagé, e	clear	libre	libero, a	livre
freigebig	généreux, se	generous	generoso, a	generoso, a	generoso, a
Freiheit(f)	liberté	liberty, freedom	libertad	libertà	liberdade
frei = lassen	relâcher	release	soltar	rilasciare	libertar
frei = machen	dégager	clear	despejar	sgomberare	desimpedir
Freitag(m)	vendredi	Friday	viernes	venerdì	sexta-feira
freiwillig	volontaire	voluntary	voluntario, a	volontario, a	voluntário, a
Freiwillige(r)m f	volontaire	volunteer	voluntario, a	volontario, a	voluntário, a
Freizeit(f)	loisir	leisure	tiempo libre	tempo libero, hobby	tempo livre
Frequenz(f)	fréquence	frequency	frecuencia	frequenza	frequência
Freude(f)	joie	joy	alegría	gioia	alegria
Freude machen	plaisir(faire)	please	gusto(dar)	piacere(fare)	gosto(dar)
Freund(in f)m	ami, e	friend	amigo, a	amico, a	amigo, a
Freundschaft(f)	amitié	friendship	amistad	amicizia	amizade
freundschaftlich	amical, e	friendly	amistoso, a	amichevole	amigável
Frieden(m)	paix	peace	paz	pace	paz
Friedhof(m)	cimetière	cemetery	cementerio	cimitero	cemitério
friedlich	pacifique	peaceful, pacific	pacífico, a	pacifico, a	pacífico, a
friedlich, ruhig	paisible	peaceful, quiet	apacible	pacifico, a; placido, a	pacífico, a
frieren	geler	freeze	helar	gelare	gelar
frieren	froid(avoir)	cold(to be)	frío(tener)	freddo(avere)	frio(ter)
frisch	frais, fraîche	fresh	fresco, a	fresco, a	fresco, a
Friseur(m), Friseuse f	coiffeur, se	hairdresser	peluquero, a	parrucchiere, a	cabeleireiro, a
Friseurladen(m)	salon(coiffure)	salon	peluquería	parrucchiere, a(da)	salão
frisieren, sich	coiffer(se)	hair(do one's)	peinar(se)	pettinare(-rsi)	pentear-se
Frist(f)	délai	delay	plazo	termine	prazo
Frisur(f)	coiffure	hair-style	peinado	pettinatura	penteado
frivol, leichtsinnig	frivole	frivolous	frívolo, a	frivolo, a	frívolo, a

G

German	French	English	Spanish	Italian	Portuguese
froh, erfreut	content, e	glad, happy, pleased	contento, a	contento, a	contente
froh	content, e	pleased, glad	contento, a	contento, a	contente
froh	gai, e	happy, merry	alegre	allegro, a	alegre
Fröhlichkeit(f)	réjouissance	rejoicing	regocijo	gioia, giubilo	regozijo; alegria
Frömmigkeit(f)	dévotion	devotion	devoción	devozione	devoção
Front(f)	devant	front, fore	frente, delantera	davanti	frente(a)
Frosch(m)	grenouille	frog	rana	rana	rã
Frostbeule(f)	engelure	chilblain	sabañón	gelone	frieira
Frucht(f)	fruit(s)	fruit	fruta	frutto; frutta	fruta
fruchtbar	fertile	fertile	fértil	fertile	fértil
Fruchtbarkeit(f)	fécondité	fertility	fecundidad	fecondità	fecundidade
früh	matinal, e	early	matutino, a	mattutino, a	matinal
früh	tôt	early	temprano	presto	cedo
früher	autrefois	past(in the)	antaño	volta(una)	antigamente
früher	antérieur, e	prior	anterior	anteriore	anterior
Frühgeburt(f)	prématuré, e	premature(baby)	prematuro, a	prematuro, a	prematuro, a
Frühling(m)	printemps	spring	primavera	primavera	primavera
frühreif, frühzeitig	précoce	precocious	precoz	precoce	precoce
Frühstück(n)	déjeuner(petit)	breakfast	desayuno	colazione(prima)	almoço(pequeno)
Fuchs(m)	renard	fox(-es)	zorro	volpe	raposa
fühlen	sentir	feel	sentir	sentire	sentir
führen	guider	guide	guiar	guidare	guiar
führen	mener, conduire	lead	guiar, conducir	condurre	levar, conduzir
führen zu	aboutir à	lead to	conducir a	arrivare a	conduzir a
Führer(in f)m	guide	guide	guía	guida	guia
Führer(in f)m	leader, chef	leader	jefe, guía	capo, guida	chefe
Führer(Reise-)(m)	guide	guide-book	guía	guida	guia
Führerschein(m)	permis(auto)	driving licence	permiso conducir	patente di guida	carta de condução
füllen	remplir	fill	llenar	riempire	encher
Füller(m)	stylo	pen, fountain-pen	estilográfica	stilografica	caneta
füllig, fettleibig	obèse	obese	obeso, a	obeso, a	obeso, a
fundamental	fondamental, e	fundamental	fundamental	fondamentale	fundamental
fünf	cinq	five	cinco	cinque	cinco
fünfzehn	quinze	fifteen	quince	quindici	quinze
fünfzig	cinquante	fifty	cincuenta	cinquanta	cinquenta
Funken(m)	étincelle	spark	chispa	scintilla	faísca
Funkspruch(m)	aérogramme	aerogram	aerograma	aerogramma	aerograma
Funktion(f)	fonction	function	función	funzione	função
funktionieren	fonctionner	function, work, run	funcionar	funzionare	funcionar
für	pour	for	para; por	per	para; por
für	pour	for	por	per	por
Furche(f)	sillon	furrow	surco	solco	rego
Furcht(f)	crainte	fear	temor, miedo	timore	temor, receio
Furcht(f)	appréhension	apprehension	aprensión, recelo	apprensione	apreensão
furchtbar	redoutable	formidable	temible	temibile	temível
Furunkel(m)	furoncle	boil	furúnculo	foruncolo	furúnculo
Fürwort(n)	pronom	pronoun	pronombre	pronome	pronome
fuschen, mogeln	tricher	cheat	trampas(hacer)	barare	batota(fazer)
Fuß(m)	pied	foot(feet pl.)	pie	piede	pé
Fußball(m)	football	football, soccer	fútbol	calcio	futebol
Fußboden(m)	plancher	floor	suelo	pavimento	soalho, sobrado
Fußgänger(m)	piéton	pedestrian	peatón	pedone	peão
Fußpfleger(in f)m	pédicure	chiropodist	pedicuro, a	pedicure	pedicuro
Fußtritt(m)	coup de pied	kick	patada	calcio	pontapé
Futter(n)	fourrage	fodder	forraje	foraggio	forragem

G

German	French	English	Spanish	Italian	Portuguese
Gabel(f)	fourchette	fork	tenedor	forchetta	garfo
Gabel(f)(Heu-; Mist-)	fourche	pitchfork, fork	horca	forca	forcado
gähnen	bâiller	yawn	bostezar	sbadigliare	bocejar
galant	galant, e	gallant	galante	galante	galante
Galaxie(f)	galaxie	galaxy	galaxia	galassia	galáxia
Galerie, Ausstellung	galerie	gallery	galería	galleria	galeria
Galone(f)	galon	stripe	galón	gallone, grado	galão
Galopp(m)	galop	gallop	galope	galoppo	galope
Ganglien(pl.)	ganglion	ganglion, gland	ganglio	ganglio	gânglio
Gangster(m)	gangster	gangster	gángster	gangster	gangster
Ganove(m), Gauner(m)	truand, e	crook	granuja, bandido	teppista	bandido
Gans(f)	oie	goose(geese pl.)	oca	oca	ganso
ganz	entier, ière	whole, entire	entero, a	intero, a	inteiro, a
ganz	toute	whole(the)	toda	tutta	toda
ganz	entièrement	entirely	completamente	interamente	inteiramente
ganz; Gesamt-	total, e	total	total	totale	total
ganz	tout à fait	quite	totalmente	affatto	totalmente
Ganze(n); Gesamtheit f	ensemble	whole; all the	conjunto	insieme	conjunto
gar, gekocht	cuit, e	cooked	cocido, a	cotto, a	cozido, a
Garage(f)	garage	garage	garaje, garage	garage	garagem
Garantie(f)	garantie	guarantee; warranty	garantía	garanzia	garantia
Garderobe(f)	vestiaire	cloak-room	vestuario	vestiario	vestiário
gären	fermenter	ferment	fermentar	fermentare	fermentar
garnieren	garnir	garnish	guarnecer	guarnire	guarnecer
Garten(m)	jardin	garden	jardín	giardino	jardim
Gartenbau(m)	horticulture	horticulture	horticultura	orticultura	horticultura
Gärtner(in f)m	jardinier, ière	gardener	jardinero, a	giardiniere, a	jardineiro, a
Gas(n)	gaz	gas	gas	gas	gás
gasförmig	gazeux, se	gaseous	gaseoso, a	gassoso, a	gasoso, a
Gäßchen(n), Gasse(f)	ruelle	alley	callejuela	viuzza, vicolo	viela
Gast(m)	invité, e	guest	invitado, a	invitato, a	convidado, a
Gast(m)	convive	guest	convidado, a	commensale	conviva
Gast(m)	hôte	guest	huésped, a	ospite	hóspede
gastfreundlich	accueillant, e	hospitable	acogedor, a	accogliente	acolhedor, a
Gastfreundlichkeit(f)	hospitalité	hospitality	hospitalidad	ospitalità	hospitalidade
Gastgeber(m); Gast(m)	hôte, tesse	host; guest	anfitrión; huésped	ospite	anfitrião; hóspede, a
Gasthaus(n)	auberge	inn	posada; albergue	locanda	estalagem
Gasthaus(n)	pension	guest-house	pensión	pensione	pensão
Gastronomie(f)	gastronomie	gastronomy	gastronomía	gastronomia	gastronomia
Gatte, Mann, Ehemann m	époux	husband	esposo	sposo, consorte	esposo
Gattin, Frau, Ehefrau f	épouse	wife(wives)	esposa	sposa, consorte	esposa
Gattung(f), Art(f)	espèce	kind, sort	especie	specie	espécie
Gauner(m)	escroc	crook, swindler	estafador	imbroglione	gatuno, escroque
Gebärmutter(f)	utérus	uterus, womb	útero	utero	útero
Gebäude(n)	bâtiment	building	edificio	edificio, palazzo	edifício
Gebäude(n)	édifice	edifice, building	edificio	edificio	edifício
Gebäude(n)	immeuble	block of flats	inmueble	palazzo, edificio	edifício, imóvel
Gebäude(n), Lokal(n)	local	premises	local	locale	local
geben	donner	give	dar	dare	dar
Gebet(n)	prière	prayer	oración	preghiera	oração
Gebiet(n), Land(n)	territoire	territory	territorio	territorio	território
gebildet	cultivé, e	cultured, learned	culto, a	colto, a	culto, a
Gebirge(n), Berg(m)	montagne	mountain	montaña	montagna	montanha
Gebiß(n)	dentier	denture	dentadura	dentiera	dentadura
geboren	né, e	born(be)	nacido, a	nato, a	nascido, a
geboren werden	naître	born(be)	nacer	nascere	nascer
Gebrauch(m)	usage	usage, use	uso, empleo	uso	uso
Gebrauch(m)	emploi	use	uso, empleo	uso	uso
gebräuchlich	usuel, le	usual	usual	usuale	usual
gebraucht	occasion	second-hand, used	segunda mano	seconda mano	segunda mão(em)
Gebühr(f)	redevance	tax; royalty	impuesto, tasa	cànone	taxa

293

German	French	English	Spanish	Italian	Portuguese
Geburt(f)	naissance	birth	nacimiento	nascita	nascimento
Geburtenrate(f)	natalité	birth-rate	natalidad	natalità	natalidade
gebürtig	natif, ive	native	nativo, a	nativo, a	nativo, a
gebürtig	originaire	native(of)	oriundo, a	originario, a	oriundo, a
Geburtstag(m)	anniversaire	birthday	cumpleaños	compleanno	aniversário
Gebüsch(n)	buisson	bush	matorral	cespuglio	moita
Gedächtnis(n)	mémoire	memory	memoria	memoria	memória
Gedächtnisschwund(m)	amnésie	amnesia	amnesia	amnesia	amnésia
Gedanke(m)	pensée	thought	pensamiento	pensiero	pensamento
Gedankenstrich(m)	tiret	dash	raya, guión	trattino	travessão, hífen
Gedeck(n)	couvert	table(lay the)	cubierto	coperto	talher
gedenken	commémorer	commemorate	conmemorar	commemorare	comemorar
Gedicht(n)	poème	poem	poema	poema	poema
Gedränge(n)	affluence	crowd	afluencia	afflusso	afluência
Gedränge(n)	encombrement	congestion, jam	estorbo	affollamento, ingorgo	engarrafamento
Geduld(f)	patience	patience	paciencia	pazienza	paciência
geduldig	patient, e	patient	paciente	paziente	paciente
Gefahr(f)	danger	danger	peligro	pericolo	perigo
Gefahr(f)	péril	peril, danger	peligro, riesgo	pericolo	perigo
gefährlich	dangereux, se	dangerous	peligroso, a	pericoloso, a	perigoso, a
gefallen(jdm)	plaire	please; like	gustar, agradar	piacere	agradar
gefällig	plaisant, e	pleasant	agradable	piacevole	agradável
Gefangene(r)mf	prisonnier, ière	prisoner	prisionero, a	prigioniero, a	prisioneiro, a
Gefängnis(n)	prison	prison, jail	prisión, cárcel	prigione, carcere	prisão, cadeia
Gefäß(Blut-)(n)	vaisseau	vessel(blood)	vaso(sanguíneo)	vaso(sanguigno)	vaso(sanguíneo)
Gefäß-	vasculaire	vascular	vascular	vascolare	vascular
Gefecht(n)	bataille	battle	batalla	battaglia	batalha
Geflügel(n)	volaille	poultry	aves de corral	pollame	aves de capoeira
Gefolge(n)	escorte	escort	escolta	scorta	escolta
gefräßig, gierig	vorace	voracious	voraz	vorace	voraz
Gefreiter(m); Korporal	caporal	corporal	cabo(mil.)	caporale	cabo
Gefühl(n)	sentiment	feeling	sentimiento	sentimento	sentimento
gegen, an	contre	against	contra	contro	encostado a
gegen, in Richtung	vers	towards, to	hacia	verso	direcção a(em)
Gegenangriff(m)	contre-attaque	counter-attack	contraataque	contro-attacco	contra-ataque
Gegenangriff(m)	riposte	counter-attack	réplica	risposta	réplica
Gegend(f)	région	region, area	región	regione	região
Gegensatz(m)	contraste	contrast	contraste	contrasto	contraste
gegenseitig	mutuel, le	mutual	mútuo, a	mutuo, a	mútuo, a
Gegenteil(n)	contraire	opposite, contrary	contrario	contrario	contrário
gegenüberliegend	opposé, e	opposite	opuesto, a	opposto, a	oposto, a
Gegenwart(f)	présent	present	presente	presente	presente
gegenwärtig, aktuell	présent, e	present	presente, actual	presente, attuale	presente, actual
Gegner(in f)m	adversaire	opponent	adversario, a	avversario, a	adversário, a
geheim	secret, ète	secret	secreto, a	segreto, a	secreto, a
Geheimnis(n)	secret	secret	secreto	segreto	segredo
Geheimnis(n); Rätsel n	mystère	mystery	misterio	mistero	mistério
gehen, fahren nach	aller	go	ir(a, por, hacia)	andare, recarsi	ir
gehen	marcher	walk	andar	andare	andar
Gehilfe(m); Hilfs-	adjoint, e	assistant	adjunto, a	aggiunto, a; vice	adjunto, a
Gehirn(n)	cerveau	brain	cerebro	cervello	cérebro
Gehirn-; zerebral	cérébral, e	cerebral	cerebral	cerebrale	cerebral
Gehör(n)	ouïe	hearing, audition	oído	udito	ouvido
gehorchen	obéir	obey	obedecer	obbedire	obedecer
gehören	appartenir(à)	belong to	pertenecer	appartenere	pertencer
gehorsam	docile	docile	dócil	docile	dócil, manso
Geier(m)	vautour	vulture	buitre	avvoltoio	abutre
Geige(f)	violon	violin	violín	violino	violino
Geisel(f)	otage	hostage	rehén	ostaggio	refém
Geist(m)	esprit	spirit	espíritus	spirito	espírito
geistig	mental, e	mental	mental	mentale	mental
geistreich	spirituel, le	spiritual	espiritual	spirituale	espiritual
geizig	avare	miserly, mean	avaro, a	avaro, a	avarento, a
gelähmt	paralysé, e	paralysed	paralítico, a	paralitico, a	paralítico, a
Gelände(n)	terrain	ground	terreno	terreno	terreno
Geländer(n)	rampe	banister, handrail	barandilla	rampa	corrimão
gelangen zu/kommen an	accéder	accede to	acceder	assurgere	chegar
geläufig	courant, e	common	corriente	corrente, comune	corrente

German	French	English	Spanish	Italian	Portuguese
gelb	jaune	yellow	amarillo, a	giallo, a	amarelo, a
Gelbsucht(f)	jaunisse	jaundice	ictericia	itterizia	ictericia
Geld(n)	argent	money	dinero	denaro; soldi	dinheiro
Geld(n)	monnaie	money	moneda, dinero	moneta	moeda
Geldbörse(f)	porte-monnaie	purse	monedero	portamonete	porta-moedas
Geldschein(m)	billet(banque)	bank-note	billete(de banco)	banconota	nota(de banco)
Geldstrafe(f)	amende	fine	multa	multa	multa
Geldstück(n)	pièce	coin	moneda	spiccioli, moneta	moeda
Gelee(n)	gelée	jelly	jalea	gelatina	geleia
gelegen	situé, e	located	situado, a	situato, a	situado, a
Gelegenheit(f)	occasion	opportunity	oportunidad	occasione	oportunidade
gelegentlich	occasionnel, le	occasional	ocasional	occasionale	ocasional
gelehrt	érudit, e	erudite, learned	erudito, a	erudito, a	erudito, a
Gelehrte(r)mf	érudit, e	scholar	erudito, a	dotto, a; erudito, a	erudito, a
Gelehrte(r)mf	savant	scientist	científico	scienziato	cientista
Gelenk(n)	articulation	joint	articulación	articolazione	articulação
Geliebte(r)mf	amant, e	lover	amante	amante	amante
gelingen	réussir	succeed	lograr, conseguir	riuscire	conseguir
Gelübde(n)	voeu	vow	voto	voto	promessa
Gemälde(n)	tableau	painting, picture	cuadro	dipinto, quadro	quadro
Gemälde(n)(Leinwand)	toile	canvas, painting	lienzo, cuadro	tela, dipinto	tela, quadro
gemäß	selon	according to	según	secondo	segundo
gemäßigt	tempéré, e	temperate	templado, a	temperato, a	temperado, a
Gemeinschaft(f)	communauté	community	comunidad	comunità	comunidade
gemeinschaftlich	collectif, ive	collective	colectivo, a	collettivo, a	colectivo, a
Gemeinschafts-	commun, e	common	común	comune	comum
gemischt	mixte	mixed	mixto, a	misto, a	misto, a
Gemüse(n)	légume	vegetable	legumbre, verdura	verdura; legume	legume
Gemüsegarten(m)	jardin	garden	huerto	orto	horta
genau, richtig	exact, e	exact, right	exacto, a	esatto, a	exacto, a
genau	précis, e	precise, accurate	preciso, a	preciso, a	exacto, a
genau, richtig; gerade	exactement	exactly	exactamente	esattamente	exactamente
genau	justement	exactly	justamente	appunto	justamente
genau	précisément	precisely	precisamente	precisamente, appunto	precisamente
genau fest = legen	préciser	specify	precisar	precisare	precisar
Genauigkeit(f)	exactitude	accuracy	exactitud	esattezza	exactidão
Genauigkeit(f)	précision	precision	precisión	precisione	precisão
Genealogie(f)	généalogie	genealogy	genealogía	genealogia	genealogia
genehmigen, zu = lassen	agréer	accept, approve	aceptar	gradire, accettare	aceitar
genehmigen	approuver	approve	aprobar	approvare	aprovar
General(m)	général	general	general	generale	general
Generation(f)	génération	generation	generación	generazione	geração
Generator(m)	générateur	generator	generador	generatore	gerador
Genesung(f)	convalescence	convalescence	convalecencia	convalescenza	convalescência
Genetik(f)	génétique	genetics	genética	genetica	genética
genial	génial, e	brilliant	genial	geniale	genial
Genie(n)	génie	genius	genio	genio	génio
genießen	jouir	enjoy	gozar	godere	gozar
Genital-	génital, e	genital	genital	genitale	genital
Genossenschaft(f)	coopérative	cooperative	cooperativa	cooperativa	cooperativa
Gentleman(m)	monsieur	man, gentleman(men)	caballero	signore	cavalheiro
genug	assez	enough; rather	bastante(s)	abbastanza	bastante
genügend	suffisant, e	sufficient	suficiente	sufficiente	suficiente
Geologie(f)	géologie	geology	geología	geologia	geologia
Geometrie(f)	géométrie	geometry	geometría	geometria	geometria
Gepäck(n)	bagage(s)	luggage, baggage	equipaje	bagaglio	bagagem
Gepäckaufbewahrung(f)	consigne(bagage)	left luggage	consigna(equipaje)	deposito bagagli	depósito(bagagem)
gepanzert	blindé, e	armoured	blindado, a	blindato, a	blindado, a
gerade	droit, e	straight	recto, a	diritto, a	recto, a
gerade	pair	even	par	pari	par
Gerade(f)	droite	straight line	recta	retta	recta
gerade = biegen	redresser	straighten out/up	enderezar	raddrizzare	endireitar
Gerät(n)	ustensile	utensil	utensilios	utensile	utensílio
geräuchert	fumé, e	smoked	ahumado, a	affumicato, a	fumado, a
geräumig	gros, se	big	grande	grosso, a	grande
Geräusch(n)	bruit	noise	ruido	rumore	ruído, barulho
gerecht	juste	just	justo, a	giusto, a	justo, a
Gerechtigkeit(f)	justice	justice	justicia	giustizia	justiça

G

295

German	French	English	Spanish	Italian	Portuguese
Gerechtigkeit(f)	équité	equity	equidad	equità	equidade
gereizt	excité, e	worked up	excitado, a	eccitato, a	excitado, a
Gericht(n)	tribunal	court, tribunal	tribunal	tribunale	tribunal
gerichtlich	judiciaire	judicial, legal	judicial	giudiziario, a	judiciário, a
gerinnen	coaguler	coagulate, clot	coagular	coagulare	coagular
gerissen, schlau	malin, igne	smart, clever	pillo, a; astuto, a	furbo, a	esperto, a; astuto, a
gern	volontiers	willingly	buena gana(de)	volentieri	bom grado(de)
gern haben	aimer	like	gustar(le)	piacere, amare	gostar(de)
Geröll(n)	éboulis	scree	escombros	detriti	escombros
Geruch(m)	odeur	odour, smell	olor	odore	cheiro, odor
Geruchssinn(m)	odorat	smell(sense of)	olfato	odorato	olfacto
Gerücht(n)	rumeur	rumour	rumor	voce, diceria	rumor
gerührt	ému, e	moved, affected	emocionado, a	commosso, a	comovido, a
Gerüst(n)	échafaudage	scaffolding	andamio	impalcatura	andaime
Gesamt-	total, e	overall	total	complessivo, a	total
Gesamt-; pauschal	global, e	global, overall	global	globale	global
Gesäß(n), Po(m)	fesse	bottom, buttock	nalga	natica	nádega
Geschädigte(r)mf	sinistré, e	victim(disaster -)	siniestrado, a	sinistrato, a	sinistrado, a
Geschäft(n)	commerce	shop, business	tienda, negocio	negozio	loja
Geschäft(n)	boutique	boutique, shop	tienda	negozio, boutique	loja
Geschäft(n), Laden(m)	magasin	shop	tienda	negozio; bottega	loja
Geschäfte(n, pl.)	affaires	business	negocios	affari	negócios
geschäftlich	commercial, e	commercial	comercial	commerciale	comercial
Geschäftsführer(m)	gérant, e	manager	gerente	gerente, gestore	gerente
Geschäftsmann(m)/frau	commerçant, e	tradesman(-men)	comerciante	commerciante	comerciante
geschehen	arriver	occur, happen	ocurrir, suceder	succedere	acontecer
Geschenk(n)	cadeau	present, gift	regalo	regalo	prenda, presente
Geschichte(f)	histoire	history	historia	storia	História
Geschichte(f)	histoire	story	historia	storia	história
Geschichtschreiber(m)	historien	historian	historiador	storico	historiador
Geschick(n)	savoir-faire	know-how	tacto, maña	savoir-faire	habilidade
Geschicklichkeit(f)	habileté	ability, skill	habilidad	abilità	habilidade
geschickt	adroit, e	skilled	diestro, a	abile	destro, a; hábil
geschickt	habile	clever, skilful	hábil; diestro, a	abile	hábil; destro, a
Geschirr(n)	vaisselle	crockery, dishes	vajilla	stoviglie, vasellame	loiça, louça
Geschirr(n)	harnais	harness	arnés	finimenti	arnês
Geschlecht(n)	sexe	sex	sexo	sesso	sexo
geschlechtlich	sexuel, le	sexual	sexual	sessuale	sexual
Geschlechts-	vénérien, ne	venereal	venéreo, a	venereo, a	venéreo, a
Geschmack(m)	goût	taste	gusto	gusto, sapore	gosto
Geschmack(m)	saveur	flavour	sabor	sapore	sabor
geschmolzen	fondu, e	melted	derretido, a	sciolto, a	derretido, a
geschnitten	coupé, e	cut	cortado, a	tagliato, a	cortado, a
Geschoß(n), Granate(f)	obus	shell	obús	proiettile	obus
Geschoß(n)	projectile	projectile	proyectil	proiettile	projéctil
geschwätzig	bavard, e	talkative	parlanchín, a	chiacchierone, a	falador, a
Geschwindigkeit(f)	vitesse	speed	velocidad	velocità	velocidade
Geschworene(r)mf	juré	juryman, juror	jurado	giurato	jurado
Geschwür(n)	ulcère	ulcer	úlcera	ulcera	úlcera
Geschwür(n)	abcès	abscess(-es)	absceso	ascesso	abcesso
gesellig	sociable	sociable	sociable	socievole	sociável
Gesellschaft(f)	compagnie	company	compañía	compagnia	companhia
Gesellschaft(f)	société	company, firm	sociedad	società	sociedade
Gesellschaft(f)	société	society	sociedad	società	sociedade
Gesellschaft(in)	compagnie(en)	company of(in the)	compañía(en)	compagnia(in)	companhia(em)
Gesetz(n)	loi	law	ley	legge	lei
Gesetzesartikel(m)	article	article	artículo	articolo	artigo
gesetzgebend	législatif, ive	legislative	legislativo, a	legislativo, a	legislativo, a
Gesetzgebung(f)	législation	legislation	legislación	legislazione	legislação
gesetzlich	légal, e	legal	legal	legale	legal
gesetzlich	institutionnel	institutional	institucional	istituzionale	institucional
Gesicht(n)	visage	face	rostro, cara	viso	cara
Gesicht(n)	figure	face	rostro	faccia	rosto
Gesicht(n)	face	face	cara	faccia	face; cara
Gesichtsausdruck(m)	physionomie	physiognomy	fisionomía	fisionomia	fisionomia
Gesichtswasser(n)	lotion	lotion	loción	lozione	loção
gespannt	tendu, e	tight	tenso, a	teso, a	esticado, a
Gespenst(n)	fantôme	ghost	fantasma	fantasma	fantasma

German	French	English	Spanish	Italian	Portuguese
gesperrt	barré, e	blocked	cortado, a	sbarrato, a	impedido, a
Gespräch(n)	conversation	conversation	conversación	conversazione	conversação
Gespräch(n)	entretien	talk, conversation	conversación	colloquio	entrevista
Gesprächspartner/in	interlocuteur	interlocutor	interlocutor, a	interlocutore, trice	interlocutor, a
Geständnis(n)	aveu	confession	confesión	confessione	confissão
Gestank(m)	puanteur	stench, stink	hedor, peste	puzza, fetore	fedor
Geste(f)	geste	gesture	gesto	gesto	gesto
gestehen	avouer	confess, admit	confesar	confessare	confessar
gestern	hier	yesterday	ayer	ieri	ontem
gestreift	rayures(à)	striped	rayas(a)	righe(a)	riscas(às)
Gestrüpp(n)	broussaille	undergrowth	zarzal, maleza	macchia, cespugli	mato, brenha
gesund	sain, e	healthy	sano, a	sano, a	são, sã
Gesundheit(f)	santé	health	salud	salute	saúde
Gesundheits-	sanitaire	sanitary-	sanitario, a	sanitario, a	sanitário, a
getötet	tué, e	killed	muerto, a	ucciso, a	morto, a
Getränk(n)	boisson	drink	bebida	bibita; bevanda	bebida
Getreide(n)	céréale	cereal	cereal	cereale	cereal
gewählt	élu, e	elected, chosen	elegido, a	eletto, a	eleito, a
gewährleisten	garantir	guarantee, warrant	garantizar	garantire	garantir
Gewalt(f); Kraft(f)	force	force	fuerza	forza	força
Gewalt(f)	violence	violence	violencia	violenza	violência
gewalttätig, gewaltsam	violent, e	violent	violento, a	violento, a	violento, a
Gewand(n)	vêtement	garment	vestido, prenda	abito, vestito	peça de roupa
Gewehr(n)	fusil	shot-gun, rifle	fusil	fucile	espingarda
Gewehr(n), Karabiner m	carabine	rifle	carabina	carabina	espingarda
Gewehrkolben(m)	crosse	butt; grip, handle	culata	calcio	coronha
Gewerkschaft(f)	syndicat	trade union	sindicato	sindacato	sindicato
Gewerkschaftswesen	syndicalisme	trade unionism	sindicalismo	sindacalismo	sindicalismo
Gewicht(n)	poids	weight	peso	peso	peso
Gewinn(m)	profit	profit, benefit	ganancia	profitto, guadagno	lucro
Gewinn(m)	gain(s)	earnings	ganancia(s)	lucro, profitto	lucro
Gewinn(m)	bénéfice	benefit; profit	beneficio	beneficio; utile	lucro, proveito
gewinnen	gagner	win	ganar	vincere	ganhar
gewiß, sicherlich	sûrement	surely, certainly	ciertamente	sicuramente	certamente
Gewissensbiß(m)	remords	remorse	remordimiento	rimorso	remorso
Gewißheit(f)	certitude	certainty	certeza	certezza	certeza
Gewitter(n)	orage	storm, thunderstorm	tormenta	temporale	tempestade
gewöhnen, sich	habituer(s')	get used to	acostumbrarse	abituarsi	habituar-se
Gewohnheit(f)	habitude	habit	costumbre	abitudine	hábito, costume
gewöhnlich	habituel, le	usual	habitual	abituale	habitual
gewöhnlich	ordinaire	ordinary	ordinario, a	ordinario, a	ordinário, a
gewöhnlich	commun, e	common, usual	común	comune	comum
Gewöhnung(f)	accoutumance	habituation	hábito	abitudine	habituação
Gewölbe(n)	voûte	vault, arch	bóveda	arco, volta	abóbada
gewölbt	bombé, e	convex	abombado, a	convesso, a	convexo, a
gewollt, absichtlich	délibéré, e	deliberate	deliberado, a	deliberato, a	deliberado, a
Gewürz(n)	épice(s)	spice	especia	spezie	especiaria
gewürzt, würzig	épicé, e	spicy	picante	piccante	picante
Gezeiten(pl.)	marée	tide	marea	marea	maré
gießen, begießen	arroser	water	regar	innaffiare	regar
Gift(n)	poison	poison	veneno	veleno	veneno
Gift(n)	venin	venom, poison	veneno	veleno	veneno
giftig	vénéneux, se	poisonous	venenoso, a	velenoso, a	venenoso, a
giftig	toxique	toxic	tóxico, a	tossico, a	tóxico, a
gigantisch, riesig	gigantesque	gigantic, huge	gigantesco, a	gigantesco, a	gigantesco, a
Gipfel(m)	sommet	summit, top	cumbre; cima	cima; vetta	cimo; cume
Gipfel(m)	cime	summit, peak, top	cima	cima, vetta	cimo, cume
Gipfel(m)	pic	peak	pico	picco	pico
Gips(m)	plâtre	plaster	yeso	gesso	gesso
Giraffe(f)	girafe	giraffe	jirafa	giraffa	girafa
Girlande(f)	guirlande	garland	guirnalda	ghirlanda	grinalda
Gitarre(f)	guitare	guitar	guitarra	chitarra	guitarra
Gitter(n)	grillage	wire fencing	reja	reticolato	gradeamento
glänzen	briller	shine	brillar	brillare	brilhar
glänzend	brillant, e	bright, shining	brillante	brillante	brilhante
glänzend	splendide	splendid	espléndido, a	splendido, a	esplêndido, a
Glanzleistung(f)	exploit	exploit	hazaña	impresa, prodezza	proeza, feito
glanzlos, matt	mat, e	dull, matt	mate	opaco, a	mate

G

297

German	French	English	Spanish	Italian	Portuguese
Glas(n)	verre	glass	vidrio	vetro	vidro
Glas(n)	verre	glass(-es)	vaso	bicchiere	copo
Glasgefäß(n)	bocal	jar	tarro, bocal	boccale, vaso	boião
glatt	lisse	smooth	liso, a	liscio, a	liso, a
glätten, ab = flachen	aplatir	flatten	allanar, aplastar	appiattire	achatar, alisar
glatzköpfig	chauve	bald	calvo, a	calvo, a	calvo, a; careca
Glaube(m)	foi	faith	fe	fede	fé
Glaube(m)	croyance	belief	creencia	credenza	crença
glauben	croire	believe	creer	credere	crer
Gläubige(r)mf	croyant, e	believer	creyente	credente	crente
gleich	égal, e	equal	igual	uguale	igual
gleich, wie	pareil, le	same, similar, like	igual	uguale, pari	igual
gleichförmig	uniforme	uniform	uniforme	uniforme	uniforme
Gleichgewicht(n)	équilibre	balance	equilibrio	equilibrio	equilibrio
gleichgültig	indifférent, e	indifferent	indiferente	indifferente	indiferente
Gleichheit(f)	égalité	equality	igualdad	uguaglianza	igualdade
gleichwertig	équivalent, e	equivalent	equivalente	equivalente	equivalente
gleichzeitig	simultané, e	simultaneous	simultáneo, a	simultaneo, a	simultâneo, a
Gleitschiene(f)	glissière	slide	corredera, guía	guida, scivolo	corrediça
Gletscher(m)	glacier	glacier	glaciar	ghiacciaio	glaciar
Glied(n)	membre	limb	miembro	membro, arto	membro
Globus(m)	globe	globe	globo	globo	globo
Glocke(f)	cloche	bell	campana	campana	sino
glorreich	glorieux, se	glorious	glorioso, a	glorioso, a	glorioso, a
Glossar(n)	glossaire	glossary	glosario	glossario	glossário
Glück(n)	bonheur	happiness	felicidad	felicità	felicidade
Glück(n), Chance(f)	chance	luck; chance	suerte, fortuna	fortuna	sorte
Glück haben	chance(avoir)	fortunate(be)	suerte(tener)	fortuna(avere)	sorte(ter)
glücklich	heureux, se	happy, glad	feliz	felice	feliz
glücklicherweise	heureusement	fortunately	afortunadamente	fortunatamente	felizmente
Glückspilz(m)	chanceux, se	lucky	afortunado, a	fortunato, a	afortunado, a
Glückwunsch!	félicitations!	congratulations!	enhorabuena(!)	congratulazioni!	parabéns!
Glückwunschkarte(f)	carte de voeux	greeting(s) card	postal, carta	biglietto di auguri	cartão(festas)
Glühbirne(f)	ampoule	bulb	bombilla	lampadina	lâmpada
glühend	incandescent, e	incandescent	incandescente	incandescente	incandescente
Glut(f)	braise	embers	brasa	brace	brasa
Gnade(f); Anmut(f)	grâce	grace	gracia	grazia	graça
Gold(n)	or	gold	oro	oro	ouro
Golf(n)	golf	golf	golf	golf	golfe
Golf(m)	golfe	gulf	golfo	golfo	golfo
Golfplatz(m)	golf(terrain)	golf course	golf	golf	campo de golfe
Gorilla(m)	gorille	gorilla	gorila	gorilla	gorila
Gott!(Mein Gott!)	Dieu(mon)	Goodness(my)	Dios(mío)	Dio(mio)	Deus(meu)
Gott(m)	dieu	God	dios, Dios	dio, Dio (dio, dei)	Deus
göttlich	divin, e	divine	divino, a	divino, a	divino, a
Gouverneur(m)	gouverneur	governor	gobernador	governatore	governador
Grab(n)	tombe	grave	tumba	tomba	túmulo, sepultura
Grab(n)	sépulture	burial(-place)	sepultura	sepoltura	sepultura
graben	creuser	dig	cavar	scavare	cavar
Graben(m)	fossé	ditch	cuneta	fossato, fosso	fosso
Graben(m)	tranchée	trench	trinchera, zanja	trincea	trincheira
Grabmal(n)	tombeau	tomb	tumba	tomba	túmulo
Grad(m)	degré	degree	grado	grado	grau
Grammatik(f)	grammaire	grammar	gramática	grammatica	gramática
Graphik(f)	graphique	graph	gráfico, a	grafico	gráfico
Graphologie(f)	graphologie	graphology	grafología	grafologia	grafologia
Gras(n)	herbe	grass	hierba, yerba	erba	erva
Gräte(f)	arête	fish-bone, bone	espina	lisca	espinha
gratulieren	féliciter	congratulate	felicitar	congratularsi	felicitar
gratulieren	congratuler	congratulate	congratular	congratulare	congratular
grau	gris, e	grey	gris	grigio, a	cinzento, a
grausam	cruel, le	cruel	cruel	crudele	cruel
grausam	atroce	atrocious	atroz	atroce	atroz
Grausen(n)	horreur	horror	horror	orrore	horror
grausig	horrible	horrible	horrible	orribile, orrendo, a	horrível
Gravieren(n)	gravure	engraving	grabado	incisione	gravura
Gravur(f)	gravure	print	grabado	stampa	gravura
graziös	gracieux, se	graceful	gracioso, a	grazioso, a	gracioso, a

German	French	English	Spanish	Italian	Portuguese
greifen	empoigner, saisir	grab, grasp	empuñar	agguantare	agarrar
greifen, packen	serrer	grip, hold tight	apretar	stringere	apertar
Grenze(f)	limite	limit	límite	limite	limite
Grenze(f)	frontière	border, frontier	frontera	confine, frontiera	fronteira
Grenze(f)	frontière, limite	boundary	frontera, límite	frontiera, limite	fronteira, limite
Griff(m)	poignée	handle	manilla, mango	maniglia	fecho
Griff(m)	poignée	handle	asa, mango	manico	asa
Griff(m)	manette	handle	manecilla	leva	manípulo
Griff(m)	anse	handle	asa	ansa	asa
grillen	griller	grill	asar(parrilla)	arrostire	grelhar
Grimasse(f)	grimace	grimace	mueca	smorfia	careta
grinsen, kichern	ricaner	snigger	burlarse	sogghignare	troçar
Grippe(f)	grippe	flu, influenza	gripe	influenza	gripe
grob	grossier, ière	rude; crude	grosero, a	grossolano, a	grosseiro, a
Groll(m), Trotz(m)	dépit	spite; vexation	despecho	dispetto	despeito
groß	grand, e	tall	alto, a	alto, a	alto, a; grande
groß	grand, e	big	gran, grande	grande	grande
groß	gros, se	big	grueso, a; grande	grosso, a; grande	grande
groß	grand, e	great	gran, grande	grand(e)	grande
großartig	superbe	superb	soberbio, a	splendido, a	soberbo, a
großartig	formidable	tremendous	formidable	formidabile	formidável
großartig	fameux, se	excellent	famoso, a	ottimo, a	famoso, a
großartig, fabelhaft	épatant, e	wonderful, super	estupendo, a	straordinario, a	estupendo, a
Größe(f)	taille, grandeur	height, size	talla, estatura	statura	estatura
Größe(f)	taille	size	tamaño	misura	tamanho
Größe(f)	taille	size	talla, número	taglia, misura	tamanho
Größe(f)	pointure	size	número	numero	tamanho; número
Großeltern(pl.)	grands-parents	grandparents	abuelos	nonni	avós
Großmutter(f)	grand-mère	grandmother	abuela	nonna	avó
Großvater(m)	grand-père	grandfather	abuelo	nonno	avô
Grotte(f)	grotte	cave, grotto	cueva, gruta	grotta	gruta
Grube(f)	fosse	pit	fosa, hoyo	fossa; buca	fossa
Grube(f)	trou	pit, hole	hoyo	buca	cova
grün	vert, e	green	verde	verde	verde
Grün(n)	verdure	greenery	verdor, verdura	verdura	verdura
Grund(m)	raison	reason	razón, causa	ragione	razão
Grund(m)(der--für)	pourquoi(le--de)	reason(the--for)	porqué(el--de)	perché(il--di)	porquê(o--de)
Grundbuch(n)	cadastre	land register	catastro	catasto	cadastro
gründen	fonder	found	fundar	fondare	fundar
Gründer(in f)m	fondateur, trice	founder	fundador, a	fondatore, trice	fundador, a
Grundlage(f)	base	base	base	base	base
Grundsatz(m)	principe	principle	principio	principio	princípio
Grundschullehrer/in	instituteur	teacher(primary)	maestro, a	maestro, a	professor primário
Grund-; Grundlage	base(de)	basic	básico, a	base	base(de)
Gruppe(f)	groupe	group	grupo	gruppo	grupo
Guerilla(f)	guérilla	guerilla	guerrilla	guerriglia	guerrilha
Gulli, Abwasserkanäle	égout	sewer, drain	cloaca	fogna	esgoto
gültig; annehmbar	valable	valid, good	válido, a; valedero	valido, a	válido, a
Gültigkeit(f)	validité	validity	validez	validità	validade
Gummi(m, n)	caoutchouc	rubber	caucho	gomma	borracha
Gummiband(n)	élastique	rubber band	goma elástica	elastico	elástico
Gunst(f)	faveur	favour	favor	favore	favor
günstig	favorable	favourable	favorable	favorevole	favorável
günstig	propice	favourable	propicio, a	propizio, a	propício, a
günstig	opportun, e	opportune	oportuno, a	opportuno, a	oportuno, a
Gürtel(m)	ceinture	belt	cinturón	cintura	cinto
gut	bon, ne	good	bueno, a	buono, a	bom, boa
gut	bien	well	bien	bene	bem
Gut(n)	bien	good	bien	bene	bem
Gut(n), Besitzung(f)	domaine	domain, estate	dominio, terreno	tenuta, fondo	terreno
gutartig	bénin, bénigne	benign	benigno, a	benigno, a	benigno, a
Güte(f)	bonté	kindness	bondad	bontà	bondade
gute Nacht	bonne nuit	good night	buenas noches	buona notte	boa noite
gute Reise	bon voyage	good trip(have a)	buen viaje	buon viaggio	boa viagem
guten Abend	bonsoir	good evening	buenas tardes	buonasera	boa tarde
Guten Appetit !	bon appétit !	enjoy your meal !	que aproveche(!)	buon appetito !	bom proveito !
guten Morgen !/-Tag	bonjour !	good morning !/aft-	hola(!)	buongiorno !	bom dia !
guten Tag !	bonjour !	good afternoon !	hola(!)	buona sera !	bom dia !

G

299

German	French	English	Spanish	Italian	Portuguese
guten Tag	bonjour	hello	buenos días	buongiorno	bom dia
gütig, liebvoll	bon, aimable	kind, kindly	bueno, a	buono, a	bom, boa
Gutsherr(-sbesitzer)	propriétaire	landowner	propietario, a	proprietario, a	proprietário, a
Gymnasium(n)	lycée	comprehensive sch.	instituto, liceo	liceo	liceu
Gymnastik(f)	gymnastique	gymnastics	gimnasia	ginnastica	ginástica
Gynäkologie(f)	gynécologie	gynaecology	ginecología	ginecologia	ginecologia

H

German	French	English	Spanish	Italian	Portuguese
Haar(n)	cheveu(x)	hair	pelo, cabello	capello	cabelo
Haar(n)	poil	hair	pelo	pelo	pêlo
Haarknoten(m)	chignon	chignon, bun	moño	crocchia	carrapicho
Haarspray(m, n)	laque	hair-spray	laca	lacca	laca
haben	avoir	have	haber; tener	avere	haver; ter
haben	avoir	have	tener	avere	ter, possuir
Habicht(m)	épervier	sparrow-hawk	gavilán	sparviere	gavião
Hafen(m)	port	port, harbour	puerto	porto	porto
Hafendamm(m), Mole(f)	jetée	jetty	escollera	molo, gettata	molhe
Haft(f)	détention	detention	detención	detenzione	detenção
Haft(f), Verhaftung(f)	emprisonnement	imprisonment	encarcelamiento	incarcerazione	prisão
haftbar	responsable	liable(to be)	responsable	responsabile	responsável
Häftling(m)	détenu, e	prisoner	detenido, a; preso, a	detenuto, a	preso, a; detido, a
Hagel(m)	grêle	hail	granizo	grandine	granizo
Hahn(m)	coq	cock	gallo	gallo	galo
Hahn(m)(Wasser-; Gas-)	robinet	cock, tap	llave, grifo	rubinetto	torneira
Hähnchen, Hühnchen(n)	poulet	chicken	pollo	pollo	frango
Hai(m)	requin	shark	tiburón	squalo	tubarão
Haken(m)	crochet	hook	gancho	gancio, uncino	gancho
halb	demi, e	half	medio, a	mezzo, a	meio, a
halb	semi	semi, half	semi	semi	semi
halb-	mi-	half(-); mid-	medio, a	semi-; mezzo-	meio, a
halbamtlich	officieux, se	unofficial	oficioso, a	ufficioso, a	oficioso, a
halbe Stunde	demi-heure	half an hour	media hora	mezz'ora	meia-hora
Halbinsel(f)	péninsule	peninsula	península	penisola	península
Halbkreis(m)	arc	arc	arco	arco	arco
Halbkreis(m)	hémisphère	hemisphere	hemisferio	emisfero	hemisfério
Hälfte(f)	moitié	half(-lves)	mitad	metà	metade
Hallo!; tschüs!; tschüß	salut!	hi!, hello!	hola(!)	ciao!	olá!
Hals(m), Nacken(m)	cou	neck	cuello	collo	pescoço
Hals(m)	gorge	throat	garganta	gola	garganta
Hals(m)(Flaschen)	goulot	neck(bottle)	gollete	collo	gargalo
Halsentzündung(f)	laryngite	laryngitis	laringitis	laringite	laringite
Halskette(f); Kette(f)	collier	necklace	collar	collana	colar
Halsschmerzen(m, pl)	mal de gorge	sore throat	dolor de garganta	mal di gola	dor de garganta
Halstuch(n), Schal(m)	écharpe	scarf	bufanda	sciarpa	cachecol, cachené
Halt(m)	halte, arrêt	halt, stop	alto, parada	sosta, fermata	alto, paragem
halten	tenir	hold	tener	tenere	ter, segurar
halten(an-, auf-)	arrêter	stop	parar	fermare	parar
Haltung(f)	attitude	attitude	actitud	atteggiamento	atitude
Hammer(m)	marteau	hammer	martillo	martello	martelo
Hämorrhoiden(f, pl)	hémorroïde(s)	haemorrhoids	hemorroides	emorroide	hemorróidas
Hampelmann(m)	pantin	puppet	títere	burattino	fantoche
Hand(f)	main	hand	mano	mano	mão
Handel(m)	commerce	trade, commerce	comercio	commercio	comércio
handeln	agir	act	actuar	agire	agir
Handfläche(f)	paume	palm	palma	palma	palma
Handgelenk(n)	poignet	wrist	muñeca	polso	punho

German	French	English	Spanish	Italian	Portuguese
Handgepäck(n)	bagages à main	hand luggage	equipaje de mano	bagaglio a mano	bagagem de mão
handgeschrieben	manuscrit, e	handwritten	manuscrito, a	manoscritto, a	manuscrito, a
Handgranate(f)	grenade	grenade	granada	bomba a mano	granada
Handikap(n)	handicap	handicap	hándicap	handicap	handicap
Handkurbel(f)	manivelle	crank	manivela	manovella	manivela
Händler(in f)m	marchand, e	tradesman, dealer	vendedor, a	mercante	negociante
handlich	maniable	handy, manageable	manuable	maneggevole	manejável
Handlung(f)	acte	action, act	acto	atto	acto, acção
Handschellen(f, pl)	menottes	handcuffs	esposas	manette	algemas
Handschuh(m)	gant	glove	guante	guanto	luva
Hand schütteln	serrer la main	shake hands	estrechar la mano	stringere la mano	apertar a mão
Handtasche(f)	sac à main	handbag	bolso	borsetta	carteira
Handtuch(n)	serviette	towel	toalla	asciugamano	toalha
Handvoll(f)	poignée	handful	puñado	manciata, pugno	punhado
Handwerker(in f)m	artisan	craftsman(-men)	artesano	artigiano	artesão
Hang(m), Abhang(m)	pente, côte	slope	declive	pendio, discesa	declive
Hängematte(f)	hamac	hammock	hamaca	amaca	rede
hängen, auf = hängen	pendre	hang	colgar	appendere	pendurar
Harem(m)	harem	harem	harén	harem	harém
Harfe(f)	harpe	harp	arpa	arpa	harpa
harmlos	inoffensif, ive	inoffensive	inofensivo, a	inoffensivo, a	inofensivo, a
Harmonie(f)	harmonie	harmony	armonía	armonia	harmonia
harmonisch	harmonieux, se	harmonious	armonioso, a	armonioso, a	harmonioso, a
Harnblase(f)	vessie	bladder	vejiga	vescica	bexiga
Harnstoff(m)	urée	urea	urea	urea	ureia
Harpune(f)	harpon	harpoon	arpón	arpione	arpão
hart	dur, e	hard	duro, a	duro, a	duro, a
Hartnäckigkeit(f)	ténacité	tenacity	tenacidad	tenacità; tenacia	tenacidade
Harz(m)	résine	resin	resina	resina	resina
Haß(m)	haine	hate	odio	odio	ódio
hassen	haïr	hate, detest	odiar	odiare	odiar
hassen	détester	detest, hate	detestar, odiar	detestare, odiare	detestar
häßlich, gräßlich	laid, e; moche	ugly, hideous	feo, a	brutto, a	feio, a
Hauch(m), Atemzug(m)	bouffée	puff, breath	bocanada	ventata	baforada
Häufchen(n), Kot(m)	crotte	dropping, dung	caca	sterco	bosta
Haufen(m)	tas	pile	montón	mucchio	montão, pilha
Haufen(m)	amas	pile	montón	mucchio	amontoado
häufig	fréquent, e	frequent	frecuente	frequente	frequente
Hauptmann(m); Kapitän	capitaine	captain	capitán	capitano	capitão
Hauptsache(f)	essentiel	main thing(the)	esencial	essenziale	essencial
hauptsächlich	principal, e	principal, main	principal	principale	principal
Hauptstadt(f)	capitale	capital	capital	capitale	capital(a)
Hauptwort(n)	nom, substantif	noun	nombre	nome, sostantivo	substantivo
Hauptwort(n)	substantif	substantive, noun	sustantivo	sostantivo	substantivo
Haus(n)	maison	house	casa	casa	casa
Haus-	domestique	domestic, home	doméstico, a	domestico, a	doméstico, a
Hausangestellte(r)mf	domestique	servant	criado, a	domestico, a	empregado, a
Hause(zu)	maison(à la)	home(at)	casa(en)	casa(a)	casa(em)
Hausfrau(f)	ménagère	housewife(-ives)	ama de casa	casalinga	dona de casa
Haushalt(m)	ménage	housework	limpieza	pulizie	limpeza
Haushaltshilfe(f)	bonne	maid	criada	domestica	criada
Hausmeister(in f)m	concierge	porter, caretaker	conserje	portiere, a	porteiro, a
Haut(f)	peau	skin	piel	pelle	pele
Haut-	cutané, e	cutaneous, skin	cutáneo, a	cutaneo, a	cutâneo, a
Hebamme(f)	sage-femme	midwife(-ives)	comadrona	levatrice	parteira
Hebel(m)	levier	lever	palanca	leva	alavanca
heben	lever	lift(up), raise	levantar	alzare	levantar
Hecke(f)	haie	hedge	seto, valla	siepe	sebe
Heft(n)	cahier	exercise book	cuaderno	quaderno	caderno
heftig, stark	violent, e	violent	violento, a	violento, a	violento, a
heftig, stark	intense	intense	intenso, a	intenso, a	intenso, a
Heftzwecke(f)	punaise	drawing-pin	chincheta	puntina(disegno)	percevejo
Heide(f)	lande	moor, heath	landa	landa	charneca
heilen	guérir	cure, heal	curar	guarire	curar
Heilgymnastik(f)	rééducation	therapy	reeducación	rieducazione	reeducação
heilig	saint, e	holy	santo, a; san	santo, a	santo, a
heilig	sacré, e	holy; sacred	sagrado, a	sacro, a	sagrado, a
Heilige(r)mf	saint, e	saint	santo, a	santo, a	santo, a

German	French	English	Spanish	Italian	Portuguese
Heiligtum(n)	sanctuaire	sanctuary	santuario	santuario	santuário
Heilmittel(n)	remède	remedy	remedio	rimedio	remédio
Heilpraktiker(in f)m	guérisseur, se	healer	curandero, a	guaritore, -trice	curandeiro, a
Heilung(f)	guérison	cure, recovery	curación	guarigione	cura
Heim(n)	foyer	home	hogar	focolare	lar
Heimat-; Geburts-	natal, e	native	natal	natale	natal
heimlich	clandestin, e	clandestine	clandestino, a	clandestino, a	clandestino, a
heim = suchen; betrüben	affliger	distress, afflict	afligir	affliggere	afligir
heimtückisch	perfide	treacherous	pérfido, a	perfido, a	pérfido, a
Heimweh(n)	nostalgie	homesickness	nostalgia	nostalgia	nostalgia
heiraten	marier(se)	married(get)	casarse	sposarsi	casar-se
heiser	enroué, e	hoarse	ronco, a	rauco, a	rouco, a
heiß	chaud, e	hot	caliente	caldo, a	quente
heißen	nommer(se)	called(be)	llamarse	chiamarsi	chamar-se
Heißluftballon(m)	ballon	balloon	globo	pallone	balão
heiter	serein, e	serene	sereno, a	sereno, a	sereno, a
Heiterkeit(f)	sérénité	serenity	serenidad	serenità	serenidade
Heiterkeit(f)	allégresse	elation	júbilo, alegría	esultanza	júbilo, alegria
heizen	chauffer	heat	calentar	riscaldare	aquecer
Heizkörper(m)	radiateur	radiator, heater	radiador	termosifone	aquecedor
Heizöl(n)	mazout	fuel oil	fuel-oil	nafta	fuel, óleo
Heizung(f)	chauffage	heating	calefacción	riscaldamento	aquecimento
Hektar(m)	hectare	hectare	hectárea	ettaro	hectare
Held(m), Heldin(f)	héros, héroïne	hero, heroine	héroe, heroína	eroe, eroina	herói, heroína
heldenhaft	héroïque	heroic	heroico, a	eroico, a	heróico, a
helfen	aider	help, assist, aid	ayudar	aiutare	ajudar
helfen	secourir	help, assist, aid	socorrer	soccorrere	socorrer
hell	clair, e	light	claro, a	chiaro, a	claro, a
Helligkeit(f)	clarté	brightness	claridad	chiarezza	claridade
Helm(m)	casque	helmet	casco	casco, elmetto	capacete
Hemd(n)	chemise	shirt	camisa	camicia	camisa
Hepatitis, Gelbsucht f	hépatite	hepatitis	hepatitis	epatite	hepatite
heran = rücken	rapprocher	bring nearer	acercar	avvicinare	acercar
heraus = fordern	défier	challenge	desafiar	sfidare	desafiar
heraus = fordern, reizen	provoquer	provoke	provocar	provocare	provocar
Herausforderung(f)	provocation	provocation	provocación	provocazione	provocação
Herausforderung(f)	défi	challenge	desafío	sfida	desafio
Herausgeber(in f)m	éditeur, trice	publisher; editor	editor, a	editore, trice	editor, a
heraus = ziehen, ziehen	extraire	extract	extraer	estrarre	extrair
Herbst(m)	automne	autumn	otoño	autunno	outono
Herd(m)	cuisinière	cooker, stove	cocina	cucina	fogão
Herde(f)	troupeau	herd	ganado	branco	manada
Herde(f)	troupeau	flock	rebaño	gregge	rebanho
herein!	entrez!	come in!	pase(!), adelante!	avanti!, prego!	entre!
Hering(m)	hareng	herring	arenque	aringa	arenque
Herkunft(f)	provenance	origin	procedencia	provenienza	proveniência
hermetisch	hermétique	hermetic	hermético, a	ermetico, a	hermético, a
Heroin(n)	héroïne	heroin	heroína	eroina	heroína
Herr(in f)m	maître, esse	master, mistress	señor, señora	maestro, a; padrone, a	dono, a; senhor, a
Herr(m)	monsieur	Sir	señor	signore	senhor
Herr(m)	monsieur(Mr)	Mr	señor	signor	senhor
Herr(m)	monsieur(Mr)	Mr	Don	Signor	Senhor
Herr(m)	Seigneur	Lord	Señor	Signore	Senhor
Herrensitz(m), -haus n	manoir, château	mansion	mansión, morada	maniero, castello	mansão, palacete
Herrenzimmer(n)	salon	lounge	sala	salotto	sala de estar
Herrschaft(f)	règne	reign	reino	regno	reinado
Herrscher(in f)m	souverain, e	sovereign, monarch	soberano, a; monarca	sovrano, a; monarca	soberano, a; monarca
Herrscherhaus(n)	dynastie	dynasty	dinastía	dinastia	dinastia
her = stellen	produire	produce	producir	produrre	produzir
her = stellen	fabriquer	manufacture, make	fabricar	fabbricare	fabricar
Hersteller(in f)m	fabricant, e	manufacturer	fabricante	fabbricante	fabricante
Hersteller(in f)m	producteur, trice	producer	productor, a	produttore, trice	produtor, a
Herstellung(f)	fabrication	manufacture	fabricación	fabbricazione	fabrico
Herumstreicher(m)	rôdeur, se	prowler	vagabundo, a	vagabondo, a	vagabundo, a
herunter = gehen	descendre	go down, descend	descender, bajar	scendere	descer, baixar
herunter = lassen	baisser, abaisser	lower	bajar	calare, abbassare	baixar, abaixar
hervorragend	éminent, e	eminent	eminente	eminente	eminente
hervor = stehen	dépasser	protrude	sobresalir	sporgere	sobressair

| --- | --- | --- | --- | --- | --- |
Herz(n)	coeur	heart	corazón	cuore	coração
Herzattacke(f)	crise cardiaque	heart attack	crisis cardíaca	infarto	ataque
Herzjagen(n)	tachycardie	tachycardia	taquicardia	tachicardia	taquicardia
Herzklopfen(n)	palpitation	palpitation	palpitación	palpitazione	palpitação
herzkrank	cardiaque	heart-trouble...	cardíaco, a	cardiaco, a	cardíaco, a
herzlich	chaleureux, se	hearty, warm	caluroso, a	caloroso, a	caloroso, a
herzlich, freundlich	cordial, e	cordial, hearty	cordial	cordiale	cordial
Herzog(m), Herzogin(f)	duc, duchesse	duke, duchess	duque, duquesa	duca, duchessa	duque, duquesa
heterosexuell	hétérosexuel, le	heterosexual	heterosexual	eterosessuale	heterossexual
Heuchelei(f)	hypocrisie	hypocrisy	hipocresía	ipocrisia	hipocrisia
Heuchler(in f)m	hypocrite	hypocrite	hipócrita	ipocrita	hipócrita
heulen	hurler	howl	aullar	ululare, guaire	uivar; urrar
heute	aujourd'hui	today	hoy	oggi	hoje
heute abend	soir(ce)	tonight	noche(esta)	sera(questa)	noite(esta)
Hexenschuß(m)	lumbago	lumbago	lumbago	lombaggine	lumbago
Hexer(m); Hexe(f)	sorcier, ière	wizard; witch	brujo, a	stregone, strega	bruxo, a
Hexerei(f)	sorcellerie	witchcraft	brujería	stregoneria	bruxaria
hier	ici	here	aquí	qui	aqui
hier(ist/sind)	voici	here is; here are	he aquí	ecco	aqui está
Hierarchie(f)	hiérarchie	hierarchy	jerarquía	gerarchia	hierarquia
hierarchisch	hiérarchique	hierarchical	jerárquico, a	gerarchico, a	hierárquico, a
Hilfe(f)	aide	help	ayuda	aiuto	ajuda
Hilfe(f)	secours	help, aid	socorro	soccorso	socorro
Hilfe(f)	assistance	assistance	asistencia	assistenza	assistência
Hilfs-; Hilfe(f)	auxiliaire	auxiliary	auxiliar	ausiliare	auxiliar
Hilfsarbeiter(in f)m	manoeuvre	labourer	peón, obrero	manovale	servente
Himmel(m)	ciel	sky	cielo	cielo	céu
Himmel(m)	ciel, paradis	heaven	cielo, paraíso	cielo, paradiso	céu, paraíso
himmlisch	céleste	heavenly	celeste	celeste	celeste
hinaus = lehnen	pencher(se)	lean out	asomarse	sporgersi	debruçar-se
Hindernis(n)	obstacle	obstacle	obstáculo	ostacolo	obstáculo
hinken	boiter	limp	cojear	zoppicare	coxear
hin = knien, sich	agenouiller(s')	kneel	arrodillarse	inginocchiare(-rsi)	ajoelhar-se
hin = legen, sich	allonger(s')	lie down	acostarse	sdraiarsi	estender-se
Hinrichtung(f)	exécution	execution	ejecución	esecuzione	execução
hinten, zurück	arrière, derrière	behind, back	atrás	dietro, posteriore	atrás
hinter	derrière	behind	detrás, tras	dietro	atrás, detrás
Hinter-, Rückseite(f)	derrière, arrière	back, rear	trasero, a	retro	trazeiro
hinter, nach	suite(à la)	following	después de	seguito a(in)	seguir a(a)
Hinterhalt(m)	embuscade	ambush	emboscada	imboscata	emboscada
Hinternvoll(m)	fessée	spanking	azotaina, paliza	sculacciata	surra, açoite
hinunter	bas	down	abajo	giù	baixo
hinzu = fügen	ajouter	add	añadir	aggiungere	ajuntar, juntar
hinzugefügt	additionnel, le	additional	adicional	addizionale	adicional
Hippie(m)	hippie, y	hippy	hippy, jipi	capellone, hippy	hippie
historisch	historique	historic(al)	histórico, a	storico, a	histórico, a
Hitze(f)	chaleur	heat	calor	caldo; calore	calor
Hobby(n)	passe-temps	hobby, pastime	pasatiempo	passatempo	passatempo
hoch	haut, e	high, tall	alto, a	alto, a	alto, a
hoch	grand, e	high	alto, a	forte; alto, a	alto, a
hoch, erhöht	élevé, e	high	alto, a	elevato, a; alto, a	alto, a
hoch, schrill	aigu, ë	sharp, shrill	agudo, a	acuto, a	agudo, a
Hochebene(f)	plateau	plateau	meseta	altipiano	planalto
hocherfreut	ravi, e	delighted	encantado, a	lietissimo, a	encantado, a
hochkompliziert	sophistiqué, e	sophisticated	sofisticado, a	sofisticato, a	sofisticado, a
Hochzeit(f); Heirat(f)	mariage	wedding; marriage	matrimonio	matrimonio	casamento
Hochzeit(f)	noce	wedding	boda	nozze	boda
Hocker(m)	tabouret	stool	taburete	sgabello	escabelo, banco
Hockeyspiel(n)	hockey	hockey	hockey	hockey	hóquei
Hoden(m)	testicule	testicle	testículo	testicolo	testículo
Hof(m)	cour	yard	patio	cortile	pátio
Hof(m)	cour	court	corte	corte	corte
hoffen	espérer	hope	esperar, desear	sperare	esperar, desejar
Hoffnung(f)	espoir	hope	esperanza	speranza	esperança
höflich	poli, e	polite	educado, a; cortés	educato, a	educado, a
höflich	courtois, e	courteous	cortés	cortese	cortês
Höflichkeit(f)	politesse	politeness	cortesía	educazione	delicadeza
Höhe(f)	hauteur	height	altura	altezza	altura

German	French	English	Spanish	Italian	Portuguese
Höhe(f)	altitude	altitude, height	altitud, altura	altitudine	altitude
höher, besser	supérieur, e	superior	superior, a	superiore	superior, a
hohl	creux, se	hollow	hueco, a	vuoto, a; cavo, a	oco, a
Höhle(f)	caverne	cave, cavern	caverna	caverna	caverna
Höhlenforschung(f)	spéléologie	pot-holing	espeleología	speleologia	espeleologia
Hohlraum(m)	cavité	cavity	cavidad	cavità	cavidade
holen, suchen	chercher	seek	buscar, investigar	cercare	procurar, buscar
Hölle(f)	enfer	hell	infierno	inferno	inferno
Höllen-; höllisch	infernal, e	infernal	infernal	infernale	infernal
Holz(n)	bois	timber	madera	legno	madeira
Holzgerüst(n)	charpente	framework	armazón	ossatura, travatura	madeiramento
homogen	homogène	homogeneous	homogéneo, a	omogeneo, a	homogéneo, a
Homonym(n)	homonyme	homonym	homónimo, a	omonimo, a	homónimo, a
Homöopathie(f)	homéopathie	homoeopathy	homeopatía	omeopatia	homeopatia
homosexuell	homosexuel, le	homosexual	homosexual	omosessuale	homossexual
Honig(m)	miel	honey	miel	miele	mel
Honorar(n)	honoraires	fee	honorarios	onorario	honorários
Honorar(n); Gage(f)	cachet	fee	remuneración	cachet, compenso	remuneração
hören	entendre	hear	oír	sentire	ouvir
Horizont(m)	horizon	horizon, sky-line	horizonte	orizzonte	horizonte
Hormon(n)	hormone	hormone	hormona	ormone	hormona
Horn(n)	corne	horn	cuerno	corno	corno; chifre
Horoskop(n)	horoscope	horoscope	horóscopo	oroscopo	horóscopo
Hose(f)	pantalon	trousers	pantalón	pantalone	calças
Hosenträger(m)	bretelle(s)	braces	tirantes	bretella	suspensórios
Hospiz(n)	hospice	hospice; home	hospicio	ospizio	hospício, asilo
Hotel(n)	hôtel	hotel	hotel	albergo, hotel	hotel
Hotelwesen(n)	hôtellerie	hotel trade	hostelería	alberghiera(indust-)	hotelaria
Hotelzimmer(n)	chambre d'hôtel	room, hotel room	habitación	camera	quarto
hübsch	joli, e	pretty	bonito, a	carino, a	bonito, a
Hubschrauber(m)	hélicoptère	helicopter	helicóptero	elicottero	helicóptero
Huf(m)	sabot	hoof	pezuña, casco	zoccolo	casco
Hüfte(f)	hanche	hip	cadera	anca	anca
Hügel(m)	colline	hill	colina	collina	colina
Huhn(n)	poule	hen	gallina	gallina	galinha
Huldigung(f); Ehrung f	hommage	homage, tribute	homenaje	omaggio	homenagem
Hülle(f)	gaine	sheath	funda, estuche	guaina, astuccio	invólucro
Hummer(m)	homard	lobster	bogavante	gambero(di mare)	lavagante
Humor(m)	humour	humour	humor	umorismo	humor
humoristisch	humoristique	humorous	humorístico, a	umoristico, a	humorístico, a
Hund(m)	chien, ne	dog, bitch(-es)	perro, a	cane, cagna	cão, cadela
Hundert(n)	centaine	hundred(about a)	centena	centinaio	centena
hundert	cent	hundred(one)	cien, ciento	cento	cem, cento
Hunger(m)(haben)	faim(avoir)	hunger(hungry be)	hambre(tener)	fame(aver)	fome(ter)
Hungersnot(f)	famine	famine	hambre	fame, carestia	fome
hungrig	affamé, e	starving, hungry	hambriento, a	affamato, a	esfomeado, a
Hupe(f)	klaxon	horn, hooter	claxon, bocina	clacson	buzina
hupen	klaxonner	hoot	pitar	suonare(clacson)	buzinar
Husten(m)	toux	cough	tos	tosse	tosse
husten	tousser	cough	toser	tossire	tossir
Hut(m)	chapeau	hat	sombrero	cappello	chapéu
hüten	garder	look after	vigilar, guardar	custodire	cuidar de, vigiar
hüten, bewachen	garder	guard, watch over	guardar	custodire, guardare	guardar, vigiar
Hütte(f)	case	hut	cabaña	capanna	palhota
Hyäne(f)	hyène	hyena	hiena	iena	hiena
hydraulisch	hydraulique	hydraulic	hidráulico, a	idraulico, a	hidráulico, a
Hygiene(f)	hygiène	hygiene	higiene	igiene	higiene
hygienisch	hygiénique	hygienic	higiénico, a	igienico, a	higiénico, a
Hymne(f)	hymne	hymn	himno	inno	hino
Hypnose(f)	hypnose	hypnosis	hipnosis	ipnosi	hipnose
Hypnotismus(m)	hypnotisme	hypnotism	hipnotismo	ipnotismo	hipnotismo
Hypothek(f)	hypothèque	mortgage	hipoteca	ipoteca	hipoteca
Hypothese(f)	hypothèse	hypothesis(-es)	hipótesis	ipotesi	hipótese
hysterisch	hystérique	hysteric(al)	histérico, a	isterico, a	histérico, a

I

German	French	English	Spanish	Italian	Portuguese
ich	je	I	yo	io	eu
ideal	idéal, e	ideal	ideal	ideale	ideal
Ideal(n)	idéal	ideal	ideal	ideale	ideal
Idee(f)	idée	idea	idea	idea	ideia
identifizieren	identifier	identify	identificar	identificare	identificar
identisch	identique	identical	idéntico, a	identico, a	idêntico, a
Identität(f)	identité	identity	identidad	identità	identidade
Ideologie(f)	idéologie	ideology	ideología	ideologia	ideologia
Idiot(m), Dummkopf(m)	idiot, e	idiot, fool	idiota	idiota; scemo, a	idiota
Idiot(in f)m	imbécile	fool, idiot	imbécil	imbecille	imbecil, parvo
idiotisch, dumm	idiot, e	idiotic, stupid	idiota; tonto, a	idiota; stupido, a	idiota
Idol(n)	idole	idol	ídolo	idolo	ídolo
Iglu(n)	igloo	igloo	iglú	igloo	iglu
ihm, ihr, ihm	lui	him, her, it	le, él; ella; se	lui; gli; le	ele(a); lhe
ihnen	leur	them(to -)	les	loro; gli	lhes
ihr; Sie	vous	you	vosotros; ustedes	voi; lei	vós; você
ihr/ihre	leur(s)	their	su, sus, suyo	loro(il/la, i/le)	seu, sua, deles
ihrige(der, die, das)	leur(le, la)	theirs	suyo, a(el, la)	loro(il, la)	seu(o), a sua; dele, a
Ihr(e); euer, eure	votre	your	vuestro, a	vostro, a(il, la)	vosso, a
illegal	illégal, e	illegal	ilegal	illegale	ilegal
Illusion(f)	illusion	illusion	ilusión	illusione	ilusão
Illustration(f)	illustration	illustration	ilustración	illustrazione	ilustração
illustriert	illustré, e	illustrated	ilustrado, a	illustrato, a	ilustrado, a
Illustrierte(f)	magazine	magazine	revista	rivista	revista
immer	toujours	always	siempre	sempre	sempre
immer noch	toujours	still	todavía	sempre	ainda
immer(für)	toujours(pour)	forever	siempre(para, por)	sempre(per)	sempre(para)
immergrün; ausdauernd	vivace	hardy	vivaz	vivace	vivaz
Immobilien(f, pl)	immobilier	property	inmobiliario	immobiliare	imobiliário
immunisieren	immuniser	immunize	inmunizar	immunizzare	imunizar
Immunität(f)	immunité	immunity	inmunidad	immunità	imunidade
Imperialismus(m)	impérialisme	imperialism	imperialismo	imperialismo	imperialismo
Impfstoff(m)	vaccin	vaccine	vacuna	vaccino	vacina
Impfung(f)	vaccination	vaccination	vacunación	vaccinazione	vacinação
imprägnieren	imprégner	impregnate	impregnar	impregnare	impregnar
improvisieren	improviser	improvise	improvisar	improvvisare	improvisar
Impuls(m)	impulsion	impulse	impulso	impulso	impulso
in	dans	in, into	dentro, en	in	dentro(de), em
in	à	in	en	a	em
in	en	in	en	in	em
in Betrieb sein	marcher	work, run	marchar	funzionare	funcionar
Index(m)	index	index	índice	indice	índice
Index m(Preisindex m)	indice	index	índice	indice	índice
indirekt	indirect, e	indirect	indirecto, a	indiretto, a	indirecto, a
Indiskretion(f)	indiscrétion	indiscretion	indiscreción	indiscrezione	indiscrição
individuell	individuel, le	individual	individual	individuale	individual
Individuum(n)	individu	individual	individuo	individuo	indivíduo
indoktrinieren	endoctriner	indoctrinate	adoctrinar	addottrinare	doutrinar
Industrie(f)	industrie	industry	industria	industria	indústria
industriell	industriel, le	industrial	industrial	industriale	industrial
Industrielle(m)	industriel	industrialist	industrial	industriale	industrial
Infarkt(m)	infarctus	coronary	infarto	infarto	enfarte
Infektion(f)	infection	infection	infección	infezione	infecção
Infinitiv(m)	infinitif	infinitive	infinitivo	infinito	infinitivo
Inflation(f)	inflation	inflation	inflación	inflazione	inflação
Informatik(f)	informatique	data processing	informática	informatica	informática
Information(f)	information	information	información	informazione	informação
informieren	informer	inform	informar	imformare	informar
Ingenieur(in f)m	ingénieur	engineer	ingeniero, a	ingegnere	engenheiro, a
Ingenieurkunst(f)	ingénierie	engineering	ingeniería	ingegneria	engenharia
Inhaber(in f)m	titulaire	holder	titular	titolare	titular

G

German	French	English	Spanish	Italian	Portuguese
Inhalt(m)	contenu	content(s)	contenido	contenuto	conteúdo
Initiative(f)	initiative	initiative	iniciativa	iniziativa	iniciativa
inklusiv	inclus, e	included	incluido, a	incluso, a	incluso, a
Inkompetenz(f)	incompétence	incompetence	incompetencia	incompetenza	incompetência
Innen-	intérieur, e	domestic, home	interior	interno, a	interno, a
inner	intérieur, e	inner, interior	interior	interiore	interior
innere(r, s); innen	intérieur, e	inside, inner	interior	interno, a	interior
Innere(n)	intérieur	interior	interior	interiore	interior
innovieren, erneuern	innover	innovate	innovar	innovare	inovar
Inschrift(f)	inscription	inscription	inscripción	iscrizione	inscrição
Insekt(n)	insecte	insect	insecto	insetto	insecto
Insel(f)	île	island, isle	isla	isola	ilha
Inselchen(n)	îlot	islet	islote	isolotto	ilhéu, ilhota
Inselgruppe(f)	archipel	archipelago	archipiélago	arcipelago	arquipélago
Inspektor(in f)m	inspecteur, trice	inspector	inspector, a	ispettore, trice	inspector, a
Instandhaltung(f)	entretien	upkeep	cuidado	mantenimento	manutenção
Instinkt(m)	instinct	instinct	instinto	istinto	instinto
instinktiv	instinctif, ive	instinctive	instintivo, a	istintivo, a	instintivo, a
Institut(n)	institut	institute	instituto	istituto	instituto
Institution(f)	institution	institution	institución	istituzione	instituição
Instrument(n)	instrument	instrument	instrumento	strumento	instrumento
Insulin(n)	insuline	insulin	insulina	insulina	insulina
intakt	intact, e	intact	intacto, a	intatto, a	intacto, a
integrieren	intégrer	integrate	integrar	integrare	integrar
Integrität(f)	intégrité	integrity	integridad	integrità	integridade
intellektuell	intellectuel, le	intellectual	intelectual	intellettuale	intelectual
intelligent	intelligent, e	intelligent	inteligente	intelligente	inteligente
Intelligenz(f)	intelligence	intelligence	inteligencia	intelligenza	inteligência
Intensität(f)	intensité	intensity	intensidad	intensità	intensidade
intensiv	intensif, ive	intensive	intensivo, a	intensivo, a	intensivo, a
interessant	intéressant, e	interesting	interesante	interessante	interessante
Interesse(n)	intérêt	interest	interés	interesse	interesse
interessieren, sich	intéresser(s')	interested in(be)	interesarse	interessarsi	interessar-se
intern	interne	internal, inner	interno, a	interno, a	interno, a
international	international, e	international	internacional	internazionale	internacional
Internatsschüler(m)	pensionnaire	boarder	interno, a	collegiale	interno, a
Interview(n)	interview	interview	interviú	intervista	entrevista
intim	intime	close, intimate	íntimo, a	intimo, a	íntimo, a
Intoleranz(f)	intolérance	intolerance	intolerancia	intolleranza	intolerância
Intrige(f)	intrigue	intrigue	intriga	intrigo	intriga
intrigieren	intriguer	intrigue	intrigar	intrigare	intrigar
Intuition(f)	intuition	intuition	intuición	intuizione	intuição
Invasion(f)	invasion	invasion	invasión	invasione	invasão
Inventar(n)	inventaire	inventory	inventario	inventario	inventário
Inventur(f)	inventaire	stock-list(taking)	inventario	inventario	inventário
investieren	investir	invest	invertir	investire	investir
Investition(f)	investissement	investment	inversión	investimento	investimento
Investitur(f)	investiture	investiture	investidura	investitura	investidura
Inzucht(f)	inceste	incest	incesto	incesto	incesto
inzwischen	entre-temps	meanwhile, meantime	entretanto	intanto, frattanto	entretanto
inzwischen	attendant(en)	meanwhile	mientras	attesa(in)	entretanto
irdisch	terrestre	terrestrial	terrestre	terrestre	terrestre
irgendwo	quelque part	somewhere	alguna parte(en)	qualche parte(da)	algures
Iris(f)	iris	iris	iris	iride	íris
Ironie(f)	ironie	irony	ironía	ironia	ironia
Irrenhaus(n)	asile	mental hospital	manicomio	manicomio	manicômio
Irrtum(m), Fehler(m)	erreur	error, mistake	error	errore	erro
Irrtum(m)(machen)	erreur(faire)	mistake(make a)	error(cometer un)	errore(fare un)	erro(dar um)
Ischias(m)	sciatique	sciatica	ciática	sciatica	ciática
islamisch	islamique	Islamic	islámico, a	islamico, a	islâmico, a
isolieren	isoler	insulate; isolate	aislar	isolare	isolar
Isolierung(f)	isolation	insulation	aislamiento	isolamento	isolação

J

German	French	English	Spanish	Italian	Portuguese
ja	oui	yes	sí	sì	sim
Ja, bitte?	allô!	hello!	dígame(!)	pronto!	está lá?; estou?
Jacke(f)	veste	jacket	chaqueta	giacca	jaqueta, casaco
Jagd(f)	chasse	hunting	caza	caccia	caça
jagen	chasser	hunt	cazar	cacciare	caçar
Jäger(in f)m	chasseur	hunter	cazador	cacciatore	caçador
Jahr(n)	an	year	año	anno	ano
Jahr(n)	année	year	año	annata, anno	ano
Jahrestag(m)	anniversaire	anniversary	aniversario	anniversario	aniversário
Jahreszeit(f)	saison	season	estación	stagione	estação
Jahrgang(m)	millésime	vintage	cosecha(año)	annata	vintage
Jahrhundert(n)	siècle	century	siglo	secolo	século
jährlich	annuel, le	yearly, annual	anual	annuale	anual
Jahrzehnt(n)	décennie	decade	decenio, década	decennio	década
jammern	lamenter(se)	lament	lamentarse	lamentarsi	lamentar-se
Januar(m)	janvier	January	enero	gennaio	Janeiro
Jazz(m)	jazz	jazz	jazz	jazz	jazz
jede(r, s)	chaque	every, each	cada	ogni	cada
jeder, jede	chacun, e; chaque	each, every(one)	cada uno(una)	ciascuno, a	cada um(uma)
jeder	quiconque	anyone(who)	quienquiera	chiunque	qualquer(um)
jedoch	cependant	however, but	sin embargo	eppure, tuttavia	todavia, porém
jedoch	toutefois	however	sin embargo	tuttavia	todavia
jemand	quelqu'un, e	someone, somebody	alguien	qualcuno, a	alguém
jenseits	au-delà de	beyond	más allá de	al di là	além de(para)
jetzt	maintenant	now	ahora	ora, adesso	agora
Jockey(m)	jockey	jockey	jockey	jockey, fantino	jockey
Journalismus(m)	journalisme	journalism	periodismo	giornalismo	jornalismo
Journalist(in f)m	journaliste	journalist	periodista	giornalista	jornalista
Juckreiz(m)	démangeaison	itch, itching	picazón	prurito	comichão
Jude(m), Jüdin(f)	juif, juive	Jew, Jewess(-es)	judío, judía	ebreo, a	judeu, judia
Judo(n)	judo	judo	judo, yudo	judò	judo
Jugend(f)	jeunesse	youth	juventud	gioventù, giovinezza	juventude
Jugendliche(r)mf	adolescent, e	teenager	adolescente	adolescente	adolescente
Juli(m)	juillet	July	julio	luglio	Julho
jung	jeune	young	joven	giovane	jovem
Junge(m)	garçon	boy	muchacho, mozo	ragazzo	rapaz
jungen Leute(pl)	jeunes	young people	jóvenes	giovani	jovens
Jünger(m)	disciple	disciple	discípulo	discepolo	discípulo
Jüngere(r)mf	cadet, te	younger; youngest	menor	cadetto, a	novo, a(o, a mais)
Jungfräulichkeit(f)	virginité	virginity	virginidad	verginità	virgindade
Junggeselle m/-sellin	célibataire	bachelor; single -	soltero, a	scapolo, nubile	solteiro, a
Juni(m)	juin	June	junio	giugno	Junho
Junta(f)	junte	junta	junta	giunta	junta
Jurist(in f)m	juriste	jurist; lawyer	jurista	giurista	jurista
juristisch	juridique	juridical, legal	jurídico, a	giuridico, a	jurídico, a
Jury(f)	jury	jury	jurado; tribunal	giuria	júri
Juwel, Schmuckstück(n)	joyau	jewel	joya	gioiello	jóia

G

K

German	French	English	Spanish	Italian	Portuguese
Kabarett(n)	cabaret	cabaret; nightclub	cabaret	cabaret	cabaret
Kabel(n)	câble	cable	cable	cavo	cabo
Kabine(f)	cabine	cabin	cabina	cabina	cabine
Kabinett(n)	cabinet(pol.)	cabinet	gabinete	gabinetto	gabinete
Kaffee(m)	café	coffee	café	caffè	café
Kaffeelöffel(m)	cuiller à café	teaspoon	cucharilla	cucchiaino	colher de chá
Kaffeemaschine(f)	cafetière	coffee-pot	cafetera	caffettiera	cafeteira
Käfig(m)	cage	cage	jaula	gabbia	gaiola, jaula
Kai((m)	quai	quay	muelle	molo	cais
Kaiser(m)	empereur	emperor	emperador	imperatore	imperador
Kaiserin(f)	impératrice	empress	emperatriz	imperatrice	imperatriz
Kaiserschnitt(m)	césarienne	Caesarean	cesárea	taglio cesareo	cesariana
Kajak(m)	kayac	kayak	kayac, piragua	kayak	kayac
Kakao(m)	cacao	cocoa, cacao	cacao	cacao	cacau
Kalb(n)	veau	calf(-lves); veal	becerro; ternera	vitello(a)	bezerro; vitelo
Kalender(m)	calendrier	calendar	calendario	calendario	calendário
Kaliber(n)	calibre	bore, calibre	calibre	calibro	calibre
Kalorie(f)	calorie	calorie	caloría	caloria	caloria
kalt	froid, e	cold	frío, a	freddo, a	frio, a
Kaltblütigkeit(f)	sang-froid	cool, calm	sangre fría	sangue freddo	sangue-frio
Kalzium(n)	calcium	calcium	calcio	calcio	cálcio
Kamel(n)	chameau	camel	camello	cammello	camelo
Kamera(f)	appareil photo	camera	cámara fotográfica	macchina fotografica	máquina fotográfica
Kamera(f)	caméra	cine-camera	cámara	cinepresa	câmara
Kamerad(in f)m	camarade	friend	compañero, a	compagno, a	camarada
Kamin(m)	cheminée	chimney; fire-place	chimenea	camino	chaminé
Kamm(m)	peigne	comb	peine	pettine	pente
Kamm(m)	crête	crest	cresta	cresta	crista, cimo
kämmen	peigner(se)	comb(one's hair)	peinar(se)	pettinarsi	pentear-se
Kammer(f)	chambre	chamber	cámara	camera	câmara
Kampf(m)	lutte	struggle, fight	lucha	lotta	luta
Kampf(m)	combat	combat, fight	combate	combattimento	combate
Kampfbahn(f)	arène(s)	bull ring, arena	plaza de toros	arena	praça de touros
kämpfen	lutter	fight, struggle	luchar	lottare	lutar
kämpfen	battre(se)	fight	pelearse	battersi, lottare	lutar
kämpfen für	militer	militate	militar	militare	militar
Kämpfer(m)	combattant, e	fighting-man	combatiente	combattente	combatente
Kämpfer(m); Ringer(m)	lutteur, se	wrestler; fighter	luchador, a	lottatore, trice	lutador, a
Kanal(m)	canal	canal	canal	canale	canal
Kandidat(in f)m	candidat, e	candidate	candidato, a	candidato, a	candidato, a
Känguruh(n)	kangourou	kangaroo	canguro	canguro	cangurú
Kaninchen(n)	lapin, e	rabbit	conejo, a	coniglio, a	coelho, a
Kanister(m)	bidon	can	bidón, lata	bidone	cantil
Kanone(f)	canon	cannon	cañón	cannone	canhão
Kanu(n)	canoë	canoe	canoa	canoa	canoa
Kanzler(in f)m	chancelier	chancellor	canciller	cancelliere	chanceler
Kap(n)	cap	cape	cabo	capo	cabo
Kapelle(f)	chapelle	chapel	capilla	cappella	capela
Kapital(n)	capital	capital, assets	capital	capitale	capital(o)
Kapitalismus(m)	capitalisme	capitalism	capitalismo	capitalismo	capitalismo
Kapitel(n)	chapitre	chapter	capítulo	capitolo	capítulo
kapitulieren	capituler	capitulate	capitular	capitolare	capitular
Kappe(f)	capuchon, capsule cap		capuchón	cappuccio	capuz
Karaffe(f)	carafe	jug, carafe	jarra	caraffa	jarro, caneca
Karat(n)	carat	carat	quilate	carato	quilate
Karate(n)	karaté	karate	karate	karatè	karaté
Kardinal(m)	cardinal	cardinal	cardenal	cardinale	cardeal
Kardiologie(f)	cardiologie	cardiology	cardiología	cardiologia	cardiologia
Karies(f)	carie	tooth decay	caries	carie	cárie
karikieren	caricaturer	caricature	caricaturar	caricaturare	caricaturar
Karneval(m)	carnaval	carnival	carnaval	carnevale	carnaval

German	French	English	Spanish	Italian	Portuguese
Karosserie(f)	carrosserie	body(-work)	carrocería	carrozzeria	carroçaria
Karre(f)	chariot	trolley	carro	carrello	carroça, carro
Karren(m)	charrette	cart	carreta, carro	carretta	carroça, carreta
Karriere(f)	carrière	career	carrera	carriera	carreira
Karte(f)	carte	card, ticket	tarjeta	tessera	bilhete
Karte(f); Fahrkarte(f)	ticket	ticket	ticket, billete	biglietto	bilhete
Karte(f)(Speisekarte)	carte(resto)	menu	menú	menù, carta	lista
Kartei(f)	fichier	card-index	fichero	schedario	ficheiro
Karteikarte(f)	fiche	card	ficha	scheda, cartella	ficha
Kartoffel(f)	pomme de terre	potato(-es)	patata	patata	batata
Karussell(n)	manège	roundabout	tiovivo, noria	giostra	carrossel
Käse(m)	fromage	cheese	queso	formaggio	queijo
Kaserne(f)	caserne	barracks	cuartel	caserma	quartel
Kasino(n)	casino	casino	casino	casinò	casino
Kasse(f)	caisse	cash-desk	caja	cassa	caixa
Kassette(f)	cassette	cassette	casete	cassetta	cassete
Kassettenrecorder(m)	magnétophone	tape recorder	magnetófono	registratore	gravador
kassieren(ein =)	toucher	cash, earn, win	cobrar	incassare	receber
Kassierer(in f)m	caissier, ière	cashier	cajero, a	cassiere, a	caixa(o)
kastanienbraun	châtain	chestnut brown	castaño, a	castano, a	castanho, a
Kaste(f)	caste	caste	casta	casta	casta
Katalog(m)	catalogue	catalogue	catálogo	catalogo	catálogo
Katastrophe(f)	catastrophe	catastrophe	catástrofe	catastrofe	catástrofe
Katastrophe(f)	cataclysme	cataclysm	cataclismo	cataclisma	cataclismo
Kategorie(f)	catégorie	category	categoría	categoria	categoria
Kater(m), Katze(f)	chat, te	cat	gato, a	gatto, a	gato, a
Kathedrale(f), Dom(m)	cathédrale	cathedral	catedral	cattedrale, duomo	catedral
katholisch	catholique	Catholic	católico, a	cattolico, a	católico, a
kauen	mâcher	chew	masticar	masticare	mastigar
Kauf(m)	achat	purchase	compra	acquisto	compra
kaufen	acheter	buy	comprar	comprare	comprar
Käufer(in f)m	acheteur, se	buyer	comprador, a	acquirente	comprador, a
Kaufmann m, Kauffrau f	commerçant, e	shop-keeper	tendero, a	negoziante	comerciante
Kaufmann m, Kauffrau f	marchand, e	shop-keeper	vendedor, a	negoziante	comerciante
Kaviar(m)	caviar	caviar	caviar	caviale	caviar
Kegel(m)	cône	cone	cono	cono	cone
Kegel(f)	quille	skittle	bolos(juego)	birillo	paulitos
kegelförmig	conique	conical	cónico, a	conico, a	cónico, a
Kehlkopf(m)	larynx	larynx	laringe	laringe	laringe
Keil(m)	cale	wedge, chock	cuña	zeppa	cunha
Keim(m)	germe	germ, seed	germen	germe	germe
Keim(m)	germe	seed	germen, grano	germoglio	germe
keiner, keine	aucun, e	no, not any; no one	ningún, o, a	nessuno, a	nenhum, a
Keks(m)	biscuit	biscuit	galleta	biscotto	biscoito
Kelch(m), Schale(f)	coupe	glass(-es)	copa	calice	taça
Keller(m)	cave	cellar	bodega, sótano	cantina	adega
Kellner(in f)m	serveur, se	waiter, waitress	camarero, a	cameriere, a	criado, moço
kennen	connaître	know	conocer, saber	conoscere, sapere	conhecer, saber
Kenntnis(f)	connaissance	knowledge	conocimiento	conoscenza	conhecimento
Kenntnis(f), Begriff m	notion	notion	noción	nozione	noção
kentern, um = kippen	chavirer	capsize	zozobrar	capovolgersi	soçobrar
Kerbe(f), Einschnitt m	encoche	notch	muesca	tacca, intacco	entalhe
Kerbe(f)	entaille	cut, nick, notch	cortadura	incisione	incisão, golpe
Kern(m)	pépin	pip	pepita	seme	caroço
Kern(m)	noyau	stone	hueso	nocciolo	caroço
Kern(m)	noyau	nucleus(-ei)	núcleo	nucleo	núcleo
Kern-, Atom-	nucléaire	nuclear	nuclear	nucleare	nuclear
Kerze(f)	bougie	candle	vela	candela	vela
Kerze(f)	cierge	candle	cirio	cero	círio
Kette(f)	chaîne	chain	cadena	catena	cadeia, corrente
keuchen	haleter	pant, gasp	jadear	ansimare	arquejar
keusch	chaste	pure	casto, a	casto, a	casto, a
keusch	pudique	modest	púdico, a	pudico, a	púdico, a
KFZ-Schein(m)	carte grise	log-book	cédula id-fiscal	libretto di circola-	livrete(circulação)
Kiefer(m)	mâchoire	jaw	mandíbula	mascella	maxila
Kielwasser(n)	sillage	wake	estela	scia	esteira
Kies(m)	gravier	gravel	grava	ghiaia	cascalho
Kieselstein(m)	galet	pebble	canto rodado	ciottolo	seixo

G

Kilo(gramm n)n	kilogramme	kilogram(me)	kilogramo	chilogrammo, chilo	quilograma, quilo
Kilometer(m)	kilomètre	kilometre	kilómetro	chilometro	quilómetro
Kimono(m)	kimono	kimono	quimono, kimono	chimono	quimono
Kind(n)	enfant	child, children(pl)	niño, a; chico, a	bambino, a	criança
Kind(n)	gamin, e	kid, child	chiquillo, a	ragazzino, a	miúdo
Kinderarzt(m)/-ärztin	pédiatre	paediatrician	pediatra	pediatra	pediatra
Kinderlähmung(f)	poliomyélite	polio(myelitis)	poliomielitis	poliomelite	poliomielite
Kindermädchen(n)	nurse	nanny	niñera	bambinaia	ama
Kinderwagen(m)	landau	pram	cochecito	carrozzina	carrinho(bebé)
Kinder-, kindisch	infantile	infantile, child	infantil	infantile	infantil
Kindheit(f)	enfance	childhood	infancia	infanzia	infância
Kinn(n)	menton	chin	barbilla	mento	queixo
Kino(n)	cinéma	cinema	cine	cinema	cinema
Kirche(f)	église	church(-es)	iglesia	chiesa	igreja
Kirsche(f)	cerise	cherry	cereza	ciliegia	cereja
Kissen(n)	coussin	cushion	cojín	cuscino	almofada
Kiste(f)	caisse	chest, case	cajón, caja	cassa	caixa
Kitt(m)	mastic	putty	masilla	mastice	betume
Kittel(m)	blouse	overall	bata, blusa	blusa, camice	bata
Kitzeln(n)	chatouille(s)	tickle	cosquillas	solletico	cócegas
Klage(f)	plainte	complaint	queja	lamento	queixume, queixa
Klammer(f)	parenthèse	bracket	paréntesis	parentesi	parêntesis
Klappe(f)	vanne	gate; valve	compuerta	saracinesca	comporta
Klappenventil(n)	clapet	valve	válvula	valvola	válvula
Klappstuhl(m)	strapontin	folding seat	traspuntín	strapuntino	banco dobrável
klar	clair, e	clear	claro, a	chiaro, a; limpido, a	claro, a
klar	lucide	lucid	lúcido, a	lucido, a	lúcido, a
klären	clarifier	clarify	clarificar	chiarificare	clarificar
Klarinette(f)	clarinette	clarinet	clarinete	clarinetto	clarinete
Klarstellung(f)	précision	clarification	aclaración	precisazione	explicação, precisão
Klasse(f)	classe	class	clase	classe, ceto	classe
Klassenstufe(f)	classe	class, form	clase, curso	classe	classe
Klassenzimmer(n)	classe(salle)	classroom	aula	aula	aula(sala de)
klassisch	classique	classical	clásico, a	classico, a	clássico, a
klatschen	applaudir	applaud, clap	aplaudir	applaudire	aplaudir
Klausel(f)	clause	clause	cláusula	clausola	cláusula
Klavier(n)	piano	piano	piano	pianoforte	piano
kleben	coller	stick, glue	pegar	incollare	colar, pegar
klebrig, anhaftend	adhésif, ive	adhesive	adhesivo, a	adesivo, a	adesivo, a
klebrig	gluant, e	sticky	viscoso, a	viscido, a	viscoso, a
Klebstoff(m)	colle	glue	cola, pegamento	colla	cola
Kleid(n)	robe	dress	vestido	vestito	vestido
Kleiderständer(m)	portemanteau	hat stand	colgador, percha	attaccapanni	cabide
Kleidung(f)	habit(s)	clothes	vestido, traje	vestito(i), abiti	fato, traje
Kleidung(f)	vêtements	clothes	ropa, prenda	vestiti	roupa(s)
Kleidungsstück(n)	vêtement	garment	traje, ropa	vestito	peça de roupa
klein	petit, e	small, little	pequeño, a	piccolo, a	pequeno, a
klein	petit, e	little	pequeño, a	piccolo, a	pequeno, a
kleiner Junge(m)	garçon, enfant	boy	chico	ragazzo, bambino	rapaz
Kleingeld(n); Klein-	monnaie	change	cambio	resto	troco
Klempner(m)	plombier	plumber	fontanero	idraulico	canalizador
Klerus(m)	clergé	clergy	clero	clero	clero
klettern	grimper	climb	escalar, subir	arrampicarsi	trepar, escalar
Klient(in f)m	client, e	client	cliente	cliente	cliente
Klima(n)	climat	climate	clima	clima	clima
Klimaanlage(f)	climatiseur	air conditioner	climatizador	condizionatore	climatizador
Klimpern, Klingeln(n)	tintement	ringing, jingle	tañido	tintinnio	tilintar
Klingel(f)	sonnette	bell	timbre	campanello	campainha
Klingel(f)	sonnerie	ring	campana, timbre	squillo, soneria	campainha, toque
klingeln	sonner	ring	sonar, tocar	suonare, sonare	soar, tocar
klingen	résonner	resound, sound	resonar	rimbombare	ressoar, ecoar
Klinik(f)	clinique	nursing-home	clínica	clinica	clínica
Kloster(n)	couvent	convent	convento	convento	convento
Kloster(n)	monastère	monastery	monasterio	monastero	mosteiro
Klub(m)	club	club	club	club	clube
klug, gescheit	intelligent, e	clever	inteligente	intelligente	inteligente
knabbern	croquer	crunch	mascar	sgranocchiare	trincar
knabbern	grignoter	nibble	mordisquear	sgranocchiare	petiscar

German	French	English	Spanish	Italian	Portuguese
Knall(m)	détonation	detonation	detonación	detonazione	detonação
Knall(m), Explosion(f)	déflagration	explosion	deflagración	deflagrazione	deflagração
Knallkörper(m)	pétard	banger, cracker	petardo	petardo	bomba, foguete
kneifen	pincer	pinch, nip	pellizcar	pizzicare	beliscar
Kneipe(f)	bar	bar, pub	bar, café	bar	bar, café
kneten	pétrir	knead	amasar	impastare	amassar
Knie(n)	genou	knee	rodilla	ginocchio	joelho
Kniescheibe(f)	rotule	knee-cap	rótula	rotula	rótula
knirschen	grincer	grind, grate	chirriar	stridere	ranger
Knöchel(m)	cheville	ankle	tobillo	caviglia	tornozelo
Knochen(m)	os	bone	hueso	osso	osso
Knopf(m)	bouton	button	botón	bottone	botão
Knopf(m)	bouton	knob	botón	manopola, pomello	botão
Knorpel(m)	cartilage	cartilage	cartílago	cartilagine	cartilagem
Knospe(f)	bourgeon	bud	brote, botón	gemma	rebento, botão
Knoten(m)	noeud	knot	nudo	nodo	nó, laço
Koalition(f)	coalition	coalition	coalición	coalizione	coligação
Kobra(f)	cobra	cobra	cobra	cobra	cobra
Koch(m), Köchin(f)	cuisinier, ière	cook; chef	cocinero, a	cuoco, a	cozinheiro, a
kochen	bouillir	boil	hervir	bollire	ferver
kochen	cuire	cook	cocer	cuocere	cozer
kochen	cuisiner	cook	cocinar	cucinare	cozinhar
Kochen(n)	ébullition	boiling	ebullición	ebollizione	fervura
Kochen(n), Sieden(n)	cuisson	cooking	cocción	cottura	cozedura, cocção
kochend	bouillant, e	boiling	hirviente	bollente	fervente
Kocher(m)	réchaud	stove	hornillo	fornello	fogão
Kochtopf(m)	marmite	cooking-pot	marmita, olla	pentola, marmitta	marmita
Kod(m)	code	code	código	codice	código
Köder(m)	appât	bait	cebo	esca	engodo, isca
kodifizieren	codifier	codify	codificar	codificare	codificar
Koeffizient(m)	coefficient	coefficient	coeficiente	coefficiente	coeficiente
Koffer(großer)(m)	malle	trunk	baúl	baule	mala
Koffer(m)	valise	suitcase, case	maleta	valigia	mala
Kofferraum(m)	coffre	boot	maletero	bagagliaio	mala
Kohl(m)	chou	cabbage	col	cavolo	couve
Kohle(f)	charbon	coal	carbón	carbone	carvão
Kohlenförderung(f)	extraction	extraction	extracción	estrazione	extracção
Kohlensäure(f)	carbonique	carbonic	carbónico, a	carbonico, a	carbónico, a
Kohlenstoff(m)	carbone	carbon	carbono	carbonio	carbono
Kokain(m)	cocaïne	cocaine	cocaína	cocaina	cocaína
kokett; eitel	coquet, te	pretty; coquettish	presumido, a	civettuolo, a	vaidoso, a
Kokosnuß(f)	noix de coco	coconut	coco	noce di cocco	coco
Kokuspalme(f)	cocotier	coconut palm(tree)	cocotero	palma da cocco	coqueiro
Kolben(m)	piston	piston	pistón	pistone	pistão
Kolik(f)	colique	colic	cólico	colica	cólica
Kollege(m), Kollegin f	collègue	colleague	colega	collega	colega
Kollegium(n)	collège	college	colegio	collegio	colégio
Kollektion(f)	collection	collection	colección	collezione	colecção
Kolonie(f)	colonie	colony	colonia	colonia	colónia
Kolonisierung(f)	colonisation	colonization	colonización	colonizzazione	colonização
Koma(n)	coma	coma	coma	coma	coma
Kombination(f)	combinaison	combination	combinación	combinazione	combinação
Komet(m)	comète	comet	cometa	cometa	cometa
Komiker(in f)m	comique	comedian, comic	cómico, a	comico	cómico
komisch	comique	comic, funny	cómico, a	comico, a	cómico, a
Komitee(n), Ausschuß m	comité	committee	comité	comitato	comissão
Komma(n)	virgule	comma	coma	virgola	vírgula
Kommandant(m), Major m	commandant	major	comandante	comandante	comandante
Kommando(n)	commando	commando	comando	commando	comando
kommen	venir	come	venir	venire	vir
kommen Sie!	venez!	come(on)!	venga(!)	venga!, venite!	venha!
kommen Sie her!	venez ici!	come here!	venga aquí(!)	venga qui!, venite!	venha cá!
Kommentar(m)	commentaire	commentary	comentario	commentario	comentário
Kommissariat(n)	commissariat	police station	comisaría	commissariato	esquadra(polícia)
Kommission(f)	commission	commission	comisión	commissione	comissão
Kommunismus(m)	communisme	communism	comunismo	comunismo	comunismo
Komödiant(in f)m	comédien, ne	comedian, -dienne	comediante, a	commediante	comediante, a
Komödie(f)	comédie	comedy	comedia	commedia	comédia

G

German	French	English	Spanish	Italian	Portuguese
kompakt	compact, e	compact	compacto, a	compatto, a	compacto, a
Kompaß(m)	boussole	compass	brújula	bussola	bússola
Kompaß(m)	compas	compass(es)	compás	compasso	compasso
Kompensation(f)	compensation	compensation	compensación	compenso	compensação
kompetent	compétent, e	competent	competente, capaz	competente	competente, capaz
Komplex(m)	complexe	complex	complejo	complesso	complexo
Kompliment(n)	compliment	compliment	cumplido	complimento	cumprimento
Komplize(m), Komplizin	complice	accomplice	cómplice	complice	cúmplice
kompliziert	compliqué, e	complicated	complicado, a	complicato, a	complicado, a
Komplott(n)	conspiration	plot, conspiracy	conspiración	cospirazione	conspiração
Komponist(in f)m	compositeur	composer	compositor	compositore	compositor
Kompott(n)	compote	stewed fruit	compota	frutta cotta	compota
Kompromiß(m)	compromis	compromise	compromiso	compromesso	compromisso
Kompromittierung(f)	compromission	compromising	compromiso	compromissione	comprometimento
Kondensierung(f)	condensation	condensation	condensación	condensazione	condensação
Konditorei(f)	pâtisserie	cake shop	pastelería	pasticceria	pastelaria
Konferenz(f)	conférence	conference; lecture	conferencia	conferenza	conferência
Konflikt(m)	conflit	conflict	conflicto	conflitto	conflito
Konfrontation(f)	affrontement	confrontation	enfrentamiento	affrontamento	afrontamento
konfrontieren	confronter	confront	confrontar	confrontare	confrontar
Kongress(m)	congrès	congress	congreso	congresso	congresso
König(m)	roi	king	rey	re	rei
Königin(f)	reine	queen	reina	regina	rainha
königlich	royal, e	royal	real	reale	real
Königreich(n)	royaume	kingdom	reino	reame	reino
Königstum(n)	royauté	royalty, monarchy	realeza	sovranità	realeza
Konjugation(f)	conjugaison	conjugation	conjugación	coniugazione	conjugação
Konjunktur(f)	conjoncture	conjuncture	coyuntura	congiuntura	conjuntura
konkret	concret, ète	concrete	concreto, a	concreto, a	concreto, a
konkurrent(in f)m	concurrent, e	competitor	competidor, a	concorrente	concorrente
Konkurrenz(f)	concurrence	competition	competencia	concorrenza	concorrência
Konkurs(m)	faillite	failure; bankruptcy	quiebra, ruina	fallimento	falência
können	pouvoir	can, able to(be)	poder	potere	poder
Konsequenz(f)	conséquence	consequence	consecuencia	conseguenza	consequência
Konserve(f)	conserve(s)	tinned food	conserva	conserva	conserva
konservieren	conserver	preserve, keep	conservar	conservare	conservar
Konservierung(f)	conservation	conservation	conservación	conservazione	conservação
Konstellation(f)	constellation	constellation	constelación	costellazione	constelação
Konsul(m)	consul	consul	cónsul	console	cônsul
Konsulat(n)	consulat	consulate	consulado	consolato	consulado
Kontakt(m)	contact	contact	contacto	contatto	contacto
Kontakt(auf = nehmen)	contact(prendre)	contact	contacto(entrar en)	contattare	contactar
Kontaktlinse(f)	lentille	lens(contact -)	lentilla	lente a contatto	lente
Kontinent(m)	continent	continent	continente	continente	continente
Konto(n)	compte	account	cuenta	conto	conta
Kontoauszug(m)	relevé(compte)	statement(bank)	estado(cuentas)	estratto conto	extracto(conta)
Kontra geben	contrer	counter	oponerse(a)	opporsi(a)	contrariar
Kontrolle(f)	contrôle	examination	control	controllo	controlo
Kontrolleur(m)	contrôleur	inspector	revisor	controllore	revisor; fiscal
kontrollieren	contrôler	control, check	controlar	controllare	controlar
konvergieren	converger	converge	converger	convergere	convergir
konvertieren	convertir(se)	convert	convertirse	convertirsi	converter-se
Konvoi(m)	convoi	convoy	convoy	convoglio	comboio
konzentrieren	concentrer	concentrate	concentrar	concentrare	concentrar
konzentrieren, sich	concentrer(se)	concentrate	concentrar(se)	concentrarsi	concentrar-se
Konzeption(f)	conception	conception	concepción	concezione	concepção
Konzert(n)	concert	concert	concierto	concerto	concerto
Konzert(n), Vortrag(m)	récital	recital	recital	recital	recital
koordinieren	coordonner	coordinate	coordinar	coordinare	coordenar
Kopf(m)	tête	head	cabeza	testa, capo	cabeça
Kopfhörer(m)	écouteurs, casque	ear/headphones	casco	cuffia	auscultadores
Kopfkissen(n)	oreiller	pillow	almohada	guanciale	travesseiro
Kopfsalat(m)	laitue, salade	lettuce	lechuga	lattuga	alface
Kopfschmerzen(m, pl)	mal de tête	headache	dolor de cabeza	mal di testa	dor de cabeça
Kopfsprung(m)	plongeon	dive	zambullida	tuffo	mergulho
Kopie(f)	copie	copy	copia	copia	cópia
kopieren	copier	copy	copiar	copiare	copiar
Koralle(f)	corail	coral	coral	corallo	coral

German	French	English	Spanish	Italian	Portuguese
Koran(der)	Coran	Koran	Corán	Corano	Alcorão
Korb(m)	panier	basket	cesto	paniere, cesto	cesto
Korb(m)(Papierkorb m)	corbeille	basket; bin	cesto(a); cestillo	cestino	cesto, a
Kordel(f)	cordon	cord, string	cordón, cable	cordone	cordão
Kork(m)	liège	cork	corcho	sughero	cortiça
Korken(m)	bouchon	cork	corcho	tappo, turacciolo	rolha
Korkenzieher(m)	tire-bouchon	corkscrew	sacacorchos	cavatappi	saca-rolhas
Korn(n)	grain	grain	grano	chicco, grano	grão
Körnchen(n)	granule	granule	gránulo	granulo	grânulo
Körper(m)	corps	body	cuerpo	corpo	corpo
körperlich	corporel, le	bodily	corporal	corporale	corporal
Körperschaft(f)	corporation	corporation	corporación	corporazione	corporação
Korrespondenz(f)	correspondance	correspondence	correspondencia	corrispondenza	correspondência
korrigieren	corriger	correct, rectify	corregir	correggere	corrigir
Korrosion(f)	corrosion	corrosion	corrosión	corrosione	corrosão
Korruption(f)	corruption	corruption	corrupción	corruzione	corrupção
Korsett(n)	gaine	girdle	faja	guaina, corsetto	cinta elástica
Kosmetik(f)	cosmétique	cosmetic	cosmético	cosmetico	cosmético
kosmopolitisch	cosmopolite	cosmopolitan	cosmopolita	cosmopolita	cosmopolita
kosten	goûter	taste	probar	assaggiare	provar
kosten	déguster	taste, sample	saborear, catar	gustare	provar
kosten, genießen	savourer	savour	saborear	assaporare	saborear
kosten	coûter	cost	costar	costare	custar
Kosten(pl.)	coût	cost	costo, coste	costo	custo, preço
Kosten(pl.)	frais	expenses	gastos	spese(le)	gastos, despesas
Kosten(pl.)	frais(scolarité)	fee	gastos(escolares)	spese	despesas
kostenlos	gratuit, e	free	gratis; gratuito, a	gratuito, a; gratis	grátis; gratuito, a
Kostenvoranschlag(m)	devis	estimate	presupuesto	preventivo	orçamento
köstlich	délicieux, se	delicious	delicioso, a	delizioso, a	delicioso, a
Kostüm(n)	tailleur	suit	traje	tailleur	saia-casaco
Krabbe(f)	crevette	prawn, shrimp	gamba, camarón	gamberetto	camarão
Krach(m)	vacarme	uproar, din	alboroto, jaleo	chiasso	barulho
krachen	craquer	crack	crujir	scricchiolare	estalar
Kraft(f)	vigueur	vigour	vigor	vigore	vigor
Kraft(f)	force, puissance	strength, power	fuerza	forza	força, potência
Kraft(in), geltend	vigueur(en)	force(in), current	vigente	vigore(in), vigente	vigente
kräftig, fest	robuste, solide	sturdy	vigoroso, a; fuerte	robusto, a; forte	robusto, a; forte
kräftig, stark	puissant, e	potent, powerful	potente	potente	potente
Kraftwerk(n), Zentrale	centrale	power-station	central	centrale	central
Kragen(m)	col	collar	cuello	collo, colletto	colarinho; gola
Kralle(f), Klaue(f)	griffe	claw	garra	artiglio	garra
Krampf(m)	crampe	cramp	calambre	crampo	cãibra
Krampf(m)	spasme	spasm	espasmo	spasma	espasmo
Kramwarenhandel(m)	droguerie	hardware shop	droguería	mesticheria	drogaria
Kran(m)	grue	crane	grúa	gru	grua
krank	malade	ill	enfermo, a	malato, a	doente; enfermo, a
Kranke(f, m)	malade	sick person	enfermo, a	malato, a	doente
kränken	blesser, offenser	hurt, offend	lastimar, ofender	ferire, offendere	magoar, ofender
Krankenhaus(n)	hôpital	hospital	hospital	ospedale	hospital
Krankenpfleger(in f)m	infirmier, ière	nurse	enfermero, a	infermiere, a	enfermeiro, a
Krankenraum(m)	infirmerie	infirmary	enfermería	infermeria	enfermaria
Krankenwagen(m)	ambulance	ambulance	ambulancia	ambulanza	ambulância
Krankheit(f)	maladie	illness	enfermedad	malattia	doença
Krapfen, Pfannkuchen	beignets	fritters	buñuelos	frittella	pastéis
Krater(m)	cratère	crater	cráter	cratere	cratera
Krätze(f)	gale	scabies	sarna	scabbia, rogna	sarna
kratzen	gratter	scrape, scratch	raspar, rascar	grattare	raspar
kratzen	griffer	scratch, claw	arañar	graffiare	arranhar
kratzen, schrammen	égratigner	scratch	rasguñar	scalfire	arranhar
kratzen, sich	gratter(se)	scratch oneself	rascarse	grattarsi	coçar-se
Kratzer(m), Schramme f	éraflure	scratch, graze	rasguño	scalfittura	arranhadura
Kraut(n), Kräuter(pl.)	herbe(s)	herb(s)	hierbas	erbe(aromatiche)	erva
Kräutertee(m)	tisane	herb tea	tisana	tisana	tisana
Kravatte(f)	cravate	tie	corbata	cravatta	gravata
Krebs(m)	cancer	cancer	cáncer	cancro	cancro
Krebs(m)	crabe	crab	cangrejo	granchio	caranguejo
krebsartig	cancéreux, se	cancerous	canceroso, a	canceroso, a	canceroso, a
Kredit(m)	crédit	credit	crédito	credito	crédito

German	French	English	Spanish	Italian	Portuguese
Kreditkarte(f)	carte de crédit	credit card	carta de crédito	carta di credito	cartão de crédito
Kreis(m)	cercle	circle	círculo	cerchio	círculo
Kreislauf(m)	circulation	circulation	circulación	circolazione	circulação
Kreisumfang(m)	circonférence	circumference	circunferencia	circonferenza	circunferência
Kreisverkehr(m)	rond-point	roundabout	glorieta	rotonda, rotatoria	rotunda
Kreuz(n)	croix	cross(-es)	cruz	croce	cruz
kreuzen	croiser	interbreed, cross	cruzar	incrociare	cruzar
kreuzen, sich	croiser(se)	cross, intersect	cruzarse	incrociarsi	cruzar-se
Kreuzfahrt(f)	croisière	cruise	crucero	crociera	cruzeiro
Kreuzung(f)	croisement	crossing	cruce	incrocio	cruzamento
Kreuzung(f)	carrefour	cross-road(s)	encrucijada	incrocio	cruzamento
Kreuzung(f)	intersection	intersection	intersección	intersezione	intersecção
Kreuzworträtsel(n)	mots croisés	crossword	crucigrama	cruciverba	palavras cruzadas
kriechen	ramper	crawl	arrastrarse	strisciare	rastejar
Krieg(m)	guerre	war	guerra	guerra	guerra
kriegerisch	belliqueux, se	aggressive	belicoso, a	bellicoso, a	belicoso, a
Kriegskunst(f)	arts martiaux	martial arts	artes marciales	arti marziali	artes marciais
Kriegsschiff(n)	cuirassé	warship	acorazado	corazzata	couraçado
Kriminalität(f)	délinquance	delinquency	delincuencia	delinquenza	delinquência
Kriminalroman(m)	roman policier	detective novel	novela policíaca	giallo	romance policial
Kriminelle(r)mf	délinquant, e	delinquent	delincuente	delinquente	delinquente
Krise(f)	crise	crisis(-ses)	crisis	crisi	crise
Kristall(n)	cristal	crystal	cristal	cristallo	cristal
Kriterium(n)	critère	criterion(-ia)	criterio	criterio	critério
Kritik(f)	critique	criticism	crítica	critica	crítica
kritisieren	critiquer	criticize	criticar	criticare	criticar
Krokodil(n)	crocodile	crocodile	cocodrilo	coccodrillo	crocodilo
Krone(f)	couronne	crown	corona	corona	coroa
Krücke(f)	béquille	crutch(-es)	muleta	stampella	muleta
krumm, gebeugt	cambré, e	arched	arqueado, a	inarcato, a; arcuato, a	arqueado, a
Krümmung(f)	courbure	bend, curve	curvatura	curvatura	curvatura
Kruste(f)	croûte	crust	costra, corteza	crosta	crosta
Küche(f)	cuisine	kitchen	cocina	cucina	cozinha
Kuchen(m)	gâteau	cake; pastry	pastel	dolce	bolo
Kugel(f)	boule	bowl	bola	boccia	bola
Kugel(f)	bille	ball	bola	sfera	esfera
Kugel(f)	balle	bullet	bala	pallottola	bala
Kugelschreiber(m)	stylo à bille	ball-point pen	bolígrafo	penna a sfera	esferográfica
Kuh(f)	vache	cow	vaca	vacca, mucca	vaca
Kühlschrank(m)	frigo, frigidaire	fridge	frigorífico	frigorifero	frigorífico
Kühlschrank(m)	réfrigérateur	refrigerator	nevera	frigorifero	frigorífico
Kühltruhe(f)	congélateur	freezer	congelador	congelatore	congelador
Kühl-; kalt, kühl	frigorifique	refrigerating	frigorífico, a	frigorífero, a	frigorífico, a
kühn, mutig	intrépide	intrepid	intrépido, a	intrepido, a	intrépido, a
Kühnheit(f)	audace	audacity	audacia	audacia	audácia
Küken(n)	poussin	chick	pollito	pulcino	pinto
Kulisse(f)	coulisses	wings	bastidores	quinte(le)	bastidores
Kult(m)	culte	worship	culto	culto	culto
Kultur(f)	culture	culture	cultura	cultura	cultura
kulturell	culturel, le	cultural	cultural	culturale	cultural
Kummer(m)	chagrin	grief, sorrow	pena	dispiacere	desgosto, pena
kümmern sich/um	occuper(s')	look after	ocuparse	occuparsi	tomar conta
Kunde(m), Kundin(f)	client, e	customer	cliente	cliente	cliente
Kunst(f)	art	art	arte	arte	arte
Kunst(f)	beaux-arts	fine arts	bellas artes	belle arti	belas-artes
Künstler(in f)m	artiste	artist	artista	artista	artista
künstlich	artificiel, le	artificial	artificial	artificiale	artificial
Kupfer(n)	cuivre	copper	cobre	rame	cobre
Kuppel(f)	coupole	dome	cúpula, bóveda	cupola	cúpula
Kuppel(f)	dôme	dome	cúpula	duomo	cúpula
Kuppelei(f)	proxénétisme	pimping	proxenetismo	prossenetismo	proxenetismo
kuppeln, verbinden	connecter	connect	conectar	connettere	ligar
Kupplung(f)	embrayage	clutch	embrague	frizione	embraiagem
Kur(f)	cure	treatment	cura	cura	cura
Kurs(m)	cap	head for	rumbo a	rotta	rumo
Kurs(m)	cours	rate, quotation	cotización	corso	índice, tabela
Kurswert(m)	cotation	quotation	cotización	quotazione	cotação
Kurve(f)	courbe	curve	curva	curva	curva

German	French	English	Spanish	Italian	Portuguese
Kurve(f)	virage	bend, turn	curva	curva	curva
kurvenreich	sinueux, se	winding, sinuous	sinuoso, a	sinuoso, a	sinuoso, a
kurz	court, e	short	corto, a	corto, a	curto, a
kurz	bref, brève	brief, short	breve	breve	breve
kurze Hose(f)	short	shorts	pantalón corto	shorts, calzoncini	calções; calção
kürzlich	récemment	recently	recientemente	recentemente	recentemente
kurzsichtig	myope	short-sighted	miope	miope	míope
Kuß(m)	baiser	kiss	beso(dar un)	bacio	beijo
Küßchen(n)	bise	kiss	besito	bacio	beijinho
küssen, umarmen	embrasser	kiss; embrace	abrazar, besar	baciare	abraçar, beijar
Küste(f)	côte	coast	costa	costa	costa
Küste(f)	bord de mer	sea-side	orilla del mar	riva	beira mar
Küsten-	côtier, ère	coastal	costero, a	costiero, a	costeiro, a
Küstenstreifen(m)	littoral	coast	litoral	litorale	litoral
Küstenstrich(m)	rivage	shore	orilla	riva	beira-mar

L

German	French	English	Spanish	Italian	Portuguese
Labor(n)	laboratoire	laboratory	laboratorio	laboratorio	laboratório
Labyrinth(n)	labyrinthe	labyrinth, maze	laberinto	labirinto	labirinto
lächeln	sourire	smile	sonreír	sorridere	sorrir
Lächeln(n)	sourire	smile	sonrisa	sorriso	sorriso
lächelnd	souriant, e	cheerful	sonriente	sorridente	sorridente
lachen	rire	laugh	reir	ridere	rir
Lachen(n)	rire	laugh, laughter	risa	riso, ridere	riso
lächerlich	ridicule	ridiculous	ridículo, a	ridicolo, a	ridículo, a
Lachs(m)	saumon	salmon	salmón	salmone	salmão
Lack(m)	laque	lacquer	laca	lacca	laca
Lack(m)	vernis	varnish	barniz	vernice	verniz
laden	charger	load	cargar	caricare	carregar
Ladentisch(m)	comptoir	counter	mostrador	banco	balcão
Laderaum(m)	cale	hold	bodega	stiva	porão
Ladung(f)	chargement	load, loading	cargamento	carico	carregamento
Ladung(f)	cargaison	cargo, freight	cargamento	carico	carga
Lage(f)	situation	situation	situación	situazione	situação
Lage(f)	situation	location, position	situación	situazione	situação
Lage(f), Stelle(f)	emplacement	location, site	sitio	posto, sito, luogo	lugar; sítio
Lager(n)	entrepôt	warehouse	almacén	magazzino	armazém
lagern	stocker	stock, store	almacenar	immagazzinare	armazenar
Lähmung(f)	paralysie	paralysis	parálisis	paralisi	paralisia
Laken(n)	drap	sheet	sábana	lenzuolo	lençol
Lama(n)	lama	llama	llama	lama	lama
Lamm(n)	agneau	lamb	cordero	agnello	cordeiro
Lampe(f)	lampe	lamp	lámpara	lampada	candeeiro
lancieren, starten	lancer	launch, start up	lanzar	lanciare	lançar
Land(n)	terre	land	tierra	terra	terra
Land(n)	pays	country	país	paese	país
Land(n)	campagne	country(side)	campo	campagna	campo
landen	atterrir	land	aterrizar	atterrare	aterrar
Land gehen(an)	débarquer	disembark, land	desembarcar	sbarcare	desembarcar
Landkarte(f)	carte(géo)	map	mapa	mappa, carta	mapa
ländlich	rural, e	rural	rural	rurale	rural
ländlich, einfach	rustique	rustic	rústico, a	rustico, a	rústico, a
Landschaft(f)	paysage	landscape	paisaje	paesaggio	paisagem
Landstraße(f)	route nationale	main/trunk road	carretera	strada statale	estrada
Landstreicher(in f)m	vagabond, e	vagabond; tramp	vagabundo, a	vagabondo, a	vagabundo, a
Landwirt(in f)m	agriculteur	farmer	agricultor, a	agricoltore	agricultor, a

German	French	English	Spanish	Italian	Portuguese
Landwirt(in f)m	cultivateur	farmer	cultivador, a	coltivatore, trice	lavrador, a
Landwirtschaft(f)	agriculture	agriculture	agricultura	agricoltura	agricultura
landwirtschaftlich	agricole	agricultural	agrícola	agricolo, a	agrícola
lang	long, longue	long	largo, a	lungo, a	longo, a
lange	longtemps	long time(a)	mucho tiempo	molto/molto tempo	muito tempo
Länge(f)	longueur	length	longitud	lunghezza	comprimento
Längengrad(m)	longitude	longitude	longitud	longitudine	longitude
Langeweile(f)	ennui	boredom	aburrimiento	noia	aborrecimento
Längs-	longitudinal, e	longitudinal	longitudinal	longitudinale	longitudinal
langsam	lent, e	slow	lento, a	lento, a	lento, a
langsam	lentement	slowly	lentamente	lentamente	lentamente
langsam, sanft	doucement	gently; slowly	despacio	piano, adagio	devagar
Languste(f)	langouste	crayfish	langosta	aragosta	lagosta
Langustine(f)	langoustine	Dublin Bay prawn	langostino	scampo	lagostim
langweilen, sich	ennuyer(s')	bored(be)	aburrir(se)	annoiarsi	aborrecer-se
langweilig	ennuyeux, se	boring; annoying	aburrido, a	noioso, a	aborrecido, a
Lanze(f)	lance	spear, lance	lanza	lancia	lança
Lappen(m)	chiffon	rag	trapo	straccio	trapo
Larve(f)	larve	larva(-vae)	larva	larva	larva
Laser(m)	laser	laser	láser	laser	laser
lassen	laisser	let; leave	dejar	lasciare	deixar
lassen(zurück = -, ver-)	laisser	leave	dejar	lasciare	deixar
lässig, entspannt	décontracté, e	relaxed	relajado, a	rilassato, a	descontraído, a
Last(f)	charge	load	carga, peso	carico	carga, peso
Last(f)	fardeau	burden	carga	fardello	fardo
Laster(n)	vice	vice	vicio	vizio	vício
lasterhaft	vicieux, se	vicious	vicioso, a	vizioso, a	vicioso, a
Lästerung(f)(Gottes-)	blasphème	blasphemy	blasfemia	bestemmia	blasfémia
Lastwagen(m)	camion	lorry	camión	camion	camião
Laterne(f)	lanterne	lantern	linterna	lanterna	lanterna
laufen	courir	run	correr	correre	correr
laufen, gehen	marcher, cheminer	walk	caminar	camminare	caminhar
laufend, heutig	courant, e	current	corriente	corrente	corrente, vulgar
Läufer(in f)m	coureur, se	runner	corredor, a	corridore	corredor, a
Laune(f)	humeur	mood	humor	umore	humor
Laune(f)	caprice	caprice, whim	capricho	capriccio	capricho, birra
laut	fort, e	loud	fuerte; alto, a	forte; alto, a	forte; alto, a
laut	bruyant, e	noisy; loud	ruidoso, a	rumoroso, a	barulhento, a
Lautsprecher(m)	baffle	speaker	altavoz	altoparlante	alto-falante
Lautsprecher(m)	haut-parleur	loud-speaker	altavoz	altoparlante	alto-falante
lauwarm, lau	tiède	lukewarm, tepid	tibio, a	tiepido, a	tépido, a; morno, a
Lawine(f)	avalanche	avalanche	avalancha	valanga	avalanche
Leben(n)	vie	life(lives)	vida	vita	vida
leben	vivre	live	vivir	vivere	viver
lebendig	vivant, e	alive	vivo, a	vivo, a; vivente	vivo, a
lebendig	vif, vive	lively	vivo, a	vivace; vivo, a	vivo, a
Lebensbeschreibung(f)	biographie	biography	biografía	biografia	biografia
Lebenskraft(f)	vitalité	vitality	vitalidad	vitalità	vitalidade
Lebensmittel(n, pl)	aliment	food	alimento	alimento, cibo	alimento
Lebensmittelhändler m	épicier, ière	grocer	tendero, a	droghiere, a	merceeiro, a
Lebensmittelladen(m)	épicerie	grocer's(shop)	ultramarinos	drogheria	mercearia
Lebensmittelladen(m)	alimentation	food shop	alimentación	alimentari(negozio)	mercearia
Leber(f)	foie	liver	hígado	fegato	fígado
lebhaft	animé, e	lively	animado, a	animato, a	animado, a
Leck(n)	fuite	leak	escape	perdita	fuga
lecken	lécher	lick	lamer	leccare	lamber
Leder(n)	cuir	leather	cuero	cuoio, pelle	couro
ledig	célibataire	single, unmarried	soltero, a	scapolo; nubile	solteiro, a
leer	vide	empty	vacío, a	vuoto, a	vazio, a
leeren	vider	empty	vaciar	vuotare	esvaziar
legen	mettre, placer	lay	poner, colocar	porre, mettere	pôr, colocar
legen, stellen	mettre	put	poner	mettere	pôr
legen	poser	put, lay(down)	poner, colocar	posare, porre	pôr, colocar
legen, stellen	déposer	put down, lay down	depositar	depositare, porre	pousar
Legende(f)	légende	legend	leyenda	leggenda	lenda
Legierung(f)	alliage	alloy	aleación	lega	liga
legitim	légitime	legitimate	legítimo, a	legittimo, a	legítimo, a
Lehre(f), Lehrjahre(f)	apprentissage	apprenticeship	aprendizaje	apprendistato	aprendizagem

German	French	English	Spanish	Italian	Portuguese
Lehre(f)	doctrine	doctrine	doctrina	dottrina	doutrina
lehren, unterrichten	enseigner	teach	enseñar	insegnare	ensinar
Lehrer(in f)m	professeur	teacher	profesor, a	professore, essa	professor, a
Lehrer(in f)m	enseignant, e	teacher	profesor, a	insegnante	professor, a
Lehrsatz(m)	théorème	theorem	teorema	teorema	teorema
Leiche(f)	cadavre	corpse	cadáver	cadavere	cadáver
Leiche(f)	macchabée	corpse	cadáver	cadavere	cadáver
Leichenschauhaus(n)	morgue	mortuary	depósito(cadáver.)	obitorio	morgue
leicht	léger, ère	light	ligero, a	leggero, a	ligeiro, a; leve
leicht	légèrement	lightly, slightly	ligeramente	leggermente	ligeiramente
leicht	facile	easy	fácil	facile	fácil
leicht	facilement	easily	fácilmente	facilemente	fácilmente
Leichtathletik(f)	athlétisme	athletics	atletismo	atletismo	atletismo
leiden	souffrir	suffer	sufrir	soffrire	sofrer
Leiden(n)	souffrance	suffering	sufrimiento	sofferenza	sofrimento
Leidenschaft(f)	passion	passion	pasión	passione	paixão
leidenschaftlich	passionné, e	interested(very)	apasionado, a	appassionato, a	apaixonado, a
leid tun	navré, e	sorry	desconsolado, a	spiacente	desolado, a
leihen, verleihen	prêter	lend	prestar	prestare	emprestar
leisten, sich	permettre(se)	afford	permitirse	permettersi	permitir-se
Leistung(f)	performance	performance	proeza, hazaña	prestazione	desempenho
leistungsfähig	productif, ive	productive	productivo, a	produttivo, a	produtivo, a
Leitartikel(m)	éditorial	editorial	editorial	editoriale	editorial
leiten, führen	diriger	manage, run	dirigir	dirigere	dirigir
leitende Angestellte	cadre	executive	ejecutivo	dirigente	quadro
Leiter(m), Führer(m)	chef, dirigeant	leader	jefe	capo, dirigente	chefe, líder
Leiter(m), Führer(m)	dirigeant, e	leader, manager	dirigente	dirigente	dirigente
Leiter/in, Unterhalter	animateur, trice	leader, organiser	animador, a	animatore, trice	animador, a
Leiter/in; Lehrer/in	moniteur, trice	instructor	monitor, a	istruttore, trice	monitor, a
Leiter(f)	échelle	ladder	escalera	scala	escada
Leitung(f)(-snetz n)	canalisation	pipe	canalización	canalizzazione	canalização
lernen	apprendre	learn	aprender	imparare	aprender
Lernen(n)	apprentissage	learning	estudio	tirocinio	aprendizagem
lesbisch	lesbienne	lesbian	lesbiana	lesbica	lésbica
Lesen(n)	lecture	reading	lectura	lettura	leitura
lesen	lire	read	leer	leggere	ler
Leser(in f)m	lecteur, trice	reader	lector, a	lettore, trice	leitor, a
leserlich	lisible	legible	legible	leggibile	legível
Letzte(f, m)	dernier	last	último, a	ultimo, a	último, a
letzte, Schluß-	final, e	final	final	finale	final
letzte(r, s); End-	terminal, e	terminal, final	terminal	terminale	terminal
letzter, letzte	dernier, ière	last	último, a	ultimo, a	último, a
leuchtend, hell	lumineux, se	luminous	luminoso, a	luminoso, a	luminoso, a
leuchtend	luisant, e	shining, bright	reluciente	brillante	brilhante
Leuchtturm(m)	phare	lighthouse	faro	faro	farol
Leukämie(f)	leucémie	leukaemia	leucemia	leucemia	leucemia
Leute(pl.)	gens	people	gente	gente(la)	gente, pessoas
Leutnant(m)	lieutenant	lieutenant	teniente	tenente	tenente
liberal	libéral, e	liberal	liberal	liberale	liberal
Liberalismus(m)	libéralisme	liberalism	liberalismo	liberalismo	liberalismo
Libido(f)	libido	libido	líbido	libido	líbido
Licht(n)	lumière	light	luz	luce	luz
Lid(n)	paupière	eyelid	párpado	palpebra	pálpebra
lieb, nett	aimable, gentil	nice	amable	amabile	amável
lieb	gracieux, se	good natured	simpático, a	grazioso, a	gracioso, a
Liebe(f)	amour	love	amor	amore	amor
liebe(r)	cher, ère	dear	querido, a	caro, a	caro, a; querido, a
lieben	aimer	love	amar, querer	amare, volere bene	amar, gostar de
liebenswert	charmant, e	charming, lovely	encantador, a	affascinante	encantador, a
liebevoll	affectueux, se	affectionate	afectuoso, a	affettuoso, a	afectuoso, a
Liebhaber(in f)m	amateur de	lover of	amante de	appassionato, a	apreciador, a
liebkosen, streicheln	caresser	caress	acariciar	accarezzare	acariciar
Liebling(m)	chéri, e	dear, darling	querido, a	caro, a	querido, a
Lieblings-	préféré, e	favourite	preferido, a	preferito, a	preferido, a
Lied(n)	chanson, chant	song	canción; cante	canzone; canto	canção; canto
Lieferant(in f)m	fournisseur, se	supplier	abastecedor, a	fornitore, trice	fornecedor, a
liefern	livrer, délivrer	deliver	entregar	consegnare	entregar
Lieferung(f)	livraison	delivery	entrega	consegna	entrega

German	French	English	Spanish	Italian	Portuguese
Lieferung(f)	fourniture	supply(ing)	abastecimiento	fornitura	fornecimento
liegend	gisant, e	lying	yacente	giacente	jacente
Liegeplatz(m)	couchette	couchette	litera	cuccetta	couchette
Liegestuhl(m)	chaise longue	deck-chair	hamaca	sdraio	preguiceira
Likör(m)	liqueur	liqueur	licor	liquore	licor
lindern	soulager	relieve	aliviar	sollevare, lenire	aliviar
Lineal(n)	règle	ruler	regla	riga	régua
linear	linéaire	linear	lineal	lineare	linear
Linie(f)	ligne	line	línea	linea	linha
links; linke(r, s)	gauche	left	izquierdo, a	sinistro, a	esquerdo, a
Linse(f)(Pflanze)	lentille	lentil	lenteja	lenticchia	lentilha
Lippe(f)	lèvre	lip	labio	labbro(a)	lábio
Lippenstift(m)	rouge à lèvres	lipstick	barra de labios	rossetto	baton
liquidieren	liquider	liquidate	liquidar	liquidare	liquidar
List(f)	ruse	trick, craftiness	ardid; astucia	furbizia	astúcia
List(f), Trick(m)	astuce	trick	astucia	astuzia	astúcia
Liste(f)	liste	list	lista	lista	lista
Liste(f)	barème	scale	baremo	tariffario	tabela
Liter(m, n)	litre	litre	litro	litro	litro
literarisch	littéraire	literary	literario	letterario, a	literário, a
Literatur(f)	littérature	literature	literatura	letteratura	literatura
Lizenz(f)	licence	licence	licencia	licenza	licença
Lizenz(f)	licence	degree	licenciatura	laurea	licenciatura
Lob(n)	éloge	praise	elogio	elogio	elogio
Loch(n)	trou	hole	agujero	buco(a), foro	buraco, furo
Locke(f)	boucle	curl	rizo	ricciolo	caracóis
Locke(f)	mèche	lock(of hair)	mechón	ciocca	madeixa
locker, lose	lâche, détendu, e	loose, slack	flojo, a	allentato, a	frouxo, a
lockern	desserrer	loosen	aflojar	allentare	desapertar
lockern	relâcher	loosen	aflojar	allentare	largar; soltar
lockig	frisé, e	curly	rizado, a	ricciuto, a	ondulado, a
Lockmittel(n)	leurre, appât	lure, bait	señuelo	esca	isca, engodo
Löffel(m)	cuillère	spoon	cuchara	cucchiaio	colher
Loge(f)	loge	box	camerino	camerino	camarim
logisch	logique	logical	lógico, a	logico, a	lógico, a
Lohn(m)	paie(paye)	pay	paga	paga, stipendio	paga, ordenado
Lohn(m), Gehalt(n)	salaire	salary, wage	salario	salario	salário
lokal	local, e	local	local	locale	local
lokalisieren	localiser	localize; locate	localizar	localizzare	localizar
lokalisieren	repérer	locate	localizar	localizzare	localizar
Lokomotive(f)	locomotive	locomotive	locomotiva	locomotiva	locomotiva
Los(n)	lot	prize	premio	premio	prémio
Los(n)	billet	ticket	billete	biglietto	bilhete
löschen	éteindre	extinguish	apagar	spegnere	apagar
Löschen(Aus-)(n)	extinction	extinction	extinción	estinzione	extinção
Lösegeld(n)	rançon	ransom	rescate	riscatto	resgate
lösen	desserrer	loosen	aflojar	allentare	afrouxar
lösen, ab = trennen	détacher	detach, unfasten	desatar	staccare	desatar
lösen	résoudre	solve, resolve	resolver	risolvere	resolver
lösen	solutionner	solve	solucionar	risolvere	solucionar
los = lassen	lâcher	release	soltar	lasciare	soltar
löslich	soluble	soluble	soluble	solubile	solúvel
Lösung(f)	solution	solution	solución	soluzione	solução
Lösungsmittel(n)	dissolvant	solvent, remover	disolvente	solvente	acetona
Lotterie(f)	loterie	lottery	lotería	lotteria	lotaria
Löwe(m), Löwin(f)	lion, ne	lion, lioness	león, leona	leone, leonessa	leão, leoa
loyal, treu	loyal, e	loyal	leal	leale	leal
Luft(f)	air	air	aire	aria	ar
Luft(f), Puste(f)	souffle	breath	soplo, aliento	fiato, soffio	sopro, fôlego
Luft-	aérien, ne	aerial, air	aéreo, a	aereo, a	aéreo, a
lüften	aérer	air, ventilate	airear, ventilar	arieggiare	arejar, ventilar
Luftfahrt(f)	aviation	aviation	aviación	aviazione	aviação
Luftfahrt(f)	aéronautique	aeronautics	aeronáutica	aeronautica	aeronáutica
Luft raus = lassen	dégonfler	deflate	desinflar	sgonfiare	desinchar
Luftröhre(f)	trachée-artère	trachea	traquearteria	trachea	traqueia
Lüge(f)	mensonge	lie, fib	mentira	bugia	mentira
lügen	mentir	lie	mentir	mentire	mentir
Lügner(in f)m	menteur, se	liar	mentiroso, a	bugiardo, a	mentiroso, a

German	French	English	Spanish	Italian	Portuguese
Lump(m)	crapule	crook, villain	granuja; pillo, a	canaglia	crápula
Lunge(f)	poumon	lung	pulmón	polmone	pulmão
Lungenentzündung(f)	pneumonie	pneumonia	neumonía	polmonite	pneumonia
Lupe(f)	loupe	magnifying-glass	lupa	lente(ingrandimento)	lupa
Lust(f)	envie	desire	ganas	voglia	vontade
lustig, amüsant	amusant, e	funny, amusing	divertido, a	buffo, a; divertente	divertido, a
lustig, fröhlich	joyeux, se	merry, joyful	alegre	allegro, a; felice	alegre
lustig	drôle	funny	gracioso, a	buffo, a	divertido, a
lutschen	sucer	suck	chupar	succhiare	chupar
Lutscher(m)	sucette	lollipop	pirulí	lecca lecca	chupa-chupa
Luxus(m)	luxe	luxury	lujo	lusso	luxo
lynchen	lyncher	lynch	linchar	linciare	linchar

M

German	French	English	Spanish	Italian	Portuguese
machen, tun	faire	make, do	hacer	fare	fazer
Macht(f)	pouvoir	power	poder	potere	poder
Macht(f); Kraft(f)	puissance; force	power; strength	potencia; fuerza	potenza; forza	potência; poder
mächtig, kräftig	puissant, e	powerful, strong	poderoso, a	poderoso, a; potente	poderoso, a
machtlos	impuissant, e	powerless	impotente	impotente	impotente
Mädchen(n)	fille	girl	chica	ragazza	rapariga
Mafia(f)	mafia	Mafia	mafia	mafia	mafia
Magen(m)	estomac	stomach	estómago	stomaco	estômago
Magen-	gastrique	gastric	gástrico, a	gastrico, a	gástrico, a
mager	maigre	thin	delgado, a	magro, a	magro, a
magisch	magique	magic	mágico, a	magico, a	mágico, a
Magistrat(m)	magistrat	magistrate	magistrado	magistrato	magistrado
Magnet(m)	aimant	magnet	imán	calamita	íman
magnetisch	magnétique	magnetic	magnético, a	magnetico, a	magnético, a
mahlen	moudre	grind	moler	macinare	moer
mahlen	broyer	crush, grind	triturar	stritolare, macinare	triturar; moer
Mahlzeit(f)	repas	meal	comida	pasto	refeição
Mähne(f)	crinière	mane	crines, melena	criniera	crina
Mai(m)	mai	May	mayo	maggio	Maio
Mais(m)	maïs	maize, corn	maíz	granturco, mais	milho
Majestät(f)	majesté	majesty	majestad	maestà	majestade
majestätisch	majestueux, se	majestic	majestuoso, a	maestoso, a	majestoso, a
makaber	macabre	macabre	macabro, a	macabro, a	macabro, a
Makrele(f)	maquereau	mackerel	caballa	sgombro	cavala
Mal(n)	fois	time	vez	volta	vez
malen	peindre	paint	pintar	dipingere	pintar
Malerei(f)	peinture	painting	pintura	pittura; dipinto	pintura
malerisch	pittoresque	picturesque	pintoresco, a	pittoresco, a	pitoresco, a
Mama(f)	maman	Mummy, Mum	mamá	mamma	mamã
Manager(m)	imprésario	impresario	empresario	impresario	empresário
manche	certaines	certain; some	algunos, as	certi, e; alcuni, e	certos, as
manchmal	quelquefois	sometimes	a veces	qualche volta	às vezes
manchmal	parfois	sometimes	a veces	talvolta	às vezes
Mandarine(f)	mandarine	tangerine	mandarina	mandarino	tangerina
Mandel(f)	amande	almond	almendra	mandorla	amêndoa
Mandeln(f, pl)	amygdale(s)	tonsils	amígdalas	tonsilla	amígdala
Mangel(m)	manque	lack, shortage	falta, carencia	mancanza	falta, carência
Mangel(m)	pénurie	shortage	penuria, escasez	penuria	penúria
mangelhaft	déficient, e	deficient	deficiente	deficiente	deficiente
Maniküre(f)	manucure	manicure	manicura	manicure	manicura
manipulieren	manipuler	manipulate	manipular	manipolare	manipular
Mann(m), Mensch(m)	homme	man(men)	hombre	uomo; uomini	homem

G

319

German	French	English	Spanish	Italian	Portuguese
Männchen(n)	mâle	male	macho	maschio	macho
Mannequin(n)	mannequin	model	maniquí, modelo	indossatore, trice	modelo
mannigfach	divers, e	various, varied	vario, a	vario, a	variado, a
männlich	masculin, e	masculine, male	masculino, a	maschile	masculino, a
männlich, mannhaft	viril, e	virile, manly	viril	virile	viril
Männlichkeit(f)	virilité	virility	virilidad	virilità	virilidade
Mannschaft(f), Team(n)	équipe	team	equipo	squadra; équipe	equipa, grupo
Manöver(n)	manoeuvre	manoeuvre	maniobra	manovra	manobra
Mantel(m)	manteau	coat	abrigo	cappotto	casaco, manto
Mantel(m)	pardessus	overcoat	abrigo	soprabito	sobretudo
manuell; Hand-	manuel, elle	manual; hand-	manual	manuale	manual
Marathonlauf(m)	marathon	marathon	maratón	maratona	maratona
Märchen(n)	conte	tale, story	cuento	racconto, fiaba	conto
Marine(f)	marine	navy	marina	marina	marinha
Mark(n)	moelle	marrow(-bone)	médula, tuétano	midollo	medula, tutano
Marke(f)	marque	brand, make	marca	marchio, marca	marca
markieren	marquer	mark	marcar	segnare, marcare	marcar
Markierung(f)	repère	mark, landmark	señal, indicio	contrassegno	sinal, marca
Markt(m)	marché	market	mercado	mercato	mercado
Marmelade(f)	confiture	jam	mermelada	marmellata	doce, compota
Marmor(m)	marbre	marble	mármol	marmo	mármore
Märtyrer(in f)m	martyr, e	martyr	mártir	martire	mártir
Marxismus(m)	marxisme	Marxism	marxismo	marxismo	marxismo
März(m)	mars	March	marzo	marzo	Março
Maschine(f)	machine	machine	máquina	macchina	máquina
Masern(pl.)	rougeole	measles	sarampión	morbillo	sarampo
Maske(f)	masque	mask	máscara	maschera	máscara
Maß(n)	dimension	dimension, size	dimensión	dimensione	dimensão
Massage(f)	massage	massage	masaje	massaggio	massagem
Masse(f)	masse	mass	masa	massa	massa
Massenauswanderung(f)	exode	exodus	éxodo	esodo	êxodo
mäßigen	modérer	moderate	moderar	moderare	moderar
massiv	massif, ive	massive; solid	masivo, a	massiccio, a	maciço, a
Mast(m)	mât	mast	mástil	albero	mastro
Matador(m)	matador	matador	matador	matador	matador
Material(n)	matériel	material	material	materiale	material
Material(n)	matériau	material	material	materiale	material
Material(n)	matière	material	material; materia	materiale; materia	material; matéria
Materie(f)	substance	matter, material	materia	materia	matéria
Mathematik(f)	mathématique(s)	mathematics	matemáticas	matematica	matemáticas
Matraze(f)	matelas	mattress(-es)	colchón	materasso	colchão
Matrikel(f)	matricule	roll, register	matrícula	matricola	matrícula
Matrose(m)	matelot	sailor	marinero	marinaio	marinheiro
matt	terne	dull	sin brillo, mate	spento, a; smorto, a	baço, a
matt	faible	dim	flojo, a	debole	fraco, a
Mauer(f)	mur	wall	muro, pared	muro	muro, parede
Maul(n)	gueule	mouth	hocico	muso	goela, garganta
Maurer(m)	maçon	builder	albañil	muratore	pedreiro, trolha
Maus(f)	souris	mouse(mice pl.)	ratón	topo	rato
Maximum(n)	maximum	maximum	máximo	massimo	máximo
Mäzen(m), Sponsor(m)	mécène	patron	mecenas	mecenate	mecenas
Mechanik(f)	mécanique	mechanics	mecánica	meccanica	mecânica
Mechaniker(in f)m	mécanicien, ne	mechanic	mecánico, a	meccanico, a	mecânico, a
mechanisch	mécanique	mechanical	mecánico, a	meccanico, a	mecânico, a
Mechanismus(m)	mécanisme	mechanism	mecanismo	meccanismo	mecanismo
meckern, murren	rouspéter	grouse, moan	refunfuñar	brontolare	rezingar
Medaille(f)	médaille	medal	medalla	medaglia	medalha
Medikament(n)	médicament	drug, medicine	medicina	medicina	medicamento
Medizin(f)	médecine	medicine	medicina	medicina	medicina
medizinisch	médical, e	medical	médico, a	medico, a	médico, a
Meer(n)	mer	sea	mar	mare	mar
Meerenge(f)	détroit	strait	estrecho	stretto	estreito
Meeresfrüchte(f, pl.)	fruits de mer	seafood	marisco	frutti di mare	marisco
Mehl(n)	farine	flour	harina	farina	farinha
mehr	plus	more	más	più	mais
mehr	davantage, plus	more	más	più, di più	mais
mehrere	plusieurs	several	varios, as	parecchi	vários, as
Mehrheit(f)	majorité	majority	mayoría	maggioranza	maioria

320

German	French	English	Spanish	Italian	Portuguese
Mehrzahl(f)	pluriel	plural	plural	plurale	plural
mein	mon	my	mi	mio, mia(il, la)	meu, minha
meine	ma	my	mi	mia(la)	minha
meine	mes	my	mis	miei, mie(i, le)	meus
meine, meiner	mien, ne	mine	mío, mía	mio(il); mia(la)	meu, minha
meine Damen	mesdames	ladies	señoras	signore	senhoras
meine Herren	messieurs	gentlemen	señores	signori	senhores
Meinung(f)	avis	opinion	opinión	avviso, parere	opinião, parecer
Meinung(f)	opinion	opinion	opinión	opinione	opinião
meisten(die)	plupart(la)	most(of the)	mayoría(la)	maggior parte(la)	maior parte(a)
Meister(in f)m	champion, ne	champion	campeón, a	campione, -essa	campeão, campeã
Meister(m), Virtuose m	virtuose	virtuoso	virtuoso, a	virtuoso, a	virtuoso, a
Meisterschaft(f)	championnat	championship	campeonato	campionato	campeonato
Meisterwerk(n)	chef-d'oeuvre	masterpiece	obra maestra	capolavoro	obra-prima
melden; an = zeigen	signaler	point out	señalar	segnalare	assinalar
Melodie(f)	mélodie	melody, tune	melodía	melodia	melodia
Melodie(f)	air	tune	melodía	melodia	melodia
Melone(f)	melon	melon	melón	melone	melão
Membran(f)	membrane	membrane	membrana	membrana	membrana
Menge(f)	multitude	multitude	multitud	moltitudine	multidão
Menge(f)	foule	crowd	muchedumbre	folla	multidão
Menge(f)	cohue, foule	crush, crowd	barullo, jaleo	ressa, affollamento	multidão, confusão
Menschheit(f)	humanité	humanity	humanidad	umanità	humanidade
menschlich	humain, e	human	humano, a	umano, a	humano, a
Mentalität(f)	mentalité	mentality	mentalidad	mentalità	mentalidade
Menü(n), Speisekarte f	menu	menu	menú	menù	ementa
Meridian(m)	méridien	meridian	meridiano	meridiano	meridiano
Merkmal(n)	caractéristique	feature	característica	caratteristica	característica
Messe(f)	messe	mass	misa	messa	missa
Messe(f)	foire	fair	feria	fiera	feira
Messe(f)	salon	show, exhibition	salón	salone	salão
messen	mesurer	measure	medir	misurare	medir
Messer(n)	couteau	knife(-ives)	cuchillo	coltello	faca
Metal(n)	métal	metal	metal	metallo	metal
metallisch	métallique	metallic	metálico, a	metallico, a	metálico, a
Meter(m, n)	mètre	metre	metro	metro	metro
Methode(f)	méthode	method	método	metodo	método
metrisch	métrique	metric	métrico, a	metrico, a	métrico, a
Metzgerei(f)	boucherie	butcher's(shop)	carnicería	macelleria	talho
Metzgerei(f)	charcuterie	delicatessen shop	salchichería	salumeria	salsicharia
miauen	miauler	mew	maullar	miagolare	miar
mich; mir	me, m'; moi	me	me	mi, me	me
mich; mir; ich	moi	me; I	mí; me; yo	io; me	eu; me; mim
Miete(f)	loyer	rent	alquiler	affitto	aluguer
mieten; vermieten	louer	hire, rent	alquilar	noleggiare	alugar
mieten; pachten	louer à bail	lease	arrendar	noleggiare	arrendar, alugar
Mieter(in f)m	locataire	tenant	inquilino, a	inquilino, a	inquilino, a
Migräne(f)	migraine	migraine, headache	jaqueca	emicrania	enxaqueca
Mikrobe(f)	microbe	germ, microbe	microbio	microbo	micróbio
Mikrophon(n)	micro(phone)	microphone, mike	micrófono	microfono	microfone
Mikroskop(n)	microscope	microscope	microscopio	microscopio	microscópio
Milch(f)	lait	milk	leche	latte	leite
mild	doux, ce	mild	templado, a	mite	ameno, a
Mildtätigkeit(f)	charité	charity	caridad	carità	caridade
Milieu(n)	milieu	milieu, background	ambiente, medio	ambiente	meio
Militant(m)	militant, e	militant	militante	militante	militante
militärisch	militaire	military	militar	militare	militar
Miliz(f)	milice	militia	milicia	milizia	milícia
Milliarde(f)	milliard	thousand million	mil millones	miliardo	bilião
Million(f)	million	million	millón	milione	milhão
Milz(f)	rate	spleen	bazo	milza	baço
Minderheit(f)	minorité	minority	minoría	minoranza	minoria
Minderjährige(r)mf	mineur, e	minor	menor	minore, minorenne	menor
minderwertig	inférieur, e	inferior	inferior	inferiore	inferior
mineralisch	minéral, e	mineral	mineral	minerale	mineral
Miniatur(f)	miniature	miniature	miniatura	miniatura	miniatura
Minimum(n)	minimum	minimum	mínimo, a	minimo, a	mínimo, a
Minister(in f)m	ministre	minister	ministro	ministro	ministro

G

German	French	English	Spanish	Italian	Portuguese
Ministerium(n)	ministère	ministry	ministerio	ministero	ministério
Ministerpräsident(m)	premier ministre	prime minister	primer ministro	primo ministro	primeiro ministro
Minute(f)	minute	minute	minuto	minuto	minuto
Minze(f)	menthe	mint	menta	menta	hortelã
mir	moi(à)	mine, to me	mío, a(el, la)	mio, mia(è)	meu(é)
mischen	mélanger	mix	mezclar	mescolare	misturar
Mischling(m)	métis, se	half-caste	mestizo, a	meticcio, a	mestiço, a
Mischung(f)	mélange	mixture; mixing	mezcla	miscuglio	mistura
Mischung(f)	mélange	blend, mixture	mezcla	mescolanza	mistura
mißachten	dédaigner	disdain	desdeñar	disprezzare	desdenhar
Mißbildung(f)	déformation	distortion	deformación	deformazione	deformação
mißbilligen	désapprouver	disapprove	desaprobar	disapprovare	desaprovar
Mißbrauch(m)	abus	abuse, misuse	abuso	abuso	abuso
mißbrauchen	abuser	take advantage of	abusar	abusare	abusar
Mißerfolg(m)	échec	failure	fracaso, revés	smacco, sconfitta	fracasso
Missetäter(in f)m	malfaiteur	criminal	malhechor	malvivente	malfeitor
Mißgeschick(n)	mésaventure	mishap	contratiempo	disavventura	contratempo
Mißhandlung(f)	sévices	cruelty	malos tratos	sevizie	sevícias
Mission(f)	mission	mission	misión	missione	missão
mißlingen	rater	fail	fallar	mancare	falhar
mißtrauen	méfier(se)	mistrust	desconfiar	diffidare	desconfiar
Mißtrauen(n)	méfiance	distrust, mistrust	desconfianza	diffidenza	desconfiança
mißtrauisch	méfiant, e	suspicious	desconfiado, a	diffidente	desconfiado, a
Mist(m)	fumier	manure	estiércol	letame	estrume
mit	avec	with	con	con	com
Mitarbeit(f)	collaboration	collaboration	colaboración	collaborazione	colaboração
Mitarbeit(f)	coopération	cooperation	cooperación	cooperazione	cooperação
mit = arbeiten	coopérer	cooperate	cooperar	cooperare	cooperar
Mitarbeiter(in f)m	collaborateur	assistant	colaborador, a	collaboratore, -trice	colaborador, a
mit = bringen	amener	bring	traer	portare	trazer
mit = fühlen	compatir	sympathize	compadecer	compatire	apiedar-se
Mitglied(n)	membre(de)	member(of)	miembro, a; socio, a	membro, i	membro, a; sócio, a
Mitglied(n)	adhérent, e	member	adherente	aderente, socio	aderente
Mitglied werden	adhérer	join	adherir a	aderire a	aderir a
Mitlaut(m)	consonne	consonant	consonante	consonante	consoante
Mitleid(n)	pitié	pity	piedad	pietà	piedade
mit = nehmen	emporter	take(away)	llevar	portar via	levar
mit = nehmen	emmener	take	llevar	portare, condurre	levar
mit sich bringen	entraîner	entail	ocasionar	comportare	acarretar
Mittag(m)	midi	midday, noon	mediodía	mezzogiorno	meio-dia
Mittag essen(zu)	déjeuner	have lunch, lunch	almorzar	pranzare	almoçar
Mittagsschlaf(m)	sieste	nap, snooze	siesta	siesta, riposino	sesta
Mitte(f)	milieu	middle	medio	mezzo	meio
Mitte(f)	centre	centre	centro	centro	centro
mitteilen	communiquer	communicate	comunicar	comunicare	comunicar
Mitteilung(f)	avis	notice	aviso	avviso	aviso, notícia
mittel	moyen, ne	middle	medio, a	medio, a	médio, a
Mittel(n)	moyen	means	medio(s)	mezzo	meio
Mittel(n, pl)	ressource(s)	resources	recurso	risorsa	recurso
mittelmäßig, schlecht	médiocre	mediocre	mediocre	mediocre	mediocre
Mittelohrentzündung f	otite	ear-ache	otitis	otite	otite
Mittelpunkt(m)	centre	hub	centro	centro	centro
Mitternacht(f)	minuit	midnight	medianoche	mezzanotte	meia-noite
mittlere(r, s)	moyen, ne	medium	medio, a	medio, a	médio, a
Mittwoch(m)	mercredi	Wednesday	miércoles	mercoledì	quarta-feira
Mitwirkung(unter)	concours	cooperation, help	ayuda	concorso	colaboração
Möbel(pl)	mobilier	furniture	mobiliario	mobilio	mobiliário
Möbelstück(n)	meuble	furniture	mueble	mobile	móvel
mobilisieren	mobiliser	mobilize	mobilizar	mobilitare	mobilizar
möchte(ich)	voudrais(je)	would like(I)	quisiera(yo)	vorrei	gostava
Mode(f)	mode	fashion	moda	moda	moda
Modell(n)	modèle	model, pattern	modelo	modello	modelo
Modell(n)	maquette	model	maqueta	modello	maqueta
Modell stehen	poser(photo)	pose	posar	posare	posar
modern	moderne	modern	moderno, a	moderno, a	moderno, a
Mofa(n)	mobylette	moped	velomotor	motorino, scooter	motorizada
mögen; gern mögen	aimer	enjoy	gustar	piacere	gostar
möglich	possible	possible	posible	possibile	possível

German	French	English	Spanish	Italian	Portuguese
möglich	éventuel, le	possible	eventual	eventuale	eventual
Möglichkeit(f)	possibilité	possibility	posibilidad	possibilità	possibilidade
Mohammedaner(in f)m	musulman, e	Moslem, Muslim	musulmán, a	musulmano, a	muçulmano, a
Möhre(f)	carotte	carrot	zanahoria	carota	cenoura
Molekül(n)	molécule	molecule	molécula	molecola	molécula
Moment(m)	moment, instant	while, time	rato	attimo, momento	momento, instante
Moment(m)	instant	moment, instant	instante	istante	instante
Moment bitte!	attendez!	wait!	espere(!)	aspetti!	espere!
Monarchie(f)	monarchie	monarchy	monarquía	monarchia	monarquia
Monat(m)	mois	month	mes	mese	mês
monatlich	mensuel, le	monthly	mensual	mensile	mensal
Mönch(m)	moine	monk	monje, fraile	monaco, frate	monge, frade
Mond(m)	lune	moon	luna	luna	lua
Monogamie(f)	monogamie	monogamy	monogamia	monogamia	monogamia
Monopol(n)	monopole	monopoly	monopolio	monopolio	monopólio
monoton, eintönig	monotone	monotonous	monótono, a	monotono, a	monótono, a
Monster(n)	monstre	monster	monstruo	mostro	monstro
Monsun(m)	mousson	monsoon	monzón	monsone	monção
Montag(m)	lundi	Monday	lunes	lunedì	segunda-feira
Montage(f)	montage	mounting, assembly	montaje	montaggio	montagem
Montage(f)	assemblage	assembly	ensambladura	assemblaggio	montagem
Moos(n)	mousse	moss	musgo	muschio	musgo
Moral(f)	morale	moral	moral	morale	moral
moralisch	moral, e	moral	moral	morale	moral
Mord(m)	meurtre	murder	asesinato	assassinio	homicídio, crime
Mord(m)	assassinat	murder	asesinato	assassinio	assassínio
Mörder(in f)m	assassin	murderer	asesino, a	assassino, a	assassino, a
Mörder(in f)m	meurtrier, ière	murderer	homicida	omicida	assassino, a
Mörder(in f)m	tueur, se	killer	asesino, a	assassino, a	assassino, a
Morgen(m)	matin	morning	mañana	mattino	manhã
morgen	demain	tomorrow	mañana	domani	amanhã
Morgendämmerung(f)	aube	dawn	alba	alba	amanhecer
Morgenmantel(m)	peignoir	dressing gown	bata	accappatoio	roupão
Morgenröte(f)	aurore	dawn	aurora	aurora	aurora
Morphium(n)	morphine	morphine	morfina	morfina	morfina
Morphologie(f)	morphologie	morphology	morfología	morfologia	morfologia
Mörtel(m)	mortier	mortar	argamasa	malta, calcina	argamassa
Mosaik(n)	mosaïque	mosaic	mosaico	mosaico	mosaico
Moschee(f)	mosquée	mosque	mezquita	moschea	mesquita
Motel(n)	motel	motel	motel	motel	motel
Motiv(n)	motif	motive	motivo	motivo	motivo
motivieren	motiver	motivate	motivar	motivare	motivar
Motor(m)	moteur	engine; motor	motor	motore	motor
Motorhaube(f)	capot	bonnet, hood	capó	cofano	capota
Motorrad(n)	moto	motor-bike	moto	moto	mota
Motorradfahrer(in f)m	motard	motorcyclist	motorista	motociclista	motociclista
Möve(f)	mouette	seagull	gaviota	gabbiano	gaivota
Mücke(f)	moustique	mosquito(-es)	mosquito	zanzara	mosquito
müde, ermüdet	fatigué, e	tired	cansado, a	stanco, a	cansado, a
Müdigkeit(f)	fatigue	tiredness	cansancio	stanchezza	fatiga, cansaço
Mühle(f)	moulin	mill	molino	mulino	moinho
mühsam, schwierig	pénible	hard, arduous	penoso, a; duro, a	penoso, a	penoso, a
multiplizieren	multiplier	multiply	multiplicar	moltiplicare	multiplicar
Mumps(m)	oreillons	mumps	paperas	orecchioni	trasorelho
Mund(m)	bouche	mouth	boca	bocca	boca
mündlich	oral, e	oral	oral	orale	oral
Munition(f)	munitions	ammunition	municiones	munizioni	munições
Murmel(f)	bille	marble	bola	biglia	berlinde
Muschel(f)	coquillage	shell-fish; shell	marisco	conchiglia	concha
Muschel(f)	moule	mussel	mejillón	cozza	mexilhão
Museum(n)	musée	museum	museo	museo	museu
Musik(f)	musique	music	música	musica	música
musikalisch	musical, e	musical	musical	musicale	musical
Musiker(in f)m	musicien, ne	musician	músico, a	musicista	músico, a
Muskel(m)	muscle	muscle	músculo	muscolo	músculo
Muskel-	musculaire	muscular	muscular	muscolare	muscular
muskulös	musclé, e	muscular	musculoso, a	muscoloso, a	musculado, a
müssen	falloir	have to, must	necesario(ser)	bisognare	preciso(ser)

G

German	French	English	Spanish	Italian	Portuguese
müssen	devoir	must, have to	deber	dovere	dever
Muster(n)	modèle	pattern	modelo	modello	modelo
Muster(n), Modell(n)	modèle	design	modelo, patrón	modello	modelo
Muster(n); Exemplar(n)	spécimen	specimen	espécimen	specimen	espécime
Mut(m)	courage	courage	valentía	coraggio	coragem
mutig	courageux, brave	brave	valiente, valeroso	coraggioso, a	corajoso, a
mutlos, verzagt	découragé, e	disheartened	desalentado, a	scoraggiato, a	desalentado, a
Mutter(f)	mère	mother	madre	madre	mãe
Mutter(f)(Schrauben-)	écrou	nut	tuerca	dado	porca
mütterlich	maternel, le	maternal, motherly	materno, a; maternal	materno, a	maternal
Mütze(f)	casquette	cap	gorra	berretto	boné
Mütze(f)	bonnet	cap, hat	gorro	berretto, cuffia	barrete
mysteriös	mystérieux, se	mysterious	misterioso, a	misterioso, a	misterioso, a
mystisch	mystique	mystic(al)	místico, a	mistico, a	místico, a
Mythos(m); Sage(f)	mythe	myth	mito	mito	mito

N

German	French	English	Spanish	Italian	Portuguese

German	French	English	Spanish	Italian	Portuguese
Nabel(m)	nombril	navel	ombligo	ombelico	umbigo
nach	à	to	a; en	a	a; para
nach, zu	vers	to, towards	hacia	verso	para
nach	après	after; afterwards	después	dopo	depois
nach = ahmen	imiter	imitate	imitar	imitare	imitar
Nachahmung(f)	imitation	imitation	imitación	imitazione	imitação
Nachbar(in f)m	voisin, e	neighbour	vecino, a	vicino, a	vizinho, a
Nachbarschaft(f)	voisinage	neighbourhood	vecindario	vicinanza	vizinhança
nach = denken, sinnen	méditer	meditate	meditar	meditare	meditar
nach = folgen	succéder	succeed	suceder	succedere	suceder
Nachfolger(in f)m	successeur	successor	sucesor	successore	sucessor
Nachkomme(m)	progéniture	offspring	progenitura	progenitura	progenitura
Nachkommenschaft(f)	descendance	descendants	descendencia	discendenza	descendência
Nachlaß, Ermäßigung	remise, rabais	reduction	descuento	rimessa, sconto	desconto
nachlässig	négligent, e	careless	descuidado, a	negligente	descuidado, a
Nachlässigkeit(f)	négligence	negligence	negligencia	negligenza	negligência
Nachmittag(m)	après-midi	afternoon	tarde	pomeriggio	tarde
Nachricht(f)	message	message	mensaje	messaggio	mensagem, recado
Nachrichten(pl.)	actualités(T.V)	news	telediario	telegiornale	telejornal
Nachrichten(f, pl)	nouvelles	news	noticias	notizie	notícias
Nachsicht(f)	indulgence	indulgence	indulgencia	indulgenza	indulgência
nächste	prochain, e	next	próximo, a	prossimo, a	próximo, a
nächste	suivant, e	following, next	siguiente	seguente	seguinte
Nacht(f)	nuit	night	noche	notte	noite
Nachteil(m)	désavantage	disadvantage	desventaja	svantaggio	desvantagem
Nachteil(m)	inconvénient	disadvantage	inconveniente	inconveniente	inconveniente
Nachthemd(n)	chemise de nuit	nightdress(-es)	camisón	camicia da notte	camisa de noite
Nachtisch(m)	dessert	dessert	postre	dessert	sobremesa
nächtlich	nocturne	nocturnal, night-	nocturno, a	notturno, a	nocturno, a
nach = trauern(jdm/etw)	regretter	regret	lamentar, añorar	rimpiangere	lamentar
Nacken(m)	nuque	nape of the neck	nuca	nuca	nuca
nackt	nu, e	naked; bare	desnudo, a	nudo, a	nu, nua
Nadel(f)	aiguille	needle	aguja	ago	agulha
Nadelbaum(m)	conifère	conifer	conífera	conifera	conífera
Nagel(m)	clou	nail	clavo	chiodo	prego
nageln	clouer	nail	clavar	inchiodare	pregar, cravar
nah(e)	près, proche	near, close to	cerca	vicino, a	perto
nah(e)	proche	near, close	cercano, a; próximo	prossimo, a	próximo, a; perto
Nähe(f)	proximité	proximity	proximidad	prossimità	proximidade

German	French	English	Spanish	Italian	Portuguese
nahe bei	proximité(à)	close, near	cerca de	vicinanze(nelle)	próximo a
nähen	coudre	sew	coser	cucire	coser
nähern, sich	approcher(s')	approach	acercar(se)	avvicinarsi	aproximar-se
nahrhaft	nutritif, ive	nutritious	nutritivo, a	nutritivo, a	nutritivo, a
Nahrung(f)	nourriture	food	alimento	cibo; nutrimento	alimentação
Naht(f)	couture	sewing	costura	cucito	costura
naiv	naïf, ive	naïve	ingenuo, a	ingenuo, a	ingénuo, a
naiv, aufrichtig	candide	ingenuous	cándido, a	candido, a	cândido, a
Name(m)	nom	name	nombre	nome	nome
Narbe(f)	cicatrice	scar	cicatriz	cicatrice	cicatriz
Narkose(f)	anesthésie	anaesthetic	anestesia	anestesia	anestesia
nasal	nasal, e	nasal	nasal	nasale	nasal
Nascherei(f)	friandise	delicacy	golosina	dolciume	guloseima
Nase(f)	nez	nose	nariz	naso	nariz
Nase putzen	moucher(se)	blow one's nose	sonarse	soffiarsi il naso	assoar-se
Nasenloch(n)	narine	nostril	nariz	narice	narina
naß	mouillé, e; humide wet	mojado, a; húmedo, a bagnato, a; umido, a	molhado, a; húmido, a
Nation(f)	nation	nation	nación	nazione	nação
national	national, e	national	nacional	nazionale	nacional
Nationalismus(m)	nationalisme	nationalism	nacionalismo	nazionalismo	nacionalismo
Nationalität(f)	nationalité	nationality	nacionalidad	nazionalità	nacionalidade
Natur(f)	nature	nature	naturaleza	natura	natureza
natürlich	naturel, le	natural	natural	naturale	natural
natürlich	évidemment	of course	desde luego	evidentemente	evidentemente
natürlich	bien sûr	of course	claro	certamente	claro
Naturschutz(m)	écologie	ecology	ecología	ecologia	ecologia
nautisch, Wasser-	nautique	nautical, water-	náutico, a	nautico, a	náutico, a
Nebel(m)	brouillard	fog	niebla	nebbia	nevoeiro
Nebel(m)	brume	mist, haze	bruma	foschia	bruma
neben, daneben	à côté	next to, beside	al lado	accanto; vicino, a	ao lado
nebensächlich	secondaire	secondary	secundario, a	secondario, a	secundário, a
necken	taquiner	tease	hacer rabiar	stuzzicare	arreliar
Neffe(m)	neveu	nephew	sobrino	nipote	sobrinho
negativ	négatif, ive	negative	negativo, a	negativo, a	negativo, a
Negativ(n)	cliché, négatif	negative	cliché	negativo	cliché
Neger(in f)m	nègre, esse	negro(-ress), black	negro, a	negro, a	negro, a
nehmen	prendre	take	tomar, coger	prendere	tomar
nehmen	prendre(leçon)	have(a lesson)	recibir(clases)	prendere(lezione)	ter(lição)
neigen	pencher	tilt, lean	inclinar	inclinare	inclinar
neigen	incliner	incline, tilt	inclinar	inclinare	inclinar
Neigung(f), Gefälle(n)	inclinaison	slant, incline	inclinación	inclinazione	inclinação
Neigung(f)	tendance	trend, tendency	inclinación	inclinazione	inclinação
nein	non	no	no	no	não
nein, danke	non merci	no thank you	no, gracias	no, grazie	não, obrigado
nennen	nommer	name	llamar	chiamare	chamar
Nerv(m)	nerf	nerve	nervio	nervo	nervo
Nervenzusammenbruch m	dépression	breakdown	depresión	esaurimento(nerv.)	depressão
nervös; Nerven-	nerveux, se	nervous	nervioso, a	nervoso, a	nervoso, a
nervös	nerveux, se	nervy	nervioso, a	nervoso, a	nervoso, a
Nerz(m)	vison	mink	visón	visone	marta
Nest(n)	nid	nest	nido	nido	ninho
nett	gentil, le	kind, nice	gentil, amable	gentile	gentil, amável
nett	joli, e	nice	lindo, a	bello, a	bonito, a
Netz(n)	filet	net	red	rete	rede
Netz(n)	réseau	network	red	rete	rede
Netzhaut(f)	rétine	retina	retina	retina	retina
neu	nouveau, nouvelle	new	nuevo, a	nuovo, a	novo, a
neu	neuf, neuve	new	nuevo, a	nuovo, a	novo, a
neu	récent, e	recent	reciente	recente	recente
Neuerung(f)(Er-)	innovation	innovation	innovación	innovazione	inovação
Neugeborene(n)	nouveau-né, e	new-born baby	recién nacido, a	neonato, a	recém-nascido, a
neugierig	curieux, se	curious	curioso, a	curioso, a	curioso, a
Neuheit(f)	nouveauté	novelty	novedad	novità	novidade
Neuling(m)	novice, débutant	novice	novicio, a; novato, a	novizio, a	principiante
neun	neuf	nine	nueve	nove	nove
neunzehn	dix-neuf	nineteen	diecinueve	diciannove	dezanove
neunzig	quatre-vingt-dix	ninety	noventa	novanta	noventa
Neurologie(f)	neurologie	neurology	neurología	neurologia	neurologia

German	French	English	Spanish	Italian	Portuguese
Neurose(f)	névrose	neurosis(-ses)	neurosis	nevrosi	nevrose
neutral	neutre	neutral	neutro, a	neutro, a	neutro, a
neutralisieren	neutraliser	neutralize	neutralizar	neutralizzare	neutralizar
nicht	pas	not	no	non	não, nem
nicht existierend	inexistant, e	non-existent	inexistente	inesistente	inexistente
nicht wissen	ignorer	ignorant of(be)	ignorar	ignorare	ignorar
Nichte(f)	nièce	niece	sobrina	nipote	sobrinha
Nichtraucher(m)	non-fumeur	non-smoker	no-fumadores	non-fumatore	não-fumador
nichts	rien	nothing	nada	niente, nulla	nada
Nickel(n)	nickel	nickel	níquel	nichel	níquel
Niederlage(f)	défaite	defeat	derrota	sconfitta	derrota
nieder = lassen	abaisser	lower	bajar	abbassare	abaixar
nieder = lassen, sich	installer(s')	settle	instalarse	stabilirsi	instalar-se
Niederlassung	implantation	setting up(of)	implantación	impianto	implantação
nieder = schlagen	assommer	knock out	dejar k.o.	stordire	espancar
niederträchtig	infâme	vile, infamous	infame	infame	infame
niedrig	bas, basse	low	bajo, a	basso, a	baixo, a
niemals, jemals	jamais	never; ever	jamás, nunca	mai	nunca, jamais
niemand	personne	nobody, no one	nadie	nessuno	ninguém
Niere(f)	rein	kidney	riñón	rene	rim
niesen	éternuer	sneeze	estornudar	starnutire	espirrar
Nikotin(n)	nicotine	nicotine	nicotina	nicotina	nicotina
Nilpferd(n)	hippopotame	hippopotamus	hipopótamo	ippopotamo	hipopótamo
noch, wieder	encore	still	todavía, aún	ancora	ainda
noch, noch mehr	encore	still; yet	aún	ancora	ainda
noch	encore	more	más	ancora	mais
noch einmal	encore	again	otra vez	ancora	mais(uma vez)
noch(nicht)	encore(pas)	yet(not)	todavía no	ancora(non)	ainda não
Nomade(m)	nomade	nomad	nómada	nomade	nómada
Nonne(f), Schwester(f)	soeur	nun, sister	monja	suora	freira
Norden(m)	Nord	North	Norte	Nord	Norte
nordisch; nördlich	nordique	nordic; northern	nórdico, a	nordico, a	nórdico, a
nörgeln	râler	moan, groan	refunfuñar	brontolare	resmungar
Norm(f)	norme	norm, standard	norma	norma	norma
normal	normal, e	normal; usual	normal	normale	normal
Notar(m)	notaire	solicitor, lawyer	notario	notaio	notário
Notausgang(m)	sortie(secours)	emergency exit	salida(emergencia)	uscita(sicurezza)	saída de emergência
Note(f)	note	note	nota	nota	nota
Note(f)	note	mark	nota	voto	nota
Notfall(m)	urgence	emergency, urgency	urgencia	urgenza	urgência
notieren; bemerken	noter	note; notice	anotar	notare	anotar, notar
nötig, notwendig	nécessaire	necessary	necesario, a	necessario, a	necessário, a
Notizbuch(n)	carnet	note-book	libreta	taccuino	bloco, canhenho
Notwendigkeit(f)	nécessité	necessity	necesidad	necessità	necessidade
November(m)	novembre	November	noviembre	novembre	Novembro
Nudeln(f, pl)	pâtes	pasta, noodles	pastas(aliment.)	pasta	massa
Nudeln(f, pl)	nouilles	noodles	macarrones	tagliatelle, pasta	massa
Nudist(in f)m	naturiste	nudist	naturista	nudista	naturista
Null(f)	zéro	zero, nought	cero	zero	zero
numerisch	numérique	numerical	numérico, a	numerico, a	numérico, a
Nummer(f)	numéro	number	número	numero	número
Nummer(f)(wählen)	composer(n°tél)	dial	marcar un número	comporre(numero)	discar, marcar
nur	seulement	only	solamente, sólo	solo, soltanto	somente, só
nützlich	utile	useful	útil	utile	útil
nutzlos	inutile	useless	inútil	inutile	inútil
Nylon(m)	nylon	nylon	nilón	nylon	nylon

O

German	French	English	Spanish	Italian	Portuguese
Oase(f)	oasis	oasis(oases pl.)	oasis	oasi	oásis
ob	si	whether	si	se	se
Obdach(n), Schutz(m)	abri, refuge	shelter	abrigo, refugio	riparo, rifugio	abrigo, refúgio
oben	haut(en)	upstairs	arriba	alto(in)	cima(em)
oben	au-dessus	overhead	arriba	sopra, in alto	cima(por, em)
oben(-stehend)	ci-dessus	above	arriba(más)	sopra(qui)	acima
Oben-; Hoch-; auf	haut	up	arriba	alto, a	cima(em, para)
Ober(m)	garçon	waiter	camarero	cameriere	criado
obere(r, s); Ober-	supérieur, e	upper	superior, a	superiore	superior, a
Oberfläche(f)	surface	surface	superficie	superficie	superfície
Oberfläche(f)	superficie	area	superficie	superficie	superfície
Obergewalt(f)	suprématie	supremacy	supremacía	supremazia	supremacia
Oberhaut(f), Haut(f)	épiderme	epidermis, skin	epidermis	epidermide	epiderme
Oberkellner(m)	maître d'hôtel	head-waiter	jefe de hotel	capocameriere	mordomo
Oberkörper(m)	buste	bust	busto	busto	busto
Oberschule(f)	collège	comprehensive(Jnr)	escuela(EGB)	scuola media	escola preparatória
Oberst(m)	colonel	colonel	coronel	colonnello	coronel
oberst-, höchst-	suprême	supreme	supremo, a	supremo, a	supremo, a
Oberteil(n)	dessus	top	superior(parte)	disopra	cima(parte de)
Oberteil(n)	haut	top	alto	alto	alto, cimo
obgleich, obwohl	quoique	although, though	aunque	sebbene	embora
Objekt(n), Ding(n)	objet	object	objeto	oggetto	objecto
objektiv, sachlich	objectif, ive	objective	objetivo, a	oggettivo, a	objectivo, a
Objektiv(n), Ziel(n)	objectif	objective	objetivo	obiettivo	objectivo
Objektiv(n)	objectif	lens	objetivo	obiettivo	objectiva
obligatorisch	obligatoire	compulsory	obligatorio, a	obbligatorio, a	obrigatório, a
obligatorisch	obligatoire	mandatory	obligatorio, a	obbligatorio, a	obrigatório, a
Obstsaft(m)	jus de fruit	fruit-juice	zumo de fruta	succo di frutta	sumo de fruta
obszön	obscène	obscene	obsceno, a	osceno, a	obsceno, a
obwohl, obgleich	bien que	though, although	aunque	benché	ainda que
Ochse(m); Rind(n)	boeuf	bullock; beef	buey; carne de vaca	bue; manzo	boi; carne de vaca
öde; einsam	désertique	desert, barren	desértico, a	desertico, a	desértico, a
oder	ou	or	o; u	o	ou
Ofen(m)	poêle	stove	estufa	stufa	fogão
Ofen(m)	four	oven	horno	forno	forno
offen; geöffnet	ouvert, e	open	abierto, a	aperto, a	aberto, a
offen, ehrlich	franc, che	frank	franco, a	franco, a; sincero, a	franco, a
offenbar	évident, e	evident	evidente	evidente	evidente
Offenkundigkeit(f)	notoriété	notoriety	notoriedad	notorietà	notoriedade
offensichtlich	évident, e	obvious, evident	evidente	evidente	evidente
Offensive(f)	offensive	offensive	ofensiva	offensiva	ofensiva
öffentlich	public, ique	public	público, a	pubblico, a	público, a
offiziell	officiel, le	official	oficial	ufficiale	oficial
Offizier(m)	officier	officer	oficial	ufficiale	oficial
öffnen	ouvrir	open	abrir	aprire	abrir
Öffnung(f), Mündung(f)	orifice	orifice, aperture	orificio	orifizio	orifício
Öffnungszeiten(f, pl)	ouverture	opening	apertura	apertura	abertura
oft	souvent	often	frecuentemente	spesso	frequentemente
ohne	sans	without	sin	senza	sem
Ohnmacht(f)	syncope	black-out	síncope	sincope	síncope
ohnmächtig werden	évanouir(s')	faint	desmayarse	svenire	desmaiar
Ohr(n)	oreille	ear	oreja	orecchio	orelha
Ohrfeige(f)	claque	slap	bofetada	schiaffo	bofetada
Ohrfeige(f)	gifle	slap	bofetada	schiaffo	bofetada
Ohrläppchen(n)	lobe	lobe	lóbulo	lobo	lóbulo
Ohrring(m)	boucle(s)	earring	pendientes	orecchini	brincos, argolas
Oktober(m)	octobre	October	octubre	ottobre	Outubro
Öl(n); Speiseöl(n)	huile	oil	aceite	olio	óleo; azeite
Öl(n); Motoröl(n)	huile	oil	aceite; óleo	olio	óleo
Olive(f)	olive	olive	aceituna, oliva	oliva	azeitona
olympisch	olympique	Olympic	olímpico, a	olimpico, a	olímpico, a

German	French	English	Spanish	Italian	Portuguese
Onkel(m)	oncle	uncle	tío	zio	tio
Oper(f)	opéra	opera	ópera	opera	ópera
Operation(f)	opération	operation	operación	operazione	operação
Operette(f)	opérette	operetta	zarzuela, opereta	operetta	opereta
operieren	opérer	operate(on)	operar	operare	operar
Opfer(n)	sacrifice	sacrifice	sacrificio	sacrificio	sacrifício
Opfer(n)	victime	victim	víctima	vittima	vítima
opfern	sacrifier	sacrifice	sacrificar	sacrificare	sacrificar
Opposition(f)	opposition	opposition	oposición	opposizione	oposição
Optiker(in f)m	opticien, ne	optician	óptico, a	ottico	oculista
optimistisch	optimiste	optimistic	optimista	ottimista	optimista
optisch	optique	optic(al)	óptico, a	ottico, a	óptico, a
orangefarben	orange	orange	anaranjado, a	arancione	cor-de-laranja
Orchester(n)	orchestre	orchestra; band	orquesta	orchestra	orquestra
Orchidee(f)	orchidée	orchid	orquídea	orchidea	orquídia
ordentlich	rangé, e	tidy	ordenado, a	ordinato, a	arrumado, a
ordnen	classer	classify, file	clasificar	classificare	classificar
Ordner(m)	classeur	file	clasificador	schedario	classificador
Ordnung(f)	ordre	order	orden	ordine	ordem
Organ(n)	organe	organ	órgano	organo	órgão
Organisation(f)	organisation	organization	organización	organizzazione	organização
Organisator(in f)m	organisateur	organizer	organizador, a	organizzatore, trice	organizador, a
organisch	organique	organic	orgánico, a	organico, a	orgânico, a
organisieren	organiser	organize	organizar	organizzare	organizar
Organismus(m)	organisme	organism	organismo	organismo	organismo
Orgasmus(m)	orgasme	orgasm	orgasmo	orgasmo	orgasmo
Orgel(f)	orgue	organ	órgano	organo	órgão
Orgie(f)	orgie	orgy	orgía	orgia	orgia
orientalisch	oriental, e	oriental	oriental	orientale	oriental
orientieren	orienter	position	orientar	orientare	orientar
Orientierung(f)	orientation	orientation	orientación	orientamento	orientação
original	original, e	original	original	originale	original
Original(n)	original	original	original	originale	original
Orkan(m)	ouragan	hurricane	huracán	uragano	furacão
Ort(m)	lieu	place, spot	lugar	luogo	lugar
Ort(m), Platz(m)	place, endroit	place	lugar	posto	lugar; sítio
Ort(m), Lage(f)	site	site	paraje, vista	sito	sítio
orthodox	orthodoxe	orthodox	ortodoxo, a	ortodosso, a	ortodoxo, a
Ortschaft(f)	localité	locality	localidad	località	localidade
Osten(m)	Est	East	Este	Est	Este, Leste
Ostern(n)	Pâques	Easter	Pascua	Pasqua	Páscoa
oval	ovale	oval	oval, ovalado, a	ovale	oval
Oxydierung(f)	oxydation	oxidization	oxidación	ossidazione	oxidação
Ozean(m)	océan	ocean	océano	oceano	oceano
ozeanisch	océanique	oceanic	oceánico, a	oceanico, a	oceânico, a
Ozon(n)	ozone	ozone	ozono	ozono	ozone

P

German	French	English	Spanish	Italian	Portuguese
Paar(n)	paire	pair(of)	par	paio	par
Paar(n)	couple	couple	pareja	coppia	casal
paaren, sich	accoupler(s')	mate	aparearse	accoppiarsi	acasalar-se
Packeis(n)	banquise	ice-floe	banco de hielo	banchisa	campo de gelo
Page(m), Hotelboy(m)	chasseur(hôtel)	page(boy), bellboy	botones	fattorino	paquete
Paket(n)	paquet	packet; package	paquete	pacco	pacote
Paket(n)	colis	parcel	paquete	pacco, collo	pacote
Pakt(m)	pacte	pact	pacto	patto	pacto

German	French	English	Spanish	Italian	Portuguese
Palast(m)	palais	palace	palacio	palazzo	palácio
Palme(f)	palmier	palm-tree	palmera	palma	palmeira
Pampelmuse(f)	pamplemousse	grapefruit	pomelo	pompelmo	toranja
Panik(f)	panique	panic	pánico	panico	pânico
Panik(f)	affolement	panic	pánico	panico	pânico
Panik geraten(in)	affoler(s')	panic	ponerse nervioso, a	disorientarsi	afligir-se
Panne(f)	panne	breakdown	avería	guasto, panna	avaria
Panther(m)	panthère	panther	pantera	pantera	pantera
Pantoffel(m)	pantoufle	slipper	zapatilla	pantofola	pantufa, chinelo
Papa	papa	Daddy, Dad	papá	papà, babbo	papá
Papagei(m)	perroquet	parrot	loro	pappagallo	papagaio
Papier(n)	papier	paper	papel	carta	papel
Papiere(pl); Ausweise	papiers(les)	papers	documentación	documenti	documentos
Pappe(f)	carton	cardboard	cartón	cartone	cartão
pappig	pâteux, se	pasty	pastoso, a	pastoso, a	pastoso, a
Papst(m)	Pape	Pope	Papa	Papa	Papa
Parade(f)	défilé	parade	desfile	sfilata	desfile
Parade(f)	parade	parade	parada, desfile	parata	parada
Paradies(n)	paradis	paradise	paraíso	paradiso	paraíso
Paradox(n)	paradoxe	paradox	paradoja	paradosso	paradoxo
parallel	parallèle	parallel	paralelo, a	parallelo, a	paralelo, a
Paranoia(f)	paranoïa	paranoia	paranoia	paranoia	paranóia
Parasit(m)	parasite	parasite	parásito	parassita	parasita
Parfüm(n)	parfum	perfume, scent	perfume	profumo	perfume
Parfümerie(f)	parfumerie	perfume shop	perfumería	profumeria	perfumaria
Park(m)	parc	park	parque	parco	parque
parken	garer	park	aparcar	posteggiare	estacionar
parken	stationner	park	estacionarse	stazionare	estacionar
Parken(n)	stationnement	parking	estacionamiento	sosta	estacionamento
Parkplatz(m)	parking	car park	aparcamiento	parcheggio	p.estacionamento
Parlament(n)	parlement	parliament	parlamento	parlamento	parlamento
Partei(f)	parti	party	partido	partito	partido
Partitur(f)	partition	score(music)	partitura	spartito	partitura
Partner(in f)m	partenaire	partner	pareja	socio, a; partner	parceiro, a
Party(f)	cocktail	party(cocktail -)	cóctel	party	recepção
Parzelle(f)	parcelle	plot	parcela	parcella	parcela
Paß(m)	col	pass	puerto	colle, passo	desfiladeiro
Paß(m)	passeport	passport	pasaporte	passaporto	passaporte
Passage(f)	galerie	arcade	galería	galleria	galeria
Passagier(in f)m	passager, ère	passenger	pasajero, a	passeggero, a	passageiro, a
Passagierdampfer(m)	paquebot	liner	buque	transatlantico	paquete
passen	convenir	suit, fit	convenir	convenire	estar bem
passend	adéquat, e	appropriate	adecuado, a	adeguato, a	adequado, a
passieren	produire(se)	happen, occur	suceder, ocurrir	accadere	ocorrer
passiv	passif, ive	passive	pasivo, a	passivo, a	passivo, a
Paste(f); Masse(f)	pâte	paste	masa, pasta	impasto, pasta	massa
Pastete(f)	pâté	paté	paté	patè	paté
Pastete(f)	tourte	pie	pastel, tortada	torta salata	empada
Pastor(in f)m	pasteur	vicar, minister	pastor	pastore	padre; pastor
Pate(m)	parrain	godfather	padrino	padrino	padrinho
Patent(n)	brevet	patent	patente	brevetto	patente
Patin(f)	marraine	godmother	madrina	madrina	madrinha
Patriarch(m)	patriarche	patriarch	patriarca	patriarca	patriarca
Patrone(f)	cartouche	cartridge	cartucho	cartuccia	cartucho
Patrouille(f), Streife	patrouille	patrol	patrulla	pattuglia	patrulha
pauschal	forfaitaire	inclusive	global; convenido, a	forfettario, a	preço fixo(a)
Pause(f)	pause	pause, break	pausa	pausa	pausa
Pause(f), Stillstand	arrêt	stop	parada	fermata	paragem
Pause(f)	récréation	break	recreo	ricreazione	recreio
Pause(f)	entracte	interval	intermedio	intervallo	intervalo
Pazifik(m)	Pacifique	Pacific Ocean	Pacífico	Pacifico	Pacífico
Pech(n), Unglück(n)	malchance	ill luck, bad luck	mala suerte	sfortuna	má sorte
Pedal(n)	pédale	pedal	pedal	pedale	pedal
pedantisch	pédant, e	pedantic	pedante	pedante	pedante; vaidoso, a
Peitsche(f)	fouet	whip	látigo	frusta	chicote
Pelz(m)	fourrure	fur	piel	pelliccia	pele; peliça
Penizillin(n)	pénicilline	penicillin	penicilina	penicillina	penicilina
Penner(m)	clochard, e	tramp	vagabundo, a	barbone, a; vagabondo	vagabundo, a

G

329

German	French	English	Spanish	Italian	Portuguese
Pension(f)	pension	pension; allowance	pensión	pensione	pensão
pensioniert sein	retraité, e(être)	retired(be)	jubilado, a(estar)	pensione(essere in)	reformado, a(estar)
Pensionierung(f)	retraite	retirement	jubilación	pensione	reforma
Pensionsgast(m)	pensionnaire	resident	pensionista	pensionante	hóspede
per	par	per	por	per	por
Periode(f)	période	period	período	periodo	período
periodisch	périodique	periodic(al)	periódico, a	periodico, a	periódico, a
Perle(f)	perle	pearl	perla	perla	pérola
Person(f)	personne	person	persona	persona	pessoa
Personal(n)	personnel	staff, personnel	personal, plantilla	personale	pessoal
Personalausweis(m)	carte d'identité	identity card	carné de identidad	carta d'identità	bilhete(identidade)
Personalbestand(m)	effectif	number of people	efectivo	effettivo	efectivo
persönlich	personnel, le	personal	personal	personale	pessoal
Persönlichkeit(f)	personnalité	personality	personalidad	personalità	personalidade
Perspektive(f)	perspective	perspective	perspectiva	prospettiva	perspectiva
Perücke(f)	perruque	wig	peluca	parrucca	peruca
pervers	pervers, e	perverse	perverso, a	perverso, a	perverso, a
pessimistisch	pessimiste	pessimistic	pesimista	pessimista	pessimista
Pfahl(m)	piquet	post, stake, peg	estaca	picchetto	estaca
Pfahl(m)	pieu, poteau	stake, post	estaca	palo, piolo	estaca
Pfand(n)	gage	pledge	prenda	pegno	penhor
Pfanne(f)	poêle	frying pan	sartén	padella	frigideira
Pfeffer(m)	poivre	pepper	pimienta	pepe	pimenta
Pfeife(f)	sifflet	whistle	pito	fischietto	apito
Pfeife(f)	pipe	pipe	pipa	pipa	cachimbo
pfeifen	siffler	whistle	silbar	fischiare	assobiar
Pfeil(m)	flèche	arrow	flecha	freccia	flecha, seta
Pfeiler(m)	pilier	pillar	pilar	pilastro	pilar
Pferd(n)	cheval	horse	caballo	cavallo	cavalo
Pferderennen(n)	courses	races	carreras	corsa	corridas
Pferdestall(m)	écurie	stable	cuadra	scuderia	cavalariça
Pfirsich(m)	pêche	peach	melocotón	pesca	pêssego
Pflanze(f)	plante	plant	planta	pianta	planta
Pflanze(f)	végétal	vegetable, plant	vegetal	vegetale	vegetal
pflanzen	planter	plant	plantar	piantare	plantar
Pflanzenwuchs(m)	végétation	vegetation	vegetación	vegetazione	vegetação
Pflaster(n)	sparadrap	plaster	esparadrapo	cerotto	esparadrapo
Pflasterstein(m)	pavé	paving-stone	adoquín	selce, selciato	pedra de calçada
Pflaume(f)	prune	plum	ciruela	prugna, susina	ameixa
Pflege(f)	soin	care	cuidado	cura	cuidado
pflegen	soigner	nurse; tend; treat	curar	curare	cuidar
Pflicht(f)	devoir	duty	deber	dovere	dever
pflücken	cueillir	pick, gather	coger, recoger	cogliere, raccogliere	colher
Pforte(f)	porte	gate	puerta, entrada	porta, uscita	porta
Pfosten(m)	poteau	post, pole	poste	palo	poste
Pfote(f); Bein(n)	patte	paw; leg; foot	pata	zampa	pata
Pfropfen(m), Stöpsel	bouchon	cap, plug	tapón	tappo	rolha; tampa
Phänomen(n)	phénomène	phenomenon(-mena)	fenómeno	fenomeno	fenómeno
Phantasievorstellung	fantasme	fantasy	fantasma	fantasia	fantasma
phantastisch	fantastique	fantastic	fantástico, a	fantastico, a	fantástico, a
phantastisch	fabuleux, se	fabulous	fabuloso, a	favoloso, a	fabuloso, a
Phase(f)	phase	phase, stage	fase	fase	fase
Philosophie(f)	philosophie	philosophy	filosofia	filosofia	filosofia
phonetisch	phonétique	phonetic	fonético, a	fonetico, a	fonético, a
Physik(f)	physique	physics	física	fisica	fisíca
Physiker(in f)m	physicien, ne	physicist	físico, a	fisico, a	físico, a
physisch	physique	physical	físico, a	fisico, a	físico, a
Pianist(in f)m	pianiste	pianist	pianista	pianista	pianista
Pickel(m)	bouton	spot, pimple	grano	brufolo, foruncolo	borbulha
Pilger(in f)m	pèlerin	pilgrim	peregrino	pellegrino, a	peregrino
Pille(f)	pilule	pill	píldora	pillola	pílula
Pilot(m)	pilote	pilot	piloto	pilota	piloto
Pilz(m)	champignon	mushroom	champiñón, seta	fungo	cogumelo
Pinsel(m)	pinceau	brush	pincel	pennello	pincel
Pionier, Bahnbrecher	pionnier	pioneer	pionero	pioniere	pioneiro
Pirat(in f)m	pirate	pirate	pirata	pirata	pirata
Piroge(f), Kanu(n)	pirogue	pirogue	piragua	piroga	piroga
Piste(f)	piste	slope	pista	pista	pista

German	French	English	Spanish	Italian	Portuguese
Pistole(f)	pistolet	gun, pistol	pistola	pistola	pistola
plädieren	plaider	plead	litigar	patrocinare	defender(causa)
Plakat(n)	affiche	poster, placard	cartel	manifesto	cartaz
Plakat(n)	poster	poster	cartel, póster	poster, manifesto	cartaz
Plakat(n), Schild(n)	pancarte	sign, notice	pancarta	cartello	cartaz
Plan(m)	plan	plan; drawing	plan; plano	piano; schema	plano; desenho
Plan(m)	plan, projet	scheme, plan	plan, proyecto	schema, piano	plano, projecto
Plan(m)	projet	plan	plan, proyecto	progetto	projecto
Plan(m)(Stadtplan m)	plan	map	plano	pianta; stradario	planta
Plane(f)	bâche	cover	toldo, lona	telone	toldo
planen	projeter	plan	proyectar, planear	progettare	projectar
Planet(m)	planète	planet	planeta	pianeta	planeta
Plastik(n)	plastique	plastic	plástico	plastica	plástico
plastisch	plastique	plastic	plástico, a	plastico, a	plástico, a
platt	plat, e	flat	llano, a	piatto, a	plano, a
platt, ohne Luft	dégonflé, e	deflated, flat	desinflado, a	sgonfio, a	vazio, a
Platte(f)	plaque	plate, plaque	placa	lastra, piastra	placa
Plattenspieler(m)	tourne-disque	record-player	tocadiscos	giradischi	gira-discos
Plattform(f)	plate-forme	platform	plataforma	piattaforma	plataforma
Platz(m)	place	square	plaza	piazza	praça
Platz(m)	place	room	sitio, espacio	spazio	espaço
platzen	éclater	burst	reventar	scoppiare	rebentar
platzen, bersten	crever	puncture, burst	reventar	bucare, scoppiare	rebentar; furar
plötzlich	soudain	sudden(ly)	pronto(de)	ad un tratto	súbito(de)
Plünderung(f)	pillage	plunder, pillage	saqueo	saccheggio	pilhagem
plus	plus	plus	más	più	mais
Pocken(f, pl)	variole	smallpox	viruela	vaiolo	varíola
Podest(n)	podium	podium, stage	podio	podio	estrado
Poesie(f)	poésie	poetry	poesia	poesia	poesia
Pokal(m)	coupe	cup	copa	coppa	taça
Pol(m)	pôle	pole	polo	polo	polo
polar; Polar-	polaire	polar	polar	polare	polar
Polemik(f)	polémique	controversy	polémica	polemica	polémica
polieren	polir	polish	pulir	lucidare, levigare	polir
polieren, wachsen	cirer	polish	dar crema	lucidare	encerar
poliert	poli, e	polished	pulido, a	levigato, a	polido, a
Politik(f)	politique	politics	política	politica	política
Politik(f)	politique	policy	política	politica	política
Politiker(in f)m	homme politique	politician	político	uomo politico	político
Politiker(in f)m	politicien, ne	politician	político, a	politico, a	político, a
politisch	politique	political	político, a	politico, a	político, a
Polizeiwache(f)	poste de police	police station	cuartelillo	posto di guardia	esquadra
Polizist(in f)m	policier	policeman(-men)	policía	poliziotto	polícia
Polizist(in f)m	gendarme	policeman(-men)	guardia civil	carabiniere	guarda-republicano
Polygamie(f)	polygamie	polygamy	poligamia	poligamia	poligamia
Polyp(m)	polype	polyp	pólipo	polipo	pólipo
Pommes Frites	frites	chips	patatas fritas	patatine fritte	batatas fritas
populär	populaire	popular	popular	popolare	popular
Pore(f)	pore	pore	poro	poro	poro
Pornographie(f)	pornographie	pornography	pornografía	pornografia	pornografia
porös	poreux, se	porous	poroso, a	poroso, a	poroso, a
Portal(n)	porche	porch	soportal, porche	atrio, portico	pórtico
Portier(m)	portier	porter	portero	portiere	porteiro
Porto(-kosten)(n/pl)	port	postage	porte	porto	porte
portofrei	franco de port	carriage-paid	porte pago	porto franco	porte pago
Portrait(n)	portrait	portrait	retrato	ritratto	retrato
Porzellan(n)	porcelaine	porcelain, china	porcelana	porcellana	porcelana
Position(f)	position	position	posición	posizione	posição
positiv	positif, ive	positive	positivo, a	positivo, a	positivo, a
Post(f)	poste	post-office	correos	posta	correios
Post(f)	courrier	mail, post	correo	posta	correio
Postanweisung(f)	mandat-lettre	postal order	giro postal	vaglia(postale)	vale postal
Postkarte(f)	carte postale	post-card	tarjeta postal	cartolina	bilhete-postal
potentiell	potentiel, le	potential	potencial	potenziale	potencial
prächtig	somptueux, se	sumptuous	suntuoso, a	sontuoso, a	sumptuoso, a
prächtig	magnifique	magnificent	magnífico, a	magnifico, a	magnífico, a
prächtig, brillant	brillant, e	brilliant	brillante	brillante	brilhante

G

German	French	English	Spanish	Italian	Portuguese
prahlen	vanter(se)	boast	jactarse	vantarsi	gabar-se
Praktikant(in f)m	stagiaire	trainee	cursillista	apprendista	estagiário
Praktikum(n)	stage	training period	cursillo	tirocinio, stage	estágio
praktisch	pratique	practical	práctico, a	pratico, a	prático, a
praktisch	commode	convenient	cómodo, a	comodo, a	cómodo, a
Präposition(f)	préposition	preposition	preposición	preposizione	preposição
Präservativ(n)	préservatif	condom, sheath	preservativo	preservativo	preservativo
Präsident(in f)m	président, e	president	presidente	presidente, essa	presidente
Präsidium n, Vorsitz m	présidence	presidency	presidencia	presidenza	presidência
Praxis(f)(Arztpraxis)	cabinet(médecin)	surgery	consulta(-torio)	studio(medico)	consultório
predigen	prêcher	preach	predicar	predicare	pregar
Preis(m)	prix	price	precio	prezzo	preço
Preis(m)	prix	prize	premio	premio	prémio
preis = geben; auf = geben	abandonner	abandon, leave	abandonar	abbandonare	abandonar
Preisstopp(m)	blocage	freeze	congelación	blocco	congelamento
Preisträger(in f)m	lauréat, e	prize-winner	galardonado, a	premiato, a	galardoado, a
Preisträgerliste(f)	palmarès	list of winners	lista de premios	albo dei premiati	quadro de honra
Premierminister(m)	premier ministre	prime minister	primer ministro	primo ministro	primeiro ministro
Presse(f)	presse	press	prensa	stampa	imprensa
Priester(m)	prêtre	priest	sacerdote, padre	prete	padre
Primär-	primaire	primary	primario, a	primario, a	primário, a
primitiv	primitif, ive	primitive	primitivo, a	primitivo, a	primitivo, a
Prinz(m)	prince	prince	príncipe	principe	príncipe
Prinzessin(f)	princesse	princess(-es)	princesa	principessa	princesa
privat	privé, e	private	privado, a	privato, a	privado, a
Privatmann(m)	particulier	individual	particular	privato	particular
Probe(f), Muster(n)	échantillon	sample	muestra	campione	amostra
Problem(n)	problème	problem	problema	problema	problema
Produkt(n)	produit	product	producto	prodotto	produto
Produktion(f)	production	production	producción	produzione	produção
Produzent(in f)m	producteur, trice	producer	productor, a	produttore, trice	produtor, a
produzieren	produire	produce	producir	produrre	produzir
professionell	professionnel, le	professional	profesional	professionale	profissional
Professor(in f)m	professeur	professor	catedrático, a	professore, essa	professor, a
Profi(m)	professionnel	professional	profesional	professionista	profissional
Profil(n)	profil	profile	perfil	profilo	perfil
profitieren	profiter	take advantage of	aprovechar	approfittare	aproveitar
profitieren, gewinnen	bénéficier	profit, benefit	beneficiar	beneficiare	beneficiar
Prognose(f)	pronostic	prognosis(-ses)	pronóstico	prognosi	prognóstico
Programm(n)	programme	programme	programa	programma	programa
Programm, Fernseh-	chaîne	channel	cadena	canale	canal
Programmierer(in f)m	programmeur, se	programmer	programador, a	programmatore, trice	programador, a
Prominente(r)mf	sommité	V.I.P	eminencia	sommità	sumidade
Propaganda(f)	propagande	propaganda	propaganda	propaganda	propaganda
Propeller(m)	hélice	propeller	hélice	elica	hélice
Prostata(f)	prostate	prostate	próstata	prostata	próstata
Prostituierte(f)	prostituée	prostitute	prostituta	prostituta	prostituta
Prostitution(f)	prostitution	prostitution	prostitución	prostituzione	prostituição
Protestant(in f)m	protestant, e	Protestant	protestante	protestante	protestante
protestieren	protester	protest, contest	protestar	protestare	protestar
Prothese(f)	prothèse	artificial-, false-	prótesis	protesi	prótese
Protokoll(n)	procès-verbal	minutes, report	acta	verbale	acta
Protokoll(n)	protocole	protocol	protocolo	protocollo	protocolo
Prototyp(m)	prototype	prototype	prototipo	prototipo	protótipo
Provinz(f)	province	province	provincia	provincia	província
provisorisch	provisoire	provisional	provisional	provvisorio, a	provisório, a
Prozent(n)	pour cent	per cent	por ciento	per cento	por cento
Prozent(n)	degré(alcool)	proof(per cent)	graduación	grado	grau
Prozentsatz(m)	pourcentage	percentage	porcentaje	percentuale	percentagem
Prozeß(m)	procès	lawsuit, trial	proceso, juicio	processo	processo
Prozeß(m)	procès	lawsuit	pleito	causa	pleito, processo
Prozession(f)	procession	procession	procesión	processione	procissão
prüfen, erforschen	étudier, examiner	investigate	estudiar	studiare	estudar, examinar
Prüfung(f)	examen	examination, exam	examen	esame	exame
Prüfung(f)	concours	competitive exam	oposiciones	concorso	concurso
prügeln	matraquer	beat up, club	aporrear	manganellare	espancar
prunkvoll	fastueux, se	sumptuous	ostentoso, a	fastoso, a	faustoso, a
Pseudonym(n)	pseudonyme	pseudonym	seudónimo	pseudonimo	pseudónimo

German	French	English	Spanish	Italian	Portuguese
pst!	chut!	hush!, sh!	chitón(!)	sst!, zitto!	chut!
Psychiater(in f)m	psychiatre	psychiatrist	siquiatra	psichiatra	psiquiatra
psychisch	psychique	psychological	síquico, a	psichico, a	psíquico, a
Psychoanalytiker(m)	psychanalyste	psychoanalyst	sicoanalista	psicanalista	psicanalista
Psychologe(m)/-gin(f)	psychologue	psychologist	sicólogo, a	psicologo, a	psicólogo, a
Psychologie(f)	psychologie	psychology	sicología	psicologia	psicologia
Psychose(f)	psychose	psychosis(-ses)	sicosis	psichosi	psicose
Pubertät(f)	puberté	puberty	pubertad	pubertà	puberdade
Publikum(n)	public	public; audience	público	pubblico	público
Puder(m); Pulver(n)	poudre	powder	polvo	polvere	pó
Pullover(m)	pull-over	pullover, sweater	jersey	maglione, pullover	pulover
Pullover(m)	chandail	jumper, sweater	jersey	maglione	camisola
Puls(m)	pouls	pulse	pulso	polso	pulso
Pulsschlag(m)	pulsation	beating, pulsation	pulsación	pulsazione	pulsação
Pulver(n)(Schieß-)	poudre	powder	pólvora	polvere	pólvora
Pumpe(f)	pompe	pump	bomba	pompa	bomba
Punkt(m)	point	point	punto	punto	ponto
Punkt(m)	point	dot	punto	punto	ponto
Punktion(f)	ponction	puncture	punción	puntura, prelievo	punção
pünktlich	ponctuel, le	punctual	puntual	puntuale	pontual
Punktzahl(f)	score	score	marca, tanteo	punteggio	resultado
Pupille(f)	pupille	pupil	pupila	pupilla	pupila
Puppe(f)	poupée	doll	muñeca	bambola	boneca
Putzfrau(f)	femme de ménage	domestic help	asistenta	donna di servizio	mulher a dias
Puzzle(n)	puzzle	jigsaw(puzzle)	rompecabezas	puzzle	puzzle
Pyramide(f)	pyramide	pyramid	pirámide	piramide	pirâmide
Python(m)	python	python	pitón	pitone	jibóia

G

Q

German	French	English	Spanish	Italian	Portuguese
Qual(f)	supplice	torture	suplicio	supplizio	suplício
quälen	tourmenter	torment	atormentar	tormentare	atormentar
quälen	harceler	harass	acosar	assillare	perseguir
qualifiziert	qualifié, e	qualified	calificado, a	qualificato, a	qualificado, a
Qualität(f)	qualité	quality	calidad; cualidad	qualità	qualidade
Quantität(f)	quantité	quantity, amount	cantidad	quantità	quantidade
Quartett(n)	quatuor	quartet	cuarteto	quartetto	quarteto
Quecksilber(n)	mercure	mercury	mercurio	mercurio	mercúrio
Quelle(f)	source	spring	fuente	sorgente	fonte, nascente
quengelig	grognon, ne	grumpy	gruñon, a	brontolone	rabugento, a
Quer-; schräg	transversal, e	transversal	transversal	trasversale	transversal
Quetschung(f)	contusion	bruise	contusión	contusione	contusão
Quittung(f)	quittance	receipt	recibo	ricevuta	recibo
Quittung(f)	reçu	receipt	recibo	ricevuta	recibo
Quote(f)	quota	quota	cuota	quota	cota
Quotient(m), Bruch(m)	quotient	quotient	cociente	quoziente	quociente

R

German	French	English	Spanish	Italian	Portuguese
Rabatt(m)	rabais, remise	discount	rebaja, descuento	ribasso, sconto	desconto, saldo
Rabbiner(m)	rabbin	rabbi	rabino	rabbino	rabino
Rabe(m)	corbeau	crow	cuervo	corvo	corvo
Rache(f)	vengeance	revenge	venganza	vendetta	vingança
Rachen(m)	pharynx	pharynx	faringe	faringe	faringe
rächen	venger	avenge	vengar	vendicare	vingar
rachitisch	rachitique	rickety	raquítico, a	rachitico, a	raquítico, a
Rachsucht(f)	rancune	grudge, spite	rencor	rancore	rancor
Rad(n)	roue	wheel	rueda	ruota	roda
Radar(m)	radar	radar	radar	radar	radar
Radfahren(n)	cyclisme	cycling	ciclismo	ciclismo	ciclismo
Radfahrer(in f)m	cycliste	cyclist	ciclista	ciclista	ciclista
radieren	effacer	erase, rub out	borrar	cancellare	apagar
Radiergummi(m)	gomme	rubber	goma	gomma	borracha
Radio(n)	radio	radio	radio	radio	rádio
Radio(n)	poste radio	radio set	aparato de radio	radio	rádio
Radioaktivität(f)	radioactivité	radioactivity	radiactividad	radioattività	radioactividade
Radioübertragung(f)	radiodiffusion	broadcasting	radiodifusión	radiodiffusione	radiodifusão
Radius(m)	rayon	radius(-ii)	radio	raggio	raio
Rahmen(m)	cadre	frame	marco	cornice, quadro	moldura
Rahmen(m), Chassis(n)	châssis	frame, chassis	chasis	telaio	chassis
Rakete(f)	fusée	rocket	cohete	razzo	foguete
Rakete(f)	missile	missile	misil	missile	míssil
Ramadan(m)	ramadan	Ramadan	ramadán	ramadan	ramadão
Rand(m)	bord	side; edge	borde	bordo, riva, orlo	borda
Rand(m)	bordure	edge, border	bordura; ribete	bordo, lungo	borda, orla
Rand(m)	marge	margin	margen	margine	margem«
Rang(m)	rang	rank	puesto	rango	posição
Rang(m)	grade	rank	grado	grado	grau
Rangordnung(f)	ordre	order	orden	ordine	ordem
Ranzen(m)	cartable	briefcase; satchel	cartera	cartella	pasta
rasch	vite	fast, quickly	pronto; rápido, a	presto	depressa; rápido, a
Rasen(m)	gazon	grass	césped	prato, erba	relva
Rasenfläche(f)	pelouse	lawn	césped	prato inglese	relvado
Rasierapparat(m)	rasoir	razor	navaja de afeitar	rasoio	navalha, gilete
rasieren, sich	raser(se)	shave	afeitar(se)	radersi	barbear-se
Rasse(f)	race	race, breed	raza	razza	raça
Rasse(f)	race	breed	casta, raza	razza	casta, raça
rassisch	racial, e	racial	racial	raziale	racial
Rassismus(m)	racisme	racism	racismo	razzismo	racismo
Rat(m)	conseil	advice	consejo	consiglio	conselho
Rat(m)(Stadtrat m)	conseil	council	concejo	giunta, consiglio	município
Rat(m)(Europrat m)	conseil	council	consejo	consiglio	conselho
Rat(m)(Staatsrat m)	conseiller, ère	councillor	concejal, a	consigliere, a	conselheiro, a
Rate(f)	taux	rate	tasa	tasso	taxa
raten	deviner	guess	adivinar	indovinare	adivinhar
Rathaus(n)	mairie	town hall	ayuntamiento	municipio, comune	câmara
ratifizieren	ratifier	ratify	ratificar	ratificare	ratificar
Ration(f); Stück(n)	ration, portion	ration	ración	razione	ração
rational	rationnel, le	rational	racional	razionale	racional
Rationierung(f)	rationnement	rationing	racionamiento	razionamento	racionamento
ratlos	désemparé, e	distraught	desamparado, a	smarrito, a; sgomento	desamparado, a
Rätsel(n)	énigme	enigma	enigma	enigma	enigma
Ratte(f)	rat	rat	rata	topo, ratto	rato, a
Räuber(in f)m	brigand	bandit	maleante	brigante	bandido
Raubüberfall(m)	hold-up	hold-up	atraco	rapina	assalto
Raubvogel(m)	rapace	bird of prey	rapaz	rapace	ave de rapina
Rauch(m)	fumée	smoke	humo	fumo	fumo
Rauch(m)	fumée	smoke, fumes	humo	smog, fumo	fumo
rauchen	fumer	smoke	fumar	fumare	fumar
Raucher(in f)m	fumeurs	smokers	fumadores	fumatore, trice	fumadores

German	French	English	Spanish	Italian	Portuguese
rauh	rugueux, se	rough, harsh	rugoso, a	rugoso, a	rugoso, a
rauh, heiser	rauque	hoarse	ronco, a	rauco, a	rouco, a
Raum(m)	espace	space	espacio	spazio	espaço
Raum(m)	pièce	room	cuarto	stanza	divisão
Raum-	spatial, e	space	espacial	spaziale	espacial
räumen, leeren	évacuer	evacuate	evacuar	evacuare	evacuar
Rauschgiftsüchtige(r)	toxicomane	drug addict	drogadicto, a	tossicomane	toxicómano, drogado
raus = ziehen	débrancher	unplug	desenchufar	staccare	desligar
Raute(f), Rhombus(m)	losange	diamond-shaped	rombo	rombo	losango
Razzia(f)	rafle	raid, round-up	redada	retata	rusga
reagieren	réagir	react	reaccionar	reagire	reagir
Reaktion(f)	réaction	reaction	reacción	reazione	reacção
reaktionär	réactionnaire	reactionary	reaccionario, a	reazionario, a	reaccionário, a
Reaktor(m)	réacteur	reactor; engine	reactor	reattore	reactor
Rebell(m)	rebelle	rebel	rebelde	ribelle	rebelde
Rechen(m)	râteau	rake	rastrillo	rastrello	ancinho
Rechenmaschine(f)	calculatrice	calculator	calculadora	calcolatrice	calculadora
rechnen, berechnen	calculer	calculate, reckon	calcular	calcolare	calcular
rechnen, mit etwas	attendre à(s')	expect	esperar(se)	aspettarsi	esperar
Rechnung(f)	note	bill	cuenta	conto	conta
Rechnung(f)	facture	invoice, bill	factura	fattura	factura
Rechnung(f)	compte	account	cuenta	conto	conta
Recht(n)	droit	law	derecho	diritto	direito
Recht(n)	droit	right	derecho	diritto	direito
Recht(n)(haben)	raison(avoir)	right(to be)	razón(tener)	ragione(avere)	razão(ter)
rechte(r, s); rechts	droit, e	right	derecho, a; destra, a	destro, a	direito, a
Rechteck(n)	rectangle	rectangle	rectángulo	rettangolo	rectângulo
Rechtfertigung(f)	justification	justification	justificación	giustificazione	justificação
rechtmäßig	judiciaire, légal	legal	judicial	giudiziario, a	judicial
rechtmäßig	légitime, légal	rightful, lawful	legítimo, a	legittimo, a	legítimo, a
Rechtmäßigkeit(f)	légalité	legality	legalidad	legalità	legalidade
Rechtschreibung(f)	orthographe	spelling	ortografía	ortografia	ortografia
Rechtsprechung(f)	jurisprudence	jurisprudence	jurisprudencia	giurisprudenza	jurisprudência
Redaktion(f)	rédaction	editorial staff	redacción	redazione	redacção
Rede(f)	discours	speech, talk	discurso	discorso	discurso
Redegewandtheit(f)	éloquence	eloquence	elocuencia	eloquenza	eloquência
reden(mit jdm)	parler à	talk to, speak to	hablar con	parlare a	falar com
Redensart(f)	locution	phrase, locution	locución	locuzione	locução
Redner(in f)m	orateur, trice	speaker, orator	orador, a; locutor, a	oratore, trice	orador, a
reduzieren	réduire	reduce	reducir	ridurre	reduzir
Reeder(m)	armateur	ship-owner	armador	armatore	armador
Referat(n)	exposé	talk, commentary	exposición	relazione; esposto	exposição
Referenz(f)	référence	reference	referencia	riferimento	referência
reflektieren	réfléchir(se)	reflected(be)	reflejar	riflettere(-ersi)	reflectir
Reflex(m)	réflexe	reflex	reflejo	riflesso	reflexo
Reform(f)	réforme	reform	reforma	riforma	reforma
Refrain(m)	refrain	refrain, chorus	estribillo	ritornello	refrão
Regal(n)	étagère	shelf(-ves)	estantería	scaffale	prateleira
Regel(f)	règle	rule	regla, norma	regola, norma	regra, norma
regelmäßig	régulier, ière	regular	regular	regolare	regular
regeln; erledigen	régler	settle	resolver	risolvere	resolver
Regelung(f)	réglementation	regulation(s)	reglamentación	regolamentazione	regulamentação
Regen(m)	pluie	rain	lluvia	pioggia	chuva
Regenbogen(m)	arc-en-ciel	rainbow	arco iris	arcobaleno	arco-íris
Regenmantel(m)	imperméable	rain-coat, mac	gabardina	impermeabile	gabardina
Regenschirm(m)	parapluie	umbrella	paraguas	ombrello	chapéu de chuva
regieren	gouverner	govern	gobernar	governare	governar
Regierung(f)	gouvernement	government	gobierno	governo	governo
Regime(n)	régime	régime	régimen	regime	regime
Regiment(n)	régiment	regiment	regimiento	reggimento	regimento
Register(n)	registre	register	registro	registro	registo
Registrierung(f)	enregistrement	registration	registro	registrazione	registo
regnen	pleuvoir	rain	llover	piovere	chover
regnerisch	pluvieux, se	rainy	lluvioso, a	piovoso, a	chuvoso, a
Regulierung(f)	régularisation	regularization	regularización	regolarizzazione	regularização
regungslos	inerte	inert	inerte	inerte	inerte
reiben	frotter	rub	frotar	strofinare, sfregare	esfregar
Reibung(f)	frottement	friction, rubbing	frotamiento	strofinìo	fricção

G

German	French	English	Spanish	Italian	Portuguese
Reich(n)	empire	empire	imperio	impero	império
reich	riche	rich, wealthy	rico, a	ricco, a	rico, a
reichlich	copieux, se	copious	copioso, a	abbondante	copioso, a
reichlich	abondant, e	plentiful, abundant	abundante	abbondante	abundante
Reichtum(m)	richesse	wealth, richness	riqueza	ricchezza	riqueza
Reichweite(f)	portée	range, reach	alcance	portata, gittata	alcance
Reif(m)	givre	frost	escarcha	brina	geada
reif	mûr, e	ripe	maduro, a	maturo, a	maduro, a
reif	mûr, e	mature	maduro, a	maturo, a	maduro, a
Reife(f)	maturité	maturity	madurez	maturità	maturidade
Reifen(m)	pneu	tyre	neumático	pneumatico, gomma	pneu
Reifenpanne(f)	crevaison	puncture	pinchazo	foratura	furo
Reihe(f)	rangée	row	hilera, fila	fila	fileira, renque
Reihe(f)	tour	turn	turno	turno	vez
rein	pur, e	pure	puro, a	puro, a	puro, a
reinigen	nettoyer	clean	limpiar	pulire	limpar
reinigen	purifier	purify	purificar	purificare	purificar
Reinigung(f)	nettoyage	cleaning	limpieza	pulizia	limpeza
Reinlichkeit(f)	propreté	clean(li)ness	limpieza	pulizia	limpeza
Reis(m)	riz	rice	arroz	riso	arroz
Reise(f)	voyage	trip; journey	viaje	viaggio	viagem
Reisebus(m)	autocar	coach	autocar	pullman	autocarro
reisen	voyager	travel	viajar	viaggiare	viajar
Reisende(r)mf	voyageur, se	traveller	viajero, a	viaggiatore, trice	viajante
Reisetasche(f)	sac de voyage	travel-bag	bolso de viaje	borsa da viaggio	saco de viagem
Reiten(n)	équitation	riding(horse -)	equitación	equitazione	equitação
Reiter(in f)m	cavalier, ière	rider	jinete, a	cavaliere	cavaleiro, a
Reiter-	équestre	equestrian	ecuestre	equestre	equestre
reizen, irritieren	irriter	irritate	irritar	irritare	irritar
reizen, an = regen	stimuler	stimulate	estimular	stimolare	estimular
reizend	adorable	adorable, lovely	adorable	adorabile	adorável
reizend, anziehend	séduisant, e	attractive	atractivo, a	seducente	atraente
Reklame(f)	réclame(s), pub	advertisement	publicidad	reclame	publicidade
Rekord(m)	record	record	récord	record	recorde
Rekrutierung(f)	recrutement	recruitment	reclutamiento	reclutamento	recrutamento
relativ	relatif, ive	relative	relativo, a	relativo, a	relativo, a
Relief(n)	relief	relief	relieve	rilievo	relevo
Religion(f)	religion	religion	religión	religione	religião
religiös	religieux, se	religious	religioso, a	religioso, a	religioso, a
Rennen(n)	course	race	carrera	corsa	corrida
Rennwagen(m)	voiture(course)	racing car	coche de carreras	macchina da corsa	carro de corrida
Renovation(f)	rénovation	renovation	renovación	rinnovazione	restauração
Rentabilität(f)	rentabilité	profitability	rentabilidad	redditività	rentabilidade
Rentner(in f)m	retraité, e	retired person	retirado, a	pensionato, a	reformado, a
Reparation(f)	réparation	repair	reparación	riparazione	reparação
reparieren	réparer	repair, mend	reparar	riparare	reparar
Repatriierung(f)	rapatriement	repatriation	repatriación	rimpatrio	repatriação
Repertoire(n)	répertoire	index; repertoire	repertorio	repertorio	repertório
Reportage(f)	reportage	report	reportaje	cronaca	reportagem
Reproduktion(f)	reproduction	reproduction	reproducción	riproduzione	reprodução
reproduzieren	reproduire	reproduce	reproducir	riprodurre	reproduzir
Reptil(n)	reptile	reptile	reptil	rettile	réptil
Republik(f)	république	republic	república	repubblica	república
Reserve(f)	réserve	reserve	reserva	riserva	reserva
reservieren	réserver	reserve	reservar	riservare	reservar
reserviert	réservé, e	reserved	reservado, a	prenotato, a	reservado, a
Reservierung(f)	réservation	reservation	reservación	prenotazione	reserva
Respekt(m)	respect	respect	respeto	rispetto	respeito
respektieren	respecter	respect	respetar	rispettare	respeitar
Rest(m)	reste	rest, remainder	resto	resto	resto
Restaurant(n)	restaurant	restaurant	restaurante	ristorante	restaurante
retten	sauver	save	salvar	salvare	salvar
retten	secourir	rescue	socorrer	soccorrere	socorrer
Retter(in f)m	sauveteur	rescuer	socorrista	soccorritore	socorrista
Rettung(f)	sauvetage	rescue	salvamento	salvataggio	salvamento
Rettungsring(m)	bouée	lifebelt	salvavidas	salvagente	bóia
Revision(f)	révision	revision	revisión	revisione	revisão
Revolte(f)	révolte	revolt	revuelta	rivolta	revolta

German	French	English	Spanish	Italian	Portuguese
Revolution(f)	révolution	revolution	revolución	rivoluzione	revolução
revolutionär	révolutionnaire	revolutionary	revolucionario, a	rivoluzionario, a	revolucionário, a
Revolver(m)	révolver	revolver, gun	revólver	revolver	revólver
Rezept(n)	recette	recipe	receta	ricetta	receita
Rezept(n)	ordonnance	prescription	receta	ricetta medica	receita
Rezeption(f)	réception	reception	recepción	reception	recepção
Rheumatismus(m)	rhumatisme	rheumatism	reumatismo	reumatismo	reumatismo
Rhythmus(m)	cadence	rate, rhythm	cadencia	cadenza	cadência
richten auf	braquer	aim	apuntar	puntare	apontar
richten, steuern	diriger	direct, guide, point	dirigir, guiar	dirigere	dirigir
Richter(in f)m	juge	judge	juez	giudice	juíz
richtig	juste, exact, e	right	exacto, a	giusto, a	certo, a
richtig	correct, e	correct, proper	correcto, a	corretto, a	correcto, a
richtig	correctement	properly	correctamente	correttamente	correctamente
Richtung(f)	direction	direction	dirección	direzione	direcção
Richtung(f)	sens	direction, way	sentido	senso	sentido
riechen	sentir	smell	oler	odorare, annusare	cheirar
Riegel(m), Schloß(n)	verrou	bolt, lock	cerrojo	catenaccio	ferrolho
Riemen(m)	courroie	belt; strap	correa	cinghia	correia
Riemen(m), Gurt(m)	sangle	strap	cincha, correa	cinghia	correia
riesig	colossal, e	colossal	colosal	colossale	colossal
riesig, gigantisch	géant, e	giant	gigante	gigante	gigante
riesig	énorme	enormous, huge	enorme	enorme	enorme
Riff(n)	récif	reef	arrecife	scoglio	recife
Rille(f), Nute(f)	rainure	groove	ranura	scanalatura	ranhura
Rinde(f)	écorce	bark	corteza	scorza, buccia	casca
Ring(m)	anneau	ring	anilla, anillo	anello	anel
Ring(m)	bague	ring	anillo, sortija	anello	anel
ringförmig	annulaire	annular, ring-	anular	anulare	anelar
Rinnstein(m)	caniveau	gutter	arroyo	canaletto di scolo	valeta
Rippe(f)	côte	rib	costilla	costola	costela
Risiko(n)	risque	risk	riesgo	rischio	risco
riskieren	risquer	risk	arriesgar	rischiare	arriscar
Riß(m), Spalte(f)	fissure, fente	crack, fissure	fisura, grieta	fessura, crepa	fissura; fenda
Riß(m), Hautriß(m)	gerçure	chap(ped)	grieta	screpolatura	greta
rissig	craquelé, e	crackled, cracked	agrietado, a	screpolato, a	estalado, a
Rivale(m), Rivalin(f)	rival, e	rival; competitor	rival	rivale	rival
Rivalität(f)	rivalité	rivalry	rivalidad	rivalità	rivalidade
Roboter(m)	robot	robot	robot	robot	robot
robust, stark	robuste	robust, sturdy	robusto, a	robusto, a	robusto, a
Rock(m)	jupe	skirt	falda	gonna	saia
Roggen(m)	seigle	rye	centeno	segale	centeio
roh	cru, e	raw	crudo, a	crudo, a	cru, a
roh	brut, e	raw; crude	bruto, a	grezzo, a	bruto, a
Rohkost(f)	crudité	salad, crudité	ensalada	insalata mista	salada
Röhre(f), Leitung(f)	conduit(e)	pipe	caño, conducto	condotto(a)	cano, tubo
Röhre(f), Schlauch(m)	tuyau(terie)	pipe	tubo, caño	tubo, tubazione	tubo, cano
Rolle(f)	rôle	role, part	cometido, función	ruolo, parte	função
Rolle(f)	rôle	role	papel	parte, ruolo	papel
Rolle(f), Walze(f)	rouleau	roll	rollo	rotolo; rullo	rolo
rollen	rouler	roll	rodar	rotolare	rolar
Roman(m)	roman	novel	novela	romanzo	romance
romantisch	romantique	romantic	romántico, a	romantico, a	romântico, a
Röntgenbild(n)	radiographie	X-ray; radiography	radiografía	radiografia	radiografia
rosafarben	rose	pink	rosa	rosa	cor-de-rosa
Rose(f)	rose	rose	rosa	rosa	rosa
Rost(m)	rouille	rust	herrumbre	ruggine	ferrugem
rot	rouge	red	rojo, a	rosso, a	vermelho, a
Röteln(pl)	rubéole	German measles	rubéola	rosolia	rubéola
rothaarig	roux, rousse	auburn; reddish	pelirrojo, a	rosso, a	ruivo, a
Route(f), Strecke(f)	itinéraire	itinerary, route	itinerario	itinerario	itinerário
Route(f), Weg(m)	itinéraire, route	route	ruta, itinerario	rotta, itinerario	caminho, rota
Routine(f)	routine	routine	rutina	routine, tran tran	rotina
Rubin(m)	rubis	ruby	rubí	rubino	rubi
Ruck(m), Stoß(m)	secousse	jolt, jerk	sacudida	scossa	abalo
Rück-; Hinter-	derrière, arrière	rear	trasero, a; de atrás	dietro, indietro	traseiro, a
Rücken(m)	dos	back	espalda	schiena	costas
Rückfahrkarte(f)	billet A/R	return ticket	billete ida/vuelta	andata e ritorno	bilhete ida/volta

G

German	French	English	Spanish	Italian	Portuguese
Rückgang(m)	régression	regression	regresión	regresso	regressão
Rückkehr(f)	retour	return	regreso, vuelta	ritorno	regresso, volta
Rückruf(m)	rappel	recall	recuerdo	richiamo	lembrança
Rucksack(m)	sac à dos	rucksack	mochila	zaino	mochila
Rückschluß(m)	déduction	deduction	deducción	deduzione	dedução
Rückseite(f)	envers	reverse, back	revés	rovescio	avesso
Rückspiegel(m)	rétroviseur	rear-view mirror	retrovisor	retrovisore	retrovisor
Rückstand(m)	résidu	residue	residuo	residuo	resíduo
Rückstoß(m)	recul	recoil	retroceso	rinculo	recuo
Rücktritt(m)	démission	resignation	dimisión	dimissione	demissão
rückwärts	arrière(en)	backward(s)	atrás(para)	indietro	trás(para)
Rückzahlung(f)	remboursement	repayment	reembolso	rimborso	reembolso
Ruder(n)	rame	oar	remo	remo	remo
Ruder(n), Steur(n)	gouvernail	rudder	timón	timone	leme
rudern	ramer	row	remar	remare	remar
Rudersport(m)	aviron	rowing	remo; piragua	canottaggio	remo
Ruf(m)(Zu-, An-)	appel	call	llamada	chiamata	chamada
rufen(an =), heißen	appeler	call	llamar	chiamare	chamar
Rüge(f)	blâme	blame; reprimand	reprobación	biasimo	censura
Ruhe(f)	repos	rest	descanso	riposo	descanço
Ruhe(f), Stille(f)	calme	calm, quiet, still	calma, sosiego	calma, quiete	calma, sossego
ruhig	tranquille	quiet, still, calm	tranquilo, a	tranquillo, a	tranquilo, a
ruhig, still	calme	calm, quiet, still	tranquilo, a	calmo, a	calmo, a
Ruhm(m)	gloire	glory	gloria	gloria	glória
Ruhm(m)	renommée	fame	fama	fama	fama
rühren	remuer	stir	remover	mescolare	mexer
rühren	émouvoir	move	conmover	commuovere	comover
rühren	toucher, émouvoir	affect	afectar	commuovere	afectar
Rührung(f)	émotion	emotion	emoción	emozione	emoção
Ruine(f)	ruine	ruin	ruina	rovina	ruína
ruinieren	ruiner	ruin	arruinar	rovinare	arruinar
Rumpf(m)	coque	hull	casco	scafo	casco
rund	rond, e	round	redondo, a	rotondo, a	redondo, a
rund	circulaire	circular	circular	circolare	circular
Rundfahrt(f)(-reise)	circuit	tour	circuito	giro, circuito	circuito
rüstig, kräftig	vigoureux, se	vigorous, strong	vigoroso, a	vigoroso, a	vigoroso, a
Rutschbahn(f)	toboggan	slide, chute	tobogán	scivolo	escorrega
rutschen	glisser	slip, slide	resbalar	scivolare	escorregar

S

German	French	English	Spanish	Italian	Portuguese
Saal(m), Raum(m)	salle	room	sala	sala, stanza	sala
sabbern	baver	dribble	babear	sbavare	babar-se
Säbel(m)	sabre	sabre	sable	sciabola	sabre
Sabotage(f)	sabotage	sabotage	sabotaje	sabotaggio	sabotagem
sabotieren	saboter	sabotage	sabotear	sabotare	sabotar
Sachen(pl)	affaires	things	cosas	roba, oggetti	coisas
Sack(m)	sac	sack	saco	sacco	saco
Sadist(in f)m	sadique	sadist	sádico, a	sadico, a	sádico, a
sadistisch	sadique	sadistic	sádico, a	sadico, a	sádico, a
säen	semer	sow	sembrar	seminare	semear
Safe(m)	coffre-fort	safe	caja fuerte	cassaforte	cofre-forte
Saft(m)	sève	sap	savia	linfa	seiva
Saft(m)	jus	juice	jugo	succo	sumo
Saft(m), Sirup(m)	sirop	cordial, squash	almíbar	sciroppo	xarope
Säge(f)	scie	saw	sierra	sega	serra
sagen	dire	say	decir	dire	dizer

German	French	English	Spanish	Italian	Portuguese
sagen	dire	tell	decir	dire	contar
sägen	scier	saw	serrar, aserrar	segare	serrar
Sahne(f)	crème	cream	crema	crema	creme
saisonbedingt	saisonnier, ière	seasonal	temporero, a	stagionale	sazonal
Salat(m); Kopfsalat(m)	salade	salad; lettuce	ensalada; lechuga	insalata	salada
Salbe(f)	pommade	ointment, cream	pomada	pomata	pomada
Salve(f)	rafale	burst, hail	ráfaga	raffica	rajada
Salz(n)	sel	salt	sal	sale	sal
salzig	salé, e	salty	salado, a	salato, a	salgado, a
Samen(m)	semence	seed	simiente	seme, semente	semente
Samenkorn(n)	graine	seed	semilla	seme	semente
Sammelbecken(n)	réceptacle	receptacle	receptáculo	ricettacolo	receptáculo
sammeln	rassembler	gather(together)	juntar	radunare	juntar
sammeln	réunir	gather(together)	reunir	riunire	reunir
sammeln	collectionner	collect	coleccionar	collezionare	coleccionar
Sammlung(f)	collection	collection	colección	collezione	colecção
Samstag(m)	samedi	Saturday	sábado	sabato	sábado
Samt(m)	velours	velvet	terciopelo	velluto	veludo
Sand(m)	sable	sand	arena	sabbia	areia
Sandale(f)	sandale	sandal	sandalia	sandalo	sandália
sanft	doux, ce	soft	suave	morbido, a	macio, a
Sänger(in f)m	chanteur, se	singer	cantante	cantante	cantor, a
Saphir(m)	saphir	sapphire	zafiro	zaffiro	safira
Sardine(f)	sardine	sardine	sardina	sardina	sardinha
Sarg(m)	cercueil	coffin	ataúd	bara	caixão
Satellit(m)	satellite	satellite	satélite	satellite	satélite
Satin(m)	satin	satin	raso, satén	raso	cetim
Sattel(m)	selle	saddle	silla	sella	sela
Sattel(m)	selle	saddle	sillín	sellino	selim
sättigen	saturer	saturate	saturar	saturare	saturar
Satz(m)	phrase	sentence	frase	frase	frase
Satz(m)	ensemble	set	conjunto	insieme	conjunto
Satz(m)	dépôt	deposit	depósito	deposito	depósito
sauber	propre	clean	limpio, a	pulito, a	limpo, a
Säuberungsaktion(f)	purge	purge	purga	purga	purga
sauer	aigre	sour	agrio, a	aspro, a; agro, a	azedo, a
Sauerstoff(m)	oxygène	oxygen	oxígeno	ossigeno	oxigénio
saugen	téter	suck	mamar	poppare	mamar
Säugetier(n)	mammifère	mammal	mamífero	mammifero	mamífero
Saugnapf(m)	ventouse	suction disc	ventosa	ventosa	ventosa
Säule(f)	colonne	column	columna	colonna	coluna
Saum(m)	couture	seam	costura	cucito	costura
Sauna(f)	sauna	sauna	sauna	sauna	sauna
Säure(f)	acide	acid	ácido	acido	ácido
Savanne(f)	savane	savannah	sabana	savana	savana
schäbig	sordide	sordid	sórdido, a	squallido, a	sórdido, a
Schachspiel(n)	échecs	chess	ajedrez	scacchi	xadrês
Schachtel(f)	boîte	box	caja	scatola	caixa
schade!	dommage(c'est)	pity(it is a)	pena(es una)	peccato(è)	pena(e')
schade!(wie ---)	dommage(quel)	pity(what a)	lástima(qué)	peccato(che)	pena(que)
Schädel(m)	crâne	skull	cráneo	cranio	crâneo
Schaden(m)	dégât(s)	damage	daño(s), estrago(s)	danno	estrago
Schaden(m)	dommage	damage	perjuicio, daño	danno	prejuízo, dano
Schaden(m)	préjudice	wrong, harm	perjuicio	pregiudizio, danno	prejuízo
Schadenersatz(m)	indemnité	allowance	dietas	indennità	ajuda de custo
schädlich	nuisible	harmful	dañino, a	nocivo, a	nocivo, a
schädlich	nocif, ive	harmful	nocivo, a	nocivo, a	nocivo, a
Schaf(n)	mouton	sheep; mutton	carnero; oveja	pecora; montone	carneiro; ovelha
Schaf-	ovin	ovine	ovino	ovino	ovino
Schäfer(in f)m	berger, ère	shepherd, -ess	pastor, a	pastore, pastorella	pastor, a
Schal(m)	cache-nez	scarf	bufanda	sciarpa	cachecol
Schal(m)	châle	shawl	chal	scialle	xale
Schale(f)	cuvette	basin, bowl	palangana	catino	bacia
Schale(f), Muschel(f)	coquille	shell	concha	conchiglia	concha
Schale(f)	coquille, coque	shell	cáscara	guscio	casca
schälen	peler	peel	mondar	sbucciare	descascar
schälen	éplucher	peel	pelar	sbucciare	descascar
Schalentier(n)	crustacé	shell-fish	crustáceo	crostaceo	crustáceo

German	French	English	Spanish	Italian	Portuguese
schalldicht	insonore	sound-proof	insonoro, a	insonoro, a	insonoro, a
Schallplatte(f)	disque	record	disco	disco	disco
Schalter(m)	bouton	switch	interruptor, botón	bottone, pulsante	interruptor
Schalter(m)	interrupteur	switch	interruptor	interruttore	interruptor
Schalter(m)	commutateur	switch	conmutador	commutatore	comutador
Schalter(m)	guichet	counter, position	ventanilla	sportello	guichê, postigo
Scham(f), Schande(f)	honte	shame	vergüenza	vergogna	vergonha
schämen, sich	honte(avoir)	ashamed(be)	vergüenza(tener)	vergognarsi	vergonha(ter)
Schande(f)	déshonneur	dishonour	deshonor	disonore	desonra
scharf	vif, vive	keen	agudo, a; vivo, a	vivo, a	vivo, a
scharf	aiguisé, e	sharp	afilado, a	affilato, a	afiado, a
scharf	piquant, e	spicy, hot	picante	piccante	picante
schärfen	aiguiser	sharpen	afilar	affilare	afiar
scharfsinnig	judicieux, se	judicious	juicioso, a	giudizioso, a	judicioso, a
scharfsinnig, listig	subtil, e	subtle	sutil	sottile	subtil
Scharnier(n)	charnière	hinge	bisagra	cerniera	gonzo, dobradiça
Schatten(m)	ombre	shadow	sombra	ombra	sombra
Schatz(m)	trésor	treasure	tesoro	tesoro	tesouro
schätzen	estimer	estimate, value	valorar, estimar	stimare, valutare	estimar
schätzen	apprécier	appreciate	apreciar	apprezzare	apreciar
Schatzmeister(in f)m	trésorier, ière	treasurer	tesorero, a	tesoriere, a	tesoureiro, a
Schätzung(f)	évaluation	assessment	evaluación	valutazione	avaliação
Schätzung(f)	estimation	estimate	estimación	stima, valutazione	estimativa
Schau, Ausstellung(f)	exhibition	exhibition	exhibición	esibizione	exibição
schauen, an = sehen	regarder	look(at)	mirar	guardare	olhar
Schauer(m)	frisson	shiver	escalofrío	brivido	arrepio
Schaufel(f); Spaten(m)	pelle	spade; shovel	pala	pala	pá
Schaufenster(n)	vitrine	shop-window	escaparate	vetrina	montra, vitrina
Schaufensterpuppe(f)	mannequin	dummy; model	maniquí	manichino	manequim
Schaukel(f)	balançoire	swing; see-saw	columpio	altalena	baloiço
schaukeln	tanguer	pitch	cabecear	beccheggiare	balouçar-se
Schaum(m), Gischt(f)	écume	foam, froth	espuma	schiuma	espuma
Schaum(m)	mousse	froth, foam	espuma	schiuma	espuma
Schauspieler(in f)m	acteur, actrice	actor, actress	actor, actriz	attore, attrice	actor, actriz
Schauspieler(in f)m	comédien, ne	actor, actress	actor, actriz	attore, attrice	actor, actriz
Scheck(m)	chèque	cheque	cheque, talón	assegno	cheque
Scheckheft(n)	chéquier	cheque book	talonario(cheques)	libretto di assegni	livro de cheques
Scheibe(f)	rondelle	washer	arandela	rondella	anilha
Scheibe(f)	rondelle	slice	rodaja	fettina, fetta	rodela
Scheibe(f)	tranche	slice	rebanada	fetta	fatia
Scheibe(f); Spiegel(m)	glace; miroir	window; mirror	cristal; luna	vetro; specchio	vidro; espelho
Scheibe(f)(Fenster-)	vitre	pane, window	cristal, vidrio	vetro	vidro
Scheide(f)(Anat.)	vagin	vagina	vagina	vagina	vagina
scheiden lassen, sich	divorcer	divorce	divorciar(se)	divorziare	divorciar-se
Scheidung(f)	divorce	divorce	divorcio	divorzio	divórcio
Schein(m), Genehmigung	permis	licence; permit	permiso	permesso, licenza	licença
scheinen	sembler	seem	parecer	sembrare	parecer
scheinen, erscheinen	paraître	seem, appear, look	parecer	parere, sembrare	parecer
Scheinwerfer(m)	projecteur	projector	proyector	proiettore	projector
Scheinwerfer(m)	phare(s)	headlight	faro(s)	fanale, faro(-ri)	faróis
Scheit(n)	bûche	log	leño	tronco, ceppo	acha
scheitern	échouer	fail	fracasar	fallire	falhar
Schellfisch(m)	morue	cod	bacalao	baccalà; merluzzo	bacalhau
schelmisch	coquin, e	mischievous	travieso, a	birbante, birichino, a	travesso, a; maroto, a
Schema(n)	schéma	diagram	esquema	schema	esquema
Schenkel(m)	cuisse	leg	muslo; pierna	coscia	perna
Schenkel(m)	cuisse	thigh	muslo	coscia	coxa
schenken, an = bieten	offrir	give; offer	ofrecer	offrire, regalare	oferecer
Schere(f)	ciseaux	scissors	tijeras	forbici	tesoura
scherzen	plaisanter	joke	bromear	scherzare	gracejar
Scheune(f)	grange	barn	granero	fienile	celeiro
scheußlich	abominable	awful	abominable	abominevole	abominável
Schicht(f)	couche	layer	capa	strato	camada
schick	chic, élégant	smart, chic	elegante	elegante	elegante
schicken, senden(ab =)	envoyer	send	enviar	inviare	enviar
Schicksal(n)	destinée	destiny	destino	destino	destino
Schicksal(n)	destin	fate, destiny	destino, sino	destino	destino
Schicksal(n)	sort	fate	suerte, destino	sorte, destino	sorte, destino

German	French	English	Spanish	Italian	Portuguese
Schicksal(n)	fatalité	fatality, fate	fatalidad	fatalità	fatalidade
schieben, stoßen	pousser	push	empujar	spingere	empurrar
Schiedsrichter(in f)m	arbitre	referee	árbitro	arbitro	árbitro
schief	travers(de)	askew	través(de)	traverso(di)	través(de)
Schiefer(m)	ardoise	slate	pizarra	ardesia	ardósia, lousa
schielen	loucher	squint	bizquear	strabico(essere)	estrábico(ser)
Schienbein(n)	tibia	tibia	tibia	tibia	tíbia
Schiene(f)	rail	rail; track	carril	rotaia	carril
schießen, feuern	tirer	shoot, fire	disparar	tirare, sparare	atirar, disparar
schießen(Tor-)	marquer	score	marcar	segnare	marcar
Schießen(n)	tir	shooting, firing	tiro	tiro	tiro
Schiff(n)	navire	ship	navío	nave	navio
Schiff(n)	bateau	boat, ship	barco	imbarcazione, nave	barco
Schiff(n)	vaisseau	vessel, ship	nave, navío	vascello, nave	navio
Schiffbruch(m)	naufrage	wreck	naufragio	naufragio	naufrágio
Schild(n)	panneau	sign, notice	señal, letrero	cartello	sinal
Schild(m)(Reklame-)	enseigne	sign	letrero	insegna	letreiro
Schild(n)	étiquette	label, tag	etiqueta	etichetta	rótulo
Schilddrüse(f)	thyroïde	thyroid(gland)	tiroides	tiroide	tiróide
Schildkröte(f)	tortue	tortoise; turtle	tortuga	tartaruga	tartaruga
Schimmer(m)	lueur	gleam, glow	resplandor	chiarore, luce	luz, clarão
schimpfen	gronder	scold, tell off	regañar	sgridare	ralhar
Schimpfwort(n)	gros mot	bad word	palabrota	parolaccia	palavrão
Schinken(m)	jambon	ham	jamón	prosciutto	fiambre
Schlaf(m)	sommeil	sleep	sueño	sonno	sono
Schlafanzug(m)	pyjama	pyjamas	pijama	pigiama	pijama
Schläfe(f)	tempe	temple	sien	tempia	têmpora
schlafen	dormir	sleep	dormir	dormire	dormir
schlafend	endormi, e	asleep	dormido, a	addormentato, a	adormecido, a
schlafen gehen	coucher(se)	go to bed	ir a la cama	andare a letto	deitar-se
schlaff, lose	desserré, e	slack	flojo, a	allentato, a	frouxo, a
schlaff, lose	détendu, e	slack, loose	aflojado, a	allentato, a	frouxo, a; lasso, a
schlaff	mou, molle	lethargic	fofo, a	molle; fiacco, a	mole; fraco, a
Schlaflosigkeit(f)	insomnie	insomnia	insomnio	insonnia	insónia
Schläfrigkeit(f)	somnolence	drowsiness	somnolencia	sonnolenza	sonolência
Schlafrock(m)	robe de chambre	dressing gown	bata	vestaglia	roupão
Schlafsack(m)	sac de couchage	sleeping bag	saco de dormir	sacco a pelo	saco-cama
Schlaftablette(f)	somnifère	sleeping tablet	somnífero	sonnifero	soporífero
Schlafwandler(in f)m	somnambule	sleep-walker	sonámbulo, a	sonnambulo, a	sonâmbulo, a
Schlag(m)	coup	knock, blow	golpe	colpo	golpe
schlagen	battre	beat	batir	battere	bater
Schlag(m)	tape, fessée	smack	cachete	schiaffo	palmada
schlagen, prügeln	frapper	hit, knock, strike	golpear	picchiare	bater
Schläger(Tennis-)(m)	raquette	racket	raqueta	racchetta	raqueta
Schläger(m)	raquette	bat	raqueta, pala	racchetta	raqueta
Schlägerei(f)	bagarre	fight	riña	rissa, zuffa	briga
Schlamm(m)	boue	mud	barro	fango, melma	lama
Schlamm(m)	vase	sludge, mud	limo, fango	melma	lodo
Schlange(f)	serpent	snake	serpiente	serpente	serpente
Schlange(f)	file	queue, line	fila	fila, coda	fila, bicha
Schlange(f)	queue	queue	cola	coda, fila	bicha; fila
schlank	svelte	slim, slender	esbelto, a	slanciato, a; snello, a	esbelto, a
schlank	mince	slim; slender	delgado, a	snello, a	magro, a; delgado, a
schlau, gerissen	rusé, e	crafty, cunning	astuto, a	astuto, a	astuto, a; fino, a
Schlauch(m)	tuyau	hose	manguera	tubo	mangueira
schlecht	mauvais, e	bad	malo, a	cattivo, a	mau, má
schlecht	mal	badly	mal	male	mal
Schleife(f)	boucle	loop	lazo	cappio; occhiello	laço
Schleier(m)	voile	veil	velo	velo	véu
schleppen	traîner	drag, trail, haul	arrastrar	trascinare	arrastar
schleudern	déraper	skid	patinar	slittare	derrapar
schließen	fermer	close, shut	cerrar	chiudere	fechar, cerrar
schließen, abschließen	conclure	conclude	concluir	concludere	concluir
Schließfach(n)	consigne	luggage lockers	consigna	cassetta, deposito	depósito
schlimmer	pire	worse	peor	peggio	pior
Schlitten(m)	traîneau	sleigh, sledge	trineo	slitta	trenó
Schlittschuh laufen	patiner	skate	patinar	pattinare	patinar
Schlitz(m)	fente	slit	raja	fessura; spacco	fenda

G

341

German	French	English	Spanish	Italian	Portuguese
Schloß(n)	château	castle; mansion	castillo	castello	castelo
Schloß(Tür-)(n)	serrure	lock	cerradura	serratura	fechadura
Schlucht(f); Graben(m)	ravin	ravine	barranco	burrone	barranco
Schluchzer(m)	sanglot	sob	sollozo	singhiozzo	soluço
schlucken	avaler	swallow	tragar	inghiottire, ingoiare	engolir
schlummern	sommeiller	doze	dormitar	sonnecchiare	dormitar
Schluß(m)(Abschluß m)	clôture	closure, closing	clausura	chiusura	encerramento
Schlüssel(m)	clef, clé	key	llave	chiave	chave
Schlüsselbein(n)	clavicule	collar-bone	clavícula	clavicola	clavícula
Schlüsselring(m)	porte-clefs	key-ring	llavero	portachiavi	porta-chaves
schmackhaft	savoureux, se	tasty	sabroso, a	saporito, a	saboroso, a
schmeicheln	flatter	flatter	halagar	adulare	lisonjear
schmelzen	fondre	melt	fundir	fondere	fundir
Schmelzen(n)(Ver-)	fusion	fusion, melting	fusión	fusione	fusão
Schmerz(m)	douleur	pain, ache	dolor	dolore	dor
Schmerz(m), Kummer(m)	peine	sorrow, grief	pena	pena; dolore	pena; tristeza
Schmerz(m), Weh(n)	mal	ache, pain	dolor	male	dor
Schmerzen haben	mal(avoir)	hurts(it)	dolerle a uno	male(aver)	doer
schmerzhaft	douloureux, se	painful, aching	doloroso, a	doloroso, a	doloroso, a
schmerzlindernd	sédatif, ive	sedative	sedativo, a	sedativo, a	sedativo, a
schmerzlos	indolore	painless	indoloro, a	indolore	indolor
Schmetterling(m)	papillon	butterfly	mariposa	farfalla	borboleta
Schmiere(f)	graisse	grease	grasa	grasso	massa
Schmiergelder(pl.)	pot-de-vin	bribe	soborno	bustarella	suborno
schmierig, fettig	graisseux, se	fatty, greasy	grasiento, a	unto, a	gorduroso, a
Schmierzettel(m)	brouillon	rough paper	borrador	brutta copia	rascunho
schmilzen	fondre	melt	derretir	sciogliere(-rsi)	derreter
Schminke(f)	maquillage	make-up	maquillaje	trucco	maquilhagem
schminken, sich	maquiller(se)	make-up(put on)	maquillarse	truccarsi	maquilhar-se
Schmiß(m), Schnitt(m)	balafre	gash	cuchillada	sfregio	corte, cutilada
Schmuck(m)	parure	finery, jewellery	adorno	parure	adorno
Schmuck(m)(-stück n)	bijou(x)	jewel	joya	gioiello	jóia
schmücken	décorer	decorate	decorar, adornar	ornare, adornare	ornar, adornar
Schmuckgeschäft(n)	bijouterie	jeweller's	joyería	gioielleria	joalharia
Schmuckkasten(m)	coffret	box, case	estuche	portagioie	estojo
Schmuggel(m)	contrebande	smuggling	contrabando	contrabbando	contrabando
Schmutz(m)	saleté	dirt	suciedad	sporcizia	sujidade, porcaria
Schnabel(m)	bec	beak	pico	becco	bico
Schnalle(f)	boucle	buckle	hebilla	fibbia	fivela; argola
Schnaps(m)	eau-de-vie	spirits	aguardiente	grappa, acquavite	aguardente
schnarchen	ronfler	snore	roncar	russare	ressonar, roncar
Schnauze(f)	museau	muzzle	hocico	muso	focinho
Schnecke(f)	escargot	snail	caracol	lumaca, chiocciola	caracol
Schnee(m)	neige	snow	nieve	neve	neve
Schneide(f)	lame	blade	hoja	lama	lâmina
schneiden	couper	cut	cortar	tagliare	cortar
schneiden	sectionner	cut, divide	seccionar	sezionare	seccionar
Schneider(m)	tailleur	tailor	sastre	sarto	alfaiate
Schneider(in f)m	couturier, ière	dressmaker, tailor	modista	sarto, a	costureiro, a
schnell, rasch	vite	quickly, fast	rápido, pronto	fretta(in), presto	rápido, a; depressa
schnell	rapide	rapid, fast, quick	rápido, a	rapido, a; veloce	rápido, a
schnell, rasch	prompt, e	quick, prompt	pronto, a	pronto, a	pronto, a
Schnelligkeit(f)	vélocité, vitesse	velocity	velocidad	velocità	velocidade
Schnitt(m)	coupure(peau)	cut	corte, tajo	taglio	corte, golpe
Schnitt(m)	forme	design, style	hechura	taglio, stile	corte, design
Schnitt(m)	section	section	sección	sezione	secção
schnüffeln	renifler	sniff	resoplar	tirar su col naso	fungar
Schnuller(m)	sucette	dummy	chupete	succhiotto	chupeta
Schnupfen(m)	rhume	cold	resfriado	raffreddore	constipação
Schnur(f)	ficelle	string, cord	cordel	spago	cordel, guita
Schnurrbart(m)	moustache	moustache	bigote	baffo	bigode
Schnürsenkel(m)	lacet	lace	cordón	laccio	cordão
Schock(m)	choc	shock	choque	choc, colpo	choque
Schokolade(f)	chocolat	chocolate	chocolate	cioccolato, a	chocolate
schon	déjà	already	ya	giá	já
schön	beau, belle	beautiful, fine	hermoso, a; bello, a	bello, a	belo, a; bonito, a
schön	belle	beautiful	bella	bella	bela
schön, e, er, es	belle	beautiful, fine	hermosa	bella	bonita, bela

German	French	English	Spanish	Italian	Portuguese
schönes Wetter	beau temps	fine weather	buen tiempo	bel tempo	bom tempo
Schönheit(f)	beauté	beauty	belleza	bellezza	beleza
Schönheitspflege(f)	soins de beauté	beauty treatment	cosmética	cura	tratamento
schöpfen	puiser	draw(from)	sacar	attingere	tirar, extrair
schöpfen	créer	create	crear	creare	criar
Schöpfer(in f)m	créateur, trice	creator(creative)	creador, a	creatore, trice	criador, a
schräg, schief	oblique	oblique, slanting	oblicuo, a	obliquo, a	oblíquo, a
Schrank(m)(Kleider-)	armoire	wardrobe	armario	armadio	armário
Schrank(m)	armoire	cupboard	armario	armadio	armário
Schranke(f)	barrière	barrier; gate	barrera	barriera	barreira
Schraube(f)	vis	screw	tornillo	vite	parafuso
Schraubenschlüssel(m)	clé	spanner, wrench	llave	chiave	chave
Schraubenzieher(m)	tournevis	screwdriver	destornillador	cacciavite	chave de parafusos
Schreck(m), Angst(f)	frayeur	fright	espanto	spavento	temor
Schrecken(m)	terreur	terror	terror	terrore	terror
schrecklich	terrible	terrible	terrible	terribile	terrível
schrecklich	affreux, se	awful	horrendo, a	spaventoso, a	horrível
Schrei(m)	cri	shout	grito	grido	grito
schreiben	écrire	write	escribir	scrivere	escrever
Schreibtisch(m)	bureau	desk	escritorio	scrivania	secretária
Schreibwarenladen(m)	papeterie	stationer's	papelería	cartoleria	papelaria
schreien	crier	shout, scream	gritar	gridare	gritar
Schrift(f)	écriture	writing	escritura	scrittura	escrita
Schriftsteller(in f)m	écrivain	writer	escritor, a	scrittore, -trice	escritor, a
Schriftsteller(in f)m	romancier, ière	novelist	novelista	romanziere, a	romancista
Schrifttyp(m)	caractère	letter; character	letra	carattere, lettera	carácter
Schritt(m)	pas	step; pace	paso	passo	passo
schrumpfen	rétrécir	shrink	encoger	restringere	encolher
Schubkarre(f)	brouette	wheelbarrow	carretilla	carriola	carro de mão
Schublade(f)	tiroir	drawer	cajón	cassetto	gaveta
schüchtern	timide	shy, timid	tímido, a	timido, a	tímido, a
Schüchternheit(f)	timidité	shyness, timidity	timidez	timidezza	timidez
Schuh(m)	chaussure	shoe	calzado	scarpa, e.	sapato
Schuh(m)	soulier	shoe	zapato	scarpa	sapato
Schuhe anziehen, sich	chausser(se)	put on(shoes)	calzarse	calzarsi	calçar-se
Schuld(f)	dette	debt	deuda	debito	dívida
Schuld(f)	culpabilité	guilt	culpabilidad	colpevolezza	culpabilidade
schuldig	coupable	guilty	culpable	colpevole	culpado, a
schuldig	fautif, ive	wrong(in the)	culpable	colpevole	culpado, a
Schuldirektor(m)	directeur(école)	headmaster	director(escuela)	direttore(scuola)	director(escola)
Schule(f)	école	school	escuela	scuola	escola
Schüler(in f)m	élève	pupil	alumno, a	alunno, a	aluno, a
Schüler(in f)m	écolier, ière	schoolboy/girl	colegial, a	scolaro, a	aluno, a
Schulter(f)	épaule	shoulder	hombro	spalla	ombro
Schulzeit(f)	scolarité	schooling	escolaridad	scolarità	escolaridade
Schuppe(f)	écaille	scale	escama	squama	escama
Schuppe(f)	pellicule	dandruff	caspa	forfora	caspa
Schuppen(m)	hangar	shed	cobertizo	hangar, capannone	alpendre
Schürze(f)	tablier	apron	delantal	grembiule	avental
Schüssel(f)	plat	dish, plate	fuente, plato	vassoio, piatto	travessa
schütteln	secouer	shake	sacudir	scuotere	sacudir
schütteln	agiter	shake	agitar	agitare	agitar
Schutz(m)	protection	protection	protección	protezione	protecção
schwach	faible	weak	débil	debole, fragile	fraco, a
Schwäche(f)	faiblesse	weakness(-es)	debilidad	debolezza	fraqueza
Schwäche(f), Versagen	défaillance	weakness(-es)	desfallecimiento	svenimento	desfalecimento
schwächen	affaiblir	weaken	debilitar	indebolire	enfraquecer
schwächlich, kümmer-	chétif, ive	puny, weak	endeble	gracile	débil
Schwadron; Eskadron(f)	escadron	squadron	escuadrón	squadrone; squadra	esquadrão
Schwager(m)	beau-frère	brother-in-law	cuñado	cognato	cunhado
Schwägerin(f)	belle-soeur	sister-in-law	cuñada	cognata	cunhada
Schwalbe(f)	hirondelle	swallow	golondrina	rondine	andorinha
Schwamm(m)	éponge	sponge	esponja	spugna	esponja
schwammig	spongieux, se	spongy	esponjoso, a	spugnoso, a	esponjoso, a
Schwan(m)	cygne	swan	cisne	cigno	cisne
schwanger	enceinte	pregnant	encinta	incinta	grávida
Schwangerschaft(f)	grossesse	pregnancy	embarazo	gravidanza	gravidez
Schwanken(n)	fluctuation	fluctuation	fluctuación	fluttuazione	flutuação

German	French	English	Spanish	Italian	Portuguese
schwanken	osciller	oscillate	oscilar	oscillare	oscilar
Schwanz(m)	queue	tail	rabo	coda	cauda
schwarz	noir, e	black	negro, a	nero, a	preto, a
Schwarze(f, m)	noir, e	black(person)	negro, a	negro, a	negro, a
Schwarzhändler(in f)m	trafiquant, e	trafficker; pedlar	traficante	trafficante	traficante
schwätzen, schwatzen	bavarder	chat, talk	charlar	chiacchierare	falar, conversar
schweben, gleiten	planer	glide	planear	planare	planar
schweigen	taire(se)	silent(to be)	callarse	tacere	calar-se
Schwein(n)	porc	pig; pork(meat)	cerdo	porco, maiale	porco
Schweiß(m)	sueur	sweat	sudor	sudore	suor
Schweiß(m)	transpiration	perspiration	transpiración	traspirazione	transpiração
Schweißen(n)	soudure	welding	soldadura	saldatura	soldadura
schwenken	agiter	wave	agitar	agitare	agitar
schwenken	pivoter	revolve, pivot	girar	girare, ruotare	girar; rodar
schwer	lourd, e	heavy	pesado, a	pesante	pesado, a
schwer; ernst	grave	grave, serious	grave	grave	grave
schwer	difficile	difficult	difícil	difficile	difícil
Schwere(f)	gravité	gravity	gravedad	gravità	gravidade
Schwert(n)	épée	sword	espada	spada	espada
Schwester(f)	soeur	sister	hermana	sorella	irmã
Schwiegereltern(pl.)	beaux-parents	parents-in-law	suegros	suoceri	sogros
Schwiegermutter(f)	belle-mère	mother-in-law	suegra	suocera	sogra
Schwiegersohn(m)	gendre	son-in-law	yerno	genero	genro
Schwiegertochter(f)	belle-fille	daughter-in-law	nuera	nuora	nora
Schwiegervater(m)	beau-père	father-in-law	suegro	suocero	sogro
schwierig	délicat, e	delicate	delicado, a	delicato, a	delicado, a
Schwierigkeit(f)	difficulté	difficulty	dificultad	difficoltà	dificuldade
Schwimmbad(n)	piscine	swimming-pool	piscina	piscina	piscina
schwimmen, treiben	flotter	float	flotar	galleggiare	flutuar
schwimmen	nager	swim	nadar	nuotare	nadar
Schwimmen(n)	natation, nage	swimming	natación	nuoto	natação
Schwimmer(in f)m	nageur, se	swimmer	nadador, a	nuotatore, trice	nadador, a
Schwindel(m)	vertige	dizziness	vértigo	vertigine	vertigem
Schwindel(m), Gaunerei	escroquerie	swindle	estafa, timo	truffa, imbroglio	trapaça, burla
schwingen	vibrer	vibrate	vibrar	vibrare	vibrar
schwitzen	transpirer	perspire, sweat	transpirar	traspirare	transpirar
schwitzen	suer	sweat	sudar	sudare	suar
schwören	jurer	swear	jurar	giurare	jurar
Schwung(m)	entrain	liveliness	vivacidad	brio	entusiasmo
sechs	six	six	seis	sei	seis
sechzehn	seize	sixteen	dieciséis	sedici	dezasseis
sechzig	soixante	sixty	sesenta	sessanta	sessenta
See(f)	mer	sea	mar	mare	mar
See-	maritime	maritime, sea-	marítimo, a	marittimo, a	marítimo, a
See-	naval, e	naval	naval	navale	naval
See(m)	lac	lake	lago	lago	lago
Seefahrer(m)	navigateur	navigator	navegante	navigatore	navegador
Seefahrt(f)	navigation	navigation	navegación	navigazione	navegação
Seehund(m)	phoque	seal	foca	foca	foca
Seekrankheit(f)	mal de mer	sea-sickness	mareo	mal di mare	enjôo
Seele(f)	âme	soul	alma	anima	alma
Seemann(m)	marin	sailor	marino	marinaio	marinheiro
Segel(n)	voile	sail	vela	vela	vela
Segelboot(n)	voilier	yacht, sailing boat	velero	veliero	veleiro
Segelflugzeug(n)	planeur	glider	planeador	aliante	planador
Segeln(n)	voile	sailing	vela	vela	vela
segnen	bénir	bless	bendecir	benedire	benzer
sehen	voir	see	ver	vedere	ver
Sehkraft(f)	vue	sight	vista	vista	vista
sehr	très	very	muy	molto	muito
seht!, schauen Sie!	regardez!	look!	mire(!)	guardi!, guardate!	olhe!
Seide(f)	soie	silk	seda	seta	seda
Seidentuch, Halstuch	foulard	scarf	fular, pañuelo	foulard	lenço, cachecol
Seife(f)	savon	soap	jabón	sapone	sabão
Seilbahn(f)	téléphérique	cable-car	teleférico	teleferica	teleférico
sein	être	be	ser, estar	essere	ser, estar
sein	être	be	estar	essere	estar
sein, e; ihr, ihre	sa	her; his; its	su	sua(la)	sua

344

German	French	English	Spanish	Italian	Portuguese
sein, seine, ihr, ihre	son	his; her; its	su	suo(il)	seu
seine; ihre	ses	his; her; its	sus	suoi(i); sue(le)	seus, suas
seine, ihre	sien, ne	his; hers; its	suyo, suya	suo, sua(il, la)	seu, sua
seismisch	sismique	seismic	sísmico, a	sismico, a	sísmico, a
seit	depuis	since; for	desde	da	desde
Seite(f)	côté	side	lado	lato	lado
Seite(f)	face	side	cara	faccia	face; lado
Seite(f)	page	page	página	pagina	página
seitlich	latéral, e	lateral	lateral	laterale	lateral
Sekretär(in f)m	secrétaire	secretary	secretario, a	segretario, a	secretário, a
Sekte(f)	secte	sect	secta	setta	seita
Sekunde(f)	seconde	second	segundo	secondo	segundo
selbe; gleich(der -)	même	same	mismo, a	stesso, a	mesmo, a
selbst(er, sie, es)	même(lui, elle)	self(him, her, it)	mismo, a(él, ella)	stesso, a(lui, lei)	próprio, a(ele, a)
Selbstmord(m)	suicide	suicide	suicidio	suicidio	suicídio
selten	rare	rare	raro, a	raro, a	raro, a
seltsam	étrange	strange, odd	extraño, a; raro, a	strano, a	estranho, a
seltsam	bizarre	strange, odd	raro, a	strano, a	estranho, a
seltsam, ungewohnt	insolite	unusual	insólito, a	insolito, a	insólito, a
Senat(m), Bundesrat(m)	sénat	senate	senado	senato	senado
Senator(m)	sénateur	senator	senador	senatore	senador
senden	envoyer	send	mandar, enviar	mandare, inviare	mandar, enviar
senden	diffuser	broadcast	difundir	trasmettere	transmitir
Sender(m)	émetteur	transmitter	emisor	emittente	emissor
Sendung(f), Versand(m)	envoi	sending	envío	invio	envio
Sendung(f)	émission	sending	envío	emissione	envio
Sendung(f)	émission	programme	emisión	programma	emissão
Senf(m)	moutarde	mustard	mostaza	senape	mostarda
senken	baisser	drop, lower; fall	rebajar	abbassare, calare	baixar
senkrecht	vertical, e	vertical	vertical	verticale	vertical
senkrecht	perpendiculaire	perpendicular	perpendicular	perpendicolare	perpendicular
Senkung(f)	baisse	fall, drop	baja	calo	baixa
Senkung(f)	réduction	reduction	rebaja	riduzione	desconto
sensibilisieren	sensibiliser	sensitive(make sb)	sensibilizar	sensibilizzare	sensibilizar
Sensibilität(f)	sensibilité	sensitivity	sensibilidad	sensibilità	sensibilidade
sentimental	sentimental, e	sentimental	sentimental	sentimentale	sentimental
September(m)	septembre	September	septiembre	settembre	Setembro
Serie(f)	série	series	serie	serie	série
Serum(n)	sérum	serum	suero	siero	soro
Serviette(f)	serviette	serviette, napkin	servilleta	tovagliolo	guardanapo
Sessel(m)	fauteuil	arm-chair	sillón	poltrona	poltrona
setzen, sich	asseoir(s')	sit(down)	sentarse	sedersi	sentar-se
setzen, stellen	mettre, placer	set	poner, colocar	porre, mettere	pôr, colocar
setzen, stellen	placer	place, install	colocar	collocare, porre	colocar; pôr
Seuche(f)	épidémie	epidemic	epidemia	epidemia	epidemia
seufzen	soupirer	sigh	suspirar	sospirare	suspirar
Sexualität(f)	sexualité	sexuality	sexualidad	sessualità	sexualidade
Shampoo(n)	shampooing	shampoo	champú	shampoo	champô
sich, selbst	soi(-même)	oneself	sí(mismo)	se(stesso)	si(mesmo)
sicher	sûr, e; certain, e	sure, certain	seguro, a	sicuro, a	seguro, a
sicher	assuré, e	assured	seguro, a	sicuro, a; certo, a	certo, a
sicher	certain, e	certain, sure	cierto, a	certo, a; sicuro, a	certo, a
sicher	sauf, ve	safe	salvo, a	salvo, a	salvo, a
Sicherheit(f)	sûreté	safety	seguridad	sicurezza	segurança
Sicherheit(f)	sécurité	security; safety	seguridad	sicurezza	segurança
sicherlich	certainement	certainly	ciertamente	certamente	certamente
Sicht(-weite)(f)	visibilité	visibility	visibilidad	visibilità	visibilidade
sichtbar	visible	visible	visible	visibile	visível
sichtbar machen	visualiser	display	visualizar	visualizzare	visualizar
sie	elle	she	ella	essa; lei; ella	ela
sie	elles	they	ellas	esse, loro	elas
sie	ils	they	ellos	essi; loro	eles
Sie	vous	you	usted(es)	lei, loro(pl.)	você
sieben	sept	seven	siete	sette	sete
siebzehn	dix-sept	seventeen	diecisiete	diciassette	dezassete
siebzig	soixante-dix	seventy	setenta	settanta	setenta
Sieg(m)	victoire	victory	victoria	vittoria	vitória
Siegel(n)	sceau	seal	sello	sigillo	selo

G

German	French	English	Spanish	Italian	Portuguese
Sieger(in f)m	vainqueur	winner; victor	vencedor, a	vincitore, trice	vencedor, a
Signal(n)	signal	signal	señal	segnale	sinal
Silbe(f)	syllabe	syllable	sílaba	sillaba	sílaba
Silber(n)	argent	silver	plata	argento	prata
Silbermöwe(f)	goéland	gull	gaviota	gabbiano	gaivota
Silhouette(f)	silhouette	outline	silueta	sagoma; silhouette	silhueta
singen	chanter	sing	cantar	cantare	cantar
sinken, versenken	couler, enfoncer	sink	hundir	affondare	afundar
Sinn(m)	esprit	mind	espíritu	mente	espírito
Sinnestäuschung(f)	hallucination	hallucination	alucinación	allucinazione	alucinação
sinnlich	sensuel, le	sensual	sensual	sensuale	sensual
Sinnlichkeit(f)	sensualité	sensuality	sensualidad	sensualità	sensualidade
sinnreich	ingénieux, se	ingenious	ingenioso, a	ingegnoso, a	engenhoso, a
Sippe(f)	clan	clan	clan	clan	clã
Sirene(f)	sirène	siren	sirena	sirena	sirene
Sirup(m)	sirop	syrup, medicine	jarabe	sciroppo	xarope
Sitten(f, pl)	moeurs	morals	costumbres	costumi	costumes
Sitz(m)	siège	seat	asiento	sedia	assento
sitzen	assis, e	seated	sentado, a	seduto, a	sentado, a
Sitzplatz(m)	place	seat	sitio, asiento	posto	lugar
Sitzung(f)	séance	session; meeting	sesión	seduta	sessão
Sitzung(f)	session	session	sesión	sessione	sessão
Skalpell(n)	bistouri	scalpel, bistoury	bisturí	bisturi	bisturi
Skandal(m)	scandale	scandal	escándalo	scandalo	escândalo
Skelett(n)	squelette	skeleton	esqueleto	scheletro	esqueleto
skeptisch	sceptique	sceptic(al)	escéptico, a	scettico, a	céptico, a
Ski(m)	ski	ski	esquí	sci	esqui
skifahren	skier	ski	esquiar	sciare	esquiar
Skizze(f)	croquis	sketch(-es)	croquis	schizzo	esboço
Sklave(m), Sklavin(f)	esclave	slave	esclavo, a	schiavo, a	escravo, a
Sklaverei(f)	esclavage	slavery	esclavitud	schiavitù	escravatura
Sklerose(f)	sclérose	sclerosis(-ses)	esclerósis	sclerosi	esclerose
Skoliose(f)	scoliose	scoliosis	escoliosis	scoliosi	escoliose
Skonto(m)	escompte	discount	descuento	sconto	desconto
Skorpion(m)	scorpion	scorpion	escorpión	scorpione	escorpião
Skrupel(m)	scrupule	scruple	escrúpulo	scrupolo	escrúpulo
Skulptur(f)	sculpture	sculpture	escultura	scultura	escultura
Smaragd(m)	émeraude	emerald	esmeralda	smeraldo	esmeralda
Smoking(m)	smoking	dinner-jacket	esmoquin	smoking	smoking
Snobismus(m)	snobisme	snobbery	esnobismo	snobismo	snobismo
so	ainsi	so, thus	así	così	assim
so	si	so	tan	così	tão
so(sehr), derartig	tellement, si	so(-much, -many)	tanto, a; tan	talmente	tanto, a
so viel, e	tant	so much, so many	tanto, tan	tanto	tanto
sobald	dès(que)	as soon as	desde	fin da	logo que
Socke(f), Strumpf(m)	chaussette(s)	sock	calcetín(es)	calza, e; calzini	peúga
Socke(f)	socquette	sock(ankle-)	calcetín	calzino	meias
Sockel(m)	socle	base	zócalo	zoccolo	soco, pedestal
Sofa(n)	canapé	sofa	sofá, canapé	divano, canapè	canapé, sofá
sofort	immédiatement	immediately	immediatamente	immediatamente	imediatamente
sofort, sogleich	aussitôt	straight away	seguida(en)	subito, appena	imediatamente
Software(f)	logiciel	software	logicial	software	software
sogar; selbst	même	even	aun; incluso	anche; perfino	mesmo(que)
sogleich, sofort	suite(tout de)	once(at)	seguida(en)	subito	imediatamente
Sohle(f)	semelle	sole	suela	suola	sola
Sohn(m)	fils	son	hijo	figlio	filho
solche(r, s); so ein	tel, le	such a, such(pl.)	tal	tale	tal
Soldat(m)	soldat	soldier	soldado	soldato	soldado
Söldner(m)	mercenaire	mercenary	mercenario	mercenario	mercenário
Solidarität(f)	solidarité	solidarity	solidaridad	solidarietà	solidaridade
solide, fest	solide	solid, strong	sólido, a	solido, a	sólido, a
Sommer(m)	été	summer	verano	estate	verão
sommerlich	estival, e	summer	estival	estivo, a	estival
Sonate(f)	sonate	sonata	sonata	sonata	sonata
Sonde(f)	sonde	probe	sonda	sonda	sonda
Sonderangebot(n)	réclame(en)	offer(on)	reclamo(de)	offerta(in)	promoção(em)
Sonne(f)	soleil	sun	sol	sole	sol
Sonne scheint(die)	soleil(il fait)	sunny(it's)	sol(hace)	sole(c'è il)	sol(está)

German	French	English	Spanish	Italian	Portuguese
Sonnen-	solaire	solar	solar	solare	solar
Sonnenbrand(m)	coup de soleil	sunburn	insolación	scottatura	insolação
Sonnenschirm(m)	ombrelle	sunshade, parasol	sombrilla	ombrello, parasole	sombrinha
Sonnenschirm(m)	parasol	parasol, sunshade	parasol	ombrellone	guarda-sol
Sonnenstich(m)	insolation	sunstroke	insolación	insolazione	insolação
Sonnenuntergang(m)	coucher(soleil)	sunset	puesta de sol	tramonto	pôr do sol
sonnig	ensoleillé, e	sunny	soleado, a	soleggiato, a	soalheiro, a
Sonntag(m)	dimanche	Sunday	domingo	domenica	domingo
Sorge(f)	souci	worry	preocupación	preoccupazione	preocupação
Sorge(f)	inquiétude	anxiety, worry	inquietud	inquietudine	inquietação
sorgen, sich; plagen, s.	soucier(se)	worry	preocuparse	preoccuparsi	preocupar-se
sorgenvoll	soucieux, se	worried	preocupado, a	preoccupato, a	preocupado, a
Sorgfalt(f)	attention	care, caution	cuidado	accuratezza	atenção, cuidado
sorgfältig	méticuleux, se	meticulous	meticuloso, a	meticoloso, a	meticuloso, a
sorgfältig	soigneux, se	neat, tidy	cuidadoso, a	accurato, a	cuidadoso, a
Sorte(f), Art(f)	sorte, espèce	sort, kind, type	especie, género	specie, genere	espécie, género
sortieren	trier	sort(out)	escoger, separar	scegliere, smistare	escolher, triar
Sortiment(n)	assortiment	assortment, set	surtido	assortimento	sortimento
Soße(f)	sauce	sauce	salsa	sugo; salsa	molho
Souveränität(f)	souveraineté	sovereignty	soberanía	sovranità	soberania
sozial	social, e	social	social	sociale	social
Sozialismus(m)	socialisme	socialism	socialismo	socialismo	socialismo
Soziologie(f)	sociologie	sociology	sociología	sociologia	sociologia
Spachtel(f)	spatule	spatula	espátula	spatola	espátula
Spalt(m)	fente	split; slot; slit	grieta	fessura	fenda
Spalt(m), Bresche(f)	brèche	breach, gap	brecha	breccia	brecha
Spalte(f)	crevasse	crevice	grieta	crepa, crepaccio	fenda
Spalte(f)	faille	break, fault	falla	faglia	falha
spalten	fendre	split, slit	rajar, partir	spaccare	fender, rachar
Spaltung(f)(Atom)	fission	fission	fisión	fissione	fissão
spannen	tendre	tighten; stretch	tender	tendere	estender, esticar
spannend	passionnant, e	fascinating	apasionante	appassionante	apaixonante
Spannung(f)	tension	tension	tensión	tensione	tensão
Spannung(f)	suspense	suspense	suspense	suspense	suspense
sparen	épargner	save	ahorrar	risparmiare	poupar
sparen	économiser	save, economise	economizar	economizzare	economizar
sparen	gagner	save	ganar	guadagnare	ganhar
Sparer(in f)m	épargnant, e	saver, investor	ahorrador, a	risparmiatore, trice	aforrador, a
spät	tard	late	tarde	tardi	tarde
später	ultérieur, e	later	ulterior	ulteriore	ulterior
später	plus tard	later	más tarde	più tardi	mais tarde
spätere(r, s)	postérieur, e	later	posterior	posteriore	posterior
Spatz(m)	moineau	sparrow	gorrión	passero	pardal
spazieren = gehen	promener	walk(go for a)	pasear	passeggiare	passear
Spaziergang(m)	promenade	walk; drive; ride	paseo	passeggiata	passeio
Speiche(f)	rayon	spoke	radio	raggio	raio
Speichel(m)	salive	saliva	saliva	saliva	saliva
Speicher(m), Dachboden	grenier	attic, loft	desván	solaio; granaio	sótão
Speiseröhre(f)	oesophage	oesophagus	esófago	esofago	esófago
Spekulation(f)	spéculation	speculation	especulación	speculazione	especulação
Sperma(n)	sperme	sperm	esperma	sperma	esperma
Sperre(f)	barrage	blockade	cordón(policía)	posto di blocco	barreira
sperrig, lästig	encombrant, e	bulky, cumbersome	voluminoso, a	imgombrante	volumoso, a
Spezialist(in f)m	spécialiste	specialist	especialista	specialista	especialista
Spezialität(f)	spécialité	speciality	especialidad	specialità	especialidade
speziell, eigen	spécial, e	special	especial	speciale	especial
spezifieren	spécifier	specify, state	especificar	specificare	especificar
spezifisch	spécifique	specific	específico, a	specifico, a	específico, a
Sphäre(f)	sphère	sphere	esfera	sfera	esfera
Spiegel(m)	miroir	mirror	espejo	specchio	espelho
Spiel(n)	jeu	game	juego	gioco	jogo
Spiel(n)	partie	game	partida	partita	jogada, jogo
Spiel(n)	match	match(-es), game	partido	partita	desafio, partida
spielen	jouer	play	tocar	suonare	tocar
spielen	jouer	play	jugar	giocare	jogar, brincar
spielen	jouer	act	desempeñar	recitare	representar
spielen	jouer	gamble	jugar	giocare	jogar
Spieler(in f)m	joueur, se	player	jugador, a	giocatore, trice	jogador, a

G

German	French	English	Spanish	Italian	Portuguese
Spielerei(f)	fantaisie	fancy; fantasy	fantasía	fantasia	fantasia
Spielerei(f)	gadget	gadget	chisme, mecanismo	gadget	aparelho
Spielkarte(f)	carte à jouer	card	carta	carta da gioco	carta
Spielmarke(f)	jeton	counter, token	ficha	gettone	ficha
Spielzeug(n)	jouet	toy	juguete	giocattolo	brinquedo
Spieß(m)	broche	spit	asador	spiedo	espeto
Spinne(f)	araignée	spider	araña	ragno	aranha
Spion(m), Spionin(f)	espion, ne	spy	espía	spia	espião, espia
Spionage(f)	espionnage	spying, espionage	espionaje	spionaggio	espionagem
Spirale(f)	spirale	spiral	espiral	spirale	espiral
Spirale(f)	stérilet	coil	espiral	spirale	esterilete
spitz	pointu, e	pointed, sharp	puntiagudo, a	appuntito, a	pontiagudo, a
Spitze(f)	pointe	point	punta	punta	ponta
Spitze(f)	dentelle	lace	puntilla	merletto	renda
Spitzname(m)	surnom	nickname	apodo, mote	soprannome	alcunha, apelido
Sponsor(m)	sponsor	sponsor	patrocinador	sponsor	patrocinador
sponsorisieren	parrainer	sponsor	patrocinar	sponsorizzare	apadrinhar
spontan	spontané, e	spontaneous	espontáneo, a	spontaneo, a	espontâneo, a
Sport(m)	sport	sport	deporte	sport	desporto
Sportler(in f)m	sportif, ive	sportsman/-woman	deportista	sportivo, a	desportista
sportlich; Sport-	sportif, ive	sporty, athletic	deportivo, a	sportivo, a	desportivo, a
Sportplatz(m)	terrain(sport)	field; court	campo	terreno	campo
Sportwagen(m)	poussette	push-chair	silla de bebé	passeggino	cadeira de bebé
Spott(m)	moquerie	mockery	burla, mofa	canzonatura, beffa	zombaria, troça
Sprache(f)	langage	language	lenguaje	linguaggio	linguagem
Sprache(f)	langue	language	idioma, lengua	lingua	língua, idioma
sprechen, reden	parler	speak, talk	hablar	parlare	falar
Sprechen(n); Sprache f	parler(le)	speech	habla(el)	parlare(il)	fala(a)
Sprechweise(f)	élocution	elocution	elocución	eloquio	elocução
sprengen	exploser, sauter	blow up	estallar, saltar	scoppiare, saltare	explodir
Sprichwort(n)	proverbe	proverb	proverbio	proverbio	provérbio
Springbrunnen(m)	fontaine	fountain	fuente	fontana	fonte
springen	sauter	jump	saltar	saltare	saltar, pular
springen	bondir	jump, leap	saltar	saltare, balzare	saltar
springen; sprudeln	jaillir	spring	brotar, surgir	schizzare	brotar
Spritze(f)	seringue	syringe	jeringa	siringa	seringa
Spritze(f)	piqûre	injection	inyección	iniezione	injecção
spritzen	gicler, jaillir	squirt, spurt	salpicar	sprizzare, schizzare	salpicar
spritzen, ein = spritzen	injecter	inject	inyectar	iniettare	injectar
sprudelnd; Sprudel-	gazeux, se	fizzy, sparkling	gaseoso, a	gassato, a	gasoso, a
Sprudelwasser(n)	eau gazeuse	sparkling water	gaseosa	acqua gassata	água gaseificada
sprühen	vaporiser	spray	vaporizar	vaporizzare	vaporizar
Sprühregen(m)	bruine	drizzle	llovizna	pioggerella	chuvisco
Sprung(m)	saut, bond	jump, leap, spring	salto, brinco	salto, balzo	salto, pulo
Sprung(m), Riß(m)	félure	crack	raja, grieta	incrinatura	estaladela
spucken	cracher	spit	escupir	sputare	cuspir
Spülbecken(n)	évier	sink	fregadero	acquaio, lavandino	pia, banca
Spule(f)	bobine	reel	bobina, carrete	bobina	bobina
Spur(f)	trace	trace, track	huella, rastro	traccia	traço; vestígio
Spur(f)	piste	track	pista	pista	pista
Spur(f)	marque	mark	señal, marca	segno, marca	marca, vestígio
Spur(f)	file	lane	fila	fila, corsia	fila
Spur(f)(Straßen-)	voie	lane	vía	corsia	faixa(rua)
spüren, fühlen	éprouver	feel	sentir	provare	sentir
Staat(m)	état	state	estado	stato	estado
staatlich geprüft	diplômé, e	qualified	graduado, a	diplomato, a	diplomado, a
staatsbürgerlich	civique	civic	cívico, a	civico, a	cívico, a
Staatsoberhaupt(n)	chef d'état	head of state	jefe de estado	capo di stato	chefe de estado
Stabilität(f)	stabilité	stability	estabilidad	stabilità	estabilidade
Stadium(n)	stade	stadium	estadio	stadio	estádio
Stadt(f)	ville	town	ciudad	città	cidade
Stadt(f)	cité	city	ciudad	città	cidade
Städtebau(m)	urbanisme	town-planning	urbanismo	urbanistica	urbanismo
Städter(in f)m	citadin, e	town/city dweller	ciudadano, a	cittadino, a	citadino, a
städtisch, Stadt-	urbain, e	urban	urbano, a	urbano, a	urbano, a
städtisch; Stadt-	municipal, e	municipal; town -	municipal	municipale	municipal
Stadtzentrum(n)	centre ville	city/town centre	centro(ciudad)	centro della città	centro(cidade)
Stahl(m)	acier	steel	acero	acciaio	aço

German	French	English	Spanish	Italian	Portuguese
Stamm(m)	tronc	trunk	tronco	tronco	tronco
Stamm(m)	tribu	tribe	tribu	tribù	tribo
Stammbaum(Tier-)(m)	pédigree	pedigree	pedigrí	pedigree	pedigree
stammeln	bafouiller	splutter, stammer	balbucear	farfugliare	balbuciar
Stand(m), Niveau(n)	niveau	level	nivel	livello	nível
Standard(m)	niveau(de vie)	standard of living	nivel(de vida)	tenore(di vita)	nível(de vida)
ständig	continuel, le	continual	continuo, a	continuo, a	contínuo, a
Stange(f)	barre	bar	barra	sbarra	barra
Stange(f)	tige	rod	tallo, vástago	asta, barra	haste
Stapel(m)	pile	pile	pila	pila	pilha, montão
stapeln	empiler	pile up, stack	apilar, amontonar	accatastare	empilhar, amontoar
stapeln	entasser	pile up	amontonar	ammucchiare	amontoar
Star(m)	vedette	star	estrella; divo, a	vedette; divo, a	vedeta, estrela
stark	fort, e	strong	fuerte	forte	forte
Stärke(f)	force	strength	fuerza	forza	força
Stärke(f), Dicke(f)	épaisseur	thickness	espesor	spessore	espessura
Stärkungsmittel(n)	fortifiant	tonic	fortificante	ricostituente	fortificante
starr, steif	raide	stiff	tieso, a; rígido, a	rigido, a	teso, a; hirto, a
starr	inflexible	inflexible	inflexible	inflessibile	inflexível
Starrkrampf(m)	tétanie	tetany	tetania	tetania	tetania
Start(m)	lancement	launch(ing)	lanzamiento	lancio	lançamento
starten	démarrer	start	arrancar	avviare, iniziare	arrancar
Starter(m)	démarreur	starter	arranque	motorino(avviamento)	motor de arranque
Station(f)	station	station	estación	stazione	estação
statisch	statique	static	estático, a	statico, a	estático, a
Statistik(f)	statistique(s)	statistics	estadística	statistica	estatística
Statue(f)	statue	statue	estatua	statua	estátua
Status(m); Statut(n)	statut	status; statute	estatuto	statuto	estatuto
Staub(m)	poussière	dust	polvo	polvere	poeira
Staubsauger(m)	aspirateur	vacuum-cleaner	aspirador	aspirapolvere	aspirador
stechen	piquer	prick, sting	pinchar	pungere	picar
Steckdose(f)	prise	plug; socket	enchufe	presa	tomada
Stecknadel(f)	épingle	pin	alfiler	spillo	alfinete
stehen = bleiben	arrêter(s')	stop	pararse	fermarsi	parar
stehend, aufrecht	debout	standing(up)	de pie, en pie	in piedi	de pé, em pé
stehlen	voler	steal, rob	robar	rubare	roubar
steif	rigide	rigid, stiff	rígido, a	rigido, a	rígido, a
Steigeisen(n)	crampons	crampons, irons	crampones	rampone	grampo
steigen	monter	climb; rise; go up	subir	salire	subir
Steigerung(f)	hausse	rise, increase	subida	aumento	subida
Steigung(f)	montée	rise	subida	salita	subida
steil	raide; escarpé, e	steep	empinado, a	ripido, a	empinado, a
steil	escarpé, e	steep	escarpado, a	scosceso, a	escarpado, a
steil	abrupt, e	steep	abrupto, a	ripido, a; scosceso, a	abrupto, a
Steilküste(f)	falaise	cliff	acantilado	scogliera	falésia
Stein(m)	pierre	stone	piedra	pietra	pedra
Stein(m)	caillou	stone, pebble	piedra	sasso	calhau
Stein(m)(Spiel)	pion(dames)	draught	ficha(damas)	pedina(dama)	peça, tábula(dama)
Steinbruch(m)	carrière	quarry	cantera	cava	pedreira
Steindruck(m)	lithographie	lithograph(y)	litografía	litografia	litografia
Stelle(f)	endroit	place, spot	lugar, sitio	luogo, posto	lugar, sítio
Stelle(f)	emploi	employment	empleo	impiego	emprego
stellen	poser, placer	place	poner, colocar	collocare	pôr, colocar
stellen, setzen	situer	situate, locate	situar, localizar	situare, localizzare	situar, localizar
Stellung, Position(f)	situation	position, job	situación	situazione	situação
Stellung(f), Amt(n)	fonction	function	función	funzione	função
Stellvertreter(in f)m	remplacant, e	substitute	sustituto, a	sostituto, a	substituto, a
Stellvertreter(in f)m	suppléant, e	substitute	suplente, a	supplente	suplente
Stellvertreter(in f)m	adjoint, e	deputy	substituto, a	assessore	adjunto, a
Stempel(m), Siegel(n)	cachet	postmark, seal	sello	sigillo, bollo	selo
stempeln	tamponner	stamp	sellar	timbrare	carimbar
Steppe(f)	steppe	steppe	estepa	steppa	estepe
sterben	mourir	die	morir	morire	morrer
Sterblichkeit(f)	mortalité	mortality	mortalidad	mortalità	mortalidade
Stereo(f)	stéréo	stereo	estéreo	stereo	estereofonia
steril	stérile	sterile	estéril	sterile	estéril
Stern(m)	étoile	star	estrella	stella	estrela
Stern(m), Gestirn(n)	astre	star	astro	astro	astro

G

German	French	English	Spanish	Italian	Portuguese
Steuer(n)	volant	steering-wheel	volante	volante	volante
Steuer(f)	impôt	tax	impuesto	tassa	imposto
Steuer(f)	taxe	tax; duty	tasa, impuesto	tassa, imposta	taxa, imposto
steuerfrei	détaxé, e	duty(tax)-free	desgravado, a	sgravio fiscale	isento de taxa
Steuerhinterziehung f	fraude(fiscale)	tax evasion	fraude(fiscal)	frode(fiscale)	fraude(fiscal)
Steuerwesen(n)	fiscalité	tax system	fiscalidad	fiscalità	fiscalidade
Stewardess(f)	hôtesse	hostess(air -)	azafata	hostess	hospedeira
Stich(m)	piqûre	sting, bite	picadura	puntura	picada
Stich(m); Masche(f)	point	stitch	puntada	punto	ponto
sticken	broder	embroider	bordar	ricamare	bordar
Stiefel(m)	botte	boot	bota	stivale	bota
Stiel(m)	manche	handle	mango(el)	manico	cabo
Stiel(m)	tige	stem	tallo	stelo	caule
Stier(m)	taureau	bull	toro	toro	touro; toiro
Stierkampf(m)	corrida	bull-fight	corrida	corrida	toirada
Stierkämpfer(m)	toréador	bull-fighter	torero	torero	toureiro
Stil(m)	style	style	estilo	stile	estilo
still	calme, tranquille	still	quieto, a; tranquilo	calmo, a; silenzioso, a	quieto, a
still, leise, ruhig	silencieux, se	silent, quiet	silencioso, a	silenzioso, a	silencioso, a
Stille(f)	silence	silence	silencio	silenzio	silêncio
stillen	allaiter	feed	pecho(dar el)	allattare	aleitar
Stillgestanden!	garde-à-vous!	attention!	firmes(!)	attenti!	sentido!
Stillstand(m)	arrêt, cessation	stop, cessation	cese	cessazione, tregua	cessação
Stimm-	vocal, e	vocal	vocal	vocale	vocal
Stimme(f)	voix	voice	voz	voce	voz
stimmlos, heiser	aphone	lose one's voice	afónico, a	afono, a	áfono, a
stimmt!	exact(c'est)	right(that 's)	exacto(es)	esatto(è)	exacto(é)
Stimmung(f)	ambiance	atmosphere	ambiente	atmosfera	ambiente
Stimmung(f), Moral(f)	moral	morale	moral, ánimo	morale	moral
Stimmung machen	animer	liven up	animar	animare	animar
stinken	puer	stink	apestar	puzzare	cheirar mal
Stipendium(n)	bourse	grant; scholarship	beca	borsa di studio	bolsa
Stirn(f)	front	forehead	frente	fronte	testa
Stock(m)	bâton	stick	palo	bastone	pau, bastão
Stock(m)	canne	stick	bastón	bastone	bengala
Stöckchen(n)	baguette	stick	varilla	bacchetta	vara
Stoff(m)	étoffe	material	tejido, tela	stoffa	tecido, estofo
Stoff(m)	tissu	material, fabric	tela	tessuto	tecido
Stoff(m), Material(n)	matière	matter, material	materia	materia	matéria
stöhnen	gémir	moan	gemir	gemere	gemer
stolpern	trébucher	stumble, trip	tropezar	inciampare	tropeçar
Stolz(m)	fierté	pride	orgullo	fierezza	orgulho
Stolz(m)	orgueil	pride, arrogance	orgullo	orgoglio	orgulho
stolz	fier, fière	proud	altivo, a	fiero, a	altivo, a
stolz, arrogant	orgueilleux, se	proud, arrogant	orgulloso, a	orgoglioso, a	orgulhoso, a
Stoppuhr(f)	chronomètre	chronometer	cronómetro	cronometro	cronómetro
stören	troubler	disturb; trouble	perturbar	turbare, disturbare	perturbar
stören	déranger	disturb, bother	molestar	disturbare	incomodar
stören	gêner	obstruct	molestar	imbarazzare	incomodar
stören	perturber	disturb, perturb	perturbar	perturbare	perturbar
stören	incommoder	bother	incomodar	incomodare	incomodar
Störung(f)	obstruction	obstruction	obstrucción	ostruzione	obstrucção
Stoß(m), Aufprall(m)	choc	shock, impact	choque	urto, scontro	choque
Stoß(m)	impact	impact	impacto	impatto	impacto
Stoßdämpfer(m)	amortisseur	shock absorber	amortiguador	ammortizzatore	amortecedor
stoßen	heurter	knock(against)	tropezar con	urtare	chocar, bater
stoßen, sich	cogner(se)	knock	golpe(darse un)	sbattere	chocar com
stottern	bégayer	stutter, stammer	tartamudear	balbettare	gaguejar
Strafe(f)	punition	punishment	castigo	punizione	castigo
Strafe(f)	sanction	sanction	sanción	sanzione	sanção
Strafe(f), Strafpunkt	pénalité	penalty	penalidad	penalità	penalidade
Strafmandat(n)	procès-verbal	ticket, penalty	multa	contravvenzione	multa
strafrechtlich	pénal, e	penal	penal	penale	penal
Strahl(m)(Licht)	faisceau, rayon	beam	haz	fascio	foco
Strahl(m)	rayon	ray	rayo	raggio	raio
Strahl(m)	jet	spray, jet	surtidor, chorro	getto, zampillo	jacto, repuxo
Strahlung(f)	rayonnement	radiance	irradiación	irradiazione	irradiação
Strand(m)	plage	beach(-es)	playa	spiaggia	praia

German	French	English	Spanish	Italian	Portuguese
Straße(f)	route	road	carretera	strada	estrada
Straße(f)	rue	street	calle	via	rua
Straßenbahn(f)	tramway	tram-car	tranvía	tram	carro eléctrico
Straßenlaterne(f)	lampadaire	street-lamp	lámpara de pie	lampione	candeeiro
Strategie(f)	stratégie	strategy	estrategia	strategia	estratégia
Strauß(m)	bouquet	bunch; bouquet	ramo	mazzo	ramo
Strecke(f)	étape	stage	etapa	tappa	etapa
Strecke(f)	trajet	journey, trip	trayecto	tragitto	trajecto
Strecke(f)(Renn-)	circuit	circuit	circuito	circuito	circuito
Strecke(f), Route(f)	parcours	journey, course	recorrido	percorso	percurso
Streich(m)	farce	joke; farce	broma	scherzo	partida
streicheln	caresser	stroke	acariciar	carezzare	afagar
Streicheln(n)	caresse	caress	caricia	carezza	carícia
streichen	peindre	paint	pintar	imbiancare	pintar
streichen	annuler	delete	borrar	annullare	suprimir
Streichholz(n)	allumette	match(-es)	cerilla	fiammifero	fósforo
Streichung(f)	rature	deletion	tachadura	cancellatura	rasura
Streifen(m)	bande	band, strip	faja, tira	striscia	tira
Streik(m)	grève	strike	huelga	sciopero	greve
Streit(m)	dispute	dispute, argument	disputa	disputa, lite	disputa
streiten, kämpfen	combattre	fight	combatir	combattere	combater
streiten, sich	disputer(se)	quarrel, argue	reñir(con)	litigare	disputar-se
Streitfall(m)	litige	litigation	litigio	litigio	litígio
streng	sévère	severe, strict	severo, a	severo, a	severo, a
streng	rigoureux, se	rigorous	riguroso, a	rigoroso, a	rigoroso, a
streng, hart	austère	austere	austero, a	austero, a	austero, a
streng	strict, e	strict	estricto, a	stretto, a	estrito, a
Strich(m)	trait	line	raya	tratto, riga	traço, risco
Strich(m)	raie	line	raya	riga	linha; risca
stricken	tricoter	knit	hacer punto	lavorare a maglia	tricotar
Stroh(n)	paille	straw	paja	paglia	palha
Strohhütte(f)	paillotte	hut(straw-hut)	choza	capanna	palhota
Strolch(m)	voyou	hooligan	canalla	mascalzone, a	patife
Strom(m)	fleuve	river	río	fiume	rio
Strom(m)	courant	current	corriente	corrente	corrente
Stromkreis(m)	circuit	circuit, system	circuito	circuito	circuito
Struktur(f)	structure	structure	estructura	struttura	estrutura
Struktur(f)	ossature	structure	armazón	ossatura	ossatura
Strumpf(m)(Nylon-)	bas	stocking	media	calza	meias
Strumpfhose(f)	collants	tights(pair of)	pantys	collant	meias
Stück(n)	pièce	play	obra	commedia	peça
Stück(n)	morceau, bout	piece, bit	pedazo	pezzo	pedaço
Stück(n), Portion(f)	portion	portion, piece	porción	porzione	porção
Student(in f)m	étudiant, e	student	estudiante	studente, -essa	estudante
Studie(f)	étude	study; survey	estudio	studio	estudo
studieren	étudier	study	estudiar	studiare	estudar
Studio(n)	studio	studio	estudio	studio	estúdio
Stufe(f)	marche	step	peldaño, escalón	scalino	degrau
Stuhl(m)	chaise	chair	silla	sedia	cadeira
stumm	muet, te	dumb; silent	mudo, a	muto, a	mudo, a
Stunde(f); Zeit(f)	heure	hour; time	hora	ora	hora
Stunde(f); Lektion(f)	leçon	lesson	lección	lezione	lição
stürzen, sich	précipiter(se)	rush	precipitarse	precipitarsi	precipitar-se
Stütze(f)	appui	support	apoyo	appoggio	apoio
Stütze(f)	support	support	soporte	supporto	suporte
stützen, unterstützen	supporter	support	soportar	sopportare	suportar
stützen, sich	appuyer(s')	lean on(against)	apoyar(se)	appoggiarsi	apoiar-se
Stützpunkt(m)	base(militaire)	base	base(militar)	base(militare)	base(militar)
Subjekt(n)	sujet	subject	sujeto	soggetto	sujeito
Subskription(f)	souscription	subscription	suscripción	sottoscrizione	subscrição
Substanz(f)	substance	substance	sustancia	sostanza	substância
Subtraktion(f)	soustraction	subtraction	resta	sottrazione	subtração
Subvention(f)	subvention	subsidy	subvención	sussidio	subvenção
Suche(f)	recherche	search	busca	ricerca	busca
suchen	chercher	look for, search -	buscar	cercare	procurar; buscar
suchen	rechercher	search/look for	buscar, indagar	ricercare	buscar, procurar
suchen, durchsuchen	fouiller	search	registrar	frugare	rebuscar
Sucht(f)	manie	mania	manía	mania	mania

German	French	English	Spanish	Italian	Portuguese
Süden(m)	Sud	South	Sur	Sud	Sul
Suite(f)	suite	suite	suite	appartamento	suite
Sultan(m)	sultan	sultan	sultán	sultano	sultão
Summe(f)	somme	sum, amount	suma; cantidad	somma	soma; quantia
Summe(f), Ganze(s)(n)	total	total	total	totale	total
Sumpf(m)	marais	marsh	pantano	palude	pântano
Sumpffieber(n)	paludisme	malaria	paludismo	malaria, paludismo	paludismo
sumpfig	marécageux, se	marshy, boggy	pantanoso, a	paludoso, a	pantanoso, a
Sünde(f)	péché	sin	pecado	peccato	pecado
Superbenzin(n)	essence super	four-star petrol	supercarburante	benzina super	super
Supermarkt(m)	supermarché	supermarket	supermercado	supermercato	supermercado
Suppe(f)	soupe	soup	sopa	minestra	sopa
süß	doux, ce	sweet	dulce	dolce	doce
süß	sucré, e	sweet	azucarado, a	zuccherato, a	açucarado, a; doce
Süßwarenladen(m)	confiserie	sweet shop	confitería	confetteria	confeitaria
Symbol(n)	symbole	symbol	símbolo	simbolo	símbolo
symbolisch	symbolique	symbolic(al)	simbólico, a	simbolico, a	simbólico, a
Symetrie(f)	symétrie	symmetry	simetría	simmetria	simetria
sympathisch	sympathique	pleasant, nice	simpático, a	simpatico, a	simpático, a
Symphonie(f)	symphonie	symphony	sinfonía	sinfonia	sinfonia
Symposium(n)	colloque	symposium	coloquio	colloquio	colóquio
Symptom(n)	symptôme	symptom	síntoma	sintomo	sintoma
Synagoge(f)	synagogue	synagogue	sinagoga	sinagoga	sinagoga
synchronisieren	synchroniser	synchronize	sincronizar	sincronizzare	sincronizar
Synonym(n)	synonyme	synonym	sinónimo	sinonimo	sinónimo
Syntax(f), Satzlehre f	syntaxe	syntax	sintaxis	sintassi	sintaxe
Synthese(f)	synthèse	synthesis(-ses)	síntesis	sintesi	síntese
synthetisch	synthétique	synthetic	sintético, a	sintetico, a	sintético, a
Syphilis(f)	syphilis	syphilis	sífilis	sifilide	sífilis
System(n)	système	system	sistema	sistema	sistema
systematisch	systématique	systematic	sistemático, a	sistematico, a	sistemático, a
Szene(f)	scène	scene	escena	scena	cena
Szene(f), Bühne(f)	scène	stage	escena	scena	cena

T

German	French	English	Spanish	Italian	Portuguese
Tabak(m)	tabac	tobacco	tabaco	tabacco	tabaco
Tabakladen(m)	bureau de tabac	tobacconist's	estanco	tabaccheria	estanco, tabacaria
Tabelle(f), Skala(f)	échelle	scale	escala	scala	escala
Tablett(n), Platte(f)	plateau	tray	bandeja	vassoio	tabuleiro
Tablette(f)	comprimé	tablet, pill	comprimido	compressa	comprimido
Tablette(f)	cachet	tablet	pastilla	pastiglia	comprimido
Tafel(f)	tableau	board, panel	tablero, tablón	pannello, quadro	painel, quadro
Tafel(f)	tableau noir	blackboard	pizarra	lavagna	quadro
Tag(m)	jour, journée	day	día; jornada	giorno; giornata	dia
Tageszeitung(f)	quotidien	daily	diario	quotidiano	diário
täglich	journalier, ière	daily	diario, a	giornaliero, a	diário, a
täglich	quotidien, ne	daily	cotidiano, a	quotidiano, a	quotidiano, a
Taifun(m)	typhon	typhoon	tifón	tifone	tufão
Taille(f)	taille	waist	cintura, talle	vita	cinta
Takt(m), Rhythmus(m)	rythme	rhythm	ritmo	ritmo	ritmo
Takt(m)	tact	tact	tacto	tatto	tacto
Taktik(f)	tactique	tactic	táctica	tattica	táctica
taktisch	tactique	tactical	táctico, a	tattico, a	táctico, a
Tal(n)	vallée	valley	valle	valle	vale
Talent(n)	talent	talent	talento	talento	talento
Talent(n)	don	gift, talent	don, talento	dono	dom, talento

German	French	English	Spanish	Italian	Portuguese
Tank(m)	réservoir	tank	depósito	serbatoio	depósito
Tankstelle(f)	poste d'essence	petrol station	gasolinera	distributore(benzina)	bomba de gasolina
Tankstelle(f)	station-service	service station	estación(servicio)	stazione di servizio	estação de serviço
Tanne(f)	sapin	fir-tree	abeto	abete	abeto
Tante(f)	tante	aunt	tía	zia	tia
Tanz(m)	danse	dance	danza, baile	ballo, danza	dança
tanzen	danser	dance	bailar	ballare	dançar, bailar
Tänzer(in f)m	danseur, se	dancer	bailarín, a	ballerino, a	bailarino, a
Tanzlokal(n)	dancing	dance-hall	sala de baile	sala da ballo	dancing
Tapete(f)	tapisserie	wallpaper	empapelado	carta da parati	papel de parede
tapfer	vaillant, e	brave	valiente	valoroso, a	valente; bravo, a
Tarif(m)	tarif	tariff, price	tarifa	tariffa	tarifa
Tarif(m)	tarif	fare	tarifa	tariffa	tarifa
Tasche(f)	poche	pocket	bolsillo	tasca	bolso
Tasche(f)	sac	bag	bolsa, saco	borsa	saco
Tasche(f)(Umhänge-)	sacoche	bag	cartera	saccoccia, borsa	saco
Taschenkalender(m)	agenda	diary	agenda	agenda	agenda
Taschenlampe(f)	lampe de poche	torch	linterna	lampadina tascabile	pilha
Taschentuch(n)	mouchoir	handkerchief	pañuelo	fazzoletto	lenço
Tasse(f)	tasse	cup	taza	tazza	chávena
Tastatur(f)	clavier	keyboard	teclado	tastiera	teclado
Taste(f)	touche	key	tecla	tasto	tecla
Taste(f)	bouton	button	pulsador	pulsante, bottone	botão
Tätigkeit(f)	activité	activity	actividad	attività	actividade
Tatkraft(f), Schwung m	dynamisme	dynamism	dinamismo	dinamismo	dinamismo
Tätowierung(f)	tatouage	tattoo	tatuaje	tatuaggio	tatuagem
Tatsache(f)	fait	fact	hecho	fatto	facto
tatsächlich, wirklich	effectif, ive	effective	efectivo, a	effettivo, a	efectivo, a
tatsächlich	effet(en)	indeed	efecto(en)	infatti	efeito(com)
Tau(m)	rosée	dew	rocío	rugiada	orvalho
Tau(n)	corde	rope	cuerda	corda	corda
taub	sourd, e	deaf	sordo, a	sordo, a	surdo, a
Taube(f)	pigeon	pigeon	paloma	piccione	pombo, a
Taubheit(f)	surdité	deafness	sordera	sordità	surdez
taubstumm	sourd-muet, te	deaf and dumb	sordomudo, a	sordomuto, a	surdo-mudo, a
tauchen	plonger	plunge, dive	zambullirse	tuffarsi	mergulhar
Taucheranzug(m)	scaphandre	diving-suit	escafandra	scafandro	escafandro
Taufe(f)	baptême	baptism	bautizo	battesimo	baptismo
taumeln	chanceler	stagger	tambalearse	barcollare	vacilar
taumeln	vaciller	sway, wobble	vacilar	vacillare	vacilar
Tausch(Aus-, Um-)(m)	échange	exchange	cambio	scambio	troca; câmbio
tauschen	échanger	exchange	intercambiar	scambiare	trocar
täuschen, sich	tromper(se)	mistaken(be)	equivocarse	sbagliarsi	enganar-se
tausend	mille	thousand	mil	mille; mila(pl.)	mil
Tausend(n)	millier	thousand	millar	migliaio(a)	milhar
tausendste	millième	thousandth	milésimo, a	millesimo, a	milésimo, a
Taxi(n)	taxi	taxi, cab	taxi	taxi, tassì	táxi
Taxifahrer(in f)m	chauffeur(taxi)	taxi-driver	taxista	tassista	motorista
Techniker(in f)m	technicien, ne	technician	técnico, a	tecnico, a	técnico, a
technisch	technique	technical	técnico, a	tecnico, a	técnico, a
Technokrat(m)	technocrate	technocrat	tecnócrata	tecnocrate	tecnocrata
Technologie(f)	technologie	technology	tecnología	tecnologia	tecnologia
Tee(m)	thé	tea	té	tè	chá
Teekanne(f)	théière	teapot	tetera	teiera	bule
Teer(m)	goudron	tar	alquitrán	asfalto	alcatrão
Teich(m)	étang	pond	estanque	stagno	lago; tanque
Teig(m)	pâte	pastry, dough	masa	pasta	massa
Teil(m n)	partie, part	part	parte	pezzo, parte	parte
Teil(n)	pièce	part, component	pieza	pezzo	peça
Teilchen(n)	particule	particle	partícula	particella	partícula
teilen	diviser	divide	dividir	dividere	dividir
teilen	partager	share, divide	repartir	dividere	repartir
Teilhaber(in f)m	associé, e	associate, partner	socio, a, asociado	socio, a	sócio, a
teil = nehmen	participer(à)	take part(in)	participar(en)	partecipare(a)	participar(em)
Teint(m)	teint	complexion, colour	tez, color	carnagione	tez
Telefon(n)	téléphone	telephone, phone	teléfono	telefono	telefone
telefonieren	téléphoner	phone, ring, call	telefonear	telefonare	telefonar
Telefonzelle(f)	cabine(téléph.)	phone box	cabina(telefónica)	cabina(telefonica)	cabine(telefónica)

G

353

German	French	English	Spanish	Italian	Portuguese
Telefonzelle(f)	taxi-/publiphone	public call-box	teléfono público	telefono pubblico	telefone público
Telegramm(n)	télégramme	telegram, cable	telegrama	telegramma	telegrama
Telepathie(f)	télépathie	telepathy	telepatía	telepatia	telepatia
Teleskop(n)	télescope	telescope	telescopio	telescopio	telescópio
Telex(n)	télex	telex	telex	telex	telex
Teller(m)	assiette	plate	plato	piatto	prato
Tempel(m)	temple	temple	templo	tempio	templo
Temperament(n)	tempérament	temperament	temperamento	temperamento	temperamento
Temperatur(f)	température	temperature	temperatura	temperatura	temperatura
Tendenz(f), Neigung(f)	tendance	tendency; trend	tendencia	tendenza	tendência
Tennis(n)	tennis	tennis	tenis	tennis	ténis
Tenor(m)	ténor	tenor	tenor	tenore	tenor
Teppich(m)	tapis	mat, rug, carpet	alfombra, tapiz	tappeto	tapete, carpete
Teppichboden(m)	moquette, tapis	carpet	moqueta	moquette	alcatifa
terrorisieren	terroriser	terrorize	aterrorizar	terrorizzare	aterrorizar
Terrorismus(m)	terrorisme	terrorism	terrorismo	terrorismo	terrorismo
Terrorist(in f)m	terroriste	terrorist	terrorista	terrorista	terrorista
Tesafilm(m)	scotch	sellotape	papel celo	scotch	fita adesiva
Test(m), Probe(f)	épreuve, test	test	prueba	prova, test	prova
Testament(n)	testament	will, testament	testamento	testamento	testamento
testen	tester	test	ensayar, probar	testare	testar
Tetanus(m)	tétanos	tetanus	tétanos	tetano	tétano
teuer	cher, ère	expensive, dear	caro, a	caro, a	caro, a
teuer	coûteux, se	costly, expensive	costoso, a	costoso, a	custoso, a
Teufel(m)	diable	devil	diablo	diavolo	diabo
Teufel(m)	démon	demon, devil	demonio	demonio	demónio
Text(m)	texte	text	texto	testo	texto
Textil-; Web-	textile	textile	textil	tessile	textil
Theater(n)	théâtre	theatre	teatro	teatro	teatro
Theke(f)	comptoir	counter, bar	barra	banco	balcão
Thema(n)	thème	theme	tema	tema	tema
Thema(n)	matière	subject matter	materia, tema	materia, tema	assunto
Thema(n)	sujet, thème	subject, theme	tema	tema	assunto, tema
Thema(n), Objekt(n)	objet, thème	theme, subject	objeto, tema	oggetto, scopo	tema, assunto
Theologie(f)	théologie	theology	teología	teologia	teologia
theoretisch	théorique	theoretical	teórico, a	teorico, a	teórico, a
Theorie(f)	théorie	theory	teoría	teoria	teoria
Therapie(f)	thérapie	therapy	terapia	terapia	terapia
Thermal-	thermal, e	thermal	termal	termale	termal
thermisch	thermique	thermic, thermal	térmico, a	termico, a	térmico, a
Thermometer(n)	thermomètre	thermometer	termómetro	termometro	termómetro
These(f)	thèse	thesis(theses)	tesis	tesi	tese
Thron(m)	trône	throne	trono	trono	trono
Thunfisch(m)	thon	tuna(fish)	atún, bonito	tonno	atum
Tick(m)	tic	twitch(ing)	tic	tic	tique
tief	profond, e	deep	profundo, a	profondo, a	profundo, a
Tief(n)	dépression(atm.)	depression	depresión	depressione	depressão
Tiefe(f)	profondeur	depth	profundidad	profondità	profundidade
Tiefkühlkost(f)	surgelés	frozen food	congelados	surgelati	congelados
Tier(n)	animal	animal	animal	animale	animal
Tierarzt(m)	vétérinaire	vet	veterinario	veterinario	veterinário
Tiger(m)	tigre	tiger	tigre	tigre	tigre
Tinte(f)	encre	ink	tinta	inchiostro	tinta
Tisch(m)	table	table	mesa	tavolo; tavola	mesa
Tischdecke(f)	nappe	table-cloth	mantel	tovaglia	toalha
Tischler(m)	menuisier	joiner, carpenter	carpintero	falegname	carpinteiro
Tischtennis(n)	tennis de table	table-tennis	ping-pong	ping pong	ténis de mesa
Titel(m)	titre	title	título	titolo	título
Toast(m)	pain grillé	toast	tostadas	pane tostato	pão torrado
toasten	griller	toast	tostar	abbrustolire	torrar
Tochter(f)	fille	daughter	hija	figlia	filha
Tochtergeschwulst(f)	métastase	metastasis(-es)	metástasis	metastasi	metástase
Tod(m)	mort	death	muerte	morte	morte
Tod(m)	décès	death	fallecimiento	decesso	falecimento
Todeskampf(m), Agonie	agonie	agony	agonía	agonia	agonia
tödlich	mortel, le	mortal; deadly	mortal	mortale	mortal
tödlich	mortel, le	fatal	mortal	mortale	mortal
tödlich	fatal, e	fatal	fatal	fatale	fatal

German	French	English	Spanish	Italian	Portuguese
Toilette(f)	water-closet	toilets	water, retretes	WC; gabinetto	retrete, sanita
Toiletten(f pl)	toilettes(W.C)	toilet, lavatory	servicios(W.C)	toilettes; W.C	lavabos; sanita
Toilettenpapier(n)	papier toilette	toilet paper	papel higiénico	carta igienica	papel higiénico
Toleranz(f)	tolérance	tolerance	tolerancia	tolleranza	tolerância
Tollwut(f)	rage	rabies	rabia	rabbia	raiva
Tomate(f)	tomate	tomato(-es)	tomate	pomodoro	tomate
Ton(m), Lehm(m)	argile	clay	arcilla	argilla	argila
Ton(m)	son	sound	sonido	suono	som
Ton(m), Klang(m)	ton, son, timbre	tone	tono, sonido	tono	tom, som, timbre
Tonart, Klangfarbe(f)	tonalité	tonality, tone	tonalidad	tonalità	tonalidade
Tonfall(m)	intonation	intonation	entonación	intonazione	entoação
Tonleiter(f)	solfège	sol-fa, theory	solfeo	solfeggio	solfejo
Tonne(f)	tonne	ton	tonelada	tonnellata	tonelada
Topas(m)	topaze	topaz	topacio	topazio	topázio
Topf(m)	pot	pot	maceta	vaso	vaso; pote
Topf(m)	casserole	pan, saucepan	cazo, cacerola	casseruola	tacho, caçarola
Tor(n)	portail	gate	portal	portone	portal
Tor(n)	but	goal	gol	goal, rete	golo
Torpedo(m)	torpille	torpedo(-es)	torpedo	torpedine	torpedo
Torte(f)	tarte	tart	tarta	torta, crostata	torta
Torwärter(m)	goal	goalkeeper	portero	portiere	guarda-redes
tot	mort, e	dead	muerto, a	morto, a	morto, a
Tote(r)mf	mort, e	dead man/woman	muerto, a	morto, a	morto, a
töten	tuer	kill	matar	uccidere	matar
Totschlag(m)	homicide	murder, homicide	homicidio	omicidio	homicídio
Tour(f), Fußtour(f)	randonnée	ramble	caminata, paseo	gita, escursione	caminhada
Tourismus(m)	tourisme	tourism	turismo	turismo	turismo
Tourist(m)	touriste	tourist	turista	turista	turista
Toxikologie(f)	toxicologie	toxicology	toxicología	tossicologia	toxicologia
traben	trotter	trot	trotar	trottare	trotar
Tradition(f)	tradition	tradition	tradición	tradizione	tradição
tragbar	portatif, ive	portable	portátil	portatile	portátil
tragen	porter	carry	llevar	portare	levar
tragen	porter	wear	llevar	indossare, portare	usar; trazer
Trägheit(f)	inertie	inertia	inercia	inerzia	inércia
tragisch	tragique	tragic	trágico, a	tragico, a	trágico, a
Tragödie(f)	tragédie	tragedy	tragedia	tragedia	tragédia
Trainer(m)	entraîneur	trainer	entrenador	allenatore	treinador
Training(n)	entraînement	training, practice	entrenamiento	allenamento	treino
Traktor(m)	tracteur	tractor	tractor	trattore	tractor
trampen	auto-stop	hitch-hiking	autostop, a dedo	autostop	boleia(pedir)
Träne(f)	larme	tear	lágrima	lacrima	lágrima
Tränengas(n)	lacrymogène	tear-gas	lacrimógeno	lacrimogeno	lacrimogéneo
Transaktion(f)	transaction	transaction	transacción	transazione	transacção
Transfusion(f)	transfusion	transfusion	transfusión	trasfusione	transfusão
Transport(m)	transport	transport	transporte	trasporto	transporte
transportieren	transporter	transport, carry	transportar	trasportare	transportar
Transvestit(m)	travesti	transvestite	travesti	travestito	travesti
Trapez(n)	trapèze	trapezium; trapeze	trapecio	trapezio	trapézio
Traube(f)	grappe	bunch	racimo	grappolo	cacho
Traube(f)(Wein-)	raisin	grape	uva(s)	uva	uva
Traubenzucker(m)	glucose	glucose	glucosa	glucosio	glicose
Trauer(f)	deuil	mourning(be in)	duelo; luto	lutto	luto
Traum(m)	rêve	dream	sueño	sogno	sonho
Trauma(n)	traumatisme	traumatism	traumatismo	trauma	traumatismo
träumen	rêver	dream	soñar	sognare	sonhar
traurig	triste	sad, unhappy	triste	triste	triste
Traurigkeit(f)	tristesse	sadness	tristeza	tristezza	tristeza
Treffen(n), Gespräch n	entrevue	interview	entrevista	intervista	entrevista
treffen	rencontrer	meet	encontrar	incontrare	encontrar
treffen, sich	réunir(se)	meet	reunirse	riunirsi	reunir-se
Treffen(n)	réunion	meeting; reunion	reunión	riunione	reunião
Treibstoff(m)	carburant	fuel	carburante	carburante	carburante
trennen	séparer	separate, part	separar	separare, dividere	separar
trennen	dissocier	dissociate	disociar	dissociare	dissociar
Trennung(f)	séparation	separation	separación	separazione	separação
Trennung(f)	division	partition	división	divisione	partilha
Trennung(f)	ségrégation	segregation	segregación	segregazione	segregação

G

355

German	French	English	Spanish	Italian	Portuguese
Trennwand(f)	cloison	partition	tabique	tramezzo	tabique
Treppe(f)	escalier	staircase, stairs	escalera	scala	escada
treu	fidèle	faithful	fiel	fedele	fiel
Treuhandschaft(f)	tutelle	trusteeship	tutela	tutela	tutela
Trichter(m)	entonnoir	funnel	embudo	imbuto	funil
Trickaufnahme(f)	truquage	faking	falsificación	trucco	falsificação
Trickfilm(m)Zeichen-	dessin animé	cartoon	dibujo animado	cartone animato	desenho animado
Trikot(m), Strickweste	tricot	sweater, jumper	prenda de punto	maglia	malha
Trikot(n)	maillot de corps	vest	camiseta	maglia intima	camisola interior
trinkbar, genießbar	potable	drinking	potable	potabile	potável
trinken	boire	drink	beber	bere	beber
Trinker(in f)m	buveur, se	drinker	bebedor, a	bevitore, trice	bebedor, a
Trinkgeld(n)	pourboire	tip	propina	mancia	gorgeta
Trinkschale(f)	bol	bowl	tazón	scodella	tigela; malga
Triumph(m)	triomphe	triumph	triunfo	trionfo	triunfo
trocken	sec, sèche	dry	seco, a	secco, a; asciutto, a	seco, a
Trockenheit(f)	sécheresse	drought	sequía	siccità	seca
trocknen	sécher	dry	secar	asciugare; seccare	secar
Trommelfell(n)	tympan	eardrum	tímpano	timpano	tímpano
Trompete(f)	trompette	trumpet	trompeta	trombetta	trombeta
Tropfen(m)	goutte	drop	gota	goccia	gota
Trophäe(f)	trophée	trophy	trofeo	trofeo	troféu
tropisch	tropical, e	tropical	tropical	tropicale	tropical
trösten	consoler	console, comfort	consolar	consolare	consolar
tröstlich	réconfortant, e	comforting	reconfortante	riconfortante	reconfortante
trotz	malgré	despite	a pesar de	malgrado	apesar de
trotzen	braver	defy	desafiar	sfidare	defrontar
trüb	trouble	cloudy, muddy	turbio, a	torbido, a	turvo, a
Trübsinn(m)	cafard	miserable(feel)	melancolía	malinconia	tristeza
Truhe(f)	bahut, coffre	chest	arca, cajón	cassone	baú, arca, armário
Trümmer(m, pl)	ruine	ruin	ruina	rovina	ruína
Trümmer(m, pl)	débris, restes	remains, debris	resto, residuo	resti, cocci	resto, destroços
Trümmer(m, pl)	décombres	ruins	escombros	macerie, rovine	escombros
Trumpf(m), Vorteil(m)	atout, avantage	asset	ventaja	vantaggio	vantagem
Trunkenbold(m)	ivrogne	drunkard	borracho, a	ubriaco, a	bêbedo, a; ébrio, a
Trunkenheit(f)	ivresse	drunkenness	ebriedad	ubriachezza	embriaguez
Truppe(f)	troupe	troop	tropa	truppa	tropa
tschüs!; tschüß!	salut!	hi!; hello!	hola(!)	ciao!	salvé!
tschüß!, lebe wohl!	adieu!	good bye!	adiós(!)	addio!	adeus!
Tube(f)	tube	tube	tubo	tubo	tubo
Tuberkulose(f)	tuberculose	tuberculosis, T.B.	tuberculosis	tubercolosi	tuberculose
Tuch(n)	toile	canvas, material	tela, lienzo	tela	tela
tüchtig, fähig	efficace	efficient	eficiente	efficiente	eficiente
Tugend(f)	vertu	virtue	virtud	virtù	virtude
tugendhaft	vertueux, se	virtuous	virtuoso, a	virtuoso, a	virtuoso, a
Tulpe(f)	tulipe	tulip	tulipán	tulipano	tulipa
Tumor(m)	tumeur	tumour	tumor	tumore	tumor
Tümpel(m)	mare	pond, pool	charca	stagno	charco
Tumult(m)	tumulte	tumult, uproar	tumulto	tumulto	tumulto
tun, machen	faire	do, make	hacer	fare	fazer
Tunika(f)	tunique	tunic	túnica	tunica	túnica
Tunnel(m)	tunnel	tunnel	túnel	tunnel	túnel
Tür(f)	porte	door	puerta	porta	porta
Turbine(f)	turbine	turbine	turbina	turbina	turbina
Turbulenz(f)	turbulence	turbulence	turbulencia	turbolenza	turbulência
Turm(m)	tour	tower	torre	torre	torre
Turnier(n)	tournoi	tournament	torneo	torneo	torneio
Typ(m)	type	type	tipo	tipo	tipo
Typhus(m)	typhoïde	typhoid	tifoidea	tifoide	tifóide
typisch	typique	typical	típico, a	tipico, a	típico, a
Tyrann(m)	tyran	tyrant	tirano, a	tiranno, a	tirano, a

U

German	French	English	Spanish	Italian	Portuguese
U-Bahn(f)	métro	underground, tube	metro	metropolitana	metropolitano
übel	mauvais, mal	evil, bad	malo, a	cattivo, a; male	mau, má
üben; trainieren	entraîner(s')	train, practise	entrenarse	allenare(-rsi)	treinar-se
über	au-dessus	above	encima(por, de)	sopra(al di)	cima(por); acima de
über; auf	sur	on, upon	sobre	sopra, su	sobre
über	dessus(au-, par-)	above, on, over	arriba, encima	sopra	em cima, sobre
überall	partout	everywhere	por todas partes	dappertutto	por toda a parte
Überarbeitung(f)	surmenage	overwork(ing)	agotamiento	esaurimento	esgotamento
überdies, ferner	plus(de)	moreover, further	más de	più(di, in)	além do mais
über die Ufer treten	déborder	overflow	salirse de madre	straripare	extravasar
Überdosis(f)	surdose	overdose	sobredosis	overdose	overdose
überein = kommen	convenir	agree	acordar	convenire	convir, combinar
überein = stimmen	concorder	tally, agree	concordar	concordare	concordar
überein = stimmen	accord(être d')	agree	acuerdo(estar de)	accordo(essere d')	acordo(estar de)
Übereinstimmung(f)	convention	agreement	convención	convenzione	convenção
Überfall(m)	incursion	incursion	incursión	incursione	incursão
Überfliegen(n)	survol	flight over	sobrevuelo	sorvolo	sobrevôo
Überfluß(m)	abondance	abundance	abundancia	abbondanza	abundância
überführen	transférer	transfer	transferir	trasferire	transferir
übergenau sein	maniaque	fussy	maniático, a	pignolo, a	meticuloso, a
überholen	dépasser	go beyond, exceed	sobresalir	oltrepassare	ultrapassar
überholen	doubler	overtake	adelantar	sorpassare	ultrapassar
Überholung(f)	révision	service, overhaul	revisión	revisione	revisão
überirdisch	surnaturel, le	supernatural	sobrenatural	soprannaturale	sobrenatural
über = laufen	déborder	overflow	desbordar	traboccare	transbordar
Überläufer(in f)m	transfuge	defector	transfuga	transfuga	trânsfuga
überleben	survivre	survive	sobrevivir	sopravvivere	sobreviver
Überlebende(r)mf	rescapé, e	survivor	superviviente	scampato, a	sobrevivente
Überlebende(r)mf	survivant, e	survivor	superviviente	superstite	sobrevivente
überlegen	réfléchir(à)	reflect, think	reflexionar	riflettere	reflectir; pensar
Überlegenheit(f)	supériorité	superiority	superioridad	superiorità	superioridade
Überlegung(f)	raisonnement	reasoning	razonamiento	ragionamento	raciocínio
Übermaß(n)	excès	excess	exceso	eccesso	excesso
übermäßig	excessif, ive	excessive	excesivo, a	eccessivo, a	excessivo, a
übernehmen, nehmen	assumer	assume	asumir	assumere	assumir
überprüfen	vérifier	check, verify	comprobar	verificare	verificar
überprüfen	superviser	supervise	supervisar	soprintendere	supervisar
Überprüfung(f)	vérification	verification	verificación	verifica	verificação
Überprüfung(f)	inspection	inspection	inspección	ispezione	inspecção
überqueren	traverser	cross	atravesar, cruzar	attraversare	atravessar
überqueren	franchir	cross	atravesar	varcare, passare	atravessar
überraschen	étonner	astonish, amaze	sorprender	sorprendere	espantar
überrascht	surpris, e	surprised	sorprendido, a	sorpreso, a	surpreendido, a
Überraschung(f)	surprise	surprise	sorpresa	sorpresa	surpresa
überreden	persuader	persuade	persuadir	persuadere	persuadir
überrennen	culbuter	somersault	volcar	ribaltare	cambalhotas(dar)
Überrest(m)	vestige	remains	vestigio	vestigia	vestígio
Übersättigung(f)	saturation	saturation	saturación	saturazione	saturação
Überschall-	supersonique	supersonic	supersónico, a	supersonico, a	supersónico, a
überschlagen, sich	renverser(se)	overturn	volcarse	rovesciarsi	virar; cair
überschreiten	dépasser	exceed	adelantar	superare	ultrapassar
Überschuß(m)	excédent	surplus, excess	excedente	eccedente	excedente
Überschwemmung(f)	inondation	flooding, flood	inundación	inondazione	inundação
Überschwemmung(f)	déluge	flood; downpour	diluvio	diluvio	dilúvio
überseeisch	outre-mer	overseas	ultramar	oltremare	ultramar
übersenden	expédier, livrer	consign	enviar, expedir	inviare	enviar, expedir
Übersetzer(in f)m	traducteur, trice	translator	traductor, a	traduttore, trice	tradutor, a
Übersetzung(f)	traduction	translation	traducción	traduzione	tradução
übertragen	transmettre	transmit	transmitir	trasmettere	transmitir
übertragen	téléviser	televise	televisar	teletrasmettere	televisionar
Übertragung(f)	transmission	transmission	transmisión	trasmissione	transmissão

G

357

German	French	English	Spanish	Italian	Portuguese
übertreiben	exagérer	exaggerate	exagerar	esagerare	exagerar
überwachen	surveiller	watch; supervise	vigilar	sorvegliare	vigiar
Überwachung(f)	surveillance	watch; supervision	vigilancia	sorveglianza	vigilância
überwinden	surmonter	overcome	superar	superare	superar
überzeugen	convaincre	convince	convencer	convincere	convencer
überzeugen, sich	assurer(s')	make sure	cerciorarse	accertarsi	verificar
Überzeugung(f)	conviction	conviction	convicción	convinzione	convicção
üblich, gewönhnlich	habituellement	usually	generalmente	abitualmente	habitualmente
übrig = bleiben, bleiben	rester	left(be), remain	quedar	rimanere, avanzare	sobrar
übrigens	ailleurs(d')	moreover, besides	por otra parte	del resto, d'altronde	aliás
Übung(f)	exercice	exercise	ejercicio	esercizio	exercício
Ufer(n)	rive	bank	orilla, margen	riva	margem
Ufer(n)	berge	bank	ribera, orilla	sponda	margem
Uhr(f)	horloge	clock	reloj	orologio	relógio
Uhr(f), Armbanduhr(f)	montre	watch	reloj	orologio	relógio
Ulk(m), Witz(m)	canular	joke, hoax	broma	scherzo, burla	partida
um	autour	around	alrededor	intorno, attorno	redor de(em)
um...zu	afin de	in order to	a fin de	per; allo scopo di	a fim de
um = bringen, sich	suicider(se)	commit suicide	suicidarse	suicidarsi	suicidar-se
Umdrehung(f)	tour	turn	vuelta	giro	volta, giro
Umfang(m)	périmètre	perimeter	perímetro	perimetro	perímetro
Umfang(m)	étendue	extent	extensión, amplitud	estensione, ampiezza	extensão
Umfrage(f)	enquête, étude	survey	encuesta	inchiesta	inquérito
Umfrage(f)	sondage	poll(opinion)	sondeo	sondaggio	sondagem
um = geben	entourer	surround	rodear	circondare	rodear, cercar
Umgebung(f)	alentours	surroundings	alrededores	dintorni	arredores
Umgebung(f)	environnement	surroundings	ambiente(medio)	ambiente	ambiente
umgehen	contourner	bypass	contornear	aggirare	contornar
umgekehrt	inverse	opposite	inverso, a	inverso, a	inverso, a
umher = gehen	circuler	circulate	circular	circolare	circular
um = kehren	inverser	reverse, invert	invertir	invertire	inverter
Umkehrung(f)	inversion	inversion	inversión	inversione	inversão
Umkreis(m), Umfang(m)	périphérie	periphery	periferia	periferia	periferia
Umkreis(m)	pourtour	periphery	contorno	giro, circuito	perímetro
Umlaufbahn(f)	orbite	orbit	órbita	orbita	órbita
um = leiten	dévier	divert	desviar	deviare	desviar
Umleitung(f)	déviation	diversion	desviación	deviazione	desvio
Umriß(m)	contour	outline, contour	contorno	contorno	contorno
Umsatz(m)	chiffre(affaire)	turnover	volumen(negocios)	fatturato	volume(negócios)
Umschlag(m)(Brief-)	enveloppe	envelope	sobre	busta	envelope
Umstand(m)	circonstance	circumstance	circunstancia	circostanza	circunstância
Umstandswort, Adverb	adverbe	adverb	adverbio	avverbio	advérbio
Umstellung(f)	déplacement	transfer, moving	desplazamiento	spostamento	deslocação
Umstellung(f)	réadaptation	readjustment	readaptación	riadattamento	readaptação
um = stoßen	renverser	knock over/down	derribar	travolgere	derrubar
um = ziehen	déménager	move	mudar(se)	traslocare	mudar, mudar-se
Umzug(m), Festzug(m)	cortège	procession	cortejo	corteo	cortejo
unabhängig	indépendant, e	independent	independiente	indipendente	independente
Unabhängigkeit(f)	indépendance	independence	independencia	indipendenza	independência
Unachtsamkeit(f)	inattention	carelessness	descuido	disattenzione	distracção
unangenehm	désagréable	unpleasant	desagradable	sgradevole	desagradável
unangenehm	déplaisant, e	unpleasant	desagradable	sgradevole	desagradável
unanständig	indécent, e	indecent	indecente	indecente	indecente
unaufmerksam	dissipé, e	unruly	indisciplinado, a	indisciplinato, a	indisciplinado, a
unbarmherzig	impitoyable	pitiless	despiadado, a	spietato, a	impiedoso, a
unbedeutend	insignifiant, e	insignificant	insignificante	insignificante	insignificante
unbedeutend	mineur, e	minor	menor	minore	menor
unbedingt	absolu, e	absolute	absoluto, a	assoluto, a	absoluto, a
unbedingt, absolut	absolument	absolutely	absolutamente	assolutamente	absolutamente
unbekannt	inconnu, e	unknown	desconocido, a	sconosciuto, a	desconhecido, a
unbekümmert	insouciant, e	carefree	despreocupado, a	noncurante	descuidado, a
unbelebt, leblos	inanimé, e	lifeless	inanimado, a	inanimato, a	inanimado, a
unbeliebt	impopulaire	unpopular	impopular	impopolare	impopular
unberührt	vierge	virgin	virgen	vergine	virgem
unbesiegbar	invincible	invincible	invencible	invincibile	invencível
unbeständig	instable	unstable	inestable	instabile	instável
unbestimmt	indéfini, e	indefinite	indefinido, a	indefinito, a	indefinido, a
unbestraft	impuni, e	unpunished	impune	impunito, a	impune

German	French	English	Spanish	Italian	Portuguese
unbestreitbar	incontestable	incontestable	indiscutible	incontestabile	incontestável
unbeweglich	immobile	motionless	inmóvil	immobile	imóvel
unbewußt	inconscient, e	unconscious	inconsciente	incosciente	inconsciente
unbrennbar	ininflammable	fire-proof	ininflamable	ininfiammabile	prova de fogo(à)
und	et	and	y	e, ed	e
und, plus	plus	plus	más	più	mais
undankbar	ingrat, e	ungrateful	ingrato, a	ingrato, a	ingrato, a
undenkbar	impensable	unthinkable	increíble	impensabile	impensável
undenkbar	inimaginable	inconceivable	inimaginable	inimmaginabile	inimaginável
undurchlässig	étanche	watertight(air-)	estanco, a	stagno, a	estanque
undurchsichtig; trüb	opaque	opaque	opaco, a	opaco, a	opaco, a
uneben	inégal, e	uneven	desigual	disuguale	desigual
Unebenheit(f); Buckel	bosse	bump	bache	gobba, dosso, cunetta	bossa; alto
unehelich	illégitime	illegitimate	ilegítimo, a	illegittimo, a	ilegítimo, a
unehrlich	malhonnête	dishonest	deshonesto, a	disonesto, a	desonesto, a
Uneinigkeit(f), Streit	désaccord	disagreement	discrepancia	disaccordo	desacordo
unempfindlich	insensible	insensitive	insensible	insensibile	insensível
unendlich	infini, e	infinite	infinito, a	infinito, a	infinito, a
unendlich groß	immense	immense, vast	inmenso, a	immenso, a	imenso, a
unentbehrlich	indispensable	indispensable	indispensable	indispensabile	indispensável
unentgeltlich	bénévole	voluntary	benévolo, a	benevolo, a	benévolo, a
unermüdlich	infatigable	tireless	incansable	instancabile	infatigável
unerreichbar	inaccessible	inaccessible	inaccesible	inaccessibile	inacessível
unerwartet, unverhofft	inespéré, e	unexpected	inesperado, a	insperato, a	inesperado, a
unfähig, untauglich	incapable	incapable, unable	incapaz	incapace	incapaz
Unfall(m)	accident	accident	accidente	incidente	acidente
unfehlbar	infaillible	infallible	infalible	infallibile	infalível
ungebildet	illettré, e	illiterate	analfabeto, a	analfabeta	iletrado, a
Ungeduld(f)	impatience	impatience	impaciencia	impazienza	impaciência
ungeduldig	impatient, e	impatient	impaciente	impaziente	impaciente
ungeeignet	inadapté, e	unsuitable	inadaptado, a	inadatto, a	inadaptado, a
ungeeignet	inapte	unsuited, unfit	inapto, a	inabile	inapto, a
ungefähr	approximatif, ive	approximate	aproximativo, a	approssimativo, a	aproximado, a
ungefähr	environ	about	aproximadamente	circa	cerca de
ungehorsam sein	désobéir	disobey	desobedecer	disobbedire	desobedecer
ungenau	inexact, e	inexact, inaccurate	inexacto, a	inesatto, a	inexacto, a
ungenügend	insuffisant, e	insufficient	insuficiente	insufficiente	insuficiente
ungerade	impair	odd	impar	dispari	impar
Ungerechtigkeit(f)	injustice	injustice	injusticia	ingiustizia	injustiça
ungeschickt	maladroit, e	clumsy, awkward	torpe	maldestro, a	desajeitado, a
ungestüm, stürmisch	impétueux, se	impetuous	impetuoso, a	impetuoso, a	impetuoso, a
ungesund	malsain, e	unhealthy	malsano, a	malsano, a	doentio, a
unglaublich	incroyable	unbelievable	increíble	incredibile	incrível
ungleich	inégal, e	unequal	desigual	ineguale	desigual
Ungleichheit(f)	inégalité	inequality	desigualdad	disuguaglianza	desigualdade
Unglück(n)	malheur	misfortune	desgracia	disgrazia	desgraça
Unglück(n)	malchance	misfortune	mala suerte	sventura, sfortuna	desventura
unglücklich	malheureux, se	unfortunate	desgraciado, a	disgraziato, a	infeliz
unglücklich	malchanceux, se	unlucky	desafortunado, a	sfortunato, a	azarento, a
unglücklich, betrübt	malheureux, se	unhappy, miserable	desgraciado, a	infelice	infeliz
Ungnade(f)	disgrâce	disgrace	desgracia	disgrazia	desvalimento
ungültig erklären	annuler	annul	anular	annullare	anular
Unheil(n)	désastre	disaster	desastre	disastro	desastre
unheilbar	incurable	incurable	incurable	incurabile	incurável
unheilvoll	sinistre	sinister	siniestro, a	sinistro, a	sinistro, a
unhöflich	impoli, e	impolite, rude	maleducado, a	maleducato, a	mal educado, a
Uniform(f)	uniforme	uniform	uniforme	uniforme; divisa	uniforme
unitarisch	unitaire	unitary, per unit	unitario, a	unitario, a	unitário, a
universell	universel, le	universal	universal	universale	universal
Universität(f)	université	university	universidad	università	universidade
Universität-	universitaire	academic	universitario, a	universitario, a	universitário, a
Universum(n)	univers	universe	universo	universo	universo
unlogisch	illogique	illogical	ilógico, a	illogico, a	ilógico, a
unmenschlich	inhumain, e	inhuman	inhumano, a	inumano, a	desumano, a
unmöglich	impossible	impossible	imposible	impossibile	impossível
Unordnung(f)	désordre	disorder, mess	desorden	disordine	desordem
unparteiisch	impartial, e	impartial	imparcial	imparziale	imparcial
Unrat(m)	détritus	rubbish, garbage	desperdicios	detrito	detrito, lixo

German	French	English	Spanish	Italian	Portuguese
Unrecht(haben)	tort(avoir)	wrong(to be)	culpa(tener)	torto(aver)	razão(não ter)
unregelmäßig	irrégulier, e	irregular	irregular	irregolare	irregular
Unreinheit(f)	impureté	impurity	impureza	impurità	impureza
unrichtig, falsch	incorrect, e	incorrect, wrong	incorrecto, a	scorretto, a	incorrecto, a
Unruhen(f, pl)	troubles	troubles	disturbios	disordini	perturbação
uns	nous	us	nos	ci, ce	nos
unschuldig	innocent, e	innocent	inocente	innocente	inocente
unser, unsere	notre	our	nuestro, a	nostro, a(il, la)	nosso, a
unsere(der, die, das)	nôtre(le, la)	ours	nuestro, a(el, la)	nostro, a(il, la)	nosso, a(o, a)
unser(e)	nos	our	nuestros, nuestras	nostri, e(i, le)	nossos, nossas
unsicher	incertain, e	uncertain	inseguro, a	incerto, a	incerto, a
unsicher, ungewiß	aléatoire	aleatory, uncertain	aleatorio, a	aleatorio, a	aleatório, a; incerto
unsichtbar	invisible	invisible	invisible	invisibile	invisível
unsinnig	absurde	absurd	absurdo, a	assurdo, a	absurdo, a
unsterblich	immortel, le	immortal	inmortal	immortale	imortal
untätig, inaktiv	inactif, ive	inactive	inactivo, a	inattivo, a	inactivo, a
untätig	inoccupé, e	unoccupied	desocupado, a	inoperoso, a	desocupado, a
unten; hinunter	bas(en)	downstairs	abajo	basso, giù	baixo(de)
unten(-stehend)	ci-dessous	below	abajo(más)	sotto(qui)	abaixo
unter	sous	under	debajo, bajo	sotto	debaixo, sob
unter(halb); unten	sous, au-dessous	beneath	bajo; debajo; abajo	sotto	baixo; baixo(de-; a-)
unter	au-dessous	below, under(neath)	debajo(de)	sotto(al di)	baixo(por); abaixo
unter	dessous	under, beneath	debajo, abajo	sotto	debaixo, sob
unter	parmi	among	entre	fra, tra	entre
Unterarm(m)	avant-bras	fore-arm	antebrazo	avambraccio	antebraço
Unterbewußtsein(n)	subconscient	subconscious	subconsciente	subcosciente	subconsciente
Unterboden(m)	sous-sol	subsoil	subsuelo	sottosuolo	sub-solo
unterbrechen	interrompre	interrupt	interrumpir	interrompere	interromper
Unterbrechung(f)	interruption	interruption	interrupción	interruzione	interrupção
unter = bringen	loger	accommodate	alojar	alloggiare	alojar, morar
Unterbringung(f)	hébergement	accommodation	alojamiento	alloggio	alojamento
unterdrückt	opprimé, e	oppressed	oprimido, a	oppresso, a	oprimido, a
Unterdrückung(f)	répression	repression	represión	repressione	repressão
untere(r)	inférieur, e	lower	inferior	inferiore	inferior
Unterernährung(f)	malnutrition	malnutrition	desnutrición	malnutrizione	malnutrição
Untergang(m)	déclin	decline	decadencia, ocaso	declino	declínio
Untergang(m), Verfall	déchéance	downfall	decaimiento	decadenza	decadência
Untergebene(f m)	subordonné, e	subordinate	subordinado, a	subalterno, a	subordinado, a
Untergeschoß(n)	sous-sol	basement	sótano	scantinato	cave
unterhalten	distraire	entertain	entretener	distrarre	distrair
Unterhaltung(f)	spectacles	entertainment	espectáculos	spettacoli	espectáculos
Unterhändler(in f)m	négociateur	negotiator	negociador, a	negoziatore, trice	negociador, a
Unterhose(f)	slip	briefs, pants	calzoncillos	mutande, slip	cuecas
Unterhose(f), Slip(m)	culotte	briefs, knickers	bragas	mutandine, slip	cuecas
unterirdisch	souterrain, e	underground	subterráneo, a	sotterraneo, a	subterrâneo, a
Unterleib(m)	abdomen	abdomen	abdomen	addome	abdómen
Untermieter(in f)m	pensionnaire	lodger	huésped	ospite	hóspede
Unternehmen(n)	entreprise	company, firm	empresa	impresa, ditta	empresa
unternehmen	entreprendre	undertake	emprender	intraprendere	empreender
Unternehmer(in f)m	entrepreneur	contractor	empresario	imprenditore	empresário
Unternehmer(in f)m	patron	manager, boss	director, jefe	manager, padrone	director, patrão
Unteroffizier(m)	sergent	sergeant	sargento	sergente	sargento
Unterricht(m)	cours	lesson	curso, clase	corso, lezione	curso, aula
Unterricht(m), Lehre f	enseignement	teaching	enseñanza	insegnamento	ensino
Unterrock(m)	jupon	petticoat, slip	enagua	sottana	saiote
Unterrock(m)	combinaison	slip	combinación	sottoveste	combinação
unterscheiden	distinguer	distinguish	distinguir	distinguere	distinguir
unterscheiden	discerner	discern	discernir	discernere	discernir
Unterschied(m)	différence	difference	diferencia	differenza	diferença
unterschreiben	signer	sign	firmar	firmare	assinar
Unterschrift(f)	signature	signature	firma	firma	assinatura
Unterseeboot(n)	sous-marin	submarine	submarino	sottomarino	submarino
unterstreichen	souligner	underline	subrayar	sottolineare	sublinhar
unterstützen	soutenir	support	sostener	sostenere	sustentar
Unterstützung(f)	soutien, appui	support	sostén, apoyo	sostegno, appoggio	apoio, socorro
untersuchen	examiner	examine, inspect	examinar	esaminare	examinar
untersuchen	enquêter	investigate	investigar	investigare, indagare	investigar
Untersuchung(f)	examen(médical)	examination	examen, chequeo	esame	exame

German	French	English	Spanish	Italian	Portuguese
Untersuchung(f)	enquête	inquiry, inquest	investigación	indagine, inchiesta	inquérito
Untertasse(f)	soucoupe	saucer	platillo	piattino	pires
Unterteil(n)	dessous	lower part	inferior(parte)	sotto, disotto	baixo(parte de)
Untertiteln(mit)	sous-titré, e	subtitled	subtitulado, a	didascalie(con)	legendado, a
Unterwelt(f)	pègre	underworld	hampa	teppa, malviventi	súcia, ladroagem
unterwerfen	soumettre	submit	someter	sottomettere	submeter
unterwerfen	assujettir	subject(to)	someter, sujetar	assoggettare	sujeitar
Unterwerfung(f)	soumission	submission	sumisión	sottomissione	submissão
untreu	infidèle	unfaithful	infiel	infedele	infiel
ununterbrochen	continu, e	continuous	continuo, a	continuo, a	contínuo, a
unveränderlich	invariable	invariable	invariable	invariabile	invariável
unverändert	inchangé, e	unchanged	inalterado, a	immutato, a	inalterado, a
unverdaulich	indigeste	indigestible	indigesto, a	indigesto, a	indigesto, a
unvereinbar	incompatible	incompatible	incompatible	incompatibile	incompatível
unveröffentlicht	inédit, e	unpublished	inédito, a	inedito, a	inédito, a
unverschämt	impertinent, e	impertinent	impertinente	impertinente	impertinente
unverschämt, frech	insolent, e	insolent	insolente	insolente	insolente
unverzüglich	immédiat, e	immediate	inmediato, a	immediato, a	imediato, a
Unvollkommenheit(f)	imperfection	imperfection	imperfección	imperfezione	imperfeição
unvollständig	incomplet, ète	incomplete	incompleto, a	incompleto, a	incompleto, a
unvorhergesehen	imprévu, e	unexpected	imprevisto, a	imprevisto, a	imprevisto, a
unvorsichtig	imprudent, e	careless	imprudente	imprudente	imprudente
Unvorsichtigkeit(f)	imprudence	imprudence	imprudencia	imprudenza	imprudência
Unwetter(n)	tempête	storm	tempestad	tempesta	tempestade
unwirksam, unfähig	inefficace	inefficient	ineficaz	inefficace	ineficaz
Unwissenheit(f)	ignorance	ignorance	ignorancia	ignoranza	ignorância
Unwohlsein, Schwäche	malaise	faintness	malestar	malessere	indisposição
unwürdig	indigne	unworthy	indigno, a	indegno, a	indigno, a
unzufrieden	mécontent, e	displeased	descontento, a	scontento, a	descontente
unzufrieden	insatisfait, e	not satisfied	insatisfecho, a	insoddisfatto, a	insatisfeito, a
Unzufriedenheit(f)	mécontentement	displeasure	descontento	scontento	descontentamento
unzulässig	inadmissible	inadmissible	inadmisible	inammissibile	inadmissível
üppig	luxueux, se	luxurious	lujoso, a	lussuoso, a	luxuoso, a
üppig	luxuriant, e	luxuriant, lush	exuberante	lussureggiante	luxuriante
Uran(n)	uranium	uranium	uranio	uranio	urânio
Urin(m)	urine	urine	orina	urina	urina
Urlaub(m)	congé	holiday, vacation	vacaciones	ferie(le)	férias
Urlaubstag(m)	jour de congé	day off	día libre	giorno di vacanza	dia de folga
Ursache(f), Grund(m)	cause	cause	causa	causa	causa
Ursprung(m)	origine	origin	origen	origine	origem
Ursprung(m)	source, origine	source	fuente, origen	fonte, origine	fonte, origem
Urteil(n)	jugement	judgement	juicio	giudizio	julgamento
Urteil(n)	jugement	sentence	sentencia	sentenza	sentença
Urteil(n)	verdict	verdict	veredicto	verdetto	veredicto
utopisch	utopique	Utopian	utópico, a	utopico, a	utópico, a

V

German	French	English	Spanish	Italian	Portuguese
Vakuum(n), Leere(f)	vide	vacuum; void	vacío	vuoto	vazio, vácuo
Vanille(f)	vanille	vanilla	vainilla	vaniglia	baunilha
variieren	diversifier	diversify	diversificar	diversificare	diversificar
Vase(f)	vase	vase	jarrón	vaso	jarra
Vaseline(f)	vaseline	vaseline	vaselina	vasellina	vaselina
Vater(m)	père	father	padre	padre	pai
Vaterland(n)	patrie	native land	patria	patria	pátria
väterlich	paternel, le	paternal	paterno, a	paterno, a	paterno, a
Vene(f)	veine	vein	vena	vena	veia

German	French	English	Spanish	Italian	Portuguese
Ventilator(m)	ventilateur	fan, ventilator	ventilador	ventilatore	ventilador
Verabredung(f)	rendez-vous	appointment	cita	appuntamento	encontro
Verachtung(f)	mépris	contempt, scorn	desprecio	disprezzo	desprezo
veraltet	démodé, e; désuet	obsolete	anticuado, a	antiquato, a	antiquado, a
veränderlich	variable	variable	variable	variabile	variável
verändern	modifier	modify	modificar	modificare	modificar
verändern	transformer	transform, change	transformar	trasformare	transformar
Veränderung(f)	changement	change	cambio	cambiamento	mudança
Veränderung(f)	transformation	transformation	transformación	trasformazione	transformação
veranlassen	induire	induce	inducir	indurre	induzir
verantwortlich	responsable	responsible	responsable	responsabile	responsável
Verantwortliche(r)mf	responsable	person in charge	encargado, a	responsabile	responsável
Verantwortung(f)	responsabilité	responsibility	responsabilidad	responsabilità	responsabilidade
Verb(n)	verbe	verb	verbo	verbo	verbo
Verband(m)	pansement	plaster, bandage	cura, vendaje	medicazione	penso, curativo
Verband(m)	association	association	asociación	associazione	associação
Verband(m)	fédération	federation	federación	federazione	federação
verbannen	bannir	banish	desterrar	bandire	desterrar
Verbannte(r)mf	exilé, e	exile	exiliado, a	esiliato, a	exilado, a
Verbannung(f)	exil	exile	exilio	esilio	exílio
verbergen, verhehlen	dissimuler	conceal	disimular	dissimulare	dissimular
verbergen, verhehlen	cacher	conceal	esconder, ocultar	nascondere	ocultar
verbessern	améliorer	improve	mejorar	migliorare	melhorar
verbessern, ändern	amender	amend	enmendar	emendare	emendar
Verbesserung(f)	amélioration	improvement	mejora; mejoría	miglioramento	melhoramento
Verbesserung(f)	correction	correction	corrección	correzione	correcção
verbiegen, verdrehen	tordre	twist	torcer	torcere, piegare	torcer
verbieten	défendre	forbid	prohibir	proibire	proibir
verbieten	interdire	forbid, ban	prohibir	vietare, proibire	proibir
verbinden	relier	link, connect	enlazar, unir	collegare	ligar
verbinden	associer	combine, associate	asociar	associare	associar
Verbindung(f)	liaison	link	enlace	collegamento	conexão
Verbindung(f)	liaison	connection, link	relación; enlace	collegamento	ligação, junção
Verbindung; Anschluß	connexion	connection	conexión	connessione	conexão
Verbindung, Anschluß	correspondance	connection	empalme	coincidenza	correspondência
verblüfft	stupéfait, e	amazed	estupefacto, a	stupefatto, a	estupefacto, a
verbogen	gondolé, e	warped, buckled	combado, a	incurvato, a	empenado, a
Verbot(n)	interdiction	ban	prohibición	proibizione	proibição
verboten	interdit, e	forbidden	prohibido, a	proibito, a	proibido, a
Verbrauch(m)	consommation	consumption	consumo	consumo	consumo
verbrauchen	consommer	consume	consumir	consumare	consumir
Verbraucher(in f)m	consommateur	consumer	consumidor, a	consumatore, trice	consumidor, a
verbraucht	usé, e	worn, worn out	usado, a	logoro, a	usado, a
Verbrechen(n)	crime	crime	crimen	crimine	crime
Verbrecher(in f)m	criminel, le	criminal	criminal	criminale	criminoso, a
verbreiten	diffuser	diffuse	difundir	diffondere	difundir
verbreiten	propager	spread	propagar	propagare	propagar
verbreiten	élargir	widen, enlarge	ensanchar	allargare	alargar
Verbreitung; Sendung	diffusion	diffusion	difusión	diffusione	difusão
verbrennbar	combustible	combustible	combustible	combustibile	combustível
verbrennen	brûler	burn	quemar	bruciare	queimar, arder
Verbrennung(f)	brûlure	burn	quemadura	bruciatura	queimadura
verbringen	passer	spend	pasar	trascorrere	passar
verbünden	allier	ally	aliar, unir	alleare, unire	aliar, unir
Verbundenheit(f)	attachement	attachment	apego, cariño	attaccamento	apego
verdächtig	suspect, e	suspicious	sospechoso, a	sospetto, a	suspeito, a
verdächtigen	soupçonner	suspect	sospechar	sospettare	suspeitar
verdammen	damner	damn	condenar	dannare	condenar
verdammt	maudit, e	cursed, damned	maldito, a	maledetto, a	maldito, a
Verdauung(f)	digestion	digestion	digestión	digestione	digestão
verdienen	gagner	earn; win	ganar	guadagnare	ganhar
verdienen	mériter	deserve, merit	merecer	meritare	merecer
Verdienst(n)	mérite	merit, worth	mérito	merito	mérito
verdorben, korrupt	corrompu, e	corrupt	corrompido, a	corrotto, a	corrupto, a
Verdruß(m)	contrariété	annoyance	molestia	seccatura	contrariedade
verdünnen	diluer	dilute	diluir	diluire	diluir
Verdunstung(f)	évaporation	evaporation	evaporación	evaporazione	evaporação
verdutzt	ahuri, e	stupefied	espantado, a	attonito, a	pasmado, a

German	French	English	Spanish	Italian	Portuguese
Veredelung; Pfropfen	greffe	graft	injerto	innesto	enxerto
vereinen	unir	unite	unir	unire	unir, juntar
vereinfachen	simplifier	simplify	simplificar	semplificare	simplificar
vereinigt	unifié, e	unified, united	unificado, a	unificato, a	unificado, a
Vereinigung(f), Fusion	fusion	merger	fusión	fusione, alleanza	fusão
verengen	resserrer	narrow	estrechar	ristringere	estreitar
Vererbung(f)	hérédité	heredity	herencia	ereditarietà	hereditariedade
Verfahren(n)	procédé	process	procedimiento	procedimento	procedimento
Verfahren(n)	procédure	procedure	procedimiento	procedimento	procedimento
Verfall(m), Untergang	décadence	decadence, decline	decadencia	decadenza	decadência
verfallen	périmé, e	expired	caducado, a	scaduto, a	caducado, a
Verfassung(f)	constitution	constitution	constitución	costituzione	constituição
Verfassung(f)	forme	form	forma(en)	forma	forma
verfaulen	pourrir	rot	pudrir	marcire	apodrecer
verfault	pourri, e	rotten	podrido, a	marcio, a	podre
verflucht	hanté, e	haunted	embrujado, a	spiritato, a	assombrado, a
verfolgen	poursuivre	pursue	perseguir	inseguire	perseguir
verfolgen	persécuter	persecute	perseguir	perseguitare	perseguir
verfolgen, quälen	obséder	obsess	obsesionar	ossessionare	obcecar
verformen	déformer	distort, deform	deformar	deformare	deformar
verfügbar	disponible	available	disponible	disponibile	disponível
verführen	attirer, séduire	entice	atraer, seducir	attirare, sedurre	atrair, seduzir
verführen, verleiten	séduire	charm; seduce	seducir	sedurre	seduzir
Verführung(f)	séduction	seduction	seducción	seduzione	sedução
vergangen	passé, e	past	pasado, a	passato, a	passado, a
Vergangenheit(f)	passé	past	pasado	passato	passado
vergänglich	éphémère	ephemeral	efímero, a	effimero, a	efémero, a
Vergaser(m)	carburateur	carburettor	carburador	carburatore	carburador
Vergebung(f)	pardon	forgiveness	perdón	scusa, perdono	perdão
Vergehen(n), Delikt(n)	délit	offence	delito	delitto	delito
vergehen, verfließen	écouler(s')	elapse	transcurrir	trascorrere	decorrer
Vergeltung(f)	représaille(s)	reprisal	represalia	rappresaglia	represália
vergessen	oublier	forget	olvidar	dimenticare	esquecer
vergewaltigen	violer	rape	violar	violentare	violentar
Vergewaltigung(f)	viol	rape	violación	stupro	violação
Vergiftung(f)	empoisonnement	poisoning	envenenamiento	avvelenamento	envenenamento
Vergiftung(f)	intoxication	poisoning	intoxicación	intossicazione	intoxicação
vergleichen	comparer	compare	comparar	paragonare	comparar
Vergnügen(n)	plaisir	pleasure	placer	piacere	prazer
Vergnügen(n)	amusement	amusement, fun	diversión	divertimento	divertimento
vergrößern	agrandir	enlarge	ampliar	ingrandire	ampliar
Verhaftung(f)	arrestation	arrest	arresto	arresto	detenção
Verhalten(n)	comportement	behaviour	comportamiento	comportamento	comportamento
Verhältnis(n)	proportion	proportion, ratio	proporción	proporzione	proporção
verhandeln	négocier	negotiate	negociar	negoziare	negociar
verhandeln	argumenter	argue	argüir, argumentar	argomentare	argumentar
Verhandlung(f)	négociation	negotiation	negociación	negoziato	negociação
Verhandlungen(pl)	pourparlers	talks	negociaciones	trattative	negociações
verheiratet	marié, e	married	casado, a	sposato, a	casado, a
verhindern	empêcher	prevent	impedir	impedire	impedir
Verhütungsmittel(n)	contraceptif	contraceptive	anticonceptivo	anticoncezionale	contraceptivo
Verkauf(m)	vente	sale	venta	vendita	venda
verkaufen	vendre	sell	vender	vendere	vender
Verkäufer(in f)m	vendeur, se	sales assistant	vendedor, a	commesso, a	vendedor, a
Verkäufer(in f)m	vendeur, se	salesman(-men)	vendedor, a	venditore, trice	vendedor, a
Verkehr(m)	circulation	traffic	tráfico	traffico	trânsito
Verkehr(m)	trafic	traffic	tráfico	traffico	tráfego, tráfico
verkleiden	déguiser	disguise	disfrazar	mascherare	disfarçar
verkrüppelt	estropié, e	crippled	lisiado, a	storpio, a	aleijado, a
Verlagswesen(n)	édition	publishing	industria editor-	edizione	indústria livro
verlangen, fordern	exiger, demander	demand	exigir, demandar	esigere, domandare	exigir, pedir
verlängern	allonger	lengthen	alargar	allungare	alongar
verlängern	prolonger	extend	prolongar	prolungare	prolongar
Verlängerung(f)	prolongation	prolongation	prolongación	prolungazione	prolongamento
Verlängerung(f)	prolongement	extension	prolongamiento	prolungamento	prolongamento
verlangsamen	ralentir	slow down	aminorar	rallentare	abrandar
verlassen	quitter	leave	dejar, abandonar	lasciare	deixar
Verlegenheit(f)	gêne	embarrassment	molestia	disagio, imbarazzo	embaraço

German	French	English	Spanish	Italian	Portuguese
Verlegenheit(f)	embarras	embarrassment	apuro	imbarazzo	embaraço
Verlegung(f)	transfert	transfer	transferencia	trasferimento	transferência
verletzen	blesser	injure, wound	herir	ferire	ferir
verletzen, sich	blesser(se)	injured(to be)	herir(se)	ferirsi	ferir-se
verletzen, brechen	violer	violate, break	violar	violare	violar
Verletzung(f)	blessure	injury, wound	herida	ferita	ferida
Verletzung(f)	lésion	lesion, injury	lesión	lesione	lesão
verleugnen, verneinen	renier	disown; renounce	renegar	rinnegare	renegar
verleumden	dénigrer	denigrate	denigrar	denigrare	denegrir
Verleumdung(f)	calomnie	slander	calumnia	calunnia	calúnia
Verleumdung(f)	diffamation	slander	difamación	diffamazione	difamação
verliebt	amoureux, se	love(in)	enamorado, a	innamorato, a	apaixonado, a
verlieren	perdre	lose	perder	perdere	perder
verloben, sich	fiancer(se)	engaged(get)	prometerse	fidanzarsi	ficar noivo, a
Verlobte(r)mf	fiancé, e	fiancé(e)	novio, a	fidanzato, a	noivo, a
verloren	perdu, e	lost	perdido, a	perso, a; smarrito, a	perdido, a
Verlust(m)	perte	loss, waste	pérdida	perdita	perda, prejuizo
Verlust(m), Defizit(n)	déficit	deficit	déficit	deficit	défice
vermachen	léguer	bequeath, leave	legar	legare	legar
vermarkten	commercialiser	market	comercializar	commercializzare	comercializar
vermehren	grossir	increase	agrandar	ingrandire	aumentar
vermehren, sich	proliférer	proliferate	proliferar	prolificare	proliferar
vermeiden	éviter	avoid	evitar	evitare	evitar
Vermerk(m)	note	note	nota	appunto	nota
Vermerk(m)	mention	mention	mención	menzione	menção
vermieten; mieten	louer	rent	alquilar	affittare	alugar
Vermietung(f)	location	rental, hiring	alquiler	noleggio, affitto	aluguer
Verminderung(f)	diminution	reduction	disminución	diminuzione	diminuição
Vermögen(n)	fortune	fortune	fortuna	fortuna	fortuna
vermuten	présumer	presume	presumir	presumere	presumir
vernachlässigen	négliger	neglect	descuidar	trascurare	descuidar
verneinen, leugnen	nier	deny	negar	negare	negar
vernichten	anéantir	annihilate, destroy	aniquilar	annientare	aniquilar
vernünftig	raisonnable	reasonable	razonable	ragionevole	razoável
vernünftig	sensé, e	sensible	sensato, a	sensato, a	sensato, a
veröffentlichen	publier	publish, issue	publicar	pubblicare	publicar
Veröffentlichung(f)	publication	publication	publicación	pubblicazione	publicação
Verpackung(f)	emballage	packing, wrapping	embalaje, envase	imballaggio	embalagem
verpassen	manquer	miss	perder	perdere; mancare	perder
verpassen	rater	miss	perder	perdere; mancare	perder
Verpflanzung(f)	greffe	transplant, graft	trasplante	trapianto	enxerto
Verpflichtung(f)	obligation	obligation	obligación	obbligo	obrigação
Verpflichtung(f)	engagement	commitment	compromiso	impegno	compromisso
Verrat(m)	trahison	betrayal; treason	traición	tradimento	traição
verraten	trahir	betray	traicionar	tradire	trair
verraten	violer	violate	violar	violare	violar
Verräter(in f)m	traître, esse	traitor, -tress	traidor, a	traditore, trice	traidor, a
Verrenkung(f)	entorse	sprain	esguince	storta	entorse
verringern	diminuer	reduce, decrease	disminuir	diminuire	diminuir
Verringerung(f)	réduction	reduction	reducción	riduzione	redução
verrückt	fou, folle	mad, foolish, crazy	loco, a	matto, a; pazzo, a	louco, a; maluco, a
verrückt	dément, e	insane, crazy, mad	demente	demente	demente
verrückt	cinglé, e	mad, nuts, barmy	chiflado, a	tocco, a; picchiato, a	doido, a; louco, a
verrückt; schwach	débile	crazy, mad	débil	scemo, a; minorato, a	parvo, a
Verrückte(r)mf	maniaque	maniac	maníaco, a	maniaco, a	maníaco, a
Verruf bringen(in)	discréditer	discredit	desacreditar	discreditare	desacreditar
Vers(m)	vers	line	verso	verso	verso
Versagen(n)	défaillance	failure, fault	fallo	difetto	falha
versammeln	assembler	assemble	reunir	radunare, riunire	reunir
Versammlung(f)	rassemblement	gathering	concentración	raduno, adunanza	ajuntamento
Versammlung(f)	assemblée	meeting, assembly	asamblea	assemblea	assembleia
verscheiden	expirer	die	expirar	spirare	expirar
verschicken	expédier	dispatch, send	expedir	spedire	expedir
verschieben	reporter	postpone	postergar	rinviare	adiar
verschieben	suspendre	suspend, defer	suspender	sospendere	suspender
verschieden	différent, e	different	diferente	differente	diferente
verschieden	divers, e	diverse, various	diverso, a	diverso, a	diverso, a
Verschiedenheit(f)	diversité	diversity	diversidad	diversità	diversidade

German	French	English	Spanish	Italian	Portuguese
verschimmeln	moisir	mouldy(to go)	enmohecer	ammuffire	bolor(criar)
Verschlechterung(f)	détérioration	deterioration	deterioración	deteriorazione	deterioração
verschlimmern	aggraver	worsen, aggravate	empeorar	aggravare	agravar
verschlingen	dévorer	devour	devorar	divorare	devorar
verschlüsseln	coder	code, encode	codificar	cifrare	codificar
verschmitzt, schlau	astucieux, se	astute, clever	astuto, a	astuto, a	astucioso, a
verschmutzen	salir	dirty	ensuciar	sporcare	sujar
Verschmutzung(f)	pollution	pollution	contaminación	inquinamento	poluição
verschütten	renverser	spill, knock over	derramar, volcar	rovesciare	entornar
verschütten	répandre	spread; spill	derramar	spargere	espalhar
verschwenden	gaspiller, perdre	waste	despilfarrar	sprecare	desperdiçar
verschwenden	gaspiller	waste	desperdiciar	sperperare	desperdiçar
Verschwendung(f)	gaspillage	waste	despilfarro	spreco	desperdício
verschwinden	disparaître	disappear	desaparecer	sparire	desaparecer
verschwommen	flou, e	fuzzy, blurred	borroso, a	sfumato, a	vago, a
Verschwörung(f)	complot	conspiracy, plot	complot	complotto	conspiração
versenken	immerger	immerse	sumergir	immergere	imergir
Versenkung(f)	immersion	immersion	inmersión	immersione	imersão
versetzen, -schieben	déplacer	shift, move	trasladar	spostare	deslocar
Versetzung(f)	mutation	transfer	traslado	trasferimento	transferência
versichern; zu = sichern	assurer(s')	ensure; insure	asegurarse	assicurarsi	assegurar-se
versichert	assuré, e	insured	asegurado, a	assicurato, a	segurado, a
Versicherung(f)	assurance	insurance	seguro	assicurazione	seguro
Versöhnung(f)	réconciliation	reconciliation	reconciliación	riconciliazione	reconciliação
versorgen, liefern	fournir	provide	proveer	fornire	fornecer
versorgen	approvisionner	supply	aprovisionar	rifornire	abastecer
versorgen	ravitailler	supply	abastecer	rifornire	abastecer
Versorgung(f)	alimentation	supplying	abastecimiento	rifornimento	abastecimento
Verspätung(f)	retard	delay; lateness	atraso	ritardo	atraso
verspotten	moquer(se)	make fun of, mock	mofarse, burlarse	burlarsi	troçar
Versprechen(n)	promesse	promise	promesa	promessa	promessa
versprechen	promettre	promise	prometer	promettere	prometer
versprochen	promis, e	promised	prometido, a	promesso, a	prometido, a
Verständigung(f)	communication	communication	comunicación	comunicazione	comunicação
verstärken	renforcer	reinforce	reforzar	rinforzare	reforçar
verstärken	consolider	strengthen	consolidar	consolidare	consolidar
Verstärkung(f)	renfort	reinforcement	refuerzo	rinforzo	reforço
Verstauchung(f)	foulure	sprain	esguince	slogatura	entorse
Versteck(n)	affût	wait for(in)	acecho(al)	agguato	espreita de(à)
verstecken	cacher	hide	esconder	nascondere	esconder
verstehen	comprendre	understand	comprender	capire	compreender
Versteigerung(f)	adjudication	auction	adjudicación	aggiudicazione	adjudicação
versterben, sterben	décéder	die	fallecer	decedere	falecer
Verstopfung(f)	constipation	constipation	estreñimiento	stitichezza	prisão de ventre
Verstorbene(f, m)	défunt, e	deceased person	difunto, a	defunto, a	defunto, a
Verstoß(m)	infraction	offence, violation	infracción	infrazione	infracção
Verstoß(m)	violation	violation	violación	violazione	violação
verstümmelt	mutilé, e	disabled	mutilado, a	mutilato, a	mutilado, a
Versuch(m)	essai	trial, test	prueba	prova, collaudo	ensaio
Versuch(m)	tentative	attempt	tentativa	tentativo	tentativa
Versuch(m)	expérience	experiment	experimento	esperimento	experiência
versuchen	essayer	try	probar, intentar	provare	tentar; provar
versuchen; wagen	tenter	attempt, try	intentar	tentare	tentar
Versuchskaninchen(n)	cobaye	guinea-pig(be a)	conejillo(Indias)	cavia	cobaia
Versuchung(f)	tentation	temptation	tentación	tentazione	tentação
vertagen	ajourner	postpone, adjourn	aplazar	rimandare, aggiornare	adiar
vertauschen	substituer	substitute	sustituir	sostituire	substituir
verteidigen	défendre	defend	defender	difendere	defender
Verteidigung(f)	défense	defence	defensa	difesa	defesa
verteilen	distribuer	distribute; deal	distribuir	distribuire	distribuir
Verteilung(f)	distribution	distribution	distribución	distribuzione	distribuição
Verteilung(f)	répartition	distribution	reparto	ripartizione	repartição
Vertrag(m), Kontrakt m	contrat	contract	contrato	contratto	contrato
Vertrag(m)	traité	treaty	tratado	trattato	tratado
Vertrauen(n)	confiance	confidence, trust	confianza	fiducia	confiança
vertrauen(jdm.)	confiance(avoir)	trust	confianza(tener)	fiducia(aver)	confiar
Vertrauen(im)	confidence	confidence, secret	confidencia	confidenza	confidência
vertraulich	confidentiel, le	confidential	confidencial	confidenziale	confidencial

G

German	French	English	Spanish	Italian	Portuguese
vertraut, intim	intime	intimate	íntimo, a	intimo, a	íntimo, a
Vertreibung(f)	expatriation	expatriation	expatriación	espatrio	expatriação
Vertreter(in f)m	représentant, e	representative, rep	representante	rappresentante	representante
Verunglückte(r)mf	accidenté, e	injured person	accidentado, a	accidentato, a	acidentado, a
verunreinigen	polluer	pollute	contaminar	inquinare	poluir
verursachen	causer, provoquer	cause	causar, provocar	causare, provocare	causar, provocar
verursachen	occasionner	cause, bring about	ocasionar, causar	causare	ocasionar, causar
verurteilen	condamner	condemn	condenar	condannare	condenar
verurteilen	condamner	convict, sentence	condenar	condannare	condenar
Verurteilung(f)	condamnation	sentence	condenación	condanna	condenação
vervollkommnen	perfectionner	improve; perfect	perfeccionar	perfezionare	aperfeiçoar
verwackelt	trouble	blurred	desenfocado, a	sfocato, a	tremido, a
verwalten	administrer	manage, run	administrar	amministrare	administrar
verwalten, führen	gérer	manage	administrar	amministrare	gerir
Verwalter(in f)m	gestionnaire	manager	gestor, a	gestore	gestor, a
Verwalter(in f)m	gérant, e	manager	gerente, director, a	gestore, gerente	gerente, director, a
Verwaltung(f)	administration	administration	administración	amministrazione	administração
Verwaltung(f)	gestion	management	gestión	gestione	gestão
Verwaltungs-	administratif, ve	administrative	administrativo, a	amministrativo, a	administrativo, a
Verwandlung(f)	métamorphose	metamorphosis(-es)	metamorfosis	metamorfosi	metamorfose
verwandt	parent, e	relative, relation	pariente	parente	parente
Verwandtschaft(f)	parenté	relationship	parentesco	parentela	parentesco
verwechseln	confondre	confuse, mistake	confundir	confondere	confundir
Verwechslung(f)	confusion	confusion	confusión	confusione	confusão
verweigern	refuser	refuse	rehusar	rifiutare	recusar
Verweigerung(f)	refus	refusal	rechazo	rifiuto	recusa
verwelken	flétrir	wilt, wither	marchitar	appassire	murchar
verwickeln	impliquer	involve	implicar	implicare	implicar
verwickeln, verwirren	emmêler(s')	tangle(up)	enmarañar(se)	aggrovigliare(-rsi)	emaranhar-se
Verwicklung(f)	implication	implication	implicación	implicazione	implicação
verwirklichen	réaliser	carry out, perform	realizar	realizzare	realizar, fazer
Verwirklichung(f)	réalisation	realization	realización	realizzazione	realização
verwirrend	déconcertant, e	disconcerting	desconcertante	sconcertante	desconcertante
verworren	trouble	troubled	confuso, a; torbido, a	confuso, a
verwundbar	vulnérable	vulnerable	vulnerable	vulnerabile	vulnerável
verwüsten, zerstören	dévaster	ravage, devastate	devastar	devastare	devastar
verwüsten	ravager	devastate, ravage	asolar, devastar	devastare	assolar
verwüsten	saccager	ransack	saquear	saccheggiare	saquear
Verwüstung(f)	ravage	devastation	destrozo	devastazione	estrago
verzehren	absorber	absorb	absorber	assorbire	absorver
verzeihen, vergeben	pardonner	forgive, pardon	perdonar	perdonare	perdoar
Verzeihung!	pardon!	sorry!, excuse me!	perdón(!), disculpe	scusi!	perdão!, desculpe!
verziehen, sich	dissiper	dissipate, clear	disipar	dissipare	dissipar
Verzierung; Schmuck	ornement	ornament	adorno	ornamento	ornamento
verzögern	retarder	delay	retrasar, demorar	ritardare	atrasar, demorar
verzollen	dédouaner	clear(customs)	retirar aduana	sdoganare	desalfandegar
Verzweiflung(f)	désespoir	despair	desesperación	disperazione	desespero
Verzweiflung(f)	détresse	distress	angustia	sconforto	aflição, angústia
Veto(n)	veto	veto	veto	veto	veto
Videorecorder(m)	magnétoscope	video recorder	magnetoscopio	videoregistratore	gravador video
Vieh(n)	bétail, bestiaux	cattle	ganado	bestiame	gado
viel(e)	beaucoup	much, many	mucho	molto	muito
viel(e)	beaucoup	lots of, a lot of	mucho, a	molto, a, i, e	muito, a
viel-; vielfältig	multiple	multiple, numerous	múltiple	multiplo, a	múltiplo, a
viele	beaucoup	many	muchos, as	molti	muitos, as
Vielfalt(f)	variété	variety	variedad	varietà	variedade
vielfältig	varié, e	varied, various	variado, a	vario, a	variado, a
viel Glück	bonne chance	good luck	buena suerte	buona fortuna	boa sorte
vielleicht	peut-être	perhaps, maybe	quizá(s)	forse	talvez
vielseitig	polyvalent, e	polyvalent	polivalente	polivalente	polivalente
vier	quatre	four	cuatro	quattro	quatro
Viereck(n)	carré	square	cuadrado	quadrato	quadrado
Viertel(n)	quart	quarter	cuarto	quarto	quarto
Viertel(n)	quartier	district	barrio	quartiere	bairro
Vierteljahr(n)	trimestre	term; quarter	trimestre	trimestre	trimestre
vierteljährlich	trimestriel, le	quarterly	trimestral	trimestrale	trimestral
vierzehn	quatorze	fourteen	catorce	quattordici	catorze
vierzig	quarante	forty	cuarenta	quaranta	quarenta

German	French	English	Spanish	Italian	Portuguese
violett, lila	violet, te	violet, purple	violeta	viola	roxo, a; violeta
Viper(f), Otter(f)	vipère	viper	víbora	vipera	víbora
Virus(m)	virus	virus	virus	virus	vírus
Visitenkarte(f)	carte de visite	visiting card	tarjeta de visita	biglietto da visita	cartão de visita
visuell	visuel, le	visual	visual	visivo, a; visuale	visual
Visum(n)	visa	visa	visado	visto	visto
Vitamin(n)	vitamine	vitamin	vitamina	vitamina	vitamina
Vize-Präsident(m)	vice-président	vice-president	vicepresidente	vicepresidente	vice-presidente
Vogel(m)	oiseau	bird	pájaro, ave	uccello	pássaro, ave
Vokabular(n)	vocabulaire	vocabulary	vocabulario	vocabolario	vocabulário
Vokal(m), Selbstlaut m	voyelle	vowel	vocal	vocale	vogal
Volk(n)	peuple	people	pueblo	popolo	povo
Völkermord(m)	génocide	genocide	genocidio	genocidio	genocídio
Volkswirt(in f)m	économiste	economist	economista	economista	economista
Volkszählung(f)	recensement	census	censo	censimento	recenseamento
voll	plein, e	full	lleno, a	pieno, a	cheio, a
vollbringen	accomplir	achieve	ejecutar, realizar	realizzare, compiere	realizar
vollführen	accomplir	accomplish	realizar, efectuar	compiere, effettuare	realizar
völlig	complètement	completely	completamente	completamente	completamente
Vollkommenheit(f)	perfection	perfection	perfección	perfezione	perfeição
vollständig, voll	complet, ète	complete, full	completo, a	completo, a	completo, a
vollständig	intégral, e	integral	íntegro, a	integrale	integral
Volumen(n)	volume	volume	volumen	volume	volume
von	de	of	de	di; del; dello, a	de
vor	devant	in front(ahead)of	delante, ante	davanti a	diante de
vor, vorher	avant	before	antes(de)	prima	antes(de)
vor	il y a	ago	hace	fa	há
voran, voraus	avant(en)	ahead	adelante	avanti	adiante
voran = gehen, voraus = -	précéder	precede	preceder	precedere	preceder
voran = gehen; vorrücken	avancer	advance	adelantar	avanzare	adiantar
vorbei = kommen	passer	call, drop in	pasar	passare	passar
vor = bereiten	préparer	prepare	preparar	preparare	preparar
Vorbereitung(f)	préparation	preparation	preparación	preparazione	preparação
vor = bestellen	réserver	book, reserve	reservar	prenotare	reservar
Vorderteil(n)	avant	front, fore	delantero, a	anteriore	dianteira
Vorführung(f)	présentation	presentation	presentación	presentazione	apresentação
Vorführung(f)	démonstration	demonstration	demostración	dimostrazione	demonstração
Vorgänger(in f)m	prédécesseur	predecessor	predecesor, a	predecessore	predecessor, a
Vorgehen(n), Handlung	action	action	acción	azione	acção
Vorgeschichte(f)	préhistoire	prehistory	prehistoria	preistoria	pré-história
Vorgesetzte(r)mf	supérieur	superior	superior	superiore	superior
vor = greifen	anticiper	anticipate	anticipar	anticipare	antecipar
Vorhaben(n)	projet	project, plan	proyecto, plan	progetto	projecto
Vorhang(m)	rideau	curtain	cortina	tenda, tapparella	cortina
Vorhang m; Jalousie f	store	blind; shade	toldo; persiana	tapparella	estore
Vorhängeschloß(n)	cadenas	padlock	candado	lucchetto, catenaccio	cadeado
vorher, zuvor	auparavant	before	antes	prima	dantes
vorhergehend	antérieur, e	previous, former	anterior	anteriore	anterior
vorhergehend	préalable	preliminary	previo, a	preliminare	prévio, a
vorhergehend	antécédent, e	previous	antecedente	antecedente	antecedente
vorherig	précédent, e	previous	precedente	precedente	precedente
vor = herrschen	prévaloir	prevail	prevalecer	prevalere	prevalecer
vorherrschend	prédominant, e	predominant	predominante	predominante	predominante
Vorhersage(f)	prévision	forecast	previsión	previsione	previsão
Vorhersage(f)	pronostic	forecast	pronóstico	pronostico	prognóstico
vorher = sagen	prédire	predict	predecir	predire	predizer
vorher = sehen; planen	prévoir	foresee; plan	prever	prevedere	prever
vor = laden	convoquer	summon; invite	convocar	convocare	convocar
Vorlesung(f), Vortrag	conférence	lecture	conferencia	conferenza	conferência
Vorliebe(f)	préférence	preference	preferencia	preferenza	preferência
vorliegenden Fall(im)	occurence(en l')	case(in this)	caso(en este)	nella circostanza	caso(neste)
Vormund(m)	tuteur, tutrice	guardian	tutor, a	tutore, trice	tutor, a
Vorname(m)	prénom	first name	nombre	nome	nome próprio
Vorort(m)	banlieue	suburbs	afueras	periferia	arredores
Vorrang(m)	priorité	priority	prioridad	precedenza; priorità	prioridade
vorrangig; Prioritäts-	prioritaire	priority(have)	prioritario, a	prioritario, a	prioritário, o
Vorrat(m)	provision	stock, supply	provisión	provvista	provisão
Vorrecht(n)	privilège	privilege	privilegio	privilegio	privilégio

G

German	French	English	Spanish	Italian	Portuguese
vorsätzlich	prémédité, e	premeditated	premeditado, a	premeditato, a	premeditado, a
Vorschlag(m)	proposition	proposal	propuesta	proposta	proposta
vor = schlagen	proposer	propose; offer	proponer	proporre	propor
vor = schlagen	suggérer	suggest	sugerir	suggerire	sugerir, propôr
vor = schreiben	prescrire	prescribe	prescribir	prescrivere	prescrever
vor = setzen	préméditer	premeditate	premeditar	premeditare	premeditar
Vorsicht(f)	précaution	precaution	precaución	precauzione	precaução
Vorsicht(f)	prudence	caution, prudence	prudencia	prudenza	prudência
vorsichtig	prudent, e	careful, prudent	prudente	prudente	prudente
Vorsilbe(f)	préfixe	prefix	prefijo	prefisso	prefixo
Vorsitzende(r)mf	président, e	chairman/-woman	presidente	presidente, essa	presidente
Vorspeise(f)	hors-d'oeuvre	starter	entremeses	antipasto	acepipe, entrada
Vorsprung(m)	avance	advance	adelanto	anticipo	avanço
Vorstadt(f)	faubourg	suburb	suburbio	sobborgo	subúrbio
vor = stellen	présenter	introduce	presentar	presentare	apresentar
vor = stellen	introduire	introduce	presentar	introdurre	apresentar
vor = stellen, sich	imaginer	imagine	imaginar	immaginare	imaginar
vor = stellen, sich	concevoir	conceive(of)	concebir	concepire	conceber
Vorstellung(f)	représentation	performance	representación	rappresentazione	representação
Vortäuschung(f)	simulation	simulation	simulación	simulazione	simulação
Vorteil(m)	avantage	advantage	ventaja	vantaggio	vantagem
Vortrag(m)	récitation	recitation	recitación	recita	recitação
vorübergehend	temporaire	temporary	temporario, a	temporaneo, a	temporário, a
Vorurteil(n)	préjugé	prejudice	prejuicio	pregiudizio	preconceito
Vorwählnummer(f)	indicatif(tél.)	dialling code	prefijo	prefisso	indicativo, prefixo
vorwärts	avant	forward(s)	adelante(hacia)	davanti	frente(para a)
vor = werfen	reprocher	reproach	reprochar	rimproverare	censurar
Vorwort(n)	préface	preface	prefacio	prefazione	prefácio
vor = zeigen, - = stellen	présenter	present	presentar	presentare	apresentar
vorzüglich	excellent, e	excellent	excelente	eccellente	excelente
vulgär	vulgaire	vulgar	vulgar	volgare	vulgar
Vulkan(m)	volcan	volcano(-es)	volcán	vulcano	vulcão

W

German	French	English	Spanish	Italian	Portuguese
Waage(f)	balance	scales	balanza	bilancia	balança
Waage(f)	bascule	scales	báscula	basculla, bilancia	báscula
waagerecht	horizontal, e	horizontal	horizontal	orizzontale	horizontal
Wache(f)	garde	guard	guardia	guardia, custodia	guarda
Wache(f)	sentinelle	sentry	centinela	sentinella	sentinela
wach = rufen, erinnern	évoquer	evoke	evocar	evocare	evocar
Wachs(n)	cire	wax, polish	cera	cera	cera
wachsam	vigilant, e	vigilant	vigilante	vigilante	vigilante
wachsen	croître	grow, increase	crecer	crescere	crescer
wachsen	grandir	grow	crecer	crescere	crescer
wachsen	pousser, croître	grow	crecer	crescere	crescer
Wachstum(n)	croissance	growth	crecimiento	crescita	crescimento
Wächter(in f)m	gardien, ne; garde	guard; keeper	guardián, guarda	guardiano, a; custode	guarda
Wächter(m), Hüter(m)	garde	guard	guarda	guardia	guarda
Wade(f)	mollet	calf(-lves)	pantorrilla	polpaccio	barriga(perna)
Waffe(f)	arme	weapon, arm	arma	arma	arma
Waffe(f)	arme	arm	arma	arma; armi	arma
Waffenstillstand(m)	trêve	truce	tregua	tregua	trégua
wagen	oser	dare	osar, atreverse	osare	ousar, atrever-se
Wagen(m)	voiture	car	coche	macchina, auto	carro
Wagen(m)	wagon	coach, carriage	vagón	vagone, carrozza	vagão
Wagenheber(m)	cric	jack	gato	cric, cricco	macaco

German	French	English	Spanish	Italian	Portuguese
Wagentür(f)	portière	door(car)	puerta	sportello	porta
Waggon(m)(Güterwagen)	wagon	truck, wag(g)on	vagón	vagone	vagão
waghalsig	téméraire	rash, reckless	temerario, a	temerario, a	temerário, a
Wahl(f)	choix	choice	escogimiento	scelta	escolha
Wahl(f)	option, choix	option	opción	opzione	opção
Wahl(f)	élection	election	elección	elezione	eleição
Wahl(f), Abstimmung(f)	scrutin, vote	poll; ballot	escrutinio	scrutinio	escrutínio
Wahl(f)	vote	vote	voto	voto	voto
Wahl(f)	suffrage	vote	sufragio	suffragio	sufrágio
wählen	élire	elect	elegir	eleggere	eleger
wählen	voter	vote	votar	votare	votar
Wähler(in f)m	électeur, trice	voter	elector, a	elettore, -trice	eleitor, a
wahlfrei, beliebig	facultatif, ive	optional	facultativo, a	facoltativo, a	facultativo, a
Wahlkampf(m)	campagne	campaign	campaña	campagna	campanha
Wahnsinn(m)	démence	insanity, madness	demencia	demenza, follia	demência
Wahnsinn(m), Wahn(m)	folie	madness, folly	locura	follia, pazzia	loucura
wahr	vrai, e	true	verdadero, a	vero, a	verdadeiro, a
während	pendant, durant	for; during	durante	durante	durante
während	durant, pendant	during, for	durante	durante	durante
während	pendant que	while	mientras	mentre; già che	enquanto
während	tandis que	while, whilst	mientras	mentre	enquanto
wahrhaftig	véritable	real, genuine	verdadero, a	vero, a	verdadeiro, a
Wahrheit(f)	vérité	truth	verdad	verità	verdade
wahrnehmbar	perceptible	perceptible	perceptible	percettibile	perceptível
wahr = nehmen	percevoir	perceive	percibir	percepire	perceber
wahrscheinlich	vraisemblable	likely, probable	verosímil	verosimile	verosímil
wahrscheinlich	probablement	probably	probablemente	probabilmente	provavelmente
wahrscheinlich	probable	probable, likely	probable	probabile	provável
Währung(f)	devise	currency	divisa	valuta	moeda, divisa
Währung(f), Devisen pl	monnaie	currency	moneda	valuta; moneta	moeda
Währungs-, Geld-	monétaire	monetary	monetario, a	monetario, a	monetário, a
Waise(f)	orphelin, e	orphan	huérfano, a	orfano, a	órfão, órfã
Wal(m)	baleine	whale	ballena	balena	baleia
Wald(m)	forêt	forest	bosque	foresta, bosco	floresta, bosque
Wald(m)	bois	wood	bosque	bosco	bosque
Wallfahrt(f)	pèlerinage	pilgrimage	peregrinación	pellegrinaggio	peregrinação
Walnuß(f)	noix	walnut	nuez	noce	noz
Walzer(m)	valse	waltz	vals	valzer	valsa
Wand(f)	paroi, mur	wall	pared	parete	parede
wandernd; Wander-	migrateur, trice	migrant	migratorio, a	migratore, trice	migrador, a
Wanderung(f)	marche	walk(ing)	marcha	marcia	marcha
Wanderung(f)	migration	migration	migración	migrazione	migração
Wandschirm(m)	écran	screen	pantalla	schermo	painel
Wandschrank(m)	placard	cupboard	armario	armadio a muro	armário
Wandteppich; Gobelin m	tapisserie	tapestry	tapiz; tapicería	arazzo; tappezzeria	tapeçaria
Wange(f)	joue	cheek	mejilla	guancia	bochecha, face
wanken	tituber	stagger	titubear	barcollare	titubear
wann	quand	when	cuándo, cuando	quando	quando
Wanne(f), Faß(n)	cuve	tank; vat	cuba	tino	cuba
Wanne(f); Schüssel(f)	bassine	bowl	barreño	bacinella	bacia
Ware(f)	marchandise	goods, merchandise	mercancía	merce	mercadoria
Warenlager(n)	magasin	store	almacén	magazzino; negozio	armazém
warm	chaud, e	warm	cálido, a	caldo, a	cálido, a
warnen	avertir	warn	advertir	avvertire	avisar, prevenir
warnen	prévenir	warn, inform	prevenir, avisar	prevenire	prevenir, avisar
Warnung(f)	avertissement	warning	advertencia	ammonizione	aviso
warten	attendre	wait(for)	esperar	aspettare	esperar
Warten(n)	attente	wait(ing)	espera	attesa	espera
Wärter(in f)m	gardien, ne	keeper, caretaker	guardián, ana	custode, guardia	guarda
Wartezimmer(n)	salle d'attente	waiting-room	sala de espera	sala d'attesa	sala de espera
Wartung(f)	entretien	maintenance	mantenimiento	manutenzione	manutenção
warum	pourquoi	why	por qué	perché	porquê
Warze(f)	verrue	wart	verruga	verruca, porro	verruga
was, das	que	that; whom; which	que, qué	che	que
was	quoi	what	que, qué	cosa, che cosa	quê
was auch immer	quel que soit	whatever	cualquiera que sea	qualunque sia	seja qual for
Waschbecken(n)	lavabo	wash-basin	lavabo	lavabo, lavandino	lavabo
Wäsche(f)	linge	linen	ropa	biancheria	roupa

G

German	French	English	Spanish	Italian	Portuguese
waschen	laver	wash	lavar	lavare	lavar
waschen, sich	laver(se)	wash	lavarse	lavarsi	lavar-se
Waschen(n)	lavage	washing	lavado	lavaggio	lavagem
Wäscherei(f)	blanchisserie	laundry	lavandería	lavanderia	lavandaria
Waschlappen(m)	gant	flannel	manopla	guanto	luva
Waschpulver(n)	lessive	washing powder	detergente	detersivo	detergente
Wasser(n)	eau	water	agua	acqua	água
Wasser-	aquatique	aquatic	acuático, a	acquatico, a	aquático, a
wasserdicht	imperméable	water-proof	impermeable	impermeabile	impermeável
Wasserfall(m)	cascade	waterfall	cascada	cascata	cascata
Wasserfläche(f)	nappe(eau)	sheet, expanse	capa(de agua)	falda	lençol(de água)
Wasserhahn(m), Hahn(m)	robinet	tap; stop-cock	grifo	rubinetto	torneira
Wasserkessel(m)	bouilloire	kettle	hervidor	bollitore	chaleira
Wasserski(m)	ski nautique	water-skiing	esquí acuático	sci nautico	esqui aquático
Wasserstoff(m)	hydrogène	hydrogen	hidrógeno	idrogeno	hidrogénio
weben	tisser	weave	tejer	tessere	tecer
Wechsel(m)(Geld-)	change	exchange	cambio	cambio	câmbio
Wechseljahre(n, pl)	ménopause	menopause	menopausia	menopausa	menopausa
wechseln	changer	shift	cambiar	cambiare	mudar; remover
wecken	réveiller	wake(up)	despertar	svegliare	acordar
Wecker(m)	réveil	alarm clock	despertador	sveglia	despertador
weder, noch	ni	neither, nor	ni	né	nem
Weg(m)	chemin	path; way	camino	cammino	caminho
Weg(m)	voie	way; track	vía; camino	via; binario	via; caminho
Weg(m)	chemin, voie	way	camino	cammino, strada	caminho
Weg(m)	sentier	footpath, path	sendero, senda	sentiero	vereda, atalho
weg(fort); weit weg	loin(au)	away, far away	lejos(a lo)	lontano	longe(ao)
weg = gehen	partir	leave, go away	salir, marcharse	partire	partir, abalar
weg = räumen	débarrasser	clear, rid	quitar, tirar	sbarazzare	desembaraçar
weg = reißen, aus = reißen	arracher	tear out; tear off	arrancar	strappare, togliere	arrancar
weg = werfen	jeter	throw away(out)	echar, tirar	buttare	deitar fora
weg = werfen, auf = geben	larguer	let go, release	largar	lasciare, mollare	largar, deixar
Weh(n)	mal	harm, hurt	daño	male	mal
weh tun, schmerzen	mal(faire)	ache, hurt	doler	male(fare)	doer
wehen	souffler	blow	soplar	soffiare	soprar
Wehmut(f)	mélancolie	melancholy	melancolía	malinconia	melancolia
Weibchen(n)	femelle	female	hembra	femmina	fêmea
weiblich	féminin	feminine	femenino	femminile	feminino
weich	mou, molle	soft	blando, a	molle; tenero, a	mole
weich	tendre	soft; tender	blando, a	morbido, a; tenero, a	tenro, a
Weichtier(n)	mollusque	mollusc	molusco	mollusco	molusco
Weide(f), Wiese(f)	pré	meadow, field	prado	prato	prado
Weihe(f)	consécration	consecration	consagración	consacrazione	consagração
weihen	consacrer	consecrate	consagrar	consacrare	consagrar
Weihnachten(n)	Noël	Christmas	Navidad	Natale	Natal
Weihwasser(n)	eau bénite	holy water	agua bendita	acqua santa	água benta
weil, da	parce que	because	porque	perché	porque
weil, denn	car	because, for	porque, pues	perché	porque, pois
Wein(m)	vin	wine	vino	vino	vinho
weinen	pleurer	cry	llorar	piangere	chorar
Weinkarte(f)	carte des vins	wine-list	carta de vinos	lista dei vini	lista dos vinhos
Weise(f), Art(f)	façon, manière	way, manner, fashion	modo, manera	modo, maniera	modo, maneira
Weise(f)	mode, manière	mode, manner	modo, manera	modo, maniera	modo, maneira
Weise(m)	sage	sage, wise man	sabio	saggio, a; savio, a	sábio
weiß	blanc, blanche	white	blanco, a	bianco, a	branco, a
weit	vaste	vast	vasto, a	vasto, a	vasto, a
weit	ample	ample; loose	amplio, a	ampio, a	amplo, a
weit, breit	large	wide; broad	ancho, a	largo, a	largo, a
weit	grand, e	large, big	gran, grande	grande, ampio, a	grande
weit, fern	loin	far(away), distant	lejos	lontano, a	longe
Weite(f), Größe(f)	ampleur	scale, size	amplitud	ampiezza	amplidão
weiter	autre	further; other	otro, a	altro, a	mais
weiter	plus loin	further	más lejos	più in là	mais longe
weiter = gehen	avancer	advance, move fwd	avanzar	procedere	avançar
weiträumig	spacieux, se	spacious	espacioso, a	spazioso, a	espaçoso, a
weitsichtig	presbyte	long-sighted	présbita	presbite	présbita
Weizen(m)	blé	corn	trigo	grano	trigo
welch(e, er, es)	quel, le	what; which	cuál; que	quale; che	qual; que

German	French	English	Spanish	Italian	Portuguese
welche	laquelle	which; who; whom	cual(la)	quale(la)	qual(a)
welcher	lequel	which; who; whom	cúal, cual	quale(il)	qual(o)
Welle(f); Flut(f)	flot	wave; flood	oleada	flutto	corrente
Welle(f)	onde	wave	onda	onda	onda
Welle(f)	vague	wave	ola	onda	onda, vaga
Welle(f)	lame	wave	ola	ondata	vaga
Welt(f)	monde	world	mundo	mondo	mundo
weltlich	mondial, e	world-wide, world	mundial	mondiale	mundial
Weltraumfahrt(f)	astronautique	astronautics	astronáutica	astronautica	astronáutica
wenden	tourner	turn	girar	svoltare, girare	virar
wenig(e)	peu	little, few	poco, a	poco, a	pouco, a
weniger	moins	less	menos	meno	menos
wenigsten(am)	moins(le)	least(the)	menos(lo)	meno(il)	menos(o)
wenn; ob	si	if; whether	si	se	se
wenn nur, sofern, daß	pourvu que	provided that	ojalá	purché	oxalá
wer; wen	qui	who(m); which; that	quién, que	chi, che	quem
Werbung(f), Anzeige(f)	publicité	advertising	publicidad	pubblicità	publicidade
werden	devenir	become	volverse	diventare	tornar-se
werden	devenir	become	llegar a ser	diventare	vir a ser
werden	devenir	become	ponerse	diventare	pôr-se
werfen	jeter	throw	arrojar, lanzar	gettare	atirar, lançar
werfen	lancer	throw	lanzar	lanciare	lançar; atirar
Werk(n)	ouvrage	work	obra	lavoro	obra
Werk(n)	oeuvre, travail	work	obra	opera	obra
Werkstatt(f)	atelier	workshop	taller	officina	oficina
Werkzeug(n)	outil	tool	herramienta	attrezzo	ferramenta
Werkzeug(n)	outillage	tools, equipment	herramientas	attrezzatura	ferramentas
Wert(m)	valeur	value, worth	valor	valore	valor
Wert(m)	valeur, mérite	worth, merit	valor, mérito	valore, merito	valor, mérito
wert sein	valoir	worth(be)	valer	valere	valer
wertlos	nul, le	worthless; useless	nulo, a	nullo, a	nulo, a
Wertsachen(f pl)	objets de valeur	valuables	objetos de valor	oggetti di valore	objectos de valor
wertvoll, kostbar	précieux, se	precious	precioso, a	prezioso, a	precioso, a
wesentlich	essentiel, le	essential	esencial	essenziale	essencial
wesentlich	vital, e	vital	vital	vitale	vital
Wespe(f)	guêpe	wasp	avispa	vespa	vespa
Weste(f), Jacke(f)	gilet	cardigan	chaleco	gilè; golf	casaco de malha
Westen(m)	Ouest	West	Oeste	Ovest	Oeste
westlich	occidental, e	Western	occidental	occidentale	ocidental
Wettbewerb(m)	concours	competition	concurso	concorso	concurso
Wettbewerb(m)	concours	contest	concurso	gara	concurso
Wettbewerb(m)	compétition	competition	competición	competizione, gara	competição
Wette(f)	pari	bet	apuesta	scommessa	aposta
Wetter(n)	temps	weather	tiempo	tempo	tempo
Wetterberuhigung(f)	accalmie	lull	calma	schiarita, tregua	acalmia
Wetterkunde(f)	météorologie	weather forecast	meteorología	meteorologia	meteorologia
Wettkampf(m)	challenge	challenge, contest	trofeo, challenge	gara, sfida	desafio, torneio
Wettrennen(n)	course	running	carrera	corsa	corrida
wichtig	important, e	important	importante	importante	importante
wider, gegen	contre	against	contra(en)	contro	contra
widerlegen	réfuter	refute	refutar	confutare	refutar
Widerschein(m), Reflex	reflet	reflection	reflejo	riflesso	reflexo
widersetzen, sich	opposer(s')	oppose	oponerse	opporsi	opor-se
widersprechen	contredire	contradict	contradecir	contraddire	contradizer
Widerspruch(m)	contradiction	contradiction	contradicción	contraddizione	contradição
Widerstand(m)	résistance	resistance	resistencia	resistenza	resistência
widerstandsfähig	résistant, e	resistant	resistente	resistente	resistente
widerstehen	résister	resist; withstand	resistir	resistere	resistir
widerstehen	résister à	withstand	resistir a	resistere a	resistir a
widerwärtig	odieux, se	odious, obnoxious	odioso, a	odioso, a	odioso, a
widmen	consacrer	devote	dedicar	dedicare	dedicar
widmen	dédier	dedicate	dedicar	dedicare	dedicar
wie	comment	how	cómo	come	como
wie	comme	as; like	como	come	como
wie bitte?	comment?	pardon?	cómo(?)	come?, come dice?	como disse?
wieder = bekommen	récupérer	recover, get back	recuperar	recuperare	recuperar
Wiederbelebung(f)	réanimation	resuscitation	reanimación	rianimazione	reanimação
wieder = bringen	ramener	bring back	devolver, traer	riportare	trazer

G

German	French	English	Spanish	Italian	Portuguese
wiederein = setzen	réintégrer	reinstate	rehabilitar	reintegrare	reintegrar
wiederher = stellen	restaurer	restore	restaurar	restaurare	restaurar
wieder = holen	répéter	repeat	repetir	ripetere	repetir
wieder montieren	remonter	reassemble	volver a montar	rimontare	tornar a montar
wieder = sehen	revoir	see again	volver a ver	rivedere	voltar a ver
Wiege(f)	berceau	cradle	cuna	culla	berço
wiegen	bercer	rock	mecer	cullare	embalar
wiegen	peser	weigh	pesar	pesare	pesar
Wiese(f)	prairie	meadow	pradera	prateria	pradaria, prado
wieviel	combien	how much, how many	cuánto; cuanto	quanto	quanto
wild	sauvage	wild	salvaje	selvaggio, a	selvagem
wild	farouche	wild	feroz	selvatico, a	arisco, a
wild, furchtbar	féroce	ferocious, fierce	feroz	feroce	feroz
Wild(n)	gibier	game	caza	selvaggina	caça
Wildbach(m)	torrent	torrent	torrente	torrente	torrente
wilde Ehe(f)	concubinage	co-habitation	concubinato	concubinato	concubinato
Wille(m)	volonté	will, determination	voluntad	volontà	vontade
Willkommen(n)	bienvenu, e	welcome(to be)	bienvenido, a	benvenuto, a	bem-vindo, a
willkürlich	arbitraire	arbitrary	arbitrario, a	arbitrario, a	arbitrário, a
wimmeln	grouiller	crawl with	hormiguear	brulicare	pulular
Wimper(f)	cil	eyelash	pestaña	ciglio(a)	pestana
Wind(m)	vent	wind	viento	vento	vento
Winde(f)	vérin, cric	jack	gato, cric	martinetto, binda	macaco
Windpocken(f, pl)	varicelle	chicken-pox	varicela	varicella	varicela
Windschutzscheibe(f)	pare-brise	windscreen	parabrisas	parabrezza	pára-brisas
Windstoß(m)	rafale	gust, gale	ráfaga	raffica	rajada
Windstoß(m)	bourrasque	squall	borrasca	burrasca	borrasca
Windsurfen(n)	planche à voile	windsurf(ing)	tabla a vela, surf	windsurf	wind-surf
Winkel(m)	angle	angle	ángulo	angolo	ângulo
Winter(m)	hiver	winter	invierno	inverno	inverno
winzig	minuscule	minute, tiny	minúsculo, o	minuscolo, a	minúsculo, a
wir	nous	we	nosotros	noi	nós
Wirbel(m)	remous	eddy, swirl	remolino	mulinello, gorgo	redemoinho
Wirbel(wind)(m)	tourbillon	whirlwind, swirl	torbellino	vortice	turbilhão
Wirbel(m)	vertèbre	vertebra(-ae)	vértebra	vertebra	vértebra
Wirbelsäule(f)	colonne(vertéb-)	spine	columna vertebral	colonna vertebrale	coluna vertebral
Wirbelsturm(m)	tornade	tornado(-es)	tornado	tornado	tornado
Wirbelwind(m)	cyclone	cyclone	ciclón	ciclone	ciclone
wirken	opérer	operate	efectuar	operare	fazer
wirklich	réel, le	real, actual	real	reale; vero, a	real
wirklich	réellement	truly	realmente	realmente	realmente
wirklich	vraiment	really	verdaderamente	veramente	verdadeiramente
Wirklichkeit(f)	réalité	reality	realidad	realtà	realidade
Wirkung(f)	effet	effect	efecto	effetto	efeito
wirkungsvoll	efficace	effective	eficaz	efficace	eficaz
Wirtschaft(f)	économie	economy	economía	economia	economia
wirtschaftlich	économique	economic(al)	económico, a	economico, a	económico, a
wissen	savoir	know	saber	sapere	saber
Wissen(n)	savoir	knowledge	saber	sapere	sabedoria
Wissenschaft(f)	science	science	ciencia	scienza	ciência
Wissenschaftler(m)	savant, e	learned person	sabio, a	studioso, a; dotto, a	sábio, a
Wissenschaftler(m)	scientifique	scientist	científico	scienziato	cientista
wissenschaftlich	scientifique	scientific	científico, a	scientifico, a	científico, a
wittern, schnüffeln	flairer	sniff; scent; sense	olfatear, husmear	annusare	farejar, cheirar
Witwer(m), Witwe(f)	veuf, veuve	widower, widow	viudo, a	vedovo, a	viúvo, a
Witz(m)	blague	joke	chiste	scherzo	anedota, chalaça
Witz(m)	plaisanterie	joke	chiste, gracia	scherzo	brincadeira
wo	où	where	donde, dónde	dove	onde
woanders	ailleurs	somewhere else	otra parte(en)	altrove	noutro sítio
Woche(f)	semaine	week	semana	settimana	semana
Wochenende(n)	week-end	weekend	fin de semana	fine settimana	fim de semana
wöchentlich	hebdomadaire	weekly	semanal	settimanale	semanal
wohl	bien	well	bien	bene	bem
Wohlbefinden(n)	bien-être	well-being	bienestar	benessere	bem-estar
wohl fühlen, sich	aise(être à l')	ease(be at)	gusto(estar a)	agio(essere a)	vontade(estar à)
wohlwollend	bienveillant, e	benevolent	benévolo, a	benevolo, a	benévolo, a
wohnen, bleiben	demeurer	live, stay, remain	residir, vivir	dimorare, stare	habitar
wohnen	résider	reside	residir	risiedere	residir

German	French	English	Spanish	Italian	Portuguese
Wohnsitz(m), Wohnort m	domicile	home	domicilio	domicilio	domicílio
Wohnsitz(m)	résidence	residence	residencia	residenza	residência
Wohnung(f)	logement	accommodation	alojamiento	alloggio	alojamento
Wohnung(f)	appartement	flat, apartment	piso	appartamento	apartamento
Wohnung(f)	habitation	dwelling; living	vivienda, morada	abitazione	habitação, morada
Wohnung(f), Haus(n)	demeure	residence, dwelling	morada, casa	dimora	habitação, casa
Wohnwagen(m)	caravane	caravan	caravana	roulotte	caravana
Wohnzimmer(n)	salle de séjour	living-room	sala de estar	soggiorno	sala de estar
Wolf(m)	loup	wolf(-lves)	lobo	lupo	lobo
Wolke(f)	nuage	cloud	nube	nuvola	nuvem
Wolkenkratzer(m)	gratte-ciel	skyscraper	rascacielos	grattacielo	arranha-céus
Wolle(f)	laine	wool	lana	lana	lã
wollen	vouloir	want	querer	volere	querer
Wort(n)	mot	word	palabra	parola	palavra
Wort(n)	parole	word; speech	palabra	parola	palavra
Worte(pl.)	propos	words, talk	palabras	parole, discorsi	fala, conversa
Wörterbuch(n)	dictionnaire	dictionary	diccionario	dizionario	dicionário
Wrack(n)	épave	wreck	ruina, restos	relitto	destroços
Wunde(f)	plaie	wound; cut	llaga, herida	piaga	ferida
Wunder(n)	miracle	miracle	milagro	miracolo	milagre
wunderbar	merveilleux, se	marvellous	maravilloso, a	meraviglioso, a	maravilhoso, a
wunderbar	merveilleux, se	wonderful	maravilloso, a	meraviglioso, a	maravilhoso, a
wunderbar	prestigieux, se	prestigious	prestigioso, a	prestigioso, a	prestigioso, a
wunderbar	prodigieux, se	prodigious	prodigioso, a	prodigioso, a	prodigioso, a
wundern, sich	étonner(s')	astonished(be -)	sorprenderse	meravigliarsi	espantar-se
Wunsch(m)	désir	wish(-es)	deseo	desiderio	desejo
Wunsch(m)	voeu	wish(-es)	deseo	augurio	voto
wünschen	désirer	desire, want	desear	desiderare	desejar
wünschen	souhaiter	wish, desire	desear	augurare	desejar
Würde(f)	dignité	dignity	dignidad	dignità	dignidade
würdig	digne	worthy; dignified	digno, a	degno, a	digno, a
Würfel(m)	cube	cube	cubo	cubo	cubo
Würfel(m)	dé(jeux)	die(dice)	dado	dado	dado
Wurm(m)	ver	worm	gusano	verme	verme
Wurst(f)	saucisse	sausage	salchicha	salsiccia	salsicha
Würze(f)	assaisonnement	seasoning	aliño	condimento	tempero
Wurzel(f)	racine	root	raíz	radice	raiz
Wüste(f)	désert	desert	desierto	deserto	deserto
Wut(f)	colère	anger(be angry)	cólera, ira	collera, ira	cólera, ira
Wut(f)	fureur	fury	furor	furore	furor
Wut(f)	rage, fureur	rage	rabia, furia	rabbia	raiva, furor
wütend	furieux, se	furious	furioso, a	furioso, a	furioso, a

Y

German	French	English	Spanish	Italian	Portuguese
Yoga(n), Joga(n)	yoga	yoga	yoga	yoga	yoga

Z

German	French	English	Spanish	Italian	Portuguese
zähflüssig	visqueux, se	viscous	viscoso, a	vischioso, a	viscoso, a
Zahl(f), Ziffer(f)	chiffre	figure, number	cifra, número	cifra, numero	número
zählen	compter	count	contar	contare	contar
zählen, auf jdn	compter sur	rely on	contar con	contare su	contar com
Zähler(m)	compteur	meter	contador	contatore	contador
zahlreich	nombreux, se	numerous, many	numeroso, a	numeroso, a	numeroso, a
Zahlung(f)	payement	payment	abono, pago	pagamento	pagamento
zähmen	apprivoiser	tame	domesticar	addomesticare	domesticar
zähmen	dompter	tame	domar	domare	domar
Zahn(m)	dent	tooth(teeth)	diente	dente	dente
Zahnarzt(in f)m	dentiste	dentist	dentista	dentista	dentista
Zahnbürste(f)	brosse à dents	toothbrush	cepillo de dientes	spazzolino	escova de dentes
Zahnfleisch(n)	gencive	gum	encía	gengiva	gengiva
Zahnpasta(f)	dentifrice	tooth-paste	dentífrico	dentifricio	dentífrico
Zahnschmerzen(m, pl)	mal aux dents	toothache	dolor de dientes	mal di denti	dor de dentes
Zahnstocher(m)	cure-dents	tooth-pick	palillo	stuzzicadenti	palito
Zahnziehen(n)	extraction	extraction	extracción	estrazione	extracção
Zange(f)	pince	pincers, pliers	pinza(s), tenazas	pinza	pinça, alicate
Zangen(pl)	pinces	pliers, pincers	alicates, tenazas	pinze	alicate; tenaz
Zäpfchen(n)	suppositoire	suppository	supositorio	supposta	supositório
zart; fein	délicat, e	delicate	delicado, a	delicato, a	delicado, a
zärtlich	tendre	tender	tierno, a	tenero, a	terno, a
Zärtlichkeit(f)	tendresse	tenderness	ternura	tenerezza	ternura
Zauberei(f)	magie	magic	magia	magia	magia
Zaun(m)	clôture	fence, railings	valla, cerca	recinzione, muro	cerca, vedação
Zebra(n)	zèbre	zebra	cebra	zebra	zebra
Zehe(f)	orteil	toe	dedo del pie	dito del piede	dedo do pé
zehn	dix	ten	diez	dieci	dez
zehnte	dixième	tenth	décimo, a	decimo, a	décimo, a
Zeichen(n), Abzeichen	insigne	badge	insignia	distintivo	insígnia
Zeichen(n)	signe	sign	signo	segno	sinal, signo
Zeichendreieck(n)	équerre	square(set -)	escuadra	squadra	esquadro
Zeichensetzung(f)	ponctuation	punctuation	puntuación	punteggiatura	pontuação
zeichnen	dessiner	draw; design	dibujar; diseñar	disegnare	desenhar
Zeichner(in f)m	dessinateur	drawer; designer	dibujante	disegnatore, trice	desenhador, a
Zeichnung(f)	dessin	drawing; design	dibujo; diseño	disegno	desenho
zeigen	montrer	show	enseñar, mostrar	mostrare	mostrar
Zeit(f)	temps	time	tiempo	tempo	tempo
zeitgenössisch	contemporain, e	contemporary	contemporáneo, a	contemporaneo, a	contemporâneo, a
Zeitschrift, Revue(f)	revue, magazine	review, magazine	revista	rivista, periodico	revista
Zeitung(f)	journal	newspaper, paper	periódico, diario	giornale	jornal
Zeitungskiosk(m)	kiosque	news-stand	quiosco	edicola; chiosco	quiosque
Zeitvertreib(m)	distraction(s)	entertainment	distracción	svago, distrazione	distracção, -ões
Zellulitis(f)	cellulite	fat, cellulitis	celulitis	cellulite	celulite
Zelt(n)	tente	tent	tienda	tenda	tenda
zelten	camper	camp	acampar	campeggiare	acampar
Zement(m)	ciment	cement	cemento	cemento	cimento
Zensur(f)	censure	censorship	censura	censura	censura
Zentimeter(n, m)	centimètre	centimetre	centímetro	centimetro	centímetro
zentral	central, e	central	central	centrale	central
zentrifugal	centrifuge	centrifugal	centrífugo, a	centrifugo, a	centrífugo, a
Zentrum(n)	centre	centre	centro	centro	centro
zerbrechen	casser, briser	break	romper	rompere	quebrar, partir
zerbrechlich	fragile	fragile	frágil	fragile	frágil
Zeremonie(f)	cérémonie	ceremony	ceremonia	cerimonia	cerimónia
zerkratzt	rayé, e	scratched	rayado, a	rigato, a	riscado, a
zerlegen	décomposer	decompose	descomponer	decomporre	decompor
Zerlegung(f), Abbau(m)	démontage	dismantling	desmontaje	smontaggio	desmontagem
zernagen	ronger	gnaw	roer	rodere	roer
zerquetschen	écraser	crush, flatten	aplastar	schiacciare	esmagar
zerreißen	déchirer	tear	rasgar, romper	strappare	rasgar

German	French	English	Spanish	Italian	Portuguese
zerschneiden	découper	cut up	recortar	tagliare	recortar
Zerstäuber(m)	atomiseur	spray, atomizer	atomizador	nebulizzatore	pulverizador
Zerstäubung(f)	pulvérisation	spraying	pulverización	nebulizzazione	pulverização
zerstören	détruire	destroy	destruir	distruggere	destruir
zerstören	démolir	demolish	demoler	demolire	demolir
Zerstörung(f)	destruction	destruction	destrucción	distruzione	destruição
zerstreuen	disperser	disperse; scatter	dispersar	disperdere	dispersar
zerstreut	distrait, e	absent-minded	distraído, a	distratto, a	distraído, a
zerstückeln	déchiqueter	tear to pieces	despedazar	dilaniare	despedaçar
Zeuge(m), Zeugin(f)	témoin	witness	testigo	testimone	testemunha
zeugen, erzeugen	engendrer	generate	engendrar	generare	engendrar
zeugen, bezeugen	témoigner	witness	atestiguar	testificare	testemunhar
Zeugenaussage(f)	témoignage	testimony, evidence	testimonio	testimonianza	testemunho
Zeugung(f)	procréation	procreation	procreación	procreazione	procriação
Ziege(f)	chèvre	goat	cabra	capra	cabra
Ziegel(m)	brique	brick	ladrillo	mattone	tijolo
Ziegel(m)	tuile	tile	teja	tegola	telha
ziehen	tirer	pull	tirar	tirare	puxar
Ziel(n)	but	aim, purpose	propósito	scopo	fim, intento
zielen	viser	aim	apuntar	mirare	apontar
Zielscheibe(f)	cible	target	blanco	bersaglio	alvo
Zifferblatt(n)	cadran	dial	esfera	quadrante	mostrador
Zigarette(f)	cigarette	cigarette	cigarrillo	sigaretta	cigarro
Zigarre(f)	cigare	cigar	cigarro, puro	sigaro	charuto
Zimmer(n)(Schlaf-)	chambre	bedroom, room	cuarto	camera, stanza	quarto
Zimmermädchen(n)	femme de chambre	chambermaid	camarera	cameriera	empregada
Zimmermann(m)	charpentier	carpenter	carpintero	carpentiere	carpinteiro
Zinn(n)	étain	tin; pewter	estaño	stagno	estanho
Zins(m)	intérêt	interest	interés	interesse	juro
Zipfel(m), Ende(n)	bout	end, tip	punta	punta, estremità	ponta
zirkulieren	circuler	circulate	circular	circolare	circular
Zirkus(m)	cirque	circus	circo	circo	circo
Zirrhose(f)	cirrhose	cirrhosis	cirrosis	cirrosi	cirrose
zitieren	citer	quote	citar	citare	citar
Zitrone(f)	citron	lemon	limón	limone	limão
zittern	trembler	tremble	temblar	tremare	tremer
zittern	grelotter	shiver	tiritar	tremare(di freddo)	tiritar
zivil	civil, e	civil	civil	civile	civil
Zivilisation(f)	civilisation	civilization	civilización	civiltà	civilização
zivilisieren	civiliser	civilize	civilizar	civilizzare	civilizar
Zögern(n)	hésitation	hesitation	vacilación	esitazione	hesitação
zögern	hésiter	hesitate	dudar	esitare	hesitar
Zoll(m)	douane	customs	aduana	dogana	alfândega
zollfrei	hors-taxe	duty-free	libre impuestos	duty-free	sem imposto
Zöllner(m), Zollbeamte	douanier	customs officer	aduanero	doganiere	guarda-fiscal
Zone(f)	zone	zone	zona	zona	zona
Zoo(m)	zoo	zoo	zoológico	zoo	jardim zoológico
zoologisch	zoologique	zoological	zoológico, a	zoologico, a	zoológico, a
Zopf(m)	tresse	plait, braid	trenza	treccia	trança
Zopf(m)	natte	plait	trenza	treccia	trança
zu	à, en, pour, chez	to, at, by, for	en, a, por	a, in, da	em, a, para
zu früh (sein)	avance(être en)	early(to be)	adelantado(estar)	anticipo(essere in)	adiantado(estar)
zu spät kommen	retard(être en)	late(to be)	retrasado, a(estar)	ritardo(essere in)	atrasado, a(estar)
zu, geschlossen	fermé, e	closed, shut	cerrado, a	chiuso, a	fechado, a
Zubehör(n)	accessoire	accessory	accesorio	accessorio	acessório
Zucht(f); Aufzucht(f)	élevage	breeding; rearing	ganadería	allevamento	criação de gado
züchten	élever	breed, rear	criar	allevare	criar
Zucker(m)	sucre	sugar	azúcar	zucchero	açúcar
Zuckerkrankheit(f)	diabète	diabetes	diabetes	diabete	diabetes
Zuckung(f), Krampf(m)	convulsion	convulsion	convulsión	convulsione	convulsão
zu = decken	couvrir	cover	cubrir	coprire	cobrir
zu = erkennen, erteilen	décerner	award	otorgar	conferire	atribuir
Zufall(m)	hasard	chance, luck	azar, casualidad	caso	acaso, azar
Zufall(m)	aléa	hazard	riesgo, azar	rischio	acaso
Zuflucht(f), Berufung	recours	recourse	recurso	ricorso	recurso
Zufluchtsort(m)	refuge, asile	refuge	refugio, asilo	rifugio, asilo	refúgio, asilo
zufrieden	satisfait, e	satisfied	satisfecho, a	soddisfatto, a	satisfeito, a
Zufriedenheit(f)	satisfaction	satisfaction	satisfacción	soddisfazione	satisfação

German	French	English	Spanish	Italian	Portuguese
Zug(m), Eisenbahn(f)	train	train	tren	treno	comboio
Zug(m)(Gesichts-)	trait(s)	feature	rasgos	tratto, lineamento	feição
Zugang(m)	accès	access	acceso	accesso	acesso
Zugang haben zu	accéder à	reach	llegar a	accedere a	chegar a
zugänglich	accessible	accessible	accesible	accessibile	acessível
zu = geben; zu = lassen	admettre	admit	admitir	ammettere	admitir
zugunsten von	profit(au--de)	in aid of	beneficio(en--de)	beneficio(al--di)	proveito(em--de)
Zuhälter(m)	proxénète	pimp	proxeneta	ruffiano, prosseneta	proxeneta
zu helfen wissen, sich	débrouiller(se)	manage	desenredarse	cavarsela	desenredar-se
zu = hören, horchen	écouter	listen(to)	escuchar	ascoltare	escutar
Zuhörer(in f)m	auditeur, trice	listener	auditor, a	uditore, uditrice	ouvinte
zu = jubeln	acclamer	cheer	aclamar	acclamare	aclamar
Zukunft(f)	avenir	future	porvenir, futuro	avvenire	futuro
Zukunft(f)	futur	future	futuro	futuro	futuro
zukünftig	futur, e	future	futuro, a	futuro, a	futuro, a
Zulage(f)	prime	bonus	prima	premio, sussidio	gratificação
zulässig, annehmbar	admissible	admissible	admisible	ammissibile	admissível
Zulassung, Einweisung	admission	admission	admisión	ammissione	admissão
Zulassung(f)	homologation	certification	homologación	omologazione	homologação
zu = machen	fermer	shut	cerrar	chiudere	fechar
zunächst	abord(d')	first(at)	primero	anzitutto	primeiro
Zunahme(f)	augmentation	increase, rise	aumento	aumento	aumento
Zunahme(f)	augmentation	increment	incremento	incremento	incremento
Zündkerze(f)	bougie	sparking plug	bujía	candela	vela
Zündung(f)	allumage	ignition	encendido	accensione	ignição
zu = nehmen	accroître	increase	incrementar	accrescere	aumentar
zu = nehmen	augmenter	increase, raise	aumentar	aumentare	aumentar
zu = nehmen	grossir	put on weight	engordar	ingrassare	engordar
Zuneigung(f)	affection	affection, love	afecto; afección	affetto	afeição; afecto
Zunge(f)	langue	tongue	lengua	lingua	língua
zur Zeit	actuellement	now, at present	actualmente	attualmente	actualmente
zurück = bringen	rapporter	bring back	traer	riportare	trazer
zurück = erstatten	restituer	return	restituir	restituire	restituir
zurück = geben	rendre	give back	devolver	rendere	devolver
zurück = gehen	retourner	return(to)	regresar	tornare	voltar(a)
zurück = gehen	reculer	move back, reverse	retroceder	indietreggiare	recuar
zurück = halten	retenir	hold back; retain	retener	trattenere	reter
zurück = kehren	réintégrer	return	reintegrar	reintegrare	voltar
zurück = kommen	revenir	come back, return	volver	ritornare	voltar
zurück = kommen	rentrer	go back, come back	regresar	tornare, rientrare	voltar
zurück = schicken	renvoyer	send back, return	devolver	rinviare	devolver
zurück = treten	désister(se)	withdraw, give up	desistir	desistere, rinunziare	desistir
zurück = treten	démissionner	resign	dimitir	dimettere(-rsi)	demitir-se
zurück = zahlen	rembourser	pay back, reimburse	reembolsar	rimborsare	reembolsar
zurück = ziehen	retirer	withdraw	retirar	ritirare	retirar
zusammen	ensemble	together	juntos	insieme	junto
Zusammenarbeit(f)	concertation	cooperation	concertación	concertazione	concertação
zusammen = brechen	écrouler(s')	collapse, crumble	derrumbar(se)	crollare	desmoronar-se
zusammen = brechen	effondrer(s')	collapse	hundirse	crollare	desabar
Zusammenfassung(f)	résumé	summary	resumen	riassunto	resumo
zusammengefügt	joint, e	joined, linked	junto, a	giunto, a	junto, a
Zusammenhalt(m)	cohésion	cohesion	cohesión	coesione	coesão
zusammenhängend	cohérent, e	coherent	coherente	coerente	coerente
zusammenklappbar	escamotable	fold-away	plegable	ribaltabile	escamoteável
zusammen = setzen	assembler	assemble	ensamblar	assemblare	juntar
Zusammensetzen(n)	remontage	reassembly	volver a montar	rimontaggio	nova montagem
Zusammensetzung(f)	composition	composition	composición	composizione	composição
zusammen = stellen	composer	compose	componer	comporre	compor
Zusammenstoß(m)	collision	collision	colisión, choque	collisione	colisão, choque
zusammen = stoßen	tamponner	bump, crash into	chocar con	tamponare	chocar, esbarrar
Zusammentreffen(n)	coincidence	coincidence	coincidencia	coincidenza	coincidência
Zusammenziehen(n)	contraction	contraction	contracción	contrazione	contracção
zusätzlich	supplémentaire	additional, extra	suplementario, a	supplementare	suplementar
Zuschauer(in f)m	spectateur, trice	spectator	espectador, a	spettatore, trice	espectador, a
Zuschuß(m)	subvention	grant, subsidy	subvención	sovvenzione	subvenção
Zustand(m)	état	condition	condición	condizione	estado
Zuständigkeit(f)	compétence	competence	competencia	competenza	competência
zu = stimmen	consentir	consent	consentir	consentire	consentir

German	French	English	Spanish	Italian	Portuguese
Zustimmung(f)(verbal)	agrément	approval, consent	consentimiento	consenso	consentimento
zu = teilen	attribuer	assign	asignar	assegnare	destinar
zu = teilen, bewilligen	allouer	allocate	conceder	assegnare	conceder
zuverlässig	fiable	reliable	fiable, seguro, a	sicuro, a; affidabile	seguro, a
zuviel	trop	too(much, many)	demasiado, a	troppo, a	demasiado, a
Zuwachs(m)	accroissement	increase	crecimiento	crescita	crescimento
Zwang(m)	contrainte	restraint	obligación	costrizione	obrigação
Zwangsvorstellung(f)	hantise	obsessive fear	obsesión	ossessione	obsessão
zwanzig	vingt	twenty	veinte	venti	vinte
zwei	deux	two	dos	due	dois, duas
zweideutig, mehrdeutig	ambigu, ë	ambiguous	ambiguo, a	ambiguo, a	ambíguo, a
zweideutig	équivoque	equivocal	equívoco, a	equivoco, a	equívoco, a
Zweifel(m)	doute	doubt	duda	dubbio	dúvida
zweifelhaft	douteux, se	dubious; doubtful	dudoso, a	dubbio, a	duvidoso, a
zweifeln	douter	doubt	dudar	dubitare	duvidar
Zweigstelle(f)	succursale	branch(-es)	sucursal	succursale	sucursal
zweisprachig	bilingue	bilingual	bilingüe	bilingue	bilingue
zweite	deuxième	second	segundo, a	secondo, a	segundo, a
zweite	second, e	second	segundo, a	secondo, a	segundo, a
Zwerchfell(n)	diaphragme	diaphragm	diafragma	diaframma	diafragma
Zwerg(m)	nain, e	dwarf	enano, a	nano, a	anão, anã
Zwiebel(f)	oignon	onion	cebolla	cipolla	cebola
Zwilling(m)	jumeau, jumelle	twin	gemelo, a	gemello, a	gémeo, a
zwingen	forcer	force	forzar	forzare	forçar
zwingen	contraindre	force, compel	obligar a	costringere	obrigar
zwingen	obliger	oblige, force	obligar	obbligare	obrigar
zwischen	entre	between	entre	tra, fra	entre
Zwischen-; Mittel-	intermédiaire	intermediate	intermediario, a	intermediario, a	intermediário, a
Zwischenfall(m)	incident	incident	incidente	incidente	incidente
Zwischenlandung(f)	escale	stop(over)	escala	scalo	escala
Zwischenraum(m)	espace	space, gap	espacio	spazio	espaço
zwitterhaft	hybride	hybrid	híbrido, a	ibrido, a	híbrido, a
zwölf	douze	twelve	doce	dodici	doze
Zyklus(m)	cycle	cycle	ciclo	ciclo	ciclo
Zylinder(m)	cylindre	cylinder	cilindro	cilindro	cilindro
zylindrisch	cylindrique	cylindrical	cilíndrico, a	cilindrico, a	cilíndrico, a
zynisch	cynique	cynical	cínico, a	cinico, a	cínico, a
Zyste(f)	kyste	cyst	quiste	ciste	quisto

G

Notes

Notes

G

Notes

Notes

G

Notes

Notes

Notes

A

Spanish	French	English	German	Portuguese	Italian
a	à; dans; chez; de	at; to; in; by; on	zu; in; nach; auf; an; bei	a; para; de; com; em	a; da; con; in; di
abadía	abbaye	abbey	Abtei(f)	abadia	abbazia, badia
abajo	bas	down	hinunter	baixo	giù
abajo	bas(en)	downstairs	unten; hinunter	baixo(de)	basso, giù
abajo(más)	ci-dessous	below	unten(-stehend)	abaixo	sotto(qui)
abandonar	abandonner	abandon, leave	preis = geben; auf = geben	abandonar	abbandonare
abanico	éventail	fan	Fächer(m)	leque	ventaglio
abastecedor, a	fournisseur, se	supplier	Lieferant(in f)m	fornecedor, a	fornitore, trice
abastecer	ravitailler	supply	versorgen	abastecer	rifornire
abastecimiento	alimentation	supplying	Versorgung(f)	abastecimento	rifornimento
abastecimiento	fourniture	supply(ing)	Lieferung(f)	fornecimento	fornitura
abdicar	abdiquer	abdicate	ab = danken	abdicar	abdicare
abdomen	abdomen	abdomen	Unterleib(m)	abdómen	addome
abeja	abeille	bee	Biene(f)	abelha	ape
abeto	sapin	fir-tree	Tanne(f)	abeto	abete
abierto, a	ouvert, e	open	offen; geöffnet	aberto, a	aperto, a
abismo, sima	gouffre	chasm, pit	Abgrund(m), Kluft(f)	abismo	baratro
abogado, a	avocat, e	lawyer, barrister	Anwalt(m), Anwältin(f)	advogado, a	avvocato, tessa
abolir	abolir	abolish	ab = schaffen	abolir	abolire
abombado, a	bombé, e	convex	gewölbt	convexo, a	convesso, a
abominable	abominable	awful	scheußlich	abominável	abominevole
abono, pago	payement	payment	Zahlung(f)	pagamento	pagamento
abono	engrais	fertilizer, manure	Dünger(m)	adubo	concime
abordar	accoster	berth	an = legen	acostar	accostare, attraccare
a bordo	à bord	aboard	an Bord	a bordo	a bordo
abortar	avorter	abort	ab = treiben	abortar	abortire
aborto	avortement	abortion	Abtreibung(f)	aborto	aborto
abrazar, besar	embrasser	kiss; embrace	küssen, umarmen	abraçar, beijar	baciare
abrelatas	ouvre-boîte(s)	tin/can opener	Büchsenöffner(m)	abre-latas	apriscatole
abreviatura	abréviation	abbreviation	Abkürzung(f)(Wort)	abreviatura	abbreviazione
abrigo	manteau	coat	Mantel(m)	casaco, manto	cappotto
abrigo	pardessus	overcoat	Mantel(m)	sobretudo	soprabito
abrigo, refugio	abri, refuge	shelter	Obdach(n), Schutz(m)	abrigo, refúgio	riparo, rifugio
abril	avril	April	April(m)	Abril	aprile
abrir	ouvrir	open	öffnen	abrir	aprire
abrirse	éclore	hatch	aus = schlüpfen	abrir-se	schiudere, uscire
abrupto, a	abrupt, e	steep	steil	abrupto, a	ripido, a; scosceso, a
absceso	abcès	abscess(-es)	Geschwür(n)	abcesso	ascesso
absolutamente	absolument	absolutely	unbedingt, absolut	absolutamente	assolutamente
absoluto, a	absolu, e	absolute	unbedingt	absoluto, a	assoluto, a
absorber	absorber	absorb	verzehren	absorver	assorbire
abstracto, a	abstrait, e	abstract	abstrakt	abstracto, a	astratto, a
absurdo, a	absurde	absurd	unsinnig	absurdo, a	assurdo, a
abuchear	huer	boo	aus = pfeifen	vaiar	fischiare
abuela	grand-mère	grandmother	Großmutter(f)	avó	nonna
abuelo	grand-père	grandfather	Großvater(m)	avô	nonno
abuelos	grands-parents	grandparents	Großeltern(pl.)	avós	nonni
abundancia	abondance	abundance	Überfluß(m)	abundância	abbondanza
abundante	abondant, e	plentiful, abundant	reichlich	abundante	abbondante
aburrido, a	ennuyeux, se	boring; annoying	langweilig	aborrecido, a	noioso, a
aburrimiento	ennui	boredom	Langeweile(f)	aborrecimento	noia
aburrir(se)	ennuyer(s')	bored(be)	langweilen, sich	aborrecer-se	annoiarsi
abusar	abuser	take advantage of	mißbrauchen	abusar	abusare
abuso	abus	abuse, misuse	Mißbrauch(m)	abuso	abuso
acabar	achever	complete, finish	beenden	acabar	terminare, finire
acabar, terminar	finir, terminer	finish, end	beenden	acabar, terminar	finire
academia	académie	academy	Akademie(f)	academia	accademia

Spanish	French	English	German	Portuguese	Italian
acampar	camper	camp	zelten	acampar	campeggiare
acantilado	falaise	cliff	Steilküste(f)	falésia	scogliera
acaparar	cumuler	accumulate	an = häufen	acumular	cumulare
acariciar	caresser	stroke	streicheln	afagar	carezzare
acariciar	caresser	caress	liebkosen, streicheln	acariciar	accarezzare
acceder	accéder	accede to	gelangen zu/kommen an	chegar	assurgere
accesible	accessible	accessible	zugänglich	acessível	accessibile
acceso	accès	access	Zugang(m)	acesso	accesso
accesorio	accessoire	accessory	Zubehör(n)	acessório	accessorio
accidentado, a	accidenté, e	injured person	Verunglückte(f, m)	acidentado, a	accidentato, a
accidente	accident	accident	Unfall(m)	acidente	incidente
acción	action	action	Vorgehen(n), Handlung	acçâo	azione
acción	action	share	Aktie(f)	acçâo	azione
accionista	actionnaire	shareholder	Aktionär(m)	accionista	azionista
acecho(al)	affût	wait for(in)	Versteck(n)	espreita de(à)	agguato
aceite	huile	oil	Öl(n); Speiseöl(n)	óleo; azeite	olio
aceite; óleo	huile	oil	Öl(n); Motoröl(n)	óleo	olio
aceituna, oliva	olive	olive	Olive(f)	azeitona	oliva
acelerar	accélérer	accelerate	beschleunigen	acelerar	accelerare
acento	accent(')	accent	Akzent(m)	acento	accento
acentuación	accentuation	stress(ing)	Betonung(f)	acentuação	accentazione
aceptar	accepter	accept, agree	akzeptieren, an = nehmen	aceitar	accettare
aceptar	agréer	accept, approve	genehmigen, zu = lassen	aceitar	gradire, accettare
acera	trottoir	pavement	Bürgersteig(m)	passeio	marciapiede
acercar(se)	approcher(s')	approach	nähern, sich	aproximar-se	avvicinarsi.
acercar	rapprocher	bring nearer	heran = rücken	acercar	avvicinare
acero	acier	steel	Stahl(m)	aço	acciaio
ácido	acide	acid	Säure(f)	ácido	acido
aclamar	acclamer	cheer	zu = jubeln	aclamar	acclamare
aclaración	précision	clarification	Klarstellung(f)	explicação, precisão	precisazione
acogedor, a	accueillant, e	hospitable	gastfreundlich	acolhedor, a	accogliente
acoger, recibir	accueillir	welcome	empfangen, auf = nehmen	acolher, receber	accogliere
acompañar	accompagner	accompany	begleiten	acompanhar	accompagnare
acondicionar	aménager	fit out; convert	ein = richten	arranjar, dispor	sistemare
aconsejar	conseiller	advise	beraten	aconselhar	consigliare
acontecimiento	événement	event	Ereignis(n)	acontecimento	avvenimento
acorazado	cuirassé	warship	Kriegsschiff(n)	couraçado	corazzata
acordar	convenir	agree	überein = kommen	convir, combinar	convenire
acordarse	souvenir(se)	remember, recall	erinnern, sich	recordar-se	ricordarsi
acosar	harceler	harass	quälen	perseguir	assillare
acostarse	allonger(s')	lie down	hin = legen, sich	estender-se	sdraiarsi
acostumbrarse	habituer(s')	get used to	gewöhnen, sich	habituar-se	abituarsi
acrílico	acrylique	acrylic	Akryl(n)	acrílico	acrilico
acrobacia	acrobatie	acrobatics, stunts	Akrobatik(f)	acrobacia	acrobazia
acróbata	acrobate	acrobat	Akrobat(in f)m	acrobata	acrobata
acta	procès-verbal	minutes, report	Protokoll(n)	acta	verbale
actitud	attitude	attitude	Haltung(f)	atitude	atteggiamento
activar	activer	activate	beschleunigen	activar	attivare
actividad	activité	activity	Tätigkeit(f)	actividade	attività
activo, a	actif, ive	active	aktiv, tatkräftig	activo, a	attivo, a
acto	acte	action, act	Handlung(f)	acto, acçâo	atto
actor, actriz	acteur, actrice	actor, actress	Schauspieler(in f)m	actor, actriz	attore, attrice
actor, actriz	comédien, ne	actor, actress	Schauspieler(in f)m	actor, actriz	attore, attrice
actual	actuel, le	present, current	aktuell, gegenwärtig	actual	attuale
actualizar	actualiser	update	aktualisieren	actualizar	attualizzare
actualmente	actuellement	now, at present	zur Zeit	actualmente	attualmente
actuar	agir	act	handeln	agir	agire
acuario	aquarium	aquarium	Aquarium(n)	aquário	acquario
acuático, a	aquatique	aquatic	Wasser-	aquático, a	acquatico, a
acuerdo	accord	agreement	Einverständnis(n)	acordo	accordo
acuerdo(estar de)	accord(être d')	agree	überein = stimmen	acordo(estar de)	accordo(essere d')
acumular	accumuler	accumulate	an = häufen	acumular	accumulare
acupuntura	acuponcture	acupuncture	Akupunktur(f)	acupunctura	agopuntura
acurrucar(se)	blottir(se).	huddle	an = schmiegen, sich	aninhar-se	rannicchiarsi
acusación	accusation	accusation, charge	Anklage(f)	acusação	accusa
acusado, a; reo	accusé, e	accused(the)	Angeklagte(f, m)	acusado, a; réu(ré)	accusato, a
acusar	accuser	accuse	an = klagen	acusar	accusare
acústica	acoustique	acoustics	Akustik(f)	acústica	acustica

Spanish	French	English	German	Portuguese	Italian
adaptación	adaptation	adaptation	Anpassung(f)	adaptação	adattamento
adaptar	adapter	adapt, adjust	an = passen	adaptar	adattare
adaptarse(a)	adapter(s')	adapt(to)	an = passen, sich	adaptar-se(a)	adattarsi(a)
adecuado, a	adéquat, e	appropriate	passend	adequado, a	adeguato, a
adelantado(estar)	avance(être en)	early(to be)	zu früh (sein)	adiantado(estar)	anticipo(essere in)
adelantar	avancer	advance	voran = gehen; vorrücken	adiantar	avanzare
adelantar	dépasser	exceed	überschreiten	ultrapassar	superare
adelantar	doubler	overtake	überholen	ultrapassar	sorpassare
adelante	avant(en)	ahead	voran, voraus	adiante	avanti
adelante(hacia)	avant	forward(s)	vorwärts	frente(para a)	davanti
adelanto	avance	advance	Vorsprung(m)	avanço	anticipo
adelgazar	maigrir	lose weight	ab = nehmen	emagrecer	dimagrire
además	plus(de)	further, moreover	ferner, überdies	além disso	più(di, in)
además(de)	de plus, en outre	besides	außerdem; außer	além disso; além de	inoltre
adepto, a; seguidor	adepte	follower	Anhänger(in f)m	adepto, a; seguidor, a	seguace, adepto, a
adherente	adhérent, e	member	Mitglied(n)	aderente	aderente, socio
adherir a	adhérer	join	Mitglied werden	aderir a	aderire a
adhesión	adhésion	membership	Beitritt(m)	adesão	adesione
adhesivo, a	adhésif, ive	adhesive	klebrig, anhaftend	adesivo, a	adesivo, a
adición, suma	addition, somme	addition, sum	Addition(f), Summe(f)	adição, soma	addizione, somma
adicional	additionnel, le	additional	hinzugefügt	adicional	addizionale
adicto, dependencia	accoutumance	addiction	Abhängigkeit(f)	dependência	assuefazione
adiós(!)	adieu!, bonjour!	good bye!	tschüß!, lebe wohl!	adeus!	addio!
adivinar	deviner	guess	raten	adivinhar	indovinare
adjetivo	adjectif	adjective	Adjektiv(n)	adjectivo	aggettivo
adjudicación	adjudication	auction	Versteigerung(f)	adjudicação	aggiudicazione
adjunto, a	adjoint, e	assistant	Gehilfe(m); Hilfs-	adjunto, a	aggiunto, a; vice
adjunto, a	ci-joint, e	enclosed	anbei	anexo(em)	allegato, a
administración	administration	administration	Verwaltung(f)	administração	amministrazione
administrar	administrer	manage, run	verwalten	administrar	amministrare
administrar	gérer	manage	verwalten, führen	gerir	amministrare
administrativo, a	administratif, ve	administrative	Verwaltungs-	administrativo, a	amministrativo, a
admiración	admiration	admiration	Bewunderung(f)	admiração	ammirazione
admirador, a	admirateur, trice	admirer, fan	Bewunderer(in f)m	admirador, a	ammiratore, trice
admisible	admissible	admissible	zulässig, annehmbar	admissível	ammissibile
admisión	admission	admission	Zulassung, Einweisung	admissão	ammissione
admitir	admettre	admit	zu = geben; zu = lassen	admitir	ammettere
adoctrinar	endoctriner	indoctrinate	indoktrinieren	doutrinar	addottrinare
adolescente	adolescent, e	teenager	Jugendliche(m, f)	adolescente	adolescente
adoptar	adopter	adopt	adoptieren	adoptar	adottare
adoquín	pavé	paving-stone	Pflasterstein(m)	pedra de calçada	selce, selciato
adorable	adorable	adorable, lovely	reizend	adorável	adorabile
adorar	adorer	adore	an = beten	adorar	adorare
adornar	ornement	ornament	Verzierung; Schmuck	ornamento	ornamento
adorno	parure	finery, jewellery	Schmuck(m)	adorno	parure
adquirido, a	acquis, e	acquired	erworben	adquirido, a	acquisito, a
adquirir	acquérir	acquire	erwerben; erlangen	adquirir, obter	acquistare
aduana	douane	customs	Zoll(m)	alfândega	dogana
aduanero	douanier	customs officer	Zöllner(m)	guarda-fiscal	doganiere
adulterio	adultère	adultery	Ehebruch(m)	adultério	adulterio
adulto, a	adulte	adult	Erwachsene(f, m)	adulto, a	adulto, a
adverbio	adverbe	adverb	Umstandswort, Adverb	advérbio	avverbio
adversario, a	adversaire	opponent	Gegner(in f)m	adversário, a	avversario, a
adverso, a	adverse	adverse, opposing	feindlich, gegnerisch	adverso, a	avverso, a
advertencia	avertissement	warning	Warnung(f)	aviso	ammonizione
advertir	avertir	warn	warnen	avisar, prevenir	avvertire
aéreo, a	aérien, ne	aerial, air	Luft-	aéreo, a	aereo, a
aerograma	aérogramme	aerogram	Funkspruch(m)	aerograma	aerogramma
aeronáutica	aéronautique	aeronautics	Luftfahrt(f)	aeronáutica	aeronautica
aeropuerto	aéroport	airport	Flughafen(m)	aeroporto	aeroporto
afectar	toucher, émouvoir	affect	rühren	afectar	commuovere
afecto; afección	affection	affection, love	Zuneigung(f)	afeição; afecto	affetto
afectuoso, a	affectueux, se	affectionate	liebevoll	afectuoso, a	affettuoso, a
afeitar(se)	raser(se)	shave	rasieren, sich	barbear-se	radersi
aficionado, a	amateur	amateur	Amateur(in f)m	amador, a	dilettante
afilado, a	aiguisé, e	sharp	scharf	afiado, a	affilato, a
afilar	aiguiser	sharpen	schärfen	afiar	affilare
a fin de	afin de	in order to	um...zu	a fim de	per; allo scopo di

Spanish	French	English	German	Portuguese	Italian
a fin de que	afin que	so that	damit	a fim de que	affinché
afinidad	affinité	affinity	Ähnlichkeit(f)	afinidade	affinità
afirmar	affirmer	assert, maintain	behaupten	afirmar	affermare
afligir	affliger	distress, afflict	heim = suchen; betrüben	afligir	affliggere
aflojado, a	détendu, e	slack, loose	schlaff, lose	frouxo, a; lasso, a	allentato, a
aflojar	relâcher	loosen	lockern	largar; soltar	allentare
aflojar	desserrer	loosen	lockern	desapertar	allentare
aflojar	desserrer	loosen	lösen	afrouxar	allentare
afluencia	affluence	crowd	Gedränge(n)	afluência	afflusso
afluencia	affluence	rush	Andrang(m)	afluência	affluenza
afónico, a	aphone	lose one's voice	stimmlos, heiser	áfono, a	afono, a
afortunadamente	heureusement	fortunately	glücklicherweise	felizmente	fortunatamente
afortunado, a	chanceux, se	lucky	Glückspilz(m)	afortunado, a	fortunato, a
afrontar	affronter	confront, face	entgegen = treten	afrontar	affrontare
afueras	banlieue	suburbs	Vorort(m)	arredores	periferia
agacharse	baisser(se)	bend down	bücken, sich	baixar-se	abbassarsi
agarrar, coger	attraper	catch	fangen	agarrar, apanhar	acchiappare
agencia	agence	agency	Agentur(f); Filiale(f)	agência	agenzia
agenda	agenda	diary	Taschenkalender(m)	agenda	agenda
agente	agent	agent	Agent(in f)m	agente	agente
ágil	agile	agile, nimble	flink	ágil	agile
agitación	agitation	agitation; unrest	Aufregung(f); Unruhe f	agitação	agitazione
agitar	agiter	shake	schütteln	agitar	agitare
agitar	agiter	wave	schwenken	agitar	agitare
agonía	agonie	agony	Todeskampf(m), Agonie	agonia	agonia
agosto	août	August	August(m)	Agosto	agosto
agotado, a	épuisé, e	exhausted	erschöpft	esgotado, a	esausto, a
agotado, a	épuisé, e	exhausted, run out	ausverkauft	esgotado, a	esaurito, a
agotamiento	surmenage	overwork(ing)	Überarbeitung(f)	esgotamento	esaurimento
agradable	agréable	pleasant, nice	angenehm	agradável	gradevole, piacevole
agradable	plaisant, e	pleasant	gefällig	agradável	piacevole
agradecer	remercier	thank	danken; bedanken, sich	agradecer	ringraziare
agradecido, a	reconnaissant, e	grateful	dankbar	reconhecido, a	grato, a
agradecimiento	remerciement	thanks	Dank(m)	agradecimento	ringraziamento
agrandar	grossir	increase	vermehren	aumentar	ingrandire
agredir	agresser	attack, assault	an = greifen	agredir	aggredire
agregado, a	attaché, e	attaché	Attaché(m)	adido, a	addetto, a
agresión	agression	attack	Aggression(f), Angriff	agressão	aggressione
agresor, a	agresseur	attacker	Angreifer(in f)m	agressor, a	aggressore
agrícola	agricole	agricultural	landwirtschaftlich	agrícola	agricolo, a
agricultor, a	agriculteur	farmer	Landwirt(in f)m	agricultor, a	agricoltore
agricultura	agriculture	agriculture	Landwirtschaft(f)	agricultura	agricoltura
agrietado, a	craquelé, e	crackled, cracked	rissig	estalado, a	screpolato, a
agrio, a	aigre	sour	sauer	azedo, a	aspro, a; agro, a
agua	eau	water	Wasser(n)	água	acqua
agua bendita	eau bénite	holy water	Weihwasser(n)	água benta	acqua santa
aguamarina	aigue-marine	aquamarine	Aquamarin(m)	água marinha	acquamarina
aguantar, pasar	endurer	endure, bear	aus = halten, ertragen	aguentar	patire, resistere
aguardiente	eau-de-vie	spirits	Schnaps(m)	aguardente	grappa, acquavite
agudo, a	aigu, ë	sharp, shrill	hoch, schrill	agudo, a	acuto, a
agudo, a; vivo, a	vif, vive	keen	scharf	vivo, a	vivo, a
águila	aigle	eagle	Adler(m)	águia	aquila
aguja	aiguille	needle	Nadel(f)	agulha	ago
agujero	trou	hole	Loch(n)	buraco, furo	buco(a), foro
ahí; allí	là	there	da	aí; ali; lá	là
ahogar(se)	noyer(se)	drown	ertrinken	afogar-se	annegare
ahora	maintenant	now	jetzt	agora	ora, adesso
ahorrador, a	épargnant, e	saver, investor	Sparer(in f)m	aforrador, a	risparmiatore, trice
ahorrar	épargner	save	sparen	poupar	risparmiare
ahumado, a	fumé, e	smoked	geräuchert	fumado, a	affumicato, a
aire	air	air	Luft(f)	ar	aria
airear, ventilar	aérer	air, ventilate	lüften	arejar, ventilar	arieggiare
aislado, a	isolé, e	isolated, lonely	allein, einsam	isolado, a; só, a	isolato, a
aislado, a; solo, a	seul, e	lonely	einsam	isolado, a	isolato, a; solo, a
aislamiento	isolation	insulation	Isolierung(f)	isolação	isolamento
aislar	isoler	isolate	ab = sondern; isolieren	isolar	isolare
aislar	isoler	insulate; isolate	isolieren	isolar	isolare
ajedrez	échecs	chess	Schachspiel(n)	xadrês	scacchi

Spanish	French	English	German	Portuguese	Italian
ajustar	ajuster	adjust	ein = stellen	ajustar	aggiustare
ajustar, arreglar	régler	adjust, tune	ein = stellen	afinar, regular	regolare
ala	aile	wing	Flügel(m)	asa	ala
alambre	fil(de fer)	wire	Draht(m)	arame	filo(di ferro)
alargar	allonger	lengthen	verlängern	alongar	allungare
alarma	alarme	alarm	Alarm(m)	alarme	allarme
alba	aube	dawn	Morgendämmerung(f)	amanhecer	alba
albañil	maçon	builder	Maurer(m)	pedreiro, trolha	muratore
alboroto, jaleo	vacarme	uproar, din	Krach(m)	barulho	chiasso
álbum	album	album	Album(n)	álbum	album
alcalde	maire	mayor	Bürgermeister(m)	President.da Câmara	sindaco
alcance	portée	range, reach	Reichweite(f)	alcance	portata, gittata
alcanzar, lograr	atteindre	reach	erreichen	atingir	raggiungere
alcohol	alcool	alcohol	Alkohol(m)	álcool	alcol, alcool
alcohol	alcool(s)	spirit(s)	Alkohol(m)	álcool	alcolico
alcoholismo	alcoolisme	alcoholism	Alkoholmißbrauch(m)	alcoolismo	alcolismo
aldea, pueblo	village	village	Dorf(n)	aldeia, povoado	paese, villaggio
aleación	alliage	alloy	Legierung(f)	liga	lega
aleatorio, a	aléatoire	aleatory, uncertain	unsicher, ungewiß	aleatório, a; incerto	aleatorio, a
alegrarse	réjouir(se)	delighted(be)	erfreuen, sich	alegrar-se	rallegrare(-arsi)
alegre	gai, e	happy, merry	froh	alegre	allegro, a
alegre	joyeux, se	merry, joyful	lustig, fröhlich	alegre	allegro, a; felice
alegría	joie	joy	Freude(f)	alegria	gioia
alejamiento	éloignement	distance	Entfernung(f)	afastamento	lontananza
alentar, animar	encourager	encourage, urge	ermutigen	encorajar	incoraggiare
alergia	allergie	allergy	Allergie(f)	alergia	allergia
alerta	alerte	alert	Alarm(m)	alerta, alarme	allarme
aleta	nageoire	fin	Flosse(f)	barbatana	pinna
aleta	palme	flipper	Flosse(f)	barbatanas	pinna
alfabeto	alphabet	alphabet	Alphabet(n)	alfabeto	alfabeto
alfiler	épingle	pin	Stecknadel(f)	alfinete	spillo
alfombra, tapiz	tapis	mat, rug, carpet	Teppich(m)	tapete, carpete	tappeto
alga	algue	seaweed, alga(ae)	Alge(f)	alga	alga
álgebra	algèbre	algebra	Algebra(f)	álgebra	algebra
algo	quelque chose	something	etwas	qualquer coisa	qualche cosa
algodón	coton	cotton	Baumwolle(f)	algodão	cotone
alguien	quelqu'un, e	someone, somebody	jemand	alguém	qualcuno, a
alguna parte(en)	quelque part	somewhere	irgendwo	algures	qualche parte(da)
alguno, a	quelque	some, any	einige	algum, a	qualche
algunos, as	quelques	few(a), some	einige	alguns, algumas	alcuni, e
algunos, as	certaines	certain; some	manche	certos, as	certi, e; alcuni, e
alianza	alliance	alliance	Bündnis(n)	aliança	alleanza
aliar, unir	allier	ally	verbünden	aliar, unir	alleare, unire
alicates, tenazas	pinces	pliers, pincers	Zangen(pl)	alicate; tenaz	pinze
aliento	haleine	breath	Atem(m)	hálito	alito
alimentación	alimentation	feeding; food	Ernährung(f)	alimentação	alimentazione
alimentación	alimentation	food shop	Lebensmittelladen(m)	mercearia	alimentari(negozio)
alimentar	nourrir	feed, nourish	ernähren	alimentar	nutrire
alimento	nourriture	food	Nahrung(f)	alimentação	cibo; nutrimento
alimento	aliment	food	Lebensmittel(n, pl)	alimento	alimento, cibo
alineación	alignement	alignment	Ausrichtung(f)	alinhamento	allineamento
aliño	assaisonnement	seasoning	Würze(f)	tempero	condimento
aliviar	alléger	lighten	erleichtern	aliviar	alleggerire
aliviar	soulager	relieve	erleichtern	aliviar	alleggerire
aliviar	soulager	relieve	lindern	aliviar	sollevare, lenire
alivio, desahogo	soulagement	relief	Erleichterung(f)	alívio	sollievo
al lado	à côté	next to, beside	neben, daneben	ao lado	accanto; vicino, a
alma	âme	soul	Seele(f)	alma	anima
almacén	magasin	store	Warenlager(n)	armazém	magazzino; negozio
almacén	entrepôt	warehouse	Lager(n)	armazém	magazzino
almacenar	stocker	stock, store	lagern	armazenar	immagazzinare
almendra	amande	almond	Mandel(f)	amêndoa	mandorla
almíbar	sirop	cordial, squash	Saft(m), Sirup(m)	xarope	sciroppo
almirante	amiral	admiral	Admiral(m)	almirante	ammiraglio
almohada	oreiller	pillow	Kopfkissen(n)	travesseiro	guanciale
almorzar	déjeuner	have lunch, lunch	Mittag essen(zu)	almoçar	pranzare
alocución	allocution	speech(short)	Ansprache(kurze)(f)	alocução	allocuzione
alojamiento	logement	accommodation	Wohnung(f)	alojamento	alloggio

Spanish	French	English	German	Portuguese	Italian
alojamiento	hébergement	accommodation	Unterbringung(f)	alojamento	alloggio
alojar	loger	accommodate	unter = bringen	alojar, morar	alloggiare
alopatía	allopathie	allopathy	Allopathie(f)	alopatia	allopatia
alpinista	alpiniste	mountaineer	Alpinist(m)	alpinista	alpinista
alquilar	louer	hire, rent	mieten; vermieten	alugar	noleggiare
alquilar	louer	rent	vermieten; mieten	alugar	affittare
alquiler	location	rental, hiring	Vermietung(f)	aluguer	noleggio, affitto
alquiler	loyer	rent	Miete(f)	aluguer	affitto
alquitrán	goudron	tar	Teer(m)	alcatrão	asfalto
alrededor	autour	around	um	redor de(em)	intorno, attorno
alrededores	alentours	surroundings	Umgebung(f)	arredores	dintorni
altavoz	haut-parleur	loud-speaker	Lautsprecher(m)	alto-falante	altoparlante
altavoz	baffle	speaker	Lautsprecher(m)	alto-falante	altoparlante
alternar	alterner	alternate	ab = wechseln	alternar	alternare
alternativo, a	alternatif, ive	alternating(ive)	alternativ	alternativo, a	alternativo, a
altitud, altura	altitude	altitude, height	Höhe(f)	altitude	altitudine
altivo, a	fier, fière	proud	stolz	altivo, a	fiero, a
alto, a	haut, e	high, tall	hoch	alto, a	alto, a
alto, a	élévé, e	high	hoch, erhöht	alto, a	elevato, a; alto, a
alto, a	grand, e	high	hoch	alto, a	forte; alto, a
alto, a	grand, e	tall	groß	alto, a; grande	alto, a
alto	haut	top	Oberteil(n)	alto, cimo	alto
alto, parada	halte, arrêt	halt, stop	Halt(m)	alto, paragem	sosta, fermata
altura	hauteur	height	Höhe(f)	altura	altezza
alucinación	hallucination	hallucination	Sinnestäuschung(f)	alucinação	allucinazione
aluminio	aluminium	aluminium	Aluminium(n)	alumínio	alluminio
alumno, a	élève	pupil	Schüler(in f)m	aluno, a	alunno, a
allá	là-bas	over there	da; dort	além, acolá	là; laggiù
allanar, aplastar	aplatir	flatten	glätten, ab = flachen	achatar, alisar	appiattire
allí; allá	là	there	da; dort	aí; lá	là; lì
amable	aimable	nice	lieb, nett	amável	amabile
ama de casa	ménagère	housewife(-ives)	Hausfrau(f)	dona de casa	casalinga
amaestrar	dresser	train	ab = richten, dressieren	amestrar	addestrare
amanecer	lever(se)	rise	auf = gehen	nascer	sorgere
amanecer	lever(se)	break, dawn	an = brechen	nascer	sorgere
amante	amant, e	lover	Geliebte(f, m)	amante	amante
amante de	amateur de	lover of	Liebhaber(in f)m	apreciador, a	appassionato, a
amar, querer	aimer	love	lieben	amar, gostar de	amare, volere bene
amargo, a	amer, ère	bitter	bitter; sauer	amargo, a	amaro, a
amarillo, a	jaune	yellow	gelb	amarelo, a	giallo, a
amasar	pétrir	knead	kneten	amassar	impastare
ambición	ambition	ambition	Ehrgeiz(m)	ambição	ambizione
ambicioso, a	ambitieux, se	ambitious	ehrgeizig	ambicioso, a	ambizioso, a
ambiente	ambiance	atmosphere	Stimmung(f)	ambiente	atmosfera
ambiente(medio)	environnement	surroundings	Umgebung(f)	ambiente	ambiente
ambiente, medio	milieu	milieu, background	Milieu(n)	meio	ambiente
ambiguo, a	ambigu, ë	ambiguous	zweideutig, mehrdeutig	ambíguo, a	ambiguo, a
ambos, ambas	à la fois	both	beide, beides	ambos, os dois	entrambi
ambulancia	ambulance	ambulance	Krankenwagen(m)	ambulância	ambulanza
amenaza	menace	threat	Drohung(f)	ameaça	minaccia
amenazar	menacer	threaten	bedrohen	ameaçar	minacciare
amígdalas	amygdale(s)	tonsils	Mandeln(f, pl)	amígdala	tonsilla
amigo, a	ami, e	friend	Freund(in f)m	amigo, a	amico, a
aminorar	ralentir	slow down	verlangsamen	abrandar	rallentare
amistad	amitié	friendship	Freundschaft(f)	amizade	amicizia
amistoso, a	amical, e	friendly	freundschaftlich	amigável	amichevole
amnesia	amnésie	amnesia	Gedächtnisschwund(m)	amnésia	amnesia
amnistía	amnistie	amnesty	Amnestie(f)	amnistia	amnistia
amontonar	entasser	pile up	stapeln	amontoar	ammucchiare
amor	amour	love	Liebe(f)	amor	amore
amortiguador	amortisseur	shock absorber	Stoßdämpfer(m)	amortecedor	ammortizzatore
amortiguar	amortir	absorb, cushion	dämpfen	amortecer	attutire
amovible	amovible	removable	auswechselbar	amovível	amovibile
ampliar	agrandir	enlarge	vergrößern	ampliar	ingrandire
amplio, a	ample	ample; loose	weit	amplo, a	ampio, a
amplitud	ampleur	scale, size	Weite(f), Größe(f)	amplidão	ampiezza
amplitud	amplitude	amplitude	Amplitude(f)	amplitude	ampiezza
ampolla	ampoule	blister	Blase(f)	empola	bolla, vescica

Spanish	French	English	German	Portuguese	Italian
ampolla	cloque	blister	Blase(f)(Brandblase)	bolha	vescica
amputar	amputer	amputate	amputieren	amputar	amputare
analfabeto, a	illettré, e	illiterate	ungebildet	iletrado, a	analfabeta
análisis	analyse	analysis(-ses)	Analyse(f)	análise	analisi
analizar	analyser	analyse	analysieren	analisar	analizzare
análogo, a	analogue	analogous, similar	analog	análogo, a	analogo, a
anaranjado, a	orange	orange	orangefarben	cor-de-laranja	arancione
anarquía	anarchie	anarchy	Anarchie(f)	anarquia	anarchia
anatomía	anatomie	anatomy	Anatomie(f)	anatomia	anatomia
anciano, a	âgé, e	old	alt	idoso, a	anziano, a
ancla	ancre	anchor	Anker(m)	âncora	àncora
ancho, a	large	wide, broad	weit, breit	largo, a	largo, a
ancho, a	large	broad	breit, weit	largo, a; amplo, a	largo, a; ampio, a
anchura	largeur	width, breadth	Breite(f)	largura	larghezza
andamio	échafaudage	scaffolding	Gerüst(n)	andaime	impalcatura
andar	marcher	walk	gehen	andar	andare
andén	quai	platform	Bahnsteig(m)	plataforma	binario, marciapiede
anécdota	anecdote	anecdote	Anekdote(f)	anedota	aneddoto
anemia	anémie	anaemia	Blutarmut(f)	anemia	anemia
anestesia	anesthésie	anaesthetic	Narkose(f)	anestesia	anestesia
anexo; anejo	annexe	annexe	Anhang(m), Anlage(f)	anexo	annesso
anfitrión; huésped	hôte, tesse	host; guest	Gastgeber(m); Gast(m)	anfitrião; hóspede, a	ospite
ángel	ange	angel	Engel(m)	anjo	angelo
angina	angine	sore throat	Angina(f)	angina	angina, tonsillite
ángulo	angle	angle	Winkel(m)	ângulo	angolo
angustia	angoisse	anguish, distress	Angst(f)	angústia	angoscia
angustia	détresse	distress	Verzweiflung(f)	aflição, angústia	sconforto
anilla, anillo	anneau	ring	Ring(m)	anel	anello
anillo, sortija	bague	ring	Ring(m)	anel	anello
animado, a	animé, e	lively	lebhaft	animado, a	animato, a
animador, a	animateur, trice	leader, organiser	Leiter/in, Unterhalter	animador, a	animatore, trice
animal	animal	animal	Tier(n)	animal	animale
animar	animer	animate	beleben	animar	animare
animar	animer	liven up	Stimmung machen	animar	animare
aniquilar	anéantir	annihilate, destroy	vernichten	aniquilar	annientare
aniversario	anniversaire	anniversary	Jahrestag(m)	aniversário	anniversario
anomalía	anomalie	anomaly	Anomalie(f)	anomalia	anomalia
anonimato	anonymat	anonymity	Anonymität(f)	anonimato	anonimato
anónimo, a	anonyme	anonymous	anonym, unbekannt	anónimo, a	anonimo, a
anormal	anormal, e	not normal	anormal	anormal	anormale
anotar	noter	note; notice	notieren; bemerken	anotar, notar	notare
ansioso, a	anxieux, se	anxious	ängstlich	ansioso, a	ansioso, a
antaño	autrefois	past(in the)	früher	antigamente	volta(una)
antebrazo	avant-bras	fore-arm	Unterarm(m)	antebraço	avambraccio
antecedente	antécédent, e	previous	vorhergehend	antecedente	antecedente
antena	antenne	aerial, antenna(e)	Antenne(f)	antena	antenna
antepasado, a	ancêtre	ancestor	Ahn(m)	antepassado, a	antenato, a
antepasados	aieux	ancestors	Ahnen(pl.)	antepassados	antenati
anterior	antérieur, e	previous, former	vorhergehend	anterior	anteriore
anterior	antérieur, e	prior	früher	anterior	anteriore
antes(de)	avant	before	vor, vorher	antes(de)	prima
antes	auparavant	before	vorher, zuvor	dantes	prima
antibiótico	antibiotique	antibiotic	Antibiotikum(n)	antibiótico	antibiotico
anticipar	anticiper	anticipate	vor = greifen	antecipar	anticipare
anticonceptivo	contraceptif	contraceptive	Verhütungsmittel(n)	contraceptivo	anticoncezionale
anticuado, a	démodé, e; désuet	obsolete	veraltet	antiquado, a	antiquato, a
anticuario	antiquités	antique shop	Antiquität(en)	antiguidades	antiquariato
antigüedad	antiquité	antiquity	Antiquität(f)	antiguidade	antichità
antiguo, a	antique	antique, ancient	antik	antigo, a	antico, a
antiguo, a	ancien, ne	old	alt	antigo, a	vecchio, a; antico, a
antiguo, a	ancien, ne	ancient	alt	antigo, a	antico, a
antirrobo	antivol	anti-theft lock	Diebstahlsicherung(f)	alarme	antifurto
antiséptico, a	antiseptique	antiseptic	antiseptisch	antiséptico, a	antisettico, a
antorcha	torche	torch	Fackel(f)	tocha, archote	torcia
anual	annuel, le	yearly, annual	jährlich	anual	annuale
anuario, guía	annuaire	directory	Adreßbuch; Telefonbuch	anuário	elenco, annuario
anular	annuler	annul	ungültig erklären	anular	annullare
anular	annuler	quash	auf = heben	anular	annullare

Spanish	French	English	German	Portuguese	Italian
anular	annulaire	annular, ring-	ringförmig	anelar	anulare
anunciar	annoncer	announce	an = kündigen	anunciar	annunciare
anunciar	afficher	post up, put up	an = schlagen	afixar	affiggere
anuncio	annonce	notice	Anzeige(f)	anúncio	annuncio
anuncios(fijación)	affichage	putting up posters	Anschlag, Plakatierung	afixação	affissione
añadir	ajouter	add	hinzu = fügen	ajuntar, juntar	aggiungere
año	an	year	Jahr(n)	ano	anno
año	année	year	Jahr(n)	ano	annata, anno
anzuelo	hameçon	hook	Angelhaken(m)	anzol	amo
apacible	paisible	peaceful, quiet	friedlich, ruhig	pacífico, a	pacifico, a; placido, a
apaciguar	apaiser	calm, soothe	beruhigen	acalmar	calmare
apagar	éteindre	turn/switch off	aus = schalten	apagar	spegnere
apagar	éteindre	extinguish	löschen	apagar	spegnere
aparador	buffet	dresser; sideboard	Büfett(n)	aparador	credenza, buffè
aparato	appareil	appliance, device	Apparat(m)	aparelho	apparecchio
aparato de radio	poste radio	radio set	Radio(n)	rádio	radio
aparcamiento	parking	car park	Parkplatz(m)	p.estacionamento	parcheggio
aparcar	garer	park	parken	estacionar	posteggiare
aparearse	accoupler(s')	mate	paaren, sich	acasalar-se	accoppiarsi
aparecer	apparaître	appear	erscheinen	aparecer	apparire
apariencia	apparence	appearance, look	Aussehen(n)	aparência	apparenza
apartar	écarter	separate, part	entfernen	afastar	allontanare; scartare
apasionado, a	passionné, e	interested(very)	leidenschaftlich	apaixonado, a	appassionato, a
apasionante	passionnant, e	fascinating	spannend	apaixonante	appassionante
apego, cariño	attachement	attachment	Verbundenheit(f)	apego	attaccamento
apelación	appel	appeal	Berufung(f)	apelação	appello
apellido	nom	surname	Familienname(m)	apelido	cognome
aperitivo	apéritif	aperitif, drink	Apéritif(m)	aperitivo	aperitivo
apertura	ouverture	opening	Öffnungszeiten(f, pl)	abertura	apertura
a pesar de	malgré	despite	trotz	apesar de	malgrado
apestar	puer	stink	stinken	cheirar mal	puzzare
apetito	appétit	appetite	Appetit(m)	apetite	appetito
apilar, amontonar	empiler	pile up, stack	stapeln	empilhar, amontoar	accatastare
aplanar	aplanir	level	ebnen	aplanar	spianare
aplastar	écraser	crush, flatten	zerquetschen	esmagar	schiacciare
aplaudir	applaudir	applaud, clap	klatschen	aplaudir	applaudire
aplazar	ajourner	postpone, adjourn	vertagen	adiar	rimandare, aggiornare
aplicar	appliquer	apply	an = wenden	aplicar	applicare
apodo, mote	surnom	nickname	Spitzname(m)	alcunha, apelido	soprannome
aporrear	matraquer	beat up, club	prügeln	espancar	manganellare
apoyar(se)	appuyer(s')	lean on(against)	stützen, sich	apoiar-se	appoggiarsi
apoyo	appui	support	Stütze(f)	apoio	appoggio
apreciación	appréciation	appreciation	Beurteilung(f)	apreciação	giudizio
apreciar	apprécier	appreciate	schätzen	apreciar	apprezzare
aprender	apprendre	learn	lernen	aprender	imparare
aprendizaje	apprentissage	apprenticeship	Lehre(f), Lehrjahre(f)	aprendizagem	apprendistato
aprensión, recelo	appréhension	apprehension	Furcht(f)	apreensão	apprensione
apretar	serrer	grip, hold tight	greifen, packen	apertar	stringere
apretar	presser	press, squeeze	drücken(zusammen-)	prensar	premere
apretar	serrer, resserrer	tighten	an = ziehen	apertar	stringere
aprobar	approuver	approve	genehmigen	aprovar	approvare
aprovechar	profiter	take advantage of	profitieren	aproveitar	approfittare
aprovisionar	approvisionner	supply	versorgen	abastecer	rifornire
aproximadamente	environ	about	ungefähr	cerca de	circa
aproximativo, a	approximatif, ive	approximate	ungefähr	aproximado, a	approssimativo, a
aptitud(es)	aptitude	ability, aptitude	Fähigkeit(f)	aptidão, talento	attitudine
apto, a	apte, compétent, e	able, qualified	fähig; tauglich	apto, a	adatto, a
apuesta	pari	bet	Wette(f)	aposta	scommessa
apuesta	enjeu	stake	Einsatz(m)(Spiel-)	aposta	posta
apuntar	braquer	aim	richten auf	apontar	puntare
apuntar	viser	aim	zielen	apontar	mirare
apuro	embarras	embarrassment	Verlegenheit(f)	embaraço	imbarazzo
aquí	ici	here	hier	aqui	qui
arandela	rondelle	washer	Scheibe(f)	anilha	rondella
araña	araignée	spider	Spinne(f)	aranha	ragno
arañar	griffer	scratch, claw	kratzen	arranhar	graffiare
arbitrario, a	arbitraire	arbitrary	willkürlich	arbitrário, a	arbitrario, a
árbitro	arbitre	referee	Schiedsrichter(in f)m	árbitro	arbitro

Spanish	French	English	German	Portuguese	Italian
árbol	arbre	tree	Baum(m)	árvore	albero
arca, cajón	bahut, coffre	chest	Truhe(f)	baú, arca, armário	cassone
arca	arche	arch	Bogen(m), Gewölbe(n)	arco	arco, volta
arcaico, a	archaïque	archaic	archaisch	arcaico, a	arcaico, a
arcilla	argile	clay	Ton(m), Lehm(m)	argila	argilla
arco	arc	bow	Bogen(m)	arco	arco
arco	arc	arc	Halbkreis(m)	arco	arco
arco iris	arc-en-ciel	rainbow	Regenbogen(m)	arco-íris	arcobaleno
archipiélago	archipel	archipelago	Inselgruppe(f)	arquipélago	arcipelago
archivos	archives	archives	Archiv(n)	arquivo	archivi
ardid; astucia	ruse	trick, craftiness	List(f)	astúcia	furbizia
ardiente	brûlant, e	boiling hot	brennend, kochend	ardente	ardente, bollente
ardilla	écureuil	squirrel	Eichhörnchen(n)	esquilo	scoiattolo
área, zona	aire, zone	area	Bereich(m), Gebiet(n)	área, zona	area, zona
arena	sable	sand	Sand(m)	areia	sabbia
arena	arène	arena	Arena(f)	arena	arena
arenque	hareng	herring	Hering(m)	arenque	aringa
argamasa	mortier	mortar	Mörtel(m)	argamassa	malta, calcina
argüir, argumentar	argumenter	argue	verhandeln	argumentar	argomentare
argumento	argument	argument	Argument(n)	argumento	argomento
árido, a	aride	arid	dürr, trocken	árido, a	arido, a
aristócrata	aristocrate	aristocrat	Adlige(f, m)	aristocrata	aristocratico, a
aritmética	arithmétique	arithmetic	Arithmetik(f)	aritmética	aritmetica
arma	arme	weapon, arm	Waffe(f)	arma	arma
arma	arme	arm	Waffe(f)	arma	arma; armi
armador	armateur	ship-owner	Reeder(m)	armador	armatore
armamento	armement	armament, weapons	Bewaffnung(f)	armamento	armamento
armario	armoire	wardrobe	Schrank(m)(Kleider-)	armário	armadio
armario	armoire	cupboard	Schrank(m)	armário	armadio
armario	placard	cupboard	Wandschrank(m)	armário	armadio a muro
armazón	ossature	structure	Struktur(f)	ossatura	ossatura
armazón	charpente	framework	Holzgerüst(n)	madeiramento	ossatura, travatura
armonía	harmonie	harmony	Harmonie(f)	harmonia	armonia
armonioso, a	harmonieux, se	harmonious	harmonisch	harmonioso, a	armonioso, a
arnés	harnais	harness	Geschirr(n)	arnês	finimenti
aroma	arôme	aroma	Aroma(n)	aroma, cheiro	aroma
arpa	harpe	harp	Harfe(f)	harpa	arpa
arpón	harpon	harpoon	Harpune(f)	arpão	arpione
arqueado, a	cambré, e	arched	krumm, gebeugt	arqueado, a	inarcato, a; arcuato, a
arqueología	archéologie	archaeology	Archeologie(f)	arqueologia	archeologia
arquitecto, a	architecte	architect	Architekt(in f)m	arquitecto, a	architetto
arquitectura	architecture	architecture	Architektur(f)	arquitectura	architettura
arrancar	arracher	tear out; tear off	weg = reißen, aus = reißen	arrancar	strappare, togliere
arrancar	démarrer	start	starten	arrancar	avviare, iniziare
arranque	démarreur	starter	Starter(m)	motor de arranque	motorino(avviamento)
arrastrar	traîner	drag, trail, haul	schleppen	arrastar	trascinare
arrastrarse	ramper	crawl	kriechen	rastejar	strisciare
arrecife	récif	reef	Riff(n)	recife	scoglio
arreglar	arranger	arrange	arrangieren	arranjar	sistemare
arreglo	arrangement	arrangement	Anordnung(f)	arranjo	ordinamento
arreglo, acuerdo	arrangement	arrangement	Abmachung(f)	compromisso	accordo
arrendar	louer à bail	lease	mieten; pachten	arrendar, alugar	noleggiare
arresto	arrestation	arrest	Verhaftung(f)	detenção	arresto
arriate	parterre	flower-bed	Beet(n)	canteiro	aiuola
arriba	haut(en)	upstairs	oben	cima(em)	alto(in)
arriba	là-haut	up there	da oben	lá em cima	in alto
arriba, encima	dessus(au-, par-)	above, on, over	über	em cima, sobre	sopra
arriba	au-dessus	overhead	oben	cima(por, em)	sopra, in alto
arriba(más)	ci-dessus	above	oben(-stehend)	acima	sopra(qui)
arriba	haut	up	Oben-; Hoch-; auf	cima(em, para)	alto, a
arriesgar	risquer	risk	riskieren	arriscar	rischiare
arrodillarse	agenouiller(s')	kneel	hin = knien, sich	ajoelhar-se	inginocchiare(-rsi)
arrojar, lanzar	jeter	throw	werfen	atirar, lançar	gettare
arroyo	caniveau	gutter	Rinnstein(m)	valeta	canaletto di scolo
arroz	riz	rice	Reis(m)	arroz	riso
arruga	ride	wrinkle	Falte(f)	ruga	ruga
arruinar	ruiner	ruin	ruinieren	arruinar	rovinare
arsenal	arsenal	arsenal, armoury	Arsenal(n)	arsenal	arsenale

S

Spanish	French	English	German	Portuguese	Italian
arte	art	art	Kunst(f)	arte	arte
arteria	artère	artery	Ader(f); Arterie(f)	artéria	arteria
artesano	artisan	craftsman(-men)	Handwerker(in f)m	artesão	artigiano
artes marciales	arts martiaux	martial arts	Kriegskunst(f)	artes marciais	arti marziali
articulación	articulation	joint	Gelenk(n)	articulação	articolazione
artículo	article	article	Artikel(m)	artigo	articolo
artículo	article	article	Gesetzesartikel(m)	artigo	articolo
artículo	article	item	Artikel(m)	artigo	articolo
artificial	artificiel, le	artificial	künstlich	artificial	artificiale
artista	artiste	artist	Künstler(in f)m	artista	artista
artrosis	arthrose	arthritis	Arthrose(f)	artrose	artrosi
asa	anse	handle	Griff(m)	asa	ansa
asa, mango	poignée	handle	Griff(m)	asa	manico
asado	rôti	roast; joint	Braten(m)	assado	arrosto
asador	broche	spit	Spieß(m)	espeto	spiedo
asalariado, a	salarié, e	salaried employee	Arbeitnehmer(in f)m	assalariado, a	salariato, a
asalto	assaut	assault, attack	Angriff(m)	assalto	assalto
asamblea	assemblée	meeting, assembly	Versammlung(f)	assembleia	assemblea
asar(parrilla)	griller	grill	grillen	grelhar	arrostire
ascensor	ascenseur	lift, elevator	Aufzug(m)	elevador	ascensore
asco(dar)	dégoûter	disgust	an = widern	enojar	disgustare
asegurado, a	assuré, e	insured	versichert	segurado, a	assicurato, a
asegurarse	assurer(s')	ensure; insure	versichern; zu = sichern	assegurar-se	assicurarsi
asesinato	assassinat	murder	Mord(m)	assassínio	assassinio
asesinato	meurtre	murder	Mord(m)	homicídio, crime	assassinio
asesino, a	assassin	murderer	Mörder(in f)m	assassino, a	assassino, a
asesino, a	tueur, se	killer	Mörder(in f)m	assassino, a	assassino, a
asfalto	bitume	asphalt, tarmac	Asphalt(m)	asfalto	bitume
asfixia	asphyxie	suffocation	Ersticken(n)	asfixia	asfissia
así	ainsi	so, thus	so	assim	cosi
asiento	siège	seat	Sitz(m)	assento	sedia
asignar	attribuer	assign	zu = teilen	destinar	assegnare
asignatura	matière	subject	Fach(n)	matéria	materia
asilo	asile	asylum(political)	Asyl(n)	asilo	asilo
asistencia	assistance	assistance	Hilfe(f)	assistência	assistenza
asistenta	femme de ménage	domestic help	Putzfrau(f)	mulher a dias	donna di servizio
asistente, a	assistant, e	assistant	Assistent(in f)m	assistente	assistente
asistir	assister	attend	assistieren	assistir	assistere
asma	asthme	asthma	Asthma(n)	asma	asma
asociación	association	association	Verband(m)	associação	associazione
asociar	associer	combine, associate	verbinden	associar	associare
asociarse(a, con)	associer à(s')	join	an = schließen, sich	associar-se a	associarsi(a, con)
asolar, devastar	ravager	devastate, ravage	verwüsten	assolar	devastare
asomarse	pencher(se)	lean out	hinaus = lehnen	debruçar-se	sporgersi
asombroso, a	étonnant, e	surprising	erstaunlich	espantoso, a	sorprendente
aspecto	aspect	aspect	Aussehen(n)	aspecto	aspetto
aspirador	aspirateur	vacuum-cleaner	Staubsauger(m)	aspirador	aspirapolvere
aspirar	aspirer	inhale, suck in(up)	ein = atmen, saugen	aspirar	aspirare
aspirina	aspirine	aspirin	Aspirin(n)	aspirina	aspirina
asquear	écoeurer	disgust	an = ekeln, an = widern	enjoar	nauseare
asqueroso, a	dégoûtant, e	disgusting	ekelhaft	nojento, a	disgustoso, a
asqueroso, a	infect, e	foul, vile	ekelhaft, stinkig	asqueroso, a	fetido, a
astro	astre	star	Stern(m), Gestirn(n)	astro	astro
astrología	astrologie	astrology	Astrologie(f)	astrologia	astrologia
astronáutica	astronautique	astronautics	Weltraumfahrt(f)	astronáutica	astronautica
astronomía	astronomie	astronomy	Astronomie(f)	astronomia	astronomia
astucia	astuce	trick	List(f), Trick(m)	astúcia	astuzia
astuto, a	astucieux, se	astute, clever	verschmitzt, schlau	astucioso, a	astuto, a
astuto, a	rusé, e	crafty, cunning	schlau, gerissen	astuto, a; fino, a	astuto, a
asumir	assumer	assume	übernehmen, nehmen	assumir	assumere
asunto	affaire	affair, matter	Affäre(f), Sache(f)	assunto	faccenda, affare
asustar	effrayer	frighten	erschrecken	assustar	spaventare
atacar	attaquer	attack	an = greifen	atacar	attaccare
atajo	raccourci	short cut	Abkürzung(f)	atalho	scorciatoia
ataque	attaque	attack	Angriff(m)	ataque	attacco
atar	attacher	attach, tie, fasten	fest = binden, binden	atar	legare
atar, fijar	attacher	fasten	befestigen	atar, amarrar	attaccare, legare
ataúd	cercueil	coffin	Sarg(m)	caixão	bara

Spanish	French	English	German	Portuguese	Italian
atención a(en)	attention(à l')	attention	Aufmerksamkeit(f)	cuidado(ao)	attenzione
atentado	attentat	attempt, attack	Attentat(n)	atentado	attentato
atento, a	attentif, ive	attentive, careful	aufmerksam	atento, a	attento, a
atenuar	atténuer	attenuate	ab = schwächen; lindern	atenuar	attenuare
aterrizar	atterrir	land	landen	aterrar	atterrare
aterrorizar	terroriser	terrorize	terrorisieren	aterrorizar	terrorizzare
atestiguar	témoigner	witness	zeugen, bezeugen	testemunhar	testificare
Atlántico	Atlantique	Atlantic	Atlantik(m)	Atlântico	Atlantico
atleta	athlète	athlete	Athlet(in f)m	atleta	atleta
atletismo	athlétisme	athletics	Leichtathletik(f)	atletismo	atletismo
atmósfera	atmosphère	atmosphere	Atmosphäre(f)	atmosfera	atmosfera
atolón	atoll	atoll	Atoll(n)	atol	atollo
atómico, a	atomique	atomic	atomar	atómico, a	atomico, a
atomizador	atomiseur	spray, atomizer	Zerstäuber(m)	pulverizador	nebulizzatore
átomo	atome	atom	Atom(n)	átomo	atomo
atormentado, a	tourmenté, e	tormented	beunruhigt	atormentado, a	tormentato, a
atormentar	tourmenter	torment	quälen	atormentar	tormentare
atracción	attraction	attraction	Anziehung(f)	atracção	attrazione
atraco	hold-up	hold-up	Raubüberfall(m)	assalto	rapina
atractivo, a	séduisant, e	attractive	reizend, anziehend	atraente	seducente
atraer	attirer	attract	an = ziehen	atrair	attirare
atraer, seducir	attirer, séduire	entice	verführen	atrair, seduzir	attirare, sedurre
atrás	arrière, derrière	behind, back	hinten, zurück	atrás	dietro, posteriore
atrás(para)	arrière(en)	backward(s)	rückwärts	trás(para)	indietro
atraso	retard	delay; lateness	Verspätung(f)	atraso	ritardo
atravesar, cruzar	traverser	cross	überqueren	atravessar	attraversare
atravesar	franchir	cross	überqueren	atravessar	varcare, passare
atravesar	transpercer	pierce	durchbohren	trespassar	trapassare
atrayente	attirant, e	attractive	anziehend	atraente	attraente
atribuir	attribuer	attribute	bei = messen	atribuir	attribuire
atroz	atroce	atrocious	grausam	atroz	atroce
atún, bonito	thon	tuna(fish)	Thunfisch(m)	atum	tonno
aturdidor, a	étourdissant, e	deafening	betäubend	atroador, a	sbalorditivo, a
aturdir; atontar	étourdir	stun, daze	betäuben	aturdir; atordoar	stordire
audacia	audace	audacity	Kühnheit(f)	audácia	audacia
audiencia	audience	audience	Audienz(f)	audiência	udienza
auditor, a	auditeur, trice	listener	Zuhörer(in f)m	ouvinte	uditore, uditrice
auge, desarrollo	essor	expansion, boom	Aufschwung(m)	progresso	sviluppo
aula	classe(salle)	classroom	Klassenzimmer(n)	aula(sala de)	aula
aullar	hurler	howl	heulen	uivar; urrar	ululare, guaire
aumentar	augmenter	increase, raise	zu = nehmen	aumentar	aumentare
aumento	augmentation	increase, rise	Zunahme(f)	aumento	aumento
aun; incluso	même	even	sogar; selbst	mesmo(que)	anche; perfino
aún	encore, toujours	still; yet	noch, noch mehr	ainda	ancora
aunque	quoique	although, though	obgleich, obwohl	embora	sebbene
aunque	bien que	though, although	obwohl, obgleich	ainda que	benché
aurora	aurore	dawn	Morgenröte(f)	aurora	aurora
auscultar	ausculter	examine	ab = horchen	auscultar	auscultare
ausente	absent, e	absent	abwesend	ausente	assente
austero, a	austère	austere	streng, hart	austero, a	austero, a
auténtico, a	authentique	authentic, genuine	authentisch	autêntico, a	autentico, a
autobús	autobus	bus	Bus(m)	autocarro	autobus
autocar	autocar	coach	Reisebus(m)	autocarro	pullman
autógrafo	autographe	autograph	Autogramm(n)	autógrafo	autografo
autómata	automate	automaton	Automat(m)	autómato	automa
automático, a	automatique	automatic	automatisch	automático, a	automatico, a
automóvil	automobile	car	Auto(n)	automóvel	automobile
autonomía	autonomie	autonomy	Autonomie(f)	autonomia	autonomia
autónomo, a	autonome	autonomous	autonom; unabhängig	autónomo, a	autonomo, a
autopista	autoroute	motorway	Autobahn(f)	auto-estrada	autostrada
autopsia	autopsie	autopsy	Autopsie(f)	autópsia	autopsia
autor, a	auteur	author	Autor(in f)m	autor, a	autore, autrice
autoridad	autorité	authority	Autorität(f)	autoridade	autorità
autoritario, a	autoritaire	authoritarian	autoritär	autoritário, a	autoritario, a
autorizar	autoriser	authorize	erlauben	autorizar	autorizzare
autostop, a dedo	auto-stop	hitch-hiking	trampen	boleia(pedir)	autostop
auxiliar	auxiliaire	auxiliary	Hilfs-; Hilfe(f)	auxiliar	ausiliare
avalancha	avalanche	avalanche	Lawine(f)	avalanche	valanga

S

Spanish	French	English	German	Portuguese	Italian
avanzar	avancer	advance, move fwd	weiter = gehen	avançar	procedere
avaro, a	avare	miserly, mean	geizig	avarento, a	avaro, a
ave, pájaro	oiseau	bird	Vogel(m)	ave	uccello
avenida	avenue	avenue	Allee(f)	avenida	viale
aventura	aventure	adventure	Abenteuer(n)	aventura	avventura
avería	panne	breakdown	Panne(f)	avaria	guasto, panna
aves de corral	volaille	poultry	Geflügel(n)	aves de capoeira	pollame
aviación	aviation	aviation	Luftfahrt(f)	aviação	aviazione
aviador, a	aviateur, trice	aviator	Flieger(m), Pilot(m)	aviador, a	aviatore, trice
avión	avion	plane, aeroplane	Flugzeug(n)	avião	aereo
aviso	avis	notice	Mitteilung(f)	aviso, notícia	avviso
avispa	guêpe	wasp	Wespe(f)	vespa	vespa
avistar, divisar	apercevoir	perceive, notice	bemerken	avistar	scorgere
ayer	hier	yesterday	gestern	ontem	ieri
ayuda	aide	help	Hilfe(f)	ajuda	aiuto
ayuda	concours	cooperation, help	Mitwirkung(unter)	colaboração	concorso
ayudar	aider	help, assist, aid	helfen	ajudar	aiutare
ayuntamiento	mairie	town hall	Rathaus(n)	câmara	municipio, comune
azafata	hôtesse de l'air	hostess(air -)	Stewardess(f)	hospedeira	hostess
azar, casualidad	hasard	chance, luck	Zufall(m)	acaso, azar	caso
azar(al)	hasard(au)	random(at)	aufs Geratewohl	acaso(ao)	casaccio(a)
azotaina, paliza	fessée	spanking	Hinternvoll(m)	surra, açoite	sculacciata
azúcar	sucre	sugar	Zucker(m)	açúcar	zucchero
azucarado, a	sucré, e	sweet	süß	açucarado, a; doce	zuccherato, a
azul	bleu, e	blue	blau	azul	blu

B

Spanish	French	English	German	Portuguese	Italian
babear	baver	dribble	sabbern	babar-se	sbavare
bacalao	morue	cod	Schellfisch(m)	bacalhau	baccalà; merluzzo
bacteria	bactérie	bacterium(-eria)	Bakterie(f)	bactéria	batterio
bache	bosse	bump	Unebenheit(f); Buckel	bossa; alto	gobba, dosso, cunetta
bachillerato	baccalauréat	G.C.E. A.Level(s)	Abitur(n)	bacharelato	maturità
bahía	baie	bay	Bucht(f)	baía	baia
bailar	danser	dance	tanzen	dançar, bailar	ballare
bailarín, a	danseur, se	dancer	Tänzer(in f)m	bailarino, a	ballerino, a
baile	bal	dance, ball	Ball(m)	baile	ballo
baja	baisse	fall, drop	Senkung(f)	baixa	calo
bajar	baisser, abaisser	lower	herunter = lassen	baixar, abaixar	calare, abbassare
bajar	abaisser	lower	nieder = lassen	abaixar	abbassare
bajar	descendre	fall, drop	fallen	baixar	abbassare
bajarse	descendre	get out of; get off	aus = steigen	descer	scendere
bajo, a	bas, basse	low	niedrig	baixo, a	basso, a
bala	balle	bullet	Kugel(f)	bala	pallottola
balance	bilan	balance-sheet	Bilanz(f)	balanço	bilancio
balanza	balance	scales	Waage(f)	balança	bilancia
balbucear	bafouiller	splutter, stammer	stammeln	balbuciar	farfugliare
balcón	balcon	balcony	Balkon(m)	varanda	balcone
baldosa, azulejo	carreau	tile	Fliese(f), Kachel(f)	ladrilho, azulejo	piastrella
balón	ballon	ball	Ball(m)(Fußball m)	bola	pallone
baloncesto	basket-ball	basket-ball	Basketball(m)	basquetebol	pallacanestro
balsa	radeau	raft	Floß(n)	jangada	zattera
ballena	baleine	whale	Wal(m)	baleia	balena
ballet	ballet	ballet	Ballett(n)	ballet, bailado	balletto
bancario, a	bancaire	bank, banking	Bank-	bancário, a	bancario, a
banco	banc	bench	Bank(f)	banco	panca; panchina
banco, banca	banque	bank	Bank(f)	banco	banca

Spanish	French	English	German	Portuguese	Italian
banco de hielo	banquise	ice-floe	Packeis(n)	campo de gelo	banchisa
banda	fanfare	brass band	Fanfare(f)	fanfarra, banda	banda
bandeja	plateau	tray	Tablett(n), Platte(f)	tabuleiro	vassoio
bandera	drapeau	flag	Fahne(f)	bandeira	bandiera
bandera	drapeau	flag	Flagge(f)	bandeira	bandiera
bandido	bandit	bandit	Bandit(m)	bandido	bandito
banquero	banquier	banker	Bankier(m)	banqueiro	banchiere
banquete	banquet	banquet	Bankett(n)	banquete	banchetto
bañarse	baigner(se)	bathe; swim	baden; schwimmen	banho(tomar)	bagno(fare il)
bañera	baignoire	bath	Badewanne(f)	banheira	vasca da bagno
baño	bain	bath	Bad(n)	banho	bagno
baño	baignade	swimming, bathing	Baden(n)	banho	bagno
bar, café	bar	bar, pub	Kneipe(f)	bar, café	bar
barandilla	rampe	banister, handrail	Geländer(n)	corrimão	rampa
barato, a	bon marché	cheap	billig	barato, a	buon prezzo
barba	barbe	beard	Bart(m)	barba	barba
bárbaro, a	barbare	barbaric	barbarisch	bárbaro, a	barbaro, a
barbilla	menton	chin	Kinn(n)	queixo	mento
barca	barque	boat(small)	Barke(f), Kahn(m)	barca	barca
barco	bateau	boat, ship	Schiff(n)	barco	imbarcazione, nave
baremo	barème	scale	Liste(f)	tabela	tariffario
barniz	vernis	varnish	Lack(m)	verniz	vernice
barómetro	baromètre	barometer	Barometer(n)	barómetro	barometro
barón, baronesa	baron, ne	baron, baroness	Baron(in, f)m	barão, baronesa	barone, baronessa
barra	barre	bar	Stange(f)	barra	sbarra
barra	comptoir	counter, bar	Theke(f)	balcão	banco
barra de labios	rouge à lèvres	lipstick	Lippenstift(m)	baton	rossetto
barranco	ravin	ravine	Schlucht(f); Graben(m)	barranco	burrone
barreño	bassine	bowl	Wanne(f); Schüssel(f)	bacia	bacinella
barrer	balayer	sweep	fegen	varrer	spazzare
barrera	barrière	barrier; gate	Schranke(f)	barreira	barriera
barricada	barricade	barricade	Barrikade(f)	barricada	barricata
barriga, vientre	ventre	stomach, abdomen	Bauch(m)	barriga	pancia, ventre
barril	fût	barrel	Faß(n)	barril	fusto, barile
barrio	quartier	district	Viertel(n)	bairro	quartiere
barro	boue	mud	Schlamm(m)	lama	fango, melma
barullo, jaleo	cohue, foule	crush, crowd	Menge(f)	multidão, confusão	ressa, affollamento
báscula	bascule	scales	Waage(f)	báscula	basculla, bilancia
base	base	base	Grundlage(f)	base	base
base(militar)	base(militaire)	base	Stützpunkt(m)	base(militar)	base(militare)
básico	base(de)	basic	Grund-; Grundlage	base(de)	base
basta(!)	assez!; suffit!	enough!(that's)	das langt, jetzt langt	basta!, chega!	basta così!
bastante(s)	assez	enough; rather	genug	bastante	abbastanza
bastidores	coulisses	wings	Kulisse(f)	bastidores	quinte(le)
bastón	canne	stick	Stock(m)	bengala	bastone
basura	ordure(s)	rubbish, garbage	Abfall(m)	lixo	immondizia
bata	robe de chambre	dressing gown	Schlafrock(m)	roupão	vestaglia
bata	peignoir	dressing gown	Morgenmantel(m)	roupão	accappatoio
bata, blusa	blouse	overall	Kittel(m)	bata	blusa, camice
batalla	bataille	battle	Gefecht(n)	batalha	battaglia
batería	batterie	battery	Batterie(f)	bateria	batteria
batir	battre	beat	schlagen	bater	battere
baúl	malle	trunk	Koffer(großer)(m)	mala	baule
bautizo	baptême	baptism	Taufe(f)	baptismo	battesimo
bazo	rate	spleen	Milz(f)	baço	milza
bebé	bébé	baby	Baby(n)	bebé	bebè, bambino, a
bebedor, a	buveur, se	drinker	Trinker(in f)m	bebedor, a	bevitore, trice
beber	boire	drink	trinken	beber	bere
bebida	boisson	drink	Getränk(n)	bebida	bibita; bevanda
beca	bourse	grant; scholarship	Stipendium(n)	bolsa	borsa di studio
becerro; ternera	veau	calf(-lves); veal	Kalb(n)	bezerro; vitelo	vitello(a)
belicoso, a	belliqueux, se	aggressive	kriegerisch	belicoso, a	bellicoso, a
bella	belle	beautiful	schön	bela	bella
bellas artes	beaux-arts	fine arts	Kunst(f)	belas-artes	belle arti
belleza	beauté	beauty	Schönheit(f)	beleza	bellezza
bello, a	beau, belle	handsome	ansehnlich, schön	bonito, a	bello, a
bendecir	bénir	bless	segnen	benzer	benedire
beneficiar	bénéficier	profit, benefit	profitieren, gewinnen	beneficiar	beneficiare

Spanish	French	English	German	Portuguese	Italian
beneficio	bénéfice	benefit; profit	Gewinn(m)	lucro, proveito	beneficio; utile
beneficio(en--de)	profit(au--de)	in aid of	zugunsten von	proveito(em--de)	beneficio(al--di)
benévolo, a	bénévole	voluntary	unentgeltlich	benévolo, a	benevolo, a
benévolo, a	bienveillant, e	benevolent	wohlwollend	benévolo, a	benevolo, a
benigno, a	bénin, bénigne	benign	gutartig	benigno, a	benigno, a
besito	bise	kiss	Küßchen(n)	beijinho	bacio
beso(dar un)	baiser	kiss	Kuß(m)	beijo	bacio
bestia	bête	animal, beast	Biest(n), Tier(n)	bicho, animal	bestia
biberón	biberon	bottle(baby's -)	Fläschchen(n)	biberão	biberon
Biblia	Bible	Bible	Bibel(f)	Bíblia	Bibbia
bibliografía	bibliographie	bibliography	Bibliographie(f)	bibliografia	bibliografia
biblioteca	bibliothèque	library	Bibliothek(f)	biblioteca	biblioteca
biblioteca	bibliothèque	bookcase	Bücherschrank(m)	estante	libreria
bíceps	biceps	biceps	Bizeps(m)	biceps	bicipite
bici	vélo	bike	Fahrrad(n)	bicicleta	bici, bicicletta
bicicleta	bicyclette	bicycle	Fahrrad(n)	bicicleta	bicicletta
bidón, lata	bidon	can	Kanister(m)	cantil	bidone
bien	bien	well	wohl	bem	bene
bien	bien	well	gut	bem	bene
bien	bien	good	Gut(n)	bem	bene
bienes	biens	possessions, estate	Besitz(m), Güter(pl)	bens	beni; averi
bienestar	bien-être	well-being	Wohlbefinden(n)	bem-estar	benessere
bienvenido, a	bienvenu, e	welcome(to be)	Willkommen(n)	bem-vindo, a	benvenuto, a
bigote	moustache	moustache	Schnurrbart(m)	bigode	baffo
bilingüe	bilingue	bilingual	zweisprachig	bilingue	bilingue
billar	billard	billiards	Billard(n)	bilhar	biliardo
billete	billet	ticket	Fahrkarte(f)	bilhete	biglietto
billete(de banco)	billet(banque)	bank-note	Geldschein(m)	nota(de banco)	banconota
billete	billet	ticket	Los(n)	bilhete	biglietto
billete de ida	billet simple	single ticket	einfache Fahrkarte(f)	bilhete de ida	andata
billete ida/vuelta	billet aller/R	return ticket	Rückfahrkarte(f)	bilhete ida/volta	andata e ritorno
biografía	biographie	biography	Lebensbeschreibung(f)	biografia	biografia
biología	biologie	biology	Biologie(f)	biologia	biologia
bisagra	charnière	hinge	Scharnier(n)	gonzo, dobradiça	cerniera
bistec	bifteck	steak	Beefsteak(n)	bife	bistecca
bisturí	bistouri	scalpel, bistoury	Skalpell(n)	bisturi	bisturi
bizquear	loucher	squint	schielen	estrábico(ser)	strabico(essere)
blanco, a	blanc, che	white	weiß	branco, a	bianco, a
blanco	cible	target	Zielscheibe(f)	alvo	bersaglio
blando, a	mou, molle	soft	weich	mole	molle; tenero, a
blando, a	tendre	soft; tender	weich	tenro, a	morbido, a; tenero, a
blasfemia	blasphème	blasphemy	Lästerung(f)(Gottes-)	blasfémia	bestemmia
blindado, a	blindé, e	armoured	gepanzert	blindado, a	blindato, a
bloc	bloc	pad	Block(m)	bloco	blocco
bloque	bloc	block	Block(m)	bloco	blocco
bloquear	bloquer	block	blockieren	bloquear	bloccare
bloqueo	blocage	jamming	Blockierung(f), Sperre	bloqueamento	bloccaggio
bloqueo	blocus	blockade	Blockade(f)	bloqueio	blocco
bobina, carrete	bobine	reel	Spule(f)	bobina	bobina
boca	bouche	mouth	Mund(m)	boca	bocca
bocadillo	sandwich	sandwich(-es)	Butterbrot(n)	sande, sanduiche	panino
bocado	bouchée	mouthful	Bissen(m)	bocado	boccone
bocanada	bouffée	puff, breath	Hauch(m), Atemzug(m)	baforada	ventata
boda	noce	wedding	Hochzeit(f)	boda	nozze
bodega, sótano	cave	cellar	Keller(m)	adega	cantina
bodega	cale	hold	Laderaum(m)	porão	stiva
bofetada	claque	slap	Ohrfeige(f)	bofetada	schiaffo
bofetada	gifle	slap	Ohrfeige(f)	bofetada	schiaffo
bogavante	homard	lobster	Hummer(m)	lavagante	gambero(di mare)
bola	boule	bowl	Kugel(f)	bola	boccia
bola	boule	ball	Ball(m)(Schneeball)	bola	palla
bola	bille	marble	Murmel(f)	berlinde	biglia
bola	bille	ball	Kugel(f)	esfera	sfera
boletín	bulletin	bulletin, report	Bericht(m)	boletim	bollettino, bolletta
bolígrafo	stylo à bille	ball-point pen	Kugelschreiber(m)	esferográfica	penna a sfera
bolos(juego)	quille	skittle	Kegel(f)	paulitos	birillo
bolsa, saco	sac	bag	Tasche(f)	saco	borsa
Bolsa	Bourse(la)	Stock Exchange	Börse(f)	Bolsa	Borsa

Spanish	French	English	German	Portuguese	Italian
bolsillo	poche	pocket	Tasche(f)	bolso	tasca
bolsita	sachet	bag(small), sachet	Beutel(m), Tütchen(n)	pacote; carteira	bustina
bolso	sac à main	handbag	Handtasche(f)	carteira	borsetta
bolso de viaje	sac de voyage	travel-bag	Reisetasche(f)	saco de viagem	borsa da viaggio
bomba	pompe	pump	Pumpe(f)	bomba	pompa
bomba	bombe	bomb	Bombe(f)	bomba	bomba
bombero	pompier(sapeur-)	fireman(-men)	Feuerwehrmann(m)	bombeiro	pompiere
bombilla	ampoule	bulb	Glühbirne(f)	lâmpada	lampadina
bondad	bonté	kindness	Güte(f)	bondade	bontà
bonito, a	joli, e	pretty	hübsch	bonito, a	carino, a
bordar	broder	embroider	sticken	bordar	ricamare
borde	bord	side; edge	Rand(m)	borda	bordo, riva, orlo
bordura; ribete	bordure	edge, border	Rand(m)	borda, orla	bordo, lungo
borracho, a	ivrogne	drunkard	Trunkenbold(m)	bêbedo, a; ébrio, a	ubriaco, a
borrador	brouillon	rough paper	Schmierzettel(m)	rascunho	brutta copia
borrar	effacer	erase, rub out	radieren	apagar	cancellare
borrar	annuler	delete	streichen	suprimir	annullare
borrasca	bourrasque	squall	Windstoß(m)	borrasca	burrasca
borroso, a	flou, e	fuzzy, blurred	verschwommen	vago, a	sfumato, a
bosque	bois	wood	Wald(m)	bosque	bosco
bosque	forêt	forest	Wald(m)	floresta, bosque	foresta, bosco
bostezar	bâiller	yawn	gähnen	bocejar	sbadigliare
bota	botte	boot	Stiefel(m)	bota	stivale
botánica	botanique	botany	Botanik(f)	botânica	botanica
bote	canot	dinghy	Boot(n)	canoa	canotto
botella	bouteille	bottle	Flasche(f)	garrafa	bottiglia
botín	butin	spoils	Beute(f)	despojo	bottino
botón	bouton	button	Knopf(m)	botão	bottone
botón	bouton	knob	Knopf(m)	botão	manopola, pomello
botones	chasseur(hôtel)	page(boy), bellboy	Page(m), Hotelboy(m)	paquete	fattorino
bóveda	voûte	vault, arch	Gewölbe(n)	abóbada	arco, volta
boxeador	boxeur	boxer	Boxer(m)	pugilista	pugile
boxeo	boxe	boxing	Boxen(n)	boxe	pugilato
boya	bouée	buoy	Boje(f)	bóia	boa
bragas	culotte	briefs, knickers	Unterhose(f), Slip(m)	cuecas	mutandine, slip
brasa	braise	embers	Glut(f)	brasa	brace
brazo	bras	arm	Arm(m)	braço	braccio
brecha	brèche	breach, gap	Spalt(m), Bresche(f)	brecha	breccia
breve	bref, brève	brief, short	kurz	breve	breve
bricolage, maña	bricolage	odd-jobs	Basteln(n)	bricolage	bricolage
brigada	brigade	brigade	Brigade(f)	brigada	brigata, squadra
brillante	brillant, e	bright, shining	glänzend	brilhante	brillante
brillante	brillant, e	brilliant	prächtig, brillant	brilhante	brillante
brillar	briller	shine	glänzen	brilhar	brillare
broche	broche	brooch	Brosche(f)	broche	spilla
broma	farce, blague	joke; farce	Streich(m)	partida	scherzo
broma	canular	joke, hoax	Ulk(m), Witz(m)	partida	scherzo, burla
bromear	plaisanter	joke	scherzen	gracejar	scherzare
bronce	bronze	bronze	Bronze(f)	bronze	bronzo
bronceado	bronzage	sun-tan	Bräune(f)	bronzeamento	abbronzatura
broncear	bronzer	tan	bräunen	bronzear	abbronzare
bronquios	bronche(s)	bronchial tubes	Bronchie(f)	brônquios	bronco(bronchi)
bronquitis	bronchite	bronchitis	Bronchitis(f)	bronquite	bronchite
brotar, surgir	jaillir	spring	springen; sprudeln	brotar	schizzare
brote, botón	bourgeon	bud	Knospe(f)	rebento, botão	gemma
brujería	sorcellerie	witchcraft	Hexerei(f)	bruxaria	stregoneria
brujo, a	sorcier, ière	wizard; witch	Hexer(m); Hexe(f)	bruxo, a	stregone, strega
brújula	boussole	compass	Kompaß(m)	bússola	bussola
bruma	brume	mist, haze	Nebel(m)	bruma	foschia
brusco, a	brusque	abrupt, sudden	brüsk	brusco, a	brusco, a
brutal	brutal, e	brutal	brutal	brutal	brutale
brutalidad	brutalité	brutality	Brutalität, Roheit(f)	brutalidade	brutalità
bruto, a	brut, e	raw; crude	roh	bruto, a	grezzo, a
buen tiempo	beau temps	fine weather	schönes Wetter	bom tempo	bel tempo
buen viaje	bon voyage	good trip(have a)	gute Reise	boa viagem	buon viaggio
buena gana(de)	volontiers	willingly	gern	bom grado(de)	volentieri
buena suerte	bonne chance	good luck	viel Glück	boa sorte	buona fortuna
buenas noches	bonne nuit	good night	gute Nacht	boa noite	buona notte

Spanish	French	English	German	Portuguese	Italian
buenas tardes	bonsoir	good evening	guten Abend	boa tarde	buonasera
bueno, a	bon, ne	good	gut	bom, boa	buono, a
bueno, a	bon, aimable	kind, kindly	gütig, liebvoll	bom, boa	buono, a
bueno, a	sage	good	brav	ajuizado, a	buono, a; bravo, a
bueno, a	brave	decent, nice	brav, nett, angenehm	amável	bravo, a
buenos días	bonjour	hello	guten Tag	bom dia	buongiorno
buey; carne de vaca	boeuf	bullock; beef	Ochse(m); Rind(n)	boi; carne de vaca	bue; manzo
bufanda	écharpe	scarf	Halstuch(n), Schal(m)	cachecol, cachené	sciarpa
bufanda	cache-nez	scarf	Schal(m)	cachecol	sciarpa
buitre	vautour	vulture	Geier(m)	abutre	avvoltoio
bujía	bougie	sparking plug	Zündkerze(f)	vela	candela
bulevar	boulevard	boulevard	Boulevard(m)	avenida	viale
buñuelos	beignets	fritters	Krapfen, Pfannkuchen	pastéis	frittella
buque	paquebot	liner	Passagierdampfer(m)	paquete	transatlantico
buqué, aroma, boca	bouquet	bouquet	Blume(f), Bukett(n)	aroma	bouquet, aroma
burbuja	bulle	bubble	Blase(f)	bolha	bolla
burgués, a	bourgeois, e	middle class	Bürger(in f)m	burguês, a	borghese
burguesía	bourgeoisie	middle class	Bürgertum(n)	burguesia	borghesia
burla, mofa	moquerie	mockery	Spott(m)	zombaria, troça	canzonatura, beffa
burlarse	ricaner	snigger	grinsen, kichern	troçar	sogghignare
busca	recherche	search	Suche(f)	busca	ricerca
buscar	chercher	look for, search -	suchen	procurar; buscar	cercare
buscar, investigar	chercher	seek	holen, suchen	procurar, buscar	cercare
buscar, indagar	rechercher	search/look for	suchen	buscar, procurar	ricercare
busto	buste	bust	Oberkörper(m)	busto	busto
buzón	boîte(lettres)	letter box	Briefkasten(m)	caixa do correio	buca delle lettere

C

Spanish	French	English	German	Portuguese	Italian
caballa	maquereau	mackerel	Makrele(f)	cavala	sgombro
caballero	monsieur	man, gentleman(men)	Gentleman(m)	cavalheiro	signore
caballo	cheval	horse	Pferd(n)	cavalo	cavallo
cabaña	case	hut	Hütte(f)	palhota	capanna
cabaret	cabaret	cabaret; nightclub	Kabarett(n)	cabaret	cabaret
cabecear	tanguer	pitch	schaukeln	baloucar-se	beccheggiare
cabeza	tête	head	Kopf(m)	cabeça	testa, capo
cabina	cabine	cabin	Kabine(f)	cabine	cabina
cabina(telefónica)	cabine(téléph.)	phone box	Telefonzelle(f)	cabine(telefónica)	cabina(telefonica)
cable	câble	cable	Kabel(n)	cabo	cavo
cabo	bout, extrémité	end, tip	Ende(n)	cabo	capo, estremità
cabo	cap	cape	Kap(n)	cabo	capo
cabo(mil.)	caporal	corporal	Gefreiter(m); Korporal	cabo	caporale
cabra	chèvre	goat	Ziege(f)	cabra	capra
caca	crotte	dropping, dung	Häufchen(n), Kot(m)	bosta	sterco
cacahuete, maní	cacahuète	peanut	Erdnuß(f)	amendoim	arachide
cacao	cacao	cocoa, cacao	Kakao(m)	cacau	cacao
cachete	tape, fessée	smack	Schlag(m)	palmada	schiaffo
cada	chaque	every, each	jede(r, s)	cada	ogni
cada uno(una)	chacun, e; chaque	each, every(one)	jeder, jede	cada um(uma)	ciascuno, a
cadáver	cadavre	corpse	Leiche(f)	cadáver	cadavere
cadáver	macchabée	corpse	Leiche(f)	cadáver	cadavere
cadena	chaîne	chain	Kette(f)	cadeia, corrente	catena
cadena	chaîne	channel	Programm, Fernseh-	canal	canale
cadencia	cadence	rate, rhythm	Rhythmus(m)	cadência	cadenza
cadera	hanche	hip	Hüfte(f)	anca	anca
caducado, a	périmé, e	expired	verfallen	caducado, a	scaduto, a
caer	tomber	fall	fallen	cair	cadere

Spanish	French	English	German	Portuguese	Italian
caer(dejar)	tomber(laisser)	drop	fallenlassen	cair(deixar)	cadere(lasciar)
café	café	coffee	Kaffee(m)	café	caffè
cafetera	cafetière	coffee-pot	Kaffeemaschine(f)	cafeteira	caffettiera
caída	chute	fall	Fall(m)	queda	caduta
caja	boîte	box	Schachtel(f)	caixa	scatola
caja	caisse	cash-desk	Kasse(f)	caixa	cassa
caja fuerte	coffre-fort	safe	Safe(m)	cofre-forte	cassaforte
cajero, a	caissier, ière	cashier	Kassierer(in f)m	caixa(o)	cassiere, a
cajón, caja	caisse	chest, case	Kiste(f)	caixa	cassa
cajón	tiroir	drawer	Schublade(f)	gaveta	cassetto
calambre	crampe	cramp	Krampf(m)	câibra	crampo
calcetín(es)	chaussette(s)	sock	Socke(f), Strumpf(m)	peúga	calza, e; calzini
calcetín	socquette	sock(ankle-)	Socke(f)	meias	calzino
calcio	calcium	calcium	Kalzium(n)	cálcio	calcio
calculadora	calculatrice	calculator	Rechenmaschine(f)	calculadora	calcolatrice
calcular	calculer	calculate, reckon	rechnen, berechnen	calcular	calcolare
cálculo	calcul	calculation	Berechnung(f)	cálculo	calcolo
caldo	bouillon	stock, broth	Brühe(f)	caldo	brodo
calefacción	chauffage	heating	Heizung(f)	aquecimento	riscaldamento
calendario	calendrier	calendar	Kalender(m)	calendário	calendario
calentamiento	échauffement	heating	Aufwärmen(n)	aquecimento	riscaldamento
calentar	chauffer	heat	heizen	aquecer	riscaldare
calibre	calibre	bore, calibre	Kaliber(n)	calibre	calibro
calidad; cualidad	qualité	quality	Qualität(f)	qualidade	qualità
cálido, a	chaud, e	warm	warm	cálido, a	caldo, a
caliente	chaud, e	hot	heiß	quente	caldo, a
calificado, a	qualifié, e	qualified	qualifiziert	qualificado, a	qualificato, a
calma, sosiego	calme	calm, quiet, still	Ruhe(f), Stille(f)	calma, sossego	calma, quiete
calma	accalmie	lull	Wetterberuhigung(f)	acalmia	schiarita, tregua
calmante	calmant	sedative	Beruhigungsmittel(n)	calmante	calmante
calmar	calmer	calm	beruhigen	acalmar	calmare
calor	chaleur	heat	Hitze(f)	calor	caldo; calore
caloría	calorie	calorie	Kalorie(f)	caloria	caloria
calumnia	calomnie	slander	Verleumdung(f)	calúnia	calunnia
caluroso, a	chaleureux, se	hearty, warm	herzlich	caloroso, a	caloroso, a
calvo, a	chauve	bald	glatzköpfig	calvo, a; careca	calvo, a
calzada	chaussée	road	Fahrbahn(f)	calçada	carreggiata
calzado	chaussure	shoe	Schuh(m)	sapato	scarpa, e
calzarse	chausser(se)	put on(shoes)	Schuhe anziehen, sich	calçar-se	calzarsi
calzoncillos	slip	briefs, pants	Unterhose(f)	cuecas	mutande, slip
callarse	taire(se)	silent(to be)	schweigen	calar-se	tacere
calle	rue	street	Straße(f)	rua	via
callejuela	ruelle	alley	Gäßchen(n), Gasse(f)	viela	viuzza, vicolo
cama	lit	bed	Bett(n)	cama	letto
cama de campaña	lit de camp	camp-bed	Feldbett(n)	cama de campismo	letto da campo
cámara	chambre	chamber	Kammer(f)	câmara	camera
cámara(diputados)	Chambre(députés)	House, Chamber	Abgeordnetenhaus(n)	câmara	camera
cámara	caméra	cine-camera	Kamera(f)	câmara	cinepresa
cámara fotográfica	appareil photo	camera	Kamera(f)	máquina fotográfica	macchina fotografica
camarera	femme de chambre	chambermaid	Zimmermädchen(n)	empregada	cameriera
camarero	garçon	waiter	Ober(m)	criado	cameriere
camarero, a	serveur, se	waiter, waitress	Kellner(in f)m	criado, a; moço	cameriere, a
cambiar	changer	shift	wechseln	mudar; remover	cambiare
cambio	échange	exchange	Tausch(Aus-, Um-)(m)	troca; câmbio	scambio
cambio	change	exchange	Wechsel(m)(Geld-)	câmbio	cambio
cambio	monnaie	change	Kleingeld(n); Klein-	troco	resto
cambio	changement	change	Veränderung(f)	mudança	cambiamento
camello	chameau	camel	Kamel(n)	camelo	cammello
camerino	loge	box	Loge(f)	camarim	camerino
camilla	civière	stretcher	Bahre(f)	maca	barella
caminar	marcher, cheminer	walk	laufen, gehen	caminhar	camminare
caminata, paseo	randonnée	ramble	Tour(f), Fußtour(f)	caminhada	gita, escursione
camino	chemin, voie	way	Weg(m)	caminho	cammino, strada
camino	chemin	path; way	Weg(m)	caminho	cammino
camión	camion	lorry	Lastwagen(m)	camião	camion
camisa	chemise	shirt	Hemd(n)	camisa	camicia
camiseta	maillot de corps	vest	Trikot(n)	camisola interior	maglia intima
camisón	chemise de nuit	nightdress(-es)	Nachthemd(n)	camisa de noite	camicia da notte

S

Spanish	French	English	German	Portuguese	Italian
campana	cloche	bell	Glocke(f)	sino	campana
campana, timbre	sonnerie	ring	Klingel(f)	campainha, toque	squillo, soneria
campaña	campagne	campaign	Wahlkampf(m)	campanha	campagna
campeón, a	champion, ne	champion	Meister(in f)m	campeão, campeã	campione, -essa
campeonato	championnat	championship	Meisterschaft(f)	campeonato	campionato
campesino, a	paysan, ne	farmer	Bauer(m), Bäuerin(f)	camponês, a	contadino, a
camping	camping(aire de)	camp(ing) site	Campingplatz(m)	campismo	campeggio
campo	campagne	country(side)	Land(n)	campo	campagna
campo	champ	field	Feld(n)	campo	campo
campo, área	domaine	field, scope	Bereich(m)	domínio	campo, settore
campo	terrain(sport)	field; court	Sportplatz(m)	campo	terreno
canal	canal	canal	Kanal(m)	canal	canale
canal	chenal	channel	Fahrwasser(n)	canal	canale
canalización	canalisation	pipe	Leitung(f)(-snetz n)	canalização	canalizzazione
canalón	gouttière	gutter	Dachrinne(f)	goteira	grondaia
canalla	voyou	hooligan	Strolch(m)	patife	mascalzone, a
cancelar, anular	annuler	cancel	annullieren	anular	annullare
cáncer	cancer	cancer	Krebs(m)	cancro	cancro
canceroso, a	cancéreux, se	cancerous	krebsartig	canceroso, a	canceroso, a
canciller	chancelier	chancellor	Kanzler(in f)m	chanceler	cancelliere
canción; cante	chanson, chant	song	Lied(n)	canção; canto	canzone; canto
candado	cadenas	padlock	Vorhängeschloß(n)	cadeado	lucchetto, catenaccio
candidato, a	candidat, e	candidate	Kandidat(in f)m	candidato, a	candidato, a
candidatura	candidature	application	Bewerbung(f)	candidatura	candidatura
cándido, a	candide	ingenuous	naiv, aufrichtig	cândido, a	candido, a
cangrejo	crabe	crab	Krebs(m)	caranguejo	granchio
cangrejo(de río)	écrevisse	crayfish	Flußkrebs(m)	caranguejo	gambero(di fiume)
canguro	kangourou	kangaroo	Känguruh(n)	cangurú	canguro
canoa	canoë	canoe	Kanu(n)	canoa	canoa
cansado, a	fatigué, e	tired	müde, ermüdet	cansado, a	stanco, a
cansancio	fatigue	tiredness	Müdigkeit(f)	fatiga, cansaço	stanchezza
cansar, fatigar	fatiguer	tire, make tired	ermüden	cansar, fatigar	stancare
cantante	chanteur, se	singer	Sänger(in f)m	cantor, a	cantante
cantar	chanter	sing	singen	cantar	cantare
cantera	carrière	quarry	Steinbruch(m)	pedreira	cava
cantidad	quantité	quantity, amount	Quantität(f)	quantidade	quantità
canto rodado	galet	pebble	Kieselstein(m)	seixo	ciottolo
caña	ligne	line	Angelschnur(f)	linha	lenza
caña de pescar	canne à pêche	fishing rod	Angelrute(f)	cana de pesca	canna da pesca
caño, conducto	conduit(e)	pipe	Röhre(f), Leitung(f)	cano, tubo	condotto(a)
cañón	canon	cannon	Kanone(f)	canhão	cannone
capa	couche	coat	Anstrich(m)	camada	strato
capa	couche	layer	Schicht(f)	camada	strato
capa(de agua)	nappe(eau)	sheet, expanse	Wasserfläche(f)	lençol(de água)	falda
capacidad	contenance	capacity, content	Fassungsvermögen(n)	capacidade	capacità
capaz de	capable de	able to(be)	fähig	capaz de	capace di
capilla	chapelle	chapel	Kapelle(f)	capela	cappella
capital	capital	capital, assets	Kapital(n)	capital(o)	capitale
capital	capitale	capital	Hauptstadt(f)	capital(a)	capitale
capitalismo	capitalisme	capitalism	Kapitalismus(m)	capitalismo	capitalismo
capitán	capitaine	captain	Hauptmann(m); Kapitän	capitão	capitano
capitular	capituler	capitulate	kapitulieren	capitular	capitolare
capítulo	chapitre	chapter	Kapitel(n)	capítulo	capitolo
capó	capot	bonnet, hood	Motorhaube(f)	capota	cofano
capricho	caprice	caprice, whim	Laune(f)	capricho, birra	capriccio
capturar	capturer	capture	fangen	capturar	catturare
capuchón	capuchon	cap	Kappe(f)	capuz	cappuccio
cara	face	face	Gesicht(n)	face; cara	faccia
cara	face	side	Seite(f)	face; lado	faccia
carabina	carabine	rifle	Gewehr(n), Karabiner m	espingarda	carabina
caracol	escargot	snail	Schnecke(f)	caracol	lumaca, chiocciola
carácter	caractère	character	Charakter(m)	carácter	carattere
característica	caractéristique	feature	Merkmal(n)	característica	caratteristica
característico, a	caractéristique	characteristic	charakteristisch	característico, a	caratteristico, a
caramelo; bombón	bonbon	sweet	Bonbon(n, m)	rebuçado	caramella
caravana	caravane	caravan	Wohnwagen(m)	caravana	roulotte
carbón	charbon	coal	Kohle(f)	carvão	carbone
carbónico, a	carbonique	carbonic	Kohlensäure(f)	carbónico, a	carbonico, a

carbono	carbone	carbon	Kohlenstoff(m)	carbono	carbonio
carburador	carburateur	carburettor	Vergaser(m)	carburador	carburatore
carburante	carburant	fuel	Treibstoff(m)	carburante	carburante
cardenal	cardinal	cardinal	Kardinal(m)	cardeal	cardinale
cardíaco, a	cardiaque	heart-trouble...	herzkrank	cardíaco, a	cardiaco, a
cardiología	cardiologie	cardiology	Kardiologie(f)	cardiologia	cardiologia
carencia	carence	deficiency	Fehlen(n), Mangel(m)	carência	carenza
carga, peso	charge	load	Last(f)	carga, peso	carico
carga	charge	contribution	Abgaben(pl.)	encargo	onere
carga	fardeau	burden	Last(f)	fardo	fardello
cargamento	chargement	load, loading	Ladung(f)	carregamento	carico
cargamento	cargaison	cargo, freight	Ladung(f)	carga	carico
cargar	charger	load	laden	carregar	caricare
cargo	charge	charge	Anklage(f)(punkt m)	acusação	indizio
carguero, buque	cargo	cargo(-boat)	Frachter(m)	cargueiro	cargo, nave da carico
caricaturar	caricaturer	caricature	karikieren	caricaturar	caricaturare
caricia	caresse	caress	Streicheln(n)	carícia	carezza
caridad	charité	charity	Mildtätigkeit(f)	caridade	carità
caries	carie	tooth decay	Karies(f)	cárie	carie
carnaval	carnaval	carnival	Karneval(m)	carnaval	carnevale
carne	chair	flesh	Fleisch(n)	carne	carne
carne	viande	meat	Fleisch(n)	carne	carne
carné de identidad	carte d'identité	identity card	Personalausweis(m)	bilhete(identidade)	carta d'identità
carnero; oveja	mouton	sheep; mutton	Schaf(n)	carneiro; ovelha	pecora; montone
carnicería	boucherie	butcher's(shop)	Metzgerei(f)	talho	macelleria
carnívoro, a	carnivore	carnivorous	fleischfressend	carnívoro, a	carnivoro, a
caro, a	cher, ère	expensive, dear	teuer	caro, a	caro, a
carpintero	menuisier	joiner, carpenter	Tischler(m)	carpinteiro	falegname
carpintero	charpentier	carpenter	Zimmermann(m)	carpinteiro	carpentiere
carrera	carrière	career	Karriere(f)	carreira	carriera
carrera	course	race	Rennen(n)	corrida	corsa
carrera	course	running	Wettrennen(n)	corrida	corsa
carreras	courses	races	Pferderennen(n)	corridas	corsa
carreta, carro	charrette	cart	Karren(m)	carroça, carreta	carretta
carretera	route	road	Straße(f)	estrada	strada
carretera	route nationale	main/trunk road	Landstraße(f)	estrada	strada statale
carretilla	brouette	wheelbarrow	Schubkarre(f)	carro de mão	carriola
carril	rail	rail; track	Schiene(f)	carril	rotaia
carro	chariot	trolley	Karre(f)	carroça, carro	carrello
carrocería	carrosserie	body(-work)	Karosserie(f)	carroçaria	carrozzeria
carta	lettre	letter	Brief(m)	carta	lettera
carta	carte à jouer	card	Spielkarte(f)	carta	carta da gioco
carta de crédito	carte de crédit	credit card	Kreditkarte(f)	cartão de crédito	carta di credito
carta de vinos	carte des vins	wine-list	Weinkarte(f)	lista dos vinhos	lista dei vini
cartel	affiche	poster, placard	Plakat(n)	cartaz	manifesto
cartel, póster	poster	poster	Plakat(n)	cartaz	poster, manifesto
cartera	portefeuille	wallet	Brieftasche(f)	carteira	portafoglio
cartera	cartable	briefcase; satchel	Ranzen(m)	pasta	cartella
cartera	sacoche	bag	Tasche(f)(Umhänge-)	saco	saccoccia, borsa
cartero, a	facteur, trice	postman/-woman	Briefträger(in f)m	carteiro, a	postino, a
cartílago	cartilage	cartilage	Knorpel(m)	cartilagem	cartilagine
cartón	carton	cardboard	Pappe(f)	cartão	cartone
cartucho	cartouche	cartridge	Patrone(f)	cartucho	cartuccia
casa	maison	house	Haus(n)	casa	casa
casa(en)	maison(à la)	home(at)	Hause(zu)	casa(em)	casa(a)
casado, a	marié, e	married	verheiratet	casado, a	sposato, a
casarse	marier(se)	married(get)	heiraten	casar-se	sposarsi
cascada	cascade	waterfall	Wasserfall(m)	cascata	cascata
cáscara	coquille, coque	shell	Schale(f)	casca	guscio
casco	casque	helmet	Helm(m)	capacete	casco, elmetto
casco	écouteurs, casque	ear/headphones	Kopfhörer(m)	auscultadores	cuffia
casco	coque	hull	Rumpf(m)	casco	scafo
casete	cassette	cassette	Kassette(f)	cassete	cassetta
casi	presque	almost, nearly	fast	quase	quasi
casino	casino	casino	Kasino(n)	casino	casinò
caso	cas	case	Fall(m)	caso	caso
caso(en este)	occurence(en l')	case(in this)	vorliegenden Fall(im)	caso(neste)	nella circostanza
caspa	pellicule	dandruff	Schuppe(f)	caspa	forfora

S

Spanish	French	English	German	Portuguese	Italian
casta, raza	race	breed	Rasse(f)	casta, raça	razza
casta	caste	caste	Kaste(f)	casta	casta
castaño, a	châtain	chestnut brown	kastanienbraun	castanho, a	castano, a
castigar	punir	punish	bestrafen	castigar	punire
castigo	punition	punishment	Strafe(f)	castigo	punizione
castigo	châtiment	punishment	Bestrafung(f)	castigo	castigo
castillo	château	castle; mansion	Schloß(n)	castelo	castello
casto, a	chaste	pure	keusch	casto, a	casto, a
cataclismo	cataclysme	cataclysm	Katastrophe(f)	cataclismo	cataclisma
catálogo	catalogue	catalogue	Katalog(m)	catálogo	catalogo
catastro	cadastre	land register	Grundbuch(n)	cadastro	catasto
catástrofe	catastrophe	catastrophe	Katastrophe(f)	catástrofe	catastrofe
catedral	cathédrale	cathedral	Kathedrale(f), Dom(m)	catedral	cattedrale, duomo
catedrático, a	professeur	professor	Professor(in f)m	professor, a	professore, essa
categoría	catégorie	category	Kategorie(f)	categoria	categoria
católico, a	catholique	Catholic	katholisch	católico, a	cattolico, a
catorce	quatorze	fourteen	vierzehn	catorze	quattordici
caucho	caoutchouc	rubber	Gummi(m, n)	borracha	gomma
causa	cause	cause	Ursache(f), Grund(m)	causa	causa
causar, provocar	causer, provoquer	cause	verursachen	causar, provocar	causare, provocare
cavar	creuser	dig	graben	cavar	scavare
caverna	caverne	cave, cavern	Höhle(f)	caverna	caverna
caviar	caviar	caviar	Kaviar(m)	caviar	caviale
cavidad	cavité	cavity	Hohlraum(m)	cavidade	cavità
caza	chasse	hunting	Jagd(f)	caça	caccia
caza	gibier	game	Wild(n)	caça	selvaggina
cazador	chasseur	hunter	Jäger(in f)m	caçador	cacciatore
cazar	chasser	hunt	jagen	caçar	cacciare
cazo, cacerola	casserole	pan, saucepan	Topf(m)	tacho, caçarola	casseruola
cebo	appât	bait	Köder(m)	engodo, isca	esca
cebolla	oignon	onion	Zwiebel(f)	cebola	cipolla
cebra	zèbre	zebra	Zebra(n)	zebra	zebra
ceder	céder, renoncer	give up	auf = geben; nach = geben	ceder	cedere
cédula iden-fiscal	carte grise	log-book	KFZ-Schein(m)	livrete(circulação)	libretto di circola-
ceja	sourcil	eyebrow	Augenbraue(f)	sobrolho	sopracciglio(a)
celebrar	célébrar	celebrate	feiern	celebrar	celebrare
célebre, famoso, a	célèbre	famous, well-known	berühmt	célèbre	celebre; famoso, a
celeste	céleste	heavenly	himmlisch	celeste	celeste
celos	jalousie	jealousy	Eifersucht(f)	ciúme	gelosia
celoso, a	jaloux, se	jealous	eifersüchtig	ciumento, a	geloso, a
celulitis	cellulite	fat, cellulitis	Zellulitis(f)	celulite	cellulite
cementerio	cimetière	cemetery	Friedhof(m)	cemitério	cimitero
cemento	ciment	cement	Zement(m)	cimento	cemento
cena	dîner	dinner	Abendessen(n)	jantar	cena
cenar	dîner	dinner(have)	Abend essen(zu)	jantar	cenare
cenar	souper	supper(have)	Abend essen(zu)	cear	cenare
cenicero	cendrier	ash-tray	Aschenbecher(m)	cinzeiro	portacenere
ceniza(s)	cendre(s)	ash(es)	Asche(f)	cinza	cenere(-ri)
censo	recensement	census	Volkszählung(f)	recenseamento	censimento
censura	censure	censorship	Zensur(f)	censura	censura
centellear	scintiller	sparkle	flimmern	cintilar	scintillare
centena	centaine	hundred(about a)	Hundert(n)	centena	centinaio
centeno	seigle	rye	Roggen(m)	centeio	segale
centímetro	centimètre	centimetre	Zentimeter(n, m)	centímetro	centimetro
centinela	sentinelle	sentry	Wache(f)	sentinela	sentinella
central	central, e	central	zentral	central	centrale
central	centrale	power-station	Kraftwerk(n), Zentrale	central	centrale
centrífugo, a	centrifuge	centrifugal	zentrifugal	centrífuga, a	centrifugo, a
centro	centre	centre	Mitte(f)	centro	centro
centro	centre	centre	Zentrum(m)	centro	centro
centro	centre	hub	Mittelpunkt(m)	centro	centro
centro(ciudad)	centre ville	city/town centre	Stadtzentrum(n)	centro(cidade)	centro della città
cepillo	brosse	brush	Bürste(f)	escova	spazzola
cepillo de dientes	brosse à dents	toothbrush	Zahnbürste(f)	escova de dentes	spazzolino
cera	cire	wax, polish	Wachs(n)	cera	cera
cerca	près, proche	near, close to	nah(e)	perto	vicino, a
cerca de	auprès de	close to	bei	perto de	vicino a
cerca de	proximité(à)	close, near	nahe bei	próximo a	vicinanze(nelle)

Spanish	French	English	German	Portuguese	Italian
cercano, a; próximo	proche	near, close	nah(e)	próximo, a; perto	prossimo, a
cerciorarse	assurer(s')	make sure	überzeugen, sich	verificar	accertarsi
cerdo	porc	pig; pork(meat)	Schwein(n)	porco	porco, maiale
cereal	céréale	cereal	Getreide(n)	cereal	cereale
cerebral	cérébral, e	cerebral	Gehirn-; zerebral	cerebral	cerebrale
cerebro	cerveau	brain	Gehirn(n)	cérebro	cervello
ceremonia	cérémonie	ceremony	Zeremonie(f)	cerimónia	cerimonia
cereza	cerise	cherry	Kirsche(f)	cereja	ciliegia
cerilla	allumette	match(-es)	Streichholz(n)	fósforo	fiammifero
cero	zéro	zero, nought	Null(f)	zero	zero
cerrado, a	fermé, e	closed, shut	zu, geschlossen	fechado, a	chiuso, a
cerradura	serrure	lock	Schloß(Tür-)(n)	fechadura	serratura
cerrar	fermer	close, shut	schließen	fechar, cerrar	chiudere
cerrar	fermer	shut	zu = machen	fechar	chiudere
cerrar con llave	fermer à clé	lock	ab = schließen	fechar à chave	chiudere a chiave
cerrojo	verrou	bolt, lock	Riegel(m), Schloß(n)	ferrolho	catenaccio
certeza	certitude	certainty	Gewißheit(f)	certeza	certezza
certificado	certificat	certificate	Bescheinigung(f)	certificado	certificato
certificar	certifier	certify	bescheinigen	certificar	certificare
cerveza	bière	beer	Bier(n)	cerveja	birra
cesar, parar	cesser	stop, cease	auf = hören	cessar, parar	cessare, smettere
cesárea	césarienne	Caesarean	Kaiserschnitt(m)	cesariana	taglio cesareo
cese	arrêt, cessation	stop, cessation	Stillstand(m)	cessação	cessazione, tregua
césped	gazon	grass	Rasen(m)	relva	prato, erba
césped	pelouse	lawn	Rasenfläche(f)	relvado	prato inglese
cesto	panier	basket	Korb(m)	cesto	paniere, cesto
cesto(a); cestillo	corbeille	basket; bin	Korb(m)(Papierkorb m)	cesto, a	cestino
ciática	sciatique	sciatica	Ischias(m)	ciática	sciatica
cicatriz	cicatrice	scar	Narbe(f)	cicatriz	cicatrice
ciclismo	cyclisme	cycling	Radfahren(n)	ciclismo	ciclismo
ciclista	cycliste	cyclist	Radfahrer(in f)m	ciclista	ciclista
ciclo	cycle	cycle	Zyklus(m)	ciclo	ciclo
ciclón	cyclone	cyclone	Wirbelwind(m)	ciclone	ciclone
ciego, a	aveugle	blind	blind	cego, a	cieco, a
cielo	ciel	sky	Himmel(m)	céu	cielo
cielo, paraíso	ciel, paradis	heaven	Himmel(m)	céu, paraíso	cielo, paradiso
cien, ciento	cent	hundred(one)	hundert	cem, cento	cento
ciencia	science	science	Wissenschaft(f)	ciência	scienza
científico, a	scientifique	scientific	wissenschaftlich	científico, a	scientifico, a
científico	scientifique	scientist	Wissenschaftler(m)	cientista	scienziato
científico	savant	scientist	Gelehrte(r)m	cientista	scienziato
ciertamente	certainement	certainly	sicherlich	certamente	certamente
ciertamente	sûrement	surely, certainly	gewiß, sicherlich	certamente	sicuramente
cierto, a	certain, e	certain, sure	sicher	certo, a	certo, a; sicuro, a
cifra, número	chiffre	figure, number	Zahl(f), Ziffer(f)	número	cifra, numero
cigarrillo	cigarette	cigarette	Zigarette(f)	cigarro	sigaretta
cigarro, puro	cigare	cigar	Zigarre(f)	charuto	sigaro
cilíndrico, a	cylindrique	cylindrical	zylindrisch	cilíndrico, a	cilindrico, a
cilindro	cylindre	cylinder	Zylinder(m)	cilindro	cilindro
cima	cime	summit, peak, top	Gipfel(m)	cimo, cume	cima, vetta
cinco	cinq	five	fünf	cinco	cinque
cincuenta	cinquante	fifty	fünfzig	cinquenta	cinquanta
cincha, correa	sangle	strap	Riemen(m), Gurt(m)	correia	cinghia
cine	cinéma	cinema	Kino(n)	cinema	cinema
cineasta	cinéaste	film-producer	Filmproduzent(in f)m	cineasta	cineasta
cínico, a	cynique	cynical	zynisch	cínico, a	cinico, a
cinta, banda	ruban	ribbon; tape; band	Band(n)	fita	nastro
cinta	bande	tape	Band(n)	fita	nastro
cintura, talle	taille	waist	Taille(f)	cinta	vita
cinturón	ceinture	belt	Gürtel(m)	cinto	cintura
circo	cirque	circus	Zirkus(m)	circo	circo
circuito	circuit	circuit	Strecke(f)(Renn-)	circuito	circuito
circuito	circuit	circuit, system	Stromkreis(m)	circuito	circuito
circuito	circuit	tour	Rundfahrt(f)(-reise)	circuito	giro, circuito
circulación	circulation	circulation	Kreislauf(m)	circulação	circolazione
circular	circuler	circulate	umher = gehen	circular	circolare
circular	circuler	circulate	zirkulieren	circular	circolare
circular	circulaire	circular	rund	circular	circolare

S

Spanish	French	English	German	Portuguese	Italian
círculo	cercle	circle	Kreis(m)	círculo	cerchio
circunferencia	circonférence	circumference	Kreisumfang(m)	circunferência	circonferenza
circunstancia	circonstance	circumstance	Umstand(m)	circunstância	circostanza
cirio	cierge	candle	Kerze(f)	círio	cero
cirrosis	cirrhose	cirrhosis	Zirrhose(f)	cirrose	cirrosi
ciruela	prune	plum	Pflaume(f)	ameixa	prugna, susina
cirugía	chirurgie	surgery	Chirurgie(f)	cirurgia	chirurgia
cirujano	chirurgien	surgeon	Chirurg(in f)m	cirurgião	chirurgo
cisne	cygne	swan	Schwan(m)	cisne	cigno
cita	rendez-vous	appointment	Verabredung(f)	encontro	appuntamento
citar	citer	quote	zitieren	citar	citare
ciudad	ville	town	Stadt(f)	cidade	città
ciudad	cité	city	Stadt(f)	cidade	città
ciudadano, a	citadin, e	town/city dweller	Städter(in f)m	citadino, a	cittadino, a
ciudadano, a	citoyen, ne	citizen	Bürger(in f)m	cidadão, cidadã	cittadino, a
cívico, a	civique	civic	staatsbürgerlich	cívico, a	civico, a
civil	civil, e	civil	zivil	civil	civile
civilización	civilisation	civilization	Zivilisation(f)	civilização	civiltà
civilizar	civiliser	civilize	zivilisieren	civilizar	civilizzare
clan	clan	clan	Sippe(f)	clã	clan
clandestino, a	clandestin, e	clandestine	heimlich	clandestino, a	clandestino, a
claridad	clarté	brightness	Helligkeit(f)	claridade	chiarezza
clarificar	clarifier	clarify	klären	clarificar	chiarificare
clarinete	clarinette	clarinet	Klarinette(f)	clarinete	clarinetto
claro	bien sûr	of course	natürlich	claro	certamente
claro, a	clair, e	clear	klar	claro, a	chiaro, a; límpido, a
claro, a	clair, e	light	hell	claro, a	chiaro, a
clase, curso	classe	class, form	Klassenstufe(f)	classe	classe
clase	classe	class	Klasse(f)	classe	classe, ceto
clásico, a	classique	classical	klassisch	clássico, a	classico, a
clasificación	classement	filing	Einorden(n)	classificação	classificazione
clasificador	classeur	file	Ordner(m)	classificador	schedario
clasificar	classer	classify, file	ordnen	classificar	classificare
cláusula	clause	clause	Klausel(f)	cláusula	clausola
clausura	clôture	closure, closing	Schluß(m)(Abschluß m)	encerramento	chiusura
clavar	clouer	nail	nageln	pregar, cravar	inchiodare
clavar	enfoncer	drive in	ein = schlagen	cravar	piantare
clavícula	clavicule	collar-bone	Schlüsselbein(n)	clavícula	clavícola
clavo	clou	nail	Nagel(m)	prego	chiodo
claxon, bocina	klaxon	horn, hooter	Hupe(f)	buzina	clacson
clero	clergé	clergy	Klerus(m)	clero	clero
cliché	cliché, négatif	negative	Negativ(n)	cliché	negativo
cliente	client, e	customer	Kunde(m), Kundin(f)	cliente	cliente
cliente	client, e	client	Klient(in f)m	cliente	cliente
clima	climat	climate	Klima(n)	clima	clima
climatizador	climatiseur	air conditioner	Klimaanlage(f)	climatizador	condizionatore
clínica	clinique	nursing-home	Klinik(f)	clínica	clinica
cloaca	égout	sewer, drain	Gulli, Abwasserkanäle	esgoto	fogna
club	club	club	Klub(m)	clube	club
coagular	coaguler	coagulate, clot	gerinnen	coagular	coagulare
coágulo	caillot	clot	Blutgerinnsel(n)	coágulo	grumo
coalición	coalition	coalition	Koalition(f)	coligação	coalizione
coartada	alibi	alibi	Alibi(n)	alibi	alibi
cobarde	lâche	cowardly	feig(e)	cobarde	vigliacco, a
cobardía	lâcheté	cowardliness	Feigheit(f)	cobardia	vigliaccheria
cobertizo	hangar	shed	Schuppen(m)	alpendre	hangar, capannone
cobra	cobra	cobra	Kobra(f)	cobra	cobra
cobrar	encaisser	cash	ein = kassieren	receber	incassare
cobrar	toucher	cash, earn, win	kassieren(ein =)	receber	incassare
cobre	cuivre	copper	Kupfer(n)	cobre	rame
cocaína	cocaïne	cocaine	Kokain(n)	cocaína	cocaina
cocción	cuisson	cooking	Kochen(n), Sieden(n)	cozedura, cocção	cottura
cocer	cuire	cook	kochen	cozer	cuocere
cocido, a	cuit, e	cooked	gar, gekocht	cozido, a	cotto, a
cociente	quotient	quotient	Quotient(m), Bruch(m)	quociente	quoziente
cocina	cuisine	kitchen	Küche(f)	cozinha	cucina
cocina	cuisinière	cooker, stove	Herd(m)	fogão	cucina
cocinar	cuisiner	cook	kochen	cozinhar	cucinare

Spanish	French	English	German	Portuguese	Italian
cocinero, a	cuisinier, ière	cook; chef	Koch(m), Köchin(f)	cozinheiro, a	cuoco, a
coco	noix de coco	coconut	Kokosnuß(f)	coco	noce di cocco
cocodrilo	crocodile	crocodile	Krokodil(n)	crocodilo	coccodrillo
cocotero, coco	cocotier	coconut palm(tree)	Kokuspalme(f)	coqueiro	palma da cocco
cóctel	cocktail	cocktail	Cocktail(m)	coquetel	cocktail
cóctel	cocktail	party(cocktail -)	Party(f)	recepção	party
coche	voiture	car	Wagen(m)	carro	macchina, auto
coche de carreras	voiture(course)	racing car	Rennwagen(m)	carro de corrida	macchina da corsa
cochecito	landau	pram	Kinderwagen(m)	carrinho(bebé)	carrozzina
codiciar	convoiter	covet	begehren	cobiçar	ambire, desiderare
codificar	codifier	codify	kodifizieren	codificar	codificare
codificar	coder	code, encode	verschlüsseln	codificar	cifrare
código	code	code	Kod(m)	código	codice
codo	coude	elbow	Ellenbogen(m)	cotovelo	gomito
coeficiente	coefficient	coefficient	Koeffizient(m)	coeficiente	coefficiente
coger, agarrar	saisir, prendre	seize	ergreifen	agarrar	afferrare
coger, recoger	cueillir	pick, gather	pflücken	colher	cogliere, raccogliere
coherente	cohérent, e	coherent	zusammenhängend	coerente	coerente
cohesión	cohésion	cohesion	Zusammenhalt(m)	coesão	coesione
cohete	fusée	rocket	Rakete(f)	foguete	razzo
coincidencia	coincidence	coincidence	Zusammentreffen(n)	coincidência	coincidenza
cojear	boiter	limp	hinken	coxear	zoppicare
cojín	coussin	cushion	Kissen(n)	almofada	cuscino
col	chou	cabbage	Kohl(m)	couve	cavolo
cola	queue	queue	Schlange(f)	bicha; fila	coda, fila
cola, pegamento	colle	glue	Klebstoff(m)	cola	colla
colaboración	collaboration	collaboration	Mitarbeit(f)	colaboração	collaborazione
colaborador, a	collaborateur	assistant	Mitarbeiter(in f)m	colaborador, a	collaboratore, -trice
colchón	matelas	mattress(-es)	Matraze(f)	colchão	materasso
colección	collection	collection	Kollektion(f)	colecção	collezione
colección	collection	collection	Sammlung(f)	colecção	collezione
coleccionar	collectionner	collect	sammeln	coleccionar	collezionare
colectivo, a	collectif, ive	collective	gemeinschaftlich	colectivo, a	collettivo, a
colega	collègue	colleague	Kollege(m), Kollegin f	colega	collega
colegial, a	écolier, ière	schoolboy/girl	Schüler(in f)m	aluno, a	scolaro, a
colegio	collège	college	Kollegium(n)	colégio	collegio
cólera, ira	colère	anger(be angry)	Wut(f)	cólera, ira	collera, ira
cólera	choléra	cholera	Cholera(f)	cólera	colera
colgador, percha	portemanteau	hat stand	Kleiderständer(m)	cabíde	attaccapanni
colgar	pendre	hang	hängen, auf = hängen	pendurar	appendere
colgar, suspender	suspendre	hang up	auf = hängen	pendurar	appendere
colgar	accrocher	hang	auf = hängen	pendurar	appendere
cólico	colique	colic	Kolik(f)	cólica	colica
colina	colline	hill	Hügel(m)	colina	collina
colisión, choque	collision	collision	Zusammenstoß(m)	colisão, choque	collisione
colmena	ruche	hive	Bienenstock(m)	colmeia	alveare
colocar	placer	place, install	setzen, stellen	colocar; pôr	collocare, porre
colonia	colonie	colony	Kolonie(f)	colónia	colonia
colonia(agua de)	eau de toilette	toilet water	Eau de Toilette(n)	água de colónia	acqua di toeletta
colonización	colonisation	colonization	Kolonisierung(f)	colonização	colonizzazione
coloquio	colloque	symposium	Symposium(n)	colóquio	colloquio
color	couleur	colour	Farbe(f)	côr	colore
colorante	colorant	colouring	Farbstoff(m)	corante	colorante
colorear	colorier	colour(in)	an = malen	colorir	colorare
colosal	colossal, e	colossal	riesig	colossal	colossale
columna	colonne	column	Säule(f)	coluna	colonna
columna vertebral	colonne(vertéb-)	spine	Wirbelsäule(f)	coluna vertebral	colonna vertebrale
columpio	balançoire	swing; see-saw	Schaukel(f)	baloiço	altalena
collar	collier	necklace	Halskette(f); Kette(f)	colar	collana
coma	coma	coma	Koma(n)	coma	coma
coma	virgule	comma	Komma(n)	vírgula	virgola
comadrona	sage-femme	midwife(-ives)	Hebamme(f)	parteira	levatrice
comandante	commandant	major	Kommandant(m), Major m	comandante	comandante
comando	commando	commando	Kommando(n)	comando	commando
combado, a	gondolé, e	warped, buckled	verbogen	empenado, a	incurvato, a
combate	combat	combat, fight	Kampf(m)	combate	combattimento
combatiente	combattant, e	fighting-man	Kämpfer(m)	combatente	combattente
combatir	combattre	fight	streiten, kämpfen	combater	combattere

S

Spanish	French	English	German	Portuguese	Italian
combinación	combinaison	combination	Kombination(f)	combinação	combinazione
combinación	combinaison	slip	Unterrock(m)	combinação	sottoveste
combustible	combustible	combustible	verbrennbar	combustível	combustibile
comedia	comédie	comedy	Komödie(f)	comédia	commedia
comediante, a	comédien, ne	comedian	Komödiant(in f)m	comediante, a	commediante
comedor	salle à manger	dining-room	Eßzimmer(n)	sala de jantar	sala da pranzo
comentar	commenter	comment(on)	erläutern	comentar	commentare
comentario	commentaire	comment	Anmerkung(f)	comentário	commento
comentario	commentaire	commentary	Kommentar(m)	comentário	commentario
comenzar	commencer	begin, start	an = fangen	começar	cominciare
comer	manger	eat	essen	comer	mangiare
comercial	commercial, e	commercial	geschäftlich	comercial	commerciale
comercializar	commercialiser	market	vermarkten	comercializar	commercializzare
comerciante	commerçant, e	tradesman(-men)	Geschäftsmann(m)	comerciante	commerciante
comerciar, tratar	négocier, traiter	deal	handeln	negociar, tratar	negoziare, trattare
comercio	commerce	trade, commerce	Handel(m)	comércio	commercio
comestible	comestible	edible	eßbar	comestível	commestibile
comestibles	denrée	foodstuff	Eßware(f)	género; víveres	derrata
cometa	comète	comet	Komet(m)	cometa	cometa
cometer	commettre	commit	begehen, verüben	cometer	commettere
cometido, función	rôle	role, part	Rolle(f)	função	ruolo, parte
cómico, a	comique	comic, funny	komisch	cómico, a	comico, a
cómico	comique	comedian, comic	Komiker(in f)m	cómico	comico
comics, tebeos	bande dessinée	cartoon(strip)	Comic Strip(m)	banda desenhada	fumetto
comida	repas	meal	Mahlzeit(f)	refeição	pasto
comienzo	début	beginning	Anfang(m)	princípio	inizio
comienzo, principio	commencement	beginning	Anfang(m)	começo, princípio	principio, inizio
comisaría	commissariat	police station	Kommissariat(n)	esquadra(polícia)	commissariato
comisión	commission	commission	Kommission(f)	comissão	commissione
comisión	commission	committee	Ausschuß(m)	comissão	commissione
comité	comité	committee	Komitee(n), Ausschuß m	comissão	comitato
como	comme	as; like	wie	como	come
cómo	comment	how	wie	como	come
cómo(?)	comment?	pardon?	wie bitte?	como disse?	come?, come dice?
cómodo, a	confortable	comfortable	bequem	confortável	confortevole
cómodo, a	commode	convenient	praktisch	cómodo, a	comodo, a
compacto, a	compact, e	compact	kompakt	compacto, a	compatto, a
compadecer	compatir	sympathize	mit = fühlen	apiedar-se	compatire
compadecer	plaindre	pity	bedauern	lastimar	compatire
compañero, a	compagnon, agne	companion	Begleiter(in f)m	companheiro, a	compagno, a
compañero, a	camarade	friend	Kamerad(in f)m	camarada	compagno, a
compañía	compagnie	company	Gesellschaft(f)	companhia	compagnia
compañía(en)	compagnie(en)	company of(in the)	Gesellschaft(in)	companhia(em)	compagnia(in)
comparar	comparer	compare	vergleichen	comparar	paragonare
compartimiento	compartiment	compartment	Abteil(n)	compartimento	compartimento
compás	compas	compass(es)	Kompaß(m)	compasso	compasso
compensación	compensation	compensation	Kompensation(f)	compensação	compenso
competencia	compétence	competence	Zuständigkeit(f)	competência	competenza
competencia	concurrence	competition	Konkurrenz(f)	concorrência	concorrenza
competente, capaz	compétent, e	competent	kompetent	competente, capaz	competente
competición	compétition	competition	Wettbewerb(m)	competição	competizione, gara
competidor, a	concurrent, e	competitor	konkurrent(in f)m	concorrente	concorrente
complejo	complexe	complex	Komplex(m)	complexo	complesso
complemento	complément	complement	Ergänzung(f)	complemento	complemento
completamente	complètement	completely	völlig	completamente	completamente
completamente	entièrement	entirely	ganz	inteiramente	interamente
completo, a	complet, ète	complete, full	vollständig, voll	completo, a	completo, a
complicado, a	compliqué, e	complicated	kompliziert	complicado, a	complicato, a
cómplice	complice	accomplice	Komplize m, Komplizin	cúmplice	complice
complot	complot	conspiracy, plot	Verschwörung(f)	conspiração	complotto
componente	composant	component	Bestandteil(m)	componente	componente
componer	composer	compose	zusammen = stellen	compor	comporre
comportamiento	comportement	behaviour	Verhalten(n)	comportamento	comportamento
composición	composition	composition	Zusammensetzung(f)	composição	composizione
compositor	compositeur	composer	Komponist(in f)m	compositor	compositore
compota	compote	stewed fruit	Kompott(n)	compota	frutta cotta
compra	achat	purchase	Kauf(m)	compra	acquisto
comprador, a	acheteur, se	buyer; shopper	Käufer(in f)m	comprador, a	acquirente

Spanish	French	English	German	Portuguese	Italian
comprar	acheter	buy	kaufen	comprar	comprare
compras	courses	shopping	Einkäufe(pl)	compras	spesa
comprender	comprendre	comprise	ein = begreifen	compreender	comprendere
comprender	comprendre	understand	verstehen	compreender	capire
compresión	compression	compression	Druck(m)	compressão	compressione
comprimido	comprimé	tablet, pill	Tablette(f)	comprimido	compressa
comprimir	comprimer	compress	drücken	comprimir	comprimere
comprobar	vérifier	check, verify	überprüfen	verificar	verificare
comprometer	compromettre	compromise	bloß = stellen(jdn.)	comprometer	compromettere
comprometerse	engager(s')	commit oneself	engagieren, sich	comprometer-se	impegnarsi a
compromiso	compromis	compromise	Kompromiß(m)	compromisso	compromesso
compromiso	compromission	compromising	Kompromittierung(f)	comprometimento	compromissione
compromiso	engagement	commitment	Verpflichtung(f)	compromisso	impegno
compuerta	vanne	gate; valve	Klappe(f)	comporta	saracinesca
común	commun, e	common, usual	gewöhnlich	comum	comune
común	commun, e	common	Gemeinschafts-	comum	comune
común	banal, e	banal	banal	banal	banale
comunicación	communication	communication	Verständigung(f)	comunicação	comunicazione
comunicar	communiquer	communicate	mitteilen	comunicar	comunicare
comunidad	communauté	community	Gemeinschaft(f)	comunidade	comunità
comunismo	communisme	communism	Kommunismus(m)	comunismo	comunismo
con	avec	with	mit	com	con
concebir	concevoir	design	entwerfen	conceber	ideare
concebir	concevoir	conceive(of)	vor = stellen, sich	conceber	concepire
conceder	accorder	grant	bewilligen	conceder	concedere, accordare
conceder	allouer	allocate	zu = teilen, bewilligen	conceder	assegnare
concejal, a	conseiller, ère	councillor	Rat(m)(Staatsrat m)	conselheiro, a	consigliere, a
concejo	conseil	council	Rat(m)(Stadtrat m)	município	giunta, consiglio
concentración	rassemblement	gathering	Versammlung(f)	ajuntamento	raduno, adunanza
concentrar(se)	concentrer(se)	concentrate	konzentrieren, sich	concentrar-se	concentrarsi
concentrar	concentrer	concentrate	konzentrieren	concentrar	concentrare
concepción	conception	conception	Konzeption(f)	concepção	concezione
concepto	concept	concept	Begriff(m)	conceito	concetto
concernir	concerner	concern	betreffen	dizer respeito a	riguardare
concertación	concertation	cooperation	Zusammenarbeit(f)	concertação	concertazione
conciencia	conscience	conscience	Bewußtsein(n)	consciência	coscienza
concierto	concert	concert	Konzert(n)	concerto	concerto
concluir	conclure	conclude	schließen, abschließen	concluir	concludere
conclusión	conclusion	conclusion	Abschluß(m)	conclusão	conclusione
concordar	concorder	tally, agree	überein = stimmen	concordar	concordare
concreto, a	concret, ète	concrete	konkret	concreto, a	concreto, a
concubinato	concubinage	co-habitation	wilde Ehe(f)	concubinato	concubinato
concurrir a	assister	attend	bei = wohnen	assistir a	presenziare
concurso	concours	competition	Wettbewerb(m)	concurso	concorso
concurso	concours	contest	Wettbewerb(m)	concurso	gara
concha	coquille	shell	Schale(f), Muschel(f)	concha	conchiglia
condecorar	décorer	decorate	aus = zeichnen	condecorar	decorare
condenación	condamnation	sentence	Verurteilung(f)	condenação	condanna
condenar	condamner	condemn	verurteilen	condenar	condannare
condenar	condamner	convict, sentence	verurteilen	condenar	condannare
condenar	damner	damn	verdammen	condenar	dannare
condensación	condensation	condensation	Kondensierung(f)	condensação	condensazione
condición	condition	condition	Bedingung(f)	condição	condizione
condición	état	condition	Zustand(m)	estado	condizione
conducir	conduire	drive	fahren	conduzir	guidare
conducir a	aboutir à	lead to	führen zu	conduzir a	arrivare a
conductor, a	conducteur, trice	driver	Fahrer(in f)m	condutor, a	conducente
conectar	connecter	connect	kuppeln, verbinden	ligar	connettere
conejillo(Indias)	cobaye	guinea-pig(be a)	Versuchskaninchen(n)	cobaia	cavia
conejo, a	lapin, e	rabbit	Kaninchen(n)	coelho, a	coniglio, a
conexión	connexion	connection	Verbindung; Anschluß	conexão	connessione
confección	confection	clothing industry	Anfertigung(f)	confecção	confezione
conferencia	conférence	conference; lecture	Konferenz(f)	conferência	conferenza
conferencia	conférence	lecture	Vorlesung(f), Vortrag	conferência	conferenza
confesar	avouer	confess, admit	gestehen	confessar	confessare
confesión	aveu	confession	Geständnis(n)	confissão	confessione
confianza	confiance	confidence, trust	Vertrauen(n)	confiança	fiducia
confianza(tener)	confiance(avoir)	trust	vertrauen(jdm.)	confiar	fiducia(aver)

S

Spanish	French	English	German	Portuguese	Italian
confiar	confier	entrust	an = vertrauen	confiar	affidare
confidencia	confidence	confidence, secret	Vertrauen(im)	confidência	confidenza
confidencial	confidentiel, le	confidential	vertraulich	confidencial	confidenziale
confirmar	confirmer	confirm	bestätigen	confirmar	confermare
confitería	confiserie	sweet shop	Süßwarenladen(m)	confeitaria	confetteria
conflicto	conflit	conflict	Konflikt(m)	conflito	conflitto
conforme a/con	conforme à	in accordance with	entsprechend	conforme com	conforme a
confort	confort	comfort	Bequemlichkeit(f)	conforto	comodità
confrontar	confronter	confront	konfrontieren	confrontar	confrontare
confundir	confondre	confuse, mistake	verwechseln	confundir	confondere
confusión	confusion	confusion	Verwechslung(f)	confusão	confusione
confuso, a	trouble	troubled	verworren	confuso, a	confuso, a; torbido, a
congelación	blocage	freeze	Preisstopp(m)	congelamento	blocco
congelador	congélateur	freezer	Kühltruhe(f)	congelador	congelatore
congelados	surgelés	frozen food	Tiefkühlkost(f)	congelados	surgelati
congestión	congestion	congestion	Blutandrang(m)	congestão	congestione
congratular	congratuler	congratulate	gratulieren	congratular	congratulare
congreso	congrès	congress	Kongress(m)	congresso	congresso
cónico, a	conique	conical	kegelförmig	cónico, a	conico, a
conífera	conifère	conifer	Nadelbaum(m)	conífera	conifera
conjugación	conjugaison	conjugation	Konjugation(f)	conjugação	coniugazione
conjunto	ensemble	whole; all the	Ganze(n); Gesamtheit f	conjunto	insieme
conjunto	ensemble	set	Satz(m)	conjunto	insieme
conmemorar	commémorer	commemorate	gedenken	comemorar	commemorare
conmocionado, a	bouleversé, e	overwhelmed	erschüttert	perturbado, a	sconvolto, a
conmover	émouvoir	move	rühren	comover	commuovere
conmutador	commutateur	switch	Schalter(m)	comutador	commutatore
cono	cône	cone	Kegel(m)	cone	cono
conocer, saber	connaître	know	kennen	conhecer, saber	conoscere, sapere
conocimiento	connaissance	knowledge	Kenntnis(f)	conhecimento	conoscenza
conquista	conquête	conquest	Eroberung(f)	conquista	conquista
consagración	consécration	consecration	Weihe(f)	consagração	consacrazione
consagración a	dévouement	devotion	Ergebenheit(f)	dedicação	dedizione
consagrar	consacrer	consecrate	weihen	consagrar	consacrare
consciente	conscient, e	conscious	bewußt	consciente	cosciente, conscio, a
consecuencia	conséquence	consequence	Konsequenz(f)	consequência	conseguenza
consecutivo, a	consécutif, ive	consecutive	folgend	consecutivo, a	consecutivo, a
conseguir	parvenir	reach, arrive at	erreichen	chegar; conseguir	giungere
consejero, a	conseiller, ère	adviser	Berater(in f)m	conselheiro, a	consigliere, a
consejo	conseil	advice	Rat(m)	conselho	consiglio
consejo	conseil	council	Rat(m)(Europrat m)	conselho	consiglio
consentimiento	agrément	approval, consent	Zustimmung(f)(verbal)	consentimento	consenso
consentir	consentir	agree	ein = willigen	consentir	consentire
consentir	consentir	consent	zu = stimmen	consentir	consentire
conserje	concierge	porter, caretaker	Hausmeister(in f)m	porteiro, a	portiere, a
conserva	conserve(s)	tinned food	Konserve(f)	conserva	conserva
conservación	conservation	conservation	Konservierung(f)	conservação	conservazione
conservar	conserver	preserve, keep	konservieren	conservar	conservare
considerable	considérable	considerable	erheblich	considerável	considerevole
consideración	considération	consideration	Betrachtung(f)	consideração	considerazione
considerar	considérer	consider	an = sehen(als)	considerar	considerare
considerar	considérer	regard	betrachten	considerar	considerare
consigna, orden	consigne	orders, instruction	Anweisung(f)	ordem, instruções	direttiva, ordine
consigna	consigne	luggage lockers	Schließfach(n)	depósito	cassetta, deposito
consigna(equipaje)	consigne(bagage)	left luggage	Gepäckaufbewahrung(f)	depósito(bagagem)	deposito bagagli
consiguiente(por)	conséquent(par)	therefore	folglich; deshalb	conseguinte(por)	perciò
consistir en	consister à	consist(in, of)	bestehen aus	consistir em	consistere in
consolar	consoler	console, comfort	trösten	consolar	consolare
consolidar	consolider	strengthen	verstärken	consolidar	consolidare
consonante	consonne	consonant	Mitlaut(m)	consoante	consonante
conspiración	conspiration	plot, conspiracy	Komplott(n)	conspiração	cospirazione
constante	constant, e	constant	beständig	constante	costante
constatar	constater	state; note	fest = stellen	constatar	constatare
constelación	constellation	constellation	Konstellation(f)	constelação	costellazione
constipar(se)	enrhumer(s')	catch a cold	erkälten, sich	constipar-se	raffreddarsi
constitución	constitution	constitution	Verfassung(f)	constituição	costituzione
constituir	constituer	constitute	bilden	constituir	costituire
construcción	construction	construction	Bau(m)	construção	costruzione

Spanish	French	English	German	Portuguese	Italian
construir	construire	construct, build	bauen	construir	costruire
cónsul	consul	consul	Konsul(m)	cônsul	console
consulado	consulat	consulate	Konsulat(n)	consulado	consolato
consulta(-torio)	cabinet(médecin)	surgery	Praxis(f)(Arztpraxis)	consultório	studio(medico)
consultar	consulter	consult	befragen	consultar	consultare
consumidor, a	consommateur	consumer	Verbraucher(in f)m	consumidor, a	consumatore, trice
consumir	consommer	consume	verbrauchen	consumir	consumare
consumo	consommation	consumption	Verbrauch(m)	consumo	consumo
contabilidad	comptabilité	accountancy	Buchhaltung(f)	contabilidade	contabilità
contable	comptable	accountant	Buchhalter(in f)m	contabilista	ragioniere
contacto	contact	contact	Kontakt(m)	contacto	contatto
contacto(entrar en)	contact(prendre)	contact	Kontakt(auf – nehmen)	contactar	contattare
contado(al)	comptant	cash	Barzahlung(f)	pronto(a)	contanti
contador	compteur	meter	Zähler(m)	contador	contatore
contagio	contagion	contagion	Ansteckung(f)	contágio	contagio
contagioso, a	contagieux, se	contagious	ansteckend	contagioso, a	contagioso, a
contaminación	contamination	contamination	Ansteckung(f)	contaminação	contaminazione
contaminación	pollution	pollution	Verschmutzung(f)	poluição	inquinamento
contaminar	polluer	pollute	verunreinigen	poluir	inquinare
contar	compter	count	zählen	contar	contare
contar	raconter	relate, tell	erzählen	contar	raccontare
contar con	compter sur	rely on	zählen, auf jdn	contar com	contare su
contemplar	contempler	contemplate	betrachten	contemplar	contemplare
contemporáneo, a	contemporain, e	contemporary	zeitgenössisch	contemporâneo, a	contemporaneo, a
contener	contenir	contain	enthalten	conter	contenere
contenido	contenu	content(s)	Inhalt(m)	conteúdo	contenuto
contento, a	content, e	pleased, glad	froh	contente	contento, a
contento, a	content, e	glad, happy, pleased	froh, erfreut	contente	contento, a
contestación(en)	suite à	further to	Anschluß an(im)	consequência(em)	seguito(facendo)
contestar	répondre	answer, reply	antworten	responder	rispondere
continente	continent	continent	Kontinent(m)	continente	continente
continuación	suite	continuation	Folge(f)	continuação	seguito
continuar	continuer	continue, go on	fort – setzen	continuar	continuare
continuo, a	continu, e	continuous	ununterbrochen	contínuo, a	continuo, a
continuo, a	continuel, le	continual	ständig	contínuo, a	continuo, a
contornear	contourner	bypass	umgehen	contornar	aggirare
contorno	contour	outline, contour	Umriß(m)	contorno	contorno
contorno	pourtour	periphery	Umkreis(m)	perímetro	giro, circuito
contra	contre	against	gegen, an	encostado a	contro
contra(en)	contre	against	wider, gegen	contra	contro
contraataque	contre-attaque	counter-attack	Gegenangriff(m)	contra-ataque	contro-attacco
contrabando	contrebande	smuggling	Schmuggel(m)	contrabando	contrabbando
contracción	contraction	contraction	Zusammenziehen(n)	contracção	contrazione
contradecir	contredire	contradict	widersprechen	contradizer	contraddire
contradicción	contradiction	contradiction	Widerspruch(m)	contradição	contraddizione
contrariado, a	contrarié, e	upset	ärgerlich sein	contrariado, a	contrariato, a
contrario, a	contraire	contrary	entgegengesetzt	contrário, a	contrario, a
contrario	contraire	opposite, contrary	Gegenteil(n)	contrário	contrario
contraste	contraste	contrast	Gegensatz(m)	contraste	contrasto
contratar, reclutar	recruter	recruit	an – werben	recrutar	assumere
contratiempo	mésaventure	mishap	Mißgeschick(n)	contratempo	disavventura
contrato	contrat	contract	Vertrag(m), Kontrakt m	contrato	contratto
contribuir	contribuer	contribute	bei – tragen	contribuir	contribuire
control	contrôle	control, check	Aufsicht(f), Prüfung f	controlo	controllo
control	contrôle	examination	Kontrolle(f)	controlo	controllo
controlar	contrôler	control, check	kontrollieren	controlar	controllare
controlar, examinar	contrôler	inspect	besichtigen	examinar	esaminare
contusión	contusion	bruise	Quetschung(f)	contusão	contusione
convalecencia	convalescence	convalescence	Genesung(f)	convalescência	convalescenza
convencer	convaincre	convince	überzeugen	convencer	convincere
convención	convention	agreement	Übereinstimmung(f)	convenção	convenzione
conveniente	convenable	suitable, fitting	angemessen	conveniente	conveniente
convenir	convenir	suit, fit	passen	estar bem	convenire
convento	couvent	convent	Kloster(n)	convento	convento
converger	converger	converge	konvergieren	convergir	convergere
conversación	conversation	conversation	Gespräch(n)	conversação	conversazione
conversación	entretien	talk, conversation	Gespräch(n)	entrevista	colloquio
convertirse	convertir(se)	convert	konvertieren	converter-se	convertirsi

S

Spanish	French	English	German	Portuguese	Italian
convicción	conviction	conviction	Überzeugung(f)	convicção	convinzione
convidado, a	convive	guest	Gast(m)	conviva	commensale
convocar	convoquer	summon; invite	vor = laden	convocar	convocare
convocatoria	convocation	notification	Einberufung(f); Ladung	convocação	convocazione
convoy	convoi	convoy	Konvoi(m)	comboio	convoglio
convulsión	convulsion	convulsion	Zuckung(f), Krampf(m)	convulsão	convulsione
conyugal	conjugal, e	married, marriage-	ehelich	conjugal	coniugale
cooperación	coopération	cooperation	Mitarbeit(f)	cooperação	cooperazione
cooperar	coopérer	cooperate	mit = arbeiten	cooperar	cooperare
cooperativa	coopérative	cooperative	Genossenschaft(f)	cooperativa	cooperativa
coordinar	coordonner	coordinate	koordinieren	coordenar	coordinare
copa	coupe	glass(-es)	Kelch(m), Schale(f)	taça	calice
copa	coupe	cup	Pokal(m)	taça	coppa
copia	copie	copy	Kopie(f)	cópia	copia
copiar	copier	copy	kopieren	copiar	copiare
copioso, a	copieux, se	copious	reichlich	copioso, a	abbondante
copo	flocon	flake	Flocke(f)	floco	fiocco
coral	corail	coral	Koralle(f)	coral	corallo
Corán	Coran	Koran	Koran(der)	Alcorão	Corano
corazón	coeur	heart	Herz(n)	coração	cuore
corbata	cravate	tie	Kravatte(f)	gravata	cravatta
corcho	liège	cork	Kork(m)	cortiça	sughero
corcho	bouchon	cork	Korken(m)	rolha	tappo, turacciolo
cordel	ficelle	string, cord	Schnur(f)	cordel, guita	spago
cordero	agneau	lamb	Lamm(n)	cordeiro	agnello
cordial	cordial, e	cordial, hearty	herzlich, freundlich	cordial	cordiale
cordón, cable	cordon	cord, string	Kordel(f)	cordão	cordone
cordón	lacet	lace	Schnürsenkel(m)	cordão	laccio
cordón(policía)	barrage	blockade	Sperre(f)	barreira	posto di blocco
coro	choeur	choir	Chor(m)	coro	coro
corona	couronne	crown	Krone(f)	coroa	corona
coronel	colonel	colonel	Oberst(m)	coronel	colonnello
corporación	corporation	corporation	Körperschaft(f)	corporação	corporazione
corporal	corporel, le	bodily	körperlich	corporal	corporale
correa	courroie	belt; strap	Riemen(m)	correia	cinghia
correa	bracelet	strap	Armband(n)	pulseira	cinturino
corrección	correction	correction	Verbesserung(f)	correcção	correzione
correctamente	correctement	properly	richtig	correctamente	correttamente
correcto, a	correct, e	correct, proper	richtig	correcto, a	corretto, a
corredera, guía	glissière	slide	Gleitschiene(f)	corrediça	guida, scivolo
corredor, a	coureur, se	runner	Läufer(in f)m	corredor, a	corridore
corregir	corriger	correct, rectify	korrigieren	corrigir	correggere
corregir	corriger	rectify, correct	berichtigen	rectificar	correggere
correo	courrier	mail, post	Post(f)	correio	posta
correos	poste	post-office	Post(f)	correios	posta
correr	courir	run	laufen	correr	correre
correr, fluir	couler	flow, run	fließen	correr	scorrere
correr, fluir	écouler(s')	run, flow	ab = fließen	escorrer	scorrere, defluire
correr, rodar	rouler	run, drive, go	fahren	andar; rolar	correre, andare
correspondencia	correspondance	correspondence	Korrespondenz(f)	correspondência	corrispondenza
corresponder	correspondre	correspond, tally	entsprechen	corresponder	corrispondere
corrida	corrida	bull-fight	Stierkampf(m)	toirada	corrida
corriente	courant, e	common	geläufig	corrente	corrente, comune
corriente	courant, e	current	laufend, heutig	corrente, vulgar	corrente
corriente	courant	current	Strom(m)	corrente	corrente
corrompido, a	corrompu, e	corrupt	verdorben, korrupt	corrupto, a	corrotto, a
corrosión	corrosion	corrosion	Korrosion(f)	corrosão	corrosione
corrupción	corruption	corruption	Korruption(f)	corrupção	corruzione
cortado, a	coupé, e	cut	geschnitten	cortado, a	tagliato, a
cortado, a	barré, e	blocked	gesperrt	impedido, a	sbarrato, a
cortadura	entaille	cut, nick, notch	Kerbe(f)	incisão, golpe	incisione
cortar	couper	cut	schneiden	cortar	tagliare
corte, tajo	coupure(peau)	cut	Schnitt(m)	corte, golpe	taglio
corte	cour	court	Hof(m)	corte	corte
cortejo	cortège	procession	Umzug(m), Festzug(m)	cortejo	corteo
cortés	courtois, e	courteous	höflich	cortês	cortese
cortesía	politesse	politeness	Höflichkeit(f)	delicadeza	educazione
corteza	écorce	bark	Rinde(f)	casca	scorza, buccia

Spanish	French	English	German	Portuguese	Italian
cortina	rideau	curtain	Vorhang(m)	cortina	tenda, tapparella
corto, a	court, e	short	kurz	curto, a	corto, a
cosa	chose	thing	Ding(n)	coisa	cosa
cosas	affaires	things	Sachen(pl)	coisas	roba, oggetti
cosecha	récolte	crop; harvest	Ernte(f)	colheita	raccolta
cosecha	moisson	harvest	Ernte(f)	ceifa, colheita	mietitura
cosecha(año)	millésime	vintage	Jahrgang(m)	vintage	annata
cosechar, recoger	récolter	harvest, gather	ernten	colher, apanhar	raccogliere
coser	coudre	sew	nähen	coser	cucire
cosmética	soins de beauté	beauty treatment	Schönheitspflege(f)	tratamento	cura
cosmético	cosmétique	cosmetic	Kosmetik(f)	cosmético	cosmetico
cosmonauta	cosmonaute	astronaut	Astronaut(m)	cosmonauta	cosmonauta
cosmopolita	cosmopolite	cosmopolitan	kosmopolitisch	cosmopolita	cosmopolita
cosquillas	chatouille(s)	tickle	Kitzeln(n)	cócegas	solletico
costa	côte	coast	Küste(f)	costa	costa
costar	coûter	cost	kosten	custar	costare
costero, a	côtier, ère	coastal	Küsten-	costeiro, a	costiero, a
costilla	côte	rib	Rippe(f)	costela	costola
costo, coste	coût	cost	Kosten(pl)	custo, preço	costo
costoso, a	coûteux, se	costly, expensive	teuer	custoso, a	costoso, a
costra, corteza	croûte	crust	Kruste(f)	crosta	crosta
costumbre	coutume	custom	Brauch(m)	costume	costume, usanza
costumbre	habitude	habit	Gewohnheit(f)	hábito, costume	abitudine
costumbres	moeurs	morals	Sitten(f, pl)	costumes	costumi
costura	couture	sewing	Naht(f)	costura	cucito
costura	couture	seam	Saum(m)	costura	cucito
cotidiano, a	quotidien, ne	daily	täglich	quotidiano, a	quotidiano, a
cotización	cotisation	contribution	Beitrag(m)	contribuição	contributo
cotización	cours	rate, quotation	Kurs(m)	índice, tabela	corso
cotización	cotation	quotation	Kurswert(m)	cotação	quotazione
coyuntura	conjoncture	conjuncture	Konjunktur(f)	conjuntura	congiuntura
crampones	crampons	crampons, irons	Steigeisen(n)	grampo	rampone
cráneo	crâne	skull	Schädel(m)	crâneo	cranio
cráter	cratère	crater	Krater(m)	cratera	cratere
creación	création	creation	Erschaffung; Schöpfung	criação	creazione, creato
creador, a	créateur, trice	creator(creative)	Schöpfer(in f)m	criador, a	creatore, trice
crear	créer	create	schöpfen	criar	creare
crecer	grandir	grow	wachsen	crescer	crescere
crecer	croître	grow, increase	wachsen	crescer	crescere
crecer	pousser, croître	grow	wachsen	crescer	crescere
crecimiento	croissance	growth	Wachstum(n)	crescimento	crescita
crecimiento	accroissement	increase	Zuwachs(m)	crescimento	crescita
crédito	crédit	credit	Kredit(m)	crédito	credito
creencia	croyance	belief	Glaube(m)	crença	credenza
creer	croire	believe	glauben	crer	credere
crema	crème	cream	Sahne(f)	creme	crema
crema	crème(peau)	cream	Creme(f)	creme	crema
crema, beis	beige	beige	beige	bege	beige
crepúsculo	crépuscule	twilight, dusk	Abenddämmerung(f)	crepúsculo	crepuscolo
cresta	crête	crest	Kamm(m)	crista, cimo	cresta
creyente	croyant, e	believer	Gläubige(f, m)	crente	credente
criada	bonne	maid	Haushaltshilfe(f)	criada	domestica
criado, a	domestique	servant	Hausangestellte(m, f)	empregado, a	domestico, a
criar, educar	élever	bring up	erziehen, auf = ziehen	criar, educar	allevare, educare
criar	élever	breed, rear	züchten	criar	allevare
crimen	crime	crime	Verbrechen(n)	crime	crimine
criminal	criminel, le	criminal	Verbrecher(in f)m	criminoso, a	criminale
crines, melena	crinière	mane	Mähne(f)	crina	criniera
crisis	crise	crisis(-ses)	Krise(f)	crise	crisi
crisis cardíaca	crise cardiaque	heart attack	Herzattacke(f)	ataque	infarto
cristal	cristal	crystal	Kristall(n)	cristal	cristallo
cristal, vidrio	vitre	pane, window	Scheibe(f)(Fenster-)	vidro	vetro
cristiano, a	chrétien, ne	Christian	Christ(in f)m	cristão, cristã	cristiano, a
criterio	critère	criterion(-ia)	Kriterium(n)	critério	criterio
crítica	critique	criticism	Kritik(f)	crítica	critica
criticar	critiquer	criticize	kritisieren	criticar	criticare
cromosoma	chromosome	chromosome	Chromosom(n)	cromossoma	cromosoma
crónico, a	chronique	chronic	chronisch	crónico, a	cronico, a

S

Spanish	French	English	German	Portuguese	Italian
crónica	chronique	chronicle	Chronik(f)	crónica	cronaca
cronología	chronologie	chronology	Chronologie(f)	cronologia	cronologia
cronómetro	chronomètre	chronometer	Stoppuhr(f)	cronómetro	cronometro
croquis	croquis	sketch(-es)	Skizze(f)	esboço	schizzo
cruce	croisement	crossing	Kreuzung(f)	cruzamento	incrocio
crucero	croisière	cruise	Kreuzfahrt(f)	cruzeiro	crociera
crucigrama	mots croisés	crossword	Kreuzworträtsel(n)	palavras cruzadas	cruciverba
crudo, a	cru, e	raw	roh	cru, a	crudo, a
cruel	cruel, le	cruel	grausam	cruel	crudele
crujir	craquer	crack	krachen	estalar	scricchiolare
crupier	croupier, ière	croupier	Croupier(m)	croupier	croupier
crustáceo	crustacé	shell-fish	Schalentier(n)	crustáceo	crostaceo
cruz	croix	cross(-es)	Kreuz(n)	cruz	croce
cruzar	croiser	interbreed, cross	kreuzen	cruzar	incrociare
cruzarse	croiser(se)	cross, intersect	kreuzen, sich	cruzar-se	incrociarsi
cuaderno	cahier	exercise book	Heft(n)	caderno	quaderno
cuadra	écurie	stable	Pferdestall(m)	cavalariça	scuderia
cuadrado	carré	square	Viereck(n)	quadrado	quadrato
cuadro	tableau	painting, picture	Gemälde(n)	quadro	dipinto, quadro
cúal, cual	lequel	which; who; whom	welcher	qual(o)	quale(il)
cual(la)	laquelle	which; who; whom	welche	qual(a)	quale(la)
cuál; que	quel, le	what; which	welch(e, er, es)	qual; que	quale; che
cualidad	qualité	quality	Eigenschaft(f)	qualidade	qualità
cualquier(a)	quelconque	any, whatever	beliebig	qualquer	qualunque
cualquiera que sea	quel que soit	whatever	was auch immer	seja qual for	qualunque sia
cuando	quand, lorsque	when; as	als; wenn	quando	quando
cuándo, cuando	quand	when	wann	quando	quando
cuánto; cuanto	combien	how much, how many	wieviel	quanto	quanto
cuarenta	quarante	forty	vierzig	quarenta	quaranta
cuartel	caserne	barracks	Kaserne(f)	quartel	caserma
cuartelillo	poste de police	police station	Polizeiwache(f)	esquadra	posto di guardia
cuarteto	quatuor	quartet	Quartett(n)	quarteto	quartetto
cuarto, a	quart; quatrième	quarter	Viertel(n)	quarto	quarto
cuarto	chambre	bedroom, room	Zimmer(n)(Schlaf-)	quarto	camera, stanza
cuarto	pièce	room	Raum(m)	divisão	stanza
cuarto de baño	salle de bains	bathroom	Badezimmer(n)	quarto de banho	bagno
cuatro	quatre	four	vier	quatro	quattro
cuba	cuve	tank; vat	Wanne(f), Faß(n)	cuba	tino
cubierto	couvert	table(lay the)	Gedeck(n)	talher	coperto
cubo	seau	bucket, pail	Eimer(m)	balde	secchio
cubo	cube	cube	Würfel(m)	cubo	cubo
cubo de basura	poubelle	bin, dustbin	Abfalleimer(m)	caixote do lixo	pattumiera
cubrir	couvrir	cover	zu = decken	cobrir	coprire
cuchara	cuillère	spoon	Löffel(m)	colher	cucchiaio
cucharilla	cuiller à café	teaspoon	Kaffeelöffel(m)	colher de chá	cucchiaino
cuchillada	balafre	gash	Schmiß(m), Schnitt(m)	corte, cutilada	sfregio
cuchillo	couteau	knife(-ives)	Messer(n)	faca	coltello
cuello	cou	neck	Hals(m), Nacken(m)	pescoço	collo
cuello	col	collar	Kragen(m)	colarinho; gola	collo, colletto
cuenta	compte	account	Konto(n)	conta	conto
cuenta	compte	account	Rechnung(f)	conta	conto
cuenta	note	bill	Rechnung(f)	conta	conto
cuento	conte	tale, story	Märchen(n)	conto	racconto, fiaba
cuerda	corde	rope	Tau(n)	corda	corda
cuerno	corne	horn	Horn(n)	corno; chifre	corno
cuero	cuir	leather	Leder(n)	couro	cuoio, pelle
cuerpo	corps	body	Körper(m)	corpo	corpo
cuervo	corbeau	crow	Rabe(m)	corvo	corvo
cuesta	côte	hill, slope	Abhang(m), Steigung(f)	ladeira, encosta	salita, pendio
cuestión	question	question	Frage(f)	questão	questione
cueva, gruta	grotte	cave, grotto	Grotte(f)	gruta	grotta
cuidado	soin	care	Pflege(f)	cuidado	cura
cuidado	entretien	upkeep	Instandhaltung(f)	manutenção	mantenimento
cuidado	attention	care, caution	Sorgfalt(f)	atenção, cuidado	accuratezza
cuidado(!)	attention!	careful!(be)	Achtung!(f)	atenção!, cuidado!	attenzione!, attento!
cuidadoso, a	soigneux, se	neat, tidy	sorgfältig	cuidadoso, a	accurato, a
culata	crosse	butt; grip, handle	Gewehrkolben(m)	coronha	calcio
culpa	faute	fault	Fehler(m)	culpa	colpa

Spanish	French	English	German	Portuguese	Italian
culpa(tener)	tort(avoir)	wrong(to be)	Unrecht(haben)	razão(não ter)	torto(aver)
culpabilidad	culpabilité	guilt	Schuld(f)	culpabilidade	colpevolezza
culpable	coupable	guilty	schuldig	culpado, a	colpevole
culpable	fautif, ive	wrong(in the)	schuldig	culpado, a	colpevole
cultivador, a	cultivateur	farmer	Landwirt(in f)m	lavrador, a	coltivatore, trice
cultivar	cultiver	cultivate	bebauen, züchten	cultivar	coltivare
cultivar	cultiver	cultivate, grow	an = bauen, an = pflanzen	cultivar	coltivare
cultivo	culture	cultivation	Anbau(m)	cultura	coltura
culto, a	cultivé, e	cultured, learned	gebildet	culto, a	colto, a
culto	culte	worship	Kult(m)	culto	culto
cultura	culture	culture	Kultur(f)	cultura	cultura
cultural	culturel, le	cultural	kulturell	cultural	culturale
cumbre; cima	sommet	summit, top	Gipfel(m)	cimo; cume	cima; vetta
cumpleaños	anniversaire	birthday	Geburtstag(m)	aniversário	compleanno
cumplido	compliment	compliment	Kompliment(n)	cumprimento	complimento
cumplir, realizar	accomplir	perform, accomplish	aus = führen, vollenden	realizar	compiere
cuna	berceau	cradle	Wiege(f)	berço	culla
cuneta	fossé	ditch	Graben(m)	fosso	fossato, fosso
cuña	cale	wedge, chock	Keil(m)	cunha	zeppa
cuñada	belle-soeur	sister-in-law	Schwägerin(f)	cunhada	cognata
cuñado	beau-frère	brother-in-law	Schwager(m)	cunhado	cognato
cuota	quota	quota	Quote(f)	cota	quota
cuota	cotisation	subscription, dues	Beitrag m(Mitglieds-)	quota	quota
cúpula, bóveda	coupole	dome	Kuppel(f)	cúpula	cupola
cúpula	dôme	dome	Kuppel(f)	cúpula	duomo
cura	cure	treatment	Kur(f)	cura	cura
cura, vendaje	pansement	plaster, bandage	Verband(m)	penso, curativo	medicazione
curación	guérison	cure, recovery	Heilung(f)	cura	guarigione
curandero, a	guérisseur, se	healer	Heilpraktiker(in f)m	curandeiro, a	guaritore, -trice
curar	guérir	cure, heal	heilen	curar	guarire
curar	soigner	nurse; tend; treat	pflegen	cuidar	curare
curioso, a	curieux, se	curious	neugierig	curioso, a	curioso, a
cursillista	stagiaire	trainee	Praktikant(in f)m	estagiário	apprendista
cursillo	stage	training period	Praktikum(n)	estágio	tirocinio, stage
curso, clase	cours	lesson	Unterricht(m)	curso, aula	corso, lezione
curva	courbe	curve	Kurve(f)	curva	curva
curva	virage	bend, turn	Kurve(f)	curva	curva
curvatura	courbure	bend, curve	Krümmung(f)	curvatura	curvatura
cutáneo, a	cutané, e	cutaneous, skin	Haut-	cutâneo, a	cutaneo, a
cuyo, a; del cual	dont	whose, of which	dessen; deren	cujo, a; do qual	di cui

S

CH

Spanish	French	English	German	Portuguese	Italian
chabolas	bidonville	shanty-town	Elendsviertel(n)	bairro de lata	bidonville
chal	châle	shawl	Schal(m)	xale	scialle
chaleco	gilet	cardigan	Weste(f), Jacke(f)	casaco de malha	gilè; golf
champaña	champagne	champagne	Champagner(m)	champanhe	champagne
champiñón, seta	champignon	mushroom	Pilz(m)	cogumelo	fungo
champú	shampooing	shampoo	Shampoo(n)	champô	shampoo
chapa	tôle	sheet-metal	Blech(n)	chapa	lamiera
chaqueta	veste	jacket	Jacke(f)	jaqueta, casaco	giacca
charca	mare	pond, pool	Tümpel(m)	charco	stagno
charlar	bavarder	chat, talk	schwätzen, schwatzen	falar, conversar	chiacchierare
chasis	châssis	frame, chassis	Rahmen(m), Chassis(n)	chassis	telaio
chatarra	ferraille	scrap iron	Alteisen(n)	sucata	ferraglia, rottame
cheque, talón	chèque	cheque	Scheck(m)	cheque	assegno
chica	fille	girl	Mädchen(n)	rapariga	ragazza
chico	garçon, enfant	boy	kleiner Junge(m)	rapaz	ragazzo, bambino

Spanish	French	English	German	Portuguese	Italian
chichón	bosse	lump, bump	Beule(f)	bossa; alto	bernoccolo, gobba
chiflado, a	cinglé, e	mad, nuts, barmy	verrückt	doido, a; louco, a	tocco, a; picchiato, a
chillar	hurler	scream, yell	brüllen	gritar; berrar	urlare
chimenea	cheminée	chimney; fire-place	Kamin(m)	chaminé	camino
chincheta	punaise	drawing-pin	Heftzwecke(f)	percevejo	puntina(disegno)
chiquillo, a	gamin, e	kid, child	Kind(n)	miúdo	ragazzino, a
chirriar	grincer	grind, grate	knirschen	ranger	stridere
chisme, mecanismo	gadget	gadget	Spielerei(f)	aparelho	gadget
chispa	étincelle	spark	Funken(m)	faísca	scintilla
chiste	blague	joke	Witz(m)	anedota, chalaça	scherzo
chiste, gracia	plaisanterie	joke	Witz(m)	brincadeira	scherzo
chitón(!)	chut!	hush!, sh!	pst!	chut!	sst!, zitto!
chocante	choquant, e	shocking	anstößig	chocante	urtante
chocar con	tamponner	bump, crash into	zusammen = stoßen	chocar, esbarrar	tamponare
chocolate	chocolat	chocolate	Schokolade(f)	chocolate	cioccolato, a
chófer	chauffeur	driver; chauffeur	Fahrer m; Chauffeur m	motorista	autista
choque	choc	shock, impact	Stoß(m), Aufprall(m)	choque	urto, scontro
choque	choc	shock	Schock(m)	choque	choc, colpo
choza	paillotte	hut(straw-hut)	Strohhütte(f)	palhota	capanna
chupar	sucer	suck	lutschen	chupar	succhiare
chupete	sucette	dummy	Schnuller(m)	chupeta	succhiotto

D

Spanish	French	English	German	Portuguese	Italian
dado	dé(jeux)	die(dice)	Würfel(m)	dado	dado
danza, baile	danse	dance	Tanz(m)	dança	ballo, danza
dañar	endommager	damage	beschädigen	estragar	danneggiare
dañino, a	nuisible	harmful	schädlich	nocivo, a	nocivo, a
daño	mal	harm, hurt	Weh(n)	mal	male
daño(s), estrago(s)	dégât(s)	damage	Schaden(m)	estrago	danno
dar	donner	give	geben	dar	dare
dar a luz	accoucher	birth(give)	entbinden	dar à luz	partorire
dar crema	cirer	polish	polieren, wachsen	encerar	lucidare
dar trabajo	embaucher	employ, take on	ein = stellen	empregar	assumere
darse cuenta	réaliser	realize	begreifen	aperceber-se	realizzare
darse prisa	dépêcher(se)	hurry(up)	beeilen, sich	despachar-se	sbrigarsi
dátil	datte	date	Dattel(f)	tâmara	dattero
datos	donnée(s)	data	Daten(pl)	dados	dati
de	de	of	von	de	di; del; dello, a
de, desde	de	from	aus; von	de	da
debajo, abajo	dessous	under, beneath	unter	debaixo, sob	sotto
debajo, bajo	sous	under	unter	debaixo, sob	sotto
debajo(de)	au-dessous	below, under(neath)	unter	baixo(por); abaixo	sotto(al di)
debate	débat	debate	Debatte(f)	debate	dibattito
deber	devoir	must, have to	müssen	dever	dovere
deber	devoir	duty	Pflicht(f)	dever	dovere
deber, tarea	devoir	homework; exercise	Aufgabe(f)	dever	compito
débil	débile	crazy, mad	verrückt; schwach	parvo, a	scemo, a; minorato, a
débil	faible	weak	schwach	fraco, a	debole, fragile
debilidad	faiblesse	weakness(-es)	Schwäche(f)	fraqueza	debolezza
debilitar	affaiblir	weaken	schwächen	enfraquecer	indebolire
decadencia	décadence	decadence, decline	Verfall(m), Untergang	decadência	decadenza
decadencia, ocaso	déclin	decline	Untergang(m)	declínio	declino
decaído, a	déchu, e	fallen, deposed	abgesetzt, verfallen	decaído, a	destituito, a
decaimiento	déchéance	downfall	Untergang(m), Verfall	decadência	decadenza
decano, a	doyen, ne	oldest person	Älteste(f, m)	decano, a	decano, a
decenio, década	décennie	decade	Jahrzehnt(n)	década	decennio
decente	décent, e	decent	anständig	decente	decente
decepción	déception	disappointment	Enttäuschung(f)	decepção	delusione

Spanish	French	English	German	Portuguese	Italian
decepcionado, a	déçu, e	disappointed	enttäuscht	desiludido, a	deluso, a
decepcionar	décevoir	disappoint	enttäuschen	desapontar	deludere
decidir	décider	decide	entscheiden	decidir	decidere
decimal	décimal, e	decimal	dezimal	decimal	decimale
décimo, a	dixième	tenth	zehnte	décimo, a	decimo, a
decir	dire	say	sagen	dizer	dire
decir	dire	tell	sagen	contar	dire
decisión	décision	decision	Entscheidung(f)	decisão	decisione
declaración	déclaration	declaration	Erklärung(f)	declaração	dichiarazione
declarar	déclarer	declare	bekannt = geben	declarar	dichiarare
declive	pente	slope	Hang(m), Abhang(m)	declive	pendio, discesa
decoración	décoration	decoration	Dekoration(f)	decoração	decorazione
decorado	décors	set, scenery	Dekor(m), Bühnenbild n	cenários	scenografia
decorar, adornar	décorer	decorate	schmücken	ornar, adornar	ornare, adornare
decrecer	décroître	decrease	ab = nehmen	decrescer	decrescere
decreciente	dégressif, ive	decreasing	abnehmend	decrescente	decrescente
decreto	décret	decree	Erlaß(m), Verordnung f	decreto	decreto
dedicar	dédier	dedicate	widmen	dedicar	dedicare
dedicar	consacrer	devote	widmen	dedicar	dedicare
dedicarse a	occuper(s')	deal with	beschäftigen, sich	tratar de	occuparsi
dedo	doigt	finger	Finger(m)	dedo	dito
dedo del pie	orteil	toe	Zehe(f)	dedo do pé	dito del piede
deducción	déduction	deduction	Abzug(m)	dedução	deduzione
deducción	déduction	deduction	Rückschluß(m)	dedução	deduzione
deducir	déduire	deduct	folgern, schließen aus	deduzir	detrarre
defecto	défaut	defect, fault	Fehler(m)	defeito	difetto
defectuoso, a	défectueux, se	defective, faulty	defekt	defeituoso, a	difettoso, a
defender	défendre	defend	verteidigen	defender	difendere
defensa	défense	defence	Verteidigung(f)	defesa	difesa
deficiente	déficient, e	deficient	mangelhaft	deficiente	deficiente
déficit	déficit	deficit	Verlust(m), Defizit(n)	défice	deficit
definición	définition	definition	Definition(f)	definição	definizione
definir	définir	define	definieren	definir	definire
definitivo, a	définitif, ive	definitive, final	endgültig	definitivo, a	definitivo, a
deflación	déflation	deflation	Deflation(f)	deflação	deflazione
deflagración	déflagration	explosion	Knall(m), Explosion(f)	deflagração	deflagrazione
deformación	déformation	distortion	Mißbildung(f)	deformação	deformazione
deformar	déformer	distort, deform	verformen	deformar	deformare
degenerar	dégénérer	degenerate	degenerieren	degenerar	degenerare
degradación	dégradation	degradation	Beschädigung(f)	degradação	degradazione
degradar	dégrader	degrade	degradieren	degradar	degradare
dejar	laisser	let; leave	lassen	deixar	lasciare
dejar	laisser	leave	lassen(zurück = -, ver-)	deixar	lasciare
dejar, abandonar	quitter	leave	verlassen	deixar	lasciare
dejar k.o.	assommer	knock out	nieder = schlagen	espancar	stordire
dejo	accent	accent	Akzent(m), Tonfall(m)	sotaque	accento
delantal	tablier	apron	Schürze(f)	avental	grembiule
delante, ante	devant	in front(ahead)of	vor	diante de	davanti a
delantero, a	avant	front, fore	Vorderteil(n)	dianteira	anteriore
delegación	délégation	delegation	Delegation(f)	delegação	delegazione
delegado, a	délégué, e	delegate	Abgesandte(f, m)	delegado, a	delegato, a
delegar	déléguer	delegate	beauftragen	delegar	delegare
deletrear	épeler	spell	buchstabieren	soletrar	compitare, sillabare
delfín	dauphin	dolphin	Delphin(m)	golfinho	delfino
delgado, a	mince	thin	dünn	fino, a	sottile
delgado, a	mince	slim; slender	schlank	magro, a; delgado, a	snello, a
delgado, a	maigre	thin	mager	magro, a	magro, a
deliberado, a	délibéré, e	deliberate	gewollt, absichtlich	deliberado, a	deliberato, a
deliberar	délibérer	deliberate	beraten	deliberar	deliberare
delicadeza	délicatesse	delicacy	Aufmerksamkeit(f)	delicadeza	delicatezza
delicado, a	délicat, e	delicate	schwierig	delicado, a	delicato, a
delicado, a	délicat, e	delicate	zart; fein	delicado, a	delicato, a
delicioso, a	délicieux, se	delicious	köstlich	delicioso, a	delizioso, a
delicioso, a	charmant, e	delightful	entzückend, reizend	delicioso, a	delizioso, a
delimitar	délimiter	delimit	ab = grenzen	delimitar	delimitare
delincuencia	délinquance	delinquency	Kriminalität(f)	delinquência	delinquenza
delincuente	délinquant, e	delinquent	Kriminelle(f, m)	delinquente	delinquente
delirio	délire	delirium	Fieberwahn(m)	delírio	delirio

S

417

Spanish	French	English	German	Portuguese	Italian
delito	délit	offence	Vergehen(n), Delikt(n)	delito	delitto
demagogia	démagogie	demagogy	Demagogie(f)	demagogia	demagogia
demanda	requête	request	Ersuchen(n), Gesuch(n)	pedido	richiesta
demasiado, a	trop	too(much, many)	zuviel	demasiado, a	troppo, a
demencia	démence	insanity, madness	Wahnsinn(m)	demência	demenza, follia
demente	dément, e	insane, crazy, mad	verrückt	demente	demente
democracia	démocratie	democracy	Demokratie(f)	democracia	democrazia
demócrata	démocrate	democrat	Demokrat(in f)m	democrata	democratico, a
demografía	démographie	demography	Demographie(f)	demografia	demografia
demoler	démolir	demolish	zerstören	demolir	demolire
demonio	démon	demon, devil	Teufel(m)	demónio	demonio
demostración	démonstration	demonstration	Vorführung(f)	demonstração	dimostrazione
demostrar	démontrer	demonstrate	beweisen	demonstrar	dimostrare
denigrar	dénigrer	denigrate	verleumden	denegrir	denigrare
densidad	densité	density	Dichte(f)	densidade	densità
denso, a	dense	dense	dicht	denso, a	denso, a
dentadura	dentier	denture	Gebiß(n)	dentadura	dentiera
dentífrico	dentifrice	tooth-paste	Zahnpasta(f)	dentífrico	dentifricio
dentista	dentiste	dentist	Zahnarzt(in f)m	dentista	dentista
dentro, en	dans	in, into	in	dentro(de), em	in
dentro, adentro	dedans	inside	in, drinnen, innen	dentro	dentro
denunciar	dénoncer	denounce	denunzieren	denunciar	denunziare
denunciar	plainte(porter)	complaint(lodge a)	an = zeigen	queixa(apresentar)	querelare
departamento	département	department	Bezirk(m), Bereich(m)	departamento	dipartimento
depender	dépendre(de)	depend(on)	ab = hängen	depender	dipendere
dependiente	dépendant, e	dependent(on)	abhängig	dependente	dipendente
depilar	épiler	remove hair	enthaaren	depilar	depilare
deplorable	déplorable	deplorable	beklagenswert	deplorável	deplorevole
deplorar	déplorer	deplore	beklagen	deplorar	deplorare
deportación	déportation	deportation	Deportation(f)	deportação	deportazione
deporte	sport	sport	Sport(m)	desporto	sport
deportista	sportif, ive	sportsman/-woman	Sportler(in f)m	desportista	sportivo, a
deportivo, a	sportif, ive	sporty, athletic	sportlich; Sport-	desportivo, a	sportivo, a
deposición	déposition	statement	Aussage(f)	deposição	deposizione
depositar	déposer	deposit	deponieren	depositar	depositare
depositar	déposer	put down, lay down	legen, stellen	pousar	depositare, porre
depósito	dépôt	deposit	Satz(m)	depósito	deposito
depósito	réservoir	tank	Tank(m)	depósito	serbatoio
depósito(cadáver.)	morgue	mortuary	Leichenschauhaus(n)	morgue	obitorio
depresión	dépression	breakdown	Nervenzusammenbruch m	depressão	esaurimento(nerv.)
depresión	dépression(atm.)	depression	Tief(n)	depressão	depressione
deprimido, a	déprimé, e	depressed	deprimiert	deprimido, a	depresso, a
derecho, a	droit, e	right	rechte(r, s); rechts	direito, a	destro, a
derecho	droit	law	Recht(n)	direito	diritto
derecho	droit	right	Recht(n)	direito	diritto
derivar	dériver	drift	ab = treiben	derivar	derivare
derramar	répandre	spread; spill	verschütten	espalhar	spargere
derramar, volcar	renverser	spill, knock over	verschütten	entornar	rovesciare
derrame, flujo	écoulement	flow, outflow	Abfluß(m)	escoamento	deflusso, scolo
derretido, a	fondu, e	melted	geschmolzen	derretido, a	sciolto, a
derretir	fondre	melt	schmilzen	derreter	sciogliere(-rsi)
derribar	renverser	knock over/down	um = stoßen	derrubar	travolgere
derrota	défaite	defeat	Niederlage(f)	derrota	sconfitta
derrumbar(se)	écrouler(s')	collapse, crumble	zusammen = brechen	desmoronar-se	crollare
desabrochar	dégrafer	undo, unfasten	auf = machen	desapertar	slacciare
desaconsejar	déconseiller	advise against	ab = raten	desaconselhar	sconsigliare
desacreditar	discréditer	discredit	Verruf bringen(in)	desacreditar	discreditare
desactivar	désamorcer	defuse	entschärfen	despoletar	disinnescare
desafiar	défier	challenge	heraus = fordern	desafiar	sfidare
desafiar	braver	defy	trotzen	defrontar	sfidare
desafío	défi	challenge	Herausforderung(f)	desafio	sfida
desafortunado, a	malchanceux, se	unlucky	unglücklich	azarento, a	sfortunato, a
desagradable	désagréable	unpleasant	unangenehm	desagradável	sgradevole
desagradable	déplaisant, e	unpleasant	unangenehm	desagradável	sgradevole
desalentado, a	découragé, e	disheartened	mutlos, verzagt	desalentado, a	scoraggiato, a
desalentador, a	décourageant, e	discouraging	entmutigend	desanimador, a	scoraggiante
desalentar	décourager	discourage	entmutigen	desalentar	scoraggiare
desamparado, a	désemparé, e	distraught	ratlos	desamparado, a	smarrito, a; sgomento

Spanish	French	English	German	Portuguese	Italian
desangramiento	saignement	bleeding	Blutung(f)	perda de sangue	emorragia
desanimado, a	découragé, e	discouraged	entmutigt	desalentado, a	scoraggiato, a
desaparecer	disparaître	disappear	verschwinden	desaparecer	sparire
desaprobar	désapprouver	disapprove	mißbilligen	desaprovar	disapprovare
desarmar	désarmer	disarm	ab = rüsten, entwaffnen	desarmar	disarmare
desarme	désarmement	disarmament	Abrüstung(f)	desarmamento	disarmo
desarrollar	développer	develop	entwickeln	desenvolver	sviluppare
desarrollo	développement	development	Entwicklung(f)	desenvolvimento	sviluppo
desastre	désastre	disaster	Unheil(n)	desastre	disastro
desatar	détacher	detach, unfasten	lösen, ab = trennen	desatar	staccare
desayuno	déjeuner(petit)	breakfast	Frühstück(n)	almoço(pequeno)	colazione(prima)
desbloquear	débloquer	release	deblockieren, lösen	desbloquear	sbloccare
desbordar	déborder	overflow	über = laufen	transbordar	traboccare
descansado, a	détendu, e	relaxed	entspannt	descontraído, a	disteso, a; rilassato
descansar	reposer(se)	rest	aus = ruhen, sich	descançar	riposarsi
descanso	repos	rest	Ruhe(f)	descanço	riposo
descarga	déchargement	unloading	Ausladen(n)	descarga	scarico
descargar	décharger	unload	ab = laden, aus = laden	descarregar	scaricare
descargar	débarquer	unload	aus = laden	descarregar	sbarcare
descendencia	descendance	descendants	Nachkommenschaft(f)	descendência	discendenza
descender, bajar	descendre	go down, descend	herunter = gehen	descer, baixar	scendere
descenso, bajada	descente	descent	Abstieg(m)	descida	discesa
descifrar	décoder	decode	dekodieren	decifrar	decifrare
descolonizar	décoloniser	decolonize	entkolonisieren	descolonizar	decolonizzare
descoloramiento	décoloration	discolouration	Entfärbung(f)	descoloração	decolorazione
descomponer	décomposer	decompose	zerlegen	decompor	decomporre
desconcertante	déconcertant, e	disconcerting	verwirrend	desconcertante	sconcertante
desconfiado, a	méfiant, e	suspicious	mißtrauisch	desconfiado, a	diffidente
desconfianza	méfiance	distrust, mistrust	Mißtrauen(n)	desconfiança	diffidenza
desconfiar	méfier(se)	mistrust	mißtrauen	desconfiar	diffidare
descongelar	décongeler	thaw	auf = tauen	descongelar	scongelare
descongelar	dégivrer	de-ice; defrost	ab = tauen	descongelar	sbrinare
desconocido, a	inconnu, e	unknown	unbekannt	desconhecido, a	sconosciuto, a
desconsolado, a	navré, e	sorry	leid tun	desolado, a	spiacente
descontaminar	décontaminer	decontaminate	entseuchen	descontaminar	decontaminare
descontento	mécontentement	displeasure	Unzufriedenheit(f)	descontentamento	scontento
descontento, a	mécontent, e	displeased	unzufrieden	descontente	scontento, a
descosido, a	décousu, e	unstitched	abgetrennt	descosido, a	scucito, a
describir	décrire	describe	beschreiben	descrever	descrivere
descripción	description	description	Beschreibung(f)	descrição	descrizione
descubrimiento	découverte	discovery	Entdeckung(f)	descoberta	scoperta
descubrir	découvrir	discover	entdecken	descobrir	scoprire
descubrir	déceler	discover; reveal	auf = decken, entdecken	descobrir	svelare, scoprire
descuento	escompte	discount	Skonto(m)	desconto	sconto
descuento	remise, rabais	reduction	Nachlaß, Ermäßigung	desconto	rimessa, sconto
descuidado, a	négligent, e	careless	nachlässig	descuidado, a	negligente
descuidar	négliger	neglect	vernachlässigen	descuidar	trascurare
descuido	inattention	carelessness	Unachtsamkeit(f)	distracção	disattenzione
desde	depuis	since; for	seit	desde	da
desde	dès(que)	as soon as	sobald	logo que	fin da
desde luego	évidemment	of course	natürlich	evidentemente	evidentemente
desdeñar	dédaigner	disdain	mißachten	desdenhar	disprezzare
desdoblar	déplier	unfold	auf = falten	desdobrar	spiegare, aprire
desear	désirer	desire, want	wünschen	desejar	desiderare
desear	souhaiter	wish, desire	wünschen	desejar	augurare
desembarcar	débarquer	disembark, land	Land gehen(an)	desembarcar	sbarcare
desembolsar	débourser	spend	aus = geben	desembolsar	sborsare
desempeñar	jouer	act	spielen	representar	recitare
desenchufar	débrancher	unplug	raus = ziehen	desligar	staccare
desenchufar	débrancher	disconnect, unplug	aus = machen, abschalten	desligar	disinserire
desenfocado, a	trouble	blurred	verwackelt	tremido, a	sfocato, a
desenredar	débrouiller	clear up	entwirren	desenredar	sbrogliare
desenredarse	débrouiller(se)	manage	zu helfen wissen, sich	desenredar-se	cavarsela
desenrollar	dérouler	unroll	ab = rollen	desenrolar	svolgere, srotolare
desenterrar	déterrer	dig up	aus = graben	desenterrar	dissotterrare
deseo	désir	wish(-es)	Wunsch(m)	desejo	desiderio
deseo	voeu	wish(-es)	Wunsch(m)	voto	augurio
deseoso, a	avide, impatient	eager	begierig	ávido, a; desejoso, a	desideroso, a

Spanish	French	English	German	Portuguese	Italian
desértico, a	désertique	desert, barren	öde; einsam	desértico, a	desertico, a
desesperación	désespoir	despair	Verzweiflung(f)	desespero	disperazione
desfallecimiento	défaillance	weakness(-es)	Schwäche(f), Versagen	desfalecimento	svenimento
desfavorecido, a	défavorisé, e	underprivileged	benachteiligt	desfavorecido, a	svantaggiato, a
desfile	défilé	parade	Parade(f)	desfile	sfilata
desgaste	usure	wear	Abnützung(f)	usura, desgaste	usura; logorio
desgracia	malheur	misfortune	Unglück(n)	desgraça	disgrazia
desgracia	disgrâce	disgrace	Ungnade(f)	desvalimento	disgrazia
desgraciado, a	malheureux, se	unhappy, miserable	unglücklich, betrübt	infeliz	infelice
desgraciado, a	malheureux, se	unfortunate	unglücklich	infeliz	disgraziato, a
desgravado, a	détaxé, e	duty(tax)-free	steuerfrei	isento de taxa	sgravio fiscale
deshacer	défaire	dismantle, undo	ab = bauen	desfazer	disfare
desheredar	déshériter	disinherit	enterben	deserdar	diseredare
deshidratar	déshydrater	dehydrate	aus = trocknen	desidratar	disidratare
deshielo	dégel	thaw	Auftauen(n)	degelo	disgelo
deshonesto, a	malhonnête	dishonest	unehrlich	desonesto, a	disonesto, a
deshonor	déshonneur	dishonour	Schande(f)	desonra	disonore
desierto	désert	desert	Wüste(f)	deserto	deserto
designar	désigner	appoint	ernennen	designar	designare
desigual	inégal, e	unequal	ungleich	desigual	ineguale
desigual	inégal, e	uneven	uneben	desigual	disuguale
desigualdad	inégalité	inequality	Ungleichheit(f)	desigualdade	disuguaglianza
desinfectar	désinfecter	disinfect	desinfizieren	desinfectar	disinfettare
desinflado, a	dégonflé, e	deflated, flat	platt, ohne Luft	vazio, a	sgonfio, a
desinflar	dégonfler	deflate	Luft raus = lassen	desinchar	sgonfiare
desintegrar	désintégrer	disintegrate	auf = lösen	desintegrar	disintegrare
desistir	désister(se)	withdraw, give up	zurück = treten	desistir	desistere, rinunziare
deslumbrar	éblouir	dazzle, glare	blenden	encandear	abbagliare
desmayarse	évanouir(s')	faint	ohnmächtig werden	desmaiar	svenire
desmentir	démentir	refute, deny	dementieren, leugnen	desmentir	smentire
desmontaje	démontage	dismantling	Zerlegung(f), Abbau(m)	desmontagem	smontaggio
desmontar	démonter	remove, dismantle	ab = bauen	desmontar	smontare
desmoralizar	démoraliser	demoralize	entmutigen	desmoralizar	demoralizzare
desmovilizar	démobiliser	demobilize	demobilisieren	desmobilizar	smobilitare
desnudar	dénuder	strip, bare	entblößen	desnudar	denudare
desnudar(se)	déshabiller(se)	undress	aus = ziehen, sich	despir-se	svestire(-irsi)
desnudo, a	nu, e	naked; bare	nackt	nu, nua	nudo, a
desnutrición	malnutrition	malnutrition	Unterernährung(f)	malnutrição	malnutrizione
desobedecer	désobéir	disobey	ungehorsam sein	desobedecer	disobbedire
desocupado, a	inoccupé, e	unoccupied	untätig	desocupado, a	inoperoso, a
desodorante	déodorant	deodorant	Deo(n)	desodorisante	deodorante
desodorante	désodorisant	air-freshener	Deodorant(n)	desodorisante	deodorante
desolado, a	désolé, e	sorry	betrübt	desolado, a	spiacente
desorden	désordre	disorder, mess	Unordnung(f)	desordem	disordine
desorganizar	désorganiser	disorganize	desorganisieren	desorganizar	disorganizzare
despacio	doucement	gently; slowly	langsam, sanft	devagar	piano, adagio
despacho	bureau	office	Büro(n)	escritório	ufficio
despacho; bufete	cabinet(avocat)	practice	Büro(n)(Anwaltsbüro)	escritório	studio(avvocato)
despecho	dépit	spite; vexation	Groll(m), Trotz(m)	despeito	dispetto
despedazar	déchiqueter	tear to pieces	zerstückeln	despedaçar	dilaniare
despedir	renvoyer	dismiss	entlassen	despedir	dimettere
despedir	licencier	lay off, dismiss	entlassen	despedir	licenziare
despegar	décoller	unstick	ab = lösen	descolar	staccare, scollare
despegar	décoller	take off	ab = heben	descolar	decollare
despejar	dégager	clear	frei = machen	desimpedir	sgomberare
desperdiciar	gaspiller	waste	verschwenden	desperdiçar	sperperare
desperdicios	détritus	rubbish, garbage	Unrat(m)	detrito, lixo	detrito
despertador	réveil	alarm clock	Wecker(m)	despertador	sveglia
despertar(se)	éveiller(s')	wake up	auf = wachen	despertar	svegliarsi
despertar	réveiller	wake(up)	wecken	acordar	svegliare
despiadado, a	impitoyable	pitiless	unbarmherzig	impiedoso, a	spietato, a
despido	licenciement	dismissal, lay-off	Entlassung(f)	despedimento	licenziamento
despilfarrar	gaspiller, perdre	waste	verschwenden	desperdiçar	sprecare
despilfarro	gaspillage	waste	Verschwendung(f)	desperdício	spreco
desplazamiento	déplacement	transfer, moving	Umstellung(f)	deslocação	spostamento
desplazar(se)	déplacer(se)	move, shift	bewegen, sich	deslocar-se	spostare(-arsi)
déspota	despote	despot	Despot(m)	déspota	despota
desprecio	mépris	contempt, scorn	Verachtung(f)	desprezo	disprezzo

420

Spanish	French	English	German	Portuguese	Italian
desprendimiento	éboulement	landslide	Erdrutsch(m)	desmoronamento	frana, slavina
despreocupado, a	insouciant, e	carefree	unbekümmert	descuidado, a	noncurante
después	après	after; afterwards	nach	depois	dopo
después	ensuite	then, next	danach	em seguida	poi, dopo
después	puis, ensuite	then	dann	depois	poi
después de	suite(à la)	following	hinter, nach	seguir a(a)	seguito a(in)
desterrar	bannir	banish	verbannen	desterrar	bandire
destilación	distillation	distillation	Destillation(f)	distilação	distillazione
destinación	destination	destination	Bestimmungsort(m)	destino	destinazione
destinar	destiner	intended to(be)	bestimmen für	destinar	destinare
destinatario, a	destinataire	addressee	Empfänger(in f)m	destinatário, a	destinatario, a
destino	destinée	destiny	Schicksal(n)	destino	destino
destino, sino	destin	fate, destiny	Schicksal(n)	destino	destino
destituir	limoger	dismiss	entlassen	destituir	silurare
destornillador	tournevis	screwdriver	Schraubenzieher(m)	chave de parafusos	cacciavite
destrozo	ravage	devastation	Verwüstung(f)	estrago	devastazione
destrucción	destruction	destruction	Zerstörung(f)	destruição	distruzione
destruir	détruire	destroy	zerstören	destruir	distruggere
desusado, a	désuet, ète	obsolete	altmodisch	desusado, a	antiquato, a; desueto
desvalijar	dévaliser	rob, burgle	aus = rauben	roubar	svaligiare
desván	grenier	attic, loft	Speicher(m), Dachboden	sótão	solaio; granaio
desventaja	désavantage	disadvantage	Nachteil(m)	desvantagem	svantaggio
desviación	déviation	diversion	Umleitung(f)	desvio	deviazione
desviar	dévier	divert	um = leiten	desviar	deviare
detallado, a	détaillé, e	detailed	einzelnen(im)	detalhado, a	dettagliato, a
detalle	détail	detail	Einzelheit(f)	pormenor	particolare
detección	détection	detection	Aufspüren(n)	detecção	rivelazione
detective	détective	detective	Detektiv(m)	detective	detective
detector	détecteur	detector	Anzeiger(m)	detector	rivelatore
detención	détention	detention	Haft(f)	detenção	detenzione
detenido, a; preso, a	détenu, e	prisoner	Häftling(m)	preso, a; detido, a	detenuto, a
detergente	lessive	washing powder	Waschpulver(n)	detergente	detersivo
deterioración	détérioration	deterioration	Verschlechterung(f)	deterioração	deteriorazione
determinar	déterminer	determine	fest = legen	determinar	determinare
detestar, odiar	détester	detest, hate	hassen	detestar	detestare, odiare
detonación	détonation	detonation	Knall(m)	detonação	detonazione
detrás, tras	derrière	behind	hinter	atrás, detrás	dietro
deuda	dette	debt	Schuld(f)	dívida	debito
devaluación	dévaluation	devaluation	Abwertung(f)	desvalorização	svalutazione
devaluar	dévaluer	devalue	entwerten, ab = werten	desvalorizar	svalutare
devastar	dévaster	ravage, devastate	verwüsten, zerstören	devastar	devastare
devoción	dévotion	devotion	Frömmigkeit(f)	devoção	devozione
devolver	rendre	give back	zurück = geben	devolver	rendere
devolver	renvoyer	send back, return	zurück = schicken	devolver	rinviare
devolver, traer	ramener	bring back	wieder = bringen	trazer	riportare
devorar	dévorer	devour	verschlingen	devorar	divorare
día; jornada	jour, journée	day	Tag(m)	dia	giorno; giornata
día libre	jour de congé	day off	Urlaubstag(m)	dia de folga	giorno di vacanza
día siguiente	lendemain	next day	folgenden Tag(m)	dia seguinte	indomani(l')
diabetes	diabète	diabetes	Zuckerkrankheit(f)	diabetes	diabete
diablo	diable	devil	Teufel(m)	diabo	diavolo
diafragma	diaphragme	diaphragm	Zwerchfell(n)	diafragma	diaframma
diagnóstico	diagnostic	diagnosis(-oses)	Diagnose(f)	diagnóstico	diagnosi
diagonal	diagonal, e	diagonal	diagonal	diagonal	diagonale
diagrama	diagramme	diagram	Diagramm(n)	diagrama	diagramma
dialecto	dialecte	dialect	Dialekt(m)	dialecto	dialetto
diálogo	dialogue	dialogue	Dialog(m)	diálogo	dialogo
diamante	diamant	diamond	Diamant(m)	diamante	diamante
diámetro	diamètre	diameter	Durchmesser(m)	diâmetro	diametro
diapositiva	diapo(sitives)	slide	Diapositiv(n), Dia(n)	diapositivos	diapositiva
diario, a	journalier, ière	daily	täglich	diário, a	giornaliero, a
diario	quotidien	daily	Tageszeitung(f)	diário	quotidiano
diarrea	diarrhée	diarrhoea	Durchfall(m)	diarreia	diarrea
dibujante	dessinateur	drawer; designer	Zeichner(in f)m	desenhador, a	disegnatore, trice
dibujar; diseñar	dessiner	draw; design	zeichnen	desenhar	disegnare
dibujo; diseño	dessin	drawing; design	Zeichnung(f)	desenho	disegno
dibujo animado	dessin animé	cartoon	Trickfilm(m)Zeichen-	desenho animado	cartone animato
diccionario	dictionnaire	dictionary	Wörterbuch(n)	dicionário	dizionario

S

Spanish	French	English	German	Portuguese	Italian
diciembre	décembre	December	Dezember(m)	Dezembro	dicembre
dictador	dictateur	dictator	Diktator(m)	ditador	dittatore
dictadura	dictature	dictatorship	Diktatur(f)	ditadura	dittatura
diecinueve	dix-neuf	nineteen	neunzehn	dezanove	diciannove
dieciocho	dix-huit	eighteen	achtzehn	dezoito	diciotto
dieciséis	seize	sixteen	sechzehn	dezasseis	sedici
diecisiete	dix-sept	seventeen	siebzehn	dezassete	diciassette
diente	dent	tooth(teeth)	Zahn(m)	dente	dente
diesel	diesel	diesel	Diesel(m)	diesel	diesel
diestro, a	adroit, e	skilled	geschickt	destro, a; hábil	abile
dieta	régime	diet(be on a)	Diät(f)	dieta	dieta
dietas	indemnité	allowance	Schadenersatz(m)	ajuda de custo	indennità
dietético, a	diététique	dietetic	diätetisch	dietético, a	dietetico, a
diez	dix	ten	zehn	dez	dieci
difamación	diffamation	slander	Verleumdung(f)	difamação	diffamazione
diferencia	différence	difference	Unterschied(m)	diferença	differenza
diferencia, margen	écart	gap, margin	Abstand(m)	desvio, margem	margine, differenza
diferente	différent, e	different	verschieden	diferente	differente
diferir, demorar	différer	postpone	auf = schieben	diferir, adiar	differire, rimandare
difícil	difficile	difficult	schwer	difícil	difficile
dificultad	difficulté	difficulty	Schwierigkeit(f)	dificuldade	difficoltà
dificultad	peine	trouble, effort	Anstrengung(f)	esforço	fatica
difteria	diphtérie	diphtheria	Diphterie(f)	difteria	difterite
difundir	diffuser	broadcast	senden	transmitir	trasmettere
difundir	diffuser	diffuse	verbreiten	difundir	diffondere
difunto, a	défunt, e	deceased person	Verstorbene(f, m)	defunto, a	defunto, a
difusión	diffusion	diffusion	Verbreitung; Sendung	difusão	diffusione
dígame(!)	allô!	hello!	Ja, bitte?	está lá?; estou?	pronto!
digestión	digestion	digestion	Verdauung(f)	digestão	digestione
dignidad	dignité	dignity	Würde(f)	dignidade	dignità
digno, a	digne	worthy; dignified	würdig	digno, a	degno, a
dilatación	dilatation	expansion	Ausdehnung(f)	dilatação	dilatazione
diluir	diluer	dilute	verdünnen	diluir	diluire
diluvio	déluge	flood; downpour	Überschwemmung(f)	dilúvio	diluvio
dimensión	dimension	dimension, size	Maß(n)	dimensão	dimensione
dimisión	démission	resignation	Rücktritt(m)	demissão	dimissione
dimitir	démissionner	resign	zurück = treten	demitir-se	dimettere(-rsi)
dinámico, a	dynamique	dynamic	dynamisch	dinâmico, a	dinamico, a
dinamismo	dynamisme	dynamism	Tatkraft(f), Schwung m	dinamismo	dinamismo
dinamita	dynamite	dynamite	Dynamit(n)	dinamite	dinamite
dinastía	dynastie	dynasty	Herrscherhaus(n)	dinastia	dinastia
dinero	argent	money	Geld(n)	dinheiro	denaro; soldi
dios, Dios	dieu	God	Gott(m)	Deus	dio, Dio (dio, dei)
Dios(mío)	Dieu(mon)	Goodness(my)	Gott!(Mein Gott!)	Deus(meu)	Dio(mio)
diploma, título	diplôme	diploma	Diplom(n)	diploma	diploma
diplomacia	diplomatie	diplomacy	Diplomatie(f)	diplomacia	diplomazia
diplomático	diplomate	diplomat	Diplomat(in f)m	diplomata	diplomatico
diplomático, a	diplomatique	diplomatic	diplomatisch	diplomático, a	diplomatico, a
diputado	député	Member(Parliament)	Abgeordnete(m, f)	deputado	deputato
dirección	direction	direction	Richtung(f)	direcção	direzione
dirección	direction	management	Direktion(f)	direcção	direzione
dirección	adresse	address	Anschrift(f), Adresse	endereço, morada	indirizzo
dirección única	sens unique	one-way	Einbahnstraße(f)	sentido único	senso unico
directamente	directement	directly	direkt	directamente	direttamente
directo, a	direct, e	direct	direkt	directo, a	diretto, a
director, a	directeur, trice	director, head	Direktor(in f)m	director, a	direttore, -trice
director, jefe	patron	manager, boss	Unternehmer(in f)m	director, patrão	manager, padrone
director(escuela)	directeur(école)	headmaster	Schuldirektor(m)	director(escola)	direttore(scuola)
director(orquesta)	chef(orchestre)	conductor	Dirigent(in f)m	maestro(orquestra)	direttore(orchestra)
dirigente	dirigeant, e	leader, manager	Leiter(m), Führer(m)	dirigente	dirigente
dirigir	diriger	manage, run	leiten, führen	dirigir	dirigere
dirigir, guiar	diriger	direct, guide, point	richten, steuern	dirigir	dirigere
discernir	discerner	discern	unterscheiden	discernir	discernere
disciplina	discipline	discipline	Disziplin(f)	disciplina	disciplina
discípulo	disciple	disciple	Jünger(m)	discípulo	discepolo
disco	disque	record	Schallplatte(f)	disco	disco
discoteca	discothèque	disco(theque)	Diskothek(f)	discoteca	discoteca
discoteca	boîte de nuit	night-club	Diskothek(f)	boîte	discoteca, night

Spanish	French	English	German	Portuguese	Italian
discrepancia	désaccord	disagreement	Uneinigkeit(f), Streit	desacordo	disaccordo
discreto, a	discret, éte	discreet	diskret	discreto, a	discreto, a
disculpar(se)	excuser(s')	apologize	entschuldigen, sich	desculpar-se	scusarsi
discurso	discours	speech, talk	Rede(f)	discurso	discorso
discusión	discussion	discussion, talk	Diskussion(f)	discussão	discussione
discutir	discuter	discuss	besprechen	discutir	discutere
diseño	dessin, plan	design	Entwurf(m)	desenho	disegno
disfrazar	déguiser	disguise	verkleiden	disfarçar	mascherare
disidente	dissident, e	dissident	Dissident(m)	dissidente	dissidente
disimular	dissimuler	conceal	verbergen, verhehlen	dissimular	dissimulare
disipar	dissiper	dissipate, clear	verziehen, sich	dissipar	dissipare
disminución	diminution	reduction	Verminderung(f)	diminuição	diminuzione
disminuir	diminuer	reduce, decrease	verringern	diminuir	diminuire
disociar	dissocier	dissociate	trennen	dissociar	dissociare
disolvente	dissolvant	solvent, remover	Lösungsmittel(n)	acetona	solvente
disolver	dissoudre	dissolve	auf = lösen	dissolver	sciogliere
disparar	tirer	shoot, fire	schießen, feuern	atirar, disparar	tirare, sparare
dispersar	disperser	disperse; scatter	zerstreuen	dispersar	disperdere
disponer	disposer	arrange	auf = stellen	dispor	disporre
disponible	disponible	available	verfügbar	disponível	disponibile
disposición	disposition	arrangement	Anordnung(f)	disposição	disposizione
disposición	agencement	layout	Anlage(f)	disposição	disposizione
dispuesto, a	prêt, e	ready	fertig	pronto, a	pronto, a
disputa	dispute	dispute, argument	Streit(m)	disputa	disputa, lite
distancia	distance	distance	Entfernung(f)	distância	distanza
distinguir	distinguer	distinguish	unterscheiden	distinguir	distinguere
distinto, a	distinct, e	distinct	deutlich	distinto, a	distinto, a
distracción	distraction(s)	entertainment	Zeitvertreib(m)	distracção, -ões	svago, distrazione
distraer	distraire	distract, divert	ab = lenken	distrair	distrarre
distraído, a	distrait, e	absent-minded	zerstreut	distraído, a	distratto, a
distribución	distribution	distribution	Verteilung(f)	distribuição	distribuzione
distribuir	distribuer	distribute; deal	verteilen	distribuir	distribuire
distrito, área	district, région	district	Bezirk(m)	distrito	distretto
disturbios	troubles	troubles	Unruhen(f, pl)	perturbação	disordini
disuadir	dissuader	dissuade	ab = raten	dissuadir	dissuadere
disuasión	dissuasion	dissuasion	Abschreckung(f)	dissuasão	dissuasione
diván	divan	couch(-es)	Couch(f), Sofa(n)	divã	divano
divergir	diverger	diverge	ab = weichen	divergir	divergere
diversidad	diversité	diversity	Verschiedenheit(f)	diversidade	diversità
diversificar	diversifier	diversify	variieren	diversificar	diversificare
diversión	amusement	amusement, fun	Vergnügen(n)	divertimento	divertimento
diverso, a	divers, e	diverse, various	verschieden	diverso, a	diverso, a
divertido, a	amusant, e	funny, amusing	lustig, amüsant	divertido, a	buffo, a; divertente
divertido, a	amusant, e	amusing, funny	amüsant, drollig	engraçado, a	divertente
divertir(se)	amuser(s')	fun(have)	amüsieren, sich	divertir-se	divertire(-rsi)
dividir	diviser	divide	teilen	dividir	dividere
divino, a	divin, e	divine	göttlich	divino, a	divino, a
divisa	devise	currency	Währung(f)	moeda, divisa	valuta
división	division	division	Division(f)	divisão	divisione
división	division	partition	Trennung(f)	partilha	divisione
divorciar(se)	divorcer	divorce	scheiden lassen, sich	divorciar-se	divorziare
divorcio	divorce	divorce	Scheidung(f)	divórcio	divorzio
divulgar	divulguer	divulge, reveal	aus = plaudern	divulgar	divulgare
doblar	plier	fold	falten	dobrar	piegare
doble	double	double	doppelt	duplo, a	doppio, a
doble	double	dual	doppelt	duplo, a	doppio, a
doce	douze	twelve	zwölf	doze	dodici
docena	douzaine	dozen	Dutzend(n)	dúzia	dozzina
dócil	docile	docile	gehorsam	dócil, manso	docile
doctor, a	docteur(toresse)	doctor	Arzt(m); Doktor(m)	doutor, a	dottore, -essa
doctor, a	docteur	doctor	Doktor(m)	doutor, a	dottore, -essa
doctrina	doctrine	doctrine	Lehre(f)	doutrina	dottrina
documentación	documentation	documentation	Dokumentation(f)	documentação	documentazione
documentación	papiers(les)	papers	Papiere(pl); Ausweise	documentos	documenti
documento	document	document	Dokument(n)	documento	documento
dogmático, a	dogmatique	dogmatic	dogmatisch	dogmático, a	dogmatico, a
doler	mal(faire)	ache, hurt	weh tun, schmerzen	doer	male(fare)
dolerle a uno	mal(avoir)	hurts(it)	Schmerzen haben	doer	male(aver)

Spanish	French	English	German	Portuguese	Italian
dolor	douleur	pain, ache	Schmerz(m)	dor	dolore
dolor	mal	ache, pain	Schmerz(m), Weh(n)	dor	male
dolor de cabeza	mal de tête	headache	Kopfschmerzen(m, pl)	dor de cabeça	mal di testa
dolor de dientes	mal aux dents	toothache	Zahnschmerzen(m, pl)	dor de dentes	mal di denti
dolor de garganta	mal de gorge	sore throat	Halsschmerzen(m, pl)	dor de garganta	mal di gola
doloroso, a	douloureux, se	painful, aching	schmerzhaft	doloroso, a	doloroso, a
domar	dompter	tame	zähmen	domar	domare
domesticar	apprivoiser	tame	zähmen	domesticar	addomesticare
doméstico, a	domestique	domestic, home	Haus-	doméstico, a	domestico, a
domicilio	domicile	home	Wohnsitz(m), Wohnort m	domicílio	domicilio
dominar	dominer	dominate, rule	beherrschen	dominar	dominare
dominar	maîtriser	control, master	beherrschen	dominar	dominare
domingo	dimanche	Sunday	Sonntag(m)	domingo	domenica
dominio, terreno	domaine	domain, estate	Gut(n), Besitzung(f)	terreno	tenuta, fondo
Don	monsieur(Mr)	Mr	Herr(m)	Senhor	Signor
don, talento	don	gift, talent	Talent(n)	dom, talento	dono
donde, dónde	où	where	wo	onde	dove
doparse	doper(se)	take stimulants	dopen, sich	drogar-se	drogarsi
dormido, a	endormi, e	asleep	schlafend	adormecido, a	addormentato, a
dormir	dormir	sleep	schlafen	dormir	dormire
dormitar	sommeiller	doze	schlummern	dormitar	sonnecchiare
dos	deux	two	zwei	dois, duas	due
dosificación	dosage	proportion	Dosierung(f)	dosagem	dosaggio, dose
dosis	dose	dose	Dosis(f)	dose	dose
dotado, a	doué, e	gifted, talented	begabt	dotado, a; capaz	dotato, a
drama	drame	drama	Drama(n)	drama	dramma
dramático, a	dramatique	dramatic	dramatisch	dramático, a	drammatico, a
drenar	drainer	drain	entwässern	drenar	drenare
droga	drogue	drug	Droge(f)	droga	droga
drogadicto, a	toxicomane	drug addict	Rauschgiftsüchtige(r)	toxicómano, drogado	tossicomane
drogado, a	drogué, é	drug addict	Drogenabhängige(m, f)	drogado, a	drogato, a
droguería	droguerie	hardware shop	Kramwarenhandel(m)	drogaria	mesticheria
ducha	douche	shower	Dusche(f)	duche, chuveiro	doccia
duda	doute	doubt	Zweifel(m)	dúvida	dubbio
dudar	douter	doubt	zweifeln	duvidar	dubitare
dudar	douter, hésiter	hesitate	zögern	hesitar	esitare
dudoso, a	douteux, se	dubious; doubtful	zweifelhaft	duvidoso, a	dubbio, a
duelo	duel	duel	Duell(n)	duelo	duello
duelo; luto	deuil	mourning(be in)	Trauer(f)	luto	lutto
dueño, a	propriétaire	landlord	Besitzer/in; (Haus-)	senhorio, a; dono, a	proprietario, a
dulce	doux, ce	sweet	süß	doce	dolce
duna	dune	dune	Düne(f)	duna	duna
duque, duquesa	duc, duchesse	duke, duchess	Herzog(m), Herzogin(f)	duque, duquesa	duca, duchessa
duración	durée	duration, length	Dauer(f)	duração	durata
durante	pendant	during; for	während	durante	durante
durante	durant, pendant	during, for	während	durante	durante
durar	durer	last	dauern	durar	durare
duro, a	dur, e	hard	hart	duro, a	duro, a

E

Spanish	French	English	German	Portuguese	Italian
ebriedad	ivresse	drunkenness	Trunkenheit(f)	embriaguez	ubriachezza
ebullición	ébullition	boiling	Kochen(n)	fervura	ebollizione
eclipse	éclipse	eclipse	Finsternis(f)	eclipse	eclisse
eco	écho	echo(-es)	Echo(n)	eco	eco
ecología	écologie	ecology	Naturschutz(m)	ecologia	ecologia
economía, ahorro	économie, épargne	saving	Ersparnis(f)	economia	risparmio
economía	économie	economy	Wirtschaft(f)	economia	economia

Spanish	French	English	German	Portuguese	Italian
económico, a	économique	economic(al)	wirtschaftlich	económico, a	economico, a
economista	économiste	economist	Volkswirt(in f)m	economista	economista
economizar	économiser	save, economise	sparen	economizar	economizzare
ecuador	équateur	equator	Äquator(m)	equador	equatore
ecuatorial	équatorial, e	equatorial	äquatorial	equatorial	equatoriale
ecuestre	équestre	equestrian	Reiter-	equestre	equestre
eczema	eczéma	eczema	Ekzem(n)	eczema	eczema
echar, tirar	jeter	throw away(out)	weg = werfen	deitar fora	buttare
echar al correo	poster	post, mail	ein = werfen	pôr no correio	impostare, imbucare
edad	âge	age	Alter(n)	idade	età
edición	édition	edition	Auflage(f), Ausgabe(f)	edição	edizione
edificar	bâtir	build	bauen	construir	costruire
edificio	édifice	edifice, building	Gebäude(n)	edifício	edificio
edificio	bâtiment	building	Gebäude(n)	edifício	edificio, palazzo
editor, a	éditeur, trice	publisher; editor	Herausgeber(in f)m	editor, a	editore, trice
editorial	éditorial	editorial	Leitartikel(m)	editorial	editoriale
educación	éducation	education	Erziehung(f)	educação	educazione
educado, a; cortés	poli, e	polite	höflich	educado, a	educato, a
educador, a	éducateur, trice	instructor	Erzieher(in f)m	educador, a	educatore, trice
educar	éduquer	educate	erziehen, bilden	educar	educare
efectivo, a	effectif, ive	effective	tatsächlich, wirklich	efectivo, a	effettivo, a
efectivo	effectif	number of people	Personalbestand(m)	efectivo	effettivo
efecto	effet	effect	Wirkung(f)	efeito	effetto
efecto(en)	effet(en)	indeed	tatsächlich	efeito(com)	infatti
efectuar	effectuer	carry out, perform	aus = führen	efectuar	effettuare
efectuar	opérer	operate	wirken	fazer	operare
eficaz	efficace	effective	wirkungsvoll	eficaz	efficace
eficiente	efficace	efficient	tüchtig, fähig	eficiente	efficiente
efímero, a	éphémère	ephemeral	vergänglich	efémero, a	effimero, a
egoísta	égoïste	selfish	egoistisch	egoísta	egoista
eje	axe	axis	Achse(f)	eixo	asse
ejecución	exécution	execution	Hinrichtung(f)	execução	esecuzione
ejecutar	exécuter	perform, carry out	aus = führen	executar	eseguire
ejecutar, realizar	accomplir	achieve	vollbringen	realizar	realizzare, compiere
ejecutivo, a	exécutif, ive	executive	ausübend, vollziehend	executivo, a	esecutivo, a
ejecutivo	cadre	executive	leitende Angestellte	quadro	dirigente
ejemplo	exemple	example	Beispiel(n)	exemplo	esempio
ejemplo(por)	exemple(par)	instance(for)	Beispiel(zum)	exemplo(por)	esempio(per)
ejercicio	exercice	exercise	Übung(f)	exercício	esercizio
ejercitar	exercer	exercise, practise	aus = üben	exercitar	esercitare
ejército	armée	army	Armee(f)	exército	esercito
el, lo, los	le, l', les	the	der, die, das, die	o, os	il, lo, l'; i, gli
él	il	he; it	er; es	ele	egli, lui, esso
él, la	celui, celle	the one	derjenige, die-, das-	o, a	quello, a
elaborar	élaborer	elaborate	aus = arbeiten	elaborar	elaborare
elástico, a	élastique	elastic; flexible	elastisch	elástico, a	elastico, a
elección	élection	election	Wahl(f)	eleição	elezione
elector, a	électeur, trice	voter	Wähler(in f)m	eleitor, a	elettore, -trice
electricidad	électricité	electricity	Elektrizität(f)	electricidade	elettricità
electricista	électricien	electrician	Elektriker(in f)m	electricista	elettricista
eléctrico, a	électrique	electric(al)	elektrisch	eléctrico, a	elettrico, a
electrónica	électronique	electronics	Elektronik(f)	electrónica	elettronica
electrónico, a	électronique	electronic	elektronisch	electrónico, a	elettronico, a
elefante	éléphant	elephant	Elefant(m)	elefante	elefante
elegancia	élégance	elegance	Eleganz(f)	elegância	eleganza
elegante	élégant, e	elegant, smart	elegant	elegante	elegante
elegante	chic	smart, chic	schick	elegante	elegante
elegido, a	élu, e	elected, chosen	gewählt	eleito, a	eletto, a
elegir	élire	elect	wählen	eleger	eleggere
elemento	élément	element	Element(n)	elemento	elemento
elevar	élever, hausser	raise	an = heben	elevar	elevare, alzare
elevar, alzar	élever	elevate	erhöhen	elevar	elevare
eliminación	élimination	elimination	Beseitigung(f)	eliminação	eliminazione
eliminar	éliminer	eliminate	aus = scheiden	eliminar	eliminare
elipse	ellipse	ellipse	Ellipse(f)	elipse	ellisse
élite	élite	élite	Elite(f)	elite	elite
elocución	élocution	elocution	Sprechweise(f)	elocução	eloquio
elocuencia	éloquence	eloquence	Redegewandtheit(f)	eloquência	eloquenza

S

Spanish	French	English	German	Portuguese	Italian
elogio	éloge	praise	Lob(n)	elogio	elogio
ella	elle	she	sie	ela	essa; lei; ella
ellas	elles	they	sie	elas	esse, loro
ello	cela	it	es	isto; isso	ció; questo
ellos	ils	they	sie	eles	essi; loro
embajada	ambassade	embassy	Botschaft(f)	embaixada	ambasciata
embajador	ambassadeur	ambassador	Botschafter(in f)m	embaixador	ambasciatore
embalaje, envase	emballage	packing, wrapping	Verpackung(f)	embalagem	imballaggio
embaldosado	carrelage	tiling; tiles	Fliesen(n); Fliese(f)	ladrilho	pavimento
embalse, presa	barrage	dam	Damm(m)	barragem	diga
embarazo	grossesse	pregnancy	Schwangerschaft(f)	gravidez	gravidanza
embarcar	embarquer	board, embark	ein = steigen	embarcar	imbarcare
embarcar	embarquer	load	ein = laden	carregar	imbarcare
embargo	embargo	embargo	Embargo(n)	embargo	embargo
emblema	emblème	emblem	Emblem(n)	emblema	emblema
emboscada	embuscade	ambush	Hinterhalt(m)	emboscada	imboscata
embrague	embrayage	clutch	Kupplung(f)	embraiagem	frizione
embriagado, a	soûl, e; saoul, e	drunk	betrunken	bêbado, a; ébrio, a	ubriaco, a
embrión	embryon	embryo	Embryo(n)	embrião	embrione
embrujado, a	hanté, e	haunted	verflucht	assombrado, a	spiritato, a
embrutecer	abrutir	exhaust; stupefy	ab = stumpfen	embrutecer	abbrutire
embudo	entonnoir	funnel	Trichter(m)	funil	imbuto
emerger	émerger	emerge	auf = tauchen	emergir	emergere
emigración	émigration	emigration	Auswanderung(f)	emigração	emigrazione
emigrante	émigré, e	emigrant	Emigrant(in f)m	emigrante	emigrato, a
emigrar	émigrer	emigrate	aus = wandern	emigrar	emigrare
eminencia	sommité	V.I.P.	Prominente(f, m)	sumidade	sommità
eminente	éminent, e	eminent	hervorragend	eminente	eminente
emisario	émissaire	emissary	Bote(m)	emissário	emissario
emisión	émission	programme	Sendung(f)	emissão	programma
emisor	émetteur	transmitter	Sender(m)	emissor	emittente
emitir	émettre	emit	aus = strahlen	emitir	emettere
emoción	émotion	emotion	Rührung(f)	emoção	emozione
emocionado, a	ému, e	moved, affected	gerührt	comovido, a	commosso, a
emocionante	émouvant, e	moving	ergreifend	comovente	commovente
emotivo, a	émotif, ive	emotional	empfindsam	emotivo, a	emotivo, a
empalmar	brancher	connect	an = schließen	ligar	allacciare
empalme	correspondance	connection	Verbindung, Anschluß	correspondência	coincidenza
empapar	imbiber	soak	durchtränken	embeber	imbevere
empapelado	tapisserie	wallpaper	Tapete(f)	papel de parede	carta da parati
empaquetar	empaqueter	pack, wrap	ein = packen, verpacken	empacotar	impacchettare
empeñar	engager	engage	engagieren	empenhar	impegnare
empeñarse	acharner(s')	persist	beharren	insistir	accanirsi
empeorar	aggraver	worsen, aggravate	verschlimmern	agravar	aggravare
emperador	empereur	emperor	Kaiser(m)	imperador	imperatore
emperatriz	impératrice	empress	Kaiserin(f)	imperatriz	imperatrice
empinado, a	raide; escarpé, e	steep	steil	empinado, a	ripido, a
empleado, a	employé, e	employee	Angestellte(f, m)	empregado, a	impiegato, a
emplear	employer	employ	an = stellen	empregar	impiegare
empleo	emploi	job, work	Beruf(m)	emprego	impiego
empleo	emploi	employment	Stelle(f)	emprego	impiego
empotrar	encastrer	set in	ein = setzen	embutir	incastrare
emprender	entreprendre	undertake	unternehmen	empreender	intraprendere
empresa	entreprise	company, firm	Unternehmen(n)	empresa	impresa, ditta
empresario	entrepreneur	contractor	Unternehmer(in f)m	empresário	imprenditore
empresario	imprésario	impresario	Manager(m)	empresário	impresario
empujar	pousser	push	schieben, stoßen	empurrar	spingere
empujar	bousculer	push	drängeln	empurrar	spingere, urtare
empuñar	empoigner, saisir	grab, grasp	greifen	agarrar	agguantare
emulsión	émulsion	emulsion	Emulsion(f)	emulsão	emulsione
en	en; dans; à; de; sur	in; into; at; to; by	in; nach; an; auf; im; aus	em; a; para; com	in; di; da; a
en, encima, sobre	sur	on	auf	em cima de; sobre	sopra, su
en casa de	chez	at, to	bei	em casa de	da
en vez de/lugar de	au lieu de	instead(of)	anstatt	em vez de/lugar de	invece di
enagua	jupon	petticoat, slip	Unterrock(m)	saiote	sottana
enamorado, a	amoureux, se	love(in)	verliebt	apaixonado, a	innamorato, a
enano, a	nain, e	dwarf	Zwerg(m)	anão, anã	nano, a
encantado, a	ravi, e	delighted	hocherfreut	encantado, a	lietissimo, a

Spanish	French	English	German	Portuguese	Italian
encantador, a	ravissant, e	ravishing, lovely	entzückend	encantador, a	incantevole
encantador, a	charmant, e	charming, lovely	liebenswert	encantador, a	affascinante
encanto	charme	charm	Charme(m), Reiz(m)	encanto	fascino
encarcelamiento	emprisonnement	imprisonment	Haft(f), Verhaftung(f)	prisão	incarcerazione
encarcelar	incarcérer	imprison	ein = sperren	encarcerar	incarcerare
encargado, a	responsable	person in charge	Verantwortliche(f, m)	responsável	responsabile
encargo, pedido	commande	order	Bestellung(f)	encomenda	ordinazione
encender	allumer	switch on	an = machen	acender	accendere
encender	allumer	light	an = zünden	acender	accendere
encendido	allumage	ignition	Zündung(f)	ignição	accensione
encerrar	enfermer	shut in	ein = schließen	encerrar, fechar	rinchiudere
encía	gencive	gum	Zahnfleisch(n)	gengiva	gengiva
enciclopedia	encyclopédie	encyclopaedia	Enzyklopädie(f)	enciclopédia	enciclopedia
encima(por, de)	au-dessus	above	über	cima(por); acima de	sopra(al di)
encinta	enceinte	pregnant	schwanger	grávida	incinta
encoger	rétrécir	shrink	schrumpfen	encolher	restringere
encontrar	trouver	find	finden	achar, encontrar	trovare
encontrar	rencontrer	meet	treffen	encontrar	incontrare
encrucijada	carrefour	cross-road(s)	Kreuzung(f)	cruzamento	incrocio
encuadernación	reliure	binding(book-)	Einband(m)	encadernação	rilegatura
encuentro	rencontre	meeting	Begegnung(f)	encontro	incontro
encuesta	enquête, étude	survey	Umfrage(f)	inquérito	inchiesta
enchufar	brancher	plug in	ein = stecken	ligar	innestare
enchufe	prise	plug; socket	Steckdose(f)	tomada	presa
endeble	chétif, ive	puny, weak	schwächlich, kümmer-	débil	gracile
enderezar	redresser	straighten out/up	gerade = biegen	endireitar	raddrizzare
enemigo, a	ennemi, e	enemy	Feind(in f)m	inimigo, a	nemico, a
energía	énergie	energy	Energie(f)	energia	energia
enero	janvier	January	Januar(m)	Janeiro	gennaio
enfermedad	maladie	illness	Krankheit(f)	doença	malattia
enfermería	infirmerie	infirmary	Krankenraum(m)	enfermaria	infermeria
enfermero, a	infirmier, ière	nurse	Krankenpfleger(in f)m	enfermeiro, a	infermiere, a
enfermo, a	malade	ill	krank	doente; enfermo, a	malato, a
enfermo, a	malade	sick person	Kranke(f, m)	doente	malato, a
enfocar	envisager	envisage	beabsichtigen	encarar	prevedere
enfrentamiento	affrontement	confrontation	Konfrontation(f)	afrontamento	affrontamento
enfriar	refroidir	cool(down)	ab = kühlen	arrefecer	raffreddare
enganchar	accrocher	connect, link	an = hängen	engatar	agganciare
engañar	tromper	deceive, cheat	betrügen	enganar	ingannare
engendrar	engendrer	generate	zeugen, erzeugen	engendrar	generare
engendrar	générer	generate	erzeugen	gerar	generare
engordar	grossir	put on weight	zu = nehmen	engordar	ingrassare
engranar	enclencher	engage	ein = legen, = schalten	engrenar	ingranare, avviare
enhorabuena(!)	félicitations!	congratulations!	Glückwunsch!	parabéns!	congratulazioni!
enigma	énigme	enigma	Rätsel(n)	enigma	enigma
enlace	liaison	link	Verbindung(f)	conexão	collegamento
enlazar, unir	relier	link, connect	verbinden	ligar	collegare
enmarañar(se)	emmêler(s')	tangle(up)	verwickeln, verwirren	emaranhar-se	aggrovigliare(-rsi)
enmendar	amender	amend	verbessern, ändern	emendar	emendare
enmohecer	moisir	mouldy(to go)	verschimmeln	bolor(criar)	ammuffire
enorme	énorme	enormous, huge	riesig	enorme	enorme
enriquecer	enrichir	enrich	bereichern	enriquecer	arricchire
enrollar	enrouler	roll up	auf = wickeln	enrolar	arrotolare
ensalada; lechuga	salade	salad; lettuce	Salat(m); Kopfsalat(m)	salada	insalata
ensalada	crudité	salad, crudité	Rohkost(f)	salada	insalata mista
ensambladura	assemblage	assembly	Montage(f)	montagem	assemblaggio
ensamblar	assembler	assemble	zusammen = setzen	juntar	assemblare
ensanchar	élargir	widen, enlarge	verbreiten	alargar	allargare
ensayar, probar	tester	test	testen	testar	testare
enseñanza	enseignanta	teaching	Unterricht(m), Lehre f	ensino	insegnamento
enseñar	enseigner	teach	lehren, unterrichten	ensinar	insegnare
enseñar, mostrar	montrer	show	zeigen	mostrar	mostrare
ensuciar	salir	dirty	verschmutzen	sujar	sporcare
entender	comprendre	understand	begreifen, verstehen	entender	comprendere
enterarse	apprendre	hear(of)	erfahren	saber	apprendere, sapere
entero, a	entier, ière	whole, entire	ganz	inteiro, a	intero, a
entierro	enterrement	burial, funeral	Beerdigung(f)	enterro	funerale
entonación	intonation	intonation	Tonfall(m)	entoação	intonazione

Spanish	French	English	German	Portuguese	Italian
entonces	alors	then	dann	então	allora
entrada	entrée	entry, entrance	Eintritt(m), Eingang m	entrada	ingresso
entrada	entrée	admission	Eintrittskarte(f)	entrada, bilhete	ingresso
entrar	entrer	enter, come/go in	ein = treten	entrar	entrare
entre	entre	between	zwischen	entre	tra, fra
entre	parmi	among	unter	entre	fra, tra
entrega	livraison	delivery	Lieferung(f)	entrega	consegna
entregar	livrer	deliver	liefern	entregar	consegnare
entremeses	hors-d'oeuvre	starter	Vorspeise(f)	acepipe, entrada	antipasto
entrenador	entraîneur	trainer	Trainer(m)	treinador	allenatore
entrenamiento	entraînement	training, practice	Training(n)	treino	allenamento
entrenarse	entraîner(s')	train, practise	üben; trainieren	treinar-se	allenare(-rsi)
entretanto	entre-temps	meanwhile, meantime	inzwischen	entretanto	intanto, frattanto
entretener	distraire	entertain	unterhalten	distrair	distrarre
entrever	entrevoir	glimpse	flüchtig sehen	entrever	intravedere
entrevista	entrevue	interview	Treffen(n), Gespräch n	entrevista	intervista
entusiasmo	enthousiasme	enthusiasm	Begeisterung(f)	entusiasmo	entusiasmo
enumerar	énumérer	enumerate	auf = zählen	enumerar	enumerare
envenenamiento	empoisonnement	poisoning	Vergiftung(f)	envenenamento	avvelenamento
enviar	envoyer	send	schicken, senden(ab =)	enviar	inviare
enviar, expedir	expédier, livrer	consign	übersenden	enviar, expedir	inviare
envío	envoi	sending	Sendung(f), Versand(m)	envio	invio
envío	émission	sending	Sendung(f)	envio	emissione
envolver	envelopper	wrap, envelop	ein = hüllen, ein = packen	envolver	avvolgere
epidemia	épidémie	epidemic	Seuche(f)	epidemia	epidemia
epidermis	épiderme	epidermis, skin	Oberhaut(f), Haut(f)	epiderme	epidermide
epilepsia	épilepsie	epilepsy	Epilepsie(f)	epilepsia	epilessia
episodio	épisode	episode	Episode(f)	episódio	episodio
época	époque	epoch, era, time	Epoche(f), Ära(f), Zeit	época	epoca
epopeya	épopée	epic	Epos(n)	epopeia	epopea
equidad	équité	equity	Gerechtigkeit(f)	equidade	equità
equilibrar	équilibrer	balance	aus = gleichen	equilibrar	equilibrare
equilibrio	équilibre	balance	Gleichgewicht(n)	equilíbrio	equilibrio
equipaje	bagage(s)	luggage, baggage	Gepäck(n)	bagagem	bagaglio
equipaje de mano	bagages à main	hand luggage	Handgepäck(n)	bagagem de mão	bagaglio a mano
equipar	équiper	equip, fit out	aus = rüsten	equipar	equipaggiare
equipo	équipe	team	Mannschaft(f), Team(n)	equipa, grupo	squadra; équipe
equipo	équipement	equipment	Ausstattung(f)	equipamento	equipaggiamento
equitación	équitation	riding(horse -)	Reiten(n)	equitação	equitazione
equivalente	équivalent, e	equivalent	gleichwertig	equivalente	equivalente
equivocarse	tromper(se)	mistaken(be)	täuschen, sich	enganar-se	sbagliarsi
equívoco, a	équivoque	equivocal	zweideutig	equívoco, a	equivoco, a
era	ère	era	Ära(f)	era	era
erigir, levantar	ériger	erect	errichten	erigir	erigere
erigir	dresser	erect, put up	auf = richten, errichten	erigir, erguer	drizzare
ermitaño	ermite	hermit	Einsiedler(in f)m	eremita	eremita
erosión	érosion	erosion	Abtragung(f)	erosão	erosione
erótico, a	érotique	erotic	erotisch	erótico, a	erotico, a
erotismo	érotisme	eroticism	Erotik(f)	erotismo	erotismo
error	erreur	error, mistake	Irrtum(m), Fehler(m)	erro	errore
error(cometer un)	erreur(faire)	mistake(make a)	Irrtum(m)(machen)	erro(dar um)	errore(fare un)
eructar	roter	burp	auf = stoßen, rülpsen	arrotar	ruttare
erudito, a	érudit, e	erudite, learned	gelehrt	erudito, a	erudito, a
erudito, a	érudit, e	scholar	Gelehrte(f, m)	erudito, a	dotto, a; erudito, a
erupción	éruption	eruption	Ausbruch(m)	erupção	eruzione
esbelto, a	svelte	slim, slender	schlank	esbelto, a	slanciato, a; snello, a
escafandra	scaphandre	diving-suit	Taucheranzug(m)	escafandro	scafandro
escala	échelle	scale	Tabelle(f), Skala(f)	escala	scala
escala	escale	stop(over)	Zwischenlandung(f)	escala	scalo
escalar, subir	grimper	climb	klettern	trepar, escalar	arrampicarsi
escalera	échelle	ladder	Leiter(f)	escada	scala
escalera	escalier	staircase, stairs	Treppe(f)	escada	scala
escalofrío	frisson	shiver	Schauer(m)	arrepio	brivido
escama	écaille	scale	Schuppe(f)	escama	squama
escándalo	scandale	scandal	Skandal(m)	escândalo	scandalo
escapar(se)	échapper(s')	escape	fliehen	escapar-se	scappare
escaparate	vitrine	shop-window	Schaufenster(n)	montra, vitrina	vetrina
escape	fuite	leak	Leck(n)	fuga	perdita

Spanish	French	English	German	Portuguese	Italian
escarcha	givre	frost	Reif(m)	geada	brina
escarpado, a	escarpé, e	steep	steil	escarpado, a	scosceso, a
escena	scène	scene	Szene(f)	cena	scena
escena	scène	stage	Szene(f), Bühne(f)	cena	scena
escéptico, a	sceptique	sceptic(al)	skeptisch	céptico, a	scettico, a
esclavitud	esclavage	slavery	Sklaverei(f)	escravatura	schiavitú
esclavo, a	esclave	slave	Sklave(m), Sklavin(f)	escravo, a	schiavo, a
esclerósis	sclérose	sclerosis(-ses)	Sklerose(f)	esclerose	sclerosi
escoba	balai	brush, broom	Besen(m)	vassoura	scopa
escoger	choisir	choose, select	aus = wählen	escolher	scegliere
escoger, separar	trier	sort(out)	sortieren	escolher, triar	scegliere, smistare
escogimiento	choix	choice	Wahl(f)	escolha	scelta
escolaridad	scolarité	schooling	Schulzeit(f)	escolaridade	scolarità
escoliosis	scoliose	scoliosis	Skoliose(f)	escoliose	scoliosi
escolta	escorte	escort	Gefolge(n)	escolta	scorta
escollera	jetée	jetty	Hafendamm(m), Mole(f)	molhe	molo, gettata
escombros	décombres	ruins	Trümmer(m, pl)	escombros	macerie, rovine
escombros	éboulis	scree	Geröll(n)	escombros	detriti
esconder	cacher	hide	verstecken	esconder	nascondere
esconder, ocultar	cacher	conceal	verbergen, verhehlen	ocultar	nascondere
escorpión	scorpion	scorpion	Skorpion(m)	escorpião	scorpione
escribir	écrire	write	schreiben	escrever	scrivere
escritor, a	écrivain	writer	Schriftsteller(in f)m	escritor, a	scrittore, -trice
escritorio	bureau	desk	Schreibtisch(m)	secretária	scrivania
escritura	écriture	writing	Schrift(f)	escrita	scrittura
escrúpulo	scrupule	scruple	Skrupel(m)	escrúpulo	scrupolo
escrutinio	scrutin, vote	poll; ballot	Wahl(f), Abstimmung(f)	escrutínio	scrutinio
escuadra	équerre	square(set -)	Zeichendreieck(n)	esquadro	squadra
escuadrón	escadron	squadron	Schwadron; Eskadron(f)	esquadrão	squadrone; squadra
escuchar	écouter	listen(to)	zu = hören, horchen	escutar	ascoltare
escudriñar	scruter	scan, scrutinize	erforschen	perscrutar	scrutare
escuela	école	school	Schule(f)	escola	scuola
escuela(EGB)	collège	comprehensive(Jnr)	Oberschule(f)	escola preparatória	scuola media
escultura	sculpture	sculpture	Skulptur(f)	escultura	scultura
escupir	cracher	spit	spucken	cuspir	sputare
es decir	c'est-à-dire	that is(to say)	das heißt	quer dizer	cioè
ese, esa, esos(as)	ce, cette, ces	that, those	dieser, diese, dieses	este, esta, estes	quello, a; questo, a
ése, ésa, éso(s)	celui-là, celle-	that one	der(jenige); die( )	esse(a); aquele(a)	quello, quella
esencial	essentiel, le	essential	wesentlich	essencial	essenziale
esencial	essentiel	main thing(the)	Hauptsache(f)	essencial	essenziale
esfera	sphère	sphere	Sphäre(f)	esfera	sfera
esfera	cadran	dial	Zifferblatt(n)	mostrador	quadrante
esfuerzo	effort	effort	Anstrengung(f)	esforço	sforzo
esgrima	escrime	fencing	Fechten(n)	esgrima	scherma
esguince	entorse	sprain	Verrenkung(f)	entorse	storta
esguince	foulure	sprain	Verstauchung(f)	entorse	slogatura
esmalte	émail	enamel	Emaille(f), Glasur(f)	esmalte	smalto
esmeralda	émeraude	emerald	Smaragd(m)	esmeralda	smeraldo
esmoquin	smoking	dinner-jacket	Smoking(m)	smoking	smoking
esnobismo	snobisme	snobbery	Snobismus(m)	snobismo	snobismo
eso, aquello	cela, ça	that	das, jene(r, s)	isso, aquilo	ciò, questo, quello
esófago	oesophage	oesophagus	Speiseröhre(f)	esófago	esofago
esos, aquellos	ceux, celles, ces	these, those	diese	aqueles, aquelas	questi, e
espacial	spatial, e	space	Raum-	espacial	spaziale
espacio	espace	space, gap	Zwischenraum(m)	espaço	spazio
espacio	espace	space	Raum(m)	espaço	spazio
espacioso, a	spacieux, se	spacious	weiträumig	espaçoso, a	spazioso, a
espada	épée	sword	Schwert(n)	espada	spada
espalda	dos	back	Rücken(m)	costas	schiena
espantado, a	ahuri, e	stupefied	verdutzt	pasmado, a	attonito, a
espantar, asustar	effarer, effrayer	terrify	erschrecken	apavorar	sgomentare
espanto	frayeur	fright	Schreck(m), Angst(f)	temor	spavento
esparadrapo	sparadrap	plaster	Pflaster(n)	esparadrapo	cerotto
espasmo	spasme	spasm	Krampf(m)	espasmo	spasma
espátula	spatule	spatula	Spachtel(f)	espátula	spatola
especia	épice(s)	spice	Gewürz(n)	especiaria	spezie
especial	spécial, e	special	speziell, eigen	especial	speciale
especialidad	spécialité	speciality	Spezialität(f)	especialidade	specialità

S

Spanish	French	English	German	Portuguese	Italian
especialista	spécialiste	specialist	Spezialist(in f)m	especialista	specialista
especialista	spécialiste	expert, specialist	Fachmann(m)	especialista	specialista
especialmente	particulièrement	especially	besonders	especialmente	particolarmente
especie	espèce	species	Art(f)	espécie	specie
especie	espèce	kind, sort	Gattung(f), Art(f)	espécie	specie
especie, género	sorte, espèce	sort, kind, type	Sorte(f), Art(f)	espécie, género	specie, genere
especificar	spécifier	specify, state	spezifieren	especificar	specificare
específico, a	spécifique	specific	spezifisch	específico, a	specifico, a
espécimen	spécimen	specimen	Muster(n); Exemplar(n)	espécime	specimen
espectáculo	spectacle	show	Aufführung(f)	espectáculo	spettacolo
espectáculos	spectacles	entertainment	Unterhaltung(f)	espectáculos	spettacoli
espectador, a	spectateur, trice	spectator	Zuschauer(in f)m	espectador, a	spettatore, trice
especulación	spéculation	speculation	Spekulation(f)	especulação	speculazione
espejismo	mirage	mirage	Fata Morgana(f)	miragem	miraggio
espejo	miroir	mirror	Spiegel(m)	espelho	specchio
espeleología	spéléologie	pot-holing	Höhlenforschung(f)	espeleologia	speleologia
espera	attente	wait(ing)	Warten(n)	espera	attesa
esperanza	espoir	hope	Hoffnung(f)	esperança	speranza
esperar	attendre	wait(for)	warten	esperar	aspettare
esperar	attendre	expect	erwarten	esperar	aspettare
esperar, desear	espérer	hope	hoffen	esperar, desejar	sperare
esperar(se)	attendre à(s')	expect	rechnen, mit etwas	esperar	aspettarsi
espere(!)	attendez!	wait!	Moment bitte!	espere!	aspetti!
esperma	sperme	sperm	Sperma(n)	esperma	sperma
espeso, a	épais, se	thick	dick	espesso, a	spesso, a
espesor	épaisseur	thickness	Stärke(f), Dicke(f)	espessura	spessore
espía	espion, ne	spy	Spion(m), Spionin(f)	espião, espia	spia
espina	épine	thorn	Dorn(m); Stachel(m)	espinho	spina
espina	arête	fish-bone, bone	Gräte(f)	espinha	lisca
espionaje	espionnage	spying, espionage	Spionage(f)	espionagem	spionaggio
espiral	spirale	spiral	Spirale(f)	espiral	spirale
espiral	stérilet	coil	Spirale(f)	esterilete	spirale
espirar	expirer	breathe out	aus = atmen	expirar	espirare
espíritu	esprit	mind	Sinn(m)	espírito	mente
espiritual	spirituel, le	spiritual	geistreich	espiritual	spirituale
espíritus	esprit	spirit	Geist(m)	espírito	spirito
espléndido, a	splendide	splendid	glänzend	esplêndido, a	splendido, a
esponja	éponge	sponge	Schwamm(m)	esponja	spugna
esponjoso, a	spongieux, se	spongy	schwammig	esponjoso, a	spugnoso, a
espontáneo, a	spontané, e	spontaneous	spontan	espontâneo, a	spontaneo, a
esposa	épouse	wife(wives)	Gattin, Frau, Ehefrau f	esposa	sposa, consorte
esposas	menottes	handcuffs	Handschellen(f, pl)	algemas	manette
esposo	époux	husband	Gatte, Mann, Ehemann(m)	esposo	sposo, consorte
espuma	écume	foam, froth	Schaum(m), Gischt(f)	espuma	schiuma
espuma	mousse	froth, foam	Schaum(m)	espuma	schiuma
esqueleto	squelette	skeleton	Skelett(n)	esqueleto	scheletro
esquema	schéma	diagram	Schema(n)	esquema	schema
esquí	ski	ski	Ski(m)	esqui	sci
esquí acuático	ski nautique	water-skiing	Wasserski(m)	esqui aquático	sci nautico
esquiar	skier	ski	skifahren	esquiar	sciare
esquimal	esquimau	Eskimo	Eskimo(m)	esquimó	eschimese
esquina, rincón	coin	corner	Ecke(f)	canto, esquina	angolo
estabilidad	stabilité	stability	Stabilität(f)	estabilidade	stabilità
establecer	établir	establish	festsetzen, aufstellen	estabelecer	stabilire
establecerse	établir(s')	settle; set up	an = siedeln, sich	estabelecer-se	stabilirsi
establecimiento	établissement	establishment	Anstalt(f)	estabelecimento	stabilimento
estaca	pieu, poteau	stake, post	Pfahl(m)	estaca	palo, piolo
estaca	piquet	post, stake, peg	Pfahl(m)	estaca	picchetto
estación	gare	station	Bahnhof(m)	estação, gare	stazione
estación	saison	season	Jahreszeit(f)	estação	stagione
estación	station	station	Station(f)	estação	stazione
estación	station	resort	Erholungsort(m)	estação	stazione
estación(servicio)	station-service	service station	Tankstelle(f)	estação de serviço	stazione di servizio
estacionamiento	stationnement	parking	Parken(n)	estacionamento	sosta
estacionarse	stationner	park	parken	estacionar	stazionare
estadio	stade	stadium	Stadium(n)	estádio	stadio
estadística	statistique(s)	statistics	Statistik(f)	estatística	statistica
estado	état	state	Staat(m)	estado	stato

Spanish	French	English	German	Portuguese	Italian
estado(cuentas)	relevé(compte)	statement(bank)	Kontoauszug(m)	extracto(conta)	estratto conto
estafa, timo	escroquerie	swindle	Schwindel(m), Gaunerei	trapaça, burla	truffa, imbroglio
estafador	escroc	crook, swindler	Gauner(m)	gatuno, escroque	imbroglione
estallar, reventar	crever, éclater	burst	bersten	furar, rebentar	scoppiare
estallar	exploser	explode, blow up	explodieren	explodir	esplodere
estancia	séjour	stay	Aufenthalt(m)	estadia, estada	soggiorno
estanco	bureau de tabac	tobacconist's	Tabakladen(m)	estanco, tabacaria	tabaccheria
estanco, a	étanche	watertight(air-)	undurchlässig	estanque	stagno, a
estanque	étang	pond	Teich(m)	lago; tanque	stagno
estanque	bassin	pond	Bassin(n), Teich(m)	lago	bacino
estantería	étagère	shelf(-ves)	Regal(n)	prateleira	scaffale
estaño	étain	tin; pewter	Zinn(n)	estanho	stagno
estar	être	be	sein	estar	essere
estático, a	statique	static	statisch	estático, a	statico, a
estatua	statue	statue	Statue(f)	estátua	statua
estatuto	statut	status; statute	Status(m); Statut(n)	estatuto	statuto
este; esta; estos, as	ce, cette	this, that	dieser, diese	este, a; esse, a	questo, a; quello, a
éste; ésta; éstos	cet, cette	this, that	dieser, diese	este; esta; estes, as	questo, a; quello, a
éste; ésta	celui-ci, celle-	this one	diese(r, s)(hier)	este, esta	questo, questa
Este	Est	East	Osten(m)	Este, Leste	Est
estela	sillage	wake	Kielwasser(n)	esteira	scia
estepa	steppe	steppe	Steppe(f)	estepe	steppa
estéreo	stéréo	stereo	Stereo(f)	estereofonia	stereo
estéril	stérile	sterile	steril	estéril	sterile
estético, a	esthétique	aesthetic	ästhetisch	estético, a	estetico, a
estiércol	fumier	manure	Mist(m)	estrume	letame
estilo	style	style	Stil(m)	estilo	stile
estilográfica	stylo	pen, fountain-pen	Füller(m)	caneta	stilografica
estima	estime	esteem	Achtung(f)	estima	stima
estimación	estimation	estimate	Schätzung(f)	estimativa	stima, valutazione
estimular	stimuler	stimulate	reizen, an = regen	estimular	stimolare
estirar	étirer	stretch	aus = dehnen	esticar	stirare
estival	estival, e	summer	sommerlich	estival	estivo, a
esto	ceci	this	dies(es); das	isto	questo, ciò
estómago	estomac	stomach	Magen(m)	estômago	stomaco
estorbo	encombrement	congestion, jam	Gedränge(n)	engarrafamento	affollamento, ingorgo
estornudar	éternuer	sneeze	niesen	espirrar	starnutire
estos, as; esos, as	ces	these, those	diese(pl)	estes, as; esses, as	questi, e
éstos; ésos	ceux-ci, celles-	these; those	diese; jene	estes(as); esses(as)	questi; quelli
estrangulación	étranglement	strangling	Erwürgen(n)	estrangulamento	strangolamento
estrategia	stratégie	strategy	Strategie(f)	estratégia	strategia
estrechar	resserrer	narrow	verengen	estreitar	ristringere
estrechar(se)	rétrécir(se)	narrow	enger machen/werden	estreitar-se	restringersi
estrechar la mano	serrer la main	shake hands	Hand schütteln	apertar a mão	stringere la mano
estrecho, a	étroit, e	narrow	eng	estreito, a	stretto, a
estrecho	détroit	strait	Meerenge(f)	estreito	stretto
estrella	étoile	star	Stern(m)	estrela	stella
estrella; divo, a	vedette	star	Star(m)	vedeta, estrela	vedette; divo, a
estrellarse	écraser(s')	crash	ab = stürzen	esmagar-se	schiantare
estreñimiento	constipation	constipation	Verstopfung(f)	prisão de ventre	stitichezza
estribillo	refrain	refrain, chorus	Refrain(m)	refrão	ritornello
estricto, a	strict, e	strict	streng	estrito, a	stretto, a
estropear	abîmer	damage, spoil, ruin	beschädigen	estragar	sciupare, rovinare
estructura	structure	structure	Struktur(f)	estrutura	struttura
estuche	coffret	box, case	Schmuckkasten(m)	estojo	portagioie
estuche	étui	case	Etui(n)	estojo	astuccio
estudiante	étudiant, e	student	Student(in f)m	estudante	studente, -essa
estudiar	étudier	study	studieren	estudar	studiare
estudiar	étudier, examiner	investigate	prüfen, erforschen	estudar, examinar	studiare
estudio	étude	study; survey	Studie(f)	estudo	studio
estudio	apprentissage	learning	Lernen(n)	aprendizagem	tirocinio
estudio	studio	studio	Studio(n)	estúdio	studio
estudioso, a	studieux, se	studious	fleißig	estudioso, a	studioso, a
estufa	poêle	stove	Ofen(m)	fogão	stufa
estupefacto, a	stupéfait, e	amazed	verblüfft	estupefacto, a	stupefatto, a
estupendo, a	épatant, e	wonderful, super	großartig, fabelhaft	estupendo, a	straordinario, a
estupidez	bêtise	stupid thing(do a)	Dummheit(f)	asneira	sciocchezza
estúpido, a	stupide	stupid, silly	dumm	estúpido, a	stupido, a

Spanish	French	English	German	Portuguese	Italian
estupor	stupeur	stupor	Erstaunen(n)	estupefacção	stupore
etapa	étape	stage	Strecke(f)	etapa	tappa
eternidad	éternité	eternity	Ewigkeit(f)	eternidade	eternità
eterno, a	éternel, le	eternal	ewig	eterno, a	eterno, a
ético, a	éthique	ethical	ethisch	ético, a	etico, a
etiqueta	étiquette	label, tag	Schild(n)	rótulo	etichetta
étnico, a	ethnique	ethnic(al)	ethnisch	étnico, a	etnico, a
eufórico, a	euphorique	euphoric	euphorisch	eufórico, a	euforico, a
eutanasia	euthanasie	euthanasia	Euthanasie(f)	eutanásia	eutanasia
evacuar	évacuer	evacuate	räumen, leeren	evacuar	evacuare
evaluación	évaluation	assessment	Schätzung(f)	avaliação	valutazione
evaporación	évaporation	evaporation	Verdunstung(f)	evaporação	evaporazione
evasión	évasion	escape	Flucht(f)	evasão	evasione
eventual	éventuel, le	possible	möglich	eventual	eventuale
eventualidad	éventualité	contingency	Eventualität(f)	eventualidade	eventualità
evidencia, prueba	évidence, preuve	evidence, proof	Beweis(m)	evidência, prova	testimonianza, prova
evidente	évident, e	obvious, evident	offensichtlich	evidente	evidente
evitar	éviter	avoid	vermeiden	evitar	evitare
evocar	évoquer	evoke	wach = rufen, erinnern	evocar	evocare
evolución	évolution	evolution	Entwicklung(f)	evolução	evoluzione
evolucionar	évoluer	evolve	entwickeln, sich	evoluir	evolvere
ex, antiguo, a	ancien, ne	former	ehemalig	antigo, a	ex
exactamente	exactement	exactly	genau, richtig; gerade	exactamente	esattamente
exactitud	exactitude	accuracy	Genauigkeit(f)	exactidão	esattezza
exacto, a	exact, e	exact, right	genau, richtig	exacto, a	esatto, a
exacto, a	exact, e	accurate	genau; richtig	exacto, a	accurato, a
exacto, a	juste, exact, e	right	richtig	certo, a	giusto, a
exacto(es)	exact(c'est)	right(that 's)	stimmt!	exacto(é)	esatto(è)
exagerar	exagérer	exaggerate	übertreiben	exagerar	esagerare
examen	examen	examination, exam	Prüfung(f)	exame	esame
examen, chequeo	examen(médical)	examination	Untersuchung(f)	exame	esame
examinar	examiner	examine, inspect	untersuchen	examinar	esaminare
excavar	fouiller	excavate	aus = graben	escavar	scavare
excedente	excédent	surplus, excess	Überschuß(m)	excedente	eccedente
Excelencia(Su)	Excellence, Votre	Excellency(Your)	Exzellenz(f)	Excelência(Vossa)	Eccellenza(Sua)
excelente	excellent, e	excellent	vorzüglich	excelente	eccellente
excepción	exception	exception	Ausnahme(f)	excepção	eccezione
excepcional	exceptionnel, le	exceptional	außergewöhnlich	excepcional	eccezionale
excepto, salvo	excepté	except	außer	excepto	tranne
excepto	sauf	except	außer	salvo, excepto	salvo
excesivo, a	excessif, ive	excessive	übermäßig	excessivo, a	eccessivo, a
exceso	excès	excess	Übermaß(n)	excesso	eccesso
excitado, a	excité, e	worked up	gereizt	excitado, a	eccitato, a
excitado, a	énervé, e	edgy, worked up	erregt, nervös	enervado, a	nervoso, a
excitante	excitant, e	exciting	aufregend	excitante	eccitante
excitar	exciter	excite	auf = regen	excitar	eccitare
exclamar	exclamer(s')	exclaim	aus = rufen	exclamar	esclamare
excluir	exclure	exclude	aus = schließen	excluir	escludere
exclusiva(-ividad)	exclusivité	exclusive rights	Alleinvertrieb(m)	exclusividade	esclusività
exclusivo, a	exclusif, ive	exclusive	ausschließlich	exclusivo, a	esclusivo, a
excremento	excrément	excrement	Ausscheidung(f)	excremento	escremento
excursión	excursion	excursion	Ausflug(m)	excursão	gita, escursione
excusa, disculpa	excuse	excuse; apology	Entschuldigung(f)	desculpa	scusa
exhibición	exhibition	exhibition	Schau, Ausstellung(f)	exibição	esibizione
exigencia	exigence	demand, requirement	Forderung(f)	exigência	esigenza
exigir	exiger, réclamer	demand, require	fordern	exigir	esigere
exigir	exiger, demander	demand	verlangen, fordern	exigir, pedir	esigere, domandare
exiliado, a	exilé, e	exile	Verbannte(f, m)	exilado, a	esiliato, a
exilio	exil	exile	Verbannung(f)	exílio	esilio
existencia	existence	existence, life	Dasein(n)	existência	esistenza
existir	exister	exist	existieren	existir	esistere
éxito	succès	success(-es)	Erfolg(m)	sucesso, êxito	successo
éxito, logro	réussite	success(-es)	Erfolg(m)	êxito	riuscita
éxodo	exode	exodus	Massenauswanderung(f)	êxodo	esodo
exótico, a	exotique	exotic	exotisch	exótico, a	esotico, a
expansión	expansion	expansion	Ausdehnung(f)	expansão	espansione
expatriación	expatriation	expatriation	Vertreibung(f)	expatriação	espatrio
expatriarse	expatrier(s')	expatriate	aus = wandern	expatriar-se	espatriarse

| --- | --- | --- | --- | --- | --- |
expedición	expédition	expedition	Expedition(f)	expedição	spedizione
expediente	dossier	record, file	Akte(f)	processo	dossier
expedir	expédier	dispatch, send	verschicken	expedir	spedire
experiencia	expérience	experience	Erfahrung(f)	experiência	esperienza
experimentación	Experimentation	experimentation	Experimentieren(n)	experimentação	sperimentazione
experimental	expérimental, e	experimental	experimentell	experimental	sperimentale
experimento	expérience	experiment	Versuch(m)	experiência	esperimento
experto, a; perito, a	expert, e	expert	Experte(m), Expertin f	perito, a	esperto, a
expirar; vencer	expirer	expire	ab = laufen	expirar	scadere
expirar	expirer	die	verscheiden	expirar	spirare
explicación	explication	explanation	Erklärung(f)	explicação	spiegazione
explicar	expliquer	explain	erklären	explicar	spiegare
exploración	exploration	exploration	Erforschung(f)	exploração	esplorazione
explorador, a	explorateur	explorer	Forscher(in f)m	explorador, a	esploratore, trice
explorar	explorer	explore	erforschen	explorar	esplorare
explosión	explosion	explosion	Explosion(f)	explosão	esplosione
explotar	exploiter	exploit	aus = nutzen	explorar	sfruttare
exponer	étaler	spread(out)	aus = breiten	expor	stendere, spalmare
exportación	exportation	export(ing)	Export(m), Ausfuhr(f)	exportação	esportazione
exportar	exporter	export	exportieren	exportar	esportare
exposición	exposition	exhibition, show	Ausstellung(f)	exposição	esposizione, mostra
exposición	exposé	talk, commentary	Referat(n)	exposição	relazione; esposto
expositor, a	exposant, e	exhibitor	Aussteller(in f)m	expositor, a	espositore, trice
expresamente	exprès	purpose(on)	absichtlich	propósito(de)	apposta
expresar(se)	exprimer(s')	express oneself	aus = drücken, sich	exprimir-se	esprimersi
expresión	expression	expression	Ausdruck(m)	expressão	espressione
expulsar	expulser	expel, eject	aus = weisen	expulsar	espellere
éxtasis	extase	ecstasy	Entzückung(f)	êxtase	estasi
extender	étendre	extend, spread	aus = breiten	estender	stendere
extender(se)	étendre, agrandir	expand	aus = dehnen	estender	estendere
extenderse	étendre(s')	stretch	erstrecken, sich	estender-se	estendersi
extensión	extension	extension	Ausdehnung(f)	extensão	estensione
extensión, amplitud	étendue	extent	Umfang(m)	extensão	estensione, ampiezza
extenuado, a	exténué, e	exhausted	erschöpft	extenuado, a	spossato, a
exterior	extérieur	outside; exterior	Außenseite(f)	exterior	esterno
exterior	extérieur, e	foreign	Außen-	exterior	estero, a
exterior	extérieur, e	outside	äußer; Außen-	exterior	esteriore
externo, a	externe	external	äußerlich	externo, a	esterno, a
externo, a	extérieur, e	outer, outside	äußere	exterior; externo, a	esterno, a
extinción	extinction	extinction	Löschen(Aus-)(n)	extinção	estinzione
extintor	extincteur	extinguisher	Feuerlöscher(m)	extintor	estintore
extorsión	racket	racket(-eering)	Erpressung(f)	vigarice	racket
extracción	extraction	extraction	Kohlenförderung(f)	extracção	estrazione
extracción	extraction	extraction	Zahnziehen(n)	extracção	estrazione
extracto	relevé	statement	Aufstellung(f)machen	levantamento	estratto
extraer	extraire	extract	heraus = ziehen, ziehen	extrair	estrarre
extranjero, a	étranger, ère	foreigner	Ausländer(in f)m	estrangeiro, a	straniero, a
extranjero, a	étranger, ère	foreign	ausländisch	estrangeiro, a	estero, a
extranjero	étranger(l')	foreign country	Ausland(n)	estrangeiro	estero
extranjero(en el)	étranger(à l')	abroad	Ausland(im)	estrangeiro(ao)	estero(all')
extraño, a; raro, a	étrange	strange, odd	seltsam	estranho, a	strano, a
extraordinario, a	extraordinaire	extraordinary	außergewöhnlich	extraordinário, a	straordinario, a
extremidad	extrémité	extremity, end	Extremität(f)	extremidade	estremità
extremo, a	extrême	extreme	extrem	extremo, a	estremo, a
exuberante	luxuriant, e	luxuriant, lush	üppig	luxuriante	lussureggiante
eyectar, expulsar	éjecter	eject	aus = stoßen	expelir	espellere

S

433

F

Spanish	French	English	German	Portuguese	Italian
fábrica	usine	factory, plant	Fabrik(f)	fábrica	fabbrica
fabricación	fabrication	manufacture	Herstellung(f)	fabrico	fabbricazione
fabricante	fabricant, e	manufacturer	Hersteller(in f)m	fabricante	fabbricante
fabricar	fabriquer	manufacture, make	her = stellen	fabricar	fabbricare
fabuloso, a	fabuleux, se	fabulous	phantastisch	fabuloso, a	favoloso, a
fácil	facile	easy	leicht	fácil	facile
fácilmente	facilement	easily	leicht	fácilmente	facilmente
factor	facteur	factor	Faktor(m)	factor	fattore
factura	facture	invoice, bill	Rechnung(f)	factura	fattura
facultad	faculté	possibility	Fähigkeit(f)	faculdade	facoltà
facultad	faculté	Faculty	Fakultät(f)	faculdade	facoltà
facultativo, a	facultatif, ive	optional	wahlfrei, beliebig	facultativo, a	facoltativo, a
fachada	façade	front(age)	Fassade(f)	fachada	facciata
faisán	faisan	pheasant	Fasan(m)	faisão	fagiano
faja, tira	bande	band, strip	Streifen(m)	tira	striscia
faja	gaine	girdle	Korsett(n)	cinta elástica	guaina, corsetto
falda	jupe	skirt	Rock(m)	saia	gonna
falsificación	truquage	faking	Trickaufnahme(f)	falsificação	trucco
falsificar	falsifier	falsify	fälschen	falsificar	falsificare
falso, a	faux, fausse	wrong, false	falsch	falso, a	falso, a
falta, carencia	manque	lack, shortage	Mangel(m)	falta, carência	mancanza
falta, error	faute	mistake, error	Fehler(m), Irrtum(m)	falta, erro	fallo, errore
faltar	manquer	lack, be short of	fehlen	falta(ter)	mancare
falla	faille	break, fault	Spalte(f)	falha	faglia
fallar	rater	fail	mißlingen	falhar	mancare
fallecer	décéder	die	versterben, sterben	falecer	decedere
fallecimiento	décès	death	Tod(m)	falecimento	decesso
fallo	défaillance	failure, fault	Versagen(n)	falha	difetto
fama	renommée	fame	Ruhm(m)	fama	fama
familia	famille	family	Familie(f)	família	famiglia
familiar	familial, e	family	Familien-	familiar	familiare
familiar	familier, ière	familiar	familiär	familiar	familiare
famoso, a	fameux, se	excellent	großartig	famoso, a	ottimo, a
fanático, a	fanatique	fanatic(al)	fanatisch	fanático, a	fanatico, a
fantasía	fantaisie	fancy; fantasy	Spielerei(f)	fantasia	fantasia
fantasma	fantôme	ghost	Gespenst(n)	fantasma	fantasma
fantasma	fantasme	fantasy	Phantasievorstellung	fantasma	fantasia
fantástico, a	fantastique	fantastic	phantastisch	fantástico, a	fantastico, a
faringe	pharynx	pharynx	Rachen(m)	faringe	faringe
farmacéutico, a	pharmacien, ne	chemist, pharmacist	Apotheker(in f)m	farmacêutico, a	farmacista
farmacia	pharmacie	chemist's	Apotheke(f)	farmácia	farmacia
faro	phare	lighthouse	Leuchtturm(m)	farol	faro
faro(s)	phare(s)	headlight	Scheinwerfer(m)	faróis	fanale, faro(-ri)
fascinado, a	fasciné, e	fascinated	fasziniert	fascinado, a	affascinato, a
fascinante	fascinant, e	fascinating	faszinierend	fascinante	affascinante
fascista	fasciste	fascist	Faschist(in f)m	fascista	fascista
fase	phase	phase, stage	Phase(f)	fase	fase
fastidiar	embêter	bother, annoy	ärgern	aborrecer	infastidire
fastidio	agacement	irritation	Ärger(m)	irritação	irritazione
fatal	fatal, e	fatal	tödlich	fatal	fatale
fatalidad	fatalité	fatality, fate	Schicksal(n)	fatalidade	fatalità
fatigante	fatigant, e	tiring	anstrengend	cansativo, a	faticoso, a
fauna	faune	fauna	Fauna(f), Tierwelt(f)	fauna	fauna
favor	faveur	favour	Gunst(f)	favor	favore
favorable	favorable	favourable	günstig	favorável	favorevole
favorecer	favoriser	favour	begünstigen	favorecer	favorire
favorito, a	favori, ite	favourite	Favorit(in f)m	favorito, a	favorito, a
fe	foi	faith	Glaube(m)	fé	fede
febrero	février	February	Februar(m)	Fevereiro	febbraio
fecundación	fécondation	fertilization	Befruchtung(f)	fecundação	fecondazione
fecundidad	fécondité	fertility	Fruchtbarkeit(f)	fecundidade	fecondità

Spanish	French	English	German	Portuguese	Italian
fecha	date	date	Datum(n)	data	data
federación	fédération	federation	Verband(m)	federação	federazione
felicidad	bonheur	happiness	Glück(n)	felicidade	felicità
felicitar	féliciter	congratulate	gratulieren	felicitar	congratularsi
feliz	heureux, se	happy, glad	glücklich	feliz	felice
femenino, a	féminin, e	feminine	fraulich	feminino, a	femminile
femenino	féminin	feminine	weiblich	feminino	femminile
fenómeno	phénomène	phenomenon(-mena)	Phänomen(n)	fenómeno	fenomeno
feo, a	laid, e; moche	ugly, hideous	häßlich, gräßlich	feio, a	brutto, a
feria	foire	fair	Messe(f)	feira	fiera
fermentar	fermenter	ferment	gären	fermentar	fermentare
feroz	féroce	ferocious, fierce	wild, furchtbar	feroz	feroce
feroz	farouche	wild	wild	arisco, a	selvatico, a
ferretería	quincaillerie	ironmonger's	Eisenwarenhandlung(f)	loja de ferragens	ferramenta
ferrocarril	chemin de fer	railway	Eisenbahn(f)	caminho de ferro	ferrovia
fértil	fertile	fertile	fruchtbar	fértil	fertile
festín	festin	feast, banquet	Festmahl(n)	festim, banquete	festino
festival	festival	festival	Festspiel(n)	festival	festival
festivo(día)	férié(jour)	public holiday	Feiertag(m)	feriado(dia)	festivo(giorno)
feto	foetus	foetus	Fötus(m)	feto	feto
fiable, seguro, a	fiable	reliable	zuverlässig	seguro, a	sicuro, a; affidabile
fibra	fibre	fibre	Faser(f)	fibra	fibra
ficción	fiction	fiction	Fiktion(f)	ficção	finzione
ficha	fiche	card	Karteikarte(f)	ficha	scheda, cartella
ficha	jeton	counter, token	Spielmarke(f)	ficha	gettone
ficha(damas)	pion(dames)	draught	Stein(m)(Spiel)	peça, tábula(dama)	pedina(dama)
fichero	fichier	card-index	Kartei(f)	ficheiro	schedario
fiebre	fièvre	fever, temperature	Fieber(n)	febre	febbre
fiel	fidèle	faithful	treu	fiel	fedele
fiesta	fête	celebration	Feier(f)	festa	festa
figura	figure	figure	Figur(f)	figura	figura
fijación	fixation	fixing, fixation	Befestigung(f)	fixação	fissazione
fijar	fixer	fix, attach	befestigen	fixar	fissare
fijo, a	fixe	fixed	fest	fixo, a	fisso, a
fila	file	lane	Spur(f)	fila	fila, corsia
fila	file	queue, line	Schlange(f)	fila, bicha	fila, coda
filamento	filament	filament	Faser(f), Faden(m)	filamento	filamento
filial, sucursal	filiale	subsidiary	Filiale(f)	filial, sucursal	filiale
filosofía	philosophie	philosophy	Philosophie(f)	filosofia	filosofia
filtro	filtre	filter	Filter(m)	filtro	filtro
fin	fin	end	Ende(n)	fim	fine
final	final, e	final	letzte, Schluß-	final	finale
financiación	financement	financing	Finanzierung(f)	financiamento	finanziamento
financiar	financer	finance	finanzieren	financiar	finanziare
financiero, a	financier, ière	financial	finanziell	financeiro, a	finanziario, a
finanza	finance	finance	Finanzwelt, Finanzen	finança	finanza
fin de semana	week-end	weekend	Wochenende(n)	fim de semana	fine settimana
fino, a	fin, e	fine, thin	fein, dünn	fino, a	fine, sottile
firma	firme	firm	Firma(f)	firma	firma, ditta, azienda
firma	signature	signature	Unterschrift(f)	assinatura	firma
firmar	signer	sign	unterschreiben	assinar	firmare
firme	ferme	firm	fest	firme	fermo, a; solido, a
firmes(!)	garde-à-vous!	attention!	Stillgestanden!	sentido!	attenti!
firmeza	fermeté	firmness	Entschlossenheit(f)	firmeza	fermezza
fiscal	fiscal, e	fiscal, tax	fiskalisch, Steuer-	fiscal	fiscale
fiscalidad	fiscalité	tax system	Steuerwesen(n)	fiscalidade	fiscalità
fisco	fisc	Inland Revenue	Fiskus(m), Finanzamt	fisco	fisco
físico, a	physique	physical	physisch	físico, a	fisico, a
físico, a	physicien, ne	physicist	Physiker(in f)m	físico, a	fisico, a
física	physique	physics	Physik(f)	física	fisica
físico	physique	physique	Äußere(n), Aussehen(n)	físico	fisico
fisión	fission	fission	Spaltung(f)(Atom)	fissão	fissione
fisionomía	physionomie	physiognomy	Gesichtsausdruck(m)	fisionomia	fisionomia
fisura, grieta	fissure, fente	crack, fissure	Riß(m), Spalte(f)	fissura; fenda	fessura, crepa
flash	flash	flash	Blitz(m)	flash	flash
flauta	flûte	flute	Flöte(f)	flauta	flauto
flecha	flèche	arrow	Pfeil(m)	flecha, seta	freccia
flete	fret	freight	Fracht(f)	frete	nolo, carico

S

Spanish	French	English	German	Portuguese	Italian
flexibilidad	souplesse	suppleness	Biegsamkeit(f)	flexibilidade	flessibilità
flexible	flexible	flexibel	flexibel	flexível	flessibile
flexible	souple	supple; flexible	biegsam	maleável	flessibile
flojo, a	lâche, détendu, e	loose, slack	locker, lose	frouxo, a	allentato, a
flojo, a	desserré, e	slack	schlaff, lose	frouxo, a	allentato, a
flojo, a	faible	dim	matt	fraco, a	debole
flor	fleur	flower	Blume(f)	flor	fiore
flora	flore	flora	Flora(f), Pflanzenwelt	flora	flora
florista	fleuriste	florist	Blumenhändler(in f)m	florista	fioraio
flota	flotte	fleet	Flotte(f)	frota	flotta
flotar	flotter	float	schwimmen, treiben	flutuar	galleggiare
fluctuación	fluctuation	fluctuation	Schwanken(n)	flutuação	fluttuazione
fluido	fluide	fluid	Flüssigkeit(f)	fluido	fluido
flujo	flux	flow	Fluß(m), Strömung(f)	fluxo	flusso
foca	phoque	seal	Seehund(m)	foca	foca
fofo, a	mou, molle	lethargic	schlaff	mole; fraco, a	molle; fiacco, a
folklore	folklore	folklore	Folklore(f)	folclore	folclore
folleto	prospectus	leaflet	Flugblatt(n)	prospecto	prospetto
follón, lío	pagaille	mess	Durcheinander(n)	desordem	caos, confusione
fondo	fond	bottom; back	Boden(m), Grund(m)	fundo	fondo
fondos	fonds	funds	Fonds(m), Kapital(n)	fundos, capital	fondi
fonético, a	phonétique	phonetic	phonetisch	fonético, a	fonetico, a
fontanero	plombier	plumber	Klempner(m)	canalizador	idraulico
forma	forme	shape, form	Form(f), Aussehen(n)	forma	forma
forma(en)	forme	form	Verfassung(f)	forma	forma
formación	formation	formation	Entstehung(f)	formação	formazione
formación	formation	training	Ausbildung(f)	formação	formazione
formalidad	formalité	formality	Formalität(f)	formalidade	formalità
formar	former	form	bilden, formen	formar	formare
formato, tamaño	format	format, size	Format(n)	formato	formato
formidable	formidable	tremendous	großartig	formidável	formidabile
fórmula	formule	formula	Formel(f)	fórmula	formula
formulario	formulaire	form	Formular(n), Vordruck	formulário	modulo, formulario
forraje	fourrage	fodder	Futter(n)	forragem	foraggio
fortificante	fortifiant	tonic	Stärkungsmittel(n)	fortificante	ricostituente
fortuna	fortune	fortune	Vermögen(n)	fortuna	fortuna
forzar	forcer	force	zwingen	forçar	forzare
fosa, hoyo	fosse	pit	Grube(f)	fossa	fossa; buca
fósil	fossile	fossil	Fossil(n)	fóssil	fossile
foto	photo	photo(graph)	Foto(n)	fotografia	foto, fotografia
fotografía	photographie	photography	Fotografie(f)	fotografia	fotografia
fotografiar	photographier	take a photo	fotografieren	fotografar	fotografare
fracasar	échouer	fail	scheitern	falhar	fallire
fracaso, revés	échec	failure	Mißerfolg(m)	fracasso	smacco, sconfitta
fracción	fraction	fraction	Bruchteil(m)	fracção	frazione
fractura	fracture	fracture	Bruch(m)	fractura	frattura
frágil	fragile	fragile	zerbrechlich	frágil	fragile
fragmento	fragment	fragment	Fragment(n)	fragmento	frammento
franco, a	franc, che	frank	offen, ehrlich	franco, a	franco, a; sincero, a
franquear	affranchir	stamp	frankieren, freimachen	franquear	affrancare
frasco	flacon	bottle(small)	Fläschchen(n)	frasco	boccetta
frase	phrase	sentence	Satz(m)	frase	frase
fraternidad	fraternité	brotherhood	Brüderlichkeit(f)	fraternidade	fraternità
fraude	fraude	fraud	Betrug(m)	fraude	frode
fraude(fiscal)	fraude(fiscale)	tax evasion	Steuerhinterziehung f	fraude(fiscal)	frode(fiscale)
frecuencia	fréquence	frequency	Frequenz(f)	frequência	frequenza
frecuente	fréquent, e	frequent	häufig	frequente	frequente
frecuentemente	souvent	often	oft	frequentemente	spesso
fregadero	évier	sink	Spülbecken(n)	pia, banca	acquaio, lavandino
freír	frire	fry	braten	fritar	friggere
frenar	freiner	brake	bremsen	travar	frenare
freno	frein	brake	Bremse(f)	travão	freno
frente	front	forehead	Stirn(f)	testa	fronte
frente, delantera	devant	front, fore	Front(f)	frente(a)	davanti
fresa	fraise	strawberry	Erdbeere(f)	morango	fragola
fresco, a	frais, fraîche	fresh	frisch	fresco, a	fresco, a
frigorífico, a	frigorifique	refrigerating	Kühl-; kalt, kühl	frigorífico, a	frigorifero, a
frigorífico	frigo, frigidaire	fridge	Kühlschrank(m)	frigorífico	frigorifero

Spanish	French	English	German	Portuguese	Italian
frío, a	froid, e	cold	kalt	frio, a	freddo, a
frío(tener)	froid(avoir)	cold(to be)	frieren	frio(ter)	freddo(avere)
frívolo, a	frivole	frivolous	frivol, leichtsinnig	frívolo, a	frivolo, a
frontera	frontière	border, frontier	Grenze(f)	fronteira	confine, frontiera
frontera, límite	frontière, limite	boundary	Grenze(f)	fronteira, limite	frontiera, limite
frotamiento	frottement	friction, rubbing	Reibung(f)	fricção	strofinio
frotar	frotter	rub	reiben	esfregar	strofinare, sfregare
frustración	frustration	frustration	Enttäuschung(f)	frustração	frustrazione
fruta	fruit(s)	fruit	Frucht(f)	fruta	frutto; frutta
fuego	feu	fire	Feuer(n)	fogo	fuoco
fuel-oil	mazout	fuel oil	Heizöl(n)	fuel, óleo	nafta
fuente	fontaine	fountain	Springbrunnen(m)	fonte	fontana
fuente	source	spring	Quelle(f)	fonte, nascente	sorgente
fuente, origen	source, origine	source	Ursprung(m)	fonte, origem	fonte, origine
fuente, plato	plat	dish, plate	Schüssel(f)	travessa	vassoio, piatto
fuera, afuera	dehors	outside, outdoors	draußen	fora	fuori
fuera borda	hors-bord	speed-boat	Außenbordmotor(m)	fora de borda	fuoribordo
fuera de	hors de	out of	außer(+dat)	fora de	fuori, fuori di
fuerte	fort, e	strong	stark	forte	forte
fuerte; alto, a	fort, e	loud	laut	forte; alto, a	forte; alto, a
fuerza	force	strength	Stärke(f), Kraft(f)	força	forza
fuerza	force	force	Gewalt(f); Kraft(f)	força	forza
fugitivo, a	fugitif, ive	fugitive	flüchtig	fugitivo, a	fuggitivo, a
fular, pañuelo	foulard	scarf	Seidentuch, Halstuch	lenço, cachecol	foulard
fumadores	fumeurs	smokers	Raucher(m)	fumadores	fumatore, trice
fumar	fumer	smoke	rauchen	fumar	fumare
función	fonction	function	Funktion(f)	função	funzione
función	fonction	function	Stellung(f), Amt(n)	função	funzione
funcionamiento	fonctionnement	functioning	Betrieb(m)	funcionamento	funzionamento
funcionar	fonctionner	function, work, run	funktionieren	funcionar	funzionare
funcionar(hacer)	marcher(faire)	operate	bedienen	funcionar(fazer)	funzionare(fare)
funcionario, a	fonctionnaire	state employee	Beamter(m), Beamtin(f)	funcionário, a	impiegato statale
funcionario, a	fonctionnaire	civil servant	Beamte(r)m, Beamtin(f)	funcionário, a	funzionario, a
funda, estuche	gaine	sheath	Hülle(f)	invólucro	guaina, astuccio
funda	housse	cover	Bezug(m)	cobertura	fodera
fundador, a	fondateur, trice	founder	Gründer(in f)m	fundador, a	fondatore, trice
fundamental	fondamental, e	fundamental	fundamental	fundamental	fondamentale
fundar	fonder	found	gründen	fundar	fondare
fundir	fondre	melt	schmelzen	fundir	fondere
funerales	funérailles	funeral	Begräbnis(n)	funeral	funerale
furioso, a	furieux, se	furious	wütend	furioso, a	furioso, a
furor	fureur	fury	Wut(f)	furor	furore
furúnculo	furoncle	boil	Furunkel(m)	furúnculo	foruncolo
fusil	fusil	shot-gun, rifle	Gewehr(n)	espingarda	fucile
fusión	fusion	fusion, melting	Schmelzen(n)(Ver-)	fusão	fusione
fusión	fusion	merger	Vereinigung(f), Fusion	fusão	fusione, alleanza
fútbol	football	football, soccer	Fußball(m)	futebol	calcio
futuro, a	futur, e	future	zukünftig	futuro, a	futuro, a
futuro	futur	future	Zukunft(f)	futuro	futuro

G

Spanish	French	English	German	Portuguese	Italian
gabardina	imperméable	rain-coat, mac	Regenmantel(m)	gabardina	impermeabile
gabinete	cabinet(pol.)	cabinet	Kabinett(n)	gabinete	gabinetto
gafas	lunettes	glasses	Brille(f)	óculos	occhiali
galante	galant, e	gallant	galant	galante	galante
galardonado, a	lauréat, e	prize-winner	Preisträger(in f)m	galardoado, a	premiato, a
galaxia	galaxie	galaxy	Galaxie(f)	galáxia	galassia
galería	galerie	arcade	Passage(f)	galeria	galleria

S

Spanish	French	English	German	Portuguese	Italian
galería	galerie	gallery	Galerie, Ausstellung	galeria	galleria
galón	galon	stripe	Galone(f)	galão	gallone, grado
galope	galop	gallop	Galopp(m)	galope	galoppo
galleta	biscuit	biscuit	Keks(m)	biscoito	biscotto
gallina	poule	hen	Huhn(n)	galinha	gallina
gallo	coq	cock	Hahn(m)	galo	gallo
gamba, camarón	crevette	prawn, shrimp	Krabbe(f)	camarão	gamberetto
ganadería	élevage	breeding; rearing	Zucht(f); Aufzucht(f)	criação de gado	allevamento
ganado	bétail, bestiaux	cattle	Vieh(n)	gado	bestiame
ganado	troupeau	herd	Herde(f)	manada	branco
ganancia	gain, bénéfice	earnings	Gewinn(m)	lucro	lucro, profitto
ganancia	profit	profit, benefit	Gewinn(m)	lucro	profitto, guadagno
ganar	gagner	win	gewinnen	ganhar	vincere
ganar	gagner	earn; win	verdienen	ganhar	guadagnare
ganar	gagner	save	sparen	ganhar	guadagnare
ganas	envie	desire	Lust(f)	vontade	voglia
gancho	crochet	hook	Haken(m)	gancho	gancio, uncino
ganglio	ganglion	ganglion, gland	Ganglien(pl.)	gânglio	ganglio
gangrena	gangrène	gangrene	Brand(m), Wundbrand(m)	gangrena	cancrena
gángster	gangster	gangster	Gangster(m)	gangster	gangster
garaje, garage	garage	garage	Garage(f)	garagem	garage
garajista	garagiste	garage mechanic	Autoschlosser(m)	garagista	garagista
garantía	garantie	guarantee; warranty	Garantie(f)	garantia	garanzia
garantizar	garantir	guarantee, warrant	gewährleisten	garantir	garantire
garganta	gorge	throat	Hals(m)	garganta	gola
garra	griffe	claw	Kralle(f), Klaue(f)	garra	artiglio
gas	gaz	gas	Gas(n)	gás	gas
gaseosa	eau gazeuse	sparkling water	Sprudelwasser(n)	água gaseificada	acqua gassata
gaseoso, a	gazeux, se	gaseous	gasförmig	gasoso, a	gassoso, a
gaseoso, a	gazeux, se	fizzy, sparkling	sprudelnd; Sprudel-	gasoso, a	gassato, a
gasoil	gas-oil	diesel oil	Diesel(n), Dieselöl(n)	gasóleo	gasolio
gasolina	essence	petrol	Benzin(n)	gasolina	benzina
gasolinera	poste d'essence	petrol station	Tankstelle(f)	bomba de gasolina	distributore(benzina)
gastar	dépenser	spend	aus = geben	gastar	spendere
gasto	dépense	expenditure	Ausgabe(f)	despesa, gasto	spesa
gastos	frais	expenses	Kosten(pl.)	gastos, despesas	spese(le)
gastos(escolares)	frais(scolarité)	fee	Kosten(pl.)	despesas	spese
gástrico, a	gastrique	gastric	Magen-	gástrico, a	gastrico, a
gastronomía	gastronomie	gastronomy	Gastronomie(f)	gastronomia	gastronomia
gatillo	gâchette	trigger	Abzug(m)	gatilho	grilletto
gato, a	chat, te	cat	Kater(m), Katze(f)	gato, a	gatto, a
gato	cric	jack	Wagenheber(m)	macaco	cric, cricco
gato, cric	vérin, cric	jack	Winde(f)	macaco	martinetto, binda
gavilán	épervier	sparrow-hawk	Habicht(m)	gavião	sparviere
gaviota	mouette	seagull	Möve(f)	gaivota	gabbiano
gaviota	goéland	gull	Silbermöwe(f)	gaivota	gabbiano
gemelo, a	jumeau, jumelle	twin	Zwilling(m)	gémeo, a	gemello, a
gemelos	jumelles	binoculars	Fernglas(n)	binóculos	binocolo
gemir	gémir	moan	stöhnen	gemer	gemere
genealogía	généalogie	genealogy	Genealogie(f)	genealogia	genealogia
generación	génération	generation	Generation(f)	geração	generazione
generador	générateur	generator	Generator(m)	gerador	generatore
general, e	général, e	general	allgemein, generell	geral	generale
general(en)	général(en)	usually, in general	allgemeinen(im)	geral(em)	genere(in)
general	général	general	General(m)	general	generale
generalmente	habituellement	usually	üblich, gewöhnlich	habitualmente	abitualmente
género	genre	kind, sort	Art(f), Sorte(f)	género	genere
generoso, a	généreux, se	generous	freigebig	generoso, a	generoso, a
genética	génétique	genetics	Genetik(f)	genética	genetica
genial	génial, e	brilliant	genial	genial	geniale
genio	génie	genius	Genie(n)	génio	genio
genital	génital, e	genital	Genital-	genital	genitale
genocidio	génocide	genocide	Völkermord(m)	genocídio	genocidio
gente	gens	people	Leute(pl.)	gente, pessoas	gente(la)
gentil, amable	gentil, le	kind, nice	nett	gentil, amável	gentile
genuino, a	authentique	genuine	echt	autêntico, a	genuino, a
geografía	géographie	geography	Erdkunde(f)	geografia	geografia
geología	géologie	geology	Geologie(f)	geologia	geologia

Spanish	French	English	German	Portuguese	Italian
geometría	géométrie	geometry	Geometrie(f)	geometria	geometria
gerente	gérant, e	manager	Geschäftsführer(m)	gerente	gerente, gestore
gerente, director, a	gérant, e	manager	Verwalter(in f)m	gerente, director, a	gestore, gerente
germen	germe	germ, seed	Keim(m)	germe	germe
germen, grano	germe	seed	Keim(m)	germe	germoglio
gestión	gestion	management	Verwaltung(f)	gestão	gestione
gesto	geste	gesture	Geste(f)	gesto	gesto
gestor, a	gestionnaire	manager	Verwalter(in f)m	gestor, a	gestore
gigante	géant, e	giant	riesig, gigantisch	gigante	gigante
gigantesco, a	gigantesque	gigantic, huge	gigantisch, riesig	gigantesco, a	gigantesco, a
gimnasia	gymnastique	gymnastics	Gymnastik(f)	ginástica	ginnastica
ginecología	gynécologie	gynaecology	Gynäkologie(f)	ginecologia	ginecologia
girar	tourner	turn	drehen	girar; rodar	girare
girar	tourner	turn	wenden	virar	svoltare, girare
girar	pivoter	revolve, pivot	schwenken	girar; rodar	girare, ruotare
girar(hacer)	tourner(faire)	rotate, revolve	drehen	girar(fazer)	roteare
giro postal	mandat-lettre	postal order	Postanweisung(f)	vale postal	vaglia(postale)
glaciar	glacier	glacier	Gletscher(m)	glaciar	ghiacciaio
glándula	glande	gland	Drüse(f)	glândula	ghiandola
global	global, e	global, overall	Gesamt-; pauschal	global	globale
global; convenido, a	forfaitaire	inclusive	pauschal	preço fixo(a)	forfettario, a
globo	globe	globe	Globus(m)	globo	globo
globo	ballon	balloon	Heißluftballon(m)	balão	pallone
glóbulo	globule(sang)	corpuscle, globule	Blutkörperchen(n)	glóbulo	globulo
gloria	gloire	glory	Ruhm(m)	glória	gloria
glorieta	rond-point	roundabout	Kreisverkehr(m)	rotunda	rotonda, rotatoria
glorioso, a	glorieux, se	glorious	glorreich	glorioso, a	glorioso, a
glosario	glossaire	glossary	Glossar(n)	glossário	glossario
glucosa	glucose	glucose	Traubenzucker(m)	glicose	glucosio
gobernador	gouverneur	governor	Gouverneur(m)	governador	governatore
gobernar	gouverner	govern	regieren	governar	governare
gobierno	gouvernement	government	Regierung(f)	governo	governo
gol	but	goal	Tor(n)	golo	goal, rete
golf	golf	golf	Golf(n)	golfe	golf
golf	golf(terrain)	golf course	Golfplatz(m)	campo de golfe	golf
golfo	golfe	gulf	Golf(m)	golfo	golfo
golondrina	hirondelle	swallow	Schwalbe(f)	andorinha	rondine
golosina	friandise	delicacy	Nascherei(f)	guloseima	dolciume
goloso, a	gourmand, e	greedy	erpicht auf	guloso, a	goloso, a
golpe	coup	knock, blow	Schlag(m)	golpe	colpo
golpe(darse un)	cogner(se)	knock	stoßen, sich	chocar com	sbattere
golpear	frapper	hit, knock, strike	schlagen, prügeln	bater	picchiare
golpear	battre	beat, hit	schlagen	golpear	picchiare
gollete	goulot	neck(bottle)	Hals(m)(Flaschen)	gargalo	collo
goma	gomme	rubber	Radiergummi(m)	borracha	gomma
goma elástica	élastique	rubber band	Gummiband(n)	elástico	elastico
gordo; grasa	graisse	fat	Fett(n)	gordura	grasso
gorila	gorille	gorilla	Gorilla(m)	gorila	gorilla
gorra	casquette	cap	Mütze(f)	boné	berretto
gorrión	moineau	sparrow	Spatz(m)	pardal	passero
gorro	bonnet	cap, hat	Mütze(f)	barrete	berretto, cuffia
gota	goutte	drop	Tropfen(m)	gota	goccia
gozar	jouir	enjoy	genießen	gozar	godere
grabación	enregistrement	recording	Aufnahme(f)	gravação	registrazione
grabado	gravure	engraving	Gravieren(n)	gravura	incisione
grabado	gravure	print	Gravur(f)	gravura	stampa
grabar	enregistrer	record	auf = nehmen	gravar	registrare
gracia	grâce	grace	Gnade(f); Anmut(f)	graça	grazia
gracias	merci	thank you, thanks	danke	obrigado, a	grazie
gracias a	grâce à	thanks to	dank	graças a	grazie a
gracioso, a	drôle	funny	lustig	divertido, a	buffo, a
gracioso, a	gracieux, se	graceful	graziös	gracioso, a	grazioso, a
grado	degré	degree	Grad(m)	grau	grado
grado	grade	rank	Rang(m)	grau	grado
graduación	degré(alcool)	proof(per cent)	Prozent(n)	grau	grado
graduado, a	diplômé, e	qualified	staatlich geprüft	diplomado, a	diplomato, a
gráfico, a	graphique	graph	Graphik(f)	gráfico	grafico
grafología	graphologie	graphology	Graphologie(f)	grafologia	grafologia

S

Spanish	French	English	German	Portuguese	Italian
gramática	grammaire	grammar	Grammatik(f)	gramática	grammatica
gran, grande	grand, e	large, big	weit	grande	grande, ampio, a
gran, grande	grand, e	big	groß	grande	grande
gran, grande	grand, e	great	groß	grande	grand(e)
granada	grenade	grenade	Handgranate(f)	granada	bomba a mano
grande	gros, se	big	geräumig	grande	grosso, a
granero	grange	barn	Scheune(f)	celeiro	fienile
granizo	grêle	hail	Hagel(m)	granizo	grandine
granja	ferme	farm	Bauernhof(m)	quinta	fattoria
granjero, a	fermier, ière	farmer	Bauer(m), Bäuerin(f)	caseiro, a	contadino, a
grano	grain	grain	Korn(n)	grão	chicco, grano
grano	grain(café)	bean(coffee-)	Bohne(Kaffee-)(f)	grão	chicco
grano	bouton	spot, pimple	Pickel(m)	borbulha	brufolo, foruncolo
granuja; pillo, a	crapule	crook, villain	Lump(m)	crápula	canaglia
granuja, bandido	truand, e	crook	Ganove(m), Gauner(m)	bandido	teppista
gránulo	granule	granule	Körnchen(n)	grânulo	granulo
grasa	graisse	grease	Schmiere(f)	massa	grasso
grasiento, a	graisseux, se	fatty, greasy	schmierig, fettig	gorduroso, a	unto, a
graso, a	gras, se	fat(ty), greasy	fett	gordo, a	grasso, a
gratis; gratuito, a	gratuit, e	free	kostenlos	grátis; gratuito, a	gratuito, a; gratis
gratitud	gratitude	gratitude	Dankbarkeit(f)	gratidão	gratitudine
grava	gravier	gravel	Kies(m)	cascalho	ghiaia
grave	grave	grave, serious	schwer; ernst	grave	grave
gravedad	gravité	gravity	Schwere(f)	gravidade	gravità
grieta	crevasse	crevice	Spalte(f)	fenda	crepa, crepaccio
grieta	fente	split; slot; slit	Spalt(m)	fenda	fessura
grieta	gerçure	chap(ped)	Riß(m), Hautriß(m)	greta	screpolatura
grifo	robinet	tap; stop-cock	Wasserhahn(m), Hahn(m)	torneira	rubinetto
gripe	grippe	flu, influenza	Grippe(f)	gripe	influenza
gris	gris, e	grey	grau	cinzento, a	grigio, a
gritar	crier	shout, scream	schreien	gritar	gridare
grito	cri	shout	Schrei(m)	grito	grido
grosero, a	grossier, ière	rude; crude	grob	grosseiro, a	grossolano, a
grúa	grue	crane	Kran(m)	grua	gru
grueso, a; grande	gros, se	big	groß	grande	grosso, a; grande
grueso, a; gordo, a	gros, se	fat	dick	gordo, a	grosso, a
gruñon, a	grognon, ne	grumpy	quengelig	rabugento, a	brontolone
grupo	groupe	group	Gruppe(f)	grupo	gruppo
guante	gant	glove	Handschuh(m)	luva	guanto
guarda	garde	guard	Wächter(m), Hüter(m)	guarda	guardia
guardar	garder	keep	behalten	guardar	tenere
guardar	garder	guard, watch over	hüten, bewachen	guardar, vigiar	custodire, guardare
guardia	garde	guard	Wache(f)	guarda	guardia, custodia
guardia civil	gendarme	policeman(-men)	Polizist(in f)m	guarda-republicano	carabiniere
guardián, ana	gardien, ne	keeper, caretaker	Wärter(in f)m	guarda	custode, guardia
guardián, guarda	gardien, ne; garde	guard; keeper	Wächter(in f)m	guarda	guardiano, a; custode
guarnecer	garnir	garnish	garnieren	guarnecer	guarnire
guerra	guerre	war	Krieg(m)	guerra	guerra
guerrilla	guérilla	guerilla	Guerilla(f)	guerrilha	guerriglia
guía	guide	guide	Führer(in f)m	guia	guida
guía	guide	guide-book	Führer(Reise-)(m)	guia	guida
guiar	guider	guide	führen	guiar	guidare
guiar, conducir	mener, conduire	lead	führen	levar, conduzir	condurre
guión	scénario	script(film -)	Drehbuch(n)	guião	scenario
guionista	scénariste	script-writer	Drehbuchautor(in f)m	cenarista	scenarista
guirnalda	guirlande	garland	Girlande(f)	grinalda	ghirlanda
guitarra	guitare	guitar	Gitarre(f)	guitarra	chitarra
gusano	ver	worm	Wurm(m)	verme	verme
gustar	aimer	enjoy	mögen; gern mögen	gostar	piacere
gustar(le)	aimer	like	gern haben	gostar(de)	piacere, amare
gustar, agradar	plaire	please; like	gefallen(jdm)	agradar	piacere
gusto	goût	taste	Geschmack(m)	gosto	gusto, sapore
gusto(dar)	plaisir(faire)	please	Freude machen	gosto(dar)	piacere(fare)
gusto(estar a)	aise(être à l')	ease(be at)	wohl fühlen, sich	vontade(estar à)	agio(essere a)

H

Spanish	French	English	German	Portuguese	Italian
haber; tener	avoir	have	haben	haver; ter	avere
hábil; diestro, a	habile	clever, skilful	geschickt	hábil; destro, a	abile
habilidad	habileté	ability, skill	Geschicklichkeit(f)	habilidade	abilità
habitación	chambre d'hôtel	room, hotel room	Hotelzimmer(n)	quarto	camera
habitación(1 cama)	chambre à 1 lit	single room	Einzelzimmer(n)	quarto individual	camera singola
habitante	habitant, e	inhabitant	Einwohner(in f)m	habitante	abitante
hábito	accoutumance	habituation	Gewöhnung(f)	habituação	abitudine
habitual	habituel, le	usual	gewöhnlich	habitual	abituale
habla(el)	parler(le)	speech	Sprechen(n); Sprache f	fala(a)	parlare(il)
hablar	parler	speak, talk	sprechen, reden	falar	parlare
hablar con	parler à	talk to, speak to	reden(mit jdm)	falar com	parlare a
hace	il y a	ago	vor	há	fa
hacer	faire	do, make	tun, machen	fazer	fare
hacer	faire	make, do	machen, tun	fazer	fare
hacer punto	tricoter	knit	stricken	tricotar	lavorare a maglia
hacer rabiar	taquiner	tease	necken	arreliar	stuzzicare
hacia	vers	to, towards	nach, zu	para	verso
hacia	vers	towards, to	gegen, in Richtung	direcção a(em)	verso
hacha	hache	axe	Axt(f)	machado	ascia
hada	fée	fairy	Fee(f)	fada	fata
halagar	flatter	flatter	schmeicheln	lisonjear	adulare
hamaca	hamac	hammock	Hängematte(f)	rede	amaca
hamaca	chaise longue	deck-chair	Liegestuhl(m)	preguiceira	sdraio
hambre(tener)	faim(avoir)	hunger(hungry be)	Hunger(m)(haben)	fome(ter)	fame(aver)
hambre	famine	famine	Hungersnot(f)	fome	fame, carestia
hambriento, a	affamé, e	starving, hungry	hungrig	esfomeado, a	affamato, a
hampa	pègre	underworld	Unterwelt(f)	súcia, ladroagem	teppa, malviventi
hándicap	handicap	handicap	Handikap(n)	handicap	handicap
harén	harem	harem	Harem(m)	harém	harem
harina	farine	flour	Mehl(n)	farinha	farina
hasta	jusqu'à	until, till	bis	até	fino a, sino a
hasta	jusqu'à	as far as	bis	até	fino
hasta luego	au revoir	good bye, bye-bye	auf Wiedersehen	até logo, adeus!	arrivederci
hasta pronto	à bientôt	see you soon, bye	bis bald	até breve; até já	a presto
hay	il y a	there is, there are	es gibt	há	c'è; ci sono
haz	faisceau	beam	Strahl(m)(Licht)	foco	fascio
hazaña	exploit	exploit	Glanzleistung(f)	proeza, feito	impresa, prodezza
he aquí	voici	here is; here are	hier(ist/sind)	aqui está	ecco
hebilla	boucle	buckle	Schnalle(f)	fivela; argola	fibbia
hectárea	hectare	hectare	Hektar(m)	hectare	ettaro
hecho	fait	fact	Tatsache(f)	facto	fatto
hechura	forme	design, style	Schnitt(m)	corte, design	taglio, stile
hedor, peste	puanteur	stench, stink	Gestank(m)	fedor	puzza, fetore
helado	glace	ice cream	Eis(n)	gelado	gelato
helado, a	glacé, e; gelé, e	icy	eisig	gelado, a	gelato, a; ghiacciato
heladura	gélure	frostbite	Erfrierung(f)	frieira	congelamento
helar	geler	freeze	frieren	gelar	gelare
helecho	fougère	fern	Farn(-kraut n)m	feto	felce
hélice	hélice	propeller	Propeller(m)	hélice	elica
helicóptero	hélicoptère	helicopter	Hubschrauber(m)	helicóptero	elicottero
hembra	femelle	female	Weibchen(n)	fêmea	femmina
hemisferio	hémisphère	hemisphere	Halbkreis(m)	hémisfério	emisfero
hemorragia	hémorragie	haemorrhage	Blutsturz(m)	hemorragia	emorragia
hemorroides	hémorroïde(s)	haemorrhoids	Hämorrhoiden(f, pl)	hemorróidas	emorroide
hepatitis	hépatite	hepatitis	Hepatitis, Gelbsucht f	hepatite	epatite
heredero, a	héritier, ière	heir, heiress	Erbe(m), Erbin(f)	herdeiro, a	erede
hereditario, a	héréditaire	hereditary	erblich	hereditário, a	ereditario, a
herencia	hérédité	heredity	Vererbung(f)	hereditariedade	ereditarietà
herencia	héritage	inheritance, legacy	Erbschaft(f)	herança	eredità
herida	blessure	injury, wound	Verletzung(f)	ferida	ferita
herir	blesser	injure, wound	verletzen	ferir	ferire

S

Spanish	French	English	German	Portuguese	Italian
herir(se)	blesser(se)	injured(to be)	verletzen, sich	ferir-se	ferirsi
hermana	soeur	sister	Schwester(f)	irmã	sorella
hermano	frère	brother	Bruder(m)	irmão	fratello
hermético, a	hermétique	hermetic	hermetisch	hermético, a	ermetico, a
hermoso, a; bello, a	beau, belle	beautiful, fine	schön	belo, a; bonito, a	bello, a
hermosa	belle	beautiful, fine	schön, e, er, es	bonita, bela	bella
hernia	hernie	hernia	Bruch(m)	hérnia	ernia
héroe, heroína	héros, héroïne	hero, heroine	Held(m), Heldin(f)	herói, heroína	eroe, eroina
heroico, a	héroïque	heroic	heldenhaft	heróico, a	eroico, a
heroína	héroïne	heroin	Heroin(n)	heroína	eroina
herramienta	outil	tool	Werkzeug(n)	ferramenta	attrezzo
herramientas	outillage	tools, equipment	Werkzeug(n)	ferramentas	attrezzatura
herrumbre	rouille	rust	Rost(m)	ferrugem	ruggine
hervidor	bouilloire	kettle	Wasserkessel(m)	chaleira	bollitore
hervir	bouillir	boil	kochen	ferver	bollire
heterosexual	hétérosexuel, le	heterosexual	heterosexuell	heterossexual	eterosessuale
híbrido, a	hybride	hybrid	zwitterhaft	híbrido, a	ibrido, a
hidráulico, a	hydraulique	hydraulic	hydraulisch	hidráulico, a	idraulico, a
hidrógeno	hydrogène	hydrogen	Wasserstoff(m)	hidrogénio	idrogeno
hielo	glace	ice	Eis(n)	gelo	ghiaccio
hiena	hyène	hyena	Hyäne(f)	hiena	iena
hierba, yerba	herbe	grass	Gras(n)	erva	erba
hierbas	herbe(s)	herb(s)	Kraut(n), Kräuter(pl.)	erva	erbe(aromatiche)
hierro	fer	iron	Eisen(n)	ferro	ferro
hígado	foie	liver	Leber(f)	fígado	fegato
higiene	hygiène	hygiene	Hygiene(f)	higiene	igiene
higiénico, a	hygiénique	hygienic	hygienisch	higiénico, a	igienico, a
hija	fille	daughter	Tochter(f)	filha	figlia
hijo	fils	son	Sohn(m)	filho	figlio
hilera, fila	rangée	row	Reihe(f)	fileira, renque	fila
hilo	fil	thread	Faden(m)	fio	filo
himno	hymne	hymn	Hymne(f)	hino	inno
hinchar	enfler	swell	an = schwellen	inchar	gonfiare
hipertensión	hypertension	blood pressure	Bluthochdruck(m)	hipertensão	ipertensione
hipnosis	hypnose	hypnosis	Hypnose(f)	hipnose	ipnosi
hipnotismo	hypnotisme	hypnotism	Hypnotismus(m)	hipnotismo	ipnotismo
hipocresía	hypocrisie	hypocrisy	Heuchelei(f)	hipocrisia	ipocrisia
hipócrita	hypocrite	hypocrite	Heuchler(in f)m	hipócrita	ipocrita
hipopótamo	hippopotame	hippopotamus	Nilpferd(n)	hipopótamo	ippopotamo
hipoteca	hypothèque	mortgage	Hypothek(f)	hipoteca	ipoteca
hipótesis	hypothèse	hypothesis(-es)	Hypothese(f)	hipótese	ipotesi
hippy, jipi	hippie, y	hippy	Hippie(m)	hippie	capellone, hippy
hirviente	bouillant, e	boiling	kochend	fervente	bollente
histérico, a	hystérique	hysteric(al)	hysterisch	histérico, a	isterico, a
historia	histoire	story	Geschichte(f)	história	storia
historia	histoire	history	Geschichte(f)	História	storia
historiador	historien	historian	Geschichtschreiber(m)	historiador	storico
histórico, a	historique	historic(al)	historisch	histórico, a	storico, a
hocico	museau	muzzle	Schnauze(f)	focinho	muso
hocico	gueule	mouth	Maul(n)	goela, garganta	muso
hockey	hockey	hockey	Hockeyspiel(n)	hóquei	hockey
hogar	foyer	home	Heim(n)	lar	focolare
hogar, chimenea	foyer, âtre	fire-place, hearth	Feuerstelle(f), Herd m	lareira	focolare
hoja	feuille	leaf(leaves)	Blatt(n)	folha	foglia
hoja	feuille	sheet	Blatt(n)	folha	foglio
hoja	lame	blade	Schneide(f)	lâmina	lama
hola(!)	bonjour!	good morning!/aft-	guten Morgen!/-Tag	bom dia!	buongiorno!
hola(!)	bonjour!	good afternoon!	guten Tag!	bom dia!	buona sera!
hola(!)	salut!	hi!, hello!	Hallo!; tschüs!, tschüß	olá!	ciao!
holgazán, a	fainéant, e	lazy	faul	preguiçoso, a	fannullone, a
hombre	homme	man(men)	Mann(m), Mensch(m)	homem	uomo; uomini
hombro	épaule	shoulder	Schulter(f)	ombro	spalla
homenaje	hommage	homage, tribute	Huldigung(f); Ehrung f	homenagem	omaggio
homeopatía	homéopathie	homoeopathy	Homöopathie(f)	homeopatia	omeopatia
homicida	meurtrier, ière	murderer	Mörder(in f)m	assassino, a	omicida
homicidio	homicide	murder, homicide	Totschlag(m)	homicídio	omicidio
homogéneo, a	homogène	homogeneous	homogen	homogéneo, a	omogeneo, a
homologación	homologation	certification	Zulassung(f)	homologação	omologazione

Spanish	French	English	German	Portuguese	Italian
homónimo, a	homonyme	homonym	Homonym(n)	homónimo, a	omonimo, a
homosexual	homosexuel, le	homosexual	homosexuell	homossexual	omosessuale
honor	honneur	honour	Ehre(f)	honra	onore
honorable	honorable	honourable	ehrwürdig	honroso, a	onorabile
honorarios	honoraires	fee	Honorar(n)	honorários	onorario
honrado, a	honnête	honest	ehrlich	honesto, a	onesto, a
hora	heure	hour; time	Stunde(f); Zeit(f)	hora	ora
horario(s)	horaire(s)	timetable	Fahrplan(m)	horário	orario
horca	fourche	pitchfork, fork	Gabel(f)(Heu-; Mist-)	forcado	forca
horizontal	horizontal, e	horizontal	waagerecht	horizontal	orizzontale
horizonte	horizon	horizon, sky-line	Horizont(m)	horizonte	orizzonte
hormiga	fourmi	ant	Ameise(f)	formiga	formica
hormigón	béton	concrete	Beton(m)	betão	calcestruzzo
hormiguear	grouiller	crawl with	wimmeln	pulular	brulicare
hormona	hormone	hormone	Hormon(m)	hormona	ormone
hornillo	réchaud	stove	Kocher(m)	fogão	fornello
horno	four	oven	Ofen(m)	forno	forno
horóscopo	horoscope	horoscope	Horoskop(n)	horóscopo	oroscopo
horrendo, a	affreux, se	awful	schrecklich	horrível	spaventoso, a
horrible	horrible	horrible	grausig	horrível	orribile, orrendo, a
horror	horreur	horror	Grausen(n)	horror	orrore
horroroso, a	épouvantable	dreadful	entsetzlich	horroroso, a	spaventoso, a
horticultura	horticulture	horticulture	Gartenbau(m)	horticultura	orticultura
hospicio	hospice	hospice; home	Hospiz(n)	hospício, asilo	ospizio
hospital	hôpital	hospital	Krankenhaus(n)	hospital	ospedale
hospitalidad	hospitalité	hospitality	Gastfreundlichkeit(f)	hospitalidade	ospitalità
hostelería	hôtellerie	hotel trade	Hotelwesen(n)	hotelaria	alberghiera(indust-)
hostil	hostile	hostile	feindlich	hostil	ostile
hotel	hôtel	hotel	Hotel(n)	hotel	albergo, hotel
hoy	aujourd'hui	today	heute	hoje	oggi
hoyo	trou	pit, hole	Grube(f)	cova	buca
hueco, a	creux, se	hollow	hohl	oco, a	vuoto, a; cavo, a
huelga	grève	strike	Streik(m)	greve	sciopero
huella, rastro	trace	trace, track	Spur(f)	traço; vestígio	traccia
huella	empreinte	print	Abdruck(m)	impressão; marca	impronta
huérfano, a	orphelin, e	orphan	Waise(f, m)	órfão, órfã	orfano, a
huerto	jardin	garden	Gemüsegarten(m)	horta	orto
hueso	os	bone	Knochen(m)	osso	osso
hueso	noyau	stone	Kern(m)	caroço	nocciolo
huésped	pensionnaire	lodger	Untermieter(in f)m	hóspede	ospite
huésped, a	hôte	guest	Gast(m)	hóspede, a	ospite
huevo	oeuf	egg	Ei(n)	ovo	uovo(a)
huída	fuite	flight, escape	Flucht(f)	fuga	fuga
huir	fuir	run away, flee	fliehen	fugir	fuggire
huir	enfuir(s')	run away	fliehen	fugir	fuggire
humanidad	humanité	humanity	Menschheit(f)	humanidade	umanità
humano, a	humain, e	human	menschlich	humano, a	umano, a
humedad	humidité	humidity	Feuchtigkeit(f)	humidade	umidità
húmedo, a	humide	damp, humid, moist	feucht	húmido, a	umido, a
humillar	humilier	humiliate	erniedrigen	humilhar	umiliare
humo	fumée	smoke	Rauch(m)	fumo	fumo
humo	fumée	smoke, fumes	Rauch(m)	fumo	smog, fumo
humor	humeur	mood	Laune(f)	humor	umore
humor	humour	humour	Humor(m)	humor	umorismo
humorístico, a	humoristique	humorous	humoristisch	humorístico, a	umoristico, a
hundir	couler, enfoncer	sink	sinken, versenken	afundar	affondare
hundirse	effondrer(s')	collapse	zusammen = brechen	desabar	crollare
huracán	ouragan	hurricane	Orkan(m)	furacão	uragano

S

I

Spanish	French	English	German	Portuguese	Italian
iceberg	iceberg	iceberg	Eisberg(m)	iceberg	iceberg
ictericia	jaunisse	jaundice	Gelbsucht(f)	ictericia	itterizia
idea	idée	idea	Idee(f)	ideia	idea
ideal	idéal, e	ideal	ideal	ideal	ideale
ideal	idéal	ideal	Ideal(n)	ideal	ideale
idéntico, a	identique	identical	identisch	idêntico, a	identico, a
identidad	identité	identity	Identität(f)	identidade	identità
identificar	identifier	identify	identifizieren	identificar	identificare
ideología	idéologie	ideology	Ideologie(f)	ideologia	ideologia
idioma, lengua	langue	language	Sprache(f)	língua, idioma	lingua
idiota; tonto, a	idiot, e	idiotic, stupid	idiotisch, dumm	idiota	idiota; stupido, a
idiota	idiot, e	idiot, fool	Idiot(m), Dummkopf(m)	idiota	idiota; scemo, a
idiotez	idiotie	stupidity	Dummheit(f)	idiotice, asneira	idiozia
ídolo	idole	idol	Idol(n)	ídolo	idolo
iglesia	église	church(-es)	Kirche(f)	igreja	chiesa
iglú	igloo	igloo	Iglu(n)	iglu	igloo
ignorancia	ignorance	ignorance	Unwissenheit(f)	ignorância	ignoranza
ignorar	ignorer	ignorant of(be)	nicht wissen	ignorar	ignorare
igual	égal, e	equal	gleich	igual	uguale
igual	pareil, le	same, similar, like	gleich, wie	igual	uguale, pari
igualdad	égalité	equality	Gleichheit(f)	igualdade	uguaglianza
igualmente	également, aussi	too, also, as well	ebenfalls, auch	igualmente	ugualmente
ilegal	illégal, e	illegal	illegal	ilegal	illegale
ilegítimo, a	illégitime	illegitimate	unehelich	ilegítimo, a	illegittimo, a
ilógico, a	illogique	illogical	unlogisch	ilógico, a	illogico, a
iluminación	éclairage	lighting	Beleuchtung(f)	iluminação	illuminazione
iluminado, a	illuminé, e	illuminated	erleuchtet	iluminado, a	illuminato, a
iluminar	éclairer	light; illuminate	beleuchten	iluminar	illuminare
ilusión	illusion	illusion	Illusion(f)	ilusão	illusione
ilustración	illustration	illustration	Illustration(f)	ilustração	illustrazione
ilustrado, a	illustré, e	illustrated	illustriert	ilustrado, a	illustrato, a
ilustre	illustre	illustrious	berühmt	ilustre	illustre
imagen	image	image, picture	Bild(n)	imagem	immagine
imagen	image	picture	Bild(n)	gravura	illustrazione
imaginación	imagination	imagination	Einbildung(f)	imaginação	immaginazione
imaginar	imaginer	imagine	vor = stellen, sich	imaginar	immaginare
imaginario, a	imaginaire	imaginary	eingebildet	imaginário, a	immaginario, a
imaginarse	imaginer(s')	imagine	ein = bilden, sich	julgar	immaginarsi
imán	aimant	magnet	Magnet(m)	íman	calamita
imbécil	imbécile	fool, idiot	Idiot(in f)m	imbecil; parvo, a	imbecille
imitación	imitation	imitation	Nachahmung(f)	imitação	imitazione
imitar	imiter	imitate	nach = ahmen	imitar	imitare
impaciencia	impatience	impatience	Ungeduld(f)	impaciência	impazienza
impaciente	impatient, e	impatient	ungeduldig	impaciente	impaziente
impacto	impact	impact	Stoß(m)	impacto	impatto
impacto	impact	impact	Einfluß(m)	impacto	impatto
impar	impair	odd	ungerade	ímpar	dispari
imparcial	impartial, e	impartial	unparteiisch	imparcial	imparziale
impedir	empêcher	prevent	verhindern	impedir	impedire
imperativo, a	impératif, ive	imperative, urgent	bindend, zwingend	imperativo, a	imperativo, a
imperfección	imperfection	imperfection	Unvollkommenheit(f)	imperfeição	imperfezione
imperialismo	impérialisme	imperialism	Imperialismus(m)	imperialismo	imperialismo
imperio	empire	empire	Reich(n)	império	impero
impermeable	imperméable	water-proof	wasserdicht	impermeável	impermeabile
impertinente	impertinent, e	impertinent	unverschämt	impertinente	impertinente
impetuoso, a	impétueux, se	impetuous	ungestüm, stürmisch	impetuoso, a	impetuoso, a
implantación	implantation	setting up(of)	Niederlassung	implantação	impianto
implantar	implanter	establish, set up	etablieren, gründen	implantar	impiantare
implicación	implication	implication	Verwicklung(f)	implicação	implicazione
implicar	impliquer	involve	verwickeln	implicar	implicare
implicar	impliquer	imply	bedeuten; an = deuten	implicar	implicare

Spanish	French	English	German	Portuguese	Italian
implicarse	mêler de(se)	interfere	ein = mischen, sich	envolver-se	immischiare(-rsi)
implorar	implorer	implore, beg	an = flehen	implorar	implorare
imponer	imposer	impose	auf = zwingen	impor	imporre
imponerse	imposer(s')	impose oneself on	auf = drängen, sich	impor-se	imporsi
impopular	impopulaire	unpopular	unbeliebt	impopular	impopolare
importación	importation	import; importing	Einfuhr(f)	importação	importazione
importancia	importance	importance	Bedeutung(f)	importância	importanza
importante	important, e	important	wichtig	importante	importante
importar	importer	import	ein = führen	importar	importare
importe	montant	amount	Betrag(m)	montante	ammontare
imposible	impossible	impossible	unmöglich	impossível	impossibile
impotente	impuissant, e	powerless	machtlos	impotente	impotente
impregnar	imprégner	impregnate	imprägnieren	impregnar	impregnare
imprenta	imprimerie	printing works	Druckerei(f)	tipografia	tipografia
impresión	impression	impression	Eindruck(m)	impressão	impressione
impresión	impression	printing	Druck(m)	impressão	stampa
impresionante	impressionnant, e	impressive	beeindruckend	impressionante	impressionante
impresionar	impressionner	impress	beeindrucken	impressionar	impressionare
impreso	imprimé	printed form	Formular(n)	impresso	stampato
imprevisto, a	imprévu, e	unexpected	unvorhergesehen	imprevisto, a	imprevisto, a
imprimir	imprimer	print	drucken	imprimir	stampare
improvisar	improviser	improvise	improvisieren	improvisar	improvvisare
imprudencia	imprudence	imprudence	Unvorsichtigkeit(f)	imprudência	imprudenza
imprudente	imprudent, e	careless	unvorsichtig	imprudente	imprudente
impuesto	impôt	tax	Steuer(f)	imposto	tassa
impuesto, tasa	redevance	tax; royalty	Gebühr(f)	taxa	cànone
impugnar, objetar	contester	contest	bestreiten	contestar	contestare
impulso	impulsion	impulse	Impuls(m)	impulso	impulso
impulso	élan	spring, bound	Anlauf(m), Schwung(m)	impulso	slancio
impune	impuni, e	unpunished	unbestraft	impune	impunito, a
impureza	impureté	impurity	Unreinheit(f)	impureza	impurità
inaccesible	inaccessible	inaccessible	unerreichbar	inacessível	inaccessibile
inactivo, a	inactif, ive	inactive	untätig, inaktiv	inactivo, a	inattivo, a
inadaptado, a	inadapté, e	unsuitable	ungeeignet	inadaptado, a	inadatto, a
inadmisible	inadmissible	inadmissible	unzulässig	inadmissível	inammissibile
inalterado, a	inchangé, e	unchanged	unverändert	inalterado, a	immutato, a
inanimado, a	inanimé, e	lifeless	unbelebt, leblos	inanimado, a	inanimato, a
inapto, a	inapte	unsuited, unfit	ungeeignet	inapto, a	inabile
inauguración	inauguration	inauguration	Einweihung(f)	inauguração	inaugurazione
inaugurar	inaugurer	inaugurate	ein = weihen	inaugurar	inaugurare
incandescente	incandescent, e	incandescent	glühend	incandescente	incandescente
incansable	infatigable	tireless	unermüdlich	infatigável	instancabile
incapaz	incapable	incapable, unable	unfähig, untauglich	incapaz	incapace
incendio	incendie	fire	Brand(m)	incêndio	incendio
incesto	inceste	incest	Inzucht(f)	incesto	incesto
incidente	incident	incident	Zwischenfall(m)	incidente	incidente
incinerar	incinérer	incinerate	ein = äschern	incinerar	incenerire
incitar	inciter	incite	an = regen	incitar	incitare
inclinación	inclinaison	slant, incline	Neigung(f), Gefälle(n)	inclinação	inclinazione
inclinación	tendance	trend, tendency	Neigung(f)	inclinação	inclinazione
inclinar	incliner	incline, tilt	neigen	inclinar	inclinare
inclinar	pencher	tilt, lean	neigen	inclinar	inclinare
inclinarse	pencher(se)	bend, lean	bücken, sich	inclinar-se	chinarsi
incluido, a	inclus, e	included	inklusiv	incluso, a	incluso, a
incluir	inclure	include	ein = schließen	incluir	includere
incoloro, a	incolore	colourless	farblos	incolor	incolore
incomodar	incommoder	bother	stören	incomodar	incomodare
incompatible	incompatible	incompatible	unvereinbar	incompatível	incompatibile
incompetencia	incompétence	incompetence	Inkompetenz(f)	incompetência	incompetenza
incompleto, a	incomplet, ète	incomplete	unvollständig	incompleto, a	incompleto, a
inconsciente	inconscient, e	unconscious	unbewußt	inconsciente	incosciente
inconveniente	inconvénient	disadvantage	Nachteil(m)	inconveniente	inconveniente
incorporación	incorporation	incorporation	Eingliederung(f)	incorporação	incorporazione
incorporar	incorporer	incorporate	ein = verleiben	incorporar	incorporare
incorrecto, a	incorrect, e	incorrect, wrong	unrichtig, falsch	incorrecto, a	scorretto, a
increíble	incroyable	unbelievable	unglaublich	incrível	incredibile
increíble	impensable	unthinkable	undenkbar	impensável	impensabile
incrementar	accroître	increase	zu = nehmen	aumentar	accrescere

S

Spanish	French	English	German	Portuguese	Italian
incremento	augmentation	increment	Zunahme(f)	incremento	incremento
incriminar	incriminer	incriminate	beschuldigen	incriminar	incriminare
inculpado, a	inculpé, e	accused(the)	Angeklagte(f, m)	acusado, a	imputato, a
inculpar, acusar	inculper	charge, accuse	beschuldigen	inculpar, acusar	incolpare, accusare
incurable	incurable	incurable	unheilbar	incurável	incurabile
incursión	incursion	incursion	Überfall(m)	incursão	incursione
indecente	indécent, e	indecent	unanständig	indecente	indecente
indefinido, a	indéfini, e	indefinite	unbestimmt	indefinido, a	indefinito, a
indemnidad	indemnité	compensation	Entschädigung(f)	indemnização	risarcimento
indemnizar	indemniser	compensate	entschädigen	indemnizar	indennizzare
indemnizar	dédommager	compensate	entschädigen	indemnizar	indennizzare
independencia	indépendance	independence	Unabhängigkeit(f)	independência	indipendenza
independiente	indépendant, e	independent	unabhängig	independente	indipendente
indicador	indicateur	indicator	Anzeiger(m)	indicador	indicatore
indicación	indication	indication	Angabe(f), Hinweis(m)	indicação	indicazione
indicar	indiquer	indicate, show	an = deuten, zeigen	indicar	indicare
índice	indice	index	Index m(Preisindex m)	índice	indice
índice	index	index	Index(m)	índice	indice
indicio	indice	indication, sign	Anzeichen(n)	indício	indizio
indiferente	indifférent, e	indifferent	gleichgültig	indiferente	indifferente
indígena	indigène	native, indigenous	Eingeborene(f, m)	indígena	indigeno, a
indigesto, a	indigeste	indigestible	unverdaulich	indigesto, a	indigesto, a
indignación	indignation	indignation	Empörung(f)	indignação	indignazione
indigno, a	indigne	unworthy	unwürdig	indigno, a	indegno, a
indirecto, a	indirect, e	indirect	indirekt	indirecto, a	indiretto, a
indisciplinado, a	dissipé, e	unruly	unaufmerksam	indisciplinado, a	indisciplinato, a
indiscreción	indiscrétion	indiscretion	Indiskretion(f)	indiscrição	indiscrezione
indiscutible	incontestable	incontestable	unbestreitbar	incontestável	incontestabile
indispensable	indispensable	indispensable	unentbehrlich	indispensável	indispensabile
individual	individuel, le	individual	individuell	individual	individuale
individuo	individu	individual	Individuum(n)	indivíduo	individuo
indoloro, a	indolore	painless	schmerzlos	indolor	indolore
inducir	induire	induce	veranlassen	induzir	indurre
indulgencia	indulgence	indulgence	Nachsicht(f)	indulgência	indulgenza
industria	industrie	industry	Industrie(f)	indústria	industria
industria editor-	édition	publishing	Verlagswesen(n)	indústria livro	edizione
industrial	industriel, le	industrial	industriell	industrial	industriale
industrial	industriel	industrialist	Industrielle(m)	industrial	industriale
inédito, a	inédit, e	unpublished	unveröffentlicht	inédito, a	inedito, a
ineficaz	inefficace	inefficient	unwirksam, unfähig	ineficaz	inefficace
inercia	inertie	inertia	Trägheit(f)	inércia	inerzia
inerte	inerte	inert	regunglos	inerte	inerte
inesperado, a	inespéré, e	unexpected	unerwartet, unverhofft	inesperado, a	insperato, a
inestable	instable	unstable	unbeständig	instável	instabile
inexacto, a	inexact, e	inexact, inaccurate	ungenau	inexacto, a	inesatto, a
inexistente	inexistant, e	non-existent	nicht existierend	inexistente	inesistente
infalible	infaillible	infallible	unfehlbar	infalível	infallibile
infame	infâme	vile, infamous	niederträchtig	infame	infame
infancia	enfance	childhood	Kindheit(f)	infância	infanzia
infantil	infantile	infantile, child	Kinder-, kindisch	infantil	infantile
infarto	infarctus	coronary	Infarkt(m)	enfarte	infarto
infección	infection	infection	Infektion(f)	infecção	infezione
infeliz, triste	malheureux, se	unhappy, sorrowful	betrübt, unglücklich	infeliz, triste	infelice, triste
inferior	inférieur, e	inferior	minderwertig	inferior	inferiore
inferior	inférieur, e	lower	untere(r)	inferior	inferiore
inferior(parte)	dessous	lower part	Unterteil(n)	baixo(parte de)	sotto, disotto
infernal	infernal, e	infernal	Höllen-; höllisch	infernal	infernale
infiel	infidèle	unfaithful	untreu	infiel	infedele
infierno	enfer	hell	Hölle(f)	inferno	inferno
infiltración	infiltration	infiltration	Einsickern(n)	infiltração	infiltrazione
infinitivo	infinitif	infinitive	Infinitiv(m)	infinitivo	infinito
infinito, a	infini, e	infinite	unendlich	infinito, a	infinito, a
inflación	inflation	inflation	Inflation(f)	inflação	inflazione
inflamable	inflammable	inflammable	brennbar	inflamável	infiammabile
inflar	gonfler	inflate, blow up	auf = blasen	inchar, encher	gonfiare
inflexible	inflexible	inflexible	starr	inflexível	inflessibile
infligir	infliger	inflict	auf = erlegen	infligir	infliggere
influencia	influence	influence	Einfluß(m)	influência	influenza

Spanish	French	English	German	Portuguese	Italian
influyente	influent, e	influential	einflußreich	influente	influente
información	information	information	Information(f)	informação	informazione
información	renseignement	information	Auskunft(f)	informação	informazione
informar	informer	inform	informieren	informar	informare
informar(se)	renseigner(se)	inquire	erkundigen, sich	informar-se	informare(-arsi)
informarse	informer(s')	inquire	erkundigen, sich	informar-se	informarsi
informática	informatique	data processing	Informatik(f)	informática	informatica
informe	rapport	report	Bericht(m)	relatório	rapporto, relazione
informe, acta	compte rendu	report, minutes	Bericht(m)	relatório, acta	resoconto
infracción	infraction	offence, violation	Verstoß(m)	infracção	infrazione
ingeniería	ingénierie	engineering	Ingenieurkunst(f)	engenharia	ingegneria
ingeniero, a	ingénieur	engineer	Ingenieur(in f)m	engenheiro, a	ingegnere
ingenioso, a	ingénieux, se	ingenious	sinnreich	engenhoso, a	ingegnoso, a
ingenuo, a	naïf, ïve	naïve	naiv	ingénuo, a	ingenuo, a
ingerencia	ingérence	interference	Einmischung(f)	ingerência	ingerenza
ingrato, a	ingrat, e	ungrateful	undankbar	ingrato, a	ingrato, a
ingresar, meterse	engager(s')	join, enter	bei = treten	aderir, ligar-se	impegnarsi
ingresar	verser	pay(in)	ein = zahlen	pagar	versare
ingresos	recette	receipts; takings	Einnahmen(f, pl)	receita	incasso
inhalar	inhaler, respirer	inhale	ein = atmen	inalar	inalare
inhumano, a	inhumain, e	inhuman	unmenschlich	desumano, a	inumano, a
iniciación	initiation	initiation	Einführung(f)	iniciação	iniziazione
inicial	initial, e	initial	anfänglich; Anfangs-	inicial	iniziale
iniciar	déclencher	trigger off	aus = lösen	desencadear	scattare, attivare
iniciativa	initiative	initiative	Initiative(f)	iniciativa	iniziativa
inimaginable	inimaginable	inconceivable	undenkbar	inimaginável	inimmaginabile
ininflamable	ininflammable	fire-proof	unbrennbar	prova de fogo(à)	ininfiammabile
injerto	greffe	graft	Veredelung; Pfropfen	enxerto	innesto
injuria	injure	insult	Beleidigung(f)	injúria	ingiuria
injusticia	injustice	injustice	Ungerechtigkeit(f)	injustiça	ingiustizia
inmediatamente	immédiatement	immediately	sofort	imediatamente	immediatamente
inmediato, a	immédiat, e	immediate	unverzüglich	imediato, a	immediato, a
inmenso, a	immense	immense, vast	unendlich groß	imenso, a	immenso, a
inmersión	immersion	immersion	Versenkung(f)	imersão	immersione
inmigración	immigration	immigration	Einwanderung(f)	imigração	immigrazione
inmigrado, a	immigré, e	immigrant	Einwanderer(in f)m	imigrante	immigrato, a
inmobiliario	immobilier	property	Immobilien(f, pl)	imobiliário	immobiliare
inmortal	immortel, le	immortal	unsterblich	imortal	immortale
inmóvil	immobile	motionless	unbeweglich	imóvel	immobile
inmueble	immeuble	block of flats	Gebäude(n)	edifício, imóvel	palazzo, edificio
inmunidad	immunité	immunity	Immunität(f)	imunidade	immunità
inmunizar	immuniser	immunize	immunisieren	imunizar	immunizzare
innato, a	inné, e	innate	angeboren	inato, a	innato, a
innovación	innovation	innovation	Neuerung(f)(Er-)	inovação	innovazione
innovar	innover	innovate	innovieren, erneuern	inovar	innovare
inocente	innocent, e	innocent	unschuldig	inocente	innocente
inofensivo, a	inoffensif, ive	inoffensive	harmlos	inofensivo, a	inoffensivo, a
inorgánico, a	inorganique	inorganic	anorganisch	inorgânico, a	inorganico, a
inquieto, a	inquiet, ète	worried	besorgt	inquieto, a	inquieto, a
inquietud	inquiétude	anxiety, worry	Sorge(f)	inquietação	inquietudine
inquilino, a	locataire	tenant	Mieter(in f)m	inquilino, a	inquilino, a
insatisfecho, a	insatisfait, e	not satisfied	unzufrieden	insatisfeito, a	insoddisfatto, a
inscribir	inscrire, noter	note, write	ein = schreiben	inscrever	iscrivere
inscribirse	inscrire(s')	join	bei = treten	inscrever-se	iscriversi
inscripción	inscription	inscription	Inschrift(f)	inscrição	iscrizione
insecto	insecte	insect	Insekt(n)	insecto	insetto
inseguro, a	incertain, e	uncertain	unsicher	incerto, a	incerto, a
inseminación	insémination	insemination	Befruchtung(f)	inseminação	inseminazione
insensible	insensible	insensitive	unempfindlich	insensível	insensibile
inserción	insertion	insertion	Einfügung(f)	inserção	inserzione
insertar	insérer	insert	ein = setzen, ein = fügen	inserir	inserire
insignia	insigne	badge	Zeichen(n), Abzeichen	insígnia	distintivo
insignificante	insignifiant, e	insignificant	unbedeutend	insignificante	insignificante
insistir	insister	insist	bestehen, beharren	insistir	insistere
insolación	insolation	sunstroke	Sonnenstich(m)	insolação	insolazione
insolación	coup de soleil	sunburn	Sonnenbrand(m)	insolação	scottatura
insolencia	insolence	insolence	Frechheit(f)	insolência	insolenza
insolente	insolent, e	insolent	unverschämt, frech	insolente	insolente

Spanish	French	English	German	Portuguese	Italian
insólito, a	insolite	unusual	seltsam, ungewohnt	insólito, a	insolito, a
insomnio	insomnie	insomnia	Schlaflosigkeit(f)	insónia	insonnia
insonoro, a	insonore	sound-proof	schalldicht	insonoro, a	insonoro, a
inspección	inspection	inspection	Überprüfung(f)	inspecção	ispezione
inspector, a	inspecteur, trice	inspector	Inspektor(in f)m	inspector, a	ispettore, trice
inspiración	inspiration	inspiration	Anregung(f)	inspiração	ispirazione
instalación	installation	installation	Einrichtung(f)	instalação	installazione
instalar	installer	install	ein = richten	instalar	installare
instalarse	installer(s')	settle	nieder = lassen, sich	instalar-se	stabilirsi
instante	instant	moment, instant	Moment(m)	instante	istante
instintivo, a	instinctif, ive	instinctive	instinktiv	instintivo, a	istintivo, a
instinto	instinct	instinct	Instinkt(m)	instinto	istinto
institución	institution	institution	Institution(f)	instituição	istituzione
institucional	institutionnel	institutional	gesetzlich	institucional	istituzionale
instituto	institut	institute	Institut(n)	instituto	istituto
instituto, liceo	lycée	comprehensive sch.	Gymnasium(n)	liceu	liceo
instrucción	instruction	instruction	Ausbildung(f)	instrução	istruzione
instructor	instructeur	instructor	Ausbilder(m)	instrutor, a	istruttore, trice
instruir	instruire	teach	aus = bilden	instruir	istruire
instrumento	instrument	instrument	Instrument(n)	instrumento	strumento
insuficiente	insuffisant, e	insufficient	ungenügend	insuficiente	insufficiente
insulina	insuline	insulin	Insulin(n)	insulina	insulina
insultar	insulter	insult	beleidigen	insultar	insultare
insulto	insulte	insult	Beleidigung(f)	insulto	insulto
intacto, a	intact, e	intact	intakt	intacto, a	intatto, a
integrar	intégrer	integrate	integrieren	integrar	integrare
integridad	intégrité	integrity	Integrität(f)	integridade	integrità
íntegro, a	intégral, e	integral	vollständig	integral	integrale
intelectual	intellectuel, le	intellectual	intellektuell	intelectual	intellettuale
inteligencia	intelligence	intelligence	Intelligenz(f)	inteligência	intelligenza
inteligente	intelligent, e	intelligent	intelligent, gescheit	inteligente	intelligente
intención	intention	intention	Absicht(f)	intenção	intenzione
intención	intention, but	purpose, aim, goal	Absicht(f)	intenção	intento, fine, scopo
intención(tener)	intention(avoir)	intend	beabsichtigen	tencionar	intenzione(avere)
intensidad	intensité	intensity	Intensität(f)	intensidade	intensità
intensivo, a	intensif, ive	intensive	intensiv	intensivo, a	intensivo, a
intenso, a	intense	intense	heftig, stark	intenso, a	intenso, a
intentar	tenter	attempt, try	versuchen; wagen	tentar	tentare
intercambiar	échanger	exchange	tauschen	trocar	scambiare
interceptar	intercepter	intercept	auf = fangen, ab = fangen	interceptar	intercettare
interés	intérêt	interest	Interesse(n)	interesse	interesse
interés	intérêt	interest	Zins(m)	juro	interesse
interesante	intéressant, e	interesting	interessant	interessante	interessante
interesarse	intéresser(s')	interested in(be)	interessieren, sich	interessar-se	interessarsi
interferencia	interférence	interference	Einmischung; Störung	interferência	interferenza
interior	intérieur, e	inside, inner	innere(r, s); innen	interior	interno, a
interior	intérieur, e	inner, interior	inner	interior	interiore
interior	intérieur, e	domestic, home	Innen-	interno, a	interno, a
interior	intérieur	interior	Innere(n)	interior	interiore
interlocutor, a	interlocuteur	interlocutor	Gesprächspartner/in	interlocutor, a	interlocutore, trice
intermediario, a	intermédiaire	intermediate	Zwischen-, Mittel-	intermediário, a	intermediario, a
intermedio	entracte	interval	Pause(f)	intervalo	intervallo
intermitente	intermittent, e	intermittent	aussetzend	intermitente	intermittente
intermitente	clignotant	indicator	Blinklicht(n)	pisca	freccia
internacional	international, e	international	international	internacional	internazionale
interno, a	interne	internal, inner	intern	interno, a	interno, a
interno, a	pensionnaire	boarder	Internatsschüler(m)	interno, a	collegiale
interpretar	interpréter	interpret	deuten, aus = legen	interpretar	interpretare
intérprete	interprète	interpreter	Dolmetscher(in f)m	intérprete	interprete
interrogar	interroger	question, ask	fragen, befragen	interrogar	interrogare
interrumpir	interrompre	interrupt	unterbrechen	interromper	interrompere
interrupción	interruption	interruption	Unterbrechung(f)	interrupção	interruzione
interruptor	interrupteur	switch	Schalter(m)	interruptor	interruttore
interruptor, botón	bouton	switch	Schalter(m)	interruptor	bottone, pulsante
intersección	intersection	intersection	Kreuzung(f)	intersecção	intersezione
intervalo	intervalle	interval	Abstand(m)	intervalo	intervallo
intervalo	intervalle	gap	Abstand(m)	intervalo	intervallo
intervención	intervention	intervention	Eingriff(m)	intervenção	intervento

Spanish	French	English	German	Portuguese	Italian
intervenir	intervenir	intervene	dazwischen = treten	intervir	intervenire
interviú	interview	interview	Interview(n)	entrevista	intervista
intestino	intestin	intestine	Darm(m)	intestino	intestino
intimidar	intimider	intimidate	ein = schüchtern	intimidar	intimidire
íntimo, a	intime	close, intimate	intim	íntimo, a	intimo, a
íntimo, a	intime	intimate	vertraut, intim	íntimo, a	intimo, a
intolerancia	intolérance	intolerance	Intoleranz(f)	intolerância	intolleranza
intoxicación	intoxication	poisoning	Vergiftung(f)	intoxicação	intossicazione
intrépido, a	intrépide	intrepid	kühn, mutig	intrépido, a	intrepido, a
intriga	intrigue	intrigue	Intrige(f)	intriga	intrigo
intrigar	intriguer	intrigue	intrigieren	intrigar	intrigare
introducir	introduire	insert; introduce	ein = führen	introduzir	introdurre
intrusión	intrusion	intrusion	Eindringen(n)	intrusão	intrusione
intuición	intuition	intuition	Intuition(f)	intuição	intuizione
inundación	inondation	flooding, flood	Überschwemmung(f)	inundação	inondazione
inútil	inutile	useless	nutzlos	inútil	inutile
invadir	envahir	invade	ein = fallen	invadir	invadere
inválido, a	invalide	disabled	behindert	inválido, a	invalido, a
inválido, a	infirme	disabled	behindert	doente	infermo, a
invariable	invariable	invariable	unveränderlich	invariável	invariabile
invasión	invasion	invasion	Invasion(f)	invasão	invasione
invencible	invincible	invincible	unbesiegbar	invencível	invincibile
invención	invention	invention	Erfindung(f)	invenção	invenzione
inventar	inventer	invent	erfinden	inventar	inventare
inventario	inventaire	inventory	Inventar(n)	inventário	inventario
inventario	inventaire	stock-list(taking)	Inventur(f)	inventário	inventario
inventor	inventeur	inventor	Erfinder(in f)m	inventor	inventore
inversión	inversion	inversion	Umkehrung(f)	inversão	inversione
inversión	investissement	investment	Investition(f)	investimento	investimento
inverso, a	inverse	opposite	umgekehrt	inverso, a	inverso, a
invertir	inverser	reverse, invert	um = kehren	inverter	invertire
invertir	investir	invest	investieren	investir	investire
invertir	placer	invest	an = legen	pôr a render	investire
investidura	investiture	investiture	Investitur(f)	investidura	investitura
investigación	enquête	inquiry, inquest	Untersuchung(f)	inquérito	indagine, inchiesta
investigación	recherche	research	Forschung(f)	investigação	ricerca
investigador, a	chercheur, euse	research worker	Forscher(in f)m	investigador, a	cercatore
investigar	enquêter	investigate	untersuchen	investigar	investigare, indagare
invierno	hiver	winter	Winter(m)	inverno	inverno
invisible	invisible	invisible	unsichtbar	invisível	invisibile
invitación	invitation	invitation	Einladung(f)	convite	invito
invitado, a	invité, e	guest	Gast(m)	convidado, a	invitato, a
invitar	inviter	invite	ein = laden	convidar	invitare
invocar	invoquer	invoke	beziehen auf, sich	invocar	invocare
inyección	piqûre	injection	Spritze(f)	injecção	iniezione
inyectar	injecter	inject	spritzen, ein = spritzen	injectar	iniettare
ir(a, por, hacia)	aller	go	gehen, fahren nach	ir	andare, recarsi
ir a buscar	aller chercher	go to fetch/get	ab = holen	ir buscar	andare a prendere
ir a la cama	coucher(se)	go to bed	schlafen gehen	deitar-se	andare a letto
iris	iris	iris	Iris(f)	íris	iride
ironía	ironie	irony	Ironie(f)	ironia	ironia
irradiación	irradiation	irradiation	Bestrahlung(f)	irradiação	irradiazione
irradiación	rayonnement	radiance	Strahlung(f)	irradiação	irradiazione
irregular	irrégulier, e	irregular	unregelmäßig	irregular	irregolare
irrigar	irriguer	irrigate	bewässern	irrigar	irrigare
irritante	irritant, e	irritating	ärgerlich; aufregend	irritante	irritante
irritar	irriter	irritate	reizen, irritieren	irritar	irritare
irrupción	irruption	irruption	Eindringen(n)	irrupção	irruzione
irse, escaparse	échapper	drop	entgleiten	escapar	sfuggire, scappare
isla	île	island, isle	Insel(f)	ilha	isola
islámico, a	islamique	Islamic	islamisch	islâmico, a	islamico, a
islote	îlot	islet	Inselchen(n)	ilhéu, ilhota	isolotto
itinerario	itinéraire	itinerary, route	Route(f), Strecke(f)	itinerário	itinerario
izquierdo, a	gauche	left	links; linke(r, s)	esquerdo, a	sinistro, a

S

J

Spanish	French	English	German	Portuguese	Italian
jabón	savon	soap	Seife(f)	sabão	sapone
jactarse	vanter(se)	boast	prahlen	gabar-se	vantarsi
jadear	haleter	pant, gasp	keuchen	arquejar	ansimare
jalea	gelée	jelly	Gelee(n)	geleia	gelatina
jamás, nunca	jamais	never; ever	niemals, jemals	nunca, jamais	mai
jamón	jambon	ham	Schinken(m)	fiambre	prosciutto
jaqueca	migraine	migraine, headache	Migräne(f)	enxaqueca	emicrania
jarabe	sirop	syrup, medicine	Sirup(m)	xarope	sciroppo
jardín	jardin	garden	Garten(m)	jardim	giardino
jardinero, a	jardinier, ière	gardener	Gärtner(in f)m	jardineiro, a	giardiniere, a
jarra	carafe	jug, carafe	Karaffe(f)	jarro, caneca	caraffa
jarrón	vase	vase	Vase(f)	jarra	vaso
jaula	cage	cage	Käfig(m)	gaiola, jaula	gabbia
jazz	jazz	jazz	Jazz(m)	jazz	jazz
jefe	chef	head; chief; leader	Chef(in f)m	chefe	capo
jefe	chef, dirigeant	leader	Leiter(m), Führer(m)	chefe, líder	capo, dirigente
jefe de empresa	chef(entreprise)	manager, head	Betriebsführer(m)	chefe de empresa	dirigente d'azienda
jefe de estado	chef d'état	head of state	Staatsoberhaupt(n)	chefe de estado	capo di stato
jefe de hotel	maître d'hôtel	head-waiter	Oberkellner(m)	mordomo	capocameriere
jerarquía	hiérarchie	hierarchy	Hierarchie(f)	hierarquia	gerarchia
jerárquico, a	hiérarchique	hierarchical	hierarchisch	hierárquico, a	gerarchico, a
jerga	jargon	jargon	Fachsprache(f)	calão, gíria	gergo
jeringa	seringue	syringe	Spritze(f)	seringa	siringa
jersey	pull-over	pullover, sweater	Pullover(m)	pulover	maglione, pullover
jersey	chandail	jumper, sweater	Pullover(m)	camisola	maglione
jinete, a	cavalier, ière	rider	Reiter(in f)m	cavaleiro, a	cavaliere, a
jirafa	girafe	giraffe	Giraffe(f)	girafa	giraffa
jockey	jockey	jockey	Jockey(m)	jockey	jockey, fantino
jorobado, a	bossu, e	hunch-backed	buckelig	corcunda	gobbo, a
joven	jeune	young	jung	jovem	giovane
jóvenes	jeunes	young people	jungen Leute(pl)	jovens	giovani
joya	bijou(x)	jewel	Schmuck(m)(-stück n)	jóia	gioiello
joya	joyau	jewel	Juwel(n), Schmuckstück	jóia	gioiello
joyería	bijouterie	jeweller's	Schmuckgeschäft(n)	joalharia	gioielleria
jubilación	retraite	retirement	Pensionierung(f)	reforma	pensione
jubilado, a(estar)	retraité, e(être)	retired(be)	pensioniert sein	reformado, a(estar)	pensione(essere in)
júbilo, alegría	allégresse	elation	Heiterkeit(f)	júbilo, alegria	esultanza
judía	haricot	bean	Bohne(f)	feijão	fagiolo; fagiolino
judicial	judiciaire	judicial, legal	gerichtlich	judiciário, a	giudiziario, a
judicial	judiciaire, légal	legal	rechtmäßig	judicial	giudiziario, a
judío, judía	juif, juive	Jew, Jewess(-es)	Jude(m), Jüdin(f)	judeu, judia	ebreo, a
judo, yudo	judo	judo	Judo(n)	judo	judò
juego	jeu	game	Spiel(n)	jogo	gioco
jueves	jeudi	Thursday	Donnerstag(m)	quinta-feira	giovedì
juez	juge	judge	Richter(in f)m	juíz	giudice
jugador, a	joueur, se	player	Spieler(in f)m	jogador, a	giocatore, trice
jugar	jouer	play	spielen	jogar, brincar	giocare
jugar	jouer	gamble	spielen	jogar	giocare
jugo	jus	juice	Saft(m)	sumo	succo
juguete	jouet	toy	Spielzeug(n)	brinquedo	giocattolo
juicio	jugement	judgement	Urteil(n)	julgamento	giudizio
juicioso, a	judicieux, se	judicious	scharfsinnig	judicioso, a	giudizioso, a
julio	juillet	July	Juli(m)	Julho	luglio
junio	juin	June	Juni(m)	Junho	giugno
junta	assemblée	meeting, conference	Versammlung(f)	assembleia, reunião	assemblea
junta	junte	junta	Junta(f)	junta	giunta
junta	joint	joint, join. seal	Dichtung(f)	junta, anilha	giunto, guarnizione
juntar	rassembler	gather(together)	sammeln	juntar	radunare
juntarse con	joindre à(se)	join	an = schließen, sich	juntar-se	unirsi, associarsi
junto, a	joint, e	joined, linked	zusammengefügt	junto, a	giunto, a
juntos	ensemble	together	zusammen	junto	insieme

Spanish	French	English	German	Portuguese	Italian
jurado	juré	juryman, juror	Geschworene(f, m)	jurado	giurato
jurado; tribunal	jury	jury	Jury(f)	júri	giuria
juramento	serment	oath, pledge	Eid(m)	juramento	giuramento
juramento, taco	juron	swear-word	Fluch(m)	palavrão	bestemmia
jurar	jurer	swear	schwören	jurar	giurare
jurídico, a	juridique	juridical, legal	juristisch	jurídico, a	giuridico, a
jurisprudencia	jurisprudence	jurisprudence	Rechtsprechung(f)	jurisprudência	giurisprudenza
jurista	juriste	jurist; lawyer	Jurist(in f)m	jurista	giurista
justamente	justement	exactly	genau	justamente	appunto
justicia	justice	justice	Gerechtigkeit(f)	justiça	giustizia
justificación	justification	justification	Rechtfertigung(f)	justificação	giustificazione
justificar	justifier	justify	begründen, belegen	justificar	giustificare
justo, a	juste	just	gerecht	justo, a	giusto, a
juventud	jeunesse	youth	Jugend(f)	juventude	gioventù, giovinezza
juzgar	juger	judge	beurteilen	julgar	giudicare

K

Spanish	French	English	German	Portuguese	Italian
karate	karaté	karate	Karate(n)	karaté	karatè
kayac, piragua	kayac	kayak	Kajak(m)	kayac	kayak
kilogramo	kilogramme	kilogram(me)	Kilo(gramm)n)n	quilograma, quilo	chilogrammo, chilo
kilómetro	kilomètre	kilometre	Kilometer(m)	quilómetro	chilometro

L

Spanish	French	English	German	Portuguese	Italian
la, las	la, l', les	the	die	a, as	la; l'; le
laberinto	labyrinthe	labyrinth, maze	Labyrinth(n)	labirinto	labirinto
labio	lèvre	lip	Lippe(f)	lábio	labbro(a)
laboratorio	laboratoire	laboratory	Labor(n)	laboratório	laboratorio
labranza	labour	ploughing	Feldarbeit(f)	lavoura	aratura
laca	laque	lacquer	Lack(m)	laca	lacca
laca	laque	hair-spray	Haarspray(m, n)	laca	lacca
lacrimógeno	lacrymogène	tear-gas	Tränengas(n)	lacrimogéneo	lacrimogeno
ladera	coteau	hill(side)	Anhöhe(f), Hang(m)	encosta; colina	colle, collinetta
lado	côté	side	Seite(f)	lado	lato
ladrar	aboyer	bark	bellen	ladrar	abbaiare
ladrillo	brique	brick	Ziegel(m)	tijolo	mattone
ladrón, a	voleur, se	thief(-ves), robber	Dieb(in f)m	ladrão, ladra	ladro, a
lagarto	lézard	lizard	Eidechse(f)	lagarto	lucertola
lago	lac	lake	See(m)	lago	lago
lágrima	larme	tear	Träne(f)	lágrima	lacrima
laguna	lagune	lagoon	Binnensee(m)	laguna	laguna
lamentar, añorar	regretter	regret	nach – trauern(jdm/etw)	lamentar	rimpiangere
lamentarse	lamenter(se)	lament	jammern	lamentar-se	lamentarsi
lamento(lo)	regret	regret	Bedauern(n)	pena; pesar	rimpianto
lamer	lécher	lick	lecken	lamber	leccare
lámpara	lampe	lamp	Lampe(f)	candeeiro	lampada
lámpara de pie	lampadaire	street-lamp	Straßenlaterne(f)	candeeiro	lampione
lana	laine	wool	Wolle(f)	lã	lana

Spanish	French	English	German	Portuguese	Italian
landa	lande	moor, heath	Heide(f)	charneca	landa
langosta	langouste	crayfish	Languste(f)	lagosta	aragosta
langostino	langoustine	Dublin Bay prawn	Langustine(f)	lagostim	scampo
lanza	lance	spear, lance	Lanze(f)	lança	lancia
lanzamiento	lancement	launch(ing)	Start(m)	lançamento	lancio
lanzar	lancer	throw	werfen	lançar; atirar	lanciare
lanzar	lancer	launch, start up	lancieren, starten	lançar	lanciare
lápiz	crayon	pencil	Bleistift(m)	lápis	matita, lapis
largar	larguer	let go, release	weg = werfen, auf = geben	largar, deixar	lasciare, mollare
largo, a	long, longue	long	lang	longo, a	lungo, a
largo(a lo)	long(le)	along	entlang	longo(ao)	lungo
laringe	larynx	larynx	Kehlkopf(m)	laringe	laringe
laringitis	laryngite	laryngitis	Halsentzündung(f)	laringite	laringite
larva	larve	larva(-vae)	Larve(f)	larva	larva
láser	laser	laser	Laser(m)	laser	laser
lástima(qué)	dommage(quel)	pity(what a)	schade !(wie ---)	pena(que)	peccato(che)
lastimar, ofender	blesser, offenser	hurt, offend	kränken	magoar, ofender	ferire, offendere
lata	boîte	tin	Dose(f)	lata	latta, scatola
lateral	latéral, e	lateral	seitlich	lateral	laterale
látigo	fouet	whip	Peitsche(f)	chicote	frusta
latitud	latitude	latitude	Breitengrad(m)	latitude	latitudine
lavabo	lavabo	wash-basin	Waschbecken(n)	lavabo	lavabo, lavandino
lavado	lavage	washing	Waschen(n)	lavagem	lavaggio
lavandería	blanchisserie	laundry	Wäscherei(f)	lavandaria	lavanderia
lavar	laver	wash	waschen	lavar	lavare
lavarse	laver(se)	wash	waschen, sich	lavar-se	lavarsi
laxante	laxatif, ive	laxative	abführend	laxante	lassativo, a
lazo	boucle	loop	Schleife(f)	laço	cappio; occhiello
le, él; ella; se	lui	him, her, it	ihm, ihr, ihm	ele(a); lhe	lui; gli; le
leal	loyal, e	loyal	loyal, treu	leal	leale
lección	leçon	lesson	Stunde(f); Lektion(f)	lição	lezione
lector, a	lecteur, trice	reader	Leser(in f)m	leitor, a	lettore, trice
lectura	lecture	reading	Lesen(n)	leitura	lettura
leche	lait	milk	Milch(f)	leite	latte
lechuga	laitue, salade	lettuce	Kopfsalat(m)	alface	lattuga
leer	lire	read	lesen	ler	leggere
legal	légal, e	legal	gesetzlich	legal	legale
legalidad	légalité	legality	Rechtmäßigkeit(f)	legalidade	legalità
legar	léguer	bequeath, leave	vermachen	legar	legare
legible	lisible	legible	leserlich	legível	leggibile
legislación	législation	legislation	Gesetzgebung(f)	legislação	legislazione
legislativo, a	législatif, ive	legislative	gesetzgebend	legislativo, a	legislativo, a
legítimo, a	légitime	legitimate	legitim	legítimo, a	legittimo, a
legítimo, a	légitime, légal	rightful, lawful	rechtmäßig	legítimo, a	legittimo, a
legumbre, verdura	légume	vegetable	Gemüse(n)	legume	verdura; legume
lejos	loin	far(away), distant	weit, fern	longe	lontano, a
lejos(a lo)	loin(au)	away, far away	weg(fort); weit weg	longe(ao)	lontano
lengua	langue	tongue	Zunge(f)	língua	lingua
lenguaje	langage	language	Sprache(f)	linguagem	linguaggio
lentamente	lentement	slowly	langsam	lentamente	lentamente
lenteja	lentille	lentil	Linse(f)(Pflanze)	lentilha	lenticchia
lentejuela	paillette	glitter, spangle	Flitter(m)	lentejoula	lustrino
lentilla	lentille	lens(contact -)	Kontaktlinse(f)	lente	lente a contatto
lento, a	lent, e	slow	langsam	lento, a	lento, a
lento	slow	smooch, slow dance	Blues(m), Slow(m)	slow	lento, slow
leña	bois	wood	Brennholz(n)	lenha	legna
leño	bûche	log	Scheit(n)	acha	tronco, ceppo
león, leona	lion, ne	lion, lioness	Löwe(m), Löwin(f)	leão, leoa	leone, leonessa
les	leur	them(to -)	ihnen	lhes	loro; gli
lesbiana	lesbienne	lesbian	lesbisch	lésbica	lesbica
lesión	lésion	lesion, injury	Verletzung(f)	lesão	lesione
letra	lettre	letter	Buchstabe(m)	letra	lettera
letra	caractère	letter, character	Schrifttyp(m)	carácter	carattere, lettera
letrero	enseigne	sign	Schild(m)(Reklame-)	letreiro	insegna
leucemia	leucémie	leukaemia	Leukämie(f)	leucemia	leucemia
levantar	lever	lift(up), raise	heben	levantar	alzare
levantar, elevar	soulever	lift, raise	an = heben, hoch = heben	levantar, erguer	sollevare
levantar(se)	lever(se)	get up	erheben, sich	levantar-se	alzarsi

Spanish	French	English	German	Portuguese	Italian
levantarse	lever(se)	stand up, get up	auf = stehen	levantar-se	alzarsi
ley	loi	law	Gesetz(n)	lei	legge
leyenda	légende	legend	Legende(f)	lenda	leggenda
liberal	libéral, e	liberal	liberal	liberal	liberale
liberalismo	libéralisme	liberalism	Liberalismus(m)	liberalismo	liberalismo
liberar	libérer	liberate, free	befreien	libertar	liberare
libertad	liberté	liberty, freedom	Freiheit(f)	liberdade	libertà
libertar	délivrer	free	befreien	libertar	rilasciare, liberare
líbido	libido	libido	Libido(f)	líbido	libido
libre	libre	free	frei	livre	libero, a
libre	libre	clear	frei	livre	libero, a
libre impuestos	hors-taxe	duty-free	zollfrei	sem imposto	duty-free
librería	librairie	book-shop	Buchhandlung(f)	livraria	libreria
libreta	carnet	note-book	Notizbuch(n)	bloco, canhenho	taccuino
libro	livre	book	Buch(n)	livro	libro
licencia	licence	licence	Lizenz(f)	licença	licenza
licenciatura	licence	degree	Lizenz(f)	licenciatura	laurea
licor	liqueur	liqueur	Likör(m)	licor	liquore
lienzo, cuadro	toile	canvas, painting	Gemälde(n)(Leinwand)	tela, quadro	tela, dipinto
ligar, amarrar	lier	tie, bind	binden, verbinden	ligar	legare
ligeramente	légèrement	lightly, slightly	leicht	ligeiramente	leggermente
ligero, a	léger, ère	light	leicht	ligeiro, a; leve	leggero, a
lima	lime	file	Feile(f)	lima	lima
limitar	limiter	limit	begrenzen	limitar	limitare
límite	limite	limit	Grenze(f)	limite	limite
limítrofe	limitrophe	border(ing)	angrenzend	limítrofe	limitrofo
limo, fango	vase	sludge, mud	Schlamm(m)	lodo	melma
limón	citron	lemon	Zitrone(f)	limão	limone
limpiar	nettoyer	clean	reinigen	limpar	pulire
limpiar, secar	essuyer	wipe, dry	ab = wischen, abtrocknen	limpar, secar	asciugare
limpieza	propreté	clean(li)ness	Reinlichkeit(f)	limpeza	pulizia
limpieza	nettoyage	cleaning	Reinigung(f)	limpeza	pulizia
limpieza	ménage	housework	Haushalt(m)	limpeza	pulizie
limpio, a	propre	clean	sauber	limpo, a	pulito, a
linchar	lyncher	lynch	lynchen	linchar	linciare
lindo, a	joli, e	nice	nett	bonito, a	bello, a
línea	ligne	line	Linie(f)	linha	linea
lineal	linéaire	linear	linear	linear	lineare
lingote	lingot	ingot, bullion	Barren(m)	lingote	lingotto
linterna	lanterne	lantern	Laterne(f)	lanterna	lanterna
linterna	lampe de poche	torch	Taschenlampe(f)	pilha	lampadina tascabile
liquidación	règlement	settlement	Begleichung(f)	pagamento	saldo
liquidar	liquider	liquidate	liquidieren	liquidar	liquidare
liquidar, pagar	régler	settle	bezahlen	pagar	regolare, saldare
líquido, a	liquide	liquid	flüssig	líquido, a	liquido, a
líquido	liquide	liquid	Flüssigkeit(f)	líquido	liquido
lisiado, a	estropié, e	crippled	verkrüppelt	aleijado, a	storpio, a
liso, a	lisse	smooth	glatt	liso, a	liscio, a
lista	liste	list	Liste(f)	lista	lista
lista de premios	palmarès	list of winners	Preisträgerliste(f)	quadro de honra	albo dei premiati
litera	couchette	couchette	Liegeplatz(m)	couchette	cuccetta
literario, a	littéraire	literary	literarisch	literário, a	letterario, a
literatura	littérature	literature	Literatur(f)	literatura	letteratura
litigar	plaider	plead	plädieren	defender(causa)	patrocinare
litigio	litige	litigation	Streitfall(m)	litígio	litigio
litografía	lithographie	lithograph(y)	Steindruck(m)	litografia	litografia
litoral	littoral	coast	Küstenstreifen(m)	litoral	litorale
litro	litre	litre	Liter(m, n)	litro	litro
lívido, a	livide	livid, pallid	blaß, fahl	lívido, a	livido, a
lo	le	the	das	o	lo
lobo	loup	wolf(-lves)	Wolf(m)	lobo	lupo
lóbulo	lobe	lobe	Ohrläppchen(n)	lóbulo	lobo
local	local, e	local	lokal	local	locale
local	local	premises	Gebäude(n), Lokal(n)	local	locale
localidad	localité	locality	Ortschaft(f)	localidade	località
localizar	localiser	localize; locate	lokalisieren	localizar	localizzare
localizar	repérer	locate	lokalisieren	localizar	localizzare
loción	lotion	lotion	Gesichtswasser(n)	loção	lozione

S

Spanish	French	English	German	Portuguese	Italian
loco, a	fou, folle	mad, foolish, crazy	verrückt	louco, a; maluco, a	matto, a; pazzo, a
locomotiva	locomotive	locomotive	Lokomotive(f)	locomotiva	locomotiva
locución	locution	phrase, locution	Redensart(f)	locução	locuzione
locura	folie	madness, folly	Wahnsinn(m), Wahn(m)	loucura	follia, pazzia
logicial	logiciel	software	Software(f)	software	software
lógico, a	logique	logical	logisch	lógico, a	logico, a
lograr, conseguir	réussir	succeed	gelingen	conseguir	riuscire
lograr, alcanzar	arriver(à)	attain	erlangen, erreichen	alcançar, atingir	raggiungere
lograr, triunfar	remporter, gagner	achieve	erringen	alcançar, obter	raggiungere, ottenere
longitud	longueur	length	Länge(f)	comprimento	lunghezza
longitud	longitude	longitude	Längengrad(m)	longitude	longitudine
longitudinal	longitudinal, e	longitudinal	Längs-	longitudinal	longitudinale
loro	perroquet	parrot	Papagei(m)	papagaio	pappagallo
los, las	les	the	die	os, as	i, gli; le
lote	lot	batch, assortment	Assortiment(n)	lote	assortimento
lotería	loterie	lottery	Lotterie(f)	lotaria	lotteria
lúcido, a	lucide	lucid	klar	lúcido, a	lucido, a
lucha	lutte	struggle, fight	Kampf(m)	luta	lotta
luchador, a	lutteur, se	wrestler; fighter	Kämpfer(m); Ringer(m)	lutador, a	lottatore, trice
luchar	lutter	fight, struggle	kämpfen	lutar	lottare
lugar	lieu	place, spot	Ort(m)	lugar	luogo
lugar	place	place	Ort(m), Platz(m)	lugar; sítio	posto
lugar, sitio	endroit	place, spot	Stelle(f)	lugar, sítio	luogo, posto
lugar, punto	point	spot	Fleck(m); Ort; Stelle	ponto	punto
lujo	luxe	luxury	Luxus(m)	luxo	lusso
lujoso, a	luxueux, se	luxurious	üppig	luxuoso, a	lussuoso, a
lumbago	lumbago	lumbago	Hexenschuß(m)	lumbago	lombaggine
luminoso, a	lumineux, se	luminous	leuchtend, hell	luminoso, a	luminoso, a
luna	lune	moon	Mond(m)	lua	luna
luna; cristal	glace; miroir	window; mirror	Scheibe(f); Spiegel(m)	vidro; espelho	vetro; specchio
lunes	lundi	Monday	Montag(m)	segunda-feira	lunedì
lupa	loupe	magnifying-glass	Lupe(f)	lupa	lente(ingrandimento)
luz	lumière	light	Licht(n)	luz	luce

LL

Spanish	French	English	German	Portuguese	Italian
llaga, herida	plaie	wound; cut	Wunde(f)	ferida	piaga
llama	flamme	flame	Flamme(f)	chama	fiamma
llama	lama	llama	Lama(n)	lama	lama
llamada	appel	call	Ruf(m)(Zu-, An-)	chamada	chiamata
llamada	rappel	reminder	Erinnerung(f); Mahnung	aviso; lembrança	richiamo
llamar	appeler	call	rufen(an=), heißen	chamar	chiamare
llamar	frapper	knock	an= klopfen	bater	bussare
llamar	nommer	name	nennen	chamar	chiamare
llamarse	nommer(se)	called(be)	heißen	chamar-se	chiamarsi
llano, a	plat, e	flat	platt	plano, a	piatto, a
llanta	jante	rim	Felge(f), Radkranz(m)	jante, camba	cerchione
llanura, llano	plaine	plain	Ebene(f)	planície	pianura
llave	clef, clé	key	Schlüssel(m)	chave	chiave
llave	clé	spanner, wrench	Schraubenschlüssel(m)	chave	chiave
llave, grifo	robinet	cock, tap	Hahn(m)(Wasser-; Gas-)	torneira	rubinetto
llavero	porte-clefs	key-ring	Schlüsselring(m)	porta-chaves	portachiavi
llegada; meta	arrivée	arrival	Ankunft(f)	chegada	arrivo
llegar	arriver	arrive, come	an= kommen	chegar	arrivare
llegar a	accéder à	reach	Zugang haben zu	chegar a	accedere a
llegar a ser	devenir	become	werden	vir a ser	diventare
llenar	remplir	fill	füllen	encher	riempire
lleno, a	plein, e	full	voll	cheio, a	pieno, a
llevar	porter	carry	tragen	levar	portare

Spanish	French	English	German	Portuguese	Italian
llevar	emporter	take(away)	mit = nehmen	levar	portar via
llevar	emmener	take	mit = nehmen	levar	portare, condurre
llevar	porter	wear	tragen	usar; trazer	indossare, portare
llorar	pleurer	cry	weinen	chorar	piangere
llover	pleuvoir	rain	regnen	chover	piovere
llovizna	bruine	drizzle	Sprühregen(m)	chuvisco	pioggerella
lluvia	pluie	rain	Regen(m)	chuva	pioggia
lluvioso, a	pluvieux, se	rainy	regnerisch	chuvoso, a	piovoso, a

M

Spanish	French	English	German	Portuguese	Italian
macabro, a	macabre	macabre	makaber	macabro, a	macabro, a
macarrones	nouilles	noodles	Nudeln(f, pl)	massa	tagliatelle, pasta
maceta	pot	pot	Topf(m)	vaso; pote	vaso
macho	mâle	male	Männchen(n)	macho	maschio
madera	bois	timber	Holz(n)	madeira	legno
madre	mère	mother	Mutter(f)	mãe	madre
madrina	marraine	godmother	Patin(f)	madrinha	madrina
madurez	maturité	maturity	Reife(f)	maturidade	maturità
maduro, a	mûr, e	ripe	reif	maduro, a	maturo, a
maduro, a	mûr, e	mature	reif	maduro, a	maturo, a
maestro, a	instituteur	teacher(primary)	Grundschullehrer/in	professor primário	maestro, a
maestro(natación)	maître-nageur	life-guard	Bademeister(in f)m	nadador-salvador	bagnino
mafia	mafia	Mafia	Mafia(f)	mafia	mafia
magia	magie	magic	Zauberei(f)	magia	magia
mágico, a	magique	magic	magisch	mágico, a	magico, a
magistrado	magistrat	magistrate	Magistrat(m)	magistrado	magistrato
magnético, a	magnétique	magnetic	magnetisch	magnético, a	magnetico, a
magnetófono	magnétophone	tape recorder	Kassettenrecorder(m)	gravador	registratore
magnetoscopio	magnétoscope	video recorder	Videorecorder(m)	gravador video	videoregistratore
magnífico, a	magnifique	magnificent	prächtig	magnífico, a	magnifico, a
maíz	maïs	maize, corn	Mais(m)	milho	granturco, mais
majestad	majesté	majesty	Majestät(f)	majestade	maestà
majestuoso, a	majestueux, se	majestic	majestätisch	majestoso, a	maestoso, a
mal	mal	evil	Böse(n)	mal	male
mal	mal	badly	schlecht	mal	male
mala suerte	malchance	misfortune	Unglück(n)	desventura	sventura, sfortuna
mala suerte	malchance	ill luck, bad luck	Pech(n), Unglück(n)	má sorte	sfortuna
maldito, a	maudit, e	cursed, damned	verdammt	maldito, a	maledetto, a
maleante	brigand	bandit	Räuber(in f)m	bandido	brigante
maleducado, a	impoli, e	impolite, rude	unhöflich	mal educado, a	maleducato, a
malestar	malaise	faintness	Unwohlsein, Schwäche	indisposição	malessere
maleta	valise	suitcase, case	Koffer(m)	mala	valigia
maletero	coffre	boot	Kofferraum(m)	mala	bagagliaio
maletín	attaché-case	attaché-case	Aktenkoffer(m)	maleta	valigetta
maletín, estuche	trousse	kit, case, bag	Etui(n), Tasche(f)	estojo	borsa, astuccio
malevolencia	malveillance	ill will	Böswilligkeit(f)	malevolência	malanimo
malévolo, a	malveillant, e	malevolent	böswillig	malévolo, a	malevolo, a
maleza	brousse	bush(the)	Busch(m)	mato	boscaglia
malhechor	malfaiteur	criminal	Missetäter(in f)m	malfeitor	malvivente
malo, a	mauvais, mal	evil, bad	übel	mau, má	cattivo, a; male
malo, a	mauvais, e	bad	schlecht	mau, má	cattivo, a
malo, a	méchant, e	naughty	böse, boshaft	mau, má	cattivo, a
malos tratos	sévices	cruelty	Mißhandlung(f)	sevícias	sevizie
malsano, a	malsain, e	unhealthy	ungesund	doentio, a	malsano, a
mama, teta	mamelle	udder	Euter(n)	mama	mammella
mamá	maman	Mummy, Mum	Mama(f)	mamã	mamma
mamar	téter	suck	saugen	mamar	poppare
mamífero	mammifère	mammal	Säugetier(n)	mamífero	mammifero

Spanish	French	English	German	Portuguese	Italian
mancha	tache	stain	Fleck(m)	mancha, nódoa	macchia
mandar, ordenar	ordonner	command, order	befehlen, beherrschen	mandar, ordenar	comandare, ordinare
manchar	tacher	stain, dirty	beflecken, beschmutzen	manchar, sujar	macchiare
mandar, enviar	envoyer	send	senden	mandar, enviar	mandare, inviare
mandarina	mandarine	tangerine	Mandarine(f)	tangerina	mandarino
mandíbula	mâchoire	jaw	Kiefer(m)	maxila	mascella
mando	commandement	command	Befehl(m)(-sgewalt f)	comando	comando
manecilla	manette	handle	Griff(m)	manípulo	leva
manera, modo	manière	manner, way	Art(f)	maneira, modo	maniera, modo
manga(la)	manche	sleeve	Ärmel(m)	manga	manica
mango(el)	manche	handle	Stiel(m)	cabo	manico
manguera	tuyau	hose	Schlauch(m)	mangueira	tubo
manguilla	épuisette	fishing net	Fangnetz(n)	rede	guadino, retino
manía	manie	mania	Sucht(f)	mania	mania
maníaco, a	maniaque	maniac	Verrückte(f, m)	maníaco, a	maniaco, a
maniático, a	maniaque	fussy	übergenau sein	meticuloso, a	pignolo, a
manicomio	asile	mental hospital	Irrenhaus(n)	manicômio	manicomio
manicura	manucure	manicure	Maniküre(f)	manicura	manicure
manifestación	manifestation	demonstration	Demonstration(f)	manifestação	manifestazione
manifestante	manifestant, e	demonstrator	Demonstrant(in f)m	manifestante	manifestante
manilla, mango	poignée	handle	Griff(m)	fecho	maniglia
maniobra	manoeuvre	manoeuvre	Manöver(n)	manobra	manovra
manipular	manipuler	manipulate	manipulieren	manipular	manipolare
maniquí	mannequin	dummy; model	Schaufensterpuppe(f)	manequim	manichino
maniquí, modelo	mannequin	model	Mannequin(n)	modelo	indossatore, trice
manivela	manivelle	crank	Handkurbel(f)	manivela	manovella
mano	main	hand	Hand(f)	mão	mano
mano de obra	main-d'oeuvre	manpower, labour	Arbeitskräfte(pl.)	mão-de-obra	manodopera
mano de obra	main-d'oeuvre	workforce, labour	Arbeitskraft(f)	mão-de-obra	manodopera
manopla	gant	flannel	Waschlappen(m)	luva	guanto
mansión, morada	manoir, château	mansion	Herrensitz(m), -haus n	mansão, palacete	maniero, castello
manta	couverture	blanket; cover	Decke(f)(Woll-, Bett-)	manta, cobertor	coperta
mantel	nappe	table-cloth	Tischdecke(f)	toalha	tovaglia
mantener	maintenir	maintain	erhalten	manter	mantenere
mantenimiento	entretien	maintenance	Wartung(f)	manutenção	manutenzione
mantequilla	beurre	butter	Butter(f)	manteiga	burro
manuable	maniable	handy, manageable	handlisch	manejável	maneggevole
manual	manuel, elle	manual; hand-	manuell; Hand-	manual	manuale
manuscrito, a	manuscrit, e	handwritten	handgeschrieben	manuscrito, a	manoscritto, a
mañana	matin	morning	Morgen(m)	manhã	mattino
mañana	demain	tomorrow	morgen	amanhã	domani
manzana	pomme	apple	Apfel(m)	maçã	mela
mapa	carte(géo)	map	Landkarte(f)	mapa	mappa, carta
maqueta	maquette	model	Modell(n)	maqueta	modello
maquillaje	maquillage	make-up	Schminke(f)	maquilhagem	trucco
maquillarse	maquiller(se)	make-up(put on)	schminken, sich	maquilhar-se	truccarsi
máquina	machine	machine	Maschine(f)	máquina	macchina
mar	mer	sea	Meer(n)	mar	mare
mar	mer	sea	See(f)	mar	mare
maratón	marathon	marathon	Marathonlauf(m)	maratona	maratona
maravillar	émerveiller	amaze	entzücken	maravilhar	meravigliare
maravilloso, a	merveilleux, se	marvellous	wunderbar	maravilhoso, a	meraviglioso, a
maravilloso, a	merveilleux, se	wonderful	wunderbar	maravilhoso, a	meraviglioso, a
marca	marque	brand, make	Marke(f)	marca	marchio, marca
marca, tanteo	score	score	Punktzahl(f)	resultado	punteggio
marcar	marquer	mark	markieren	marcar	segnare, marcare
marcar	cocher	tick	an = kreuzen	marcar	segnare
marcar	marquer	score	schießen(Tor-)	marcar	segnare
marcar un número	composer(n°tél)	dial	Nummer(f)(wählen)	discar, marcar	comporre(numero)
marco	cadre	frame	Rahmen(m)	moldura	cornice, quadro
marcha	marche	walk(ing)	Wanderung(f)	marcha	marcia
marchar	marcher	work, run	in Betrieb sein	funcionar	funzionare
marchitar	flétrir	wilt, wither	verwelken	murchar	appassire
marea	marée	tide	Gezeiten(pl.)	maré	marea
marejada	houle	swell, surge	Brandung(f)	vaga	ondosità
mareo	mal de mer	sea-sickness	Seekrankheit(f)	enjôo	mal di mare
marfil	ivoire	ivory	Elfenbein(n)	marfim	avorio
margen	marge	margin	Rand(m)	margem	margine

Spanish	French	English	German	Portuguese	Italian
marginal	marginal, e	fringe(on the)	Außenseiter(in f)m	marginal	marginale
marido	mari	husband	Ehemann(m)	marido	marito
marina	marine	navy	Marine(f)	marinha	marina
marinero	matelot	sailor	Matrose(m)	marinheiro	marinaio
marino	marin	sailor	Seemann(m)	marinheiro	marinaio
mariposa	papillon	butterfly	Schmetterling(m)	borboleta	farfalla
marisco	coquillage	shell-fish; shell	Muschel(f)	concha	conchiglia
marisco	fruits de mer	seafood	Meeresfrüchte(f, pl.)	marisco	frutti di mare
marítimo, a	maritime	maritime, sea-	See-	marítimo, a	marittimo, a
marmita, olla	marmite	cooking-pot	Kochtopf(m)	marmita	pentola, marmitta
mármol	marbre	marble	Marmor(m)	mármore	marmo
martes	mardi	Tuesday	Dienstag(m)	terça-feira	martedì
martillo	marteau	hammer	Hammer(m)	martelo	martello
mártir	martyr, e	martyr	Märtyrer(in f)m	mártir	martire
marxismo	marxisme	Marxism	Marxismus(m)	marxismo	marxismo
marzo	mars	March	März(m)	Março	marzo
más	plus	plus	und, plus	mais	più
más	plus	plus	plus	mais	più
más	plus	more	mehr	mais	più
más	davantage, plus	more	mehr	mais	più, di più
más	encore	more	noch	mais	ancora
más(de)	supplément(en)	extra-, additional-	Extra-; Neben-	mais(a)	più(in)
más allá de	au-delà de	beyond	jenseits	além de(para)	al di là
más bien	plutôt	rather	eher, lieber	antes; mais	piuttosto
más de	plus(de)	moreover, further	überdies, ferner	além do mais	più(di, in)
más lejos	plus loin	further	weiter	mais longe	più in là
más tarde	plus tard	later	später	mais tarde	più tardi
masa	masse	mass	Masse(f)	massa	massa
masa	pâte	pastry; dough	Teig(m)	massa	pasta
masa, pasta	pâte	paste	Paste(f); Masse(f)	massa	impasto, pasta
masacre	massacre	slaughter	Blutbad(n)	massacre	massacro
masaje	massage	massage	Massage(f)	massagem	massaggio
mascar	croquer	crunch	knabbern	trincar	sgranocchiare
máscara	masque	mask	Maske(f)	máscara	maschera
masculino, a	masculin, e	masculine, male	männlich	masculino, a	maschile
masilla	mastic	putty	Kitt(m)	betume	mastice
masivo, a	massif, ive	massive; solid	massiv	maciço, a	massiccio, a
masticar	mâcher	chew	kauen	mastigar	masticare
mástil	mât	mast	Mast(m)	mastro	albero
matador	matador	matador	Matador(m)	matador	matador
matar	tuer	kill	töten	matar	uccidere
mate	mat, e	dull, matt	glanzlos, matt	mate	opaco, a
matemáticas	mathématique(s)	mathematics	Mathematik(f)	matemáticas	matematica
materia	matière	matter, material	Stoff(m), Material(n)	matéria	materia
materia	substance	matter, material	Materie(f)	matéria	materia
materia, tema	matière	subject matter	Thema(n)	assunto	materia, tema
material; materia	matière	material	Material(n)	material; matéria	materiale; materia
material	matériau	material	Material(n)	material	materiale
material	matériel	material	Material(n)	material	materiale
materno, a; maternal	maternel, le	maternal, motherly	mütterlich	maternal	materno, a
matiz	nuance, ton	shade, nuance	Farbenton(m)	matiz, tom	sfumatura
matorral	buisson	bush	Gebüsch(n)	moita	cespuglio
matrícula	matricule	roll, register	Matrikel(f)	matrícula	matricola
matrícula	inscription	registration	Einschreibung(f)	matrícula	iscrizione
matrícula	immatriculation	registration	Eintragung(f)	matrícula	immatricolazione
matricularse	inscrire(s')	register	ein = schreiben, sich	matricular-se	iscriversi
matrimonio	mariage	wedding; marriage	Hochzeit(f); Heirat(f)	casamento	matrimonio
matutino, a	matinal, e	early	früh	matinal	mattutino, a
maullar	miauler	mew	miauen	miar	miagolare
máximo	maximum	maximum	Maximum(n)	máximo	massimo
mayo	mai	May	Mai(m)	Maio	maggio
mayoría	majorité	majority	Mehrheit(f)	maioria	maggioranza
mayoría(la)	plupart(la)	most(of the)	meisten(die)	maior parte(a)	maggior parte(la)
me	me, m'; moi	me	mich; mir	me	mi, me
mecánica	mécanique	mechanics	Mechanik(f)	mecânica	meccanica
mecánico, a	mécanique	mechanical	mechanisch	mecânico, a	meccanico, a
mecánico, a	mécanicien, ne	mechanic	Mechaniker(in f)m	mecânico, a	meccanico, a
mecanismo	mécanisme	mechanism	Mechanismus(m)	mecanismo	meccanismo

S

Spanish	French	English	German	Portuguese	Italian
mecenas	mécène	patron	Mäzen(m), Sponsor(m)	mecenas	mecenate
mecer	bercer	rock	wiegen	embalar	cullare
mechero	briquet	lighter	Feuerzeug(n)	isqueiro	accendino
mechón	mèche	lock(of hair)	Locke(f)	madeixa	ciocca
medalla	médaille	medal	Medaille(f)	medalha	medaglia
media	bas	stocking	Strumpf(m)(Nylon-)	meias	calza
media	moyenne	average	Durchschnitt(m)	média	media
media hora	demi-heure	half an hour	halbe Stunde	meia-hora	mezz'ora
medianoche	minuit	midnight	Mitternacht(f)	meia-noite	mezzanotte
medicina	médecine	medicine	Medizin(f)	medicina	medicina
medicina	médicament	drug, medicine	Medikament(n)	medicamento	medicina
médico, a	médical, e	medical	medizinisch	médico, a	medico, a
médico	médecin	doctor	Arzt(m), Ärztin(f)	médico	medico
medio	milieu	middle	Mitte(f)	meio	mezzo
medio, a	demi, e	half	halb	meio, a	mezzo, a
medio, a	mi-	half(-); mid-	halb-	meio, a	semi-; mezzo-
medio, a	moyen, ne	middle	mittel	médio, a	medio, a
medio, a	moyen, ne	medium	mittlere(r, s)	médio, a	medio, a
medio(s)	moyen	means	Mittel(n)	meio	mezzo
mediocre	médiocre	mediocre	mittelmäßig, schlecht	medíocre	mediocre
mediodía	midi	midday, noon	Mittag(m)	meio-dia	mezzogiorno
medir	mesurer	measure	messen	medir	misurare
meditar	méditer	meditate	nach = denken, sinnen	meditar	meditare
médula, tuétano	moelle	marrow(-bone)	Mark(n)	medula, tutano	midollo
mejilla	joue	cheek	Wange(f)	bochecha, face	guancia
mejillón	moule	mussel	Muschel(f)	mexilhão	cozza
mejor	meilleur, e	better	besser(sein)	melhor	migliore
mejor	mieux	better	besser	melhor	meglio
mejor	meilleur, e	best	Beste(f, m)	melhor	migliore
mejora; mejoría	amélioration	improvement	Verbesserung(f)	melhoramento	miglioramento
mejorar	améliorer	improve	verbessern	melhorar	migliorare
melancolía	mélancolie	melancholy	Wehmut(f)	melancolia	malinconia
melancolía	cafard	miserable(feel)	Trübsinn(m)	tristeza	malinconia
melocotón	pêche	peach	Pfirsich(m)	pêssego	pesca
melodía	mélodie	melody, tune	Melodie(f)	melodia	melodia
melodía	air	tune	Melodie(f)	melodia	melodia
melón	melon	melon	Melone(f)	melão	melone
membrana	membrane	membrane	Membran(f)	membrana	membrana
memoria	mémoire	memory	Gedächtnis(n)	memória	memoria
mención	mention	mention	Vermerk(m)	menção	menzione
mendigo, a	mendiant, e	beggar	Bettler(in f)m	mendigo, a	mendicante
menopausia	ménopause	menopause	Wechseljahre(n, pl)	menopausa	menopausa
menor	mineur, e	minor	unbedeutend	menor	minore
menor	mineur, e	minor	Minderjährige(f, m)	menor	minore, minorenne
menor	cadet, te	younger; youngest	Jüngere(m, f)	novo, a(o, a mais)	cadetto, a
menos	moins	less	weniger	menos	meno
menos(lo)	moins(le)	least(the)	wenigsten(am)	menos(o)	meno(il)
mensaje	message	message	Nachricht(f)	mensagem, recado	messaggio
mensual	mensuel, le	monthly	monatlich	mensal	mensile
menta	menthe	mint	Minze(f)	hortelã	menta
mental	mental, e	mental	geistig	mental	mentale
mentalidad	mentalité	mentality	Mentalität(f)	mentalidade	mentalità
mentir	mentir	lie	lügen	mentir	mentire
mentira	mensonge	lie, fib	Lüge(f)	mentira	bugia
mentiroso, a	menteur, se	liar	Lügner(in f)m	mentiroso, a	bugiardo, a
menú	menu	menu	Menü(n), Speisekarte f	ementa	menù
menú	carte(resto)	menu	Karte(f)(Speisekarte)	lista	menù, carta
mercado	marché	market	Markt(m)	mercado	mercato
mercancía	marchandise	goods, merchandise	Ware(f)	mercadoria	merce
mercenario	mercenaire	mercenary	Söldner(m)	mercenário	mercenario
mercurio	mercure	mercury	Quecksilber(n)	mercúrio	mercurio
merecer	mériter	deserve, merit	verdienen	merecer	meritare
meridiano	méridien	meridian	Meridian(m)	meridiano	meridiano
mérito	mérite	merit, worth	Verdienst(n)	mérito	merito
mermelada	confiture	jam	Marmelade(f)	doce, compota	marmellata
mes	mois	month	Monat(m)	mês	mese
mesa	table	table	Tisch(m)	mesa	tavolo; tavola
meseta	plateau	plateau	Hochebene(f)	planalto	altipiano

458

Spanish	French	English	German	Portuguese	Italian
mestizo, a	métis, se	half-caste	Mischling(m)	mestiço, a	meticcio, a
metal	métal	metal	Metal(n)	metal	metallo
metálico, a	métallique	metallic	metallisch	metálico, a	metallico, a
metamorfosis	métamorphose	metamorphosis(-es)	Verwandlung(f)	metamorfose	metamorfosi
metástasis	métastase	metastasis(-es)	Tochtergeschwulst(f)	metástase	metastasi
meteorología	météorologie	weather forecast	Wetterkunde(f)	meteorologia	meteorologia
meticuloso, a	méticuleux, se	meticulous	sorgfältig	meticuloso, a	meticoloso, a
método	méthode	method	Methode(f)	método	metodo
métrico, a	métrique	metric	metrisch	métrico, a	metrico, a
metro	métro	underground, tube	U-Bahn(f)	metropolitano	metropolitana
metro	mètre	metre	Meter(m, n)	metro	metro
mezcla	mélange	mixture; mixing	Mischung(f)	mistura	miscuglio
mezcla	mélange	blend, mixture	Mischung(f)	mistura	mescolanza
mezclar	mélanger	mix	mischen	misturar	mescolare
mezquita	mosquée	mosque	Moschee(f)	mesquita	moschea
mi	mon	my	mein	meu, minha	mio, mia(il, la)
mi	ma	my	meine	minha	mia(la)
mí, me; yo	moi	me; I	mich; mir; ich	eu; me; mim	io; me
microbio	microbe	germ, microbe	Mikrobe(f)	micróbio	microbo
micrófono	micro(phone)	microphone, mike	Mikrophon(n)	microfone	microfono
microscopio	microscope	microscope	Mikroskop(n)	microscópio	microscopio
miedo	peur	fear	Angst(f)	medo	paura
miedo(tener)	peur(avoir)	afraid(to be)	Angst(haben)	medo(ter)	paura(avere)
miel	miel	honey	Honig(m)	mel	miele
miembro	membre	limb	Glied(n)	membro	membro, arto
miembro, a; socio, a	membre(de)	member(of)	Mitglied(n)	membro, a; sócio, a	membro, i
mientras	pendant que	while	während	enquanto	mentre; già che
mientras	tandis que	while, whilst	während	enquanto	mentre
mientras	attendant(en)	meanwhile	inzwischen	entretanto	attesa(in)
miércoles	mercredi	Wednesday	Mittwoch(m)	quarta-feira	mercoledì
migración	migration	migration	Wanderung(f)	migração	migrazione
migratorio, a	migrateur, trice	migrant	wandernd; Wander-	migrador, a	migratore, trice
mil	mille	thousand	tausend	mil	mille; mila(pl.)
milagro	miracle	miracle	Wunder(n)	milagre	miracolo
milésimo, a	millième	thousandth	tausendste	milésimo, a	millesimo, a
milicia	milice	militia	Miliz(f)	milícia	milizia
militante	militant, e	militant	Militant(m)	militante	militante
militar	militaire	military	militärisch	militar	militare
militar	militer	militate	kämpfen für	militar	militare
mil millones	milliard	thousand million	Milliarde(f)	bilião	miliardo
millar	millier	thousand	Tausend(n)	milhar	migliaio(a)
millón	million	million	Million(f)	milhão	milione
mina	mine	mine	Bergwerk(n)	mina	miniera
mineral	minéral, e	mineral	mineralisch	mineral	minerale
mineral	minerai	ore	Erz(n)	minério	minerale
miniatura	miniature	miniature	Miniatur(f)	miniatura	miniatura
mínimo, a	minimum	minimum	Minimum(n)	mínimo, a	minimo, a
ministerio	ministère	ministry	Ministerium(n)	ministério	ministero
ministro	ministre	minister	Minister(in f)m	ministro	ministro
minoría	minorité	minority	Minderheit(f)	minoria	minoranza
minúsculo, a	minuscule	minute, tiny	winzig	minúsculo, a	minuscolo, a
minusválido, a	handicapé, e	handicapped	behindert	deficiente	andicappato, a
minuto	minute	minute	Minute(f)	minuto	minuto
mío, mía	mien, ne	mine	meine, meiner	meu, minha	mio(il); mia(la)
mío, a(el, la)	moi(à)	mine, to me	mir	meu(é)	mio, mia(è)
miope	myope	short-sighted	kurzsichtig	míope	miope
mirada	regard	look, expression	Blick(m)	olhar	sguardo
mirar	regarder	look(at)	schauen, an = sehen	olhar	guardare
mirar	regarder	watch, look(at)	fern = sehen	ver	guardare
mire(!)	regardez!	look!	seht!, schauen Sie!	olhe!	guardi!, guardate!
mis	mes	my	meine	meus	miei, mie(i, le)
misa	messe	mass	Messe(f)	missa	messa
miseria	misère	poverty	Elend(n)	miséria	miseria
misil	missile	missile	Rakete(f)	míssil	missile
misión	mission	mission	Mission(f)	missão	missione
mismo, a	même	same	selbe; gleich(der -)	mesmo, a	stesso, a
mismo, a(él, ella)	même(lui, elle)	self(him, her, it)	selbst(er, sie, es)	próprio, a(ele, a)	stesso, a(lui, lei)
misterio	mystère	mystery	Geheimnis(n); Rätsel n	mistério	mistero

S

Spanish	French	English	German	Portuguese	Italian
misterioso, a	mystérieux, se	mysterious	mysteriös	misterioso, a	misterioso, a
místico, a	mystique	mystic(al)	mystisch	místico, a	mistico, a
mitad	moitié	half(-lves)	Hälfte(f)	metade	metà
mito	mythe	myth	Mythos(m); Sage(f)	mito	mito
mixto, a	mixte	mixed	gemischt	misto, a	misto, a
mobiliario	mobilier	furniture	Möbel(pl)	mobiliário	mobilio
mobiliario	ameublement	furnishing	Einrichtung(f)	mobiliário	arredamento, mobilio
mobilidad	mobilité	mobility	Beweglichkeit(f)	mobilidade	mobilità
mobilizar	mobiliser	mobilize	mobilisieren	mobilizar	mobilitare
mochila	sac à dos	rucksack	Rucksack(m)	mochila	zaino
moda	mode	fashion	Mode(f)	moda	moda
modelo	modèle	model, pattern	Modell(n)	modelo	modello
modelo	modèle	pattern	Muster(n)	modelo	modello
modelo, patrón	modèle	design	Muster(n), Modell(n)	modelo	modello
moderar	modérer	moderate	mäßigen	moderar	moderare
moderno, a	moderne	modern	modern	moderno, a	moderno, a
modesto, a	modeste	modest	bescheiden	modesto, a	modesto, a
modificación	modification	modification	Abänderung(f)	modificação	modifica
modificar	modifier	modify	verändern	modificar	modificare
modista	couturier, ière	dressmaker, tailor	Schneider(in f)m	costureiro, a	sarto, a
modo, manera	façon, manière	way, manner, fashion	Weise(f), Art(f)	modo, maneira	modo, maniera
modo, manera	mode, manière	mode, manner	Weise(f)	modo, maneira	modo, maniera
mofarse, burlarse	moquer(se)	make fun of, mock	verspotten	troçar	burlarsi
mojado, a	mouillé, e	wet	naß	molhado, a	bagnato, a
mojar	mouiller	wet	an = feuchten	molhar	bagnare
mojar	tremper	soak	ein = weichen	molhar	inzuppare
molar	molaire	molar	Backenzahn(m)	molar	molare
molde	moule	mould	Form(f)	molde; forma	stampo, forma
molécula	molécule	molecule	Molekül(n)	molécula	molecola
moler	moudre	grind	mahlen	moer	macinare
molestar	gêner	obstruct	stören	incomodar	imbarazzare
molestar	déranger	disturb, bother	stören	incomodar	disturbare
molestia	gêne	embarrassment	Verlegenheit(f)	embaraço	disagio, imbarazzo
molestia	contrariété	annoyance	Verdruß(m)	contrariedade	seccatura
molino	moulin	mill	Mühle(f)	moinho	mulino
molusco	mollusque	mollusc	Weichtier(n)	molusco	mollusco
momento	moment	moment	Augenblick(m)	momento	momento, attimo
monarquía	monarchie	monarchy	Monarchie(f)	monarquia	monarchia
monasterio	monastère	monastery	Kloster(n)	mosteiro	monastero
mondar	peler	peel	schälen	descascar	sbucciare
moneda, dinero	monnaie	money	Geld(n)	moeda	moneta
moneda	pièce	coin	Geldstück(n)	moeda	spiccioli, moneta
moneda	monnaie	currency	Währung(f), Devisen pl	moeda	valuta; moneta
monedero	porte-monnaie	purse	Geldbörse(f)	porta-moedas	portamonete
monetario, a	monétaire	monetary	Währungs-, Geld-	monetário, a	monetario, a
monitor, a	moniteur, trice	instructor	Leiter/in; Lehrer/in	monitor, a	istruttore, trice
monja	soeur	nun, sister	Nonne(f), Schwester(f)	freira	suora
monje, fraile	moine	monk	Mönch(m)	monge, frade	monaco, frate
mono	singe	monkey	Affe(m)	macaco	scimmia
monogamia	monogamie	monogamy	Monogamie(f)	monogamia	monogamia
monopolio	monopole	monopoly	Monopol(n)	monopólio	monopolio
monótono, a	monotone	monotonous	monoton, eintönig	monótono, a	monotono, a
monstruo	monstre	monster	Monster(n)	monstro	mostro
montaje	montage	mounting, assembly	Montage(f)	montagem	montaggio
montaña	montagne	mountain	Gebirge(n), Berg(m)	montanha	montagna
monte	mont, montagne	mount	Berg(m)	monte	monte
montón	amas	pile	Haufen(m)	amontoado	mucchio
montón	tas	pile	Haufen(m)	montão, pilha	mucchio
monumento	monument	monument	Denkmal(n)	monumento	monumento
moño	chignon	chignon, bun	Haarknoten(m)	carrapicho	crocchia
monzón	mousson	monsoon	Monsun(m)	monção	monsone
moqueta	moquette	carpet	Teppichboden(m)	alcatifa	moquette
morada, casa	demeure	residence, dwelling	Wohnung(f), Haus(n)	habitação, casa	dimora
moral	moral, e	moral	moralisch	moral	morale
moral, ánimo	moral	morale	Stimmung(f), Moral(f)	moral	morale
moral	morale	moral	Moral(f)	moral	morale
morder	mordre	bite	beißen	morder	mordere
mordisquear	grignoter	nibble	knabbern	petiscar	sgranocchiare

Spanish	French	English	German	Portuguese	Italian
morfina	morphine	morphine	Morphium(n)	morfina	morfina
morfología	morphologie	morphology	Morphologie(f)	morfologia	morfologia
morir	mourir	die	sterben	morrer	morire
mortal	mortel, le	mortal; deadly	tödlich	mortal	mortale
mortal	mortel, le	fatal	tödlich	mortal	mortale
mortalidad	mortalité	mortality	Sterblichkeit(f)	mortalidade	mortalità
mosaico	mosaïque	mosaic	Mosaik(n)	mosaico	mosaico
mosca	mouche	fly	Fliege(f)	mosca	mosca
mosquito	moustique	mosquito(-es)	Mücke(f)	mosquito	zanzara
mostaza	moutarde	mustard	Senf(m)	mostarda	senape
mostrador	comptoir	counter	Ladentisch(m)	balcão	banco
motel	motel	motel	Motel(n)	motel	motel
motín	émeute	riot	Aufruhr(m)	motim	sommossa
motivar	motiver	motivate	motivieren	motivar	motivare
motivo	motif	motive	Motiv(n)	motivo	motivo
moto	moto	motor-bike	Motorrad(n)	mota	moto
motor	moteur	engine; motor	Motor(m)	motor	motore
motorista	motard	motorcyclist	Motorradfahrer(in f)m	motociclista	motociclista
mover	remuer	move	bewegen, sich	mexer-se	muovere(-rsi)
moverse	bouger	move	bewegen	mexer-se	muovere
móvil, movible	mobile	mobile, movable	beweglich, mobil	móvel	mobile
movimiento	mouvement	movement, motion	Bewegung(f)	movimento	movimento
muchacho, mozo	garçon	boy	Junge(m)	rapaz	ragazzo
muchedumbre	foule	crowd	Menge(f)	multidão	folla
mucho	beaucoup	much, many	viel(e)	muito	molto
mucho, a	beaucoup	lots of, a lot of	viel(e)	muito, a	molto, a, i, e
mucho tiempo	longtemps	long time(a)	lange	muito tempo	molto/molto tempo
muchos, as	beaucoup	many	viele	muitos, as	molti
mudar	changer	change	ändern	mudar; trocar	cambiare
mudar(se)	déménager	move	um = ziehen	mudar, mudar-se	traslocare
mudo, a	muet, te	dumb; silent	stumm	mudo, a	muto, a
mueble	meuble	furniture	Möbelstück(n)	móvel	mobile
mueca	grimace	grimace	Grimasse(f)	careta	smorfia
muelle	quai	quay	Kai((m)	cais	molo
muelle	ressort	spring	Feder(f)(Sprung-)	mola	molla
muerte	mort	death	Tod(m)	morte	morte
muerto, a	mort, e	dead	tot	morto, a	morto, a
muerto, a	tué, e	killed	getötet	morto, a	ucciso, a
muerto, a	mort, e	dead man/woman	Tote(f, m)	morto, a	morto, a
muesca	encoche	notch	Kerbe(f), Einschnitt m	entalhe	tacca, intacco
muestra	échantillon	sample	Probe(f), Muster(n)	amostra	campione
mujer	femme	woman(women)	Frau(f)	mulher	donna
mujer	femme, épouse	wife(wives)	Ehefrau(f), Frau(f)	mulher	moglie
muleta	béquille	crutch(-es)	Krücke(f)	muleta	stampella
multa	amende	fine	Geldstrafe(f)	multa	multa
multa	procès-verbal	ticket, penalty	Strafmandat(n)	multa	contravvenzione
múltiple	multiple	multiple, numerous	viel-; vielfältig	múltiplo, a	multiplo, a
multiplicar	multiplier	multiply	multiplizieren	multiplicar	moltiplicare
multitud	multitude	multitude	Menge(f)	multidão	moltitudine
mundial	mondial, e	world-wide, world	weltlich	mundial	mondiale
mundo	monde	world	Welt(f)	mundo	mondo
municiones	munitions	ammunition	Munition(f)	munições	munizioni
municipal	municipal, e	municipal; town -	städtisch; Stadt-	municipal	municipale
muñeca	poignet	wrist	Handgelenk(n)	punho	polso
muñeca	poupée	doll	Puppe(f)	boneca	bambola
muralla	enceinte	fence; enclosure	Einzäunung(f)	muralha, recinto	cinta, recinto
murmurar	murmurer	murmur, whisper	flüstern	murmurar	mormorare
muro, pared	mur	wall	Mauer(f)	muro, parede	muro
muscular	musculaire	muscular	Muskel-	muscular	muscolare
músculo	muscle	muscle	Muskel(m)	músculo	muscolo
musculoso, a	musclé, e	muscular	muskulös	musculado, a	muscoloso, a
museo	musée	museum	Museum(n)	museu	museo
musgo	mousse	moss	Moos(n)	musgo	muschio
música	musique	music	Musik(f)	música	musica
musical	musical, e	musical	musikalisch	musical	musicale
músico, a	musicien, ne	musician	Musiker(in f)m	músico, a	musicista
muslo	cuisse	thigh	Schenkel(m)	coxa	coscia
muslo; pierna	cuisse	leg	Schenkel(m)	perna	coscia

S

Spanish	French	English	German	Portuguese	Italian
musulmán, a	musulman, e	Moslem, Muslim	Mohammedaner(in f)m	muçulmano, a	musulmano, a
mutilado, a	mutilé, e	disabled	verstümmelt	mutilado, a	mutilato, a
mútuo, a	mutuel, le	mutual	gegenseitig	mútuo, a	mutuo, a
muy	très	very	sehr	muito	molto

N

Spanish	French	English	German	Portuguese	Italian
nacer	naître	born(be)	geboren werden	nascer	nascere
nacido, a	né, e	born(be)	geboren	nascido, a	nato, a
nacimiento	naissance	birth	Geburt(f)	nascimento	nascita
nación	nation	nation	Nation(f)	nação	nazione
nacional	national, e	national	national	nacional	nazionale
nacionalidad	nationalité	nationality	Nationalität(f)	nacionalidade	nazionalità
nacionalismo	nationalisme	nationalism	Nationalismus(m)	nacionalismo	nazionalismo
nacionalizado, a	naturalisé, e	naturalized	eingebürgert	naturalizado, a	naturalizzato, a
nada	rien	nothing	nichts	nada	niente, nulla
nadador, a	nageur, se	swimmer	Schwimmer(in f)m	nadador, a	nuotatore, trice
nadar	nager	swim	schwimmen	nadar	nuotare
nadie	personne	nobody, no one	niemand	ninguém	nessuno
nalga	fesse	bottom, buttock	Gesäß(n), Po(m)	nádega	natica
naranja	orange	orange	Apfelsine(f)	laranja	arancia
narcótico	narcotique	narcotic	Betäubungsmittel(n)	narcótico	narcotico
narcótico	stupéfiant	narcotic	Betäubungsmittel(n)	narcótico	stupefacente
nariz	nez	nose	Nase(f)	nariz	naso
nariz	narine	nostril	Nasenloch(n)	narina	narice
narración	récit	story	Bericht(m)	narração	racconto
nasal	nasal, e	nasal	nasal	nasal	nasale
natación	natation, nage	swimming	Schwimmen(n)	natação	nuoto
natal	natal, e	native	Heimat-; Geburts-	natal	natale
natalidad	natalité	birth-rate	Geburtenrate(f)	natalidade	natalità
nativo, a	natif, ive	native	gebürtig	nativo, a	nativo, a
natural	naturel, le	natural	natürlich	natural	naturale
naturaleza	nature	nature	Natur(f)	natureza	natura
naturista	naturiste	nudist	Nudist(in f)m	naturista	nudista
naufragio	naufrage	wreck	Schiffbruch(m)	naufrágio	naufragio
náusea	nausée	nausea, feel sick	Brechreiz(m)	naúsea	nausea
náutico, a	nautique	nautical, water-	nautisch, Wasser-	naútico, a	nautico, a
navaja de afeitar	rasoir	razor	Rasierapparat(m)	navalha, gilete	rasoio
naval	naval, e	naval	See-	naval	navale
nave, navío	vaisseau	vessel, ship	Schiff(n)	navio	vascello, nave
navegación	navigation	navigation	Seefahrt(f)	navegação	navigazione
navegante	navigateur	navigator	Seefahrer(m)	navegador	navigatore
Navidad	Noël	Christmas	Weihnachten(n)	Natal	Natale
navío	navire	ship	Schiff(n)	navio	nave
necesario, a	nécessaire	necessary	nötig, notwendig	necessário, a	necessario, a
necesario(ser)	falloir	have to, must	müssen	preciso(ser)	bisognare
necesidad	besoin	need	Bedürfnis(n)	necessidade	bisogno
necesidad	nécessité	necessity	Notwendigkeit(f)	necessidade	necessità
necesitar	besoin(avoir)	require, need	brauchen	necessidade(ter)	bisogno(avere)
negar	nier	deny	verneinen, leugnen	negar	negare
negativo, a	négatif, ive	negative	negativ	negativo, a	negativo, a
negligencia	négligence	negligence	Nachlässigkeit(f)	negligência	negligenza
negociación	négociation	negotiation	Verhandlung(f)	negociação	negoziato
negociaciones	pourparlers	talks	Verhandlungen(pl)	negociações	trattative
negociador, a	négociateur	negotiator	Unterhändler(in f)m	negociador, a	negoziatore, trice
negociar	négocier	negotiate	verhandeln	negociar	negoziare
negocios	affaires	business	Geschäfte(n, pl.)	negócios	affari
negro, a	noir, e	black	schwarz	preto, a	nero, a

Spanish	French	English	German	Portuguese	Italian
negro, a	noir, e	black(person)	Schwarze(f, m)	negro, a	negro, a
negro, a	nègre, esse	negro(-ress), black	Neger(in f)m	negro, a	negro, a
nervio	nerf	nerve	Nerv(m)	nervo	nervo
nervioso, a	nerveux, se	nervous	nervös; Nerven-	nervoso, a	nervoso, a
nervioso, a	nerveux, se	nervy	nervös	nervoso, a	nervoso, a
neumático	pneu	tyre	Reifen(m)	pneu	pneumatico, gomma
neumonía	pneumonie	pneumonia	Lungenentzündung(f)	pneumonia	polmonite
neurología	neurologie	neurology	Neurologie(f)	neurologia	neurologia
neurosis	névrose	neurosis(-ses)	Neurose(f)	nevrose	nevrosi
neutralizar	neutraliser	neutralize	neutralisieren	neutralizar	neutralizzare
neutro, a	neutre	neutral	neutral	neutro, a	neutro, a
nevera	réfrigérateur	refrigerator	Kühlschrank(m)	frigorífico	frigorifero
ni	ni	neither, nor	weder, noch	nem	né
nicotina	nicotine	nicotine	Nikotin(n)	nicotina	nicotina
nido	nid	nest	Nest(n)	ninho	nido
niebla	brouillard	fog	Nebel(m)	nevoeiro	nebbia
nieto, a	petit-fils/fille	grandson/-daughter	Enkel(m), Enkelin(f)	neto, a	nipote
nieve	neige	snow	Schnee(m)	neve	neve
nilón	nylon	nylon	Nylon(m)	nylon	nylon
ningún, o, a	aucun, e	no, not any; no one	keiner, keine	nenhum, a	nessuno, a
niñera	nurse	nanny	Kindermädchen(n)	ama	bambinaia
niño, a; chico, a	enfant	child, children(pl)	Kind(n)	criança	bambino, a
níquel	nickel	nickel	Nickel(n)	níquel	nichel
nivel	niveau	level	Stand(m), Niveau(n)	nível	livello
nivel(de vida)	niveau(de vie)	standard of living	Standard(m)	nível(de vida)	tenore(di vita)
no	non	no	nein	não	no
no-fumadores	non-fumeur	non-smoker	Nichtraucher(m)	não-fumador	non-fumatore
no, gracias	non merci	no thank you	nein, danke	não, obrigado	no, grazie
no	pas	not	nicht	não, nem	non
noble	noble	noble	edel; nobel	nobre	nobile
noble	noble	nobleman(-men)	Edelmann m, Edelfrau f	nobre	nobile
noción	notion	notion	Kenntnis(f), Begriff m	noção	nozione
nocivo, a	nocif, ive	harmful	schädlich	nocivo, a	nocivo, a
nocturno, a	nocturne	nocturnal, night-	nächtlich	nocturno, a	notturno, a
noche	nuit	night	Nacht(f)	noite	notte
noche(esta)	soir(ce)	tonight	heute abend	noite(esta)	sera(questa)
nómada	nomade	nomad	Nomade(m)	nómada	nomade
nombramiento	nomination	nomination	Ernennung(f)	nomeação	nomina
nombrar	nommer	appoint	ernennen	nomear	nominare
nombre	nom, substantif	noun	Hauptwort(n)	substantivo	nome, sostantivo
nombre	nom	name	Name(m)	nome	nome
nombre	prénom	first name	Vorname(m)	nome próprio	nome
nórdico, a	nordique	nordic; northern	nordisch; nördlich	nórdico, a	nordico, a
norma	norme	norm, standard	Norm(f)	norma	norma
normal	normal, e	normal; usual	normal	normal	normale
Norte	Nord	North	Norden(m)	Norte	Nord
nos	nous	us	uns	nos	ci, ce
nosotros	nous	we	wir	nós	noi
nostalgia	nostalgie	homesickness	Heimweh(n)	nostalgia	nostalgia
nota	note	note	Vermerk(m)	nota	appunto
nota	note	note	Note(f)	nota	nota
nota	note	mark	Note(f)	nota	voto
notable	remarquable	remarkable	bemerkenswert	notável	notevole
notar, señalar	remarquer	notice	bemerken	notar, reparar	notare, osservare
notario	notaire	solicitor, lawyer	Notar(m)	notário	notaio
noticias	nouvelles	news	Nachrichten(f, pl)	notícias	notizie
notificar	notifier	notify	bekannt = geben	notificar	notificare
notoriedad	notoriété	notoriety	Offenkundigkeit(f)	notoriedade	notorietà
novedad	nouveauté	novelty	Neuheit(f)	novidade	novità
novela	roman	novel	Roman(m)	romance	romanzo
novela policíaca	roman policier	detective novel	Kriminalroman(m)	romance policial	giallo
novelista	romancier, ière	novelist	Schriftsteller(in f)m	romancista	romanziere, a
noventa	quatre-vingt-dix	ninety	neunzig	noventa	novanta
novicio, a; novato, a	novice, débutant	novice	Neuling(m)	principiante	novizio, a
noviembre	novembre	November	November(m)	Novembro	novembre
novio, a	fiancé, e	fiancé(e)	Verlobte(f, m)	noivo, a	fidanzato, a
novio, novia	marié, mariée	bridegroom, bride-	Bräutigam(m), Braut(f)	noivo, noiva	sposo, sposa
nube	nuage	cloud	Wolke(f)	nuvem	nuvola

S

Spanish	French	English	German	Portuguese	Italian
nuca	nuque	nape of the neck	Nacken(m)	nuca	nuca
nuclear	nucléaire	nuclear	Kern-, Atom-	nuclear	nucleare
núcleo	noyau	nucleus(-ei)	Kern(m)	núcleo	nucleo
nudo	noeud	knot	Knoten(m)	nó, laço	nodo
nuera	belle-fille	daughter-in-law	Schwiegertochter(f)	nora	nuora
nuestro, a	notre	our	unser, unsere	nosso, a	nostro, a(il, la)
nuestro, a(el, la)	nôtre(le, la)	ours	unsere(der, die, das)	nosso, a(o, a)	nostro, a(il, la)
nuestros, nuestras	nos	our	unser(e)	nossos, nossas	nostri, e(i, le)
nueve	neuf	nine	neun	nove	nove
nuevo, a	nouveau, nouvelle	new	neu	novo, a	nuovo, a
nuevo, a	neuf, neuve	new	neu	novo, a	nuovo, a
nuez	noix	walnut	Walnuß(f)	noz	noce
nulo, a	nul, le	worthless; useless	wertlos	nulo, a	nullo, a
numerario	titulaire	tenured	festangestellt	titular	titolare
numérico, a	numérique	numerical	numerisch	numérico, a	numerico, a
número	nombre	number	Anzahl(f), Zahl(f)	número	numero
número	numéro	number	Nummer(f)	número	numero
número	pointure	size	Größe(f)	tamanho; número	numero
número, edición	numéro, tirage	issue	Auflage(f)	número	numero, pubblicazione
numeroso, a	nombreux, se	numerous, many	zahlreich	numeroso, a	numeroso, a
nutritivo, a	nutritif, ive	nutritious	nahrhaft	nutritivo, a	nutritivo, a

O

Spanish	French	English	German	Portuguese	Italian
o; u	ou	or	oder	ou	o
oasis	oasis	oasis(oases pl.)	Oase(f)	oásis	oasi
obedecer	obéir	obey	gehorchen	obedecer	obbedire
obeso, a	obèse	obese	füllig, fettleibig	obeso, a	obeso, a
obispo	évêque	bishop	Bischof(m)	bispo	vescovo
objeción, reparo	objection	objection, protest	Einwand(m)	objecção	obiezione
objetivo, a	objectif, ive	objective	objektiv, sachlich	objectivo, a	oggettivo, a
objetivo	objectif	objective	Objektiv(n), Ziel(n)	objectivo	obiettivo
objetivo	objectif	lens	Objektiv(n)	objectiva	obiettivo
objeto	objet	object	Objekt(n), Ding(n)	objecto	oggetto
objeto, tema	objet, thème	theme, subject	Thema(n), Objekt(n)	tema, assunto	oggetto, scopo
objetos de valor	objets de valeur	valuables	Wertsachen(f pl)	objectos de valor	oggetti di valore
oblicuo, a	oblique	oblique, slanting	schräg, schief	oblíquo, a	obliquo, a
obligación	obligation	obligation	Verpflichtung(f)	obrigação	obbligo
obligación	contrainte	restraint	Zwang(m)	obrigação	costrizione
obligar	obliger	oblige, force	zwingen	obrigar	obbligare
obligar a	contraindre	force, compel	zwingen	obrigar	costringere
obligatorio, a	obligatoire	compulsory	obligatorisch	obrigatório, a	obbligatorio, a
obligatorio, a	obligatoire	mandatory	obligatorisch	obrigatório, a	obbligatorio, a
obra	oeuvre, travail	work	Werk(n)	obra	opera
obra	ouvrage	work	Werk(n)	obra	lavoro
obra	chantier	work-site	Baustelle(f)	obra	cantiere
obra	pièce	play	Stück(n)	peça	commedia
obra maestra	chef-d'oeuvre	masterpiece	Meisterwerk(n)	obra-prima	capolavoro
obrero, a	ouvrier, ière	worker, workman	Arbeiter(in f)m	operário, a	operaio, a
obsceno, a	obscène	obscene	obszön	obsceno, a	osceno, a
observación	remarque	remark, comment	Bemerkung(f)	observação	osservazione
observador, a	observateur	observer	Beobachter(in f)m	observador, a	osservatore, trice
observar	observer	observe	beobachten	observar	osservare
obsesión	obsession	obsession	fixe Idee(f)	obsessão	ossessione
obsesión	hantise	obsessive fear	Zwangsvorstellung(f)	obsessão	ossessione
obsesionar	obséder	obsess	verfolgen, quälen	obcecar	ossessionare
obseso, a	obsédé, e	maniac	Besessene(f, m)	obcecado, a	maniaco, a
obstáculo	obstacle	obstacle	Hindernis(n)	obstáculo	ostacolo
obstrucción	obstruction	obstruction	Störung(f)	obstrucção	ostruzione

| --- | --- | --- | --- | --- | --- |
obtener	obtenir	obtain, get	erhalten	obter	ottenere
obtener	obtenir, recevoir	get, obtain	bekommen	obter	ottenere
obús	obus	shell	Geschoß(n), Granate(f)	obus	proiettile
oca	oie	goose(geese pl.)	Gans(f)	ganso	oca
ocasional	occasionnel, le	occasional	gelegentlich	ocasional	occasionale
ocasionar, causar	occasionner	cause, bring about	verursachen	ocasionar, causar	causare
ocasionar	entraîner	entail	mit sich bringen	acarretar	comportare
occidental	occidental, e	Western	westlich	ocidental	occidentale
oceánico, a	océanique	oceanic	ozeanisch	oceânico, a	oceanico, a
océano	océan	ocean	Ozean(m)	oceano	oceano
octavilla	tract	handout, leaflet	Flugblatt(n)	panfleto	volantino
octubre	octobre	October	Oktober(m)	Outubro	ottobre
oculista	oculiste	oculist	Augenarzt m/-ärztin f	oftalmologista	oculista
ocupado, a	occupé, e	busy	beschäftigt	ocupado, a	impegnato, a
ocupado, a	occupé, e	engaged; taken	besetzt	ocupado, a	occupato, a
ocupado, a	occupé, e	occupied	besetzt	ocupado, a	occupato, a
ocupar	occuper	occupy, fill	ein = nehmen	ocupar	occupare
ocuparse	occuper(s')	look after	kümmern sich/um	tomar conta	occuparsi
ocurrir, suceder	arriver	occur, happen	geschehen	acontecer	succedere
ochenta	quatre-vingts	eighty	achtzig	oitenta	ottanta
ocho	huit	eight	acht	oito	otto
odiar	haïr	hate, detest	hassen	odiar	odiare
odio	haine	hate	Haß(m)	ódio	odio
odioso, a	odieux, se	odious, obnoxious	widerwärtig	odioso, a	odioso, a
Oeste	Ouest	West	Westen(m)	Oeste	Ovest
ofender, picar	vexer	offend, vex	beleidigen	ofender	offendere
ofenderse	vexer(se)	get upset	beleidigt sein	ofender-se	offendersi
ofensiva	offensive	offensive	Offensive(f)	ofensiva	offensiva
oferta	offre	offer	Angebot(n)	oferta	offerta
oficial	officiel, le	official	offiziell	oficial	ufficiale
oficial	officier	officer	Offizier(m)	oficial	ufficiale
oficinista	employé, e	clerk	Angestellte(f, m)	empregado, a	impiegato, a
oficio	métier	profession, job	Beruf(m)	ofício	mestiere
oficioso, a	officieux, se	unofficial	halbamtlich	oficioso, a	ufficioso, a
ofrecer	offrir	give; offer	schenken, an = bieten	oferecer	offrire, regalare
oftalmología	ophtalmologie	ophthalmology	Augenheilkunde(f)	oftalmologia	oftalmologia
oído	ouïe	hearing, audition	Gehör(n)	ouvido	udito
oír	entendre	hear	hören	ouvir	sentire
ojalá	pourvu que	provided that	wenn nur, sofern, daß	oxalá	purché
ojeada	regard	glance	Blick(m)	olhada	occhiata
ojeras	cerne	ring, circle	Augenringe(pl.)	olheiras	occhiaia
ojo	oeil	eye	Auge(n)	olho	occhio
ojos	yeux	eyes	Augen(n, pl)	olhos	occhi
ola	vague	wave	Welle(f)	onda, vaga	onda
ola	lame	wave	Welle(f)	vaga	ondata
oleada	flot	wave; flood	Welle(f); Flut(f)	corrente	flutto
oler	sentir	smell	riechen	cheirar	odorare, annusare
olfatear, husmear	flairer	sniff; scent; sense	wittern, schnüffeln	farejar, cheirar	annusare
olfato	odorat	smell(sense of)	Geruchssinn(m)	olfacto	odorato
olímpico, a	olympique	Olympic	olympisch	olímpico, a	olimpico, a
olor	odeur	odour, smell	Geruch(m)	cheiro, odor	odore
olvidar	oublier	forget	vergessen	esquecer	dimenticare
ombligo	nombril	navel	Nabel(m)	umbigo	ombelico
omitir	omettre	omit	aus = lassen	omitir	omettere
once	onze	eleven	elf	onze	undici
onda	onde	wave	Welle(f)	onda	onda
opaco, a	opaque	opaque	undurchsichtig; trüb	opaco, a	opaco, a
opción	option, choix	option	Wahl(f)	opção	opzione
ópera	opéra	opera	Oper(f)	ópera	opera
operación	opération	operation	Operation(f)	operação	operazione
operar	opérer	operate(on)	operieren	operar	operare
opinión	opinion	opinion	Meinung(f)	opinião	opinione
opinión	avis	opinion	Meinung(f)	opinião, parecer	avviso, parere
oponerse	opposer(s')	oppose	widersetzen, sich	opor-se	opporsi
oponerse(a)	contrer	counter	Kontra geben	contrariar	opporsi(a)
oportunidad	occasion	opportunity	Gelegenheit(f)	oportunidade	occasione
oportuno, a	opportun, e	opportune	günstig	oportuno, a	opportuno, a
oposición	opposition	opposition	Opposition(f)	oposição	opposizione

S

Spanish	French	English	German	Portuguese	Italian
oposiciones	concours	competitive exam	Prüfung(f)	concurso	concorso
oprimido, a	opprimé, e	oppressed	unterdrückt	oprimido, a	oppresso, a
óptico, a	opticien, ne	optician	Optiker(in f)m	oculista	ottico
óptico, a	optique	optic(al)	optisch	óptico, a	ottico, a
optimista	optimiste	optimistic	optimistisch	optimista	ottimista
opuesto, a	opposé, e	opposing	entgegengesetzt	oposto, a	opposto, a
opuesto, a	opposé, e	opposite	gegenüberliegend	oposto, a	opposto, a
opuesto, a	opposé, e	opposed to	entgegengesetzt	contra(ser)	opposto, a
oración	prière	prayer	Gebet(n)	oração	preghiera
orador, a; locutor, a	orateur, trice	speaker, orator	Redner(in f)m	orador, a	oratore, trice
oral	oral, e	oral	mündlich	oral	orale
órbita	orbite	orbit	Umlaufbahn(f)	órbita	orbita
orden	ordre	order	Ordnung(f)	ordem	ordine
orden	ordre	order	Rangordnung(f)	ordem	ordine
orden	ordre	order	Befehl(m)	ordem	ordine
orden, pedido	bon	form, slip, voucher	Bestellschein(m)	nota	bolla, buono, bolletta
ordenado, a	rangé, e	tidy	ordentlich	arrumado, a	ordinato, a
ordenador	ordinateur	computer	Computer(m)	computador	computer
ordenar	ranger	tidy up	auf = räumen	ordenar	ordinare
ordenar	ordonner	order	befehlen, verordnen	ordenar	ordinare
ordenar, mandar	commander	command	befehlen, befehligen	comandar	comandare
ordenar, colocar	ranger, ordonner	tidy, put in order	ein = räumen	arrumar	sistemare
ordinario, a	ordinaire	ordinary	gewöhnlich	ordinário, a	ordinario, a
oreja	oreille	ear	Ohr(n)	orelha	orecchio
orgánico, a	organique	organic	organisch	orgânico, a	organico, a
organismo	organisme	organism	Organismus(m)	organismo	organismo
organización	organisation	organization	Organisation(f)	organização	organizzazione
organizador, a	organisateur	organizer	Organisator(in f)m	organizador, a	organizzatore, trice
organizar	organiser	organize	organisieren	organizar	organizzare
órgano	organe	organ	Organ(n)	órgão	organo
órgano	orgue	organ	Orgel(f)	órgão	organo
orgasmo	orgasme	orgasm	Orgasmus(m)	orgasmo	orgasmo
orgía	orgie	orgy	Orgie(f)	orgia	orgia
orgullo	orgueil	pride, arrogance	Stolz(m)	orgulho	orgoglio
orgullo	fierté	pride	Stolz(m)	orgulho	fierezza
orgulloso, a	orgueilleux, se	proud, arrogant	stolz, arrogant	orgulhoso, a	orgoglioso, a
orientación	orientation	orientation	Orientierung(f)	orientação	orientamento
oriental	oriental, e	oriental	orientalisch	oriental	orientale
orientar	orienter	position	orientieren	orientar	orientare
orificio	orifice	orifice, aperture	Öffnung(f), Mündung(f)	orifício	orifizio
origen	origine	origin	Ursprung(m)	origem	origine
original	original, e	original	original	original	originale
original	original	original	Original(n)	original	originale
orilla, margen	rive	bank	Ufer(n)	margem	riva
orilla	rivage	shore	Küstenstrich(m)	beira-mar	riva
orilla del mar	bord de mer	sea-side	Küste(f)	beira-mar	riva
orina	urine	urine	Urin(m)	urina	urina
oriundo, a	originaire	native(of)	gebürtig	oriundo, a	originario, a
oro	or	gold	Gold(n)	ouro	oro
orquesta	orchestre	orchestra; band	Orchester(n)	orquestra	orchestra
orquídea	orchidée	orchid	Orchidee(f)	orquídia	orchidea
ortodoxo, a	orthodoxe	orthodox	orthodox	ortodoxo, a	ortodosso, a
ortografía	orthographe	spelling	Rechtschreibung(f)	ortografia	ortografia
os; les; le; te	vous; te	you	euch; Sie; Ihnen	vos; vosco; lhe	vi; ve; le; ti; te
osar, atreverse	oser	dare	wagen	ousar, atrever-se	osare
oscilar	osciller	oscillate	schwanken	oscilar	oscillare
oscilar, vacilar	vaciller	flicker	flackern	tremer	vacillare
oscuridad	obscurité	darkness	Dunkelheit(f)	obscuridade	oscurità, buio
oscuro, a	sombre; obscur, e	dark	dunkel	escuro, a; sombrio, a	scuro, a
oso	ours	bear	Bär(m)	urso	orso
ostentoso, a	fastueux, se	sumptuous	prunkvoll	faustoso, a	fastoso, a
ostra	huître	oyster	Auster(f)	ostra	ostrica
otitis	otite	ear-ache	Mittelohrentzündung f	otite	otite
otoño	automne	autumn	Herbst(m)	outono	autunno
otorgar	décerner	award	zu = erkennen, erteilen	atribuir	conferire
otro, a	autre	other	andere, sonstige	outro, a	altro, a
otro, a	autre(d')	else	ander; anders	outro, a	altro, a
otro, a	autre	further; other	weiter	mais	altro, a

Spanish	French	English	German	Portuguese	Italian
otro modo(de)	autrement	otherwise	anders; sonst	outro modo(de)	altrimenti
otra parte(en)	ailleurs	somewhere else	woanders	noutro sítio	altrove
otra vez	encore	again	noch einmal	mais(uma vez)	ancora
oval, ovalado, a	ovale	oval	oval	oval	ovale
ovario	ovaire	ovary	Eierstock(m)	ovário	ovaia
ovino	ovin	ovine	Schaf-	ovino	ovino
óvulo	ovule	ovule	Ei(zelle f)n	óvulo	ovulo
oxidación	oxydation	oxidization	Oxydierung(f)	oxidação	ossidazione
oxígeno	oxygène	oxygen	Sauerstoff(m)	oxigénio	ossigeno
ozono	ozone	ozone	Ozon(n)	ozone	ozono

P

Spanish	French	English	German	Portuguese	Italian
paciencia	patience	patience	Geduld(f)	paciência	pazienza
paciente	patient, e	patient	geduldig	paciente	paziente
pacífico, a	pacifique	peaceful, pacific	friedlich	pacífico, a	pacifico, a
Pacífico	Pacifique	Pacific Ocean	Pazifik(m)	Pacífico	Pacifico
pacto	pacte	pact	Pakt(m)	pacto	patto
padre	père	father	Vater(m)	pai	padre
padres	parents	parents	Eltern(pl)	pais	genitori
padrino	parrain	godfather	Pate(m)	padrinho	padrino
paga	paie(paye)	pay	Lohn(m)	paga, ordenado	paga, stipendio
pagar	payer	pay	bezahlen	pagar	pagare
página	page	page	Seite(f)	página	pagina
pago, abono	paiement	payment	Bezahlung(f)	pagamento	pagamento
pais	pays	country	Land(n)	país	paese
paisaje	paysage	landscape	Landschaft(f)	paisagem	paesaggio
paja	paille	straw	Stroh(n)	palha	paglia
pajarita	noeud papillon	bow tie	Fliege(f)	laço	papillon
pájaro	oiseau	bird	Vogel(m)	pássaro	uccello
pala	pelle	spade; shovel	Schaufel(f); Spaten(m)	pá	pala
palabra	parole	word; speech	Wort(n)	palavra	parola
palabra	mot	word	Wort(n)	palavra	parola
palabras	propos	words, talk	Worte(pl.)	fala, conversa	parole, discorsi
palabrota	gros mot	bad word	Schimpfwort(n)	palavrão	parolaccia
palacio	palais	palace	Palast(m)	palácio	palazzo
palanca	levier	lever	Hebel(m)	alavanca	leva
palangana	cuvette	basin, bowl	Schale(f)	bacia	catino
pálido, a	pâle	pale	blaß	pálido, a	pallido, a
palillo	cure-dents	tooth-pick	Zahnstocher(m)	palito	stuzzicadenti
palma	paume	palm	Handfläche(f)	palma	palma
palmera	palmier	palm-tree	Palme(f)	palmeira	palma
palo	bâton	stick	Stock(m)	pau, bastão	bastone
paloma	pigeon	pigeon	Taube(f)	pombo, a	piccione
palpar	palper, tâter	feel, finger	betasten	apalpar	palpare
palpitación	palpitation	palpitation	Herzklopfen(n)	palpitação	palpitazione
paludismo	paludisme	malaria	Sumpffieber(n)	paludismo	malaria, paludismo
pan	pain	bread	Brot(n)	pão	pane
panadería	boulangerie	baker's(shop)	Bäckerei(f)	padaria	panificio
pancarta	pancarte	sign, notice	Plakat(n), Schild(n)	cartaz	cartello
pandilla	bande	gang	Bande(f)	quadrilha	banda
pánico	panique	panic	Panik(f)	pânico	panico
pánico	affolement	panic	Panik(f)	pânico	panico
pantalón	pantalon	trousers	Hose(f)	calças	pantalone
pantalón corto	short	shorts	kurze Hose(f)	calções; calção	shorts, calzoncini
pantalla	écran	screen	Wandschirm(m)	painel	schermo
pantalla	écran	screen	Bildschirm; Leinwand	écran	schermo
pantano	marais	marsh	Sumpf(m)	pântano	palude
pantanoso, a	marécageux, se	marshy, boggy	sumpfig	pantanoso, a	paludoso, a

Spanish	French	English	German	Portuguese	Italian
pantera	panthère	panther	Panther(m)	pantera	pantera
pantorrilla	mollet	calf(-lves)	Wade(f)	barriga(perna)	polpaccio
pantys	collants	tights(pair of)	Strumpfhose(f)	meias	collant
panza	panse	belly, paunch	Bauch(m); Pansen(m)	pança	pancia
pañuelo	mouchoir	handkerchief	Taschentuch(n)	lenço	fazzoletto
Papa	Pape	Pope	Papst(m)	Papa	Papa
papá	papa	Daddy, Dad	Papa	papá	papà, babbo
papel	papier	paper	Papier(n)	papel	carta
papel	rôle	role	Rolle(f)	papel	parte, ruolo
papel celo	scotch	sellotape	Tesafilm(m)	fita adesiva	scotch
papelería	papeterie	stationer's	Schreibwarenladen(m)	papelaria	cartoleria
papel higiénico	papier toilette	toilet paper	Toilettenpapier(n)	papel higiénico	carta igienica
paperas	oreillons	mumps	Mumps(m)	trasorelho	orecchioni
paquete	paquet	packet; package	Paket(n)	pacote	pacco
paquete	colis	parcel	Paket(n)	pacote	pacco, collo
par	paire	pair(of)	Paar(n)	par	paio
par	pair	even	gerade	par	pari
para; por	pour	for	für	para; por	per
parabrisas	pare-brise	windscreen	Windschutzscheibe(f)	pára-brisas	parabrezza
paracaídas	parachute	parachute	Fallschirm(m)	pára-quedas	paracadute
parada	arrêt	stop	Pause(f), Stillstand	paragem	fermata
parada, desfile	parade	parade	Parade(f)	parada	parata
parado, a	chômeur, euse	unemployed person	Arbeitslose(f, m)	desempregado, a	disoccupato, a
paradoja	paradoxe	paradox	Paradox(n)	paradoxo	paradosso
paraguas	parapluie	umbrella	Regenschirm(m)	chapéu de chuva	ombrello
paraíso	paradis	paradise	Paradies(n)	paraíso	paradiso
paraje, vista	site	site	Ort(m), Lage(f)	sítio	sito
paralelo, a	parallèle	parallel	parallel	paralelo, a	parallelo, a
parálisis	paralysie	paralysis	Lähmung(f)	paralisia	paralisi
paralítico, a	paralysé, e	paralysed	gelähmt	paralítico, a	paralitico, a
paranoia	paranoïa	paranoia	Paranoia(f)	paranóia	paranoia
parar	arrêter	stop	halten(an-, auf-)	parar	fermare
pararse	arrêter(s')	stop	stehen = bleiben	parar	fermarsi
parásito	parasite	parasite	Parasit(m)	parasita	parassita
parasol	parasol	parasol, sunshade	Sonnenschirm(m)	guarda-sol	ombrellone
parcela	parcelle	plot	Parzelle(f)	parcela	parcella
pardo, a	brun, ne	brown	braun	castanho, a	bruno, a
parecer	paraître	seem, appear, look	scheinen, erscheinen	parecer	parere, sembrare
parecer	sembler	seem	scheinen	parecer	sembrare
parecerse(a)	ressembler(à)	look like	ähneln, aussehen wie	parecer-se	somigliare a
parecido	ressemblance	resemblance	Ähnlichkeit(f)	semelhança	somiglianza
pared	paroi, mur	wall	Wand(f)	parede	parete
pareja	couple	couple	Paar(n)	casal	coppia
pareja	partenaire	partner	Partner(in f)m	parceiro, a	socio, a; partner
parentesco	parenté	relationship	Verwandtschaft(f)	parentesco	parentela
paréntesis	parenthèse	bracket	Klammer(f)	parêntesis	parentesi
pariente	parent, e	relative, relation	verwandt	parente	parente
parlamento	parlement	parliament	Parlament(n)	parlamento	parlamento
parlanchín, a	bavard, e	talkative	geschwätzig	falador, a	chiacchierone, a
paro, desempleo	chômage	unemployment	Arbeitslosigkeit(f)	desemprego	disoccupazione
párpado	paupière	eyelid	Lid(n)	pálpebra	palpebra
parque	parc	park	Park(m)	parque	parco
párrafo	paragraphe	paragraph	Absatz(m), Abschnitt m	parágrafo	paragrafo
parte	partie, part	part	Teil(m n)	parte	pezzo, parte
parte	part, partie	share; part	Anteil(m); Teil(m, n)	parte	parte
participar(en)	participer(à)	take part(in)	teil = nehmen	participar(em)	partecipare(a)
participar en	participer à	participate in	beteiligen, sich	participar em	partecipare a
partícula	particule	particle	Teilchen(n)	partícula	particella
particular	particulier, ière	particular	eigentümlich	particular	particolare
particular	particulier	individual	Privatmann(m)	particular	privato
particularmente	notamment	particular(in)	besonders, nämlich	particularmente	particolarmente
partida	partie	game	Spiel(n)	jogada, jogo	partita
partidario, a	partisan, e	partisan	Anhänger(in f)m	partidário, a	partigiano, a
partido	parti	party	Partei(f)	partido	partito
partido	match	match(-es), game	Spiel(n)	desafio, partida	partita
partitura	partition	score(music)	Partitur(f)	partitura	spartito
parto	accouchement	delivery; birth	Entbindung(f)	parto	parto
pasado, a	passé, e	past	vergangen	passado, a	passato, a

Spanish	French	English	German	Portuguese	Italian
pasado	passé	past	Vergangenheit(f)	passado	passato
pasado de moda	démodé, e	old-fashioned	altmodisch	fora de moda	passato di moda
pasaje, paso	passage	passage	Durchgang(m)	passagem	passaggio
pasaje, trozo	extrait	extract	Auszug(m)	excerto, trecho	brano, estratto
pasajero, a	passager, ère	passenger	Passagier(in f)m	passageiro, a	passeggero, a
pasaporte	passeport	passport	Paß(m)	passaporte	passaporto
pasar	passer	pass, go(through)	fahren über	passar(por; em)	passare
pasar	passer	call, drop in	vorbei = kommen	passar	passare
pasar	passer	spend	verbringen	passar	trascorrere
pasar(un examen)	passer(examen)	take(an exam)	ab = legen(Prüfung f)	fazer(exame)	dare(un esame)
pasatiempo	passe-temps	hobby, pastime	Hobby(n)	passatempo	passatempo
Pascua	Pâques	Easter	Ostern(n)	Páscoa	Pasqua
pase(!), adelante!	entrez!	come in!	herein!	entre!	avanti!, prego!
pasear	promener	walk(go for a)	spazieren = gehen	passear	passeggiare
paseo	promenade	walk; drive; ride	Spaziergang(m)	passeio	passeggiata
paseo, calle	allée	path, lane	Allee(f)	alameda	viale
pasillo	couloir	corridor	Flur(m)	corredor	corridoio
pasión	passion	passion	Leidenschaft(f)	paixão	passione
pasivo, a	passif, ive	passive	passiv	passivo, a	passivo, a
paso	pas	step; pace	Schritt(m)	passo	passo
pastas(aliment.)	pâtes	pasta, noodles	Nudeln(f, pl)	massa	pasta
pastel	gâteau	cake; pastry	Kuchen(m)	bolo	dolce
pastel, tortada	tourte	pie	Pastete(f)	empada	torta salata
pastelería	pâtisserie	cake shop	Konditorei(f)	pastelaria	pasticceria
pasteles	pâtisserie(s)	pastry, cake	Backwaren(f, pl)	pastelaria	dolci
pastilla	cachet	tablet	Tablette(f)	comprimido	pastiglia
pastor, a	berger, ère	shepherd, -ess	Schäfer(in f)m	pastor, a	pastore, pastorella
pastor	pasteur	vicar, minister	Pastor(in f)m	padre; pastor	pastore
pastoso, a	pâteux, se	pasty	pappig	pastoso, a	pastoso, a
pata	patte	paw; leg; foot	Pfote(f); Bein(n)	pata	zampa
patada	coup de pied	kick	Fußtritt(m)	pontapé	calcio
patata	pomme de terre	potato(-es)	Kartoffel(f)	batata	patata
patatas fritas	frites	chips	Pommes Frites	batatas fritas	patatine fritte
paté	pâté	paté	Pastete(f)	paté	patè
patente	brevet	patent	Patent(n)	patente	brevetto
paterno, a	paternel, le	paternal	väterlich	paterno, a	paterno, a
patinaje	patinage	skating	Eiskunstlauf(m)	patinagem	pattinaggio
patinar	patiner	skate	Schlittschuh laufen	patinar	pattinare
patinar	déraper	skid	schleudern	derrapar	slittare
patio	cour	yard	Hof(m)	pátio	cortile
pato	canard	duck	Ente(f)	pato, a	anatra
patria	patrie	native land	Vaterland(n)	pátria	patria
patriarca	patriarche	patriarch	Patriarch(m)	patriarca	patriarca
patrimonio	patrimoine	patrimony	Familiengut(n)	património	patrimonio
patrocinador	sponsor	sponsor	Sponsor(m)	patrocinador	sponsor
patrocinar	parrainer	sponsor	sponsorisieren	apadrinhar	sponsorizzare
patrón, a; dueño, a	patron, ne	boss; employer	Chef(m), Arbeitgeber m	patrão, patroa	padrone, a
patrón	employeur	employer	Arbeitgeber(in f)m	patrão	datore di lavoro
patrulla	patrouille	patrol	Patrouille(f), Streife	patrulha	pattuglia
pausa	pause	pause, break	Pause(f)	pausa	pausa
payaso	clown	clown	Clown(m)	palhaço	pagliaccio, clown
paz	paix	peace	Frieden(m)	paz	pace
peaje	péage	toll	Autobahngebühr(f)	portagem	pedaggio
peatón	piéton	pedestrian	Fußgänger(m)	peão	pedone
pecado	péché	sin	Sünde(f)	pecado	peccato
pecho	poitrine	chest; breast	Brust(f)	peito	petto
pecho(dar el)	allaiter	feed	stillen	aleitar	allattare
pedal	pédale	pedal	Pedal(n)	pedal	pedale
pedante	pédant, e	pedantic	pedantisch	pedante; vaidoso, a	pedante
pedazo, trozo	morceau, bout	piece, bit	Stück(n)	pedaço	pezzo
pediatra	pédiatre	paediatrician	Kinderarzt m/-ärztin	pediatra	pediatra
pedicuro, a	pédicure	chiropodist	Fußpfleger(in f)m	pedicuro	pedicure
pedido	demande	request	Anfrage(f)	pedido	richiesta
pedigrí	pédigree	pedigree	Stammbaum(Tier-)(m)	pedigree	pedigree
pedir	demander	ask(for)	fragen	pedir	chiedere
pedir	demander	beg	bitten	pedir	domandare
pedir, encargar	commander	order	bestellen	encomendar	ordinare
pedir prestado	emprunter	borrow	borgen	pedir emprestado	prendere in prestito

Spanish	French	English	German	Portuguese	Italian
pegar	coller	stick, glue	kleben	colar, pegar	incollare
peinado	coiffure	hair-style	Frisur(f)	penteado	pettinatura
peinar(se)	coiffer(se)	hair(do one's)	frisieren, sich	pentear-se	pettinare(-rsi)
peinar(se)	peigner(se)	comb(one's hair)	kämmen	pentear-se	pettinarsi
peine	peigne	comb	Kamm(m)	pente	pettine
pelaje, pelo	pelage	coat, fur	Fell(n)	pêlo	pelo
pelar	éplucher	peel	schälen	descascar	sbucciare
peldaño, escalón	marche	step	Stufe(f)	degrau	scalino
pelearse	battre(se)	fight	kämpfen	lutar	battersi, lottare
película	pellicule	film	Film(m)	película	pellicola
película	film	film, movie	Film(m)	filme	film
peligro	danger	danger	Gefahr(f)	perigo	pericolo
peligro, riesgo	péril	peril, danger	Gefahr(f)	perigo	pericolo
peligroso, a	dangereux, se	dangerous	gefährlich	perigoso, a	pericoloso, a
pelirrojo, a	roux, rousse	auburn; reddish	rothaarig	ruivo, a	rosso, a
pelo	poil	hair	Haar(n)	pêlo	pelo
pelo, cabello	cheveu(x)	hair	Haar(n)	cabelo	capello
pelota	balle	ball	Ball(m)	bola	palla
peluca	perruque	wig	Perücke(f)	peruca	parrucca
peludo, a	poilu, e	hairy	behaart	peludo, a	peloso, a
peluquería	salon(coiffure)	salon	Friseurladen(m)	salão	parrucchiere, a(da)
peluquero, a	coiffeur, se	hairdresser	Friseur(m), Friseuse f	cabeleireiro, a	parrucchiere, a
pellizcar	pincer	pinch, nip	kneifen	beliscar	pizzicare
pena	peine	sorrow, grief	Schmerz(m), Kummer(m)	pena; tristeza	pena; dolore
pena	chagrin	grief, sorrow	Kummer(m)	desgosto, pena	dispiacere
pena, castigo	peine	sentence	Bestrafung(f)	pena	punizione, castigo
pena(es una)	dommage(c'est)	pity(it is a)	schade!	pena(e')	peccato(è)
penal	pénal, e	penal	strafrechtlich	penal	penale
penalidad	pénalité	penalty	Strafe(f), Strafpunkt	penalidade	penalità
pendientes	boucle(s)	earring	Ohrring(m)	brincos, argolas	orecchini
penetrar	pénétrer	enter, penetrate	ein = dringen	penetrar	penetrare
penicilina	pénicilline	penicillin	Penizillin(n)	penicilina	penicillina
península	péninsule	peninsula	Halbinsel(f)	península	penisola
penoso, a; duro, a	pénible	hard, arduous	mühsam, schwierig	penoso, a	penoso, a
pensamiento	pensée	thought	Gedanke(m)	pensamento	pensiero
pensar	penser	think	denken	pensar	pensare
pensión	pension	pension; allowance	Pension(f)	pensão	pensione
pensión	pension	guest-house	Gasthaus(n)	pensão	pensione
pensionista	pensionnaire	resident	Pensionsgast(m)	hóspede	pensionante
penuria, escasez	pénurie	shortage	Mangel(m)	penúria	penuria
peñasco, roca	rocher	rock	Felsen(m)	rochedo, rocha	masso, roccia
peón, obrero	manoeuvre	labourer	Hilfsarbeiter(in f)m	servente	manovale
peón(ajedrez)	pion(échecs)	pawn(chess)	Bauer(m)(Schach)	peão(xadrez)	pedone(scacchi)
peor	pire	worse	schlimmer	pior	peggio
pepita	pépin	pip	Kern(m)	caroço	seme
pequeño, a	petit, e	small, little	klein	pequeno, a	piccolo, a
pequeño, a	petit, e	little	klein	pequeno, a	piccolo, a
pera	poire	pear	Birne(f)	pêra	pera
perceptible	perceptible	perceptible	wahrnehmbar	perceptível	percettibile
percibir	percevoir	perceive	wahr = nehmen	perceber	percepire
percha	cintre	hanger, coat-hanger	Bügel(m)	cabide	gruccia, attaccapanni
perder	perdre	lose	verlieren	perder	perdere
perder	rater	miss	verpassen	perder	perdere; mancare
perder	manquer	miss	verpassen	perder	perdere; mancare
pérdida	perte	loss, waste	Verlust(m)	perda, prejuizo	perdita
perdido, a	perdu, e	lost	verloren	perdido, a	perso, a; smarrito, a
perdón	pardon	forgiveness	Vergebung(f)	perdão	scusa, perdono
perdón(!), disculpe	pardon!	sorry!, excuse me!	Verzeihung!	perdão!, desculpe!	scusi!
perdonar	pardonner	forgive, pardon	verzeihen, vergeben	perdoar	perdonare
perdone(!)	excusez-moi!	excuse me!; sorry!	Entschuldigung!	desculpe!; perdão!	scusi!
peregrinación	pèlerinage	pilgrimage	Wallfahrt(f)	peregrinação	pellegrinaggio
peregrino	pèlerin	pilgrim	Pilger(in f)m	peregrino	pellegrino, a
perezoso, a	paresseux, se	lazy	faul	preguiçoso, a	pigro, a
perfección	perfection	perfection	Vollkommenheit(f)	perfeição	perfezione
perfeccionar	perfectionner	improve; perfect	vervollkommnen	aperfeiçoar	perfezionare
perfecto, a	parfait, e	perfect	einwandfrei	perfeito, a	perfetto, a
pérfido, a	perfide	treacherous	heimtückisch	pérfido, a	perfido, a
perfil	profil	profile	Profil(n)	perfil	profilo

Spanish	French	English	German	Portuguese	Italian
perforación	forage	boring	Bohrung(f)	perfuração	perforazione
perforar	perforer	perforate	durchbohren	perfurar	perforare
perforar	percer	drill; pierce	bohren	furar	bucare, forare
perfume	parfum	perfume, scent	Parfüm(n)	perfume	profumo
perfumería	parfumerie	perfume shop	Parfümerie(f)	perfumaria	profumeria
periferia	périphérie	periphery	Umkreis(m), Umfang(m)	periferia	periferia
perímetro	périmètre	perimeter	Umfang(m)	perímetro	perimetro
periódico, a	périodique	periodic(al)	periodisch	periódico, a	periodico, a
periódico, diario	journal	newspaper, paper	Zeitung(f)	jornal	giornale
periodismo	journalisme	journalism	Journalismus(m)	jornalismo	giornalismo
periodista	journaliste	journalist	Journalist(in f)m	jornalista	giornalista
período	période	period	Periode(f)	período	periodo
perjuicio	préjudice	wrong, harm	Schaden(m)	prejuízo	pregiudizio
perjuicio, daño	dommage	damage	Schaden(m)	prejuízo, dano	danno
perla	perle	pearl	Perle(f)	pérola	perla
permanente	permanent, e	permanent	andauernd	permanente	permanente
permiso	permission	permission	Erlaubnis(f)	permissão	permesso
permiso	permis	licence; permit	Schein(m), Genehmigung	licença	permesso, licenza
permiso conducir	permis(auto)	driving licence	Führerschein(m)	carta de condução	patente di guida
permitir	permettre	allow, enable	erlauben	permitir	permettere
permitirse	permettre(se)	afford	leisten, sich	permitir-se	permettersi
perno, tornillo	boulon	bolt	Bolzen(m)	parafuso; cavilha	bullone
pero; sino; mas	mais	but	aber	mas	ma
pero	mais, cependant	but, yet, however	aber, jedoch	porém	però
perpendicular	perpendiculaire	perpendicular	senkrecht	perpendicular	perpendicolare
perpetuo, a	perpétuel, le	perpetual	fortdauernd	perpétuo, a	perpetuo, a
perro, a	chien, ne	dog, bitch(-es)	Hund(m)	cão, cadela	cane, cagna
perseguir	poursuivre	pursue	verfolgen	perseguir	inseguire
perseguir	persécuter	persecute	verfolgen	perseguir	perseguitare
perseverancia	persévérance	perseverance	Ausdauer(f)	perseverança	perseveranza
perseverar	persévérer	persevere	beharren, aus = halten	perseverar	perseverare
persistencia	persistance	persistence	Beharrlichkeit(f)	persistência	persistenza
persona	personne	person	Person(f)	pessoa	persona
personal	personnel, le	personal	persönlich	pessoal	personale
personal	personnel	staff, personnel	Personal(n)	pessoal	personale
personalidad	personnalité	personality	Persönlichkeit(f)	personalidade	personalità
perspectiva	perspective	prospect	Aussicht(f)	perspectiva	prospettiva
perspectiva	perspective	perspective	Perspektive(f)	perspectiva	prospettiva
persuadir	persuader	persuade	überreden	persuadir	persuadere
pertenecer	appartenir(à)	belong to	gehören	pertencer	appartenere
perturbar	perturber	disturb, perturb	stören	perturbar	perturbare
perturbar	troubler	disturb; trouble	stören	perturbar	turbare, disturbare
perverso, a	pervers, e	perverse	pervers	perverso, a	perverso, a
pesadilla	cauchemar	nightmare	Alptraum(m)	pesadelo	incubo
pesado, a	lourd, e	heavy	schwer	pesado, a	pesante
pesado(hacer)	alourdir	make heavy	erschweren	pesado(tornar)	appesantire
pesar	peser	weigh	wiegen	pesar	pesare
pesca	pêche	fishing, angling	Fischen n; Fischfang m	pesca	pesca
pesca(con caña)	pêche	angling	Angeln(n)	pesca(à linha)	pesca(con lenza)
pescadería	poissonnerie	fishmonger's	Fischgeschäft(n)	peixaria	pescheria
pescado	poisson	fish	Fisch(m)	peixe	pesce
pescador	pêcheur	fisherman(-men)	Fischer(m)	pescador	pescatore
pesimista	pessimiste	pessimistic	pessimistisch	pessimista	pessimista
peso	poids	weight	Gewicht(n)	peso	peso
pestaña	cil	eyelash	Wimper(f)	pestana	ciglio(a)
pestañear	clignoter	flash	blinken	piscar	lampeggiare
pétalo	pétale	petal	Blütenblatt(n)	pétala	petalo
petardo	pétard	banger, cracker	Knallkörper(m)	bomba, foguete	petardo
petición	demande	request; demand	Bitte(f); Gesuch(n)	pedido	richiesta
petición	pétition	petition	Bittschrift(f), Gesuch	petição	petizione
petróleo	pétrole	oil	Erdöl(n)	petróleo	petrolio
pezuña, casco	sabot	hoof	Huf(m)	casco	zoccolo
pianista	pianiste	pianist	Pianist(in f)m	pianista	pianista
piano	piano	piano	Klavier(n)	piano	pianoforte
picadura	piqûre	sting, bite	Stich(m)	picada	puntura
picante	piquant, e	spicy, hot	scharf	picante	piccante
picante	épicé, e	spicy	gewürzt, würzig	picante	piccante
picazón	démangeaison	itch, itching	Juckreiz(m)	comichão	prurito

Spanish	French	English	German	Portuguese	Italian
pico	bec	beak	Schnabel(m)	bico	becco
pico	pic	peak	Gipfel(m)	pico	picco
pie	pied	foot(feet pl.)	Fuß(m)	pé	piede
pie(de), en pie	debout	standing(up)	stehend, aufrecht	de pé, em pé	in piedi
piedad	pitié	pity	Mitleid(n)	piedade	pietà
piedra	pierre	stone	Stein(m)	pedra	pietra
piedra	caillou	stone, pebble	Stein(m)	calhau	sasso
piel	peau	skin	Haut(f)	pele	pelle
piel	fourrure	fur	Pelz(m)	pele; peliça	pelliccia
pierna	jambe	leg	Bein(n)	perna	gamba
pieza	pièce	part, component	Teil(n)	peça	pezzo
pijama	pyjama	pyjamas	Schlafanzug(m)	pijama	pigiama
pila	pile	pile	Stapel(m)	pilha, montão	pila
pila	pile	battery	Batterie(f)	pilha	pila
pilar	pilier	pillar	Pfeiler(m)	pilar	pilastro
píldora	pilule	pill	Pille(f)	pílula	pillola
pilotar	piloter	pilot; fly; drive	fliegen; lotsen; fahren	pilotar	pilotare
piloto	pilote	pilot	Pilot(m)	piloto	pilota
pillo, a; astuto, a	malin, igne	smart, clever	gerissen, schlau	esperto, a; astuto, a	furbo, a
pimienta	poivre	pepper	Pfeffer(m)	pimenta	pepe
pincel	pinceau	brush	Pinsel(m)	pincel	pennello
pinchar	piquer	prick, sting	stechen	picar	pungere
pinchazo	crevaison	puncture	Reifenpanne(f)	furo	foratura
ping-pong	tennis de table	table-tennis	Tischtennis(n)	ténis de mesa	ping pong
pintar	peindre	paint	malen	pintar	dipingere
pintar	peindre	paint	streichen	pintar	imbiancare
pintor, a	peintre	painter	Anstreicher; Maler(m)	pintor, a	pittore, trice
pintoresco, a	pittoresque	picturesque	malerisch	pitoresco, a	pittoresco, a
pintura	peinture	painting	Malerei(f)	pintura	pittura; dipinto
pintura	peinture	paint	Farbe(f)	tinta	vernice, pittura
piña	ananas	pineapple	Ananas(f)	ananás	ananas
pinza(s), tenazas	pince	pincers, pliers	Zange(f)	pinça, alicate	pinza
pionero	pionnier	pioneer	Pionier, Bahnbrecher	pioneiro	pioniere
pipa	pipe	pipe	Pfeife(f)	cachimbo	pipa
piragua	pirogue	pirogue	Piroge(f), Kanu(n)	piroga	piroga
pirámide	pyramide	pyramid	Pyramide(f)	pirâmide	piramide
pirata	pirate	pirate	Pirat(in f)m	pirata	pirata
pirulí	sucette	lollipop	Lutscher(m)	chupa-chupa	lecca lecca
piscina	piscine	swimming-pool	Schwimmbad(n)	piscina	piscina
piso	appartement	flat, apartment	Wohnung(f)	apartamento	appartamento
piso, planta	étage	floor, storey	Etage(f)	andar	piano
pista	piste	track	Spur(f)	pista	pista
pista	piste	runway	Bahn(Lande-, Start-)	pista	pista
pista	piste	slope	Piste(f)	pista	pista
pista de patinar	patinoire	skating rink	Eisbahn(f)	pista de patinagem	pista da pattinaggio
pistola	pistolet	gun, pistol	Pistole(f)	pistola	pistola
pistón	piston	piston	Kolben(m)	pistão	pistone
pitar	klaxonner	hoot	hupen	buzinar	suonare(clacson)
pito	sifflet	whistle	Pfeife(f)	apito	fischietto
pitón	python	python	Python(m)	jibóia	pitone
pizarra	ardoise	slate	Schiefer(m)	ardósia, lousa	ardesia
pizarra	tableau noir	blackboard	Tafel(f)	quadro	lavagna
placa	plaque	plate, plaque	Platte(f)	placa	lastra, piastra
placer	plaisir	pleasure	Vergnügen(n)	prazer	piacere
plan; plano	plan	plan; drawing	Plan(m)	plano; desenho	piano; schema
plan, proyecto	plan, projet	scheme, plan	Plan(m)	plano, projecto	schema, piano
plan, proyecto	projet	plan	Plan(m)	projecto	progetto
plancha	fer à repasser	iron	Bügeleisen(n)	ferro de passar	ferro da stiro
planchado	repassage	ironing	Bügeln(n)	passar a ferro	stirare
planeador	planeur	glider	Segelflugzeug(n)	planador	aliante
planear	planer	glide	schweben, gleiten	planar	planare
planeta	planète	planet	Planet(m)	planeta	pianeta
plano	plan	map	Plan(m)(Stadtplan m)	planta	pianta; stradario
planta, fábrica	plante	plant	Pflanze(f)	planta	pianta
planta, fábrica	usine	plant	Anlage(f)	fábrica	fabbrica
planta baja, bajo	rez-de-chaussée	ground floor	Erdgeschoß(n)	rés-do-chão	piano terra
plantar	planter	plant	pflanzen	plantar	piantare
plantilla	personnel	staff	Personal(n)	pessoal	personale

Spanish	French	English	German	Portuguese	Italian
plástico, a	plastique	plastic	plastisch	plástico, a	plastico, a
plástico	plastique	plastic	Plastik(n)	plástico	plastica
plata	argent	silver	Silber(n)	prata	argento
plataforma	plate-forme	platform	Plattform(f)	plataforma	piattaforma
plátano, banana	banane	banana	Banane(f)	banana	banana
platillo	soucoupe	saucer	Untertasse(f)	pires	piattino
plato	assiette	plate	Teller(m)	prato	piatto
playa	plage	beach(-es)	Strand(m)	praia	spiaggia
plaza	place	square	Platz(m)	praça	piazza
plaza de toros	arène(s)	bull ring, arena	Kampfbahn(f)	praça de touros	arena
plazo	délai	delay	Frist(f)	prazo	termine
plegable	escamotable	fold-away	zusammenklappbar	escamoteável	ribaltabile
plegar, doblar	plier	bend	biegen	vergar	piegare
pleito	procès	lawsuit	Prozeß(m)	pleito, processo	causa
pliegue	pli	fold; pleat	Falte(f); Kniff(m)	prega	piega
plomo	plomb	lead	Blei(n)	chumbo	piombo
pluma	plume	feather	Feder(f)	pluma; pena	penna, piuma
plural	pluriel	plural	Mehrzahl(f)	plural	plurale
población	population	population	Bevölkerung(f)	população	popolazione
poblado, a	peuplé, e	populated	bevölkert	povoado, a	popolato, a
pobre	pauvre	poor	arm	pobre	povero, a
pobreza	pauvreté	poverty	Armut(f)	pobreza	povertà
poco	peu	some; a little	etwas; wenig	pouco	poco, pó
poco, a	peu	little, few	wenig(e)	pouco, a	poco, a
poder	pouvoir	can, able to(be)	können	poder	potere
poder	pouvoir	power	Macht(f)	poder	potere
poderoso, a	puissant, e	powerful, strong	mächtig, kräftig	poderoso, a	poderoso, a; potente
podio	podium	podium, stage	Podest(n)	estrado	podio
podrido, a	pourri, e	rotten	verfault	podre	marcio, a
poema	poème	poem	Gedicht(n)	poema	poema
poesía	poésie	poetry	Poesie(f)	poesia	poesia
polar	polaire	polar	polar; Polar-	polar	polare
polea	poulie	pulley	Flaschenzug(m)	polia	puleggia
polémica	polémique	controversy	Polemik(f)	polémica	polemica
policía	police	police	Polizei(f)	polícia	polizia
policía	policier	policeman(-men)	Polizist(in f)m	polícia	poliziotto
poligamia	polygamie	polygamy	Polygamie(f)	poligamia	poligamia
poliomielitis	poliomyélite	polio(myelitis)	Kinderlähmung(f)	poliomielite	poliomelite
pólipo	polype	polyp	Polyp(m)	pólipo	polipo
política	politique	politics	Politik(f)	política	politica
política	politique	policy	Politik(f)	política	politica
político, a	politique	political	politisch	político, a	politico, a
político	homme politique	politician	Politiker(in f)m	político	uomo politico
político, a	politicien, ne	politician	Politiker(in f)m	político, a	politico, a
polivalente	polyvalent, e	polyvalent	vielseitig	polivalente	polivalente
polo	pôle	pole	Pol(m)	polo	polo
polvo	poussière	dust	Staub(m)	poeira	polvere
polvo	poudre	powder	Puder(m); Pulver(n)	pó	polvere
pólvora	poudre	powder	Pulver(n)(Schieß-).	pólvora	polvere
pollada	couvée	brood	Brut(f)	ninhada	covata
pollito	poussin	chick	Küken(n)	pinto	pulcino
pollo	poulet	chicken	Hähnchen, Hühnchen(n)	frango	pollo
pomada	pommade	ointment, cream	Salbe(f)	pomada	pomata
pomelo	pamplemousse	grapefruit	Pampelmuse(f)	toranja	pompelmo
poner	mettre	put	legen, stellen	pôr	mettere
poner, colocar	mettre, placer	set	setzen, stellen	pôr, colocar	porre, mettere
poner, colocar	mettre, placer	lay	legen	pôr, colocar	porre, mettere
poner, colocar	poser, placer	place	stellen	pôr, colocar	collocare
poner, colocar	poser	put, lay(down)	legen	pôr, colocar	posare, porre
poner(huevos)	pondre	lay	Eier legen	pôr(ovos)	fare l'uovo
ponerse	devenir	become	werden	pôr-se	diventare
ponerse nervioso, a	affoler(s')	panic	Panik geraten(in)	afligir-se	disorientarsi
ponerse nervioso, a	énerver(s')	edgy, irritable(be)	auf = regen, sich	enervar-se	innervosirsi
popular	populaire	popular	populär	popular	popolare
por	par	by, through	durch	por	per, da
por	par	per	per	por	per
por	pour	for	für	por	per
porcelana	porcelaine	porcelain, china	Porzellan(n)	porcelana	porcellana

Spanish	French	English	German	Portuguese	Italian
porcentaje	pourcentage	percentage	Prozentsatz(m)	percentagem	percentuale
por ciento	pour cent	per cent	Prozent(n)	por cento	per cento
porción	portion	portion, piece	Stück(n), Portion(f)	porção	porzione
por favor(!)	s'il vous plaît!	please!	bitte!	se faz favor!	per favore!
pornografía	pornographie	pornography	Pornographie(f)	pornografia	pornografia
poro	pore	pore	Pore(f)	poro	poro
poroso, a	poreux, se	porous	porös	poroso, a	poroso, a
por otra parte	ailleurs(d')	moreover, besides	übrigens	por outro lado	del resto, d'altronde
porque	parce que	because	weil, da	porque	perché
porque, pues	car	because, for	weil, denn	porque, pois	perché
por qué	pourquoi	why	warum	porquê	perché
porqué(el--de)	pourquoi(le--de)	reason(the--for)	Grund(m)(der--für)	porquê(o--de)	perché(il--di)
portadocumentos	porte-documents	document case	Aktenmappe(f)	carteira	portadocumenti
portal	portail	gate	Tor(n)	portal	portone
por tanto, pues	donc	therefore; so	also	portanto, pois	dunque
portátil	portatif, ive	portable	tragbar	portátil	portatile
porte	port	postage	Porto(-kosten)(n/pl)	porte	porto
porte pago	franco de port	carriage-paid	portofrei	porte pago	porto franco
portero	portier	porter	Portier(m)	porteiro	portiere
portero	goal	goalkeeper	Torwärter(m)	guarda-redes	portiere
por todas partes	partout	everywhere	überall	por toda a parte	dappertutto
porvenir, futuro	avenir	future	Zukunft(f)	futuro	avvenire
posada; albergue	auberge	inn	Gasthaus(n)	estalagem	locanda
posar	poser(photo)	pose	Modell stehen	posar	posare
poseer	posséder	own, possess	besitzen	possuír	possedere
posibilidad	possibilité	possibility	Möglichkeit(f)	possibilidade	possibilità
posible	possible	possible	möglich	possível	possibile
posición	position	position	Position(f)	posição	posizione
positivo, a	positif, ive	positive	positiv	positivo, a	positivo, a
postal, carta	carte de voeux	greeting(s) card	Glückwunschkarte(f)	cartão(festas)	biglietto di auguri
poste	poteau	post, pole	Pfosten(m)	poste	palo
postergar	reporter	postpone	verschieben	adiar	rinviare
posterior	postérieur, e	later	später(r, s)	posterior	posteriore
postre	dessert	dessert	Nachtisch(m)	sobremesa	dessert
potable	potable	drinking	trinkbar, genießbar	potável	potabile
potencia, fuerza	puissance, force	power, strength	Macht(f), Kraft(f)	potência, poder	potenza, forza
potencial	potentiel, le	potential	potentiell	potencial	potenziale
potente	puissant, e	potent, powerful	kräftig, stark	potente	potente
potro	poulain	foal	Fohlen(n)	potro	puledro
pozo	puits	well	Brunnen(m)	poço	pozzo
practicar	pratiquer	practise	betreiben, üben	praticar	praticare
práctico, a	pratique	practical	praktisch	prático, a	pratico, a
pradera	prairie	meadow	Wiese(f)	pradaria, prado	prateria
prado	pré	meadow, field	Weide(f), Wiese(f)	prado	prato
precaución	précaution	precaution	Vorsicht(f)	precaução	precauzione
precedente	précédent, e	previous	vorherig	precedente	precedente
preceder	précéder	precede	voran = gehen, voraus = -	preceder	precedere
precio	prix	price	Preis(m)	preço	prezzo
precioso, a	précieux, se	precious	wertvoll, kostbar	precioso, a	prezioso, a
precipicio	précipice	precipice	Abgrund(m)	precipício	precipizio
precipitación	précipitation	hurry, haste	Eile(f), Hast(f)	precipitação	precipitazione
precipitarse	précipiter(se)	rush	stürzen, sich	precipitar-se	precipitarsi
precisamente	précisément	precisely	genau	precisamente	precisamente, appunto
precisar	préciser	specify	genau fest = legen	precisar	precisare
precisión	précision	precision	Genauigkeit(f)	precisão	precisione
preciso, a	précis, e	precise, accurate	genau	exacto, a	preciso, a
precoz	précoce	precocious	frühreif, frühzeitig	precoce	precoce
predecesor, a	prédécesseur	predecessor	Vorgänger(in f)m	predecessor, a	predecessore
predecir	prédire	predict	vorher = sagen	predizer	predire
predicar	prêcher	preach	predigen	pregar	predicare
predominante	prédominant, e	predominant	vorherrschend	predominante	predominante
prefacio	préface	preface	Vorwort(n)	prefácio	prefazione
preferencia	préférence	preference	Vorliebe(f)	preferência	preferenza
preferido, a	préféré, e	favourite	Lieblings-	preferido, a	preferito, a
preferir	préférer	prefer	bevorzugen	preferir	preferire
prefijo	préfixe	prefix	Vorsilbe(f)	prefixo	prefisso
prefijo	indicatif(tél.)	dialling code	Vorwählnummer(f)	indicativo, prefixo	prefisso
pregunta	question	question	Frage(f)	pergunta	domanda

Spanish	French	English	German	Portuguese	Italian
preguntar	demander	ask	fragen	perguntar	domandare
preguntar	poser(question)	ask	fragen	perguntar	porre(domanda)
preguntarse	demander(se)	wonder	fragen, sich	perguntar-se	domandarsi
prehistoria	préhistoire	prehistory	Vorgeschichte(f)	pré-história	preistoria
prejuicio	préjugé	prejudice	Vorurteil(n)	preconceito	pregiudizio, danno
preliminar	préliminaire	preliminary	einleitend	preliminar	preliminare
prematuro, a	prématuré, e	premature(baby)	Frühgeburt(f)	prematuro, a	prematuro, a
premeditado, a	prémédité, e	premeditated	vorsätzlich	premeditado, a	premeditato, a
premeditar	préméditer	premeditate	vor = setzen	premeditar	premeditare
premio	prix	prize	Preis(m)	prémio	premio
premio	lot	prize	Los(n)	prémio	premio
prenda	gage	pledge	Pfand(n)	penhor	pegno
prenda de punto	tricot	sweater, jumper	Trikot(m), Strickweste	malha	maglia
prensa	presse	press	Presse(f)	imprensa	stampa
preocupación	souci	worry	Sorge(f)	preocupação	preoccupazione
preocupado, a	soucieux, se	worried	sorgenvoll	preocupado, a	preoccupato, a
preocupar	préoccuper	worry, preoccupy	beunruhigen	preocupar	preoccupare
preocuparse	inquiéter(s')	worry	beunruhigen, sich	preocupar-se	preoccuparsi
preocuparse	soucier(se)	worry	sorgen, sich; plagen, s.	preocupar-se	preoccuparsi
preparación	préparation	preparation	Vorbereitung(f)	preparação	preparazione
preparar	préparer	prepare	vor = bereiten	preparar	preparare
preposición	préposition	preposition	Präposition(f)	preposição	preposizione
presa	proie	prey	Beute(f)	presa	preda
présbita	presbyte	long-sighted	weitsichtig	présbita	presbite
prescribir	prescrire	prescribe	vor = schreiben	prescrever	prescrivere
presencia	présence	presence	Anwesenheit(f)	presença	presenza
presentación	présentation	presentation	Vorführung(f)	apresentação	presentazione
presentar	présenter	present	vor = zeigen, - = stellen	apresentar	presentare
presentar	présenter	introduce	vor = stellen	apresentar	presentare
presentar	introduire	introduce	vor = stellen	apresentar	introdurre
presente	présent, e	present	anwesend	presente	presente
presente, actual	présent, e	present	gegenwärtig, aktuell	presente, actual	presente, attuale
presente	présent, e	present	Gegenwart(f)	presente	presente
preservativo	préservatif	condom, sheath	Präservativ(n)	preservativo	preservativo
presidencia	présidence	presidency	Präsidium n, Vorsitz m	presidência	presidenza
presidente	président, e	president	Präsident(in f)m	presidente	presidente, essa
presidente	président, e	chairman/-woman	Vorsitzende(m, f)	presidente	presidente, essa
presión	pression	pressure	Druck(m)	pressão	pressione
préstamo	prêt	loan	Darlehen(n)	empréstimo	prestito
préstamo	emprunt	loan	Anleihe(f)	empréstimo	prestito
prestar	prêter	lend	leihen, verleihen	emprestar	prestare
prestigio	prestige	prestige	Ansehen(n)	prestigio	prestigio
prestigioso, a	prestigieux, se	prestigious	wunderbar	prestigioso, a	prestigioso, a
presumido, a	coquet, te	pretty; coquettish	kokett; eitel	vaidoso, a	civettuolo, a
presumir	présumer	presume	vermuten	presumir	presumere
presuntuoso, a	prétentieux, se	pretentious	eingebildet	pretencioso, a	pretenzioso, a
presupuesto	budget	budget	Budget(n)	orçamento	bilancio
presupuesto	devis	estimate	Kostenvoranschlag(m)	orçamento	preventivo
prevalecer	prévaloir	prevail	vor = herrschen	prevalecer	prevalere
prevenir, avisar	prévenir	warn, inform	warnen	prevenir, avisar	prevenire
prever	prévoir	foresee; plan	vorher = sehen; planen	prever	prevedere
previo, a	préalable	preliminary	vorhergehend	prévio, a	preliminare
previsión	prévision	forecast	Vorhersage(f)	previsão	previsione
prima	prime	bonus	Zulage(f)	gratificação	premio, sussidio
primario, a	primaire	primary	Primär-	primário, a	primario, a
primavera	printemps	spring	Frühling(m)	primavera	primavera
primer ministro	premier ministre	prime minister	Ministerpräsident(m)	primeiro ministro	primo ministro
primer ministro	premier ministre	prime minister	Premierminister(m)	primeiro ministro	primo ministro
primero	abord(d')	first(at)	zunächst	primeiro	anzitutto
primero, a; primer	premier, ière	first	erste(r, s)	primeiro, a	primo, a
primitivo, a	primitif, ive	primitive	primitiv	primitivo, a	primitivo, a
primo, a	cousin, e	cousin	Cousin(m), Cousine(f)	primo, a	cugino, a
primogénito, a	aîné, e	oldest, eldest	Ältere(f, m)	velho, a(o, a mais)	primogenito, a
princesa	princesse	princess(-es)	Prinzessin(f)	princesa	principessa
principal	principal, e	principal, main	hauptsächlich	principal	principale
príncipe	prince	prince	Prinz(m)	príncipe	principe
principiante	débutant, e	beginner	Anfänger(in f)m	principiante	principiante
principiar	commencer	start	an = fangen	principiar, começar	cominciare

475

Spanish	French	English	German	Portuguese	Italian
principiar	débuter	begin, start	an = fangen	principiar	esordire
principio	principe	principle	Grundsatz(m)	princípio	principio
prioridad	priorité	priority	Vorrang(m)	prioridade	precedenza; priorità
prioritario, a	prioritaire	priority(have)	vorrangig; Prioritäts-	prioritário, a	prioritario, a
prisa	hâte	haste, hurry	Eile(f)	pressa	fretta
prisa(tener)	pressé, e(être)	hurry(be in a)	eilig(es...haben)	pressa(ter)	fretta(avere)
prisión, cárcel	prison	prison, jail	Gefängnis(n)	prisão, cadeia	prigione, carcere
prisionero, a	prisonnier, ière	prisoner	Gefangene(f, m)	prisioneiro, a	prigioniero, a
privado, a	privé, e	private	privat	privado, a	privato, a
privar	priver	deprive	berauben, entziehen	privar	privare
privilegiado, a	privilégié, e	privileged	bevorzugt	privilegiado, a	privilegiato, a
privilegio	privilège	privilege	Vorrecht(n)	privilégio	privilegio
probable	probable	probable, likely	wahrscheinlich	provável	probabile
probablemente	probablement	probably	wahrscheinlich	provavelmente	probabilmente
probar	prouver	prove	beweisen	provar	provare
probar, intentar	essayer	try	versuchen	tentar; provar	provare
probar	goûter	taste	kosten	provar	assaggiare
problema	problème	problem	Problem(n)	problema	problema
problema	ennui, problème	trouble, problem	Ärger(m)	aborrecimento	guaio
procedencia	provenance	origin	Herkunft(f)	proveniência	provenienza
procedimiento	procédé	process	Verfahren(n)	procedimento	procedimento
procedimiento	procédure	procedure	Verfahren(n)	procedimento	procedimento
procesión	procession	procession	Prozession(f)	procissão	processione
proceso, juicio	procès	lawsuit, trial	Prozeß(m)	processo	processo
proclamar	proclamer	proclaim	bekannt = geben	proclamar	proclamare
procreación	procréation	procreation	Zeugung(f)	procriação	procreazione
procrear	procréer	procreate	erzeugen	procriar	procreare
procurarse	procurer(se)	obtain, get	besorgen, sich	arranjar; obter	procurarsi
prodigioso, a	prodigieux, se	prodigious	wunderbar	prodigioso, a	prodigioso, a
producción	production	production	Produktion(f)	produção	produzione
producir	produire	produce	produzieren	produzir	produrre
producir	produire	produce	her = stellen	produzir	produrre
productivo, a	productif, ive	productive	leistungsfähig	produtivo, a	produttivo, a
producto	produit	product	Produkt(n)	produto	prodotto
productor, a	producteur, trice	producer	Hersteller(in f)m	produtor, a	produttore, trice
productor, a	producteur, trice	producer	Produzent(in f)m	produtor, a	produttore, trice
proeza, hazaña	performance	performance	Leistung(f)	desempenho	prestazione
profanar	profaner	desecrate	entweihen	profanar	profanare
profesión	profession	profession	Beruf(m)	profissão	professione
profesional	professionnel, le	professional	professionell	profissional	professionale
profesional	professionnel	professional	Profi(m)	profissional	professionista
profesor, a	enseignant, e	teacher	Lehrer(in f)m	professor, a	insegnante
profesor, a	professeur	teacher	Lehrer(in f)m	professor, a	professore, essa
profundidad	profondeur	depth	Tiefe(f)	profundidade	profondità
profundo, a	profond, e	deep	tief	profundo, a	profondo, a
progenitura	progéniture	offspring	Nachkomme(m)	progenitura	progenitura
programa	programme	programme	Programm(n)	programa	programma
programador, a	programmeur, se	programmer	Programmierer(in f)m	programador, a	programmatore, trice
progresión	progression	progression	Fortschreiten(n)	progressão	progressione
progresivo, a	progressif, ive	progressive	fortschreitend	progressivo, a	progressivo, a
progreso	progrès	progress	Fortschritt(m)	progresso	progresso
prohibición	interdiction	ban	Verbot(n)	proibição	proibizione
prohibido, a	interdit, e	forbidden	verboten	proibido, a	proibito, a
prohibir	défendre	forbid	verbieten	proibir	proibire
prohibir	interdire	forbid, ban	verbieten	proibir	vietare, proibire
proliferar	proliférer	proliferate	vermehren, sich	proliferar	prolificare
prolongación	prolongation	prolongation	Verlängerung(f)	prolongamento	prolungazione
prolongamiento	prolongement	extension	Verlängerung(f)	prolongamento	prolungamento
prolongar	prolonger	extend	verlängern	prolongar	prolungare
promesa	promesse	promise	Versprechen(n)	promessa	promessa
prometer	promettre	promise	versprechen	prometer	promettere
prometerse	fiançer(se)	engaged(get)	verloben, sich	ficar noivo, a	fidanzarsi
prometido, a	promis, e	promised	versprochen	prometido, a	promesso, a
promoción	promotion	promotion	Beförderung(f)	promoção	promozione
promover	promouvoir	promote	befördern	promover	promuovere
pronombre	pronom	pronoun	Fürwort(n)	pronome	pronome
pronóstico	pronostic	forecast	Vorhersage(f)	prognóstico	pronostico
pronóstico	pronostic	prognosis(-ses)	Prognose(f)	prognóstico	prognosi

Spanish	French	English	German	Portuguese	Italian
pronto	bientôt	soon	bald	logo, brevemente	presto
pronto, a	prompt, e	quick, prompt	schnell, rasch	pronto, a	pronto, a
pronto(de)	soudain	sudden(ly)	plötzlich	súbito(de)	ad un tratto
pronto; rápido, a	vite	fast, quickly	rasch	depressa; rápido, a	presto
pronunciar	prononcer	pronounce	aus = sprechen	pronunciar	pronunziare
propaganda	propagande	propaganda	Propaganda(f)	propaganda	propaganda
propagar	propager	spread	verbreiten	propagar	propagare
propicio, a	propice	favourable	günstig	propício, a	propizio, a
propiedad	propriété	property	Eigentum(n)	propriedade	proprietà
propietario, a	propriétaire	owner	Eigentümer(in f)m	proprietário, a	proprietario, a
propietario, a	propriétaire	landowner	Gutsherr(-sbesitzer)	proprietário, a	proprietario, a
propina	pourboire	tip	Trinkgeld(n)	gorgeta	mancia
propio, a	propre	own	eigen	próprio, a	proprio, a
proponer	proposer	propose; offer	vor = schlagen	propor	proporre
proporción	proportion	proportion, ratio	Verhältnis(n)	proporção	proporzione
proporcionar	rapporter	bring in, yield	ein = bringen	render	fruttare
propósito	but	aim, purpose	Ziel(n)	fim, intento	scopo
propósito	dessein	purpose, aim	Absicht(f)	propósito	proposito
propósito	propos, intention	intention, aim	Absicht(f)	propósito	proposito
propuesta	proposition	proposal	Vorschlag(m)	proposta	proposta
propulsión	propulsion	propulsion	Antrieb(m)	propulsão	propulsione
próspero, a	prospère	flourishing	erfolgreich, blühend	próspero, a	prospero, a
próstata	prostate	prostate	Prostata(f)	próstata	prostata
prostitución	prostitution	prostitution	Prostitution(f)	prostituição	prostituzione
prostituta	prostituée	prostitute	Prostituierte(f)	prostituta	prostituta
protección	protection	protection	Schutz(m)	protecção	protezione
proteger	protéger	protect	beschützen	proteger	proteggere
prótesis	prothèse	artificial-, false-	Prothese(f)	prótese	protesi
protestante	protestant, e	Protestant	Protestant(in f)m	protestante	protestante
protestar	protester	protest, contest	protestieren	protestar	protestare
protocolo	protocole	protocol	Protokoll(n)	protocolo	protocollo
prototipo	prototype	prototype	Prototyp(m)	protótipo	prototipo
protuberancia	protubérance	protuberance	Beule(f), Buckel(m)	protuberância	protuberanza
proveer	fournir	provide	versorgen, liefern	fornecer	fornire
proveer, dar	fournir	supply, provide	beliefern	fornecer	fornire
proverbio	proverbe	proverb	Sprichwort(n)	provérbio	proverbio
provincia	province	province	Provinz(f)	província	provincia
provisión	provision	stock, supply	Vorrat(m)	provisão	provvista
provisional	provisoire	provisional	provisorisch	provisório, a	provvisorio, a
provocación	provocation	provocation	Herausforderung(f)	provocação	provocazione
provocar	provoquer	provoke	heraus = fordern, reizen	provocar	provocare
proxeneta	proxénète	pimp	Zuhälter(m)	proxeneta	ruffiano, prosseneta
proxenetismo	proxénétisme	pimping	Kuppelei(f)	proxenetismo	prossenetismo
proximidad	proximité	proximity	Nähe(f)	proximidade	prossimità
próximo, a	prochain, e	next	nächste	próximo, a	prossimo, a
proyectar, planear	projeter	plan	planen	projectar	progettare
proyectil	projectile	projectile	Geschoß(n)	projéctil	proiettile
proyecto, plan	projet	project, plan	Vorhaben(n)	projecto	progetto
proyector	projecteur	projector	Scheinwerfer(m)	projector	proiettore
prudencia	prudence	caution, prudence	Vorsicht(f)	prudência	prudenza
prudente	prudent, e	careful, prudent	vorsichtig	prudente	prudente
prueba	preuve	proof, evidence	Beweis(m)	prova	prova
prueba	épreuve	test	Test(m), Probe(f)	prova	prova, test
prueba	essai	trial, test	Versuch(m)	ensaio	prova, collaudo
pubertad	puberté	puberty	Pubertät(f)	puberdade	pubertà
publicación	publication	publication	Veröffentlichung(f)	publicação	pubblicazione
publicar	publier	publish, issue	veröffentlichen	publicar	pubblicare
publicidad	publicité	advertising	Werbung(f), Anzeige(f)	publicidade	pubblicità
publicidad	réclame(s)	advertisement	Reklame(f)	publicidade	reclame
público, a	public, ique	public	öffentlich	público, a	pubblico, a
público	public	public; audience	Publikum(n)	público	pubblico
púdico, a	pudique	modest	keusch	púdico, a	pudico, a
pudrir	pourrir	rot	verfaulen	apodrecer	marcire
pueblo	peuple	people	Volk(n)	povo	popolo
pueblo	village	village	Dorf(n)	povoado, aldeia	villaggio, paese
puente	pont	bridge	Brücke(f)	ponte	ponte
puente	pont	deck; bridge	Deck(n)	convés	ponte
puerta	porte	door	Tür(f)	porta	porta

Spanish	French	English	German	Portuguese	Italian
puerta	portière	door(car)	Wagentür(f)	porta	sportello
puerta, entrada	porte	gate	Pforte(f)	porta	porta, uscita
puerto	port	port, harbour	Hafen(m)	porto	porto
puerto	col	pass	Paß(m)	desfiladeiro	colle, passo
puesta de sol	coucher(soleil)	sunset	Sonnenuntergang(m)	pôr do sol	tramonto
puesto	rang	rank	Rang(m)	posição	rango
pulga	puce	flea	Floh(m)	pulga	pulce
pulgar	pouce	thumb	Daumen(m)	polegar	pollice
pulido, a	poli, e	polished	poliert	polido, a	levigato, a
pulir	polir	polish	polieren	polir	lucidare, levigare
pulmón	poumon	lung	Lunge(f)	pulmão	polmone
pulsación	pulsation	beating, pulsation	Pulsschlag(m)	pulsação	pulsazione
pulsador	bouton	button	Taste(f)	botão	pulsante, bottone
pulsera	bracelet	bracelet	Armband(n)	pulseira	braccialetto
pulso	pouls	pulse	Puls(m)	pulso	polso
pulverización	pulvérisation	spraying	Zerstäubung(f)	pulverização	nebulizzazione
punción	ponction	puncture	Punktion(f)	punção	puntura, prelievo
punta	pointe	point	Spitze(f)	ponta	punta
punta	bout	tip, end	Zipfel(m), Ende(n)	ponta	punta, estremità
punta; remate	embout	tip, end	Endstück(n)	ponta; remate	estremità; punta
puntada	point	stitch	Stich(m); Masche(f)	ponto	punto
puntiagudo, a	pointu, e	pointed, sharp	spitz	pontiagudo, a	appuntito, a
puntilla	dentelle	lace	Spitze(f)	renda	merletto
punto	point	point	Punkt(m)	ponto	punto
punto	point	dot	Punkt(m)	ponto	punto
punto de vista	point de vue	viewpoint	Aussichtspunkt(m)	ponto de vista	punto di vista
puntuación	ponctuation	punctuation	Zeichensetzung(f)	pontuação	punteggiatura
puntual	ponctuel, le	punctual	pünktlich	pontual	puntuale
puñado	poignée	handful	Handvoll(f)	punhado	manciata, pugno
puñal	poignard	dagger	Dolch(m)	punhal	pugnale
puñetazo	coup de poing	punch	Faustschlag(m)	soco; murro	pugno
puño	poing	fist	Faust(f)	punho	pugno
pupila	pupille	pupil	Pupille(f)	pupila	pupilla
purga	purge	purge	Säuberungsaktion(f)	purga	purga
purificar	purifier	purify	reinigen	purificar	purificare
puro, a	pur, e	pure	rein	puro, a	puro, a
pus	pus	pus	Eiter(m)	pus	pus

Q

Spanish	French	English	German	Portuguese	Italian
que, qué	que	that; whom; which	was, das	que	che
que, qué	quoi	what	was	quê	cosa, che cosa
que aproveche(!)	bon appétit!	enjoy your meal!	Guten Appetit!	bom proveito!	buon appetito!
quebradizo, a	cassant, e	brittle	brüchig, spröde	quebradiço, a	fragile
quedar	rester	left(be), remain	übrig = bleiben, bleiben	sobrar	rimanere, avanzare
quedarse	rester	stay, remain	bleiben	ficar	restare
queja	plainte	complaint	Klage(f)	queixume, queixa	lamento
quejarse	plaindre(se)	complain	beklagen, sich	queixar-se	lamentarsi
quemadura	brûlure	burn	Verbrennung(f)	queimadura	bruciatura
quemar	brûler	burn	verbrennen	queimar, arder	bruciare
querer	vouloir	want	wollen	querer	volere
querido, a	chéri, e	dear, darling	Liebling(m)	querido, a	caro, a
querido, a	cher, ère	dear	liebe(r)	caro, a; querido, a	caro, a
queso	fromage	cheese	Käse(m)	queijo	formaggio
quiebra, ruina	faillite	failure; bankruptcy	Konkurs(m)	falência	fallimento
quiebra(hacer)	faillite(faire)	bankrupt(go)	bankrott sein	falir	fallire
quién, que	qui	who(m); which; that	wer; wen	quem	chi, che
quienquiera	quiconque	anyone(who)	jeder	qualquer(um)	chiunque
quieto, a	calme, tranquille	still	still	quieto, a	calmo, a

Spanish	French	English	German	Portuguese	Italian
quilate	carat	carat	Karat(n)	quilate	carato
química	chimie	chemistry	Chemie(f)	química	chimica
químico, a	chimique	chemical	chemisch	químico, a	chimico, a
quimono, kimono	kimono	kimono	Kimono(m)	quimono	chimono
quince	quinze	fifteen	fünfzehn	quinze	quindici
quiosco	kiosque	news-stand	Zeitungskiosk(m)	quiosque	edicola; chiosco
quisiera(yo)	voudrais(je)	would like(I)	möchte(ich)	gostava	vorrei
quiste	kyste	cyst	Zyste(f)	quisto	ciste
quitar, retirar	enlever, retirer	remove	ab = nehmen	remover, retirar	rimuovere
quitar	ôter, enlever	remove, take away	ab = nehmen	tirar	togliere
quitar	enlever	take off	aus = ziehen	tirar	togliere
quitar, tirar	débarrasser	clear, rid	weg = räumen	desembaraçar	sbarazzare
quitarse	débarrasser(se)	get rid of	beseitigen	livrar-se	liberarsi
quizá(s)	peut-être	perhaps, maybe	vielleicht	talvez	forse

R

Spanish	French	English	German	Portuguese	Italian
rabia, furia	rage, fureur	rage	Wut(f)	raiva, furor	rabbia
rabia	rage	rabies	Tollwut(f)	raiva	rabbia
rabino	rabbin	rabbi	Rabbiner(m)	rabino	rabbino
rabo	queue	tail	Schwanz(m)	cauda	coda
racial	racial, e	racial	rassisch	racial	raziale
racimo	grappe	bunch	Traube(f)	cacho	grappolo
ración	ration, portion	ration	Ration(f); Stück(n)	ração	razione
racional	rationnel, le	rational	rational	racional	razionale
racionamiento	rationnement	rationing	Rationierung(f)	racionamento	razionamento
racismo	racisme	racism	Rassismus(m)	racismo	razzismo
radar	radar	radar	Radar(m)	radar	radar
radiación	radiation	radiation	Bestrahlung(f)	radiação	radiazione
radiactividad	radioactivité	radioactivity	Radioaktivität(f)	radioactivade	radioattività
radiador	radiateur	radiator, heater	Heizkörper(m)	aquecedor	termosifone
radio	rayon	radius(-ii)	Radius(m)	raio	raggio
radio	rayon	spoke	Speiche(f)	raio	raggio
radio	radio	radio	Radio(n)	rádio	radio
radiodifusión	radiodiffusion	broadcasting	Radioübertragung(f)	radiodifusão	radiodiffusione
radiografía	radiographie	X-ray; radiography	Röntgenbild(n)	radiografia	radiografia
ráfaga	rafale	gust, gale	Windstoß(m)	rajada	raffica
ráfaga	rafale	burst, hail	Salve(f)	rajada	raffica
raíz	racine	root	Wurzel(f)	raiz	radice
raja, grieta	fente, fissure	slit	Schlitz(m)	fenda	fessura; spacco
raja, grieta	félure	crack	Sprung(m), Riß(m)	estaladela	incrinatura
rajar, partir	fendre	split, slit	spalten	fender, rachar	spaccare
rajar, hender	fendre	slit	auf = schlitzen	rachar, fender	fendere
rama	branche	branch	Ast(m)	ramo	ramo
ramadán	ramadan	Ramadan	Ramadan(m)	ramadão	ramadan
ramo	bouquet	bunch; bouquet	Strauß(m)	ramo	mazzo
rana	grenouille	frog	Frosch(m)	rã	rana
ranura	rainure	groove	Rille(f), Nute(f)	ranhura	scanalatura
rapaz	rapace	bird of prey	Raubvogel(m)	ave de rapina	rapace
rápido, a	rapide	rapid, fast, quick	schnell	rápido, a	rapido, a; veloce
rápido, pronto	vite	quickly, fast	schnell, rasch	rápido, a; depressa	fretta(in), presto
raqueta	raquette	racket	Schläger(Tennis-)(m)	raqueta	racchetta
raqueta, pala	raquette	bat	Schläger(m)	raqueta	racchetta
raquítico, a	rachitique	rickety	rachitisch	raquítico, a	rachitico, a
raro, a	rare	rare	selten	raro, a	raro, a
raro, a	bizarre	strange, odd	seltsam	estranho, a	strano, a
rascacielos	gratte-ciel	skyscraper	Wolkenkratzer(m)	arranha-céus	grattacielo
rascarse	gratter(se)	scratch oneself	kratzen, sich	coçar-se	grattarsi

Spanish	French	English	German	Portuguese	Italian
rasgar, romper	déchirer	tear	zerreißen	rasgar	strappare
rasgos	trait(s)	feature	Zug(m)(Gesichts-)	feição	tratto, lineamento
rasguñar	égratigner	scratch	kratzen, schrammen	arranhar	scalfire
rasguño	éraflure	scratch, graze	Kratzer(m), Schramme f	arranhadura	scalfittura
raso, satén	satin	satin	Satin(m)	cetim	raso
raspar, rascar	gratter	scrape, scratch	kratzen	raspar	grattare
rastrillo	râteau	rake	Rechen(m)	ancinho	rastrello
rata	rat	rat	Ratte(f)	rato, a	topo, ratto
ratificar	ratifier	ratify	ratifizieren	ratificar	ratificare
rato	moment, instant	while, time	Moment(m)	momento, instante	attimo, momento
ratón	souris	mouse(mice pl.)	Maus(f)	rato	topo
raya	raie	line	Strich(m)	linha; risca	riga
raya	trait	line	Strich(m)	traço, risco	tratto, riga
raya, guión	tiret	dash	Gedankenstrich(m)	travessão, hífen	trattino
rayado, a	rayé, e	scratched	zerkratzt	riscado, a	rigato, a
rayar	rayer	cross out	durch = streichen	riscar; cortar	cancellare
rayas(a)	rayures(à)	striped	gestreift	riscas(às)	righe(a)
rayo	rayon	ray	Strahl(m)	raio	raggio
rayo	foudre	lightning	Blitz(m)	raio	fulmine
raza	race	race, breed	Rasse(f)	raça	razza
razón, causa	raison	reason	Grund(m)	razão	ragione
razón(tener)	raison(avoir)	right(to be)	Recht(n)(haben)	razão(ter)	ragione(avere)
razón, relación	rapport	ratio, proportion	Beziehung(f)	razão	rapporto
razonable	raisonnable	reasonable	vernünftig	razoável	ragionevole
razonamiento	raisonnement	reasoning	Überlegung(f)	raciocínio	ragionamento
reacción	réaction	reaction	Reaktion(f)	reacção	reazione
reaccionar	réagir	react	reagieren	reagir	reagire
reaccionario, a	réactionnaire	reactionary	reaktionär	reaccionário, a	reazionario, a
reactor	réacteur	reactor; engine	Reaktor(m)	reactor	reattore
readaptación	réadaptation	readjustment	Umstellung(f)	readaptação	riadattamento
real	réel, le	real, actual	wirklich	real	reale; vero, a
real	royal, e	royal	königlich	real	reale
realeza	royauté	royalty, monarchy	Königstum(n)	realeza	sovranità
realidad	réalité	reality	Wirklichkeit(f)	realidade	realtà
realización	réalisation	realization	Verwirklichung(f)	realização	realizzazione
realizar	réaliser	carry out, perform	verwirklichen	realizar, fazer	realizzare
realizar, efectuar	accomplir	accomplish	vollführen	realizar	compiere, effettuare
realmente	réellement	truly	wirklich	realmente	realmente
reanimación	réanimation	resuscitation	Wiederbelebung(f)	reanimação	rianimazione
rebaja	réduction	reduction	Senkung(f)	desconto	riduzione
rebaja, descuento	rabais, remise	discount	Rabatt(m)	desconto, saldo	ribasso, sconto
rebajar	baisser	drop, lower; fall	senken	baixar	abbassare, calare
rebanada	tranche	slice	Scheibe(f)	fatia	fetta
rebanada de pan	tartine de pain	slice of bread	Brotscheibe(f)	fatia de pão	fetta di pane
rebaño	troupeau	flock	Herde(f)	rebanho	gregge
rebelarse	insurger(s')	rebel(against)	empören, sich	insurgir-se	ribellarsi
rebelde	rebelle	rebel	Rebell(m)	rebelde	ribelle
rebelión	rébellion	rebellion	Aufstand(m)	rebelião	ribellione
rebotar	rebondir	bounce, rebound	ab = prallen, aufprallen	ressaltar	rimbalzare
recalcar, subrayar	souligner	emphasize	betonen	acentuar	accentuare
recalentar	réchauffer	warm, (re)heat	auf = wärmen	aquecer	riscaldare
recepción	accueil	reception; welcome	Empfang(m), Aufnahme f	recepção	accoglienza
recepción	réception	reception	Empfang(m)	recepção	ricezione
recepción	réception	reception	Rezeption(f)	recepção	reception
recepción	réception	party, reception	Empfang(m)	recepção	ricevimento
receptáculo	réceptacle	receptacle	Sammelbecken(n)	receptáculo	ricettacolo
receptor	récepteur	receiver	Empfänger(m)	receptor	ricevitore
receta	recette	recipe	Rezept(n)	receita	ricetta
receta	ordonnance	prescription	Rezept(n)	receita	ricetta medica
recibir	recevoir	receive, get	empfangen	receber	ricevere
recibir(clases)	prendre(leçon)	have(a lesson)	nehmen	ter(lição)	prendere(lezione)
recibo	reçu	receipt	Quittung(f)	recibo	ricevuta
recibo	quittance	receipt	Quittung(f)	recibo	ricevuta
recibo	réception	receipt	Empfang(m)	recepção	ricevuta
recién nacido, a	nouveau-né, e	new-born baby	Neugeborene(n)	recém-nascido, a	neonato, a
reciente	récent, e	recent	neu	recente	recente
recientemente	récemment	recently	kürzlich	recentemente	recentemente
recipiente	récipient	container	Behälter(m)	recipiente	recipiente

Spanish	French	English	German	Portuguese	Italian
recitación	récitation	recitation	Vortrag(m)	recitação	recita
recital	récital	recital	Konzert(n), Vortrag(m)	recital	recital
reclamación	réclamation	complaint, claim	Beschwerde(f)	reclamação	reclamo
reclamar	réclamer à	ask(for)	bitten um	reclamar	reclamare
reclamo(de)	réclame(en)	offer(on)	Sonderangebot(n)	promoção(em)	offerta(in)
reclutamiento	recrutement	recruitment	Rekrutierung(f)	recrutamento	reclutamento
recoger	ramasser	pick up	auf = heben	apanhar, recolher	raccogliere
recomendación	recommandation	recommendation	Empfehlung(f)	recomendação	raccomandazione
recompensa	récompense	reward; award	Belohnung(f)	recompensa	ricompensa
reconciliación	réconciliation	reconciliation	Versöhnung(f)	reconciliação	riconciliazione
reconfortante	réconfortant, e	comforting	tröstlich	reconfortante	riconfortante
reconocer	reconnaître	recognize	erkennen	reconhecer	riconoscere
récord	record	record	Rekord(m)	recorde	record
recordar, acordarse	rappeler(se)	recall, remember	erinnern, sich	lembrar-se	ricordarsi
recorrido	parcours	journey; course	Strecke(f), Route(f)	percurso	percorso
recortar	découper	cut up	zerschneiden	recortar	tagliare
recreo	récréation	break	Pause(f)	recreio	ricreazione
recta	droite	straight line	Gerade(f)	recta	retta
rectángulo	rectangle	rectangle	Rechteck(n)	rectângulo	rettangolo
rectificar	rectifier	rectify	berichtigen	rectificar	rettificare
recto, a	droit, e	straight	gerade	recto, a	diritto, a
recuerdo	souvenir	memory	Erinnerung(f)	recordação	ricordo
recuerdo	rappel	recall	Rückruf(m)	lembrança	richiamo
recuerdo	souvenir	souvenir	Andenken(n)	recordação	ricordo, souvenir
recuperar	récupérer	recover, get back	wieder = bekommen	recuperar	recuperare
recurrir, apelar	recourir à	appeal to	Berufung(f)ein = legen	recorrer, apelar	ricorrere, appellarsi
recurso	recours	recourse	Zuflucht(f), Berufung	recurso	ricorso
recurso	ressource(s)	resources	Mittel(n, pl)	recurso	risorsa
rechazar	refuser, rejeter	reject	ab = lehnen, verwerfen	rejeitar	rigettare
rechazo	refus	refusal	Verweigerung(f)	recusa	rifiuto
red	filet	net	Netz(n)	rede	rete
red	réseau	network	Netz(n)	rede	rete
redacción	rédaction	editorial staff	Redaktion(f)	redacção	redazione
redada	rafle	raid, round-up	Razzia(f)	rusga	retata
redondo, a	rond, e	round	rund	redondo, a	rotondo, a
reducción	réduction	reduction	Verringerung(f)	redução	riduzione
reducir	réduire	reduce	reduzieren	reduzir	ridurre
reducir, aminorar	décélérer	decelerate	ab = bremsen	desacelerar	decelerare
reembolsar	rembourser	pay back, reimburse	zurück = zahlen	reembolsar	rimborsare
reembolso	remboursement	repayment	Rückzahlung(f)	reembolso	rimborso
referencia	référence	reference	Referenz(f)	referência	riferimento
referirse	référer(se)	refer to	beziehen, sich	referir-se	riferirsi
reflejar	réfléchir(se)	reflected(be)	reflektieren	reflectir	riflettere(-ersi)
reflejo	réflexe	reflex	Reflex(m)	reflexo	riflesso
reflejo	reflet	reflection	Widerschein(m), Reflex	reflexo	riflesso
reflexionar	réfléchir(à)	reflect, think	überlegen	reflectir; pensar	riflettere
reflexivo, a	réfléchi, e	thoughtful	bedächtig	ponderado, a	riflessivo, a
reflujo	reflux	ebb	Ebbe(f)	refluxo	riflusso
reforma	réforme	reform	Reform(f)	reforma	riforma
reforzar	renforcer	reinforce	verstärken	reforçar	rinforzare
refrescar	rafraîchir	cool	ab = kühlen	refrescar	rinfrescare
refuerzo	renfort	reinforcement	Verstärkung(f)	reforço	rinforzo
refugiado, a	réfugié, e	refugee	Flüchtling(m)	refugiado, a	rifugiato, a
refugio, asilo	refuge, asile	refuge	Zufluchtsort(m)	refúgio, asilo	rifugio, asilo
refunfuñar	râler	moan, groan	nörgeln	resmungar	brontolare
refunfuñar	rouspéter	grouse, moan	meckern, murren	rezingar	brontolare
refutar	réfuter	refute	widerlegen	refutar	confutare
regalo	cadeau	present, gift	Geschenk(n)	prenda, presente	regalo
regañar	gronder	scold, tell off	schimpfen	ralhar	sgridare
regar	arroser	water	gießen, begießen	regar	innaffiare
regatear	marchander	bargain, haggle	feilschen, handeln	regatear	contrattare
régimen	régime	régime	Regime(n)	regime	regime
régimen	régime	speed	Drehzahl(f)	velocidade	regime
regimiento	régiment	regiment	Regiment(n)	regimento	reggimento
región	région	region, area	Gegend(f)	região	regione
registrar	fouiller	search	suchen, durchsuchen	rebuscar	frugare
registrar	enregistrer	register, check in	auf = geben	registar	registrare

S

481

Spanish	French	English	German	Portuguese	Italian
registro	enregistrement	registration	Registrierung(f)	registo	registrazione
registro	registre	register	Register(n)	registo	registro
regla	règle	ruler	Lineal(n)	régua	riga
regla, norma	règle	rule	Regel(f)	regra, norma	regola, norma
reglaje, ajuste	réglage	adjustment	Einstellung(f)	afinação	regolazione
reglamentación	réglementation	regulation(s)	Regelung(f)	regulamentação	regolamentazione
reglamento	règlement	regulation	Bestimmung(f)	regulamento	regolamento
regocijo	réjouissance	rejoicing	Fröhlichkeit(f)	regozijo; alegria	gioia, giubilo
regresar	rentrer	go back, come back	zurück = kommen	voltar	tornare, rientrare
regresar	retourner	return(to)	zurück = gehen	voltar(a)	tornare
regresión	régression	regression	Rückgang(m)	regressão	regresso
regreso, vuelta	retour	return	Rückkehr(f)	regresso, volta	ritorno
regular	régulier, ière	regular	regelmäßig	regular	regolare
regularización	régularisation	regularization	Regulierung(f)	regularização	regolarizzazione
rehabilitar	réintégrer	reinstate	wiederein = setzen	reintegrar	reintegrare
rehén	otage	hostage	Geisel(f)	refém	ostaggio
rehusar	refuser	refuse	verweigern	recusar	rifiutare
reina	reine	queen	Königin(f)	rainha	regina
reino	royaume	kingdom	Königreich(n)	reino	reame
reino	règne	reign	Herrschaft(f)	reinado	regno
reintegrar	réintégrer	return	zurück = kehren	voltar	reintegrare
reir	rire	laugh	lachen	rir	ridere
reivindicación	revendication	claim, demand	Forderung(f)	reivindicação	rivendicazione
reivindicar	revendiquer	claim	beanspruchen	reivindicar	rivendicare
reja	grillage	wire fencing	Gitter(n)	gradeamento	reticolato
relación	relation	relation(-ship)	Beziehung(f)	relação	relazione
relación; enlace	liaison	connection, link	Verbindung(f)	ligação, junção	collegamento
relajado, a	décontracté, e	relaxed	lässig, entspannt	descontraído, a	rilassato, a
relajamiento	relaxation	relaxation	Entspannung(f)	relaxação	rilassamento
relámpago	éclair	lightning; flash	Blitz(m)	relâmpago	lampo
relatar	relater	relate, recount	erzählen	relatar	riferire
relativo, a	relatif, ive	relative	relativ	relativo, a	relativo, a
relieve	relief	relief	Relief(n)	relevo	rilievo
religión	religion	religion	Religion(f)	religião	religione
religioso, a	religieux, se	religious	religiös	religioso, a	religioso, a
reloj	montre	watch	Uhr(f), Armbanduhr(f)	relógio	orologio
reloj	horloge	clock	Uhr(f)	relógio	orologio
reluciente	luisant, e	shining, bright	leuchtend	brilhante	brillante
remar	ramer	row	rudern	remar	remare
remedio	remède	remedy	Heilmittel(n)	remédio	rimedio
remiendo	raccommodage	mending	Flicken(n)	remendo	rammendo
remitente	expéditeur	sender	Absender(in f)m	expedidor	mittente
remo	rame	oar	Ruder(n)	remo	remo
remo; piragua	aviron	rowing	Rudersport(m)	remo	canottaggio
remolcar	remorquer	tow	ab = schleppen	rebocar	rimorchiare
remolino	remous	eddy, swirl	Wirbel(m)	redemoinho	mulinello, gorgo
remolque	remorque	trailer	Anhänger(m)	reboque	rimorchio
remordimiento	remords	remorse	Gewissensbiß(m)	remorso	rimorso
remover	remuer	stir	rühren	mexer	mescolare
remuneración	rémunération	remuneration	Entlohnung(f), Lohn(m)	remuneração	rimunerazione
remuneración	cachet	fee	Honorar(n), Gage(f)	remuneração	cachet, compenso
rencor	rancune	grudge, spite	Rachsucht(f)	rancor	rancore
rendimiento	rendement	output, yield	Ertrag(m), Leistung(f)	rendimento	rendimento
rendimiento	rendement	yield	Ertrag(m)	rendimento; produto	rendimento
renegar	renier	disown; renounce	verleugnen, verneinen	renegar	rinnegare
renovación	rénovation	renovation	Renovation(f)	restauração	rinnovazione
renovación	renouvellement	renewal	Erneuerung(f)	renovação	rinnovo
renovar	renouveler	renew	erneuern	renovar	rinnovare
renta, ingresos	revenu	income, revenue	Einkommen(n)	rendimento	reddito
renta; ganancia	rapport	yield, return	Ertrag(m)	renda; ganho	frutto, rendita
renta	rente	income, pension	Einkommen(n)	renda	rendita
rentabilidad	rentabilité	profitability	Rentabilität(f)	rentabilidade	redditività
rentable	rentable	profitable	einträglich	rentável	redditizio, a
renunciar	renoncer	give up	auf = geben	desistir; renunciar	rinunciare
reñir(con)	disputer(se)	quarrel, argue	streiten, sich	disputar-se	litigare
reparación	réparation	repair	Reparation(f)	reparação	riparazione
reparar	réparer	repair, mend	reparieren	reparar	riparare
repartir	répartir	share out	auf = teilen	repartir	ripartire

482

Spanish	French	English	German	Portuguese	Italian
repartir	partager	share, divide	teilen	repartir	dividere
reparto	répartition	distribution	Verteilung(f)	repartição	ripartizione
repatriación	rapatriement	repatriation	Repatriierung(f)	repatriação	rimpatrio
repertorio	répertoire	index; repertoire	Repertoire(n)	repertório	repertorio
repetir	répéter	repeat	wieder = holen	repetir	ripetere
réplica	riposte	counter-attack	Gegenangriff(m)	réplica	risposta
replicar	répliquer	reply	erwidern, entgegnen	replicar	replicare
reportaje	reportage	report	Reportage(f)	reportagem	cronaca
represalia	représaille(s)	reprisal	Vergeltung(f)	represália	rappresaglia
representación	représentation	representation	Darstellung(f)	representação	rappresentazione
representación	représentation	performance	Vorstellung(f)	representação	rappresentazione
representante	représentant, e	representative, rep	Vertreter(in f)m	representante	rappresentante
representar	représenter	represent	dar = stellen	representar	rappresentare
represión	répression	repression	Unterdrückung(f)	repressão	repressione
reprobación	blâme	blame; reprimand	Rüge(f)	censura	biasimo
reprochar	reprocher	reproach	vor = werfen	censurar	rimproverare
reproducción	reproduction	reproduction	Reproduktion(f)	reprodução	riproduzione
reproducir	reproduire	reproduce	reproduzieren	reproduzir	riprodurre
reproducir(se)	reproduire(se)	breed(animals)	fort = pflanzen, sich	reproduzir-se	riprodurre(-rsi)
reptil	reptile	reptile	Reptil(n)	réptil	rettile
república	république	republic	Republik(f)	república	repubblica
reputación, fama	réputation	reputation	Ansehen(n), Ruf(m)	reputação, fama	reputazione, fama
requisitoria	réquisitoire	indictment	Anklagerede(f)	requisitório	requisitoria
resbalar	glisser	slip, slide	rutschen	escorregar	scivolare
rescate	rançon	ransom	Lösegeld(n)	resgate	riscatto
reserva	réserve	reserve	Reserve(f)	reserva	riserva
reserva	réservation	reservation	Reservierung(f)	reserva	prenotazione
reservado, a	réservé, e	reserved	reserviert	reservado, a	prenotato, a
reservar	réserver	reserve	reservieren	reservar	riservare
reservar	réserver	book, reserve	vor = bestellen	reservar	prenotare
resfriado	rhume	cold	Schnupfen(m)	constipação	raffreddore
residencia	résidence	residence	Wohnsitz(m)	residência	residenza
residir	résider	reside	wohnen	residir	risiedere
residir, vivir	demeurer	live, stay, remain	wohnen, bleiben	habitar	dimorare, stare
residuo	résidu	residue	Rückstand(m)	resíduo	residuo
residuo	déchet	waste	Abfall(m)	resíduo	scarto
resignarse	résigner(se)	resign oneself	entsagen, ergeben, sich	resignar-se	rassegnarsi
resina	résine	resin	Harz(m)	resina	resina
resistencia	résistance	resistance	Widerstand(m)	resistência	resistenza
resistencia	endurance	endurance	Ausdauer(f)	resistência	resistenza
resistente	résistant, e	resistant	widerstandsfähig	resistente	resistente
resistir	résister	resist; withstand	widerstehen	resistir	resistere
resistir a	résister à	withstand	widerstehen	resistir a	resistere a
resolver	résoudre	solve, resolve	lösen	resolver	risolvere
resolver	régler	settle	regeln; erledigen	resolver	risolvere
resonar	résonner	resound, sound	klingen	ressoar, ecoar	rimbombare
resoplar	renifler	sniff	schnüffeln	fungar	tirar su col naso
respectivamente	respectivement	respectively	beziehungsweise	respectivamente	rispettivamente
respetable	respectable	respectable	achtbar	respeitável	rispettabile
respetar	respecter	respect	respektieren	respeitar	rispettare
respeto	respect	respect	Respekt(m)	respeito	rispetto
respiración	respiration	breathing	Atmung(f)	respiração	respirazione
respirar	respirer	breathe	atmen	respirar	respirare
resplandor	lueur	gleam, glow	Schimmer(m)	luz, clarão	chiarore, luce
responder	répondre	reply, answer	erwidern	responder	rispondere
responsabilidad	responsabilité	responsibility	Verantwortung(f)	responsabilidade	responsabilità
responsable	responsable	responsible	verantwortlich	responsável	responsabile
responsable	responsable	liable(to be)	haftbar	responsável	responsabile
respuesta	réponse	answer, reply	Antwort(f)	resposta	risposta
resta	soustraction	subtraction	Subtraktion(f)	subtração	sottrazione
restaurante	restaurant	restaurant	Restaurant(n)	restaurante	ristorante
restaurar	restaurer	restore	wiederher = stellen	restaurar	restaurare
restituir	restituer	return	zurück = erstatten	restituir	restituire
resto	reste	rest, remainder	Rest(m)	resto	resto
resto, residuo	débris, restes	remains, debris	Trümmer(m, pl)	resto, destroços	resti, cocci
restricción	restriction	restriction	Einschränkung(f)	restrição	restrizione
restringir	restreindre	restrict	beschränken	restringir	restringere
resultado	résultat	result	Ergebnis(n)	resultado	risultato, esito

S

Spanish	French	English	German	Portuguese	Italian
resultar	résulter, être	result, be	ergeben, sich	resultar	risultare
resumen	résumé	summary	Zusammenfassung(f)	resumo	riassunto
retener	retenir	hold back; retain	zurück = halten	reter	trattenere
retina	rétine	retina	Netzhaut(f)	retina	retina
retirado, a	retraité, e	retired person	Rentner(in f)m	reformado, a	pensionato, a
retirar	retirer	withdraw	zurück = ziehen	retirar	ritirare
retirar aduana	dédouaner	clear(customs)	verzollen	desalfandegar	sdoganare
retrasado, a(estar)	retard(être en)	late(to be)	zu spät kommen	atrasado, a(estar)	ritardo(essere in)
retrasar, demorar	retarder	delay	verzögern	atrasar, demorar	ritardare
retrato	portrait	portrait	Portrait(n)	retrato	ritratto
retroceder	reculer	move back, reverse	zurück = gehen	recuar	indietreggiare
retroceso	recul	recoil	Rückstoß(m)	recuo	rinculo
retrovisor	rétroviseur	rear-view mirror	Rückspiegel(m)	retrovisor	retrovisore
reumatismo	rhumatisme	rheumatism	Rheumatismus(m)	reumatismo	reumatismo
reunión	réunion	meeting; reunion	Treffen(n)	reunião	riunione
reunir	réunir	gather(together)	sammeln	reunir	riunire
reunir	assembler	assemble	versammeln	reunir	radunare, riunire
reunirse	réunir(se)	meet	treffen, sich	reunir-se	riunirsi
reunirse con	rejoindre	rejoin, return to	an = schließen, sich	reunir-se	raggiungere
revelar	révéler	reveal	auf = decken	revelar	rivelare
reventar	crever	puncture, burst	platzen, bersten	rebentar; furar	bucare, scoppiare
reventar	éclater	burst	platzen	rebentar	scoppiare
revés	envers	reverse, back	Rückseite(f)	avesso	rovescio
revisión	révision	revision	Revision(f)	revisão	revisione
revisión	révision	service, overhaul	Überholung(f)	revisão	revisione
revisor	contrôleur	inspector	Kontrolleur(m)	revisor; fiscal	controllore
revista	magazine	magazine	Illustrierte(f)	revista	rivista
revista	revue, magazine	review, magazine	Zeitschrift, Revue(f)	revista	rivista, periodico
revocar	révoquer	dismiss	ab = setzen, entlassen	demitir	revocare
revolución	révolution	revolution	Revolution(f)	revolução	rivoluzione
revolucionario, a	révolutionnaire	revolutionary	revolutionär	revolucionário, a	rivoluzionario, a
revólver	révolver	revolver, gun	Revolver(m)	revólver	revolver
revuelta	révolte	revolt	Revolte(f)	revolta	rivolta
rey	roi	king	König(m)	rei	re
rezar	prier	pray	beten	rezar, orar	pregare
riachuelo, arroyo	ruisseau	stream, brook	Bach(m)	regato, ribeiro	ruscello
riada	ruée	rush	Ansturm(m)	corrida	ressa
ribera, orilla	berge	bank	Ufer(n)	margem	sponda
rico, a	riche	rich, wealthy	reich	rico, a	ricco, a
ridículo, a	ridicule	ridiculous	lächerlich	ridículo, a	ridicolo, a
riesgo	risque	risk	Risiko(n)	risco	rischio
riesgo, azar	aléa	hazard	Zufall(m)	acaso	rischio
rígido, a	rigide	rigid, stiff	steif	rígido, a	rigido, a
riguroso, a	rigoureux, se	rigorous	streng	rigoroso, a	rigoroso, a
riña	bagarre	fight	Schlägerei(f)	briga	rissa, zuffa
riñón	rein	kidney	Niere(f)	rim	rene
río	fleuve	river	Strom(m)	rio	fiume
río, ribera	rivière	river	Fluß(m)	rio, ribeira	fiume
riqueza	richesse	wealth, richness	Reichtum(m)	riqueza	ricchezza
risa	rire	laugh, laughter	Lachen(n)	riso	riso, ridere
ritmo	rythme	rhythm	Takt(m), Rhythmus(m)	ritmo	ritmo
rito	rite	rite; ritual	Brauch(m), Ritus(m)	rito	rito
rival	rival, e	rival; competitor	Rivale(m), Rivalin(f)	rival	rivale
rivalidad	rivalité	rivalry	Rivalität(f)	rivalidade	rivalità
rizado, a	frisé, e	curly	lockig	ondulado, a	ricciuto, a
rizo	boucle	curl	Locke(f)	caracóis	ricciolo
robar	voler	steal, rob	stehlen	roubar	rubare
robar	dérober	steal	entwenden	roubar, furtar	derubare
robo	vol	theft, robbery	Diebstahl(m)	roubo	furto
robo, atraco	cambriolage	burglary	Einbruch(m)	roubo, assalto	furto con scasso
robot	robot	robot	Roboter(m)	robot	robot
robusto, a	robuste	robust, sturdy	robust, stark	robusto, a	robusto, a
roca	roche, rocher	rock	Fels(m)	rocha	roccia
rocío	rosée	dew	Tau(m)	orvalho	rugiada
rodaja	rondelle	slice	Scheibe(f)	rodela	fettina, fetta
rodaje	rodage	running in	Einfahren(n)	rodagem	rodaggio
rodaje	tournage	shooting	Filmaufnahme(f)	filmagem	riprese
rodar	rouler	roll	rollen	rolar	rotolare

Spanish	French	English	German	Portuguese	Italian
rodar, filmar	filmer	film	filmen	filmar	filmare
rodear	entourer	surround	um = geben	rodear, cercar	circondare
rodilla	genou	knee	Knie(n)	joelho	ginocchio
roer	ronger	gnaw	zernagen	roer	rodere
rojo, a	rouge	red	rot	vermelho, a	rosso, a
rollo	rouleau	roll	Rolle(f), Walze(f)	rolo	rotolo; rullo
romántico, a	romantique	romantic	romantisch	romântico, a	romantico, a
rombo	losange	diamond-shaped	Raute(f), Rhombus(m)	losango	rombo
rompecabezas	puzzle	jigsaw(puzzle)	Puzzle(n)	puzzle	puzzle
romper	casser, briser	break	zerbrechen	quebrar, partir	rompere
romper	briser	break	brechen, zerbrechen	quebrar	spezzare, rompere
romper	rompre	break	brechen(ab = -; zer-)	romper	rompere
romper	déferler	break	branden	quebrar-se	infrangersi
roncar	ronfler	snore	schnarchen	ressonar, roncar	russare
ronco, a	enroué, e	hoarse	heiser	rouco, a	rauco, a
ronco, a	rauque	hoarse	rauh, heiser	rouco, a	rauco, a
roña, mugre	crasse	filth, dirt	Dreck(m)	sujidade	sporcizia
ropa, prenda	vêtements	clothes	Kleidung(f)	roupa(s)	vestiti
ropa	habillement	clothing	Bekleidung(f)	vestuário	abbigliamento
ropa	linge	linen	Wäsche(f)	roupa	biancheria
rosa	rose	pink	rosafarben	cor-de-rosa	rosa
rosa	rose	rose	Rose(f)	rosa	rosa
rostro, cara	visage	face	Gesicht(n)	cara	viso
rostro	figure	face	Gesicht(n)	rosto	faccia
rotación	rotation	rotation	Drehung(f)	rotação	rotazione
rótula	rotule	knee-cap	Kniescheibe(f)	rótula	rotula
rotulador	crayon-feutre	felt-tip pen	Filzschreiber(m)	marcador	pennarello
rotura	cassure, rupture	break	Bruch(m)	ruptura, quebra	frattura, rottura
rubéola	rubéole	German measles	Röteln(pl)	rubéola	rosolia
rubí	rubis	ruby	Rubin(m)	rubi	rubino
rubio(pelo)	blond, e	fair, blond	blond	louro, a	biondo, a
rueda	roue	wheel	Rad(n)	roda	ruota
rugoso, a	rugueux, se	rough, harsh	rauh	rugoso, a	rugoso, a
ruido	bruit	noise	Geräusch(n)	ruído, barulho	rumore
ruidoso, a	bruyant, e	noisy; loud	laut	barulhento, a	rumoroso, a
ruina	ruine	ruin	Ruine(f)	ruína	rovina
ruina	ruine	ruin	Trümmer(m, pl)	ruína	rovina
ruina, restos	épave	wreck	Wrack(n)	destroços	relitto
rumbo a	cap	head for	Kurs(m)	rumo	rotta
rumor	rumeur	rumour	Gerücht(n)	rumor	voce, diceria
ruptura	rupture	rupture	Bruch(m)	ruptura	rottura
rural	rural, e	rural	ländlich	rural	rurale
rústico, a	rustique	rustic	ländlich, einfach	rústico, a	rustico, a
ruta, itinerario	itinéraire, route	route	Route(f), Weg(m)	caminho, rota	rotta, itinerario
rutina	routine	routine	Routine(f)	rotina	routine, tran tran

S

Spanish	French	English	German	Portuguese	Italian
sábado	samedi	Saturday	Samstag(m)	sábado	sabato
sabana	savane	savannah	Savanne(f)	savana	savana
sábana	drap	sheet	Laken(n)	lençol	lenzuolo
sabañón	engelure	chilblain	Frostbeule(f)	frieira	gelone
saber	savoir	know	wissen	saber	sapere
saber	savoir	knowledge	Wissen(n)	sabedoria	sapere
sabio	sage	sage, wise man	Weise(m)	sábio	saggio, a; savio, a
sabio, a	savant, e	learned person	Wissenschaftler(m)	sábio, a	studioso, a; dotto, a
sable	sabre	sabre	Säbel(m)	sabre	sciabola
sabor	saveur	flavour	Geschmack(m)	sabor	sapore
saborear	savourer	savour	kosten, genießen	saborear	assaporare

Spanish	French	English	German	Portuguese	Italian
saborear, catar	déguster	taste, sample	kosten	provar	gustare
sabotaje	sabotage	sabotage	Sabotage(f)	sabotagem	sabotaggio
sabotear	saboter	sabotage	sabotieren	sabotar	sabotare
sabroso, a	savoureux, se	tasty	schmackhaft	saboroso, a	saporito, a
sacacorchos	tire-bouchon	corkscrew	Korkenzieher(m)	saca-rolhas	cavatappi
sacar, quitar	enlever	take away, remove	entfernen	retirar, tirar	togliere
sacar	prélever	take from	entnehmen	tirar	prelevare
sacar	puiser	draw(from)	schöpfen	tirar, extraír	attingere
sacar	retirer	draw out, withdraw	ab = heben	levantar	prelevare
sacerdote, padre	prêtre	priest	Priester(m)	padre	prete
saco	sac	sack	Sack(m)	saco	sacco
saco de dormir	sac de couchage	sleeping bag	Schlafsack(m)	saco-cama	sacco a pelo
sacrificar	sacrifier	sacrifice	opfern	sacrificar	sacrificare
sacrificio	sacrifice	sacrifice	Opfer(n)	sacrifício	sacrificio
sacrilegio	sacrilège	sacrilege	Entweihung(f)	sacrilégio	sacrilegio
sacudida	secousse	jolt, jerk	Ruck(m), Stoß(m)	abalo	scossa
sacudir	secouer	shake	schütteln	sacudir	scuotere
sádico, a	sadique	sadistic	sadistisch	sádico, a	sadico, a
sádico, a	sadique	sadist	Sadist(in f)m	sádico, a	sadico, a
sagrado, a	sacré, e	holy; sacred	heilig	sagrado, a	sacro, a
sal	sel	salt	Salz(n)	sal	sale
sala	salle	room	Saal(m), Raum(m)	sala	sala, stanza
sala	salon	lounge	Herrenzimmer(n)	sala de estar	salotto
sala de baile	dancing	dance-hall	Tanzlokal(n)	dancing	sala da ballo
sala de espera	salle d'attente	waiting-room	Wartezimmer(n)	sala de espera	sala d'attesa
sala de estar	salle de séjour	living-room	Wohnzimmer(n)	sala de estar	soggiorno
salado, a	salé, e	salty	salzig	salgado, a	salato, a
salario	salaire	salary, wage	Lohn(m), Gehalt(n)	salário	salario
salchicha	saucisse	sausage	Wurst(f)	salsicha	salsiccia
salchichería	charcuterie	delicatessen shop	Metzgerei(f)	salsicharia	salumeria
saldar	solder	sell off	aus = verkaufen	saldar	saldare, liquidare
saldos, rebajas	soldes	sales	Ausverkauf(m)	saldos	saldi
salida	sortie	exit, way out	Ausgang(m)	saída	uscita
salida, partida	départ	departure, start	Abfahrt(f)	partida	partenza
salida	issue(sortie)	way out, exit	Ausgang(m)	saída	uscita
salida(emergencia)	sortie(secours)	emergency exit	Notausgang(m)	saída de emergência	uscita(sicurezza)
salir	sortir	go out, come out	aus = gehen	sair	uscire
salir, marcharse	partir	leave, go away	weg = gehen	partir, abalar	partire
salirse de madre	déborder	overflow	über die Ufer treten	extravasar	straripare
saliva	salive	saliva	Speichel(m)	saliva	saliva
salmón	saumon	salmon	Lachs(m)	salmão	salmone
salón	salon	show, exhibition	Messe(f)	salão	salone
salón de té	salon de thé	tea-room	Café(n), Konditorei(f)	casa de chá	sala da tè
salpicar	gicler, jaillir	squirt, spurt	spritzen	salpicar	sprizzare, schizzare
salsa	sauce	sauce	Soße(f)	molho	sugo; salsa
saltar	sauter	jump	springen	saltar, pular	saltare
saltar	bondir	jump, leap	springen	saltar	saltare, balzare
salto, brinco	saut, bond	jump, leap, spring	Sprung(m)	salto, pulo	salto, balzo
salud	santé	health	Gesundheit(f)	saúde	salute
saludar	saluer	greet; say hello	begrüßen	saudar	salutare
salvaje	sauvage	wild	wild	selvagem	selvaggio, a
salvamento	sauvetage	rescue	Rettung(f)	salvamento	salvataggio
salvamento	sauvetage	salvage	Bergung(f)	salvamento	salvataggio
salvar	sauver	save	retten	salvar	salvare
salvavidas	bouée	lifebelt	Rettungsring(m)	bóia	salvagente
salvo, a	sauf, ve	safe	sicher	salvo, a	salvo, a
salvoconducto	laissez-passer	pass	Ausweis(m)	salvo-conduto	lascia-passare
sanción	sanction	sanction	Strafe(f)	sanção	sanzione
sandalia	sandale	sandal	Sandale(f)	sandália	sandalo
sangrar	saigner	bleed	bluten	sangrar	sanguinare
sangre	sang	blood	Blut(n)	sangue	sangue
sangre fría	sang-froid	cool, calm	Kaltblütigkeit(f)	sangue-frio	sangue freddo
sanitario, a	sanitaire	sanitary	Gesundheits-	sanitário, a	sanitario, a
sano, a	sain, e	healthy	gesund	são, sã	sano, a
santo, a; san	saint, e	holy	heilig	santo, a	santo, a
santo, a	saint, e	saint	Heilige(m, f)	santo, a	santo, a
santuario	sanctuaire	sanctuary	Heiligtum(n)	santuário	santuario
saquear	saccager	ransack	verwüsten	saquear	saccheggiare

Spanish	French	English	German	Portuguese	Italian
saqueo	pillage	plunder, pillage	Plünderung(f)	pilhagem	saccheggio
sarampión	rougeole	measles	Masern(pl.)	sarampo	morbillo
sardina	sardine	sardine	Sardine(f)	sardinha	sardina
sargento	sergent	sergeant	Unteroffizier(m)	sargento	sergente
sarna	gale	scabies	Krätze(f)	sarna	scabbia, rogna
sartén	poêle	frying pan	Pfanne(f)	frigideira	padella
sastre	tailleur	tailor	Schneider(m)	alfaiate	sarto
satélite	satellite	satellite	Satellit(m)	satélite	satellite
satisfacción	satisfaction	satisfaction	Zufriedenheit(f)	satisfação	soddisfazione
satisfecho, a	satisfait, e	satisfied	zufrieden	satisfeito, a	soddisfatto, a
saturación	saturation	saturation	Übersättigung(f)	saturação	saturazione
saturar	saturer	saturate	sättigen	saturar	saturare
sauna	sauna	sauna	Sauna(f)	sauna	sauna
savia	sève	sap	Saft(m)	seiva	linfa
secador	sèche-cheveux	hair-dryer	Fön(m), Haartrockner m	secador	asciugacapelli
secar	sécher	dry	trocknen	secar	asciugare; seccare
sección	section	section	Schnitt(m)	secção	sezione
sección	rayon	department	Abteilung(f)	secção	reparto
seccionar	sectionner	cut, divide	schneiden	seccionar	sezionare
seco, a	sec, sèche	dry	trocken	seco, a	secco, a; asciutto, a
secreción	sécrétion	secretion	Ausscheidung(f)	secreção	secrezione
secretario, a	secrétaire	secretary	Sekretär(in f)m	secretário, a	segretario, a
secreto, a	secret, ète	secret	geheim	secreto, a	segreto, a
secreto	secret	secret	Geheimnis(n)	segredo	segreto
secta	secte	sect	Sekte(f)	seita	setta
sector	secteur	sector	Bereich(m)	sector	settore
secuencia	séquence	sequence	Folge(f), Sequenz(f)	sequência	sequenza
secuestrar	séquestrer	lock away	ein = sperren	sequestrar	sequestrare
secuestrar	kidnapper	kidnap	entführen	raptar	rapire
secuestrar	détourner	hijack	entführen	sequestrar	dirottare
secundario, a	secondaire	secondary	nebensächlich	secundário, a	secondario, a
sed	soif	thirst	Durst(m)	sede	sete
seda	soie	silk	Seide(f)	seda	seta
sedativo, a	sédatif, ive	sedative	schmerzlindernd	sedativo, a	sedativo, a
sede	siège	head office	Firmensitz(m)	sede	sede
seducción	séduction	seduction	Verführung(f)	sedução	seduzione
seducir	séduire	charm; seduce	verführen, verleiten	seduzir	sedurre
segmento	segment	segment	Abschnitt(m)	segmento	segmento
segregación	ségrégation	segregation	Trennung(f)	segregação	segregazione
seguida(en)	aussitôt	straight away	sofort, sogleich	imediatamente	subito, appena
seguida(en)	suite(tout de)	once(at)	sogleich, sofort	imediatamente	subito
seguir	suivre	follow	folgen	seguir	seguire
según	selon	according to	gemäß	segundo	secondo
segunda mano	occasion	second-hand, used	gebraucht	segunda mão(em)	seconda mano
segundo, a	deuxième	second	zweite	segundo, a	secondo, a
segundo, a	second, e	second	zweite	segundo, a	secondo, a
segundo	seconde	second	Sekunde(f)	segundo	secondo
seguridad	sûreté	safety	Sicherheit(f)	segurança	sicurezza
seguridad	sécurité	security; safety	Sicherheit(f)	segurança	sicurezza
seguro	assurance	insurance	Versicherung(f)	seguro	assicurazione
seguro, a	sûr, e; certain, e	sure, certain	sicher	seguro, a	sicuro, a
seguro, a	assuré, e	assured	sicher	certo, a	sicuro, a; certo, a
seis	six	six	sechs	seis	sei
seismo	séisme	earthquake	Erdbeben(n)	sismo	sisma
selección	sélection	selection	Auslese(f); Auswahl(f)	selecção	selezione
seleccionar	sélectionner	select	aus = lesen	seleccionar	selezionare
selva, jungla	jungle	jungle	Dschungel(m)	selva	giungla
sellar	tamponner	stamp	stempeln	carimbar	timbrare
sello	cachet	postmark; seal	Stempel(m), Siegel(n)	selo	sigillo, bollo
sello	sceau	seal	Siegel(n)	selo	sigillo
sello	timbre(-poste)	stamp	Briefmarke(f)	selo	francobollo
semana	semaine	week	Woche(f)	semana	settimana
semanal	hebdomadaire	weekly	wöchentlich	semanal	settimanale
semblante, cara	mine	look	Aussehen(n)	aparência	cera, aspetto
sembrar	semer	sow	säen	semear	seminare
semejante	semblable	similar	ähnlich	semelhante	simile, uguale
semi	semi	semi, half	halb	semi	semi
semilla	graine	seed	Samenkorn(n)	semente	seme

S

Spanish	French	English	German	Portuguese	Italian
senado	sénat	senate	Senat(m), Bundesrat(m)	senado	senato
senador	sénateur	senator	Senator(m)	senador	senatore
sencillez	simplicité	simplicity	Einfachheit(f)	simplicidade	semplicità
sendero, senda	sentier	footpath, path	Weg(m)	vereda, atalho	sentiero
seno, pecho	sein(s)	breast	Busen(m)	seio	seno
sensación	sensation	sensation; feeling	Empfindung(f)	sensação	sensazione
sensato, a	sensé, e	sensible	vernünftig	sensato, a	sensato, a
sensibilidad	sensibilité	sensitivity	Sensibilität(f)	sensibilidade	sensibilità
sensibilizar	sensibiliser	sensitive(make sb)	sensibilisieren	sensibilizar	sensibilizzare
sensible	sensible	sensitive	empfindlich	sensível	sensibile
sensual	sensuel, le	sensual	sinnlich	sensual	sensuale
sensualidad	sensualité	sensuality	Sinnlichkeit(f)	sensualidade	sensualità
sentado, a	assis, e	seated	sitzen	sentado, a	seduto, a
sentarse	asseoir(s')	sit(down)	setzen, sich	sentar-se	sedersi
sentencia	jugement	sentence	Urteil(n)	sentença	sentenza
sentido	sens	meaning, sense	Bedeutung(f)	sentido	senso
sentido	sens	direction, way	Richtung(f)	sentido	senso
sentimental	sentimental, e	sentimental	sentimental	sentimental	sentimentale
sentimiento	sentiment	feeling	Gefühl(n)	sentimento	sentimento
sentir	sentir	feel	fühlen	sentir	sentire
sentir	éprouver	feel	spüren, fühlen	sentir	provare
sentir	ressentir	feel	empfinden	sentir	sentire
sentir(lo)	regretter	sorry(be), regret	bedauern	sentir, lamentar	dispiacere(-ersi)
señal, marca	marque, trace	mark	Spur(f)	marca, vestígio	segno, marca
señal	signal	signal	Signal(n)	sinal	segnale
señal, indicio	repère	mark, landmark	Markierung(f)	sinal, marca	contrassegno
señal, letrero	panneau	sign, notice	Schild(n)	sinal	cartello
señal(dejar)	arrhes	deposit	Anzahlung(f)	sinal	caparra
señalar	signaler	point out	melden; an = zeigen	assinalar	segnalare
señalar, indicar	désigner	indicate	bezeichnen	indicar	indicare
señalización	signalisation	sign	Beschilderung(f)	sinalização	segnalazione
señor	monsieur(Mr)	Mr	Herr(m)	senhor	signor
señor	monsieur	Sir	Herr(m)	senhor	signore
señor, señora	maître, esse	master, mistress	Herr(in f)m	dono, a; senhor, a	maestro, a; padrone, a
Señor	Seigneur	Lord	Herr(m)	Senhor	Signore
señora	madame	Mrs; Madam	Frau(f)	senhora	signora
señora	dame	lady	Dame(f)	senhora	signora
señoras	mesdames	ladies	meine Damen	senhoras	signore
señores	messieurs	gentlemen	meine Herren	senhores	signori
señorita	mademoiselle	Miss	Fräulein(n)	menina	signorina
señuelo	leurre, appât	lure, bait	Lockmittel(n)	isca, engodo	esca
separación	séparation	separation	Trennung(f)	separação	separazione
separar	séparer	separate, part	trennen	separar	separare, dividere
septiembre	septembre	September	September(m)	Setembro	settembre
sepultura	sépulture	burial(-place)	Grab(n)	sepultura	sepoltura
sequía	sécheresse	drought	Trockenheit(f)	seca	siccità
ser, estar	être	be	sein	ser, estar	essere
serenidad	sérénité	serenity	Heiterkeit(f)	serenidade	serenità
sereno, a	serein, e	serene	heiter	sereno, a	sereno, a
serie	série	series	Serie(f)	série	serie
serio, a	sérieux, se	serious	ernst, ernsthaft	sério, a	serio, a
serpiente	serpent	snake	Schlange(f)	serpente	serpente
serrar, aserrar	scier	saw	sägen	serrar	segare
servicial	dévoué, e	devoted	ergeben	dedicado, a	devoto, a
servicio	service	service	Dienstleistung(f)	serviço	servizio
servicio	service	service	Bedienung(f)	serviço	servizio
servicios(W.C)	toilettes(W.C)	toilet, lavatory	Toiletten(f pl)	lavabos; sanita	toilettes; W.C
servilleta	serviette	serviette, napkin	Serviette(f)	guardanapo	tovagliolo
servir	servir	serve	dienen, bedienen	servir	servire
servirse	servir de(se)	use	benutzen	servir-se	adoperare
sesenta	soixante	sixty	sechzig	sessenta	sessanta
sesión	session	session	Sitzung(f)	sessão	sessione
sesión	séance	session; meeting	Sitzung(f)	sessão	seduta
seta	champignon	mushroom	Pilz(m), Champignon(m)	cogumelo	fungo
setenta	soixante-dix	seventy	siebzig	setenta	settanta
seto, valla	haie	hedge	Hecke(f)	sebe	siepe
seudónimo	pseudonyme	pseudonym	Pseudonym(n)	pseudónimo	pseudonimo
severo, a	sévère	severe, strict	streng	severo, a	severo, a

Spanish	French	English	German	Portuguese	Italian
sexo	sexe	sex	Geschlecht(n)	sexo	sesso
sexual	sexuel, le	sexual	geschlechtlich	sexual	sessuale
sexualidad	sexualité	sexuality	Sexualität(f)	sexualidade	sessualità
si	si	if; whether	wenn; ob	se	se
sí	oui	yes	ja	sim	sì
sí(mismo)	soi(-même)	oneself	sich, selbst	si(mesmo)	se(stesso)
sicoanalista	psychanalyste	psychoanalyst	Psychoanalytiker(m)	psicanalista	psicanalista
sicología	psychologie	psychology	Psychologie(f)	psicologia	psicologia
sicólogo, a	psychologue	psychologist	Psychologe(m)/-gin(f)	psicólogo, a	psicologo, a
sicosis	psychose	psychosis(-ses)	Psychose(f)	psicose	psichosi
sidra	cidre	cider	Apfelwein(m)	sidra	sidro
siempre	toujours	always	immer	sempre	sempre
siempre(para, por)	toujours(pour)	forever	immer(für)	sempre(para)	sempre(per)
sien	tempe	temple	Schläfe(f)	têmpora	tempia
siento(lo)	excuse(je m')	sorry(I am)	es tut mir leid	desculpe!	scusi(mi)
siento(lo)	désolé, e	regret(I)	bedauern	lamento(eu)	rammaricato, a
sierra	scie	saw	Säge(f)	serra	sega
sierra	chaîne(montagne)	range(mountain)	Bergkette(f)	serra	catena(monti)
siesta	sieste	nap, snooze	Mittagsschlaf(m)	sesta	siesta, riposino
siete	sept	seven	sieben	sete	sette
sífilis	syphilis	syphilis	Syphilis(f)	sífilis	sifilide
sigla	sigle	initials	Abkürzung(f)	sigla	sigla
siglo	siècle	century	Jahrhundert(n)	século	secolo
significación	signification	meaning	Bedeutung(f)	significação	significato
significar	signifier	mean, signify	bedeuten	significar	significare
significativo, a	significatif, ive	significant	bezeichnend	significativo, a	significativo, a
signo	signe	sign	Zeichen(n)	sinal, signo	segno
siguiente	suivant, e	following, next	nächste	seguinte	seguente
silaba	syllabe	syllable	Silbe(f)	sílaba	sillaba
silbar	siffler	whistle	pfeifen	assobiar	fischiare
silencio	silence	silence	Stille(f)	silêncio	silenzio
silencioso, a	silencieux, se	silent, quiet	still, leise, ruhig	silencioso, a	silenzioso, a
silueta	silhouette	outline	Silhouette(f)	silhueta	sagoma; silhouette
silla	chaise	chair	Stuhl(m)	cadeira	sedia
silla	selle	saddle	Sattel(m)	sela	sella
silla de bebé	poussette	push-chair	Sportwagen(m)	cadeira de bebé	passeggino
sillín	selle	saddle	Sattel(m)	selim	sellino
sillón	fauteuil	arm-chair	Sessel(m)	poltrona	poltrona
simbólico, a	symbolique	symbolic(al)	symbolisch	simbólico, a	simbolico, a
símbolo	symbole	symbol	Symbol(n)	símbolo	simbolo
simetría	symétrie	symmetry	Symetrie(f)	simetria	simmetria
simiente	semence	seed	Samen(m)	semente	seme, semente
similar	similaire	similar	ähnlich, gleichartig	similar	similare
simpático, a	sympathique	pleasant, nice	sympathisch	simpático, a	simpatico, a
simpático, a	gracieux, se	good natured	lieb	gracioso, a	grazioso, a
simple	simple	simple	einfach	simples	semplice
simplemente	simplement	simply	einfach	simplesmente	semplicemente
simplificar	simplifier	simplify	vereinfachen	simplificar	semplificare
simulación	simulation	simulation	Vortäuschung(f)	simulação	simulazione
simultáneo, a	simultané, e	simultaneous	gleichzeitig	simultâneo, a	simultaneo, a
sin	sans	without	ohne	sem	senza
sin brillo, mate	terne	dull	matt	baço, a	spento, a; smorto, a
sin embargo	cependant	however, but	jedoch	todavia, porém	eppure, tuttavia
sin embargo	pourtant	yet, however	dennoch, doch	contudo, todavia	però, tuttavia
sin embargo	toutefois	however	jedoch	todavia	tuttavia
sinagoga	synagogue	synagogue	Synagoge(f)	sinagoga	sinagoga
sincero, a	sincère	sincere, candid	aufrichtig	sincero, a	sincero, a
síncope	syncope	black-out	Ohnmacht(f)	síncope	sincope
sincronizar	synchroniser	synchronize	synchronisieren	sincronizar	sincronizzare
sindicalismo	syndicalisme	trade unionism	Gewerkschaftswesen	sindicalismo	sindacalismo
sindicato	syndicat	trade union	Gewerkschaft(f)	sindicato	sindacato
sinfonía	symphonie	symphony	Symphonie(f)	sinfonia	sinfonia
singular	singulier	singular	Einzahl(f)	singular	singolare
siniestrado, a	sinistré, e	victim(disaster -)	Geschädigte(r)m f	sinistrado, a	sinistrato, a
siniestro, a	sinistre	sinister	unheilvoll	sinistro, a	sinistro, a
si no	sinon	otherwise, or else	andernfalls, sonst	senão	se no; altrimenti
sinónimo	synonyme	synonym	Synonym(n)	sinónimo	sinonimo
sintaxis	syntaxe	syntax	Syntax(f), Satzlehre f	sintaxe	sintassi

Spanish	French	English	German	Portuguese	Italian
síntesis	synthèse	synthesis(-ses)	Synthese(f)	síntese	sintesi
sintético, a	synthétique	synthetic	synthetisch	sintético, a	sintetico, a
síntoma	symptôme	symptom	Symptom(n)	sintoma	sintomo
sinuoso, a	sinueux, se	winding, sinuous	kurvenreich	sinuoso, a	sinuoso, a
siquiatra	psychiatre	psychiatrist	Psychiater(in f)m	psiquiatra	psichiatra
síquico, a	psychique	psychological	psychisch	psíquico, a	psichico, a
siquiera(ni)	même pas	even(not)	einmal(nicht)	sequer(nem)	neanche
sirena	sirène	siren	Sirene(f)	sirene	sirena
sísmico, a	sismique	seismic	seismisch	sísmico, a	sismico, a
sistema	système	system	System(n)	sistema	sistema
sistemático, a	systématique	systematic	systematisch	sistemático, a	sistematico, a
sitio	emplacement	location, site	Lage(f), Stelle(f)	lugar; sítio	posto, sito, luogo
sitio, espacio	place	room	Platz(m)	espaço	spazio
sitio, asiento	place	seat	Sitzplatz(m)	lugar	posto
sitio	siège	siege	Belagerung(f)	cerco	assedio
situación	situation	situation	Lage(f)	situação	situazione
situación	situation	location, position	Lage(f)	situação	situazione
situación	situation	position, job	Stellung, Position(f)	situação	situazione
situado, a	situé, e	located	gelegen	situado, a	situato, a
situar, localizar	situer	situate, locate	stellen, setzen	situar, localizar	situare, localizzare
soberanía	souveraineté	sovereignty	Souveränität(f)	soberania	sovranità
soberano, a; monarca	souverain, e	sovereign, monarch	Herrscher(in f)m	soberano, a; monarca	sovrano, a; monarca
soberbio, a	superbe	superb	großartig	soberbo, a	splendido, a
soborno	pot-de-vin	bribe	Schmiergelder(pl.)	suborno	bustarella
sobrar, quedar	rester	remain	bleiben	sobejar, sobrar	restare, rimanere
sobre	sur; au-dessus de	on, upon	über; auf	sobre	sopra, su
sobre	enveloppe	envelope	Umschlag(m)(Brief-)	envelope	busta
sobredosis	surdose	overdose	Überdosis(f)	overdose	overdose
sobrenatural	surnaturel, le	supernatural	überirdisch	sobrenatural	soprannaturale
sobreponer	superposer	superpose	aufeinander = legen	sobrepor	sovrapporre
sobresalir	dépasser	protrude	hervor = stehen	sobressair	sporgere
sobresalir	dépasser	go beyond, exceed	überholen	ultrapassar	oltrepassare
sobre todo	surtout	above all	besonders	sobretudo	soprattutto
sobrevivir	survivre	survive	überleben	sobreviver	sopravvivere
sobrevuelo	survol	flight over	Überfliegen(n)	sobrevôo	sorvolo
sobrina	nièce	niece	Nichte(f)	sobrinha	nipote
sobrino	neveu	nephew	Neffe(m)	sobrinho	nipote
sociable	sociable	sociable	gesellig	sociável	socievole
social	social, e	social	sozial	social	sociale
socialismo	socialisme	socialism	Sozialismus(m)	socialismo	socialismo
sociedad	société	society	Gesellschaft(f)	sociedade	società
sociedad	société	company, firm	Gesellschaft(f)	sociedade	società
socio, a, asociado	associé, e	associate, partner	Teilhaber(in f)m	sócio, a	socio, a
sociología	sociologie	sociology	Soziologie(f)	sociologia	sociologia
socorrer	secourir	help, assist, aid	helfen	socorrer	soccorrere
socorrer	secourir	rescue	retten	socorrer	soccorrere
socorrista	sauveteur	rescuer	Retter(in f)m	socorrista	soccorritore
socorro	secours	help, aid	Hilfe(f)	socorro	soccorso
sofá, canapé	canapé	sofa	Sofa(n)	canapé, sofá	divano, canapè
sofisticado, a	sophistiqué, e	sophisticated	hochkompliziert	sofisticado, a	sofisticato, a
sofocar, ahogar	étouffer	suffocate; choke	ersticken	sufocar	soffocare
sol	soleil	sun	Sonne(f)	sol	sole
sol(hace)	soleil(il fait)	sunny(it's)	Sonne scheint(die)	sol(está)	sole(c'è il)
solamente, sólo	seulement	only	nur	somente, só	solo, soltanto
solar	solaire	solar	Sonnen-	solar	solare
soldado	soldat	soldier	Soldat(m)	soldado	soldato
soldadura	soudure	welding	Schweißen(n)	soldadura	saldatura
soleado, a	ensoleillé, e	sunny	sonnig	soalheiro, a	soleggiato, a
soledad	solitude	loneliness	Einsamkeit(f)	solidão	solitudine
solemne	solennel, le	solemn	feierlich	solene	solenne
solfeo	solfège	sol-fa, theory	Tonleiter(f)	solfejo	solfeggio
solicitar	solliciter	appeal to, request	ersuchen	solicitar	sollecitare
solicitud	demande(emploi)	application	Bewerbung(f)	pedido	domanda
solidaridad	solidarité	solidarity	Solidarität(f)	solidaridade	solidarietà
sólido, a	solide	solid, strong	solide, fest	sólido, a	solido, a
solitario, a	solitaire	solitary, lonely	einsam	solitário, a	solitario, a
solo, a	seul, e	alone	allein	só	solo, a
solo, a; único, a	un, e(à)	single	einzeln; einzig	único, a	singolo, a

Spanish	French	English	German	Portuguese	Italian
solo, a	seul, e	only	einzig	só	solo, a
soltar	lâcher	release	los = lassen	soltar	lasciare
soltar	relâcher	release	frei = lassen	libertar	rilasciare
soltero, a	célibataire	single, unmarried	ledig	solteiro, a	scapolo; nubile
soltero, a	célibataire	bachelor; single -	Junggeselle m/-sellin	solteiro, a	scapolo, nubile
soltura(con)	couramment	fluently	fließend	fluentemente	correntemente
soluble	soluble	soluble	löslich	solúvel	solubile
solución	solution	solution	Lösung(f)	solução	soluzione
solucionar	solutionner	solve	lösen	solucionar	risolvere
sollozo	sanglot	sob	Schluchzer(m)	soluço	singhiozzo
sombra	ombre	shadow	Schatten(m)	sombra	ombra
sombrero	chapeau	hat	Hut(m)	chapéu	cappello
sombrilla	ombrelle	sunshade, parasol	Sonnenschirm(m)	sombrinha	ombrello, parasole
someter	soumettre	submit	unterwerfen	submeter	sottomettere
someter, sujetar	assujettir	subject(to)	unterwerfen	sujeitar	assoggettare
somnífero	somnifère	sleeping tablet	Schlaftablette(f)	soporífero	sonnifero
somnolencia	somnolence	drowsiness	Schläfrigkeit(f)	sonolência	sonnolenza
sonámbulo, a	somnambule	sleep-walker	Schlafwandler(in f)m	sonâmbulo, a	sonnambulo, a
sonar, tocar	sonner	ring	klingeln	soar, tocar	suonare, sonare
sonarse	moucher(se)	blow one's nose	Nase putzen	assoar-se	soffiarsi il naso
sonata	sonate	sonata	Sonate(f)	sonata	sonata
sonda	sonde	probe	Sonde(f)	sonda	sonda
sondeo	sondage	poll(opinion)	Umfrage(f)	sondagem	sondaggio
sonido	son	sound	Ton(m)	som	suono
sonreír	sourire	smile	lächeln	sorrir	sorridere
sonriente	souriant, e	cheerful	lächelnd	sorridente	sorridente
sonrisa	sourire	smile	Lächeln(n)	sorriso	sorriso
sonrojarse	rougir	blush, flush	erröten	corar	arrossire
soñar	rêver	dream	träumen	sonhar	sognare
sopa	soupe	soup	Suppe(f)	sopa	minestra
soplar	souffler	blow	blasen	soprar	soffiare
soplar	souffler	blow	wehen	soprar	soffiare
soplo, aliento	souffle	breath	Luft(f), Puste(f)	sopro, fôlego	fiato, soffio
soportal, porche	porche	porch	Portal(n)	pórtico	atrio, portico
soportar	supporter	support	stützen, unterstützen	suportar	sopportare
soporte	support	support	Stütze(f)	suporte	supporto
sordera	surdité	deafness	Taubheit(f)	surdez	sordità
sórdido, a	sordide	sordid	schäbig	sórdido, a	squallido, a
sordo, a	sourd, e	deaf	taub	surdo, a	sordo, a
sordomudo, a	sourd-muet, te	deaf and dumb	taubstumm	surdo-mudo, a	sordomuto, a
sorprender	étonner	astonish, amaze	überraschen	espantar	sorprendere
sorprenderse	étonner(s')	astonished(be -)	wundern, sich	espantar-se	meravigliarsi
sorprendido, a	surpris, e	surprised	überrascht	surpreendido, a	sorpreso, a
sorpresa	surprise	surprise	Überraschung(f)	surpresa	sorpresa
sosia	sosie	double	Doppelgänger(in f)m	sósia	sosia
sospecha	soupçon	suspicion	Argwohn(m), Verdacht m	suspeita	sospetto
sospechar	soupçonner	suspect	verdächtigen	suspeitar	sospettare
sospechar	douter(se)	suspect, mistrust	ahnen, vermuten	suspeitar	sospettare
sospechoso, a	suspect, e	suspicious	verdächtig	suspeito, a	sospetto, a
sostén, apoyo	soutien, appui	support	Unterstützung(f)	apoio, socorro	sostegno, appoggio
sostén	soutien-gorge	bra	Büstenhalter(m)	soutien	reggiseno
sostener	soutenir	support	unterstützen	sustentar	sostenere
sótano	sous-sol	basement	Untergeschoß(n)	cave	scantinato
su	son	his; her; its	sein, seine, ihr, ihre	seu	suo(il)
su	sa	her; his; its	sein, e; ihr, ihre	sua	sua(la)
su, sus, suyo	leur(s)	their	ihr/ihre	seu, sua, deles	loro(il/la, i/le)
suave	doux, ce	soft	sanft	macio, a	morbido, a
subasta	enchère	bid, bidding	Auktion(f); Gebot(n)	leilão	asta
subconsciente	subconscient	subconscious	Unterbewußtsein(n)	subconsciente	subcosciente
subida	montée	rise	Steigung(f)	subida	salita
subida	hausse	rise, increase	Steigerung(f)	subida	aumento
subir	monter	climb; rise; go up	steigen	subir	salire
subir	élever(s')	rise	an = steigen	subir	elevarsi
subir	monter	get into, get on	ein = steigen	subir a, entrar	salire
sublevarse	insurger(s')	rise up, revolt	auf = lehnen gegen, sich	insurgir-se	insorgere
sublime	sublime	sublime	erhaben	sublime	sublime
submarino	sous-marin	submarine	Unterseeboot(n)	submarino	sottomarino
subordinado, a	subordonné, e	subordinate	Untergebene(f m)	subordinado, a	subalterno, a

S

Spanish	French	English	German	Portuguese	Italian
subrayar	souligner	underline	unterstreichen	sublinhar	sottolineare
subscripción	abonnement	subscription	Abonnement(n)	assinatura	abbonamento
subsidio	allocation	allowance	Beihilfe(f), Zulage(f)	subsídio, abono	assegnazione; assegno
subsistir	subsister	subsist, remain	fort = bestehen	subsistir	sussistere
substituto, a	adjoint, e	deputy	Stellvertreter(in f)m	adjunto, a	assessore
subsuelo	sous-sol	subsoil	Unterboden(m)	sub-solo	sottosuolo
subterráneo, a	souterrain, e	underground	unterirdisch	subterrâneo, a	sotterraneo, a
subtitulado, a	sous-titré, e	subtitled	Untertiteln(mit)	legendado, a	didascalie(con)
suburbio	faubourg	suburb	Vorstadt(f)	subúrbio	sobborgo
subvención	subvention	grant, subsidy	Zuschuß(m)	subvenção	sovvenzione
subvención	subvention	subsidy	Subvention(f)	subvenção	sussidio
suceder	succéder	succeed	nach = folgen	suceder	succedere
suceder, ocurrir	produire(se)	happen, occur	passieren	ocorrer	accadere
sucesivo, a	successif, ive	successive	aufeinanderfolgend	sucessivo, a	successivo, a
sucesor	successeur	successor	Nachfolger(in f)m	sucessor	successore
suciedad	saleté	dirt	Schmutz(m)	sujidade, porcaria	sporcizia
sucinto, a	succinct, e	succinct, brief	bündig	sucinto, a	succinto, a
sucio, a	sale	dirty	dreckig	sujo, a	sporco, a
sucumbir	succomber	succumb	erliegen	sucumbir	soccombere
sucursal	succursale	branch(-es)	Zweigstelle(f)	sucursal	succursale
sudar	suer	sweat	schwitzen	suar	sudare
sudor	sueur	sweat	Schweiß(m)	suor	sudore
suegra	belle-mère	mother-in-law	Schwiegermutter(f)	sogra	suocera
suegro	beau-père	father-in-law	Schwiegervater(m)	sogro	suocero
suegros	beaux-parents	parents-in-law	Schwiegereltern(pl.)	sogros	suoceri
suela	semelle	sole	Sohle(f)	sola	suola
suelo	sol	ground	Boden(m)	solo	suolo
suelo	plancher	floor	Fußboden(m)	soalho, sobrado	pavimento
sueño	sommeil	sleep	Schlaf(m)	sono	sonno
sueño	rêve	dream	Traum(m)	sonho	sogno
suero	sérum	serum	Serum(n)	soro	siero
suerte, fortuna	chance	luck; chance	Glück(n), Chance(f)	sorte	fortuna
suerte(tener)	chance(avoir)	fortunate(be)	Glück haben	sorte(ter)	fortuna(avere)
suerte, destino	sort	fate	Schicksal(m)	sorte, destino	sorte, destino
suficiente	suffisant, e	sufficient	genügend	suficiente	sufficiente
sufragio	suffrage	vote	Wahl(f)	sufrágio	suffragio
sufrimiento	souffrance	suffering	Leiden(n)	sofrimento	sofferenza
sufrir	souffrir	suffer	leiden	sofrer	soffrire
sufrir, padecer	subir	undergo	ertragen	sofrer	subire
sugerir	suggérer	suggest	vor = schlagen	sugerir, propôr	suggerire
suicidarse	suicider(se)	commit suicide	um = bringen, sich	suicidar-se	suicidarsi
suicidio	suicide	suicide	Selbstmord(m)	suicídio	suicidio
suite	suite	suite	Suite(f)	suite	appartamento
sujeto	sujet	subject	Subjekt(n)	sujeito	soggetto
sultán	sultan	sultan	Sultan(m)	sultão	sultano
suma; cantidad	somme	sum, amount	Summe(f)	soma; quantia	somma
sumergir	immerger	immerse	versenken	imergir	immergere
sumergir	tremper	dip	ein = tauchen	mergulhar	intingere
sumisión	soumission	submission	Unterwerfung(f)	submissão	sottomissione
suntuoso, a	somptueux, se	sumptuous	prächtig	sumptuoso, a	sontuoso, a
superar	surmonter	overcome	überwinden	superar	superare
supercarburante	essence super	four-star petrol	Superbenzin(n)	super	benzina super
superficie	superficie	area	Oberfläche(f)	superfície	superficie
superficie	surface	surface	Oberfläche(f)	superfície	superficie
superior, a	supérieur, e	superior	höher, besser	superior, a	superiore
superior, a	supérieur, e	upper	obere(r, s); Ober-	superior, a	superiore
superior	supérieur	superior	Vorgesetzte(f, m)	superior	superiore
superior(parte)	dessus	top	Oberteil(n)	cima(parte de)	disopra
superioridad	supériorité	superiority	Überlegenheit(f)	superioridade	superiorità
supermercado	supermarché	supermarket	Supermarkt(m)	supermercado	supermercato
supersónico, a	supersonique	supersonic	Überschall-	supersónico, a	supersonico, a
supersticioso, a	superstitieux, se	superstitious	abergläubisch	supersticioso, a	superstizioso, a
supervisar	superviser	supervise	überprüfen	supervisar	soprintendere
superviviente	survivant, e	survivor	Überlebende(f, m)	sobrevivente	superstite
superviviente	rescapé, e	survivor	Überlebende(f, m)	sobrevivente	scampato, a
suplementario, a	supplémentaire	additional, extra	zusätzlich	suplementar	supplementare
suplemento	supplément	supplement	Ergänzung(f); Zulage f	suplemento	supplemento
suplente, a	suppléant, e	substitute	Stellvertreter(in f)m	suplente	supplente

Spanish	French	English	German	Portuguese	Italian
suplicar	supplier	implore	an = flehen	suplicar	supplicare
suplicio	supplice	torture	Qual(f)	suplício	supplizio
suponer	supposer	suppose	an = nehmen	supor	supporre
supositorio	suppositoire	suppository	Zäpfchen(n)	supositório	supposta
supremacía	suprématie	supremacy	Obergewalt(f)	supremacia	supremazia
supremo, a	suprême	supreme	oberst-, höchst-	supremo, a	supremo, a
suprimir	supprimer	delete	beseitigen	suprimir	sopprimere
suprimir	supprimer	suppress	ab = schaffen	suprimir	sopprimere
Sur	Sud	South	Süden(m)	Sul	Sud
surco	sillon	furrow	Furche(f)	rego	solco
surtido	assortiment	assortment, set	Sortiment(n)	sortimento	assortimento
surtidor, chorro	jet	spray, jet	Strahl(m)	jacto, repuxo	getto, zampillo
sus	ses	his; her; its	seine; ihre	seus, suas	suoi(i); sue(le)
suscripción	souscription	subscription	Subskription(f)	subscrição	sottoscrizione
suscriptor, a	abonné, e	subscriber	Abonnent(m)	assinante	abbonato, a
suspender	suspendre	suspend, defer	verschieben	suspender	sospendere
suspender	échouer(examen)	fail	durch = fallen	ficar mal(exame)	bocciare
suspense	suspense	suspense	Spannung(f)	suspense	suspense
suspensión	suspension	suspension	Federung(f)	suspensão	sospensione
suspirar	soupirer	sigh	seufzen	suspirar	sospirare
sustancia	substance	substance	Substanz(f)	substância	sostanza
sustantivo	substantif	substantive, noun	Hauptwort(n)	substantivo	sostantivo
sustituir	substituer	substitute	vertauschen	substituir	sostituire
sustituir	remplacer	replace	ersetzen	substituir	sostituire
sustituto, a	remplacant, e	substitute	Stellvertreter(in f)m	substituto, a	sostituto, a
sustraer, restar	soustraire	subtract	ab = ziehen	subtrair, deduzir	sottrarre
susurrar	chuchoter	whisper	flüstern	sussurrar	bisbigliare
sutil	subtil, e	subtle	scharfsinnig, listig	subtil	sottile
suyo, suya	sien, ne	his; hers; its	seine, ihre	seu, sua	suo, sua(il, la)
suyo, a(el, la)	leur(le, la)	theirs	ihrige(der, die, das)	seu(o), a sua; dele, a	loro(il, la)

T

Spanish	French	English	German	Portuguese	Italian
tabaco	tabac	tobacco	Tabak(m)	tabaco	tabacco
tabique	cloison	partition	Trennwand(f)	tabique	tramezzo
tabla	planche	board	Brett(n)	tábua	tavola, asse
tabla a vela, surf	planche à voile	windsurf(ing)	Windsurfen(n)	wind-surf	windsurf
tablero	panneau	panel	Brett(n)	painel	cartello
tablero, tablón	tableau	board, panel	Tafel(f)	painel, quadro	pannello, quadro
taburete	tabouret	stool	Hocker(m)	escabelo, banco	sgabello
táctica	tactique	tactic	Taktik(f)	táctica	tattica
táctico, a	tactique	tactical	taktisch	táctico, a	tattico, a
tacto	tact	tact	Takt(m)	tacto	tatto
tacto, maña	savoir-faire	know-how	Geschick(n)	habilidade	savoir-faire
tachadura	rature	deletion	Streichung(f)	rasura	cancellatura
tal	tel, le	such a, such(pl.)	solche(r, s); so ein	tal	tale
talento	talent	talent	Talent(n)	talento	talento
talón	talon	heel	Ferse(f); Absatz(m)	calcanhar	tallone
talonario(cheques)	chéquier	cheque book	Scheckheft(n)	livro de cheques	libretto di assegni
talla, estatura	taille, grandeur	height, size	Größe(f)	estatura	statura
talla, número	taille	size	Größe(f)	tamanho	taglia, misura
taller	atelier	workshop	Werkstatt(f)	oficina	officina
tallo	tige	stem	Stiel(m)	caule	stelo
tallo, vástago	tige	rod	Stange(f)	haste	asta, barra
tamaño	taille	size	Größe(f)	tamanho	misura
tambalearse	chanceler	stagger	taumeln	vacilar	barcollare
también	aussi	also, too; as	auch	também	anche, pure
tan	si	so	so	tão	così

Spanish	French	English	German	Portuguese	Italian
tangente	tangent, e	tangent	berührend	tangente	tangente
tantear	tâter	feel, touch	berühren	tatear, apalpar	tastare
tanto, tan	tant	so much, so many	so viel, e	tanto	tanto
tanto, a; tan	tellement	so(-much, -many)	so(sehr), derartig	tanto, a	talmente
tañido	tintement	ringing, jingle	Klimpern, Klingeln(n)	tilintar	tintinnio
tapa, tapadera	couvercle	lid, cover	Deckel(m)	tampa	coperchio
tapiz; tapicería	tapisserie	tapestry	Wandteppich; Gobelin m	tapeçaria	arazzo; tappezzeria
tapón	bouchon	cap, plug	Pfropfen(m), Stöpsel	rolha; tampa	tappo
taquicardia	tachycardie	tachycardia	Herzjagen(n)	taquicardia	tachicardia
taquilla	guichet	booking office	Fahrkartenschalter(m)	bilheteira	biglietteria
tarde	après-midi	afternoon	Nachmittag(m)	tarde	pomeriggio
tarde, noche	soir	evening	Abend(m)	tarde, noite	sera
tarde	tard	late	spät	tarde	tardi
tarea	tâche	task	Aufgabe(f)	tarefa	compito
tarea, trabajo	ouvrage	work	Arbeit(f)	obra, trabalho	opera, lavoro
tarifa	tarif	tariff, price	Tarif(m)	tarifa	tariffa
tarifa	tarif	fare	Tarif(m)	tarifa	tariffa
tarjeta	carte	card, ticket	Karte(f)	bilhete	tessera
tarjeta de visita	carte de visite	visiting card	Visitenkarte(f)	cartão de visita	biglietto da visita
tarjeta postal	carte postale	post-card	Postkarte(f)	bilhete-postal	cartolina
tarro, bocal	bocal	jar	Glasgefäß(n)	boião	boccale, vaso
tarta	tarte	tart	Torte(f)	torta	torta, crostata
tartamudear	bégayer	stutter, stammer	stottern	gaguejar	balbettare
tasa, impuesto	taxe	tax; duty	Steuer(f)	taxa, imposto	tassa, imposta
tasa	taux	rate	Rate(f)	taxa	tasso
tasar, valorar	évaluer, estimer	assess	ein = schätzen	avaliar, fixar	valutare, stimare
tatuaje	tatouage	tattoo	Tätowierung(f)	tatuagem	tatuaggio
taxi	taxi	taxi, cab	Taxi(n)	táxi	taxi, tassì
taxista	chauffeur(taxi)	taxi-driver	Taxifahrer(in f)m	motorista	tassista
taza	tasse	cup	Tasse(f)	chávena	tazza
tazón	bol	bowl	Trinkschale(f)	tigela; malga	scodella
te	te, t'	you	dich; dir	te	ti, te
té	thé	tea	Tee(m)	chá	tè
teatro	théâtre	theatre	Theater(n)	teatro	teatro
tecla	touche	key	Taste(f)	tecla	tasto
teclado	clavier	keyboard	Tastatur(f)	teclado	tastiera
técnico, a	technique	technical	technisch	técnico, a	tecnico, a
técnico, a	technicien, ne	technician	Techniker(in f)m	técnico, a	tecnico, a
tecnócrata	technocrate	technocrat	Technokrat(m)	tecnocrata	tecnocrate
tecnología	technologie	technology	Technologie(f)	tecnologia	tecnologia
techo	plafond	ceiling	Decke(f)(Zimmer-)	tecto	soffitto
teja	tuile	tile	Ziegel(m)	telha	tegola
tejado	toit	roof	Dach(n)	telhado	tetto
tejer	tisser	weave	weben	tecer	tessere
tejido, tela	étoffe	material	Stoff(m)	tecido, estofo	stoffa
tela	tissu	material, fabric	Stoff(m)	tecido	tessuto
tela, lienzo	toile	canvas, material	Tuch(n)	tela	tela
telediario	actualités(T.V)	news	Nachrichten(pl.)	telejornal	telegiornale
teleférico	téléphérique	cable-car	Seilbahn(f)	teleférico	teleferica
telefonear	téléphoner	phone, ring, call	telefonieren	telefonar	telefonare
teléfono	téléphone	telephone, phone	Telefon(n)	telefone	telefono
teléfono público	taxi-/publiphone	public call-box	Telefonzelle(f)	telefone público	telefono pubblico
telegrama	télégramme	telegram, cable	Telegramm(n)	telegrama	telegramma
telemando	télécommande	remote control	Fernsteuerung(f)	telecomando	telecomando
telepatía	télépathie	telepathy	Telepathie(f)	telepatia	telepatia
telescopio	télescope	telescope	Teleskop(n)	telescópio	telescopio
telespectador, a	télespectateur	viewer	Fernsehzuschauer/in	telespectador, a	telespettatore, trice
televisar	téléviser	televise	übertragen	televisionar	teletrasmettere
televisión	télévision	television	Fernsehen(n)	televisão; TV	televisione
televisor	téléviseur	television set	Fernseher(m)	televisor	televisore
telex	télex	telex	Telex(n)	telex	telex
tema	thème	theme	Thema(n)	tema	tema
tema	sujet, thème	subject, theme	Thema(n)	assunto, tema	tema
temblar	trembler	tremble	zittern	tremer	tremare
temer, tener miedo	craindre	fear, be afraid of	befürchten, fürchten	temer	temere
temerario, a	téméraire	rash, reckless	waghalsig	temerário, a	temerario, a
temible	redoutable	formidable	furchtbar	temível	temibile
temor, miedo	crainte	fear	Furcht(f)	temor, receio	timore

| --- | --- | --- | --- | --- | --- |
temperamento	tempérament	temperament	Temperament(n)	temperamento	temperamento
temperatura	température	temperature	Temperatur(f)	temperatura	temperatura
tempestad	tempête	storm	Unwetter(n)	tempestade	tempesta
templado, a	tempéré, e	temperate	gemäßigt	temperado, a	temperato, a
templado, a	doux, ce	mild	mild	ameno, a	mite
templo	temple	temple	Tempel(m)	templo	tempio
temporario, a	temporaire	temporary	vorübergehend	temporário, a	temporaneo, a
temporero, a	saisonnier, ière	seasonal	saisonbedingt	sazonal	stagionale
temprano	tôt	early	früh	cedo	presto
tenacidad	ténacité	tenacity	Hartnäckigkeit(f)	tenacidade	tenacità; tenacia
tendencia	tendance	tendency; trend	Tendenz(f), Neigung(f)	tendência	tendenza
tender	tendre	tighten; stretch	spannen	estender, esticar	tendere
tendero, a	commerçant, e	shop-keeper	Kaufmann m, Kauffrau f	comerciante	negoziante
tendero, a	épicier, ière	grocer	Lebensmittelhändler m	merceeiro, a	droghiere, a
tenedor	fourchette	fork	Gabel(f)	garfo	forchetta
tener	avoir	have	haben	ter, possuir	avere
tener	tenir	hold	halten	ter, segurar	tenere
teniente	lieutenant	lieutenant	Leutnant(m)	tenente	tenente
tenis	tennis	tennis	Tennis(n)	ténis	tennis
tenor	ténor	tenor	Tenor(m)	tenor	tenore
tensión	tension	tension	Spannung(f)	tensão	tensione
tenso, a	tendu, e	tight	gespannt	esticado, a	teso, a
tentación	tentation	temptation	Versuchung(f)	tentação	tentazione
tentáculo	tentacule	tentacle	Fangarm(m)	tentáculo	tentacolo
tentativa	tentative	attempt	Versuch(m)	tentativa	tentativo
teñir	teindre, colorer	dye	färben	tingir	tingere
teología	théologie	theology	Theologie(f)	teologia	teologia
teorema	théorème	theorem	Lehrsatz(m)	teorema	teorema
teoría	théorie	theory	Theorie(f)	teoria	teoria
teórico, a	théorique	theoretical	theoretisch	teórico, a	teorico, a
terapia	thérapie	therapy	Therapie(f)	terapia	terapia
tercer mundo	tiers-monde	third world	dritte Welt(f)	terceiro mundo	terzo mondo
tercero, a	troisième	third	dritte	terceiro, a	terzo, a
tercio, a; tercero	tiers	third	Drittel(n)	terço, a; terceiro	terzo, a
terciopelo	velours	velvet	Samt(m)	veludo	velluto
termal	thermal, e	thermal	Thermal-	termal	termale
térmico, a	thermique	thermic, thermal	thermisch	térmico, a	termico, a
terminal	terminal, e	terminal, final	letzte(r, s); End-	terminal	terminale
terminar	terminer	end, finish	beenden	terminar	terminare
término	terme	term	Ausdruck(m)	termo	parola
término	terme	end	Ende(n), Ziel(n)	termo	termine
termómetro	thermomètre	thermometer	Thermometer(n)	termómetro	termometro
ternura	tendresse	tenderness	Zärtlichkeit(f)	ternura	tenerezza
terremoto	séisme	earthquake	Erdbeben(n)	terremoto	terremoto
terreno	terrain	ground	Gelände(n)	terreno	terreno
terrestre	terrestre	terrestrial	irdisch	terrestre	terrestre
terrible	terrible	terrible	schrecklich	terrível	terribile
territorio	territoire	territory	Gebiet(n), Land(n)	território	territorio
terror	terreur	terror	Schrecken(m)	terror	terrore
terrorismo	terrorisme	terrorism	Terrorismus(m)	terrorismo	terrorismo
terrorista	terroriste	terrorist	Terrorist(in f)m	terrorista	terrorista
tesis	thèse	thesis(theses)	These(f)	tese	tesi
tesorero, a	trésorier, ière	treasurer	Schatzmeister(in f)m	tesoureiro, a	tesoriere, a
tesoro	trésor	treasure	Schatz(m)	tesouro	tesoro
testamento	testament	will, testament	Testament(n)	testamento	testamento
testículo	testicule	testicle	Hoden(m)	testículo	testicolo
testigo	témoin	witness	Zeuge(m), Zeugin(f)	testemunha	testimone
testimoniar	témoigner	testify	aus = sagen	testemunhar	testimoniare
testimonio	témoignage	testimony, evidence	Zeugenaussage(f)	testemunho	testimonianza
tetania	tétanie	tetany	Starrkrampf(m)	tetania	tetania
tétanos	tétanos	tetanus	Tetanus(m)	tétano	tetano
tetera	théière	teapot	Teekanne(f)	bule	teiera
textil	textile	textile	Textil-; Web-	textil	tessile
texto	texte	text	Text(m)	texto	testo
tez, color	teint	complexion, colour	Teint(m)	tez	carnagione
tía	tante	aunt	Tante(f)	tia	zia
tibia	tibia	tibia	Schienbein(n)	tíbia	tibia
tibio, a	tiède	lukewarm, tepid	lauwarm, lau	tépido, a; morno, a	tiepido, a

Spanish	French	English	German	Portuguese	Italian
tiburón	requin	shark	Hai(m)	tubarão	squalo
tic	tic	twitch(ing)	Tick(m)	tique	tic
ticket, billete	ticket	ticket	Karte(f); Fahrkarte(f)	bilhete	biglietto
tiempo	temps	time	Zeit(f)	tempo	tempo
tiempo	temps	weather	Wetter(n)	tempo	tempo
tiempo libre	loisir	leisure	Freizeit(f)	tempo livre	tempo libero, hobby
tienda	boutique	boutique, shop	Geschäft(n)	loja	negozio, boutique
tienda	magasin	shop	Geschäft(n), Laden(m)	loja	negozio; bottega
tienda, negocio	commerce	shop, business	Geschäft(n)	loja	negozio
tienda	tente	tent	Zelt(n)	tenda	tenda
tierno, a	tendre	tender	zärtlich	terno, a	tenero, a
tierra	terre	earth	Erde(f)	Terra	terra
tierra	terre	land	Land(n)	terra	terra
tierra	terre	soil	Erde(f)	terra	terra
tieso, a; rígido, a	raide	stiff	starr, steif	teso, a; hirto, a	rigido, a
tifoidea	typhoïde	typhoid	Typhus(m)	tifóide	tifoide
tifón	typhon	typhoon	Taifun(m)	tufão	tifone
tigre	tigre	tiger	Tiger(m)	tigre	tigre
tijeras	ciseaux	scissors	Schere(f)	tesoura	forbici
timbre	sonnette	bell	Klingel(f)	campainha	campanello
timidez	timidité	shyness, timidity	Schüchternheit(f)	timidez	timidezza
tímido, a	timide	shy, timid	schüchtern	tímido, a	timido, a
timón	gouvernail	rudder	Ruder(n), Steur(n)	leme	timone
tímpano	tympan	eardrum	Trommelfell(n)	tímpano	timpano
tinieblas	ténèbres	darkness	Finsternis(f)	trevas	tenebre
tinta	encre	ink	Tinte(f)	tinta	inchiostro
tinte, color	teinte	tint, colour	Färbung(f), Farbe(f)	tinta	tinta
tío	oncle	uncle	Onkel(m)	tio	zio
tiovivo, noria	manège	roundabout	Karussell(n)	carrossel	giostra
típico, a	typique	typical	typisch	típico, a	tipico, a
tipo	type	type	Typ(m)	tipo	tipo
tirano, a	tyran	tyrant	Tyrann(m)	tirano, a	tiranno, a
tirantes	bretelle(s)	braces	Hosenträger(m)	suspensórios	bretella
tirar	tirer	pull, draw	ziehen	puxar	tirare
tirar	tracter	tug, tow	ab = schleppen	puxar	trainare, tirare
tirar	tirer	fire, shoot	feuern, schießen	disparar, atirar	sparare, tirare
tiritar	grelotter	shiver	zittern	tiritar	tremare(di freddo)
tiro	tir	shooting, firing	Schießen(n)	tiro	tiro
tiroides	thyroïde	thyroid(gland)	Schilddrüse(f)	tiróide	tiroide
tisana	tisane	herb tea	Kräutertee(m)	tisana	tisana
títere	pantin	puppet	Hampelmann(m)	fantoche	burattino
titubear	tituber	stagger	wanken	titubear	barcollare
titulado, a	diplômé, e	graduate	Diplom-	diplomado, a	diplomato, a
titular	titulaire	holder	Inhaber(in f)m	titular	titolare
título	titre	title	Titel(m)	título	titolo
toalla	serviette	towel	Handtuch(n)	toalha	asciugamano
tobillo	cheville	ankle	Knöchel(m)	tornozelo	caviglia
tobogán	toboggan	slide, chute	Rutschbahn(f)	escorrega	scivolo
tocadiscos	tourne-disque	record-player	Plattenspieler(m)	gira-discos	giradischi
tocar	toucher	touch	an = fassen, berühren	tocar	toccare
tocar	jouer	play	spielen	tocar	suonare
toda	toute	whole(the)	ganz	toda	tutta
todavía, aún	encore	still	noch, wieder	ainda	ancora
todavía	toujours	still	immer noch	ainda	sempre
todavía no	encore(pas)	yet(not)	noch(nicht)	ainda não	ancora(non)
todo, a	tout, e	all(the)	alles	todo, a	tutto, a
todos	tous	all(the)	alle	todos	tutti
toldo, lona	bâche	cover	Plane(f)	toldo	telone
toldo; persiana	store	blind; shade	Vorhang m; Jalousie f	estore	tapparella
tolerancia	tolérance	tolerance	Toleranz(f)	tolerância	tolleranza
tolerar	tolérer	tolerate	dulden, ertragen	tolerar	tollerare
tomar, coger	prendre	take	nehmen	tomar	prendere
tomate	tomate	tomato(-es)	Tomate(f)	tomate	pomodoro
tonalidad	tonalité	tonality, tone	Tonart(f), Klangfarbe	tonalidade	tonalità
tonel; barril	tonneau	barrel	Faß(n)	tonel; barril	botte, barile
tonelada	tonne	ton	Tonne(f)	tonelada	tonnellata
tono, sonido	ton, son, timbre	tone	Ton(m), Klang(m)	tom, som, timbre	tono
tontería	sottise	silliness	Dummheit(f)	estupidez	sciocchezza

Spanish	French	English	German	Portuguese	Italian
tonto, a	bête; sot, te	silly, foolish	dumm	tolo, a; burro, a	sciocco, a
topacio	topaze	topaz	Topas(m)	topázio	topazio
tórax	thorax	thorax	Brustkasten(m)	tórax	torace
torbellino	tourbillon	whirlwind, swirl	Wirbel(wind)(m)	turbilhão	vortice
torcer	tordre	twist	verbiegen, verdrehen	torcer	torcere, piegare
torero	toréador	bull-fighter	Stierkämpfer(m)	toureiro	torero
tormenta	orage	storm, thunderstorm	Gewitter(n)	tempestade	temporale
tornado	tornade	tornado(-es)	Wirbelsturm(m)	tornado	tornado
torneo	tournoi	tournament	Turnier(n)	torneio	torneo
tornillo	vis	screw	Schraube(f)	parafuso	vite
toro	taureau	bull	Stier(m)	touro; toiro	toro
torpe	maladroit, e	clumsy, awkward	ungeschickt	desajeitado, a	maldestro, a
torpedo	torpille	torpedo(-es)	Torpedo(m)	torpedo	torpedine
torpor	torpeur	torpor	Erstarrungszustand(m)	torpor	torpore
torre	tour	tower	Turm(m)	torre	torre
torrente	torrent	torrent	Wildbach(m)	torrente	torrente
torsión	torsion	twist(ing)	Drehung(f), Torsion(f)	torção	torsione
tortuga	tortue	tortoise; turtle	Schildkröte(f)	tartaruga	tartaruga
tortura	torture	torture	Folter(f)	tortura	tortura
tos	toux	cough	Husten(m)	tosse	tosse
toser	tousser	cough	husten	tossir	tossire
tostadas	pain grillé	toast	Toast(m)	pão torrado	pane tostato
tostar	griller	toast	toasten	torrar	abbrustolire
total	total, e	total	ganz; Gesamt-	total	totale
total	total, e	overall	Gesamt-	total	complessivo, a
total	total	total	Summe(f), Ganze(s)(n)	total	totale
totalmente	tout à fait	quite	ganz	totalmente	affatto
tóxico, a	toxique	toxic	giftig	tóxico, a	tossico, a
toxicología	toxicologie	toxicology	Toxikologie(f)	toxicologia	tossicologia
tozudo, a	têtu, e	stubborn	dickköpfig	cabeçudo, a	testardo, a
trabajador, a	travailleur, se	worker	Arbeiter(in)m	trabalhador, a	lavoratore, trice
trabajar	travailler	work	arbeiten	trabalhar	lavorare
trabajo	travail	work	Arbeit(f)	trabalho	lavoro
trabajo	travail	labour	Arbeit(f)	trabalho	lavoro
tractor	tracteur	tractor	Traktor(m)	tractor	trattore
tradición	tradition	tradition	Tradition(f)	tradição	tradizione
traducción	traduction	translation	Übersetzung(f)	tradução	traduzione
traductor, a	traducteur, trice	translator	Übersetzer(in f)m	tradutor, a	traduttore, trice
traer	apporter	bring	bringen	trazer	apportare, portare
traer	amener	bring	mit = bringen	trazer	portare
traer	rapporter	bring back	zurück = bringen	trazer	riportare
traficante	trafiquant, e	trafficker; pedlar	Schwarzhändler(in f)m	traficante	trafficante
tráfico	trafic	traffic	Verkehr(m)	tráfego, tráfico	traffico
tráfico	circulation	traffic	Verkehr(m)	trânsito	traffico
tragar	avaler	swallow	schlucken	engolir	inghiottire, ingoiare
tragedia	tragédie	tragedy	Tragödie(f)	tragédia	tragedia
trágico, a	tragique	tragic	tragisch	trágico, a	tragico, a
traición	trahison	betrayal; treason	Verrat(m)	traição	tradimento
traicionar	trahir	betray	verraten	trair	tradire
traidor, a	traître, esse	traitor, -tress	Verräter(in f)m	traidor, a	traditore, trice
traje, ropa	vêtement	garment	Kleidungsstück(n)	peça de roupa	vestito
traje	costume	suit	Anzug(m)	fato, traje	abito, vestito
traje	tailleur	suit	Kostüm(n)	saia-casaco	tailleur
traje	combinaison	suit(ski-)	Anzug(m)(Ski-)	fato	tuta, completo
traje(espacial)	combinaison	suit(space-)	Anzug(Raum-)(m)	fato(espacial)	tuta(spaziale)
traje de baño	maillot de bain	swimsuit; trunks	Badeanzug(m)	fato de banho	costume da bagno
traje de noche	robe de soirée	evening dress	Abendkleid(n)	vestido de noite	abito da sera
trampa	piège	trap, snare	Falle(f)	armadilha	trappola
trampas(hacer)	tricher	cheat	fuschen, mogeln	batota(fazer)	barare
tranquilizante	tranquillisant	tranquillizer	Beruhigungsmittel(n)	tranquilizante	tranquillante
tranquilizar	rassurer	reassure	beruhigen	tranquilizar	rassicurare
tranquilo, a	tranquille	quiet, still, calm	ruhig	tranquilo, a	tranquillo, a
tranquilo, a	calme	calm, quiet, still	ruhig, still	calmo, a	calmo, a
transacción	transaction	transaction	Transaktion(f)	transacção	transazione
transbordador	bac	ferry	Fähre(f)	barco	traghetto, ferry
transcurrir	écouler(s')	elapse	vergehen, verfließen	decorrer	trascorrere
transferencia	transfert	transfer	Verlegung(f)	transferência	trasferimento
transferir	transférer	transfer	überführen	transferir	trasferire

Spanish	French	English	German	Portuguese	Italian
transformación	transformation	transformation	Veränderung(f)	transformação	trasformazione
transformar	transformer	transform, change	verändern	transformar	trasformare
transfuga	transfuge	defector	Überläufer(in f)m	trânsfuga	transfuga
transfusión	transfusion	transfusion	Transfusion(f)	transfusão	trasfusione
transmisión	transmission	transmission	Übertragung(f)	transmissão	trasmissione
transmitir	transmettre	transmit	übertragen	transmitir	trasmettere
transparente	transparent, e	transparent	durchsichtig	transparente	trasparente
transpiración	transpiration	perspiration	Schweiß(m)	transpiração	traspirazione
transpirar	transpirer	perspire, sweat	schwitzen	transpirar	traspirare
transportar	transporter	transport, carry	transportieren	transportar	trasportare
transporte	transport	transport	Transport(m)	transporte	trasporto
transversal	transversal, e	transversal	Quer-; schräg	transversal	trasversale
tranvía	tramway	tram-car	Straßenbahn(f)	carro eléctrico	tram
trapecio	trapèze	trapezium; trapeze	Trapez(n)	trapézio	trapezio
trapo	chiffon	rag	Lappen(m)	trapo	straccio
traquearteria	trachée-artère	trachea	Luftröhre(f)	traqueia	trachea
trasero, a; de atrás	derrière, arrière	rear	Rück-; Hinter-	traseiro, a	dietro, indietro
trasero, a	derrière	back, rear	Hinter-, Rückseite(f)	trazeiro	retro
trasladar	déplacer	shift, move	versetzen, -schieben	deslocar	spostare
traslado	mutation	transfer	Versetzung(f)	transferência	trasferimento
trasplante	greffe	transplant, graft	Verpflanzung(f)	enxerto	trapianto
traspuntín	strapontin	folding seat	Klappstuhl(m)	banco dobrável	strapuntino
tratado	traité	treaty	Vertrag(m)	tratado	trattato
tratamiento	traitement	treatment	Behandlung(f)	tratamento	trattamento
tratar	traiter	treat; deal with	behandeln	tratar	trattare
tratar, curar	soigner	treat	behandeln	tratar, cuidar	curare
traumatismo	traumatisme	traumatism	Trauma(n)	traumatismo	trauma
través(de)	travers(de)	askew	schief	través(de)	traverso(di)
través de(a)	travers(à)	across; through	durch	através de	attraverso
travesti	travesti	transvestite	Transvestit(m)	travesti	travestito
travieso, a	coquin, e	mischievous	schelmisch	travesso, a; maroto, a	birbante, birichino, a
trayecto	trajet	journey, trip	Strecke(f)	trajecto	tragitto
trayectoria	trajectoire	trajectory	Bahn(f), Kurs(m)	trajectória	traiettoria
trazar	tracer	draw	entwerfen	traçar	tracciare
trece	treize	thirteen	dreizehn	treze	tredici
tregua	trêve	truce	Waffenstillstand(m)	trégua	tregua
tregua, respiro	répit	respite	Atempause(f)	trégua, espera	tregua, riposo
treinta	trente	thirty	dreißig	trinta	trenta
tren	train	train	Zug(m), Eisenbahn(f)	comboio	treno
trenza	natte	plait	Zopf(m)	trança	treccia
trenza	tresse	plait, braid	Zopf(m)	trança	treccia
tres	trois	three	drei	três	tre
triángulo	triangle	triangle	Dreieck(n)	triângulo	triangolo
tribu	tribu	tribe	Stamm(m)	tribo	tribù
tribunal	tribunal	court, tribunal	Gericht(n)	tribunal	tribunale
trigo	blé	corn	Weizen(m)	trigo	grano
trimestral	trimestriel, le	quarterly	vierteljährlich	trimestral	trimestrale
trimestre	trimestre	term; quarter	Vierteljahr(n)	trimestre	trimestre
trinchera, zanja	tranchée	trench	Graben(m)	trincheira	trincea
trineo	traîneau	sleigh, sledge	Schlitten(m)	trenó	slitta
tripulación	équipage	crew	Besatzung(f)	equipagem	equipaggio
triste	triste	sad, unhappy	traurig	triste	triste
tristeza	tristesse	sadness	Traurigkeit(f)	tristeza	tristezza
triturar	broyer	crush, grind	mahlen	triturar; moer	stritolare, macinare
triunfo	triomphe	triumph	Triumph(m)	triunfo	trionfo
trofeo	trophée	trophy	Trophäe(f)	troféu	trofeo
trofeo, challenge	challenge	challenge, contest	Wettkampf(m)	desafio, torneio	gara, sfida
trompeta	trompette	trumpet	Trompete(f)	trombeta	trombetta
tronco	tronc	trunk	Stamm(m)	tronco	tronco
trono	trône	throne	Thron(m)	trono	trono
tropa	troupe	troop	Truppe(f)	tropa	truppa
tropezar	trébucher	stumble, trip	stolpern	tropeçar	inciampare
tropezar con	heurter	knock(against)	stoßen	chocar, bater	urtare
tropical	tropical, e	tropical	tropisch	tropical	tropicale
trotar	trotter	trot	traben	trotar	trottare
trucha	truite	trout	Forelle(f)	truta	trota
trueno	tonnerre	thunder	Donner(m)	trovão	tuono
tu	ton	your	dein(e)	teu	tuo(il)

Spanish	French	English	German	Portuguese	Italian
tu	ta	your	dein(e)	tua, teu	tua(la)
tú	tu	you	du	tu	tu
tú; te	toi	you	du; dich	tu; ti	tu; te
tuberculosis	tuberculose	tuberculosis, T.B.	Tuberkulose(f)	tuberculose	tubercolosi
tubo	tube	tube	Tube(f)	tubo	tubo
tubo, caño	tuyau(terie)	pipe	Röhre(f), Schlauch(m)	tubo, cano	tubo, tubazione
tuerca	écrou	nut	Mutter(f)(Schrauben-)	porca	dado
tuerto, a	borgne	one-eyed	einäugig	zarolho, a	guercio, a
tugurio	taudis	slum	Bruchbude(f)	antro, tugúrio	topaia
tulipán	tulipe	tulip	Tulpe(f)	tulipa	tulipano
tumba	tombe	grave	Grab(n)	túmulo, sepultura	tomba
tumba	tombeau	tomb	Grabmal(n)	túmulo	tomba
tumor	tumeur	tumour	Tumor(m)	tumor	tumore
tumulto	tumulte	tumult, uproar	Tumult(m)	tumulto	tumulto
túnel	tunnel	tunnel	Tunnel(m)	túnel	tunnel
túnica	tunique	tunic	Tunika(f)	túnica	tunica
turbina	turbine	turbine	Turbine(f)	turbina	turbina
turbio, a	trouble	cloudy; muddy	trüb	turvo, a	torbido, a
turbulencia	turbulence	turbulence	Turbulenz(f)	turbulência	turbolenza
turismo	tourisme	tourism	Tourismus(m)	turismo	turismo
turista	touriste	tourist	Tourist(m)	turista	turista
turno	tour	turn	Reihe(f)	vez	turno
tus	tes	your	deine	teus, tuas	tuoi, tue(i, le)
tutela	tutelle	trusteeship	Treuhandschaft(f)	tutela	tutela
tutor, a	tuteur, tutrice	guardian	Vormund(m)	tutor, a	tutore, trice
tuyo, a	toi(à)	yours	dir	teu, tua	tuo, a; tuoi, tue
tuyo, a	tien, ne	yours	deine(r, s), deine	teu, tua	tuo, a

U

Spanish	French	English	German	Portuguese	Italian
úlcera	ulcère	ulcer	Geschwür(n)	úlcera	ulcera
ulterior	ultérieur, e	later	später	ulterior	ulteriore
último, a	dernier, ière	last	letzter, letzte	último, a	ultimo, a
último, a	ultime	ultimate, final	allerletzte(r, s)	último, a	ultimo, a
último, a	dernier	last	Letzte(f, m)	último, a	ultimo, a
ultramar	outre-mer	overseas	überseeisch	ultramar	oltremare
ultramarinos	épicerie	grocer's(shop)	Lebensmittelladen(m)	mercearia	drogheria
un, uno	un	one	eins	um	un, uno
unánime	unanime	unanimous	einstimmig	unânime	unanime
únicamente	uniquement	only	ausschließlich	somente	unicamente
único, a	unique	unique, exceptional	einmalig	único, a	unico, a
único, a	unique	unique; only	einzig, einzeln	único, a	unico, a
unidad	unité	unity	Einigkeit(f)	unidade	unità
unidad	unité	unit	Einheit(f)	unidade	unità
unificado, a	unifié, e	unified, united	vereinigt	unificado, a	unificato, a
uniforme	uniforme	uniform	gleichförmig	uniforme	uniforme
uniforme	uniforme	uniform	Uniform(f)	uniforme	uniforme; divisa
unión	union	union	Bund(m), Vereinigung f	união	unione
unir	unir	unite	vereinen	unir, juntar	unire
unitario, a	unitaire	unitary, per unit	unitarisch	unitário, a	unitario, a
universal	universel, le	universal	universell	universal	universale
universidad	université	university	Universität(f)	universidade	università
universitario, a	universitaire	academic	Universität-	universitário, a	universitario, a
universo	univers	universe	Universum(n)	universo	universo
uno, una	un, e	a, an	ein, e	um, uma	uno, una
uno u otro, cada	un(l')ou l'autre	either	eine(der) der andere	um ou outro, cada	uno(l') o l'altro
untuoso, a	onctueux, se	unctuous	cremig, sahnig	untuoso, a	untuoso, a

Spanish	French	English	German	Portuguese	Italian
uña	ongle	nail	Fingernagel(m)	unha	unghia
uranio	uranium	uranium	Uran(n)	urânio	uranio
urbanismo	urbanisme	town-planning	Städtebau(m)	urbanismo	urbanistica
urbano, a	urbain, e	urban	städtisch, Stadt-	urbano, a	urbano, a
urea	urée	urea	Harnstoff(m)	ureia	urea
urgencia	urgence	emergency, urgency	Notfall(m)	urgência	urgenza
urgencia	urgence	urgency	Dringlichkeit(f)	urgência	urgenza
urgente	urgent, e	urgent	dringend	urgente	urgente
usado, a	usé, e	worn, worn out	verbraucht	usado, a	logoro, a
usar, emplear	employer	use	benützen	usar	usare, adoperare
uso, empleo	usage	usage, use	Gebrauch(m)	uso	uso
uso, empleo	emploi	use	Gebrauch(m)	uso	uso
usted(es)	vous	you	Sie	você	lei, loro(pl.)
usual	usuel, le	usual	gebräuchlich	usual	usuale
usuario, a	usager, ère	user	Benutzer(in f)m	utente	utente
utensilios	ustensile	utensil	Gerät(n)	utensílio	utensile
útero	utérus	uterus, womb	Gebärmutter(f)	útero	utero
útil	utile	useful	nützlich	útil	utile
utilización	utilisation	utilization, use	Benutzung(f)	utilização	utilizzazione
utilizador, a	utilisateur	user	Benutzer(in f)m	utilizador, a	utilizzatore, trice
utilizar	utiliser	use	benutzen	utilizar	utilizzare
utópico, a	utopique	Utopian	utopisch	utópico, a	utopico, a
uva(s)	raisin	grape	Traube(f)(Wein-)	uva	uva

V

Spanish	French	English	German	Portuguese	Italian
vaca	vache	cow	Kuh(f)	vaca	vacca, mucca
vacaciones	vacances	holidays	Ferien(pl.)	férias	vacanze
vacaciones	vacances	vacation	Ferien(pl.)	férias	vacanze
vacaciones	congé	holiday, vacation	Urlaub(m)	férias	ferie(le)
vaciar	vider	empty	leeren	esvaziar	vuotare
vacilación	hésitation	hesitation	Zögern(n)	hesitação	esitazione
vacilar	vaciller	sway, wobble	taumeln	vacilar	vacillare
vacío, a	vide	empty	leer	vazio, a	vuoto, a
vacío	vide	vacuum; void	Vakuum(n), Leere(f)	vazio, vácuo	vuoto
vacuna	vaccin	vaccine	Impfstoff(m)	vacina	vaccino
vacunación	vaccination	vaccination	Impfung(f)	vacinação	vaccinazione
vagabundo, a	vagabond, e	vagabond; tramp	Landstreicher(in f)m	vagabundo, a	vagabondo, a
vagabundo, a	rôdeur, se	prowler	Herumstreicher(m)	vagabundo, a	vagabondo, a
vagabundo, a	clochard, e	tramp	Penner(m)	vagabundo, a	barbone, a; vagabondo
vagina	vagin	vagina	Scheide(f)(Anat.)	vagina	vagina
vagón	wagon	coach, carriage	Wagen(m)	vagão	vagone, carrozza
vagón	wagon	truck, wag(g)on	Waggon(m)(Güterwagen)	vagão	vagone
vainilla	vanille	vanilla	Vanille(f)	baunilha	vaniglia
vajilla	vaisselle	crockery, dishes	Geschirr(n)	loiça, louça	stoviglie, vasellame
vale, de acuerdo	accord(d')	all right, O.K	einverstanden, okay	acordo(de)	accordo(d')
vale la pena	vaut la peine	worthwhile	der Mühe wert	vale a pena	vale la pena
valentía	courage	courage	Mut(m)	coragem	coraggio
valer	valoir	worth(be)	wert sein	valer	valere
validez	validité	validity	Gültigkeit(f)	validade	validità
válido, a; valedero	valable	valid, good	gültig; annehmbar	válido, a	valido, a
valiente	vaillant, e	brave	tapfer	valente; bravo, a	valoroso, a
valiente, valeroso	courageux, brave	brave	mutig	corajoso, a	coraggioso, a
valor	valeur	value, worth	Wert(m)	valor	valore
valor, mérito	valeur, mérite	worth, merit	Wert(m)	valor, mérito	valore, merito
valoración	évaluation	assessment	Einschätzung(f)	avaliação	valutazione
valorar, estimar	estimer	estimate, value	schätzen	estimar	stimare, valutare

Spanish	French	English	German	Portuguese	Italian
vals	valse	waltz	Walzer(m)	valsa	valzer
válvula	clapet	valve	Klappenventil(n)	válvula	valvola
valla, cerca	clôture	fence, railings	Zaun(m)	cerca, vedação	recinzione, muro
valle	vallée	valley	Tal(n)	vale	valle
vanidad	vanité	vanity	Eitelkeit(f)	vaidade	vanità
vapor	vapeur	steam	Dampf(m)	vapor	vapore
vapor	vapeur	vapour, fumes	Dunst(m)	vapor	vapore
vaporizar	vaporiser	spray	sprühen	vaporizar	vaporizzare
variable	variable	variable	veränderlich	variável	variabile
variación	variation	variation	Abwandlung(f)	variação	variazione
variado, a	varié, e	varied, various	vielfältig	variado, a	vario, a
varicela	varicelle	chicken-pox	Windpocken(f, pl)	varicela	varicella
variedad	variété	variety	Vielfalt(f)	variedade	varietà
varilla	baguette	stick	Stöckchen(n)	vara	bacchetta
vario, a	divers, e	various, varied	mannigfach	variado, a	vario, a
varios, as	plusieurs	several	mehrere	vários, as	parecchi
vascular	vasculaire	vascular	Gefäß-	vascular	vascolare
vaselina	vaseline	vaseline	Vaseline(f)	vaselina	vasellina
vaso	verre	glass(-es)	Glas(n)	copo	bicchiere
vaso(sanguíneo)	vaisseau	vessel(blood)	Gefäß(Blut-)(n)	vaso(sanguíneo)	vaso(sanguigno)
vasto, a	vaste	vast	weit	vasto, a	vasto, a
veces(a)	parfois	sometimes	manchmal	às vezes	talvolta
veces(a)	quelquefois	sometimes	manchmal	às vezes	qualche volta
vecindario	voisinage	neighbourhood	Nachbarschaft(f)	vizinhança	vicinanza
vecino, a	voisin, e	neighbour	Nachbar(in f)m	vizinho, a	vicino, a
vegetación	végétation	vegetation	Pflanzenwuchs(m)	vegetação	vegetazione
vegetal	végétal	vegetable, plant	Pflanze(f)	vegetal	vegetale
vehículo	véhicule	vehicle	Fahrzeug(n)	veículo	veicolo
veinte	vingt	twenty	zwanzig	vinte	venti
veintiún(o)	vingt-et-un	twenty one	einundzwanzig	vinte e um	ventuno
vejación	vexation	vexation	Ärger(m)	vexame	vessazione
vejiga	vessie	bladder	Harnblase(f)	bexiga	vescica
vela	bougie	candle	Kerze(f)	vela	candela
vela	voile	sailing	Segeln(n)	vela	vela
vela	voile	sail	Segel(n)	vela	vela
velero	voilier	yacht, sailing boat	Segelboot(n)	veleiro	veliero
velo	voile	veil	Schleier(m)	véu	velo
velocidad	vitesse	speed	Geschwindigkeit(f)	velocidade	velocità
velocidad	vélocité, vitesse	velocity	Schnelligkeit(f)	velocidade	velocità
velomotor	mobylette	moped	Mofa(n)	motorizada	motorino, scooter
vena	veine	vein	Vene(f)	veia	vena
vencedor, a	vainqueur	winner; victor	Sieger(in f)m	vencedor, a	vincitore, trice
vencer	vaincre	defeat	besiegen	vencer	vincere
vencimiento	échéance	expiration	Fälligkeitstermin(m)	vencimento	scadenza
vendaje, venda	bandage	bandage	Bandage(f), Verband(m)	ligadura	fasciatura
vendedor, a	vendeur, se	salesman(-men)	Verkäufer(in f)m	vendedor, a	venditore, trice
vendedor, a	vendeur, se	sales assistant	Verkäufer(in f)m	vendedor, a	commesso, a
vendedor, a	marchand, e	shop-keeper	Kaufmann m, Kauffrau f	comerciante	negoziante
vendedor, a	marchand, e	tradesman, dealer	Händler(in f)m	negociante	mercante
vender	vendre	sell	verkaufen	vender	vendere
veneno	poison	poison	Gift(n)	veneno	veleno
veneno	venin	venom, poison	Gift(n)	veneno	veleno
venenoso, a	vénéneux, se	poisonous	giftig	venenoso, a	velenoso, a
venéreo, a	vénérien, ne	venereal	Geschlechts-	venéreo, a	venereo, a
venga(!)	venez!	come(on)!	kommen Sie!	venha!	venga!, venite!
venga aquí(!)	venez ici!	come here!	kommen Sie her!	venha cá!	venga qui!, venite!
venganza	vengeance	revenge	Rache(f)	vingança	vendetta
vengar	venger	avenge	rächen	vingar	vendicare
venir	venir	come	kommen	vir	venire
venta	vente	sale	Verkauf(m)	venda	vendita
ventaja	avantage	advantage	Vorteil(m)	vantagem	vantaggio
ventaja	atout, avantage	asset	Trumpf(m), Vorteil(m)	vantagem	vantaggio
ventana	fenêtre	window	Fenster(n)	janela	finestra
ventanilla	hublot	window	Bullauge(n), Luke(f)	vigia	oblò
ventanilla	guichet	counter, position	Schalter(m)	guichê, postigo	sportello
ventilación	ventilation	ventilation	Belüftung(f)	ventilação	ventilazione
ventilador	ventilateur	fan, ventilator	Ventilator(m)	ventilador	ventilatore
ventosa	ventouse	suction disc	Saugnapf(m)	ventosa	ventosa

S

Spanish	French	English	German	Portuguese	Italian
ver	voir	see	sehen	ver	vedere
verano	été	summer	Sommer(m)	verão	estate
verbo	verbe	verb	Verb(n)	verbo	verbo
verdad	vérité	truth	Wahrheit(f)	verdade	verità
verdaderamente	vraiment	really	wirklich	verdadeiramente	veramente
verdadero, a	vrai, e	true	wahr	verdadeiro, a	vero, a
verdadero, a	véritable	real, genuine	wahrhaftig	verdadeiro, a	vero, a
verde	vert, e	green	grün	verde	verde
verdor, verdura	verdure	greenery	Grün(n)	verdura	verdura
veredicto	verdict	verdict	Urteil(n)	veredicto	verdetto
vergonzoso, a	honteux, se	shameful	beschämend	vergonhoso, a	vergognoso, a
vergüenza	honte	shame	Scham(f), Schande(f)	vergonha	vergogna
vergüenza(tener)	honte(avoir)	ashamed(be)	schämen, sich	vergonha(ter)	vergognarsi
verificación	vérification	verification	Überprüfung(f)	verificação	verifica
verosímil	vraisemblable	likely, probable	wahrscheinlich	verosímil	verosimile
verruga	verrue	wart	Warze(f)	verruga	verruca, porro
verso	vers	line	Vers(m)	verso	verso
vértebra	vertèbre	vertebra(-ae)	Wirbel(m)	vértebra	vertebra
verter	verser	pour	aus = gießen	verter	versare
verter	déverser	pour out, tip	aus = gießen	despejar	riversare, scaricare
vertical	vertical, e	vertical	senkrecht	vertical	verticale
vértigo	vertige	dizziness	Schwindel(m)	vertigem	vertigine
vesícula	vésicule	gall-bladder	Blase(f)	vesícula	cistifellea
vestíbulo	hall	foyer, hall	Eingangshalle(f)	vestíbulo	hall, ingresso
vestíbulo	vestibule	hall	Flur(m)	vestíbulo; hall	ingresso, anticamera
vestido, a	habillé, e	dressed	angezogen	vestido, a	vestito, a
vestido, traje	habit(s)	clothes	Kleidung(f)	fato, traje	vestito(i), abiti
vestido	robe	dress	Kleid(n)	vestido	vestito
vestido, prenda	vêtement	garment	Gewand(n)	peça de roupa	abito, vestito
vestigio	vestige	remains	Überrest(m)	vestígio	vestigia
vestir	vêtir	clothe, dress	an = ziehen, an = kleiden	vestir	vestire
vestirse	habiller(s')	dress	an = ziehen, sich	vestir-se	vestirsi
vestirse, ataviar	habiller(s')	dress up	an = kleiden	vestir-se	vestire(-rsi)
vestuario	vestiaire	cloak-room	Garderobe(f)	vestiário	vestiario
veterinario	vétérinaire	vet	Tierarzt(m)	veterinário	veterinario
veto	veto	veto	Veto(n)	veto	veto
vez	fois	time	Mal(n)	vez	volta
vez(una)	fois(une)	once	einmal	vez(uma)	volta(una)
vía; camino	voie	way; track	Weg(m)	via; caminho	via; binario
vía	voie	lane	Spur(f)(Straßen-)	faixa(rua)	corsia
viajar	voyager	travel	reisen	viajar	viaggiare
viaje	voyage	trip; journey	Reise(f)	viagem	viaggio
viajero, a	voyageur, se	traveller	Reisende(r)m f	viajante	viaggiatore, trice
víbora	vipère	viper	Viper(f), Otter(f)	víbora	vipera
vibrar	vibrer	vibrate	schwingen	vibrar	vibrare
vicepresidente	vice-président	vice-president	Vize-Präsident(m)	vice-presidente	vicepresidente
vicio	vice	vice	Laster(n)	vício	vizio
vicioso, a	vicieux, se	vicious	lasterhaft	vicioso, a	vizioso, a
víctima	victime	victim	Opfer(n)	vítima	vittima
victoria	victoire	victory	Sieg(m)	vitória	vittoria
vida	vie	life(lives)	Leben(n)	vida	vita
vidrio	verre	glass	Glas(n)	vidro	vetro
viejo, a	vieux, vieille	old	alt	velho, a	vecchio, a
viejo, anciano	vieillard	old man(men)	Alte(m), alter Mann(m)	velho, ancião	vecchio, anziano
viento	vent	wind	Wind(m)	vento	vento
viernes	vendredi	Friday	Freitag(m)	sexta-feira	venerdì
viga	poutre	beam	Balken(m)	trave	trave
vigente	vigueur(en)	force(in), current	Kraft(in), geltend	vigente	vigore(in), vigente
vigilancia	surveillance	watch; supervision	Überwachung(f)	vigilância	sorveglianza
vigilante	vigilant, e	vigilant	wachsam	vigilante	vigilante
vigilante	surveillant, e	supervisor	Aufseher m, Supervisor	vigia	sorvegliante
vigilar	surveiller	watch; supervise	überwachen	vigiar	sorvegliare
vigilar, guardar	garder	look after	hüten	cuidar de, vigiar	custodire
vigor	vigueur	vigour	Kraft(f)	vigor	vigore
vigoroso, a	vigoureux, se	vigorous, strong	rüstig, kräftig	vigoroso, a	vigoroso, a
vigoroso, a; fuerte	robuste, solide	sturdy	kräftig, fest	robusto, a; forte	robusto, a; forte
vinagre	vinaigre	vinegar	Essig(m)	vinagre	aceto
vino	vin	wine	Wein(m)	vinho	vino

Spanish	French	English	German	Portuguese	Italian
violación	viol	rape	Vergewaltigung(f)	violação	stupro
violación	violation	violation	Verstoß(m)	violação	violazione
violar	violer	rape	vergewaltigen	violentar	violentare
violar	violer	violate	verraten	violar	violare
violencia	violence	violence	Gewalt(f)	violência	violenza
violento, a	violent, e	violent	heftig, stark	violento, a	violento, a
violento, a	violent, e	violent	gewalttätig, gewaltsam	violento, a	violento, a
violeta	violet, te	violet, purple	violett, lila	roxo, a; violeta	viola
violín	violon	violin	Geige(f)	violino	violino
violoncelo	violoncelle	cello	Cello(n)	violoncelo	violoncello
virgen	vierge	virgin	unberührt	virgem	vergine
virginidad	virginité	virginity	Jungfräulichkeit(f)	virgindade	verginità
viril	viril, e	virile, manly	männlich, mannhaft	viril	virile
virilidad	virilité	virility	Männlichkeit(f)	virilidade	virilità
virtud	vertu	virtue	Tugend(f)	virtude	virtù
virtuoso, a	vertueux, se	virtuous	tugendhaft	virtuoso, a	virtuoso, a
virtuoso, a	virtuose	virtuoso	Meister(m), Virtuose m	virtuoso, a	virtuoso, a
viruela	variole	smallpox	Pocken(f, pl)	varíola	vaiolo
virus	virus	virus	Virus(m)	vírus	virus
visado	visa	visa	Visum(n)	visto	visto
viscoso, a	visqueux, se	viscous	zähflüssig	viscoso, a	vischioso, a
viscoso, a	gluant, e	sticky	klebrig	viscoso, a	viscido, a
visibilidad	visibilité	visibility	Sicht(-weite)(f)	visibilidade	visibilità
visible	visible	visible	sichtbar	visível	visibile
visita	visite	visit	Besuch(m)	visita	visita
visitante	visiteur, se	visitor	Besucher(in f)m	visitante	visitatore, trice
visitar	visiter	visit	besuchen	visitar	andare a trovare
visitar	visiter	visit	besichtigen, reisen	visitar	visitare
visón	vison	mink	Nerz(m)	marta	visone
vista	vue	sight	Sehkraft(f)	vista	vista
vista	vue	view	Ausblick(m)	vista	veduta
visual	visuel, le	visual	visuell	visual	visivo, a; visuale
visualizar	visualiser	display	sichtbar machen	visualizar	visualizzare
visualizar	afficher(s')	display	erscheinen	mostrar, dar	apparire
vital	vital, e	vital	wesentlich	vital	vitale
vitalidad	vitalité	vitality	Lebenskraft(f)	vitalidade	vitalità
vitamina	vitamine	vitamin	Vitamin(n)	vitamina	vitamina
viudo, a	veuf, veuve	widower, widow	Witwer(m), Witwe(f)	viúvo, a	vedovo, a
viva(!)	vive!	hurrah!; Long live!	Es lebe!; Lang lebe!	viva!	viva!, evviva!
vivacidad	entrain	liveliness	Schwung(m)	entusiasmo	brio
vivaque	bivouac	bivouac	Biwak(m)	acampamento	bivacco
vivaz	vivace	hardy	immergrün; ausdauernd	vivaz	vivace
vivienda, morada	habitation	dwelling; living	Wohnung(f)	habitação, morada	abitazione
vivir	vivre	live	leben	viver	vivere
vivir, habitar	habiter	live(in), inhabit	bewohnen, wohnen	morar	abitare
vivo, a	vivant, e	alive	lebendig	vivo, a	vivo, a; vivente
vivo, a	vif, vive	lively	lebendig	vivo, a	vivace; vivo, a
vocabulario	vocabulaire	vocabulary	Vokabular(n)	vocabulário	vocabolario
vocación	vocation	vocation	Berufung(f)	vocação	vocazione
vocal	vocal, e	vocal	Stimm-	vocal	vocale
vocal	voyelle	vowel	Vokal(m), Selbstlaut m	vogal	vocale
volante	volant	steering-wheel	Steuer(n)	volante	volante
volar	voler	fly	fliegen	voar	volare
volcán	volcan	volcano(-es)	Vulkan(m)	vulcão	vulcano
volcar	culbuter	somersault	überrennen	cambalhotas(dar)	ribaltare
volcarse	renverser(se)	overturn	überschlagen, sich	virar; cair	rovesciarsi
volumen	volume	volume	Volumen(n)	volume	volume
volumen(negocios)	chiffre(affaire)	turnover	Umsatz(m)	volume(negócios)	fatturato
voluminoso, a	encombrant, e	bulky, cumbersome	sperrig, lästig	volumoso, a	imgombrante
voluntad	volonté	will	Wille(m)	vontade	volontà
voluntario, a	volontaire	voluntary	freiwillig	voluntário, a	volontario, a
voluntario, a	volontaire	volunteer	Freiwillige(f, m)	voluntário, a	volontario, a
volver	tourner	turn	drehen	virar	girare
volver	revenir	come back, return	zurück = kommen	voltar	ritornare
volver a montar	remonter	reassemble	wieder montieren	tornar a montar	rimontare
volver a montar	remontage	reassembly	Zusammensetzen(n)	nova montagem	rimontaggio
volver a ver	revoir	see again	wieder = sehen	voltar a ver	rivedere
volverse	devenir	become	werden	tornar-se	diventare

Spanish	French	English	German	Portuguese	Italian
vomitar	vomir	vomit	erbrechen, sich	vomitar	vomitare
voraz	vorace	voracious	gefräßig, gierig	voraz	vorace
vosotros; ustedes	vous	you	ihr; Sie	vós; você	voi; lei
votar	voter	vote	wählen	votar	votare
voto	voeu	vow	Gelübde(n)	promessa	voto
voto	vote	vote	Wahl(f)	voto	voto
voz	voix	voice	Stimme(f)	voz	voce
vuelo	vol	flight	Flug(m)	voo	volo
vuelta	tour	turn	Umdrehung(f)	volta, giro	giro
vuestro, a	votre	your	Ihr(e); euer, eure	vosso, a	vostro, a(il, la)
vuestro, a; suyo, a	vôtre(le, la)	yours	eure(r, s); Ihre(r, s)	vosso, a; seu, sua	vostro, a; suo, sua
vuestros, as	vos	your	eure, Ihre	vossos, as	vostri, e
vulgar	vulgaire	vulgar	vulgär	vulgar	volgare
vulnerable	vulnérable	vulnerable	verwundbar	vulnerável	vulnerabile

W

Spanish	French	English	German	Portuguese	Italian
water, retretes	water-closet	toilets	Toilette(f)	retrete, sanita	WC; gabinetto

Y

Spanish	French	English	German	Portuguese	Italian
y	et	and	und	e	e, ed
ya	déjà	already	schon	já	giá
ya que; pues	puisque	since	da, weil	já que	poichè
yacente	gisant, e	lying	liegend	jacente	giacente
yerno	gendre	son-in-law	Schwiegersohn(m)	genro	genero
yeso	plâtre	plaster	Gips(m)	gesso	gesso
yo	je	I	ich	eu	io
yoga	yoga	yoga	Yoga(n), Joga(n)	yoga	yoga

Z

Spanish	French	English	German	Portuguese	Italian
zafarrancho	branle-bas	upheaval	Durcheinander(n)	agitação	scompiglio
zafiro	saphir	sapphire	Saphir(m)	safira	zaffiro
zambullida	plongeon	dive	Kopfsprung(m)	mergulho	tuffo

Spanish	French	English	German	Portuguese	Italian
zambullirse	plonger	plunge, dive	tauchen	mergulhar	tuffarsi
zanahoria	carotte	carrot	Möhre(f)	cenoura	carota
zapatilla	pantoufle	slipper	Pantoffel(m)	pantufa, chinelo	pantofola
zapato	soulier	shoe	Schuh(m)	sapato	scarpa
zarzal, maleza	broussaille	undergrowth	Gestrüpp(n)	mato, brenha	macchia, cespugli
zarzuela, opereta	opérette	operetta	Operette(f)	opereta	operetta
zócalo	socle	base	Sockel(m)	soco, pedestal	zoccolo
zona	zone	zone	Zone(f)	zona	zona
zoológico	zoo	zoo	Zoo(m)	jardim zoológico	zoo
zoológico, a	zoologique	zoological	zoologisch	zoológico, a	zoologico, a
zorro	renard	fox(-es)	Fuchs(m)	raposa	volpe
zozobrar	chavirer	capsize	kentern, um = kippen	soçobrar	capovolgersi
zumo de fruta	jus de fruit	fruit-juice	Obstsaft(m)	sumo de fruta	succo di frutta

S

Notes

Notes

Notes

Notes

509

Notes

S

Notes

A

Italian	French	English	German	Spanish	Portuguese
a	à; en; de; par; chez at; to; in; by; on	zu; in; nach; auf; an; bei	a; en; de; por; con	a; em; para; de; com
abbagliare	éblouir	dazzle, glare	blenden	deslumbrar	encandear
abbaiare	aboyer	bark	bellen	ladrar	ladrar
abbandonare	abandonner	abandon, leave	preis = geben; auf = geben	abandonar	abandonar
abbassamento	baisse, chute	drop, fall	Sinken(n), Fallen(n)	baja	baixa
abbassare	abaisser	lower	nieder = lassen	bajar	abaixar
abbassare, calare	baisser	drop, lower; fall	senken	rebajar	baixar
abbassare	descendre	fall, drop	fallen	bajar	baixar
abbassarsi	baisser(se)	bend down	bücken, sich	agacharse	baixar-se
abbastanza	assez	enough; rather	genug	bastante(s)	bastante
abbazia, badia	abbaye	abbey	Abtei(f)	abadía	abadia
abbigliamento	habillement	clothing	Bekleidung(f)	ropa	vestuário
abbonamento	abonnement	subscription	Abonnement(n)	subscripción	assinatura
abbonato, a	abonné, e	subscriber	Abonnent(m)	suscriptor, a	assinante
abbondante	abondant, e	plentiful, abundant	reichlich	abundante	abundante
abbondante	copieux, se	copious	reichlich	copioso, a	copioso, a
abbondanza	abondance	abundance	Uberfluß(m)	abundancia	abundância
abbreviazione	abréviation	abbreviation	Abkürzung(f)(Wort)	abreviatura	abreviatura
abbronzare	bronzer	tan	bräunen	broncear	bronzear
abbronzatura	bronzage	sun-tan	Bräune(f)	bronceado	bronzeamento
abbrustolire	griller	toast	toasten	tostar	torrar
abbrutire	abrutir	exhaust; stupefy	ab = stumpfen	embrutecer	embrutecer
abdicare	abdiquer	abdicate	ab = danken	abdicar	abdicar
abete	sapin	fir-tree	Tanne(f)	abeto	abeto
abile	habile	clever, skilful	geschickt	hábil; diestro, a	hábil; destro, a
abile	adroit, e	skilled	geschickt	diestro, a	destro, a; hábil
abilità	habileté	ability, skill	Geschicklichkeit(f)	habilidad	habilidade
abitante	habitant, e	inhabitant	Einwohner(in f)m	habitante	habitante
abitare	habiter	live(in), inhabit	bewohnen, wohnen	vivir, habitar	morar
abitazione	habitation	dwelling; living	Wohnung(f)	vivienda, morada	habitação, morada
abito, vestito	costume	suit	Anzug(m)	traje	fato, traje
abito da sera	robe de soirée	evening dress	Abendkleid(n)	traje de noche	vestido de noite
abituale	habituel, le	usual	gewöhnlich	habitual	habitual
abitualmente	habituellement	usually	üblich, gewöhnlich	generalmente	habitualmente
abituarsi	habituer(s')	get used to	gewöhnen, sich	acostumbrarse	habituar-se
abitudine	habitude	habit	Gewohnheit(f)	costumbre	hábito, costume
abitudine	accoutumance	habituation	Gewöhnung(f)	hábito	habituação
abolire	abolir	abolish	ab = schaffen	abolir	abolir
abominevole	abominable	awful	scheußlich	abominable	abominável
a bordo	à bord	aboard	an Bord	a bordo	a bordo
abortire	avorter	abort	ab = treiben	abortar	abortar
aborto	avortement	abortion	Abtreibung(f)	aborto	aborto
abusare	abuser	take advantage of	mißbrauchen	abusar	abusar
abuso	abus	abuse, misuse	Mißbrauch(m)	abuso	abuso
accademia	académie	academy	Akademie(f)	academia	academia
accadere	produire(se)	happen, occur	passieren	suceder, ocurrir	ocorrer
accanirsi	acharner(s')	persist	beharren	empeñarse	insistir
accanto; vicino	à côté	next to, beside	neben, daneben	al lado	ao lado
accappatoio	peignoir	dressing gown	Morgenmantel(m)	bata	roupão
accarezzare	caresser	caress	liebkosen, streicheln	acariciar	acariciar
accatastare	empiler	pile up, stack	stapeln	apilar, amontonar	empilhar, amontoar
accedere a	accéder à	reach	Zugang haben zu	llegar a	chegar a
accelerare	accélérer	accelerate	beschleunigen	acelerar	acelerar
accendere	allumer	switch on	an = machen	encender	acender
accendere	allumer	light	an = zünden	encender	acender
accendino	briquet	lighter	Feuerzeug(n)	mechero	isqueiro
accensione	allumage	ignition	Zündung(f)	encendido	ignição

Italian	French	English	German	Spanish	Portuguese
accentazione	accentuation	stress(ing)	Betonung(f)	acentuación	acentuação
accento	accent	accent	Akzent(m), Tonfall(m)	dejo	sotaque
accento	accent(')	accent	Akzent(m)	acento	acento
accentuare	souligner	emphasize	betonen	recalcar, subrayar	acentuar
accertarsi	assurer(s')	make sure	überzeugen, sich	cerciorarse	verificar
accessibile	accessible	accessible	zugänglich	accesible	acessível
accesso	accès	access	Zugang(m)	acceso	acesso
accessorio	accessoire	accessory	Zubehör(n)	accesorio	acessório
accettare	accepter	accept, agree	akzeptieren, an=nehmen	aceptar	aceitar
acchiappare	attraper	catch	fangen	agarrar, coger	agarrar, apanhar
acciaio	acier	steel	Stahl(m)	acero	aço
accidentato, a	accidenté, e	injured person	Verunglückte(f, m)	accidentado, a	acidentado, a
acclamare	acclamer	cheer	zu=jubeln	aclamar	aclamar
accogliente	accueillant, e	hospitable	gastfreundlich	acogedor, a	acolhedor, a
accoglienza	accueil	reception; welcome	Empfang(m), Aufnahme f	recepción	recepção
accogliere	accueillir	welcome	empfangen, auf=nehmen	acoger, recibir	acolher, receber
accompagnare	accompagner	accompany	begleiten	acompañar	acompanhar
accoppiarsi	accoupler(s')	mate	paaren, sich	aparearse	acasalar-se
accordo	accord	agreement	Einverständnis(n)	acuerdo	acordo
accordo	arrangement	arrangement	Abmachung(f)	arreglo, acuerdo	compromisso
accordo(d')	accord(d')	all right, O.K	einverstanden, okay	vale, de acuerdo	acordo(de)
accordo(essere d')	accord(être d')	agree	überein=stimmen	acuerdo(estar de)	acordo(estar de)
accostare, attraccare	accoster	berth	an=legen	abordar	acostar
accrescere	accroître	increase	zu=nehmen	incrementar	aumentar
accumulare	accumuler	accumulate	an=häufen	acumular	acumular
accuratezza	attention	care, caution	Sorgfalt(f)	cuidado	atenção, cuidado
accurato, a	soigneux, se	neat, tidy	sorgfältig	cuidadoso, a	cuidadoso, a
accurato, a	exact, e	accurate	genau; richtig	exacto, a	exacto, a
accusa	accusation	accusation, charge	Anklage(f)	acusación	acusação
accusare	accuser	accuse	an=klagen	acusar	acusar
accusato, a	accusé, e	accused(the)	Angeklagte(f, m)	acusado, a; reo	acusado, a; réu(ré)
aceto	vinaigre	vinegar	Essig(m)	vinagre	vinagre
acido	acide	acid	Säure(f)	ácido	ácido
acqua	eau	water	Wasser(n)	agua	água
acqua di toeletta	eau de toilette	toilet water	Eau de Toilette(n)	colonia(agua de)	água de colónia
acqua gassata	eau gazeuse	sparkling water	Sprudelwasser(n)	gaseosa	água gaseificada
acqua santa	eau bénite	holy water	Weihwasser(n)	agua bendita	água benta
acquaio, lavandino	évier	sink	Spülbecken(n)	fregadero	pia, banca
acquamarina	aigue-marine	aquamarine	Aquamarin(m)	aguamarina	água marinha
acquario	aquarium	aquarium	Aquarium(n)	acuario	aquário
acquatico, a	aquatique	aquatic	Wasser-	acuático, a	aquático, a
acquirente	acheteur, se	buyer; shopper	Käufer(in f)m	comprador, a	comprador, a
acquisito, a	acquis, e	acquired	erworben	adquirido, a	adquirido, a
acquistare	acquérir	acquire	erwerben; erlangen	adquirir	adquirir, obter
acquisto	achat	purchase	Kauf(m)	compra	compra
acrilico	acrylique	acrylic	Akryl(n)	acrílico	acrílico
acrobata	acrobate	acrobat	Akrobat(in f)m	acróbata	acrobata
acrobazia	acrobatie	acrobatics, stunts	Akrobatik(f)	acrobacia	acrobacia
acustica	acoustique	acoustics	Akustik(f)	acústica	acústica
acuto, a	aigu, ë	sharp, shrill	hoch, schrill	agudo, a	agudo, a
ad un tratto	soudain	sudden(ly)	plötzlich	pronto(de)	súbito(de)
adattamento	adaptation	adaptation	Anpassung(f)	adaptación	adaptação
adattare	adapter	adapt, adjust	an=passen	adaptar	adaptar
adattarsi(a)	adapter(s')	adapt(to)	an=passen, sich	adaptarse(a)	adaptar-se(a)
adatto, a	apte	able, qualified	fähig; tauglich	apto, a	apto, a
addestrare	dresser	train	ab=richten, dressieren	amaestrar	amestrar
addetto, a	attaché, e	attaché	Attaché(m)	agregado, a	adido, a
addio!	adieu!	good bye!	tschüß!, lebe wohl!	adiós(!)	adeus!
addizionale	additionnel, le	additional	hinzugefügt	adicional	adicional
addizione, somma	addition, somme	addition, sum	Addition(f), Summe(f)	adición, suma	adição, soma
addome	abdomen	abdomen	Unterleib(m)	abdomen	abdómen
addomesticare	apprivoiser	tame	zähmen	domesticar	domesticar
addormentato, a	endormi, e	asleep	schlafend	dormido, a	adormecido, a
addottrinare	endoctriner	indoctrinate	indoktrinieren	adoctrinar	doutrinar
adeguato, a	adéquat, e	appropriate	passend	adecuado, a	adequado, a
aderente, socio	adhérent, e	member	Mitglied(n)	adherente	aderente
aderire a	adhérer	join	Mitglied werden	adherir a	aderir a
adesione	adhésion	membership	Beitritt(m)	adhesión	adesão

Italian	French	English	German	Spanish	Portuguese
adesivo, a	adhésif, ive	adhesive	klebrig, anhaftend	adhesivo, a	adesivo, a
adolescente	adolescent, e	teenager	Jugendliche(m, f)	adolescente	adolescente
adoperare	servir de(se)	use	benutzen	servirse	servir-se
adorabile	adorable	adorable, lovely	reizend	adorable	adorável
adorare	adorer	adore	an = beten	adorar	adorar
adottare	adopter	adopt	adoptieren	adoptar	adoptar
adulare	flatter	flatter	schmeicheln	halagar	lisonjear
adulterio	adultère	adultery	Ehebruch(m)	adulterio	adultério
adulto, a	adulte	adult	Erwachsene(f, m)	adulto, a	adulto, a
aereo, a	aérien, ne	aerial, air	Luft-	aéreo, a	aéreo, a
aereo	avion	plane, aeroplane	Flugzeug(n)	avión	avião
aerogramma	aérogramme	aerogram	Funkspruch(m)	aerograma	aerograma
aeronautica	aéronautique	aeronautics	Luftfahrt(f)	aeronáutica	aeronáutica
aeroporto	aéroport	airport	Flughafen(m)	aeropuerto	aeroporto
affamato, a	affamé, e	starving, hungry	hungrig	hambriento, a	esfomeado, a
affari	affaires	business	Geschäfte(n, pl.)	negocios	negócios
affascinante	fascinant, e	fascinating	faszinierend	fascinante	fascinante
affascinante	charmant, e	charming, lovely	liebenswert	encantador, a	encantador, a
affascinato, a	fasciné, e	fascinated	fasziniert	fascinado, a	fascinado, a
affatto	tout à fait	quite	ganz	totalmente	totalmente
affermare	affirmer	assert, maintain	behaupten	afirmar	afirmar
afferrare	saisir	seize	ergreifen	coger, agarrar	agarrar
affetto	affection	affection, love	Zuneigung(f)	afecto; afección	afeição; afecto
affettuoso, a	affectueux, se	affectionate	liebevoll	afectuoso, a	afectuoso, a
affidare	confier	entrust	an = vertrauen	confiar	confiar
affiggere	afficher	post up, put up	an = schlagen	anunciar	afixar
affilare	aiguiser	sharpen	schärfen	afilar	afiar
affilato, a	aiguisé, e	sharp	scharf	afilado, a	afiado, a
affinché	afin que	so that	damit	a fin de que	a fim de que
affinità	affinité	affinity	Ähnlichkeit(f)	afinidad	afinidade
affissione	affichage	putting up posters	Anschlag, Plakatierung	anuncios(fijación)	afixação
affittare	louer	rent	vermieten; mieten	alquilar	alugar
affitto	loyer	rent	Miete(f)	alquiler	aluguer
affliggere	affliger	distress, afflict	heim = suchen; betrüben	afligir	afligir
affluenza	affluence	rush	Andrang(m)	afluencia	afluência
afflusso	affluence	crowd	Gedränge(n)	afluencia	afluência
affollamento, ingorgo	encombrement	congestion, jam	Gedränge(n)	estorbo	engarrafamento
affondare	couler, enfoncer	sink	sinken, versenken	hundir	afundar
affrancare	affranchir	stamp	frankieren, freimachen	franquear	franquear
affrontamento	affrontement	confrontation	Konfrontation(f)	enfrentamiento	afrontamento
affrontare	affronter	confront, face	entgegen = treten	afrontar	afrontar
affumicato, a	fumé, e	smoked	geräuchert	ahumado, a	fumado, a
afono, a	aphone	lose one's voice	stimmlos, heiser	afónico, a	áfono, a
agenda	agenda	diary	Taschenkalender(m)	agenda	agenda
agente	agent	agent	Agent(in f)m	agente	agente
agenzia	agence	agency	Agentur(f); Filiale(f)	agencia	agência
agganciare	accrocher	connect, link	an = hängen	enganchar	engatar
aggettivo	adjectif	adjective	Adjektiv(n)	adjetivo	adjectivo
aggirare	contourner	bypass	umgehen	contornear	contornar
aggiudicazione	adjudication	auction	Versteigerung(f)	adjudicación	adjudicação
aggiungere	ajouter	add	hinzu = fügen	añadir	ajuntar, juntar
aggiunto, a; vice	adjoint, e	assistant	Gehilfe(m); Hilfs-	adjunto, a	adjunto, a
aggiustare	ajuster	adjust	ein = stellen	ajustar	ajustar
aggravare	aggraver	worsen, aggravate	verschlimmern	empeorar	agravar
aggredire	agresser	attack, assault	an = greifen	agredir	agredir
aggressione	agression	attack	Aggression(f), Angriff	agresión	agressão
aggressore	agresseur	attacker	Angreifer(in f)m	agresor, a	agressor, a
aggrovigliare(-rsi)	emmêler(s')	tangle(up)	verwickeln, verwirren	enmarañar(se)	emaranhar-se
agguantare	empoigner, saisir	grab, grasp	greifen	empuñar	agarrar
agguato	affût	wait for(in)	Versteck(n)	acecho(al)	espreita de(à)
agile	agile	agile, nimble	flink	ágil	ágil
agio(essere a)	aise(être à l')	ease(be at)	wohl fühlen, sich	gusto(estar a)	vontade(estar à)
agire	agir	act	handeln	actuar	agir
agitare	agiter	shake	schütteln	agitar	agitar
agitare	agiter	wave	schwenken	agitar	agitar
agitazione	agitation	agitation; unrest	Aufregung(f); Unruhe f	agitación	agitação
agnello	agneau	lamb	Lamm(n)	cordero	cordeiro
ago	aiguille	needle	Nadel(f)	aguja	agulha

Italian	French	English	German	Spanish	Portuguese
agonia	agonie	agony	Todeskampf(m), Agonie	agonía	agonia
agopuntura	acuponcture	acupuncture	Akupunktur(f)	acupuntura	acupunctura
agosto	août	August	August(m)	agosto	Agosto
agricolo, a	agricole	agricultural	landwirtschaftlich	agrícola	agrícola
agricoltore	agriculteur	farmer	Landwirt(in f)m	agricultor, a	agricultor, a
agricoltura	agriculture	agriculture	Landwirtschaft(f)	agricultura	agricultura
aiuola	parterre	flower-bed	Beet(n)	arriate	canteiro
aiutare	aider	help, assist, aid	helfen	ayudar	ajudar
aiuto	aide	help	Hilfe(f)	ayuda	ajuda
al di là	au-delà de	beyond	jenseits	más allá de	além de(para)
ala	aile	wing	Flügel(m)	ala	asa
alba	aube	dawn	Morgendämmerung(f)	alba	amanhecer
alberghiera(indust-)	hôtellerie	hotel trade	Hotelwesen(n)	hostelería	hotelaria
albergo, hotel	hôtel	hotel	Hotel(n)	hotel	hotel
albero	arbre	tree	Baum(m)	árbol	árvore
albero	mât	mast	Mast(m)	mástil	mastro
albo dei premiati	palmarès	list of winners	Preisträgerliste(f)	lista de premios	quadro de honra
album	album	album	Album(n)	álbum	álbum
alcol, alcool	alcool	alcohol	Alkohol(m)	alcohol	álcool
alcolico	alcool(s)	spirit(s)	Alkohol(m)	alcohol	álcool
alcolismo	alcoolisme	alcoholism	Alkoholmißbrauch(m)	alcoholismo	alcoolismo
alcuni, e	quelques	few(a), some	einige	algunos, as	alguns, algumas
aleatorio, a	aléatoire	aleatory, uncertain	unsicher, ungewiß	aleatorio, a	aleatório, a; incerto
alfabeto	alphabet	alphabet	Alphabet(n)	alfabeto	alfabeto
alga	algue	seaweed, alga(ae)	Alge(f)	alga	alga
algebra	algèbre	algebra	Algebra(f)	álgebra	álgebra
aliante	planeur	glider	Segelflugzeug(n)	planeador	planador
alibi	alibi	alibi	Alibi(n)	coartada	alibi
alimentari(negozio)	alimentation	food shop	Lebensmittelladen(m)	alimentación	mercearia
alimentazione	alimentation	feeding; food	Ernährung(f)	alimentación	alimentação
alimento, cibo	aliment	food	Lebensmittel(n, pl)	alimento	alimento
alito	haleine	breath	Atem(m)	aliento	hálito
allacciare	brancher	connect	an = schließen	empalmar	ligar
allargare	élargir	widen, enlarge	verbreiten	ensanchar	alargar
allarme	alarme	alarm	Alarm(m)	alarma	alarme
allarme	alerte	alert	Alarm(m)	alerta	alerta, alarme
allattare	allaiter	feed	stillen	pecho(dar el)	aleitar
alleanza	alliance	alliance	Bündnis(n)	alianza	aliança
alleare, unire	allier	ally	verbünden	aliar, unir	aliar, unir
allegato, a	ci-joint, e	enclosed	anbei	adjunto, a	anexo(em)
alleggerire	alléger	lighten	erleichtern	aliviar	aliviar
alleggerire	soulager	relieve	erleichtern	aliviar	aliviar
allegro, a	gai, e	happy, merry	froh	alegre	alegre
allegro, a; felice	joyeux, se	merry, joyful	lustig, fröhlich	alegre	alegre
allenamento	entraînement	training, practice	Training(n)	entrenamiento	treino
allenare(-rsi)	entraîner(s')	train, practise	üben; trainieren	entrenarse	treinar-se
allenatore	entraîneur	trainer	Trainer(m)	entrenador	treinador
allentare	desserrer	loosen	lösen	aflojar	afrouxar
allentare	desserrer	loosen	lockern	aflojar	desapertar
allentare	relâcher	loosen	lockern	aflojar	largar; soltar
allentato, a	desserré, e	slack	schlaff, lose	flojo, a	frouxo, a
allentato, a	détendu, e	slack, loose	schlaff, lose	aflojado, a	frouxo, a; lasso, a
allentato, a	lâche, détendu, e	loose, slack	locker, lose	flojo, a	frouxo, a
allergia	allergie	allergy	Allergie(f)	alergia	alergia
allevamento	élevage	breeding; rearing	Zucht(f); Aufzucht(f)	ganadería	criação de gado
allevare, educare	élever	bring up	erziehen, auf = ziehen	criar, educar	criar, educar
allevare	élever	breed, rear	züchten	criar	criar
allineamento	alignement	alignment	Ausrichtung(f)	alineación	alinhamento
allocuzione	allocution	speech(short)	Ansprache(kurze)(f)	alocución	alocução
alloggiare	loger	accommodate	unter = bringen	alojar	alojar, morar
alloggio	logement	accommodation	Wohnung(f)	alojamiento	alojamento
alloggio	hébergement	accommodation	Unterbringung(f)	alojamiento	alojamento
allontanare; scartare	écarter	separate, part	entfernen	apartar	afastar
allopatia	allopathie	allopathy	Allopathie(f)	alopatía	alopatia
allora	alors	then	dann	entonces	então
allucinazione	hallucination	hallucination	Sinnestäuschung(f)	alucinación	alucinação
alluminio	aluminium	aluminium	Aluminium(n)	aluminio	alumínio
allungare	allonger	lengthen	verlängern	alargar	alongar

Italian	French	English	German	Spanish	Portuguese
alpinista	alpiniste	mountaineer	Alpinist(m)	alpinista	alpinista
altalena	balançoire	swing; see-saw	Schaukel(f)	columpio	baloiço
alternare	alterner	alternate	ab = wechseln	alternar	alternar
alternativo, a	alternatif, ive	alternating(ive)	alternativ	alternativo, a	alternativo, a
altezza	hauteur	height	Höhe(f)	altura	altura
altipiano	plateau	plateau	Hochebene(f)	meseta	planalto
altitudine	altitude	altitude, height	Höhe(f)	altitud, altura	altitude
alto, a	haut, e	high, tall	hoch	alto, a	alto, a
alto, a	haut	up	Oben-; Hoch-; auf	arriba	cima(em, para)
alto, a	grand, e	tall	groß	alto, a	alto, a; grande
alto	haut	top	Oberteil(n)	alto	alto, cimo
alto(in)	haut(en)	upstairs	oben	arriba	cima(em)
altoparlante	haut-parleur	loud-speaker	Lautsprecher(m)	altavoz	alto-falante
altoparlante	baffle	speaker	Lautsprecher(m)	altavoz	alto-falante
altrimenti	autrement	otherwise	anders; sonst	otro modo(de)	outro modo(de)
altro, a	autre	other	andere, sonstige	otro, a	outro, a
altro, a	autre(d')	else	ander; anders	otro, a	outro, a
altro, a	autre	further; other	weiter	otro, a	mais
altronde(d')	ailleurs(d')	moreover, besides	übrigens	por otra parte	aliás
altrove	ailleurs	somewhere else	woanders	otra parte(en)	noutro sítio
alunno, a	élève	pupil	Schüler(in f)m	alumno, a	aluno, a
alveare	ruche	hive	Bienenstock(m)	colmena	colmeia
alzare	lever	lift(up), raise	heben	levantar	levantar
alzarsi	lever(se)	stand up, get up	auf = stehen	levantarse	levantar-se
alzarsi	lever(se)	get up	erheben, sich	levantar(se)	levantar-se
amabile	aimable	nice	lieb, nett	amable	amável
amaca	hamac	hammock	Hängematte(f)	hamaca	rede
amante	amant, e	lover	Geliebte(f, m)	amante	amante
amare, volere bene	aimer	love	lieben	amar, querer	amar, gostar de
amaro, a	amer, ère	bitter	bitter; sauer	amargo, a	amargo, a
ambasciata	ambassade	embassy	Botschaft(f)	embajada	embaixada
ambasciatore	ambassadeur	ambassador	Botschafter(in f)m	embajador	embaixador
ambiente	milieu	milieu, background	Milieu(n)	ambiente, medio	meio
ambiente	environnement	surroundings	Umgebung(f)	ambiente(medio)	ambiente
ambiguo, a	ambigu, ë	ambiguous	zweideutig, mehrdeutig	ambiguo, a	ambíguo, a
ambire, desiderare	convoiter	covet	begehren	codiciar	cobiçar
ambizione	ambition	ambition	Ehrgeiz(m)	ambición	ambição
ambizioso, a	ambitieux, se	ambitious	ehrgeizig	ambicioso, a	ambicioso, a
ambulanza	ambulance	ambulance	Krankenwagen(m)	ambulancia	ambulância
amichevole	amical, e	friendly	freundschaftlich	amistoso, a	amigável
amicizia	amitié	friendship	Freundschaft(f)	amistad	amizade
amico, a	ami, e	friend	Freund(in f)m	amigo, a	amigo, a
ammettere	admettre	admit	zu = geben; zu = lassen	admitir	admitir
amministrare	administrer	manage, run	verwalten	administrar	administrar
amministrare	gérer	manage	verwalten, führen	administrar	gerir
amministrativo, a	administratif, ve	administrative	Verwaltungs-	administrativo, a	administrativo, a
amministrazione	administration	administration	Verwaltung(f)	administración	administração
ammiraglio	amiral	admiral	Admiral(m)	almirante	almirante
ammiratore, trice	admirateur, trice	admirer, fan	Bewunderer(in f)m	admirador, a	admirador, a
ammirazione	admiration	admiration	Bewunderung(f)	admiración	admiração
ammissibile	admissible	admissible	zulässig, annehmbar	admissible	admissível
ammissione	admission	admission	Zulassung, Einweisung	admisión	admissão
ammonizione	avertissement	warning	Warnung(f)	advertencia	aviso
ammontare	montant	amount	Betrag(m)	importe	montante
ammortizzatore	amortisseur	shock absorber	Stoßdämpfer(m)	amortiguador	amortecedor
ammucchiare	entasser	pile up	stapeln	amontonar	amontoar
ammuffire	moisir	mouldy(to go)	verschimmeln	enmohecer	bolor(criar)
amnesia	amnésie	amnesia	Gedächtnisschwund(m)	amnesia	amnésia
amnistia	amnistie	amnesty	Amnestie(f)	amnistía	amnistia
amo	hameçon	hook	Angelhaken(m)	anzuelo	anzol
amore	amour	love	Liebe(f)	amor	amor
amovibile	amovible	removable	auswechselbar	amovible	amovível
ampiezza	ampleur	scale, size	Weite(f), Größe(f)	amplitud	amplidão
ampiezza	amplitude	amplitude	Amplitude(f)	amplitud	amplitude
ampio, a	ample	ample; loose	weit	amplio, a	amplo, a
amputare	amputer	amputate	amputieren	amputar	amputar
analfabeta	illettré, e	illiterate	ungebildet	analfabeto, a	iletrado, a
analisi	analyse	analysis(-ses)	Analyse(f)	análisis	análise

Italian	French	English	German	Spanish	Portuguese
analizzare	analyser	analyse	analysieren	analizar	analisar
analogo, a	analogue	analogous, similar	analog	análogo, a	análogo, a
ananas	ananas	pineapple	Ananas(f)	piña	ananás
anarchia	anarchie	anarchy	Anarchie(f)	anarquía	anarquia
anatomia	anatomie	anatomy	Anatomie(f)	anatomía	anatomia
anatra	canard	duck	Ente(f)	pato	pato, a
anca	hanche	hip	Hüfte(f)	cadera	anca
anche, pure	aussi	also, too; as	auch	también	também
anche; perfino	même	even	sogar; selbst	aun; incluso	mesmo(que)
àncora	ancre	anchor	Anker(m)	ancla	âncora
ancora	encore	still	noch, wieder	todavía, aún	ainda
ancora	encore	again	noch einmal	otra vez	mais(uma vez)
ancora	encore	more	noch	más	mais
ancora	encore	still; yet	noch, noch mehr	aún	ainda
ancora(non)	encore(pas)	yet(not)	noch(nicht)	todavía no	ainda não
andare, recarsi	aller	go	gehen, fahren nach	ir(a, por, hacia)	ir
andare	marcher	walk	gehen	andar	andar
andare a letto	coucher(se)	go to bed	schlafen gehen	ir a la cama	deitar-se
andare a prendere	aller chercher	go to fetch/get	ab = holen	ir a buscar	ir buscar
andare a trovare	visiter	visit	besuchen	visitar	visitar
andata	billet simple	single ticket	einfache Fahrkarte(f)	billete de ida	bilhete de ida
andata e ritorno	billet aller/R	return ticket	Rückfahrkarte(f)	billete ida/vuelta	bilhete ida/volta
andicappato, a	handicapé, e	handicapped	behindert	minusválido, a	deficiente
aneddoto	anecdote	anecdote	Anekdote(f)	anécdota	anedota
anello	bague	ring	Ring(m)	anillo, sortija	anel
anello	anneau	ring	Ring(m)	anilla, anillo	anel
anemia	anémie	anaemia	Blutarmut(f)	anemia	anemia
anestesia	anesthésie	anaesthetic	Narkose(f)	anestesia	anestesia
angelo	ange	angel	Engel(m)	ángel	anjo
angina	angine	sore throat	Angina(f)	angina	angina
angolo	angle	angle	Winkel(m)	ángulo	ângulo
angolo	coin	corner	Ecke(f)	esquina, rincón	canto, esquina
angoscia	angoisse	anguish, distress	Angst(f)	angustia	angústia
anima	âme	soul	Seele(f)	alma	alma
animale	animal	animal	Tier(n)	animal	animal
animare	animer	animate	beleben	animar	animar
animare	animer	liven up	Stimmung machen	animar	animar
animato, a	animé, e	lively	lebhaft	animado, a	animado, a
animatore, trice	animateur, trice	leader, organiser	Leiter/in, Unterhalter	animador, a	animador, a
annata, anno	année	year	Jahr(n)	año	ano
annata	millésime	vintage	Jahrgang(m)	cosecha(año)	vintage
annegare	noyer(se)	drown	ertrinken	ahogar(se)	afogar-se
annesso	annexe	annexe	Anhang(m), Anlage(f)	anexo; anejo	anexo
annientare	anéantir	annihilate, destroy	vernichten	aniquilar	aniquilar
anniversario	anniversaire	anniversary	Jahrestag(m)	aniversario	aniversário
anno	an	year	Jahr(n)	año	ano
annoiarsi	ennuyer(s')	bored(be)	langweilen, sich	aburrir(se)	aborrecer-se
annuale	annuel, le	yearly, annual	jährlich	anual	anual
annullare	annuler	cancel	annullieren	cancelar, anular	anular
annullare	annuler	delete	streichen	borrar	suprimir
annullare	annuler	quash	auf = heben	anular	anular
annullare	annuler	annul	ungültig erklären	anular	anular
annunciare	annoncer	announce	an = kündigen	anunciar	anunciar
annuncio	annonce	notice	Anzeige(f)	anuncio	anúncio
annusare	flairer	sniff; scent; sense	wittern, schnüffeln	olfatear, husmear	farejar, cheirar
anomalia	anomalie	anomaly	Anomalie(f)	anomalía	anomalia
anonimato	anonymat	anonymity	Anonymität(f)	anonimato	anonimato
anonimo, a	anonyme	anonymous	anonym, unbekannt	anónimo, a	anónimo, a
anormale	anormal, e	not normal	anormal	anormal	anormal
ansa	anse	handle	Griff(m)	asa	asa
ansimare	haleter	pant, gasp	keuchen	jadear	arquejar
ansioso, a	anxieux, se	anxious	ängstlich	ansioso, a	ansioso, a
antecedente	antécédent, e	previous	vorhergehend	antecedente	antecedente
antenati	aïeux	ancestors	Ahnen(pl.)	antepasados	antepassados
antenato, a	ancêtre	ancestor	Ahn(m)	antepasado, a	antepassado, a
antenna	antenne	aerial, antenna(e)	Antenne(f)	antena	antena
anteriore	antérieur, e	previous, former	vorhergehend	anterior	anterior
anteriore	antérieur, e	prior	früher	anterior	anterior

Italian	French	English	German	Spanish	Portuguese
anteriore	avant	front, fore	Vorderteil(n)	delantero, a	dianteira
antibiotico	antibiotique	antibiotic	Antibiotikum(n)	antibiótico	antibiótico
antichità	antiquité	antiquity	Antiquität(f)	antigüedad	antiguidade
anticipare	anticiper	anticipate	vor = greifen	anticipar	antecipar
anticipo	avance	advance	Vorsprung(m)	adelanto	avanço
anticipo(essere in)	avance(être en)	early(to be)	zu früh (sein)	adelantado(estar)	adiantado(estar)
antico, a	ancien, ne	ancient	alt	antiguo, a	antigo, a
antico, a	antique	antique, ancient	antik	antiguo, a	antigo, a
anticoncezionale	contraceptif	contraceptive	Verhütungsmittel(n)	anticonceptivo	contraceptivo
antifurto	antivol	anti-theft lock	Diebstahlsicherung(f)	antirrobo	alarme
antipasto	hors-d'oeuvre	starter	Vorspeise(f)	entremeses	acepipe, entrada
antiquariato	antiquités	antique shop	Antiquitäten	anticuario	antiguidades
antiquato, a	démodé, e; désuet	obsolete	veraltet	anticuado, a	antiquado, a
antiquato, a; desueto	désuet, ète	obsolete	altmodisch	desusado, a	desusado, a
antisettico, a	antiseptique	antiseptic	antiseptisch	antiséptico, a	antiséptico, a
anulare	annulaire	annular, ring-	ringförmig	anular	anelar
anziano, a	âgé, e	old	alt	anciano, a	idoso, a
anzitutto	abord(d')	first(at)	zunächst	primero	primeiro
ape	abeille	bee	Biene(f)	abeja	abelha
aperitivo	apéritif	aperitif, drink	Apéritif(m)	aperitivo	aperitivo
aperto, a	ouvert, e	open	offen; geöffnet	abierto, a	aberto, a
apertura	ouverture	opening	Öffnungszeiten(f, pl)	apertura	abertura
apparecchio	appareil	appliance, device	Apparat(m)	aparato	aparelho
apparenza	apparence	appearance, look	Aussehen(n)	apariencia	aparência
apparire	apparaître	appear	erscheinen	aparecer	aparecer
apparire	afficher(s')	display	erscheinen	visualizar	mostrar, dar
appartamento	appartement	flat, apartment	Wohnung(f)	piso	apartamento
appartamento	suite	suite	Suite(f)	suite	suite
appartenere	appartenir(à)	belong to	gehören	pertenecer	pertencer
appassionante	passionnant, e	fascinating	spannend	apasionante	apaixonante
appassionato, a	passionné, e	interested(very)	leidenschaftlich	apasionado, a	apaixonado, a
appassionato, a	amateur de	lover of	Liebhaber(in f)m	amante de	apreciador, a
appassire	flétrir	wilt, wither	verwelken	marchitar	murchar
appello	appel	appeal	Berufung(f)	apelación	apelação
appendere	accrocher	hang	auf = hängen	colgar	pendurar
appendere	pendre	hang	hängen, auf = hängen	colgar	pendurar
appendere	suspendre	hang up	auf = hängen	colgar, suspender	pendurar
appesantire	alourdir	make heavy	erschweren	pesado(hacer)	pesado(tornar)
appetito	appétit	appetite	Appetit(m)	apetito	apetite
appiattire	aplatir	flatten	glätten, ab = flachen	allanar, aplastar	achatar, alisar
applaudire	applaudir	applaud, clap	klatschen	aplaudir	aplaudir
applicare	appliquer	apply	an = wenden	aplicar	aplicar
appoggiarsi	appuyer(s')	lean on(against)	stützen, sich	apoyar(se)	apoiar-se
appoggio	appui	support	Stütze(f)	apoyo	apoio
apportare, portare	apporter	bring	bringen	traer	trazer
apposta	exprès	purpose(on)	absichtlich	expresamente	propósito(de)
apprendere, sapere	apprendre	hear(of)	erfahren	enterarse	saber
apprendista	stagiaire	trainee	Praktikant(in f)m	cursillista	estagiário
apprendistato	apprentissage	apprenticeship	Lehre(f), Lehrjahre(f)	aprendizaje	aprendizagem
apprensione	appréhension	apprehension	Furcht(f)	aprensión, recelo	apreensão
apprezzare	apprécier	appreciate	schätzen	apreciar	apreciar
approfittare	profiter	take advantage of	profitieren	aprovechar	aproveitar
approssimativo, a	approximatif, ive	approximate	ungefähr	aproximativo, a	aproximado, a
approvare	approuver	approve	genehmigen	aprobar	aprovar
appuntamento	rendez-vous	appointment	Verabredung(f)	cita	encontro
appuntito, a	pointu, e	pointed, sharp	spitz	puntiagudo, a	pontiagudo, a
appunto	note	note	Vermerk(m)	nota	nota
appunto	justement	exactly	genau	justamente	justamente
a presto	à bientôt	see you soon, bye	bis bald	hasta pronto	até breve; até já
aprile	avril	April	April(m)	abril	Abril
aprire	ouvrir	open	öffnen	abrir	abrir
apriscatole	ouvre-boîte(s)	tin/can opener	Büchsenöffner(m)	abrelatas	abre-latas
aquila	aigle	eagle	Adler(m)	águila	águia
arachide	cacahuète	peanut	Erdnu0(f)	cacahuete, maní	amendoim
aragosta	langouste	crayfish	Languste(f)	langosta	lagosta
arancia	orange	orange	Apfelsine(f)	naranja	laranja
arancione	orange	orange	orangefarben	anaranjado, a	cor-de-laranja
aratura	labour	ploughing	Feldarbeit(f)	labranza	lavoura

I

arazzo; tappezzeria	tapisserie	tapestry	Wandteppich; Gobelin m	tapiz; tapicería	tapeçaria
arbitrario, a	arbitraire	arbitrary	willkürlich	arbitrario, a	arbitrário, a
arbitro	arbitre	referee	Schiedsrichter(in f)m	árbitro	árbitro
arcaico, a	archaïque	archaic	archaisch	arcaico, a	arcaico, a
archeologia	archéologie	archaeology	Archeologie(f)	arqueología	arqueologia
architetto	architecte	architect	Architekt(in f)m	arquitecto, a	arquitecto, a
architettura	architecture	architecture	Architektur(f)	arquitectura	arquitectura
archivi	archives	archives	Archiv(n)	archivos	arquivo
arcipelago	archipel	archipelago	Inselgruppe(f)	archipiélago	arquipélago
arco	arc	bow	Bogen(m)	arco	arco
arco	arc	arc	Halbkreis(m)	arco	arco
arco, volta	arche	arch	Bogen(m), Gewölbe(n)	arca	arco
arco, volta	voûte	vault, arch	Gewölbe(f)	bóveda	abóbada
arcobaleno	arc-en-ciel	rainbow	Regenbogen(m)	arco iris	arco-íris
ardente, bollente	brûlant, e	boiling hot	brennend, kochend	ardiente	ardente
ardesia	ardoise	slate	Schiefer(m)	pizarra	ardósia, lousa
area, zona	aire, zone	area	Bereich(m), Gebiet(n)	área, zona	área, zona
arena	arène	arena	Arena(f)	arena	arena
arena	arène(s)	bull ring, arena	Kampfbahn(f)	plaza de toros	praça de touros
argento	argent	silver	Silber(n)	plata	prata
argilla	argile	clay	Ton(m), Lehm(m)	arcilla	argila
argomentare	argumenter	argue	verhandeln	argüir, argumentar	argumentar
argomento	argument	argument	Argument(n)	argumento	argumento
aria	air	air	Luft(f)	aire	ar
arido, a	aride	arid	dürr, trocken	árido, a	árido, a
arieggiare	aérer	air, ventilate	lüften	airear, ventilar	arejar, ventilar
aringa	hareng	herring	Hering(m)	arenque	arenque
aristocratico, a	aristocrate	aristocrat	Adlige(f, m)	aristócrata	aristocrata
aritmetica	arithmétique	arithmetic	Arithmetik(f)	aritmética	aritmética
arma	arme	weapon, arm	Waffe(f)	arma	arma
arma; armi(pl.)	arme	arm	Waffe(f)	arma	arma
armadio	armoire	wardrobe	Schrank(m)(Kleider-)	armario	armário
armadio	armoire	cupboard	Schrank(m)	armario	armário
armadio a muro	placard	cupboard	Wandschrank(m)	armario	armário
armamento	armement	armament, weapons	Bewaffnung(f)	armamento	armamento
armatore	armateur	ship-owner	Reeder(m)	armador	armador
armonia	harmonie	harmony	Harmonie(f)	armonía	harmonia
armonioso, a	harmonieux, se	harmonious	harmonisch	armonioso, a	harmonioso, a
aroma	arôme	aroma	Aroma(n)	aroma	aroma, cheiro
arpa	harpe	harp	Harfe(f)	arpa	harpa
arpione	harpon	harpoon	Harpune(f)	arpón	arpão
arrampicarsi	grimper	climb	klettern	escalar, subir	trepar, escalar
arredamento, mobilia	ameublement	furnishing	Einrichtung(f)	mobiliario	mobiliário
arresto	arrestation	arrest	Verhaftung(f)	arresto	detenção
arricchire	enrichir	enrich	bereichern	enriquecer	enriquecer
arrivare a	arriver	arrive, come	an = kommen	llegar	chegar
arrivare a	aboutir à	lead to	führen zu	conducir a	conduzir a
arrivederci	au revoir	good bye, bye-bye	auf Wiedersehen	hasta luego	até logo, adeus!
arrivo	arrivée	arrival	Ankunft(f)	llegada; meta	chegada
arrossire	rougir	blush, flush	erröten	sonrojarse	corar
arrostire	griller	grill	grillen	asar(parrilla)	grelhar
arrosto	rôti	roast; joint	Braten(m)	asado	assado
arrotolare	enrouler	roll up	auf = wickeln	enrollar	enrolar
arsenale	arsenal	arsenal, armoury	Arsenal(n)	arsenal	arsenal
arte	art	art	Kunst(f)	arte	arte
arteria	artère	artery	Ader(f); Arterie(f)	arteria	artéria
articolazione	articulation	joint	Gelenk(n)	articulación	articulação
articolo	article	article	Artikel(m)	artículo	artigo
articolo	article	article	Gesetzesartikel(m)	artículo	artigo
articolo	article	item	Artikel(m)	artículo	artigo
artificiale	artificiel, le	artificial	künstlich	artificial	artificial
artigiano	artisan	craftsman(-men)	Handwerker(in f)m	artesano	artesão
artiglio	griffe	claw	Kralle(f), Klaue(f)	garra	garra
arti marziali	arts martiaux	martial arts	Kriegskunst(f)	artes marciales	artes marciais
artista	artiste	artist	Künstler(in f)m	artista	artista
artrosi	arthrose	arthritis	Arthrose(f)	artrosis	artrose
ascensore	ascenseur	lift, elevator	Aufzug(m)	ascensor	elevador
ascesso	abcès	abscess(-es)	Geschwür(n)	absceso	abcesso

Italian	French	English	German	Spanish	Portuguese
ascia	hache	axe	Axt(f)	hacha	machado
asciugacapelli	sèche-cheveux	hair-dryer	Fön(m), Haartrockner m	secador	secador
asciugamano	serviette	towel	Handtuch(n)	toalla	toalha
asciugare	essuyer	wipe, dry	ab = wischen, abtrocknen	limpiar, secar	limpar, secar
asciugare; seccare	sécher	dry	trocknen	secar	secar
ascoltare	écouter	listen(to)	zu = hören, horchen	escuchar	escutar
asfalto	goudron	tar	Teer(m)	alquitrán	alcatrão
asfissia	asphyxie	suffocation	Ersticken(n)	asfixia	asfixia
asilo	asile	asylum(political)	Asyl(n)	asilo	asilo
asma	asthme	asthma	Asthma(n)	asma	asma
aspettare	attendre	wait(for)	warten	esperar	esperar
aspettare	attendre	expect	erwarten	esperar	esperar
aspettarsi	attendre à(s')	expect	rechnen, mit etwas	esperar(se)	esperar
aspetti!	attendez!	wait!	Moment bitte!	espere(!)	espere!
aspetto	aspect	aspect	Aussehen(n)	aspecto	aspecto
aspirapolvere	aspirateur	vacuum-cleaner	Staubsauger(m)	aspirador	aspirador
aspirare	aspirer	inhale, suck in(up)	ein = atmen, saugen	aspirar	aspirar
aspirina	aspirine	aspirin	Aspirin(n)	aspirina	aspirina
aspro, a; agro, a	aigre	sour	sauer	agrio, a	azedo, a
assaggiare	goûter	taste	kosten	probar	provar
assai; molto	beaucoup; très	much	sehr; viel(e)	mucho; muy	muito
assalto	assaut	assault, attack	Angriff(m)	asalto	assalto
assaporare	savourer	savour	kosten, genießen	saborear	saborear
assassinio	assassinat	murder	Mord(m)	asesinato	assassínio
assassinio	meurtre	murder	Mord(m)	asesinato	homicídio, crime
assassino, a	assassin	murderer	Mörder(in f)m	asesino, a	assassino, a
assassino, a	tueur, se	killer	Mörder(in f)m	asesino, a	assassino, a
asse	axe	axis	Achse(f)	eje	eixo
assedio	siège	siege	Belagerung(f)	sitio	cerco
assegnare	allouer	allocate	zu = teilen, bewilligen	conceder	conceder
assegnare	attribuer	assign	zu = teilen	asignar	destinar
assegnazione; assegno	allocation	allowance	Beihilfe(f), Zulage(f)	subsidio	subsídio, abono
assegno	chèque	cheque	Scheck(m)	cheque, talón	cheque
assemblaggio	assemblage	assembly	Montage(f)	ensambladura	montagem
assemblare	assembler	assemble	zusammen = setzen	ensamblar	juntar
assemblea	assemblée	meeting, assembly	Versammlung(f)	asamblea	assembleia
assente	absent, e	absent	abwesend	ausente	ausente
assessore	adjoint, e	deputy	Stellvertreter(in f)m	substituto, a	adjunto, a
assicurarsi	assurer(s')	ensure; insure	versichern; zu = sichern	asegurarse	assegurar-se
assicurato, a	assuré, e	insured	versichert	asegurado, a	segurado, a
assicurazione	assurance	insurance	Versicherung(f)	seguro	seguro
assillare	harceler	harass	quälen	acosar	perseguir
assistente	assistant, e	assistant	Assistent(in f)m	asistente, a	assistente
assistenza	assistance	assistance	Hilfe(f)	asistencia	assistência
assistere	assister	attend	assistieren	asistir	assistir
associare	associer	combine, associate	verbinden	asociar	associar
associarsi(a, con)	associer à(s')	join	an = schließen, sich	asociarse(a, con)	associar-se a
associazione	association	association	Verband(m)	asociación	associação
assoggettare	assujettir	subject(to)	unterwerfen	someter, sujetar	sujeitar
assolutamente	absolument	absolutely	unbedingt, absolut	absolutamente	absolutamente
assoluto, a	absolu, e	absolute	unbedingt	absoluto, a	absoluto, a
assorbire	absorber	absorb	verzehren	absorber	absorver
assortimento	assortiment	assortment	Sortiment(n)	surtido	sortimento
assortimento	lot	batch, assortment	Assortiment(n)	lote	lote
assuefazione	accoutumance	addiction	Abhängigkeit(f)	adicto, dependencia	dependência
assumere	assumer	assume	übernehmen, nehmen	asumir	assumir
assumere	embaucher	employ, take on	ein = stellen	dar trabajo	empregar
assumere	recruter	recruit	an = werben	contratar, reclutar	recrutar
assurdo, a	absurde	absurd	unsinnig	absurdo, a	absurdo, a
assurgere	accéder	accede to	gelangen zu/kommen an	acceder	chegar
asta	enchère	bid, bidding	Auktion(f); Gebot(n)	subasta	leilão
asta, barra	tige	rod	Stange(f)	tallo, vástago	haste
astratto, a	abstrait, e	abstract	abstrakt	abstracto, a	abstracto, a
astro	astre	star	Stern(m), Gestirn(n)	astro	astro
astrologia	astrologie	astrology	Astrologie(f)	astrología	astrologia
astronautica	astronautique	astronautics	Weltraumfahrt(f)	astronáutica	astronáutica
astronomia	astronomie	astronomy	Astronomie(f)	astronomía	astronomia
astuccio	étui	case	Etui(n)	estuche	estojo

I

Italian	French	English	German	Spanish	Portuguese
astuto, a	astucieux, se	astute, clever	verschmitzt, schlau	astuto, a	astucioso, a
astuto, a	rusé, e	crafty, cunning	schlau, gerissen	astuto, a	astuto, a; fino, a
astuzia	astuce	trick	List(f), Trick(m)	astucia	astúcia
Atlantico	Atlantique	Atlantic	Atlantik(m)	Atlántico	Atlântico
atleta	athlète	athlete	Athlet(in f)m	atleta	atleta
atletismo	athlétisme	athletics	Leichtathletik(f)	atletismo	atletismo
atmosfera	atmosphère	atmosphere	Atmosphäre(f)	atmósfera	atmosfera
atmosfera	ambiance	atmosphere	Stimmung(f)	ambiente	ambiente
atollo	atoll	atoll	Atoll(n)	atolón	atol
atomico, a	atomique	atomic	atomar	atómico, a	atómico, a
atomo	atome	atom	Atom(n)	átomo	átomo
atrio, portico	porche	porch	Portal(n)	soportal, porche	pórtico
atroce	atroce	atrocious	grausam	atroz	atroz
attaccamento	attachement	attachment	Verbundenheit(f)	apego, cariño	apego
attaccapanni	portemanteau	hat stand	Kleiderständer(m)	colgador, percha	cabide
attaccare	attaquer	attack	an = greifen	atacar	atacar
attaccare, legare	attacher	fasten	befestigen	atar, fijar	atar, amarrar
attacco	attaque	attack	Angriff(m)	ataque	ataque
atteggiamento	attitude	attitude	Haltung(f)	actitud	atitude
attentato	attentat	attempt, attack	Attentat(n)	atentado	atentado
attenti!	garde-à-vous!	attention!	Stillgestanden!	firmes(!)	sentido!
attento, a	attentif, ive	attentive, careful	aufmerksam	atento, a	atento, a
attenuare	atténuer	attenuate	ab = schwächen; lindern	atenuar	atenuar
attenzione	attention(à l')	attention	Aufmerksamkeit(f)	atención a(en)	cuidado(ao)
attenzione!, attento!	attention!	careful!(be)	Achtung!(f)	cuidado(!)	atenção!, cuidado!
aterrare	atterrir	land	landen	aterrizar	aterrar
attesa	attente	wait(ing)	Warten(n)	espera	espera
attesa(in)	attendant(en)	meanwhile	inzwischen	mientras	entretanto
attimo, momento	moment, instant	while, time	Moment(m)	rato	momento, instante
attingere	puiser	draw(from)	schöpfen	sacar	tirar, extraír
attirare	attirer	attract	an = ziehen	atraer	atrair
attirare, sedurre	attirer, séduire	entice	verführen	atraer, seducir	atrair, seduzir
attitudine	aptitude	ability, aptitude	Fähigkeit(f)	aptitud(es)	aptidão, talento
attivare	activer	activate	beschleunigen	activar	activar
attività	activité	activity	Tätigkeit(f)	actividad	actividade
attivo, a	actif, ive	active	aktiv, tatkräftig	activo, a	activo, a
atto	acte	action, act	Handlung(f)	acto	acto, acção
attonito, a	ahuri, e	stupefied	verdutzt	espantado, a	pasmado, a
attore, attrice	acteur, actrice	actor, actress	Schauspieler(in f)m	actor, actriz	actor, actriz
attore, attrice	comédien, ne	actor, actress	Schauspieler(in f)m	actor, actriz	actor, actriz
attraente	attirant, e	attractive	anziehend	atrayente	atraente
attraversare	traverser	cross	überqueren	atravesar, cruzar	atravessar
attraverso	travers(à)	across; through	durch	través de(a)	através de
attrazione	attraction	attraction	Anziehung(f)	atracción	atracção
attrezzatura	outillage	tools, equipment	Werkzeug(n)	herramientas	ferramentas
attrezzo	outil	tool	Werkzeug(n)	herramienta	ferramenta
attribuire	attribuer	attribute	bei = messen	atribuir	atribuir
attuale	actuel, le	present, current	aktuell, gegenwärtig	actual	actual
attualizzare	actualiser	update	aktualisieren	actualizar	actualizar
attualmente	actuellement	now, at present	zur Zeit	actualmente	actualmente
attutire	amortir	absorb, cushion	dämpfen	amortiguar	amortecer
audacia	audace	audacity	Kühnheit(f)	audacia	audácia
augurare	souhaiter	wish, desire	wünschen	desear	desejar
augurio	voeu	wish(-es)	Wunsch(m)	deseo	voto
aula	classe(salle)	classroom	Klassenzimmer(n)	aula	aula(sala de)
aumentare	augmenter	increase, raise	zu = nehmen	aumentar	aumentar
aumento	augmentation	increase, rise	Zunahme(f)	aumento	aumento
aumento	hausse	rise, increase	Steigerung(f)	subida	subida
aurora	aurore	dawn	Morgenröte(f)	aurora	aurora
auscultare	ausculter	examine	ab = horchen	auscultar	auscultar
ausiliare	auxiliaire	auxiliary	Hilfs-; Hilfe(f)	auxiliar	auxiliar
austero, a	austère	austere	streng, hart	austero, a	austero, a
autentico, a	authentique	authentic, genuine	authentisch	auténtico, a	autêntico, a
autista	chauffeur	driver; chauffeur	Fahrer m; Chauffeur m	chófer	motorista
autobus	autobus	bus	Bus(m)	autobús	autocarro
autografo	autographe	autograph	Autogramm(n)	autógrafo	autógrafo
automa	automate	automaton	Automat(m)	autómata	autómato
automatico, a	automatique	automatic	automatisch	automático, a	automático, a

Italian	French	English	German	Spanish	Portuguese
automobile	automobile	car	Auto(n)	automóvil	automóvel
autonomia	autonomie	autonomy	Autonomie(f)	autonomía	autonomia
autonomo, a	autonome	autonomous	autonom; unabhängig	autónomo, a	autónomo, a
autopsia	autopsie	autopsy	Autopsie(f)	autopsia	autópsia
autore, autrice	auteur	author	Autor(in f)m	autor, a	autor, a
autorità	autorité	authority	Autorität(f)	autoridad	autoridade
autoritario, a	autoritaire	authoritarian	autoritär	autoritario, a	autoritário, a
autorizzare	autoriser	authorize	erlauben	autorizar	autorizar
autostop	auto-stop	hitch-hiking	trampen	autostop, a dedo	boleia(pedir)
autostrada	autoroute	motorway	Autobahn(f)	autopista	auto-estrada
autunno	automne	autumn	Herbst(m)	otoño	outono
avambraccio	avant-bras	fore-arm	Unterarm(m)	antebrazo	antebraço
avanti	avant(en)	ahead	voran, voraus	adelante	adiante
avanti!, prego!	entrez!	come in!	herein!	pase(!), adelante!	entre!
avanzare	avancer	advance	voran = gehen; vorrücken	adelantar	adiantar
avaro, a	avare	miserly, mean	geizig	avaro, a	avarento, a
avere	avoir	have	haben	haber; tener	haver; ter
avere	avoir	have	haben	tener	ter, possuir
aviatore, trice	aviateur, trice	aviator	Flieger(m), Pilot(m)	aviador, a	aviador, a
aviazione	aviation	aviation	Luftfahrt(f)	aviación	aviação
avorio	ivoire	ivory	Elfenbein(n)	marfil	marfim
avvelenamento	empoisonnement	poisoning	Vergiftung(f)	envenenamiento	envenenamento
avvenimento	événement	event	Ereignis(n)	acontecimiento	acontecimento
avvenire	avenir	future	Zukunft(f)	porvenir, futuro	futuro
avventura	aventure	adventure	Abenteuer(n)	aventura	aventura
avverbio	adverbe	adverb	Umstandswort, Adverb	adverbio	advérbio
avversario, a	adversaire	opponent	Gegner(in f)m	adversario, a	adversário, a
avverso, a	adverse	adverse, opposing	feindlich, gegnerisch	adverso, a	adverso, a
avvertire	avertir	warn	warnen	advertir	avisar, prevenir
avviare, iniziare	démarrer	start	starten	arrancar	arrancar
avvicinare	rapprocher	bring nearer	heran = rücken	acercar	acercar
avvicinarsi	approcher(s')	approach	nähern, sich	acercar(se)	aproximar-se
avviso, parere	avis	opinion	Meinung(f)	opinión	opinião, parecer
avviso	avis	notice	Mitteilung(f)	aviso	aviso, notícia
avvocato, tessa	avocat, e	lawyer, barrister	Anwalt(m), Anwältin(f)	abogado, a	advogado, a
avvolgere	envelopper	wrap, envelop	ein = hüllen, ein = packen	envolver	envolver
avvoltoio	vautour	vulture	Geier(m)	buitre	abutre
azione	action	action	Vorgehen(n), Handlung	acción	acção
azione	action	share	Aktie(f)	acción	acção
azionista	actionnaire	shareholder	Aktionär(m)	accionista	accionista

B

Italian	French	English	German	Spanish	Portuguese
baccalà; merluzzo	morue	cod	Schellfisch(m)	bacalao	bacalhau
bacchetta	baguette	stick	Stöckchen(n)	varilla	vara
baciare	embrasser	kiss; embrace	küssen, umarmen	abrazar, besar	abraçar, beijar
bacinella	bassine	bowl	Wanne(f); Schüssel(f)	barreño	bacia
bacino	bassin	pond	Bassin(n), Teich(m)	estanque	lago
bacio	baiser	kiss	Kuß(m)	beso(dar un)	beijo
bacio	bise	kiss	Küßchen(n)	besito	beijinho
baffo	moustache	moustache	Schnurrbart(m)	bigote	bigode
bagagliaio	coffre	boot	Kofferraum(m)	maletero	mala
bagaglio	bagage(s)	luggage, baggage	Gepäck(n)	equipaje	bagagem
bagaglio a mano	bagages à main	hand luggage	Handgepäck(n)	equipaje de mano	bagagem de mão
bagnare	mouiller	wet	an = feuchten	mojar	molhar
bagnato, a	mouillé, e	wet	naß	mojado, a	molhado, a
bagnino	maître-nageur	life-guard	Bademeister(in f)m	maestro(natación)	nadador-salvador

Italian	French	English	German	Spanish	Portuguese
bagno	bain	bath	Bad(n)	baño	banho
bagno	baignade	swimming, bathing	Baden(n)	baño	banho
bagno(fare il)	baigner(se)	bathe; swim	baden; schwimmen	bañarse	banho(tomar)
bagno	salle de bains	bathroom	Badezimmer(n)	cuarto de baño	quarto de banho
baia	baie	bay	Bucht(f)	bahía	baía
balbettare	bégayer	stutter, stammer	stottern	tartamudear	gaguejar
balcone	balcon	balcony	Balkon(m)	balcón	varanda
balena	baleine	whale	Wal(m)	ballena	baleia
ballare	danser	dance	tanzen	bailar	dançar, bailar
ballerino, a	danseur, se	dancer	Tänzer(in f)m	bailarín, a	bailarino, a
balletto	ballet	ballet	Ballet(n)	ballet	ballet, bailado
ballo, danza	danse	dance	Tanz(m)	danza, baile	dança
ballo	bal	dance, ball	Ball(m)	baile	baile
bambinaia	nurse	nanny	Kindermädchen(n)	niñera	ama
bambino, a	enfant	child, children(pl)	Kind(n)	niño, a; chico, a	criança
bambola	poupée	doll	Puppe(f)	muñeca	boneca
banale	banal, e	banal	banal	común	banal
banana	banane	banana	Banane(f)	plátano, banana	banana
banca	banque	bank	Bank(f)	banco, banca	banco
bancario, a	bancaire	bank, banking	Bank-	bancario, a	bancário, a
banchetto	banquet	banquet	Bankett(n)	banquete	banquete
banchiere	banquier	banker	Bankier(m)	banquero	banqueiro
banchisa	banquise	ice-floe	Packeis(n)	banco de hielo	campo de gelo
banco	comptoir	counter	Ladentisch(m)	mostrador	balcão
banco	comptoir	counter, bar	Theke(f)	barra	balcão
banconota	billet(banque)	bank-note	Geldschein(m)	billete(de banco)	nota(de banco)
banda	bande	gang	Bande(f)	pandilla	quadrilha
banda	fanfare	brass band	Fanfare(f)	banda	fanfarra, banda
bandiera	drapeau	flag	Fahne(f)	bandera	bandeira
bandiera	drapeau	flag	Flagge(f)	bandera	bandeira
bandire	bannir	banish	verbannen	desterrar	desterrar
bandito	bandit	bandit	Bandit(m)	bandido	bandido
bar	bar	bar, pub	Kneipe(f)	bar, café	bar, café
bara	cercueil	coffin	Sarg(m)	ataúd	caixão
barare	tricher	cheat	fuschen, mogeln	trampas(hacer)	batota(fazer)
baratro	gouffre	chasm, pit	Abgrund(m), Kluft(f)	abismo, sima	abismo
barba	barbe	beard	Bart(m)	barba	barba
barbaro, a	barbare	barbaric	barbarisch	bárbaro, a	bárbaro, a
barbone, a; vagabondo	clochard, e	tramp	Penner(m)	vagabundo, a	vagabundo, a
barca	barque	boat(small)	Barke(f), Kahn(m)	barca	barca
barcollare	chanceler	stagger	taumeln	tambalearse	vacilar
barcollare	tituber	stagger	wanken	titubear	titubear
barella	civière	stretcher	Bahre(f)	camilla	maca
barometro	baromètre	barometer	Barometer(m)	barómetro	barómetro
barone, baronessa	baron, ne	baron, baroness	Baron(in, f)m	barón, baronesa	barão, baronesa
barricata	barricade	barricade	Barrikade(f)	barricada	barricada
barriera	barrière	barrier; gate	Schranke(f)	barrera	barreira
bascula, bilancia	bascule	scales	Waage(f)	báscula	báscula
base	base	base	Grundlage(f)	base	base
base	base(de)	basic	Grund-; Grundlage	básico	base(de)
base(militare)	base(militaire)	base	Stützpunkt(m)	base(militar)	base(militar)
basso, a	bas, basse	low	niedrig	bajo, a	baixo, a
basso, giù	bas(en)	downstairs	unten; hinunter	abajo	baixo(de)
basta così!	assez!; suffit!	enough !(that's)	das langt, jetzt langt	basta(!)	basta!, chega!
bastone	bâton	stick	Stock(m)	palo	pau, bastão
bastone	canne	stick	Stock(m)	bastón	bengala
battaglia	bataille	battle	Gefecht(n)	batalla	batalha
battere	battre	beat	schlagen	batir	bater
battello	bateau	boat	barco	Boot(n)	barco
batteria	batterie	battery	Batterie(f)	batería	bateria
batterio	bactérie	bacterium(-eria)	Bakterie(f)	bacteria	bactéria
battersi, lottare	battre(se)	fight	kämpfen	pelearse	lutar
battesimo	baptême	baptism	Taufe(f)	bautizo	baptismo
baule	malle	trunk	Koffer(großer)(m)	baúl	mala
bebè, bambino, a	bébé	baby	Baby(n)	bebé	bebé
beccheggiare	tanguer	pitch	schaukeln	cabecear	balouçar-se
becco	bec	beak	Schnabel(m)	pico	bico
beige	beige	beige	beige	crema, beis	bege

Italian	French	English	German	Spanish	Portuguese
bella	belle	beautiful	schön	bella	bela
bella	belle	beautiful, fine	schön, e, er, es	hermosa	bonita, bela
belle arti	beaux-arts	fine arts	Kunst(f)	bellas artes	belas-artes
bellezza	beauté	beauty	Schönheit(f)	belleza	beleza
bellicoso, a	belliqueux, se	aggressive	kriegerisch	belicoso, a	belicoso, a
bello, a	beau, belle	beautiful, fine	schön	hermoso, a; bello, a	belo, a; bonito, a
bello, a	joli, e	nice	nett	lindo, a	bonito, a
bello, a	beau, belle	handsome	ansehnlich, schön	bello, a	bonito, a
bel tempo	beau temps	fine weather	schönes Wetter	buen tiempo	bom tempo
benché	bien que	though, although	obwohl, obgleich	aunque	ainda que
bene	bien	well	wohl	bien	bem
bene	bien	well	gut	bien	bem
bene	bien	good	Gut(n)	bien	bem
benedire	bénir	bless	segnen	bendecir	benzer
beneficiare	bénéficier	profit, benefit	profitieren, gewinnen	beneficiar	beneficiar
beneficio; utile	bénéfice	benefit; profit	Gewinn(m)	beneficio	lucro, proveito
beneficio(al--di)	profit(au--de)	in aid of	zugunsten von	beneficio(en--de)	proveito(em--de)
benessere	bien-être	well-being	Wohlbefinden(n)	bienestar	bem-estar
benevolo, a	bienveillant, e	benevolent	wohlwollend	benévolo, a	benévolo, a
benevolo, a	bénévole	voluntary	unentgeltlich	benévolo, a	benévolo, a
beni; averi	biens	possessions, estate	Besitz(m), Güter(pl)	bienes	bens
benigno, a	bénin, bénigne	benign	gutartig	benigno, a	benigno, a
benvenuto, a	bienvenu, e	welcome(to be)	Willkommen(n)	bienvenido, a	bem-vindo, a
benzina	essence	petrol	Benzin(n)	gasolina	gasolina
benzina super	essence super	four-star petrol	Superbenzin(n)	supercarburante	super
bere	boire	drink	trinken	beber	beber
bernoccolo, gobba	bosse	lump, bump	Beule(f)	chichón	bossa; alto
berretto, cuffia	bonnet	cap, hat	Mütze(f)	gorro	barrete
berretto	casquette	cap	Mütze(f)	gorra	boné
bersaglio	cible	target	Zielscheibe(f)	blanco	alvo
bestemmia	blasphème	blasphemy	Lästerung(f)(Gottes-)	blasfemia	blasfémia
bestemmia	juron	swear-word	Fluch(m)	juramento, taco	palavrão
bestia	bête	animal, beast	Biest(n), Tier(n)	bestia	bicho, animal
bestiame	bétail, bestiaux	cattle	Vieh(n)	ganado	gado
bevanda, bibita	boisson	drink	Getränk(n)	bebida	bebida
bevitore, trice	buveur, se	drinker	Trinker(in f)m	bebedor, a	bebedor, a
biancheria	linge	linen	Wäsche(f)	ropa	roupa
bianco, a	blanc, che	white	weiß	blanco, a	branco, a
biasimo	blâme	blame; reprimand	Rüge(f)	reprobación	censura
Bibbia	Bible	Bible	Bibel(f)	Biblia	Bíblia
biberon	biberon	bottle(baby's -)	Fläschchen(n)	biberón	biberão
bibita	boisson	drink	Getränk(n)	bebida	bebida
bibliografia	bibliographie	bibliography	Bibliographie(f)	bibliografía	bibliografia
biblioteca	bibliothèque	library	Bibliothek(f)	biblioteca	biblioteca
bicchiere	verre	glass(-es)	Glas(n)	vaso	copo
bici, bicicletta	vélo	bike	Fahrrad(n)	bici	bicicleta
bicicletta	bicyclette	bicycle	Fahrrad(n)	bicicleta	bicicleta
bicipite	biceps	biceps	Bizeps(m)	bíceps	biceps
bidone	bidon	can	Kanister(m)	bidón, lata	cantil
bidonville	bidonville	shanty-town	Elendsviertel(n)	chabolas	bairro de lata
biglia	bille	marble	Murmel(f)	bola	berlinde
biglietteria	guichet	booking office	Fahrkartenschalter(m)	taquilla	bilheteira
biglietto	billet	ticket	Fahrkarte(f)	billete	bilhete
biglietto	ticket	ticket	Karte(f); Fahrkarte(f)	ticket, billete	bilhete
biglietto	billet	ticket	Los(n)	billete	bilhete
biglietto da visita	carte de visite	visiting card	Visitenkarte(f)	tarjeta de visita	cartão de visita
biglietto di auguri	carte de voeux	greeting(s) card	Glückwunschkarte(f)	postal, carta	cartão(festas)
bilancia	balance, bascule	scales	Waage(f)	balanza	balança
bilancio	budget	budget	Budget(n)	presupuesto	orçamento
bilancio	bilan	balance-sheet	Bilanz(f)	balance	balanço
biliardo	billard	billiards	Billard(n)	billar	bilhar
bilingue	bilingue	bilingual	zweisprachig	bilingüe	bilingue
binario, marciapiede	quai	platform	Bahnsteig(m)	andén	plataforma
binocolo	jumelles	binoculars	Fernglas(n)	gemelos	binóculos
biografia	biographie	biography	Lebensbeschreibung(f)	biografía	biografia
biologia	biologie	biology	Biologie(f)	biología	biologia
biondo, a	blond, e	fair, blond	blond	rubio(pelo)	louro, a
birbante, birichino, a	coquin, e	mischievous	schelmisch	travieso, a	travesso, a; maroto, a

Italian	French	English	German	Spanish	Portuguese
birillo	quille	skittle	Kegel(f)	bolos(juego)	paulitos
birra	bière	beer	Bier(n)	cerveza	cerveja
bisbigliare	chuchoter	whisper	flüstern	susurrar	sussurrar
biscotto	biscuit	biscuit	Keks(m)	galleta	biscoito
bisognare	falloir	have to, must	müssen	necesario(ser)	preciso(ser)
bisogno	besoin	need	Bedürfnis(n)	necesidad	necessidade
bisogno(avere)	besoin(avoir)	require, need	brauchen	necesitar	necessidade(ter)
bistecca	bifteck	steak	Beefsteak(n)	bistec	bife
bisturi	bistouri	scalpel, bistoury	Skalpell(n)	bisturí	bisturi
bitume	bitume	asphalt, tarmac	Asphalt(m)	asfalto	asfalto
bivacco	bivouac	bivouac	Biwak(m)	vivaque	acampamento
blindato, a	blindé, e	armoured	gepanzert	blindado, a	blindado, a
bloccaggio	blocage	jamming	Blockierung(f), Sperre	bloqueo	bloqueamento
bloccare	bloquer	block	blockieren	bloquear	bloquear
blocco	bloc	block	Block(m)	bloque	bloco
blocco	bloc	pad	Block(m)	bloc	bloco
blocco	blocage	freeze	Preisstopp(m)	congelación	congelamento
blocco	blocus	blockade	Blockade(f)	bloqueo	bloqueio
blu	bleu, e	blue	blau	azul	azul
blusa, camice	blouse	overall	Kittel(m)	bata, blusa	bata
boa	bouée	buoy	Boje(f)	boya	bóia
bobina	bobine	reel	Spule(f)	bobina, carrete	bobina
bocca	bouche	mouth	Mund(m)	boca	boca
boccale, vaso	bocal	jar	Glasgefäß(n)	tarro, bocal	boião
boccetta	flacon	bottle(small)	Fläschchen(n)	frasco	frasco
boccia	boule	bowl	Kugel(f)	bola	bola
bocciare	échouer(examen)	fail	durch = fallen	suspender	ficar mal(exame)
boccone	bouchée	mouthful	Bissen(m)	bocado	bocado
bolla	bulle	bubble	Blase(f)	burbuja	bolha
bolla, vescica	ampoule	blister	Blase(f)	ampolla	empola
bolla, buono, bolletta	bon	form, slip, voucher	Bestellschein(m)	orden, pedido	nota
bollente	bouillant, e	boiling	kochend	hirviente	fervente
bollettino	bulletin	bulletin, report	Bericht(m)	boletín	boletim
bollire	bouillir	boil	kochen	hervir	ferver
bollitore	bouilloire	kettle	Wasserkessel(m)	hervidor	chaleira
bomba	bombe	bomb	Bombe(f)	bomba	bomba
bomba a mano	grenade	grenade	Handgranate(f)	granada	granada
bontà	bonté	kindness	Güte(f)	bondad	bondade
bordo, riva, orlo	bord	side; edge	Rand(m)	borde	borda
bordo, lungo	bordure	edge, border	Rand(m)	bordura; ribete	borda, orla
borghese	bourgeois, e	middle class	Bürger(in f)m	burgués, a	burguês, a
borghesia	bourgeoisie	middle class	Bürgertum(n)	burguesía	burguesia
borsa	sac	bag	Tasche(f)	bolsa, saco	saco
borsa, astuccio	trousse	kit, case, bag	Etui(n), Tasche(f)	maletín, estuche	estojo
Borsa	Bourse(la)	Stock Exchange	Börse(f)	Bolsa	Bolsa
borsa da viaggio	sac de voyage	travel-bag	Reisetasche(f)	bolso de viaje	saco de viagem
borsa di studio	bourse	grant; scholarship	Stipendium(n)	beca	bolsa
borsetta	sac à main	handbag	Handtasche(f)	bolso	carteira
boscaglia	brousse	bush(the)	Busch(m)	maleza	mato
bosco	bois	wood	Wald(m)	bosque	bosque
botanica	botanique	botany	Botanik(f)	botánica	botânica
botte, barile	tonneau	barrel	Faß(n)	tonel; barril	tonel; barril
bottega	magasin, boutique	shop	Laden(m)	tienda, comercio	loja
bottiglia	bouteille	bottle	Flasche(f)	botella	garrafa
bottino	butin	spoils	Beute(f)	botín	despojo
bottone	bouton	button	Knopf(m)	botón	botão
bottone, pulsante	bouton	switch	Schalter(m)	interruptor, botón	interruptor
bouquet, aroma	bouquet	bouquet	Blume(f), Bukett(n)	buqué, aroma, boca	aroma
braccialetto	bracelet	bracelet	Armband(n)	pulsera	pulseira
braccio	bras	arm	Arm(m)	brazo	braço
brace	braise	embers	Glut(f)	brasa	brasa
branco	troupeau	herd	Herde(f)	ganado	manada
brano, estratto	extrait	extract	Auszug(m)	pasaje, trozo	excerto, trecho
bravo, a	brave	decent, nice	brav, nett, angenehm	bueno, a	amável
breccia	brèche	breach, gap	Spalt(m), Bresche(f)	brecha	brecha
bretella	bretelle(s)	braces	Hosenträger(m)	tirantes	suspensórios
breve	bref, brève	brief, short	kurz	breve	breve
brevetto	brevet	patent	Patent(n)	patente	patente

Italian	French	English	German	Spanish	Portuguese
bricolage	bricolage	odd-jobs	Basteln(n)	bricolage, maña	bricolage
brigante	brigand	bandit	Räuber(in f)m	maleante	bandido
brigata, squadra	brigade	brigade	Brigade(f)	brigada	brigada
brillante	brillant, e	bright, shining	glänzend	brillante	brilhante
brillante	luisant, e	shining, bright	leuchtend	reluciente	brilhante
brillante	brillant, e	brilliant	prächtig, brillant	brillante	brilhante
brillare	briller	shine	glänzen	brillar	brilhar
brina	givre	frost	Reif(m)	escarcha	geada
brio	entrain	liveliness	Schwung(m)	vivacidad	entusiasmo
brivido	frisson	shiver	Schauer(m)	escalofrío	arrepio
brodo	bouillon	stock, broth	Brühe(f)	caldo	caldo
bronchite	bronchite	bronchitis	Bronchitis(f)	bronquitis	bronquite
bronco(bronchi)	bronche(s)	bronchial tubes	Bronchie(f)	bronquios	brônquios
brontolare	râler	moan, groan	nörgeln	refunfuñar	resmungar
brontolare	rouspéter	grouse, moan	meckern, murren	refunfuñar	rezingar
brontolone	grognon, ne	grumpy	quengelig	gruñón, a	rabugento, a
bronzo	bronze	bronze	Bronze(f)	bronce	bronze
bruciare	brûler	burn	verbrennen	quemar	queimar, arder
bruciatura	brûlure	burn	Verbrennung(f)	quemadura	queimadura
brufolo, foruncolo	bouton	spot, pimple	Pickel(m)	grano	borbulha
brulicare	grouiller	crawl with	wimmeln	hormiguear	pulular
bruno, a	brun, ne	brown	braun	pardo, a	castanho, a
brusco, a	brusque	abrupt, sudden	brüsk	brusco, a	brusco, a
brutale	brutal, e	brutal	brutal	brutal	brutal
brutalità	brutalité	brutality	Brutalität, Roheit(f)	brutalidad	brutalidade
brutta copia	brouillon	rough paper	Schmierzettel(m)	borrador	rascunho
brutto, a	laid, e; moche	ugly, hideous	häßlich, gräßlich	feo, a	feio, a
buca	trou	pit, hole	Grube(f)	hoyo	cova
buca delle lettere	boîte(lettres)	letter box	Briefkasten(m)	buzón	caixa do correio
bucare	trouer	hole, pierce	durchlöchern	agujerear	furar, esburacar
bucare, forare	percer	drill; pierce	bohren	perforar	furar
bucare, scoppiare	crever	puncture, burst	platzen, bersten	reventar	rebentar; furar
buco(a), foro	trou	hole	Loch(n)	agujero	buraco, furo
bue; manzo	boeuf	bullock; beef	Ochse(m); Rind(n)	buey; carne de vaca	boi; carne de vaca
buffo, a	drôle	funny	lustig	gracioso, a	divertido, a
buffo, a; divertente	amusant, e	funny, amusing	lustig, amüsant	divertido, a	divertido, a
bugia	mensonge	lie, fib	Lüge(f)	mentira	mentira
bugiardo, a	menteur, se	liar	Lügner(in f)m	mentiroso, a	mentiroso, a
bullone	boulon	bolt	Bolzen(m)	perno, tornillo	parafuso; cavilha
buon appetito!	bon appétit!	enjoy your meal!	Guten Appetit!	que aproveche(!)	bom proveito!
buon prezzo	bon marché	cheap	billig	barato, a	barato, a
buon viaggio	bon voyage	good trip(have a)	gute Reise	buen viaje	boa viagem
buona fortuna	bonne chance	good luck	viel Glück	buena suerte	boa sorte
buona notte	bonne nuit	good night	gute Nacht	buenas noches	boa noite
buonasera	bonsoir	good evening	guten Abend	buenas tardes	boa tarde
buona sera!	bonjour!	good afternoon!	guten Tag!	hola(!)	bom dia!
buongiorno!	bonjour!	good morning!/aft-	guten Morgen!/-Tag	hola(!)	bom dia!
buongiorno	bonjour	hello	guten Tag	buenos días	bom dia
buono, a	bon, ne	good	gut	bueno, a	bom, boa
buono, a	bon, aimable	kind, kindly	gütig, liebvoll	bueno, a	bom, boa
buono, a; bravo, a	sage	good	brav	bueno, a	ajuizado, a
burattino	pantin	puppet	Hampelmann(m)	títere	fantoche
burlarsi	moquer(se)	make fun of, mock	verspotten	mofarse, burlarse	troçar
burrasca	bourrasque	squall	Windstoß(m)	borrasca	borrasca
burro	beurre	butter	Butter(f)	mantequilla	manteiga
burrone	ravin	ravine	Schlucht(f); Graben(m)	barranco	barranco
bussare	frapper	knock	an = klopfen	llamar	bater
bussola	boussole	compass	Kompaß(m)	brújula	bússola
busta	enveloppe	envelope	Umschlag(m)(Brief-)	sobre	envelope
bustarella	pot-de-vin	bribe	Schmiergelder(pl.)	soborno	suborno
bustina	sachet	bag(small), sachet	Beutel(m), Tütchen(n)	bolsita	pacote; carteira
busto	buste	bust	Oberkörper(m)	busto	busto
buttare	jeter	throw away(out)	weg = werfen	echar, tirar	deitar fora

I

C

Italian	French	English	German	Spanish	Portuguese
cabaret	cabaret	cabaret; nightclub	Kabarett(n)	cabaret	cabaret
cabina	cabine	cabin	Kabine(f)	cabina	cabine
cabina(telefonica)	cabine(téléph.)	phone box	Telefonzelle(f)	cabina(telefónica)	cabine(telefónica)
cacao	cacao	cocoa, cacao	Kakao(m)	cacao	cacau
caccia	chasse	hunting	Jagd(f)	caza	caça
cacciare	chasser	hunt	jagen	cazar	caçar
cacciatore	chasseur	hunter	Jäger(in f)m	cazador	caçador
cacciavite	tournevis	screwdriver	Schraubenzieher(m)	destornillador	chave de parafusos
cachet, compenso	cachet	fee	Honorar(n); Gage(f)	remuneración	remuneração
cadavere	cadavre	corpse	Leiche(f)	cadáver	cadáver
cadavere	macchabée	corpse	Leiche(f)	cadáver	cadáver
cadenza	cadence	rate, rhythm	Rhythmus(m)	cadencia	cadência
cadere	tomber	fall	fallen	caer	cair
cadere(lasciar)	tomber(laisser)	drop	fallenlassen	caer(dejar)	cair(deixar)
cadetto, a	cadet, te	younger; youngest	Jüngere(m, f)	menor	novo, a(o, a mais)
caduta	chute	fall	Fall(m)	caída	queda
caffè	café	coffee	Kaffee(m)	café	café
caffettiera	cafetière	coffee-pot	Kaffeemaschine(f)	cafetera	cafeteira
calamita	aimant	magnet	Magnet(m)	imán	íman
calare, abbassare	baisser, abaisser	lower	herunter = lassen	bajar	baixar, abaixar
calcestruzzo	béton	concrete	Beton(m)	hormigón	betão
calcio	coup de pied	kick	Fußtritt(m)	patada	pontapé
calcio	football	football, soccer	Fußball(m)	fútbol	futebol
calcio	crosse	butt; grip, handle	Gewehrkolben(m)	culata	coronha
calcio	calcium	calcium	Kalzium(n)	calcio	cálcio
calcolare	calculer	calculate, reckon	rechnen, berechnen	calcular	calcular
calcolatrice	calculatrice	calculator	Rechenmaschine(f)	calculadora	calculadora
calcolo	calcul	calculation	Berechnung(f)	cálculo	cálculo
caldo	chaleur	heat	Hitze(f)	calor	calor
caldo, a	chaud, e	hot	heiß	caliente	quente
caldo, a	chaud, e	warm	warm	cálido, a	cálido, a
calendario	calendrier	calendar	Kalender(m)	calendario	calendário
calibro	calibre	bore, calibre	Kaliber(n)	calibre	calibre
calice	coupe	glass(-es)	Kelch(m), Schale(f)	copa	taça
calma, quiete	calme	calm, quiet, still	Ruhe(f), Stille(f)	calma, sosiego	calma, sossego
calmante	calmant	sedative	Beruhigungsmittel(n)	calmante	calmante
calmare	calmer	calm	beruhigen	calmar	acalmar
calmare	apaiser	calm, soothe	beruhigen	apaciguar	acalmar
calmo, a	calme	calm, quiet, still	ruhig, still	tranquilo, a	calmo, a
calmo, a; silenzioso, a	calme, tranquille	still	still	quieto, a; tranquilo	quieto, a
calo	baisse	fall, drop	Senkung(f)	baja	baixa
calore; caldo	chaleur	heat	Hitze(f)	calor	calor
caloria	calorie	calorie	Kalorie(f)	caloría	caloria
caloroso, a	chaleureux, se	hearty, warm	herzlich	caluroso, a	caloroso, a
calunnia	calomnie	slander	Verleumdung(f)	calumnia	calúnia
calvo, a	chauve	bald	glatzköpfig	calvo, a	calvo, a; careca
calza	bas	stocking	Strumpf(m)(Nylon-)	media	meias
calza, e; calzini	chaussette(s)	sock	Socke(f), Strumpf(m)	calcetín(es)	peúga
calzarsi	chausser(se)	put on(shoes)	Schuhe anziehen, sich	calzarse	calçar-se
calzino	socquette	sock(ankle-)	Socke(f)	calcetín	meias
cambiamento	changement	change	Veränderung(f)	cambio	mudança
cambiare	changer	change	ändern	mudar	mudar; trocar
cambiare	changer	shift	wechseln	cambiar	mudar; remover
cambio	change	exchange	Wechsel(m)(Geld-)	cambio	câmbio
camera, stanza	chambre	bedroom, room	Zimmer(n)(Schlaf-)	cuarto	quarto
camera	chambre d'hôtel	room, hotel room	Hotelzimmer(n)	habitación	quarto
camera	chambre	chamber	Kammer(f)	cámara	câmara
camera	Chambre(députés) House, Chamber		Abgeordnetenhaus(n)	cámara(diputados)	câmara
camera singola	chambre à 1 lit	single room	Einzelzimmer(n)	habitación(I cama)	quarto individual
cameriera	femme de chambre chambermaid		Zimmermädchen(n)	camarera	empregada
cameriere	garçon	waiter	Ober(m)	camarero	criado

Italian	French	English	German	Spanish	Portuguese
cameriere, a	serveur, se	waiter, waitress	Kellner(in f)m	camarero, a	criado, a; moço
camerino	loge	box	Loge(f)	camerino	camarim
camicia	chemise	shirt	Hemd(n)	camisa	camisa
camicia da notte	chemise de nuit	nightdress(-es)	Nachthemd(n)	camisón	camisa de noite
camino	cheminée	chimney; fire-place	Kamin(m)	chimenea	chaminé
camion	camion	lorry	Lastwagen(m)	camión	camião
cammello	chameau	camel	Kamel(n)	camello	camelo
camminare	marcher, cheminer	walk	laufen, gehen	caminar	caminhar
cammino	chemin	path; way	Weg(m)	camino	caminho
cammino, strada	chemin, voie	way	Weg(m)	camino	caminho
campagna	campagne	country(side)	Land(n)	campo	campo
campagna	campagne	campaign	Wahlkampf(m)	campaña	campanha
campana	cloche	bell	Glocke(f)	campana	sino
campanello	sonnette	bell	Klingel(f)	timbre	campainha
campeggiare	camper	camp	zelten	acampar	acampar
campeggio	camping(aire de)	camp(ing) site	Campingplatz(m)	camping	campismo
campionato	championnat	championship	Meisterschaft(f)	campeonato	campeonato
campione, -essa	champion, ne	champion	Meister(in f)m	campeón, a	campeão, campeã
campione	échantillon	sample	Probe(f), Muster(n)	muestra	amostra
campo	champ	field	Feld(n)	campo	campo
campo, settore	domaine	field, scope	Bereich(m)	campo, área	domínio
canaglia	crapule	crook, villain	Lump(m)	granuja; pillo, a	crápula
canale	canal	canal	Kanal(m)	canal	canal
canale	chaîne	channel	Programm, Fernseh-	cadena	canal
canale	chenal	channel	Fahrwasser(n)	canal	canal
canaletto di scolo	caniveau	gutter	Rinnstein(m)	arroyo	valeta
canalizzazione	canalisation	pipe	Leitung(f)(-snetz n)	canalización	canalização
cancellare	effacer	erase, rub out	radieren	borrar	apagar
cancellare	rayer	cross out	durch = streichen	rayar	riscar; cortar
cancellatura	rature	deletion	Streichung(f)	tachadura	rasura
cancelliere	chancelier	chancellor	Kanzler(in f)m	canciller	chanceler
canceroso, a	cancéreux, se	cancerous	krebsartig	canceroso, a	canceroso, a
cancrena	gangrène	gangrene	Brand(m), Wundbrand(m)	gangrena	gangrena
cancro	cancer	cancer	Krebs(m)	cáncer	cancro
candela	bougie	candle	Kerze(f)	vela	vela
candela	bougie	sparking plug	Zündkerze(f)	bujía	vela
candidato, a	candidat, e	candidate	Kandidat(in f)m	candidato, a	candidato, a
candidatura	candidature	application	Bewerbung(f)	candidatura	candidatura
candido, a	candide	ingenuous	naiv, aufrichtig	cándido, a	cândido, a
cane, cagna	chien, ne	dog, bitch(-es)	Hund(m)	perro, a	cão, cadela
canguro	kangourou	kangaroo	Känguruh(n)	canguro	cangurú
canna da pesca	canne à pêche	fishing rod	Angelrute(f)	caña de pescar	cana de pesca
cannone	canon	cannon	Kanone(f)	cañón	canhão
canoa	canoë	canoe	Kanu(n)	canoa	canoa
cànone	redevance	tax; royalty	Gebühr(f)	impuesto, tasa	taxa
canottaggio	aviron	rowing	Rudersport(m)	remo, piragua	remo
canotto	canot	dinghy	Boot(n)	bote	canoa
cantante	chanteur, se	singer	Sänger(in f)m	cantante	cantor, a
cantare	chanter	sing	singen	cantar	cantar
cantiere	chantier	work-site	Baustelle(f)	obra	obra
cantina	cave	cellar	Keller(m)	bodega, sótano	adega
canzonatura, beffa	moquerie	mockery	Spott(m)	burla, mofa	zombaria, troça
canzone; canto	chanson, chant	song	Lied(n)	canción; cante	canção; canto
caos, confusione	pagaille	mess	Durcheinander(n)	follón, lío	desordem
capace di	capable de	able to(be)	fähig	capaz de	capaz de
capacità	contenance	capacity, content	Fassungsvermögen(n)	capacidad	capacidade
capanna	case	hut	Hütte(f)	cabaña	palhota
capanna	paillotte	hut(straw-hut)	Strohhütte(f)	choza	palhota
caparra	arrhes	deposit	Anzahlung(f)	señal(dejar)	sinal
capello	cheveu(x)	hair	Haar(n)	pelo, cabello	cabelo
capellone, hippy	hippie, y	hippy	Hippie(m)	hippy, jipi	hippie
capire	comprendre	understand	verstehen	comprender	compreender
capitale	capitale	capital	Hauptstadt(f)	capital	capital(a)
capitale	capital	capital, assets	Kapital(n)	capital	capital(o)
capitalismo	capitalisme	capitalism	Kapitalismus(m)	capitalismo	capitalismo
capitano	capitaine	captain	Hauptmann(m); Kapitän	capitán	capitão
capitolare	capituler	capitulate	kapitulieren	capitular	capitular
capitolo	chapitre	chapter	Kapitel(n)	capítulo	capítulo

Italian	French	English	German	Spanish	Portuguese
capo	tête	head	Kopf(m)	cabeza	cabeça
capo	chef	head; chief; leader	Chef(in f)m	jefe	chefe
capo, dirigente	chef, dirigeant	leader	Leiter(m), Führer(m)	jefe	chefe, líder
capo, estremità	bout, extrémité	end, tip	Ende(n)	cabo	cabo
capo	cap	cape	Kap(n)	cabo	cabo
capocameriere	maître d'hôtel	head-waiter	Oberkellner(m)	jefe de hotel	mordomo
capo di stato	chef d'état	head of state	Staatsoberhaupt(n)	jefe de estado	chefe de estado
capolavoro	chef-d'oeuvre	masterpiece	Meisterwerk(n)	obra maestra	obra-prima
caporale	caporal	corporal	Gefreiter(m); Korporal	cabo(mil.)	cabo
capovolgersi	chavirer	capsize	kentern, um = kippen	zozobrar	soçobrar
cappella	chapelle	chapel	Kapelle(f)	capilla	capela
cappello	chapeau	hat	Hut(m)	sombrero	chapéu
cappio; occhiello	boucle	loop	Schleife(f)	lazo	laço
cappotto	manteau	coat	Mantel(m)	abrigo	casaco, manto
cappuccio	capuchon	cap	Kappe(f)	capuchón	capuz
capra	chèvre	goat	Ziege(f)	cabra	cabra
capriccio	caprice	caprice, whim	Laune(f)	capricho	capricho, birra
carabina	carabine	rifle	Gewehr(n), Karabiner m	carabina	espingarda
carabiniere	gendarme	policeman(-men)	Polizist(in f)m	guardia civil	guarda-republicano
caraffa	carafe	jug, carafe	Karaffe(f)	jarra	jarro, caneca
caramella	bonbon	sweet	Bonbon(n, m)	caramelo; bombón	rebuçado
carato	carat	carat	Karat(n)	quilate	quilate
carattere	caractère	character	Charakter(m)	carácter	carácter
carattere, lettera	caractère	letter, character	Schrifttyp(m)	letra	carácter
caratteristico, a	caractéristique	characteristic	charakteristisch	característico, a	característico, a
caratteristica	caractéristique	feature	Merkmal(n)	característica	característica
carbone	charbon	coal	Kohle(f)	carbón	carvão
carbonico, a	carbonique	carbonic	Kohlensäure(f)	carbónico, a	carbónico, a
carbonio	carbone	carbon	Kohlenstoff(m)	carbono	carbono
carburante	carburant	fuel	Treibstoff(m)	carburante	carburante
carburatore	carburateur	carburettor	Vergaser(m)	carburador	carburador
cardiaco, a	cardiaque	heart-trouble...	herzkrank	cardíaco, a	cardíaco, a
cardinale	cardinal	cardinal	Kardinal(m)	cardenal	cardeal
cardiologia	cardiologie	cardiology	Kardiologie(f)	cardiología	cardiologia
carenza	carence	deficiency	Fehlen(n), Mangel(m)	carencia	carência
carezza	caresse	caress	Streicheln(n)	caricia	carícia
carezzare	caresser	stroke	streicheln	acariciar	afagar
cargo, nave da carico	cargo	cargo(-boat)	Frachter(m)	carguero, buque	cargueiro
caricare	charger	load	laden	cargar	carregar
caricaturare	caricaturer	caricature	karikieren	caricaturar	caricaturar
carico	charge	load	Last(m)	carga, peso	carga, peso
carico	chargement	load, loading	Ladung(f)	cargamento	carregamento
carico	cargaison	cargo, freight	Ladung(f)	cargamento	carga
carie	carie	tooth decay	Karies(f)	caries	cárie
carino, a	joli, e	pretty	hübsch	bonito, a	bonito, a
carità	charité	charity	Mildtätigkeit(f)	caridad	caridade
carnagione	teint	complexion, colour	Teint(m)	tez, color	tez
carne	chair	flesh	Fleisch(m)	carne	carne
carne	viande	meat	Fleisch(n)	carne	carne
carnevale	carnaval	carnival	Karneval(m)	carnaval	carnaval
carnivoro, a	carnivore	carnivorous	fleischfressend	carnívoro, a	carnívoro, a
caro, a	cher, ère	expensive, dear	teuer	caro, a	caro, a
caro, a	cher, ère	dear	liebe(r)	querido, a	caro, a; querido, a
caro, a	chéri, e	dear, darling	Liebling(m)	querido, a	querido, a
carota	carotte	carrot	Möhre(f)	zanahoria	cenoura
carpentiere	charpentier	carpenter	Zimmermann(m)	carpintero	carpinteiro
carreggiata	chaussée	road	Fahrbahn(f)	calzada	calçada
carrello	chariot	trolley	Karre(f)	carro	carroça, carro
carretta	charrette	cart	Karren(m)	carreta, carro	carroça, carreta
carriera	carrière	career	Karriere(f)	carrera	carreira
carriola	brouette	wheelbarrow	Schubkarre(f)	carretilla	carro de mão
carrozzeria	carrosserie	body(-work)	Karosserie(f)	carrocería	carroçaria
carrozzina	landau	pram	Kinderwagen(m)	cochecito	carrinho(bebé)
carta	papier	paper	Papier(n)	papel	papel
carta da gioco	carte à jouer	card	Spielkarte(f)	carta	carta
carta da parati	tapisserie	wallpaper	Tapete(f)	empapelado	papel de parede
carta di credito	carte de crédit	credit card	Kreditkarte(f)	carta de crédito	cartão de crédito
carta d'identità	carte d'identité	identity card	Personalausweis(m)	carné de identidad	bilhete(identidade)

Italian	French	English	German	Spanish	Portuguese
carta igienica	papier toilette	toilet paper	Toilettenpapier(n)	papel higiénico	papel higiénico
cartella	cartable	briefcase; satchel	Ranzen(m)	cartera	pasta
cartello	panneau	panel	Brett(n)	tablero	painel
cartello	panneau	sign, notice	Schild(n)	señal, letrero	sinal
cartello	pancarte	sign, notice	Plakat(n), Schild(n)	pancarta	cartaz
cartilagine	cartilage	cartilage	Knorpel(m)	cartílago	cartilagem
cartoleria	papeterie	stationer's	Schreibwarenladen(m)	papelería	papelaria
cartolina	carte postale	post-card	Postkarte(f)	tarjeta postal	bilhete-postal
cartone	carton	cardboard	Pappe(f)	cartón	cartão
cartone animato	dessin animé	cartoon	Trickfilm(m)Zeichen-	dibujo animado	desenho animado
cartuccia	cartouche	cartridge	Patrone(f)	cartucho	cartucho
casa	maison	house	Haus(n)	casa	casa
casa(a)	maison(à la)	home(at)	Hause(zu)	casa(en)	casa(em)
casaccio(a)	hasard(au)	random(at)	aufs Geratewohl	azar(al)	acaso(ao)
casalinga	ménagère	housewife(-ives)	Hausfrau(f)	ama de casa	dona de casa
casalinghi	article ménager	kitchenware	Küchengerät(n)	utensilio(cocina)	utensílio(cozinha)
cascata	cascade	waterfall	Wasserfall(m)	cascada	cascata
casco, elmetto	casque	helmet	Helm(m)	casco	capacete
caserma	caserne	barracks	Kaserne(f)	cuartel	quartel
casinò	casino	casino	Kasino(n)	casino	casino
caso	cas	case	Fall(m)	caso	caso
caso	hasard	chance, luck	Zufall(m)	azar, casualidad	acaso, azar
cassa	caisse	chest, case	Kiste(f)	cajón, caja	caixa
cassa	caisse	cash-desk	Kasse(f)	caja	caixa
cassaforte	coffre-fort	safe	Safe(m)	caja fuerte	cofre-forte
casseruola	casserole	pan, saucepan	Topf(m)	cazo, cacerola	tacho, caçarola
cassetta	cassette	cassette	Kassette(f)	casete	cassete
cassetta, deposito	consigne	luggage lockers	Schließfach(n)	consigna	depósito
cassetto	tiroir	drawer	Schublade(f)	cajón	gaveta
cassiere, a	caissier, ière	cashier	Kassierer(in f)m	cajero, a	caixa(o)
cassone	bahut, coffre	chest	Truhe(f)	arca, cajón	baú, arca, armário
casta	caste	caste	Kaste(f)	casta	casta
castano, a	châtain	chestnut brown	kastanienbraun	castaño, a	castanho, a
castello	château	castle; mansion	Schloß(n)	castillo	castelo
castigo	châtiment	punishment	Bestrafung(f)	castigo	castigo
casto, a	chaste	pure	keusch	casto, a	casto, a
cataclisma	cataclysme	cataclysm	Katastrophe(f)	cataclismo	cataclismo
catalogo	catalogue	catalogue	Katalog(m)	catálogo	catálogo
catasto	cadastre	land register	Grundbuch(n)	catastro	cadastro
catastrofe	catastrophe	catastrophe	Katastrophe(f)	catástrofe	catástrofe
categoria	catégorie	category	Kategorie(f)	categoría	categoria
catena	chaîne	chain	Kette(f)	cadena	cadeia, corrente
catena(monti)	chaîne(montagne)	range(mountain)	Bergkette(f)	sierra	serra
catenaccio	verrou	bolt, lock	Riegel(m), Schloß(n)	cerrojo	ferrolho
catino	cuvette	basin, bowl	Schale(f)	palangana	bacia
cattedrale, duomo	cathédrale	cathedral	Kathedrale(f), Dom(m)	catedral	catedral
cattivo, a	mauvais, e	bad	schlecht	malo, a	mau, má
cattivo, a; male	mauvais, mal	evil, bad	übel	malo, a	mau, má
cattivo, a	méchant, e	naughty	böse, boshaft	malo, a	mau, má
cattolico, a	catholique	Catholic	katholisch	católico, a	católico, a
catturare	capturer	capture	fangen	capturar	capturar
causa	cause	cause	Ursache(f), Grund(m)	causa	causa
causa	procès	lawsuit	Prozeß(m)	pleito	pleito, processo
causare, provocare	causer, provoquer	cause	verursachen	causar, provocar	causar, provocar
causare	occasionner	cause, bring about	verursachen	ocasionar, causar	ocasionar, causar
cava	carrière	quarry	Steinbruch(m)	cantera	pedreira
cavaliere, a	cavalier, ière	rider	Reiter(in f)m	jinete, a	cavaleiro, a
cavallo	cheval	horse	Pferd(n)	caballo	cavalo
cavarsela	débrouiller(se)	manage	zu helfen wissen, sich	desenredarse	desenredar-se
cavatappi	tire-bouchon	corkscrew	Korkenzieher(m)	sacacorchos	saca-rolhas
caverna	caverne	cave, cavern	Höhle(f)	caverna	caverna
cavia	cobaye	guinea-pig(be a)	Versuchskaninchen(n)	conejillo(Indias)	cobaia
caviale	caviar	caviar	Kaviar(m)	caviar	caviar
caviglia	cheville	ankle	Knöchel(m)	tobillo	tornozelo
cavità	cavité	cavity	Hohlraum(m)	cavidad	cavidade
cavo	câble	cable	Kabel(n)	cable	cabo
cavolo	chou	cabbage	Kohl(m)	col	couve
c'è; ci sono	il y a	there is, there are	es gibt	hay	há

Italian	French	English	German	Spanish	Portuguese
cedere	céder, renoncer	give up	auf = geben; nach = geben	ceder	ceder
celebrare	célébrer	celebrate	feiern	celebrar	celebrar
celebre; famoso, a	célèbre	famous, well-known	berühmt	célèbre, famoso, a	célèbre
celeste	céleste	heavenly	himmlisch	celeste	celeste
cellulite	cellulite	fat, cellulitis	Zellulitis(f)	celulitis	celulite
cemento	ciment	cement	Zement(m)	cemento	cimento
cena	dîner	dinner	Abendessen(n)	cena	jantar
cenare	dîner	dinner(have)	Abend essen(zu)	cenar	jantar
cenare	souper	supper(have)	Abend essen(zu)	cenar	cear
cenere(-ri)	cendre(s)	ash(es)	Asche(f)	ceniza(s)	cinza
censimento	recensement	census	Volkszählung(f)	censo	recenseamento
censura	censure	censorship	Zensur(f)	censura	censura
centimetro	centimètre	centimetre	Zentimeter(n, m)	centímetro	centímetro
centinaio	centaine	hundred(about a)	Hundert(n)	centena	centena
cento	cent	hundred(one)	hundert	cien, ciento	cem, cento
centrale	central, e	central	zentral	central	central
centrale	centrale	power-station	Kraftwerk(n), Zentrale	central	central
centrifugo, a	centrifuge	centrifugal	zentrifugal	centrífugo, a	centrífugo, a
centro	centre	centre	Mitte(f)	centro	centro
centro	centre	centre	Zentrum(n)	centro	centro
centro	centre	hub	Mittelpunkt(m)	centro	centro
centro della città	centre ville	city/town centre	Stadtzentrum(n)	centro(ciudad)	centro(cidade)
ceppo, tronco	bûche	log	Scheit(n)	leño	acha
cera	cire	wax, polish	Wachs(n)	cera	cera
cera, aspetto	mine	look	Aussehen(n)	semblante, cara	aparência
cercare	chercher	look for, search -	suchen	buscar	procurar; buscar
cercare	chercher	seek	holen, suchen	buscar, investigar	procurar, buscar
cercatore	chercheur, euse	research worker	Forscher(in f)m	investigador, a	investigador, a
cerchio	cercle	circle	Kreis(m)	círculo	círculo
cerchione	jante	rim	Felge(f), Radkranz(m)	llanta	jante, camba
cereale	céréale	cereal	Getreide(n)	cereal	cereal
cerebrale	cérébral, e	cerebral	Gehirn-; zerebral	cerebral	cerebral
cerimonia	cérémonie	ceremony	Zeremonie(f)	ceremonia	cerimónia
cerniera	charnière	hinge	Scharnier(n)	bisagra	gonzo, dobradiça
cero	cierge	candle	Kerze(f)	cirio	círio
cerotto	sparadrap	plaster	Pflaster(n)	esparadrapo	esparadrapo
certamente	bien sûr	of course	natürlich	claro	claro
certamente	certainement	certainly	sicherlich	ciertamente	certamente
certezza	certitude	certainty	Gewißheit(f)	certeza	certeza
certi, e; alcuni, e	certaines	certain; some	manche	algunos, as	certos, as
certificare	certifier	certify	bescheinigen	certificar	certificar
certificato	certificat	certificate	Bescheinigung(f)	certificado	certificado
certo, a; sicuro, a	certain, e	certain, sure	sicher	cierto, a	certo, a
cervello	cerveau	brain	Gehirn(n)	cerebro	cérebro
cespuglio	buisson	bush	Gebüsch(n)	matorral	moita
cessare, smettere	cesser	stop, cease	auf = hören	cesar, parar	cessar, parar
cessazione, tregua	arrêt, cessation	stop, cessation	Stillstand(m)	cese	cessação
cestino	corbeille	basket; bin	Korb(m)(Papierkorb m)	cesto(a); cestillo	cesto, a
champagne	champagne	champagne	Champagner(m)	champaña	champanhe
che	que	that; whom; which	was, das	que, qué	que
chi, che	qui	who(m); which; that	wer; wen	quién, que	quem
chiacchierare	bavarder	chat, talk	schwätzen, schwatzen	charlar	falar, conversar
chiacchierone, a	bavard, e	talkative	geschwätzig	parlanchín, a	falador, a
chiamare	appeler	call	rufen(an =), heißen	llamar	chamar
chiamare	nommer	name	nennen	llamar	chamar
chiamarsi	nommer(se)	called(be)	heißen	llamarse	chamar-se
chiamata	appel	call	Ruf(m)(Zu-, An-)	llamada	chamada
chiarezza	clarté	brightness	Helligkeit(f)	claridad	claridade
chiarificare	clarifier	clarify	klären	clarificar	clarificar
chiaro, a; limpido, a	clair, e	clear	klar	claro, a	claro, a
chiaro, a	clair, e	light	hell	claro, a	claro, a
chiarore, luce	lueur	gleam, glow	Schimmer(m)	resplandor	luz, clarão
chiasso	vacarme	uproar, din	Krach(m)	alboroto, jaleo	barulho
chiave	clef, clé	key	Schlüssel(m)	llave	chave
chiave	clé	spanner, wrench	Schraubenschlüssel(m)	llave	chave
chicco, grano	grain	grain	Korn(n)	grano	grão
chicco	grain(café)	bean(coffee-)	Bohne(Kaffee-)(f)	grano	grão
chiedere	demander	ask(for)	fragen	pedir	pedir

Italian	French	English	German	Spanish	Portuguese
chiesa	église	church(-es)	Kirche(f)	iglesia	igreja
chilogrammo, chilo	kilogramme	kilogram(me)	Kilo(gramm n)n	kilogramo	quilograma, quilo
chilometro	kilomètre	kilometre	Kilometer(m)	kilómetro	quilómetro
chimica	chimie	chemistry	Chemie(f)	química	química
chimico, a	chimique	chemical	chemisch	químico, a	químico, a
chimono	kimono	kimono	Kimono(m)	quimono, kimono	quimono
chinare	pencher	bend, incline	niegen; biegen	inclinar(se)	inclinar
chinarsi	pencher(se)	bend, lean	bücken, sich	inclinarse	inclinar-se
chiodo	clou	nail	Nagel(m)	clavo	prego
chirurgia	chirurgie	surgery	Chirurgie(f)	cirugía	cirurgia
chirurgo	chirurgien	surgeon	Chirurg(in f)m	cirujano	cirurgião
chitarra	guitare	guitar	Gitarre(f)	guitarra	guitarra
chiudere	fermer	close, shut	schließen	cerrar	fechar, cerrar
chiudere	fermer	shut	zu = machen	cerrar	fechar
chiudere a chiave	fermer à clé	lock	ab = schließen	cerrar con llave	fechar à chave
chiunque	quiconque	anyone(who)	jeder	quienquiera	qualquer(um)
chiuso, a	fermé, e	closed, shut	zu, geschlossen	cerrado, a	fechado, a
chiusura	clôture	closure, closing	Schluß(m)(Abschluß m)	clausura	encerramento
choc, colpo	choc	shock	Schock(m)	choque	choque
ci, ce	nous	us	uns	nos	nos
ciao!	salut!	hi!, hello!	Hallo!; tschüs!; tschüß	hola(!)	olá!
ciascuno, a	chacun, e; chaque	each, every(one)	jeder, jede	cada uno(una)	cada um(uma)
cibo; nutrimento	nourriture	food	Nahrung(f)	alimento	alimentação
cicatrice	cicatrice	scar	Narbe(f)	cicatriz	cicatriz
ciclismo	cyclisme	cycling	Radfahren(n)	ciclismo	ciclismo
ciclista	cycliste	cyclist	Radfahrer(in f)m	ciclista	ciclista
ciclo	cycle	cycle	Zyklus(m)	ciclo	ciclo
ciclone	cyclone	cyclone	Wirbelwind(m)	ciclón	ciclone
cieco, a	aveugle	blind	blind	ciego, a	cego, a
cielo	ciel	sky	Himmel(m)	cielo	céu
cielo, paradiso	ciel, paradis	heaven	Himmel(m)	cielo, paraíso	céu, paraíso
cifra, numero	chiffre	figure, number	Zahl(f), Ziffer(f)	cifra, número	número
cifrare	coder	code, encode	verschlüsseln	codificar	codificar
ciglio	cil	eyelash	Wimper(f)	pestaña	pestana
cigno	cygne	swan	Schwan(m)	cisne	cisne
ciliegia	cerise	cherry	Kirsche(f)	cereza	cereja
cilindrico, a	cylindrique	cylindrical	zylindrisch	cilíndrico, a	cilíndrico, a
cilindro	cylindre	cylinder	Zylinder(m)	cilindro	cilindro
cima, vetta	cime	summit, peak, top	Gipfel(m)	cima	cimo, cume
cima; vetta	sommet	summit, top	Gipfel(m)	cumbre; cima	cimo; cume
cimitero	cimetière	cemetery	Friedhof(m)	cementerio	cemitério
cineasta	cinéaste	film-producer	Filmproduzent(in f)m	cineasta	cineasta
cinema	cinéma	cinema	Kino(n)	cine	cinema
cinepresa	caméra	cine-camera	Kamera(f)	cámara	câmara
cinghia	courroie	belt; strap	Riemen(m)	correa	correia
cinghia	sangle	strap	Riemen(m), Gurt(m)	cincha, correa	correia
cinico, a	cynique	cynical	zynisch	cínico, a	cínico, a
cinquanta	cinquante	fifty	fünfzig	cincuenta	cinquenta
cinque	cinq	five	fünf	cinco	cinco
cinta, recinto	enceinte	fence; enclosure	Einzäunung(f)	muralla	muralha, recinto
cintura	ceinture	belt	Gürtel(m)	cinturón	cinto
cinturino	bracelet	strap	Armband(n)	correa	pulseira
ciò, questo, quello	cela, ça	that	das, jene(r, s)	eso, aquello, ello	isso, aquilo
ciocca	mèche	lock(of hair)	Locke(f)	mechón	madeixa
cioccolato, a	chocolat	chocolate	Schokolade(f)	chocolate	chocolate
cioè	c'est-à-dire	that is(to say)	das heißt	es decir	quer dizer
ciottolo	galet	pebble	Kieselstein(m)	canto rodado	seixo
cipolla	oignon	onion	Zwiebel(f)	cebolla	cebola
circa	environ	about	ungefähr	aproximadamente	cerca de
circo	cirque	circus	Zirkus(m)	circo	circo
circolare	circuler	circulate	umher = gehen	circular	circular
circolare	circuler	circulate	zirkulieren	circular	circular
circolare	circulaire	circular	rund	circular	circular
circolazione	circulation	circulation	Kreislauf(m)	circulación	circulação
circondare	entourer	surround	um = geben	rodear	rodear, cercar
circonferenza	circonférence	circumference	Kreisumfang(m)	circunferencia	circunferência
circostanza	circonstance	circumstance	Umstand(m)	circunstancia	circunstância
circuito	circuit	circuit	Strecke(f)(Renn-)	circuito	circuito

I

Italian	French	English	German	Spanish	Portuguese
circuito	circuit	circuit, system	Stromkreis(m)	circuito	circuito
cirrosi	cirrhose	cirrhosis	Zirrhose(f)	cirrosis	cirrose
ciste	kyste	cyst	Zyste(f)	quiste	quisto
cistifellea	vésicule	gall-bladder	Blase(f)	vesícula	vesícula
citare	citer	quote	zitieren	citar	citar
città	ville	town	Stadt(f)	ciudad	cidade
città	cité	city	Stadt(f)	ciudad	cidade
cittadino, a	citadin, e	town/city dweller	Städter(in f)m	ciudadano, a	citadino, a
cittadino, a	citoyen, ne	citizen	Bürger(in f)m	ciudadano, a	cidadão, cidadã
civettuolo, a	coquet, te	pretty; coquettish	kokett; eitel	presumido, a	vaidoso, a
civico, a	civique	civic	staatsbürgerlich	cívico, a	cívico, a
civile	civil, e	civil	zivil	civil	civil
civilizzare	civiliser	civilize	zivilisieren	civilizar	civilizar
civiltà	civilisation	civilization	Zivilisation(f)	civilización	civilização
clacson	klaxon	horn, hooter	Hupe(f)	claxon, bocina	buzina
clan	clan	clan	Sippe(f)	clan	clã
clandestino, a	clandestin, e	clandestine	heimlich	clandestino, a	clandestino, a
clarinetto	clarinette	clarinet	Klarinette(f)	clarinete	clarinete
classe, ceto	classe	class	Klasse(f)	clase	classe
classe	classe	class, form	Klassenstufe(f)	clase, curso	classe
classico, a	classique	classical	klassisch	clásico, a	clássico, a
classificare	classer	classify, file	ordnen	clasificar	classificar
classificazione	classement	filing	Einorden(n)	clasificación	classificação
clausola	clause	clause	Klausel(f)	cláusula	cláusula
clavicola	clavicule	collar-bone	Schlüsselbein(n)	clavícula	clavícula
clero	clergé	clergy	Klerus(m)	clero	clero
cliente	client, e	customer	Kunde(m), Kundin(f)	cliente	cliente
cliente	client, e	client	Klient(in f)m	cliente	cliente
clima	climat	climate	Klima(n)	clima	clima
clinica	clinique	nursing-home	Klinik(f)	clínica	clínica
club	club	club	Klub(m)	club	clube
coagulare	coaguler	coagulate, clot	gerinnen	coagular	coagular
coalizione	coalition	coalition	Koalition(f)	coalición	coligação
cobra	cobra	cobra	Kobra(f)	cobra	cobra
cocaina	cocaïne	cocaine	Kokain(n)	cocaína	cocaína
coccodrillo	crocodile	crocodile	Krokodil(n)	cocodrilo	crocodilo
cocktail	cocktail	cocktail	Cocktail(m)	cóctel	coquetel
coda	queue	tail	Schwanz(m)	rabo	cauda
coda, fila	queue	queue	Schlange(f)	cola	bicha; fila
codice	code	code	Kod(m)	código	código
codificare	codifier	codify	kodifizieren	codificar	codificar
coefficiente	coefficient	coefficient	Koeffizient(m)	coeficiente	coeficiente
coerente	cohérent, e	coherent	zusammenhängend	coherente	coerente
coesione	cohésion	cohesion	Zusammenhalt(m)	cohesión	coesão
cofano	capot	bonnet, hood	Motorhaube(f)	capó	capota
cogliere, raccogliere	cueillir	pick, gather	pflücken	coger, recoger	colher
cognata	belle-soeur	sister-in-law	Schwägerin(f)	cuñada	cunhada
cognato	beau-frère	brother-in-law	Schwager(m)	cuñado	cunhado
cognome	nom	surname	Familienname(m)	apellido	apelido
coincidenza	coincidence	coincidence	Zusammentreffen(n)	coincidencia	coincidência
coincidenza	correspondance	connection	Verbindung, Anschluß	empalme	correspondência
colazione(prima)	déjeuner(petit)	breakfast	Frühstück(n)	desayuno	almoço(pequeno)
colera	choléra	cholera	Cholera(f)	cólera	cólera
colica	colique	colic	Kolik(f)	cólico	cólica
colla	colle	glue	Klebstoff(m)	cola, pegamento	cola
collaboratore, trice	collaborateur	assistant	Mitarbeiter(in f)m	colaborador, a	colaborador, a
collaborazione	collaboration	collaboration	Mitarbeit(f)	colaboración	colaboração
collana	collier	necklace	Halskette(f); Kette(f)	collar	colar
collant	collants	tights(pair of)	Strumpfhose(f)	pantys	meias
colle, collinetta	coteau	hill(side)	Anhöhe(f), Hang(m)	ladera	encosta; colina
colle, passo	col	pass	Paß(m)	puerto	desfiladeiro
collega	collègue	colleague	Kollege(m), Kollegin f	colega	colega
collegamento	liaison	connection, link	Verbindung(f)	relación; enlace	ligação, junção
collegamento	liaison	link	Verbindung(f)	enlace	conexão
collegare	relier	link, connect	verbinden	enlazar, unir	ligar
collegiale	pensionnaire	boarder	Internatsschüler(m)	interno, a	interno, a
collegio	collège	college	Kollegium(n)	colegio	colégio
collera, ira	colère	anger(be angry)	Wut(f)	cólera, ira	cólera, ira

Italian	French	English	German	Spanish	Portuguese
collettivo, a	collectif, ive	collective	gemeinschaftlich	colectivo, a	colectivo, a
collezionare	collectionner	collect	sammeln	coleccionar	coleccionar
collezione	collection	collection	Kollektion(f)	colección	colecção
collezione	collection	collection	Sammlung(f)	colección	colecção
collina	colline	hill	Hügel(m)	colina	colina
collisione	collision	collision	Zusammenstoß(m)	colisión, choque	colisão, choque
collo	cou	neck	Hals(m), Nacken(m)	cuello	pescoço
collo, colletto	col	collar	Kragen(m)	cuello	colarinho; gola
collo	goulot	neck(bottle)	Hals(m)(Flaschen)	gollete	gargalo
collocare, porre	placer, disposer	place, install	setzen, stellen	colocar	colocar; pôr
collocare	placer, poser	place	stellen	poner, colocar	pôr, colocar
colloquio	entretien	talk, conversation	Gespräch(n)	conversación	entrevista
colloquio	colloque	symposium	Symposium(n)	coloquio	colóquio
colonia	colonie	colony	Kolonie(f)	colonia	colónia
colonizzazione	colonisation	colonization	Kolonisierung(f)	colonización	colonização
colonna	colonne	column	Säule(f)	columna	coluna
colonna vertebrale	colonne(vertéb-)	spine	Wirbelsäule(f)	columna vertebral	coluna vertebral
colonnello	colonel	colonel	Oberst(m)	coronel	coronel
colorante	colorant	colouring	Farbstoff(m)	colorante	corante
colorare	colorier	colour(in)	an = malen	colorear	colorir
colore	couleur	colour	Farbe(f)	color	côr
colossale	colossal, e	colossal	riesig	colosal	colossal
colpa	faute	fault	Fehler(m)	culpa	culpa
colpevole	coupable	guilty	schuldig	culpable	culpado, a
colpevole	fautif, ive	wrong(in the)	schuldig	culpable	culpado, a
colpevolezza	culpabilité	guilt	Schuld(f)	culpabilidad	culpabilidade
colpo	coup	knock, blow	Schlag(m)	golpe	golpe
coltello	couteau	knife(-ives)	Messer(n)	cuchillo	faca
coltivare	cultiver	cultivate	bebauen, züchten	cultivar	cultivar
coltivare	cultiver	cultivate, grow	an = bauen, an = pflanzen	cultivar	cultivar
coltivatore, trice	cultivateur	farmer	Landwirt(in f)m	cultivador, a	lavrador, a
colto, a	cultivé, e	cultured, learned	gebildet	culto, a	culto, a
coltura	culture	cultivation	Anbau(m)	cultivo	cultura
coma	coma	coma	Koma(n)	coma	coma
comandante	commandant	major	Kommandant(m), Major m	comandante	comandante
comandare	commander	command	befehlen, befehligen	ordenar, mandar	comandar
comandare, ordinare	ordonner	command, order	befehlen, beherrschen	mandar, ordenar	mandar, ordenar
comando	commandement	command	Befehl(m)(-sgewalt f)	mando	comando
combattente	combattant, e	fighting-man	Kämpfer(m)	combatiente	combatente
combattere	combattre	fight	streiten, kämpfen	combatir	combater
combattimento	combat	combat, fight	Kampf(m)	combate	combate
combinazione	combinaison	combination	Kombination(f)	combinación	combinação
combustibile	combustible	combustible	verbrennbar	combustible	combustível
come	comme	as; like	wie	como	como
come	comment	how	wie	cómo	como
come?, come dice?	comment?	pardon?	wie bitte?	cómo(?)	como disse?
cometa	comète	comet	Komet(m)	cometa	cometa
comico, a	comique	comic, funny	komisch	cómico, a	cómico, a
comico	comique	comedian, comic	Komiker(in f)m	cómico	cómico
cominciare	commencer	begin, start	an = fangen	comenzar	começar
comitato	comité	committee	Komitee(n), Ausschuß m	comité	comissão
commando	commando	commando	Kommando(n)	comando	comando
commedia	comédie	comedy	Komödie(f)	comedia	comédia
commedia	pièce	play	Stück(n)	obra	peça
commediante	comédien, ne	comedian	Komödiant(in f)m	comediante, a	comediante, a
commemorare	commémorer	commemorate	gedenken	conmemorar	comemorar
commensale	convive	guest	Gast(m)	convidado, a	conviva
commentare	commenter	comment(on)	erläutern	comentar	comentar
commentario	commentaire	commentary	Kommentar(m)	comentario	comentário
commento	commentaire	comment	Anmerkung(f)	comentario	comentário
commerciale	commercial	commercial	geschäftlich	comercial	comercial
commercializzare	commercialiser	market	vermarkten	comercializar	comercializar
commerciante	commerçant, e	tradesman(-men)	Geschäftsmann(m)	comerciante	comerciante
commercio	commerce	trade, commerce	Handel(m)	comercio	comércio
commesso, a	vendeur, se	sales assistant	Verkäufer(in f)m	vendedor, a	vendedor, a
commestibile	comestible	edible	eßbar	comestible	comestível
commettere	commettre	commit	begehen, verüben	cometer	cometer
commissariato	commissariat	police station	Kommissariat(n)	comisaría	esquadra(polícia)

I

Italian	French	English	German	Spanish	Portuguese
commissione	commission	commission	Kommission(f)	comisión	comissão
commissione	commission	committee	Ausschuß(m)	comisión	comissão
commosso, a	ému, e	moved, affected	gerührt	emocionado, a	comovido, a
commovente	émouvant, e	moving	ergreifend	emocionante	comovente
commuovere	émouvoir	move	rühren	conmover	comover
commuovere	toucher, émouvoir	affect	rühren	afectar	afectar
commutatore	commutateur	switch	Schalter(m)	conmutador	comutador
comodità	confort	comfort	Bequemlichkeit(f)	confort	conforto
comodo, a	commode	convenient	praktisch	cómodo, a	cómodo, a
compagnia	compagnie	company	Gesellschaft(f)	compañía	companhia
compagnia(in)	compagnie(en)	company of(in the)	Gesellschaft(in)	compañía(en)	companhia(em)
compagno, a	compagnon, agne	companion	Begleiter(in f)m	compañero, a	companheiro, a
compagno, a	camarade	friend	Kamerad(in f)m	compañero, a	camarada
comparire	paraître	appear	erscheinen	parecer, aparecer	parecer, aparecer
compartimento	compartiment	compartment	Abteil(n)	compartimiento	compartimento
compasso	compas	compass(es)	Kompaß(m)	compás	compasso
compatire	compatir	sympathize	mit = fühlen	compadecer	apiedar-se
compatire	plaindre	pity	bedauern	compadecer	lastimar
compatto, a	compact, e	compact	kompakt	compacto, a	compacto, a
compenso	compensation	compensation	Kompensation(f)	compensación	compensação
competente	compétent, e	competent	kompetent	competente, capaz	competente, capaz
competenza	compétence	competence	Zuständigkeit(f)	competencia	competência
competizione, gara	compétition	competition	Wettbewerb(m)	competición	competição
compiere	accomplir	perform, accomplish	aus = führen, vollenden	cumplir, realizar	realizar
compiere, effettuare	accomplir	accomplish	vollführen	realizar, efectuar	realizar
compiere, realizzare	accomplir	achieve	vollbringen	ejecutar, realizar	realizar
compitare, sillabare	épeler	spell	buchstabieren	deletrear	soletrar
compito	devoir	homework; exercise	Aufgabe(f)	deber, tarea	dever
compito	tâche	task	Aufgabe(f)	tarea	tarefa
compleanno	anniversaire	birthday	Geburtstag(m)	cumpleaños	aniversário
complemento	complément	complement	Ergänzung(f)	complemento	complemento
complessivo, a	total, e	overall	Gesamt-	total	total
complesso	complexe	complex	Komplex(m)	complejo	complexo
completamente	complètement	completely	völlig	completamente	completamente
completo, a	complet, ète	complete, full	vollständig, voll	completo, a	completo, a
complicato, a	compliqué, e	complicated	kompliziert	complicado, a	complicado, a
complice	complice	accomplice	Komplize m, Komplizin	cómplice	cúmplice
complimenti!	félicitations!	congratulations!	Glückwunsch!	enhorabuena(!)	parabéns!
complimento	compliment	compliment	Kompliment(n)	cumplido	cumprimento
complotto	complot	conspiracy, plot	Verschwörung(f)	complot	conspiração
componente	composant	component	Bestandteil(m)	componente	componente
comporre	composer	compose	zusammen = stellen	componer	compor
comporre(numero)	composer(n°tél)	dial	Nummer(f)(wählen)	marcar un número	discar, marcar
comportamento	comportement	behaviour	Verhalten(n)	comportamiento	comportamento
comportare	entraîner	entail	mit sich bringen	ocasionar	acarretar
compositore	compositeur	composer	Komponist(in f)m	compositor	compositor
composizione	composition	composition	Zusammensetzung(f)	composición	composição
comprare	acheter	buy	kaufen	comprar	comprar
comprendere	comprendre	comprise	ein = begreifen	comprender	compreender
comprendere	comprendre	understand	begreifen, verstehen	entender	entender
compressa	comprimé	tablet, pill	Tablette(f)	comprimido	comprimido
compressione	compression	compression	Druck(m)	compresión	compressão
comprimere	comprimer	compress	drücken	comprimir	comprimir
compromesso	compromis	compromise	Kompromiß(m)	compromiso	compromisso
compromettere	compromettre	compromise	bloß = stellen(jdn.)	comprometer	comprometer
compromissione	compromission	compromising	Kompromittierung(f)	compromiso	comprometimento
computer	ordinateur	computer	Computer(m)	ordenador	computador
comune	commun, e	common, usual	gewöhnlich	común	comum
comune	commun, e	common	Gemeinschafts-	común	comum
comunicare	communiquer	communicate	mitteilen	comunicar	comunicar
comunicazione	communication	communication	Verständigung(f)	comunicación	comunicação
comunismo	communisme	communism	Kommunismus(m)	comunismo	comunismo
comunità	communauté	community	Gemeinschaft(f)	comunidad	comunidade
con	avec	with	mit	con	com
concedere, accordare	accorder	grant	bewilligen	conceder	conceder
concentrare	concentrer	concentrate	konzentrieren	concentrar	concentrar
concentrarsi	concentrer(se)	concentrate	konzentrieren, sich	concentrar(se)	concentrar-se
concepire	concevoir	conceive(of)	vor = stellen, sich	concebir	conceber

Italian	French	English	German	Spanish	Portuguese
concertazione	concertation	cooperation	Zusammenarbeit(f)	concertación	concertação
concerto	concert	concert	Konzert(n)	concierto	concerto
concetto	concept	concept	Begriff(m)	concepto	conceito
concezione	conception	conception	Konzeption(f)	concepción	concepção
conchiglia	coquille	shell	Schale(f), Muschel(f)	concha	concha
conchiglia	coquillage	shell-fish; shell	Muschel(f)	marisco	concha
concime	engrais	fertilizer, manure	Dünger(m)	abono	adubo
concludere	conclure	conclude	schließen, abschließen	concluir	concluir
conclusione	conclusion	conclusion	Abschluß(m)	conclusión	conclusão
concordare	concorder	tally, agree	überein = stimmen	concordar	concordar
concorrente	concurrent, e	competitor	konkurrent(in f)m	competidor, a	concorrente
concorrenza	concurrence	competition	Konkurrenz(f)	competencia	concorrência
concorso	concours	competition	Wettbewerb(m)	concurso	concurso
concorso	concours	competitive exam	Prüfung(f)	oposiciones	concurso
concorso	concours	cooperation, help	Mitwirkung(unter)	ayuda	colaboração
concreto, a	concret, ète	concrete	konkret	concreto, a	concreto, a
concubinato	concubinage	co-habitation	wilde Ehe(f)	concubinato	concubinato
condanna	condamnation	sentence	Verurteilung(f)	condenación	condenação
condannare	condamner	condemn	verurteilen	condenar	condenar
condannare	condamner	convict, sentence	verurteilen	condenar	condenar
condensazione	condensation	condensation	Kondensierung(f)	condensación	condensação
condimento	assaisonnement	seasoning	Würze(f)	aliño	tempero
condizionatore	climatiseur	air conditioner	Klimaanlage(f)	climatizador	climatizador
condizione	condition	condition	Bedingung(f)	condición	condição
condizione	état	condition	Zustand(m)	condición	estado
condotto(a)	conduit(e)	pipe	Röhre(f), Leitung(f)	caño, conducto	cano, tubo
conducente	conducteur, trice	driver	Fahrer(in f)m	conductor, a	condutor, a
condurre	mener, conduire	lead	führen	guiar, conducir	levar, conduzir
conferenza	conférence	conference; lecture	Konferenz(f)	conferencia	conferência
conferenza	conférence	lecture	Vorlesung(f), Vortrag	conferencia	conferência
conferire	décerner	award	zu = erkennen, erteilen	otorgar	atribuir
confermare	confirmer	confirm	bestätigen	confirmar	confirmar
confessare	avouer	confess, admit	gestehen	confesar	confessar
confessione	aveu	confession	Geständnis(n)	confesión	confissão
confetteria	confiserie	sweet shop	Süßwarenladen(m)	confitería	confeitaria
confezione	confection	clothing industry	Anfertigung(f)	confección	confecção
confidenza	confidence	confidence, secret	Vertrauen(im)	confidencia	confidência
confidenziale	confidentiel, le	confidential	vertraulich	confidencial	confidencial
confine, frontiera	frontière	border, frontier	Grenze(f)	frontera	fronteira
conflitto	conflit	conflict	Konflikt(m)	conflicto	conflito
confondere	confondre	confuse, mistake	verwechseln	confundir	confundir
conforme a	conforme à	in accordance with	entsprechend	conforme a/con	conforme com
confortevole	confortable	comfortable	bequem	cómodo, a	confortável
confrontare	confronter	confront	konfrontieren	confrontar	confrontar
confusione	confusion	confusion	Verwechslung(f)	confusión	confusão
confuso, a; torbido, a	trouble	troubled	verworren	confuso, a	confuso, a
confutare	réfuter	refute	widerlegen	refutar	refutar
congelamento	gélure	frostbite	Erfrierung(f)	heladura	frieira
congelatore	congélateur	freezer	Kühltruhe(f)	congelador	congelador
congestione	congestion	congestion	Blutandrang(m)	congestión	congestão
congiuntura	conjoncture	conjuncture	Konjunktur(f)	coyuntura	conjuntura
congratulare	congratuler	congratulate	gratulieren	congratular	congratular
congratularsi	féliciter	congratulate	gratulieren	felicitar	felicitar
congratulazioni!	félicitations!	congratulations!	Glückwunsch!	enhorabuena(!)	parabéns!
congresso	congrès	congress	Kongress(m)	congreso	congresso
conico, a	conique	conical	kegelförmig	cónico, a	cónico, a
conifera	conifère	conifer	Nadelbaum(m)	conifera	conifera
coniglio, a	lapin, e	rabbit	Kaninchen(n)	conejo, a	coelho, a
coniugale	conjugal, e	married, marriage-	ehelich	conyugal	conjugal
coniugazione	conjugaison	conjugation	Konjugation(f)	conjugación	conjugação
connessione	connexion	connection	Verbindung; Anschluß	conexión	conexão
connettere	connecter	connect	kuppeln, verbinden	conectar	ligar
cono	cône	cone	Kegel(m)	cono	cone
conoscenza	connaissance	knowledge	Kenntnis(f)	conocimiento	conhecimento
conoscere, sapere	connaître	know	kennen	conocer, saber	conhecer, saber
conquista	conquête	conquest	Eroberung(f)	conquista	conquista
consacrare	consacrer	consecrate	weihen	consagrar	consagrar
consacrazione	consécration	consecration	Weihe(f)	consagración	consagração

Italian	French	English	German	Spanish	Portuguese
consecutivo, a	consécutif, ive	consecutive	folgend	consecutivo, a	consecutivo, a
consegna	livraison	delivery	Lieferung(f)	entrega	entrega
consegnare	livrer	deliver	liefern	entregar	entregar
conseguenza	conséquence	consequence	Konsequenz(f)	consecuencia	consequência
consenso	agrément	approval, consent	Zustimmung(f)(verbal)	consentimiento	consentimento
consentire	consentir	agree	ein = willigen	consentir	consentir
consentire	consentir	consent	zu = stimmen	consentir	consentir
conserva	conserve(s)	tinned food	Konserve(f)	conserva	conserva
conservare	conserver	preserve, keep	konservieren	conservar	conservar
conservazione	conservation	conservation	Konservierung(f)	conservación	conservação
considerare	considérer	consider	an = sehen(als)	considerar	considerar
considerare	considérer	regard	betrachten	considerar	considerar
considerazione	considération	consideration	Betrachtung(f)	consideración	consideração
considerevole	considérable	considerable	erheblich	considerable	considerável
consigliare	conseiller	advise	beraten	aconsejar	aconselhar
consigliere, a	conseiller, ère	adviser	Berater(in f)m	consejero, a	conselheiro, a
consigliere, a	conseiller, ère	councillor	Rat(m)(Staatsrat m)	concejal, a	conselheiro, a
consiglio	conseil	advice	Rat(m)	consejo	conselho
consiglio	conseil	council	Rat(m)(Europrat m)	consejo	conselho
consistere in	consister à	consist(in, of)	bestehen aus	consistir en	consistir em
consolare	consoler	console, comfort	trösten	consolar	consolar
consolato	consulat	consulate	Konsulat(n)	consulado	consulado
console	consul	consul	Konsul(m)	cónsul	cônsul
consolidare	consolider	strengthen	verstärken	consolidar	consolidar
consonante	consonne	consonant	Mitlaut(m)	consonante	consoante
constatare	constater	state; note	fest = stellen	constatar	constatar
consultare	consulter	consult	befragen	consultar	consultar
consumare	consommer	consume	verbrauchen	consumir	consumir
consumatore, trice	consommateur	consumer	Verbraucher(in f)m	consumidor, a	consumidor, a
consumo	consommation	consumption	Verbrauch(m)	consumo	consumo
contabilità	comptabilité	accountancy	Buchhaltung(f)	contabilidad	contabilidade
contadino, a	paysan, ne	farmer	Bauer(m), Bäuerin(f)	campesino, a	camponês, a
contadino, a; fattore	fermièr, ière	farmer	Bauer(m), Bäuerin(f)	granjero, a	caseiro, a
contagio	contagion	contagion	Ansteckung(f)	contagio	contágio
contagioso, a	contagieux, se	contagious	ansteckend	contagioso, a	contagioso, a
contaminazione	contamination	contamination	Ansteckung(f)	contaminación	contaminação
contanti	comptant	cash	Barzahlung(f)	contado(al)	pronto(a)
contare	compter	count	zählen	contar	contar
contare su	compter sur	rely on	zählen, auf jdn	contar con	contar com
contatore	compteur	meter	Zähler(m)	contador	contador
contattare	contact(prendre)	contact	Kontakt(auf = nehmen)	contacto(entrar en)	contactar
contatto	contact	contact	Kontakt(m)	contacto	contacto
contemplare	contempler	contemplate	betrachten	contemplar	contemplar
contemporaneo, a	contemporain, e	contemporary	zeitgenössisch	contemporáneo, a	contemporâneo, a
contenere	contenir	contain	enthalten	contener	conter
contento, a	content, e	glad, happy, pleased	froh, erfreut	contento, a	contente
contento, a	content, e	pleased, glad	froh	contento, a	contente
contenuto	contenu	content(s)	Inhalt(m)	contenido	conteúdo
contestare	contester	contest	bestreiten	impugnar, objetar	contestar
continente	continent	continent	Kontinent(m)	continente	continente
continuare	continuer	continue, go on	fort = setzen	continuar	continuar
continuo, a	continu, e	continuous	ununterbrochen	continuo, a	contínuo, a
continuo, a	continuel, le	continual	ständig	continuo, a	contínuo, a
conto	compte	account	Konto(n)	cuenta	conta
conto	compte	account	Rechnung(f)	cuenta	conta
conto	note	bill	Rechnung(f)	cuenta	conta
contorno	contour	outline, contour	Umriß(m)	contorno	contorno
contrabbando	contrebande	smuggling	Schmuggel(m)	contrabando	contrabando
contraddire	contredire	contradict	widersprechen	contradecir	contradizer
contraddizione	contradiction	contradiction	Widerspruch(m)	contradicción	contradição
contrariato, a	contrarié, e	upset	ärgerlich sein	contrariado, a	contrariado, a
contrario, a	contraire	contrary	entgegengesetzt	contrario, a	contrário, a
contrario	contraire	opposite, contrary	Gegenteil(n)	contrario	contrário
contrassegno	repère	mark, landmark	Markierung(f)	señal, indicio	sinal, marca
contrasto	contraste	contrast	Gegensatz(m)	contraste	contraste
contrattare	marchander	bargain, haggle	feilschen, handeln	regatear	regatear
contratto	contrat	contract	Vertrag(m), Kontrakt m	contrato	contrato
contravvenzione	procès-verbal	ticket, penalty	Strafmandat(n)	multa	multa

Italian	French	English	German	Spanish	Portuguese
contrazione	contraction	contraction	Zusammenziehen(n)	contracción	contracção
contribuire	contribuer	contribute	bei = tragen	contribuir	contribuir
contributo	cotisation	contribution	Beitrag(m)	cotización	contribuição
contro	contre	against	gegen, an	contra	encostado a
contro	contre	against	wider, gegen	contra(en)	contra
contro-attacco	contre-attaque	counter-attack	Gegenangriff(m)	contraataque	contra-ataque
controllare	contrôler	control, check	kontrollieren	controlar	controlar
controllo	contrôle	control, check	Aufsicht(f), Prüfung f	control	controlo
controllo	contrôle	examination	Kontrolle(f)	control	controlo
controllore	contrôleur	inspector	Kontrolleur(m)	revisor	revisor; fiscal
contusione	contusion	bruise	Quetschung(f)	contusión	contusão
convalescenza	convalescence	convalescence	Genesung(f)	convalecencia	convalescência
conveniente	convenable	suitable, fitting	angemessen	conveniente	conveniente
convenire	convenir	agree	überein = kommen	acordar	convir, combinar
convenire	convenir	suit, fit	passen	convenir	estar bem
convento	couvent	convent	Kloster(n)	convento	convento
convenzione	convention	agreement	Übereinstimmung(f)	convención	convenção
convergere	converger	converge	konvergieren	converger	convergir
conversazione	conversation	conversation	Gespräch(n)	conversación	conversação
convertirsi	convertir(se)	convert	konvertieren	convertirse	converter-se
convesso, a	bombé, e	convex	gewölbt	abombado, a	convexo, a
convincere	convaincre	convince	überzeugen	convencer	convencer
convinzione	conviction	conviction	Überzeugung(f)	convicción	convicção
convocare	convoquer	summon; invite	vor = laden	convocar	convocar
convocazione	convocation	notification	Einberufung(f); Ladung	convocatoria	convocação
convoglio	convoi	convoy	Konvoi(m)	convoy	comboio
convulsione	convulsion	convulsion	Zuckung(f), Krampf(m)	convulsión	convulsão
cooperare	coopérer	cooperate	mit = arbeiten	cooperar	cooperar
cooperativa	coopérative	cooperative	Genossenschaft(f)	cooperativa	cooperativa
cooperazione	coopération	cooperation	Mitarbeit(f)	cooperación	cooperação
coordinare	coordonner	coordinate	koordinieren	coordinar	coordenar
coperchio	couvercle	lid, cover	Deckel(m)	tapa, tapadera	tampa
coperta	couverture	blanket; cover	Decke(f)(Woll-, Bett-)	manta	manta, cobertor
coperto	couvert	table(lay the)	Gedeck(n)	cubierto	talher
copia	copie	copy	Kopie(f)	copia	cópia
copiare	copier	copy	kopieren	copiar	copiar
coppa	coupe	cup	Pokal(m)	copa	taça
coppia	couple	couple	Paar(n)	pareja	casal
coprire	couvrir	cover	zu = decken	cubrir	cobrir
coraggio	courage	courage	Mut(m)	valentía	coragem
coraggioso, a	courageux, brave	brave	mutig	valiente, valeroso	corajoso, a
corallo	corail	coral	Koralle(f)	coral	coral
Corano	Coran	Koran	Koran(der)	Corán	Alcorão
corazzata	cuirassé	warship	Kriegsschiff(n)	acorazado	couraçado
corda	corde	rope	Tau(n)	cuerda	corda
cordiale	cordial, e	cordial, hearty	herzlich, freundlich	cordial	cordial
cordone	cordon	cord, string	Kordel(f)	cordón, cable	cordão
cornice, quadro	cadre	frame	Rahmen(m)	marco	moldura
corno	corne	horn	Horn(n)	cuerno	corno; chifre
coro	choeur	choir	Chor(m)	coro	coro
corona	couronne	crown	Krone(f)	corona	coroa
corpo	corps	body	Körper(m)	cuerpo	corpo
corporale	corporel, le	bodily	körperlich	corporal	corporal
corporazione	corporation	corporation	Körperschaft(f)	corporación	corporação
correggere	corriger	correct, rectify	korrigieren	corregir	corrigir
correggere	corriger	rectify, correct	berichtigen	corregir	rectificar
corrente, comune	courant, e	common	geläufig	corriente	corrente
corrente	courant, e	current	laufend, heutig	corriente	corrente, vulgar
corrente	courant	current	Strom(m)	corriente	corrente
correntemente	couramment	fluently	fließend	soltura(con)	fluentemente
correre	courir	run	laufen	correr	correr
correre, andare	rouler	run, drive, go	fahren	correr, rodar	andar; rolar
correttamente	correctement	properly	richtig	correctamente	correctamente
corretto, a	correct, e	correct, proper	richtig	correcto, a	correcto, a
correzione	correction	correction	Verbesserung(f)	corrección	correcção
corrida	corrida	bull-fight	Stierkampf(m)	corrida	toirada
corridoio	couloir	corridor	Flur(m)	pasillo	corredor
corridore	coureur, se	runner	Läufer(in f)m	corredor, a	corredor, a

539

Italian	French	English	German	Spanish	Portuguese
corrispondenza	correspondance	correspondence	Korrespondenz(f)	correspondencia	correspondência
corrispondere	correspondre	correspond, tally	entsprechen	corresponder	corresponder
corrosione	corrosion	corrosion	Korrosion(f)	corrosión	corrosão
corrotto, a	corrompu, e	corrupt	verdorben, korrupt	corrompido, a	corrupto, a
corruzione	corruption	corruption	Korruption(f)	corrupción	corrupção
corsa	course	race	Rennen(n)	carrera	corrida
corsa	course	running	Wettrennen(n)	carrera	corrida
corsa	courses	races	Pferderennen(n)	carreras	corridas
corsia	voie	lane	Spur(f)(Straßen-)	vía	faixa(rua)
corso	cours	rate, quotation	Kurs(m)	cotización	índice, tabela
corso, lezione	cours	lesson	Unterricht(m)	curso, clase	curso, aula
corte	cour	court	Hof(m)	corte	corte
corteo	cortège	procession	Umzug(m), Festzug(m)	cortejo	cortejo
cortese	courtois, e	courteous	höflich	cortés	cortês
cortile	cour	yard	Hof(m)	patio	pátio
corto, a	court, e	short	kurz	corto, a	curto, a
corvo	corbeau	crow	Rabe(m)	cuervo	corvo
cosa	chose	thing	Ding(n)	cosa	coisa
cosa, che cosa	quoi	what	was	que, qué	quê
coscia	cuisse	thigh	Schenkel(m)	muslo	coxa
coscia	cuisse	leg	Schenkel(m)	muslo; pierna	perna
cosciente, conscio, a	conscient, e	conscious	bewußt	consciente	consciente
coscienza	conscience	conscience	Bewußtsein(n)	conciencia	consciência
così	ainsi	so, thus	so	así	assim
così	si	so	so	tan	tão
cosmetico	cosmétique	cosmetic	Kosmetik(f)	cosmético	cosmético
cosmonauta	cosmonaute	astronaut	Astronaut(m)	cosmonauta	cosmonauta
cosmopolita	cosmopolite	cosmopolitan	kosmopolitisch	cosmopolita	cosmopolita
cospirazione	conspiration	plot, conspiracy	Komplott(n)	conspiración	conspiração
costa	côte	coast	Küste(f)	costa	costa
costante	constant, e	constant	beständig	constante	constante
costare	coûter	cost	kosten	costar	custar
costellazione	constellation	constellation	Konstellation(f)	constelación	constelação
costiero, a	côtier, ère	coastal	Küsten-	costero, a	costeiro, a
costituire	constituer	constitute	bilden	constituir	constituir
costituzione	constitution	constitution	Verfassung(f)	constitución	constituição
costo	coût	cost	Kosten(pl)	costo, coste	custo, preço
costola	côte	rib	Rippe(f)	costilla	costela
costoso, a	coûteux, se	costly, expensive	teuer	costoso, a	custoso, a
costringere	contraindre	force, compel	zwingen	obligar a	obrigar
costrizione	contrainte	restraint	Zwang(m)	obligación	obrigação
costruire	construire	construct, build	bauen	construir	construir
costruire	bâtir	build	bauen	edificar	construir
costruzione	construction	construction	Bau(m)	construcción	construção
costume, usanza	coutume	custom	Brauch(m)	costumbre	costume
costume da bagno	maillot de bain	swimsuit; trunks	Badeanzug(m)	traje de baño	fato de banho
costumi	moeurs	morals	Sitten(f, pl)	costumbres	costumes
cotone	coton	cotton	Baumwolle(f)	algodón	algodão
cotto, a	cuit, e	cooked	gar, gekocht	cocido, a	cozido, a
cottura	cuisson	cooking	Kochen(n), Sieden(n)	cocción	cozedura, cocção
covata	couvée	brood	Brut(f)	pollada	ninhada
cozza	moule	mussel	Muschel(f)	mejillón	mexilhão
crampo	crampe	cramp	Krampf(m)	calambre	cãibra
cranio	crâne	skull	Schädel(m)	cráneo	crâneo
cratere	cratère	crater	Krater(m)	cráter	cratera
cravatta	cravate	tie	Kravatte(f)	corbata	gravata
creare	créer	create	schöpfen	crear	criar
creatore, trice	créateur, trice	creator(creative)	Schöpfer(in f)m	creador, a	criador, a
creazione, creato	création	creation	Erschaffung; Schöpfung	creación	criação
credente	croyant, e	believer	Gläubige(f, m)	creyente	crente
credenza	croyance	belief	Glaube(m)	creencia	crença
credenza, buffè	buffet	dresser; sideboard	Büfett(n)	aparador	aparador
credere	croire	believe	glauben	creer	crer
credito	crédit	credit	Kredit(m)	crédito	crédito
crema	crème	cream	Sahne(f)	crema	creme
crema	crème(peau)	cream	Creme(f)	crema	creme
crepa, crepaccio	crevasse	crevice	Spalte(f)	grieta	fenda
crepuscolo	crépuscule	twilight, dusk	Abenddämmerung(f)	crepúsculo	crepúsculo

Italian	French	English	German	Spanish	Portuguese
crescere	grandir	grow	wachsen	crecer	crescer
crescere	pousser, croître	grow	wachsen	crecer	crescer
crescere	croître	grow, increase	wachsen	crecer	crescer
crescita	croissance	growth	Wachstum(n)	crecimiento	crescimento
crescita	accroissement	increase	Zuwachs(m)	crecimiento	crescimento
cresta	crête	crest	Kamm(m)	cresta	crista, cimo
cric, cricco	cric	jack	Wagenheber(m)	gato	macaco
criminale	criminel, le	criminal	Verbrecher(in f)m	criminal	criminoso, a
crimine	crime	crime	Verbrechen(n)	crimen	crime
criniera	crinière	mane	Mähne(f)	crines, melena	crina
crisi	crise	crisis(-ses)	Krise(f)	crisis	crise
cristallo	cristal	crystal	Kristall(n)	cristal	cristal
cristiano, a	chrétien, ne	Christian	Christ(in f)m	cristiano, a	cristão, cristã
criterio	critère	criterion(-ia)	Kriterium(n)	criterio	critério
critica	critique	criticism	Kritik(f)	crítica	crítica
criticare	critiquer	criticize	kritisieren	criticar	criticar
crocchia	chignon	chignon, bun	Haarknoten(m)	moño	carrapicho
croce	croix	cross(-es)	Kreuz(n)	cruz	cruz
crociera	croisière	cruise	Kreuzfahrt(f)	crucero	cruzeiro
crollare	écrouler(s')	collapse, crumble	zusammen = brechen	derrumbar(se)	desmoronar-se
crollare	effondrer(s')	collapse	zusammen = brechen	hundirse	desabar
cromosoma	chromosome	chromosome	Chromosom(n)	cromosoma	cromossoma
cronaca	chronique	chronicle	Chronik(f)	crónica	crónica
cronaca	reportage	report	Reportage(f)	reportaje	reportagem
cronico, a	chronique	chronic	chronisch	crónico, a	crónico, a
cronologia	chronologie	chronology	Chronologie(f)	cronología	cronologia
cronometro	chronomètre	chronometer	Stoppuhr(f)	cronómetro	cronómetro
crosta	croûte	crust	Kruste(f)	costra, corteza	crosta
crostaceo	crustacé	shell-fish	Schalentier(n)	crustáceo	crustáceo
croupier	croupier, ière	croupier	Croupier(m)	crupier	croupier
cruciverba	mots croisés	crossword	Kreuzworträtsel(n)	crucigrama	palavras cruzadas
crudele	cruel, le	cruel	grausam	cruel	cruel
crudo, a	cru, e	raw	roh	crudo, a	cru, a
cubo	cube	cube	Würfel(m)	cubo	cubo
cuccetta	couchette	couchette	Liegeplatz(m)	litera	couchette
cucchiaino	cuiller à café	teaspoon	Kaffeelöffel(m)	cucharilla	colher de chá
cucchiaio	cuillère	spoon	Löffel(m)	cuchara	colher
cucina	cuisine	kitchen	Küche(f)	cocina	cozinha
cucina	cuisinière	cooker, stove	Herd(m)	cocina	fogão
cucinare	cuisiner	cook	kochen	cocinar	cozinhar
cucire	coudre	sew	nähen	coser	coser
cucito	couture	sewing	Naht(f)	costura	costura
cucito	couture	seam	Saum(m)	costura	costura
cuffia	écouteurs, casque	ear/headphones	Kopfhörer(m)	casco	auscultadores
cugino, a	cousin, e	cousin	Cousin(m), Cousine(f)	primo, a	primo, a
culla	berceau	cradle	Wiege(f)	cuna	berço
cullare	bercer	rock	wiegen	mecer	embalar
culto	culte	worship	Kult(m)	culto	culto
cultura	culture	culture	Kultur(f)	cultura	cultura
culturale	culturel, le	cultural	kulturell	cultural	cultural
cumulare	cumuler	accumulate	an = häufen	acaparar	acumular
cuocere	cuire	cook	kochen	cocer	cozer
cuoco, a	cuisinier, ière	cook; chef	Koch(m), Köchin(f)	cocinero, a	cozinheiro, a
cuoio, pelle	cuir	leather	Leder(n)	cuero	couro
cuore	coeur	heart	Herz(n)	corazón	coração
cupola	coupole	dome	Kuppel(f)	cúpula, bóveda	cúpula
cura	soin	care	Pflege(f)	cuidado	cuidado
cura	cure	treatment	Kur(f)	cura	cura
cura	soins de beauté	beauty treatment	Schönheitspflege(f)	cosmética	tratamento
curare	soigner	nurse; tend; treat	pflegen	curar	cuidar
curioso, a	curieux, se	curious	neugierig	curioso, a	curioso, a
curva	courbe	curve	Kurve(f)	curva	curva
curva	virage	bend, turn	Kurve(f)	curva	curva
curvatura	courbure	bend, curve	Krümmung(f)	curvatura	curvatura
cuscino	coussin	cushion	Kissen(n)	cojín	almofada
custode, guardia	gardien, ne	keeper, caretaker	Wärter(in f)m	guardián, ana	guarda
custodire	garder	look after	hüten	vigilar, guardar	cuidar de, vigiar
custodire, guardare	garder	guard, watch over	hüten, bewachen	guardar	guardar, vigiar

Italian	French	English	German	Spanish	Portuguese
cutaneo, a	cutané, e	cutaneous, skin	Haut-	cutáneo, a	cutâneo, a

D

Italian	French	English	German	Spanish	Portuguese
da	de	from	aus; von	de, desde	de
da	chez	at, to	bei	en casa de	em casa de
da	depuis	since; for	seit	desde	desde
dado	dé(jeux)	die(dice)	Würfel(m)	dado	dado
dado	écrou	nut	Mutter(f)(Schrauben-)	tuerca	porca
dannare	damner	damn	verdammen	condenar	condenar
danneggiare	endommager	damage	beschädigen	dañar	estragar
danno	dommage	damage	Schaden(m)	perjuicio, daño	prejuízo, dano
danno	dégât(s)	damage	Schaden(m)	daño(s), estrago(s)	estrago
dappertutto	partout	everywhere	überall	por todas partes	por toda a parte
dare	donner	give	geben	dar	dar
dare(un esame)	passer(examen)	take(an exam)	ab = legen(Prüfung f)	pasar(un examen)	fazer(exame)
data	date	date	Datum(n)	fecha	data
dati	donnée(s)	data	Daten(pl)	datos	dados
datore di lavoro	employeur	employer	Arbeitgeber(in f)m	patrón	patrão
dattero	datte	date	Dattel(f)	dátil	tâmara
davanti	avant	forward(s)	vorwärts	adelante(hacia)	frente(para a)
davanti	devant	front, fore	Front(f)	frente, delantera	frente(a)
davanti a	devant	in front(ahead)of	vor	delante, ante	diante de
debito	dette	debt	Schuld(f)	deuda	dívida
debole, fragile	faible	weak	schwach	débil	fraco, a
debole	faible	dim	matt	flojo, a	fraco, a
debolezza	faiblesse	weakness(-es)	Schwäche(f)	debilidad	fraqueza
decadenza	décadence	decadence, decline	Verfall(m), Untergang	decadencia	decadência
decadenza	déchéance	downfall	Untergang(m), Verfall	decaimiento	decadência
decano, a	doyen, ne	oldest person	Älteste(f, m)	decano, a	decano, a
decedere	décéder	die	versterben, sterben	fallecer	falecer
decelerare	décélérer	decelerate	ab = bremsen	reducir, aminorar	desacelerar
decennio	décennie	decade	Jahrzehnt(n)	decenio, década	década
decente	décent, e	decent	anständig	decente	decente
decesso	décès	death	Tod(m)	fallecimiento	falecimento
decidere	décider	decide	entscheiden	decidir	decidir
decifrare	décoder	decode	dekodieren	descifrar	decifrar
decimale	décimal, e	decimal	dezimal	decimal	decimal
decimo, a	dixième	tenth	zehnte	décimo, a	décimo, a
decisione	décision	decision	Entscheidung(f)	decisión	decisão
declino	déclin	decline	Untergang(m)	decadencia, ocaso	declínio
decollare	décoller	take off	ab = heben	despegar	descolar
decolonizzare	décoloniser	decolonize	entkolonisieren	descolonizar	descolonizar
decolorazione	décoloration	discolouration	Entfärbung(f)	descoloramiento	descoloração
decomporre	décomposer	decompose	zerlegen	descomponer	decompor
decontaminare	décontaminer	decontaminate	entseuchen	descontaminar	descontaminar
decorare	décorer	decorate	aus = zeichnen	condecorar	condecorar
decorazione	décoration	decoration	Dekoration(f)	decoración	decoração
decrescente	dégressif, ive	decreasing	abnehmend	decreciente	decrescente
decrescere	décroître	decrease	ab = nehmen	decrecer	decrescer
decreto	décret	decree	Erlaß(m), Verordnung f	decreto	decreto
dedicare	dédier	dedicate	widmen	dedicar	dedicar
dedicare	consacrer	devote	widmen	dedicar	dedicar
dedizione	dévouement	devotion	Ergebenheit(f)	consagración a	dedicação
deduzione	déduction	deduction	Abzug(m)	deducción	dedução
deduzione	déduction	deduction	Rückschluß(m)	deducción	dedução
deficiente	déficient, e	deficient	mangelhaft	deficiente	deficiente

Italian	French	English	German	Spanish	Portuguese
deficit	déficit	deficit	Verlust(m), Defizit(n)	déficit	défice
definire	définir	define	definieren	definir	definir
definitivo, a	définitif, ive	definitive, final	endgültig	definitivo, a	definitivo, a
definizione	définition	definition	Definition(f)	definición	definição
deflagrazione	déflagration	explosion	Knall(m), Explosion(f)	deflagración	deflagração
deflazione	déflation	deflation	Deflation(f)	deflación	deflação
deflusso, scolo	écoulement	flow, outflow	Abfluß(m)	derrame, flujo	escoamento
deformare	déformer	distort, deform	verformen	deformar	deformar
deformazione	déformation	distortion	Mißbildung(f)	deformación	deformação
defunto, a	défunt, e	deceased person	Verstorbene(f, m)	difunto, a	defunto, a
degenerare	dégénérer	degenerate	degenerieren	degenerar	degenerar
degno, a	digne	worthy; dignified	würdig	digno, a	digno, a
degradare	dégrader	degrade	degradieren	degradar	degradar
degradazione	dégradation	degradation	Beschädigung(f)	degradación	degradação
delegare	déléguer	delegate	beauftragen	delegar	delegar
delegato, a	délégué, e	delegate	Abgesandte(f, m)	delegado, a	delegado, a
delegazione	délégation	delegation	Delegation(f)	delegación	delegação
delfino	dauphin	dolphin	Delphin(m)	delfín	golfinho
deliberare	délibérer	deliberate	beraten	deliberar	deliberar
deliberato, a	délibéré, e	deliberate	gewollt, absichtlich	deliberado, a	deliberado, a
delicatezza	délicatesse	delicacy	Aufmerksamkeit(f)	delicadeza	delicadeza
delicato, a	délicat, e	delicate	schwierig	delicado, a	delicado, a
delicato, a	délicat, e	delicate	zart; fein	delicado, a	delicado, a
delimitare	délimiter	delimit	ab = grenzen	delimitar	delimitar
delinquente	délinquant, e	delinquent	Kriminelle(f, m)	delincuente	delinquente
delinquenza	délinquance	delinquency	Kriminalität(f)	delincuencia	delinquência
delirio	délire	delirium	Fieberwahn(m)	delirio	delírio
delitto	délit	offence	Vergehen(n), Delikt(n)	delito	delito
delizioso, a	délicieux, se	delicious	köstlich	delicioso, a	delicioso, a
delizioso, a	charmant, e	delightful	entzückend, reizend	delicioso, a	delicioso, a
deludere	décevoir	disappoint	enttäuschen	decepcionar	desapontar
delusione	déception	disappointment	Enttäuschung(f)	decepción	decepção
deluso, e	déçu, e	disappointed	enttäuscht	decepcionado, a	desiludido, a
demagogia	démagogie	demagogy	Demagogie(f)	demagogia	demagogia
demente	dément, e	insane, crazy, mad	verrückt	demente	demente
demenza, follia	démence	insanity, madness	Wahnsinn(m)	demencia	demência
democratico, a	démocrate	democrat	Demokrat(in f)m	demócrata	democrata
democrazia	démocratie	democracy	Demokratie(f)	democracia	democracia
demografia	démographie	demography	Demographie(f)	demografía	demografia
demolire	démolir	demolish	zerstören	demoler	demolir
demonio	démon	demon, devil	Teufel(m)	demonio	demónio
demoralizzare	démoraliser	demoralize	entmutigen	desmoralizar	desmoralizar
denaro; soldi	argent	money	Geld(n)	dinero	dinheiro
denigrare	dénigrer	denigrate	verleumden	denigrar	denegrir
densità	densité	density	Dichte(f)	densidad	densidade
denso, a	dense	dense	dicht	denso, a	denso, a
dente	dent	tooth(teeth)	Zahn(m)	diente	dente
dentiera	dentier	denture	Gebiß(n)	dentadura	dentadura
dentifricio	dentifrice	tooth-paste	Zahnpasta(f)	dentífrico	dentífrico
dentista	dentiste	dentist	Zahnarzt(in f)m	dentista	dentista
dentro	dedans	inside	in, drinnen, innen	dentro, adentro	dentro
denudare	dénuder	strip, bare	entblößen	desnudar	desnudar
denunziare	dénoncer	denounce	denunzieren	denunciar	denunciar
deodorante	déodorant	deodorant	Deo(n)	desodorante	desodorisante
deodorante	désodorisant	air-freshener	Deodorant(n)	desodorante	desodorisante
depilare	épiler	remove hair	enthaaren	depilar	depilar
deplorare	déplorer	deplore	beklagen	deplorar	deplorar
deplorevole	déplorable	deplorable	beklagenswert	deplorable	deplorável
deportazione	déportation	deportation	Deportation(f)	deportación	deportação
depositare	déposer	deposit	deponieren	depositar	depositar
depositare, porre	déposer	put down, lay down	legen, stellen	depositar	pousar
deposito	dépôt	deposit	Satz(m)	depósito	depósito
deposito bagagli	consigne(bagage)	left luggage	Gepäckaufbewahrung(f)	consigna(equipaje)	depósito(bagagem)
deposizione	déposition	statement	Aussage(f)	deposición	deposição
depressione	dépression(atm.)	depression	Tief(n)	depresión	depressão
depresso, a	déprimé, e	depressed	deprimiert	deprimido, a	deprimido, a
deputato	député	Member(Parliament)	Abgeordnete(m, f)	diputado	deputado
derivare	dériver	drift	ab = treiben	derivar	derivar

Italian	French	English	German	Spanish	Portuguese
derrata	denrée	foodstuff	Eßware(f)	comestibles	género; víveres
derubare	dérober	steal	entwenden	robar	roubar, furtar
descrivere	décrire	describe	beschreiben	describir	descrever
descrizione	description	description	Beschreibung(f)	descripción	descrição
desertico, a	désertique	desert, barren	öde; einsam	desértico, a	desértico, a
deserto	désert	desert	Wüste(f)	desierto	deserto
desiderare	désirer	desire, want	wünschen	desear	desejar
desiderio	désir	wish(-es)	Wunsch(m)	deseo	desejo
desideroso, a	avide, impatient	eager	begierig	deseoso, a	ávido, a; desejoso, a
designare	désigner	appoint	ernennen	designar	designar
desistere, rinunziare	désister(se)	withdraw, give up	zurück = treten	desistir	desistir
despota	despote	despot	Despot(m)	déspota	déspota
dessert	dessert	dessert	Nachtisch(m)	postre	sobremesa
destinare	destiner	intended to(be)	bestimmen für	destinar	destinar
destinatario, a	destinataire	addressee	Empfänger(in f)m	destinatario, a	destinatário, a
destinazione	destination	destination	Bestimmungsort(m)	destinación	destino
destino	destin	fate, destiny	Schicksal(n)	destino, sino	destino
destino	destinée	destiny	Schicksal(n)	destino	destino
destituito, a	déchu, e	fallen, deposed	abgesetzt, verfallen	decaído, a	decaído, a
destro, a	droit, e	right	rechte(r, s); rechts	derecho, a	direito, a
detective	détective	detective	Detektiv(m)	detective	detective
detenuto, a	détenu, e	prisoner	Häftling(m)	detenido, a; preso, a	preso, a; detido, a
detenzione	détention	detention	Haft(f)	detención	detenção
deteriorazione	détérioration	deterioration	Verschlechterung(f)	deterioración	deterioração
determinare	déterminer	determine	fest = legen	determinar	determinar
detersivo	lessive	washing powder	Waschpulver(n)	detergente	detergente
detestare, odiare	détester	detest, hate	hassen	detestar, odiar	detestar
detonazione	détonation	detonation	Knall(m)	detonación	detonação
detrarre	déduire	deduct	folgern, schließen aus	deducir	deduzir
detriti	éboulis	scree	Geröll(n)	escombros	escombros
detrito	détritus	rubbish, garbage	Unrat(m)	desperdicios	detrito, lixo
dettagliato, a	détaillé, e	detailed	einzelnen(im)	detallado, a	detalhado, a
devastare	dévaster	ravage, devastate	verwüsten, zerstören	devastar	devastar
devastare	ravager	devastate, ravage	verwüsten	asolar, devastar	assolar
devastazione	ravage	devastation	Verwüstung(f)	destrozo	estrago
deviare	dévier	divert	um = leiten	desviar	desviar
deviazione	déviation	diversion	Umleitung(f)	desviación	desvio
devoto, a	dévoué, e	devoted	ergeben	servicial	dedicado, a
devozione	dévotion	devotion	Frömmigkeit(f)	devoción	devoção
di; del; dello, a	de	of	von	de	de
di cui	dont	whose, of which	dessen; deren	cuyo, a; del cual	cujo, a; do qual
diabete	diabète	diabetes	Zuckerkrankheit(f)	diabetes	diabetes
diaframma	diaphragme	diaphragm	Zwerchfell(n)	diafragma	diafragma
diagnosi	diagnostic	diagnosis(-oses)	Diagnose(f)	diagnóstico	diagnóstico
diagonale	diagonal, e	diagonal	diagonal	diagonal	diagonal
diagramma	diagramme	diagram	Diagramm(n)	diagrama	diagrama
dialetto	dialecte	dialect	Dialekt(m)	dialecto	dialecto
dialogo	dialogue	dialogue	Dialog(m)	diálogo	diálogo
diamante	diamant	diamond	Diamant(m)	diamante	diamante
diametro	diamètre	diameter	Durchmesser(m)	diámetro	diâmetro
diapositiva	diapo(sitives)	slide	Diapositiv(n), Dia(n)	diapositiva	diapositivos
diarrea	diarrhée	diarrhoea	Durchfall(m)	diarrea	diarreia
diavolo	diable	devil	Teufel(m)	diablo	diabo
dibattito	débat	debate	Debatte(f)	debate	debate
dicembre	décembre	December	Dezember(m)	diciembre	Dezembro
dichiarare	déclarer	declare	bekannt = geben	declarar	declarar
dichiarazione	déclaration	declaration	Erklärung(f)	declaración	declaração
diciannove	dix-neuf	nineteen	neunzehn	diecinueve	dezanove
diciassette	dix-sept	seventeen	siebzehn	diecisiete	dezassete
diciotto	dix-huit	eighteen	achtzehn	dieciocho	dezoito
didascalie(con)	sous-titré, e	subtitled	Untertiteln(mit)	subtitulado, a	legendado, a
dieci	dix	ten	zehn	diez	dez
diesel	diesel	diesel	Diesel(m)	diesel	diesel
dieta	régime	diet(be on a)	Diät(f)	dieta	dieta
dietetico, a	diététique	dietetic	diätetisch	dietético, a	dietético, a
dietro, indietro	derrière, arrière	rear	Rück-; Hinter-	trasero, a; de atrás	traseiro, a
dietro	derrière	behind	hinter	detrás, tras	atrás, detrás
dietro, posteriore	arrière, derrière	behind, back	hinten, zurück	atrás	atrás

Italian	French	English	German	Spanish	Portuguese
difendere	défendre	defend	verteidigen	defender	defender
difesa	défense	defence	Verteidigung(f)	defensa	defesa
difetto	défaut	defect, fault	Fehler(m)	defecto	defeito
difetto	défaillance	failure, fault	Versagen(n)	fallo	falha
difettoso, a	défectueux, se	defective, faulty	defekt	defectuoso, a	defeituoso, a
diffamazione	diffamation	slander	Verleumdung(f)	difamación	difamação
differente	différent, e	different	verschieden	diferente	diferente
differenza	différence	difference	Unterschied(m)	diferencia	diferença
differire, rimandare	différer	postpone	auf = schieben	diferir, demorar	diferir, adiar
difficile	difficile	difficult	schwer	difícil	difícil
difficoltá	difficulté	difficulty	Schwierigkeit(f)	dificultad	dificuldade
diffidare	méfier(se)	mistrust	mißtrauen	desconfiar	desconfiar
diffidente	méfiant, e	suspicious	mißtrauisch	desconfiado, a	desconfiado, a
diffidenza	méfiance	distrust, mistrust	Mißtrauen(n)	desconfianza	desconfiança
diffondere	diffuser	diffuse	verbreiten	difundir	difundir
diffusione	diffusion	diffusion	Verbreitung; Sendung	difusión	difusão
difterite	diphtérie	diphtheria	Diphterie(f)	difteria	difteria
diga	barrage	dam	Damm(m)	embalse, presa	barragem
digestione	digestion	digestion	Verdauung(f)	digestión	digestão
dignità	dignité	dignity	Würde(f)	dignidad	dignidade
dilaniare	déchiqueter	tear to pieces	zerstückeln	despedazar	despedaçar
dilatazione	dilatation	expansion	Ausdehnung(f)	dilatación	dilatação
dilettante	amateur	amateur	Amateur(in f)m	aficionado, a	amador, a
diluire	diluer	dilute	verdünnen	diluir	diluir
diluvio	déluge	flood; downpour	Überschwemmung(f)	diluvio	dilúvio
dimagrire	maigrir	lose weight	ab = nehmen	adelgazar	emagrecer
dimensione	dimension	dimension, size	Maß(n)	dimensión	dimensão
dimenticare	oublier	forget	vergessen	olvidar	esquecer
dimettere	renvoyer	dismiss	entlassen	despedir	despedir
dimettere(-rsi)	démissionner	resign	zurück = treten	dimitir	demitir-se
diminuire	diminuer	reduce, decrease	verringern	disminuir	diminuir
diminuzione	diminution	reduction	Verminderung(f)	disminución	diminuição
dimissione	démission	resignation	Rücktritt(m)	dimisión	demissão
dimora	demeure	residence, dwelling	Wohnung(f), Haus(n)	morada, casa	habitação, casa
dimorare, stare	demeurer	live, stay, remain	wohnen, bleiben	residir, vivir	habitar
dimostrare	démontrer	demonstrate	beweisen	demostrar	demonstrar
dimostrazione	démonstration	demonstration	Vorführung(f)	demostración	demonstração
dinamico, a	dynamique	dynamic	dynamisch	dinámico, a	dinâmico, a
dinamismo	dynamisme	dynamism	Tatkraft(f), Schwung m	dinamismo	dinamismo
dinamite	dynamite	dynamite	Dynamit(n)	dinamita	dinamite
dinastia	dynastie	dynasty	Herrscherhaus(n)	dinastía	dinastia
dintorni	alentours	surroundings	Umgebung(f)	alrededores	arredores
dio, Dio (dio, dei)	dieu	God	Gott(m)	dios, Dios	Deus
Dio(mio)	Dieu(mon)	Goodness(my)	Gott!(Mein Gott!)	Dios(mío)	Deus(meu)
dipartimento	département	department	Bezirk(m), Bereich(m)	departamento	departamento
dipendente	dépendant, e	dependent(on)	abhängig	dependiente	dependente
dipendere	dépendre(de)	depend(on)	ab = hängen	depender	depender
dipingere	peindre	paint	malen	pintar	pintar
dipinto, quadro	tableau	painting, picture	Gemälde(n)	cuadro	quadro
diploma	diplôme	diploma	Diplom(n)	diploma, título	diploma
diplomatico, a	diplomatique	diplomatic	diplomatisch	diplomático, a	diplomático, a
diplomatico	diplomate	diplomat	Diplomat(in f)m	diplomático	diplomata
diplomato, a	diplômé, e	qualified	staatlich geprüft	graduado, a	diplomado, a
diplomato, a	diplômé, e	graduate	Diplom-	titulado, a	diplomado, a
diplomazia	diplomatie	diplomacy	Diplomatie(f)	diplomacia	diplomacia
dire	dire	say	sagen	decir	dizer
dire	dire	tell	sagen	decir	contar
direttamente	directement	directly	direkt	directamente	directamente
direttiva, ordine	consigne	orders, instruction	Anweisung(f)	consigna, orden	ordem, instruções
diretto, a	direct, e	direct	direkt	directo, a	directo, a
direttore, -trice	directeur, trice	director, head	Direktor(in f)m	director, a	director, a
direttore(scuola)	directeur(école)	headmaster	Schuldirektor(m)	director(escuela)	director(escola)
direttore(orchestra)	chef(orchestre)	conductor	Dirigent(in f)m	director(orquesta)	maestro(orquestra)
direzione	direction	direction	Richtung(f)	dirección	direcção
direzione	direction	management	Direktion(f)	dirección	direcção
dirigente	dirigeant, e	leader, manager	Leiter(m), Führer(m)	dirigente	dirigente
dirigente	cadre	executive	leitende Angestellte	ejecutivo	quadro
dirigente d'azienda	chef(entreprise)	manager, head	Betriebsführer(m)	jefe de empresa	chefe de empresa

I

Italian	French	English	German	Spanish	Portuguese
dirigere	diriger	direct, guide, point	richten, steuern	dirigir, guiar	dirigir
dirigere	diriger	manage, run	leiten, führen	dirigir	dirigir
diritto, a	droit, e	straight	gerade	recto, a	recto, a
diritto	droit	law	Recht(n)	derecho	direito
diritto	droit	right	Recht(n)	derecho	direito
dirottare	détourner	hijack	entführen	secuestrar	sequestrar
disaccordo	désaccord	disagreement	Uneinigkeit(f), Streit	discrepancia	desacordo
disagio, imbarazzo	gêne	embarrassment	Verlegenheit(f)	molestia	embaraço
disapprovare	désapprouver	disapprove	mißbilligen	desaprobar	desaprovar
disarmare	désarmer	disarm	ab = rüsten, entwaffnen	desarmar	desarmar
disarmo	désarmement	disarmament	Abrüstung(f)	desarme	desarmamento
disastro	désastre	disaster	Unheil(n)	desastre	desastre
disattenzione	inattention	carelessness	Unachtsamkeit(f)	descuido	distracção
disavventura	mésaventure	mishap	Mißgeschick(n)	contratiempo	contratempo
discendenza	descendance	descendants	Nachkommenschaft(f)	descendencia	descendência
discepolo	disciple	disciple	Jünger(m)	discípulo	discípulo
discernere	discerner	discern	unterscheiden	discernir	discernir
discesa	descente	descent	Abstieg(m)	descenso, bajada	descida
disciplina	discipline	discipline	Disziplin(f)	disciplina	disciplina
disco	disque	record	Schallplatte(f)	disco	disco
discorso	discours	speech, talk	Rede(f)	discurso	discurso
discoteca	discothèque	disco(theque)	Diskothek(f)	discoteca	discoteca
discoteca, night	boîte de nuit	night-club	Diskothek(f)	discoteca	boîte
discreditare	discréditer	discredit	Verruf bringen(in)	desacreditar	desacreditar
discreto, a	discret, ète	discreet	diskret	discreto, a	discreto, a
discussione	discussion	discussion, talk	Diskussion(f)	discusión	discussão
discutere	discuter	discuss	besprechen	discutir	discutir
disegnare	dessiner	draw; design	zeichnen	dibujar; diseñar	desenhar
disegnatore, trice	dessinateur	drawer; designer	Zeichner(in f)m	dibujante	desenhador, a
disegno	dessin	drawing; design	Zeichnung(f)	dibujo; diseño	desenho
disegno	dessin, plan	design	Entwurf(m)	diseño	desenho
diseredare	déshériter	disinherit	enterben	desheredar	deserdar
disfare	défaire	dismantle, undo	ab = machen	deshacer	desfazer
disgelo	dégel	thaw	Auftauen(n)	deshielo	degelo
disgrazia	disgrâce	disgrace	Ungnade(f)	desgracia	desvalimento
disgrazia	malheur	misfortune	Unglück(n)	desgracia	desgraça
disgraziato, a	malheureux, se	unfortunate	unglücklich	desgraciado, a	infeliz
disgustare	dégoûter	disgust	an = widern	asco(dar)	enojar
disgustoso, a	dégoûtant, e	disgusting	ekelhaft	asqueroso, a	nojento, a
disidratare	déshydrater	dehydrate	aus = trocknen	deshidratar	desidratar
disinfettare	désinfecter	disinfect	desinfizieren	desinfectar	desinfectar
disinnescare	désamorcer	defuse	entschärfen	desactivar	despoletar
disinserire	débrancher	disconnect, unplug	aus = machen, abschalten	desenchufar	desligar
disintegrare	désintégrer	disintegrate	auf = lösen	desintegrar	desintegrar
disobbedire	désobéir	disobey	ungehorsam sein	desobedecer	desobedecer
disoccupato, a	chômeur, euse	unemployed person	Arbeitslose(f, m)	parado, a	desempregado, a
disoccupazione	chômage	unemployment	Arbeitslosigkeit(f)	paro, desempleo	desemprego
disonesto, a	malhonnête	dishonest	unehrlich	deshonesto, a	desonesto, a
disonore	déshonneur	dishonour	Schande(f)	deshonor	desonra
disopra	dessus	top	Oberteil(n)	superior(parte)	cima(parte de)
disordine	désordre	disorder, mess	Unordnung(f)	desorden	desordem
disordini	troubles	troubles	Unruhen(f, pl)	disturbios	perturbação
disorganizzare	désorganiser	disorganize	desorganisieren	desorganizar	desorganizar
disorientarsi	affoler(s')	panic	Panik geraten(in)	ponerse nervioso, a	afligir-se
dispari	impair	odd	ungerade	impar	ímpar
disperazione	désespoir	despair	Verzweiflung(f)	desesperación	desespero
disperdere	disperser	disperse; scatter	zerstreuen	dispersar	dispersar
dispetto	dépit	spite; vexation	Groll(m), Trotz(m)	despecho	despeito
dispiacere	chagrin	grief, sorrow	Kummer(m)	pena	desgosto, pena
dispiacere(-ersi)	regretter	sorry(be), regret	bedauern	sentir(lo)	sentir, lamentar
disponibile	disponible	available	verfügbar	disponible	disponível
disporre	disposer	arrange	auf = stellen	disponer	dispor
disposizione	agencement	layout	Anlage(f)	disposición	disposição
disposizione	disposition	arrangement	Anordnung(f)	disposición	disposição
disprezzare	dédaigner	disdain	mißachten	desdeñar	desdenhar
disprezzo	mépris	contempt, scorn	Verachtung(f)	desprecio	desprezo
disputa, lite	dispute	dispute, argument	Streit(m)	disputa	disputa
dissidente	dissident, e	dissident	Dissident(m)	disidente	dissidente

Italian	French	English	German	Spanish	Portuguese
dissimulare	dissimuler	conceal	verbergen, verhehlen	disimular	dissimular
dissipare	dissiper	dissipate, clear	verziehen, sich	disipar	dissipar
dissociare	dissocier	dissociate	trennen	disociar	dissociar
dissotterrare	déterrer	dig up	aus = graben	desenterrar	desenterrar
dissuadere	dissuader	dissuade	ab = raten	disuadir	dissuadir
dissuasione	dissuasion	dissuasion	Abschreckung(f)	disuasión	dissuasão
distanza	distance	distance	Entfernung(f)	distancia	distância
disteso, a; rilassato	détendu, e	relaxed	entspannt	descansado, a	descontraído, a
distillazione	distillation	distillation	Destillation(f)	destilación	distilação
distinguere	distinguer	distinguish	unterscheiden	distinguir	distinguir
distintivo	insigne	badge	Zeichen(n), Abzeichen	insignia	insígnia
distinto, a	distinct, e	distinct	deutlich	distinto, a	distinto, a
distrarre	distraire	distract, divert	ab = lenken	distraer	distrair
distrarre	distraire	entertain	unterhalten	entretener	distrair
distratto, a	distrait, e	absent-minded	zerstreut	distraído, a	distraído, a
distretto	district, région	district	Bezirk(m)	distrito, área	distrito
distribuire	distribuer	distribute; deal	verteilen	distribuir	distribuir
distributore(benzina)	poste d'essence	petrol station	Tankstelle(f)	gasolinera	bomba de gasolina
distribuzione	distribution	distribution	Verteilung(f)	distribución	distribuição
distruggere	détruire	destroy	zerstören	destruir	destruir
distruzione	destruction	destruction	Zerstörung(f)	destrucción	destruição
disturbare	déranger	disturb, bother	stören	molestar	incomodar
disuguaglianza	inégalité	inequality	Ungleichheit(f)	desigualdad	desigualdade
disuguale	inégal, e	uneven	uneben	desigual	desigual
dito	doigt	finger	Finger(m)	dedo	dedo
dito del piede	orteil	toe	Zehe(f)	dedo del pie	dedo do pé
ditta, firma, azienda	firme	firm	Firma(f)	firma	firma
dittatore	dictateur	dictator	Diktator(m)	dictador	ditador
dittatura	dictature	dictatorship	Diktatur(f)	dictadura	ditadura
divano	divan	couch(-es)	Couch(f), Sofa(n)	diván	divã
divano, canapè	canapé	sofa	Sofa(n)	sofá, canapé	canapé, sofá
diventare	devenir	become	werden	volverse	tornar-se
diventare	devenir	become	werden	llegar a ser	vir a ser
diventare	devenir	become	werden	ponerse	pôr-se
divergere	diverger	diverge	ab = weichen	divergir	divergir
diversificare	diversifier	diversify	variieren	diversificar	diversificar
diversità	diversité	diversity	Verschiedenheit(f)	diversidad	diversidade
diverso, a	divers, e	diverse, various	verschieden	diverso, a	diverso, a
divertente	amusant, e	amusing, funny	amüsant, drollig	divertido, a	engraçado, a
divertimento	amusement	amusement, fun	Vergnügen(n)	diversión	divertimento
divertire(-rsi)	amuser(s')	fun(have)	amüsieren, sich	divertir(se)	divertir-se
dividere	diviser	divide	teilen	dividir	dividir
dividere	partager	share, divide	teilen	repartir	repartir
divino, a	divin, e	divine	göttlich	divino, a	divino, a
divisione	division	division	Division(f)	división	divisão
divisione	division	partition	Trennung(f)	división	partilha
divorare	dévorer	devour	verschlingen	devorar	devorar
divorziare	divorcer	divorce	scheiden lassen, sich	divorciar(se)	divorciar-se
divorzio	divorce	divorce	Scheidung(f)	divorcio	divórcio
divulgare	divulguer	divulge, reveal	aus = plaudern	divulgar	divulgar
dizionario	dictionnaire	dictionary	Wörterbuch(n)	diccionario	dicionário
doccia	douche	shower	Dusche(f)	ducha	duche, chuveiro
docile	docile	docile	gehorsam	dócil	dócil, manso
documentazione	documentation	documentation	Dokumentation(f)	documentación	documentação
documenti	papiers(les)	papers	Papiere(pl); Ausweise	documentación	documentos
documento	document	document	Dokument(n)	documento	documento
dodici	douze	twelve	zwölf	doce	doze
dogana	douane	customs	Zoll(m)	aduana	alfândega
doganiere	douanier	customs officer	Zöllner(m)	aduanero	guarda-fiscal
dogmatico, a	dogmatique	dogmatic	dogmatisch	dogmático, a	dogmático, a
dolce	doux, ce	sweet	süß	dulce	doce
dolce	gâteau	cake; pastry	Kuchen(m)	pastel	bolo
dolci	pâtisserie(s)	pastry, cake	Backwaren(f, pl)	pasteles	pastelaria
dolciume	friandise	delicacy	Nascherei(f)	golosina	guloseima
dolore	douleur	pain, ache	Schmerz(m)	dolor	dor
doloroso, a	douloureux, se	painful, aching	schmerzhaft	doloroso, a	doloroso, a
domanda	question	question	Frage(f)	pregunta	pergunta
domanda	demande(emploi)	application	Bewerbung(f)	solicitud	pedido

547

Italian	French	English	German	Spanish	Portuguese
domandare	demander	ask; beg	fragen; bitten	preguntar	perguntar
domandare, chiedere	demander	beg	bitten	pedir	pedir
domandarsi	demander(se)	wonder	fragen, sich	preguntarse	perguntar-se
domani	demain	tomorrow	morgen	mañana	amanhã
domare	dompter	tame	zähmen	domar	domar
domenica	dimanche	Sunday	Sonntag(m)	domingo	domingo
domestica	bonne	maid	Haushaltshilfe(f)	criada	criada
domestico, a	domestique	domestic, home	Haus-	doméstico, a	doméstico, a
domestico, a	domestique	servant	Hausangestellte(m, f)	criado, a	empregado, a
domicilio	domicile	home	Wohnsitz(m), Wohnort m	domicilio	domicílio
dominare	dominer	dominate, rule	beherrschen	dominar	dominar
dominare	maîtriser	control, master	beherrschen	dominar	dominar
donna	femme	woman(women)	Frau(f)	mujer	mulher
donna di servizio	femme de ménage	domestic help	Putzfrau(f)	asistenta	mulher a dias
dono	don	gift, talent	Talent(n)	don, talento	dom, talento
dopo	après	after; afterwards	nach	después	depois
doppio, a	double	double	doppelt	doble	duplo, a
doppio, a	double	dual	doppelt	doble	duplo, a
dormire	dormir	sleep	schlafen	dormir	dormir
dose	dose	dose	Dosis(f)	dosis	dose
dosaggio, dose	dosage	proportion	Dosierung(f)	dosificación	dosagem
dossier	dossier	record, file	Akte(f)	expediente	processo
dotato, a	doué, e	gifted, talented	begabt	dotado, a	dotado, a; capaz
dotto, a; erudito, a	érudit, e	scholar	Gelehrte(f, m)	erudito, a	erudito, a
dottore, -essa	docteur(toresse)	doctor	Arzt(m); Doktor(m)	doctor, a	doutor, a
dottore, -essa	docteur	doctor	Doktor(m)	doctor, a	doutor, a
dottrina	doctrine	doctrine	Lehre(f)	doctrina	doutrina
dove	où	where	wo	donde, dónde	onde
dovere	devoir	must, have to	müssen	deber	dever
dovere	devoir	duty	Pflicht(f)	deber	dever
dozzina	douzaine	dozen	Dutzend(n)	docena	dúzia
dramma	drame	drama	Drama(n)	drama	drama
drammatico, a	dramatique	dramatic	dramatisch	dramático, a	dramático, a
drenare	drainer	drain	entwässern	drenar	drenar
drizzare	dresser	erect, put up	auf = richten, errichten	erigir	erigir, erguer
droga	drogue	drug	Droge(f)	droga	droga
drogarsi	doper(se)	take stimulants	dopen, sich	doparse	drogar-se
drogato, a	drogué, e	drug addict	Drogenabhängige(m, f)	drogado, a	drogado, a
drogheria	épicerie	grocer's(shop)	Lebensmittelladen(m)	ultramarinos	mercearia
droghiere, a	épicier, ière	grocer	Lebensmittelhändler m	tendero, a	merceeiro, a
dubbio, a	douteux, se	dubious; doubtful	zweifelhaft	dudoso, a	duvidoso, a
dubbio	doute	doubt	Zweifel(m)	duda	dúvida
dubitare	douter	doubt	zweifeln	dudar	duvidar
duca, duchessa	duc, duchesse	duke, duchess	Herzog(m), Herzogin(f)	duque, duquesa	duque, duquesa
due	deux	two	zwei	dos	dois, duas
duello	duel	duel	Duell(n)	duelo	duelo
duna	dune	dune	Düne(f)	duna	duna
dunque	donc	therefore; so	also	por tanto, pues	portanto, pois
duomo	dôme	dome	Kuppel(f)	cúpula	cúpula
durante	durant, pendant	during, for	während	durante	durante
durante	pendant	during; for	während	durante	durante
durare	durer	last	dauern	durar	durar
durata	durée	duration, length	Dauer(f)	duración	duração
duro, a	dur, e	hard	hart	duro, a	duro, a
duty-free	hors-taxe	duty-free	zollfrei	libre impuestos	sem imposto

E

Italian	French	English	German	Spanish	Portuguese
e, ed	et	and	und	y	e
ebollizione	ébullition	boiling	Kochen(n)	ebullición	fervura
ebreo, a	juif, juive	Jew, Jewess(-es)	Jude(m), Jüdin(f)	judío, judía	judeu, judia
eccedente	excédent	surplus, excess	Überschuß(m)	excedente	excedente
eccellente	excellent, e	excellent	vorzüglich	excelente	excelente
Eccellenza(Sua)	Excellence, Votre	Excellency(Your)	Exzellenz(f)	Excelencia(Su)	Excelência(Vossa)
eccessivo, a	excessif, ive	excessive	übermäßig	excesivo, a	excessivo, a
eccesso	excès	excess	Übermaß(n)	exceso	excesso
eccezionale	exceptionnel, le	exceptional	außergewöhnlich	excepcional	excepcional
eccezione	exception	exception	Ausnahme(f)	excepción	excepção
eccitante	excitant, e	exciting	aufregend	excitante	excitante
eccitare	exciter	excite	auf = regen	excitar	excitar
eccitato, a	excité, e	worked up	gereizt	excitado, a	excitado, a
ecco	voici	here is; here are	hier(ist/sind)	he aquí	aqui está
eclisse	éclipse	eclipse	Finsternis(f)	eclipse	eclipse
eco	écho	echo(-es)	Echo(n)	eco	eco
ecologia	écologie	ecology	Naturschutz(m)	ecología	ecologia
economia	économie	economy	Wirtschaft(f)	economía	economia
economico, a	économique	economic(al)	wirtschaftlich	económico, a	económico, a
economista	économiste	economist	Volkswirt(in f)m	economista	economista
economizzare	économiser	save, economise	sparen	economizar	economizar
eczema	eczéma	eczema	Ekzem(n)	eczema	eczema
edicola; chiosco	kiosque	news-stand	Zeitungskiosk(m)	quiosco	quiosque
edificio	édifice	edifice, building	Gebäude(n)	edificio	edifício
edificio, palazzo	bâtiment	building	Gebäude(n)	edificio	edifício
editore, trice	éditeur, trice	publisher; editor	Herausgeber(in f)m	editor, a	editor, a
editoriale	éditorial	editorial	Leitartikel(m)	editorial	editorial
edizione	édition	publishing	Verlagswesen(n)	industria editor-	indústria livro
edizione	édition	edition	Auflage(f), Ausgabe(f)	edición	edição
educare	éduquer	educate	erziehen, bilden	educar	educar
educato, a	poli, e	polite	höflich	educado, a; cortés	educado, a
educatore, trice	éducateur, trice	instructor	Erzieher(in f)m	educador, a	educador, a
educazione	éducation	education	Erziehung(f)	educación	educação
educazione	politesse	politeness	Höflichkeit(f)	cortesía	delicadeza
effettivo, a	effectif, ive	effective	tatsächlich, wirklich	efectivo, a	efectivo, a
effettivo	effectif	number of people	Personalbestand(m)	efectivo	efectivo
effetto	effet	effect	Wirkung(f)	efecto	efeito
effettuare	effectuer	carry out, perform	aus = führen	efectuar	efectuar
efficace	efficace	effective	wirkungsvoll	eficaz	eficaz
efficiente	efficace	efficient	tüchtig, fähig	eficiente	eficiente
effimero, a	éphémère	ephemeral	vergänglich	efímero, a	efémero, a
egli, lui, esso	il	he; it	er; es	él	ele
egoista	égoïste	selfish	egoistisch	egoísta	egoísta
elaborare	élaborer	elaborate	aus = arbeiten	elaborar	elaborar
elastico, a	élastique	elastic; flexible	elastisch	elástico, a	elástico, a
elastico	élastique	rubber band	Gummiband(n)	goma elástica	elástico
elefante	éléphant	elephant	Elefant(m)	elefante	elefante
elegante	élégant, e	elegant, smart	elegant	elegante	elegante
elegante	chic	smart, chic	schick	elegante	elegante
eleganza	élégance	elegance	Eleganz(f)	elegancia	elegância
eleggere	élire	elect	wählen	elegir	eleger
elemento	élément	element	Element(n)	elemento	elemento
elenco, annuario	annuaire	directory	Adreßbuch; Telefonbuch	anuario, guía	anuário
eletto, a	élu, e	elected, chosen	gewählt	elegido, a	eleito, a
elettore, -trice	électeur, trice	voter	Wähler(in f)m	elector, a	eleitor, a
elettricista	électricien	electrician	Elektriker(in f)m	electricista	electricista
elettricità	électricité	electricity	Elektrizität(f)	electricidad	electricidade
elettrico, a	électrique	electric(al)	elektrisch	eléctrico, a	eléctrico, a
elettronica	électronique	electronics	Elektronik(f)	electrónica	electrónica
elettronico, a	électronique	electronic	elektronisch	electrónico, a	electrónico, a
elevare	élever	elevate	erhöhen	elevar, alzar	elevar

Italian	French	English	German	Spanish	Portuguese
elevare, alzare	élever, hausser	raise	an = heben	elevar	elevar
elevarsi	élever(s')	rise	an = steigen	subir	subir
elevato, a; alto, a	élevé, e	high	hoch, erhöht	alto, a	alto, a
elezione	élection	election	Wahl(f)	elección	eleição
elica	hélice	propeller	Propeller(m)	hélice	hélice
elicottero	hélicoptère	helicopter	Hubschrauber(m)	helicóptero	helicóptero
eliminare	éliminer	eliminate	aus = scheiden	eliminar	eliminar
eliminazione	élimination	elimination	Beseitigung(f)	eliminación	eliminação
elite	élite	élite	Elite(f)	élite	elite
ellisse	ellipse	ellipse	Ellipse(f)	elipse	elipse
elogio	éloge	praise	Lob(n)	elogio	elogio
eloquenza	éloquence	eloquence	Redegewandtheit(f)	elocuencia	eloquência
eloquio	élocution	elocution	Sprechweise(f)	elocución	elocução
embargo	embargo	embargo	Embargo(n)	embargo	embargo
emblema	emblème	emblem	Emblem(n)	emblema	emblema
embrione	embryon	embryo	Embryo(m)	embrión	embrião
emendare	amender	amend	verbessern, ändern	enmendar	emendar
emergere	émerger	emerge	auf = tauchen	emerger	emergir
emettere	émettre	emit	aus = strahlen	emitir	emitir
emicrania	migraine	migraine, headache	Migräne(f)	jaqueca	enxaqueca
emigrare	émigrer	emigrate	aus = wandern	emigrar	emigrar
emigrato, a	émigré, e	emigrant	Emigrant(in f)m	emigrante	emigrante
emigrazione	émigration	emigration	Auswanderung(f)	emigración	emigração
eminente	éminent, e	eminent	hervorragend	eminente	eminente
emisfero	hémisphère	hemisphere	Halbkreis(m)	hemisferio	hémisfério
emissario	émissaire	emissary	Bote(m)	emisario	emissário
emissione	émission	sending	Sendung(f)	envío	envio
emittente	émetteur	transmitter	Sender(m)	emisor	emissor
emorragia	hémorragie	haemorrhage	Blutsturz(m)	hemorragia	hemorragia
emorragia	saignement	bleeding	Blutung(f)	desangramiento	perda de sangue
emorroide	hémorroïde(s)	haemorrhoids	Hämorrhoiden(f, pl)	hemorroides	hemorróidas
emotivo, a	émotif, ive	emotional	empfindsam	emotivo, a	emotivo, a
emozione	émotion	emotion	Rührung(f)	emoción	emoção
emulsione	émulsion	emulsion	Emulsion(f)	emulsión	emulsão
enciclopedia	encyclopédie	encyclopaedia	Enzyklopädie(f)	enciclopedia	enciclopédia
energia	énergie	energy	Energie(f)	energía	energia
enigma	énigme	enigma	Rätsel(n)	enigma	enigma
enorme	énorme	enormous, huge	riesig	enorme	enorme
entrambi	à la fois	both	beide, beides	ambos, ambas	ambos, os dois
entrare	entrer	enter, come/go in	ein = treten	entrar	entrar
entusiasmo	enthousiasme	enthusiasm	Begeisterung(f)	entusiasmo	entusiasmo
enumerare	énumérer	enumerate	auf = zählen	enumerar	enumerar
epatite	hépatite	hepatitis	Hepatitis, Gelbsucht f	hepatitis	hepatite
epidemia	épidémie	epidemic	Seuche(f)	epidemia	epidemia
epidermide	épiderme	epidermis, skin	Oberhaut(f), Haut(f)	epidermis	epiderme
epilessia	épilepsie	epilepsy	Epilepsie(f)	epilepsia	epilepsia
episodio	épisode	episode	Episode(f)	episodio	episódio
epoca	époque	epoch, era, time	Epoche(f), Ära(f), Zeit	época	época
epopea	épopée	epic	Epos(n)	epopeya	epopeia
eppure, tuttavia	cependant	however, but	jedoch	sin embargo	todavia, porém
equatore	équateur	equator	Äquator(m)	ecuador	equador
equatoriale	équatorial, e	equatorial	äquatorial	ecuatorial	equatorial
equestre	équestre	equestrian	Reiter-	ecuestre	equestre
equilibrare	équilibrer	balance	aus = gleichen	equilibrar	equilibrar
equilibrio	équilibre	balance	Gleichgewicht(n)	equilibrio	equilíbrio
equipaggiamento	équipement	equipment	Ausstattung(f)	equipo	equipamento
equipaggiare	équiper	equip, fit out	aus = rüsten	equipar	equipar
equipaggio	équipage	crew	Besatzung(f)	tripulación	equipagem
equità	équité	equity	Gerechtigkeit(f)	equidad	equidade
equitazione	équitation	riding(horse -)	Reiten(n)	equitación	equitação
equivalente	équivalent, e	equivalent	gleichwertig	equivalente	equivalente
equivoco, a	équivoque	equivocal	zweideutig	equívoco, a	equívoco, a
era	ère	era	Ära(f)	era	era
erba	herbe	grass	Gras(n)	hierba, yerba	erva
erbe(aromatiche)	herbe(s)	herb(s)	Kraut(n), Kräuter(pl.)	hierbas	erva
erede	héritier, ière	heir, heiress	Erbe(m), Erbin(f)	heredero, a	herdeiro, a
eredità	héritage	inheritance, legacy	Erbschaft(f)	herencia	herança
ereditarietà	hérédité	heredity	Vererbung(f)	herencia	hereditariedade

Italian	French	English	German	Spanish	Portuguese
ereditario, a	héréditaire	hereditary	erblich	hereditario, a	hereditário, a
eremita	ermite	hermit	Einsiedler(in f)m	ermitaño	eremita
erigere	ériger	erect	errichten	erigir, levantar	erigir
ermetico, a	hermétique	hermetic	hermetisch	hermético, a	hermético, a
ernia	hernie	hernia	Bruch(m)	hernia	hérnia
eroe, eroina	héros, héroïne	hero, heroine	Held(m), Heldin(f)	héroe, heroína	herói, heroína
eroico, a	héroïque	heroic	heldenhaft	heroico, a	heróico, a
eroina	héroïne	heroin	Heroin(n)	heroína	heroína
erosione	érosion	erosion	Abtragung(f)	erosión	erosão
erotico, a	érotique	erotic	erotisch	erótico, a	erótico, a
erotismo	érotisme	eroticism	Erotik(f)	erotismo	erotismo
errore	erreur, faute	error, mistake	Irrtum(m), Fehler(m)	error	erro
errore(fare un)	erreur(faire)	mistake(make a)	Irrtum(m)(machen)	error(cometer un)	erro(dar um)
erudito, a	érudit, e	erudite, learned	gelehrt	erudito, a	erudito, a
eruzione	éruption	eruption	Ausbruch(m)	erupción	erupção
esagerare	exagérer	exaggerate	übertreiben	exagerar	exagerar
esame	examen	examination, exam	Prüfung(f)	examen	exame
esame	examen(médical)	examination	Untersuchung(f)	examen, chequeo	exame
esaminare	contrôler	inspect	besichtigen	controlar, examinar	examinar
esaminare	examiner	examine, inspect	untersuchen	examinar	examinar
esattamente	exactement	exactly	genau, richtig; gerade	exactamente	exactamente
esattezza	exactitude	accuracy	Genauigkeit(f)	exactitud	exactidão
esatto, a	exact, e	exact, right	genau, richtig	exacto, a	exacto, a
esatto(è)	exact(c'est)	right(that 's)	stimmt!	exacto(es)	exacto(é)
esaurimento(nerv.)	dépression	breakdown	Nervenzusammenbruch m	depresión	depressão
esaurimento	surmenage	overwork(ing)	Überarbeitung(f)	agotamiento	esgotamento
esaurito, a	épuisé, e	exhausted, run out	ausverkauft	agotado, a	esgotado, a
esausto, a	épuisé, e	exhausted	erschöpft	agotado, a	esgotado, a
esca	appât	bait	Köder(m)	cebo	engodo, isca
esca	leurre, appât	lure, bait	Lockmittel(n)	señuelo	isca, engodo
eschimese	esquimau	Eskimo	Eskimo(m)	esquimal	esquimó
esclamare	exclamer(s')	exclaim	aus = rufen	exclamar	exclamar
escludere	exclure	exclude	aus = schließen	excluir	excluir
esclusività	exclusivité	exclusive rights	Alleinvertrieb(m)	exclusiva(-ividad)	exclusividade
esclusivo, a	exclusif, ive	exclusive	ausschließlich	exclusivo, a	exclusivo, a
escremento	excrément	excrement	Ausscheidung(f)	excremento	excremento
esecutivo, a	exécutif, ive	executive	ausübend, vollziehend	ejecutivo, a	executivo, a
esecuzione	exécution	execution	Hinrichtung(f)	ejecución	execução
eseguire	exécuter	perform, carry out	aus = führen	ejecutar	executar
esempio	exemple	example	Beispiel(n)	ejemplo	exemplo
esempio(per)	exemple(par)	instance(for)	Beispiel(zum)	ejemplo(por)	exemplo(por)
esercitare	exercer	exercise, practise	aus = üben	ejercitar	exercitar
esercito	armée	army	Armee(f)	ejército	exército
esercizio	exercice	exercise	Übung(f)	ejercicio	exercício
esibizione	exhibition	exhibition	Schau, Ausstellung(f)	exhibición	exibição
esigenza	exigence	demand, requirement	Forderung(f)	exigencia	exigência
esigere	exiger, réclamer	demand, require	fordern	exigir	exigir
esigere, domandare	exiger, demander	demand	verlangen, fordern	exigir, demandar	exigir, pedir
esiliato, a	exilé, e	exile	Verbannte(f, m)	exiliado, a	exilado, a
esilio	exil	exile	Verbannung(f)	exilio	exílio
esistenza	existence	existence, life	Dasein(n)	existencia	existência
esistere	exister	exist	existieren	existir	existir
esitare	hésiter	hesitate	zögern	dudar	hesitar
esitazione	hésitation	hesitation	Zögern(n)	vacilación	hesitação
esodo	exode	exodus	Massenauswanderung(f)	èxodo	èxodo
esofago	oesophage	oesophagus	Speiseröhre(f)	esófago	esófago
esordire	débuter	begin, start	an = fangen	principiar	principiar
esotico, a	exotique	exotic	exotisch	exótico, a	exótico, a
espansione	expansion	expansion	Ausdehnung(f)	expansión	expansão
espatriare	expatrier(s')	expatriate	aus = wandern	expatriarse	expatriar-se
espatrio	expatriation	expatriation	Vertreibung(f)	expatriación	expatriação
espellere	expulser	expel, eject	aus = weisen	expulsar	expulsar
espellere	éjecter	eject	aus = stoßen	eyectar, expulsar	expelir
esperienza	expérience	experience	Erfahrung(f)	experiencia	experiência
esperimento	expérience	experiment	Versuch(m)	experimento	experiência
esperto, a	expert, e	expert	Experte(m), Expertin f	experto, a; perito, a	perito, a
espirare	expirer	breathe out	aus = atmen	espirar	expirar
esplodere	exploser	explode, blow up	explodieren	estallar	explodir

551

Italian	French	English	German	Spanish	Portuguese
esplorare	explorer	explore	erforschen	explorar	explorar
esploratore, trice	explorateur	explorer	Forscher(in f)m	explorador, a	explorador, a
esplorazione	exploration	exploration	Erforschung(f)	exploración	exploração
esplosione	explosion	explosion	Explosion(f)	explosión	explosão
esportare	exporter	export	exportieren	exportar	exportar
esportazione	exportation	export(ing)	Export(m), Ausfuhr(f)	exportación	exportação
espositore, trice	exposant, e	exhibitor	Aussteller(in f)m	expositor, a	expositor, a
esposizione, mostra	exposition	exhibition, show	Ausstellung(f)	exposición	exposição
espressione	expression	expression	Ausdruck(m)	expresión	expressão
esprimersi	exprimer(s')	express oneself	aus = drücken, sich	expresar(se)	exprimir-se
essa; lei; ella	elle	she	sie	ella	ela
esse, loro	elles	they	sie	ellas	elas
essenziale	essentiel, le	essential	wesentlich	esencial	essencial
essenziale	essentiel	main thing(the)	Hauptsache(f)	esencial	essencial
essere	être	be	sein	ser, estar	ser, estar
essere	être	be	sein	estar	estar
essi; loro	ils	they	sie	ellos	eles
Est	Est	East	Osten(m)	Este	Este, Leste
estasi	extase	ecstasy	Entzückung(f)	éxtasis	êxtase
estate	été	summer	Sommer(m)	verano	verão
estendere	étendre, agrandir	expand	aus = dehnen	extender(se)	estender
estendersi	étendre(s')	stretch	erstrecken, sich	extenderse	estender-se
estensione	extension	extension	Ausdehnung(f)	extensión	extensão
estensione, ampiezza	étendue	extent	Umfang(m)	extensión, amplitud	extensão
esteriore	extérieur, e	outside	äußer; Außen-	exterior	exterior
esterno, a	extérieur, e	outer, outside	äußere	externo, a	exterior; externo, a
esterno, a	externe	external	äußerlich	externo, a	externo, a
esterno	extérieur	outside; exterior	Außenseite(f)	exterior	exterior
estero, a	étranger, ère	foreign	ausländisch	extranjero, a	estrangeiro, a
estero, a	extérieur, e	foreign	Außen-	exterior	exterior
estero	étranger(l')	foreign country	Ausland(n)	extranjero	estrangeiro
estero(all')	étranger(à l')	abroad	Ausland(im)	extranjero(en el)	estrangeiro(ao)
estetico, a	esthétique	aesthetic	ästhetisch	estético, a	estético, a
estintore	extincteur	extinguisher	Feuerlöscher(m)	extintor	extintor
estinzione	extinction	extinction	Löschen(Aus-)(n)	extinción	extinção
estivo, a	estival, e	summer	sommerlich	estival	estival
estrarre	extraire	extract	heraus = ziehen, ziehen	extraer	extrair
estratto	relevé	statement	Aufstellung(f)machen	extracto	levantamento
estratto conto	relevé(compte)	statement(bank)	Kontoauszug(m)	estado(cuentas)	extracto(conta)
estrazione	extraction	extraction	Kohlenförderung(f)	extracción	extracção
estrazione	extraction	extraction	Zahnziehen(n)	extracción	extracção
estremità	extrémité	extremity, end	Extremität(f)	extremidad	extremidade
estremità; punta	embout	tip, end	Endstück(n)	punta; remate	ponta; remate
estremo, a	extrême	extreme	extrem	extremo, a	extremo, a
esultanza	allégresse	elation	Heiterkeit(f)	júbilo, alegría	júbilo, alegria
età	âge	age	Alter(n)	edad	idade
eternità	éternité	eternity	Ewigkeit(f)	eternidad	eternidade
eterno, a	éternel, le	eternal	ewig	eterno, a	eterno, a
eterosessuale	hétérosexuel, le	heterosexual	heterosexuell	heterosexual	heterossexual
etichetta	étiquette	label, tag	Schild(n)	etiqueta	rótulo
etico, a	éthique	ethical	ethisch	ético, a	ético, a
etnico, a	ethnique	ethnic(al)	ethnisch	étnico, a	étnico, a
ettaro	hectare	hectare	Hektar(m)	hectárea	hectare
euforico, a	euphorique	euphoric	euphorisch	eufórico, a	eufórico, a
eutanasia	euthanasie	euthanasia	Euthanasie(f)	eutanasia	eutanásia
evacuare	évacuer	evacuate	räumen, leeren	evacuar	evacuar
evaporazione	évaporation	evaporation	Verdunstung(f)	evaporación	evaporação
evasione	évasion	escape	Flucht(f)	evasión	evasão
eventuale	éventuel, le	possible	möglich	eventual	eventual
eventualità	éventualité	contingency	Eventualität(f)	eventualidad	eventualidade
evidenza, prova	évidence, preuve	evidence, proof	Beweis(m)	evidencia, prueba	evidência, prova
evidente	évident, e	obvious, evident	offensichtlich	evidente	evidente
evidentemente	évidemment	of course	natürlich	desde luego	evidentemente
evitare	éviter	avoid	vermeiden	evitar	evitar
evocare	évoquer	evoke	wach = rufen, erinnern	evocar	evocar
evoluzione	évolution	evolution	Entwicklung(f)	evolución	evolução
evolvere	évoluer	evolve	entwickeln, sich	evolucionar	evoluir
ex	ancien, ne	former	ehemalig	ex, antiguo, a	antigo, a

F

Italian	French	English	German	Spanish	Portuguese
fa	il y a	ago	vor	hace	há
fabbrica	usine	factory, plant	Fabrik(f)	fábrica	fábrica
fabbrica	usine	plant	Anlage(f)	fábrica	fábrica
fabbricante	fabricant, e	manufacturer	Hersteller(in f)m	fabricante	fabricante
fabbricare	fabriquer	manufacture, make	her = stellen	fabricar	fabricar
fabbricazione	fabrication	manufacture	Herstellung(f)	fabricación	fabrico
faccenda, affare	affaire	affair, matter	Affäre(f), Sache(f)	asunto	assunto
faccia	face	face	Gesicht(n)	cara	face; cara
faccia	face	side	Seite(f)	cara	face; lado
faccia	figure	face	Gesicht(n)	rostro	rosto
facciata	façade	front(age)	Fassade(f)	fachada	fachada
facile	facile	easy	leicht	fácil	fácil
facilmente	facilement	easily	leicht	fácilmente	fácilmente
facoltà	faculté	possibility	Fähigkeit(f)	facultad	faculdade
facoltà	faculté	Faculty	Fakultät(f)	facultad	faculdade
facoltativo, a	facultatif, ive	optional	wahlfrei, beliebig	facultativo, a	facultativo, a
fagiano	faisan	pheasant	Fasan(m)	faisán	faisão
fagiolo; fagiolino	haricot	bean	Bohne(f)	judía	feijão
faglia	faille	break, fault	Spalte(f)	falla	falha
falda	nappe(eau)	sheet, expanse	Wasserfläche(f)	capa(de agua)	lençol(de água)
falegname	menuisier	joiner, carpenter	Tischler(m)	carpintero	carpinteiro
fallimento	faillite	failure; bankruptcy	Konkurs(m)	quiebra, ruina	falência
fallire	faillite(faire)	bankrupt(go)	bankrott sein	quiebra(hacer)	falir
fallire	échouer	fail	scheitern	fracasar	falhar
fallo, errore	faute, erreur	mistake, error	Fehler(m), Irrtum(m)	falta, error	falta, erro
falsificare	falsifier	falsify	fälschen	falsificar	falsificar
falso, a	faux, fausse	wrong, false	falsch	falso, a	falso, a
fama	renommée	fame	Ruhm(m)	fama	fama
fame(aver)	faim(avoir)	hunger(hungry be)	Hunger(m)(haben)	hambre(tener)	fome(ter)
fame, carestia	famine	famine	Hungersnot(f)	hambre	fome
famiglia	famille	family	Familie(f)	familia	família
familiare	familial, e	family	Familien-	familiar	familiar
familiare	familier, ière	familiar	familiär	familiar	familiar
fanale, faro(-ri)	phare(s)	headlight	Scheinwerfer(m)	faro(s)	faróis
fanatico, a	fanatique	fanatic(al)	fanatisch	fanático, a	fanático, a
fango, melma	boue	mud	Schlamm(m)	barro	lama
fannullone, a	fainéant, e	lazy	faul	holgazán, a	preguiçoso, a
fantasia	fantaisie	fancy; fantasy	Spielerei(f)	fantasía	fantasia
fantasia	fantasme	fantasy	Phantasievorstellung	fantasma	fantasma
fantasma	fantôme	ghost	Gespenst(n)	fantasma	fantasma
fantastico, a	fantastique	fantastic	phantastisch	fantástico, a	fantástico, a
fardello	fardeau	burden	Last(f)	carga	fardo
fare	faire	do, make	tun, machen	hacer	fazer
fare	faire	make, do	machen, tun	hacer	fazer
fare l'uovo	pondre	lay	Eier legen	poner(huevos)	pôr(ovos)
farfalla	papillon	butterfly	Schmetterling(m)	mariposa	borboleta
farfugliare	bafouiller	splutter, stammer	stammeln	balbucear	balbuciar
farina	farine	flour	Mehl(n)	harina	farinha
faringe	pharynx	pharynx	Rachen(m)	faringe	faringe
farmacia	pharmacie	chemist's	Apotheke(f)	farmacia	farmácia
farmacista	pharmacien, ne	chemist, pharmacist	Apotheker(in f)m	farmacéutico, a	farmacêutico, a
faro	phare	lighthouse	Leuchtturm(m)	faro	farol
fasciatura	bandage	bandage	Bandage(f), Verband(m)	vendaje, venda	ligadura
fascino	charme	charm	Charme(m), Reiz(m)	encanto	encanto
fascio	faisceau	beam	Strahl(m)(Licht)	haz	foco
fascista	fasciste	fascist	Faschist(in f)m	fascista	fascista
fase	phase	phase, stage	Phase(f)	fase	fase
fastoso, a	fastueux, se	sumptuous	prunkvoll	ostentoso, a	faustoso, a
fata	fée	fairy	Fee(f)	hada	fada
fatale	fatal, e	fatal	tödlich	fatal	fatal
fatalità	fatalité	fatality, fate	Schicksal(n)	fatalidad	fatalidade

I

553

Italian	French	English	German	Spanish	Portuguese
fatica	peine	trouble, effort	Anstrengung(f)	dificultad	esforço
faticoso, a	fatigant, e	tiring	anstrengend	fatigante	cansativo, a
fatto	fait	fact	Tatsache(f)	hecho	facto
fattore	facteur	factor	Faktor(m)	factor	factor
fattore, essa	fermier, ière	farmer	Bauer(m), Bäuerin(f)	granjero, a	caseiro, a
fattoria	ferme	farm	Bauernhof(m)	granja	quinta
fattorino	chasseur(hôtel)	page(boy), bellboy	Page(m), Hotelboy(m)	botones	paquete
fattura	facture	invoice, bill	Rechnung(f)	factura	factura
fatturato	chiffre(affaire)	turnover	Umsatz(m)	volumen(negocios)	volume(negócios)
fauna	faune	fauna	Fauna(f), Tierwelt(f)	fauna	fauna
favoloso, a	fabuleux, se	fabulous	phantastisch	fabuloso, a	fabuloso, a
favore	faveur	favour	Gunst(f)	favor	favor
favorevole	favorable	favourable	günstig	favorable	favorável
favorire	favoriser	favour	begünstigen	favorecer	favorecer
favorito, a	favori, ite	favourite	Favorit(in f)m	favorito, a	favorito, a
fazzoletto	mouchoir	handkerchief	Taschentuch(n)	pañuelo	lenço
febbraio	février	February	Februar(m)	febrero	Fevereiro
febbre	fièvre	fever, temperature	Fieber(n)	fiebre	febre
fecondazione	fécondation	fertilization	Befruchtung(f)	fecundación	fecundação
fecondità	fécondité	fertility	Fruchtbarkeit(f)	fecundidad	fecundidade
fede	foi	faith	Glaube(m)	fe	fé
fedele	fidèle	faithful	treu	fiel	fiel
federazione	fédération	federation	Verband(m)	federación	federação
fegato	foie	liver	Leber(f)	hígado	fígado
felce	fougère	fern	Farn(-kraut n)m	helecho	feto
felice	heureux, se	happy, glad	glücklich	feliz	feliz
felicità	bonheur	happiness	Glück(n)	felicidad	felicidade
femmina	femelle	female	Weibchen(n)	hembra	fêmea
femminile	féminin	feminine	weiblich	femenino	feminino
femminile	féminin, e	feminine	fraulich	femenino, a	feminino, a
fendere	fendre	slit	auf = schlitzen	rajar, hender	rachar, fender
fenomeno	phénomène	phenomenon(-mena)	Phänomen(n)	fenómeno	fenómeno
ferie(le)	congé	holiday, vacation	Urlaub(m)	vacaciones	férias
ferire	blesser	injure, wound	verletzen	herir	ferir
ferire, offendere	blesser, offenser	hurt, offend	kränken	lastimar, ofender	magoar, ofender
ferirsi	blesser(se)	injured(to be)	verletzen, sich	herir(se)	ferir-se
ferita	blessure	injury, wound	Verletzung(f)	herida	ferida
fermare	arrêter	stop	halten(an-, auf-)	parar	parar
fermarsi	arrêter(s')	stop	stehen = bleiben	pararse	parar
fermata	arrêt	stop	Pause(f), Stillstand	parada	paragem
fermentare	fermenter	ferment	gären	fermentar	fermentar
fermezza	fermeté	firmness	Entschlossenheit(f)	firmeza	firmeza
fermo, a; solido, a	ferme	firm	fest	firme	firme
feroce	féroce	ferocious, fierce	wild, furchtbar	feroz	feroz
ferraglia, rottame	ferraille	scrap iron	Alteisen(n)	chatarra	sucata
ferramenta	quincaillerie	ironmonger's	Eisenwarenhandlung(f)	ferretería	loja de ferragens
ferro	fer	iron	Eisen(n)	hierro	ferro
ferro da stiro	fer à repasser	iron	Bügeleisen(n)	plancha	ferro de passar
ferrovia	chemin de fer	railway	Eisenbahn(f)	ferrocarril	caminho de ferro
fertile	fertile	fertile	fruchtbar	fértil	fértil
fessura	fente	split; slot; slit	Spalt(m)	grieta	fenda
fessura; spacco	fente	slit	Schlitz(m)	raja	fenda
fessura, crepa	fissure, fente	crack, fissure	Riß(m), Spalte(f)	fisura, grieta	fissura; fenda
festa	fête	celebration	Feier(f)	fiesta	festa
festino	festin	feast, banquet	Festmahl(n)	festín	festim, banquete
festival	festival	festival	Festspiel(n)	festival	festival
festivo(giorno)	férié(jour)	public holiday	Feiertag(m)	festivo(día)	feriado(dia)
fetido, a	infect, e	foul, vile	ekelhaft, stinkig	asqueroso, a	asqueroso, a
feto	foetus	foetus	Fötus(m)	feto	feto
fetta	tranche	slice	Scheibe(f)	rebanada	fatia
fetta di pane	tartine de pain	slice of bread	Brotscheibe(f)	rebanada de pan	fatia de pão
fettina, fetta	rondelle	slice	Scheibe(f)	rodaja	rodela
fiamma	flamme	flame	Flamme(f)	llama	chama
fiammifero	allumette	match(-es)	Streichholz(n)	cerilla	fósforo
fiato, soffio	souffle	breath	Luft(f), Puste(f)	soplo, aliento	sopro, fôlego
fibbia	boucle	buckle	Schnalle(f)	hebilla	fivela; argola
fibra	fibre	fibre	Faser(f)	fibra	fibra
fidanzarsi	fiancer(se)	engaged(get)	verloben, sich	prometerse	ficar noivo, a

Italian	French	English	German	Spanish	Portuguese
fidanzato, a	fiancé, e	fiancé(e)	Verlobte(f, m)	novio, a	noivo, a
fiducia	confiance	confidence, trust	Vertrauen(n)	confianza	confiança
fiducia(aver)	confiance(avoir)	trust	vertrauen(jdm.)	confianza(tener)	confiar
fienile	grange	barn	Scheune(f)	granero	celeiro
fiera	foire	fair	Messe(f)	feria	feira
fierezza	fierté	pride	Stolz(m)	orgullo	orgulho
fiero, a	fier, fière	proud	stolz	altivo, a	altivo, a
figlia	fille	daughter	Tochter(f)	hija	filha
figlio	fils	son	Sohn(m)	hijo	filho
figura	figure	figure	Figur(f)	figura	figura
fila, corsia	file	lane	Spur(f)	fila	fila
fila, coda	file	queue, line	Schlange(f)	fila	fila, bicha
fila	rangée	row	Reihe(f)	hilera, fila	fileira, renque
filamento	filament	filament	Faser(f), Faden(m)	filamento	filamento
filiale	filiale	subsidiary	Filiale(f)	filial, sucursal	filial, sucursal
film	film	film, movie	Film(m)	película	filme
filmare	filmer	film	filmen	rodar, filmar	filmar
filo	fil	thread	Faden(m)	hilo	fio
filo(di ferro)	fil(de fer)	wire	Draht(m)	alambre	arame
filosofia	philosophie	philosophy	Philosophie(f)	filosofía	filosofia
filtro	filtre	filter	Filter(m)	filtro	filtro
fin da	dès(que)	as soon as	sobald	desde	logo que
finale	final, e	final	letzte, Schluß-	final	final
finanza	finance	finance	Finanzwelt, Finanzen	finanza	finança
finanziamento	financement	financing	Finanzierung(f)	financiación	financiamento
finanziare	financer	finance	finanzieren	financiar	financiar
finanziario, a	financier, ière	financial	finanziell	financiero, a	financeiro, a
fine	fin	end	Ende(n)	fin	fim
fine, sottile	fin, e	fine, thin	fein, dünn	fino, a	fino, a
fine settimana	week-end	weekend	Wochenende(n)	fin de semana	fim de semana
finestra	fenêtre	window	Fenster(n)	ventana	janela
finimenti	harnais	harness	Geschirr(n)	arnés	arnês
finire	finir	finish, end	beenden	acabar, terminar	acabar, terminar
fino	jusqu'à	as far as	bis	hasta	até
fino a, sino a	jusqu'à	until, till	bis	hasta	até
finzione	fiction	fiction	Fiktion(f)	ficción	ficção
fiocco	flocon	flake	Flocke(f)	copo	floco
fioraio	fleuriste	florist	Blumenhändler(in f)m	florista	florista
fiore	fleur	flower	Blume(f)	flor	flor
firma	signature	signature	Unterschrift(f)	firma	assinatura
firmare	signer	sign	unterschreiben	firmar	assinar
fiscale	fiscal, e	fiscal, tax	fiskalisch, Steuer-	fiscal	fiscal
fiscalità	fiscalité	tax system	Steuerwesen(n)	fiscalidad	fiscalidade
fischiare	siffler	whistle	pfeifen	silbar	assobiar
fischiare, urlare	huer	boo	aus = pfeifen	abuchear	vaiar
fischietto	sifflet	whistle	Pfeife(f)	pito	apito
fisco	fisc	Inland Revenue	Fiskus(m), Finanzamt	fisco	fisco
fisica	physique	physics	Physik(f)	física	física
fisico, a	physique	physical	physisch	físico, a	físico, a
fisico, a	physicien, ne	physicist	Physiker(in f)m	físico, a	físico, a
fisico	physique	physique	Äußere(n), Aussehen(n)	físico	físico
fisionomia	physionomie	physiognomy	Gesichtsausdruck(m)	fisionomía	fisionomia
fissare	fixer	fix, attach	befestigen	fijar	fixar
fissazione	fixation	fixing, fixation	Befestigung(f)	fijación	fixação
fissione	fission	fission	Spaltung(f)(Atom)	fisión	fissão
fisso, a	fixe	fixed	fest	fijo, a	fixo, a
fiume	fleuve	river	Strom(m)	río	rio
fiume	rivière	river	Fluß(m)	río, ribera	rio, ribeira
flash	flash	flash	Blitz(m)	flash	flash
flauto	flûte	flute	Flöte(f)	flauta	flauta
flessibile	flexible	flexible	flexibel	flexible	flexível
flessibile	souple	supple; flexible	biegsam	flexible	maleável
flessibilità	souplesse	suppleness	Biegsamkeit(f)	flexibilidad	flexibilidade
flora	flore	flora	Flora(f), Pflanzenwelt	flora	flora
flotta	flotte	fleet	Flotte(f)	flota	frota
fluido	fluide	fluid	Flüssigkeit(f)	fluido	fluido
flusso	flux	flow	Fluß(m), Strömung(f)	flujo	fluxo
flutto	flot	wave; flood	Welle(f); Flut(f)	oleada	corrente

I

Italian	French	English	German	Spanish	Portuguese
fluttuazione	fluctuation	fluctuation	Schwanken(n)	fluctuación	flutuação
foca	phoque	seal	Seehund(m)	foca	foca
focolare	foyer	home	Heim(n)	hogar	lar
focolare	foyer, âtre	fire-place, hearth	Feuerstelle(f), Herd m	hogar, chimenea	lareira
fodera	housse	cover	Bezug(m)	funda	cobertura
foglia	feuille	leaf(leaves)	Blatt(n)	hoja	folha
foglio	feuille	sheet	Blatt(n)	hoja	folha
fogna	égout	sewer, drain	Gulli, Abwasserkanäle	cloaca	esgoto
folclore	folklore	folklore	Folklore(f)	folklore	folclore
folla	foule	crowd	Menge(f)	muchedumbre	multidão
follia, pazzia	folie	madness, folly	Wahnsinn(m), Wahn(m)	locura	loucura
fondamentale	fondamental, e	fundamental	fundamental	fundamental	fundamental
fondare	fonder	found	gründen	fundar	fundar
fondatore, trice	fondateur, trice	founder	Gründer(in f)m	fundador, a	fundador, a
fondere	fondre	melt	schmelzen	fundir	fundir
fondi	fonds	funds	Fonds(m), Kapital(n)	fondos	fundos, capital
fondo	fond	bottom; back	Boden(m), Grund(m)	fondo	fundo
fonetico, a	phonétique	phonetic	phonetisch	fonético, a	fonético, a
fontana	fontaine	fountain	Springbrunnen(m)	fuente	fonte
fonte, origine	source, origine	source	Ursprung(m)	fuente, origen	fonte, origem
foraggio	fourrage	fodder	Futter(n)	forraje	forragem
foratura	crevaison	puncture	Reifenpanne(f)	pinchazo	furo
forbici	ciseaux	scissors	Schere(f)	tijeras	tesoura
forca	fourche	pitchfork, fork	Gabel(f)(Heu-; Mist-)	horca	forcado
forchetta	fourchette	fork	Gabel(f)	tenedor	garfo
foresta, bosco	forêt	forest	Wald(m)	bosque	floresta, bosque
forfettario, a	forfaitaire	inclusive	pauschal	global; convenido, a	preço fixo(a)
forfora	pellicule	dandruff	Schuppe(f)	caspa	caspa
forma	forme	shape, form	Form(f), Aussehen(n)	forma	forma
forma	forme	form	Verfassung(f)	forma(en)	forma
formaggio	fromage	cheese	Käse(m)	queso	queijo
formalità	formalité	formality	Formalität(f)	formalidad	formalidade
formare	former	form	bilden, formen	formar	formar
formato	format	format, size	Format(n)	formato, tamaño	formato
formazione	formation	formation	Entstehung(f)	formación	formação
formazione	formation	training	Ausbildung(f)	formación	formação
formica	fourmi	ant	Ameise(f)	hormiga	formiga
formidabile	formidable	tremendous	großartig	formidable	formidável
formula	formule	formula	Formel(f)	fórmula	fórmula
fornello	réchaud	stove	Kocher(m)	hornillo	fogão
fornire	fournir	supply, provide	beliefern	proveer, dar	fornecer
fornire	fournir	provide	versorgen, liefern	proveer	fornecer
fornitore, trice	fournisseur, se	supplier	Lieferant(in f)m	abastecedor, a	fornecedor, a
fornitura	fourniture	supply(ing)	Lieferung(f)	abastecimiento	fornecimento
forno	four	oven	Ofen(m)	horno	forno
forse	peut-être	perhaps, maybe	vielleicht	quizá(s)	talvez
forte	fort, e	strong	stark	fuerte	forte
forte; alto, a	fort, e	loud	laut	fuerte; alto, a	forte; alto, a
forte; alto, a	grand, e	high	hoch	alto, a	alto, a
fortuna	fortune	fortune	Vermögen(n)	fortuna	fortuna
fortuna	chance	luck; chance	Glück(m), Chance(f)	suerte, fortuna	sorte
fortuna(avere)	chance(avoir)	fortunate(be)	Glück haben	suerte(tener)	sorte(ter)
fortunatamente	heureusement	fortunately	glücklicherweise	afortunadamente	felizmente
fortunato, a	chanceux, se	lucky	Glückspilz(m)	afortunado, a	afortunado, a
foruncolo	furoncle	boil	Furunkel(m)	furúnculo	furúnculo
forza	force	strength	Stärke(f), Kraft(f)	fuerza	força
forza	force	force	Gewalt(f); Kraft(f)	fuerza	força
forzare	forcer	force	zwingen	forzar	forçar
foschia	brume	mist, haze	Nebel(m)	bruma	bruma
fossa; buca	fosse	pit	Grube(f)	fosa, hoyo	fossa
fossato, fosso	fossé	ditch	Graben(m)	cuneta	fosso
fossile	fossile	fossil	Fossil(n)	fósil	fóssil
foto, fotografia	photo	photo(graph)	Foto(n)	foto	fotografia
fotografare	photographier	take a photo	fotografieren	fotografiar	fotografar
fotografia	photographie	photography	Fotografie(f)	fotografía	fotografia
foulard	foulard	scarf	Seidentuch, Halstuch	fular, pañuelo	lenço, cachecol
fra, tra	parmi	among	unter	entre	entre
fragile	fragile	fragile	zerbrechlich	frágil	frágil

Italian	French	English	German	Spanish	Portuguese
fragile	cassant, e	brittle	brüchig, spröde	quebradizo, a	quebradiço, a
fragola	fraise	strawberry	Erdbeere(f)	fresa	morango
frammento	fragment	fragment	Fragment(n)	fragmento	fragmento
frana, slavina	éboulement	landslide	Erdrutsch(m)	desprendimiento	desmoronamento
franco, a; sincero, a	franc, che	frank	offen, ehrlich	franco, a	franco, a
francobollo	timbre(-poste)	stamp	Briefmarke(f)	sello	selo
frase	phrase	sentence	Satz(m)	frase	frase
fratello	frère	brother	Bruder(m)	hermano	irmão
fraternità	fraternité	brotherhood	Brüderlichkeit(f)	fraternidad	fraternidade
frattura	fracture	fracture	Bruch(m)	fractura	fractura
frattura, rottura	cassure, rupture	break	Bruch(m)	rotura	ruptura, quebra
frazione	fraction	fraction	Bruchteil(m)	fracción	fracção
freccia	flèche	arrow	Pfeil(m)	flecha	flecha, seta
freccia	clignotant	indicator	Blinklicht(n)	intermitente	pisca
freddo, a	froid, e	cold	kalt	frío, a	frio, a
freddo(avere)	froid(avoir)	cold(to be)	frieren	frío(tener)	frio(ter)
frenare	freiner	brake	bremsen	frenar	travar
freno	frein	brake	Bremse(f)	freno	travão
frequente	fréquent, e	frequent	häufig	frecuente	frequente
frequenza	fréquence	frequency	Frequenz(f)	frecuencia	frequência
fresco, a	frais, fraîche	fresh	frisch	fresco, a	fresco, a
fretta	hâte	haste, hurry	Eile(f)	prisa	pressa
fretta(avere)	pressé, e(être)	hurry(be in a)	eilig(es...haben)	prisa(tener)	pressa(ter)
fretta(in), presto	vite	quickly, fast	schnell, rasch	rápido, pronto	rápido, a; depressa
friggere	frire	fry	braten	freír	fritar
frigorifero, a	frigorifique	refrigerating	Kühl-; kalt, kühl	frigorífico, a	frigorífico, a
frigorifero	frigo, frigidaire	fridge	Kühlschrank(m)	frigorífico	frigorífico
frigorifero	réfrigérateur	refrigerator	Kühlschrank(m)	nevera	frigorífico
frittella	beignets	fritters	Krapfen, Pfannkuchen	buñuelos	pastéis
frivolo, a	frivole	frivolous	frivol, leichtsinnig	frívolo, a	frívolo, a
frizione	embrayage	clutch	Kupplung(f)	embrague	embraiagem
frode	fraude	fraud	Betrug(m)	fraude	fraude
frode(fiscale)	fraude(fiscale)	tax evasion	Steuerhinterziehung f	fraude(fiscal)	fraude(fiscal)
fronte	front	forehead	Stirn(f)	frente	testa
frontiera, limite	frontière, limite	boundary	Grenze(f)	frontera, límite	fronteira, limite
frugare	fouiller	search	suchen, durchsuchen	registrar	rebuscar
frusta	fouet	whip	Peitsche(f)	látigo	chicote
frustrazione	frustration	frustration	Enttäuschung(f)	frustración	frustração
frutta cotta	compote	stewed fruit	Kompott(n)	compota	compota
fruttare	rapporter	bring in, yield	ein = bringen	proporcionar	render
frutti di mare	fruits de mer	seafood	Meeresfrüchte(f, pl.)	marisco	marisco
frutto; frutta	fruit(s)	fruit	Frucht(f)	fruta	fruta
frutto, rendita	rapport	yield, return	Ertrag(m)	renta; ganancia	renda; ganho
fucile	fusil	shot-gun, rifle	Gewehr(n)	fusil	espingarda
fuga	fuite	flight, escape	Flucht(f)	huída	fuga
fuggire	fuir	run away, flee	fliehen	huir	fugir
fuggire	enfuir(s')	run away	fliehen	huir	fugir
fuggitivo, a	fugitif, ive	fugitive	flüchtig	fugitivo, a	fugitivo, a
fulmine	foudre	lightning	Blitz(m)	rayo	raio
fumare	fumer	smoke	rauchen	fumar	fumar
fumatore, trice	fumeurs	smokers	Raucher(m)	fumadores	fumadores
fumetto	bande dessinée	cartoon(strip)	Comic Strip(m)	comics, tebeos	banda desenhada
fumo	fumée	smoke	Rauch(m)	humo	fumo
funerale	enterrement	burial, funeral	Beerdigung(f)	entierro	enterro
funerale	funérailles	funeral	Begräbnis(n)	funerales	funeral
fungo	champignon	mushroom	Pilz(m)	champiñón, seta	cogumelo
funzionamento	fonctionnement	functioning	Betrieb(m)	funcionamiento	funcionamento
funzionare	fonctionner	function, work, run	funktionieren	funcionar	funcionar
funzionare	marcher	work, run	in Betrieb sein	marchar	funcionar
funzionare(fare)	marcher(faire)	operate	bedienen	funcionar(hacer)	funcionar(fazer)
funzionario, a	fonctionnaire	civil servant	Beamte(r)m, Beamtin(f)	funcionario, a	funcionário, a
funzione	fonction	function	Funktion(f)	función	função
funzione	fonction	function	Stellung(f), Amt(n)	función	função
fuoco	feu	fire	Feuer(n)	fuego	fogo
fuori	dehors	outside, outdoors	draußen	fuera, afuera	fora
fuori, fuori di	hors de	out of	außer(+dat)	fuera de	fora de
fuoribordo	hors-bord	speed-boat	Außenbordmotor(m)	fuera borda	fora de borda
furbizia	ruse	trick, craftiness	List(f)	ardid; astucia	astúcia

Italian	French	English	German	Spanish	Portuguese
furbo, a	malin, igne	smart, clever	gerissen, schlau	pillo, a; astuto, a	esperto, a; astuto, a
furioso, a	furieux, se	furious	wütend	furioso, a	furioso, a
furore	fureur	fury	Wut(f)	furor	furor
furto	vol	theft, robbery	Diebstahl(m)	robo	roubo
furto con scasso	cambriolage	burglary	Einbruch(m)	robo, atraco	roubo, assalto
fusione	fusion	fusion, melting	Schmelzen(n)(Ver-)	fusión	fusão
fusione, alleanza	fusion	merger	Vereinigung(f), Fusion	fusión	fusão
fusto, barile	fût	barrel	Faß(n)	barril	barril
futuro, a	futur, e	future	zukünftig	futuro, a	futuro, a
futuro	futur	future	Zukunft(f)	futuro	futuro

G

Italian	French	English	German	Spanish	Portuguese
gabbia	cage	cage	Käfig(m)	jaula	gaiola, jaula
gabbiano	mouette	seagull	Möve(f)	gaviota	gaivota
gabbiano	goéland	gull	Silbermöwe(f)	gaviota	gaivota
gabinetto	cabinet(pol.)	cabinet	Kabinett(n)	gabinete	gabinete
gadget	gadget	gadget	Spielerei(f)	chisme, mecanismo	aparelho
galante	galant, e	gallant	galant	galante	galante
galassia	galaxie	galaxy	Galaxie(f)	galaxia	galáxia
galleggiare	flotter	float	schwimmen, treiben	flotar	flutuar
galleria	galerie	arcade	Passage(f)	galería	galeria
galleria	galerie	gallery	Galerie, Ausstellung	galería	galeria
gallina	poule	hen	Huhn(n)	gallina	galinha
gallo	coq	cock	Hahn(m)	gallo	galo
gallone, grado	galon	stripe	Galone(f)	galón	galão
galoppo	galop	gallop	Galopp(m)	galope	galope
gamba	jambe	leg	Bein(n)	pierna	perna
gamberetto	crevette	prawn, shrimp	Krabbe(f)	gamba, camarón	camarão
gambero(di mare)	homard	lobster	Hummer(m)	bogavante	lavagante
gambero(di fiume)	écrevisse	crayfish	Flußkrebs(m)	cangrejo(de río)	caranguejo
gancio, uncino	crochet	hook	Haken(m)	gancho	gancho
ganglio	ganglion	ganglion, gland	Ganglien(pl.)	ganglio	gânglio
gangster	gangster	gangster	Gangster(m)	gángster	gangster
gara	concours	contest	Wettbewerb(m)	concurso	concurso
gara, sfida	challenge	challenge, contest	Wettkampf(m)	trofeo, challenge	desafio, torneio
garage	garage	garage	Garage(f)	garaje, garage	garagem
garagista	garagiste	garage mechanic	Autoschlosser(m)	garajista	garagista
garantire	garantir	guarantee, warrant	gewährleisten	garantizar	garantir
garanzia	garantie	guarantee; warranty	Garantie(f)	garantía	garantia
gas	gaz	gas	Gas(n)	gas	gás
gasolio	gas-oil	diesel oil	Diesel(n), Dieselöl(n)	gasoil	gasóleo
gassato, a	gazeux, se	fizzy, sparkling	sprudelnd; Sprudel-	gaseoso, a	gasoso, a
gassoso, a	gazeux, se	gaseous	gasförmig	gaseoso, a	gasoso, a
gastrico, a	gastrique	gastric	Magen-	gástrico, a	gástrico, a
gastronomia	gastronomie	gastronomy	Gastronomie(f)	gastronomía	gastronomia
gatto, a	chat, te	cat	Kater(m), Katze(f)	gato, a	gato, a
gelare	geler	freeze	frieren	helar	gelar
gelatina	gelée	jelly	Gelee(n)	jalea	geleia
gelato, a; ghiacciato	glacé, e; gelé, e	icy	eisig	helado, a	gelado, a
gelato	glace	ice cream	Eis(n)	helado	gelado
gelone	engelure	chilblain	Frostbeule(f)	sabañón	frieira
gelosia	jalousie	jealousy	Eifersucht(f)	celos	ciúme
geloso, a	jaloux, se	jealous	eifersüchtig	celoso, a	ciumento, a
gemello, a	jumeau, jumelle	twin	Zwilling(m)	gemelo, a	gémeo, a
gemere	gémir	moan	stöhnen	gemir	gemer
gemma	bourgeon	bud	Knospe(f)	brote, botón	rebento, botão

Italian	French	English	German	Spanish	Portuguese
genealogia	généalogie	genealogy	Genealogie(f)	genealogía	genealogia
generale	général, e	general	allgemein, generell	general	geral
generale	général	general	General(m)	general	general
generare	engendrer	generate	zeugen, erzeugen	engendrar	engendrar
generare	générer	generate	erzeugen	engendrar	gerar
generatore	générateur	generator	Generator(m)	generador	gerador
generazione	génération	generation	Generation(f)	generación	geração
genere	genre	kind, sort	Art(f), Sorte(f)	género	género
genere(in)	général(en)	usually, in general	allgemeinen(im)	general(en)	geral(em)
genero	gendre	son-in-law	Schwiegersohn(m)	yerno	genro
generoso, a	généreux, se	generous	freigebig	generoso, a	generoso, a
genetica	génétique	genetics	Genetik(f)	genética	genética
gengiva	gencive	gum	Zahnfleisch(n)	encía	gengiva
geniale	génial, e	brilliant	genial	genial	genial
genio	génie	genius	Genie(n)	genio	génio
genitale	génital, e	genital	Genital-	genital	genital
genitori	parents	parents	Eltern(pl)	padres	pais
gennaio	janvier	January	Januar(m)	enero	Janeiro
genocidio	génocide	genocide	Völkermord(m)	genocidio	genocídio
gente(la)	gens	people	Leute(pl.)	gente	gente, pessoas
gentile	gentil, le	kind, nice	nett	gentil, amable	gentil, amável
genuino, a	authentique	genuine	echt	genuino, a	autêntico, a
geografia	géographie	geography	Erdkunde(f)	geografía	geografia
geologia	géologie	geology	Geologie(f)	geología	geologia
geometria	géométrie	geometry	Geometrie(f)	geometría	geometria
gerarchia	hiérarchie	hierarchy	Hierarchie(f)	jerarquía	hierarquia
gerarchico, a	hiérarchique	hierarchical	hierarchisch	jerárquico, a	hierárquico, a
gerente, gestore	gérant, e	manager	Geschäftsführer(m)	gerente	gerente
gergo	jargon	jargon	Fachsprache(f)	jerga	calão, gíria
germe	germe	germ, seed	Keim(m)	germen	germe
germoglio	germe	seed	Keim(m)	germen, grano	germe
gesso	plâtre	plaster	Gips(m)	yeso	gesso
gestione	gestion	management	Verwaltung(f)	gestión	gestão
gesto	geste	gesture	Geste(f)	gesto	gesto
gestore	gestionnaire	manager	Verwalter(in f)m	gestor, a	gestor, a
gestore, gerente	gérant, e	manager	Verwalter(in f)m	gerente, director, a	gerente, director, a
gettare	jeter	throw	werfen	arrojar, lanzar	atirar, lançar
gettata, molo	jetée	jetty	Hafendamm(m)	escollera	molhe
getto, zampillo	jet	spray, jet	Strahl(m)	surtidor, chorro	jacto, repuxo
gettone	jeton	counter, token	Spielmarke(f)	ficha	ficha
ghiacciaio	glacier	glacier	Gletscher(m)	glaciar	glaciar
ghiaccio	glace	ice	Eis(n)	hielo	gelo
ghiaia	gravier	gravel	Kies(m)	grava	cascalho
ghiandola	glande	gland	Drüse(f)	glándula	glândula
ghirlanda	guirlande	garland	Girlande(f)	guirnalda	grinalda
giá	déjà	already	schon	ya	já
giacca	veste	jacket	Jacke(f)	chaqueta	jaqueta, casaco
giacente	gisant, e	lying	liegend	yacente	jacente
giallo, a	jaune	yellow	gelb	amarillo, a	amarelo, a
giallo	roman policier	detective novel	Kriminalroman(m)	novela policíaca	romance policial
giardiniere, a	jardinier, ière	gardener	Gärtner(in f)m	jardinero, a	jardineiro, a
giardino	jardin	garden	Garten(m)	jardín	jardim
gigante	géant, e	giant	riesig, gigantisch	gigante	gigante
gigantesco, a	gigantesque	gigantic, huge	gigantisch, riesig	gigantesco, a	gigantesco, a
gilè; golf	gilet	cardigan	Weste(f), Jacke(f)	chaleco	casaco de malha
ginecologia	gynécologie	gynaecology	Gynäkologie(f)	ginecología	ginecologia
ginnastica	gymnastique	gymnastics	Gymnastik(f)	gimnasia	ginástica
ginocchio	genou	knee	Knie(n)	rodilla	joelho
giocare	jouer	play	spielen	jugar	jogar, brincar
giocare	jouer	gamble	spielen	jugar	jogar
giocatore, trice	joueur, se	player	Spieler(in f)m	jugador, a	jogador, a
giocattolo	jouet	toy	Spielzeug(n)	juguete	brinquedo
gioco	jeu	game	Spiel(n)	juego	jogo
gioia	joie	joy	Freude(f)	alegría	alegria
gioia, giubilo	réjouissance	rejoicing	Fröhlichkeit(f)	regocijo	regozijo; alegria
gioielleria	bijouterie	jeweller's	Schmuckgeschäft(n)	joyería	joalharia
gioiello	bijou(x)	jewel	Schmuck(m)(-stück n)	joya	jóia
gioiello	joyau	jewel	Juwel(n), Schmuckstück	joya	jóia

I

Italian	French	English	German	Spanish	Portuguese
giornale	journal	newspaper, paper	Zeitung(f)	periódico, diario	jornal
giornaliero, a	journalier, ière	daily	täglich	diario, a	diário, a
giornalismo	journalisme	journalism	Journalismus(m)	periodismo	jornalismo
giornalista	journaliste	journalist	Journalist(in f)m	periodista	jornalista
giorno; giornata	jour, journée	day	Tag(m)	día; jornada	dia
giorno di vacanza	jour de congé	day off	Urlaubstag(m)	día libre	dia de folga
giostra	manège	roundabout	Karussell(n)	tiovivo, noria	carrossel
giovane	jeune	young	jung	joven	jovem
giovani	jeunes	young people	jungen Leute(pl)	jóvenes	jovens
giovedì	jeudi	Thursday	Donnerstag(m)	jueves	quinta-feira
gioventù, giovinezza	jeunesse	youth	Jugend(f)	juventud	juventude
giradischi	tourne-disque	record-player	Plattenspieler(m)	tocadiscos	gira-discos
giraffa	girafe	giraffe	Giraffe(f)	jirafa	girafa
girare, ruotare	pivoter	revolve, pivot	schwenken	girar	girar; rodar
girare	tourner	turn	drehen	girar	girar; rodar
girare	tourner	turn	drehen	volver	virar
giro	tour	turn	Umdrehung(f)	vuelta	volta, giro
giro, circuito	circuit	tour	Rundfahrt(f)(-reise)	circuito	circuito
giro, circuito	pourtour	periphery	Umkreis(m)	contorno	perímetro
gita, escursione	excursion	excursion	Ausflug(m)	excursión	excursão
gita, escursione	randonnée	ramble	Tour(f), Fußtour(f)	caminata, paseo	caminhada
giù	bas	down	hinunter	abajo	baixo
giudicare	juger	judge	beurteilen	juzgar	julgar
giudice	juge	judge	Richter(in f)m	juez	juíz
giudiziario, a	judiciaire	judicial, legal	gerichtlich	judicial	judiciário, a
giudiziario, a	judiciaire, légal	legal	rechtmäßig	judicial	judicial
giudizio	jugement	judgement	Urteil(n)	juicio	julgamento
giudizio	appréciation	appreciation	Beurteilung(f)	apreciación	apreciação
giudizioso, a	judicieux, se	judicious	scharfsinnig	juicioso, a	judicioso, a
giugno	juin	June	Juni(m)	junio	Junho
giungere	parvenir	reach, arrive at	erreichen	conseguir	chegar; conseguir
giungla	jungle	jungle	Dschungel(m)	selva, jungla	selva
giunta, consiglio	conseil	council	Rat(m)(Stadtrat m)	concejo	município
giunta	junte	junta	Junta(f)	junta	junta
giunto, a	joint, e	joined, linked	zusammengefügt	junto, a	junto, a
giunto, guarnizione	joint	joint, join, seal	Dichtung(f)	junta	junta, anilha
giuramento	serment	oath, pledge	Eid(m)	juramento	juramento
giurare	jurer	swear	schwören	jurar	jurar
giurato	juré	juryman, juror	Geschworene(f, m)	jurado	jurado
giuria	jury	jury	Jury(f)	jurado; tribunal	júri
giuridico, a	juridique	juridical, legal	juristisch	jurídico, a	jurídico, a
giurisprudenza	jurisprudence	jurisprudence	Rechtsprechung(f)	jurisprudencia	jurisprudência
giurista	juriste	jurist; lawyer	Jurist(in f)m	jurista	jurista
giustificare	justifier	justify	begründen, belegen	justificar	justificar
giustificazione	justification	justification	Rechtfertigung(f)	justificación	justificação
giustizia	justice	justice	Gerechtigkeit(f)	justicia	justiça
giusto, a	juste	right	richtig	exacto, a	certo, a
giusto, a	juste	just	gerecht	justo, a	justo, a
globale	global, e	global, overall	Gesamt-; pauschal	global	global
globo	globe	globe	Globus(m)	globo	globo
globulo	globule(sang)	corpuscle, globule	Blutkörperchen(n)	glóbulo	glóbulo
gloria	gloire	glory	Ruhm(m)	gloria	glória
glorioso, a	glorieux, se	glorious	glorreich	glorioso, a	glorioso, a
glossario	glossaire	glossary	Glossar(n)	glosario	glossário
glucosio	glucose	glucose	Traubenzucker(m)	glucosa	glicose
goal, rete	but	goal	Tor(n)	gol	golo
gobba, dosso, cunetta	bosse	bump	Unebenheit(f); Buckel	bache	bossa; alto
gobbo, a	bossu, e	hunch-backed	buckelig	jorobado, a	corcunda
goccia	goutte	drop	Tropfen(m)	gota	gota
godere	jouir	enjoy	genießen	gozar	gozar
gola	gorge	throat	Hals(m)	garganta	garganta
golf	golf	golf	Golf(n)	golf	golfe
golf	golf(terrain)	golf course	Golfplatz(m)	golf	campo de golfe
golfo	golfe	gulf	Golf(m)	golfo	golfo
goloso, a	gourmand, e	greedy	erpicht auf	goloso, a	guloso, a
gomito	coude	elbow	Ellenbogen(m)	codo	cotovelo
gomma	gomme	rubber	Radiergummi(m)	goma	borracha
gomma	caoutchouc	rubber	Gummi(m, n)	caucho	borracha

Italian	French	English	German	Spanish	Portuguese
gonfiare	gonfler	inflate, blow up	auf = blasen	inflar	inchar, encher
gonfiare	enfler	swell	an = schwellen	hinchar	inchar
gonna	jupe	skirt	Rock(m)	falda	saia
gorilla	gorille	gorilla	Gorilla(m)	gorila	gorila
governare	gouverner	govern	regieren	gobernar	governar
governatore	gouverneur	governor	Gouverneur(m)	gobernador	governador
governo	gouvernement	government	Regierung(f)	gobierno	governo
gracile	chétif, íve	puny, weak	schwächlich, kümmer-	endeble	débil
gradevole, piacevole	agréable	pleasant, nice	angenehm	agradable	agradável
gradire, accettare	agréer	accept, approve	genehmigen, zu = lassen	aceptar	aceitar
grado	degré	degree	Grad(m)	grado	grau
grado	degré(alcool)	proof(per cent)	Prozent(n)	graduación	grau
grado	grade	rank	Rang(m)	grado	grau
graffiare	griffer	scratch, claw	kratzen	arañar	arranhar
grafico	graphique	graph	Graphik(f)	gráfico, a	gráfico
grafologia	graphologie	graphology	Graphologie(f)	grafología	grafologia
grammatica	grammaire	grammar	Grammatik(f)	gramática	gramática
granchio	crabe	crab	Krebs(m)	cangrejo	caranguejo
grand(e)	grand, e	great	groß	gran, grande	grande
grande; ampio, a	grand, e	large, big	weit	gran, grande	grande
grande	grand, e	big	groß	gran, grande	grande
grandine	grêle	hail	Hagel(m)	granizo	granizo
grano	blé	corn	Weizen(m)	trigo	trigo
granturco, mais	maïs	maize, corn	Mais(m)	maíz	milho
granulo	granule	granule	Körnchen(n)	gránulo	grânulo
grappa, acquavite	eau-de-vie	spirits	Schnaps(m)	aguardiente	aguardente
grappolo	grappe	bunch	Traube(f)	racimo	cacho
grasso, a	gras, se	fat(ty), greasy	fett	graso, a	gordo, a
grasso	graisse	fat	Fett(n)	gordo; grasa	gordura
grasso	graisse	grease	Schmiere(f)	grasa	massa
gratitudine	gratitude	gratitude	Dankbarkeit(f)	gratitud	gratidão
grato, a	reconnaissant, e	grateful	dankbar	agradecido, a	reconhecido, a
grattacielo	gratte-ciel	skyscraper	Wolkenkratzer(m)	rascacielos	arranha-céus
grattare	gratter	scrape, scratch	kratzen	raspar, rascar	raspar
grattarsi	gratter(se)	scratch oneself	kratzen, sich	rascarse	coçar-se
gratuito, a; gratis	gratuit, e	free	kostenlos	gratis; gratuito, a	grátis; gratuito, a
grave	grave	grave, serious	schwer; ernst	grave	grave
gravidanza	grossesse	pregnancy	Schwangerschaft(f)	embarazo	gravidez
gravità	gravité	gravity	Schwere(f)	gravedad	gravidade
grazia	grâce	grace	Gnade(f); Anmut(f)	gracia	graça
grazie	merci	thank you, thanks	danke	gracias	obrigado, a
grazie a	grâce à	thanks to	dank	gracias a	graças a
grazioso, a	gracieux, se	good natured	lieb	simpático, a	gracioso, a
grazioso, a	gracieux, se	graceful	graziös	gracioso, a	gracioso, a
gregge	troupeau	flock	Herde(f)	rebaño	rebanho
grembiule	tablier	apron	Schürze(f)	delantal	avental
grezzo, a	brut, e	raw; crude	roh	bruto, a	bruto, a
gridare	crier	shout, scream	schreien	gritar	gritar
grido	cri	shout	Schrei(m)	grito	grito
grigio, a	gris, e	grey	grau	gris	cinzento, a
grilletto	gâchette	trigger	Abzug(m)	gatillo	gatilho
grondaia	gouttière	gutter	Dachrinne(f)	canalón	goteira
grosso, a; grande	gros, se	big	groß	grueso, a; grande	grande
grosso, a	gros, se	fat	dick	grueso, a; gordo, a	gordo, a
grosso, a	gros, se	big	geräumig	grande	grande
grossolano, a	grossier, ière	rude; crude	grob	grosero, a	grosseiro, a
grotta	grotte	cave, grotto	Grotte(f)	cueva, gruta	gruta
gru	grue	crane	Kran(m)	grúa	grua
gruccia, attaccapanni	cintre	hanger, coat-hanger	Bügel(m)	percha	cabide
grumo	caillot	clot	Blutgerinnsel(n)	coágulo	coágulo
gruppo	groupe	group	Gruppe(f)	grupo	grupo
guadagnare	gagner	earn; win	verdienen	ganar	ganhar
guadagnare	gagner	save	sparen	ganar	ganhar
guadino, retino	épuisette	fishing net	Fangnetz(n)	manguilla	rede
guaina, astuccio	gaine	sheath	Hülle(f)	funda, estuche	invólucro
guaina, corsetto	gaine	girdle	Korsett(n)	faja	cinta elástica
guaio	ennui, problème	trouble, problem	Ärger(m)	problema	aborrecimento
guancia	joue	cheek	Wange(f)	mejilla	bochecha, face

Italian	French	English	German	Spanish	Portuguese
guanciale	oreiller	pillow	Kopfkissen(n)	almohada	travesseiro
guanto	gant	glove	Handschuh(m)	guante	luva
guanto	gant	flannel	Waschlappen(m)	manopla	luva
guardare	regarder	look(at)	schauen, an = sehen	mirar	olhar
guardare	regarder	watch, look(at)	fern = sehen	mirar	ver
guardi!, guardate!	regardez!	look!	seht!, schauen Sie!	mire(!)	olhe!
guardia	garde	guard	Wächter(m), Hüter(m)	guarda	guarda
guardia, custodia	garde	guard	Wache(f)	guardia	guarda
guardiano, a; custode	gardien, ne; garde	guard; keeper	Wächter(in f)m	guardián, guarda	guarda
guarigione	guérison	cure, recovery	Heilung(f)	curación	cura
guarire	guérir	cure, heal	heilen	curar	curar
guaritore, -trice	guérisseur, se	healer	Heilpraktiker(in f)m	curandero, a	curandeiro, a
guarnire	garnir	garnish	garnieren	guarnecer	guarnecer
guasto, panna	panne	breakdown	Panne(f)	avería	avaria
guercio, a	borgne	one-eyed	einäugig	tuerto, a	zarolho, a
guerra	guerre	war	Krieg(m)	guerra	guerra
guerriglia	guérilla	guerilla	Guerilla(f)	guerrilla	guerrilha
guida	guide	guide	Führer(in f)m	guía	guia
guida	guide	guide-book	Führer(Reise-)(m)	guía	guia
guida, scivolo	glissière	slide	Gleitschiene(f)	corredera, guía	corrediça
guidare	guider	guide	führen	guiar	guiar
guidare	conduire	drive	fahren	conducir	conduzir
guscio	coquille, coque	shell	Schale(f)	cáscara	casca
gustare	déguster	taste, sample	kosten	saborear, catar	provar
gusto, sapore	goût	taste	Geschmack(m)	gusto	gosto

H

Italian	French	English	German	Spanish	Portuguese
hall, ingresso	hall	foyer, hall	Eingangshalle(f)	vestíbulo	vestíbulo
handicap	handicap	handicap	Handikap(n)	hándicap	handicap
hangar, capannone	hangar	shed	Schuppen(m)	cobertizo	alpendre
harem	harem	harem	Harem(m)	harén	harém
hockey	hockey	hockey	Hockeyspiel(n)	hockey	hóquei
hostess	hôtesse de l'air	hostess(air -)	Stewardess(f)	azafata	hospedeira

I

Italian	French	English	German	Spanish	Portuguese
i, gli; le	les	the	die	los, las	os, as
ibrido, a	hybride	hybrid	zwitterhaft	híbrido, a	híbrido, a
iceberg	iceberg	iceberg	Eisberg(m)	iceberg	iceberg
idea	idée	idea	Idee(f)	idea	ideia
ideale	idéal, e	ideal	ideal	ideal	ideal
ideale	idéal	ideal	Ideal(n)	ideal	ideal
ideare	concevoir	design	entwerfen	concebir	conceber
identico, a	identique	identical	identisch	idéntico, a	idêntico, a
identificare	identifier	identify	identifizieren	identificar	identificar

Italian	French	English	German	Spanish	Portuguese
identità	identité	identity	Identität(f)	identidad	identidade
ideologia	idéologie	ideology	Ideologie(f)	ideología	ideologia
idiota; stupido, a	idiot, e	idiotic, stupid	idiotisch, dumm	idiota; tonto, a	idiota
idiota; scemo, a	idiot, e	idiot, fool	Idiot(m), Dummkopf(m)	idiota	idiota
idiozia	idiotie	stupidity	Dummheit(f)	idiotez	idiotice, asneira
idolo	idole	idol	Idol(n)	ídolo	ídolo
idraulico, a	hydraulique	hydraulic	hydraulisch	hidráulico, a	hidráulico, a
idraulico	plombier	plumber	Klempner(m)	fontanero	canalizador
idrogeno	hydrogène	hydrogen	Wasserstoff(m)	hidrógeno	hidrogénio
iena	hyène	hyena	Hyäne(f)	hiena	hiena
ieri	hier	yesterday	gestern	ayer	ontem
igiene	hygiène	hygiene	Hygiene(f)	higiene	higiene
igienico, a	hygiénique	hygienic	hygienisch	higiénico, a	higiénico, a
igloo	igloo	igloo	Iglu(n)	iglú	iglu
ignoranza	ignorance	ignorance	Unwissenheit(f)	ignorancia	ignorância
ignorare	ignorer	ignorant of(be)	nicht wissen	ignorar	ignorar
il, lo, l'; i, gli	le, l', les	the	der, die, das, die	el, lo, los	o, os
illegale	illégal, e	illegal	illegal	ilegal	ilegal
illegittimo, a	illégitime	illegitimate	unehelich	ilegítimo, a	ilegítimo, a
illogico, a	illogique	illogical	unlogisch	ilógico, a	ilógico, a
illuminare	éclairer	light; illuminate	beleuchten	iluminar	iluminar
illuminato, a	illuminé, e	illuminated	erleuchtet	iluminado, a	iluminado, a
illuminazione	éclairage	lighting	Beleuchtung(f)	iluminación	iluminação
illusione	illusion	illusion	Illusion(f)	ilusión	ilusão
illustrato, a	illustré, e	illustrated	illustriert	ilustrado, a	ilustrado, a
illustrazione	illustration	illustration	Illustration(f)	ilustración	ilustração
illustrazione	image	picture	Bild(n)	imagen	gravura
illustre	illustre	illustrious	berühmt	ilustre	ilustre
imballaggio	emballage	packing, wrapping	Verpackung(f)	embalaje, envase	embalagem
imbarazzare	gêner	obstruct	stören	molestar	incomodar
imbarazzo	embarras	embarrassment	Verlegenheit(f)	apuro	embaraço
imbarcare	embarquer	board, embark	ein = steigen	embarcar	embarcar
imbarcare	embarquer	load	ein = laden	embarcar	carregar
imbarcazione, nave	bateau	boat, ship	Schiff(n)	barco	barco
imbecille	imbécile	fool, idiot	Idiot(in f)m	imbécil	imbecíl; parvo, a
imbevere	imbiber	soak	durchtränken	empapar	embeber
imbiancare	peindre	paint	streichen	pintar	pintar
imboscata	embuscade	ambush	Hinterhalt(m)	emboscada	emboscada
imbroglione	escroc	crook, swindler	Gauner(m)	estafador	gatuno, escroque
imbuto	entonnoir	funnel	Trichter(m)	embudo	funil
imformare	informer	inform	informieren	informar	informar
imgombrante	encombrant, e	bulky, cumbersome	sperrig, lästig	voluminoso, a	volumoso, a
imitare	imiter	imitate	nach = ahmen	imitar	imitar
imitazione	imitation	imitation	Nachahmung(f)	imitación	imitação
immagazzinare	stocker	stock, store	lagern	almacenar	armazenar
immaginare	imaginer	imagine	vor = stellen, sich	imaginar	imaginar
immaginario, a	imaginaire	imaginary	eingebildet	imaginario, a	imaginário, a
immaginarsi	imaginer(s')	imagine	ein = bilden, sich	imaginarse	julgar
immaginazione	imagination	imagination	Einbildung(f)	imaginación	imaginação
immagine	image	image, picture	Bild(n)	imagen	imagem
immatricolazione	immatriculation	registration	Eintragung(f)	matrícula	matrícula
immediatamente	immédiatement	immediately	sofort	inmediatamente	imediatamente
immediato, a	immédiat, e	immediate	unverzüglich	inmediato, a	imediato, a
immenso, a	immense	immense, vast	unendlich groß	inmenso, a	imenso, a
immergere	immerger	immerse	versenken	sumergir	imergir
immersione	immersion	immersion	Versenkung(f)	inmersión	imersão
immigrato, a	immigré, e	immigrant	Einwanderer(in f)m	inmigrado, a	imigrante
immigrazione	immigration	immigration	Einwanderung(f)	inmigración	imigração
immischiare(-rsi)	mêler de(se)	interfere	ein = mischen, sich	implicarse	envolver-se
immobile	immobile	motionless	unbeweglich	inmóvil	imóvel
immobiliare	immobilier	property	Immobilien(f, pl)	inmobiliario	imobiliário
immondizia	ordure(s)	rubbish, garbage	Abfall(m)	basura	lixo
immortale	immortel, le	immortal	unsterblich	inmortal	imortal
immunità	immunité	immunity	Immunität(f)	inmunidad	imunidade
immunizzare	immuniser	immunize	immunisieren	inmunizar	imunizar
immutato, a	inchangé, e	unchanged	unverändert	inalterado, a	inalterado, a
impacchettare	empaqueter	pack, wrap	ein = packen, verpacken	empaquetar	empacotar
impalcatura	échafaudage	scaffolding	Gerüst(n)	andamio	andaime

I

563

Italian	French	English	German	Spanish	Portuguese
imparare	apprendre	learn	lernen	aprender	aprender
imparziale	impartial, e	impartial	unparteiisch	imparcial	imparcial
impastare	pétrir	knead	kneten	amasar	amassar
impasto, pasta	pâte	paste	Paste(f); Masse(f)	masa, pasta	massa
impatto	impact	impact	Stoß(m)	impacto	impacto
impatto	impact	impact	Einfluß(m)	impacto	impacto
impaziente	impatient, e	impatient	ungeduldig	impaciente	impaciente
impazienza	impatience	impatience	Ungeduld(f)	impaciencia	impaciência
impedire	empêcher	prevent	verhindern	impedir	impedir
impegnare	engager	engage	engagieren	empeñar	empenhar
impegnarsi	engager(s')	join, enter	bei = treten	ingresar, meterse	aderir, ligar-se
impegnarsi a	engager(s')	commit oneself	engagieren, sich	comprometerse	comprometer-se
impegnato, a	occupé, e	busy	beschäftigt	ocupado, a	ocupado, a
impegno	engagement	commitment	Verpflichtung(f)	compromiso	compromisso
impensabile	impensable	unthinkable	undenkbar	increíble	impensável
imperativo, a	impératif, ive	imperative, urgent	bindend, zwingend	imperativo, a	imperativo, a
imperatore	empereur	emperor	Kaiser(m)	emperador	imperador
imperatrice	impératrice	empress	Kaiserin(f)	emperatriz	imperatriz
imperfezione	imperfection	imperfection	Unvollkommenheit(f)	imperfección	imperfeição
imperialismo	impérialisme	imperialism	Imperialismus(m)	imperialismo	imperialismo
impermeabile	imperméable	water-proof	wasserdicht	impermeable	impermeável
impermeabile	imperméable	rain-coat, mac	Regenmantel(m)	gabardina	gabardina
impero	empire	empire	Reich(n)	imperio	império
impertinente	impertinent, e	impertinent	unverschämt	impertinente	impertinente
impetuoso, a	impétueux, se	impetuous	ungestüm, stürmisch	impetuoso, a	impetuoso, a
impiantare	implanter	establish, set up	etablieren, gründen	implantar	implantar
impianto	implantation	setting up(of)	Niederlassung	implantación	implantação
impiegare	employer	employ	an = stellen	emplear	empregar
impiegato, a	employé, e	employee	Angestellte(f, m)	empleado, a	empregado, a
impiegato, a	employé, e	clerk	Angestellte(f, m)	oficinista	empregado, a
impiegato statale	fonctionnaire	state employee	Beamter(m), Beamtin(f)	funcionario, a	funcionário, a
impiego	emploi	job, work	Beruf(m)	empleo	emprego
impiego	emploi	employment	Stelle(f)	empleo	emprego
implicare	impliquer	involve	verwickeln	implicar	implicar
implicare	impliquer	imply	bedeuten; an = deuten	implicar	implicar
implicazione	implication	implication	Verwicklung(f)	implicación	implicação
implorare	implorer	implore, beg	an = flehen	implorar	implorar
impopolare	impopulaire	unpopular	unbeliebt	impopular	impopular
imporre	imposer	impose	auf = zwingen	imponer	impor
imporsi	imposer(s')	impose oneself on	auf = drängen, sich	imponerse	impor-se
importante	important, e	important	wichtig	importante	importante
importanza	importance	importance	Bedeutung(f)	importancia	importância
importare	importer	import	ein = führen	importar	importar
importazione	importation	import; importing	Einfuhr(f)	importación	importação
impossibile	impossible	impossible	unmöglich	imposible	impossível
impostare, imbucare	poster	post, mail	ein = werfen	echar al correo	pôr no correio
impotente	impuissant, e	powerless	machtlos	impotente	impotente
impregnare	imprégner	impregnate	imprägnieren	impregnar	impregnar
imprenditore	entrepreneur	contractor	Unternehmer(in f)m	empresario	empresário
impresa, ditta	entreprise	company, firm	Unternehmen(n)	empresa	empresa
impresa, prodezza	exploit	exploit	Glanzleistung(f)	hazaña	proeza, feito
impresario	imprésario	impresario	Manager(m)	empresario	empresário
impressionante	impressionnant, e	impressive	beeindruckend	impresionante	impressionante
impressionare	impressionner	impress	beeindrucken	impresionar	impressionar
impressione	impression	impression	Eindruck(m)	impresión	impressão
imprevisto, a	imprévu, e	unexpected	unvorhergesehen	imprevisto, a	imprevisto, a
impronta	empreinte	print	Abdruck(m)	huella	impressão; marca
improvvisare	improviser	improvise	improvisieren	improvisar	improvisar
imprudente	imprudent, e	careless	unvorsichtig	imprudente	imprudente
imprudenza	imprudence	imprudence	Unvorsichtigkeit(f)	imprudencia	imprudência
impulso	impulsion	impulse	Impuls(m)	impulso	impulso
impunito, a	impuni, e	unpunished	unbestraft	impune	impune
impurità	impureté	impurity	Unreinheit(f)	impureza	impureza
imputato, a	inculpé, e	accused(the)	Angeklagte(f, m)	inculpado, a	acusado, a
in	dans	in, into	in	dentro, en	dentro(de), em
in	en	in	in	en	em
inabile	inapte	unsuited, unfit	ungeeignet	inapto, a	inapto, a
inaccessibile	inaccessible	inaccessible	unerreichbar	inaccesible	inacessível

Italian	French	English	German	Spanish	Portuguese
inadatto, a	inadapté, e	unsuitable	ungeeignet	inadaptado, a	inadaptado, a
inalare	inhaler, respirer	inhale	ein = atmen	inhalar	inalar
in alto	là-haut	up there	da oben	arriba	lá em cima
inammissibile	inadmissible	inadmissible	unzulässig	inadmisible	inadmissível
inanimato, a	inanimé, e	lifeless	unbelebt, leblos	inanimado, a	inanimado, a
inarcato, a; arcuato, a	cambré, e	arched	krumm, gebeugt	arqueado, a	arqueado, a
inattivo, a	inactif, ive	inactive	untätig, inaktiv	inactivo, a	inactivo, a
inaugurare	inaugurer	inaugurate	ein = weihen	inaugurar	inaugurar
inaugurazione	inauguration	inauguration	Einweihung(f)	inauguración	inauguração
incandescente	incandescent, e	incandescent	glühend	incandescente	incandescente
incantevole	ravissant, e	ravishing, lovely	entzückend	encantador, a	encantador, a
incapace	incapable	incapable, unable	unfähig, untauglich	incapaz	incapaz
incarcerare	incarcérer	imprison	ein = sperren	encarcelar	encarcerar
incarcerazione	emprisonnement	imprisonment	Haft(f), Verhaftung(f)	encarcelamiento	prisão
incassare	encaisser	cash	ein = kassieren	cobrar	receber
incassare	toucher	cash, earn, win	kassieren(ein =)	cobrar	receber
incasso	recette	receipts; takings	Einnahmen(f, pl)	ingresos	receita
incastrare	encastrer	set in	ein = setzen	empotrar	embutir
incendio	incendie	fire	Brand(m)	incendio	incêndio
incenerire	incinérer	incinerate	ein = äschern	incinerar	incinerar
incerto, a	incertain, e	uncertain	unsicher	inseguro, a	incerto, a
incesto	inceste	incest	Inzucht(f)	incesto	incesto
inchiesta	enquête, étude	survey	Umfrage(f)	encuesta	inquérito
inchiodare	clouer	nail	nageln	clavar	pregar, cravar
inchiostro	encre	ink	Tinte(f)	tinta	tinta
inciampare	trébucher	stumble, trip	stolpern	tropezar	tropeçar
incidente	accident	accident	Unfall(m)	accidente	acidente
incidente	incident	incident	Zwischenfall(m)	incidente	incidente
incinta	enceinte	pregnant	schwanger	encinta	grávida
incisione	gravure	engraving	Gravieren(n)	grabado	gravura
incisione	entaille	cut, nick, notch	Kerbe(f)	cortadura	incisão, golpe
incitare	inciter	incite	an = regen	incitar	incitar
inclinare	incliner	incline, tilt	neigen	inclinar	inclinar
inclinare	pencher	tilt, lean	neigen	inclinar	inclinar
inclinazione	inclinaison	slant, incline	Neigung(f), Gefälle(n)	inclinación	inclinação
inclinazione	tendance	trend, tendency	Neigung(f)	inclinación	inclinação
includere	inclure	include	ein = schließen	incluir	incluir
incluso, a	inclus, e	included	inklusiv	incluido, a	incluso, a
incollare	coller	stick, glue	kleben	pegar	colar, pegar
incolore	incolore	colourless	farblos	incoloro, a	incolor
incolpare, accusare	inculper	charge, accuse	beschuldigen	inculpar, acusar	inculpar, acusar
incomodare	incommoder	bother	stören	incomodar	incomodar
incompatibile	incompatible	incompatible	unvereinbar	incompatible	incompatível
incompetenza	incompétence	incompetence	Inkompetenz(f)	incompetencia	incompetência
incompleto, a	incomplet, ète	incomplete	unvollständig	incompleto, a	incompleto, a
incontestabile	incontestable	incontestable	unbestreitbar	indiscutible	incontestável
incontrare	rencontrer	meet	treffen	encontrar	encontrar
incontro	rencontre	meeting	Begegnung(f)	encuentro	encontro
inconveniente	inconvénient	disadvantage	Nachteil(m)	inconveniente	inconveniente
incoraggiare	encourager	encourage, urge	ermutigen	alentar, animar	encorajar
incorporare	incorporer	incorporate	ein = verleiben	incorporar	incorporar
incorporazione	incorporation	incorporation	Eingliederung(f)	incorporación	incorporação
incosciente	inconscient, e	unconscious	unbewußt	inconsciente	inconsciente
incredibile	incroyable	unbelievable	unglaublich	increíble	incrível
incremento	augmentation	increment	Zunahme(f)	incremento	incremento
incriminare	incriminer	incriminate	beschuldigen	incriminar	incriminar
incrinatura	félure	crack	Sprung(m), Riß(m)	raja, grieta	estaladela
incrociare	croiser	interbreed, cross	kreuzen	cruzar	cruzar
incrociarsi	croiser(se)	cross, intersect	kreuzen, sich	cruzarse	cruzar-se
incrocio	croisement	crossing	Kreuzung(f)	cruce	cruzamento
incrocio	carrefour	cross-road(s)	Kreuzung(f)	encrucijada	cruzamento
incubo	cauchemar	nightmare	Alptraum(m)	pesadilla	pesadelo
incurabile	incurable	incurable	unheilbar	incurable	incurável
incursione	incursion	incursion	Überfall(m)	incursión	incursão
incurvato, a	gondolé, e	warped, buckled	verbogen	combado, a	empenado, a
indagine, inchiesta	enquête	inquiry, inquest	Untersuchung(f)	investigación	inquérito
indebolire	affaiblir	weaken	schwächen	debilitar	enfraquecer
indecente	indécent, e	indecent	unanständig	indecente	indecente

I

565

Italian	French	English	German	Spanish	Portuguese
indefinito, a	indéfini, e	indefinite	unbestimmt	indefinido, a	indefinido, a
indegno, a	indigne	unworthy	unwürdig	indigno, a	indigno, a
indennità	indemnité	allowance	Schadenersatz(m)	dietas	ajuda de custo
indennizzare	indemniser	compensate	entschädigen	indemnizar	indemnizar
indennizzare	dédommager	compensate	entschädigen	indemnizar	indemnizar
indicare	indiquer	indicate, show	an = deuten, zeigen	indicar	indicar
indicare	désigner	indicate	bezeichnen	señalar, indicar	indicar
indicatore	indicateur	indicator	Anzeiger(m)	indicador	indicador
indicazione	indication	indication	Angabe(f), Hinweis(m)	indicación	indicação
indice	indice	index	Index m(Preisindex m)	índice	índice
indice	index	index	Index(m)	índice	índice
indietreggiare	reculer	move back, reverse	zurück = gehen	retroceder	recuar
indietro	arrière(en)	backward(s)	rückwärts	atrás(para)	trás(para)
indifferente	indifférent, e	indifferent	gleichgültig	indiferente	indiferente
indigeno, a	indigène	native, indigenous	Eingeborene(f, m)	indígena	indígena
indigesto, a	indigeste	indigestible	unverdaulich	indigesto, a	indigesto, a
indignazione	indignation	indignation	Empörung(f)	indignación	indignação
indipendente	indépendant, e	independent	unabhängig	independiente	independente
indipendenza	indépendance	independence	Unabhängigkeit(f)	independencia	independência
indiretto, a	indirect, e	indirect	indirekt	indirecto, a	indirecto, a
indirizzo	adresse	address	Anschrift(f), Adresse	dirección	endereço, morada
indisciplinato, a	dissipé, e	unruly	unaufmerksam	indisciplinado, a	indisciplinado, a
indiscrezione	indiscrétion	indiscretion	Indiskretion(f)	indiscreción	indiscrição
indispensabile	indispensable	indispensable	unentbehrlich	indispensable	indispensável
individuale	individuel, le	individual	individuell	individual	individual
individuo	individu	individual	Individuum(n)	individuo	indivíduo
indizio	indice	indication, sign	Anzeichen(n)	indicio	indício
indizio	charge	charge	Anklage(f)(punkt m)	cargo	acusação
indolore	indolore	painless	schmerzlos	indoloro, a	indolor
indomani(l')	lendemain	next day	folgenden Tag(m)	día siguiente	dia seguinte
indossare, portare	porter	wear	tragen	llevar	usar; trazer
indossatore, trice	mannequin	model	Mannequin(n)	maniquí, modelo	modelo
indovinare	deviner	guess	raten	adivinar	adivinhar
indulgenza	indulgence	indulgence	Nachsicht(f)	indulgencia	indulgência
indurre	induire	induce	veranlassen	inducir	induzir
industria	industrie	industry	Industrie(f)	industria	indústria
industriale	industriel, le	industrial	industriell	industrial	industrial
industriale	industriel	industrialist	Industrielle(m)	industrial	industrial
inedito, a	inédit, e	unpublished	unveröffentlicht	inédito, a	inédito, a
inefficace	inefficace	inefficient	unwirksam, unfähig	ineficaz	ineficaz
ineguale	inégal, e	unequal	ungleich	desigual	desigual
inerte	inerte	inert	regungslos	inerte	inerte
inerzia	inertie	inertia	Trägheit(f)	inercia	inércia
inesatto, a	inexact, e	inexact, inaccurate	ungenau	inexacto, a	inexacto, a
inesistente	inexistant, e	non-existent	nicht existierend	inexistente	inexistente
infallibile	infaillible	infallible	unfehlbar	infalible	infalível
infame	infâme	vile, infamous	niederträchtig	infame	infame
infantile	infantile	infantile, child	Kinder-, kindisch	infantil	infantil
infanzia	enfance	childhood	Kindheit(f)	infancia	infância
infarto	infarctus	coronary	Infarkt(m)	infarto	enfarte
infarto	crise cardiaque	heart attack	Herzattacke(f)	crisis cardíaca	ataque
infastidire	embêter	bother, annoy	ärgern	fastidiar	aborrecer
infatti	effet(en)	indeed	tatsächlich	efecto(en)	efeito(com)
infedele	infidèle	unfaithful	untreu	infiel	infiel
infelice	malheureux, se	unhappy, miserable	unglücklich, betrübt	desgraciado, a	infeliz
infelice, triste	malheureux, se	unhappy, sorrowful	betrübt, unglücklich	infeliz, triste	infeliz, triste
inferiore	inférieur, e	inferior	minderwertig	inferior	inferior
inferiore	inférieur, e	lower	untere(r)	inferior	inferior
infermeria	infirmerie	infirmary	Krankenraum(m)	enfermería	enfermaria
infermiere, a	infirmier, ière	nurse	Krankenpfleger(in f)m	enfermero, a	enfermeiro, a
infermo, a	infirme	disabled	behindert	inválido, a	doente
infernale	infernal, e	infernal	Höllen-; höllisch	infernal	infernal
inferno	enfer	hell	Hölle(f)	infierno	inferno
infezione	infection	infection	Infektion(f)	infección	infecção
infiammabile	inflammable	inflammable	brennbar	inflamable	inflamável
infiltrazione	infiltration	infiltration	Einsickern(n)	infiltración	infiltração
infinito, a	infini, e	infinite	unendlich	infinito, a	infinito, a
infinito	infinitif	infinitive	Infinitiv(m)	infinitivo	infinitivo

Italian	French	English	German	Spanish	Portuguese
inflazione	inflation	inflation	Inflation(f)	inflación	inflação
inflessibile	inflexible	inflexible	starr	inflexible	inflexível
infliggere	infliger	inflict	auf = erlegen	infligir	infligir
influente	influent, e	influential	einflußreich	influyente	influente
influenza	influence	influence	Einfluß(m)	influencia	influência
influenza(-arsi)	grippe	flu, influenza	Grippe(f)	gripe	gripe
informare(-arsi)	renseigner(se)	inquire	erkundigen, sich	informar(se)	informar-se
informarsi	informer(s')	inquire	erkundigen, sich	informarse	informar-se
informatica	informatique	data processing	Informatik(f)	informática	informática
informazione	information	information	Information(f)	información	informação
informazione	renseignement	information	Auskunft(f)	información	informação
infrangersi	déferler	break	branden	romper	quebrar-se
infrazione	infraction	offence, violation	Verstoß(m)	infracción	infracção
ingannare	tromper	deceive, cheat	betrügen	engañar	enganar
ingegnere	ingénieur	engineer	Ingenieur(in f)m	ingeniero, a	engenheiro, a
ingegneria	ingénierie	engineering	Ingenieurkunst(f)	ingeniería	engenharia
ingegnoso, a	ingénieux, se	ingenious	sinnreich	ingenioso, a	engenhoso, a
ingenuo, a	naif, ïve	naive	naiv	ingenuo, a	ingênuo, a
ingerenza	ingérence	interference	Einmischung(f)	ingerencia	ingerência
inghiottire, ingoiare	avaler	swallow	schlucken	tragar	engolir
inginocchiare(-rsi)	agenouiller(s')	kneel	hin = knien, sich	arrodillarse	ajoelhar-se
ingiuria	injure	insult	Beleidigung(f)	injuria	injúria
ingiustizia	injustice	injustice	Ungerechtigkeit(f)	injusticia	injustiça
ingranare, avviare	enclencher	engage	ein = legen, = schalten	engranar	engrenar
ingrandire	agrandir	enlarge	vergrößern	ampliar	ampliar
ingrandire	grossir	increase	vermehren	agrandar	aumentar
ingrassare	grossir	put on weight	zu = nehmen	engordar	engordar
ingrato, a	ingrat, e	ungrateful	undankbar	ingrato, a	ingrato, a
ingresso	entrée	entry, entrance	Eintritt(m), Eingang m	entrada	entrada
ingresso	entrée	admission	Eintrittskarte(f)	entrada	entrada, bilhete
ingresso, anticamera	vestibule	hall	Flur(m)	vestíbulo	vestíbulo; hall
iniettare	injecter	inject	spritzen, ein = spritzen	inyectar	injectar
iniezione	piqûre	injection	Spritze(f)	inyección	injecção
inimmaginabile	inimaginable	inconceivable	undenkbar	inimaginable	inimaginável
ininfiammabile	ininflammable	fire-proof	unbrennbar	ininflamable	prova de fogo(à)
iniziale	initial, e	initial	anfänglich; Anfangs-	inicial	inicial
iniziativa	initiative	initiative	Initiative(f)	iniciativa	iniciativa
iniziazione	initiation	initiation	Einführung(f)	iniciación	iniciação
inizio	début	beginning	Anfang(m)	comienzo	princípio
innaffiare	arroser	water	gießen, begießen	regar	regar
innamorato, a	amoureux, se	love(in)	verliebt	enamorado, a	apaixonado, a
innato, a	inné, e	innate	angeboren	innato, a	inato, a
innervosirsi	énerver(s')	edgy, irritable(be)	auf = regen, sich	ponerse nervioso, a	enervar-se
innestare	brancher	plug in	ein = stecken	enchufar	ligar
innesto	greffe	graft	Veredelung; Pfropfen	injerto	enxerto
inno	hymne	hymn	Hymne(f)	himno	hino
innocente	innocent, e	innocent	unschuldig	inocente	inocente
innovare	innover	innovate	innovieren, erneuern	innovar	inovar
innovazione	innovation	innovation	Neuerung(f)(Er-)	innovación	inovação
inoffensivo, a	inoffensif, ive	inoffensive	harmlos	inofensivo, a	inofensivo, a
inoltre	de plus, en outre	besides	außerdem; außer	además(de)	além disso; além de
inondazione	inondation	flooding, flood	Überschwemmung(f)	inundación	inundação
inoperoso, a	inoccupé, e	unoccupied	untätig	desocupado, a	desocupado, a
inorganico, a	inorganique	inorganic	anorganisch	inorgánico, a	inorgânico, a
in piedi	debout	standing(up)	stehend, aufrecht	de pie, en pie	de pé, em pé
inquieto, a	inquiet, ète	worried	besorgt	inquieto, a	inquieto, a
inquietudine	inquiétude	anxiety, worry	Sorge(f)	inquietud	inquietação
inquilino, a	locataire	tenant	Mieter(in f)m	inquilino, a	inquilino, a
inquinamento	pollution	pollution	Verschmutzung(f)	contaminación	poluição
inquinare	polluer	pollute	verunreinigen	contaminar	poluir
insalata	salade	salad; lettuce	Salat(m); Kopfsalat(m)	ensalada; lechuga	salada
insalata mista	crudité	salad, crudité	Rohkost(f)	ensalada	salada
insegna	enseigne	sign	Schild(m)(Reklame-)	letrero	letreiro
insegnamento	enseignement	teaching	Unterricht(m), Lehre f	enseñanza	ensino
insegnante	enseignant, e	teacher	Lehrer(in f)m	profesor, a	professor, a
insegnare	enseigner	teach	lehren, unterrichten	enseñar	ensinar
inseguire	poursuivre	pursue	verfolgen	perseguir	perseguir
inseminazione	insémination	insemination	Befruchtung(f)	inseminación	inseminação

Italian	French	English	German	Spanish	Portuguese
insensibile	insensible	insensitive	unempfindlich	insensible	insensível
inserire	insérer	insert	ein = setzen, ein = fügen	insertar	inserir
inserzione	insertion	insertion	Einfügung(f)	inserción	inserção
insetto	insecte	insect	Insekt(n)	insecto	insecto
insieme	ensemble	together	zusammen	juntos	junto
insieme	ensemble	whole; all the	Ganze(n); Gesamtheit f	conjunto	conjunto
insieme	ensemble	set	Satz(m)	conjunto	conjunto
insignificante	insignifiant, e	insignificant	unbedeutend	insignificante	insignificante
insistere	insister	insist	bestehen, beharren	insistir	insistir
insoddisfatto, a	insatisfait, e	not satisfied	unzufrieden	insatisfecho, a	insatisfeito, a
insolazione	insolation	sunstroke	Sonnenstich(m)	insolación	insolação
insolente	insolent, e	insolent	unverschämt, frech	insolente	insolente
insolenza	insolence	insolence	Frechheit(f)	insolencia	insolência
insolito, a	insolite	unusual	seltsam, ungewohnt	insólito, a	insólito, a
insonnia	insomnie	insomnia	Schlaflosigkeit(f)	insomnio	insónia
insonoro, a	insonore	sound-proof	schalldicht	insonoro, a	insonoro, a
insorgere	insurger(s')	rise up, revolt	auf = lehnen gegen, sich	sublevarse	insurgir-se
insperato, a	inespéré, e	unexpected	unerwartet, unverhofft	inesperado, a	inesperado, a
instabile	instable	unstable	unbeständig	inestable	instável
installare	installer	install	ein = richten	instalar	instalar
installazione	installation	installation	Einrichtung(f)	instalación	instalação
instancabile	infatigable	tireless	unermüdlich	incansable	infatigável
insufficiente	insuffisant, e	insufficient	ungenügend	insuficiente	insuficiente
insulina	insuline	insulin	Insulin(n)	insulina	insulina
insultare	insulter	insult	beleidigen	insultar	insultar
insulto	insulte	insult	Beleidigung(f)	insulto	insulto
intanto, frattanto	entre-temps	meanwhile, meantime	inzwischen	entretanto	entretanto
intatto, a	intact, e	intact	intakt	intacto, a	intacto, a
integrale	intégral, e	integral	vollständig	íntegro, a	integral
integrare	intégrer	integrate	integrieren	integrar	integrar
integrità	intégrité	integrity	Integrität(f)	integridad	integridade
intellettuale	intellectuel, le	intellectual	intellektuell	intelectual	intelectual
intelligente	intelligent, e	intelligent	intelligent, gescheit	inteligente	inteligente
intelligenza	intelligence	intelligence	Intelligenz(f)	inteligencia	inteligência
intensità	intensité	intensity	Intensität(f)	intensidad	intensidade
intensivo, a	intensif, ive	intensive	intensiv	intensivo, a	intensivo, a
intenso, a	intense	intense	heftig, stark	intenso, a	intenso, a
intento, fine, scopo	intention, but	purpose, aim, goal	Absicht(f)	intención	intenção
intenzione	intention	intention	Absicht(f)	intención	intenção
intenzione(avere)	intention(avoir)	intend	beabsichtigen	intención(tener)	tencionar
interamente	entièrement	entirely	ganz	completamente	inteiramente
intercettare	intercepter	intercept	auf = fangen, ab = fangen	interceptar	interceptar
interessante	intéressant, e	interesting	interessant	interesante	interessante
interessarsi	intéresser(s')	interested in(be)	interessieren, sich	interesarse	interessar-se
interesse	intérêt	interest	Interesse(n)	interés	interesse
interesse	intérêt	interest	Zins(m)	interés	juro
interferenza	interférence	interference	Einmischung; Störung	interferencia	interferência
interiore	intérieur, e	inner, interior	inner	interior	interior
interiore	intérieur	interior	Innere(n)	interior	interior
interlocutore, trice	interlocuteur	interlocutor	Gesprächspartner/in	interlocutor, a	interlocutor, a
intermediario, a	intermédiaire	intermediate	Zwischen-, Mittel-	intermediario, a	intermediário, a
intermittente	intermittent, e	intermittent	aussetzend	intermitente	intermitente
internazionale	international, e	international	international	internacional	internacional
interno, a	interne	internal, inner	intern	interno, a	interno, a
interno, a	intérieur, e	inside, inner	innere(r, s); innen	interior	interior
interno, a	intérieur, e	domestic, home	Innen-	interior	interno, a
intero, a	entier, ière	whole, entire	ganz	entero, a	inteiro, a
interpretare	interpréter	interpret	deuten, aus = legen	interpretar	interpretar
interprete	interprète	interpreter	Dolmetscher(in f)m	intérprete	intérprete
interrogare	interroger	question, ask	fragen, befragen	interrogar	interrogar
interrompere	interrompre	interrupt	unterbrechen	interrumpir	interromper
interruttore	interrupteur	switch	Schalter(m)	interruptor	interruptor
interruzione	interruption	interruption	Unterbrechung(f)	interrupción	interrupção
intersezione	intersection	intersection	Kreuzung(f)	intersección	intersecção
intervallo	intervalle	interval	Abstand(m)	intervalo	intervalo
intervallo	intervalle	gap	Abstand(m)	intervalo	intervalo
intervallo	entracte	interval	Pause(f)	intermedio	intervalo
intervenire	intervenir	intervene	dazwischen = treten	intervenir	intervir

568

Italian	French	English	German	Spanish	Portuguese
intervento	intervention	intervention	Eingriff(m)	intervención	intervenção
intervista	entrevue	interview	Treffen(n), Gespräch n	entrevista	entrevista
intervista	interview	interview	Interview(n)	interviú	entrevista
intestino	intestin	intestine	Darm(m)	intestino	intestino
intimidire	intimider	intimidate	ein = schüchtern	intimidar	intimidar
intimo, a	intime	close, intimate	intim	íntimo, a	íntimo, a
intimo, a	intime	intimate	vertraut, intim	íntimo, a	íntimo, a
intingere	tremper	dip	ein = tauchen	sumergir	mergulhar
intolleranza	intolérance	intolerance	Intoleranz(f)	intolerancia	intolerância
intonazione	intonation	intonation	Tonfall(m)	entonación	entoação
intorno, attorno	autour	around	um	alrededor	redor de(em)
intossicazione	intoxication	poisoning	Vergiftung(f)	intoxicación	intoxicação
intraprendere	entreprendre	undertake	unternehmen	emprender	empreender
intravedere	entrevoir	glimpse	flüchtig sehen	entrever	entrever
intrepido, a	intrépide	intrepid	kühn, mutig	intrépido, a	intrépido, a
intrigare	intriguer	intrigue	intrigieren	intrigar	intrigar
intrigo	intrigue	intrigue	Intrige(f)	intriga	intriga
introdurre	introduire	introduce	vor = stellen	presentar	apresentar
introdurre	introduire	insert; introduce	ein = führen	introducir	introduzir
intrusione	intrusion	intrusion	Eindringen(n)	intrusión	intrusão
intuizione	intuition	intuition	Intuition(f)	intuición	intuição
inumano, a	inhumain, e	inhuman	unmenschlich	inhumano, a	desumano, a
inutile	inutile	useless	nutzlos	inútil	inútil
invadere	envahir	invade	ein = fallen	invadir	invadir
invalido, a	invalide	disabled	behindert	inválido, a	inválido, a
invariabile	invariable	invariable	unveränderlich	invariable	invariável
invasione	invasion	invasion	Invasion(f)	invasión	invasão
invece di	au lieu de	instead(of)	anstatt	en vez de/lugar de	em vez de/lugar de
inventare	inventer	invent	erfinden	inventar	inventar
inventario	inventaire	inventory	Inventar(n)	inventario	inventário
inventario	inventaire	stock-list(taking)	Inventur(f)	inventario	inventário
inventore	inventeur	inventor	Erfinder(in f)m	inventor	inventor
invenzione	invention	invention	Erfindung(f)	invención	invenção
inverno	hiver	winter	Winter(m)	invierno	inverno
inversione	inversion	inversion	Umkehrung(f)	inversión	inversão
inverso, a	inverse	opposite	umgekehrt	inverso, a	inverso, a
invertire	inverser	reverse, invert	um = kehren	invertir	inverter
investigare, indagare	enquêter	investigate	untersuchen	investigar	investigar
investimento	investissement	investment	Investition(f)	inversión	investimento
investire	investir	invest	investieren	invertir	investir
investire	placer	invest	an = legen	invertir	pôr a render
investitura	investiture	investiture	Investitur(f)	investidura	investidura
inviare	envoyer	send	schicken, senden(ab =)	enviar	enviar
inviare	expédier, livrer	consign	übersenden	enviar, expedir	enviar, expedir
invincibile	invincible	invincible	unbesiegbar	invencible	invencível
invio	envoi	sending	Sendung(f), Versand(m)	envío	envio
invisibile	invisible	invisible	unsichtbar	invisible	invisível
invitare	inviter	invite	ein = laden	invitar	convidar
invitato, a	invité, e	guest	Gast(m)	invitado, a	convidado, a
invito	invitation	invitation	Einladung(f)	invitación	convite
invocare	invoquer	invoke	beziehen auf, sich	invocar	invocar
inzuppare	tremper	soak	ein = weichen	mojar	molhar
io	je	I	ich	yo	eu
io; me	moi	me; I	mich; mir; ich	mí, me; yo	eu; me; mim
ipertensione	hypertension	blood pressure	Bluthochdruck(m)	hipertensión	hipertensão
ipnosi	hypnose	hypnosis	Hypnose(f)	hipnosis	hipnose
ipnotismo	hypnotisme	hypnotism	Hypnotismus(m)	hipnotismo	hipnotismo
ipocrisia	hypocrisie	hypocrisy	Heuchelei(f)	hipocresía	hipocrisia
ipocrita	hypocrite	hypocrite	Heuchler(in f)m	hipócrita	hipócrita
ipoteca	hypothèque	mortgage	Hypothek(f)	hipoteca	hipoteca
ipotesi	hypothèse	hypothesis(-es)	Hypothese(f)	hipótesis	hipótese
ippopotamo	hippopotame	hippopotamus	Nilpferd(n)	hipopótamo	hipopótamo
iride	iris	iris	Iris(f)	iris	íris
ironia	ironie	irony	Ironie(f)	ironía	ironia
irradiazione	rayonnement	radiance	Strahlung(f)	irradiación	irradiação
irradiazione	irradiation	irradiation	Bestrahlung(f)	irradiación	irradiação
irregolare	irrégulier, e	irregular	unregelmäßig	irregular	irregular
irrigare	irriguer	irrigate	bewässern	irrigar	irrigar

I

569

Italian	French	English	German	Spanish	Portuguese
irritante	irritant, e	irritating	ärgerlich; aufregend	irritante	irritante
irritare	irriter	irritate	reizen, irritieren	irritar	irritar
irritazione	agacement	irritation	Ärger(m)	fastidio	irritação
irruzione	irruption	irruption	Eindringen(n)	irrupción	irrupção
iscrivere	inscrire, noter	note, write	ein = schreiben	inscribir	inscrever
iscriversi	inscrire(s')	register	ein = schreiben, sich	matricularse	matricular-se
iscriversi	inscrire(s')	join	bei = treten	inscribirse	inscrever-se
iscrizione	inscription	inscription	Inschrift(f)	inscripción	inscrição
iscrizione	inscription	registration	Einschreibung(f)	matrícula	matrícula
islamico, a	islamique	Islamic	islamisch	islámico, a	islâmico, a
isola	île	island, isle	Insel(f)	isla	ilha
isolamento	isolation	insulation	Isolierung(f)	aislamiento	isolação
isolare	isoler	isolate	ab = sondern; isolieren	aislar	isolar
isolare	isoler	insulate; isolate	isolieren	aislar	isolar
isolato, a	isolé, e	isolated, lonely	allein, einsam	aislado, a	isolado, a; só, a
isolato, a; solo, a	seul, e	lonely	einsam	aislado, a; solo, a	isolado, a
isolotto	îlot	islet	Inselchen(n)	islote	ilhéu, ilhota
ispettore, trice	inspecteur, trice	inspector	Inspektor(in f)m	inspector, a	inspector, a
ispezione	inspection	inspection	Überprüfung(f)	inspección	inspecção
ispirazione	inspiration	inspiration	Anregung(f)	inspiración	inspiração
istante	instant	moment, instant	Moment(m)	instante	instante
isterico, a	hystérique	hysteric(al)	hysterisch	histérico, a	histérico, a
istintivo, a	instinctif, ive	instinctive	instinktiv	instintivo, a	instintivo, a
istinto	instinct	instinct	Instinkt(m)	instinto	instinto
istituto	institut	institute	Institut(n)	instituto	instituto
istituzionale	institutionnel	institutional	gesetzlich	institucional	institucional
istituzione	institution	institution	Institution(f)	institución	instituição
istruire	instruire	teach	aus = bilden	instruir	instruir
istruttore, trice	instructeur	instructor	Ausbilder(m)	instructor	instrutor, a
istruttore, trice	moniteur, trice	instructor	Leiter/in; Lehrer/in	monitor, a	monitor, a
istruzione	instruction	instruction	Ausbildung(f)	instrucción	instrução
itinerario	itinéraire	itinerary, route	Route(f), Strecke(f)	itinerario	itinerário
itterizia	jaunisse	jaundice	Gelbsucht(f)	ictericia	ictericia

J

Italian	French	English	German	Spanish	Portuguese
jazz	jazz	jazz	Jazz(m)	jazz	jazz
jockey, fantino	jockey	jockey	Jockey(m)	jockey	jockey
judò	judo	judo	Judo(n)	judo, yudo	judo

K

Italian	French	English	German	Spanish	Portuguese
karatè	karaté	karate	Karate(n)	karate	karaté
kayak	kayac	kayak	Kajak(m)	kayac, piragua	kayac

L

Italian	French	English	German	Spanish	Portuguese
la, l', le	la, l', les	the	die	la, las	a, as
là	là	there	da	ahí; allí	aí; ali; lá
là; lì	là	there	da; dort	allí; allá	aí; lá
là, laggiù	là-bas	over there	da; dort	allá	além, acolá
labbro(a)	lèvre	lip	Lippe(f)	labio	lábio
labirinto	labyrinthe	labyrinth, maze	Labyrinth(n)	laberinto	labirinto
laboratorio	laboratoire	laboratory	Labor(n)	laboratorio	laboratório
lacca	laque	lacquer	Lack(m)	laca	laca
lacca	laque	hair-spray	Haarspray(m, n)	laca	laca
laccio	lacet	lace	Schnürsenkel(m)	cordón	cordão
lacrima	larme	tear	Träne(f)	lágrima	lágrima
lacrimogeno	lacrymogène	tear-gas	Tränengas(n)	lacrimógeno	lacrimogéneo
ladro, a	voleur, se	thief(-ves), robber	Dieb(in f)m	ladrón, a	ladrão, ladra
lago	lac	lake	See(m)	lago	lago
laguna	lagune	lagoon	Binnensee(m)	laguna	laguna
lama	lame	blade	Schneide(f)	hoja	lâmina
lama	lama	llama	Lama(n)	llama	lama
lamentarsi	plaindre(se)	complain	beklagen, sich	quejarse	queixar-se
lamentarsi	lamenter(se)	lament	jammern	lamentarse	lamentar-se
lamento	plainte	complaint	Klage(f)	queja	queixume, queixa
lamiera	tôle	sheet-metal	Blech(n)	chapa	chapa
lampada	lampe	lamp	Lampe(f)	lámpara	candeeiro
lampadina	ampoule	bulb	Glühbirne(f)	bombilla	lâmpada
lampadina tascabile	lampe de poche	torch	Taschenlampe(f)	linterna	pilha
lampeggiare	clignoter	flash	blinken	pestañear	piscar
lampione	lampadaire	street-lamp	Straßenlaterne(f)	lámpara de pie	candeeiro
lampo	éclair	lightning; flash	Blitz(m)	relámpago	relâmpago
lana	laine	wool	Wolle(f)	lana	lã
lancia	lance	spear, lance	Lanze(f)	lanza	lança
lanciare	lancer	throw	werfen	lanzar	lançar; atirar
lanciare	lancer	launch, start up	lancieren, starten	lanzar	lançar
lancio	lancement	launch(ing)	Start(m)	lanzamiento	lançamento
landa	lande	moor, heath	Heide(f)	landa	charneca
lanterna	lanterne	lantern	Laterne(f)	linterna	lanterna
larghezza	largeur	width, breadth	Breite(f)	anchura	largura
largo, a	large	wide, broad	weit, breit	ancho, a	largo, a
largo, a; ampio, a	large	broad	breit, weit	ancho, a	largo, a; amplo, a
laringe	larynx	larynx	Kehlkopf(m)	laringe	laringe
laringite	laryngite	laryngitis	Halsentzündung(f)	laringitis	laringite
larva	larve	larva(-vae)	Larve(f)	larva	larva
lascia-passare	laissez-passer	pass	Ausweis(m)	salvoconducto	salvo-conduto
lasciare	laisser	let; leave	lassen	dejar	deixar
lasciare	laisser	leave	lassen(zurück = -, ver-)	dejar	deixar
lasciare	quitter	leave	verlassen	dejar, abandonar	deixar
lasciare	lâcher	release	los = lassen	soltar	soltar
lasciare, mollare	larguer	let go, release	weg = werfen, auf = geben	largar	largar, deixar
laser	laser	laser	Laser(m)	láser	laser
lassativo, a	laxatif, ive	laxative	abführend	laxante	laxante
lastra, piastra	plaque	plate, plaque	Platte(f)	placa	placa
laterale	latéral, e	lateral	seitlich	lateral	lateral
latitudine	latitude	latitude	Breitengrad(m)	latitud	latitude
lato	côté	side	Seite(f)	lado	lado
latta, scatola	boîte	tin	Dose(f)	lata	lata
latte	lait	milk	Milch(f)	leche	leite
lattuga	laitue, salade	lettuce	Kopfsalat(m)	lechuga	alface
laurea	licence	degree	Lizenz(f)	licenciatura	licenciatura
lavabo, lavandino	lavabo	wash-basin	Waschbecken(n)	lavabo	lavabo
lavaggio	lavage	washing	Waschen(n)	lavado	lavagem
lavagna	tableau noir	blackboard	Tafel(f)	pizarra	quadro
lavanderia	blanchisserie	laundry	Wäscherei(f)	lavandería	lavandaria
lavandino, acquaio	évier	sink	Ausguß m, Spülbecken n	fregadero, pila	lavadouro

I

Italian	French	English	German	Spanish	Portuguese
lavare	laver	wash	waschen	lavar	lavar
lavarsi	laver(se)	wash	waschen, sich	lavarse	lavar-se
lavorare	travailler	work	arbeiten	trabajar	trabalhar
lavorare a maglia	tricoter	knit	stricken	hacer punto	tricotar
lavoratore, trice	travailleur, se	worker	Arbeiter(in f)m	trabajador, a	trabalhador, a
lavoro	travail	work	Arbeit(f)	trabajo	trabalho
lavoro	travail	labour	Arbeit(f)	trabajo	trabalho
lavoro, opera	ouvrage, oeuvre	work	Werk(n)	obra	obra
leale	loyal, e	loyal	loyal, treu	leal	leal
lecca lecca	sucette	lollipop	Lutscher(m)	pirulí	chupa-chupa
leccare	lécher	lick	lecken	lamer	lamber
lega	alliage	alloy	Legierung(f)	aleación	liga
legale	légal, e	legal	gesetzlich	legal	legal
legalità	légalité	legality	Rechtmäßigkeit(f)	legalidad	legalidade
legare	lier	tie, bind	binden, verbinden	ligar, amarrar	ligar
legare	attacher	attach, tie, fasten	fest = binden, binden	atar	atar
legare	léguer	bequeath, leave	vermachen	legar	legar
legge	loi	law	Gesetz(n)	ley	lei
leggenda	légende	legend	Legende(f)	leyenda	lenda
leggere	lire	read	lesen	leer	ler
leggermente	légèrement	lightly, slightly	leicht	ligeramente	ligeiramente
leggero, a	léger, ère	light	leicht	ligero, a	ligeiro, a; leve
leggibile	lisible	legible	leserlich	legible	legível
legislativo, a	législatif, ive	legislative	gesetzgebend	legislativo, a	legislativo, a
legislazione	législation	legislation	Gesetzgebung(f)	legislación	legislação
legittimo, a	légitime	legitimate	legitim	legítimo, a	legítimo, a
legittimo, a	légitime, légal	rightful, lawful	rechtmäßig	legítimo, a	legítimo, a
legna	bois	wood	Brennholz(n)	leña	lenha
legno	bois	timber	Holz(n)	madera	madeira
lei, loro(pl.)	vous	you	Sie	usted(es)	você
lentamente	lentement	slowly	langsam	lentamente	lentamente
lente(ingrandimento)	loupe	magnifying-glass	Lupe(f)	lupa	lupa
lente a contatto	lentille	lens(contact -)	Kontaktlinse(f)	lentilla	lente
lenticchia	lentille	lentil	Linse(f)(Pflanze)	lenteja	lentilha
lento, a	lent, e	slow	langsam	lento, a	lento, a
lento, slow	slow	smooch, slow dance	Blues(m), Slow(m)	lento	slow
lenza	ligne	line	Angelschnur(f)	caña	linha
lenzuolo	drap	sheet	Laken(n)	sábana	lençol
leone, leonessa	lion, ne	lion, lioness	Löwe(m), Löwin(f)	león, leona	leão, leoa
lesbica	lesbienne	lesbian	lesbisch	lesbiana	lésbica
lesione	lésion	lesion, injury	Verletzung(f)	lesión	lesão
letame	fumier	manure	Mist(m)	estiércol	estrume
lettera	lettre	letter	Buchstabe(m)	letra	letra
lettera	lettre	letter	Brief(m)	carta	carta
letterario, a	littéraire	literary	literarisch	literario, a	literário, a
letteratura	littérature	literature	Literatur(f)	literatura	literatura
letto	lit	bed	Bett(n)	cama	cama
letto da campo	lit de camp	camp-bed	Feldbett(n)	cama de campaña	cama de campismo
lettore, trice	lecteur, trice	reader	Leser(in f)m	lector, a	leitor, a
lettura	lecture	reading	Lesen(n)	lectura	leitura
leucemia	leucémie	leukaemia	Leukämie(f)	leucemia	leucemia
leva	levier	lever	Hebel(m)	palanca	alavanca
leva	manette	handle	Griff(m)	manecilla	manípulo
levatrice	sage-femme	midwife(-ives)	Hebamme(f)	comadrona	parteira
levigato, a	poli, e	polished	poliert	pulido, a	polido, a
lezione	leçon	lesson	Stunde(f); Lektion(f)	lección	lição
liberale	libéral, e	liberal	liberal	liberal	liberal
liberalismo	libéralisme	liberalism	Liberalismus(m)	liberalismo	liberalismo
liberare	libérer	liberate, free	befreien	liberar	libertar
liberarsi	débarrasser(se)	get rid of	beseitigen	quitarse	livrar-se
libero, a	libre	free	frei	libre	livre
libero, a	libre	clear	frei	libre	livre
libertà	liberté	liberty, freedom	Freiheit(f)	libertad	liberdade
libido	libido	libido	Libido(f)	libido	líbido
libreria	librairie	book-shop	Buchhandlung(f)	librería	livraria
libreria	bibliothèque	bookcase	Bücherschrank(m)	biblioteca	estante
libretto di circola-	carte grise	log-book	KFZ-Schein(m)	cédula iden-fiscal	livrete(circulação)
libretto di assegni	chéquier	cheque book	Scheckheft(n)	talonario(cheques)	livro de cheques

Italian	French	English	German	Spanish	Portuguese
libro	livre	book	Buch(n)	libro	livro
licenza	licence	licence	Lizenz(f)	licencia	licença
licenziamento	licenciement	dismissal, lay-off	Entlassung(f)	despido	despedimento
licenziare	licencier	lay off, dismiss	entlassen	despedir	despedir
liceo	lycée	comprehensive sch.	Gymnasium(n)	instituto, liceo	liceu
lietissimo, a	ravi, e	delighted	hocherfreut	encantado, a	encantado, a
lima	lime	file	Feile(f)	lima	lima
limitare	limiter	limit	begrenzen	limitar	limitar
limite	limite	limit	Grenze(f)	límite	limite
limitrofo	limitrophe	border(ing)	angrenzend	limítrofe	limítrofe
limone	citron	lemon	Zitrone(f)	limón	limão
linciare	lyncher	lynch	lynchen	linchar	linchar
linea	ligne	line	Linie(f)	línea	linha
lineare	linéaire	linear	linear	lineal	linear
linfa	sève	sap	Saft(m)	savia	seiva
lingotto	lingot	ingot, bullion	Barren(m)	lingote	lingote
lingua	langue	tongue	Zunge(f)	lengua	língua
lingua	langue	language	Sprache(f)	idioma, lengua	língua, idioma
linguaggio	langage	language	Sprache(f)	lenguaje	linguagem
liquidare	liquider	liquidate	liquidieren	liquidar	liquidar
liquido, a	liquide	liquid	flüssig	líquido, a	líquido, a
liquido	liquide	liquid	Flüssigkeit(f)	líquido	líquido
liquore	liqueur	liqueur	Likör(m)	licor	licor
lisca	arête	fish-bone, bone	Gräte(f)	espina	espinha
liscio, a	lisse	smooth	glatt	liso, a	liso, a
lista	liste	list	Liste(f)	lista	lista
lista dei vini	carte des vins	wine-list	Weinkarte(f)	carta de vinos	lista dos vinhos
litigare	disputer(se)	quarrel, argue	streiten, sich	reñir(con)	disputar-se
litigio	litige	litigation	Streitfall(m)	litigio	litígio
litografia	lithographie	lithograph(y)	Steindruck(m)	litografía	litografia
litorale	littoral	coast	Küstenstreifen(m)	litoral	litoral
litro	litre	litre	Liter(m, n)	litro	litro
livello	niveau	level	Stand(m), Niveau(n)	nivel	nível
livido, a	livide	livid, pallid	blaß, fahl	lívido, a	lívido, a
lo	le	the	das	lo	o
lobo	lobe	lobe	Ohrläppchen(n)	lóbulo	lóbulo
locale	local, e	local	lokal	local	local
locale	local	premises	Gebäude(n), Lokal(n)	local	local
località	localité	locality	Ortschaft(f)	localidad	localidade
localizzare	localiser	localize; locate	lokalisieren	localizar	localizar
localizzare	repérer	locate	lokalisieren	localizar	localizar
locanda	auberge	inn	Gasthaus(n)	posada; albergue	estalagem
locomotiva	locomotive	locomotive	Lokomotive(f)	locomotiva	locomotiva
locuzione	locution	phrase, locution	Redensart(f)	locución	locução
logico, a	logique	logical	logisch	lógico, a	lógico, a
logoro, a	usé, e	worn, worn out	verbraucht	usado, a	usado, a
lombaggine	lumbago	lumbago	Hexenschuß(m)	lumbago	lumbago
longitudinale	longitudinal, e	longitudinal	Längs-	longitudinal	longitudinal
longitudine	longitude	longitude	Längengrad(m)	longitud	longitude
lontananza	éloignement	distance	Entfernung(f)	alejamiento	afastamento
lontano, a	loin	far(away), distant	weit, fern	lejos	longe
lontano	loin(au)	away, far away	weg(fort); weit weg	lejos(a lo)	longe(ao)
loro(il/la, i/le)	leur(s)	their	ihr/ihre	su, sus, suyo	seu, sua, deles
loro(il, la)	leur(le, la)	theirs	ihrige(der, die, das)	suyo, a(el, la)	seu(o), a sua; dele, a
loro; gli	leur	them(to -)	ihnen	les	lhes
lotta	lutte	struggle, fight	Kampf(m)	lucha	luta
lottare	lutter	fight, struggle	kämpfen	luchar	lutar
lottatore, trice	lutteur, se	wrestler; fighter	Kämpfer(m); Ringer(m)	luchador, a	lutador, a
lotteria	loterie	lottery	Lotterie(f)	lotería	lotaria
lozione	lotion	lotion	Gesichtswasser(n)	loción	loção
lucchetto, catenaccio	cadenas	padlock	Vorhängeschloß(n)	candado	cadeado
luce	lumière	light	Licht(n)	luz	luz
lucertola	lézard	lizard	Eidechse(f)	lagarto	lagarto
lucidare	cirer	polish	polieren, wachsen	dar crema	encerar
lucidare, levigare	polir	polish	polieren	pulir	polir
lucido, a	lucide	lucid	klar	lúcido, a	lúcido, a
lucro, profitto	gain(s)	earnings	Gewinn(m)	ganancia(s)	lucro
luglio	juillet	July	Juli(m)	julio	Julho

I

Italian	French	English	German	Spanish	Portuguese
lui; gli; le	lui	him, her, it	ihm, ihr, ihm	le, él; ella; se	ele(a); lhe
lumaca, chiocciola	escargot	snail	Schnecke(f)	caracol	caracol
luminoso, a	lumineux, se	luminous	leuchtend, hell	luminoso, a	luminoso, a
luna	lune	moon	Mond(m)	luna	lua
lunedì	lundi	Monday	Montag(m)	lunes	segunda-feira
lunghezza	longueur	length	Länge(f)	longitud	comprimento
lungo, a	long, longue	long	lang	largo, a	longo, a
lungo	long(le)	along	entlang	largo(a lo)	longo(ao)
luogo	lieu	place, spot	Ort(m)	lugar	lugar
luogo, posto	endroit	place, spot	Stelle(f)	lugar, sitio	lugar, sítio
lupo	loup	wolf(-lves)	Wolf(m)	lobo	lobo
lusso	luxe	luxury	Luxus(m)	lujo	luxo
lussuoso, a	luxueux, se	luxurious	üppig	lujoso, a	luxuoso, a
lussureggiante	luxuriant, e	luxuriant, lush	üppig	exuberante	luxuriante
lustrino	paillette	glitter, spangle	Flitter(m)	lentejuela	lentejoula
lutto	deuil	mourning(be in)	Trauer(f)	duelo; luto	luto

M

Italian	French	English	German	Spanish	Portuguese
ma	mais	but	aber	pero; sino; mas	mas
macabro, a	macabre	macabre	makaber	macabro, a	macabro, a
macchia	tache	stain	Fleck(m)	mancha	mancha, nódoa
macchia, cespugli	broussaille	undergrowth	Gestrüpp(n)	zarzal, maleza	mato, brenha
macchiare	tacher	stain, dirty	beflecken, beschmutzen	manchar	manchar, sujar
macchina	machine	machine	Maschine(f)	máquina	máquina
macchina, auto	voiture	car	Wagen(m)	coche	carro
macchina da corsa	voiture(course)	racing car	Rennwagen(m)	coche de carreras	carro de corrida
macchina fotografica	appareil photo	camera	Kamera(f)	cámara fotográfica	máquina fotográfica
macelleria	boucherie	butcher's(shop)	Metzgerei(f)	carnicería	talho
macerie, rovine	décombres	ruins	Trümmer(m, pl)	escombros	escombros
macinare	moudre	grind	mahlen	moler	moer
madre	mère	mother	Mutter(f)	madre	mãe
madrina	marraine	godmother	Patin(f)	madrina	madrinha
maestà	majesté	majesty	Majestät(f)	majestad	majestade
maestoso, a	majestueux, se	majestic	majestätisch	majestuoso, a	majestoso, a
maestro, a; padrone, a	maître, esse	master, mistress	Herr(in f)m	señor, señora	dono, a; senhor, a
maestro, a	instituteur	teacher(primary)	Grundschullehrer/in	maestro, a	professor primário
mafia	mafia	Mafia	Mafia(f)	mafia	mafia
magazzino; negozio	magasin	store	Warenlager(n)	almacén	armazém
magazzino	entrepôt	warehouse	Lager(n)	almacén	armazém
maggio	mai	May	Mai(m)	mayo	Maio
maggioranza	majorité	majority	Mehrheit(f)	mayoría	maioria
maggior parte(la)	plupart(la)	most(of the)	meisten(die)	mayoría(la)	maior parte(a)
magia	magie	magic	Zauberei(f)	magia	magia
magico, a	magique	magic	magisch	mágico, a	mágico, a
magistrato	magistrat	magistrate	Magistrat(m)	magistrado	magistrado
maglia	tricot	sweater, jumper	Trikot(m), Strickweste	prenda de punto	malha
maglia intima	maillot de corps	vest	Trikot(n)	camiseta	camisola interior
maglione	chandail	jumper, sweater	Pullover(m)	jersey	camisola
maglione, pullover	pull-over	pullover, sweater	Pullover(m)	jersey	pulover
magnetico, a	magnétique	magnetic	magnetisch	magnético, a	magnético, a
magnifico, a	magnifique	magnificent	prächtig	magnífico, a	magnífico, a
magro, a	maigre	thin	mager	delgado, a	magro, a
mai	jamais	never; ever	niemals, jemals	jamás, nunca	nunca, jamais
malanimo	malveillance	ill will	Böswilligkeit(f)	malevolencia	malevolência
malaria, paludismo	paludisme	malaria	Sumpffieber(n)	paludismo	paludismo
malato, a	malade	ill	krank	enfermo, a	doente; enfermo, a

Italian	French	English	German	Spanish	Portuguese
malato, a	malade	sick person	Kranke(f, m)	enfermo, a	doente
malattia	maladie	illness	Krankheit(f)	enfermedad	doença
maldestro, a	maladroit, e	clumsy, awkward	ungeschickt	torpe	desajeitado, a
mal di denti	mal aux dents	toothache	Zahnschmerzen(m, pl)	dolor de dientes	dor de dentes
mal di gola	mal de gorge	sore throat	Halsschmerzen(m, pl)	dolor de garganta	dor de garganta
mal di mare	mal de mer	sea-sickness	Seekrankheit(f)	mareo	enjôo
mal di testa	mal de tête	headache	Kopfschmerzen(m, pl)	dolor de cabeza	dor de cabeça
male	mal	evil	Böse(n)	mal	mal
male	mal	harm, hurt	Weh(n)	daño	mal
male	mal	ache, pain	Schmerz(m), Weh(n)	dolor	dor
male	mal	badly	schlecht	mal	mal
male(fare)	mal(faire)	ache, hurt	weh tun, schmerzen	doler	doer
male(aver)	mal(avoir)	hurts(it)	Schmerzen haben	dolerle a uno	doer
maledetto, a	maudit, e	cursed, damned	verdammt	maldito, a	maldito, a
maleducato, a	impoli, e	impolite, rude	unhöflich	maleducado, a	mal educado, a
malessere	malaise	faintness	Unwohlsein, Schwäche	malestar	indisposição
malevolo, a	malveillant, e	malevolent	böswillig	malévolo, a	malévolo, a
malgrado	malgré	despite	trotz	a pesar de	apesar de
malinconia	mélancolie	melancholy	Wehmut(f)	melancolía	melancolia
malinconia	cafard	miserable(feel)	Trübsinn(m)	melancolía	tristeza
malnutrizione	malnutrition	malnutrition	Unterernährung(f)	desnutrición	malnutrição
malsano, a	malsain, e	unhealthy	ungesund	malsano, a	doentio, a
malta, calcina	mortier	mortar	Mörtel(m)	argamasa	argamassa
malvivente	malfaiteur	criminal	Missetäter(in f)m	malhechor	malfeitor
mamma	maman	Mummy, Mum	Mama(f)	mamá	mamã
mammella	mamelle	udder	Euter(n)	mama, teta	mama
mammifero	mammifère	mammal	Säugetier(n)	mamífero	mamífero
manager, padrone	patron, dirigeant	manager, boss	Unternehmer(in f)m	director, jefe	director, patrão
mancanza	manque	lack, shortage	Mangel(m)	falta, carencia	falta, carência
mancare	manquer	lack, be short of	fehlen	faltar	falta(ter)
mancare	rater	fail	mißlingen	fallar	falhar
mancia	pourboire	tip	Trinkgeld(n)	propina	gorgeta
manciata, pugno	poignée	handful	Handvoll(f)	puñado	punhado
mandare, inviare	envoyer	send	senden	mandar, enviar	mandar, enviar
mandarino	mandarine	tangerine	Mandarine(f)	mandarina	tangerina
mandorla	amande	almond	Mandel(f)	almendra	amêndoa
maneggevole	maniable	handy, manageable	handlich	manuable	manejável
manette	menottes	handcuffs	Handschellen(f, pl)	esposas	algemas
manganellare	matraquer	beat up, club	prügeln	aporrear	espancar
mangiare	manger	eat	essen	comer	comer
mania	manie	mania	Sucht(f)	manía	mania
maniaco, a	maniaque	maniac	Verrückte(f, m)	maníaco, a	maníaco, a
maniaco, a	obsédé, e	maniac	Besessene(f, m)	obseso, a	obcecado, a
manica	manche	sleeve	Ärmel(m)	manga(la)	manga
manichino	mannequin	dummy; model	Schaufensterpuppe(f)	maniquí	manequim
manico	manche	handle	Stiel(m)	mango(el)	cabo
manico	poignée	handle	Griff(m)	asa, mango	asa
manicomio	asile	mental hospital	Irrenhaus(n)	manicomio	manicômio
manicure	manucure	manicure	Maniküre(f)	manicura	manicura
maniera, modo	manière	manner, way	Art(f)	manera, modo	maneira, modo
maniero, castello	manoir, château	mansion	Herrensitz(m), -haus n	mansión, morada	mansão, palacete
manifestante	manifestant, e	demonstrator	Demonstrant(in f)m	manifestante	manifestante
manifestazione	manifestation	demonstration	Demonstration(f)	manifestación	manifestação
manifesto	affiche	poster, placard	Plakat(n)	cartel	cartaz
maniglia	poignée	handle	Griff(m)	manilla, mango	fecho
manipolare	manipuler	manipulate	manipulieren	manipular	manipular
mano	main	hand	Hand(f)	mano	mão
manodopera	main-d'oeuvre	workforce, labour	Arbeitskraft(f)	mano de obra	mão-de-obra
manodopera	main-d'oeuvre	manpower, labour	Arbeitskräfte(pl.)	mano de obra	mão-de-obra
manopola, pomello	bouton	knob	Knopf(m)	botón	botão
manoscritto, a	manuscrit, e	handwritten	handgeschrieben	manuscrito, a	manuscrito, a
manovale	manoeuvre	labourer	Hilfsarbeiter(in f)m	peón, obrero	servente
manovella	manivelle	crank	Handkurbel(f)	manivela	manivela
manovra	manoeuvre	manoeuvre	Manöver(n)	maniobra	manobra
mantenere	maintenir	maintain	erhalten	mantener	manter
mantenimento	entretien	upkeep	Instandhaltung(f)	cuidado	manutenção
manuale	manuel, elle	manual; hand-	manuell; Hand-	manual	manual
manutenzione	entretien	maintenance	Wartung(f)	mantenimiento	manutenção

I

Italian	French	English	German	Spanish	Portuguese
mappa, carta	carte(géo)	map	Landkarte(f)	mapa	mapa
maratona	marathon	marathon	Marathonlauf(m)	maratón	maratona
marchio, marca	marque	brand, make	Marke(f)	marca	marca
marcia	marche	walk(ing)	Wanderung(f)	marcha	marcha
marciapiede	trottoir	pavement	Bürgersteig(m)	acera	passeio
marcio, a	pourri, e	rotten	verfault	podrido, a	podre
marcire	pourrir	rot	verfaulen	pudrir	apodrecer
mare	mer	sea	Meer(n)	mar	mar
mare	mer	sea	See(f)	mar	mar
marea	marée	tide	Gezeiten(pl.)	marea	maré
marginale	marginal, e	fringe(on the)	Außenseiter(in f)m	marginal	marginal
margine	marge	margin	Rand(m)	margen	margem
margine, differenza	écart	gap, margin	Abstand(m)	diferencia, margen	desvio, margem
marina	marine	navy	Marine(f)	marina	marinha
marinaio	marin	sailor	Seemann(m)	marino	marinheiro
marinaio	matelot	sailor	Matrose(m)	marinero	marinheiro
marito	mari	husband	Ehemann(m)	marido	marido
marittimo, a	maritime	maritime, sea-	See-	marítimo, a	marítimo, a
marmellata	confiture	jam	Marmelade(f)	mermelada	doce, compota
marmo	marbre	marble	Marmor(m)	mármol	mármore
martedì	mardi	Tuesday	Dienstag(m)	martes	terça-feira
martello	marteau	hammer	Hammer(m)	martillo	martelo
martinetto, binda	vérin, cric	jack	Winde(f)	gato, cric	macaco
martire	martyr, e	martyr	Märtyrer(in f)m	mártir	mártir
marxismo	marxisme	Marxism	Marxismus(m)	marxismo	marxismo
marzo	mars	March	März(m)	marzo	Março
mascalzone, a	voyou	hooligan	Strolch(m)	canalla	patife
mascella	mâchoire	jaw	Kiefer(m)	mandíbula	maxila
maschera	masque	mask	Maske(f)	máscara	máscara
mascherare	déguiser	disguise	verkleiden	disfrazar	disfarçar
maschile	masculin, e	masculine, male	männlich	masculino, a	masculino, a
maschio	mâle	male	Männchen(n)	macho	macho
massa	masse	mass	Masse(f)	masa	massa
massacro	massacre	slaughter	Blutbad(n)	masacre	massacre
massaggio	massage	massage	Massage(f)	masaje	massagem
massiccio, a	massif, ive	massive; solid	massiv	masivo, a	maciço, a
massimo	maximum	maximum	Maximum(n)	máximo	máximo
masso, roccia	rocher	rock	Felsen(m)	peñasco, roca	rochedo, rocha
masticare	mâcher	chew	kauen	masticar	mastigar
mastice	mastic	putty	Kitt(m)	masilla	betume
matador	matador	matador	Matador(m)	matador	matador
matematica	mathématique(s)	mathematics	Mathematik(f)	matemáticas	matemáticas
materasso	matelas	mattress(-es)	Matraze(f)	colchón	colchão
materia	matière	matter, material	Stoff(m), Material(n)	materia	matéria
materia	substance	matter, material	Materie(f)	materia	matéria
materia	matière	subject	Fach(n)	asignatura	matéria
materia, tema	matière	subject-matter	Thema(n)	materia, tema	assunto
materiale	matériel	material	Material(n)	material	material
materiale	matériau	material	Material(n)	material	material
materiale; materia	matériel	material	Material(n)	material; materia	material; matéria
materno, a	maternel, le	maternal, motherly	mütterlich	materno, a; maternal	maternal
matita, lapis	crayon	pencil	Bleistift(m)	lápiz	lápis
matricola	matricule	roll, register	Matrikel(f)	matrícula	matrícula
matrimonio	mariage	wedding; marriage	Hochzeit(f); Heirat(f)	matrimonio	casamento
mattino	matin	morning	Morgen(m)	mañana	manhã
matto, a; pazzo, a	fou, folle	mad, foolish, crazy	verrückt	loco, a	louco, a; maluco, a
mattone	brique	brick	Ziegel(m)	ladrillo	tijolo
mattutino, a	matinal, e	early	früh	matutino, a	matinal
maturità	maturité	maturity	Reife(f)	madurez	maturidade
maturità	baccalauréat	G.C.E. A.Level(s)	Abitur(n)	bachillerato	bacharelato
maturo, a	mûr, e	ripe	reif	maduro, a	maduro, a
maturo, a	mûr, e	mature	reif	maduro, a	maduro, a
mazzo	bouquet	bunch; bouquet	Strauß(m)	ramo	ramo
meccanica	mécanique	mechanics	Mechanik(f)	mecánica	mecânica
meccanico, a	mécanique	mechanical	mechanisch	mecánico, a	mecânico, a
meccanico, a	mécanicien, ne	mechanic	Mechaniker(in f)m	mecánico, a	mecânico, a
meccanismo	mécanisme	mechanism	Mechanismus(m)	mecanismo	mecanismo
mecenate	mécène	patron	Mäzen(m), Sponsor(m)	mecenas	mecenas

Italian	French	English	German	Spanish	Portuguese
medaglia	médaille	medal	Medaille(f)	medalla	medalha
media	moyenne	average	Durchschnitt(m)	media	média
medicazione	pansement	plaster, bandage	Verband(m)	cura, vendaje	penso, curativo
medicina	médecine	medicine	Medizin(f)	medicina	medicina
medicina	médicament	drug, medicine	Medikament(n)	medicina	medicamento
medico	médecin	doctor	Arzt(m), Ärztin(f)	médico	médico
medico, a	médical, e	medical	medizinisch	médico, a	médico, a
medio, a	moyen, ne	middle	mittel	medio, a	médio, a
medio, a	moyen, ne	medium	mittlere(r, s)	medio, a	médio, a
mediocre	médiocre	mediocre	mittelmäßig, schlecht	mediocre	medíocre
meditare	méditer	meditate	nach = denken, sinnen	meditar	meditar
meglio	mieux	better	besser	mejor	melhor
mela	pomme	apple	Apfel(m)	manzana	maçã
melma	vase	sludge, mud	Schlamm(m)	limo, fango	lodo
melodia	mélodie	melody, tune	Melodie(f)	melodía	melodia
melodia	air	tune	Melodie(f)	melodía	melodia
melone	melon	melon	Melone(f)	melón	melão
membrana	membrane	membrane	Membran(f)	membrana	membrana
membro, arto	membre	limb	Glied(n)	miembro	membro
membro, i	membre(de)	member(of)	Mitglied(n)	miembro, a; socio, a	membro, a; sócio, a
memoria	mémoire	memory	Gedächtnis(n)	memoria	memória
mendicante	mendiant, e	beggar	Bettler(in f)m	mendigo, a	mendigo, a
meno	moins	less	weniger	menos	menos
meno(il)	moins(le)	least(the)	wenigsten(am)	menos(lo)	menos(o)
menopausa	ménopause	menopause	Wechseljahre(n, pl)	menopausia	menopausa
mensile	mensuel, le	monthly	monatlich	mensual	mensal
menta	menthe	mint	Minze(f)	menta	hortelã
mentale	mental, e	mental	geistig	mental	mental
mentalità	mentalité	mentality	Mentalität(f)	mentalidad	mentalidade
mente	esprit	mind	Sinn(m)	espíritu	espírito
mentire	mentir	lie	lügen	mentir	mentir
mento	menton	chin	Kinn(n)	barbilla	queixo
mentre; già che	pendant que	while	während	mientras	enquanto
mentre	tandis que	while, whilst	während	mientras	enquanto
menù	menu	menu	Menü(n), Speisekarte f	menú	ementa
menù, carta	carte(f)(resto)	menu	Karte(f)(Speisekarte)	menú	lista
menzione	mention	mention	Vermerk(m)	mención	menção
meravigliare	émerveiller	amaze	entzücken	maravillar	maravilhar
meravigliarsi	étonner(s')	astonished(be -)	wundern, sich	sorprenderse	espantar-se
meraviglioso, a	merveilleux, se	marvellous	wunderbar	maravilloso, a	maravilhoso, a
meraviglioso, a	merveilleux, se	wonderful	wunderbar	maravilloso, a	maravilhoso, a
mercante	marchand, e	tradesman, dealer	Händler(in f)m	vendedor, a	negociante
mercato	marché	market	Markt(m)	mercado	mercado
merce	marchandise	goods, merchandise	Ware(f)	mercancía	mercadoria
mercenario	mercenaire	mercenary	Söldner(m)	mercenario	mercenário
mercoledì	mercredi	Wednesday	Mittwoch(m)	miércoles	quarta-feira
mercurio	mercure	mercury	Quecksilber(n)	mercurio	mercúrio
meridiano	méridien	meridian	Meridian(m)	meridiano	meridiano
meritare	mériter	deserve, merit	verdienen	merecer	merecer
merito	mérite	merit, worth	Verdienst(n)	mérito	mérito
merletto	dentelle	lace	Spitze(f)	puntilla	renda
mescolanza	mélange	blend, mixture	Mischung(f)	mezcla	mistura
mescolare	mélanger	mix	mischen	mezclar	misturar
mescolare	remuer	stir	rühren	remover	mexer
mese	mois	month	Monat(m)	mes	mês
messa	messe	mass	Messe(f)	misa	missa
messaggio	message	message	Nachricht(f)	mensaje	mensagem, recado
mesticheria	droguerie	hardware shop	Kramwarenhandel(m)	droguería	drogaria
mestiere	métier	profession, job	Beruf(m)	oficio	ofício
metà	moitié	half(-lves)	Hälfte(f)	mitad	metade
metallico, a	métallique	metallic	metallisch	metálico, a	metálico, a
metallo	métal	metal	Metal(n)	metal	metal
metamorfosi	métamorphose	metamorphosis(-es)	Verwandlung(f)	metamorfosis	metamorfose
metastasi	métastase	metastasis(-es)	Tochtergeschwulst(f)	metástasis	metástase
meteorologia	météorologie	weather forecast	Wetterkunde(f)	meteorología	meteorologia
meticcio, a	métis, se	half-caste	Mischling(m)	mestizo, a	mestiço, a
meticoloso, a	méticuleux, se	meticulous	sorgfältig	meticuloso, a	meticuloso, a
metodo	méthode	method	Methode(f)	método	método

I

Italian	French	English	German	Spanish	Portuguese
metrico, a	métrique	metric	metrisch	métrico, a	métrico, a
metro	mètre	metre	Meter(m, n)	metro	metro
metropolitana	métro	underground, tube	U-Bahn(f)	metro	metropolitano
mettere	mettre	put	legen, stellen	poner	pôr
mezzanotte	minuit	midnight	Mitternacht(f)	medianoche	meia-noite
mezzo, a	demi, e	half	halb	medio, a	meio, a
mezzo	milieu	middle	Mitte(f)	medio	meio
mezzo	moyen	means	Mittel(n)	medio(s)	meio
mezzogiorno	midi	midday, noon	Mittag(m)	mediodía	meio-dia
mezz'ora	demi-heure	half an hour	halbe Stunde	media hora	meia-hora
mi, me	me, m'; moi	me	mich; mir	me	me
mia(la)	ma	my	meine	mi	minha
miagolare	miauler	mew	miauen	maullar	miar
microbo	microbe	germ, microbe	Mikrobe(f)	microbio	micróbio
microfono	micro(phone)	microphone, mike	Mikrophon(n)	micrófono	microfone
microscopio	microscope	microscope	Mikroskop(n)	microscopio	microscópio
midollo	moelle	marrow(-bone)	Mark(n)	médula, tuétano	medula, tutano
miei, mie(i, le)	mes	my	meine	mis	meus
miele	miel	honey	Honig(m)	miel	mel
mietitura	moisson	harvest	Ernte(f)	cosecha	ceifa, colheita
migliaio(a)	millier	thousand	Tausend(n)	millar	milhar
miglioramento	amélioration	improvement	Verbesserung(f)	mejora; mejoría	melhoramento
migliorare	améliorer	improve	verbessern	mejorar	melhorar
migliore	meilleur, e	better	besser(sein)	mejor	melhor
migliore	meilleur, e	best	Beste(f, m)	mejor	melhor
migratore, trice	migrateur, trice	migrant	wandernd; Wander-	migratorio, a	migrador, a
migrazione	migration	migration	Wanderung(f)	migración	migração
miliardo	milliard	thousand million	Milliarde(f)	mil millones	bilião
milione	million	million	Million(f)	millón	milhão
militante	militant, e	militant	Militant(m)	militante	militante
militare	militer	militate	kämpfen für	militar	militar
militare	militaire	military	militärisch	militar	militar
milizia	milice	militia	Miliz(f)	milicia	milícia
mille; mila(pl.)	mille	thousand	tausend	mil	mil
millesimo, a	millième	thousandth	tausendste	milésimo, a	milésimo, a
milza	rate	spleen	Milz(f)	bazo	baço
minaccia	menace	threat	Drohung(f)	amenaza	ameaça
minacciare	menacer	threaten	bedrohen	amenazar	ameaçar
minerale	minéral, e	mineral	mineralisch	mineral	mineral
minerale	minerai	ore	Erz(n)	mineral	minério
minestra	soupe	soup	Suppe(f)	sopa	sopa
miniatura	miniature	miniature	Miniatur(f)	miniatura	miniatura
miniera	mine	mine	Bergwerk(n)	mina	mina
minimo, a	minimum	minimum	Minimum(n)	mínimo, a	mínimo, a
ministero	ministère	ministry	Ministerium(n)	ministerio	ministério
ministro	ministre	minister	Minister(in f)m	ministro	ministro
minoranza	minorité	minority	Minderheit(f)	minoría	minoria
minore, minorenne	mineur, e	minor	Minderjährige(f, m)	menor	menor
minore	mineur, e	minor	unbedeutend	menor	menor
minuscolo, a	minuscule	minute, tiny	winzig	minúsculo, a	minúsculo, a
minuto	minute	minute	Minute(f)	minuto	minuto
mio, mia(il, la)	mon	my	mein	mi	meu, minha
mio, mia(è)	moi(à)	mine, to me	mir	mío, a(el, la)	meu(é)
mio(il); mia(la)	mien, ne	mine	meine, meiner	mío, mía	meu, minha
miope	myope	short-sighted	kurzsichtig	miope	míope
miracolo	miracle	miracle	Wunder(n)	milagro	milagre
miraggio	mirage	mirage	Fata Morgana(f)	espejismo	miragem
mirare	viser	aim	zielen	apuntar	apontar
miscuglio	mélange	mixture; mixing	Mischung(f)	mezcla	mistura
miseria	misère	poverty	Elend(n)	miseria	miséria
missile	missile	missile	Rakete(f)	misil	míssil
missione	mission	mission	Mission(f)	misión	missão
misterioso, a	mystérieux, se	mysterious	mysteriös	misterioso, a	misterioso, a
mistero	mystère	mystery	Geheimnis(n); Rätsel n	misterio	mistério
mistico, a	mystique	mystic(al)	mystisch	místico, a	místico, a
misto, a	mixte	mixed	gemischt	mixto, a	misto, a
misura	taille	size	Größe(f)	tamaño	tamanho
misurare	mesurer	measure	messen	medir	medir

Italian	French	English	German	Spanish	Portuguese
mite	doux, ce	mild	mild	templado, a	ameno, a
mito	mythe	myth	Mythos(m); Sage(f)	mito	mito
mittente	expéditeur	sender	Absender(in f)m	remitente	expedidor
mobile	mobile	mobile, movable	beweglich, mobil	móvil, movible	móvel
mobile	meuble	furniture	Möbelstück(n)	mueble	móvel
mobilio	mobilier	furniture	Möbel(pl)	mobiliario	mobiliário
mobilità	mobilité	mobility	Beweglichkeit(f)	mobilidad	mobilidade
mobilitare	mobiliser	mobilize	mobilisieren	mobilizar	mobilizar
moda	mode	fashion	Mode(f)	moda	moda
modello	modèle	model, pattern	Modell(n)	modelo	modelo
modello	modèle	design	Muster(n), Modell(n)	modelo, patrón	modelo
modello	modèle	pattern	Muster(n)	modelo	modelo
modello	maquette	model	Modell(n)	maqueta	maqueta
moderare	modérer	moderate	mäßigen	moderar	moderar
moderno, a	moderne	modern	modern	moderno, a	moderno, a
modesto, a	modeste	modest	bescheiden	modesto, a	modesto, a
modifica	modification	modification	Abänderung(f)	modificación	modificação
modificare	modifier	modify	verändern	modificar	modificar
modo, maniera	façon, manière	way, manner, fashion	Weise(f), Art(f)	modo, manera	modo, maneira
modo, maniera	mode, manière	mode, manner	Weise(f)	modo, manera	modo, maneira
modulo, formulario	formulaire	form	Formular(n), Vordruck	formulario	formulário
moglie	femme, épouse	wife(wives)	Ehefrau(f), Frau(f)	mujer	mulher
molare	molaire	molar	Backenzahn(m)	molar	molar
molecola	molécule	molecule	Molekül(n)	molécula	molécula
molla	ressort	spring	Feder(f)(Sprung-)	muelle	mola
molle; tenero, a	mou, molle	soft	weich	blando, a	mole
molle; fiacco, a	mou, molle	lethargic	schlaff	fofo, a	mole; fraco, a
mollusco	mollusque	mollusc	Weichtier(n)	molusco	molusco
molo	quai	quay	Kai(m)	muelle	cais
molti	beaucoup	many	viele	muchos, as	muitos, as
moltiplicare	multiplier	multiply	multiplizieren	multiplicar	multiplicar
moltitudine	multitude	multitude	Menge(f)	multitud	multidão
molto	beaucoup	much, many	viel(e)	mucho	muito
molto, a, i, e	beaucoup	lots of, a lot of	viel(e)	mucho, a	muito, a
molto, assai	très	very	sehr	muy	muito
molto/molto tempo	longtemps	long time(a)	lange	mucho tiempo	muito tempo
momento, attimo	moment	moment	Augenblick(m)	momento	momento
monaco, frate	moine	monk	Mönch(m)	monje, fraile	monge, frade
monarchia	monarchie	monarchy	Monarchie(f)	monarquía	monarquia
monastero	monastère	monastery	Kloster(n)	monasterio	mosteiro
mondiale	mondial, e	world-wide, world	weltlich	mundial	mundial
mondo	monde	world	Welt(f)	mundo	mundo
moneta	monnaie	money	Geld(n)	moneda, dinero	moeda
monetario, a	monétaire	monetary	Währungs-, Geld-	monetario, a	monetário, a
monogamia	monogamie	monogamy	Monogamie(f)	monogamia	monogamia
monopolio	monopole	monopoly	Monopol(n)	monopolio	monopólio
monotono, a	monotone	monotonous	monoton, eintönig	monótono, a	monótono, a
monsone	mousson	monsoon	Monsun(m)	monzón	monção
montaggio	montage	mounting, assembly	Montage(f)	montaje	montagem
montagna	montagne	mountain	Gebirge(n), Berg(m)	montaña	montanha
monte	mont, montagne	mount	Berg(m)	monte	monte
monumento	monument	monument	Denkmal(n)	monumento	monumento
moquette	moquette	carpet	Teppichboden(m)	moqueta	alcatifa
morale	moral	morale	Stimmung(f), Moral(f)	moral, ánimo	moral
morale	moral, e	moral	moralisch	moral	moral
morale	morale	moral	Moral(f)	moral	moral
morbido, a	doux, ce	soft	sanft	suave	macio, a
morbido, a; tenero, a	tendre	soft; tender	weich	blando, a	tenro, a
morbillo	rougeole	measles	Masern(pl.)	sarampión	sarampo
mordere	mordre	bite	beißen	morder	morder
morfina	morphine	morphine	Morphium(n)	morfina	morfina
morfologia	morphologie	morphology	Morphologie(f)	morfología	morfologia
morire	mourir	die	sterben	morir	morrer
mormorare	murmurer	murmur, whisper	flüstern	murmurar	murmurar
mortale	mortel, le	mortal; deadly	tödlich	mortal	mortal
mortale	mortel, le	fatal	tödlich	mortal	mortal
mortalità	mortalité	mortality	Sterblichkeit(f)	mortalidad	mortalidade
morte	mort	death	Tod(m)	muerte	morte

Italian	French	English	German	Spanish	Portuguese
morto, a	mort, e	dead	tot	muerto, a	morto, a
morto, a	mort, e	dead man/woman	Tote(f, m)	muerto, a	morto, a
mosaico	mosaïque	mosaic	Mosaik(n)	mosaico	mosaico
mosca	mouche	fly	Fliege(f)	mosca	mosca
moschea	mosquée	mosque	Moschee(f)	mezquita	mesquita
mostra, esposizione	exposition	show	Ausstellung(f)	exposición	exibição
mostrare	montrer	show	zeigen	enseñar, mostrar	mostrar
mostro	monstre	monster	Monster(n)	monstruo	monstro
motel	motel	motel	Motel(n)	motel	motel
motivare	motiver	motivate	motivieren	motivar	motivar
motivo	motif	motive	Motiv(n)	motivo	motivo
moto	moto	motor-bike	Motorrad(n)	moto	mota
motociclista	motard	motorcyclist	Motorradfahrer(in f)m	motorista	motociclista
motore	moteur	engine; motor	Motor(m)	motor	motor
motorino(avviamento)	démarreur	starter	Starter(m)	arranque	motor de arranque
motorino, scooter	mobylette	moped	Mofa(n)	velomotor	motorizada
movimento	mouvement	movement, motion	Bewegung(f)	movimiento	movimento
mucchio	tas	pile	Haufen(m)	montón	montão, pilha
mucchio	amas	pile	Haufen(m)	montón	amontoado
mulinello, gorgo	remous	eddy, swirl	Wirbel(m)	remolino	redemoinho
mulino	moulin	mill	Mühle(f)	molino	moinho
multa	amende	fine	Geldstrafe(f)	multa	multa
multiplo, a	multiple	multiple, numerous	viel-; vielfältig	múltiple	múltiplo, a
municipale	municipal, e	municipal; town -	städtisch; Stadt-	municipal	municipal
municipio, comune	mairie	town hall	Rathaus(n)	ayuntamiento	câmara
munizioni	munitions	ammunition	Munition(f)	municiones	munições
muovere	bouger	move	bewegen	moverse	mexer-se
muovere(-rsi)	remuer	move	bewegen, sich	mover	mexer-se
muratore	maçon	builder	Maurer(m)	albañil	pedreiro, trolha
muro	mur	wall	Mauer(f)	muro, pared	muro, parede
muschio	mousse	moss	Moos(n)	musgo	musgo
muscolare	musculaire	muscular	Muskel-	muscular	muscular
muscolo	muscle	muscle	Muskel(m)	músculo	músculo
muscoloso, a	musclé, e	muscular	muskulös	musculoso, a	musculado, a
museo	musée	museum	Museum(n)	museo	museu
musica	musique	music	Musik(f)	música	música
musicale	musical, e	musical	musikalisch	musical	musical
musicista	musicien, ne	musician	Musiker(in f)m	músico, a	músico, a
muso	museau	muzzle	Schnauze(f)	hocico	focinho
muso	gueule	mouth	Maul(n)	hocico	goela, garganta
musulmano, a	musulman, e	Moslem, Muslim	Mohammedaner(in f)m	musulmán, a	muçulmano, a
mutande, slip	slip	briefs, pants	Unterhose(f)	calzoncillos	cuecas
mutandine, slip	culotte	briefs, knickers	Unterhose(f), Slip(m)	bragas	cuecas
mutilato, a	mutilé, e	disabled	verstümmelt	mutilado, a	mutilado, a
muto, a	muet, te	dumb; silent	stumm	mudo, a	mudo, a
mutuo, a	mutuel, le	mutual	gegenseitig	mútuo, a	mútuo, a

N

Italian	French	English	German	Spanish	Portuguese
nafta	mazout	fuel oil	Heizöl(n)	fuel-oil	fuel, óleo
nano, a	nain, e	dwarf	Zwerg(m)	enano, a	anão, anã
narcotico	narcotique	narcotic	Betäubungsmittel(n)	narcótico	narcótico
narice	narine	nostril	Nasenloch(n)	nariz	narina
nasale	nasal, e	nasal	nasal	nasal	nasal
nascere	naître	born(be)	geboren werden	nacer	nascer
nascita	naissance	birth	Geburt(f)	nacimiento	nascimento
nascondere	cacher	hide	verstecken	esconder	esconder

Italian	French	English	German	Spanish	Portuguese
nascondere	cacher	conceal	verbergen, verhehlen	esconder, ocultar	ocultar
naso	nez	nose	Nase(f)	nariz	nariz
nastro	ruban	ribbon; tape; band	Band(n)	cinta, banda	fita
nastro	bande	tape	Band(n)	cinta	fita
natale	natal, e	native	Heimat-; Geburts-	natal	natal
Natale	Noël	Christmas	Weihnachten(n)	Navidad	Natal
natalità	natalité	birth-rate	Geburtenrate(f)	natalidad	natalidade
natica	fesse	bottom, buttock	Gesäß(n), Po(m)	nalga	nádega
nativo, a	natif, ive	native	gebürtig	nativo, a	nativo, a
nato, a	né, e	born(be)	geboren	nacido, a	nascido, a
natura	nature	nature	Natur(f)	naturaleza	natureza
naturale	naturel, le	natural	natürlich	natural	natural
naturalizzato, a	naturalisé, e	naturalized	eingebürgert	nacionalizado, a	naturalizado, a
naufragio	naufrage	wreck	Schiffbruch(m)	naufragio	naufrágio
nausea	nausée	nausea, feel sick	Brechreiz(m)	náusea	naúsea
nauseare	écoeurer	disgust	an = ekeln, an = widern	asquear	enjoar
nautico, a	nautique	nautical, water-	nautisch, Wasser-	náutico, a	naútico, a
navale	naval, e	naval	See-	naval	naval
nave	navire	ship	Schiff(n)	navío	navio
navigatore	navigateur	navigator	Seefahrer(m)	navegante	navegador
navigazione	navigation	navigation	Seefahrt(f)	navegación	navegação
nazionale	national, e	national	national	nacional	nacional
nazionalismo	nationalisme	nationalism	Nationalismus(m)	nacionalismo	nacionalismo
nazionalità	nationalité	nationality	Nationalität(f)	nacionalidad	nacionalidade
nazione	nation	nation	Nation(f)	nación	nação
né	ni	neither, nor	weder, noch	ni	nem
neanche	même pas	even(not)	einmal(nicht)	siquiera(ni)	sequer(nem)
nebbia	brouillard	fog	Nebel(m)	niebla	nevoeiro
nebulizzatore	atomiseur	spray, atomizer	Zerstäuber(m)	atomizador	pulverizador
nebulizzazione	pulvérisation	spraying	Zerstäubung(f)	pulverización	pulverização
necessario, a	nécessaire	necessary	nötig, notwendig	necesario, a	necessário, a
necessità	nécessité	necessity	Notwendigkeit(f)	necesidad	necessidade
negare	nier	deny	verneinen, leugnen	negar	negar
negativo, a	négatif, ive	negative	negativ	negativo, a	negativo, a
negativo	cliché, négatif	negative	Negativ(n)	cliché	cliché
negligente	négligent, e	careless	nachlässig	descuidado, a	descuidado, a
negligenza	négligence	negligence	Nachlässigkeit(f)	negligencia	negligência
negoziante	commerçant, e	shop-keeper	Kaufmann m, Kauffrau f	tendero, a	comerciante
negoziante	marchand, e	shop-keeper	Kaufmann m, Kauffrau f	vendedor, a	comerciante
negoziare	négocier	negotiate	verhandeln	negociar	negociar
negoziatore, trice	négociateur	negotiator	Unterhändler(in f)m	negociador, a	negociador, a
negoziare, trattare	négocier, traiter	deal	handeln	comerciar, tratar	negociar, tratar
negoziato(-ziazione)	négociation	negotiation	Verhandlung(f)	negociación	negociação
negozio; bottega	magasin	shop	Geschäft(n), Laden(m)	tienda	loja
negozio, boutique	boutique	boutique, shop	Geschäft(n)	tienda	loja
negozio	commerce	shop, business	Geschäft(n)	tienda, negocio	loja
negro, a	nègre, esse	negro(-ress), black	Neger(in f)m	negro, a	negro, a
negro, a	noir, e	black(person)	Schwarze(f, m)	negro, a	negro, a
nella circostanza	occurence(en l')	case(in this)	vorliegenden Fall(im)	caso(en este)	caso(neste)
nemico, a	ennemi, e	enemy	Feind(in f)m	enemigo, a	inimigo, a
neonato, a	nouveau-né, e	new-born baby	Neugeborene(n)	recién nacido, a	recém-nascido, a
nero, a	noir, e	black	schwarz	negro, a	preto, a
nervo	nerf	nerve	Nerv(m)	nervio	nervo
nervoso, a	nerveux, se	nervous	nervös; Nerven-	nervioso, a	nervoso, a
nervoso, a	énervé, e	edgy, worked up	erregt, nervös	excitado, a	enervado, a
nervoso, a	nerveux, se	nervy	nervös	nervioso, a	nervoso, a
nessuno, a	aucun, e	no, not any; no one	keiner, keine	ningún, o, a	nenhum, a
nessuno	personne	nobody, no one	niemand	nadie	ninguém
neurologia	neurologie	neurology	Neurologie(f)	neurología	neurologia
neutralizzare	neutraliser	neutralize	neutralisieren	neutralizar	neutralizar
neutro, a	neutre	neutral	neutral	neutro, a	neutro, a
neve	neige	snow	Schnee(m)	nieve	neve
nevrosi	névrose	neurosis(-ses)	Neurose(f)	neurosis	nevrose
nichel	nickel	nickel	Nickel(n)	níquel	níquel
nicotina	nicotine	nicotine	Nikotin(n)	nicotina	nicotina
nido	nid	nest	Nest(n)	nido	ninho
niente, nulla	rien	nothing	nichts	nada	nada
nipote(il)	neveu	nephew	Neffe(m)	sobrino	sobrinho

I

Italian	French	English	German	Spanish	Portuguese
nipote(la)	nièce	niece	Nichte(f)	sobrina	sobrinha
nipote	petit-fils/fille	grandson/-daughter	Enkel(m), Enkelin(f)	nieto, a	neto, a
no	non	no	nein	no	não
no, grazie	non merci	no thank you	nein, danke	no, gracias	não, obrigado
nobile	noble	noble	edel; nobel	noble	nobre
nobile	noble	nobleman(-men)	Edelmann m, Edelfrau f	noble	nobre
nocciolo	noyau	stone	Kern(m)	hueso	caroço
noce	noix	walnut	Walnuß(f)	nuez	noz
noce di cocco	noix de coco	coconut	Kokosnuß(f)	coco	coco
nocivo, a	nocif, ive	harmful	schädlich	nocivo, a	nocivo, a
nocivo, a	nuisible	harmful	schädlich	dañino, a	nocivo, a
nodo	noeud	knot	Knoten(m)	nudo	nó, laço
noi	nous	we	wir	nosotros	nós
noia	ennui	boredom	Langeweile(f)	aburrimiento	aborrecimento
noioso, a	ennuyeux, se	boring; annoying	langweilig	aburrido, a	aborrecido, a
noleggiare	louer	hire, rent	mieten; vermieten	alquilar	alugar
noleggiare	louer à bail	lease	mieten; pachten	arrendar	arrendar, alugar
noleggio, affitto	location	rental, hiring	Vermietung(f)	alquiler	aluguer
nolo, carico	fret	freight	Fracht(f)	flete	frete
nomade	nomade	nomad	Nomade(m)	nómada	nómada
nome, sostantivo	nom, substantif	noun	Hauptwort(n)	nombre	substantivo
nome	nom	name	Name(m)	nombre	nome
nome	prénom	first name	Vorname(m)	nombre	nome próprio
nomina	nomination	nomination	Ernennung(f)	nombramiento	nomeação
nominare	nommer	appoint	ernennen	nombrar	nomear
non	pas	not	nicht	no	não, nem
noncurante	insouciant, e	carefree	unbekümmert	despreocupado, a	descuidado, a
non-fumatore	non-fumeur	non-smoker	Nichtraucher(m)	no-fumadores	não-fumador
nonna	grand-mère	grandmother	Großmutter(f)	abuela	avó
nonni	grands-parents	grandparents	Großeltern(pl.)	abuelos	avós
nonno	grand-père	grandfather	Großvater(m)	abuelo	avô
Nord	Nord	North	Norden(m)	Norte	Norte
nordico, a	nordique	nordic; northern	nordisch; nördlich	nórdico, a	nórdico, a
norma	norme	norm, standard	Norm(f)	norma	norma
normale	normal, e	normal; usual	normal	normal	normal
nostalgia	nostalgie	homesickness	Heimweh(n)	nostalgia	nostalgia
nostri, e(i, le)	nos	our	unser(e)	nuestros, nuestras	nossos, nossas
nostro, a(il, la)	notre	our	unser, unsere	nuestro, a	nosso, a
nostro, a(il, la)	nôtre(le, la)	ours	unsere(der, die, das)	nuestro, a(el, la)	nosso, a(o, a)
nota	note	note	Note(f)	nota	nota
notaio	notaire	solicitor, lawyer	Notar(m)	notario	notário
notare	noter	note; notice	notieren; bemerken	anotar	anotar, notar
notare, osservare	remarquer	notice	bemerken	notar, señalar	notar, reparar
notevole	remarquable	remarkable	bemerkenswert	notable	notável
notificare	notifier	notify	bekannt = geben	notificar	notificar
notizie	nouvelles	news	Nachrichten(f, pl)	noticias	notícias
notorietà	notoriété	notoriety	Offenkundigkeit(f)	notoriedad	notoriedade
notte	nuit	night	Nacht(f)	noche	noite
notturno, a	nocturne	nocturnal, night-	nächtlich	nocturno, a	nocturno, a
novanta	quatre-vingt-dix	ninety	neunzig	noventa	noventa
nove	neuf	nine	neun	nueve	nove
novembre	novembre	November	November(m)	noviembre	Novembro
novità	nouveauté	novelty	Neuheit(f)	novedad	novidade
novizio, a	novice, débutant	novice	Neuling(m)	novicio, a; novato, a	principiante
nozione	notion	notion	Kenntnis(f), Begriff m	noción	noção
nozze	noce	wedding	Hochzeit(f)	boda	boda
nuca	nuque	nape of the neck	Nacken(m)	nuca	nuca
nucleare	nucléaire	nuclear	Kern-, Atom-	nuclear	nuclear
nucleo	noyau	nucleus(-ei)	Kern(m)	núcleo	núcleo
nudista	naturiste	nudist	Nudist(in f)m	naturista	naturista
nudo, a	nu, e	naked; bare	nackt	desnudo, a	nu, nua
nullo, a	nul, le	worthless; useless	wertlos	nulo, a	nulo, a
numerico, a	numérique	numerical	numerisch	numérico, a	numérico, a
numero	nombre	number	Anzahl(f), Zahl(f)	número	número
numero	numéro	number	Nummer(f)	número	número
numero	pointure	size	Größe(f)	número	tamanho; número
numero, pubblicazione	numéro, tirage	issue	Auflage(f)	número, edición	número
numeroso, a	nombreux, se	numerous, many	zahlreich	numeroso, a	numeroso, a

Italian	French	English	German	Spanish	Portuguese
nuora	belle-fille	daughter-in-law	Schwiegertochter(f)	nuera	nora
nuotare	nager	swim	schwimmen	nadar	nadar
nuotatore, trice	nageur, se	swimmer	Schwimmer(in f)m	nadador, a	nadador, a
nuoto	natation, nage	swimming	Schwimmen(n)	natación	natação
nuovo, a	nouveau, nouvelle	new	neu	nuevo, a	novo, a
nuovo, a	neuf, neuve	new	neu	nuevo, a	novo, a
nutrire	nourrir	feed, nourish	ernähren	alimentar	alimentar
nutritivo, a	nutritif, ive	nutritious	nahrhaft	nutritivo, a	nutritivo, a
nuvola	nuage	cloud	Wolke(f)	nube	nuvem
nylon	nylon	nylon	Nylon(m)	nilón	nylon

O

Italian	French	English	German	Spanish	Portuguese
o	ou	or	oder	o; u	ou
oasi	oasis	oasis(oases pl.)	Oase(f)	oasis	oásis
obbedire	obéir	obey	gehorchen	obedecer	obedecer
obbligare	obliger	oblige, force	zwingen	obligar	obrigar
obbligatorio, a	obligatoire	compulsory	obligatorisch	obligatorio, a	obrigatório, a
obbligatorio, a	obligatoire	mandatory	obligatorisch	obligatorio, a	obrigatório, a
obbligo	obligation	obligation	Verpflichtung(f)	obligación	obrigação
obeso, a	obèse	obese	füllig, fettleibig	obeso, a	obeso, a
obiettivo	objectif	objective	Objektiv(n), Ziel(n)	objetivo	objectivo
obiettivo	objectif	lens	Objektiv(n)	objetivo	objectiva
obiezione	objection	objection, protest	Einwand(m)	objeción, reparo	objecção
obitorio	morgue	mortuary	Leichenschauhaus(n)	depósito(cadáver.)	morgue
obliquo, a	oblique	oblique, slanting	schräg, schief	oblicuo, a	oblíquo, a
oblò	hublot	window	Bullauge(n), Luke(f)	ventanilla	vigia
oca	oie	goose(geese pl.)	Gans(f)	oca	ganso
occasionale	occasionnel, le	occasional	gelegentlich	ocasional	ocasional
occasione	occasion	opportunity	Gelegenheit(f)	oportunidad	oportunidade
occhi	yeux	eyes	Augen(n, pl)	ojos	olhos
occhiaia	cerne	ring, circle	Augenringe(pl.)	ojeras	olheiras
occhiali	lunettes	glasses	Brille(f)	gafas	óculos
occhiata	regard	glance	Blick(m)	ojeada	olhada
occhio	oeil	eye	Auge(n)	ojo	olho
occidentale	occidental, e	Western	westlich	occidental	ocidental
occupare	occuper	occupy, fill	ein = nehmen	ocupar	ocupar
occuparsi	occuper(s')	deal with	beschäftigen, sich	dedicarse a	tratar de
occuparsi	occuper(s')	look after	kümmern sich/um	ocuparse	tomar conta
occupato, a	occupé, e	engaged; taken	besetzt	ocupado, a	ocupado, a
occupato, a	occupé, e	occupied	besetzt	ocupado, a	ocupado, a
oceanico, a	océanique	oceanic	ozeanisch	oceánico, a	oceânico, a
oceano	océan	ocean	Ozean(m)	océano	oceano
oculista	oculiste	oculist	Augenarzt m/-ärztin f	oculista	oftalmologista
odiare	haïr	hate, detest	hassen	odiar	odiar
odio	haine	hate	Haß(m)	odio	ódio
odioso, a	odieux, se	odious, obnoxious	widerwärtig	odioso, a	odioso, a
odorare, annusare	sentir	smell	riechen	oler	cheirar
odorato	odorat	smell(sense of)	Geruchssinn(m)	olfato	olfacto
odore	odeur	odour, smell	Geruch(m)	olor	cheiro, odor
offendere	vexer	offend, vex	beleidigen	ofender, picar	ofender
offendersi	vexer(se)	get upset	beleidigt sein	ofenderse	ofender-se
offensiva	offensive	offensive	Offensive(f)	ofensiva	ofensiva
offerta	offre	offer	Angebot(n)	oferta	oferta
offerta(in)	réclame(en)	offer(on)	Sonderangebot(n)	reclamo(de)	promoção(em)
officina	atelier	workshop	Werkstatt(f)	taller	oficina
offrire, regalare	offrir	give; offer	schenken, an = bieten	ofrecer	oferecer

Italian	French	English	German	Spanish	Portuguese
oftalmologia	ophtalmologie	ophthalmology	Augenheilkunde(f)	oftalmología	oftalmologia
oggetti di valore	objets de valeur	valuables	Wertsachen(f pl)	objetos de valor	objectos de valor
oggettivo, a	objectif, ive	objective	objektiv, sachlich	objetivo, a	objectivo, a
oggetto	objet	object	Objekt(n), Ding(n)	objeto	objecto
oggetto, scopo	objet, thème	theme, subject	Thema(n), Objekt(n)	objeto, tema	tema, assunto
oggi	aujourd'hui	today	heute	hoy	hoje
ogni	chaque	every, each	jede(r, s)	cada	cada
olimpico, a	olympique	Olympic	olympisch	olímpico, a	olímpico, a
olio	huile	oil	Öl(n); Speiseöl(n)	aceite	óleo; azeite
olio	huile	oil	Öl(n); Motoröl(n)	aceite; óleo	óleo
oliva	olive	olive	Olive(f)	aceituna, oliva	azeitona
oltremare	outre-mer	overseas	überseeisch	ultramar	ultramar
oltrepassare	dépasser	go beyond, exceed	überholen	sobresalir	ultrapassar
omaggio	hommage	homage, tribute	Huldigung(f); Ehrung f	homenaje	homenagem
ombelico	nombril	navel	Nabel(m)	ombligo	umbigo
ombra	ombre	shadow	Schatten(m)	sombra	sombra
ombrello	parapluie	umbrella	Regenschirm(m)	paraguas	chapéu de chuva
ombrello, parasole	ombrelle	sunshade, parasol	Sonnenschirm(m)	sombrilla	sombrinha
ombrellone	parasol	parasol, sunshade	Sonnenschirm(m)	parasol	guarda-sol
omeopatia	homéopathie	homoeopathy	Homöopathie(f)	homeopatía	homeopatia
omettere	omettre	omit	aus = lassen	omitir	omitir
omicida	meurtrier, ière	murderer	Mörder(in f)m	homicida	assassino, a
omicidio	homicide	murder, homicide	Totschlag(m)	homicidio	homicídio
omogeneo, a	homogène	homogeneous	homogen	homogéneo, a	homogéneo, a
omologazione	homologation	certification	Zulassung(f)	homologación	homologação
omonimo, a	homonyme	homonym	Homonym(n)	homónimo, a	homónimo, a
omosessuale	homosexuel, le	homosexual	homosexuell	homosexual	homossexual
onda	vague	wave	Welle(f)	ola	onda, vaga
onda	onde	wave	Welle(f)	onda	onda
ondata	lame	wave	Welle(f)	ola	vaga
ondosità	houle	swell, surge	Brandung(f)	marejada	vaga
onere	charge	contribution	Abgaben(pl.)	carga	encargo
onesto, a	honnête	honest	ehrlich	honrado, a	honesto, a
onorabile	honorable	honourable	ehrwürdig	honorable	honroso, a
onorario	honoraires	fee	Honorar(n)	honorarios	honorários
onore	honneur	honour	Ehre(f)	honor	honra
opaco, a	opaque	opaque	undurchsichtig; trüb	opaco, a	opaco, a
opaco, a	mat, e	dull, matt	glanzlos, matt	mate	mate
opera	opéra	opera	Oper(f)	ópera	ópera
opera	oeuvre, travail	work	Werk(n)	obra	obra
opera, lavoro	ouvrage	work	Arbeit(f)	tarea, trabajo	obra, trabalho
operaio, a	ouvrier, ière	worker, workman	Arbeiter(in f)m	obrero, a	operário, a
operare	opérer	operate	wirken	efectuar	fazer
operare	opérer	operate(on)	operieren	operar	operar
operazione	opération	operation	Operation(f)	operación	operação
operetta	opérette	operetta	Operette(f)	zarzuela, opereta	opereta
opinione	opinion	opinion	Meinung(f)	opinión	opinião
opporsi	opposer(s')	oppose	widersetzen, sich	oponerse	opor-se
opporsi(a)	contrer	counter	Kontra geben	oponerse(a)	contrariar
opportuno, a	opportun, e	opportune	günstig	oportuno, a	oportuno, a
opposizione	opposition	opposition	Opposition(f)	oposición	oposição
opposto, a	opposé, e	opposing	entgegengesetzt	opuesto, a	oposto, a
opposto, a	opposé, e	opposite	gegenüberliegend	opuesto, a	oposto, a
opposto, a	opposé, e	opposed to	entgegengesetzt	opuesto, a	contra(ser)
oppresso, a	opprimé, e	oppressed	unterdrückt	oprimido, a	oprimido, a
opzione, scelta	option, choix	option	Wahl(f)	opción	opção
ora	heure	hour; time	Stunde(f); Zeit(f)	hora	hora
ora, adesso	maintenant	now	jetzt	ahora	agora
orale	oral, e	oral	mündlich	oral	oral
orario	horaire(s)	timetable	Fahrplan(m)	horario(s)	horário
oratore, trice	orateur, trice	speaker, orator	Redner(in f)m	orador, a; locutor, a	orador, a
orbita	orbite	orbit	Umlaufbahn(f)	órbita	órbita
orchestra	orchestre	orchestra; band	Orchester(n)	orquesta	orquestra
orchidea	orchidée	orchid	Orchidee(f)	orquídea	orquídia
ordinamento	arrangement	arrangement	Anordnung(f)	arreglo	arranjo
ordinare	ranger	tidy up	auf = räumen	ordenar	ordenar
ordinare	ordonner	order	befehlen, verordnen	ordenar	ordenar
ordinare	commander	order	bestellen	pedir, encargar	encomendar

Italian	French	English	German	Spanish	Portuguese
ordinario, a	ordinaire	ordinary	gewöhnlich	ordinario, a	ordinário, a
ordinato, a	rangé, e	tidy	ordentlich	ordenado, a	arrumado, a
ordinazione	commande	order	Bestellung(f)	encargo, pedido	encomenda
ordine	ordre	order	Ordnung(f)	orden	ordem
ordine	ordre	order	Rangordnung(f)	orden	ordem
ordine	ordre	order	Befehl(m)	orden	ordem
orecchini	boucle(s)	earring	Ohrring(m)	pendientes	brincos, argolas
orecchio	oreille	ear	Ohr(n)	oreja	orelha
orecchioni	oreillons	mumps	Mumps(m)	paperas	trasorelho
orfano, a	orphelin, e	orphan	Waise(f, m)	huérfano, a	órfão, órfã
organico, a	organique	organic	organisch	orgánico, a	orgânico, a
organismo	organisme	organism	Organismus(m)	organismo	organismo
organizzare	organiser	organize	organisieren	organizar	organizar
organizzatore, trice	organisateur	organizer	Organisator(in f)m	organizador, a	organizador, a
organizzazione	organisation	organization	Organisation(f)	organización	organização
organo	organe	organ	Organ(n)	órgano	órgão
organo	orgue	organ	Orgel(f)	órgano	órgão
orgasmo	orgasme	orgasm	Orgasmus(m)	orgasmo	orgasmo
orgia	orgie	orgy	Orgie(f)	orgía	orgia
orgoglio	orgueil	pride, arrogance	Stolz(m)	orgullo	orgulho
orgoglioso, a	orgueilleux, se	proud, arrogant	stolz, arrogant	orgulloso, a	orgulhoso, a
orientale	oriental, e	oriental	orientalisch	oriental	oriental
orientamento	orientation	orientation	Orientierung(f)	orientación	orientação
orientare	orienter	position	orientieren	orientar	orientar
orifizio	orifice	orifice, aperture	Öffnung(f), Mündung(f)	orificio	orifício
originale	original, e	original	original	original	original
originale	original	original	Original(n)	original	original
originario, a	originaire	native(of)	gebürtig	oriundo, a	oriundo, a
origine	origine	origin	Ursprung(m)	origen	origem
orizzontale	horizontal, e	horizontal	waagerecht	horizontal	horizontal
orizzonte	horizon	horizon, sky-line	Horizont(m)	horizonte	horizonte
ormone	hormone	hormone	Hormon(n)	hormona	hormona
ornamento	ornement	ornament	Verzierung; Schmuck	adorno	ornamento
ornare, adornare	décorer	decorate	schmücken	decorar, adornar	ornar, adornar
oro	or	gold	Gold(n)	oro	ouro
orologio	horloge	clock	Uhr(f)	reloj	relógio
orologio	montre	watch	Uhr(f), Armbanduhr(f)	reloj	relógio
oroscopo	horoscope	horoscope	Horoskop(n)	horóscopo	horóscopo
orribile, orrendo, a	horrible	horrible	grausig	horrible	horrível
orrore	horreur	horror	Grausen(n)	horror	horror
orso	ours	bear	Bär(m)	oso	urso
orticultura	horticulture	horticulture	Gartenbau(m)	horticultura	horticultura
orto	jardin	garden	Gemüsegarten(m)	huerto	horta
ortodosso, a	orthodoxe	orthodox	orthodox	ortodoxo, a	ortodoxo, a
ortografia	orthographe	spelling	Rechtschreibung(f)	ortografía	ortografia
osare	oser	dare	wagen	osar, atreverse	ousar, atrever-se
osceno, a	obscène	obscene	obszön	obsceno, a	obsceno, a
oscillare	osciller	oscillate	schwanken	oscilar	oscilar
oscurità, buio	obscurité	darkness	Dunkelheit(f)	oscuridad	obscuridade
ospedale	hôpital	hospital	Krankenhaus(n)	hospital	hospital
ospitalità	hospitalité	hospitality	Gastfreundlichkeit(f)	hospitalidad	hospitalidade
ospite	hôte	guest	Gast(m)	huésped, a	hóspede, a
ospite	hôte, tesse	host; guest	Gastgeber(m); Gast(m)	anfitrión; huésped	anfitrião; hóspede, a
ospite	pensionnaire	lodger	Untermieter(in f)m	huésped	hóspede
ospizio	hospice	hospice; home	Hospiz(n)	hospicio	hospício, asilo
ossatura	ossature	structure	Struktur(f)	armazón	ossatura
ossatura, travatura	charpente	framework	Holzgerüst(n)	armazón	madeiramento
osservare	observer	observe	beobachten	observar	observar
osservatore, trice	observateur	observer	Beobachter(in f)m	observador, a	observador, a
osservazione	remarque	remark, comment	Bemerkung(f)	observación	observação
ossessionare	obséder	obsess	verfolgen, quälen	obsesionar	obcecar
ossessione	obsession	obsession	fixe Idee(f)	obsesión	obsessão
ossessione	hantise	obsessive fear	Zwangsvorstellung(f)	obsesión	obsessão
ossidazione	oxydation	oxidization	Oxydierung(f)	oxidación	oxidação
ossigeno	oxygène	oxygen	Sauerstoff(m)	oxígeno	oxigénio
osso	os	bone	Knochen(m)	hueso	osso
ostacolo	obstacle	obstacle	Hindernis(n)	obstáculo	obstáculo
ostaggio	otage	hostage	Geisel(f)	rehén	refém

Italian	French	English	German	Spanish	Portuguese
ostile	hostile	hostile	feindlich	hostil	hostil
ostrica	huître	oyster	Auster(f)	ostra	ostra
ostruzione	obstruction	obstruction	Störung(f)	obstrucción	obstrucção
otite	otite	ear-ache	Mittelohrentzündung f	otitis	otite
ottanta	quatre-vingts	eighty	achtzig	ochenta	oitenta
ottenere	obtenir	obtain, get	erhalten	obtener	obter
ottenere	obtenir, recevoir	get, obtain	bekommen	obtener	obter
ottico, a	optique	optic(al)	optisch	óptico, a	óptico, a
ottico	opticien, ne	optician	Optiker(in f)m	óptico, a	oculista
ottimista	optimiste	optimistic	optimistisch	optimista	optimista
ottimo, a	fameux, se	excellent	großartig	famoso, a	famoso, a
otto	huit	eight	acht	ocho	oito
ottobre	octobre	October	Oktober(m)	octubre	Outubro
ovaia	ovaire	ovary	Eierstock(m)	ovario	ovário
ovale	ovale	oval	oval	oval, ovalado, a	oval
overdose	surdose	overdose	Überdosis(f)	sobredosis	overdose
Ovest	Ouest	West	Westen(m)	Oeste	Oeste
ovino	ovin	ovine	Schaf-	ovino	ovino
ovulo	ovule	ovule	Ei(zelle f)n	óvulo	óvulo
ozono	ozone	ozone	Ozon(n)	ozono	ozone

P

Italian	French	English	German	Spanish	Portuguese
pacco	paquet	packet; package	Paket(n)	paquete	pacote
pacco, collo	colis	parcel	Paket(n)	paquete	pacote
pace	paix	peace	Frieden(m)	paz	paz
pacifico, a	pacifique	peaceful, pacific	friedlich	pacifico, a	pacífico, a
pacifico, a; placido, a	paisible	peaceful, quiet	friedlich, ruhig	apacible	pacífico, a
Pacifico	Pacifique	Pacific Ocean	Pazifik(m)	Pacífico	Pacífico
padella	poêle	frying pan	Pfanne(f)	sartén	frigideira
padre	père	father	Vater(m)	padre	pai
padrino	parrain	godfather	Pate(m)	padrino	padrinho
padrone, a	patron, ne	boss; employer	Chef(m), Arbeitgeber m	patrón, a; dueño, a	patrão, patroa
paesaggio	paysage	landscape	Landschaft(f)	paisaje	paisagem
paese	pays	country	Land(n)	país	país
paese, villaggio	village	village	Dorf(n)	aldea, pueblo	aldeia, povoado
paga, stipendio	paie(paye)	pay	Lohn(m)	paga	paga, ordenado
pagamento	paiement	payment	Bezahlung(f)	pago, abono	pagamento
pagamento	payement	payment	Zahlung(f)	abono, pago	pagamento
pagare	payer	pay	bezahlen	pagar	pagar
pagina	page	page	Seite(f)	página	página
paglia	paille	straw	Stroh(n)	paja	palha
pagliaccio, clown	clown	clown	Clown(m)	payaso	palhaço
paio	paire	pair(of)	Paar(n)	par	par
pala	pelle	spade; shovel	Schaufel(f); Spaten(m)	pala	pá
palazzo	palais	palace	Palast(m)	palacio	palácio
palazzo, edificio	immeuble	block of flats	Gebäude(n)	inmueble	edifício, imóvel
palla	boule	ball	Ball(m)(Schneeball)	bola	bola
palla	balle	ball	Ball(m)	pelota	bola
pallacanestro	basket-ball	basket-ball	Basketball(m)	baloncesto	basquetebol
pallido, a	pâle	pale	blaß	pálido, a	pálido, a
pallone	ballon	ball	Ball(m)(Fußball m)	balón	bola
pallone	ballon	balloon	Heißluftballon(m)	globo	balão
pallottola	balle	bullet	Kugel(f)	bala	bala
palma	paume	palm	Handfläche(f)	palma	palma
palma	palmier	palm-tree	Palme(f)	palmera	palmeira
palma da cocco	cocotier	coconut palm(tree)	Kokuspalme(f)	cocotero	coqueiro

palo, piolo	pieu, poteau	stake, post	Pfahl(m)	estaca	estaca
palo	poteau	post, pole	Pfosten(m)	poste	poste
palpare	palper, tâter	feel, finger	betasten	palpar	apalpar
palpebra	paupière	eyelid	Lid(n)	párpado	pálpebra
palpitazione	palpitation	palpitation	Herzklopfen(n)	palpitación	palpitação
palude	marais	marsh	Sumpf(m)	pantano	pântano
paludoso, a	marécageux, se	marshy, boggy	sumpfig	pantanoso, a	pantanoso, a
panca, panchina	banc	bench	Bank(f)	banco	banco
pancia, ventre	ventre	stomach, abdomen	Bauch(m)	barriga, vientre	barriga
pancia	panse	belly, paunch	Bauch(m); Pansen(m)	panza	pança
pane	pain	bread	Brot(n)	pan	pão
pane tostato	pain grillé	toast	Toast(m)	tostadas	pão torrado
panico	panique	panic	Panik(f)	pánico	pânico
panico	affolement	panic	Panik(f)	pánico	pânico
paniere, cesto	panier	basket	Korb(m)	cesto	cesto
panificio	boulangerie	baker's(shop)	Bäckerei(f)	panadería	padaria
panino	sandwich	sandwich(-es)	Butterbrot(n)	bocadillo	sande, sanduiche
pannello, quadro	tableau	board, panel	Tafel(f)	tablero, tablón	painel, quadro
pantalone	pantalon	trousers	Hose(f)	pantalón	calças
pantera	panthère	panther	Panther(m)	pantera	pantera
pantofola	pantoufle	slipper	Pantoffel(m)	zapatilla	pantufa, chinelo
papà, babbo	papa	Daddy, Dad	Papa	papá	papá
Papa	Pape	Pope	Papst(m)	Papa	Papa
papillon	noeud papillon	bow tie	Fliege(f)	pajarita	laço
pappagallo	perroquet	parrot	Papagei(m)	loro	papagaio
parabrezza	pare-brise	windscreen	Windschutzscheibe(f)	parabrisas	pára-brisas
paracadute	parachute	parachute	Fallschirm(m)	paracaídas	pára-quedas
paradiso	paradis	paradise	Paradies(n)	paraíso	paraíso
paradosso	paradoxe	paradox	Paradox(n)	paradoja	paradoxo
paragonare	comparer	compare	vergleichen	comparar	comparar
paragrafo	paragraphe	paragraph	Absatz(m), Abschnitt m	párrafo	parágrafo
paralisi	paralysie	paralysis	Lähmung(f)	parálisis	paralisia
paralitico, a	paralysé, e	paralysed	gelähmt	paralítico, a	paralítico, a
parallelo, a	parallèle	parallel	parallel	paralelo, a	paralelo, a
paranoia	paranoïa	paranoia	Paranoia(f)	paranoia	paranóia
parassita	parasite	parasite	Parasit(m)	parásito	parasita
parata	parade	parade	Parade(f)	parada, desfile	parada
parcella	parcelle	plot	Parzelle(f)	parcela	parcela
parcheggio	parking	car park	Parkplatz(m)	aparcamiento	p.estacionamento
parco	parc	park	Park(m)	parque	parque
parecchi	plusieurs	several	mehrere	varios, as	vários, as
parente	parent, e	relative, relation	verwandt	pariente	parente
parentela	parenté	relationship	Verwandtschaft(f)	parentesco	parentesco
parentesi	parenthèse	bracket	Klammer(f)	paréntesis	parêntesis
parere, sembrare	paraître	seem, appear, look	scheinen, erscheinen	parecer	parecer
parete	paroi, mur	wall	Wand(f)	pared	parede
pari	pair	even	gerade	par	par
parlamento	parlement	parliament	Parlament(n)	parlamento	parlamento
parlare	parler	speak, talk	sprechen, reden	hablar	falar
parlare a	parler à	talk to, speak to	reden(mit jdm)	hablar con	falar com
parlare(il)	parler(le)	speech	Sprechen(n); Sprache f	habla(el)	fala(a)
parola	mot	word	Wort(n)	palabra	palavra
parola	terme	term	Ausdruck(m)	término	termo
parola	parole	word; speech	Wort(n)	palabra	palavra
parolaccia	gros mot	bad word	Schimpfwort(n)	palabrota	palavrão
parole, discorsi	propos	words, talk	Worte(pl.)	palabras	fala, conversa
parrucca	perruque	wig	Perücke(f)	peluca	peruca
parrucchiere, a	coiffeur, se	hairdresser	Friseur(m), Friseuse f	peluquero, a	cabeleireiro, a
parrucchiere, a(da)	salon(coiffure)	salon	Friseurladen(m)	peluquería	salão
parte	part, partie	share; part	Anteil(m); Teil(m, n)	parte	parte
parte, ruolo	rôle	role	Rolle(f)	papel	papel
partecipare(a)	participer(à)	take part(in)	teil = nehmen	participar(en)	participar(em)
partecipare a	participer à	participate in	beteiligen, sich	participar en	participar em
partenza	départ	departure, start	Abfahrt(f)	salida, partida	partida
particella	particule	particle	Teilchen(n)	partícula	partícula
particolare	particulier, ière	particular	eigentümlich	particular	particular
particolare	détail	detail	Einzelheit(f)	detalle	pormenor
particolarmente	particulièrement	especially	besonders	especialmente	especialmente

Italian	French	English	German	Spanish	Portuguese
particolarmente	notamment	particular(in)	besonders, nämlich	particularmente	particularmente
partigiano, a	partisan, e	partisan	Anhänger(in f)m	partidario, a	partidário, a
partire	partir	leave, go away	weg = gehen	salir, marcharse	partir, abalar
partita	partie	game	Spiel(n)	partida	jogada, jogo
partita	match	match(-es), game	Spiel(n)	partido	desafio, partida
partito	parti	party	Partei(f)	partido	partido
partner; socio, a	partenaire	partner	Partner(in f)m	pareja	parceiro, a
parto	accouchement	delivery; birth	Entbindung(f)	parto	parto
partorire	accoucher	birth(give)	entbinden	dar a luz	dar à luz
party	cocktail	party(cocktail -)	Party(f)	cóctel	recepção
parure	parure	finery, jewellery	Schmuck(m)	adorno	adorno
Pasqua	Pâques	Easter	Ostern(n)	Pascua	Páscoa
passaggio	passage	passage	Durchgang(m)	pasaje, paso	passagem
passaporto	passeport	passport	Paß(m)	pasaporte	passaporte
passare	passer	pass, go(through)	fahren über	pasar	passar(por; em)
passare	passer	call, drop in	vorbei = kommen	pasar	passar
passatempo	passe-temps	hobby, pastime	Hobby(n)	pasatiempo	passatempo
passato, a	passé, e	past	vergangen	pasado, a	passado, a
passato	passé	past	Vergangenheit(f)	pasado	passado
passato di moda	démodé, e	old-fashioned	altmodisch	pasado de moda	fora de moda
passeggero, a	passager, ère	passenger	Passagier(in f)m	pasajero, a	passageiro, a
passeggiare	promener	walk(go for a)	spazieren = gehen	pasear	passear
passeggiata	promenade	walk; drive; ride	Spaziergang(m)	paseo	passeio
passeggino	poussette	push-chair	Sportwagen(m)	silla de bebé	cadeira de bebé
passero	moineau	sparrow	Spatz(m)	gorrión	pardal
passione	passion	passion	Leidenschaft(f)	pasión	paixão
passivo, a	passif, ive	passive	passiv	pasivo, a	passivo, a
passo	pas	step; pace	Schritt(m)	paso	passo
pasta	pâte	pastry; dough	Teig(m)	masa	massa
pasta	pâtes	pasta, noodles	Nudeln(f, pl)	pastas(aliment.)	massa
pasticceria	pâtisserie	cake shop	Konditorei(f)	pastelería	pastelaria
pastiglia	cachet	tablet	Tablette(f)	pastilla	comprimido
pasto	repas	meal	Mahlzeit(f)	comida	refeição
pastore, pastorella	berger, ère	shepherd, -ess	Schäfer(in f)m	pastor, a	pastor, a
pastore	pasteur	vicar, minister	Pastor(in f)m	pastor	padre; pastor
pastoso, a	pâteux, se	pasty	pappig	pastoso, a	pastoso, a
patata	pomme de terre	potato(-es)	Kartoffel(f)	patata	batata
patatine fritte	frites	chips	Pommes Frites	patatas fritas	batatas fritas
patè	pâté	paté	Pastete(f)	paté	paté
patente di guida	permis(auto)	driving licence	Führerschein(m)	permiso conducir	carta de condução
paterno, a	paternel, le	paternal	väterlich	paterno, a	paterno, a
patire, resistere	endurer	endure, bear	aus = halten, ertragen	aguantar, pasar	aguentar
patria	patrie	native land	Vaterland(n)	patria	pátria
patriarca	patriarche	patriarch	Patriarch(m)	patriarca	patriarca
patrimonio	patrimoine	patrimony	Familiengut(n)	patrimonio	património
patrocinare	plaider	plead	plädieren	litigar	defender(causa)
pattinaggio	patinage	skating	Eiskunstlauf(m)	patinaje	patinagem
pattinare	patiner	skate	Schlittschuh laufen	patinar	patinar
patto	pacte	pact	Pakt(m)	pacto	pacto
pattuglia	patrouille	patrol	Patrouille(f), Streife	patrulla	patrulha
pattumiera	poubelle	bin, dustbin	Abfalleimer(m)	cubo de basura	caixote do lixo
paura	peur	fear	Angst(f)	miedo	medo
paura(avere)	peur(avoir)	afraid(to be)	Angst(haben)	miedo(tener)	medo(ter)
pausa	pause	pause, break	Pause(f)	pausa	pausa
pavimento	carrelage	tiling; tiles	Fliesen(n); Fliese(f)	embaldosado	ladrilho
pavimento	plancher	floor	Fußboden(m)	suelo	soalho, sobrado
paziente	patient, e	patient	geduldig	paciente	paciente
pazienza	patience	patience	Geduld(f)	paciencia	paciência
peccato	péché	sin	Sünde(f)	pecado	pecado
peccato(è)	dommage(c'est)	pity(it is a)	schade !	pena(es una)	pena(e')
peccato(che)	dommage(quel)	pity(what a)	schade !(wie ---)	lástima(qué)	pena(que)
pecora; montone	mouton	sheep; mutton	Schaf(n)	carnero; oveja	carneiro; ovelha
pedaggio	péage	toll	Autobahngebühr(f)	peaje	portagem
pedale	pédale	pedal	Pedal(n)	pedal	pedal
pedante	pédant, e	pedantic	pedantisch	pedante	pedante; vaidoso, a
pediatra	pédiatre	paediatrician	Kinderarzt m/-ärztin	pediatra	pediatra
pedicure	pédicure	chiropodist	Fußpfleger(in f)m	pedicuro, a	pedicuro
pedigree	pédigree	pedigree	Stammbaum(Tier-)(m)	pedigrí	pedigree

Italian	French	English	German	Spanish	Portuguese
pedina(dama)	pion(dames)	draught	Stein(m)(Spiel)	ficha(damas)	peça, tábula(dama)
pedone	piéton	pedestrian	Fußgänger(m)	peatón	peão
pedone(scacchi)	pion(échecs)	pawn(chess)	Bauer(m)(Schach)	peón(ajedrez)	peão(xadrez)
peggio	pire	worse	schlimmer	peor	pior
pegno	gage	pledge	Pfand(n)	prenda	penhor
pelle	peau	skin	Haut(f)	piel	pele
pellegrinaggio	pèlerinage	pilgrimage	Wallfahrt(f)	peregrinación	peregrinação
pellegrino, a	pèlerin	pilgrim	Pilger(in f)m	peregrino	peregrino
pelliccia	fourrure	fur	Pelz(m)	piel	pele; peliça
pellicola	pellicule	film	Film(m)	película	película
pelo	poil	hair	Haar(n)	pelo	pêlo
pelo	pelage	coat, fur	Fell(n)	pelaje, pelo	pêlo
peloso, a	poilu, e	hairy	behaart	peludo, a	peludo, a
pena; dolore	peine	sorrow, grief	Schmerz(m), Kummer(m)	pena	pena; tristeza
penale	pénal, e	penal	strafrechtlich	penal	penal
penalità	pénalité	penalty	Strafe(f), Strafpunkt	penalidad	penalidade
pendio, discesa	pente	slope	Hang(m), Abhang(m)	declive	declive
penetrare	pénétrer	enter, penetrate	ein = dringen	penetrar	penetrar
penicillina	pénicilline	penicillin	Penizilin(n)	penicilina	penicilina
penisola	péninsule	peninsula	Halbinsel(f)	península	península
penna, piuma	plume	feather	Feder(f)	pluma	pluma; pena
penna a sfera	stylo à bille	ball-point pen	Kugelschreiber(m)	bolígrafo	esferográfica
pennarello	crayon-feutre	felt-tip pen	Filzschreiber(m)	rotulador	marcador
pennello	pinceau	brush	Pinsel(m)	pincel	pincel
penoso, a	pénible	hard, arduous	mühsam, schwierig	penoso, a; duro, a	penoso, a
pensare	penser	think	denken	pensar	pensar
pensiero	pensée	thought	Gedanke(m)	pensamiento	pensamento
pensionante	pensionnaire	resident	Pensionsgast(m)	pensionista	hóspede
pensionato, a	retraité, e	retired person	Rentner(in f)m	retirado, a	reformado, a
pensione	pension	guest-house	Gasthaus(n)	pensión	pensão
pensione	retraite	retirement	Pensionierung(f)	jubilación	reforma
pensione	pension	pension; allowance	Pension(f)	pensión	pensão
pensione(essere in)	retraité, e(être)	retired(be)	pensioniert sein	jubilado, a(estar)	reformado, a(estar)
pentola, marmitta	marmite	cooking-pot	Kochtopf(m)	marmita, olla	marmita
penuria	pénurie	shortage	Mangel(m)	penuria, escasez	penúria
pepe	poivre	pepper	Pfeffer(m)	pimienta	pimenta
per; allo scopo di	afin de	in order to	um...zu	a fin de	a fim de
per, da	par	by, through	durch	por	por
per	par	per	per	por	por
per	pour	for	für	por	por
per	pour	for	für	para; por	para; por
pera	poire	pear	Birne(f)	pera	pêra
per cento	pour cent	per cent	Prozent(n)	por ciento	por cento
percentuale	pourcentage	percentage	Prozentsatz(m)	porcentaje	percentagem
percepire	percevoir	perceive	wahr = nehmen	percibir	perceber
percettibile	perceptible	perceptible	wahrnehmbar	perceptible	perceptível
perché	car	because, for	weil, denn	porque, pues	porque, pois
perché	pourquoi	why	warum	por qué	porquê
perché	parce que	because	weil, da	porque	porque
perché(il--di)	pourquoi(le--de)	reason(the--for)	Grund(m)(der--für)	porqué(el--de)	porquê(o--de)
perciò	conséquent(par)	therefore	folglich, deshalb	consiguiente(por)	conseguinte(por)
percorso	parcours	journey; course	Strecke(f), Route(f)	recorrido	percurso
perdere	perdre	lose	verlieren	perder	perder
perdere; mancare	manquer	miss	verpassen	perder	perder
perdere; mancare	rater	miss	verpassen	perder	perder
perdita	perte	loss, waste	Verlust(m)	pérdida	perda, prejuizo
perdita	fuite	leak	Leck(n)	escape	fuga
perdonare	pardonner	forgive, pardon	verzeihen, vergeben	perdonar	perdoar
per favore!	s'il vous plaît !	please!	bitte!	por favor(!)	se faz favor !
perfetto, a	parfait, e	perfect	einwandfrei	perfecto, a	perfeito, a
perfezionare	perfectionner	improve; perfect	vervollkommnen	perfeccionar	aperfeiçoar
perfezione	perfection	perfection	Vollkommenheit(f)	perfección	perfeição
perfido, a	perfide	treacherous	heimtückisch	pérfido, a	pérfido, a
perforare	perforer	perforate	durchbohren	perforar	perfurar
perforazione	forage	boring	Bohrung(f)	perforación	perfuração
pericolo	danger	danger	Gefahr(f)	peligro	perigo
pericolo	péril	peril, danger	Gefahr(f)	peligro, riesgo	perigo
pericoloso, a	dangereux, se	dangerous	gefährlich	peligroso, a	perigoso, a

Italian	French	English	German	Spanish	Portuguese
periferia	banlieue	suburbs	Vorort(m)	afueras	arredores
periferia	périphérie	periphery	Umkreis(m), Umfang(m)	periferia	periferia
perimetro	périmètre	perimeter	Umfang(m)	perímetro	perímetro
periodico, a	périodique	periodic(al)	periodisch	periódico, a	periódico, a
periodo	période	period	Periode(f)	período	período
perla	perle	pearl	Perle(f)	perla	pérola
permanente	permanent, e	permanent	andauernd	permanente	permanente
permesso	permission	permission	Erlaubnis(f)	permiso	permissão
permesso, licenza	permis	licence; permit	Schein(m), Genehmigung	permiso	licença
permettere	permettre	allow, enable	erlauben	permitir	permitir
permettersi	permettre(se)	afford	leisten, sich	permitirse	permitir-se
però	mais, cependant	but, yet, however	aber, jedoch	pero	porém
però, tuttavia	pourtant	yet, however	dennoch, doch	sin embargo	contudo, todavia
perpendicolare	perpendiculaire	perpendicular	senkrecht	perpendicular	perpendicular
perpetuo, a	perpétuel, le	perpetual	fortdauernd	perpetuo, a	perpétuo, a
perseguitare	persécuter	persecute	verfolgen	perseguir	perseguir
perseveranza	persévérance	perseverance	Ausdauer(f)	perseverancia	perseverança
perseverare	persévérer	persevere	beharren, aus = halten	perseverar	perseverar
persistenza	persistance	persistence	Beharrlichkeit(f)	persistencia	persistência
perso, a; smarrito, a	perdu, e	lost	verloren	perdido, a	perdido, a
persona	personne	person	Person(f)	persona	pessoa
personale	personnel, le	personal	persönlich	personal	pessoal
personale	personnel	staff, personnel	Personal(m)	personal, plantilla	pessoal
personalità	personnalité	personality	Persönlichkeit(f)	personalidad	personalidade
persuadere	persuader	persuade	überreden	persuadir	persuadir
perturbare	perturber	disturb, perturb	stören	perturbar	perturbar
perverso, a	pervers, e	perverse	pervers	perverso, a	perverso, a
pesante	lourd, e	heavy	schwer	pesado, a	pesado, a
pesare	peser	weigh	wiegen	pesar	pesar
pesca	pêche	peach	Pfirsich(m)	melocotón	pêssego
pesca	pêche	fishing, angling	Fischen n; Fischfang m	pesca	pesca
pesca(con lenza)	pêche	angling	Angeln(n)	pesca(con caña)	pesca(à linha)
pescatore	pêcheur	fisherman(-men)	Fischer(m)	pescador	pescador
pesce	poisson	fish	Fisch(m)	pescado	peixe
pescheria	poissonnerie	fishmonger's	Fischgeschäft(n)	pescadería	peixaria
peso	poids	weight	Gewicht(n)	peso	peso
pessimista	pessimiste	pessimistic	pessimistisch	pesimista	pessimista
petalo	pétale	petal	Blütenblatt(n)	pétalo	pétala
petardo	pétard	banger, cracker	Knallkörper(m)	petardo	bomba, foguete
petizione	pétition	petition	Bittschrift(f), Gesuch	petición	petição
petrolio	pétrole	oil	Erdöl(n)	petróleo	petróleo
pettinare(-rsi)	coiffer(se)	hair(do one's)	frisieren, sich	peinar(se)	pentear-se
pettinarsi	peigner(se)	comb(one's hair)	kämmen	peinar(se)	pentear-se
pettinatura	coiffure	hair-style	Frisur(f)	peinado	penteado
pettine	peigne	comb	Kamm(m)	peine	pente
petto	poitrine	chest; breast	Brust(f)	pecho	peito
pezzo	morceau, bout	piece, bit	Stück(n)	pedazo, trozo	pedaço
pezzo, parte	partie, part	part	Teil(m n)	parte	parte
pezzo	pièce	part, component	Teil(n)	pieza	peça
piacere, amare	aimer	like	gern haben	gustar(le)	gostar(de)
piacere	aimer	enjoy	mögen; gern mögen	gustar	gostar
piacere	plaire	please; like	gefallen(jdm)	gustar, agradar	agradar
piacere(fare)	plaisir(faire)	please	Freude machen	gusto(dar)	gosto(dar)
piacere	plaisir	pleasure	Vergnügen(n)	placer	prazer
piacevole	plaisant, e	pleasant	gefällig	agradable	agradável
piaga	plaie	wound; cut	Wunde(f)	llaga, herida	ferida
pianeta	planète	planet	Planet(m)	planeta	planeta
piangere	pleurer	cry	weinen	llorar	chorar
pianista	pianiste	pianist	Pianist(in f)m	pianista	pianista
piano, adagio	doucement	gently; slowly	langsam, sanft	despacio	devagar
piano	étage	floor, storey	Etage(f)	piso, planta	andar
piano; schema	plan	plan; drawing	Plan(m)	plan; plano	plano; desenho
pianoforte	piano	piano	Klavier(n)	piano	piano
piano terra	rez-de-chaussée	ground floor	Erdgeschoß(n)	planta baja, bajo	rés-do-chão
pianta	plante	plant	Pflanze(f)	planta	planta
pianta; stradario	plan	map	Plan(m)(Stadtplan m)	plano	planta
piantare	planter	plant	pflanzen	plantar	plantar
piantare	enfoncer	drive in	ein = schlagen	clavar	cravar

Italian	French	English	German	Spanish	Portuguese
pianura	plaine	plain	Ebene(f)	llanura, llano	planície
piastrella	carreau	tile	Fliese(f), Kachel(f)	baldosa, azulejo	ladrilho, azulejo
piattaforma	plate-forme	platform	Plattform(f)	plataforma	plataforma
piattino	soucoupe	saucer	Untertasse(f)	platillo	pires
piatto, a	plat, e	flat	platt	llano, a	plano, a
piatto	assiette, plat	plate	Teller(m)	plato	prato
piazza	place	square	Platz(m)	plaza	praça
piccante	piquant, e	spicy, hot	scharf	picante	picante
piccante	épicé, e	spicy	gewürzt, würzig	picante	picante
picchetto	piquet	post, stake, peg	Pfahl(m)	estaca	estaca
picchiare	frapper	hit, knock, strike	schlagen, prügeln	golpear	bater
picchiare	battre, frapper	beat, hit	schlagen	golpear	golpear
piccione	pigeon	pigeon	Taube(f)	paloma	pombo, a
picco	pic	peak	Gipfel(m)	pico	pico
piccolo, a	petit, e	small, little	klein	pequeño, a	pequeno, a
piccolo, a	petit, e	little	klein	pequeño, a	pequeno, a
piede	pied	foot(feet pl.)	Fuß(m)	pie	pé
piega	pli	fold; pleat	Falte(f); Kniff(m)	pliegue	prega
piegare	plier	fold	falten	doblar	dobrar
piegare	plier	bend	biegen	plegar, doblar	vergar
pieno, a	plein, e	full	voll	lleno, a	cheio, a
pietà	pitié	pity	Mitleid(n)	piedad	piedade
pietra	pierre	stone	Stein(m)	piedra	pedra
pigiama	pyjama	pyjamas	Schlafanzug(m)	pijama	pijama
pignolo, a	maniaque	fussy	übergenau sein	maniático, a	meticuloso, a
pigro, a	paresseux, se	lazy	faul	perezoso, a	preguiçoso, a
pila	pile	pile	Stapel(m)	pila	pilha, montão
pila	pile	battery	Batterie(f)	pila	pilha
pilastro	pilier	pillar	Pfeiler(m)	pilar	pilar
pillola	pilule	pill	Pille(f)	píldora	pílula
pilota	pilote	pilot	Pilot(m)	piloto	piloto
pilotare	piloter	pilot; fly; drive	fliegen; lotsen; fahren	pilotar	pilotar
ping pong	tennis de table	table-tennis	Tischtennis(n)	ping-pong	ténis de mesa
pinna	nageoire	fin	Flosse(f)	aleta	barbatana
pinna	palme	flipper	Flosse(f)	aleta	barbatanas
pinza	pince	pincers, pliers	Zange(f)	pinza(s), tenazas	pinça, alicate
pinze	pinces	pliers, pincers	Zangen(pl)	alicates, tenazas	alicate; tenaz
pioggerella	bruine	drizzle	Sprühregen(m)	llovizna	chuvisco
pioggia	pluie	rain	Regen(m)	lluvia	chuva
piombo	plomb	lead	Blei(n)	plomo	chumbo
pioniere	pionnier	pioneer	Pionier, Bahnbrecher	pionero	pioneiro
piovere	pleuvoir	rain	regnen	llover	chover
piovoso, a	pluvieux, se	rainy	regnerisch	lluvioso, a	chuvoso, a
pipa	pipe	pipe	Pfeife(f)	pipa	cachimbo
piramide	pyramide	pyramid	Pyramide(f)	pirámide	pirâmide
pirata	pirate	pirate	Pirat(in f)m	pirata	pirata
piroga	pirogue	pirogue	Piroge(f), Kanu(n)	piragua	piroga
piscina	piscine	swimming-pool	Schwimmbad(n)	piscina	piscina
pista	piste	track	Spur(f)	pista	pista
pista	piste	slope	Piste(f)	pista	pista
pista	piste	runway	Bahn(Lande-, Start-)	pista	pista
pista da pattinaggio	patinoire	skating rink	Eisbahn(f)	pista de patinar	pista de patinagem
pistola	pistolet	gun, pistol	Pistole(f)	pistola	pistola
pistone	piston	piston	Kolben(m)	pistón	pistão
pitone	python	python	Python(m)	pitón	jibóia
pittore, trice	peintre	painter	Anstreicher; Maler(m)	pintor, a	pintor, a
pittoresco, a	pittoresque	picturesque	malerisch	pintoresco, a	pitoresco, a
pittura; dipinto	peinture	painting	Malerei(f)	pintura	pintura
più	plus	more	mehr	más	mais
più, di più	davantage, plus	more	mehr	más	mais
più	plus	plus	und, plus	más	mais
più	plus	plus	plus	más	mais
più(di, in)	plus(de)	further, moreover	ferner, überdies	además	além disso
più(di, in)	plus(de)	moreover, further	überdies, ferner	más de	além do mais
più(in)	supplément(en)	extra-, additional-	Extra-; Neben-	más(de)	mais(a)
più in là	plus loin	further	weiter	más lejos	mais longe
più tardi	plus tard	later	später	más tarde	mais tarde
piuttosto	plutôt	rather	eher, lieber	más bien	antes; mais

Italian	French	English	German	Spanish	Portuguese
pizzicare	pincer	pinch, nip	kneifen	pellizcar	beliscar
planare	planer	glide	schweben, gleiten	planar	planar
plastico, a	plastique	plastic	plastisch	plástico, a	plástico, a
plastica	plastique	plastic	Plastik(n)	plástico	plástico
plurale	pluriel	plural	Mehrzahl(f)	plural	plural
pneumatico, gomma	pneu	tyre	Reifen(m)	neumático	pneu
poco, pó	peu	some; a little	etwas; wenig	poco	pouco
poco, a	peu	little, few	wenig(e)	poco, a	pouco, a
poderoso, a; potente	puissant, e	powerful, strong	mächtig, kräftig	poderoso, a	poderoso, a
podio	podium	podium, stage	Podest(n)	podio	estrado
poema	poème	poem	Gedicht(n)	poema	poema
poesia	poésie	poetry	Poesie(f)	poesía	poesia
poi, dopo	ensuite	then, next	danach	después	em seguida
poi	puis, ensuite	then	dann	después	depois
poichè	puisque	since	da, weil	ya que; pues	já que
polare	polaire	polar	polar; Polar-	polar	polar
polemica	polémique	controversy	Polemik(f)	polémica	polémica
poligamia	polygamie	polygamy	Polygamie(f)	poligamia	poligamia
poliomelite	poliomyélite	polio(myelitis)	Kinderlähmung(f)	poliomielitis	poliomielite
polipo	polype	polyp	Polyp(m)	pólipo	pólipo
politico, a	politique	political	politisch	político, a	político, a
politica	politique	politics	Politik(f)	política	política
politica	politique	policy	Politik(f)	política	política
politico, a	politicien, ne	politician	Politiker(in f)m	político, a	político, a
polivalente	polyvalent, e	polyvalent	vielseitig	polivalente	polivalente
polizia	police	police	Polizei(f)	policía	polícia
poliziotto	policier	policeman(-men)	Polizist(in f)m	policía	polícia
pollame	volaille	poultry	Geflügel(n)	aves de corral	aves de capoeira
pollice	pouce	thumb	Daumen(m)	pulgar	polegar
pollo	poulet	chicken	Hähnchen, Hühnchen(n)	pollo	frango
polmone	poumon	lung	Lunge(f)	pulmón	pulmão
polmonite	pneumonie	pneumonia	Lungenentzündung(f)	neumonía	pneumonia
polo	pôle	pole	Pol(m)	polo	polo
polpaccio	mollet	calf(-lves)	Wade(f)	pantorrilla	barriga(perna)
polso	poignet	wrist	Handgelenk(n)	muñeca	punho
polso	pouls	pulse	Puls(m)	pulso	pulso
poltrona	fauteuil	arm-chair	Sessel(m)	sillón	poltrona
polvere	poussière	dust	Staub(m)	polvo	poeira
polvere	poudre	powder	Puder(m); Pulver(n)	polvo	pó
polvere	poudre	powder	Pulver(n)(Schieß-)	pólvora	pólvora
pomata	pommade	ointment, cream	Salbe(f)	pomada	pomada
pomeriggio	après-midi	afternoon	Nachmittag(m)	tarde	tarde
pomodoro	tomate	tomato(-es)	Tomate(f)	tomate	tomate
pompa	pompe	pump	Pumpe(f)	bomba	bomba
pompelmo	pamplemousse	grapefruit	Pampelmuse(f)	pomelo	toranja
pompiere	pompier(sapeur-)	fireman(-men)	Feuerwehrmann(m)	bombero	bombeiro
ponte	pont	bridge	Brücke(f)	puente	ponte
ponte	pont	deck; bridge	Deck(n)	puente	convés
popolare	populaire	popular	populär	popular	popular
popolato, a	peuplé, e	populated	bevölkert	poblado, a	povoado, a
popolazione	population	population	Bevölkerung(f)	población	população
popolo	peuple	people	Volk(n)	pueblo	povo
poppare	téter	suck	saugen	mamar	mamar
porcellana	porcelaine	porcelain, china	Porzellan(n)	porcelana	porcelana
porco, maiale	porc	pig; pork(meat)	Schwein(n)	cerdo	porco
pornografia	pornographie	pornography	Pornographie(f)	pornografía	pornografia
poro	pore	pore	Pore(f)	poro	poro
poroso, a	poreux, se	porous	porös	poroso, a	poroso, a
porre, mettere	mettre, placer	lay	legen	poner, colocar	pôr, colocar
porre, mettere	mettre, placer	set	setzen, stellen	poner, colocar	pôr, colocar
porre(domanda)	poser(question)	ask	fragen	preguntar	perguntar
porta	porte	door	Tür(f)	puerta	porta
porta, uscita	porte	gate	Pforte(f)	puerta, entrada	porta
portacenere	cendrier	ash-tray	Aschenbecher(m)	cenicero	cinzeiro
portachiavi	porte-clefs	key-ring	Schlüsselring(m)	llavero	porta-chaves
portadocumenti	porte-documents	document case	Aktenmappe(f)	portadocumentos	carteira
portafoglio	portefeuille	wallet	Brieftasche(f)	cartera	carteira
portagioie	coffret	box, case	Schmuckkasten(m)	estuche	estojo

Italian	French	English	German	Spanish	Portuguese
portamonete	porte-monnaie	purse	Geldbörse(f)	monedero	porta-moedas
portare	porter	carry	tragen	llevar	levar
portare	amener	bring	mit = bringen	traer	trazer
portare, condurre	emmener	take	mit = nehmen	llevar	levar
portar via	emporter	take(away)	mit = nehmen	llevar	levar
portata, gittata	portée	range, reach	Reichweite(f)	alcance	alcance
portatile	portatif, ive	portable	tragbar	portátil	portátil
portiere	portier	porter	Portier(m)	portero	porteiro
portiere, a	concierge	porter, caretaker	Hausmeister(in f)m	conserje	porteiro, a
portiere	goal	goalkeeper	Torwärter(m)	portero	guarda-redes
porto	port	port, harbour	Hafen(m)	puerto	porto
porto	port	postage	Porto(-kosten)(n/pl)	porte	porte
porto franco	franco de port	carriage-paid	portofrei	porte pago	porte pago
portone	portail	gate	Tor(n)	portal	portal
porzione	portion	portion, piece	Stück(n), Portion(f)	porción	porção
posare, porre	poser	put, lay(down)	legen	poner, colocar	pôr, colocar
posare	poser(photo)	pose	Modell stehen	posar	posar
positivo, a	positif, ive	positive	positiv	positivo, a	positivo, a
posizione	position	position	Position(f)	posición	posição
possedere	posséder	own, possess	besitzen	poseer	possuír
possibile	possible	possible	möglich	posible	possível
possibilità	possibilité	possibility	Möglichkeit(f)	posibilidad	possibilidade
posta	poste	post-office	Post(f)	correos	correios
posta	courrier	mail, post	Post(f)	correo	correio
posta	enjeu	stake	Einsatz(m)(Spiel-)	apuesta	aposta
posteggiare	garer	park	parken	aparcar	estacionar
poster	poster	poster	Plakat(n)	cartel, póster	cartaz
posteriore	postérieur, e	later	spätere(r, s)	posterior	posterior
postino, a	facteur, trice	postman/-woman	Briefträger(in f)m	cartero, a	carteiro, a
posto	place	place	Ort(m), Platz(m)	lugar	lugar; sítio
posto, sito, luogo	emplacement	location, site	Lage(f), Stelle(f)	sitio	lugar; sítio
posto	place	seat	Sitzplatz(m)	sitio, asiento	lugar
posto di blocco	barrage	blockade	Sperre(f)	cordón(policía)	barreira
posto di guardia	poste de police	police station	Polizeiwache(f)	cuartelillo	esquadra
potabile	potable	drinking	trinkbar, genießbar	potable	potável
potente	puissant, e	potent, powerful	kräftig, stark	potente	potente
potenza, forza	puissance, force	power, strength	Macht(f), Kraft(f)	potencia, fuerza	potência, poder
potenziale	potentiel, le	potential	potentiell	potencial	potencial
potere	pouvoir	can, able to(be)	können	poder	poder
potere	pouvoir	power	Macht(f)	poder	poder
povero, a	pauvre	poor	arm	pobre	pobre
povertà	pauvreté	poverty	Armut(f)	pobreza	pobreza
pozzo	puits	well	Brunnen(m)	pozo	poço
pranzare	déjeuner	have lunch, lunch	Mittag essen(zu)	almorzar	almoçar
prateria	prairie	meadow	Wiese(f)	pradera	pradaria, prado
praticare	pratiquer	practise	betreiben, üben	practicar	praticar
pratico, a	pratique	practical	praktisch	práctico, a	prático, a
prato	pré	meadow, field	Weide(f), Wiese(f)	prado	prado
prato, erba	gazon	grass	Rasen(m)	césped	relva
prato inglese	pelouse	lawn	Rasenfläche(f)	césped	relvado
precauzione	précaution	precaution	Vorsicht(f)	precaución	precaução
precedente	précédent, e	previous	vorherig	precedente	precedente
precedenza; priorità	priorité	priority	Vorrang(m)	prioridad	prioridade
precedere	précéder	precede	voran = gehen, voraus = -	preceder	preceder
precipitarsi	précipiter(se)	rush	stürzen, sich	precipitarse	precipitar-se
precipitazione	précipitation	hurry, haste	Eile(f), Hast(f)	precipitación	precipitação
precipizio	précipice	precipice	Abgrund(m)	precipicio	precipício
precisamente, appunto	précisément	precisely	genau	precisamente	precisamente
precisare	préciser	specify	genau fest = legen	precisar	precisar
precisazione	précision	clarification	Klarstellung(f)	aclaración	explicação, precisão
precisione	précision	precision	Genauigkeit(f)	precisión	precisão
preciso, a	précis, e	precise, accurate	genau	preciso, a	exacto, a
precoce	précoce	precocious	frühreif, frühzeitig	precoz	precoce
preda	proie	prey	Beute(f)	presa	presa
predecessore	prédécesseur	predecessor	Vorgänger(in f)m	predecesor, a	predecessor, a
predicare	prêcher	preach	predigen	predicar	pregar
predire	prédire	predict	vorher = sagen	predecir	predizer
predominante	prédominant, e	predominant	vorherrschend	predominante	predominante

Italian	French	English	German	Spanish	Portuguese
prefazione	préface	preface	Vorwort(n)	prefacio	prefácio
preferenza	préférence	preference	Vorliebe(f)	preferencia	preferência
preferire	préférer	prefer	bevorzugen	preferir	preferir
preferito, a	préféré, e	favourite	Lieblings-	preferido, a	preferido, a
prefisso	préfixe	prefix	Vorsilbe(f)	prefijo	prefixo
prefisso	indicatif(tél.)	dialling code	Vorwählnummer(f)	prefijo	indicativo, prefixo
pregare	prier	pray	beten	rezar	rezar, orar
preghiera	prière	prayer	Gebet(n)	oración	oração
pregiudizio	préjugé	prejudice	Vorurteil(n)	prejuicio	preconceito
pregiudizio, danno	préjudice	wrong, harm	Schaden(m)	perjuicio	prejuízo
preistoria	préhistoire	prehistory	Vorgeschichte(f)	prehistoria	pré-história
prelevare	prélever	take from	entnehmen	sacar	tirar
prelevare	retirer	draw out, withdraw	ab = heben	sacar	levantar
preliminare	préliminaire	preliminary	einleitend	preliminar	preliminar
preliminare	préalable	preliminary	vorhergehend	previo, a	prévio, a
prematuro, a	prématuré, e	premature(baby)	Frühgeburt(f)	prematuro, a	prematuro, a
premeditare	préméditer	premeditate	vor = setzen	premeditar	premeditar
premeditato, a	prémédité, e	premeditated	vorsätzlich	premeditado, a	premeditado, a
premere	presser	press, squeeze	drücken(zusammen-)	apretar	prensar
premiato, a	lauréat, e	prize-winner	Preisträger(in f)m	galardonado, a	galardoado, a
premio	prix	prize	Preis(m)	premio	prémio
premio	lot	prize	Los(n)	premio	prémio
premio, sussidio	prime	bonus	Zulage(f)	prima	gratificação
prendere	prendre	take	nehmen	tomar, coger	tomar
prendere(lezione)	prendre(leçon)	have(a lesson)	nehmen	recibir(clases)	ter(lição)
prendere in prestito	emprunter	borrow	borgen	pedir prestado	pedir emprestado
prenotare	réserver	book, reserve	vor = bestellen	reservar	reservar
prenotato, a	réservé, e	reserved	reserviert	reservado, a	reservado, a
prenotazione	réservation	reservation	Reservierung(f)	reserva	reserva
preoccupare	préoccuper	worry, preoccupy	beunruhigen	preocupar	preocupar
preoccuparsi	inquiéter(s')	worry	beunruhigen, sich	preocuparse	preocupar-se
preoccuparsi	soucier(se)	worry	sorgen, sich; plagen, s.	preocuparse	preocupar-se
preoccupato, a	soucieux, se	worried	sorgenvoll	preocupado, a	preocupado, a
preoccupazione	souci	worry	Sorge(f)	preocupación	preocupação
preparare	préparer	prepare	vor = bereiten	preparar	preparar
preparazione	préparation	preparation	Vorbereitung(f)	preparación	preparação
preposizione	préposition	preposition	Präposition(f)	preposición	preposição
presa	prise	plug; socket	Steckdose(f)	enchufe	tomada
presbite	presbyte	long-sighted	weitsichtig	présbita	présbita
prescrivere	prescrire	prescribe	vor = schreiben	prescribir	prescrever
presentare	présenter	present	vor = zeigen, - = stellen	presentar	apresentar
presentare	présenter	introduce	vor = stellen	presentar	apresentar
presentazione	présentation	presentation	Vorführung(f)	presentación	apresentação
presente	présent, e	present	anwesend	presente	presente
presente, attuale	présent, e	present	gegenwärtig, aktuell	presente, actual	presente, actual
presente	présent	present	Gegenwart(f)	presente	presente
presenza	présence	presence	Anwesenheit(f)	presencia	presença
presenziare	assister	attend	bei = wohnen	concurrir a	assistir a
preservativo	préservatif	condom, sheath	Präservativ(n)	preservativo	preservativo
presidente, essa	président, e	president	Präsident(in f)m	presidente	presidente
presidente, essa	président, e	chairman/-woman	Vorsitzende(m, f)	presidente	presidente
presidenza	présidence	presidency	Präsidium n, Vorsitz m	presidencia	presidência
pressione	pression	pressure	Druck(m)	presión	pressão
prestare	prêter	lend	leihen, verleihen	prestar	emprestar
prestazione	performance	performance	Leistung(f)	proeza, hazaña	desempenho
prestigio	prestige	prestige	Ansehen(n)	prestigio	prestigio
prestigioso, a	prestigieux, se	prestigious	wunderbar	prestigioso, a	prestigioso, a
prestito	prêt	loan	Darlehen(n)	préstamo	empréstimo
prestito	emprunt	loan	Anleihe(f)	préstamo	empréstimo
presto	bientôt	soon	bald	pronto	logo, brevemente
presto	vite	fast, quickly	rasch	pronto; rápido, a	depressa; rápido, a
presto	tôt	early	früh	temprano	cedo
presumere	présumer	presume	vermuten	presumir	presumir
prete	prêtre	priest	Priester(m)	sacerdote, padre	padre
pretenzioso, a	prétentieux, se	pretentious	eingebildet	presuntuoso, a	pretencioso, a
prevalere	prévaloir	prevail	vor = herrschen	prevalecer	prevalecer
prevedere	prévoir	foresee; plan	vorher = sehen; planen	prever	prever
prevedere	envisager	envisage	beabsichtigen	enfocar	encarar

Italian	French	English	German	Spanish	Portuguese
prevenire	prévenir	warn, inform	warnen	prevenir, avisar	prevenir, avisar
preventivo	devis	estimate	Kostenvoranschlag(m)	presupuesto	orçamento
previsione	prévision	forecast	Vorhersage(f)	previsión	previsão
prezioso, a	précieux, se	precious	wertvoll, kostbar	precioso, a	precioso, a
prezzo	prix	price	Preis(m)	precio	preço
prigione, carcere	prison	prison, jail	Gefängnis(n)	prisión, cárcel	prisão, cadeia
prigioniero, a	prisonnier, ière	prisoner	Gefangene(f, m)	prisionero, a	prisioneiro, a
prima	avant	before	vor, vorher	antes(de)	antes(de)
prima	auparavant	before	vorher, zuvor	antes	dantes
primario, a	primaire	primary	Primär-	primario, a	primário, a
primavera	printemps	spring	Frühling(m)	primavera	primavera
primitivo, a	primitif, ive	primitive	primitiv	primitivo, a	primitivo, a
primo, a	premier, ière	first	erste(r, s)	primero, a; primer	primeiro, a
primogenito, a	aîné, e	oldest, eldest	Ältere(f, m)	primogénito, a	velho, a(o, a mais)
primo ministro	premier ministre	prime minister	Premierminister(m)	primer ministro	primeiro ministro
primo ministro	premier ministre	prime minister	Ministerpräsident(m)	primer ministro	primeiro ministro
principale	principal, e	principal, main	hauptsächlich	principal	principal
principe	prince	prince	Prinz(m)	príncipe	príncipe
principessa	princesse	princess(-es)	Prinzessin(f)	princesa	princesa
principiante	débutant, e	beginner	Anfänger(in f)m	principiante	principiante
principio, inizio	commencement	beginning, start	Anfang(m)	comienzo, principio	começo, princípio
principio	principe	principle	Grundsatz(m)	principio	princípio
priorità	priorité	priority	Vorrang(m), Priorität	prioridad	prioridade
prioritario, a	prioritaire	priority(have)	vorrangig; Prioritäts-	prioritario, a	prioritário, a
privare	priver	deprive	berauben, entziehen	privar	privar
privato, a	privé, e	private	privat	privado, a	privado, a
privato	particulier	individual	Privatmann(m)	particular	particular
privilegiato, a	privilégié, e	privileged	bevorzugt	privilegiado, a	privilegiado, a
privilegio	privilège	privilege	Vorrecht(n)	privilegio	privilégio
probabile	probable	probable, likely	wahrscheinlich	probable	provável
probabilmente	probablement	probably	wahrscheinlich	probablemente	provavelmente
problema	problème	problem	Problem(n)	problema	problema
procedere	avancer	advance, move fwd	weiter = gehen	avanzar	avançar
procedimento	procédé	process	Verfahren(n)	procedimiento	procedimento
procedimento	procédure	procedure	Verfahren(n)	procedimiento	procedimento
processione	procession	procession	Prozession(f)	procesión	procissão
processo	procès	lawsuit, trial	Prozeß(m)	proceso, juicio	processo
proclamare	proclamer	proclaim	bekannt = geben	proclamar	proclamar
procreare	procréer	procreate	erzeugen	procrear	procriar
procreazione	procréation	procreation	Zeugung(f)	procreación	procriação
procurarsi	procurer(se)	obtain, get	besorgen, sich	procurarse	arranjar; obter
prodigioso, a	prodigieux, se	prodigious	wunderbar	prodigioso, a	prodigioso, a
prodotto	produit	product	Produkt(n)	producto	produto
produrre	produire	produce	produzieren	producir	produzir
produrre	produire	produce	her = stellen	producir	produzir
produttivo, a	productif, ive	productive	leistungsfähig	productivo, a	produtivo, a
produttore, trice	producteur, trice	producer	Hersteller(in f)m	productor, a	produtor, a
produttore, trice	producteur, trice	producer	Produzent(in f)m	productor, a	produtor, a
produzione	production	production	Produktion(f)	producción	produção
profanare	profaner	desecrate	entweihen	profanar	profanar
professionale	professionnel, le	professional	professionell	profesional	profissional
professione	profession	profession	Beruf(m)	profesión	profissão
professionista	professionnel	professional	Profi(m)	profesional	profissional
professore, essa	professeur	teacher	Lehrer(in f)m	profesor, a	professor, a
professore, essa	professeur	professor	Professor(in f)m	catedrático, a	professor, a
profilo	profil	profile	Profil(n)	perfil	perfil
profitto, guadagno	profit	profit, benefit	Gewinn(m)	ganancia	lucro
profondità	profondeur	depth	Tiefe(f)	profundidad	profundidade
profondo, a	profond, e	deep	tief	profundo, a	profundo, a
profumeria	parfumerie	perfume shop	Parfümerie(f)	perfumería	perfumaria
profumo	parfum	perfume, scent	Parfüm(m)	perfume	perfume
progenitura	progéniture	offspring	Nachkomme(m)	progenitura	progenitura
progettare	projeter	plan	planen	proyectar, planear	projectar
progetto	projet	project, plan	Vorhaben(n)	proyecto, plan	projecto
progetto	projet	plan	Plan(m)	plan, proyecto	projecto
prognosi	pronostic	prognosis(-ses)	Prognose(f)	pronóstico	prognóstico
programma	programme	programme	Programm(n)	programa	programa
programma	émission	programme	Sendung(f)	emisión	emissão

Italian	French	English	German	Spanish	Portuguese
programmatore, trice	programmeur, se	programmer	Programmierer(in f)m	programador, a	programador, a
progressione	progression	progression	Fortschreiten(n)	progresión	progressão
progressivo, a	progressif, ive	progressive	fortschreitend	progresivo, a	progressivo, a
progresso	progrès	progress	Fortschritt(m)	progreso	progresso
proibire	défendre	forbid	verbieten	prohibir	proibir
proibito, a	interdit, e	forbidden	verboten	prohibido, e	proibido, a
proibizione	interdiction	ban	Verbot(n)	prohibición	proibição
proiettile	projectile	projectile	Geschoß(n)	proyectil	projéctil
proiettile	obus	shell	Geschoß(n), Granate(f)	obús	obus
proiettore	projecteur	projector	Scheinwerfer(m)	proyector	projector
prolificare	proliférer	proliferate	vermehren, sich	proliferar	proliferar
prolungamento	prolongement	extension	Verlängerung(f)	prolongamiento	prolongamento
prolungare	prolonger	extend	verlängern	prolongar	prolongar
prolungazione	prolongation	prolongation	Verlängerung(f)	prolongación	prolongamento
promessa	promesse	promise	Versprechen(n)	promesa	promessa
promesso, a	promis, e	promised	versprochen	prometido, a	prometido, a
promettere	promettre	promise	versprechen	prometer	prometer
promozione	promotion	promotion	Beförderung(f)	promoción	promoção
promuovere	promouvoir	promote	befördern	promover	promover
pronome	pronom	pronoun	Fürwort(n)	pronombre	pronome
pronostico	pronostic	forecast	Vorhersage(f)	pronóstico	prognóstico
pronto!	allô!	hello!	Ja, bitte?	dígame(!)	está lá?; estou?
pronto, a	prêt, e	ready	fertig	dispuesto, a	pronto, a
pronto, a	prompt, e	quick, prompt	schnell, rasch	pronto, a	pronto, a
pronunziare	prononcer	pronounce	aus=sprechen	pronunciar	pronunciar
propaganda	propagande	propaganda	Propaganda(f)	propaganda	propaganda
propagare	propager	spread	verbreiten	propagar	propagar
propizio, a	propice	favourable	günstig	propicio, a	propício, a
proporre	proposer	propose; offer	vor=schlagen	proponer	propor
proporzione	proportion	proportion, ratio	Verhältnis(n)	proporción	proporção
proposito	dessein	purpose, aim	Absicht(f)	propósito	propósito
proposito	propos, intention	intention, aim	Absicht(f)	propósito	propósito
proposta	proposition	proposal	Vorschlag(m)	propuesta	proposta
proprietà	propriété	property	Eigentum(n)	propiedad	propriedade
proprietario, a	propriétaire	owner	Eigentümer(in f)m	propietario, a	proprietário, a
proprietario, a	propriétaire	landowner	Gutsherr(-sbesitzer)	propietario, a	proprietário, a
proprietario, a	propriétaire	landlord	Besitzer/in; (Haus-)	dueño, a	senhorio, a; dono, a
proprio, a	propre	own	eigen	propio, a	próprio, a
propulsione	propulsion	propulsion	Antrieb(m)	propulsión	propulsão
prosciutto	jambon	ham	Schinken(m)	jamón	fiambre
prospero, a	prospère	flourishing	erfolgreich, blühend	próspero, a	próspero, a
prospettiva	perspective	prospect	Aussicht(f)	perspectiva	perspectiva
prospettiva	perspective	perspective	Perspektive(f)	perspectiva	perspectiva
prospetto	prospectus	leaflet	Flugblatt(n)	folleto	prospecto
prossenetismo	proxénétisme	pimping	Kuppelei(f)	proxenetismo	proxenetismo
prossimità	proximité	proximity	Nähe(f)	proximidad	proximidade
prossimo, a	prochain, e	next	nächste	próximo, a	próximo, a
prossimo, a	proche	near, close	nah(e)	cercano, a; próximo	próximo, a; perto
prostata	prostate	prostate	Prostata(f)	próstata	próstata
prostituta	prostituée	prostitute	Prostituierte(f)	prostituta	prostituta
prostituzione	prostitution	prostitution	Prostitution(f)	prostitución	prostituição
proteggere	protéger	protect	beschützen	proteger	proteger
protesi	prothèse	artificial-, false-	Prothese(f)	prótesis	prótese
protestante	protestant, e	Protestant	Protestant(in f)m	protestante	protestante
protestare	protester	protest, contest	protestieren	protestar	protestar
protezione	protection	protection	Schutz(m)	protección	protecção
protocollo	protocole	protocol	Protokoll(n)	protocolo	protocolo
prototipo	prototype	prototype	Prototyp(m)	prototipo	protótipo
protuberanza	protubérance	protuberance	Beule(f), Buckel(m)	protuberancia	protuberância
prova	preuve	proof, evidence	Beweis(m)	prueba	prova
prova, test	épreuve, essai	test	Test(m), Probe(f)	prueba	prova
prova, collaudo	essai	trial, test	Versuch(m)	prueba	ensaio
provare	essayer	try	versuchen	probar, intentar	tentar; provar
provare	prouver	prove	beweisen	probar	provar
provare	éprouver	feel	spüren, fühlen	sentir	sentir
provenienza	provenance	origin	Herkunft(f)	procedencia	proveniência
proverbio	proverbe	proverb	Sprichwort(n)	proverbio	provérbio
provincia	province	province	Provinz(f)	provincia	província

Italian	French	English	German	Spanish	Portuguese
provocare	provoquer	provoke	heraus = fordern, reizen	provocar	provocar
provocazione	provocation	provocation	Herausforderung(f)	provocación	provocação
provvisorio, a	provisoire	provisional	provisorisch	provisional	provisório, a
provvista	provision	stock, supply	Vorrat(m)	provisión	provisão
prudente	prudent, e	careful, prudent	vorsichtig	prudente	prudente
prudenza	prudence	caution, prudence	Vorsicht(f)	prudencia	prudência
prugna, susina	prune	plum	Pflaume(f)	ciruela	ameixa
prurito	démangeaison	itch, itching	Juckreiz(m)	picazón	comichão
pseudonimo	pseudonyme	pseudonym	Pseudonym(n)	seudónimo	pseudónimo
psicanalista	psychanalyste	psychoanalyst	Psychoanalytiker(m)	sicoanalista	psicanalista
psichiatra	psychiatre	psychiatrist	Psychiater(in f)m	siquiatra	psiquiatra
psichico, a	psychique	psychological	psychisch	síquico, a	psíquico, a
psicosi	psychose	psychosis(-ses)	Psychose(f)	sicosis	psicose
psicologia	psychologie	psychology	Psychologie(f)	sicología	psicologia
psicologo, a	psychologue	psychologist	Psychologe(m)/-gin(f)	sicólogo, a	psicólogo, a
pubblicare	publier	publish, issue	veröffentlichen	publicar	publicar
pubblicazione	publication	publication	Veröffentlichung(f)	publicación	publicação
pubblicità	publicité	advertising	Werbung(f), Anzeige(f)	publicidad	publicidade
pubblico, a	public, ique	public	öffentlich	público, a	público, a
pubblico	public	public; audience	Publikum(n)	público	público
pubertà	puberté	puberty	Pubertät(f)	pubertad	puberdade
pudico, a	pudique	modest	keusch	púdico, a	púdico, a
pugilato	boxe	boxing	Boxen(n)	boxeo	boxe
pugile	boxeur	boxer	Boxer(m)	boxeador	pugilista
pugnale	poignard	dagger	Dolch(m)	puñal	punhal
pugno	poing	fist	Faust(f)	puño	punho
pugno	coup de poing	punch	Faustschlag(m)	puñetazo	soco; murro
pulce	puce	flea	Floh(m)	pulga	pulga
pulcino	poussin	chick	Küken(n)	pollito	pinto
puledro	poulain	foal	Fohlen(n)	potro	potro
puleggia	poulie	pulley	Flaschenzug(m)	polea	polia
pulire	nettoyer	clean	reinigen	limpiar	limpar
pulito, a	propre	clean	sauber	limpio, a	limpo, a
pulizia	propreté	clean(li)ness	Reinlichkeit(f)	limpieza	limpeza
pulizia	nettoyage	cleaning	Reinigung(f)	limpieza	limpeza
pulizie	ménage	housework	Haushalt(m)	limpieza	limpeza
pullman	autocar	coach	Reisebus(m)	autocar	autocarro
pulsante, bottone	bouton	button	Taste(f)	pulsador	botão
pulsazione	pulsation	beating, pulsation	Pulsschlag(m)	pulsación	pulsação
pungere	piquer	prick, sting	stechen	pinchar	picar
punire	punir	punish	bestrafen	castigar	castigar
punizione	punition	punishment	Strafe(f)	castigo	castigo
punizione, castigo	peine	sentence	Bestrafung(f)	pena, castigo	pena
punta	pointe	point	Spitze(f)	punta	ponta
punta, estremità	bout	tip, end	Zipfel(m), Ende(n)	punta	ponta
puntare	braquer	aim	richten auf	apuntar	apontar
punteggiatura	ponctuation	punctuation	Zeichensetzung(f)	puntuación	pontuação
punteggio	score	score	Punktzahl(f)	marca, tanteo	resultado
puntina(disegno)	punaise	drawing-pin	Heftzwecke(f)	chincheta	percevejo
punto	point	point	Punkt(m)	punto	ponto
punto	point	dot	Punkt(m)	punto	ponto
punto	point	spot	Fleck(m); Ort; Stelle	lugar, punto	ponto
punto	point	stitch	Stich(m); Masche(f)	puntada	ponto
punto di vista	point de vue	viewpoint	Aussichtspunkt(m)	punto de vista	ponto de vista
puntuale	ponctuel, le	punctual	pünktlich	puntual	pontual
puntura	piqûre	sting, bite	Stich(m)	picadura	picada
puntura, prelievo	ponction	puncture	Punktion(f)	punción	punção
pupilla	pupille	pupil	Pupille(f)	pupila	pupila
purché	pourvu que	provided that	wenn nur, sofern, daß	ojalá	oxalá
pure	aussi	also; too, as well	auch	también	também
purga	purge	purge	Säuberungsaktion(f)	purga	purga
purificare	purifier	purify	reinigen	purificar	purificar
puro, a	pur, e	pure	rein	puro, a	puro, a
pus	pus	pus	Eiter(m)	pus	pus
puzza, fetore	puanteur	stench, stink	Gestank(m)	hedor, peste	fedor
puzzare	puer	stink	stinken	apestar	cheirar mal
puzzle	puzzle	jigsaw(puzzle)	Puzzle(n)	rompecabezas	puzzle

I

Q

Italian	French	English	German	Spanish	Portuguese
quaderno	cahier	exercise book	Heft(n)	cuaderno	caderno
quadrante	cadran	dial	Zifferblatt(n)	esfera	mostrador
quadrato	carré	square	Viereck(n)	cuadrado	quadrado
qualche	quelque	some, any	einige	alguno, a	algum, a
qualche cosa	quelque chose	something	etwas	algo	qualquer coisa
qualche parte(da)	quelque part	somewhere	irgendwo	alguna parte(en)	algures
qualche volta	quelquefois	sometimes	manchmal	a veces	às vezes
qualcuno, a	quelqu'un, e	someone, somebody	jemand	alguien	alguém
quale; che	quel, le	what; which	welch(e, er, es)	cuál; que	qual; que
quale(il)	lequel	which; who; whom	welcher	cúal, cual	qual(o)
quale(la)	laquelle	which; who; whom	welche	cual(la)	qual(a)
qualificato, a	qualifié, e	qualified	qualifiziert	calificado, a	qualificado, a
qualità	qualité	quality	Qualität(f)	calidad; cualidad	qualidade
qualità	qualité	quality	Eigenschaft(f)	cualidad	qualidade
qualunque	quelconque	any, whatever	beliebig	cualquier(a)	qualquer
qualunque sia	quel que soit	whatever	was auch immer	cualquiera que sea	seja qual for
quando	quand	when	wann	cuándo, cuando	quando
quando	lorsque	when; as	als; wenn	cuando	quando
quantità	quantité	quantity, amount	Quantität(f)	cantidad	quantidade
quanto	combien	how much, how many	wieviel	cuánto; cuanto	quanto
quaranta	quarante	forty	vierzig	cuarenta	quarenta
quartetto	quatuor	quartet	Quartett(n)	cuarteto	quarteto
quartiere	quartier	district	Viertel(n)	barrio	bairro
quarto	quart	quarter	Viertel(n)	cuarto	quarto
quasi	presque	almost, nearly	fast	casi	quase
quattordici	quatorze	fourteen	vierzehn	catorce	catorze
quattro	quatre	four	vier	cuatro	quatro
quello, a; questo, a	ce, cette, ces	that, those	dieser, diese, dieses	ese, esa, esos(as)	este, esta, estes
quello, a	celui, celle	the one	derjenige, die-, das-	él, la	o, a
quello, quella	celui-là, celle-	that one	der(jenige); die( )	ése, ésa, éso(s)	esse(a); aquele(a)
querelare	plainte(porter)	complaint(lodge a)	an = zeigen	denunciar	queixa(apresentar)
questi, e	ces	these, those	diese(pl)	estos, as; esos, as	estes, as; esses, as
questi, e	ceux, celles, ces	these, those	diese	esos, aquellos	aqueles, aquelas
questi; quelli	ceux-ci, celles-	these; those	diese; jene	éstos; ésos	estes(as); esses(as)
questione	question	question	Frage(f)	cuestión	questão
questo, a; quello, a	ce, cette	this, that	dieser, diese	este; esta; estos, as	este, a; esse, a
questo, a; quello, a	cet, cette	this, that	dieser, diese	éste; ésta; éstos	este; esta; estes, as
questo, questa	celui-ci, celle-	this one	diese(r, s)(hier)	éste, ésta	este, esta
questo, ciò	ceci	this	dies(es); das	esto	isto
qui	ici	here	hier	aquí	aqui
quindici	quinze	fifteen	fünfzehn	quince	quinze
quinte(le)	coulisses	wings	Kulisse(f)	bastidores	bastidores
quota	quota	quota	Quote(f)	cuota	cota
quota	cotisation	subscription, dues	Beitrag m(Mitglieds-)	cuota	quota
quotazione	cotation	quotation	Kurswert(m)	cotización	cotação
quotidiano, a	quotidien, ne	daily	täglich	cotidiano, a	quotidiano, a
quotidiano	quotidien	daily	Tageszeitung(f)	diario	diário
quoziente	quotient	quotient	Quotient(m), Bruch(m)	cociente	quociente

R

Italian	French	English	German	Spanish	Portuguese
rabbia	rage	rabies	Tollwut(f)	rabia	raiva
rabbia	rage, fureur	rage	Wut(f)	rabia, furia	raiva, furor
rabbino	rabbin	rabbi	Rabbiner(m)	rabino	rabino
racchetta	raquette	racket	Schläger(Tennis-)(m)	raqueta	raqueta
racchetta	raquette	bat	Schläger(m)	raqueta, pala	raqueta
raccogliere	ramasser	pick up	auf = heben	recoger	apanhar, recolher
raccogliere	récolter	harvest, gather	ernten	cosechar, recoger	colher, apanhar
raccolta	récolte	crop; harvest	Ernte(f)	cosecha	colheita
raccomandazione	recommandation	recommendation	Empfehlung(f)	recomendación	recomendação
raccontare	raconter	relate, tell	erzählen	contar	contar
racconto	récit	story	Bericht(m)	narración	narração
racconto, fiaba	conte	tale, story	Märchen(n)	cuento	conto
rachitico, a	rachitique	rickety	rachitisch	raquítico, a	raquítico, a
racket	racket	racket(-eering)	Erpressung(f)	extorsión	vigarice
radar	radar	radar	Radar(m)	radar	radar
raddrizzare	redresser	straighten out/up	gerade = biegen	enderezar	endireitar
radersi	raser(se)	shave	rasieren, sich	afeitar(se)	barbear-se
radiazione	radiation	radiation	Bestrahlung(f)	radiación	radiação
radice	racine	root	Wurzel(f)	raíz	raiz
radio	radio	radio	Radio(n)	radio	rádio
radio	poste radio	radio set	Radio(n)	aparato de radio	rádio
radioattività	radioactivité	radioactivity	Radioaktivität(f)	radiactividad	radioactividade
radiodiffusione	radiodiffusion	broadcasting	Radioübertragung(f)	radiodifusión	radiodifusão
radiografia	radiographie	X-ray; radiography	Röntgenbild(n)	radiografía	radiografia
radunare	rassembler	gather(together)	sammeln	juntar	juntar
radunare, riunire	assembler, réunir	assemble	versammeln	reunir	reunir
raduno, adunanza	rassemblement	gathering	Versammlung(f)	concentración	ajuntamento
raffica	rafale	gust, gale	Windstoß(m)	ráfaga	rajada
raffica	rafale	burst, hail	Salve(f)	ráfaga	rajada
raffreddare	refroidir	cool(down)	ab = kühlen	enfriar	arrefecer
raffreddarsi	enrhumer(s')	catch a cold	erkälten, sich	constipar(se)	constipar-se
raffreddore	rhume	cold	Schnupfen(m)	resfriado	constipação
ragazza	fille	girl	Mädchen(n)	chica	rapariga
ragazzino, a	gamin, e	kid, child	Kind(n)	chiquillo, a	miúdo
ragazzo	garçon	boy	Junge(m)	muchacho, mozo	rapaz
ragazzo, bambino	garçon, enfant	boy	kleiner Junge(m)	chico	rapaz
raggio	rayon	radius(-ii)	Radius(m)	radio	raio
raggio	rayon	ray	Strahl(m)	rayo	raio
raggio	rayon	spoke	Speiche(f)	radio	raio
raggiungere	atteindre	reach	erreichen	alcanzar, lograr	atingir
raggiungere	arriver(à)	attain	erlangen, erreichen	lograr, alcanzar	alcançar, atingir
raggiungere	rejoindre	rejoin, return to	an = schließen, sich	reunirse con	reunir-se
raggiungere, ottenere	remporter, gagner	achieve	erringen	lograr, triunfar	alcançar, obter
ragionamento	raisonnement	reasoning	Überlegung(f)	razonamiento	raciocínio
ragione	raison	reason	Grund(m)	razón, causa	razão
ragione(avere)	raison(avoir)	right(to be)	Recht(n)(haben)	razón(tener)	razão(ter)
ragionevole	raisonnable	reasonable	vernünftig	razonable	razoável
ragioniere	comptable	accountant	Buchhalter(in f)m	contable	contabilista
ragno	araignée	spider	Spinne(f)	araña	aranha
rallegrare(-arsi)	réjouir(se)	delighted(be)	erfreuen, sich	alegrarse	alegrar-se
rallentare	ralentir	slow down	verlangsamen	aminorar	abrandar
ramadan	ramadan	Ramadan	Ramadan(m)	ramadán	ramadão
rame	cuivre	copper	Kupfer(n)	cobre	cobre
rammaricato, a	désolé, e	regret(I)	bedauern	siento(lo)	lamento(eu)
rammendo	raccommodage	mending	Flicken(n)	remiendo	remendo
ramo	branche	branch	Ast(m)	rama	ramo
rampa	rampe	banister, handrail	Geländer(n)	barandilla	corrimão
rampone	crampons	crampons, irons	Steigeisen(n)	crampones	grampo
rana	grenouille	frog	Frosch(m)	rana	rã
rancore	rancune	grudge, spite	Rachsucht(f)	rencor	rancor
rango	rang	rank	Rang(m)	puesto	posição

599

Italian	French	English	German	Spanish	Portuguese
rannicchiarsi	blottir(se)	huddle	an = schmiegen, sich	acurrucar(se)	aninhar-se
rapace	rapace	bird of prey	Raubvogel(m)	rapaz	ave de rapina
rapido, a; veloce	rapide	rapid, fast, quick	schnell	rápido, a	rápido, a
rapina	hold-up	hold-up	Raubüberfall(m)	atraco	assalto
rapire	kidnapper	kidnap	entführen	secuestrar	raptar
rapporto	rapport	ratio, proportion	Beziehung(f)	razón, relación	razão
rapporto, relazione	rapport	report	Bericht(m)	informe	relatório
rappresaglia	représaille(s)	reprisal	Vergeltung(f)	represalia	represália
rappresentante	représentant, e	representative, rep	Vertreter(in f)m	representante	representante
rappresentare	représenter	represent	dar = stellen	representar	representar
rappresentazione	représentation	representation	Darstellung(f)	representación	representação
rappresentazione	représentation	performance	Vorstellung(f)	representación	representação
raro, a	rare	rare	selten	raro, a	raro, a
raso	satin	satin	Satin(m)	raso, satén	cetim
rasoio	rasoir	razor	Rasierapparat(m)	navaja de afeitar	navalha, gilete
rassegnarsi	résigner(se)	resign oneself	entsagen, ergeben, sich	resignarse	resignar-se
rassicurare	rassurer	reassure	beruhigen	tranquilizar	tranquilizar
rastrello	râteau	rake	Rechen(m)	rastrillo	ancinho
ratificare	ratifier	ratify	ratifizieren	ratificar	ratificar
rauco, a	rauque	hoarse	rauh, heiser	ronco, a	rouco, a
rauco, a	enroué, e	hoarse	heiser	ronco, a	rouco, a
raziale	racial, e	racial	rassisch	racial	racial
razionale	rationnel, le	rational	rational	racional	racional
razionamento	rationnement	rationing	Rationierung(f)	racionamiento	racionamento
razione	ration, portion	ration	Ration(f); Stück(n)	ración	ração
razza	race	race, breed	Rasse(f)	raza	raça
razza	race	breed	Rasse(f)	casta, raza	casta, raça
razzismo	racisme	racism	Rassismus(m)	racismo	racismo
razzo	fusée	rocket	Rakete(f)	cohete	foguete
re	roi	king	König(m)	rey	rei
reagire	réagir	react	reagieren	reaccionar	reagir
reale; vero, a	réel, le	real, actual	wirklich	real	real
reale	royal, e	royal	königlich	real	real
realizzare	réaliser	realize	begreifen	darse cuenta	aperceber-se
realizzare	réaliser	carry out, perform	verwirklichen	realizar	realizar, fazer
realizzazione	réalisation	realization	Verwirklichung(f)	realización	realização
realmente	réellement	truly	wirklich	realmente	realmente
realtà	réalité	reality	Wirklichkeit(f)	realidad	realidade
reame	royaume	kingdom	Königreich(n)	reino	reino
reattore	réacteur	reactor; engine	Reaktor(m)	reactor	reactor
reazionario, a	réactionnaire	reactionary	reaktionär	reaccionario, a	reaccionário, a
reazione	réaction	reaction	Reaktion(f)	reacción	reacção
recente, e	récent, e	recent	neu	reciente	recente
recentemente	récemment	recently	kürzlich	recientemente	recentemente
reception	réception	reception	Rezeption(f)	recepción	recepção
recinzione, muro	clôture	fence, railings	Zaun(m)	valla, cerca	cerca, vedação
recipiente	récipient	container	Behälter(m)	recipiente	recipiente
recita	récitation	recitation	Vortrag(m)	recitación	recitação
recital	récital	recital	Konzert(n), Vortrag(m)	recital	recital
recitare	jouer	act	spielen	desempeñar	representar
reclamare	réclamer à	ask(for)	bitten um	reclamar	reclamar
reclame	réclame(s)	advertisement	Reklame(f)	publicidad	publicidade
reclamo	réclamation	complaint, claim	Beschwerde(f)	reclamación	reclamação
reclutamento	recrutement	recruitment	Rekrutierung(f)	reclutamiento	recrutamento
record	record	record	Rekord(m)	récord	recorde
recuperare	récupérer	recover, get back	wieder = bekommen	recuperar	recuperar
redazione	rédaction	editorial staff	Redaktion(f)	redacción	redacção
redditività	rentabilité	profitability	Rentabilität(f)	rentabilidad	rentabilidade
redditizio, a	rentable	profitable	einträglich	rentable	rentável
reddito	revenu	income, revenue	Einkommen(n)	renta, ingresos	rendimento
regalo	cadeau	present, gift	Geschenk(n)	regalo	prenda, presente
reggimento	régiment	regiment	Regiment(n)	regimiento	regimento
reggiseno	soutien-gorge	bra	Büstenhalter(m)	sostén	soutien
regime	régime	régime	Regime(n)	régimen	regime
regime	régime	speed	Drehzahl(f)	régimen	velocidade
regina	reine	queen	Königin(f)	reina	rainha
regione	région	region, area	Gegend(f)	región	região
registrare	enregistrer	record	auf = nehmen	grabar	gravar

Italian	French	English	German	Spanish	Portuguese
registrare	enregistrer	register, check in	auf = geben	registrar	registar
registratore	magnétophone	tape recorder	Kassettenrecorder(m)	magnetófono	gravador
registrazione	enregistrement	recording	Aufnahme(f)	grabación	gravação
registrazione	enregistrement	registration	Registrierung(f)	registro	registo
registro	registre	register	Register(n)	registro	registo
regno	règne	reign	Herrschaft(f)	reino	reinado
regola, norma	règle	rule	Regel(f)	regla, norma	regra, norma
regolamentazione	réglementation	regulation(s)	Regelung(f)	reglamentación	regulamentação
regolamento	règlement	regulation	Bestimmung(f)	reglamento	regulamento
regolare	régulier, ière	regular	regelmäßig	regular	regular
regolare	régler	adjust, tune	ein = stellen	ajustar, arreglar	afinar, regular
regolare, saldare	régler	settle	bezahlen	liquidar, pagar	pagar
regolarizzazione	régularisation	regularization	Regulierung(f)	regularización	regularização
regolazione	réglage	adjustment	Einstellung(f)	reglaje, ajuste	afinação
regresso	régression	regression	Rückgang(m)	regresión	regressão
reintegrare	réintégrer	return	zurück = kehren	reintegrar	voltar
reintegrare	réintégrer	reinstate	wiederein = setzen	rehabilitar	reintegrar
relativo, a	relatif, ive	relative	relativ	relativo, a	relativo, a
relazione	relation	relation(-ship)	Beziehung(f)	relación	relação
relazione; esposto	exposé	talk, commentary	Referat(n)	exposición	exposição
religione	religion	religion	Religion(f)	religión	religião
religioso, a	religieux, se	religious	religiös	religioso, a	religioso, a
relitto	épave	wreck	Wrack(n)	ruina, restos	destroços
remare	ramer	row	rudern	remar	remar
remo	rame	oar	Ruder(n)	remo	remo
rendere	rendre	give back	zurück = geben	devolver	devolver
rendimento	rendement	output, yield	Ertrag(m), Leistung(f)	rendimiento	rendimento
rendimento	rendement	yield	Ertrag(m)	rendimiento	rendimento; produto
rendita	rente	income, pension	Einkommen(n)	renta	renda
rene	rein	kidney	Niere(f)	riñón	rim
reparto	rayon	department	Abteilung(f)	sección	secção
repertorio	répertoire	index; repertoire	Repertoire(n)	repertorio	repertório
replicare	répliquer	reply	erwidern, entgegnen	replicar	replicar
repressione	répression	repression	Unterdrückung(f)	represión	repressão
repubblica	république	republic	Republik(f)	república	república
reputazione, fama	réputation	reputation	Ansehen(n), Ruf(m)	reputación, fama	reputação, fama
requisitoria	réquisitoire	indictment	Anklagerede(f)	requisitoria	requisitório
residenza	résidence	residence	Wohnsitz(m)	residencia	residência
residuo	résidu	residue	Rückstand(m)	residuo	resíduo
resina	résine	resin	Harz(m)	resina	resina
resistente	résistant, e	resistant	widerstandsfähig	resistente	resistente
resistenza	résistance	resistance	Widerstand(m)	resistencia	resistência
resistenza	endurance	endurance	Ausdauer(f)	resistencia	resistência
resistere	résister	resist; withstand	widerstehen	resistir	resistir
resistere a	résister à	withstand	widerstehen	resistir a	resistir a
resoconto	compte rendu	report, minutes	Bericht(m)	informe, acta	relatório, acta
respirare	respirer	breathe	atmen	respirar	respirar
respirazione	respiration	breathing	Atmung(f)	respiración	respiração
responsabile	responsable	responsible	verantwortlich	responsable	responsável
responsabile	responsable	liable(to be)	haftbar	responsable	responsável
responsabile	responsable	person in charge	Verantwortliche(f, m)	encargado, a	responsável
responsabilità	responsabilité	responsibility	Verantwortung(f)	responsabilidad	responsabilidade
ressa, affollamento	cohue, foule	crush, crowd	Menge(f)	barullo, jaleo	multidão, confusão
ressa	ruée	rush	Ansturm(m)	riada	corrida
restare, rimanere	rester	remain	bleiben	sobrar, quedar	sobejar, sobrar
restare	rester	stay, remain	bleiben	quedarse	ficar
restaurare	restaurer	restore	wiederher = stellen	restaurar	restaurar
resti, cocci	débris, restes	remains, debris	Trümmer(m, pl)	resto, residuo	resto, destroços
restituire	restituer	return	zurück = erstatten	restituir	restituir
resto	reste	rest, remainder	Rest(m)	resto	resto
resto	monnaie	change	Kleingeld(n); Klein-	cambio	troco
restringere	rétrécir	shrink	schrumpfen	encoger	encolher
restringere	restreindre	restrict	beschränken	restringir	restringir
restringersi	rétrécir(se)	narrow	enger machen/werden	estrechar(se)	estreitar-se
restrizione	restriction	restriction	Einschränkung(f)	restricción	restrição
retata	rafle	raid, round-up	Razzia(f)	redada	rusga
rete	filet	net	Netz(n)	red	rede
rete	réseau	network	Netz(n)	red	rede

Italian	French	English	German	Spanish	Portuguese
reticolato	grillage	wire fencing	Gitter(n)	reja	gradeamento
retina	rétine	retina	Netzhaut(f)	retina	retina
retro	derrière, arrière	back, rear	Hinter-, Rückseite(f)	trasero, a	trazeiro
retrovisore	rétroviseur	rear-view mirror	Rückspiegel(m)	retrovisor	retrovisor
retta	droite	straight line	Gerade(f)	recta	recta
rettangolo	rectangle	rectangle	Rechteck(n)	rectángulo	rectângulo
rettificare	rectifier	rectify	berichtigen	rectificar	rectificar
rettile	reptile	reptile	Reptil(n)	reptil	réptil
reumatismo	rhumatisme	rheumatism	Rheumatismus(m)	reumatismo	reumatismo
revisione	révision	revision	Revision(f)	revisión	revisão
revisione	révision	service, overhaul	Überholung(f)	revisión	revisão
revocare	révoquer	dismiss	ab = setzen, entlassen	revocar	demitir
revolver	révolver	revolver, gun	Revolver(m)	revólver	revólver
riadattamento	réadaptation	readjustment	Umstellung(f)	readaptación	readaptação
rianimazione	réanimation	resuscitation	Wiederbelebung(f)	reanimación	reanimação
riassunto	résumé	summary	Zusammenfassung(f)	resumen	resumo
ribaltabile	escamotable	fold-away	zusammenklappbar	plegable	escamoteável
ribaltare	culbuter	somersault	überrennen	volcar	cambalhotas(dar)
ribasso, sconto	rabais, remise	discount	Rabatt(m)	rebaja, descuento	desconto, saldo
ribellarsi	insurger(s')	rebel(against)	empören, sich	rebelarse	insurgir-se
ribelle	rebelle	rebel	Rebell(m)	rebelde	rebelde
ribellione	rébellion	rebellion	Aufstand(m)	rebelión	rebelião
ricamare	broder	embroider	sticken	bordar	bordar
ricchezza	richesse	wealth, richness	Reichtum(m)	riqueza	riqueza
ricciolo	boucle	curl	Locke(f)	rizo	caracóis
ricciuto, a	frisé, e	curly	lockig	rizado, a	ondulado, a
ricco, a	riche	rich, wealthy	reich	rico, a	rico, a
ricerca	recherche	research	Forschung(f)	investigación	investigação
ricerca	recherche	search	Suche(f)	busca	busca
ricercare	rechercher	search/look for	suchen	buscar, indagar	buscar, procurar
ricetta	recette	recipe	Rezept(n)	receta	receita
ricettacolo	réceptacle	receptacle	Sammelbecken(n)	receptáculo	receptáculo
ricetta medica	ordonnance	prescription	Rezept(n)	receta	receita
ricevere	recevoir	receive, get	empfangen	recibir	receber
ricevimento	réception	party, reception	Empfang(m)	recepción	recepção
ricevitore	récepteur	receiver	Empfänger(m)	receptor	receptor
ricevuta	reçu	receipt	Quittung(f)	recibo	recibo
ricevuta	quittance	receipt	Quittung(f)	recibo	recibo
ricevuta	réception	receipt	Empfang(m)	recibo	recepção
ricezione	réception	reception	Empfang(m)	recepción	recepção
richiamo	rappel	recall	Rückruf(m)	recuerdo	lembrança
richiamo	rappel	reminder	Erinnerung(f); Mahnung	llamada	aviso; lembrança
richiesta	demande	request	Anfrage(f)	pedido	pedido
richiesta	demande	request; demand	Bitte(f); Gesuch(n)	petición	pedido
richiesta	requête	request	Ersuchen(n), Gesuch(n)	demanda	pedido
ricompensa	récompense	reward; award	Belohnung(f)	recompensa	recompensa
riconciliazione	réconciliation	reconciliation	Versöhnung(f)	reconciliación	reconciliação
riconfortante	réconfortant, e	comforting	tröstlich	reconfortante	reconfortante
riconoscere	reconnaître	recognize	erkennen	reconocer	reconhecer
ricordarsi	rappeler(se)	recall, remember	erinnern, sich	recordar, acordarse	lembrar-se
ricordarsi	souvenir(se)	remember, recall	erinnern, sich	acordarse	recordar-se
ricordo	souvenir	memory	Erinnerung(f)	recuerdo	recordação
ricordo, souvenir	souvenir	souvenir	Andenken(n)	recuerdo	recordação
ricorrere, appellarsi	recourir à	appeal to	Berufung(f)ein = legen	recurrir, apelar	recorrer, apelar
ricorso	recours	recourse	Zuflucht(f), Berufung	recurso	recurso
ricostituente	fortifiant	tonic	Stärkungsmittel(n)	fortificante	fortificante
ricreazione	récréation	break	Pause(f)	recreo	recreio
ridere	rire	laugh	lachen	reir	rir
ridicolo, a	ridicule	ridiculous	lächerlich	ridículo, a	ridículo, a
ridurre	réduire	reduce	reduzieren	reducir	reduzir
riduzione	réduction	reduction	Verringerung(f)	reducción	redução
riduzione	réduction	reduction	Senkung(f)	rebaja	desconto
rieducazione	rééducation	therapy	Heilgymnastik(f)	reeducación	reeducação
riempire	remplir	fill	füllen	llenar	encher
riferimento	référence	reference	Referenz(f)	referencia	referência
riferire	relater	relate, recount	erzählen	relatar	relatar
riferirsi	référer(se)	refer to	beziehen, sich	referirse	referir-se
rifiutare	refuser	refuse	verweigern	rehusar	recusar

Italian	French	English	German	Spanish	Portuguese
rifiuto	refus	refusal	Verweigerung(f)	rechazo	recusa
riflessivo, a	réfléchi, e	thoughtful	bedächtig	reflexivo, a	ponderado, a
riflesso	reflet	reflection	Widerschein(m), Reflex	reflejo	reflexo
riflesso	réflexe	reflex	Reflex(m)	reflejo	reflexo
riflettere	réfléchir(à)	reflect, think	überlegen	reflexionar	reflectir; pensar
riflettere(-ersi)	réfléchir(se)	reflected(be)	reflektieren	reflejar	reflectir
riflusso	reflux	ebb	Ebbe(f)	reflujo	refluxo
riforma	réforme	reform	Reform(f)	reforma	reforma
rifornimento	alimentation	supplying	Versorgung(f)	abastecimiento	abastecimento
rifornire	approvisionner	supply	versorgen	aprovisionar	abastecer
rifornire	ravitailler	supply	versorgen	abastecer	abastecer
rifugiato, a	réfugié, e	refugee	Flüchtling(m)	refugiado, a	refugiado, a
rifugio, asilo	refuge, asile	refuge	Zufluchtsort(m)	refugio, asilo	refúgio, asilo
riga	raie	line	Strich(m)	raya	linha; risca
riga	règle	ruler	Lineal(n)	regla	régua
rigato, a	rayé, e	scratched	zerkratzt	rayado, a	riscado, a
rigettare	refuser, rejeter	reject	ab = lehnen, verwerfen	rechazar	rejeitar
righe(a)	rayures(à)	striped	gestreift	rayas(a)	riscas(às)
rigido, a	rigide	rigid, stiff	steif	rígido, a	rígido, a
rigido, a	raide	stiff	starr, steif	tieso, a; rígido, a	teso, a; hirto, a
rigoroso, a	rigoureux, se	rigorous	streng	riguroso, a	rigoroso, a
riguardare	concerner	concern	betreffen	concernir	dizer respeito a
rilasciare	relâcher	release	frei = lassen	soltar	libertar
rilasciare, liberare	délivrer	free	befreien	libertar	libertar
rilassamento	relaxation	relaxation	Entspannung(f)	relajamiento	relaxação
rilassato, a	décontracté, e	relaxed	lässig, entspannt	relajado, a	descontraído, a
rilegatura	reliure	binding(book-)	Einband(m)	encuadernación	encadernação
rilievo	relief	relief	Relief(n)	relieve	relevo
rimandare, aggiornare	ajourner	postpone, adjourn	vertagen	aplazar	adiar
rimanere, avanzare	rester	left(be), remain	übrig = bleiben, bleiben	quedar	sobrar
rimbalzare	rebondir	bounce, rebound	ab = prallen, aufprallen	rebotar	ressaltar
rimbombare	résonner	resound, sound	klingen	resonar	ressoar, ecoar
rimborsare	rembourser	pay back, reimburse	zurück = zahlen	reembolsar	reembolsar
rimborso	remboursement	repayment	Rückzahlung(f)	reembolso	reembolso
rimedio	remède	remedy	Heilmittel(n)	remedio	remédio
rimessa, sconto	remise, rabais	reduction	Nachlaß, Ermäßigung	descuento	desconto
rimontaggio	remontage	reassembly	Zusammensetzen(n)	volver a montar	nova montagem
rimontare	remonter	reassemble	wieder montieren	volver a montar	tornar a montar
rimorchiare	remorquer	tow	ab = schleppen	remolcar	rebocar
rimorchio	remorque	trailer	Anhänger(m)	remolque	reboque
rimorso	remords	remorse	Gewissensbiß(m)	remordimiento	remorso
rimpatrio	rapatriement	repatriation	Repatriierung(f)	repatriación	repatriação
rimpiangere	regretter	regret	nach = trauern(jdm/etw)	lamentar, añorar	lamentar
rimpianto	regret	regret	Bedauern(n)	lamento(lo)	pena; pesar
rimproverare	reprocher	reproach	vor = werfen	reprochar	censurar
rimunerazione	rémunération	remuneration	Entlohnung(f), Lohn(m)	remuneración	remuneração
rimuovere	enlever, retirer	remove	ab = nehmen	quitar, retirar	remover, retirar
rinchiudere	enfermer	shut in	ein = schließen	encerrar	encerrar, fechar
rinculo	recul	recoil	Rückstoß(m)	retroceso	recuo
rinforzare	renforcer	reinforce	verstärken	reforzar	reforçar
rinforzo	renfort	reinforcement	Verstärkung(f)	refuerzo	reforço
rinfrescare	rafraîchir	cool	ab = kühlen	refrescar	refrescar
ringraziamento	remerciement	thanks	Dank(m)	agradecimiento	agradecimento
ringraziare	remercier	thank	danken; bedanken, sich	agradecer	agradecer
rinnegare	renier	disown; renounce	verleugnen, verneinen	renegar	renegar
rinnovare	renouveler	renew	erneuern	renovar	renovar
rinnovazione	rénovation	renovation	Renovation(f)	renovación	restauração
rinnovo	renouvellement	renewal	Erneuerung(f)	renovación	renovação
rinunciare	renoncer	give up	auf = geben	renunciar	desistir; renunciar
rinviare	renvoyer	send back, return	zurück = schicken	devolver	devolver
rinviare	reporter	postpone	verschieben	postergar	adiar
riparare	réparer	repair, mend	reparieren	reparar	reparar
riparazione	réparation	repair	Reparation(f)	reparación	reparação
riparo, rifugio	abri, refuge	shelter	Obdach(n), Schutz(m)	abrigo, refugio	abrigo, refúgio
ripartire	répartir	share out	auf = teilen	repartir	repartir
ripartizione	répartition	distribution	Verteilung(f)	reparto	repartição
ripetere	répéter	repeat	wieder = holen	repetir	repetir
ripido, a	raide, escarpé, e	steep	steil	empinado, a	empinado, a

I

Italian	French	English	German	Spanish	Portuguese
ripido, a; scosceso, a	abrupt, e	steep	steil	abrupto, a	abrupto, a
riportare	rapporter	bring back	zurück = bringen	traer	trazer
riportare	ramener	bring back	wieder = bringen	devolver, traer	trazer
riposarsi	reposer(se)	rest	aus = ruhen, sich	descansar	descançar
riposo	repos	rest	Ruhe(f)	descanso	descanço
riprese	tournage	shooting	Filmaufnahme(f)	rodaje	filmagem
riprodurre	reproduire	reproduce	reproduzieren	reproducir	reproduzir
riprodurre(-rsi)	reproduire(se)	breed(animals)	fort = pflanzen, sich	reproducir(se)	reproduzir-se
riproduzione	reproduction	reproduction	Reproduktion(f)	reproducción	reprodução
risarcimento	indemnité	compensation	Entschädigung(f)	indemnidad	indemnização
riscaldamento	échauffement	heating	Aufwärmen(n)	calentamiento	aquecimento
riscaldamento	chauffage	heating	Heizung(f)	calefacción	aquecimento
riscaldare	réchauffer	warm, (re)heat	auf = wärmen	recalentar	aquecer
riscaldare	chauffer	heat	heizen	calentar	aquecer
riscatto	rançon	ransom	Lösegeld(n)	rescate	resgate
rischiare	risquer	risk	riskieren	arriesgar	arriscar
rischio	risque	risk	Risiko(n)	riesgo	risco
rischio	aléa	hazard	Zufall(m)	riesgo, azar	acaso
riserva	réserve	reserve	Reserve(f)	reserva	reserva
riservare	réserver	reserve	reservieren	reservar	reservar
risiedere	résider	reside	wohnen	residir	residir
riso, ridere	rire	laugh, laughter	Lachen(n)	risa	riso
riso	riz	rice	Reis(m)	arroz	arroz
risolvere	résoudre	solve, resolve	lösen	resolver	resolver
risolvere	régler	settle	regeln; erledigen	resolver	resolver
risolvere	solutionner	solve	lösen	solucionar	solucionar
risorsa	ressource(s)	resources	Mittel(n, pl)	recurso	recurso
risparmiare	épargner	save	sparen	ahorrar	poupar
risparmiatore, trice	épargnant, e	saver, investor	Sparer(in f)m	ahorrador, a	aforrador, a
risparmio	économie, épargne	saving	Ersparnis(f)	economía, ahorro	economia
rispettabile	respectable	respectable	achtbar	respetable	respeitável
rispettare	respecter	respect	respektieren	respetar	respeitar
rispettivamente	respectivement	respectively	beziehungsweise	respectivamente	respectivamente
rispetto	respect	respect	Respekt(m)	respeto	respeito
rispondere	répondre	answer, reply	antworten	contestar	responder
rispondere	répondre	reply, answer	erwidern	responder	responder
risposta	réponse	answer, reply	Antwort(f)	respuesta	resposta
risposta	riposte	counter-attack	Gegenangriff(m)	réplica	réplica
rissa, zuffa	bagarre	fight	Schlägerei(f)	riña	briga
ristorante	restaurant	restaurant	Restaurant(n)	restaurante	restaurante
ristringere	resserrer	narrow	verengen	estrechar	estreitar
risultare	résulter, être	result, be	ergeben, sich	resultar	resultar
risultato, esito	résultat	result	Ergebnis(n)	resultado	resultado
ritardare	retarder	delay	verzögern	retrasar, demorar	atrasar, demorar
ritardo	retard	delay; lateness	Verspätung(f)	atraso	atraso
ritardo(essere in)	retard(être en)	late(to be)	zu spät kommen	retrasado, a(estar)	atrasado, a(estar)
ritirare	retirer	withdraw	zurück = ziehen	retirar	retirar
ritmo	rythme	rhythm	Takt(m), Rhythmus(m)	ritmo	ritmo
rito	rite	rite; ritual	Brauch(m), Ritus(m)	rito	rito
ritornare	revenir	come back, return	zurück = kommen	volver	voltar
ritornello	refrain	refrain, chorus	Refrain(m)	estribillo	refrão
ritorno	retour	return	Rückkehr(f)	regreso, vuelta	regresso, volta
ritratto	portrait	portrait	Porträt(n)	retrato	retrato
riunione	réunion	meeting; reunion	Treffen(n)	reunión	reunião
riunire	réunir	gather(together)	sammeln	reunir	reunir
riunirsi	réunir(se)	meet	treffen, sich	reunirse	reunir-se
riuscire	réussir	succeed	gelingen	lograr, conseguir	conseguir
riuscita	réussite	success(-es)	Erfolg(m)	éxito, logro	êxito
riva	rive	bank	Ufer(n)	orilla, margen	margem
riva	rivage	shore	Küstenstrich(m)	orilla	beira-mar
riva	bord de mer	sea-side	Küste(f)	orilla del mar	beira-mar
rivale	rival, e	rival; competitor	Rivale(m), Rivalin(f)	rival	rival
rivalità	rivalité	rivalry	Rivalität(f)	rivalidad	rivalidade
rivedere	revoir	see again	wieder = sehen	volver a ver	voltar a ver
rivelare	révéler	reveal	auf = decken	revelar	revelar
rivelatore	détecteur	detector	Anzeiger(m)	detector	detector
rivelazione	détection	detection	Aufspüren(n)	detección	detecção
rivendicare	revendiquer	claim	beanspruchen	reivindicar	reivindicar

Italian	French	English	German	Spanish	Portuguese
rivendicazione	revendication	claim, demand	Forderung(f)	reivindicación	reivindicação
riversare, scaricare	déverser	pour out, tip	aus=gießen	verter	despejar
rivista, periodico	revue, magazine	review, magazine	Zeitschrift, Revue(f)	revista	revista
rivista	magazine	magazine	Illustrierte(f)	revista	revista
rivolta	révolte	revolt	Revolte(f)	revuelta	revolta
rivoluzionario, a	révolutionnaire	revolutionary	revolutionär	revolucionario, a	revolucionário, a
rivoluzione	révolution	revolution	Revolution(f)	revolución	revolução
roba, oggetti	affaires	things	Sachen(pl)	cosas	coisas
robot	robot	robot	Roboter(m)	robot	robot
robusto, a	robuste	robust, sturdy	robust, stark	robusto, a	robusto, a
robusto, a; forte	robuste, solide	sturdy	kräftig, fest	vigoroso, a; fuerte	robusto, a; forte
roccia	roche, rocher	rock	Fels(m)	roca	rocha
rodaggio	rodage	running in	Einfahren(n)	rodaje	rodagem
rodere	ronger	gnaw	zernagen	roer	roer
romantico, a	romantique	romantic	romantisch	romántico, a	romântico, a
romanziere, a	romancier, ière	novelist	Schriftsteller(in f)m	novelista	romancista
romanzo	roman	novel	Roman(m)	novela	romance
rombo	losange	diamond-shaped	Raute(f), Rhombus(m)	rombo	losango
rompere	rompre	break	brechen(ab=-; zer-)	romper	romper
rompere	casser, briser	break	zerbrechen	romper	quebrar, partir
rondella	rondelle	washer	Scheibe(f)	arandela	anilha
rondine	hirondelle	swallow	Schwalbe(f)	golondrina	andorinha
rosa	rose	rose	Rose(f)	rosa	rosa
rosa	rose	pink	rosafarben	rosa	cor-de-rosa
rosolia	rubéole	German measles	Röteln(pl)	rubéola	rubéola
rossetto	rouge à lèvres	lipstick	Lippenstift(m)	barra de labios	baton
rosso, a	rouge	red	rot	rojo, a	vermelho, a
rosso, a	roux, rousse	auburn; reddish	rothaarig	pelirrojo, a	ruivo, a
rotaia	rail	rail; track	Schiene(f)	carril	carril
rotazione	rotation	rotation	Drehung(f)	rotación	rotação
roteare	tourner(faire)	rotate, revolve	drehen	girar(hacer)	girar(fazer)
rotolare	rouler	roll	rollen	rodar	rolar
rotolo; rullo	rouleau	roll	Rolle(f), Walze(f)	rollo	rolo
rotonda, rotatoria	rond-point	roundabout	Kreisverkehr(m)	glorieta	rotunda
rotondo, a	rond, e	round	rund	redondo, a	redondo, a
rotta, itinerario	itinéraire, route	route	Route(f), Weg(m)	ruta, itinerario	caminho, rota
rotta	cap	head for	Kurs(m)	rumbo a	rumo
rottura	rupture	rupture	Bruch(m)	ruptura	ruptura
rotula	rotule	knee-cap	Kniescheibe(f)	rótula	rótula
roulotte	caravane	caravan	Wohnwagen(m)	caravana	caravana
routine, tran tran	routine	routine	Routine(f)	rutina	rotina
rovesciare	renverser	spill, knock over	verschütten	derramar, volcar	entornar
rovesciarsi	renverser(se)	overturn	überschlagen, sich	volcarse	virar; cair
rovescio	envers	reverse, back	Rückseite(f)	revés	avesso
rovina	ruine	ruin	Ruine(f)	ruina	ruína
rovina	ruine	ruin	Trümmer(m, pl)	ruina	ruína
rovinare	ruiner	ruin	ruinieren	arruinar	arruinar
rubare	voler	steal, rob	stehlen	robar	roubar
rubinetto	robinet	tap; stop-cock	Wasserhahn(m), Hahn(m)	grifo	torneira
rubinetto	robinet	cock, tap	Hahn(m)(Wasser-; Gas-)	llave, grifo	torneira
rubino	rubis	ruby	Rubin(m)	rubí	rubi
ruffiano, prosseneta	proxénète	pimp	Zuhälter(m)	proxeneta	proxeneta
ruga	ride	wrinkle	Falte(f)	arruga	ruga
ruggine	rouille	rust	Rost(m)	herrumbre	ferrugem
rugiada	rosée	dew	Tau(m)	rocío	orvalho
rugoso, a	rugueux, se	rough, harsh	rauh	rugoso, a	rugoso, a
rumore	bruit	noise	Geräusch(n)	ruido	ruído, barulho
rumoroso, a	bruyant, e	noisy; loud	laut	ruidoso, a	barulhento, a
ruolo, parte	rôle	role, part	Rolle(f)	cometido, función	função
ruota	roue	wheel	Rad(n)	rueda	roda
rurale	rural, e	rural	ländlich	rural	rural
ruscello	ruisseau	stream, brook	Bach(m)	riachuelo, arroyo	regato, ribeiro
russare	ronfler	snore	schnarchen	roncar	ressonar, roncar
rustico, a	rustique	rustic	ländlich, einfach	rústico, a	rústico, a
ruttare	roter	burp	auf=stoßen, rülpsen	eructar	arrotar

S

Italian	French	English	German	Spanish	Portuguese
sabato	samedi	Saturday	Samstag(m)	sábado	sábado
sabbia	sable	sand	Sand(m)	arena	areia
sabotaggio	sabotage	sabotage	Sabotage(f)	sabotaje	sabotagem
sabotare	saboter	sabotage	sabotieren	sabotear	sabotar
saccheggiare	saccager	ransack	verwüsten	saquear	saquear
saccheggio	pillage	plunder, pillage	Plünderung(f)	saqueo	pilhagem
sacco	sac	sack	Sack(m)	saco	saco
sacco a pelo	sac de couchage	sleeping bag	Schlafsack(m)	saco de dormir	saco-cama
saccoccia, borsa	sacoche	bag	Tasche(f)(Umhänge-)	cartera	saco
sacrificare	sacrifier	sacrifice	opfern	sacrificar	sacrificar
sacrificio	sacrifice	sacrifice	Opfer(n)	sacrificio	sacrifício
sacrilegio	sacrilège	sacrilege	Entweihung(f)	sacrilegio	sacrilégio
sacro, a	sacré, e	holy; sacred	heilig	sagrado, a	sagrado, a
sadico, a	sadique	sadistic	sadistisch	sádico, a	sádico, a
sadico, a	sadique	sadist	Sadist(in f)m	sádico, a	sádico, a
saggio, a; savio, a	sage	sage, wise man	Weise(m)	sabio	sábio
sagoma; silhouette	silhouette	outline	Silhouette(f)	silueta	silhueta
sala, stanza	salle	room	Saal(m), Raum(m)	sala	sala
sala da ballo	dancing	dance-hall	Tanzlokal(n)	sala de baile	dancing
sala da pranzo	salle à manger	dining-room	Eßzimmer(n)	comedor	sala de jantar
sala da tè	salon de thé	tea-room	Café(n), Konditorei(f)	salón de té	casa de chá
sala d'attesa	salle d'attente	waiting-room	Wartezimmer(n)	sala de espera	sala de espera
salariato, a	salarié, e	salaried employee	Arbeitnehmer(in f)m	asalariado, a	assalariado, a
salario	salaire	salary, wage	Lohn(m), Gehalt(n)	salario	salário
salato, a	salé, e	salty	salzig	salado, a	salgado, a
saldare, liquidare	solder	sell off	aus = verkaufen	saldar	saldar
saldatura	soudure	welding	Schweißen(n)	soldadura	soldadura
saldi	soldes	sales	Ausverkauf(m)	saldos, rebajas	saldos
saldo	règlement	settlement	Begleichung(f)	liquidación	pagamento
sale	sel	salt	Salz(n)	sal	sal
salire	monter	climb; rise; go up	steigen	subir	subir
salire	monter	get into, get on	ein = steigen	subir	subir a, entrar
salita, pendio	côte	hill, slope	Abhang(m), Steigung(f)	cuesta	ladeira, encosta
salita	montée	rise	Steigung(f)	subida	subida
saliva	salive	saliva	Speichel(m)	saliva	saliva
salmone	saumon	salmon	Lachs(m)	salmón	salmão
salone	salon	show, exhibition	Messe(f)	salón	salão
salotto	salon	lounge	Herrenzimmer(n)	sala	sala de estar
salsiccia	saucisse	sausage	Wurst(f)	salchicha	salsicha
saltare	sauter	jump	springen	saltar	saltar, pular
saltare, balzare	bondir	jump, leap	springen	saltar	saltar
salto, balzo	saut, bond	jump, leap, spring	Sprung(m)	salto, brinco	salto, pulo
salumeria	charcuterie	delicatessen shop	Metzgerei(f)	salchichería	salsicharia
salutare	saluer	greet; say hello	begrüßen	saludar	saudar
salute	santé	health	Gesundheit(f)	salud	saúde
salvagente	bouée	lifebelt	Rettungsring(m)	salvavidas	bóia
salvare	sauver	save	retten	salvar	salvar
salvataggio	sauvetage	rescue	Rettung(f)	salvamento	salvamento
salvataggio	sauvetage	salvage	Bergung(f)	salvamento	salvamento
salvo	sauf	except	außer	excepto	salvo, excepto
salvo, a	sauf, ve	safe	sicher	salvo, a	salvo, a
sandalo	sandale	sandal	Sandale(f)	sandalia	sandália
sangue	sang	blood	Blut(n)	sangre	sangue
sangue freddo	sang-froid	cool, calm	Kaltblütigkeit(f)	sangre fría	sangue-frio
sanguinare	saigner	bleed	bluten	sangrar	sangrar
sanitario, a	sanitaire	sanitary	Gesundheits-	sanitario, a	sanitário, a
sano, a	sain, e	healthy	gesund	sano, a	são, sã
santo, a	saint, e	holy	heilig	santo, a; san	santo, a
santo, a	saint, e	saint	Heilige(m, f)	santo, a	santo, a
santuario	sanctuaire	sanctuary	Heiligtum(n)	santuario	santuário
sanzione	sanction	sanction	Strafe(f)	sanción	sanção

sapere	savoir	know	wissen	saber	saber
sapere	savoir	knowledge	Wissen(n)	saber	sabedoria
sapone	savon	soap	Seife(f)	jabón	sabão
sapore	saveur	flavour	Geschmack(m)	sabor	sabor
saporito, a	savoureux, se	tasty	schmackhaft	sabroso, a	saboroso, a
saracinesca	vanne	gate; valve	Klappe(f)	compuerta	comporta
sardina	sardine	sardine	Sardine(f)	sardina	sardinha
sarto, a	couturier, ière	dressmaker, tailor	Schneider(in f)m	modista	costureiro, a
sarto	tailleur	tailor	Schneider(m)	sastre	alfaiate
sasso	caillou	stone, pebble	Stein(m)	piedra	calhau
satellite	satellite	satellite	Satellit(m)	satélite	satélite
saturare	saturer	saturate	sättigen	saturar	saturar
saturazione	saturation	saturation	Übersättigung(f)	saturación	saturação
sauna	sauna	sauna	Sauna(f)	sauna	sauna
savana	savane	savannah	Savanne(f)	sabana	savana
savoir-faire	savoir-faire	know-how	Geschick(n)	tacto, maña	habilidade
sbadigliare	bâiller	yawn	gähnen	bostezar	bocejar
sbagliarsi	tromper(se)	mistaken(be)	täuschen, sich	equivocarse	enganar-se
sbalorditivo, a	étourdissant, e	deafening	betäubend	aturdidor, a	atroador, a
sbarazzare	débarrasser	clear, rid	weg = räumen	quitar, tirar	desembaraçar
sbarcare	débarquer	disembark, land	Land gehen(an)	desembarcar	desembarcar
sbarcare	débarquer	unload	aus = laden	descargar	descarregar
sbarra	barre	bar	Stange(f)	barra	barra
sbarrato, a	barré, e	blocked	gesperrt	cortado, a	impedido, a
sbattere	cogner(se)	knock	stoßen, sich	golpe(darse un)	chocar com
sbavare	baver	dribble	sabbern	babear	babar-se
sbloccare	débloquer	release	deblockieren, lösen	desbloquear	desbloquear
sborsare	débourser	spend	aus = geben	desembolsar	desembolsar
sbrigarsi	dépêcher(se)	hurry(up)	beeilen, sich	darse prisa	despachar-se
sbrinare	dégivrer	de-ice; defrost	ab = tauen	descongelar	descongelar
sbrogliare	débrouiller	clear up	entwirren	desenredar	desenredar
sbucciare	éplucher	peel	schälen	pelar	descascar
sbucciare	peler	peel	schälen	mondar	descascar
scabbia, rogna	gale	scabies	Krätze(f)	sarna	sarna
scacchi	échecs	chess	Schachspiel(n)	ajedrez	xadrês
scadenza	échéance	expiration	Fälligkeitstermin(m)	vencimiento	vencimento
scadere	expirer	expire	ab = laufen	expirar; vencer	expirar
scaduto, a	périmé, e	expired	verfallen	caducado, a	caducado, a
scafandro	scaphandre	diving-suit	Taucheranzug(m)	escafandra	escafandro
scaffale	étagère	shelf(-ves)	Regal(n)	estantería	prateleira
scafo	coque	hull	Rumpf(m)	casco	casco
scala	escalier	staircase, stairs	Treppe(f)	escalera	escada
scala	échelle	ladder	Leiter(f)	escalera	escada
scala	échelle	scale	Tabelle(f), Skala(f)	escala	escala
scalfire	égratigner	scratch	kratzen, schrammen	rasguñar	arranhar
scalfittura	éraflure	scratch, graze	Kratzer(m), Schramme f	rasguño	arranhadura
scalino	marche	step	Stufe(f)	peldaño, escalón	degrau
scalo	escale	stop(over)	Zwischenlandung(f)	escala	escala
scambiare	échanger	exchange	tauschen	intercambiar	trocar
scambio	échange	exchange	Tausch(Aus-, Um-)(m)	cambio	troca; câmbio
scampato, a	rescapé, e	survivor	Überlebende(f, m)	superviviente	sobrevivente
scampo	langoustine	Dublin Bay prawn	Langustine(f)	langostino	lagostim
scanalatura	rainure	groove	Rille(f), Nute(f)	ranura	ranhura
scandalo	scandale	scandal	Skandal(m)	escándalo	escândalo
scantinato	sous-sol	basement	Untergeschoß(n)	sótano	cave
scapolo; nubile	célibataire	single, unmarried	ledig	soltero, a	solteiro, a
scapolo, nubile	célibataire	bachelor; single -	Junggeselle m/-sellin	soltero, a	solteiro, a
scappare	échapper(s')	escape	fliehen	escapar(se)	escapar-se
scaricare	décharger	unload	ab = laden, aus = laden	descargar	descarregar
scarico	déchargement	unloading	Ausladen(n)	descarga	descarga
scarpa, e	chaussure	shoe	Schuh(m)	calzado	sapato
scarpa	soulier	shoe	Schuh(m)	zapato	sapato
scarto	déchet	waste	Abfall(m)	residuo	resíduo
scatola	boîte	box	Schachtel(f)	caja	caixa
scattare, attivare	déclencher	trigger off	aus = lösen	iniciar	desencadear
scavare	creuser	dig	graben	cavar	cavar
scavare	fouiller	excavate	aus = graben	excavar	escavar
scegliere	choisir	choose, select	aus = wählen	escoger	escolher

Italian	French	English	German	Spanish	Portuguese
scelta	choix	choice	Wahl(f)	escogimiento	escolha
scemo, a; minorato, a	débile	crazy, mad	verrückt; schwach	débil	parvo, a
scena	scène	scene	Szene(f)	escena	cena
scena	scène	stage	Szene(f), Bühne(f)	escena	cena
scenario	scénario	script(film -)	Drehbuch(n)	guión	guião
scenarista	scénariste	script-writer	Drehbuchautor(in f)m	guionista	cenarista
scendere	descendre	go down, descend	herunter = gehen	descender, bajar	descer, baixar
scendere	descendre	get out of; get off	aus = steigen	bajarse	descer
scenografia	décors	set, scenery	Dekor(m), Bühnenbild n	decorado	cenários
scettico, a	sceptique	sceptic(al)	skeptisch	escéptico, a	céptico, a
scheda, cartella	fiche	card	Karteikarte(f)	ficha	ficha
schedario	fichier	card-index	Kartei(f)	fichero	ficheiro
schedario	classeur	file	Ordner(m)	clasificador	classificador
scheletro	squelette	skeleton	Skelett(n)	esqueleto	esqueleto
schema	schéma	diagram	Schema(n)	esquema	esquema
schema, piano	plan, projet	scheme, plan	Plan(m)	plan, proyecto	plano, projecto
scherma	escrime	fencing	Fechten(n)	esgrima	esgrima
schermo	écran	screen	Bildschirm; Leinwand	pantalla	écran
schermo	écran	screen	Wandschirm(m)	pantalla	painel
scherzare	plaisanter	joke	scherzen	bromear	gracejar
scherzo	plaisanterie	joke	Witz(m)	chiste, gracia	brincadeira
scherzo	blague	joke	Witz(m)	chiste	anedota, chalaça
scherzo	farce	joke; farce	Streich(m)	broma	partida
scherzo, burla	canular	joke, hoax	Ulk(m), Witz(m)	broma	partida
schiacciare	écraser	crush, flatten	zerquetschen	aplastar	esmagar
schiaffo	claque	slap	Ohrfeige(f)	bofetada	bofetada
schiaffo	gifle	slap	Ohrfeige(f)	bofetada	bofetada
schiantare	écraser(s')	crash	ab = stürzen	estrellarse	esmagar-se
schiarita, tregua	accalmie	lull	Wetterberuhigung(f)	calma	acalmia
schiavitú	esclavage	slavery	Sklaverei(f)	esclavitud	escravatura
schiavo, a	esclave	slave	Sklave(m), Sklavin(f)	esclavo, a	escravo, a
schiena	dos	back	Rücken(m)	espalda	costas
schiudere, uscire	éclore	hatch	aus = schlüpfen	abrirse	abrir-se
schiuma	mousse	froth, foam	Schaum(m)	espuma	espuma
schiuma	écume	foam, froth	Schaum(m), Gischt(f)	espuma	espuma
schizzare	jaillir	spring	springen; sprudeln	brotar, surgir	brotar
schizzo	croquis	sketch(-es)	Skizze(f)	croquis	esboço
sci	ski	ski	Ski(m)	esquí	esqui
sci nautico	ski nautique	water-skiing	Wasserski(m)	esquí acuático	esqui aquático
scia	sillage	wake	Kielwasser(n)	estela	esteira
sciabola	sabre	sabre	Säbel(m)	sable	sabre
schiaffo	tape, fessée	smack	Schlag(m)	cachete	palmada
scialle	châle	shawl	Schal(m)	chal	xale
sciare	skier	ski	skifahren	esquiar	esquiar
sciarpa	écharpe	scarf	Halstuch(n), Schal(m)	bufanda	cachecol, cachené
sciarpa	cache-nez	scarf	Schal(m)	bufanda	cachecol
sciatica	sciatique	sciatica	Ischias(m)	ciática	ciática
scientifico, a	scientifique	scientific	wissenschaftlich	científico, a	científico, a
scienza	science	science	Wissenschaft(f)	ciencia	ciência
scienziato	scientifique	scientist	Wissenschaftler(m)	científico	cientista
scienziato	savant	scientist	Gelehrte(f, m)	científico	cientista
scimmia	singe	monkey	Affe(m)	mono	macaco
scintilla	étincelle	spark	Funken(m)	chispa	faísca
scintillare	scintiller	sparkle	flimmern	centellear	cintilar
sciocchezza	bêtise	stupid thing(do a)	Dummheit(f)	estupidez	asneira
sciocchezza	sottise	silliness	Dummheit(f)	tontería	estupidez
sciocco, a	bête; sot, te	silly, foolish	dumm	tonto, a	tolo, a; burro, a
sciogliere	dissoudre	dissolve	auf = lösen	disolver	dissolver
sciogliere(-rsi)	fondre	melt	schmelzen	derretir	derreter
sciolto, a	fondu, e	melted	geschmolzen	derretido, a	derretido, a
sciopero	grève	strike	Streik(m)	huelga	greve
sciroppo	sirop	cordial, squash	Saft(m), Sirup(m)	almíbar	xarope
sciroppo	sirop	syrup, medicine	Sirup(m)	jarabe	xarope
sciupare, rovinare	abîmer	damage, spoil, ruin	beschädigen	estropear	estragar
scivolare	glisser	slip, slide	rutschen	resbalar	escorregar
scivolo	toboggan	slide, chute	Rutschbahn(f)	tobogán	escorrega
sclerosi	sclérose	sclerosis(-ses)	Sklerose(f)	esclerósis	esclerose
scodella	bol	bowl	Trinkschale(f)	tazón	tigela; malga

Italian	French	English	German	Spanish	Portuguese
scogliera	falaise	cliff	Steilküste(f)	acantilado	falésia
scoglio	récif	reef	Riff(n)	arrecife	recife
scoiattolo	écureuil	squirrel	Eichhörnchen(n)	ardilla	esquilo
scolarità	scolarité	schooling	Schulzeit(f)	escolaridad	escolaridade
scolaro, a	écolier, ière	schoolboy/girl	Schüler(in f)m	colegial, a	aluno, a
scoliosi	scoliose	scoliosis	Skoliose(f)	escoliosis	escoliose
scommessa	pari	bet	Wette(f)	apuesta	aposta
scompartimento	compartiment	compartment	Abteil(n)	compartimiento	compartimento
scompiglio	branle-bas	upheaval	Durcheinander(n)	zafarrancho	agitação
sconcertante	déconcertant, e	disconcerting	verwirrend	desconcertante	desconcertante
sconfitta	défaite	defeat	Niederlage(f)	derrota	derrota
sconforto	détresse	distress	Verzweiflung(f)	angustia	aflição, angústia
scongelare	décongeler	thaw	auf = tauen	descongelar	descongelar
sconosciuto, a	inconnu, e	unknown	unbekannt	desconocido, a	desconhecido, a
sconsigliare	déconseiller	advise against	ab = raten	desaconsejar	desaconselhar
scontento	mécontentement	displeasure	Unzufriedenheit(f)	descontento	descontentamento
scontento, a	mécontent, e	displeased	unzufrieden	descontento, a	descontente
sconto	escompte	discount	Skonto(m)	descuento	desconto
sconvolto, a	bouleversé, e	overwhelmed	erschüttert	conmocionado, a	perturbado, a
scopa	balai	brush, broom	Besen(m)	escoba	vassoura
scoperta	découverte	discovery	Entdeckung(f)	descubrimiento	descoberta
scopo	but	aim, purpose	Ziel(n)	propósito	fim, intento
scoppiare	crever, éclater	burst	bersten	estallar, reventar	furar, rebentar
scoppiare	éclater	burst	platzen	reventar	rebentar
scoprire	découvrir	discover	entdecken	descubrir	descobrir
scoraggiante	décourageant, e	discouraging	entmutigend	desalentador, a	desanimador, a
scoraggiare	décourager	discourage	entmutigen	desalentar	desalentar
scoraggiato, a	découragé, e	discouraged	entmutigt	desanimado, a	desalentado, a
scoraggiato, a	découragé, e	disheartened	mutlos, verzagt	desalentado, a	desalentado, a
scorciatoia	raccourci	short cut	Abkürzung(f)	atajo	atalho
scorgere	apercevoir	perceive, notice	bemerken	avistar, divisar	avistar
scorpione	scorpion	scorpion	Skorpion(m)	escorpión	escorpião
scorrere	couler	flow, run	fließen	correr, fluir	correr
scorrere, defluire	écouler(s')	run, flow	ab = fließen	correr, fluir	escorrer
scorretto, a	incorrect, e	incorrect, wrong	unrichtig, falsch	incorrecto, a	incorrecto, a
scorta	escorte	escort	Gefolge(n)	escolta	escolta
scorza, buccia	écorce	bark	Rinde(f)	corteza	casca
scosceso, a	escarpé, e	steep	steil	escarpado, a	escarpado, a
scossa	secousse	jolt, jerk	Ruck(m), Stoß(m)	sacudida	abalo
scotch	scotch	sellotape	Tesafilm(m)	papel celo	fita adesiva
scottatura	coup de soleil	sunburn	Sonnenbrand(m)	insolación	insolação
screpolato, a	craquelé, e	crackled, cracked	rissig	agrietado, a	estalado, a
screpolatura	gerçure	chap(ped)	Riß(m), Hautriß(m)	grieta	greta
scricchiolare	craquer	crack	krachen	crujir	estalar
scrittore, -trice	écrivain	writer	Schriftsteller(in f)m	escritor, a	escritor, a
scrittura	écriture	writing	Schrift(f)	escritura	escrita
scrivania	bureau	desk	Schreibtisch(m)	escritorio	secretária
scrivere	écrire	write	schreiben	escribir	escrever
scrupolo	scrupule	scruple	Skrupel(m)	escrúpulo	escrúpulo
scrutare	scruter	scan, scrutinize	erforschen	escudriñar	perscrutar
scrutinio	scrutin, vote	poll; ballot	Wahl(f), Abstimmung(f)	escrutinio	escrutínio
scucito, a	décousu, e	unstitched	abgetrennt	descosido, a	descosido, a
scuderia	écurie	stable	Pferdestall(m)	cuadra	cavalariça
sculacciata	fessée	spanking	Hinternvoll(m)	azotaina, paliza	surra, açoite
scultura	sculpture	sculpture	Skulptur(f)	escultura	escultura
scuola	école	school	Schule(f)	escuela	escola
scuola media	collège	comprehensive(Jnr)	Oberschule(f)	escuela(EGB)	escola preparatória
scuotere	secouer	shake	schütteln	sacudir	sacudir
scuro, a	sombre; obscur, e	dark	dunkel	oscuro, a	escuro, a; sombrio, a
scusa	excuse	excuse; apology	Entschuldigung(f)	excusa, disculpa	desculpa
scusa, perdono	pardon	forgiveness	Vergebung(f)	perdón	perdão
scusarsi	excuser(s')	apologize	entschuldigen, sich	disculpar(se)	desculpar-se
scusi(mi)	excuse(je m')	sorry(I am)	es tut mir leid	siento(lo)	desculpe!
scusi!	excusez-moi!	excuse me!; sorry!	Entschuldigung!	perdone(!)	desculpe!; perdão!
scusi!	pardon!	sorry!, excuse me!	Verzeihung!	perdón(!), disculpe	perdão!, desculpe!
sdoganare	dédouaner	clear(customs)	verzollen	retirar aduana	desalfandegar
sdraiarsi	allonger(s')	lie down	hin = legen, sich	acostarse	estender-se
sdraio	chaise longue	deck-chair	Liegestuhl(m)	hamaca	preguiceira

Italian	French	English	German	Spanish	Portuguese
se	si	if; whether	wenn; ob	si	se
se(stesso)	soi(-même)	oneself	sich, selbst	si(mismo)	si(mesmo)
sebbene	quoique	although, though	obgleich, obwohl	aunque	embora
seccatura	contrariété	annoyance	Verdruß(m)	molestia	contrariedade
secchio	seau	bucket, pail	Eimer(m)	cubo	balde
secco, a; asciutto, a	sec, sèche	dry	trocken	seco, a	seco, a
secolo	siècle	century	Jahrhundert(n)	siglo	século
seconda mano	occasion	second-hand, used	gebraucht	segunda mano	segunda mão(em)
secondario, a	secondaire	secondary	nebensächlich	secundario, a	secundário, a
secondo, a	second, e	second	zweite	segundo, a	segundo, a
secondo, a	deuxième	second	zweite	segundo, a	segundo, a
secondo	seconde	second	Sekunde(f)	segundo	segundo
secondo	selon	according to	gemäß	según	segundo
secrezione	sécrétion	secretion	Ausscheidung(f)	secreción	secreção
sedativo, a	sédatif, ive	sedative	schmerzlindernd	sedativo, a	sedativo, a
sede	siège	head office	Firmensitz(m)	sede	sede
sedersi	asseoir(s')	sit(down)	setzen, sich	sentarse	sentar-se
sedia	chaise	chair	Stuhl(m)	silla	cadeira
sedia	siège	seat	Sitz(m)	asiento	assento
sedici	seize	sixteen	sechzehn	dieciséis	dezasseis
seducente	séduisant, e	attractive	reizend, anziehend	atractivo, a	atraente
sedurre	séduire	charm; seduce	verführen, verleiten	seducir	seduzir
seduta	séance	session; meeting	Sitzung(f)	sesión	sessão
seduto, a	assis, e	seated	sitzen	sentado, a	sentado, a
seduzione	séduction	seduction	Verführung(f)	seducción	sedução
sega	scie	saw	Säge(f)	sierra	serra
segale	seigle	rye	Roggen(m)	centeno	centeio
segare	scier	saw	sägen	serrar, aserrar	serrar
segmento	segment	segment	Abschnitt(m)	segmento	segmento
segnalare	signaler	point out	melden; an = zeigen	señalar	assinalar
segnalazione	signalisation	sign	Beschilderung(f)	señalización	sinalização
segnale	signal	signal	Signal(n)	señal	sinal
segnare	cocher, noter	tick	an = kreuzen	marcar	marcar
segnare, marcare	marquer, pointer	mark	markieren	marcar	marcar
segnare	marquer	score	schießen(Tor-)	marcar	marcar
segno	signe	sign	Zeichen(n)	signo	sinal, signo
segno, marca	marque, trace	mark	Spur(f)	señal, marca	marca, vestígio
segregazione	ségrégation	segregation	Trennung(f)	segregación	segregação
segretario, a	secrétaire	secretary	Sekretär(in f)m	secretario, a	secretário, a
segreto, a	secret, ète	secret	geheim	secreto, a	secreto, a
segreto	secret	secret	Geheimnis(n)	secreto	segredo
seguace, adepto, a	adepte	follower	Anhänger(in f)m	adepto, a; seguidor	adepto, a; seguidor, a
seguente	suivant, e	following, next	nächste	siguiente	seguinte
seguire	suivre	follow	folgen	seguir	seguir
seguito	suite	continuation	Folge(f)	continuación	continuação
seguito(facendo)	suite à	further to	Anschluß an(im)	contestación(en)	consequência(em)
seguito a(in)	suite(à la)	following	hinter, nach	después de	seguir a(a)
sei	six	six	sechs	seis	seis
selce, selciato	pavé	paving-stone	Pflasterstein(m)	adoquín	pedra de calçada
selezionare	sélectionner	select	aus = lesen	seleccionar	seleccionar
selezione	sélection	selection	Auslese(f); Auswahl(f)	selección	selecção
sella	selle	saddle	Sattel(m)	silla	sela
sellino	selle	saddle	Sattel(m)	sillín	selim
selvaggina	gibier	game	Wild(n)	caza	caça
selvaggio, a	sauvage	wild	wild	salvaje	selvagem
selvatico, a	farouche	wild	wild	feroz	arisco, a
sembrare	sembler	seem	scheinen	parecer	parecer
seme	graine	seed	Samenkorn(n)	semilla	semente
seme, semente	semence	seed	Samen(m)	simiente	semente
seme	pépin	pip	Kern(m)	pepita	caroço
semi	semi	semi, half	halb	semi	semi
semi-; mezzo-	mi-	half(-); mid-	halb-	medio, a	meio, a
seminare	semer	sow	säen	sembrar	semear
semplice	simple	simple	einfach	simple	simples
semplicemente	simplement	simply	einfach	simplemente	simplesmente
semplicità	simplicité	simplicity	Einfachheit(f)	sencillez	simplicidade
semplificare	simplifier	simplify	vereinfachen	simplificar	simplificar
sempre	toujours	always	immer	siempre	sempre

Italian	French	English	German	Spanish	Portuguese
sempre	toujours	still	immer noch	todavía	ainda
sempre(per)	toujours(pour)	forever	immer(für)	siempre(para, por)	sempre(para)
senape	moutarde	mustard	Senf(m)	mostaza	mostarda
senato	sénat	senate	Senat(m), Bundesrat(m)	senado	senado
senatore	sénateur	senator	Senator(m)	senador	senador
seno	sein(s)	breast	Busen(m)	seno, pecho	seio
se no; altrimenti	sinon	otherwise, or else	andernfalls, sonst	si no	senão
sensato, a	sensé, e	sensible	vernünftig	sensato, a	sensato, a
sensazione	sensation	sensation; feeling	Empfindung(f)	sensación	sensação
sensibile	sensible	sensitive	empfindlich	sensible	sensível
sensibilità	sensibilité	sensitivity	Sensibilität(f)	sensibilidad	sensibilidade
sensibilizzare	sensibiliser	sensitive(make sb)	sensibilisieren	sensibilizar	sensibilizar
senso	sens	meaning, sense	Bedeutung(f)	sentido	sentido
senso	sens	direction, way	Richtung(f)	sentido	sentido
senso unico	sens unique	one-way	Einbahnstraße(f)	dirección única	sentido único
sensuale	sensuel, le	sensual	sinnlich	sensual	sensual
sensualità	sensualité	sensuality	Sinnlichkeit(f)	sensualidad	sensualidade
sentenza	jugement	sentence	Urteil(n)	sentencia	sentença
sentiero	sentier	footpath, path	Weg(m)	sendero, senda	vereda, atalho
sentimentale	sentimental, e	sentimental	sentimental	sentimental	sentimental
sentimento	sentiment	feeling	Gefühl(n)	sentimiento	sentimento
sentinella	sentinelle	sentry	Wache(f)	centinela	sentinela
sentire	entendre, écouter	hear	hören	oír	ouvir
sentire	sentir	feel	fühlen	sentir	sentir
sentire	ressentir	feel	empfinden	sentir	sentir
senza	sans	without	ohne	sin	sem
separare, dividere	séparer	separate, part	trennen	separar	separar
separazione	séparation	separation	Trennung(f)	separación	separação
sepoltura	sépulture	burial(-place)	Grab(n)	sepultura	sepultura
sequenza	séquence	sequence	Folge(f), Sequenz(f)	secuencia	sequência
sequestrare	séquestrer	lock away	ein = sperren	secuestrar	sequestrar
sera	soir	evening	Abend(m)	tarde, noche	tarde, noite
sera(questa)	soir(ce)	tonight	heute abend	noche(esta)	noite(esta)
serbatoio	réservoir	tank	Tank(m)	depósito	depósito
serenità	sérénité	serenity	Heiterkeit(f)	serenidad	serenidade
sereno, a	serein, e	serene	heiter	sereno, a	sereno, a
sergente	sergent	sergeant	Unteroffizier(m)	sargento	sargento
serie	série	series	Serie(f)	serie	série
serio, a	sérieux, se	serious	ernst, ernsthaft	serio, a	sério, a
serpente	serpent	snake	Schlange(f)	serpiente	serpente
serratura	serrure	lock	Schloß(Tür-)(n)	cerradura	fechadura
servire	servir	serve	dienen, bedienen	servir	servir
servizio	service	service	Dienstleistung(f)	servicio	serviço
servizio	service	service	Bedienung(f)	servicio	serviço
sessanta	soixante	sixty	sechzig	sesenta	sessenta
sessione	session	session	Sitzung(f)	sesión	sessão
sesso	sexe	sex	Geschlecht(n)	sexo	sexo
sessuale	sexuel, le	sexual	geschlechtlich	sexual	sexual
sessualità	sexualité	sexuality	Sexualität(f)	sexualidad	sexualidade
seta	soie	silk	Seide(f)	seda	seda
sete	soif	thirst	Durst(m)	sed	sede
setta	secte	sect	Sekte(f)	secta	seita
settanta	soixante-dix	seventy	siebzig	setenta	setenta
sette	sept	seven	sieben	siete	sete
settembre	septembre	September	September(m)	septiembre	Setembro
settimana	semaine	week	Woche(f)	semana	semana
settimanale	hebdomadaire	weekly	wöchentlich	semanal	semanal
settore	secteur	sector	Bereich(m)	sector	sector
severo, a	sévère	severe, strict	streng	severo, a	severo, a
sevizie	sévices	cruelty	Mißhandlung(f)	malos tratos	sevícias
sezionare	sectionner	cut, divide	schneiden	seccionar	seccionar
sezione	section	section	Schnitt(m)	sección	secção
sfera	sphère	sphere	Sphäre(f)	esfera	esfera
sfera	bille	ball	Kugel(f)	bola	esfera
sfida	défi	challenge	Herausforderung(f)	desafío	desafio
sfidare	défier	challenge	heraus = fordern	desafiar	desafiar
sfidare	braver	defy	trotzen	desafiar	defrontar
sfilata	défilé	parade	Parade(f)	desfile	desfile

Italian	French	English	German	Spanish	Portuguese
sfocato, a	trouble	blurred	verwackelt	desenfocado, a	tremido, a
sfortuna	malchance	ill luck, bad luck	Pech(n), Unglück(n)	mala suerte	má sorte
sfortunato, a	malchanceux, se	unlucky	unglücklich	desafortunado, a	azarento, a
sforzo	effort	effort	Anstrengung(f)	esfuerzo	esforço
sfregio	balafre	gash	Schmiß(m), Schnitt(m)	cuchillada	corte, cutilada
sfruttare	exploiter	exploit	aus = nutzen	explotar	explorar
sfuggire, scappare	échapper	drop	entgleiten	irse, escaparse	escapar
sfumato, a	flou, e	fuzzy, blurred	verschwommen	borroso, a	vago, a
sfumatura	nuance, ton	shade, nuance	Farbenton(m)	matiz	matiz, tom
sgabello	tabouret	stool	Hocker(m)	taburete	escabelo, banco
sgomberare	dégager	clear	frei = machen	despejar	desimpedir
sgombro	maquereau	mackerel	Makrele(f)	caballa	cavala
sgomentare	effarer, effrayer	terrify	erschrecken	espantar, asustar	apavorar
sgonfiare	dégonfler	deflate	Luft raus = lassen	desinflar	desinchar
sgonfio, a	dégonflé, e	deflated, flat	platt, ohne Luft	desinflado, a	vazio, a
sgradevole	déplaisant, e	unpleasant	unangenehm	desagradable	desagradável
sgradevole	désagréable	unpleasant	unangenehm	desagradable	desagradável
sgranocchiare	croquer	crunch	knabbern	mascar	trincar
sgranocchiare	grignoter	nibble	knabbern	mordisquear	petiscar
sgravio fiscale	détaxé, e	duty(tax)-free	steuerfrei	desgravado, a	isento de taxa
sgridare	gronder	scold, tell off	schimpfen	regañar	ralhar
sguardo	regard	look, expression	Blick(m)	mirada	olhar
shampoo	shampooing	shampoo	Shampoo(n)	champú	champô
shorts, calzoncini	short	shorts	kurze Hose(f)	pantalón corto	calções; calção
sì	oui	yes	ja	sí	sim
siccità	sécheresse	drought	Trockenheit(f)	sequía	seca
sicuramente	sûrement	surely, certainly	gewiß, sicherlich	ciertamente	certamente
sicurezza	sûreté	safety	Sicherheit(f)	seguridad	segurança
sicurezza	sécurité	security; safety	Sicherheit(f)	seguridad	segurança
sicuro, a	sûr, e; certain, e	sure, certain	sicher	seguro, a	seguro, a
sicuro, a; certo, a	assuré, e	assured	sicher	seguro, a	certo, a
sicuro, a; affidabile	fiable	reliable	zuverlässig	fiable, seguro, a	seguro, a
sidro	cidre	cider	Apfelwein(m)	sidra	sidra
siepe	haie	hedge	Hecke(f)	seto, valla	sebe
siero	sérum	serum	Serum(n)	suero	soro
siesta, riposino	sieste	nap, snooze	Mittagsschlaf(m)	siesta	sesta
sifilide	syphilis	syphilis	Syphilis(f)	sífilis	sífilis
sigaretta	cigarette	cigarette	Zigarette(f)	cigarrillo	cigarro
sigaro	cigare	cigar	Zigarre(f)	cigarro, puro	charuto
sigillo, bollo	cachet	postmark; seal	Stempel(m), Siegel(n)	sello	selo
sigillo	sceau	seal	Siegel(n)	sello	selo
sigla	sigle	initials	Abkürzung(f)	sigla	sigla
significare	signifier	mean, signify	bedeuten	significar	significar
significativo, a	significatif, ive	significant	bezeichnend	significativo, a	significativo, a
significato	signification	meaning	Bedeutung(f)	significación	significação
signora	dame	lady	Dame(f)	señora	senhora
signora	madame	Mrs; Madam	Frau(f)	señora	senhora
signore	mesdames	ladies	meine Damen	señoras	senhoras
signor	monsieur(Mr)	Mr	Herr(m)	señor	senhor
signor	monsieur(Mr)	Mr	Herr(m)	Don	Senhor
signore	monsieur	man, gentleman(men)	Gentleman(m)	caballero	cavalheiro
signore	monsieur	Sir	Herr(m)	señor	senhor
Signore	Seigneur	Lord	Herr(m)	Señor	Senhor
signori	messieurs	gentlemen	meine Herren	señores	senhores
signorina	mademoiselle	Miss	Fräulein(n)	señorita	menina
silenzio	silence	silence	Stille(f)	silencio	silêncio
silenzioso, a	silencieux, se	silent, quiet	still, leise, ruhig	silencioso, a	silencioso, a
sillaba	syllabe	syllable	Silbe(f)	sílaba	sílaba
silurare	limoger	dismiss	entlassen	destituir	destituir
simbolico, a	symbolique	symbolic(al)	symbolisch	simbólico, a	simbólico, a
simbolo	symbole	symbol	Symbol(n)	símbolo	símbolo
similare	similaire	similar	ähnlich, gleichartig	similar	similar
simile, uguale	semblable	similar	ähnlich	semejante	semelhante
simmetria	symétrie	symmetry	Symetrie(f)	simetría	simetria
simpatico, a	sympathique	pleasant, nice	sympathisch	simpático, a	simpático, a
simulazione	simulation	simulation	Vortäuschung(f)	simulación	simulação
simultaneo, a	simultané, e	simultaneous	gleichzeitig	simultáneo, a	simultâneo, a
sinagoga	synagogue	synagogue	Synagoge(f)	sinagoga	sinagoga

sincero, a	sincère	sincere, candid	aufrichtig	sincero, a	sincero, a
sincope	syncope	black-out	Ohnmacht(f)	síncope	síncope
sincronizzare	synchroniser	synchronize	synchronisieren	sincronizar	sincronizar
sindacalismo	syndicalisme	trade unionism	Gewerkschaftswesen	sindicalismo	sindicalismo
sindacato	syndicat	trade union	Gewerkschaft(f)	sindicato	sindicato
sindaco	maire	mayor	Bürgermeister(m)	alcalde	President.da Câmara
sinfonia	symphonie	symphony	Symphonie(f)	sinfonía	sinfonia
singhiozzo	sanglot	sob	Schluchzer(m)	sollozo	soluço
singolare	singulier	singular	Einzahl(f)	singular	singular
singolo, a	un, e(à)	single	einzeln; einzig	solo, a; único, a	único, a
sinistrato, a	sinistré, e	victim(disaster -)	Geschädigte(r)m f	siniestrado, a	sinistrado, a
sinistro, a	gauche	left	links; linke(r, s)	izquierdo, a	esquerdo, a
sinistro, a	sinistre	sinister	unheilvoll	siniestro, a	sinistro, a
sinonimo	synonyme	synonym	Synonym(n)	sinónimo	sinónimo
sintassi	syntaxe	syntax	Syntax(f), Satzlehre f	sintaxis	sintaxe
sintesi	synthèse	synthesis(-ses)	Synthese(f)	síntesis	síntese
sintetico, a	synthétique	synthetic	synthetisch	sintético, a	sintético, a
sintomo	symptôme	symptom	Symptom(n)	síntoma	sintoma
sinuoso, a	sinueux, se	winding, sinuous	kurvenreich	sinuoso, a	sinuoso, a
sirena	sirène	siren	Sirene(f)	sirena	sirene
siringa	seringue	syringe	Spritze(f)	jeringa	seringa
sisma	séisme	earthquake	Erdbeben(n)	seismo	sismo
sismico, a	sismique	seismic	seismisch	sísmico, a	sísmico, a
sistema	système	system	System(n)	sistema	sistema
sistemare	ranger, ordonner	tidy, put in order	ein = räumen	ordenar, colocar	arrumar
sistemare	arranger	arrange	arrangieren	arreglar	arranjar
sistemare	aménager	fit out; convert	ein = richten	acondicionar	arranjar, dispor
sistematico, a	systématique	systematic	systematisch	sistemático, a	sistemático, a
sito	site	site	Ort(m), Lage(f)	paraje, vista	sítio
situare, localizzare	situer	situate, locate	stellen, setzen	situar, localizar	situar, localizar
situato, a	situé, e	located	gelegen	situado, a	situado, a
situazione	situation	situation	Lage(f)	situación	situação
situazione	situation	location, position	Lage(f)	situación	situação
situazione	situation	position, job	Stellung, Position(f)	situación	situação
slacciare	dégrafer	undo, unfasten	auf = machen	desabrochar	desapertar
slanciato, a; snello, a	svelte	slim, slender	schlank	esbelto, a	esbelto, a
slancio	élan	spring, bound	Anlauf(m), Schwung(m)	impulso	impulso
slitta	traîneau	sleigh, sledge	Schlitten(m)	trineo	trenó
slittare	déraper	skid	schleudern	patinar	derrapar
slogatura	foulure	sprain	Verstauchung(f)	esguince	entorse
smacco, sconfitta	échec	failure	Mißerfolg(m)	fracaso, revés	fracasso
smalto	émail	enamel	Emaille(f), Glasur(f)	esmalte	esmalte
smarrito, a; sgomento	désemparé, e	distraught	ratlos	desamparado, a	desamparado, a
smentire	démentir	refute, deny	dementieren, leugnen	desmentir	desmentir
smeraldo	émeraude	emerald	Smaragd(m)	esmeralda	esmeralda
smistare, scegliere	trier	sort(out)	sortieren	escoger, separar	escolher, triar
smobilitare	démobiliser	demobilize	demobilisieren	desmovilizar	desmobilizar
smog, fumo	fumée	smoke, fumes	Rauch(m)	humo	fumo
smoking	smoking	dinner-jacket	Smoking(m)	esmoquin	smoking
smontaggio	démontage	dismantling	Zerlegung(f), Abbau(m)	desmontaje	desmontagem
smontare	démonter	remove, dismantle	ab = bauen	desmontar	desmontar
smorfia	grimace	grimace	Grimasse(f)	mueca	careta
snello, a	mince	slim; slender	schlank	delgado, a	magro, a; delgado, a
snobismo	snobisme	snobbery	Snobismus(m)	esnobismo	snobismo
sobborgo	faubourg	suburb	Vorstadt(f)	suburbio	subúrbio
soccombere	succomber	succumb	erliegen	sucumbir	sucumbir
soccorrere	secourir	help, assist, aid	helfen	socorrer	socorrer
soccorrere	secourir	rescue	retten	socorrer	socorrer
soccorritore	sauveteur	rescuer	Retter(in f)m	socorrista	socorrista
soccorso	secours	help, aid	Hilfe(f)	socorro	socorro
sociale	social, e	social	sozial	social	social
socialismo	socialisme	socialism	Sozialismus(m)	socialismo	socialismo
società	société	society	Gesellschaft(f)	sociedad	sociedade
società	société	company, firm	Gesellschaft(f)	sociedad	sociedade
socievole	sociable	sociable	gesellig	sociable	sociável
socio, a	associé, e	associate, partner	Teilhaber(in f)m	socio, a, asociado	sócio, a
sociologia	sociologie	sociology	Soziologie(f)	sociología	sociologia
soddisfatto, a	satisfait, e	satisfied	zufrieden	satisfecho, a	satisfeito, a

I

Italian	French	English	German	Spanish	Portuguese
soddisfazione	satisfaction	satisfaction	Zufriedenheit(f)	satisfacción	satisfação
sofferenza	souffrance	suffering	Leiden(n)	sufrimiento	sofrimento
soffiare	souffler	blow	blasen	soplar	soprar
soffiare	souffler	blow	wehen	soplar	soprar
soffiarsi il naso	moucher(se)	blow one's nose	Nase putzen	sonarse	assoar-se
soffitto	plafond	ceiling	Decke(f)(Zimmer-)	techo	tecto
soffocare	étouffer	suffocate; choke	ersticken	sofocar, ahogar	sufocar
soffrire	souffrir	suffer	leiden	sufrir	sofrer
sofisticato, a	sophistiqué, e	sophisticated	hochkompliziert	sofisticado, a	sofisticado, a
software	logiciel	software	Software(f)	logicial	software
soggetto	sujet	subject	Subjekt(n)	sujeto	sujeito
sogghignare	ricaner	snigger	grinsen, kichern	burlarse	troçar
soggiorno	séjour	stay	Aufenthalt(m)	estancia	estadia, estada
soggiorno	salle de séjour	living-room	Wohnzimmer(n)	sala de estar	sala de estar
sognare	rêver	dream	träumen	soñar	sonhar
sogno	rêve	dream	Traum(m)	sueño	sonho
solaio; granaio	grenier	attic, loft	Speicher(m), Dachboden	desván	sótão
solare	solaire	solar	Sonnen-	solar	solar
solco	sillon	furrow	Furche(f)	surco	rego
soldato	soldat	soldier	Soldat(m)	soldado	soldado
sole	soleil	sun	Sonne(f)	sol	sol
sole(c'è il)	soleil(il fait)	sunny(it's)	Sonne scheint(die)	sol(hace)	sol(está)
soleggiato, a	ensoleillé, e	sunny	sonnig	soleado, a	soalheiro, a
solenne	solennel, le	solemn	feierlich	solemne	solene
solfeggio	solfège	sol-fa, theory	Tonleiter(f)	solfeo	solfejo
solidarietà	solidarité	solidarity	Solidarität(f)	solidaridad	solidaridade
solido, a	solide	solid, strong	solide, fest	sólido, a	sólido, a
solitario, a	solitaire	solitary, lonely	einsam	solitario, a	solitário, a
solitudine	solitude	loneliness	Einsamkeit(f)	soledad	solidão
sollecitare	solliciter	appeal to, request	ersuchen	solicitar	solicitar
solletico	chatouille(s)	tickle	Kitzeln(n)	cosquillas	cócegas
sollevare	soulever	lift, raise	an = heben, hoch = heben	levantar, elevar	levantar, erguer
sollevare, lenire	soulager	relieve	lindern	aliviar	aliviar
sollievo	soulagement	relief	Erleichterung(f)	alivio, desahogo	alívio
solo, a	seul, e	alone	allein	solo, a	só
solo, a	seul, e	only	einzig	solo, a	só
solo; soltanto	seulement	only	nur	solamente, sólo	somente, só
solubile	soluble	soluble	löslich	soluble	solúvel
soluzione	solution	solution	Lösung(f)	solución	solução
solvente	dissolvant	solvent, remover	Lösungsmittel(n)	disolvente	acetona
somiglianza	ressemblance	resemblance	Ähnlichkeit(f)	parecido	semelhança
somigliare a	ressembler(à)	look like	ähneln, aussehen wie	parecerse(a)	parecer-se
somma	somme	sum, amount	Summe(f)	suma; cantidad	soma; quantia
sommità	sommité	V.I.P	Prominente(f, m)	eminencia	sumidade
sommossa	émeute	riot	Aufruhr(m)	motín	motim
sonata	sonate	sonata	Sonate(f)	sonata	sonata
sonda	sonde	probe	Sonde(f)	sonda	sonda
sondaggio	sondage	poll(opinion)	Umfrage(f)	sondeo	sondagem
sonnambulo, a	somnambule	sleep-walker	Schlafwandler(in f)m	sonámbulo, a	sonâmbulo, a
sonnecchiare	sommeiller	doze	schlummern	dormitar	dormitar
sonnifero	somnifère	sleeping tablet	Schlaftablette(f)	somnífero	soporífero
sonno	sommeil	sleep	Schlaf(m)	sueño	sono
sonnolenza	somnolence	drowsiness	Schläfrigkeit(f)	somnolencia	sonolência
sontuoso, a	somptueux, se	sumptuous	prächtig	suntuoso, a	sumptuoso, a
sopportare	supporter	support	stützen, unterstützen	soportar	suportar
sopprimere	supprimer	suppress	ab = schaffen	suprimir	suprimir
sopprimere	supprimer	delete	beseitigen	suprimir	suprimir
sopra, su	sur	on, upon	über; auf	sobre, en, encima	sobre; em cima de
sopra	dessus(au-, par-)	above, on, over	über	arriba, encima	em cima, sobre
sopra(al di)	au-dessus	above	über	encima(por, de)	cima(por); acima de
sopra, in alto	au-dessus	overhead	oben	arriba	cima(por, em)
sopra(qui)	ci-dessus	above	oben(-stehend)	arriba(más)	acima
soprabito	pardessus	overcoat	Mantel(m)	abrigo	sobretudo
sopracciglio	sourcil	eyebrow	Augenbraue(f)	ceja	sobrolho
soprannaturale	surnaturel, le	supernatural	überirdisch	sobrenatural	sobrenatural
soprannome	surnom	nickname	Spitzname(m)	apodo, mote	alcunha, apelido
soprattutto	surtout	above all	besonders	sobre todo	sobretudo
sopravvivere	survivre	survive	überleben	sobrevivir	sobreviver

Italian	French	English	German	Spanish	Portuguese
soprintendere	superviser	supervise	überprüfen	supervisar	supervisar
sordità	surdité	deafness	Taubheit(f)	sordera	surdez
sordo, a	sourd, e	deaf	taub	sordo, a	surdo, a
sordomuto, a	sourd-muet, te	deaf and dumb	taubstumm	sordomudo, a	surdo-mudo, a
sorella	soeur	sister	Schwester(f)	hermana	irmã
sorgente	source	spring	Quelle(f)	fuente	fonte, nascente
sorgere	lever(se)	rise	auf = gehen	amanecer	nascer
sorgere	lever(se)	break, dawn	an = brechen	amanecer	nascer
sorpassare	doubler	overtake	überholen	adelantar	ultrapassar
sorprendente	étonnant, e	surprising	erstaunlich	asombroso, a	espantoso, a
sorprendere	étonner	astonish, amaze	überraschen	sorprender	espantar
sorpresa	surprise	surprise	Überraschung(f)	sorpresa	surpresa
sorpreso, a	surpris, e	surprised	überrascht	sorprendido, a	surpreendido, a
sorridente	souriant, e	cheerful	lächelnd	sonriente	sorridente
sorridere	sourire	smile	lächeln	sonreír	sorrir
sorriso	sourire	smile	Lächeln(n)	sonrisa	sorriso
sorte, destino	sort	fate	Schicksal(n)	suerte, destino	sorte, destino
sorvegliante	surveillant, e	supervisor	Aufseher m, Supervisor	vigilante	vigia
sorveglianza	surveillance	watch; supervision	Überwachung(f)	vigilancia	vigilância
sorvegliare	surveiller	watch; supervise	überwachen	vigilar	vigiar
sorvolo	survol	flight over	Überfliegen(n)	sobrevuelo	sobrevôo
sosia	sosie	double	Doppelgänger(in f)m	sosia	sósia
sospendere	suspendre	suspend, defer	verschieben	suspender	suspender
sospensione	suspension	suspension	Federung(f)	suspensión	suspensão
sospettare	soupçonner	suspect	verdächtigen	sospechar	suspeitar
sospettare	douter(se)	suspect, mistrust	ahnen, vermuten	sospechar	suspeitar
sospetto, a	suspect, e	suspicious	verdächtig	sospechoso, a	suspeito, a
sospetto	soupçon; méfiance	suspicion	Argwohn(m), Verdacht m	sospecha	suspeita
sospirare	soupirer	sigh	seufzen	suspirar	suspirar
sosta, fermata	halte, arrêt	halt, stop	Halt(m)	alto, parada	alto, paragem
sosta	stationnement	parking	Parken(n)	estacionamiento	estacionamento
sostantivo	substantif	substantive, noun	Hauptwort(n)	sustantivo	substantivo
sostanza	substance	substance	Substanz(f)	sustancia	substância
sostegno, appoggio	soutien, appui	support	Unterstützung(f)	sostén, apoyo	apoio, socorro
sostenere	soutenir	support	unterstützen	sostener	sustentar
sostituire	substituer	substitute	vertauschen	sustituir	substituir
sostituire	remplacer	replace	ersetzen	sustituir	substituir
sostituto, a	remplacant, e	substitute	Stellvertreter(in f)m	sustituto, a	substituto, a
sottana	jupon	petticoat, slip	Unterrock(m)	enagua	saiote
sotterraneo, a	souterrain, e	underground	unterirdisch	subterráneo, a	subterrâneo, a
sottile	mince	thin	dünn	delgado, a	fino, a
sottile	subtil, e	subtle	scharfsinnig, listig	sutil	subtil
sotto	sous	under	unter	debajo, bajo	debaixo, sob
sotto	dessous	under, beneath	unter	debajo, abajo	debaixo, sob
sotto(al di)	au-dessous	below, under(neath)	unter	debajo(de)	baixo(por); abaixo
sotto(qui)	ci-dessous	below	unten(-stehend)	abajo(más)	abaixo
sotto, disotto	dessous	lower part	Unterteil(m)	inferior(parte)	baixo(parte de)
sottolineare	souligner	underline	unterstreichen	subrayar	sublinhar
sottomarino	sous-marin	submarine	Unterseeboot(n)	submarino	submarino
sottomettere	soumettre	submit	unterwerfen	someter	submeter
sottomissione	soumission	submission	Unterwerfung(f)	sumisión	submissão
sottoscrizione	souscription	subscription	Subskription(f)	suscripción	subscrição
sottosuolo	sous-sol	subsoil	Unterboden(m)	subsuelo	sub-solo
sottoveste	combinaison	slip	Unterrock(m)	combinación	combinação
sottrarre	soustraire	subtract	ab = ziehen	sustraer, restar	subtrair, deduzir
sottrazione	soustraction	subtraction	Subtraktion(f)	resta	subtração
sovranità	royauté	royalty, monarchy	Königstum(n)	realeza	realeza
sovranità	souveraineté	sovereignty	Souveränität(f)	soberanía	soberania
sovrano, a; monarca	souverain, e	sovereign, monarch	Herrscher(in f)m	soberano, a; monarca	soberano, a; monarca
sovrapporre	superposer	superpose	aufeinander = legen	sobreponer	sobrepor
sovvenzione	subvention	grant, subsidy	Zuschuß(m)	subvención	subvenção
spaccare	fendre	split, slit	spalten	rajar, partir	fender, rachar
spada	épée	sword	Schwert(n)	espada	espada
spago	ficelle	string, cord	Schnur(f)	cordel	cordel, guita
spalla	épaule	shoulder	Schulter(f)	hombro	ombro
sparare, tirare	tirer	fire, shoot	feuern, schießen	tirar	disparar, atirar
spargere	répandre	spread; spill	verschütten	derramar	espalhar
sparire	disparaître	disappear	verschwinden	desaparecer	desaparecer

I

615

Italian	French	English	German	Spanish	Portuguese
spartito	partition	score(music)	Partitur(f)	partitura	partitura
sparviere	épervier	sparrow-hawk	Habicht(m)	gavilán	gavião
spasma	spasme	spasm	Krampf(m)	espasmo	espasmo
spatola	spatule	spatula	Spachtel(f)	espátula	espátula
spaventare	effrayer	frighten	erschrecken	asustar	assustar
spavento	frayeur	fright	Schreck(m), Angst(f)	espanto	temor
spaventoso, a	épouvantable	dreadful	entsetzlich	horroroso, a	horroroso, a
spaventoso, a	affreux, se	awful	schrecklich	horrendo, a	horrível
spaziale	spatial, e	space	Raum-	espacial	espacial
spazio	espace	space	Raum(m)	espacio	espaço
spazio	place	room	Platz(m)	sitio, espacio	espaço
spazio	espace	space, gap	Zwischenraum(m)	espacio	espaço
spazioso, a	spacieux, se	spacious	weiträumig	espacioso, a	espaçoso, a
spazzare	balayer	sweep	fegen	barrer	varrer
spazzola	brosse	brush	Bürste(f)	cepillo	escova
spazzolino	brosse à dents	toothbrush	Zahnbürste(f)	cepillo de dientes	escova de dentes
specchio	miroir	mirror	Spiegel(m)	espejo	espelho
speciale	spécial, e	special	speziell, eigen	especial	especial
specialista	spécialiste	specialist	Spezialist(in f)m	especialista	especialista
specialista	spécialiste	expert, specialist	Fachmann(m)	especialista	especialista
specialità	spécialité	speciality	Spezialität(f)	especialidad	especialidade
specie	espèce	species	Art(f)	especie	espécie
specie	espèce	kind, sort	Gattung(f), Art(f)	especie	espécie
specie, genere	sorte	sort, kind, type	Sorte(f), Art(f)	especie, género	espécie, género
specificare	spécifier	specify, state	spezifieren	especificar	especificar
specifico, a	spécifique	specific	spezifisch	específico, a	específico, a
specimen	spécimen	specimen	Muster(n); Exemplar(n)	espécimen	espécime
speculazione	spéculation	speculation	Spekulation(f)	especulación	especulação
spedire	expédier	dispatch, send	verschicken	expedir	expedir
spedizione	expédition	expedition	Expedition(f)	expedición	expedição
spegnere	éteindre	turn/switch off	aus = schalten	apagar	apagar
spegnere	éteindre	extinguish	löschen	apagar	apagar
speleologia	spéléologie	pot-holing	Höhlenforschung(f)	espeleología	espeleologia
spendere	dépenser	spend	aus = geben	gastar	gastar
spento, a; smorto, a	terne	dull	matt	sin brillo, mate	baço, a
speranza	espoir	hope	Hoffnung(f)	esperanza	esperança
sperare	espérer	hope	hoffen	esperar, desear	esperar, desejar
sperimentale	expérimental, e	experimental	experimentell	experimental	experimental
sperimentazione	expérimentation	experimentation	Experimentieren(n)	experimentación	experimentação
sperma	sperme	sperm	Sperma(n)	esperma	esperma
sperperare	gaspiller	waste	verschwenden	desperdiciar	desperdiçar
spesa	dépense	expenditure	Ausgabe(f)	gasto	despesa, gasto
spesa	courses	shopping	Einkäufe(pl)	compras	compras
spese	frais	expenses	Kosten(pl.)	gastos	gastos, despesas
spese	frais(scolarité)	fee	Kosten(pl.)	gastos(escolares)	despesas
spesso, a	épais, se	thick	dick	espeso, a	espesso, a
spesso	souvent	often	oft	frecuentemente	frequentemente
spessore	épaisseur	thickness	Stärke(f), Dicke(f)	espesor	espessura
spettacoli	spectacles	entertainment	Unterhaltung(f)	espectáculos	espectáculos
spettacolo	spectacle	show	Aufführung(f)	espectáculo	espectáculo
spettatore, trice	spectateur, trice	spectator	Zuschauer(in f)m	espectador, a	espectador, a
spezie	épice(s)	spice	Gewürz(n)	especia	especiaria
spezzare, rompere	briser	break	brechen, zerbrechen	romper	quebrar
spia	espion, ne	spy	Spion(in f)m	espía	espião, espia
spiacente	désolé, e	sorry	betrübt	desolado, a	desolado, a
spiacente	navré, e	sorry	leid tun	desconsolado, a	desolado, a
spiaggia	plage	beach(-es)	Strand(m)	playa	praia
spianare	aplanir	level	ebnen	aplanar	aplanar
spiccioli, moneta	pièce	coin	Geldstück(n)	moneda	moeda
spiedo	broche	spit	Spieß(m)	asador	espeto
spiegare, aprire	déplier	unfold	auf = falten	desdoblar	desdobrar
spiegare	expliquer	explain	erklären	explicar	explicar
spiegazione	explication	explanation	Erklärung(f)	explicación	explicação
spietato, a	impitoyable	pitiless	unbarmherzig	despiadado, a	impiedoso, a
spilla	broche	brooch	Brosche(f)	broche	broche
spillo	épingle	pin	Stecknadel(f)	alfiler	alfinete
spina	épine	thorn	Dorn(m); Stachel(m)	espina	espinho
spingere	pousser	push	schieben, stoßen	empujar	empurrar

Italian	French	English	German	Spanish	Portuguese
spingere, urtare	bousculer	push	drängeln	empujar	empurrar
spionaggio	espionnage	spying, espionage	Spionage(f)	espionaje	espionagem
spirale	spirale	spiral	Spirale(f)	espiral	espiral
spirale	stérilet	coil	Spirale(f)	espiral	esterilete
spirare	expirer	die	verscheiden	expirar	expirar
spiritato, a	hanté, e	haunted	verflucht	embrujado, a	assombrado, a
spirito	esprit	spirit	Geist(m)	espíritus	espírito
spirituale	spirituel, le	spiritual	geistreich	espiritual	espiritual
splendido, a	splendide	splendid	glänzend	espléndido, a	esplêndido, a
splendido, a	superbe	superb	großartig	soberbio, a	soberbo, a
sponda	berge	bank	Ufer(n)	ribera, orilla	margem
sponsor	sponsor	sponsor	Sponsor(m)	patrocinador	patrocinador
sponsorizzare	parrainer	sponsor	sponsorisieren	patrocinar	apadrinhar
spontaneo, a	spontané, e	spontaneous	spontan	espontáneo, a	espontâneo, a
sporcare	salir	dirty	verschmutzen	ensuciar	sujar
sporcizia	saleté	dirt	Schmutz(m)	suciedad	sujidade, porcaria
sporcizia	crasse	filth, dirt	Dreck(m)	roña, mugre	sujidade
sporco, a	sale	dirty	dreckig	sucio, a	sujo, a
sporgere	dépasser	protrude	hervor = stehen	sobresalir	sobressair
sporgersi	pencher(se)	lean out	hinaus = lehnen	asomarse	debruçar-se
sport	sport	sport	Sport(m)	deporte	desporto
sportello	portière	door(car)	Wagentür(f)	puerta	porta
sportello	guichet	counter, position	Schalter(m)	ventanilla	guichê, postigo
sportivo, a	sportif, ive	sporty, athletic	sportlich; Sport-	deportivo, a	desportivo, a
sportivo, a	sportif, ive	sportsman/-woman	Sportler(in f)m	deportista	desportista
sposa, consorte	épouse	wife(wives)	Gattin, Frau, Ehefrau f	esposa	esposa
sposarsi	marier(se)	married(get)	heiraten	casarse	casar-se
sposato, a	marié, e	married	verheiratet	casado, a	casado, a
sposo, consorte	époux	husband	Gatte, Mann, Ehemann m	esposo	esposo
sposo, sposa	marié, mariée	bridegroom, bride	Bräutigam(m), Braut(f)	novio, novia	noivo, noiva
spossato, a	exténué, e	exhausted	erschöpft	extenuado, a	extenuado, a
spostamento	déplacement	transfer, moving	Umstellung(f)	desplazamiento	deslocação
spostare	déplacer	shift, move	versetzen, -schieben	trasladar	deslocar
spostare(-arsi)	déplacer(se)	move, shift	bewegen, sich	desplazar(se)	deslocar-se
sprecare	gaspiller, perdre	waste	verschwenden	despilfarrar	desperdiçar
spreco	gaspillage	waste	Verschwendung(f)	despilfarro	desperdício
sprizzare, schizzare	gicler, jaillir	squirt, spurt	spritzen	salpicar	salpicar
spugna	éponge	sponge	Schwamm(m)	esponja	esponja
spugnoso, a	spongieux, se	spongy	schwammig	esponjoso, a	esponjoso, a
sputare	cracher	spit	spucken	escupir	cuspir
squadra; équipe	équipe, groupe	team	Mannschaft(f), Team(n)	equipo	equipa, grupo
squadra	équerre	square(set -)	Zeichendreieck(n)	escuadra	esquadro
squadrone; squadra	escadron	squadron	Schwadron; Eskadron(f)	escuadrón	esquadrão
squallido, a	sordide	sordid	schäbig	sórdido, a	sórdido, a
squalo	requin	shark	Hai(m)	tiburón	tubarão
squama	écaille	scale	Schuppe(f)	escama	escama
squillo, soneria	sonnerie	ring	Klingel(f)	campana, timbre	campainha, toque
sst!, zitto!	chut!	hush!, sh!	pst!	chitón(!)	chut!
stabilimento	établissement	establishment	Anstalt(f)	establecimiento	estabelecimento
stabilire	établir	establish	festsetzen, aufstellen	establecer	estabelecer
stabilirsi	établir(s')	settle; set up	an = siedeln, sich	establecerse	estabelecer-se
stabilirsi	installer(s')	settle	nieder = lassen, sich	instalarse	instalar-se
stabilità	stabilité	stability	Stabilität(f)	estabilidad	estabilidade
staccare	détacher	detach, unfasten	lösen, ab = trennen	desatar	desatar
staccare, scollare	décoller	unstick	ab = lösen	despegar	descolar
staccare	débrancher	unplug	raus = ziehen	desenchufar	desligar
stadio	stade	stadium	Stadium(n)	estadio	estádio
stagionale	saisonnier, ière	seasonal	saisonbedingt	temporero, a	sazonal
stagione	saison	season	Jahreszeit(f)	estación	estação
stagno	étang	pond	Teich(m)	estanque	lago; tanque
stagno	mare	pond, pool	Tümpel(m)	charca	charco
stagno, a	étanche	watertight(air-)	undurchlässig	estanco, a	estanque
stagno	étain	tin; pewter	Zinn(n)	estaño	estanho
stampa	presse	press	Presse(f)	prensa	imprensa
stampa	gravure	print	Gravur(f)	grabado	gravura
stampa	impression	printing	Druck(m)	impresión	impressão
stampare	imprimer	print	drucken	imprimir	imprimir
stampato	imprimé	printed form	Formular(n)	impreso	impresso

617

Italian	French	English	German	Spanish	Portuguese
stampella	béquille	crutch(-es)	Krücke(f)	muleta	muleta
stampo, forma	moule	mould	Form(f)	molde	molde; forma
stancare	fatiguer	tire, make tired	ermüden	cansar, fatigar	cansar, fatigar
stanchezza	fatigue	tiredness	Müdigkeit(f)	cansancio	fatiga, cansaço
stanco, a	fatigué, e	tired	müde, ermüdet	cansado, a	cansado, a
stanza	pièce	room	Raum(m)	cuarto	divisão
starnutire	éternuer	sneeze	niesen	estornudar	espirrar
statico, a	statique	static	statisch	estático, a	estático, a
statistica	statistique(s)	statistics	Statistik(f)	estadística	estatística
stato	état	state	Staat(m)	estado	estado
statua	statue	statue	Statue(f)	estatua	estátua
statura	taille, grandeur	height, size	Größe(f)	talla, estatura	estatura
statuto	statut	status; statute	Status(m); Statut(n)	estatuto	estatuto
stazionare	stationner	park	parken	estacionarse	estacionar
stazione	station	station	Station(f)	estación	estação
stazione	station	resort	Erholungsort(m)	estación	estação
stazione	gare	station	Bahnhof(m)	estación	estação, gare
stazione di servizio	station-service	service station	Tankstelle(f)	estación(servicio)	estação de serviço
stella	étoile	star	Stern(m)	estrella	estrela
stelo	tige	stem	Stiel(m)	tallo	caule
stendere	étendre	extend, spread	aus = breiten	extender	estender
stendere, spalmare	étaler	spread(out)	aus = breiten	exponer	expor
steppa	steppe	steppe	Steppe(f)	estepa	estepe
sterco	crotte	dropping, dung	Häufchen(n), Kot(m)	caca	bosta
stereo	stéréo	stereo	Stereo(f)	estéreo	estereofonia
sterile	stérile	sterile	steril	estéril	estéril
stesso, a	même	same	selbe; gleich(der -)	mismo, a	mesmo, a
stesso, a(lui, lei)	même(lui, elle)	self(him, her, it)	selbst(er, sie, es)	mismo, a(él, ella)	próprio, a(ele, a)
stile	style	style	Stil(m)	estilo	estilo
stilografica	stylo	pen, fountain-pen	Füller(m)	estilográfica	caneta
stima	estime	esteem	Achtung(f)	estima	estima
stima, valutazione	estimation	estimate	Schätzung(f)	estimación	estimativa
stimare, valutare	estimer	estimate, value	schätzen	valorar, estimar	estimar
stimolare	stimuler	stimulate	reizen, an = regen	estimular	estimular
stirare	étirer	stretch	aus = dehnen	estirar	esticar
stirare	repassage	ironing	Bügeln(n)	planchado	passar a ferro
stitichezza	constipation	constipation	Verstopfung(f)	estreñimiento	prisão de ventre
stiva	cale	hold	Laderaum(m)	bodega	porão
stivale	botte	boot	Stiefel(m)	bota	bota
stoffa	étoffe	material	Stoff(m)	tejido, tela	tecido, estofo
stomaco	estomac	stomach	Magen(m)	estómago	estômago
stordire	étourdir	stun, daze	betäuben	aturdir; atontar	aturdir; atordoar
stordire	assommer	knock out	nieder = schlagen	dejar k.o.	espancar
storia	histoire	history	Geschichte(f)	historia	História
storia	histoire	story	Geschichte(f)	historia	história
storico, a	historique	historic(al)	historisch	histórico, a	histórico, a
storico	historien	historian	Geschichtschreiber(m)	historiador	historiador
storpio, a	estropié, e	crippled	verkrüppelt	lisiado, a	aleijado, a
storta	entorse	sprain	Verrenkung(f)	esguince	entorse
stoviglie, vasellame	vaisselle	crockery, dishes	Geschirr(n)	vajilla	loiça, louça
strabico, a(essere)	loucher	squint	schielen	bizquear	estrábico, a(ser)
straccio	chiffon	rag	Lappen(m)	trapo	trapo
strada	route	road	Straße(f)	carretera	estrada
strada statale	route nationale	main/trunk road	Landstraße(f)	carretera	estrada
strangolamento	étranglement	strangling	Erwürgen(n)	estrangulación	estrangulamento
straniero, a	étranger, ère	foreigner	Ausländer(in f)m	extranjero, a	estrangeiro, a
strano, a	étrange	strange, odd	seltsam	extraño, a; raro, a	estranho, a
strano, a	bizarre	strange, odd	seltsam	raro, a	estranho, a
straordinario, a	extraordinaire	extraordinary	außergewöhnlich	extraordinario, a	extraordinário, a
straordinario, a	épatant, e	wonderful, super	großartig, fabelhaft	estupendo, a	estupendo, a
strappare, togliere	arracher	tear out; tear off	weg = reißen, aus = reißen	arrancar	arrancar
strappare	déchirer	tear	zerreißen	rasgar, romper	rasgar
strapuntino	strapontin	folding seat	Klappstuhl(m)	traspuntín	banco dobrável
straripare	déborder	overflow	über die Ufer treten	salirse de madre	extravasar
strategia	stratégie	strategy	Strategie(f)	estrategia	estratégia
strato	couche	coat	Anstrich(m)	capa	camada
strato	couche	layer	Schicht(f)	capa	camada
stregone, strega	sorcier, ière	wizard; witch	Hexer(m); Hexe(f)	brujo, a	bruxo, a

stregoneria	sorcellerie	witchcraft	Hexerei(f)	brujería	bruxaria
stretto, a	étroit, e	narrow	eng	estrecho, a	estreito, a
stretto, a; rigido, a	strict, e	strict	streng	estricto, a	estrito, a
stretto	détroit	strait	Meerenge(f)	estrecho	estreito
stridere	grincer	grind, grate	knirschen	chirriar	ranger
stringere	serrer	grip, hold tight	greifen, packen	apretar	apertar
stringere	serrer, resserrer	tighten	an = ziehen	apretar	apertar
stringere la mano	serrer la main	shake hands	Hand schütteln	estrechar la mano	apertar a mão
striscia	bande	band, strip	Streifen(m)	faja, tira	tira
strisciare	ramper	crawl	kriechen	arrastrarse	rastejar
stritolare, macinare	broyer	crush, grind	mahlen	triturar	triturar; moer
strofinare, sfregare	frotter	rub	reiben	frotar	esfregar
strofinio	frottement	friction, rubbing	Reibung(f)	frotamiento	fricção
strumento	instrument	instrument	Instrument(n)	instrumento	instrumento
struttura	structure	structure	Struktur(f)	estructura	estrutura
studente, -essa	étudiant, e	student	Student(in f)m	estudiante	estudante
studiare	étudier	study	studieren	estudiar	estudar
studiare	étudier, examiner	investigate	prüfen, erforschen	estudiar	estudar, examinar
studio	étude	study; survey	Studie(f)	estudio	estudo
studio(medico)	cabinet(médecin)	surgery	Praxis(f)(Arztpraxis)	consulta(-torio)	consultório
studio(avvocato)	cabinet(avocat)	practice	Büro(n)(Anwaltsbüro)	despacho; bufete	escritório
studio	studio	studio	Studio(n)	estudio	estúdio
studioso, a	studieux, se	studious	fleißig	estudioso, a	estudioso, a
studioso, a; dotto, a	savant, e	learned person	Wissenschaftler(m)	sabio, a	sábio, a
stufa	poêle	stove	Ofen(m)	estufa	fogão
stupefacente	stupéfiant	narcotic	Betäubungsmittel(n)	narcótico	narcótico
stupefatto, a	stupéfait, e	amazed	verblüfft	estupefacto, a	estupefacto, a
stupido, a	stupide	stupid, silly	dumm	estúpido, a	estúpido, a
stupore	stupeur	stupor	Erstaunen(n)	estupor	estupefacção
stupro	viol	rape	Vergewaltigung(f)	violación	violação
stuzzicadenti	cure-dents	tooth-pick	Zahnstocher(m)	palillo	palito
stuzzicare	taquiner	tease	necken	hacer rabiar	arreliar
su, sopra	sur	on, upon	über; auf	sobre	sobre
sua(la)	sa	her; his; its	sein, e; ihr, ihre	su	sua
subalterno, a	subordonné, e	subordinate	Untergebene(f m)	subordinado, a	subordinado, a
subcosciente	subconscient	subconscious	Unterbewußtsein(n)	subconsciente	subconsciente
subire	subir	undergo	ertragen	sufrir, padecer	sofrer
subito	suite(tout de)	once(at)	sogleich, sofort	seguida(en)	imediatamente
subito, appena	aussitôt	straight away	sofort, sogleich	seguida(en)	imediatamente
sublime	sublime	sublime	erhaben	sublime	sublime
succedere	succéder	succeed	nach = folgen	suceder	suceder
succedere	arriver	occur, happen	geschehen	ocurrir, suceder	acontecer
successivo, a	successif, ive	successive	aufeinanderfolgend	sucesivo, a	sucessivo, a
successo	succès	success(-es)	Erfolg(m)	éxito	sucesso, êxito
successore	successeur	successor	Nachfolger(in f)m	sucesor	sucessor
succhiare	sucer	suck	lutschen	chupar	chupar
succhiotto	sucette	dummy	Schnuller(m)	chupete	chupeta
succinto, a	succinct, e	succinct, brief	bündig	sucinto, a	sucinto, a
succo	jus	juice	Saft(m)	jugo	sumo
succo di frutta	jus de fruit	fruit-juice	Obstsaft(m)	zumo de fruta	sumo de fruta
succursale	succursale	branch(-es)	Zweigstelle(f)	sucursal	sucursal
Sud	Sud	South	Süden(m)	Sur	Sul
sudare	suer	sweat	schwitzen	sudar	suar
sudore	sueur	sweat	Schweiß(m)	sudor	suor
sufficiente	suffisant, e	sufficient	genügend	suficiente	suficiente
suffragio	suffrage	vote	Wahl(f)	sufragio	sufrágio
suggerire	suggérer	suggest	vor = schlagen	sugerir	sugerir, propôr
sughero	liège	cork	Kork(m)	corcho	cortiça
sugo; salsa	sauce	sauce	Soße(f)	salsa	molho
suicidarsi	suicider(se)	commit suicide	um = bringen, sich	suicidarse	suicidar-se
suicidio	suicide	suicide	Selbstmord(m)	suicidio	suicídio
sultano	sultan	sultan	Sultan(m)	sultán	sultão
suo(il)	son	his; her; its	sein, seine, ihr, ihre	su	seu
suo, sua(il, la)	sien, ne	his; hers; its	seine, ihre	suyo, suya	seu, sua
suocera	belle-mère	mother-in-law	Schwiegermutter(f)	suegra	sogra
suoceri	beaux-parents	parents-in-law	Schwiegereltern(pl.)	suegros	sogros
suocero	beau-père	father-in-law	Schwiegervater(m)	suegro	sogro
suoi(i); sue(le)	ses	his; her; its	seine; ihre	sus	seus, suas

Italian	French	English	German	Spanish	Portuguese
suola	semelle	sole	Sohle(f)	suela	sola
suolo	sol	ground	Boden(m)	suelo	solo
suonare, sonare	jouer	play	spielen	tocar	tocar
suonare, sonare	sonner	ring	klingeln	sonar, tocar	soar, tocar
suonare(clacson)	klaxonner	hoot	hupen	pitar	buzinar
suono	son	sound	Ton(m)	sonido	som
suora	soeur	nun, sister	Nonne(f), Schwester(f)	monja	freira
superare	dépasser	exceed	überschreiten	adelantar	ultrapassar
superare	surmonter	overcome	überwinden	superar	superar
superficie	superficie	area	Oberfläche(f)	superficie	superfície
superficie	surface	surface	Oberfläche(f)	superficie	superfície
superiore	supérieur, e	superior	höher, besser	superior, a	superior, a
superiore	supérieur, e	upper	obere(r, s); Ober-	superior, a	superior, a
superiore	supérieur	superior	Vorgesetzte(f, m)	superior	superior
superiorità	supériorité	superiority	Überlegenheit(f)	superioridad	superioridade
supermercato	supermarché	supermarket	Supermarkt(m)	supermercado	supermercado
supersonico, a	supersonique	supersonic	Überschall-	supersónico, a	supersónico, a
superstite	survivant, e	survivor	Überlebende(f, m)	superviviente	sobrevivente
superstizioso, a	superstitieux, se	superstitious	abergläubisch	supersticioso, a	supersticioso, a
supplente	suppléant, e	substitute	Stellvertreter(in f)m	suplente, a	suplente
supplementare	supplémentaire	additional, extra	zusätzlich	suplementario, a	suplementar
supplemento	supplément	supplement	Ergänzung(f); Zulage f	suplemento	suplemento
supplicare	supplier	implore	an = flehen	suplicar	suplicar
supplizio	supplice	torture	Qual(f)	suplicio	suplício
supporre	supposer	suppose	an = nehmen	suponer	supor
supporto	support	support	Stütze(f)	soporte	suporte
supposta	suppositoire	suppository	Zäpfchen(n)	supositorio	supositório
supremazia	suprématie	supremacy	Obergewalt(f)	supremacía	supremacia
supremo, a	suprême	supreme	oberst-, höchst-	supremo, a	supremo, a
surgelati	surgelés	frozen food	Tiefkühlkost(f)	congelados	congelados
suspense	suspense	suspense	Spannung(f)	suspense	suspense
sussidio	subvention	subsidy	Subvention(f)	subvención	subvenção
sussistere	subsister	subsist, remain	fort = bestehen	subsistir	subsistir
svago, distrazione	distraction(s)	entertainment	Zeitvertreib(m)	distracción	distracção, -ões
svaligiare	dévaliser	rob, burgle	aus = rauben	desvalijar	roubar
svalutare	dévaluer	devalue	entwerten, ab = werten	desvaluar	desvalorizar
svalutazione	dévaluation	devaluation	Abwertung(f)	devaluación	desvalorização
svantaggiato, a	défavorisé, e	underprivileged	benachteiligt	desfavorecido, a	desfavorecido, a
svantaggio	désavantage	disadvantage	Nachteil(m)	desventaja	desvantagem
sveglia	réveil	alarm clock	Wecker(m)	despertador	despertador
svegliare	réveiller	wake(up)	wecken	despertar	acordar
svegliarsi	éveiller(s')	wake up	auf = wachen	despertar(se)	despertar
svelare, scoprire	déceler	discover; reveal	auf = decken, entdecken	descubrir	descobrir
svenimento	défaillance	weakness(-es)	Schwäche(f), Versagen	desfallecimiento	desfalecimento
svenire	évanouir(s')	faint	ohnmächtig werden	desmayarse	desmaiar
sventura, sfortuna	malchance	misfortune	Unglück(n)	mala suerte	desventura
svestire(-irsi)	déshabiller(se)	undress	aus = ziehen, sich	desnudar(se)	despir-se
sviluppare	développer	develop	entwickeln	desarrollar	desenvolver
sviluppo	développement	development	Entwicklung(f)	desarrollo	desenvolvimento
sviluppo	essor	expansion, boom	Aufschwung(m)	auge, desarrollo	progresso
svolgere, srotolare	dérouler	unroll	ab = rollen	desenrollar	desenrolar
svoltare, girare	tourner	turn	wenden	girar	virar

T

Italian	French	English	German	Spanish	Portuguese
tabaccheria	bureau de tabac	tobacconist's	Tabakladen(m)	estanco	estanco, tabacaria
tabacco	tabac	tobacco	Tabak(m)	tabaco	tabaco

Italian	French	English	German	Spanish	Portuguese
tacca, intacco	encoche	notch	Kerbe(f), Einschnitt m	muesca	entalhe
taccuino	carnet	note-book	Notizbuch(n)	libreta	bloco, canhenho
tacere	taire(se)	silent(to be)	schweigen	callarse	calar-se
tachicardia	tachycardie	tachycardia	Herzjagen(n)	taquicardia	taquicardia
taglia, misura	taille	size	Größe(f)	talla, número	tamanho
tagliare	couper	cut	schneiden	cortar	cortar
tagliare	découper	cut up	zerschneiden	recortar	recortar
tagliatelle, pasta	nouilles	noodles	Nudeln(f, pl)	macarrones	massa
tagliato, a	coupé, e	cut	geschnitten	cortado, a	cortado, a
taglio	coupure(peau)	cut	Schnitt(m)	corte, tajo	corte, golpe
taglio, stile	forme	design, style	Schnitt(m)	hechura	corte, design
taglio cesareo	césarienne	Caesarean	Kaiserschnitt(m)	cesárea	cesariana
tailleur	tailleur	suit	Kostüm(n)	traje	saia-casaco
tale	tel, le	such a, such(pl.)	solche(r, s); so ein	tal	tal
talento	talent	talent	Talent(n)	talento	talento
tallone	talon	heel	Ferse(f); Absatz(m)	talón	calcanhar
talmente	tellement	so(-much, -many)	so(sehr), derartig	tanto, a; tan	tanto, a
talvolta	parfois	sometimes	manchmal	a veces	às vezes
tamponare	tamponner	bump, crash into	zusammen = stoßen	chocar con	chocar, esbarrar
tangente	tangent, e	tangent	berührend	tangente	tangente
tanto	tant	so much, so many	so viel, e	tanto, tan	tanto
tappa	étape	stage	Strecke(f)	etapa	etapa
tapparella	store	blind; shade	Vorhang m; Jalousie f	toldo; persiana	estore
tappeto	tapis	mat, rug, carpet	Teppich(m)	alfombra, tapiz	tapete, carpete
tappo, turacciolo	bouchon	cork	Korken(m)	corcho	rolha
tappo	bouchon	cap, plug	Pfropfen(m), Stöpsel	tapón	rolha; tampa
tardi	tard	late	spät	tarde	tarde
tariffa	tarif	tariff, price	Tarif(m)	tarifa	tarifa
tariffa	tarif	fare	Tarif(m)	tarifa	tarifa
tariffario	barème	scale	Liste(f)	baremo	tabela
tartaruga	tortue	tortoise; turtle	Schildkröte(f)	tortuga	tartaruga
tasca	poche	pocket	Tasche(f)	bolsillo	bolso
tassa, imposta	taxe	tax; duty	Steuer(f)	tasa, impuesto	taxa, imposto
tassa	impôt	tax	Steuer(f)	impuesto	imposto
tassista	chauffeur(taxi)	taxi-driver	Taxifahrer(in f)m	taxista	motorista
tasso	taux	rate	Rate(f)	tasa	taxa
tastare	tâter	feel, touch	berühren	tantear	tatear, apalpar
tastiera	clavier	keyboard	Tastatur(f)	teclado	teclado
tasto	touche	key	Taste(f)	tecla	tecla
tattica	tactique	tactic	Taktik(f)	táctica	táctica
tattico, a	tactique	tactical	taktisch	táctico, a	táctico, a
tatto	tact	tact	Takt(m)	tacto	tacto
tatuaggio	tatouage	tattoo	Tätowierung(f)	tatuaje	tatuagem
tavola, asse	planche	board	Brett(n)	tabla	tábua
tavolo; tavola	table	table	Tisch(m)	mesa	mesa
taxi, tassì	taxi	taxi, cab	Taxi(n)	taxi	táxi
tazza	tasse	cup	Tasse(f)	taza	chávena
tè	thé	tea	Tee(m)	té	chá
teatro	théâtre	theatre	Theater(n)	teatro	teatro
tecnico, a	technique	technical	technisch	técnico, a	técnico, a
tecnico, a	technicien, ne	technician	Techniker(in f)m	técnico, a	técnico, a
tecnocrate	technocrate	technocrat	Technokrat(m)	tecnócrata	tecnocrata
tecnologia	technologie	technology	Technologie(f)	tecnología	tecnologia
tegola	tuile	tile	Ziegel(m)	teja	telha
teiera	théière	teapot	Teekanne(f)	tetera	bule
tela	toile	canvas, material	Tuch(n)	tela, lienzo	tela
tela, dipinto	toile	canvas, painting	Gemälde(n)(Leinwand)	lienzo, cuadro	tela, quadro
telaio	châssis	frame, chassis	Rahmen(m), Chassis(n)	chasis	chassis
telecomando	télécommande	remote control	Fernsteuerung(f)	telemando	telecomando
teleferica	téléphérique	cable-car	Seilbahn(f)	teleférico	teleférico
telefonare	téléphoner	phone, ring, call	telefonieren	telefonear	telefonar
telefono	téléphone	telephone, phone	Telefon(n)	teléfono	telefone
telefono pubblico	taxi-/publiphone	public call-box	Telefonzelle(f)	teléfono público	telefone público
telegiornale	actualités(T.V)	news	Nachrichten(pl.)	telediario	telejornal
telegramma	télégramme	telegram, cable	Telegramm(n)	telegrama	telegrama
telepatia	télépathie	telepathy	Telepathie(f)	telepatía	telepatia
telescopio	télescope	telescope	Teleskop(n)	telescopio	telescópio
telespettatore, trice	téléspectateur	viewer	Fernsehzuschauer/in	telespectador, a	telespectador, a

Italian	French	English	German	Spanish	Portuguese
teletrasmettere	téléviser	televise	übertragen	televisar	televisionar
televisione	télévision	television	Fernsehen(n)	televisión	televisão; TV
televisore	téléviseur	television set	Fernseher(m)	televisor	televisor
telex	télex	telex	Telex(n)	telex	telex
telone	bâche	cover	Plane(f)	toldo, lona	toldo
tema	thème	theme	Thema(n)	tema	tema
tema	sujet, thème	subject, theme	Thema(n)	tema	assunto, tema
temerario, a	téméraire	rash, reckless	waghalsig	temerario, a	temerário, a
temere	craindre	fear, be afraid of	befürchten, fürchten	temer, tener miedo	temer
temibile	redoutable	formidable	furchtbar	temible	temível
temperamento	tempérament	temperament	Temperament(n)	temperamento	temperamento
temperato, a	tempéré, e	temperate	gemäßigt	templado, a	temperado, a
temperatura	température	temperature	Temperatur(f)	temperatura	temperatura
tempesta	tempête	storm	Unwetter(n)	tempestad	tempestade
tempia	tempe	temple	Schläfe(f)	sien	têmpora
tempio	temple	temple	Tempel(m)	templo	templo
tempo	temps	weather	Wetter(n)	tiempo	tempo
tempo	temps	time	Zeit(f)	tiempo	tempo
tempo libero, hobby	loisir	leisure	Freizeit(f)	tiempo libre	tempo livre
temporale	orage	storm, thunderstorm	Gewitter(n)	tormenta	tempestade
temporaneo, a	temporaire	temporary	vorübergehend	temporario, a	temporário, a
tenacità; tenacia	ténacité	tenacity	Hartnäckigkeit(f)	tenacidad	tenacidade
tenda, tapparella	rideau, store	curtain	Vorhang(m)	cortina	cortina
tenda	tente	tent	Zelt(n)	tienda	tenda
tendenza	tendance	tendency; trend	Tendenz(f), Neigung(f)	tendencia	tendência
tendere	tendre	tighten; stretch	spannen	tender	estender, esticar
tenebre	ténèbres	darkness	Finsternis(f)	tinieblas	trevas
tenente	lieutenant	lieutenant	Leutnant(m)	teniénte	tenente
tenere	tenir	hold	halten	tener	ter, segurar
tenere	garder	keep	behalten	guardar	guardar
tenerezza	tendresse	tenderness	Zärtlichkeit(f)	ternura	ternura
tenero, a	tendre	tender	zärtlich	tierno, a	terno, a
tennis	tennis	tennis	Tennis(n)	tenis	ténis
tenore(di vita)	niveau(de vie)	standard of living	Standard(m)	nivel(de vida)	nível(de vida)
tenore	ténor	tenor	Tenor(m)	tenor	tenor
tensione	tension	tension	Spannung(f)	tensión	tensão
tentacolo	tentacule	tentacle	Fangarm(m)	tentáculo	tentáculo
tentare	tenter	attempt, try	versuchen; wagen	intentar	tentar
tentativo	tentative	attempt	Versuch(m)	tentativa	tentativa
tentazione	tentation	temptation	Versuchung(f)	tentación	tentação
tenuta, fondo	domaine	domain, estate	Gut(n), Besitzung(f)	dominio, terreno	terreno
teologia	théologie	theology	Theologie(f)	teología	teologia
teorema	théorème	theorem	Lehrsatz(m)	teorema	teorema
teoria	théorie	theory	Theorie(f)	teoría	teoria
teorico, a	théorique	theoretical	theoretisch	teórico, a	teórico, a
teppa, malviventi	pègre	underworld	Unterwelt(f)	hampa	súcia, ladroagem
teppista	truand, e	crook	Ganove(m), Gauner(m)	granuja, bandido	bandido
terapia	thérapie	therapy	Therapie(f)	terapia	terapia
termale	thermal, e	thermal	Thermal-	termal	termal
termico, a	thermique	thermic, thermal	thermisch	térmico, a	térmico, a
terminale	terminal, e	terminal, final	letzte(r, s); End-	terminal	terminal
terminare	terminer	end, finish	beenden	terminar	terminar
terminare, finire	achever	complete, finish	beenden	acabar	acabar
termine	terme, fin	end	Ende(n), Ziel(n)	término	termo
termine	délai	delay	Frist(f)	plazo	prazo
termometro	thermomètre	thermometer	Thermometer(n)	termómetro	termómetro
termosifone	radiateur	radiator, heater	Heizkörper(m)	radiador	aquecedor
terra	terre	earth	Erde(f)	tierra	Terra
terra	terre	land	Land(n)	tierra	terra
terra	terre	soil	Erde(f)	tierra	terra
terremoto	séisme	earthquake	Erdbeben(n)	terremoto	terremoto
terreno	terrain	ground	Gelände(n)	terreno	terreno
terreno	terrain(sport)	field; court	Sportplatz(m)	campo	campo
terrestre	terrestre	terrestrial	irdisch	terrestre	terrestre
terribile	terrible	terrible	schrecklich	terrible	terrível
territorio	territoire	territory	Gebiet(n), Land(n)	territorio	território
terrore	terreur	terror	Schrecken(m)	terror	terror
terrorismo	terrorisme	terrorism	Terrorismus(m)	terrorismo	terrorismo

Italian	French	English	German	Spanish	Portuguese
terrorista	terroriste	terrorist	Terrorist(in f)m	terrorista	terrorista
terrorizzare	terroriser	terrorize	terrorisieren	aterrorizar	aterrorizar
terzo, a	troisième	third	dritte	tercero, a	terceiro, a
terzo, a	tiers	third	Drittel(n)	tercio, a; tercero	terço, a; terceiro
terzo mondo	tiers-monde	third world	dritte Welt(f)	tercer mundo	terceiro mundo
tesi	thèse	thesis(theses)	These(f)	tesis	tese
teso, a	tendu, e	tight	gespannt	tenso, a	esticado, a
tesoriere	trésorier, ière	treasurer	Schatzmeister(in f)m	tesorero, a	tesoureiro, a
tesoro	trésor	treasure	Schatz(m)	tesoro	tesouro
tessera	carte	card, ticket	Karte(f)	tarjeta	bilhete
tessere	tisser	weave	weben	tejer	tecer
tessile	textile	textile	Textil-; Web-	textil	têxtil
tessuto	tissu	material, fabric	Stoff(m)	tela	tecido
testa, capo	tête	head	Kopf(m)	cabeza	cabeça
testamento	testament	will, testament	Testament(n)	testamento	testamento
testardo, a	têtu, e	stubborn	dickköpfig	tozudo, a	cabeçudo, a
testare	tester	test	testen	ensayar, probar	testar
testicolo	testicule	testicle	Hoden(m)	testículo	testículo
testificare	témoigner	witness	zeugen, bezeugen	atestiguar	testemunhar
testimone	témoin	witness	Zeuge(m), Zeugin(f)	testigo	testemunha
testimonianza	témoignage	testimony, evidence	Zeugenaussage(f)	testimonio	testemunho
testimoniare	témoigner	testify	aus = sagen	testimoniar	testemunhar
testo	texte	text	Text(m)	texto	texto
tetania	tétanie	tetany	Starrkrampf(m).	tetania	tetania
tetano	tétanos	tetanus	Tetanus(m)	tétanos	tétano
tetto	toit	roof	Dach(n)	tejado	telhado
ti, te	te, t'	you	dich; dir	te	te
tibia	tibia	tibia	Schienbein(n)	tibia	tíbia
tic	tic	twitch(ing)	Tick(m)	tic	tique
tiepido, a	tiède	lukewarm, tepid	lauwarm, lau	tibio, a	tépido, a; morno, a
tifoide	typhoïde	typhoid	Typhus(m)	tifoidea	tifóide
tifone	typhon	typhoon	Taifun(m)	tifón	tufão
tigre	tigre	tiger	Tiger(m)	tigre	tigre
timbrare	tamponner	stamp	stempeln	sellar	carimbar
timidezza	timidité	shyness, timidity	Schüchternheit(f)	timidez	timidez
timido, a	timide	shy, timid	schüchtern	tímido, a	tímido, a
timone	gouvernail	rudder	Ruder(n), Steur(n)	timón	leme
timore	crainte	fear	Furcht(f)	temor, miedo	temor, receio
timpano	tympan	eardrum	Trommelfell(n)	tímpano	tímpano
tingere	teindre, colorer	dye	färben	teñir	tingir
tino	cuve	tank; vat	Wanne(f), Faß(n).	cuba	cuba
tinta	teinte	tint, colour	Färbung(f), Farbe(f)	tinte, color	tinta
tintinnio	tintement	ringing, jingle	Klimpern, Klingeln(n)	tañido	tilintar
tipico, a	typique	typical	typisch	típico, a	típico, a
tipo	type	type	Typ(m)	tipo	tipo
tipografia	imprimerie	printing works	Druckerei(f)	imprenta	tipografia
tiranno, a	tyran	tyrant	Tyrann(m)	tirano, a	tirano, a
tirare	tirer	pull, draw	ziehen	tirar	puxar
tirare, sparare	tirer	shoot, fire	schießen, feuern	disparar	atirar, disparar
tirar su col naso	renifler	sniff	schnüffeln	resoplar	fungar
tiro	tir	shooting, firing	Schießen(n)	tiro	tiro
tirocinio	apprentissage	learning	Lernen(n)	estudio	aprendizagem
tirocinio, stage	stage	training period	Praktikum(n).	cursillo	estágio
tiroide	thyroïde	thyroid(gland)	Schilddrüse(f)	tiroides	tiróide
tisana	tisane	herb tea	Kräutertee(m)	tisana	tisana
titolare	titulaire	holder	Inhaber(in f)m	titular	titular
titolare	titulaire	tenured	festangestellt	numerario	titular
titolo	titre	title	Titel(m)	título	título
toccare	toucher	touch	an = fassen, berühren	tocar	tocar
tocco, a; picchiato, a	cinglé, e	mad, nuts, barmy	verrückt	chiflado, a	doido, a; louco, a
togliere	enlever	take off	aus = ziehen	quitar	tirar
togliere	enlever	take away, remove	entfernen	sacar, quitar	retirar, tirar
togliere; W.C	ôter, enlever	remove, take away	ab = nehmen	quitar	tirar
toilettes; W.C	toilettes(W.C)	toilet, lavatory	Toiletten(f pl)	servicios(W.C)	lavabos; sanita
tolleranza	tolérance	tolerance	Toleranz(f)	tolerancia	tolerância
tollerare	tolérer	tolerate	dulden, ertragen	tolerar	tolerar
tomba	tombe	grave	Grab(n)	tumba	túmulo, sepultura
tomba	tombeau	tomb	Grabmal(n)	tumba	túmulo

I

Italian	French	English	German	Spanish	Portuguese
tonalità	tonalité	tonality, tone	Tonart(f), Klangfarbe	tonalidad	tonalidade
tonnellata	tonne	ton	Tonne(f)	tonelada	tonelada
tonno	thon	tuna(fish)	Thunfisch(m)	atún, bonito	atum
tono	ton, son, timbre	tone	Ton(m), Klang(m)	tono, sonido	tom, som, timbre
tonsilla	amygdale(s)	tonsils	Mandeln(f, pl)	amígdalas	amígdala
topaia	taudis	slum	Bruchbude(f)	tugurio	antro, tugúrio
topazio	topaze	topaz	Topas(m)	topacio	topázio
topo, ratto	rat	rat	Ratte(f)	rata	rato, a
topo	souris	mouse(mice pl.)	Maus(f)	ratón	rato
torace	thorax	thorax	Brustkasten(m)	tórax	tórax
torbido, a	trouble	cloudy; muddy	trüb	turbio, a	turvo, a
torcere, piegare	tordre	twist	verbiegen, verdrehen	torcer	torcer
torcia	torche	torch	Fackel(f)	antorcha	tocha, archote
torero	toréador	bull-fighter	Stierkämpfer(m)	torero	toureiro
tormentare	tourmenter	torment	quälen	atormentar	atormentar
tormentato, a	tourmenté, e	tormented	beunruhigt	atormentado, a	atormentado, a
tornado	tornade	tornado(-es)	Wirbelsturm(m)	tornado	tornado
tornare	retourner	return(to)	zurück = gehen	regresar	voltar(a)
tornare, rientrare	rentrer	go back, come back	zurück = kommen	regresar	voltar
torneo	tournoi	tournament	Turnier(n)	torneo	torneio
toro	taureau	bull	Stier(m)	toro	touro; toiro
torpedine	torpille	torpedo(-es)	Torpedo(m)	torpedo	torpedo
torpore	torpeur	torpor	Erstarrungszustand(m)	torpor	torpor
torre	tour	tower	Turm(m)	torre	torre
torrente	torrent	torrent	Wildbach(m)	torrente	torrente
torsione	torsion	twist(ing)	Drehung(f), Torsion(f)	torsión	torção
torta, crostata	tarte	tart	Torte(f)	tarta	torta
torta salata	tourte	pie	Pastete(f)	pastel, tortada	empada
torto(aver)	tort(avoir)	wrong(to be)	Unrecht(haben)	culpa(tener)	razão(não ter)
tortura	torture	torture	Folter(f)	tortura	tortura
tosse	toux	cough	Husten(m)	tos	tosse
tossico, a	toxique	toxic	giftig	tóxico, a	tóxico, a
tossicologia	toxicologie	toxicology	Toxikologie(f)	toxicología	toxicologia
tossicomane	toxicomane	drug addict	Rauschgiftsüchtige(r)	drogadicto, a	toxicómano, drogado
tossire	tousser	cough	husten	toser	tossir
totale	total, e	total	ganz; Gesamt-	total	total
totale	total	total	Summe(f), Ganze(s)(n)	total	total
tovaglia	nappe	table-cloth	Tischdecke(f)	mantel	toalha
tovagliolo	serviette	serviette, napkin	Serviette(f)	servilleta	guardanapo
tra, fra	entre	between	zwischen	entre	entre
traboccare	déborder	overflow	über = laufen	desbordar	transbordar
traccia	trace	trace, track	Spur(f)	huella, rastro	traço; vestígio
tracciare	tracer	draw	entwerfen	trazar	traçar
trachea	trachée-artère	trachea	Luftröhre(f)	traquearteria	traqueia
tradimento	trahison	betrayal; treason	Verrat(m)	traición	traição
tradire	trahir	betray	verräten	traicionar	trair
traditore, trice	traître, esse	traitor, -tress	Verräter(in f)m	traidor, a	traidor, a
tradizione	tradition	tradition	Tradition(f)	tradición	tradição
traduttore, trice	traducteur, trice	translator	Übersetzer(in f)m	traductor, a	tradutor, a
traduzione	traduction	translation	Übersetzung(f)	traducción	tradução
trafficante	trafiquant, e	trafficker; pedlar	Schwarzhändler(in f)m	traficante	traficante
traffico	trafic	traffic	Verkehr(m)	tráfico	tráfego, tráfico
traffico	circulation	traffic	Verkehr(m)	tráfico	trânsito
tragedia	tragédie	tragedy	Tragödie(f)	tragedia	tragédia
traghetto, ferry	bac	ferry	Fähre(f)	transbordador	barco
tragico, a	tragique	tragic	tragisch	trágico, a	trágico, a
tragitto	trajet	journey, trip	Strecke(f)	trayecto	trajecto
traiettoria	trajectoire	trajectory	Bahn(f), Kurs(m)	trayectoria	trajectória
trainare, tirare	tracter	tug, tow	ab = schleppen	tirar	puxar
tram	tramway	tram-car	Straßenbahn(f)	tranvía	carro eléctrico
tramezzo	cloison	partition	Trennwand(f)	tabique	tabique
tramonto	coucher(soleil)	sunset	Sonnenuntergang(m)	puesta de sol	pôr do sol
tranne	excepté, sauf	except	außer	excepto, salvo	excepto
tranquillante	tranquillisant	tranquillizer	Beruhigungsmittel(n)	tranquilizante	tranquilizante
tranquillo, a	tranquille	quiet, still, calm	ruhig	tranquilo, a	tranquilo, a
transatlantico	paquebot	liner	Passagierdampfer(m)	buque	paquete
transazione	transaction	transaction	Transaktion(f)	transacción	transacção
transfuga	transfuge	defector	Überläufer(in f)m	transfuga	trânsfuga

Italian	French	English	German	Spanish	Portuguese
trapassare	transpercer	pierce	durchbohren	atravesar	trespassar
trapezio	trapèze	trapezium; trapeze	Trapez(n)	trapecio	trapézio
trapianto	greffe	transplant, graft	Verpflanzung(f)	trasplante	enxerto
trappola	piège	trap, snare	Falle(f)	trampa	armadilha
trascinare	traîner	drag, trail, haul	schleppen	arrastrar	arrastar
trascorrere	passer	spend	verbringen	pasar	passar
trascorrere	écouler(s')	elapse	vergehen, verfließen	transcurrir	decorrer
trascurare	négliger	neglect	vernachlässigen	descuidar	descuidar
trasferimento	mutation	transfer	Versetzung(f)	traslado	transferência
trasferimento	transfert	transfer	Verlegung(f)	transferencia	transferência
trasferire	transférer	transfer	überführen	transferir	transferir
trasformare	transformer	transform, change	verändern	transformar	transformar
trasformazione	transformation	transformation	Veränderung(f)	transformación	transformação
trasfusione	transfusion	transfusion	Transfusion(f)	transfusión	transfusão
traslocare	déménager	move	um = ziehen	mudar(se)	mudar, mudar-se
trasmettere	transmettre	transmit	übertragen	transmitir	transmitir
trasmettere	diffuser	broadcast	senden	difundir	transmitir
trasmissione	transmission	transmission	Übertragung(f)	transmisión	transmissão
trasparente	transparent, e	transparent	durchsichtig	transparente	transparente
traspirare	transpirer	perspire, sweat	schwitzen	transpirar	transpirar
traspirazione	transpiration	perspiration	Schweiß(m)	transpiración	transpiração
trasportare	transporter	transport, carry	transportieren	transportar	transportar
trasporto	transport	transport	Transport(m)	transporte	transporte
trasversale	transversal, e	transversal	Quer-; schräg	transversal	transversal
trattamento	traitement	treatment	Behandlung(f)	tratamiento	tratamento
trattare	traiter	treat; deal with	behandeln	tratar	tratar
trattative	pourparlers	talks	Verhandlungen(pl)	negociaciones	negociações
trattato	traité	treaty	Vertrag(m)	tratado	tratado
trattenere	retenir	hold back; retain	zurück = halten	retener	reter
trattino	tiret	dash	Gedankenstrich(m)	raya, guión	travessão, hífen
tratto, riga	trait	line	Strich(m)	raya	traço, risco
tratto, lineamento	trait(s)	feature	Zug(m)(Gesichts-)	rasgos	feição
trattore	tracteur	tractor	Traktor(m)	tractor	tractor
trauma	traumatisme	traumatism	Trauma(n)	traumatismo	traumatismo
trave	poutre	beam	Balken(m)	viga	trave
traverso(di)	travers(de)	askew	schief	través(de)	través(de)
travestito	travesti	transvestite	Transvestit(m)	travesti	travesti
travolgere	renverser	knock over/down	um = stoßen	derribar	derrubar
tre	trois	three	drei	tres	três
treccia	natte	plait	Zopf(m)	trenza	trança
treccia	tresse	plait, braid	Zopf(m)	trenza	trança
tredici	treize	thirteen	dreizehn	trece	treze
tregua	trêve	truce	Waffenstillstand(m)	tregua	trégua
tregua, riposo	répit	respite	Atempause(f)	tregua, respiro	trégua, espera
tremare(di freddo)	grelotter	shiver	zittern	tiritar	tiritar
tremare	trembler	tremble	zittern	temblar	tremer
treno	train	train	Zug(m), Eisenbahn(f)	tren	comboio
trenta	trente	thirty	dreißig	treinta	trinta
triangolo	triangle	triangle	Dreieck(n)	triángulo	triângulo
tribù	tribu	tribe	Stamm(m)	tribu	tribo
tribunale	tribunal	court, tribunal	Gericht(n)	tribunal	tribunal
trimestrale	trimestriel, le	quarterly	vierteljährlich	trimestral	trimestral
trimestre	trimestre	term; quarter	Vierteljahr(n)	trimestre	trimestre
trincea	tranchée	trench	Graben(m)	trinchera, zanja	trincheira
trionfo	triomphe	triumph	Triumph(m)	triunfo	triunfo
triste	triste	sad, unhappy	traurig	triste	triste
tristezza	tristesse	sadness	Traurigkeit(f)	tristeza	tristeza
trofeo	trophée	trophy	Trophäe(f)	trofeo	troféu
trombetta	trompette	trumpet	Trompete(f)	trompeta	trombeta
tronco	tronc	trunk	Stamm(m)	tronco	tronco
trono	trône	throne	Thron(m)	trono	trono
tropicale	tropical, e	tropical	tropisch	tropical	tropical
troppo, a	trop	too(much, many)	zuviel	demasiado, a	demasiado, a
trota	truite	trout	Forelle(f)	trucha	truta
trottare	trotter	trot	traben	trotar	trotar
trovare	trouver	find	finden	encontrar	achar, encontrar
truccarsi	maquiller(se)	make-up(put on)	schminken, sich	maquillarse	maquilhar-se
trucco	maquillage	make-up	Schminke(f)	maquillaje	maquilhagem

Italian	French	English	German	Spanish	Portuguese
trucco	truquage	faking	Trickaufnahme(f)	falsificación	falsificação
truffa, imbroglio	escroquerie	swindle	Schwindel(m), Gaunerei	estafa, timo	trapaça, burla
truppa	troupe	troop	Truppe(f)	tropa	tropa
tu	tu	you	du	tú	tu
tu; te	toi	you	du; dich	tú; te	tu; ti
tua(la)	ta	your	dein(e)	tu	tua, teu
tubercolosi	tuberculose	tuberculosis, T.B.	Tuberkulose(f)	tuberculosis	tuberculose
tubo	tube	tube	Tube(f)	tubo	tubo
tubo	tuyau	hose	Schlauch(m)	manguera	mangueira
tubo, tubazione	tuyau(terie)	pipe	Röhre(f), Schlauch(m)	tubo, caño	tubo, cano
tuffarsi	plonger	plunge, dive	tauchen	zambullirse	mergulhar
tuffo	plongeon	dive	Kopfsprung(m)	zambullida	mergulho
tulipano	tulipe	tulip	Tulpe(f)	tulipán	tulipa
tumore	tumeur	tumour	Tumor(m)	tumor	tumor
tumulto	tumulte	tumult, uproar	Tumult(m)	tumulto	tumulto
tunica	tunique	tunic	Tunika(f)	túnica	túnica
tunnel	tunnel	tunnel	Tunnel(m)	túnel	túnel
tuo(il)	ton	your	dein(e)	tu	teu
tuo, a; tuoi, tue	toi(à)	yours	dir	tuyo, a	teu, tua
tuo, a	tien, ne	yours	deine(r, s), deine	tuyo, a	teu, tua
tuoi, tue(i, le)	tes	your	deine	tus	teus, tuas
tuono	tonnerre	thunder	Donner(m)	trueno	trovão
turbare, disturbare	troubler	disturb; trouble	stören	perturbar	perturbar
turbina	turbine	turbine	Turbine(f)	turbina	turbina
turbolenza	turbulence	turbulence	Turbulenz(f)	turbulencia	turbulência
turismo	tourisme	tourism	Tourismus(m)	turismo	turismo
turista	touriste	tourist	Tourist(m)	turista	turista
turno	tour	turn	Reihe(f)	turno	vez
tuta(spaziale)	combinaison	suit(space-)	Anzug(Raum-)(m)	traje(espacial)	fato(espacial)
tuta, completo	combinaison	suit(ski-)	Anzug(m)(Ski-)	traje	fato
tutela	tutelle	trusteeship	Treuhandschaft(f)	tutela	tutela
tutore, trice	tuteur, tutrice	guardian	Vormund(m)	tutor, a	tutor, a
tutta	toute	whole(the)	ganz	toda	toda
tuttavia	toutefois	however	jedoch	sin embargo	todavia
tutti	tous	all(the)	alle	todos	todos
tutto, a	tout, e	all(the)	alles	todo, a	todo, a

U

Italian	French	English	German	Spanish	Portuguese
ubriachezza	ivresse	drunkenness	Trunkenheit(f)	ebriedad	embriaguez
ubriaco, a	soûl, e; ivre	drunk	betrunken	embriagado, a	bêbado, a; ébrio, a
ubriaco, a	ivrogne	drunkard	Trunkenbold(m)	borracho, a	bêbedo, a; ébrio, a
uccello	oiseau	bird	Vogel(m)	pájaro, ave	pássaro, ave
uccidere	tuer	kill	töten	matar	matar
ucciso, a	tué, e	killed	getötet	muerto, a	morto, a
udienza	audience	audience	Audienz(f)	audiencia	audiência
udito	ouïe	hearing, audition	Gehör(n)	oído	ouvido
uditore, uditrice	auditeur, trice	listener	Zuhörer(in f)m	auditor, a	ouvinte
ufficiale	officiel, le	official	offiziell	oficial	oficial
ufficiale	officier	officer	Offizier(m)	oficial	oficial
ufficio	bureau	office	Büro(n)	despacho	escritório
ufficioso, a	officieux, se	unofficial	halbamtlich	oficioso, a	oficioso, a
uguaglianza	égalité	equality	Gleichheit(f)	igualdad	igualdade
uguale	égal, e	equal	gleich	igual	igual
uguale, pari	pareil, le	same, similar, like	gleich, wie	igual	igual
ugualmente	également	too, also, as well	ebenfalls, auch	igualmente	igualmente
ulcera	ulcère	ulcer	Geschwür(n)	úlcera	úlcera

ulteriore	ultérieur, e	later	später	ulterior	ulterior
ultimo, a	dernier, ière	last	letzter, letzte	último, a	último, a
ultimo, a	ultime	ultimate, final	allerletzte(r, s)	último, a	último, a
ultimo, a	dernier	last	Letzte(f, m)	último, a	último, a
ululare, guaire	hurler	howl	heulen	aullar	uivar; urrar
umanità	humanité	humanity	Menschheit(f)	humanidad	humanidade
umano, a	humain, e	human	menschlich	humano, a	humano, a
umidità	humidité	humidity	Feuchtigkeit(f)	humedad	humidade
umido, a	humide	damp, humid, moist	feucht	húmedo, a	húmido, a
umiliare	humilier	humiliate	erniedrigen	humillar	humilhar
umore	humeur	mood	Laune(f)	humor	humor
umorismo	humour	humour	Humor(m)	humor	humor
umoristico, a	humoristique	humorous	humoristisch	humorístico, a	humorístico, a
un, uno	un	one	eins	un, uno	um
unanime	unanime	unanimous	einstimmig	unánime	unânime
undici	onze	eleven	elf	once	onze
unghia	ongle	nail	Fingernagel(m)	uña	unha
unicamente	uniquement	only	ausschließlich	únicamente	somente
unico, a	unique	unique; only	einzig, einzeln	único, a	único, a
unico, a	unique	unique, exceptional	einmalig	único, a	único, a
unificato, a	unifié, e	unified, united	vereinigt	unificado, a	unificado, a
uniforme	uniforme	uniform	gleichförmig	uniforme	uniforme
uniforme; divisa	uniforme	uniform	Uniform(f)	uniforme	uniforme
unione	union	union	Bund(m), Vereinigung f	unión	união
unire	unir	unite	vereinen	unir	unir, juntar
unirsi, associarsi	joindre à(se)	join	an = schließen, sich	juntarse con	juntar-se
unità	unité	unity	Einigkeit(f)	unidad	unidade
unità	unité	unit	Einheit(f)	unidad	unidade
unitario, a	unitaire	unitary, per unit	unitarisch	unitario, a	unitário, a
universale	universel, le	universal	universell	universal	universal
università	université	university	Universität(f)	universidad	universidade
universitario, a	universitaire	academic	Universität-	universitario, a	universitário, a
universo	univers	universe	Universum(n)	universo	universo
uno, una	un, e	a, an	ein, e	uno, una	um, uma
uno(l') o l'altro	un(l')ou l'autre	either	eine(der) der andere	uno u otro, cada	um ou outro, cada
unto, a	graisseux, se	fatty, greasy	schmierig, fettig	grasiento, a	gorduroso, a
untuoso, a	onctueux, se	unctuous	cremig, sahnig	untuoso, a	untuoso, a
uomo; uomini	homme	man(men)	Mann(m), Mensch(m)	hombre	homem
uomo politico	homme politique	politician	Politiker(in f)m	político	político
uovo(a)	oeuf	egg	Ei(n)	huevo	ovo
uragano	ouragan	hurricane	Orkan(m)	huracán	furacão
uranio	uranium	uranium	Uran(n)	uranio	urânio
urbanistica	urbanisme	town-planning	Städtebau(m)	urbanismo	urbanismo
urbano, a	urbain, e	urban	städtisch, Stadt-	urbano, a	urbano, a
urea	urée	urea	Harnstoff(m)	urea	ureia
urgente	urgent, e	urgent	dringend	urgente	urgente
urgenza	urgence	urgency	Dringlichkeit(f)	urgencia	urgência
urgenza	urgence	emergency, urgency	Notfall(m)	urgencia	urgência
urina	urine	urine	Urin(m)	orina	urina
urlare	hurler	scream, yell	brüllen	chillar	gritar; berrar
urtante	choquant, e	shocking	anstößig	chocante	chocante
urtare	heurter	knock(against)	stoßen	tropezar con	chocar, bater
urto, scontro	choc	shock, impact	Stoß(m), Aufprall(m)	choque	choque
usare, adoperare	employer	use	benützen	usar, emplear	usar
uscire	sortir	go out, come out	aus = gehen	salir	sair
uscita	sortie	exit, way out	Ausgang(m)	salida	saída
uscita(sicurezza)	sortie(secours)	emergency exit	Notausgang(m)	salida(emergencia)	saída de emergência
uscita	issue(sortie)	way out, exit	Ausgang(m)	salida	saída
uso	usage	usage, use	Gebrauch(m)	uso, empleo	uso
uso	emploi	use	Gebrauch(m)	uso, empleo	uso
usuale	usuel, le	usual	gebräuchlich	usual	usual
usura; logorio	usure	wear	Abnützung(f)	desgaste	usura, desgaste
utensile	ustensile	utensil	Gerät(n)	utensilios	utensílio
utente	usager, ère	user	Benutzer(in f)m	usuario, a	utente
utero	utérus	uterus, womb	Gebärmutter(f)	útero	útero
utile	utile	useful	nützlich	útil	útil
utilizzare	utiliser	use	benutzen	utilizar	utilizar
utilizzatore, trice	utilisateur	user	Benutzer(in f)m	utilizador, a	utilizador, a

I

Italian	French	English	German	Spanish	Portuguese
utilizzazione	utilisation	utilization, use	Benutzung(f)	utilización	utilização
utopico, a	utopique	Utopian	utopisch	utópico, a	utópico, a
uva	raisin	grape	Traube(f)(Wein-)	uva(s)	uva

V

Italian	French	English	German	Spanish	Portuguese
vacanze	vacances	holidays	Ferien(pl.)	vacaciones	férias
vacanze	vacances	vacation	Ferien(pl.)	vacaciones	férias
vacca, mucca	vache	cow	Kuh(f)	vaca	vaca
vaccinazione	vaccination	vaccination	Impfung(f)	vacunación	vacinação
vaccino	vaccin	vaccine	Impfstoff(m)	vacuna	vacina
vacillare	vaciller	sway, wobble	taumeln	vacilar	vacilar
vacillare	vaciller	flicker	flackern	oscilar, vacilar	tremer
vagabondo, a	vagabond, e	vagabond; tramp	Landstreicher(in f)m.	vagabundo, a	vagabundo, a
vagabondo, a	rôdeur, se	prowler	Herumstreicher(m)	vagabundo, a	vagabundo, a
vagina	vagin	vagina	Scheide(f)(Anat.)	vagina	vagina
vaglia(postale)	mandat-lettre	postal order	Postanweisung(f)	giro postal	vale postal
vagone	wagon	truck, wag(g)on	Waggon(m)(Güterwagen)	vagón	vagão
vagone, carrozza	wagon	coach, carriage	Wagen(m)	vagón	vagão
vaiolo	variole	smallpox	Pocken(f, pl)	viruela	varíola
valanga	avalanche	avalanche	Lawine(f)	avalancha	avalanche
vale la pena	vaut la peine	worthwhile	der Mühe wert	vale la pena	vale a pena
valere	valoir	worth(be)	wert sein	valer	valer
validità	validité	validity	Gültigkeit(f)	validez	validade
valido, a	valable	valid, good	gültig; annehmbar	válido, a; valedero	válido, a
valigetta	attaché-case	attaché-case	Aktenkoffer(m)	maletín	maleta
valigia	valise	suitcase, case	Koffer(m)	maleta	mala
valle	vallée	valley	Tal(n)	valle	vale
valore	valeur	value, worth	Wert(m)	valor	valor
valore, merito	valeur, mérite	worth, merit	Wert(m)	valor, mérito	valor, mérito
valoroso, a	vaillant, e	brave	tapfer	valiente	valente; bravo, a
valuta	devise	currency	Währung(f)	divisa	moeda, divisa
valuta; moneta	monnaie	currency	Währung(f), Devisen pl	moneda	moeda
valutare, stimare	évaluer, estimer	assess	ein = schätzen	tasar, valorar	avaliar, fixar
valutazione	évaluation	assessment	Einschätzung(f)	valoración	avaliação
valutazione	évaluation	assessment	Schätzung(f)	evaluación	avaliação
valvola	clapet	valve	Klappenventil(n)	válvula	válvula
valzer	valse	waltz	Walzer(m)	vals	valsa
vaniglia	vanille	vanilla	Vanille(f)	vainilla	baunilha
vanità	vanité	vanity	Eitelkeit(f)	vanidad	vaidade
vantaggio	avantage	advantage	Vorteil(m)	ventaja	vantagem
vantaggio	atout, avantage	asset	Trumpf(m), Vorteil(m)	ventaja	vantagem
vantarsi	vanter(se)	boast	prahlen	jactarse	gabar-se
vapore	vapeur	steam	Dampf(m)	vapor	vapor
vapore	vapeur	vapour, fumes	Dunst(m)	vapor	vapor
vaporizzare	vaporiser	spray	sprühen	vaporizar	vaporizar
varcare, passare	franchir	cross	überqueren	atravesar	atravessar
variabile	variable	variable	veränderlich	variable	variável
variazione	variation	variation	Abwandlung(f)	variación	variação
varicella	varicelle	chicken-pox	Windpocken(f, pl)	varicela	varicela
varietà	variété	variety	Vielfalt(f)	variedad	variedade
vario, a	varié, e	varied, various	vielfältig	variado, a	variado, a
vario, a	divers, e	various, varied	mannigfach	vario, a	variado, a
vasca da bagno	baignoire	bath	Badewanne(f)	bañera	banheira
vascello, nave	vaisseau	vessel, ship	Schiff(n)	nave, navío	navio
vascolare	vasculaire	vascular	Gefäß	vascular	vascular
vasellina	vaseline	vaseline	Vaseline(f)	vaselina	vaselina

Italian	French	English	German	Spanish	Portuguese
vaso	vase	vase	Vase(f)	jarrón	jarra
vaso	pot	pot	Topf(m)	maceta	vaso; pote
vaso(sanguigno)	vaisseau	vessel(blood)	Gefäß(Blut-)(n)	vaso(sanguíneo)	vaso(sanguíneo)
vassoio	plateau	tray	Tablett(n), Platte(f)	bandeja	tabuleiro
vassoio, piatto	plat	dish, plate	Schüssel(f)	fuente, plato	travessa
vasto, a	vaste	vast	weit	vasto, a	vasto, a
vecchio, a	vieux, vieille	old	alt	viejo, a	velho, a
vecchio, a; antico, a	ancien, ne	old	alt	antiguo, a	antigo, a
vecchio, anziano	vieillard	old man(men)	Alte(m), alter Mann(m)	viejo, anciano	velho, ancião
vedere	voir	see	sehen	ver	ver
vedette; divo, a	vedette	star	Star(m)	estrella; divo, a	vedeta, estrela
vedovo, a	veuf, veuve	widower, widow	Witwer(m), Witwe(f)	viudo, a	viúvo, a
veduta	vue	view	Ausblick(m)	vista	vista
vegetale	végétal	vegetable, plant	Pflanze(f)	vegetal	vegetal
vegetazione	végétation	vegetation	Pflanzenwuchs(m)	vegetación	vegetação
veicolo	véhicule	vehicle	Fahrzeug(n)	vehículo	veículo
vela	voile	sail	Segel(n)	vela	vela
vela	voile	sailing	Segeln(n)	vela	vela
veleno	poison	poison	Gift(n)	veneno	veneno
veleno	venin	venom, poison	Gift(n)	veneno	veneno
velenoso, a	vénéneux, se	poisonous	giftig	venenoso, a	venenoso, a
veliero	voilier	yacht, sailing boat	Segelboot(n)	velero	veleiro
velluto	velours	velvet	Samt(m)	terciopelo	veludo
velo	voile	veil	Schleier(m)	velo	véu
velocità	vitesse	speed	Geschwindigkeit(f)	velocidad	velocidade
velocità	vélocité, vitesse	velocity	Schnelligkeit(f)	velocidad	velocidade
vena	veine	vein	Vene(f)	vena	veia
vendere	vendre	sell	verkaufen	vender	vender
vendetta	vengeance	revenge	Rache(f)	venganza	vingança
vendicare	venger	avenge	rächen	vengar	vingar
vendita	vente	sale	Verkauf(m)	venta	venda
venditore, trice	vendeur, se	salesman(-men)	Verkäufer(in f)m	vendedor, a	vendedor, a
venerdì	vendredi	Friday	Freitag(m)	viernes	sexta-feira
venereo, a	vénérien, ne	venereal	Geschlechts-	venéreo, a	venéreo, a
venga!, venite!	venez!	come(on)!	kommen Sie!	venga(!)	venha!
venga qui!, venite!	venez ici!	come here!	kommen Sie her!	venga aquí (!)	venha cá!
venire	venir	come	kommen	venir	vir
ventaglio	éventail	fan	Fächer(m)	abanico	leque
ventata	bouffée	puff, breath	Hauch(m), Atemzug(m)	bocanada	baforada
venti	vingt	twenty	zwanzig	veinte	vinte
ventilatore	ventilateur	fan, ventilator	Ventilator(m)	ventilador	ventilador
ventilazione	ventilation	ventilation	Belüftung(f)	ventilación	ventilação
vento	vent	wind	Wind(m)	viento	vento
ventosa	ventouse	suction disc	Saugnapf(m)	ventosa	ventosa
ventuno	vingt-et-un	twenty one	einundzwanzig	veintiún(o)	vinte e um
veramente	vraiment	really	wirklich	verdaderamente	verdadeiramente
verbale	procès-verbal	minutes, report	Protokoll(n)	acta	acta
verbo	verbe	verb	Verb(n)	verbo	verbo
verde	vert, e	green	grün	verde	verde
verdetto	verdict	verdict	Urteil(n)	veredicto	veredicto
verdura; legume	légume	vegetable	Gemüse(n)	legumbre, verdura	legume
verdura	verdure	greenery	Grün(n)	verdor, verdura	verdura
vergine	vierge	virgin	unberührt	virgen	virgem
verginità	virginité	virginity	Jungfräulichkeit(f)	virginidad	virgindade
vergogna	honte	shame	Scham(f), Schande(f)	vergüenza	vergonha
vergognarsi	honte(avoir)	ashamed(be)	schämen, sich	vergüenza(tener)	vergonha(ter)
vergognoso, a	honteux, se	shameful	beschämend	vergonzoso, a	vergonhoso, a
verifica	vérification	verification	Überprüfung(f)	verificación	verificação
verificare	vérifier	check, verify	überprüfen	comprobar	verificar
verità	vérité	truth	Wahrheit(f)	verdad	verdade
verme	ver	worm	Wurm(m)	gusano	verme
vernice, pittura	peinture	paint	Farbe(f)	pintura	tinta
vernice	vernis	varnish	Lack(m)	barniz	verniz
vero, a	vrai, e	true	wahr	verdadero, a	verdadeiro, a
vero, a	véritable	real, genuine	wahrhaftig	verdadero, a	verdadeiro, a
verosimile	vraisemblable	likely, probable	wahrscheinlich	verosímil	verosímil
verruca, porro	verrue	wart	Warze(f)	verruga	verruga
versare	verser	pour	aus = gießen	verter	verter

I

629

Italian	French	English	German	Spanish	Portuguese
versare	verser	pay(in)	ein = zahlen	ingresar	pagar
verso	vers	to, towards	nach, zu	hacia	para
verso	vers	towards, to	gegen, in Richtung	hacia	direcção a(em)
verso	vers	line	Vers(m)	verso	verso
vertebra	vertèbre	vertebra(-ae)	Wirbel(m)	vértebra	vértebra
verticale	vertical, e	vertical	senkrecht	vertical	vertical
vertigine	vertige	dizziness	Schwindel(m)	vértigo	vertigem
vescica	vessie	bladder	Harnblase(f)	vejiga	bexiga
vescica	cloque, ampoule	blister	Blase(f)(Brandblase)	ampolla	bolha
vescovo	évêque	bishop	Bischof(m)	obispo	bispo
vespa	guêpe	wasp	Wespe(f)	avispa	vespa
vessazione	vexation	vexation	Ärger(m)	vejación	vexame
vestaglia	robe de chambre	dressing gown	Schlafrock(m)	bata	roupão
vestiario	vestiaire	cloak-room	Garderobe(f)	vestuario	vestiário
vestigia	vestige	remains	Überrest(m)	vestigio	vestígio
vestire	vêtir	clothe, dress	an = ziehen, an = kleiden	vestir	vestir
vestire(-rsi)	habiller(s')	dress up	an = kleiden	vestirse, ataviar	vestir-se
vestirsi	habiller(s')	dress	an = ziehen, sich	vestirse	vestir-se
vestiti	vêtements	clothes	Kleidung(f)	ropa, prenda	roupa(s)
vestito(i), abiti	habit(s)	clothes	Kleidung(f)	vestido, traje	fato, traje
vestito, a	habillé, e	dressed	angezogen	vestido, a	vestido, a
vestito	vêtement	garment	Kleidungsstück(n)	traje, ropa	peça de roupa
vestito	robe	dress	Kleid(n)	vestido	vestido
veterinario	vétérinaire	vet	Tierarzt(m)	veterinario	veterinário
veto	veto	veto	Veto(n)	veto	veto
vetrina	vitrine	shop-window	Schaufenster(n)	escaparate	montra, vitrina
vetro	verre	glass	Glas(n)	vidrio	vidro
vetro	vitre	pane, window	Scheibe(f)(Fenster-)	cristal, vidrio	vidro
vetro; specchio	glace; miroir	window; mirror	Scheibe(f); Spiegel(m)	cristal; luna	vidro; espelho
vi; ve; le; ti; te	vous; te	you	euch; Sie; Ihnen	os; les; le; te	vos; vosco; lhe
via	rue	street	Straße(f)	calle	rua
via; binario	voie	way; track	Weg(m)	vía; camino	via; caminho
viaggiare	voyager	travel	reisen	viajar	viajar
viaggiatore, trice	voyageur, se	traveller	Reisende(r)m f	viajero, a	viajante
viaggio	voyage	trip; journey	Reise(f)	viaje	viagem
viale	avenue	avenue	Allee(f)	avenida	avenida
viale	boulevard	boulevard	Boulevard(m)	bulevar	avenida
viale	allée	path, lane	Allee(f)	paseo, calle	alameda
vibrare	vibrer	vibrate	schwingen	vibrar	vibrar
vicepresidente	vice-président	vice-president	Vize-Präsident(m)	vicepresidente	vice-presidente
vicinanza	voisinage	neighbourhood	Nachbarschaft(f)	vecindario	vizinhança
vicinanze(nelle)	proximité(à)	close, near	nahe bei	cerca de	próximo a
vicino, a	voisin, e	neighbour	Nachbar(in f)m	vecino, a	vizinho, a
vicino, a	près, proche	near, close to	nah(e)	cerca	perto
vicino a	auprès de	close to	bei	cerca de	perto de
videoregistratore	magnétoscope	video recorder	Videorecorder(m)	magnetoscopio	gravador vídeo
vietare, proibire	interdire	forbid, ban	verbieten	prohibir	proibir
vigilante	vigilant, e	vigilant	wachsam	vigilante	vigilante
vigliaccheria	lâcheté	cowardliness	Feigheit(f)	cobardía	cobardia
vigliacco, a	lâche	cowardly	feig(e)	cobarde	cobarde
vigore	vigueur	vigour	Kraft(f)	vigor	vigor
vigore(in), vigente	vigueur(en)	force(in), current	Kraft(in), geltend	vigente	vigente
vigoroso, a	vigoureux, se	vigorous, strong	rüstig, kräftig	vigoroso, a	vigoroso, a
vincere	gagner	win	gewinnen	ganar	ganhar
vincere	vaincre	defeat	besiegen	vencer	vencer
vincitore, trice	vainqueur	winner; victor	Sieger(in f)m	vencedor, a	vencedor, a
vino	vin	wine	Wein(m)	vino	vinho
viola	violet, te	violet, purple	violett, lila	violeta	roxo, a; violeta
violare	violer	violate	verraten	violar	violar
violazione	violation	violation	Verstoß(m)	violación	violação
violentare	violer	rape	vergewaltigen	violentar	violentar
violento, a	violent, e	violent	gewalttätig, gewaltsam	violento, a	violento, a
violento, a	violent, e	violent	heftig, stark	violento, a	violento, a
violenza	violence	violence	Gewalt(f)	violencia	violência
violino	violon	violin	Geige(f)	violín	violino
violoncello	violoncelle	cello	Cello(n)	violoncelo	violoncelo
vipera	vipère	viper	Viper(f), Otter(f)	víbora	víbora
virgola	virgule	comma	Komma(n)	coma	vírgula

Italian	French	English	German	Spanish	Portuguese
virile	viril, e	virile, manly	männlich, mannhaft	viril	viril
virilità	virilité	virility	Männlichkeit(f)	virilidad	virilidade
virtù	vertu	virtue	Tugend(f)	virtud	virtude
virtuoso, a	vertueux, se	virtuous	tugendhaft	virtuoso, a	virtuoso, a
virtuoso, a	virtuose	virtuoso	Meister(m), Virtuose m	virtuoso, a	virtuoso, a
virus	virus	virus	Virus(m)	virus	vírus
vischioso, a	visqueux, se	viscous	zähflüssig	viscoso, a	viscoso, a
viscido, a	gluant, e	sticky	klebrig	viscoso, a	viscoso, a
visibile	visible	visible	sichtbar	visible	visivel
visibilità	visibilité	visibility	Sicht(-weite)(f)	visibilidad	visibilidade
visita	visite	visit	Besuch(m)	visita	visita
visitare	visiter	visit	besichtigen, reisen	visitar	visitar
visitatore, trice	visiteur, se	visitor	Besucher(in f)m	visitante	visitante
visivo, a; visuale	visuel, le	visual	visuell	visual	visual
viso	visage	face	Gesicht(n)	rostro, cara	cara
visone	vison	mink	Nerz(m)	visón	marta
vista	vue	sight	Sehkraft(f)	vista	vista
visto	visa	visa	Visum(n)	visado	visto
visualizzare	visualiser	display	sichtbar machen	visualizar	visualizar
vita	vie, existence	life(lives)	Leben(n)	vida	vida
vita	taille	waist	Taille(f)	cintura, talle	cinta
vitale	vital, e	vital	wesentlich	vital	vital
vitalità	vitalité	vitality	Lebenskraft(f)	vitalidad	vitalidade
vitamina	vitamine	vitamin	Vitamin(n)	vitamina	vitamina
vite	vis	screw	Schraube(f)	tornillo	parafuso
vitello(a)	veau	calf(-lves); veal	Kalb(n)	becerro; ternera	bezerro; vitelo
vittima	victime	victim	Opfer(n)	víctima	vítima
vittoria	victoire	victory	Sieg(m)	victoria	vitória
viuzza, vicolo	ruelle	alley	Gäßchen(n), Gasse(f)	callejuela	viela
viva!, evviva!	vive!	hurrah!; Long live!	Es lebe!; Lang lebe!	viva(!)	viva!
vivace; vivo, a	vif, vive	lively	lebendig	vivo, a	vivo, a
vivace	vivace	hardy	immergrün; ausdauernd	vivaz	vivaz
vivere	vivre	live	leben	vivir	viver
vivo, a	vif, vive	keen	scharf	agudo, a; vivo, a	vivo, a
vivo, a; vivente	vivant, e	alive	lebendig	vivo, a	vivo, a
vizio	vice	vice	Laster(n)	vicio	vício
vizioso, a	vicieux, se	vicious	lasterhaft	vicioso, a	vicioso, a
vocabolario	vocabulaire	vocabulary	Vokabular(n)	vocabulario	vocabulário
vocale	vocal, e	vocal	Stimm-	vocal	vocal
vocale	voyelle	vowel	Vokal(m), Selbstlaut m	vocal	vogal
vocazione	vocation	vocation	Berufung(f)	vocación	vocação
voce	voix	voice	Stimme(f)	voz	voz
voce, diceria	rumeur, bruit	rumour	Gerücht(n)	rumor	rumor
voglia	envie	desire	Lust(f)	ganas	vontade
voi; lei	vous	you	ihr; Sie	vosotros; ustedes	vós; você
volante	volant	steering-wheel	Steuer(n)	volante	volante
volantino	tract	handout, leaflet	Flugblatt(n)	octavilla	panfleto
volare	voler	fly	fliegen	volar	voar
volentieri	volontiers	willingly	gern	buena gana(de)	bom grado(de)
volere	vouloir	want	wollen	querer	querer
volgare	vulgaire	vulgar	vulgär	vulgar	vulgar
volo	vol	flight	Flug(m)	vuelo	voo
volontà	volonté	will, determination	Wille(m)	voluntad	vontade
volontario, a	volontaire	voluntary	freiwillig	voluntario, a	voluntário, a
volontario, a	volontaire	volunteer	Freiwillige(r)m f	voluntario, a	voluntário, a
volpe	renard	fox(-es)	Fuchs(m)	zorro	raposa
volta	fois	time	Mal(n)	vez	vez
volta(una)	fois(une)	once	einmal	vez(una)	vez(uma)
volta(una)	autrefois	past(in the)	früher	antaño	antigamente
volume	volume	volume	Volumen(n)	volumen	volume
vomitare	vomir	vomit	erbrechen, sich	vomitar	vomitar
vorace	vorace	voracious	gefräßig, gierig	voraz	voraz
vorrei	voudrais(je)	would like(I)	möchte(ich)	quisiera(yo)	gostava
vortice	tourbillon	whirlwind, swirl	Wirbel(wind)(m)	torbellino	turbilhão
vostri, e	vos	your	eure, Ihre	vuestros, as	vossos, as
vostro, a(il, la)	votre	your	Ihr(e); euer, eure	vuestro, a	vosso, a
vostro, a; suo, sua	vôtre(le, la)	yours	eure(r, s); Ihre(r, s)	vuestro, a; suyo, a	vosso, a; seu, sua
votare	voter	vote	wählen	votar	votar

631

Italian	French	English	German	Spanish	Portuguese
voto	voeu	vow	Gelübde(n)	voto	promessa
voto	vote	vote	Wahl(f)	voto	voto
voto	note	mark	Note(f)	nota	nota
vulcano	volcan	volcano(-es)	Vulkan(m)	volcán	vulcão
vulnerabile	vulnérable	vulnerable	verwundbar	vulnerable	vulnerável
vuotare	vider	empty	leeren	vaciar	esvaziar
vuoto, a	vide	empty	leer	vacío, a	vazio, a
vuoto, a; cavo, a	creux, se	hollow	hohl	hueco, a	oco, a
vuoto	vide	vacuum; void	Vakuum(n), Leere(f)	vacío	vazio, vácuo

W

Italian	French	English	German	Spanish	Portuguese
WC; gabinetto	water-closet	toilets	Toilette(f)	water, retretes	retrete, sanita
windsurf	planche à voile	windsurf(ing)	Windsurfen(n)	tabla a vela, surf	wind-surf

Y

Italian	French	English	German	Spanish	Portuguese
yoga	yoga	yoga	Yoga(n), Joga(n)	yoga	yoga

Z

Italian	French	English	German	Spanish	Portuguese
zaffiro	saphir	sapphire	Saphir(m)	zafiro	safira
zaino	sac à dos	rucksack	Rucksack(m)	mochila	mochila
zampa	patte	paw; leg; foot	Pfote(f); Bein(n)	pata	pata
zanzara	moustique	mosquito(-es)	Mücke(f)	mosquito	mosquito
zattera	radeau	raft	Floß(n)	balsa	jangada
zebra	zèbre	zebra	Zebra(n)	cebra	zebra
zeppa	cale	wedge, chock	Keil(m)	cuña	cunha
zero	zéro	zero, nought	Null(f)	cero	zero
zia	tante	aunt	Tante(f)	tía	tia
zio	oncle	uncle	Onkel(m)	tío	tio
zoccolo	sabot	hoof	Huf(m)	pezuña, casco	casco
zoccolo	socle	base	Sockel(m)	zócalo	soco, pedestal
zona	zone	zone	Zone(f)	zona	zona
zoo	zoo	zoo	Zoo(m)	zoológico	jardim zoológico

Italian	French	English	German	Spanish	Portuguese
zoologico, a	zoologique	zoological	zoologisch	zoológico, a	zoológico, a
zoppicare	boiter	limp	hinken	cojear	coxear
zuccherato, a	sucré, e	sweet	süß	azucarado, a	açucarado, a; doce
zucchero	sucre	sugar	Zucker(m)	azúcar	açúcar

I

Notes

Notes

Notes

Notes

Notes

A

Portuguese	French	English	German	Spanish	Italian
a, as	la, l', les	the	die	la, las	la; l'; le
a	à; en; de; par; chez	at; to; in; by; on	zu; in; nach; auf; an; bei	a; de; en; por; con	a; da; di; con; in; per
abadia	abbaye	abbey	Abtei(f)	abadía	abbazia, badia
abaixar	abaisser	lower	nieder = lassen	bajar	abbassare
abaixo	ci-dessous	below	unten(-stehend)	abajo(más)	sotto(qui)
abalo	secousse	jolt, jerk	Ruck(m), Stoß(m)	sacudida	scossa
abandonar	abandonner	abandon, leave	preis = geben; auf = geben	abandonar	abbandonare
abastecer	approvisionner	supply	versorgen	aprovisionar	rifornire
abastecer	ravitailler	supply	versorgen	abastecer	rifornire
abastecimento	alimentation	supplying	Versorgung(f)	abastecimiento	rifornimento
abcesso	abcès	abscess(-es)	Geschwür(n)	absceso	ascesso
abdicar	abdiquer	abdicate	ab = danken	abdicar	abdicare
abdómen	abdomen	abdomen	Unterleib(m)	abdomen	addome
abelha	abeille	bee	Biene(f)	abeja	ape
aberto, a	ouvert, e	open	offen; geöffnet	abierto, a	aperto, a
abertura	ouverture	opening	Öffnungszeiten(f, pl)	apertura	apertura
abeto	sapin	fir-tree	Tanne(f)	abeto	abete
abismo	gouffre	chasm, pit	Abgrund(m), Kluft(f)	abismo, sima	baratro
abóbada	voûte	vault, arch	Gewölbe(n)	bóveda	arco, volta
abolir	abolir	abolish	ab = schaffen	abolir	abolire
abominável	abominable	awful	scheußlich	abominable	abominevole
a bordo	à bord	aboard	an Bord	a bordo	a bordo
aborrecer	embêter	bother, annoy	ärgern	fastidiar	infastidire
aborrecer-se	ennuyer(s')	bored(be)	langweilen, sich	aburrir(se)	annoiarsi
aborrecido, a	ennuyeux, se	boring; annoying	langweilig	aburrido, a	noioso, a
aborrecimento	ennui	boredom	Langeweile(f)	aburrimiento	noia
aborrecimento	ennui, problème	trouble, problem	Ärger(m)	problema	guaio
abortar	avorter	abort	ab = treiben	abortar	abortire
aborto	avortement	abortion	Abtreibung(f)	aborto	aborto
abraçar, beijar	embrasser	kiss; embrace	küssen, umarmen	abrazar, besar	baciare
abrandar	ralentir	slow down	verlangsamen	aminorar	rallentare
abre-latas	ouvre-boîte(s)	tin/can opener	Büchsenöffner(m)	abrelatas	apriscatole
abreviatura	abréviation	abbreviation	Abkürzung(f)(Wort)	abreviatura	abbreviazione
abrigo, refúgio	abri, refuge	shelter	Obdach(n), Schutz(m)	abrigo, refugio	riparo, rifugio
Abril	Avril	April	April(m)	Abril	Aprile
abrir	ouvrir	open	öffnen	abrir	aprire
abrir-se	éclore	hatch	aus = schlüpfen	abrirse	schiudere, uscire
abrupto, a	abrupt, e	steep	steil	abrupto, a	ripido, a; scosceso, a
absolutamente	absolument	absolutely	unbedingt, absolut	absolutamente	assolutamente
absoluto, a	absolu, e	absolute	unbedingt	absoluto, a	assoluto, a
absorver	absorber	absorb	verzehren	absorber	assorbire
abstracto, a	abstrait, e	abstract	abstrakt	abstracto, a	astratto, a
absurdo, a	absurde	absurd	unsinnig	absurdo, a	assurdo, a
abundância	abondance	abundance	Überfluß(m)	abundancia	abbondanza
abundante	abondant, e	plentiful, abundant	reichlich	abundante	abbondante
abusar	abuser	take advantage of	mißbrauchen	abusar	abusare
abuso	abus	abuse, misuse	Mißbrauch(m)	abuso	abuso
abutre	vautour	vulture	Geier(m)	buitre	avvoltoio
acabar, terminar	finir	finish, end	beenden	acabar, terminar	finire
acabar	achever	complete, finish	beenden	acabar	terminare, finire
academia	académie	academy	Akademie(f)	academia	accademia
acalmar	calmer	calm	beruhigen	calmar	calmare
acalmar	apaiser	calm, soothe	beruhigen	apaciguar	calmare
acalmia	accalmie	lull	Wetterberuhigung(f)	calma	schiarita, tregua
acampamento	bivouac	bivouac	Biwak(m)	vivaque	bivacco
acampar	camper	camp	zelten	acampar	campeggiare
acariciar	caresser	caress	liebkosen, streicheln	acariciar	accarezzare

Portuguese	French	English	German	Spanish	Italian
acarretar	entraîner	entail	mit sich bringen	ocasionar	comportare
acasalar-se	accoupler(s')	mate	paaren, sich	aparearse	accoppiarsi
acaso	aléa	hazard	Zufall(m)	riesgo, azar	rischio
acaso, azar	hasard	chance, luck	Zufall(m)	azar, casualidad	caso
acaso(ao)	hasard(au)	random(at)	aufs Geratewohl	azar(al)	casaccio(a)
acção	action	action	Vorgehen(n), Handlung	acción	azione
acção	action	share	Aktie(f)	acción	azione
accionista	actionnaire	shareholder	Aktionär(m)	accionista	azionista
aceitar	accepter	accept, agree	akzeptieren, an = nehmen	aceptar	accettare
aceitar	agréer	accept, approve	genehmigen, zu = lassen	aceptar	gradire, accettare
acelerar	accélérer	accelerate	beschleunigen	acelerar	accelerare
acender	allumer	switch on	an = machen	encender	accendere
acender	allumer	light	an = zünden	encender	accendere
acento	accent(')	accent	Akzent(m)	acento	accento
acentuação	accentuation	stress(ing)	Betonung(f)	acentuación	accentazione
acentuar	souligner	emphasize	betonen	recalcar, subrayar	accentuare
acepipe, entrada	hors-d'oeuvre	starter	Vorspeise(f)	entremeses	antipasto
acercar	rapprocher	bring nearer	heran = rücken	acercar	avvicinare
acessível	accessible	accessible	zugänglich	accesible	accessibile
acesso	accès	access	Zugang(m)	acceso	accesso
acessório	accessoire	accessory	Zubehör(n)	accesorio	accessorio
acetona	dissolvant	solvent, remover	Lösungsmittel(n)	disolvente	solvente
acha	bûche	log	Scheit(n)	leño	tronco, ceppo
achar, encontrar	trouver	find	finden	encontrar	trovare
achatar, alisar	aplatir	flatten	glätten, ab = flachen	allanar, aplastar	appiattire
acidentado, a	accidenté, e	injured person	Verunglückte(f, m)	accidentado, a	accidentato, a
acidente	accident	accident	Unfall(m)	accidente	incidente
ácido	acide	acid	Säure(f)	ácido	acido
acima	ci-dessus	above	oben(-stehend)	arriba(más)	sopra(qui)
aclamar	acclamer	cheer	zu = jubeln	aclamar	acclamare
aço	acier	steel	Stahl(m)	acero	acciaio
acolhedor, a	accueillant, e	hospitable	gastfreundlich	acogedor, a	accogliente
acolher, receber	accueillir	welcome	empfangen, auf = nehmen	acoger, recibir	accogliere
acompanhar	accompagner	accompany	begleiten	acompañar	accompagnare
aconselhar	conseiller	advise	beraten	aconsejar	consigliare
acontecer	arriver	occur, happen	geschehen	ocurrir, suceder	succedere
acontecimento	événement	event	Ereignis(n)	acontecimiento	avvenimento
acordar	réveiller	wake(up)	wecken	despertar	svegliare
acordo	accord	agreement	Einverständnis(n)	acuerdo	accordo
acordo(de)	accord(d')	all right, O.K	einverstanden, okay	vale, de acuerdo	accordo(d')
acordo(estar de)	accord(être d')	agree	überein = stimmen	acuerdo(estar de)	accordo(essere d')
acostar	accoster	berth	an = legen	abordar	accostare, attraccare
acrílico	acrylique	acrylic	Akryl(n)	acrílico	acrilico
acrobata	acrobate	acrobat	Akrobat(in f)m	acróbata	acrobata
acrobacia	acrobatie	acrobatics, stunts	Akrobatik(f)	acrobacia	acrobazia
acta	procès-verbal	minutes, report	Protokoll(n)	acta	verbale
activar	activer	activate	beschleunigen	activar	attivare
actividade	activité	activity	Tätigkeit(f)	actividad	attività
activo, a	actif, ive	active	aktiv, tatkräftig	activo, a	attivo, a
acto, acção	acte	action, act	Handlung(f)	acto	atto
actor, actriz	acteur, actrice	actor, actress	Schauspieler(in f)m	actor, actriz	attore, attrice
actor, actriz	comédien, ne	actor, actress	Schauspieler(in f)m	actor, actriz	attore, attrice
actual	actuel, le	present, current	aktuell, gegenwärtig	actual	attuale
actualizar	actualiser	update	aktualisieren	actualizar	attualizzare
actualmente	actuellement	now, at present	zur Zeit	actualmente	attualmente
açúcar	sucre	sugar	Zucker(m)	azúcar	zucchero
açucarado, a; doce	sucré, e	sweet	süß	azucarado, a	zuccherato, a
acumular	accumuler	accumulate	an = häufen	acumular	accumulare
acumular	cumuler	accumulate	an = häufen	acaparar	cumulare
acupunctura	acuponcture	acupuncture	Akupunktur(f)	acupuntura	agopuntura
acusação	accusation	accusation, charge	Anklage(f)	acusación	accusa
acusação	charge	charge	Anklage(f)(punkt m)	cargo	indizio
acusado, a; réu(ré)	accusé, e	accused(the)	Angeklagte(f, m)	acusado, a; reo	accusato, a
acusado, a	inculpé, e	accused(the)	Angeklagte(f, m)	inculpado, a	imputato, a
acusar	accuser	accuse	an = klagen	acusar	accusare
acústica	acoustique	acoustics	Akustik(f)	acústica	acustica
adaptação	adaptation	adaptation	Anpassung(f)	adaptación	adattamento
adaptar	adapter	adapt, adjust	an = passen	adaptar	adattare

Portuguese	French	English	German	Spanish	Italian
adaptar-se(a)	adapter(s')	adapt(to)	an = passen, sich	adaptarse(a)	adattarsi(a)
adega	cave	cellar	Keller(m)	bodega, sótano	cantina
adepto, a; seguidor, a	adepte	follower	Anhänger(in f)m	adepto, a; seguidor	seguace, adepto, a
adequado, a	adéquat, e	appropriate	passend	adecuado, a	adeguato, a
aderente	adhérent, e	member	Mitglied(n)	adherente	aderente, socio
aderir a	adhérer	join	Mitglied werden	adherir a	aderire a
aderir, ligar-se	engager(s')	join, enter	bei = treten	ingresar, meterse	impegnarsi
adesão	adhésion	membership	Beitritt(m)	adhesión	adesione
adesivo, a	adhésif, ive	adhesive	klebrig, anhaftend	adhesivo, a	adesivo, a
adeus!	adieu!	good bye!	tschüß!, lebe wohl!	adiós(!)	addio!
adiantado(estar)	avance(être en)	early(to be)	zu früh (sein)	adelantado(estar)	anticipo(essere in)
adiantar	avancer	advance	voran = gehen; vorrücken	adelantar	avanzare
adiante	avant(en)	ahead	voran, voraus	adelante	avanti
adiar	ajourner	postpone, adjourn	vertagen	aplazar	rimandare, aggiornare
adiar	reporter	postpone	verschieben	postergar	rinviare
adição, soma	addition, somme	addition, sum	Addition(f), Summe(f)	adición, suma	addizione, somma
adicional	additionnel, le	additional	hinzugefügt	adicional	addizionale
adido	attaché	attaché	Attaché(m)	agregado	addetto, a
adivinhar	deviner	guess	raten	adivinar	indovinare
adjectivo	adjectif	adjective	Adjektiv(n)	adjetivo	aggettivo
adjudicação	adjudication	auction	Versteigerung(f)	adjudicación	aggiudicazione
adjunto, a	adjoint, e	assistant	Gehilfe(m); Hilfs-	adjunto, a	aggiunto, a; vice
adjunto, a	adjoint, e	deputy	Stellvertreter(in f)m	substituto, a	assessore
administração	administration	administration	Verwaltung(f)	administración	amministrazione
administrar	administrer	manage, run	verwalten	administrar	amministrare
administrativo, a	administratif, ve	administrative	Verwaltungs-	administrativo, a	amministrativo, a
admiração	admiration	admiration	Bewunderung(f)	admiración	ammirazione
admirador, a	admirateur, trice	admirer, fan	Bewunderer(in f)m	admirador, a	ammiratore, trice
admissão	admission	admission	Zulassung, Einweisung	admisión	ammissione
admissível	admissible	admissible	zulässig, annehmbar	admisible	ammissibile
admitir	admettre	admit	zu = geben; zu = lassen	admitir	ammettere
adolescente	adolescent, e	teenager	Jugendliche(m, f)	adolescente	adolescente
adoptar	adopter	adopt	adoptieren	adoptar	adottare
adorar	adorer	adore	an = beten	adorar	adorare
adorável	adorable	adorable, lovely	reizend	adorable	adorabile
adormecido, a	endormi, e	asleep	schlafend	dormido, a	addormentato, a
adorno	parure	finery, jewellery	Schmuck(m)	adorno	parure
adquirido, a	acquis, e	acquired	erworben	adquirido, a	acquisito, a
adquirir, obter	acquérir	acquire	erwerben; erlangen	adquirir	acquistare
adubo	engrais	fertilizer, manure	Dünger(m)	abono	concime
adultério	adultère	adultery	Ehebruch(m)	adulterio	adulterio
adulto, a	adulte	adult	Erwachsene(f, m)	adulto, a	adulto, a
advérbio	adverbe	adverb	Umstandswort, Adverb	adverbio	avverbio
adversário, a	adversaire	opponent	Gegner(in f)m	adversario, a	avversario, a
adverso, a	adverse	adverse, opposing	feindlich, gegnerisch	adverso, a	avverso, a
advogado, a	avocat, e	lawyer, barrister	Anwalt(m), Anwältin(f)	abogado, a	avvocato, tessa
aéreo, a	aérien, ne	aerial, air	Luft-	aéreo, a	aereo, a
aerograma	aérogramme	aerogram	Funkspruch(m)	aerograma	aerogramma
aeronáutica	aéronautique	aeronautics	Luftfahrt(f)	aeronáutica	aeronautica
aeroporto	aéroport	airport	Flughafen(m)	aeropuerto	aeroporto
afagar	caresser	stroke	streicheln	acariciar	carezzare
afastamento	éloignement	distance	Entfernung(f)	alejamiento	lontananza
afastar	écarter	separate, part	entfernen	apartar	allontanare; scartare
afectar	toucher, émouvoir	affect	rühren	afectar	commuovere
afectuoso, a	affectueux, se	affectionate	liebevoll	afectuoso, a	affettuoso, a
afeição; afecto	affection	affection, love	Zuneigung(f)	afecto; afección	affetto
afiado, a	aiguisé, e	sharp	scharf	afilado, a	affilato, a
afiar	aiguiser	sharpen	schärfen	afilar	affilare
a fim de	afin de	in order to	um...zu	a fin de	per; allo scopo di
a fim de que	afin que	so that	damit	a fin de que	affinché
afinação	réglage	adjustment	Einstellung(f)	reglaje, ajuste	regolazione
afinar, regular	régler	adjust, tune	ein = stellen	ajustar, arreglar	regolare
afinidade	affinité	affinity	Ähnlichkeit(f)	afinidad	affinità
afirmar	affirmer	assert, maintain	behaupten	afirmar	affermare
afixação	affichage	putting up posters	Anschlag, Plakatierung	anuncios(fijación)	affissione
afixar	afficher	post up, put up	an = schlagen	anunciar	affiggere
aflição, angústia	détresse	distress	Verzweiflung(f)	angustia	sconforto
afligir	affliger	distress, afflict	heim = suchen; betrüben	afligir	affliggere

643

Portuguese	French	English	German	Spanish	Italian
afligir-se	affoler(s')	panic	Panik geraten(in)	ponerse nervioso, a	disorientarsi
afluência	affluence	rush	Andrang(m)	afluencia	affluenza
afluência	affluence	crowd	Gedränge(n)	afluencia	afflusso
afogar-se	noyer(se)	drown	ertrinken	ahogar(se)	annegare
áfono, a	aphone	lose one's voice	stimmlos, heiser	afónico, a	afono, a
aforrador, a	épargnant, e	saver, investor	Sparer(in f)m	ahorrador, a	risparmiatore, trice
afortunado, a	chanceux, se	lucky	Glückspilz(m)	afortunado, a	fortunato, a
afrontamento	affrontement	confrontation	Konfrontation(f)	enfrentamiento	affrontamento
afrontar	affronter	confront, face	entgegen = treten	afrontar	affrontare
afrouxar	desserrer	loosen	lösen	aflojar	allentare
afundar	couler, enfoncer	sink	sinken, versenken	hundir	affondare
agarrar, apanhar	attraper	catch	fangen	agarrar, coger	acchiappare
agarrar	saisir	seize	ergreifen	coger, agarrar	afferrare
agarrar	empoigner, saisir	grab, grasp	greifen	empuñar	agguantare
agência	agence	agency	Agentur(f); Filiale(f)	agencia	agenzia
agenda	agenda	diary	Taschenkalender(m)	agenda	agenda
agente	agent	agent	Agent(in f)m	agente	agente
ágil	agile	agile, nimble	flink	ágil	agile
agir	agir	act	handeln	actuar	agire
agitação	agitation	agitation; unrest	Aufregung(f); Unruhe f	agitación	agitazione
agitação	branle-bas	upheaval	Durcheinander(n)	zafarrancho	scompiglio
agitar	agiter	shake	schütteln	agitar	agitare
agitar	agiter	wave	schwenken	agitar	agitare
agonia	agonie	agony	Todeskampf(m), Agonie	agonía	agonia
agora	maintenant	now	jetzt	ahora	ora, adesso
Agosto	Août	August	August(m)	Agosto	Agosto
agradar	plaire	please; like	gefallen(jdm)	gustar, agradar	piacere
agradável	agréable	pleasant, nice	angenehm	agradable	gradevole, piacevole
agradável	plaisant, e	pleasant	gefällig	agradable	piacevole
agradecer	remercier	thank	danken; bedanken, sich	agradecer	ringraziare
agradecimento	remerciement	thanks	Dank(m)	agradecimiento	ringraziamento
agravar	aggraver	worsen, aggravate	verschlimmern	empeorar	aggravare
agredir	agresser	attack, assault	an = greifen	agredir	aggredire
agressão	agression	attack	Aggression(f), Angriff	agresión	aggressione
agressor, a	agresseur	attacker	Angreifer(in f)m	agresor, a	aggressore
agrícola	agricole	agricultural	landwirtschaftlich	agrícola	agricolo, a
agricultor, a	agriculteur	farmer	Landwirt(in f)m	agricultor, a	agricoltore
agricultura	agriculture	agriculture	Landwirtschaft(f)	agricultura	agricoltura
água benta	eau	water	Wasser(n)	agua	acqua
água benta	eau bénite	holy water	Weihwasser(n)	agua bendita	acqua santa
água de colónia	eau de toilette	toilet water	Eau de Toilette(n)	colonia(agua de)	acqua di toeletta
água gaseificada	eau gazeuse	sparkling water	Sprudelwasser(n)	gaseosa	acqua gassata
água marinha	aigue-marine	aquamarine	Aquamarin(m)	aguamarina	acquamarina
aguardente	eau-de-vie	spirits	Schnaps(m)	aguardiente	grappa, acquavite
agudo, a	aigu, ë	sharp, shrill	hoch, schrill	agudo, a	acuto, a
aguentar	endurer	endure, bear	aus = halten, ertragen	aguantar, pasar	patire, resistere
águia	aigle	eagle	Adler(m)	águila	aquila
agulha	aiguille	needle	Nadel(f)	aguja	ago
aí; lá	là	there	da; dort	allí; allá	là; lì
ai; ali; lá	là	there	da	ahí; allí	là
ainda	encore	still	noch, wieder	todavía, aún	ancora
ainda	encore	still; yet	noch, noch mehr	aún	ancora
ainda	toujours	still	immer noch	todavía	sempre
ainda não	encore(pas)	yet(not)	noch(nicht)	todavía no	ancora(non)
ainda que	bien que	though, although	obwohl, obgleich	aunque	benché
ajoelhar-se	agenouiller(s')	kneel	hin = knien, sich	arrodillarse	inginocchiare(-rsi)
ajuda	aide	help	Hilfe(f)	ayuda	aiuto
ajuda de custo	indemnité	allowance	Schadenersatz(m)	dietas	indennità
ajudar	aider	help, assist, aid	helfen	ayudar	aiutare
ajuizado, a	sage	good	brav	bueno, a	buono, a; bravo, a
ajuntamento	rassemblement	gathering	Versammlung(f)	concentración	raduno, adunanza
ajuntar, juntar	ajouter	add	hinzu = fügen	añadir	aggiungere
ajustar	ajuster	adjust	ein = stellen	ajustar	aggiustare
alameda	allée	path, lane	Allee(f)	paseo, calle	viale
alargar	élargir	widen, enlarge	verbreiten	ensanchar	allargare
alarme	alarme	alarm	Alarm(m)	alarma	allarme
alarme	antivol	anti-theft lock	Diebstahlsicherung(f)	antirrobo	antifurto
alavanca	levier	lever	Hebel(m)	palanca	leva

| --- | --- | --- | --- | --- | --- |
álbum	album	album	Album(n)	álbum	album
alcançar, atingir	arriver(à)	attain	erlangen, erreichen	lograr, alcanzar	raggiungere
alcançar, obter	remporter, gagner	achieve	erringen	lograr, triunfar	raggiungere, ottenere
alcance	portée	range, reach	Reichweite(f)	alcance	portata, gittata
alcatifa	moquette	carpet	Teppichboden(m)	moqueta	moquette
alcatrão	goudron	tar	Teer(m)	alquitrán	asfalto
álcool	alcool	alcohol	Alkohol(m)	alcohol	alcol, alcool
álcool	alcool(s)	spirit(s)	Alkohol(m)	alcohol	alcolico
alcoolismo	alcoolisme	alcoholism	Alkoholmißbrauch(m)	alcoholismo	alcolismo
Alcorão	Coran	Koran	Koran(der)	Corán	Corano
alcunha, apelido	surnom	nickname	Spitzname(m)	apodo, mote	soprannome
aldeia, povoado	village	village	Dorf(n)	aldea, pueblo	paese, villaggio
aleatório, a; incerto	aléatoire	aleatory, uncertain	unsicher, ungewiß	aleatorio, a	aleatorio, a
alegrar-se	réjouir(se)	delighted(be)	erfreuen, sich	alegrarse	rallegrare(-arsi)
alegre	joyeux, se	merry, joyful	lustig, fröhlich	alegre	allegro, a; felice
alegre	gai, e	happy, merry	froh	alegre	allegro, a
alegria	joie	joy	Freude(f)	alegría	gioia
aleijado, a	estropié, e	crippled	verkrüppelt	lisiado, a	storpio, a
aleitar	allaiter	feed	stillen	pecho(dar el)	allattare
além, acolá	là-bas	over there	da; dort	allá	là, laggiù
além de(para)	au-delà de	beyond	jenseits	más allá de	al di là
além disso	plus(de)	further, moreover	ferner, überdies	además	più(di, in)
além disso; além de	de plus, en outre	besides	außerdem, außer	además(de)	inoltre
além do mais	plus(de)	moreover, further	überdies, ferner	más de	più(di, in)
alergia	allergie	allergy	Allergie(f)	alergia	allergia
alerta, alarme	alerte	alert	Alarm(m)	alerta	allarme
alfabeto	alphabet	alphabet	Alphabet(n)	alfabeto	alfabeto
alface	laitue, salade	lettuce	Kopfsalat(m)	lechuga	lattuga
alfaiate	tailleur	tailor	Schneider(m)	sastre	sarto
alfândega	douane	customs	Zoll(m)	aduana	dogana
alfinete	épingle	pin	Stecknadel(f)	alfiler	spillo
alga	algue	seaweed, alga(ae)	Alge(f)	alga	alga
álgebra	algèbre	algebra	Algebra(f)	álgebra	algebra
algemas	menottes	handcuffs	Handschellen(f, pl)	esposas	manette
algodão	coton	cotton	Baumwolle(f)	algodón	cotone
alguém	quelqu'un, e	someone, somebody	jemand	alguien	qualcuno, a
algum, a	quelque	some, any	einige	alguno, a	qualche
alguns, algumas	quelques	few(a), some	einige	algunos, as	alcuni, e
algures	quelque part	somewhere	irgendwo	alguna parte(en)	qualche parte(da)
aliança	alliance	alliance	Bündnis(n)	alianza	alleanza
aliar, unir	allier	ally	verbünden	aliar, unir	alleare, unire
aliás	ailleurs(d')	moreover, besides	übrigens	por otra parte	del resto, d'altronde
alibi	alibi	alibi	Alibi(n)	coartada	alibi
alicate; tenaz	pinces	pliers, pincers	Zangen(pl)	alicates, tenazas	pinze
alimentação	alimentation	feeding; food	Ernährung(f)	alimentación	alimentazione
alimentação	nourriture	food	Nahrung(f)	alimento	cibo; nutrimento
alimentar	nourrir	feed, nourish	ernähren	alimentar	nutrire
alimento	aliment	food	Lebensmittel(n, pl)	alimento	alimento, cibo
alinhamento	alignement	alignment	Ausrichtung(f)	alineación	allineamento
aliviar	alléger	lighten	erleichtern	aliviar	alleggerire
aliviar	soulager	relieve	erleichtern	aliviar	alleggerire
aliviar	soulager	relieve	lindern	aliviar	sollevare, lenire
alívio	soulagement	relief	Erleichterung(f)	alivio, desahogo	sollievo
alma	âme	soul	Seele(f)	alma	anima
almirante	amiral	admiral	Admiral(m)	almirante	ammiraglio
almoçar	déjeuner	have lunch, lunch	Mittag essen(zu)	almorzar	pranzare
almoço(pequeno)	déjeuner(petit)	breakfast	Frühstück(n)	desayuno	colazione(prima)
almofada	coussin	cushion	Kissen(n)	cojín	cuscino
alocução	allocution	speech(short)	Ansprache(kurze)(f)	alocución	allocuzione
alojamento	logement	accommodation	Wohnung(f)	alojamiento	alloggio
alojamento	hébergement	accommodation	Unterbringung(f)	alojamiento	alloggio
alojar, morar	loger	accommodate	unter = bringen	alojar	alloggiare
alongar	allonger	lengthen	verlängern	alargar	allungare
alopatia	allopathie	allopathy	Allopathie(f)	alopatía	allopatia
alpendre	hangar	shed	Schuppen(m)	cobertizo	hangar, capannone
alpinista	alpiniste	mountaineer	Alpinist(m)	alpinista	alpinista
alternar	alterner	alternate	ab = wechseln	alternar	alternare
alternativo, a	alternatif, ive	alternating(ive)	alternativ	alternativo, a	alternativo, a

Portuguese	French	English	German	Spanish	Italian
altitude	altitude	altitude, height	Höhe(f)	altitud, altura	altitudine
altivo, a	fier, fière	proud	stolz	altivo, a	fiero, a
alto, a	haut, e	high, tall	hoch	alto, a	alto, a
alto, a	grand, e	high	hoch	alto, a	forte; alto, a
alto, a	élevé, e	high	hoch, erhöht	alto, a	elevato, a; alto, a
alto, a; grande	grand, e	tall	groß	alto, a	alto, a
alto, cimo	haut	top	Oberteil(n)	alto	alto
alto, paragem	halte, arrêt	halt, stop	Halt(m)	alto, parada	sosta, fermata
alto-falante	baffle	speaker	Lautsprecher(m)	altavoz	altoparlante
alto-falante	haut-parleur	loud-speaker	Lautsprecher(m)	altavoz	altoparlante
altura	hauteur	height	Höhe(f)	altura	altezza
alucinação	hallucination	hallucination	Sinnestäuschung(f)	alucinación	allucinazione
alugar	louer	rent	vermieten; mieten	alquilar	affittare
alugar	louer	hire, rent	mieten; vermieten	alquilar	noleggiare
aluguer	loyer	rent	Miete(f)	alquiler	affitto
aluguer	location	rental, hiring	Vermietung(f)	alquiler	noleggio, affitto
alumínio	aluminium	aluminium	Aluminium(n)	aluminio	alluminio
aluno, a	élève	pupil	Schüler(in f)m	alumno, a	alunno, a
aluno, a	écolier, ière	schoolboy/girl	Schüler(in f)m	colegial, a	scolaro, a
alvo	cible	target	Zielscheibe(f)	blanco	bersaglio
ama	nurse	nanny	Kindermädchen(n)	niñera	bambinaia
amador, a	amateur	amateur	Amateur(in f)m	aficionado, a	dilettante
amanhã	demain	tomorrow	morgen	mañana	domani
amanhecer	aube	dawn	Morgendämmerung(f)	alba	alba
amante	amant, e	lover	Geliebte(f, m)	amante	amante
amar, gostar de	aimer	love	lieben	amar, querer	amare, volere bene
amarelo, a	jaune	yellow	gelb	amarillo, a	giallo, a
amargo, a	amer, ère	bitter	bitter; sauer	amargo, a	amaro, a
amassar	pétrir	knead	kneten	amasar	impastare
amável	aimable	nice	lieb, nett	amable	amabile
amável	brave	decent, nice	brav, nett, angenehm	bueno, a	bravo, a
ambição	ambition	ambition	Ehrgeiz(m)	ambición	ambizione
ambicioso, a	ambitieux, se	ambitious	ehrgeizig	ambicioso, a	ambizioso, a
ambiente	ambiance	atmosphere	Stimmung(f)	ambiente	atmosfera
ambiente	environnement	surroundings	Umgebung(f)	ambiente(medio)	ambiente
ambíguo, a	ambigu, ë	ambiguous	zweideutig, mehrdeutig	ambiguo, a	ambiguo, a
ambos, os dois	à la fois	both	beide, beides	ambos, ambas	entrambi
ambulância	ambulance	ambulance	Krankenwagen(m)	ambulancia	ambulanza
ameaça	menace	threat	Drohung(f)	amenaza	minaccia
ameaçar	menacer	threaten	bedrohen	amenazar	minacciare
ameixa	prune	plum	Pflaume(f)	ciruela	prugna, susina
amêndoa	amande	almond	Mandel(f)	almendra	mandorla
amendoim	cacahuète	peanut	Erdnuß(f)	cacahuete, maní	arachide
ameno, a	doux, ce	mild	mild	templado, a	mite
amestrar	dresser	train	ab = richten, dressieren	amaestrar	addestrare
amigável	amical, e	friendly	freundschaftlich	amistoso, a	amichevole
amígdala	amygdale(s)	tonsils	Mandeln(f, pl)	amígdalas	tonsilla
amigo, a	ami, e	friend	Freund(in f)m	amigo, a	amico, a
amizade	amitié	friendship	Freundschaft(f)	amistad	amicizia
amnésia	amnésie	amnesia	Gedächtnisschwund(m)	amnesia	amnesia
amnistia	amnistie	amnesty	Amnestie(f)	amnistía	amnistia
amontoado	amas	pile	Haufen(m)	montón	mucchio
amontoar	entasser	pile up	stapeln	amontonar	ammucchiare
amor	amour	love	Liebe(f)	amor	amore
amortecedor	amortisseur	shock absorber	Stoßdämpfer(m)	amortiguador	ammortizzatore
amortecer	amortir	absorb, cushion	dämpfen	amortiguar	attutire
amostra	échantillon	sample	Probe(f), Muster(n)	muestra	campione
amovível	amovible	removable	auswechselbar	amovible	amovibile
ampliar	agrandir	enlarge	vergrößern	ampliar	ingrandire
amplidão	ampleur	scale, size	Weite(f), Größe(f)	amplitud	ampiezza
amplitude	amplitude	amplitude	Amplitude(f)	amplitud	ampiezza
amplo, a	ample	ample; loose	weit	amplio, a	ampio, a
amputar	amputer	amputate	amputieren	amputar	amputare
analisar	analyser	analyse	analysieren	analizar	analizzare
análise	analyse	analysis(-ses)	Analyse(f)	análisis	analisi
análogo, a	analogue	analogous, similar	analog	análogo, a	analogo, a
ananás	ananas	pineapple	Ananas(f)	piña	ananas
anão, anã	nain, e	dwarf	Zwerg(m)	enano, a	nano, a

Portuguese	French	English	German	Spanish	Italian
anarquia	anarchie	anarchy	Anarchie(f)	anarquía	anarchia
anatomia	anatomie	anatomy	Anatomie(f)	anatomía	anatomia
anca	hanche	hip	Hüfte(f)	cadera	anca
ancinho	râteau	rake	Rechen(m)	rastrillo	rastrello
âncora	ancre	anchor	Anker(m)	ancla	àncora
andaime	échafaudage	scaffolding	Gerüst(n)	andamio	impalcatura
andar	marcher, aller	walk	gehen	andar	andare
andar; rolar	rouler	run, drive, go	fahren	correr, rodar	correre, andare
andar	étage	floor, storey	Etage(f)	piso, planta	piano
andorinha	hirondelle	swallow	Schwalbe(f)	golondrina	rondine
anedota	anecdote	anecdote	Anekdote(f)	anécdota	aneddoto
anedota, chalaça	blague	joke	Witz(m)	chiste	scherzo
anel	anneau	ring	Ring(m)	anilla, anillo	anello
anel	bague	ring	Ring(m)	anillo, sortija	anello
anelar	annulaire	annular, ring-	ringförmig	anular	anulare
anemia	anémie	anaemia	Blutarmut(f)	anemia	anemia
anestesia	anesthésie	anaesthetic	Narkose(f)	anestesia	anestesia
anexo	annexe	annexe	Anhang(m), Anlage(f)	anexo; anejo	annesso
anexo(em)	ci-joint, e	enclosed	anbei	adjunto, a	allegato, a
anfitrião; hóspede, a	hôte, tesse	host; guest	Gastgeber(m); Gast(m)	anfitrión; huésped	ospite
angina	angine	sore throat	Angina(f)	angina	angina, tonsillite
ângulo	angle	angle	Winkel(m)	ángulo	angolo
angústia	angoisse	anguish, distress	Angst(f)	angustia	angoscia
anilha	rondelle	washer	Scheibe(f)	arandela	rondella
animado, a	animé, e	lively	lebhaft	animado, a	animato, a
animador, a	animateur, trice	leader, organiser	Leiter/in, Unterhalter	animador, a	animatore, trice
animal	animal	animal	Tier(n)	animal	animale
animar	animer	animate	beleben	animar	animare
animar	animer	liven up	Stimmung machen	animar	animare
aninhar-se	blottir(se)	huddle	an = schmiegen, sich	acurrucar(se)	rannicchiarsi
aniquilar	anéantir	annihilate, destroy	vernichten	aniquilar	annientare
aniversário	anniversaire	birthday	Geburtstag(m)	cumpleaños	compleanno
aniversário	anniversaire	anniversary	Jahrestag(m)	aniversario	anniversario
anjo	ange	angel	Engel(m)	ángel	angelo
ano	an	year	Jahr(n)	año	anno
ano	année	year	Jahr(n)	año	annata, anno
anomalia	anomalie	anomaly	Anomalie(f)	anomalía	anomalia
anonimato	anonymat	anonymity	Anonymität(f)	anonimato	anonimato
anónimo, a	anonyme	anonymous	anonym, unbekannt	anónimo, a	anonimo, a
anormal	anormal, e	not normal	anormal	anormal	anormale
anotar, notar	noter	note; notice	notieren; bemerken	anotar	notare
ansioso, a	anxieux, se	anxious	ängstlich	ansioso, a	ansioso, a
antebraço	avant-bras	fore-arm	Unterarm(m)	antebrazo	avambraccio
antecedente	antécédent, e	previous	vorhergehend	antecedente	antecedente
antecipar	anticiper	anticipate	vor = greifen	anticipar	anticipare
antena	antenne	aerial, antenna(e)	Antenne(f)	antena	antenna
antepassado, a	ancêtre	ancestor	Ahn(m)	antepasado, a	antenato, a
antepassados	aïeux	ancestors	Ahnen(pl.)	antepasados	antenati
anterior	antérieur, e	previous, former	vorhergehend	anterior	anteriore
anterior	antérieur, e	prior	früher	anterior	anteriore
antes(de)	avant	before	vor, vorher	antes(de)	prima
antes; mais	plutôt	rather	eher, lieber	más bien	piuttosto
antibiótico	antibiotique	antibiotic	Antibiotikum(n)	antibiótico	antibiotico
antigamente	autrefois	past(in the)	früher	antaño	volta(una)
antigo, a	ancien, ne	old	alt	antiguo, a	vecchio, a; antico, a
antigo, a	ancien, ne	ancient	alt	antiguo, a	antico, a
antigo, a	ancien, ne	former	ehemalig	ex, antiguo, a	ex
antigo, a	antique	antique, ancient	antik	antiguo, a	antico, a
antiguidade	antiquité	antiquity	Antiquität(f)	antigüedad	antichità
antiguidades	antiquités	antique shop	Antiquitäten	anticuario	antiquariato
antiquado, a	démodé, e; désuet	obsolete	veraltet	anticuado, a	antiquato, a
antiséptico, a	antiseptique	antiseptic	antiseptisch	antiséptico, a	antisettico, a
antro, tugúrio	taudis	slum	Bruchbude(f)	tugurio	topaia
anual	annuel, le	yearly, annual	jährlich	anual	annuale
anuário	annuaire	directory	Adreßbuch; Telefonbuch	anuario, guía	elenco, annuario
anular	annuler	cancel	annullieren	cancelar, anular	annullare
anular	annuler	quash	auf = heben	anular	annullare
anular	annuler	annul	ungültig erklären	anular	annullare

Portuguese	French	English	German	Spanish	Italian
anunciar	annoncer	announce	an = kündigen	anunciar	annunciare
anúncio	annonce	notice	Anzeige(f)	anuncio	annuncio
anzol	hameçon	hook	Angelhaken(m)	anzuelo	amo
ao lado	à côté	next to, beside	neben, daneben	al lado	accanto; vicino, a
apadrinhar	parrainer	sponsor	sponsorisieren	patrocinar	sponsorizzare
apagar	éteindre	turn/switch off	aus = schalten	apagar	spegnere
apagar	éteindre	extinguish	löschen	apagar	spegnere
apagar	effacer	erase, rub out	radieren	borrar	cancellare
apaixonado, a	passionné, e	interested(very)	leidenschaftlich	apasionado, a	appassionato, a
apaixonado, a	amoureux, se	love(in)	verliebt	enamorado, a	innamorato, a
apaixonante	passionnant, e	fascinating	spannend	apasionante	appassionante
apalpar	palper, tâter	feel, finger	betasten	palpar	palpare
apanhar, recolher	ramasser	pick up	auf = heben	recoger	raccogliere
aparador	buffet	dresser; sideboard	Büfett(n)	aparador	credenza, buffè
aparecer	apparaître	appear	erscheinen	aparecer	apparire
aparelho	appareil	appliance, device	Apparat(m)	aparato	apparecchio
aparelho	gadget	gadget	Spielerei(f)	chisme, mecanismo	gadget
aparência	apparence	appearance, look	Aussehen(n)	apariencia	apparenza
aparência	mine	look	Aussehen(n)	semblante, cara	cera, aspetto
apartamento	appartement	flat, apartment	Wohnung(f)	piso	appartamento
apavorar	effarer, effrayer	terrify	erschrecken	espantar, asustar	sgomentare
apego	attachement	attachment	Verbundenheit(f)	apego, cariño	attaccamento
apelação	appel	appeal	Berufung(f)	apelación	appello
apelido	nom	surname	Familienname(m)	apellido	cognome
aperceber-se	réaliser	realize	begreifen	darse cuenta	realizzare
aperfeiçoar	perfectionner	improve; perfect	vervollkommnen	perfeccionar	perfezionare
aperitivo	apéritif	aperitif, drink	Apéritif(m)	aperitivo	aperitivo
apertar	serrer	grip, hold tight	greifen, packen	apretar	stringere
apertar	serrer, resserrer	tighten	an = ziehen	apretar	stringere
apertar a mão	serrer la main	shake hands	Hand schütteln	estrechar la mano	stringere la mano
apesar de	malgré	despite	trotz	a pesar de	malgrado
apetite	appétit	appetite	Appetit(m)	apetito	appetito
apiedar-se	compatir	sympathize	mit = fühlen	compadecer	compatire
apito	sifflet	whistle	Pfeife(f)	pito	fischietto
aplanar	aplanir	level	ebnen	aplanar	spianare
aplaudir	applaudir	applaud, clap	klatschen	aplaudir	applaudire
aplicar	appliquer	apply	an = wenden	aplicar	applicare
apodrecer	pourrir	rot	verfaulen	pudrir	marcire
apoiar-se	appuyer(s')	lean on(against)	stützen, sich	apoyar(se)	appoggiarsi
apoio	appui	support	Stütze(f)	apoyo	appoggio
apoio, socorro	soutien, appui	support	Unterstützung(f)	sostén, apoyo	sostegno, appoggio
apontar	viser	aim	zielen	apuntar	mirare
apontar	braquer	aim	richten auf	apuntar	puntare
aposta	pari	bet	Wette(f)	apuesta	scommessa
aposta	enjeu	stake	Einsatz(m)(Spiel-)	apuesta	posta
apreciação	appréciation	appreciation	Beurteilung(f)	apreciación	giudizio
apreciador, a	amateur de	lover of	Liebhaber(in f)m	amante de	appassionato, a
apreciar	apprécier	appreciate	schätzen	apreciar	apprezzare
apreensão	appréhension	apprehension	Furcht(f)	aprensión, recelo	apprensione
aprender	apprendre	learn	lernen	aprender	imparare
aprendizagem	apprentissage	apprenticeship	Lehre(f), Lehrjahre(f)	aprendizaje	apprendistato
aprendizagem	apprentissage	learning	Lernen(n)	estudio	tirocinio
apresentação	présentation	presentation	Vorführung(f)	presentación	presentazione
apresentar	présenter	present	vor = zeigen, - = stellen	presentar	presentare
apresentar	présenter	introduce	vor = stellen	presentar	presentare
apresentar	introduire	introduce	vor = stellen	presentar	introdurre
aprovar	approuver	approve	genehmigen	aprobar	approvare
aproveitar	profiter	take advantage of	profitieren	aprovechar	approfittare
aproximado, a	approximatif, ive	approximate	ungefähr	aproximativo, a	approssimativo, a
aproximar-se	approcher(s')	approach	nähern, sich	acercar(se)	avvicinarsi
aptidão, talento	aptitude	ability, aptitude	Fähigkeit(f)	aptitud(es)	attitudine
apto, a	apte	able, qualified	fähig; tauglich	apto, a	adatto, a
aquário	aquarium	aquarium	Aquarium(n)	acuario	acquario
aquático, a	aquatique	aquatic	Wasser-	acuático, a	acquatico, a
aquecedor	radiateur	radiator, heater	Heizkörper(m)	radiador	termosifone
aquecer	chauffer	heat	heizen	calentar	riscaldare
aquecer	réchauffer	warm, (re)heat	auf = wärmen	recalentar	riscaldare
aquecimento	chauffage	heating	Heizung(f)	calefacción	riscaldamento

Portuguese	French	English	German	Spanish	Italian
aquecimento	échauffement	heating	Aufwärmen(n)	calentamiento	riscaldamento
aqueles, aquelas	ceux, celles, ces	these, those	diese	esos, aquellos	questi, e
aqui	ici	here	hier	aquí	qui
aqui está	voici	here is; here are	hier(ist/sind)	he aquí	ecco
ar	air	air	Luft(f)	aire	aria
arame	fil(de fer)	wire	Draht(m)	alambre	filo(di ferro)
aranha	araignée	spider	Spinne(f)	araña	ragno
arbitrário, a	arbitraire	arbitrary	willkürlich	arbitrario, a	arbitrario, a
árbitro	arbitre	referee	Schiedsrichter(in f)m	árbitro	arbitro
arcaico, a	archaïque	archaic	archaisch	arcaico, a	arcaico, a
arco	arc	bow	Bogen(m)	arco	arco
arco	arc	arc	Halbkreis(m)	arco	arco
arco	arche	arch	Bogen(m), Gewölbe(n)	arca	arco, volta
arco-íris	arc-en-ciel	rainbow	Regenbogen(m)	arco iris	arcobaleno
ardente	brûlant, e	boiling hot	brennend, kochend	ardiente	ardente, bollente
ardósia, lousa	ardoise	slate	Schiefer(m)	pizarra	ardesia
área, zona	aire, zone	area	Bereich(m), Gebiet(n)	área, zona	area, zona
areia	sable	sand	Sand(m)	arena	sabbia
arejar, ventilar	aérer	air, ventilate	lüften	airear, ventilar	arieggiare
arena	arène	arena	Arena(f)	arena	arena
arenque	hareng	herring	Hering(m)	arenque	aringa
argamassa	mortier	mortar	Mörtel(m)	argamasa	malta, calcina
argila	argile	clay	Ton(m), Lehm(m)	arcilla	argilla
argumentar	argumenter	argue	verhandeln	argüir, argumentar	argomentare
argumento	argument	argument	Argument(n)	argumento	argomento
árido, a	aride	arid	dürr, trocken	árido, a	arido, a
arisco, a	farouche	wild	wild	feroz	selvatico, a
aristocrata	aristocrate	aristocrat	Adlige(f, m)	aristócrata	aristocratico, a
aritmética	arithmétique	arithmetic	Arithmetik(f)	aritmética	aritmetica
arma	arme	weapon, arm	Waffe(f)	arma	arma
arma	arme	arm	Waffe(f)	arma	arma; armi
armadilha	piège	trap, snare	Falle(f)	trampa	trappola
armador	armateur	ship-owner	Reeder(m)	armador	armatore
armamento	armement	armament, weapons	Bewaffnung(f)	armamento	armamento
armário	armoire	wardrobe	Schrank(m)(Kleider-)	armario	armadio
armário	armoire	cupboard	Schrank(m)	armario	armadio
armário	placard	cupboard	Wandschrank(m)	armario	armadio a muro
armazém	magasin	store	Warenlager(n)	almacén	magazzino; negozio
armazém	entrepôt	warehouse	Lager(n)	almacén	magazzino
armazenar	stocker	stock, store	lagern	almacenar	immagazzinare
arnês	harnais	harness	Geschirr(n)	arnés	finimenti
aroma, cheiro	arôme	aroma	Aroma(n)	aroma	aroma
aroma	bouquet	bouquet	Blume(f), Bukett(n)	buqué, aroma, boca	bouquet, aroma
arpão	harpon	harpoon	Harpune(f)	arpón	arpione
arqueado, a	cambré, e	arched	krumm, gebeugt	arqueado, a	inarcato, a; arcuato, a
arquejar	haleter	pant, gasp	keuchen	jadear	ansimare
arqueologia	archéologie	archaeology	Archeologie(f)	arqueología	archeologia
arquipélago	archipel	archipelago	Inselgruppe(f)	archipiélago	arcipelago
arquitecto, a	architecte	architect	Architekt(in f)m	arquitecto, a	architetto
arquitectura	architecture	architecture	Architektur(f)	arquitectura	architettura
arquivo	archives	archives	Archiv(n)	archivos	archivi
arrancar	arracher	tear out; tear off	weg = reißen, aus = reißen	arrancar	strappare, togliere
arrancar	démarrer	start	starten	arrancar	avviare, iniziare
arranha-céus	gratte-ciel	skyscraper	Wolkenkratzer(m)	rascacielos	grattacielo
arranhadura	éraflure	scratch, graze	Kratzer(m), Schramme f	rasguño	scalfittura
arranhar	égratigner	scratch	kratzen, schrammen	rasguñar	scalfire
arranhar	griffer	scratch, claw	kratzen	arañar	graffiare
arranjar	arranger	arrange	arrangieren	arreglar	sistemare
arranjar, dispor	aménager	fit out; convert	ein = richten	acondicionar	sistemare
arranjar; obter	procurer(se)	obtain, get	besorgen, sich	procurarse	procurarsi
arranjo	arrangement	arrangement	Anordnung(f)	arreglo	ordinamento
arrastar	traîner	drag, trail, haul	schleppen	arrastrar	trascinare
arredores	alentours	surroundings	Umgebung(f)	alrededores	dintorni
arredores	banlieue	suburbs	Vorort(m)	afueras	periferia
arrefecer	refroidir	cool(down)	ab = kühlen	enfriar	raffreddare
arreliar	taquiner	tease	necken	hacer rabiar	stuzzicare
arrendar, alugar	louer à bail	lease	mieten; pachten	arrendar	noleggiare
arrepio	frisson	shiver	Schauer(m)	escalofrío	brivido

Portuguese	French	English	German	Spanish	Italian
arriscar	risquer	risk	riskieren	arriesgar	rischiare
arrotar	roter	burp	auf = stoßen, rülpsen	eructar	ruttare
arroz	riz	rice	Reis(m)	arroz	riso
arruinar	ruiner	ruin	ruinieren	arruinar	rovinare
arrumado, a	rangé, e	tidy	ordentlich	ordenado, a	ordinato, a
arrumar	ranger, ordonner	tidy, put in order	ein = räumen	ordenar, colocar	sistemare
arsenal	arsenal	arsenal, armoury	Arsenal(n)	arsenal	arsenale
arte	art	art	Kunst(f)	arte	arte
artéria	artère	artery	Ader(f); Arterie(f)	arteria	arteria
artesão	artisan	craftsman(-men)	Handwerker(in f)m	artesano	artigiano
artes marciais	arts martiaux	martial arts	Kriegskunst(f)	artes marciales	arti marziali
articulação	articulation	joint	Gelenk(n)	articulación	articolazione
artificial	artificiel, le	artificial	künstlich	artificial	artificiale
artigo	article	article	Artikel(m)	artículo	articolo
artigo	article	article	Gesetzesartikel(m)	artículo	articolo
artigo	article	item	Artikel(m)	artículo	articolo
artista	artiste	artist	Künstler(in f)m	artista	artista
artrose	arthrose	arthritis	Arthrose(f)	artrosis	artrosi
árvore	arbre	tree	Baum(m)	árbol	albero
asa	aile	wing	Flügel(m)	ala	ala
asa	anse	handle	Griff(m)	asa	ansa
asa	poignée	handle	Griff(m)	asa, mango	manico
asfalto	bitume	asphalt, tarmac	Asphalt(m)	asfalto	bitume
asfixia	asphyxie	suffocation	Ersticken(n)	asfixia	asfissia
asilo	asile	asylum(political)	Asyl(n)	asilo	asilo
asma	asthme	asthma	Asthma(n)	asma	asma
asneira	bêtise	stupid thing(do a)	Dummheit(f)	estupidez	sciocchezza
aspecto	aspect	aspect	Aussehen(n)	aspecto	aspetto
aspirador	aspirateur	vacuum-cleaner	Staubsauger(m)	aspirador	aspirapolvere
aspirar	aspirer	inhale, suck in(up)	ein = atmen, saugen	aspirar	aspirare
aspirina	aspirine	aspirin	Aspirin(n)	aspirina	aspirina
asqueroso, a	infect, e	foul, vile	ekelhaft, stinkig	asqueroso, a	fetido, a
assado	rôti	roast; joint	Braten(m)	asado	arrosto
assalariado, a	salarié, e	salaried employee	Arbeitnehmer(in f)m	asalariado, a	salariato, a
assalto	assaut	assault, attack	Angriff(m)	asalto	assalto
assalto	hold-up	hold-up	Raubüberfall(m)	atraco	rapina
assassínio	assassinat	murder	Mord(m)	asesinato	assassinio
assassino, a	assassin	murderer	Mörder(in f)m	asesino, a	assassino, a
assassino, a	meurtrier, ière	murderer	Mörder(in f)m	homicida	omicida
assassino, a	tueur, se	killer	Mörder(in f)m	asesino, a	assassino, a
assegurar-se	assurer(s')	ensure; insure	versichern; zu = sichern	asegurarse	assicurarsi
assembleia	assemblée	meeting, assembly	Versammlung(f)	asamblea	assemblea
assento	siège	seat	Sitz(m)	asiento	sedia
assim	ainsi	so, thus	so	así	così
assinalar	signaler	point out	melden; an = zeigen	señalar	segnalare
assinante	abonné, e	subscriber	Abonnent(m)	suscriptor, a	abbonato, a
assinar	signer	sign	unterschreiben	firmar	firmare
assinatura	signature	signature	Unterschrift(f)	firma	firma
assinatura	abonnement	subscription	Abonnement(n)	subscripción	abbonamento
assistência	assistance	assistance	Hilfe(f)	asistencia	assistenza
assistente	assistant, e	assistant	Assistent(in f)m	asistente, a	assistente
assistir	assister	attend	assistieren	asistir	assistere
assistir a	assister	attend	bei = wohnen	concurrir a	presenziare
assoar-se	moucher(se)	blow one's nose	Nase putzen	sonarse	soffiarsi il naso
assobiar	siffler	whistle	pfeifen	silbar	fischiare
associação	association	association	Verband(m)	asociación	associazione
associar	associer	combine, associate	verbinden	asociar	associare
associar-se a	associer à(s')	join	an = schließen, sich	asociarse(a, con)	associarsi(a, con)
assolar	ravager	devastate, ravage	verwüsten	asolar, devastar	devastare
assombrado, a	hanté, e	haunted	verflucht	embrujado, a	spiritato, a
assumir	assumer	assume	übernehmen, nehmen	asumir	assumere
assunto	matière	subject matter	Thema(n)	materia, tema	materia, tema
assunto, tema	sujet, thème	subject, theme	Thema(n)	tema	tema
assunto	affaire	affair, matter	Affäre(f), Sache(f)	asunto	faccenda, affare
assustar	effrayer	frighten	erschrecken	asustar	spaventare
astro	astre	star	Stern(m), Gestirn(n)	astro	astro
astrologia	astrologie	astrology	Astrologie(f)	astrología	astrologia
astronáutica	astronautique	astronautics	Weltraumfahrt(f)	astronáutica	astronautica

Portuguese	French	English	German	Spanish	Italian
astronomia	astronomie	astronomy	Astronomie(f)	astronomía	astronomia
astúcia	astuce	trick	List(f), Trick(m)	astucia	astuzia
astúcia	ruse	trick, craftiness	List(f)	ardid; astucia	furbizia
astucioso, a	astucieux, se	astute, clever	verschmitzt, schlau	astuto, a	astuto, a
astuto, a; fino, a	rusé, e	crafty, cunning	schlau, gerissen	astuto, a	astuto, a
atacar	attaquer	attack	an = greifen	atacar	attaccare
atalho	raccourci	short cut	Abkürzung(f)	atajo	scorciatoia
ataque	attaque	attack	Angriff(m)	ataque	attacco
ataque	crise cardiaque	heart attack	Herzattacke(f)	crisis cardíaca	infarto
atar	attacher	attach, tie, fasten	fest = binden, binden	atar	legare
atar, amarrar	attacher	fasten	befestigen	atar, fijar	attaccare, legare
até	jusqu'à	until, till	bis	hasta	fino a, sino a
até	jusqu'à	as far as	bis	hasta	fino
até breve; até já	à bientôt	see you soon, bye	bis bald	hasta pronto	a presto
até logo, adeus!	au revoir	good bye, bye-bye	auf Wiedersehen	hasta luego	arrivederci
atenção, cuidado	attention	care, caution	Sorgfalt(f)	cuidado	accuratezza
atenção!, cuidado!	attention!	careful!(be)	Achtung!(f)	cuidado(!)	attenzione!, attento!
atentado	attentat	attempt, attack	Attentat(n)	atentado	attentato
atento, a	attentif, ive	attentive, careful	aufmerksam	atento, a	attento, a
atenuar	atténuer	attenuate	ab = schwächen; lindern	atenuar	attenuare
aterrar	atterrir	land	landen	aterrizar	atterrare
aterrorizar	terroriser	terrorize	terrorisieren	aterrorizar	terrorizzare
atingir	atteindre	reach	erreichen	alcanzar, lograr	raggiungere
atirar, lançar	jeter	throw	werfen	arrojar, lanzar	gettare
atirar, disparar	tirer	shoot, fire	schießen, feuern	disparar	tirare, sparare
atitude	attitude	attitude	Haltung(f)	actitud	atteggiamento
Atlântico	Atlantique	Atlantic	Atlantik(m)	Atlántico	Atlantico
atleta	athlète	athlete	Athlet(in f)m	atleta	atleta
atletismo	athlétisme	athletics	Leichtathletik(f)	atletismo	atletismo
atmosfera	atmosphère	atmosphere	Atmosphäre(f)	atmósfera	atmosfera
atol	atoll	atoll	Atoll(n)	atolón	atollo
atómico, a	atomique	atomic	atomar	atómico, a	atomico, a
átomo	atome	atom	Atom(n)	átomo	atomo
atormentado, a	tourmenté, e	tormented	beunruhigt	atormentado, a	tormentato, a
atormentar	tourmenter	torment	quälen	atormentar	tormentare
atracção	attraction	attraction	Anziehung(f)	atracción	attrazione
atraente	attirant, e	attractive	anziehend	atrayente	attraente
atraente	séduisant, e	attractive	reizend, anziehend	atractivo, a	seducente
atrair	attirer	attract	an = ziehen	atraer	attirare
atrair, seduzir	attirer, séduire	entice	verführen	atraer, seducir	attirare, sedurre
atrás	arrière, derrière	behind, back	hinten, zurück	atrás	dietro, posteriore
atrás, detrás	derrière	behind	hinter	detrás, tras	dietro
atrasado, a(estar)	retard(être en)	late(to be)	zu spät kommen	retrasado, a(estar)	ritardo(essere in)
atrasar, demorar	retarder	delay	verzögern	retrasar, demorar	ritardare
atraso	retard	delay; lateness	Verspätung(f)	atraso	ritardo
através de	travers(à)	across; through	durch	través de(a)	attraverso
atravessar	franchir	cross	überqueren	atravesar	varcare, passare
atravessar	traverser	cross	überqueren	atravesar, cruzar	attraversare
atribuir	attribuer	attribute	bei = messen	atribuir	attribuire
atribuir	décerner	award	zu = erkennen, erteilen	otorgar	conferire
atroador, a	étourdissant, e	deafening	betäubend	aturdidor, a	sbalorditivo, a
atroz	atroce	atrocious	grausam	atroz	atroce
atum	thon	tuna(fish)	Thunfisch(m)	atún, bonito	tonno
aturdir; atordoar	étourdir	stun, daze	betäuben	aturdir; atontar	stordire
audácia	audace	audacity	Kühnheit(f)	audacia	audacia
audiência	audience	audience	Audienz(f)	audiencia	udienza
aula(sala de)	classe(salle)	classroom	Klassenzimmer(n)	aula	aula
aumentar	augmenter	increase, raise	zu = nehmen	aumentar	aumentare
aumentar	accroître	increase	zu = nehmen	incrementar	accrescere
aumentar	grossir	increase	vermehren	agrandar	ingrandire
aumento	augmentation	increase, rise	Zunahme(f)	aumento	aumento
aurora	aurore	dawn	Morgenröte(f)	aurora	aurora
auscultadores	écouteurs, casque	ear/headphones	Kopfhörer(m)	casco	cuffia
auscultar	ausculter	examine	ab = horchen	auscultar	auscultare
ausente	absent, e	absent	abwesend	ausente	assente
austero, a	austère	austere	streng, hart	austero, a	austero, a
autêntico, a	authentique	authentic, genuine	authentisch	auténtico, a	autentico, a
autêntico, a	authentique	genuine	echt	genuino, a	genuino, a

Portuguese	French	English	German	Spanish	Italian
autocarro	autobus	bus	Bus(m)	autobús	autobus
autocarro	autocar	coach	Reisebus(m)	autocar	pullman
auto-estrada	autoroute	motorway	Autobahn(f)	autopista	autostrada
autógrafo	autographe	autograph	Autogramm(n)	autógrafo	autografo
automático, a	automatique	automatic	automatisch	automático, a	automatico, a
autómato	automate	automaton	Automat(m)	autómata	automa
automóvel	automobile	car	Auto(n)	automóvil	automobile
autonomia	autonomie	autonomy	Autonomie(f)	autonomía	autonomia
autónomo, a	autonome	autonomous	autonom; unabhängig	autónomo, a	autonomo, a
autópsia	autopsie	autopsy	Autopsie(f)	autopsia	autopsia
autor, a	auteur	author	Autor(in f)m	autor, a	autore, autrice
autoridade	autorité	authority	Autorität(f)	autoridad	autorità
autoritário, a	autoritaire	authoritarian	autoritär	autoritario, a	autoritario, a
autorizar	autoriser	authorize	erlauben	autorizar	autorizzare
auxiliar	auxiliaire	auxiliary	Hilfs-; Hilfe(f)	auxiliar	ausiliare
auxiliar, ajudar	aider, assister	assist	helfen	ayudar, asistir	assistere, aiutare
avalanche	avalanche	avalanche	Lawine(f)	avalancha	valanga
avaliação	évaluation	assessment	Einschätzung(f)	valoración	valutazione
avaliação	évaluation	assessment	Schätzung(f)	evaluación	valutazione
avaliar, fixar	évaluer, estimer	assess	ein = schätzen	tasar, valorar	valutare, stimare
avançar	avancer	advance, move fwd	weiter = gehen	avanzar	procedere
avanço	avance	advance	Vorsprung(m)	adelanto	anticipo
avarento, a	avare	miserly, mean	geizig	avaro, a	avaro, a
avaria	panne	breakdown	Panne(f)	avería	guasto, panna
ave	oiseau	bird	Vogel(m)	ave, pájaro	uccello
ave de rapina	rapace	bird of prey	Raubvogel(m)	rapaz	rapace
avenida	avenue	avenue	Allee(f)	avenida	viale
avenida	boulevard	boulevard	Boulevard(m)	bulevar	viale
avental	tablier	apron	Schürze(f)	delantal	grembiule
aventura	aventure	adventure	Abenteuer(n)	aventura	avventura
aves de capoeira	volaille	poultry	Geflügel(n)	aves de corral	pollame
avesso	envers	reverse, back	Rückseite(f)	revés	rovescio
aviação	aviation	aviation	Luftfahrt(f)	aviación	aviazione
aviador, a	aviateur, trice	aviator	Flieger(m), Pilot(m)	aviador, a	aviatore, trice
avião	avion	plane, aeroplane	Flugzeug(n)	avión	aereo
ávido, a; desejoso, a	avide, impatient	eager	begierig	deseoso, a	desideroso, a
avisar, prevenir	avertir	warn	warnen	advertir	avvertire
aviso, notícia	avis	notice	Mitteilung(f)	aviso	avviso
aviso	avertissement	warning	Warnung(f)	advertencia	ammonizione
aviso; lembrança	rappel	reminder	Erinnerung(f); Mahnung	llamada	richiamo
avistar	apercevoir	perceive, notice	bemerken	avistar, divisar	scorgere
avó	grand-père	grandfather	Großvater(m)	abuelo	nonno
avó	grand-mère	grandmother	Großmutter(f)	abuela	nonna
avós	grands-parents	grandparents	Großeltern(pl.)	abuelos	nonni
azarento, a	malchanceux, se	unlucky	unglücklich	desafortunado, a	sfortunato, a
azedo, a	aigre	sour	sauer	agrio, a	aspro, a; agro, a
azeitona	olive	olive	Olive(f)	aceituna, oliva	oliva
azul	bleu, e	blue	blau	azul	blu

B

Portuguese	French	English	German	Spanish	Italian
babar-se	baver	dribble	sabbern	babear	sbavare
bacalhau	morue	cod	Schellfisch(m)	bacalao	baccalà; merluzzo
bacharelato	baccalauréat	G.C.E. A.Level(s)	Abitur(n)	bachillerato	maturità
bacia	cuvette	basin, bowl	Schale(f)	palangana	catino
bacia	bassine	bowl	Wanne(f); Schüssel(f)	barreño	bacinella
baço	rate	spleen	Milz(f)	bazo	milza

Portuguese	French	English	German	Spanish	Italian
baço, a	terne	dull	matt	sin brillo, mate	spento, a; smorto, a
bactéria	bactérie	bacterium(-eria)	Bakterie(f)	bacteria	batterio
baforada	bouffée	puff, breath	Hauch(m), Atemzug(m)	bocanada	ventata
bagagem	bagage(s)	luggage, baggage	Gepäck(n)	equipaje	bagaglio
bagagem de mão	bagages à main	hand luggage	Handgepäck(n)	equipaje de mano	bagaglio a mano
baía	baie	bay	Bucht(f)	bahía	baia
bailarino, a	danseur, se	dancer	Tänzer(in f)m	bailarín, a	ballerino, a
baile	bal	dance, ball	Ball(m)	baile	ballo
bairro	quartier	district	Viertel(n)	barrio	quartiere
bairro de lata	bidonville	shanty-town	Elendsviertel(n)	chabolas	bidonville
baixa	baisse	fall, drop	Senkung(f)	baja	calo
baixar, abaixar	baisser, abaisser	lower	herunter = lassen	bajar	calare, abbassare
baixar	baisser	drop, lower; fall	senken	rebajar	abbassare, calare
baixar	descendre	fall, drop	fallen	bajar	abbassare
baixar-se	baisser(se)	bend down	bücken, sich	agacharse	abbassarsi
baixo, a	bas, basse	low	niedrig	bajo, a	basso, a
baixo	bas	down	hinunter	abajo	giù
baixo(de)	bas(en)	downstairs	unten; hinunter	abajo	basso, giù
baixo(parte de)	dessous	lower part	Unterteil(n)	inferior(parte)	sotto, disotto
baixo(por); abaixo	au-dessous	below, under(neath)	unter	debajo(de)	sotto(al di)
bala	balle	bullet	Kugel(f)	bala	pallottola
balança	balance	scales	Waage(f)	balanza	bilancia
balanço	bilan	balance-sheet	Bilanz(f)	balance	bilancio
balão	ballon	balloon	Heißluftballon(m)	globo	pallone
balbuciar	bafouiller	splutter, stammer	stammeln	balbucear	farfugliare
balcão	comptoir	counter	Ladentisch(m)	mostrador	banco
balcão	comptoir	counter, bar	Theke(f)	barra	banco
balde	seau	bucket, pail	Eimer(m)	cubo	secchio
baleia	baleine	whale	Wal(m)	ballena	balena
ballet, bailado	ballet	ballet	Ballet(n)	ballet	balletto
baloiço	balançoire	swing; see-saw	Schaukel(f)	columpio	altalena
balouçar-se	tanguer	pitch	schaukeln	cabecear	beccheggiare
banal	banal, e	banal	banal	común	banale
banana	banane	banana	Banane(f)	plátano, banana	banana
bancário, a	bancaire	bank, banking	Bank-	bancario, a	bancario, a
banco	banque	bank	Bank(f)	banco, banca	banca
banco	banc	bench	Bank(f)	banco	panca; panchina
banco dobrável	strapontin	folding seat	Klappstuhl(m)	traspuntín	strapuntino
banda desenhada	bande dessinée	cartoon(strip)	Comic Strip(m)	comics, tebeos	fumetto
bandeira	drapeau	flag	Fahne(f)	bandera	bandiera
bandeira	drapeau	flag	Flagge(f)	bandera	bandiera
bandido	bandit	bandit	Bandit(m)	bandido	bandito
bandido	brigand	bandit	Räuber(in f)m	maleante	brigante
bandido	truand, e	crook	Ganove(m), Gauner(m)	granuja, bandido	teppista
banheira	baignoire	bath	Badewanne(f)	bañera	vasca da bagno
banho	bain	bath	Bad(n)	baño	bagno
banho	baignade	swimming, bathing	Baden(n)	baño	bagno
banho(tomar)	baigner(se)	bathe; swim	baden; schwimmen	bañarse	bagno(fare il)
banqueiro	banquier	banker	Bankier(m)	banquero	banchiere
banquete	banquet	banquet	Bankett(n)	banquete	banchetto
baptismo	baptême	baptism	Taufe(f)	bautizo	battesimo
bar, café	bar	bar, pub	Kneipe(f)	bar, café	bar
barão, baronesa	baron, ne	baron, baroness	Baron(in, f)m	barón, baronesa	barone, baronessa
barato, a	bon marché	cheap	billig	barato, a	buon prezzo
barba	barbe	beard	Bart(m)	barba	barba
bárbaro, a	barbare	barbaric	barbarisch	bárbaro, a	barbaro, a
barbatana	nageoire	fin	Flosse(f)	aleta	pinna
barbatanas	palme	flipper	Flosse(f)	aleta	pinna
barbear-se	raser(se)	shave	rasieren, sich	afeitar(se)	radersi
barca	barque	boat(small)	Barke(f), Kahn(m)	barca	barca
barco	bateau	boat, ship	Schiff(n)	barco	imbarcazione, nave
barco	bac	ferry	Fähre(f)	transbordador	traghetto, ferry
barómetro	baromètre	barometer	Barometer(n)	barómetro	barometro
barra	barre	bar	Stange(f)	barra	sbarra
barragem	barrage	dam	Damm(m)	embalse, presa	diga
barranco	ravin	ravine	Schlucht(f); Graben(m)	barranco	burrone
barreira	barrière	barrier; gate	Schranke(f)	barrera	barriera
barreira	barrage	blockade	Sperre(f)	cordón(policía)	posto di blocco

| --- | --- | --- | --- | --- | --- |
barrete	bonnet	cap, hat	Mütze(f)	gorro	berretto, cuffia
barricada	barricade	barricade	Barrikade(f)	barricada	barricata
barriga(perna)	mollet	calf(-lves)	Wade(f)	pantorrilla	polpaccio
barriga	ventre	stomach, abdomen	Bauch(m)	barriga, vientre	pancia, ventre
barril	fût	barrel	Faß(n)	barril	fusto, barile
barulhento, a	bruyant, e	noisy; loud	laut	ruidoso, a	rumoroso, a
barulho	vacarme	uproar, din	Krach(m)	alboroto, jaleo	chiasso
báscula	bascule	scales	Waage(f)	báscula	basculla, bilancia
base	base	base	Grundlage(f)	base	base
base(militar)	base(militaire)	base	Stützpunkt(m)	base(militar)	base(militare)
base(de)	base(de)	basic	Grund-; Grundlage	básico	base
basquetebol	basket-ball	basket-ball	Basketball(m)	baloncesto	pallacanestro
basta!, chega!	assez!; suffit!	enough!(that's)	das langt, jetzt langt	basta(!)	basta così!
bastante	assez	enough; rather	genug	bastante(s)	abbastanza
bastidores	coulisses	wings	Kulisse(f)	bastidores	quinte(le)
bata	blouse	overall	Kittel(m)	bata, blusa	blusa, camice
batalha	bataille	battle	Gefecht(n)	batalla	battaglia
batata	pomme de terre	potato(-es)	Kartoffel(f)	patata	patata
batatas fritas	frites	chips	Pommes Frites	patatas fritas	patatine fritte
bater	battre	beat	schlagen	batir	battere
bater	frapper	hit, knock, strike	schlagen, prügeln	golpear	picchiare
bater	frapper	knock	an – klopfen	llamar	bussare
bateria	batterie	battery	Batterie(f)	batería	batteria
baton	rouge à lèvres	lipstick	Lippenstift(m)	barra de labios	rossetto
batota(fazer)	tricher	cheat	fuschen, mogeln	trampas(hacer)	barare
baú, arca, armário	bahut, coffre	chest	Truhe(f)	arca, cajón	cassone
baunilha	vanille	vanilla	Vanille(f)	vainilla	vaniglia
bêbado, a; ébrio, a	soûl, e; saoul, e	drunk	betrunken	embriagado, a	ubriaco, a
bebé	bébé	baby	Baby(n)	bebé	bebè, bambino, a
bêbedo, a; ébrio, a	ivrogne	drunkard	Trunkenbold(m)	borracho, a	ubriaco, a
bebedor, a	buveur, se	drinker	Trinker(in f)m	bebedor, a	bevitore, trice
beber	boire	drink	trinken	beber	bere
bebida	boisson	drink	Getränk(n)	bebida	bibita, bevanda
bege	beige	beige	beige	crema, beis	beige
beijinho	bise	kiss	Küßchen(n)	besito	bacio
beijo	baiser	kiss	Kuß(m)	beso(dar un)	bacio
beira-mar	bord de mer	sea-side	Küste(f)	orilla del mar	riva
beira-mar	rivage	shore	Küstenstrich(m)	orilla	riva
bela	belle	beautiful	schön	bella	bella
belas-artes	beaux-arts	fine arts	Kunst(f)	bellas artes	belle arti
beleza	beauté	beauty	Schönheit(f)	belleza	bellezza
belicoso, a	belliqueux, se	aggressive	kriegerisch	belicoso, a	bellicoso, a
beliscar	pincer	pinch, nip	kneifen	pellizcar	pizzicare
belo, a; bonito, a	beau, belle	beautiful, fine	schön	hermoso, a; bello, a	bello, a
bem	bien	well	wohl	bien	bene
bem	bien	well	gut	bien	bene
bem	bien	good	Gut(n)	bien	bene
bem-estar	bien-être	well-being	Wohlbefinden(n)	bienestar	benessere
bem-vindo, a	bienvenu, e	welcome(to be)	Willkommen(n)	bienvenido, a	benvenuto, a
beneficiar, lucrar	bénéficier	profit, benefit	profitieren, gewinnen	beneficiar	beneficiare
benévolo, a	bénévole	voluntary	unentgeltlich	benévolo, a	benevolo, a
benévolo, a	bienveillant, e	benevolent	wohlwollend	benévolo, a	benevolo, a
bengala	canne	stick	Stock(m)	bastón	bastone
benigno, a	bénin, bénigne	benign	gutartig	benigno, a	benigno, a
bens	biens	possessions, estate	Besitz(m), Güter(pl)	bienes	beni; averi
benzer	bénir	bless	segnen	bendecir	benedire
berço	berceau	cradle	Wiege(f)	cuna	culla
berlinde	bille	marble	Murmel(f)	bola	biglia
betão	béton	concrete	Beton(m)	hormigón	calcestruzzo
betume	mastic	putty	Kitt(m)	masilla	mastice
bexiga	vessie	bladder	Harnblase(f)	vejiga	vescica
bezerro; vitelo	veau	calf(-lves); veal	Kalb(n)	becerro; ternera	vitello(a)
biberão	biberon	bottle(baby's -)	Fläschchen(n)	biberón	biberon
Bíblia	Bible	Bible	Bibel(f)	Biblia	Bibbia
bibliografia	bibliographie	bibliography	Bibliographie(f)	bibliografía	bibliografia
biblioteca	bibliothèque	library	Bibliothek(f)	biblioteca	biblioteca
biceps	biceps	biceps	Bizeps(m)	bíceps	bicipite
bicha; fila	queue	queue	Schlange(f)	cola	coda, fila

Portuguese	French	English	German	Spanish	Italian
bicho, animal	bête	animal, beast	Biest(n), Tier(n)	bestia	bestia
bicicleta	bicyclette	bicycle	Fahrrad(n)	bicicleta	bicicletta
bicicleta	vélo	bike	Fahrrad(n)	bici	bici, bicicletta
bico	bec	beak	Schnabel(m)	pico	becco
bife	bifteck	steak	Beefsteak(n)	bistec	bistecca
bigode	moustache	moustache	Schnurrbart(m)	bigote	baffo
bilhar	billard	billiards	Billard(n)	billar	biliardo
bilhete	carte	card, ticket	Karte(f)	tarjeta	tessera
bilhete	billet	ticket	Fahrkarte(f)	billete	biglietto
bilhete	ticket	ticket	Karte(f); Fahrkarte(f)	ticket, billete	biglietto
bilhete	billet	ticket	Los(n)	billete	biglietto
bilhete de ida	billet simple	single ticket	einfache Fahrkarte(f)	billete de ida	andata
bilhete(identidade)	carte d'identité	identity card	Personalausweis(m)	carné de identidad	carta d'identità
bilhete ida/volta	billet A/Retour	return ticket	Rückfahrkarte(f)	billete ida/vuelta	andata e ritorno
bilhete-postal	carte postale	post-card	Postkarte(f)	tarjeta postal	cartolina
bilheteira	guichet	booking office	Fahrkartenschalter(m)	taquilla	biglietteria
bilião	milliard	thousand million	Milliarde(f)	mil millones	miliardo
bilingue	bilingue	bilingual	zweisprachig	bilingüe	bilingue
binóculos	jumelles	binoculars	Fernglas(n)	gemelos	binocolo
biografia	biographie	biography	Lebensbeschreibung(f)	biografía	biografia
biologia	biologie	biology	Biologie(f)	biología	biologia
biscoito	biscuit	biscuit	Keks(m)	galleta	biscotto
bispo	évêque	bishop	Bischof(m)	obispo	vescovo
bisturi	bistouri	scalpel, bistoury	Skalpell(n)	bisturí	bisturi
blasfémia	blasphème	blasphemy	Lästerung(f)(Gottes-)	blasfemia	bestemmia
blindado, a	blindé, e	armoured	gepanzert	blindado, a	blindato, a
bloco	bloc	block	Block(m)	bloque	blocco
bloco	bloc	pad	Block(m)	bloc	blocco
bloco, canhenho	carnet	note-book	Notizbuch(n)	libreta	taccuino
bloqueamento	blocage	jamming	Blockierung(f), Sperre	bloqueo	bloccaggio
bloquear	bloquer	block	blockieren	bloquear	bloccare
bloqueio	blocus	blockade	Blockade(f)	bloqueo	blocco
boa noite	bonne nuit	good night	gute Nacht	buenas noches	buona notte
boa sorte	bonne chance	good luck	viel Glück	buena suerte	buona fortuna
boa tarde	bonsoir	good evening	guten Abend	buenas tardes	buonasera
boa viagem	bon voyage	good trip(have a)	gute Reise	buen viaje	buon viaggio
bobina	bobine	reel	Spule(f)	bobina, carrete	bobina
boca	bouche	mouth	Mund(m)	boca	bocca
bocado	bouchée	mouthful	Bissen(m)	bocado	boccone
bocejar	bâiller	yawn	gähnen	bostezar	sbadigliare
bochecha, face	joue	cheek	Wange(f)	mejilla	guancia
boda	noce	wedding	Hochzeit(f)	boda	nozze
bofetada	gifle	slap	Ohrfeige(f)	bofetada	schiaffo
bofetada	claque	slap	Ohrfeige(f)	bofetada	schiaffo
boi; carne de vaca	boeuf	bullock; beef	Ochse(m); Rind(n)	buey; carne de vaca	bue; manzo
bóia	bouée	lifebelt	Rettungsring(m)	salvavidas	salvagente
bóia	bouée	buoy	Boje(f)	boya	boa
boião	bocal	jar	Glasgefäß(n)	tarro, bocal	boccale, vaso
bola	boule	ball	Ball(m)(Schneeball)	bola	palla
boîte	boîte de nuit	night-club	Diskothek(f)	discoteca	discoteca, night
bola	balle	ball	Ball(m)	pelota	palla
bola	ballon	ball	Ball(m)(Fußball m)	balón	pallone
boleia(pedir)	auto-stop	hitch-hiking	trampen	autostop, a dedo	autostop
boletim	bulletin	bulletin, report	Bericht(m)	boletín	bollettino, bolletta
bolha	bulle	bubble	Blase(f)	burbuja	bolla
bolha	cloque	blister	Blase(f)(Brandblase)	ampolla	vescica
bolo	gâteau	cake; pastry	Kuchen(m)	pastel	dolce
bola	boule	bowl	Kugel(f)	bola	boccia
bolor(criar)	moisir	mouldy(to go)	verschimmeln	enmohecer	ammuffire
bolsa	bourse	grant; scholarship	Stipendium(n)	beca	borsa di studio
Bolsa	Bourse(la)	Stock Exchange	Börse(f)	Bolsa	Borsa
bolso	poche	pocket	Tasche(f)	bolsillo	tasca
bom, boa	bon, ne	good	gut	bueno, a	buono, a
bom, boa	bon, aimable	kind, kindly	gütig, liebvoll	bueno, a	buono, a
bomba	bombe	bomb	Bombe(f)	bomba	bomba
bomba, foguete	pétard	banger, cracker	Knallkörper(m)	petardo	petardo
bomba	pompe	pump	Pumpe(f)	bomba	pompa
bomba de gasolina	poste d'essence	petrol station	Tankstelle(f)	gasolinera	distributore(benzina)

P

Portuguese	French	English	German	Spanish	Italian
bombeiro	pompier(sapeur-)	fireman(-men)	Feuerwehrmann(m)	bombero	pompiere
bom dia	bonjour	hello	guten Tag	buenos días	buongiorno
bom dia!	bonjour!	good morning!/aft-	guten Morgen!/Tag	hola(!)	buongiorno!
bom dia!	bonjour!	good afternoon!	guten Tag!	hola(!)	buona sera!
bom grado(de)	volontiers	willingly	gern	buena gana(de)	volentieri
bom proveito!	bon appétit!	enjoy your meal!	Guten Appetit!	que aproveche(!)	buon appetito!
bom tempo	beau temps	fine weather	schönes Wetter	buen tiempo	bel tempo
bondade	bonté	kindness	Güte(f)	bondad	bontà
boné	casquette	cap	Mütze(f)	gorra	berretto
boneca	poupée	doll	Puppe(f)	muñeca	bambola
bonita, bela	belle	beautiful, fine	schön, e, er, es	hermosa	bella
bonito, a	joli, e	pretty	hübsch	bonito, a	carino, a
bonito, a	joli, e	nice	nett	lindo, a	bello, a
bonito, a	beau, belle	handsome	ansehnlich, schön	bello, a	bello, a
borboleta	papillon	butterfly	Schmetterling(m)	mariposa	farfalla
borbulha	bouton	spot, pimple	Pickel(m)	grano	brufolo, foruncolo
borda	bord	side; edge	Rand(m)	borde	bordo, riva, orlo
borda, orla	bordure	edge, border	Rand(m)	bordura; ribete	bordo, lungo
bordar	broder	embroider	sticken	bordar	ricamare
borracha	gomme	rubber	Radiergummi(m)	goma	gomma
borracha	caoutchouc	rubber	Gummi(m, n)	caucho	gomma
borrasca	bourrasque	squall	Windstoß(m)	borrasca	burrasca
bosque	bois	wood	Wald(m)	bosque	bosco
bossa; alto	bosse	lump, bump	Beule(f)	chichón	bernoccolo, gobba
bossa; alto	bosse	bump	Unebenheit(f); Buckel	bache	gobba, dosso, cunetta
bosta	crotte	dropping, dung	Häufchen(n), Kot(m)	caca	sterco
bota	botte	boot	Stiefel(m)	bota	stivale
botânica	botanique	botany	Botanik(f)	botánica	botanica
botão	bouton	button	Knopf(m)	botón	bottone
botão	bouton	button	Taste(f)	pulsador	pulsante, bottone
botão	bouton	knob	Knopf(m)	botón	manopola, pomello
boxe	boxe	boxing	Boxen(n)	boxeo	pugilato
braço	bras	arm	Arm(m)	brazo	braccio
branco, a	blanc, che	white	weiß	blanco, a	bianco, a
brasa	braise	embers	Glut(f)	brasa	brace
brecha	brèche	breach, gap	Spalt(m), Bresche(f)	brecha	breccia
breve	bref, brève	brief, short	kurz	breve	breve
bricolage	bricolage	odd-jobs	Basteln(n)	bricolage, maña	bricolage
briga	bagarre	fight	Schlägerei(f)	riña	rissa, zuffa
brigada	brigade	brigade	Brigade(f)	brigada	brigata, squadra
brilhante	brillant, e	bright, shining	glänzend	brillante	brillante
brilhante	brillant, e	brilliant	prächtig, brillant	brillante	brillante
brilhante	luisant, e	shining, bright	leuchtend	reluciente	brillante
brilhar	briller	shine	glänzen	brillar	brillare
brincadeira	plaisanterie	joke	Witz(m)	chiste, gracia	scherzo
brincos, argolas	boucle(s)	earring	Ohrring(m)	pendientes	orecchini
brinquedo	jouet	toy	Spielzeug(n)	juguete	giocattolo
broche	broche	brooch	Brosche(f)	broche	spilla
brônquios	bronche(s)	bronchial tubes	Bronchie(f)	bronquios	bronco(bronchi)
bronquite	bronchite	bronchitis	Bronchitis(f)	bronquitis	bronchite
bronze	bronze	bronze	Bronze(f)	bronce	bronzo
bronzeamento	bronzage	sun-tan	Bräune(f)	bronceado	abbronzatura
bronzear	bronzer	tan	bräunen	broncear	abbronzare
brotar, jorrar	jaillir	spring	springen; sprudeln	brotar, surgir	schizzare
bruma	brume	mist, haze	Nebel(m)	bruma	foschia
brusco, a	brusque	abrupt, sudden	brüsk	brusco, a	brusco, a
brutal	brutal, e	brutal	brutal	brutal	brutale
brutalidade	brutalité	brutality	Brutalität, Roheit(f)	brutalidad	brutalità
bruto, a	brut, e	raw; crude	roh	bruto, a	grezzo, a
bruxaria	sorcellerie	witchcraft	Hexerei(f)	brujería	stregoneria
bruxo, a	sorcier, ière	wizard; witch	Hexer(m); Hexe(f)	brujo, a	stregone, strega
bule	théière	teapot	Teekanne(f)	tetera	teiera
buraco, furo	trou	hole	Loch(n)	agujero	buco(a), foro
burguês, a	bourgeois, e	middle class	Bürger(in f)m	burgués, a	borghese
burguesia	bourgeoisie	middle class	Bürgertum(n)	burguesía	borghesia
busca	recherche	search	Suche(f)	busca	ricerca
buscar, procurar	rechercher	search/look for	suchen	buscar, indagar	ricercare
bússola	boussole	compass	Kompaß(m)	brújula	bussola

Portuguese	French	English	German	Spanish	Italian
busto	buste	bust	Oberkörper(m)	busto	busto
buzina	klaxon	horn, hooter	Hupe(f)	claxon, bocina	clacson
buzinar	klaxonner	hoot	hupen	pitar	suonare(clacson)

C

Portuguese	French	English	German	Spanish	Italian
cabaret	cabaret	cabaret; nightclub	Kabarett(n)	cabaret	cabaret
cabeça	tête	head	Kopf(m)	cabeza	testa, capo
cabeçudo, a	têtu, e	stubborn	dickköpfig	tozudo, a	testardo, a
cabeleireiro, a	coiffeur, se	hairdresser	Friseur(m), Friseuse f	peluquero, a	parrucchiere, a
cabelo	cheveu(x)	hair	Haar(n)	pelo, cabello	capello
cabide	portemanteau	hat stand	Kleiderständer(m)	colgador, percha	attaccapanni
cabide	cintre	hanger, coat-hanger	Bügel(m)	percha	gruccia, attaccapanni
cabine	cabine	cabin	Kabine(f)	cabina	cabina
cabine(telefónica)	cabine(téléph.)	phone box	Telefonzelle(f)	cabina(telefónica)	cabina(telefonica)
cabo	cap	cape	Kap(n)	cabo	capo
cabo	bout, extrémité	end, tip	Ende(n)	cabo	capo, estremità
cabo	câble	cable	Kabel(n)	cable	cavo
cabo	manche	handle	Stiel(m)	mango(el)	manico
cabo	caporal	corporal	Gefreiter(m); Korporal	cabo(mil.)	caporale
cabra	chèvre	goat	Ziege(f)	cabra	capra
caça	chasse	hunting	Jagd(f)	caza	caccia
caça	gibier	game	Wild(n)	caza	selvaggina
caçador	chasseur	hunter	Jäger(in f)m	cazador	cacciatore
caçar	chasser	hunt	jagen	cazar	cacciare
cacau	cacao	cocoa, cacao	Kakao(m)	cacao	cacao
cachecol	cache-nez	scarf	Schal(m)	bufanda	sciarpa
cachecol, cachené	écharpe	scarf	Halstuch(n), Schal(m)	bufanda	sciarpa
cachimbo	pipe	pipe	Pfeife(f)	pipa	pipa
cacho	grappe	bunch	Traube(f)	racimo	grappolo
cada	chaque	every, each	jede(r, s)	cada	ogni
cadastro	cadastre	land register	Grundbuch(n)	catastro	catasto
cada um(uma)	chacun, e; chaque	each, every(one)	jeder, jede	cada uno(una)	ciascuno, a
cadáver	cadavre	corpse	Leiche(f)	cadáver	cadavere
cadáver	macchabée	corpse	Leiche(f)	cadáver	cadavere
cadeado	cadenas	padlock	Vorhängeschloß(n)	candado	lucchetto, catenaccio
cadeia, corrente	chaîne	chain	Kette(f)	cadena	catena
cadeira	chaise	chair	Stuhl(m)	silla	sedia
cadeira de bebé	poussette	push-chair	Sportwagen(m)	silla de bebé	passeggino
cadência	cadence	rate, rhythm	Rhythmus(m)	cadencia	cadenza
caderno	cahier	exercise book	Heft(n)	cuaderno	quaderno
caducado, a	périmé, e	expired	verfallen	caducado, a	scaduto, a
café	café	coffee	Kaffee(m)	café	caffè
cafeteira	cafetière	coffee-pot	Kaffeemaschine(f)	cafetera	caffettiera
cãibra	crampe	cramp	Krampf(m)	calambre	crampo
cair	tomber	fall	fallen	caer	cadere
cair(deixar)	tomber(laisser)	drop	fallenlassen	caer(dejar)	cadere(lasciar)
cais	quai	quay	Kai((m)	muelle	molo
caixa	boîte	box	Schachtel(f)	caja	scatola
caixa	caisse	chest, case	Kiste(f)	cajón, caja	cassa
caixa	caisse	cash-desk	Kasse(f)	caja	cassa
caixa(o)	caissier, ière	cashier	Kassierer(in f)m	cajero, a	cassiere, a
caixa do correio	boîte(lettres)	letter box	Briefkasten(m)	buzón	buca delle lettere
caixão	cercueil	coffin	Sarg(m)	ataúd	bara
caixote do lixo	poubelle	bin, dustbin	Abfalleimer(m)	cubo de basura	pattumiera
calão, gíria	jargon	jargon	Fachsprache(f)	jerga	gergo
calar-se	taire(se)	silent(to be)	schweigen	callarse	tacere

P

| --- | --- | --- | --- | --- | --- |
calçada	chaussée	road	Fahrbahn(f)	calzada	carreggiata
calcanhar	talon	heel	Ferse(f); Absatz(m)	talón	tallone
calçar-se	chausser(se)	put on(shoes)	Schuhe anziehen, sich	calzarse	calzarsi
calças	pantalon	trousers	Hose(f)	pantalón	pantalone
cálcio	calcium	calcium	Kalzium(n)	calcio	calcio
calções; calção	short	shorts	kurze Hose(f)	pantalón corto	shorts, calzoncini
calculadora	calculatrice	calculator	Rechenmaschine(f)	calculadora	calcolatrice
calcular	calculer	calculate, reckon	rechnen, berechnen	calcular	calcolare
cálculo	calcul	calculation	Berechnung(f)	cálculo	calcolo
caldo	bouillon	stock, broth	Brühe(f)	caldo	brodo
calendário	calendrier	calendar	Kalender(m)	calendario	calendario
calhau	caillou	stone, pebble	Stein(m)	piedra	sasso
calibre	calibre	bore, calibre	Kaliber(n)	calibre	calibro
cálido, a	chaud, e	warm	warm	cálido, a	caldo, a
calma, sossego	calme	calm, quiet, still	Ruhe(f), Stille(f)	calma, sosiego	calma, quiete
calmante	calmant	sedative	Beruhigungsmittel(n)	calmante	calmante
calmo, a	calme	calm, quiet, still	ruhig, still	tranquilo, a	calmo, a
calor	chaleur	heat	Hitze(f)	calor	caldo; calore
caloria	calorie	calorie	Kalorie(f)	caloría	caloria
caloroso, a	chaleureux, se	hearty, warm	herzlich	caluroso, a	caloroso, a
calúnia	calomnie	slander	Verleumdung(f)	calumnia	calunnia
calvo, a; careca	chauve	bald	glatzköpfig	calvo, a	calvo, a
cama	lit	bed	Bett(n)	cama	letto
camada	couche	coat	Anstrich(m)	capa	strato
camada	couche	layer	Schicht(f)	capa	strato
cama de campismo	lit de camp	camp-bed	Feldbett(n)	cama de campaña	letto da campo
câmara	chambre	chamber	Kammer(f)	cámara	camera
câmara	Chambre(députés)	House, Chamber	Abgeordnetenhaus(n)	cámara(diputados)	camera
câmara	mairie	town hall	Rathaus(n)	ayuntamiento	municipio, comune
câmara	caméra	cine-camera	Kamera(f)	cámara	cinepresa
camarada	camarade	friend	Kamerad(in f)m	compañero, a	compagno, a
camarão	crevette	prawn, shrimp	Krabbe(f)	gamba, camarón	gamberetto
camarim	loge	box	Loge(f)	camerino	camerino
cambalhotas(dar)	culbuter	somersault	überrennen	volcar	ribaltare
câmbio	change	exchange	Wechsel(m)(Geld-)	cambio	cambio
camelo	chameau	camel	Kamel(n)	camello	cammello
camião	camion	lorry	Lastwagen(m)	camión	camion
caminhada	randonnée	ramble	Tour(f), Fußtour(f)	caminata, paseo	gita, escursione
caminhar	marcher, cheminer	walk	laufen, gehen	caminar	camminare
caminho	chemin	path; way	Weg(m)	camino	cammino
caminho	chemin, voie	way	Weg(m)	camino	cammino, strada
caminho, rota	itinéraire, route	route	Route(f), Weg(m)	ruta, itinerario	rotta, itinerario
caminho de ferro	chemin de fer	railway	Eisenbahn(f)	ferrocarril	ferrovia
camisa	chemise	shirt	Hemd(n)	camisa	camicia
camisa de noite	chemise de nuit	nightdress(-es)	Nachthemd(n)	camisón	camicia da notte
camisola	chandail	jumper, sweater	Pullover(m)	jersey	maglione
camisola interior	maillot de corps	vest	Trikot(n)	camiseta	maglia intima
campainha	sonnette	bell	Klingel(f)	timbre	campanello
campainha, toque	sonnerie	ring	Klingel(f)	campana, timbre	squillo, soneria
campanha	campagne	campaign	Wahlkampf(m)	campaña	campagna
campeão, campeã	champion, ne	champion	Meister(in f)m	campeón, a	campione, -essa
campeonato	championnat	championship	Meisterschaft(f)	campeonato	campionato
campismo	camping(aire de)	camp(ing) site	Campingplatz(m)	camping	campeggio
campo	campagne	country(side)	Land(n)	campo	campagna
campo	champ	field	Feld(n)	campo	campo
campo	terrain(sport)	field; court	Sportplatz(m)	campo	terreno
campo de gelo	banquise	ice-floe	Packeis(n)	banco de hielo	banchisa
campo de golfe	golf(terrain)	golf course	Golfplatz(m)	golf	golf
camponês, a	paysan, ne	farmer	Bauer(m), Bäuerin(f)	campesino, a	contadino, a
cana de pesca	canne à pêche	fishing rod	Angelrute(f)	caña de pescar	canna da pesca
canal	canal	canal	Kanal(m)	canal	canale
canal	chaîne	channel	Programm, Fernseh-	cadena	canale
canal	chenal	channel	Fahrwasser(n)	canal	canale
canalização	canalisation	pipe	Leitung(f)(-snetz n)	canalización	canalizzazione
canalizador	plombier	plumber	Klempner(m)	fontanero	idraulico
canapé, sofá	canapé	sofa	Sofa(n)	sofá, canapé	divano, canapè
canção; canto	chanson, chant	song	Lied(n)	canción; cante	canzone; canto
canceroso, a	cancéreux, se	cancerous	krebsartig	canceroso, a	canceroso, a

Portuguese	French	English	German	Spanish	Italian
cancro	cancer	cancer	Krebs(m)	cáncer	cancro
candeeiro	lampe	lamp	Lampe(f)	lámpara	lampada
candeeiro	lampadaire	street-lamp	Straßenlaterne(f)	lámpara de pie	lampione
candidato, a	candidat, e	candidate	Kandidat(in f)m	candidato, a	candidato, a
candidatura	candidature	application	Bewerbung(f)	candidatura	candidatura
cândido, a	candide	ingenuous	naiv, aufrichtig	cándido, a	candido, a
caneta	stylo	pen, fountain-pen	Füller(m)	estilográfica	stilografica
cangurú	kangourou	kangaroo	Känguruh(n)	canguro	canguro
canhão	canon	cannon	Kanone(f)	cañón	cannone
cano, tubo	conduit(e)	pipe	Röhre(f), Leitung(f)	caño, conducto	condotto(a)
canoa	canot	dinghy	Boot(n)	bote	canotto
canoa	canoë	canoe	Kanu(n)	canoa	canoa
cansado, a	fatigué, e	tired	müde, ermüdet	cansado, a	stanco, a
cansar, fatigar	fatiguer	tire, make tired	ermüden	cansar, fatigar	stancare
cansativo, a	fatigant, e	tiring	anstrengend	fatigante	faticoso, a
cantar	chanter	sing	singen	cantar	cantare
canteiro	parterre	flower-bed	Beet(n)	arriate	aiuola
cantil	bidon	can	Kanister(m)	bidón, lata	bidone
canto, esquina	coin	corner	Ecke(f)	esquina, rincón	angolo
cantor, a	chanteur, se	singer	Sänger(in f)m	cantante	cantante
cão, cadela	chien, ne	dog, bitch(-es)	Hund(m)	perro, a	cane, cagna
capacete	casque	helmet	Helm(m)	casco	casco, elmetto
capacidade	contenance	capacity, content	Fassungsvermögen(n)	capacidad	capacità
capaz de	capable de	able to(be)	fähig	capaz de	capace di
capela	chapelle	chapel	Kapelle(f)	capilla	cappella
capital(o)	capital	capital, assets	Kapital(n)	capital	capitale
capital(a)	capitale	capital	Hauptstadt(f)	capital	capitale
capitalismo	capitalisme	capitalism	Kapitalismus(m)	capitalismo	capitalismo
capitão	capitaine	captain	Hauptmann(m); Kapitän	capitán	capitano
capitular	capituler	capitulate	kapitulieren	capitular	capitolare
capítulo	chapitre	chapter	Kapitel(n)	capítulo	capitolo
capota	capot	bonnet, hood	Motorhaube(f)	capó	cofano
capricho, birra	caprice	caprice, whim	Laune(f)	capricho	capriccio
capturar	capturer	capture	fangen	capturar	catturare
capuz	capuchon	cap	Kappe(f)	capuchón	cappuccio
cara	visage	face	Gesicht(n)	rostro, cara	viso
caracóis	boucle	curl	Locke(f)	rizo	ricciolo
caracol	escargot	snail	Schnecke(f)	caracol	lumaca, chiocciola
carácter	caractère	letter, character	Schrifttyp(m)	letra	carattere, lettera
carácter	caractère	character	Charakter(m)	carácter	carattere
característica	caractéristique	feature	Merkmal(n)	característica	caratteristica
característico, a	caractéristique	characteristic	charakteristisch	característico, a	caratteristico, a
caranguejo	crabe	crab	Krebs(m)	cangrejo	granchio
caranguejo	écrevisse	crayfish	Flußkrebs(m)	cangrejo(de río)	gambero(di fiume)
caravana	caravane	caravan	Wohnwagen(m)	caravana	roulotte
carbónico, a	carbonique	carbonic	Kohlensäure(f)	carbónico, a	carbonico, a
carbono	carbone	carbon	Kohlenstoff(m)	carbono	carbonio
carburador	carburateur	carburettor	Vergaser(m)	carburador	carburatore
carburante	carburant	fuel	Treibstoff(m)	carburante	carburante
cardeal	cardinal	cardinal	Kardinal(m)	cardenal	cardinale
cardíaco, a	cardiaque	heart-trouble...	herzkrank	cardíaco, a	cardiaco, a
cardiologia	cardiologie	cardiology	Kardiologie(f)	cardiología	cardiologia
carência	carence	deficiency	Fehlen(n), Mangel(m)	carencia	carenza
careta	grimace	grimace	Grimasse(f)	mueca	smorfia
carga, peso	charge	load	Last(f)	carga, peso	carico
carga	cargaison	cargo, freight	Ladung(f)	cargamento	carico
cargueiro	cargo	cargo(-boat)	Frachter(m)	carguero, buque	cargo, nave da carico
caricaturar	caricaturer	caricature	karikieren	caricaturar	caricaturare
carícia	caresse	caress	Streicheln(n)	caricia	carezza
caridade	charité	charity	Mildtätigkeit(f)	caridad	carità
cárie	carie	tooth decay	Karies(f)	caries	carie
carimbar	tamponner	stamp	stempeln	sellar	timbrare
carnaval	carnaval	carnival	Karneval(m)	carnaval	carnevale
carne	chair	flesh	Fleisch(n)	carne	carne
carne	viande	meat	Fleisch(n)	carne	carne
carneiro; ovelha	mouton	sheep; mutton	Schaf(n)	carnero; oveja	pecora; montone
carnívoro, a	carnivore	carnivorous	fleischfressend	carnívoro, a	carnivoro, a
caro, a	cher, ère	expensive, dear	teuer	caro, a	caro, a

P

Portuguese	French	English	German	Spanish	Italian
caro, a; querido, a	cher, ère	dear	liebe(r)	querido, a	caro, a
caroço	noyau	stone	Kern(m)	hueso	nocciolo
caroço	pépin	pip	Kern(m)	pepita	seme
carpinteiro	menuisier	joiner, carpenter	Tischler(m)	carpintero	falegname
carpinteiro	charpentier	carpenter	Zimmermann(m)	carpintero	carpentiere
carrapicho	chignon	chignon, bun	Haarknoten(m)	moño	crocchia
carregamento	chargement	load, loading	Ladung(f)	cargamento	carico
carregar	charger	load	laden	cargar	caricare
carregar	embarquer	load	ein = laden	embarcar	imbarcare
carreira	carrière	career	Karriere(f)	carrera	carriera
carril	rail	rail; track	Schiene(f)	carril	rotaia
carrinho(bebé)	landau	pram	Kinderwagen(m)	cochecito	carrozzina
carro	voiture	car	Wagen(m)	coche	macchina, auto
carro de corrida	voiture(course)	racing car	Rennwagen(m)	coche de carreras	macchina da corsa
carro de mão	brouette	wheelbarrow	Schubkarre(f)	carretilla	carriola
carro eléctrico	tramway	tram-car	Straßenbahn(f)	tranvía	tram
carroça, carro	chariot	trolley	Karre(f)	carro	carrello
carroça, carreta	charrette	cart	Karren(m)	carreta, carro	carretta
carroçaria	carrosserie	body(-work)	Karosserie(f)	carrocería	carrozzeria
carrossel	manège	roundabout	Karussell(n)	tiovivo, noria	giostra
carta	lettre	letter	Brief(m)	carta	lettera
carta	carte à jouer	card	Spielkarte(f)	carta	carta da gioco
carta de condução	permis(auto)	driving licence	Führerschein(m)	permiso conducir	patente di guida
cartão	carton	cardboard	Pappe(f)	cartón	cartone
cartão(festas)	carte de voeux	greeting(s) card	Glückwunschkarte(f)	postal, carta	biglietto di auguri
cartão de crédito	carte de crédit	credit card	Kreditkarte(f)	carta de crédito	carta di credito
cartão de visita	carte de visite	visiting card	Visitenkarte(f)	tarjeta de visita	biglietto da visita
cartaz	affiche	poster, placard	Plakat(n)	cartel	manifesto
cartaz	poster	poster	Plakat(n)	cartel, póster	poster, manifesto
cartaz	pancarte	sign, notice	Plakat(n), Schild(n)	pancarta	cartello
carteira	portefeuille	wallet	Brieftasche(f)	cartera	portafoglio
carteira	porte-documents	document case	Aktenmappe(f)	portadocumentos	portadocumenti
carteira	sac à main	handbag	Handtasche(f)	bolso	borsetta
carteiro, a	facteur, trice	postman/-woman	Briefträger(in f)m	cartero, a	postino, a
cartilagem	cartilage	cartilage	Knorpel(m)	cartílago	cartilagine
cartucho	cartouche	cartridge	Patrone(f)	cartucho	cartuccia
carvão	charbon	coal	Kohle(f)	carbón	carbone
casa	maison	house	Haus(n)	casa	casa
casa(em)	maison(à la)	home(at)	Hause(zu)	casa(en)	casa(a)
casa de chá	salon de thé	tea-room	Café(n), Konditorei(f)	salón de té	sala da tè
casaco, manto	manteau	coat	Mantel(m)	abrigo	cappotto
casaco de malha	gilet	cardigan	Weste(f), Jacke(f)	chaleco	gilè; golf
casado, a	marié, e	married	verheiratet	casado, a	sposato, a
casal	couple	couple	Paar(n)	pareja	coppia
casamento	mariage	wedding; marriage	Hochzeit(f); Heirat(f)	matrimonio	matrimonio
casar-se	marier(se)	married(get)	heiraten	casarse	sposarsi
casca	écorce	bark	Rinde(f)	corteza	scorza, buccia
casca	coquille, coque	shell	Schale(f)	cáscara	guscio
cascalho	gravier	gravel	Kies(m)	grava	ghiaia
cascata	cascade	waterfall	Wasserfall(m)	cascada	cascata
casco	sabot	hoof	Huf(m)	pezuña, casco	zoccolo
casco	coque	hull	Rumpf(m)	casco	scafo
caseiro, a	fermier, ière	farmer	Bauer(m), Bäuerin(f)	granjero, a	contadino, a
casino	casino	casino	Kasino(n)	casino	casinò
caso	cas	case	Fall(m)	caso	caso
caso(neste)	occurence(en l')	case(in this)	vorliegenden Fall(im)	caso(en este)	nella circostanza
caspa	pellicule	dandruff	Schuppe(f)	caspa	forfora
cassete	cassette	cassette	Kassette(f)	casete	cassetta
casta	caste	caste	Kaste(f)	casta	casta
casta, raça	race	breed	Rasse(f)	casta, raza	razza
castanho, a	brun, ne	brown	braun	pardo, a	bruno, a
castanho, a	châtain	chestnut brown	kastanienbraun	castaño, a	castano, a
castelo	château	castle; mansion	Schloß(n)	castillo	castello
castigar	punir	punish	bestrafen	castigar	punire
castigo	punition	punishment	Strafe(f)	castigo	punizione
castigo	châtiment	punishment	Bestrafung(f)	castigo	castigo
casto, a	chaste	pure	keusch	casto, a	casto, a
cataclismo	cataclysme	cataclysm	Katastrophe(f)	cataclismo	cataclisma

Portuguese	French	English	German	Spanish	Italian
catálogo	catalogue	catalogue	Katalog(m)	catálogo	catalogo
catástrofe	catastrophe	catastrophe	Katastrophe(f)	catástrofe	catastrofe
catedral	cathédrale	cathedral	Kathedrale(f), Dom(m)	catedral	cattedrale, duomo
categoria	catégorie	category	Kategorie(f)	categoría	categoria
católico, a	catholique	Catholic	katholisch	católico, a	cattolico, a
catorze	quatorze	fourteen	vierzehn	catorce	quattordici
cauda	queue	tail	Schwanz(m)	rabo	coda
caule	tige	stem	Stiel(m)	tallo	stelo
causa	cause	cause	Ursache(f), Grund(m)	causa	causa
causar, provocar	causer, provoquer	cause	verursachen	causar, provocar	causare, provocare
cavala	maquereau	mackerel	Makrele(f)	caballa	sgombro
cavalariça	écurie	stable	Pferdestall(m)	cuadra	scuderia
cavaleiro, a	cavalier, ière	rider	Reiter(in f)m	jinete, a	cavaliere, a
cavalheiro	monsieur	man, gentleman(men)	Gentleman(m)	caballero	signore
cavalo	cheval	horse	Pferd(n)	caballo	cavallo
cavar	creuser	dig	graben	cavar	scavare
cave	sous-sol	basement	Untergeschoß(n)	sótano	scantinato
caverna	caverne	cave, cavern	Höhle(f)	caverna	caverna
caviar	caviar	caviar	Kaviar(m)	caviar	caviale
cavidade	cavité	cavity	Hohlraum(m)	cavidad	cavità
cear	souper	supper(have)	Abend essen(zu)	cenar	cenare
cebola	oignon	onion	Zwiebel(f)	cebolla	cipolla
ceder	céder, renoncer	give up	auf = geben; nach = geben	ceder	cedere
cedo	tôt	early	früh	temprano	presto
cego, a	aveugle	blind	blind	ciego, a	cieco, a
ceifa, colheita	moisson	harvest	Ernte(f)	cosecha	mietitura
celebrar	célébrer	celebrate	feiern	celebrar	celebrare
célebre	célèbre	famous, well-known	berühmt	célebre, famoso, a	celebre; famoso, a
celeiro	grange	barn	Scheune(f)	granero	fienile
celeste	céleste	heavenly	himmlisch	celeste	celeste
celulite	cellulite	fat, cellulitis	Zellulitis(f)	celulitis	cellulite
cem, cento	cent	hundred(one)	hundert	cien, ciento	cento
cemitério	cimetière	cemetery	Friedhof(m)	cementerio	cimitero
cena	scène	scene	Szene(f)	escena	scena
cena	scène	stage	Szene(f), Bühne(f)	escena	scena
cenários	décors	set, scenery	Dekor(m), Bühnenbild n	decorado	scenografia
cenarista	scénariste	script-writer	Drehbuchautor(in f)m	guionista	scenarista
cenoura	carotte	carrot	Möhre(f)	zanahoria	carota
censura	censure	censorship	Zensur(f)	censura	censura
censura	blâme	blame; reprimand	Rüge(f)	reprobación	biasimo
censurar	reprocher	reproach	vor = werfen	reprochar	rimproverare
centeio	seigle	rye	Roggen(m)	centeno	segale
centena	centaine	hundred(about a)	Hundert(n)	centena	centinaio
centímetro	centimètre	centimetre	Zentimeter(n, m)	centímetro	centimetro
central	central, e	central	zentral	central	centrale
central	centrale	power-station	Kraftwerk(n), Zentrale	central	centrale
centrífugo, a	centrifuge	centrifugal	zentrifugal	centrífugo, a	centrifugo, a
centro	centre	centre	Mitte(f)	centro	centro
centro	centre	centre	Zentrum(n)	centro	centro
centro	centre	hub	Mittelpunkt(m)	centro	centro
centro(cidade)	centre ville	city/town centre	Stadtzentrum(n)	centro(ciudad)	centro della città
céptico, a	sceptique	sceptic(al)	skeptisch	escéptico, a	scettico, a
cera	cire	wax, polish	Wachs(n)	cera	cera
cerca, vedação	clôture	fence, railings	Zaun(m)	valla, cerca	recinzione, muro
cerca de	environ	about	ungefähr	aproximadamente	circa
cerco	siège	siege	Belagerung(f)	sitio	assedio
cereal	céréale	cereal	Getreide(n)	cereal	cereale
cerebral	cérébral, e	cerebral	Gehirn-; zerebral	cerebral	cerebrale
cérebro	cerveau	brain	Gehirn(n)	cerebro	cervello
cereja	cerise	cherry	Kirsche(f)	cereza	ciliegia
cerimónia	cérémonie	ceremony	Zeremonie(f)	ceremonia	cerimonia
certamente	certainement	certainly	sicherlich	ciertamente	certamente
certamente	sûrement	surely, certainly	gewiß, sicherlich	ciertamente	sicuramente
certeza	certitude	certainty	Gewißheit(f)	certeza	certezza
certificado	certificat	certificate	Bescheinigung(f)	certificado	certificato
certificar	certifier	certify	bescheinigen	certificar	certificare
certo, a	certain, e	certain, sure	sicher	cierto, a	certo, a; sicuro, a
certo, a	juste; exact, e	right	richtig	exacto, a	giusto, a

661

P

| --- | --- | --- | --- | --- | --- |
certo, a	assuré, e	assured	sicher	seguro, a	sicuro, a; certo, a
certos, as	certaines	certain; some	manche	algunos, as	certi, e; alcuni, e
cerveja	bière	beer	Bier(n)	cerveza	birra
cesariana	césarienne	Caesarean	Kaiserschnitt(m)	cesárea	taglio cesareo
cessação	arrêt, cessation	stop, cessation	Stillstand(m)	cese	cessazione, tregua
cessar, parar	cesser	stop, cease	auf = hören	cesar, parar	cessare, smettere
cesto, a	corbeille	basket; bin	Korb(m)(Papierkorb m)	cesto(a); cestillo	cestino
cesto	panier	basket	Korb(m)	cesto	paniere, cesto
cetim	satin	satin	Satin(m)	raso, satén	raso
céu	ciel	sky	Himmel(m)	cielo	cielo
céu, paraíso	ciel, paradis	heaven	Himmel(m)	cielo, paraíso	cielo, paradiso
chá	thé	tea	Tee(m)	té	tè
chaleira	bouilloire	kettle	Wasserkessel(m)	hervidor	bollitore
chama	flamme	flame	Flamme(f)	llama	fiamma
chamada	appel	call	Ruf(m)(Zu-, An-)	llamada	chiamata
chamar	appeler	call	rufen(an =), heißen	llamar	chiamare
chamar	nommer	name	nennen	llamar	chiamare
chamar-se	nommer(se)	called(be)	heißen	llamarse	chiamarsi
chaminé	cheminée	chimney; fire-place	Kamin(m)	chimenea	camino
champanhe	champagne	champagne	Champagner(m)	champaña	champagne
champô	shampooing	shampoo	Shampoo(n)	champú	shampoo
chanceler	chancelier	chancellor	Kanzler(in f)m	canciller	cancelliere
chapa	tôle	sheet-metal	Blech(n)	chapa	lamiera
chapéu	chapeau	hat	Hut(m)	sombrero	cappello
chapéu de chuva	parapluie	umbrella	Regenschirm(m)	paraguas	ombrello
charco	mare	pond, pool	Tümpel(m)	charca	stagno
charneca	lande	moor, heath	Heide(f)	landa	landa
charuto	cigare	cigar	Zigarre(f)	cigarro, puro	sigaro
chassis	châssis	frame, chassis	Rahmen(m), Chassis(n)	chasis	telaio
chave	clef, clé	key	Schlüssel(m)	llave	chiave
chave	clé	spanner, wrench	Schraubenschlüssel(m)	llave	chiave
chave de parafusos	tournevis	screwdriver	Schraubenzieher(m)	destornillador	cacciavite
chávena	tasse	cup	Tasse(f)	taza	tazza
chefe	chef	head; chief; leader	Chef(in f)m	jefe	capo
chefe, líder	chef, dirigeant	leader	Leiter(m), Führer(m)	jefe	capo, dirigente
chefe de empresa	chef(entreprise)	manager, head	Betriebsführer(m)	jefe de empresa	dirigente d'azienda
chefe de estado	chef d'état	head of state	Staatsoberhaupt(n)	jefe de estado	capo di stato
chegada	arrivée	arrival	Ankunft(f)	llegada; meta	arrivo
chegar	arriver	arrive, come	an = kommen	llegar	arrivare
chegar	accéder	accede to	gelangen zu/kommen an	acceder	assurgere
chegar a	accéder à	reach	Zugang haben zu	llegar a	accedere a
chegar; conseguir	parvenir	reach, arrive at	erreichen	conseguir	giungere
cheio, a	plein, e	full	voll	lleno, a	pieno, a
cheirar	sentir	smell	riechen	oler	odorare, annusare
cheirar mal	puer	stink	stinken	apestar	puzzare
cheiro, odor	odeur	odour, smell	Geruch(m)	olor	odore
cheque	chèque	cheque	Scheck(m)	cheque, talón	assegno
chicote	fouet	whip	Peitsche(f)	látigo	frusta
chocante	choquant, e	shocking	anstößig	chocante	urtante
chocar, bater	heurter	knock(against)	stoßen	tropezar con	urtare
chocar, esbarrar	tamponner	bump, crash into	zusammen = stoßen	chocar con	tamponare
chocar com	cogner(se)	knock	stoßen, sich	golpe(darse un)	sbattere
chocolate	chocolat	chocolate	Schokolade(f)	chocolate	cioccolato, a
choque	choc	shock	Schock(m)	choque	choc, colpo
choque	choc	shock, impact	Stoß(m), Aufprall(m)	choque	urto, scontro
chorar	pleurer	cry	weinen	llorar	piangere
chover	pleuvoir	rain	regnen	llover	piovere
chumbo	plomb	lead	Blei(n)	plomo	piombo
chupa-chupa	sucette	lollipop	Lutscher(m)	pirulí	lecca lecca
chupar	sucer	suck	lutschen	chupar	succhiare
chupeta	sucette	dummy	Schnuller(m)	chupete	succhiotto
chut!	chut!	hush!, sh!	pst!	chitón(!)	sst!, zitto!
chuva	pluie	rain	Regen(m)	lluvia	pioggia
chuvisco	bruine	drizzle	Sprühregen(m)	llovizna	pioggerella
chuvoso, a	pluvieux, e	rainy	regnerisch	lluvioso, a	piovoso, a
ciática	sciatique	sciatica	Ischias(m)	ciática	sciatica
cicatriz	cicatrice	scar	Narbe(f)	cicatriz	cicatrice
ciclismo	cyclisme	cycling	Radfahren(n)	ciclismo	ciclismo

Portuguese	French	English	German	Spanish	Italian
ciclista	cycliste	cyclist	Radfahrer(in f)m	ciclista	ciclista
ciclo	cycle	cycle	Zyklus(m)	ciclo	ciclo
ciclone	cyclone	cyclone	Wirbelwind(m)	ciclón	ciclone
cidadão, cidadã	citoyen, ne	citizen	Bürger(in f)m	ciudadano, a	cittadino, a
cidade	ville	town	Stadt(f)	ciudad	città
cidade	cité	city	Stadt(f)	ciudad	città
ciência	science	science	Wissenschaft(f)	ciencia	scienza
científico, a	scientifique	scientific	wissenschaftlich	científico, a	scientifico, a
cientista	scientifique	scientist	Wissenschaftler(m)	científico	scienziato
cientista	savant	scientist	Gelehrte(f, m)	científico	scienziato
cigarro	cigarette	cigarette	Zigarette(f)	cigarrillo	sigaretta
cilíndrico, a	cylindrique	cylindrical	zylindrisch	cilíndrico, a	cilindrico, a
cilindro	cylindre	cylinder	Zylinder(m)	cilindro	cilindro
cima(por); acima de	au-dessus	above	über	encima(por, de)	sopra(al di)
cima(por, em)	au-dessus	overhead	oben	arriba	sopra, in alto
cima(parte de)	dessus	top	Oberteil(n)	superior(parte)	disopra
cima(em)	haut(en)	upstairs	oben	arriba	alto(in)
cima(em, para)	haut	up	Oben-; Hoch-; auf	arriba	alto, a
cimento	ciment	cement	Zement(m)	cemento	cemento
cimo, cume	cime	summit, peak, top	Gipfel(m)	cima	cima, vetta
cimo; cume	sommet	summit, top	Gipfel(m)	cumbre; cima	cima; vetta
cinco	cinq	five	fünf	cinco	cinque
cineasta	cinéaste	film-producer	Filmproduzent(in f)m	cineasta	cineasta
cinema	cinéma	cinema	Kino(n)	cine	cinema
cínico, a	cynique	cynical	zynisch	cínico, a	cinico, a
cinquenta	cinquante	fifty	fünfzig	cincuenta	cinquanta
cinta	taille	waist	Taille(f)	cintura, talle	vita
cinta elástica	gaine	girdle	Korsett(n)	faja	guaina, corsetto
cintilar	scintiller	sparkle	flimmern	centellear	scintillare
cinto	ceinture	belt	Gürtel(m)	cinturón	cintura
cinza	cendre(s)	ash(es)	Asche(f)	ceniza(s)	cenere(-ri)
cinzeiro	cendrier	ash-tray	Aschenbecher(m)	cenicero	portacenere
cinzento, a	gris, e	grey	grau	gris	grigio, a
circo	cirque	circus	Zirkus(m)	circo	circo
circuito	circuit	circuit	Strecke(f)(Renn-)	circuito	circuito
circuito	circuit	circuit, system	Stromkreis(m)	circuito	circuito
circuito	circuit	tour	Rundfahrt(f)(-reise)	circuito	giro, circuito
circulação	circulation	circulation	Kreislauf(m)	circulación	circolazione
circular	circuler	circulate	zirkulieren	circular	circolare
circular	circuler	circulate	umher = gehen	circular	circolare
circular	circulaire	circular	rund	circular	circolare
círculo	cercle	circle	Kreis(m)	círculo	cerchio
circunferência	circonférence	circumference	Kreisumfang(m)	circunferencia	circonferenza
circunstância	circonstance	circumstance	Umstand(m)	circunstancia	circostanza
círio	cierge	candle	Kerze(f)	cirio	cero
cirrose	cirrhose	cirrhosis	Zirrhose(f)	cirrosis	cirrosi
cirurgia	chirurgie	surgery	Chirurgie(f)	cirugía	chirurgia
cirurgião	chirurgien	surgeon	Chirurg(in f)m	cirujano	chirurgo
cisne	cygne	swan	Schwan(m)	cisne	cigno
citadino, a	citadin, e	town/city dweller	Städter(in f)m	ciudadano, a	cittadino, a
citar	citer	quote	zitieren	citar	citare
ciúme	jalousie	jealousy	Eifersucht(f)	celos	gelosia
ciumento, a	jaloux, se	jealous	eifersüchtig	celoso, a	geloso, a
cívico, a	civique	civic	staatsbürgerlich	cívico, a	civico, a
civil	civil, e	civil	zivil	civil	civile
civilização	civilisation	civilization	Zivilisation(f)	civilización	civiltà
civilizar	civiliser	civilize	zivilisieren	civilizar	civilizzare
clã	clan	clan	Sippe(f)	clan	clan
clandestino, a	clandestin, e	clandestine	heimlich	clandestino, a	clandestino, a
claridade	clarté	brightness	Helligkeit(f)	claridad	chiarezza
clarificar	clarifier	clarify	klären	clarificar	chiarificare
clarinete	clarinette	clarinet	Klarinette(f)	clarinete	clarinetto
claro	bien sûr	of course	natürlich	claro	certamente
claro, a	clair, e	clear	klar	claro, a	chiaro, a; limpido, a
claro, a	clair, e	light	hell	claro, a	chiaro, a
classe	classe	class	Klasse(f)	clase	classe, ceto
classe	classe	class, form	Klassenstufe(f)	clase, curso	classe
clássico, a	classique	classical	klassisch	clásico, a	classico, a

P

Portuguese	French	English	German	Spanish	Italian
classificação	classement	filing	Einorden(n)	clasificación	classificazione
classificador	classeur	file	Ordner(m)	clasificador	schedario
classificar	classer	classify, file	ordnen	clasificar	classificare
cláusula	clause	clause	Klausel(f)	cláusula	clausola
clavícula	clavicule	collar-bone	Schlüsselbein(n)	clavícula	clavicola
clero	clergé	clergy	Klerus(m)	clero	clero
cliché	cliché, négatif	negative	Negativ(n)	cliché	negativo
cliente	client, e	customer	Kunde(m), Kundin(f)	cliente	cliente
cliente	client, e	client	Klient(in f)m	cliente	cliente
clima	climat	climate	Klima(n)	clima	clima
climatizador	climatiseur	air conditioner	Klimaanlage(f)	climatizador	condizionatore
clínica	clinique	nursing-home	Klinik(f)	clínica	clinica
clube	club	club	Klub(m)	club	club
coagular	coaguler	coagulate, clot	gerinnen	coagular	coagulare
coágulo	caillot	clot	Blutgerinnsel(n)	coágulo	grumo
cobaia	cobaye	guinea-pig(be a)	Versuchskaninchen(n)	conejillo(Indias)	cavia
cobarde	lâche	cowardly	feig(e)	cobarde	vigliacco, a
cobardia	lâcheté	cowardliness	Feigheit(f)	cobardía	vigliaccheria
cobertura	housse	cover	Bezug(m)	funda	fodera
cobiçar	convoiter	covet	begehren	codiciar	ambire, desiderare
cobra	cobra	cobra	Kobra(f)	cobra	cobra
cobre	cuivre	copper	Kupfer(n)	cobre	rame
cobrir	couvrir	cover	zu = decken	cubrir	coprire
cocaína	cocaïne	cocaine	Kokain(n)	cocaína	cocaina
coçar-se	gratter(se)	scratch oneself	kratzen, sich	rascarse	grattarsi
cócegas	chatouille(s)	tickle	Kitzeln(n)	cosquillas	solletico
coco	noix de coco	coconut	Kokosnuß(f)	coco	noce di cocco
codificar	codifier	codify	kodifizieren	codificar	codificare
codificar	coder	code, encode	verschlüsseln	codificar	cifrare
código	code	code	Kod(m)	código	codice
coeficiente	coefficient	coefficient	Koeffizient(m)	coeficiente	coefficiente
coelho, a	lapin, e	rabbit	Kaninchen(n)	conejo, a	coniglio, a
coerente	cohérent, e	coherent	zusammenhängend	coherente	coerente
coesão	cohésion	cohesion	Zusammenhalt(m)	cohesión	coesione
cofre-forte	coffre-fort	safe	Safe(m)	caja fuerte	cassaforte
cogumelo	champignon	mushroom	Pilz(m)	champiñón, seta	fungo
coincidência	coincidence	coincidence	Zusammentreffen(n)	coincidencia	coincidenza
coisa	chose	thing	Ding(n)	cosa	cosa
coisas	affaires	things	Sachen(pl)	cosas	roba, oggetti
cola	colle	glue	Klebstoff(m)	cola, pegamento	colla
colaboração	collaboration	collaboration	Mitarbeit(f)	colaboración	collaborazione
colaboração	concours	cooperation, help	Mitwirkung(unter)	ayuda	concorso
colaborador, a	collaborateur	assistant	Mitarbeiter(in f)m	colaborador, a	collaboratore, -trice
colar	collier	necklace	Halskette(f); Kette(f)	collar	collana
colar, pegar	coller	stick, glue	kleben	pegar	incollare
colarinho; gola	col	collar	Kragen(m)	cuello	collo, colletto
colchão	matelas	mattress(-es)	Matraze(f)	colchón	materasso
colecção	collection	collection	Kollektion(f)	colección	collezione
colecção	collection	collection	Sammlung(f)	colección	collezione
coleccionar	collectionner	collect	sammeln	coleccionar	collezionare
colectivo, a	collectif, ive	collective	gemeinschaftlich	colectivo, a	collettivo, a
colega	collègue	colleague	Kollege(m), Kollegin f	colega	collega
colégio	collège	college	Kollegium(n)	colegio	collegio
cólera	choléra	cholera	Cholera(f)	cólera	colera
cólera, ira	colère	anger(be angry)	Wut(f)	cólera, ira	collera, ira
colheita	récolte	crop; harvest	Ernte(f)	cosecha	raccolta
colher	cuillère	spoon	Löffel(m)	cuchara	cucchiaio
colher	cueillir	pick, gather	pflücken	coger, recoger	cogliere, raccogliere
colher, apanhar	récolter	harvest, gather	ernten	cosechar, recoger	raccogliere
colher de chá	cuiller à café	teaspoon	Kaffeelöffel(m)	cucharilla	cucchiaino
cólica	colique	colic	Kolik(f)	cólico	colica
coligação	coalition	coalition	Koalition(f)	coalición	coalizione
colina	colline	hill	Hügel(m)	colina	collina
colisão, choque	collision	collision	Zusammenstoß(m)	colisión, choque	collisione
colmeia	ruche	hive	Bienenstock(m)	colmena	alveare
colocar; pôr	placer	place, install	setzen, stellen	colocar	collocare, porre
colónia	colonie	colony	Kolonie(f)	colonia	colonia
colonização	colonisation	colonization	Kolonisierung(f)	colonización	colonizzazione

Portuguese	French	English	German	Spanish	Italian
colóquio	colloque	symposium	Symposium(n)	coloquio	colloquio
colorir	colorier	colour(in)	an = malen	colorear	colorare
colossal	colossal, e	colossal	riesig	colosal	colossale
coluna	colonne	column	Säule(f)	columna	colonna
coluna vertebral	colonne(vertéb-)	spine	Wirbelsäule(f)	columna vertebral	colonna vertebrale
com	avec	with	mit	con	con
coma	coma	coma	Koma(n)	coma	coma
comandante	commandant	major	Kommandant(m), Major m	comandante	comandante
comandar	commander	command	befehlen, befehligen	ordenar, mandar	comandare
comando	commandement	command	Befehl(m)(-sgewalt f)	mando	comando
comando	commando	commando	Kommando(n)	comando	commando
combate	combat	combat, fight	Kampf(m)	combate	combattimento
combatente	combattant, e	fighting-man	Kämpfer(m)	combatiente	combattente
combater	combattre	fight	streiten, kämpfen	combatir	combattere
combinação	combinaison	combination	Kombination(f)	combinación	combinazione
combinação	combinaison	slip	Unterrock(m)	combinación	sottoveste
comboio	convoi	convoy	Konvoi(m)	convoy	convoglio
comboio	train	train	Zug(m), Eisenbahn(f)	tren	treno
combustível	combustible	combustible	verbrennbar	combustible	combustibile
começar	commencer	begin, start	an = fangen	comenzar	cominciare
começo, princípio	commencement	beginning, start	Anfang(m)	comienzo, principio	principio, inizio
comédia	comédie	comedy	Komödie(f)	comedia	commedia
comediante, a	comédien, ne	comedian	Komödiant(in f)m	comediante, a	commediante
comemorar	commémorer	commemorate	gedenken	conmemorar	commemorare
comentar	commenter	comment(on)	erläutern	comentar	commentare
comentário	commentaire	comment	Anmerkung(f)	comentario	commento
comentário	commentaire	commentary	Kommentar(m)	comentario	commentario
comer	manger	eat	essen	comer	mangiare
comercial	commercial, e	commercial	geschäftlich	comercial	commerciale
comercializar	commercialiser	market	vermarkten	comercializar	commercializzare
comerciante	commerçant, e	tradesman(-men)	Geschäftsmann m/-frau	comerciante	commerciante
comerciante	commerçant, e	shop-keeper	Kaufmann m, Kauffrau f	tendero, a	negoziante
comerciante	marchand, e	shop-keeper	Kaufmann m, Kauffrau f	vendedor, a	negoziante
comércio	commerce	trade, commerce	Handel(m)	comercio	commercio
comestível	comestible	edible	eßbar	comestible	commestibile
cometa	comète	comet	Komet(m)	cometa	cometa
cometer	commettre	commit	begehen, verüben	cometer	commettere
comichão	démangeaison	itch, itching	Juckreiz(m)	picazón	prurito
cómico	comique	comedian, comic	Komiker(in f)m	cómico	comico
cómico, a	comique	comic, funny	komisch	cómico, a	comico, a
comissão	commission	commission	Kommission(f)	comisión	commissione
comissão	commission	committee	Ausschuß(m)	comisión	commissione
comissão	comité	committee	Komitee(n), Ausschuß m	comité	comitato
como	comme	as; like	wie	como	come
como	comment	how	wie	cómo	come
como disse?	comment?	pardon?	wie bitte?	cómo(?)	come?, come dice?
cómodo, a	commode	convenient	praktisch	cómodo, a	comodo, a
comovente	émouvant, e	moving	ergreifend	emocionante	commovente
comover	émouvoir	move	rühren	conmover	commuovere
comovido, a	ému, e	moved, affected	gerührt	emocionado, a	commosso, a
compacto, a	compact, e	compact	kompakt	compacto, a	compatto, a
companheiro, a	compagnon, agne	companion	Begleiter(in f)m	compañero, a	compagno, a
companhia	compagnie	company	Gesellschaft(f)	compañía	compagnia
companhia(em)	compagnie(en)	company of(in the)	Gesellschaft(in)	compañía(en)	compagnia(in)
comparar	comparer	compare	vergleichen	comparar	paragonare
compartimento	compartiment	compartment	Abteil(n)	compartimiento	compartimento
compasso	compas	compass(es)	Kompaß(m)	compás	compasso
compensação	compensation	compensation	Kompensation(f)	compensación	compenso
competência	compétence	competence	Zuständigkeit(f)	competencia	competenza
competente, capaz	compétent, e	competent	kompetent	competente, capaz	competente
competição	compétition	competition	Wettbewerb(m)	competición	competizione, gara
complemento	complément	complement	Ergänzung(f)	complemento	complemento
completamente	complètement	completely	völlig	completamente	completamente
completo, a	complet, ète	complete, full	vollständig, voll	completo, a	completo, a
complexo	complexe	complex	Komplex(m)	complejo	complesso
complicado, a	compliqué, e	complicated	kompliziert	complicado, a	complicato, a
componente	composant	component	Bestandteil(m)	componente	componente
compor	composer	compose	zusammen = stellen	componer	porre

P

665

Portuguese	French	English	German	Spanish	Italian
comporta	vanne	gate; valve	Klappe(f)	compuerta	saracinesca
comportamento	comportement	behaviour	Verhalten(n)	comportamiento	comportamento
composição	composition	composition	Zusammensetzung(f)	composición	composizione
compositor	compositeur	composer	Komponist(in f)m	compositor	compositore
compota	compote	stewed fruit	Kompott(n)	compota	frutta cotta
compra	achat	purchase	Kauf(m)	compra	acquisto
comprador, a	acheteur, se	buyer; shopper	Käufer(in f)m	comprador, a	acquirente
comprar	acheter	buy	kaufen	comprar	comprare
compras	courses	shopping	Einkäufe(pl)	compras	spesa
compreender	comprendre	understand	verstehen	comprender	capire
compreender	comprendre	comprise	ein = begreifen	comprender	comprendere
compressão	compression	compression	Druck(m)	compresión	compressione
comprimento	longueur	length	Länge(f)	longitud	lunghezza
comprimido	comprimé	tablet, pill	Tablette(f)	comprimido	compressa
comprimido	cachet	tablet	Tablette(f)	pastilla	pastiglia
comprimir	comprimer	compress	drücken	comprimir	comprimere
comprometer	compromettre	compromise	bloß = stellen(jdn.)	comprometer	compromettere
comprometer-se	engager(s')	commit oneself	engagieren, sich	comprometerse	impegnarsi a
comprometimento	compromission	compromising	Kompromittierung(f)	compromiso	compromissione
compromisso	compromis	compromise	Kompromiß(m)	compromiso	compromesso
compromisso	arrangement	arrangement	Abmachung(f)	arreglo, acuerdo	accordo
compromisso	engagement	commitment	Verpflichtung(f)	compromiso	impegno
computador	ordinateur	computer	Computer(m)	ordenador	computer
comum	commun, e	common	Gemeinschafts-	común	comune
comum	commun, e	common, usual	gewöhnlich	común	comune
comunicação	communication	communication	Verständigung(f)	comunicación	comunicazione
comunicar	communiquer	communicate	mitteilen	comunicar	comunicare
comunidade	communauté	community	Gemeinschaft(f)	comunidad	comunità
comunismo	communisme	communism	Kommunismus(m)	comunismo	comunismo
comutador	commutateur	switch	Schalter(m)	conmutador	commutatore
conceber	concevoir	conceive(of)	vor = stellen, sich	concebir	concepire
conceber	concevoir	design	entwerfen	concebir	ideare
conceder	accorder	grant	bewilligen	conceder	concedere, accordare
conceder	allouer	allocate	zu = teilen, bewilligen	conceder	assegnare
conceito	concept	concept	Begriff(m)	concepto	concetto
concentrar	concentrer	concentrate	konzentrieren	concentrar	concentrare
concentrar-se	concentrer(se)	concentrate	konzentrieren, sich	concentrar(se)	concentrarsi
concepção	conception	conception	Konzeption(f)	concepción	concezione
concertação	concertation	cooperation	Zusammenarbeit(f)	concertación	concertazione
concerto	concert	concert	Konzert(n)	concierto	concerto
concha	coquille	shell	Schale(f), Muschel(f)	concha	conchiglia
concha	coquillage	shell-fish; shell	Muschel(f)	marisco	conchiglia
concluir	conclure	conclude	schließen, abschließen	concluir	concludere
conclusão	conclusion	conclusion	Abschluß(m)	conclusión	conclusione
concordar	concorder	tally, agree	überein = stimmen	concordar	concordare
concorrência	concurrence	competition	Konkurrenz(f)	competencia	concorrenza
concorrente	concurrent, e	competitor	konkurrent(in f)m	competidor, a	concorrente
concreto, a	concret, ète	concrete	konkret	concreto, a	concreto, a
concubinato	concubinage	co-habitation	wilde Ehe(f)	concubinato	concubinato
concurso	concours	competition	Wettbewerb(m)	concurso	concorso
concurso	concours	contest	Wettbewerb(m)	concurso	gara
concurso	concours	competitive exam	Prüfung(f)	oposiciones	concorso
condecorar	décorer	decorate	aus = zeichnen	condecorar	decorare
condenação	condamnation	sentence	Verurteilung(f)	condenación	condanna
condenar	condamner	condemn	verurteilen	condenar	condannare
condenar	condamner	convict, sentence	verurteilen	condenar	condannare
condenar	damner	damn	verdammen	condenar	dannare
condensação	condensation	condensation	Kondensierung(f)	condensación	condensazione
condição	condition	condition	Bedingung(f)	condición	condizione
condutor, a	conducteur, trice	driver	Fahrer(in f)m	conductor, a	conducente
conduzir	conduire	drive	fahren	conducir	guidare
conduzir a	aboutir à	lead to	führen zu	conducir a	arrivare a
cone	cône	cone	Kegel(m)	cono	cono
conexão	connexion	connection	Verbindung; Anschluß	conexión	connessione
conexão	liaison	link	Verbindung(f)	enlace	collegamento
confecção	confection	clothing industry	Anfertigung(f)	confección	confezione
confeitaria	confiserie	sweet shop	Süßwarenladen(m)	confitería	confetteria
conferência	conférence	conference; lecture	Konferenz(f)	conferencia	conferenza

Portuguese	French	English	German	Spanish	Italian
conferência	conférence	lecture	Vorlesung(f), Vortrag	conferencia	conferenza
confessar	avouer	confess, admit	gestehen	confesar	confessare
confiança	confiance	confidence, trust	Vertrauen(n)	confianza	fiducia
confiar	confier	entrust	an = vertrauen	confiar	affidare
confiar	confiance(avoir)	trust	vertrauen(jdm.)	confianza(tener)	fiducia(aver)
confidência	confidence	confidence, secret	Vertrauen(im)	confidencia	confidenza
confidencial	confidentiel, le	confidential	vertraulich	confidencial	confidenziale
confirmar, comprovar	confirmer	confirm	bestätigen	confirmar	confermare
confissão	aveu	confession	Geständnis(n)	confesión	confessione
conflito	conflit	conflict	Konflikt(m)	conflicto	conflitto
conforme com	conforme à	in accordance with	entsprechend	conforme a/con	conforme a
confortável	confortable	comfortable	bequem	cómodo, a	confortevole
conforto	confort	comfort	Bequemlichkeit(f)	confort	comodità
confrontar	confronter	confront	konfrontieren	confrontar	confrontare
confundir	confondre	confuse, mistake	verwechseln	confundir	confondere
confusão	confusion	confusion	Verwechslung(f)	confusión	confusione
confuso, a	trouble	troubled	verworren	confuso, a	confuso, a; torbido, a
congelador	congélateur	freezer	Kühltruhe(f)	congelador	congelatore
congelados	surgelés	frozen food	Tiefkühlkost(f)	congelados	surgelati
congelamento	blocage	freeze	Preisstopp(m)	congelación	blocco
congestão	congestion	congestion	Blutandrang(m)	congestión	congestione
congratular	congratuler	congratulate	gratulieren	congratular	congratulare
congresso	congrès	congress	Kongress(m)	congreso	congresso
conhecer, saber	connaître	know	kennen	conocer, saber	conoscere, sapere
conhecimento	connaissance	knowledge	Kenntnis(f).	conocimiento	conoscenza
cónico, a	conique	conical	kegelförmig	cónico, a	conico, a
conífera	conifère	conifer	Nadelbaum(m)	conífera	conifera
conjugação	conjugaison	conjugation	Konjugation(f)	conjugación	coniugazione
conjugal	conjugal, e	married, marriage-	ehelich	conyugal	coniugale
conjunto	ensemble	whole; all the	Ganze(n); Gesamtheit f	conjunto	insieme
conjunto	ensemble	set	Satz(m)	conjunto	insieme
conjuntura	conjoncture	conjuncture	Konjunktur(f)	coyuntura	congiuntura
conquista	conquête	conquest	Eroberung(f)	conquista	conquista
consagração	consécration	consecration	Weihe(f)	consagración	consacrazione
consagrar	consacrer	consecrate	weihen	consagrar	consacrare
consciência	conscience	conscience	Bewußtsein(n)	conciencia	coscienza
consciente	conscient, e	conscious	bewußt	consciente	cosciente, conscio, a
consecutivo, a	consécutif, ive	consecutive	folgend	consecutivo, a	consecutivo, a
conseguinte(por)	conséquent(par)	therefore	folglich; deshalb	consiguiente(por)	perciò
conseguir	réussir	succeed	gelingen	lograr, conseguir	riuscire
conselheiro, a	conseiller, ère	adviser	Berater(in f)m	consejero, a	consigliere, a
conselheiro, a	conseiller, ère	councillor	Rat(m)(Staatsrat m)	concejal, a	consigliere, a
conselho	conseil	advice	Rat(m)	consejo	consiglio
conselho	conseil	council	Rat(m)(Europrat m)	consejo	consiglio
consentimento	agrément	approval, consent	Zustimmung(f)(verbal)	consentimiento	consenso
consentir	consentir	agree	ein = willigen	consentir	consentire
consentir	consentir	consent	zu = stimmen	consentir	consentire
consequência	conséquence	consequence	Konsequenz(f)	consecuencia	conseguenza
consequência(em)	suite à	further to	Anschluß an(im)	contestación(en)	seguito(facendo)
conserva	conserve(s)	tinned food	Konserve(f)	conserva	conserva
conservação	conservation	conservation	Konservierung(f)	conservación	conservazione
conservar	conserver	preserve, keep	konservieren	conservar	conservare
consideração	considération	consideration	Betrachtung(f)	consideración	considerazione
considerar	considérer	consider	an = sehen(als)	considerar	considerare
considerar	considérer	regard	betrachten	considerar	considerare
considerável	considérable	considerable	erheblich	considerable	considerevole
consistir em	consister à	consist(in, of)	bestehen aus	consistir en	consistere in
consoante	consonne	consonant	Mitlaut(m)	consonante	consonante
consolar	consoler	console, comfort	trösten	consolar	consolare
consolidar	consolider	strengthen	verstärken	consolidar	consolidare
conspiração	conspiration	plot, conspiracy	Komplott(n)	conspiración	cospirazione
conspiração	complot	conspiracy, plot	Verschwörung(f)	complot	complotto
constante	constant, e	constant	beständig	constante	costante
constatar	constater	state; note	fest = stellen	constatar	constatare
constelação	constellation	constellation	Konstellation(f)	constelación	costellazione
constipação	rhume	cold	Schnupfen(m)	resfriado	raffreddore
constipar-se	enrhumer(s')	catch a cold	erkälten, sich	constipar(se)	raffreddarsi
constituição	constitution	constitution	Verfassung(f)	constitución	costituzione

P

667

Portuguese	French	English	German	Spanish	Italian
constituir	constituer	constitute	bilden	constituir	costituire
construção	construction	construction	Bau(m)	construcción	costruzione
construir	construire	construct, build	bauen	construir	costruire
construir	bâtir	build	bauen	edificar	costruire
cônsul	consul	consul	Konsul(m)	cónsul	console
consulado	consulat	consulate	Konsulat(n)	consulado	consolato
consultar	consulter	consult	befragen	consultar	consultare
consultório	cabinet(médecin)	surgery	Praxis(f)(Arztpraxis)	consulta(-torio)	studio(medico)
consumidor, a	consommateur	consumer	Verbraucher(in f)m	consumidor, a	consumatore, trice
consumir	consommer	consume	verbrauchen	consumir	consumare
consumo	consommation	consumption	Verbrauch(m)	consumo	consumo
conta	compte	account	Rechnung(f)	cuenta	conto
conta	compte	account	Konto(n)	cuenta	conto
conta	note	bill	Rechnung(f)	cuenta	conto
contabilidade	comptabilité	accountancy	Buchhaltung(f)	contabilidad	contabilità
contabilista	comptable	accountant	Buchhalter(in f)m	contable	ragioniere
contactar	contact(prendre)	contact	Kontakt(auf = nehmen)	contacto(entrar en)	contattare
contacto	contact	contact	Kontakt(m)	contacto	contatto
contador	compteur	meter	Zähler(m)	contador	contatore
contágio	contagion	contagion	Ansteckung(f)	contagio	contagio
contagioso, a	contagieux, se	contagious	ansteckend	contagioso, a	contagioso, a
contaminação	contamination	contamination	Ansteckung(f)	contaminación	contaminazione
contar	compter	count	zählen	contar	contare
contar	raconter	relate, tell	erzählen	contar	raccontare
contar	dire	tell	sagen	decir	dire
contar com	compter sur	rely on	zählen, auf jdn	contar con	contare su
contemplar	contempler	contemplate	betrachten	contemplar	contemplare
contemporâneo, a	contemporain, e	contemporary	zeitgenössisch	contemporáneo, a	contemporaneo, a
contente	content, e	pleased, glad	froh	contento, a	contento, a
contente	content, e	glad, happy, pleased	froh, erfreut	contento, a	contento, a
conter	contenir	contain	enthalten	contener	contenere
contestar	contester	contest	bestreiten	impugnar, objetar	contestare
conteúdo	contenu	content(s)	Inhalt(m)	contenido	contenuto
continente	continent	continent	Kontinent(m)	continente	continente
continuação	suite	continuation	Folge(f)	continuación	seguito
continuar	continuer	continue, go on	fort = setzen	continuar	continuare
contínuo, a	continu, e	continuous	ununterbrochen	continuo, a	continuo, a
contínuo, a	continuel, le	continual	ständig	continuo, a	continuo, a
conto	conte	tale, story	Märchen(n)	cuento	racconto, fiaba
contornar	contourner	bypass	umgehen	contornear	aggirare
contorno	contour	outline, contour	Umriß(m)	contorno	contorno
contra	contre	against	wider, gegen	contra(en)	contro
contra(ser)	opposé, e	opposed to	entgegengesetzt	opuesto, a	opposto, a
contra-ataque	contre-attaque	counter-attack	Gegenangriff(m)	contraataque	contro-attacco
contrabando	contrebande	smuggling	Schmuggel(m)	contrabando	contrabbando
contracção	contraction	contraction	Zusammenziehen(n)	contracción	contrazione
contraceptivo	contraceptif	contraceptive	Verhütungsmittel(n)	anticonceptivo	anticoncezionale
contradição	contradiction	contradiction	Widerspruch(m)	contradicción	contraddizione
contradizer	contredire	contradict	widersprechen	contradecir	contraddire
contrariado, a	contrarié, e	upset	ärgerlich sein	contrariado, a	contrariato, a
contrariar	contrer	counter	Kontra geben	oponerse(a)	opporsi(a)
contrariedade	contrariété	annoyance	Verdruß(m)	molestia	seccatura
contrário, a	contraire	contrary	entgegengesetzt	contrario, a	contrario, a
contrário	contraire	opposite, contrary	Gegenteil(n)	contrario	contrario
contraste	contraste	contrast	Gegensatz(m)	contraste	contrasto
contratempo	mésaventure	mishap	Mißgeschick(n)	contratiempo	disavventura
contrato	contrat	contract	Vertrag(m), Kontrakt m	contrato	contratto
contribuição	cotisation	contribution	Beitrag(m)	cotización	contributo
contribuir	contribuer	contribute	bei = tragen	contribuir	contribuire
controlar	contrôler	control, check	kontrollieren	controlar	controllare
controlo	contrôler	control, check	Aufsicht(f), Prüfung f	control	controllo
controlo	contrôle	examination	Kontrolle(f)	control	controllo
contudo, todavia	pourtant	yet, however	dennoch, doch	sin embargo	però, tuttavia
contusão	contusion	bruise	Quetschung(f)	contusión	contusione
convalescência	convalescence	convalescence	Genesung(f)	convalecencia	convalescenza
convenção	convention	agreement	Übereinstimmung(f)	convención	convenzione
convencer	convaincre	convince	überzeugen	convencer	convincere
conveniente	convenable	suitable, fitting	angemessen	conveniente	conveniente

Portuguese	French	English	German	Spanish	Italian
convento	couvent	convent	Kloster(n)	convento	convento
convergir	converger	converge	konvergieren	converger	convergere
conversação	conversation	conversation	Gespräch(n)	conversación	conversazione
converter-se	convertir(se)	convert	konvertieren	convertirse	convertirsi
convés	pont	deck; bridge	Deck(n)	puente	ponte
convexo, a	bombé, e	convex	gewölbt	abombado, a	convesso, a
convicção	conviction	conviction	Überzeugung(f)	convicción	convinzione
convidado, a	invité, e	guest	Gast(m)	invitado, a	invitato, a
convidar	inviter	invite	ein = laden	invitar	invitare
convir, combinar	convenir	agree	überein = kommen	acordar	convenire
convite	invitation	invitation	Einladung(f)	invitación	invito
conviva	convive	guest	Gast(m)	convidado, a	commensale
convocação	convocation	notification	Einberufung(f); Ladung	convocatoria	convocazione
convocar	convoquer	summon; invite	vor = laden	convocar	convocare
convulsão	convulsion	convulsion	Zuckung(f), Krampf(m)	convulsión	convulsione
cooperação	coopération	cooperation	Mitarbeit(f)	cooperación	cooperazione
cooperar	coopérer	cooperate	mit = arbeiten	cooperar	cooperare
cooperativa	coopérative	cooperative	Genossenschaft(f)	cooperativa	cooperativa
coordenar	coordonner	coordinate	koordinieren	coordinar	coordinare
cópia	copie	copy	Kopie(f)	copia	copia
copiar	copier	copy	kopieren	copiar	copiare
copioso, a	copieux, se	copious	reichlich	copioso, a	abbondante
copo	verre	glass(-es)	Glas(n)	vaso	bicchiere
coqueiro	cocotier	coconut palm(tree)	Kokuspalme(f)	cocotero	palma da cocco
coquetel	cocktail	cocktail	Cocktail(m)	cóctel	cocktail
côr	couleur	colour	Farbe(f)	color	colore
coração	coeur	heart	Herz(n)	corazón	cuore
coragem	courage	courage	Mut(m)	valentía	coraggio
corajoso, a	courageux, brave	brave	mutig	valiente, valeroso	coraggioso, a
coral	corail	coral	Koralle(f)	coral	corallo
corante	colorant	colouring	Farbstoff(m)	colorante	colorante
corar	rougir	blush, flush	erröten	sonrojarse	arrossire
corcunda	bossu, e	hunch-backed	buckelig	jorobado, a	gobbo, a
corda	corde	rope	Tau(n)	cuerda	corda
cordão	cordon	cord, string	Kordel(f)	cordón, cable	cordone
cordão	lacet	lace	Schnürsenkel(m)	cordón	laccio
cordeiro	agneau	lamb	Lamm(n)	cordero	agnello
cordel, guita	ficelle	string, cord	Schnur(f)	cordel	spago
cor-de-laranja	orange	orange	orangefarben	anaranjado, a	arancione
cor-de-rosa	rose	pink	rosafarben	rosa	rosa
cordial	cordial, e	cordial, hearty	herzlich, freundlich	cordial	cordiale
corno; chifre	corne	horn	Horn(n)	cuerno	corno
coro	choeur	choir	Chor(m)	coro	coro
coroa	couronne	crown	Krone(f)	corona	corona
coronel	colonel	colonel	Oberst(m)	coronel	colonnello
coronha	crosse	butt; grip, handle	Gewehrkolben(m)	culata	calcio
corpo	corps	body	Körper(m)	cuerpo	corpo
corporação	corporation	corporation	Körperschaft(f)	corporación	corporazione
corporal	corporel, le	bodily	körperlich	corporal	corporale
correcção	correction	correction	Verbesserung(f)	corrección	correzione
correctamente	correctement	properly	richtig	correctamente	correttamente
correcto, a	correct, e	correct, proper	richtig	correcto, a	corretto, a
corrediça	glissière	slide	Gleitschiene(f)	corredera, guía	guida, scivolo
corredor	couloir	corridor	Flur(m)	pasillo	corridoio
corredor, a	coureur, se	runner	Läufer(in f)m	corredor, a	corridore
correia	courroie	belt; strap	Riemen(m)	correa	cinghia
correia	sangle	strap	Riemen(m), Gurt(m)	cincha, correa	cinghia
correio	courrier	mail, post	Post(f)	correo	posta
correios	poste	post-office	Post(f)	correos	posta
corrente	courant, e	common	geläufig	corriente	corrente, comune
corrente, vulgar	courant, e	current	laufend, heutig	corriente	corrente
corrente	courant	current	Strom(m)	corriente	corrente
corrente	flot	wave; flood	Welle(f); Flut(f)	oleada	flutto
correr	courir	run	laufen	correr	correre
correr	couler	flow, run	fließen	correr, fluir	scorrere
correspondência	correspondance	correspondence	Korrespondenz(f)	correspondencia	corrispondenza
correspondência	correspondance	connection	Verbindung, Anschluß	empalme	coincidenza
corresponder	correspondre	correspond, tally	entsprechen	corresponder	corrispondere

Portuguese	French	English	German	Spanish	Italian
corrida	course	running	Wettrennen(n)	carrera	corsa
corrida	course	race	Rennen(n)	carrera	corsa
corrida	ruée	rush	Ansturm(m)	riada	ressa
corridas	courses	races	Pferderennen(n)	carreras	corsa
corrigir	corriger	correct, rectify	korrigieren	corregir	correggere
corrimão	rampe	banister, handrail	Geländer(n)	barandilla	rampa
corrosão	corrosion	corrosion	Korrosion(f)	corrosión	corrosione
corrupção	corruption	corruption	Korruption(f)	corrupción	corruzione
corrupto, a	corrompu, e	corrupt	verdorben, korrupt	corrompido, a	corrotto, a
cortado, a	coupé, e	cut	geschnitten	cortado, a	tagliato, a
cortar	couper	cut	schneiden	cortar	tagliare
corte, design	forme	design, style	Schnitt(m)	hechura	taglio, stile
corte, golpe	coupure(peau)	cut	Schnitt(m)	corte, tajo	taglio
corte, cutilada	balafre	gash	Schmiß(m), Schnitt(m)	cuchillada	sfregio
corte	cour	court	Hof(m)	corte	corte
cortejo	cortège	procession	Umzug(m), Festzug(m)	cortejo	corteo
cortês	courtois, e	courteous	höflich	cortés	cortese
cortiça	liège	cork	Kork(m)	corcho	sughero
cortina	rideau	curtain	Vorhang(m)	cortina	tenda
corvo	corbeau	crow	Rabe(m)	cuervo	corvo
coser	coudre	sew	nähen	coser	cucire
cosmético	cosmétique	cosmetic	Kosmetik(f)	cosmético	cosmetico
cosmonauta	cosmonaute	astronaut	Astronaut(m)	cosmonauta	cosmonauta
cosmopolita	cosmopolite	cosmopolitan	kosmopolitisch	cosmopolita	cosmopolita
costa	côte	coast	Küste(f)	costa	costa
costas	dos	back	Rücken(m)	espalda	schiena
costeiro, a	côtier, ère	coastal	Küsten-	costero, a	costiero, a
costela	côte	rib	Rippe(f)	costilla	costola
costume	coutume	custom	Brauch(m)	costumbre	costume, usanza
costumes	moeurs	morals	Sitten(f, pl)	costumbres	costumi
costura	couture	sewing	Naht(f)	costura	cucito
costura	couture	seam	Saum(m)	costura	cucito
costureiro, a	couturier, ière	dressmaker, tailor	Schneider(in f)m	modista	sarto, a
cota	quota	quota	Quote(f)	cuota	quota
cotação	cotation	quotation	Kurswert(m)	cotización	quotazione
cotovelo	coude	elbow	Ellenbogen(m)	codo	gomito
couchette	couchette	couchette	Liegeplatz(m)	litera	cuccetta
couraçado	cuirassé	warship	Kriegsschiff(n)	acorazado	corazzata
couro	cuir	leather	Leder(n)	cuero	cuoio, pelle
couve	chou	cabbage	Kohl(m)	col	cavolo
cova	trou	pit, hole	Grube(f)	hoyo	buca
coxa	cuisse	thigh	Schenkel(m)	muslo	coscia
coxear	boiter	limp	hinken	cojear	zoppicare
cozedura, cocção	cuisson	cooking	Kochen(n), Sieden(n)	cocción	cottura
cozer	cuire	cook	kochen	cocer	cuocere
cozido, a	cuit, e	cooked	gar, gekocht	cocido, a	cotto, a
cozinha	cuisine	kitchen	Küche(f)	cocina	cucina
cozinhar	cuisiner	cook	kochen	cocinar	cucinare
cozinheiro, a	cuisinier, ière	cook; chef	Koch(m), Köchin(f)	cocinero, a	cuoco, a
crâneo	crâne	skull	Schädel(m)	cráneo	cranio
crápula	crapule	crook, villain	Lump(m)	granuja; pillo, a	canaglia
cratera	cratère	crater	Krater(m)	cráter	cratere
cravar	enfoncer	drive in	ein = schlagen	clavar	piantare
crédito	crédit	credit	Kredit(m)	crédito	credito
creme	crème	cream	Sahne(f)	crema	crema
creme	crème(peau)	cream	Creme(f)	crema	crema
crença	croyance	belief	Glaube(m)	creencia	credenza
crente	croyant, e	believer	Gläubige(f, m)	creyente	credente
crepúsculo	crépuscule	twilight, dusk	Abenddämmerung(f)	crepúsculo	crepuscolo
crer	croire	believe	glauben	creer	credere
crescer	croître	grow, increase	wachsen	crecer	crescere
crescer	grandir	grow	wachsen	crecer	crescere
crescer	pousser, croître	grow	wachsen	crecer	crescere
crescimento	croissance	growth	Wachstum(n)	crecimiento	crescita
crescimento	accroissement	increase	Zuwachs(m)	crecimiento	crescita
criação	création	creation	Erschaffung; Schöpfung	creación	creazione, creato
criação de gado	élevage	breeding; rearing	Zucht(f); Aufzucht(f)	ganadería	allevamento
criada	bonne	maid	Haushaltshilfe(f)	criada	domestica

Portuguese	French	English	German	Spanish	Italian
criado	garçon	waiter	Ober(m)	camarero	cameriere
criado, a; moço	serveur, se	waiter, waitress	Kellner(in f)m	camarero, a	cameriere, a
criador, a	créateur, trice	creator(creative)	Schöpfer(in f)m	creador, a	creatore, trice
criança	enfant	child, children(pl)	Kind(n)	niño, a; chico, a	bambino, a
criar	créer	create	schöpfen	crear	creare
criar	élever	breed, rear	züchten	criar	allevare
criar, educar	élever	bring up	erziehen, auf = ziehen	criar, educar	allevare, educare
crime	crime	crime	Verbrechen(n)	crimen	crimine
criminoso, a	criminel, le	criminal	Verbrecher(in f)m	criminal	criminale
crina	crinière	mane	Mähne(f)	crines, melena	criniera
crise	crise	crisis(-ses)	Krise(f)	crisis	crisi
crista, cimo	crête	crest	Kamm(m)	cresta	cresta
cristal	cristal	crystal	Kristall(m)	cristal	cristallo
cristão, cristã	chrétien, ne	Christian	Christ(in f)m	cristiano, a	cristiano, a
critério	critère	criterion(-ia)	Kriterium(n)	criterio	criterio
crítica	critique	criticism	Kritik(f)	crítica	critica
criticar	critiquer	criticize	kritisieren	criticar	criticare
crocodilo	crocodile	crocodile	Krokodil(n)	cocodrilo	coccodrillo
cromossoma	chromosome	chromosome	Chromosom(n)	cromosoma	cromosoma
crónica	chronique	chronicle	Chronik(f)	crónica	cronaca
crónico, a	chronique	chronic	chronisch	crónico, a	cronico, a
cronologia	chronologie	chronology	Chronologie(f)	cronología	cronologia
cronómetro	chronomètre	chronometer	Stoppuhr(f)	cronómetro	cronometro
crosta	croûte	crust	Kruste(f)	costra, corteza	crosta
croupier	croupier, ière	croupier	Croupier(m)	crupier	croupier
cru, a	cru, e	raw	roh	crudo, a	crudo, a
cruel	cruel, le	cruel	grausam	cruel	crudele
crustáceo	crustacé	shell-fish	Schalentier(n)	crustáceo	crostaceo
cruz	croix	cross(-es)	Kreuz(n)	cruz	croce
cruzamento	croisement	crossing	Kreuzung(f)	cruce	incrocio
cruzamento	carrefour	cross-road(s)	Kreuzung(f)	encrucijada	incrocio
cruzar	croiser	interbreed, cross	kreuzen	cruzar	incrociare
cruzar-se	croiser(se)	cross, intersect	kreuzen, sich	cruzarse	incrociarsi
cruzeiro	croisière	cruise	Kreuzfahrt(f)	crucero	crociera
cuba	cuve	tank; vat	Wanne(f), Faß(n)	cuba	tino
cubo	cube	cube	Würfel(m)	cubo	cubo
cuecas	culotte	briefs, knickers	Unterhose(f), Slip(m)	bragas	mutandine, slip
cuecas	slip	briefs, pants	Unterhose(f)	calzoncillos	mutande, slip
cuidado(ao)	attention(à l')	attention	Aufmerksamkeit(f)	atención a(en)	attenzione
cuidado	soin	care	Pflege(f)	cuidado	cura
cuidadoso, a	soigneux, se	neat, tidy	sorgfältig	cuidadoso, a	accurato, a
cuidar	soigner	nurse; tend; treat	pflegen	curar	curare
cuidar de, vigiar	garder	look after	hüten	vigilar, guardar	custodire
cujo; a; do qual	dont	whose, of which	dessen; deren	cuyo, a; del cual	di cui
culpa	faute	fault	Fehler(m)	culpa	colpa
culpabilidade	culpabilité	guilt	Schuld(f)	culpabilidad	colpevolezza
culpado, a	coupable	guilty	schuldig	culpable	colpevole
culpado, a	fautif, ive	wrong(in the)	schuldig	culpable	colpevole
cultivar	cultiver	cultivate	bebauen, züchten	cultivar	coltivare
cultivar	cultiver	cultivate, grow	an = bauen, an = pflanzen	cultivar	coltivare
culto	culte	worship	Kult(m)	culto	culto
culto, a	cultivé, e	cultured, learned	gebildet	culto, a	colto, a
cultura	culture	cultivation	Anbau(m)	cultivo	coltura
cultura	culture	culture	Kultur(f)	cultura	cultura
cultural	culturel, le	cultural	kulturell	cultural	culturale
cúmplice	complice	accomplice	Komplize(m), Komplizin	cómplice	complice
cumprimento	compliment	compliment	Kompliment(n)	cumplido	complimento
cunha	cale	wedge, chock	Keil(m)	cuña	zeppa
cunhada	belle-soeur	sister-in-law	Schwägerin(f)	cuñada	cognata
cunhado	beau-frère	brother-in-law	Schwager(m)	cuñado	cognato
cúpula	coupole	dome	Kuppel(f)	cúpula, bóveda	cupola
cúpula	dôme	dome	Kuppel(f)	cúpula	duomo
cura	guérison	cure, recovery	Heilung(f)	curación	guarigione
cura	cure	treatment	Kur(f)	cura	cura
curandeiro, a	guérisseur, se	healer	Heilpraktiker(in f)m	curandero, a	guaritore, -trice
curar	guérir	cure, heal	heilen	curar	guarire
curioso, a	curieux, se	curious	neugierig	curioso, a	curioso, a
curso, aula	cours	lesson	Unterricht(m)	curso, clase	corso, lezione

P

Portuguese	French	English	German	Spanish	Italian
curto, a	court, e	short	kurz	corto, a	corto, a
curva	courbe	curve	Kurve(f)	curva	curva
curva	virage	bend, turn	Kurve(f)	curva	curva
curvatura	courbure	bend, curve	Krümmung(f)	curvatura	curvatura
cuspir	cracher	spit	spucken	escupir	sputare
custar	coûter	cost	kosten	costar	costare
custo, preço	coût	cost	Kosten(pl)	costo, coste	costo
custoso, a	coûteux, se	costly, expensive	teuer	costoso, a	costoso, a
cutâneo, a	cutané, e	cutaneous, skin	Haut-	cutáneo, a	cutaneo, a

D

Portuguese	French	English	German	Spanish	Italian
dado	dé(jeux)	die(dice)	Würfel(m)	dado	dado
dados	donnée(s)	data	Daten(pl)	datos	dati
dança	danse	dance	Tanz(m)	danza, baile	ballo, danza
dançar, bailar	danser	dance	tanzen	bailar	ballare
dancing	dancing	dance-hall	Tanzlokal(n)	sala de baile	sala da ballo
dantes	auparavant	before	vorher, zuvor	antes	prima
dar	donner	give	geben	dar	dare
dar à luz	accoucher	birth(give)	entbinden	dar a luz	partorire
data	date	date	Datum(n)	fecha	data
de	de	of	von	de	di; del; dello, a
de	de	from	aus; von	de, desde	da
debaixo, sob	sous	under	unter	debajo, bajo	sotto
debaixo, sob	dessous	under, beneath	unter	debajo, abajo	sotto
debate	débat	debate	Debatte(f)	debate	dibattito
débil	chétif, ive	puny, weak	schwächlich, kümmer-	endeble	gracile
debruçar-se	pencher(se)	lean out	hinaus = lehnen	asomarse	sporgersi
década	décennie	decade	Jahrzehnt(n)	decenio, década	decennio
decadência	décadence	decadence, decline	Verfall(m), Untergang	decadencia	decadenza
decadência	déchéance	downfall	Untergang(m), Verfall	decaimiento	decadenza
decaído, a	déchu, e	fallen, deposed	abgesetzt, verfallen	decaído, a	destituito, a
decano, a	doyen, ne	oldest person	Älteste(f, m)	decano, a	decano, a
decente	décent, e	decent	anständig	decente	decente
decepção	déception	disappointment	Enttäuschung(f)	decepción	delusione
decidir	décider	decide	entscheiden	decidir	decidere
decifrar	décoder	decode	dekodieren	descifrar	decifrare
decimal	décimal, e	decimal	dezimal	decimal	decimale
décimo, a	dixième	tenth	zehnte	décimo, a	decimo, a
decisão	décision	decision	Entscheidung(f)	decisión	decisione
declaração	déclaration	declaration	Erklärung(f)	declaración	dichiarazione
declarar	déclarer	declare	bekannt = geben	declarar	dichiarare
declínio	déclin	decline	Untergang(m)	decadencia, ocaso	declino
declive	pente	slope	Hang(m), Abhang(m)	declive	pendio, discesa
decompor	décomposer	decompose	zerlegen	descomponer	decomporre
decoração	décoration	decoration	Dekoration(f)	decoración	decorazione
decorrer	écouler(s')	elapse	vergehen, verfließen	transcurrir	trascorrere
decrescente	dégressif, ive	decreasing	abnehmend	decreciente	decrescente
decrescer	décroître	decrease	ab = nehmen	decrecer	decrescere
decreto	décret	decree	Erlaß(m), Verordnung f	decreto	decreto
dedicação	dévouement	devotion	Ergebenheit(f)	consagración a	dedizione
dedicado, a	dévoué, e	devoted	ergeben	servicial	devoto, a
dedicar	dédier	dedicate	widmen	dedicar	dedicare
dedicar	consacrer	devote	widmen	dedicar	dedicare
dedo	doigt	finger	Finger(m)	dedo	dito
dedo do pé	orteil	toe	Zehe(f)	dedo del pie	dito del piede
dedução	déduction	deduction	Rückschluß(m)	deducción	deduzione

672

Portuguese	French	English	German	Spanish	Italian
dedução	déduction	deduction	Abzug(m)	deducción	deduzione
deduzir	déduire	deduct	folgern, schließen aus	deducir	detrarre
defeito	défaut	defect, fault	Fehler(m)	defecto	difetto
defeituoso, a	défectueux, se	defective, faulty	defekt	defectuoso, a	difettoso, a
defender	défendre	defend	verteidigen	defender	difendere
defender(causa)	plaider	plead	plädieren	litigar	patrocinare
defesa	défense	defence	Verteidigung(f)	defensa	difesa
défice	déficit	deficit	Verlust(m), Defizit(n)	déficit	deficit
deficiente	déficient, e	deficient	mangelhaft	deficiente	deficiente
deficiente	handicapé, e	handicapped	behindert	minusválido, a	andicappato, a
definição	définition	definition	Definition(f)	definición	definizione
definir	définir	define	definieren	definir	definire
definitivo, a	définitif, ive	definitive, final	endgültig	definitivo, a	definitivo, a
deflação	déflation	deflation	Deflation(f)	deflación	deflazione
deflagração	déflagration	explosion	Knall(m), Explosion(f)	deflagración	deflagrazione
deformação	déformation	distortion	Mißbildung(f)	deformación	deformazione
deformar	déformer	distort, deform	verformen	deformar	deformare
defrontar	braver	defy	trotzen	desafiar	sfidare
defunto, a	défunt, e	deceased person	Verstorbene(f, m)	difunto, a	defunto, a
degelo	dégel	thaw	Auftauen(n)	deshielo	disgelo
degenerar	dégénérer	degenerate	degenerieren	degenerar	degenerare
degradação	dégradation	degradation	Beschädigung(f)	degradación	degradazione
degradar	dégrader	degrade	degradieren	degradar	degradare
degrau	marche	step	Stufe(f)	peldaño, escalón	scalino
deitar fora	jeter	throw away(out)	weg = werfen	echar, tirar	buttare
deitar-se	coucher(se)	go to bed	schlafen gehen	ir a la cama	andare a letto
deixar	laisser	let; leave	lassen	dejar	lasciare
deixar	laisser	leave	lassen(zurück = -, ver-)	dejar	lasciare
deixar	quitter	leave	verlassen	dejar, abandonar	lasciare
delegação	délégation	delegation	Delegation(f)	delegación	delegazione
delegado, a	délégué, e	delegate	Abgesandte(f, m)	delegado, a	delegato, a
delegar	déléguer	delegate	beauftragen	delegar	delegare
deliberado, a	délibéré, e	deliberate	gewollt, absichtlich	deliberado, a	deliberato, a
deliberar	délibérer	deliberate	beraten	deliberar	deliberare
delicadeza	délicatesse	delicacy	Aufmerksamkeit(f)	delicadeza	delicatezza
delicadeza	politesse	politeness	Höflichkeit(f)	cortesía	educazione
delicado, a	délicat, e	delicate	schwierig	delicado, a	delicato, a
delicado, a	délicat, e	delicate	zart; fein	delicado, a	delicato, a
delicioso, a	délicieux, se	delicious	köstlich	delicioso, a	delizioso, a
delicioso, a	charmant, e	delightful	entzückend, reizend	delicioso, a	delizioso, a
delimitar	délimiter	delimit	ab = grenzen	delimitar	delimitare
delinquência	délinquance	delinquency	Kriminalität(f)	delincuencia	delinquenza
delinquente	délinquant, e	delinquent	Kriminelle(f, m)	delincuente	delinquente
delirio	délire	delirium	Fieberwahn(m)	delirio	delirio
delito	délit	offence	Vergehen(n), Delikt(n)	delito	delitto
demagogia	démagogie	demagogy	Demagogie(f)	demagogia	demagogia
demasiado, a	trop	too(much, many)	zuviel	demasiado, a	troppo, a
demência	démence	insanity, madness	Wahnsinn(m)	demencia	demenza, follia
demente	dément, e	insane, crazy, mad	verrückt	demente	demente
demissão	démission	resignation	Rücktritt(m)	dimisión	dimissione
demitir	révoquer	dismiss	ab = setzen, entlassen	revocar	revocare
demitir-se	démissionner	resign	zurück = treten	dimitir	dimettere(-rsi)
democracia	démocratie	democracy	Demokratie(f)	democracia	democrazia
democrata	démocrate	democrat	Demokrat(in f)m	demócrata	democratico, a
demografia	démographie	demography	Demographie(f)	demografía	demografia
demolir	démolir	demolish	zerstören	demoler	demolire
demónio	démon	demon, devil	Teufel(m)	demonio	demonio
demonstração	démonstration	demonstration	Vorführung(f)	demostración	dimostrazione
demonstrar	démontrer	demonstrate	beweisen	demostrar	dimostrare
denegrir	dénigrer	denigrate	verleumden	denigrar	denigrare
densidade	densité	density	Dichte(f)	densidad	densità
denso, a	dense	dense	dicht	denso, a	denso, a
dentadura	dentier	denture	Gebiß(n)	dentadura	dentiera
dente	dent	tooth(teeth)	Zahn(m)	diente	dente
dentífrico	dentifrice	tooth-paste	Zahnpasta(f)	dentífrico	dentifricio
dentista	dentiste	dentist	Zahnarzt(in f)m	dentista	dentista
dentro(de), em	dans	in, into	in	dentro, en	in
dentro	dedans	inside	in, drinnen, innen	dentro, adentro	dentro

P

Portuguese	French	English	German	Spanish	Italian
denunciar	dénoncer	denounce	denunzieren	denunciar	denunziare
departamento	département	department	Bezirk(m), Bereich(m)	departamento	dipartimento
de pé, em pé	debout	standing(up)	stehend, aufrecht	de pie, en pie	in piedi
dependência	accoutumance	addiction	Abhängigkeit(f)	adicto, dependencia	assuefazione
dependente	dépendant, e	dependent(on)	abhängig	dependiente	dipendente
depender	dépendre(de)	depend(on)	ab = hängen	depender	dipendere
depilar	épiler	remove hair	enthaaren	depilar	depilare
deplorar	déplorer	deplore	beklagen	deplorar	deplorare
deplorável	déplorable	deplorable	beklagenswert	deplorable	deplorevole
depois	après	after; afterwards	nach	después	dopo
depois	puis, ensuite	then	dann	después	poi
deportação	déportation	deportation	Deportation(f)	deportación	deportazione
deposição	déposition	statement	Aussage(f)	deposición	deposizione
depositar	déposer	deposit	deponieren	depositar	depositare
depósito	dépôt	deposit	Satz(m)	depósito	deposito
depósito	consigne	luggage lockers	Schließfach(n)	consigna	cassetta, deposito
depósito(bagagem)	consigne(bagage)	left luggage	Gepäckaufbewahrung(f)	consigna(equipaje)	deposito bagagli
depósito	réservoir	tank	Tank(m)	depósito	serbatoio
depressa; rápido, a	vite	fast, quickly	rasch	pronto; rápido, a	presto
depressão	dépression	breakdown	Nervenzusammenbruch m	depresión	esaurimento(nerv.)
depressão	dépression(atm.)	depression	Tief(n)	depresión	depressione
deprimido, a	déprimé, e	depressed	deprimiert	deprimido, a	depresso, a
deputado	député	Member(Parliament)	Abgeordnete(m, f)	diputado	deputato
derivar	dériver	drift	ab = treiben	derivar	derivare
derrapar	déraper	skid	schleudern	patinar	slittare
derreter	fondre	melt	schmilzen	derretir	sciogliere(-rsi)
derretido, a	fondu, e	melted	geschmolzen	derretido, a	sciolto, a
derrota	défaite	defeat	Niederlage(f)	derrota	sconfitta
derrubar	renverser	knock over/down	um = stoßen	derribar	travolgere
desabar	effondrer(s')	collapse	zusammen = brechen	hundirse	crollare
desacelerar	décélérer	decelerate	ab = bremsen	reducir, aminorar	decelerare
desaconselhar	déconseiller	advise against	ab = raten	desaconsejar	sconsigliare
desacordo	désaccord	disagreement	Uneinigkeit(f), Streit	discrepancia	disaccordo
desacreditar	discréditer	discredit	Verruf bringen(in)	desacreditar	discreditare
desafiar	défier	challenge	heraus = fordern	desafiar	sfidare
desafio	défi	challenge	Herausforderung(f)	desafío	sfida
desafio, torneio	challenge	challenge, contest	Wettkampf(m)	trofeo, challenge	gara, sfida
desafio, partida	match	match(-es), game	Spiel(n)	partido	partita
desagradável	désagréable	unpleasant	unangenehm	desagradable	sgradevole
desagradável	déplaisant, e	unpleasant	unangenehm	desagradable	sgradevole
desajeitado, a	maladroit, a	clumsy, awkward	ungeschickt	torpe	maldestro, a
desalentado, a	découragé, e	disheartened	mutlos, verzagt	desalentado, a	scoraggiato, a
desalentado, a	découragé, e	discouraged	entmutigt	desanimado, a	scoraggiato, a
desalentar	décourager	discourage	entmutigen	desalentar	scoraggiare
desalfandegar	dédouaner	clear(customs)	verzollen	retirar aduana	sdoganare
desamparado, a	désemparé, e	distraught	ratlos	desamparado, a	smarrito, a; sgomento
desanimador, a	décourageant, e	discouraging	entmutigend	desalentador, a	scoraggiante
desaparecer	disparaître	disappear	verschwinden	desaparecer	sparire
desapertar	desserrer	loosen	lockern	aflojar	allentare
desapertar	dégrafer	undo, unfasten	auf = machen	desabrochar	slacciare
desapontar	décevoir	disappoint	enttäuschen	decepcionar	deludere
desaprovar	désapprouver	disapprove	mißbilligen	desaprobar	disapprovare
desarmamento	désarmement	disarmament	Abrüstung(f)	desarme	disarmo
desarmar	désarmer	disarm	ab = rüsten, entwaffnen	desarmar	disarmare
desastre	désastre	disaster	Unheil(n)	desastre	disastro
desatar	détacher	detach, unfasten	lösen, ab = trennen	desatar	staccare
desbloquear	débloquer	release	deblockieren, lösen	desbloquear	sbloccare
descançar	reposer(se)	rest	aus = ruhen, sich	descansar	riposarsi
descanço	repos	rest	Ruhe(f)	descanso	riposo
descarga	déchargement	unloading	Ausladen(n)	descarga	scarico
descarregar	décharger	unload	ab = laden, aus = laden	descargar	scaricare
descarregar	débarquer	unload	aus = laden	descargar	sbarcare
descascar	peler	peel	schälen	mondar	sbucciare
descascar	éplucher	peel	schälen	pelar	sbucciare
descendência	descendance	descendants	Nachkommenschaft(f)	descendencia	discendenza
descer, baixar	descendre	go down, descend	herunter = gehen	descender, bajar	scendere
descer	descendre	get out of; get off	aus = steigen	bajarse	scendere
descida	descente	descent	Abstieg(m)	descenso, bajada	discesa

Portuguese	French	English	German	Spanish	Italian
descoberta	découverte	discovery	Entdeckung(f)	descubrimiento	scoperta
descobrir	découvrir	discover	entdecken	descubrir	scoprire
descobrir	déceler	discover; reveal	auf = decken, entdecken	descubrir	svelare, scoprire
descolar	décoller	unstick	ab = lösen	despegar	staccare, scollare
descolar	décoller	take off	ab = heben	despegar	decollare
descolonizar	décoloniser	decolonize	entkolonisieren	descolonizar	decolonizzare
descoloração	décoloration	discolouration	Entfärbung(f)	descoloramiento	decolorazione
desconcertante	déconcertant, e	disconcerting	verwirrend	desconcertante	sconcertante
desconfiado, a	méfiant, e	suspicious	mißtrauisch	desconfiado, a	diffidente
desconfiar	méfier(se)	mistrust	mißtrauen	desconfiar	diffidare
desconfiança	méfiance	distrust, mistrust	Mißtrauen(n)	desconfianza	diffidenza
descongelar	décongeler	thaw	auf = tauen	descongelar	scongelare
descongelar	dégivrer	de-ice; defrost	ab = tauen	descongelar	sbrinare
desconhecido, a	inconnu, e	unknown	unbekannt	desconocido, a	sconosciuto, a
descontaminar	décontaminer	decontaminate	entseuchen	descontaminar	decontaminare
descontentamento	mécontentement	displeasure	Unzufriedenheit(f)	descontento	scontento
descontente	mécontent, e	displeased	unzufrieden	descontento, a	scontento, a
desconto, saldo	rabais, remise	discount	Rabatt(m)	rebaja, descuento	ribasso, sconto
desconto	remise, rabais	reduction	Nachlaß, Ermäßigung	descuento	rimessa, sconto
desconto	escompte	discount	Skonto(m)	descuento	sconto
desconto	réduction	reduction	Senkung(f)	rebaja	riduzione
descontraído, a	décontracté, e	relaxed	lässig, entspannt	relajado, a	rilassato, a
descontraído, a	détendu, e	relaxed	entspannt	descansado, a	disteso, a; rilassato
descosido, a	décousu, e	unstitched	abgetrennt	descosido, a	scucito, a
descrever	décrire	describe	beschreiben	describir	descrivere
descrição	description	description	Beschreibung(f)	descripción	descrizione
descuidado, a	insouciant, e	carefree	unbekümmert	despreocupado, a	noncurante
descuidado, a	négligent, e	careless	nachlässig	descuidado, a	negligente
descuidar	négliger	neglect	vernachlässigen	descuidar	trascurare
desculpa	excuse	excuse; apology	Entschuldigung(f)	excusa, disculpa	scusa
desculpar-se	excuser(s')	apologize	entschuldigen, sich	disculpar(se)	scusarsi
desculpe!	excuse(je m')	sorry(I am)	es tut mir leid	siento(lo)	scusi(mi)
desculpe!; perdão!	excusez-moi!	excuse me!; sorry!	Entschuldigung!	perdone(!)	scusi!
desde	depuis	since; for	seit	desde	da
desdenhar	dédaigner	disdain	mißachten	desdeñar	disprezzare
desdobrar	déplier	unfold	auf = falten	desdoblar	spiegare, aprire
desejar	désirer	desire, want	wünschen	desear	desiderare
desejar	souhaiter	wish, desire	wünschen	desear	augurare
desejo	désir	wish(-es)	Wunsch(m)	deseo	desiderio
desembaraçar	débarrasser	clear, rid	weg = räumen	quitar, tirar	sbarazzare
desembarcar	débarquer	disembark, land	Land gehen(an)	desembarcar	sbarcare
desembolsar	débourser	spend	aus = geben	desembolsar	sborsare
desempenho	performance	performance	Leistung(f)	proeza, hazaña	prestazione
desempregado, a	chômeur, euse	unemployed person	Arbeitslose(f, m)	parado, a	disoccupato, a
desemprego	chômage	unemployment	Arbeitslosigkeit(f)	paro, desempleo	disoccupazione
desencadear	déclencher	trigger off	aus = lösen	iniciar	scattare, attivare
desenhador, a	dessinateur	drawer; designer	Zeichner(in f)m	dibujante	disegnatore, trice
desenhar	dessiner	draw; design	zeichnen	dibujar; diseñar	disegnare
desenho	dessin	drawing; design	Zeichnung(f)	dibujo; diseño	disegno
desenho	dessin, plan	design	Entwurf(m)	diseño	disegno
desenho animado	dessin animé	cartoon	Trickfilm(m)Zeichen-	dibujo animado	cartone animato
desenredar	débrouiller	clear up	entwirren	desenredar	sbrogliare
desenredar-se	débrouiller(se)	manage	zu helfen wissen, sich	desenredarse	cavarsela
desenrolar	dérouler	unroll	ab = rollen	desenrollar	svolgere, srotolare
desenterrar	déterrer	dig up	aus = graben	desenterrar	dissotterrare
desenvolver	développer	develop	entwickeln	desarrollar	sviluppare
desenvolvimento	développement	development	Entwicklung(f)	desarrollo	sviluppo
deserdar	déshériter	disinherit	enterben	desheredar	diseredare
desértico, a	désertique	desert, barren	öde; einsam	desértico, a	desertico, a
deserto	désert	desert	Wüste(f)	desierto	deserto
desespero	désespoir	despair	Verzweiflung(f)	desesperación	disperazione
desfalecimento	défaillance	weakness(-es)	Schwäche(f), Versagen	desfallecimiento	svenimento
desfavorecido, a	défavorisé, e	underprivileged	benachteiligt	desfavorecido, a	svantaggiato, a
desfazer	défaire	dismantle, undo	ab = bauen	deshacer	disfare
desfiladeiro	col	pass	Paß(m)	puerto	colle, passo
desfile	défilé	parade	Parade(f)	desfile	sfilata
desgosto, pena	chagrin	grief, sorrow	Kummer(m)	pena	dispiacere
desgraça	malheur	misfortune	Unglück(n)	desgracia	disgrazia

P

675

Portuguese	French	English	German	Spanish	Italian
desidratar	déshydrater	dehydrate	aus = trocknen	deshidratar	disidratare
designar	désigner	appoint	ernennen	designar	designare
desigual	inégal, e	unequal	ungleich	desigual	ineguale
desigual	inégal, e	uneven	uneben	desigual	disuguale
desigualdade	inégalité	inequality	Ungleichheit(f)	desigualdad	disuguaglianza
desiludido, a	déçu, e	disappointed	enttäuscht	decepcionado, a	deluso, a
desimpedir	dégager	clear	frei = machen	despejar	sgomberare
desinchar	dégonfler	deflate	Luft raus = lassen	desinflar	sgonfiare
desinfectar	désinfecter	disinfect	desinfizieren	desinfectar	disinfettare
desintegrar	désintégrer	disintegrate	auf = lösen	desintegrar	disintegrare
desistir	désister(se)	withdraw, give up	zurück = treten	desistir	desistere, rinunziare
desistir; renunciar	renoncer	give up	auf = geben	renunciar	rinunciare
desligar	débrancher	unplug	raus = ziehen	desenchufar	staccare
desligar	débrancher	disconnect, unplug	aus = machen, abschalten	desenchufar	disinserire
deslocação	déplacement	transfer, moving	Umstellung(f)	desplazamiento	spostamento
deslocar	déplacer	shift, move	versetzen, -schieben	trasladar	spostare
deslocar-se	déplacer(se)	move, shift	bewegen, sich	desplazar(se)	spostare(-arsi)
desmaiar	évanouir(s')	faint	ohnmächtig werden	desmayarse	svenire
desmentir	démentir	refute, deny	dementieren, leugnen	desmentir	smentire
desmobilizar	démobiliser	demobilize	demobilisieren	desmovilizar	smobilitare
desmontagem	démontage	dismantling	Zerlegung(f), Abbau(m)	desmontaje	smontaggio
desmontar	démonter	remove, dismantle	ab = bauen	desmontar	smontare
desmoralizar	démoraliser	demoralize	entmutigen	desmoralizar	demoralizzare
desmoronamento	éboulement	landslide	Erdrutsch(m)	desprendimiento	frana, slavina
desmoronar-se	écrouler(s')	collapse, crumble	zusammen = brechen	derrumbar(se)	crollare
desnudar	dénuder	strip, bare	entblößen	desnudar	denudare
desobedecer	désobéir	disobey	ungehorsam sein	desobedecer	disobbedire
desocupado, a	inoccupé, e	unoccupied	untätig	desocupado, a	inoperoso, a
desodorisante	déodorant	deodorant	Deo(n)	desodorante	deodorante
desodorisante	désodorisant	air-freshener	Deodorant(n)	desodorante	deodorante
desolado, a	désolé, e	sorry	betrübt	desolado, a	spiacente
desolado, a	navré, e	sorry	leid tun	desconsolado, a	spiacente
desonesto, a	malhonnête	dishonest	unehrlich	deshonesto, a	disonesto, a
desonra	déshonneur	dishonour	Schande(f)	deshonor	disonore
desordem	désordre	disorder, mess	Unordnung(f)	desorden	disordine
desordem	pagaille	mess	Durcheinander(n)	follón, lío	caos, confusione
desorganizar	désorganiser	disorganize	desorganisieren	desorganizar	disorganizzare
despachar-se	dépêcher(se)	hurry(up)	beeilen, sich	darse prisa	sbrigarsi
despedaçar	déchiqueter	tear to pieces	zerstückeln	despedazar	dilaniare
despedimento	licenciement	dismissal, lay-off	Entlassung(f)	despido	licenziamento
despedir	licencier	lay off, dismiss	entlassen	despedir	licenziare
despedir	renvoyer	dismiss	entlassen	despedir	dimettere
despeito	dépit; vexation	spite; vexation	Groll(m), Trotz(m)	despecho	dispetto
despejar	déverser	pour out, tip	aus = gießen	verter	riversare, scaricare
desperdiçar	gaspiller, perdre	waste	verschwenden	despilfarrar	sprecare
desperdiçar	gaspiller	waste	verschwenden	desperdiciar	sperperare
desperdício	gaspillage	waste	Verschwendung(f)	despilfarro	spreco
despertador	réveil	alarm clock	Wecker(m)	despertador	sveglia
despertar	éveiller(s')	wake up	auf = wachen	despertar(se)	svegliarsi
despesa, gasto	dépense	expenditure	Ausgabe(f)	gasto	spesa
despesas	frais(scolarité)	fee	Kosten(pl.)	gastos(escolares)	spese
despir-se	déshabiller(se)	undress	aus = ziehen, sich	desnudar(se)	svestire(-irsi)
despojo	butin	spoils	Beute(f)	botín	bottino
despoletar	désamorcer	defuse	entschärfen	desactivar	disinnescare
desportista	sportif, ive	sportsman-/-woman	Sportler(in f)m	deportista	sportivo, a
desportivo, a	sportif, ive	sporty, athletic	sportlich; Sport-	deportivo, a	sportivo, a
desporto	sport	sport	Sport(m)	deporte	sport
déspota	despote	despot	Despot(m)	déspota	despota
desprezo	mépris	contempt, scorn	Verachtung(f)	desprecio	disprezzo
desterrar	bannir	banish	verbannen	desterrar	bandire
destinar	destiner	intended to(be)	bestimmen für	destinar	destinare
destinar	attribuer	assign	zu = teilen	asignar	assegnare
destinatário, a	destinataire	addressee	Empfänger(in f)m	destinatario, a	destinatario, a
destino	destin	fate, destiny	Schicksal(n)	destino, sino	destino
destino	destinée	destiny	Schicksal(n)	destino	destino
destino	destination	destination	Bestimmungsort(m)	destinación	destinazione
destituir	limoger	dismiss	entlassen	destituir	silurare
destro, a; hábil	adroit, e	skilled	geschickt	diestro, a	abile

| --- | --- | --- | --- | --- | --- |
destroços	épave	wreck	Wrack(n)	ruina, restos	relitto
destruição	destruction	destruction	Zerstörung(f)	destrucción	distruzione
destruir	détruire	destroy	zerstören	destruir	distruggere
desumano, a	inhumain, e	inhuman	unmenschlich	inhumano, a	inumano, a
desusado, a	désuet, ète	obsolete	altmodisch	desusado, a	antiquato, a; desueto
desvalimento	disgrâce	disgrace	Ungnade(f)	desgracia	disgrazia
desvalorização	dévaluation	devaluation	Abwertung(f)	devaluación	svalutazione
desvalorizar	dévaluer	devalue	entwerten, ab = werten	devaluar	svalutare
desvantagem	désavantage	disadvantage	Nachteil(m)	desventaja	svantaggio
desventura	malchance	misfortune	Unglück(n)	mala suerte	sventura, sfortuna
desviar	dévier	divert	um = leiten	desviar	deviare
desvio	déviation	diversion	Umleitung(f)	desviación	deviazione
desvio, margem	écart	gap, margin	Abstand(m)	diferencia, margen	margine, differenza
detalhado, a	détaillé, e	detailed	einzelnen(im)	detallado, a	dettagliato, a
detecção	détection	detection	Aufspüren(n)	detección	rivelazione
detective	détective	detective	Detektiv(m)	detective	detective
detector	détecteur	detector	Anzeiger(m)	detector	rivelatore
detenção	détention	detention	Haft(f)	detención	detenzione
detenção	arrestation	arrest	Verhaftung(f)	arresto	arresto
detergente	lessive	washing powder	Waschpulver(n)	detergente	detersivo
deterioração	détérioration	deterioration	Verschlechterung(f)	deterioración	deteriorazione
determinar	déterminer	determine	fest = legen	determinar	determinare
detestar	détester	detest, hate	hassen	detestar, odiar	detestare, odiare
detonação	détonation	detonation	Knall(m)	detonación	detonazione
detrito, lixo	détritus	rubbish, garbage	Unrat(m)	desperdicios	detrito
Deus	dieu	God	Gott(m)	dios, Dios	dio, Dio (dio, dei)
Deus(meu)	Dieu(mon)	Goodness(my)	Gott!(Mein Gott!)	Dios(mío)	Dio(mio)
devagar	doucement	gently; slowly	langsam, sanft	despacio	piano, adagio
devastar	dévaster	ravage, devastate	verwüsten, zerstören	devastar	devastare
dever	devoir	must, have to	müssen	deber	dovere
dever	devoir	duty	Pflicht(f)	deber	dovere
dever	devoir	homework; exercise	Aufgabe(f)	deber, tarea	compito
devoção	dévotion	devotion	Frömmigkeit(f)	devoción	devozione
devolver	renvoyer	send back, return	zurück = schicken	devolver	rinviare
devolver	rendre	give back	zurück = geben	devolver	rendere
devorar	dévorer	devour	verschlingen	devorar	divorare
dez	dix	ten	zehn	diez	dieci
dezanove	dix-neuf	nineteen	neunzehn	diecinueve	diciannove
dezasseis	seize	sixteen	sechzehn	dieciséis	sedici
dezassete	dix-sept	seventeen	siebzehn	diecisiete	diciassette
Dezembro	Décembre	December	Dezember(m)	Diciembre	Dicembre
dezoito	dix-huit	eighteen	achtzehn	dieciocho	diciotto
dia	jour, journée	day	Tag(m)	día; jornada	giorno; giornata
dia de folga	jour de congé	day off	Urlaubstag(m)	día libre	giorno di vacanza
diabetes	diabète	diabetes	Zuckerkrankheit(f)	diabetes	diabete
diabo	diable	devil	Teufel(m)	diablo	diavolo
diafragma	diaphragme	diaphragm	Zwerchfell(n)	diafragma	diaframma
diagnóstico	diagnostic	diagnosis(-oses)	Diagnose(f)	diagnóstico	diagnosi
diagonal	diagonal, e	diagonal	diagonal	diagonal	diagonale
diagrama	diagramme	diagram	Diagramm(n)	diagrama	diagramma
dialecto	dialecte	dialect	Dialekt(m)	dialecto	dialetto
diálogo	dialogue	dialogue	Dialog(m)	diálogo	dialogo
diamante	diamant	diamond	Diamant(m)	diamante	diamante
diâmetro	diamètre	diameter	Durchmesser(m)	diámetro	diametro
diante de	devant	in front(ahead)of	vor	delante, ante	davanti a
dianteira	avant	front, fore	Vorderteil(n)	delantero, a	anteriore
diapositivos	diapo(sitives)	slide	Diapositiv(n), Dia(n)	diapositiva	diapositiva
diário, a	journalier, ière	daily	täglich	diario, a	giornaliero, a
diário	quotidien	daily	Tageszeitung(f)	diario	quotidiano
diarreia	diarrhée	diarrhoea	Durchfall(m)	diarrea	diarrea
dia seguinte	lendemain	next day	folgenden Tag(m)	día siguiente	indomani(l')
dicionário	dictionnaire	dictionary	Wörterbuch(n)	diccionario	dizionario
diesel	diesel	diesel	Diesel(m)	diesel	diesel
dieta	régime	diet(be on a)	Diät(f)	dieta	dieta
dietético, a	diététique	dietetic	diätetisch	dietético, a	dietetico, a
difamação	diffamation	slander	Verleumdung(f)	difamación	diffamazione
diferença	différence	difference	Unterschied(m)	diferencia	differenza
diferente	différent, e	different	verschieden	diferente	differente

P

Portuguese	French	English	German	Spanish	Italian
diferir, adiar	différer	postpone	auf = schieben	diferir, demorar	differire, rimandare
difícil	difficile	difficult	schwer	difícil	difficile
dificuldade	difficulté	difficulty	Schwierigkeit(f)	dificultad	difficoltá
difteria	diphtérie	diphtheria	Diphterie(f)	difteria	difterite
difundir	diffuser	diffuse	verbreiten	difundir	diffondere
difusão	diffusion	diffusion	Verbreitung; Sendung	difusión	diffusione
digestão	digestion	digestion	Verdauung(f)	digestión	digestione
dignidade	dignité	dignity	Würde(f)	dignidad	dignità
digno, a	digne	worthy; dignified	würdig	digno, a	degno, a
dilatação	dilatation	expansion	Ausdehnung(f)	dilatación	dilatazione
diluir	diluer	dilute	verdünnen	diluir	diluire
dilúvio	déluge	flood; downpour	Überschwemmung(f)	diluvio	diluvio
dimensão	dimension	dimension, size	Maß(n)	dimensión	dimensione
diminuição	diminution	reduction	Verminderung(f)	disminución	diminuzione
diminuir	diminuer	reduce, decrease	verringern	disminuir	diminuire
dinâmico, a	dynamique	dynamic	dynamisch	dinámico, a	dinamico, a
dinamismo	dynamisme	dynamism	Tatkraft(f), Schwung m	dinamismo	dinamismo
dinamite	dynamite	dynamite	Dynamit(n)	dinamita	dinamite
dinastia	dynastie	dynasty	Herrscherhaus(n)	dinastía	dinastia
dinheiro	argent	money	Geld(n)	dinero	denaro; soldi
diploma	diplôme	diploma	Diplom(n)	diploma, título	diploma
diplomacia	diplomatie	diplomacy	Diplomatie(f)	diplomacia	diplomazia
diplomado, a	diplômé, e	qualified	staatlich geprüft	graduado, a	diplomato, a
diplomado, a	diplômé, e	graduate	Diplom-	titulado, a	diplomato, a
diplomata	diplomate	diplomat	Diplomat(in f)m	diplomático	diplomatico
diplomático, a	diplomatique	diplomatic	diplomatisch	diplomático, a	diplomatico, a
direcção	direction	management	Direktion(f)	dirección	direzione
direcção	direcção	direction	Richtung(f)	dirección	direzione
direcção a(em)	vers	towards, to	gegen, in Richtung	hacia	verso
directamente	directement	directly	direkt	directamente	direttamente
directo, a	direct, e	direct	direkt	directo, a	diretto, a
director, a	directeur, trice	director, head	Direktor(in f)m	director, a	direttore, -trice
director, patrão	patron, dirigeant	manager, boss	Unternehmer(in f)m	director, jefe	manager, padrone
director(escola)	directeur(école)	headmaster	Schuldirektor(m)	director(escuela)	direttore(scuola)
direito	droit	law	Recht(n)	derecho	diritto
direito	droit	right	Recht(n)	derecho	diritto
direito, a	droit, e	right	rechte(r, s); rechts	derecho, a	destro, a
dirigente	dirigeant, e	leader, manager	Leiter(m), Führer(m)	dirigente	dirigente
dirigir	diriger	direct, guide, point	richten, steuern	dirigir, guiar	dirigere
dirigir	diriger	manage, run	leiten, führen	dirigir	dirigere
discar, marcar	composer(n°tél)	dial	Nummer(f)(wählen)	marcar un número	comporre(numero)
discernir	discerner	discern	unterscheiden	discernir	discernere
disciplina	discipline	discipline	Disziplin(f)	disciplina	disciplina
discípulo	disciple	disciple	Jünger(m)	discípulo	discepolo
disco	disque	record	Schallplatte(f)	disco	disco
discoteca	discothèque	disco(theque)	Diskothek(f)	discoteca	discoteca
discreto, a	discret, ète	discreet	diskret	discreto, a	discreto, a
discurso	discours	speech, talk	Rede(f)	discurso	discorso
discussão	discussion	discussion, talk	Diskussion(f)	discusión	discussione
discutir	discuter	discuss	besprechen	discutir	discutere
disfarçar	déguiser	disguise	verkleiden	disfrazar	mascherare
disparar, atirar	tirer	fire, shoot	feuern, schießen	tirar	sparare, tirare
dispersar	disperser	disperse; scatter	zerstreuen	dispersar	disperdere
disponível	disponible	available	verfügbar	disponible	disponibile
dispor	disposer	arrange	auf = stellen	disponer	disporre
disposição	disposition	arrangement	Anordnung(f)	disposición	disposizione
disposição	agencement	layout	Anlage(f)	disposición	disposizione
disputa	dispute	dispute, argument	Streit(m)	disputa	disputa, lite
disputar-se	disputer(se)	quarrel, argue	streiten, sich	reñir(con)	litigare
dissidente	dissident, e	dissident	Dissident(m)	disidente	dissidente
dissimular	dissimuler	conceal	verbergen, verhehlen	disimular	dissimulare
dissipar	dissiper	dissipate, clear	verziehen, sich	disipar	dissipare
dissociar	dissocier	dissociate	trennen	disociar	dissociare
dissolver	dissoudre	dissolve	auf = lösen	disolver	sciogliere
dissuadir	dissuader	dissuade	ab = raten	disuadir	dissuadere
dissuasão	dissuasion	dissuasion	Abschreckung(f)	disuasión	dissuasione
distância	distance	distance	Entfernung(f)	distancia	distanza
distilação	distillation	distillation	Destillation(f)	destilación	distillazione

Portuguese	French	English	German	Spanish	Italian
distinguir	distinguer	distinguish	unterscheiden	distinguir	distinguere
distinto, a	distinct, e	distinct	deutlich	distinto, a	distinto, a
distracção	inattention	carelessness	Unachtsamkeit(f)	descuido	disattenzione
distracção, -ões	distraction(s)	entertainment	Zeitvertreib(m)	distracción	svago, distrazione
distraído, a	distrait, e	absent-minded	zerstreut	distraído, a	distratto, a
distrair	distraire	distract, divert	ab = lenken	distraer	distrarre
distrair	distraire	entertain	unterhalten	entretener	distrarre
distribuição	distribution	distribution	Verteilung(f)	distribución	distribuzione
distribuir	distribuer	distribute; deal	verteilen	distribuir	distribuire
distrito	district, région	district	Bezirk(m)	distrito, área	distretto
ditador	dictateur	dictator	Diktator(m)	dictador	dittatore
ditadura	dictature	dictatorship	Diktatur(f)	dictadura	dittatura
divã	divan	couch(-es)	Couch(f), Sofa(n)	diván	divano
divergir	diverger	diverge	ab = weichen	divergir	divergere
diversidade	diversité	diversity	Verschiedenheit(f)	diversidad	diversità
diversificar	diversifier	diversify	variieren	diversificar	diversificare
diverso, a	divers, e	diverse, various	verschieden	diverso, a	diverso, a
divertido, a	amusant, e	funny, amusing	lustig, amüsant	divertido, a	buffo, a; divertente
divertido, a	drôle	funny	lustig	gracioso, a	buffo, a
divertimento	amusement	amusement, fun	Vergnügen(n)	diversión	divertimento
divertir-se	amuser(s')	fun(have)	amüsieren, sich	divertir(se)	divertire(-rsi)
dívida	dette	debt	Schuld(f)	deuda	debito
dividir	diviser	divide	teilen	dividir	dividere
divino, a	divin, e	divine	göttlich	divino, a	divino, a
divisão	division	division	Division(f)	división	divisione
divisão	pièce	room	Raum(m)	cuarto	stanza
divorciar-se	divorcer	divorce	scheiden lassen, sich	divorciar(se)	divorziare
divórcio	divorce	divorce	Scheidung(f)	divorcio	divorzio
divulgar	divulguer	divulge, reveal	aus = plaudern	divulgar	divulgare
dizer	dire	say	sagen	decir	dire
dizer respeito a	concerner	concern	betreffen	concernir	riguardare
dobrar	plier	fold	falten	doblar	piegare
doce	doux, ce	sweet	süß	dulce	dolce
doce, compota	confiture	jam	Marmelade(f)	mermelada	marmellata
dócil, manso	docile	docile	gehorsam	dócil	docile
documentação	documentation	documentation	Dokumentation(f)	documentación	documentazione
documento	document	document	Dokument(n)	documento	documento
documentos	papiers(les)	papers	Papiere(pl); Ausweise	documentación	documenti
doença	maladie	illness	Krankheit(f)	enfermedad	malattia
doente; enfermo, a	malade	ill	krank	enfermo, a	malato, a
doente	infirme	disabled	behindert	inválido, a	infermo, a
doente	malade	sick person	Kranke(f, m)	enfermo, a	malato, a
doentio, a	malsain, e	unhealthy	ungesund	malsano, a	malsano, a
doer	mal(faire)	ache, hurt	weh tun, schmerzen	doler	male(fare)
doer	mal(avoir)	hurts(it)	Schmerzen haben	dolerle uno	male(aver)
dogmático, a	dogmatique	dogmatic	dogmatisch	dogmático, a	dogmatico, a
doido, a; louco, a	cinglé, e	mad, nuts, barmy	verrückt	chiflado, a	tocco, a; picchiato, a
dois, duas	deux	two	zwei	dos	due
doloroso, a	douloureux, se	painful, aching	schmerzhaft	doloroso, a	doloroso, a
dom, talento	don	gift, talent	Talent(n)	don, talento	dono
domar	dompter	tame	zähmen	domar	domare
domesticar	apprivoiser	tame	zähmen	domesticar	addomesticare
doméstico, a	domestique	domestic, home	Haus-	doméstico, a	domestico, a
domicílio	domicile	home	Wohnsitz(m), Wohnort m	domicilio	domicilio
dominar	dominer	dominate, rule	beherrschen	dominar	dominare
dominar	maîtriser	control, master	beherrschen	dominar	dominare
domingo	dimanche	Sunday	Sonntag(m)	domingo	domenica
domínio	domaine	field, scope	Bereich(m)	campo, área	campo, settore
dona de casa	ménagère	housewife(-ives)	Hausfrau(f)	ama de casa	casalinga
dono, a; senhor, a	maître, esse	master, mistress	Herr(in f)m	señor, señora	maestro, a; padrone, a
dor	douleur	pain, ache	Schmerz(m)	dolor	dolore
dor	mal	ache, pain	Schmerz(m), Weh(n)	dolor	male
dor de cabeça	mal de tête	headache	Kopfschmerzen(m, pl)	dolor de cabeza	mal di testa
dor de dentes	mal aux dents	toothache	Zahnschmerzen(m, pl)	dolor de dientes	mal di denti
dor de garganta	mal de gorge	sore throat	Halsschmerzen(m, pl)	dolor de garganta	mal di gola
dormir	dormir	sleep	schlafen	dormir	dormire
dormitar	sommeiller	doze	schlummern	dormitar	sonnecchiare
dosagem	dosage	proportion	Dosierung(f)	dosificación	dosaggio, dose

P

Portuguese	French	English	German	Spanish	Italian
dose	dose	dose	Dosis(f)	dosis	dose
dotado, a; capaz	doué, e	gifted, talented	begabt	dotado, a	dotato, a
doutor, a	docteur(toresse)	doctor	Arzt(m); Doktor(m)	doctor, a	dottore, -essa
doutor, a	docteur	doctor	Doktor(m)	doctor, a	dottore, -essa
doutrina	doctrine	doctrine	Lehre(f)	doctrina	dottrina
doutrinar	endoctriner	indoctrinate	indoktrinieren	adoctrinar	addottrinare
doze	douze	twelve	zwölf	doce	dodici
drama	drame	drama	Drama(n)	drama	dramma
dramático, a	dramatique	dramatic	dramatisch	dramático, a	drammatico, a
drenar	drainer	drain	entwässern	drenar	drenare
droga	drogue	drug	Droge(f)	droga	droga
drogado, a	drogué, e	drug addict	Drogenabhängige(m, f)	drogado, a	drogato, a
drogaria	droguerie	hardware shop	Kramwarenhandel(m)	droguería	mesticheria
drogar-se	doper(se)	take stimulants	dopen, sich	doparse	drogarsi
duche, chuveiro	douche	shower	Dusche(f)	ducha	doccia
duelo	duel	duel	Duell(n)	duelo	duello
duna	dune	dune	Düne(f)	duna	duna
duplo, a	double	double	doppelt	doble	doppio, a
duplo, a	double	dual	doppelt	doble	doppio, a
duque, duquesa	duc, duchesse	duke, duchess	Herzog(m), Herzogin(f)	duque, duquesa	duca, duchessa
duração	durée	duration, length	Dauer(f)	duración	durata
durante	durant, pendant	during, for	während	durante	durante
durante	pendant	during; for	während	durante	durante
durar	durer	last	dauern	durar	durare
duro, a	dur, e	hard	hart	duro, a	duro, a
dúvida	doute	doubt	Zweifel(m)	duda	dubbio
duvidar	douter	doubt	zweifeln	dudar	dubitare
duvidoso, a	douteux, se	dubious; doubtful	zweifelhaft	dudoso, a	dubbio, a
dúzia	douzaine	dozen	Dutzend(n)	docena	dozzina

E

Portuguese	French	English	German	Spanish	Italian
e	et	and	und	y	e, ed
eclipse	éclipse	eclipse	Finsternis(f)	eclipse	eclisse
eco	écho(-es)	echo(-es)	Echo(n)	eco	eco
ecologia	écologie	ecology	Naturschutz(m)	ecología	ecologia
economia	économie	economy	Wirtschaft(f)	economía	economia
economia	économie, épargne	saving	Ersparnis(f)	economía, ahorro	risparmio
económico, a	économique	economic(al)	wirtschaftlich	económico, a	economico, a
economista	économiste	economist	Volkswirt(in f)m	economista	economista
economizar	économiser	save, economise	sparen	economizar	economizzare
écran	écran	screen	Bildschirm; Leinwand	pantalla	schermo
eczema	eczéma	eczema	Ekzem(n)	eczema	eczema
edição	édition	edition	Auflage(f), Ausgabe(f)	edición	edizione
edifício	édifice	edifice, building	Gebäude(n)	edificio	edificio
edifício	bâtiment	building	Gebäude(n)	edificio	edificio, palazzo
edifício, imóvel	immeuble	block of flats	Gebäude(n)	inmueble	palazzo, edificio
editor, a	éditeur, trice	publisher; editor	Herausgeber(in f)m	editor, a	editore, trice
editorial	éditorial	editorial	Leitartikel(m)	editorial	editoriale
educação	éducation	education	Erziehung(f)	educación	educazione
educado, a	poli, e	polite	höflich	educado, a; cortés	educato, a
educador, a	éducateur, trice	instructor	Erzieher(in f)m	educador, a	educatore, trice
educar	éduquer	educate	erziehen, bilden	educar	educare
efectivo	effectif	number of people	Personalbestand(m)	efectivo	effettivo
efectivo, a	effectif, ive	effective	tatsächlich, wirklich	efectivo, a	effettivo, a
efectuar	effectuer	carry out, perform	aus = führen	efectuar	effettuare
efeito	effet	effect	Wirkung(f)	efecto	effetto

Portuguese	French	English	German	Spanish	Italian
efeito(com)	effet(en)	indeed	tatsächlich	efecto(en)	infatti
efémero, a	éphémère	ephemeral	vergänglich	efímero, a	effimero, a
eficaz	efficace	effective	wirkungsvoll	eficaz	efficace
eficiente	efficace	efficient	tüchtig, fähig	eficiente	efficiente
egoísta	égoïste	selfish	egoistisch	egoísta	egoista
eixo	axe	axis	Achse(f)	eje	asse
ela	elle	she	sie	ella	essa; lei; ella
elaborar	élaborer	elaborate	aus = arbeiten	elaborar	elaborare
elas	elles	they	sie	ellas	esse, loro
elástico	élastique	rubber band	Gummiband(n)	goma elástica	elastico
elástico, a	élastique	elastic; flexible	elastisch	elástico, a	elastico, a
ele	il	he; it	er; es	él	egli, lui, esso
ele(a); lhe	lui	him, her, it	ihm, ihr, ihm	le, él; ella; se	lui; gli; le
electricidade	électricité	electricity	Elektrizität(f)	electricidad	elettricità
electricista	électricien	electrician	Elektriker(in f)m	electricista	elettricista
eléctrico, a	électrique	electric(al)	elektrisch	eléctrico, a	elettrico, a
electrónica	électronique	electronics	Elektronik(f)	electrónica	elettronica
electrónico, a	électronique	electronic	elektronisch	electrónico, a	elettronico, a
elefante	éléphant	elephant	Elefant(m)	elefante	elefante
elegância	élégance	elegance	Eleganz(f)	elegancia	eleganza
elegante	élégant, e	elegant, smart	elegant	elegante	elegante
elegante	chic	smart, chic	schick	elegante	elegante
eleger	élire	elect	wählen	elegir	eleggere
eleição	élection	election	Wahl(f)	elección	elezione
eleito, a	élu, e	elected, chosen	gewählt	elegido, a	eletto, a
eleitor, a	électeur, trice	voter	Wähler(in f)m	elector, a	elettore, -trice
elemento	élément	element	Element(n)	elemento	elemento
eles	ils	they	sie	ellos	essi; loro
elevador	ascenseur	lift, elevator	Aufzug(m)	ascensor	ascensore
elevar	élever	elevate	erhöhen	elevar, alzar	elevare
elevar	élever, hausser	raise	an = heben	elevar	elevare, alzare
eliminação	élimination	elimination	Beseitigung(f)	eliminación	eliminazione
eliminar	éliminer	eliminate	aus = scheiden	eliminar	eliminare
elipse	ellipse	ellipse	Ellipse(f)	elipse	ellisse
elite	élite	élite	Elite(f)	élite	elite
elocução	élocution	elocution	Sprechweise(f)	elocución	eloquio
elogio	éloge	praise	Lob(n)	elogio	elogio
eloquência	éloquence	eloquence	Redegewandtheit(f)	elocuencia	eloquenza
em	en; dans; à; de; sur	in; into; at; to; by	in; zu; nach; an; bei; auf	en; a; hacia; con; de	in; a; di; da
emagrecer	maigrir	lose weight	ab = nehmen	adelgazar	dimagrire
emaranhar-se	emmêler(s')	tangle(up)	verwickeln, verwirren	enmarañar(se)	aggrovigliare(-rsi)
embaixada	ambassade	embassy	Botschaft(f)	embajada	ambasciata
embaixador	ambassadeur	ambassador	Botschafter(in f)m	embajador	ambasciatore
embalagem	emballage	packing, wrapping	Verpackung(f)	embalaje, envase	imballaggio
embalar	bercer	rock	wiegen	mecer	cullare
embaraço	embarras	embarrassment	Verlegenheit(f)	apuro	imbarazzo
embaraço	gêne	embarrassment	Verlegenheit(f)	molestia	disagio, imbarazzo
embarcar	embarquer	board, embark	ein = steigen	embarcar	imbarcare
embargo	embargo	embargo	Embargo(n)	embargo	embargo
embeber	imbiber	soak	durchtränken	empapar	imbevere
emblema	emblème	emblem	Emblem(n)	emblema	emblema
embora	quoique	although, though	obgleich, obwohl	aunque	sebbene
emboscada	embuscade	ambush	Hinterhalt(m)	emboscada	imboscata
embraiagem	embrayage	clutch	Kupplung(f)	embrague	frizione
embriaguez	ivresse	drunkenness	Trunkenheit(f)	ebriedad	ubriachezza
embrião	embryon	embryo	Embryo(m)	embrión	embrione
embrutecer	abrutir	exhaust; stupefy	ab = stumpfen	embrutecer	abbrutire
embutir	encastrer	set in	ein = setzen	empotrar	incastrare
em casa de	chez	at, to	bei	en casa de	da
em cima de; sobre	sur	on	auf	en, encima, sobre	sopra, su
em cima, sobre	dessus(au-, par-)	above, on, over	über	arriba, encima	sopra
emendar	amender	amend	verbessern, ändern	enmendar	emendare
ementa	menu	menu	Menü(n), Speisekarte f	menú	menù
emergir	émerger	emerge	auf = tauchen	emerger	emergere
emigração	émigration	emigration	Auswanderung(f)	emigración	emigrazione
emigrante	émigré, e	emigrant	Emigrant(in f)m	emigrante	emigrato, a
emigrar	émigrer	emigrate	aus = wandern	emigrar	emigrare
eminente	éminent, e	eminent	hervorragend	eminente	eminente

Portuguese	French	English	German	Spanish	Italian
emissão	émission	programme	Sendung(f)	emisión	programma
emissário	émissaire	emissary	Bote(m)	emisario	emissario
emissor	émetteur	transmitter	Sender(m)	emisor	emittente
emitir	émettre	emit	aus = strahlen	emitir	emettere
emoção	émotion	emotion	Rührung(f)	emoción	emozione
emotivo, a	émotif, ive	emotional	empfindsam	emotivo, a	emotivo, a
empacotar	empaqueter	pack, wrap	ein = packen, verpacken	empaquetar	impacchettare
empada	tourte	pie	Pastete(f)	pastel, tortada	torta salata
empenado, a	gondolé, e	warped, buckled	verbogen	combado, a	incurvato, a
empenhar	engager	engage	engagieren	empeñar	impegnare
empilhar, amontoar	empiler	pile up, stack	stapeln	apilar, amontonar	accatastare
empinado, a	raide; escarpé, e	steep	steil	empinado, a	ripido, a
empola	ampoule	blister	Blase(f)	ampolla	bolla, vescica
empreender	entreprendre	undertake	unternehmen	emprender	intraprendere
empregada	femme de chambre	chambermaid	Zimmermädchen(n)	camarera	cameriera
empregado, a	employé, e	employee	Angestellte(f, m)	empleado, a	impiegato, a
empregado, a	employé, e	clerk	Angestellte(f, m)	oficinista	impiegato, a
empregado, a	domestique	servant	Hausangestellte(m, f)	criado, a	domestico, a
empregar	employer	employ	an = stellen	emplear	impiegare
empregar	embaucher	employ, take on	ein = stellen	dar trabajo	assumere
emprego	emploi	employment	Stelle(f)	empleo	impiego
emprego	emploi	job, work	Beruf(m)	empleo	impiego
empresa	entreprise	company, firm	Unternehmen(n)	empresa	impresa, ditta
empresário	entrepreneur	contractor	Unternehmer(in f)m	empresario	imprenditore
empresário	imprésario	impresario	Manager(m)	empresario	impresario
emprestar	prêter	lend	leihen, verleihen	prestar	prestare
empréstimo	prêt	loan	Darlehen(n)	préstamo	prestito
empréstimo	emprunt	loan	Anleihe(f)	préstamo	prestito
empurrar	bousculer	push	drängeln	empujar	spingere, urtare
empurrar	pousser	push	schieben, stoßen	empujar	spingere
em seguida	ensuite	then, next	danach	después	poi, dopo
emulsão	émulsion	emulsion	Emulsion(f)	emulsión	emulsione
em vez de/lugar de	au lieu de	instead(of)	anstatt	en vez de/lugar de	invece di
encadernação	reliure	binding(book-)	Einband(m)	encuadernación	rilegatura
encandear	éblouir	dazzle, glare	blenden	deslumbrar	abbagliare
encantado, a	ravi, e	delighted	hocherfreut	encantado, a	lietissimo, a
encantador, a	charmant, e	charming, lovely	liebenswert	encantador, a	affascinante
encantador, a	ravissant, e	ravishing, lovely	entzückend	encantador, a	incantevole
encanto	charme	charm	Charme(m), Reiz(m)	encanto	fascino
encarar	envisager	envisage	beabsichtigen	enfocar	prevedere
encarcerar	incarcérer	imprison	ein = sperren	encarcelar	incarcerare
encargo	charge	contribution	Abgaben(pl.)	carga	onere
encerar	cirer	polish	polieren, wachsen	dar crema	lucidare
encerramento	clôture	closure, closing	Schluß(m)(Abschluß m)	clausura	chiusura
encerrar, fechar	enfermer	shut in	ein = schließen	encerrar	rinchiudere
encher	remplir	fill	füllen	llenar	riempire
enciclopédia	encyclopédie	encyclopaedia	Enzyklopädie(f)	enciclopedia	enciclopedia
encolher	rétrécir	shrink	schrumpfen	encoger	restringere
encomenda	commande	order	Bestellung(f)	encargo, pedido	ordinazione
encomendar	commander	order	bestellen	pedir, encargar	ordinare
encontrar	rencontrer	meet	treffen	encontrar	incontrare
encontro	rencontre	meeting	Begegnung(f)	encuentro	incontro
encontro	rendez-vous	appointment	Verabredung(f)	cita	appuntamento
encorajar	encourager	encourage, urge	ermutigen	alentar, animar	incoraggiare
encosta; colina	coteau	hill(side)	Anhöhe(f), Hang(m)	ladera	colle, collinetta
encostado a	contre	against	gegen, an	contra	contro
endereço, morada	adresse	address	Anschrift(f), Adresse	dirección	indirizzo
endireitar	redresser	straighten out/up	gerade = biegen	enderezar	raddrizzare
energia	énergie	energy	Energie(f)	energía	energia
enervado, a	énervé, e	edgy, worked up	erregt, nervös	excitado, a	nervoso, a
enervar-se	énerver(s')	edgy, irritable(be)	auf = regen, sich	ponerse nervioso, a	innervosirsi
enfarte	infarctus	coronary	Infarkt(m)	infarto	infarto
enfermaria	infirmerie	infirmary	Krankenraum(m)	enfermería	infermeria
enfermeiro, a	infirmier, ière	nurse	Krankenpfleger(in f)m	enfermero, a	infermiere, a
enfraquecer	affaiblir	weaken	schwächen	debilitar	indebolire
enganar	tromper	deceive, cheat	betrügen	engañar	ingannare
enganar-se	tromper(se)	mistaken(be)	täuschen, sich	equivocarse	sbagliarsi
engarrafamento	encombrement	congestion, jam	Gedränge(n)	estorbo	affollamento, ingorgo

Portuguese	French	English	German	Spanish	Italian
engatar	accrocher	connect, link	an = hängen	enganchar	agganciare
engendrar	engendrer	generate	zeugen, erzeugen	engendrar	generare
engenharia	ingénierie	engineering	Ingenieurkunst(f)	ingeniería	ingegneria
engenheiro, a	ingénieur	engineer	Ingenieur(in f)m	ingeniero, a	ingegnere
engenhoso, a	ingénieux, se	ingenious	sinnreich	ingenioso, a	ingegnoso, a
engodo, isca	appât	bait	Köder(m)	cebo	esca
engolir	avaler	swallow	schlucken	tragar	inghiottire, ingoiare
engordar	grossir	put on weight	zu = nehmen	engordar	ingrassare
engraçado, a	amusant, e	amusing, funny	amüsant, drollig	divertido, a	divertente
engrenar	enclencher	engage	ein = legen, = schalten	engranar	ingranare, avviare
enigma	énigme	enigma	Rätsel(n)	enigma	enigma
enjoar	écoeurer	disgust	an = ekeln, an = widern	asquear	nauseare
enjôo	mal de mer	sea-sickness	Seekrankheit(f)	mareo	mal di mare
enojar	dégoûter	disgust	an = widern	asco(dar)	disgustare
enorme	énorme	enormous, huge	riesig	enorme	enorme
enquanto	pendant que	while	während	mientras	mentre; già che
enquanto	tandis que	while, whilst	während	mientras	mentre
enriquecer	enrichir	enrich	bereichern	enriquecer	arricchire
enrolar	enrouler	roll up	auf = wickeln	enrollar	arrotolare
ensaio	essai	trial, test	Versuch(m)	prueba	prova, collaudo
ensinar	enseigner	teach	lehren, unterrichten	enseñar	insegnare
ensino	enseignement	teaching	Unterricht(m), Lehre f	enseñanza	insegnamento
entalhe	encoche	notch	Kerbe(f), Einschnitt m	muesca	tacca, intacco
então	alors	then	dann	entonces	allora
entender	comprendre	understand	begreifen, verstehen	entender	comprendere
enterro	enterrement	burial, funeral	Beerdigung(f)	entierro	funerale
entoação	intonation	intonation	Tonfall(m)	entonación	intonazione
entornar	renverser	spill, knock over	verschütten	derramar, volcar	rovesciare
entorse	entorse	sprain	Verrenkung(f)	esguince	storta
entorse	foulure	sprain	Verstauchung(f)	esguince	slogatura
entrada	entrée	entry, entrance	Eintritt(m), Eingang m	entrada	ingresso
entrada, bilhete	entrée	admission	Eintrittskarte(f)	entrada	ingresso
entrar	entrer	enter, come/go in	ein = treten	entrar	entrare
entre!	entrez!	come in!	herein!	pase(!), adelante!	avanti!, prego!
entre	entre	between	zwischen	entre	tra, fra
entre	parmi	among	unter	entre	fra, tra
entrega	livraison	delivery	Lieferung(f)	entrega	consegna
entregar	livrer	deliver	liefern	entregar	consegnare
entretanto	attendant(en)	meanwhile	inzwischen	mientras	attesa(in)
entretanto	entre-temps	meanwhile, meantime	inzwischen	entretanto	intanto, frattanto
entrever	entrevoir	glimpse	flüchtig sehen	entrever	intravedere
entrevista	entrevue	interview	Treffen(n), Gespräch n	entrevista	intervista
entrevista	entretien	talk, conversation	Gespräch(n)	conversación	colloquio
entrevista	interview	interview	Interview(n)	interviú	intervista
entusiasmo	enthousiasme	enthusiasm	Begeisterung(f)	entusiasmo	entusiasmo
entusiasmo	entrain	liveliness	Schwung(m)	vivacidad	brio
enumerar	énumérer	enumerate	auf = zählen	enumerar	enumerare
envelope	enveloppe	envelope	Umschlag(m)(Brief-)	sobre	busta
envenenamento	empoisonnement	poisoning	Vergiftung(f)	envenenamiento	avvelenamento
enviar	envoyer	send	schicken, senden(ab =)	enviar	inviare
enviar, expedir	expédier, livrer	consign	übersenden	enviar, expedir	inviare
envio	envoi	sending	Sendung(f), Versand(m)	envío	invio
envio	émission	sending	Sendung(f)	envío	emissione
envolver	envelopper	wrap, envelop	ein = hüllen, ein = packen	envolver	avvolgere
envolver-se	mêler de(se)	interfere	ein = mischen, sich	implicarse	immischiare(-rsi)
enxaqueca	migraine	migraine, headache	Migräne(f)	jaqueca	emicrania
enxerto	greffe	graft	Veredelung; Pfropfen	injerto	innesto
enxerto	greffe	transplant, graft	Verpflanzung(f)	trasplante	trapianto
epidemia	épidémie	epidemic	Seuche(f)	epidemia	epidemia
epiderme	épiderme	epidermis, skin	Oberhaut(f), Haut(f)	epidermis	epidermide
epilepsia	épilepsie	epilepsy	Epilepsie(f)	epilepsia	epilessia
episódio	épisode	episode	Episode(f)	episodio	episodio
época	époque	epoch, era, time	Epoche(f), Ära(f), Zeit	época	epoca
epopeia	épopée	epic	Epos(n)	epopeya	epopea
equador	équateur	equator	Äquator(m)	ecuador	equatore
equatorial	équatorial, e	equatorial	äquatorial	ecuatorial	equatoriale
equestre	équestre	equestrian	Reiter-	ecuestre	equestre
equidade	équité	equity	Gerechtigkeit(f)	equidad	equità

P

Portuguese	French	English	German	Spanish	Italian
equilibrar	équilibrer	balance	aus = gleichen	equilibrar	equilibrare
equilíbrio	équilibre	balance	Gleichgewicht(n)	equilibrio	equilibrio
equipa, grupo	équipe	team	Mannschaft(f), Team(n)	equipo	squadra; équipe
equipagem	équipage	crew	Besatzung(f)	tripulación	equipaggio
equipamento	équipement	equipment	Ausstattung(f)	equipo	equipaggiamento
equipar	équiper	equip, fit out	aus = rüsten	equipar	equipaggiare
equitação	équitation	riding(horse -)	Reiten(n)	equitación	equitazione
equivalente	équivalent, e	equivalent	gleichwertig	equivalente	equivalente
equívoco, a	équivoque	equivocal	zweideutig	equívoco, a	equivoco, a
era	ère	era	Ära(f)	era	era
eremita	ermite	hermit	Einsiedler(in f)m	ermitaño	eremita
erigir	ériger	erect	errichten	erigir, levantar	erigere
erigir, erguer	dresser	erect, put up	auf = richten, errichten	erigir	drizzare
erosão	érosion	erosion	Abtragung(f)	erosión	erosione
erótico, a	érotique	erotic	erotisch	erótico, a	erotico, a
erotismo	érotisme	eroticism	Erotik(f)	erotismo	erotismo
erro	erreur	error, mistake	Irrtum(m), Fehler(m)	error	errore
erro(dar um)	erreur(faire)	mistake(make a)	Irrtum(m)(machen)	error(cometer un)	errore(fare un)
erudito, a	érudit, e	erudite, learned	gelehrt	erudito, a	erudito, a
erudito, a	érudit, e	scholar	Gelehrte(f, m)	erudito, a	dotto, a; erudito, a
erupção	éruption	eruption	Ausbruch(m)	erupción	eruzione
erva	herbe	grass	Gras(n)	hierba, yerba	erba
erva	herbe(s)	herb(s)	Kraut(n), Kräuter(pl.)	hierbas	erbe(aromatiche)
esbelto, a	svelte	slim, slender	schlank	esbelto, a	slanciato, a; snello, a
esboço	croquis	sketch(-es)	Skizze(f)	croquis	schizzo
escabelo, banco	tabouret	stool	Hocker(m)	taburete	sgabello
escada	échelle	ladder	Leiter(f)	escalera	scala
escada	escalier	staircase, stairs	Treppe(f)	escalera	scala
escafandro	scaphandre	diving-suit	Taucheranzug(m)	escafandra	scafandro
escala	échelle	scale	Tabelle(f), Skala(f)	escala	scala
escala	escale	stop(over)	Zwischenlandung(f)	escala	scalo
escama	écaille	scale	Schuppe(f)	escama	squama
escamoteável	escamotable	fold-away	zusammenklappbar	plegable	ribaltabile
escândalo	scandale	scandal	Skandal(m)	escándalo	scandalo
escapar-se	échapper	drop	entgleiten	irse, escaparse	sfuggire, scappare
escapar-se	échapper(s')	escape	fliehen	escapar(se)	scappare
escarpado, a	escarpé, e	steep	steil	escarpado, a	scosceso, a
escavar	fouiller	excavate	aus = graben	excavar	scavare
esclerose	sclérose	sclerosis(-ses)	Sklerose(f)	esclerósis	sclerosi
escoamento	écoulement	flow, outflow	Abfluß(m)	derrame, flujo	deflusso, scolo
escola	école	school	Schule(f)	escuela	scuola
escola preparatória	collège	comprehensive(Jnr)	Oberschule(f)	escuela(EGB)	scuola media
escolaridade	scolarité	schooling	Schulzeit(f)	escolaridad	scolarità
escolha	choix	choice	Wahl(f)	escogimiento	scelta
escolher	choisir	choose, select	aus = wählen	escoger	scegliere
escolher, triar	trier	sort(out)	sortieren	escoger, separar	scegliere, smistare
escoliose	scoliose	scoliosis	Skoliose(f)	escoliosis	scoliosi
escolta	escorte	escort	Gefolge(n)	escolta	scorta
escombros	décombres	ruins	Trümmer(m, pl)	escombros	macerie, rovine
escombros	éboulis	scree	Geröll(n)	escombros	detriti
esconder	cacher	hide	verstecken	esconder	nascondere
escorpião	scorpion	scorpion	Skorpion(m)	escorpión	scorpione
escorrega	toboggan	slide, chute	Rutschbahn(f)	tobogán	scivolo
escorregar	glisser	slip, slide	rutschen	resbalar	scivolare
escorrer	écouler(s')	run, flow	ab = fließen	correr, fluir	scorrere, defluire
escova	brosse	brush	Bürste(f)	cepillo	spazzola
escova de dentes	brosse à dents	toothbrush	Zahnbürste(f)	cepillo de dientes	spazzolino
escravatura	esclavage	slavery	Sklaverei(f)	esclavitud	schiavitù
escravo, a	esclave	slave	Sklave(m), Sklavin(f)	esclavo, a	schiavo, a
escrever	écrire	write	schreiben	escribir	scrivere
escrita	écriture	writing	Schrift(f)	escritura	scrittura
escritor, a	écrivain	writer	Schriftsteller(in f)m	escritor, a	scrittore, -trice
escritório	bureau	office	Büro(n)	despacho	ufficio
escritório	cabinet(avocat)	practice	Büro(n)(Anwaltsbüro)	despacho; bufete	studio(avvocato)
escrúpulo	scrupule	scruple	Skrupel(m)	escrúpulo	scrupolo
escrutínio	scrutin, vote	poll; ballot	Wahl(f), Abstimmung(f)	escrutinio	scrutinio
escultura	sculpture	sculpture	Skulptur(f)	escultura	scultura
escuro, a; sombrio, a	sombre; obscur, e	dark	dunkel	oscuro, a	scuro, a

Portuguese	French	English	German	Spanish	Italian
escutar	écouter	listen(to)	zu = hören, horchen	escuchar	ascoltare
esfera	bille	ball	Kugel(f)	bola	sfera
esfera	sphère	sphere	Sphäre(f)	esfera	sfera
esferográfica	stylo à bille	ball-point pen	Kugelschreiber(m)	bolígrafo	penna a sfera
esfomeado, a	affamé, e	starving, hungry	hungrig	hambriento, a	affamato, a
esforço	effort	effort	Anstrengung(f)	esfuerzo	sforzo
esforço	peine	trouble, effort	Anstrengung(f)	dificultad	fatica
esfregar	frotter	rub	reiben	frotar	strofinare, sfregare
esgotado, a	épuisé, e	exhausted	erschöpft	agotado, a	esausto, a
esgotado, a	épuisé, e	exhausted, run out	ausverkauft	agotado, a	esaurito, a
esgotamento	surmenage	overwork(ing)	Überarbeitung(f)	agotamiento	esaurimento
esgoto	égout	sewer, drain	Gulli, Abwasserkanäle	cloaca	fogna
esgrima	escrime	fencing	Fechten(n)	esgrima	scherma
esmagar	écraser	crush, flatten	zerquetschen	aplastar	schiacciare
esmagar-se	écraser(s')	crash	ab = stürzen	estrellarse	schiantare
esmalte	émail	enamel	Emaille(f), Glasur(f)	esmalte	smalto
esmeralda	émeraude	emerald	Smaragd(m)	esmeralda	smeraldo
esófago	oesophage	oesophagus	Speiseröhre(f)	esófago	esofago
espacial	spatial, e	space	Raum-	espacial	spaziale
espaço	espace	space, gap	Zwischenraum(m)	espacio	spazio
espaço	espace	space	Raum(m)	espacio	spazio
espaço	place	room	Platz(m)	sitio, espacio	spazio
espaçoso, a	spacieux, se	spacious	weiträumig	espacioso, a	spazioso, a
espada	épée	sword	Schwert(n)	espada	spada
espalhar	répandre	spread; spill	verschütten	derramar	spargere
espancar	assommer	knock out	nieder = schlagen	dejar k.o.	stordire
espancar	matraquer	beat up, club	prügeln	aporrear	manganellare
espantar	étonner	astonish, amaze	überraschen	sorprender	sorprendere
espantar-se	étonner(s')	astonished(be -)	wundern, sich	sorprenderse	meravigliarsi
espantoso, a	étonnant, e	surprising	erstaunlich	asombroso, a	sorprendente
esparadrapo	sparadrap	plaster	Pflaster(n)	esparadrapo	cerotto
espasmo	spasme	spasm	Krampf(m)	espasmo	spasma
espátula	spatule	spatula	Spachtel(f)	espátula	spatola
especial	spécial, e	special	speziell, eigen	especial	speciale
especialidade	spécialité	speciality	Spezialität(f)	especialidad	specialità
especialista	spécialiste	specialist	Spezialist(in f)m	especialista	specialista
especialista	spécialiste	expert, specialist	Fachmann(m)	especialista	specialista
especialmente	particulièrement	especially	besonders	especialmente	particolarmente
especiaria	épice(s)	spice	Gewürz(n)	especia	spezie
espécie	espèce	kind, sort	Gattung(f), Art(f)	especie	specie
espécie, género	sorte	sort, kind, type	Sorte(f), Art(f)	especie, género	specie, genere
espécie	espèce	species	Art(f)	especie	specie
especificar	spécifier	specify, state	spezifieren	especificar	specificare
específico, a	spécifique	specific	spezifisch	específico, a	specifico, a
espécime	spécimen	specimen	Muster(n); Exemplar(n)	espécimen	specimen
espectáculo	spectacle	show	Aufführung(f)	espectáculo	spettacolo
espectáculos	spectacles	entertainment	Unterhaltung(f)	espectáculos	spettacoli
espectador, a	spectateur, trice	spectator	Zuschauer(in f)m	espectador, a	spettatore, trice
especulação	spéculation	speculation	Spekulation(f)	especulación	speculazione
espeleologia	spéléologie	pot-holing	Höhlenforschung(f)	espeleología	speleologia
espelho	miroir	mirror	Spiegel(m)	espejo	specchio
espera	attente	wait(ing)	Warten(n)	espera	attesa
esperança	espoir	hope	Hoffnung(f)	esperanza	speranza
esperar, desejar	espérer	hope	hoffen	esperar, desear	sperare
esperar	attendre	wait(for)	warten	esperar	aspettare
esperar	attendre	expect	erwarten	esperar	aspettare
esperar	attendre à(s')	expect	rechnen, mit etwas	esperar(se)	aspettarsi
espere!	attendez!	wait!	Moment bitte!	espere(!)	aspetti!
esperma	sperme	sperm	Sperma(n)	esperma	sperma
esperto, a; astuto, a	malin, igne	smart, clever	gerissen, schlau	pillo, a; astuto, a	furbo, a
espesso, a	épais, se	thick	dick	espeso, a	spesso, a
espessura	épaisseur	thickness	Stärke(f), Dicke(f)	espesor	spessore
espeto	broche	spit	Spieß(m)	asador	spiedo
espião, espia	espion, ne	spy	Spion(m), Spionin(f)	espía	spia
espingarda	fusil	shot-gun, rifle	Gewehr(n)	fusil	fucile
espingarda	carabine	rifle	Gewehr(n), Karabiner m	carabina	carabina
espinha	arête	fish-bone, bone	Gräte(f)	espina	lisca
espinho	épine	thorn	Dorn(m); Stachel(m)	espina	spina

Portuguese	French	English	German	Spanish	Italian
espionagem	espionnage	spying, espionage	Spionage(f)	espionaje	spionaggio
espiral	spirale	spiral	Spirale(f)	espiral	spirale
espírito	esprit	mind	Sinn(m)	espíritu	mente
espírito	esprit	spirit	Geist(m)	espíritus	spirito
espiritual	spirituel, le	spiritual	geistreich	espiritual	spirituale
espirrar	éternuer	sneeze	niesen	estornudar	starnutire
esplêndido, a	splendide	splendid	glänzend	espléndido, a	splendido, a
esponja	éponge	sponge	Schwamm(m)	esponja	spugna
esponjoso, a	spongieux, se	spongy	schwammig	esponjoso, a	spugnoso, a
espontâneo, a	spontané, e	spontaneous	spontan	espontáneo, a	spontaneo, a
esposa	épouse	wife(wives)	Gattin, Frau, Ehefrau f	esposa	sposa, consorte
esposo	époux	husband	Gatte, Mann, Ehemann m	esposo	sposo, consorte
espreita de(à)	affût	wait for(in)	Versteck(n)	acecho(al)	agguato
espuma	écume	foam, froth	Schaum(m), Gischt(f)	espuma	schiuma
espuma	mousse	froth, foam	Schaum(m)	espuma	schiuma
esquadra	poste de police	police station	Polizeiwache(f)	cuartelillo	posto di guardia
esquadra(polícia)	commissariat	police station	Kommissariat(n)	comisaría	commissariato
esquadrão	escadron	squadron	Schwadron; Eskadron(f)	escuadrón	squadrone; squadra
esquadro	équerre	square(set -)	Zeichendreieck(n)	escuadra	squadra
esquecer	oublier	forget	vergessen	olvidar	dimenticare
esqueleto	squelette	skeleton	Skelett(n)	esqueleto	scheletro
esquema	schéma	diagram	Schema(n)	esquema	schema
esquerdo, a	gauche	left	links; linke(r, s)	izquierdo, a	sinistro, a
esqui	ski	ski	Ski(m)	esquí	sci
esqui aquático	ski nautique	water-skiing	Wasserski(m)	esquí acuático	sci nautico
esquiar	skier	ski	skifahren	esquiar	sciare
esquilo	écureuil	squirrel	Eichhörnchen(n)	ardilla	scoiattolo
esquimó	esquimau	Eskimo	Eskimo(m)	esquimal	eschimese
esse(a); aquele(a)	celui-là, celle-	that one	der(jenige); die( )	ése, ésa, éso(s)	quello, quella
essencial	essentiel, le	essential	wesentlich	esencial	essenziale
essencial	essentiel	main thing(the)	Hauptsache(f)	esencial	essenziale
estabelecer	établir	establish	festsetzen, aufstellen	establecer	stabilire
estabelecer-se	établir(s')	settle; set up	an = siedeln, sich	establecerse	stabilirsi
estabelecimento	établissement	establishment	Anstalt(f)	establecimiento	stabilimento
estabilidade	stabilité	stability	Stabilität(f)	estabilidad	stabilità
estaca	pieu, poteau	stake, post	Pfahl(m)	estaca	palo, piolo
estaca	piquet	post, stake, peg	Pfahl(m)	estaca	picchetto
estação	station	station	Station(f)	estación	stazione
estação	station	resort	Erholungsort(m)	estación	stazione
estação, gare	gare	station	Bahnhof(m)	estación	stazione
estação	saison	season	Jahreszeit(f)	estación	stagione
estação de serviço	station-service	service station	Tankstelle(f)	estación(servicio)	stazione di servizio
estacionamento	stationnement	parking	Parken(n)	estacionamiento	sosta
estacionar	garer	park	parken	aparcar	posteggiare
estacionar	stationner	park	parken	estacionarse	stazionare
estadia, estada	séjour	stay	Aufenthalt(m)	estancia	soggiorno
estádio	stade	stadium	Stadium(n)	estadio	stadio
estado	état	condition	Zustand(m)	condición	condizione
estado	état	state	Staat(m)	estado	stato
estagiário	stagiaire	trainee	Praktikant(in f)m	cursillista	apprendista
estágio	stage	training period	Praktikum(n).	cursillo	tirocinio, stage
está lá?; estou ?	allô!	hello!	Ja, bitte?	dígame(!)	pronto!
estaladela	félure	crack	Sprung(m), Riß(m)	raja, grieta	incrinatura
estalado, a	craquelé, e	crackled, cracked	rissig	agrietado, a	screpolato, a
estalagem	auberge	inn	Gasthaus(n)	posada; albergue	locanda
estalar	craquer	crack	krachen	crujir	scricchiolare
estanco, tabacaria	bureau de tabac	tobacconist's	Tabakladen(m)	estanco	tabaccheria
estanho	étain	tin; pewter	Zinn(n)	estaño	stagno
estanque	étanche	watertight(air-)	undurchlässig	estanco, a	stagno, a
estante	bibliothèque	bookcase	Bücherschrank(m)	biblioteca	libreria
estar	être	be	sein	estar	essere
estar bem	convenir	suit, fit	passen	convenir	convenire
estático, a	statique	static	statisch	estático, a	statico, a
estatística	statistique(s)	statistics	Statistik(f)	estadística	statistica
estátua	statue	statue	Statue(f)	estatua	statua
estatura	taille, grandeur	height, size	Größe(f)	talla, estatura	statura
estatuto	statut	status; statute	Status(m); Statut(n)	estatuto	statuto
este, a; esse, a	ce, cette	this, that	dieser, diese	este; esta; estos, as	questo, a; quello, a

Portuguese	French	English	German	Spanish	Italian
este, esta, estes	ce, cette, ces	that, those	dieser, diese, dieses	ese, esa, esos(as)	quello, a; questo, a
este; esta; estes, as	cet, cette	this, that	dieser, diese	éste; ésta; éstos	questo, a; quello, a
este, esta	celui-ci, celle-	this one	diese(r, s)(hier)	éste, ésta	questo, questa
Este, Leste	Est	East	Osten(m)	Este	Est
esteira	sillage	wake	Kielwasser(n)	estela	scia
estender	étendre	extend, spread	aus = breiten	extender	stendere
estender	étendre, agrandir	expand	aus = dehnen	extender(se)	estendere
estender, esticar	tendre	tighten; stretch	spannen	tender	tendere
estender-se	allonger(s')	lie down	hin = legen, sich	acostarse	sdraiarsi
estender-se	étendre(s')	stretch	erstrecken, sich	extenderse	estendersi
estepe	steppe	steppe	Steppe(f)	estepa	steppa
estereofonia	stéréo	stereo	Stereo(f)	estéreo	stereo
estéril	stérile	sterile	steril	estéril	sterile
esterilete	stérilet	coil	Spirale(f)	espiral	spirale
estes, as; esses, as	ces	these, those	diese(pl)	estos, as; esos, as	questi, e
estes(as); esses(as)	ceux-ci, celles-	these; those	diese; jene	éstos; ésos	questi; quelli
estético, a	esthétique	aesthetic	ästhetisch	estético, a	estetico, a
esticado, a	tendu, e	tight	gespannt	tenso, a	teso, a
esticar, estirar	étirer	stretch	aus = dehnen	estirar	stirare
estilo	style	style	Stil(m)	estilo	stile
estima	estime	esteem	Achtung(f)	estima	stima
estimar	estimer	estimate, value	schätzen	valorar, estimar	stimare, valutare
estimativa	estimation	estimate	Schätzung(f)	estimación	stima, valutazione
estimular	stimuler	stimulate	reizen, an = regen	estimular	stimolare
estival	estival, e	summer	sommerlich	estival	estivo, a
estojo	coffret	box, case	Schmuckkasten(m)	estuche	portagioie
estojo	trousse	kit, case, bag	Etui(n), Tasche(f)	maletín, estuche	borsa, astuccio
estojo	étui	case	Etui(n)	estuche	astuccio
estômago	estomac	stomach	Magen(m)	estómago	stomaco
estore	store	blind; shade	Vorhang m; Jalousie f	toldo; persiana	tapparella
estrábico, a(ser)	loucher	squint	schielen	bizquear	strabico, a(essere)
estrada	route	road	Straße(f)	carretera	strada
estrada	route nationale	main/trunk road	Landstraße(f)	carretera	strada statale
estrado	podium	podium, stage	Podest(n)	podio	podio
estragar	abîmer	damage, spoil, ruin	beschädigen	estropear	sciupare, rovinare
estragar	endommager	damage	beschädigen	dañar	danneggiare
estrago	dégât(s)	damage	Schaden(m)	daño(s), estrago(s)	danno
estrago	ravage	devastation	Verwüstung(f)	destrozo	devastazione
estrangeiro, a	étranger, ère	foreign	ausländisch	extranjero, a	estero, a
estrangeiro, a	étranger, ère	foreigner	Ausländer(in f)m	extranjero, a	straniero, a
estrangeiro	étranger(l')	foreign country	Ausland(n)	extranjero	estero
estrangeiro(ao)	étranger(à l')	abroad	Ausland(im)	extranjero(en el)	estero(all')
estrangulamento	étranglement	strangling	Erwürgen(n)	estrangulación	strangolamento
estranho, a	étrange	strange, odd	seltsam	extraño, a; raro, a	strano, a
estranho, a	bizarre	strange, odd	seltsam	raro, a	strano, a
estratégia	stratégie	strategy	Strategie(f)	estrategia	strategia
estreitar	resserrer	narrow	verengen	estrechar	ristringere
estreitar-se	rétrécir(se)	narrow	enger machen/werden	estrechar(se)	restringersi
estreito	détroit	strait	Meerenge(f)	estrecho	stretto
estreito, a	étroit, e	narrow	eng	estrecho, a	stretto, a
estrela	étoile	star	Stern(m)	estrella	stella
estrito, a	strict, e	strict	streng	estricto, a	stretto, a
estrume	fumier	manure	Mist(m)	estiércol	letame
estrutura	structure	structure	Struktur(f)	estructura	struttura
estudante	étudiant, e	student	Student(in f)m	estudiante	studente, -essa
estudar	étudier	study	studieren	estudiar	studiare
estudar, examinar	étudier, examiner	investigate	prüfen, erforschen	estudiar	studiare
estúdio	studio	studio	Studio(n)	estudio	studio
estudioso, a	studieux, se	studious	fleißig	estudioso, a	studioso, a
estudo	étude	study; survey	Studie(f)	estudio	studio
estupefacção	stupeur	stupor	Erstaunen(n)	estupor	stupore
estupefacto, a	stupéfait, e	amazed	verblüfft	estupefacto, a	stupefatto, a
estupendo, a	épatant, e	wonderful, super	großartig, fabelhaft	estupendo, a	straordinario, a
estupidez	sottise	silliness	Dummheit(f)	tontería	sciocchezza
estúpido, a	stupide	stupid, silly	dumm	estúpido, a	stupido, a
esvaziar	vider	empty	leeren	vaciar	vuotare
etapa	étape	stage	Strecke(f)	etapa	tappa
eternidade	éternité	eternity	Ewigkeit(f)	eternidad	eternità

P

Portuguese	French	English	German	Spanish	Italian
eterno, a	éternel, le	eternal	ewig	eterno, a	eterno, a
ético, a	éthique	ethical	ethisch	ético, a	etico, a
étnico, a	ethnique	ethnic(al)	ethnisch	étnico, a	etnico, a
eu	je	I	ich	yo	io
eu; me; mim	moi	me; I	mich; mir; ich	mí, me; yo	io; me
eufórico, a	euphorique	euphoric	euphorisch	eufórico, a	euforico, a
eutanásia	euthanasie	euthanasia	Euthanasie(f)	eutanasia	eutanasia
evacuar	évacuer	evacuate	räumen, leeren	evacuar	evacuare
evaporação	évaporation	evaporation	Verdunstung(f)	evaporación	evaporazione
evasão	évasion	escape	Flucht(f)	evasión	evasione
eventual	éventuel, le	possible	möglich	eventual	eventuale
eventualidade	éventualité	contingency	Eventualität(f)	eventualidad	eventualità
evidência, prova	évidence, preuve	evidence, proof	Beweis(m)	evidencia, prueba	testimonianza, prova
evidente	évident, e	obvious, evident	offensichtlich	evidente	evidente
evidentemente	évidemment	of course	natürlich	desde luego	evidentemente
evitar	éviter	avoid	vermeiden	evitar	evitare
evocar	évoquer	evoke	wach = rufen, erinnern	evocar	evocare
evolução	évolution	evolution	Entwicklung(f)	evolución	evoluzione
evoluir	évoluer	evolve	entwickeln, sich	evolucionar	evolvere
exactamente	exactement	exactly	genau, richtig; gerade	exactamente	esattamente
exactidão	exactitude	accuracy	Genauigkeit(f)	exactitud	esattezza
exacto, a	exact, e	exact, right	genau, richtig	exacto, a	esatto, a
exacto, a	précis, e	precise, accurate	genau	preciso, a	preciso, a
exacto, a	exact, e	accurate	genau; richtig	exacto, a	accurato, a
exacto(é)	exact (c'est)	right(that 's)	stimmt!	exacto(es)	esatto(è)
exagerar	exagérer	exaggerate	übertreiben	exagerar	esagerare
exame	examen	examination, exam	Prüfung(f)	examen	esame
exame	examen(médical)	examination	Untersuchung(f)	examen, chequeo	esame
examinar	examiner	examine, inspect	untersuchen	examinar	esaminare
examinar	contrôler	inspect	besichtigen	controlar, examinar	esaminare
excedente	excédent	surplus, excess	Überschuß(m)	excedente	eccedente
Excelência(Vossa)	Excellence, Votre	Excellency(Your)	Exzellenz(f)	Excelencia(Su)	Eccellenza(Sua)
excelente	excellent, e	excellent	vorzüglich	excelente	eccellente
excepção	exception	exception	Ausnahme(f)	excepción	eccezione
excepcional	exceptionnel, le	exceptional	außergewöhnlich	excepcional	eccezionale
excepto	excepté	except	außer	excepto, salvo	tranne
excerto, trecho	extrait	extract	Auszug(m)	pasaje, trozo	brano, estratto
excessivo, a	excessif, ive	excessive	übermäßig	excesivo, a	eccessivo, a
excesso	excès	excess	Übermaß(n)	exceso	eccesso
excitado, a	excité, e	worked up	gereizt	excitado, a	eccitato, a
excitante	excitant, e	exciting	aufregend	excitante	eccitante
excitar	exciter	excite	auf = regen	excitar	eccitare
exclamar	exclamer(s')	exclaim	aus = rufen	exclamar	esclamare
excluir	exclure	exclude	aus = schließen	excluir	escludere
exclusividade	exclusivité	exclusive rights	Alleinvertrieb(m)	exclusiva(-ividad)	esclusività
exclusivo, a	exclusif, ive	exclusive	ausschließlich	exclusivo, a	esclusivo, a
excremento	excrément	excrement	Ausscheidung(f)	excremento	escremento
excursão	excursion	excursion	Ausflug(m)	excursión	gita, escursione
execução	exécution	execution	Hinrichtung(f)	ejecución	esecuzione
executar	exécuter	perform, carry out	aus = führen	ejecutar	eseguire
executivo, a	exécutif, ive	executive	ausübend, vollziehend	ejecutivo, a	esecutivo, a
exemplo	exemple	example	Beispiel(n)	ejemplo	esempio
exemplo(por)	exemple(par)	instance(for)	Beispiel(zum)	ejemplo(por)	esempio(per)
exercício	exercice	exercise	Übung(f)	ejercicio	esercizio
exercitar	exercer	exercise, practise	aus = üben	ejercitar	esercitare
exército	armée	army	Armee(f)	ejército	esercito
exibição	exhibition	exhibition	Schau, Ausstellung(f)	exhibición	esibizione
exigência	exigence	demand, requirement	Forderung(f)	exigencia	esigenza
exigir	exiger, réclamer	demand, require	fordern	exigir	esigere
exigir, pedir	exiger, demander	demand	verlangen, fordern	exigir, demandar	esigere, domandare
exilado, a	exilé, e	exile	Verbannte(f, m)	exiliado, a	esiliato, a
exilio	exil	exile	Verbannung(f)	exilio	esilio
existência	existence	existence, life	Dasein(n)	existencia	esistenza
existir	exister	exist	existieren	existir	esistere
êxito	réussite	success(-es)	Erfolg(m)	éxito, logro	riuscita
êxodo	exode	exodus	Massenauswanderung(f)	éxodo	esodo
exótico, a	exotique	exotic	exotisch	exótico, a	esotico, a
expansão	expansion	expansion	Ausdehnung(f)	expansión	espansione

Portuguese	French	English	German	Spanish	Italian
expatriação	expatriation	expatriation	Vertreibung(f)	expatriación	espatrio
expatriar-se	expatrier(s')	expatriate	aus = wandern	expatriarse	espatriare
expedição	expédition	expedition	Expedition(f)	expedición	spedizione
expedidor	expéditeur	sender	Absender(in f)m	remitente	mittente
expedir	expédier	dispatch, send	verschicken	expedir	spedire
expelir	éjecter	eject	aus = stoßen	eyectar, expulsar	espellere
experiência	expérience	experience	Erfahrung(f)	experiencia	esperienza
experiência	expérience	experiment	Versuch(m)	experimento	esperimento
experimentação	expérimentation	experimentation	Experimentieren(n)	experimentación	sperimentazione
experimental	expérimental, e	experimental	experimentell	experimental	sperimentale
expirar	expirer	die	verscheiden	expirar	spirare
expirar	expirer	breathe out	aus = atmen	espirar	espirare
expirar	expirer	expire	ab = laufen	expirar; vencer	scadere
explicação	explication	explanation	Erklärung(f)	explicación	spiegazione
explicação, precisão	précision	clarification	Klarstellung(f)	aclaración	precisazione
explicar	expliquer	explain	erklären	explicar	spiegare
explodir	exploser	explode, blow up	explodieren	estallar	esplodere
exploração	exploration	exploration	Erforschung(f)	exploración	esplorazione
explorador, a	explorateur	explorer	Forscher(in f)m	explorador, a	esploratore, trice
explorar	explorer	explore	erforschen	explorar	esplorare
explorar	exploiter	exploit	aus = nutzen	explotar	sfruttare
explosão	explosion	explosion	Explosion(f)	explosión	esplosione
expor	étaler	spread(out)	aus = breiten	exponer	stendere, spalmare
exportação	exportation	export(ing)	Export(m), Ausfuhr(f)	exportación	esportazione
exportar	exporter	export	exportieren	exportar	esportare
exposição	exposition	exhibition, show	Ausstellung(f)	exposición	esposizione, mostra
exposição	exposé	talk, commentary	Referat(n)	exposición	relazione; esposto
expositor, a	exposant, e	exhibitor	Aussteller(in f)m	expositor, a	espositore, trice
expressão	expression	expression	Ausdruck(m)	expresión	espressione
exprimir-se	exprimer(s')	express oneself	aus = drücken, sich	expresar(se)	esprimersi
expulsar	expulser	expel, eject	aus = weisen	expulsar	espellere
êxtase	extase	ecstasy	Entzückung(f)	éxtasis	estasi
extensão	extension	extension	Ausdehnung(f)	extensión	estensione
extensão	étendue	extent	Umfang(m)	extensión, amplitud	estensione, ampiezza
extenuado, a	exténué, e	exhausted	erschöpft	extenuado, a	spossato, a
exterior; externo, a	extérieur, e	outer, outside	äußere	externo, a	esterno, a
exterior	extérieur, e	outside	äußer; Außen-	exterior	esteriore
exterior	extérieur, e	foreign	Außen-	exterior	estero, a
exterior	extérieur	outside; exterior	Außenseite(f)	exterior	esterno
externo, a	externe	external	äußerlich	externo, a	esterno, a
extinção	extinction	extinction	Löschen(Aus-)(n)	extinción	estinzione
extintor	extincteur	extinguisher	Feuerlöscher(m)	extintor	estintore
extracção	extraction	extraction	Kohlenförderung(f)	extracción	estrazione
extracção	extraction	extraction	Zahnziehen(n)	extracción	estrazione
extracto(conta)	relevé(compte)	statement(bank)	Kontoauszug(m)	estado(cuentas)	estratto conto
extrair	extraire	extract	heraus = ziehen, ziehen	extraer	estrarre
extraordinário, a	extraordinaire	extraordinary	außergewöhnlich	extraordinario, a	straordinario, a
extravasar	déborder	overflow	über die Ufer treten	salirse de madre	straripare
extremidade	extrémité	extremity, end	Extremität(f)	extremidad	estremità
extremo, a	extrême	extreme	extrem	extremo, a	estremo, a

F

Portuguese	French	English	German	Spanish	Italian
fábrica	usine	factory, plant	Fabrik(f)	fábrica	fabbrica
fábrica	usine	plant	Anlage(f)	fábrica	fabbrica
fabricante	fabricant, e	manufacturer	Hersteller(in f)m	fabricante	fabbricante
fabricar	fabriquer	manufacture, make	her = stellen	fabricar	fabbricare

Portuguese	French	English	German	Spanish	Italian
fabrico	fabrication	manufacture	Herstellung(f)	fabricación	fabbricazione
fabuloso, a	fabuleux, se	fabulous	phantastisch	fabuloso, a	favoloso, a
faca	couteau	knife(-ives)	Messer(n)	cuchillo	coltello
face; lado	face	side	Seite(f)	cara	faccia
face; cara	face	face	Gesicht(n)	cara	faccia
fachada	façade	front(age)	Fassade(f)	fachada	facciata
fácil	facile	easy	leicht	fácil	facile
fácilmente	facilement	easily	leicht	fácilmente	facilmente
facto	fait	fact	Tatsache(f)	hecho	fatto
factor	facteur	factor	Faktor(m)	factor	fattore
factura	facture	invoice, bill	Rechnung(f)	factura	fattura
faculdade	faculté	possibility	Fähigkeit(f)	facultad	facoltà
faculdade	faculté	Faculty	Fakultät(f)	facultad	facoltà
facultativo, a	facultatif, ive	optional	wahlfrei, beliebig	facultativo, a	facoltativo, a
fada	fée	fairy	Fee(f)	hada	fata
faisão	faisan	pheasant	Fasan(m)	faisán	fagiano
faísca	étincelle	spark	Funken(m)	chispa	scintilla
faixa(rua)	voie	lane	Spur(f)(Straßen-)	vía	corsia
fala(a)	parler(le)	speech	Sprechen(n); Sprache f	habla(el)	parlare(il)
fala, conversa	propos	words, talk	Worte(pl.)	palabras	parole, discorsi
falador, a	bavard, e	talkative	geschwätzig	parlanchín, a	chiacchierone, a
falar	parler	speak, talk	sprechen, reden	hablar	parlare
falar com	parler à	talk to, speak to	reden(mit jdm)	hablar con	parlare a
falar, conversar	bavarder	chat, talk	schwätzen, schwatzen	charlar	chiacchierare
falecer	décéder	die	versterben, sterben	fallecer	decedere
falecimento	décès	death	Tod(m)	fallecimiento	decesso
falência	faillite	failure; bankruptcy	Konkurs(m)	quiebra, ruina	fallimento
falésia	falaise	cliff	Steilküste(f)	acantilado	scogliera
falha	faille	break, fault	Spalte(f)	falla	faglia
falha	défaillance	failure, fault	Versagen(n)	fallo	difetto
falhar	rater	fail	mißlingen	fallar	mancare
falhar	échouer	fail	scheitern	fracasar	fallire
falir	faillite(faire)	bankrupt(go)	bankrott sein	quiebra(hacer)	fallire
falsificação	truquage	faking	Trickaufnahme(f)	falsificación	trucco
falsificar	falsifier	falsify	fälschen	falsificar	falsificare
falso, a	faux, fausse	wrong, false	falsch	falso, a	falso, a
falta, erro	faute, erreur	mistake, error	Fehler(m), Irrtum(m)	falta, error	fallo, errore
falta, carência	manque	lack, shortage	Mangel(m)	falta, carencia	mancanza
falta(ter)	manquer	lack, be short of	fehlen	faltar	mancare
fama	renommée	fame	Ruhm(m)	fama	fama
família	famille	family	Familie(f)	familia	famiglia
familiar	familial, e	family	Familien-	familiar	familiare
familiar	familier, ière	familiar	familiär	familiar	familiare
famoso, a	fameux, se	excellent	großartig	famoso, a	ottimo, a
fanático, a	fanatique	fanatic(al)	fanatisch	fanático, a	fanatico, a
fanfarra, banda	fanfare	brass band	Fanfare(f)	banda	banda
fantasia	fantaisie	fancy; fantasy	Spielerei(f)	fantasía	fantasia
fantasma	fantôme	ghost	Gespenst(n)	fantasma	fantasma
fantasma	fantasme	fantasy	Phantasievorstellung	fantasma	fantasia
fantástico, a	fantastique	fantastic	phantastisch	fantástico, a	fantastico, a
fantoche	pantin	puppet	Hampelmann(m)	títere	burattino
fardo	fardeau	burden	Last(f)	carga	fardello
farejar, cheirar	flairer	sniff; scent; sense	wittern, schnüffeln	olfatear, husmear	annusare
faringe	pharynx	pharynx	Rachen(m)	faringe	faringe
farinha	farine	flour	Mehl(n)	harina	farina
farmacêutico, a	pharmacien, ne	chemist, pharmacist	Apotheker(in f)m	farmacéutico, a	farmacista
farmácia	pharmacie	chemist's	Apotheke(f)	farmacia	farmacia
faróis	phare(s)	headlight	Scheinwerfer(m)	faro(s)	fanale, faro(-ri)
farol	phare	lighthouse	Leuchtturm(m)	faro	faro
fascinado, a	fasciné, e	fascinated	fasziniert	fascinado, a	affascinato, a
fascinante	fascinant, e	fascinating	faszinierend	fascinante	affascinante
fascista	fasciste	fascist	Faschist(in f)m	fascista	fascista
fase	phase	phase, stage	Phase(f)	fase	fase
fatal	fatal, e	fatal	tödlich	fatal	fatale
fatalidade	fatalité	fatality, fate	Schicksal(n)	fatalidad	fatalità
fatia	tranche	slice	Scheibe(f)	rebanada	fetta
fatia de pão	tartine de pain	slice of bread	Brotscheibe(f)	rebanada de pan	fetta di pane
fatiga, cansaço	fatigue	tiredness	Müdigkeit(f)	cansancio	stanchezza

Portuguese	French	English	German	Spanish	Italian
fato, traje	habit(s)	clothes	Kleidung(f)	vestido, traje	vestito(i), abiti
fato, traje	costume	suit	Anzug(m)	traje	abito, vestito
fato(espacial)	combinaison	suit(ski-)	Anzug(m)(Ski-)	traje	tuta, completo
fato(espacial)	combinaison	suit(space-)	Anzug(Raum-)(m)	traje(espacial)	tuta(spaziale)
fato de banho	maillot de bain	swimsuit; trunks	Badeanzug(m)	traje de baño	costume da bagno
fauna	faune	fauna	Fauna(f), Tierwelt(f)	fauna	fauna
faustoso, a	fastueux, se	sumptuous	prunkvoll	ostentoso, a	fastoso, a
favor	faveur	favour	Gunst(f)	favor	favore
favorável	favorable	favourable	günstig	favorable	favorevole
favorecer	favoriser	favour	begünstigen	favorecer	favorire
favorito, a	favori, ite	favourite	Favorit(in f)m	favorito, a	favorito, a
fazer	faire	do, make	tun, machen	hacer	fare
fazer	faire	make, do	machen, tun	hacer	fare
fazer	opérer	operate	wirken	efectuar	operare
fazer(exame)	passer(examen)	take(an exam)	ab = legen(Prüfung f)	pasar(un examen)	dare(un esame)
fé	foi	faith	Glaube(m)	fe	fede
febre	fièvre	fever, temperature	Fieber(n)	fiebre	febbre
fechado, a	fermé, e	closed, shut	zu, geschlossen	cerrado, a	chiuso, a
fechadura	serrure	lock	Schloß(Tür-)(n)	cerradura	serratura
fechar, cerrar	fermer	close, shut	schließen	cerrar	chiùdere
fechar	fermer	shut	zu = machen	cerrar	chiùdere
fechar à chave	fermer à clé	lock	ab = schließen	cerrar con llave	chiudere a chiave
fecho	poignée	handle	Griff(m)	manilla, mango	maniglia
fecundação	fécondation	fertilization	Befruchtung(f)	fecundación	fecondazione
fecundidade	fécondité	fertility	Fruchtbarkeit(f)	fecundidad	fecondità
federação	fédération	federation	Verband(m)	federación	federazione
fedor	puanteur	stench, stink	Gestank(m)	hedor, peste	puzza, fetore
feição	trait(s)	feature	Zug(m)(Gesichts-)	rasgos	tratto, lineamento
feijão	haricot	bean	Bohne(f)	judía	fagiolo; fagiolino
feio, a	laid, e; moche	ugly, hideous	häßlich, gräßlich	feo, a	brutto, a
feira	foire	fair	Messe(f)	feria	fiera
felicidade	bonheur	happiness	Glück(n)	felicidad	felicità
felicitar	féliciter	congratulate	gratulieren	felicitar	congratularsi
feliz	heureux, se	happy, glad	glücklich	feliz	felice
felizmente	heureusement	fortunately	glücklicherweise	afortunadamente	fortunatamente
fêmea	femelle	female	Weibchen(n)	hembra	femmina
feminino, a	féminin, e	feminine	fraulich	femenino, a	femminile
feminino	féminin	feminine	weiblich	femenino	femminile
fenda	crevasse	crevice	Spalte(f)	grieta	crepa, crepaccio
fenda	fente	split; slot; slit	Spalt(m)	grieta	fessura
fenda	fente	slit	Schlitz(m)	raja	fessura; spacco
fender, rachar	fendre	split, slit	spalten	rajar, partir	spaccare
fenómeno	phénomène	phenomenon(-mena)	Phänomen(n)	fenómeno	fenomeno
feriado(dia)	férié(jour)	public holiday	Feiertag(m)	festivo(día)	festivo(giorno)
férias	vacances	holidays	Ferien(pl.)	vacaciones	vacanze
férias	vacances	vacation	Ferien(pl.)	vacaciones	vacanze
férias	congé(s)	holiday, vacation	Urlaub(m)	vacaciones	ferie(le)
ferida	blessure	injury, wound	Verletzung(f)	herida	ferita
ferida	plaie	wound; cut	Wunde(f)	llaga, herida	piaga
ferir	blesser	injure, wound	verletzen	herir	ferire
ferir-se	blesser(se)	injured(to be)	verletzen, sich	herir(se)	ferirsi
fermentar	fermenter	ferment	gären	fermentar	fermentare
feroz	féroce	ferocious, fierce	wild, furchtbar	feroz	feroce
ferramenta	outil	tool	Werkzeug(n)	herramienta	attrezzo
ferramentas	outillage	tools, equipment	Werkzeug(n)	herramientas	attrezzatura
ferro	fer	iron	Eisen(n)	hierro	ferro
ferro de passar	fer à repasser	iron	Bügeleisen(n)	plancha	ferro da stiro
ferrolho	verrou	bolt, lock	Riegel(m), Schloß(n)	cerrojo	catenaccio
ferrugem	rouille	rust	Rost(m)	herrumbre	ruggine
fértil	fertile	fertile	fruchtbar	fértil	fertile
fervente	bouillant, e	boiling	kochend	hirviente	bollente
ferver	bouillir	boil	kochen	hervir	bollire
fervura	ébullition	boiling	Kochen(n)	ebullición	ebollizione
festa	fête	celebration	Feier(f)	fiesta	festa
festim, banquete	festin	feast, banquet	Festmahl(n)	festín	festino
festival	festival	festival	Festspiel(n)	festival	festival
feto	foetus	foetus	Fötus(m)	feto	feto
feto	fougère	fern	Farn(-kraut n)m	helecho	felce

P

Portuguese	French	English	German	Spanish	Italian
Fevereiro	Février	February	Februar(m)	Febrero	Febbraio
fiambre	jambon	ham	Schinken(m)	jamón	prosciutto
fibra	fibre	fibre	Faser(f)	fibra	fibra
ficar	rester	stay, remain	bleiben	quedarse	restare
ficar mal(exame)	échouer(examen)	fail	durch = fallen	suspender	bocciare
ficar noivo, a	fiançer(se)	engaged(get)	verloben, sich	prometerse	fidanzarsi
ficção	fiction	fiction	Fiktion(f)	ficción	finzione
ficha	fiche	card	Karteikarte(f)	ficha	scheda, cartella
ficha	jeton	counter, token	Spielmarke(f)	ficha	gettone
ficheiro	fichier	card-index	Kartei(f)	fichero	schedario
fiel	fidèle	faithful	treu	fiel	fedele
fígado	foie	liver	Leber(f)	hígado	fegato
figura	figure	figure	Figur(f)	figura	figura
fila	file	lane	Spur(f)	fila	fila, corsia
fila, bicha	file	queue, line	Schlange(f)	fila	fila, coda
filamento	filament	filament	Faser(f), Faden(m)	filamento	filamento
fileira, renque	rangée	row	Reihe(f)	hilera, fila	fila
filha	fille	daughter	Tochter(f)	hija	figlia
filho	fils	son	Sohn(m)	hijo	figlio
filial, sucursal	filiale	subsidiary	Filiale(f)	filial, sucursal	filiale
filmagem	tournage	shooting	Filmaufnahme(f)	rodaje	riprese
filmar	filmer	film	filmen	rodar, filmar	filmare
filme	film	film, movie	Film(m)	película	film
filosofia	philosophie	philosophy	Philosophie(f)	filosofía	filosofia
filtro	filtre	filter	Filter(m)	filtro	filtro
fim	fin	end	Ende(n)	fin	fine
fim, intento	but	aim, purpose	Ziel(n)	propósito	scopo
fim de semana	week-end	weekend	Wochenende(n)	fin de semana	fine settimana
final	final, e	final	letzte, Schluß-	final	finale
finança	finance	finance	Finanzwelt, Finanzen	finanza	finanza
financeiro, a	financier, ière	financial	finanziell	financiero, a	finanziario, a
financiamento	financement	financing	Finanzierung(f)	financiación	finanziamento
financiar	financer	finance	finanzieren	financiar	finanziare
fino, a	fin, e	fine, thin	fein, dünn	fino, a	fine, sottile
fino, a	mince	thin	dünn	delgado, a	sottile
fio	fil	thread	Faden(m)	hilo	filo
firma	firme	firm	Firma(f)	firma	firma, ditta, azienda
firme	ferme	firm	fest	firme	fermo, a; solido, a
firmeza	fermeté	firmness	Entschlossenheit(f)	firmeza	fermezza
fiscal	fiscal, e	fiscal, tax	fiskalisch, Steuer-	fiscal	fiscale
fiscalidade	fiscalité	tax system	Steuerwesen(n)	fiscalidad	fiscalità
fisco	fisc	Inland Revenue	Fiskus(m), Finanzamt	fisco	fisco
física	physique	physics	Physik(f)	física	fisica
físico, a	physique	physical	physisch	físico, a	fisico, a
físico, a	physicien, ne	physicist	Physiker(in f)m	físico, a	fisico, a
físico	physique	physique	Äußere(n), Aussehen(n)	físico	fisico
fisionomia	physionomie	physiognomy	Gesichtsausdruck(m)	fisionomía	fisionomia
fissão	fission	fission	Spaltung(f)(Atom)	fisión	fissione
fissura; fenda	fissure, fente	crack, fissure	Riß(m), Spalte(f)	fisura, grieta	fessura, crepa
fita	ruban	ribbon; tape; band	Band(n)	cinta, banda	nastro
fita	bande	tape	Band(n)	cinta	nastro
fita adesiva	scotch	sellotape	Tesafilm(m)	papel celo	scotch
fivela; argola	boucle	buckle	Schnalle(f)	hebilla	fibbia
fixação	fixation	fixing, fixation	Befestigung(f)	fijación	fissazione
fixar	fixer	fix, attach	befestigen	fijar	fissare
fixo, a	fixe	fixed	fest	fijo, a	fisso, a
flash	flash	flash	Blitz(m)	flash	flash
flauta	flûte	flute	Flöte(f)	flauta	flauto
flecha, seta	flèche	arrow	Pfeil(m)	flecha	freccia
flexibilidade	souplesse	suppleness	Biegsamkeit(f)	flexibilidad	flessibilità
flexível	flexible	flexible	flexibel	flexible	flessibile
floco	flocon	flake	Flocke(f)	copo	fiocco
flor	fleur	flower	Blume(f)	flor	fiore
flora	flore	flora	Flora(f), Pflanzenwelt	flora	flora
floresta, bosque	forêt	forest	Wald(m)	bosque	foresta, bosco
florista	fleuriste	florist	Blumenhändler(in f)m	florista	fioraio
fluentemente	couramment	fluently	fließend	soltura(con)	correntemente
fluido	fluide	fluid	Flüssigkeit(f)	fluido	fluido

Portuguese	French	English	German	Spanish	Italian
flutuação	fluctuation	fluctuation	Schwanken(n)	fluctuación	fluttuazione
flutuar	flotter	float	schwimmen, treiben	flotar	galleggiare
fluxo	flux	flow	Fluß(m), Strömung(f)	flujo	flusso
foca	phoque	seal	Seehund(m)	foca	foca
focinho	museau	muzzle	Schnauze(f)	hocico	muso
foco	faisceau	beam	Strahl(m)(Licht)	haz	fascio
fogão	poêle	stove	Ofen(m)	estufa	stufa
fogão	cuisinière	cooker, stove	Herd(m)	cocina	cucina
fogão	réchaud	stove	Kocher(m)	hornillo	fornello
fogo	feu	fire	Feuer(n)	fuego	fuoco
foguete	fusée	rocket	Rakete(f)	cohete	razzo
folclore	folklore	folklore	Folklore(f)	folklore	folclore
folha	feuille	sheet	Blatt(n)	hoja	foglio
folha	feuille	leaf(leaves)	Blatt(n)	hoja	foglia
fome(ter)	faim(avoir)	hunger(hungry be)	Hunger(m)(haben)	hambre(tener)	fame(aver)
fome	famine	famine	Hungersnot(f)	hambre	fame, carestia
fonético, a	phonétique	phonetic	phonetisch	fonético, a	fonetico, a
fonte	fontaine	fountain	Springbrunnen(m)	fuente	fontana
fonte, nascente	source	spring	Quelle(f)	fuente	sorgente
fonte, origem	source, origine	source	Ursprung(m)	fuente, origen	fonte, origine
fora	dehors	outside, outdoors	draußen	fuera, afuera	fuori
fora de	hors de	out of	außer(+dat)	fuera de	fuori, fuori di
fora de borda	hors-bord	speed-boat	Außenbordmotor(m)	fuera borda	fuoribordo
fora de moda	démodé, e	old-fashioned	altmodisch	pasado de moda	passato di moda
força	force	strength	Stärke(f), Kraft(f)	fuerza	forza
força	force	force	Gewalt(f); Kraft(f)	fuerza	forza
forcado	fourche	pitchfork, fork	Gabel(f)(Heu-; Mist-)	horca	forca
forçar	forcer	force	zwingen	forzar	forzare
forma	forme	shape, form	Form(f), Aussehen(n)	forma	forma
forma	forme	form	Verfassung(f)	forma(en)	forma
formação	formation	formation	Entstehung(f)	formación	formazione
formação	formation	training	Ausbildung(f)	formación	formazione
formalidade	formalité	formality	Formalität(f)	formalidad	formalità
formar	former	form	bilden, formen	formar	formare
formato	format	format, size	Format(n)	formato, tamaño	formato
formidável	formidable	tremendous	großartig	formidable	formidabile
formiga	fourmi	ant	Ameise(f)	hormiga	formica
fórmula	formule	formula	Formel(f)	fórmula	formula
formulário	formulaire	form	Formular(n), Vordruck	formulario	modulo, formulario
fornecedor, a	fournisseur, se	supplier	Lieferant(in f)m	abastecedor, a	fornitore, trice
fornecer	fournir	supply, provide	beliefern	proveer, dar	fornire
fornecer	fournir	provide	versorgen, liefern	proveer	fornire
fornecimento	fourniture	supply(ing)	Lieferung(f)	abastecimiento	fornitura
forno	four	oven	Ofen(m)	horno	forno
forragem	fourrage	fodder	Futter(n)	forraje	foraggio
forte	fort, e	strong	stark	fuerte	forte
forte; alto, a	fort, e	loud	laut	fuerte; alto, a	forte; alto, a
fortificante	fortifiant	tonic	Stärkungsmittel(n)	fortificante	ricostituente
fortuna	fortune	fortune	Vermögen(n)	fortuna	fortuna
fósforo	allumette	match(-es)	Streichholz(n)	cerilla	fiammifero
fossa	fosse	pit	Grube(f)	fosa, hoyo	fossa, buca
fóssil	fossile	fossil	Fossil(n)	fósil	fossile
fosso	fossé	ditch	Graben(m)	cuneta	fossato, fosso
fotografar	photographier	take a photo	fotografieren	fotografiar	fotografare
fotografia	photographie	photography	Fotografie(f)	fotografía	fotografia
fotografia	photo	photo(graph)	Foto(n)	foto	foto, fotografia
fracasso	échec	failure	Mißerfolg(m)	fracaso, revés	smacco, sconfitta
fracção	fraction	fraction	Bruchteil(m)	fracción	frazione
fraco, a	faible	weak	schwach	débil	debole, fragile
fraco, a	faible	dim	matt	flojo, a	debole
fractura	fracture	fracture	Bruch(m)	fractura	frattura
frágil	fragile	fragile	zerbrechlich	frágil	fragile
fragmento	fragment	fragment	Fragment(n)	fragmento	frammento
franco, a	franc, che	frank	offen, ehrlich	franco, a	franco, a; sincero, a
frango	poulet	chicken	Hähnchen, Hühnchen(n)	pollo	pollo
franquear	affranchir	stamp	frankieren, freimachen	franquear	affrancare
fraqueza	faiblesse	weakness(-es)	Schwäche(f)	debilidad	debolezza
frasco	flacon	bottle(small)	Fläschchen(n)	frasco	boccetta

P

693

Portuguese	French	English	German	Spanish	Italian
frase	phrase	sentence	Satz(m)	frase	frase
fraternidade	fraternité	brotherhood	Brüderlichkeit(f)	fraternidad	fraternità
fraude	fraude	fraud	Betrug(m)	fraude	frode
fraude(fiscal)	fraude(fiscale)	tax evasion	Steuerhinterziehung f	fraude(fiscal)	frode(fiscale)
freira	soeur	nun, sister	Nonne(f), Schwester(f)	monja	suora
frente(a)	devant	front, fore	Front(f)	frente, delantera	davanti
frente(para a)	avant	forward(s)	vorwärts	adelante(hacia)	davanti
frequência	fréquence	frequency	Frequenz(f)	frecuencia	frequenza
frequente	fréquent, e	frequent	häufig	frecuente	frequente
frequentemente	souvent	often	oft	frecuentemente	spesso
fresco, a	frais, fraîche	fresh	frisch	fresco, a	fresco, a
frete	fret	freight	Fracht(f)	flete	nolo, carico
fricção	frottement	friction, rubbing	Reibung(f)	frotamiento	strofinio
frieira	engelure	chilblain	Frostbeule(f)	sabañón	gelone
frieira	gélure	frostbite	Erfrierung(f)	heladura	congelamento
frigideira	poêle	frying pan	Pfanne(f)	sartén	padella
frigorífico	frigo, frigidaire	fridge	Kühlschrank(m)	frigorífico	frigorifero
frigorífico	réfrigérateur	refrigerator	Kühlschrank(m)	nevera	frigorifero
frigorífico, a	frigorifique	refrigerating	Kühl-; kalt, kühl	frigorífico, a	frigorifero, a
frio, a	froid, e	cold	kalt	frío, a	freddo, a
frio(ter)	froid(avoir)	cold(to be)	frieren	frío(tener)	freddo(avere)
fritar	frire	fry	braten	freír	friggere
frívolo, a	frivole	frivolous	frivol, leichtsinnig	frívolo, a	frivolo, a
fronteira	frontière	border, frontier	Grenze(f)	frontera	confine, frontiera
fronteira, limite	frontière, limite	boundary	Grenze(f)	frontera, límite	frontiera, limite
frota	flotte	fleet	Flotte(f)	flota	flotta
frouxo, a	lâche, détendu, e	loose, slack	locker, lose	flojo, a	allentato, a
frouxo, a; lasso, a	détendu, e	slack, loose	schlaff, lose	aflojado, a	allentato, a
frouxo, a	desserré, e	slack	schlaff, lose	flojo, a	allentato, a
frustração	frustration	frustration	Enttäuschung(f)	frustración	frustrazione
fruta	fruit(s)	fruit	Frucht(f)	fruta	frutto; frutta
fuel, óleo	mazout	fuel oil	Heizöl(n)	fuel-oil	nafta
fuga	fuite	flight, escape	Flucht(f)	huída	fuga
fuga	fuite	leak	Leck(n)	escape	perdita
fugir	fuir	run away, flee	fliehen	huir	fuggire
fugir	enfuir(s')	run away	fliehen	huir	fuggire
fugitivo, a	fugitif, ive	fugitive	flüchtig	fugitivo, a	fuggitivo, a
fumado, a	fumé, e	smoked	geräuchert	ahumado, a	affumicato, a
fumadores	fumeurs	smokers	Raucher(m)	fumadores	fumatore, trice
fumar	fumer	smoke	rauchen	fumar	fumare
fumo	fumée	smoke	Rauch(m)	humo	fumo
fumo	fumée	smoke, fumes	Rauch(m)	humo	smog, fumo
função	fonction	function	Funktion(f)	función	funzione
função	fonction	function	Stellung(f), Amt(n)	función	funzione
função	rôle	role, part	Rolle(f)	cometido, función	ruolo, parte
funcionamento	fonctionnement	functioning	Betrieb(m)	funcionamiento	funzionamento
funcionar	fonctionner	function, work, run	funktionieren	funcionar	funzionare
funcionar	marcher	work, run	in Betrieb sein	marchar	funzionare
funcionar(fazer)	marcher(faire)	operate	bedienen	funcionar(hacer)	funzionare(fare)
funcionário, a	fonctionnaire	state employee	Beamten(m), Beamtin(f)	funcionario, a	impiegato statale
funcionário, a	fonctionnaire	civil servant	Beamte(r)m, Beamtin(f)	funcionario, a	funzionario, a
fundador, a	fondateur, trice	founder	Gründer(in f)m	fundador, a	fondatore, trice
fundamental	fondamental, e	fundamental	fundamental	fundamental	fondamentale
fundar	fonder	found	gründen	fundar	fondare
fundir	fondre	melt	schmelzen	fundir	fondere
fundo	fond	bottom; back	Boden(m), Grund(m)	fondo	fondo
fundos, capital	fonds	funds	Fonds(m), Kapital(n)	fondos	fondi
funeral	funérailles	funeral	Begräbnis(n)	funerales	funerale
fungar	renifler	sniff	schnüffeln	resoplar	tirar su col naso
funil	entonnoir	funnel	Trichter(m)	embudo	imbuto
furacão	ouragan	hurricane	Orkan(m)	huracán	uragano
furar	percer	drill; pierce	bohren	perforar	bucare, forare
furar, rebentar	crever, éclater	burst	bersten	estallar, reventar	scoppiare
furioso, a	furieux, se	furious	wütend	furioso, a	furioso, a
furo	crevaison	puncture	Reifenpanne(f)	pinchazo	foratura
furor	fureur	fury	Wut(f)	furor	furore
furúnculo	furoncle	boil	Furunkel(m)	furúnculo	foruncolo
fusão	fusion	fusion, melting	Schmelzen(n)(Ver-)	fusión	fusione

Portuguese	French	English	German	Spanish	Italian
fusão	fusion	merger	Vereinigung(f), Fusion	fusión	fusione, alleanza
futebol	football	football, soccer	Fußball(m)	fútbol	calcio
futuro	avenir	future	Zukunft(f)	porvenir, futuro	avvenire
futuro	futur	future	Zukunft(f)	futuro	futuro
futuro, a	futur, e	future	zukünftig	futuro, a	futuro, a

G

Portuguese	French	English	German	Spanish	Italian
gabardina	imperméable	rain-coat, mac	Regenmantel(m)	gabardina	impermeabile
gabar-se	vanter(se)	boast	prahlen	jactarse	vantarsi
gabinete	cabinet(pol.)	cabinet	Kabinett(n)	gabinete	gabinetto
gado	bétail, bestiaux	cattle	Vieh(n)	ganado	bestiame
gaguejar	bégayer	stutter, stammer	stottern	tartamudear	balbettare
gaiola, jaula	cage	cage	Käfig(m)	jaula	gabbia
gaivota	mouette	seagull	Möve(f)	gaviota	gabbiano
gaivota	goéland	gull	Silbermöwe(f)	gaviota	gabbiano
galante	galant, e	gallant	galant	galante	galante
galão	galon	stripe	Galone(f)	galón	gallone, grado
galardoado, a	lauréat, e	prize-winner	Preisträger(in f)m	galardonado, a	premiato, a
galáxia	galaxie	galaxy	Galaxie(f)	galaxia	galassia
galeria	galerie	gallery	Galerie, Ausstellung	galería	galleria
galeria	galerie	arcade	Passage(f)	galería	galleria
galinha	poule	hen	Huhn(n)	gallina	gallina
galo	coq	cock	Hahn(m)	gallo	gallo
galope	galop	gallop	Galopp(m)	galope	galoppo
gancho	crochet	hook	Haken(m)	gancho	gancio, uncino
gânglio	ganglion	ganglion, gland	Ganglien(pl.)	ganglio	ganglio
gangrena	gangrène	gangrene	Brand(m), Wundbrand(m)	gangrena	cancrena
gangster	gangster	gangster	Gangster(m)	gángster	gangster
ganhar	gagner	win	gewinnen	ganar	vincere
ganhar	gagner	earn; win	verdienen	ganar	guadagnare
ganhar	gagner	save	sparen	ganar	guadagnare
ganso	oie	goose(geese pl.)	Gans(f)	oca	oca
garagem	garage	garage	Garage(f)	garaje, garage	garage
garagista	garagiste	garage mechanic	Autoschlosser(m)	garajista	garagista
garantia	garantie	guarantee; warranty	Garantie(f)	garantía	garanzia
garantir	garantir	guarantee, warrant	gewährleisten	garantizar	garantire
garfo	fourchette	fork	Gabel(f)	tenedor	forchetta
gargalo	goulot	neck(bottle)	Hals(m)(Flaschen)	gollete	collo
garganta	gorge	throat	Hals(m)	garganta	gola
garra	griffe	claw	Kralle(f), Klaue(f)	garra	artiglio
garrafa	bouteille	bottle	Flasche(f)	botella	bottiglia
gás	gaz	gas	Gas(n)	gas	gas
gasóleo	gas-oil	diesel oil	Diesel(n), Dieselöl(n)	gasoil	gasolio
gasolina	essence	petrol	Benzin(n)	gasolina	benzina
gasoso, a	gazeux, se	gaseous	gasförmig	gaseoso, a	gassoso, a
gasoso, a	gazeux, se	fizzy, sparkling	sprudelnd; Sprudel-	gaseoso, a	gassato, a
gastar	dépenser	spend	aus = geben	gastar	spendere
gastos, despesas	frais	expenses	Kosten(pl.)	gastos	spese(le)
gástrico, a	gastrique	gastric	Magen-	gástrico, a	gastrico, a
gastronomia	gastronomie	gastronomy	Gastronomie(f)	gastronomía	gastronomia
gatilho	gâchette	trigger	Abzug(m)	gatillo	grilletto
gato, a	chat, te	cat	Kater(m), Katze(f)	gato, a	gatto, a
gatuno, escroque	escroc	crook, swindler	Gauner(m)	estafador	imbroglione
gaveta	tiroir	drawer	Schublade(f)	cajón	cassetto
gavião	épervier	sparrow-hawk	Habicht(m)	gavilán	sparviere
geada	givre	frost	Reif(m)	escarcha	brina

Portuguese	French	English	German	Spanish	Italian
gelado	glace	ice cream	Eis(n)	helado	gelato
gelado, a	glacé, e; gelé, e	icy	eisig	helado, a	gelato, a; ghiacciato
gelar	geler	freeze	frieren	helar	gelare
geleia	gelée	jelly	Gelee(n)	jalea	gelatina
gelo	glace	ice	Eis(n)	hielo	ghiaccio
gémeo, a	jumeau, jumelle	twin	Zwilling(m)	gemelo, a	gemello, a
gemer	gémir	moan	stöhnen	gemir	gemere
genealogia	généalogie	genealogy	Genealogie(f)	genealogía	genealogia
general	général	general	General(m)	general	generale
género	genre	kind, sort	Art(f), Sorte(f)	género	genere
género; víveres	denrée	foodstuff	Eßware(f)	comestibles	derrata
generoso, a	généreux, se	generous	freigebig	generoso, a	generoso, a
genética	génétique	genetics	Genetik(f)	genética	genetica
gengiva	gencive	gum	Zahnfleisch(n)	encía	gengiva
genial	génial, e	brilliant	genial	genial	geniale
génio	génie	genius	Genie(n)	genio	genio
genital	génital, e	genital	Genital-	genital	genitale
genocídio	génocide	genocide	Völkermord(m)	genocidio	genocidio
genro	gendre	son-in-law	Schwiegersohn(m)	yerno	genero
gente, pessoas	gens	people	Leute(pl.)	gente	gente(la)
gentil, amável	gentil, le	kind, nice	nett	gentil, amable	gentile
geografia	géographie	geography	Erdkunde(f)	geografía	geografia
geologia	géologie	geology	Geologie(f)	geología	geologia
geometria	géométrie	geometry	Geometrie(f)	geometría	geometria
geração	génération	generation	Generation(f)	generación	generazione
gerador	générateur	generator	Generator(m)	generador	generatore
geral	général, e	general	allgemein, generell	general	generale
geral(em)	général(en)	usually, in general	allgemeinen(im)	general(en)	genere(in)
gerar	générer	generate	erzeugen	engendrar	generare
gerente	gérant, e	manager	Geschäftsführer(m)	gerente	gerente, gestore
gerente, director, a	gérant, e	manager	Verwalter(in f)m	gerente, director, a	gestore, gerente
gerir	gérer	manage	verwalten, führen	administrar	amministrare
germe	germe	germ, seed	Keim(m)	germen	germe
germe	germe	seed	Keim(m)	germen, grano	germoglio
gesso	plâtre	plaster	Gips(m)	yeso	gesso
gestão	gestion	management	Verwaltung(f)	gestión	gestione
gesto	geste	gesture	Geste(f)	gesto	gesto
gestor, a	gestionnaire	manager	Verwalter(in f)m	gestor, a	gestore
gigante	géant, e	giant	riesig, gigantisch	gigante	gigante
gigantesco, a	gigantesque	gigantic, huge	gigantisch, riesig	gigantesco, a	gigantesco, a
ginástica	gymnastique	gymnastics	Gymnastik(f)	gimnasia	ginnastica
ginecologia	gynécologie	gynaecology	Gynäkologie(f)	ginecología	ginecologia
gira-discos	tourne-disque	record-player	Plattenspieler(m)	tocadiscos	giradischi
girafa	girafe	giraffe	Giraffe(f)	jirafa	giraffa
girar; rodar	tourner	turn	drehen	girar	girare
girar; rodar	pivoter	revolve, pivot	schwenken	girar	girare, ruotare
girar(fazer)	tourner(faire)	rotate, revolve	drehen	girar(hacer)	roteare
glaciar	glacier	glacier	Gletscher(m)	glaciar	ghiacciaio
glândula	glande	gland	Drüse(f)	glándula	ghiandola
glicose	glucose	glucose	Traubenzucker(m)	glucosa	glucosio
global	global, e	global, overall	Gesamt-; pauschal	global	globale
globo	globe	globe	Globus(m)	globo	globo
glóbulo	globule(sang)	corpuscle, globule	Blutkörperchen(n)	glóbulo	globulo
glória	gloire	glory	Ruhm(m)	gloria	gloria
glorioso, a	glorieux, se	glorious	glorreich	glorioso, a	glorioso, a
glossário	glossaire	glossary	Glossar(n)	glosario	glossario
goela, garganta	gueule	mouth	Maul(n)	hocico	muso
golfe	golf	golf	Golf(n)	golf	golf
golfinho	dauphin	dolphin	Delphin(m)	delfín	delfino
golfo	golfe	gulf	Golf(m)	golfo	golfo
golo	but	goal	Tor(n)	gol	goal, rete
golpe	coup	knock, blow	Schlag(m)	golpe	colpo
golpear	battre, frapper	beat, hit	schlagen	golpear	picchiare
gonzo, dobradiça	charnière	hinge	Scharnier(n)	bisagra	cerniera
gordo, a	gras, se	fat(ty), greasy	fett	graso, a	grasso, a
gordo, a	gros, se	fat	dick	grueso, a; gordo, a	grosso, a
gordura	graisse	fat	Fett(n)	gordo; grasa	grasso
gorduroso, a	graisseux, se	fatty, greasy	schmierig, fettig	grasiento, a	unto, a

Portuguese	French	English	German	Spanish	Italian
gorgeta	pourboire	tip	Trinkgeld(n)	propina	mancia
gorila	gorille	gorilla	Gorilla(m)	gorila	gorilla
gostar	aimer	enjoy	mögen; gern mögen	gustar	piacere
gostar(de)	aimer	like	gern haben	gustar(le)	piacere, amare
gostava	voudrais(je)	would like(I)	möchte(ich)	quisiera(yo)	vorrei
gosto	goût	taste	Geschmack(m)	gusto	gusto, sapore
gosto(dar)	plaisir(faire)	please	Freude machen	gusto(dar)	piacere(fare)
gota	goutte	drop	Tropfen(m)	gota	goccia
goteira	gouttière	gutter	Dachrinne(f)	canalón	grondaia
governador	gouverneur	governor	Gouverneur(m)	gobernador	governatore
governar	gouverner	govern	regieren	gobernar	governare
governo	gouvernement	government	Regierung(f)	gobierno	governo
gozar	jouir	enjoy	genießen	gozar	godere
graça	grâce	grace	Gnade(f); Anmut(f)	gracia	grazia
graças a	grâce à	thanks to	dank	gracias a	grazie a
gracejar	plaisanter	joke	scherzen	bromear	scherzare
gracioso, a	gracieux, se	graceful	graziös	gracioso, a	grazioso, a
gracioso, a	gracieux, se	good natured	lieb	simpático, a	grazioso, a
gradeamento	grillage	wire fencing	Gitter(n)	reja	reticolato
gráfico	graphique	graph	Graphik(f)	gráfico, a	grafico
grafologia	graphologie	graphology	Graphologie(f)	grafología	grafologia
gramática	grammaire	grammar	Grammatik(f)	gramática	grammatica
grampo	crampons	crampons, irons	Steigeisen(n)	crampones	rampone
granada	grenade	grenade	Handgranate(f)	granada	bomba a mano
grande	grand, e	great	groß	gran, grande	grand(e)
grande	grand, e	large, big	weit	gran, grande	grande, ampio, a
grande	grand, e	big	groß	gran, grande	grande
grande	gros, se	big	groß	grueso, a; grande	grosso, a; grande
grande	gros, se	big	geräumig	grande	grosso, a
granizo	grêle	hail	Hagel(m)	granizo	grandine
grânulo	granule	granule	Körnchen(n)	gránulo	granulo
grão	grain	grain	Korn(n)	grano	chicco, grano
grão	grain(café)	bean(coffee-)	Bohne(Kaffee-)(f)	grano	chicco
gratidão	gratitude	gratitude	Dankbarkeit(f)	gratitud	gratitudine
gratificação	prime	bonus	Zulage(f)	prima	premio, sussidio
grátis; gratuito, a	gratuit, e	free	kostenlos	gratis; gratuito, a	gratuito, a; gratis
grau	degré	degree	Grad(m)	grado	grado
grau	degré(alcool)	proof(per cent)	Prozent(n)	graduación	grado
grau	grade	rank	Rang(m)	grado	grado
gravação	enregistrement	recording	Aufnahme(f)	grabación	registrazione
gravador	magnétophone	tape recorder	Kassettenrecorder(m)	magnetófono	registratore
gravador video	magnétoscope	video recorder	Videorecorder(m)	magnetoscopio	videoregistratore
gravar	enregistrer	record	auf = nehmen	grabar	registrare
gravata	cravate	tie	Kravatte(f)	corbata	cravatta
grave	grave	grave, serious	schwer; ernst	grave	grave
grávida	enceinte	pregnant	schwanger	encinta	incinta
gravidade	gravité	gravity	Schwere(f)	gravedad	gravità
gravidez	grossesse	pregnancy	Schwangerschaft(f)	embarazo	gravidanza
gravura	gravure	engraving	Gravieren(n)	grabado	incisione
gravura	gravure	print	Gravur(f)	grabado	stampa
gravura	image	picture	Bild(n)	imagen	illustrazione
grelhar	griller	grill	grillen	asar(parrilla)	arrostire
greta	gerçure	chap(ped)	Riß(m), Hautriß(m)	grieta	screpolatura
greve	grève	strike	Streik(m)	huelga	sciopero
grinalda	guirlande	garland	Girlande(f)	guirnalda	ghirlanda
gripe	grippe	flu, influenza	Grippe(f)	gripe	influenza
gritar	crier	shout, scream	schreien	gritar	gridare
gritar; berrar	hurler	scream, yell	brüllen	chillar	urlare
grito	cri	shout	Schrei(m)	grito	grido
grosseiro, a	grossier, ière	rude; crude	grob	grosero, a	grossolano, a
grua	grue	crane	Kran(m)	grúa	gru
grupo	groupe	group	Gruppe(f).	grupo	gruppo
gruta	grotte	cave, grotto	Grotte(f).	cueva, gruta	grotta
guarda	garde	guard	Wache(f)	guardia	guardia, custodia
guarda	garde	guard	Wächter(m), Hüter(m)	guarda	guardia
guarda	gardien, ne	keeper, caretaker	Wärter(in f)m	guardián, ana	custode, guardia
guarda	gardien, ne; garde	guard; keeper	Wächter(in f)m	guardián, guarda	guardiano, a; custode
guarda-fiscal	douanier	customs officer	Zöllner(m)	aduanero	doganiere

P

Portuguese	French	English	German	Spanish	Italian
guarda-republicano	gendarme	policeman(-men)	Polizist(in f)m	guardia civil	carabiniere
guardanapo	serviette	serviette, napkin	Serviette(f)	servilleta	tovagliolo
guardar	garder	keep	behalten	guardar	tenere
guardar, vigiar	garder	guard, watch over	hüten, bewachen	guardar	custodire, guardare
guarda-redes	goal	goalkeeper	Torwärter(m)	portero	portiere
guarda-sol	parasol	parasol, sunshade	Sonnenschirm(m)	parasol	ombrellone
guarnecer	garnir	garnish	garnieren	guarnecer	guarnire
guerra	guerre	war	Krieg(m)	guerra	guerra
guerrilha	guérilla	guerilla	Guerilla(f)	guerrilla	guerriglia
guia	guide	guide	Führer(in f)m	guía	guida
guia	guide	guide-book	Führer(Reise-)(m)	guía	guida
guião	scénario	script(film -)	Drehbuch(n)	guión	scenario
guiar	guider	guide	führen	guiar	guidare
guichê, postigo	guichet	counter, position	Schalter(m)	ventanilla	sportello
guitarra	guitare	guitar	Gitarre(f)	guitarra	chitarra
guloseima	friandise	delicacy	Nascherei(f)	golosina	dolciume
guloso, a	gourmand, e	greedy	erpicht auf	goloso, a	goloso, a

H

Portuguese	French	English	German	Spanish	Italian
há	il y a	there is, there are	es gibt	hay	c'è; ci sono
há	il y a	ago	vor	hace	fa
hábil; destro, a	habile; adroit, e	clever, skilful	geschickt	hábil; diestro, a	abile
habilidade	habileté	ability, skill	Geschicklichkeit(f)	habilidad	abilità
habilidade	savoir-faire	know-how	Geschick(n)	tacto, maña	savoir-faire
habitação, morada	habitation	dwelling; living	Wohnung(f)	vivienda, morada	abitazione
habitação, casa	demeure	residence, dwelling	Wohnung(f), Haus(n)	morada, casa	dimora
habitante	habitant, e	inhabitant	Einwohner(in f)m	habitante	abitante
habitar	demeurer	live, stay, remain	wohnen, bleiben	residir, vivir	dimorare, stare
hábito, costume	habitude	habit	Gewohnheit(f)	costumbre	abitudine
habituação	accoutumance	habituation	Gewöhnung(f)	hábito	abitudine
habitual	habituel, le	usual	gewöhnlich	habitual	abituale
habitualmente	habituellement	usually	üblich, gewönhlich	generalmente	abitualmente
habituar-se	habituer(s')	get used to	gewöhnen, sich	acostumbrarse	abituarsi
hálito	haleine	breath	Atem(m)	aliento	alito
handicap	handicap	handicap	Handikap(n)	hándicap	handicap
harém	harem	harem	Harem(m)	harén	harem
harmonia	harmonie	harmony	Harmonie(f)	armonía	armonia
harmonioso, a	harmonieux, se	harmonious	harmonisch	armonioso, a	armonioso, a
harpa	harpe	harp	Harfe(f)	arpa	arpa
haste	tige	rod	Stange(f)	tallo, vástago	asta, barra
haver; ter	avoir	have	haben	haber; tener	avere
hectare	hectare	hectare	Hektar(m)	hectárea	ettaro
hélice	hélice	propeller	Propeller(m)	hélice	elica
helicóptero	hélicoptère	helicopter	Hubschrauber(m)	helicóptero	elicottero
hemisfério	hémisphère	hemisphere	Halbkreis(m)	hemisferio	emisfero
hemorragia	hémorragie	haemorrhage	Blutsturz(m)	hemorragia	emorragia
hemorróidas	hémorroïde(s)	haemorrhoids	Hämorrhoiden(f, pl)	hemorroides	emorroide
hepatite	hépatite	hepatitis	Hepatitis, Gelbsucht f	hepatitis	epatite
herança	héritage	inheritance, legacy	Erbschaft(f)	herencia	eredità
herdeiro, a	héritier, ière	heir, heiress	Erbe(m), Erbin(f)	heredero, a	erede
hereditariedade	hérédité	heredity	Vererbung(f)	herencia	ereditarietà
hereditário, a	héréditaire	hereditary	erblich	hereditario, a	ereditario, a
hermético, a	hermétique	hermetic	hermetisch	hermético, a	ermetico, a
hérnia	hernie	hernia	Bruch(m)	hernia	ernia
herói, heroína	héros, héroïne	hero, heroine	Held(m), Heldin(f)	héroe, heroína	eroe, eroina
heróico, a	héroïque	heroic	heldenhaft	heroico, a	eroico, a

Portuguese	French	English	German	Spanish	Italian
heroína	héroïne	heroin	Heroin(n)	heroína	eroina
hesitação	hésitation	hesitation	Zögern(n)	vacilación	esitazione
hesitar	hésiter	hesitate	zögern	dudar	esitare
heterossexual	hétérosexuel, le	heterosexual	heterosexuell	heterosexual	eterosessuale
híbrido, a	hybride	hybrid	zwitterhaft	híbrido, a	ibrido, a
hidráulico, a	hydraulique	hydraulic	hydraulisch	hidráulico, a	idraulico, a
hidrogénio	hydrogène	hydrogen	Wasserstoff(m)	hidrógeno	idrogeno
hiena	hyène	hyena	Hyäne(f)	hiena	iena
hierarquia	hiérarchie	hierarchy	Hierarchie(f)	jerarquía	gerarchia
hierárquico, a	hiérarchique	hierarchical	hierarchisch	jerárquico, a	gerarchico, a
higiene	hygiène	hygiene	Hygiene(f)	higiene	igiene
higiénico, a	hygiénique	hygienic	hygienisch	higiénico, a	igienico, a
hino	hymne	hymn	Hymne(f)	himno	inno
hipertensão	hypertension	blood pressure	Bluthochdruck(m)	hipertensión	ipertensione
hipnose	hypnose	hypnosis	Hypnose(f)	hipnosis	ipnosi
hipnotismo	hypnotisme	hypnotism	Hypnotismus(m)	hipnotismo	ipnotismo
hipocrisia	hypocrisie	hypocrisy	Heuchelei(f)	hipocresía	ipocrisia
hipócrita	hypocrite	hypocrite	Heuchler(in f)m	hipócrita	ipocrita
hipopótamo	hippopotame	hippopotamus	Nilpferd(n)	hipopótamo	ippopotamo
hipoteca	hypothèque	mortgage	Hypothek(f)	hipoteca	ipoteca
hipótese	hypothèse	hypothesis(-es)	Hypothese(f)	hipótesis	ipotesi
hippie	hippie, y	hippy	Hippie(m)	hippy, jipi	capellone, hippy
histérico, a	hystérique	hysteric(al)	hysterisch	histérico, a	isterico, a
História	histoire	history	Geschichte(f)	historia	storia
história	histoire	story	Geschichte(f)	historia	storia
historiador	historien	historian	Geschichtschreiber(m)	historiador	storico
histórico, a	historique	historic(al)	historisch	histórico, a	storico, a
hoje	aujourd'hui	today	heute	hoy	oggi
homem	homme	man(men)	Mann(m), Mensch(m)	hombre	uomo; uomini
homenagem	hommage	homage, tribute	Huldigung(f); Ehrung f	homenaje	omaggio
homeopatia	homéopathie	homoeopathy	Homöopathie(f)	homeopatía	omeopatia
homicídio	homicide	murder, homicide	Totschlag(m)	homicidio	omicidio
homicídio, crime	meurtre	murder	Mord(m)	asesinato	assassinio
homogéneo, a	homogène	homogeneous	homogen	homogéneo, a	omogeneo, a
homologação	homologation	certification	Zulassung(f)	homologación	omologazione
homónimo, a	homonyme	homonym	Homonym(n)	homónimo, a	omonimo, a
homossexual	homosexuel, le	homosexual	homosexuell	homosexual	omosessuale
honesto, a	honnête	honest	ehrlich	honrado, a	onesto, a
honorários	honoraires	fee	Honorar(n)	honorarios	onorario
honra	honneur	honour	Ehre(f)	honor	onore
honroso, a	honorable	honourable	ehrwürdig	honorable	onorabile
hóquei	hockey	hockey	Hockeyspiel(n)	hockey	hockey
hora	heure	hour; time	Stunde(f); Zeit(f)	hora	ora
horário	horaire(s)	timetable	Fahrplan(m)	horario(s)	orario
horizontal	horizontal, e	horizontal	waagerecht	horizontal	orizzontale
horizonte	horizon	horizon, sky-line	Horizont(m)	horizonte	orizzonte
hormona	hormone	hormone	Hormon(n)	hormona	ormone
horóscopo	horoscope	horoscope	Horoskop(n)	horóscopo	oroscopo
horrível	horrible	horrible	grausig	horrible	orribile, orrendo, a
horrível	affreux, se	awful	schrecklich	horrendo, a	spaventoso, a
horror	horreur	horror	Grausen(n)	horror	orrore
horroroso, a	épouvantable	dreadful	entsetzlich	horroroso, a	spaventoso, a
horta	jardin	garden	Gemüsegarten(m)	huerto	orto
hortelã	menthe	mint	Minze(f)	menta	menta
horticultura	horticulture	horticulture	Gartenbau(m)	horticultura	orticultura
hóspede	pensionnaire	resident	Pensionsgast(m)	pensionista	pensionante
hóspede	pensionnaire	lodger	Untermieter(in f)m	huésped	ospite
hóspede, a	hôte	guest	Gast(m)	huésped, a	ospite
hospedeira	hôtesse	hostess(air -)	Stewardess(f)	azafata	hostess
hospício, asilo	hospice	hospice; home	Hospiz(n)	hospicio	ospizio
hospital	hôpital	hospital	Krankenhaus(n)	hospital	ospedale
hospitalidade	hospitalité	hospitality	Gastfreundlichkeit(f)	hospitalidad	ospitalità
hostil	hostile	hostile	feindlich	hostil	ostile
hotel	hôtel	hotel	Hotel(n)	hotel	albergo, hotel
hotelaria	hôtellerie	hotel trade	Hotelwesen(n)	hostelería	alberghiera(indust-)
humanidade	humanité	humanity	Menschheit(f)	humanidad	umanità
humano, a	humain, e	human	menschlich	humano, a	umano, a
humidade	humidité	humidity	Feuchtigkeit(f)	humedad	umidità

Portuguese	French	English	German	Spanish	Italian
húmido, a	humide	damp, humid, moist	feucht	húmedo, a	umido, a
humilhar	humilier	humiliate	erniedrigen	humillar	umiliare
humor	humeur	mood	Laune(f)	humor	umore
humor	humour	humour	Humor(m)	humor	umorismo
humorístico, a	humoristique	humorous	humoristisch	humorístico, a	umoristico, a

I

Portuguese	French	English	German	Spanish	Italian
iceberg	iceberg	iceberg	Eisberg(m)	iceberg	iceberg
icterícia	jaunisse	jaundice	Gelbsucht(f)	ictericia	itterizia
idade	âge	age	Alter(n)	edad	età
ideal	idéal	ideal	Ideal(n)	ideal	ideale
ideal	idéal, e	ideal	ideal	ideal	ideale
ideia	idée	idea	Idee(f)	idea	idea
idêntico, a	identique	identical	identisch	idéntico, a	identico, a
identidade	identité	identity	Identität(f)	identidad	identità
identificar	identifier	identify	identifizieren	identificar	identificare
ideologia	idéologie	ideology	Ideologie(f)	ideología	ideologia
idiota	idiot, e	idiotic, stupid	idiotisch, dumm	idiota; tonto, a	idiota; stupido, a
idiota	idiot, e	idiot, fool	Idiot(m), Dummkopf(m)	idiota	idiota; scemo, a
idiotice, asneira	idiotie	stupidity	Dummheit(f)	idiotez	idiozia
ídolo	idole	idol	Idol(n)	ídolo	idolo
idoso, a	âgé, e	old	alt	anciano, a	anziano, a
iglu	igloo	igloo	Iglu(n)	iglú	igloo
ignição	allumage	ignition	Zündung(f)	encendido	accensione
ignorância	ignorance	ignorance	Unwissenheit(f)	ignorancia	ignoranza
ignorar	ignorer	ignorant of(be)	nicht wissen	ignorar	ignorare
igreja	église	church(-es)	Kirche(f)	iglesia	chiesa
igual	égal, e	equal	gleich	igual	uguale
igual	pareil, le	same, similar, like	gleich, wie	igual	uguale, pari
igualdade	égalité	equality	Gleichheit(f)	igualdad	uguaglianza
igualmente	également	too, also, as well	ebenfalls, auch	igualmente	ugualmente
ilegal	illégal, e	illegal	illegal	ilegal	illegale
ilegítimo, a	illégitime	illegitimate	unehelich	ilegítimo, a	illegittimo, a
iletrado, a	illettré, e	illiterate	ungebildet	analfabeto, a	analfabeta
ilha	île	island, isle	Insel(f)	isla	isola
ilhéu, ilhota	îlot	islet	Inselchen(n)	islote	isolotto
ilógico, a	illogique	illogical	unlogisch	ilógico, a	illogico, a
iluminação	éclairage	lighting	Beleuchtung(f)	iluminación	illuminazione
iluminado, a	illuminé, e	illuminated	erleuchtet	iluminado, a	illuminato, a
iluminar	éclairer	light; illuminate	beleuchten	iluminar	illuminare
ilusão	illusion	illusion	Illusion(f)	ilusión	illusione
ilustração	illustration	illustration	Illustration(f)	ilustración	illustrazione
ilustrado, a	illustré, e	illustrated	illustriert	ilustrado, a	illustrato, a
ilustre	illustre	illustrious	berühmt	ilustre	illustre
imagem	image	image, picture	Bild(n)	imagen	immagine
imaginação	imagination	imagination	Einbildung(f)	imaginación	immaginazione
imaginar	imaginer	imagine	vor = stellen, sich	imaginar	immaginare
imaginário, a	imaginaire	imaginary	eingebildet	imaginario, a	immaginario, a
íman	aimant	magnet	Magnet(m)	imán	calamita
imbecil; parvo, a	imbécile	fool, idiot	Idiot(in f)m	imbécil	imbecille
imediatamente	immédiatement	immediately	sofort	inmediatamente	immediatamente
imediatamente	aussitôt	straight away	sofort, sogleich	seguida(en)	subito, appena
imediatamente	suite(tout de)	once(at)	sogleich, sofort	seguida(en)	subito
imediato, a	immédiat, e	immediate	unverzüglich	inmediato, a	immediato, a
imenso, a	immense	immense, vast	unendlich groß	inmenso, a	immenso, a
imergir	immerger	immerse	versenken	sumergir	immergere

Portuguese	French	English	German	Spanish	Italian
imersão	immersion	immersion	Versenkung(f)	inmersión	immersione
imigração	immigration	immigration	Einwanderung(f)	inmigración	immigrazione
imigrante	immigré, e	immigrant	Einwanderer(in f)m	inmigrado, a	immigrato, a
imitação	imitation	imitation	Nachahmung(f)	imitación	imitazione
imitar	imiter	imitate	nach = ahmen	imitar	imitare
imobiliário	immobilier	property	Immobilien(f, pl)	inmobiliario	immobiliare
imortal	immortel, le	immortal	unsterblich	inmortal	immortale
imóvel	immobile	motionless	unbeweglich	inmóvil	immobile
impaciência	impatience	impatience	Ungeduld(f)	impaciencia	impazienza
impaciente	impatient, e	impatient	ungeduldig	impaciente	impaziente
impacto	impact	impact	Stoß(m)	impacto	impatto
impacto	impact	impact	Einfluß(m)	impacto	impatto
impar	impair	odd	ungerade	impar	dispari
imparcial	impartial, e	impartial	unparteiisch	imparcial	imparziale
impedido, a	barré, e	blocked	gesperrt	cortado, a	sbarrato, a
impedir	empêcher	prevent	verhindern	impedir	impedire
impensável	impensable	unthinkable	undenkbar	increíble	impensabile
imperador	empereur	emperor	Kaiser(m)	emperador	imperatore
imperativo, a	impératif, ive	imperative, urgent	bindend, zwingend	imperativo, a	imperativo, a
imperatriz	impératrice	empress	Kaiserin(f)	emperatriz	imperatrice
imperfeição	imperfection	imperfection	Unvollkommenheit(f)	imperfección	imperfezione
imperialismo	impérialisme	imperialism	Imperialismus(m)	imperialismo	imperialismo
império	empire	empire	Reich(n)	imperio	impero
impermeável	imperméable	water-proof	wasserdicht	impermeable	impermeabile
impertinente	impertinent, e	impertinent	unverschämt	impertinente	impertinente
impetuoso, a	impétueux, se	impetuous	ungestüm, stürmisch	impetuoso, a	impetuoso, a
impiedoso, a	impitoyable	pitiless	unbarmherzig	despiadado, a	spietato, a
implantação	implantation	setting up(of)	Niederlassung	implantación	impianto
implantar	implanter	establish, set up	etablieren, gründen	implantar	impiantare
implicação	implication	implication	Verwicklung(f)	implicación	implicazione
implicar	impliquer	involve	verwickeln	implicar	implicare
implicar	impliquer	imply	bedeuten; an = deuten	implicar	implicare
implorar	implorer	implore, beg	an = flehen	implorar	implorare
impopular	impopulaire	unpopular	unbeliebt	impopular	impopolare
impor	imposer	impose	auf = zwingen	imponer	imporre
impor-se	imposer(s')	impose oneself on	auf = drängen, sich	imponerse	imporsi
importação	importation	import; importing	Einfuhr(f)	importación	importazione
importância	importance	importance	Bedeutung(f)	importancia	importanza
importante	important, e	important	wichtig	importante	importante
importar	importer	import	ein = führen	importar	importare
impossível	impossible	impossible	unmöglich	imposible	impossibile
imposto	impôt	tax	Steuer(f)	impuesto	tassa
impotente	impuissant, e	powerless	machtlos	impotente	impotente
impregnar	imprégner	impregnate	imprägnieren	impregnar	impregnare
imprensa	presse	press	Presse(f)	prensa	stampa
impressão	impression	impression	Eindruck(m)	impresión	impressione
impressão	impression	printing	Druck(m)	impresión	stampa
impressão; marca	empreinte	print	Abdruck(m)	huella	impronta
impressionante	impressionnant, e	impressive	beeindruckend	impresionante	impressionante
impressionar	impressionner	impress	beeindrucken	impresionar	impressionare
impresso	imprimé	printed form	Formular(n)	impreso	stampato
imprevisto, a	imprévu, e	unexpected	unvorhergesehen	imprevisto, a	imprevisto, a
imprimir	imprimer	print	drucken	imprimir	stampare
improvisar	improviser	improvise	improvisieren	improvisar	improvvisare
imprudência	imprudence	imprudence	Unvorsichtigkeit(f)	imprudencia	imprudenza
imprudente	imprudent, e	careless	unvorsichtig	imprudente	imprudente
impulso	impulsion	impulse	Impuls(m)	impulso	impulso
impulso	élan	spring, bound	Anlauf(m), Schwung(m)	impulso	slancio
impune	impuni, e	unpunished	unbestraft	impune	impunito, a
impureza	impureté	impurity	Unreinheit(f)	impureza	impurità
imunidade	immunité	immunity	Immunität(f)	inmunidad	immunità
imunizar	immuniser	immunize	immunisieren	inmunizar	immunizzare
inacessível	inaccessible	inaccessible	unerreichbar	inaccesible	inaccessibile
inactivo, a	inactif, ive	inactive	untätig, inaktiv	inactivo, a	inattivo, a
inadaptado, a	inadapté, e	unsuitable	ungeeignet	inadaptado, a	inadatto, a
inadmissível	inadmissible	inadmissible	unzulässig	inadmisible	inammissibile
inalar	inhaler, respirer	inhale	ein = atmen	inhalar	inalare
inalterado, a	inchangé, e	unchanged	unverändert	inalterado, a	immutato, a

Portuguese	French	English	German	Spanish	Italian
inanimado, a	inanimé, e	lifeless	unbelebt, leblos	inanimado, a	inanimato, a
inapto, a	inapte	unsuited, unfit	ungeeignet	inapto, a	inabile
inato, a	inné, e	innate	angeboren	innato, a	innato, a
inauguração	inauguration	inauguration	Einweihung(f)	inauguración	inaugurazione
inaugurar	inaugurer	inaugurate	ein = weihen	inaugurar	inaugurare
incandescente	incandescent, e	incandescent	glühend	incandescente	incandescente
incapaz	incapable	incapable, unable	unfähig, untauglich	incapaz	incapace
incêndio	incendie	fire	Brand(m)	incendio	incendio
incerto, a	incertain, e	uncertain	unsicher	inseguro, a	incerto, a
incesto	inceste	incest	Inzucht(f)	incesto	incesto
inchar	enfler	swell	an = schwellen	hinchar	gonfiare
inchar, encher	gonfler	inflate, blow up	auf = blasen	inflar	gonfiare
incidente	incident	incident	Zwischenfall(m)	incidente	incidente
incinerar	incinérer	incinerate	ein = äschern	incinerar	incenerire
incisão, golpe	entaille	cut, nick, notch	Kerbe(f)	cortadura	incisione
incitar	inciter	incite	an = regen	incitar	incitare
inclinação	inclinaison	slant, incline	Neigung(f), Gefälle(n)	inclinación	inclinazione
inclinação	tendance	trend, tendency	Neigung(f)	inclinación	inclinazione
inclinar	incliner	incline, tilt	neigen	inclinar	inclinare
inclinar	pencher	tilt, lean	neigen	inclinar	inclinare
inclinar-se	pencher(se)	bend, lean	bücken, sich	inclinarse	chinarsi
incluir	inclure	include	ein = schließen	incluir	includere
incluso, a	inclus, e	included	inklusiv	incluido, a	incluso, a
incolor	incolore	colourless	farblos	incoloro, a	incolore
incomodar	incommoder	bother	stören	incomodar	incomodare
incomodar	déranger	disturb, bother	stören	molestar	disturbare
incomodar	gêner	obstruct	stören	molestar	imbarazzare
incompatível	incompatible	incompatible	unvereinbar	incompatible	incompatibile
incompetência	incompétence	incompetence	Inkompetenz(f)	incompetencia	incompetenza
incompleto, a	incomplet, ète	incomplete	unvollständig	incompleto, a	incompleto, a
inconsciente	inconscient, e	unconscious	unbewußt	inconsciente	incosciente
incontestável	incontestable	incontestable	unbestreitbar	indiscutible	incontestabile
inconveniente	inconvénient	disadvantage	Nachteil(m)	inconveniente	inconveniente
incorporação	incorporation	incorporation	Eingliederung(f)	incorporación	incorporazione
incorporar	incorporer	incorporate	ein = verleiben	incorporar	incorporare
incorrecto, a	incorrect, e	incorrect, wrong	unrichtig, falsch	incorrecto, a	scorretto, a
incremento	augmentation	increment	Zunahme(f)	incremento	incremento
incriminar	incriminer	incriminate	beschuldigen	incriminar	incriminare
incrível	incroyable	unbelievable	unglaublich	increíble	incredibile
inculpar, acusar	inculper	charge, accuse	beschuldigen	inculpar, acusar	incolpare, accusare
incurável	incurable	incurable	unheilbar	incurable	incurabile
incursão	incursion	incursion	Überfall(m)	incursión	incursione
indecente	indécent, e	indecent	unanständig	indecente	indecente
indefinido, a	indéfini, e	indefinite	unbestimmt	indefinido, a	indefinito, a
indemnização	indemnité	compensation	Entschädigung(f)	indemnidad	risarcimento
indemnizar	indemniser	compensate	entschädigen	indemnizar	indennizzare
indemnizar	dédommager	compensate	entschädigen	indemnizar	indennizzare
independência	indépendance	independence	Unabhängigkeit(f)	independencia	indipendenza
independente	indépendant, e	independent	unabhängig	independiente	indipendente
indicação	indication	indication	Angabe(f), Hinweis(m)	indicación	indicazione
indicar	indiquer	indicate, show	an = deuten, zeigen	indicar	indicare
indicar	désigner	indicate	bezeichnen	señalar, indicar	indicare
indicativo, prefixo	indicatif(tél.)	dialling code	Vorwählnummer(f)	prefijo	prefisso
indicador	indicateur	indicator	Anzeiger(m)	indicador	indicatore
índice	indice	index	Index m(Preisindex m)	índice	indice
índice	index	index	Index(m)	índice	indice
índice, tabela	cours	rate, quotation	Kurs(m)	cotización	corso
indício	indice	indication, sign	Anzeichen(n)	indicio	indizio
indiferente	indifférent, e	indifferent	gleichgültig	indiferente	indifferente
indígena	indigène	native, indigenous	Eingeborene(f, m)	indígena	indigeno, a
indigesto, a	indigeste	indigestible	unverdaulich	indigesto, a	indigesto, a
indignação	indignation	indignation	Empörung(f)	indignación	indignazione
indigno, a	indigne	unworthy	unwürdig	indigno, a	indegno, a
indirecto, a	indirect, e	indirect	indirekt	indirecto, a	indiretto, a
indisciplinado, a	dissipé, e	unruly	unaufmerksam	indisciplinado, a	indisciplinato, a
indiscrição	indiscrétion	indiscretion	Indiskretion(f)	indiscreción	indiscrezione
indispensável	indispensable	indispensable	unentbehrlich	indispensable	indispensabile
indisposição	malaise	faintness	Unwohlsein, Schwäche	malestar	malessere

Portuguese	French	English	German	Spanish	Italian
individual	individuel, le	individual	individuell	individual	individuale
indivíduo	individu	individual	Individuum(n)	individuo	individuo
indolor	indolore	painless	schmerzlos	indoloro, a	indolore
indulgência	indulgence	indulgence	Nachsicht(f)	indulgencia	indulgenza
indústria	industrie	industry	Industrie(f)	industria	industria
industrial	industriel, le	industrial	industriell	industrial	industriale
industrial	industriel	industrialist	Industrielle(m)	industrial	industriale
indústria livro	édition	publishing	Verlagswesen(n)	industria editor-	edizione
induzir	induire	induce	veranlassen	inducir	indurre
inédito, a	inédit, e	unpublished	unveröffentlicht	inédito, a	inedito, a
ineficaz	inefficace	inefficient	unwirksam, unfähig	ineficaz	inefficace
inércia	inertie	inertia	Trägheit(f)	inercia	inerzia
inerte	inerte	inert	regungslos	inerte	inerte
inesperado, a	inespéré, e	unexpected	unerwartet, unverhofft	inesperado, a	insperato, a
inexacto, a	inexact, e	inexact, inaccurate	ungenau	inexacto, a	inesatto, a
inexistente	inexistant, e	non-existent	nicht existierend	inexistente	inesistente
infalível	infaillible	infallible	unfehlbar	infalible	infallibile
infame	infâme	vile, infamous	niederträchtig	infame	infame
infância	enfance	childhood	Kindheit(f)	infancia	infanzia
infantil	infantile	infantile, child	Kinder-, kindisch	infantil	infantile
infatigável	infatigable	tireless	unermüdlich	incansable	instancabile
infecção	infection	infection	Infektion(f)	infección	infezione
infeliz	malheureux, se	unhappy, miserable	unglücklich, betrübt	desgraciado, a	infelice
infeliz, triste	malheureux, se	unhappy, sorrowful	betrübt, unglücklich	infeliz, triste	infelice, triste
infeliz	malheureux, se	unfortunate	unglücklich	desgraciado, a	disgraziato, a
inferior	inférieur, e	inferior	minderwertig	inferior	inferiore
inferior	inférieur, e	lower	untere(r)	inferior	inferiore
infernal	infernal, e	infernal	Höllen-; höllisch	infernal	infernale
inferno	enfer	hell	Hölle(f)	infierno	inferno
infiel	infidèle	unfaithful	untreu	infiel	infedele
infiltração	infiltration	infiltration	Einsickern(n)	infiltración	infiltrazione
infinitivo	infinitif	infinitive	Infinitiv(m)	infinitivo	infinito
infinito, a	infini, e	infinite	unendlich	infinito, a	infinito, a
inflação	inflation	inflation	Inflation(f)	inflación	inflazione
inflamável	inflammable	inflammable	brennbar	inflamable	infiammabile
inflexível	inflexible	inflexible	starr	inflexible	inflessibile
infligir	infliger	inflict	auf = erlegen	infligir	infliggere
influência	influence	influence	Einfluß(m)	influencia	influenza
influente	influent, e	influential	einflußreich	influyente	influente
informação	information	information	Information(f)	información	informazione
informação	renseignement	information	Auskunft(f)	información	informazione
informar	informer	inform	informieren	informar	imformare
informar-se	informer(s')	inquire	erkundigen, sich	informarse	informarsi
informar-se	renseigner(se)	inquire	erkundigen, sich	informar(se)	informare(-arsi)
informática	informatique	data processing	Informatik(f)	informática	informatica
infracção	infraction	offence, violation	Verstoß(m)	infracción	infrazione
ingénuo, a	naïf, ïve	naive	naiv	ingenuo, a	ingenuo, a
ingerência	ingérence	interference	Einmischung(f)	ingerencia	ingerenza
ingrato, a	ingrat, e	ungrateful	undankbar	ingrato, a	ingrato, a
iniciação	initiation	initiation	Einführung(f)	iniciación	iniziazione
inicial	initial, e	initial	anfänglich; Anfangs-	inicial	iniziale
iniciativa	initiative	initiative	Initiative(f)	iniciativa	iniziativa
inimaginável	inimaginable	inconceivable	undenkbar	inimaginable	inimmaginabile
inimigo, a	ennemi, e	enemy	Feind(in f)m	enemigo, a	nemico, a
injecção	piqûre	injection	Spritze(f)	inyección	iniezione
injectar	injecter	inject	spritzen, ein = spritzen	inyectar	iniettare
injúria	injure	insult	Beleidigung(f)	injuria	ingiuria
injustiça	injustice	injustice	Ungerechtigkeit(f)	injusticia	ingiustizia
inocente	innocent, e	innocent	unschuldig	inocente	innocente
inofensivo, a	inoffensif, ive	inoffensive	harmlos	inofensivo, a	inoffensivo, a
inorgânico, a	inorganique	inorganic	anorganisch	inorgánico, a	inorganico, a
inovação	innovation	innovation	Neuerung(f)(Er-)	innovación	innovazione
inovar	innover	innovate	innovieren, erneuern	innovar	innovare
inquérito	enquête	inquiry, inquest	Untersuchung(f)	investigación	indagine, inchiesta
inquérito	enquête, étude	survey	Umfrage(f)	encuesta	inchiesta
inquietação	inquiétude	anxiety, worry	Sorge(f)	inquietud	inquietudine
inquieto, a	inquiet, ète	worried	besorgt	inquieto, a	inquieto, a
inquilino, a	locataire	tenant	Mieter(in f)m	inquilino, a	inquilino, a

P

Portuguese	French	English	German	Spanish	Italian
insatisfeito, a	insatisfait, e	not satisfied	unzufrieden	insatisfecho, a	insoddisfatto, a
inscrever	inscrire, noter	note, write	ein = schreiben	inscribir	iscrivere
inscrever-se	inscrire(s')	join	bei = treten	inscribirse	iscriversi
inscrição	inscription	inscription	Inschrift(f)	inscripción	iscrizione
insecto	insecte	insect	Insekt(n)	insecto	insetto
inseminação	insémination	insemination	Befruchtung(f)	inseminación	inseminazione
insensível	insensible	insensitive	unempfindlich	insensible	insensibile
inserção	insertion	insertion	Einfügung(f)	inserción	inserzione
inserir	insérer	insert	ein = setzen, ein = fügen	insertar	inserire
insígnia	insigne	badge	Zeichen(n), Abzeichen	insignia	distintivo
insignificante	insignifiant, e	insignificant	unbedeutend	insignificante	insignificante
insistir	insister	insist	bestehen, beharren	insistir	insistere
insistir	acharner(s')	persist	beharren	empeñarse	accanirsi
insolação	insolation	sunstroke	Sonnenstich(m)	insolación	insolazione
insolação	coup de soleil	sunburn	Sonnenbrand(m)	insolación	scottatura
insolência	insolence	insolence	Frechheit(f)	insolencia	insolenza
insolente	insolent, e	insolent	unverschämt, frech	insolente	insolente
insólito, a	insolite	unusual	seltsam, ungewohnt	insólito, a	insolito, a
insónia	insomnie	insomnia	Schlaflosigkeit(f)	insomnio	insonnia
insonoro, a	insonore	sound-proof	schalldicht	insonoro, a	insonoro, a
inspecção	inspection	inspection	Überprüfung(f)	inspección	ispezione
inspector, a	inspecteur, trice	inspector	Inspektor(in f)m	inspector, a	ispettore, trice
inspiração	inspiration	inspiration	Anregung(f)	inspiración	ispirazione
instalação	installation	installation	Einrichtung(f)	instalación	installazione
instalar	installer	install	ein = richten	instalar	installare
instalar-se	installer(s')	settle	nieder = lassen, sich	instalarse	stabilirsi
instante	instant	moment, instant	Moment(m)	instante	istante
instável	instable	unstable	unbeständig	inestable	instabile
instintivo, a	instinctif, ive	instinctive	instinktiv	instintivo, a	istintivo, a
instinto	instinct	instinct	Instinkt(m)	instinto	istinto
institucional	institutionnel	institutional	gesetzlich	institucional	istituzionale
instituição	institution	institution	Institution(f)	institución	istituzione
instituto	institut	institute	Institut(n)	instituto	istituto
instrução	instruction	instruction	Ausbildung(f)	instrucción	istruzione
instruir	instruire	teach	aus = bilden	instruir	istruire
instrumento	instrument	instrument	Instrument(n)	instrumento	strumento
instrutor, a	instructeur	instructor	Ausbilder(m)	instructor	istruttore, trice
insuficiente	insuffisant, e	insufficient	ungenügend	insuficiente	insufficiente
insulina	insuline	insulin	Insulin(n)	insulina	insulina
insultar	insulter	insult	beleidigen	insultar	insultare
insulto	insulte	insult	Beleidigung(f)	insulto	insulto
insurgir-se	insurger(s')	rebel(against)	empören, sich	rebelarse	ribellarsi
insurgir-se	insurger(s')	rise up, revolt	auf = lehnen gegen, sich	sublevarse	insorgere
intacto, a	intact, e	intact	intakt	intacto, a	intatto, a
integral	intégral, e	integral	vollständig	íntegro, a	integrale
integrar	intégrer	integrate	integrieren	integrar	integrare
integridade	intégrité	integrity	Integrität(f)	integridad	integrità
inteiramente	entièrement	entirely	ganz	completamente	interamente
inteiro, a	entier, ière	whole, entire	ganz	entero, a	intero, a
intelectual	intellectuel, le	intellectual	intellektuell	intelectual	intellettuale
inteligência	intelligence	intelligence	Intelligenz(f)	inteligencia	intelligenza
inteligente	intelligent, e	intelligent	intelligent, klug	inteligente	intelligente
intenção	intention	intention	Absicht(f)	intención	intenzione
intenção	intention, but	purpose, aim, goal	Absicht(f)	intención	intento, fine, scopo
intensidade	intensité	intensity	Intensität(f)	intensidad	intensità
intensivo, a	intensif, ive	intensive	intensiv	intensivo, a	intensivo, a
intenso, a	intense	intense	heftig, stark	intenso, a	intenso, a
interceptar	intercepter	intercept	auf = fangen, ab = fangen	interceptar	intercettare
interessante	intéressant, e	interesting	interessant	interesante	interessante
interessar-se	intéresser(s')	interested in(be)	interessieren, sich	interesarse	interessarsi
interesse	intérêt	interest	Interesse(n)	interés	interesse
interferência	interférence	interference	Einmischung; Störung	interferencia	interferenza
interior	intérieur	interior	Innere(n)	interior	interiore
interior	intérieur, e	inside, inner	innere(r, s), innen	interior	interno, a
interior	intérieur, e	inner, interior	inner	interior	interiore
interlocutor, a	interlocuteur	interlocutor	Gesprächspartner/in	interlocutor, a	interlocutore, trice
intermediário, a	intermédiaire	intermediate	Zwischen-, Mittel-	intermediario, a	intermediario, a
intermitente	intermittent, e	intermittent	aussetzend	intermitente	intermittente

Portuguese	French	English	German	Spanish	Italian
internacional	international, e	international	international	internacional	internazionale
interno, a	interne	internal, inner	intern	interno, a	interno, a
interno, a	intérieur, e	domestic, home	Innen-	interior	interno, a
interno, a	pensionnaire	boarder	Internatsschüler(m)	interno, a	collegiale
interpretar	interpréter	interpret	deuten, aus = legen	interpretar	interpretare
intérprete	interprète	interpreter	Dolmetscher(in)f)m	intérprete	interprete
interrogar	interroger	question, ask	fragen, befragen	interrogar	interrogare
interromper	interrompre	interrupt	unterbrechen	interrumpir	interrompere
interrupção	interruption	interruption	Unterbrechung(f)	interrupción	interruzione
interruptor	interrupteur	switch	Schalter(m)	interruptor	interruttore
interruptor	bouton	switch	Schalter(m)	interruptor, botón	bottone, pulsante
intersecção	intersection	intersection	Kreuzung(f)	intersección	intersezione
intervalo	entracte	interval	Pause(f)	intermedio	intervallo
intervalo	intervalle	interval	Abstand(m)	intervalo	intervallo
intervalo	intervalle	gap	Abstand(m)	intervalo	intervallo
intervenção	intervention	intervention	Eingriff(m)	intervención	intervento
intervir	intervenir	intervene	dazwischen = treten	intervenir	intervenire
intestino	intestin	intestine	Darm(m)	intestino	intestino
intimidar	intimider	intimidate	ein = schüchtern	intimidar	intimidire
íntimo, a	intime	intimate	vertraut, intim	íntimo, a	intimo, a
íntimo, a	intime	close, intimate	intim	íntimo, a	intimo, a
intolerância	intolérance	intolerance	Intoleranz(f)	intolerancia	intolleranza
intoxicação	intoxication	poisoning	Vergiftung(f)	intoxicación	intossicazione
intrépido, a	intrépide	intrepid	kühn, mutig	intrépido, a	intrepido, a
intriga	intrigue	intrigue	Intrige(f)	intriga	intrigo
intrigar	intriguer	intrigue	intrigieren	intrigar	intrigare
introduzir	introduire	insert; introduce	ein = führen	introducir	introdurre
intrusão	intrusion	intrusion	Eindringen(n)	intrusión	intrusione
intuição	intuition	intuition	Intuition(f)	intuición	intuizione
inundação	inondation	flooding, flood	Überschwemmung(f)	inundación	inondazione
inútil	inutile	useless	nutzlos	inútil	inutile
invadir	envahir	invade	ein = fallen	invadir	invadere
inválido, a	invalide	disabled	behindert	inválido, a	invalido, a
invariável	invariable	invariable	unveränderlich	invariable	invariabile
invasão	invasion	invasion	Invasion(f)	invasión	invasione
invenção	invention	invention	Erfindung(f)	invención	invenzione
invencível	invincible	invincible	unbesiegbar	invencible	invincibile
inventar	inventer	invent	erfinden	inventar	inventare
inventário	inventaire	inventory	Inventar(n)	inventario	inventario
inventário	inventaire	stock-list(taking)	Inventur(f)	inventario	inventario
inventor	inventeur	inventor	Erfinder(in f)m	inventor	inventore
inverno	hiver	winter	Winter(m)	invierno	inverno
inversão	inversion	inversion	Umkehrung(f)	inversión	inversione
inverso, a	inverse	opposite	umgekehrt	inverso, a	inverso, a
inverter	inverser	reverse, invert	um = kehren	invertir	invertire
investidura	investiture	investiture	Investitur(f)	investidura	investitura
investigação	recherche	research	Forschung(f)	investigación	ricerca
investigador, a	chercheur, euse	research worker	Forscher(in f)m	investigador, a	cercatore
investigar	enquêter	investigate	untersuchen	investigar	investigare, indagare
investimento	investissement	investment	Investition(f)	inversión	investimento
investir	investir	invest	investieren	invertir	investire
invisível	invisible	invisible	unsichtbar	invisible	invisibile
invocar	invoquer	invoke	beziehen auf, sich	invocar	invocare
invólucro	gaine	sheath	Hülle(f)	funda, estuche	guaina, astuccio
ir	aller	go	gehen, fahren nach	ir(a, por, hacia)	andare, recarsi
ir buscar	aller chercher	go to fetch/get	ab = holen	ir a buscar	andare a prendere
íris	iris	iris	Iris(f)	iris	iride
irmã	soeur	sister	Schwester(f)	hermana	sorella
irmão	frère	brother	Bruder(m)	hermano	fratello
ironia	ironie	irony	Ironie(f)	ironía	ironia
irradiação	irradiation	irradiation	Bestrahlung(f)	irradiación	irradiazione
irradiação	rayonnement	radiance	Strahlung(f)	irradiación	irradiazione
irregular	irrégulier, e	irregular	unregelmäßig	irregular	irregolare
irrigar	irriguer	irrigate	bewässern	irrigar	irrigare
irritação	agacement	irritation	Ärger(m)	fastidio	irritazione
irritante	irritant, e	irritating	ärgerlich; aufregend	irritante	irritante
irritar	irriter	irritate	reizen, irritieren	irritar	irritare
irrupção	irruption	irruption	Eindringen(n)	irrupción	irruzione

P

Portuguese	French	English	German	Spanish	Italian
isca, engodo	leurre, appât	lure, bait	Lockmittel(n)	señuelo	esca
isento de taxa	détaxé, e	duty(tax)-free	steuerfrei	desgravado, a	sgravio fiscale
islâmico, a	islamique	Islamic	islamisch	islámico, a	islamico, a
isolação	isolation	insulation	Isolierung(f)	aislamiento	isolamento
isolado, a	seul, e	lonely	einsam	aislado, a; solo, a	isolato, a; solo, a
isolado, a; só, a	isolé, e	isolated, lonely	allein, einsam	aislado, a	isolato, a
isolar	isoler	isolate	ab = sondern; isolieren	aislar	isolare
isolar	isoler	insulate; isolate	isolieren	aislar	isolare
isqueiro	briquet	lighter	Feuerzeug(n)	mechero	accendino
isso, aquilo	cela, ça	that	das, jene(r, s)	eso, aquello, ello	ciò, questo, quello
isto	ceci	this	dies(es); das	esto	questo, ciò
itinerário	itinéraire	itinerary, route	Route(f), Strecke(f)	itinerario	itinerario

J

Portuguese	French	English	German	Spanish	Italian
já	déjà	already	schon	ya	giá
jacente	gisant, e	lying	liegend	yacente	giacente
jacto, repuxo	jet	spray, jet	Strahl(m)	surtidor, chorro	getto, zampillo
Janeiro	Janvier	January	Januar(m)	Enero	Gennaio
janela	fenêtre	window	Fenster(n)	ventana	finestra
jangada	radeau	raft	Floß(n)	balsa	zattera
jantar	dîner	dinner	Abendessen(n)	cena	cena
jantar	dîner	dinner(have)	Abend essen(zu)	cenar	cenare
jante, camba	jante	rim	Felge(f), Radkranz(m)	llanta	cerchione
já que	puisque	since	da, weil	ya que; pues	poichè
jaqueta, casaco	veste	jacket	Jacke(f)	chaqueta	giacca
jardim	jardin	garden	Garten(m)	jardín	giardino
jardim zoológico	zoo	zoo	Zoo(m)	zoológico	zoo
jardineiro, a	jardinier, ière	gardener	Gärtner(in f)m	jardinero, a	giardiniere, a
jarra	vase	vase	Vase(f)	jarrón	vaso
jarro, caneca	carafe	jug, carafe	Karaffe(f)	jarra	caraffa
jazz	jazz	jazz	Jazz(m)	jazz	jazz
jibóia	python	python	Python(m)	pitón	pitone
joalharia	bijouterie	jeweller's	Schmuckgeschäft(n)	joyería	gioielleria
jockey	jockey	jockey	Jockey(m)	jockey	jockey, fantino
joelho	genou	knee	Knie(n)	rodilla	ginocchio
jogada, jogo	partie	game	Spiel(n)	partida	partita
jogador, a	joueur, se	player	Spieler(in f)m	jugador, a	giocatore, trice
jogar, brincar	jouer	play	spielen	jugar	giocare
jogar	jouer	gamble	spielen	jugar	giocare
jogo	jeu	game	Spiel(n)	juego	gioco
jóia	bijou(x)	jewel	Schmuck(m)(-stück n)	joya	gioiello
jóia	joyau	jewel	Juwel(n), Schmuckstück	joya	gioiello
jornal	journal	newspaper, paper	Zeitung(f)	periódico, diario	giornale
jornalismo	journalisme	journalism	Journalismus(m)	periodismo	giornalismo
jornalista	journaliste	journalist	Journalist(in f)m	periodista	giornalista
jorrar	jaillir	gush, spurt out	auf = spritzen	brotar	sgorgare
jovem	jeune	young	jung	joven	giovane
jovens	jeunes	young people	jungen Leute(pl)	jóvenes	giovani
júbilo, alegria	allégresse	elation	Heiterkeit(f)	júbilo, alegría	esultanza
judeu, judia	juif, juive	Jew, Jewess(-es)	Jude(m), Jüdin(f)	judío, judía	ebreo, a
judicial	judiciaire, légal	legal	rechtmäßig	judicial	giudiziario, a
judiciário, a	judiciaire	judicial, legal	gerichtlich	judicial	giudiziario, a
judicioso, a	judicieux, se	judicious	scharfsinnig	juicioso, a	giudizioso, a
judo	judo	judo	Judo(n)	judo, yudo	judò
juíz	juge	judge	Richter(in f)m	juez	giudice
julgamento	jugement	judgement	Urteil(n)	juicio	giudizio

Portuguese	French	English	German	Spanish	Italian
julgar	juger	judge	beurteilen	juzgar	giudicare
julgar	imaginer(s')	imagine	ein = bilden, sich	imaginarse	immaginarsi
Julho	Juillet	July	Juli(m)	Julio	Luglio
Junho	Juin	June	Juni(m)	Junio	Giugno
junta, anilha	joint	joint, join, seal	Dichtung(f)	junta	giunto, guarnizione
junta	junte	junta	Junta(f)	junta	giunta
juntar	assembler	assemble	zusammen = setzen	ensamblar	assemblare
juntar	rassembler	gather(together)	sammeln	juntar	radunare
juntar-se	joindre à(se)	join	an = schließen, sich	juntarse con	unirsi, associarsi
junto	ensemble	together	zusammen	juntos	insieme
junto, a	joint, e	joined, linked	zusammengefügt	junto, a	giunto, a
jurado	juré	juryman, juror	Geschworene(f, m)	jurado	giurato
juramento	serment	oath, pledge	Eid(m)	juramento	giuramento
jurar	jurer	swear	schwören	jurar	giurare
júri	jury	jury	Jury(f)	jurado; tribunal	giuria
jurídico, a	juridique	juridical, legal	juristisch	jurídico, a	giuridico, a
jurisprudência	jurisprudence	jurisprudence	Rechtsprechung(f)	jurisprudencia	giurisprudenza
jurista	juriste	jurist; lawyer	Jurist(in f)m	jurista	giurista
juro	intérêt	interest	Zins(m)	interés	interesse
justamente	justement	exactly	genau	justamente	appunto
justiça	justice	justice	Gerechtigkeit(f)	justicia	giustizia
justificação	justification	justification	Rechtfertigung(f)	justificación	giustificazione
justificar	justifier	justify	begründen, belegen	justificar	giustificare
justo, a	juste	just	gerecht	justo, a	giusto, a
juventude	jeunesse	youth	Jugend(f)	juventud	gioventù, giovinezza

K

Portuguese	French	English	German	Spanish	Italian
karaté	karaté	karate	Karate(n)	karate	karatè
kayac	kayac	kayak	Kajak(m)	kayac, piragua	kayak

L

Portuguese	French	English	German	Spanish	Italian
lá	là	there	dort	allá	là
lá em cima	là-haut	up there	da oben	arriba	in alto
lã	laine	wool	Wolle(f)	lana	lana
lábio	lèvre	lip	Lippe(f)	labio	labbro(a)
labirinto	labyrinthe	labyrinth, maze	Labyrinth(n)	laberinto	labirinto
laboratório	laboratoire	laboratory	Labor(n).	laboratorio	laboratorio
laca	laque	lacquer	Lack(m)	laca	lacca
laca	laque	hair-spray	Haarspray(m, n)	laca	lacca
laço	boucle	loop	Schleife(f)	lazo	cappio; occhiello
laço	noeud papillon	bow tie	Fliege(f)	pajarita	papillon
lacrimogéneo	lacrymogène	tear-gas	Tränengas(n)	lacrimógeno	lacrimogeno
ladeira, encosta	côte	hill, slope	Abhang(m), Steigung(f)	cuesta	salita, pendio
lado	côté	side	Seite(f)	lado	lato

P

Portuguese	French	English	German	Spanish	Italian
ladrão, ladra	voleur, se	thief(-ves), robber	Dieb(in f)m	ladrón, a	ladro, a
ladrar	aboyer	bark	bellen	ladrar	abbaiare
ladrilho, azulejo	carreau	tile	Fliese(f), Kachel(f)	baldosa, azulejo	piastrella
ladrilho	carrelage	tiling; tiles	Fliesen(n); Fliese(f)	embaldosado	pavimento
lagarto	lézard	lizard	Eidechse(f)	lagarto	lucertola
lago	lac	lake	See(m)	lago	lago
lago	bassin	pond	Bassin(n), Teich(m)	estanque	bacino
lago; tanque	étang	pond	Teich(m)	estanque	stagno
lagosta	langouste	crayfish	Languste(f)	langosta	aragosta
lagostim	langoustine	Dublin Bay prawn	Langustine(f)	langostino	scampo
lágrima	larme	tear	Träne(f)	lágrima	lacrima
laguna	lagune	lagoon	Binnensee(m)	laguna	laguna
lama	boue	mud	Schlamm(m)	barro	fango, melma
lama	lama	llama	Lama(n)	llama	lama
lamber	lécher	lick	lecken	lamer	leccare
lamentar	regretter	regret	nach = trauern(jdm/etw)	lamentar, añorar	rimpiangere
lamentar-se	lamenter(se)	lament	jammern	lamentarse	lamentarsi
lamento(eu)	désolé, e	regret(I)	bedauern	siento(lo)	rammaricato, a
lâmina	lame	blade	Schneide(f)	hoja	lama
lâmpada	ampoule	bulb	Glühbirne(f)	bombilla	lampadina
lança	lance	spear, lance	Lanze(f)	lanza	lancia
lançamento	lancement	launch(ing)	Start(m)	lanzamiento	lancio
lançar; atirar	lancer	throw	werfen	lanzar	lanciare
lançar	lancer	launch, start up	lancieren, starten	lanzar	lanciare
lanterna	lanterne	lantern	Laterne(f)	linterna	lanterna
lápis	crayon	pencil	Bleistift(m)	lápiz	matita, lapis
lar	foyer	home	Heim(n)	hogar	focolare
laranja	orange	orange	Apfelsine(f)	naranja	arancia
lareira	foyer, âtre	fire-place	Feuerstelle(f), Herd m	hogar, chimenea	focolare
largar, deixar	larguer	let go, release	weg = werfen, auf = geben	largar	lasciare, mollare
largar; soltar	relâcher	loosen	lockern	aflojar	allentare
largo, a	large	wide, broad	weit, breit	ancho, a	largo, a
largo, a; amplo, a	large	broad	breit, weit	ancho, a	largo, a; ampio, a
largura	largeur	width, breadth	Breite(f)	anchura	larghezza
laringe	larynx	larynx	Kehlkopf(m)	laringe	laringe
laringite	laryngite	laryngitis	Halsentzündung(f)	laringitis	laringite
larva	larve	larva(-vae)	Larve(f)	larva	larva
laser	laser	laser	Laser(m)	láser	laser
lastimar	plaindre	pity	bedauern	compadecer	compatire
lata	boîte	tin	Dose(f)	lata	latta, scatola
lateral	latéral, e	lateral	seitlich	lateral	laterale
latitude	latitude	latitude	Breitengrad(m)	latitud	latitudine
lavabo	lavabo	wash-basin	Waschbecken(n)	lavabo	lavabo, lavandino
lavabos; sanita	toilettes(W.C)	toilet, lavatory	Toiletten(f pl)	servicios(W.C)	toilettes; W.C
lavadouro	évier	sink	Ausguß m, Spülbecken n	fregadero, pila	lavandino, acquaio
lavagante	homard	lobster	Hummer(m)	bogavante	gambero(di mare)
lavagem	lavage	washing	Waschen(n)	lavado	lavaggio
lavandaria	blanchisserie	laundry	Wäscherei(f)	lavandería	lavanderia
lavar	laver	wash	waschen	lavar	lavare
lavar-se	laver(se)	wash	waschen, sich	lavarse	lavarsi
lavoura	labour	ploughing	Feldarbeit(f)	labranza	aratura
lavrador, a	cultivateur	farmer	Landwirt(in f)m	cultivador, a	coltivatore, trice
laxante	laxatif, ive	laxative	abführend	laxante	lassativo, a
leal	loyal, e	loyal	loyal, treu	leal	leale
leão, leoa	lion, ne	lion, lioness	Löwe(m), Löwin(f)	león, leona	leone, leonessa
legal	légal, e	legal	gesetzlich	legal	legale
legalidade	légalité	legality	Rechtmäßigkeit(f)	legalidad	legalità
legar	léguer	bequeath, leave	vermachen	legar	legare
legendado, a	sous-titré, e	subtitled	Untertiteln(mit)	subtitulado, a	didascalie(con)
legislação	législation	legislation	Gesetzgebung(f)	legislación	legislazione
legislativo, a	législatif, ive	legislative	gesetzgebend	legislativo, a	legislativo, a
legítimo, a	légitime	legitimate	legitim	legítimo, a	legittimo, a
legítimo, a	légitime, légal	rightful, lawful	rechtmäßig	legítimo, a	legittimo, a
legível	lisible	legible	leserlich	legible	leggibile
legume	légume	vegetable	Gemüse(n)	legumbre, verdura	verdura; legume
lei	loi	law	Gesetz(n)	ley	legge
leilão	enchère	bid, bidding	Auktion(f); Gebot(n)	subasta	asta
leite	lait	milk	Milch(f)	leche	latte

Portuguese	French	English	German	Spanish	Italian
leitor, a	lecteur, trice	reader	Leser(in f)m	lector, a	lettore, trice
leitura	lecture	reading	Lesen(n)	lectura	lettura
lembrança	rappel	recall	Rückruf(m)	recuerdo	richiamo
lembrar-se	rappeler(se)	recall, remember	erinnern, sich	recordar, acordarse	ricordarsi
leme	gouvernail	rudder	Ruder(n), Steur(n)	timón	timone
lenço	mouchoir	handkerchief	Taschentuch(n)	pañuelo	fazzoletto
lenço, cachecol	foulard	scarf	Seidentuch, Halstuch	fular, pañuelo	foulard
lençol	drap	sheet	Laken(n)	sábana	lenzuolo
lençol(de água)	nappe(eau)	sheet, expanse	Wasserfläche(f)	capa(de agua)	falda
lenda	légende	legend	Legende(f)	leyenda	leggenda
lenha	bois	wood	Brennholz(n)	leña	legna
lentamente	lentement	slowly	langsam	lentamente	lentamente
lente	lentille	len ;(contact -)	Kontaktlinse(f)	lentilla	lente a contatto
lentejoula	paillette	glitter, spangle	Flitter(m)	lentejuela	lustrino
lentilha	lentille	lentil	Linse(f)(Pflanze)	lenteja	lenticchia
lento, a	lent, e	slow	langsam	lento, a	lento, a
leque	éventail	fan	Fächer(m)	abanico	ventaglio
ler	lire	read	lesen	leer	leggere
lesão	lésion	lesion, injury	Verletzung(f)	lesión	lesione
lésbica	lesbienne	lesbian	lesbisch	lesbiana	lesbica
letra	lettre	letter	Buchstabe(m)	letra	lettera
letreiro	enseigne	sign	Schild(m)(Reklame-)	letrero	insegna
leucemia	leucémie	leukaemia	Leukämie(f)	leucemia	leucemia
levantamento	relevé	statement	Aufstellung(f)machen	extracto	estratto
levantar	lever	lift(up), raise	heben	levantar	alzare
levantar, erguer	soulever	lift, raise	an = heben, hoch = heben	levantar, elevar	sollevare
levantar	retirer	draw out, withdraw	ab = heben	sacar	prelevare
levantar-se	lever(se)	get up	erheben, sich	levantar(se)	alzarsi
levantar-se	lever(se)	stand up, get up	auf = stehen	levantarse	alzarsi
levar	porter	carry	tragen	llevar	portare
levar	emmener	take	mit = nehmen	llevar	portare, condurre
levar	emporter	take(away)	mit = nehmen	llevar	portar via
levar, conduzir	mener, conduire	lead	führen	guiar, conducir	condurre
lhes	leur	them(to -)	ihnen	les	loro; gli
liberal	libéral, e	liberal	liberal	liberal	liberale
liberalismo	libéralisme	liberalism	Liberalismus(m)	liberalismo	liberalismo
liberdade	liberté	liberty, freedom	Freiheit(f)	libertad	libertà
libertar	libérer	liberate, free	befreien	liberar	liberare
libertar	délivrer	free	befreien	libertar	rilasciare, liberare
libertar	relâcher	release	frei = lassen	soltar	rilasciare
líbido	libido	libido	Libido(f)	líbido	libido
lição	leçon	lesson	Stunde(f); Lektion(f)	lección	lezione
licença	licence	licence	Lizenz(f)	licencia	licenza
licença	permis	licence; permit	Schein(m), Genehmigung	permiso	permesso, licenza
licenciatura	licence	degree	Lizenz(f)	licenciatura	laurea
liceu	lycée	comprehensive sch.	Gymnasium(n)	instituto, liceo	liceo
licor	liqueur	liqueur	Likör(m)	licor	liquore
liga	alliage	alloy	Legierung(f).	aleación	lega
ligação, junção	liaison	connection, link	Verbindung(f)	relación; enlace	collegamento
ligadura	bandage	bandage	Bandage(f), Verband(m)	vendaje, venda	fasciatura
ligar	lier	tie, bind	binden, verbinden	ligar, amarrar	legare
ligar	relier	link, connect	verbinden	enlazar, unir	collegare
ligar	connecter	connect	kuppeln, verbinden	conectar	connettere
ligar	brancher	connect	an = schließen	empalmar	allacciare
ligar	brancher	plug in	ein = stecken	enchufar	innestare
ligeiramente	légèrement	lightly, slightly	leicht	ligeramente	leggermente
ligeiro, a; leve	léger, ère	light	leicht	ligero, a	leggero, a
lima	lime	file	Feile(f)	lima	lima
limão	citron	lemon	Zitrone(f)	limón	limone
limitar	limiter	limit	begrenzen	limitar	limitare
limite	limite	limit	Grenze(f)	límite	limite
limítrofe	limitrophe	border(ing)	angrenzend	limítrofe	limitrofo
limpar, secar	essuyer	wipe, dry	ab = wischen, abtrocknen	limpiar, secar	asciugare
limpar	nettoyer	clean	reinigen	limpiar	pulire
limpeza	propreté	clean(li)ness	Reinlichkeit(f)	limpieza	pulizia
limpeza	ménage	housework	Haushalt(m)	limpieza	pulizie
limpeza	nettoyage	cleaning	Reinigung(f)	limpieza	pulizia
limpo, a	propre	clean	sauber	limpio, a	pulito, a

Portuguese	French	English	German	Spanish	Italian
linchar	lyncher	lynch	lynchen	linchar	linciare
linear	linéaire	linear	linear	lineal	lineare
lingote	lingot	ingot, bullion	Barren(m)	lingote	lingotto
lingua	langue	tongue	Zunge(f)	lengua	lingua
língua, idioma	langue	language	Sprache(f)	idioma, lengua	lingua
linguagem	langage	language	Sprache(f)	lenguaje	linguaggio
linha	ligne	line	Linie(f)	línea	linea
linha	ligne	line	Angelschnur(f)	caña	lenza
linha; risca	raie	line	Strich(m)	raya	riga
liquidar	liquider	liquidate	liquidieren	liquidar	liquidare
líquido, a	liquide	liquid	flüssig	líquido, a	liquido, a
líquido	liquide	liquid	Flüssigkeit(f)	líquido	liquido
liso, a	lisse	smooth	glatt	liso, a	liscio, a
lisonjear	flatter	flatter	schmeicheln	halagar	adulare
lista	liste	list	Liste(f)	lista	lista
lista	carte(resto)	menu	Karte(f)(Speisekarte)	menú	menù, carta
lista dos vinhos	carte des vins	wine-list	Weinkarte(f)	carta de vinos	lista dei vini
literário, a	littéraire	literary	literarisch	literario, a	letterario, a
literatura	littérature	literature	Literatur(f)	literatura	letteratura
litígio	litige	litigation	Streitfall(m)	litigio	litigio
litografia	lithographie	lithograph(y)	Steindruck(m)	litografía	litografia
litoral	littoral	coast	Küstenstreifen(m)	litoral	litorale
litro	litre	litre	Liter(m, n)	litro	litro
lívido, a	livide	livid, pallid	blaß, fahl	lívido, a	livido, a
livraria	librairie	book-shop	Buchhandlung(f)	librería	libreria
livrar-se	débarrasser(se)	get rid of	beseitigen	quitarse	liberarsi
livre	libre	free	frei	libre	libero, a
livre	libre	clear	frei	libre	libero, a
livrete(circulação)	carte grise	log-book	KFZ-Schein(m)	cédula iden-fiscal	libretto di circola-
livro	livre	book	Buch(n)	libro	libro
livro de cheques	chéquier	cheque book	Scheckheft(n)	talonario(cheques)	libretto di assegni
lixo	ordure(s)	rubbish, garbage	Abfall(m)	basura	immondizia
lobo	loup	wolf(-lves)	Wolf(m)	lobo	lupo
lóbulo	lobe	lobe	Ohrläppchen(n)	lóbulo	lobo
local	local, e	local	lokal	local	locale
local	local	premises	Gebäude(n), Lokal(n)	local	locale
localidade	localité	locality	Ortschaft(f)	localidad	località
localizar	localiser	localize; locate	lokalisieren	localizar	localizzare
localizar	repérer	locate	lokalisieren	localizar	localizzare
loção	lotion	lotion	Gesichtswasser(n)	loción	lozione
locomotiva	locomotive	locomotive	Lokomotive(f)	locomotiva	locomotiva
locução	locution	phrase, locution	Redensart(f)	locución	locuzione
lodo	vase	sludge, mud	Schlamm(m)	limo, fango	melma
lógico, a	logique	logical	logisch	lógico, a	logico, a
logo, brevemente	bientôt	soon	bald	pronto	presto
logo que	dès(que)	as soon as	sobald	desde	fin da
loiça, louça	vaisselle	crockery, dishes	Geschirr(n)	vajilla	stoviglie, vasellame
loja	boutique	boutique, shop	Geschäft(n)	tienda	negozio, boutique
loja	magasin	shop	Geschäft(n), Laden(m)	tienda	negozio; bottega
loja	commerce	shop, business	Geschäft(n)	tienda, negocio	negozio
loja de ferragens	quincaillerie	ironmonger's	Eisenwarenhandlung(f)	ferretería	ferramenta
longe	loin	far(away), distant	weit, fern	lejos	lontano, a
longe(ao)	loin(au)	away, far away	weg(fort); weit weg	lejos(a lo)	lontano
longitude	longitude	longitude	Längengrad(m)	longitud	longitudine
longitudinal	longitudinal, e	longitudinal	Längs-	longitudinal	longitudinale
longo, a	long, longue	long	lang	largo, a	lungo, a
longo(ao)	long(le)	along	entlang	largo(a lo)	lungo
losango	losange	diamond-shaped	Raute(f), Rhombus(m)	rombo	rombo
lotaria	loterie	lottery	Lotterie(f)	lotería	lotteria
lote	lot	batch, assortment	Assortiment(n)	lote	assortimento
louco, a; maluco, a	fou, folle	mad, foolish, crazy	verrückt	loco, a	matto, a; pazzo, a
loucura	folie	madness, folly	Wahnsinn(m), Wahn(m)	locura	follia, pazzia
louro, a	blond, e	fair, blond	blond	rubio(pelo)	biondo, a
lua	lune	moon	Mond(m)	luna	luna
lúcido, a	lucide	lucid	klar	lúcido, a	lucido, a
lucro	gain(s)	earnings	Gewinn(m)	ganancia(s)	lucro, profitto
lucro	profit	profit, benefit	Gewinn(m)	ganancia	profitto, guadagno
lucro, proveito	bénéfice	benefit; profit	Gewinn(m)	beneficio	beneficio; utile

Portuguese	French	English	German	Spanish	Italian
lugar	lieu	place, spot	Ort(m)	lugar	luogo
lugar, sítio	endroit	place, spot	Stelle(f)	lugar, sitio	luogo, posto
lugar; sítio	emplacement	location, site	Lage(f), Stelle(f)	sitio	posto, sito, luogo
lugar; sítio	place	place	Ort(m), Platz(m)	lugar	posto
lugar	place	seat	Sitzplatz(m)	sitio, asiento	posto
lumbago	lumbago	lumbago	Hexenschuß(m)	lumbago	lombaggine
luminoso, a	lumineux, se	luminous	leuchtend, hell	luminoso, a	luminoso, a
lupa	loupe	magnifying-glass	Lupe(f)	lupa	lente(ingrandimento)
luta	lutte	struggle, fight	Kampf(m)	lucha	lotta
lutador, a	lutteur, se	wrestler; fighter	Kämpfer(m); Ringer(m)	luchador, a	lottatore, trice
lutar	lutter	fight, struggle	kämpfen	luchar	lottare
lutar	battre(se)	fight	kämpfen	pelearse	battersi, lottare
luto	deuil	mourning(be in)	Trauer(f)	duelo; luto	lutto
luva	gant	glove	Handschuh(m)	guante	guanto
luva	gant	flannel	Waschlappen(m)	manopla	guanto
luxo	luxe	luxury	Luxus(m)	lujo	lusso
luxuoso, a	luxueux, se	luxurious	üppig	lujoso, a	lussuoso, a
luxuriante	luxuriant, e	luxuriant, lush	üppig	exuberante	lussureggiante
luz	lumière	light	Licht(n)	luz	luce
luz, clarão	lueur	gleam, glow	Schimmer(m)	resplandor	chiarore, luce

M

Portuguese	French	English	German	Spanish	Italian
maca	civière	stretcher	Bahre(f)	camilla	barella
maçã	pomme	apple	Apfel(m)	manzana	mela
macabro, a	macabre	macabre	makaber	macabro, a	macabro, a
macaco	singe	monkey	Affe(m)	mono	scimmia
macaco	cric	jack	Wagenheber(m)	gato	cric, cricco
macaco	vérin, cric	jack	Winde(f)	gato, cric	martinetto, binda
machado	hache	axe	Axt(f)	hacha	ascia
macho	mâle	male	Männchen(n)	macho	maschio
maciço, a	massif, ive	massive; solid	massiv	masivo, a	massiccio, a
macio, a	doux, ce	soft	sanft	suave	morbido, a
madeira	bois	timber	Holz(n)	madera	legno
madeiramento	charpente	framework	Holzgerüst(n)	armazón	ossatura, travatura
madeixa	mèche	lock(of hair)	Locke(f)	mechón	ciocca
madrinha	marraine	godmother	Patin(f)	madrina	madrina
maduro, a	mûr, e	mature	reif	maduro, a	maturo, a
maduro, a	mûr, e	ripe	reif	maduro, a	maturo, a
mãe	mère	mother	Mutter(f)	madre	madre
maestro(orquestra)	chef(orchestre)	conductor	Dirigent(in f)m	director(orquesta)	direttore(orchestra)
mafia	mafia	Mafia	Mafia(f)	mafia	mafia
magia	magie	magic	Zauberei(f)	magia	magia
mágico, a	magique	magic	magisch	mágico, a	magico, a
magistrado	magistrat	magistrate	Magistrat(m)	magistrado	magistrato
magnético, a	magnétique	magnetic	magnetisch	magnético, a	magnetico, a
magnífico, a	magnifique	magnificent	prächtig	magnífico, a	magnifico, a
magoar, ofender	blesser, offenser	hurt, offend	kränken	lastimar, ofender	ferire, offendere
magro, a	maigre	thin	mager	delgado, a	magro, a
magro, a; delgado, a	mince	slim; slender	schlank	delgado, a	snello, a
Maio	Mai	May	Mai(m)	Mayo	Maggio
maioria	majorité	majority	Mehrheit(f)	mayoría	maggioranza
maior parte(a)	plupart(la)	most(of the)	meisten(die)	mayoría(la)	maggior parte(la)
mais	plus	plus	plus	más	più
mais	plus	plus	und, plus	más	più
mais	plus	more	mehr	más	più
mais	encore	more	noch	más	ancora

Portuguese	French	English	German	Spanish	Italian
mais	davantage, plus	more	mehr	más	più, di più
mais(uma vez)	encore	again	noch einmal	otra vez	ancora
mais(a)	supplément(en)	extra-, additional-	Extra-; Neben-	más(de)	più(in)
mais longe	plus loin	further	weiter	más lejos	più in là
mais tarde	plus tard	later	später	más tarde	più tardi
majestade	majesté	majesty	Majestät(f)	majestad	maestà
majestoso, a	majestueux, se	majestic	majestätisch	majestuoso, a	maestoso, a
mal	mal	evil	Böse(n)	mal	male
mal	mal	harm, hurt	Weh(n)	daño	male
mal	mal	badly	schlecht	mal	male
mala	malle	trunk	Koffer(großer)(m)	baúl	baule
mala	valise	suitcase, case	Koffer(m)	maleta	valigia
mala	coffre	boot	Kofferraum(m)	maletero	bagagliaio
maldito, a	maudit, e	cursed, damned	verdammt	maldito, a	maledetto, a
maleável	souple	supple; flexible	biegsam	flexible	flessibile
mal educado, a	impoli, e	impolite, rude	unhöflich	maleducado, a	maleducato, a
maleta	attaché-case	attaché-case	Aktenkoffer(m)	maletín	valigetta
malevolência	malveillance	ill will	Böswilligkeit(f)	malevolencia	malanimo
malévolo, a	malveillant, e	malevolent	böswillig	malévolo, a	malevolo, a
malfeitor	malfaiteur	criminal	Missetäter(in f)m	malhechor	malvivente
malha	tricot	sweater, jumper	Trikot(m), Strickweste	prenda de punto	maglia
malnutrição	malnutrition	malnutrition	Unterernährung(f)	desnutrición	malnutrizione
mama	mamelle	udder	Euter(n)	mama, teta	mammella
mamã	maman	Mummy, Mum	Mama(f)	mamá	mamma
mamar	téter	suck	saugen	mamar	poppare
mamífero	mammifère	mammal	Säugetier(n)	mamífero	mammifero
manada	troupeau	herd	Herde(f)	ganado	branco
mancha, nódoa	tache	stain	Fleck(m)	mancha	macchia
manchar, sujar	tacher	stain, dirty	beflecken, beschmutzen	manchar	macchiare
mandar, enviar	envoyer	send	senden	mandar, enviar	mandare, inviare
mandar, ordenar	ordonner	command, order	befehlen, beherrschen	mandar, ordenar	comandare, ordinare
maneira, modo	manière	manner, way	Art(f)	manera, modo	maniera, modo
manejável	maniable	handy, manageable	handlich	manuable	maneggevole
manequim	mannequin	dummy; model	Schaufensterpuppe(f)	maniquí	manichino
manga	manche	sleeve	Ärmel(m)	manga(la)	manica
mangueira	tuyau	hose	Schlauch(m)	manguera	tubo
manhã	matin	morning	Morgen(m)	mañana	mattino
mania	manie	mania	Sucht(f)	manía	mania
maníaco, a	maniaque	maniac	Verrückte(f, m)	maníaco, a	maniaco, a
manicômio	asile	mental hospital	Irrenhaus(n)	manicomio	manicomio
manicura	manucure	manicure	Maniküre(f)	manicura	manicure
manifestação	manifestation	demonstration	Demonstration(f)	manifestación	manifestazione
manifestante	manifestant, e	demonstrator	Demonstrant(in f)m	manifestante	manifestante
manipular	manipuler	manipulate	manipulieren	manipular	manipolare
manípulo	manette	handle	Griff(m)	manecilla	leva
manivela	manivelle	crank	Handkurbel(f)	manivela	manovella
manobra	manoeuvre	manoeuvre	Manöver(n)	maniobra	manovra
mansão, palacete	manoir, château	mansion	Herrensitz(m), -haus n	mansión, morada	maniero, castello
manta, cobertor	couverture	blanket; cover	Decke(f)(Woll-, Bett-)	manta	coperta
manteiga	beurre	butter	Butter(f)	mantequilla	burro
manter	maintenir	maintain	erhalten	mantener	mantenere
manual	manuel, elle	manual; hand-	manuell; Hand-	manual	manuale
manuscrito, a	manuscrit, e	handwritten	handgeschrieben	manuscrito, a	manoscritto, a
manutenção	entretien	upkeep	Instandhaltung(f)	cuidado	mantenimento
manutenção	entretien	maintenance	Wartung(f)	mantenimiento	manutenzione
mão	main	hand	Hand(f)	mano	mano
mão-de-obra	main-d'oeuvre	manpower, labour	Arbeitskräfte(pl.)	mano de obra	manodopera
mão-de-obra	main-d'oeuvre	workforce, labour	Arbeitskraft(f)	mano de obra	manodopera
mapa	carte(géo)	map	Landkarte(f)	mapa	mappa, carta
maqueta	maquette	model	Modell(n)	maqueta	modello
maquilhagem	maquillage	make-up	Schminke(f)	maquillaje	trucco
maquilhar-se	maquiller(se)	make-up(put on)	schminken, sich	maquillarse	truccarsi
máquina	machine	machine	Maschine(f)	máquina	macchina
máquina fotográfica	appareil photo	camera	Kamera(f)	cámara fotográfica	macchina fotografica
mar	mer	sea	Meer(n)	mar	mare
mar	mer	sea	See(f)	mar	mare
maratona	marathon	marathon	Marathonlauf(m)	maratón	maratona
maravilhar	émerveiller	amaze	entzücken	maravillar	meravigliare

Portuguese	French	English	German	Spanish	Italian
maravilhoso, a	merveilleux, se	wonderful	wunderbar	maravilloso, a	meraviglioso, a
maravilhoso, a	merveilleux, se	marvellous	wunderbar	maravilloso, a	meraviglioso, a
marca, vestígio	marque, trace	mark	Spur(f)	señal, marca	segno, marca
marca	marque	brand, make	Marke(f)	marca	marchio, marca
marcador	crayon-feutre	felt-tip pen	Filzschreiber(m)	rotulador	pennarello
marcar	marquer	mark	markieren	marcar	segnare, marcare
marcar	cocher	tick	an = kreuzen	marcar	segnare
marcar	marquer	score	schießen(Tor-)	marcar	segnare
marcha	marche	walk(ing)	Wanderung(f)	marcha	marcia
Março	Mars	March	März(m)	Marzo	Marzo
maré	marée	tide	Gezeiten(pl.)	marea	marea
marfim	ivoire	ivory	Elfenbein(n)	marfil	avorio
margem	marge	margin	Rand(m)	margen	margine
margem	rive	bank	Ufer(n)	orilla, margen	riva
margem	berge	bank	Ufer(n)	ribera, orilla	sponda
marginal	marginal, e	fringe(on the)	Außenseiter(in f)m	marginal	marginale
marido	mari	husband	Ehemann(m)	marido	marito
marinha	marine	navy	Marine(f)	marina	marina
marinheiro	marin	sailor	Seemann(m)	marino	marinaio
marinheiro	matelot	sailor	Matrose(m)	marinero	marinaio
marisco	fruits de mer	seafood	Meeresfrüchte(f, pl.)	marisco	frutti di mare
marítimo, a	maritime	maritime, sea-	See-	marítimo, a	marittimo, a
marmita	marmite	cooking-pot	Kochtopf(m)	marmita, olla	pentola, marmitta
mármore	marbre	marble	Marmor(m)	mármol	marmo
marta	vison	mink	Nerz(m)	visón	visone
martelo	marteau	hammer	Hammer(m)	martillo	martello
mártir	martyr, e	martyr	Märtyrer(in f)m	mártir	martire
marxismo	marxisme	Marxism	Marxismus(m)	marxismo	marxismo
mas	mais	but	aber	pero; sino, mas	ma
máscara	masque	mask	Maske(f)	máscara	maschera
masculino, a	masculin, e	masculine, male	männlich	masculino, a	maschile
má sorte	malchance	ill luck, bad luck	Pech(n), Unglück(n)	mala suerte	sfortuna
massa	masse	mass	Masse(f)	masa	massa
massa	pâte	paste	Paste(f); Masse(f)	masa, pasta	impasto, pasta
massa	pâte	pastry; dough	Teig(m)	masa	pasta
massa	pâtes	pasta, noodles	Nudeln(f, pl)	pastas(aliment.)	pasta
massa	nouilles	noodles	Nudeln(f, pl)	macarrones	tagliatelle, pasta
massa	graisse	grease	Schmiere(f)	grasa	grasso
massacre	massacre	slaughter	Blutbad(n)	masacre	massacro
massagem	massage	massage	Massage(f)	masaje	massaggio
mastigar	mâcher	chew	kauen	masticar	masticare
mastro	mât	mast	Mast(m)	mástil	albero
matador	matador	matador	Matador(m)	matador	matador
matar	tuer	kill	töten	matar	uccidere
mate	mat, e	dull, matt	glanzlos, matt	mate	opaco, a
matemáticas	mathématique(s)	mathematics	Mathematik(f)	matemáticas	matematica
matéria	matière	matter, material	Stoff(m), Material(n)	materia	materia
matéria	matière	subject	Fach(n)	asignatura	materia
matéria	substance	matter, material	Materie(f)	materia	materia
material	matériel	material	Material(n)	material	materiale
material	matériau	material	Material(n)	material	materiale
material; matéria	matière	material	Material(n)	material; materia	materiale; materia
maternal	maternel, le	maternal, motherly	mütterlich	materno, a; maternal	materno, a
matinal	matinal, e	early	früh	matutino, a	mattutino, a
matiz, tom	nuance, ton	shade, nuance	Farbenton(m)	matiz	sfumatura
mato, brenha	broussaille	undergrowth	Gestrüpp(n)	zarzal, maleza	macchia, cespugli
mato	brousse	bush(the)	Busch(m)	maleza	boscaglia
matrícula	matricule	roll, register	Matrikel(f)	matrícula	matricola
matrícula	inscription	registration	Einschreibung(f)	matrícula	iscrizione
matrícula	immatriculation	registration	Eintragung(f)	matrícula	immatricolazione
matricular-se	inscrire(s')	register	ein = schreiben, sich	matricularse	iscriversi
maturidade	maturité	maturity	Reife(f)	madurez	maturità
mau, má	mauvais, e	bad	schlecht	malo, a	cattivo, a
mau, má	mauvais, mal	evil, bad	übel	malo, a	cattivo, a; male
mau, má	méchant, e	naughty	böse, boshaft	malo, a	cattivo, a
maxila	mâchoire	jaw	Kiefer(m)	mandíbula	mascella
máximo	maximum	maximum	Maximum(n)	máximo	massimo
me	me, m'; moi	me	mich; mir	me	mi, me

P

Portuguese	French	English	German	Spanish	Italian
mecânica	mécanique	mechanics	Mechanik(f)	mecánica	meccanica
mecânico, a	mécanique	mechanical	mechanisch	mecánico, a	meccanico, a
mecânico, a	mécanicien, ne	mechanic	Mechaniker(in f)m	mecánico, a	meccanico, a
mecanismo	mécanisme	mechanism	Mechanismus(m)	mecanismo	meccanismo
mecenas	mécène	patron	Mäzen(m), Sponsor(m)	mecenas	mecenate
medalha	médaille	medal	Medaille(f)	medalla	medaglia
média	moyenne	average	Durchschnitt(m)	media	media
medicamento	médicament	drug, medicine	Medikament(n)	medicina	medicina
medicina	médecine	medicine	Medizin(f)	medicina	medicina
médico	médecin	doctor	Arzt(m), Ärztin(f)	médico	medico
médico, a	médical, e	medical	medizinisch	médico, a	medico, a
médio, a	moyen, ne	middle	mittel	medio, a	medio, a
médio, a	moyen, ne	medium	mittlere(r, s)	medio, a	medio, a
mediocre	médiocre	mediocre	mittelmäßig, schlecht	mediocre	mediocre
medir	mesurer	measure	messen	medir	misurare
meditar	méditer	meditate	nach = denken, sinnen	meditar	meditare
medo	peur	fear	Angst(f)	miedo	paura
medo(ter)	peur(avoir)	afraid(to be)	Angst(haben)	miedo(tener)	paura(avere)
medula, tutano	moelle	marrow(-bone)	Mark(n)	médula, tuétano	midollo
meia-hora	demi-heure	half an hour	halbe Stunde	media hora	mezz'ora
meia-noite	minuit	midnight	Mitternacht(f)	medianoche	mezzanotte
meias	bas	stocking	Strumpf(m)(Nylon-)	media	calza
meias	collants	tights(pair of)	Strumpfhose(f)	pantys	collant
meias	socquette	sock(ankle-)	Socke(f)	calcetín	calzino
meio, a	demi, e	half	halb	medio, a	mezzo, a
meio, a	mi-	half(-); mid-	halb-	medio, a	semi-; mezzo-
meio	milieu	middle	Mitte(f)	medio	mezzo
meio	moyen	means	Mittel(n)	medio(s)	mezzo
meio	milieu	milieu, background	Milieu(n)	ambiente, medio	ambiente
meio-dia	midi	midday, noon	Mittag(m)	mediodía	mezzogiorno
mel	miel	honey	Honig(m)	miel	miele
melancolia	mélancolie	melancholy	Wehmut(f)	melancolía	malinconia
melão	melon	melon	Melone(f)	melón	melone
melhor	meilleur, e	better	besser(sein)	mejor	migliore
melhor	mieux	better	besser	mejor	meglio
melhor	meilleur, e	best	Beste(f, m)	mejor	migliore
melhoramento	amélioration	improvement	Verbesserung(f)	mejora; mejoría	miglioramento
melhorar	améliorer	improve	verbessern	mejorar	migliorare
melodia	air	tune	Melodie(f)	melodía	melodia
melodia	mélodie	melody, tune	Melodie(f)	melodía	melodia
membrana	membrane	membrane	Membran(f)	membrana	membrana
membro	membre	limb	Glied(n)	miembro	membro, arto
membro, a; sócio, a	membre(de)	member(of)	Mitglied(n)	miembro, a; socio, a	membro, i
memória	mémoire	memory	Gedächtnis(n)	memoria	memoria
menção	mention	mention	Vermerk(m)	mención	menzione
mendigo, a	mendiant, e	beggar	Bettler(in f)m	mendigo, a	mendicante
menina	mademoiselle	Miss	Fräulein(n)	señorita	signorina
menopausa	ménopause	menopause	Wechseljahre(n, pl)	menopausia	menopausa
menor	mineur, e	minor	unbedeutend	menor	minore
menor	mineur, e	minor	Minderjährige(f, m)	menor	minore, minorenne
menos	moins	less	weniger	menos	meno
menos(o)	moins(le)	least(the)	wenigsten(am)	menos(lo)	meno(il)
mensagem, recado	message	message	Nachricht(f)	mensaje	messaggio
mensal	mensuel, le	monthly	monatlich	mensual	mensile
mental	mental, e	mental	geistig	mental	mentale
mentalidade	mentalité	mentality	Mentalität(f)	mentalidad	mentalità
mentir	mentir	lie	lügen	mentir	mentire
mentira	mensonge	lie, fib	Lüge(f)	mentira	bugia
mentiroso, a	menteur, se	liar	Lügner(in f)m	mentiroso, a	bugiardo, a
mercado	marché	market	Markt(m)	mercado	mercato
mercadoria	marchandise	goods	Ware(f)	mercancía	merce
mercearia	épicerie	grocer's(shop)	Lebensmittelladen(m)	ultramarinos	drogheria
mercearia	alimentation	food shop	Lebensmittelladen(m)	alimentación	alimentari(negozio)
merceeiro, a	épicier, ière	grocer	Lebensmittelhändler m	tendero, a	droghiere, a
mercenário	mercenaire	mercenary	Söldner(m)	mercenario	mercenario
mercúrio	mercure	mercury	Quecksilber(n)	mercurio	mercurio
merecer	mériter	deserve, merit	verdienen	merecer	meritare
mergulhar	plonger	plunge, dive	tauchen	zambullirse	tuffarsi

Portuguese	French	English	German	Spanish	Italian
mergulhar	tremper	dip	ein=tauchen	sumergir	intingere
mergulho	plongeon	dive	Kopfsprung(m)	zambullida	tuffo
meridiano	méridien	meridian	Meridian(m)	meridiano	meridiano
mérito	mérite	merit, worth	Verdienst(n)	mérito	merito
mês	mois	month	Monat(m)	mes	mese
mesa	table	table	Tisch(m)	mesa	tavolo; tavola
mesmo, a	même	same	selbe; gleich(der -)	mismo, a	stesso, a
mesmo(que)	même	even	sogar; selbst	aun; incluso	anche; perfino
mesquita	mosquée	mosque	Moschee(f)	mezquita	moschea
mestiço, a	métis, se	half-caste	Mischling(m)	mestizo, a	meticcio, a
metade	moitié	half(-lves)	Hälfte(f)	mitad	metà
metal	métal	metal	Metal(n)	metal	metallo
metálico, a	métallique	metallic	metallisch	metálico, a	metallico, a
metamorfose	métamorphose	metamorphosis(-es)	Verwandlung(f)	metamorfosis	metamorfosi
metástase	métastase	metastasis(-es)	Tochtergeschwulst(f)	metástasis	metastasi
meteorologia	météorologie	weather forecast	Wetterkunde(f)	meteorología	meteorologia
meticuloso, a	méticuleux, se	meticulous	sorgfältig	meticuloso, a	meticoloso, a
meticuloso, a	maniaque	fussy	übergenau sein	maniático, a	pignolo, a
método	méthode	method	Methode(f)	método	metodo
métrico, a	métrique	metric	metrisch	métrico, a	metrico, a
metro	mètre	metre	Meter(m, n)	metro	metro
metropolitano	métro	underground, tube	U-Bahn(f)	metro	metropolitana
meu, minha	mon	my	mein	mi	mio, mia(il, la)
meu, minha	mien, ne	mine	meine, meiner	mío, mía	mio(il); mia(la)
meu(é)	moi(à)	mine, to me	mir	mío, a(el, la)	mio, mia(è)
meus	mes	my	meine	mis	miei, mie(i, le)
mexer	remuer	stir	rühren	remover	mescolare
mexer-se	bouger	move	bewegen	moverse	muovere
mexer-se	remuer	move	bewegen, sich	mover	muovere(-rsi)
mexilhão	moule	mussel	Muschel(f)	mejillón	cozza
miar	miauler	mew	miauen	maullar	miagolare
micróbio	microbe	germ, microbe	Mikrobe(f)	microbio	microbo
microfone	micro(phone)	microphone, mike	Mikrophon(n)	micrófono	microfono
microscópio	microscope	microscope	Mikroskop(n)	microscopio	microscopio
migração	migration	migration	Wanderung(f)	migración	migrazione
migrador, a	migrateur, trice	migrant	wandernd; Wander-	migratorio, a	migratore, trice
mil	mille	thousand	tausend	mil	mille; mila(pl.)
milagre	miracle	miracle	Wunder(n)	milagro	miracolo
milésimo, a	millième	thousandth	tausendste	milésimo, a	millesimo, a
milhão	million	million	Million(f)	millón	milione
milhar	millier	thousand	Tausend(n)	millar	migliaio(a)
milho	maïs	maize, corn	Mais(m)	maíz	granturco, mais
milícia	milice	militia	Miliz(f)	milicia	milizia
militante	militant, e	militant	Militant(m)	militante	militante
militar	militaire	military	militärisch	militar	militare
militar	militer	militate	kämpfen für	militar	militare
mina	mine	mine	Bergwerk(n)	mina	miniera
mineral	minéral, e	mineral	mineralisch	mineral	minerale
minério	minerai	ore	Erz(n)	mineral	minerale
minha	ma	my	meine	mi	mia(la)
miniatura	miniature	miniature	Miniatur(f)	miniatura	miniatura
mínimo, a	minimum	minimum	Minimum(n)	mínimo, a	minimo, a
ministério	ministère	ministry	Ministerium(n)	ministerio	ministero
ministro	ministre	minister	Minister(in f)m	ministro	ministro
minoria	minorité	minority	Minderheit(f)	minoría	minoranza
minúsculo, a	minuscule	minute, tiny	winzig	minúsculo, a	minuscolo, a
minuto	minute	minute	Minute(f)	minuto	minuto
míope	myope	short-sighted	kurzsichtig	miope	miope
miragem	mirage	mirage	Fata Morgana(f)	espejismo	miraggio
miséria	misère	poverty	Elend(n)	miseria	miseria
missa	messe	mass	Messe(f)	misa	messa
missão	mission	mission	Mission(f)	misión	missione
míssil	missile	missile	Rakete(f)	misil	missile
mistério	mystère	mystery	Geheimnis(n); Rätsel n	misterio	mistero
misterioso, a	mystérieux, se	mysterious	mysteriös	misterioso, a	misterioso, a
místico, a	mystique	mystic(al)	mystisch	místico, a	mistico, a
misto, a	mixte	mixed	gemischt	mixto, a	misto, a
mistura	mélange	mixture; mixing	Mischung(f)	mezcla	miscuglio

mistura	mélange	blend, mixture	Mischung(f)	mezcla	mescolanza
misturar	mélanger	mix	mischen	mezclar	mescolare
mito	mythe	myth	Mythos(m); Sage(f)	mito	mito
miúdo	gamin, e	kid, child	Kind(n)	chiquillo, a	ragazzino, a
mobiliário	mobilier	furniture	Möbel(pl)	mobiliario	mobilio
mobiliário	ameublement	furnishing	Einrichtung(f)	mobiliario	arredamento, mobilio
mobilidade	mobilité	mobility	Beweglichkeit(f)	mobilidad	mobilità
mobilizar	mobiliser	mobilize	mobilisieren	mobilizar	mobilitare
mochila	sac à dos	rucksack	Rucksack(m)	mochila	zaino
moda	mode	fashion	Mode(f)	moda	moda
modelo	modèle	model, pattern	Modell(n)	modelo	modello
modelo	modèle	design	Muster(n), Modell(n)	modelo, patrón	modello
modelo	modèle	pattern	Muster(n)	modelo	modello
modelo	mannequin	model	Mannequin(n)	maniquí, modelo	indossatore, trice
moderar	modérer	moderate	mäßigen	moderar	moderare
moderno, a	moderne	modern	modern	moderno, a	moderno, a
modesto, a	modeste	modest	bescheiden	modesto, a	modesto, a
modificação	modification	modification	Abänderung(f)	modificación	modifica
modificar	modifier	modify	verändern	modificar	modificare
modo, maneira	façon, manière	way, manner, fashion	Weise(f), Art(f)	modo, manera	modo, maniera
modo, maneira	mode, manière	mode, manner	Weise(f)	modo, manera	modo, maniera
moeda, divisa	devise	currency	Währung(f)	divisa	valuta
moeda	monnaie	money	Geld(n)	moneda, dinero	moneta
moeda	monnaie	currency	Währung(f), Devisen pl	moneda	valuta; moneta
moeda	pièce	coin	Geldstück(n)	moneda	spiccioli, moneta
moer	moudre	grind	mahlen	moler	macinare
moinho	moulin	mill	Mühle(f)	molino	mulino
moita	buisson	bush	Gebüsch(n)	matorral	cespuglio
mola	ressort	spring	Feder(f)(Sprung-)	muelle	molla
molar	molaire	molar	Backenzahn(m)	molar	molare
molde; forma	moule	mould	Form(f)	molde	stampo, forma
moldura	cadre	frame	Rahmen(m)	marco	cornice, quadro
mole	mou, molle	soft	weich	blando, a	molle; tenero, a
mole; fraco, a	mou, molle	lethargic	schlaff	fofo, a	molle; fiacco, a
molécula	molécule	molecule	Molekül(n).	molécula	molecola
molhado, a; húmido, a	mouillé, e; humide	wet	naß	mojado, a; húmedo, a	bagnato, a; umido, a
molhar	mouiller	wet	an = feuchten	mojar	bagnare
molhar	tremper	soak	ein = weichen	mojar	inzuppare
molhe	jetée	jetty	Hafendamm(m), Mole(f)	escollera	molo, gettata
molho	sauce	sauce	Soße(f)	salsa	sugo; salsa
molusco	mollusque	mollusc	Weichtier(n)	molusco	mollusco
momento	moment	moment	Augenblick(m)	momento	momento, attimo
momento, instante	moment, instant	while, time	Moment(m)	rato	attimo, momento
monarquia	monarchie	monarchy	Monarchie(f)	monarquía	monarchia
monção	mousson	monsoon	Monsun(m)	monzón	monsone
monetário, a	monétaire	monetary	Währungs-, Geld-	monetario, a	monetario, a
monge, frade	moine	monk	Mönch(m)	monje, fraile	monaco, frate
monitor, a	moniteur, trice	instructor	Leiter/in; Lehrer/in	monitor, a	istruttore, trice
monogamia	monogamie	monogamy	Monogamie(f)	monogamia	monogamia
monopólio	monopole	monopoly	Monopol(n)	monopolio	monopolio
monótono, a	monotone	monotonous	monoton, eintönig	monótono, a	monotono, a
monstro	monstre	monster	Monster(n)	monstruo	mostro
montagem	montage	mounting, assembly	Montage(f)	montaje	montaggio
montagem	assemblage	assembly	Montage(f)	ensambladura	assemblaggio
montanha	montagne	mountain	Gebirge(n), Berg(m)	montaña	montagna
montante	montant	amount	Betrag(m)	importe	ammontare
montão, pilha	tas	pile	Haufen(m)	montón	mucchio
monte	mont, montagne	mount	Berg(m)	monte	monte
montra, vitrina	vitrine	shop-window	Schaufenster(n)	escaparate	vetrina
monumento	monument	monument	Denkmal(n)	monumento	monumento
moral	morale	moral	Moral(f)	moral	morale
moral	moral, e	moral	moralisch	moral	morale
moral	moral	morale	Stimmung(f), Moral(f)	moral, ánimo	morale
morango	fraise	strawberry	Erdbeere(f)	fresa	fragola
morar	habiter	live(in), inhabit	bewohnen, wohnen	vivir, habitar	abitare
morder	mordre	bite	beißen	morder	mordere
mordomo	maître d'hôtel	head-waiter	Oberkellner(m)	jefe de hotel	capocameriere
morfina	morphine	morphine	Morphium(n)	morfina	morfina

Portuguese	French	English	German	Spanish	Italian
morfologia	morphologie	morphology	Morphologie(f)	morfología	morfologia
morgue	morgue	mortuary	Leichenschauhaus(n)	depósito(cadáver.)	obitorio
morrer	mourir	die	sterben	morir	morire
mortal	mortel, le	mortal; deadly	tödlich	mortal	mortale
mortal	mortel, le	fatal	tödlich	mortal	mortale
mortalidade	mortalité	mortality	Sterblichkeit(f)	mortalidad	mortalità
morte	mort	death	Tod(m)	muerte	morte
morto, a	mort, e	dead	tot	muerto, a	morto, a
morto, a	tué, e	killed	getötet	muerto, a	ucciso, a
morto, a	mort, e	dead man/woman	Tote(f, m)	muerto, a	morto, a
mosaico	mosaïque	mosaic	Mosaik(n)	mosaico	mosaico
mosca	mouche	fly	Fliege(f)	mosca	mosca
mosquito	moustique	mosquito(-es)	Mücke(f)	mosquito	zanzara
mostarda	moutarde	mustard	Senf(m)	mostaza	senape
mosteiro	monastère	monastery	Kloster(n)	monasterio	monastero
mostrador	cadran	dial	Zifferblatt(n)	esfera	quadrante
mostrar	montrer	show	zeigen	enseñar, mostrar	mostrare
mostrar, dar	afficher(s')	display	erscheinen	visualizar	apparire
mota	moto	motor-bike	Motorrad(n)	moto	moto
motel	motel	motel	Motel(n)	motel	motel
motim	émeute	riot	Aufruhr(m)	motín	sommossa
motivar	motiver	motivate	motivieren	motivar	motivare
motivo	motif	motive	Motiv(n)	motivo	motivo
motociclista	motard	motorcyclist	Motorradfahrer(in f)m	motorista	motociclista
motor	moteur	engine; motor	Motor(m)	motor	motore
motor de arranque	démarreur	starter	Starter(m)	arranque	motorino(avviamento)
motorista	chauffeur	driver; chauffeur	Fahrer m; Chauffeur m	chófer	autista
motorista	chauffeur(taxi)	taxi-driver	Taxifahrer(in f)m	taxista	tassista
motorizada	mobylette	moped	Mofa(n)	velomotor	motorino, scooter
móvel	mobile	mobile, movable	beweglich, mobil	móvil, movible	mobile
móvel	meuble	furniture	Möbelstück(n)	mueble	mobile
movimento	mouvement	movement, motion	Bewegung(f)	movimiento	movimento
muçulmano, a	musulman, e	Moslem, Muslim	Mohammedaner(in f)m	musulmán, a	musulmano, a
mudança	changement	change	Veränderung(f)	cambio	cambiamento
mudar; trocar	changer	change	ändern	mudar	cambiare
mudar; remover	changer	shift	wechseln	cambiar	cambiare
mudar, mudar-se	déménager	move	um = ziehen	mudar(se)	traslocare
mudo, a	muet, te	dumb; silent	stumm	mudo, a	muto, a
muito	beaucoup	much, many	viel(e)	mucho	molto
muito, a	beaucoup	lots of, a lot of	viel(e)	mucho, a	molto, a, i, e
muito	très	very	sehr	muy	molto
muito tempo	longtemps	long time(a)	lange	mucho tiempo	molto/molto tempo
muitos, as	beaucoup	many	viele	muchos, as	molti
muleta	béquille	crutch(-es)	Krücke(f)	muleta	stampella
mulher	femme	woman(women)	Frau(f)	mujer	donna
mulher	femme, épouse	wife(wives)	Ehefrau(f), Frau(f)	mujer	moglie
mulher a dias	femme de ménage	domestic help	Putzfrau(f)	asistenta	donna di servizio
multa	amende	fine	Geldstrafe(f)	multa	multa
multa	procès-verbal	ticket, penalty	Strafmandat(n)	multa	contravvenzione
multidão	multitude	multitude	Menge(f)	multitud	moltitudine
multidão	foule	crowd	Menge(f)	muchedumbre	folla
multidão, confusão	cohue, foule	crush, crowd	Menge(f)	barullo, jaleo	ressa, affollamento
multiplicar	multiplier	multiply	multiplizieren	multiplicar	moltiplicare
múltiplo, a	multiple	multiple, numerous	viel-; vielfältig	múltiple	multiplo, a
mundial	mondial, e	world-wide, world	weltlich	mundial	mondiale
mundo	monde	world	Welt(f)	mundo	mondo
municipal	municipal, e	municipal; town -	städtisch; Stadt-	municipal	municipale
município	conseil	council	Rat(m)(Stadtrat m)	concejo	giunta, consiglio
munições	munitions	ammunition	Munition(f)	municiones	munizioni
muralha, recinto	enceinte	fence; enclosure	Einzäunung(f)	muralla	cinta, recinto
murchar	flétrir	wilt, wither	verwelken	marchitar	appassire
murmurar	murmurer	murmur, whisper	flüstern	murmurar	mormorare
muro, parede	mur	wall	Mauer(f)	muro, pared	muro
musculado, a	musclé, e	muscular	muskulös	musculoso, a	muscoloso, a
muscular	musculaire	muscular	Muskel-	muscular	muscolare
músculo	muscle	muscle	Muskel(m)	músculo	muscolo
museu	musée	museum	Museum(n)	museo	museo
musgo	mousse	moss	Moos(n)	musgo	muschio

Portuguese	French	English	German	Spanish	Italian
música	musique	music	Musik(f)	música	musica
musical	musical, e	musical	musikalisch	musical	musicale
músico, a	musicien, ne	musician	Musiker(in f)m	músico, a	musicista
mutilado, a	mutilé, e	disabled	verstümmelt	mutilado, a	mutilato, a
mútuo, a	mutuel, le	mutual	gegenseitig	mútuo, a	mutuo, a

N

Portuguese	French	English	German	Spanish	Italian
nação	nation	nation	Nation(f)	nación	nazione
nacional	national, e	national	national	nacional	nazionale
nacionalidade	nationalité	nationality	Nationalität(f)	nacionalidad	nazionalità
nacionalismo	nationalisme	nationalism	Nationalismus(m)	nacionalismo	nazionalismo
nada	rien	nothing	nichts	nada	niente, nulla
nadador, a	nageur, se	swimmer	Schwimmer(in f)m	nadador, a	nuotatore, trice
nadador-salvador	maître-nageur	life-guard	Bademeister(in f)m	maestro(natación)	bagnino
nadar	nager	swim	schwimmen	nadar	nuotare
nádega	fesse	bottom, buttock	Gesäß(n), Po(m)	nalga	natica
não	non	no	nein	no	no
não, nem	pas	not	nicht	no	non
não-fumador	non-fumeur	non-smoker	Nichtraucher(m)	no-fumadores	non-fumatore
não, obrigado	non merci	no thank you	nein, danke	no, gracias	no, grazie
narcótico	narcotique	narcotic	Betäubungsmittel(n)	narcótico	narcotico
narcótico	stupéfiant	narcotic	Betäubungsmittel(n)	narcótico	stupefacente
narina	narine	nostril	Nasenloch(n)	nariz	narice
nariz	nez	nose	Nase(f)	nariz	naso
narração	récit	story	Bericht(m)	narración	racconto
nasal	nasal, e	nasal	nasal	nasal	nasale
nascer	naître	born(be)	geboren werden	nacer	nascere
nascer	lever(se)	rise	auf = gehen	amanecer	sorgere
nascer	lever(se)	break, dawn	an = brechen	amanecer	sorgere
nascido, a	né, e	born(be)	geboren	nacido, a	nato, a
nascimento	naissance	birth	Geburt(f)	nacimiento	nascita
natação	natation, nage	swimming	Schwimmen(n)	natación	nuoto
natal	natal, e	native	Heimat-; Geburts-	natal	natale
Natal	Noël	Christmas	Weihnachten(n)	Navidad	Natale
natalidade	natalité	birth-rate	Geburtenrate(f)	natalidad	natalità
nativo, a	natif, ive	native	gebürtig	nativo, a	nativo, a
natural	naturel, le	natural	natürlich	natural	naturale
naturalizado, a	naturalisé, e	naturalized	eingebürgert	nacionalizado, a	naturalizzato, a
natureza	nature	nature	Natur(f)	naturaleza	natura
naturista	naturiste	nudist	Nudist(in f)m	naturista	nudista
naufrágio	naufrage	wreck	Schiffbruch(m)	naufragio	naufragio
naúsea	nausée	nausea, feel sick	Brechreiz(m)	náusea	nausea
naútico, a	nautique	nautical, water-	nautisch, Wasser-	náutico, a	nautico, a
naval	naval, e	naval	See-	naval	navale
navalha, gilete	rasoir	razor	Rasierapparat(m)	navaja de afeitar	rasoio
navegação	navigation	navigation	Seefahrt(f)	navegación	navigazione
navegador	navigateur	navigator	Seefahrer(m)	navegante	navigatore
navio	navire	ship	Schiff(n)	navío	nave
navio	vaisseau	vessel, ship	Schiff(n)	nave, navío	vascello, nave
necessário, a	nécessaire	necessary	nötig, notwendig	necesario, a	necessario, a
necessidade	nécessité	necessity	Notwendigkeit(f)	necesidad	necessità
necessidade	besoin	need	Bedürfnis(n)	necesidad	bisogno
necessidade(ter)	besoin(avoir)	require, need	brauchen	necesitar	bisogno(avere)
negar	nier	deny	verneinen, leugnen	negar	negare
negativo, a	négatif, ive	negative	negativ	negativo, a	negativo, a
negligência	négligence	negligence	Nachlässigkeit(f)	negligencia	negligenza

Portuguese	French	English	German	Spanish	Italian
negociação	négociation	negotiation	Verhandlung(f)	negociación	negoziato
negociações	pourparlers	talks	Verhandlungen(pl)	negociaciones	trattative
negociador, a	négociateur	negotiator	Unterhändler(in f)m	negociador, a	negoziatore, trice
negociante	marchand, e	tradesman, dealer	Händler(in f)m	vendedor, a	mercante
negociar	négocier	negotiate	verhandeln	negociar	negoziare
negociar, tratar	négocier, traiter	deal	handeln	comerciar, tratar	negoziare, trattare
negócios	affaires	business	Geschäfte(n, pl.)	negocios	affari
negro, a	noir, e	black(person)	Schwarze(f, m)	negro, a	negro, a
negro, a	nègre, esse	negro(-ress), black	Neger(in f)m	negro, a	negro, a
nem	ni	neither, nor	weder, noch	ni	né
nenhum, a	aucun, e	no, not any; no one	keiner, keine	ningún, o, a	nessuno, a
nervo	nerf	nerve	Nerv(m)	nervio	nervo
nervoso, a	nerveux, se	nervous	nervös; Nerven-	nervioso, a	nervoso, a
nervoso, a	nerveux, se	nervy	nervös	nervioso, a	nervoso, a
neto, a	petit-fils/fille	grandson/-daughter	Enkel(m), Enkelin(f)	nieto, a	nipote
neurologia	neurologie	neurology	Neurologie(f)	neurología	neurologia
neutralizar	neutraliser	neutralize	neutralisieren	neutralizar	neutralizzare
neutro, a	neutre	neutral	neutral	neutro, a	neutro, a
neve	neige	snow	Schnee(m)	nieve	neve
nevoeiro	brouillard	fog	Nebel(m)	niebla	nebbia
nevrose	névrose	neurosis(-ses)	Neurose(f)	neurosis	nevrosi
nicotina	nicotine	nicotine	Nikotin(n)	nicotina	nicotina
ninguém	personne	nobody, no one	niemand	nadie	nessuno
ninhada	couvée	brood	Brut(f)	pollada	covata
ninho	nid	nest	Nest(n)	nido	nido
níquel	nickel	nickel	Nickel(n)	níquel	nichel
nível	niveau	level	Stand(m), Niveau(n)	nivel	livello
nível(de vida)	niveau(de vie)	standard of living	Standard(m)	nivel(de vida)	tenore(di vita)
nó, laço	noeud	knot	Knoten(m)	nudo	nodo
nobre	noble	noble	edel; nobel	noble	nobile
nobre	noble	nobleman/-woman	Edelmann m, Edelfrau f	noble	nobile
noção	notion	notion	Kenntnis(f), Begriff m	noción	nozione
nocivo, a	nocif, ive	harmful	schädlich	nocivo, a	nocivo, a
nocivo, a	nuisible	harmful	schädlich	dañino, a	nocivo, a
nocturno, a	nocturne	nocturnal, night-	nächtlich	nocturno, a	notturno, a
noite	nuit	night	Nacht(f)	noche	notte
noite(esta)	soir(ce)	tonight	heute abend	noche(esta)	sera(questa)
noivo, a	fiancé, e	fiancé(e)	Verlobte(f, m)	novio, a	fidanzato, a
noivo, noiva	marié, mariée	bridegroom, bride	Bräutigam(m), Braut(f)	novio, novia	sposo, sposa
nojento, a	dégoûtant, e	disgusting	ekelhaft	asqueroso, a	disgustoso, a
nómada	nomade	nomad	Nomade(m)	nómada	nomade
nome	nom	name	Name(m)	nombre	nome
nomeação	nomination	nomination	Ernennung(f)	nombramiento	nomina
nomear	nommer	appoint	ernennen	nombrar	nominare
nome próprio	prénom	first name	Vorname(m)	nombre	nome
nora	belle-fille	daughter-in-law	Schwiegertochter(f)	nuera	nuora
nórdico, a	nordique	nordic; northern	nordisch; nördlich	nórdico, a	nordico, a
norma	norme	norm, standard	Norm(f)	norma	norma
normal	normal, e	normal; usual	normal	normal	normale
Norte	Nord	North	Norden(m)	Norte	Nord
nós	nous	we	wir	nosotros	noi
nos	nous	us	uns	nos	ci, ce
nosso, a	notre	our	unser, unsere	nuestro, a	nostro, a(il, la)
nosso, a(o, a)	nôtre(le, la)	ours	unsere(der, die, das)	nuestro, a(el, la)	nostro, a(il, la)
nossos, nossas	nos	our	unser(e)	nuestros, nuestras	nostri, e(i, le)
nostalgia	nostalgie	homesickness	Heimweh(n)	nostalgia	nostalgia
nota	note	note	Vermerk(m)	nota	appunto
nota	note	mark	Note(f)	nota	voto
nota	note	note	Note(f)	nota	nota
nota	bon	form, slip, voucher	Bestellschein(m)	orden, pedido	bolla, buono, bolletta
nota(de banco)	billet(banque)	bank-note	Geldschein(m)	billete(de banco)	banconota
notar, reparar	remarquer	notice	bemerken	notar, señalar	notare, osservare
notário	notaire	solicitor, lawyer	Notar(m)	notario	notaio
notável	remarquable	remarkable	bemerkenswert	notable	notevole
notícias	nouvelles	news	Nachrichten(f, pl)	noticias	notizie
notificar	notifier	notify	bekannt = geben	notificar	notificare
notoriedade	notoriété	notoriety	Offenkundigkeit(f)	notoriedad	notorietà
noutro sítio	ailleurs	somewhere else	woanders	otra parte(en)	altrove

P

Portuguese	French	English	German	Spanish	Italian
nova montagem	remontage	reassembly	Zusammensetzen(n)	volver a montar	rimontaggio
nove	neuf	nine	neun	nueve	nove
Novembro	Novembre	November	November(m)	Noviembre	Novembre
noventa	quatre-vingt-dix	ninety	neunzig	noventa	novanta
novidade	nouveauté	novelty	Neuheit(f)	novedad	novità
novo, a	nouveau, nouvelle	new	neu	nuevo, a	nuovo, a
novo, a	neuf, neuve	new	neu	nuevo, a	nuovo, a
novo, a(o, a mais)	cadet, te	younger; youngest	Jüngere(m, f)	menor	cadetto, a
noz	noix	walnut	Walnuß(f)	nuez	noce
nu, nua	nu, e	naked; bare	nackt	desnudo, a	nudo, a
nuca	nuque	nape of the neck	Nacken(m)	nuca	nuca
nuclear	nucléaire	nuclear	Kern-, Atom-	nuclear	nucleare
núcleo	noyau	nucleus(-ei)	Kern(m)	núcleo	nucleo
nulo, a	nul, le	worthless; useless	wertlos	nulo, a	nullo, a
numérico, a	numérique	numerical	numerisch	numérico, a	numerico, a
número	nombre	number	Anzahl(f), Zahl(f)	número	numero
número	numéro	number	Nummer(f)	número	numero
número	chiffre	figure, number	Zahl(f), Ziffer(f)	cifra, número	cifra, numero
número	numéro, tirage	issue	Auflage(f)	número, edición	numero, pubblicazione
numeroso, a	nombreux, se	numerous, many	zahlreich	numeroso, a	numeroso, a
nunca, jamais	jamais	never; ever	niemals, jemals	jamás, nunca	mai
nutritivo, a	nutritif, ive	nutritious	nahrhaft	nutritivo, a	nutritivo, a
nuvem	nuage	cloud	Wolke(f)	nube	nuvola
nylon	nylon	nylon	Nylon(m)	nilón	nylon

O

Portuguese	French	English	German	Spanish	Italian
o, os	le, l', les	the	der, die, das, die	el, lo, los	il, lo, l'; i, gli
o	le	the	das	lo	lo
o, a	celui, celle	the one	derjenige, die-, das-	él, la	quello, a
oásis	oasis	oasis(oases pl.)	Oase(f)	oasis	oasi
obcecado, a	obsédé, e	maniac	Besessene(m, f)	obseso, a	maniaco, a
obcecar	obséder	obsess	verfolgen, quälen	obsesionar	ossessionare
obedecer	obéir	obey	gehorchen	obedecer	obbedire
obeso, a	obèse	obese	füllig, fettleibig	obeso, a	obeso, a
objecção	objection	objection, protest	Einwand(m)	objeción, reparo	obiezione
objectiva	objectif	lens	Objektiv(n)	objetivo	obiettivo
objectivo, a	objectif, ive	objective	objektiv, sachlich	objetivo, a	oggettivo, a
objectivo	objectif	objective	Objektiv(n), Ziel(n)	objetivo	obiettivo
objecto	objet	object	Objekt(n), Ding(n)	objeto	oggetto
objectos de valor	objets de valeur	valuables	Wertsachen(f pl)	objetos de valor	oggetti di valore
oblíquo, a	oblique	oblique, slanting	schräg, schief	oblicuo, a	obliquo, a
obra	oeuvre, travail	work	Werk(n)	obra	opera
obra, trabalho	ouvrage	work	Arbeit(f)	tarea, trabajo	opera, lavoro
obra	ouvrage	work	Werk(n)	obra	lavoro
obra	chantier	work-site	Baustelle(f)	obra	cantiere
obra-prima	chef-d'oeuvre	masterpiece	Meisterwerk(n)	obra maestra	capolavoro
obrigação	obligation	obligation	Verpflichtung(f)	obligación	obbligo
obrigação	contrainte	restraint	Zwang(m)	obligación	costrizione
obrigado, a	merci	thank you, thanks	danke	gracias	grazie
obrigar	obliger	oblige, force	zwingen	obligar	obbligare
obrigar	contraindre	force, compel	zwingen	obligar a	costringere
obrigatório, a	obligatoire	compulsory	obligatorisch	obligatorio, a	obbligatorio, a
obrigatório, a	obligatoire	mandatory	obligatorisch	obligatorio, a	obbligatorio, a
obsceno, a	obscène	obscene	obszön	obsceno, a	osceno, a
obscuridade	obscurité	darkness	Dunkelheit(f)	oscuridad	oscurità, buio
observação	remarque	remark, comment	Bemerkung(f)	observación	osservazione

Portuguese	French	English	German	Spanish	Italian
observador, a	observateur	observer	Beobachter(in f)m	observador, a	osservatore, trice
observar	observer	observe	beobachten	observar	osservare
obsessão	obsession	obsession	fixe Idee(f)	obsesión	ossessione
obsessão	hantise	obsessive fear	Zwangsvorstellung(f)	obsesión	ossessione
obstáculo	obstacle	obstacle	Hindernis(n)	obstáculo	ostacolo
obstrucção	obstruction	obstruction	Störung(f)	obstrucción	ostruzione
obter	obtenir	obtain, get	erhalten	obtener	ottenere
obter	obtenir, recevoir	get, obtain	bekommen	obtener	ottenere
obus	obus	shell	Geschoß(n), Granate(f)	obús	proiettile
ocasional	occasionnel, le	occasional	gelegentlich	ocasional	occasionale
ocasionar, causar	occasionner	cause, bring about	verursachen	ocasionar, causar	causare
oceânico, a	océanique	oceanic	ozeanisch	oceánico, a	oceanico, a
oceano	océan	ocean	Ozean(m)	océano	oceano
ocidental	occidental, e	Western	westlich	occidental	occidentale
oco, a	creux, se	hollow	hohl	hueco, a	vuoto, a; cavo, a
ocorrer	produire(se)	happen, occur	passieren	suceder, ocurrir	accadere
oculista	opticien, ne	optician	Optiker(in f)m	óptico, a	ottico, a
óculos	lunettes	glasses	Brille(f)	gafas	occhiali
ocultar	cacher	conceal	verbergen, verhehlen	esconder, ocultar	nascondere
ocupado, a	occupé, e	busy	beschäftigt	ocupado, a	impegnato, a
ocupado, a	occupé, e	occupied	besetzt	ocupado, a	occupato, a
ocupado, a	occupé, e	engaged; taken	besetzt	ocupado, a	occupato, a
ocupar	occuper	occupy, fill	ein = nehmen	ocupar	occupare
odiar	haïr	hate, detest	hassen	odiar	odiare
ódio	haine	hate	Haß(m)	odio	odio
odioso, a	odieux, se	odious, obnoxious	widerwärtig	odioso, a	odioso, a
Oeste	Ouest	West	Westen(m)	Oeste	Ovest
ofender	vexer	offend, vex	beleidigen	ofender, picar	offendere
ofender-se	vexer(se)	get upset	beleidigt sein	ofenderse	offendersi
ofensiva	offensive	offensive	Offensive(f)	ofensiva	offensiva
oferecer	offrir	give; offer	schenken, an = bieten	ofrecer	offrire, regalare
oferta	offre	offer	Angebot(n)	oferta	offerta
oficial	officiel, le	official	offiziell	oficial	ufficiale
oficial	officier	officer	Offizier(m)	oficial	ufficiale
oficina	atelier	workshop	Werkstatt(f)	taller	officina
ofício	métier	profession, job	Beruf(m)	oficio	mestiere
oficioso, a	officieux, se	unofficial	halbamtlich	oficioso, a	ufficioso, a
oftalmologia	ophtalmologie	ophthalmology	Augenheilkunde(f)	oftalmología	oftalmologia
oftalmologista	oculiste	oculist	Augenarzt(m)	oculista	oculista
oitenta	quatre-vingts	eighty	achtzig	ochenta	ottanta
oito	huit	eight	acht	ocho	otto
olá!	salut!	hi!, hello!	Hallo!; tschüs!; tschüß	hola(!)	ciao!
óleo; azeite	huile	oil	Öl(n); Speiseöl(n)	aceite	olio
óleo	huile	oil	Öl(n); Motoröl(n)	aceite; óleo	olio
olfacto	odorat	smell(sense of)	Geruchssinn(m).	olfato	odorato
olhada	regard	glance	Blick(m)	ojeada	occhiata
olhar	regard	look, expression	Blick(m)	mirada	sguardo
olhar	regarder	look(at)	schauen, an = sehen	mirar	guardare
olhe!	regardez!	look!	seht!, schauen Sie!	mire(!)	guardi!, guardate!
olheiras	cerne	ring, circle	Augenringe(pl.)	ojeras	occhiaia
olho	oeil	eye	Auge(n)	ojo	occhio
olhos	yeux	eyes	Augen(n, pl)	ojos	occhi
olímpico, a	olympique	Olympic	olympisch	olímpico, a	olimpico, a
ombro	épaule	shoulder	Schulter(f)	hombro	spalla
omitir	omettre	omit	aus = lassen	omitir	omettere
onda	onde	wave	Welle(f)	onda	onda
onda, vaga	vague	wave	Welle(f)	ola	onda
onde	où	where	wo	donde, dónde	dove
ondulado, a	frisé, e	curly	lockig	rizado, a	ricciuto, a
ontem	hier	yesterday	gestern	ayer	ieri
onze	onze	eleven	elf	once	undici
opaco, a	opaque	opaque	undurchsichtig; trüb	opaco, a	opaco, a
opção	option, choix	option	Wahl(f)	opción	opzione
ópera	opéra	opera	Oper(f)	ópera	opera
operação	opération	operation	Operation(f)	operación	operazione
operar	opérer	operate(on)	operieren	operar	operare
operário, a	ouvrier, ière	worker, workman	Arbeiter(in f)m	obrero, a	operaio, a
opereta	opérette	operetta	Operette(f)	zarzuela, opereta	operetta

P

Portuguese	French	English	German	Spanish	Italian
opinião	opinion	opinion	Meinung(f)	opinión	opinione
opinião, parecer	avis	opinion	Meinung(f)	opinión	aviso, parere
opor-se	opposer(s')	oppose	widersetzen, sich	oponerse	opporsi
oportunidade	occasion	opportunity	Gelegenheit(f)	oportunidad	occasione
oportuno, a	opportun, e	opportune	günstig	oportuno, a	opportuno, a
oposição	opposition	opposition	Opposition(f)	oposición	opposizione
oposto, a	opposé, e	opposite	gegenüberliegend	opuesto, a	opposto, a
oposto, a	opposé, e	opposing	entgegengesetzt	opuesto, a	opposto, a
oprimido, a	opprimé, e	oppressed	unterdrückt	oprimido, a	oppresso, a
óptico, a	optique	optic(al)	optisch	óptico, a	ottico, a
optimista	optimiste	optimistic	optimistisch	optimista	ottimista
oração	prière	prayer	Gebet(n)	oración	preghiera
orador, a	orateur, trice	speaker, orator	Redner(in f)m	orador, a; locutor, a	oratore, trice
oral	oral, e	oral	mündlich	oral	orale
órbita	orbite	orbit	Umlaufbahn(f)	órbita	orbita
orçamento	budget	budget	Budget(n)	presupuesto	bilancio
orçamento	devis	estimate	Kostenvoranschlag(m)	presupuesto	preventivo
ordem	ordre	order	Ordnung(f)	orden	ordine
ordem	ordre	order	Rangordnung(f)	orden	ordine
ordem	ordre	order	Befehl(m)	orden	ordine
ordem, instruções	consigne	orders, instruction	Anweisung(f)	consigna, orden	direttiva, ordine
ordenar	ordonner	order	befehlen, verordnen	ordenar	ordinare
ordenar	ranger	tidy up	auf = räumen	ordenar	ordinare
ordinário, a	ordinaire	ordinary	gewöhnlich	ordinario, a	ordinario, a
orelha	oreille	ear	Ohr(n)	oreja	orecchio
órfão, órfã	orphelin, e	orphan	Waise(f, m)	huérfano, a	orfano, a
orgânico, a	organique	organic	organisch	orgánico, a	organico, a
organismo	organisme	organism	Organismus(m)	organismo	organismo
organização	organisation	organization	Organisation(f)	organización	organizzazione
organizador, a	organisateur	organizer	Organisator(in f)m	organizador, a	organizzatore, trice
organizar	organiser	organize	organisieren	organizar	organizzare
órgão	organe	organ	Organ(n)	órgano	organo
órgão	orgue	organ	Orgel(f)	órgano	organo
orgasmo	orgasme	orgasm	Orgasmus(m)	orgasmo	orgasmo
orgia	orgie	orgy	Orgie(f)	orgía	orgia
orgulho	orgueil	pride, arrogance	Stolz(m)	orgullo	orgoglio
orgulho	fierté	pride	Stolz(m)	orgullo	fierezza
orgulhoso, a	orgueilleux, se	proud, arrogant	stolz, arrogant	orgulloso, a	orgoglioso, a
orientação	orientation	orientation	Orientierung(f)	orientación	orientamento
oriental	oriental, e	oriental	orientalisch	oriental	orientale
orientar	orienter	position	orientieren	orientar	orientare
orifício	orifice	orifice, aperture	Öffnung(f), Mündung(f)	orificio	orifizio
origem	origine	origin	Ursprung(m)	origen	origine
original	original, e	original	original	original	originale
original	original	original	Original(n)	original	originale
oriundo, a	originaire	native(of)	gebürtig	oriundo, a	originario, a
ornamento	ornement	ornament	Verzierung; Schmuck	adorno	ornamento
ornar, adornar	décorer	decorate	schmücken	decorar, adornar	ornare, adornare
orquestra	orchestre	orchestra; band	Orchester(n)	orquesta	orchestra
orquídia	orchidée	orchid	Orchidee(f)	orquídea	orchidea
ortodoxo, a	orthodoxe	orthodox	orthodox	ortodoxo, a	ortodosso, a
ortografia	orthographe	spelling	Rechtschreibung(f)	ortografía	ortografia
orvalho	rosée	dew	Tau(m)	rocío	rugiada
os, as	les	the	die	los, las	i, gli; le
oscilar	osciller	oscillate	schwanken	oscilar	oscillare
ossatura	ossature	structure	Struktur(f)	armazón	ossatura
osso	os	bone	Knochen(m)	hueso	osso
ostra	huître	oyster	Auster(f)	ostra	ostrica
otite	otite	ear-ache	Mittelohrentzündung f	otitis	otite
ou	ou	or	oder	o; u	o
ouro	or	gold	Gold(n)	oro	oro
ousar, atrever-se	oser	dare	wagen	osar, atreverse	osare
outono	automne	autumn	Herbst(m)	otoño	autunno
outro, a	autre	other	andere, sonstige	otro, a	altro, a
outro, a	autre(d')	else	ander; anders	otro, a	altro, a
outro modo(de)	autrement	otherwise	anders; sonst	otro modo(de)	altrimenti
Outubro	Octobre	October	Oktober(m)	Octubre	Ottobre
ouvido	ouïe	hearing, audition	Gehör(n)	oído	udito

Portuguese	French	English	German	Spanish	Italian
ouvinte	auditeur, trice	listener	Zuhörer(in f)m	auditor, a	uditore, uditrice
ouvir	entendre	hear	hören	oír	sentire
oval	ovale	oval	oval	oval, ovalado, a	ovale
ovário	ovaire	ovary	Eierstock(m)	ovario	ovaia
overdose	surdose	overdose	Überdosis(f)	sobredosis	overdose
ovino	ovin	ovine	Schaf-	ovino	ovino
ovo	oeuf	egg	Ei(n)	huevo	uovo(a)
óvulo	ovule	ovule	Ei(zelle f)n	óvulo	ovulo
oxalá	pourvu que	provided that	wenn nur, sofern, daß	ojalá	purché
oxidação	oxydation	oxidization	Oxydierung(f)	oxidación	ossidazione
oxigénio	oxygène	oxygen	Sauerstoff(m)	oxígeno	ossigeno
ozone	ozone	ozone	Ozon(n)	ozono	ozono

P

Portuguese	French	English	German	Spanish	Italian
pá	pelle	spade; shovel	Schaufel(f); Spaten(m)	pala	pala
paciência	patience	patience	Geduld(f)	paciencia	pazienza
paciente	patient, e	patient	geduldig	paciente	paziente
pacífico, a	pacifique	peaceful, pacific	friedlich	pacífico, a	pacifico, a
pacífico, a	paisible	peaceful, quiet	friedlich, ruhig	apacible	pacifico, a; placido, a
Pacífico	Pacifique	Pacific Ocean	Pazifik(m)	Pacífico	Pacifico
pacote	paquet	packet; package	Paket(n)	paquete	pacco
pacote	colis	parcel	Paket(n)	paquete	pacco, collo
pacote; carteira	sachet	bag(small), sachet	Beutel(m), Tütchen(n)	bolsita	bustina
pacto	pacte	pact	Pakt(m)	pacto	patto
padaria	boulangerie	baker's(shop)	Bäckerei(f)	panadería	panificio
padre	prêtre	priest	Priester(m)	sacerdote, padre	prete
padre; pastor	pasteur	vicar, minister	Pastor(in f)m	pastor	pastore
padrinho	parrain	godfather	Pate(m)	padrino	padrino
paga, ordenado	paie(paye)	pay	Lohn(m)	paga	paga, stipendio
pagamento	paiement	payment	Bezahlung(f)	pago, abono	pagamento
pagamento	payement	payment	Zahlung(f)	abono, pago	pagamento
pagamento	règlement	settlement	Begleichung(f)	liquidación	saldo
pagar	payer	pay	bezahlen	pagar	pagare
pagar	régler	settle	bezahlen	liquidar, pagar	regolare, saldare
pagar	verser	pay(in)	ein = zahlen	ingresar	versare
página	page	page	Seite(f)	página	pagina
pai	père	father	Vater(m)	padre	padre
painel	panneau	panel	Brett(n)	tablero	cartello
painel	écran	screen	Wandschirm(m)	pantalla	schermo
painel, quadro	tableau	board, panel	Tafel(f)	tablero, tablón	pannello, quadro
pais	parents	parents	Eltern(pl)	padres	genitori
país	pays	country	Land(n)	país	paese
paisagem	paysage	landscape	Landschaft(f)	paisaje	paesaggio
paixão	passion	passion	Leidenschaft(f)	pasión	passione
palácio	palais	palace	Palast(m)	palacio	palazzo
palavra	mot	word	Wort(n)	palabra	parola
palavra	parole	word; speech	Wort(n)	palabra	parola
palavrão	juron	swear-word	Fluch(m)	juramento, taco	bestemmia
palavrão	gros mot	bad word	Schimpfwort(n)	palabrota	parolaccia
palavras cruzadas	mots croisés	crossword	Kreuzworträtsel(n)	crucigrama	cruciverba
palha	paille	straw	Stroh(n)	paja	paglia
palhaço	clown	clown	Clown(m)	payaso	pagliaccio, clown
palhota	case	hut	Hütte(f)	cabaña	capanna
palhota	paillotte	hut(straw-hut)	Strohhütte(f)	choza	capanna
pálido, a	pâle	pale	blaß	pálido, a	pallido, a
palito	cure-dents	tooth-pick	Zahnstocher(m)	palillo	stuzzicadenti

P

Portuguese	French	English	German	Spanish	Italian
palma	paume	palm	Handfläche(f)	palma	palma
palmada	tape, fessée	smack	Schlag(m)	cachete	schiaffo
palmeira	palmier	palm-tree	Palme(f)	palmera	palma
pálpebra	paupière	eyelid	Lid(n)	párpado	palpebra
palpitação	palpitation	palpitation	Herzklopfen(n)	palpitación	palpitazione
paludismo	paludisme	malaria	Sumpffieber(n)	paludismo	malaria, paludismo
pança	panse	belly, paunch	Bauch(m); Pansen(m)	panza	pancia
panfleto	tract	handout, leaflet	Flugblatt(n)	octavilla	volantino
pânico	panique	panic	Panik(f)	pánico	panico
pânico	affolement	panic	Panik(f)	pánico	panico
pântano	marais	marsh	Sumpf(m)	pantano	palude
pantanoso, a	marécageux, se	marshy, boggy	sumpfig	pantanoso, a	paludoso, a
pantera	panthère	panther	Panther(m)	pantera	pantera
pantufa, chinelo	pantoufle	slipper	Pantoffel(m)	zapatilla	pantofola
pão	pain	bread	Brot(n)	pan	pane
pão torrado	pain grillé	toast	Toast(m)	tostadas	pane tostato
papá	papa	Daddy, Dad	Papa	papá	papà, babbo
Papa	Pape	Pope	Papst(m)	Papa	Papa
papagaio	perroquet	parrot	Papagei(m)	loro	pappagallo
papel	papier	paper	Papier(n)	papel	carta
papel	rôle	role	Rolle(f)	papel	parte, ruolo
papelaria	papeterie	stationer's	Schreibwarenladen(m)	papelería	cartoleria
papel de parede	tapisserie	wallpaper	Tapete(f)	empapelado	carta da parati
papel higiénico	papier toilette	toilet paper	Toilettenpapier(n)	papel higiénico	carta igienica
paquete	paquebot	liner	Passagierdampfer(m)	buque	transatlantico
paquete	chasseur(hôtel)	page(boy), bellboy	Page(m), Hotelboy(m)	botones	fattorino
par	paire	pair(of)	Paar(n)	par	paio
par	pair	even	gerade	par	pari
para; por	pour	for	für	para; por	per
para	vers	to, towards	nach, zu	hacia	verso
parabéns!	félicitations!	congratulations!	Glückwunsch!	enhorabuena(!)	congratulazioni!
pára-brisas	pare-brise	windscreen	Windschutzscheibe(f)	parabrisas	parabrezza
parada	parade	parade	Parade(f)	parada, desfile	parata
paradoxo	paradoxe	paradox	Paradox(n)	paradoja	paradosso
parafuso	vis	screw	Schraube(f)	tornillo	vite
parafuso; cavilha	boulon	bolt	Bolzen(m)	perno, tornillo	bullone
paragem	arrêt	stop	Pause(f), Stillstand	parada	fermata
parágrafo	paragraphe	paragraph	Absatz(m), Abschnitt m	párrafo	paragrafo
paraíso	paradis	paradise	Paradies(n)	paraíso	paradiso
paralelo, a	parallèle	parallel	parallel	paralelo, a	parallelo, a
paralisia	paralysie	paralysis	Lähmung(f)	parálisis	paralisi
paralítico, a	paralysé, e	paralysed	gelähmt	paralítico, a	paralitico, a
paranóia	paranoia	paranoia	Paranoia(f)	paranoia	paranoia
pára-quedas	parachute	parachute	Fallschirm(m)	paracaídas	paracadute
parar	arrêter	stop	halten(an-, auf-)	parar	fermare
parar	arrêter(s')	stop	stehen = bleiben	pararse	fermarsi
parasita	parasite	parasite	Parasit(m)	parásito	parassita
parceiro, a	partenaire	partner	Partner(in f)m	pareja	socio, a; partner
parcela	parcelle	plot	Parzelle(f)	parcela	parcella
pardal	moineau	sparrow	Spatz(m)	gorrión	passero
parecer	paraître	seem, appear, look	scheinen, erscheinen	parecer	parere, sembrare
parecer	sembler	seem	scheinen	parecer	sembrare
parecer-se	ressembler(à)	look like	ähneln, aussehen wie	parecerse(a)	somigliare a
parede	paroi, mur	wall	Wand(f)	pared	parete
parente	parent, e	relative, relation	verwandt	pariente	parente
parentesco	parenté	relationship	Verwandtschaft(f)	parentesco	parentela
parêntesis	parenthèse	bracket	Klammer(f)	paréntesis	parentesi
parlamento	parlement	parliament	Parlament(n)	parlamento	parlamento
parque	parc	park	Park(m)	parque	parco
pestacionamento	parking	car park	Parkplatz(m)	aparcamiento	parcheggio
parte	partie, part	part	Teil(m n)	parte	pezzo, parte
parte	part, partie	share; part	Anteil(m); Teil(m, n)	parte	parte
parteira	sage-femme	midwife(-ives)	Hebamme(f)	comadrona	levatrice
participar(em)	participer(à)	take part(in)	teil = nehmen	participar(en)	partecipare(a)
participar em	participer à	participate in	beteiligen, sich	participar en	partecipare a
partícula	particule	particle	Teilchen(n)	partícula	particella
particular	particulier, ière	particular	eigentümlich	particular	particolare
particular	particulier	individual	Privatmann(m)	particular	privato

Portuguese	French	English	German	Spanish	Italian
particularmente	notamment	particular(in)	besonders, nämlich	particularmente	particolarmente
partida	départ	departure, start	Abfahrt(f)	salida, partida	partenza
partida	canular	joke, hoax	Ulk(m), Witz(m)	broma	scherzo, burla
partida	farce	joke; farce	Streich(m)	broma	scherzo
partidário, a	partisan, e	partisan	Anhänger(in f)m	partidário, a	partigiano, a
partido	parti	party	Partei(f)	partido	partito
partilha	division	partition	Trennung(f)	división	divisione
partir, abalar	partir	leave, go away	weg = gehen	salir, marcharse	partire
partitura	partition	score(music)	Partitur(f)	partitura	spartito
parto	accouchement	delivery; birth	Entbindung(f)	parto	parto
parvo, a	débile	crazy, mad	verrückt; schwach	débil	scemo, a; minorato, a
Páscoa	Pâques	Easter	Ostern(n)	Pascua	Pasqua
pasmado, a	ahuri, e	stupefied	verdutzt	espantado, a	attonito, a
passado, a	passé, e	past	vergangen	pasado, a	passato, a
passado	passé	past	Vergangenheit(f)	pasado	passato
passageiro, a	passager, ère	passenger	Passagier(in f)m	pasajero, a	passeggero, a
passagem	passage	passage	Durchgang(m)	pasaje, paso	passaggio
passaporte	passeport	passport	Paß(m)	pasaporte	passaporto
passar(por; em)	passer	pass, go(through)	fahren über	pasar	passare
passar	passer	call, drop in	vorbei = kommen	pasar	passare
passar	passer	spend	verbringen	pasar	trascorrere
passar a ferro	repassage	ironing	Bügeln(n)	planchado	stirare
pássaro	oiseau	bird	Vogel(m)	pájaro	uccello
passatempo	passe-temps	hobby, pastime	Hobby(n)	pasatiempo	passatempo
passear	promener	walk(go for a)	spazieren = gehen	pasear	passeggiare
passeio	promenade	walk; drive; ride	Spaziergang(m)	paseo	passeggiata
passeio	trottoir	pavement	Bürgersteig(m)	acera	marciapiede
passivo, a	passif, ive	passive	passiv	pasivo, a	passivo, a
passo	pas	step; pace	Schritt(m)	paso	passo
pasta	cartable	briefcase; satchel	Ranzen(m)	cartera	cartella
pastéis	beignets	fritters	Krapfen, Pfannkuchen	buñuelos	frittella
pastelaria	pâtisserie	cake shop	Konditorei(f)	pastelería	pasticceria
pastelaria	pâtisserie(s)	pastry, cake	Backwaren(f, pl)	pasteles	dolci
pastor, a	berger, ère	shepherd, -ess	Schäfer(in f)m	pastor, a	pastore, pastorella
pastoso, a	pâteux, se	pasty	pappig	pastoso, a	pastoso, a
pata	patte	paw; leg; foot	Pfote(f); Bein(n)	pata	zampa
paté	pâté	paté	Pastete(f)	paté	patè
patente	brevet	patent	Patent(n)	patente	brevetto
paterno, a	paternel, le	paternal	väterlich	paterno, a	paterno, a
patife	voyou	hooligan	Strolch(m)	canalla	mascalzone, a
patinagem	patinage	skating	Eiskunstlauf(m)	patinaje	pattinaggio
patinar	patiner	skate	Schlittschuh laufen	patinar	pattinare
pátio	cour	yard	Hof(m)	patio	cortile
pato, a	canard	duck	Ente(f)	pato	anatra
patrão, patroa	patron, ne	boss; employer	Chef(m), Arbeitgeber m	patrón, a; dueño, a	padrone, a
patrão	employeur	employer	Arbeitgeber(in f)m	patrón	datore di lavoro
pátria	patrie	native land	Vaterland(n)	patria	patria
patriarca	patriarche	patriarch	Patriarch(m)	patriarca	patriarca
património	patrimoine	patrimony	Familiengut(n)	patrimonio	patrimonio
patrocinador	sponsor	sponsor	Sponsor(m)	patrocinador	sponsor
patrulha	patrouille	patrol	Patrouille(f), Streife	patrulla	pattuglia
pau, bastão	bâton	stick	Stock(m)	palo	bastone
paulitos	quille	skittle	Kegel(f)	bolos(juego)	birillo
pausa	pause	pause, break	Pause(f)	pausa	pausa
paz	paix	peace	Frieden(m)	paz	pace
pé	pied	foot(feet pl.)	Fuß(m)	pie	piede
peão(xadrez)	pion(échecs)	pawn(chess)	Bauer(m)(Schach)	peón(ajedrez)	pedone(scacchi)
peão	piéton	pedestrian	Fußgänger(m)	peatón	pedone
peça	pièce	part, component	Teil(n)	pieza	pezzo
peça, tábula(dama)	pion(dames)	draught	Stein(m)(Spiel)	ficha(damas)	pedina(dama)
peça	pièce	play	Stück(m)	obra	commedia
peça de roupa	vêtement	garment	Kleidungsstück(n)	traje, ropa	vestito
pecado	péché	sin	Sünde(f)	pecado	peccato
pedaço	morceau, bout	piece, bit	Stück(n)	pedazo, trozo	pezzo
pedal	pédale	pedal	Pedal(n)	pedal	pedale
pedante; vaidoso, a	pédant, e	pedantic	pedantisch	pedante	pedante
pediatra	pédiatre	paediatrician	Kinderarzt(m)/-ärztin	pediatra	pediatra
pedicuro	pédicure	chiropodist	Fußpfleger(in f)m	pedicuro, a	pedicure

P

pedido	demande	request	Anfrage(f)	pedido	richiesta
pedido	demande	request; demand	Bitte(f); Gesuch(n)	petición	richiesta
pedido	requête	request	Ersuchen(n), Gesuch(n)	demanda	richiesta
pedido	demande(emploi)	application	Bewerbung(f)	solicitud	domanda
pedigree	pédigree	pedigree	Stammbaum(Tier-)(m)	pedigrí	pedigree
pedir	demander	ask(for)	fragen	pedir	chiedere
pedir	demander	beg	bitten	pedir	domandare
pedir emprestado	emprunter	borrow	borgen	pedir prestado	prendere in prestito
pedra	pierre	stone	Stein(m)	piedra	pietra
pedra de calçada	pavé	paving-stone	Pflasterstein(m)	adoquín	selce, selciato
pedreira	carrière	quarry	Steinbruch(m)	cantera	cava
pedreiro, trolha	maçon	builder	Maurer(m)	albañil	muratore
peito	poitrine	chest; breast	Brust(f)	pecho	petto
peixaria	poissonnerie	fishmonger's	Fischgeschäft(n)	pescadería	pescheria
peixe	poisson	fish	Fisch(m)	pescado	pesce
pele	peau	skin	Haut(f)	piel	pelle
pele; peliça	fourrure	fur	Pelz(m)	piel	pelliccia
película	pellicule	film	Film(m)	película	pellicola
pêlo	poil	hair	Haar(n)	pelo	pelo
pêlo	pelage	coat, fur	Fell(n)	pelaje, pelo	pelo
peludo, a	poilu, e	hairy	behaart	peludo, a	peloso, a
pena(que)	dommage(quel)	pity(what a)	schade!(wie ---)	lástima(qué)	peccato(che)
pena(e')	dommage(c'est)	pity(it is a)	schade!	pena(es una)	peccato(è)
pena	peine	sentence	Bestrafung(f)	pena, castigo	punizione, castigo
pena; tristeza	peine	sorrow, grief	Schmerz(m), Kummer(m)	pena	pena; dolore
pena; pesar	regret	regret	Bedauern(n)	lamento(lo)	rimpianto
penal	pénal, e	penal	strafrechtlich	penal	penale
penalidade	pénalité	penalty	Strafe(f), Strafpunkt	penalidad	penalità
pendurar	pendre	hang	hängen, auf = hängen	colgar	appendere
pendurar	accrocher	hang	auf = hängen	colgar	appendere
pendurar	suspendre	hang up	auf = hängen	colgar, suspender	appendere
penetrar	pénétrer	enter, penetrate	ein = dringen	penetrar	penetrare
penhor	gage	pledge	Pfand(n)	prenda	pegno
penicilina	pénicilline	penicillin	Penizillin(n)	penicilina	penicillina
península	péninsule	peninsula	Halbinsel(f)	península	penisola
penoso, a	pénible	hard, arduous	mühsam, schwierig	penoso, a; duro, a	penoso, a
pensamento	pensée	thought	Gedanke(m)	pensamiento	pensiero
pensão	pension	pension; allowance	Pension(f)	pensión	pensione
pensão	pension	guest-house	Gasthaus(n)	pensión	pensione
pensar	penser	think	denken	pensar	pensare
penso, curativo	pansement	plaster, bandage	Verband(m)	cura, vendaje	medicazione
pente	peigne	comb	Kamm(m)	peine	pettine
penteado	coiffure	hair-style	Frisur(f)	peinado	pettinatura
pentear-se	coiffer(se)	hair(do one's)	frisieren, sich	peinar(se)	pettinare(-rsi)
pentear-se	peigner(se)	comb(one's hair)	kämmen	peinar(se)	pettinarsi
penúria	pénurie	shortage	Mangel(m)	penuria, escasez	penuria
pequeno, a	petit, e	small, little	klein	pequeño, a	piccolo, a
pequeno, a	petit, e	little	klein	pequeño, a	piccolo, a
pêra	poire	pear	Birne(f)	pera	pera
perceber	percevoir	perceive	wahr = nehmen	percibir	percepire
percentagem	pourcentage	percentage	Prozentsatz(m)	porcentaje	percentuale
perceptível	perceptible	perceptible	wahrnehmbar	perceptible	percettibile
percevejo	punaise	drawing-pin	Heftzwecke(f)	chincheta	puntina(disegno)
percurso	parcours	journey; course	Strecke(f), Route(f)	recorrido	percorso
perda, prejuizo	perte	loss, waste	Verlust(m)	pérdida	perdita
perda de sangue	saignement	bleeding	Blutung(f)	desangramiento	emorragia
perdão	pardon	forgiveness	Vergebung(f)	perdón	scusa, perdono
perdão!, desculpe!	pardon!	sorry!, excuse me!	Verzeihung!	perdón(!), disculpe	scusi!
perder	perdre	lose	verlieren	perder	perdere
perder	manquer	miss	verpassen	perder	perdere; mancare
perder	rater	miss	verpassen	perder	perdere; mancare
perdido, a	perdu, e	lost	verloren	perdido, a	perso, a; smarrito, a
perdoar	pardonner	forgive, pardon	verzeihen, vergeben	perdonar	perdonare
peregrinação	pèlerinage	pilgrimage	Wallfahrt(f)	peregrinación	pellegrinaggio
peregrino	pèlerin	pilgrim	Pilger(in f)m	peregrino	pellegrino
perfeição	perfection	perfection	Vollkommenheit(f)	perfección	perfezione
perfeito, a	parfait, e	perfect	einwandfrei	perfecto, a	perfetto, a
pérfido, a	perfide	treacherous	heimtückisch	pérfido, a	perfido, a

Portuguese	French	English	German	Spanish	Italian
perfil	profil	profile	Profil(n)	perfil	profilo
perfumaria	parfumerie	perfume shop	Parfümerie(f)	perfumería	profumeria
perfume	parfum	perfume, scent	Parfüm(n)	perfume	profumo
perfuração	forage	boring	Bohrung(f)	perforación	perforazione
perfurar	perforer	perforate	durchbohren	perforar	perforare
pergunta	question	question	Frage(f)	pregunta	domanda
perguntar	demander	ask	fragen	preguntar	domandare
perguntar	poser(question)	ask	fragen	preguntar	porre(domanda)
perguntar-se	demander(se)	wonder	fragen, sich	preguntarse	domandarsi
periferia	périphérie	periphery	Umkreis(m), Umfang(m)	periferia	periferia
perigo	péril	peril, danger	Gefahr(f)	peligro, riesgo	pericolo
perigo	danger	danger	Gefahr(f)	peligro	pericolo
perigoso, a	dangereux, se	dangerous	gefährlich	peligroso, a	pericoloso, a
perímetro	périmètre	perimeter	Umfang(m)	perímetro	perimetro
perímetro	pourtour	periphery	Umkreis(m)	contorno	giro, circuito
periódico, a	périodique	periodic(al)	periodisch	periódico, a	periodico, a
período	période	period	Periode(f)	período	periodo
perito, a	expert, e	expert	Experte(m), Expertin f	experto, a; perito, a	esperto, a
permanente	permanent, e	permanent	andauernd	permanente	permanente
permissão	permission	permission	Erlaubnis(f)	permiso	permesso
permitir	permettre	allow, enable	erlauben	permitir	permettere
permitir-se	permettre(se)	afford	leisten, sich	permitirse	permettersi
perna	jambe	leg	Bein(n)	pierna	gamba
perna	cuisse	leg	Schenkel(m)	muslo; pierna	coscia
pérola	perle	pearl	Perle(f)	perla	perla
perpendicular	perpendiculaire	perpendicular	senkrecht	perpendicular	perpendicolare
perpétuo, a	perpétuel, le	perpetual	fortdauernd	perpetuo, a	perpetuo, a
perscrutar	scruter	scan, scrutinize	erforschen	escudriñar	scrutare
perseguir	poursuivre	pursue	verfolgen	perseguir	inseguire
perseguir	harceler	harass	quälen	acosar	assillare
perseguir	persécuter	persecute	verfolgen	perseguir	perseguitare
perseverança	persévérance	perseverance	Ausdauer(f)	perseverancia	perseveranza
perseverar	persévérer	persevere	beharren, aus = halten	perseverar	perseverare
persistência	persistance	persistence	Beharrlichkeit(f)	persistencia	persistenza
personalidade	personnalité	personality	Persönlichkeit(f)	personalidad	personalità
perspectiva	perspective	perspective	Perspektive(f)	perspectiva	prospettiva
perspectiva	perspective	prospect	Aussicht(f)	perspectiva	prospettiva
persuadir	persuader	persuade	überreden	persuadir	persuadere
pertencer	appartenir(à)	belong to	gehören	pertenecer	appartenere
perto	près, proche	near, close to	nah(e)	cerca	vicino, a
perto de	auprès de	close to	bei	cerca de	vicino a
perturbação	troubles	troubles	Unruhen(f, pl)	disturbios	disordini
perturbado, a	bouleversé, e	overwhelmed	erschüttert	conmocionado, a	sconvolto, a
perturbar	perturber	disturb, perturb	stören	perturbar	perturbare
perturbar	troubler	disturb; trouble	stören	perturbar	turbare, disturbare
peruca	perruque	wig	Perücke(f)	peluca	parrucca
perverso, a	pervers, e	perverse	pervers	perverso, a	perverso, a
pesadelo	cauchemar	nightmare	Alptraum(m)	pesadilla	incubo
pesado, a	lourd, e	heavy	schwer	pesado, a	pesante
pesado(tornar)	alourdir	make heavy	erschweren	pesado(hacer)	appesantire
pesar	peser	weigh	wiegen	pesar	pesare
pesca	pêche	fishing, angling	Fischen n; Fischfang m	pesca	pesca
pesca(à linha)	pêche	angling	Angeln(n)	pesca(con caña)	pesca(con lenza)
pescador	pêcheur	fisherman(-men)	Fischer(m)	pescador	pescatore
pescoço	cou	neck	Hals(m), Nacken(m)	cuello	collo
peso	poids	weight	Gewicht(n)	peso	peso
pêssego	pêche	peach	Pfirsich(m)	melocotón	pesca
pessimista	pessimiste	pessimistic	pessimistisch	pesimista	pessimista
pessoa	personne	person	Person(f)	persona	persona
pessoal	personnel, le	personal	persönlich	personal	personale
pessoal	personnel	staff, personnel	Personal(n)	personal, plantilla	personale
pestana	cil	eyelash	Wimper(f)	pestaña	ciglio(a)
pétala	pétale	petal	Blütenblatt(n)	pétalo	petalo
petição	pétition	petition	Bittschrift(f), Gesuch	petición	petizione
petiscar	grignoter	nibble	knabbern	mordisquear	sgranocchiare
petróleo	pétrole	oil	Erdöl(n)	petróleo	petrolio
peúga	chaussette(s)	sock	Socke(f), Strumpf(m)	calcetín(es)	calza, e; calzini
pia, banca	évier	sink	Spülbecken(n)	fregadero	acquaio, lavandino

Portuguese	French	English	German	Spanish	Italian
pianista	pianiste	pianist	Pianist(in f)m	pianista	pianista
piano	piano	piano	Klavier(n)	piano	pianoforte
picada	piqûre	sting, bite	Stich(m)	picadura	puntura
picante	piquant, e	spicy, hot	scharf	picante	piccante
picante	épicé, e	spicy	gewürzt, würzig	picante	piccante
picar	piquer	prick, sting	stechen	pinchar	pungere
pico	pic	peak	Gipfel(m)	pico	picco
piedade	pitié	pity	Mitleid(n)	piedad	pietà
pijama	pyjama	pyjamas	Schlafanzug(m)	pijama	pigiama
pilar	pilier	pillar	Pfeiler(m)	pilar	pilastro
pilha	pile	battery	Batterie(f)	pila	pila
pilha	lampe de poche	torch	Taschenlampe(f)	linterna	lampadina tascabile
pilha, montão	pile	pile	Stapel(m)	pila	pila
pilhagem	pillage	plunder, pillage	Plünderung(f)	saqueo	saccheggio
pilotar	piloter	pilot; fly; drive	fliegen; lotsen; fahren	pilotar	pilotare
piloto	pilote	pilot	Pilot(m)	piloto	pilota
pílula	pilule	pill	Pille(f)	píldora	pillola
pimenta	poivre	pepper	Pfeffer(m)	pimienta	pepe
pinça, alicate	pince	pincers, pliers	Zange(f)	pinza(s), tenazas	pinza
pincel	pinceau	brush	Pinsel(m)	pincel	pennello
pintar	peindre	paint	streichen	pintar	imbiancare
pintar	peindre	paint	malen	pintar	dipingere
pinto	poussin	chick	Küken(n)	pollito	pulcino
pintor, a	peintre	painter	Anstreicher; Maler(m)	pintor, a	pittore, trice
pintura	peinture	painting	Malerei(f)	pintura	pittura; dipinto
pioneiro	pionnier	pioneer	Pionier, Bahnbrecher	pionero	pioniere
pior	pire	worse	schlimmer	peor	peggio
pirâmide	pyramide	pyramid	Pyramide(f)	pirámide	piramide
pirata	pirate	pirate	Pirat(in f)m	pirata	pirata
pires	soucoupe	saucer	Untertasse(f)	platillo	piattino
piroga	pirogue	pirogue	Piroge(f), Kanu(n)	piragua	piroga
pisca	clignotant	indicator	Blinklicht(n)	intermitente	freccia
piscar	clignoter	flash	blinken	pestañear	lampeggiare
piscina	piscine	swimming-pool	Schwimmbad(n)	piscina	piscina
pista	piste	track	Spur(f)	pista	pista
pista	piste	runway	Bahn(Lande-, Start-)	pista	pista
pista	piste	slope	Piste(f)	pista	pista
pista de patinagem	patinoire	skating rink	Eisbahn(f)	pista de patinar	pista da pattinaggio
pistão	piston	piston	Kolben(m)	pistón	pistone
pistola	pistolet	gun, pistol	Pistole(f)	pistola	pistola
pitoresco, a	pittoresque	picturesque	malerisch	pintoresco, a	pittoresco, a
placa	plaque	plate, plaque	Platte(f)	placa	lastra, piastra
planador	planeur	glider	Segelflugzeug(n)	planeador	aliante
planalto	plateau	plateau	Hochebene(f)	meseta	altipiano
planar	planer	glide	schweben, gleiten	planear	planare
planeta	planète	planet	Planet(m)	planeta	pianeta
planície	plaine	plain	Ebene(f)	llanura, llano	pianura
plano, a	plat, e	flat	platt	llano, a	piatto, a
plano; desenho	plan	plan; drawing	Plan(m)	plan; plano	piano; schema
plano, projecto	plan, projet	scheme, plan	Plan(m)	plan, proyecto	schema, piano
planta	plante	plant	Pflanze(f)	planta	pianta
planta	plan	map	Plan(m)(Stadtplan m)	plano	pianta; stradario
plantar	planter	plant	pflanzen	plantar	piantare
plástico, a	plastique	plastic	plastisch	plástico, a	plastico, a
plástico	plastique	plastic	Plastik(n)	plástico	plastica
plataforma	plate-forme	platform	Plattform(f)	plataforma	piattaforma
plataforma	quai	platform	Bahnsteig(m)	andén	binario, marciapiede
pleito, processo	procès	lawsuit	Prozeß(m)	pleito	causa
pluma; pena	plume	feather	Feder(f)	pluma	penna, piuma
plural	pluriel	plural	Mehrzahl(f)	plural	plurale
pneu	pneu	tyre	Reifen(m)	neumático	pneumatico, gomma
pneumonia	pneumonie	pneumonia	Lungenentzündung(f)	neumonía	polmonite
pó	poudre	powder	Puder(m); Pulver(n)	polvo	polvere
pobre	pauvre	poor	arm	pobre	povero, a
pobreza	pauvreté	poverty	Armut(f)	pobreza	povertà
poço	puits	well	Brunnen(m)	pozo	pozzo
poder	pouvoir	can, able to(be)	können	poder	potere
poder	pouvoir	power	Macht(f)	poder	potere

Portuguese	French	English	German	Spanish	Italian
poderoso, a	puissant, e	powerful, strong	mächtig, kräftig	poderoso, a	poderoso, a; potente
podre	pourri, e	rotten	verfault	podrido, a	marcio, a
poeira	poussière	dust	Staub(m)	polvo	polvere
poema	poème	poem	Gedicht(n)	poema	poema
poesia	poésie	poetry	Poesie(f)	poesía	poesia
polar	polaire	polar	polar; Polar-	polar	polare
polegar	pouce	thumb	Daumen(m)	pulgar	pollice
polémica	polémique	controversy	Polemik(f)	polémica	polemica
polia	poulie	pulley	Flaschenzug(m)	polea	puleggia
polícia	police	police	Polizei(f)	policía	polizia
polícia	policier	policeman(-men)	Polizist(in f)m	policía	poliziotto
polido, a	poli, e	polished	poliert	pulido, a	levigato, a
poligamia	polygamie	polygamy	Polygamie(f)	poligamia	poligamia
poliomielite	poliomyélite	polio(myelitis)	Kinderlähmung(f)	poliomielitis	poliomelite
pólipo	polype	polyp	Polyp(m)	pólipo	polipo
polir	polir	polish	polieren	pulir	lucidare, levigare
política	politique	politics	Politik(f)	política	politica
política	politique	policy	Politik(f)	política	politica
político, a	politique	political	politisch	político, a	politico, a
político	homme politique	politician	Politiker(in f)m	político	uomo politico
político, a	politicien, ne	politician	Politiker(in f)m	político, a	politico, a
polivalente	polyvalent, e	polyvalent	vielseitig	polivalente	polivalente
polo	pôle	pole	Pol(m)	polo	polo
poltrona	fauteuil	arm-chair	Sessel(m)	sillón	poltrona
poluição	pollution	pollution	Verschmutzung(f)	contaminación	inquinamento
poluir	polluer	pollute	verunreinigen	contaminar	inquinare
pólvora	poudre	powder	Pulver(n)(Schieß-)	pólvora	polvere
pomada	pommade	ointment, cream	Salbe(f)	pomada	pomata
pombo, a	pigeon	pigeon	Taube(f)	paloma	piccione
ponderado, a	réfléchi, e	thoughtful	bedächtig	reflexivo, a	riflessivo, a
ponta	pointe	point	Spitze(f)	punta	punta
ponta	bout	tip, end	Zipfel(m), Ende(n)	punta	punta, estremità
ponta; remate	embout	tip, end	Endstück(n)	punta; remate	estremità; punta
pontapé	coup de pied	kick	Fußtritt(m)	patada	calcio
ponte	pont	bridge	Brücke(f)	puente	ponte
pontiagudo, a	pointu, e	pointed, sharp	spitz	puntiagudo, a	appuntito, a
ponto	point	point	Punkt(m)	punto	punto
ponto	point	dot	Punkt(m)	punto	punto
ponto	point	spot	Fleck(m); Ort; Stelle	lugar, punto	punto
ponto	point	stitch	Stich(m); Masche(f)	puntada	punto
ponto de vista	point de vue	viewpoint	Aussichtspunkt(m)	punto de vista	punto di vista
pontuação	ponctuation	punctuation	Zeichensetzung(f)	puntuación	punteggiatura
pontual	ponctuel, le	punctual	pünktlich	puntual	puntuale
população	population	population	Bevölkerung(f)	población	popolazione
popular	populaire	popular	populär	popular	popolare
por	par	by, through	durch	por	per, da
por	par	per	per	por	per
por	pour	for	für	por	per
por toda a parte	partout	everywhere	überall	por todas partes	dappertutto
pôr	mettre	put	legen, stellen	poner	mettere
pôr, colocar	mettre, placer	lay	legen	poner, colocar	porre, mettere
pôr, colocar	poser, placer	place	stellen	poner, colocar	collocare
pôr, colocar	poser	put, lay(down)	legen	poner, colocar	posare, porre
pôr, colocar	mettre, placer	set	setzen, stellen	poner, colocar	porre, mettere
pôr(ovos)	pondre	lay	Eier legen	poner(huevos)	fare l'uovo
porão	cale	hold	Laderaum(m)	bodega	stiva
pôr a render	placer	invest	an = legen	invertir	investire
porca	écrou	nut	Mutter(f)(Schrauben-)	tuerca	dado
porção	portion	portion, piece	Stück(n), Portion(f)	porción	porzione
porcelana	porcelaine	porcelain, china	Porzellan(n)	porcelana	porcellana
por cento	pour cent	per cent	Prozent(n)	por ciento	per cento
porco	porc	pig; pork(meat)	Schwein(n)	cerdo	porco, maiale
pôr do sol	coucher(soleil)	sunset	Sonnenuntergang(m)	puesta de sol	tramonto
porém	mais, cependant	but, yet, however	aber, jedoch	pero	però
pormenor	détail	detail	Einzelheit(f)	detalle	particolare
pôr no correio	poster	post, mail	ein = werfen	echar al correo	impostare, imbucare
pornografia	pornographie	pornography	Pornographie(f)	pornografía	pornografia
poro	pore	pore	Pore(f)	poro	poro

P

Portuguese	French	English	German	Spanish	Italian
poroso, a	poreux, se	porous	porös	poroso, a	poroso, a
porque	parce que	because	weil, da	porque	perché
porque, pois	car	because, for	weil, denn	porque, pues	perché
porquê	pourquoi	why	warum	por qué	perché
porquê(o--de)	pourquoi(le--de)	reason(the--for)	Grund(m)(der--für)	porqué(el--de)	perché(il--di)
pôr-se	devenir	become	werden	ponerse	diventare
porta	porte	door	Tür(f)	puerta	porta
porta	portière	door(car)	Wagentür(f)	puerta	sportello
porta	porte	gate	Pforte(f)	puerta, entrada	porta, uscita
porta-chaves	porte-clefs	key-ring	Schlüsselring(m)	llavero	portachiavi
portagem	péage	toll	Autobahngebühr(f)	peaje	pedaggio
portal	portail	gate	Tor(n)	portal	portone
porta-moedas	porte-monnaie	purse	Geldbörse(f)	monedero	portamonete
portanto, pois	donc	therefore; so	also	por tanto, pues	dunque
portátil	portatif, ive	portable	tragbar	portátil	portatile
porte	port	postage	Porto(-kosten)(n/pl)	porte	porto
porteiro, a	concierge	porter, caretaker	Hausmeister(in f)m	conserje	portiere, a
porteiro	portier	porter	Portier(m)	portero	portiere
porte pago	franco de port	carriage-paid	portofrei	porte pago	porto franco
pórtico	porche	porch	Portal(n)	soportal, porche	atrio, portico
porto	port	port, harbour	Hafen(m)	puerto	porto
posar	poser(photo)	pose	Modell stehen	posar	posare
posição	position	position	Position(f)	posición	posizione
posição	rang	rank	Rang(m)	puesto	rango
positivo, a	positif, ive	positive	positiv	positivo, a	positivo, a
possibilidade	possibilité	possibility	Möglichkeit(f)	posibilidad	possibilità
possível	possible	possible	möglich	posible	possibile
possuir	posséder	own, possess	besitzen	poseer	possedere
poste	poteau	post, pole	Pfosten(m)	poste	palo
posterior	postérieur, e	later	spätere(r, s)	posterior	posteriore
potável	potable	drinking	trinkbar, genießbar	potable	potabile
potência, poder	puissance, force	power, strength	Macht(f), Kraft(f)	potencia, fuerza	potenza, forza
potencial	potentiel, le	potential	potentiell	potencial	potenziale
potente	puissant, e	potent, powerful	kräftig, stark	potente	potente
potro	poulain	foal	Fohlen(n)	potro	puledro
pouco	peu	some; a little	etwas; wenig	poco	poco, pó
pouco, a	peu	little, few	wenig(e)	poco, a	poco, a
poupar	épargner	save	sparen	ahorrar	risparmiare
pousar	déposer	put down, lay down	legen, stellen	depositar	depositare, porre
povo	peuple	people	Volk(n)	pueblo	popolo
povoado, a	peuplé, e	populated	bevölkert	poblado, a	popolato, a
praça	place	square	Platz(m)	plaza	piazza
praça de touros	arène(s)	bull ring, arena	Kampfbahn(f)	plaza de toros	arena
pradaria, prado	prairie	meadow	Wiese(f)	pradera	prateria
prado	pré	meadow, field	Weide(f), Wiese(f)	prado	prato
praia	plage	beach(-es)	Strand(m)	playa	spiaggia
prata	argent	silver	Silber(n)	plata	argento
prateleira	étagère	shelf(-ves)	Regal(n)	estantería	scaffale
praticar	pratiquer	practise	betreiben, üben	practicar	praticare
prático, a	pratique	practical	praktisch	práctico, a	pratico, a
prato	assiette	plate	Teller(m)	plato	piatto
prazer	plaisir	pleasure	Vergnügen(n)	placer	piacere
prazo	délai	delay	Frist(f)	plazo	termine
precaução	précaution	precaution	Vorsicht(f)	precaución	precauzione
precedente	précédent, e	previous	vorherig	precedente	precedente
preceder	précéder	precede	voran = gehen, voraus = -	preceder	precedere
precioso, a	précieux, se	precious	wertvoll, kostbar	precioso, a	prezioso, a
precipício	précipice	precipice	Abgrund(m)	precipicio	precipizio
precipitação	précipitation	hurry, haste	Eile(f), Hast(f)	precipitación	precipitazione
precipitar-se	précipiter(se)	rush	stürzen, sich	precipitarse	precipitarsi
precisamente	précisément	precisely	genau	precisamente	precisamente, appunto
precisão	précision	precision	Genauigkeit(f)	precisión	precisione
precisar	préciser	specify	genau fest = legen	precisar	precisare
preciso(ser)	falloir	have to, must	müssen	necesario(ser)	bisognare
preço	prix	price	Preis(m)	precio	prezzo
preço fixo(a)	forfaitaire	inclusive	pauschal	global; convenido, a	forfettario, a
precoce	précoce	precocious	frühreif, frühzeitig	precoz	precoce
preconceito	préjugé	prejudice	Vorurteil(n)	prejuicio	pregiudizio

Portuguese	French	English	German	Spanish	Italian
predecessor, a	prédécesseur	predecessor	Vorgänger(in f)m	predecesor, a	predecessore
predizer	prédire	predict	vorher = sagen	predecir	predire
predominante	prédominant, e	predominant	vorherrschend	predominante	predominante
prefácio	préface	preface	Vorwort(n)	prefacio	prefazione
preferência	préférence	preference	Vorliebe(f)	preferencia	preferenza
preferido, a	préféré, e	favourite	Lieblings-	preferido, a	preferito, a
preferir	préférer	prefer	bevorzugen	preferir	preferire
prefixo	préfixe	prefix	Vorsilbe(f)	prefijo	prefisso
prega	pli	fold; pleat	Falte(f); Kniff(m)	pliegue	piega
pregar, cravar	clouer	nail	nageln	clavar	inchiodare
pregar	prêcher	preach	predigen	predicar	predicare
prego	clou	nail	Nagel(m)	clavo	chiodo
preguiceira	chaise longue	deck-chair	Liegestuhl(m)	hamaca	sdraio
preguiçoso, a	paresseux, se	lazy	faul	perezoso, a	pigro, a
preguiçoso, a	fainéant, e	lazy	faul	holgazán, a	fannullone, a
pré-história	préhistoire	prehistory	Vorgeschichte(f)	prehistoria	preistoria
prejuízo	préjudice	wrong, harm	Schaden(m)	perjuicio	pregiudizio, danno
prejuízo, dano	dommage	damage	Schaden(m)	perjuicio, daño	danno
preliminar	préliminaire	preliminary	einleitend	preliminar	preliminare
prematuro, a	prématuré, e	premature(baby)	Frühgeburt(f)	prematuro, a	prematuro, a
premeditado, a	prémédité, e	premeditated	vorsätzlich	premeditado, a	premeditato, a
premeditar	préméditer	premeditate	vor = setzen	premeditar	premeditare
prémio	prix	prize	Preis(m)	premio	premio
prémio	lot	prize	Los(n)	premio	premio
prenda, presente	cadeau	present, gift	Geschenk(n)	regalo	regalo
prensar	presser	press, squeeze	drücken(zusammen-)	apretar	premere
preocupação	souci	worry	Sorge(f)	preocupación	preoccupazione
preocupado, a	soucieux, se	worried	sorgenvoll	preocupado, a	preoccupato, a
preocupar	préoccuper	worry, preoccupy	beunruhigen	preocupar	preoccupare
preocupar-se	soucier(se)	worry	sorgen, sich; plagen, s.	preocuparse	preoccuparsi
preocupar-se	inquiéter(s')	worry	beunruhigen, sich	preocuparse	preoccuparsi
preparação	préparation	preparation	Vorbereitung(f)	preparación	preparazione
preparar	préparer	prepare	vor = bereiten	preparar	preparare
preposição	préposition	preposition	Präposition(f)	preposición	preposizione
presa	proie	prey	Beute(f)	presa	preda
présbita	presbyte	long-sighted	weitsichtig	présbita	presbite
prescrever	prescrire	prescribe	vor = schreiben	prescribir	prescrivere
presença	présence	presence	Anwesenheit(f)	presencia	presenza
presente	présent, e	present	anwesend	presente	presente
presente, actual	présent, e	present	gegenwärtig, aktuell	presente, actual	presente, attuale
presente	présent	present	Gegenwart(f)	presente	presente
preservativo	préservatif	condom, sheath	Präservativ(n)	preservativo	preservativo
presidência	présidence	presidency	Präsidium n, Vorsitz m	presidencia	presidenza
President.da Câmara	maire	mayor	Bürgermeister(m)	alcalde	sindaco
presidente	président, e	president	Präsident(in f)m	presidente	presidente, essa
presidente	président, e	chairman/-woman	Vorsitzende(f, m)	presidente	presidente, essa
preso, a; detido, a	détenu, e	prisoner	Häftling(m)	detenido, a; preso, a	detenuto, a
pressa	hâte	haste, hurry	Eile(f)	prisa	fretta
pressa(ter)	pressé, e(être)	hurry(be in a)	eilig(es...haben)	prisa(tener)	fretta(avere)
pressão	pression	pressure	Druck(m)	presión	pressione
prestigio	prestige	prestige	Ansehen(n)	prestigio	prestigio
prestigioso, a	prestigieux, se	prestigious	wunderbar	prestigioso, a	prestigioso, a
presumir	présumer	presume	vermuten	presumir	presumere
pretencioso, a	prétentieux, se	pretentious	eingebildet	presuntuoso, a	pretenzioso, a
preto, a	noir, e	black	schwarz	negro, a	nero, a
prevalecer	prévaloir	prevail	vor = herrschen	prevalecer	prevalere
prevenir, avisar	prévenir	warn, inform	warnen	prevenir, avisar	prevenire
prever	prévoir	foresee; plan	vorher = sehen; planen	prever	prevedere
prévio, a	préalable	preliminary	vorhergehend	previo, a	preliminare
previsão	prévision	forecast	Vorhersage(f)	previsión	previsione
primário, a	primaire	primary	Primär-	primario, a	primario, a
primavera	printemps	spring	Frühling(m)	primavera	primavera
primeiro, a	premier, ière	first	erste(r, s)	primero, a; primer	primo, a
primeiro	abord(d')	first(at)	zunächst	primero	anzitutto
primeiro ministro	premier ministre	prime minister	Premierminister(m)	primer ministro	primo ministro
primeiro ministro	premier ministre	prime minister	Ministerpräsident(m)	primer ministro	primo ministro
primitivo, a	primitif, ive	primitive	primitiv	primitivo, a	primitivo, a
primo, a	cousin, e	cousin	Cousin(m), Cousine(f)	primo, a	cugino, a

P

Portuguese	French	English	German	Spanish	Italian
princesa	princesse	princess(-es)	Prinzessin(f)	princesa	principessa
principal	principal, e	principal, main	hauptsächlich	principal	principale
príncipe	prince	prince	Prinz(m)	príncipe	principe
principiante	débutant, e	beginner	Anfänger(in f)m	principiante	principiante
principiante	novice, débutant	novice	Neuling(m)	novicio, a; novato, a	novizio, a
principiar, começar	commencer	start, begin	an = fangen	principiar	cominciare
principiar	débuter	begin, start	an = fangen	principiar	esordire
princípio	début	beginning	Anfang(m)	comienzo	inizio
princípio	principe	principle	Grundsatz(m)	principio	principio
prioridade	priorité	priority	Vorrang(m)	prioridad	precedenza; priorità
prioritário, a	prioritaire	priority(have)	vorrangig; Prioritäts-	prioritario, a	prioritario, a
prisão, cadeia	prison	prison, jail	Gefängnis(n)	prisión, cárcel	prigione, carcere
prisão	emprisonnement	imprisonment	Haft(f), Verhaftung(f)	encarcelamiento	incarcerazione
prisão de ventre	constipation	constipation	Verstopfung(f)	estreñimiento	stitichezza
prisioneiro, a	prisonnier, ière	prisoner	Gefangene(f, m)	prisionero, a	prigioniero, a
privado, a	privé, e	private	privat	privado, a	privato, a
privar	priver	deprive	berauben, entziehen	privar	privare
privilegiado, a	privilégié, e	privileged	bevorzugt	privilegiado, a	privilegiato, a
privilégio	privilège	privilege	Vorrecht(n)	privilegio	privilegio
problema	problème	problem	Problem(n)	problema	problema
procedimento	procédé	process	Verfahren(n)	procedimiento	procedimento
procedimento	procédure	procedure	Verfahren(n)	procedimiento	procedimento
processo	procès	lawsuit, trial	Prozeß(m)	proceso, juicio	processo
processo	dossier	record, file	Akte(f)	expediente	dossier
procissão	procession	procession	Prozession(f)	procesión	processione
proclamar	proclamer	proclaim	bekannt = geben	proclamar	proclamare
procriação	procréation	procreation	Zeugung(f)	procreación	procreazione
procriar	procréer	procreate	erzeugen	procrear	procreare
procurar; buscar	chercher	look for, search -	suchen	buscar	cercare
procurar; buscar	chercher	seek	holen, suchen	buscar, investigar	cercare
prodigioso, a	prodigieux, se	prodigious	wunderbar	prodigioso, a	prodigioso, a
produção	production	production	Produktion(f)	producción	produzione
produtivo, a	productif, ive	productive	leistungsfähig	productivo, a	produttivo, a
produto	produit	product	Produkt(n)	producto	prodotto
produtor, a	producteur, trice	producer	Hersteller(in f)m	productor, a	produttore, trice
produtor, a	producteur, trice	producer	Produzent(in f)m	productor, a	produttore, trice
produzir	produire	produce	produzieren	producir	produrre
produzir	produire	produce	her = stellen	producir	produrre
proeza, feito	exploit	exploit	Glanzleistung(f)	hazaña	impresa, prodezza
profanar	profaner	desecrate	entweihen	profanar	profanare
professor, a	enseignant, e	teacher	Lehrer(in f)m	profesor, a	insegnante
professor, a	professeur	teacher	Lehrer(in f)m	profesor, a	professore, essa
professor, a	professeur	professor	Professor(in f)m	catedrático, a	professore, essa
professor primário	instituteur	teacher(primary)	Grundschullehrer/in	maestro, a	maestro, a
profissão	profession	profession	Beruf(m)	profesión	professione
profissional	professionnel, le	professional	professionell	profesional	professionale
profissional	professionnel	professional	Profi(m)	profesional	professionista
profundidade	profondeur	depth	Tiefe(f)	profundidad	profondità
profundo, a	profond, e	deep	tief	profundo, a	profondo, a
progenitura	progéniture	offspring	Nachkomme(m)	progenitura	progenitura
prognóstico	pronostic	prognosis(-ses)	Prognose(f)	pronóstico	prognosi
prognóstico	pronostic	forecast	Vorhersage(f)	pronóstico	pronostico
programa	programme	programme	Programm(n)	programa	programma
programador, a	programmeur, se	programmer	Programmierer(in f)m	programador, a	programmatore, trice
progressão	progression	progression	Fortschreiten(n)	progresión	progressione
progressivo, a	progressif, ive	progressive	fortschreitend	progresivo, a	progressivo, a
progresso	progrès	progress	Fortschritt(m)	progreso	progresso
progresso	essor	expansion, boom	Aufschwung(m)	auge, desarrollo	sviluppo
proibição	interdiction	ban	Verbot(n)	prohibición	proibizione
proibido, a	interdit, e	forbidden	verboten	prohibido, a	proibito, a
proibir	défendre	forbid	verbieten	prohibir	proibire
proibir	interdire	forbid, ban	verbieten	prohibir	vietare, proibire
projectar	projeter	plan	planen	proyectar, planear	progettare
projéctil	projectile	projectile	Geschoß(n)	proyectil	proiettile
projecto	projet	plan	Plan(m)	plan, proyecto	progetto
projecto	projet	project, plan	Vorhaben(n)	proyecto, plan	progetto
projector	projecteur	projector	Scheinwerfer(m)	proyector	proiettore
proliferar	proliférer	proliferate	vermehren, sich	proliferar	prolificare

Portuguese	French	English	German	Spanish	Italian
prolongamento	prolongement	extension	Verlängerung(f)	prolongamiento	prolungamento
prolongamento	prolongation	prolongation	Verlängerung(f)	prolongación	prolungazione
prolongar	prolonger	extend	verlängern	prolongar	prolungare
promessa	promesse	promise	Versprechen(n)	promesa	promessa
promessa	voeu	vow	Gelübde(n)	voto	voto
prometer	promettre	promise	versprechen	prometer	promettere
prometido, a	promis, e	promised	versprochen	prometido, a	promesso, a
promoção	promotion	promotion	Beförderung(f)	promoción	promozione
promoção(em)	réclame(en)	offer(on)	Sonderangebot(n)	reclamo(de)	offerta(in)
promover	promouvoir	promote	befördern	promover	promuovere
pronome	pronom	pronoun	Fürwort(n)	pronombre	pronome
pronto, a	prompt, e	quick, prompt	schnell, rasch	pronto, a	pronto, a
pronto, a	prêt, e	ready	fertig	dispuesto, a	pronto, a
pronto(a)	comptant	cash	Barzahlung(f)	contado(al)	contanti
pronunciar	prononcer	pronounce	aus = sprechen	pronunciar	pronunziare
propaganda	propagande	propaganda	Propaganda(f)	propaganda	propaganda
propagar	propager	spread	verbreiten	propagar	propagare
propício, a	propice	favourable	günstig	propicio, a	propizio, a
propor	proposer	propose; offer	vor = schlagen	proponer	proporre
proporção	proportion	proportion, ratio	Verhältnis(n)	proporción	proporzione
propósito	propos, intention	intention, aim	Absicht(f)	propósito	proposito
propósito	dessein	purpose, aim	Absicht(f)	propósito	proposito
propósito(de)	exprès	purpose(on)	absichtlich	expresamente	apposta
proposta	proposition	proposal	Vorschlag(m)	propuesta	proposta
propriedade	propriété	property	Eigentum(n)	propiedad	proprietà
proprietário, a	propriétaire	owner	Eigentümer(in f)m	propietario, a	proprietario, a
proprietário, a	propriétaire	landowner	Gutsherr(-besitzer)	propietario, a	proprietario, a
próprio, a	propre	own	eigen	propio, a	proprio, a
próprio, a(ele, a)	même(lui, elle)	self(him, her, it)	selbst(er, sie, es)	mismo, a(él, ella)	stesso, a(lui, lei)
propulsão	propulsion	propulsion	Antrieb(m)	propulsión	propulsione
prospecto	prospectus	leaflet	Flugblatt(n)	folleto	prospetto
próspero, a	prospère	flourishing	erfolgreich, blühend	próspero, a	prospero, a
próstata	prostate	prostate	Prostata(f)	próstata	prostata
prostituição	prostitution	prostitution	Prostitution(f)	prostitución	prostituzione
prostituta	prostituée	prostitute	Prostituierte(f)	prostituta	prostituta
protecção	protection	protection	Schutz(m)	protección	protezione
proteger	protéger	protect	beschützen	proteger	proteggere
prótese	prothèse	artificial-, false-	Prothese(f)	prótesis	protesi
protestante	protestant, e	Protestant	Protestant(in f)m	protestante	protestante
protestar	protester	protest, contest	protestieren	protestar	protestare
protocolo	protocole	protocol	Protokoll(n)	protocolo	protocollo
protótipo	prototype	prototype	Prototyp(m)	prototipo	prototipo
protuberância	protubérance	protuberance	Beule(f), Buckel(m)	protuberancia	protuberanza
prova	preuve	proof, evidence	Beweis(m)	prueba	prova
prova	épreuve, essai	test	Test(m), Probe(f)	prueba	prova, test
prova de fogo(à)	ininflammable	fire-proof	unbrennbar	ininflamable	ininfiammabile
provar	prouver	prove	beweisen	probar	provare
provar	goûter	taste	kosten	probar	assaggiare
provar	déguster	taste, sample	kosten	saborear, catar	gustare
provável	probable	probable, likely	wahrscheinlich	probable	probabile
provavelmente	probablement	probably	wahrscheinlich	probablemente	probabilmente
proveito(em--de)	profit(au--de)	in aid of	zugunsten von	beneficio(en--de)	beneficio(al--di)
proveniência	provenance	origin	Herkunft(f)	procedencia	provenienza
provérbio	proverbe	proverb	Sprichwort(n)	proverbio	proverbio
província	province	province	Provinz(f)	provincia	provincia
provisão	provision	stock, supply	Vorrat(m)	provisión	provvista
provisório, a	provisoire	provisional	provisorisch	provisional	provvisorio, a
provocação	provocation	provocation	Herausforderung(f)	provocación	provocazione
provocar	provoquer	provoke	heraus = fordern, reizen	provocar	provocare
proxeneta	proxénète	pimp	Zuhälter(m)	proxeneta	ruffiano, prosseneta
proxenetismo	proxénétisme	pimping	Kuppelei(f)	proxenetismo	prossenetismo
proximidade	proximité	proximity	Nähe(f)	proximidad	prossimità
próximo, a; perto	proche	near, close	nah(e)	cercano, a; próximo	prossimo, a
próximo, a	prochain, e	next	nächste	próximo, a	prossimo, a
próximo a	proximité(à)	close, near	nahe bei	cerca de	vicinanze(nelle)
prudência	prudence	caution, prudence	Vorsicht(f)	prudencia	prudenza
prudente	prudent, e	careful, prudent	vorsichtig	prudente	prudente
pseudónimo	pseudonyme	pseudonym	Pseudonym(n)	seudónimo	pseudonimo

P

Portuguese	French	English	German	Spanish	Italian
psicanalista	psychanalyste	psychoanalyst	Psychoanalytiker(m)	sicoanalista	psicanalista
psicologia	psychologie	psychology	Psychologie(f)	sicología	psicologia
psicólogo, a	psychologue	psychologist	Psychologe(m)/-gin(f)	sicólogo, a	psicologo, a
psicose	psychose	psychosis(-ses)	Psychose(f)	sicosis	psichosi
psiquiatra	psychiatre	psychiatrist	Psychiater(in f)m	siquiatra	psichiatra
psíquico, a	psychique	psychological	psychisch	síquico, a	psichico, a
puberdade	puberté	puberty	Pubertät(f)	pubertad	pubertà
publicação	publication	publication	Veröffentlichung(f)	publicación	pubblicazione
publicar	publier	publish, issue	veröffentlichen	publicar	pubblicare
publicidade	publicité	advertising	Werbung(f), Anzeige(f)	publicidad	pubblicità
publicidade	réclame(s)	advertisement	Reklame(f)	publicidad	reclame
público	public	public; audience	Publikum(n)	público	pubblico
público, a	public, ique	public	öffentlich	público, a	pubblico, a
púdico, a	pudique	modest	keusch	púdico, a	pudico, a
pugilista	boxeur	boxer	Boxer(m)	boxeador	pugile
pulga	puce	flea	Floh(m)	pulga	pulce
pulmão	poumon	lung	Lunge(f)	pulmón	polmone
pulover	pull-over	pullover, sweater	Pullover(m)	jersey	maglione, pullover
pulsação	pulsation	beating, pulsation	Pulsschlag(m)	pulsación	pulsazione
pulseira	bracelet	bracelet	Armband(n)	pulsera	braccialetto
pulseira	bracelet	strap	Armband(n)	correa	cinturino
pulso	pouls	pulse	Puls(m)	pulso	polso
pulular	grouiller	crawl with	wimmeln	hormiguear	brulicare
pulverização	pulvérisation	spraying	Zerstäubung(f)	pulverización	nebulizzazione
pulverizador	atomiseur	spray, atomizer	Zerstäuber(m)	atomizador	nebulizzatore
punção	ponction	puncture	Punktion(f)	punción	puntura, prelievo
punhado	poignée	handful	Handvoll(f)	puñado	manciata, pugno
punhal	poignard	dagger	Dolch(m)	puñal	pugnale
punho	poing	fist	Faust(f)	puño	pugno
punho	poignet	wrist	Handgelenk(n)	muñeca	polso
pupila	pupille	pupil	Pupille(f)	pupila	pupilla
purga	purge	purge	Säuberungsaktion(f)	purga	purga
purificar	purifier	purify	reinigen	purificar	purificare
puro, a	pur, e	pure	rein	puro, a	puro, a
pus	pus	pus	Eiter(m)	pus	pus
puxar	tirer	pull	ziehen	tirar	tirare
puxar	tirer	draw	ziehen	tirar	tirare
puxar	tracter	tug, tow	ab = schleppen	tirar	trainare, tirare
puzzle	puzzle	jigsaw(puzzle)	Puzzle(n)	rompecabezas	puzzle

Q

Portuguese	French	English	German	Spanish	Italian
quadrado	carré	square	Viereck(n)	cuadrado	quadrato
quadrilha	bande	gang	Bande(f)	pandilla	banda
quadro	tableau	painting, picture	Gemälde(n)	cuadro	dipinto, quadro
quadro	tableau noir	blackboard	Tafel(f)	pizarra	lavagna
quadro	cadre	executive	leitende Angestellte	ejecutivo	dirigente
quadro de honra	palmarès	list of winners	Preisträgerliste(f)	lista de premios	albo dei premiati
qual(o)	lequel	which; who; whom	welcher	cúal, cual	quale(il)
qual(a)	laquelle	which; who; whom	welche	cual(la)	quale(la)
qual; que	quel, le	what; which	welch(e, er, es)	cuál; que	quale; che
qualidade	qualité	quality	Qualität(f)	calidad; cualidad	qualità
qualidade	qualité	quality	Eigenschaft(f)	cualidad	qualità
qualificado, a	qualifié, e	qualified	qualifiziert	calificado, a	qualificato, a
qualquer	quelconque	any, whatever	beliebig	cualquier(a)	qualunque
qualquer(um)	quiconque	anyone(who)	jeder	quienquiera	chiunque
qualquer coisa	quelque chose	something	etwas	algo	qualche cosa

Portuguese	French	English	German	Spanish	Italian
quando	quand	when	wann	cuándo, cuando	quando
quando	lorsque	when; as	als; wenn	cuando	quando
quantidade	quantité	quantity, amount	Quantität(f)	cantidad	quantità
quanto	combien	how much, how many	wieviel	cuánto; cuanto	quanto
quarenta	quarante	forty	vierzig	cuarenta	quaranta
quarta-feira	mercredi	Wednesday	Mittwoch(m)	miércoles	mercoledì
quartel	caserne	barracks	Kaserne(f)	cuartel	caserma
quarteto	quatuor	quartet	Quartett(n)	cuarteto	quartetto
quarto	quart; quatrième	quarter	Viertel(n)	cuarto	quarto
quarto	chambre	bedroom, room	Zimmer(n)(Schlaf-)	cuarto	camera, stanza
quarto	chambre d'hôtel	room, hotel room	Hotelzimmer(n)	habitación	camera
quarto de banho	salle de bains	bathroom	Badezimmer(n)	cuarto de baño	bagno
quarto individual	chambre à 1 lit	single room	Einzelzimmer(n)	habitación(l cama)	camera singola
quase	presque	almost, nearly	fast	casi	quasi
quatro	quatre	four	vier	cuatro	quattro
que	que	that; whom; which	was, das	que, qué	che
quê	quoi	what	was	que, qué	cosa, che cosa
quebradiço, a	cassant, e	brittle	brüchig, spröde	quebradizo, a	fragile
quebrar	briser	break	brechen, zerbrechen	romper	spezzare, rompere
quebrar, partir	casser, briser	break	zerbrechen	romper	rompere
quebrar-se	déferler	break	branden	romper	infrangersi
queda	chute	fall	Fall(m)	caída	caduta
queijo	fromage	cheese	Käse(m)	queso	formaggio
queimadura	brûlure	burn	Verbrennung(f)	quemadura	bruciatura
queimar, arder	brûler	burn	verbrennen	quemar	bruciare
queixa(apresentar)	plainte(porter)	complaint(lodge a)	an = zeigen	denunciar	querelare
queixar-se	plaindre(se)	complain	beklagen, sich	quejarse	lamentarsi
queixo	menton	chin	Kinn(n)	barbilla	mento
queixume, queixa	plainte	complaint	Klage(f)	queja	lamento
quem	qui	who(m); which; that	wer; wen	quién, que	chi, che
quente	chaud, e	hot	heiß	caliente	caldo, a
quer dizer	c'est-à-dire	that is(to say)	das heißt	es decir	cioè
querer	vouloir	want	wollen	querer	volere
querido, a	chéri, e	dear, darling	Liebling(m)	querido, a	caro, a
quieto, a	calme, tranquille	still	still	quieto, a	calmo, a
questão	question	question	Frage(f)	cuestión	questione
quilate	carat	carat	Karat(n)	quilate	carato
quilograma, quilo	kilogramme	kilogram(me)	Kilo(gramm n)n	kilogramo	chilogrammo, chilo
quilómetro	kilomètre	kilometre	Kilometer(m)	kilómetro	chilometro
química	chimie	chemistry	Chemie(f)	química	chimica
químico, a	chimique	chemical	chemisch	químico, a	chimico, a
quimono	kimono	kimono	Kimono(m)	quimono, kimono	chimono
quinta	ferme	farm	Bauernhof(m)	granja	fattoria
quinta-feira	jeudi	Thursday	Donnerstag(m)	jueves	giovedì
quinze	quinze	fifteen	fünfzehn	quince	quindici
quiosque	kiosque	news-stand	Zeitungskiosk(m)	quiosco	edicola; chiosco
quisto	kyste	cyst	Zyste(f)	quiste	ciste
quociente	quotient	quotient	Quotient(m), Bruch(m)	cociente	quoziente
quota	cotisation	subscription, dues	Beitrag m(Mitglieds-)	cuota	quota
quotidiano, a	quotidien, ne	daily	täglich	cotidiano, a	quotidiano, a

R

Portuguese	French	English	German	Spanish	Italian
rã	grenouille	frog	Frosch(m)	rana	rana
rabino	rabbin	rabbi	Rabbiner(m)	rabino	rabbino
rabugento, a	grognon, ne	grumpy	quengelig	gruñon, a	brontolone
raça	race	race, breed	Rasse(f)	raza	razza

Portuguese	French	English	German	Spanish	Italian
ração	ration, portion	ration	Ration(f); Stück(n)	ración	razione
rachar, fender	fendre	slit	auf = schlitzen	rajar, hender	fendere
racial	racial, e	racial	rassisch	racial	raziale
raciocínio	raisonnement	reasoning	Überlegung(f)	razonamiento	ragionamento
racional	rationnel, le	rational	rational	racional	razionale
racionamento	rationnement	rationing	Rationierung(f)	racionamiento	razionamento
racismo	racisme	racism	Rassismus(m)	racismo	razzismo
radar	radar	radar	Radar(m)	radar	radar
radiação	radiation	radiation	Bestrahlung(f)	radiación	radiazione
rádio	radio	radio	Radio(n)	radio	radio
rádio	poste radio	radio set	Radio(n)	aparato de radio	rádio
radioactividade	radioactivité	radioactivity	Radioaktivität(f)	radiactividad	radioattività
radiodifusão	radiodiffusion	broadcasting	Radioübertragung(f)	radiodifusión	radiodiffusione
radiografia	radiographie	X-ray; radiography	Röntgenbild(n)	radiografía	radiografia
rainha	reine	queen	Königin(f)	reina	regina
raio	rayon	radius(-ii)	Radius(m)	radio	raggio
raio	rayon	ray	Strahl(m)	rayo	raggio
raio	rayon	spoke	Speiche(f)	radio	raggio
raio	foudre	lightning	Blitz(m)	rayo	fulmine
raiva, furor	rage, fureur	rage	Wut(f)	rabia, furia	rabbia
raiva	rage	rabies	Tollwut(f)	rabia	rabbia
raiz	racine	root	Wurzel(f)	raíz	radice
rajada	rafale	gust, gale	Windstoß(m)	ráfaga	raffica
rajada	rafale	burst, hail	Salve(f)	ráfaga	raffica
ralhar	gronder	scold, tell off	schimpfen	regañar	sgridare
ramadão	ramadan	Ramadan	Ramadan(m)	ramadán	ramadan
ramo	branche	branch	Ast(m)	rama	ramo
ramo	bouquet	bunch; bouquet	Strauß(m)	ramo	mazzo
rancor	rancune	grudge, spite	Rachsucht(f)	rencor	rancore
ranger	grincer	grind, grate	knirschen	chirriar	stridere
ranhura	rainure	groove	Rille(f), Nute(f)	ranura	scanalatura
rapariga	fille	girl	Mädchen(n)	chica	ragazza
rapaz	garçon	boy	Junge(m)	muchacho, mozo	ragazzo
rapaz	garçon, enfant	boy	kleiner Junge(m)	chico	ragazzo, bambino
rápido, a	rapide	rapid, fast, quick	schnell	rápido, a	rapido, a; veloce
rápido, a; depressa	vite	quickly, fast	schnell, rasch	rápido, pronto	fretta(in), presto
raposa	renard	fox(-es)	Fuchs(m)	zorro	volpe
raptar	kidnapper	kidnap	entführen	secuestrar	rapire
raqueta	raquette	racket	Schläger(Tennis-)(m)	raqueta	racchetta
raqueta	raquette	bat	Schläger(m)	raqueta, pala	racchetta
raquítico, a	rachitique	rickety	rachitisch	raquítico, a	rachitico, a
raro, a	rare	rare	selten	raro, a	raro, a
rascunho	brouillon	rough paper	Schmierzettel(m)	borrador	brutta copia
rasgar	déchirer	tear	zerreißen	rasgar, romper	strappare
raspar	gratter	scrape, scratch	kratzen	raspar, rascar	grattare
rastejar	ramper	crawl	kriechen	arrastrarse	strisciare
rasura	rature	deletion	Streichung(f)	tachadura	cancellatura
ratificar	ratifier	ratify	ratifizieren	ratificar	ratificare
rato, a	rat	rat	Ratte(f)	rata	topo, ratto
rato	souris	mouse(mice pl.)	Maus(f)	ratón	topo
razão	rapport	ratio, proportion	Beziehung(f)	razón, relación	rapporto
razão	raison	reason	Grund(m)	razón, causa	ragione
razão(ter)	raison(avoir)	right(to be)	Recht(n)(haben)	razón(tener)	ragione(avere)
razão(não ter)	tort(avoir)	wrong(to be)	Unrecht(haben)	culpa(tener)	torto(aver)
razoável	raisonnable	reasonable	vernünftig	razonable	ragionevole
reacção	réaction	reaction	Reaktion(f)	reacción	reazione
reaccionário, a	réactionnaire	reactionary	reaktionär	reaccionario, a	reazionario, a
reactor	réacteur	reactor; engine	Reaktor(m)	reactor	reattore
readaptação	réadaptation	readjustment	Umstellung(f)	readaptación	riadattamento
reagir	réagir	react	reagieren	reaccionar	reagire
real	réel, le	real, actual	wirklich	real	reale; vero, a
real	royal, e	royal	königlich	real	reale
realeza	royauté	royalty, monarchy	Königstum(n)	realeza	sovranità
realidade	réalité	reality	Wirklichkeit(f)	realidad	realtà
realização	réalisation	realization	Verwirklichung(f)	realización	realizzazione
realizar, fazer	réaliser	carry out, perform	verwirklichen	realizar	realizzare
realizar	accomplir	accomplish	vollführen	realizar, efectuar	compiere, effettuare
realizar	accomplir	perform, accomplish	aus = führen, vollenden	cumplir, realizar	compiere

Portuguese	French	English	German	Spanish	Italian
realizar	accomplir	achieve	vollbringen	ejecutar, realizar	realizzare, compiere
realmente	réellement	truly	wirklich	realmente	realmente
reanimação	réanimation	resuscitation	Wiederbelebung(f)	reanimación	rianimazione
rebanho	troupeau	flock	Herde(f)	rebaño	gregge
rebelde	rebelle	rebel	Rebell(m)	rebelde	ribelle
rebelião	rébellion	rebellion	Aufstand(m)	rebelión	ribellione
rebentar	éclater	burst	platzen	reventar	scoppiare
rebentar; furar	crever	puncture, burst	platzen, bersten	reventar	bucare, scoppiare
rebento, botão	bourgeon	bud	Knospe(f)	brote, botón	gemma
rebocar	remorquer	tow	ab = schleppen	remolcar	rimorchiare
reboque	remorque	trailer	Anhänger(m)	remolque	rimorchio
rebuçado	bonbon	sweet	Bonbon(n, m)	caramelo; bombón	caramella
rebuscar	fouiller	search	suchen, durchsuchen	registrar	frugare
receber	recevoir	receive, get	empfangen	recibir	ricevere
receber	encaisser	cash	ein = kassieren	cobrar	incassare
receber	toucher	cash, earn, win	kassieren(ein =)	cobrar	incassare
receita	recette	recipe	Rezept(n)	receta	ricetta
receita	recette	receipts; takings	Einnahmen(f, pl)	ingresos	incasso
receita	ordonnance	prescription	Rezept(n)	receta	ricetta medica
recém-nascido, a	nouveau-né, e	new-born baby	Neugeborene(n)	recién nacido, a	neonato, a
recenseamento	recensement	census	Volkszählung(f)	censo	censimento
recente	récent, e	recent	neu	reciente	recente
recentemente	récemment	recently	kürzlich	recientemente	recentemente
recepção	réception	reception	Rezeption(f)	recepción	reception
recepção	réception	reception	Empfang(m)	recepción	ricezione
recepção	réception	party, reception	Empfang(m)	recepción	ricevimento
recepção	accueil	reception; welcome	Empfang(m), Aufnahme f	recepción	accoglienza
recepção	cocktail	party(cocktail -)	Party(f)	cóctel	party
recepção	réception	receipt	Empfang(m)	recibo	ricevuta
receptáculo	réceptacle	receptacle	Sammelbecken(n)	receptáculo	ricettacolo
receptor	récepteur	receiver	Empfänger(m)	receptor	ricevitore
recibo	reçu	receipt	Quittung(f)	recibo	ricevuta
recibo	quittance	receipt	Quittung(f)	recibo	ricevuta
recife	récif	reef	Riff(n)	arrecife	scoglio
recipiente	récipient	container	Behälter(m)	recipiente	recipiente
recitação	récitation	recitation	Vortrag(m)	recitación	recita
recital	récital	recital	Konzert(n), Vortrag(m)	recital	recital
reclamação	réclamation	complaint, claim	Beschwerde(f)	reclamación	reclamo
reclamar	réclamer à	ask(for)	bitten um	reclamar	reclamare
recomendação	recommandation	recommendation	Empfehlung(f)	recomendación	raccomandazione
recompensa	récompense	reward; award	Belohnung(f)	recompensa	ricompensa
reconciliação	réconciliation	reconciliation	Versöhnung(f)	reconciliación	riconciliazione
reconfortante	réconfortant, e	comforting	tröstlich	reconfortante	riconfortante
reconhecer	reconnaître	recognize	erkennen	reconocer	riconoscere
reconhecido, a	reconnaissant, e	grateful	dankbar	agradecido, a	grato, a
recordação	souvenir	memory	Erinnerung(f)	recuerdo	ricordo
recordação	souvenir	souvenir	Andenken(n)	recuerdo	ricordo, souvenir
recordar-se	souvenir(se)	remember, recall	erinnern, sich	acordarse	ricordarsi
recorde	record	record	Rekord(m)	récord	record
recorrer, apelar	recourir à	appeal to	Berufung(f)ein = legen	recurrir, apelar	ricorrere, appellarsi
recortar	découper	cut up	zerschneiden	recortar	tagliare
recreio	récréation	break	Pause(f)	recreo	ricreazione
recrutamento	recrutement	recruitment	Rekrutierung(f)	reclutamiento	reclutamento
recrutar	recruter	recruit	an = werben	contratar, reclutar	assumere
recta	droite	straight line	Gerade(f)	recta	retta
rectângulo	rectangle	rectangle	Rechteck(n)	rectángulo	rettangolo
rectificar	rectifier	rectify	berichtigen	rectificar	rettificare
rectificar	corriger	rectify, correct	berichtigen	corregir	correggere
recto, a	droit, e	straight	gerade	recto, a	diritto, a
recuar	reculer	move back, reverse	zurück = gehen	retroceder	indietreggiare
recuo	recul	recoil	Rückstoß(m)	retroceso	rinculo
recuperar	récupérer	recover, get back	wieder = bekommen	recuperar	recuperare
recurso	recours	recourse	Zuflucht(f), Berufung	recurso	ricorso
recurso	ressource(s)	resources	Mittel(n, pl)	recurso	risorsa
recusa	refus	refusal	Verweigerung(f)	rechazo	rifiuto
recusar	refuser	refuse	verweigern	rehusar	rifiutare
redacção	rédaction	editorial staff	Redaktion(f)	redacción	redazione
rede	filet	net	Netz(n)	red	rete

P

Portuguese	French	English	German	Spanish	Italian
rede	hamac	hammock	Hängematte(f)	hamaca	amaca
rede	épuisette	fishing net	Fangnetz(n)	manguilla	guadino, retino
rede	réseau	network	Netz(n)	red	rete
redemoinho	remous	eddy, swirl	Wirbel(m)	remolino	mulinello, gorgo
redondo, a	rond, e	round	rund	redondo, a	rotondo, a
redor de(em)	autour	around	um	alrededor	intorno, attorno
redução	réduction	reduction	Verringerung(f)	reducción	riduzione
reduzir	réduire	reduce	reduzieren	reducir	ridurre
reeducação	rééducation	therapy	Heilgymnastik(f)	reeducación	rieducazione
reembolsar	rembourser	pay back, reimburse	zurück = zahlen	reembolsar	rimborsare
reembolso	remboursement	repayment	Rückzahlung(f)	reembolso	rimborso
refeição	repas	meal	Mahlzeit(f)	comida	pasto
refém	otage	hostage	Geisel(f)	rehén	ostaggio
referência	référence	reference	Referenz(f)	referencia	riferimento
referir-se	référer(se)	refer to	beziehen, sich	referirse	riferirsi
reflectir; pensar	réfléchir(à)	reflect, think	überlegen	reflexionar	riflettere
reflectir	réfléchir(se)	reflected(be)	reflektieren	reflejar	riflettere(-ersi)
reflexo	réflexe	reflex	Reflex(m)	reflejo	riflesso
reflexo	réflet	reflection	Widerschein(m), Reflex	reflejo	riflesso
refluxo	reflux	ebb	Ebbe(f)	reflujo	riflusso
reforçar	renforcer	reinforce	verstärken	reforzar	rinforzare
reforço	renfort	reinforcement	Verstärkung(f)	refuerzo	rinforzo
reforma	réforme	reform	Reform(f)	reforma	riforma
reforma	retraite	retirement	Pensionierung(f)	jubilación	pensione
reformado, a	retraité, e	retired person	Rentner(in f)m	retirado, a	pensionato, a
reformado, a(estar)	retraité, e(être)	retired(be)	pensioniert sein	jubilado, a(estar)	pensione(essere in)
refrão	refrain	refrain, chorus	Refrain(m)	estribillo	ritornello
refrescar	rafraîchir	cool	ab = kühlen	refrescar	rinfrescare
refugiado, a	réfugié, e	refugee	Flüchtling(m)	refugiado, a	rifugiato, a
refúgio, asilo	refuge, asile	refuge	Zufluchtsort(m)	refugio, asilo	rifugio, asilo
refutar	réfuter	refute	widerlegen	refutar	confutare
regar	arroser	water	gießen, begießen	regar	innaffiare
regatear	marchander	bargain, haggle	feilschen, handeln	regatear	contrattare
regato, ribeiro	ruisseau	stream, brook	Bach(m)	riachuelo, arroyo	ruscello
região	région	region, area	Gegend(f)	región	regione
regime	régime	régime	Regime(n)	régimen	regime
regimento	régiment	regiment	Regiment(n)	regimiento	reggimento
registar	enregistrer	register, check in	auf = geben	registrar	registrare
registo	enregistrement	registration	Registrierung(f)	registro	registrazione
registo	registre	register	Register(n)	registro	registro
rego	sillon	furrow	Furche(f)	surco	solco
regozijo; alegria	réjouissance	rejoicing	Fröhlichkeit(f)	regocijo	gioia, giubilo
regra, norma	règle	rule	Regel(f)	regla, norma	regola, norma
regressão	régression	regression	Rückgang(m)	regresión	regresso
regresso, volta	retour	return	Rückkehr(f)	regreso, vuelta	ritorno
régua	règle	ruler	Lineal(n)	regla	riga
regulamentação	réglementation	regulation(s)	Regelung(f)	reglamentación	regolamentazione
regulamento	règlement	regulation	Bestimmung(f)	reglamento	regolamento
regular	régulier, ière	regular	regelmäßig	regular	regolare
regularização	régularisation	regularization	Regulierung(f)	regularización	regolarizzazione
rei	roi	king	König(m)	rey	re
reinado	règne	reign	Herrschaft(f)	reino	regno
reino	royaume	kingdom	Königreich(n)	reino	reame
reintegrar	réintégrer	reinstate	wiederein = setzen	rehabilitar	reintegrare
reivindicação	revendication	claim, demand	Forderung(f)	reivindicación	rivendicazione
reivindicar	revendiquer	claim	beanspruchen	reivindicar	rivendicare
rejeitar	refuser, rejeter	reject	ab = lehnen, verwerfen	rechazar	rigettare
relação	relation	relation(-ship)	Beziehung(f)	relación	relazione
relâmpago	éclair	lightning; flash	Blitz(m)	relámpago	lampo
relatar	relater	relate, recount	erzählen	relatar	riferire
relativo, a	relatif, ive	relative	relativ	relativo, a	relativo, a
relatório	rapport	report	Bericht(m)	informe	rapporto, relazione
relatório, acta	compte rendu	report, minutes	Bericht(m)	informe, acta	resoconto
relaxação	relaxation	relaxation	Entspannung(f)	relajamiento	rilassamento
relevo	relief	relief	Relief(m)	relieve	rilievo
religião	religion	religion	Religion(f)	religión	religione
religioso, a	religieux, se	religious	religiös	religioso, a	religioso, a
relógio	horloge	clock	Uhr(f)	reloj	orologio

Portuguese	French	English	German	Spanish	Italian
relógio	montre	watch	Uhr(f), Armbanduhr(f)	reloj	orologio
relva	gazon	grass	Rasen(m)	césped	prato, erba
relvado	pelouse	lawn	Rasenfläche(f)	césped	prato inglese
remar	ramer	row	rudern	remar	remare
remédio	remède	remedy	Heilmittel(n)	remedio	rimedio
remendo	raccommodage	mending	Flicken(n)	remiendo	rammendo
remo	rame	oar	Ruder(n)	remo	remo
remo	aviron	rowing	Rudersport(m)	remo, piragua	canottaggio
remorso	remords	remorse	Gewissensbiß(m)	remordimiento	rimorso
remover, retirar	enlever, retirer	remove	ab = nehmen	quitar, retirar	rimuovere
remuneração	rémunération	remuneration	Entlohnung(f), Lohn(m)	remuneración	rimunerazione
remuneração	cachet	fee	Honorar(n); Gage(f)	remuneración	cachet, compenso
renda	dentelle	lace	Spitze(f)	puntilla	merletto
renda; ganho	rapport	yield, return	Ertrag(m)	renta; ganancia	frutto, rendita
renda	rente	income, pension	Einkommen(n)	renta	rendita
render	rapporter	bring in, yield	ein = bringen	proporcionar	fruttare
rendimento	rendement	output, yield	Ertrag(m), Leistung(f)	rendimiento	rendimento
rendimento; produto	rendement	yield	Ertrag(m)	rendimiento	rendimento
rendimento	revenu	income, revenue	Einkommen(n)	renta, ingresos	reddito
renegar	renier	disown; renounce	verleugnen, verneinen	renegar	rinnegare
renovação	renouvellement	renewal	Erneuerung(f)	renovación	rinnovo
renovar	renouveler	renew	erneuern	renovar	rinnovare
rentabilidade	rentabilité	profitability	Rentabilität(f)	rentabilidad	redditività
rentável	rentable	profitable	einträglich	rentable	redditizio, a
reparação	réparation	repair	Reparation(f)	reparación	riparazione
reparar	réparer	repair, mend	reparieren	reparar	riparare
repartição	répartition	distribution	Verteilung(f)	reparto	ripartizione
repartir	répartir	share out	auf = teilen	repartir	ripartire
repartir	partager	share, divide	teilen	repartir	dividere
repatriação	rapatriement	repatriation	Repatriierung(f)	repatriación	rimpatrio
repertório	répertoire	index; repertoire	Repertoire(n)	repertorio	repertorio
repetir	répéter	repeat	wieder = holen	repetir	ripetere
réplica	riposte	counter-attack	Gegenangriff(m)	réplica	risposta
replicar	répliquer	reply	erwidern, entgegnen	replicar	replicare
reportagem	reportage	report	Reportage(f)	reportaje	cronaca
represália	représaille(s)	reprisal	Vergeltung(f)	represalia	rappresaglia
representação	représentation	representation	Darstellung(f)	representación	rappresentazione
representação	représentation	performance	Vorstellung(f)	representación	rappresentazione
representante	représentant, e	representative, rep	Vertreter(in f)m	representante	rappresentante
representar	représenter	represent	dar = stellen	representar	rappresentare
representar	jouer	act	spielen	desempeñar	recitare
repressão	répression	repression	Unterdrückung(f)	represión	repressione
reprodução	reproduction	reproduction	Reproduktion(f)	reproducción	riproduzione
reproduzir	reproduire	reproduce	reproduzieren	reproducir	riprodurre
reproduzir-se	reproduire(se)	breed(animals)	fort = pflanzen, sich	reproducir(se)	riprodurre(-rsi)
réptil	reptile	reptile	Reptil(n)	reptil	rettile
república	république	republic	Republik(f)	república	repubblica
reputação, fama	réputation	reputation	Ansehen(n), Ruf(m)	reputación, fama	reputazione, fama
requisitório	réquisitoire	indictment	Anklagerede(f)	requisitoria	requisitoria
rés-do-chão	rez-de-chaussée	ground floor	Erdgeschoß(n)	planta baja, bajo	piano terra
reserva	réserve	reserve	Reserve(f)	reserva	riserva
reserva	réservation	reservation	Reservierung(f)	reserva	prenotazione
reservado, a	réservé, e	reserved	reserviert	reservado, a	prenotato, a
reservar	réserver	reserve	reservieren	reservar	riservare
reservar	réserver	book, reserve	vor = bestellen	reservar	prenotare
resgate	rançon	ransom	Lösegeld(n)	rescate	riscatto
residência	résidence	residence	Wohnsitz(m)	residencia	residenza
residir	résider	reside	wohnen	residir	risiedere
resíduo	résidu	residue	Rückstand(m)	residuo	residuo
resíduo	déchet	waste	Abfall(m)	residuo	scarto
resignar-se	résigner(se)	resign oneself	entsagen, ergeben, sich	resignarse	rassegnarsi
resina	résine	resin	Harz(m)	resina	resina
resistência	résistance	resistance	Widerstand(m)	resistencia	resistenza
resistência	endurance	endurance	Ausdauer(f)	resistencia	resistenza
resistente	résistant, e	resistant	widerstandsfähig	resistente	resistente
resistir	résister	resist; withstand	widerstehen	resistir	resistere
resistir a	résister à	withstand	widerstehen	resistir a	resistere a
resmungar	râler	moan, groan	nörgeln	refunfuñar	brontolare

Portuguese	French	English	German	Spanish	Italian
resolver	résoudre	solve, resolve	lösen	resolver	risolvere
resolver	régler	settle	regeln; erledigen	resolver	risolvere
respectivamente	respectivement	respectively	beziehungsweise	respectivamente	rispettivamente
respeitar	respecter	respect	respektieren	respetar	rispettare
respeitável	respectable	respectable	achtbar	respetable	rispettabile
respeito	respect	respect	Respekt(m)	respeto	rispetto
respiração	respiration	breathing	Atmung(f)	respiración	respirazione
respirar	respirer	breathe	atmen	respirar	respirare
responder	répondre	answer, reply	antworten	contestar	rispondere
responder	répondre	reply, answer	erwidern	responder	rispondere
responsabilidade	responsabilité	responsibility	Verantwortung(f)	responsabilidad	responsabilità
responsável	responsable	responsible	verantwortlich	responsable	responsabile
responsável	responsable	liable(to be)	haftbar	responsable	responsabile
responsável	responsable	person in charge	Verantwortliche(f, m)	encargado, a	responsabile
resposta	réponse	answer, reply	Antwort(f)	respuesta	risposta
ressaltar	rebondir	bounce, rebound	ab = prallen, aufprallen	rebotar	rimbalzare
ressoar, ecoar	résonner	resound, sound	klingen	resonar	rimbombare
ressonar, roncar	ronfler	snore	schnarchen	roncar	russare
restauração	rénovation	renovation	Renovation(f)	renovación	rinnovazione
restaurante	restaurant	restaurant	Restaurant(n)	restaurante	ristorante
restaurar	restaurer	restore	wiederher = stellen	restaurar	restaurare
restituir	restituer	return	zurück = erstatten	restituir	restituire
resto	reste	rest, remainder	Rest(m)	resto	resto
resto, destroços	débris, restes	remains, debris	Trümmer(m, pl)	resto, residuo	resti, cocci
restrição	restriction	restriction	Einschränkung(f)	restricción	restrizione
restringir	restreindre	restrict	beschränken	restringir	restringere
resultado	résultat	result	Ergebnis(n)	resultado	risultato, esito
resultado	score	score	Punktzahl(f)	marca, tanteo	punteggio
resultar	résulter, être	result, be	ergeben, sich	resultar	risultare
resumo	résumé	summary	Zusammenfassung(f)	resumen	riassunto
reter	retenir	hold back; retain	zurück = halten	retener	trattenere
retina	rétine	retina	Netzhaut(f)	retina	retina
retirar	retirer	withdraw	zurück = ziehen	retirar	ritirare
retirar, tirar	enlever	take away, remove	entfernen	sacar, quitar	togliere
retrato	portrait	portrait	Portrait(n)	retrato	ritratto
retrete, sanita	water-closet	toilets	Toilette(f)	water, retretes	WC; gabinetto
retrovisor	rétroviseur	rear-view mirror	Rückspiegel(m)	retrovisor	retrovisore
reumatismo	rhumatisme	rheumatism	Rheumatismus(m)	reumatismo	reumatismo
reunião	réunion	meeting; reunion	Treffen(n)	reunión	riunione
reunir	réunir	gather(together)	sammeln	reunir	riunire
reunir	assembler	assemble	versammeln	reunir	radunare, riunire
reunir-se	réunir(se)	meet	treffen, sich	reunirse	riunirsi
reunir-se	rejoindre	rejoin, return to	an = schließen, sich	reunirse con	raggiungere
revelar	révéler	reveal	auf = decken	revelar	rivelare
revisão	révision	revision	Revision(f)	revisión	revisione
revisão	révision	service, overhaul	Überholung(f)	revisión	revisione
revisor; fiscal	contrôleur	inspector	Kontrolleur(m)	revisor	controllore
revista	revue, magazine	review, magazine	Zeitschrift, Revue(f)	revista	rivista, periodico
revista	magazine	magazine	Illustrierte(f)	revista	rivista
revolta	révolte	revolt	Revolte(f)	revuelta	rivolta
revolução	révolution	revolution	Revolution(f)	revolución	rivoluzione
revolucionário, a	révolutionnaire	revolutionary	revolutionär	revolucionario, a	rivoluzionario, a
revólver	révolver	revolver, gun	Revolver(m)	revólver	revolver
rezar, orar	prier	pray	beten	rezar	pregare
rezingar	rouspéter	grouse, moan	meckern, murren	refunfuñar	brontolare
rico, a	riche	rich, wealthy	reich	rico, a	ricco, a
ridículo, a	ridicule	ridiculous	lächerlich	ridículo, a	ridicolo, a
rígido, a	rigide	rigid, stiff	steif	rígido, a	rigido, a
rigoroso, a	rigoureux, se	rigorous	streng	riguroso, a	rigoroso, a
rim	rein	kidney	Niere(f)	riñón	rene
rio	fleuve	river	Strom(m)	río	fiume
rio, ribeira	rivière	river	Fluß(m)	río, ribera	fiume
riqueza	richesse	wealth, richness	Reichtum(m)	riqueza	ricchezza
rir	rire	laugh	lachen	reir	ridere
riscado, a	rayé, e	scratched	zerkratzt	rayado, a	rigato, a
riscar; cortar	rayer	cross out	durch = streichen	rayar	cancellare
riscas(às)	rayures(à)	striped	gestreift	rayas(a)	righe(a)
risco	risque	risk	Risiko(n)	riesgo	rischio

Portuguese	French	English	German	Spanish	Italian
riso	rire	laugh, laughter	Lachen(n)	risa	riso, ridere
ritmo	rythme	rhythm	Takt(m), Rhythmus(m)	ritmo	ritmo
rito	rite	rite; ritual	Brauch(m), Ritus(m)	rito	rito
rival	rival, e	rival; competitor	Rivale(m), Rivalin(f)	rival	rivale
rivalidade	rivalité	rivalry	Rivalität(f)	rivalidad	rivalità
robot	robot	robot	Roboter(m)	robot	robot
robusto, a	robuste	robust, sturdy	robust, stark	robusto, a	robusto, a
robusto, a; forte	robuste, solide	sturdy	kräftig, fest	vigoroso, a; fuerte	robusto, a; forte
rocha	roche, rocher	rock	Fels(m)	roca	roccia
rochedo, rocha	rocher	rock	Felsen(m)	peñasco, roca	masso, roccia
roda	roue	wheel	Rad(n)	rueda	ruota
rodagem	rodage	running in	Einfahren(n)	rodaje	rodaggio
rodear, cercar	entourer	surround	um = geben	rodear	circondare
rodela	rondelle	slice	Scheibe(f)	rodaja	fettina, fetta
roer	ronger	gnaw	zernagen	roer	rodere
rolar	rouler	roll	rollen	rodar	rotolare
rolha	bouchon	cork	Korken(m)	corcho	tappo, turacciolo
rolha; tampa	bouchon	cap, plug	Pfropfen(m), Stöpsel	tapón	tappo
rolo	rouleau	roll	Rolle(f), Walze(f)	rollo	rotolo; rullo
romance	roman	novel	Roman(m)	novela	romanzo
romance policial	roman policier	detective novel	Kriminalroman(m)	novela policíaca	giallo
romancista	romancier, ière	novelist	Schriftsteller(in f)m	novelista	romanziere, a
romântico, a	romantique	romantic	romantisch	romántico, a	romantico, a
romper	rompre	break	brechen(ab = -; zer-)	romper	rompere
rosa	rose	rose	Rose(f)	rosa	rosa
rosto	figure	face	Gesicht(n)	rostro	faccia
rotação	rotation	rotation	Drehung(f)	rotación	rotazione
rotina	routine	routine	Routine(f)	rutina	routine, tran tran
rótula	rotule	knee-cap	Kniescheibe(f)	rótula	rotula
rótulo	étiquette	label, tag	Schild(n)	etiqueta	etichetta
rotunda	rond-point	roundabout	Kreisverkehr(m)	glorieta	rotonda, rotatoria
roubar	voler	steal, rob	stehlen	robar	rubare
roubar, furtar	dérober	steal	entwenden	robar	derubare
roubar	dévaliser	rob, burgle	aus = rauben	desvalijar	svaligiare
roubo	vol	theft, robbery	Diebstahl(m)	robo	furto
roubo, assalto	cambriolage	burglary	Einbruch(m)	robo, atraco	furto con scasso
rouco	rauque	hoarse	rauh, heiser	ronco, a	rauco, a
rouco, a	enroué, e	hoarse	heiser	ronco, a	rauco, a
roupa	linge	linen	Wäsche(f)	ropa	biancheria
roupa(s)	vêtements	clothes	Kleidung(f)	ropa, prenda	vestiti
roupão	peignoir	dressing gown	Morgenmantel(m)	bata	accappatoio
roupão	robe de chambre	dressing gown	Schlafrock(m)	bata	vestaglia
roxo, a; violeta	violet, te	violet, purple	violett, lila	violeta	viola
rua	rue	street	Straße(f)	calle	via
rubéola	rubéole	German measles	Röteln(pl)	rubéola	rosolia
rubi	rubis	ruby	Rubin(m)	rubí	rubino
ruga	ride	wrinkle	Falte(f)	arruga	ruga
rugoso, a	rugueux, se	rough, harsh	rauh	rugoso, a	rugoso, a
ruído, barulho	bruit	noise	Geräusch(n)	ruido	rumore
ruína	ruine	ruin	Trümmer(m, pl)	ruina	rovina
ruína	ruine	ruin	Ruine(f)	ruina	rovina
ruivo, a	roux, rousse	auburn; reddish	rothaarig	pelirrojo, a	rosso, a
rumo	cap	head for	Kurs(m)	rumbo a	rotta
rumor	rumeur	rumour	Gerücht(n)	rumor	voce, diceria
ruptura	rupture	rupture	Bruch(m)	ruptura	rottura
ruptura, quebra	cassure, rupture	break	Bruch(m)	rotura	frattura, rottura
rural	rural, e	rural	ländlich	rural	rurale
rusga	rafle	raid, round-up	Razzia(f)	redada	retata
rústico, a	rustique	rustic	ländlich, einfach	rústico, a	rustico, a

P

S

Portuguese	French	English	German	Spanish	Italian
sábado	samedi	Saturday	Samstag(m)	sábado	sabato
sabão	savon	soap	Seife(f)	jabón	sapone
sabedoria	savoir	knowledge	Wissen(n)	saber	sapere
saber	savoir	know	wissen	saber	sapere
saber	apprendre	hear(of)	erfahren	enterarse	apprendre, sapere
sábio, a	savant, e	learned person	Wissenschaftler(m)	sabio, a	studioso, a; dotto, a
sábio	sage	sage, wise man	Weise(m)	sabio	saggio, a; savio, a
sabor	saveur	flavour	Geschmack(m)	sabor	sapore
saborear	savourer	savour	kosten, genießen	saborear	assaporare
saboroso, a	savoureux, se	tasty	schmackhaft	sabroso, a	saporito, a
sabotagem	sabotage	sabotage	Sabotage(f)	sabotaje	sabotaggio
sabotar	saboter	sabotage	sabotieren	sabotear	sabotare
sabre	sabre	sabre	Säbel(m)	sable	sciabola
saca-rolhas	tire-bouchon	corkscrew	Korkenzieher(m)	sacacorchos	cavatappi
saco	sac	bag	Tasche(f)	bolsa, saco	borsa
saco	sacoche	bag	Tasche(f)(Umhänge-)	cartera	saccoccia, borsa
saco	sac	sack	Sack(m)	saco	sacco
saco-cama	sac de couchage	sleeping bag	Schlafsack(m)	saco de dormir	sacco a pelo
saco de viagem	sac de voyage	travel-bag	Reisetasche(f)	bolso de viaje	borsa da viaggio
sacrificar	sacrifier	sacrifice	opfern	sacrificar	sacrificare
sacrifício	sacrifice	sacrifice	Opfer(n)	sacrificio	sacrificio
sacrilégio	sacrilège	sacrilege	Entweihung(f)	sacrilegio	sacrilegio
sacudir	secouer	shake	schütteln	sacudir	scuotere
sádico, a	sadique	sadistic	sadistisch	sádico, a	sadico, a
sádico, a	sadique	sadist	Sadist(in f)m	sádico, a	sadico, a
safira	saphir	sapphire	Saphir(m)	zafiro	zaffiro
sagrado, a	sacré, e	holy; sacred	heilig	sagrado, a	sacro, a
saia	jupe	skirt	Rock(m)	falda	gonna
saia-casaco	tailleur	suit	Kostüm(n)	traje	tailleur
saída	sortie	exit, way out	Ausgang(m)	salida	uscita
saída	issue(sortie)	way out, exit	Ausgang(m)	salida	uscita
saída de emergência	sortie(secours)	emergency exit	Notausgang(m)	salida(emergencia)	uscita(sicurezza)
saiote	jupon	petticoat, slip	Unterrock(m)	enagua	sottana
sair	sortir	go out, come out	aus = gehen	salir	uscire
sal	sel	salt	Salz(n)	sal	sale
sala	salle	room	Saal(m), Raum(m)	sala	sala, stanza
salada	salade	salad; lettuce	Salat(m); Kopfsalat(m)	ensalada; lechuga	insalata
salada	crudité	salad, crudité	Rohkost(f)	ensalada	insalata mista
sala de espera	salle d'attente	waiting-room	Wartezimmer(n)	sala de espera	sala d'attesa
sala de estar	salle de séjour	living-room	Wohnzimmer(n)	sala de estar	soggiorno
sala de estar	salon	lounge	Herrenzimmer(n)	sala	salotto
sala de jantar	salle à manger	dining-room	Eßzimmer(n)	comedor	sala da pranzo
salão	salon(coiffure)	salon	Friseurladen(m)	peluquería	parrucchiere, a(da)
salão	salon	show, exhibition	Messe(f)	salón	salone
salário	salaire	salary, wage	Lohn(m), Gehalt(n)	salario	salario
saldar	solder	sell off	aus = verkaufen	saldar	saldare, liquidare
saldos	soldes	sales	Ausverkauf(m)	saldos, rebajas	saldi
salgado, a	salé, e	salty	salzig	salado, a	salato, a
saliva	salive	saliva	Speichel(m)	saliva	saliva
salmão	saumon	salmon	Lachs(m)	salmón	salmone
salpicar	gicler, jaillir	squirt, spurt	spritzen	salpicar	sprizzare, schizzare
salsicha	saucisse	sausage	Wurst(f)	salchicha	salsiccia
salsicharia	charcuterie	delicatessen shop	Metzgerei(f)	salchichería	salumeria
saltar, pular	sauter	jump	springen	saltar	saltare
saltar	bondir	jump, leap	springen	saltar	saltare, balzare
salto, pulo	saut, bond	jump, leap, spring	Sprung(m)	salto, brinco	salto, balzo
salvamento	sauvetage	salvage	Bergung(f)	salvamento	salvataggio
salvamento	sauvetage	rescue	Rettung(f)	salvamento	salvataggio
salvar	sauver	save	retten	salvar	salvare
salvo, excepto	sauf	except	außer	excepto	salvo
salvo, a	sauf, ve	safe	sicher	salvo, a	salvo, a

Portuguese	French	English	German	Spanish	Italian
salvo-conduto	laissez-passer	pass	Ausweis(m)	salvoconducto	lascia-passare
sanção	sanction	sanction	Strafe(f)	sanción	sanzione
sandália	sandale	sandal	Sandale(f)	sandalia	sandalo
sande, sanduiche	sandwich	sandwich(-es)	Butterbrot(n)	bocadillo	panino
sangrar	saigner	bleed	bluten	sangrar	sanguinare
sangue	sang	blood	Blut(n)	sangre	sangue
sangue-frio	sang-froid	cool, calm	Kaltblütigkeit(f)	sangre fría	sangue freddo
sanitário, a	sanitaire	sanitary	Gesundheits-	sanitario, a	sanitario, a
santo, a	saint, e	holy	heilig	santo, a; san	santo, a
santo, a	saint, e	saint	Heilige(m, f)	santo, a	santo, a
santuário	sanctuaire	sanctuary	Heiligtum(n)	santuario	santuario
são, sã	sain, e	healthy	gesund	sano, a	sano, a
sapato	soulier	shoe	Schuh(m)	zapato	scarpa
sapato	chaussure	shoe	Schuh(m)	calzado	scarpa, e
saquear	saccager	ransack	verwüsten	saquear	saccheggiare
sarampo	rougeole	measles	Masern(pl.)	sarampión	morbillo
sardinha	sardine	sardine	Sardine(f)	sardina	sardina
sargento	sergent	sergeant	Unteroffizier(m)	sargento	sergente
sarna	gale	scabies	Krätze(f)	sarna	scabbia, rogna
satélite	satellite	satellite	Satellit(m)	satélite	satellite
satisfação	satisfaction	satisfaction	Zufriedenheit(f)	satisfacción	soddisfazione
satisfeito, a	satisfait, e	satisfied	zufrieden	satisfecho, a	soddisfatto, a
saturação	saturation	saturation	Übersättigung(f)	saturación	saturazione
saturar	saturer	saturate	sättigen	saturar	saturare
saudar	saluer	greet; say hello	begrüßen	saludar	salutare
saúde	santé	health	Gesundheit(f)	salud	salute
sauna	sauna	sauna	Sauna(f)	sauna	sauna
savana	savane	savannah	Savanne(f)	sabana	savana
sazonal	saisonnier, ière	seasonal	saisonbedingt	temporero, a	stagionale
se	si	if; whether	wenn; ob	si	se
sebe	haie	hedge	Hecke(f)	seto, valla	siepe
seca	sécheresse	drought	Trockenheit(f)	sequía	siccità
secador	sèche-cheveux	hair-dryer	Fön(m), Haartrockner m	secador	asciugacapelli
secar	sécher	dry	trocknen	secar	asciugare; seccare
secção	section	section	Schnitt(m)	sección	sezione
secção	rayon	department	Abteilung(f)	sección	reparto
seccionar	sectionner	cut, divide	schneiden	seccionar	sezionare
seco, a	sec, sèche	dry	trocken	seco, a	secco, a; asciutto, a
secreção	sécrétion	secretion	Ausscheidung(f)	secreción	secrezione
secretária	bureau	desk	Schreibtisch(m)	escritorio	scrivania
secretário, a	secrétaire	secretary	Sekretär(in f)m	secretario, a	segretario, a
secreto, a	secret, ète	secret	geheim	secreto, a	segreto, a
sector	secteur	sector	Bereich(m)	sector	settore
século	siècle	century	Jahrhundert(n)	siglo	secolo
secundário, a	secondaire	secondary	nebensächlich	secundario, a	secondario, a
seda	soie	silk	Seide(f)	seda	seta
sedativo, a	sédatif, ive	sedative	schmerzlindernd	sedativo, a	sedativo, a
sede	siège	head office	Firmensitz(m)	sede	sede
sede	soif	thirst	Durst(m)	sed	sete
sedução	séduction	seduction	Verführung(f)	seducción	seduzione
seduzir	séduire	charm; seduce	verführen, verleiten	seducir	sedurre
se faz favor!	s'il vous plaît!	please!	bitte!	por favor(!)	per favore!
segmento	segment	segment	Abschnitt(m)	segmento	segmento
segredo	secret	secret	Geheimnis(n)	secreto	segreto
segregação	ségrégation	segregation	Trennung(f)	segregación	segregazione
seguinte	suivant, e	following, next	nächste	siguiente	seguente
seguir	suivre	follow	folgen	seguir	seguire
seguir a(a)	suite(à la)	following	hinter, nach	después de	seguito a(in)
segunda-feira	lundi	Monday	Montag(m)	lunes	lunedi
segunda mão(em)	occasion	second-hand, used	gebraucht	segunda mano	seconda mano
segundo, a	deuxième	second	zweite	segundo, a	secondo, a
segundo, a	second, e	second	zweite	segundo, a	secondo, a
segundo	selon	according to	gemäß	según	secondo
segundo	seconde	second	Sekunde(f)	segundo	secondo
segurado, a	assuré, e	insured	versichert	asegurado, a	assicurato, a
segurança	sûreté	safety	Sicherheit(f)	seguridad	sicurezza
segurança	sécurité	security; safety	Sicherheit(f)	seguridad	sicurezza
seguro	assurance	insurance	Versicherung(f)	seguro	assicurazione

P

Portuguese	French	English	German	Spanish	Italian
seguro, a	sûr, e; certain, e	sure, certain	sicher	seguro, a	sicuro, a
seguro, a	fiable	reliable	zuverlässig	fiable, seguro, a	sicuro, a; affidabile
seio	sein(s)	breast	Busen(m)	seno, pecho	seno
seis	six	six	sechs	seis	sei
seita	secte	sect	Sekte(f)	secta	setta
seiva	sève	sap	Saft(m)	savia	linfa
seixo	galet	pebble	Kieselstein(m)	canto rodado	ciottolo
seja qual for	quel que soit	whatever	was auch immer	cualquiera que sea	qualunque sia
sela	selle	saddle	Sattel(m)	silla	sella
selecção	sélection	selection	Auslese(f); Auswahl(f)	selección	selezione
seleccionar	sélectionner	select	aus = lesen	seleccionar	selezionare
selim	selle	saddle	Sattel(m)	sillín	sellino
selo	cachet	postmark; seal	Stempel(m), Siegel(n)	sello	sigillo, bollo
selo	sceau	seal	Siegel(n)	sello	sigillo
selo	timbre(-poste)	stamp	Briefmarke(f)	sello	francobollo
selva	jungle	jungle	Dschungel(m)	selva, jungla	giungla
selvagem	sauvage	wild	wild	salvaje	selvaggio, a
sem	sans	without	ohne	sin	senza
semana	semaine	week	Woche(f)	semana	settimana
semanal	hebdomadaire	weekly	wöchentlich	semanal	settimanale
semear	semer	sow	säen	sembrar	seminare
semelhança	ressemblance	resemblance	Ähnlichkeit(f)	parecido	somiglianza
semelhante	semblable	similar	ähnlich	semejante	simile, uguale
semente	semence	seed	Samen(m)	simiente	seme, semente
semente	graine	seed	Samenkorn(n)	semilla	seme
semi	semi	semi, half	halb	semi	semi
sem imposto	hors-taxe	duty-free	zollfrei	libre impuestos	duty-free
sempre	toujours	always	immer	siempre	sempre
sempre(para)	toujours(pour)	forever	immer(für)	siempre(para, por)	sempre(per)
senado	sénat	senate	Senat(m), Bundesrat(m)	senado	senato
senador	sénateur	senator	Senator(m)	senador	senatore
senão	sinon	otherwise, or else	andernfalls, sonst	si no	se no; altrimenti
senhor	monsieur(Mr)	Mr	Herr(m)	señor	signor
senhor	monsieur(Mr)	Mr	Herr(m)	Don	Signor
senhor	monsieur	Sir	Herr(m)	señor	signore
Senhor	Seigneur	Lord	Herr(m)	Señor	Signore
senhora	madame	Mrs; Madam	Frau(f)	señora	signora
senhora	dame	lady	Dame(f)	señora	signora
senhoras	mesdames	ladies	meine Damen	señoras	signore
senhores	messieurs	gentlemen	meine Herren	señores	signori
senhorio, a; dono, a	propriétaire	landlord	Besitzer/in; (Haus-)	dueño, a	proprietario, a
sensação	sensation	sensation; feeling	Empfindung(f)	sensación	sensazione
sensato, a	sensé, e	sensible	vernünftig	sensato, a	sensato, a
sensibilidade	sensibilité	sensitivity	Sensibilität(f)	sensibilidad	sensibilità
sensibilizar	sensibiliser	sensitive(make sb)	sensibilisieren	sensibilizar	sensibilizzare
sensível	sensible	sensitive	empfindlich	sensible	sensibile
sensual	sensuel, le	sensual	sinnlich	sensual	sensuale
sensualidade	sensualité	sensuality	Sinnlichkeit(f)	sensualidad	sensualità
sentado, a	assis, e	seated	sitzen	sentado, a	seduto, a
sentar-se	asseoir(s')	sit(down)	setzen, sich	sentarse	sedersi
sentença	jugement	sentence	Urteil(n)	sentencia	sentenza
sentido!	garde-à-vous!	attention!	Stillgestanden!	firmes(!)	attenti!
sentido, significado	sens	meaning, sense	Bedeutung(f)	sentido	senso
sentido	sens	direction, way	Richtung(f)	sentido	senso
sentido único	sens unique	one-way	Einbahnstraße(f)	dirección única	senso unico
sentimental	sentimental, e	sentimental	sentimental	sentimental	sentimentale
sentimento	sentiment	feeling	Gefühl(n)	sentimiento	sentimento
sentinela	sentinelle	sentry	Wache(f)	centinela	sentinella
sentir	sentir	feel	fühlen	sentir	sentire
sentir	ressentir	feel	empfinden	sentir	sentire
sentir	éprouver	feel	spüren, fühlen	sentir	provare
sentir, lamentar	regretter	sorry(be), regret	bedauern	sentir(lo)	dispiacere(-ersi)
separação	séparation	separation	Trennung(f)	separación	separazione
separar	séparer	separate, part	trennen	separar	separare, dividere
sepultura	sépulture	burial(-place)	Grab(n)	sepultura	sepoltura
sequência	séquence	sequence	Folge(f), Sequenz(f)	secuencia	sequenza
sequer(nem)	même pas	even(not)	einmal(nicht)	siquiera(ni)	neanche
sequestrar	séquestrer	lock away	ein = sperren	secuestrar	sequestrare

Portuguese	French	English	German	Spanish	Italian
sequestrar	détourner	hijack	entführen	secuestrar	dirottare
ser, estar	être	be	sein	ser, estar	essere
serenidade	sérénité	serenity	Heiterkeit(f)	serenidad	serenità
sereno, a	serein, e	serene	heiter	sereno, a	sereno, a
série	série	series	Serie(f)	serie	serie
seringa	seringue	syringe	Spritze(f)	jeringa	siringa
sério, a	sérieux, se	serious	ernst, ernsthaft	serio, a	serio, a
serpente	serpent	snake	Schlange(f)	serpiente	serpente
serra	scie	saw	Säge(f)	sierra	sega
serra	chaîne(montagne)	range(mountain)	Bergkette(f)	sierra	catena(monti)
serrar	scier	saw	sägen	serrar, aserrar	segare
servente	manoeuvre	labourer	Hilfsarbeiter(in f)m	peón, obrero	manovale
serviço	service	service	Dienstleistung(f)	servicio	servizio
serviço	service	service	Bedienung(f)	servicio	servizio
servir	servir	serve	dienen, bedienen	servir	servire
servir-se	servir de(se)	use	benutzen	servirse	adoperare
sessão	séance	session; meeting	Sitzung(f)	sesión	seduta
sessão	session	session	Sitzung(f)	sesión	sessione
sessenta	soixante	sixty	sechzig	sesenta	sessanta
sesta	sieste	nap, snooze	Mittagsschlaf(m)	siesta	siesta, riposino
sete	sept	seven	sieben	siete	sette
Setembro	Septembre	September	September(m)	Septiembre	Settembre
setenta	soixante-dix	seventy	siebzig	setenta	settanta
seu	son	his; her; its	sein, seine, ihr, ihre	su	suo(il)
seu, sua, deles	leur(s)	their	ihr/ihre	su, sus, suyo	loro(il/la, i/le)
seu(o), a sua; dele, a	leur(le, la)	theirs	ihrige(der, die, das)	suyo, a(el, la)	loro(il, la)
seu, sua	sien, ne	his; hers; its	seine, ihre	suyo, suya	suo, sua(il, la)
seus, suas	ses	his; her; its	seine; ihre	sus	suoi(i); sue(le)
severo, a	sévère	severe, strict	streng	severo, a	severo, a
sevícias	sévices	cruelty	Mißhandlung(f)	malos tratos	sevizie
sexo	sexe	sex	Geschlecht(n)	sexo	sesso
sexta-feira	vendredi	Friday	Freitag(m)	viernes	venerdì
sexual	sexuel, le	sexual	geschlechtlich	sexual	sessuale
sexualidade	sexualité	sexuality	Sexualität(f)	sexualidad	sessualità
si(mesmo)	soi(-même)	oneself	sich, selbst	si(mismo)	se(stesso)
sidra	cidre	cider	Apfelwein(m)	sidra	sidro
sífilis	syphilis	syphilis	Syphilis(f)	sífilis	sifilide
sigla	sigle	initials	Abkürzung(f)	sigla	sigla
significação	signification	meaning	Bedeutung(f)	significación	significato
significar	signifier	mean, signify	bedeuten	significar	significare
significativo, a	significatif, ive	significant	bezeichnend	significativo, a	significativo, a
sílaba	syllabe	syllable	Silbe(f)	sílaba	sillaba
silêncio	silence	silence	Stille(f)	silencio	silenzio
silencioso, a	silencieux, se	silent, quiet	still, leise, ruhig	silencioso, a	silenzioso, a
silhueta	silhouette	outline	Silhouette(f)	silueta	sagoma; silhouette
sim	oui	yes	ja	sí	sì
simbólico, a	symbolique	symbolic(al)	symbolisch	simbólico, a	simbolico, a
símbolo	symbole	symbol	Symbol(n)	símbolo	simbolo
simetria	symétrie	symmetry	Symetrie(f)	simetría	simmetria
similar	similaire	similar	ähnlich, gleichartig	similar	similare
simpático, a	sympathique	pleasant, nice	sympathisch	simpático, a	simpatico, a
simples	simple	simple	einfach	simple	semplice
simplesmente	simplement	simply	einfach	simplemente	semplicemente
simplicidade	simplicité	simplicity	Einfachheit(f)	sencillez	semplicità
simplificar	simplifier	simplify	vereinfachen	simplificar	semplificare
simulação	simulation	simulation	Vortäuschung(f)	simulación	simulazione
simultâneo, a	simultané, e	simultaneous	gleichzeitig	simultáneo, a	simultaneo, a
sinagoga	synagogue	synagogue	Synagoge(f)	sinagoga	sinagoga
sinal, signo	signe	sign	Zeichen(n)	signo	segno
sinal	signal	signal	Signal(n)	señal	segnale
sinal, marca	repère	mark, landmark	Markierung(f)	señal, indicio	contrassegno
sinal	panneau	sign, notice	Schild(n)	señal, letrero	cartello
sinal	arrhes	deposit	Anzahlung(f)	señal(dejar)	caparra
sinalização	signalisation	sign	Beschilderung(f)	señalización	segnalazione
sincero, a	sincère	sincere, candid	aufrichtig	sincero, a	sincero, a
síncope	syncope	black-out	Ohnmacht(f)	síncope	sincope
sincronizar	synchroniser	synchronize	synchronisieren	sincronizar	sincronizzare
sindicalismo	syndicalisme	trade unionism	Gewerkschaftswesen	sindicalismo	sindacalismo

P

Portuguese	French	English	German	Spanish	Italian
sindicato	syndicat	trade union	Gewerkschaft(f)	sindicato	sindacato
sinfonia	symphonie	symphony	Symphonie(f)	sinfonía	sinfonia
singular	singulier	singular	Einzahl(f)	singular	singolare
sinistrado, a	sinistré, e	victim(disaster -)	Geschädigte(r)m f	siniestrado, a	sinistrato, a
sinistro, a	sinistre	sinister	unheilvoll	siniestro, a	sinistro, a
sino	cloche	bell	Glocke(f)	campana	campana
sinónimo	synonyme	synonym	Synonym(n)	sinónimo	sinonimo
sintaxe	syntaxe	syntax	Syntax(f), Satzlehre f	sintaxis	sintassi
síntese	synthèse	synthesis(-ses)	Synthese(f)	síntesis	sintesi
sintético, a	synthétique	synthetic	synthetisch	sintético, a	sintetico, a
sintoma	symptôme	symptom	Symptom(n)	síntoma	sintomo
sinuoso, a	sinueux, se	winding, sinuous	kurvenreich	sinuoso, a	sinuoso, a
sirene	sirène	siren	Sirene(f)	sirena	sirena
sísmico, a	sismique	seismic	seismisch	sísmico, a	sismico, a
sismo	séisme	earthquake	Erdbeben(n)	seismo	sisma
sistema	système	system	System(n)	sistema	sistema
sistemático, a	systématique	systematic	systematisch	sistemático, a	sistematico, a
sítio	site	site	Ort(m), Lage(f)	paraje, vista	sito
situação	situation	situation	Lage(f)	situación	situazione
situação	situation	location, position	Lage(f)	situación	situazione
situação	situation	position, job	Stellung, Position(f)	situación	situazione
situado, a	situé, e	located	gelegen	situado, a	situato, a
situar, localizar	situer	situate, locate	stellen, setzen	situar, localizar	situare, localizzare
slow	slow	smooch, slow dance	Blues(m), Slow(m)	lento	lento, slow
smoking	smoking	dinner-jacket	Smoking(m)	esmoquin	smoking
snobismo	snobisme	snobbery	Snobismus(m)	esnobismo	snobismo
só	seul, e	only	einzig	solo, a	solo, a
só	seul, e	alone	allein	solo, a	solo, a
soalheiro, a	ensoleillé, e	sunny	sonnig	soleado, a	soleggiato, a
soalho, sobrado	plancher	floor	Fußboden(m)	suelo	pavimento
soar, tocar	sonner	ring	klingeln	sonar, tocar	suonare, sonare
sobejar, sobrar	rester	remain	bleiben	sobrar, quedar	restare, rimanere
soberania	souveraineté	sovereignty	Souveränität(f)	soberanía	sovranità
soberano, a; monarca	souverain, e	sovereign, monarch	Herrscher(in f)m	soberano, a; monarca	sovrano, a; monarca
soberbo, a	superbe	superb	großartig	soberbio, a	splendido, a
sobrar	rester	left(be), remain	übrig – bleiben, bleiben	quedar	rimanere, avanzare
sobre	sur	on, upon	über; auf	sobre	sopra, su
sobremesa	dessert	dessert	Nachtisch(m)	postre	dessert
sobrenatural	surnaturel, le	supernatural	überirdisch	sobrenatural	soprannaturale
sobrepor	superposer	superpose	aufeinander – legen	sobreponer	sovrapporre
sobressair	dépasser	protrude	hervor = stehen	sobresalir	sporgere
sobretudo	pardessus	overcoat	Mantel(m)	abrigo	soprabito
sobretudo	surtout	above all	besonders	sobre todo	soprattutto
sobrevivente	survivant, e	survivor	Überlebende(f, m)	superviviente	superstite
sobrevivente	rescapé, e	survivor	Überlebende(f, m)	superviviente	scampato, a
sobreviver	survivre	survive	überleben	sobrevivir	sopravvivere
sobrevôo	survol	flight over	Überfliegen(n)	sobrevuelo	sorvolo
sobrinha	nièce	niece	Nichte(f)	sobrina	nipote
sobrinho	neveu	nephew	Neffe(m)	sobrino	nipote
sobrolho	sourcil	eyebrow	Augenbraue(f)	ceja	sopracciglio(a)
social	social, e	social	sozial	social	sociale
socialismo	socialisme	socialism	Sozialismus(m)	socialismo	socialismo
sociável	sociable	sociable	gesellig	sociable	socievole
sociedade	société	society	Gesellschaft(f)	sociedad	società
sociedade	société	company, firm	Gesellschaft(f)	sociedad	società
sócio, a	associé, e	associate, partner	Teilhaber(in f)m	socio, a, asociado	socio, a
sociologia	sociologie	sociology	Soziologie(f)	sociología	sociologia
soco, pedestal	socle	base	Sockel(m)	zócalo	zoccolo
soco; murro	coup de poing	punch	Faustschlag(m)	puñetazo	pugno
soçobrar	chavirer	capsize	kentern, um = kippen	zozobrar	capovolgersi
socorrer	secourir	help, assist, aid	helfen	socorrer	soccorrere
socorrer	secourir	rescue	retten	socorrer	soccorrere
socorrista	sauveteur	rescuer	Retter(in f)m	socorrista	soccorritore
socorro	secours	help, aid	Hilfe(f)	socorro	soccorso
sofisticado, a	sophistiqué, e	sophisticated	hochkompliziert	sofisticado, a	sofisticato, a
sofrer	souffrir	suffer	leiden	sufrir	soffrire
sofrer	subir	undergo	ertragen	sufrir, padecer	subire
sofrimento	souffrance	suffering	Leiden(n)	sufrimiento	sofferenza

Portuguese	French	English	German	Spanish	Italian
software	logiciel	software	Software(f)	logicial	software
sogra	belle-mère	mother-in-law	Schwiegermutter(f)	suegra	suocera
sogro	beau-père	father-in-law	Schwiegervater(m)	suegro	suocero
sogros	beaux-parents	parents-in-law	Schwiegereltern(pl.)	suegros	suoceri
sol	soleil	sun	Sonne(f)	sol	sole
sol(está)	soleil(il fait)	sunny(it's)	Sonne scheint(die)	sol(hace)	sole(c'è il)
sola	semelle	sole	Sohle(f)	suela	suola
solar	solaire	solar	Sonnen-	solar	solare
soldado	soldat	soldier	Soldat(m)	soldado	soldato
soldadura	soudure	welding	Schweißen(n)	soldadura	saldatura
solene	solennel, le	solemn	feierlich	solemne	solenne
soletrar	épeler	spell	buchstabieren	deletrear	compitare
solfejo	solfège	sol-fa, theory	Tonleiter(f)	solfeo	solfeggio
solicitar	solliciter	appeal to, request	ersuchen	solicitar	sollecitare
solidão	solitude	loneliness	Einsamkeit(f)	soledad	solitudine
solidariedade	solidarité	solidarity	Solidarität(f)	solidaridad	solidarietà
sólido, a	solide	solid, strong	solide, fest	sólido, a	solido, a
solitário, a	solitaire	solitary, lonely	einsam	solitario, a	solitario, a
solo	sol	ground	Boden(m)	suelo	suolo
soltar	lâcher	release	los = lassen	soltar	lasciare
solteiro, a	célibataire	bachelor; single -	Junggeselle m/-sellin	soltero	scapolo, nubile
solteiro, a	célibataire	single, unmarried	ledig	soltero, a	scapolo; nubile
solução	solution	solution	Lösung(f)	solución	soluzione
solucionar	solutionner	solve	lösen	solucionar	risolvere
soluço	sanglot	sob	Schluchzer(m)	sollozo	singhiozzo
solúvel	soluble	soluble	löslich	soluble	solubile
som	son	sound	Ton(m)	sonido	suono
soma; quantia	somme	sum, amount	Summe(f)	suma; cantidad	somma
sombra	ombre	shadow	Schatten(m)	sombra	ombra
sombrinha	ombrelle	sunshade, parasol	Sonnenschirm(m)	sombrilla	ombrello, parasole
somente, só	seulement	only	nur	solamente, sólo	solo, soltanto
somente	uniquement	only	ausschließlich	únicamente	unicamente
sonâmbulo, a	somnambule	sleep-walker	Schlafwandler(in f)m	sonámbulo, a	sonnambulo, a
sonata	sonate	sonata	Sonate(f)	sonata	sonata
sonda	sonde	probe	Sonde(f)	sonda	sonda
sondagem	sondage	poll(opinion)	Umfrage(f)	sondeo	sondaggio
sonhar	rêver	dream	träumen	soñar	sognare
sonho	rêve	dream	Traum(m)	sueño	sogno
sono	sommeil	sleep	Schlaf(m)	sueño	sonno
sonolência	somnolence	drowsiness	Schläfrigkeit(f)	somnolencia	sonnolenza
sopa	soupe	soup	Suppe(f)	sopa	minestra
soporífero	somnifère	sleeping tablet	Schlaftablette(f)	somnífero	sonnifero
soprar	souffler	blow	blasen	soplar	soffiare
soprar	souffler	blow	wehen	soplar	soffiare
sopro, fôlego	souffle	breath	Luft(f), Puste(f)	soplo, aliento	fiato, soffio
sórdido, a	sordide	sordid	schäbig	sórdido, a	squallido, a
soro	sérum	serum	Serum(n)	suero	siero
sorridente	souriant, e	cheerful	lächelnd	sonriente	sorridente
sorrir	sourire	smile	lächeln	sonreír	sorridere
sorriso	sourire	smile	Lächeln(n)	sonrisa	sorriso
sorte, destino	sort	fate	Schicksal(n)	suerte, destino	sorte, destino
sorte	chance	luck; chance	Glück(n), Chance(f)	suerte, fortuna	fortuna
sorte(ter)	chance(avoir)	fortunate(be)	Glück haben	suerte(tener)	fortuna(avere)
sortimento	assortiment	assortment	Sortiment(n)	surtido	assortimento
sósia	sosie	double	Doppelgänger(in f)m	sosia	sosia
sótão	grenier	attic, loft	Speicher(m), Dachboden	desván	solaio; granaio
sotaque	accent	accent	Akzent(m), Tonfall(m)	dejo	accento
soutien	soutien-gorge	bra	Büstenhalter(m)	sostén	reggiseno
sua	sa	her; his; its	sein, e; ihr, ihre	su	sua(la)
suar	suer	sweat	schwitzen	sudar	sudare
subconsciente	subconscient	subconscious	Unterbewußtsein(n)	subconsciente	subcosciente
subida	montée	rise	Steigung(f)	subida	salita
subida	hausse	rise, increase	Steigerung(f)	subida	aumento
subir	monter	climb; rise; go up	steigen	subir	salire
subir	élever(s')	rise	an = steigen	subir	elevarsi
subir a, entrar	monter	get into, get on	ein = steigen	subir	salire
súbito(de)	soudain	sudden(ly)	plötzlich	pronto(de)	ad un tratto
sublime	sublime	sublime	erhaben	sublime	sublime

747

P

French	English	German	Spanish	Italian
..........souligner ....underline		unterstreichen	subrayar............	sottolineare
........sous-marin .....submarine		Unterseeboot(n)	submarino	sottomarino
..........soumettre .....submit		unterwerfen	someter	sottomettere
........soumission .....submission		Unterwerfung(f)	sumisión	sottomissione
...ordinado, a ....subordonné, e ....subordinate		Untergebene(f m)	subordinado, a	subalterno, a
.uborno ....pot-de-vin ....bribe...........		Schmiergelder(pl.)........	soborno	bustarella
subscrição ......souscription ....subscription		Subskription(f)	suscripción	sottoscrizione
subsídio, abono ....allocation ......allowance........		Beihilfe(f), Zulage(f)	subsidio	assegnazione; assegno
subsistir ....subsister .....subsist, remain ...		fort = bestehen	subsistir	sussistere
sub-solo ....sous-sol .....subsoil		Unterboden(m)	subsuelo	sottosuolo
substância ....substance .....substance		Substanz(f)	sustancia	sostanza
substantivo ....substantif .....substantive, noun ..		Hauptwort(n)	sustantivo	sostantivo
substantivo ....nom, substantif...noun.............		Hauptwort(n)	nombre	nome, sostantivo
substituir ....substituer .....substitute		vertauschen	sustituir	sostituire
substituir ....remplacer ......replace		ersetzen	sustituir	sostituire
substituto, a ....remplacant, e ....substitute		Stellvertreter(in f)m	sustituto, a	sostituto, a
subterrâneo, a .....souterrain, e .....underground		unterirdisch	subterráneo, a	sotterraneo, a
subtil ....subtil, e .....subtle		scharfsinnig, listig......	sutil	sottile
subtração ....soustraction .....subtraction		Subtraktion(f)	resta	sottrazione
subtrair, deduzir ....soustraire ......subtract		ab = ziehen	sustraer, restar	sottrarre
subúrbio ....faubourg ......suburb		Vorstadt(f)	suburbio	sobborgo
subvenção ....subvention .....grant, subsidy ...		Zuschuß(m)	subvención	sovvenzione
subvenção ....subvention .....subsidy		Subvention(f)	subvención	sussidio
sucata ....ferraille ......scrap iron		Alteisen(n)	chatarra	ferraglia, rottame
suceder ....succéder .....succeed		nach = folgen	suceder	succedere
sucessivo, a ....successif, ive ....successive		aufeinanderfolgend	sucesivo, a	successivo, a
sucesso, êxito ......succès ......success(-es)		Erfolg(m)	éxito	successo
sucessor ....successeur .....successor		Nachfolger(in f)m	sucesor	successore
súcia, ladroagem ...pègre ......underworld		Unterwelt(f)	hampa	teppa, malviventi
sucinto, a ....succinct, e .....succinct, brief ...		bündig	sucinto, a	succinto, a
sucumbir ....succomber .....succumb		erliegen	sucumbir	soccombere
sucursal ....succursale .....branch(-es)		Zweigstelle(f)	sucursal	succursale
suficiente ....suffisant, e .....sufficient		genügend	suficiente	sufficiente
sufocar ....étouffer ......suffocate; choke ...		ersticken	sofocar, ahogar	soffocare
sufrágio ....suffrage ......vote		Wahl(f)	sufragio	suffragio
sugerir, propôr ....suggérer .....suggest		vor = schlagen	sugerir	suggerire
suicidar-se ....suicider(se) .....commit suicide ...		um = bringen, sich	suicidarse	suicidarsi
suicídio ....suicide ......suicide		Selbstmord(m)	suicidio	suicidio
suite ....suite ......suite		Suite(f)	suite	appartamento
sujar ....salir ......dirty		verschmutzen	ensuciar	sporcare
sujeitar ....assujettir .....subject(to)		unterwerfen	someter, sujetar	assoggettare
sujeito ....sujet ......subject		Subjekt(n)	sujeto	soggetto
sujidade, porcaria ..saleté ......dirt		Schmutz(m)	suciedad	sporcizia
sujidade ....crasse ......filth, dirt		Dreck(m)	roña, mugre	sporcizia
sujo, a ....sale ......dirty		dreckig	sucio, a	sporco, a
Sul ....Sud ......South		Süden(m)	Sur	Sud
sultão ....sultan ......sultan		Sultan(m)	sultán	sultano
sumidade ....sommité .....V.I.P		Prominente(f, m)	eminencia	sommità
sumo ....jus ......juice		Saft(m)	jugo	succo
sumo de fruta ......jus de fruit ....fruit-juice		Obstsaft(m)	zumo de fruta	succo di frutta
sumptuoso, a ......somptueux, se ....sumptuous		prächtig	suntuoso, a	sontuoso, a
suor ....sueur ......sweat		Schweiß(m)	sudor	sudore
super ....essence super ....four-star petrol ...		Superbenzin(n)	supercarburante	benzina super
superar............surmonter .....overcome		überwinden	superar......	superare
superfície ....superficie .....area		Oberfläche(f)	superficie	superficie
superfície ....surface ......surface		Oberfläche(f)	superficie	superficie
superior, a ....supérieur, e ....superior		höher, besser	superior, a	superiore
superior, a ....supérieur, e ....upper		obere(r, s); Ober-	superior, a	superiore
superior ....supérieur .....superior		Vorgesetzte(f, m)	superior	superiore
superioridade ......supériorité .....superiority		Überlegenheit(f)	superioridad	superiorità
supermercado ......supermarché ....supermarket		Supermarkt(m)	supermercado	supermercato
supersónico, a .....supersonique ....supersonic		Überschall-	supersónico, a	supersonico, a
supersticioso, a ....superstitieux, se ..superstitious		abergläubisch	supersticioso, a	superstizioso, a
supervisar ....superviser .....supervise		überprüfen	supervisar	soprintendere
suplementar ....supplémentaire ..additional, extra ...		zusätzlich	suplementario, a	supplementare
suplemento ....supplément .....supplement		Ergänzung(f); Zulage f	suplemento	supplemento
suplente ....suppléant, e ....substitute		Stellvertreter(in f)m	suplente, a	supplente
suplicar ....supplier ......implore		an = flehen	suplicar	supplicare

Portuguese	French	English	German	Spanish	Italian
suplício	supplice	torture	Qual(f)	suplicio	supplizio
supor	supposer	suppose	an = nehmen	suponer	supporre
suportar	supporter	support	stützen, unterstützen	soportar	sopportare
suporte	support	support	Stütze(f)	soporte	supporto
supositório	suppositoire	suppository	Zäpfchen(n)	supositorio	supposta
supremacia	suprématie	supremacy	Obergewalt(f)	supremacía	supremazia
supremo, a	suprême	supreme	oberst-, höchst-	supremo, a	supremo, a
suprimir	supprimer	delete	beseitigen	suprimir	sopprimere
suprimir	supprimer	suppress	ab = schaffen	suprimir	sopprimere
suprimir	annuler	delete	streichen	borrar	annullare
surdez	surdité	deafness	Taubheit(f)	sordera	sordità
surdo, a	sourd, e	deaf	taub	sordo, a	sordo, a
surdo-mudo, a	sourd-muet, te	deaf and dumb	taubstumm	sordomudo, a	sordomuto, a
surpreendido, a	surpris, e	surprised	überrascht	sorprendido, a	sorpreso, a
surpresa	surprise	surprise	Überraschung(f)	sorpresa	sorpresa
surra, açoite	fessée	spanking	Hinternvoll(m)	azotaina, paliza	sculacciata
suspeita	soupçon	suspicion	Argwohn(m), Verdacht m	sospecha	sospetto
suspeitar	soupçonner	suspect	verdächtigen	sospechar	sospettare
suspeitar	douter(se)	suspect, mistrust	ahnen, vermuten	sospechar	sospettare
suspeito, a	suspect, e	suspicious	verdächtig	sospechoso, a	sospetto, a
suspender	suspendre	suspend, defer	verschieben	suspender	sospendere
suspensão	suspension	suspension	Federung(f)	suspensión	sospensione
suspense	suspense	suspense	Spannung(f)	suspense	suspense
suspensórios	bretelle(s)	braces	Hosenträger(m)	tirantes	bretella
suspirar	soupirer	sigh	seufzen	suspirar	sospirare
sussurrar	chuchoter	whisper	flüstern	susurrar	bisbigliare
sustentar	soutenir	support	unterstützen	sostener	sostenere

T

Portuguese	French	English	German	Spanish	Italian
tabaco	tabac	tobacco	Tabak(m)	tabaco	tabacco
tabela	barème	scale	Liste(f)	baremo	tariffario
tabique	cloison	partition	Trennwand(f)	tabique	tramezzo
tábua	planche	board	Brett(n)	tabla	tavola, asse
tabuleiro	plateau	tray	Tablett(n), Platte(f)	bandeja	vassoio
taça	coupe	glass(-es)	Kelch(m), Schale(f)	copa	calice
taça	coupe	cup	Pokal(m)	copa	coppa
tacho, caçarola	casserole	pan, saucepan	Topf(m)	cazo, cacerola	casseruola
táctica	tactique	tactic	Taktik(f)	táctica	tattica
táctico, a	tactique	tactical	taktisch	táctico, a	tattico, a
tacto	tact	tact	Takt(m)	tacto	tatto
tal	tel, le	such a, such(pl.)	solche(r, s); so ein	tal	tale
talento	talent	talent	Talent(n)	talento	talento
talher	couvert	table(lay the)	Gedeck(n)	cubierto	coperto
talho	boucherie	butcher's(shop)	Metzgerei(f)	carnicería	macelleria
talvez	peut-être	perhaps, maybe	vielleicht	quizá(s)	forse
tamanho	taille	size	Größe(f)	tamaño	misura
tamanho	taille	size	Größe(f)	talla, número	taglia, misura
tamanho; número	pointure	size	Größe(f)	número	numero
tâmara	datte	date	Dattel(f)	dátil	dattero
também	aussi	also, too; as	auch	también	anche, pure
tampa	couvercle	lid, cover	Deckel(m)	tapa, tapadera	coperchio
tangente	tangent, e	tangent	berührend	tangente	tangente
tangerina	mandarine	tangerine	Mandarine(f)	mandarina	mandarino
tanto	tant	so much, so many	so viel, e	tanto, tan	tanto
tanto, a	tellement	so(-much, -many)	so(sehr), derartig	tanto, a; tan	talmente
tão	si	so	so	tan	così

P

Portuguese	French	English	German	Spanish	Italian
tapeçaria	tapisserie	tapestry	Wandteppich; Gobelin m	tapiz; tapicería	arazzo; tappezzeria
tapete, carpete	tapis	mat, rug, carpet	Teppich(m)	alfombra, tapiz	tappeto
taquicardia	tachycardie	tachycardia	Herzjagen(n)	taquicardia	tachicardia
tarde	après-midi	afternoon	Nachmittag(m)	tarde	pomeriggio
tarde, noite	soir	evening	Abend(m)	tarde, noche	sera
tarde	tard	late	spät	tarde	tardi
tarefa	tâche	task	Aufgabe(f)	tarea	compito
tarifa	tarif	tariff, price	Tarif(m)	tarifa	tariffa
tarifa	tarif	fare	Tarif(m)	tarifa	tariffa
tartaruga	tortue	tortoise; turtle	Schildkröte(f)	tortuga	tartaruga
tatear, apalpar	tâter	feel, touch	berühren	tantear	tastare
tatuagem	tatouage	tattoo	Tätowierung(f)	tatuaje	tatuaggio
taxa	redevance	tax; royalty	Gebühr(f)	impuesto, tasa	cànone
taxa, imposto	taxe	tax; duty	Steuer(f)	tasa, impuesto	tassa, imposta
taxa	taux	rate	Rate(f)	tasa	tasso
táxi	taxi	taxi, cab	Taxi(n)	taxi	taxi, tassi
te	te, t'	you	dich; dir	te	ti, te
teatro	théâtre	theatre	Theater(n)	teatro	teatro
tecer	tisser	weave	weben	tejer	tessere
tecido	tissu	material, fabric	Stoff(m)	tela	tessuto
tecido, estofo	étoffe	material	Stoff(m)	tejido, tela	stoffa
tecla	touche	key	Taste(f)	tecla	tasto
teclado	clavier	keyboard	Tastatur(f)	teclado	tastiera
técnico, a	technique	technical	technisch	técnico, a	tecnico, a
técnico, a	technicien, ne	technician	Techniker(in f)m	técnico, a	tecnico, a
tecnocrata	technocrate	technocrat	Technokrat(m)	tecnócrata	tecnocrate
tecnologia	technologie	technology	Technologie(f)	tecnología	tecnologia
tecto	plafond	ceiling	Decke(f)(Zimmer-)	techo	soffitto
tela	toile	canvas, material	Tuch(n)	tela, lienzo	tela
tela, quadro	toile	canvas, painting	Gemälde(n)(Leinwand)	lienzo, cuadro	tela, dipinto
telecomando	télécommande	remote control	Fernsteuerung(f)	telemando	telecomando
teleférico	téléphérique	cable-car	Seilbahn(f)	teleférico	teleferica
telefonar	téléphoner	phone, ring, call	telefonieren	telefonear	telefonare
telefone	téléphone	telephone, phone	Telefon(n)	teléfono	telefono
telefone público	taxi-/publiphone	public call-box	Telefonzelle(f)	teléfono público	telefono pubblico
telegrama	télégramme	telegram, cable	Telegramm(n)	telegrama	telegramma
telejornal	actualités(T.V)	news	Nachrichten(pl.)	telediario	telegiornale
telepatia	télépathie	telepathy	Telepathie(f)	telepatía	telepatia
telescópio	télescope	telescope	Teleskop(n)	telescopio	telescopio
telespectador, a	télespectateur	viewer	Fernsehzuschauer/in	telespectador, a	telespettatore, trice
televisão; TV	télévision	television	Fernsehen(n)	televisión	televisione
televisionar	téléviser	televise	übertragen	televisar	teletrasmettere
televisor	téléviseur	television set	Fernseher(m)	televisor	televisore
telex	télex	telex	Telex(n)	telex	telex
telha	tuile	tile	Ziegel(m)	teja	tegola
telhado	toit	roof	Dach(n)	tejado	tetto
tema	thème	theme	Thema(n)	tema	tema
tema, assunto	objet, thème	theme, subject	Thema(n), Objekt(n)	objeto, tema	oggetto, scopo
temer	craindre	fear, be afraid of	befürchten, fürchten	temer, tener miedo	temere
temerário, a	téméraire	rash, reckless	waghalsig	temerario, a	temerario, a
temível	redoutable	formidable	furchtbar	temible	temibile
temor, receio	crainte	fear	Furcht(f)	temor, miedo	timore
temor	frayeur	fright	Schreck(m), Angst(f)	espanto	spavento
temperado, a	tempéré, e	temperate	gemäßigt	templado, a	temperato, a
temperamento	tempérament	temperament	Temperament(n)	temperamento	temperamento
temperatura	température	temperature	Temperatur(f)	temperatura	temperatura
tempero	assaisonnement	seasoning	Würze(f)	aliño	condimento
tempestade	tempête	storm	Unwetter(n)	tempestad	tempesta
tempestade	orage	storm, thunderstorm	Gewitter(n)	tormenta	temporale
templo	temple	temple	Tempel(m)	templo	tempio
tempo	temps	weather	Wetter(n)	tiempo	tempo
tempo	temps	time	Zeit(f)	tiempo	tempo
tempo livre	loisir	leisure	Freizeit(f)	tiempo libre	tempo libero, hobby
têmpora	tempe	temple	Schläfe(f)	sien	tempia
temporário, a	temporaire	temporary	vorübergehend	temporario, a	temporaneo, a
tenacidade	ténacité	tenacity	Hartnäckigkeit(f)	tenacidad	tenacità; tenacia
tencionar	intention(avoir)	intend	beabsichtigen	intención(tener)	intenzione(avere)
tenda	tente	tent	Zelt(n)	tienda	tenda

Portuguese	French	English	German	Spanish	Italian
tendência	tendance	tendency; trend	Tendenz(f), Neigung(f)	tendencia	tendenza
tenente	lieutenant	lieutenant	Leutnant(m)	teniente	tenente
ténis	tennis	tennis	Tennis(n)	tenis	tennis
ténis de mesa	tennis de table	table-tennis	Tischtennis(n)	ping-pong	ping pong
tenor	ténor	tenor	Tenor(m)	tenor	tenore
tenro, a	tendre	soft; tender	weich	blando, a	morbido, a; tenero, a
tensão	tension	tension	Spannung(f)	tensión	tensione
tentação	tentation	temptation	Versuchung(f)	tentación	tentazione
tentáculo	tentacule	tentacle	Fangarm(m)	tentáculo	tentacolo
tentar	tenter	attempt, try	versuchen; wagen	intentar	tentare
tentar; provar	essayer	try	versuchen	probar, intentar	provare
tentativa	tentative	attempt	Versuch(m)	tentativa	tentativo
teologia	théologie	theology	Theologie(f)	teología	teologia
teorema	théorème	theorem	Lehrsatz(m)	teorema	teorema
teoria	théorie	theory	Theorie(f)	teoría	teoria
teórico, a	théorique	theoretical	theoretisch	teórico, a	teorico, a
tépido; a; morno, a	tiède	lukewarm, tepid	lauwarm, lau	tibio, a	tiepido, a
ter, possuir	avoir	have	haben	tener	avere
ter, segurar	tenir	hold	halten	tener	tenere
ter(lição)	prendre(leçon)	have(a lesson)	nehmen	recibir(clases)	prendere(lezione)
terapia	thérapie	therapy	Therapie(f)	terapia	terapia
terça-feira	mardi	Tuesday	Dienstag(m)	martes	martedì
terceiro, a	troisième	third	dritte	tercero, a	terzo, a
terceiro mundo	tiers-monde	third world	dritte Welt(f)	tercer mundo	terzo mondo
terço, a; terceiro	tiers	third	Drittel(n)	tercio, a; tercero	terzo, a
termal	thermal, e	thermal	Thermal-	termal	termale
térmico, a	thermique	thermic, thermal	thermisch	térmico, a	termico, a
terminal	terminal, e	terminal, final	letzte(r, s); End-	terminal	terminale
terminar	terminer	end, finish	beenden	terminar	terminare
termo	terme	term	Ausdruck(m)	término	parola
termo	terme	end	Ende(n), Ziel(n)	término	termine
termómetro	thermomètre	thermometer	Thermometer(n)	termómetro	termometro
terno, a	tendre	tender	zärtlich	tierno, a	tenero, a
ternura	tendresse	tenderness	Zärtlichkeit(f)	ternura	tenerezza
Terra	terre	earth	Erde(f)	tierra	terra
terra	terre	land	Land(n)	tierra	terra
terra	terre	soil	Erde(f)	tierra	terra
terremoto	séisme	earthquake	Erdbeben(n)	terremoto	terremoto
terreno	terrain	ground	Gelände(n)	terreno	terreno
terreno	domaine	domain, estate	Gut(n), Besitzung(f)	dominio, terreno	tenuta, fondo
terrestre	terrestre	terrestrial	irdisch	terrestre	terrestre
território	territoire	territory	Gebiet(n), Land(n)	territorio	territorio
terrível	terrible	terrible	schrecklich	terrible	terribile
terror	terreur	terror	Schrecken(m)	terror	terrore
terrorismo	terrorisme	terrorism	Terrorismus(m)	terrorismo	terrorismo
terrorista	terroriste	terrorist	Terrorist(in f)m	terrorista	terrorista
tese	thèse	thesis(theses)	These(f)	tesis	tesi
teso, a; hirto, a	raide	stiff	starr, steif	tieso, a; rígido, a	rigido, a
tesoura	ciseaux	scissors	Schere(f)	tijeras	forbici
tesoureiro, a	trésorier, ière	treasurer	Schatzmeister(in f)m	tesorero, a	tesoriere, a
tesouro	trésor	treasure	Schatz(m)	tesoro	tesoro
testa	front	forehead	Stirn(f)	frente	fronte
testamento	testament	will, testament	Testament(n)	testamento	testamento
testar	tester	test	testen	ensayar, probar	testare
testemunha	témoin	witness	Zeuge(m), Zeugin(f)	testigo	testimone
testemunhar	témoigner	testify	aus = sagen	testimoniar	testimoniare
testemunhar	témoigner	witness	zeugen, bezeugen	atestiguar	testificare
testemunho	témoignage	testimony, evidence	Zeugenaussage(f)	testimonio	testimonianza
testículo	testicule	testicle	Hoden(m)	testículo	testicolo
tetania	tétanie	tetany	Starrkrampf(m)	tetania	tetania
tétano	tétanos	tetanus	Tetanus(m)	tétanos	tetano
teu	ton	your	dein(e)	tu	tuo(il)
teu, tua	toi(à)	yours	dir	tuyo, a	tuo, a; tuoi, tue
teu, tua	tien, ne	yours	deine(r, s), deine	tuyo, a	tuo, a
teus, tuas	tes	your	deine	tus	tuoi, tue(i, le)
textil	textile	textile	Textil-; Web-	textil	tessile
texto	texte	text	Text(m)	texto	testo
tez	teint	complexion, colour	Teint(m)	tez, color	carnagione

P

Portuguese	French	English	German	Spanish	Italian
tia	tante	aunt	Tante(f)	tía	zia
tíbia	tibia	tibia	Schienbein(n)	tibia	tibia
tifóide	typhoïde	typhoid	Typhus(m)	tifoidea	tifoide
tigela; malga	bol	bowl	Trinkschale(f)	tazón	scodella
tigre	tigre	tiger	Tiger(m)	tigre	tigre
tijolo	brique	brick	Ziegel(m)	ladrillo	mattone
tilintar	tintement	ringing, jingle	Klimpern, Klingeln(n)	tañido	tintinnio
timidez	timidité	shyness, timidity	Schüchternheit(f)	timidez	timidezza
tímido, a	timide	shy, timid	schüchtern	tímido, a	timido, a
tímpano	tympan	eardrum	Trommelfell(n)	tímpano	timpano
tingir	teindre, colorer	dye	färben	teñir	tingere
tinta	encre	ink	Tinte(f)	tinta	inchiostro
tinta	peinture	paint	Farbe(f)	pintura	vernice, pittura
tinta	teinte	tint, colour	Färbung(f), Farbe(f)	tinte, color	tinta
tio	oncle	uncle	Onkel(m)	tío	zio
típico, a	typique	typical	typisch	típico, a	típico, a
tipo	type	type	Typ(m)	tipo	tipo
tipografia	imprimerie	printing works	Druckerei(f)	imprenta	tipografia
tique	tic	twitch(ing)	Tick(m)	tic	tic
tira	bande	band, strip	Streifen(m)	faja, tira	striscia
tirano, a	tyran	tyrant	Tyrann(m)	tirano, a	tiranno, a
tirar	enlever	take off	aus = ziehen	quitar	togliere
tirar	ôter, enlever	remove, take away	ab = nehmen	quitar	togliere
tirar	prélever	take from	entnehmen	sacar	prelevare
tirar, extrair	puiser	draw(from)	schöpfen	sacar	attingere
tiritar	grelotter	shiver	zittern	tiritar	tremare(di freddo)
tiro	tir	shooting, firing	Schießen(n)	tiro	tiro
tiróide	thyroïde	thyroid(gland)	Schilddrüse(f)	tiroides	tiroide
tisana	tisane	herb tea	Kräutertee(m)	tisana	tisana
titubear	tituber	stagger	wanken	titubear	barcollare
titular	titulaire	holder	Inhaber(in f)m	titular	titolare
titular	titulaire	tenured	festangestellt	numerario	titolare
título	titre	title	Titel(m)	título	titolo
toalha	nappe	table-cloth	Tischdecke(f)	mantel	tovaglia
toalha	serviette	towel	Handtuch(n)	toalla	asciugamano
tocar	toucher	touch	an = fassen, berühren	tocar	toccare
tocar	jouer	play	spielen	tocar	suonare
tocha, archote	torche	torch	Fackel(f)	antorcha	torcia
toda	toute	whole(the)	ganz	toda	tutta
todavia	toutefois	however	jedoch	sin embargo	tuttavia
todavia, porém	cependant	however, but	jedoch	sin embargo	eppure, tuttavia
todo, a	tout, e	all(the)	alles	todo, a	tutto, a
todos	tous	all(the)	alle	todos	tutti
toirada	corrida	bull-fight	Stierkampf(m)	corrida	corrida
toldo	bâche	cover	Plane(f)	toldo, lona	telone
tolerância	tolérance	tolerance	Toleranz(f)	tolerancia	tolleranza
tolerar	tolérer	tolerate	dulden, ertragen	tolerar	tollerare
tolo, a; burro, a	bête; sot, te	silly, foolish	dumm	tonto, a	sciocco, a
tom, som, timbre	ton, son, timbre	tone	Ton(m), Klang(m)	tono, sonido	tono
tomada	prise	plug; socket	Steckdose(f)	enchufe	presa
tomar	prendre	take	nehmen	tomar, coger	prendere
tomar conta	occuper(s')	look after	kümmern sich/um	ocuparse	occuparsi
tomate	tomate	tomato(-es)	Tomate(f)	tomate	pomodoro
tonalidade	tonalité	tonality, tone	Tonart(f), Klangfarbe	tonalidad	tonalità
tonel; barril	tonneau	barrel	Faß(n)	tonel; barril	botte, barile
tonelada	tonne	ton	Tonne(f)	tonelada	tonnellata
topázio	topaze	topaz	Topas(m)	topacio	topazio
toranja	pamplemousse	grapefruit	Pampelmuse(f)	pomelo	pompelmo
tórax	thorax	thorax	Brustkasten(m)	tórax	torace
torção	torsion	twist(ing)	Drehung(f), Torsion(f)	torsión	torsione
torcer	tordre	twist	verbiegen, verdrehen	torcer	torcere, piegare
tornado	tornade	tornado(-es)	Wirbelsturm(m)	tornado	tornado
tornar a montar	remonter	reassemble	wieder montieren	volver a montar	rimontare
tornar-se	devenir	become	werden	volverse	diventare
torneio	tournoi	tournament	Turnier(n)	torneo	torneo
torneira	robinet	tap; stop-cock	Wasserhahn(m), Hahn(m)	grifo	rubinetto
torneira	robinet	cock, tap	Hahn(m)(Wasser-; Gas-)	llave, grifo	rubinetto
tornozelo	cheville	ankle	Knöchel(m)	tobillo	caviglia

Portuguese	French	English	German	Spanish	Italian
torpedo	torpille	torpedo(-es)	Torpedo(m)	torpedo	torpedine
torpor	torpeur	torpor	Erstarrungszustand(m)	torpor	torpore
torrar	griller	toast	toasten	tostar	abbrustolire
torre	tour	tower	Turm(m)	torre	torre
torrente	torrent	torrent	Wildbach(m)	torrente	torrente
torta	tarte	tart	Torte(f)	tarta	torta, crostata
tortura	torture	torture	Folter(f)	tortura	tortura
tosse	toux	cough	Husten(m)	tos	tosse
tossir	tousser	cough	husten	toser	tossire
total	total, e	total	ganz; Gesamt-	total	totale
total	total, e	overall	Gesamt-	total	complessivo, a
total	total	total	Summe(f), Ganze(s)(n)	total	totale
totalmente	tout à fait	quite	ganz	totalmente	affatto
toureiro	toréador	bull-fighter	Stierkämpfer(m)	torero	torero
touro; toiro	taureau	bull	Stier(m)	toro	toro
tóxico, a	toxique	toxic	giftig	tóxico, a	tossico, a
toxicologia	toxicologie	toxicology	Toxikologie(f)	toxicología	tossicologia
toxicómano, drogado	toxicomane	drug addict	Rauschgiftsüchtige(r)	drogadicto, a	tossicomane
trabalhador, a	travailleur, se	worker	Arbeiter(in f)m	trabajador, a	lavoratore, trice
trabalhar	travailler	work	arbeiten	trabajar	lavorare
trabalho	travail	work	Arbeit(f)	trabajo	lavoro
trabalho	travail	labour	Arbeit(f)	trabajo	lavoro
traçar	tracer	draw	entwerfen	trazar	tracciare
traço, risco	trait	line	Strich(m)	raya	tratto, riga
traço; vestígio	trace	trace, track	Spur(f)	huella, rastro	traccia
tractor	tracteur	tractor	Traktor(m)	tractor	trattore
tradição	tradition	tradition	Tradition(f)	tradición	tradizione
tradução	traduction	translation	Übersetzung(f)	traducción	traduzione
tradutor, a	traducteur, trice	translator	Übersetzer(in f)m	traductor, a	traduttore, trice
tráfego, tráfico	trafic	traffic	Verkehr(m)	tráfico	traffico
traficante	trafiquant, e	trafficker; pedlar	Schwarzhändler(in f)m	traficante	trafficante
tragédia	tragédie	tragedy	Tragödie(f)	tragedia	tragedia
trágico, a	tragique	tragic	tragisch	trágico, a	tragico, a
traição	trahison	betrayal; treason	Verrat(m)	traición	tradimento
traidor, a	traître, esse	traitor, -tress	Verräter(in f)m	traidor, a	traditore, trice
trair	trahir	betray	verraten	traicionar	tradire
trajecto	trajet	journey, trip	Strecke(f)	trayecto	tragitto
trajectória	trajectoire	trajectory	Bahn(f), Kurs(m)	trayectoria	traiettoria
trança	natte	plait	Zopf(m)	trenza	treccia
trança	tresse	plait, braid	Zopf(m)	trenza	treccia
tranquilizante	tranquillisant	tranquillizer	Beruhigungsmittel(n)	tranquilizante	tranquillante
tranquilizar	rassurer	reassure	beruhigen	tranquilizar	rassicurare
tranquilo, a	tranquille	quiet, still, calm	ruhig	tranquilo, a	tranquillo, a
transacção	transaction	transaction	Transaktion(f)	transacción	transazione
transbordar	déborder	overflow	über = laufen	desbordar	traboccare
transferência	transfert	transfer	Verlegung(f)	transferencia	trasferimento
transferência	mutation	transfer	Versetzung(f)	traslado	trasferimento
transferir	transférer	transfer	überführen	transferir	trasferire
transformação	transformation	transformation	Veränderung(f)	transformación	trasformazione
transformar	transformer	transform, change	verändern	transformar	trasformare
trânsfuga	transfuge	defector	Überläufer(in f)m	transfuga	transfuga
transfusão	transfusion	transfusion	Transfusion(f)	transfusión	trasfusione
trânsito	circulation	traffic	Verkehr(m)	tráfico	traffico
transmissão	transmission	transmission	Übertragung(f)	transmisión	trasmissione
transmitir	transmettre	transmit	übertragen	transmitir	trasmettere
transmitir	diffuser	broadcast	senden	difundir	trasmettere
transparente	transparent, e	transparent	durchsichtig	transparente	trasparente
transpiração	transpiration	perspiration	Schweiß(m)	transpiración	traspirazione
transpirar	transpirer	perspire, sweat	schwitzen	transpirar	traspirare
transportar	transporter	transport, carry	transportieren	transportar	trasportare
transporte	transport	transport	Transport(m)	transporte	trasporto
transversal	transversal, e	transversal	Quer-; schräg	transversal	trasversale
trapaça, burla	escroquerie	swindle	Schwindel(m), Gaunerei	estafa, timo	truffa, imbroglio
trapézio	trapèze	trapezium; trapeze	Trapez(n)	trapecio	trapezio
trapo	chiffon	rag	Lappen(m)	trapo	straccio
traqueia	trachée-artère	trachea	Luftröhre(f)	traquearteria	trachea
trás(para)	arrière(en)	backward(s)	rückwärts	atrás(para)	indietro
traseiro, a	derrière, arrière	rear	Rück-; Hinter-	trasero, a; de atrás	dietro, indietro

P

Portuguese	French	English	German	Spanish	Italian
trasorelho	oreillons	mumps	Mumps(m)	paperas	orecchioni
tratado	traité	treaty	Vertrag(m)	tratado	trattato
tratamento	traitement	treatment	Behandlung(f)	tratamiento	trattamento
tratamento	soins de beauté	beauty treatment	Schönheitspflege(f)	cosmética	cura
tratar	traiter	treat; deal with	behandeln	tratar	trattare
tratar, cuidar	soigner	treat	behandeln	tratar, curar	curare
tratar de	occuper(s')	deal with	beschäftigen, sich	dedicarse a	occuparsi
traumatismo	traumatisme	traumatism	Trauma(n)	traumatismo	trauma
travão	frein	brake	Bremse(f)	freno	freno
travar	freiner	brake	bremsen	frenar	frenare
trave	poutre	beam	Balken(m)	viga	trave
través(de)	travers(de)	askew	schief	través(de)	traverso(di)
travessa	plat	dish, plate	Schüssel(f)	fuente, plato	vassoio, piatto
travessão, hífen	tiret	dash	Gedankenstrich(m)	raya, guión	trattino
travesseiro	oreiller	pillow	Kopfkissen(n)	almohada	guanciale
travesso, a; maroto, a	coquin, e	mischievous	schelmisch	travieso, a	birbante, birichino, a
travesti	travesti	transvestite	Transvestit(m)	travesti	travestito
trazeiro	derrière	back, rear	Hinter-, Rückseite(f)	trasero, a	retro
trazer	apporter	bring	bringen	traer	apportare, portare
trazer	amener	bring	mit = bringen	traer	portare
trazer	rapporter	bring back	zurück = bringen	traer	riportare
trazer	ramener	bring back	wieder = bringen	devolver, traer	riportare
trégua	trêve	truce	Waffenstillstand(m)	tregua	tregua
trégua, espera	répit	respite	Atempause(f)	tregua, respiro	tregua, riposo
treinador	entraîneur	trainer	Trainer(m)	entrenador	allenatore
treinar-se	entraîner(s')	train, practise	üben; trainieren	entrenarse	allenare(-rsi)
treino	entraînement	training, practice	Training(n)	entrenamiento	allenamento
tremer	trembler	tremble	zittern	temblar	tremare
tremer	vaciller	flicker	flackern	oscilar, vacilar	vacillare
tremido, a	trouble	blurred	verwackelt	desenfocado, a	sfocato, a
trenó	traîneau	sleigh, sledge	Schlitten(m)	trineo	slitta
trepar, escalar	grimper	climb	klettern	escalar, subir	arrampicarsi
três	trois	three	drei	tres	tre
trespassar	transpercer	pierce	durchbohren	atravesar	trapassare
trevas	ténèbres	darkness	Finsternis(f)	tinieblas	tenebre
treze	treize	thirteen	dreizehn	trece	tredici
triângulo	triangle	triangle	Dreieck(n)	triángulo	triangolo
tribo	tribu	tribe	Stamm(m)	tribu	tribù
tribunal	tribunal	court, tribunal	Gericht(n)	tribunal	tribunale
tricotar	tricoter	knit	stricken	hacer punto	lavorare a maglia
trigo	blé	corn	Weizen(m)	trigo	grano
trimestral	trimestriel, le	quarterly	vierteljährlich	trimestral	trimestrale
trimestre	trimestre	term; quarter	Vierteljahr(n)	trimestre	trimestre
trincar	croquer	crunch	knabbern	mascar	sgranocchiare
trincheira	tranchée	trench	Graben(m)	trinchera, zanja	trincea
trinta	trente	thirty	dreißig	treinta	trenta
triste	triste	sad, unhappy	traurig	triste	triste
tristeza	tristesse	sadness	Traurigkeit(f)	tristeza	tristezza
tristeza	cafard	miserable(feel)	Trübsinn(m)	melancolía	malinconia
triturar; moer	broyer	crush, grind	mahlen	triturar	stritolare, macinare
triunfo	triomphe	triumph	Triumph(m)	triunfo	trionfo
troca; câmbio	échange	exchange	Tausch(Aus-, Um-)(m)	cambio	scambio
trocar	échanger	exchange	tauschen	intercambiar	scambiare
troçar	moquer(se)	make fun of, mock	verspotten	mofarse, burlarse	burlarsi
troçar	ricaner	snigger	grinsen, kichern	burlarse	sogghignare
troco	monnaie	change	Kleingeld(n); Klein-	cambio	resto
troféu	trophée	trophy	Trophäe(f)	trofeo	trofeo
trombeta	trompette	trumpet	Trompete(f)	trompeta	trombetta
tronco	tronc	trunk	Stamm(m)	tronco	tronco
trono	trône	throne	Thron(m)	trono	trono
tropa	troupe	troop	Truppe(f)	tropa	truppa
tropeçar	trébucher	stumble, trip	stolpern	tropezar	inciampare
tropical	tropical, e	tropical	tropisch	tropical	tropicale
trotar	trotter	trot	traben	trotar	trottare
trovão	tonnerre	thunder	Donner(m)	trueno	tuono
truta	truite	trout	Forelle(f)	trucha	trota
tu	tu	you	du	tú	tu
tua, teu	ta	your	dein(e)	tu	tua(la)

Portuguese	French	English	German	Spanish	Italian
tu; ti	toi	you	du; dich	tú; te	tu; te
tubarão	requin	shark	Hai(m)	tiburón	squalo
tuberculose	tuberculose	tuberculosis, T.B.	Tuberkulose(f)	tuberculosis	tubercolosi
tubo	tube	tube	Tube(f)	tubo	tubo
tubo, cano	tuyau(terie)	pipe	Röhre(f), Schlauch(m)	tubo, caño	tubo, tubazione
tufão	typhon	typhoon	Taifun(m)	tifón	tifone
tulipa	tulipe	tulip	Tulpe(f)	tulipán	tulipano
tumor	tumeur	tumour	Tumor(m)	tumor	tumore
túmulo	tombeau	tomb	Grabmal(n)	tumba	tomba
túmulo, sepultura	tombe	grave	Grab(n)	tumba	tomba
tumulto	tumulte	tumult, uproar	Tumult(m)	tumulto	tumulto
túnel	tunnel	tunnel	Tunnel(m)	túnel	tunnel
túnica	tunique	tunic	Tunika(f)	túnica	tunica
turbilhão	tourbillon	whirlwind, swirl	Wirbel(wind)(m)	torbellino	vortice
turbina	turbine	turbine	Turbine(f)	turbina	turbina
turbulência	turbulence	turbulence	Turbulenz(f)	turbulencia	turbolenza
turismo	tourisme	tourism	Tourismus(m)	turismo	turismo
turista	touriste	tourist	Tourist(m)	turista	turista
turvo, a	trouble	cloudy; muddy	trüb	turbio, a	torbido, a
tutela	tutelle	trusteeship	Treuhandschaft(f)	tutela	tutela
tutor, a	tuteur, tutrice	guardian	Vormund(m)	tutor, a	tutore, trice

U

Portuguese	French	English	German	Spanish	Italian
uivar; urrar	hurler	howl	heulen	aullar	ululare, guaire
úlcera	ulcère	ulcer	Geschwür(n)	úlcera	ulcera
ulterior	ultérieur, e	later	später	ulterior	ulteriore
último, a	ultime	ultimate, final	allerletzte(r, s)	último, a	ultimo, a
último, a	dernier, ière	last	letzter, letzte	último, a	ultimo, a
último, a	dernier	last	Letzte(f, m)	último, a	ultimo, a
ultramar	outre-mer	overseas	überseeisch	ultramar	oltremare
ultrapassar	dépasser	go beyond, exceed	überholen	sobresalir	oltrepassare
ultrapassar	dépasser	exceed	überschreiten	adelantar	superare
ultrapassar	doubler	overtake	überholen	adelantar	sorpassare
um, uma	un, e	a, an	ein, e	uno, una	uno, una
um	un	one	eins	un, uno	un, uno
um ou outro, cada	un(l')ou l'autre	either	eine(der) der andere	uno u otro, cada	uno(l') o l'altro
umbigo	nombril	navel	Nabel(m)	ombligo	ombelico
unânime	unanime	unanimous	einstimmig	unánime	unanime
unha	ongle	nail	Fingernagel(m)	uña	unghia
união	union	union	Bund(m), Vereinigung f	unión	unione
único, a	unique	unique; only	einzig, einzeln	único, a	unico, a
único, a	unique	unique, exceptional	einmalig	único, a	unico, a
único, a	un, e(à)	single	einzeln; einzig	solo, a; único, a	singolo, a
unidade	unité	unity	Einigkeit(f)	unidad	unità
unidade	unité	unit	Einheit(f)	unidad	unità
unificado, a	unifié, e	unified, united	vereinigt	unificado, a	unificato, a
uniforme	uniforme	uniform	gleichförmig	uniforme	uniforme
uniforme	uniforme	uniform	Uniform(f)	uniforme	uniforme; divisa
unir, juntar	unir	unite	vereinen	unir	unire
unitário, a	unitaire	unitary, per unit	unitarisch	unitario, a	unitario, a
universal	universel, le	universal	universell	universal	universale
universidade	université	university	Universität(f)	universidad	università
universitário, a	universitaire	academic	Universität-	universitario, a	universitario, a
universo	univers	universe	Universum(n)	universo	universo
untuoso, a	onctueux, se	unctuous	cremig, sahnig	untuoso, a	untuoso, a
urânio	uranium	uranium	Uran(n)	uranio	uranio

P

Portuguese	French	English	German	Spanish	Italian
urbanismo	urbanisme	town-planning	Städtebau(m)	urbanismo	urbanistica
urbano, a	urbain, e	urban	städtisch, Stadt-	urbano, a	urbano, a
ureia	urée	urea	Harnstoff(m)	urea	urea
urgência	urgence	emergency, urgency	Notfall(m)	urgencia	urgenza
urgência	urgence	urgency	Dringlichkeit(f)	urgencia	urgenza
urgente	urgent, e	urgent	dringend	urgente	urgente
urina	urine	urine	Urin(m)	orina	urina
urso	ours	bear	Bär(m)	oso	orso
usado, a	usé, e	worn, worn out	verbraucht	usado, a	logoro, a
usar	employer	use	benützen	usar, emplear	usare, adoperare
usar; trazer	porter	wear	tragen	llevar	indossare, portare
uso	usage	usage, use	Gebrauch(m)	uso, empleo	uso
uso	emploi	use	Gebrauch(m)	uso, empleo	uso
usual	usuel, le	usual	gebräuchlich	usual	usuale
usura, desgaste	usure	wear	Abnützung(f)	desgaste	usura; logorio
utensílio	ustensile	utensil	Gerät(n)	utensilios	utensile
utente	usager, ère	user	Benutzer(in f)m	usuario, a	utente
útero	utérus	uterus, womb	Gebärmutter(f)	útero	utero
útil	utile	useful	nützlich	útil	utile
utilização	utilisation	utilization, use	Benutzung(f)	utilización	utilizzazione
utilizador, a	utilisateur	user	Benutzer(in f)m	utilizador, a	utilizzatore, trice
utilizar	utiliser	use	benutzen	utilizar	utilizzare
utópico, a	utopique	Utopian	utopisch	utópico, a	utopico, a
uva	raisin	grape	Traube(f)(Wein-)	uva(s)	uva

V

Portuguese	French	English	German	Spanish	Italian
vaca	vache	cow	Kuh(f)	vaca	vacca, mucca
vacilar	vaciller	sway, wobble	taumeln	vacilar	vacillare
vacilar	chanceler	stagger	taumeln	tambalearse	barcollare
vacina	vaccin	vaccine	Impfstoff(m)	vacuna	vaccino
vacinação	vaccination	vaccination	Impfung(f)	vacunación	vaccinazione
vaga	vague, houle	swell, surge	Brandung(f)	marejada	ondosità
vaga	lame	wave	Welle(f)	ola	ondata
vagabundo, a	vagabond, e	vagabond; tramp	Landstreicher(in f)m	vagabundo, a	vagabondo, a
vagabundo, a	rôdeur, se	prowler	Herumstreicher(m)	vagabundo, a	vagabondo, a
vagabundo, a	clochard, e	tramp	Penner(m)	vagabundo, a	barbone, a; vagabondo
vagão	wagon	coach, carriage	Wagen(m)	vagón	vagone, carrozza
vagão	wagon	truck, wag(g)on	Waggon(m)(Güterwagen)	vagón	vagone
vagina	vagin	vagina	Scheide(f)(Anat.)	vagina	vagina
vago, a	flou, e	fuzzy, blurred	verschwommen	borroso, a	sfumato, a
vaiar	huer	boo	aus = pfeifen	abuchear	fischiare, urlare
vaidade	vanité	vanity	Eitelkeit(f)	vanidad	vanità
vaidoso, a	coquet, te	pretty; coquettish	kokett; eitel	presumido, a	civettuolo, a
vale	vallée	valley	Tal(n)	valle	valle
vale a pena	vaut la peine	worthwhile	der Mühe wert	vale la pena	vale la pena
valente; bravo, a	vaillant, e	brave	tapfer	valiente	valoroso, a
vale postal	mandat-lettre	postal order	Postanweisung(f)	giro postal	vaglia(postale)
valer	valoir	worth(be)	wert sein	valer	valere
valeta	caniveau	gutter	Rinnstein(m)	arroyo	canaletto di scolo
validade	validité	validity	Gültigkeit(f)	validez	validità
válido, a	valable	valid, good	gültig; annehmbar	válido, a; valedero	valido, a
valor	valeur	value, worth	Wert(m)	valor	valore
valor, mérito	valeur, mérite	worth, merit	Wert(m)	valor, mérito	valore, merito
valsa	valse	waltz	Walzer(m)	vals	valzer
válvula	clapet	valve	Klappenventil(n)	válvula	valvola
vantagem	avantage	advantage	Vorteil(m)	ventaja	vantaggio

Portuguese	French	English	German	Spanish	Italian
vantagem	atout, avantage	asset	Trumpf(m), Vorteil(m)	ventaja	vantaggio
vapor	vapeur	steam	Dampf(m)	vapor	vapore
vapor	vapeur	vapour, fumes	Dunst(m)	vapor	vapore
vaporizar	vaporiser	spray	sprühen	vaporizar	vaporizzare
vara	baguette	stick	Stöckchen(n)	varilla	bacchetta
varanda	balcon	balcony	Balkon(m)	balcón	balcone
variação	variation	variation	Abwandlung(f)	variación	variazione
variado, a	divers, e	various, varied	mannigfach	vario, a	vario, a
variado, a	varié, e	varied, various	vielfältig	variado, a	vario, a
variável	variable	variable	veränderlich	variable	variabile
varicela	varicelle	chicken-pox	Windpocken(f, pl)	varicela	varicella
variedade	variété	variety	Vielfalt(f)	variedad	varietà
varíola	variole	smallpox	Pocken(f, pl)	viruela	vaiolo
vários, as	plusieurs	several	mehrere	varios, as	parecchi
varrer	balayer	sweep	fegen	barrer	spazzare
vascular	vasculaire	vascular	Gefäß-	vascular	vascolare
vaselina	vaseline	vaseline	Vaseline(f)	vaselina	vasellina
vaso; pote	pot	pot	Topf(m)	maceta	vaso
vaso(sanguíneo)	vaisseau	vessel(blood)	Gefäß(Blut-)(n)	vaso(sanguíneo)	vaso(sanguigno)
vassoura	balai	brush, broom	Besen(m)	escoba	scopa
vasto, a	vaste	vast	weit	vasto, a	vasto, a
vazio, a	vide	empty	leer	vacío, a	vuoto, a
vazio, a	dégonflé, e	deflated, flat	platt, ohne Luft	desinflado, a	sgonfio, a
vazio, vácuo	vide	vacuum; void	Vakuum(n), Leere(f)	vacío	vuoto
vedeta, estrela	vedette	star	Star(m)	estrella; divo, a	vedette; divo, a
vegetação	végétation	vegetation	Pflanzenwuchs(m)	vegetación	vegetazione
vegetal	végétal	vegetable, plant	Pflanze(f)	vegetal	vegetale
veia	veine	vein	Vene(f)	vena	vena
veículo	véhicule	vehicle	Fahrzeug(n)	vehículo	veicolo
vela	bougie	candle	Kerze(f)	vela	candela
vela	bougie	sparking plug	Zündkerze(f)	bujía	candela
vela	voile	sail	Segel(n)	vela	vela
vela	voile	sailing	Segeln(n)	vela	vela
veleiro	voilier	yacht, sailing boat	Segelboot(n)	velero	veliero
velho, a	vieux, vieille	old	alt	viejo, a	vecchio, a
velho, ancião	vieillard	old man(men)	Alte(m), alter Mann(m)	viejo, anciano	vecchio, anziano
velho, a(o, a mais)	aîné, e	oldest, eldest	Ältere(f, m)	primogénito, a	primogenito, a
velocidade	vitesse	speed	Geschwindigkeit(f)	velocidad	velocità
velocidade	vélocité, vitesse	velocity	Schnelligkeit(f)	velocidad	velocità
velocidade	régime	speed	Drehzahl(f)	régimen	regime
veludo	velours	velvet	Samt(m)	terciopelo	velluto
vencedor, a	vainqueur	winner; victor	Sieger(in f)m	vencedor, a	vincitore, trice
vencer	vaincre	defeat	besiegen	vencer	vincere
vencimento	échéance	expiration	Fälligkeitstermin(m)	vencimiento	scadenza
venda	vente	sale	Verkauf(m)	venta	vendita
vendedor, a	vendeur, se	sales assistant	Verkäufer(in f)m	vendedor, a	commesso, a
vendedor, a	vendeur, se	salesman(-men)	Verkäufer(in f)m	vendedor, a	venditore, trice
vender	vendre	sell	verkaufen	vender	vendere
veneno	poison	poison	Gift(n)	veneno	veleno
veneno	venin	venom, poison	Gift(n)	veneno	veleno
venenoso, a	vénéneux, se	poisonous	giftig	venenoso, a	velenoso, a
venéreo, a	vénérien, ne	venereal	Geschlechts-	venéreo, a	venereo, a
venha!	venez!	come(on)!	kommen Sie!	venga(!)	venga!, venite!
venha cá!	venez ici!	come here!	kommen Sie her!	venga aquí(!)	venga qui!, venite!
ventilação	ventilation	ventilation	Belüftung(f)	ventilación	ventilazione
ventilador	ventilateur	fan, ventilator	Ventilator(m)	ventilador	ventilatore
vento	vent	wind	Wind(m)	viento	vento
ventosa	ventouse	suction disc	Saugnapf(m)	ventosa	ventosa
ver	voir	see	sehen	ver	vedere
ver	regarder	watch, look(at)	fern = sehen	mirar	guardare
verão	été	summer	Sommer(m)	verano	estate
verbo	verbe	verb	Verb(n)	verbo	verbo
verdade	vérité	truth	Wahrheit(f)	verdad	verità
verdadeiramente	vraiment	really	wirklich	verdaderamente	veramente
verdadeiro, a	vrai, e	true	wahr	verdadero, a	vero, a
verdadeiro, a	véritable	real, genuine	wahrhaftig	verdadero, a	vero, a
verde	vert, e	green	grün	verde	verde
verdura	verdure	greenery	Grün(n)	verdor, verdura	verdura

P

Portuguese	French	English	German	Spanish	Italian
vereda, atalho	sentier	footpath, path	Weg(m)	sendero, senda	sentiero
veredicto	verdict	verdict	Urteil(n)	veredicto	verdetto
vergar	plier	bend	biegen	plegar, doblar	piegare
vergonha	honte	shame	Scham(f), Schande(f)	vergüenza	vergogna
vergonha(ter)	honte(avoir)	ashamed(be)	schämen, sich	vergüenza(tener)	vergognarsi
vergonhoso, a	honteux, se	shameful	beschämend	vergonzoso, a	vergognoso, a
verificação	vérification	verification	Überprüfung(f)	verificación	verifica
verificar	vérifier	check, verify	überprüfen	comprobar	verificare
verificar	assurer(s')	make sure	überzeugen, sich	cerciorarse	accertarsi
verme	ver	worm	Wurm(m)	gusano	verme
vermelho, a	rouge	red	rot	rojo, a	rosso, a
verniz	vernis	varnish	Lack(m)	barniz	vernice
verosímil	vraisemblable	likely, probable	wahrscheinlich	verosímil	verosimile
verruga	verrue	wart	Warze(f)	verruga	verruca, porro
verso	vers	line	Vers(m)	verso	verso
vértebra	vertèbre	vertebra(-ae)	Wirbel(m)	vértebra	vertebra
verter	verser	pour	aus = gießen	verter	versare
vertical	vertical, e	vertical	senkrecht	vertical	verticale
vertigem	vertige	dizziness	Schwindel(m)	vértigo	vertigine
vesícula	vésicule	gall-bladder	Blase(f)	vesícula	cistifellea
vespa	guêpe	wasp	Wespe(f)	avispa	vespa
vestiário	vestiaire	cloak-room	Garderobe(f)	vestuario	vestiario
vestíbulo	hall	foyer, hall	Eingangshalle(f)	vestíbulo	hall, ingresso
vestíbulo; hall	vestibule	hall	Flur(m)	vestíbulo	ingresso, anticamera
vestido, a	habillé, e	dressed	angezogen	vestido, a	vestito, a
vestido	robe	dress	Kleid(n)	vestido	vestito
vestido de noite	robe de soirée	evening dress	Abendkleid(n)	traje de noche	abito da sera
vestígio	vestige	remains	Überrest(m)	vestigio	vestigia
vestir	vêtir	clothe, dress	an = ziehen, an = kleiden	vestir	vestire
vestir-se	habiller(s')	dress	an = ziehen, sich	vestirse	vestirsi
vestir-se	habiller(s')	dress up	an = kleiden	vestirse, ataviar	vestire(-rsi)
vestuário	habillement	clothing	Bekleidung(f)	ropa	abbigliamento
veterinário	vétérinaire	vet	Tierarzt(m)	veterinario	veterinario
veto	veto	veto	Veto(n)	veto	veto
véu	voile	veil	Schleier(m)	velo	velo
vexame	vexation	vexation	Ärger(m)	vejación	vessazione
vez	fois	time	Mal(n)	vez	volta
vez(uma)	fois(une)	once	einmal	vez(una)	volta(una)
vez	tour	turn	Reihe(f)	turno	turno
vezes(às), às vezes	parfois	sometimes	manchmal	a veces	talvolta
vezes(às), às vezes	quelquefois	sometimes	manchmal	a veces	qualche volta
via; caminho	voie	way; track	Weg(m)	vía; camino	via; binario
viagem	voyage	trip; journey	Reise(f)	viaje	viaggio
viajante	voyageur, se	traveller	Reisende(r)m f	viajero, a	viaggiatore, trice
viajar	voyager	travel	reisen	viajar	viaggiare
víbora	vipère	viper	Viper(f), Otter(f)	víbora	vipera
vibrar	vibrer	vibrate	schwingen	vibrar	vibrare
vice-presidente	vice-président	vice-president	Vize-Präsident(m)	vicepresidente	vicepresidente
vício	vice	vice	Laster(n)	vicio	vizio
vicioso, a	vicieux, se	vicious	lasterhaft	vicioso, a	vizioso, a
vida	vie	life(lives)	Leben(n)	vida	vita
vidro	verre	glass	Glas(n)	vidrio	vetro
vidro; espelho	vitre	pane, window	Scheibe(f)(Fenster-)	cristal, vidrio	vetro
vidro; espelho	glace; miroir	window; mirror	Scheibe(f); Spiegel(m)	luna; cristal	vetro; specchio
viela	ruelle	alley	Gäßchen(n), Gasse(f)	callejuela	viuzza, vicolo
vigarice	racket	racket(-eering)	Erpressung(f)	extorsión	racket
vigente	vigueur(en)	force(in), current	Kraft(in), geltend	vigente	vigore(in), vigente
vigia	hublot	window	Bullauge(n), Luke(f)	ventanilla	obló
vigia	surveillant, e	supervisor	Aufseher m, Supervisor	vigilante	sorvegliante
vigiar	surveiller	watch; supervise	überwachen	vigilar	sorvegliare
vigilância	surveillance	watch; supervision	Überwachung(f)	vigilancia	sorveglianza
vigilante	vigilant, e	vigilant	wachsam	vigilante	vigilante
vigor	vigueur	vigour	Kraft(f)	vigor	vigore
vigoroso, a	vigoureux, se	vigorous, strong	rüstig, kräftig	vigoroso, a	vigoroso, a
vinagre	vinaigre	vinegar	Essig(m)	vinagre	aceto
vingança	vengeance	revenge	Rache(f)	venganza	vendetta
vingar	venger	avenge	rächen	vengar	vendicare
vinho	vin	wine	Wein(m)	vino	vino

Portuguese	French	English	German	Spanish	Italian
vintage	millésime	vintage	Jahrgang(m)	cosecha(año)	annata
vinte	vingt	twenty	zwanzig	veinte	venti
vinte e um	vingt-et-un	twenty one	einundzwanzig	veintiún(o)	ventuno
violação	violation	violation	Verstoß(m)	violación	violazione
violação	viol	rape	Vergewaltigung(f)	violación	stupro
violar	violer	violate	verraten	violar	violare
violência	violence	violence	Gewalt(f)	violencia	violenza
violentar	violer	rape	vergewaltigen	violar	violentare
violento, a	violent, e	violent	gewalttätig, gewaltsam	violento, a	violento, a
violento, a	violent, e	violent	heftig, stark	violento, a	violento, a
violino	violon	violin	Geige(f)	violín	violino
violoncelo	violoncelle	cello	Cello(n)	violoncelo	violoncello
vir	venir	come	kommen	venir	venire
vir a ser	devenir	become	werden	llegar a ser	diventare
virar	tourner	turn	drehen	volver	girare
virar	tourner	turn	wenden	girar	svoltare, girare
virar; cair	renverser(se)	overturn	überschlagen, sich	volcarse	rovesciarsi
virgem	vierge	virgin	unberührt	virgen	vergine
virgindade	virginité	virginity	Jungfräulichkeit(f)	virginidad	verginità
vírgula	virgule	comma	Komma(n)	coma	virgola
viril	viril, e	virile, manly	männlich, mannhaft	viril	virile
virilidade	virilité	virility	Männlichkeit(f)	virilidad	virilità
virtude	vertu	virtue	Tugend(f)	virtud	virtù
virtuoso, a	vertueux, se	virtuous	tugendhaft	virtuoso, a	virtuoso, a
virtuoso, a	virtuose	virtuoso	Meister(m), Virtuose m	virtuoso, a	virtuoso, a
vírus	virus	virus	Virus(m)	virus	virus
viscoso, a	visqueux, se	viscous	zähflüssig	viscoso, a	vischioso, a
viscoso, a	gluant, e	sticky	klebrig	viscoso, a	viscido, a
visibilidade	visibilité	visibility	Sicht(-weite)(f)	visibilidad	visibilità
visita	visite	visit	Besuch(m)	visita	visita
visitante	visiteur, se	visitor	Besucher(in f)m	visitante	visitatore, trice
visitar	visiter	visit	besichtigen, reisen	visitar	visitare
visitar	visiter	visit	besuchen	visitar	andare a trovare
visível	visible	visible	sichtbar	visible	visibile
vista	vue	sight	Sehkraft(f)	vista	vista
vista	vue	view	Ausblick(m)	vista	veduta
visto	visa	visa	Visum(n)	visado	visto
visual	visuel, le	visual	visuell	visual	visivo, a; visuale
visualizar	visualiser	display	sichtbar machen	visualizar	visualizzare
vital	vital, e	vital	wesentlich	vital	vitale
vitalidade	vitalité	vitality	Lebenskraft(f)	vitalidad	vitalità
vitamina	vitamine	vitamin	Vitamin(n)	vitamina	vitamina
vítima	victime	victim	Opfer(n)	víctima	vittima
vitória	victoire	victory	Sieg(m)	victoria	vittoria
viúvo, a	veuf, veuve	widower, widow	Witwer(m), Witwe(f)	viudo, a	vedovo, a
viva!	vive!	hurrah!; Long live!	Es lebe!; Lang lebe!	viva(!)	viva!, evviva!
vivaz	vivace	hardy	immergrün; ausdauernd	vivaz	vivace
viver	vivre	live	leben	vivir	vivere
vivo, a	vif, vive	lively	lebendig	vivo, a	vivace; vivo, a
vivo, a	vif, vive	keen	scharf	agudo, a; vivo, a	vivo, a
vivo, a	vivant, e	alive	lebendig	vivo, a	vivo, a; vivente
vizinhança	voisinage	neighbourhood	Nachbarschaft(f)	vecindario	vicinanza
vizinho, a	voisin, e	neighbour	Nachbar(in f)m	vecino, a	vicino, a
voar	voler	fly	fliegen	volar	volare
vocabulário	vocabulaire	vocabulary	Vokabular(n)	vocabulario	vocabolario
vocação	vocation	vocation	Berufung(f)	vocación	vocazione
vocal	vocal, e	vocal	Stimm-	vocal	vocale
você	vous	you	Sie	usted(es)	lei, loro(pl.)
vogal	voyelle	vowel	Vokal(m), Selbstlaut m	vocal	vocale
volante	volant	steering-wheel	Steuer(n)	volante	volante
volta, giro	tour	turn	Umdrehung(f)	vuelta	giro
voltar	revenir	come back, return	zurück = kommen	volver	ritornare
voltar(a)	retourner	return(to)	zurück = gehen	regresar	tornare
voltar	rentrer	go back, come back	zurück = kommen	regresar	tornare, rientrare
voltar	réintégrer	return	zurück = kehren	reintegrar	reintegrare
voltar a ver	revoir	see again	wieder = sehen	volver a ver	rivedere
volume	volume	volume	Volumen(n)	volumen	volume
volume(negócios)	chiffre(affaire)	turnover	Umsatz(m)	volumen(negocios)	fatturato

P

Portuguese	French	English	German	Spanish	Italian
volumoso, a	encombrant, e	bulky, cumbersome	sperrig, lästig	voluminoso, a	imgombrante
voluntário, a	volontaire	voluntary	freiwillig	voluntario, a	volontario, a
voluntário, a	volontaire	volunteer	Freiwillige(r)m f	voluntario, a	volontario, a
vomitar	vomir	vomit	erbrechen, sich	vomitar	vomitare
vontade	volonté	will	Wille(m)	voluntad	volontà
vontade	envie	desire	Lust(f)	ganas	voglia
vontade(estar à)	aise(être à l')	ease(be at)	wohl fühlen, sich	gusto(estar a)	agio(essere a)
voo	vol	flight	Flug(m)	vuelo	volo
voraz	vorace	voracious	gefräßig, gierig	voraz	vorace
vós; você	vous	you	ihr; Sie	vosotros; ustedes	voi; lei
vos; vosco; lhe	vous; te	you	euch; Sie; Ihnen	os; les; le; te	vi; ve; le; ti; te
vosso, a	votre	your	Ihr(e); euer, eure	vuestro, a	vostro, a(il, la)
vosso, a; seu, sua	vôtre(le, la)	yours	eure(r, s); Ihre(r, s)	vuestro, a; suyo, a	vostro, a; suo, sua
vossos, as	vos	your	eure, Ihre	vuestros, as	vostri, e
votar	voter	vote	wählen	votar	votare
voto	voeu	wish(-es)	Wunsch(m)	deseo	augurio
voto	vote	vote	Wahl(f)	voto	voto
voz	voix	voice	Stimme(f)	voz	voce
vulcão	volcan	volcano(-es)	Vulkan(m)	volcán	vulcano
vulgar	vulgaire	vulgar	vulgär	vulgar	volgare
vulnerável	vulnérable	vulnerable	verwundbar	vulnerable	vulnerabile

W

Portuguese	French	English	German	Spanish	Italian
wind-surf	planche à voile	windsurf(ing)	Windsurfen(n)	tabla a vela, surf	windsurf

X

Portuguese	French	English	German	Spanish	Italian
xadrês	échecs	chess	Schachspiel(n)	ajedrez	scacchi
xale	châle	shawl	Schal(m)	chal	scialle
xarope	sirop	cordial, squash	Saft(m), Sirup(m)	almíbar	sciroppo
xarope	sirop	syrup, medicine	Sirup(m)	jarabe	sciroppo

Y

Portuguese	French	English	German	Spanish	Italian
yoga	yoga	yoga	Yoga(n), Joga(n)	yoga	yoga

Z

Portuguese	French	English	German	Spanish	Italian
zarolho, a	borgne	one-eyed	einäugig	tuerto, a	guercio, a
zebra	zèbre	zebra	Zebra(n)	cebra	zebra
zero	zéro	zero, nought	Null(f)	cero	zero
zombaria, troça	moquerie	mockery	Spott(m)	burla, mofa	canzonatura, beffa
zona	zone	zone	Zone(f)	zona	zona
zoológico, a	zoologique	zoological	zoologisch	zoológico, a	zoologico, a

P

Notes

Notes

Notes

Notes